Neu

Preiswert

Zuverlässig

Dieses neue Taschenbuch ist ein ganz außergewöhnliches Wörterbuch. Sein Inhalt basiert auf den zweisprachigen Wörterbüchern des Verlages Langenscheidt — des bedeutendsten Verlages auf diesem Gebiet. Es enthält über 40000 Stichwörter, gibt die Aussprache in beiden Teilen in Internationaler Lautschrift und besitzt besondere Anhänge für Eigennamen, Abkürzungen und Maße und Gewichte.

Neu und einzigartig ist die Fülle der grammatischen Informationen: Mehr als 15000 deutsche Substantive und Verben haben Angaben zur Deklination und Konjugation. Über die unregelmäßigen Verben in beiden Sprachen gibt der Hauptteil und der Anhang zuverlässig Auskunft.

Dieses Wörterbuch ist somit ein modernes und handliches Nachschlagewerk für jeden, der in seinem Beruf, beim Lernen oder Lehren mit der englischen und deutschen Sprache zu tun hat.

LANGENSCHEIDTS

DEUTSCH-ENGLISCHES
ENGLISCH-DEUTSCHES
WÖRTERBUCH

Beide Teile in einem Band

Bearbeitet und herausgegeben

von der

LANGENSCHEIDT-REDAKTION

 WASHINGTON SQUARE PRESS · NEW YORK

LANGENSCHEIDT'S

GERMAN-ENGLISH
ENGLISH-GERMAN
DICTIONARY

Two Volumes in One

Edited by
THE LANGENSCHEIDT
EDITORIAL STAFF

 WASHINGTON SQUARE PRESS · NEW YORK

LANGENSCHEIDT'S GERMAN-ENGLISH
ENGLISH-GERMAN DICTIONARY

A *Washington Square Press* edition

1st printing.......................January, 1953
37th printing.....................August, 1969

New Revised and Enlarged Edition

1st printing.......................January, 1970

This WASHINGTON SQUARE PRESS edition is published by
arrangement with Langenscheidt KG, Publishers, Berlin
and Munich, Germany, and is printed from brand-new
plates made from newly set, clear, easy-to-read type.

WSP

L

Published by Washington Square Press,
a division of Simon & Schuster, Inc., 630 Fifth Avenue, New York, N.Y.

WASHINGTON SQUARE PRESS editions are distributed in the
U.S. by Simon & Schuster, Inc., 630 Fifth Avenue, New
York, N.Y. 10020 and in Canada by Simon & Schuster
of Canada, Ltd., Richmond Hill, Ontario, Canada.

Preface

For over 100 years Langenscheidt's bilingual dictionaries have been an essential tool of the language student. For several decades Langenscheidt's German-English dictionaries have been used in all walks of life as well as in schools.

However, languages are in a constant process of change. To bring you abreast of these changes Langenscheidt has compiled this entirely new dictionary. Many new words which have entered the German and English languages in the last few years have been included in the vocabulary: e.g., Mondfähre, Mehrwertsteuer, Einwegflasche, Antirakete; lunar probe, heart transplant, non-violence.

Langenscheidt's German-English Dictionary contains another new and long desired feature for the English-speaking user: it provides clear answers to questions of declension and conjugation in over 15,000 German noun and verb entries (see pp. 7 to 8).

The phonetic transcription of the German and English headwords follows the principles laid down by the International Phonetic Association (IPA).

In addition to the vocabulary this Dictionary contains special quick-reference sections of proper names — up-to-date with names like Wankel, Mössbauer, Henze —, abbreviations and weights and measures.

Designed for the widest possible variety of uses, this Dictionary, with its more than 40,000 entries in all, will be of great value to students, teachers, and tourists as well as in home and office libraries.

Contents

Arrangement of the Dictionary and Guide for the User

1. Arrangement. Strict alphabetical order has been maintained throughout this Dictionary. The irregular plural forms of English nouns as well as the principal parts (infinitive, preterite, and past participle) of the irregular English and German verbs have also been given in their proper alphabetical order; e.g. *man – men; bite – bit – bitten; beißen – biß – gebissen.*

2. Pronunciation. Pronunciation is given in square brackets by means of the symbols of the International Phonetic Association. No transcription of compounds is given if the parts appear as separate headwords. The German suffixes as given on page 12 are not transcribed unless they are parts of catchwords.

3. Explanatory additions have been printed in italics; e.g. *abstract Inhalt* kurz zs.-fassen; *Abbau* pulling down *(of structure); abbauen* pull down *(structure); durchsichtig glass, etc.:* transparent.

4. Subject Labels. The field of knowledge from which a headword or some of its meanings are taken is, where possible, indicated by figurative or abbreviated labels or by other labels written out in full. A figurative or abbreviated label placed immediately after a headword applies to all translations. Any label preceding an individual translation refers to this only. In Part I, any abbreviated label with a colon applies to all following translations. An F placed before a German illustrative phrase or its English equivalent indicates that the phrase in question is colloquial usage. An F: placed before a German phrase applies to that phrase and its translation(s). Figurative labels have always, other labels sometimes, been placed between illustrative phrases and their translations.

5. Translations of similar meanings have been subdivided by **commas,** the various senses by **semicolons.**

6. American spelling has been given in the following ways: *theat|re, Am. -er, defen|ce, Am. -se; council(l)or, hono(u)r, judg(e)ment; plough, Am. plow.*

7. Grammatical References in Part I. Parts of speech (adjective, verb, etc.) have been indicated throughout. Entries have been subdivided by Arabic numerals to distinguish the various parts of speech.

I. Nouns. The inflectional forms *(genitive singular / nominative plural)* follow immediately after the indication of gender. No forms are given for compounds if the parts appear as separate headwords.

The horizontal stroke replaces that part of the word which remains unchanged in the inflexion: *Affe m (-n/-n); Affäre f (-/-n).*

The sign ⁼ indicates that an Umlaut appears in the inflected form in question: *Blatt n (-[e]s/⁼er).*

II. Verbs. Verbs have been treated in the following ways:

a) *bändigen v/t. (ge-, h):* The past participle of this verb is formed by means of the prefix ge- and the auxiliary verb *haben: er hat gebändigt.*

b) *abfassen v/t. (sep., -ge-, h):* In conjugation the prefix *ab* must be separated from the primary verb *fassen: er faßt ab; er hat abgefaßt.*

c) *verderben v/i. (irr., no -ge-, sein): irr.* following the verb refers the reader to the list of irregular German verbs in the appendix (p. 573) for the principal parts of this particular verb: *es verdarb; es ist verdorben.*

d) *abfallen v/i. (irr. fallen, sep., -ge-, sein):* A reference such as *irr. fallen* indicates that the compound verb *abfallen* is conjugated exactly like the primary verb *fallen* as given in the list of irregular verbs: *er fiel ab; er ist abgefallen.*

e) *sieden v/t. and v/i. ([irr.,] ge-, h):* The square brackets indicate that *sieden* can be treated as a regular or irregular verb: *er siedete or er sott; er hat gesiedet or er hat gesotten.*

III. Prepositions. Prepositions governing a headword are given in both languages. The grammatical construction following a German preposition is indicated only if the preposition governs two different cases. If a German preposition applies to all translations it is given only with the first whereas its English equivalents are given after each translation: *schützen* ... protect (*gegen, vor dat.* against, from), defend (against, from), guard (against, from); shelter (from).

IV. Subdivision. Entries have been subdivided by Arabic numerals
a) to distinguish the various parts of speech: *laut 1. adj.* ...; *2. adv.* ...; *3. prp.* ...; *4. ♀ m* ...;
b) to distinguish between the transitive and intransitive meanings of a verb if these differ in their translations;
c) to show that in case of change of meaning a noun or verb may be differently inflected or conjugated: *Bau m 1.* (-[e]s/*no pl.*)...; *2.* (-[e]s/-ten) ...; *3.* (-[e]s/-e) ...; *schwimmen v/i.* (*irr.*, ge-) *1.* (*sein*) ...; *2.* (*h*) ...

If grammatical indications come before the subdivision they refer to all translations following: *Alte* (-*n*/-*n*) *1. m* ...; *2. f* ...; *humpeln v/i.* (ge-) *1.* (*sein*) ...; *2.* (*h*) ...

8. Grammatical References in Part II. Parts of speech (adjective, verb, etc.) have been indicated only in cases of doubt. Entries have been subdivided by Arabic numerals to distinguish the various parts of speech.

a) (~*ally*) after an English adjective means that the adverb is formed by affixing ...*ally*: *automatic* (~*ally*) = *automatically*.

b) *irr.* following a verb refers the reader to the list of irregular English verbs in the appendix (p. 575) for the principal parts of this particular verb. A reference such as *irr. fall* indicates that the compound verb, e.g. *befall*, is conjugated exactly like the primary verb *fall*.

Symbols and Abbreviations Used in This Dictionary

1. Symbols

The swung dash or tilde (~ ♀, ~ ♀) serves as a mark of repetition within an entry. The tilde in bold type (~) represents either the complete word at the beginning of the entry or the unchanged part of that word which is followed by a vertical line (|). The simple tilde (~) represents: a) the headword immediately preceding, which itself may contain a tilde in bold type; b) in phonetic transcription, any part of the preceding transcription that remains unchanged.

When the initial letter changes from small to capital or vice versa, the usual tilde is replaced by ♀ or ♀.

Examples: *abandon* [ə'bændən], ~*ment* [~nmənt = ə'bændənmənt]; *certi|ficate,* ~*fication,* ~*fy,* ~*tude. Drama,* ~*tiker,* ♀*tisch; Haus|flur,* ~*frau; fassen: sich kurz* ~.

□ after an English adjective means that an adverb may be formed regularly from it by adding ...*ly,* or by changing ...*le* into ...*ly,* or ...*y* into ...*ily;* e.g.: *rich* □ = *richly; acceptable* □ = *acceptably; happy* □ = *happily.*

F   *familiar,* familiär; *colloquial usage,* Umgangssprache.

P   *low colloquialism,* populär, Sprache des Volkes.

V   *vulgar,* vulgär.

†   *archaic,* veraltet.

 ✒ *rare, little used,* selten.

ⓤ *scientific term,* wissenschaftlich.

♀ *botany,* Botanik.

⊕ *engineering,* Technik; *handicraft,* Handwerk.

⚒ *mining,* Bergbau.

✕ *military term,* militärisch.

⚓ *nautical term,* Schiffahrt.

† *commercial term,* Handelswesen.

🚃 *railway, railroad,* Eisenbahn.

✈ *aviation,* Flugwesen.

📯 *postal affairs,* Postwesen.

♪   *musical term*, Musik.
△   *architecture*, Architektur.
⚡   *electrical engineering*, Elektrotechnik.
ⓈⓈ   *legal term*, Rechtswissenschaft.

⅄   *mathematics*, Mathematik.
⚘   *farming*, Landwirtschaft.
♏   *chemistry*, Chemie.
☤   *medicine*, Medizin.

2. Abbreviations

a.   *also*, auch.
abbr.   *abbreviation*, Abkürzung.
acc.   *accusative (case)*, Akkusativ.
adj.   *adjective*, Adjektiv.
adv.   *adverb*, Adverb.
allg.   *commonly*, allgemein.
Am.   *American English*, amerikanisches Englisch.
anat.   *anatomy*, Anatomie.
appr.   *approximately*, etwa.
art.   *article*, Artikel.
ast.   *astronomy*, Astronomie.
attr.   *attributively*, attributiv.

biol.   *biology*, Biologie.
Brt.   *British English*, britisches Englisch.
b.s.   *bad sense*, in schlechtem Sinne.
bsd.   *especially*, besonders.

cj.   *conjunction*, Konjunktion.
co.   *comic(al)*, scherzhaft.
coll.   *collectively*, als Sammelwort.
comp.   *comparative*, Komparativ.
contp.   *contemptuously*, verächtlich.

dat.   *dative (case)*, Dativ.
dem.   *demonstrative*, Demonstrativ...

ea.   *one another, each other*, einander.
eccl.   *ecclesiastical*, kirchlich.
e-e, e-e, e-e a(n), eine.
e-m, e-m, e-m to a(n), einem.
e-n, e-n, e-n a(n), einen.
engS.   *more strictly taken*, in engerem Sinne.
e-r, e-r, e-r of a(n), to a(n), einer.
e-s, e-s, e-s of a(n), eines.
esp.   *especially*, besonders.
et., et., et. something, etwas.
etc.   *et cetera, and so on*, und so weiter.

f   *feminine*, weiblich.
fig.   *figuratively*, bildlich.
frz.   *French*, französisch.

gen.   *genitive (case)*. Genitiv.
geogr.   *geography*, Geographie.
geol.   *geology*, Geologie.
geom.   *geometry*, Geometrie.
ger.   *gerund*, Gerundium.
Ggs.   *antonym*, Gegensatz.
gr.   *grammar*, Grammatik.

h   *have*, haben.
hist.   *history*, Geschichte.
hunt.   *hunting*, Jagdwesen.

ichth.   *ichthyology*, Ichthyologie.
impers.   *impersonal*, unpersönlich.
indef.   *indefinite*, Indefinit...
inf.   *infinitive (mood)*, Infinitiv.
int.   *interjection*, Interjektion.
interr.   *interrogative*, Interrogativ...
iro.   *ironically*, ironisch.
irr.   *irregular*, unregelmäßig.

j., j., j. someone, jemand.
j-m, j-m, j-m to s.o. jemandem.
j-n, j-n, j-n someone, jemanden.
j-s, j-s, j-s, someone's, jemandes.

konkr.   *concretely*, konkret.

ling.   *linguistics*, Linguistik.
lit.   *literary*, nur in der Schriftsprache vorkommend.

m   *masculine*, männlich.
m-e, m-e, m-e my, meine.
m-r   *of my, to my*, meiner.
metall.   *metallurgy*, Metallurgie.
meteor.   *meteorology*, Meteorologie.
min.   *mineralogy*, Mineralogie.
mot.   *motoring*, Kraftfahrwesen.
mount.   *mountaineering*, Bergsteigerei.
mst   *mostly, usually*, meistens.
myth.   *mythology*, Mythologie.

n   *neuter*, sächlich.
nom.   *nominative (case)*, Nominativ.
npr.   *proper name*, Eigenname.

od.   *or*, oder.
opt.   *optics*, Optik.

orn.	ornithology, Ornithologie.
o.s.	oneself, sich.
P.,	person, Person.
p.	person, Person.
paint.	painting, Malerei.
parl.	parliamentary term, parlamentarischer Ausdruck.
pass.	passive voice, Passiv.
pers.	personal, Personal...
pharm.	pharmacy, Pharmazie.
phls.	philosophy, Philosophie.
phot.	photography, Photographie.
phys.	physics, Physik.
physiol.	physiology, Physiologie.
pl.	plural, Plural.
poet.	poetry, Dichtung.
pol.	politics, Politik.
poss.	possessive, Possessiv...
p.p.	past participle, Partizip Perfekt.
p.pr.	present participle, Partizip Präsens.
pred.	predicative, prädikativ.
pres.	present, Präsens.
pret.	preterit(e), Präteritum.
pron.	pronoun, Pronomen.
prov.	provincialism, Provinzialismus.
prp.	preposition, Präposition.
psych.	psychology, Psychologie.
refl.	reflexive, reflexiv.
rel.	relative, Relativ...
rhet.	rhetoric, Rhetorik.
S., S.	thing, Sache.
s.	see, refer to, siehe.
schott.	Scotch, schottisch.
s-e, s-e,	s-e his, one's, seine.
sep.	separable, abtrennbar.
sg.	singular, Singular.

sl.	slang, Slang.
s-m, s-m,	s-m to his, to one's, seinem.
s-n, s-n,	s-n his, one's, seinen.
s.o., s.o.,	s.o. someone, jemand(en).
s-r, s-r,	s-r of his, of one's, to his, to one's, seiner.
s-s, s-s,	s-s of his, of one's, seines.
s.th., s.th.,	s.th. something, etwas.
subj.	subjunctive (mood), Konjunktiv.
sup.	superlative, Superlativ.
surv.	surveying, Landvermessung.
tel.	telegraphy, Telegraphie.
teleph.	telephony, Fernsprechwesen.
thea.	theat|re, Am. -er, Theater.
typ.	typography, Typographie.
u., u.	and, und.
univ.	university, Hochschulwesen, Studentensprache.
v/aux.	auxiliary verb, Hilfsverb.
vb.	verb, Verb.
vet.	veterinary medicine, Veterinärmedizin.
vgl.	confer, vergleiche.
v/i.	verb intransitive, intransitives Verb.
v/refl.	verb reflexive, reflexives Verb.
v/t.	verb transitive, transitives Verb.
weitS.	more widely taken, in weiterem Sinne.
z.B.	for example, zum Beispiel.
zo.	zoology, Zoologie.
zs.	together, zusammen.
Zssg(n).	compound word(s), Zusammensetzung(en).

Guide to Pronunciation
for the German-English Part

The length of vowels is indicated by [ː] following the vowel symbol, the stress by [ˈ] preceding the stressed syllable. The glottal stop [ʔ] is the forced stop between one word or syllable and a following one beginning with a vowel, as in *unentbehrlich* [unˈʔɛntˈbeːrlɪç].

A. Vowels

[a] as in French *carte*: Mann [man].

[ɑː] as in *father*: Wagen [ˈvɑːgən].

[e] as in *bed*: Edikt [eˈdikt].

[eː] resembles the sound in *day*: Weg [veːk].

[ə] unstressed e as in *ago*: Bitte [ˈbitə].

[ɛ] as in *fair*: männlich [ˈmɛnlɪç], Geld [gɛlt].

[ɛː] same sound but long: zählen [ˈtsɛːlən].

[i] as in *Wind* [vint].

[iː] as in *meet*: hier [hiːr].

[ɔ] as in *long*: Ort [ɔrt].

[ɔː] same sound but long as in *draw*: Komfort [kɔmˈfɔːr].

[o] as in *molest*: Moral [moˈrɑːl].

[oː] resembles the English sound in *go* [gou] but without the [u]: Boot [boːt].

[øː] as in French *feu*. The sound may be acquired by saying [e] through closely rounded lips: schön [ʃøːn].

[ø] same sound but short: Ökonomie [økonoˈmiː].

[œ] as in French *neuf*. The sound resembles the English vowel in *her*. Lips, however, must be well rounded as for [ɔ]: öffnen [ˈœfnən].

[u] as in *book*: Mutter [ˈmutər].

[uː] as in *boot*: Uhr [uːr].

[y] almost like the French u as in *sur*. It may be acquired by saying [i] through fairly closely rounded lips: Glück [glyk].

[yː] same sound but long: führen [ˈfyːrən].

B. Diphthongs

[aɪ] as in *like*: Mai [maɪ].
[au] as in *mouse*: Maus [maus].

[ɔʏ] as in *boy*: Beute [ˈbɔʏtə], Läufer [ˈlɔʏfər].

C. Consonants

[b] as in *better*: besser [ˈbɛsər].

[d] as in *dance*: du [duː].

[f] as in *find*: finden [ˈfindən], Vater [ˈfɑːtər], Philosoph [filoˈzoːf].

[g] as in *gold*: Gold [gɔlt], Geld [gɛlt].

[ʒ] as in *measure*: Genie [ʒeˈniː], Journalist [ʒurnaˈlist].

[h] as in *house* but not aspirated: Haus [haus].

[ç] an approximation to this sound may be acquired by assuming the mouth-configuration for [i] and emitting a strong current of breath: Licht [liçt], Mönch [mœnç], lustig [ˈlustiç].

[x] as in Scotch *loch*. Whereas [ç] is pronounced at the front of the mouth, [x] is pronounced in the throat: Loch [lɔx].

[j] as in *year*: ja [jɑː].

[k] as in *kick*: keck [kɛk], Tag [tɑːk], Chronist [kroˈnist], Café [kaˈfeː].

[l] as in *lump*. Pronounced like English initial "clear l": lassen [ˈlasən].

[m] as in *mouse*: Maus [maus].

[n] as in *not*: nein [naɪn].

[ŋ] as in *sing, drink*: singen [ˈziŋən], trinken [ˈtriŋkən].

[p] as in *pass*: Paß [pas], Weib [vaɪp], obgleich [ɔpˈglaɪç].

[r] as in *rot*. There are two pronunciations: the frontal or lingual r and the uvular r (the latter unknown in England): *rot* [ro:t].

[s] as in *miss*. Unvoiced when final, doubled, or next a voiceless consonant: *Glas* [glɑ:s], *Masse* ['masə], *Mast* [mast], *naß* [nas].

[z] as in *zero*. S voiced when initial in a word or syllable: *Sohn* [zo:n], *Rose* ['ro:zə].

[ʃ] as in *ship*: *Schiff* [ʃif], *Charme* [ʃarm], *Spiel* [ʃpi:l], *Stein* [ʃtaɪn].

[t] as in *tea*: *Tee* [te:], *Thron* [tro:n], *Stadt* [ʃtat], *Bad* [bɑ:t], *Findling* ['fintliŋ], *Wind* [vint].

[v] as in *vast*: *Vase* ['vɑ:zə], *Winter* ['vintər].

[ã, ɛ̃, õ] are nasalized vowels. Examples: *Ensemble* [ã'sã:bəl], *Terrain* [tɛ'rɛ̃:], *Bonbon* [bõ'bõ:].

List of Suffixes

often given without phonetic transcription

-bar	[-bɑ:r]		-ist	[-ist]
-chen	[-çən]		-keit	[-kaɪt]
-d	[-t]		-lich	[-liç]
-de	[-də]		-ling	[-liŋ]
-ei	[-aɪ]		-losigkeit	[-lo:ziçkaɪt]
-en	[-ən]		-nis	[-nis]
-end	[-ənt]		-sal	[-zɑ:l]
-er	[-ər]		-sam	[-zɑ:m]
-haft	[-haft]		-schaft	[-ʃaft]
-heit	[-haɪt]		-sieren	[-zi:rən]
-ie	[-i:]		-ste	[-stə]
-ieren	[-i:rən]		-tät	[-tɛ:t]
-ig	[-iç]		-tum	[-tu:m]
-ik	[-ik]		-ung	[-uŋ]
-in	[-in]		-ungs-	[-uŋs-]
-isch	[-iʃ]			

Erläuterung der phonetischen Umschrift im englisch-deutschen Teil

A. Vokale und Diphthonge

[ɑ:] reines langes a, wie in Vater, kam, Schwan: *far* [fɑ:], *father* ['fɑ:ðə].

[ʌ] kommt im Deutschen nicht vor. Kurzes dunkles a, bei dem die Lippen nicht gerundet sind. Vorn und offen gebildet: *butter* ['bʌtə], *come* [kʌm], *colour* ['kʌlə], *blood* [blʌd], *flourish* ['flʌriʃ], *twopence* ['tʌpəns].

[æ] heller, ziemlich offener, nicht zu kurzer Laut. Raum zwischen Zunge und Gaumen noch größer als bei ä in Ähre: *fat* [fæt], *man* [mæn].

[ɛə] nicht zu offenes halblanges ä; im Englischen nur vor r, das als ein dem ä nachhallendes ə erscheint: *bare* [bɛə], *pair* [pɛə], *there* [ðɛə].

[ai] Bestandteile: helles, zwischen ɑ und æ liegendes a und schwächeres offenes i. Die Zunge hebt sich halbwegs zur i-Stellung: *I* [ai], *lie* [lai], *dry* [drai].

[au] Bestandteile: helles, zwischen ɑ und æ liegendes a und schwächeres offenes u: *house* [haus], *now* [nau].

[ei] halboffenes e, nach i auslautend, indem die Zunge sich halbwegs zur i-Stellung hebt: *date* [deit], *play* [plei], *obey* [ə'bei].

[e] halboffenes kurzes e, etwas geschlossener als das e in Bett: *bed* [bed], *less* [les].

[ə] flüchtiger Gleitlaut, ähnlich dem deutschen flüchtig gesprochenen e in Gelage: *about* [ə'baut], *butter* ['bʌtə], *nation* ['neiʃən], *connect* [kə'nekt].

[i:] langes i wie in lieb, Bibel, aber etwas offener einsetzend als im Deutschen; wird in Südengland doppellautig gesprochen, indem sich die Zunge allmählich zur i-Stellung hebt: *scene* [si:n], *sea* [si:], *feet* [fi:t], *ceiling* ['si:liŋ].

[i] kurzes offenes i wie in bin, mit: *big* [big], *city* ['siti].

[iə] halboffenes halblanges i mit nachhallendem ə: *here* [hiə], *hear* [hiə], *inferior* [in'fiəriə].

[ou] halboffenes langes o, in schwaches u auslautend; keine Rundung der Lippen, kein Heben der Zunge: *note* [nout], *boat* [bout], *below* [bi'lou].

[ɔ:] offener langer, zwischen a und o schwebender Laut: *fall* [fɔ:l], *nought* [nɔ:t], *or* [ɔ:], *before* [bi'fɔ:].

[ɔ] offener kurzer, zwischen a und o schwebender Laut, offener als das o in Motto: *god* [gɔd], *not* [nɔt], *wash* [wɔʃ], *hobby* ['hɔbi].

[ə:] im Deutschen fehlender Laut; offenes langes ö, etwa wie gedehnt gesprochenes ö in öffnen, Mörder; kein Vorstülpen oder Runden der Lippen, kein Heben der Zunge: *word* [wə:d], *girl* [gə:l], *learn* [lə:n], *murmur* ['mə:mə].

[ɔi] Bestandteile: offenes o und schwächeres offenes i. Die Zunge hebt sich halbwegs zur i-Stellung: *voice* [vɔis], *boy* [bɔi], *annoy* [ə'nɔi].

[u:] langes u wie in Buch, doch ohne Lippenrundung; vielfach diphthongisch als halboffenes langes u mit nachhallendem geschlossenen u: *fool* [fu:l], *shoe* [ʃu:], *you* [ju:], *rule* [ru:l], *canoe* [kə'nu:].

[uə] halboffenes halblanges u mit nachhallendem ə: *poor* [puə], *sure* [ʃuə], *allure* [ə'ljuə].

[u] flüchtiges u: *put* [put], *look* [luk], *full* [ful].

Die **Länge eines Vokals** wird durch [:] bezeichnet, z.B. *ask* [ɑ:sk], *astir* [ə'stə:].

Vereinzelt werden auch die folgenden französischen Nasallaute gebraucht: [ã] wie in frz. *blanc*, [õ] wie in frz. *bonbon* und [ɛ̃] wie in frz. *vin*.

B. Konsonanten

[r] nur vor Vokalen gesprochen. Völlig verschieden vom deutschen Zungenspitzen- oder Zäpfchen-r. Die Zungenspitze bildet mit der oberen Zahnwulst eine Enge, durch die der Ausatmungsstrom mit Stimmton hindurchgetrieben wird, ohne den Laut zu rollen. Am Ende eines Wortes wird r nur bei Bindung mit dem Anlautvokal des folgenden Wortes gesprochen: *rose* [rouz], *pride* [praid], *there is* [ðɛərˈiz].

[ʒ] stimmhaftes sch, wie g in Genie, j in Journal: *azure* [ˈæʒə], *jazz* [dʒæz], *jeep* [dʒiːp], *large* [lɑːdʒ].

[ʃ] stimmloses sch, wie im Deutschen Schnee, rasch: *shake* [ʃeik], *washing* [ˈwɔʃiŋ], *lash* [læʃ].

[θ] im Deutschen nicht vorhandener stimmloser Lispellaut; durch Anlegen der Zunge an die oberen Schneidezähne hervorgebracht: *thin* [θin], *path* [pɑː θ], *method* [ˈmeθəd].

[ð] derselbe Laut wie θ, nur stimmhaft, d.h. mit Stimmton: *there* [ðɛə], *breathe* [briːð], *father* [ˈfɑːðə].

[s] stimmloser Zischlaut, entsprechend dem deutschen ß in Spaß, reißen: *see* [siː], *hats* [hæts], *decide* [diˈsaid].

[z] stimmhafter Zischlaut wie im Deutschen sausen: *zeal* [ziːl], *rise* [raiz], *horizon* [həˈraizn].

[ŋ] wird wie der deutsche Nasenlaut in fangen, singen gebildet: *ring* [riŋ], *singer* [ˈsiŋə].

[ŋk] derselbe Laut mit nachfolgendem k wie im Deutschen senken, Wink: *ink* [iŋk], *tinker* [ˈtiŋkə].

[w] flüchtiges, mit Lippe an Lippe gesprochenes w, aus der Mundstellung für u: gebildet: *will* [wil], *swear* [swɛə], *queen* [kwiːn].

[f] stimmloser Lippenlaut wie im Deutschen flott, Pfeife: *fat* [fæt], *tough* [tʌf], *effort* [ˈefət].

[v] stimmhafter Lippenlaut wie im Deutschen Vase, Ventil: *vein* [vein], *velvet* [ˈvelvit].

[j] flüchtiger zwischen j und i schwebender Laut: *onion* [ˈʌnjən], *yes* [jes], *filial* [ˈfiljəl].

Die Betonung der englischen Wörter wird durch das Zeichen [ˈ] vor der zu betonenden Silbe angegeben, z.B. *onion* [ˈʌnjən]. Sind zwei Silben eines Wortes mit Tonzeichen versehen, so sind beide gleichmäßig zu betonen, z.B. *unsound* [ˈʌnˈsaund].

Um Raum zu sparen, werden die Endung -ed* und das Plural-s** der englischen Stichwörter hier im Vorwort einmal mit Lautschrift gegeben, erscheinen dann aber im Wörterverzeichnis ohne Lautschrift, sofern keine Ausnahmen vorliegen.

* [-d] nach Vokalen und stimmhaften Konsonanten; [-t] nach stimmlosen Konsonanten; [-id] nach auslautendem d und t.

** [-z] nach Vokalen und stimmhaften Konsonanten; [-s] nach stimmlosen Konsonanten.

Numerals

Cardinal Numbers

0	null *nought, zero, cipher*	51	einundfünfzig *fifty-one*
1	eins *one*	60	sechzig *sixty*
2	zwei *two*	61	einundsechzig *sixty-one*
3	drei *three*	70	siebzig *seventy*
4	vier *four*	71	einundsiebzig *seventy-one*
5	fünf *five*	80	achtzig *eighty*
6	sechs *six*	81	einundachtzig *eighty-one*
7	sieben *seven*	90	neunzig *ninety*
8	acht *eight*	91	einundneunzig *ninety-one*
9	neun *nine*	100	hundert *a* or *one hundred*
10	zehn *ten*	101	hundert(und)eins *a hundred and one*
11	elf *eleven*		
12	zwölf *twelve*	200	zweihundert *two hundred*
13	dreizehn *thirteen*	300	dreihundert *three hundred*
14	vierzehn *fourteen*	572	fünfhundert(und)zweiundsiebzig *five hundred and seventy-two*
15	fünfzehn *fifteen*		
16	sechzehn *sixteen*		
17	siebzehn *seventeen*	1000	tausend *a* or *one thousand*
18	achtzehn *eighteen*	1972	neunzehnhundertzweiundsiebzig *nineteen hundred and seventy-two*
19	neunzehn *nineteen*		
20	zwanzig *twenty*		
21	einundzwanzig *twenty-one*	500 000	fünfhunderttausend *five hundred thousand*
22	zweiundzwanzig *twenty-two*		
23	dreiundzwanzig *twenty-three*	1 000 000	eine Million *a* or *one million*
30	dreißig *thirty*		
31	einunddreißig *thirty-one*	2 000 000	zwei Millionen *two million*
40	vierzig *forty*		
41	einundvierzig *forty-one*	1 000 000 000	eine Milliarde *a* or *one milliard (Am. billion)*
50	fünfzig *fifty*		

Ordinal Numbers

1.	erste *first (1st)*	16.	sechzehnte *sixteenth*
2.	zweite *second (2nd)*	17.	siebzehnte *seventeenth*
3.	dritte *third (3rd)*	18.	achtzehnte *eighteenth*
4.	vierte *fourth (4th)*	19.	neunzehnte *nineteenth*
5.	fünfte *fifth (5th), etc.*	20.	zwanzigste *twentieth*
6.	sechste *sixth*	21.	einundzwanzigste *twenty-first*
7.	siebente *seventh*	22.	zweiundzwanzigste *twenty-second*
8.	achte *eighth*		
9.	neunte *ninth*	23.	dreiundzwanzigste *twenty-third*
10.	zehnte *tenth*		
11.	elfte *eleventh*	30.	dreißigste *thirtieth*
12.	zwölfte *twelfth*	31.	einunddreißigste *thirty-first*
13.	dreizehnte *thirteenth*	40.	vierzigste *fortieth*
14.	vierzehnte *fourteenth*	41.	einundvierzigste *forty-first*
15.	fünfzehnte *fifteenth*	50.	fünfzigste *fiftieth*

51. einundfünfzigste *fifty-first*
60. sechzigste *sixtieth*
61. einundsechzigste *sixty-first*
70. siebzigste *seventieth*
71. einundsiebzigste *seventy-first*
80. achtzigste *eightieth*
81. einundachtzigste *eighty-first*
90. neunzigste *ninetieth*
100. hundertste (*one*) *hundredth*
101. hundert(und)erste (*one*) *hundred and first*
200. zweihundertste *two hundredth*

300. dreihundertste *three hundredth*
572. fünfhundert(und)zweiund-siebzigste *five hundred and seventy-second*
1000. tausendste (*one*) *thousandth*
1970. neunzehnhundert(und)sieb-zigste *nineteen hundred and seventy*
500000. fünfhunderttausendste *five hundred thousandth*
1000000. millionste (*one*) *millionth*
2000000. zweimillionste *two millionth*

Fractional Numbers and other Numerical Values

$1/2$ halb *one* or *a half*
$1/2$ eine halbe Meile *half a mile*
$1\frac{1}{2}$ anderthalb *or* eineinhalb *one and a half*
$2\frac{1}{2}$ zweieinhalb *two and a half*
$1/3$ ein Drittel *one* or *a third*
$2/3$ zwei Drittel *two thirds*
$1/4$ ein Viertel *one fourth, one* or *a quarter*
$3/4$ drei Viertel *three fourths, three quarters*
$1\frac{1}{4}$ ein und eine viertel Stunde *one hour and a quarter*
$1/5$ ein Fünftel *one* or *a fifth*
$3\frac{4}{5}$ drei vier Fünftel *three and four fifths*
0,4 null Komma vier *point four (.4)*
2,5 zwei Komma fünf *two point five (2.5)*

einfach *single*
zweifach *double, twofold*
dreifach *threefold, treble, triple*
vierfach *fourfold, quadruple*
fünffach *fivefold, quintuple*

einmal *once*
zweimal *twice*
drei-, vier-, fünfmal *three* or *four* or *five times*
zweimal soviel(e) *twice as much* or *many*

erstens, zweitens, drittens *first(ly), secondly, thirdly; in the first* or *second* or *third place*

$2 \times 3 = 6$ zwei mal drei ist sechs, zwei multipliziert mit drei ist sechs *twice three are* or *make six, two multiplied by three are* or *make six*

$7 + 8 = 15$ sieben plus acht ist fünf-zehn *seven plus eight are fifteen*

$10 - 3 = 7$ zehn minus drei ist sieben *ten minus three are seven*

$20 : 5 = 4$ zwanzig (dividiert) durch fünf ist vier *twenty divided by five make four*

PART I

GERMAN-ENGLISH
DICTIONARY

A

Aal *ichth.* [ɑ:l] *m* (-[e]s/-e) eel; **'⌐-glatt** *adj.* (as) slippery as an eel.

Aas [ɑ:s] *n* 1. (-es/⌐-e) carrion, carcass; 2. *fig.* (-es/Äser) beast; **'⌐geier** *orn. m* vulture.

ab [ap] 1. *prp.* (*dat.*): ⌐ Brüssel from Brussels onwards; ⌐ Fabrik, Lager etc. ✝ ex works, warehouse, *etc.*; 2. *prp.* (*dat.*, ✝ *acc.*): ⌐ erstem or ersten März from March 1st, on and after March 1st; 3. ✝ *prp.* (*gen.*) less; ⌐ Unkosten less charges; 4. *adv. time:* von jetzt ⌐ from now on, in futur⌐; ⌐ und zu from time to time, now and then; von da ⌐ from that time forward; *space: thea.* exit, *pl.* exeunt; von da ⌐ from there (on).

abä⌐i⌐er|n ['apʔ-] *v/t.* (*sep.*, -ge-, h) al⌐er, modify; *parl.* amend; **'⌐ung** *f* alteration, modification; *parl.* amendment (*to bill, etc.*); **'⌐ungsantrag** *parl. m* amendment.

abarbeiten ['apʔ-] *v/t.* (*sep.*, -ge-, h) work off (*debt*); sich ⌐ drudge, toil.

Abart ['apʔ-] *f* variety.

'Abbau *m* 1. (-[e]s/*no pl.*) pulling down, demolition (*of structure*); dismantling (*of machine, etc.*); dismissal, discharge (*of personnel*); reduction (*of staff, prices, etc.*); cut (*of prices, etc.*); 2. ⚒ (-[e]s/-e) working, exploitation; **'⌐en** *v/t.* (*sep.*, -ge-, h) pull or take down, demolish (*structure*); dismantle (*machine, etc.*); dismiss, discharge (*personnel*); reduce (*staff, prices, etc.*); cut (*prices, etc.*); ⚒ work, exploit.

'ab|beißen *v/t.* (*irr.* beißen, *sep.*, -ge-, h) bite off; **'⌐bekommen** *v/t.* (*irr.* kommen, *sep.*, no -ge-, h) get off; s-n Teil or et. ⌐ get one's share; et. ⌐ be hurt, get hurt.

abberuf|en *v/t.* (*irr.* rufen, *sep.*, no -ge-, h) recall; **'⌐ung** *f* recall.

'ab|bestellen *v/t.* (*sep.*, no -ge-, h) countermand, cancel one's order for (*goods, etc.*); cancel one's subscription to, discontinue (*newspaper, etc.*); **'⌐biegen** *v/i.* (*irr.* biegen, *sep.*, -ge-, sein) *p.* turn off; *road:* turn off, bend; nach rechts (links) ⌐ turn right (left); von e-r Straße ⌐ turn off a road.

'Abbild *n* likeness; image; **'⌐en** ['⌐dən] *v/t.* (*sep.*, -ge-, h) figure, represent; sie ist auf der ersten Seite abgebildet her picture is on the front page; **⌐ung** ['⌐duŋ] *f* picture, illustration.

'abbinden *v/t.* (*irr.* binden, *sep.*,

-ge-, h) untie, unbind, remove; ⚕ ligate, tie up.

'Abbitte *f* apology; ⌐ leisten or tun make one's apology (*bei j-m wegen et. to s.o. for s.th.*); **'⌐n** *v/t.* (*irr.* bitten, *sep.*, -ge-, h): j-m et. ⌐ apologize to s.o. for s.th.

'ab|blasen *v/t.* (*irr.* blasen, *sep.*, -ge-, h) blow off (*dust, etc.*); call off (*strike, etc.*), cancel; ✗ break off (*attack*); **'⌐blättern** *v/i.* (*sep.*, -ge-, sein) paint, *etc.*: scale, peel (off); ⚕ *skin:* desquamate; ♃ shed the leaves; **'⌐blenden** (*sep.*, -ge-, h) 1. *v/t.* screen (*light*); *mot.* dim, dip (*headlights*); 2. *v/i. mot.* dim or dip the headlights; *phot.* stop down; **'⌐blitzen** ✝ *v/i.* (*sep.*, -ge-, sein) meet with a rebuff; ⌐ lassen snub; **'⌐brausen** (*sep.*, -ge-) 1. *v/refl.* (h) have a shower(-bath), douche; 2. ✝ *v/i.* (sein) rush off; **'⌐brechen** (*irr.* brechen, *sep.*, -ge-) 1. *v/t.* (h) break off (*a. fig.*); pull down, demolish (*building, etc.*); strike (*tent*); *fig.* stop; das Lager ⌐ break up camp, strike tents; 2. *v/i.* (sein) break off; 3. *fig. v/i.* (h) stop; **'⌐bremsen** *v/t.* and *v/i.* (*sep.*, -ge-, h) slow down; brake; **'⌐brennen** (*irr.* brennen, *sep.*, -ge-) 1. *v/t.* (h) burn down (*building, etc.*); let or set off (*firework*); 2. *v/i.* (sein) burn away or down; s. abgebrannt; **'⌐bringen** *v/t.* (*irr.* bringen, *sep.*, -ge-, h) get off; j-n ⌐ von argue s.o. out of; dissuade s.o. from; **'⌐bröckeln** *v/i.* (*sep.*, -ge-, sein) crumble (*a. ✝*).

'Abbruch *m* pulling down, demolition (*of building, etc.*); rupture (*of relations*); breaking off (*of negotiations, etc.*); *fig.* damage, injury; j-m ⌐ tun damage s.o.

'ab|brühen *v/t.* (*sep.*, -ge-, h) scald; s. abgebrüht; **'⌐bürsten** *v/t.* (*sep.*, -ge-, h) brush off (*dirt, etc.*); brush (*coat, etc.*); **'⌐büßen** *v/t.* (*sep.*, -ge-, h) expiate, atone for (*sin, etc.*); serve (*sentence*). [bet.]

Abc [ɑːbeˈtseː] *n* (-/-) ABC, alpha-]

'abdank|en *v/i.* (*sep.*, -ge-, h) resign; *ruler:* abdicate; **'⌐ung** *f* (-/-en) resignation, abdication.

'ab|decken *v/t.* (*sep.*, -ge-, h) uncover; untile (*roof*); unroof (*building*); clear (*table*); cover; **'⌐dichten** *v/t.* (*sep.*, -ge-, h) make tight; seal up (*window, etc.*); ⊕ pack (*gland, etc.*); **'⌐dienen** *v/t.* (*sep.*, -ge-, h): s-e Zeit ⌐ ✗ serve one's time; **'⌐drängen** *v/t.* (*sep.*, -ge-, h) push aside; **'⌐drehen** (*sep.*, -ge-, h)

2*

1. *v/t.* twist off (*wire*); turn off (*water*, *gas*, *etc.*); ⚡ switch off (*light*); **2.** ⚓, ≷ *v/i.* change one's course; '⸜drosseln *mot. v/t.* (*sep.*, -ge-, *h*) throttle.

'**Abdruck** *m* (-[e]s/⸜e) impression, print, mark; cast; '⸜en *v/t.* (*sep.*, -ge-, *h*) print; publish (*article*).

'**abdrücken** (*sep.*, -ge-, *h*) **1.** *v/t.* fire (*gun*, *etc.*); F hug *or* squeeze affectionately; *sich* ⸜ leave an impression *or* a mark; **2.** *v/i.* pull the trigger.

Abend ['ɑːbənt] *m* (-s/-e) evening; *am* ⸜ in the evening, at night; *heute* **abend** tonight; *morgen* (*gestern*) **abend** tomorrow (last) night; *s.* essen; '⸜anzug *m* evening dress; '⸜blatt *n* evening paper; '⸜brot *n* supper, dinner; '⸜dämmerung *f* (evening) twilight, dusk; '⸜essen *n* *s.* Abendbrot; '⸜gesellschaft *f* evening party; '⸜kasse *thea. f* box-office; '⸜kleid *n* evening dress *or* gown; '⸜land *n* (-[e]s/*no pl.*) the Occident; ⸜ländisch *adj.* ['⸜lendiʃ] western, occidental; '⸜mahl *eccl. n* (-[e]s/-e) the (Holy) Communion, the Lord's Supper; '⸜rot *n* evening *or* sunset glow. [evening.)

abends *adv.* ['ɑːbənts] in the)
'**Abend|schule** *f* evening school, night-school; '⸜sonne *f* setting sun; '⸜toilette *f* evening dress; '⸜wind *m* evening breeze; '⸜zeitung *f* evening paper.

Abenteu|er ['ɑːbəntɔʏər] *n* (-s/-) adventure; ⸜erlich *adj.* adventurous; *fig.*: strange; wild, fantastic; ⸜rer ['⸜ɔʏrər] *m* (-s/-) adventurer.

aber ['ɑːbər] **1.** *adv.* again; *Tausende und* ⸜ *Tausende* thousands upon thousands; **2.** *cj.* but; *oder* ⸜ otherwise, (or) else; **3.** *int.*: ⸜! now then!; ⸜, ⸜! come, come!; ⸜ *nein*! no!, on the contrary!; **4.** ⸟ *n* (-s/-) but.

'**Aber|glaube** *m* superstition; ⸟-gläubisch *adj.* ['⸜ɡlɔʏbiʃ] superstitious.

aberkenn|en ['ap⁹-] *v/t.* (*irr.* kennen, *sep.*, *no* -ge-, *h*): *j-m et.* ⸜ deprive s.o. of s.th. (*a.* ⚖); dispossess s.o. of s.th.; '⸟ung *f* (-/-en) deprivation (*a.* ⚖); dispossession.

aber|malig *adj.* ['ɑːbərmɑːliç] repeated; ⸜mals *adv.* ['⸜s] again, once more.

ab|ernten ['ap⁹-] *v/t.* (*sep.*, -ge-, *h*) reap, harvest; ⸜essen ['ap⁹-] (*irr.* essen, *sep.*, -ge-, *h*) **1.** *v/t.* clear (*plate*). **2.** *v/i.* finish eating; '⸜fahren (*irr.* fahren, *sep.*, -ge-) **1.** *v/i.* (*sein*) leave (*nach her*), depart (for), start (for); set out *or* off (for); **2.** *v/t.* (*h*) carry *or* cart away (*load*).

'**Abfahrt** *f* departure (*nach her*), start (for); setting out *or* off (for); *skiing*: downhill run; '⸜sbahnsteig *m* departure platform; '⸜slauf *m* *skiing*: downhill race; '⸜ssignal *n* starting-signal; '⸜szeit *f* time of departure; ⚓ *a.* time of sailing.

'**Abfall** *m* defection (von from), falling away (from); *esp. pol.* secession (from); *eccl.* apostasy (from); *often* **Abfälle** *pl.* waste, refuse, rubbish, *Am. a.* garbage; ⊕ clippings *pl.*, shavings *pl.*; *at butcher's*: offal; '⸜eimer *m* dust-bin, *Am.* ash can; '⸟en *v/i.* (*irr.* fallen, *sep.*, -ge-, *sein*) *leaves*, *etc.*: fall (off); *ground*, *etc.*: slope (down); *fig.* fall away (von from); *esp. pol.* secede (from); *eccl.* apostatize (from); ⸜ *gegen* come off badly by comparison with, be inferior to; '⸜erzeugnis *n* waste product; by-product.

'**abfällig** *adj.* judgement, *etc.*: adverse, unfavo(u)rable; *remark*: disparaging, depreciatory.

'**Abfallprodukt** *n* by-product; waste product.

'**ab|fangen** *v/t.* (*irr.* fangen, *sep.*, -ge-, *h*) catch; snatch (*ball*, *etc.*); intercept (*letter*, *etc.*); △, ✗ prop; ✗ check (*attack*); ✈ flatten out; *mot.*, ≷ right; '⸜färben *v/i.* (*sep.*, -ge-, *h*): *der Pullover färbt ab* the colo(u)r of the pull-over runs (*auf acc.* on); ⸜ *auf* (*acc.*) influence, affect.

'**abfass|en** *v/t.* (*sep.*, -ge-, *h*) compose, write, pen; catch (*thief, etc.*); '⸟ung *f* composition; wording.

'**ab|faulen** *v/i.* (*sep.*, -ge-, *sein*) rot off; '⸜fegen *v/t.* (*sep.*, -ge-, *h*) sweep off; '⸜feilen *v/t.* (*sep.*, -ge-, *h*) file off.

abfertig|en ['apfɛrtiɡən] *v/t.* (*sep.*, -ge-, *h*) dispatch (*a.* ✉); *customs*: clear; serve, attend to (*customer*); *j-n kurz* ⸜ snub s.o.; '⸟ung *f* (-/-en) dispatch; *customs*: clearance; *schroffe* ⸜ snub. [(off), discharge.)

'**abfeuern** *v/t.* (*sep.*, -ge-, *h*) fire)
'**abfind|en** *v/t.* (*irr.* finden, *sep.*, -ge-, *h*) satisfy, pay off (*creditor*); compensate; *sich mit et.* ⸜ resign o.s. to s.th.; put up with s.th.; '⸟ung *f* (-/-en) settlement; satisfaction; compensation; ⸟ung(ssumme) *f* indemnity; compensation.

'**ab|flachen** *v/t.* and *v/refl.* (*sep.*, -ge-, *h*) flatten; '⸜flauen *v/i.* (*sep.*, -ge-, *sein*) *wind*, *etc.*: abate; *interest*, *etc.*: flag; ⚓ *business*: slacken; '⸜fliegen *v/i.* (*irr.* fliegen, *sep.*, -ge-, *sein*) leave by plane; ≷ take off, start; '⸜fließen *v/i.* (*irr.* fließen, *sep.*, -ge-, *sein*) drain *or* flow off *or* away. [parture.)

'**Abflug** ≷ *m* take-off, start, de-)
'**Abfluß** *m* flowing *or* draining off *or* away; discharge (*a.* ✇); drain (*a. fig.*); sink; outlet (*of lake*, *etc.*).

'**abfordern** *v/t.* (*sep.*, -ge-, *h*): *j-m et.* ⸜ demand s.th. of *or* from s.o.

Abfuhr ['apfuːr] f (-/-en) removal; fig. rebuff.

'abführ|en (sep., -ge-, h) **1.** v/t. lead off or away; march (prisoner) off; pay over (money) (an acc. to); **2.** ◯ v/i. purge (the bowels), loosen the bowels; **~end** ◯ adj. purgative, aperient, laxative; **'2mittel** ◯ n purgative, aperient, laxative.

'abfüllen v/t. (sep., -ge-, h) decant; in Flaschen ~ bottle; Bier in Fässer ~ rack casks with beer.

'Abgabe f sports: pass; casting (of one's vote); sale (of shares, etc.); mst ~n pl. taxes pl.; rates pl., Am. local taxes pl.; duties pl.; **'2frei** adj. tax-free; duty-free; **'2pflichtig** adj. taxable; dutiable; liable to tax or duty.

'Abgang m departure; start; thea. exit (a. fig.); retirement (from a job); loss, wastage; deficiency (in weight, etc.); ◯ discharge; ◯ miscarriage; nach ~ von der Schule after leaving school.

'abgängig adj. missing.

'Abgangszeugnis n (school-)leaving certificate, Am. a. diploma.

'Abgas n waste gas; esp. mot. exhaust gas. [toil-worn, worn-out.\

abgearbeitet adj. ['apgəʔarbaɪtət]\

'abgeben v/t. (irr. geben, sep., -ge-, h) leave (bei, an dat. at); hand in (paper, etc.); deposit, leave (luggage); cast (one's vote); sports: pass (ball, etc.); sell, dispose of (goods); give off (heat, etc.); e-e Erklärung ~ make a statement; s-e Meinung ~ express one's opinion (über acc. on); j-m et. ~ von et. give s.o. some of s.th.; e-n guten Gelehrten ~ make a good scholar; sich ~ mit occupy o.s. with s.th.; sie gibt sich gern mit Kindern ab she loves to be among children.

'abge|brannt adj. burnt down; F fig. hard up, sl. broke; **~brüht** fig. adj. ['~bryːt] hardened, callous; **'~droschen** adj. trite, hackneyed; **~feimt** adj. ['~faɪmt] cunning, crafty; **'~griffen** adj. worn; book: well-thumbed; **~härtet** adj. ['~hertət] hardened (gegen to), inured (to); **~härmt** adj. ['~hermt] care-worn.

'abgehen (irr. gehen, sep., -ge-) **1.** v/i. (sein) go off or away; leave, start, depart; letter, etc.: be dispatched; post: go; thea. make one's exit; side-road: branch off; goods: sell; button, etc.: come off; stain, etc.: come out; ◯ be discharged; (von e-m Amt) ~ give up a post; retire; von der Schule ~ leave school; ~ von digress from (main subject); deviate from (rule); alter, change (one's opinion); relinquish (plan, etc.); diese Eigenschaft geht ihm ab he lacks this quality; gut ~ end well, pass off well; hiervon geht or gehen

... ab † less, minus; **2.** v/t. (h) measure by steps; patrol.

abge|hetzt adj. ['apgəhetst] harassed; exhausted; run down; breathless; **~kartet** F adj. ['~kartət]: ~e Sache prearranged affair, put-up job; **'~legen** adj. remote, distant; secluded; out-of-the-way; **~macht** adj. ['~maxt]: ~! it's a bargain or deal!; **~magert** adj. ['~maːgərt] emaciated; **~neigt** adj. ['~naɪkt] disinclined (dat. for s.th.; zu tun to do), averse (to; from doing), unwilling (zu tun to do); **~nutzt** adj. ['~nutst] worn-out.

Abgeordnete ['apgəʔɔrdnətə] m, f (-n/-n) deputy, delegate; in Germany: member of the Bundestag or Landtag; Brt. Member of Parliament, Am. Representative.

'abgerissen fig. adj. ragged; shabby; style, speech: abrupt, broken.

'Abgesandte m, f (-n/-n) envoy; emissary; ambassador.

'abgeschieden fig. adj. isolated, secluded, retired; **'2heit** f (-/-en) seclusion; retirement.

'abgeschlossen adj. flat: self-contained; training, etc.: complete.

abgeschmackt adj. ['apgəʃmakt] tasteless; tactless; **'2heit** f (-/-en) tastelessness; tactlessness.

'abgesehen adj.: ~ von apart from, Am. a. aside from.

abge|spannt fig. adj. ['apgəʃpant] exhausted, tired, run down; **'~standen** adj. stale, flat; **'~storben** adj. numb; dead; **~stumpft** adj. ['~ʃtumpft] blunt(ed); fig. indifferent (gegen to); **'~tragen** adj. worn-out; threadbare, shabby.

'abgewöhnen v/t. (sep., -ge-, h): j-m et. ~ break or cure s.o. of s.th.; sich das Rauchen ~ give up smoking.

abgezehrt adj. ['apgətseːrt] emaciated, wasted.

'abgießen v/t. (irr. gießen, sep., -ge-, h) pour off; ◯ decant; ⊕ cast.

'Abglanz m reflection (a. fig.).

'abgleiten v/i. (irr. gleiten, sep., -ge-, sein) slip off; slide off; glide\

'Abgott m idol. [off.\

abgöttisch adv. ['apgœtiʃ]: j-n ~ lieben idolize or worship s.o.; ~ (up)on s.o.

'ab|grasen v/t. (sep., -ge-, h) graze; fig. scour; **'~grenzen** v/t. (sep., -ge-, h) mark off, delimit; demarcate (a. fig.); fig. define.

'Abgrund m abyss; precipice; chasm, gulf; am Rande des ~s on the brink of disaster.

'Abguß m cast.

'ab|hacken v/t. (sep., -ge-, h) chop or cut off; **'~haken** fig. v/t. (sep., -ge-, h) tick or check off; **'~halten** v/t. (irr. halten, sep., -ge-, h) hold (meeting, examination, etc.); keep out (rain); j-n von der Arbeit ~ keep

s.o. from his work; *j-n davon* ～ *et. zu tun* keep *or* restrain s.o. from doing s.th.; *et. von j-m* ～ keep s.th. away from s.o.; '～**handeln** *v/t.* (*sep.*, -ge-, *h*) discuss, treat; *j-m et.* ～ bargain s.th. out of s.o.
abhanden *adv.* [ap'handən]: ～ *kommen* get lost.
'**Abhandlung** *f* treatise (*über acc.* [up]on), dissertation ([up]on, concerning); essay.
'**Abhang** *m* slope, incline; declivity.
'**abhängen 1.** *v/t.* (*sep.*, -ge-, *h*) take down (*picture, etc.*); 🖾 uncouple; **2.** *v/i.* (*irr.* hängen, *sep.*, -ge-, *h*): ～ *von* depend (up)on.
abhängig *adj.* ['apheŋiç]: ～ *von* dependent (up)on; '2**keit** *f* (-/*no pl.*) dependence (*von* [up]on).
ab|härmen ['aphermən] *v/refl.* (*sep.*, -ge-, *h*) pine away (*über acc.* at); '～**härten** *v/t.* (*sep.*, -ge-, *h*) harden (*gegen* to), inure (to); *sich* ～ harden o.s. (*gegen* to), inure o.s. (to); '～**hauen** (*irr.* hauen, *sep.*, -ge-) **1.** *v/t.* (*h*) cut *or* chop off; **2.** F *v/i.* (*sein*) be off; *hau ab! sl.* beat it!, scram!; '～**häuten** *v/t.* (*sep.*, -ge-, *h*) skin, flay; '～**heben** (*irr.* heben, *sep.*, -ge-, *h*) **1.** *v/t.* lift *or* take off; *teleph.* lift (*receiver*); (with)draw (*money*); *sich* ～ *von* stand out against; *fig. a.* contrast with; **2.** *v/i.* cut (the cards); *teleph.* lift the receiver; '～**heilen** *v/i.* (*sep.*, -ge-, *sein*) heal (up); '～**helfen** *v/i.* (*irr.* helfen, *sep.*, -ge-, *h*): *e-m Übel* ～ cure *or* redress an evil; *dem ist nicht abzuhelfen* there is nothing to be done about it; '～**hetzen** *v/refl.* (*sep.*, -ge-, *h*) tire o.s. out; rush, hurry.
'**Abhilfe** *f* remedy, redress, relief; ～ *schaffen* take remedial measures.
'**abhobeln** *v/t.* (*sep.*, -ge-, *h*) plane (away, down).
abhold *adj.* ['aphɔlt] averse (*dat.* to *s.th.*); ill-disposed (towards *s.o.*).
'**ab|holen** *v/t.* (*sep.*, -ge-, *h*) fetch; call for, come for; *j-n von der Bahn* ～ go to meet s.o. at the station; '～**holzen** *v/t.* (*sep.*, -ge-, *h*) fell, cut down (*trees*); deforest; '～**horchen** 🖾 *v/t.* (*sep.*, -ge-, *h*) auscultate, sound; '～**hören** *v/t.* (*sep.*, -ge-, *h*) listen in to, intercept (*telephone conversation*); *e-n Schüler* ～ hear a pupil's lesson.
Abitur [abi'tuːr] *n* (-s/🔾-e) school-leaving examination (*qualifying for university entrance*).
'**ab|jagen** *v/t.* (*sep.*, -ge-, *h*): *j-m et.* ～ recover s.th. from s.o.; '～**kanzeln** F *v/t.* (*sep.*, -ge-, *h*) reprimand, F tell *s.o.* off; '～**kaufen** *v/t.* (*sep.*, -ge-, *h*): *j-m et.* ～ buy *or* purchase s.th. from s.o.

Abkehr *fig.* ['apkeːr] *f* (-/*no pl.*) estrangement (*von* from); withdrawal (from); '2**en** *v/t.* (*sep.*, -ge-, *h*) sweep off; *sich* ～ *von* turn away from; *fig.*: take no further interest in; become estranged from; withdraw from.
'**ab|klingen** *v/i.* (*irr.* klingen, *sep.*, -ge-, *sein*) fade away; *pain, etc.*: die down; *pain, illness*: ease off; '～**klopfen** (*sep.*, -ge-, *h*) **1.** *v/t.* knock (*dust, etc.*) off; dust (*coat, etc.*); 🖾 sound, percuss; **2.** *v/i. conductor*: stop the orchestra; '～**knicken** *v/t.* (*sep.*, -ge-, *h*) snap *or* break off; bend off; '～**knöpfen** *v/t.* (*sep.*, -ge-, *h*) unbutton; F *j-m Geld* ～ get money out of s.o.; '～**kochen** (*sep.*, -ge-, *h*) **1.** *v/t.* boil; scald (*milk*); **2.** *v/i.* cook in the open air (*a.* 🖾); '～**kommandieren** 🖾 *v/t.* (*sep.*, *no* -ge-, *h*) detach, detail; second (*officer*).
Abkomme ['apkɔmə] *m* (-n/-n) descendant.
'**abkommen 1.** *v/i.* (*irr.* kommen, *sep.*, -ge-, *sein*) come away, get away *or* off; *von e-r Ansicht* ～ change one's opinion; *von e-m Thema* ～ digress from a topic; *vom Wege* ～ lose one's way; **2.** 2 *n* (-s/-) agreement.
abkömm|lich *adj.* ['apkœmliç] dispensable; available; *er ist nicht* ～ he cannot be spared; 2**ling** ['～liŋ] *m* (-s/-e) descendant.
'**ab|koppeln** *v/t.* (*sep.*, -ge-, *h*) uncouple; '～**kratzen** (*sep.*, -ge-) **1.** *v/t.* (*h*) scrape off; **2.** *sl. v/i.* (*sein*) kick the bucket; '～**kühlen** *v/t.* (*sep.*, -ge-, *h*) cool; refrigerate; *sich* ～ cool down (*a. fig.*).
Abkunft ['apkunft] *f* (-/🔾-e) descent; origin, extraction; birth.
'**abkürz|en** *v/t.* (*sep.*, -ge-, *h*) shorten; abbreviate (*word, story, etc.*); *den Weg* ～ take a short cut; 2**ung** *f* (-/-en) abridgement; abbreviation; short cut.
'**abladen** *v/t.* (*irr.* laden, *sep.*, -ge-, *h*) unload; dump (*rubbish, etc.*).
'**Ablage** *f* place of deposit; filing tray; files *pl.*; cloak-room.
'**ab|lagern** (*sep.*, -ge-) **1.** *v/t.* (*h*) season (*wood, wine*); age (*wine*); *sich* ～ settle; be deposited; **2.** *v/i.* (*sein*) *wood, wine*: season; *wine*: age; '～**lassen** (*irr.* lassen, *sep.*, -ge-, *h*) **1.** *v/t.* let (*liquid*) run off; let off (*steam*); drain (*pond, etc.*); **2.** *v/i.* leave off (*von et.* [doing] s.th.).
'**Ablauf** *m* running off; outlet, drain; *sports*: start; *fig.* expiration, end; *nach* ～ *von* at the end of; '2**en** (*irr.* laufen, *sep.*, -ge-) **1.** *v/i.* (*sein*) run off; drain off; *period of time*: expire; ✝ *bill of exchange*: fall due; *clock, etc.*: run down; *thread, film*: unwind; *spool*: run out; *gut* ～ *end*

well; **2.** *v/t.* (*h*) wear out (*shoes*); scour (*region, etc.*); *sich die Beine ~* run one's legs off; *s. Rang.*

'Ableben *n* (*-s/ no pl.*) death, decease (*esp.* 🏛️), 🏛️ demise.

'ab|lecken *v/t.* (*sep., -ge-, h*) lick (off); **'~legen** (*sep., -ge-, h*) **1.** *v/t.* take off (*garments*); leave off (*garments*); give up, break o.s. of (*habit*); file (*documents, letters, etc.*); make (*confession, vow*); take (*oath, examination*); *Zeugnis ~* bear witness (*für* to; *von* of); *s. Rechenschaft;* **2.** *v/i.* take off one's (hat and) coat.

'Ableger ♀ *m* (*-s/-*) layer, shoot.

'ablehn|en (*sep., -ge-, h*) **1.** *v/t.* decline, refuse; reject (*doctrine, candidate, etc.*); turn down (*proposal, etc.*); **2.** *v/i.* decline; *dankend ~* decline with thanks; **'~end** *adj.* negative; **'2ung** *f* (*-/-en*) refusal; rejection.

ableit|en *v/t.* (*sep., -ge-, h*) divert (*river, etc.*); drain off *or* away (*water, etc.*); *gr.*, ♪, *fig.* derive (*aus, von* from); *fig.* infer (from); **'2ung** *f* diversion; drainage; *gr.*, ♪ derivation (*a. fig.*).

'ab|lenken *v/t.* (*sep., -ge-, h*) turn aside; divert (*suspicion, etc.*) (*von* from); *phys., etc.*: deflect (*rays, etc.*); *j-n von der Arbeit ~* distract s.o. from his work; **'~lesen** *v/t.* (*irr. lesen, sep., -ge-, h*) read (*speech, etc.*); read (off) (*values from instruments*); **'~leugnen** *v/t.* (*sep., -ge-, h*) deny, disavow, disown.

'abliefer|n *v/t.* (*sep., -ge-, h*) deliver; hand over; surrender; **'2ung** *f* delivery.

'ablöschen *v/t.* (*sep., -ge-, h*) blot (up) (*ink*); ⊕ temper (*steel*).

'ablös|en *v/t.* (*sep., -ge-, h*) detach; take off; ✂, *etc.*: relieve; supersede (*predecessor in office*); discharge (*debt*); redeem (*obligation*); *sich ~* come off; *fig.* alternate, take turns; **'2ung** *f* detachment; ✂, *etc.*: relief; *fig.* supersession; discharge; redemption.

'abmach|en *v/t.* (*sep., -ge-, h*) remove, detach; *fig.* settle, arrange (*business, etc.*); agree (up)on (*price, etc.*); **'2ung** *f* (*-/-en*) arrangement, settlement; agreement.

'abmager|n *v/i.* (*sep., -ge-, sein*) lose flesh; grow lean *or* thin; **'2ung** *f* (*-/-en*) emaciation.

'ab|mähen *v/t.* (*sep., -ge-, h*) mow (off); **'~malen** *v/t.* (*sep., -ge-, h*) copy.

'Abmarsch *m* start; ✕ marching off; **'2ieren** *v/i.* (*sep., no -ge-, sein*) start; ✕ march off.

'abmeld|en *v/t.* (*sep., -ge-, h*): *j-n von der Schule ~* give notice of the withdrawal of a pupil (from school); *sich polizeilich ~* give notice to the police of one's departure (from

town, etc.); **'2ung** *f* notice of withdrawal; notice of departure.

'abmess|en *v/t.* (*irr. messen, sep., -ge-, h*) measure; **'2ung** *f* (*-/-en*) measurement.

'ab|montieren *v/t.* (*sep., no -ge-, h*) disassemble; dismantle, strip (*machinery*); remove (*tyre, etc.*); **'~mühen** *v/refl.* (*sep., -ge-, h*) drudge, toil; **'~nagen** *v/t.* (*sep., -ge-, h*) gnaw off; pick (*bone*).

Abnahme [ˈapnaːmə] *f* (*-/ -n*) taking off; removal; ⚕ amputation; ♈ taking delivery; ♈ purchase; ♈ sale; ⊕ acceptance (*of machine, etc.*); administering (*of oath*); decrease, diminution; loss (*of weight*).

'abnehm|en (*irr. nehmen, sep., -ge-, h*) **1.** *v/t.* take off; remove; *teleph.* lift (*receiver*); ⚕ amputate; gather (*fruit*); ⊕ accept (*machine, etc.*); *j-m et. ~* take s.th. from s.o.; ♈ *a.* buy *or* purchase s.th. from s.o.; *j-m zuviel ~* overcharge s.o.; **2.** *v/i.* decrease, diminish; decline; lose weight; *moon:* wane; *storm:* abate; *days:* grow shorter; **'2er** ♈ *m* (*-s/-*) buyer; customer; consumer.

'Abneigung *f* aversion (*gegen* to); disinclination (to); dislike (to, of, for); antipathy (against, to).

abnorm *adj.* [apˈnɔrm] abnormal; anomalous; exceptional; **2i'tät** *f* (*-/-en*) abnormality; anomaly.

'abnötigen *v/t.* (*sep., -ge-, h*): *j-m et. ~* extort s.th. from s.o.

'ab|nutzen *v/t. and v/refl.* (*sep., -ge-, h*), **'~nützen** *v/t. and v/refl.* (*sep., -ge-, h*) wear out; **'2nutzung** *f*, **'2nützung** *f* (*-/-en*) wear (and tear).

Abonn|ement [abɔn(ə)ˈmãː] *n* (*-s/ -s*) subscription (*auf acc.* to); **~ent** [~ˈnɛnt] *m* (*-en/-en*) subscriber; **2ieren** [~ˈniːrən] *v/t.* (*no -ge-, h*) subscribe to (*newspaper*); **2iert** *adj.* [~ˈniːrt]: *~ sein auf* (*acc.*) take in (*newspaper, etc.*).

abordn|en [ˈapˀ-] *v/t.* (*sep., -ge-, h*) depute, delegate, *Am. a.* deputize; **'2ung** *f* delegation, deputation.

Abort [aˈbɔrt] *m* (*-[e]s/-e*) lavatory, toilet.

'ab|passen *v/t.* (*sep., -ge-, h*) fit, adjust; watch for, wait for (*s.o., opportunity*); waylay *s.o.*; **'~pflücken** *v/t.* (*sep., -ge-, h*) pick, pluck (off), gather; **'~plagen** *v/refl.* (*sep., -ge-, h*) toil; **'~platzen** *v/i.* (*sep., -ge-, sein*) burst off; fly off; **'~prallen** *v/i.* (*sep., -ge-, sein*) rebound, bounce (off); ricochet; **'~putzen** *v/t.* (*sep., -ge-, h*) clean (off, up); wipe off; polish; **'~raten** *v/i.* (*irr. raten, sep., -ge-, h*): *j-m ~ von* dissuade s.o. from, advise s.o. against; **'~räumen** *v/t.* (*sep., -ge-, h*) clear (away); **'~reagieren** *v/t.* (*sep., no -ge-, h*) work off (*one's anger, etc.*); *sich ~* F *a.* let off steam.

'abrechn|en (*sep.*, *-ge-*, *h*) **1.** *v/t.* deduct; settle (*account*); **2.** *v/i.*: mit j-m ~ settle with s.o.; *fig.* settle (accounts) with s.o., F get even with s.o.; **'2ung** *f* settlement (of accounts); deduction, discount.

'Abrede *f*: in ~ stellen deny *or* question *s.th.*

'abreib|en *v/t.* (*irr. reiben*, *sep.*, *-ge-*, *h*) rub off; rub down (*body*); polish; **'2ung** *f* rub-down; F *fig.* beating.

'Abreise *f* departure (*nach her*); **'2n** *v/i.* (*sep.*, *-ge-*, *sein*) depart (*nach for*), leave (for), start (for), set out (for).

'abreiß|en (*irr. reißen*, *sep.*, *-ge-*) **1.** *v/t.* (*h*) tear *or* pull off; pull down (*building*); *s.* abgerissen; **2.** *v/i.* (*sein*) break off; *button, etc.*: come off; **'2kalender** *m* tear-off calendar.

'ab|richten *v/t.* (*sep.*, *-ge-*, *h*) train (*animal*), break (*horse*) (in); **'~riegeln** *v/t.* (*sep.*, *-ge-*, *h*) bolt, bar (*door*); block (*road*).

'Abriß *m* draft; summary, abstract; (*brief*) outlines *pl.*; brief survey.

'ab|rollen (*sep.*, *-ge-*) *v/t.* (*h*) *and* *v/i.* (*sein*) unroll; uncoil; unwind, unreel; roll off; **'~rücken** (*sep.*, *-ge-*) **1.** *v/t.* (*h*) move off *or* away (*von from*), remove; **2.** ✗ *v/i.* (*sein*) march off, withdraw.

'Abruf *m* call; recall; *auf* ~ ✝ on call; **'2en** *v/t.* (*irr. rufen*, *sep.*, *-ge-*, *h*) call off (a. ✝), call away; recall; ✗ call out.

'ab|runden *v/t.* (*sep.*, *-ge-*, *h*) round (off); **'~rupfen** *v/t.* (*sep.*, *-ge-*, *h*) pluck off.

abrupt *adj.* [ap'rupt] abrupt.

'abrüst|en ✗ *v/i.* (*sep.*, *-ge-*, *h*) disarm; **'2ung** ✗ *f* disarmament.

'abrutschen *v/i.* (*sep.*, *-ge-*, *sein*) slip off, glide down; ✈ skid.

'Absage *f* cancellation; refusal; **'2n** (*sep.*, *-ge-*, *h*) **1.** *v/t.* cancel, call off; refuse; recall (*invitation*); **2.** *v/i.* *guest*: decline; j-m ~ cancel one's appointment with s.o.

'absägen *v/t.* (*sep.*, *-ge-*, *h*) saw off; F *fig.* sack *s.o.*

'Absatz *m* stop, pause; typ. paragraph; ✝ sale; heel (*of shoe*); landing (*of stairs*); **'2fähig** ✝ *adj.* saleable, marketable; **'~markt** ✝ *m* market, outlet; **'~möglichkeit** ✝ *f* opening, outlet.

'abschaben *v/t.* (*sep.*, *-ge-*, *h*) scrape off.

'abschaff|en *v/t.* (*sep.*, *-ge-*, *h*) abolish; abrogate (*law*); dismiss (*servants*); **'2ung** *f* (*-/-en*) abolition; abrogation; dismissal.

'ab|schälen *v/t.* (*sep.*, *-ge-*, *h*) peel (off), pare; bark (*tree*); **'~schalten** *v/t.* (*sep.*, *-ge-*, *h*) switch off, turn off *or* out; ✦ disconnect.

'abschätz|en *v/t.* (*sep.*, *-ge-*, *h*) esti-

mate; value; assess; **'2ung** *f* valuation; estimate; assessment.

'Abschaum *m* (*-[e]s/no pl.*) scum; *fig. a.* dregs *pl.*

'Abscheu *m* (*-[e]s/no pl.*) horror (*vor dat.* of), abhorrence (of); loathing (of); disgust (for).

'abscheuern *v/t.* (*sep.*, *-ge-*, *h*) scour (off); wear out; chafe, abrade.

abscheulich *adj.* [ap'ʃɔʏlɪç] abominable, detestable, horrid; **2keit** *f* (*-/-en*) detestableness; atrocity.

'ab|schicken *v/t.* (*sep.*, *-ge-*, *h*) send off, dispatch; ✉ post, *esp. Am.* mail; **'~schieben** *v/t.* (*irr. schieben*, *sep.*, *-ge-*, *h*) push *or* shove off.

Abschied ['apʃiːt] *m* (*-[e]s/*❨*-e*) departure; parting, leave-taking, farewell; dismissal, ✗ discharge; ~ nehmen take leave (*von* of), bid farewell (to); j-m den ~ geben dismiss s.o., ✗ discharge s.o.; s-n ~ nehmen resign, retire; **'~sfeier** *f* farewell party; **'~sgesuch** *n* resignation.

'ab|schießen *v/t.* (*irr. schießen*, *sep.*, *-ge-*, *h*) shoot off; shoot, discharge, fire (off) (*fire-arm*); launch (*rocket*); kill, shoot; (shoot *or* bring) down (*aircraft*); *s. Vogel*; **'~schinden** *v/refl.* (*irr. schinden*, *sep.*, *-ge-*, *h*) toil and moil, slave, drudge; **'~schirmen** *v/t.* (*sep.*, *-ge-*, *h*) shield (*gegen from*); screen (from), screen off (from); **'~schlachten** *v/t.* (*sep.*, *-ge-*, *h*) slaughter, butcher.

'Abschlag ✝ *m* reduction (*in price*); *auf* ~ on account; **2en** ['~gən] *v/t.* (*irr. schlagen*, *sep.*, *-ge-*, *h*) knock off, beat off, strike off; cut off (*head*); refuse (*request*); repel (*attack*).

abschlägig *adj.* ['apʃlɛːgɪç] negative; ~e Antwort refusal, denial.

'Abschlagszahlung *f* payment on account; instal(l)ment.

'abschleifen *v/t.* (*irr. schleifen*, *sep.*, *-ge-*, *h*) grind off; *fig.* refine, polish.

'Abschlepp|dienst *mot. m* towing service, *Am. a.* wrecking service; **2en** *v/t.* (*sep.*, *-ge-*, *h*) drag off; *mot.* tow off.

'abschließen (*irr. schließen*, *sep.*, *-ge-*, *h*) **1.** *v/t.* lock (up); ⊕ seal (up); conclude (*letter, etc.*); settle (*account*); balance (*the books*); effect (*insurance*); contract (*loan*); *fig.* seclude, isolate; e-n Handel ~ strike a bargain; *sich* ~ seclude o.s.; **2.** *v/i.* conclude; **'~d 1.** *adj.* concluding; final; **2.** *adv.* in conclusion.

'Abschluß *m* settlement; conclusion; ⊕ seal; **'~prüfung** *f* final examination, finals *pl.*, *Am. a.* graduation; **'~zeugnis** *n* leaving certificate; diploma.

'ab|schmeicheln *v/t.* (*sep.*, *-ge-*, *h*): j-m et. ~ coax s.th. out of s.o.; **'~schmelzen** (*irr. schmelzen*, *sep.*,

-ge-) v/t. (h) and v/i. (sein) melt (off); ⊕ fuse; '~schmieren ⊕ v/t. (sep., -ge-, h) lubricate, grease; '~schnallen v/t. (sep., -ge-, h) unbuckle; take off (ski, etc.); '~schneiden (irr. schneiden, sep., -ge-, h) 1. v/t. cut (off); slice off; den Weg ~ take a short cut; j-m das Wort ~ cut s.o. short; 2. v/i.: gut ~ come out or off well.

'Abschnitt m ⅋ segment; ⫟ coupon; typ. section, paragraph; counterfoil, Am. a. stub (of cheque, etc.); stage (of journey); phase (of development); period (of time).

'ab|schöpfen v/t. (sep., -ge-, h) skim (off); '~schrauben v/t. (sep., -ge-, h) unscrew, screw off.

'abschrecken v/t. (sep., -ge-, h) deter (von from); scare away; '~d adj. deterrent; repulsive, forbidding.

'abschreib|en (irr. schreiben, sep., -ge-, h) 1. v/t. copy; write off (debt, etc.); plagiarize; in school: crib; 2. v/i. send a refusal; '2er m copyist; plagiarist; '2ung ⫟ f (-/-en) depreciation.

'abschreiten v/t. (irr. schreiten, sep., -ge-, h) pace (off); e-e Ehrenwache ~ inspect a guard of hono(u)r.

'Abschrift f copy, duplicate.

'abschürf|en v/t. (sep., -ge-, h) graze, abrade (skin); '2ung f (-/-en) abrasion.

'Abschuß m discharge (of fire-arm); launching (of rocket); hunt. shooting; shooting down, downing (of aircraft); '~rampe f launching platform.

abschüssig adj. ['apʃysiç] sloping; steep.

'ab|schütteln v/t. (sep., -ge-, h) shake off (a. fig.); fig. get rid of; '~schwächen v/t. (sep., -ge-, h) weaken, lessen, diminish; '~schweifen v/i. (sep., -ge-, sein) deviate; fig. digress; '~schwenken v/i. (sep., -ge-, sein) swerve; ⚔ wheel; '~schwören v/i. (irr. schwören, sep., -ge-, h) abjure; forswear; '~segeln v/i. (sep., -ge-, sein) set sail, sail away.

abseh|bar adj. ['apze:ba:r]: in ~er Zeit in the not-too-distant future; '~en (irr. sehen, sep., -ge-, h) 1. v/t. (fore)see; j-m et. ~ learn s.th. by observing s.o.; es abgesehen haben auf (acc.) have an eye on, be aiming at; 2. v/i.: ~ von refrain from; disregard.

abseits ['apzaɪts] 1. adv. aside, apart; football, etc.: off side; 2. prp. (gen.) aside from; off (the road).

'absend|en v/t. ([irr. senden,] sep., -ge-, h) send off, dispatch; ⅋ post, esp. Am. mail; '2er ⅋ m sender.

'absengen v/t. (sep., -ge-, h) singe off.

'Absenker ⅋ m (-s/-) layer, shoot.

'absetz|en (sep., -ge-, h) 1. v/t. set or put down, deposit; deduct (sum); take off (hat); remove, dismiss (official); depose, dethrone (king); drop, put down (passenger); ⫟ sell (goods); typ. set up (in type); thea.: ein Stück ~ take off a play; 2. v/i. break off, stop, pause; '2ung f (-/-en) deposition; removal, dismissal.

'Absicht f (-/-en) intention, purpose, design; '2lich 1. adj. intentional; 2. adv. on purpose.

'absitzen (irr. sitzen, sep., -ge-) 1. v/i. (sein) rider: dismount; 2. v/t. (h) serve (sentence), F do (time).

absolut adj. [apzo'lu:t] absolute.

absolvieren [apzɔl'vi:rən] v/t. (no -ge-, h) absolve; complete (studies); get through, graduate from (school).

'absonder|n v/t. (sep., -ge-, h) separate; ⚕ secrete; sich ~ withdraw; '2ung f (-/-en) separation; ⚕ secretion.

ab|sorbieren [apzɔr'bi:rən] v/t. (no -ge-, h) absorb; '~speisen fig. v/t. (sep., -ge-, h) put s.o. off.

abspenstig adj. ['apʃpɛnstiç]: ~ machen entice away (von from).

'absperr|en v/t. (sep., -ge-, h) lock; shut off; bar (way); block (road); turn off (gas, etc.); '2hahn m stopcock.

'ab|spielen v/t. (sep., -ge-, h) play (record, etc.); play back (tape recording); sich ~ happen, take place; '~sprechen v/t. (irr. sprechen, sep., -ge-, h) deny; arrange, agree; '~springen v/i. (irr. springen, sep., -ge-, sein) jump down or off; ⚙ jump, bale out, (Am. only) bail out; rebound.

'Absprung m jump; sports: take-off.

'abspülen v/t. (sep., -ge-, h) wash up; rinse.

'abstamm|en v/i. (sep., -ge-, sein) be descended; gr. be derived (both: von from); '2ung f (-/-en) descent; gr. derivation.

'Abstand m distance; interval; ⫟ compensation, indemnification; ~ nehmen von desist from.

'ab|statten v/t. (sep., -ge-, h): e-n Besuch ~ pay a visit; Dank ~ return or render thanks; '~stauben v/t. (sep., -ge-, h) dust.

'abstech|en (irr. stechen, sep., -ge-, h) 1. v/t. cut (sods); stick (pig, sheep, etc.); stab (animal); 2. v/i. contrast (von with); '2er m (-s/-) excursion, trip; detour.

'ab|stecken v/t. (sep., -ge-, h) unpin, undo; fit, pin (dress); surv. mark out; '~stehen v/i. (irr. stehen, sep., -ge-, h) stand off; stick out, protrude; s. abgestanden; '~steigen v/i. (irr. steigen, sep., -ge-, sein) descend; alight (von from) (carriage); get off, dismount (from) (horse); put up (in dat. at) (hotel); **'∼stellen** v/t. (sep., -ge-, h) put down; stop, turn off (gas, etc.); park (car), fig. put an end to s.th.; **'∼stempeln** v/t. (sep., -ge-, h) stamp; **'∼sterben** v/i. (irr. sterben, sep., -ge-, sein) die off; limb: mortify.

Abstieg ['apʃtiːk] m (-[e]s/-e) descent; fig. decline.

'abstimm|en (sep., -ge-, h) **1.** v/i. vote; **2.** v/t. tune in (radio); fig.: harmonize; time; ♣ balance (books); **'2ung** f voting; vote; tuning.

Abstinenzler [apstiˈnɛntslər] m (-s/-) teetotal(l)er.

'abstoppen (sep., -ge-, h) **1.** v/t. stop; slow down; sports: clock, time; **2.** v/i. stop.

'abstoßen v/t. (irr. stoßen, sep., -ge-, h) knock off; push off; clear off (goods), fig. repel; sich die Hörner ∼ sow one's wild oats; **'∼d** fig. adj. repulsive.

abstrakt adj. [apˈstrakt] abstract.

'ab|streichen v/t. (irr. streichen, sep., -ge-, h) take or wipe off; **'∼streifen** v/t. (sep., -ge-, h) strip off; take or pull off (glove, etc.); slip off (dress); wipe (shoes); **'∼streiten** v/t. (irr. streiten, sep., -ge-, h) contest, dispute; deny.

'Abstrich m deduction, cut; ✄ swab.

'ab|stufen v/t. (sep., -ge-, h) graduate; gradate; **'∼stumpfen** (sep., -ge-) **1.** v/t. (h) blunt; fig. dull (mind); **2.** fig. v/i. (sein) become dull.

'Absturz m fall; ✗ crash.

'ab|stürzen v/i. (sep., -ge-, sein) fall down; ✗ crash; **'∼suchen** v/t. (sep., -ge-, h) search (nach for); scour or comb (area) (for).

absurd adj. [apˈzurt] absurd, preposterous.

Abszeß ✗ [apsˈtsɛs] m (Abszesses/Abszesse) abscess.

Abt [apt] m (-[e]s/∓e) abbot.

'abtakeln ♣ v/t. (sep., -ge-, h) unrig, dismantle, strip.

Abtei [apˈtai] f (-/-en) abbey.

Ab|'teil 🚂 n compartment; **'2teilen** v/t. (sep., -ge-, h) divide; △ partition off; **'∼teilung** f division; **∼'teilung** f department; ward (of hospital); compartment; ✗ detachment; **∼'teilungsleiter** m head of a department.

'abtelegraphieren v/i. (sep., no -ge-, h) cancel a visit, etc. by telegram.

Äbtissin [ɛpˈtisin] f (-/-nen) abbess.

'ab|töten v/t. (sep., -ge-, h) destroy, kill (bacteria, etc.); **'∼tragen** v/t. (irr. tragen, sep., -ge-, h) carry off; pull down (building); wear out (garment); pay (debt).

abträglich adj. ['aptrɛːkliç] injurious, detrimental.

'abtreib|en (irr. treiben, sep., -ge-) **1.** v/t. (h) drive away or off; ein Kind ∼ procure abortion; **2.** ♣, ✗ v/i. (sein) drift off; **'2ung** f (-/-en) abortion.

'abtrennen v/t. (sep., -ge-, h) detach; separate; sever (limbs, etc.); take (trimmings) off (dress).

'abtret|en (irr. treten, sep., -ge-) **1.** v/t. (h) wear down (heels); wear out (steps, etc.); fig. cede, transfer; **2.** v/i. (sein) retire, withdraw; resign; thea. make one's exit; **'2er** m (-s/-) doormat; **'2ung** f (-/-en) cession, transfer.

'ab|trocknen (sep., -ge-) **1.** v/t. (h) dry (up); wipe (dry); sich ∼ dry oneself, rub oneself down; **2.** v/i. (sein) dry up, become dry; **'∼tropfen** v/i. (sep., -ge-, sein) liquid: drip; dishes, vegetables: drain.

abtrünnig adj. ['aptrynɪç] unfaithful, disloyal; eccl. apostate; **2e** ['∼gə] m (-n/-n) deserter; eccl. apostate.

'ab|tun v/t. (irr. tun, sep., -ge-, h) take off; settle (matter); fig.: dispose of; dismiss; **∼urteilen** ['ap⁹-] v/t. (sep., -ge-, h) pass sentence on s.o.; **'∼wägen** v/t. ([irr. wägen,] sep., -ge-, h) weigh (out); fig. consider carefully; **'∼wälzen** v/t. (sep., -ge-, h) roll away; fig. shift; **'∼wandeln** v/t. (sep., -ge-, h) vary, modify; **'∼wandern** v/i. (sep., -ge-, sein) wander away; migrate (von from).

'Abwandlung f modification, variation.

'abwarten (sep., -ge-, h) **1.** v/t. wait for, await; s-e Zeit ∼ bide one's time; **2.** v/i. wait.

abwärts adv. ['apvɛrts] down, downward(s).

'abwaschen v/t. (irr. waschen, sep., -ge-, h) wash (off, away); bathe; sponge off; wash up (dishes, etc.).

'abwechseln (sep., -ge-, h) **1.** v/t. vary; alternate; **2.** v/i. vary; alternate; mit j-m ∼ take turns; **'∼d** adj. alternate.

'Abwechs(e)lung f (-/-en) change; alternation; variation; diversion; zur ∼ for a change.

'Abweg m: auf ∼e geraten go astray; **2ig** adj. ['∼gɪç] erroneous, wrong.

'Abwehr f defen|ce, Am. -se; warding off (of thrust, etc.); **'∼dienst** ✗ m counter-espionage service; **'2en** v/t. (sep., -ge-, h) ward off; avert; repulse, repel; ward off (attack, enemy).

'abweich|en v/i. (irr. weichen, sep., -ge-, sein) deviate (von from), swerve (from); differ (from); compass-needle: deviate; **'2ung** f (-/-en) deviation; difference; deflexion, (Am. only) deflection.

'abweiden v/t. (sep., -ge-, h) graze.

'abweis|en v/t. (irr. weisen, sep., -ge-, h) refuse, reject; repel (a. ✗);

rebuff; '~end adj. unfriendly, cool; '2ung f refusal, rejection; repulse (a. ⚔); rebuff.

'ab|wenden v/t. ([irr. wenden,] sep., -ge-, h) turn away; avert (disaster, etc.); parry (thrust); sich ~ turn away (von from); '~werfen v/t. (irr. werfen, sep., -ge-, h) throw off; ⚔ drop (bombs); shed, cast (skin, etc.); shed (leaves); yield (profit).

'abwert|en v/t. (sep., -ge-, h) devaluate; '2ung f devaluation.

abwesen|d adj. ['apve:zənt] absent; '2heit f (-/⚓ -en) absence.

'ab|wickeln v/t. (sep., -ge-, h) unwind, unreel, wind off; transact (business); '~wiegen v/t. (irr. wiegen, sep., -ge-, h) weigh (out) (goods); '~wischen v/t. (sep., -ge-, h) wipe (off); '~würgen v/t. (sep., -ge-, h) strangle, throttle, choke; mot. stall; '~zahlen v/t. (sep., -ge-, h) pay off; pay by instal(l)ments; '~zählen v/t. (sep., -ge-, h) count (out, over).

'Abzahlung f instal(l)ment, payment on account; '~sgeschäft n hire-purchase.

'abzapfen v/t. (sep., -ge-, h) tap, draw off.

'Abzehrung f (-/-en) wasting away, emaciation; 🕮 consumption.

'Abzeichen n badge; ⚔ marking.

'ab|zeichnen v/t. (sep., -ge-, h) copy, draw; mark off; initial; tick off; sich ~ gegen stand out against; '~ziehen (irr. ziehen, sep., -ge-) 1. v/t. (h) take off, remove; ⅋ subtract; strip (bed); bottle (wine); phot. print (film); typ. pull (proof); take out (key); das Fell ~ skin (animal); 2. v/i. (sein) go away; ⚔ march off; smoke: escape; thunderstorm, clouds: move on.

'Abzug m departure; ⚔ withdrawal, retreat; ⊕ drain; outlet; deduction (of sum); phot. print; typ. proof (-sheet).

abzüglich prp. (gen.) ['aptsy:kliç] less, minus, deducting.

'Abzugsrohr n waste-pipe.

abzweig|en ['aptsvaɪgən] (sep.,-ge-) 1. v/t. (h) branch; divert (money); sich ~ branch off; 2. v/i. (sein) branch off; '2ung f (-/-en) branch; road-junction.

ach int. [ax] oh!, ah!, alas!; ~ so! oh, I see!

Achse ['aksə] f (-/-n) axis; ⊕: axle; shaft; axle(-tree) (of carriage); auf der ~ on the move.

Achsel ['aksəl] f (-/-n) shoulder; die ~n zucken shrug one's shoulders; '2höhle f armpit.

acht[1] [axt] 1. adj. eight; in ~ Tagen today week, this day week; vor ~ Tagen a week ago; 2. 2 f (-/-en) (figure) eight.

Acht[2] [~] f (-/no pl.) ban, outlawry; attention; außer acht lassen dis-

regard; sich in acht nehmen be careful; be on one's guard (vor j-m or et. against s.o. or s.th.); look out (for s.o. or s.th.).

'achtbar adj. respectable.

'achte adj. eighth; 2I ['~əl] n (-s/-) eighth (part).

'achten (ge-, h) 1. v/t. respect, esteem; regard; 2. v/i.: ~ auf (acc.) pay attention to; achte auf meine Worte mark or mind my words; darauf ~, daß see to it that, take care that.

ächten ['ɛçtən] v/t. (ge-, h) outlaw, proscribe; ban.

'Achter m (-s/-) rowing: eight.

achtfach adj. ['axtfax] eightfold.

'achtgeben v/i. (irr. geben, sep., -ge-, h) be careful; pay attention (auf acc. to); take care (of); gib acht! look or watch out!, be careful!

'achtlos adj. inattentive, careless, heedless.

Acht'stundentag m eight-hour day.

'Achtung f (-/no pl.) attention; respect, esteem, regard; ~! look out!, ⚔ attention!; ~ Stufe! mind the step!; '2svoll adj. respectful.

'achtzehn adj. eighteen; ~te adj. ['~tə] eighteenth.

achtzig adj. ['axtsiç] eighty; '~ste adj. eightieth.

ächzen ['ɛçtsən] v/i. (ge-, h) groan, moan.

Acker ['akər] m (-s/⸚) field; '~bau m agriculture; farming; '2bautreibend adj. agricultural, farming; '~geräte n/pl. farm implements pl.; '~land n arable land; '2n v/t. and v/i. (ge-, h) plough, till, Am. plow.

addi|eren [a'di:rən] v/t. (no -ge-, h) add (up); 2tion [adi'tsjo:n] f (-/-en) addition, adding up.

Adel ['a:dəl] m (-s/no pl.) nobility, aristocracy; '2ig adj. noble; '2n v/t. (ge-, h) ennoble (a. fig.); Brt.: knight, raise to the peerage; '~stand m nobility; aristocracy; Brt. peerage.

Ader ['a:dər] f (-/-n) ⚔, wood, etc.: vein; anat.: vein; artery; zur ~ lassen bleed.

adieu int. [a'djø:] good-bye, farewell, adieu, F cheerio.

Adjektiv gr. ['atjɛkti:f] n (-s/-e) adjective.

Adler orn. ['a:dlər] m (-s/-) eagle; '~nase f aquiline nose.

adlig adj. ['a:dliç] noble; 2e ['~gə] m (-n/-n) nobleman, peer.

Admiral ⚓ [atmi'ra:l] m (-s/-e, ⸚e) admiral.

adopt|ieren [adɔp'ti:rən] v/t. (no -ge-, h) adopt; 2ivkind [~'ti:f-] n adopted child.

Adressat [adrɛ'sa:t] m (-en/-en) addressee; consignee (of goods).

Adreßbuch [a'drɛs-] n directory.

Adress|e [a'drɛsə] *f* (-/-n) address; direction; *per* ~ care of (*abbr.* c/o); **2ieren** [~'si:rən] *v/t.* (*no* -ge-, *h*) address, direct; ✝ consign; *falsch* ~ misdirect.

adrett *adj.* [a'drɛt] smart, neat.

Adverb *gr.* [at'vɛrp] *n* (-s/-ien) adverb.

Affäre [a'fɛ:rə] *f* (-/-n) (love) affair; matter, business, incident.

Affe *zo.* ['afə] *m* (-n/-n) ape; monkey.

Affekt [a'fɛkt] *m* (-[e]s/-e) emotion; passion; **2iert** *adj.* [~'ti:rt] affected.

'affig F *adj.* foppish; affected; silly.

Afrikan|er [afri'ka:nər] *m* (-s/-) African; **2isch** *adj.* African.

After *anat.* ['aftər] *m* (-s/-) anus.

Agent [a'gɛnt] *m* (-en/-en) agent; broker; *pol.* (secret) agent; **~ur** [~'tu:r] *f* (-/-en) agency.

aggressiv *adj.* [agrɛ'si:f] aggressive.

Agio ✝ ['a:ʒio] *n* (-s/*no pl.*) agio, premium.

Agitator [agi'ta:tɔr] *m* (-s/-en) agitator. [brooch.\]

Agraffe [a'grafə] *f* (-/-n) clasp;\]

agrarisch *adj.* [a'gra:riʃ] agrarian.

Ägypt|er [ɛ:'gyptər] *m* (-s/-) Egyptian; **2isch** *adj.* Egyptian.

ah *int.* [a:] ah!

aha *int.* [a'ha] aha!, I see!

Ahle ['a:lə] *f* (-/-n) awl, pricker; punch.

Ahn [a:n] *m* (-[e]s, -en/-en) ancestor; ~*en pl. a.* forefathers *pl.*

ähneln ['ɛ:nəln] *v/i.* (ge-, *h*) be like, resemble.

ahnen ['a:nən] *v/t.* (ge-, *h*) have a presentiment of *or* that; suspect; divine.

ähnlich *adj.* ['ɛ:nliç] like, resembling; similar (*dat.* to); *iro.*: *das sieht ihm* ~ that's just like him; **'2keit** *f* (-/-en) likeness, resemblance; similarity.

Ahnung ['a:nuŋ] *f* (-/-en) presentiment; foreboding; notion, idea; **'2slos** *adj.* unsuspecting; **'2svoll** *adj.* full of misgivings.

Ahorn ♀ ['a:hɔrn] *m* (-s/-e) maple (-tree).

Ähre ♀ ['ɛ:rə] *f* (-/-n) ear, head; spike; ~*n lesen* glean.

Akademi|e [akadə'mi:] *f* (-/-n) academy, society; ~**ker** [~'de:mikər] *m* (-s/-) university man, *esp. Am.* university graduate; **2sch** *adj.* [~'de:miʃ] academic.

Akazie ♀ [a'ka:tsjə] *f* (-/-n) acacia.

akklimatisieren [aklimati'zi:rən] *v/t. and v/refl.* (*no* -ge-, *h*) acclimatize, *Am.* acclimate.

Akkord [a'kɔrt] *m* (-[e]s/-e) ♪ chord; ✝: contract; agreement; composition; *im* ~ ✝ by the piece *or* job; ~**arbeit** *f* piece-work; ~**arbeiter** *m* piece-worker; ~**lohn** *m* piece-wages *pl.*

akkredit|ieren [akredi'ti:rən] *v/t.* (*no* -ge-, *h*) accredit (*bei* to); **2iv** [~'ti:f] *n* (-s/-e) credentials *pl.*; ✝ letter of credit.

Akku F ⊕ ['aku] *m* (-s/-s), ~**mulator** ⊕ [~mu'la:tɔr] *m* (-s/-en) accumulator, (storage-)battery.

Akkusativ *gr.* ['akuzati:f] *m* (-s/-e) accusative (case). [acrobat.\]

Akrobat [akro'ba:t] *m* (-en/-en)\]

Akt [akt] *m* (-[e]s/-e) act(ion), deed; *thea.* act; *paint.* nude.

Akte ['aktə] *f* (-/-n) document, deed; file; ~*n pl.* records *pl.*, papers *pl.*; deeds *pl.*, documents *pl.*; files *pl.*; *zu den* ~*n* to be filed; *zu den* ~*n legen* file; '~**ndeckel** *m* folder; '~**nmappe** *f*, '~**ntasche** *f* portfolio; briefcase; '~**nzeichen** *n* reference *or* file number.

Aktie ✝ ['aktsjə] *f* (-/-n) share, *Am.* stock; ~*n besitzen* hold shares, *Am.* hold stock; '~**nbesitz** *m* shareholdings *pl.*, *Am.* stockholdings *pl.*; '~**ngesellschaft** *f* *appr.* joint-stock company, *Am.* (stock) corporation; '~**nkapital** *n* share-capital, *Am.* capital stock.

Aktion [ak'tsjo:n] *f* (-/-en) action; activity; *pol., etc.*: campaign, drive; ⚒ operation; ~**är** [~'nɛ:r] *m* (-s/-e) shareholder, *Am.* stockholder.

aktiv *adj.* [ak'ti:f] active.

Aktiv|a ✝ [ak'ti:va] *n/pl.* assets *pl.*; ~**posten** [~'ti:f-] *m* asset (*a. fig.*).

aktuell *adj.* [aktu'ɛl] current, present-day, up-to-date, topical.

Akust|ik [a'kustik] *f* (-/*no pl.*) acoustics *sg., pl.*; **2isch** *adj.* acoustic.

akut *adj.* [a'ku:t] acute.

Akzent [ak'tsɛnt] *m* (-[e]s/-e) accent; stress; **2uieren** [~'tu:i:rən] *v/t.* (*no* -ge-, *h*) accent(uate); stress.

Akzept ✝ [ak'tsɛpt] *n* (-[e]s/-e) acceptance; ~**ant** ✝ [~'tant] *m* (-en/-en) acceptor; **2ieren** [~'ti:rən] *v/t.* (*no* -ge-, *h*) accept.

Alarm [a'larm] *m* (-[e]s/-e) alarm; ~ *blasen or schlagen* ⚒ sound *or* give the alarm; ~**bereitschaft** *f*: *in* ~ *sein* stand by; **2ieren** [~'mi:rən] *v/t.* (*no* -ge-, *h*) alarm.

Alaun ♏ [a'laun] *m* (-[e]s/-e) alum.

albern *adj.* ['albərn] silly, foolish.

Album ['album] *n* (-s/*Alben*) album.

Alge ♀ ['algə] *f* (-/-n) alga, seaweed.

Algebra ♉ ['algebra] *f* (-/*no pl.*) algebra.

Alibi ♊ ['a:libi] *n* (-s/-s) alibi.

Alimente ♊ [ali'mɛntə] *pl.* alimony.

Alkohol ['alkohol] *m* (-s/-e) alcohol; '2**frei** *adj.* non-alcoholic, *esp. Am.* soft; ~*es Restaurant* temperance restaurant; ~**iker** [~'ho:likər] *m* (-s/-) alcoholic; **2isch** *adj.* [~'ho:liʃ] alcoholic; '~**schmuggler** *m* liquor-smuggler, *Am.* bootlegger; '~**verbot** *n* prohibition; '~**vergiftung** *f* alcoholic poisoning.

all¹ [al] **1.** *pron.* all; ～e everybody; ～es in ～em on the whole; vor ～em first of all; **2.** *adj.* all; every, each; any; ～e beide both of them; auf ～e Fälle in any case, at all events; ～e Tage every day; ～e zwei Minuten every two minutes.

All² [～] *n* (-s/no *pl.*) the universe.

'alle F *adj.* all gone; ～ werden come to an end; supplies, *etc.*: run out.

Allee [a'le:] *f* (-/-n) avenue; (tree-lined) walk.

allein [a'laın] **1.** *adj.* alone; single; unassisted; **2.** *adv.* alone; only; **3.** *cj.* yet, only, but, however; 2be-rechtigung *f* exclusive right; 2be-sitz *m* exclusive possession; 2herr-scher *m* absolute monarch, auto-crat; dictator; ～ig *adj.* only, ex-clusive, sole; 2sein *n* loneliness, solitariness, solitude; ～stehend *adj. p.*: alone in the world; single; building, *etc.*: isolated, detached; 2verkauf *m* exclusive sale; monop-oly; 2vertreter *m* sole represent-ative or agent; 2vertrieb *m* sole distributors *pl.*

allemal *adv.* ['alə'mɑːl] always; ein für ～ once (and for all).

'allen'falls *adv.* if need be; pos-sibly, perhaps; at best.

allenthalben † *adv.* ['alənt'halbən] everywhere.

'aller|'best *adj.* best ... of all, very best; ～dings *adv.* ['～'diŋs] indeed; to be sure; ～! certainly!, Am. F sure!; '～'erst **1.** *adj.* first ... of all, very first; foremost; **2.** *adv.*: zu ～ first of all.

Allergie ♊ [alɛr'giː] *f* (-/-n) allergy.

'aller|'hand *adj.* of all kinds or sorts; F das ist ja ～! F I say!; sl. that's the limit!; '2'heiligen *n* (-/no *pl.*) All Saints' Day; ～lei *adj.* ['～'laı] of all kinds or sorts; '2'lei *n* (-s/-s) medley; '～'letzt **1.** *adj.* last of all, very last; latest (news, fashion, *etc.*); **2.** *adv.*: zu ～ last of all; '～'liebst **1.** *adj.* dearest of all; (most) lovely; **2.** *adv.*: am ～en best of all; '～'meist **1.** *adj.* most; **2.** *adv.*: am ～en mostly; chiefly; '～'nächst *adj.* very next; '～'neu(e)st *adj.* the very latest; '2'seelen *n* (-/no *pl.*) All Souls' Day; '～'seits *adv.* on all sides; universally; '～'wenigst *adv.*: am ～en least of all.

'alle|'samt *adv.* one and all, all together; '～'zeit *adv.* always, at all times, for ever.

'all|'gegenwärtig *adj.* omnipresent, ubiquitous; ～'ge'mein **1.** *adj.* general; common; universal; **2.** *adv.*: im ～en in general, generally; 2ge-'meinheit *f* (-/no *pl.*) generality; universality; general public; 2'heil-mittel *n* panacea, cure-all (both a. fig.).

Allianz [ali'ants] *f* (-/-en) alliance.

alli'ier|en *v/refl.* (no -ge-, h) ally o.s. (mit to, with); 2te *m* (-n/-n) ally.

'all|'jährlich 1. *adj.* annual; **2.** *adv.* annually, every year; '2macht *f* (-/no *pl.*) omnipotence; ～'mächtig *adj.* omnipotent, almighty; ～mäh-lich [～'mɛːliç] **1.** *adj.* gradual; **2.** *adv.* gradually, by degrees.

Allopathie ♊ [alopa'tiː] allopathy.

all|seitig *adj.* ['alzaıtiç] universal; all-round; '2strom ⚡ *m* (-[e]s/no *pl.*) alternating current/direct cur-rent (abbr. A.C./D.C.); '2tag *m* workday; week-day; fig. everyday life, daily routine; ～'täglich *adj.* daily; fig. common, trivial; '2tags-leben *n* (-s/no *pl.*) everyday life; '～'wissend *adj.* omniscient; '2'wis-senheit *f* (-/no *pl.*) omniscience; '～'wöchentlich *adj.* weekly; '～zu *adv.* (much) too; '～zu'viel *adv.* too much.

Alm [alm] *f* (-/-en) Alpine pasture, alp.

Almosen ['almoːzən] *n* (-s/-) alms; ～ *pl.* alms *pl.*, charity.

Alp|druck ['alp-] *m* (-[e]s/⁼e), '～drücken *n* (-s/no *pl.*) night-mare.

Alpen ['alpən] *pl.* Alps *pl.*

Alphabet [alfa'beːt] *n* (-[e]s/-e) alphabet; 2isch *adj.* alphabetic(al).

'Alptraum *m* nightmare.

als *cj.* [als] than; as, like; (in one's capacity) as; but, except; temporal: after, when; as; ～ ob as if, as though; so viel ～ as much as; er ist zu dumm, ～ daß er es verstehen könnte he is too stupid to under-stand it; ～'bald *adv.* immediately; ～'dann *adv.* then.

also ['alzo] **1.** *adv.* thus, so; **2.** *cj.* therefore, so, consequently; na ～! there you are!

alt¹ *adj.* [alt] old; aged; ancient; antique; stale; second-hand.

Alt² ♪ [～] *m* (-s/-e) alto, contralto.

Altar [al'taːr] *m* (-[e]s/⁼e) altar.

Alteisen ['alt⁹-] *n* scrap-iron.

'Alte (-n/-n) **1.** *m* old man; F: der ～ the governor; hist.: die ～n *pl.* the ancients *pl.*; **2.** *f* old woman.

'Alter *n* (-s/-) age; old age; seniority; er ist in meinem ～ he is my age; von mittlerem ～ middle-aged.

älter *adj.* ['ɛltər] older; senior; der ～e Bruder the elder brother.

altern ['altərn] *v/i.* (ge-, h, sein) grow old, age.

Alternative [altɛrna'tiːvə] *f* (-/-n) alternative; keine ～ haben have no choice.

'Alters|grenze *f* age-limit; retire-ment age; '～heim *n* old people's home; '～rente *f* old-age pension; '2schwach *adj.* decrepit; senile; '～schwäche *f* decrepitude; '～ver-sorgung *f* old-age pension.

Altertum ['altərtu:m] *n* **1.** (-s/*no pl.*) antiquity; **2.** (-s/ᵕer) *mst* Altertümer *pl.* antiquities *pl.*

altertümlich *adj.* ['altərty:mliç] ancient, antique, archaic.

'Altertums|forscher *m* arch(a)eologist; **'ᵕkunde** *f* arch(a)eology.

ältest *adj.* ['ɛltəst] oldest; eldest (*sister, etc.*); earliest (*recollections*); **'Ꝗe** *m* (-n/-n) elder; senior; *mein ᵕr* my eldest (son).

Altistin *♪* [al'tistin] *f* (-/-nen) altosinger, contralto-singer.

'altklug *adj.* precocious, forward.

ältlich *adj.* ['ɛltliç] elderly, oldish.

'Alt|material *n* junk, scrap; salvage; **'ᵕmeister** *m* doyen, dean, F Grand Old Man (*a. sports*); *sports:* ex-champion; **'Ꝗmodisch** *adj.* old-fashioned; **'ᵕpapier** *n* waste paper; **'ᵕphilologe** *m* classical philologist *or* scholar; **'ᵕstadt** *f* old town *or* city; **'ᵕwarenhändler** *m* second-hand dealer; **ᵕ'weibersommer** *m* Indian summer; gossamer.

Aluminium ⁿⁱⁿ [alu'mi:njum] *n* (-s/*no pl.*) aluminium, *Am.* aluminum.

am *prp.* [am] = **an dem.**

Amateur [ama'tø:r] *m* (-s/-e) amateur.

Amboß ['ambɔs] *m* (Ambosses/Ambosse) anvil.

ambulan|t ♨ *adj.* [ambu'lant]: ᵕ *Behandelter* out-patient; **Ꝗz** [ᵕts] *f* (-/-en) ambulance.

Ameise *zo.* ['a:maɪzə] *f* (-/-n) ant; **'ᵕnhaufen** *m* ant-hill.

Amerikan|er [ameri'ka:nər] *m* (-s/-), **ᵕerin** *f* (-/-nen) American; **Ꝗisch** *adj.* American.

Amme ['amə] *f* (-/-n) (wet-)nurse.

Amnestie [amnɛs'ti:] *f* (-/-n) amnesty, general pardon.

Amor ['a:mɔr] *m* (-s/*no pl.*) Cupid.

Amortis|ation [amɔrtiza'tsjo:n] *f* (-/-en) amortization, redemption; **Ꝗieren** [ᵕ'zi:rən] *v/t.* (*no -ge-, h*) amortize, redeem; pay off.

Ampel ['ampəl] *f* (-/-n) hanging lamp; traffic light.

Amphibie *zo.* [am'fi:bjə] *f* (-/-n) amphibian.

Ampulle [am'pulə] *f* (-/-n) ampoule.

Amput|ation ♨ [amputa'tsjo:n] *f* (-/-en) amputation; **Ꝗieren** ♨ [ᵕ'ti:rən] *v/t.* (*no -ge-, h*) amputate; **ᵕierte** *m* (-n/-n) amputee.

Amsel *orn.* ['amzəl] *f* (-/-n) blackbird.

Amt [amt] *n* (-[e]s/ᵕer) office; post; charge; office, board; official duty, function; (telephone) exchange; **Ꝗieren** [ᵕ'ti:rən] *v/i.* (*no -ge-, h*) hold office; officiate; **Ꝗlich** *adj.* official; **ᵕmann** *m* district administrator; *hist.* bailiff.

'Amts|arzt *m* medical officer of health; **'ᵕbefugnis** *f* competence, authority; **'ᵕbereich** *m*, **'ᵕbezirk** *m* jurisdiction; **'ᵕblatt** *n* gazette; **'ᵕeid** *m* oath of office; **'ᵕeinführung** *f* inauguration; **'ᵕführung** *f* administration; **'ᵕgeheimnis** *n* official secret; **'ᵕgericht** *n* appr. district court; **'ᵕgeschäfte** *n/pl.* official duties *pl.*; **'ᵕgewalt** *f* (official) authority; **'ᵕhandlung** *f* official act; **'ᵕniederlegung** *f* (-/ᵕ-en) resignation; **'ᵕrichter** *m* appr. district court judge; **'ᵕsiegel** *n* official seal; **'ᵕvorsteher** *m* head official.

Amulett [amu'lɛt] *n* (-[e]s/-e) amulet, charm.

amüs|ant *adj.* [amy'zant] amusing, entertaining; **ᵕieren** [ᵕ'zi:rən] *v/t.* (*no -ge-, h*) amuse, entertain; *sich ᵕ* amuse *or* enjoy o.s., have a good time.

an [an] **1.** *prp.* (*dat.*) at; on, upon; in; against; to; by, near, close to; ᵕ *der Themse* on the Thames; ᵕ *der Wand* on *or* against the wall; *es ist ᵕ dir zu inf.* it is up to you to *inf.*; *am Leben* alive; *am 1. März* on March 1st; *am Morgen* in the morning; **2.** *prp.* (*acc.*) to; on; on to; at; against; about; *bis ᵕ* as far as, up to; **3.** *adv.* on; *von heute ᵕ* from this day forth, from today; *von nun or jetzt ᵕ* from now on.

analog *adj.* [ana'lo:k] analogous (*dat. or* zu to, with).

Analphabet [an'(ˀ)alfa'be:t] *m* (-en/-en) illiterate (person).

Analys|e [ana'ly:zə] *f* (-/-n) analysis; **Ꝗieren** [ᵕ'zi:rən] *v/t.* (*no -ge-, h*) analy|se, *Am.* -ze.

Anämie [anɛ'mi:] *f* (-/-n) an(a)emia.

Ananas ['ananas] *f* (-/-, -se) pineapple.

Anarchie [anar'çi:] *f* (-/-n) anarchy.

Anatom|ie [anato'mi:] *f* (-/*no pl.*) anatomy; **Ꝗisch** *adj.* [ᵕ'to:miʃ] anatomical.

'anbahnen *v/t.* (*sep., -ge-, h*) pave the way for, initiate; open up; *sich ᵕ* be opening up.

'Anbau *m* **1.** ♀ (-[e]s/*no pl.*) cultivation; **2.** △ (-[e]s/-ten) outbuilding, annex, extension, addition; **'Ꝗen** *v/t.* (*sep., -ge-, h*) ♀ cultivate, grow; △ add (*an acc.* to); **'ᵕfläche** ♀ *f* arable land.

'anbehalten *v/t.* (*irr.* halten, *sep., no -ge-, h*) keep (*garment, etc.*) on.

an'bei ✝ *adv.* enclosed.

'an|beißen (*irr.* beißen, *sep., -ge-, h*) **1.** *v/t.* bite into; **2.** *v/i. fish:* bite; **'ᵕbellen** *v/t.* (*sep., -ge-, h*) bark at; **ᵕberaumen** ['ᵕbəraumən] *v/t.* (*sep., no -ge-, h*) appoint, fix; **'ᵕbeten** *v/t.* (*sep., -ge-, h*) adore, worship.

'Anbetracht *m*: *in ᵕ* considering, in consideration of.

'**anbetteln** *v/t.* (*sep.*, -ge-, *h*) beg from, solicit alms of.
'**Anbetung** *f* (-/%-en) worship, adoration; '**Qswürdig** *adj.* adorable.
'**an|bieten** *v/t.* (*irr. bieten, sep.*, -ge-, *h*) offer; '**~binden** *v/t.* (*irr. binden, sep.*, -ge-, *h*) bind, tie (up); ~ **an** (*dat.*, *acc.*) tie to; *s.* angebunden; '**~blasen** *v/t.* (*irr. blasen, sep.*, -ge-, *h*) blow at *or* (up)on.
'**Anblick** *m* look; view; sight, aspect; '**Qen** *v/t.* (*sep.*, -ge-, *h*) look at; glance at; view; eye.
'**an|blinzeln** *v/t.* (*sep.*, -ge-, *h*) wink at; '**~brechen** (*irr. brechen, sep.*, -ge-) 1. *v/t.* (*h*) break into (*provisions, etc.*); open (*bottle, etc.*); 2. *v/i.* (*sein*) begin; *day*: break, dawn; '**~brennen** (*irr. brennen, sep.*, -ge-) 1. *v/t.* (*h*) set on fire; light (*cigar, etc.*); 2. *v/i.* (*sein*) catch fire; burn; '**~bringen** *v/t.* (*irr. bringen, sep.*, -ge-, *h*) bring; fix (*an dat.* to), attach (to); place; † dispose of (*goods*); lodge (*complaint*); *s.* angebracht.
'**Anbruch** *m* (-[e]s/*no pl.*) beginning; break (*of day*).
'**anbrüllen** *v/t.* (*sep.*, -ge-, *h*) roar at.
Andacht ['andaxt] *f* (-/-en) devotion(*s pl.*); prayers *pl.*
andächtig *adj.* ['andɛçtiç] devout.
'**andauern** *v/i.* (*sep.*, -ge-, *h*) last, continue, go on.
'**Andenken** *n* (-s/-) memory, remembrance; keepsake, souvenir; **zum ~ an** (*acc.*) in memory of.
ander *adj.* ['andər] other; different; next; opposite; **am ~en Tag** (on) the next day; **e-n Tag um den ~en** every other day; **ein ~er Freund** another friend; **nichts ~es** nothing else.
andererseits *adv.* ['andərər'zaits] on the other hand.
ändern ['ɛndərn] *v/t.* (ge-, *h*) alter; change; **ich kann es nicht ~** I can't help it; **sich ~** alter; change.
'**andern'falls** *adv.* otherwise, else.
anders *adv.* ['andərs] otherwise; differently (*als* from); else; *j.* ~ somebody else; **ich kann nicht ~, ich muß weinen** I cannot help crying; **~ werden** change.
'**ander'seits** *adv. s.* andererseits.
'**anders'wo** *adv.* elsewhere.
anderthalb *adj.* ['andərt'halp] one and a half.
'**Änderung** *f* (-/-en) change, alteration.
ander|wärts *adv.* ['andər'vɛrts] elsewhere; '**~'weitig 1.** *adj.* other; 2. *adv.* otherwise.
'**andeut|en** *v/t.* (*sep.*, -ge-, *h*) indicate; hint; intimate; imply; suggest; '**Qung** *f* intimation; hint; suggestion.
'**Andrang** *m* rush; ⚕ congestion.
andre *adj.* ['andrə] *s.* andere.

'**andrehen** *v/t.* (*sep.*, -ge-, *h*) turn on (*gas, etc.*); ⚡ switch on (*light*).
'**androh|en** *v/t.* (*sep.*, -ge-, *h*): *j-m* **et. ~** threaten s.o. with s.th.; '**Qung** *f* threat.
aneignen ['an⁹-] *v/refl.* (*sep.*, -ge-, *h*) appropriate; acquire; adopt; seize; usurp.
aneinander *adv.* [an⁹ai'nandər] together; '**~geraten** *v/i.* (*irr. raten, sep.*, *no* -ge-, *sein*) clash (*mit* with).
anekeln ['an⁹-] *v/t.* (*sep.*, -ge-, *h*) disgust, sicken.
Anerbieten ['an⁹-] *n* (-s/-) offer.
anerkannt *adj.* ['an⁹-] acknowledged, recognized.
anerkenn|en ['an⁹-] *v/t.* (*irr. kennen, sep.*, *no* -ge-, *h*) acknowledge (*als* as), recognize; appreciate; own (*child*); hono(u)r (*bill*); '**Qung** *f* (-/-en) acknowledgement; recognition; appreciation.
'**anfahr|en** (*irr. fahren, sep.*, -ge-) 1. *v/i.* (*sein*) start; ✗ descend; **angefahren kommen** drive up; 2. *v/t.* (*h*) run into; carry, convey; *j-n* ~ let fly at s.o.; '**Qt** *f* approach; drive.
'**Anfall** ✗ *m* fit, attack; '**Qen** (*irr. fallen, sep.*, -ge-) 1. *v/t.* (*h*) attack; assail; 2. *v/i.* (*sein*) accumulate; *money*: accrue.
anfällig *adj.* ['anfɛliç] susceptible (*für* to); prone to (*diseases, etc.*).
'**Anfang** *m* beginning, start, commencement; ~ **Mai** at the beginning of May, early in May; '**Qen** *v/t. and v/i.* (*irr. fangen, sep.*, -ge-, *h*) begin, start, commence.
Anfäng|er ['anfɛŋər] *m* (-s/-) beginner; '**Qlich 1.** *adj.* initial; 2. *adv.* in the beginning.
anfangs *adv.* ['anfaŋs] in the beginning; '**Qbuchstabe** *m* initial (letter); **großer ~** capital letter; **Qgründe** ['~gryndə] *m/pl.* elements *pl.*
'**anfassen** (*sep.*, -ge-, *h*) 1. *v/t.* seize; touch; handle; 2. *v/i.* lend a hand.
anfecht|bar *adj.* ['anfɛçtba:r] contestable; '**~en** *v/t.* (*irr. fechten, sep.*, -ge-, *h*) contest; dispute; ⚖ avoid (*contract*); '**Qung** *f* (-/-en) contestation; ⚖ avoidance; *fig.* temptation.
an|fertigen ['anfɛrtigən] *v/t.* (*sep.*, -ge-, *h*) make, manufacture; '**~feuchten** *v/t.* (*sep.*, -ge-, *h*) moisten, wet, damp; '**~feuern** *v/t.* (*sep.*, -ge-, *h*) fire; heat; *sports*: cheer; *fig.* encourage; '**~flehen** *v/t.* (*sep.*, -ge-, *h*) implore; '**~fliegen** ✈ *v/t.* (*irr. fliegen, sep.*, -ge-, *h*) approach, head for (*airport, etc.*); '**Qflug** *m* ✈ approach (flight); *fig.* touch, tinge.
'**anforder|n** *v/t.* (*sep.*, -ge-, *h*) demand; request; claim; '**Qung** *f* demand; request; claim.
'**Anfrage** *f* inquiry; '**Qn** *v/i.* (*sep.*, -ge-, *h*) ask (*bei j-m* s.o.); inquire (*bei j-m nach* et. of s.o. about s.th.).

an|freunden ['anfrɔʏndən] *v/refl.* (*sep.*, *-ge-*, *h*): *sich* ~ *mit* make friends with; '**~frieren** *v/i.* (*irr. frieren*, *sep.*, *-ge-*, *sein*) freeze on (*an dat. or acc.* to); '**~fügen** *v/t.* (*sep.*, *-ge-*, *h*) join, attach (*an acc.* to); '**~fühlen** *v/t.* (*sep.*, *-ge-*, *h*) feel, touch; *sich* ~ feel.

Anfuhr f ['anfuːr] *f* (*-/-en*) conveyance, carriage.

'**anführ|en** *v/t.* (*sep.*, *-ge-*, *h*) lead; allege; ✗ command; quote, cite (*authority, passage, etc.*); dupe, fool, trick; '**Ωer** *m* (ring)leader; '**Ωungszeichen** *n/pl.* quotation marks *pl.*, inverted commas *pl.*

'**Angabe** f declaration; statement; instruction; F *fig.* bragging, showing off.

'**angeb|en** (*irr. geben*, *sep.*, *-ge-*, *h*) **1.** *v/t.* declare; state; specify; allege; give (*name, reason*); ✝ quote (*prices*); denounce, inform against; **2.** *v/i. cards*: deal first; F *fig.* brag, show off, *Am.* blow; '**Ωer** *m* (*-s/-*) informer; F braggart, *Am.* blowhard; '**~lich** *adj.* ['~pliç] supposed; pretended, alleged.

'**angeboren** *adj.* innate, inborn; ✗ congenital.

'**Angebot** *n* offer (*a.* ✝); *at auction sale*: bid; ✝ supply.

'**ange|bracht** *adj.* appropriate, suitable; well-timed; '**~bunden** *adj.*: *kurz* ~ *sein* be short (*gegen* with).

'**angehen** (*irr. gehen*, *sep.*, *-ge-*) **1.** *v/i.* (*sein*) begin; *meat, etc.*: go bad, go off; *es geht an* it will do; **2.** *v/t.* (*h*): *j-n* ~ concern s.o.; *das geht dich nichts an* that is no business of yours.

'**angehör|en** *v/i.* (*sep.*, *no -ge-*, *h*) belong to; '**Ωige** ['~iɡə] *m, f* (*-n/-n*): *seine* ~*n pl.* his relations *pl.*; *die nächsten* ~*n pl.* the next of kin.

Angeklagte ✗✗ ['angəklaːktə] *m, f* (*-n/-n*) *the* accused; prisoner (at the bar); defendant.

Angel ['aŋəl] *f* (*-/-n*) hinge; fishing-tackle, fishing-rod.

'**angelegen** *adj.*: *sich et.* ~ *sein lassen* make s.th. one's business; '**Ω-heit** f business, concern, affair, matter.

'**Angel|gerät** *n* fishing-tackle; '**Ωn** (*ge-*, *h*) **1.** *v/i.* fish (*nach* for), angle (*for*) (*both a. fig.*); ~ *in* fish (*river, etc.*); **2.** *v/t.* fish (*trout*); '**~punkt** *fig. m* pivot.

'**Angel|sachse** *m* Anglo-Saxon; '**Ω-sächsisch** *adj.* Anglo-Saxon.

'**Angelschnur** f fishing-line.

'**ange|messen** *adj.* suitable, appropriate; reasonable; adequate; '**~nehm** *adj.* pleasant, agreeable, pleasing; *sehr* ~*!* glad *or* pleased to meet you; **~regt** *adj.* ['~reːkt] stimulated; *discussion*: animated, lively; '**~sehen** *adj.* respected, esteemed.

'**Angesicht** *n* (*-[e]s/-er*, *-e*) face, countenance; *von* ~ *zu* ~ face to face; '**Ωs** *prp.* (*gen.*) in view of.

angestammt *adj.* ['angəʃtamt] hereditary, innate.

Angestellte ['angəʃteltə] *m, f* (*-n/-n*) employee; *die* ~*n pl.* the staff.

'**ange|trunken** *adj.* tipsy; **~wandt** *adj.* ['~vant] applied; '**~wiesen** *adj.*: ~ *sein auf* (*acc.*) be dependent *or* thrown (up)on.

'**angewöhnen** *v/t.* (*sep.*, *-ge-*, *h*): *j-m et.* ~ accustom s.o. to s.th.; *sich et.* ~ get into the habit of s.th.; take to (*smoking*).

'**Angewohnheit** f custom, habit.

Angina ✗ [aŋˈɡiːna] *f* (*-/Anginen*) angina; tonsillitis.

'**angleichen** (*irr. gleichen*, *sep.*, *-ge-*, *h*) assimilate (*an acc.* to, with), adjust (to); *sich* ~ *an* (*acc.*) assimilate to *or* with, adjust *or* adapt o.s. to.

Angler ['aŋlər] *m* (*-s/-*) angler.

'**angliedern** *v/t.* (*sep.*, *-ge-*, *h*) join; annex; affiliate.

Anglist [aŋˈɡlist] *m* (*-en/-en*) professor *or* student of English, Angli(ci)st.

'**angreif|en** *v/t.* (*irr. greifen*, *sep.*, *-ge-*, *h*) touch; draw upon (*capital, provisions*); attack; affect (*health, material*); ✗ corrode; exhaust; '**Ωer** *m* (*-s/-*) aggressor, assailant.

'**angrenzend** *adj.* adjacent; adjoining.

'**Angriff** *m* attack, assault; *in* ~ *nehmen* set about; '**~skrieg** *m* offensive war; '**Ωslustig** *adj.* aggressive.

Angst [aŋst] f (*-/-ⸯe*) fear; anxiety; anguish; *ich habe* ~ I am afraid (*vor dat.* of); '**~hase** *m* coward.

ängstigen ['ɛŋstiɡən] *v/t.* (*ge-*, *h*) frighten, alarm; *sich* ~ be afraid (*vor dat.* of); be alarmed (*um* about).

ängstlich *adj.* ['ɛŋstliç] uneasy, nervous; anxious; afraid; scrupulous; timid; '**Ωkeit** f (*-/no pl.*) anxiety; scrupulousness; timidity.

'**an|haben** *v/t.* (*irr. haben*, *sep.*, *-ge-*, *h*) have (*garment*) on; *das kann mir nichts* ~ that can't do me any harm; '**~haften** *v/i.* (*sep.*, *-ge-*, *h*) stick, adhere (*dat.* to); '**~haken** *v/t.* (*sep.*, *-ge-*, *h*) hook on; tick (off), *Am.* check (off) (*name, item*).

'**anhalten** (*irr. halten*, *sep.*, *-ge-*, *h*) **1.** *v/t.* stop; *j-n* ~ *zu et.* keep s.o. to s.th.; *den Atem* ~ hold one's breath; **2.** *v/i.* continue, last; stop; *um ein Mädchen* ~ propose to a girl; '**~d** *adj.* continuous; persevering.

'**Anhaltspunkt** *m* clue.

'**Anhang** *m* appendix, supplement (*to book, etc.*); followers *pl.*, adherents *pl.*

'**anhäng|en** (*sep.*, *-ge-*, *h*) **1.** *v/t.* hang on; affix, attach, join; add; couple (on) (*coach, vehicle*); **2.** *v/i.*

(*irr. hängen*) adhere to; '₂er *m* (-s/-)
adherent, follower; pendant (*of
necklace, etc.*); label, tag; trailer
(*behind car, etc.*).
anhänglich *adj.* ['anhɛŋliç] devoted,
attached; '₂keit *f* (-/no *pl.*) devotion, attachment.
Anhängsel ['anhɛŋzəl] *n* (-s/-) ap-
pendage.
'**anhauchen** *v/t.* (*sep.*, -ge-, *h*)
breathe on; blow (*fingers*).
'**anhäuf|en** *v/t. and v/refl.* (*sep.*,
-ge-, *h*) pile up, accumulate; '₂ung
f accumulation.
'**an|heben** *v/t.* (*irr. heben, sep.*, -ge-,
h) lift, raise; '₊heften *v/t.* (*sep.*,
-ge-, *h*) fasten (*an acc.* to); stitch
(to).
an'heim|fallen *v/i.* (*irr. fallen, sep.*,
-ge-, *sein*): j-m ~ fall to s.o.; ₊stel-
len *v/t.* (*sep.*, -ge-, *h*): j-m et. ~
leave s.th. to s.o.
'**Anhieb** *m*: auf ~ at the first go.
'**Anhöhe** *f* rise, elevation, hill.
'**anhören** *v/t.* (*sep.*, -ge-, *h*) listen to;
sich ~ sound.
Anilin ₊ [ani'li:n] *n* (-s/no *pl.*)
anilin(e).
'**ankämpfen** *v/i.* (*sep.*, -ge-, *h*): ~
gegen struggle against.
'**Ankauf** *m* purchase.
Anker ₊ ['aŋkər] *m* (-s/-) anchor;
vor ~ gehen cast anchor; '₊kette ₊
f cable; '₂n ₊ *v/t. and v/i.* (ge-, *h*)
anchor; '₊uhr *f* lever watch.
'**anketten** *v/t.* (*sep.*, -ge-, *h*) chain
(*an dat. or acc.* to).
'**Anklage** *f* accusation, charge; ₊₊
a. indictment; '₂n *v/t.* (*sep.*, -ge-, *h*)
accuse (*gen. or wegen of*), charge
(with); ₊₊ *a.* indict (for).
'**Ankläger** *m* accuser; öffentlicher ~
₊₊ public prosecutor, *Am.* district
attorney.
'**anklammern** *v/t.* (*sep.*, -ge-, *h*)
clip *s.th.* on; *sich* ~ cling (*an dat.
or acc.* to).
'**Anklang** *m*: ~ an (*acc.*) suggestion
of; ~ finden meet with approval.
'**an|kleben** *v/t.* (*sep.*, -ge-, *h*) stick
on (*an dat. or acc.* to); glue on (to);
paste on (to); gum on (to); '₊klei-
den *v/t.* (*sep.*, -ge-, *h*) dress; *sich* ~
dress (o.s.); '₊klopfen *v/i.* (*sep.*,
-ge-, *h*) knock (*an acc.* at); '₊knip-
sen ₊ *v/t.* (*sep.*, -ge-, *h*) turn or
switch on; '₊knüpfen (*sep.*, -ge-, *h*)
1. *v/t.* tie (*an dat. or acc.* to); *fig.*
begin; Verbindungen ~ form con-
nexions *or* (*Am. only*) connections;
2. *v/i.* refer (*an acc.* to); '₊kommen
v/i. (*irr. kommen, sep.*, -ge-, *sein*)
arrive; ~ auf (*acc.*) depend (up)on;
es darauf ~ lassen run the risk, risk
it; darauf kommt es an that is the
point; es kommt nicht darauf an it
does not matter.
Ankömmling ['ankœmliŋ] *m* (-s/-e)
new-comer, new arrival.

3 SW E II

'**ankündig|en** *v/t.* (*sep.*, -ge-, *h*) an-
nounce; advertise; '₂ung *f* announcement; advertisement.
Ankunft ['ankunft] *f* (-/no *pl.*)
arrival.
'**an|kurbeln** *v/t.* (*sep.*, -ge-, *h*) *mot.*
crank up; die Wirtschaft ~ F boost
the economy; '₊lächeln *v/t.* (*sep.*,
-ge-, *h*), '₊lachen *v/t.* (*sep.*, -ge-, *h*)
smile at.
'**Anlage** *f* construction; installation;
⊕ plant; grounds *pl.*, park; plan,
arrangement, layout; enclosure (*to
letter*); ₊ investment; talent; pre-
disposition, tendency; öffentliche
~n *pl.* public gardens *pl.*; '₊kapital
₊ *n* invested capital.
'**anlangen** (*sep.*, -ge-) 1. *v/i.* (*sein*)
arrive at; 2. *v/t.* (*h*) F touch; concern; was mich anlangt as far as I
am concerned, (speaking) for myself.
Anlaß ['anlas] *m* (Anlasses/Anlässe)
occasion; ohne allen ~ without any
reason.
'**anlass|en** *v/t.* (*irr. lassen, sep.*, -ge-,
h) F leave or keep (*garment, etc.*) on;
leave (*light, etc.*) on; ⊕ start, set
going; sich gut ~ promise well;
'₂er *mot. m* (-s/-) starter.
anläßlich *prp.* (*gen.*) ['anlɛsliç] on
the occasion of.
'**Anlauf** *m* start, run; '₂en (*irr. laufen, sep.*, -ge-) 1. *v/i.* (*sein*) run up;
start; tarnish, (grow) dim; ~ gegen
run against; 2. ₊ *v/t.* (*h*) call or
touch at (*port*).
'**an|legen** (*sep.*, -ge-, *h*) 1. *v/t.* put
(*an acc.* to, against); lay out (*garden*);
invest (*money*); level (*gun*); put on
(*garment*); found (*town*); ₊ apply
(*dressing*); lay in (*provisions*); Feuer
~ an (*acc.*) set fire to; 2. *v/i.* ₊ :
land; moor; ~ auf (*acc.*) aim at;
'₊lehnen *v/t.* (*sep.*, -ge-, *h*) lean (*an
acc.* against); leave *or* set (*door*)
ajar; sich ~ an (*acc.*) lean against
or on.
Anleihe ['anlaɪə] *f* (-/-n) loan.
'**anleit|en** *v/t.* (*sep.*, -ge-, *h*) guide
(zu to); instruct (*in dat.* in); '₂ung
f guidance, instruction; guide.
'**Anliegen** *n* (-s/-) desire, request.
'**an|locken** *v/t.* (*sep.*, -ge-, *h*) allure,
entice; decoy; '₊machen *v/t.* (*sep.*,
-ge-, *h*) fasten (*an acc.* to), fix (to);
make, light (*fire*); ₊ switch on
(*light*); dress (*salad*); '₊malen *v/t.*
(*sep.*, -ge-, *h*) paint.
'**Anmarsch** *m* approach.
anmaß|en ['anma:sən] *v/refl.* (*sep.*,
-ge-, *h*) arrogate *s.th.* to o.s.; assume
(*right*); presume; '₊end *adj.*
arrogant; '₂ung *f* (-/-en) arrogance, presumption.
'**anmeld|en** *v/t.* (*sep.*, -ge-, *h*) an-
nounce, notify; sich ~ bei make an
appointment with; '₂ung *f* announcement, notification.

'anmerk|en v/t. (sep., -ge-, h) mark; note down; j-m et. ~ observe or perceive s.th. in s.o.; 'Qung f (-/-en) remark; note; annotation; comment.

'anmessen v/t. (irr. messen, sep., -ge-, h): j-m e-n Anzug ~ measure s.o. for a suit; s. angemessen.

'Anmut f (-/no pl.) grace, charm, loveliness; 'Qig adj. charming, graceful, lovely.

'an|nageln v/t. (sep., -ge-, h) nail on (an acc. to); '~nähen v/t. (sep., -ge-, h) sew on (an acc. to).

annäher|nd adj. ['annɛːərnt] approximate; 'Qung f (-/-en) approach.

Annahme ['annɑːmə] f (-/-n) acceptance; receiving-office; fig. assumption, supposition.

'annehm|bar adj. acceptable; price: reasonable; '~en (irr. nehmen, sep., -ge-, h) 1. v/t. accept, take; fig.: suppose, take it, Am. guess; assume; contract (habit); adopt (child); parl. pass (bill); sich (gen.) ~ attend to s.th.; befriend s.o.; 2. v/i. accept; 'Qlichkeit f (-/-en) amenity, agreeableness.

Annexion [anɛkˈsjoːn] f (-/-en) annexation.

Annonce [a'nõːsə] f (-/-n) advertisement.   [mous.
anonym adj. [ano'nyːm] anony-]
anordn|en ['anˀ-] v/t. (sep., -ge-, h) order; arrange; direct; 'Qung f arrangement; direction; order.

'anpacken v/t. (sep., -ge-, h) seize, grasp; fig. tackle.

'anpass|en v/t. (sep., -ge-, h) fit, adapt, suit; adjust; try or fit (garment) on; sich ~ adapt o.s. (dat. to); 'Qung f (-/-en) adaptation; '~ungsfähig adj. adaptable.

'anpflanz|en v/t. (sep., -ge-, h) cultivate, plant; 'Qung f cultivation; plantation.

Anprall ['anpral] m (-[e]s/~-e) impact; 'Qen v/i. (sep., -ge-, sein) strike (an acc. against).

'anpreisen v/t. (irr. preisen, sep., -ge-, h) commend, praise; boost, push.

'Anprobe f try-on, fitting.

'an|probieren v/t. (sep., no -ge-, h) try or fit on; '~raten v/t. (irr. raten, sep., -ge-, h) advise; '~rechnen v/t. (sep., -ge-, h) charge; hoch ~ value highly.

'Anrecht n right, title, claim (auf acc. to).

'Anrede f address; 'Qn v/t. (sep., -ge-, h) address, speak to.

'anreg|en v/t. (sep., -ge-, h) stimulate; suggest; '~end adj. stimulative, stimulating; suggestive; 'Qung f stimulation; suggestion.

'Anreiz m incentive; 'Qen v/t. (sep., -ge-, h) stimulate; incite.

'an|rennen v/i. (irr. rennen, sep., -ge-, sein): ~ gegen run against; angerannt kommen come running; '~richten v/t. (sep., -ge-, h) prepare, dress (food, salad); cause, do (damage).

anrüchig adj. ['anryçiç] disreputable.

'anrücken v/i. (sep., -ge-, sein) approach.

'Anruf m call (a. teleph.); 'Qen v/t. (irr. rufen, sep., -ge-, h) call (zum Zeugen to witness); teleph. ring up, F phone, Am. call up; hail (ship); invoke (God, etc.); appeal to (s.o.'s help).

'anrühren v/t. (sep., -ge-, h) touch; mix.

'Ansage f announcement; 'Qn v/t. (sep., -ge-, h) announce; '~r m (-s/-) announcer; compère, Am. master of ceremonies.

'ansammeln v/t. (sep., -ge-, h) collect, gather; accumulate, amass; sich ~ collect, gather; accumulate.

ansässig adj. ['anzɛsiç] resident.

'Ansatz m start.

'an|schaffen v/t. (sep., -ge-, h) procure, provide; purchase; sich et. ~ provide or supply o.s. with s.th.; '~schalten ƒ v/t. (sep., -ge-, h) connect; switch on (light).

'anschau|en v/t. (sep., -ge-, h) look at, view; '~lich adj. clear, vivid; graphic.

'Anschauung f (-/-en) view; perception; conception; intuition; contemplation; '~smaterial n illustrative material; '~sunterricht ['anʃauuŋs?-] m visual instruction, object-lessons pl.; '~svermögen n intuitive faculty.

'Anschein m (-[e]s/no pl.) appearance; 'Qend adj. apparent, seeming.

'an|schicken v/refl. (sep., -ge-, h): sich ~, et. zu tun get ready for s.th.; prepare for s.th.; set about doing s.th.; ~schirren ['~ʃirən] v/t. (sep., -ge-, h) harness.

'Anschlag m ⊕ stop, catch; ♩ touch; notice; placard, poster, bill; estimate; calculation; plot; e-n ~ auf j-n verüben make an attempt on s.o.'s life; ~brett ['~k-] n noticeboard, Am. bulletin board; Qen ['~gən] (irr. schlagen, sep., -ge-, h) 1. v/t. strike (an dat. or acc. against), knock (against); post up (bill); ♩ touch; level (gun); estimate, rate; 2. v/i. strike (an acc. against), knock (against); dog: bark; ♪ take (effect); food: agree (bei with); ~säule ['~k-] f advertising pillar; ~zettel ['~k-] m notice; placard, poster, bill.

'anschließen v/t. (irr. schließen, sep., -ge-, h) fix with a lock; join, attach, annex; ⊕, ƒ connect; sich j-m ~ join s.o.; sich e-r Meinung ~

follow an opinion; **∼d** *adj.* adjacent (*an acc.* to); subsequent (to).

'Anschluß *m* joining; 🚂, ⚡, *teleph.*, *gas, etc.*: connexion, (*Am. only*) connection; ∼ **haben an** (*acc.*) 🚂, *boat*: connect with; 🚂 run in connexion with; ∼ **finden** make friends (*an acc.* with), F **pal up** (with); *teleph.*: ∼ **bekommen** get through; **'∼dose** ⚡ *f* (wall) socket; **'∼zug** 🚂 *m* connecting train, connexion.

'an|schmiegen *v/refl.* (*sep.*, -ge-, *h*): **sich ∼ an** (*acc.*) nestle to; **'∼schmieren** *v/t.* (*sep.*, -ge-, *h*) (be)smear, grease; F *fig.* cheat; **'∼schnallen** *v/t.* (*sep.*, -ge-, *h*) buckle on; **bitte ∼!** 🚗 fasten seat-belts, please!; **'∼schnauzen** F *v/t.* (*sep.*, -ge-, *h*) snap at, blow *s.o.* up, *Am. a.* bawl *s.o.* out; **'∼schneiden** *v/t.* (*irr. schneiden, sep.*, -ge-, *h*) cut; broach (*subject*).

'Anschnitt *m* first cut *or* slice.

'an|schrauben *v/t.* (*sep.*, -ge-, *h*) screw on (*an dat. or acc.* to); **'∼schreiben** *v/t.* (*irr. schreiben, sep.*, -ge-, *h*) write down; *sports, games*: score; *et.* ∼ **lassen** have s.th. charged to one's account; buy s.th. on credit; **'∼schreien** *v/t.* (*irr. schreien, sep.*, -ge-, *h*) shout at.

'Anschrift *f* address.

an|schuldigen ['anʃuldigən] *v/t.* (*sep.*, -ge-, *h*) accuse, incriminate; **'∼schwärzen** *v/t.* (*sep.*, -ge-, *h*) blacken; *fig. a.* defame.

an|schwellen (*irr. schwellen, sep.*, -ge-) **1.** *v/i.* (*sein*) swell; increase, rise; **2.** *v/t.* (*h*) swell; **'Qung** *f* swelling.

anschwemm|en ['anʃvɛmən] *v/t.* (*sep.*, -ge-, *h*) wash ashore; *geol.* deposit (*alluvium*); **'Qung** *f* (-/-en) wash; *geol.* alluvial deposits *pl.*, alluvium.

'ansehen 1. *v/t.* (*irr. sehen, sep.*, -ge-, *h*) (take a) look at; view; regard, consider (*als* as); *et. mit* ∼ witness s.th.; ∼ **für** take for; *man sieht ihm sein Alter nicht an* he does not look his age; **2.** Q *n* (-s/*no pl.*) authority, prestige; respect; F appearance, aspect.

ansehnlich *adj.* ['anze:nliç] considerable; good-looking.

'an|seilen *mount. v/t. and v/refl.* (*sep.*, -ge-, *h*) rope; **'∼sengen** *v/t.* (*sep.*, -ge-, *h*) singe; **'∼setzen** (*sep.*, -ge-, *h*) **1.** *v/t.* put (*an acc.* to); add (to); fix, appoint (*date*); rate; fix, quote (*prices*); charge; put forth (*leaves, etc.*); put on (*flesh*); put (*food*) on (*to boil*); *Rost* ∼ rust; **2.** *v/i.* try; start; get ready.

'Ansicht *f* (-/-en) sight; view; *fig.* view, opinion; *meiner* ∼ *nach* in my opinion; *zur* ∼ ✝ on approval; **'∼(post)karte** *f* picture postcard; **'∼ssache** *f* matter of opinion.

'ansied|eln *v/t. and v/refl.* (*sep.*, -ge-, *h*) settle; **'Qler** *m* settler; **'Q-lung** *f* settlement.

'Ansinnen *n* (-s/-) request, demand.

'anspann|en *v/t.* (*sep.*, -ge-, *h*) stretch; put *or* harness (*horses, etc.*) to the carriage, *etc.*; *fig.* strain, exert; **'Qung** *fig. f* strain, exertion.

'anspeien *v/t.* (*irr. speien, sep.*, -ge-, *h*) spit upon *or* at.

'anspiel|en *v/i.* (*sep.*, -ge-, *h*) *cards*: lead; *sports*: lead off; *football*: kick off; ∼ *auf* (*acc.*) allude to, hint at; **'Qung** *f* (-/-en) allusion, hint.

'anspitzen *v/t.* (*sep.*, -ge-, *h*) point, sharpen.

'Ansporn *m* (-[e]s/🔧 -e) spur; **'Qen** *v/t.* (*sep.*, -ge-, *h*) spur *s.o.* on.

'Ansprache *f* address, speech; *e-e* ∼ *halten* deliver an address.

'ansprechen *v/t.* (*irr. sprechen, sep.*, -ge-, *h*) speak to, address; appeal to; **'∼d** *adj.* appealing.

'an|springen (*irr. springen, sep.*, -ge-) **1.** *v/i.* (*sein*) *engine*: start; **2.** *v/t.* (*h*) jump (up)on, leap at; **'∼spritzen** *v/t.* (*sep.*, -ge-, *h*) splash (*j-n mit et.* s.th. on s.o.); (be)sprinkle.

'Anspruch *m* claim (*a.* ⚖️) (*auf acc.* to), pretension (to); ⚖️ title (to); ∼ *haben auf* (*acc.*) be entitled to; *in* ∼ *nehmen* claim s.th.; *Zeit in* ∼ *nehmen* take up time; **'Qslos** *adj.* unpretentious; unassuming; **'Qsvoll** *adj.* pretentious.

'an|spülen *v/t.* (*sep.*, -ge-, *h*) *s. anschwemmen*; **'∼stacheln** *v/t.* (*sep.*, -ge-, *h*) goad (on).

Anstalt ['anʃtalt] *f* (-/-en) establishment, institution; ∼*en treffen zu* make arrangements for.

'Anstand *m* **1.** (-[e]s/🔧e) *hunt.* stand; objection; **2.** (-[e]s/🔧 🔧e) good manners *pl.*; decency, propriety.

anständig *adj.* ['anʃtendiç] decent; respectable; *price*: fair, handsome; **'Qkeit** *f* (-/🔧 -en) decency.

'Anstands|gefühl *n* sense of propriety; tact; **'Qlos** *adv.* unhesitatingly.

'anstarren *v/t.* (*sep.*, -ge-, *h*) stare *or* gaze at.

anstatt *prp.* (*gen.*) *and cj.* [an'ʃtat] instead of.

'anstaunen *v/t.* (*sep.*, -ge-, *h*) gaze at *s.o. or s.th.* in wonder.

'ansteck|en *v/t.* (*sep.*, -ge-, *h*) pin on; put on (*ring*); 💉 infect; set on fire; kindle (*fire*); light (*candle, etc.*); **'∼end** *adj.* infectious; contagious; *fig. a.* catching; **'Qung** 💉 *f* (-/-en) infection; contagion.

'an|stehen *v/i.* (*irr. stehen, sep.*, -ge-, *h*) queue up (*nach* for), *Am.* stand in line (for); **'∼steigen** *v/i.* (*irr. steigen, sep.*, -ge-, *sein*) ground; rise, ascend; *fig.* increase.

'anstell|en *v/t.* (*sep.*, -ge-, *h*) engage, employ, hire; make (*ex-*

periments); draw (*comparison*); turn on (*light, etc.*); manage; *sich ~* queue up (*nach* for), *Am.* line up (for); *sich dumm ~* set about *s.th.* stupidly; '**.ig** *adj.* handy, skil(l)ful; '**Qung** *f* place, position, job; employment.

Anstieg ['anʃtiːk] *m* (-[e]s/-e) ascent.

'**anstift|en** *v/t.* (*sep., -ge-, h*) instigate; '**Qer** *m* instigator; '**Qung** *f* instigation.

'**anstimmen** *v/t.* (*sep., -ge-, h*) strike up (*tune*).

'**Anstoß** *m football*: kick-off; *fig.* impulse; offen|ce, *Am.* -se; *~ erregen* give offence (*bei* to); *~ nehmen an* (*dat.*) take offence at; *~ geben zu et.* start s.th., initiate s.th.; '**Qen** (*irr.* stoßen, *sep., -ge-*) 1. *v/t.* (h) push, knock (*acc. or an* against); nudge; 2. *v/i.* (sein) knock (*an acc.* against); border (on, upon); adjoin; 3. *v/i.* (h): *mit der Zunge ~* lisp; *auf j-s Gesundheit ~* drink (to) s.o.'s health; '**Qend** *adj.* adjoining.

anstößig *adj.* ['anʃtøːsiç] shocking.

'**an|strahlen** *v/t.* (*sep., -ge-, h*) illuminate; floodlight (*building, etc.*); *fig.* beam at s.o.; '**.streben** *v/t.* (*sep., -ge-, h*) aim at, aspire to, strive for.

'**anstreich|en** *v/t.* (*irr.* streichen, *sep., -ge-, h*) paint; whitewash; mark; underline (*mistake*); '**Qer** *m* (-s/-) house-painter; decorator.

anstreng|en ['anʃtrɛŋən] *v/t.* (*sep., -ge-, h*) exert; try (*eyes*); fatigue; *Prozeß ~* bring an action (*gegen j-n* against s.o.); *sich ~* exert o.s.; '**.end** *adj.* strenuous; trying (*für* to); '**Qung** *f* (-/-en) exertion, strain, effort.

'**Anstrich** *m* paint, colo(u)r; coat (-ing); *fig.*: tinge; air.

'**Ansturm** *m* assault; onset; *~ auf* (*acc.*) rush for; ✝ run on (*bank*).

'**anstürmen** *v/i.* (*sep., -ge-, sein*) storm, rush.

'**Anteil** *m* share, portion; *~ nehmen an* (*dat.*) take an interest in; sympathize with; **.nahme** ['.naː-mə] *f* (-/*no pl.*) sympathy; interest; '**.schein** ✝ *m* share-certificate.

Antenne [an'tɛnə] *f* (-/-n) aerial.

Antialkoholiker [anti'ʔalkoˈhoːlikər, '~] *m* (-s/-) teetotaller.

antik *adj.* [an'tiːk] antique.

Antilope *zo.* [anti'loːpə] *f* (-/-n) antelope.

Antipathie [antipa'tiː] *f* (-/-n) antipathy.

'**antippen** F *v/t.* (*sep., -ge-, h*) tap.

Antiquar [anti'kvaːr] *m* (-s/-e) second-hand bookseller; **.iat** [.arˈjaːt] *n* (-[e]s/-e) second-hand bookshop; **Qisch** *adj.* and *adv.* [.'kvaːriʃ] second-hand.

Antiquitäten [antikviˈtɛːtən] *f/pl.* antiques *pl.*

'**Anti-Rakete** *f* anti-ballistic missile.

antiseptisch ⚕ *adj.* [antiˈzɛptiʃ] antiseptic.

Antlitz ['antlits] *n* (-es/⚔ -e) face, countenance.

Antrag ['antraːk] *m* (-[e]s/ꞙe) offer, proposal; application, request; *parl.* motion; *~ stellen auf* (*acc.*) make an application for; *parl.* put a motion for; '**.steller** *m* (-s/-) applicant; *parl.* mover; ⚖ petitioner.

'**an|treffen** *v/t.* (*irr.* treffen, *sep., -ge-, h*) meet with, find; '**.treiben** (*irr.* treiben, *sep., -ge-*) 1. *v/i.* (sein) drift ashore; 2. *v/t.* (h) drive (on); *fig.* impel; '**.treten** (*irr.* treten, *sep., -ge-*) 1. *v/t.* (h) enter upon (*office*); take up (*position*); set out on (*journey*); enter upon take possession of (*inheritance*); 2. *v/i.* (sein) take one's place; ⚔ fall in.

'**Antrieb** *m* motive, impulse; ⊕ drive, propulsion.

'**Antritt** *m* (-[e]s/⚔ -e) entrance (*into office*); taking up (*of position*); setting out (*on journey*); entering into possession (*of inheritance*).

'**antun** *v/t.* (*irr.* tun, *sep., -ge-, h*): *j-m et. ~* do s.th. to s.o.; *sich et. ~* lay hands on o.s.

'**Antwort** *f* (-/-en) answer, reply (*auf acc.* to); '**Qen** (*ge-, h*) 1. *v/i.* answer (*j-m* s.o.), reply (*j-m* to s.o.); *both*: *auf acc.* to); 2. *v/t.* answer (*auf acc.* to), reply (to); '**.schein** *m* (international) reply coupon.

'**an|vertrauen** *v/t.* (*sep., no -ge-, h*): *j-m et. ~* (en)trust s.o. with s.th., entrust s.th. to s.o.; confide s.th. to s.o.; '**.wachsen** *v/i.* (*irr.* wachsen, *sep., -ge-, sein*) take root; *fig.* increase; *~ an* (*acc.*) grow on to.

Anwalt ['anvalt] *m* (-[e]s/ꞙe) lawyer; solicitor, *Am.* attorney; counsel; barrister, *Am.* counsel(l)or; *fig.* advocate.

'**Anwandlung** *f* fit; impulse.

'**Anwärter** *m* candidate, aspirant; expectant.

Anwartschaft ['anvartʃaft] *f* (-/-en) expectancy; candidacy; prospect (*auf acc.* of).

'**anweis|en** *v/t.* (*irr.* weisen, *sep., -ge-, h*) assign; instruct; direct; *s. angewiesen*; '**Qung** *f* assignment; instruction; direction; ✝: cheque, *Am.* check; draft; *s. Postanweisung.*

'**anwend|en** *v/t.* ([*irr.* wenden], *sep., -ge-, h*) employ, use; apply (*auf acc.* to); *s. angewandt*; '**Qung** *f* application.

'**anwerben** *v/t.* (*irr.* werben, *sep., -ge-, h*) ⚔ enlist, enrol(l); engage.

'**Anwesen** *n* estate; property.

'**anwesen|d** *adj.* present; '**Qheit** *f* (-/*no pl.*) presence.

'**Anzahl** *f* (-/*no pl.*) number; quantity.

'**anzahl|en** v/t. (sep., -ge-, h) pay on account; pay a deposit; '**ung** f (first) instal(l)ment; deposit.

'**anzapfen** v/t. (sep., -ge-, h) tap.

'**Anzeichen** n symptom; sign.

Anzeige ['antsaɪgə] f (-/-n) notice, announcement; ⚓ advice; advertisement; ⚓ information; '**2n** v/t. (sep., -ge-, h) announce, notify; ⚓ advise; advertise; indicate; ⊕ instrument: indicate, show; thermometer: read (degrees); j-n ∼ denounce s.o., inform against s.o.

'**anziehen** (irr. ziehen, sep., -ge-, h) 1. v/t. draw, pull; draw (rein); tighten (screw); put on (garment); dress; fig. attract; 2. v/i. draw; prices: rise; '**∼d** adj. attractive, interesting.

'**Anziehung** f attraction; '**∼skraft** f attractive power; attraction.

'**Anzug** m 1. (-[e]s/∼e) dress; suit; 2. (-[e]s/no pl.): im ∼ sein storm: be gathering; danger: be impending.

anzüglich adj. ['antsy:kliç] personal; '**2keit** f (-/-en) personality.

'**anzünden** v/t. (sep., -ge-, h) light, kindle; strike (match); set (building) on fire.

apathisch adj. [a'pɑ:tiʃ] apathetic.

Apfel ['apfəl] m (-s/∼) apple; '**∼mus** n apple-sauce; '**∼sine** [∼'zi:nə] f (-/-n) orange; '**∼wein** m cider.

Apostel [a'pɔstəl] m (-s/-) apostle.

Apostroph [apo'stro:f] m (-s/-e) apostrophe.

Apotheke [apo'te:kə] f (-/-n) chemist's shop, pharmacy, Am. drugstore; '**∼r** m (-s/-) chemist, Am. druggist, pharmacist.

Apparat [apa'rɑ:t] m (-[e]s/-e) apparatus; device; teleph.: am ∼! speaking!; teleph.: am ∼ bleiben hold the line.

Appell [a'pɛl] m (-s/-e) ✕: roll-call; inspection; parade; fig. appeal (an acc. to); **2ieren** [∼'li:rən] v/i. (no -ge-, h) appeal (an acc. to).

Appetit [ape'ti:t] m (-[e]s/-e) appetite; **2lich** adj. appetizing, savo(u)ry, dainty.

Applaus [a'plaus] m (-es/✎ -e) applause.

Aprikose [apri'ko:zə] f (-/-n) apricot.

April [a'pril] m (-[s]/-e) April.

Aquarell [akva'rɛl] n (-s/-e) watercolo(u)r (painting), aquarelle.

Aquarium [a'kvɑ:rium] n (-s/ Aquarien) aquarium.

Äquator [ɛ'kvɑ:tɔr] m (-s/✎ -en) equator.

Ära ['ɛ:ra] f (-/✎ Ären) era.

Arab|er ['arabər] m (-s/-) Arab; **2isch** adj. [a'rɑ:biʃ] Arabian, Arab(ic).

Arbeit ['arbaɪt] f (-/-en) work; labo(u)r, toil; employment; job;

task; paper; workmanship; bei der ∼ at work; sich an die ∼ machen, an die ∼ gehen set to work; (keine) ∼ haben be in (out of) work; die ∼ niederlegen stop work, down tools; '**2en** (ge-, h) 1. v/i. work; labo(u)r, toil; 2. v/t. work; make.

'**Arbeiter** m (-s/-) worker; workman, labo(u)rer, hand; '**∼in** f (-/-nen) female worker; working woman, workwoman; '**∼klasse** f working class(es pl.); '**∼partei** f Labo(u)r Party; '**∼schaft** f (-/-en), '**∼stand** m working class(es pl.), labo(u)r.

'**Arbeit|geber** m (-s/-), '**∼geberin** f (-/-nen) employer; '**∼nehmer** m (-s/-), '**∼nehmerin** f (-/-nen) employee.

'**arbeitsam** adj. industrious.

'**Arbeits|amt** n labo(u)r exchange; '**∼anzug** m overall; '**∼beschaffung** f (-/-en) provision of work; '**∼bescheinigung** f certificate of employment; '**∼einkommen** n earned income; '**2fähig** adj. able to work; '**∼gericht** n labo(u)r or industrial court; '**∼kleidung** f working clothes pl.; '**∼kraft** f working power; worker, hand; Arbeitskräfte pl. a. labo(u)r; '**∼leistung** f efficiency; power (of engine); output (of factory); '**∼lohn** m wages pl., pay; '**2los** adj. out of work, unemployed; '**∼lose** m (-n/-n): die ∼n pl. the unemployed pl.; '**∼losenunterstützung** f unemployment benefit; ∼ beziehen F be on the dole; '**∼losigkeit** f (-/no pl.) unemployment; '**∼markt** m labo(u)r market; '**∼minister** m Minister of Labour, Am. Secretary of Labor; '**∼nachweis(stelle** f) m employment registry office, Am. labor registry office; '**∼niederlegung** f (-/-en) strike, Am. F a. walkout; '**∼pause** f break, intermission; '**∼platz** m place of work; job; '**∼raum** m workroom; '**2scheu** adj. work-shy; '**∼scheu** f aversion to work; '**∼schutzgesetz** n protective labo(u)r law; '**∼tag** m working day, workday; '**2unfähig** adj. incapable of working; disabled; '**∼weise** f practice, method of working; '**∼willige** m (-n/-n) non-striker; '**∼zeit** f working time; working hours pl.; '**∼zeug** n tools pl.; '**∼zimmer** n workroom; study.

Archäo|loge [arçeo'lo:gə] m (-n/-n) arch(a)eologist; '**∼logie** [∼o'gi:] f (-/no pl.) arch(a)eology.

Arche ['arçə] f (-/-n) ark.

Architekt [arçi'tɛkt] m (-en/-en) architect; '**∼ur** [∼'tu:r] f (-/-en) architecture.

Archiv [ar'çi:f] n (-s/-e) archives pl.; record office.

Areal [are'ɑ:l] n (-s/-e) area.

Arena [a'reːna] f (-/Arenen) arena; bullring; (circus-)ring.

arg adj. [ark] bad; wicked; gross.

Ärger ['ɛrgər] m (-s/no pl.) vexation, annoyance; anger; **'₂lich** adj. vexed, F mad, angry (auf, über acc. at s.th., with s.o.); annoying, vexatious; **'₂n** v/t. (ge-, h) annoy, vex, irritate, fret; bother; sich ~ feel angry or vexed (über acc. at, about s.th.; with s.o.); **'~nis** n (-ses/-se) scandal, offen|ce, Am. -se.

'Arg|list f (-/no pl.) cunning, craft (-iness); **'₂listig** adj. crafty, cunning; **'₂los** adj. guileless; artless, unsuspecting; **~wohn** ['~voːn] m (-[e]s/no pl.) suspicion; **₂wöhnen** ['~vøːnən] v/t. (ge-, h) suspect; **'₂wöhnisch** adj. suspicious.

Arie ♪ ['aːrjə] f (-/-n) aria.

Aristokrat [aristoˈkraːt] m (-en/-en), **~in** f (-/-nen) aristocrat; **~ie** [~kraˈtiː] f (-/-n) aristocracy.

Arkade [arˈkaːdə] f (-/-n) arcade.

arm¹ adj. [arm] poor.

Arm² [~] m (-[e]s/-e) arm; branch (of river, etc.); F: j-n auf den ~ nehmen pull s.o.'s leg.

Armaturenbrett [armaˈtuːrənbrɛt] n instrument board, dash-board.

'Arm|band n bracelet; **~banduhr** ['armbantˀ-] f wrist watch; **'~bruch** m fracture of the arm.

Armee [arˈmeː] f (-/-n) army.

Ärmel ['ɛrməl] m (-s/-) sleeve; **'~kanal** m the (English) Channel.

'Armen|haus n alms-house, Brt. a. workhouse; **'~pflege** f poor relief; **'~pfleger** m guardian of the poor; welfare officer; **'~unterstützung** f poor relief.

ärmlich adj. ['ɛrmliç] s. armselig.

'armselig adj. poor; wretched; miserable; shabby; paltry.

Armut ['armuːt] f (-/no pl.) poverty.

Aroma [aˈroːma] n (-s/Aromen, Aromata, -s) aroma, flavo(u)r; fragrance.

Arrest [aˈrɛst] m (-es/-e) arrest; confinement; seizure (of goods); detention (of pupil, etc.); ~ bekommen be kept in.

Art [aːrt] f (-/-en) kind, sort; ♀, zo. species; manner, way; nature; manners pl.; breed, race (of animals); auf die(se) ~ in this way; **'₂en** v/i. (ge-, sein): ~ nach take after. [artery.\]

Arterie anat. [arˈteːrjə] f (-/-n)\

artig adj. ['aːrtiç] good, well-behaved; civil, polite; **'₂keit** f (-/-en) good behavio(u)r; politeness; civility, a. civilities pl.

Artikel [arˈtiːkəl] m (-s/-) article; commodity.

Artillerie [artiləˈriː] f (-/-n) artillery.

Artist [arˈtist] m (-en/-en), **~in** f (-/-nen) circus performer.

Arznei [arts'naɪ] f (-/-en) medicine, F physic; **~kunde** f (-/no pl.) pharmaceutics; **~mittel** n medicine, drug.

Arzt [aːrtst] m (-es/⁼e) doctor, medical man; physician.

Ärztin ['ɛːrtstin] f (-/-nen) woman or lady doctor.

ärztlich adj. ['ɛːrtstliç] medical.

As [as] n (-ses/-se) ace.

Asche ['aʃə] f (-/-n) ash(es pl.); **'~nbahn** f sports: cinder-track, mot. dirt-track; **'~nbecher** m ash-tray; **~nbrödel** ['~nbrøːdəl] n (-s/no pl.), **~nputtel** ['~nputəl] n 1. (-s/no pl.) Cinderella; 2. (-s/-) drudge.

Ascher'mittwoch m Ash Wednesday.

'asch'grau adj. ash-grey, ashy, Am. ash-gray.

äsen hunt. ['ɛːzən] v/i. (ge-, h) graze, browse.

Asiat [azˈjaːt] m (-en/-en), **~in** f (-/-nen) Asiatic, Asian; **₂isch** adj. Asiatic, Asian.

Asket [asˈkeːt] m (-en/-en) ascetic.

Asphalt [asˈfalt] m (-[e]s/-e) asphalt; **₂ieren** [~ˈtiːrən] v/t. (no -ge-, h) asphalt.

aß [aːs] pret. of essen.

Assistent [asisˈtɛnt] m (-en/-en), **~in** f (-/-nen) assistant.

Ast [ast] m (-es/⁼e) branch, bough; knot (in timber); **'~loch** n knot-hole.

Astro|naut [astroˈnaut] m (-en/-en) astronaut; **~nom** [~ˈnoːm] m (-en/-en) astronomer.

Asyl [aˈzyːl] n (-s/-e) asylum; fig. sanctuary.

Atelier [atəˈljeː] n (-s/-s) studio.

Atem ['aːtəm] m (-s/no pl.) breath; außer ~ out of breath; **'₂los** adj. breathless; **'~not** ⚕ f difficulty in breathing; **'~pause** f breathing-space; **'~zug** m breath, respiration.

Äther ['ɛːtər] m 1. (-s/no pl.) the ether; 2. ⚗ (-s/-) ether; **₂isch** adj. [ɛˈteːriʃ] ethereal, etheric.

Athlet [atˈleːt] m (-en/-en), **~in** f (-/-nen) athlete; **~ik** f (-/no pl.) athletics mst sg.; **₂isch** adj. athletic.

atlantisch adj. [atˈlantiʃ] Atlantic.

Atlas ['atlas] m 1. geogr. (-/no pl.) Atlas; 2. (-, -ses/-se, Atlanten) maps: atlas; 3. (-, -ses/-se) textiles: satin.

atmen ['aːtmən] v/i. and v/t. (ge-, h) breathe.

Atmosphär|e [atmoˈsfɛːrə] f (-/-n) atmosphere; **₂isch** adj. atmospheric.

'Atmung f (-/-en) breathing, respiration.

Atom [aˈtoːm] n (-s/-e) atom; **₂ar** adj. [atoˈmaːr] atomic; **~bombe** f atomic bomb, atom-bomb, A-bomb; **~energie** f atomic or nuclear energy; **~forschung** f atomic or nuclear research; **~kern** m atomic nucleus; **~kraftwerk** n nuclear power station; **~meiler** *m* atomic pile, nuclear reactor; **~physiker** *m* atomic physicist; **~reaktor** *m* nuclear reactor, atomic pile; **~versuch** *m* atomic test; **~waffe** *f* atomic or nuclear weapon; **~wissenschaftler** *m* atomic scientist; **~zeitalter** *n* atomic age.

Attent|at [atɛn'tɑːt] *n* (-[e]s/-e) (attempted) assassination; *fig.* outrage; **~äter** [ˌ~ɛːtər] *m* (-s/-) assailant, assassin.

Attest [a'tɛst] *n* (-es/-e) certificate; **²ieren** [ˌ~'tiːrən] *v/t.* (*no* -ge-, *h*) attest, certify.

Attraktion [atrak'tsjoːn] *f* (-/-en) attraction.

Attrappe [a'trapə] *f* (-/-n) dummy.

Attribut [atri'buːt] *n* (-[e]s/-e) attribute; *gr.* attributive.

ätz|en ['ɛtsən] *v/t.* (ge-, *h*) corrode; **~** cauterize; etch (*metal plate*); **~end** *adj.* corrosive; caustic (*a. fig.*); **²ung** *f* (-/-en) corrosion; **~** cauterization; etching.

au *int.* [au] oh!; ouch!

auch *cj.* [aux] also, too, likewise; even; **~** *nicht* neither, nor; *wo* **~** (*immer*) wher(eso)ever; *ist es* **~** *wahr?* is it really true?

Audienz [audi'ɛnts] *f* (-/-en) audience, hearing.

auf [auf] **1.** *prp.* (*dat.*) (up)on; in; at; of; by; **~** *dem Tisch* (up)on the table; **~** *dem Markt* in the market; **~** *der Universität* at the university; **~** *e-m Ball* at a ball; **2.** *prp.* (*acc.*) on; in; at; to; towards (*a.* **~** *... zu*); up; **~** *deutsch* in German; **~** *e-e Entfernung von* at a range of; **~** *die Post etc.* gehen go to the post-office, *etc.*; **~** *ein Pfund gehen 20 Schilling* 20 shillings go to a pound; *es geht* **~** *neun* it is getting on to nine; **~** *... hin* on the strength of; **3.** *adv.* up(wards); **~** *und ab gehen* walk up and down *or* to and fro; **4.** *cj.*: **~** *daß* (in order) that; **~** *daß nicht* that not, lest; **5.** *int.*: **~***!* up!

auf|arbeiten ['auf⁹-] *v/t.* (*sep.*, -ge-, *h*) work off (*arrears of work*); furbish up; F do up (*garments*); **~atmen** *fig.* ['auf⁹-] *v/i.* (*sep.*, -ge-, *h*) breathe again.

'Aufbau *m* (-[e]s/*no pl.*) building up; construction (*of play, etc.*); F *esp. Am.* setup (*of organization*); *mot.* body (*of car, etc.*); **'²en** *v/t.* (*sep.*, -ge-, *h*) erect, build up; construct.

'auf|bauschen *v/t.* (*sep.*, -ge-, *h*) puff out; *fig.* exaggerate; **'~beißen** *v/t.* (*irr.* beißen, *sep.*, -ge-, *h*) crack; **'~bekommen** *v/t.* (*irr.* kommen, *sep.*, *no* -ge-, *h*) get open (*door*); be given (*a task*); **'~bessern** *v/t.* (*sep.*, -ge-, *h*) raise (*salary*); **'~bewahren** *v/t.* (*sep.*, *no* -ge-, *h*) keep; preserve;

'~bieten *v/t.* (*irr.* bieten, *sep.*, -ge-, *h*) summon; exert; ✕ raise; **'~binden** *v/t.* (*irr.* binden, *sep.*, -ge-, *h*) untie; **'~bleiben** *v/i.* (*irr.* bleiben, *sep.*, -ge-, *sein*) sit up; door, *etc.*: remain open; **'~blenden** (*sep.*, -ge-, *h*) **1.** *mot. v/i.* turn up the headlights; **2.** *v/t.* fade in (*scene*); **'~blicken** *v/i.* (*sep.*, -ge-, *h*) look up; raise one's eyes; **'~blitzen** *v/i.* (*sep.*, -ge-, *h*, *sein*) flash (up); **'~blühen** *v/i.* (*sep.*, -ge-, *sein*) bloom; flourish.

'aufbrausen *fig. v/i.* (*sep.*, -ge-, *sein*) fly into a passion; **'~d** *adj.* hottempered.

'auf|brechen (*irr.* brechen, *sep.*, -ge-) **1.** *v/t.* (*h*) break open; force open; **2.** *v/i.* (*sein*) burst open; set out (*nach* for); **'~bringen** *v/t.* (*irr.* bringen, *sep.*, -ge-, *h*) raise (*money, troops*); capture (*ship*); rouse *or* irritate *s.o.*

'Aufbruch *m* departure, start.

'auf|bügeln *v/t.* (*sep.*, -ge-, *h*) iron; **'~bürden** *v/t.* (*sep.*, -ge-, *h*): *j-m et.* **~** impose s.th. on s.o.; **'~decken** *v/t.* (*sep.*, -ge-, *h*) uncover; spread (*cloth*); *fig.* disclose; **'~drängen** *v/t.* (*sep.*, -ge-, *h*) force, obtrude (*j-m* [up]on s.o.); **'~drehen** *v/t.* (*sep.*, -ge-, *h*) turn on (*gas, etc.*).

'aufdringlich *adj.* obtrusive.

'Aufdruck *m* (-[e]s/-e) imprint; surcharge.

'aufdrücken *v/t.* (*sep.*, -ge-, *h*) impress.

aufeinander *adv.* [auf⁹ar'nandər] one after *or* upon another; **²folge** *f* succession; **~folgend** *adj.* successive.

Aufenthalt ['aufɛnthalt] *m* (-[e]s/-e) stay; residence; delay; ⚙ stop; **'~sgenehmigung** *f* residence permit.

auferlegen ['auf⁹ɛrleˑgən] *v/t.* (*sep.*, *no* -ge-, *h*) impose (*j-m on s.o.*).

auferstehen ['auf⁹ɛrʃteˑən] *v/i.* (*irr.* stehen, *sep.*, *no* -ge-, *sein*) rise (from the dead); **'²ung** *f* (-/-en) resurrection.

auf|essen ['auf⁹-] *v/t.* (*irr.* essen, *sep.*, -ge-, *h*) eat up; **'~fahren** *v/i.* (*irr.* fahren, *sep.*, -ge-, *sein*) ascend; start up; *fig.* fly out; ⚓ run aground; *mot.* drive *or* run (*auf acc.* against, into).

'Auffahrt *f* ascent; driving up; approach; drive, *Am.* driveway; **'~srampe** *f* ramp.

'auf|fallen *v/i.* (*irr.* fallen, *sep.*, -ge-, *sein*) be conspicuous; *j-m* **~** strike s.o.; **'~fallend** *adj.*; **'~fällig** *adj.* striking; conspicuous; flashy.

'auffangen *v/t.* (*irr.* fangen, *sep.*, -ge-, *h*) catch (up); parry (*thrust*).

'auffass|en *v/t.* (*sep.*, -ge-, *h*) conceive; comprehend; interpret; **'²ung** *f* conception; interpretation; grasp.

'**auffinden** v/t. (irr. finden, sep., -ge-, h) find, trace, discover, locate.
'**aufforder|n** v/t. (sep., -ge-, h) ask, invite; call (up)on; esp. ⚔ summon; call (up)on; esp. ⚔ summon; '**~ung** f invitation; esp. ⚔ summons.
'**auffrischen** (sep., -ge-) 1. v/t. (h) freshen up, touch up; brush up (knowledge); revive; 2. v/i. (sein) wind: freshen.
'**aufführ|en** v/t. (sep., -ge-, h) thea. represent, perform, act; enumerate; enter (in list); einzeln ~ specify, Am. itemize; sich ~ behave; '**~ung** f thea. performance; enumeration; entry; specification; conduct.
'**Aufgabe** f task; problem; school: homework; posting, Am. mailing (of letter); booking (of luggage), Am. checking (of baggage); resignation (from office); abandonment; giving up (business); es sich zur ~ machen make it one's business.
'**Aufgang** m ascent; ast. rising; staircase.
'**aufgeben** (irr. geben, sep., -ge-, h) 1. v/t. give up, abandon; resign from (office); insert (advertisement); post, Am. mail (letter); book (luggage), Am. check (baggage); hand in, send (telegram); ✝ give (order); set, Am. assign (homework); set (riddle); 2. v/i. give up or in.
'**Aufgebot** n public notice; ⚔ levy; fig. array; banns pl. (of marriage).
'**aufgehen** v/i. (irr. gehen, sep., -ge-, sein) open; ♈ leave no remainder; sewing: come apart; paste, star, curtain: rise; seed: come up; ~ in (dat.) be merged in; fig. be devoted to (work); in Flammen ~ go up in flames.
aufgeklärt adj. ['aufgəklɛːrt] enlightened; '**~heit** f (-/no pl.) enlightenment.
'**Aufgeld** ✝ n agio, premium.
'**aufge|legt** adj. ['aufgəleːkt] disposed (zu for); in the mood (zu inf. for ger., to inf.); gut (schlecht) ~ in a good (bad) humo(u)r; '**~schlossen** fig. adj. open-minded; '**~weckt** fig. adj. ['~vɛkt] bright.
'**auf|gießen** v/t. (irr. gießen, sep., -ge-, h) pour (on); make (tea); '**~greifen** v/t. (irr. greifen, sep., -ge-, h) snatch up, fig. take up;
'**Aufguß** m infusion.   [seize.]
'**auf|haben** (irr. haben, sep., -ge-, h) 1. v/t. have on (hat); have open (door); have to do (task); 2. F v/i.: das Geschäft hat auf the shop is open; '**~haken** v/t. (sep., -ge-, h) unhook; '**~halten** v/t. (irr. halten, sep., -ge-, h) keep open; stop, detain, delay; hold up (traffic); sich ~ stay; sich ~ bei dwell on; sich ~ mit spend one's time on; '**~hängen** v/t. (irr. hängen, sep., -ge-, h) hang (up); ⊕ suspend.

'**aufheb|en** v/t. (irr. heben, sep., -ge-, h) lift (up), raise; pick up; raise (siege); keep, preserve; cancel, annul, abolish; break off (engagement); break up (meeting); sich ~ neutralize; die Tafel ~ rise from the table; gut aufgehoben sein be well looked after; viel Aufhebens machen make a fuss (von about); '**~ung** f (-/-en) raising; abolition; annulment; breaking up.
'**auf|heitern** v/t. (sep., -ge-, h) cheer up; sich ~ weather: clear up; face: brighten; '**~hellen** v/t. and v/refl. (sep., -ge-, h) brighten.
'**aufhetz|en** v/t. (sep., -ge-, h) incite, instigate s.o.; '**~ung** f (-/-en) instigation, incitement.
'**auf|holen** (sep., -ge-, h) 1. v/t. make up (for); ♃ haul up; 2. v/i. gain (gegen on); pull up (to); '**~hören** v/i. (sep., -ge-, h) cease, stop; Am. quit (all: zu tun doing); F: da hört (sich) doch alles auf! that's the limit!, Am. that beats everything!; '**~kaufen** v/t. (sep., -ge-, h) buy up.
'**aufklär|en** v/t. (sep., -ge-, h) clear up; enlighten (über acc. on); ⚔ reconnoit|re (sep. -er; sich ~ clear up; '**~ung** f enlightenment; ⚔ reconnaissance.
'**auf|kleben** v/t. (sep., -ge-, h) paste on, stick on, affix on; '**~klinken** v/t. (sep., -ge-, h) unlatch; '**~knöpfen** v/t. (sep., -ge-, h) unbutton.
'**aufkommen** 1. v/i. (irr. kommen, sep., -ge-, sein) rise; recover (from illness); come up; come into fashion or use; thought: arise; ~ für et. answer for s.th.; ~ gegen prevail against s.o.; 2. ♀ n (-s/no pl.) rise; recovery.
'**auf|krempeln** ['aufkrɛmpəln] v/t. (sep., -ge-, h) turn up, roll up; tuck up; '**~lachen** v/i. (sep., -ge-, h) burst out laughing; '**~laden** v/t. (irr. laden, sep., -ge-, h) load; ⚡ charge.
'**Auflage** f edition (of book); circulation (of newspaper); ⊕ support.
'**auf|lassen** v/t. (irr. lassen, sep., -ge-, h) F leave open (door, etc.); F keep on (hat); ⚔ cede; '**~lauern** v/i. (sep., -ge-, h): j-m ~ lie in wait for s.o.
'**Auflauf** m concourse; riot; dish: soufflé; '**~en** v/i. (irr. laufen, sep., -ge-, sein) interest: accrue; ♃ run aground.
'**auflegen** (sep., -ge-, h) 1. v/t. put on, lay on; apply (auf acc. to); print, publish (book); teleph. hang up; 2. teleph. v/i. ring off.
'**auflehn|en** v/t. (sep., -ge-, h) lean (on); sich ~ lean (on); fig. rebel, revolt (gegen against); '**~ung** f (-/-en) rebellion.

'**auf|lesen** v/t. (irr. lesen, sep., -ge-, h) gather, pick up; '**~leuchten** v/i. (sep., -ge-, h) flash (up); '**~liegen** v/i. (irr. liegen, sep., -ge-, h) lie (auf dat. on).

'**auflös|bar** adj. (dis)soluble; '**~en** v/t. (sep., -ge-, h) undo (knot); break up (meeting); dissolve (salt, etc.; marriage, business, Parliament, etc.); solve (X, riddle); disintegrate; fig. aufgelöst upset; '**~ung** f (dis-) solution; disintegration.

'**aufmach|en** v/t. (sep., -ge-, h) open; undo (dress, parcel); put up (umbrella); make up, get up; sich ~ wind: rise; set out (nach acc. for); make for; die Tür ~ answer the door; '**~ung** f (-/-en) make-up, get-up.

'**aufmarschieren** v/i. (sep., no -ge-, sein) form into line; ~ lassen ✗ deploy.

'**aufmerksam** adj. attentive (gegen to); j-n ~ machen auf (acc.) call s.o.'s attention to; '**~keit** f (-/-en) attention; token.

'**aufmuntern** v/t. (sep., -ge-, h) rouse; encourage; cheer up.

Aufnahme ['aufnaːmə] f (-/-n) taking up (of work); reception; admission; phot.: taking; photograph, shot; shooting (of a film); '**~fähig** adj. capable of absorbing; mind: receptive (für of); '**~gebühr** f admission fee; '**~gerät** n phot. camera; recorder; '**~prüfung** f entrance examination.

'**aufnehmen** v/t. (irr. nehmen, sep., -ge-, h) take up; pick up; take s.o. in; take down (dictation, etc.); take s.th. in (mentally); receive (guests); admit; raise, borrow (money); draw up, record; shoot (film); phot. take (picture); gut (übel) ~ take well (ill); es ~ mit be a match for.

aufopfer|n ['auf?-] v/t. (sep., -ge-, h) sacrifice; '**~ung** f sacrifice.

'**auf|passen** v/i. (sep., -ge-, h) attend (auf acc. to); watch; at school: be attentive; look out; ~ auf (acc.) take care of; '**~platzen** v/i. (sep., -ge-, sein) burst (open); '**~polieren** v/t. (sep., no -ge-, h) polish up; '**~prallen** v/i. (sep., -ge-, sein): auf den Boden ~ strike the ground; '**~pumpen** v/t. (sep., -ge-, h) blow up (tyre, etc.); '**~raffen** v/t. (sep., -ge-, h) snatch up; sich ~ rouse o.s. (zu for); muster up one's energy; '**~räumen** (sep., -ge-, h) 1. v/t. put in order; tidy (up), Am. straighten up; clear away; 2. v/i. tidy up; ~ mit do away with.

'**aufrecht** adj. and adv. upright (a. fig.), erect; '**~erhalten** v/t. (irr. halten, sep., no -ge-, h) maintain, uphold; '**~erhaltung** f (-/no pl.) maintenance.

'**aufreg|en** (sep., -ge-, h) stir up,

excite; sich ~ get excited or upset (über acc. about); aufgeregt excited; upset; '**~ung** f excitement, agitation.

'**auf|reiben** v/t. (irr. reiben, sep., -ge-, h) chafe (skin, etc.); fig.: destroy; exhaust, wear s.o. out; '**~reißen** (irr. reißen, sep., -ge-) 1. v/t. (h) rip or tear up or open; fling open (door); open (eyes) wide; 2. v/i. (sein) split open, burst.

'**aufreiz|en** v/t. (sep., -ge-, h) incite, stir up; '**~end** adj. provocative; '**~ung** f instigation.

'**aufrichten** v/t. (sep., -ge-, h) set up, erect; sich ~ stand up; straighten; sit up (in bed).

'**aufrichtig** adj. sincere, candid; '**~keit** f sincerity, cando(u)r.

'**aufriegeln** v/t. (sep., -ge-, h) unbolt.

'**Aufriß** △ m elevation.

'**aufrollen** v/t. and v/refl. (sep., -ge-, h) roll up; unroll.

'**Aufruf** m call, summons; '**~en** v/t. (irr. rufen, sep., -ge-, h) call up; call on s.o.

Aufruhr ['aufruːr] m (-[e]s/-e) uproar, tumult; riot, rebellion.

'**aufrühr|en** v/t. (sep., -ge-, h) stir up; revive; fig. rake up; '**~er** m (-s/-) rebel; '**~erisch** adj. rebellious.

'**Aufrüstung** ✗ f (re)armament.

'**auf|rütteln** v/t. (sep., -ge-, h) shake up; rouse; '**~sagen** v/t. (sep., -ge-, h) say, repeat; recite.

aufsässig adj. ['aufzɛsiç] rebellious.

'**Aufsatz** m essay; composition; ⊕ top.

'**auf|saugen** v/t. (sep., -ge-, h) suck up; ⌀ absorb; '**~scheuchen** v/t. (sep., -ge-, h) scare (away); disturb; rouse; '**~scheuern** v/t. (sep., -ge-, h) scour; ✗ chafe; '**~schichten** v/t. (sep., -ge-, h) pile up; '**~schieben** v/t. (irr. schieben, sep., -ge-, h) slide open; fig.: put off; defer, postpone; adjourn.

'**Aufschlag** m striking; impact; additional or extra charge; facing (on coat), lapel (of coat); cuff (on sleeve); turn-up (on trousers); tennis: service; '**~en** ['~gən] (irr. schlagen, sep., -ge-) 1. v/t. (h) open; turn up (sleeve, etc.); take up (abode); pitch (tent); raise (prices); cut (one's knee) open; 2. v/i. (sein) strike, hit; ✝ rise, go up (in price); tennis: serve.

'**auf|schließen** v/t. (irr. schließen, sep., -ge-, h) unlock, open; '**~schlitzen** v/t. (sep., -ge-, h) slit or rip open.

'**Aufschluß** fig. m information.

'**auf|schnallen** v/t. (sep., -ge-, h) unbuckle; '**~schnappen** (sep., -ge-) 1. v/t. (h) snatch; fig. pick up; 2. v/i. (sein) snap open; '**~schnei-**

den (irr. schneiden, sep., -ge-, h) **1.** v/t. cut open; cut up (meat); **2.** fig. v/i. brag, boast.

'**Aufschnitt** m (slices pl. of) cold meat, Am. cold cuts pl.

'**auf|schnüren** v/t. (sep., -ge-, h) untie; unlace; '**~schrauben** v/t. (sep., -ge-, h) screw (auf acc. on); unscrew; '**~schrecken** (sep., -ge-) **1.** v/t. (h) startle; **2.** v/i. (irr. schrecken, sein) start (up).

'**Aufschrei** m shriek, scream; fig. outcry.

'**auf|schreiben** v/t. (irr. schreiben, sep., -ge-, h) write down; '**~schreien** v/i. (irr. schreien, sep., -ge-, h) cry out, scream.

'**Aufschrift** f inscription; address, direction (on letter); label.

'**Aufschub** m deferment; delay; adjournment; respite.

'**auf|schürfen** v/t. (sep., -ge-, h) graze (skin); '**~schwingen** v/refl. (irr. schwingen, sep., -ge-, h) soar, rise; sich zu et. ~ bring o.s. to do s.th.

'**Aufschwung** m fig. rise, Am. upswing; † boom.

'**aufsehen 1.** v/i. (irr. sehen, sep., -ge-, h) look up; **2.** 2 n (-s/no pl.) sensation; ~ erregen cause a sensation; '**~erregend** adj. sensational.

'**Aufseher** m overseer; inspector.

'**aufsetzen** (sep., -ge-, h) **1.** v/t. set up; put on (hat, countenance); draw up (document); sich ~ sit up; **2.** ✈ v/i. touch down.

'**Aufsicht** f (-/-en) inspection, supervision; store: shopwalker, Am. floorwalker; '**~sbehörde** f board of control; '**~srat** m board of directors.

'**auf|sitzen** v/i. (irr. sitzen, sep., -ge-, h) rider: mount; '**~spannen** v/t. (sep., -ge-, h) stretch; put up (umbrella); spread (sails); '**~sparen** v/t. (sep., -ge-, h) save; fig. reserve; '**~speichern** v/t. (sep., -ge-, h) store up; '**~sperren** v/t. (sep., -ge-, h) open wide; '**~spielen** (sep., -ge-, h) **1.** v/t. and v/i. strike up; **2.** v/refl. show off; sich ~ als set up for; '**~spießen** v/t. (sep., -ge-, h) pierce; with horns: gore; run through, spear; '**~springen** v/i. (irr. springen, sep., -ge-, sein) jump up; door: fly open; crack; skin: chap; '**~spüren** v/t. (sep., -ge-, h) hunt up; track down; '**~stacheln** fig. v/t. (sep., -ge-, h) goad; incite, instigate; '**~stampfen** v/t. (sep., -ge-, h) stamp (one's foot).

'**Aufstand** m insurrection; rebellion; uprising, revolt.

aufständisch adj. ['aufʃtendiʃ] rebellious; '2e m (-n/-n) insurgent, rebel.

'**auf|stapeln** v/t. (sep., -ge-, h) pile up; † store (up); '**~stechen** v/t. (irr. stechen, sep., -ge-, h) puncture,

prick open; ⚔ lance; '**~stecken** v/t. (sep., -ge-, h) pin up; put up (hair); '**~stehen** v/i. (irr. stehen, sep., -ge-) **1.** (sein) stand up; rise, get up; revolt; **2.** F (h) stand open; '**~steigen** v/i. (irr. steigen, sep., -ge-, sein) rise, ascend; ✈ take off; rider: mount.

'**aufstell|en** v/t. (sep., -ge-, h) set up, put up; ⚒ draw up; post (sentries); make (assertion); set (example); erect (column); set (trap); nominate (candidate); draw up (bill); lay down (rule); make out (list); set up, establish (record); '**2ung** f putting up; drawing up; erection; nomination; † statement; list.

Aufstieg ['aufʃtiːk] m (-[e]s/-e) ascent, Am. a. ascension; fig. rise.

'**auf|stöbern** fig. v/t. (sep., -ge-, h) hunt up; '**~stoßen** (irr. stoßen, sep., -ge-) **1.** v/t. (h) push open; ~ auf (acc.) knock against; **2.** v/i. (h, sein) of food: rise, repeat; belch; '**~streichen** v/t. (irr. streichen, sep., -ge-, h) spread (butter).

'**Aufstrich** m spread (for bread).

'**auf|stützen** v/t. (sep., -ge-, h) prop up, support s.th.; sich ~ auf (acc.) lean on; '**~suchen** v/t. (sep., -ge-, h) visit (places); go to see s.o., look s.o. up.

'**Auftakt** m ♩ upbeat; fig. prelude, preliminaries pl.

'**auf|tauchen** v/i. (sep., -ge-, sein) emerge, appear, turn up; '**~tauen** (sep., -ge-) **1.** v/t. (h) thaw; **2.** v/i. (sein) thaw (a. fig.); '**~teilen** v/t. (sep., -ge-, h) divide (up), share.

Auftrag ['auftraːk] m (-[e]s/⸚e) commission; instruction; mission; ⚖ mandate; † order; 2en ['gən] v/t. (irr. tragen, sep., -ge-, h) serve (up) (meal); lay on (paint); wear out (dress); j-m et. ~ charge s.o. with s.th.; '**~geber** ['k-] m (-s/-) employer; customer; principal; '**~serteilung** ['ks'ertailuŋ] f (-/-en) placing of an order.

'**auf|treffen** v/i. (irr. treffen, sep., -ge-, sein) strike, hit; '**~treiben** v/t. (irr. treiben, sep., -ge-, h) hunt up; raise (money); '**~trennen** v/t. (sep., -ge-, h) rip; unstitch (seam).

'**auftreten 1.** v/i. (irr. treten, sep., -ge-, sein) tread; thea., witness, etc.: appear (als as); behave, act; difficulties: arise; **2.** 2 n (-s/no pl.) appearance; occurrence (of events); behavio(u)r.

'**Auftrieb** m phys. and fig. buoyancy; ✈ lift; fig. impetus.

'**Auftritt** m thea. scene (a. fig.); appearance (of actor).

'**auf|trumpfen** fig. v/i. (sep., -ge-, h) put one's foot down; '**~tun** v/t. (irr. tun, sep., -ge-, h) open; sich ~ open; chasm: yawn; society: form; '**~türmen** v/t. (sep., -ge-, h) pile or heap up; sich ~ tower up; pile up; *difficulties*: accumulate; '~wachen *v/i.* (*sep.*, -ge-, sein) awake, wake up; '~wachsen *v/i.* (*irr.* wachsen, *sep.*, -ge-, sein) grow up.

'Aufwallung *f* ebullition, surge.

Aufwand ['aufvant] *m* (-[e]s/*no pl.*) expense, expenditure (*an dat.* of); pomp; splendid *or* great display (*of words, etc.*).

'aufwärmen *v/t.* (*sep.*, -ge-, h) warm up.

'Aufwarte|frau *f* charwoman, *Am. a.* cleaning woman; '2n *v/i.* (*sep.*, -ge-, h) wait (up)on *s.o.*, attend on *s.o.*; wait (at table).

aufwärts *adv.* ['aufverts] upward(s).

'Aufwartung *f* attendance; visit; *j-m s-e ~ machen* pay one's respects to s.o., call on s.o.

'aufwasch|en *v/t.* (*irr.* waschen, *sep.*, -ge-, h) wash up; '2wasser *n* dish-water.

'auf|wecken *v/t.* (*sep.*, -ge-, h) awake(n), wake (up); '~weichen (*sep.*, -ge-) 1. *v/t.* (h) soften; soak; 2. *v/i.* (sein) soften, become soft; '~weisen *v/t.* (*irr.* weisen, *sep.*, -ge-, h) show, exhibit; produce; '~wenden *v/t.* ([*irr.* wenden,] *sep.*, -ge-, h) spend; *Mühe ~* take pains; '~werfen *v/t.* (*irr.* werfen, *sep.*, -ge-, h) raise (*a.* question).

'aufwert|en *v/t.* (*sep.*, -ge-, h) revalorize; revalue; '2ung *f* revalorization; revaluation.

'aufwickeln *v/t. and v/refl.* (*sep.*, -ge-, h) wind up, roll up.

aufwiegel|n ['aufvi:gəln] *v/t.* (*sep.*, -ge-, h) stir up, incite, instigate; '2ung *f* (-/-en) instigation.

'aufwiegen *fig. v/t.* (*irr.* wiegen, *sep.*, -ge-, h) make up for.

Aufwiegler ['aufvi:glər] *m* (-s/-) agitator; instigator.

'aufwirbeln (*sep.*, -ge-) 1. *v/t.* (h) whirl up; raise (*dust*); *fig. viel Staub ~* create a sensation; 2. *v/i.* (sein) whirl up.

'aufwisch|en *v/t.* (*sep.*, -ge-, h) wipe up; '2lappen *m* floor-cloth.

'aufwühlen *v/t.* (*sep.*, -ge-, h) turn up; *fig.* stir.

'aufzähl|en *v/t.* (*sep.*, -ge-, h) count up; *fig.* enumerate, *Am. a.* call off; specify, *Am.* itemize; '2ung *f* (-/-en) enumeration; specification.

'auf|zäumen *v/t.* (*sep.*, -ge-, h) bridle; '~zehren *v/t.* (*sep.*, -ge-, h) consume.

'aufzeichn|en *v/t.* (*sep.*, -ge-, h) draw; note down; record; '2ung *f* note; record.

'auf|zeigen *v/t.* (*sep.*, -ge-, h) show; demonstrate; point out (*mistakes, etc.*); disclose; '~ziehen (*irr.* ziehen, *sep.*, -ge-) 1. *v/t.* (h) draw *or* pull up; (pull) open; hoist (*flag*); bring up (*child*); mount (*picture*);

wind (up) (*clock, etc.*); *j-n ~* tease s.o., pull s.o.'s leg; *Saiten auf e-e Violine ~* string a violin; 2. *v/i.* (sein) ✕ draw up; *storm*: approach.

'Aufzucht *f* rearing, breeding.

'Aufzug *m* ⊕ hoist; lift, *Am.* elevator; *thea.* act; attire; show.

'aufzwingen *v/t.* (*irr.* zwingen, *sep.*, -ge-, h): *j-m et. ~* force s.th. upon s.o.

Augapfel ['auk⁹-] *m* eyeball.

Auge ['augə] *n* (-s/-n) eye; sight; ⚘ bud; *in meinen ~n* in my view; *im ~ behalten* keep an eye on; keep in mind; *aus den ~n verlieren* lose sight of; *ein ~ zudrücken* turn a blind eye (*bei* to); *ins ~ fallen* strike the eye; *große ~n machen* open one's eyes wide; *unter vier ~n* face to face, privately; *kein ~ zutun* not to get a wink of sleep.

'Augen|arzt *m* oculist, eye-doctor; '~blick *m* moment, instant; '2blicklich 1. *adj.* instantaneous; momentary; present; 2. *adv.* instant(aneous)ly; at present; '~braue *f* eyebrow; '~entzündung ⚕ *f* inflammation of the eye; '~heilkunde *f* ophthalmology; '~klinik *f* ophthalmic hospital; '~leiden ⚕ *n* eye-complaint; '~licht *n* eyesight; '~lid *n* eyelid; '~maß *n*: *ein gutes ~* a sure eye; *nach dem ~* by eye; '~merk ['~merk] *n* (-[e]s/*no pl.*): *sein ~ richten auf (acc.)* turn one's attention to; *have s.th. in* view; '~schein *m* appearance; *in ~ nehmen* examine, view, inspect; '2scheinlich *adj.* evident; '~wasser *n* eyewash, eye-lotion; '~wimper *f* eyelash; '~zeuge *m* eyewitness.

August [au'gust] *m* (-[e]s, - /-e) August.

Auktion [auk'tsjo:n] *f* (-/-en) auction; ~ator [~o'na:tɔr] *m* (-s/-en) auctioneer.

Aula ['aula] *f* (-/*Aulen*, -s) (assembly) hall, *Am.* auditorium.

aus [aus] 1. *prp.* (*dat.*) out of; from; of; by; for; in; *~ Achtung* out of respect; *~ London kommen* come from London; *~ diesem Grunde* for this reason; *~ Ihrem Brief ersehe ich* I see from your letter; 2. *adv.* out; over; *die Schule ist ~* school is over; F: *von mir ~* for all I care; *auf et. ~ sein* be keen on s.th.; *es ist ~ mit ihm* it is all over with him; *das Spiel ist ~!* the game is up!; *er weiß weder ein noch ~* he is at his wit's end; *on instruments, etc.*: *an — ~ on —* off.

ausarbeit|en ['aus⁹-] *v/t.* (*sep.*, -ge-, h) work out; elaborate; '2ung *f* (-/-en) working-out; elaboration; composition.

aus|arten ['aus⁹-] *v/i.* (*sep.*, -ge-, sein) degenerate; get out of hand; ~atmen ['aus⁹-] (*sep.*, -ge-, h)

1. v/i. breathe out; **2.** v/t. breathe out; exhale (vapour, etc.); '~baggern v/t. (sep., -ge-, h) dredge (river, etc.); excavate (ground).

'Ausbau m (-[e]s/-ten) extension; completion; development; '2en v/t. (sep., -ge-, h) develop; extend; finish, complete; ⊕ dismantle (engine).

'ausbedingen v/t. (irr. bedingen, sep., no -ge-, h) stipulate.

'ausbesser|n v/t. (sep., -ge-, h) mend, repair, Am. F a. fix; '2ung f repair, mending.

'Ausbeut|e f (-/~-n) gain, profit; yield; ⚔ output; '2en v/t. (sep., -ge-, h) exploit; sweat (workers); '~ung f (-/-en) exploitation.

'ausbild|en v/t. (sep., -ge-, h) form, develop; train; instruct, educate; ⚔ drill; '2ung f development; training; instruction; education; ⚔ drill.

'ausbitten v/t. (irr. bitten, sep., -ge-, h): sich et. ~ request s.th.; insist on s.th.

'ausbleiben **1.** v/i. (irr. bleiben, sep., -ge-, sein) stay away, fail to appear; **2.** 2 n (-s/no pl.) non-arrival, non-appearance; absence.

'Ausblick m outlook (auf acc. over, on), view (of), prospect (of); fig. outlook (on).

'aus|bohren v/t. (sep., -ge-, h) bore, drill; '~brechen (irr. brechen, sep., -ge-) **1.** v/t. (h) break out; vomit; **2.** v/i. (sein) break out; fig. burst out (laughing, etc.).

'ausbreit|en v/t. (sep., -ge-, h) spread (out); stretch (out) (arms, wings); display; sich ~ spread; '2ung f (-/~-en) spreading.

'ausbrennen (irr. brennen, sep., -ge-) **1.** v/t. (h) burn out; ⚕ cauterize; **2.** v/i. (sein) burn out.

'Ausbruch m outbreak; eruption (of volcano); escape (from prison); outburst (of emotion).

'aus|brüten v/t. (sep., -ge-, h) hatch (a. fig.); '~bürgern v/t. (sep., -ge-, h) denationalize, expatriate.

'Ausdauer f perseverance; '2nd adj. persevering; ♣ perennial.

'ausdehn|en v/t. and v/refl. (sep., -ge-, h) extend (auf acc. to); expand; stretch; '2ung f expansion; extension; extent.

'aus|denken v/t. (irr. denken, sep., -ge-, h) think s.th. out, Am. a. think s.th. up, contrive, devise, invent; imagine; '~dörren v/t. (sep., -ge-, h) dry up; parch; '~drehen v/t. (sep., -ge-, h) turn off (radio, gas); ≠ turn out, switch off (light).

'Ausdruck m **1.** (-[e]s/no pl.) expression; **2.** (-[e]s/~e) expression; term.

'ausdrück|en v/t. (sep., -ge-, h) press, squeeze (out); stub out (cig-arette); fig. express; '~lich adj. express, explicit.

'ausdrucks|los adj. inexpressive, expressionless; blank; '~voll adj. expressive; '2weise f mode of expression; style.

'Ausdünstung f (-/-en) exhalation; perspiration; odo(u)r, smell.

auseinander adv. [aus'?aɪ'nandər] asunder, apart; separate(d); ~bringen v/t. (irr. bringen, sep., -ge-, h) separate, sever; ~gehen v/i. (irr. gehen, sep., -ge-, sein) meeting, crowd: break up; opinions: differ; friends: part; crowd: disperse; roads: diverge; ~nehmen v/t. (irr. nehmen, sep. -ge-, h) take apart or to pieces; ⊕ disassemble, dismantle; ~setzen fig. v/t. (sep., -ge-, h) explain; sich mit j-m ~ ⚕ compound with s.o.; argue with s.o.; have it out with s.o.; sich mit e-m Problem ~ get down to a problem; come to grips with a problem; 2setzung f (-/-en) explanation; discussion; settlement (with creditors, etc.); kriegerische ~ armed conflict.

auserlesen adj. ['aus?-] exquisite, choice; select(ed).

auserwählen ['aus?-] v/t. (sep., no -ge-, h) select, choose.

'ausfahr|en (irr. fahren, sep., -ge-) **1.** v/i. (sein) drive out, go for a drive; ⚓ leave (port); **2.** v/t. (h) take (baby) out (in pram); take s.o. for a drive; rut (road); ⚔ lower (undercarriage); '2t f drive; excursion; way out, exit (of garage, etc.); gateway; departure.

'Ausfall m falling out; ⚕: loss; deficit; '2en v/i. (irr. fallen, sep., -ge-, sein) fall out; not to take place; turn out, prove; ~ lassen drop; cancel; die Schule fällt aus there is no school; '2end adj. offensive, insulting.

'aus|fasern v/i. (sep., -ge-, sein) ravel out, fray; '~fegen v/t. (sep., -ge- h) sweep (out).

ausfertig|en ['ausfɛrtɪgən] v/t. (sep., -ge-, h) draw up (document); make out (bill, etc.); issue (passport); '2ung f (-/-en) drawing up; issue; draft; copy; in doppelter ~ in duplicate. [chen find out; discover.]

ausfindig adj. ['ausfɪndɪç]: ~ ma-)

'Ausflucht f (-/~e) excuse, evasion, shift, subterfuge.

'Ausflug m trip, excursion, outing.

Ausflügler ['ausfly:klər] m (-s/-) excursionist, tripper, tourist.

'Ausfluß m flowing out; discharge (a. ⚕); outlet, outfall.

'aus|fragen v/t. (sep., -ge-, h) interrogate, Am. a. quiz; sound; '~fransen v/i. (sep., -ge-, sein) fray.

Ausfuhr ⚕ ['ausfu:r] f (-/-en) export(ation); '~artikel ⚕ m export (article).

'ausführ|bar *adj.* practicable; ⚓ exportable; '~en *v/t.* (*sep.*, -ge-, *h*) execute, carry out, perform, *Am. a.* fill; ⚓ export; explain; *j-n* ~ take *s.o.* out.

'Ausfuhr|genehmigung *f* export permit; '~handel *m* export trade.

'ausführlich 1. *adj.* detailed; comprehensive; circumstantial; 2. *adv.* in detail, at (some) length; '2keit *f* (-/no *pl.*) minuteness of detail; particularity; comprehensiveness; copiousness.

'Ausführung *f* execution, performance; workmanship; type, make; explanation; '~sbestimmungen ⚓ *f/pl.* export regulations *pl.*

'Ausfuhr|verbot *n* embargo on exports; '~waren *f/pl.* exports *pl.*; '~zoll *m* export duty.

'ausfüllen *v/t.* (*sep.*, -ge-, *h*) fill out *or* up; fill in, complete (*form*); *Am.* fill out (*blank*).

'Ausgabe *f* distribution; edition (*of book*); expense, expenditure; issue (*of shares, etc.*); issuing office.

'Ausgang *m* going out; exit; way out; outlet; end; result; '~skapital ⚓ *n* original capital; '~spunkt *m* starting-point; '~stellung *f* starting-position.

'ausgeben *v/t.* (*irr.* geben, *sep.*, -ge-, *h*) give out; spend (*money*); issue (*shares, etc.*); *sich* ~ *für* pass *o.s.* off for, pretend to be.

ausge|beult *adj.* ['ausgəbɔylt] baggy; ~bombt *adj.* ['~bɔmpt] bombed out; ~dehnt *adj.* ['~de:nt] expansive, vast, extensive; ~dient *adj.* ['~di:nt] worn out; superannuated; retired, pensioned off; ~er Soldat ex-serviceman, veteran; '~fallen *fig. adj.* odd, queer, unusual.

'ausgehen *v/i.* (*irr.* gehen, *sep.*, -ge-, *sein*) go out; take a walk; end; *colour*: fade; *hair*: fall out; *money*, *provisions*: run out; *uns gehen die Vorräte aus* we run out of provisions; *darauf* ~ aim at; *gut etc.* ~ turn out well, *etc.*; *leer* ~ come away empty-handed; *von et.* ~ start from s.th.

'ausge|lassen *fig. adj.* frolicsome, boisterous; '~nommen *prp.* 1. (*acc.*) except (for); 2. (*nom.*): *Anwesende* ~ present company excepted; ~prägt *adj.* ['~pre:kt] marked, pronounced; ~rechnet *fig. adv.* ['~rɛçnət] just; ~ *er* he of all people; ~ *heute* today of all days; '~schlossen *fig. adj.* impossible.

'ausgestalten *v/t.* (*sep.*, *no* -ge-, *h*) arrange (*celebration*); *et. zu et.* ~ develop *or* turn s.th. into s.th.

ausge|sucht *fig. adj.* ['ausgəzu:xt] exquisite, choice; '~wachsen *adj.* full-grown; ~zeichnet *fig. adj.* ['~tsaɪçnət] excellent.

ausgiebig *adj.* ['ausgi:biç] abundant, plentiful; *meal*: substantial.

'ausgießen *v/t.* (*irr.* gießen, *sep.*, -ge-, *h*) pour out.

Ausgleich ['ausglaɪç] *m* (-[e]s/-e) compromise; compensation; ⚓ settlement; *sports*: equalization (*of score*); *tennis*: deuce (*score of 40 all*); '2en *v/t.* (*irr.* gleichen, *sep.*, -ge-, *h*) equalize; compensate (*loss*); ⚓ balance.

'aus|gleiten *v/i.* (*irr.* gleiten, *sep.*, -ge-, *sein*) slip, slide; '~graben *v/t.* (*irr.* graben, *sep.*, -ge-, *h*) dig out *or* up (*a. fig.*); excavate; exhume (*body*).

Ausguck ⚓ ['ausguk] *m* (-[e]s/-e) look-out.

'Ausguß *m* sink; '~eimer *m* slop-pail.

'aus|haken *v/t.* (*sep.*, -ge-, *h*) unhook; '~halten (*irr.* halten, *sep.*, -ge-, *h*) 1. *v/t.* endure, bear, stand; ♪ sustain (*note*); 2. *v/i.* hold out; last; ~händigen ['~hendigən] *v/t.* (*sep.*, -ge-, *h*) deliver up, hand over, surrender.

'Aushang *m* notice, placard, poster.

'aushänge|n 1. *v/t.* (*sep.*, -ge-, *h*) hang *or* put out; unhinge (*door*); 2. *v/i.* (*irr.* hängen, *sep.*, -ge-, *h*) have been hung *or* put out; '2schild *n* signboard.

aus|harren ['ausharən] *v/i.* (*sep.*, -ge-, *h*) persevere; hold out; '~hauchen *v/t.* (*sep.*, -ge-, *h*) breathe out, exhale; '~heben (*irr.* heben, *sep.*, -ge-, *h*) dig (*trench*); unhinge (*door*); recruit, levy (*soldiers*); excavate (*earth*); rob (*nest*); clean out, raid (*nest of criminals*); '~helfen *v/i.* (*irr.* helfen, *sep.*, -ge-, *h*) help out.

'Aushilf|e *f* (temporary) help *or* assistance; *sie hat e-e* ~ she has s.o. to help out; '2sweise *adv.* as a makeshift; temporarily.

'aushöhl|en *v/t.* (*sep.*, -ge-, *h*) hollow out; '2ung *f* hollow.

'aus|holen (*sep.*, -ge-, *h*) 1. *v/i.* raise one's hand (*as if to strike*); *weit* ~ go far back (*in narrating s.th.*); 2. *v/t.* sound, pump *s.o.*; '~horchen *v/t.* (*sep.*, -ge-, *h*) sound, pump *s.o.*; '~hungern *v/t.* (*sep.*, -ge-, *h*) starve (out); '~husten *v/t.* (*sep.*, -ge-, *h*) cough up; '~kennen *v/refl.* (*irr.* kennen, *sep.*, -ge-, *h*) know one's way (*about place*); be well versed, be at home (*in subject*); *er kennt sich aus* he knows what's what; '~kleiden *v/t.* (*sep.*, -ge-, *h*) undress; ⊕ line, coat; *sich* ~ undress; '~klopfen *v/t.* (*sep.*, -ge-, *h*) beat (out); dust (*garment*), knock out (*pipe*); '~klügeln ['~kly:gəln] *v/t.* (*sep.*, -ge-, *h*) work s.th. out; contrive; puzzle s.th. out.

'auskommen 1. *v/i.* (*irr.* kommen, *sep.*, -ge-, *sein*) get out; escape; ~

mit manage with *s.th.*; get on with *s.o.*; ~ *ohne* do without; *mit dem Geld* ~ make both ends meet; **2.** ♀ *n* (-*s*/*no pl.*) competence, competency.

'**auskundschaften** *v/t.* (*sep.*, -ge-, *h*) explore; ⚔ reconnoit|re, *Am.* -er, scout.

Auskunft ['auskunft] *f* (-/-̈e) information; inquiry office, inquiries *pl.*, *Am.* information desk; '~**sstelle** *f* inquiry office, inquiries *pl.*, *Am.* information bureau.

'**aus|lachen** *v/t.* (*sep.*, -ge-, *h*) laugh at, deride; '~**laden** *v/t.* (*irr. laden*, *sep.*, -ge-, *h*) unload; discharge (*cargo from ship*); cancel *s.o.'s* invitation, put off (*guest*).

'**Auslage** *f* display, show (*of goods*); *in der* ~ in the (shop) window; ~*n pl.* expenses *pl.*

'**Ausland** *n* (-[e]*s*/*no pl.*): *das* ~ foreign countries *pl.*; *ins* ~, *im* ~ abroad.

Ausländ|er ['auslɛndər] *m* (-*s*/-), '~**erin** *f* (-/-nen) foreigner; alien; '**2isch** *adj.* foreign; ♀, *zo.* exotic.

'**Auslandskorrespondent** *m* foreign correspondent.

'**auslass|en** *v/t.* (*irr. lassen*, *sep.*, -ge-, *h*) let out (*water*); melt (down) (*butter*); render down (*fat*); let out (*garment*); let down (*hem*); leave out, omit (*word*); cut *s.th.* out; miss or cut out (*meal*); miss (*dance*); *s-n Zorn an j-m* ~ vent one's anger on *s.o.*; *sich* ~ *über* (*acc.*) say *s.th.* about; express one's opinion about; '**2ung** *f* (-/-en) omission; remark, utterance; '**2ungszeichen** *gr. n* apostrophe.

'**aus|laufen** *v/i.* (*irr. laufen*, *sep.*, -ge-, *sein*) run or leak out (*aus et.* of *s.th.*); leak; end (*in s.th.*); *machine*: run down; ⚓ (set) sail; '~**leeren** *v/t.* (*sep.*, -ge-, *h*) empty; ⚕ evacuate (*bowels*).

'**ausleg|en** *v/t.* (*sep.*, -ge-, *h*) lay out; display (*goods*); explain, interpret; advance (*money*); '**2ung** *f* (-/-en) explanation, interpretation.

'**aus|leihen** *v/t.* (*irr. leihen*, *sep.*, -ge-, *h*) lend (out), *esp. Am.* loan; '~**lernen** *v/i.* (*sep.*, -ge-, *h*) finish one's apprenticeship; *man lernt nie aus* we live and learn.

'**Auslese** *f* choice, selection; *fig.* pick; '**2n** *v/t.* (*irr. lesen*, *sep.*, -ge-, *h*) pick out, select; finish reading (*book*).

'**ausliefer|n** *v/t.* (*sep.*, -ge-, *h*) hand or turn over, deliver (up); extradite (*criminal*); *ausgeliefert sein* (*dat.*) be at the mercy of; '**2ung** *f* delivery; extradition.

'**aus|liegen** *v/i.* (*irr. liegen*, *sep.*, -ge-, *h*) be displayed, be on show; '~**löschen** *v/t.* (*sep.*, -ge-, *h*) put out, switch off (*light*); extinguish (*fire*) (*a. fig.*); efface (*word*); wipe

out, erase; '~**losen** *v/t.* (*sep.*, -ge-, *h*) draw (lots) for.

'**auslös|en** *v/t.* (*sep.*, -ge-, *h*) ⊕ release; redeem, ransom (*prisoner*); redeem (*from pawn*); *fig.* cause, start; arouse (*applause*); '**2er** *m* (-*s*/-) ⊕ release, *esp. phot.* trigger.

'**aus|lüften** *v/t.* (*sep.*, -ge-, *h*) air, ventilate; '~**machen** *v/t.* (*sep.*, -ge-, *h*) make out, sight, spot; *sum*: amount to; constitute, make up; put out (*fire*); ⚡ turn out, switch off (*light*); agree on, arrange; settle; *es macht nichts aus* it does not matter; *würde es Ihnen et.* ~, *wenn* ...? would you mind (*ger.*) ...?; '~**malen** *v/t.* (*sep.*, -ge-, *h*) paint; *sich et.* ~ picture *s.th.* to *o.s.*, imagine *s.th.*

'**Ausmaß** *n* dimension(s *pl.*), measurement(s *pl.*); *fig.* extent.

aus|mergeln ['ausmɛrgəln] *v/t.* (*sep.*, -ge-, *h*) emaciate; exhaust; ~**merzen** ['~mɛrtsən] *v/t.* (*sep.*, -ge-, *h*) eliminate; eradicate; '~**messen** *v/t.* (*irr. messen*, *sep.*, -ge-, *h*) measure.

Ausnahm|e ['ausnaːmə] *f* (-/-n) exception; '**2sweise** *adv.* by way of exception; exceptionally.

'**ausnehmen** *v/t.* (*irr. nehmen*, *sep.*, -ge-, *h*) take out; draw (*fowl*); F fleece *s.o.*; *fig.* except, exempt; '~**d 1.** *adj.* exceptional; **2.** *adv.* exceedingly.

'**aus|nutzen** *v/t.* (*sep.*, -ge-, *h*) utilize; take advantage of; *esp.* ⚒, ⚔ exploit; '~**packen** *v/t.* (*sep.*, -ge-, *h*) **1.** *v/t.* unpack; **2.** F *fig. v/i.* speak one's mind; '~**pfeifen** *thea. v/t.* (*irr. pfeifen*, *sep.*, -ge-, *h*) hiss; '~**plaudern** *v/t.* (*sep.*, -ge-, *h*) blab or let out; '~**polstern** *v/t.* (*sep.*, -ge-, *h*) stuff, pad; wad; '~**probieren** *v/t.* (*sep.*, *no* -ge-, *h*) try, test.

Auspuff *mot.* ['auspuf] *m* (-[e]*s*/-*e*) exhaust; '~**gas** *mot. n* exhaust gas; '~**rohr** *mot. n* exhaust-pipe; '~**topf** *mot. m* silencer, *Am.* muffler.

'**aus|putzen** *v/t.* (*sep.*, -ge-, *h*) clean; '~**quartieren** *v/t.* (*sep.*, *no* -ge-, *h*) dislodge; ⚔ billet out; '~**radieren** *v/t.* (*sep.*, *no* -ge-, *h*) erase; '~**rangieren** *v/t.* (*sep.*, *no* -ge-, *h*) discard; '~**rauben** *v/t.* (*sep.*, -ge-, *h*) rob; ransack; '~**räumen** *v/t.* (*sep.*, -ge-, *h*) empty, clear (out); remove (*furniture*); '~**rechnen** *v/t.* (*sep.*, -ge-, *h*) calculate, compute; reckon (out), *Am.* figure out or up (*all a. fig.*).

'**Ausrede** *f* excuse, evasion, subterfuge; '**2n** (*sep.*, -ge-, *h*) **1.** *v/i.* finish speaking; ~ *lassen* hear *s.o.* out; **2.** *v/t.*: *j-m et.* ~ dissuade *s.o.* from *s.th.*

'**ausreichen** *v/i.* (*sep.*, -ge-, *h*) suffice; '~**d** *adj.* sufficient.

'**Ausreise** *f* departure; ⚓ voyage out.

'ausreiß|en (*irr. reißen, sep., -ge-*) **1.** *v/t.* (*h*) pull *or* tear out; **2.** *v/i.* (*sein*) run away; **'2er** *m* runaway.
aus|renken ['ausrɛŋkən] *v/t.* (*sep., -ge-, h*) dislocate; **'~richten** *v/t.* (*sep., -ge-, h*) straighten; ⚔ dress; adjust; deliver (*message*); do, effect; accomplish; obtain; arrange (*feast*); *richte ihr e-n Gruß von mir aus!* remember me to her!; **~rotten** ['~rɔtən] *v/t.* (*sep., -ge-, h*) root out; *fig.* extirpate, exterminate.
'Ausruf *m* cry; exclamation; **'2en** (*irr. rufen, sep., -ge-,h*) **1.** *v/i.* cry out, exclaim; **2.** *v/t.* proclaim; **'~ezeichen** *n* exclamation mark, *Am. a.* exclamation point; **'~ung** *f* (*-/-en*) proclamation; **'~ungszeichen** *n s. Ausrufezeichen.*
'ausruhen *v/i., v/t. and v/refl.* (*sep., -ge-, h*) rest.
'ausrüst|en *v/t.* (*sep., -ge-, h*) fit out; equip; **'2ung** *f* outfit, equipment, fittings *pl.*
'aussäen *v/t.* (*sep., -ge-, h*) sow; *fig.* disseminate.
'Aussage *f* statement; declaration; ⚖ evidence; *gr.* predicate; **'2n** (*sep., -ge-, h*) **1.** *v/t.* state, declare; ⚖ depose; **2.** ⚖ *v/i.* give evidence.
'Aussatz ⚕ *m* (*-es/no pl.*) leprosy.
'aus|saugen *v/t.* (*sep., -ge-, h*) suck (out); *fig.* exhaust (*land*); **'~schalten** *v/t.* (*sep., -ge-, h*) eliminate; ⚡ cut out, switch off, turn off *or* out (*light*).
Ausschank ['ausʃaŋk] *m* (*-[e]s/⸚e*) retail (*of alcoholic drinks*); public house, F pub.
'Ausschau *f* (*-/no pl.*): *~ halten nach* be on the look-out for, watch for.
'ausscheid|en (*irr. scheiden, sep., -ge-*) **1.** *v/t.* (*h*) separate; ⚗, ⚗, *physiol.* eliminate; ⚕ secrete; **2.** *v/i.* (*sein*) retire; withdraw; *sports:* drop out; **'2ung** *f* separation; elimination (*a. sports*); ⚕ secretion.
'aus|schiffen *v/t. and v/refl.* (*sep., -ge-, h*) disembark; **'~schimpfen** *v/t.* (*sep., -ge-, h*) scold, tell *s.o.* off, berate; **~schirren** ['~ʃirən] *v/t.* (*sep., -ge-, h*) unharness; **'~schlachten** *v/t.* (*sep., -ge-, h*) cut up; cannibalize (*car, etc.*); *fig.* exploit, make the most of; **'~schlafen** (*irr. schlafen, sep., -ge-, h*) **1.** *v/i.* sleep one's fill; **2.** *v/t.* sleep off (*effects of drink, etc.*).
'Ausschlag *m* ⚕ eruption, rash; deflexion (*of pointer*); *den ~ geben* settle it; **2en** ['~gən] (*irr. schlagen, sep., -ge-*) **1.** *v/t.* (*h*) knock *or* beat out; line; refuse, decline; **2.** *v/i.* (*h*) *horse:* kick; *pointer:* deflect; **3.** *v/i.* (*h, sein*) bud; **2gebend** *adj.* ['~k-] decisive.
'ausschließ|en *v/t.* (*irr. schließen, sep., -ge-, h*) shut *or* lock out; *fig.:* exclude; expel; *sports:* disqualify; **'~lich** *adj.* exclusive.
'Ausschluß *m* exclusion; expulsion; *sports:* disqualification.
'ausschmücken *v/t.* (*sep., -ge-, h*) adorn, decorate; *fig.* embellish.
'Ausschnitt *m* cut; décolleté, (low) neck (*of dress*); cutting, *Am.* clipping (*from newspaper*); *fig.* part, section.
'ausschreib|en *v/t.* (*irr. schreiben, sep., -ge-, h*) write out; copy; write out (*word*) in full; make out (*invoice*); announce; advertise; **'2ung** *f* (*-/-en*) announcement; advertisement.
'ausschreit|en (*irr. schreiten, sep., -ge-*) **1.** *v/i.* (*sein*) step out, take long strides; **2.** *v/t.* (*h*) pace (*room*), measure by steps; **'2ung** *f* (*-/-en*) excess; *~en pl.* riots *pl.*
'Ausschuß *m* refuse, waste, rubbish; committee, board.
'aus|schütteln *v/t.* (*sep., -ge-, h*) shake out; **'~schütten** *v/t.* (*sep., -ge-, h*) pour out; spill; ⚕ distribute (*dividend*); *j-m sein Herz ~* pour out one's heart to s.o.; **'~schwärmen** *v/i.* (*sep., -ge-, sein*) swarm out; *~ (lassen)* ⚔ extend, deploy.
'ausschweif|end *adj.* dissolute; **'2ung** *f* (*-/-en*) debauchery, excess.
'ausschwitzen *v/t.* (*sep., -ge-, h*) exude.
'aussehen 1. *v/i.* (*irr. sehen, sep., -ge-, h*) look; *wie sieht er aus?* what does he look like?; *es sieht nach Regen aus* it looks like rain; **2.** **2** *n* (*-s/ no pl.*) look(s *pl.*), appearance.
außen *adv.* ['ausən] (on the) outside; *von ~ her* from (the) outside; *nach ~ (hin)* outward(s); **'2aufnahme** *f film:* outdoor shot; **'2bordmotor** *m* outboard motor.
'aussenden *v/t.* (*[irr. senden,] sep., -ge-, h*) send out.
'Außen|hafen *m* outport; **'~handel** *m* foreign trade; **'~minister** *m* foreign minister; Foreign Secretary, *Am.* Secretary of State; **'~ministerium** *n* foreign ministry; Foreign Office, *Am.* State Department; **'~politik** *f* foreign policy; **'2politisch** *adj.* of *or* referring to foreign affairs; **'~seite** *f* outside, surface; **'~seiter** *m* (*-s/-*) outsider; **~stände** ⚕ ['~ʃtɛndə] *pl.* outstanding debts *pl.*, *Am.* accounts *pl.* receivable; **'~welt** *f* outer *or* outside world.
außer ['ausər] **1.** *prp.* (*dat.*) out of; beside(s), *Am.* aside from; except; *~ sich sein* be beside o.s. (*vor Freude* with joy); **2.** *cj.:* *~ daß* except that; *~ wenn* unless; **'~dem** *cj.* besides, moreover.
äußere ['ɔysərə] **1.** *adj.* exterior, outer, external, outward; **2.** **2** *n* (*Äußer[e]n/no pl.*) exterior, outside, outward appearance.
'außer|gewöhnlich *adj.* extra-

ordinary; exceptional; **'~halb 1.** *prp.* (*gen.*) outside, out of; beyond; **2.** *adv.* on the outside.

äußerlich *adj.* ['ɔysərliç] external, outward; **'2keit** *f* (-/-en) superficiality; formality.

äußern ['ɔysərn] *v/t.* (*ge-, h*) utter, express; advance; *sich ~ matter*: manifest itself; *p.* express o.s.

'außer'ordentlich *adj.* extraordinary.

äußerst ['ɔysərst] **1.** *adj.* outermost; *fig.* utmost, extreme; **2.** *adv.* extremely, highly.

außerstande *adj.* [ausər'ʃtandə] unable, not in a position.

'Äußerung *f* (-/-en) utterance, remark.

'aussetz|en (*sep., -ge-, h*) **1.** *v/t.* set or put out; lower (*boat*); promise (*reward*); settle (*pension*); bequeath; expose (*child*); expose (*dat.* to); et. ~ *an* (*dat.*) find fault with; **2.** *v/i.* intermit; fail; *activity*: stop; suspend; *mot.* misfire; **'2ung** *f* (-/-en) exposure (*of child, to weather, etc.*) (*a.* ⚕).

'Aussicht *f* (-/-en) view (*auf acc.* of); *fig.* prospect (of), chance (of); *in ~ haben* have in prospect; **'2slos** *adj.* hopeless, desperate; **'2sreich** *adj.* promising, full of promise.

aussöhn|en ['auszø:nən] *v/t.* (*sep., -ge-, h*) reconcile *s.o.* (*mit* to *s.th.*, with *s.o.*); *sich ~* reconcile o.s. (to *s.th.*, with *s.o.*); **'2ung** *f* (-/-en) reconciliation.

'aussondern *v/t.* (*sep., -ge-, h*) single out; separate.

'aus|spannen (*sep., -ge-, h*) **1.** *v/t.* stretch, extend; F *fig.* steal (*s.o.'s girl friend*); unharness (*draught animal*); **2.** *fig.* *v/i.* (take a) rest, relax; **'~speien** *v/t. and v/i.* (*irr. speien, sep., -ge-, h*) spit out.

'aussperr|en *v/t.* (*sep., -ge-, h*) shut out; lock out (*workmen*); **'2ung** *f* (-/-en) lock-out.

'aus|spielen (*sep., -ge-, h*) **1.** *v/t.* play (*card*); **2.** *v/i. at cards*: lead; *er hat ausgespielt* he is done for; **'~spionieren** *v/t.* (*sep., no -ge-,* h) spy out. [*cent*; discussion.\]

'Aussprache *f* pronunciation, ac-\

'aussprechen (*irr. sprechen, sep., -ge-, h*) **1.** *v/t.* pronounce, express; *sich ~ für* (*gegen*) declare o.s. for (against); **2.** *v/i.* finish speaking.

'Ausspruch *m* utterance; saying; remark.

'aus|spucken *v/i. and v/t.* (*sep., -ge-, h*) spit out; **'~spülen** *v/t.* (*sep., -ge-, h*) rinse.

'Ausstand *m* strike, *Am.* F *a.* walk-out; *in den ~ treten* go on strike, *Am.* F *a.* walk out.

ausstatt|en ['ausʃtatən] *v/t.* (*sep., -ge-, h*) fit out, equip; furnish; supply (*mit* with); give a dowry to

(*daughter*); get up (*book*); **'2ung** *f* (-/-en) outfit, equipment; furniture; supply; dowry; get-up (*of book*).

'aus|stechen *v/t.* (*irr. stechen, sep., -ge-, h*) cut out (*a. fig.*); put out (*eye*); **'~stehen** (*irr. stehen, sep., -ge-, h*) **1.** *v/i. payments*: be outstanding; **2.** *v/t.* endure, bear; **'~steigen** *v/i.* (*irr. steigen, sep., -ge-, sein*) get out or off, alight.

'ausstell|en *v/t.* (*sep., -ge-, h*) exhibit; make out (*invoice*); issue (*document*); draw (*bill*); **'2er** *m* (-s/-) exhibitor; drawer; **'2ung** *f* exhibition, show; **'2ungsraum** *m* show-room.

'aussterben *v/i.* (*irr. sterben, sep., -ge-, sein*) die out; become extinct.

'Aussteuer *f* trousseau, dowry.

'ausstopfen *v/t.* (*sep., -ge-, h*) stuff; wad, pad.

'ausstoß|en *v/t.* (*irr. stoßen, sep., -ge-, h*) thrust out, eject; expel; utter (*cry*); heave (*sigh*); ⚔ cashier; **'2ung** *f* (-/-en) expulsion.

'aus|strahlen *v/t. and v/i.* (*sep., -ge-, h*) radiate; **'~strecken** *v/t.* (*sep., -ge-, h*) stretch (out); **'~streichen** *v/t.* (*irr. streichen, sep., -ge-, h*) strike out; smooth (down); **'~streuen** *v/t.* (*sep., -ge-, h*) scatter; spread (*rumours*); **'~strömen** (*sep., -ge-*) **1.** *v/i.* (sein) stream out; *gas, light*: emanate; *gas, steam*: escape; **2.** *v/t.* (h) pour (out); **'~suchen** *v/t.* (*sep., -ge-, h*) choose, select.

'Austausch *m* exchange; **'2bar** *adj.* exchangeable; **'2en** *v/t.* (*sep., -ge-, h*) exchange.

'austeil|en *v/t.* (*sep., -ge-, h*) distribute; deal out (*blows*); **'2ung** *f* distribution.

Auster *zo.* ['austər] *f* (-/-n) oyster.

'austragen *v/t.* (*irr. tragen, sep., -ge-, h*) deliver (*letters, etc.*); hold (*contest*).

Austral|ier [au'stra:liər] *m* (-s/-) Australian; **2isch** *adj.* Australian.

'austreib|en *v/t.* (*irr. treiben, sep., -ge-, h*) drive out; expel; **'2ung** *f* (-/-en) expulsion.

'aus|treten (*irr. treten, sep., -ge-*) **1.** *v/t.* (h) tread or stamp out; wear out (*shoes*); wear down (*steps*); **2.** *v/i.* (sein) emerge, come out; *river*: overflow its banks; retire (*aus* from); F ease o.s.; *~ aus* leave (*society, etc.*); **'~trinken** (*irr. trinken, sep., -ge-, h*) **1.** *v/t.* drink up; empty, drain; **2.** *v/i.* finish drinking; **'2tritt** *m* leaving; retirement; **'~trocknen** (*sep., -ge-*) **1.** *v/t.* (h) dry up; drain (*land*); parch (*throat, earth*); **2.** *v/i.* (sein) dry up.

ausüb|en ['aus?-] *v/t.* (*sep., -ge-, h*) exercise; practi|se, *Am.* -ce (*profession*); exert (*influence*); **'2ung** *f* practice; exercise.

Ausverkauf † *m* selling off *or* out (*of stock*); sale; '2t †, *thea.* sold out; *theatre notice:* 'full house'.

Auswahl *f* choice; selection; † assortment. [choose, select.]

auswählen *v/t.* (*sep.*, -ge-, h)]

Auswander|er *m* emigrant; '2n *v/i.* (*sep.*, -ge-, sein) emigrate; '~ung *f* emigration.

auswärt|ig *adj.* ['ausvertiç] out-of-town; non-resident; foreign; *das Auswärtige Amt s. Außenministerium*; ~s *adv.* ['~s] outward(s); out of doors; out of town; abroad; ~ essen dine out.

'auswechseln 1. *v/t.* (*sep.*, -ge-, h) exchange; change; replace; **2.** 2 *n* (-s/*no pl.*) exchange; replacement.

'Ausweg *m* way out (*a. fig.*); outlet; *fig.* expedient.

'ausweichen *v/i.* (*irr.* weichen, *sep.*, -ge-, sein) make way (for); *fig.* evade, avoid; '~d *adj.* evasive.

Ausweis ['ausvais] *m* (-es/-e) (bank) return; identity card, *Am.* identification (card); 2en ['~zən] *v/t.* (*irr.* weisen, *sep.*, -ge-, h) turn out, expel; evict; deport; show, prove; *sich* ~ prove one's identity; '~papiere *n/pl.* identity papers *pl.*; ~ung ['~zuŋ] *f* expulsion; '~ungsbefehl *m* expulsion order.

'ausweiten *v/t. and v/refl.* (*sep.*, -ge-, h) widen, stretch, expand.

'auswendig 1. *adj.* outward, outside; **2.** *adv.* outwardly, outside; *fig.* by heart.

'aus|werfen *v/t.* (*irr.* werfen, *sep.*, -ge-, h) throw out, cast; eject; 💰 expectorate; allow (*sum of money*); '~werten *v/t.* (*sep.*, -ge-, h) evaluate; analyze, interpret; utilize, exploit; '~wickeln *v/t.* (*sep.*, -ge-, h) unwrap; '~wiegen *v/t.* (*irr.* wiegen, *sep.*, -ge-, h) weigh out; '~wirken *v/refl.* (*sep.*, -ge-, h) take effect, operate; *sich* ~ *auf* (*acc.*) affect; '2wirkung *f* effect; '~wischen *v/t.* (*sep.*, -ge-, h) wipe out, efface; '~wringen *v/t.* (*irr.* wringen, *sep.*, -ge-, h) wring out.

'Auswuchs *m* excrescence, outgrowth (*a. fig.*), protuberance.

'Auswurf *m* 💰 expectoration; *fig.* refuse, dregs *pl.*

'aus|zahlen *v/t.* (*sep.*, -ge-, h) pay out; pay *s.o.* off; '~zählen *v/t.* (*sep.*, -ge-, h) count out.

'Auszahlung *f* payment.

'Auszehrung *f* (-/-en) consumption.

'auszeichn|en *v/t.* (*sep.*, -ge-, h) mark (out); *fig.* distinguish (*sich o.s.*); '2ung *f* marking; distinction; hono(u)r; decoration.

'auszieh|en (*irr.* ziehen, *sep.*, -ge-) **1.** *v/t.* (h) draw out, extract; take off (*garment*); *sich* ~ undress; **2.** *v/i.* (sein) set out; move (out), remove, move house; '2platte *f* leaf (*of table*).

'Auszug *m* departure; 🛠 marching out; removal; extract, excerpt (*from book*); summary; † statement (of account). [tic, genuine.]

authentisch *adj.* [au'tentiʃ] authen-]

Auto ['auto] *n* (-s/-s) (motor-)car, *Am. a.* automobile; ~ fahren drive, motor; '~bahn *f* motorway, autobahn; '2biogra'phie *f* autobiography; ~bus ['~bus] *m* (-ses/-se) (motor-)bus; (motor) coach; '~bushaltestelle *f* bus stop; '~didakt [~di'dakt] *m* (-en/-en) autodidact, self-taught person; '~droschke *f* taxi(-cab), *Am.* cab; '~fahrer *m* motorist; ~'gramm *n* autograph; ~'grammjäger *m* autograph hunter; '~händler *m* car dealer; '~kino *n* drive-in cinema; ~'krat *m* (-en/-en) autocrat; ~kratie [~a-'ti:] *f* (-/-n) autocracy; ~mat [~'ma:t] *m* (-en/-en) automaton, slot-machine, vending machine; ~'matenrestaurant *n* self-service restaurant, *Am.* automat; ~'mation ⊕ [~ma'tsjo:n] *f* (-/*no pl.*) automation; 2'matisch *adj.* automatic; '~mechaniker *m* car mechanic; ~'mobil [~mo'bi:l] *n* (-s/-e) *s. Auto*; 2nom *adj.* [~'no:m] autonomous; ~nomie [~o'mi:] *f* (-/-n) autonomy.

Autor ['autɔr] *m* (-s/-en) author.

'Autoreparaturwerkstatt *f* car repair shop, garage. [thor(ess).]

Autorin [au'to:rin] *f* (-/-nen) au-]

autori|sieren [autori'zi:rən] *v/t.* (*no* -ge-, h) authorize; ~tär *adj.* [~'tɛ:r] authoritarian; 2'tät *f* (-/-en) authority.

'Auto|straße *f* motor-road; '~vermietung *f* (-/-en) car hire service.

avisieren † [avi'zi:rən] *v/t.* (*no* -ge-, h) advise.

Axt [akst] *f* (-/̈e) ax(e).

Azetylen 🔬 [atsety'le:n] *n* (-s/*no pl.*) acetylene. [2n *adj.* azure.]

Azur [a'tsu:r] *m* (-s/*no pl.*) azure;]

B

Bach [bax] *m* (-[e]s/̈e) brook, *Am. a.* run. [port.]

Backbord ⚓ ['bak-] *n* (-[e]s/-e)]

Backe ['bakə] *f* (-/-n) cheek.

backen ['bakən] (*irr.*, ge-, h) **1.** *v/t.* bake; fry; dry (*fruit*); **2.** *v/i.* bake; fry.

'Backen|bart *m* (side-)whiskers *pl.*, *Am. a.* sideburns *pl.*; '~zahn *m* molar (tooth), grinder.

Bäcker ['bɛkər] *m* (-s/-) baker; **~ei** [ˌ'raɪ] *f* (-/-en) baker's (shop), bakery.

'Back|fisch *m* fried fish; *fig.* girl in her teens, teenager, *Am. a.* bobby soxer; **'~obst** *n* dried fruit; **'~ofen** *m* oven; **'~pflaume** *f* prune; **'~pulver** *n* baking-powder; **'~stein** *m* brick; **'~ware** *f* baker's ware.

Bad [baːt] *n* (-[e]s/∸er) bath; *in river, etc.*: a. bathe; *s. Badeort; ein ~ nehmen* take *or* have a bath.

Bade|anstalt ['baːdəʔ-] *f* (public swimming) baths *pl.*; **'~anzug** *m* bathing-costume, bathing-suit; **'~hose** *f* bathing-drawers *pl.*, (bathing) trunks *pl.*; **'~kappe** *f* bathing-cap; **'~kur** *f* spa treatment; **'~mantel** *m* bathing-gown, *Am.* bathrobe; **'~meister** *m* bath attendant; swimming-instructor; **'2n** (ge-, h) **1.** *v/t.* bath (*baby, etc.*); bathe (*eyes, etc.*); **2.** *v/i.* bath, tub; have *or* take a bath; *in river, etc.*: bathe; *~ gehen* go swimming; **'~ofen** *m* geyser, boiler, *Am. a.* water heater; **'~ort** *m* watering-place; spa; seaside resort; **'~salz** *n* bath-salt; **'~strand** *m* bathing-beach; **'~tuch** *n* bath-towel; **'~wanne** *f* bath-tub; **'~zimmer** *n* bathroom.

Bagatell|e [baga'tɛlə] *f* (-/-en) trifle, trifling matter, bagatelle; **2i'sieren** *v/t.* (no -ge-, h) minimize (the importance of), *Am. a.* play down.

Bagger ['bagər] *m* (-s/-) excavator; dredge(r); **'2n** *v/i. and v/t.* (ge-, h) excavate; dredge.

Bahn [baːn] *f* (-/-en) course; path; ⛖ railway, *Am.* railroad; *mot.* lane; trajectory (*of bullet, etc.*); *ast.* orbit; *sports*: track, course, lane; *skating*: rink; *bowling*: alley; **'2brechend** *adj.* pioneer(ing), epoch-making; *art*: avant-gardist; **'~damm** *m* railway embankment, *Am.* railroad embankment; **'2en** *v/t.* (ge-, h) clear, open (up) (*way*); *den Weg ~* prepare *or* pave the way (*dat.* for); *sich e-n Weg ~* force *or* work *or* elbow one's way; **'~hof** *m* (railway-) station, *Am.* (railroad-)station; **'~linie** *f* railway-line, *Am.* railroad line; **'~steig** *m* platform; **'~steigkarte** *f* platform ticket; **'~übergang** *m* level crossing, *Am.* grade crossing.

Bahre ['baːrə] *f* (-/-n) stretcher, litter; bier.

Bai [baɪ] *f* (-/-en) bay; creek.

Baisse ✝ ['bɛːs(ə)] *f* (-/-n) depression (on the market); fall (in prices); *auf ~ spekulieren* ✝ bear, speculate for a fall, *Am.* sell short; **'~spekulant** *m* bear.

Bajonett ⚔ [bajo'nɛt] *n* (-[e]s/-e) bayonet; *das ~ aufpflanzen* fix the bayonet.

Bake ['baːkə] *f* (-/-n) ⚓ beacon; ⛖ warning-sign.

Bakterie [bak'teːrjə] *f* (-/-n) bacterium, microbe, germ.

bald *adv.* [balt] soon; shortly; before long; F almost, nearly; early; *so ~ als möglich* as soon as possible; *~ hier, ~ dort* now here, now there; **~ig** *adj.* ['~dɪç] speedy; **~e** *Antwort* ✝ early reply.

Baldrian ['baldriaːn] *m* (-s/-e) valerian.

Balg [balk] **1.** *m* (-[e]s/∸e) skin; body (*of doll*); bellows *pl.*; **2.** F *m, n* (-[e]s/∸er) brat, urchin; **2en** ['balgən] *v/refl.* (ge-, h) scuffle (*um* for), wrestle (for).

Balken ['balkən] *m* (-s/-) beam; rafter.

Balkon [bal'kõː; ~'koːn] *m* (-s/-s; -s/-e) balcony; *thea.* dress circle, *Am.* balcony; **~tür** *f* French window.

Ball [bal] *m* (-[e]s/∸e) ball; *geogr., ast. a.* globe; ball, dance; *auf dem ~* at the ball.

Ballade [ba'laːdə] *f* (-/-n) ballad.

Ballast ['balast] *m* (-es/✝-e) ballast; *fig.* burden, impediment; dead weight.

'ballen[1] *v/t.* (ge-, h) (form into a) ball; clench (*fist*); *sich ~* (form into a) ball; cluster.

'Ballen[2] *m* (-s/-) bale; *anat.* ball; *~ Papier* ten reams *pl.*

Ballett [ba'lɛt] *n* (-[e]s/-e) ballet; **~änzer** [ba'lɛtɛntsər] *m* (-s/-) ballet-dancer.

ball|förmig *adj.* ['balfœrmɪç] ball-shaped, globular; **'2kleid** *n* ball-dress.

Ballon [ba'lõː; ~ɔ'ɔːn] *m* (-s/-s; -s/-s, -e) balloon.

'Ball|saal *m* ball-room; **'~spiel** *n* ball-game, game of ball.

Balsam ['balzaːm] *m* (-s/-e) balsam, balm (*a. fig.*); **2ieren** [ˌ'mˑiːrən] *v/t.* (no -ge-, h) embalm.

Balz [balts] *f* (-/-en) mating season; display (*by cock-bird*).

Bambus ['bambus] *m* (-ses/-se) bamboo; **'~rohr** *n* bamboo, cane.

banal *adj.* [ba'naːl] commonplace, banal, trite; trivial; **2ität** [ˌli'tɛːt] *f* (-/-en) banality; commonplace; triviality.

Banane [ba'naːnə] *f* (-/-n) banana; **~nstecker** ⚡ *m* banana plug.

Band [bant] **1.** *m* (-[e]s/∸e) volume; **2.** *n* (-[e]s/∸er) band; ribbon; tape; *anat.* ligament; **3.** *fig. n* (-[e]s/-e) bond, tie; **4.** ⚙ *pret. of binden*.

Bandag|e [ban'daːʒə] *f* (-/-n) bandage; **2ieren** [ˌ'ʒiːrən] *v/t.* (no -ge-, h) (apply a) bandage.

Bande ['bandə] *f* (-/-n) *billiards*: cushion; *fig.* gang, band.

bändigen ['bɛndigən] *v/t.* (ge-, h)

tame; break in (*horse*); subdue (*a. fig.*); *fig.* restrain; master.

Bandit [ban'di:t] *m* (-en/-en) bandit.

'**Band|maß** *n* tape measure; '**~säge** *f* band-saw; '**~scheibe** *anat. f* intervertebral disc; '**~wurm** *zo. m* tapeworm.

bang *adj.* [baŋ], **~e** *adj.* ['~ə] anxious (*um about*), uneasy (*about*), concerned (*for*); *mir ist* ~ I am afraid (*vor dat.* of); *j-m bange machen* frighten *or* scare s.o.; '**~en** *v/i.* (ge-, h) be anxious *or* worried (*um about*).

Bank [baŋk] *f* 1. (-/ᵘe) bench; *school*: desk; F *durch die* ~ without exception, all through; *auf die lange* ~ *schieben* put off, postpone; shelve; 2. ✝ (-/-en) bank; *Geld auf der* ~ money in the bank; '**~anweisung** *f* cheque, *Am.* check; '**~ausweis** *m* bank return *or* statement; '**~beamte** *m* bank clerk *or* official; '**~einlage** *f* deposit.

Bankett [baŋ'kɛt] *n* (-[e]s/-e) banquet.

'**Bank|geheimnis** *n* banker's duty of secrecy; '**~geschäft** ✝ *n* bank (-ing) transaction, banking operation; '**~haus** *n* bank(ing-house).

Bankier [baŋk'je:] *m* (-s/-s) banker.

'**Bank|konto** *n* bank(ing) account; '**~note** *f* (bank) note, *Am.* (bank) bill.

bankrott [baŋ'krɔt] 1. *adj.* bankrupt; 2. ♀ *m* (-[e]s/-e) bankruptcy, insolvency, failure; ~ *machen* fail, go *or* become bankrupt.

'**Bankwesen** *n* banking.

Bann [ban] *m* (-[e]s/-e) ban; *fig.* spell; *eccl.* excommunication; '♀**en** *v/t.* (ge-, h) banish (*a. fig.*); exorcize (*devil*); avert (*danger*); *eccl.* excommunicate; spellbind.

Banner ['banər] *n* (-s/-) banner (*a. fig.*); standard; '**~träger** *m* standard-bearer.

'**Bann|fluch** *m* anathema; '**~meile** *f* precincts *pl.*; ⚖ *area around government buildings within which processions and meetings are prohibited.*

bar¹ [ba:r] 1. *adj.*: *e-r Sache* ~ destitute *or* devoid of s.th.; *~es Geld* ready money, cash; *~er Unsinn* sheer nonsense; 2. *adv.*: ~ *bezahlen* pay in cash, pay money down.

Bar² [~] *f* (-/-s) bar; night-club.

Bär [bɛ:r] *m* (-en/-en) bear; *j-m e-n ~en aufbinden* hoax s.o.

Baracke [ba'rakə] *f* (-/-n) barrack; **~nlager** *n* hutment.

Barbar [bar'ba:r] *m* (-en/-en) barbarian; **~ei** [~a'raɪ] *f* (-/-en) barbarism; barbarity; ♀**isch** [~'ba:riʃ] *adj.* barbarian; barbarous; *art*, *taste*: barbaric.

'**Bar|bestand** *m* cash in hand; '**~betrag** *m* amount in cash.

'**Bärenzwinger** *m* bear-pit.

barfuß *adj. and adv.* ['ba:r-], **~füßig** *adj. and adv.* ['~fy:siç] barefoot.

barg [bark] *pret. of* bergen.

'**Bar|geld** *n* cash, ready money; '♀**geldlos** *adj.* cashless; **~er** *Zahlungsverkehr* cashless money transfers *pl.*; ♀**häuptig** *adj. and adv.* ['~hɔyptiç] bare-headed, uncovered.

Bariton ['ba:ritɔn] *m* (-s/-e) baritone.

Barkasse ⚓ [bar'kasə] *f* (-/-n) [launch.]

barmherzig *adj.* [barm'hɛrtsiç] merciful, charitable; *der ~e Samariter* the good Samaritan; ♀**e** *Schwester* Sister of Mercy *or* Charity; ♀**keit** *f* (-/-en) mercy, charity.

Barometer [baro'-] *n* barometer.

Baron [ba'ro:n] *m* (-s/-e) baron; **~in** *f* (-/-nen) baroness.

Barre ['barə] *f* (-/-n) bar.

Barren ['barən] *m* (-s/-) *metall.* bar, ingot, bullion; *gymnastics*: parallel bars *pl.*

Barriere [bar'jɛ:rə] *f* (-/-n) barrier.

Barrikade [bari'ka:də] *f* (-/-n) barricade; **~n** *errichten* raise barricades.

barsch *adj.* [barʃ] rude, gruff, rough.

'**Bar|schaft** *f* (-/-en) ready money, cash; '**~scheck** ✝ *m* open cheque, *Am.* open check.

barst [barst] *pret. of* bersten.

Bart [ba:rt] *m* (-[e]s/ᵘe) beard; bit (*of key*); *sich e-n* ~ *wachsen lassen* grow a beard.

bärtig *adj.* ['bɛ:rtiç] bearded.

'**bartlos** *adj.* beardless.

'**Barzahlung** *f* cash payment; *nur gegen* ~ ✝ terms strictly cash.

Basis ['ba:zis] *f* (-/*Basen*) base; *fig.* basis.

Baß ♪ [bas] *m* (*Basses/Bässe*) bass; '**~geige** *f* bass-viol.

Bassist [ba'sist] *m* (-en/-en) bass (singer).

Bast [bast] *m* (-es/-e) bast; velvet (*on antlers*).

Bastard ['bastart] *m* (-[e]s/-e) bastard; half-breed; *zo.*, ⚘ hybrid.

bast|eln ['bastəln] (ge-, h) 1. *v/t.* build, F rig up; 2. *v/i.* build; '♀**ler** *m* (-s/-) amateur craftsman, do-it-yourself man.

bat [ba:t] *pret. of* bitten.

Bataillon [batal'jo:n] *n* (-s/-e) battalion.

Batist [ba'tist] *m* (-[e]s/-e) cambric.

Batterie ✕, ⚡ [batə'ri:] *f* (-/-n) battery.

Bau [bau] *m* 1. (-[e]s/*no pl.*) building, construction; build, frame; 2. (-[e]s/-ten) building, edifice; 3. (-[e]s/-e) burrow, den (*a. fig.*), earth.

'**Bau|arbeiter** *m* workman in the building trade; '**~art** *f* architecture, style; method of construction; *mot.* type, model.

Bauch [baux] *m* (-[e]s/ᵘe) *anat.* abdomen, belly; paunch; *ship:* bottom; **¦ig** *adj.* big-bellied, bulgy; **˷landung** *f* belly landing; **˷red-ner** *m* ventriloquist; **˷schmerzen** *m/pl.*, **˷weh** *n* (-s/*no pl.*) belly-ache, stomach-ache.

bauen ['bauən] (ge-, *h*) **1.** *v/t.* build, construct; erect, raise; build, make (*nest*); make (*violin, etc.*); **2.** *v/i.* build; **˷** *auf* (*acc.*) trust (in); rely *or* count *or* depend on.

Bauer ['bauər] **1.** *m* (-n, -s/-n) farmer; peasant, countryman; *chess:* pawn; **2.** *n, m* (-s/-) (bird-)cage.

Bäuerin ['bɔyərin] *f* (-/-nen) farmer's wife; peasant woman.

Bauerlaubnis ['bau⁹-] *f* building permit.

bäuerlich *adj.* ['bɔyərliç] rural, rustic.

Bauern|fänger *contp.* ['bauərn-fɛŋər] *m* (-s/-) trickster, confidence man; **˷haus** *n* farm-house; **˷hof** *m* farm.

'**bau|fällig** *adj.* out of repair, dilapidated; **¦gerüst** *n* scaffold (-ing); **¦handwerker** *m* craftsman in the building trade; **¦herr** *m* owner; **¦holz** *n* timber, *Am.* lumber; **¦jahr** *n* year of construction; **˷** *1969* 1969 model *or* make; **¦kasten** *m* box of bricks; **¦kunst** *f* architecture.

'**baulich** *adj.* architectural; structural; *in gutem* **˷***en Zustand* in good repair.

Baum [baum] *m* (-[e]s/ᵘe) tree.

'**Baumeister** *m* architect.

baumeln ['bauməln] *v/i.* (ge-, *h*) dangle, swing; *mit den Beinen* **˷** dangle *or* swing one's legs.

'**Baum|schere** *f* (*eine a pair of*) pruning-shears *pl.*; **˷schule** *f* nursery (*of young trees*); **˷stamm** *m* trunk; **˷wolle** *f* cotton; **¦wollen** *adj.* (made of) cotton.

'**Bau|plan** *m* architect's *or* building plan; **˷platz** *m* building plot *or* site, *Am.* location; **˷polizei** *f* Board of Surveyors.

Bausch [bauʃ] *m* (-es/-e, ᵘe) pad; bolster; wad; *in* **˷** *und Bogen* altogether, wholesale, in the lump; **¦en** *v/t.* (ge-, *h*) swell; *sich* **˷** bulge, swell out, billow (out).

'**Bau|stein** *m* brick, building stone; building block; *fig.* element; **˷stelle** *f* building site; **˷stil** *m* (architectural) style; **˷stoff** *m* building material; **˷unternehmer** *m* building contractor; **˷zaun** *m* hoarding.

Bay|er ['baɪər] *m* (-n/-n) Bavarian; **¦(e)risch** *adj.* Bavarian.

Bazill|enträger ⚕ [ba'tsilən-] *m* (germ-)carrier; **˷us** [˷us] *m* (-/*Ba-zillen*) bacillus, germ.

beabsichtigen [bə'apçiçtigən] *v/t.*

(*no* -ge-, *h*) intend, mean, propose (*zu tun* to do, doing).

be'acht|en *v/t.* (*no* -ge-, *h*) pay attention to; notice; observe; **˷ens-wert** *adj.* noteworthy, remarkable; **˷lich** *adj.* remarkable; considerable; **¦ung** *f* attention; consideration; notice; observance.

Beamte [bə'amtə] *m* (-n/-n) official, officer, *Am. a.* officeholder; functionary; Civil Servant.

be'ängstigend *adj.* alarming, disquieting.

beanspruch|en [bə'anʃpruxən] *v/t.* (*no* -ge-, *h*) claim, demand; require (*efforts, time, space, etc.*); ⊕ stress; **¦ung** *f* (-/-en) claim; demand (*gen.* on); ⊕ stress, strain.

beanstand|en [bə'anʃtandən] *v/t.* (*no* -ge-, *h*) object to; **¦ung** *f* (-/-en) objection (*gen.* to).

beantragen [bə'antraːgən] *v/t.* (*no* -ge-, *h*) apply for; ⚖, *parl.* move, make a motion; propose.

be'antwort|en *v/t.* (*no* -ge-, *h*) answer (*a. fig.*), reply to; **¦ung** *f* (-/-en) answer, reply; *in* **˷** (*gen.*) in answer *or* reply to.

be'arbeit|en *v/t.* (*no* -ge-, *h*) work; ♪ till; dress (*leather*); hew (*stone*); process; ⚒ treat; ⚖ be in charge of (*case*); edit, revise (*book*); adapt (*nach* from); *esp.* ♪ arrange; *j-n* **˷** work on s.o.; batter s.o.; **¦ung** *f* (-/-en) working; revision (*of book*); *thea.* adaptation; *esp.* ♪ arrangement; processing; ⚒ treatment.

be'argwöhnen *v/t.* (*no* -ge-, *h*) suspect, be suspicious of.

beaufsichtig|en [bə'aufziçtigən] *v/t.* (*no* -ge-, *h*) inspect, superintend, supervise, control; look after (*child*); **¦ung** *f* (-/-en) inspection, supervision, control.

be'auftrag|en *v/t.* (*no* -ge-, *h*) commission (*zu inf.* to *inf.*), charge (*mit* with); **¦te** [˷ktə] *m* (-n/-n) commissioner; representative; deputy; proxy.

be'bauen *v/t.* (*no* -ge-, *h*) 🜨 build on; ♪ cultivate.

beben ['beːbən] *v/i.* (ge-, *h*) shake (*vor dat.* with), tremble (with); shiver (with); *earth:* quake.

Becher ['bɛçər] *m* (-s/-) cup (*a. fig.*).

Becken ['bɛkən] *n* (-s/-) basin, *Am. a.* bowl; ♪ cymbal(s *pl.*); *anat.* pelvis.

bedacht *adj.* [bə'daxt]: **˷** *sein auf* (*acc.*) look after, be concerned about, be careful *or* mindful of; *darauf* **˷** *sein zu inf.* be anxious to *inf.*

bedächtig *adj.* [bə'dɛçtiç] deliberate.

bedang [bə'daŋ] *pret. of* bedingen.

be'danken *v/refl.* (*no* -ge-, *h*): *sich bei j-m für et.* **˷** thank s.o. for s.th.

Bedarf [bə'darf] *m* (-[e]s/*no pl.*) need (*an dat.* of), want (of); † demand (for); ~sartikel [bə'darfs?-] *m/pl.* necessaries *pl.*, requisites *pl.*

bedauerlich *adj.* [bə'dauərliç] regrettable, deplorable.

be'dauern 1. *v/t.* (*no -ge-, h*) feel or be sorry for *s.o.*; pity *s.o.*; regret, deplore *s.th.*; **2.** ♀ *n* (-s/*no pl.*) regret; pity; ~swert *adj.* pitiable, deplorable.

be'deck|en *v/t.* (*no -ge-, h*) cover; ⚔ escort; ⚓ convoy; ~t *adj.* *sky:* overcast; ♀ung *f* cover(ing); ⚔ escort; ⚓ convoy.

be'denken 1. *v/t.* (*irr.* denken, *no -ge-, h*) consider; think *s.th.* over; j-n in s-m *Testament* ~ remember s.o. in one's will; **2.** ♀ *n* (-s/-) consideration; objection; hesitation; scruple; ~los *adj.* unscrupulous.

be'denklich *adj.* doubtful; *character: a.* dubious; *situation, etc.:* dangerous, critical; delicate; risky.

Be'denkzeit *f* time for reflection; *ich gebe dir e-e Stunde* ~ I give you one hour to think it over.

be'deut|en *v/t.* (*no -ge-, h*) mean, signify; stand for; ~end *adj.* important, prominent; *sum, etc.* considerable; ~sam *adj.* significant.

Be'deutung *f* meaning, significance; importance; ♀slos *adj.* insignificant; meaningless; ♀svoll *adj.* significant; ~swandel *ling.* *m* semantic change.

be'dien|en (*no -ge-, h*) **1.** *v/t.* serve; wait on; ⊕ operate, work (*machine*); ⚔ serve (*gun*); answer (*telephone*); *sich* ~ *at table:* help o.s.; **2.** *v/i.* serve; wait (at table); *cards:* follow suit; ♀ung *f* (-/-en) service, *esp.* † attendance; *in restaurant, etc.:* service; waiter, waitress; shop assistant(s *pl.*).

beding|en [bə'diŋən] *v/t.* ([*irr.*,] *no -ge-, h*) condition; stipulate; require; cause; imply; ~t *adj.* conditional (*durch* on); restricted; ~ *sein durch* be conditioned by; ♀ung *f* (-/-en) condition; stipulation; ~en *pl.* † terms *pl.*; ~ungslos *adj.* unconditional.

be'dräng|en *v/t.* (*no -ge-, h*) press hard, beset; ♀nis *f* (-/-se) distress.

be'droh|en *v/t.* (*no -ge-, h*) threaten; menace; ~lich *adj.* threatening; ♀ung *f* threat, menace (*gen.* to).

be'drück|en *v/t.* (*no -ge-, h*) oppress; depress; deject; ♀ung *f* (-/-en) oppression; depression; dejection.

bedungen [bə'duŋən] *p.p.* of **bedingen**.

be'dürf|en *v/i.* (*irr.* dürfen, *no -ge-, h*): *e-r Sache* ~ need or want or require s.th.; ♀nis *n* (-ses/-se) need, want, requirement; *sein* ~ *verrichten* relieve o.s. or nature; ♀nisan-

stalt [bə'dyrfnis?-] *f* public convenience, *Am.* comfort station; ~tig *adj.* needy, poor, indigent.

be'ehren *v/t.* (*no -ge-, h*) hono(u)r, favo(u)r; *ich beehre mich zu inf.* I have the hono(u)r to *inf.*

be'eilen *v/refl.* (*no -ge-, h*) hasten, hurry, make haste, *Am.* F *a.* hustle.

beeindrucken [bə'aindrukən] *v/t.* (*no -ge-, h*) impress, make an impression on.

beeinfluss|en [bə'ainflusən] *v/t.* (*no -ge-, h*) influence; affect; *parl.* lobby; ♀ung *f* (-/-en) influence; *parl.* lobbying.

beeinträchtig|en [bə'aintreçtigən] *v/t.* (*no -ge-, h*) impair, injure, affect (adversely); ♀ung *f* (-/-en) impairment (*gen.* of); injury (to).

be'end|en *v/t.* (*no -ge-, h*), ~igen [~igən] *v/t.* (*no -ge-, h*) (bring to an) end, finish, terminate; ♀igung [~iguŋ] *f* (-/-en) ending, termination.

beengt *adj.* [bə'eŋkt] *space:* narrow, confined, cramped; *sich* ~ *fühlen* feel cramped (for room); feel oppressed or uneasy.

be'erben *v/t.* (*no -ge-, h*): *j-n* ~ be s.o.'s heir.

beerdig|en [bə'e:rdigən] *v/t.* (*no -ge-, h*) bury; ♀ung *f* (-/-en) burial, funeral.

Beere ['be:rə] *f* (-/-n) berry.

Beet ⚘ [be:t] *n* (-[e]s/-e) bed.

befähig|en [bə'fɛ:igən] *v/t.* (*no -ge-, h*) enable (*zu inf.* to *inf.*); qualify (*für, zu* for); ~t *adj.* [~çt] (cap)able; ♀ung *f* (-/-en) qualification; capacity.

befahl [bə'fa:l] *pret.* of **befehlen**.

be'fahr|bar *adj.* [bə'fa:rba:r] passable, practicable, trafficable; ⚓ navigable; ~en *v/t.* (*irr.* fahren, *no -ge-, h*) drive or travel on; ⚓ navigate (*river*).

be'fallen *v/t.* (*irr.* fallen, *no -ge-, h*) attack; befall; *disease: a.* strike; *fear:* seize.

be'fangen *adj.* embarrassed; self-conscious; prejudiced (*a.* ⚖); ⚖ bias(s)ed; ♀heit *f* (-/-en) embarrassment; self-consciousness; ⚖ bias, prejudice.

be'fassen *v/refl.* (*no -ge-, h*): *sich* ~ *mit* occupy o.s. with; engage in; attend to; deal with.

Befehl [bə'fe:l] *m* (-[e]s/-e) command (*über acc.* of); order; ♀en (*irr., no -ge-, h*) **1.** *v/t.* command; order; **2.** *v/i.* command; ♀igen ⚔ [~igən] *v/t.* (*no -ge-, h*) command.

Be'fehlshaber *m* (-s/-) commander(-in-chief); ♀isch *adj.* imperious.

be'festig|en *v/t.* (*no -ge-, h*) fasten (*an dat.* to), fix (to), attach (to); ⚔ fortify; *fig.* strengthen; ♀ung *f* (-/-en) fixing, fastening; ⚔ fortification; *fig.* strengthening.

be'feuchten v/t. (no -ge-, h) moisten, damp; wet.

be'finden 1. v/refl. (irr. finden, no -ge-, h) be; **2.** ♀ n (-s/no pl.) (state of) health.

be'flaggen v/t. (no -ge-, h) flag.

be'flecken v/t. (no -ge-, h) spot, stain (a. fig.); fig. sully.

beflissen adj. [bə'flisən] studious; **♀heit** f (-/no pl.) studiousness, assiduity.

befohlen [bə'fo:lən] p.p. of befehlen.

be'folg|en v/t. (no -ge-, h) follow, take (advice), obey (rule); adhere to (principle); **♀ung** f (-/♀-en) observance (of); adherence (to).

be'förder|n v/t. (no -ge-, h) convey, carry; haul (goods), transport; forward; ✝ ship (a. ♠); promote (to be) (a. ✖.); **♀ung** f conveyance, transport(ation), forwarding; promotion; **♀ungsmittel** n (means of) transport, Am. (means of) transportation.

be'fragen v/t. (no -ge-, h) question, interview; interrogate.

be'frei|en v/t. (no -ge-, h) (set) free (von from); liberate (nation, mind, etc.) (from); rescue (captive) (from); exempt s.o. (from); deliver s.o. (aus, von from); **♀er** m liberator; **♀ung** f (-/-en) liberation, deliverance; exemption.

Befremden [bə'frɛmdən] n (-s/ no pl.) surprise.

befreund|en [bə'frɔyndən] v/refl. (no -ge-, h): sich mit j-m ~ make friends with s.o.; sich mit et. ~ get used to s.th., reconcile o.s. to s.th.; **~et** adj. friendly; on friendly terms; ~ sein be friends.

befriedig|en [bə'fri:digən] v/t. (no -ge-, h) satisfy; appease (hunger); meet (expectations, demand); pay off (creditor); **~end** adj. satisfactory; **♀ung** f (-/-en) satisfaction.

be'fristen v/t. (no -ge-, h) set a time-limit.

be'frucht|en v/t. (no -ge-, h) fertilize; fructify; fecundate; impregnate; **♀ung** f (-/-en) fertilization; fructification; fecundation; impregnation.

Befug|nis [bə'fu:knis] f (-/-se) authority, warrant; esp. ⚖ competence; **♀t** adj. authorized; competent.

be'fühlen v/t. (no -ge-, h) feel; touch, handle, finger.

Be'fund m (-[e]s/-e) result; finding(s pl.) ✱ diagnosis.

be'fürcht|en v/t. (no -ge-, h) fear, apprehend; suspect; **♀ung** f (-/-en) fear, apprehension, suspicion.

befürworten [bə'fy:rvɔrtən] v/t. (no -ge-, h) plead for, advocate.

begab|t adj. [bə'gɑ:pt] gifted, talented; **♀ung** f (-/-en) gift, talent(s pl.).

begann [bə'gan] pret. of beginnen.

be'geben v/t. (irr. geben, no -ge-, h) ✝ negotiate (bill of exchange); sich ~ happen; sich ~ nach go to, make for; sich in Gefahr ~ expose o.s. to danger.

begegn|en [bə'ge:gnən] v/i. (no -ge-, sein) meet s.o. or s.th., meet with; incident: happen to; anticipate, prevent; **♀ung** f (-/-en) meeting.

be'gehen v/t. (irr. gehen, no -ge-, h) walk (on); inspect; celebrate (birthday, etc.); commit (crime); make (mistake); ein Unrecht ~ do wrong.

begehr|en [bə'ge:rən] v/t. (no -ge-, h) demand, require; desire, crave (for); long for; **~lich** adj. desirous, covetous.

begeister|n [bə'gaistərn] v/t. (no -ge-, h) inspire, fill with enthusiasm; sich ~ für feel enthusiastic about; **♀ung** f (-/no pl.) enthusiasm, inspiration.

Be'gier f, **~de** [~də] f (-/-n) desire (nach for), appetite (for); concupiscence; **♀ig** adj. eager (nach for, auf acc. for; zu inf. to inf.), desirous (nach of; zu inf. to inf.), anxious (zu inf. to inf.).

be'gießen v/t. (irr. gießen, no -ge-, h) water; baste (roasting meat); F wet (bargain).

Beginn [bə'gin] m (-[e]s/no pl.) beginning, start, commencement; origin; **♀en** v/t. and v/i. (irr. no -ge-, h) begin, start, commence.

beglaubig|en [bə'glaubigən] v/t. (no -ge-, h) attest, certify; legalize, authenticate; **♀ung** f (-/-en) attestation, certification; legalization; **♀ungsschreiben** n credentials pl.

be'gleichen ✝ v/t. (irr. gleichen, no -ge-, h) pay, settle (bill, debt).

be'gleit|en v/t. (no -ge-, h) accompany (a. ♪ auf dat. on), escort; attend (a. fig.); see (s.o. home, etc.); **♀er** m (-s/-) companion, attendant; escort; ♪ accompanist; **♀erscheinung** f attendant symptom; **♀schreiben** n covering letter; **♀ung** f (-/-en) company; attendants pl., retinue (of sovereign, etc.); esp. ✖ escort; ♠, ✖ convoy; ♪ accompaniment.

be'glückwünschen v/t. (no -ge-, h) congratulate (zu on).

begnadig|en [bə'gnɑ:digən] v/t. (no -ge-, h) pardon; pol. amnesty; **♀ung** f (-/-en) pardon; pol. amnesty.

begnügen [bə'gny:gən] v/refl. (no -ge-, h): sich ~ mit content o.s. with, be satisfied with.

begonnen [bə'gɔnən] p.p. of beginnen.

be'graben v/t. (irr. graben, no -ge-, h) bury (a. fig.); inter.

Begräbnis [bə'grɛ:pnis] n (-ses/-se) burial; funeral, obsequies pl.

begradigen [bə'grɑ:digən] v/t. (no -ge-, h) straighten (road, frontier, etc.).

be'greif|en v/t. (irr. greifen, no -ge-, h) comprehend, understand; **~lich** adj. comprehensible.

be'grenz|en v/t. (no -ge-, h) bound, border; fig. limit; **2theit** f (-/-en) limitation (of knowledge); narrowness (of mind); **2ung** f (-/-en) boundary; bound, limit; limitation.

Be'griff m idea, notion, conception; comprehension; im ~ sein zu inf. be about or going to inf.

be'gründ|en v/t. (no -ge-, h) establish, found; give reasons for, substantiate (claim charge); **2ung** f establishment, foundation; fig. substantiation (of claim or charge); reason.

be'grüß|en v/t. (no -ge-, h) greet, welcome; salute; **2ung** f (-/-en) greeting, welcome; salutation.

begünstig|en [bə'gynstigən] v/t. (no -ge-, h) favo(u)r; encourage; patronize; **2ung** (-/-en) f favo(u)r; encouragement; patronage.

begutachten [bə'gu:t?-] v/t. (no -ge-, h) give an opinion on; examine; ~ lassen obtain expert opinion on, submit s.th. to an expert.

begütert adj. [bə'gy:tərt] wealthy, well-to-do.

be'haart adj. hairy.

behäbig adj. [bə'hɛ:biç] phlegmatic, comfort-loving; figure: portly.

be'haftet adj. afflicted (with disease, etc.).

behag|en [bə'hɑ:gən] 1. v/i. (no -ge-, h) please or suit s.o.; 2. 2 n (-s/no pl.) comfort, ease; **~lich** adj. [~k-] comfortable; cosy, snug.

be'halten v/t. (irr. halten, no -ge-, h) re·ain; keep (für sich to o.s.); remember.

Behälter [bə'hɛltər] m (-s/-) container, receptacle; box; for liquid: reservoir; for oil, etc.: tank.

be'hand|eln v/t. (no -ge-, h) treat; deal with (a. subject); ⊕ process; ⚕ treat; dress (wound); **2lung** f treatment; handling; ⊕ processing.

be'hängen v/t. (no -ge-, h) hang, drape (mit with); sich ~ mit cover or load o.s. with (jewellery).

beharr|en [bə'harən] v/i. (no -ge-, h) persist (auf dat. in); **~lich** adj. persistent; **2lichkeit** f (-/no pl.) persistence.

be'hauen v/t. (no -ge-, h) hew; trim (wood).

behaupt|en [bə'hauptən] v/t. (no -ge-, h) assert; maintain; **2ung** f (-/-en) assertion; statement.

Behausung [bə'hauzuŋ] f (-/-en) habitation; lodging.

Be'helf m (-[e]s/-e) expedient, (make)shift; s. Notbehelf; **2en** v/refl. (irr. helfen, no -ge-, h): sich

~ mit make shift with; sich ~ ohne do without; **~sheim** n temporary home.

behend adj. [bə'hɛnt], **~e** adj. [~də] nimble, agile; smart; **2igkeit** [~d-] f (-/no pl.) nimbleness, agility; smartness. [lodge, shelter.]

be'herbergen v/t. (no -ge-, h)

be'herrsch|en v/t. (no -ge-, h) rule (over), govern; command (situation, etc.); have command of (language); sich ~ control o.s.; **2er** m ruler (gen. over, of); **2ung** f (-/-en) command, control.

beherzigen [bə'hɛrtsigən] v/t. (no -ge-, h) take to heart, (bear in) mind.

be'hexen v/t. (no -ge-, h) bewitch.

be'hilflich adj.: j-m ~ sein help s.o. (bei in).

be'hindern v/t. (no -ge-, h) hinder, hamper, impede; handicap; obstruct (a. traffic, etc.).

Behörde [bə'hø:rdə] f (-/-n) authority, mst authorities pl.; board; council.

be'hüten v/t. (no -ge-, h) guard, preserve (vor dat. from).

behutsam adj. [bə'hu:tzɑ:m] cautious, careful; **2keit** f (-/no pl.) caution.

bei prp. (dat.) address: ~ Schmidt care of (abbr. c/o) Schmidt; **~m** Buchhändler at the bookseller's; ~ uns with us; ~ der Hand nehmen take by the hand; ich habe kein Geld ~ mir I have no money about or on me; ~ der Kirche near the church; ~ guter Gesundheit in good health; wie es ~ Schiller heißt as Schiller says; die Schlacht ~ Waterloo the Battle of Waterloo; ~ e-m Glase Wein over a glass of wine; ~ alledem for all that; Stunden nehmen ~ take lessons from or with; ~ günstigem Wetter weather permitting.

'beibehalten v/t. (irr. halten, sep., no -ge-, h) keep up, retain.

'Beiblatt n supplement (zu to).

'beibringen v/t. (irr. bringen, sep., -ge-, h) bring forward; produce (witness, etc.); j-m et. ~ impart (news, etc.) to s.o.; teach s.o. s.th.; inflict (defeat, wound, etc.) on s.o.

Beichte ['baiçtə] f (-/-n) confession; **2n** v/t. and v/i. (ge-, h) confess.

beide adj. ['baidə] both; nur wir ~ just the two of us; in ~n Fällen in either case.

beider|lei adj. ['baidərlai] of both kinds; ~ Geschlechts of either sex; **'~seitig** 1. adj. on both sides; mutual; 2. adv. mutually; **'~seits** 1. prp. on both sides (gen. of); 2. adv. mutually.

'Beifahrer m (-s/-) (front-seat) passenger; assistant driver; motor racing: co-driver.

'**Beifall** *m* (-[e]s/*no pl.*) approbation; applause; cheers *pl.*

'**beifällig** *adj.* approving; favo(u)rable.

'**Beifallsruf** *m* acclaim; ~e *pl.* cheers *pl.*

'**beifügen** *v/t.* (*sep.*, -ge-, *h*) add; enclose.

'**Beigeschmack** *m* (-[e]s/*no pl.*) slight flavo(u)r; smack (of) (*a. fig.*).

'**Beihilfe** *f* aid; allowance; *for study:* grant; *for project:* subsidy; ₤ aiding and abetting; j-m ~ leisten ₤ aid and abet s.o.

'**beikommen** *v/i.* (*irr.* kommen, *sep.*, -ge-, *sein*) get at.

Beil [baɪl] *n* (-[e]s/-e) hatchet; chopper; cleaver; ax(e).

'**Beilage** *f* supplement (*to newspaper*); F trimming~ *pl.* (*of meal*); vegetables *pl.*

beiläufig *adj.* ['baɪlɔyfiç] casual; incidental.

'**beileg|en** *v/t.* (*sep.*, -ge-, *h*) add (*dat.* to); enclose; settle (*dispute*); '2ung *f* (-/-en) settlement.

Beileid ['baɪlaɪt] *n* condolence; j-m sein ~ bezeigen condole with s.o. (zu on, upon).

'**beiliegen** *v/i.* (*irr.* liegen, *sep.*, -ge-, *h*) be enclosed (*dat.* with).

'**beimessen** *v/t.* (*irr.* messen, *sep.*, -ge-, *h*) attribute (*dat.* to), ascribe (to); attach (*importance*) (to).

'**beimisch|en** *v/t.* (*sep.*, -ge-, *h*): e-r Sache et. ~ mix s.th. with s.th.; '2ung *f* admixture.

Bein [baɪn] *n* (-[e]s/-e) leg; bone.

'**beinah(e)** *adv.* almost, nearly.

'**Beiname** *m* appellation; nickname.

'**Beinbruch** *m* fracture of the leg.

beiordnen ['baɪ ~] *v/t.* (*sep.*, -ge-, *h*) adjoin; co-ordinate (*a. gr.*).

'**beipflichten** *v/i.* (*sep.*, -ge-, *h*) agree with s.o.; assent to s.th.

'**Beirat** *m* (-[e]s/=e) adviser, counsel(l)or; advisory board.

be'irren *v/t.* (*no* -ge-, *h*) confuse.

beisammen *adv.* [baɪ'zamən] together.

'**Beisein** *n* presence; im ~ (*gen.*) or von in the presence of s.o., in s.o.'s presence.

bei'seite *adv.* aside ,apart; Spaß ~! joking apart!

'**beisetz|en** *v/t.* (*sep.*, -ge-, *h*) bury, inter; '2ung *f* (-/-en) burial, funeral.

'**Beisitzer** ₤ *m* (-s/-) assessor; associate judge; member (*of committee*).

'**Beispiel** *n* example, instance; zum ~ for example or instance; '2haft *adj.* exemplary; '2los *adj.* unprecedented, unparalleled; unheard of.

beißen ['baɪsən] (*irr.*, ge-, *h*) **1.** *v/t.* bite; *fleas, etc.:* bite; sting, **2.** *v/i.* bite (*auf acc.* on; *in acc.* into); *fleas, etc.:* bite, sting; *smoke:* bite, burn (*in dat.* in); *pepper, etc.:* bite,

burn (*auf dat.* on); '~d *adj.* biting, pungent (*both a. fig.*); *pepper, etc.:* hot.

'**Beistand** *m* assistance.

'**beistehen** *v/i.* (*irr.* stehen, *sep.*, -ge-, *h*): j-m ~ stand by or assist or help s.o.

'**beisteuern** *v/t.* and *v/i.* (*sep.*, -ge-, *h*) contribute (zu to).

Beitrag ['baɪtra:k] *m* (-[e]s/=e) contribution; share; subscription, *Am.* dues *pl.*; article (*in newspaper, etc.*).

'**bei'treten** *v/i.* (*irr.* treten, *sep.*, -ge-, *sein*) join (*political party, etc.*); '2tritt *m* joining.

'**Beiwagen** *m* side-car (*of motorcycle*); trailer (*of tram*).

'**Beiwerk** *n* accessories *pl.*

'**beiwohnen** *v/i.* (*sep.*, -ge-, *h*) assist or be present at, attend.

bei'zeiten *adv.* early; in good time.

beizen ['baɪtsən] *v/t.* (ge-, *h*) corrode; *metall.* pickle; bate (*hides*); stain (*wood*); ✗ cauterize; *hunt.* hawk.

bejahen [bə'ja:ən] *v/t.* (*no* -ge-, *h*) answer in the affirmative, affirm; ~d *adj.* affirmative.

be'jahrt *adj.* aged.

Bejahung *f* (-/-en) affirmation, affirmative answer; *fig.* acceptance.

be'jammern *s.* beklagen.

be'kämpfen *v/t.* (*no* -ge-, *h*) fight (against), combat; *fig.* oppose.

bekannt *adj.* [bə'kant] known (*dat.* to); j-n mit j-m ~ machen introduce s.o. to s.o.; 2e *m, f* (-n/-n) acquaintance, *mst* friend; ~lich *adv.* as you know; ~machen *v/t.* (*sep.*, -ge-, *h*) make known; 2machung *f* (-/-en) publication; public notice; 2schaft *f* (-/-en) acquaintance.

be'kehr|en *v/t.* (*no* -ge-, *h*) convert; 2te *m, f* (-n/-n) convert; 2ung *f* (-/-en) conversion (zu to).

be'kenn|en *v/t.* (*irr.* kennen, *no* -ge-, *h*) admit; confess; sich schuldig ~ ₤ plead guilty; sich ~ zu declare o.s. for; profess s.th.; 2tnis *n* (-ses/-se) confession; creed.

be'klagen *v/t.* (*no* -ge-, *h*) lament, deplore; sich ~ complain (*über acc.* of, about); ~swert *adj.* deplorable, pitiable.

Beklagte [bə'kla:ktə] *m, f* (-n/-n) *civil case:* defendant, *the* accused.

be'klatschen *v/t.* (*no* -ge-, *h*) applaud, clap.

be'kleben *v/t.* (*no* -ge-, *h*) glue or stick s.th. on s.th.; mit Etiketten ~ label s.th.; mit Papier ~ paste s.th. up with paper; e-e Mauer mit Plakaten ~ paste (up) posters on a wall.

bekleckern F [bə'klɛkərn] *v/t.* (*no* -ge-, *h*) stain (*garment*); sich ~ soil one's clothes.

be'klecksen *v/t.* (*no* -ge-, *h*) stain, daub; blot.

be'kleid|en v/t. (no -ge-, h) clothe, dress; hold, fill (office, etc.); ~ mit invest with; 2ung f clothing, clothes pl.

be'klemm|en v/t. (no -ge-, h) oppress; 2ung f (-/-en) oppression; anguish, anxiety.

be'kommen (irr. kommen, no -ge-) 1. v/t. (h) get, receive; obtain; get, catch (illness); have (baby); catch (train, etc.); Zähne ~ teethe, cut one's teeth; 2. v/i. (sein): j-m (gut) ~ agree with s.o.; j-m nicht or schlecht ~ disagree with s.o.

bekömmlich adj. [bə'kœmliç] wholesome (dat. to).

beköstig|en [bə'kœstigən] v/t. (no -ge-, h) board, feed; 2ung f (-/-en) board(ing).

be'kräftig|en v/t. (no -ge-, h) confirm; 2ung f (-/-en) confirmation.

be'kränzen v/t. (no -ge-, h) wreathe; festoon.

be'kritteln v/t. (no -ge-, h) carp at, criticize.

be'kümmern v/t. (no -ge-, h) afflict, grieve; trouble; s. kümmern.

be'laden v/t. (irr. laden, no -ge-, h) load; fig. burden.

Belag [bə'la:k] m (-[e]s/-e) covering; ⊕ coat(ing); surface (of road); foil (of mirror); 🌶 fur (on tongue); (slices of) ham, etc. (on bread); filling (of roll).

Belager|er [bə'la:gərər] m (-s/-) besieger; 2n v/t. (no -ge-, h) besiege, beleaguer; ~ung f siege.

Belang [bə'laŋ] m (-[e]s/-e) importance; ~e pl. interests pl.; 2en v/t. (no -ge-, h) concern; ⅛ sue; 2los adj. unimportant; ~losigkeit f (-/-en) insignificance.

be'lasten v/t. (no -ge-, h) load; fig. burden; ⅛ incriminate; mortgage (estate, etc.); j-s Konto (mit e-r Summe) ~ ✝ charge or debit s.o.'s account (with a sum).

belästig|en [bə'lestigən] v/t. (no -ge-, h) molest; trouble, bother; 2ung f molestation; trouble.

Be'lastung f (-/-en) load (a. 🌡, ⊕); fig. burden; ✝ debit; encumbrance; ⅛ incrimination; erbliche ~ hereditary taint; ~szeuge ⅛ m witness for the prosecution.

be'laufen v/refl. (irr. laufen, no -ge-, h): sich ~ auf (acc.) amount to.

be'lauschen v/t. (no -ge-, h) overhear, eavesdrop on s.o.

be'leb|en fig. v/t. (no -ge-, h) enliven, animate; stimulate; ~t adj. street: busy, crowded; stock exchange: brisk; conversation: lively, animated.

Beleg [bə'le:k] m (-[e]s/-e) proof; ⅛ (supporting) evidence; document; voucher; 2en v/t. [-gən] (no -ge-, h) cover; reserve (seat, etc.); prove, verify; univ. enrol(l) or register for,

Am. a. sign up for (course of lectures, term); ein Brötchen mit et. ~ put s.th. on a roll, fill a roll with s.th.; ~schaft f (-/-en) personnel, staff; labo(u)r force; ~stelle f reference; 2t adj. engaged, occupied; hotel, etc.: full; voice: thick, husky; tongue: coated, furred; ~es Brot (open) sandwich.

be'lehr|en v/t. (no -ge-, h) instruct, inform; sich ~ lassen take advice; ~end adj. instructive; 2ung f (-/-en) instruction; information; advice.

beleibt adj. [bə'laipt] corpulent, stout, bulky, portly.

beleidig|en [bə'laidigən] v/t. (no -ge-, h) offend (s.o.; ear, eye, etc.); insult; ~end adj. offensive; insulting; 2ung f (-/-en) offen|ce, Am. -se; insult.

be'lesen adj. well-read.

be'leucht|en v/t. (no -ge-, h) light (up), illuminate (a. fig.); fig. shed or throw light on; 2ung f (-/-en) light(ing); illumination; 2ungskörper m lighting appliance.

be'licht|en phot. v/t. (no -ge-, h) expose; 2ung phot. f exposure.

Be'lieb|en n (-s/no pl.) will, choice; nach ~ at will; es steht in Ihrem ~ I leave it to you to; 2ig 1. adj. any; jeder ~e anyone; 2. adv. at pleasure; ~ viele as many as you like; 2t adj. [~pt] popular (bei with); ~theit f (-/no pl.) popularity.

be'liefer|n v/t. (no -ge-, h) supply, furnish (mit with); 2ung f (-/no pl.) supply.

bellen ['belən] v/i. (ge-, h) bark.

belobigen [bə'lo:bigən] v/t. (no -ge-, h) commend, praise.

be'lohn|en v/t. (no -ge-, h) reward; recompense; 2ung f (-/-en) reward; recompense.

be'lügen v/t. (irr. lügen, no -ge-, h): j-n ~ lie to s.o.

belustig|en [bə'lustigən] v/t. (no -ge-, h) amuse, entertain; sich ~ amuse o.s.; 2ung f (-/-en) amusement, entertainment.

bemächtigen [bə'mɛçtigən] v/refl. (no -ge-, h): sich e-r Sache ~ take hold of s.th., seize s.th.; sich e-r Person ~ lay hands on s.o., seize s.o.

be'malen v/t. (no -ge-, h) cover with paint; paint; daub.

bemängeln [bə'mɛŋəln] v/t. (no -ge-, h) find fault with, cavil at.

be'mannen v/t. (no -ge-, h) man.

be'merk|bar adj. perceptible; ~en v/t. (no -ge-, h) notice, perceive; remark, mention; ~enswert adj. remarkable (wegen for); 2ung f (-/-en) remark.

bemitleiden [bə'mitlaidən] v/t. (no -ge-, h) pity, commiserate (with); ~swert adj. pitiable.

be'müh|en v/t. (no -ge-, h) trouble (j-n in or wegen et. s.o. about s.th.);

sich ~ trouble o.s.; endeavo(u)r; *sich um e-e Stelle* ~ apply for a position; 2ung *f* (-/-en) trouble; endeavo(u)r, effort.

be'nachbart *adj.* neighbo(u)ring; adjoining, adjacent (to).

benachrichtig|en [bə'naːxriçtigən] *v/t.* (*no -ge-*, *h*) inform, notify; †'advise; 2ung *f* (-/-en) information; notification; †'advice.

benachteilig|en [bə'naːxtailigən] *v/t.* (*no -ge-*, *h*) place *s.o.* at a disadvantage, discriminate against *s.o.*; handicap; *sich benachteiligt fühlen* feel handicapped *or* at a disadvantage; 2ung *f* (-/-en) disadvantage; discrimination; handicap.

be'nehmen 1. *v/refl.* (*irr.* nehmen, *no -ge-*, *h*) behave (o.s.); 2. 2 *n* (*-s/no pl.*) behavio(u)r, conduct.

be'neiden *v/t.* (*no -ge-*, *h*) envy (*j-n um et.* s.o. s.th.); ~swert *adj.* enviable.

be'nennen *v/t.* (*irr.* nennen, *no -ge-*, *h*) name. [rascal; urchin.]

Bengel ['bɛŋəl] *m* (-s/-) (little)]

benommen *adj.* [bə'nɔmən] bemused, dazed, stunned; ~ *sein* be in a daze.

be'nötigen *v/t.* (*no -ge-*, *h*) need, require, want.

be'nutzen *v/t.* (*no -ge-*, *h*) use (*a. patent, etc.*); make use of; avail o.s. of (*opportunity*); take (*tram, etc.*); 2ung *f* use.

Benzin [ben'tsiːn] *n* (-s/-e) ⚛ benzine; *mot.* petrol, F juice, *Am.* gasoline, F gas; ~motor *m* petrol engine, *Am.* gasoline engine; *s.* Tank.

beobacht|en [bə'oːbaxtən] *v/t.* (*no -ge-*, *h*) observe; watch; *police:* shadow; 2er *m* (-s/-) observer; 2ung *f* (-/-en) observation.

beordern [bə'ɔrdərn] *v/t.* (*no -ge-*, *h*) order, command.

be'packen *v/t.* (*no -ge-*, *h*) load (*mit* with). [(*mit* with).]

be'pflanzen *v/t.* (*no -ge-*, *h*) plant]

bequem *adj.* [bə'kveːm] convenient; comfortable; *p.:* easy-going; lazy; ~en *v/refl.* (*no -ge-*, *h*): *sich* ~ zu condescend to; consent to; 2lichkeit *f* (-/-en) convenience; comfort, ease; indolence.

be'rat|en (*irr.* raten, *no -ge-*, *h*) 1. *v/t.* advise *s.o.*; consider, debate, discuss *s.th.*; *sich* ~ confer (*mit j-m* with s.o.; *über et.* on *or* about s.th.); 2. *v/i.* confer; *über et.* ~ consider, debate, discuss s.th., confer on *or* about s.th.; 2er *m* (-s/-) adviser, counsel(l)or; consultant; ~schlagen [~n] 1. *v/i. s.* beraten 2; 2. *v/refl.* confer (*mit j-m* with s.o.; *über et.* on *or* about s.th.); 2ung *f* (-/-en) advice; debate; consultation; conference; 2ungsstelle *f* advisory bureau.

be'raub|en *v/t.* (*no -ge-*, *h*) rob, deprive (*gen.* of); 2ung *f* (-/-en) robbery, deprivation.

be'rauschen *v/t.* (*no -ge-*, *h*) intoxicate (*a. fig.*).

be'rechn|en *v/t.* (*no -ge-*, *h*) calculate; †'charge (*zu* at); ~end *adj.* calculating, selfish; 2ung *f* calculation.

berechtig|en [bə'rɛçtigən] *v/t.* (*no -ge-*, *h*) *j-n* ~ *zu* entitle s.o. to; authorize s.o. to; ~t *adj.* [~çt] entitled (*zu* to); qualified (to); *claim:* legitimate; 2ung *f* (-/-en) title (*zu* to); authorization.

be'red|en *v/t.* (*no -ge-*, *h*) talk *s.th.* over; persuade *s.o.*; gossip about *s.o.*; 2samkeit [~tzaːmkart] *f* (-/*no pl.*) eloquence; ~t *adj.* [~t] eloquent (*a. fig.*).

Be'reich *m, n* (-[e]s/-e) area; reach; *fig.* scope, sphere; *science, etc.:* field, province; 2ern *v/t.* (*no -ge-*, *h*) enrich; *sich* ~ enrich o.s.; ~erung *f* (-/-en) enrichment.

be'reif|en *v/t.* (*no -ge-*, *h*) hoop (*barrel*); tyre, (*Am. only*) tire (*wheel*); 2ung *f* (-/-en) (set of) tyres *pl.*, (*Am. only*) (set of) tires *pl.*

be'reisen *v/t.* (*no -ge-*, *h*) tour (in), travel (over); *commercial traveller:* cover (*district*).

bereit *adj.* [bə'rart] ready, prepared; ~en *v/t.* (*no -ge-*, *h*) prepare; give (*joy, trouble, etc.*); ~s *adv.* already; 2schaft *f* (-/-en) readiness; *police:* squad; ~stellen *v/t.* (*sep.*, *-ge-*, *h*) place *s.th.* ready; provide; 2ung *f* (-/-en) preparation; ~willig *adj.* ready, willing; 2willigkeit *f* (-/*no pl.*) readiness, willingness.

be'reuen *v/t.* (*no -ge-*, *h*) repent (of); regret, rue.

Berg [bɛrk] *m* (-[e]s/-e) mountain; hill; ~e *pl. von* F heaps *pl.* of, piles *pl.* of; *über den* ~ *sein* be out of the wood, *Am.* be out of the woods; *über alle* ~e off and away; *die Haare standen ihm zu* ~e his hair stood on end; 2'ab *adv.* downhill (*a. fig.*); 2'an *adv. s.* bergauf; '~arbeiter *m* miner; 2'auf *adv.* uphill (*a. fig.*); '~bahn ⚒ *f* mountain railway; '~bau *m* (-[e]s/*pl.*) mining.

bergen ['bɛrgən] *v/t.* (*irr.*, *ge-*, *h*) save; rescue *s.o.*; ⚓ salvage, salve.

bergig *adj.* ['bɛrgiç] mountainous, hilly.

'Berg|kette *f* mountain chain *or* range; '~mann ⚒ *m* (-[e]s/Bergleute) miner; '~predigt *f* (-/*no pl.*) *the* Sermon on the Mount; '~recht *n* mining laws *pl.*; '~mot. *n* mountain race; '~rücken *m* ridge; '~rutsch *m* landslide, landslip; '~spitze *f* mountain peak; '~steiger *m* (-s/-) mountaineer; '~sturz *m s.* Bergrutsch.

'**Bergung** f (-/-en) ⚓ salvage; rescue; ~**sarbeiten** ['bɛrguŋs°-] f/pl. salvage operations pl.; rescue work.

'**Bergwerk** n mine; ~**saktien** ['bɛrkverks°-] f/pl. mining shares pl.

Bericht [bə'rɪçt] m (-[e]s/-e) report (über acc. on); account (of); 2**en** (no -ge-, h) 1. v/t. report; j-m et. ~ inform s.o. of s.th.; tell s.o. about s.th.; 2. v/i. report (über acc. on); journalist: a. cover (über et. s.th.); ~**erstatter** m (-s/-) reporter; correspondent; ~**erstattung** f reporting; report(s pl.).

berichtig|en [bə'rɪçtɪgən] v/t. (no -ge-, h) correct (s.o.; error, mistake, etc.); put right (mistake); emend (corrupt text); † settle (claim, debt, etc.); 2**ung** f (-/-en) correction; emendation; settlement.

be'riechen v/t. (irr. riechen, no -ge-, h) smell or sniff at.

Berliner [bɛr'liːnər] 1. m (-s/-) Berliner; 2. adj. (of) Berlin.

Bernstein ['bɛrnʃtaɪn] m amber; schwarzer ~ jet.

bersten ['bɛrstən] v/i. (irr., ge-, sein) burst (fig. vor dat. with).

berüchtigt adj. [bə'rʏçtɪçt] notorious (wegen for), ill-famed.

berücksichtig|en [bə'rʏkzɪçtɪgən] v/t. (no -ge-, h) take s.th. into consideration, pay regard to s.th.; consider s.o.; 2**ung** f (-/-en) consideration; regard.

Beruf [bə'ruːf] m (-[e]s/-e) calling; profession; vocation; trade; occupation; 2**en** 1. v/t. (irr. rufen, no -ge-, h): j-n zu e-m Amt ~ appoint s.o. to an office; sich auf j-n ~ refer to s.o.; 2. adj. competent; qualified; 2**lich** adj. professional; vocational.

Be'rufs|ausbildung f vocational or professional training; ~**beratung** f vocational guidance; ~**kleidung** f work clothes pl.; ~**krankheit** f occupational disease; ~**schule** f vocational school; ~**spieler** m sports: professional (player); 2**tätig** adj. working; ~**tätige** [~gə] pl. working people pl.

Be'rufung f (-/-en) appointment (zu to); ᵗᵗ appeal (bei dat. to); reference (auf acc. to); ~**sgericht** n court of appeal.

be'ruhen v/i. (no -ge-, h): ~ auf (dat.) rest or be based on; et. auf sich ~ lassen let a matter rest.

beruhig|en [bə'ruːɪgən] v/t. (no -ge-, h) quiet, calm; soothe; sich ~ calm down; 2**ung** f (-/-en) calming (down); soothing; comfort; 2**ungsmittel** ᵍ n sedative.

berühmt adj. [bə'ryːmt] famous (wegen for); celebrated; 2**heit** f (-/-en) fame, renown; famous or celebrated person, celebrity; person of note.

be'rühr|en v/t. (no -ge-, h) touch (a. fig.); touch (up)on (subject); 2**ung** f (-/-en) contact; touch; in ~ kommen mit come into contact with.

be'sag|en v/t. (no -ge-, h) say; mean, signify; ~**t** adj. [~kt] (afore-) said; above(-mentioned).

besänftigen [bə'zɛnftɪgən] v/t. (no -ge-, h) appease, calm, soothe.

Be'satz m (-es/⁼e) trimming; braid.

Be'satzung f ✕ occupation troops pl.; ✕ garrison; ⚓, 🚢 crew; ~**smacht** ✕ f occupying power.

be'schädig|en v/t. (no -ge-, h) damage, injure; 2**ung** f damage, injury (gen. to).

be'schaffen 1. v/t. (no -ge-, h) procure; provide; raise (money); 2. adj.: gut (schlecht) ~ sein be in good (bad) condition or state; 2**heit** f (-/-en) state, condition; properties pl.

beschäftig|en [bə'ʃɛftɪgən] v/t. (no -ge-, h) employ, occupy; keep busy; sich ~ occupy or busy o.s.; 2**ung** f (-/-en) employment; occupation.

be'schäm|en v/t. (no -ge-, h) (put to) shame, make s.o. feel ashamed; ~**end** adj. shameful; humiliating; ~**t** adj. ashamed (über acc. of); 2**ung** f (-/-en) shame; humiliation.

beschatten [bə'ʃatən] v/t. (no -ge-, h) shade; fig. shadow s.o., Am. sl. tail s.o.

be'schau|en v/t. (no -ge-, h) look at, view; examine, inspect (goods, etc.); ~**lich** adj. contemplative, meditative.

Bescheid [bə'ʃaɪt] m (-[e]s/-e) answer; ᵗᵗ decision; information (über acc. on, about); ~ geben let s.o. know; ~ bekommen be informed or notified; ~ hinterlassen leave word (bei with, at); ~ wissen be informed, know, F be in the know.

bescheiden adj. [bə'ʃaɪdən] modest, unassuming; 2**heit** f (-/no pl.) modesty.

bescheinig|en [bə'ʃaɪnɪgən] v/i. (no -ge-, h) certify, attest; den Empfang ~ acknowledge receipt; es wird hiermit bescheinigt, daß this is to certify that; 2**ung** f (-/-en) certification, attestation; certificate; receipt; acknowledgement.

be'schenken v/t. (no -ge-, h): j-n ~ make s.o. a present; j-n mit et. ~ present s.o. with s.th.; j-n reichlich ~ shower s.o. with gifts.

be'scher|en v/t. (no -ge-, h): j-n ~ give s.o. presents (esp. for Christmas); 2**ung** f (-/-en) presentation of gifts; F fig. mess.

be'schieß|en v/t. (irr. schießen, no -ge-, h) fire or shoot at or on; bombard (a. phys.), shell; 2**ung** f (-/-en) bombardment.

be'schimpf|en v/t. (no -ge-, h) abuse, insult; call s.o. names; 2**ung** f (-/-en) abuse; insult, affront.

be'schirmen *v/t.* (*no* -ge-, *h*) shelter, shield, guard, protect (*vor dat.* from); defend (against).

be'schlafen *v/t.* (*irr. schlafen, no* -ge-, *h*): et. ~ sleep on a matter, take counsel of one's pillow.

Be'schlag *m* ⊕ metal fitting(s *pl.*); furnishing(s *pl.*) (*of door, etc.*); shoe (*of wheel, etc.*); (horse)shoe; ₰ₜ₂ seizure, confiscation; *in* ~ *nehmen, mit* ~ *belegen* seize; ₰ₜ₂ seize, attach (*real estate, salary, etc.*); confiscate (*goods, etc.*); monopolize *s.o.'s* attention.

be'schlagen 1. *v/t.* (*irr. schlagen, no* -ge-, *h*) cover (*mit* with); ⊕ fit, mount; shoe (*horse*); hobnail (*shoe*); 2. *v/i.* (*irr. schlagen, no* -ge-, *h*) window, wall, *etc.*: steam up; *mirror, etc.*: cloud *or* film over; 3. *adj.* windows, *etc.*: steamed-up; *fig.* well versed (*auf, in dat.* in).

Beschlagnahme [bə'ʃlaːknaːmə] *f* (-/-*n*) seizure; confiscation (*of contraband goods, etc.*); ₰ₜ₂ sequestration, distraint (*of property*); ✕ requisition (*of houses, etc.*); embargo, detention (*of ship*); ₰n *v/t.* (*no* -ge-, *h*) seize; attach (*real estate*); confiscate; ₰ₜ₂ sequestrate, distrain upon (*property*); ✕ requisition; ⚓ embargo.

beschleunig|en [bə'ʃlɔʏnigən] *v/t.* (*no* -ge-, *h*) mot. accelerate; hasten, speed up; *s-e Schritte* ~ quicken one's steps; ₰ung *f* (-/-*en*) acceleration.

be'schließen *v/t.* (*irr. schließen, no* -ge-, *h*) end, close, wind up; resolve, decide.

Be'schluß *m* decision, resolution, *Am. a.* resolve; ₰ₜ₂ decree; ₰fähig *adj.*: ~ *sein* form *or* have a quorum; ₰fassung *f* (passing of a) resolution.

be'schmieren *v/t.* (*no* -ge-, *h*) (be)smear (*with grease, etc.*).

be'schmutzen *v/t.* (*no* -ge-, *h*) soil (*a. fig.*), dirty; bespatter.

be'schneiden *v/t.* (*irr. schneiden, no* -ge-, *h*) clip, cut; lop (*tree*); trim, clip (*hair, hedge, etc.*); dress (*vinestock, etc.*); *fig.* cut down, curtail, F slash.

beschönig|en [bə'ʃøːnigən] *v/t.* (*no* -ge-, *h*) gloss over, palliate; ₰ung *f* (-/-*en*) gloss, palliation.

beschränk|en [bə'ʃrɛŋkən] *v/t.* (*no* -ge-, *h*) confine, limit, restrict, *Am. a.* curb; *sich* ~ *auf* (*acc.*) confine o.s. to; ~t *fig. adj.* of limited intelligence; ₰ung *f* (-/-*en*) limitation, restriction.

be'schreib|en *v/t.* (*irr. schreiben, no* -ge-, *h*) write on (*piece of paper, etc.*), cover with writing; describe, give a description of; ₰ung *f* (-/-*en*) description; account.

be'schrift|en *v/t.* (*no* -ge-, *h*) inscribe; letter; ₰ung *f* (-/-*en*) inscription; lettering.

beschuldig|en [bə'ʃuldigən] *v/t.* (*no* -ge-, *h*) accuse (*gen.* of [*doing*] *s.th.*), *esp.* ₰ₜ₂ charge (with); ₰te [~ktə] *m, f* (-*n*/-*n*) the accused; ₰ung *f* (-/-*en*) accusation, charge.

Be'schuß *m* (*Beschusses*/*no pl.*) bombardment.

be'schütz|en *v/t.* (*no* -ge-, *h*) protect, shelter, guard (*vor dat.* from); ₰er *m* (-s/-) protector; ₰ung *f* (-/-*en*) protection.

be'schwatzen *v/t.* (*no* -ge-, *h*) talk *s.o.* into (*doing*) *s.th.*, coax *s.o.* into (*doing s.th.*).

Beschwerde [bə'ʃveːrdə] *f* (-/-*n*) trouble; ✍ complaint; complaint (*über acc.* about); ₰ₜ₂ objection (*gegen* to); ₰buch *n* complaints book.

beschwer|en [bə'ʃveːrən] *v/t.* (*no* -ge-, *h*) burden (*a. fig.*); weight (*loose sheets, etc.*); lie heavy on (*stomach*); weigh on (*mind, etc.*); *sich* ~ complain (*über acc.* about, of; *bei* to); ₰lich *adj.* troublesome.

beschwichtigen [bə'ʃviçtigən] *v/t.* (*no* -ge-, *h*) appease, calm (down), soothe.

be'schwindeln *v/t.* (*no* -ge-, *h*) tell a fib *or* lie; cheat, F diddle (*um* out of).

be'schwipst F *adj.* tipsy.

be'schwör|en *v/t.* (*irr. schwören, no* -ge-, *h*) take an oath on *s.th.*; implore *or* entreat *s.o.*; conjure (up), invoke (*spirit*); ₰ung *f* (-/-*en*) conjuration.

be'seelen *v/t.* (*no* -ge-, *h*) animate, inspire.

be'sehen *v/t.* (*irr. sehen, no* -ge-, *h*) look at; inspect; *sich et.* ~ look at *s.th.*; inspect *s.th.*

beseitig|en [bə'zaɪtigən] *v/t.* (*no* -ge-, *h*) remove, do away with; ₰ung *f* (-/-*en*) removal.

Besen ['beːzən] *m* (-s/-) broom; ₰stiel *n* broomstick.

besessen *adj.* [bə'zesən] obsessed, possessed (*von* by, with); *wie* ~ like mad; ₰e *m, f* (-*n*/-*n*) demoniac.

be'setz|en *v/t.* (*no* -ge-, *h*) occupy (*seat, table, etc.*); fill (*post, etc.*); man (*orchestra*); *thea.* cast (*play*); ✕ occupy; trim (*dress, etc.*); set (*crown with jewels, etc.*); ₰t *adj.* engaged, occupied; *seat:* taken; F *bus, etc.:* full up; *hotel:* full; *teleph.* engaged, *Am.* busy; ₰ung *f* (-/-*en*) *thea.* cast; ✕ occupation.

besichtig|en [bə'ziçtigən] *v/t.* (*no* -ge-, *h*) view, look over; inspect (*a.* ✕); visit; ₰ung *f* (-/-*en*) sightseeing; visit (*gen.* to); inspection (*a.* ✕).

be'sied|eln *v/t.* (*no* -ge-, *h*) colonize, settle; populate; ₰lung *f* (-/-*en*) colonization, settlement.

be'siegeln v/t. (no -ge-, h) seal (a. fig.).

be'siegen v/t. (no -ge-, h) conquer; defeat, beat (a. sports).

be'sinn|en v/refl. (irr. sinnen, no -ge-, h) reflect, consider; sich ~ auf (acc.) remember, think of; ~lich adj. reflective, contemplative.

Be'sinnung f (-/no pl.) reflection; consideration; consciousness; (wieder) zur ~ kommen recover consciousness; fig. come to one's senses; 2slos adj. unconscious.

Be'sitz m possession; in ~ nehmen, ~ ergreifen von take possession of; 2anzeigend gr. adj. possessive; 2en v/t. (irr. sitzen, no -ge-, h) possess; ~er m (-s/-) possessor, owner, proprietor; den ~ wechseln change hands; ~ergreifung f taking possession (von of), occupation; ~tum n (-s/~er), ~ung f (-/-en) possession; property; estate.

be'sohlen v/t. (no -ge-, h) sole.

besold|en [bə'zɔldən] v/t. (no -ge-, h) pay a salary to (civil servant, etc.); pay (soldier); 2ung f (-/-en) pay; salary.

besonder adj. particular, special; peculiar; separate; 2heit f (-/-en) particularity; peculiarity; ~s adv. especially, particularly; chiefly, mainly; separately.

besonnen adj. [bə'zɔnən] sensible, considerate, level-headed; prudent; discreet; 2heit f (-/no pl.) considerateness; prudence; discretion; presence of mind.

be'sorg|en v/t. (no -ge-, h) get (j-m et. s.o. s.th.), procure (s.th. for s.o.); do, manage; 2nis [~knis] f (-/-se) apprehension, fear, anxiety, concern (über acc. about, at); ~niserregend adj. alarming; ~t adj. [~kt] uneasy (um about); worried (about), concerned (about); anxious (um for, about); 2ung f (-/-en) procurement; management; errand; ~en machen go shopping.

be'sprech|en v/t. (irr. sprechen, no -ge-, h) discuss, talk s.th. over; arrange; review (book, etc.); sich ~ mit confer with (über acc. about); 2ung f (-/-en) discussion; review; conference.

be'spritzen v/t. (no -ge-, h) splash, (be)spatter.

besser ['besər] 1. adj. better; superior; 2. adv. better; '~n v/t. (ge-, h) (make) better, improve; reform; sich ~ get or become better, improve, change for the better; mend one's ways; '2ung f (-/-en) improvement; change for the better; reform (of character); 𝖘 improvement, recovery; gute ~! I wish you a speedy recovery!

best [best] 1. adj. best; der erste ~e (just) anybody; ~en Dank thank

you very much; sich von s-r ~en Seite zeigen be on one's best behavio(u)r; 2. adv. best; am ~en best; aufs ~e, ~ens in the best way possible; zum ~en geben recite (poem), tell (story), oblige with (song); j-n zum ~en haben or halten make fun of s.o., F pull s.o.'s leg; ich danke ~ens! thank you very much!

Be'stand m (continued) existence; continuance; stock; 🕈 stock-in-trade; 🕈 cash in hand; ~ haben be lasting, last.

be'ständig adj. constant, steady; lasting; continual; weather: settled; 2keit f (-/-en) constancy, steadiness; continuance.

Bestand|saufnahme 🕈 [bə-'ʃtants?-] f stock-taking, Am. inventory; ~teil m component, constituent; element, ingredient; part.

be'stärken v/t. (no -ge-, h) confirm, strengthen, encourage (in dat. in).

bestätig|en [bə'ʃtɛːtigən] v/t. confirm (a. 🕃🕃 verdict, 🕈 order); attest; verify (statement, etc.); ratify (law, treaty); 🕈 acknowledge (receipt); 2ung f (-/-en) confirmation; attestation; verification; ratification; acknowledgement.

bestatt|en [bə'ʃtatən] v/t. (no -ge-, h) bury, inter; 2ung f (-/-en) burial, interment; funeral; 2ungsinstitut [bə'ʃtatuŋs?-] n undertakers pl.

'Beste 1. n (-n/no pl.) the best (thing); zu deinem ~n in your interest; zum ~n der Armen for the benefit of the poor; das ~ daraus machen make the best of it; 2. m, f (-n/-n): er ist der ~ in s-r Klasse he is the best in his class.

Besteck [bə'ʃtɛk] n (-[e]s/-e) 🕃🕃 (case or set of) surgical instruments pl.; (single set of) knife, fork and spoon; (complete set of) cutlery, Am. a. flatware.

be'stehen 1. v/t. (irr. stehen, no -ge-, h) come off victorious in (combat, etc.); have (adventure); stand, undergo (well) (test, trial); pass (test, examination); 2. v/i. (irr. stehen, no -ge-, h) be, exist; continue, last; ~ auf (dat.) insist (up)on; ~ aus consist of; 3. 2 n (-s/no pl.) existence; continuance; passing.

be'stehlen v/t. (irr. stehlen, no -ge-, h) steal from, rob.

be'steig|en v/t. (irr. steigen, no -ge-, h) climb (up) (mountain, tree, etc.); mount (horse, bicycle, etc.); ascend (throne); get into or on, board (bus, train, plane); 2ung f ascent; accession (to throne).

be'stell|en v/t. (no -ge-, h) order; 🕈 a. place an order for; subscribe to (newspaper, etc.); book, reserve (room, seat, etc.); make an appointment with s.o.; send for (taxi, etc.); cultivate, till (soil, etc.); give (mes-

sage, greetings); *j-n zu sich* ~ send for s.o.; 2ung *f* order; subscription (to); booking, *esp. Am.* reservation; ✔ cultivation; message.

'besten'falls *adv.* at (the) best.

be'steuer|n *v/t. (no -ge-, h)* tax; 2ung *f* taxation.

besti|alisch *adj.* [best'ja:liʃ] bestial; brutal; inhuman; *weather, etc.*: F beastly; 2e ['~jə] *f (-/-n)* beast; *fig.* brute, beast, inhuman person.

be'stimmen *(no -ge-, h)* **1.** *v/t.* determine, decide; fix *(date, place, price, etc.)*; appoint *(date, time, place, etc.)*; prescribe; define *(species, word, etc.)*; *j-n für or zu et.* ~ designate *or* intend s.o. for s.th.; **2.** *v/i.*: ~ *über (acc.)* dispose of.

be'stimmt **1.** *adj.* voice, *manner, etc.*: decided, determined, firm; *time, etc.*: appointed, fixed; *point, number. etc.*: certain; *answer, etc.*: positive; *tone, answer, intention, idea*: definite *(a. gr.)*; ~ *nach* ⊕ ✗ bound for; **2.** *adv.* certainly, surely; 2heit *f (-/-en)* determination, firmness; certainty.

Be'stimmung *f* determination; destination *(of s.o. for the church, etc.)*; designation, appointment *(of s.o. as successor, etc.)*; definition; ⅌ provision *(in document)*; *(amtliche)* ~en *pl.* (official) regulations *pl.*; ~sort [bə'ʃtimuŋˢ-] *m* destination.

be'straf|en *v/t. (no -ge-, h)* punish *(wegen, für for; mit with)*; 2ung *f (-/-en)* punishment.

be'strahl|en *v/t. (no -ge-, h)* irradiate *(a. ✗)*; 2ung *f* irradiation; ✗ ray treatment, radiotherapy.

Bc'streb|en *n (-s/no pl.)*, ~ung *f (-/-en)* effort, endeavo(u)r.

be'streichen *v/t. (irr. streichen, no -ge-, h)* coat, cover; spread; *mit Butter* ~ butter.

be'streiten *v/t. (irr. streiten, no -ge-, h)* contest, dispute, challenge *(point, right, etc.)*; deny *(facts, guilt, etc.)*; defray *(expenses, etc.)*; fill *(programme)*.

be'streuen *v/t. (no -ge-, h)* strew, sprinkle *(mit with)*; *mit Mehl* ~ flour; *mit Zucker* ~ sugar.

be'stürmen *v/t. (no -ge-, h)* storm, assail *(a. fig.)*; pester, plague *(s.o. with questions, etc.)*.

be'stürz|t *adj.* dismayed, struck with consternation *(über acc. at)*; 2ung *f (-/-en)* consternation, dismay.

Besuch [bə'zu:x] *m (-[e]s/-e)* visit *(gen., bei, in dat. to)*; call *(bei on; in dat.* at); attendance *(gen.* at) *(lecture, church, etc.)*; visitor(s *pl.*), company; 2en *v/t. (no -ge-, h)* visit; call on, go to see; attend *(school, etc.)*; frequent; ~er *m* visitor, caller; ~szeit *f* visiting hours *pl.*

be'tasten *v/t. (no -ge-, h)* touch, feel, finger; ✗ palpate.

betätigen [bə'tɛ:tigən] *v/t. (no -ge-, h)* ⊕ operate *(machine, etc.)*; put on, apply *(brake)*; *sich* ~ *als* act *or* work as; *sich poli'isch* ~ dabble in politics.

betäub|en [bə'tɔybən] *v/t. (no -ge-, h)* stun *(a. fig.)*, daze *(by blow, noise, etc.)*; deafen *(by noise, etc.)*; slaughtering: stun *(animal)*; ✗ an(a)esthetize; 2ung *f (-/-en)* ✗ an(a)esthetization; ✗ an(a)esthesia; *fig.* stupefaction; 2ungsmittel ✗ *n* narcotic, an(a)esthetic.

beteilig|en [bə'tailgən] *v/t. (no -ge-, h)*: *j-n* ~ give s.o. a share *(an dat.* in); *sich* ~ take part *(an dat., bei* in), participate *(a. ⅌, ✝)* (in); 2te [~çtə] *m, f (-n/-n)* person *or* party concerned; 2ung *f (-/-en)* participation *(a. ⅌, ✝)*, partnership; share, interest *(a. ✝)*.

beten ['be:tən] *v/i. (ge-, h)* pray *(um* for), say one's prayers; *at table*: say grace

be'teuer|n *v/t. (no -ge- h)* protest *(one's innocence)*; swear *(to s.th.; that)*; 2ung *f* protestation; solemn declaration.

be'titeln *v/t. (no -ge-, h)* entitle *(book, etc.)*; style *(s.o. 'baron', etc.)*.

Beton ⊕ [be'tõ:; be'to:n] *m (-s/-s; -s/-e)* concrete.

be'tonen *v/t. (no -ge-, h)* stress; *fig. a.* emphasize.

betonieren [beto'ni:rən] *v/t. (no -ge-, h)* concrete.

Be'tonung *f (-/-en)* stress; emphasis.

betör|en [bə'tø:rən] *v/t. (no -ge-, h)* dazzle; infatuate, bewitch; 2ung *f (-/-en)* infatuation.

Betracht [bə'traxt] *m (-[e]s/no pl.)*: *in* ~ *ziehen* take into consideration; *(nicht) in* ~ *kommen* (not to) come into question; 2en *v/t. (no -ge-, h)* view; contemplate; *fig. a.* consider.

beträchtlich *adj.* [bə'treçtliç] considerable.

Be'trachtung *f (-/-en)* view; contemplation; consideration.

Betrag [bə'traːk] *m (-[e]s/ᵘe)* amount, sum; 2en [~gən] **1.** *v/t. (irr. tragen, no -ge-, h)* amount to; **2.** *v/refl. (irr. tragen, no -ge-, h)* behave (o.s.); **3.** 2 *n (-s/no pl.)* behavio(u)r, conduct.

be'trauen *v/t. (no -ge-, h)*: *j-n mit et.* ~ entrust *or* charge s.o. with s.th.

be'trauern *v/t. (no -ge-, h)* mourn (for, over).

Betreff [bə'trεf] *m (-[e]s/-e) at head of letter*: reference; 2en *v/t. (irr. treffen, no -ge-, h)* befall; refer to; concern; *was ... betrifft* as for, as to; 2end *adj.* concerning; *das* ~e *Geschäft* the business referred to *or* in question; 2s *prp. (gen.)* concerning; as to.

be'treiben 1. v/t. (irr. treiben, no -ge-, h) carry on (business, etc.); pursue (one's studies); operate (railway line, etc.); **2.** 2 n (-s/no pl.): auf ~ von at or by s.o.'s instigation.

be'treten 1. v/t. (irr. treten, no -ge-, h) step on; enter (room, etc.); **2.** adj. embarrassed, abashed.

betreu|en [bə'trɔʏən] v/t. (no -ge-, h) look after; attend to; care for; **2ung** f (-/no pl.) care (gen. of, for).

Betrieb [bə'tri:p] m (-[e]s/-e) working, running, esp. Am. operation; business, firm, enterprise; plant, works sg.; workshop, Am. a. shop; fig. bustle; in ~ working; 2sam adj. active; industrious.

Be'triebs|anleitung f operating instructions pl.; **~ausflug** m firm's outing; **~ferien** pl. (firm's, works) holiday; **~führer** m s. Betriebsleiter; **~kapital** n working capital; **~kosten** pl. working expenses pl., Am. operating costs pl. **~leiter** m (works) manager, superintendent; **~leitung** f management; **~material** n working materials pl.; 🔗 rolling stock; **~rat** m works council; **2sicher** adj. safe to operate; foolproof; **~störung** f breakdown; **~unfall** m industrial accident, accident while at work.

be'trinken v/refl. (irr. trinken, no -ge-, h) get drunk.

betroffen adj. [bə'trɔfən] afflicted (von by), stricken (with); fig. disconcerted.

be'trüben v/t. (no -ge-, h) grieve, afflict.

Be'trug m cheat(ing); fraud (a. 🏛🏛); deceit.

be'trüg|en v/t. (irr. trügen, no -ge-, h) deceive; cheat (a. at games); defraud; F skin; 2er m (-s/-) cheat, deceiver, impostor, confidence man, swindler, trickster; **~erisch** adj. deceitful, fraudulent.

be'trunken adj. drunken; pred. drunk; 2e m (-n/-n) drunk(en man).

Bett [bɛt] n (-[e]s/-en) bed; '**~bezug** m plumeau case; '**~decke** f blanket; bedspread, coverlet.

Bettel|brief ['bɛtəl-] m begging letter; **~ei** [~'laɪ] f (-/-en) begging, mendicancy; '2n v/i. (ge-, h) beg (um for); ~ gehen go begging; '**~stab** m: an den ~ bringen reduce to beggary.

'**Bett|gestell** n bedstead; 2lägerig adj. ['~lɛːgərɪç] bedridden, confined to bed, Am. a. bedfast; '**~laken** n sheet.

Bettler ['bɛtlər] m (-s/-) beggar, Am. sl. panhandler.

'**Bett|überzug** m plumeau case; **~uch** ['bɛttuːx] n sheet; '**~vorleger** m bedside rug; '**~wäsche** f bedlinen; '**~zeug** n bedding.

be'tupfen v/t. (no -ge-, h) dab.

beug|en ['bɔʏgən] v/t. (ge-, h) bend, bow; fig. humble, break (pride); gr. inflect (word), decline (noun, adjective); sich ~ bend (vor dat. to), bow (to); **2ung** f (-/-en) bending; gr. inflection, declension.

Beule ['bɔʏlə] f (-/-en) bump, swelling; boil; on metal, etc.: dent.

beunruhig|en [bə'unruːigən] v/t. (no -ge-, h) disturb, trouble, disquiet, alarm; sich ~ über (acc.) be uneasy about, worry about; **2ung** f (-/no pl.) disturbance; alarm; uneasiness.

beurkund|en [bə'uːrkundən] v/t. (no -ge-, h) attest, certify, authenticate; **2ung** f (-/-en) attestation, certification, authentication.

beurlaub|en [bə'uːrlaʊbən] v/t. (no -ge-, h) give or grant s.o. leave (of absence); give s.o. time off; suspend (civil servant, etc.); **2ung** f (-/-en) leave (of absence); suspension.

beurteil|en [bə'urtaɪlən] v/t. (no -ge-, h) judge (nach by); **2ung** f (-/-en) judg(e)ment.

Beute ['bɔʏtə] f (-/no pl.) booty, spoil(s pl.); loot; prey; hunt. bag; fig. prey, victim (gen. to).

Beutel ['bɔʏtəl] m (-s/-) bag; purse; pouch.

'**Beutezug** m plundering expedition.

bevölker|n [bə'fœlkərn] v/t. (no -ge-, h) people, populate; **2ung** f (-/-en) population.

bevollmächtig|en [bə'fɔlmɛçtigən] v/t. (no -ge-, h) authorize, empower; **2te** [~çtə] m, f (-n/-n) authorized person or agent, deputy; pol. plenipotentiary; **2ung** f (-/-en) authorization.

be'vor cj. before.

bevormund|en fig. [bə'foːrmundən] v/t. (no -ge-, h) patronize, keep in tutelage; **2ung** fig. f (-/-en) patronizing, tutelage.

be'vorstehen v/i. (irr. stehen, sep., -ge-, h) be approaching, be near; crisis, etc.: be imminent; j-m ~ be in store for s.o., await s.o.; **~d** adj. approaching; imminent.

bevorzug|en [bə'foːrtsuːgən] v/t. (no -ge-, h) prefer; favo(u)r; 🏛🏛 privilege; **2ung** f (-/-en) preference.

be'wach|en v/t. (no -ge-, h) guard, watch; **2ung** f (-/-en) guard; escort.

bewaffn|en [bə'vafnən] v/t. (no -ge-, h) arm; **2ung** f (-/-en) armament; arms pl.

be'wahren v/t. (no -ge-, h) keep, preserve (mst fig.: secret, silence, etc.).

be'währen v/refl. (no -ge-, h) stand the test, prove a success; sich ~ als prove o.s. (as) (a good teacher, etc.); sich ~ in prove o.s. efficient in (one's profession, etc.); sich nicht ~ prove a failure.

be'wahrheiten v/refl. (no -ge-, h) prove (to be) true; *prophecy, etc.*: come true.

be'währt adj. friend, etc.: tried; solicitor, etc.: experienced; friendship, etc.: long-standing; remedy, etc.: proved, proven.

Be'währung f ɪ̵ɪ̵ probation; *in Zeiten der ~* in times of trial; s. bewähren; **~sfrist** f ɪ̵ɪ̵ f probation.

bewaldet adj. [bə'valdət] wooded, woody, *Am. a.* timbered.

bewältigen [bə'vɛltigən] v/t. (no -ge-, h) overcome (*obstacle*); master (*difficulty*); accomplish (*task*).

be'wandert adj. (well) versed (*in dat.* in), proficient (in); *in e-m Fach gut ~ sein* have a thorough knowledge of a subject.

be'wässer|n v/t. (no -ge-, h) water (*garden, lawn, etc.*); irrigate (*land, etc.*); **2ung** f (-/-en) watering; irrigation.

bewegen[1] [bə've:gən] v/t. (irr., no -ge-, h): *j-n ~ zu* induce or get s.o. to.

beweg|en[2] [~] v/t. and v/refl. (no -ge-, h) move, stir; **2grund** [~k-] m motive (*gen.*, für for); **~lich** adj. [~k-] movable; p., mind, etc.: agile, versatile; active; **2lichkeit** [~k-] f (-/no pl.) mobility; agility, versatility; **~t** adj. [~kt] sea: rough, heavy, fig. moved, touched; voice: choked, trembling; life: eventful; etc.: stirring, stormy; **2ung** f (-/-en) movement; motion (a. phys.); fig. emotion; *in ~ setzen* set going or in motion; **~ungslos** adj. motionless, immobile.

be'weinen v/t. (no -ge-, h) weep or cry over; lament (for, over).

Beweis [bə'vais] m (-es/-e) proof (für of); **~e** (pl.) evidence (esp. ɪ̵ɪ̵); **2en** [~zən] v/t. (irr. weisen, no -ge-, h) prove; show (*interest, etc.*); **~führung** f argumentation; **~grund** m argument; **~material** n evidence; **~stück** n (piece of) evidence; ɪ̵ɪ̵ exhibit. [leave it at that.\
be'wenden vb.: *es dabei ~ lassen*]
be'werb|en v/refl. (irr. werben, no -ge-, h): *sich ~ um* apply for, *Am.* run for; stand for; compete for (*prize*); court (*woman*); **2er** m (-s/-) applicant (um for); candidate; competitor; suitor; **2ung** f application; candidature; competition; courtship; **2ungsschreiben** n (letter of) application.

bewerkstelligen [bə'vɛrkʃtɛligən] v/t. (no -ge-, h) manage, effect, bring about.

be'wert|en v/t. (no -ge-, h) value (*auf acc.* at; *nach* by); **2ung** f valuation.

bewillig|en [bə'viligən] v/t. (no -ge-, h) grant, allow; **2ung** f (-/-en) grant, allowance.

be'wirken v/t. (no -ge-, h) cause; bring about, effect.

be'wirt|en v/t. (no -ge-, h) entertain; **~schaften** v/t. (no -ge-, h) farm (*land*); ✔ cultivate (*field*); manage (*farm, etc.*); ration (*food, etc.*); control (*foreign exchange, etc.*); **2ung** f (-/-en) entertainment; hospitality.

bewog [bə'vo:k] pret. of bewegen[1], **~en** [bə'vo:gən] p.p. of bewegen[1].

be'wohn|en v/t. (no -ge-, h) inhabit, live in; occupy; **2er** m (-s/-) inhabitant; occupant.

bewölk|en [bə'vœlkən] v/refl. (no -ge-, h) sky: cloud up or over; brow: cloud over, darken; **~t** adj. sky: clouded, cloudy, overcast; brow: clouded, darkened; **2ung** f (-/no pl.) clouds pl.

be'wunder|n v/t. (no -ge-, h) admire (*wegen* for); **~nswert** adj. admirable; **2ung** f (-/-en) admiration.

bewußt adj. [bə'vust] deliberate, intentional; *sich e-r Sache ~ sein* be conscious or aware of s.th.; *die ~e Sache* the matter in question; **~los** adj. unconscious; **2sein** n (-s/no pl.) consciousness.

be'zahl|en (no -ge-, h) **1.** v/t. pay; pay for (*s.th. purchased*); pay off, settle (*debt*); **2.** v/i. pay (für for); **2ung** f payment; settlement.

be'zähmen v/t. (no -ge-, h) tame (*animal*); restrain (*one's anger, etc.*); *sich ~* control or restrain o.s.

be'zauber|n v/t. (no -ge-, h) bewitch, enchant (a. fig.); fig. charm, fascinate; **2ung** f (-/-en) enchantment, spell; fascination.

be'zeichn|en v/t. (no -ge-, h) mark; describe (*als* as), call; **~end** adj. characteristic, typical (für of); **2ung** f indication (of direction, etc.); mark, sign, symbol; name, designation, denomination.

be'zeugen v/t. (no -ge-, h) ɪ̵ɪ̵ testify to, bear witness to (*both a. fig.*); attest.

be'zieh|en v/t. (irr. ziehen, no -ge-, h) cover (*upholstered furniture, etc.*); put cover on (*cushion, etc.*); move into (*flat, etc.*); enter (*university*); draw (*salary, pension, etc.*); get, be supplied with (*goods*); take in (*newspaper, etc.*); *sich ~* sky: cloud over; *sich ~ auf* (acc.) refer to; **2er** m (-s/-) subscriber (*gen.* to).

Be'ziehung f relation (*zu* et. to s.th.; *zu* j-m with s.o.); connexion, (*Am. only*) connection (*zu* with); *in dieser ~* in this respect; **2sweise** adv. respectively; or rather.

Bezirk [bə'tsirk] m (-[e]s/-e) district, *Am. a.* precinct; s. *Wahlbezirk*.

Bezogene † [bə'tso:gənə] m (-n/-n) drawee.

Bezug [bə'tsu:k] m cover(ing), case; purchase (*of goods*); subscription (*to newspaper*); in ~ *auf* (*acc.*) with regard *or* reference to, as to; ~ *nehmen auf* (*acc.*) refer to, make reference to.

bezüglich [bə'tsy:kliç] 1. *adj.* relative, relating (*both: auf acc.* to); 2. *prp.* (*gen.*) regarding, concerning.

Be'zugsbedingungen † *f/pl.* terms *pl.* of delivery.

be'zwecken *v/t.* (*no* -ge-, *h*) aim at; ~ *mit* intend by.

be'zweifeln *v/t.* (*no* -ge-, *h*) doubt, question.

be'zwing|en *v/t.* (*irr.* zwingen, *no* -ge-, *h*) conquer (*fortress, mountain, etc.*); overcome, master (*feeling, difficulty, etc.*); *sich* ~ keep o.s. under control, restrain o.s.; **ꝥung** *f* (-/-en) conquest; mastering.

Bibel ['bi:bəl] *f* (-/-n) Bible.

Biber *zo.* ['bi:bər] *m* (-s/-) beaver.

Bibliothek [biblio'te:k] *f* (-/-en) library; **~ar** [~e'ka:r] *m* (-s/-e) librarian.

biblisch *adj.* ['bi:bliʃ] biblical, scriptural; **~e** *Geschichte* Scripture.

bieder *adj.* ['bi:dər] honest, upright, worthy (*a. iro.*); simple-minded; **'ꝥkeit** *f* (-/*no pl.*) honesty, uprightness; simple-mindedness.

bieg|en ['bi:gən] (*irr.*, ge-) 1. *v/t.* (*h*) bend; 2. *v/refl.* (*h*) bend; *sich vor Lachen* ~ double up with laughter; 3. *v/i.* (*sein*): *um e-e Ecke* ~ turn (round) a corner; **~sam** *adj.* ['bi:kza:m] *wire, etc.*: flexible; *body*: lithe, supple; pliant (*a. fig.*); **'ꝥsamkeit** *f* (-/*no pl.*) flexibility; suppleness; pliability; **'ꝥung** *f* (-/-en) bend, wind (*of road, river*); curve (*of road, arch*).

Biene *zo.* ['bi:nə] *f* (-/-n) bee; '~n-königin *f* queen bee; '~nkorb *m* (bee)hive; '~nschwarm *m* swarm of bees; '~nstock *m* (bee)hive; '~nzucht *f* bee-keeping; '~nzüchter *m* bee-keeper.

Bier [bi:r] *n* (-[e]s/-e) beer; *helles* ~ pale beer, ale; *dunkles* ~ dark beer; stout, porter; ~ *vom Faß* beer on draught; '~brauer *m* brewer; '~brauerei *f* brewery; '~garten *m* beer-garden; '~krug *m* beer-mug, *Am.* stein.

Biest [bi:st] *n* (-es/-er) beast, brute.

bieten ['bi:tən] (*irr.*, ge-, *h*) 1. *v/t.* offer; † *at auction sale*: bid; *sich* ~ *opportunity, etc.*: offer itself, arise, occur; 2. † *v/i. at auction sale*: bid.

Bigamie [biga'mi:] *f* (-/-n) bigamy.

Bilanz [bi'lants] *f* (-/-en) balance; balance-sheet, *Am. a.* statement; *fig.* result, outcome; *die* ~ *ziehen* strike a balance; *fig.* take stock (*of one's life, etc.*).

Bild [bilt] *n* (-[e]s/-er) picture; image; illustration; portrait; *fig.* idea, notion; '~bericht *m* press: picture story.

bilden ['bildən] *v/t.* (ge-, *h*) form; shape; *fig.*: educate, train (*s.o., mind, etc.*); develop (*mind, etc.*); form, be, constitute (*obstacle, etc.*); *sich* ~ form; *fig.* educate o.s., improve one's mind; *sich e-e Meinung* ~ form an opinion.

Bilder|buch ['bildər-] *n* picture-book; '~galerie *f* picture-gallery; '~rätsel *n* rebus.

'Bild|fläche *f*: F *auf der* ~ *erscheinen* appear on the scene; F *von der* ~ *verschwinden* disappear (from the scene); '~funk *m* radio picture transmission; television; '~hauer *m* (-s/-) sculptor; ~**hauerei** [~'rai] *f* (-/-en) sculpture; 'ꝥlich *adj.* pictorial; *word, etc.*: figurative; '~nis *n* (-ses/-se) portrait; '~röhre *f* picture *or* television tube; '~säule *f* statue; '~schirm *m* (television) screen; 'ꝥschön *adj.* most beautiful; '~seite *f* face, head (*of coin*); '~streifen *m* picture *or* film strip; '~telegraphie *f* (-/*no pl.*) photo-telegraphy.

'Bildung *f* (-/-en) forming, formation (*both a. gr.*: *of plural, etc.*); constitution (*of committee, etc.*); education; culture; (good) breeding.   [*sg.*; billiard-table.]

Billard ['biljart] *n* (-s/-e) billiards]

billig *adj.* ['biliç] just, equitable; fair; *price*: reasonable, moderate; *goods*: cheap, inexpensive; *recht und* ~ right and proper; **~en** ['~gən] *v/t.* (ge-, *h*) approve of, *Am. a.* approbate; 'ꝥkeit *f* (-/*no pl.*) justness, equity; fairness; reasonableness, moderateness; 'ꝥung *f* ['~guŋ] *f* (-/ꝥ-en) approval, sanction.

Binde ['bində] *f* (-/-n) band; tie; ꝸ bandage; (arm-)sling; *s. Damenbinde*; '~gewebe *anat. n* connective tissue; '~glied *n* connecting link; '~haut *anat. f* conjunctiva; '~hautentzündung ꝸ *f* conjunctivitis; '~n (*irr.*, ge-, *h*) 1. *v/t.* bind, tie (*an acc.* to); bind (*book, etc.*); make (*broom, wreath, etc.*); knot (*tie*); *sich* ~ bind *or* commit *or* engage o.s.; 2. *v/i.* bind; unite; ⊕ *cement, etc.*: set, harden; '~strich *m* hyphen; '~wort *gr. n* (-[e]s/=er) conjunction.

Bindfaden ['bint-] *m* string; pack-thread.

'Bindung *f* (-/-en) binding (*a. of ski*); ♪ slur, tie, ligature; *fig.* commitment (*a. pol.*); engagement; ~en *pl.* bonds *pl.*, ties *pl.*

binnen *prp.* (*dat., a. gen.*) ['binən] within; ~ *kurzem* before long.

'Binnen|gewässer *n* inland water; '~hafen *m* close port; '~handel *m* domestic *or* home trade, *Am.* domestic commerce; '~land *n* inland, interior; '~verkehr *m* inland traffic *or* transport.

Binse ♀ ['binzə] f (-/-n) rush; F: *in die ~n gehen* go to pot; '**~nwahrheit** f, '**~nweisheit** f truism.

Biochemie [bioçe'miː] f (-/no pl.) biochemistry.

Biograph|ie [biogra'fiː] f (-/-n) biography; **Qisch** adj. [~'graːfiʃ] biographic(al).

Biolog|ie [biolo'giː] f (-/no pl.) biology; **Qisch** adj. [~'loːgiʃ] biological.

Birke ♀ ['birkə] f (-/-n) birch(-tree).

Birne ♀ ['birnə] f (-/-n) ♀ pear; ⚡ (electric) bulb; *fig. sl.* nob, *Am.* bean.

bis [bis] **1.** *prp.* (*acc.*) *space*: to, as far as; *time*: till, until, by; *zwei ~ drei* two or three, two to three; *~ auf weiteres* until further orders, for the meantime; *~ vier zählen* count up to four; *alle ~ auf drei* all but *or* except three; **2.** *cj.* till, until.

Bisamratte zo. ['biːzam-] f muskrat.

Bischof ['biʃɔf] m (-s/≈e) bishop.

bischöflich adj. ['biʃøfliç] episcopal.

bisher adv. [bis'heːr] hitherto, up to now, so far; '**~ig** adj. until now; hitherto existing; former.

Biß [bis] **1.** m (*Bisses/Bisse*) bite; **2.** ♀ *pret.* of *beißen*.

bißchen ['bisçən] **1.** adj.: *ein ~* a little, a (little) bit of; **2.** adv.: *ein ~* a little (bit).

Bissen ['bisən] m (-s/-) mouthful; morsel; bite.

'**bissig** adj. biting (*a. fig.*); *remark*: cutting; *Achtung, ~er Hund!* beware of the dog!

Bistum ['bistuːm] n (-s/≈er) bishopric, diocese.

bisweilen adv. [bis'vaɪlən] sometimes, at times, now and then.

Bitte ['bitə] f (-/-n) request (*um* for); entreaty; *auf j-s ~ (hin)* at s.o.'s request.

'**bitten** (*irr.*, ge-, h) **1.** v/t.: j-n *um et. ~* ask *or* beg s.o. for s.th.; *j-n um Entschuldigung ~* beg s.o.'s pardon; *dürfte ich Sie um Feuer ~?* may I trouble you for a light?; *bitte* please; (*wie*) *bitte?* (I beg your) pardon?; *bitte! offering s.th.*: (please,) help yourself, (please,) do take some *or* one; *danke (schön) — bitte (sehr)!* thank you — not at all, you're welcome, don't mention it, F that's all right; **2.** v/i.: *um et. ~* ask *or* beg for s.th.

bitter adj. ['bitər] bitter (*a. fig.*); *frost*: sharp; '**Qkeit** f (-/-en) bitterness; *fig. a.* acrimony; '**~lich** adv. bitterly.

'**Bitt|gang** *eccl.* m procession; '**~schrift** f petition; '**~steller** m (-s/-) petitioner.

bläh|en ['blɛːən] (ge-, h) **1.** v/t. inflate, distend, swell out; belly (out),

swell out (*sails*); *sich ~ sails*: belly (out), swell out; *skirt*: balloon out; **2.** ⚓ v/i. cause flatulence; '**~end** ⚓ adj. flatulent; '**Qung** ⚓ f (-/-en) flatulence, F wind.

Blam|age [bla'maːʒə] f (-/-n) disgrace, shame; **Qieren** [~'miːrən] v/t. (no -ge-, h) make a fool of s.o., disgrace; *sich ~* make a fool of o.s.

blank adj. [blaŋk] shining, shiny, bright; polished; F *fig.* broke.

blanko ✝ ['blaŋko] **1.** adj. form, etc.: blank, not filled in; in blank; **2.** adv.: *~ verkaufen stock exchange*: sell short; '**Qscheck** m blank cheque, *Am.* blank check; '**Qunterschrift** f blank signature; '**Qvollmacht** f full power of attorney, carte blanche.

Bläschen ⚕ ['blɛːsçən] n (-s/-) vesicle, small blister.

Blase ['blaːzə] f (-/-n) bubble; blister (*a.* ⚕); *anat.* bladder; bleb (*in glass*); ⊕ flaw; '**~balg** m (*ein a pair of*) bellows *pl.*; '**Qn** (*irr.*, ge-, h) **1.** v/t. blow; blow, sound; play (*wind-instrument*); **2.** v/i. blow.

Blas|instrument ♪ ['blaːs-] n wind-instrument; '**~kapelle** f brass band.

blaß adj. [blas] pale (*vor dat.* with); *~ werden* turn pale; *keine blasse Ahnung* not the faintest idea.

Blässe ['blɛsə] f (-/no pl.) paleness.

Blatt [blat] n (-[e]s/≈er) leaf (*of book*, ♀); petal (*of flower*); leaf, sheet (*of paper*); ♪ sheet; blade (*of oar, saw, airscrew, etc.*); sheet (*of metal*); *cards*: hand; (news)paper.

Blattern ⚕ ['blatərn] pl. smallpox.

blättern ['blɛtərn] v/i. (ge-, h): *in e-m Buch ~* leaf through a book, thumb a book.

'**Blattnarb|e** f pock-mark; '**Qig** adj. pock-marked.

'**Blätterteig** m puff paste.

'**Blatt|gold** n gold-leaf, gold-foil; '**~laus** zo. f plant-louse; '**~pflanze** f foliage plant.

blau [blau] **1.** adj. blue; F *fig.* drunk, tight, boozy; *~er Fleck* bruise; *~es Auge* black eye; *mit e-m ~en Auge davonkommen* get off cheaply; **2.** ♀ n (-s/no pl.) blue (colo[u]r); *Fahrt ins ~e* mystery tour. [blue.)

bläuen ['blɔyən] v/t. (ge-, h) (dye))

'**blau|grau** adj. bluish grey; '**Qjacke** ⚓ f bluejacket, sailor.

'**bläulich** adj. bluish.

'**Blausäure** ⚗ f (-/no pl.) hydrocyanic *or* prussic acid.

Blech [blɛç] n (-[e]s/-e) sheet metal; metal sheet, plate; F *fig.* balderdash, rubbish, *Am. sl. a.* baloney; '**~büchse** f tin, *Am.* can; '**Qern** adj. (of) tin; *sound*: brassy; *sound, voice*: tinny; '**~musik** f brass-band music; '**~waren** f/pl. tinware.

Blei [blaɪ] n (-[e]s/-e) **1.** n lead; **2.** F n, m (lead) pencil.

bleiben ['blaɪbən] *v/i.* (*irr.*, *ge-*, *sein*) remain, stay; be left; *ruhig* ~ keep calm; ~ *bei* keep to *s.th.*, stick to *s.th.*; *bitte bleiben Sie am Apparat teleph.* hold the line, please; '~**d** *adj.* lasting, permanent; '~**lassen** *v/t.* (*irr. lassen, sep., no -ge-, h*) leave *s.th.* alone; *laß das bleiben!* don't do it!; leave it alone!; stop that (*noise, etc.*)!

bleich *adj.* [blaɪç] pale (*vor dat.* with); '~**en** (*ge-*) 1. *v/t.* (*h*) make pale; bleach; blanch; 2. *v/i.* (*irr.*, *sein*) bleach; lose colo(u)r, fade; '~**süchtig** ✻ *adj.* chlorotic, green-sick.

'**bleiern** *adj.* (of) lead, leaden (*a. fig.*).

'**Blei|rohr** *n* lead pipe; '~**soldat** *m* tin soldier; '~**stift** *m* (lead) pencil; '~**stifthülse** *f* pencil cap; '~**stiftspitzer** *m* (*-s/-*) pencil-sharpener; '~**vergiftung** ✻ *f* lead-poisoning.

Blend|e ['blɛndə] *f* (*-/-n*) *phot.* diaphragm, stop; △ blind *or* sham window; '**2en** (*ge-*, *h*) 1. *v/t.* blind; dazzle (*both a. fig.*); 2. *v/i. light:* dazzle the eyes; ~**laterne** ['blɛnt-] *f* dark lantern.

blich [blɪç] *pret. of* bleichen 2.

Blick [blɪk] *m* (*-[e]s/-e*) glance, look; view (*auf acc.* of); *auf den ersten* ~ at first sight; *ein böser* ~ an evil *or* angry look; '**2en** *v/i.* (*ge-*, *h*) look, glance (*auf acc.*, *nach* at); '~**fang** *m* eye-catcher.

blieb [bliːp] *pret. of* bleiben.

blies [bliːs] *pret. of* blasen.

blind *adj.* [blɪnt] blind (*a. fig.*: *gegen*, *für* to; *vor dat.* with); *metal:* dull, tarnished; *window:* opaque (*with age, dirt*); *mirror:* clouded, dull; *cartridge:* blank; ~*er Alarm* false alarm; ~*er Passagier* stowaway; *auf e-m Auge* ~ blind in one eye.

'**Blinddarm** *anat. m* blind gut; appendix; '~**entzündung** ✻ *f* appendicitis.

Blinde ['blɪndə] (*-n/-n*) 1. *m* blind man; 2. *f* blind woman; ~**nanstalt** ['blɪndən⁹-] *f* institute for the blind; '~**nheim** *n* home for the blind; '~**nhund** *m* guide dog, *Am. a.* seeing-eye dog; '~**nschrift** *f* braille.

'**blind|fliegen** ✈ (*irr. fliegen, sep.*, *-ge-*) *v/t.* (*h*) *and v/i.* (*sein*) fly blind *or* on instruments; '**2flug** ✈ *m* blind flying *or* flight; '**2gänger** *m* ✖ blind shell, dud; *F fig.* washout; '**2heit** *f* (*-/no pl.*) blindness; '~**lings** *adv.* ['~lɪŋs] blindly; at random; '**2schleiche** *zo. f* (*-/-n*) slow-worm, blind-worm; '~**schreiben** *v/t. and v/i.* (*irr. schreiben, sep.*, *-ge-*, *h*) touch-type.

blink|en ['blɪŋkən] *v/i.* (*ge-*, *h*) star, light: twinkle; *metal, leather, glass, etc.*: shine; signal (with lamps),

flash; '**2er** *mot. m* (*-s/-*) flashing indicator; '**2feuer** *n* flashing light.

blinzeln ['blɪntsəln] *v/i.* (*ge-*, *h*) blink (*at light, etc.*); wink.

Blitz [blɪts] *m* (*-es/-e*) lightning; '~**ableiter** *m* (*-s/-*) lightning-conductor; '**2en** *v/i.* (*ge-*, *h*) flash; *es blitzt* it is lightening; '~**gespräch** *teleph. n* special priority call; '~**licht** *phot. n* flash-light; '**2schnell** *adv.* with lightning speed; '~**strahl** *m* flash of lightning.

Block [blɔk] *m* 1. (*-[e]s/*⁓e) block; slab (*of cooking chocolate*); block, log (*of wood*); ingot (*of metal*); *parl., pol.*, ♣ bloc; 2. (*-[e]s/*⁓e, *-s*) block (*of houses*); pad, block (*of paper*); ~**ade** ✖, ⚓ [~'kɑːdə] *f* (*-/-n*) blockade; ~**adebrecher** *m* (*-s/-*) blockade-runner; '~**haus** *n* log cabin; **2ieren** [~'kiːrən] (*no -ge-*, *h*) 1. *v/t.* block (up); lock (*wheel*); 2. *v/i. brakes, etc.*: jam.

blöd *adj.* [bløːt], ~**e** *adj.* ['~də] imbecile; stupid, dull; silly; '**2heit** *f* (*-/-en*) imbecility; stupidity, dullness; silliness; '**2sinn** *m* imbecility; rubbish, nonsense; '~**sinnig** *adj.* imbecile; idiotic, stupid, foolish.

blöken ['bløːkən] *v/i.* (*ge-*, *h*) *sheep, calf:* bleat.

blond *adj.* [blɔnt] blond, fair (*-haired*).

bloß [bloːs] 1. *adj.* bare, naked; mere; ~*e Worte* mere words; *mit dem* ~*en Auge wahrnehmbar* visible to the naked eye; 2. *adv.* only, merely, simply, just.

Blöße ['bløːsə] *f* (*-/-n*) bareness, nakedness; *fig.* weak point *or* spot; *sich e-e* ~ *geben* give o.s. away; lay o.s. open to attack; *keine* ~ *bieten* be invulnerable.

'**bloß|legen** *v/t.* (*sep.*, *-ge-*, *h*) lay bare, expose; '~**stellen** *v/t.* (*sep.*, *-ge-*, *h*) expose, compromise, unmask; *sich* ~ compromise o.s.

blühen ['blyːən] *v/i.* (*ge-*, *h*) blossom, flower, bloom; *fig.* flourish, thrive, prosper; ♣ boom.

Blume ['bluːmə] *f* (*-/-n*) flower; *wine:* bouquet; *beer:* froth.

'**Blumen|beet** *n* flower-bed; '~**blatt** *n* petal; '~**händler** *m* florist; '~**strauß** *m* bouquet *or* bunch of flowers; '~**topf** *m* flowerpot; '~**zucht** *f* floriculture.

Bluse ['bluːzə] *f* (*-/-n*) blouse.

Blut [bluːt] *n* (*-[e]s/no pl.*) blood; ~ *vergießen* shed blood; *böses* ~ *machen* breed bad blood; '~**andrang** ✻ *m* congestion; '~**arm** *adj.* bloodless; ✻ an(a)emic; '~**armut** ✻ *f* an(a)emia; '~**bad** *n* carnage, massacre; '~**bank** ✻ *f* blood bank; '~**blase** *f* blood blister; '~**druck** *m* blood pressure; **2dürstig** *adj.* ['~dyrstiç] bloodthirsty.

Blüte ['blyːtə] *f* (*-/-n*) blossom,

bloom, flower; *esp. fig.* flower; prime, heyday (*of life*).

Blutegel ['blu:t⁹e:gəl] *m* (-s/-) leech.

'bluten *v/i.* (ge-, *h*) bleed (*aus* from); *aus der Nase* ~ bleed at the nose.

Bluterguß ✍ ['blu:t⁹-] *m* effusion of blood.

'Blütezeit *f* flowering period *or* time; *fig. a.* prime, heyday.

'Blut|gefäß *anat. n* blood-vessel; **~gerinnsel** ✍ ['~gərinzəl] *n* (-s/-) clot of blood; **'~gruppe** *f* blood group; **'~hund** *zo. m* bloodhound.

'blutig *adj.* bloody, blood-stained; *es ist mein* ~*er Ernst* I am dead serious; ~*er Anfänger* mere beginner, F greenhorn.

Blut|körperchen ['blu:tkœrpərçən] *n* (-s/-) blood corpuscle; **'~kreislauf** *m* (blood) circulation; **'~lache** *f* pool of blood; **'2leer** *adj.,* **'2los** *adj.* bloodless; **'~probe** *f* blood test; **'~rache** *f* blood feud *or* revenge *or* vengeance, vendetta; **'2-'rot** *adj.* blood-red; crimson; 2rünstig *adj.* ['~rynstiç] bloodthirsty; bloody; **'~schande** *f* incest; **'~spender** *m* blood-donor; **'2stillend** *adj.* blood-sta(u)nching; **'~sturz** ✍ *m* h(a)emorrhage; **'2sverwandt** *adj.* related by blood (*mit* to); **'~s-verwandtschaft** *f* blood-relationship, consanguinity; **'~übertragung** *f* blood-transfusion; **'~ung** *f* (-/-en) bleeding, h(a)emorrhage; **'2unterlaufen** *adj. eye:* bloodshot; **'~vergießen** *n* bloodshed; **'~vergiftung** *f* blood-poisoning.

Bö [bø] *f* (-/-en) gust, squall.

Bock [bɔk] *m* (-[e]s/⁼e) deer, hare, rabbit: buck; he-goat, F billy-goat; *sheep:* ram; *gymnastics:* buck; *e-n* ~ *schießen* commit a blunder, *sl.* commit a bloomer; *den* ~ *zum Gärtner machen* set the fox to keep the geese; **'2en** *v/i.* (ge-, *h*) *horse:* buck; *child:* sulk; *p.* be obstinate *or* refractory; *mot.* move jerkily, *Am.* F *a.* buck; **'2ig** *adj.* stubborn, obstinate, pigheaded; **'~sprung** *m* leap-frog; *gymnastics:* vault over the buck; *Bocksprünge machen* caper, cut capers.

Boden ['bo:dən] *m* (-s/⁼) ground; ✍ soil; bottom; floor; loft; **'~kammer** *f* garret, attic; **'2los** *adj.* bottomless; *fig.* enormous, unheard-of; **'~personal** ✈ *n* ground personnel *or* staff, *Am.* ground crew; **'~reform** *f* land reform; **'~satz** *m* grounds *pl.,* sediment; **'~schätze** *f* ['~ʃetsə] *m/pl.* mineral resources *pl.;* **'2ständig** *adj.* native, indigenous.

bog [bo:k] *pret. of* biegen.

Bogen ['bo:gən] *m* (-s/-, ⁼) bow, bend, curve; ↗ arc; △ arch; *skiing:* turn; *skating:* curve; sheet (*of* paper); **'2förmig** *adj.* arched; **'~gang** △ *m* arcade; **'~lampe** ⚡ *f* arc-lamp; **'~schütze** *m* archer, bowman.

Bohle ['bo:lə] *f* (-/-n) thick plank, board.

Bohne ['bo:nə] *f* (-/-n) bean; *grüne* ~*n pl.* French beans *pl., Am.* string beans *pl.; weiße* ~*n pl.* haricot beans *pl.;* F *blaue* ~*n pl.* bullets *pl.;* **'~n-stange** *f* beanpole (*a.* F *fig.*).

bohnern ['bo:nərn] *v/t.* (ge-, *h*) polish (*floor, etc.*), (bees)wax (*floor*).

bohr|en ['bo:rən] (ge-, *h*) **1.** *v/t.* bore, drill (*hole*); sink, bore (*well, shaft*); bore, cut, drive (*tunnel, etc.*); **2.** *v/i.* drill (*a. dentistry*); bore; **'2er** ⊕ *m* (-s/-) borer, drill.

'böig *adj.* squally, gusty; ✈ bumpy.

Boje ['bo:jə] *f* (-/-n) buoy.

Bollwerk ✕ ['bɔlverk] *n* bastion, bulwark (*a. fig.*).

Bolzen ⊕ ['bɔltsən] *m* (-s/-) bolt.

Bombard|ement [bɔmbardə'mã:] *n* (-s/-s) bombardment; bombing; shelling; **2ieren** [~'di:rən] *v/t.* (no -ge-, *h*) bomb; shell; bombard (*a. fig.*).

Bombe ['bɔmbə] *f* (-/-n) bomb; *fig.* bomb-shell; **2nsicher** *adj.* bomb-proof; F *fig.* dead sure; **'~nschaden** *m* bomb damage; **'~r** ✕: ✈ *m* (-s/-) bomber.

Bon † [bõ:] *m* (-s/-s) coupon; voucher; credit note.

Bonbon [bõ:'bõ:] *m, n* (-s/-s) sweet (-meat), bon-bon, F goody, *Am.* candy.

Bonze F ['bɔntsə] *m* (-n/-n) bigwig, *Am. a.* big shot.

Boot [bo:t] *n* (-[e]s/-e) boat; **'~shaus** *n* boat-house; **'~smann** *m* (-[e]s/*Bootsleute*) boatswain.

Bord [bɔrt] (-[e]s/-e) **1.** *n* shelf; **2.** ⚓, ✈ *m: an* ~ *on board, aboard (ship, aircraft, etc.);* *über* ~ overboard; *von* ~ *gehen* go ashore; **'~funker** ⚓, ✈ *m* wireless *or* radio operator; **'~stein** *m* kerb, *Am.* curb.

borgen ['bɔrgən] *v/t.* (ge-, *h*) borrow (*von, bei* from, of); lend, *Am. a.* loan (*j-m et.* s.th. to s.o.).

Borke ['bɔrkə] *f* (-/-n) bark (*of tree*).

borniert *adj.* [bɔr'ni:rt] narrow-minded, of restricted intelligence.

Borsalbe ['bo:r-] *f* boracic ointment.

Börse ['bœrzə] *f* (-/-n) purse; † stock exchange; stock-market; money-market; **'~nbericht** *m* market report; **'2nfähig** *adj.* stock: negotiable on the stock exchange; **'~nkurs** *m* quotation; **'~nmakler** *m* stock-broker; **'~nnotierung** *f* (official, stock exchange) quotation; **'~npapiere** *n/pl.* listed securities *pl.;* **'~nspekulant** *m* stock-jobber; **'~nzeitung** *f* financial newspaper.

Borst|e ['bɔrstə] f (-/-n) bristle (*of hog or brush, etc.*); **'⁀ig** adj. bristly.

Borte ['bɔrtə] f (-/-n) border (*of carpet, etc.*); braid, lace.

'bösartig adj. malicious, vicious; ⚕ malignant; **'⁀keit** f (-/-en) viciousness; ⚕ malignity.

Böschung ['bœʃuŋ] f (-/-en) slope; embankment (*of railway*); bank (*of river*).

böse ['bøːzə] **1.** adj. bad, evil, wicked; malevolent, spiteful; angry (*über acc.* at, about; *auf j-n* with s.o.); *er meint es nicht* ⁀ he means no harm; **2.** ⚥ n (-n/no pl.) evil; **⁀wicht** ['⁀viçt] m (-[e]s/-er, -e) villain, rascal.

bos|haft adj. ['boːshaft] wicked; spiteful; malicious; **'⁀heit** f (-/-en) wickedness; malice; spite.

'böswillig adj. malevolent; ⁀e *Absicht* ⚖ malice prepense; ⁀es *Verlassen* ⚖ wilful desertion; **'⁀keit** f (-/-en) malevolence.

bot [boːt] pret. of **bieten**.

Botan|ik [bo'taːnik] f (-/no pl.) botany; **⁀iker** m (-s/-) botanist; **⁀isch** adj. botanical.

Bote ['boːtə] m (-n/-n) messenger; **'⁀ngang** m errand; *Botengänge machen* run errands.

'Botschaft f (-/-en) message; pol. embassy; **'⁀er** m (-s/-) ambassador; *in British Commonwealth countries*: High Commissioner.

Bottich ['bɔtiç] m (-[e]s/-e) tub; wash-tub; *brewing*: tun. vat.

Bouillon [bu'ljõ:] f (-/-s) beef tea.

Bowle ['boːlə] f (-/-n) vessel: bowl; *cold drink consisting of fruit, hock and champagne or soda-water*: appr. punch.

box|en ['bɔksən] **1.** v/i. (ge-, h) box; **2.** v/t. (ge-, h) punch s.o.; **3.** ⚥ n (-s/no pl.) boxing; pugilism; **'⁀er** m (-s/-) boxer; pugilist; **'⁀handschuh** m boxing-glove; **'⁀kampf** m boxing-match, bout, fight; **'⁀sport** m boxing.

Boykott [bɔy'kɔt] (-[e]s/-e) boycott; **⁀ieren** [⁀'tiːrən] v/t. (no -ge-, h) boycott.

brach [braːx] **1.** pret. of **brechen**; **2.** ⚥ adv. fallow; uncultivated (*both a. fig.*).

brachte ['braxtə] pret. of **bringen**.

Branche † ['brãːʃə] f (-/-n) line (*of business*), trade; branch.

Brand [brant] m (-[e]s/⁀e) burning; fire, blaze; ⚕ gangrene; ♣, ♠ blight, smut, mildew; **'⁀blase** f blister; **'⁀bombe** f incendiary bomb; **⚥en** ['⁀dən] v/i. (ge-, h) surge (*a. fig.*), break (*an acc.*, *gegen* against); **'⁀fleck** m burn; **⚥ig** adj. ['⁀diç] ♣, ♠ blighted, smutted; ⚕ gangrenous; **'⁀mal** n brand; fig. stigma, blemish; **'⚥marken** v/t. (ge-, h) brand (*animal*); fig. brand

or stigmatize s.o.; **'⁀mauer** f fire (-proof) wall; **'⁀schaden** m damage caused *or* loss suffered by fire; **'⚥schatzen** v/t. (ge-, h) lay (*town*) under contribution; sack, pillage; **'⁀stätte** f, **'⁀stelle** f scene of fire; **'⁀stifter** m incendiary, *Am.* F a. firebug; **'⁀stiftung** f arson; **⁀ung** ['⁀duŋ] f (-/-en) surf, surge, breakers pl.; **'⁀wache** f fire-watch; **'⁀wunde** f burn; scald; **'⁀zeichen** n brand.

brannte ['brantə] pret. of **brennen**.

Branntwein ['brantvaın] m brandy, spirits pl.; whisk(e)y; gin; **'⁀brennerei** f distillery.

braten ['braːtən] **1.** v/t. (irr., ge-, h) *in oven*: roast; grill; *in frying-pan*: fry; bake (*apple*); *am Spieß* ⁀ roast on a spit, barbecue; **2.** v/i. (irr., ge-, h) roast; grill; fry; *in der Sonne* ⁀ p. roast *or* grill in the sun; **3.** ⚥ m (-s/-) roast (meat); joint; **'⚥fett** n dripping; **'⚥soße** f gravy.

'Brat|fisch m fried fish; **'⁀hering** m grilled herring; **'⁀huhn** n roast chicken; **'⁀kartoffeln** pl. fried potatoes pl.; **'⁀ofen** m (kitchen) oven; **'⁀pfanne** f frying-pan, *Am. a.* skillet; **'⁀röhre** f s. *Bratofen*.

Brauch [braux] m (-[e]s/⁀e) custom, usage; use, habit; practice; **'⚥bar** adj. p., thing: useful; p. capable, able; thing: serviceable; **'⚥en** (h) **1.** v/t. (ge-) need, want; require; take (*time*); use; **2.** v/aux. (no -ge-): *du brauchst es nur zu sagen* you only have to say so; *er hätte nicht zu kommen* ⁀ he need not have come; **'⁀tum** n (-[e]s/⁀er) custom; tradition; folklore.

Braue ['brauə] f (-/-n) eyebrow.

brau|en ['brauən] v/t. (ge-, h) brew; **'⚥er** m (-s/-) brewer; **⚥erei** [⁀'raɪ] f (-/-en) brewery; **'⚥haus** n brewery.

braun adj. [braun] brown; *horse*: bay; ⁀ *werden* get a tan (*on one's skin*).

Bräune ['brɔynə] f (-/no pl.) brown colo(u)r; (sun) tan; **'⚥n** (ge-, h) **1.** v/t. make *or* dye brown; *sun*: tan; **2.** v/i. tan.

'Braunkohle f brown coal, lignite.

'bräunlich adj. brownish.

Brause ['brauzə] f (-/-n) rose, sprinkling-nozzle (*of watering can*); s. *Brausebad*; s. *Brauselimonade*; **'⁀bad** n shower(-bath); **'⁀limonade** f fizzy lemonade; **'⚥n** v/i. (ge-, h) *wind, water, etc.*: roar; rush; *have a* shower(-bath); **'⁀pulver** n effervescent powder.

Braut [braut] f (-/⁀e) fiancée; *on wedding-day*: bride; **'⁀führer** m best man.

Bräutigam ['brɔytigam] m (-s/-e) fiancé; *on wedding-day*: bridegroom, *Am. a.* groom.

'Braut|jungfer f bridesmaid; **'⁀**

kleid n wedding-dress; '~kranz m bridal wreath; '~leute pl., '~paar n engaged couple; on wedding-day: bride and bridegroom; '~schleier m bridal veil.

brav adj. [bra:f] honest, upright; good, well-behaved; brave.

bravo int. ['bra:vo] bravo!, well done!

Bravour [bra'vu:r] f (-/no pl.) bravery, courage; brilliance.

Brecheisen ['breç?-] n crowbar; (burglar's) jemmy, Am. a. jimmy.

'brechen (irr., ge-) **1.** v/t. (h) break; pluck (flower); refract (ray, etc.); fold (sheet of paper); quarry (stone); vomit; die Ehe ~ commit adultery; sich ~ break (one's leg, etc.); opt. be refracted; **2.** v/i. (h) break; vomit; mit j-m ~ break with s.o.; **3.** v/i. (sein) break, get broken; bones: break, fracture.

'Brech|mittel ⚕ n emetic; F fig. sickener; '~reiz m nausea; '~stange f crowbar, Am. a. pry; '~ung opt. f (-/-en) refraction.

Brei [braɪ] m (-[e]s/-e) paste; pulp; mash; pap (for babies); made of oatmeal: porridge; (rice, etc.) pudding; 'ig adj. pasty; pulpy; pappy.

breit adj. [braɪt] broad, wide; zehn Meter ~ ten metres wide; ~e Schichten der Bevölkerung large sections of or the bulk of the population; '~beinig **1.** adj. with legs wide apart; **2.** adv.: ~ gehen straddle.

Breite ['braɪtə] f (-/-n) breadth, width; ast., geogr. latitude; '2n v/t. (ge-, h) spread; '~ngrad m degree of latitude; '~nkreis m parallel (of latitude).

'breit|machen v/refl. (sep., -ge-, h) spread o.s.; take up room; '~schlagen v/t. (irr. schlagen, sep., -ge-, h): F j-n ~ persuade s.o.; F j-n zu et. ~ talk s.o. into (doing) s.th.; '2seite ⚓ f broadside.

Bremse ['bremzə] f (-/-n) zo. gadfly; horse-fly; ⊕ brake; '2n (ge-, h) v/i. brake, put on the brakes; slow down; **2.** v/t. brake, put on the brakes to; slow down; fig. curb.

'Brems|klotz m brake-block; 🦫 wheel chock; '~pedal n brake pedal; '~vorrichtung f brake-mechanism; '~weg m braking distance.

brenn|bar adj. ['brɛnbaːr] combustible, burnable; '2dauer f burning time; '~en (irr., ge-, h) **1.** v/t. burn; distil(l) (brandy); roast (coffee); bake (brick, etc.); **2.** v/i. burn; be ablaze, be on fire; wound, eye: smart, burn; nettle: sting; vor Ungeduld ~ burn with impatience; F darauf ~ zu inf. be burning to inf.; es brennt! fire!

'Brenn|er m (-s/-) p. distiller; fixture: burner; ~essel ['brɛnnəsəl] f

stinging nettle; '~glas n burning glass; '~holz n firewood; '~material n fuel; '~öl n lamp-oil; fuel-oil; '~punkt m focus, focal point; in den ~ rücken bring into focus (a. fig.); im ~ des Interesses stehen be the focus of interest; '~schere f curling-tongs pl.; '~spiritus m methylated spirit; '~stoff m combustible; mot. fuel.

brenzlig ['brentsliç] **1.** adj. burnt; matter: dangerous; situation: precarious; ~er Geruch burnt smell, smell of burning; **2.** adv.: es riecht ~ it smells of burning.

Bresche ['brɛʃə] f (-/-n) breach (a. fig.), gap; in die ~ springen help s.o. out of a dilemma.

Brett [brɛt] n (-[e]s/-er) board; plank; shelf; spring-board; '~spiel n game played on a board.

Brezel ['bre:tsəl] f (-/-n) pretzel.

Brief [briːf] m (-[e]s/-e) letter; '~aufschrift f address (on a letter); '~beschwerer m (-s/-) paperweight; '~bogen m sheet of notepaper; '~geheimnis n secrecy of correspondence; '~karte f correspondence card (with envelope); '~kasten m letter-box; pillar-box; Am. mailbox; '2lich adj. and adv. by letter, in writing; '~marke f (postage) stamp; '~markensammlung f stamp-collection; '~öffner m letter-opener; '~ordner m letter-file; '~papier n notepaper; '~porto n postage; '~post f mail, post; '~tasche f wallet, Am. a. billfold; '~taube f carrier pigeon, homing pigeon, homer; '~träger m postman, Am. mailman; '~umschlag m envelope; '~waage f letter-balance; '~wechsel m correspondence; '~zensur f postal censorship.

briet [briːt] pret. of braten.

Brikett [bri'kɛt] n (-[e]s/-s) briquet (-te).

Brillant [bril'jant] **1.** m (-en/-en) brilliant, cut diamond; **2.** ♀ adj. brilliant; ~ring m diamond ring.

Brille ['brilə] f (-/-n) (eine a pair of) glasses pl. or spectacles pl.; goggles pl.; lavatory seat; '~nfutteral n spectacle-case; '~nträger m person who wears glasses.

bringen ['brɪŋən] v/t. (irr., ge-, h) bring; take; see (s.o. home, etc.); put (in order); make (sacrifice); yield (interest); an den Mann ~ dispose of, get rid of; j-n dazu ~, et. zu tun make or get s.o. to do s.th.; et. mit sich ~ involve s.th.; j-n um et. ~ deprive s.o. of s.th.; j-n zum Lachen ~ make s.o. laugh.

Brise ['briːzə] f (-/-n) breeze.

Brit|e ['briːtə] m (-n/-n) Briton, Am. a. Britisher; die ~n pl. the British pl.; '2isch adj. British.

bröckeln ['brœkəln] v/i. (ge-, h) crumble; become brittle.

Brocken ['brɔkən] 1. m (-s/-) piece; lump (of earth or stone, etc.); morsel (of food); F ein harter ~ a hard nut; 2. ♀ v/t. (ge-, h): Brot in die Suppe ~ break bread into soup.

brodeln ['broːdəln] v/i. (ge-, h) bubble, simmer.

Brombeer|e ['brɔm-] f blackberry; '~strauch m blackberry bush.

Bronch|ialkatarrh ♀ [brɔnçiˈɑːl-katar] m bronchial catarrh; '~ien anat. f/pl. bronchi(a) pl.; ~itis [~ˈçiːtis] f (-/Bronchitiden) bronchitis.

Bronze ['brõːsə] f (-/-n) bronze; '~medaille f bronze medal.

Brosche ['brɔʃə] f (-/-n) brooch.

broschier|en [brɔˈʃiːrən] v/t. (no -ge-, h) sew, stitch (book); ~t adj. book: paper-backed, paper-bound; fabric: figured.

Broschüre [brɔˈʃyːrə] f (-/-n) booklet; brochure; pamphlet.

Brot [broːt] n (-[e]s/-e) bread; loaf; sein ~ verdienen earn one's living; '~aufstrich m spread.

Brötchen ['brøːtçən] n (-s/-) roll.

'Brot|korb m: j-m den ~ höher hängen put s.o. on short allowance; '♀los fig. adj. unemployed; unprofitable; '~rinde f crust; '~schneidemaschine f bread-cutter; '~schnitte f slice of bread; '~studium n utilitarian study; '~teig m bread dough.

Bruch [brux] (-[e]s/♯e) break(ing); breach; ♀ fracture (of bones); ♀ hernia; crack; fold (in paper); crease (in cloth); split (in silk); ♉ fraction; breach (of promise); violation (of oath, etc.); violation, infringement (of law, etc.); '~band ♯ n truss.

brüchig adj. ['bryçiç] fragile; brittle, voice: cracked.

'Bruch|landung ✈ f crash-landing; '~rechnung f fractional arithmetic, F fractions pl.; '~strich ♉ m fraction bar; '~stück n fragment (a. fig.); '~teil m fraction; im ~ er Sekunde in a split second; '~zahl f fraction(al) number.

Brücke ['brykə] f (-/-n) bridge; carpet: rug; sports: bridge; e-e ~ schlagen über (acc.) build or throw a bridge across, bridge (river); '~n-kopf ✕ m bridge-head; '~npfeiler m pier (of bridge).

Bruder ['bruːdər] m (-s/♯) brother; eccl. (lay) brother, friar; '~krieg m fratricidal or civil war; '~kuß m fraternal kiss.

brüderlich ['bryːdərliç] 1. adj. brotherly, fraternal; 2. adv.: ~ teilen share and share alike; '♀keit f (-/no pl.) brotherliness, fraternity.

Brüh|e ['bryːə] f (-/-n) broth; stock;

beef tea; F dirty water; drink: F dishwater; '♀heiß adj. scalding hot; '~würfel m beef cube.

brüllen ['brylən] v/i. (ge-, h) roar; bellow; cattle: low; bull: bellow; vor Lachen ~ roar with laughter; ~des Gelächter roar with laughter.

brumm|en ['brumən] v/i. (ge-, h) p. speak in a deep voice, mumble; growl (a. fig.); insect: buzz; engine: buzz, boom; fig. grumble, Am. F grouch; mir brummt der Schädel my head is buzzing; '♀bär fig. m grumbler, growler, Am. F grouch; '♀er m (-s/-) bluebottle; dung-beetle; '~ig adj. grumbling, Am. F grouchy.

brünett adj. [bryˈnɛt] woman: brunette.

Brunft hunt. [brunft] f (-/♯e) rut; '~zeit f rutting season.

Brunnen ['brunən] m (-s/-) well; spring; fountain (a. fig.); e-n ~ graben sink a well; '~wasser n pump-water, well-water.

Brunst [brunst] f (-/♯e) zo. rut (of male animal), heat (of female animal); lust, sexual desire.

brünstig adj. ['brynstiç] zo. rutting, in heat; lustful.

Brust [brust] f (-/♯e) chest, anat. thorax; breast; (woman's) breast(s pl.), bosom; aus voller ~ at the top of one's voice, lustily; '~bild n half-length portrait.

brüsten ['brystən] v/refl. (ge-, h) boast, brag.

'Brust|fell anat. n pleura; '~fell-entzündung ♀ f pleurisy; '~kasten m, '~korb m chest, anat. thorax; '~schwimmen n (-s/no pl.) breast-stroke.

Brüstung ['brystuŋ] f (-/-en) balustrade, parapet.

'Brustwarze anat. f nipple.

Brut [bruːt] f (-/-en) brooding, sitting; brood; hatch; fry, spawn (of fish); fig. F brood, (bad) lot.

brutal adj. [bruˈtɑːl] brutal; ♀ität [~aliˈtɛːt] f (-/-en) brutality.

Brutapparat zo. ['bruːtʔ-] m incubator.

brüten ['bryːtən] v/i. (ge-, h) brood, sit (on egg); incubate; ~ über (dat.) brood over.

'Brutkasten ♯ m incubator.

brutto ✝ adv. ['bruto] gross; '♀gewicht n gross weight; '♀register-tonne f gross register ton; '♀verdienst m gross earnings pl.

Bube ['buːbə] m (-n/-n) boy, lad; knave, rogue; cards: knave, jack; '~nstreich m, '~nstück n boyish prank; knavish trick.

Buch [buːx] n (-[e]s/♯er) book; volume; '~binder m (book-)binder; '~drucker m printer; '~druckerei [~ˈraɪ] f printing; printing-office, Am. print shop.

Buche ⚲ ['buːxə] f (-/-n) beech.
buchen ['buːxən] v/t. (ge-, h) book, reserve (*passage, flight, etc.*); *book-keeping*: book (*item, sum*), enter (*transaction*) in the books; **et. als Erfolg ~** count s.th. as a success.
Bücher|abschluß ✝ ['byːçər-] m closing of or balancing of books; **'~brett** n bookshelf; **~ei** [~'raɪ] f (-/-en) library; **'~freund** m book-lover, bibliophil(e); **'~revisor** ✝ m (-s/-en) auditor; accountant; **'~schrank** m bookcase; **'~wurm** m bookworm.
'Buch|fink orn. m chaffinch; **'~halter** m (-s/-) book-keeper; **'~haltung** f book-keeping; **'~handel** m book-trade; **'~händler** m bookseller; **'~handlung** f bookshop, *Am.* bookstore.
Büchse ['byksə] f (-/-n) box, case; tin, *Am.* can; rifle; **~nfleisch** n tinned meat, *Am.* canned meat; **'~nöffner** ['byksən⁹-] m tin-opener, *Am.* can opener.
Buchstab|e ['buːxʃtaːbə] m (-n/-n) letter, character; *typ.* type; ♀**ieren** [~a'biːrən] v/t. (*no* -ge-, h) spell.
buchstäblich ['buːxʃtɛːplɪç] 1. *adj.* literal; 2. *adv.* literally; word for word.
Bucht [buxt] f (-/-en) bay; bight; creek, inlet.
'Buchung f (-/-en) booking, reservation; *book-keeping*: entry.
Buckel ['bukəl] 1. m (-s/-) hump, hunch; humpback, hunchback; boss, stud, knob; 2. f (-/-n) boss, stud, knob.
'buckelig *adj. s.* bucklig.
bücken ['bykən] v/refl. (ge-, h) bend (down), stoop.
bucklig *adj.* ['buklɪç] humpbacked, hunchbacked.
Bückling ['byklɪŋ] m (-s/-e) bloater, red herring; *fig.* bow.
Bude ['buːdə] f (-/-n) stall, booth; hut, cabin, *Am.* shack; F: place; den; (*student's, etc.*) digs *pl.*
Budget [by'dʒeː] n (-s/-s) budget.
Büfett [by'feː; by'fɛt] n (-[e]s/-s; -[e]s/-e) sideboard, buffet; buffet, bar, *Am. a.* counter; *kaltes* ~ buffet supper *or* lunch.
Büffel ['byfəl] m (-s/-) zo. buffalo; F *fig.* lout, blockhead.
Bug [buːk] m (-[e]s/-e) ⊕ bow; ✈ nose; fold; (sharp) crease.
Bügel ['byːgəl] m (-s/-) bow (*of spectacles, etc.*); handle (*of handbag, etc.*); coat-hanger; stirrup; **'~brett** n ironing-board; **'~eisen** n (flat-)iron; **'~falte** f crease; **♀n** v/t. (ge-, h) iron (*shirt, etc.*), press (*suit, skirt, etc.*).
Bühne ['byːnə] f (-/-n) platform (*a.* ⊕); scaffold; *thea.* stage; *fig.*: die ~ the stage; *die politische* ~ the political scene; **~nanweisungen** ['byː-

nən⁹-] f/pl. stage directions pl.; **'~nbild** n scene(ry); décor; stage design; **'~ndichter** m playwright, dramatist; **'~nlaufbahn** f stage career; **'~nstück** n stage play.
buk [buːk] *pret. of* backen.
Bull|auge ⊕ ['bul-] n porthole, bull's eye; **'~dogge** zo. f bulldog.
Bulle ['bulə] 1. zo. m (-n/-n) bull; 2. *eccl.* f (-/-n) bull.
Bummel F ['buməl] m (-s/-) stroll; spree, pub-crawl, *sl.* binge; **~ei** [~'laɪ] f (-/-en) dawdling; negligence; **'♀n** v/i. (ge-) 1. (*sein*) stroll, saunter; pub-crawl; 2. (h) dawdle (*on way, at work*), waste time; **'~streik** m go-slow (strike), *Am.* slowdown; **'~zug** m slow train, *Am.* way train.
Bummler ['bumlər] m (-s/-) saunterer, stroller; loafer, *Am.* F *a.* bum; dawdler.
Bund [bunt] 1. m (-[e]s/⸚e) *pol.* union, federation, confederacy; (waist-, neck-, wrist)band; 2. n (-[e]s/-e) bundle (*of faggots*); bundle, truss (*of hay or straw*); bunch (*of radishes, etc.*).
Bündel ['byndəl] n (-s/-) bundle, bunch; **'♀n** v/t. (ge-, h) make into a bundle, bundle up.
Bundes|bahn ['bundəs-] f Federal Railway(s *pl.*); **'~bank** f Federal Bank; **'~genosse** m ally; **'~gerichtshof** m Federal Supreme Court; **'~kanzler** m Federal Chancellor; **'~ministerium** n Federal Ministry; **'~post** f Federal Postal Administration; **'~präsident** m President of the Federal Republic; **'~rat** m Bundesrat, Upper House of German Parliament; **'~republik** f Federal Republic; **'~staat** m federal state; confederation; **'~tag** m Bundestag, Lower House of German Parliament.
bündig *adj.* ['byndɪç] *style, speech*: concise, to the point, terse.
Bündnis ['byntnɪs] n (-ses/-se) alliance; agreement.
Bunker ['buŋkər] m (-s/-) ⚒, coal, fuel, *etc.*: bunker; bin; air-raid shelter; ✕ bunker, pill-box; ⊕ (submarine) pen.
bunt *adj.* [bunt] (multi-)colo(u)red, colo(u)rful; motley; *bird, flower, etc.*: variegated; bright, gay; *fig.* mixed, motley; full of variety; **'♀druck** m colo(u)r-print(ing); **'♀stift** m colo(u)red pencil, crayon.
Bürde ['byrdə] f (-/-n) burden (*a. fig.*: *für j-n* to s.o.), load.
Burg [burk] f (-/-en) castle; fortress, citadel (*a. fig.*).
Bürge ㉛ ['byrgə] m (-n/-n) guarantor, security, surety, bailsman; sponsor; **'♀n** v/i. (ge-, h): *für j-n* ~ stand guarantee *or* surety *or* security for s.o., *Am. a.* bond s.o.; stand

bail for s.o.; vouch *or* answer for s.o.; sponsor s.o.; *für et.* ~ stand security for s.th. guarantee s.th.; vouch *or* answer for s.th.

Bürger ['byrgər] *m* (-s/-) citizen; townsman; '~**krieg** *m* civil war.

'**bürgerlich** *adj.* civic, civil; ~**e** Küche plain cooking; *Verlust der* ~**en** *Ehrenrechte* loss of civil rights; *Bürgerliches Gesetzbuch* German Civil Code; '**2e** *m* (-n/-n) commoner.

'**Bürger|meister** *m* mayor; *in Germany: a.* burgomaster; *in Scotland:* provost; '~**recht** *n* civic rights *pl.*; citizenship; '~**schaft** *f* (-/-en) citizens *pl.*; '~**steig** *m* pavement, *Am.* sidewalk; '~**wehr** *f* militia.

Bürgschaft ['byrkʃaft] *f* (-/-en) security; bail; guarantee.

Büro [by'ro:] *n* (-s/-s) office; ~**an-gestellte** *m, f* (-n/-n) clerk; ~**ar-beit** *f* office-work; ~**klammer** *f* paper-clip; ~**krat** [~o'kra:t] *m* (-en/-en) bureaucrat; ~**kratie** [~o-kra'ti:] *f* (-/-n) bureaucracy; red tape; **2kratisch** *adj.* [~o'kra:tiʃ] bureaucratic; ~**stunden** *f/pl.* office hours *pl.*; ~**vorsteher** *m* head *or* senior clerk.

Bursch [burʃ] *m* (-en/-en), ~**e** ['~ə] *m* (-n/-n) boy, lad, youth; F chap, *Am. a.* guy; *ein übler* ~ a bad lot, F a bad egg.

burschikos *adj.* [burʃi'ko:s] free and easy; *esp. girl:* boyish, unaffected, hearty.

Bürste ['byrstə] *f* (-/-n) brush; '**2n** *v/t.* (ge-, *h*) brush.

Busch [buʃ] *m* (-es/~e) bush, shrub.

Büschel ['byʃəl] *n* (-s/-) bunch;

tuft, handful (*of* hair); wisp (*of* straw *or* hair).

'**Busch|holz** *n* brushwood, underwood; '**2ig** *adj.* hair, eyebrows, *etc.*: bushy, shaggy; covered with bushes *or* scrub, bushy; '~**messer** *n* bushknife; machete; '~**neger** *m* maroon; '~**werk** *n* bushes *pl.*, shrubbery, *Am. a.* brush.

Busen ['bu:zən] *m* (-s/-) bosom, breast (*esp. of woman*); *fig.* bosom, heart; *geog.* bay, gulf; '~**freund** *m* bosom friend.

Bussard *orn.* ['busart] *m* (-[e]s/-e) buzzard.

Buße ['bu:sə] *f* (-/-n) atonement (*for sins*), penance; repentance; satisfaction; fine; ~ *tun* do penance.

büßen ['by:sən] (ge-, *h*) 1. *v/t.* expiate, atone for (*sin, crime*); *er mußte es mit s-m Leben* ~ he paid for it with his life; *das sollst du mir* ~*l* you'll pay for that!; 2. *v/i.* atone, pay (*für* for).

'**Büßer** *m* (-s/-) penitent.

'**buß|fertig** *adj.* penitent, repentant, contrite; '**2fertigkeit** *f* (-/no *pl.*) repentance, contrition; '**2tag** *m* day of repentance; *Buß- und Bettag* day of prayer and repentance.

Büste ['bystə] *f* (-/-n) bust; '~**n-halter** *m* (-s/-) brassière; F bra.

Büttenpapier ['bytən-] *n* handmade paper.

Butter ['butər] *f* (-/no *pl.*) butter; '~**blume** ♀ *f* buttercup; '~**brot** *n* (slice *or* piece of) bread and butter; F: *für ein* ~ for a song; '~**brotpa-pier** *n* greaseproof paper; '~**dose** *f* butter-dish; '~**faß** *n* butter-churn; '~**milch** *f* buttermilk; '**2n** *v/i.* (ge-, *h*) churn.

C

Café [ka'fe:] *n* (-s/-s) café, coffeehouse.

Cape [ke:p] *n* (-s/-s) cape.

Cell|ist ♩ [tʃɛ'list] *m* (-en/-en) violoncellist, (')cellist; ~**o** ♩ ['~o] *n* (-s/-s, Celli) violoncello, (')cello.

Celsius ['tselzius]: 5 *Grad* ~ (*abbr.* 5° C) five degrees centigrade.

Chaiselongue [ʃɛz(ə)'lɔ̃:] *f* (-/-n, -s) chaise longue, lounge, couch.

Champagner [ʃam'panjər] *m* (-s/-) champagne.

Champignon ♀ ['ʃampinjõ] *m* (-s/-s) champignon, (common) mushroom.

Chance ['ʃɑ̃:s(ə)] *f* (-/-n) chance; *keine* ~ *haben* not to stand a chance; *sich eine* ~ *entgehen lassen* miss a chance *or* an opportunity; *die* ~*n sind gleich* the chances *or* odds are even.

Chaos ['ka:ɔs] *n* (-/no *pl.*) chaos.

Charakter [ka'raktər] *m* (-s/-e) character; nature; ~**bild** *n* character (sketch); ~**darsteller** *thea. m* character actor; ~**fehler** *m* fault in *s.o.'s* character; **2fest** *adj.* of firm *or* strong character; **2i'sieren** *v/t.* (*no* -ge-, *h*) characterize, describe (*als acc.* as); ~**i'sierung** *f* (-/-en), ~**istik** [~'ristik] *f* (-/-en) characterization; **2istisch** *adj.* [~'ristiʃ] characteristic *or* typical (*für* of); **2lich** *adj.* of *or* concerning (the) character; **2los** *adj.* characterless, without (strength of) character, spineless; ~**rolle** *thea. f* character role; ~**zug** *m* characteristic, feature, trait.

charm|ant *adj.* [ʃar'mant] charming, winning; '**2e** [ʃarm] *m* (-s/no *pl.*) charm, grace.

Chassis [ʃa'si:] n (-/-) mot., radio: frame, chassis.

Chauffeur [ʃo'føːr] m (-s/-e) chauffeur, driver.

Chaussee [ʃo'se:] f (-/-n) highway, (high) road.

Chauvinismus [ʃovi'nismus] m (-/ no pl.) jingoism; chauvinism.

Chef [ʃɛf] m (-s/-s) head, chief; ✝ principal, F boss; senior partner.

Chemie [çe'mi:] f (-/no pl.) chemistry; ~iefaser f chemical fib|re, Am. -er; ~ikalien [~i'kaːljən] f/pl. chemicals pl.; ~iker ['çeːmikər] m (-s/-) (analytical) chemist; ℒisch adj. ['çeːmiʃ] chemical.

Chiffre ['ʃifːr] f (-/-n) number; cipher; in advertisement: box number; ℒieren [ʃi'friːrən] v/t. (no -ge-, h) cipher, code (message, etc.); write in code or cipher.

Chinese [çi'neːzə] m (-n/-n) Chinese, contp. Chinaman; ℒisch adj. Chinese.

Chinin ⚗ [çi'niːn] n (-s/no pl.) quinine.

Chirurg [çi'rurk] m (-en/-en) surgeon; ~ie [~'giː] f (-/-n) surgery; ℒisch adj. [~giʃ] surgical.

Chlor ⚗ [kloːr] n (-s/no pl.) chlorine; 'ℒen v/t. (ge-, h) chlorinate (water); '~kalk ⚗ m chloride of lime.

Chloroform ⚗ [kloro'fɔrm] n (-/no pl.) chloroform; ℒieren ⚗ [~'miːrən] v/t. (no -ge-, h) chloroform.

Cholera ⚗ ['koːləra] f (-/no pl.) cholera.

cholerisch adj. [ko'leːriʃ] choleric, irascible.

Chor [koːr] m 1. 🔺 Δ a. n (-[e]s/-e, ᵘe) chancel, choir; (organ-)loft; 2. (-[e]s/ᵘe) in drama: chorus; singers: choir chorus; piece of music: chorus; ~al [ko'raːl] m (-s/ᵘe) choral(e); hymn; '~gesang m choral singing, chorus; '~sänger m member oɩ a choir; chorister.

Christ [krist] m (-en/-en) Christian; '~baum m Chɩistmas-tree; '~enheit f (-/no ɒl.): die ~ Christendom; '~entum n (-s/n ɔl.) Christianity; '~kind n (-[e]s/no pl.) Christ-child, Infant Jesus; '2lich adj. Christian.

Chrom [kroːm] n (-s/no pl.) metal: chromium; pigment: chrome.

chromatisch ♩, opt. adj. [kro'maːtiʃ] chromatic.

Chronik ['kroːnik] f (-/-en) chronicle.

chronisch adj. ['kroːniʃ] disease: chronic (a. fig.).

Chronist [kro'nist] m (-en/-en) chronicleɩ.

chronologisch adj. [krono'loːgiʃ] chronological.

circa adv. ['tsirka] about, approximately.

Clique ['kliːkə] f (-/-n) clique, set, group, coterie; '~nwirtschaft f (-/no pl.) cliquism.

Conférencier [kõferã'sje:] m (-s/-s) compère, Am. master of ceremonies.

Couch [kautʃ] f (-/-es) couch.

Coupé [ku'pe:] n (-s/-s) mot. coupé; ⚒ 🚃 compartment.

Couplet [ku'ple:] n (-s/-s) comic or music-hall song.

Coupon [ku'põ:] m (-s/-s) coupon; dividend-warrant; counterfoil.

Courtage ✝ [kur'taːʒə] f (-/-n) brokerage.

Cousin [ku'zɛ̃] m (-s/-s), ~e [~i:nə] f (-/-n) cousin.

Creme [kreːm, kre:m] f (-/-s) cream (a. fig.: only sg.).

Cut [kœt, kat] m (-s/-s), ~away ['kœtəve:, 'katəve:] m (-s/-s) cutaway (coat), morning coat.

D

da [da:] 1. adv. space: there; ~ wo where; hier und ~ here and there; ~ bin ich here I am; ~ haben wir's! there we are!; von ~ an from there; time: ~ erst only then, not till then; von ~ an from that time (on), since then; hier und ~ now and then or again; 2. cj. time: as, when, while; nun, ~ du es einmal gesagt hast now (that) you have mentioned it; causal: as, since, because; ~ ich krank war, konnte ich nicht kommen as or since I was ill I couldn't come.

dabei adv. [da'baɪ, when emphatic: 'daːbaɪ] near (at hand), by; about, going (zu inf. to inf.), on the point (of ger.); besides; nevertheless, yet, for all that; was ist schon ~? what does it matter?; lassen wir es ~ let's leave it at that; ~ bleiben stick to one's point, persist in it.

da'bei|bleiben v/i. (irr. bleiben, sep., -ge-, sein) stay with it or them; ~sein v/i. (irr. sein, sep., -ge-, sein) be present or there; ~stehen v/i. (irr. stehen, sep., -ge-, h) stand by or near.

'dableiben v/i. (iɩr. bleiben, sep., -ge-, sein) stay, remain.

da capo adv. ['da'kaːpo] at opera, etc.: encore.

Dach [dax] n (-[e]s/ᵘer) roof; fig. shelter; '~antenne f roof aerial;

'**~decker** m (-s/-) roofer; tiler; slater; '**~fenster** n skylight; dormer window; '**~garten** m roofgarden; '**~gesellschaft †** f holding company; '**~kammer** f attic, garret; '**~pappe** f roofing felt; '**~rinne** f gutter, eaves pl.

dachte ['daxtə] pret. of denken.

Dachs zo. [daks] m (-es/-e) badger; '**~bau** m (-[e]s/-e) badger's earth.

'**Dach|sparren** m rafter; '**~stube** f attic, garret; '**~stuhl** m roof framework; '**~ziegel** m (roofing) tile.

dadurch [da'durç, when emphatic: 'da:durç] 1. adv. for this reason, in this manner or way, thus; by it or that; 2. cj.: ~, daß owing to (the fact that), because; by ger.

dafür [da'fy:r, when emphatic: 'da:fy:r] for it or that; instead (of it); in return (for it), in exchange; ~ sein in favo(u)r of it; ~ sein zu inf. be for ger., be in favo(u)r of ger.; er kann nichts ~ it is not his fault; ~ sorgen, daß see to it that.

Da'fürhalten n (-s/no pl.): nach meinem ~ in my opinion.

dagegen [da'ge:gən. when emphatic: 'da:ge:gən] 1. adv. against it or that; in comparison with it, compared to it; ~ sein be against it, be opposed to it; ich habe nichts ~ I have no objection (to it); 2. cj. on the other hand, however.

daheim adv. [da'haɪm] at home.

daher [da'he:r, when emphatic: 'da:he:r] 1. adv. from there; prefixed to verbs of motion: along; fig. from this, hence; ~ kam es, daß thus it happened that; 2. cj. therefore; that is (the reason) why.

dahin adv. [da'hin, when emphatic: 'da:hin] there, to that place; gone, past; prefixed to verbs of motion: along; j-n ~ bringen, daß induce s.o. to inf.; m-e Meinung geht ~, daß my opinion is that.

da'hingestellt adj.: es ~ sein lassen (,ob) leave it undecided (whether).

dahinter adv. [da'hintər, when emphatic: 'da:hintər] behind it or that, at the back of it; es steckt nichts ~ there is nothing in it.

da'hinterkommen v/i. (irr kommen, sep., -ge-, sein) find out about it.

damal|ig adj. ['da:ma:liç] then, of that time; der ~e Besitzer the then owner; '**~s** adv. then, at that time.

Damast [da'mast] m (-es/-e) damask.

Dame ['da:mə] f (-/-n) lady; dancing, etc.: partner; cards, chess: queen; s. Damespiel; '**~brett** n draught-board, Am. checkerboard.

'**Damen|binde** f (woman's) sanitary towel, Am. sanitary napkin; '**~doppel** n tennis: women's doubles pl.; '**~einzel** n tennis: women's

singles pl.; '**~haft** adj. ladylike; '**~konfektion** f ladies' ready-made clothes pl.; '**~mannschaft** f sports: women's team; '**~schneider** m ladies' tailor, dressmaker.

'**Damespiel** n (game of) draughts pl., Am. (game of) checkers pl.

damit 1. adv. [da'mit, when emphatic: 'da:mit] with it or that, therewith, herewith; by it or that; was will er ~ sagen? what does he mean by it?; wie steht es ~? how about it?; ~ einverstanden sein agree to it; 2. cj. (in order) that, in order to inf.; so (that); ~ nicht lest, (so as) to avoid that; for fear that (all with subjunctive).

dämlich F adj. ['dɛ:mliç] silly, asinine.

Damm [dam] m (-[e]s/⁺e) dam; dike, dyke; 🚆 embankment; embankment, Am. levee (of river); roadway; fig. barrier; '**~bruch** m bursting of a dam or dike.

dämmer|ig adj. ['dɛməriç] dusky; '**Qlicht** n twilight; '**~n** v/i. (ge-, h) dawn (a. fig.: F j-m on s.o.); grow dark or dusky; '**Qung** f (-/-en) twilight, dusk; in the morning: dawn.

Dämon ['dɛ:mɔn] m (-s/-en) demon; '**Qisch** adj. [dɛ'mo:nɪʃ] demoniac(al).

Dampf [dampf] m (-[e]s/⁺e) steam; vapo(u)r; '**~bad** n vapo(u)r-bath; '**~boot** n steamboat; '**Qen** v/i. (ge-, h) steam.

dämpfen ['dɛmpfən] v/t. (ge-, h) deaden (pain, noise, force of blow); muffle (bell, drum, oar); damp (sound, oscillation, fig. enthusiasm); ♪ mute (stringed instrument); soften (colour, light); attenuate (wave); steam (cloth, food); stew (meat, fruit); fig. suppress, curb (emotion).

'**Dampfer** m (-s/-) steamer, steamship.

'**Dämpfer** m (-s/-) damper (a. ♪ of piano); ♪ mute (for violin, etc.).

'**Dampf|heizung** f steam-heating; '**~kessel** m (steam-)boiler; '**~maschine** f steam-engine; '**~schiff** n steamer, steamship; '**~walze** f steam-roller.

danach adv. [da'na:x, when emphatic: 'da:na:x] after it or that; afterwards; subsequently; accordingly; ich fragte ihn ~ I asked him about it; iro. er sieht ganz ~ aus he looks very much like it.

Däne ['dɛ:nə] m (-n/-n) Dane.

daneben adv. [da'ne:bən, when emphatic: 'da:ne:bən] next to it or that, beside it or that; besides, moreover; beside the mark.

da'nebengehen F v/i. (irr. gehen, sep., -ge-, sein) bullet, etc.: miss the target or mark; remark, etc.: miss one's effect, F misfire.

daniederliegen [da'ni:dər-] v/i.

(*irr.* liegen, *sep.*, -ge-: *h*) be laid up (*an dat.* with); *trade*: be depressed.

dänisch *adj.* ['dɛːniʃ] Danish.

Dank [daŋk] **1.** *m* (-[e]s/*no pl.*) thanks *pl.*, gratitude; reward; *j-m* ~ *sagen* thank s.o.; *Gott sei* ~! thank God!; **2.** ♀ *prp.* (*dat.*) owing *or* thanks to; '♀**bar** *adj.* thankful, grateful (*j-m* to s.o.; *für* for); profitable; '~**barkeit** *f* (-/*no pl.*) gratitude; '♀**en** *v/i.* (ge-, h) thank (*j-m für et.* s.o. for s.th.); *danke* (*schön*)! thank you (very much)!; *danke* thank you; ‖*nein, danke* no, thank you; *nichts zu* ~ don't mention it; '♀**enswert** *adj. thing*: one can be grateful for; *efforts, etc.*: kind; *task, etc.*: rewarding, worth-while; '~**gebet** *n* thanksgiving (prayer); '~**schreiben** *n* letter of thanks.

dann *adv.* [dan] then; ~ *und wann* (every) now and then.

daran *adv.* [da'ran, *when emphatic*: 'daːran] at (*or* by, in, on, to) it *or* that; *sich* ~ *festhalten* hold on tight to it; ~ *festhalten* stick to it; *nahe* ~ *sein zu inf.* be on the point or verge of *ger.*

da'rangehen *v/i.* (*irr.* gehen, *sep.*, -ge-, sein) set to work; set about *ger.*

darauf *adv.* [da'rauf, *when emphatic*: 'daːrauf] *space*: on (top of) it *or* that; *time*: thereupon, after it *or* that; *am Tage* ~ the day after, the next *or* following day; *zwei Jahre* ~ two years later; ~ *kommt es an* that's what matters; ~**hin** *adv.* [darauf'hin, *when emphatic*: 'daːrauf'hin] thereupon.

daraus *adv.* [da'raus, *when emphatic*: 'daːraus] out of it *or* that, from it *or* that; ~ *folgt* hence it follows; *was ist* ~ *geworden?* what has become of it?; *ich mache mir nichts* ~ I don't care *or* mind (about it).

darben ['darbən] *v/i.* (ge-, h) suffer want; starve.

darbiet|en ['daːr-] *v/t.* (*irr.* bieten, *sep.*, -ge-, h) offer, present; perform; '♀**ung** *f* (-/-en) *thea., etc.*: performance.

'**darbringen** *v/t.* (*irr.* bringen, *sep.*, -ge-, h) offer; make (*sacrifice*).

darein *adv.* [da'rain, *when emphatic*: 'daːrain] into it *or* that, therein.

da'rein|finden *v/refl.* (*irr.* finden, *sep.*, -ge-, h) put up with it; ~**mischen** *v/refl.* (*sep.*, -ge-, h) interfere (with it); ~**reden** *v/i.* (*sep.*, -ge-, h) interrupt; *fig.* interfere.

darin *adv.* [da'rin, *when emphatic*: 'daːrin] in it *or* that; therein; *es war nichts* ~ there was nothing in it *or* them.

darleg|en ['daːr-] *v/t.* (*sep.*, -ge-, h)

lay open, expose, disclose; show; explain; demonstrate; point out; '♀**ung** *f* (-/-en) exposition; explanation; statement.

Darlehen ['daːrleːən] *n* (-s/-) loan.

Darm [darm] *m* (-[e]s/♀e) gut, *anat.* intestine; (sausage-)skin; *Därme pl.* intestines *pl.*, bowels *pl.*

'**darstell|en** *v/t.* (*sep.*, -ge-, h) represent; show, depict; delineate; describe; *actor*: interpret (*character, part*), represent (*character*); *graphic arts*: graph, plot (*curve, etc.*); '♀**er** *thea. m* (-s/-) interpreter (*of a part*); actor; '♀**ung** *f* representation; *thea.* performance.

'**dartun** *v/t.* (*irr.* tun, *sep.*, -ge-, h) prove; demonstrate; set forth.

darüber *adv.* [da'ryːbər, *when emphatic*: 'daːryːbər] over it *or* that; across it; in the meantime; ~ *werden Jahre vergehen* it will take years; *wir sind* ~ *hinweg* we got over it; *ein Buch* ~ *schreiben* write a book about it.

darum [da'rum, *when emphatic*: 'daːrum] **1.** *adv.* around it *or* that; *er kümmert sich nicht* ~ he does not care; *es handelt sich* ~ *zu inf.* the point is to *inf.*; **2.** *cj.* therefore, for that reason; ~ *ist er nicht gekommen* that's (the reason) why he hasn't come.

darunter *adv.* [da'runtər, *when emphatic*: 'daːruntər] under it *or* that; beneath it; among them; less; *zwei Jahre und* ~ two years and under; *was verstehst du* ~? what do you understand by it?

das [das] *s.* der.

dasein ['daː-] **1.** *v/i.* (*irr.* sein, *sep.*, -ge-, sein) be there *or* present; exist; **2.** ♀ *n* (-s/*no pl.*) existence; life; being.

daß *cj.* [das] that; ~ *nicht* less; *es sei denn*, ~ unless; *ohne* ~ without *ger.*; *nicht* ~ *ich wüßte* not that I know of.

'**dastehen** *v/i.* (*irr.* stehen, *sep.*, -ge-, h) stand (there).

Daten ['daːtən] *pl.* data *pl.* (*a.* ⊕), facts *pl.*; particulars *pl.*; '~**verarbeitung** *f* (-/-en) data processing.

datieren [da'tiːrən] *v/t. and v/i.* (*no* -ge-, h) date. [(case).)

Dativ *gr.* ['daːtiːf] *m* (-s/-e) dative)

Dattel ['datəl] *f* (-/-n) date.

Datum ['daːtum] *n* (-s/Daten) date.

Dauer ['dauər] *f* (-/*no pl.*) length, duration; continuance; *auf die* ~ in the long run; *für die* ~ *von* for a period *or* term of; *von* ~ *sein* last well; '♀**haft** *adj.* peace, *etc.*: lasting; *material, etc.*: durable; *colour, dye*: fast; '~**karte** *f* season ticket, *Am.* commutation ticket; '~**lauf** *m* jog-trot; endurance-run; '♀**n** *v/i.* (ge-, h) continue, last; take (*time*); '~**welle** *f* permanent wave, F perm.

Daumen ['daumən] *m* (-s/-) thumb; *j-m* den ~ halten keep one's fingers crossed (for s.o.); '~abdruck *m* (-[e]s/~e) thumb-print.

Daune ['daunə] *f* (-/-n): ~(n *pl.*) down; '~ndecke *f* eiderdown (quilt).

davon *adv.* [da'fɔn, *when emphatic:* 'da:fɔn] of it *or* that; thereof; from it *or* that; off, away; *was habe ich* ~? what do I get from it?; *das kommt* ~! it serves you right!

da'von|kommen *v/i.* (*irr.* kommen, *sep.*, -ge-, *sein*) escape, get off; ~laufen *v/i.* (*irr.* laufen, *sep.*, -ge-, *sein*) run away.

davor *adv.* [da'fo:r, *when emphatic:* 'da:fo:r] *space:* before it *or* that, in front of it *or* that; *er fürchtet sich* ~ he is afraid of it.

dazu *adv.* [da'tsu:, *when emphatic:* 'da:tsu:] to it *or* that; for it *or* that; for that purpose; in addition to that; *noch* ~ at that; ~ *gehört Zeit* it requires time.

da'zu|gehörig *adj.* belonging to it; ~kommen *v/i.* (*irr.* kommen, *sep.*, -ge-, *sein*) appear (on the scene); find time.

dazwischen *adv.* [da'tsviʃən] between (them), in between; ~kommen *v/i.* (*irr.* kommen, *sep.*, -ge-, *sein*) *thing:* intervene, happen.

Debatt|e [de'batə] *f* (-/-n) debate; 2ieren [~'ti:rən] (*no* -ge-, *h*) 1. *v/t.* discuss; debate; 2. *v/i.* debate (*über acc.* on).

Debüt [de'by:] *n* (-s/-s) first appearance, début.

dechiffrieren [deʃi'fri:rən] *v/t.* (*no* -ge-, *h*) decipher, decode.

Deck ⚓ [dɛk] *n* (-[e]s/-s, ⚓-e) deck; '~adresse *f* cover (address); '~bett *n* feather bed.

Decke ['dɛkə] *f* (-/-n) cover(ing); blanket; (travel[l]ing) rug; ceiling; '~l *m* (-s/-) lid, cover (*of box or pot, etc.*); lid (*of piano*); (book-)cover; '2n (ge-, *h*) 1. *v/t.* cover; *den Tisch* ~ lay the table; 2. *v/i.* paint: cover.

'Deck|mantel *m* cloak, mask, disguise; '~name *m* assumed name, pseudonym; '~ung *f* (-/-en) cover; security.

defekt [de'fɛkt] 1. *adj.* defective, faulty; 2. ♀ *m* (-[e]s/-e) defect, fault.

defin|ieren [defi'ni:rən] *v/t.* (*no* -ge-, *h*) define; 2ition [~i'tsjo:n] *f* (-/-en) definition; ~itiv *adj.* [~i'ti:f] definite; definitive.

Defizit ✝ ['de:fitsit] *n* (-s/-e) deficit, deficiency.

Degen ['de:gən] *m* (-s/-) sword; *fencing:* épée.

degradieren [degra'di:rən] *v/t.* (*no* -ge-, *h*) degrade, *Am. a.* demote.

dehn|bar *adj.* ['de:nba:r] extensible; elastic; *metal:* ductile; *notion,*

etc.: vague; '~en *v/t.* (ge-, *h*) extend; stretch; '2ung *f* (-/-en) extension; stretch(ing).

Deich [daiç] *m* (-[e]s/-e) dike, dyke.

Deichsel ['daiksəl] *f* (-/-n) pole, shaft.

dein *poss. pron.* [dain] your; *der (die, das)* ~e yours; *ich bin* ~ I am yours; *die Deinen pl.* your family; ~erseits *adv.* ['~ər'zaits] for *or* on your part; '~es'gleichen *pron.* your like, your (own) kind, F the like(s) of you.

Dekan *eccl. and univ.* [de'ka:n] *m* (-s/-e) dean.

Deklam|ation [deklama'tsjo:n] *f* (-/-en) declamation; reciting; 2ieren [~'mi:rən] *v/t. and v/i.* (*no* -ge-, *h*) recite; declaim.

Deklin|ation *gr.* [deklina'tsjo:n] *f* (-/-en) declension; 2ieren *gr.* [~'ni:rən] *v/t.* (*no* -ge-, *h*) decline.

Dekor|ateur [dekora'tø:r] *m* (-s/-e) decorator; window-dresser; *thea.* scene-painter; ~ation [~'tsjo:n] *f* (-/-en) decoration; (window-)dressing; *thea.* scenery; 2ieren [~'ri:rən] *v/t.* (*no* -ge-, *h*) decorate; dress (*window*).

Dekret [de'kre:t] *n* (-[e]s/-e) decree.

delikat *adj.* [deli'ka:t] delicate (*a. fig.*); delicious; *fig.* ticklish; 2esse [~a'tɛsə] *f* (-/-n) delicacy; dainty.

Delphin *zo.* [dɛl'fi:n] *m* (-s/-e) dolphin.

Dement|i [de'mɛnti] *n* (-s/-s) (formal) denial; 2ieren [~'ti:rən] *v/t.* (*no* -ge-, *h*) deny, give a (formal) denial of.

'dem|entsprechend *adv.*, '~gemäß *adv.* correspondingly, accordingly; '~nach *adv.* therefore, hence; accordingly; '~'nächst *adv.* soon, shortly, before long.

demobili'sier|en (*no* -ge-, *h*) 1. *v/t.* demobilize; disarm; 2. *v/i.* disarm; 2ung *f* (-/-en) demobilization.

Demokrat [demo'kra:t] *m* (-en/-en) democrat; ~ie [~a'ti:] *f* (-/-n) democracy; 2isch *adj.* [~'kra:tiʃ] democratic.

demolieren [demo'li:rən] *v/t.* (*no* -ge-, *h*) demolish.

Demonstr|ation [demɔnstra'tsjo:n] *f* (-/-en) demonstration; 2ieren [~'stri:rən] *v/t. and v/i.* (*no* -ge-, *h*) demonstrate.

Demont|age [demɔn'ta:ʒə] *f* (-/-n) disassembly; dismantling; 2ieren [~'ti:rən] *v/t.* (*no* -ge-, *h*) disassemble; dismantle.

Demut ['de:mu:t] *f* (-/*no pl.*) humility, humbleness.

demütig *adj.* ['de:my:tiç] humble; ~en ['~gən] *v/t.* (ge-, *h*) humble, humiliate.

denk|bar ['dɛŋkba:r] 1. *adj.* conceivable; thinkable, imaginable; 2. *adv.*: ~ *einfach* most simple;

'**~en** (*irr.*, ge-, h) **1.** *v/i.* think; *~ an*
(*acc.*) think of; remember; *~ über*
(*acc.*) think about; *j-m zu ~ geben*
set s.o. thinking; **2.** *v/t.* think; *sich
et. ~* imagine *or* fancy s.th.; *das
habe ich mir gedacht* I thought as
much; '**Omal** *n* monument; memorial; '**Oschrift** *f* memorandum;
memoir; '**Ostein** *m* memorial stone;
'**~würdig** *adj.* memorable; '**Ozettel**
fig. m lesson.

denn [den] **1.** *cj.* for; *mehr ~ je* more
than ever; **2.** *adv.* then; *es sei ~,
daß* unless, except; *wieso ~?* how so.

dennoch *cj.* ['dɛnɔx] yet, still,
nevertheless; though.

Denunz|iant [denun'tsjant] *m* (-en/
-en) informer; **~iation** [~'tsjoːn] *f*
(-/-en) denunciation; **Oieren** [~'tsiː-
rən] *v/t.* (*no* -ge-, h) inform against,
denounce.

Depesche [de'pɛʃə] *f* (-/-n) dispatch; telegram, F wire; wireless.

deponieren [depo'niːrən] *v/t.* (*no*
-ge-, h) deposit.

Depositen ✝ [depo'ziːtən] *pl.* de-
posits *fig.*; **~bank** *f* deposit bank.

der [deːr], **die** [diː], **das** [das] **1.** *art.*
the; **2.** *dem. pron.* that, this; he,
she, it; *die pl.* these, those, they,
them; **3.** *rel. pron.* who, which, that.

'**der'artig** *adj.* such, of such a kind
of this *or* that kind.

derb *adj.* [dɛrp] *cloth:* coarse, rough;
shoes, etc.: stout, strong; *ore, etc.:*
massive; *p.:* sturdy; rough; *food:*
coarse; *p., manners:* rough, coarse;
way of speaking: blunt, unrefined;
joke: crude; *humour:* broad.

der'gleichen *adj.* such, of that
kind; *used as a noun:* the like, such
a thing; *und ~* and the like; *nichts
~* nothing of the kind.

der- ['deːrjeːnigə], '**die-**, '**dasjenige**
dem. pron. he *who*, she *who*, that
which; *diejenigen pl.* those *who*,
those *which*.

der- [deːr'zɛlbə], **die-**, **das'selbe**
dem. pron. the same; he, she, it.

Desert|eur [dezer'tøːr] *m* (-s/-e)
deserter; **Oieren** [~'tiːrən] *v/i.* (*no*
-ge-, sein) desert.

desgleichen [dɛs'glaɪçən] **1.** *dem.
pron.* such a thing; **2.** *cj.* likewise.

deshalb ['dɛshalp] **1.** *cj.* for this *or*
that reason; therefore; **2.** *adv.:* *ich
tat es nur ~, weil* I did it only because.

desinfizieren [dɛsʔinfi'tsiːrən] *v/t.*
(*no* -ge-, h) disinfect.

Despot [dɛs'poːt] *m* (-en/-en) despot; **Oisch** *adj.* despotic.

destillieren [dɛsti'liːrən] *v/t.* (*no*
-ge-, h) distil.

desto *adv.* ['dɛsto] (all, so much)
the; *~ besser* all the better; *~ er-
staunter* (all) the more astonished.

deswegen *cj. and adv.* ['dɛs've:gən]
s. deshalb.

Detail [de'taɪ] *n* (-s/-s) detail.

Detektiv [detɛk'tiːf] *m* (-s/-e) de-
tective.

deuten ['dɔytən] (ge-, h) **1.** *v/t.*
interpret; read (*stars, dream, etc.*);
2. *v/i.:* *~ auf* (*acc.*) point at.

'**deutlich** *adj.* clear, distinct, plain.

deutsch *adj.* [dɔytʃ] German; '**Oe**
m, f (-n/-n) German.

'**Deutung** *f* (-/-en) interpretation,
explanation.

Devise [de'viːzə] *f* (-/-n) motto; *~n
pl.* ✝ foreign exchange *or* currency.

Dezember [de'tsɛmbər] *m* (-[-s]/-)
December.

dezent *adj.* [de'tsɛnt] *attire, etc.:*
decent, modest; *literature, etc.:* decent; *behaviour:* decent, proper;
music, colour: soft, restrained; *lighting, etc.:* subdued.

Dezernat [detsɛr'naːt] *n* (-[e]s/-e)
(administrative) department.

dezimal *adj.* [detsi'maːl] decimal;
Obruch *m* decimal fraction; **Ostelle**
f decimal place.

dezi'mieren *v/t.* (*no* -ge-, h) deci-
mate; *fig. a.* reduce (drastically).

Diadem [dia'deːm] *n* (-s/-e) diadem.

Diagnose [dia'gnoːzə] *f* (-/-n) diagnosis.

diagonal *adj.* [diago'naːl] diagonal;
Oe *f* (-/-n) diagonal.

Dialekt [dia'lɛkt] *m* (-[e]s/-e) dialect; **Oisch** *adj.* dialectal.

Dialog [dia'loːk] *m* (-[e]s/-e) dialogue, *Am. a.* dialog.

Diamant [dia'mant] *m* (-en/-en)
diamond.

Diät [di'ɛːt] *f* (-/*no pl.*) diet; *diät
leben* live on a diet.   [yourself.\

dich *pers. pron.* [diç] you; *~ (selbst)*\

dicht [diçt] **1.** *adj.* fog, rain, etc.:
dense; *fog, forest, hair:* thick; *eye-
brows:* bushy, thick; *crowd:* thick,
dense; *shoe, etc.:* (water)tight;
2. *adv.:* *~ an* (*dat.*) *or* bei close to.

'**dichten**[1] *v/t.* (ge-, h) make tight.

'**dichten**[2] (ge-, h) **1.** *v/t.* compose,
write; **2.** *v/i.* compose *or* write
poetry; '**Oer** *m* (-s/-) poet; author;
'**~erisch** *adj.* poetic(al); '**Okunst** *f*
poetry.

'**Dichtung**[1] ⊕ *f* (-/-en) seal(ing).

'**Dichtung**[2] *f* (-/-en) poetry; fiction;
poem, poetic work.

dick *adj.* [dik] *wall, material, etc.:*
thick; *book:* thick, bulky; *p.* fat,
stout; '**Oe** *f* (-/-n) thickness; bulk-
iness; *p.* fatness, stoutness; '**~fellig**
adj. p. thick-skinned; '**~flüssig** *adj.*
thick; viscid, viscous, syrupy; **Oicht**
['~içt] *n* (-[e]s/-e) thicket; '**Okopf** *m*
stubborn person, F pig-headed
person; '**~leibig** *adj.* ['~laɪbiç] corpulent; *fig.* bulky.

die [diː] *s. der.*

Dieb [diːp] *m* (-[e]s/-e) thief, *Am.*
F *a.* crook; **~erei** [diːbə'raɪ] *f* (-/-en)
thieving, thievery.

Diebes|bande ['di:bəs-] f band of thieves; **'~gut** n stolen goods pl.

dieb|isch adj. ['di:biʃ] thievish; fig. malicious; **2stahl** ['di:p-] m (-[e]s/ *e) theft, *tˢ* *mst* larceny.

Diele ['di:lə] f (-/-n) board, plank; hall, Am. a. hallway.

dienen ['di:nən] v/i. (ge-, h) serve (j-m s.o.; als as; zu for; dazu, zu inf. to inf.); womit kann ich ~? what can I do for you?

'Diener m (-s/-) (man-, domestic) servant; fig. bow (vor dat. to); **'~in** f (-/-nen) (woman-)servant, maid; **'~schaft** f (-/-en) servants pl.

'dienlich adj. useful, convenient; expedient, suitable.

Dienst [di:nst] m (-es/-e) service; duty; employment; ~ haben be on duty; im (außer) ~ on (off) duty.

Dienstag ['di:nsta:k] m (-[e]s/-e) Tuesday.

'Dienst|alter n seniority, length of service; **'2bar** adj. subject (j-m to s.o.); subservient (to); **'~bote** m domestic (servant), Am. help; **'2eifrig** adj. (over-)eager (in one's duty); **'2frei** adj. off duty; ~er Tag day off; **'~herr** m master; employer; **'~leistung** f service; **'2lich** adj. official; **'~mädchen** n maid, Am. help; **'~mann** m (street-)porter; **'~stunden** f/pl. office hours pl.; **'2tauglich** adj. fit for service or duty; **2tuend** adj. ['~tu:ənt] on duty; **'2untauglich** adj. unfit for service or duty; **'~weg** m official channels pl.; **'~wohnung** f official residence.

dies [di:s], **~er** ['di:zər], **~e** ['di:zə], **~es** ['di:zəs] adj. and dem. pron. this; diese pl. these; dieser Tage one of these days; used as a noun: this one; he, she, it; diese pl. they.

Dieselmotor ['di:zəl-] m Diesel engine.

dies|jährig adj. ['di:sjɛ:riç] of this year, this year's; **'~mal** adv. this time; for (this) once; **~seits** ['~zaɪts] 1. adv. on this side; 2. prp. (gen.) on this side of.

Dietrich ['di:triç] m (-s/-e) skeleton key; picklock.

Differenz [difə'rɛnts] f (-/-en) difference; disagreement.

Diktat [dik'ta:t] n (-[e]s/-e) dictation; nach ~ at or from dictation; **~or** [~ɔr] m (-s/-en) dictator; **2orisch** adj. [~a'to:riʃ] dictatorial; **~ur** [~a'tu:r] f (-/-en) dictatorship.

dik'tieren v/t. and v/i. (no -ge-, h) dictate.

Dilettant [dile'tant] m (-en/-en) dilettante, dabbler; amateur.

Ding [diŋ] n (-[e]s/-e) thing; guter ~e in good spirits; vor allen ~en first of all, above all.

Diphtherie *ₛ* [diftɛ'ri:] f (-/-n) diphtheria.

Diplom [di'plo:m] n (-[e]s/-e) diploma, certificate.

Diplomat [diplo'ma:t] m (-en/-en) diplomate; diplomatist; **~ie** [~a'ti:] f (-/no pl.) diplomacy; **2isch** adj. [~'ma:tiʃ] diplomatic (a. fig.).

dir pers. pron. [di:r] (to) you.

direkt [di'rɛkt] 1. adj. direct; ~er Wagen ￼ through carriage, Am. through car; 2. adv. direct(ly); **2ion** [~'tsjo:n] f (-/-en) direction; management; board of directors; **2or** [di'rɛktɔr] m (-s/-en) director; manager; headmaster, Am. principal; **2orin** [~'to:rin] f (-/-nen) headmistress, Am. principal; **2rice** [~'tri:s(ə)] f (-/-n) directress; manageress.

Dirig|ent ♪ [diri'gɛnt] m (-en/-en) conductor; **2ieren** [~'gi:rən] v/t. and v/i. (no -ge-, h) conduct.

Dirne ['dirnə] f (-/-n) prostitute.

Disharmon|ie ♪ [disharmo'ni:] f (-/-n) disharmony, dissonance (both a. fig.); **2isch** adj. [~'mo:niʃ] discordant, dissonant.

Diskont † [dis'kɔnt] m (-s/-e) discount; **2ieren** [~'ti:rən] v/t. (no -ge-, h) discount.

diskret [dis'kre:t] adj. discreet; **2ion** [~e'tsjo:n] f (-/no pl.) discretion.

Disku|ssion [disku'sjo:n] f (-/-en) discussion, debate; **2'tieren** (no -ge-, h) 1. v/t. discuss, debate; 2. v/i.: ~ über (acc.) have a discussion about, debate (up)on.

dispo|nieren [dispo'ni:rən] v/i. (no -ge-, h) make arrangements; plan ahead; dispose (über acc. of); **2sition** [~zi'tsjo:n] f (-/-en) disposition; arrangement; disposal.

Distanz [di'stants] f (-/-en) distance (a. fig.); **2ieren** [~'tsi:rən] v/refl. (no -ge-, h): sich ~ von dis(as)sociate o.s. from.

Distel ♀ ['distəl] f (-/-n) thistle.

Distrikt [di'strikt] m (-[e]s/-e) district; region; area.

Disziplin [distsi'pli:n] f (-/-en) discipline.

Divid|ende † [divi'dɛndə] f (-/-n) dividend; **2ieren** [~'di:rən] v/t. (no -ge-, h) divide (durch by).

Diwan ['di:va:n] m (-s/-e) divan.

doch [dɔx] 1. cj. but, though; however, yet; 2. adv. in answer to negative question: yes; bist du noch nicht fertig? — ~! aren't you ready yet? — yes, I am; also ~! I knew it!, I was right after all!; komm ~ herein! do come in!; nicht ~! don't!

Docht [dɔxt] m (-[e]s/-e) wick.

Dock ⚓ [dɔk] n (-[e]s/-s) dock.

Dogge zo. ['dɔgə] f (-/-n) Great Dane.

Dohle orn. ['do:lə] f (-/-n) (jack)daw.

Doktor ['dɔktɔr] m (-s/-en) doctor.

Dokument [doku'mɛnt] n (-[e]s/-e)

document; §'z instrument; **~arfilm** [~'tɑ:r-] *m* documentary (film).

Dolch [dɔlç] *m* (-[e]s/-e) dagger; poniard; **'~stoß** *m* dagger-thrust.

Dollar ['dɔlar] *m* (-s/-s) dollar.

dolmetsch|en ['dɔlmɛtʃən] *v/i. and v/t.* (ge-, h) interpret; **'2er** *m* (-s/-) interpreter.

Dom [do:m] *m* (-[e]s/-e) cathedral.

Domäne [do'mɛ:nə] *f* (-/-n) domain (*a. fig.*); province.

Domino ['do:mino] (-s/-s) **1.** *m* domino; **2.** *n* (game of) dominoes *pl.*

Donner ['dɔnər] *m* (-s/-) thunder; **'2n** *v/i.* (ge-, h) thunder (*a. fig.*); **'~schlag** *m* thunderclap (*a. fig.*); **'~stag** *m* Thursday; **'~wetter** *n* thunderstorm; F *fig.* telling off; F: ~! my word!, by Jove!; F *zum* ~! F confound it!, *sl.* damn it.

Doppel ['dɔpəl] *n* (-s/-) duplicate; *tennis, etc.*: double, *Am.* doubles *pl.*; **'~bett** *n* double bed; **'~decker** *m* (-s/-) ✈ biplane; double-decker (bus); **'~ehe** *f* bigamy; **'~gänger** ['~gɛŋər] *m* (-s/-) double; **'~punkt** *m* colon; **'~sinn** *m* double meaning, ambiguity; **'2sinnig** *adj.* ambiguous, equivocal; **'~stecker** ⚡ *m* two-way adapter; **'2t 1.** *adj.* double; **2.** *adv.* doubly; twice; **'~zentner** *m* quintal; **2züngig** *adj.* ['~tsyŋiç] two-faced.

Dorf [dɔrf] *n* (-[e]s/ʺer) village; **'~bewohner** *m* villager.

Dorn [dɔrn] *m* **1.** (-[e]s/-en) thorn (*a. fig.*), prickle, spine; *j-m ein* ~ *im Auge sein* be a thorn in s.o.'s flesh *or* side; **2.** (-[e]s/-e) tongue (*of buckle*); spike (*of running-shoe, etc.*); ⊕ punch; **'2ig** *adj.* thorny (*a. fig.*).

dörr|en ['dœrən] *v/t.* (ge-, h) dry; **'2fleisch** *n* dried meat; **'2gemüse** *n* dried vegetables *pl.*; **'2obst** *n* dried fruit.

Dorsch *ichth.* [dɔrʃ] *m* (-es/-e) cod(fish).

dort *adv.* [dɔrt] there; over there; **'~her** *adv.* from there; **'~hin** *adv.* there, to that place; **'~ig** *adj.* there, in *or* of that place.

Dose ['do:zə] *f* (-/-n) box; tin, *Am.* can; **~nöffner** ['do:zən?-] *m* (-s/-) tin-opener, *Am.* can opener.

Dosis ['do:zis] *f* (-/Dosen) dose (*a. fig.*).

dotieren [do'ti:rən] *v/t.* (no -ge-, h) endow.

Dotter ['dɔtər] *m, n* (-s/-) yolk.

Dozent [do'tsɛnt] *m* (-en/-en) (university) lecturer, *Am.* assistant professor.

Drache ['draxə] *m* (-n/-n) dragon; **'~n** *m* (-s/-) kite; *fig.* termagant, shrew, battle-axe.

Dragoner [dra'go:nər] *m* (-s/-) ✗ dragoon (*a. fig.*).

Draht [drɑ:t] *m* (-[e]s/ʺe) wire; **'2en**

v/t. (ge-, h) telegraph, wire; **'~geflecht** *n* (-[e]s/-e) wire netting; **'~hindernis** ✗ *n* wire entanglement; **'2ig** *adj. p.* wiry; **'2los** *adj.* wireless; **~seilbahn** *f* funicular (railway); **'~stift** *m* wire tack; **'~zieher** F *fig. m* (-s/-) wire-puller.

drall *adj.* [dral] *girl, legs, etc.*: plump; *woman*: buxom.

Drama ['drɑ:ma] *n* (-s/Dramen) drama; **~tiker** [dra'mɑ:tikər] *m* (-s/-) dramatist; **2tisch** *adj.* [dra-'mɑ:tiʃ] dramatic.

dran F *adv.* [dran] *s.* daran; *er ist gut (übel)* ~ he's well (badly) off; *ich bin* ~ it's my turn.

Drang [draŋ] **1.** *m* (-[e]s/ʺe) pressure, rush; *fig.* urge; **2.** ⚰ *pret. of* dringen.

drängen ['drɛŋən] (ge-, h) **1.** *v/t.* press (*a. fig.*), push; *fig.* urge; *creditor*: dun; *sich* ~ crowd, throng; **2.** *v/i.* press, be pressing *or* urgent.

drangsalieren [draŋza'li:rən] *v/t.* (no -ge-, h) harass, vex, plague.

drastisch *adj.* ['drastiʃ] drastic.

drauf F *adv.* [drauf] *s.* darauf; ~ *und dran sein zu inf.* be on the point of *ger.*; **2gänger** ['~gɛŋər] *m* (-s/-) dare-devil, *Am. sl. a.* go-getter.

draus F *adv.* [draus] *s.* daraus.

draußen *adv.* ['drausən] outside; out of doors; abroad; out at sea.

drechs|eln ['drɛksəln] *v/t.* (ge-, h) turn (*wood, etc.*); **2ler** ['~slər] *m* (-s/-) turner.

Dreck F [drɛk] *m* (-[e]s/*no pl.*) dirt; mud; filth (*a. fig.*); *fig.* trash; F ~ *am Stecken haben* not to have a clean slate; F *das geht dich einen* ~ *an* that's none of your business; **'2ig** *adj.* dirty; filthy.

Dreh|bank ['dre:-] *f* (-/ʺe) (turning-) lathe; **2bar** *adj.* revolving, rotating; **'~bleistift** *m* propelling pencil; **'~buch** *n* scenario; script; **'~bühne** *thea. f* revolving stage; **'2en** *v/t.* (ge-, h) turn; shoot (*film*); roll (*cigarette*); *es dreht sich darum zu inf.* it is a matter of *ger.*; *sich* ~ turn; **'~kreuz** *n* turnstile; **'~orgel** *f* barrel-organ; **'~punkt** *m* ⊕ centre of rotation, *Am.* center of rotation, pivot (*a. fig.*); **'~strom** ⚡ *m* three-phase current; **'~stuhl** *m* swivel-chair; **'~tür** *f* revolving door; **'~ung** *f* (-/-en) turn; rotation.

drei *adj.* [drai] three; **'~beinig** *adj.* three-legged; **'2eck** *n* triangle; **'~eckig** *adj.* triangular; **~erlei** *adj.* ['~ər'lai] of three kinds *or* sorts; **~fach** *adj.* ['~fax] threefold, treble; triple; **'~farbig** *adj.* three-col-o(u)r(ed); **'2fuß** *m* tripod; **~jährig** *adj.* ['~jɛ:riç] three-year-old; triennial; **'~mal** *adv.* three times; **'~malig** *adj.* done *or* repeated three times; three; **'2meilenzone** ⚓, §'z *f* three-mile limit; **'2rad** *n* tricycle;

'**~seitig** adj. three-sided; trilateral; '**~silbig** adj. trisyllabic.

dreißig adj. ['draɪsɪç] thirty; '**~ste** adj. thirtieth.

dreist adj. [draɪst] bold, audacious; cheeky, saucy; '**2igkeit** f (-/-en) boldness, audacity; cheek, sauciness.

'**drei|stimmig** ♪ adj. for or in three voices; **~tägig** adj. ['~tɛ:gɪç] three-day; '**~teilig** adj. in three parts, tripartite; '**~zehn(te)** adj. thirteen(th).

dresch|en ['drɛʃən] v/t. and v/i. (irr., ge-, h) thresh; thrash; '**2flegel** m flail; '**2maschine** f threshing-machine.

dressieren [drɛ'si:rən] v/t. (no -ge-, h) train; break in (horse).

drillen ✕, ⚓ ['drɪlən] v/t. (ge-, h) drill.

Drillinge ['drɪlɪŋə] m/pl. triplets pl.

drin F adv. [drɪn] s. darin.

dringen ['drɪŋən] v/i. (irr., ge-) **1.** (sein): ~ durch force one's way through s.th., penetrate or pierce s.th.; ~ aus break forth from s.th.; noise: come from; ~ in (acc.) penetrate into; in j-n ~ urge or press s.o.; an die Öffentlichkeit ~ get abroad; **2.** (h): ~ auf (acc.) insist on, press for; '**~d** adj. urgent, pressing; suspicion: strong.

'**dringlich** adj. urgent, pressing; '**2keit** f (-/no pl.) urgency.

drinnen adv. ['drɪnən] inside; indoors.

dritt|e adj. ['drɪtə] third; '**2el** n (-s/-) third; '**~ens** adv. thirdly; '**~letzt** adj. last but two.

Drog|e ['dro:gə] f (-/-n) drug; **~erie** [drogə'ri:] f (-/-n) chemist's (shop), Am. drugstore; **~ist** [dro-'gɪst] m (-en/-en) (retail pharmaceutical) chemist.

drohen ['dro:ən] v/i. (ge-, h) threaten, menace.

Drohne ['dro:nə] f (-/-n) zo. drone (a. fig.).

dröhnen ['drø:nən] v/i. (ge-, h) voice, etc.: resound; cannon, drum, etc.: roar; voice, cannon: boom.

Drohung ['dro:ʊŋ] f (-/-en) threat, menace.

drollig adj. ['drɔlɪç] amusing, quaint, comical.

Dromedar zo. [dromə'da:r] n (-s/-e) dromedary.

drosch [drɔʃ] pret. of dreschen.

Droschke ['drɔʃkə] f (-/-n) taxi (-cab), Am. a. cab, hack; '**~nkutscher** m cabman, driver, Am. a. hackman.

Drossel orn. ['drɔsəl] f (-/-n) thrush; '**2n** ⊕ v/t. (ge-, h) throttle.

drüben adv. ['dry:bən] over there, yonder.

drüber F adv. ['dry:bər] s. darüber.

Druck [druk] m **1.** (-[e]s/⁼e) pres-

---

sure; squeeze (of hand, etc.); **2.** typ. (-[e]s/-e) print(ing); '**~bogen** m printed sheet; '**~buchstabe** m block letter.

drucken ['drukən] v/t. (ge-, h) print; ~ lassen have s.th. printed, publish.

drücken ['drykən] (ge-, h) **1.** v/t. press; squeeze (hand, etc.); force down (prices, wages, etc.); lower (record); press, push (button, etc.). F sich ~ vor (dat.) or von shirk (work, etc.); **2.** v/i. shoe: pinch.

'**Drucker** m (-s/-) printer.

'**Drücker** m (-s/-) door-handle; trigger.

Drucker|ei [drukə'raɪ] f (-/-en) printing office, Am. printery, print shop; '**~schwärze** f printer's or printing-ink.

'**Druck|fehler** m misprint; '**~fehlerverzeichnis** n errata pl.; '**2fertig** adj. ready for press; '**~kammer** f pressurized cabin; '**~knopf** m patent fastener, snap-fastener; ⚡ push-button; '**~luft** f compressed air; '**~pumpe** f pressure pump; '**~sache(n** pl.) ⅋ f printed matter, Am. a. second-class or third-class matter; '**~schrift** f block letters; publication; '**~taste** f press key.

drum F adv., cj. [drum] s. darum.

drunter F adv. ['druntər] s. darunter.

Drüse anat. ['dry:zə] f (-/-n) gland.

du pers. pron. [du:] you.

Dublette [du'blɛtə] f (-/-n) duplicate.

ducken ['dukən] v/refl. (ge-, h) duck, crouch; fig. cringe (vor dat. to, before).

Dudelsack ♪ ['du:dəl-] m bagpipes pl.

Duell [du'ɛl] n (-s/-e) duel; **2ieren** [due'li:rən] v/refl. (no -ge-, h) (fight a) duel (mit with).

Duett ♪ [du'ɛt] n (-[e]s/-e) duet.

Duft [duft] m (-[e]s/⁼e) scent, fragrance, perfume; '**2en** v/i. (ge-, h) smell, have a scent, be fragrant; '**2end** adj. fragrant; '**2ig** adj. dainty, fragrant.

duld|en ['duldən] (ge-, h) **1.** v/t. bear, stand, endure, suffer (pain, grief, etc.); tolerate, put up with; **2.** v/i. suffer; '**~sam** adj. ['~t-] tolerant; '**2samkeit** f (-/no pl.) tolerance; **2ung** ['~dʊŋ] f (-/⁼-en) toleration; sufferance.

dumm adj. [dum] stupid, dull, Am. F dumb; '**2heit** f (-/-en) stupidity, dullness; stupid or foolish action; '**2kopf** m fool, blockhead, Am. sl. a. dumbbell.

dumpf adj. [dumpf] smell, air, etc.: musty, fusty; atmosphere: stuffy, heavy; sound, sensation, etc.: dull; '**~ig** adj. cellar, etc.: damp, musty.

Düne ['dy:nə] f (-/-n) dune, sand-hill.

Dung [duŋ] *m* (-[e]s/*no pl.*) dung, manure.

düngen ['dyŋən] *v/t.* (ge-, h) dung, manure; fertilize; **'2r** *m* (-s/-) *s. Dung*; fertilizer.

dunkel ['duŋkəl] **1.** *adj.* dark; dim; *fig.* obscure; *idea, etc.*: dim, faint, vague; **2.** **2** *n* (-s/*no pl.*) *s.* Dunkel-heit.

Dünkel ['dyŋkəl] *m* (-s/*no pl.*) conceit, arrogance; **'2haft** *adj.* conceited, arrogant.

'Dunkel|heit *f* (-/*no pl.*) darkness (*a. fig.*); *fig.* obscurity; **'~kammer** *phot. f* dark-room; **'2n** *v/i.* (ge-, h) grow dark, darken.

dünn *adj.* [dyn] *paper, material, voice, etc.*: thin; *hair, population, etc.*: thin, sparse; *liquid*: thin, watery; *air*: rare(fied).

Dunst [dunst] *m* (-es/=e) vapo(u)r; haze, mist; fume.

dünsten ['dynstən] (ge-. h) **1.** *v/t.* steam (*fish, etc.*); stew (*fruit, etc.*); **2.** *v/i.* steam.

'dunstig *adj.* vaporous; hazy.

Duplikat [dupli'ka:t] *n* (-[e]s/-e) duplicate.

Dur ♪ [du:r] *n* (-/-) major.

durch [durç] **1.** *prp.* (*acc.*) through; **2.** *adv.:* die ganze Nacht ~ all night long; ~ und ~ through and through; thoroughly.

durcharbeiten ['durç⁹-] (*sep.*, -ge-, h) **1.** *v/t.* study thoroughly; sich ~ durch work through (*book, etc.*); **2.** *v/i.* work without a break.

durch'aus *adv.* through and through; thoroughly; by all means; absolutely, quite; ~ nicht not at all, by no means.

'durch|biegen *v/t.* (*irr.* biegen, *sep.*, -ge-, h) bend; deflect (*beam, etc.*); sich ~ *beam, etc.*: deflect, sag; **'~blättern** *v/t.* (*sep.*, -ge-, h) glance *or* skim through (*book, etc.*), *Am.* thumb through, skim; **'2blick** *m*: ~ auf (*acc.*) view through to, vista over, view of; **'~blicken** *v/i.* (*sep.*, -ge-, h) look through; ~ lassen, daß give to understand that.

durch|'bluten *v/t.* (*no* -ge-, h) supply with blood; **~'bohren** *v/t.* (*no* -ge-, h) pierce; perforate; mit Blicken ~ look daggers at *s.o.*

'durch|braten *v/t.* (*irr.* braten, *sep.*, -ge-, h) roast thoroughly; **~brechen** (*irr.* brechen) **1.** ['~brɛçən] *v/t.* (*sep.*, -ge-, sein) break through *or* apart; **2.** ['~] *v/t.* (*sep.*, -ge-, h) break apart *or* in two; **3.** ['~brɛçən] *v/t.* (*no* -ge-, h) break through, breach; run (*blockade*); crash (*sound barrier*); **'~brennen** *v/i.* (*irr.* brennen, *sep.*, -ge-, sein) ⚡ fuse: blow; F *fig.* run away; *woman*: elope; **'~bringen** *v/t.* (*irr.* bringen, *sep.*, -ge-, h) bring *or* get through; dissipate, squander (*money*); **'2bruch** *m* ✕ break-

through; rupture; breach; *fig.* ultimate success.

durch'denken *v/t.* (*irr.* denken, *no* -ge-, h) think *s.th.* over thoroughly.

'durch|drängen *v/refl.* (*sep.*, -ge-, h) force *or* push one's way through; **~dringen** (*irr.* dringen) **1.** ['~driŋən] *v/i.* (*sep.*, -ge-, sein) penetrate (through); win acceptance (mit for) (*proposal*); **2.** [~'driŋən] *v/t.* (*no* -ge-, h) penetrate, pierce; *water, smell, etc.*: permeate.

durcheinander [durç⁹aı'nandər] **1.** *adv.* in confusion *or* disorder; pell-mell; **2.** **2** *n* (-s/-) muddle, mess, confusion; **~bringen** *v/t.* (*irr.* bringen, *sep.*, -ge-, h) confuse *s.o.*; *fig.* mix (*things*) up; **~werfen** *v/t.* (*irr.* werfen, *sep.*, -ge-, h) throw into disorder; *fig.* mix up.

durchfahr|en (*irr.* fahren) **1.** ['~fa:-rən] *v/i.* (*sep.*, -ge-, sein) go *or* pass *or* drive through; **2.** [~'fa:rən] *v/t.* (*no* -ge-, h) go *or* pass *or* travel *or* drive through; traverse (*tract of country, etc.*); '2t *f* passage (through); gate(way); ~ verboten! no thoroughfare!

'Durchfall *m* 🏥 diarrh(o)ea; F *fig.* failure, *Am. a.* flunk; **2en** (*irr.* fallen) **1.** ['~falən] *v/i.* (*sep.*, -ge-, sein) fall through; fail, F get ploughed (*in examination*); *thea.* be a failure, *sl.* be a flop; ~ lassen reject, F plough; **2.** [~'falən] *v/t.* (*no* -ge-, h) fall *or* drop through (*space*).

'durch|fechten *v/t.* (*irr.* fechten, *sep.*, -ge-, h) fight *or* see *s.th.* through; **'~finden** *v/refl.* (*irr.* finden, *sep.*, -ge-, h) find one's way (through).

durch|'flechten *v/t.* (*irr.* flechten, *no* -ge-, h) interweave, intertwine; **~'forschen** *v/t.* (*no* -ge-, h) search through, investigate; explore (*region, etc.*).

'Durchfuhr ✝ *f* (-/-en) transit.

durchführ|bar *adj.* ['durçfy:rba:r] practicable, feasible, workable; **'~en** *v/t.* (*sep.*, -ge-, h) lead *or* take through *or* across; *fig.* carry out *or* through; realize; **'2ungsbestimmung** *f* (implementing) regulation.

'Durchgang *m* passage; ✝ transit; *sports*: run; **'~sverkehr** *m* through traffic; ✝ transit traffic; **'~szoll** *m* transit duty.

'durchgebraten *adj.* well done.

'durchgehen (*irr.* gehen, *sep.*, -ge-) **1.** *v/i.* (sein) go *or* walk through; *bill*: pass, be carried; run away *or* off; abscond; *woman*: elope; *horse*: bolt; **2.** *v/t.* (h) go through (*street, etc.*); **3.** *v/t.* (h, sein) go *or* look *or* read through (*work, book, etc.*); **'~d 1.** *adj.* continuous; ~ Zug through train; **2.** *adv.* generally; throughout.

durch'geistigt *adj.* spiritual.

'durch|greifen *v/i.* (*irr.* greifen,

sep., -ge-, *h*) put one's hand through; *fig.* take drastic measures *or* steps; '**~greifend** *adj.* drastic; radical, sweeping; '**~halten** (*irr. halten*, *sep.*, -ge-, *h*) 1. *v/t.* keep up (*pace*, *etc.*); 2. *v/i.* hold out; '**~hauen** *v/t.* (*irr. hauen*, *sep.*, -ge-, *h*) cut *or* chop through; *fig.* give *s.o.* a good hiding; '**~helfen** *v/i.* (*irr. helfen*, *sep.*, -ge-, *h*) help through (*a. fig.*); '**~kämpfen** *v/t.* (*sep.*, -ge-, *h*) fight out; *sich ~* fight one's way through; '**~kneten** *v/t.* (*sep.*, -ge-, *h*) knead *or* work thoroughly; '**~kommen** *v/i.* (*irr. kommen*, *sep.*, -ge-, *sein*) come *or* get *or* pass through; *sick person*: pull through; *in examination*: pass.

durch'kreuzen *v/t.* (*no* -ge-, *h*) cross, foil, thwart (*plan*, *etc.*).

Durch|laß ['durçlas] *m* (*Durchlasses/Durchlässe*) passage; '**~lassen** *v/t.* (*irr. lassen*, *sep.*, -ge-, *h*) let pass, allow to pass, let through; *Wasser ~* leak; '**~lässig** *adj.* pervious (to), permeable (to); leaky.

durchlaufen (*irr. laufen*) 1. ['**~**laufən] *v/i.* (*sep.*, -ge-, *sein*) run *or* pass through; 2. ['**~**] *v/t.* (*sep.*, -ge-, *h*) wear out (*shoes*, *etc.*); 3. [**~**'laufən] *v/t.* (*no* -ge-, *h*) pass through (*stages*, *departments*, *etc.*); *sports*: cover (*distance*).

durch'leben *v/t.* (*no* -ge-, *h*) go *or* live through.

'**durchlesen** *v/t.* (*irr. lesen*, *sep.*, -ge-, *h*) read through.

durchleuchten (*h*) 1. ['**~**lɔyçtən] *v/i.* (*sep.*, -ge-) shine through; 2. [**~**'lɔyçtən] *v/t.* (*no* -ge-) ✗ X-ray; *fig.* investigate.

durchlöchern [durç'lœçərn] *v/t.* (*no* -ge-, *h*) perforate, make holes into *s.th.*

'**durchmachen** *v/t.* (*sep.*, -ge-, *h*) go through (*difficult times*, *etc.*); undergo (*suffering*).

'**Durchmarsch** *m* march(ing) through.

'**Durchmesser** *m* (-s/-) diameter.

durch'nässen *v/t.* (*no* -ge-, *h*) wet through, soak, drench.

'**durch|nehmen** *v/t.* (*irr. nehmen*, *sep.*, -ge-, *h*) go through *or* over (*subject*); '**~pausen** *v/t.* (*sep.*, -ge-, *h*) trace, calk (*design*, *etc.*).

durchqueren [durç'kveːrən] *v/t.* (*no* -ge-, *h*) cross, traverse.

'**durch|rechnen** *v/t.* (*sep.*, -ge-, *h*) (re)calculate, check; '**Ɔreise** *f* journey *or* way through; '**~reisen** 1. ['**~**raɪzən] *v/i.* (*sep.*, -ge-, *sein*) travel *or* pass through; 2. [**~**'raɪzən] *v/t.* (*no* -ge-, *h*) travel over *or* through *or* across; '**Ɔreisende** *m*, *f* (-n/-n) person travel(l)ing through. *Am. a.* transient; 🚆 through passenger; '**~reißen** (*irr. reißen*, *sep.*, -ge-) 1. *v/t.* (*sein*) tear, break; 2. *v/t.* (*h*) tear

asunder, tear in two; **~schauen** (*h*) 1. ['**~**ʃaʊən] *v/i.* *and* *v/t.* (*sep.*, -ge-) look through; 2. *fig.* [**~**'ʃaʊən] *v/t.* (*no* -ge-) see through.

'**durchscheinen** *v/i.* (*irr. scheinen*, *sep.*, -ge-, *h*) shine through; '**~d** *adj.* translucent; transparent.

'**durchscheuern** *v/t.* (*sep.*, -ge-, *h*) rub through; **~schießen** (*irr. schießen*) 1. ['**~**ʃiːsən] *v/i.* (*sep.*, -ge-, *h*) shoot through; 2. ['**~**] *v/i.* (*sep.*, -ge-, *sein*) *water*: shoot *or* race through; 3. [**~**'ʃiːsən] *v/t.* (*no* -ge-, *h*) shoot *s.th.* through; *typ.*: space out (*lines*); interleave (*book*).

'**Durchschlag** *m* colander, strainer; carbon copy; **Ɔen** (*irr. schlagen*) 1. ['**~**ʃlaːgən] *v/t.* (*sep.*, -ge-, *h*) break *or* pass through; strain (*peas*, *etc.*); *sich ~* get along, make one's way; 2. ['**~**] *v/i.* (*sep.*, -ge-, *h*) *typ.* come through; take *or* have effect; 3. [**~**'ʃlaːgən] *v/t.* (*no* -ge-, *h*) pierce; *bullet*: penetrate; '**Ɔend** *adj.* effective, telling; **~papier** ['**~**k-] *n* copying paper.

durchschneiden *v/t.* (*irr. schneiden*, *h*) 1. ['**~**ʃnaɪdən] *v/t.* (*sep.*, -ge-) cut through; 2. [**~**'ʃnaɪdən] (*no* -ge-) cut through, cut in two.

'**Durchschnitt** *m* cutting through; ⊕ section, profile; ⋏ intersection; *fig.* average; *im ~* on an average; '**Ɔlich** 1. *adj.* average; normal; 2. *adv.* on an average; normally; '**~swert** *m* average value.

'**durch|sehen** (*irr. sehen*, *sep.*, -ge-, *h*) 1. *v/i.* see *or* look through; 2. *v/t.* see *or* look through *s.th.*; look *s.th.* over, go over *s.th.*; '**~seihen** *v/t.* (*sep.*, -ge-, *h*) filter, strain; **~setzen** *v/t.* (*h*) 1. ['**~**zɛtsən] (*sep.*, -ge-) put (*plan*, *etc.*) through; force through; *seinen Kopf ~* have one's way; *sich ~* opinion, *etc.*: gain acceptance; 2. [**~**'zɛtsən] (*no* -ge-) intersperse.

'**Durchsicht** *f* looking through *or* over; examination; correction; *typ.* reading; '**Ɔig** *adj.* glass, water, *etc.*: transparent; *fig.* clear, lucid; '**~igkeit** *f* (-/*no pl.*) transparency; *fig.* clarity, lucidity.

'**durch|sickern** *v/i.* (*sep.*, -ge-, *sein*) seep *or* ooze through; *news*, *etc.*: leak out; **~sieben** *v/t.* (*h*) 1. ['**~**ziːbən] (*sep.*, -ge-) sieve, sift; bolt (*flour*); 2. [**~**'ziːbən] (*no* -ge-) riddle (*with bullets*); '**~sprechen** *v/t.* (*irr. sprechen*, *sep.*, -ge-, *h*) discuss, talk over; **~stechen** *v/t.* (*irr. stechen*, *h*) 1. ['**~**ʃtɛçən] (*sep.*, -ge-) stick (*needle*, *etc.*) through *s.th.*; stick through *s.th.*; 2. [**~**'ʃtɛçən] (*no* -ge-) pierce; cut through (*dike*, *etc.*); '**~stecken** *v/t.* (*sep.*, -ge-, *h*) pass *or* stick through.

'**Durchstich** *m* cut(ting).

durch'stöbern *v/t.* (*no* -ge-, *h*) ransack (*room*, *pockets*, *etc.*); rummage through (*drawers, papers, etc.*).

'durchstreichen *v/t.* (*irr.* streichen, *sep.*, -ge-. *h*) strike *or* cross out, cancel.

durch'streifen *v/t.* (*no* -ge-, *h*) roam *or* wander through *or* over *or* across.

durch'such|en *v/t.* (*no* -ge-, *h*) search (*a.* ♗); ♀**ung** *f* (-/-en) search.

durchtrieben *adj.* [durç'tri:bən] cunning, artful; ♀**heit** *f* (-/*no pl.*) cunning, artfulness.

durch'wachen *v/t.* (*no* -ge-, *h*) pass (*the* night) waking.

durch'wachsen *adj. bacon:* streaky.

durchwandern 1. ['‿vandərn] *v/i.* (*sep.*, -ge-, sein) walk *or* pass through; **2.** [‿'vandərn] *v/t.* (*no* -ge-, *h*) walk *or* pass through (*place*, *area, etc.*).

durch'weben *v/t.* (*no* -ge-, *h*) interweave; *fig. a.* intersperse.

durchweg *adv.* ['durçvek] throughout, without exception.

durch|weichen 1. [‿vaiçən] *v/i.* (*sep.*, -ge-, sein) soak; **2.** [‿vaiçən] *v/t.* (*no* -ge-, *h*) soak, drench; '‿**winden** *v/refl.* (*irr.* winden, *sep.*, -ge-, *h*) worm *or* thread one's way through; ‿**wühlen** (*h*) **1.** *fig.* ['‿vy:lən] *v/refl.* (*sep.*, -ge-, *h*) work one's way through; **2.** [‿'vy:lən] *v/t.* (*no* -ge-) rummage; '‿**zählen** *v/t.* (*sep.*, -ge-, *h*) count; ‿**ziehen** (*irr.* ziehen) **1.** ['‿tsi:ən] *v/i.* (*sep.*, -ge-, sein) pass *or* go *or* come *or* march through; **2.** ['‿] *v/t.* (*sep.*, -ge-, *h*) pull (*thread, etc.*) through; **3.** [‿'tsi:ən] *v/t.* (*no* -ge-, *h*) go *or* travel through; *scent, etc.*: fill, pervade (*room, etc.*).

durch'zucken *v/t.* (*no* -ge-, *h*) flash through.

'Durchzug *m* passage through; draught, *Am.* draft.

'durchzwängen *v/refl.* (*sep.*, -ge-, *h*) squeeze *o.s.* through.

dürfen ['dyrfən] (*irr.*, *h*) **1.** *v/i.* (ge-): *ich darf* (nicht) I am (not) allowed to; **2.** *v/aux.* (*no* -ge-): *ich darf inf.* I am permitted *or* allowed to *inf.*; I may *inf.*; *du darfst nicht inf.* you must not *inf.*; *iro.*: *wenn ich bitten darf* if you please.

durfte ['durftə] *pret. of* dürfen.

dürftig *adj.* ['dyrftiç] poor; scanty.

dürr *adj.* [dyr] *wood, leaves, etc.:* dry; *land:* barren, arid; *p.* gaunt, lean, skinny; ♀**e** *f* (-/-n) dryness; barrenness; leanness.

Durst [durst] *m* (-es/*no pl.*) thirst (*nach for*); ‿ *haben* be thirsty.

dürsten ['dyrstən] *v/i.* (ge-, *h*): ‿ *nach* thirst for.

durstig *adj.* thirsty (*nach for*).

Dusche ['du:ʃə] *f* (-/-n) shower (-bath); ♀**n** *v/refl. and v/i.* (ge-, *h*) have a shower(-bath).

Düse ['dy:zə] *f* (-/-n) ⊕ nozzle; 🛩 jet; ‿**nantrieb** ['‿n⁹-] *m* jet propulsion; *mit* ‿ jet-propelled; '‿**n-flugzeug** *n* jet(-propelled) aircraft, F jet; '‿**njäger** 🛩 *m* jet fighter.

düster *adj.* ['dy:stər] dark, gloomy (*both a. fig.*); *light:* dim; *fig.:* sad; depressing; ♀**heit** *f* (-/*no pl.*), '♀**keit** *f* (-/*no pl.*) gloom(iness).

Dutzend ['dutsənt] *n* (-s/-e) dozen; *ein* ‿ *Eier* a dozen eggs; ‿*e von Leuten* dozens of people; ♀**weise** *adv.* by the dozen, in dozens.

Dynam|ik [dy'na:mik] *f* (-/*no pl.*) dynamics; ♀**isch** *adj.* dynamic(al).

Dynamit [dyna'mi:t] *n* (-s/*no pl.*) dynamite.

Dynamo [dy'na:mo] *m* (-s/-s), ‿**maschine** *f* dynamo, generator.

D-Zug ['de:tsu:k] *m* express train.

E

Ebbe ['ɛbə] *f* (-/-n) ebb(-tide); low tide; ♀**n** *v/i.* (ge-, sein) ebb.

eben ['e:bən] **1.** *adj.* even; plain; level; 🝆 plane; *zu* ‿*er Erde* on the ground floor, *Am.* on the first floor; **2.** *adv.* exactly; just; ‿ *erst* just now; '♀**bild** *n* image, likeness; ‿**bürtig** *adj.* ['‿byrtiç] of equal birth; *j-m* ‿ *sein* be a match for *s.o.*, be *s.o.'s* equal; '‿**da** *adv.*, '‿**da'selbst** *adv.* at the very (same) place, just there; *quoting books:* ibidem (*abbr.* ib., ibid.); '‿**der**, '‿**die**, '‿**das** *dem. pron.* = '‿**derselbe**, '‿**die'selbe**, '‿**das'selbe** *dem. pron.* the very (same); '‿

des'wegen *adv.* for that very reason.

Ebene ['e:bənə] *f* (-/-n) plain; 🝆 plane; *fig.* level.

'eben|erdig *adj. and adv.* at street level; on the ground floor, *Am.* on the first floor; just now. likewise; '♀**holz** *n* ebony; '‿**maß** *n* symmetry; harmony; regularity (*of features*); '‿**mäßig** *adj.* symmetrical; harmonious; regular; '‿**so** *adv.* just so; just as ...; likewise; '‿**sosehr** *adv.*, '‿**soviel** *adv.* just as much; '‿**sowenig** *adv.* just as little *or* few (*pl.*), no more.

Eber zo. ['e:bər] m (-s/-) boar; '~esche ♀ f mountain-ash.

ebnen ['e:bnən] v/t. (ge-, h) level; fig. smooth.

Echo ['ɛço] n (-s/-s) echo.

echt adj. [ɛçt] genuine; true; pure; real; colour: fast; document: authentic; '2heit f (-/no pl.) genuineness, purity; reality; fastness; authenticity.

Eck [ɛk] n (-[e]s/-e) s. Ecke; '~ball m sports: corner-kick; '~e f (-/-n) corner; edge; '2ig adj. angular; fig. awkward; '~platz m corner-seat; '~stein m corner-stone; '~zahn m canine tooth.

edel adj. ['e:dəl] noble; min. precious; organs of the body: vital; '~denkend adj. noble-minded; '~mann m nobleman; '2mut m generosity; ~mütig adj. ['~my:tiç] noble-minded, generous; '2stein m precious stone; gem.

Edikt [e'dikt] n (-[e]s/-e) edict.

Efeu ♀ ['e:fɔy] m (-s/no pl.) ivy.

Effekt [ɛ'fɛkt] m (-[e]s/-e) effect; ~en pl. effects pl.; ✝: securities pl.; ✝tocks pl.; ~enhandel m dealing in stocks; ~hascherei [~haʃə'raɪ] f (-/-en) claptrap; 2iv adj. [~'ti:v] effective; 2uieren [~u'i:rən] v/t. (no -ge-, h) effect; execute, Am. a. fill; 2voll adj. effective, striking.

egal adj. [e'ga:l] equal; F all the same.

Egge ['ɛgə] f (-/-n) harrow; '2n v/t. (ge-, h) harrow.

Egois|mus [ego'ismus] m (-/Egoismen) ego(t)ism; ~t m (-en/-en) ego(t)ist; 2tisch adj. selfish, ego(t)istic(al).

ehe¹ cj. ['e:ə] before.

Ehe² [~] f (-/-n) marriage; matrimony; '~anbahnung f (-/-en) matrimonial agency; '~brecher m (-s/-) adulterer; '~brecherin f (-/-nen) adulteress; '2brecherisch adj. adulterous; '~bruch m adultery; '~frau f wife; '~gatte m, '~gattin f spouse; '~leute pl. married people pl.; '2lich adj. conjugal; child: legitimate; '~losigkeit f (-/no pl.) celibacy; single life.

ehemalig adj. ['e:əma:liç] former, ex-...; old; '~s adv. formerly.

'Ehe|mann m husband; '~paar n married couple.

'eher adv. sooner; rather; more likely; je ~ desto besser the sooner the better.

'Ehering m wedding ring.

ehern adj. ['e:ərn] brazen, of brass.

'Ehe|scheidung f divorce; '~schließung f (-/-en) (contraction of) marriage; '~stand m (-[e]s/no pl.) married state, matrimony; '~stifter m, '~stifterin f (-/-nen) matchmaker; '~vermittlung f s. Eheanbahnung; '~versprechen n promise of marriage; '~vertrag m marriage contract.

Ehrabschneider ['e:rʔapʃnaɪdər] m (-s/-) slanderer.

'ehrbar adj. hono(u)rable, respectable; modest; '2keit f (-/no pl.) respectability; modesty.

Ehre ['e:rə] f (-/-n) hono(u)r; zu ~n (gen.) in hono(u)r of; '2n v/t. (ge-, h) hono(u)r; esteem.

'ehren|amtlich adj. honorary; '2bürger m honorary citizen; '2doktor m honorary doctor; '2erklärung f (full) apology; '2gast m guest of hono(u)r; '2gericht n court of hono(u)r; '~haft adj. hono(u)rable; '2kodex m code of hono(u)r; '2legion [~legio:n] f (-/no pl.) Legion of Hono(u)r; '2mann m man of hono(u)r; '2mitglied n honorary member; '2platz m place of hono(u)r; '2recht n: bürgerliche ~e pl. civil rights pl.; '2rettung f rehabilitation; '~rührig adj. defamatory; '2sache f affair of hono(u)r; point of hono(u)r; '~voll adj. hono(u)rable; '~wert adj. hono(u)rable; '2wort n (-[e]s/-e) word of hono(u)r.

ehr|erbietig adj. ['e:rʔɛrbi:tiç] respectful; '2erbietung f (-/-en) reverence; '2furcht f (-/✝-en) respect; awe; '~furchtgebietend adj. awe-inspiring, awesome; '~fürchtig adj. ['~fyrçtiç] respectful; '2gefühl n (-[e]s/no pl.) sense of hono(u)r; '2geiz m ambition; '~geizig adj. ambitious.

'ehrlich adj. honest; commerce, game: fair; opinion: candid; ~ währt am längsten honesty is the best policy; '2keit f (-/no pl.) honesty; fairness.

'ehrlos adj. dishono(u)rable, infamous; '2igkeit f (-/-en) dishonesty, infamy.

'ehr|sam adj. s. ehrbar; '2ung f (-/-en) hono(u)r (conferred on s.o.); '~vergessen adj. dishono(u)rable, infamous; '2verlust ✝✝ m (-es/no pl.) loss of civil rights; '~würdig adj. venerable, reverend.

ei¹ int. [aɪ] ah!, indeed!

Ei² [~] n (-[e]s/-er) egg; physiol. ovum.

Eibe ♀ ['aɪbə] f (-/-n) yew(-tree).

Eiche ♀ ['aɪçə] f (-/-n) oak(-tree); ~l [~] f (-/-n) ✝ acorn; cards: club; ~lhäher orn. ['~hɛ:ər] m (-s/-) jay.

eichen¹ ['aɪçən] v/t. (ge-, h) ga(u)ge.

eichen² adj. [~] oaken, of oak.

Eich|hörnchen zo. ['aɪçhœrnçən] n (-s/-) squirrel; '~maß n standard.

Eid [aɪt] m (-es/-e) oath; '2brüchig adj.: ~ werden break one's oath.

Eidechse zo. ['aɪdɛksə] f (-/-n) lizard.

eidesstattlich ['aɪdəs-] in lieu of (an) oath; ~e Erklärung statutory declaration.

'eidlich 1. *adj.* sworn; **2.** *adv.* on oath.

'Eidotter *m, n* yolk.

'Eier|kuchen *m* omelet(te), pancake; **'⁀schale** *f* egg-shell; **'⁀stock** *anat. m* ovary; **'⁀uhr** *f* egg-timer.

Eifer ['aɪfər] *m* (-s/no pl.) zeal; eagerness; ardo(u)r; **'⁀er** *m* (-s/-) zealot; **'⁀sucht** *f* (-/no pl.) jealousy; **'Ǝsüchtig** *adj.* jealous (*auf acc.* of).

eifrig *adj.* ['aɪfrɪç] zealous, eager; ardent.

eigen *adj.* ['aɪgən] own; particular; strange, odd; *in compounds:* ...-owned; peculiar (*dat.* to); **'Ǝart** *f* peculiarity; **'⁀artig** *adj.* peculiar; singular; **Ǝbrötler** ['⁀brøːtlər] *m* (-s/-) odd *or* eccentric person, crank; **'Ǝgewicht** *n* dead weight; **⁀händig** *adj. and adv.* ['⁀hendɪç] with one's own hands; **'Ǝheim** *n* house of one's own; homestead; **'Ǝheit** *f* (-/-en) peculiarity; oddity; *of language:* idiom; **'Ǝliebe** *f* self-love; **'Ǝlob** *n* self-praise; **'⁀mächtig** *adj.* arbitrary; **'Ǝname** *m* proper name; **⁀nützig** *adj.* ['⁀nytsɪç] self-interested; selfish; **'⁀s** *adv.* expressly, specially; on purpose.

'Eigenschaft *f* (-/-en) quality (*of s.o.*); property (*of s.th.*); *in s-r ⁀ als* in his capacity as; **'⁀swort** *gr. n* (-[e]s/⁀er) adjective.

'Eigensinn *m* (-[e]s/no pl.) obstinacy; **'Ǝig** *adj.* wil(l)ful, obstinate.

'eigentlich 1. *adj.* proper; actual; true, real; **2.** *adv.* properly (speaking).

'Eigentum *n* (-s/⁀er) property.

Eigentüm|er ['aɪgənty:mər] *m* (-s/-) owner, proprietor; **'Ǝlich** *adj.* peculiar; odd; **'⁀lichkeit** *f* (-/-en) peculiarity.

'Eigentums|recht *n* ownership; copyright; **'⁀wohnung** *f* freehold flat.

'eigenwillig *adj.* self-willed; *fig.* individual.

eign|en ['aɪgnən] *v/refl.* (ge-, h): *sich ⁀ für* be suited for; **'Ǝung** *f* (-/-en) aptitude, suitability.

'Eil|bote & *m* express messenger; *durch ⁀n* by special delivery; **'⁀brief** & *m* express letter, *Am.* special delivery letter.

Eile ['aɪlə] *f* (-/no pl.) haste, speed; hurry; **'Ǝn** *v/i.* (ge-, sein) hasten, make haste; hurry; *letter, affair:* be urgent; **Ǝnds** *adv.* ['⁀ts] quickly, speedily.

'Eil|fracht *f*, **⁀gut** *n* express goods *pl., Am.* fast freight; **'Ǝig** *adj.* hasty, speedy; urgent; *es ⁀ haben* be in a hurry.

Eimer ['aɪmər] *m* (-s/-) bucket, pail.

ein [aɪn] **1.** *adj.* one; **2.** *indef. art.* a, an.

einander *adv.* [aɪ'nandər] one another; each other.

ein|arbeiten ['aɪn⁀] *v/t.* (*sep.*, -ge-, h): *j-n ⁀ in* (*acc.*) make s.o. acquainted with; **⁀armig** *adj.* ['aɪn⁀] one-armed; **⁀äschern** ['aɪn'ɛʃərn] *v/t.* (*sep.*, -ge-, h) burn to ashes; cremate (*dead body*); **'Ǝäscherung** *f* (-/-en) cremation; **⁀atmen** ['aɪn⁀] *v/t.* (*sep.*, -ge-, h) breathe, inhale; **⁀äugig** *adj.* ['aɪn'ɔ ygɪç] one-eyed.

'Einbahnstraße *f* one-way street.

'einbalsamieren *v/t.* (*sep.*, *no* -ge-, h) embalm.

'Einband *m* (-[e]s/⁀e) binding; cover.

'ein|bauen *v/t.* (*sep.*, -ge-, h) build in; install (*engine, etc.*); **'⁀behalten** *v/t.* (*irr.* halten, *sep.*, *no* -ge- h) detain; **'⁀berufen** *v/t.* (*irr.* rufen, *sep.*, *no* -ge-, h) convene; ✕ call up, *Am.* induct.

'einbett|en *v/t.* (*sep.*, -ge-, h) embed; **'Ǝzimmer** *n* single(-bedded) room.

'einbild|en *v/refl.* (*sep.*, -ge-, h) fancy, imagine; **'Ǝung** *f* imagination, fancy; conceit.

'einbinden *v/t.* (*irr.* binden, *sep.*, -ge-, h) bind (*books*).

'Einblick *m* insight (*in acc.* into).

'einbrechen (*irr.* brechen, *sep.*, -ge-) **1.** *v/t.* (h) break open; **2.** *v/i.* (sein) break in; *of night, etc.*: set in; *⁀ in* (*acc.*) break into (*house*).

'Einbrecher *m* at night: burglar; *by day:* housebreaker.

'Einbruch *m* ✕ invasion; housebreaking, burglary; *bei ⁀ der Nacht* at nightfall; **'⁀(s)diebstahl** *m* house-breaking, burglary.

einbürger|n ['aɪnbyrgərn] *v/t.* (*sep.*, -ge-, h) naturalize; **'Ǝung** *f* (-/-en) naturalization.

'Ein|buße *f* loss; **'Ǝbüßen** *v/t.* (*sep.*, -ge-, h) lose, forfeit.

ein|dämmen ['aɪndɛmən] *v/t.* (*sep.*, -ge-, h) dam (up); embank (*river*); *fig.* check; **⁀deutig** *adj.* unequivocal; clear, plain.

'eindring|en *v/i.* (*irr.* dringen, *sep.*, -ge-, sein) enter; penetrate; intrude; *⁀ in* (*acc.*) penetrate (into); force one's way into; invade (*country*); **'⁀lich** *adj.* urgent; **Ǝling** ['⁀lɪŋ] *m* (-s/-e) intruder; invader.

'Eindruck *m* (-[e]s/⁀e) impression.

'ein|drücken *v/t.* (*sep.*, -ge-, h) press in; crush (in) (*hat*); break (*pane*); **'⁀drucksvoll** *adj.* impressive; **⁀engen** ['aɪn⁀] *v/t.* (*sep.*, -ge-, h) narrow; *fig.* limit.

ein|er¹ ['aɪnər], **⁀e**, **'⁀(e)s** *indef. pron.* one.

Einer² [⁀] *m* (-s/-) ᴀ unit, digit; *rowing:* single sculler, skiff.

einerlei ['aɪnər'laɪ] **1.** *adj.* of the same kind; immaterial; *es ist mir ⁀* it is all the same to me; **2.** *Ǝ n* (-s/no pl.) sameness; monotony; humdrum (*of one's existence*).

einerseits *adv.* ['aɪnər'zaɪts] on the one hand.

einfach *adj.* ['aɪnfax] simple; single; plain; *meal:* frugal; *ticket:* single, *Am.* one-way; '**2heit** *f* (-/no *pl.*) simplicity.

einfädeln ['aɪnfɛːdəln] *v/t.* (*sep.*, -ge-, h) thread; *fig.* start, set on foot; contrive.

'**Einfahrt** *f* entrance, entry.

'**Einfall** *m* ✗ invasion; idea, inspiration; '**2en** *v/i.* (*irr. fallen, sep.*, -ge-, *sein*) fall in, collapse; break in (*on a conversation*), interrupt, cut short; chime in; ♪ join in; invade; *j-m* ~ occur to s.o.

Ein|falt ['aɪnfalt] *f* (-/no *pl.*) simplicity, silliness; **2fältig** *adj.* ['~fɛltiç] simple; silly; '**~faltspinsel** *m* simpleton, *Am.* F sucker.

'**ein|farbig** *adj.* one-colo(u)red, uni-colo(u)red; plain; '**~fassen** *v/t.* (*sep.*, -ge-, h) border; set (*precious stone*); '**2fassung** *f* border; setting; '**~fetten** *v/t.* (*sep.*, -ge-, h) grease; oil; '**~finden** *v/refl.* (*irr. finden, sep.*, -ge-, h) appear; arrive; '**~flechten** *fig. v/t.* (*irr. flechten, sep.*,-ge-,h) put in, insert; '**~fließen** *v/i.* (*irr. fließen, sep.*, -ge-, *sein*) flow in; ~ in (*acc.*) flow into; ~ *lassen* mention in passing; '**~flößen** *v/t.* (*sep.*, -ge-, h) infuse.

'**Einfluß** *m* influx; *fig.* influence; '**2reich** *adj.* influential.

ein|förmig *adj.* ['aɪnfœrmiç] uniform; monotonous; '**~frieden** ['~friːdən] *v/t.* (*sep.*, -ge-, h) fence, enclose; '**2friedung** *f* (-/-en) enclosure; '**~frieren** (*irr. frieren, sep.*, -ge-) 1. *v/i.* (*sein*) freeze (in); 2. *v/t.* (h) freeze (*food*); '**~fügen** *v/t.* (*sep.*, -ge-, h) put in; *fig.* insert; *sich* ~ fit in.

Einfuhr ✝ ['aɪnfuːr] *f* (-/-en) import(ation); '**~bestimmungen** *f/pl.* import regulations *pl.*

'**einführen** *v/t.* (*sep.*, -ge-, h) ✝ import; introduce (*s.o., custom*); insert; initiate; install (*s.o. in an office*).

'**Einfuhrwaren** ✝ *f/pl.* imports *pl.*

'**Eingabe** *f* petition; application.

'**Eingang** *m* entrance; entry; arrival (*of goods*); *nach* ~ on receipt; '**~s-buch** ✝ *n* book of entries.

'**eingeben** *v/t.* (*irr. geben, sep.*, -ge-, h) give, administer (*medicine*) (*dat.* to); prompt, suggest (to).

'**einge|bildet** *adj.* imaginary; conceited (*auf acc.* of); '**~boren** *adj.* native; '**2borene** *m, f* (-*n*/-*n*) native.

Eingebung ['aɪngəbuŋ] *f* (-/-en) suggestion; inspiration.

einge|denk *adj.* ['aɪngədɛŋk] mindful (*gen.* of); '**~fallen** *adj.* eyes, *cheeks:* sunken, hollow; emaciated; '**~fleischt** *fig. adj.* ['~gəflaɪʃt] in-

veterate; confirmed; ~*er Junggeselle* confirmed bachelor.

'**eingehen** (*irr. gehen, sep.*, -ge-) 1. *v/i.* (*sein*) mail, goods: come in, arrive; ♀, *animal:* die; cease (to exist); *material:* shrink; ~ *auf* (*acc.*) agree to; enter into; 2. *v/t.* (h, *sein*) enter into (*relationship*); contract (*marriage*); *ein Risiko* ~ run a risk, *esp. Am.* take a chance; *e-n Vergleich* ~ come to terms; *Verbindlichkeiten* ~ incur liabilities; *e-e Wette* ~ make a bet; *eingegangene Gelder* *n/pl.* receipts *pl.*; '**~d** *adj.* detailed; thorough; *examination:* close.

Eingemachte ['aɪngəmaxtə] *n* (-*n*/ no *pl.*) preserves *pl.*; pickles *pl.*

'**eingemeinden** *v/t.* (*sep.*, no -ge-, h) incorporate (*dat.* into).

'**einge|nommen** *adj.* partial (*für* to); prejudiced (*gegen* against); *von sich* ~ conceited; '**2sandt** ✒ *n* (-*s*/-*s*) letter to the editor; '**~schnappt** F *fig. adj.* ['~gəʃnapt] offended, touchy; '**~sessen** *adj.* long-established; '**2ständnis** *n* confession, avowal; '**~stehen** *v/t.* (*irr. stehen, sep.*, no -ge-, h) confess, avow.

Eingeweide *anat.* ['aɪngəvaɪdə] *pl.* viscera *pl.*; intestines *pl.*; bowels *pl.*; *esp. of animals:* entrails *pl.*

'**einge|wöhnen** *v/refl.* (*sep.*, no -ge-, h) accustom o.s. (*in acc.* to); acclimatize o.s., *Am.* acclimate o.s. (to); get used (to).

eingewurzelt *adj.* ['aɪngəvurtsəlt] deep-rooted, inveterate.

'**eingießen** *v/t.* (*irr. gießen, sep.*, -ge-, h) pour in *or* out.

eingleisig *adj.* ['aɪnglaɪziç] single-track.

'**ein|graben** *v/t.* (*irr. graben, sep.*, -ge-, h) dig in; bury; engrave; *sich* ~ ✗ dig o.s. in, entrench o.s.; *fig.* engrave itself (*on one's memory*); '**~gravieren** *v/t.* (*sep.*, no -ge-, h) engrave.

'**eingreifen** 1. *v/i.* (*irr. greifen, sep.*, -ge-, h) intervene; ~ *in* (*acc.*) interfere with; encroach on (*s.o.'s rights*); *in die Debatte* ~ join in the debate; 2. ⊕ *n* (-*s*/no *pl.*) intervention.

'**Eingriff** *m* *fig.* encroachment; ⚕ operation.

'**einhaken** *v/t.* (*sep.*, -ge-, h) fasten; *sich bei j-m* ~ take s.o.'s arm.

'**Einhalt** *m* (-[e]*s*/no *pl.*): ~ *gebieten* (*dat.*) put a stop to; '**2en** *fig.* (*irr. halten, sep.*, -ge-, h) 1. *v/t.* observe, keep; 2. *v/i.* stop, leave off (*zu tun* doing).

'**ein|hängen** ([*irr. hängen,*] *sep.*, -ge-, h) 1. *v/t.* hang in; hang up, replace (*receiver*); *sich bei j-m* ~ take s.o.'s arm, link arms with s.o.; 2. *teleph. v/i.* hang up; '**~heften** *v/t.* (*sep.*, -ge-, h) sew *or* stitch in.

'**einheimisch** *adj.* native (*in dat.*

to), indigenous (to) (*a.* ♀); ♃ endemic; *product*: home-grown; '₂e *m, f* (*-n/-n*) native; resident.

'**Einheit** *f* (*-/-en*) unity; oneness; ♃, *phys.*, ✗ unit; '₂lich *adj.* uniform; '₂spreis *m* standard price.

'**einheizen** (*sep.*, *-ge-*, *h*) **1.** *v/i.* make a fire; **2.** *v/t.* heat (*stove*).

einhellig *adj.* ['aɪnhɛlɪç] unanimous.

'**einholen** (*sep.*, *-ge-*, *h*) **1.** *v/t.* catch up with, overtake; make up for (*lost time*); make (*inquiries*); take (*order*); seek (*advice*); ask for (*permission*); buy; **2.** *v/i.*: ~ gehen go shopping.

'**Einhorn** *zo. n* unicorn.

'**einhüllen** *v/t.* (*sep.*, *-ge-*, *h*) wrap (up *or* in); envelop.

einig *adj.* ['aɪnɪç] united; ~ sein agree; nicht ~ sein differ (*über acc.* about); ~e *indef. pron.* ['~gə] several; some; ~en ['~ɪgən] *v/t.* (*sep.*, *h*) unite; sich ~ come to terms; ~ermaßen *adv.* ['~gər'ma:sən] in some measure; somewhat; ~es *indef. pron.* ['~gəs] something; '₂keit *f* (*-/no pl.*) unity; concord; ₂ung ['~g-] *f* (*-/-en*) union; agreement.

ein|impfen ['aɪn⁹-] *v/t.* (*sep.*, *-ge-*, *h*) ♃ inoculate (*a. fig.*); '~jagen *v/t.* (*sep.*, *-ge-*, *h*): j-m Furcht ~ scare s.o.

einjährig *adj.* ['aɪnjɛːrɪç] one-year-old; *esp.* ♀ annual; *animal*: yearling.

'**ein|kalkulieren** *v/t.* (*sep.*, *no -ge-*, *h*) take into account, allow for; '~kassieren *v/t.* (*sep.*, *no -ge-*, *h*) cash; collect.

'**Einkauf** *m* purchase; Einkäufe machen s. einkaufen 2; '₂en (*sep.*, *-ge-*, *h*) **1.** *v/t.* buy, purchase; **2.** *v/i.* make purchases, go shopping.

'**Einkäufer** *m* buyer.

'**Einkaufs|netz** *n* string bag; '~preis ♃ *m* purchase price; '~tasche *f* shopping-bag.

'**ein|kehren** *v/i.* (*sep.*, *-ge-*, *sein*) put up *or* stop (*at an inn*); '~kerben *v/t.* (*sep.*, *-ge-*, *h*) notch; '~kerkern *v/t.* (*sep.*, *-ge-*, *h*) imprison; '~klagen *v/t.* (*sep.*, *-ge-*, *h*) sue for; '~klammern *v/t.* (*sep.*, *-ge-*, *h*) *typ.* bracket; put in brackets.

'**Einklang** *m* unison; harmony.

'**ein|kleiden** *v/t.* (*sep.*, *-ge-*, *h*) clothe; fit out; '~klemmen *v/t.* (*sep.*, *-ge-*, *h*) squeeze (in); jam; '~klinken (*sep.*, *-ge-*) **1.** *v/t.* (*h*) latch; **2.** *v/i.* (*sein*) latch; engage; '~knicken (*sep.*, *-ge-*) *v/t.* (*h*) *and* *v/i.* (*sein*) bend in, break; '~kochen (*sep.*, *-ge-*) **1.** *v/t.* (*h*) preserve; **2.** *v/i.* (*sein*) boil down *or* away.

'**Einkommen** *n* (*-s/-*) income, revenue; '~steuer *f* income-tax.

'**einkreisen** *v/t.* (*sep.*, *-ge-*, *h*) encircle.

Einkünfte ['aɪnkynftə] *pl.* income, revenue.

'**einlad|en** *v/t.* (*irr. laden, sep.*, *-ge-*, *h*) load (in) (*goods*); *fig.* invite; '₂ung *f* invitation.

'**Einlage** *f* enclosure (*in letter*); ♃ investment; deposit (*of money*); *gambling*: stake; inserted piece; ♃ arch-support; temporary filling (*of tooth*); '₂rn ♃ *v/t.* (*sep.*, *-ge-*, *h*) store (up).

Einlaß ['aɪnlas] *m* (*Einlasses/Einlässe*) admission, admittance.

'**einlassen** *v/t.* (*irr. lassen, sep.*, *-ge-*, *h*) let in, admit; ~ in (*acc.*) ⊕ imbed in; sich ~ in *or* auf (*both acc.*) engage in, enter into.

'**ein|laufen** *v/i.* (*irr. laufen, sep.*, *-ge-*, *sein*) come in, arrive; *ship*: enter; *material*: shrink; '~leben *v/refl.* (*sep.*, *-ge-*, *h*) accustom o.s. (*in acc.* to).

'**einlege|n** *v/t.* (*sep.*, *-ge-*, *h*) lay *or* put in; insert; ⊕ inlay; deposit (*money*); pickle; preserve (*fruit*); Berufung ~ lodge an appeal (*bei* to); Ehre ~ mit gain hono(u)r *or* credit by; '₂sohle *f* insole, sock.

'**einleit|en** *v/t.* (*sep.*, *-ge-*, *h*) start; introduce; '~end *adj.* introductory; '₂ung *f* introduction.

'**ein|lenken** *fig. v/i.* (*sep.*, *-ge-*, *h*) come round; '~leuchten *v/i.* (*sep.*, *-ge-*, *h*) be evident *or* obvious; '~liefern *v/t.* (*sep.*, *-ge-*, *h*) deliver (up); in ein Krankenhaus ~ take to a hospital, *Am.* hospitalize; '~lösen *v/t.* (*sep.*, *-ge-*, *h*) ransom (*prisoner*); redeem (*pledge*); ♃ hono(u)r (*bill*); cash (*cheque*); ♃ meet (*bill*); '~machen *v/t.* (*sep.*, *-ge-*, *h*) preserve (*fruit*); tin, *Am.* can.

'**einmal** *adv.* once; one day; auf ~ all at once; es war ~ once (upon a time) there was; nicht ~ not even; '₂eins *n* (*-/-*) multiplication table; '~ig *adj.* single; unique.

'**Einmarsch** *m* marching in, entry; '₂ieren *v/i.* (*sep.*, *no -ge-*, *sein*) march in, enter.

'**ein|mengen** *v/refl.* (*sep.*, *-ge-*, *h*), '~mischen *v/refl.* (*sep.*, *-ge-*, *h*) meddle, interfere (*in acc.* with), *esp. Am. sl.* butt in.

'**Einmündung** *f* junction (*of roads*); mouth (*of river*).

einmütig *adj.* ['aɪnmyːtɪç] unanimous; '₂keit *f* (*-/no pl.*) unanimity.

Einnahme ['aɪnnaːmə] *f* (*-/-n*) ✗ taking, capture; *mst* ~n *pl.* takings *pl.*, receipts *pl.*

'**einnehmen** *v/t.* (*irr. nehmen, sep.*, *-ge-*, *h*) take (*meal, position*, ✗); ♃ take (*money*); ♃ earn, make (*money*); take up, occupy (*room*); *fig.* captivate; '~d *adj.* taking, engaging, captivating.

'**einnicken** *v/i.* (*sep.*, *-ge-*, *sein*) doze *or* drop off.

Einöde ['aɪnǭ-] f desert, solitude.

ein|ordnen ['aɪnǭ-] v/t. (sep., -ge-, h) arrange in proper order; classify; file (letters, etc.); **~packen** v/t. (sep., -ge-, h) pack up; wrap up; '**~pferchen** v/t. (sep., -ge-, h) pen in; fig. crowd, cram; '**~pflanzen** v/t. (sep., -ge-, h) plant; fig. implant; '**~pökeln** v/t. (sep., -ge-, h) pickle, salt; '**~prägen** v/t. (sep., -ge-, h) imprint; impress; sich ~ imprint itself; commit s.th. to one's memory; '**~quartieren** v/t. (sep., no -ge-, h) quarter, billet; '**~rahmen** v/t. (sep., -ge-, h) frame; '**~räumen** fig. v/t. (sep., -ge-, h) grant, concede; '**~rechnen** v/t. (sep., -ge-, h) comprise, include; **~reden** (sep., -ge-, h) 1. v/t.: j-m ~ persuade or talk s.o. into (doing) s.th.; 2. v/i.: auf j-n ~ talk insistently to s.o.; '**~reichen** v/t. (sep., -ge-, h) hand in, send in, present; '**~reihen** v/t. (sep., -ge-, h) insert (unter acc. in); class (with); place (among); sich ~ take one's place.

einreihig adj. ['aɪnraɪç] jacket: single-breasted.

'Einreise f entry; '**~erlaubnis** f, '**~genehmigung** f entry permit.

'ein|reißen (irr. reißen, sep., -ge-) 1. v/t. (h) tear; pull down (building); 2. v/i. (sein) tear; abuse, etc.: spread; **~renken** ['~rɛŋkən] v/t. (sep., -ge-, h) ⚕ set; fig. set right.

'einricht|en v/t. (sep., -ge-, h) establish; equip; arrange; set up (shop); furnish (flat); es ~ manage; sich ~ establish o.s., settle down; economize; sich ~ auf (acc.) prepare for; '**2ung** f establishment; arrangement, esp. Am. setup; equipment; furniture; fittings pl. (of shop); institution.

'ein|rollen v/t. (sep., -ge-, h) roll up or in; sich ~ roll up; curl up; '**~rosten** v/i. (sep., -ge-, sein) rust; screw, etc.: rust in; '**~rücken** (sep., -ge-) 1. v/i. (sein) enter, march in; ⚔ join the army; 2. v/t. (h) insert (advertisement in a paper); typ. indent (line, word, etc.); '**~rühren** v/t. (sep., -ge-, h) stir (in).

eins adj. [aɪns] one.

'einsam adj. lonely, solitary; '**2keit** f (-/⚕ -en) loneliness, solitude.

'einsammeln v/t. (sep., -ge-, h) gather; collect.

'Einsatz m inset; insertion (of piece of material); gambling: stake, pool; ♪ striking in, entry; employment; engagement (a. ⚔); ⚔ action, operation; unter ~ s-s Lebens at the risk of one's life.

'ein|saugen v/t. (sep., -ge-, h) suck in; fig. imbibe; '**~schalten** v/t. (sep., -ge-, h) insert; ⚡ switch or turn on; den ersten Gang ~ mot. go into first or bottom gear; sich ~

intervene; '**~schärfen** v/t. (sep., -ge-, h) inculcate (dat. upon); '**~schätzen** v/t. (sep., -ge-, h) assess, appraise, estimate (auf acc. at); value (a. fig.); '**~schenken** v/t. (sep., -ge-, h) pour in or out; '**~schicken** v/t. (sep., -ge-, h) send in; **~schieben** v/t. (irr. schieben, sep., -ge-, h) insert; '**~schiffen** v/t. and v/refl. (sep., -ge-, h) embark; '**2schiffung** f (-/-en) embarkation; '**~schlafen** v/i. (irr. schlafen, sep., -ge-, sein) fall asleep; **~schläfern** ['~ʃlɛːfərn] v/t. (sep., -ge-, h) lull to sleep; ⚗ narcotize.

'Einschlag m striking (of lightning); impact (of missile); fig. touch; '**2en** (irr. schlagen, sep., -ge-, h) 1. v/t. drive in (nail); break (in); smash (in); wrap up; take (road); tuck in (hem, etc.); enter upon (career); 2. v/i. shake hands; lightning, missile: strike; fig. be a success; nicht ~ fail; (wie e-e Bombe) ~ cause a sensation; auf j-n ~ belabour s.o.

einschlägig adj. ['aɪnʃlɛːgɪç] relevant, pertinent.

'Einschlagpapier n wrapping-paper.

'ein|schleichen v/refl. (irr. schleichen, sep., -ge-, h) creep or sneak in; '**~schleppen** v/t. (sep., -ge-, h) ⚓ tow in; import (disease); '**~schleusen** fig. v/t. (sep., -ge-, h) channel or let in; '**~schließen** v/t. (irr. schließen, sep., -ge-, h) lock in or up; enclose; ⚔ surround, encircle; fig. include; '**~schließlich** prp. (gen.) inclusive of; including, comprising; '**~schmeicheln** v/refl. (sep., -ge-, h) ingratiate o.s. (bei with); '**~schmeichelnd** adj. insinuating; '**~schmuggeln** v/t. (sep., -ge-, h) smuggle in; '**~schnappen** v/i. (sep., -ge-, sein) catch; fig. s. eingeschnappt; '**~schneidend** fig. adj. incisive, drastic.

'Einschnitt m cut, incision; notch.

'ein|schnüren v/t. (sep., -ge-, h) lace (up); '**~schränken** ['~ʃrɛŋkən] v/t. (sep., -ge-, h) restrict, confine; reduce (expenses); sich ~ economize; '**2schränkung** f (-/-en) restriction; reduction.

'Einschreibe|brief m registered letter; '**2n** v/t. (irr. schreiben, sep., -ge-, h) enter; book; enrol(l); ⚔ enlist, enrol(l); ✉ register; ~ lassen have registered; sich ~ enter one's name.

'einschreiten 1. fig. v/i. (irr. schreiten, sep., -ge-, sein) step in, interpose, intervene; take action (gegen against); 2. ♀ n (-s/no pl.) intervention.

'ein|schrumpfen v/i. (sep., -ge-, sein) shrink; '**~schüchtern** v/t. (sep., -ge-, h) intimidate; bully; '**2schüchterung** f (-/-en) intimidation; '~schulen v/t. (sep., -ge-, h) put to school.

'Einschuß m bullet-hole; ✝ invested capital.

'ein|segnen v/t. (sep., -ge-, h) consecrate; confirm (children); '2segnung f consecration; confirmation.

'einsehen 1. v/t. (irr. sehen, sep., -ge-, h) look into; fig.: see, comprehend; realize; 2. 2 n (-s/no pl.): ein ~ haben show consideration.

'einseifen v/t. (sep., -ge-, h) soap; lather (beard); F fig. humbug (s.o.).

einseitig adj. ['aınzaıtiç] one-sided; ⚕, pol., ⚖ unilateral.

'einsend|en v/t. ([irr. senden], sep., -ge-, h) send in; '2er m (-s/-) sender; contributor (to a paper).

'einsetz|en (sep., -ge-, h) 1. v/t. set or put in; stake (money); insert; institute; instal(l), appoint (s.o.); fig. use, employ, risk (one's life); sich ~ für stand up for; 2. v/i. fever, flood, weather: set in; ♪ strike in; '2ung f (-/-en) insertion; appointment, installation.

'Einsicht f (-/-en) inspection; fig. insight, understanding; judiciousness; '2ig adj. judicious, sensible.

'einsickern v/i. (sep., -ge-, sein) soak in; infiltrate.

'Einsiedler m hermit.

einsilbig adj. ['aınzılbıç] monosyllabic; fig. taciturn; '2keit f (-/no pl.) taciturnity.

'einsinken v/i. (irr. sinken, sep., -ge-, sein) sink (in).

Einspänn|er ['aınʃpɛnər] m (-s/-) one-horse carriage; '2ig adj. one-horse.

'ein|sparen v/t. (sep., -ge-, h) save, economize; '~sperren v/t. (sep., -ge-, h) imprison; lock up, confine; '~springen v/i. (irr. springen, sep., -ge-, sein) ⊕ catch; fig. step in, help out; für j-n ~ substitute for s.o.; '~spritzen v/t. (sep., -ge-, h) inject; '2spritzung f (-/-en) injection.

'Einspruch m objection, protest, veto; appeal; '~srecht n veto.

'einspurig adj. single-track.

einst adv. [aınst] once; one or some day.

'Einstand m entry; tennis: deuce.

'ein|stecken v/t. (sep., -ge-, h) put in; pocket; plug in; '~steigen v/i. (irr. steigen, sep., -ge-, sein) get in; ~! 🚂 take your seats!, Am. all aboard!

'einstell|en v/t. (sep., -ge-, h) put in; ⚔ enrol(l), enlist, Am. muster in; engage, employ, Am. a. hire; give up; stop, cease, Am. a. quit (payment, etc.); adjust (mechanism) (auf acc. to); tune in (radio) (on); opt., focus (on) (a. fig.); die Arbeit ~ cease working; strike, Am. a. walk out; sich ~ appear; sich ~ auf (acc.) be

prepared for; adapt o.s. to; '2ung f ⚔ enlistment; engagement; adjustment; focus; (mental) attitude, mentality.

'einstimm|en ♪ v/i. (sep., -ge-, h) join in; '~ig adj. unanimous; '2igkeit f (-/no pl.) unanimity.

einstöckig adj. ['aınʃtœkıç] onestoried.

'ein|streuen fig. v/t. (sep., -ge-, h) intersperse; '~studieren v/t. (sep., no -ge-, h) study; thea. rehearse; '~stürmen v/i. (sep., -ge-, sein): auf j-n ~ rush at s.o.; '2sturz m falling in, collapse; '~stürzen v/i. (sep., -ge-, sein) fall in, collapse.

einst|weilen adv. ['aınst'vaılən] for the present; in the meantime; '~weilig adj. temporary.

'ein|tauschen v/t. (sep., -ge-, h) exchange (gegen for); '~teilen v/t. (sep., -ge-, h) divide (in acc. into); classify; '~teilig adj. one-piece; '2teilung f division; classification.

eintönig adj. ['aıntø:nıç] monotonous; '2keit f (-/⚒ -en) monotony.

'Eintopf(gericht n) m hot-pot; stew.

'Eintracht f (-/no pl.) harmony, concord.

einträchtig adj. ['aıntrɛçtıç] harmonious.

'eintragen v/t. (irr. tragen, sep., -ge-, h) enter; register; bring in, yield (profit); sich ~ in (acc.) sign.

einträglich adj. ['aıntrɛ:klıç] profitable.

'Eintragung f (-/-en) entry; registration.

'ein|treffen v/i. (irr. treffen, sep., -ge-, sein) arrive; happen; come true; '~treiben v/t. (irr. treiben, sep., -ge-, h) drive in or home; collect (debts, taxes); '~treten (irr. treten, sep., -ge-, h) 1. v/i. (sein) enter; occur, happen, take place; ~ für stand up for; ~ in (acc.) enter into (rights); enter upon (possession); enter (room); join (the army, etc.); 2. v/t. (h) kick in (door); sich ed. ~ run s.th. into one's foot.

'Eintritt m entry, entrance; admittance; beginning, setting-in (of winter, etc.); ~ frei! admission free!; ~ verboten! no admittance!; '~sgeld n entrance or admission fee; sports: gate money; '~skarte f admission ticket.

'ein|trocknen v/i. (sep., -ge-, sein) dry (up); '~trüben v/refl. (sep., -ge-, h) become cloudy or overcast; ~üben ['aın²-] v/t. (sep., -ge-, h) practi|se, Am. -ce s.th.; train s.o.

einver|leiben ['aınfɛrlaıbən] v/t. ([sep.], no -ge-, h) incorporate (dat. in); annex (to); F sich et. ~ eat or drink s.th.; '2nehmen n (-s/no pl.) agreement, understanding; in gutem ~ on friendly terms; '~standen *adj.*: ~ *sein* agree; '2**ständnis** *n* agreement.

'**Einwand** *m* (-[e]s/-e) objection (*gegen* to).

'**Einwander|er** *m* immigrant; '2**n** *v/i.* (*sep.*, *-ge-*, *sein*) immigrate; '**~ung** *f* immigration.

'**einwandfrei** *adj.* unobjectionable; perfect; faultless; *alibi*: sound.

einwärts *adv.* ['aɪnvɛrts] inward(s).

'**Einwegflasche** *f* one-way bottle, non-return bottle.

'**einweih|en** *v/t.* (*sep.*, *-ge-*, *h*) *eccl.* consecrate; inaugurate; ~ *in* (*acc.*) initiate *s.o.* into; '**~ung** *f* (-/-en) consecration; inauguration; initiation.

'**einwend|en** *v/t.* ([*irr.* wenden,] *sep.*, *-ge-*, *h*) object; '2**ung** *f* objection.

'**einwerfen** (*irr.* werfen, *sep.*, *-ge-*, *h*) **1.** *v/t.* throw in (*a. fig.*); smash, break (*window-pane*); post, *Am.* mail (*letter*); interject (*remark*); **2.** *v/i.* football: throw in.

'**einwickel|n** *v/t.* (*sep.*, *-ge-*, *h*) wrap (up), envelop; '2**papier** *n* wrapping-paper.

einwillig|en ['aɪnvɪligən] *v/i.* (*sep.*, *-ge-*, *h*) consent, agree (*in acc.* to); '2**ung** *f* (-/-en) consent, agreement.

'**einwirk|en** *v/i.* (*sep.*, *-ge-*, *h*): ~ *auf* (*acc.*) act (up)on; influence; effect; '2**ung** *f* influence; effect.

Einwohner ['aɪnvoːnər] *m* (-s/-), '**~in** *f* (-/-nen) inhabitant, resident.

'**Einwurf** *m* throwing in; football: throw-in; *fig.* objection; slit (*for letters, etc.*); slot (*for coins*).

'**Einzahl** *gr. f* (-/~-en) singular (number); '2**en** *v/t.* (*sep.*, *-ge-*, *h*) pay in; '**~ung** *f* payment; deposit (*at bank*).

einzäunen ['aɪntsɔʏnən] *v/t.* (*sep.*, *-ge-*, *h*) fence in.

Einzel ['aɪntsəl] *n* (-s/-) *tennis*: single, *Am.* singles *pl.*; **~gänger** ['~gɛŋər] *m* (-s/-) outsider; F lone wolf; '**~handel** † *m* retail trade; '**~händler** † *m* retailer, retail dealer; '**~heit** *f* (-/-en) detail, item; **~en** *pl.* particulars *pl.*, details *pl.*; '2**n 1.** *adj.* single; particular; individual; separate; *of shoes, etc.*: odd; *im* **~en** in detail; **2.** *adv.*: ~ *angeben* or *aufführen* specify, *esp. Am.* itemize; '**~ne** *m* (-n/-n) *the* individual; '**~verkauf** *m* retail sale; '**~wesen** *n* individual.

'**einziehen** (*irr.* ziehen, *sep.*, *-ge-*) **1.** *v/t.* (*h*) draw in; *esp.* ⊕ retract; ✗ call up, *Am.* draft, induct; ⚔ seize, confiscate; make (*inquiries*) (*über acc.* on, about); **2.** *v/i.* (*sein*) enter; move in; *liquid*: soak in; ~ *in* (*acc.*) move into (*flat, etc.*).

einzig *adj.* ['aɪntsɪç] only; single; sole; unique; '**~artig** *adj.* unique, singular.

'**Einzug** *m* entry, entrance; moving in.

'**einzwängen** *v/t.* (*sep.*, *-ge-*, *h*) squeeze, jam.

Eis [aɪs] *n* (-es/*no pl.*) ice; ice-cream; '**~bahn** *f* skating-rink; '**~bär** *zo. m* polar bear; '**~bein** *n* pickled pork shank; '**~berg** *m* iceberg; '**~decke** *f* sheet of ice; '**~diele** *f* ice-cream parlo(u)r.

Eisen ['aɪzən] *n* (-s/-) iron.

'**Eisenbahn** *f* railway, *Am.* railroad; *mit der* ~ by rail, by train; '**~er** *m* (-s/-) railwayman; '**~fahrt** *f* railway journey; '**~knotenpunkt** *m* (railway) junction; '**~unglück** *n* railway accident; '**~wagen** *m* railway carriage, *Am.* railroad car; coach.

'**Eisen|blech** *n* sheet-iron; '**~erz** *n* iron-ore; '**~gießerei** *f* iron-foundry; '2**haltig** *adj.* ferruginous; '**~hütte** *f* ironworks *sg., pl.*; '**~waren** *f/pl.* ironmongery, *esp. Am.* hardware; '**~warenhändler** *m* ironmonger, *esp. Am.* hardware dealer.

eisern *adj.* ['aɪzərn] iron, of iron.

'**Eis|gang** *m* breaking up of the ice; ice-drift; 2**gekühlt** *adj.* ['~gəkyːlt] iced; '2**grau** *adj.* hoary; '**~hockey** *n* ice-hockey; 2**ig** *adj.* ['aɪzɪç] icy; '2'**kalt** *adj.* icy (cold); '**~kunstlauf** *m* figure-skating; '**~lauf** *m*, '**~laufen** *n* (-s/*no pl.*) skating; skate; '**~läufer** *m* skater; '**~meer** *n* polar sea; '**~schnellauf** *m* speed-skating; '**~scholle** *f* ice-floe; '**~schrank** *m s. Kühlschrank*; '**~vogel** *orn. m* kingfisher; '**~zapfen** *m* icicle; '**~zeit** *geol. f* ice-age.

eitel *adj.* ['aɪtəl] vain (*auf acc.* of); conceited; mere; '2**keit** *f* (-/-en) vanity.

Eiter ⚕ ['aɪtər] *m* (-s/*no pl.*) matter, pus; '**~beule** ⚕ *f* abscess; '2**ig** ⚕ *adj.* purulent; '2**n** ⚕ *v/i.* (*sep.*, *-ge-*, *h*) fester, suppurate; '**~ung** ⚕ *f* (-/-en) suppuration.

eitrig ⚕ *adj.* ['aɪtrɪç] purulent.

'**Eiweiß** *n* (-es/-e) white of egg; ⚕ albumen; '2**haltig** ⚕ *adj.* albuminous.

'**Eizelle** *f* egg-cell, ovum.

Ekel ['eːkəl] **1.** *m* (-s/*no pl.*) disgust (*vor dat.* at), loathing, aversion; ⚕ nausea; **2.** F *n* (-s/-) nasty person; '2**erregend** *adj.* nauseating, sickening; '2**haft** *adj.*, '2**ig** *adj.* revolting; *fig.* disgusting; '2**n** *v/refl.* (*sep.*, *-ge-*, *h*): *sich* ~ be nauseated (*vor dat.* at); *fig.* be or feel disgusted (at).

eklig *adj.* ['eːklɪç] *s. ekelhaft*.

elasti|sch *adj.* [e'lastɪʃ] elastic; 2**zität** [~tsi'tɛːt] *f* (-/*no pl.*) elasticity.

Elch *zo.* [ɛlç] *m* (-[e]s/-e) elk; moose.

Elefant *zo.* [ele'fant] *m* (-en/-en) elephant.

elegan|t adj. [ele'gant] elegant; smart; **2z** [~ts] f (-/no pl.) elegance.

elektrifizier|en [elektrifi'tsi:rən] v/t. (no -ge-, h) electrify; **2ung** f (-/-en) electrification.

Elektri|ker [e'lektrikər] m (-s/-) electrician; **2sch** adj. electric(al); **2sieren** [~'zi:rən] v/t. (no -ge-, h) electrify.

Elektrizität [elektritsi'tɛ:t] f (-/no pl.) electricity; **~sgesellschaft** f electricity supply company; **~swerk** n (electric) power station, power-house, Am. power plant.

Elektrode [elek'tro:də] f (-/-n) electrode.

Elektro|gerät [e'lektro-] n electric appliance; **~lyse** [~'ly:zə] f (-/-n) electrolysis.

Elektron ⚡ [e'lektron] n (-s/-en) electron; **~engehirn** [~'tro:nən-] n electronic brain; **~ik** [~'tro:nik] f (-/no pl.) electronics sg.

Elektro'technik f electrical engineering; **~er** m electrical engineer.

Element [ele'ment] n (-[e]s/-e) element.

elementar adj. [elemen'ta:r] elementary; **2schule** elementary or primary school, Am. grade school.

Elend ['e:lent] **1.** n (-[e]s/no pl.) misery; need, distress; **2.** ⚓ adj. miserable, wretched; needy, distressed; **'~sviertel** n slums pl.

elf [elf] **1.** adj. eleven; **2.** ⚓ f (-/-en) eleven (a. sports).

Elf [~] m (-en/-en), **~e** ['elfə] f (-/-n) elf, fairy.

'Elfenbein n (-[e]s/⚓-e) ivory; **2ern** adj. ivory.

Elf'meter m football: penalty kick; **~marke** f penalty spot.

'elfte adj. eleventh.

Elite [e'li:tə] f (-/-n) élite.

'Ellbogen anat. m (-s/-) elbow.

Elle ['ɛlə] f (-/-n) yard; anat. ulna.

Elster orn. ['ɛlstər] f (-/-n) magpie.

elter|lich adj. ['ɛltərliç] parental; **'2n** pl. parents pl.; **~nlos** adj. parentless, orphaned; **'2nteil** m parent. [(-/-n) enamel.]

Email [e'ma:j] n (-s/-s), **~le** [~] f)

Emanzipation [emantsipa'tsjo:n] f (-/-en) emancipation.

Embargo [em'bargo] n (-s/-s) embargo.

Embolie ⚓ [ɛmbo'li:] f (-/-n) embolism.

Embryo biol. ['ɛmbryo] m (-s/-s, -nen) embryo.

Emigrant [emi'grant] m (-en/-en) emigrant.

empfahl [ɛm'pfa:l] pret. of empfehlen.

Empfang [ɛm'pfaŋ] m (-[e]s/⚓e) reception (a. radio); on receipt (of s.th.); nach or bei ~ on receipt; **'2en** v/t. (irr. fangen, no -ge-, h) receive; welcome; conceive (child).

Empfänger [ɛm'pfɛŋər] m (-s/-) receiver, recipient; payee (of money); addressee (of letter); ⚓ consignee (of goods).

em'pfänglich adj. susceptible (für to); **2keit** f (-/no pl.) susceptibility.

Em'pfangs|dame f receptionist; **~gerät** n receiver, receiving set; **~schein** m receipt; **~zimmer** n reception-room.

empfehl|en [ɛm'pfe:lən] v/t. (irr., no -ge-, h) recommend; commend; ~ Sie mich (dat.) please remember me to; **~enswert** adj. (re)commendable; **2ung** f (-/-en) recommendation; compliments pl.

empfinden [ɛm'pfindən] v/t. (irr. finden, no -ge-, h) feel; perceive.

empfindlich adj. [ɛm'pfintliç] sensitive (a. phot., ⚓) (für, gegen to); pred. a. susceptible (gegen to); delicate; tender; p.: touchy, sensitive; cold: severe; pain, loss, etc.: grievous; pain: acute; **2keit** f (-/-en) sensitivity; sensibility; touchiness; delicacy.

empfindsam adj. [ɛm'pfintza:m] sensitive; sentimental; **2keit** f (-/-en) sensitiveness; sentimentality.

Empfindung [ɛm'pfinduŋ] f (-/-en) perception; sensation; sentiment; **2slos** adj. insensible; esp. fig. unfeeling; **~svermögen** n faculty of perception.

empfohlen [ɛm'pfo:lən] p.p. of empfehlen.

empor adv. [ɛm'po:r] up, upwards.

empören [ɛm'pø:rən] v/t. (no -ge-, h) incense; shock; sich ~ revolt (a. fig.), rebel; grow furious (über acc. at); empört indignant, shocked (both: über acc. at).

em'por|kommen v/i. (irr. kommen, sep., -ge-, sein) rise (in the world); **2kömmling** [~kœmliŋ] m (-s/-e) upstart; **~ragen** v/i. (sep., -ge-, h) tower, rise; **~steigen** v/i. (irr. steigen, sep., -ge-, sein) rise, ascend.

Em'pörung f (-/-en) rebellion, revolt; indignation.

emsig adj. ['emziç] busy, industrious, diligent; **2keit** f (-/no pl.) busyness, industry, diligence.

Ende ['ɛndə] n (-s/-n) end; am ~ at or in the end; after all; eventually; zu ~ gehen end; expire; run short; **'2n** v/i. (ge-, h) end; cease, finish.

end|gültig adj. ['entgyltiç] final, definitive; **'~lich** adv. finally, at last; **~los** adj. ['~lo:s] endless; **'2punkt** m final point; **'2runde** f sports: final; **'2station** ⚓ f terminus, Am. terminal; **'2summe** f (sum) total.

Endung ling. ['enduŋ] f (-/-en) ending, termination.

Endzweck ['ent-] m ultimate object.

Energie [enɛr'giː] *f* (-/-n) energy;
2los *adj.* lacking (in) energy.
e'nergisch *adj.* vigorous; energetic.
eng *adj.* [ɛŋ] narrow; *clothes:* tight;
close; intimate; *im ~eren Sinne*
strictly speaking.
engagieren [ãga'ʒiːrən] *v/t.* (*no*
-ge-, h) engage, *Am. a.* hire.
Enge ['ɛŋə] *f* (-/-n) narrowness; *fig.*
straits *pl.*
Engel ['ɛŋəl] *m* (-s/-) angel.
'**engherzig** *adj.* ungenerous, petty.
Engländer ['ɛŋlɛndər] *m* (-s/-)
Englishman; *die ~ pl.* the English
pl.; '**~in** *f* (-/-nen) Englishwoman.
englisch *adj.* ['ɛŋliʃ] English;
British.
'**Engpaß** *m* defile, narrow pass, *Am.*
a. notch; *fig.* bottle-neck.
en gros † *adv.* [ãˈgroː] wholesale.
En'groshandel † *m* wholesale
trade.
'**engstirnig** *adj.* narrow-minded.
Enkel ['ɛŋkəl] *m* (-s/-) grandchild;
grandson; '**~in** *f* (-/-nen) grand-
daughter.
enorm *adj.* [e'nɔrm] enormous; *F*
fig. tremendous.
Ensemble *thea.*, *♪* [ã'sãːbəl] *n*
(-s/-s) ensemble; company.
entart|en [ɛnt'aːrtən] *v/i.* (*no -ge-,*
sein) degenerate; **2ung** *f* (-/-en)
degeneration.
entbehr|en [ɛnt'beːrən] *v/t.* (*no*
-ge-, h) lack; miss, want; do without; **~lich** *adj.* dispensable; superfluous; **2ung** *f* (-/-en) want, privation.
ent'bind|en (*irr. binden, no -ge-, h*)
1. *v/t.* dispense, release (*von* from);
deliver (*of a child*); **2.** *v/i.* be confined; **2ung** *f* dispensation, release;
2ungsheim *n* maternity
hospital.
ent'blöß|en *v/t.* (*no -ge-, h*) bare,
strip; uncover (*head*); **~t** *adj.* bare.
ent'deck|en *v/t.* (*no -ge-, h*) dis-
cover; detect; disclose; **~er** *m* (-s/-)
discoverer; **2ung** *f* discovery.
Ente ['ɛntə] *f* (-/-n) *orn.* duck; *false*
report: F canard, hoax.
ent'ehr|en *v/t.* (*no -ge-, h*) dis-
hono(u)r; **2ung** *f* degradation; rape.
ent'eign|en *v/t.* (*no -ge-, h*) ex-
propriate; dispossess; **2ung** *f* ex-
propriation; dispossession.
ent'erben *v/t.* (*no -ge-, h*) disinherit.
entern ['ɛntərn] *v/t.* (ge-, h) board,
grapple (*ship*).
ent|'fachen *v/t.* (*no -ge-, h*) kindle;
fig. a. rouse (*passions*); **~'fallen** *v/i.*
(*irr. fallen, no -ge-, sein*): *j-m ~*
escape s.o.; *fig.* slip s.o.'s memory;
auf j-n ~ fall to s.o.'s share; *s. weg-*
fallen; **~'falten** *v/t.* (*no -ge-, h*)
unfold; *fig.:* develop; display; *sich ~*
unfold; *fig.* develop (*zu* into).
ent'fern|en *v/t.* (*no -ge-, h*) remove;
sich ~ withdraw; **~t** *adj.* distant,

remote (*both a. fig.*); **2ung** *f* (-/-en)
removal; distance; range; **2ungs-**
messer *phot. m* (-s/-) range-finder.
ent'flammen (*no -ge-*) *v/t.* (h) *and*
v/i. (*sein*) inflame; **~'fliehen** *v/i.*
(*irr. fliehen, no -ge-, sein*) flee,
escape (*aus or dat.* from); **~'frem-**
den *v/t.* (*no -ge-, h*) estrange,
alienate (*j-m* from s.o.).
ent'führ|en *v/t.* (*no -ge-, h*) abduct,
kidnap; run away with; **2er** *m*
abductor, kidnap(p)er; **2ung** *f* ab-
duction, kidnap(p)ing.
ent'gegen 1. *prp.* (*dat.*) in opposition
to, contrary to; against; **2.** *adv.*
towards; **~gehen** *v/i.* (*irr. gehen,*
sep., -ge-, sein) go to meet; **~ge-**
setzt *adj.* opposite; *fig.* contrary;
~halten *v/t.* (*irr. halten, sep., -ge-,*
h) hold out; *fig.* object; **~kommen**
v/i. (*irr. kommen, sep., -ge-, sein*)
come to meet; *fig.* meet s.o.('s
wishes) halfway; **2kommen** *n*
(-s/*no pl.*) obligingness; **~kommend**
adj. obliging; **~nehmen** *v/t.* (*irr.*
nehmen, sep., -ge-, h) accept,
receive; **~sehen** *v/i.* (*dat.*) (*irr.*
sehen, sep., -ge-, h) await; look forward to; **~setzen** *v/t.* (*sep., -ge-, h*)
oppose; **~stehen** *v/i.* (*irr. stehen,*
sep., -ge-, h) be opposed (*dat.* to);
~strecken *v/t.* (*sep., -ge-, h*) hold
or stretch out (*dat.* to); **~treten** *v/i.*
(*dat.*) (*irr. treten, sep., -ge-, sein*)
step up to s.o.; oppose; face (*danger*).
entgegn|en [ɛnt'geːgnən] *v/i.* (*no*
-ge-, h) reply; return; retort; **2ung**
f (-/-en) reply; retort.
ent'gehen *v/i.* (*irr. gehen, no -ge-,*
sein) escape.
entgeistert *adj.* [ɛnt'gaɪstərt] a-
ghast, thunderstruck, flabbergasted.
Entgelt [ɛnt'gɛlt] *n* (-[e]s/*no pl.*)
recompense; **2en** *v/t.* (*irr. gelten,*
no -ge-, h) atone or suffer or pay for.
entgleis|en [ɛnt'glaɪzən] *v/i.* (*no*
-ge-, sein) run off the rails, be
derailed; *fig.* (make a) slip; **2ung** *f*
(-/-en) derailment; *fig.* slip.
ent'gleiten *v/i.* (*irr. gleiten, no -ge-,*
sein) slip (*dat.* from).
ent'halt|en *v/t.* (*irr. halten, no*
-ge-, h) contain, hold, include;
sich ~ (*gen.*) abstain or refrain from;
~sam *adj.* abstinent; **2samkeit** *f*
(-/*no pl.*) abstinence; **2ung** *f* (-/-en)
abstention.
ent'haupten *v/t.* (*no -ge-, h*) behead,
decapitate.
ent'hüll|en *v/t.* (*no -ge-, h*) un-
cover; unveil; *fig.* reveal, disclose;
2ung *f* (-/-en) uncovering; unveil-
ing; *fig.* revelation, disclosure.
Enthusias|mus [ɛntuzi'asmus] *m*
(-/*no pl.*) enthusiasm; **~t** *m* (-en/-en)
enthusiast; *film, sports:* F fan;
2tisch *adj.* enthusiastic.
ent'kleiden *v/t. and v/refl.* (*no -ge-,*
h) undress.

ent'kommen 1. v/i. (irr. kommen, no -ge-, sein) escape (j-m s.o.; aus from), get away or off; 2. 2 n (-s/no pl.) escape.

entkräft|en [ɛnt'krɛftən] v/t. (no -ge-, h) weaken, debilitate; fig. refute; 2ung f (-/-en) weakening; debility; fig. refutation.

ent'lad|en v/t. (irr. laden, no -ge-, h) unload; esp. ∉ discharge; explode; sich ~ esp. ∉ discharge; gun: go off; anger: vent itself; 2ung f unloading; esp. ∉ discharge; explosion.

ent'lang 1. prp. (dat.; acc.) along; 2. adv. along; er geht die Straße ~ he goes along the street.

ent'larven v/t. (no -ge-, h) unmask; fig. a. expose.

ent'lass|en v/t. (irr. lassen, no -ge-, h) dismiss, discharge; F give s.o. the sack, Am. a. fire; 2ung f (-/-en) dismissal, discharge; 2ungsgesuch n resignation.

ent'lasten v/t. (no -ge-, h) unburden; ⅌ exonerate, clear (from suspicion).

Ent'lastung f (-/-en) relief; discharge; exoneration; ~sstraße f by-pass (road); ~szeuge m witness for the defen|ce, Am. -se.

ent'|laufen v/i. (irr. laufen, no -ge-, sein) run away (dat. from); ~ledigen [~'le:digən] v/refl. (gen.) (no -ge-, h): rid o.s. of s.th., get rid of s.th.; acquit o.s. of (duty); execute (orders); ~'leeren v/t. (no -ge-, h) empty.   [of-the-way.]

ent'legen adj. remote, distant, out-

ent'|lehnen v/t. (no -ge-, h) borrow (dat. or aus from); ~'locken v/t. (no -ge-, h) draw, elicit (dat. from); ~'lohnen v/t. (no -ge-, h) pay (off); ~'lüften v/t. (no -ge-, h) ventilate; ~militarisieren [~militari'zi:rən] v/t. (no -ge-, h) demilitarize; ~mutigen [~'mu:tigən] v/t. (no -ge-, h) discourage; ~'nehmen v/t. (irr. nehmen, no -ge-, h) take (dat. from); ~ aus (with)draw from; fig. gather or learn from; ~'rätseln v/t. (no -ge-, h) unriddle; ~'reißen v/t. (irr. reißen, no -ge-, h) snatch away (dat. from); ~'richten v/t. (no -ge-, h) pay; ~'rinnen v/i. (irr. rinnen, no -ge-, sein) escape (dat. from); ~'rollen v/t. (no -ge-, h) unroll; ~'rücken v/t. (no -ge-, h) remove (dat. from), carry off or away; ~'rückt adj. entranced; lost in thought.

ent'rüst|en v/t. (no -ge-, h) fill with indignation; sich ~ become angry or indignant (über acc. at s.th., with s.o.); ~et adj. indignant (über acc. at s.th., with s.o.); 2ung f indignation.

ent'sag|en v/i. (no -ge-, h) renounce, resign; 2ung f (-/-en) renunciation, resignation.

ent'schädig|en v/t. (no -ge-, h) indemnify, compensate; 2ung f indemnification, indemnity; compensation.

ent'scheid|en (irr. scheiden, no -ge-, h) 1. v/t. decide; sich ~ question, etc.: be decided; p.: decide (für for; gegen against; über acc. on); come to a decision; 2. v/i. decide; ~end adj. decisive; crucial; 2ung f decision.

entschieden adj. [ɛnt'ʃi:dən] decided; determined, resolute; 2heit f (-/no pl.) determination.

ent'schließen v/refl. (irr. schließen, no -ge-, h) resolve, decide, determine (zu on s.th.; zu inf. to inf.), make up one's mind (zu inf. to inf.).

ent'schlossen adj. resolute, determined; 2heit f (-/no pl.) resoluteness.

ent'schlüpfen v/i. (no -ge-, sein) escape, slip (dat. from).

Ent'schluß m resolution, resolve, decision, determination.

entschuldig|en [ɛnt'ʃuldigən] v/t. (no -ge-, h) excuse; sich ~ apologize (bei to; für for); sich ~ lassen beg to be excused; 2ung f (-/-en) excuse; apology; ich bitte (Sie) um ~ I beg your pardon.

ent'senden v/t. (irr. senden, no -ge-, h) send off, dispatch; delegate, depute.

ent'setz|en 1. v/t. (no -ge-, h) dismiss (from a position); ✗ relieve; frighten; sich ~ be terrified or shocked (über acc. at); 2. 2 n (-/no pl.) horror, fright; ~lich adj. horrible, dreadful, terrible, shocking.

ent'sinnen v/refl. (gen.) (irr. sinnen, no -ge-, h) remember or recall s.o., s.th.

ent'spann|en v/t. (no -ge-, h) relax; unbend; sich ~ relax; political situation: ease; 2ung f relaxation; pol. détente.

ent'sprech|en v/i. (irr. sprechen, no -ge-, h) answer (description, etc.); correspond to; meet (demand); ~end adj. corresponding; appropriate; 2ung f (-/-en) equivalent.

ent'springen v/i. (irr. springen, no -ge-, sein) escape (dat. from); river: rise, Am. head; s. entstehen.

ent'stammen v/i. (no -ge-, sein) be descended from; come from or of, originate from.

ent'steh|en v/i. (irr. stehen. no -ge-, sein) arise, originate (both: aus from); 2ung f (-/-en) origin.

ent'stell|en v/t. (no -ge-, h) disfigure; deface, deform; distort; 2ung f disfigurement; distortion, misrepresentation.

ent'täusch|en v/t. (no -ge-, h) disappoint; 2ung f disappointment.

ent'thronen v/t. (no -ge-, h) dethrone.

entvölker|n [ɛnt'fœlkərn] v/t. (no

-ge-, *h*) depopulate; 2**ung** *f* (-/-en) depopulation.

ent'wachsen *v/i.* (*irr.* wachsen, *no* -ge-, sein) outgrow.

entwaffn|en [ɛnt'vafnən] *v/t.* (*no* -ge-, *h*) disarm; 2**ung** *f* (-/-en) disarmament.

ent'warnen *v/i.* (*no -ge-, h*) *civil defence*: sound the all-clear (signal).

ent'wässer|n *v/t.* (*no -ge-, h*) drain; 2**ung** *f* (-/-en) drainage; ⚗ dehydration.

ent'weder *cj.*: ~ ... *oder* either ... or.

ent|'weichen *v/i.* (*irr.* weichen, *no* -ge-, sein) escape (*aus* from); ~'**weihen** *v/t.* (*no -ge-, h*) desecrate, profane; ~'**wenden** *v/t.* (*no -ge-, h*) pilfer, purloin (*j-m et.* s.th. from s.o.); ~'**werfen** *v/t.* (*irr.* werfen, *no* -ge-, *h*) draft, draw up (*document*); design; sketch, trace out, outline; plan.

ent'wert|en *v/t.* (*no -ge-, h*) depreciate, devaluate; cancel (*stamp*); 2**ung** *f* depreciation, devaluation; cancellation.

ent'wickeln *v/t.* (*no -ge-, h*) develop (*a. phot.*); evolve; *sich* ~ develop.

Entwicklung [ɛnt'vikluŋ] *f* (-/-en) development; evolution; ~**shilfe** *f* development aid.

ent|'wirren *v/t.* (*no -ge-, h*) disentangle, unravel; ~'**wischen** *v/i.* (*no* -ge-, sein) slip away, escape (*j-m* [from] s.o.; *aus* from); *j-m* ~ give s.o. the slip; ~'**wöhnen** [~'vø:nən] *v/t.* (*no -ge-, h*) wean.

Ent'wurf *m* sketch; design; plan; draft.

ent|'wurzeln *v/t.* (*no -ge-, h*) uproot; ~'**ziehen** *v/t.* (*irr.* ziehen, *no* -ge-, *h*) deprive (*j-m et.* s.o. of s.th.); withdraw (*dat.* from); *sich* ~ avoid, elude; evade (*responsibility*); ~'**ziffern** *v/t.* (*no -ge-, h*) decipher, make out; *tel.* decode.

ent'zück|en 1. *v/t.* (*no -ge-, h*) charm, delight; **2.** 2 *n* (-s/no *pl.*) delight, rapture(s *pl.*), transport(s *pl.*).

ent'zückend *adj.* delightful; charming.

Ent'zug *m* (-[e]s/*no pl.*) withdrawal; cancellation (*of licence*); deprivation.

entzünd|bar *adj.* [ɛnt'tsyntbɑːr] (in)flammable; ~**en** *v/t.* (*no -ge-, h*) inflame (*a.* ⚗), kindle; *sich* ~ catch fire; ⚗ become inflamed; 2**ung** *f* ⚗ inflammation.

ent'zwei *adv.* asunder, in two, to pieces; ~**en** *v/t.* (*no -ge-, h*) disunite, set at variance; *sich* ~ quarrel, fall out (*both*: *mit* with); ~**gehen** *v/i.* (*irr.* gehen, *sep.*, -ge-, sein) break, go to pieces; 2**ung** *f* (-/-en) disunion.

Enzian ⚘ ['ɛntsjɑːn] *m* (-s/-e) gentian.

Enzyklopädie [ɛntsyklopɛ'diː] *f* (-/-n) (en)cyclop(a)edia.

Epidemie ⚗ [epide'miː] *f* (-/-n) epidemic (disease).

Epilog [epi'loːk] *m* (-s/-e) epilog(ue).

episch *adj.* ['eːpiʃ] epic.

Episode [epi'zoːdə] *f* (-/-n) episode.

Epoche [e'pɔxə] *f* (-/-n) epoch.

Epos ['eːpɔs] *n* (-/Epen) epic (poem).

er *pers. pron.* [eːr] he.

erachten [ɛr'-] **1.** *v/t.* (*no -ge-, h*) consider, think, deem; **2.** 2 *n* (-s/no *pl.*) opinion; *m-s* ~*s* in my opinion.

erbarmen [ɛr'barmən] **1.** *v/refl.* (*gen.*) (*no -ge-, h*) pity *or* commiserate *s.o.*; **2.** 2 *n* (-s/no *pl.*) pity, compassion, commiseration; mercy; ~**swert** *adj.* pitiable.

erbärmlich *adj.* [ɛr'bɛrmliç] pitiful, pitiable; miserable; *behaviour*: mean.

er'barmungslos *adj.* pitiless, merciless, relentless.

er'bau|en *v/t.* (*no -ge-, h*) build (up), construct, raise; *fig.* edify; 2**er** *m* (-s/-) builder; constructor; ~**lich** *adj.* edifying; 2**ung** *fig.* *f* (-/-en) edification, *Am.* uplift.

Erbe ['ɛrbə] **1.** *m* (-n/-n) heir; **2.** *n* (-s/no *pl.*) inheritance, heritage.

er'beben *v/i.* (*no -ge-, sein*) tremble, shake, quake.

'erben *v/t.* (ge-, *h*) inherit.

er'beuten *v/t.* (*no -ge-, h*) capture.

er'bieten *v/refl.* (*irr.* bieten, *no -ge-, h*) offer, volunteer.

'Erbin *f* (-/-nen) heiress.

er'bitten *v/t.* (*irr.* bitten, *no -ge-, h*) beg *or* ask for, request, solicit.

er'bitter|n *v/t.* (*no -ge-, h*) embitter, exasperate; 2**ung** *f* (-/⚗, -en) bitterness, exasperation.

Erbkrankheit ⚗ ['ɛrp-] *f* hereditary disease.

erblassen [ɛr'blasən] *v/i.* (*no -ge-, sein*) grow *or* turn pale, lose colo(u)r.

Erblasser ⚖ ['ɛrplasər] *m* (-s/-) testator; '~**in** *f* (-/-nen) testatrix.

er'bleichen *v/i.* (*no -ge-, sein*) *s.* erblassen.

erblich *adj.* ['ɛrpliç] hereditary; 2**keit** *physiol.* *f* (-/no *pl.*) heredity.

er'blicken *v/t.* (*no -ge-, h*) perceive, see; catch sight of.

erblind|en [ɛr'blindən] *v/i.* (*no -ge-, sein*) grow blind; 2**ung** *f* (-/-en) loss of sight.

er'brechen 1. *v/t.* (*irr.* brechen, *no* -ge-, *h*) break *or* force open; vomit; *sich* ~ ⚗ vomit; **2.** 2 *n* (-s/no *pl.*) vomiting.

Erbschaft ['ɛrpʃaft] *f* (-/-en) inheritance, heritage.

Erbse ⚘ ['ɛrpsə] *f* (-/-n) pea; '~**brei** *m* pease-pudding, *Am.* pea purée; '~**nsuppe** *f* pea-soup.

Erb|stück ['ɛrp-] *n* heirloom; '~**sünde** *f* original sin; '~**teil** *n* (portion of an) inheritance.

Erd|arbeiter ['eːrt-] *m* digger, navvy; '∼ball *m* globe; '∼beben *n* (-s/-) earthquake; '∼beere & *f* strawberry; '∼boden *m* earth; ground, soil; ∼e ['eːrdə] *f* (-/∼ -n) earth; ground; soil; world; '≗en & *v/t.* (ge-, *h*) earth, ground.

er'denklich *adj.* imaginable.

Erdgeschoß ['eːrt-] *n* ground-floor, *Am.* first floor.

er'dicht|en *v/t.* (no -ge-, *h*) invent, feign; ∼et *adj.* fictitious.

erdig *adj.* ['eːrdiç] earthy.

Erd|karte ['eːrt-] *f* map of the earth; '∼kreis *m* earth, world; '∼kugel *f* globe; '∼kunde *f* geography; '∼leitung & & *f* earth-connexion, earth-wire, *Am.* ground wire; '∼nuß *f* peanut; '∼öl *n* mineral oil, petroleum.

er'dolchen *v/t.* (no -ge-, *h*) stab (with a dagger).

Erdreich ['eːrt-] *n* ground, earth.

er'dreisten *v/refl.* (no -ge-, *h*) dare, presume.

er'drosseln *v/t.* (no-ge-, *h*) strangle, throttle.

er'drücken *v/t.* (no -ge-, *h*) squeeze or crush to death; ∼d *fig. adj.* overwhelming.

Erd|rutsch ['eːrt-] *m* landslip; landslide (*a. pol.*); '∼schicht *f* layer of earth, stratum; '∼teil *m* part of the world; *geogr.* continent.

er'dulden *v/t.* (no -ge-, *h*) suffer, endure.

er'eifern *v/refl.* (no -ge-, *h*) get excited, fly into a passion.

er'eignen *v/refl.* (no -ge-, *h*) happen, come to pass, occur.

Ereignis [ɛr'aiknis] *n* (-ses/-se) event, occurrence; ≗reich *adj.* eventful.

Eremit [ere'miːt] *m* (-en/-en) hermit, anchorite.

ererbt *adj.* [ɛr'ɛrpt] inherited.

er'fahr|en 1. *v/t.* (*irr. fahren*, no -ge-, *h*) learn; hear; experience; 2. *adj.* experienced, expert, skil(l)-ful; ≗ung *f* (-/-en) experience; practice; skill.

er'fassen *v/t.* (no -ge-, *h*) grasp (*a. fig.*), seize, catch; cover; register, record.

er'find|en *v/t.* (*irr. finden*, no -ge-, *h*) invent; ≗er *m* inventor; ∼erisch *adj.* inventive; ≗ung *f* (-/-en) invention.

Erfolg [ɛr'fɔlk] *m* (-[e]s/-e) success; result; ≗en [∼gən] *v/i.* (no -ge-, sein) ensue; follow; happen; ≗los *adj.* [∼k-] unsuccessful; vain; ≗-reich *adj.* [∼k-] successful.

er'forder|lich *adj.* necessary; required; ∼n *v/t.* (no -ge-, *h*) require; demand; ≗nis *n* (-ses/-se) requirement, demand, exigence, exigency.

er'forsch|en *v/t.* (no -ge-, *h*) inquire into, investigate; explore

(*country*); ≗er *m* investigator; explorer; ≗ung *f* investigation; exploration.

er'freu|en *v/t.* (no -ge-, *h*) please; delight; gratify; rejoice; *sich e-r Sache* ∼ enjoy s.th.; ∼lich *adj.* delightful, pleasing, pleasant, gratifying.

er'frier|en *v/i.* (*irr. frieren*, no -ge-, sein) freeze to death; ≗ung *f* (-/-en) frost-bite.

er'frisch|en *v/t.* (no -ge-, *h*) refresh; ≗ung *f* (-/-en) refreshment.

er'froren *adj.* limb: frost-bitten.

er'füll|en *v/t.* (no -ge-, *h*) fill; *fig.* fulfil(l); perform (*mission*); comply with (*s.o.'s wishes*); meet (*requirements*); ≗ung *f* fulfil(l)ment; performance; compliance; ≗ungsort ✝, ✝✝ [ɛr'fylʊŋs⁹-] *m* place of performance (*of contract*).

ergänz|en [ɛr'gɛntsən] *v/t.* (no -ge-, *h*) complete, complement; supplement; replenish (*stores, etc.*); ∼end *adj.* complementary, supplementary; ≗ung *f* (-/-en) completion; supplement; replenishment; *gr.* complement; ≗ungsband *m* (-[e]s/∼e) supplementary volume.

er'geben 1. *v/t.* (*irr. geben*, no -ge-, *h*) yield, give; prove; *sich* ∼ surrender; *difficulties:* arise; devote o.s. to *s.th.*; *sich* ∼ *aus* result from; *sich* ∼ *in* (acc.) resign o.s. to; 2. *adj.* devoted (*dat.* to); ∼st *adv.* respectfully; ≗heit *f* (-/no *pl.*) devotion.

Ergeb|nis [ɛr'geːpnis] *n* (-ses/-se) result, outcome; *sports:* score; ≗ung [∼bʊŋ] *f* (-/-en) resignation; ✕ surrender.

er'gehen *v/i.* (*irr. gehen*, no -ge-, sein) be issued; ∼ *lassen* issue, publish; *über sich* ∼ *lassen* suffer, submit to; *wie ist es ihm ergangen?* how did he come off?; *sich* ∼ *in* (*dat.*) indulge in.

ergiebig *adj.* [ɛr'giːbiç] productive, rich.

er'gießen *v/refl.* (*irr. gießen*, no -ge-, *h*) flow (*in* acc. into; *über* acc. over).

er'götz|en 1. *v/t.* (no -ge-, *h*) delight; *sich* ∼ *an* (*dat.*) delight in; 2. ≗ *n* (-s/no *pl.*) delight; ∼lich *adj.* delightful.

er'greif|en *v/t.* (*irr. greifen*, no -ge-, *h*) seize; grasp; take (*possession, s.o.'s part, measures, etc.*); take to (*flight*); take up (*profession, pen, arms*); *fig.* move, affect, touch; ≗ung *f* (-/∼ -en) seizure.

Er'griffenheit *f* (-/no *pl.*) emotion.

er'gründen *v/t.* (no -ge-, *h*) fathom; *fig.* penetrate, get to the bottom of.

Er'guß *m* outpouring; effusion.

er'haben *adj.* elevated; *fig.* exalted, sublime; ∼ *sein über* (*acc.*) be above; ≗heit *f* (-/∼ -en) elevation; *fig.* sublimity.

er'halt|en 1. v/t. (irr. halten, no -ge-, h) get; obtain; receive; preserve, keep; support, maintain; sich ~ von subsist on; 2. adj.: gut ~ in good repair or condition; 2ung f preservation; maintenance.

erhältlich adj. [ɛr'hɛltlɪç] obtainable.

er'|hängen v/t. (no -ge-, h) hang; ~'härten v/t. (no -ge-, h) harden; fig. confirm; ~'haschen v/t. (no -ge-, h) snatch, catch.

er'heb|en v/t. (irr. heben, no -ge-, h) lift, raise; elevate; exalt; levy, raise, collect (taxes, etc.); Klage ~ bring an action; sich ~ rise; question, etc.: arise; ~end fig. adj. elevating; ~lich adj. [~p-] considerable; 2ung f [~buŋ] f (-/-en) elevation; levy (of taxes); revolt; rising ground.

er'|heitern v/t. (no -ge-, h) cheer up, amuse; ~'hellen v/t. (no -ge-, h) light up; fig. clear up; ~'hitzen v/t. (no -ge-, h) heat; sich ~ get or grow hot; ~'hoffen v/t. (no -ge-, h) hope for.

er'höh|en v/t. (no -ge-, h) raise; increase; 2ung f (-/-en) elevation; rise (in prices, wages); advance (in prices); increase.

er'hol|en v/refl. (no -ge-, h) recover, (take a) rest, relax; 2ung f (-/-en) recovery; recreation; relaxation; 2ungsurlaub [ɛr'ho:luŋs°-] m holiday, Am. vacation; recreation leave; ~ convalescent leave, sickleave. [(request).]

er'hören v/t. (no -ge-, h) hear; grant)

erinner|n [ɛr'inərn] v/t. (no -ge-, h): j-n ~ an (acc.) remind s.o. of; sich ~ (gen.), sich ~ an (acc.) remember s.o. or s.th., recollect s.th.; 2ung f (-/-en) remembrance; recollection; reminder; ~en pl. reminiscences pl.

er'kalten v/i. (no -ge-, sein) cool down (a. fig.), get cold.

erkält|en [ɛr'kɛltən] v/refl. (no -ge-, h): sich (sehr) ~ catch (a bad) cold; 2ung f (-/-en) cold.

er'kennen v/t. (irr. kennen, no -ge-, h) recognize (an dat. by); perceive, discern; realize.

er'kenntlich adj. perceptible; sich ~ zeigen show one's appreciation; 2keit f (-/-en) gratitude; appreciation.

Er'kenntnis 1. f perception; realization; 2. ग̈ऽ n (-ses/-se) decision, sentence, finding.

Erker ['ɛrkər] m (-s/-) bay; ~fenster n bay-window.

er'klär|en v/t. (no -ge-, h) explain; account for; declare; state; sich ~ declare (für for; gegen against); ~lich adj. explainable, explicable; ~t adj. professed, declared; 2ung f explanation; declaration.

er'klingen v/i. (irr. klingen, no -ge-, sein) (re)sound, ring (out).

erkoren adj. [ɛr'ko:rən] (s)elect, chosen.

er'krank|en v/i. (no -ge-, sein) fall ill, be taken ill (an dat. of, with); become affected; 2ung f (-/-en) illness, sickness, falling ill.

er'|kühnen v/refl. (no -ge-, h) venture, presume, make bold (zu inf. to inf.); ~'kunden v/t. (no -ge-, h) explore; ✕ reconnoit|re, Am. -er.

erkundig|en [ɛr'kundigən] v/refl. (no -ge-, h) inquire (über acc. after; nach after or for s.o.; about s.th.); 2ung f (-/-en) inquiry.

er'lahmen fig. v/i. (no -ge-, sein) grow weary, tire; slacken; interest: wane, flag; ~'langen v/t. (no -ge-, h) obtain, get.

Er'laß [ɛr'las] m (Erlasses/Erlasse) dispensation, exemption; remission (of debt, penalty, etc.); edict, decree; 2'lassen v/t. (irr. lassen, no -ge-, h) remit (debt, penalty, etc.); dispense (j-m et. s.o. from s.th.); issue (decree); enact (law).

erlauben v/t. [ɛr'laubən] v/t. (no -ge-, h) allow, permit; sich et. ~ indulge in s.th.; sich ~ zu inf. ✝ beg to inf.

Erlaubnis [ɛr'laupnis] f (-/no pl.) permission; authority; ~schein m permit.

er'läuter|n v/t. (no -ge-, h) explain, illustrate; comment (up)on; 2ung f explanation, illustration; comment.

Erle ⚘ ['ɛrlə] f (-/-n) alder.

er'leb|en v/t. (no -ge-, h) (live to) see; experience; go through; 2nis [~pnis] n (-ses/-se) experience; adventure.

erledig|en [ɛr'le:digən] v/t. (no -ge-, h) dispatch; execute; settle (matter); ~t adj. [~çt] finished, settled; fig.: played out; F done for; F: du bist für mich ~ I am through with you; 2ung [~guŋ] f (-/~-en) dispatch; settlement.

er'leichter|n v/t. (no -ge-, h) lighten (burden); fig.: make easy, facilitate; relieve; 2ung f (-/-en) ease; relief; facilitation; ~en pl. facilities pl.

er'|leiden v/t. (irr. leiden, no -ge-, h) suffer, endure; sustain (damage, loss); ~'lernen v/t. (no -ge-, h) learn, acquire.

er'leucht|en v/t. (no -ge-, h) illuminate; fig. enlighten; 2ung f (-/-en) illumination; fig. enlightenment.

er'liegen v/i. (irr. liegen, no -ge-, sein) succumb (dat. to).

erlogen adj. [ɛr'lo:gən] false, untrue.

Er'lös [ɛr'lø:s] m (-es/-e) proceeds pl.

erlosch [ɛr'lɔʃ] pret. of erlöschen; ~en 1. p.p. of erlöschen; 2. adj. extinct.

er'löschen v/i. (irr., no -ge-, sein) go out; fig. become extinct; contract: expire.

er'lös|en v/t. (no -ge-, h) redeem;

deliver; 2er *m* (-s/-) redeemer, deliverer; *eccl.* Redeemer, Saviour; 2ung *f* redemption; deliverance.

er**mächtig|en** [ɛr'mɛçtigən] *v/t.* (*no* -ge-, *h*) authorize; 2ung *f* (-/-en) authorization; authority; warrant.

er'**mahn|en** *v/t.* (*no* -ge-, *h*) admonish; 2ung *f* admonition.

er'**mangel|n** *v/i.* (*no* -ge-, *h*) be wanting (*gen.* in); 2ung *f* (-/*no pl.*): *in* ~ (*gen.*) in default of, for want of, failing.

er'**mäßig|en** *v/t.* (*no* -ge-, *h*) abate, reduce, cut (down); 2ung *f* (-/-en) abatement, reduction.

er'**matt|en** (*no* -ge-) 1. *v/t.* (*h*) fatigue, tire, exhaust; 2. *v/i.* (*sein*) tire, grow weary; *fig.* slacken; 2ung *f* (-/~ -en) fatigue, exhaustion.

er'**messen** 1. *v/t.* (*irr.* messen, *no* -ge-, *h*) judge; 2. 2 *n* (-s/*no pl.*) judg(e)ment; discretion.

er'**mitt|eln** *v/t.* (*no* -ge-, *h*) ascertain, find out; ⚖ investigate; 2(e)-lung [~(ə)luŋ] *f* (-/-en) ascertainment; inquiry; ⚖ investigation.

er'**möglichen** *v/t.* (*no* -ge-, *h*) render *or* make possible.

er'**mord|en** *v/t.* (*no* -ge-, *h*) murder; assassinate; 2ung *f* (-/-en) murder; assassination.

er'**müd|en** (*no* -ge-) 1. *v/t.* (*h*) tire, fatigue; 2. *v/i.* (*sein*) tire, get tired *or* fatigued; 2ung *f* (-/~-en) fatigue, tiredness.

er'**munter|n** *v/t.* (*no* -ge-, *h*) rouse, encourage; animate; 2ung *f* (-/-en) encouragement, animation.

er**mutig|en** [ɛr'muːtigən] *v/t.* (*no* -ge-, *h*) encourage; 2ung *f* (-/-en) encouragement.

er'**nähr|en** *v/t.* (*no* -ge-, *h*) nourish, feed; support; 2er *m* (-s/-) breadwinner, supporter; 2ung *f* (-/~-en) nourishment; support; *physiol.* nutrition.

er'**nenn|en** *v/t.* (*irr.* nennen, *no* -ge-, *h*) nominate, appoint; 2ung *f* nomination, appointment.

er'**neu|ern** *v/t.* (*no* -ge-, *h*) renew, renovate; revive; 2erung *f* renewal, renovation; revival; ~t *adv.* once more.

er**niedrig|en** [ɛr'niːdrigən] *v/t.* (*no* -ge-, *h*) degrade; humiliate, humble; 2ung *f* (-/-en) degradation; humiliation.

Ernst [ɛrnst] 1. *m* (-es/*no pl.*) seriousness; earnest(ness); gravity; *im* ~ in earnest; 2. 2 *adj.* = 2**haft** *adj.*, 2**lich** *adj.* serious, earnest; grave.

Ernte ['ɛrntə] *f* (-/-n) harvest; crop; ~'**dankfest** *n* harvest festival; 2**n** *v/t.* (ge-, *h*) harvest, gather (in), reap (*a. fig.*).

er'**nüchter|n** *v/t.* (*no* -ge-, *h*) (make) sober; *fig.* disillusion; 2ung *f* (-/-en) sobering; *fig.* disillusionment.

Er'**ober|er** *m* (-s/-) conqueror; 2n *v/t.* (*no* -ge-, *h*) conquer; ~ung *f* (-/-en) conquest.

er'**öffn|en** *v/t.* (*no* -ge-, *h*) open; inaugurate; disclose (*j-m et. s.th. to s.o.*); notify; 2ung *f* opening; inauguration; disclosure.

erörter|n [ɛr'œrtərn] *v/t.* (*no* -ge-, *h*) discuss; 2ung *f* (-/-en) discussion.

Erpel *orn.* ['ɛrpəl] *m* (-s/-) drake.

erpicht *adj.* [ɛr'piçt]: ~ *auf* (*acc.*) bent *or* intent *or* set *or* keen on.

er'**press|en** *v/t.* (*no* -ge-, *h*) extort (*von* from); blackmail; 2er *m* (-s/-) 2**erin** *f* (-/-nen) extort(ion)er; blackmailer; 2ung *f* (-/-en) extortion; blackmail.

er'**proben** *v/t.* (*no* -ge-, *h*) try, test.

erquick|en [ɛr'kvikən] *v/t.* (*no* -ge-, *h*) refresh; 2ung *f* (-/-en) refreshment.

er|'**raten** *v/t.* (*irr.* raten, *no* -ge-, *h*) guess, find out; ~'**rechnen** *v/t.* (*no* -ge-, *h*) calculate, compute, work out.

erreg|bar *adj.* [ɛr'eːkbaːr] excitable; ~en [~gən] *v/t.* (*no* -ge-, *h*) excite; cause; 2er *m* (-s/-) exciter (*a. ⚡*); 🩺 germ, virus; 2ung [~guŋ] *f* excitation; excitement.

er'**reich|bar** *adj.* attainable; within reach *or* call; ~en *v/t.* (*no* -ge-, *h*) reach; *fig.* achieve, attain; catch (*train*); come up to (*certain standard*).

er'**rett|en** *v/t.* (*no* -ge-, *h*) rescue; 2ung *f* rescue.

er'**richt|en** *v/t.* (*no* -ge-, *h*) set up, erect; establish; 2ung *f* erection; establishment.

er|'**ringen** *v/t.* (*irr.* ringen, *no* -ge-, *h*) gain, obtain; achieve (*success*); ~'**röten** *v/i.* (*no* -ge-, *sein*) blush.

Errungenschaft [ɛr'ruŋənʃaft] *f* (-/-en) acquisition; achievement.

Er'**satz** *m* (-es/*no pl.*) replacement; substitute; compensation; amends *sg.*, damages *pl.*; indemnification; *s.* Ersatzmann, Ersatzmittel; ~ **leisten** make amends; ~**mann** *m* substitute; ~**mine** *f* refill (*for pencil*); ~**mittel** *n* substitute, surrogate; ~**reifen** *mot.* *m* spare tyre, (*Am. only*) spare tire; ~**teil** ⊕ *n, m* spare part).

er'**schaff|en** *v/t.* (*irr.* schaffen, *no* -ge-, *h*) create; 2ung *f* (-/*no pl.*) creation.

er'**schallen** *v/i.* ([*irr.* schallen,] *no* -ge-, *sein*) (re)sound; ring.

er'**schein|en** 1. *v/i.* (*irr.* scheinen, *no* -ge-, *sein*) appear; 2. 2 *n* (-s/*no pl.*) appearance; 2ung *f* (-/-en) appearance; apparition; vision.

er|'**schießen** *v/t.* (*irr.* schießen, *no* -ge-, *h*) shoot (dead); ~'**schlaffen** *v/i.* (*no* -ge-, *sein*) tire; relax; *fig.* languish, slacken; ~'**schlagen** *v/t.* (*irr.* schlagen, *no* -ge-, *h*) kill, slay;

~'schließen v/t. (irr. schließen, no -ge-, h) open; open up (new market); develop (district).

er'schöpf|en v/t. (no -ge-, h) exhaust; 2ung f exhaustion.

erschrak [ɛr'ʃraːk] pret. of erschrecken 2.

er'schrecken 1. v/t. (no -ge-, h) frighten, scare; 2. v/i. (irr., no -ge-, sein) be frightened (über acc. at); ~d adj. alarming, startling.

erschrocken [ɛr'ʃrɔkən] 1. p.p. of erschrecken 2; 2. adj. frightened, terrified.

erschütter|n [ɛr'ʃytərn] v/t. (no -ge-, h) shake; fig. shock, move; 2ung f (-/-en) shock; fig. emotion; ✗ concussion; ⊕ percussion.

er'schweren v/t. (no -ge-, h) make more difficult; aggravate.

er'schwing|en v/t. (irr. schwingen, no -ge-, h) afford; ~lich adj. within s.o.'s means; prices: reasonable.

er'seh|en v/t. (irr. sehen, no -ge-, h) see, learn, gather (all: aus from); ~'sehnen v/t. (no -ge-, h) long for; ~'setzen v/t. (no -ge-, h) repair; make up for, compensate (for); replace; refund.

er'sichtlich adj. evident, obvious.

er'sinnen v/t. (irr. sinnen, no -ge-, h) contrive, devise.

er'spar|en v/t. (no -ge-, h) save; j-m et. ~ spare s.o. s.th.; 2nis f (-/-se) saving.

er'sprießlich adj. useful, beneficial.

erst [eːrst] 1. adj.: der (die, das) ~e the first; 2. adv. first; at first; only; not ... till or until.

er'starr|en v/i. (no -ge-, sein) stiffen; solidify; congeal; set; grow numb; fig. blood: run cold; ~t adj. benumbed; 2ung f (-/-en) numbness; solidification; congealment; setting.

erstatt|en [ɛr'ʃtatən] v/t. (no -ge-, h) restore; s. ersetzen; Bericht ~ (make a) report; 2ung f (-/-en) restitution.

'Erstaufführung f thea. first night or performance, premiere; film: a. first run.

er'staun|en 1. v/i. (no -ge-, sein) be astonished (über acc. at); 2. v/t. (no -ge-, h) astonish; 3. 2 n astonishment; in ~ setzen astonish; ~lich adj. astonishing, amazing.

er'stechen v/t. (irr. stechen, no -ge-, h) stab.

er'steig|en v/t. (irr. steigen, no -ge-, h) ascend, climb; 2ung f ascent.

erstens adv. ['eːrstəns] first, firstly.

er'stick|en (no -ge-) v/t. (h) and v/i. (sein) choke, suffocate; stifle; 2ung f (-/-en) suffocation. [rate, F A 1.]

'erstklassig adj. first-class, first-]

er'streben v/t. (no -ge-, h) strive after or for; ~swert adj. desirable.

er'strecken v/refl. (no -ge-, h) extend; sich ~ über (acc.) cover.

er'suchen 1. v/t. (no -ge-, h) request; 2. 2 n (-s/-) request.

er|'tappen v/t. (no -ge-, h) catch, surprise; s. frisch; ~'tönen v/i. (no -ge-, sein) (re)sound.

Ertrag [ɛr'traːk] m (-[e]s/=e) produce, yield; proceeds pl., returns pl.; ✗ output; 2en [~gən] v/t. (irr. tragen, no -ge-, h) bear, endure; suffer; stand.

erträglich adj. [ɛr'trɛːklɪç] tolerable.

er|'tränken v/t. (no -ge-, h) drown; ~'trinken v/i. (irr. trinken, no -ge-, sein) be drowned, drown; ~übrigen [ɛr'yːbrigən] v/t. (no -ge-, h) save; spare (time); sich ~ be unnecessary; ~'wachen v/i. (no -ge-, sein) awake, wake up.

er'wachs|en 1. v/i. (irr. wachsen, no -ge-, sein) arise (aus from); 2. adj. grown-up, adult; 2e m, f (-n/-n) grown-up, adult.

er'wäg|en v/t. (irr. wägen, no -ge-, h) consider, think s.th. over; 2ung f (-/-en) consideration.

er'wählen v/t. (no -ge-, h) choose, elect.

er'wähn|en v/t. (no -ge-, h) mention; 2ung f (-/-en) mention.

er'wärmen v/t. (no -ge-, h) warm, heat; sich ~ warm (up).

er'wart|en v/t. (no -ge-, h) await, wait for; fig. expect; 2ung f expectation.

er|'wecken v/t. (no -ge-, h) wake, rouse; fig. awake; cause (fear); arouse (suspicion); ~'wehren v/refl. (gen.) (no -ge-, h) keep or ward off; ~'weichen v/t. (no -ge-, h) soften; fig. move; ~'weisen v/t. (irr. weisen, no -ge-, h) prove; show (respect); render (service); do, pay (honour); do (favour).

er'weiter|n v/t. and v/refl. (no -ge-, h) expand, enlarge, extend, widen; 2ung f (-/-en) expansion, enlargement, extension.

Erwerb [ɛr'vɛrp] m (-[e]s/-e) acquisition; living; earnings pl.; business; 2en [~bən] v/t. (irr. werben, no -ge-, h) acquire; gain; earn.

erwerbs|los adj. [ɛr'vɛrpsloːs] unemployed; ~tätig adj. (gainfully) employed; ~unfähig adj. [ɛr'vɛrps?-] incapable of earning one's living; 2zweig m line of business.

Erwerbung [ɛr'vɛrbuŋ] f acquisition.

erwider|n [ɛr'viːdərn] v/t. (no -ge-, h) return; answer, reply; retort; 2ung f (-/-en) return; answer, reply.

er'wischen v/t. (no -ge-, h) catch, trap, get hold of.

er'wünscht adj. desired; desirable; welcome.

er'würgen v/t. (no -ge-, h) strangle, throttle.

Erz ⚒ [eːrts] *n* (-es/-e) ore; *poet.* brass.

er'zähl|en *v/t.* (*no* -ge-, *h*) tell; relate; narrate; **2er** *m*, **2erin** *f* (-/-nen) narrator; writer; **2ung** *f* narration; (short) story, narrative.

'Erz|bischof *eccl. m* archbishop; **'~bistum** *eccl. n* archbishopric; **'~engel** *eccl. m* archangel.

er'zeug|en *v/t.* (*no* -ge-, *h*) beget; produce; make, manufacture; **2er** *m* (-s/-) father (*of child*); † producer; **2nis** *n* produce; production; ⊕ product; **2ung** *f* production.

'Erz|feind *m* arch-enemy; **'~herzog** *m* archduke; **'~herzogin** *f* archduchess; **'~herzogtum** *n* archduchy.

er'ziehe|n *v/t.* (*irr.* ziehen, *no* -ge-, *h*) bring up, rear, raise; educate; **2r** *m* (-s/-) educator; teacher, tutor; **2rin** *f* (-/-nen) teacher; governess; **~risch** *adj.* educational, pedagogic (-al).

Er'ziehung *f* (-/⚒ -en) upbringing; breeding; education; **~sanstalt** [er'tsiːʊŋs'-] *f* reformatory, approved school; **~swesen** *n* (-s/*no pl.*) educational matters *pl.* or system.

er|'zielen *v/t.* (*no* -ge-, *h*) obtain; realize (*price*); achieve (*success*); *sports:* score (*points, goal*); **~'zürnen** *v/t.* (*no* -ge-, *h*) make angry, irritate, enrage; **~'zwingen** *v/t.* (*irr.* zwingen, *no* -ge-, *h*) (en)force; compel; extort (von from).

es *pers. pron.* [es] 1. *pers.:* it, he, she; *wo ist das Buch? — ~ ist auf dem Tisch* where is the book? — it is on the table; *das Mädchen blieb stehen, als ~ seine Mutter sah* the girl stopped when she saw her mother; 2. *impers.:* it; *~ gibt* there is, there are; *~ ist kalt* it is cold; *~ klopft* there is a knock at the door.

Esche ⚒ ['ɛʃə] *f* (-/-n) ash(-tree).

Esel *zo.* ['eːzəl] *m* (-s/-) donkey; *esp. fig.* ass; **~ei** [~'laɪ] *f* (-/-en) stupidity, stupid thing, folly; **'~sbrücke** *f at school:* crib, *Am.* pony; **~sohr** ['eːzəls'-] *n* dog's ear (*of book*).

Eskorte [ɛs'kɔrtə] *f* (-/-n) ⚒ escort; ⚓ convoy.

Espe ⚒ ['ɛspə] *f* (-/-n) asp(en).

'eßbar *adj.* eatable, edible.

Esse ['ɛsə] *f* (-/-n) chimney.

essen ['ɛsən] 1. *v/i.* (*irr.*, ge-, *h*) eat; *zu Mittag ~* (have) lunch; dine, have dinner; *zu Abend ~* dine, have dinner; *esp. late at night:* sup, have supper; *auswärts ~* eat *or* dine out; 2. *v/t.* (*irr.*, ge-, *h*) eat; *et. zu Mittag etc. ~* have s.th. for lunch, *etc.*; 3. **2** *n* (-s/-) eating; food; meal; dish; *midday meal:* lunch, dinner; *evening meal:* dinner; *last meal of the day:* supper; **'2szeit** *f* lunch-time; dinner-time; supper-time.

Essenz [ɛ'sɛnts] *f* (-/-en) essence.

Essig ['ɛsɪç] *m* (-s/-e) vinegar; **'~gurke** *f* pickled cucumber, gherkin.

'Eß|löffel *m* soup-spoon; **'~nische** *f* dining alcove, *Am.* dinette; **'~tisch** *m* dining-table; **'~waren** *f/pl.* eatables *pl.*, victuals *pl.*, food; **'~zimmer** *n* dining-room.

etablieren [eta'bliːrən] *v/t.* (*no* -ge-, *h*) establish, set up.

Etage [e'taːʒə] *f* (-/-n) floor, stor(e)y; **~nwohnung** *f* flat, *Am. a.* apartment.

Etappe [e'tapə] *f* (-/-n) ⚒ base; *fig.* stage, leg.

Etat [e'taː] *m* (-s/-s) budget, *parl. the* Estimates *pl.*; **~sjahr** *n* fiscal year. [*or sg.*]

Ethik ['eːtik] *f* (-/⚒ -en) ethics *pl.*]

Etikett [eti'ket] *n* (-[e]s/-e, -s) label, ticket; tag; *gummed: Am. a.* sticker; **~e** *f* (-/-n) etiquette; **2ieren** [~'tiːrən] *v/t.* (*no* -ge-, *h*) label.

etliche *indef. pron.* ['ɛtlɪçə] some, several.

Etui [e'tviː] *n* (-s/-s) case.

etwa *adv.* ['ɛtva] perhaps, by chance; about, around, *Am.* around; **~ig** *adj.* ['-ʔiç] possible, eventual.

etwas ['ɛtvas] 1. *indef. pron.* something; anything; 2. *adj.* some; any; 3. *adv.* somewhat; 4. **2** *n* (-/-): *das gewisse ~* that certain something.

euch *pers. pron.* [ɔʏç] you; *~* (*selbst*) yourselves.

euer *poss. pron.* ['ɔʏɐr] your; *der* (*die, das*) *eu(e)re* yours.

Eule *orn.* ['ɔʏlə] *f* (-/-n) owl; *~n nach Athen tragen* carry coals to Newcastle.

euresgleichen *pron.* ['ɔʏrəs'glaɪçən] people like you, F the likes of you.

Europä|er [ɔʏro'pɛːɐr] *m* (-s/-) European; **2isch** *adj.* European.

Euter ['ɔʏtɐr] *n* (-s/-) udder.

evakuieren [evaku'iːrən] *v/t.* (*no* -ge-, *h*) evacuate.

evangeli|sch *adj.* [evaŋ'geːliʃ] evangelic(al); Protestant; Lutheran; **2um** [~jum] *n* (-s/*Evangelien*) gospel.

eventuell [eventu'ɛl] 1. *adj.* possible; 2. *adv.* possibly, perhaps.

ewig *adj.* ['eːvɪç] eternal; everlasting; perpetual; *auf ~* for ever; **'2keit** *f* (-/-en) eternity; F: *seit e-r ~* for ages.

exakt *adj.* [ɛ'ksakt] exact; **2heit** *f* (-/-en) exactitude, exactness; accuracy.

Exam|en [ɛ'ksaːmən] *n* (-s/-, *Examina*) examination, F exam; **2inieren** [~ami'niːrən] *v/t.* (*no* -ge-, *h*) examine.

Exekutive [ɛksoku'tiːvə] *f* (-/*no pl.*) executive power.

Exempel [ɛ'ksɛmpəl] *n* (-s/-) example, instance.

Exemplar [ɛksɛm'pla:r] *n* (-s/-e) specimen; copy (*of book*).

exerzier|en ✕ [ɛksɛr'tsi:rən] *v/i.* and *v/t.* (*no* -ge-, *h*) drill; **2platz** ✕ *m* drill-ground, parade-ground.

Exil [ɛ'ksi:l] *n* (-s/-e) exile.

Existenz [ɛksiɛ'tɛnts] *f* (/-en) existence; living, livelihood; **~minimum** *n* subsistence minimum.

exis'tieren *v/i.* (*no* -ge-, *h*) exist; subsist.

exotisch *adj.* [ɛ'kso:tiʃ] exotic.

exped|ieren [ɛkspe'di:rən] *v/t.* (*no* -ge-, *h*) dispatch; **2ition** [~i'tsjo:n] *f* (-/-en) dispatch, forwarding; expedition; ✝ dispatch *or* forwarding office.

Experiment [ɛksperi'mɛnt] *n* (-[e]s/-e) experiment; **2ieren** [~'ti:rən] *v/i.* (*no* -ge-, *h*) experiment.

explo|dieren [ɛksplo'di:rən] *v/i.* (*no* -ge-, *sein*) explode; burst; **2sion** [~'zjo:n] *f* (-/-en) explosion; **~siv** *adj.* [~'zi:f] explosive.

Export [ɛks'pɔrt] *m* (-[e]s/-e) export(ation); **2ieren** [~'ti:rən] *v/t.* (*no* -ge-, *h*) export.

extra *adj.* ['ɛkstra] extra; special; **'2blatt** *n* extra edition (*of newspaper*), *Am.* extra.

Extrakt [ɛks'trakt] *m* (-[e]s/-e) extract.

Extrem [ɛks'tre:m] **1.** *n* (-s/-e) extreme; **2.** 2 *adj.* extreme.

Exzellenz [ɛkstsɛ'lɛnts] *f* (-/-en) Excellency.

exzentrisch *adj.* [ɛks'tsɛntriʃ] eccentric.

Exzeß [ɛks'tsɛs] *m* (Exzesses/Exzesse) excess.

F

Fabel ['fɑ:bəl] *f* (-/-n) fable (*a. fig.*); plot (*of story, book, etc.*); **'2haft** *adj.* fabulous; marvellous; **'2n** *v/i.* (ge-, *h*) tell (tall) stories.

Fabrik [fa'bri:k] *f* (-/-en) factory, works *sg., pl.*, mill; **~ant** [~i'kant] *m* (-en/-en) factory-owner, mill-owner; manufacturer; **~arbeit** *f* factory work; *s.* Fabrikware; **~arbeiter** *m* factory worker *or* hand; **~at** [~i'ka:t] *n* (-[e]s/-e) make; product; **~ationsfehler** [~a'tsjo:ns-] *m* flaw; **~besitzer** *m* factory-owner; **~marke** *f* trade mark; **~stadt** *f* factory *or* industrial town; **~ware** *f* manufactured article; **~zeichen** *n* *s.* Fabrikmarke.

Fach [fax] *n* (-[e]s/ᵘer) section, compartment, shelf (*of bookcase, cupboard, etc.*); pigeon-hole (*in desk*); drawer; *fig.* subject; *s.* Fachgebiet; **'~arbeiter** *m* skilled worker; **'~arzt** *m* specialist (*für* in); **'~ausbildung** *f* professional training; **'~ausdruck** *m* technical term.

fächeln ['fɛçəln] *v/t.* (ge-, *h*) fan *s.o.*

Fächer ['fɛçər] *m* (-s/-) fan; **2förmig** *adj.* ['~fœrmiç] fan-shaped.

'Fach|gebiet *n* branch, field, province; **'~kenntnisse** *f/pl.* specialized knowledge; **'~kreis** *m:* in *~en* among experts; **'2kundig** *adj.* competent, expert; **'~literatur** *f* specialized literature; **'~mann** *m* expert; **2männisch** *adj.* ['~mɛniʃ] expert; **'~schule** *f* technical school; **'~werk** △ *n* framework.

Fackel ['fakəl] *f* (-/-n) torch; **'2n** F *v/i.* (ge-, *h*) hesitate, F shilly-shally; **'~zug** *m* torchlight procession.

fad *adj.* ['fa:t], **~e** *adj.* ['fɑ:də] *food:* insipid, tasteless; stale; *p.* dull, boring.

Faden ['fɑ:dən] *m* (-s/ᵘ) thread (*a. fig.*); *fig.:* an e-m ~ hängen hang by a thread; **'~nudeln** *f/pl.* vermicelli *pl.*; **2scheinig** *adj.* ['~ʃainiç] threadbare; *excuse, etc.:* flimsy, thin.

fähig *adj.* ['fɛ:iç] capable (*zu inf.* of *ger.*; *gen.* of); able (to *inf.*); **'2keit** *f* (-/-en) (cap)ability; talent, faculty.

fahl *adj.* ['fɑ:l] pale, pallid; *colour:* faded; *complexion:* leaden, livid.

fahnd|en ['fɑ:ndən] *v/i.* (ge-, *h*): nach j-m ~ search for s.o.; **2ung** *f* (-/-en) search.

Fahne ['fɑ:nə] *f* (-/-n) flag; standard; banner; ⚓, ✕, *fig.* colo(u)rs *pl.*; *typ.* galley-proof.

'Fahnen|eid *m* oath of allegiance; **'~flucht** *f* desertion; **'2flüchtig** *adj.*: *~ werden* desert (the colo[u]rs); **'~stange** *f* flagstaff, *Am. a.* flagpole.

'Fahr|bahn *f*, **'~damm** *m* roadway.

Fähre ['fɛ:rə] *f* (-/-n) ferry(-boat).

fahren ['fɑ:rən] (*irr.*, ge-) **1.** *v/i.* (*sein*) *driver, vehicle, etc.:* drive, go, travel; *cyclist:* ride, cycle; ⚓ sail; *mot.* motor; *mit der Eisenbahn ~* go by train *or* rail; *spazieren~* go for *or* take a drive; *mit der Hand ~ über* (*acc.*) pass one's hand over; *~ lassen* let go *or* slip; *gut* (*schlecht*) *~ bei* do *or* fare well (badly) at *or* with; *er ist gut dabei gefahren* he did very well out of it; **2.** *v/t.* (*h*) carry, convey; drive (*car, train, etc.*); ride (*bicycle, etc.*).

'Fahrer *m* (-s/-) driver; **'~flucht** *f* (-/*no pl.*) hit-and-run offence, *Am.* hit-and-run offense.

'Fahr|gast *m* passenger; *in taxi*: fare; **'⁓geld** *n* fare; **'⁓gelegenheit** *f* transport facilities *pl.*; **'⁓gestell** *n mot.* chassis; ⚙ undercarriage, landing gear; **'⁓karte** *f* ticket; **'⁓kartenschalter** *m* booking-office, *Am.* ticket office; **'lässig** *adj.* careless, negligent; **'⁓lässigkeit** *f* (-/⁓-en) carelessness, negligence; **'⁓lehrer** *mot. m* driving instructor; **'⁓plan** *m* timetable, *Am. a.* schedule; **'planmäßig 1.** *adj.* regular, *Am.* scheduled; **2.** *adv.* on time, *Am. a.* on schedule; **'⁓preis** *m* fare; **'⁓rad** *n* bicycle, F bike; **'⁓schein** *m* ticket; **'⁓schule** *mot. f* driving school, school of motoring; **'⁓stuhl** *m* lift, *Am.* elevator; **'⁓stuhlführer** *m* lift-boy, lift-man, *Am.* elevator operator; **'⁓stunde** *mot. f* driving lesson.

Fahrt [fɑːrt] *f* (-/-en) ride, drive; journey; voyage, passage; trip; *⁓ ins Blaue* mystery tour; *in voller ⁓* (at) full speed.

Fährte ['fɛːrtə] *f* (-/-n) track (*a. fig.*); *auf der falschen ⁓ sein* be on the wrong track.

'Fahr|vorschrift *f* rule of the road; **'⁓wasser** *n* ⚓ navigable water; *fig.* track; **'⁓weg** *m* roadway; **'⁓zeug** *n* vehicle; ⚓ vessel.

Fakt|or ['faktɔr] *m* (-s/-en) factor; **⁓otum** [⁓'toːtum] *n* (-s/-s, *Faktoten*) factotum; **⁓ur** [⁓'tuːr] *f* (-/-en) factotum; **⁓ura** † [⁓'tuːra] *f* (-/*Fakturen*) invoice.

Fakultät *univ.* [fakul'tɛːt] *f* (-/-en) faculty.

Falke *orn.* ['falkə] *m* (-n/-n) hawk, falcon.

Fall [fal] *m* (-[e]s/⁓e) fall (*of body, stronghold, city, etc.*); gr., ♟♙ case; gesetzt den ⁓ suppose; *auf alle Fälle* at all events; *auf jeden ⁓* in any case, at any rate; *auf keinen ⁓* on no account, in no case.

Falle ['falə] *f* (-/-n) trap (*a. fig.*); pitfall (*a. fig.*); *e-e ⁓ stellen* set a trap (*j-m* for s.o.).

fallen ['falən] **1.** *v/i.* (*irr., ge-, sein*) fall, drop; ✕ be killed in action; *shot*: be heard; *flood water*: subside; *auf j-n ⁓ suspicion, etc.*: fall on s.o.; *⁓ lassen* drop (*plate, etc.*); **2.** ② *n* (-s/*no pl.*) fall(ing).

fällen ['fɛlən] *v/t.* (*ge-, h*) fell, cut down (*tree*); ✕ lower (*bayonet*); ♟♙ pass (*judgement*), give (*decision*).

'fallenlassen *v/t.* (*irr. lassen, sep., no -ge-, h*) drop (*plan, claim, etc.*).

fällig *adj.* ['fɛliç] due; payable; **'②keit** *f* (-/⁓-en) maturity; **'②keitstermin** *m* date of maturity.

'Fall|obst *n* windfall; **⁓reep** ⚓ ['⁓reːp] *n* (-[e]s/-e) gangway.

falls *cj.* [fals] if; in the event of *ger.*: in case.

'Fall|schirm *m* parachute; **'⁓**

schirmspringer *m* parachutist; **'⁓strick** *m* snare; **'⁓tür** *f* trap door.

falsch [falʃ] **1.** *adj.* false; wrong; *bank-note, etc.*: counterfeit; *money*: base; *bill of exchange, etc.*: forged; *p.* deceitful; **2.** *adv.*: *⁓ gehen watch*: go wrong; *⁓ verbunden! teleph.* sorry, wrong number.

fälsch|en ['fɛlʃən] *v/t.* (*ge-, h*) falsify; forge, fake (*document, etc.*); counterfeit (*bank-note, coin, etc.*); fake (*calculations, etc.*); tamper with (*financial account*); adulterate (*food, wine*); **'②er** *m* (-s/-) forger, faker; adulterator.

'Falsch|geld *n* counterfeit *or* bad *or* base money; **'⁓heit** *f* (-/-en) falseness, falsity; duplicity; deceitfulness; **'⁓meldung** *f* false report; **'⁓münzer** *m* (-s/-) coiner; **'⁓münzerwerkstatt** *f* coiner's den; **'②spielen** *v/i.* (*sep., -ge-, h*) cheat (at cards); **'⁓spieler** *m* cardsharper.

'Fälschung *f* (-/-en) forgery; falsification; fake; adulteration.

Falt|boot ['falt-] *n* folding canoe, *Am.* foldboat, faltboat; **⁓e** ['⁓ə] *f* (-/-n) fold; pleat (*in skirt, etc.*); crease (*in trousers*); wrinkle (*on face*); **'②en** *v/t.* (*ge-, h*) fold; clasp *or* join (*one's hands*); **'②ig** *adj.* folded; pleated; wrinkled.

Falz [falts] *m* (-es/-e) fold; rabbet (*for woodworking, etc.*); bookbinding: guard; **'②en** *v/t.* (*ge-, h*) fold; rabbet.

familiär *adj.* [famil'jɛːr] familiar; informal.

Familie [fa'miːljə] *f* (-/-n) family (*a. zo.*, ♣).

Fa'milien|angelegenheit *f* family affair; **⁓anschluß** *m*: *⁓ haben* live as one of the family; **⁓nachrichten** *f/pl. in newspaper*: birth, marriage and death announcements *pl.*; **⁓name** *m* family name, surname, *Am. a.* last name; **⁓stand** *m* marital status.

Fanati|ker [fa'nɑːtikər] *m* (-s/-) fanatic; **②sch** *adj.* fanatic(al).

Fanatismus [fana'tismus] *m* (-/*no pl.*) fanaticism.

fand [fant] *pret. of finden.*

Fanfare [fan'fɑːrə] *f* (-/-n) fanfare, flourish (of trumpets).

Fang [faŋ] *m* (-[e]s/⁓e) capture, catch(ing); *hunt.* bag; **'②en** *v/t.* (*irr. ge-, h*) catch (*animal, ball, thief, etc.*); **'⁓zahn** *m* fang (*of dog, wolf, etc.*); tusk (*of boar*).

Farb|band ['farp-] *n* (typewriter) ribbon; **⁓e** ['⁓bə] *f* (-/-n) colo(u)r; paint; dye; complexion; *cards*: suit; **②echt** *adj.* ['farpʔ-] colo(u)r-fast.

färben ['fɛrbən] *v/t.* (*ge-, h*) colo(u)r (*glass, food, etc.*); dye (*material, hair, Easter eggs, etc.*); tint (*hair,* *paper, glass*); stain (*wood, fabrics, glass, etc.*); sich ~ take on *or* assume a colo(u)r; sich rot ~ turn *or* go red.

'**farben|blind** *adj.* colo(u)r-blind; '2**druck** *m* (-[e]s/-e) colo(u)r print; '~**prächtig** *adj.* splendidly colo(u)rful.

Färber ['fɛrbər] *m* (-s/-) dyer.

Farb|fernsehen ['farp-] *n* colo(u)r television; '~**film** *m* colo(u)r film; 2**ig** *adj.* ['~bɪç] colo(u)red; *glass:* tinted, stained; *fig.* colo(u)rful; 2**los** *adj.* ['~p-] colo(u)rless; '~**photographie** *f* colo(u)r photography; '~**stift** *m* colo(u)red pencil; '~**stoff** *m* colo(u)ring matter; '~**ton** *m* tone; shade, tint.

Färbung ['fɛrbuŋ] *f* (-/-en) colo(u)ring (*a. fig.*); shade (*a. fig.*).

Farnkraut ♣ ['farnkraut] *n* fern.

Fasan *orn.* [fa'zaːn] *m* (-[e]s/-e[n]) pheasant.

Fasching ['faʃiŋ] *m* (-s/-e, -s) carnival.

Fasel|ei [faːzə'lai] *f* (-/-en) drivelling, waffling; twaddle; '2**n** *v/i.* (ge-, h) blather; F waffle.

Faser ['faːzər] *f* (-/-en) *anat.*, ♣, *fig.* fib|re, *Am.* -er; *cotton, wool, etc.:* staple; '2**ig** *adj.* fibrous; '2**n** *v/i.* (ge-, h) *wool:* shed fine hairs.

Faß [fas] *n* (*Fasses/Fässer*) cask, barrel; tub; vat; '~**bier** *n* draught beer.

Fassade △ [fa'saːdə] *f* (-/-n) façade, front (*a. fig.*); ~**nkletterer** *m* (-s/-) cat burglar.

fassen ['fasən] (ge-, h) **1.** *v/t.* seize, take hold of; catch, apprehend (*criminal*); hold; *s. einfassen*; *fig.* grasp, understand, believe; pluck up (*courage*); form (*plan*); make (*decision*); sich ~ compose o.s.; sich kurz ~ be brief; **2.** *v/i.:* ~ *nach* reach for. [ceivable.]

'**faßlich** *adj.* comprehensible, con-|

'**Fassung** *f* (-/-en) setting (*of jewels*); ∉ socket; *fig.:* composure; draft (-ing); wording, version; *die ~ verlieren* lose one's self-control; *aus der ~ bringen* disconcert; '~**kraft** *f* (powers of) comprehension, mental capacity; '~**svermögen** *n* (holding) capacity; *fig. s. Fassungskraft.*

fast *adv.* [fast] almost, nearly; ~ *nichts* next to nothing; ~ *nie* hardly ever.

fasten ['fastən] *v/i.* (ge-, h) fast; abstain from food and drink; '2**zeit** *f* Lent.

'**Fast|nacht** *f* (-/no *pl.*) Shrovetide; carnival; '~**tag** *m* fast-day.

fatal *adj.* [fa'taːl] *situation, etc.:* awkward; *business, etc.:* unfortunate; *mistake, etc.:* fatal.

fauchen ['fauxən] *v/i.* (ge-, h) cat, *etc.:* spit; F *p.* spit (*with anger*); *locomotive, etc.:* hiss.

faul *adj.* [faul] *fruit, etc.:* rotten, bad; *fish, meat:* putrid, bad; *fig.* lazy, indolent, idle; fishy; ~*e Ausrede* lame excuse; '~**en** *v/i.* (ge-, h) rot, go bad, putrefy.

faulenze|n ['faulɛntsən] *v/i.* (ge-, h) idle; laze, loaf; '2**r** *m* (-s/-) idler, sluggard, F lazy-bones.

'**Faul|heit** *f* (-/no *pl.*) idleness, laziness; '2**ig** *adj.* putrid.

Fäulnis ['foylnis] *f* (-/no *pl.*) rottenness; putrefaction; decay.

'**Faul|pelz** *m* s. Faulenzer; '~**tier** *n* zo. sloth (*a. fig.*).

Faust [faust] *f* (-/*∾e*) fist; *auf eigene ~ on* one's own initiative; '~**handschuh** *m* mitt(en); '~**schlag** *m* blow with the fist, punch, *Am.* F *a.* slug.

Favorit [favo'riːt] *m* (-en/-en) favo(u)rite.

Faxe ['faksə] *f* (-/-n): ~*n machen* (play the) fool; ~*n schneiden* pull *or* make faces.

Fazit ['faːtsit] *n* (-s/-e, -s) result, upshot; total; *das ~ ziehen* sum *or* total up.

Februar ['feːbruaːr] *m* (-[s]/-e) February.

fecht|en ['fɛçtən] *v/i.* (*irr.*, ge-, h) fight; *fenc.* fence; '2**er** *m* (-s/-) fencer.

Feder ['feːdər] *f* (-/-n) feather; (*ornamental*) plume; pen; ⊕ spring; '~**bett** *n* feather bed; '~**busch** *m* tuft of feathers; plume; '~**gewicht** *n boxing, etc.:* featherweight; '~**halter** *m* (-s/-) penholder; '~**kiel** *m* quill; '~**kraft** *f* elasticity, resilience; '~**krieg** *m* paper war; literary controversy; '2**leicht** *adj.* (as) light as a feather; '~**lesen** *n* (-s/no *pl.*): *nicht viel ~s machen* mit make short work of; '~**messer** *n* penknife; '2**n** *v/i.* (ge-, h) be elastic; '2**nd** *adj.* springy, elastic; '~**strich** *m* stroke of the pen; '~**vieh** *n* poultry; '~**zeichnung** *f* pen-and-ink drawing.

Fee [feː] *f* (-/-n) fairy.

Fegefeuer ['feːgə-] *n* purgatory.

fegen ['feːgən] *v/t.* (ge-, h) sweep; clean.

Fehde ['feːdə] *f* (-/-n) feud; private war; *in ~ liegen* be at feud; F be at daggers drawn.

Fehl [feːl] *m*: *ohne ~* without fault *or* blemish; '~**betrag** *m* deficit, deficiency.

fehlen ['feːlən] *v/i.* (ge-, h) be absent; be missing *or* lacking; do wrong; *es fehlt ihm an* (*dat.*) he lacks; *was fehlt Ihnen?* what is the matter with you?; *weit gefehlt!* far off the mark!

Fehler ['feːlər] *m* (-s/-) mistake, error, F slip; fault; ⊕ defect, flaw; '2**frei** *adj.*, '2**los** *adj.* faultless, perfect; ⊕ flawless; '2**haft** *adj.* faulty; defective; incorrect.

'**Fehl|geburt** *f* miscarriage, abortion; '₂gehen v/i. (irr. gehen, sep., -ge-, sein) go wrong; '₂griff fig. m mistake, blunder; '₂schlag fig. m failure; '₂schlagen fig. v/i. (irr. schlagen, sep., -ge-, sein) fail, miscarry; '₂schuß m miss; '₂treten v/i. (irr. treten, sep., -ge-, sein) make a false step; '₂tritt m false step; slip; fig. slip, fault; '₂urteil ⚖ n error of judg(e)ment; '₂zündung mot. f misfire, backfire.

Feier ['faɪər] f (-/-n) ceremony; celebration; festival; festivity; '₂abend m finishing or closing time; ₂ machen finish, F knock off; '₂lich adj. promise, oath, etc.: solemn; act: ceremonial; '₂lichkeit f (-/-en) solemnity; ceremony; '₂n (ge-, h) 1. v/t. hold (celebration); celebrate, observe (feast, etc.); 2. v/i. celebrate; rest (from work), make holiday; '₂tag m holiday; festive day.

feig adj. [faɪk] cowardly.

feige¹ adj. ['faɪgə] cowardly.

Feige² [₂] f (-/-n) fig; '₂nbaum ♀ m fig-tree; '₂nblatt n fig-leaf.

Feig|heit ['faɪkhaɪt] f (-/no pl.) cowardice, cowardliness; '₂ling ['₂klɪŋ] m (-s/-e) coward.

feil adj. [faɪl] for sale, to be sold; fig. venal; '₂bieten v/t. (irr. bieten, sep., -ge-, h) offer for sale.

Feile ['faɪlə] f (-/-n) file; '₂n (ge-, h) 1. v/t. file (a. fig.); fig. polish; 2. v/i. ₂ an (dat.) file (at); fig. polish (up).

feilschen ['faɪlʃən] v/i. (ge-, h) bargain (um for), haggle (for, about), Am. a. dicker (about).

fein adj. [faɪn] fine; material, etc.: high-grade; wine, etc.: choice; fabric, etc.: delicate, dainty; manners: polished; p. polite; distinction: subtle.

Feind [faɪnt] m (-[e]s/-e) enemy (a. ✕); '₂lich adj. hostile, inimical; '₂schaft f (-/-en) enmity; animosity, hostility; '₂selig adj. hostile (gegen to); '₂seligkeit f (-/-en) hostility; malevolence.

'fein|fühlend adj., '₂fühlig adj. sensitive; '₂gefühl n sensitiveness; delicacy; '₂gehalt m (monetary) standard; '₂heit f (-/-en) fineness; delicacy, daintiness; politeness; elegance; '₂kost f high-class groceries pl., Am. delicatessen; '₂mechanik f precision mechanics; '₂schmecker m (-s/-) gourmet, epicure; '₂sinnig adj. subtle.

feist adj. [faɪst] fat, stout.

Feld [fɛlt] n (-[e]s/-er) field (a. ✕, ✗, sports); ground, soil; plain; chess: square; ⚡, ⊕ panel, compartment; ins ₂ ziehen take the field; '₂arbeit f agricultural work; '₂bett n camp-bed; '₂blume f wild flower; '₂dienst ✕ m field service; '₂flasche f water-bottle;

'₂frucht f fruit of the field; '₂geschrei n war-cry, battle-cry; '₂herr m general; '₂kessel m camp-kettle; '₂lazarett ✕ n field-hospital; '₂lerche orn. f skylark; '₂marschall m Field Marshal; '₂marschmäßig ✕ adj. in full marching order; '₂maus zo. f field-mouse; '₂messer m (land) surveyor; '₂post ✕ f army postal service; '₂schlacht ✕ f battle; '₂stecher m (-s/-) (ein a pair of) field-glasses pl.; '₂stuhl m camp-stool; '₂webel ['₂ve:bəl] m (-s/-) sergeant; '₂weg m (field) path; '₂zeichen ✕ n standard; '₂zug m ✕ campaign (a. fig.), (military) expedition; Am. fig. a. drive.

Felge ['fɛlgə] f (-/-n) felloe (of cart-wheel); rim (of car wheel, etc.).

Fell [fɛl] n (-[e]s/-e) skin, pelt, fur (of dead animal); coat (of cat, etc.); fleeze (of sheep).

Fels [fɛls] m (-en/-en) rock; '₂en ['₂zən] m (-s/-) rock; '₂block ['fɛls-] m rock; boulder; ₂ig adj. ['₂zɪç] rocky.

Fenchel ♀ ['fɛnçəl] m (-s/no pl.) fennel.

Fenster ['fɛnstər] n (-s/-) window; '₂brett n window-sill; '₂flügel m casement (of casement window); sash (of sash window); '₂kreuz n cross-bar(s); '₂laden m shutter; '₂rahmen m window-frame; '₂riegel m window-fastener; '₂scheibe f (window-)pane; '₂sims m, n window-sill.

Ferien ['fe:rjən] pl. holiday(s pl.), esp. Am. vacation; leave, Am. a. furlough; parl. recess; ⚖ vacation, recess; '₂kolonie f children's holiday camp.

Ferkel ['fɛrkəl] n (-s/-) young pig; contp. p. pig.

fern [fɛrn] 1. adj. far (off), distant; remote; 2. adv. far (away); von ₂ from a distance.

'Fernamt teleph. n trunk exchange, Am. long-distance exchange.

'fernbleiben v/i. (irr. bleiben, sep., -ge-, sein) remain or stay away (dat. from); 2. ₂ n (-s/no pl.) absence (from school, etc.); absenteeism (from work).

Fern|e ['fɛrnə] f (-/-n) distance; remoteness; aus der ₂ from or at a distance; '₂er 1. adj. farther; fig.: further; future; 2. adv. further (-more), in addition, also; ₂ liefen ... also ran ...; '₂flug ☇ m long-distance flight; '₂gelenkt adj. ['₂gə-lɛŋkt] missile: guided; aircraft, etc.: remote-control(l)ed; '₂gespräch teleph. n trunk call, Am. long-distance call; '₂gesteuert adj. s. ferngelenkt; '₂glas n binoculars pl.; '₂halten v/t. and v/refl. (irr. halten, sep., -ge-, h) keep away (von from); '₂heizung f district heating; '₂la-

ster F *mot. m* long-distance lorry, *Am.* long haul truck; '~**lenkung** *f* (-/-en) remote control; '**2liegen** *v/i.* (*irr. liegen, sep., -ge-, h*): es liegt mir fern zu *inf.* I am far from *ger.*; '~**rohr** *n* telescope; '~**schreiber** *m* teleprinter, *Am.* teletypewriter; '~**sehen 1.** *n* (-s/no *pl.*) television; **2.** **2** *v/i.* (*irr. sehen, sep., -ge-, h*) watch television; '~**seher** *m* television set; *p.* television viewer, televiewer; '~**sehsendung** *f* television broadcast, telecast; '~**sicht** *f* visual range.

'**Fernsprech|amt** *n* telephone exchange, *Am. a.* central; '~**anschluß** *m* telephone connection; '~**er** *m* telephone; '~**leitung** *f* telephone line; '~**zelle** *f* telephone box.

'**fern|stehen** *v/i.* (*irr. stehen, sep., -ge-, h*) have no real (point of) contact (*dat.* with); '~**steuerung** *f s.* Fernlenkung; '**2unterricht** *m* correspondence course *or* tuition; **2verkehr** *m* long-distance traffic.

Ferse ['fɛrzə] *f* (-/-n) heel.

fertig *adj.* ['fɛrtiç] ready; *article, etc.:* finished; *clothing:* ready-made; mit et. ~ werden get s.th. finished; mit et. ~ sein have finished s.th.; '~**bringen** *v/t.* (*irr. bringen, sep., -ge-, h*) bring about; manage; '**2keit** *f* (-/-en) dexterity; skill; fluency (*in the spoken language*); '~**machen** *v/t.* (*sep., -ge-, h*) finish, complete; get *s.th.* ready; *fig.* finish, settle *s.o.'s* hash; sich ~ get ready; '**2stellung** *f* completion; '**2waren** *f/pl.* finished goods *pl. or* products *pl.*

fesch F *adj.* [fɛʃ] *hat, dress, etc.:* smart, stylish, chic; dashing.

Fessel ['fɛsəl] *f* (-/-n) chain, fetter, shackle; *vet.* fetlock; *fig.* bond, fetter, tie; '~**ballon** *m* captive balloon; '**2n** *v/t.* (ge-, h) chain, fetter, shackle; *j-n* ~ hold *or* arrest *s.o.'s* attention; fascinate *s.o.*

fest [fɛst] **1.** *adj.* firm; solid; fixed; fast; *principle:* firm, strong; *sleep:* sound; *fabric:* close; **2. 2** *n* (-es/-e) festival, celebration; holiday, *eccl.* feast; '~**binden** *v/t.* (*irr. binden, sep., -ge-, h*) fasten, tie (*an dat.* to); '**2essen** *n* banquet, feast; '~**fahren** *v/refl.* (*irr. fahren, sep., -ge-, h*) get stuck; *fig.* reach a deadlock; '**2halle** *f* (festival) hall; '~**halten** (*irr. halten, sep., -ge-, h*) **1.** *v/i.* hold fast *or* tight; ~ an (*dat.*) adhere *or* keep to; **2.** *v/t.* hold on to; hold tight; sich ~ an (*dat.*) hold on to; ~**igen** ['~igən] *v/t.* (ge-, h) consolidate (*one's position, etc.*); strengthen (*friendship, etc.*); stabilize (*currency*); **2igkeit** ['~ç-] *f* (-/no *pl.*) firmness; solidity; '**2land** *n* mainland, continent; '~**legen** *v/t.* (*sep., -ge-, h*) fix, set; sich auf et. ~

commit o.s. to s.th.; '~**lich** *adj. meal, day, etc.:* festive; *reception, etc.:* ceremonial; '**2lichkeit** *f* (-/-en) festivity; festive character; '~**machen** (*sep., -ge-, h*) **1.** *v/t.* fix, fasten, attach (*an dat.* to); 🖢 moor; **2.** 🖢 *v/i.* moor; put ashore; '**2mahl** *n* banquet, feast; '**2nahme** ['~nɑːmə] *f* (-/-n) arrest; '~**nehmen** *v/t.* (*irr. nehmen, sep., -ge-, h*) arrest, take into custody; '**2rede** *f* speech of the day; '~**setzen** *v/t.* (*sep., -ge-, h*) fix, set; sich ~ *dust, etc.:* become ingrained; *p.* settle (down); '**2spiel** *n* festival; '~**stehen** *v/i.* (*irr. stehen, sep., -ge-, h*) stand firm; *fact:* be certain; '~**stehend** *adj.* fixed, stationary; *fact:* established; '~**stellen** *v/t.* (*sep., -ge-, h*) establish (*fact, identity, etc.*); ascertain, find out (*fact, s.o.'s whereabouts, etc.*); state; see, perceive (*fact, etc.*); '**2stellung** *f* establishment; ascertainment; statement; '**2tag** *m* festive day; festival, holiday; *eccl.* feast; '**2ung** ✗ *f* (-/-en) fortress; '**2zug** *m* festive procession.

fett [fɛt] **1.** *adj.* fat; fleshy; *voice:* oily; *land, etc.:* rich; **2. 2** *n* (-[e]s/-e) fat; grease (*a.* ⊕); '**2druck** *typ. m* bold type; '**2fleck** *m* grease-spot; '~**ig** *adj.* hair, skin, *etc.:* greasy, oily; *fingers, etc.:* greasy; *substance:* fatty.

Fetzen ['fɛtsən] *m* (-s/-) shred; rag, *Am. a.* frazzle; scrap (*of paper*); in ~ in rags.

feucht *adj.* [fɔʏçt] *climate, air, etc.:* damp, moist; *air, zone, etc.:* humid; '**2igkeit** *f* (-/no *pl.*) moisture (*of substance*); dampness (*of place, etc.*); humidity (*of atmosphere, etc.*).

Feuer ['fɔʏər] *n* (-s/-) fire; light; *fig.* ardo(u)r; ~ fangen catch fire; *fig.* fall for (*girl*); '~**alarm** *m* fire alarm; '**2beständig** *adj.* fire-proof, fire-resistant; '~**bestattung** *f* cremation; '~**eifer** *m* ardo(u)r; '**2fest** *adj. s.* feuerbeständig; '**2gefährlich** *adj.* inflammable; '~**haken** *m* poker; '~**löscher** *m* (-s/-) fire extinguisher; '~**melder** *m* (-s/-) fire-alarm; '**2n** (ge-, h) **1.** ✗ *v/i.* shoot, fire (*auf acc.* at, on); **2.** F *fig. v/t.* hurl; '~**probe** *fig. f* crucial test; '**2rot** *adj.* fiery (red), (as) red as fire; '~**sbrunst** *f* conflagration; '~**schiff** 🖢 *n* lightship; '~**schutz** *m* fire prevention; ✗ covering fire; '~**sgefahr** *f* danger *or* risk of fire; '**2speiend** *adj.:* ~er Berg volcano; '~**spritze** *f* fire engine; '~**stein** *m* flint; '~**versicherung** *f* fire insurance (company); '~**wache** *f* fire station, *Am. a.* firehouse; '~**wehr** *f* fire-brigade, *Am. a.* fire department; '~**wehrmann** *m* fireman; '~**werk** *n* (display of) fireworks *pl.*; '~**werkskörper** *m* firework; '~

zange f (e-e a pair of) firetongs pl.; **~zeug** n lighter.

feurig adj. ['fɔyriç] fiery (a. fig.); fig. ardent.

Fiasko [fi'asko] n (-s/-s) (complete) failure, fiasco; sl. flop.

Fibel ['fi:bəl] f (-/-n) spelling-book, primer.

Fichte ♧ ['fiçtə] f (-/-n) spruce; **~nnadel** f pine-needle.

fidel adj. [fi'de:l] cheerful, merry, jolly, Am. F a. chipper.

Fieber ['fi:bər] n (-s/-) temperature, fever; **~ haben** have or run a temperature; **'~anfall** m attack or bout of fever; **'2haft** adj. feverish (a. fig.); febrile; **'2krank** adj. ill with fever; **'~mittel** n febrifuge; **'2n** v/i. (ge-, h) have or run a temperature; **~ nach** crave or long for; **'~schauer** m chill, shivers pl.; **'~tabelle** f temperature-chart; **'~thermometer** n clinical thermometer.

fiel [fi:l] pret. of fallen.

Figur [fi'gu:r] f (-/-en) figure; chess: chessman, piece.

figürlich adj. [fi'gy:rliç] meaning, etc.: figurative.

Filet [fi'le:] n (-s/-s) fillet (of beef, pork, etc.).

Filiale [fil'ja:lə] f (-/-n) branch.

Filigran(arbeit f) [fili'gra:n(ʔ-)] n (-s/-e) filigree.

Film [film] m (-[e]s/-e) film, thin coating (of oil, wax, etc.); phot. film; film, (moving) picture, Am. a. motion picture, F movie; e-n **~ einlegen** phot. load a camera; **'~atelier** n film studio; **'~aufnahme** f filming, shooting (of a film); film (of sporting event, etc.); **'2en** (ge-, h) 1. v/t. film, shoot (scene, etc.); 2. v/i. film, make a film; **'~gesellschaft** f film company, Am. motion-picture company; **'~kamera** f film camera, Am. motion-picture camera; **'~regisseur** m film director; **'~reklame** f screen advertising; **'~schauspieler** m film or screen actor, Am. F movie actor; **'~spule** f (film) reel; **'~streifen** m film strip; **'~theater** n cinema, Am. motion-picture or F movie theater; **'~verleih** m (-[e]s/-e) film distributors pl.; **'~vorführer** m projectionist; **'~vorstellung** f cinema performance, Am. F movie performance.

Filter ['filtər] (-s/-) 1. m (coffee-etc.) filter; 2. ⊕ n filter; **'2n** v/t. (ge-, h) filter (water, air, etc.); filtrate (water, impurities, etc.); strain (liquid); **'~zigarette** f filter-tipped cigarette.

Filz [filts] m (-es/-e) felt; fig. F skinflint; **'2ig** adj. felt-like; of felt; fig. F niggardly, stingy; **'~laus** f crab louse.

Finanz|amt [fi'nantsʔamt] n (inland) revenue office, office of the Inspector of Taxes; **~en** f/pl. finances pl.; **2iell** adj. [~'tsjel] financial; **2ieren** [~'tsi:rən] v/t. (no -ge-, h) finance (scheme, etc.); sponsor (radio programme, etc.); **~lage** f financial position; **~mann** m financier; **~minister** m minister of finance; Chancellor of the Exchequer, Am. Secretary of the Treasury; **~ministerium** n ministry of finance; Exchequer, Am. Treasury Department; **~wesen** n (-s/no pl.) finances pl.; financial matters pl.

Findelkind ['findəl-] n foundling.

finden ['findən] (irr., ge-, h) 1. v/t. find; discover, come across; find, think, consider; wie **~ Sie ...?** how do you like ...?; **sich ~** thing: be found; 2. v/i.: **~ zu** find one's way to.

'Finder m (-s/-) finder; **'~lohn** m finder's reward.

'findig adj. resourceful, ingenious.

Findling ['fintliŋ] m (-s/-e) foundling; geol. erratic block, boulder.

fing [fiŋ] pret. of fangen.

Finger ['fiŋər] m (-s/-) finger; sich die **~ verbrennen** burn one's fingers; er rührte keinen **~** he lifted no finger; **'~abdruck** m fingerprint; **'~fertigkeit** f manual skill; **'~hut** m thimble; ♧ foxglove; **'2n** v/i. (ge-, h): **~ nach** fumble for; **'~spitze** f finger-tip; **'~spitzengefühl** fig. n sure instinct; **'~übung** ♪ f finger exercise; **'~zeig** ['~tsaik] m (-[e]s/-e) hint, F pointer.

Fink orn. [fiŋk] m (-en/-en) finch.

finster adj. ['finstər] night, etc.: dark; shadows, mood, etc.: sombre; night, room, etc.: gloomy, murky; person, nature: sullen; thought, etc.: sinister, sombre, gloomy; **'2nis** f (-/no pl.) darkness, gloom.

Finte ['fintə] f (-/-n) feint; fig. a. ruse, trick.

Firma ♰ ['firma] f (-/Firmen) firm, business, company.

firmen eccl. ['firmən] v/t. (ge-, h) confirm.

'Firmen|inhaber m owner of a firm; **'~wert** m goodwill.

Firn [firn] m (-[e]s/-e) firn, névé.

First △ [first] m (-es/-e) ridge; **'~ziegel** m ridge tile.

Fisch [fiʃ] m (-es/-e) fish; **'~dampfer** m trawler; **'2en** v/t. and v/i. (ge-, h) fish; **'~er** m (-s/-) fisherman; **'~erboot** n fishing-boat; **'~erdorf** n fishing-village; **~erei** f [~'rai] f (-/-en) fishery; fishing; **'~fang** m fishing; **'~geruch** m fishy smell; **'~gräte** f fish-bone; **'~grätenmuster** n herring-bone pattern; **'~händler** m fishmonger, Am. fish dealer; **'2ig** adj. fishy; **'~laich** m spawn; **'~leim** m fish-glue; **'~mehl** n fish-meal; **'~schuppe** f scale; **'~tran** m train-oil; **'~vergiftung**

~ f fish-poisoning; **'~zucht** f pisci-culture, fish-hatching; **'~zug** m catch, haul, draught (of fish).

fiskalisch adj. [fis'kɑ:liʃ] fiscal, governmental.

Fiskus ['fiskus] m (-/~ -se, Fisken) Exchequer, esp. Am. Treasury; government.

Fistel ~ ['fistəl] f (-/-n) fistual; **'~stimme ♪** f falsetto.

Fittich ['fitiç] m (-[e]s/-e) poet. wing; j-n unter s-e ~e nehmen take s.o. under one's wing.

fix adj. [fiks] salary, price, etc.: fixed; quick, clever, smart; e-e ~e Idee an obsession; ein ~er Junge a smart fellow; **℁ierbad** phot. [fi-'ksi:rbɑ:t] n fixing bath; **~ieren** [fi'ksi:rən] v/t. (no -ge-, h) fix (a. phot.); fix one's eyes (up)on, stare at s.o.; **'℁stern** ast. m fixed star; **'℁um** n (-s/Fixa) fixed or basic salary.

flach adj. [flax] roof, etc.: flat; ground, etc.: flat, level, even; water, plate, fig.: shallow; ⅍ plane.

Fläche ['fleçə] f (-/-n) surface, ⅍ a. plane; sheet (of water, snow, etc.); geom. area; tract, expanse (of land, etc.); **~ninhalt** ⅍ ['fleçən?-] m (surface) area; **'~nmaß** n square or surface measure.

'Flach|land n plain, flat country; **'~rennen** n turf: flat race.

Flachs ♀ [flaks] m (-es/no pl.) flax.

flackern ['flakərn] v/i. (ge-, h) light, flame, eyes, etc.: flicker, wave; voice: quaver, shake.

Flagge ⚓ ['flagə] f (-/-n) flag, colo(u)rs pl.; **'℁n** v/i. (ge-, h) fly or hoist a flag; signal (with flags).

Flak ⚓ [flak] f (-/-, -s) anti-aircraft gun; anti-aircraft artillery.

Flamme ['flamə] f (-/-n) flame; blaze; **'~nmeer** n sea of flames; **'~nwerfer ⚓** m (-s/-) flame-thrower.

Flanell [fla'nɛl] m (-s/-e) flannel; **~anzug** m flannel suit; **~hose** f flannel trousers pl., flannels pl.

Flank|e ['flaŋkə] f (-/-n) flank (a. ⚔, ⊕, ⚓, mount.); side; **℁ieren** [~'ki:rən] v/t. (no -ge-, h) flank.

Flasche ['flaʃə] f (-/-n) bottle; flask. **'Flaschen|bier** n bottled beer; **'~hals** m neck of a bottle; **'~öffner** m (-s/-) bottle-opener; **'~zug** ⊕ m block and tackle.

flatter|haft adj. ['flatərhaft] girl, etc.: fickle, flighty; mind: fickle, volatile; **'~n** v/i. (ge-) **1.** (h, sein) bird, butterfly, etc.: flutter (about); bird, bat, etc.: flit (about); **2.** (h) hair, flag, garment, etc.: stream, fly; mot. wheel: shimmy, wobble; car steering: judder; **3.** (sein): auf den Boden ~ flutter to the ground.

flau adj. [flau] weak, feeble, faint; sentiment, reaction, etc.: lukewarm;

drink: stale; colour: pale, dull; **♣** market, business, etc.: dull, slack; ~e Zeit slack period.

Flaum [flaum] m (-[e]s/no pl.) down, fluff; fuzz.

Flau|s [flaus] m (-es/-e), **~sch** [~ʃ] m (-es/-e) tuft (of wool, etc.); napped coating.

Flausen F ['flauzən] f/pl. whims pl., fancies pl., (funny) ideas pl.; F fibs pl.; j-m ~ in den Kopf setzen put funny ideas into s.o.'s head; j-m ~ vormachen tell s.o. fibs.

Flaute ['flautə] f (-/-n) ⚓ dead calm; esp. ♣ dullness, slack period.

Flecht|e ['fleçtə] f (-/-n) braid, plait (of hair); ♀ lichen; ⚕ herpes; **'℁en** v/t. (irr., ge-, h) braid, plait (hair, ribbon, etc.); weave (basket, wreath, etc.); wreath (flowers); twist (rope, etc.); **'~werk** n wickerwork.

Fleck [flɛk] m (-[e]s/-e, -en) **1.** mark (of dirt, grease, etc.; zo.); spot (of grease, paint, etc.); smear (of oil, blood, etc.); stain (of wine, coffee, etc.); blot (of ink); place, spot; fig. blemish, spot, stain; **2.** patch (of material); bootmaking: heel-piece; **'~en** m (-s/-) s. Fleck 1; small (market-)town, townlet; **'~enwasser** n spot or stain remover; **'~fieber ⚕** n (epidemic) typhus; **'℁ig** adj. spotted; stained.

Fledermaus zo. ['fle:dər-] f bat.

Flegel ['fle:gəl] m (-s/-) flail; fig. lout, boor; **~ei** [~'lai] f (-/-en) rudeness; loutishness; **'℁haft** adj. rude-ill-mannered; loutish; **'~jahre** pl. awkward age.

flehen ['fle:ən] **1.** v/i. (ge-, h) entreat, implore (zu j-m s.o.; um et. s.th.); **2.** ⚕ n (-s/no pl.) supplication; imploration, entreaty.

Fleisch [flaiʃ] n (-es/no pl.) flesh; meat; ♀ pulp; **'~brühe** f meat-broth; beef tea; **'~er** m (-s/-) butcher; **~erei** [~'rai] f (-/-en) butcher's (shop), Am. butcher shop; **'~extrakt** m meat extract; **'℁fressend** adj. carnivorous; **'~hackmaschine** f mincing machine, mincer, Am. meat grinder; **'℁ig** adj. fleshy; ♀ pulpy; **'~konserven** f/pl. tinned or potted meat, Am. canned meat; **'~kost** f meat (food); **'℁lich** adj. desires, etc.: carnal, fleshly; **'℁los** adj. meatless; **'~pastete** f meat pie, Am. a. potpie; **'~speise** f meat dish; **'~vergiftung** f meat or ptomaine poisoning; **'~ware** f meat (product); **'~wolf** m s. Fleischhack-maschine.

Fleiß [flais] m (-es/no pl.) diligence, industry; **'℁ig** adj. diligent, industrious, hard-working.

fletschen ['flɛtʃən] v/t. (ge-, h): die Zähne ~ animal: bare its teeth; p. bare one's teeth.

Flicken ['flikən] **1.** m (-s/-) patch;

2. ♀ v/t. (ge-, h) patch (*dress, tyre, etc.*); repair (*shoe, roof, etc.*); cobble (*shoe*).

'Flick|schneider *m* jobbing tailor; '~schuster *m* cobbler; '~werk *n* (-[e]s/*no pl.*) patchwork.

Flieder ♀ ['fli:dər] *m* (-s/-) lilac.

Fliege ['fli:gə] *f* (-/-n) zo. fly; bow-tie.

'fliegen **1.** v/i. (*irr.*, ge-, sein) fly; go by air; **2.** v/t. (*irr.*, ge-, h) fly, pilot (*aircraft, etc.*); convey (*goods, etc.*) by air; **3.** ♀ n (-s/*no pl.*) flying; ✈ a. aviation.

Fliegen|fänger ['fli:gənfɛŋər] *m* (-s/-) fly-paper; '~fenster *n* fly-screen; '~gewicht *n* boxing, etc.: flyweight; '~klappe *f* fly-flap, Am. fly swatter; '~pilz ♀ *m* fly agaric.

'Flieger *m* (-s/-) flyer; ✈ airman, aviator; pilot; F plane, bomber; cycling: sprinter; '~abwehr ✕ *f* anti-aircraft defen|ce, Am. -se; '~alarm ✕ *m* air-raid alarm or warning; '~bombe ✕ *f* aircraft bomb; '~offizier ✕ *m* air-force officer.

flieh|en ['fli:ən] (*irr.*, ge-) **1.** v/i. (sein) flee (vor dat. from), run away; **2.** v/t. (h) flee, avoid, keep away from; '⊈kraft phys. *f* centrifugal force. [(floor-)tile.]

Fliese ['fli:zə] *f* (-/-n) (wall-)tile;]

Fließ|band ['fli:s-] *n* (-[e]s/*"er*) conveyor-belt; assembly-line; '⊈en v/i. (*irr.*, ge-, sein) river, traffic, etc.: flow; tap-water, etc.: run; '⊈end **1.** adj. water: running; traffic: moving; speech, etc.: fluent; **2.** adv.: ~ lesen (sprechen) read (speak) fluently; '~papier *n* blotting-paper.

Flimmer ['flimər] *m* (-s/-) glimmer, glitter; '⊈n v/i. (ge-, h) glimmer, glitter; television, film: flicker; es flimmert mir vor den Augen everything is dancing in front of my eyes.

flink adj. [fliŋk] quick, nimble, brisk.

Flinte ['flintə] *f* (-/-n) shotgun; die ~ ins Korn werfen throw up the sponge.

Flirt [flœrt] *m* (-es/-s) flirtation; '⊈en v/i. (ge-, h) flirt (mit with).

Flitter ['flitər] *m* (-s/-) tinsel (a. fig.), spangle; '~kram *m* cheap finery; '~wochen *pl.* honeymoon.

flitzen F ['flitsən] v/i. (ge-, sein) whisk, scamper; dash (off, etc.).

flocht [flɔxt] pret. of flechten.

Flock|e ['flɔkə] *f* (-/-n) flake (of snow, soap, etc.); flock (of wool); '⊈ig adj. fluffy, flaky.

flog [flo:k] pret. of fliegen.

floh¹ [flo:] pret. of fliehen.

Floh² zo. [~] *m* (-[e]s/*"e*) flea.

Flor [flo:r] *m* (-s/-e) bloom, blossom; fig. bloom, prime; gauze; crêpe, crape.

Florett fenc. [flo'rɛt] *n* (-[e]s/-e) foil.

florieren [flo'ri:rən] v/i. (*no* ge-, h)

business, etc.: flourish, prosper, thrive.

Floskel ['flɔskəl] *f* (-/-n) flourish; empty phrase.

floß¹ [flɔs] pret. of fließen.

Floß² [flo:s] *n* (-es/*"e*) raft, float.

Flosse ['flɔsə] *f* (-/-n) fin; flipper (of penguin, etc.).

flöß|en ['flø:sən] v/t. (ge-, h) raft, float (timber, etc.); '⊈er *m* (-s/-) rafter, raftsman.

Flöte ♪ ['flø:tə] *f* (-/-n) flute; '⊈n (ge-, h) **1.** v/i. (play the) flute; **2.** v/t. play on the flute.

flott adj. [flɔt] ♣ floating, afloat; pace, etc.: quick, brisk; music, etc.: gay, lively; dress, etc.: smart, stylish; car, etc.: sporty, racy; dancer, etc.: excellent.

Flotte ['flɔtə] *f* (-/-n) ♣ fleet; ✕ navy; '~nstützpunkt ✕ *m* naval base.

Flotille ♣ [flɔ'tiljə] *f* (-/-n) flotilla.

Flöz geol., ✕ ['flø:ts] *n* (-es/-e) seam; layer, stratum.

Fluch [flu:x] *m* (-[e]s/*"e*) curse, malediction; eccl. anathema; curse, swear-word; '⊈en v/i. (ge-, h) swear, curse.

Flucht [fluxt] *f* (-/-en) flight (vor dat. from); escape (aus dat. from); line (of windows, etc.); suite (of rooms); flight (of stairs).

flücht|en ['flyçtən] (ge-) v/i. (sein) and v/refl. (h) flee (nach, zu to); run away; escape; '~ig adj. fugitive (a. fig.); thought, etc.: fleeting; fame, etc.: transient; p. careless, superficial; ♠ volatile; ⊈ling ['~liŋ] *m* (-s/-e) fugitive; pol. refugee; '⊈lingslager *n* refugee camp.

Flug [flu:k] *m* (-[e]s/*"e*) flight; im ~(e) rapidly; quickly; '~abwehrrakete *f* anti-aircraft missile; '~bahn *f* trajectory (of rocket, etc.); ✕ flight path; '~ball *m* tennis, etc.: volley; '~blatt *n* handbill, leaflet, Am. a. flier; '~boot ✕ *n* flying-boat; '~dienst ✈ *m* air service.

Flügel ['fly:gəl] *m* (-s/-) wing (a. ♠, ✕, ✕); blade, vane (of propeller, etc.); s. Fensterflügel, Türflügel, Lungenflügel; sail (of windmill, etc.); ♪ grand piano; '~fenster ♠ *n* casement-window; '⊈lahm adj. broken-winged; '~mann ✕ *m* marker; flank man; '~tür ♠ *f* folding door.

Fluggast ['flu:k-] *m* (air) passenger.

flügge adj. ['flygə] fledged; ~ werden fledge; fig. begin to stand on one's own feet.

'Flug|hafen *m* airport; '~linie *f* ✈ air route; airline; '~platz *m* airfield, aerodrome, Am. a. airdrome; airport; '~sand geol. *m* wind-blown sand; '~schrift *f* pamphlet; '~sicherung *f* air traffic control; '~sport *m* sporting aviation; '~wesen *n* aviation, aeronautics.

'**Flugzeug** n aircraft, aeroplane, F plane, *Am. a.* airplane; '~bau m aircraft construction; '~führer m pilot; ~halle f hangar; '~rumpf m fuselage, body; '~träger m aircraft carrier, *Am. sl.* flattop; '~unglück n air crash *or* disaster.

Flunder *ichth.* ['flundər] f (-/-n) flounder.

Flunker|ei F [fluŋkə'raɪ] f (-/-en) petty lying, F fib(bing); '2n v/i. (ge-, h) F fib, tell fibs.

fluoreszieren [fluores'tsi:rən] v/i. (no -ge-, h) fluoresce.

Flur [flu:r] **1.** f (-/-en) field, meadow; *poet.* lea; **2.** m (-[e]s/-e) (entrance-)hall.

Fluß [flus] m (*Flusses/Flüsse*) river, stream; flow(ing); *fig.* fluency, flux; 2**abwärts** adv. downriver, downstream; 2**aufwärts** adv. upriver, upstream; '~bett n river bed.

flüssig adj. ['flysiç] fluid, liquid; *metal:* molten, melted; ✝ *money, capital, etc.:* available, in hand; *style:* fluent, flowing; '2keit f (-/-en) fluid, liquid; fluidity, liquidity; availability; fluency.

'**Fluß|lauf** n course of a river; '~mündung f mouth of a river; '~pferd zo. n hippopotamus; '~schiffahrt f river navigation *or* traffic.

flüstern ['flystərn] v/i. *and* v/t. (ge-, h) whisper.

Flut [flu:t] f (-/-en) flood; high tide, (flood-)tide; *fig.* flood, torrent, deluge; '2en (ge-) **1.** v/i. (*sein*) *water, crowd, etc.:* flood, surge (*über acc.* over); **2.** v/t. (h) flood (*dock, etc.*); '~welle f tidal wave.

focht [foxt] *pret. of* fechten.

Fohlen zo. ['fo:lən] **1.** n (-s/-) foal; *male:* colt; *female:* filly; **2.** 2 v/i. (ge-, h) foal.

Folge ['fɔlgə] f (-/-n) sequence, succession (*of events*); instalment, part (*of radio series, etc.*); consequence, result; series; set, suit; future; ~n pl. aftermath.

'**folgen** v/i. (dat.) (ge-, sein) follow; succeed (*j-m* s.o.; *auf acc.* to); follow, ensue (*aus* from); obey (*j-m* s.o.); ~**dermaßen** adv. ['.dərma:-sən] as follows; '~schwer adj. of grave consequence, grave.

'**folgerichtig** adj. logical; consistent.

folger|n ['fɔlgərn] v/t. (ge-, h) infer, conclude, deduce (*aus* from); '2ung f (-/-en) inference, conclusion, deduction.

'**folgewidrig** adj. illogical; inconsistent.

folglich *cj.* ['fɔlkliç] therefore, consequently.

folgsam adj. ['fɔlkza:m] obedient; '2keit f (-/no pl.) obedience.

Folie ['fo:ljə] f (-/-n) foil.

Folter ['fɔltər] f (-/-n) torture; *auf die ~ spannen* put to the rack; *fig.* F a. keep on tenterhooks; '2n v/t. (ge-, h) torture, torment; '~qual f torture, *fig. a.* torment.

Fonds ✝ [fõ:] m (-/-) fund (*a. fig.*); funds pl.

Fontäne [fɔn'tɛ:nə] f (-/-n) fountain.

foppen ['fɔpən] v/t. (ge-, h) tease, F pull s.o.'s leg; hoax, fool.

forcieren [fɔr'si:rən] v/t. (no -ge-, h) force (up).

'**Förder|band** n (-[e]s/=er) conveyor-belt; '2lich adj. conducive (*dat.* to), promotive (of); '~korb ⚒ m cage.

fordern ['fɔrdərn] v/t. (ge-, h) demand; claim (*compensation, etc.*); ask (*price, etc.*); challenge (*to duel*).

fördern ['fœrdərn] v/t. (ge-, h) further, advance, promote; ⚒ haul, raise (*coal, etc.*); *zutage ~* reveal, bring to light.

'**Forderung** f (-/-en) demand; claim; charge; challenge.

'**Förderung** f (-/-en) furtherance, advancement, promotion; ⚒ haulage; output. [trout.\]

Forelle *ichth.* [fo'rɛlə] f (-/-n)\

Form [fɔrm] f (-/-en) form; figure, shape; model; ⊕ mo(u)ld; *sports:* form, condition; 2al adj. [~'ma:l] formal; ~alität [~ali'tɛ:t] f (-/-en) formality; ~at [~'ma:t] n (-[e]s/-e) size; *von ~* of distinction; ~el ['~ɔl] f (-/-n) formula; 2ell adj. [~'mɛl] formal; 2en v/t. (ge-, h) form (*object, character, etc.*); shape, fashion (*wood, metal, etc.*); mo(u)ld (*clay, character, etc.*); '~enlehre gr. f accidence; '~fehler m informality; ⚖⚖ flaw; 2ieren [~'mi:rən] v/t. (no -ge-, h) form; draw up, line up; *sich ~* line up.

förmlich adj. ['fœrmliç] formal; ceremonious; '2keit f (-/-en) formality; ceremoniousness.

'**formlos** adj. formless, shapeless; *fig.* informal.

Formular [fɔrmu'la:r] n (-s/-e) form, *Am. a.* blank.

formu'lieren v/t. (no -ge-, h) formulate (*question, etc.*); word, phrase (*question, contract, etc.*).

forsch adj. [fɔrʃ] vigorous, energetic; smart, dashing.

forsch|en ['fɔrʃən] v/i. (ge-, h): ~ *nach* (dat.) search for *or* after; ~ *in* (dat.) search (through); '2er m (-s/-) researcher, research worker.

'**Forschung** f (-/-en) research (work); '~sreise f (exploring) expedition; '~sreisende m explorer.

Forst [fɔrst] m (-es/-e[n]) forest; '~aufseher m (forest-)keeper, gamekeeper.

Förster ['fœrstər] m (-s/-) forester; ranger.

'Forst|haus n forester's house; '~revier n forest district; '~wesen n, '~wirtschaft f forestry.

Fort¹ ⚔ [fo:r] n (-s/-s) fort.

fort² adv. [fort] away, gone; on; gone, lost; in e-m ~ continuously; und so ~ and so on or forth; s. a. weg.

'fort|bestehen v/i. (irr. stehen, sep., no -ge-, h) continue, persist; '~bewegen v/t. (sep., no -ge-, h) move (on, away); sich ~ move, walk; '2dauer f continuance; '~dauern v/i. (sep., -ge-, h) continue, last; '~fahren v/i. (irr. fahren, sep., -ge-) 1. (sein) depart, leave; drive off; 2. (h) continue, keep on (et. zu tun doing s.th.); '~führen v/t. (sep., -ge-, h) continue, carry on; '2gang m departure, leaving; continuance; '~gehen v/i. (irr. gehen, sep., -ge-, sein) go (away), leave; '~geschritten adj. advanced; '2kommen n (-s/no pl.) progress; '~laufend adj. consecutive, continuous; '~pflanzen v/t. (sep., -ge-, h) propagate; sich ~ biol. propagate, reproduce; phys., disease, rumour: be propagated; '2pflanzung f propagation; reproduction; '~reißen v/t. (irr. reißen, sep., -ge-, h) avalanche, etc.: sweep or carry away; '~schaffen v/t. (sep., -ge-, h) get or take away, remove; '~schreiten v/i. (irr. schreiten, sep., -ge-, sein) advance, proceed, progress; '~schreitend adj. progressive; '2schritt m progress; '~schrittlich adj. progressive; '~setzen v/t. (sep., -ge-, h) continue, pursue; '2setzung f (-/-en) continuation, pursuit; ~ folgt to be continued; '~während 1. adj. continual, continuous; perpetual; 2. adv. constantly, always.

Forum ['fo:rum] n (-s/Foren, Fora and -s) forum.

Foto... ['fo:to-] s. Photo...

Foyer [foa'je:] n (-s/-s) thea. foyer, Am. and parl. lobby; hotel: foyer, lounge.

Fracht [fraxt] f (-/-en) goods pl.; 🚂 carriage, freight, ⚓, ✈ freight (-age), cargo; '~brief m 🚂 consignment note, Am., ⚓ bill of lading; '~dampfer m cargo steamer, freighter; '~er m (-s/-) freighter; '2frei adj. carriage or freight paid; '~führer m carrier, Am. a. teamster; '~geld n carriage charges pl., 🚂, ⚓, Am. freight; '~gut n goods pl., freight; '~stück n package.

Frack [frak] m (-[e]s/⁻e, -s) dress coat, tail-coat, F tails; '~anzug m dress-suit.

Frag|e ['fra:gə] f (-/-n) question; gr., reth. interrogation; problem, point; e-e ~ stellen ask a question; in ~ stellen question; '~ebogen m questionnaire; form; '2en (ge-, h)

1. v/t. ask; question; es fragt sich, ob it is doubtful whether; 2. v/i. ask; '~er m (-s/-) questioner; '~ewort gr. n (-[e]s/⁻er) interrogative; '~ezeichen n question-mark, point of interrogation, Am. mst interrogation point; 2lich adj. ['fra:k-] doubtful, uncertain; in question; 2los adv. ['fra:k-] undoubtedly, unquestionably.

Fragment [frag'ment] n (-[e]s/-e) fragment.

fragwürdig adj. ['fra:k-] doubtful, dubious, questionable.

Fraktion parl. [frak'tsjo:n] f (-/-en) (parliamentary) group.

frank|ieren [fraŋ'ki:rən] v/t. (no -ge-, h) prepay, stamp; ~o adv. ['~o] free; post(age) paid; parcel: carriage paid.

Franse ['franzə] f (-/-n) fringe.

Franz|ose [fran'tso:zə] m (-n/-n) Frenchman; die ~n pl. the French pl.; ~ösin [~ø:zin] f (-/-nen) Frenchwoman; 2ösisch adj. [~ø:ziʃ] French.

fräs|en ⊕ ['frε:zən] v/t. (ge-, h) mill; 2maschine ['frε:s-] f milling-machine.

Fraß [fra:s] 1. F m (-es/-e) sl. grub; 2. 2 pret. of fressen.

Fratze ['fratsə] f (-/-n) grimace, F face; ~n schneiden make grimaces.

Frau [frau] f (-/-en) woman; lady; wife; ~ X Mrs X.

'Frauen|arzt m gyn(a)ecologist; '~klinik f hospital for women; '~rechte n/pl. women's rights pl.; '~stimmrecht pol. n women's suffrage; '~zimmer mst contp. n female, woman.

Fräulein ['frɔʏlaɪn] n (-s/-, F -s) young lady; teacher; shop-assistant; waitress; ~ X Miss X.

'fraulich adj. womanly.

frech adj. [frεç] impudent, insolent, F saucy, cheeky, Am. F a. sassy, sl. fresh; lie, etc.: brazen; thief, etc.: bold, daring; '2heit f (-/-en) impudence, insolence; F sauciness, cheek; boldness.

frei adj. [fraɪ] free (von from, of); position: vacant; field: open; parcel: carriage-paid; journalist, etc.: free-lance; liberal; candid, frank; licentious; ~ Haus ✝ franco domicile; ~er Tag day off; im Freien in the open air.

'Frei|bad n open-air bath; '~beuter ['~bɔʏtər] m (-s/-) freebooter; '2bleibend ✝ adj. price, etc.: subject to alteration; offer: conditional; '~brief m charter; fig. warrant; '~denker m (-s/-) freethinker.

Freier ['fraɪər] m (-s/-) suitor.

'Frei|exemplar n free or presentation copy; '~frau f baroness; '~gabe f release; '2geben (irr. geben, sep., -ge-, h) 1. v/t. release; give (s.o. an hour, etc.) off; 2. v/i.: j-m ~ give s.o. time off; '2gebig adj. generous, liberal; '~gebigkeit f (-/-en) generosity, liberality; '~gepäck n free luggage; '2haben v/i. (irr. haben, sep., -ge-, h) have a holiday; have a day off; '~hafen m free port; '2halten v/t. (irr. halten, sep., -ge-, h) keep free or clear; in restaurant, etc.: treat; '~handel m free trade.

'**Freiheit** f (-/-en) liberty; freedom; dichterische ~ poetic licence, Am. poetic license.

'**Frei|herr** m baron; '~karte f free (thea. a. complimentary) ticket; '2lassen v/t. (irr. lassen, sep., -ge-, h) release, set free or at liberty; gegen Kaution ~ 🏛 release on bail; '~lassung f (-/-en) release; '~lauf m free-wheel.

'**freilich** adv. indeed, certainly, of course; admittedly.

'**Frei|lichtbühne** f open-air stage or theat|re, Am. -er; '2machen v/t. (sep., -ge-, h) 🖂 prepay, stamp (letter, etc.); sich ~ undress, take one's clothes off; '~marke f stamp; '~maurer m freemason; '~maurerei [~'raɪ] f (-/no pl.) freemasonry; '~mut m frankness; '2mütig adj. ['~my:tiç] frank; '2schaffend adj.: ~er Künstler free-lance artist; ~schärler 🏛 ['~ʃɛːrlər] m (-s/-) volunteer, irregular; '~schein m licen|ce, Am. -se; '2sinnig adj. liberal; '2sprechen v/t. (irr. sprechen, sep., -ge-, h) esp. eccl. absolve (von from); 🏛 acquit (of); release (apprentice) from his articles; '~sprechung f (-/-en) esp. eccl. absolution; release from articles; = '~spruch 🏛 m acquittal; '~staat pol. m free state; '2stehen v/i. (irr. stehen, sep., -ge-, h) house, etc.: stand empty; es steht Ihnen frei zu inf. you are free or at liberty to inf.; '2stellen v/t. (sep., -ge-, h): j-n ~ exempt s.o. (von from) (a. 🗡); j-m et. ~ leave s.th. open to s.o.; '~stoß m football: free kick; '~tag m Friday; '~tod m suicide; '2tragend △ adj. cantilever; '~treppe f outdoor staircase; '2willig 1. adj. voluntary; 2. adv. a. of one's own free will; ~willige f (~'viligə) m (-n/-n) volunteer; '~zeit f free or spare or leisure time; 2zügig adj. ['~tsy:giç] free to move; '~zügigkeit f (-/no pl.) freedom of movement.

fremd adj. (fremt) strange; foreign; alien; extraneous; '~artig adj. strange; exotic.

Fremde ['fremdə] 1. f (-/no pl.) distant or foreign parts; in der ~ far away from home, abroad; 2. m, f (-n/-n) stranger; foreigner; '~buch n visitors' book; '~nführer m guide, cicerone; '~nheim n

boarding house; ~nindustrie ['fremdən⁹-] f tourist industry; ~nlegion 🗡 f Foreign Legion; ~nverkehr m tourism, tourist traffic; '~nzimmer n spare (bed-) room; tourism: room.

'**Fremd|herrschaft** f foreign rule; '~körper 🗡 m foreign body; 2ländisch adj. ['~lɛndiʃ] foreign, exotic; '~sprache f foreign language; '2sprachig adj., '2sprachlich adj. foreign-language; '~wort n (-[e]s/=er) foreign word.

Frequenz phys. [fre'kvɛnts] f (-/-en) frequency.

fressen ['frɛsən] 1. v/t. (irr., ge-, h) eat; beast of prey: devour; F p. devour, gorge; 2. v/i. (irr., ge-, h) eat; F p. gorge; 3. 2 n (-s/no pl.) feed, food.

'**Freß|gier** f voracity, gluttony; '~napf m feeding dish.

Freude ['frɔydə] f (-/-n) joy, gladness; delight; pleasure; ~ haben an (dat.) find or take pleasure in.

'**Freuden|botschaft** f glad tidings pl.; '~fest n happy occasion; '~feuer n bonfire; '~geschrei n shouts pl. of joy; '~tag m day of rejoicing, red-letter day; '~taumel m transports pl. of joy.

'**freud|estrahlend** adj. radiant with joy; '~ig adj. joyful; happy; ~es Ereignis happy event; '~los adj. ['frɔytloːs] joyless, cheerless.

freuen ['frɔyən] v/t. (ge-, h): es freut mich, daß I am glad or pleased (that); sich ~ über (acc.) be pleased about or with, be glad about; sich ~ auf (acc.) look forward to.

Freund [frɔynt] m (-es/-e) (boy-) friend; '~in [~'dɪn] f (-/-nen) (girl-) friend; '2lich adj. friendly, kind, nice; cheerful; bright; climate: mild; '~lichkeit f (-/-en) friendliness, kindness; '~schaft f (-/-en) friendship; ~ schließen make friends (mit with); '2schaftlich adj. friendly.

Frevel ['fre:fəl] m (-s/-) outrage (an dat., gegen on), crime (against); '2haft adj. wicked, outrageous; impious; '2n v/i. (ge-, h) commit a crime or outrage (gegen against).

Frevler ['fre:flər] m (-s/-) evil-doer, offender; blasphemer.

Friede(n) ['fri:də(n)] m (Friedens/ Frieden) peace; im Frieden in peace-time; laß mich in Frieden! leave me alone!

'**Friedens|bruch** m violation of (the) peace; '~stifter m peace-maker; '~störer m (-s/-) disturber of the peace; '~verhandlungen f/pl. peace negotiations pl.; '~vertrag m peace treaty.

fried|fertig adj. ['fri:t-] peaceable, peace-loving; '2hof m cemetery, graveyard; churchyard; '~lich adj.

s. friedfertig; peaceful; '∼liebend adj. peace-loving.

frieren ['fri:rən] v/i. (irr., ge-) 1. (sein) liquid: freeze, become frozen; river, etc.: freeze (over, up); window-pane, etc.: freeze over; 2. (h) be or feel cold; mich friert or ich friere an den Füßen my feet are cold.

Fries △ [fri:s] m (-es/-e) frieze.

frisch [friʃ] 1. adj. food, flowers, etc.: fresh; egg: new-laid; linen, etc.: clean; auf ∼er Tat ertappen catch red-handed; 2. adv.: ∼ gestrichen! wet paint!, Am. fresh paint!; 2e ['∼ə] f (-/no pl.) freshness.

Friseu|r [fri'zø:r] m (-s/-e) hairdresser; (men's) barber; ∼se [∼zə] f (-/-n) (woman) hairdresser.

fri'sier|en v/t. (no -ge-, h): j-n ∼ do or dress s.o.'s hair; F: einen Wagen ∼ mot. tune up or soup up or hot up a car; sich ∼ do one's hair; 2kommode f dressing-table; 2salon m hairdressing saloon; 2tisch m s. Frisierkommode.

Frist [frist] f (-/-en) (fixed or limited) period of time; time allowed; term; ✝ prescribed time; ✝ respite, grace; '2en v/t. (ge-, h): sein Dasein ∼ scrape along, scrape a living.

Frisur [fri'zu:r] f (-/-en) hair-style, hair-do, coiffure.

frivol adj. [fri'vo:l] frivolous, flippant; 2ität [∼oli'tɛ:t] f (-/-en) frivolity, flippancy.

froh adj. [fro:] joyful, glad; cheerful; happy; gay (a. colour).

fröhlich adj. ['frø:liç] gay, merry, cheerful, happy, Am. F a. chipper; '2keit f (-/% -en) gaiety, cheerfulness; merriment.

froh'locken v/i. (no -ge-, h) shout for joy, be jubilant; exult (über acc. at, in); gloat (over); '2sinn m (-[e]s/no pl.) gaiety, cheerfulness.

fromm adj. [frɔm] p. pious, religious; life, etc.: godly; prayer, etc.: devout; horse, etc.: docile; ∼e Lüge white lie; ∼er Wunsch wishful thinking, idle wish.

Frömmelei [frœmə'lai] f (-/-en) affected piety, bigotry.

'Frömmigkeit f (-/-en) piety, religiousness; godliness; devoutness.

Fron [fro:n] f (-/-en), '∼arbeit f, '∼dienst hist. m forced or compulsory labo(u)r or service; fig. drudgery.

frönen ['frø:nən] v/i. (dat.) (ge-, h) indulge in; be a slave to.

Front [frɔnt] f (-/-en) △ front, façade; face; ✕ front (line), line; pol., ✝, etc.: front.

fror [fro:r] pret. of frieren.

Frosch zo. [frɔʃ] m (-es/⁼e) frog; '∼perspektive f worm's-eye view.

Frost [frɔst] m (-es/⁼e) frost; chill; '∼beule f chilblain.

frösteln ['frœstəln] v/i. (ge-, h) feel chilly, shiver (with cold).

'frostig adj. frosty (a. fig.); fig. cold, frigid, icy.

'Frost|salbe ⚕ f chilblain ointment; '∼schaden m frost damage; '∼schutzmittel mot. n anti-freezing mixture; '∼wetter n frosty weather.

frottier|en [frɔ'ti:rən] v/t. (no -ge-, h) rub; 2(hand)tuch n Turkish towel.

Frucht [fruxt] f (-/⁼e) ⚕ fruit (a. fig.); corn; crop; fig. reward, result; '2bar adj. fruitful (esp. fig.); fertile (a. biol.); '∼barkeit f (-/no pl.) fruitfulness; fertility; '2bringend adj. fruit-bearing; fig. fruitful; '2en fig. v/i. (ge-, h) be of use; '∼knoten ⚕ m ovary; '2los adj. fruitless; fig. a. ineffective.

früh [fry:] 1. adj. early; am ∼en Morgen in the early morning; ∼es Aufstehen early rising; ∼e Anzeichen early symptoms; ∼er former; 2. adv. in the morning; ∼ aufstehen rise early; heute ∼ this morning; morgen ∼ tomorrow morning; ∼er earlier; formerly, in former times; ∼estens at the earliest; '2aufsteher m (-s/-) early riser, F early bird; '2e f (-/no pl.): in aller ∼ very early in the morning; '2geburt f premature birth; premature baby or animal; '2gottesdienst m early service; '2jahr n, 2ling ['∼lin] m (-s/-e) spring; ∼'morgens adv. early in the morning; '∼reif fig. adj. precocious; '2sport m early morning exercises; '2stück n breakfast; '∼stücken (ge-, h) 1. v/i. (have) breakfast; 2. v/t. have s.th. for breakfast; '2zug m early train.

Fuchs [fuks] m (-es/⁼e) zo. fox (a. fig.); horse: sorrel.

Füchsin zo. ['fyksin] f (-/-nen) she-fox, vixen.

'Fuchs|jagd f fox-hunt(ing); '∼pelz m fox-fur; '2rot adj. foxy-red, sorrel; '∼schwanz m foxtail; ⊕ pad-saw; ⚕ amaranth(us); '2'teufels-wild F adj. mad with rage, F hopping mad.

fuchteln ['fuxtəln] v/i. (ge-, h): ∼ mit (dat.) wave (one's hands) about.

Fuder ['fu:dər] n (-s/-) cart-load; tun (of wine). [♩ fugue.]

Fuge ['fu:gə] f (-/-n) ⊕ joint; seam;♩

füg|en ['fy:gən] v/refl. (ge-, h) submit, give in, yield (Zat., in acc. to); comply (with); ∼sam adj. ['fy:k-] (com)pliant; manageable.

fühl|bar adj. ['fy:lba:r] tangible, palpable; fig. sensible, noticeable; '∼en (ge-, h) 1. v/t. feel; be aware of; sich glücklich ∼ feel happy; 2. v/i.: mit j-m ∼ feel for or sympathize with s.o.; '2er m (-s/-) feeler

(a. fig.); '²ung f (-/-en) touch, contact (a. ✕.); ~ haben be in touch (mit with); ~ verlieren lose touch.
fuhr [fu:r] pret. of fahren.
Fuhre ['fu:rə] f (-/-n) cart-load.
führen ['fy:rən] (ge-, h) 1. v/t. lead, guide (blind person, etc.); show (zu dat. to); wield (paint-brush, etc.); ✕ command (regiment, etc.); have, bear (title, etc.); carry on (conversation, etc.); conduct (campaign, etc.); ✝ run (shop, etc.); deal in (goods); lead (life); keep (diary, etc.); ⚖ try (case); wage (war) (mit, gegen against); ~ durch show round; sich ~ conduct o.s., behave (o.s.); 2. v/i. path, etc.: lead, run, go (nach, zu to); sports, etc.: (hold the) lead, be ahead; ~ zu lead to, result in; '~d adj. leading, prominent, Am. a. banner.
'Führer m (-s/-) leader (a. pol., sports); guide(-book); '~raum ✈ m cockpit; '~schein mot. m driving licence, Am. driver's license; '~sitz m mot. driver's seat, ✈ pilot's seat; '~stand ⛿ m (driver's) cab.
'Fuhr|geld n, '~lohn m cartage, carriage; '~mann m (-[e]s/-er, -leute) carter, carrier, wag(g)oner; driver; '~park m fleet (of lorries), Am. fleet (of trucks).
'Führung f (-/-en) leadership; conduct, management; guidance; conduct, behavio(u)r; sports, etc.: lead; '~szeugnis n certificate of good conduct.
'Fuhr|unternehmer m carrier, haulage contractor, Am. a. trucker, teamster; '~werk n (horse-drawn) vehicle; cart, wag(g)on.
Fülle ['fylə] f (-/no pl.) fullness (a. fig.); corpulence, plumpness, stoutness; fig. wealth, abundance, profusion.
füllen¹ ['fylən] v/t. (ge-, h) fill (a. tooth); stuff (cushion, poultry, etc.).
Füllen² zo. [~] n (-s/-) foal; male: colt; female: filly.
'Füll|er F m (-s/-), '~feder(halter m) f fountain-pen; '~horn n horn of plenty; '~ung f (-/-en) filling; panel (of door, etc.).
Fund [funt] m (-[e]s/-e) finding, discovery; find.
Fundament [funda'mɛnt] n(-[e]s/-e) ⚖ foundation; fig. basis.
'Fund|büro n lost-property office; '~gegenstand m object found; '~grube fig. f rich source, mine.
fünf adj. [fynf] five; '²eck n pentagon; '~fach adj. ['~fax] fivefold, quintuple; '²kampf m sports: pentathlon; '²linge ['~liŋə] m/pl. quintuplets pl.; '~te adj. fifth; '²tel n (-s/-) fifth; '~tens adv. fifthly, in the fifth place; '~zehn(te) adj. fifteen(th); '~zig adj. ['~tsiç] fifty; '~zigste adj. fiftieth.

fungieren [fuŋ'gi:rən] v/i. (no -ge-, h): ~ als officiate or act as.
Funk [funk] m (-s/no pl.) radio, wireless; '~anlage f radio or wireless installation or equipment; '~bastler m do-it-yourself radio ham; '~bild n photo-radiogram.
Funke ['funkə] m (-ns/-n) spark; fig. a. glimmer.
'funkeln v/i. (ge-, h) sparkle, glitter; star: twinkle, sparkle.
'Funken¹ esp. fig. m (-s/-) s. Funke.
'funken² v/t. (ge-, h) radio, wireless, broadcast.
'Funk|er m (-s/-) radio or wireless operator; '~gerät n radio (communication) set; '~spruch m radio or wireless message; '~station f radio or wireless station; '~stille f radio or wireless silence; '~streifenwagen m radio patrol car.
Funktion [funk'tsjo:n] f (-/-en) function; ~är [~tsjo'nɛ:r] m (-s/-e) functionary, official; 2ieren [~o'ni:rən] v/i. (no -ge-, h) function, work.
'Funk|turm m radio or wireless tower; '~verkehr m radio or wireless communication; '~wagen m radio car; '~wesen n (-s/no pl.) radio communication.
für prp. (acc.) [fy:r] for; in exchange or return for; in favo(u)r of; in s.o.'s place; Schritt ~ Schritt step by step; Tag ~ Tag day after day; ich ~ meine Person ... as for me, I ...; das Für und Wider the pros and cons pl.
'Fürbitte f intercession.
Furche ['furçə] f (-/-n) furrow (a. in face); rut; ⊕ groove; '²n v/t. (ge-, h) furrow (a. face); ⊕ groove.
Furcht [furçt] f (-/no pl.) fear, dread; aus ~ vor for fear of; '²bar adj. awful, terrible, dreadful.
fürchten ['fyrçtən] (ge-, h) 1. v/t. fear, dread; sich ~ vor (dat.) be afraid or scared of; 2. v/i.: ~ um fear for.
'fürchterlich adj. s. furchtbar.
'furcht|los adj. fearless; '²losigkeit f (-/no pl.) fearlessness; '~sam adj. timid, timorous; '²samkeit f (-/no pl.) timidity.
Furie fig. ['fu:rjə] f (-/-n) fury.
Furnier ⊕ [fur'ni:r] n (-s/-e) veneer; ²en v/t. (no -ge-, h) veneer.
'Für|sorge f care; öffentliche ~ public welfare work; '~sorgeamt n welfare department; '~sorgeerziehung f corrective training for juvenile delinquents; '~sorger m (-s/-) social or welfare worker; '²sorglich adj. considerate, thoughtful, solicitous; '~sprache f intercession (für for, bei with); '~sprecher m intercessor.
Fürst [fyrst] m (-en/-en) prince; sovereign; '~enhaus n dynasty;

'**∼enstand** *m* prince's rank; '**∼entum** *n* (-s/∼er) principality; '**Ǫlich 1.** *adj.* princely (*a. fig.*), royal; *fig.* magnificent, sumptuous; **2.** *adv.*: ∼ *leben* live like a lord *or* king; '**∼lichkeiten** *f/pl.* royalties *pl.*

Furt [furt] *f* (-/-en) ford.

Furunkel [fu'ruŋkəl] *m* (-s/-) boil, furuncle.

'**Fürwort** *gr. n* (-[e]s/∼er) pronoun.

Fusel F ['fu:zəl] *m* (-s/-) low-quality spirits, F rotgut.

Fusion ✝ [fu'zjo:n] *f* (-/-en) merger, amalgamation.

Fuß [fu:s] *m* (-es/∼e) foot; ∼ *fassen* find a foothold; *fig.* become established; *auf gutem (schlechtem)* ∼ *stehen mit* be on good (bad) terms with; *zu* ∼ on foot; *zu* ∼ *gehen* walk; *gut zu* ∼ *sein* be a good walker; '**∼abstreifer** *m* (-s/-) door-scraper, door-mat; '**∼angel** *f* mantrap; '**∼ball** *m* (association) football, F *and Am.* soccer; '**∼ballspieler** *m* football player, footballer; '**∼bank** *f* footstool; '**∼bekleidung** *f* footwear, footgear; '**∼boden** *m* floor (-ing); '**∼bodenbelag** *m* floor covering; '**∼bremse** *mot. f* foot-brake;

'**Ǫen** *v/i.* (ge-, h): ∼ *auf* (*dat.*) be based *or* founded on; **∼gänger** ['∼geŋər] *m* (-s/-) pedestrian; '**∼gelenk** *anat. n* ankle joint; '**∼note** *f* footnote; '**∼pfad** *m* footpath; '**∼sack** *m* foot-muff; '**∼sohle** *anat. f* sole of the foot; '**∼soldat** ✗ *m* foot-soldier, infantryman; '**∼spur** *f* footprint; track; **∼stapfe** ['∼ʃtapfə] *f* (-/-n) footprint, *fig. a.* footstep; '**∼steig** *m* footpath; '**∼tritt** *m* kick; '**∼wanderung** *f* walking tour, hike; '**∼weg** *m* footpath.

Futter ['futər] *n* **1.** (-s/*no pl.*) food, *sl.* grub, *Am.* F *a.* chow; feed, fodder; **2.** (-s/-) lining; ⚠ casing.

Futteral [futə'ra:l] *n* (-s/-e) case (*for spectacles, etc.*); cover (*of umbrella*); sheath (*of knife*).

'**Futtermittel** *n* feeding stuff.

füttern ['fytərn] *v/t.* (ge-, h) feed; line (*dress, etc.*); ⚠ case.

'**Futter|napf** *m* feeding bowl *or* dish; '**∼neid** *fig. m* (professional) jealousy; '**∼stoff** *m* lining (material).

'**Fütterung** *f* (-/-en) feeding; lining; ⚠ casing.

Futur *gr.* [fu'tu:r] *n* (-s/-e) future (tense).

G

gab [ga:p] *pret. of geben.*

Gabe ['ga:bə] *f* (-/-n) gift, present; alms; donation; ✒ dose; talent.

Gabel ['ga:bəl] *f* (-/-n) fork; 'Ǫn *v/refl.* (ge-, h) fork, bifurcate; '**∼ung** *f* (-/-en) bifurcation.

gackern ['gakərn] *v/i.* (ge-, h) cackle.

gaffen ['gafən] *v/i.* (ge-, h) gape; stare.

Gage ['ga:ʒə] *f* (-/-n) salary, pay.

gähnen ['gɛ:nən] **1.** *v/i.* (ge-, h) yawn; **2.** Ǫ *n* (-s/*no pl.*) yawning.

Gala ['gala] *f* (-/*no pl.*) gala; *in* ∼ in full dress.

galant *adj.* [ga'lant] gallant; courteous; Ǫerie [∼ə'ri:] *f* (-/-n) gallantry; courtesy.

Galeere ⚓ [ga'le:rə] *f* (-/-n) galley.

Galerie [galə'ri:] *f* (-/-n) gallery.

Galgen ['galgən] *m* (-s/-) gallows, gibbet; '**∼frist** *f* respite; '**∼gesicht** *n* gallows-look, hangdog look; '**∼humor** *m* grim humo(u)r; '**∼strick** *m*, '**∼vogel** *m* gallows-bird, hangdog.

Galle *anat.* ['galə] *f* (-/-n) bile (*of person*); gall (*of animal*) (*a. fig.*); '**∼nblase** *anat. f* gall-bladder; '**∼nleiden** ✒ *n* bilious complaint; '**∼nstein** ✒ *m* gall-stone, bile-stone.

Gallert ['galərt] *n* (-[e]s/-e), **∼e** [ga'lɛrtə] *f* (-/-n) gelatine, jelly.

'**gallig** *fig. adj.* bilious.

Galopp [ga'lɔp] *m* (-s/-s, -e) gallop; canter; Ǫieren [∼'pi:rən] *v/i.* (*no* -ge-, *sein*) gallop; canter.

galt [galt] *pret. of gelten.*

galvani|sch *adj.* [gal'va:niʃ] galvanic; **∼sieren** [∼ani'-] *v/t.* (*no* -ge-, h) galvanize.

Gang¹ [gaŋ] *m* (-[e]s/∼e) walk; *s. Gangart; fig.* motion; running; working (*of machine*); errand; way; course (*of events, of a meal, etc.*); passage(-way); alley; corridor, gallery; *in vehicle, between seats*: gangway, *esp. Am.* aisle; 🚆 corridor, *Am.* aisle; *fencing*: pass; *anat.* duct; *mot.* gear; *erster (zweiter, dritter, vierter)* ∼ low *or* bottom (second, third, top) gear; *in* ∼ *bringen or setzen* set going *or* in motion, *Am.* operate; *in* ∼ *kommen* get going, get started; *im* ∼ *sein* be in motion; ⊕ be working *or* running; *fig.* be in progress; *in vollem* ∼ in full swing.

gang² *adj.* [∼]: ∼ *und gäbe* customary, traditional.

'**Gang|art** *f* gait, walk (*of person*); pace (*of horse*); Ǫbar *adj. road*: practicable, passable; *money*: current; ✝ *goods*: marketable; *s. gängig*.

Gängelband ['gɛŋəl-] *n* leading-strings *pl.*; *am ~ führen* keep in leading-strings, lead by the nose.

gängig *adj.* ['gɛnɪç] *money:* current; † *goods:* marketable; *~er Ausdruck* current word *or* phrase.

Gans *orn.* [gans] *f* (-/ᵘe) goose.

Gänse|blümchen ♀ ['gɛnzəbly:mçən] *n* (-s/-) daisy; *~braten m* roast goose; *~feder f* goose-quill; *~füßchen* ['~fy:sçən] *n/pl.* quotation marks *pl.*, inverted commas *pl.*; *~haut f* goose-skin; *fig. a.* gooseflesh, *Am. a.* goose pimples *pl.*; *~klein n* (-s/no *pl.*) (goose-)giblets *pl.*; *~marsch m* single *or* Indian file; *~rich orn.* ['~rɪç] *m* (-s/-e) gander; *~schmalz n* goose-grease.

ganz [gants] **1.** *adj.* all; entire, whole; complete, total, full; *den ~en Tag* all day (long); **2.** *adv.* quite; entirely, *etc.* (s. *1.*); very; *~ Auge (Ohr)* all eyes (ears); *~ und gar* wholly, totally; *~ und gar nicht* not at all; *im ~en* on the whole, generally; in all; † *in the lump;* '2e *n* (-n/no *pl.*) whole; totality; *aufs ~ gehen* go all out, *esp. Am. sl.* go the whole hog.

gänzlich *adj.* ['gɛntslɪç] complete, total, entire.

'**Ganztagsbeschäftigung** *f* fulltime job *or* employment.

gar [gɑ:r] **1.** *adj. food:* done; **2.** *adv.* quite, very; even; *~ nicht* not at all.

Garage [ga'rɑ:ʒə] *f* (-/-n) garage.

Garantie [garan'ti:] *f* (-/-n) guarantee, warranty, ⚜ guaranty; 2**ren** *v/t.* (no -ge-, h) guarantee, warrant.

Garbe ['garbə] *f* (-/-n) sheaf.

Garde ['gardə] *f* (-/-n) guard.

Garderobe [gardə'ro:bə] *f* (-/-n) wardrobe, cloakroom, *Am.* checkroom; *thea.* dressing-room; *~nfrau f* cloak-room attendant, *Am.* hatcheck girl; *~nmarke f* check; *~nschrank m* wardrobe; *~nständer m* coat-stand, hat-stand, hall-stand.

Garderobiere [gardəro'bjɛ:rə] *f* (-/-n) s. *Garderobenfrau; thea.* wardrobe mistress.

Gardine [gar'di:nə] *f* (-/-n) curtain.

gär|en ['gɛːrən] *v/i.* (*irr.*, ge-, h, sein) ferment; 2**mittel** *n* ferment.

Garn [garn] *n* (-[e]s/-e) yarn; thread; cotton; net; *j-m ins ~ gehen* fall into s.o.'s snare.

Garnele *zo.* [gar'ne:lə] *f* (-/-n) shrimp.

garnieren [gar'ni:rən] *v/t.* (no -ge-, h) trim; garnish (*esp. a dish*).

Garnison ✕ [garni'zo:n] *f* (-/-en) garrison, post.

Garnitur [garni'tu:r] *f* (-/-en) trimming; ⊕ fittings *pl.*; set.

garstig *adj.* ['garstɪç] nasty, bad; ugly.

'**Gärstoff** *m* ferment.

Garten ['gartən] *m* (-s/ᵘ) garden; *~anlage f* gardens *pl.*, park; *~ar-*

beit f gardening; '*~bau m* horticulture; '*~erde f* (garden-)mo(u)ld; '*~fest n* garden-party, *Am. a.* lawn party; '*~geräte n/pl.* gardening-tools *pl.*; '*~stadt f* garden city.

Gärtner ['gɛrtnər] *m* (-s/-) gardener; *~ei* [*~*'raɪ] *f* (-/-en) gardening, horticulture; nursery; '*~in f* (-/-nen) gardener.

Gärung ['gɛːruŋ] *f* (-/-en) fermentation.

Gas [gɑ:s] *n* (-es/-e) gas; *~ geben mot.* open the throttle, *Am.* step on the gas; '*~anstalt f* gas-works, *Am. a.* gas plant; '*~behälter m* gasometer, *Am.* gas tank *or* container; '*~beleuchtung f* gaslight; '*~brenner m* gas-burner; 2**förmig** *adj.* ['~fœrmɪç] gaseous; '*~hahn m* gas-tap; '*~herd m* gas-stove, *Am.* gas range; '*~leitung f* gas-mains *pl.*; '*~messer m* (-s/-) gas-meter; '*~ofen m* gas-oven; '*~pedal mot. n* accelerator (pedal), *Am.* gas pedal.

Gasse ['gasə] *f* (-/-n) lane, by-street, alley(-way); '*~nhauer m* (-s/-) street ballad, popular song; '*~njunge m* street arab.

Gast [gast] *m* (-es/ᵘe) guest; visitor; customer (*of public house, etc.*); *thea.:* guest (artist); guest star; '*~arbeiter m* foreign worker; '*~bett n* spare bed.

Gäste|buch ['gɛstə-] *n* visitors' book; '*~zimmer n* guest-room; spare (bed)room; s. *Gaststube.*

'**gast|freundlich** *adj.* hospitable; 2**freundschaft** *f* hospitality; '2**geber m** (-s/-) host; '2**geberin** *f* (-/-nen) hostess; '2**haus** *n*, '2**hof** *m* restaurant; inn, hotel; '2**hörer** *univ. m* guest student, *Am. a.* auditor.

gastieren *thea.* [gas'ti:rən] *v/i.* (no -ge-, h) appear as a guest.

'**gast|lich** *adj.* hospitable; '2**mahl** *n* feast, banquet; '2**recht** *n* right of *or* to hospitality; '2**rolle** *thea. f* guest part; starring part *or* role; '2**spiel** *thea. n* guest appearance *or* performance; starring (performance); '2**stätte** *f* restaurant; '2**stube** *f* taproom; restaurant; '2**wirt m** innkeeper, landlord; '2**wirtin** *f* innkeeper, landlady; '2**wirtschaft** *f* inn, public house, restaurant; '2**zimmer** *n* s. *Gästezimmer.*

'**Gas|uhr** *f* gas-meter; '*~werk n* s. *Gasanstalt.*

Gatte ['gatə] *m* (-n/-n) husband; spouse, consort.

Gatter ['gatər] *n* (-s/-) lattice; railing, grating.

'**Gattin** *f* (-/-nen) wife; spouse, consort.

Gattung ['gatuŋ] *f* (-/-en) kind; sort; type; species; genus.

gaukeln ['gaukəln] *v/i.* (ge-, h) juggle; *birds, etc.:* flutter.

Gaul [gaul] *m* (-[e]s/ᵘe) (old) nag.

Gaumen *anat.* ['gaumən] *m* (-s/-) palate.

Gauner ['gaunər] *m* (-s/-) scoundrel, swindler, sharper, *sl.* crook; ᴬei [ᴬ'raɪ] *f* (-/-en) swindling, cheating, trickery.

Gaze ['ɡɑːzə] *f* (-/-n) gauze.

Gazelle *zo.* [ga'tsɛlə] *f* (-/-n) gazelle.

Geächtete [gə'ɛçtətə] *m, f* (-n/-n) outlaw.

Gebäck [gə'bɛk] *n* (-[e]s/-e) baker's goods *pl.*; pastry; fancy cakes *pl.*

ge'backen *p.p. of* backen.

Gebälk [gə'bɛlk] *n* (-[e]s/no *pl.*) framework, timber-work; beams *pl.*

gebar [gə'baːr] *pret. of* gebären.

Gebärde [gə'bɛːrdə] *f* (-/-n) gesture; Ձn *v/refl.* (no -ge-, h) conduct o.s., behave; ᴬnspiel *n* (-[e]s/no *pl.*) gesticulation; dumb show, pantomime; ᴬnsprache *f* language of gestures.

Gebaren [gə'baːrən] *n* (-s/no *pl.*) conduct, deportment, behavio(u)r.

gebären [gə'bɛːrən] *v/t.* (irr., no -ge-, h) bear, bring forth (a. fig.); give birth to.

Ge|bäude [gə'bɔydə] *n* (-s/-) building, edifice, structure; ᴬbell [ᴬ'bɛl] *n* (-[e]s/no *pl.*) barking.

geben ['geːbən] *v/t.* (irr., ge-, h) give (*j-m* et. s.o. s.th.); present (s.o. with s.th.); put; yield *s.th.*; deal (*cards*); pledge (*one's word*); *von sich* ᴬ emit; utter (*words*); bring up, vomit (*food*); et. (*nichts*) ᴬ *auf* (*acc.*) set (no) great store by; *sich geschlagen* ᴬ give in; *sich zufrieden* ᴬ content o.s. (*mit* with); *sich zu erkennen* ᴬ make o.s. known; *es gibt* there is, there are; *was gibt es?* what is the matter?; *thea.*: *gegeben werden* be on.

Gebet [gə'beːt] *n* (-[e]s/-e) prayer.

ge'beten *p.p. of* bitten.

Gebiet [gə'biːt] *n* (-[e]s/-e) territory; district; region; area; *fig.*: field; province; sphere.

ge'biet|en (irr. bieten, no -ge-, h) **1.** *v/t.* order, command; **2.** *v/i.* rule; Ձer *m* (-s/-) master, lord, governor; Ձerin *f* (-/-nen) mistress; ᴬerisch *adj.* imperious; commanding.

Gebilde [gə'bɪldə] *n* (-s/-) form, shape; structure; Ձt *adj.* educated; cultured, cultivated.

Gebirg|e [gə'bɪrgə] *n* (-s/-) mountains *pl.*; mountain chain *or* range; Ձig *adj.* mountainous; ᴬsbewohner *m* mountaineer; ᴬszug *m* mountain range.

Ge'biß *n* (Gebisses/Gebisse) (set of) teeth; (set of) artificial *or* false teeth, denture; *harness*: bit.

ge|'bissen *p.p. of* beißen; ᴬ'blasen *p.p. of* blasen; ᴬ'blichen *p.p. of* bleichen 2; ᴬblieben [ᴬ'bliːbən] *p.p. of* bleiben; ᴬblümt *adj.*

[ᴬ'blyːmt] *pattern, design*: flowered; *material*: sprigged; ᴬ'bogen **1.** *p.p. of* biegen; **2.** *adj.* bent, curved; ᴬboren [ᴬ'boːrən] **1.** *p.p. of* gebären; **2.** *adj.* born; *ein* ᴬer *Deutscher* German by birth; ᴬe *Schmidt* née Smith.

ge'borgen 1. *p.p. of* bergen; **2.** *adj.* safe, sheltered; Ձheit *f* (-/no *pl.*) safety, security.

geborsten [gə'bɔrstən] *p.p. of* bersten.

Ge'bot *n* (-[e]s/-e) order; command; bid(ding), offer; *eccl.*: *die Zehn* ᴬe *pl.* the Ten Commandments *pl.*; Ձen *p.p. of* bieten.

ge|bracht [gə'braxt] *p.p. of* bringen; ᴬbrannt [ᴬ'brant] *p.p. of* brennen; ᴬ'braten *p.p. of* braten.

Ge'brauch *m* **1.** (-[e]s/no *pl.*) use; ⚕ application; **2.** (-[e]s/ᴬe) usage, practice; custom; Ձen *v/t.* (no -ge-, h) use, employ; Ձt *adj. clothes, etc.*: second-hand.

gebräuchlich *adj.* [gə'brɔyçliç] in use; usual, customary.

Ge'brauchs|anweisung *f* directions *pl.* or instructions *pl.* for use; ᴬartikel *m* commodity, necessary, requisite; personal article; Ձfertig *adj.* ready for use; coffee, *etc.*: instant; ᴬmuster † *n* sample; registered design.

Ge'braucht|wagen *mot. m* used car; ᴬwaren *f/pl.* second-hand articles *pl.*

Ge'brechen *n* (-s/-) defect, infirmity; affliction.

ge'brechlich *adj.* fragile; *p.*: frail, weak; infirm; Ձkeit *f* (-/-en) fragility; infirmity.

gebrochen [gə'brɔxən] *p.p. of* brechen.

Ge|brüder [gə'bryːdər] *pl.* brothers *pl.*; ᴬbrüll [ᴬ'bryl] *n* (-[e]s/no *pl.*) roaring; lowing (*of cattle*).

Gebühr [gə'byːr] *f* (-/-en) due; duty; charge; rate; fee; ᴬen *pl.* fee(s *pl.*), dues *pl.*; Ձen *v/i.* (no -ge-, h) be due (*dat.* to); *sich* ᴬ be proper *or* fitting; Ձend *adj.* due; becoming; proper; Ձenfrei *adj.* free of charge; Ձenpflichtig *adj.* liable to charges, chargeable.

gebunden [gə'bundən] **1.** *p.p. of* binden; **2.** *adj.* bound.

Geburt [gə'buːrt] *f* (-/-en) birth; ᴬenkontrolle *f*, ᴬenregelung *f* birth-control; ᴬenziffer *f* birth-rate.

gebürtig *adj.* [gə'byrtiç]: ᴬ *aus* a native of.

Ge'burts|anzeige *f* announcement of birth; ᴬfehler *m* congenital defect; ᴬhelfer *m* obstetrician; ᴬhilfe *f* obstetrics, midwifery; ᴬjahr *n* year of birth; ᴬland *n* native country; ᴬort *m* birth-place; ᴬschein *m* birth certificate; ᴬtag *m* birthday; ~urkunde f birth certificate.

Gebüsch [gə'byʃ] n (-es/-e) bushes pl., undergrowth, thicket.

gedacht [gə'daxt] p.p. of denken.

Gedächtnis [gə'dɛçtnis] n (-ses/-se) memory; remembrance, recollection; im ~ behalten keep in mind; zum ~ (gen.) in memory of; ~feier f commemoration.

Gedanke [gə'daŋkə] m (-ns/-n) thought; idea; in ~n (versunken or verloren) absorbed in thought; sich ~n machen über (acc.) worry about.

Ge'danken|gang m train of thought; ~leser m, ~leserin f (-/-nen) thought-reader; 2los adj. thoughtless; ~strich m dash; 2voll adj. thoughtful, pensive.

Gedärm [gə'dɛrm] n (-[e]s/-e) mst pl. entrails or, bowels pl., intestines pl.; ~deck [~'dɛk] n (-[e]s/-e) cover; menu; ein ~ auflegen lay a place.

gedeihen [gə'daɪən] 1. v/i. (irr., no -ge-, sein) thrive, prosper; 2. 2 n (-s/no pl.) thriving, prosperity.

ge'denken 1. v/i. (gen.) (irr. denken, no -ge-, h) think of; remember, recollect; commemorate; mention; ~ zu inf. intend to inf.; 2. 2 n (-s/no pl.) memory, remembrance (an acc. of).

Ge'denk|feier f commemoration; ~stein m memorial stone; ~tafel f commemorative or memorial tablet.

Ge'dicht n (-[e]s/-e) poem.

gediegen adj. [gə'di:gən] solid; pure; 2heit f (-/no pl.) solidity; purity.

gedieh [gə'di:] pret. of gedeihen; ~en p.p. of gedeihen.

Gedräng|e [gə'drɛŋə] n (-s/no pl.) crowd, throng; 2t adj. crowded, packed, crammed; style: concise.

ge|droschen [gə'drɔʃən] p.p. of dreschen; ~'drückt fig. adj. depressed; ~drungen [~'druŋən] 1. p.p. of dringen; 2. adj. compact; squat, stocky, thickset.

Geduld [gə'dult] f (-/no pl.) patience; 2en [~dən] v/refl. (no -ge-, h) have patience; 2ig adj. [~diç] patient.

ge|dunsen adj. [gə'dunzən] bloated; ~durft [~'durft] p.p. of dürfen 1; ~ehrt adj. [~'e:rt] hono(u)red; correspondence: Sehr ~er Herr N.! Dear Sir, Dear Mr N.; ~eignet adj. [~'aignət] fit (für, zu, als for s.th.); suitable (to, for); qualified (for).

Gefahr [gə'fa:r] f (-/-en) danger, peril; risk; auf eigene ~ at one's own risk; ~ laufen zu inf. run the risk of ger.

gefährden [gə'fɛ:rdən] v/t. (no -ge-, h) endanger; risk.

ge'fahren p.p. of fahren.

gefährlich adj. [gə'fɛ:rliç] dangerous.

ge'fahrlos adj. without risk, safe.

Gefährt|e [gə'fɛ:rtə] m (-en/-en), ~in f (-/-nen) companion, fellow.

Gefälle [gə'fɛlə] n (-s/-) fall, slope, incline, descent, gradient, esp. Am. a. grade; fall (of river, etc.).

Ge'fallen 1. m (-s/-) favo(u)r; 2. n (-s/no pl.): ~ finden an (dat.) take (a) pleasure in, take a fancy to or for; 3. 2 v/i. (irr. fallen, no -ge-, h) please (j-m s.o.); er gefällt mir I like him; sich et. ~ lassen put up with s.th.; 4. 2 p.p. of fallen.

gefällig adj. [gə'fɛliç] pleasing, agreeable; p.: complaisant, obliging; kind; 2keit f (-/~-en) complaisance, kindness; favo(u)r; ~st adv. (if you) please.

ge'fangen 1. p.p. of fangen; 2. adj. captive, imprisoned; 2e m (-n/-n), f (-/-n) prisoner, captive; 2enlager n prison(ers') camp; 2ennahme f (-/no pl.) capture; seizure, arrest; ~nehmen v/t. (irr. nehmen, sep., -ge-, h) take prisoner; fig. captivate; 2schaft f (-/no pl.) captivity, imprisonment; ~setzen v/t. (sep., -ge-, h) put in prison.

Gefängnis [gə'fɛŋnis] n (-ses/-se) prison, jail, gaol, Am. a. penitentiary; ~direktor m governor, warden; ~strafe f (sentence or term of) imprisonment; ~wärter m warder, gaoler, jailer, (prison) guard.

Gefäß [gə'fɛ:s] n (-es/-e) vessel.

gefaßt adj. [gə'fast] composed; ~ auf (acc.) prepared for.

Ge|fecht [gə'fɛçt] n (-[e]s/-e) engagement; combat, fight; action; ~fieder [~'fi:dər] n (-s/-) plumage, feathers pl.

ge|'fleckt adj. spotted; ~flochten [~'flɔxtən] p.p. of flechten; ~flogen [~'flo:gən] p.p. of fliegen; ~flohen [~'flo:ən] p.p. of fliehen; ~flossen [~'flɔsən] p.p. of fließen.

Ge|'flügel n (-s/no pl.) fowl; poultry; ~flüster [~'flystər] n (-s/no pl.) whisper(ing).

gefochten [gə'fɔxtən] p.p. of fechten.

Ge'folg|e n (-s/no pl.) retinue, train, followers pl.; attendants pl.; ~schaft [~kʃaft] f (-/-en) followers pl.

gefräßig adj. [gə'frɛ:siç] greedy, voracious; 2keit f (-/no pl.) greediness, gluttony, voracity.

ge'fressen p.p. of fressen.

ge'frier|en v/i. (irr. frieren, no -ge-, sein) congeal, freeze; 2fleisch n frozen meat; 2punkt m freezing-point; 2schutz(mittel) n) m antifreeze.

gefroren [gə'fro:rən] p.p. of frieren; 2e [~ə] n (-n/no pl.) ice-cream.

Gefüge [gə'fy:gə] n (-s/-) structure; texture.

ge'fügig adj. pliant; **2keit** f (-/no pl.) pliancy.

Gefühl [gə'fy:l] n (-[e]s/-e) feeling; touch; sense (für of); sensation; **2los** adj. unfeeling, insensible (gegen to); **2betont** adj. emotional; **2voll** adj. (full of) feeling; tender; sentimental.

ge|funden [gə'fundən] p.p. of finden; **~gangen** [~'gaŋən] p.p. of gehen.

ge'geben p.p. of geben; **~enfalls** adv. in that case; if necessary.

gegen prp. (acc.) ['ge:gən] space, time: towards; against; ₴₮ versus; about, Am. around; by; compared with; (in exchange) for; remedy: for; freundlich sein ~ be kind to (-wards); ~ bar for cash.

'Gegen|angriff m counter-attack; **'~antrag** m counter-motion; **'~antwort** f rejoinder; **'~befehl** m counter-order; **'~beschuldigung** f countercharge; **'~besuch** m return visit; **'~bewegung** f counter-movement; **'~beweis** m counter-evidence.

Gegend ['ge:gənt] f (-/-en) region; area.

'Gegen|dienst m return service, service in return; **'~druck** m counter-pressure; fig. reaction; **2ei'nander** adv. against one another or each other; **'~erklärung** f counter-statement; **'~forderung** f counter-claim; **'~frage** f counter-question; **'~geschenk** n return present; **'~gewicht** n counterbalance, counterpoise; **'~gift** 🐍 n antidote; **'~kandidat** m rival candidate; **'~klage** f countercharge; **'~leistung** f return (service), equivalent; **~lichtaufnahme** phot. ['ge:gənliçt?-] f back-lighted shot; **'~liebe** f requited love; keine ~ finden meet with no sympathy or enthusiasm; **'~maßnahme** f counter-measure; **'~mittel** n remedy (gegen for), antidote (against, for); **'~partei** f opposite party; **'~probe** f check-test; **'~satz** m contrast; opposition; im ~ zu in contrast to or with, in opposition to; **2sätzlich** adj. ['~zetsliç] contrary, opposite; **'~seite** f opposite side; **'2seitig** adj. mutual, reciprocal; **'~seitigkeit** f (-/no pl.): auf ~ assurance: mutual; auf ~ beruhen be mutual; **'~spieler** m games, sports: opponent; antagonist; **'~spionage** f counter-espionage; **'~stand** m object; subject, topic; **'~strömung** f counter-current; **'~stück** n counterpart; match; **'~teil** n contrary, reverse; im ~ on the contrary; **'2teilig** adj. contrary, opposite; **2'über 1.** adv. opposite; **2.** prp. (dat.) opposite (to); to (-wards); as against; face to face with; **~'über** n (-s/-) vis-à-vis;

2'überstehen v/i. (irr. stehen, sep., -ge-, h) (dat.) be faced with, face; **~'überstellung** esp. ₴₮ f confrontation; **'~vorschlag** m counter-proposal; **~wart** ['~vart] f (-/no pl.) presence; present time; gr. present tense; **2wärtig** ['~vertiç] **1.** adj. present; actual; **2.** adv. at present; **'~wehr** f defence, Am. -se; resistance; **'~wert** m equivalent; **'~wind** m contrary wind, head wind; **'~wirkung** f counter-effect; reaction; **'2zeichnen** v/t. (sep., -ge-, h) countersign; **'~zug** m counter-move (a. fig.); 🚂 corresponding train.

ge|gessen [gə'gesən] p.p. of essen; **~glichen** [~'gliçən] p.p. of gleichen; **~gliedert** adj. articulate, jointed; **~glitten** [~'glitən] p.p. of gleiten; **~glommen** [~'gləmən] p.p. of glimmen.

Gegner ['ge:gnər] m (-s/-) adversary, opponent; **'~schaft** f (-/-en) opposition.

ge|golten [gə'gəltən] p.p. of gelten; **~goren** [~'go:rən] p.p. of gären; **~gossen** [~'gəsən] p.p. of gießen; **~graben** p.p. of graben; **~griffen** [~'grifən] p.p. of greifen; **~habt** [~'ha:pt] p.p. of haben.

Gehalt [gə'halt] **1.** m (-[e]s/-e) contents pl.; capacity; merit; **2.** n (-[e]s/₌er) salary; **2en** p.p. of halten; **2los** [~'lo:s] adj. empty; **~s-empfänger** [gə'halts?-] m salaried employee or worker; **~serhöhung** [gə'halts?-] f rise (in salary), Am. raise; **2voll** adj. rich; substantial; wine: racy.

gehangen [gə'haŋən] p.p. of hängen 1.

gehässig adj. [gə'hesiç] malicious, spiteful; **2keit** f (-/-en) malice, spitefulness.

ge'hauen p.p. of hauen.

Ge|häuse [gə'həyzə] n (-s/-) case, box; cabinet; shell; core (of apple, etc.); **~hege** [~'he:gə] n (-s/-) enclosure.

geheim adj. [gə'haim] secret; **2dienst** m secret service.

Ge'heimnis n (-ses/-se) secret; mystery; **~krämer** m mystery-monger; **2voll** adj. mysterious.

Ge'heim|polizei f secret police; **~polizist** m detective; plain-clothes man; **~schrift** f cipher; tel. code.

ge'heißen p.p. of heißen.

gehen ['ge:ən] v/i. (irr., ge-, sein) go; walk; leave; machine: go, work; clock, watch: go; merchandise: sell; wind: blow; paste: rise; wie geht es Ihnen? how are you (getting on)?; das geht nicht that won't do; in sich ~ repent; wieviel Pfennige ~ auf e-e Mark? how many pfennigs go to a mark?; das Fenster geht nach Norden the window faces or looks north; es geht nichts über (*acc.*) there is nothing like; *wenn es nach mir ginge* if I had my way.

Geheul [gə'hɔyl] *n* (-[e]s/*no pl.*) howling.

Ge'hilf|e *m* (-n/-n), **~in** *f* (-/-nen) assistant; *fig.* helpmate.

Ge'hirn *n* (-[e]s/-e) brain(s *pl.*); **~erschütterung** ⚕ *f* concussion (of the brain); **~schlag** ⚕ *m* cerebral apoplexy.

gehoben [gə'ho:bən] **1.** *p.p. of* heben; **2.** *adj. speech, style:* elevated; **~e Stimmung** elated mood.

Gehöft [gə'hø:ft] *n* (-[e]s/-e) farm (-stead).

geholfen [gə'hɔlfən] *p.p. of* helfen.

Gehölz [gə'hœlts] *n* (-es/-e) wood, coppice, copse.

Gehör [gə'hø:r] *n* (-[e]s/*no pl.*) hearing; *ear; nach dem* **~** by ear; *j-m* **~** *schenken* lend an ear to s.o.; *sich* **~** *verschaffen* make o.s. heard.

ge'horchen *v/i.* (*no* -ge-, h) obey (*j-m* s.o.).

ge'hör|en *v/i.* (*no* -ge-, h) belong (*dat. or zu* to); *es gehört sich* it is proper *or* fit *or* right *or* suitable; *das gehört nicht hierher* that's not to the point; **~ig 1.** *adj.* belonging (*dat. or zu* to); fit, proper, right; due; F good; **2.** *adv.* duly; F thoroughly.

gehorsam [gə'ho:rza:m] **1.** *adj.* obedient; **2.** ♀ *m* (-s/*no pl.*) obedience.

'Geh|steig *m*, **~weg** *m* pavement, *Am.* sidewalk; **~werk** ⊕ *n* clockwork, works *pl.*

Geier *orn.* ['gaiər] *m* (-s/-) vulture.

Geige ♪ ['gaigə] *f* (-/-n) violin, F fiddle; (*auf der*) **~** *spielen* play (on) the violin; **~nbogen** ♪ *m* (violin-) bow; **~nkasten** ♪ *m* violin-case; **~r** ♪ *m* (-s/-), **~rin** ♪ *f* (-/-nen) violinist.

'Geigerzähler *phys. m* Geiger counter.

geil *adj.* [gail] lascivious, wanton; luxuriant.

Geisel ['gaizəl] *f* (-/-n) hostage.

Geiß *zo.* [gais] *f* (-/-en) (she-, nanny-)goat; **~blatt** ♀ *n* (-[e]s/*no pl.*) honeysuckle, woodbine; **~bock** *zo.* he-goat, billy-goat.

Geißel ['gaisəl] *f* (-/-n) whip, lash; *fig.* scourge; **'Ωn** *v/t.* (ge-, h) whip, lash; *fig.* castigate.

Geist [gaist] *m* (-es/-er) spirit; mind, intellect; wit; ghost; sprite. **'Geister|erscheinung** *f* apparition; **'Ωhaft** *adj.* ghostly.

'geistes|abwesend *adj.* absentminded; **'Ωarbeiter** *m* brainworker, white-collar worker; **'Ωblitz** *m* brain-wave, flash of genius; **'Ωgabe** *f* talent; **'Ωgegenwart** *f* presence of mind; **~gegenwärtig** *adj.* alert; quick-witted; **'~gestört** *adj.* mentally disturbed; **'~krank**

adj. insane, mentally ill; **'Ωkrankheit** *f* insanity, mental illness; **'~schwach** *adj.* feeble-minded, imbecile; **'~verwandt** *adj.* congenial; **'Ωwissenschaften** *f/pl. the Arts pl., the* Humanities *pl.*; **'Ωzustand** *m* state of mind.

'geistig *adj.* intellectual, mental; spiritual; **~e** *Getränke n/pl.* spirits *pl.*

'geistlich *adj.* spiritual; clerical; sacred; **'Ωe** *m* (-n/-n) clergyman; minister; **'Ωkeit** *f* (-/*no pl.*) clergy. **'geist|los** *adj.* spiritless; dull; stupid; **'~reich** *adj.*, **'~voll** *adj.* ingenious, spirited.

Geiz [gaits] *m* (-es/*no pl.*) avarice; **'~hals** *m* miser, niggard; **'Ωig** *adj.* avaricious, stingy, mean.

Gejammer [gə'jamər] *n* (-s/*no pl.*) lamentation(s *pl.*), wailing.

gekannt [gə'kant] *p.p. of* kennen.

Geklapper [gə'klapər] *n* (-s/*no pl.*) rattling.

Geklirr [gə'klir] *n* (-[e]s/*no pl.*), **~e** [-ə] *n* (-s/*no pl.*) clashing, clanking.

ge|klungen [-'kluŋən] *p.p. of* klingen; **~'kniffen** *p.p. of* kneifen; **~'kommen** *p.p. of* kommen; **~konnt** [-'kɔnt] *p.p. of* können 1, 2.

Ge|kreisch [gə'kraiʃ] *n* (-es/*no pl.*) screaming, screams *pl.*; shrieking; **~kritzel** [-'kritsəl] *n* (-s/*no pl.*) scrawl(ing), scribbling, scribble. **ge|krochen** [gə'krɔxən] *p.p. of* kriechen; **~künstelt** *adj.* [-'kynstəlt] affected.

Gelächter [gə'lɛçtər] *n* (-s/-) laughter.

ge'laden *p.p. of* laden.

Ge'lage *n* (-s/-) feast; drinkingbout.

Gelände [gə'lɛndə] *n* (-s/-) ground; terrain; country; area; **Ωgängig** *mot. adj.* cross-country; **~lauf** *m sports:* cross-country race *or* run. **Geländer** [gə'lɛndər] *n* (-s/-) railing, balustrade; banisters *pl.*

ge'lang *pret. of* gelingen.

ge'langen *v/i.* (*no* -ge-, sein): **~** *an* (*acc.*) *or in* (*acc.*) arrive at, get *or* come to; **~** *zu* attain (to), gain.

ge'lassen 1. *p.p. of* lassen; **2.** *adj.* calm, composed.

Gelatine [ʒela'ti:nə] *f* (-/*no pl.*) gelatin(e).

ge'laufen *p.p. of* laufen; **~läufig** *adj.* [-'lɔyfiç] current; fluent, easy; *tongue:* voluble; familiar; **~launt** *adj.* [-'launt] in a (*good, etc.*) humo(u)r *or Am.* mood.

Geläut [gə'lɔyt] *n* (-[e]s/-e), **~e** [-ə] *n* (-s/-) ringing (*of bells*); chimes *pl.* (*of church bells*).

gelb *adj.* [gɛlp] yellow; **'~lich** *adj.* yellowish; **'Ωsucht** ⚕ *f* (-/*no pl.*) jaundice.

Geld [gɛlt] *n* (-[e]s/-er) money; *im*

~ schwimmen be rolling in money; zu ~ machen turn into cash; '~anngelegenheit f money-matter; '~anlage f investment; '~ausgabe f expense; '~beutel m purse; '~entwertung f devaluation of the currency; '~erwerb m money-making; '~geber m (-s/-) financial backer, investor; '~geschäfte n/pl. money transactions pl.; '2gierig adj. greedy for money, avaricious; '~mittel n/pl. funds pl., resources pl.; '~schein m bank-note, Am. bill; '~schrank m strong-box, safe; '~sendung f remittance; '~strafe f fine; '~stück n coin; '~tasche f money-bag; notecase, Am. billfold; '~überhang m surplus money; '~umlauf m circulation of money; '~umsatz m turnover (of money); '~verlegenheit f pecuniary embarrassment; '~wechsel m exchange of money; '~wert m (-[e]s/no pl.) value of money, money value.

Gelee [ʒə'le:] n, m (-s/-s) jelly.

ge'legen 1. p.p. of liegen; 2. adj. situated, Am. a. located; convenient, opportune; 2heit f (-/-en) occasion; opportunity; chance; facility; bei ~ on occasion.

Ge'legenheits|arbeit f casual or odd job, Am. a. chore; ~arbeiter m casual labo(u)rer, odd-job man; ~kauf m bargain.

ge'legentlich 1. adj. occasional; 2. prp. (gen.) on the occasion of.

ge'lehr|ig adj. docile; 2igkeit f (-/no pl.) docility; 2samkeit f (-/no pl.) learning; ~t adj. [~t] learned; 2te [~ə] m (-n/-n) learned man, scholar.

Geleise [gə'laizə] n (-s/-) rut, track; ⚏ rails pl., line, esp. Am. tracks pl.

Geleit [gə'lait] n (-[e]s/-e) escort; attendance; j-m das ~ geben accompany s.o.; 2en v/t. (no -ge-, h) accompany, conduct; escort; ~zug ⚓ m convoy.

Gelenk anat., ⊕, ⚘ [gə'lɛŋk] n (-[e]s/-e) joint; 2ig adj. pliable, supple.

ge'lernt adj. worker: skilled; trained; ~'lesen p.p. of lesen.

Geliebte [gə'li:ptə] (-n/-n) 1. m lover; 2. f mistress, sweetheart.

geliehen [gə'li:ən] p.p. of leihen.

ge'linde 1. adj. soft, smooth, gentle; 2. adv.: gelinde gesagt to put it mildly, to say the least.

gelingen [gə'liŋən] 1. v/i. (irr., no -ge-, sein) succeed; es gelingt mir zu inf. I succeed in ger.; 2. 2 n (-s/no pl.) success.

ge'litten p.p. of leiden.

gellen ['gɛlən] (ge- h) 1. v/i. shrill; yell; of ears: ring, tingle; 2. v/t. shrill; yell; '~d adj. shrill, piercing.

ge'loben v/t. (no -ge-, h) vow, promise.

Gelöbnis [gə'lø:pnis] n (-ses/-se) promise, pledge; vow.

ge'logen p.p. of lügen.

gelt|en ['gɛltən] (irr., ge- h) 1. v/t. be worth; 2. v/i. be of value; be valid; go; count; money: be current; maxim, etc.: hold (good or true); et. ~ have credit or influence; j-m ~ concern s.o.; ~ für or als pass for, be reputed or thought or supposed to be; ~ für apply to; ~ lassen let pass, allow; ~d machen maintain, assert; s-n Einfluß bei j-m ~d machen bring one's influence to bear on s.o.; das gilt nicht that is not fair; that does not count; es galt unser Leben our life was at stake; '2ung f (-/⚘ -en) validity; value; currency; authority (of person); zur ~ kommen tell; take effect; show; '2ungsbedürfnis n desire to show off. [ise; vow.)

Gelübde [gə'lypdə] n (-s/-) prom-)

gelungen [gə'luŋən] 1. p.p. of gelingen; 2. adj. successful; amusing, funny; F: das ist ja ~! that beats everything!

gemächlich adj. [gə'mɛ:çliç] comfortable, easy; 2keit f (-/no pl.) ease, comfort.

Gemahl [gə'ma:l] m (-[e]s/-e) consort; husband.

ge'mahlen p.p. of mahlen.

Gemälde [gə'mɛ:ldə] n (-s/-) painting, picture; ~galerie f picturegallery.

gemäß prp. (dat.) [gə'mɛ:s] according to; ~igt adj. moderate; temperate (a. geogr.).

gemein adj. [gə'main] common; general; low, vulgar, mean, coarse; et. ~ haben mit have s.th. in common with.

Gemeinde [gə'maində] f (-/-n) community; parish; municipality; eccl. congregation; ~bezirk m district; municipality; ~rat m municipal council; ~steuer f rate, Am. local tax; ~vorstand m district council.

ge'mein|gefährlich adj. dangerous to the public; ~er Mensch public danger, Am. public enemy; 2heit f (-/-en) vulgarity; meanness; mean trick; ~nützig adj. of public utility; 2platz m commonplace; ~sam adj. common; joint; mutual; 2schaft f (-/-en) community; intercourse; ~schaftlich adj. s. gemeinsam; 2schaftsarbeit f [gə'mainʃafts?-] f team-work; 2sinn m (-[e]s/no pl.) public spirit; ~verständlich adj. popular; 2wesen n community; 2wohl n public welfare.

Ge'menge n (-s/-) mixture.

ge'messen 1. p.p. of messen; 2. adj. measured; formal; grave.

Gemetzel [gə'mɛtsəl] n (-s/-) slaughter, massacre.

gemieden [gə'mi:dən] *p.p. of* meiden.

Gemisch [gə'miʃ] *n* (-es/-e) mixture; ♫ₘ compound, composition.

ge|mocht [gə'mɔxt] *p.p. of* mögen;
~molken [gə'mɔlkən] *p.p. of* melken.

Gemse *zo.* ['gɛmzə] *f* (-/-n) chamois.

Gemurmel [gə'murməl] *n* (-s/*no
pl.*) murmur(ing).

Gemüse [gə'my:zə] *n* (-s/-) vegeta-
ble(s *pl.*); greens *pl.*; **~anbau** *m*
vegetable gardening, *Am.* truck
farming; **~garten** *m* kitchen garden; **~händler** *m* greengrocer.

gemußt [gə'must] *p.p. of* müssen 1.

Gemüt [gə'my:t] *n* (-[e]s/-e) mind;
feeling; soul; heart; disposition,
temper; **♫lich** *adj.* good-natured;
genial; comfortable, snug, cosy,
cozy; **~lichkeit** *f* (-/*no pl.*) snug-
ness, cosiness; easy-going; genial
temper.

Ge'müts|art *f* disposition, nature,
temper, character; **~bewegung** *f*
emotion; **♫krank** *adj.* emotionally
disturbed; melancholic; depressed;
~krankheit *f* mental disorder;
melancholy; **~ruhe** *f* composure;
~verfassung *f*, **~zustand** *m* state
of mind, humo(u)r.

ge'mütvoll *adj.* emotional; full of
feeling.

genannt [gə'nant] *p.p. of* nennen.

genas [gə'nɑ:s] *pret. of* genesen.

genau *adj.* [gə'nau] exact, accurate;
precise; strict; es ~ nehmen (mit) be
particular (about); **♫eres** full particulars *pl.*; **♫igkeit** *f* (-/-en) accuracy, exactness; precision; strictness.

genehm *adj.* [gə'ne:m] agreeable,
convenient; **~igen** [~igən] *v/t.* (*no
-ge-, h*) grant; approve (of); **♫igung**
f (-/-en) grant; approval; licen|ce,
Am. -se; permit, permission; consent.

geneigt *adj.* [gə'naikt] well disposed
(*j-m towards s.o.*); inclined (*zu* to).

General [gene'rɑ:l] *m* (-s/-e, ♫e)
general; **~bevollmächtigte** *m* chief
representative *or* agent; **~direktor**
m general manager, managing director; **~feldmarschall** ✕ *m*
field-marshal; **~intendant** *thea. m*
(artistic) director; **~konsul** *m* con-
sul-general; **~konsulat** *n* consu-
late-general; **~leutnant** ✕ *m* lieu-
tenant-general; **~major** ✕ *m*
major-general; **~probe** *thea. f* dress
rehearsal; **~stab** ✕ *m* general staff;
~stabskarte ✕ *f* ordnance (survey) map, *Am.* strategic map; **~-
streik** *m* general strike; **~ver-
sammlung** *f* general meeting; **~-
vertreter** *m* general agent; **~voll-
macht** *f* full power of attorney.

Generation [genəra'tsjo:n] *f* (-/-en)
generation.

generell *adj.* [genə'rɛl] general.

genes|en [gə'ne:zən] 1. *v/i.* (*irr., no
-ge-, sein*) recover (*von* from);
2. *p.p. of* 1; **♫ende** *m, f* (-n/-n)
convalescent; **♫ung** *f* (-/♫, -en)
recovery.

genial *adj.* [gen'jɑ:l] highly gifted,
ingenious; **♫ität** [~ali'tɛ:t] *f* (-/*no
pl.*) genius.

Genick [gə'nik] *n* (-[e]s/-e) nape (of
the neck), (back of the) neck.

Genie [ʒe'ni:] *n* (-s/-s) genius.

ge'nieren *v/t.* (*no -ge-, h*) trouble,
bother; *sich ~* feel *or* be embarrassed *or* shy; be self-conscious.

genießen [gə'ni:sən] *v/t.* (*irr., no
-ge-, h*) enjoy; eat; drink; et. ~
take some food *or* refreshments;
j-s Vertrauen ~ be in s.o.'s confidence.

Genitiv *gr.* ['ge:niti:f] *m* (-s/-e)
genitive (case); possessive (case).

ge|nommen [gə'nɔmən] *p.p. of*
nehmen; **~'normt** *adj.* standard-
ized; **~noß** [~'nɔs] *pret. of* genießen.

Genoss|e [gə'nɔsə] *m* (-n/-n) com-
panion, mate; comrade (*a. pol.*);
♫en *p.p. of* genießen; **~enschaft**
f (-/-en) company, association;
co(-)operative (society); **~in** *f*
(-/-nen) (female) companion; comrade (*a. pol.*).

genug *adj.* [gə'nu:k] enough, sufficient.

Genüg|e [gə'ny:gə] *f* (-/*no pl.*): zur
~ enough, sufficiently; **♫en** *v/i.* (*no
-ge-, h*) be enough, suffice; *das
genügt* that will do; *j-m ~* satisfy
s.o.; **♫end** *adj.* sufficient; **♫sam**
adj. [~k-] easily satisfied; frugal;
~samkeit [~k-] *f* (-/*no pl.*) modesty; frugality.

Genugtuung [gə'nu:ktu:uŋ] *f* (-/-en)
satisfaction. [gender.]

Genus *gr.* ['ge:nus] *n* (-/Genera)ʃ

Genuß [gə'nus] *m* (Genusses/Ge-
nüsse) enjoyment; pleasure; use;
consumption; taking (*of food*); fig.
treat; **~mittel** *n* semi-luxury; **~
sucht** *f* (-/*no pl.*) thirst for pleasure;
♫süchtig *adj.* pleasure-seeking.

Geo|graph [geo'grɑ:f] *m* (-/-en)
geographer; **~graphie** [~a'fi:] *f*
(-/*no pl.*) geography; **♫graphisch**
adj. [~'grɑ:fiʃ] geographic(al); **~
loge** [~'lo:gə] *m* (-n/-n) geologist;
~logie [~lo'gi:] *f* (-/*no pl.*) geology;
♫logisch *adj.* [~'lo:giʃ] geologic(al);
~metrie [~me'tri:] *f* (-/-n) geometry; **♫metrisch** *adj.* [~'me:triʃ]
geometric(al).

Gepäck [gə'pɛk] *n* (-[e]s/*no pl.*) luggage, ✕ *or Am.* baggage; **~annah-
me** *f* luggage (registration) counter,
Am. baggage (registration) counter;
~aufbewahrung *f* (-/-en) left-lug-
gage office, *Am.* checkroom; **~aus-
gabe** *f* luggage delivery office, *Am.*
baggage room; **~netz** *n* luggage-

rack, *Am.* baggage rack; **~schein** *m* luggage-ticket, *Am.* baggage check; **~träger** *m* porter, *Am. a.* redcap; *on bicycle:* carrier; **~wagen** *m* luggage van, *Am.* baggage car.

ge|pfiffen [gə'pfifən] *p.p. of pfeifen*; **~pflegt** *adj.* [~'pfle:kt] *appearance:* well-groomed; *hands, garden, etc.:* well cared-for; *garden, etc.:* well-kept.

Gepflogenheit [gə'pflo:gənhaɪt] *f* (-/-en) habit; custom; usage.

Ge|plapper [gə'plapər] *n* (-s/no pl.) babbling, chattering, **~plauder** [~-'plaudər] *n* (-s/no pl.) chatting, small talk; **~polter** [~'pɔltər] *n* (-s/no pl.) rumble; **~präge** [~'prɛ:-gə] *n* (-s/-) impression; stamp (*a. fig.*).

ge|priesen [gə'pri:zən] *p.p. of preisen*; **~quollen** [~'kvɔlən] *p.p. of quellen*.

gerade [gə'rɑ:də] **1.** *adj.* straight (*a. fig.*); *number, etc.:* even; direct; *bearing:* upright, erect; **2.** *adv.* just; er *schrieb* ~ he was (just) writing; *nun* ~ now more than ever; ~ *an dem Tage* on that very day; **3.** ♀ *f* (-n/-n) Å straight line; straight (*of race-course*); **linke** (*rechte*) ~ *boxing:* straight left (right); **~'aus** *adv.* straight on *or* ahead; **~he'raus** *adv.* frankly; **~nwegs** *adv.* [~nve:ks] directly; **~stehen** *v/i.* (*irr. stehen, sep., -ge-, h*) stand erect; ~ *für* an answer for *s.th.*; **~wegs** *adv.* [~ve:ks] straight, directly; **~'zu** *adv.* straight; almost; downright.

ge'rannt *p.p. of rennen.*

Gerassel [gə'rasəl] *n* (-s/no pl.) clanking; rattling.

Gerät [gə'rɛ:t] *n* (-[e]s/-e) tool, implement, utensil; ⊕ gear; *teleph., radio:* set; apparatus; equipment; *elektrisches* ~ electric(al) appliance.

ge'raten 1. *v/i.* (*irr. raten, no -ge-, sein*) come *or* fall *or* get (*an acc.* by, upon; *auf acc.* on, upon; *in acc.* in, into); (*gut*) ~ succeed, turn out well; *in Brand* ~ catch fire; *ins Stocken* ~ come to a standstill; *in Vergessenheit* ~ fall *or* sink into oblivion; *in Zorn* ~ fly into a passion; **2.** *p.p. of raten.*

Gerate'wohl *n: aufs* ~ at random.

geräumig *adj.* [gə'rɔymiç] spacious.

Geräusch [gə'rɔyʃ] *n* (-es/-e) noise; **2los** *adj.* noiseless; **2voll** *adj.* noisy.

gerb|en ['gɛrbən] *v/t.* (ge-, h) tan; **2er** *m* (-s/-) tanner; **2erei** [~'raɪ] *f* (-/-en) tannery.

ge'recht *adj.* just; righteous; ~ *werden* (*dat.*) do justice to; be fair to; meet; please *s.o.*; fulfil (*requirements*); **2igkeit** *f* (-/no pl.) justice; righteousness; *j-m* ~ *widerfahren lassen* do s.o. justice.

Ge'rede *n* (-s/no pl.) talk; gossip; rumo(u)r.

ge'reizt *adj.* irritable, irritated; **2-heit** *f* (-/no pl.) irritation.

ge'reuen *v/t.* (*no -ge-, h*): *es gereut mich* I repent (of) it, I am sorry for it.

Gericht [gə'riçt] *n* (-[e]s/-e) dish, course; *s. Gerichtshof; mst rhet. and fig.* tribunal; **2lich** *adj.* judicial, legal.

Ge'richts|barkeit *f* (-/-en) jurisdiction; **~bezirk** *m* jurisdiction; **~diener** *m* (court) usher; **~gebäude** *n* court-house; **~hof** *m* law-court, court of justice; **~kosten** *pl.* (law-)costs *pl.*; **~saal** *m* courtroom; **~schreiber** *m* clerk (of the court); **~stand** *m* (legal) domicile; venue; **~tag** *m* court-day; **~verfahren** *n* legal proceedings *pl.*, lawsuit; **~verhandlung** *f* (court) hearing; trial; **~vollzieher** *m* (-s/-) (court-)bailiff.

gerieben [gə'ri:bən] *p.p. of reiben.*

gering *adj.* [gə'riŋ] little, small; trifling, slight; mean, low; poor; inferior; **~achten** *v/t.* (sep., -ge-, h) think little of; disregard; **~er** *adj.* inferior. less, minor; **~fügig** *adj.* insignificant, trifling, slight; ~ **schätzen** *v/t.* (sep., -ge-, h) *s. geringachten*; **~schätzig** *adj.* disdainful, contemptuous, slighting; **2-schätzung** *f* (-/no pl.) disdain; disregard; **~st** *adj.* least; *nicht im* ~*en* not in the least.

ge'rinnen *v/i.* (*irr. rinnen, no -ge-, sein*) curdle (*a. fig.*); congeal; coagulate. clot.

Ge'rippe *n* (-s/-) skeleton (*a. fig.*); ⊕ framework.

ge|rissen [gə'risən] **1.** *p.p. of reißen*; **2.** *fig. adj.* cunning, crafty, smart; **~ritten** [~'ritən] *p.p. of reiten.*

germanis|ch *adj.* [gɛr'mɑ:niʃ] Germanic, Teutonic; **2t** [~a'nist] *m* (-en/-en) Germanist, German scholar; student of German.

gern(e) *adv.* ['gɛrn(ə)] willingly, gladly; ~ *haben or mögen* be fond of, like; er *singt* ~ he is fond of singing, he likes to sing.

ge'rochen *p.p. of riechen.*

Geröll [gə'rœl] *n* (-[e]s/-e) boulders *pl.*

geronnen [gə'rɔnən] *p.p. of rinnen.*

Gerste ♀ ['gɛrstə] *f* (-/-n) barley; **'~nkorn** *n* barleycorn; ✳ sty(e).

Gerte ['gɛrtə] *f* (-/-n) switch, twig.

Geruch [gə'rux] *m* (-[e]s/-e) smell, odo(u)r; scent; *fig.* reputation; **2los** *adj.* odo(u)rless; scentless; **~ssinn** *m* (-[e]s/ *no pl.*) sense of smell.

Gerücht [gə'ryçt] *n* (-[e]s/-e) rumo(u)r.

ge'ruchtilgend *adj.*: ~*es Mittel* deodorant.

ge'rufen *p.p. of rufen.*

ge'ruhen *v/i.* (*no -ge-, h*) deign, condescend, be pleased.

Gerümpel [gə'rympəl] *n* (-s/*no pl.*) lumber, junk.

Gerundium *gr.* [gə'rundjum] *n* (-s/Gerundien) gerund.

gerungen [gə'ruŋən] *p.p. of* ringen.

Gerüst [gə'ryst] *n* (-[e]s/-e) scaffold(ing); stage; trestle.

ge'salzen *p.p. of* salzen.

gesamt *adj.* [gə'zamt] whole, entire, total, all; ⁀ausgabe *f* complete edition; ⁀betrag *m* sum total; ⁀deutsch *adj.* all-German.

gesandt [gə'zant] *p.p. of* senden; ⁀e [⁀ə] *m* (-n/-n) envoy; ⁀schaft *f* (-/-en) legation.

Ge'sang *m* (-[e]s/⁀e) singing; song; ⁀buch *eccl. n* hymn-book; ⁀lehrer *m* singing-teacher; ⁀verein *m* choral society, *Am.* glee club.

Gesäß *anat.* [gə'zɛ:s] *n* (-es/-e) seat, buttocks *pl.*, F bottom, behind.

ge'schaffen *p.p. of* schaffen 1.

Geschäft [gə'ʃɛft] *n* (-[e]s/-e) business; transaction; affair; occupation; shop, *Am.* store; ⁀ig *adj.* busy, active; ⁀igkeit *f* (-/*no pl.*) activity; ⁀lich 1. *adj.* business ...; commercial; 2. *adv.* on business.

Ge'schäfts|bericht *m* business report; ⁀brief *m* business letter; ⁀frau *f* business woman; ⁀freund *m* business friend, correspondent; ⁀führer *m* manager; ⁀haus *n* business firm; office building; ⁀inhaber *m* owner *or* holder of a business; shopkeeper; ⁀jahr *n* financial *or* business year, *Am.* fiscal year; ⁀lage *f* business situation; ⁀leute *pl.* businessmen *pl.*; ⁀mann *m* businessman; ⁀mäßig *adj.* business-like; ⁀ordnung *f* standing orders *pl.*; rules *pl.* (of procedure); ⁀papiere *n/pl.* commercial papers *pl.*; ⁀partner *m* (business) partner; ⁀räume *m/pl.* business premises *pl.*; ⁀reise *f* business trip; ⁀reisende *m* commercial travel(l)er, *Am.* travel(l)ing salesman; ⁀schluß *m* closing-time; *nach* ⁀ *a.* after business hours; ⁀stelle *f* office; ⁀träger *m* *pol.* chargé d'affaires; ⁀ agent, representative; ⁀tüchtig *adj.* efficient, smart; ⁀unternehmen *n* business enterprise; ⁀verbindung *f* business connexion *or* connection; ⁀viertel *n* business cent|re, *Am.* -er; *Am.* downtown; shopping cent|re, *Am.* -er; ⁀zeit *f* office hours *pl.*, business hours *pl.*; ⁀zimmer *n* office, bureau; ⁀zweig *m* branch (of business), line (of business).

geschah [gə'ʃa:] *pret. of* geschehen.

geschehen [gə'ʃe:ən] 1. *v/i.* (*irr.*, *no* -ge-, *sein*) happen, occur, take place; be done; *es geschieht ihm recht* it serves him right; 2. *p.p. of*

1; 3. ⁀ *n* (-s/-) events *pl.*, happenings *pl.*

gescheit *adj.* [gə'ʃaɪt] clever, intelligent, bright.

Geschenk [gə'ʃɛŋk] *n* (-[e]s/-e) present, gift; ⁀packung *f* gift-box.

Geschicht|e [gə'ʃɪçtə] *f* 1. (-/-n) story; tale; *fig.* affair; 2. (-/*no pl.*) history; ⁀lich *adj.* historical; ⁀s-forscher *m*, ⁀sschreiber *m* historian.

Ge'schick *n* 1. (-[e]s/-e) fate; destiny; 2. (-[e]s/*no pl.*) = ⁀lichkeit *f* (-/-en) skill; dexterity; aptitude; ⁀t *adj.* skil(l)ful; dexterous; apt; clever.

ge|schieden [gə'ʃi:dən] *p.p. of* scheiden; ⁀schienen [⁀'ʃi:nən] *p.p. of* scheinen.

Geschirr [gə'ʃɪr] *n* (-[e]s/-e) vessel; dishes *pl.*; china; earthenware, crockery; service; *horse:* harness.

ge'schlafen *p.p. of* schlafen; ⁀'schlagen *p.p. of* schlagen.

Ge'schlecht *n* (-[e]s/-er) sex; kind, species; race; family; generation; *gr.* gender; ⁀lich *adj.* sexual.

Ge'schlechts|krankheit *♀ f* venereal disease; ⁀reife *f* puberty; ⁀teile *anat. n/pl.* genitals *pl.*; ⁀trieb *m* sexual instinct *or* urge; ⁀verkehr *m* (-[e]s/*no pl.*) sexual intercourse; ⁀wort *gr. n* (-[e]s/⁀er) article.

ge|schlichen [gə'ʃlɪçən] *p.p. of* schleichen; ⁀schliffen [⁀'ʃlɪfən] 1. *p.p. of* schleifen; 2. *adj. jewel:* cut; *fig.* polished; ⁀schlossen [⁀'ʃlɔsən] 1.*p.p. of* schließen; 2. *adj. formation:* close; collective; ⁀e *Gesellschaft* private party; ⁀schlungen [⁀'ʃluŋən] *p.p. of* schlingen.

Geschmack [gə'ʃmak] *m* (-[e]s/⁀e, *co.* ⁀er) taste (*a. fig.*); flavo(u)r; ⁀ *finden an* (*dat.*) take a fancy to; ⁀los *adj.* tasteless; *pred. fig.* in bad taste; ⁀(s)sache *f* matter of taste; ⁀voll *adj.* tasteful; *pred. fig.* in good taste.

ge|schmeidig *adj.* [gə'ʃmaɪdɪç] supple, pliant; ⁀schmissen [⁀'ʃmɪsən] *p.p. of* schmeißen; ⁀schmolzen [⁀'ʃmɔltsən] *p.p. of* schmelzen.

Geschnatter [gə'ʃnatər] *n* (-s/*no pl.*) cackling (*of geese*); chatter(ing) (*of girls, etc.*).

ge|schnitten [gə'ʃnɪtən] *p.p. of* schneiden; ⁀schoben [⁀'ʃo:bən] *p.p. of* schieben; ⁀scholten [⁀'ʃɔltən] *p.p. of* schelten.

Geschöpf [gə'ʃœpf] *n* (-[e]s/-e) creature.

ge'schoren *p.p. of* scheren.

Geschoß [gə'ʃɔs] *n* (Geschosses/Geschosse) projectile; missile; stor(e)y, floor.

geschossen [gə'ʃɔsən] *p.p. of* schießen.

Ge'schrei n (-[e]s/no pl.) cries pl.; shouting; fig. noise, fuss.

ge|schrieben [gə'ʃriːbən] p.p. of schreiben; **~schrie(e)n** [~'ʃriː(ə)n] p.p. of schreien; **~schritten** [~'ʃritən] p.p. of schreiten; **~schunden** [~'ʃundən] p.p. of schinden.

Geschütz ✕ [gə'ʃyts] n (-es/-e) gun, cannon; ordnance.

Geschwader ✕ [gə'ʃvaːdər] n (-s/-) ⚓ squadron; ✈ wing, Am. group.

Geschwätz [gə'ʃvɛts] n (-es/no pl.) idle talk; gossip; **2ig** adj. talkative.

geschweige cj. [gə'ʃvaɪgə]: ~ (denn) not to mention; let alone, much less.

geschwiegen [gə'ʃviːgən] p.p. of schweigen.

geschwind adj. [gə'ʃvint] fast, quick, swift; **2igkeit** [~diçkaɪt] f (-/-en) quickness; speed, pace; phys. velocity; rate; mit e-r ~ von ... at the rate of ...; **2igkeitsbegrenzung** f speed limit.

Geschwister [gə'ʃvistər] n (-s/-): ~ pl. brother(s pl.) and sister(s pl.).

ge|schwollen [gə'ʃvɔlən] **1.** p.p. of schwellen; **2.** adj. language: bombastic, pompous; **~schwommen** [~'ʃvɔmən] p.p. of schwimmen.

geschworen [gə'ʃvoːrən] p.p. of schwören; **2e** [~ə] m, f (-n/-n) juror; die ~n pl. the jury; **2engericht** n jury.

Geschwulst 🔬 [gə'ʃvulst] f (-/⁓e) swelling; tumo(u)r.

ge|schwunden [gə'ʃvundən] p.p. of schwinden; **~schwungen** [~'ʃvuŋən] p.p. of schwingen.

Geschwür 🔬 [gə'ʃvyːr] n (-[e]s/-e) abscess, ulcer.

ge'sehen p.p. of sehen.

Gesell ⚒ [gə'zɛl] m (-en/-en), **~e** [~ə] m (-n/-n) companion, fellow; ⊕ journeyman; **2en** v/refl. (no -ge-, h) associate, come together; sich zu j-m ~ join s.o.; **2ig** adj. social; sociable.

Ge'sellschaft f (-/-en) society; company (a. ✝); party; j-m ~ leisten keep s.o. company; **~er** m (-s/-) companion; ✝ partner; **~erin** f (-/-nen) (lady) companion; ✝ partner; **2lich** adj. social.

Ge'sellschafts|dame f (lady) companion; **~reise** f party tour; **~spiel** n party or round game; **~tanz** m ball-room dance.

gesessen [gə'zɛsən] p.p. of sitzen.

Gesetz [gə'zɛts] n (-es/-e) law; statute; **~buch** n code; statute-book; **~entwurf** m bill; **~eskraft** f legal force; **~essammlung** f code; **2gebend** adj. legislative; **~geber** m (-s/-) legislator; **~gebung** f (-/-en) legislation; **2lich 1.** adj. lawful, legal; **2.** adv.: ~ geschützt patented, registered; **2los** adj. lawless; **2mäßig** adj. legal; lawful.

ge'setzt 1. adj. sedate, staid; sober;

mature; **2.** cj.: ~ den Fall, (daß) ... suppose or supposing (that) ...

ge'setzwidrig adj. unlawful, illegal.

Ge'sicht n (-[e]s/-er) face; countenance; fig. character; zu ~ bekommen catch sight or a glimpse of; set eyes on.

Ge'sichts|ausdruck m (facial) expression; **~farbe** f complexion; **~kreis** m horizon; **~punkt** m point of view, viewpoint, aspect, esp. Am. angle; **~zug** m mst Gesichtszüge pl. feature(s pl.), lineament(s pl.).

Ge'sims n ledge.

Gesinde [gə'zində] n (-s/-) (domestic) servants pl.; **~l** [~l] n (-s/no pl.) rabble, mob.

ge'sinn|t adj. in compounds: ...-minded; wohl ~ well disposed (j-m towards s.o.); **2ung** f (-/-en) mind; conviction; sentiment(s pl.); opinions pl.

gesinnungs|los [gə'zinuŋsloːs] unprincipled; **~treu** adj. loyal; **2wechsel** m change of opinion; esp. pol. volte-face.

ge|sittet adj. [gə'zitət] civilized; well-bred, well-mannered; **~'soffen** p.p. of saufen; **~sogen** [~'zoːgən] p.p. of saugen; **~sonnen** [~'zɔnən] **1.** p.p. of sinnen; **2.** adj. minded, disposed; **~sotten** [~'zɔtən] p.p. of sieden; **~spalten** p.p. of spalten.

Ge'spann n (-[e]s/-e) team, Am. a. span; oxen: yoke; fig. pair, couple.

ge'spannt adj. tense (a. fig.); rope: tight, taut, fig. intent; attention: close; relations: strained; ~ sein auf (acc.) be anxious for; auf ~em Fuß on bad terms; **2heit** f (-/no pl.) tenseness, tension.

Gespenst [gə'ʃpɛnst] n (-es/-er) ghost, spect|re, Am. -er; **2isch** adj. ghostly.

Ge'spiel|e m (-n/-n), **~in** f (-/-nen) playmate.

gespien [gə'ʃpiːn] p.p. of speien.

Gespinst [gə'ʃpinst] n (-es/-e) web, tissue (both a. fig.); spun yarn.

gesponnen [gə'ʃpɔnən] p.p. of spinnen.

Gespött [gə'ʃpœt] n (-[e]s/no pl.) mockery, derision, ridicule; zum ~ der Leute werden become a laughing-stock.

Gespräch [gə'ʃprɛːç] n (-[e]s/-e) talk; conversation; teleph. call; dialogue; **2ig** adj. talkative.

ge|sprochen [gə'ʃprɔxən] p.p. of sprechen; **~'sprossen** p.p. of sprießen; **~sprungen** [~'ʃpruŋən] p.p. of springen.

Gestalt [gə'ʃtalt] f (-/-en) form, figure, shape; stature; **2en** v/t. and v/refl. (no -ge-, h) form, shape; **~ung** f (-/-en) formation; arrangement, organization.

gestanden [gə'ʃtandən] p.p. of stehen.

ge'ständ|ig adj.: ~ sein confess; **2nis** [~t-] n (-ses/-se) confession.

Ge'stank m (-[e]s/no pl.) stench.

gestatten [gə'ʃtatən] v/t. (no -ge-, h) allow, permit.

Geste ['gɛstə] f (-/-n) gesture.

ge'stehen (irr. stehen, no -ge-, h) **1.** v/t. confess, avow; **2.** v/i. confess.

Ge|'stein n (-[e]s/-e) rock, stone; **~stell** [~'ʃtɛl] n (-[e]s/-e) stand, rack, shelf; frame; trestle, horse.

gestern adv. ['gɛstərn] yesterday; ~ abend last night.

gestiegen [gə'ʃtiːgən] p.p. of steigen.

Ge'stirn n (-[e]s/-e) star; astr. constellation; **2t** adj. starry.

ge|stoben [gə'ʃtoːbən] p.p. of stieben; **~stochen** [~'ʃtɔxən] p.p. of stechen; **~stohlen** [~'ʃtoːlən] p.p. of stehlen; **~storben** [~'ʃtɔrbən] p.p. of sterben; **~stoßen** p.p. of stoßen; **~strichen** [~'ʃtriçən] p.p. of streichen.

gestrig adj. ['gɛstriç] of yesterday, yesterday's ...

ge'stritten p.p. of streiten.

Gestrüpp [gə'ʃtryp] n (-[e]s/-e) brushwood; undergrowth.

gestunken [gə'ʃtuŋkən] p.p. of stinken.

Gestüt [gə'ʃtyːt] n (-[e]s/-e) stud farm; horses kept for breeding, etc.: stud.

Gesuch [gə'zuːx] n (-[e]s/-e) application, request; petition; **2t** adj. wanted; sought-after; politeness: studied.

gesund adj. [gə'zunt] sound, healthy; salubrious; wholesome (a. fig.); **~er** Menschenverstand common sense; **~en** [~dən] v/i. (no -ge-, sein) recover.

Ge'sundheit f (-/no pl.) health (-iness); wholesomeness (a. fig.); auf j-s ~ trinken drink (to) s.o.'s health; **2lich** adj. sanitary; ~ geht es ihm gut he is in good health.

Ge'sundheits|amt n Public Health Department; **~pflege** f hygiene; public health service; **2schädlich** adj. injurious to health, unhealthy, unwholesome; **~wesen** n Public Health; **~zustand** m state of health, physical condition.

ge|sungen [gə'zuŋən] p.p. of singen; **~sunken** [~'zuŋkən] p.p. of sinken; **~tan** [~'taːn] p.p. of tun.

Getöse [gə'tøːzə] n (-s/no pl.) din, noise.

ge'tragen 1. p.p. of tragen; **2.** adj. solemn.

Getränk [gə'trɛŋk] n (-[e]s/-e) drink, beverage.

ge'trauen v/refl. (no -ge-, h) dare, venture.

Getreide [gə'traidə] n (-s/-) corn, esp. Am. grain; cereals pl.; **~(an)bau** m corn-growing, esp. Am. grain growing; **~pflanze** f cereal plant;

~speicher m granary, grain silo, Am. elevator.

ge'treten p.p. of treten.

ge'treu(lich) adj. faithful, loyal; true.

Getriebe [gə'triːbə] n (-s/-) bustle; ① gear(ing); ⊕ drive.

ge|trieben [gə'triːbən] p.p. of treiben; **~troffen** [~'trɔfən] p.p. of treffen; **~trogen** [~'troːgən] p.p. of trügen.

ge'trost adv. confidently.

ge'trunken p.p. of trinken.

Ge|tue [gə'tuːə] n (-s/no pl.) fuss; **~tümmel** [~'tyməl] n (-s/-) turmoil; **~viert** [~'fiːrt] n (-[e]s/-e) square.

Gewächs [gə'vɛks] n (-es/-e) growth (a. ♀); plant; vintage; **~haus** n greenhouse, hothouse, conservatory.

ge|'wachsen 1. p.p. of wachsen; **2.** adj.: j-m ~ sein be a match for s.o.; e-r Sache ~ sein be equal to s.th.; sich der Lage ~ zeigen rise to the occasion; **~wagt** adj. [~'vaːkt] risky; bold; **~wählt** adj. [~'vɛːlt] style: refined; **~'wahr** adj.: ~ werden (acc. or gen.) perceive s.th., become aware of s.th.; ~ werden, daß become aware that.

Gewähr [gə'vɛːr] f (-/no pl.) guarantee, warrant, security; **2en** v/t. (no -ge-, h) grant, allow; give, yield, afford; j-n ~ lassen let s.o. have his way; leave s.o. alone; **2leisten** v/t. (no -ge-, h) guarantee.

Ge'wahrsam m (-s/-e) custody, safe keeping.

Ge'währsmann m informant, source.

Gewalt [gə'valt] f (-/-en) power; authority; control; force, violence; höhere ~ act of God; mit ~ by force; **~herrschaft** f despotism, tyranny; **2ig** adj. powerful, mighty; vehement; vast; **~maßnahme** f violent measure; **2sam 1.** adi. violent; **2.** adv. a. forcibly; ~ öffnen force open; open by force; **~tat** f act of violence; **2tätig** adj. violent.

Gewand [gə'vant] n (-[e]s/ˣer) garment; robe; esp. eccl. vestment.

ge'wandt 1. p.p. of wenden 2; **2.** adj. agile, nimble, dexterous, adroit; clever; **2heit** f (-/no pl.) agility, nimbleness; adroitness, dexterity, cleverness.

ge'wann pret. of gewinnen.

Gewäsch F [gə'vɛʃ] n (-es/no pl.) twaddle, nonsense.

ge'waschen p.p. of waschen.

Gewässer [gə'vɛsər] n (-s/-) water(s pl.).

Gewebe [gə'veːbə] n (-s/-) tissue (a. anat. and fig.); fabric; web; texture.

Ge'wehr n gun; rifle; **~kolben** m (rifle-)butt; **~lauf** m (rifle-, gun-) barrel.

Geweih [gə'vaɪ] n (-[e]s/-e) horns pl., head, antlers pl.

Gewerbe [gə'vɛrbə] n (-s/-) trade, business; industry; **~freiheit** f freedom of trade; **~schein** m trade licen|ce, Am. -se; **~schule** f technical school; **~steuer** f trade tax; **2treibend** adj. carrying on a business, engaged in trade; **~treibende** m (-n/-n) tradesman.

gewerb|lich adj. [gə'vɛrplɪç] commercial, industrial; **~smäßig** adj. professional.

Ge'werkschaft f (-/-en) trade(s) union, Am. labor union; **~ler** m (-s/-) trade(s)-unionist; **2lich** adj. trade-union; **~sbund** m Trade Union Congress, Am. Federation of Labor.

ge|wesen [gə've:zən] p.p. of sein; **~wichen** [gə'vɪçən] p.p. of weichen.

Gewicht [gə'vɪçt] n (-[e]s/-e) weight, Am. F a. heft; e-r Sache **~** beimessen attach importance to s.th.; **~** haben carry weight (bei dat. with); **~** legen auf et. lay stress on s.th.; ins **~** fallen be of great weight, count, matter; **2ig** adj. weighty (a. fig.).

ge|wiesen [gə'vi:zən] p.p. of weisen; **~willt** adj. [~'vɪlt] willing.

Ge|wimmel [gə'vɪməl] n (-s/no pl.) swarm; throng; **~winde** ⊕ [~'vɪndə] n (-s/-) thread.

Gewinn [gə'vɪn] m (-[e]s/-e) gain; † gains pl.; profit; lottery ticket: prize; game: winnings pl.; **~anteil** m dividend; **~beteiligung** f profit-sharing; **2bringend** adj. profitable; **2en** (irr., no -ge-, h) 1. v/t. win; gain; get; 2. v/i. win; gain; fig. improve; **2end** adj. manner, smile: winning, engaging; **~er** m (-s/-) winner.

Ge'wirr n (-[e]s/-e) tangle, entanglement; streets: maze; voices: confusion.

gewiß [gə'vɪs] 1. adj. certain; ein gewisser Herr N. a certain Mr. N., one Mr. N.; 2. adv.: **~!** certainly!, to be sure!, Am. sure!

Ge'wissen n (-s/-) conscience; **2haft** adj. conscientious; **2los** adj. unscrupulous; **~sbisse** m/pl. remorse, pangs pl. of conscience; **~sfrage** f question of conscience.

gewissermaßen adv. [gəvɪsər-'ma:sən] to a certain extent.

Ge'wißheit f (-/-en) certainty; certitude.

Gewitter [gə'vɪtər] n (-s/-) (thunder)storm; **2n** v/i. (no -ge-, h): es gewittert there is a thunderstorm; **~regen** m thunder-shower; **~wolke** f thundercloud.

ge|woben [gə'vo:bən] p.p. of weben; **~wogen** 1. p.p. of wägen and wiegen[1]; 2. adj. (dat.) well or kindly disposed towards, favo(u)rably inclined towards.

gewöhnen [gə'vø:nən] v/t. (no -ge-, h) accustom, get used (an acc. to).

Gewohnheit [gə'vo:nhaɪt] f (-/-en) habit; custom; **2smäßig** adj. habitual.

ge'wöhnlich adj. common; ordinary; usual, customary; habitual; common, vulgar.

ge'wohnt adj. customary, habitual; (es) **~** sein zu inf. be accustomed or used to inf.

Gewölbe [gə'vœlbə] n (-s/-) vault.

ge|wonnen [gə'vɔnən] p.p. of gewinnen; **~worben** [~'vɔrbən] p.p. of werben; **~worden** [~'vɔrdən] p.p. of werden; **~worfen** [~'vɔrfən] p.p. of werfen; **~wrungen** [~'vruŋən] p.p. of wringen.

Gewühl [gə'vy:l] n (-[e]s/no pl.) bustle; milling crowd.

gewunden [gə'vundən] 1. p.p. of winden; 2. adj. twisted; winding.

Gewürz [gə'vyrts] n (-es/-e) spice; condiment; **~nelke** ♀ f clove.

ge'wußt p.p. of wissen.

Ge|'zeit f: mst **~en** pl. tide(s pl.); **~zeter** n (-s/no pl.) (shrill) clamo(u)r.

ge|'ziert adj. affected; **~zogen** [~'tso:gən] p.p. of ziehen.

Gezwitscher [gə'tsvɪtʃər] n (-s/no pl.) chirping, twitter(ing).

gezwungen [gə'tsvuŋən] 1. p.p. of zwingen; 2. adj. forced, constrained.

Gicht ♋ [gɪçt] f (-/no pl.) gout; **'2isch** ♋ adj. gouty; **'~knoten** ♋ m gouty knot.

Giebel ['gi:bəl] m (-s/-) gable(-end).

Gier [gi:r] f (-/no pl.) greed(iness) (nach for); **2ig** adj. greedy (nach for, of).

'Gießbach m torrent.

gieß|en ['gi:sən] (irr., ge-, h) 1. v/t. pour; ⊕ cast, found; water (flowers); 2. v/i.: es gießt it is pouring (with rain); **'2er** m (-s/-) founder; **2erei** [~'raɪ] f (-/-en) foundry; **'2kanne** f watering-can or -pot.

Gift [gɪft] n (-[e]s/-e) poison; venom (esp. of snakes) (a. fig.); malice, spite; **'2ig** adj. poisonous; venomous; malicious, spiteful; **'~schlange** f venomous or poisonous snake; **'~zahn** m poison-fang.

Gigant [gi'gant] m (-en/-en) giant.

Gimpel orn. ['gɪmpəl] m (-s/-) bullfinch.

ging [gɪŋ] pret. of gehen.

Gipfel ['gɪpfəl] m (-s/-) summit, top; peak; **'~konferenz** pol. f summit meeting or conference; **'2n** v/i. (ge-, h) culminate.

Gips [gɪps] m (-es/-e) min. gypsum; ⊕ plaster (of Paris); **'~abdruck** m, **'~abguß** m plaster cast; **'2en** v/t. (ge-, h) plaster; **'~verband** ♋ m plaster (of Paris) dressing.

Giraffe zo. [gi'rafə] f (-/-n) giraffe.

girieren † [ʒiˈriːrən] v/t. (no -ge-, h) endorse, indorse (bill of exchange).

Girlande [girˈlandə] f (-/-n) garland.

Giro † [ˈʒiːro] n (-s/-s) endorsement, indorsement; '∼bank f clearing-bank; '∼konto n current account.

girren [ˈgirən] v/i. (ge-, h) coo.

Gischt [giʃt] m (-es/⅞ -e) and f (-/⅞ -en) foam, froth; spray; spindrift.

Gitarre ♪ [giˈtarə] f (-/-n) guitar.

Gitter [ˈgitər] n (-s/-) grating; lattice; trellis; railing; '∼bett n crib; '∼fenster n lattice-window.

Glacéhandschuh [glaˈseː-] m kid glove.

Glanz [glants] m (-es/no pl.) brightness; lust|re, Am. -er; brilliancy; splendo(u)r.

glänzen [ˈglɛntsən] v/i. (ge-, h) glitter, shine; '∼d adj. bright, brilliant; fig. splendid.

'**Glanz|leistung** f brilliant achievement or performance; '∼papier n glazed paper; '∼punkt m highlight; '∼zeit f golden age, heyday.

Glas [glaːs] n (-es/⅌er) glass; ∼er [ˈ∼zər] m (-s/-) glazier.

gläsern adj. [ˈglɛːzərn] of glass; fig. glassy.

'**Glas|glocke** f (glass) shade or cover; globe; bell-glass; '∼hütte f glassworks sg., pl.

glasieren [glaˈziːrən] v/t. (no -ge-, h) glaze; ice, frost (cake).

glasig adj. [ˈglaːziç] glassy, vitreous.

'**Glasscheibe** f pane of glass.

Glasur [glaˈzuːr] f (-/-en) glaze, glazing; enamel; icing, frosting (on cakes).

glatt [glat] 1. adj. smooth (a. fig.); even; lie, etc.: flat, downright; road, etc.: slippery; 2. adv. smoothly; evenly; ∼ anliegen fit closely or tightly; ∼ rasiert clean-shaven; et. ∼ ableugnen deny s.th. flatly.

Glätte [ˈglɛtə] f (-/-n) smoothness; road, etc.: slipperiness.

'**Glatteis** n glazed frost, icy glaze, Am. glaze; F: j-n aufs ∼ führen lead s.o. up the garden path.

'**glätten** v/t. (ge-, h) smooth.

Glatze [ˈglatsə] f (-/-n) bald head.

Glaube [ˈglaubə] m (-ns/⅞-n) faith, belief (an acc. in); '2n (ge-, h) 1. v/t. believe; think, suppose, Am. a. guess; 2. v/i. believe (j-m s.o.; an acc. in).

'**Glaubens|bekenntnis** n creed, profession or confession of faith; '∼lehre f, '∼satz m dogma, doctrine.

glaubhaft adj. [ˈglaup-] credible; plausible; authentic.

gläubig adj. [ˈglɔybiç] believing, faithful; 2e [ˈ∼gə] m, f (-n/-n)

believer; 2er † [ˈ∼gər] m (-s/-) creditor.

glaubwürdig adj. [ˈglaup-] credible.

gleich [glaiç] 1. adj. equal (an dat. in); the same; like; even, level; in ∼er Weise likewise; zur ∼en Zeit at the same time; es ist mir ∼ it's all the same to me; das ∼e the same; as much; er ist nicht (mehr) der ∼e he is not the same man; 2. adv. alike, equally; immediately; presently, directly, at once; just; es ist ∼ acht (Uhr) it is close on or nearly eight (o'clock); ∼altrig adj. [ˈ∼altriç] (of) the same age; '∼artig adj. homogeneous; similar; uniform; '∼bedeutend adj. synonymous; equivalent (to); tantamount (mit to); '∼berechtigt adj. having equal rights; '∼bleibend adj. constant, steady; '∼en v/i. (irr., ge-, h) equal; resemble.

'**gleich|falls** adv. also, likewise; ∼förmig adj. [ˈ∼fœrmiç] uniform; '∼gesinnt adj. like-minded; '2gewicht n balance (a. fig.); equilibrium, equipoise; pol.: ∼ der Kräfte balance of power; '∼gültig adj. indifferent (gegen to); es ist mir ∼ I don't care; ∼, was du tust no matter what you do; '2gültigkeit f indifference; '2heit f (-/-en) equality; likeness; '2klang m unison; consonance, harmony; '∼kommen v/i. (irr. kommen, sep., -ge-, sein): e-r Sache ∼ amount to s.th.; j-m ∼ equal s.o.; '∼laufend adj. parallel; '∼lautend adj. consonant; identical; '∼machen v/t. (sep., -ge-, h) make equal (dat. to), equalize (to or with); '2maß n regularity; evenness; fig. equilibrium; '∼mäßig adj. equal; regular; constant; even; '2mut m equanimity; '∼mütig adj. even-tempered; calm; '∼namig adj. [ˈ∼naːmiç] of the same name; '2nis n (-ses/-se) parable; rhet. simile; '∼sam adv. as it were, so to speak; '∼schalten v/t. (sep., -ge-, h) ⊕ synchronize; pol. co-ordinate, unify; '∼seitig adj. equilateral; '∼setzen v/t. (sep., -ge-, h) equate (dat. or mit with); '∼stehen v/i. (irr. stehen, sep., -ge-, h) be equal; '∼stellen v/t. (sep., -ge-, h) equalize, equate (dat. with); put s.o. on an equal footing (with); '2stellung f equalization; equation; '2strom ⚡ m direct current; '2ung ⚡ f (-/-en) equation; '∼wertig adj. equivalent, of the same value, of equal value; '∼zeitig adj. simultaneous; synchronous; contemporary.

Gleis [glais] n (-es/-e) s. Geleise.

gleiten [ˈglaitən] v/i. (irr., ge-, sein) glide, slide.

'**Gleit|flug** m gliding flight, glide, ⚔ volplane; '∼schutzreifen m non-skid tyre, (*Am. only*) non-skid tire; '**schutz(vorrichtung** *f*) *m* anti-skid device.

Gletscher ['glɛtʃər] *m* (*-s/-*) glacier; '**spalte** *f* crevasse.

glich [gliç] *pret. of* gleichen.

Glied [gli:t] *n* (*-[e]s/-er*) *anat.* limb; member (*a. anat.*); link; ✂ rank, file; 2**ern** ['dərn] *v/t.* (*ge-,* h) joint, articulate; arrange; divide (*in acc.* into); '**erung** *f* (*-/-en*) articulation; arrangement; division; formation; '**maßen** ['tma:sən] *pl.* limbs *pl.*, extremities *pl.*

glimmen ['glimən] *v/i.* ([*irr.,*] ge-, h) *fire:* smo(u)lder (*a. fig.*); glimmer; glow.

glimpflich ['glimpfliç] **1.** *adj.* lenient, mild; **2.** *adv.:* ~ **davonkommen** get off lightly.

glitschig *adj.* ['glitʃiç] slippery.

glitt [glit] *pret. of* gleiten.

glitzern ['glitsərn] *v/i.* (ge-, h) glitter, glisten.

Globus ['glo:bus] *m* (*-, -ses/Globen, Globusse*) globe.

Glocke ['glɔkə] *f* (*-/-n*) bell; shade; (glass) cover.

'**Glocken|schlag** *m* stroke of the clock; '**spiel** *n* chime(s *pl.*); '**stuhl** *m* bell-cage; '**turm** *m* bell tower, belfry.

Glöckner ['glœknər] *m* (*-s/-*) bell-ringer.

glomm [glɔm] *pret. of* glimmen.

Glorie ['glo:rjə] *f* (*-/-n*) glory; '**schein** *fig. m* halo, aureola.

glorreich *adj.* ['glo:r-] glorious.

glotzen F ['glɔtsən] *v/i.* (ge-, h) stare.

Glück [glyk] *n* (*-[e]s/no pl.*) fortune; good luck; happiness, bliss, felicity; prosperity; *auf gut ~* on the off chance; ~ *haben* be lucky, succeed; *das ~ haben zu inf.* have the good fortune to *inf.*; *j-m ~ wünschen* congratulate s.o. (*zu* on); *viel ~!* good luck!; *zum ~* fortunately; 2**bringend** *adj.* lucky.

Glucke *orn.* ['glukə] *f* (*-/-n*) sitting hen.   [gen.]

'**glücken** *v/i.* (ge-, sein) *s.* gelin-}

gluckern ['glukərn] *v/i.* (ge-, h) *water, etc.:* gurgle.

'**glücklich** *adj.* fortunate; happy; lucky; '**er'weise** *adv.* fortunately.

'**Glücksbringer** *m* (*-s/-*) mascot.

glück'selig *adj.* blissful, blessed, happy.

glucksen ['gluksən] *v/i.* (ge-, h) gurgle.

'**Glücks|fall** *m* lucky chance, stroke of (good) luck; '**göttin** *f* Fortune; '**kind** *n* lucky person; '**pfennig** *m* lucky penny; '**pilz** *m* lucky person; '**spiel** *n* game of chance; *fig.* gamble; '**stern** *m* lucky star; '**tag** *m* happy *or* lucky day, red-letter day.

'**glück|strahlend** *adj.* radiant(ly happy); 2**wunsch** *m* congratulation, good wishes *pl.*; compliments *pl.*; ~ *zum Geburtstag* many happy returns (of the day).

Glüh|birne ⚡ ['gly:-] *f* (electric-light) bulb; 2**en** *v/i.* (ge-, h) glow; 2**end** *adj.* glowing; *iron:* red-hot; *coal:* live; *fig.* ardent, fervid; '2(end)**heiß** *adj.* burning hot; '**lampe** *f* incandescent lamp; '**wein** *m* mulled wine; **würmchen** *zo.* ['vyrmçən] *n* (*-s/-*) glow-worm.

Glut [glu:t] *f* (*-/-en*) heat, glow (*a. fig.*); glowing fire, embers *pl.*; *fig.* ardo(u)r.

Gnade ['gna:də] *f* (*-/-n*) grace; favo(u)r; mercy; clemency; pardon; ✂ quarter.

'**Gnaden|akt** *m* act of grace; '**brot** *n* (*-[e]s/no pl.*) bread of charity; '**frist** *f* reprieve; '**gesuch** *n* petition for mercy.

gnädig *adj.* ['gnɛ:diç] gracious; merciful; *address:* 2**e Frau** Madam.

Gnom [gno:m] *m* (*-en/-en*) gnome, goblin.

Gobelin [gobə'lɛ̃:] *m* (*-s/-s*) Gobelin tapestry.

Gold [gɔlt] *n* (*-[e]s/no pl.*) gold; '**barren** *m* gold bar, gold ingot, bullion; '**borte** *f* gold lace; 2**en** *adj.* ['dən] gold; *fig.* golden; '**feder** *f* gold nib; '**fisch** *m* goldfish; '2**gelb** *adj.* golden(-yellow); **gräber** ['grɛ:bər] *m* (*-s/-*) gold-digger; '**grube** *f* gold-mine; '2**haltig** *adj.* gold-bearing, containing gold; 2**ig** *fig. adj.* ['diç] sweet, lovely, *Am. a.* cute; '**mine** *f* gold-mine; '**münze** *f* gold coin; '**schmied** *m* goldsmith; '**schnitt** *m* gilt edge; *mit ~* gilt-edged; '**stück** *n* gold coin; '**waage** *f* gold-balance; '**währung** *f* gold standard.

Golf[1] *geogr.* [gɔlf] *m* (*-[e]s/-e*) gulf.

Golf[2] [~] *n* (*-s/no pl.*) golf; '**platz** *m* golf-course, (golf-)links *pl.*; '**schläger** *m* golf-club; '**spiel** *n* golf; '**spieler** *m* golfer.

Gondel ['gɔndəl] *f* (*-/-n*) gondola; ✈ *mst* car.

gönnen ['gœnən] *v/t.* (ge-, h): *j-m et.* ~ allow *or* grant *or* not to grudge s.o. s.th.

'**Gönner** *m* (*-s/-*) patron; *Am. a.* sponsor; 2**haft** *adj.* patronizing.

gor [go:r] *pret. of* gären.

Gorilla *zo.* [go'rila] *m* (*-s/-s*) gorilla.

goß [gɔs] *pret. of* gießen.

Gosse ['gɔsə] *f* (*-/-n*) gutter (*a. fig.*).

Gott [gɔt] *m* (*-es, ✝ -s/⸚er*) God; god, deity; '2**ergeben** *adj.* resigned (to the will of God).

'**Gottes|dienst** *eccl. m* (divine) service; '2**fürchtig** *adj.* godfearing; '**haus** *n* church, chapel; '**läste-**

rer *m* (-s/-) blasphemer; '**~läste-rung** *f* blasphemy.

'**Gottheit** *f* (-/-en) deity, divinity.

Göttin ['gœtin] *f* (-/-nen) goddess.

göttlich *adj.* ['gœtliç] divine.

gott|'lob *int.* thank God *or* goodness!; '**~los** *adj.* godless, impious; F *fig. deed:* unholy, wicked; 2**ver-trauen** *n* trust in God.

Götze ['gœtsə] *m* (-n/-n) idol; '**~nbild** *n* idol; '**~ndienst** *m* idolatry.

Gouvern|ante [guvɛr'nantə] *f* (-/-n) governess; '**~eur** *Am.* -er; '**~rede** *f* [guvɛr'nøːr] *m* (-s/-e) governor.

Grab [grɑːp] *n* (-[e]s/ᵘer) grave, tomb, sepulch|re, *Am.* -er.

Graben ['grɑːbən] **1.** *m* (-s/ᵘ) ditch; ✗ trench; **2.** 2 *v/t.* (*irr.*, ge-, h) dig; *animal:* burrow.

Grab|gewölbe ['grɑːp-] *n* vault, tomb; '**~mal** *n* monument; tomb, sepulch|re, *Am.* -er; '**~rede** *f* funeral sermon; funeral oration *or* address; '**~schrift** *f* epitaph; '**~stätte** *f* burial-place; grave, tomb; '**~stein** *m* tombstone; gravestone.

Grad [grɑːt] *m* (-[e]s/-e) degree; grade, rank; 15 ~ Kälte 15 degrees below zero; '**~einteilung** *f* graduation; '**~messer** *m* (-s/-) graduated scale, graduator; *fig.* criterion; '**~netz** *n map:* grid.

Graf [grɑːf] *m* (-en/-en) *in Britain:* earl; count.

Gräfin ['grɛːfin] *f* (-/-nen) countess.

'**Grafschaft** *f* (-/-en) county.

Gram [grɑːm] **1.** *m* (-[e]s/*no pl.*) grief, sorrow; **2.** 2 *adj.:* j-m ~ sein bear s.o. ill will *or* a grudge.

grämen ['grɛːmən] *v/t.* (ge-, h) grieve; *sich* ~ grieve (*über acc.* at, for, over).

Gramm [gram] *n* (-s/-e) gramme, *Am.* gram.

Grammati|k [gra'matik] *f* (-/-en) grammar; 2**sch** *adj.* grammatical.

Granat *min.* [gra'nɑːt] *m* (-[e]s/-e) garnet; '**~e** ✗ *f* (-/-n) shell; grenade; '**~splitter** ✗ *m* shell-splinter; '**~trichter** ✗ *m* shell-crater; '**~werfer** ✗ *m* (-s/-) mortar.

Granit *min.* [gra'niːt] *m* (-s/-e) granite.

Granne ♀ ['granə] *f* (-/-n) awn, beard.

Graphi|k ['grɑːfik] *f* (-/-en) graphic arts *pl.*; 2**sch** *adj.* graphic(al).

Graphit *min.* [gra'fiːt] *m* (-s/-e) graphite.

Gras ♀ [grɑːs] *n* (-es/ᵘer) grass; 2**bewachsen** *adj.* ['~bəvaksən] grass-grown, grassy; 2**en** ['~zən] *v/i.* (ge-, h) graze; '**~halm** *m* blade of grass; '**~narbe** *f* turf, sod; '**~platz** *m* grass-plot, green.

grassieren [gra'siːrən] *v/i.* (*no -ge-*, h) rage, prevail.

gräßlich *adj.* ['grɛsliç] horrible; hideous, atrocious.

Grassteppe ['grɑːs-] *f* prairie, savanna(h).

Grat [grɑːt] *m* (-[e]s/-e) edge, ridge.

Gräte ['grɛːtə] *f* (-/-n) (fish-)bone.

Gratifikation [gratifika'tsjoːn] *f* (-/-en) gratuity, bonus.

gratis *adv.* ['grɑːtis] gratis, free of charge.

Gratul|ant [gratu'lant] *m* (-en/-en) congratulator; **~ation** ['~'tsjoːn] *f* (-/-en) congratulation; 2**ieren** ['~-'liːrən] *v/i.* (*no -ge-*, h) congratulate (*j-m zu et.* s.o. on s.th.); *j-m zum Geburtstag* ~ wish s.o. many happy returns (of the day).

grau *adj.* [grau] grey, *esp. Am.* gray.

'**grauen¹** *v/i.* (ge-, h) *day:* dawn.

'**grauen²** *v/i.* (ge-, h): *mir graut vor* (*dat.*) I shudder at, I dread; **2.** 2 *n* (-s/*no pl.*) horror (*vor dat.* of); '**~erregend** *adj.*, '**~haft** *adj.*, '**~voll** *adj.* horrible, dreadful.

gräulich *adj.* ['grɔyliç] greyish, *esp. Am.* grayish.

Graupe ['graupə] *f* (-/-n) (peeled) barley, pot-barley; '**~ln 1.** *f/pl.* sleet; **2.** 2 *v/i.* (ge-, h) sleet.

'**grausam** *adj.* cruel; 2**keit** *f* (-/-en) cruelty.

grausen ['grauzən] **1.** *v/i.* (ge-, h) *s. grauen²*; **2.** 2 *n* (-s/*no pl.*) horror (*vor dat.* of).

'**grausig** *adj.* horrible; [graver.}

Graveur [gra'vøːr] *m* (-s/-e) en-

gravieren [gra'viːrən] *v/t.* (*no -ge-*, h) engrave; **~d** *fig. adj.* aggravating.

gravitätisch *adj.* [gravi'tɛːtiʃ] grave; dignified; solemn; stately.

Grazie ['grɑːtsjə] *f* (-/-n) grace(fulness).

graziös *adj.* [gra'tsjøːs] graceful.

greifen ['graifən] (*irr.*, ge-, h) **1.** *v/t.* seize, grasp, catch hold of; ♩ touch (*string*); **2.** *v/i.:* *an den Hut* ~ touch one's hat; ~ *nach* grasp *or* snatch at; *um sich* ~ spread; *j-m unter die Arme* ~ give s.o. a helping hand; *zu strengen Mitteln* ~ resort to severe measures; *zu den Waffen* ~ take up arms.

Greis [grais] *m* (-es/-e) old man; 2**enhaft** *adj.* ['~zən-] senile (*a.* ⚕); '**~in** ['~zin] *f* (-/-nen) old woman.

grell *adj.* [grɛl] *light:* glaring; *colour:* loud; *sound:* shrill.

Grenze ['grɛntsə] *f* (-/-n) limit; *territory:* boundary; *state:* frontier, borders *pl.*; e-e ~ *ziehen* draw the line; 2**n** ['~tsən] *v/i.* (ge-, h): ~ *an* (*acc.*) border on (*a. fig.*); *fig.* verge on; 2**los** *adj.* boundless.

'**Grenz|fall** *m* border-line case; '**~land** *n* borderland; '**~linie** *f* boundary *or* border line; '**~schutz** *m* frontier *or* border protection; frontier *or* border guard; '**~stein** *m* boundary stone; '**~übergang** *m* frontier *or* border crossing(-point).

Greuel ['grɔyəl] *m* (-s/-) horror;

abomination; atrocity; '**_tat** f atrocity.

Griech|e ['griːçə] m (-n/-n) Greek; '**_isch** adj. Greek; △, *features*: Grecian.

griesgrämig adj. ['griːsgrɛːmiç] morose, sullen.

Grieß [griːs] m (-es/-e) gravel (a. ⚕), grit; semolina; '**_brei** m semolina pudding.

Griff [grif] 1. m (-[e]s/-e) grip, grasp, hold; ♪ touch; handle (*of knife, etc.*); hilt (*of sword*); 2. ♀ *pret. of* greifen.

Grille ['grilə] f (-/-n) *zo.* cricket; *fig.* whim, fancy; '**_nhaft** adj. whimsical.

Grimasse [griˈmasə] f (-/-n) grimace; **_n** schneiden pull faces.

Grimm [grim] m (-[e]s/*no pl.*) fury, rage; '**_ig** adj. furious, fierce, grim.

Grind [grint] m (-[e]s/-e) scab, scurf.

grinsen ['grinzən] 1. v/i. (ge-, h) grin (*über acc.* at); sneer (at); 2. ♀ n (-s/*no pl.*) grin; sneer.

Grippe ♂ ['gripə] f (-/-n) influenza, F flu(e), grippe.

grob adj. [grɔp] coarse; gross; rude; *work, skin*: rough; '**_heit** f (-/-en) coarseness; grossness; rudeness; **_en** pl. rude things pl.

grölen F ['grøːlən] v/t. *and* v/i. (ge-, h) bawl.

Groll [grɔl] m (-[e]s/*no pl.*) grudge, ill will; '**_en** v/i. (ge-, h) *thunder*: rumble; *j-m* **_** bear s.o. ill will *or* a grudge.

Gros¹ ♀ [grɔs] n (-ses/-se) gross.

Gros² [groː] n (-/-) main body.

Groschen ['grɔʃən] m (-s/-) penny.

groß adj. [groːs] great; large; big; *figure*: tall; huge; *fig.* great, grand; *heat*: intense; *cold*: severe; *loss*: heavy; *die* ♀**en** pl. the grown-ups pl.; *im* **_en** wholesale, on a large scale; *im* **_en** (*und*) *ganzen* on the whole; *das* **_e** *Los* the first prize; *ich bin kein* **_er** *Tänzer* I am not much of a dancer; '**_artig** adj. great, grand, sublime; first-rate; '**_aufnahme** f *film*: close-up.

Größe ['grøːsə] f (-/-n) size; largeness; height, tallness; quantity (*esp.* A); *importance*: greatness; *p.* celebrity; *thea.* star.

'**Großeltern** pl. grandparents pl.

'**großenteils** adv. to a large *or* great extent, largely.

'**Größenwahn** m megalomania.

'**Groß|grundbesitz** m large landed property; '**_handel** ♀ m wholesale trade; '**_handelspreis** ♀ m wholesale price; '**_händler** ♀ m wholesale dealer, wholesaler; '**_handlung** f wholesale business; '**_herzog** m grand duke; '**_industrielle** m big industrialist.

Grossist [grɔˈsist] m (-en/-en) s. Großhändler.

groß|jährig adj. ['groːsjɛːriç] of age; **_** *werden* come of age; '**_jährigkeit** f (-/*no pl.*) majority, full (legal) age; '**_kaufmann** m wholesale merchant; '**_kraftwerk** ⚡ n super-power station; '**_macht** f great power; '**_maul** n braggart; '**_mut** f (-/*no pl.*) generosity; **_mütig** adj. ['**_myːtiç] magnanimous, generous; '**_mutter** f grandmother; '**_neffe** m great-nephew, grandnephew; '**_nichte** f great-niece, grand-niece; '**_onkel** m great-uncle, grand-uncle; '**_schreibung** f (-/-en) use of capital letters; capitalization; '**_sprecherisch** adj. boastful; '**_spurig** adj. arrogant; '**_stadt** f large town *or* city; '**_städtisch** adj. of *or* in a large town *or* city; '**_tante** f great-aunt, grand-aunt.

größtenteils adv. ['grøːstəntaɪls] mostly, chiefly, mainly.

'**groß|tun** v/i. (*irr.* tun, *sep.*, -ge-, h) swagger, boast; *sich mit et.* **_** boast *or* brag of *or* about s.th.; '**_vater** m grandfather; '**_verdiener** m (-s/-) big earner; '**_wild** n big game; '**_ziehen** v/t. (*irr.* ziehen, *sep.*, -ge-, h) bring up (*child*); rear, raise (*child, animal*); '**_zügig** adj. ['**_tsyːgiç] liberal; generous; broad-minded; *planning*: a. on a large scale.

grotesk adj. [groˈtɛsk] grotesque.

Grotte ['grɔtə] f (-/-n) grotto.

grub [gruːp] *pret. of* graben.

Grübchen ['gryːpçən] n (-s/-) dimple.

Grube ['gruːbə] f (-/-n) pit; ⚒ mine, pit.

Grübel|ei [gryːbəˈlaɪ] f (-/-en) brooding, musing, meditation; '**_n** ['**_ln] v/i. (ge-, h) muse, meditate, ponder (*all: über acc.* on, over), Am. F a. mull (over).

'**Gruben|arbeiter** ⚒ m miner; '**_gas** ⚒ n fire-damp; '**_lampe** ⚒ f miner's lamp.

Gruft [gruft] f (-/⁼e) tomb, vault.

grün [gryːn] 1. adj. green; **_er** *Hering* fresh herring; **_er** *Junge* greenhorn; **_** *und blau* schlagen beat s.o. black and blue; *vom* **_en** *Tisch aus* armchair (*strategy, etc.*); 2. ♀ n (-s/*no pl.*) green; verdure.

Grund [grunt] m (-[e]s/⁼e) ground; soil; bottom (*a. fig.*); land, estate; foundation; *fig.*: motive; reason; argument; *von* **_** *auf* thoroughly, fundamentally; '**_ausbildung** f basic instruction; ✕ basic (military) training; '**_bedeutung** f basic *or* original meaning; '**_bedingung** f basic *or* fundamental condition; '**_begriff** m fundamental *or* basic idea; **_e** pl. principles pl.; rudiments pl.; '**_besitz** m land(ed property); '~besitzer *m* landowner; '~buch *n* land register.

gründ|en ['gryndən] *v/t.* (ge-, h) establish; ✝ promote; *sich ~ auf* (*acc.*) be based or founded on; '2er *m* (-s/-) founder; ✝ promoter.

'grund|falsch *adj.* fundamentally wrong; '2farbe *f* ground-colo(u)r; *opt.* primary colo(u)r; '2fläche *f* base; area (*of room, etc.*); '2gebühr *f* basic rate or fee; flat rate; '2gedanke *m* basic or fundamental idea; '2gesetz *n* fundamental law; ₰₰ *appr.* constitution; '2kapital ✝ *n* capital (fund); '2lage *f* foundation, basis; '~legend *adj.* fundamental, basic.

gründlich *adj.* ['gryntliç] thorough; *knowledge*: profound.

'Grund|linie *f* base-line; '2los *adj.* bottomless; *fig.*: groundless; unfounded; '~mauer *f* foundation-wall. [Thursday.\

Grün'donnerstag *eccl. m* Maundy

'Grund|regel *f* fundamental rule; '~riß *m* △ ground-plan; outline; compendium; '~satz *m* principle; 2sätzlich ['~zetsliç] **1.** *adj.* fundamental; **2.** *adv.* in principle; on principle; '~schule *f* elementary or primary school; '~stein *m* △ foundation-stone; *fig.* corner-stone; '~steuer *f* land-tax; '~stock *m* basis, foundation; '~stoff *n* element; '~strich *m* down-stroke; '~stück *n* plot (of land); ₰₰ (real) estate; premises *pl.*; '~stücksmakler *m* real estate agent, *Am.* realtor; '~ton *m* ♪ keynote; ground shade.

'Gründung *f* (-/-en) foundation, establishment.

'grund|ver'schieden *adj.* entirely different; '2wasser *geol. n* (under-)ground water; '2zahl *gr.* (-/-) cardinal number; '2zug *m* main feature, characteristic.

'grünlich *adj.* greenish.

'Grün|schnabel *fig. m* greenhorn; whipper-snapper; '~span *m* (-[e]s/*no pl.*) verdigris.

grunzen ['gruntsən] *v/i. and v/t.* (ge-, h) grunt.

Grupp|e ['grupə] *f* (-/-n) group; ✕ section, *Am.* squad; 2ieren [~'pi:rən] *v/t.* (*no* -ge-, h) group, arrange in groups; *sich ~* form groups.

Gruselgeschichte ['gru:zəl-] *f* tale of horror, spine-chilling story or tale, F creepy story or tale.

Gruß [gru:s] *m* (-es/~e) salutation; greeting; *esp.* ✕, ⚓ salute; *mst* Grüße *pl.* regards *pl.*; respects *pl.*, compliments *pl.*

grüßen ['gry:sən] *v/t.* (ge-, h) greet, *esp.* ✕ salute; hail; *~ Sie ihn von mir* remember me to him; *j-n ~ lassen* send one's compliments or regards to s.o.

Grütze ['grytsə] *f* (-/-n) grits *pl.*, groats *pl.*

guck|en ['gukən] *v/i.* (ge-, h) look; peep, peer; '2loch *n* peep- or spy-hole.

Guerilla ✕ [ge'ril(j)a] *f* (-/-s) guer(r)illa war.

gültig *adj.* ['gyltiç] valid; effective, in force; legal; *coin*: current; *ticket*: available; '2keit *f* (-/*no pl.*) validity; currency (*of money*); availability (*of ticket*).

Gummi ['gumi] *n*, *m* (-s/-s) gum; (india-)rubber; '~ball *m* rubber ball; '~band *n* elastic (band); rubber band; '~baum ⚘ *m* gum-tree; (india-)rubber tree.

gum'mieren *v/t.* (*no* -ge-, h) gum.

'Gummi|handschuh *m* rubber glove; '~knüppel *m* truncheon, *Am.* club; '~schuhe *m/pl.* rubber shoes *pl.*, *Am.* rubbers *pl.*; '~sohle *f* rubber sole; '~stiefel *m* wellington (boot), *Am.* rubber boot; '~zug *m* elastic; elastic webbing.

Gunst [gunst] *f* (-/*no pl.*) favo(u)r, goodwill; *zu ~en* (*gen.*) in favo(u)r of.

günst|ig *adj.* ['gynstiç] favo(u)rable; *omen*: propitious; *im ~sten Fall* at best; *zu ~en Bedingungen* ✝ on easy terms; 2ling ['~liŋ] *m* (-s/-e) favo(u)rite.

Gurgel ['gurgəl] *f* (-/-n): *j-m an die ~ springen* leap or fly at s.o.'s throat; '2n *v/i.* (ge-, h) ⚕ gargle; gurgle.

Gurke ['gurkə] *f* (-/-n) cucumber; *pickled*: gherkin.

gurren ['gurən] *v/i.* (ge-, h) coo.

Gurt [gurt] *m* (-[e]s/-e) girdle; *harness*: girth; strap; belt.

Gürtel ['gyrtəl] *m* (-s/-) belt; girdle; *geogr.* zone.

Guß [gus] *m* (Gusses/Güsse) ⊕ founding, casting; *typ.* fount, *Am.* font; *rain*: downpour, shower; '~eisen *n* cast iron; '2eisern *adj.* cast-iron; '~stahl *m* cast steel.

gut[1] [gu:t] **1.** *adj.* good; *~e Worte* fair words; *~es Wetter* fine weather; *~er Dinge or ~en Mutes sein* be of good cheer; *~e Miene zum bösen Spiel machen* grin and bear it; *~ so!* good!, well done!; *~ werden* get well, heal; *fig.* turn out well; *ganz ~* not bad; *schon ~!* never mind!, all right!; *sei so ~ und ...* (will you) be so kind as to *inf.*; *auf ~ deutsch* in plain German; *j-m ~ sein* love or like s.o.; **2.** *adv.* well; *ein ~ gehendes Geschäft* a flourishing business; *du hast ~ lachen* it's easy or very well for you to laugh; *es ~ haben* be lucky; be well off.

Gut[2] [~] *n* (-[e]s/*~er*) possession, property; (landed) estate; ✝ goods *pl.*

'**Gut|achten** *n* (-s/-) (expert) opinion; '**~achter** *m* (-s/-) expert; consultant; '**₂artig** *adj.* good-natured; ₰ benign; **~dünken** ['~dynkən] *n* (-s/*no pl.*): *nach* ~ at discretion *or* pleasure.
Gute 1. *n* (-n/*no pl.*) *the* good; ~s *tun* do good; 2. *m*, *f* (-n/-n): *die* ~*n pl.* the good *pl.*
Güte ['gy:tə] *f* (-/*no pl.*) goodness, kindness; ✝ class, quality; *in* ~ amicably; F: *meine* ~*! good gracious!; haben Sie die* ~ *zu inf.* be so kind as to *inf.*
'**Güter|abfertigung** *f* dispatch of goods; = '**~annahme** *f* goods office, *Am.* freight office; '**~bahnhof** *m* goods station, *Am.* freight depot *or* yard; '**~gemeinschaft** ₰₰ *f* community of property; '**~trennung** ₰₰ *f* separation of property; '**~verkehr** *m* goods traffic, *Am.* freight traffic; '**~wagen** *m* (goods) wag(g)on, *Am.* freight car; *offener* ~ (goods) truck; *geschlossener* ~ (goods) van, *Am.* boxcar; '**~zug** *m* goods train, *Am.* freight train.
'**gut|gelaunt** *adj.* good-humo(u)red; '**~gläubig** *adj.* acting in good faith; *s. leichtgläubig*; '**~haben** *v/t.* (*irr.* haben, *sep.*, *-ge-*, h) have credit for (*sum of money*); '**₂haben** ✝ *n* credit (balance); '**~heißen** *v/t.* (*irr.* heißen, *sep.*, *-ge-*, h)

approve (of); '**~herzig** *adj.* good-natured, kind-hearted.
'**gütig** *adj.* good, kind(ly).
'**gütlich** *adv.*: *sich* ~ *einigen* settle *s.th.* amicably; *sich* ~ *tun an* (*dat.*) regale o.s. on.
'**gut|machen** *v/t.* (*sep.*, *-ge-*, h) make up for, compensate, repair; **~mütig** *adj.* ['~my:tiç] good-natured; '**₂mütigkeit** *f* (-/✽ -en) good nature.
'**Gutsbesitzer** *m* landowner; owner of an estate.
'**Gut|schein** *m* credit note, coupon; voucher; '**₂schreiben** *v/t.* (*irr.* schreiben, *sep.*, *-ge-*, h): *j-m e-n Betrag* ~ put a sum to s.o.'s credit; '**~schrift** ✝ *f* credit(ing).
'**Guts|haus** *n* farm-house; manor house; '**~herr** *m* lord of the manor; landowner; '**~hof** *m* farmyard; estate, farm; '**~verwalter** *m* (landlord's) manager *or* steward.
'**gutwillig** *adj.* willing; obliging.
Gymnasi|albildung [gymna'zja:l-] *f* classical education; **~ast** [~ast] *m* (-en/-en) *appr.* grammar-school boy; **~um** [~'na:zjum] *n* (-s/*Gymnasien*) *appr.* grammar-school.
Gymnasti|k [gym'nastik] *f* (-/*no pl.*) gymnastics *pl.*; **₂sch** *adj.* gymnastic.
Gynäkologe ₰ [gynɛ:ko'lo:gə] *m* (-n/-n) gyn(a)ecologist.

H

Haar [ha:r] *n* (-[e]s/-e) hair; *sich die* ~*e kämmen* comb one's hair; *sich die* ~*e schneiden lassen* have one's hair cut; *aufs* ~ to a hair; *um ein* ~ by a hair's breadth; '**~ausfall** *m* loss of hair; '**~bürste** *f* hairbrush; '**₂en** *v/i. and v/refl.* (ge-, h) lose *or* shed one's hairs; '**~esbreite** *f*: *um* ~ by a hair's breadth; '**₂'fein** *adj.* (as) fine as a hair; *fig.* subtle; '**~gefäß** *anat. n* capillary (vessel); '**₂ge'nau** *adj.* exact to a hair; '**₂ig** *adj.* hairy; *in compounds:* ...-haired; '**₂'klein** *adv.* to the last detail; '**~klemme** *f* hair grip, *Am.* bobby pin; '**~nadel** *f* hairpin; '**~nadelkurve** *f* hairpin bend; '**~netz** *n* hair-net; '**~öl** *n* hair-oil; '**₂'scharf** 1. *adj.* very sharp; *fig.* very precise; 2. *adv.* by a hair's breadth; '**~schneidemaschine** *f* (e-e a pair of) (hair) clippers *pl.*; '**~schneider** *m* barber, (men's) hairdresser; '**~schnitt** *m* haircut; '**~schwund** *m* loss of hair; ~**spalte'rei** *f* (-/-en) hair-splitting; '**₂sträubend** *adj.* hair-raising, horrifying; '**~tracht** *f* hair-style, coiffure; '**~wäsche** *f* hair-wash,

shampoo; '**~wasser** *n* hair-lotion; '**~wuchs** *m* growth of the hair; '**~wuchsmittel** *n* hair-restorer.
Habe ['ha:bə] *f* (-/*no pl.*) property; belongings *pl.*
haben ['ha:bən] 1. *v/t.* (*irr.*, ge-, h) have; F *fig.*: *sich* ~ (make a) fuss; *etwas* (*nichts*) *auf sich* ~ be of (no) consequence; *unter sich* ~ be in control of, command; *zu* ~ ✝ *goods*: obtainable, to be had; *da* ~ *wir's* / there we are!; 2. ₂ ✝ *n* (-s/-) credit (side).
Habgier ['ha:p-] *f* avarice, covetousness; '**₂ig** *adj.* avaricious, covetous.
habhaft *adj.* ['ha:phaft]: ~ *werden* (*gen.*) get hold of; catch, apprehend.
Habicht *orn.* ['ha:biçt] *m* (-[e]s/-e) (gos)hawk.
Hab|seligkeiten ['ha:p-] *f/pl.* property, belongings *pl.*; '**~sucht** *f s. Habgier;* '**₂süchtig** *adj. s. habgierig.*
Hacke ['hakə] *f* (-/-n) ₰ hoe, mattock; (pick)axe; heel.
Hacken ['hakən] 1. *m* (-s/-) heel; *die* ~ *zusammenschlagen* ✕ click one's heels; 2. ₂ *v/t.* (ge-, h) ₰

hack (*soil*); mince (*meat*); chop (*wood*).

'Hackfleisch *n* minced meat, *Am.* ground meat.

Häcksel ['hɛksəl] *n*, *m* (-s/*no pl.*) chaff, chopped straw.

Hader ['hɑːdər] *m* (-s/*no pl.*) dispute, quarrel; discord; **'2n** *v/i.* (ge-, h) quarrel (*mit* with).

Hafen ['hɑːfən] *m* (-s/ꞌ) harbo(u)r; port; **'∼anlagen** *f/pl.* docks *pl.*; **'∼arbeiter** *m* docker, *Am. a.* long-shoreman; **'∼damm** *m* jetty; pier; **'∼stadt** *f* seaport.

Hafer ['hɑːfər] *m* (-s/-) oats *pl.*; **'∼brei** *m* (oatmeal) porridge; **'∼flocken** *f/pl.* porridge oats *pl.*; **'∼grütze** *f* groats *pl.*, grits *pl.*; **'∼schleim** *m* gruel.

Haft ⁊⁊ [haft] *f* (-/*no pl.*) custody, detention, confinement; **'2bar** *adj.* responsible, ⁊⁊ liable (*für* for); **'∼befehl** *m* warrant of arrest; **'2en** *v/i.* (ge-, h) stick, adhere (*an dat.* to); **∼ für** ⁊⁊ answer for, be liable for.

Häftling ['hɛftliŋ] *m* (-s/-e) prisoner.

'Haftpflicht ⁊⁊ *f* liability; **'2ig** *adj.* liable (*für* for); **'∼versicherung** *f* third-party insurance.

'Haftung *f* (-/-en) responsibility, ⁊⁊ liability; *mit beschränkter* ∼ limited.

Hagel ['hɑːgəl] *m* (-s/-) hail; *fig. a.* shower, volley; **'∼korn** *n* hailstone; **'2n** *v/i.* (ge-, h) hail (*a. fig.*); **'∼schauer** *m* shower of hail, (brief) hailstorm.

hager *adj.* ['hɑːgər] lean, gaunt; scraggy, lank.

Hahn [hɑːn] *m* 1. *orn.* (-[e]s/Ꞌe) cock; rooster; 2. ⊕ (-[e]s/Ꞌe, -en) (stop)cock, tap, *Am. a.* faucet; **'∼enkampf** *m* cock-fight; **'∼enschrei** *m* cock-crow.

Hai *ichth.* [hai] *m* (-[e]s/-e), **'∼fisch** *m* shark.

Hain *poet.* [hain] *m* (-[e]s/-e) grove; wood.

häkel|n ['hɛːkəln] *v/t. and v/i.* (ge-, h) crochet; **'2nadel** *f* crochet needle or hook.

Haken ['hɑːkən] 1. *m* (-s/-) hook (*a. boxing*); peg; *fig.* snag, catch; 2. ♀ *v/i.* (ge-, h) get stuck, jam.

'hakig *adj.* hooked.

halb [halp] 1. *adj.* half; *eine ∼e Stunde* half an hour, a half-hour; *eine ∼e Flasche Wein* a half-bottle of wine; *ein ∼es Jahr* half a year; *∼e Note* ♪ minim, *Am. a.* half note; *∼er Ton* ♪ semitone, *Am. a.* half tone; 2. *adv.* half; *∼ voll* half full; *∼ soviel* half as much; *es schlug ∼* it struck the half-hour.

'halb|amtlich *adj.* semi-official; **'2bruder** *m* half-brother; **'2dunkel** *n* semi-darkness; dusk, twilight; **'∼er** *prp.* (*gen.*) ['halbər] on account of; for the sake of; **'2fabri-**

kat ⊕ *n* semi-finished product; **'∼gar** *adj.* underdone, *Am. a.* rare; **'2gott** *m* demigod; **'2heit** *f* (-/-en) half-measure.

halbieren [hal'biːrən] *v/t.* (*no* -ge-, h) halve, divide in half; ♔ bisect.

'Halb|insel *f* peninsula; **'∼jahr** *n* half-year, six months *pl.*; **2jährig** *adj.* ['∼jɛːriç] half-year, six months; of six months; **'2jährlich** 1. *adj.* half-yearly; 2. *adv. a.* twice a year; **'∼kreis** *m* semicircle; **'∼kugel** *f* hemisphere; **'2laut** 1. *adj.* low, subdued; 2. *adv.* in an undertone; **'2mast** *adv.* (at) half-mast, *Am. a.* (at) half-staff; **'∼messer** ♔ *m* (-s/-) radius; **'∼mond** *m* half-moon, crescent; **'2part** *adv.*: ∼ *machen* go halves, F go fifty-fifty; **'∼schuh** *m* (low) shoe; **'∼schwester** *f* half-sister; **'∼tagsbeschäftigung** *f* part-time job or employment; **'2tot** *adj.* half-dead; **2wegs** *adv.* ['∼'veːks] half-way; *fig.* to some extent, tolerably; **'∼welt** *f* demi-monde; **2wüchsig** *adj.* ['∼vyːksiç] adolescent, *Am. a.* teen-age; **'∼zeit** *f* *sports:* half(-time).

Halde ['haldə] *f* (-/-n) slope; ⚒ dump.

half [half] *pret. of* helfen.

Hälfte ['hɛlftə] *f* (-/-n) half, ⁊⁊ moiety; *die ∼ von* half of.

Halfter ['halftər] *m*, *n* (-s/-) halter.

Halle ['halə] *f* (-/-n) hall; *hotel:* lounge; *tennis:* covered court; ✈ hangar.

hallen ['halən] *v/i.* (ge-, h) (re)sound, ring, (re-)echo.

'Hallen|bad *n* indoor swimming-bath, *Am. a.* natatorium; **'∼sport** *m* indoor sports *pl.*

hallo [ha'loː] 1. *int.* hallo!, hello!, hullo!; 2. *fig. n* (-s/-s) hullabaloo.

Halm ♀ [halm] *m* (-[e]s/-e) blade; stem, stalk; straw.

Hals [hals] *m* (-es/Ꞌe) neck; throat; ∼ *über Kopf* head over heels; *auf dem ∼e haben* have on one's back, be saddled with; *sich den ∼ verrenken* crane one's neck; **'∼abschneider** *fig. m* extortioner, F shark; **'∼band** *n* necklace; collar (*for dog, etc.*); **'∼entzündung** ⚕ *f* sore throat; **'∼kette** *f* necklace; string; chain; **'∼kragen** *m* collar; **'∼schmerzen** *m/pl.*: ∼ *haben* have a sore throat; **'2starrig** *adj.* stubborn, obstinate; **'∼tuch** *n* neckerchief; scarf; **'∼weite** *f* neck size.

Halt [halt] *m* (-[e]s/-e) hold; foothold, handhold; support (*a. fig.*); *fig.:* stability; security, mainstay.

halt 1. *int.* stop!; ⚒ halt!; 2. F *adv.* just; *das ist ∼ so* that's the way it is.

'haltbar *adj. material, etc.:* durable, lasting; *colour:* fast; *fig. theory, etc.:* tenable.

'halten (*irr.*, ge-, h) 1. *v/t.* hold (*fort,*

position, water, etc.); maintain (*position, level, etc.*); keep (*promise, order, animal, etc.*); make, deliver (*speech*); give, deliver (*lecture*); take in (*newspaper*); ~ für regard as, take to be; take for; es ~ mit side with; be fond of; kurz~ keep *s.o.* short; viel (wenig) ~ von think highly (little) of; sich ~ hold out; last; *food:* keep; sich gerade ~ hold o.s. straight; sich gut ~ in examination, etc.: do well; p. be well preserved; sich ~ an (acc.) adhere or keep to; **2.** v/i. stop, halt; *ice:* bear; rope, etc.: stand the strain; ~ zu stick to or by; ~ auf (acc.) set store by, value; auf sich ~ pay attention to one's appearance; have self-respect.

'**Halte|punkt** m ⛟, etc.: wayside stop, halt; *shooting:* point of aim; *phys.* critical point; '~r m (-s/-) keeper; a. owner; *devices:* ... holder; '~stelle f stop; ⛟ station, stop; '~signal ⛟ n stop signal.

halt|los adj. ['haltlo:s] p. unsteady, unstable; *theory, etc.:* baseless, without foundation; '~machen v/i. (sep., -ge-, h) stop, halt; vor nichts ~ stick or stop; at nothing; '2ung f (-/-en) deportment, carriage; pose; *fig.* attitude (gegenüber towards); self-control; *stock exchange:* tone.

hämisch adj. ['hɛ:miʃ] spiteful, malicious.

Hammel ['haməl] m (-s/-, ⸚) wether; '~fleisch n mutton; '~keule f leg of mutton; '~rippchen n (-s/-) mutton chop.

Hammer ['hamər] m (-s/⸚) hammer; (auctioneer's) gavel; unter den ~ kommen come under the hammer.

hämmern ['hɛmərn] (ge-, h) **1.** v/t. hammer; **2.** v/i. hammer (a. an dat. at door, etc.); hammer away (auf dat. at piano); heart, etc.: throb (violently), pound.

Hämorrhoiden ⚕ [hɛːmɔroˈiːdən] f/pl. h(a)emorrhoids pl., piles pl.

Hampelmann ['hampəlman] m jumping-jack; *fig.* (mere) puppet.

Hamster zo. ['hamstər] m (-s/-) hamster; '2n v/t. and v/i. (ge-, h) hoard.

Hand [hant] f (-/⸚e) hand; j-m die ~ geben shake hands with s.o.; an ~ (gen.) or von with the help or aid of; aus erster ~ first-hand, at first hand; bei der ~, zur ~ at hand; ~ und Fuß haben be sound, hold water; seine ~ im Spiele haben have a finger in the pie; '~arbeit f manual labo(u)r or work; (handi)craft; needlework; '~arbeiter m manual labo(u)rer; '~bibliothek f reference library; '~breit **1.** f (-/-) hand's breadth; **2.** 2 adj. a hand's breadth across; '~bremse mot. f hand-brake; '~buch n manual, handbook.

Hände|druck ['hɛndə-] m (-[e]s/⸚e)

handshake; '~klatschen n (-s/no pl.) (hand-)clapping; applause.

Handel ['handəl] m **1.** (-s/no pl.) commerce; trade; business; market; traffic; transaction, deal, bargain; **2.** (-s/⸚): Händel pl. quarrels pl., contention; '2n v/i. (ge-, h) act, take action; ✝ trade (mit with s.o., in goods), deal (in goods); bargain (um for), haggle (over); ~ von treat of, deal with; es handelt sich um it concerns, it is a matter of.

'**Handels|abkommen** n trade agreement; '~bank f commercial bank; '2einig adj.: ~ werden come to terms; '~genossenschaft f traders' co-operative association; '~gericht n commercial court; '~gesellschaft f (trading) company; '~haus n business house, firm; '~kammer f Chamber of Commerce; '~marine f mercantile marine; '~minister m minister of commerce; President of the Board of Trade, Am. Secretary of Commerce; '~ministerium n ministry of commerce; Board of Trade, Am. Department of Commerce; '~reisende m commercial traveller, Am. traveling salesman, F drummer; '~schiff n merchantman; '~schiffahrt f merchant shipping; '~schule f commercial school; '~stadt f commercial town; '2üblich adj. customary in trade; '~vertrag m commercial treaty, trade agreement.

'**handeltreibend** adj. trading.

'**Hand|feger** m (-s/-) hand-brush; '~fertigkeit f manual skill; '2fest adj. sturdy, strong; *fig.* well-founded, sound; '~feuerwaffen f/pl. small arms pl.; '~fläche f flat of the hand, palm; '2gearbeitet adj. hand-made; '~geld n earnest money; ⚒ bounty; '~gelenk anat. n wrist; '~gemenge n scuffle, mêlée; '~gepäck n hand luggage, Am. hand baggage; '~granate ⚒ f hand-grenade; '2greiflich adj. violent; *fig.* tangible, palpable; ~ werden turn violent, Am. a. get tough; '~griff m grasp; handle, grip; *fig.* manipulation; '~habe fig. f handle; '2haben v/t. (ge-, h) handle, manage, operate (machine, etc.); administer (law); '~karren m hand-cart; '~koffer m suitcase, Am. a. valise; '~kuß m kiss on the hand; '~langer m (-s/-) hodman, handy man; *fig.* dog's-body, henchman.

Händler ['hɛndlər] m (-s/-) dealer, trader.

'**handlich** adj. handy; manageable.

Handlung ['handluŋ] f (-/-en) act, action; deed; *thea.* action, plot; ✝ shop, Am. store.

'**Handlungs|bevollmächtigte** m proxy; '~gehilfe m clerk; shop-assistant, *Am.* salesclerk; '~reisende *m s.* Handelsreisende; '~weise *f* conduct; way of acting.

'Hand|rücken *m* back of the hand; '~schelle *f* handcuff, manacle; '~schlag *m* handshake; '~schreiben *n* autograph letter; '~schrift *f* handwriting; manuscript; 'Qschriftlich 1. *adj.* hand-written; 2. *adv.* in one's own handwriting; '~schuh *m* glove; '~streich ⚔ *m* surprise attack, coup de main; *im* ~ *nehmen* take by surprise; '~tasche *f* handbag, *Am. a.* purse; '~tuch *n* towel; '~voll *f* (-/-) handful; '~wagen *m* hand-cart; '~werk *n* (handi)craft, trade; '~werker *m* (-s/-) (handi)craftsman, artisan, workman; '~werkzeug *n* (kit of) tools *pl.*; '~wurzel *anat. f* wrist; '~zeichnung *f* drawing.

Hanf ⚭ [hanf] *m* (-[e]s/*no pl.*) hemp.

Hang [haŋ] *m* (-[e]s/≈e) slope, incline, declivity; hillside; *fig.* inclination, propensity (*zu* for; *zu inf.* to *inf.*); tendency (to).

Hänge|boden ['hɛŋə-] *m* hangingloft; '~brücke △ *f* suspension bridge; '~lampe *f* hanging lamp; '~matte *f* hammock.

hängen ['hɛŋən] 1. *v/i.* (*irr.*, ge-, *h*) hang, be suspended; adhere, stick, cling (*an dat.* to); ~ *an* (*dat.*) be attached *or* devoted to; 2. *v/t.* (ge-, *h*) hang, suspend; '~bleiben *v/i.* (*irr.* bleiben, *sep.*, -ge-, *sein*) get caught (up) (*an dat.* on, in); *fig.* stick (in the memory).

hänseln ['hɛnzəln] *v/t.* (ge-, *h*) tease (*wegen* about), F rag.

Hansestadt ['hanzə-] *f* Hanseatic town.

Hanswurst [hans'-] *m* (-es/-e, F ≈e) merry andrew; Punch; *fig. contp.* clown, buffoon.

Hantel ['hantəl] *f* (-/-n) dumb-bell.

hantieren [han'ti:rən] *v/i.* (*no* -ge-, *h*) be busy (*mit* with); work (*an dat.* on).

Happen ['hapən] *m* (-s/-) morsel, mouthful, bite; snack.

Harfe ♪ ['harfə] *f* (-/-n) harp.

Harke ✗ ['harkə] *f* (-/-n) rake; 'Qn *v/t. and v/i.* (ge-, *h*) rake.

harmlos *adj.* ['harmlo:s] harmless, innocuous; inoffensive.

Harmon|ie [harmo'ni:] *f* (-/-n) harmony (*a. ♪*); Qieren *v/i.* (*no* -ge-, *h*) harmonize (*mit* with); *fig. a.* be in tune (with); '~ika ♪ [~'mo:nika] *f* (-/-s, *Harmoniken*) accordion; mouth-organ; Qisch *adj.* [~'mo:nif] harmonious.

Harn [harn] *m* (-[e]s/-e) urine; '~blase *anat. f* (urinary) bladder; 'Qen *v/i.* (ge-, *h*) pass water, urinate.

Harnisch ['harnif] *m* (-es/-e) armo(u)r; *in* ~ *geraten* be up in arms (*über acc.* about).

'Harnröhre *anat. f* urethra.

Harpun|e [har'pu:nə] *f* (-/-n) harpoon; Qieren [~u'ni:rən] *v/t.* (*no* -ge-, *h*) harpoon.

hart [hart] 1. *adj.* hard; *fig. a.* harsh; heavy, severe; 2. *adv.* hard; ~ *arbeiten* work hard.

Härte ['hɛrtə] *f* (-/-n) hardness; *fig. a.* hardship; severity; 'Qn (ge-, *h*) 1. *v/t.* harden (*metal*); temper (*steel*); case-harden (*iron*, *steel*); 2. *v/i. and v/refl.* harden, become *or* grow hard; *steel*: temper.

'Hart|geld *n* coin(s *pl.*), specie; '~gummi *m* hard rubber; ✝ ebonite, vulcanite; 'Qherzig *adj.* hardhearted; Qköpfig *adj.* ['~kœpfiç] stubborn, headstrong; Qnäckig *adj.* ['~nɛkiç] *p.* obstinate, obdurate; *effort*: dogged, tenacious; ✗ ailment: refractory.

Harz [ha:rts] *n* (-es/-e) resin; ♪ rosin; *mot.* gum; 'Qig *adj.* resinous.

Hasardspiel [ha'zart-] *n* game of chance; *fig.* gamble.

haschen ['hafən] (ge-, *h*) 1. *v/t.* catch (hold of), snatch; *sich* ~ *children*: play tag; 2. *v/i.*: ~ *nach* snatch at; *fig.* strain after (*effect*), fish for (*compliments*).

Hase ['ha:zə] *m* (-n/-n) *zo.* hare; *ein alter* ~ an old hand, an old-timer.

Haselnuß ⚭ ['ha:zəlnus] *f* hazelnut.

'Hasen|braten *m* roast hare; '~fuß F *fig. m* coward, F funk; '~panier F *n*: *das* ~ *ergreifen* take to one's heels; '~scharte ✗ *f* hare-lip.

Haß [has] *m* (Hasses/*no pl.*) hatred.

'hassen *v/t.* (ge-, *h*) hate.

häßlich *adj.* ['hɛsliç] ugly; *fig. a.* nasty, unpleasant.

Hast [hast] *f* (-/*no pl.*) hurry, haste; rush; *in wilder* ~ in frantic haste; 'Qen *v/i.* (ge-, *sein*) hurry, hasten; rush; 'Qig *adj.* hasty, hurried.

hätscheln ['hɛ:tfəln] *v/t.* (ge-, *h*) caress, fondle, pet; pamper, coddle.

hatte ['hatə] *pret.* of haben.

Haube ['haubə] *f* (-/-n) bonnet (*a.* ⊕, *mot.*); cap; *orn.* crest, tuft; *mot. Am. a.* hood.

Haubitze ✗ [hau'bitsə] *f* (-/-n) howitzer.

Hauch [haux] *m* (-[e]s/✿ -e) breath; *fig.*: waft, whiff (of perfume, etc.); touch, tinge (of irony, etc.); 'Qen (ge-, *h*) 1. *v/i.* breathe; 2. *v/t.* breathe, whisper; *gr.* aspirate.

Haue ['hauə] *f* (-/-n) ⚒ hoe, mattock; pick; F hiding, spanking; 'Qn (*irr.*,] ge-, *h*) 1. *v/t.* hew (*coal*, *stone*); cut up (*meat*); chop (*wood*); cut (*hole*, *steps*, etc.); beat (*child*); *sich* ~ (have a) fight; 2. *v/i.*: ~ *nach* cut at, strike out at.

Haufen ['haufən] *m* (-s/-) heap, pile (*both* F *a. fig.*); *fig.* crowd.

häufen ['hɔyfən] *v/t.* (ge-, *h*) heap

(up), pile (up); accumulate; *sich ~* pile up, accumulate; *fig.* become more frequent, increase.

'häufig *adj.* frequent; **'2keit** *f* (-/*no pl.*) frequency.

'Häufung *fig. f* (-/-en) increase, *fig.* accumulation.

Haupt [haupt] *n* (-[e]s/=er) head; *fig.* chief, head, leader; **'~altar** *m* high altar; **'~anschluß** *teleph. m* subscriber's main station; **'~bahnhof** 🚉 *m* main or central station; **'~beruf** *m* full-time occupation; **'~buch** ✝ *n* ledger; **'~darsteller** *thea. m* leading actor; **'~fach** *univ. n* main or principal subject, *Am. a.* major; **'~film** *m* feature (film); **'~geschäft** *n* main transaction; main shop; **'~geschäftsstelle** *f* head or central office; **'~gewinn** *m* first prize; **'~grund** *m* main reason; **~handelsartikel** ✝ ['haupthan-dəls²-] *m* staple.

Häuptling ['hɔyptliŋ] *m* (-s/-e) chief(tain).

'Haupt|linie 🚉 *f* main or trunk line; **'~mann** ⚔ *m* (-[e]s/*Haupt-leute*) captain; **'~merkmal** *n* characteristic feature; **'~postamt** *n* general post office, *Am.* main post office; **'~punkt** *m* main or cardinal point; **'~quartier** *n* headquarters *sg.* or *pl.*; **'~rolle** *thea. f* lead(ing part); **'~sache** *f* main thing or point; **'2sächlich** *adj.* main, chief, principal; **'~satz** *gr. m* main clause; **'~stadt** *f* capital; **'2städtisch** *adj.* metropolitan; **'~straße** *f* main street; major road; **'~treffer** *m* first prize, jackpot; **'~verkehrsstraße** *f* main road; arterial road; **'~verkehrsstunden** *f/pl.*, **'~verkehrszeit** *f* rush hour(s *pl.*), peak hour(s *pl.*); **'~versammlung** *f* general meeting; **'~wort** *gr. n* (-[e]s/=er) substantive, noun.

Haus [haus] *n* (-es/=er) house; building; home, family, household; dynasty; ✝ (business) house, firm; *parl.* House; *nach ~e* home; *zu ~e* at home, F in; **'~angestellte** *f* (-n/-n) (house-)maid; **'~apotheke** *f* (household) medicine-chest; **'~arbeit** *f* housework; **'~arrest** *m* house arrest; **'~arzt** *m* family doctor; **'~aufgaben** *f/pl.* homework, F prep; **'2backen** *fig. adj.* homely; **'~bar** *f* cocktail cabinet; **'~bedarf** *m* household requirements *pl.*; **'~besitzer** *m* house-owner; **'~diener** *m* (man-)servant; *hotel:* porter, boots *sg.*

hausen ['hauzən] *v/i.* (ge-, h) live; play or work havoc (*in* a place).

'Haus|flur *m* (entrance-)hall, *esp. Am.* hallway; **'~frau** *f* housewife; **'~halt** *m* household; **'2halten** *v/i.* (*irr. halten, sep.,* -ge-, h) be economical (*mit* with), economize (on);

~hälterin ['~hɛltərin] *f* (-/-nen) housekeeper; **'~halt(s)plan** *parl. m* budget; **'~haltung** *f* housekeeping; household, family; **'~haltwaren** *f/pl.* household articles *pl.*; **'~herr** *m* master of the family; landlord.

hausier|en [hau'zi:rən] *v/i.* (*no -ge-, h*) hawk, peddle (*mit et.* s.th.); *~ gehen* be a hawker or pedlar; **2er** *m* (-s/-) hawker, pedlar.

'Haus|kleid *n* house dress; **'~knecht** *m* boots; **'~lehrer** *m* private tutor.

häuslich *adj.* ['hɔysliç] domestic; domesticated; **'2keit** *f* (-/*no pl.*) domesticity; family life; home.

'Haus|mädchen *n* (house-)maid; **'~mannskost** *f* plain fare; **'~meister** *m* caretaker; janitor; **'~mittel** *n* popular medicine; **'~ordnung** *f* rules *pl.* of the house; **'~rat** *m* household effects *pl.*; **'~recht** *n* domestic authority; **'~sammlung** *f* house-to-house collection; **'~schlüssel** *m* latchkey; front-door key; **'~schuh** *m* slipper.

Hauss|e ✝ ['ho:s(ə)] *f* (-/-n) rise, boom; **~ier** [hos'je:] *m* (-s/-s) speculator for a rise, bull.

'Haus|stand *m* household; *e-n ~ gründen* set up house; **'~suchung** ⚖ *f* house search, domiciliary visit, *Am. a.* house check; **'~tier** *n* domestic animal; **'~tür** *f* front door; **'~verwalter** *m* steward; **'~wirt** *m* landlord; **'~wirtin** *f* (-/-nen) landlady.

Haut [haut] *f* (-/=e) skin; hide; film; *bis auf die ~* to the skin; *aus der ~ fahren* jump out of one's skin; F *e-e ehrliche ~* an honest soul; **'~abschürfung** ⚕ *f* skin abrasion; **'~arzt** *m* dermatologist; **'~ausschlag** ⚕ *m* rash; **'2eng** *adj.* garment: skin-tight; **'~farbe** *f* complexion.

Hautgout [o'gu] *m* (-s/*no pl.*) high taste.

häutig *adj.* ['hɔytiç] membranous; covered with skin.

'Haut|krankheit *f* skin disease; **'~pflege** *f* care of the skin; **'~schere** *f* (*e-e* a pair of) cuticle scissors *pl.*

Havarie ⚓ [hava'ri:] *f* (-/-n) average.

H-Bombe ⚔ ['ha:-] *f* H-bomb.

he *int.* [he:] hi!, hi there!; I say!

Hebamme ['he:p²amə] *f* midwife.

Hebe|baum ['he:bə-] *m* lever (*for raising heavy objects*); **'~bühne** *mot. f* lifting ramp; **'~eisen** *n* crowbar; **'~kran** *m* lifting crane.

Hebel ⊕ ['he:bəl] *m* (-s/-) lever; **'~arm** *m* lever arm.

heben ['he:bən] *v/t.* (*irr.,* ge-, h) lift (*a. sports*), raise (*a. fig.*); heave (*heavy load*); hoist; recover (*treas-*

ure); raise (*sunken ship*); *fig.* promote, improve, increase; *sich ~* rise, go up.

Hecht *ichth.* [heçt] *m* (-[e]s/-e) pike.

Heck [hɛk] *n* (-[e]s/-e, -s) ⚓ stern; *mot.* rear; ✈ tail.

Hecke ['hɛkə] *f* (-/-n) ⚔ hedge; *zo.* brood, hatch; '**2n** *v/t. and v/i.* (ge-, h) breed, hatch; '**~nrose** ♀ *f* dog-rose. [hallo!]

heda *int.* ['he:dɑ:] hi (there)!,)

Heer [he:r] *n* (-[e]s/-e) ⚔ army; *fig.* a. host; '**~esdienst** *m* military service; '**~esmacht** *f* military force(s *pl.*); '**~eszug** *m* military expedition; '**~führer** *m* general; '**~lager** *n* (army) camp; '**~schar** *f* army, host; '**~straße** *f* military road; highway; '**~zug** *m s.* Heereszug.

Hefe ['he:fə] *f* (-/-n) yeast; barm.

Heft [hɛft] *n* (-[e]s/-e) dagger, *etc.*: haft; *knife*: handle; *fig.* reins *pl.*; exercise book; *periodical*, *etc.*: issue, number.

'**heft|en** *v/t.* (ge-, h) fasten, fix (*an acc.* on to); affix, attach (to); pin on (to); tack, baste (*seam*, *etc.*); stitch, sew (*book*); '**2faden** *m* basting thread.

'**heftig** *adj.* *storm, anger, quarrel, etc.*: violent, fierce; *rain*, *etc.*: heavy; *pain*, *etc.*: severe; *speech, desire, etc.*: vehement, passionate; *p.* irascible; '**2keit** *f* (-/~-en) violence, fierceness; severity; vehemence; irascibility.

'**Heft|klammer** *f* paper-clip; '**~pflaster** *n* sticking plaster.

hegen ['he:gən] *v/t.* (ge-, h) preserve (*game*); nurse, tend (*plants*); have, entertain (*feelings*); harbo(u)r (*fears, suspicions, etc.*).

Hehler ⚖ ['he:lər] *m* (-s/-) receiver (of stolen goods); '**~ei** [~'raɪ] *f* (-/-en) receiving (of stolen goods).

Heide ['haɪdə] **1.** *m* (-n/-n) heathen; **2.** *f* (-/-n) heath(-land); = '**~kraut** ♀ *n* heather; '**~land** *n* heath(-land).

'**Heiden|geld** F *n* pots *pl.* of money; '**~lärm** F *m* hullabaloo; '**~spaß** F *m* capital fun; '**~tum** *n* (-s/no *pl.*) heathenism. [(-ish).)

heidnisch *adj.* ['haɪdnɪʃ] heathen)

heikel *adj.* ['haɪkəl] *p.* fastidious, particular; *problem*, *etc.*: delicate, awkward.

heil [haɪl] **1.** *adj.* *p.* safe, unhurt; whole, sound; **2.** 2 *n* (-[e]s/no *pl.*) welfare, benefit; *eccl.* salvation; **3.** *int.* hail!

Heiland *eccl.* ['haɪlant] *m* (-[e]s/-e) Saviour, Redeemer.

'**Heil|anstalt** *f* sanatorium, *Am. a.* sanitarium; '**~bad** *n* medicinal bath; spa; '**2bar** *adj.* curable; '**2en** (ge-) **1.** *v/t.* (h) cure, heal; *~ von* cure *s.o.* of; **2.** *v/i.* (sein) heal (up); '**~gehilfe** *m* male nurse.

heilig *adj.* ['haɪlɪç] holy; sacred; solemn; 2*er Abend* Christmas Eve; 2*e* ['~gə] *m, f* (-n/-n) saint; '**~gen** ['~gən] *v/t.* (ge-, h) sanctify (*a. fig.*), hallow; '**2keit** *f* (-/no *pl.*) holiness; sacredness, sanctity; '**~sprechen** *v/t.* (*irr. sprechen, sep.*, -ge-, h) canonize; '**2sprechung** *f* (-/-en) canonization; '**2tum** *n* (-[e]s/=er) sanctuary; sacred relic; 2*ung* ['~guŋ] *f* (-/-en) sanctification (*a. fig.*), hallowing.

'**Heil|kraft** *f* healing *or* curative power; '**2kräftig** *adj.* healing, curative; '**~kunde** *f* medical science; '**2los** *fig.* *adj.* confusion: utter, great; '**~mittel** *n* remedy, medicament; '**~praktiker** *m* non-medical practitioner; '**~quelle** *f* medicinal spring; '**2sam** *adj.* curative; *fig.* salutary. [Army.)

Heilsarmee ['haɪls⁹-] *f* Salvation)

'**Heil|ung** *f* (-/-en) cure, healing, successful treatment; '**~verfahren** *n* therapy.

heim [haɪm] **1.** *adv.* home; **2.** 2 *n* (-[e]s/-e) home; hostel; '**2arbeit** *f* homework, outwork.

Heimat ['haɪmɑːt] *f* (-/⁹-en) home; own country; native land; '**~land** *n* own country, native land; '**2lich** *adj.* native; '**2los** *adj.* homeless; '**~ort** *m* home town *or* village; '**~vertriebene** *m* expellee.

Heimchen *zo.* ['haɪmçən] *n* (-s/-) cricket.

'**heimisch** *adj.* trade, industry, *etc.*: home, local, domestic; ♀, *zo.*, *etc.*: native, indigenous; *~ werden* settle down; become established; *sich ~ fühlen* feel at home.

Heim|kehr ['haɪmke:r] *f* (-/no *pl.*) return (home), homecoming; '**2kehren** *v/i.* (*sep.*, -ge-, sein), '**2kommen** *v/i.* (*irr. kommen, sep.*, -ge-, sein) return home.

'**heimlich** *adj.* plan, feeling, *etc.*: secret; meeting, organization, *etc.*: clandestine; glance, movement, *etc.*: stealthy, furtive.

'**Heim|reise** *f* homeward journey; '**2suchen** *v/t.* (*sep.*, -ge-, h) disaster, *etc.*: afflict, strike; *ghost*: haunt; *God*: visit, punish; '**~tücke** *f* underhand malice, treachery; '**2tückisch** *adj.* malicious, treacherous, insidious; 2*wärts* *adv.* ['~verts] homeward(s); '**~weg** *m* way home; '**~weh** *n* homesickness, nostalgia; *~ haben* be homesick.

Heirat ['haɪrɑːt] *f* (-/-en) marriage; '**2en** (ge-, h) **1.** *v/t.* marry; **2.** *v/i.* marry, get married.

'**Heirats|antrag** *m* offer *or* proposal of marriage; '**2fähig** *adj.* marriageable; '**~kandidat** *m* possible marriage partner; '**~schwindler** *m* marriage impostor; '**~vermittler** *m* matrimonial agent.

heiser adj. ['haɪzər] hoarse; husky; '2keit f (-/no pl.) hoarseness; huskiness.

heiß adj. [haɪs] hot; fig. a. passionate, ardent; mir ist ~ I am or feel hot.

heißen ['haɪsən] (irr., ge-, h) 1. v/t.: e-n Lügner ~ call s.o. a liar; willkommen ~ welcome; 2. v/i. be called; mean; wie ~ Sie? what is your name?; was heißt das auf englisch? what's that in English?

heiter adj. ['haɪtər] day, weather: bright; sky: bright, clear; p., etc.: cheerful, gay; serene; '2keit f (-/no pl.) brightness; cheerfulness, gaiety; serenity.

heiz|en ['haɪtsən] (ge-, h) 1. v/t. heat (room, etc.); light (stove); fire (boiler); 2. v/i. stove, etc.: give out heat; turn on the heating; mit Kohlen ~ burn coal; '2er m (-s/-) stoker, fireman; '2kissen n electric heating pad; '2körper m central heating: radiator; ⚡ heating element; '2material n fuel; '2ung f (-/-en) heating.

Held [hɛlt] m (-en/-en) hero.

'Helden|gedicht n epic (poem); '2haft adj. heroic, valiant; '~mut m heroism, valo(u)r; 2mütig adj. ['~myːtɪç] heroic; '~tat f heroic or valiant deed; '~tod m hero's death; '~tum n (-[e]s/no pl.) heroism.

helfen ['hɛlfən] v/i. (dat.) (irr., ge-, h) help, assist, aid; ~ gegen be good for; sich nicht zu ~ wissen be helpless.

'Helfer m (-s/-) helper, assistant; '~shelfer m accomplice.

hell adj. [hɛl] sound, voice, light, etc.: clear; light, flame, etc.: bright; hair: fair; colour: light; ale: pale; '~blau adj. light-blue; '~blond adj. very fair; '~hörig adj. p. quick of hearing; fig. perceptive; ⚠ poorly sound-proofed; '2seher m clairvoyant.

Helm [hɛlm] m (-[e]s/-e) ⚔ helmet; 🏛 dome, cupola; ⚓ helm; '~busch m plume.

Hemd [hɛmt] n (-[e]s/-en) shirt; vest; '~bluse f shirt-blouse, Am. shirtwaist. [hemisphere.\

Hemisphäre [he:mi'sfɛːrə] f (-/-n)\

hemm|en ['hɛmən] v/t. (ge-, h) check, stop (movement, etc.); stem (stream, flow of liquid); hamper (free movement, activity); be a hindrance to; psych.: gehemmt sein be inhibited; '2nis n (-ses/-se) hindrance, impediment; '2schuh m slipper; fig. hindrance, F drag (für acc. on); '2ung f (-/-en) stoppage, check; psych.: inhibition.

Hengst zo. [hɛŋst] m (-es/-e) stallion.

Henkel ['hɛŋkəl] m (-s/-) handle, ear.

Henker ['hɛŋkər] m (-s/-) hangman, executioner; F: zum ~! hang it (all)!

Henne zo. ['hɛnə] f (-/-n) hen.

her adv. [he:r] here; hither; es ist schon ein Jahr ~, daß ... or seit ... it is a year since ...; wie lange ist es ~, seit ... how long is it since ...; hinter (dat.) ~ sein be after; ~ damit! out with it!

herab adv. [hɛ'rap] down, downward; ~lassen v/t. (irr. lassen, sep., -ge-, h) let down, lower; fig. sich ~ condescend; ~lassend adj. condescending; ~setzen v/t. (sep., -ge-, h) take down; fig. belittle, disparage s.o.; † reduce, lower, cut (price, etc.); 2setzung fig. f (-/-en) reduction; disparagement; ~steigen v/i. (irr. steigen, sep., -ge-, sein) climb down, descend; ~würdigen v/t. (sep., -ge-, h) degrade, belittle, abase.

heran adv. [hɛ'ran] close, near; up; nur ~! come on!; ~bilden v/t. (sep., -ge-, h) train, educate (zu as s.th., to be s.th.); ~kommen v/i. (irr. kommen, sep., -ge-, sein) come or draw near; approach; ~ an (acc.) come up to s.o.; measure up to; ~wachsen v/i. (irr. wachsen, sep., -ge-, sein) grow (up) (zu into).

herauf adv. [hɛ'rauf] up(wards), up here; upstairs; ~beschwören v/t. (irr. schwören, sep., no -ge-, h) evoke, call up, conjure up (spirit, etc.); fig. a. bring about, provoke; give rise to (war, etc.); ~steigen v/i. (irr. steigen, sep., -ge-, sein) climb up (here), ascend; ~ziehen (irr. ziehen, sep., -ge-) 1. v/t. (h) pull or hitch up (trousers, etc.); 2. v/i. (sein) cloud, etc.: come up.

heraus adv. [hɛ'raus] out, out here; zum Fenster ~ out of the window; ~ mit der Sprache! speak out!; ~bekommen v/t. (irr. kommen, sep., no -ge-, h) get out; get (money) back; fig. find out; ~bringen v/t. (irr. bringen, sep., -ge-, h) bring or get out; thea. stage; ~finden v/t. (irr. finden, sep., -ge-, h) find out; fig. a. discover; 2forderer m (-s/-) challenger; ~fordern v/t. (sep., -ge-, h) challenge (to a fight); provoke; 2forderung f (-/-en) challenge; provocation; ~geben (irr. geben, sep., -ge-, h) 1. v/t. surrender; hand over; restore; edit (periodical, etc.); publish (book, etc.); issue (regulations, etc.); 2. v/i. give change (auf acc. for); 2geber m (-s/-) editor; publisher; ~kommen v/i. (irr. kommen, sep., -ge-, sein) come out; fig. a. appear, be published; ~nehmen v/t. (irr. nehmen, sep., -ge-, h) take out; sich viel ~ take liberties; ~putzen v/t. (sep., -ge-, h) dress up; sich ~ dress (o.s.)

up; ⸗reden v/refl. (sep., -ge-, h) talk one's way out; ⸗stellen v/t. (sep., -ge-, h) put up; fig. emphasize, set forth; sich ⸗ emerge, turn out; ⸗strecken v/t. (sep., -ge-, h) stretch out; put out; ⸗streichen v/t. (irr. streichen, sep., -ge-, h) cross out, delete (word, etc.); fig. extol, praise; ⸗winden fig. v/refl. (irr. winden, sep., -ge-, h) extricate o.s. (aus from).

herb adj. [hɛrp] fruit, flavour, etc.: tart; wine, etc.: dry; features, etc.: austere; criticism, etc.: harsh; disappointment, etc.: bitter.

herbei adv. [hɛr'baɪ] here; ⸗! come here!; ⸗eilen [hɛr'baɪʔ-] v/i. (sep., -ge-, sein) come hurrying; ⸗führen fig. v/t. (sep., -ge-, h) cause, bring about, give rise to; ⸗schaffen v/t. (sep., -ge-, h) bring along; procure.

Herberge ['hɛrbɛrgə] f (-/-n) shelter, lodging; inn.

'Herbheit f (-/no pl.) tartness; dryness; fig.: austerity; harshness, bitterness.

Herbst [hɛrpst] m (-[e]s/-e) autumn, Am. a. fall.

Herd [he:rt] m (-[e]s/-e) hearth, fireplace; stove; fig. seat, focus.

Herde ['he:rdə] f (-/-n) herd (of cattle, pigs, etc.) (contp. a. fig.); flock (of sheep, geese, etc.).

herein [hɛ'raɪn] in (here); ⸗! come in!; ⸗brechen fig. v/i. (irr. brechen, sep., -ge-, sein) night: fall; ⸗ über (acc.) misfortune, etc.: befall; ⸗fallen fig. v/i. (irr. fallen, sep., -ge-, sein) be taken in.

'her|fallen v/i. (irr. fallen, sep., -ge-, sein): ⸗ über (acc.) attack (a. fig.), fall upon; F fig. pull to pieces; '2gang m course of events, details pl.; '⸗geben v/t. (irr. geben, sep., -ge-, h) give up, part with, return; yield; sich ⸗ zu lend o.s. to; '⸗gebracht fig. adj. traditional; customary; '⸗halten (irr. halten, sep., -ge-, h) 1. v/t. hold out; 2. v/i.: ⸗ müssen be the one to pay or suffer (für for).

Hering ichth. ['he:rɪŋ] m (-s/-e) herring.

'her|kommen v/i. (irr. kommen, sep., -ge-, sein) come or get here; come or draw near; ⸗ von come from; fig. a. be due to, be caused by; ⸗kömmlich adj. ['⸗kœmlɪç] traditional; customary; 2kunft ['⸗kunft] f (-/no pl.) origin; birth, descent; '⸗leiten v/t. (sep., -ge-, h) lead here; fig. derive (von from); '2leitung fig. f derivation.

Herold ['he:rɔlt] m (-[e]s/-e) herald.

Herr [hɛr] m (-n, ⸗ -en/-en) lord, master; eccl. the Lord; gentleman; ⸗ Maier Mr Maier; mein ⸗ Sir; m-e ⸗en gentlemen; ⸗ der Situation master of the situation.

'Herren|bekleidung f men's clothing; '⸗einzel n tennis: men's singles pl.; '⸗haus n manor-house; 2⸗los adj. ['⸗lo:s] ownerless; '⸗reiter m sports: gentleman-jockey; '⸗schneider m men's tailor; '⸗zimmer n study; smoking-room.

herrichten ['he:r-] v/t. (sep., -ge-, h) arrange, prepare.

'herrisch adj. imperious, overbearing; voice, etc.: commanding, peremptory.

'herrlich adj. excellent, glorious, magnificent, splendid; '2keit f (-/-en) glory, splendo(u)r.

'Herrschaft f (-/-en) rule, dominion (über acc. of); fig. mastery; master and mistress; m-e ⸗en! ladies and gentlemen!; '2lich adj. belonging to a master or landlord; fig. high-class, elegant.

herrsch|en ['hɛrʃən] v/i. (ge-, h) rule (über acc. over); monarch: reign (over); govern; fig. prevail, be; '2er m (-s/-) ruler; sovereign, monarch; '2sucht f thirst for power; '⸗süchtig adj. thirsting for power; imperious.

'her|rühren v/i. (sep., -ge-, h): ⸗ von come from, originate with; '⸗sagen v/t. (sep., -ge-, h) recite; say (prayer); '⸗stammen v/i. (sep., -ge-, h): ⸗ von or aus be descended from; come from; be derived from; '⸗stellen v/t. (sep., -ge-, h) place here; ✝ make, manufacture, produce; '2stellung f (-/-en) manufacture, production.

herüber adv. [hɛ'ry:bər] over (here), across.

herum adv. [hɛ'rum] (a)round; about; ⸗führen v/t. (sep., -ge-, h) show (a)round; ⸗ in (dat.) show over; ⸗lungern v/i. (sep., -ge-, h) loaf or loiter or hang about; ⸗reichen v/t. (sep., -ge-, h) pass or hand round; ⸗sprechen v/refl. (irr. sprechen, sep., -ge-, h) get about, spread; ⸗treiben v/refl. (irr. treiben, sep., -ge-, h) F gad or knock about.

herunter adv. [hɛ'runtər] down (here); downstairs; von oben ⸗ down from above; ⸗bringen v/t. (irr. bringen, sep., -ge-, h) bring down; fig. a. lower, reduce; ⸗kommen v/i. (irr. kommen, sep., -ge-, sein) come down(stairs); fig.: come down in the world; deteriorate; ⸗machen v/t. (sep., -ge-, h) take down; turn (collar, etc.) down; fig. give s.o. a dressing-down; fig. pull to pieces; ⸗reißen v/t. (irr. reißen, sep., -ge-, h) pull or tear down; fig. pull to pieces; ⸗sein F fig. v/i. (irr. sein, sep., -ge-, sein) be low in health; ⸗wirtschaften v/t. (sep., -ge-, h) run down.

hervor adv. [hɛr'fo:r] forth, out; ⸗bringen v/t. (irr. bringen, sep.,

-ge-, h) bring out, produce (a. fig.);
yield (fruit); fig. utter (word); **~
gehen** v/i. (irr. gehen, sep., -ge-,
sein) p. come (aus from); come off
(victorious) (from); fact, etc.:
emerge (from); be clear or apparent
(from); **~heben** fig. v/t. (irr. heben,
sep., -ge-, h) stress, emphasize; give
prominence to; **~holen** v/t. (sep.,
-ge-, h) produce; **~ragen** v/i. (sep.,
-ge-, h) project (über acc. over); fig.
tower (above); **~ragend** adj. pro-
jecting, prominent; fig. outstanding, excellent; **~rufen** v/t. (irr. rufen, sep., -ge-, h) thea. call for; fig.
arouse, evoke; **~stechend** fig. adj.
outstanding; striking; conspicuous.

Herz [hɛrts] n (-ens/-en) anat. heart
(a. fig.); cards: hearts pl.; fig. courage, spirit; sich ein **~** fassen take
heart; mit ganzem **~**en whole-heart-
edly; sich et. zu **~**en nehmen take
s.th. to heart; es nicht übers **~** bringen zu inf. not to have the heart to
inf.; '**~anfall** m heart attack.

'**Herzens|brecher** m (-s/-) lady-
killer; '**~lust** f: nach **~** to one's
heart's content; '**~wunsch** m
heart's desire.

'**herz|ergreifend** fig. adj. heart-
moving; '**2fehler** **♣** m cardiac defect; '**2gegend** anat. f cardiac region; '**~haft** adj. hearty, good; '**~ig**
adj. lovely, Am. a. cute; **2infarkt**
♣ ['**~**²infarkt] m (-[e]s/-e) cardiac
infarction; '**2klopfen** n (-s/no pl.)
palpitation; '**~krank** adj. having
heart trouble; '**~lich** 1. adj. heart-
felt; cordial, hearty; **~**es Beileid sincere sympathy; 2. adv.: **~** gern with
pleasure; '**~los** adj. heartless; unfeeling.

Herzog ['hɛrtso:k] m (-[e]s/**~**e, -e)
duke; '**~in** f (-/-nen) duchess; '**~
tum** n (-[e]s/**~**er) dukedom; duchy.

'**Herz|schlag** m heartbeat; **♣** heart
failure; '**~schwäche** **♣** f cardiac
insufficiency; '**~verpflanzung** **♣** f
heart transplant; '**2zerreißend** adj.
heart-rending.

Hetz|e ['hɛtsə] f (-/-n) hurry, rush;
instigation (gegen acc. against);
baiting (of); '**2en** (ge-) 1. v/t. (h)
course (hare); bait (bear, etc.);
hound: hunt, chase (animal); fig.
hurry, rush; sich **~** hurry, rush; e-n
Hund auf j-n **~** set a dog at s.o.;
2. v/i. (h) fig.: cause discord; agi-
tate (gegen against); 3. fig. v/i.
(sein) hurry, rush; '**~er** fig. m
(-s/-) instigator; agitator; '**2erisch**
adj. virulent, inflammatory; '**~jagd**
f hunt(ing); fig.: virulent campaign;
rush, hurry; '**~presse** f yellow
press.

Heu [hɔy] n (-[e]s/no pl.) hay; '**~
boden** m hayloft.

Heuchel|ei [hɔyçə'laɪ] f (-/-en)
hypocrisy; '**2n** (ge-, h) 1. v/t. sim-

ulate, feign, affect; 2. v/i. feign,
dissemble; play the hypocrite.

'**Heuchler** m (-s/-) hypocrite; '**2isch**
adj. hypocritical.

heuer ['hɔyər] 1. adv. this year;
2. **2** **♣** f (-/-n) pay, wages pl.; '**2n**
v/t. (ge-, h) hire; **♣** engage, sign
on (crew), charter (ship).

heulen ['hɔylən] v/i. (ge-, h) wind,
etc.: howl; storm, wind, etc.: roar;
siren: wail; F p. howl, cry.

'**Heu|schnupfen** **♣** m hay-fever;
'**~schrecke** zo. ['**~**ʃrɛkə] f (-/-n)
grasshopper, locust.

heut|e adv. ['hɔytə] today; **~** abend
this evening, tonight; **~** früh, **~**
morgen this morning; **~** in acht
Tagen today or this day week; **~**
vor acht Tagen a week ago today;
'**~ig** adj. this day's, today's; present; '**~zutage** adv. ['hɔyttsuta:gə]
nowadays, these days.

Hexe ['hɛksə] f (-/-n) witch, sorceress; fig.: hell-cat; hag; '**2n** v/i. (ge-,
h) practice witchcraft; F fig. work
miracles; '**~nkessel** fig. m inferno;
'**~nmeister** m wizard, sorcerer;
'**~nschuß** **♣** m lumbago; **~rei** ['**~**
'raɪ] f (-/-en) witchcraft, sorcery,
magic.

Hieb [hi:p] 1. m (-[e]s/-e) blow,
stroke, lash, cut (of whip, etc.); a.
punch (with fist); fenc. cut; **~**e pl.
hiding, thrashing; 2. **2** pret. of
hauen.

hielt [hi:lt] pret. of halten.

hier adv. [hi:r] here; in this place;
~! present!; **~** entlang! this way!

hier|an adv. ['hi:'ran, when emphatic
'hi:ran] at or by or in or on or to it
or this; **~auf** adv. ['hi:'rauf, when
emphatic 'hi:rauf] on it or this;
after this or that, then; **~aus** adv.
['hi:'raus, when emphatic 'hi:raus]
from or out of it or this; **~bei** adv.
['hi:r'baɪ, when emphatic 'hi:rbaɪ]
here; in this case, in connection
with this; **~durch** adv. ['hi:r'durç,
when emphatic 'hi:rdurç] through
here; by this, hereby; **~für** adv.
['hi:r'fy:r, when emphatic 'hi:rfy:r]
for it or this; **~her** adv. ['hi:r'he:r,
when emphatic 'hi:rhe:r] here,
hither; bis **~** as far as here; **~in** adv.
['hi:'rin, when emphatic 'hi:rin] in
it or this; in here; **~mit** adv. ['hi:r-
'mit, when emphatic 'hi:rmit] with
it or this, herewith; **~nach** adv.
['hi:r'na:x, when emphatic 'hi:rna:x]
after it or this; according to this;
~über adv. ['hi:'ry:bər, when emphatic 'hi:ry:bər] over it or this;
over here; on this (subject); **~unter**
adv. ['hi:'runtər, when emphatic
'hi:runtər] under it or this; among
these; by this or that; **~von** adv.
['hi:r'fɔn, when emphatic 'hi:rfɔn]
of or from it or this; **~zu** adv.
['hi:r'tsu:, when emphatic 'hi:rtsu:]

with it *or* this; (in addition) to this.

hiesig *adj.* ['hi:ziç] of *or* in this place *or* town, local.

hieß [hi:s] *pret. of* heißen.

Hilfe ['hilfə] *f* (-/-n) help; aid, assistance; succour; relief (für to); **~!** help!; mit **~** von with the help or aid of; **'~ruf** *m* shout *or* cry for help.

'hilf|los *adj.* helpless; **'~reich** *adj.* helpful.

'Hilfs|aktion *f* relief measures *pl.*; **'~arbeiter** *m* unskilled worker *or* labo(u)rer; **'2bedürftig** *adj.* needy, indigent; **'~lehrer** *m* assistant teacher; **'~mittel** *n* aid; device; remedy; expedient; **'~motor** *m*: Fahrrad mit **~** motor-assisted bicycle; **'~quelle** *f* resource; **'~schule** *f* elementary school for backward children; **'~werk** *n* relief organization. [berry.]

Himbeere ♀ ['himbe:rə] *f* rasp-]

Himmel ['himəl] *m* (-s/-) sky, heavens *pl.*; *eccl., fig.* heaven; **'~bett** *n* tester-bed; **'2blau** *adj.* sky-blue; **'~fahrt** *eccl. f* ascension (of Christ); Ascension-day; **'2schreiend** *adj.* crying.

'Himmels|gegend *f* region of the sky; cardinal point; **'~körper** *m* celestial body; **'~richtung** *f* point of the compass, cardinal point; direction; **'~strich** *m* region, climate zone.

'himmlisch *adj.* celestial, heavenly.

hin *adv.* [hin] there; gone, lost; **~** und her to and fro, *Am.* back and forth; **~** und wieder now and again *or* then; **~** und zurück there and back.

hinab *adv.* [hi'nap] down; **~steigen** *v/i.* (*irr.* steigen, *sep.*, -ge-, sein) climb down, descend.

hinarbeiten ['hin²-] *v/i.* (*sep.*, -ge-, h): **~** auf (*acc.*) work for *or* towards.

hinauf *adv.* [hi'nauf] up (there); upstairs; **~gehen** *v/i.* (*irr.* gehen, *sep.*, -ge-, sein) go up(stairs); *prices, wages, etc.*: go up, rise; **~steigen** *v/i.* (*irr.* steigen, *sep.*, -ge-, sein) climb up, ascend.

hinaus *adv.* [hi'naus] out; **~** mit euch! out with you!; auf (viele) Jahre **~** for (many) years (to come); **~gehen** *v/i.* (*irr.* gehen, *sep.*, -ge-, sein) go *or* walk out; **~** über (*acc.*) go beyond, exceed; **~** auf (*acc.*) *window, etc.*: look out on, overlook; *intention, etc.*: drive *or* aim at; **~laufen** *v/i.* (*irr.* laufen, *sep.*, -ge-, sein) run *or* rush out; **~** auf (*acc.*) come *or* amount to; **~schieben** *fig. v/t.* (*irr.* schieben, *sep.*, -ge-, h) put off, postpone, defer; **~werfen** *v/t.* (*irr.* werfen, *sep.*, -ge-, h) throw out (aus of); turn *or* throw *or* F chuck *s.o.* out.

'Hin|blick *m*: im **~** auf (*acc.*) in view of, with regard to; **'2bringen** *v/t.* (*irr.* bringen, *sep.*, -ge-, h) take there; while away, pass (*time*).

hinder|lich *adj.* ['hindərliç] hindering, impeding; j-m **~** sein be in s.o.'s way; **'~n** *v/t.* (ge-, h) hinder, hamper (bei, in *dat.* in); **~** an (*dat.*) prevent from; **'2nis** *n* (-ses/-se) hindrance; *sports*: obstacle; turf, *etc.*: fence; **'2nisrennen** *n* obstacle-race.

hin'durch *adv.* through; all through, throughout; across.

hinein *adv.* [hi'nain] in; **~** mit dir! in you go!; **~gehen** *v/i.* (*irr.* gehen, *sep.*, -ge-, sein) go in; **~** in (*acc.*) go into; in den Topf gehen ... hinein the pot holds *or* takes ...

'Hin|fahrt *f* journey *or* way there; **'2fallen** *v/i.* (*irr.* fallen, *sep.*, -ge-, sein) fall (down); **'2fällig** *adj. p.* frail; *regulation, etc.*: invalid; **~** machen invalidate, render invalid.

hing [hiŋ] *pret. of* hängen 1.

'Hin|gabe *f* devotion (an *acc.* to); **'2geben** *v/t.* (*irr.* geben, *sep.*, -ge-, h) give up *or* away; sich **~** (*dat.*) give o.s. to; devote o.s. to; **'~gebung** *f* (-/-en) devotion; **'2gehen** *v/i.* (*irr.* gehen, *sep.*, -ge-, sein) go *or* walk there; go (zu to); *path, etc.*: lead there; lead (zu to *a place*); **'2halten** *v/t.* (*irr.* halten, *sep.*, -ge-, h) hold out (*object, etc.*); put *s.o.* off.

hinken ['hiŋkən] *v/i.* (ge-) **1.** (h) limp (auf dem rechten Fuß with one's right leg), have a limp; **2.** (sein) limp (along).

'hin|länglich *adj.* sufficient, adequate; **'~legen** *v/t.* (*sep.*, -ge-, h) lay *or* put down; sich **~** lie down; **'~nehmen** *v/t.* (*irr.* nehmen, *sep.*, -ge-, h) accept, take; put up with; **'~raffen** *v/t.* (*sep.*, -ge-, h) *death, etc.*: snatch *s.o.* away, carry *s.o.* off; **'~reichen** *v/t.* (*sep.*, -ge-, h) **1.** *v/t.* reach *or* stretch *or* hold out (*dat.* to); **2.** *v/i.* suffice; **'~reißen** *fig. v/t.* (*irr.* reißen, *sep.*, -ge-, h) carry away; enrapture, ravish; **'~reißend** *adj.* ravishing, captivating; **'~richten** *v/t.* (*sep.*, -ge-, h) execute, put to death; **'2richtung** *f* execution; **'~setzen** *v/t.* (*sep.*, -ge-, h) set *or* put down; sich **~** sit down; **'2sicht** *f* regard, respect; in **~** auf (*acc.*) = **'~sichtlich** *prp.* (*gen.*) with regard to, as to, concerning; **'~stellen** *v/t.* (*sep.*, -ge-, h) place; put; put down; *et.* **~** als represent s.th. as; make s.th. appear (as).

hintan|setzen [hint'an-] *v/t.* (*sep.*, -ge-, h) set aside; **2setzung** *f* (-/-en) setting aside; **~stellen** *v/t.* (*sep.*, -ge-, h) set aside; **2stellung** *f* (-/-en) setting aside.

hinten *adv.* ['hintən] behind, at the

back; in the background; in the rear.

hinter *prp.* ['hɪntər] **1.** (*dat.*) behind, *Am. a.* back of; ~ *sich lassen* outdistance; **2.** (*acc.*) behind; '**⊊bein** *n* hind leg; **⊊bliebenen** *pl.* [ˌ'bli:bə-nən] *the* bereaved *pl.*; surviving dependants *pl.*; ˌ'**bringen** *v/t.* (*irr.* bringen, no -ge-, h): j-m et. ~ inform s.o. of s.th. (secretly); **ˌei'nander** *adv.* one after the other; in succession; '**⊊gedanke** *m* ulterior motive; **ˌgehen** *v/t.* (*irr.* gehen, no -ge-, h) deceive, F double-cross; ⊊'**gehung** *f* (-/-en) deception; '**⊊grund** *m* background (*a. fig.*); '**⊊halt** *m* ambush; **ˌhältig** *adj.* [ˌ'hɛltɪç] insidious; underhand; '**⊊haus** *n* back *or* rear building; **ˌher** *adv.* behind; afterwards; '**⊊hof** *m* backyard; '**⊊kopf** *m* back of the head; **ˌ'lassen** *v/t.* (*irr.* lassen, no -ge-, h) leave (behind); ⊊'**lassenschaft** *f* (-/-en) property (left), estate; **ˌ'legen** *v/t.* (no -ge-, h) deposit, lodge (*bei* with); ⊊'**legung** *f* (-/-en) deposit(ion); '**⊊list** *f* deceit; craftiness; insidiousness; **ˌlistig** *adj.* deceitful; crafty; insidious; '**⊊mann** *m* ✕ rear-rank man; *fig.*: † subsequent endorser; *pol.* backer; wire-puller; instigator; '**⊊n** F *m* (-s/-) backside, behind, bottom; '**⊊rad** *n* rear wheel; **ˌrücks** *adv.* [ˌ'ryks] from behind; *fig.* behind his, *etc.* back; '**⊊seite** *f* back; '**⊊teil** *n* back (part); rear (part); F *s.* Hintern; **ˌ'treiben** *v/t.* (*irr.* treiben, no -ge-, h) thwart, frustrate; '**⊊treppe** *f* backstairs *pl.*; '**⊊tür** *f* back door; **ˌ'ziehen** ✍ *v/t.* (*irr.* ziehen, no -ge-, h) evade (*tax, duty, etc.*); ⊊'**ziehung** *f* evasion.

hinüber *adv.* [hi'ny:bər] over (there); across.

Hin- und 'Rückfahrt *f* journey there and back, *Am.* round trip.

hinunter *adv.* [hi'nʊntər] down (there); downstairs; **ˌschlucken** *v/t.* (*sep.*, -ge-, h) swallow (down); *fig.* swallow.

'**Hinweg**[1] *m* way there *or* out.

hinweg[2] *adv.* [hɪn'vɛk] away, off; **ˌgehen** *v/i.* (*irr.* gehen, sep., -ge-sein): ~ *über* (*acc.*) go *or* walk over *or* across, *fig.* pass over, ignore; **ˌkommen** *v/i.* (*irr.* kommen, sep., -ge-, sein): ~ *über* (*acc.*) get over (*a. fig.*); **ˌsehen** *v/i.* (*irr.* sehen, sep., -ge-, h): ~ *über* (*acc.*) see *or* look over; *fig.* overlook, shut one's eyes to; **ˌsetzen** *v/refl.* (*sep.*, -ge-, h): *sich* ~ *über* (*acc.*) ignore, disregard, make light of.

Hin|weis ['hɪnvaɪs] *m* (-es/-e) reference (*auf acc.* to); hint (at); indication (*auf acc.* to); **⊊weisen** (*irr.* weisen, sep., -ge-, h) **1.** *v/t.*: j-n ~ *auf* (*acc.*) draw *or* call s.o.'s attention to; **2.** *v/i.*: ~

auf (*acc.*) point at *or* to, indicate (*a. fig.*); *fig.*: point out; hint at; '**⊊werfen** *v/t.* (*irr.* werfen, sep., -ge-, h) throw down; *fig.*: dash off (*sketch, etc.*); say *s.th.* casually; '**⊊wirken** *v/i.* (*sep.*, -ge-, h): ~ *auf* (*acc.*) work towards; use one's influence to; '**⊊ziehen** (*irr.* ziehen, sep., -ge-) **1.** *v/t.* (h) attract *or* draw there; *sich* ~ *space:* extend (*bis zu* to), stretch (to); *time:* drag on; **2.** *v/i.* (sein) go *or* move there; '**⊊zielen** *fig. v/i.* (*sep.*, -ge-, h): ~ *auf* (*acc.*) aim *or* drive at.

hin'zu *adv.* there; near; in addition; **ˌfügen** *v/t.* (*sep.*, -ge-, h) add (*zu* to) (*a. fig.*); ⊊'**fügung** *f* (-/-en) addition; **ˌkommen** *v/i.* (*irr.* kommen, sep., -ge-, sein) come up (*zu* to); supervene; be added; *es kommt (noch) hinzu, daß* add to this that, (and) moreover; **ˌrechnen** *v/t.* (*sep.*, -ge-, h) add (*zu* to), include (in, among); **ˌsetzen** *v/t.* (*sep.*, -ge-, h) *s.* hinzufügen; **ˌtreten** *v/i.* (*irr.* treten, sep., -ge-, sein) *s.* hinzukommen; join; **ˌziehen** *v/t.* (*irr.* ziehen, sep., -ge-, h) call in (*doctor, etc.*).

Hirn [hɪrn] *n* (-[e]s/-e) *anat.* brain; *fig.* brains *pl.*, mind; '**ˌgespinst** *n* figment of the mind, chimera; '**⊊los** *fig. adj.* brainless, senseless; '**ˌschale** *anat. f* brain-pan; cranium; '**ˌschlag** ✗ *m* apoplexy; '**⊊verbrannt** *adj.* ✗ crazy, F crack-brained, cracky.

Hirsch *zo.* [hɪrʃ] *m* (-es/-e) *species:* deer; stag, hart; '**ˌgeweih** *n* (stag's) antlers *pl.*; '**ˌkuh** *f* hind; '**ˌleder** *n* buckskin, deerskin.

Hirse ♀ ['hɪrzə] *f* (-/-n) millet.

Hirt [hɪrt] *m* (-en/-en), **ˌe** ['ˌə] *m* (-n/-n) herdsman; shepherd.

hissen ['hɪsən] *v/t.* (ge-, h) hoist, raise (*flag*); ⚓ *a.* trice up (*sail*).

Histori|ker [hi'sto:rikər] *m* (-s/-) historian; ⊊sch *adj.* historic(al).

Hitz|e ['hɪtsə] *f* (-/no *pl.*) heat; '**⊊ebeständig** *adj.* heat-resistant, heat-proof; '**ˌewelle** *f* heat-wave, hot spell; '**⊊ig** *adj. p.* hot-tempered, hot-headed; *discussion:* heated; '**ˌkopf** *m* hothead; '**ˌschlag** ✗ *m* heat-stroke.

hob [ho:p] *pret. of* heben.

Hobel ⊕ ['ho:bəl] *m* (-s/-) plane; '**ˌbank** *f* carpenter's bench; '**⊊n** *v/t.* (ge-, h) plane.

hoch [ho:x] **1.** *adj.* high; *church spire, tree, etc.:* tall; *position, etc.:* high, important; *guest, etc.:* distinguished; *punishment, etc.:* heavy, severe; *age:* great, old; *hohe See* open sea, high seas *pl.*; **2.** *adv.:* ~ *lebe ...!* long live ...! **3.** ⊊ *n* (-s/-s) cheer; toast; *meteorology:* high (-pressure area).

'**hoch|achten** *v/t.* (*sep.*, -ge-, h) esteem highly; '**⊊achtung** *f* high esteem or respect; '~achtungsvoll 1. adj. (most) respectful; 2. adv. correspondence: yours faithfully or sincerely, esp. Am. yours truly; '♀adel m greater or higher nobility; '♀amt eccl. n high mass; '♀antenne f overhead aerial; '♀bahn f elevated or overhead railway, Am. elevated railroad; '♀betrieb m intense activity, rush; '♀burg fig. f stronghold; '~deutsch adj. High or standard German; '♀druck m high pressure (a. fig.); mit ~ arbeiten work at high pressure; '♀ebene f plateau, tableland; '~fahrend adj. high-handed, arrogant; '~fein adj. superfine; '♀form f: in ~ in top form; '♀frequenz ⚡ f high frequency; '♀gebirge n high mountains pl.; '♀genuß m great enjoyment; '♀glanz m high polish; '♀haus n multi-stor(e)y building, skyscraper; '~herzig adj. noble-minded; generous; '♀herzigkeit f (-/-en) noble-mindedness; generosity; '♀konjunktur ✝ f boom, business prosperity; '♀land n upland(s pl.), highlands pl.; '♀mut m arrogance, haughtiness; '~mütig adj. ['~my:tiç] arrogant, haughty; ~näsig F adj. ['~nɛ:ziç] stuck-up; '♀ofen ⊕ m blast-furnace; '~rot adj. bright red; '♀saison f peak season, height of the season; '~schätzen v/t. (sep., -ge-, h) esteem highly; '♀schule f university; academy; '♀seefischerei f deep-sea fishing; '♀sommer m midsummer; '♀spannung ⚡ f high tension or voltage; '♀sprung m sports: high jump.

höchst [hø:çst] 1. adj. highest; fig. a.: supreme; extreme; 2. adv. highly, most, extremely.

Hochstap|elei [ho:xʃtɑ:pə'laɪ] f (-/-en) swindling; '~ler m (-s/-) confidence man, swindler.

höchstens adv. ['hø:çstəns] at (the) most, at best.

'**Höchst|form** f sports: top form; '~geschwindigkeit f maximum speed; speed limit; '~leistung f sports: record (performance); ⊕ maximum output (of machine, etc.); '~lohn m maximum wages pl.; '~maß n maximum; '~preis m maximum price.

'**hoch|trabend** fig. adj. high-flown; pompous; '♀verrat m high treason; '♀wald m high forest; '♀wasser n high tide or water; flood; '~wertig adj. high-grade, high-class; '♀wild n big game; '♀wohlgeboren m (-s/-) Right Hono(u)rable.

Hochzeit ['hɔxtsaɪt] f (-/-en) wedding; marriage; '♀lich adj. bridal, nuptial; '~geschenk n wedding present; '~sreise f honeymoon (trip).

Hocke ['hɔkə] f (-/-n) gymnastics: squat-vault; skiing: crouch; '♀n v/i. (ge-, h) squat, crouch; '~r m (-s/-) stool.

Höcker ['hœkər] m (-s/-) surface, etc.: bump; camel, etc.: hump; p. hump, hunch; '♀ig adj. animal: humped; p. humpbacked, hunchbacked; surface, etc.: bumpy, rough, uneven.

Hode anat. ['ho:də] m (-n/-n), f (-/-n), '~n anat. m (-s/-) testicle.

Hof [ho:f] m (-[e]s/=e) court(yard); farm; king, etc.: court; ast. halo; j-m den ~ machen court s.o.; '~dame f lady-in-waiting; '♀fähig adj. presentable at court.

Hoffart ['hɔfart] f (-/no pl.) arrogance, haughtiness; pride.

hoffen ['hɔfən] (ge-, h) 1. v/i. hope (auf acc. for); trust (in); 2. v/t.: das Beste ~ hope for the best; '~t-lich adv. it is to be hoped that, I hope, let's hope.

Hoffnung ['hɔfnuŋ] f (-/-en) hope (auf acc. for, of); in der ~ zu inf. in the hope of ger., hoping to inf.; s-e ~ setzen auf (acc.) pin one's hopes on; '♀slos adj. hopeless; '♀svoll adj. hopeful; promising.

'**Hofhund** m watch-dog.

höfisch adj. ['hø:fiʃ] courtly.

höflich adj. polite, civil, courteous (gegen to); '♀keit f (-/-en) politeness, civility, courtesy.

'**Hofstaat** m royal or princely household; suite, retinue.

Höhe ['hø:ə] f (-/-n) height; 🛰, ✈, ast., geogr. altitude; hill; peak; amount (of bill, etc.); size (of sum, fine, etc.); level (of price, etc.); severity (of punishment, etc.); ♪ pitch; in gleicher ~ mit on a level with; auf der ~ sein be up to the mark; in die ~ up(wards).

Hoheit ['ho:haɪt] f (-/-en) pol. sovereignty; title: Highness; '~s-gebiet n (sovereign) territory; '~s-gewässer n/pl. territorial waters pl.; '~szeichen n national emblem.

'**Höhen|kurort** m high-altitude health resort; '~luft f mountain air; '~sonne f mountain sun; ☀ ultra-violet lamp; '~steuer ✈ n elevator; '~zug m mountain range.

'**Höhepunkt** m highest point; ast., fig. culmination, zenith; fig. a.: climax; summit, peak.

hohl adj. [ho:l] hollow (a. fig.); cheeks, etc.: sunken; hand: cupped; sound: hollow, dull.

Höhle ['hø:lə] f (-/-n) cave, cavern; den, lair (of bear, lion, etc.) (both a. fig.); hole, burrow (of fox, rabbit, etc.); hollow; cavity.

'**Hohl|maß** n dry measure; '~raum m hollow, cavity; '~spiegel m concave mirror.

Höhlung ['høːluŋ] *f* (-/-en) excavation; hollow, cavity.

'**Hohlweg** *m* defile.

Hohn [hoːn] *m* (-[e]s/*no pl.*) scorn, disdain; derision.

höhnen ['høːnən] *v/i.* (ge-, *h*) sneer, jeer, mock, scoff (*über acc.* at).

'**Hohngelächter** *n* scornful *or* derisive laughter.

'**höhnisch** *adj.* scornful; sneering, derisive.

Höker ['høːkər] *m* (-s/-) hawker, huckster; '**⁀n** *v/i.* (ge-, *h*) huckster, hawk about.

holen ['hoːlən] *v/t.* (ge-, *h*) fetch; go for; *a.* ⁀ *lassen* send for; draw (*breath*); *sich e-e Krankheit* ⁀ catch a disease; *sich bei j-m Rat* ⁀ seek s.o.'s advice.

Holländer ['hɔlɛndər] *m* (-s/-) Dutchman.

Hölle ['hœlə] *f* (-/⁀-n) hell.

'**Höllen|angst** *fig. f*: *e-e* ⁀ *haben* be in a mortal fright *or* F blue funk; '**⁀lärm** F *fig.* *m* infernal noise; '**⁀maschine** *f* infernal machine, time bomb; '**⁀pein** F *fig. f* torment of hell.

'**höllisch** *adj.* hellish, infernal (*both a. fig.*).

holper|ig *adj.* ['hɔlpəriç] *surface, road, etc.*: bumpy, rough, uneven; *vehicle, etc.*: jolty, jerky; *verse, style, etc.*: rough, jerky; '**⁀n** (ge-) **1.** *v/i.* (sein) *vehicle*: jolt, bump; **2.** *v/i.* (*h*) *vehicle*: jolt, bump; be jolty *or* bumpy.

Holunder ♣ [ho'lundər] *m* (-s/-) elder.

Holz [hɔlts] *n* (-es/⁀er) wood; timber, *Am.* lumber; '**⁀bau** 🏠 *m* wooden structure; '**⁀bildhauer** *m* woodcarver; '**⁀blasinstrument** ♪ *n* woodwind instrument; '**⁀boden** *m* wood(en) floor; wood-loft.

hölzern *adj.* ['hœltsərn] wooden; *fig. a.* clumsy, awkward.

'**Holz|fäller** *m* (-s/-) woodcutter, woodman, *Am.* a. lumberjack, logger; '**⁀hacker** *m* (-s/-) woodchopper, woodcutter, *Am.* lumberjack; '**⁀händler** *m* wood *or* timber merchant, *Am.* lumberman; '**⁀haus** *n* wooden house, *Am.* frame house; '**⁀ig** *adj.* woody; '**⁀kohle** *f* charcoal; '**⁀platz** *m* wood *or* timber yard, *Am.* lumberyard; '**⁀schnitt** *m* woodcut, wood-engraving; '**⁀schnitzer** *m* wood-carver; '**⁀schuh** *m* wooden shoe, clog; '**⁀stoß** *m* pile *or* stack of wood; stake; '**⁀weg** *fig. m*: *auf dem* ⁀ *sein* be on the wrong track; '**⁀wolle** *f* wood-wool; fine wood shavings *pl.*, *Am. a.* excelsior.

Homöopath ✝ [homøo'paːt] *m* (-en/-en) hom(o)eopath(ist); **⁀ie** [⁀a'tiː] *f* (-/*no pl.*) hom(o)eopathy; **⁀isch** *adj.* [⁀'paːtiʃ] hom(o)eopathic.

Honig ['hoːniç] *m* (-s/-e) honey; '**⁀kuchen** *m* honey-cake; gingerbread; '**⁀süß** *adj.* honey-sweet, honeyed (*a. fig.*); '**⁀wabe** *f* honeycomb.

Honor|ar [hono'raːr] *n* (-s/-e) fee; royalties *pl.*; salary; **⁀atioren** [⁀a'tsjoːrən] *pl.* notabilities *pl.*; **⁀ieren** [⁀'riːrən] *v/t.* (*no* -ge-, *h*) fee, pay a fee to; ✝ hono(u)r, meet (*bill of exchange*).

Hopfen ['hɔpfən] *m* (-s/-) ♣ hop; *brewing*: hops *pl.*

hops|a *int.* ['hɔpsa] (wh)oops!; upsadaisy!; '**⁀en** F *v/i.* (ge-, sein) hop, jump.

hörbar *adj.* ['høːrbaːr] audible.

horch|en ['hɔrçən] *v/i.* (ge-, *h*) listen (*auf acc.* to); eavesdrop; '**⁀er** *m* (-s/-) eavesdropper.

Horde ['hɔrdə] *f* (-/-n) horde, gang.

hör|en ['høːrən] (ge-, *h*) **1.** *v/t.* hear; listen (in) to (*radio*); attend (*lecture, etc.*); hear, learn; **2.** *v/i.* hear (*von dat.* from); listen; ⁀ *auf* (*acc.*) listen to; *schwer* ⁀ be hard of hearing; ⁀ *Sie mal!* look here!; I say!; '**⁀er** *m* (-s/-) hearer; *radio*: listener(-in); *univ.* student; *teleph.* receiver; '**⁀erschaft** *f* (-/*no pl.*) audience; '**⁀gerät** *n* hearing aid; '**⁀ig** *adj.*: *j-m* ⁀ *sein* be enslaved to s.o.; '**⁀igkeit** *f* (⁀/*no pl.*) subjection.

Horizont [hori'tsɔnt] *m* (-[e]s/-e) horizon; skyline; *s-n* ⁀ *erweitern* broaden one's mind; *das geht über meinen* ⁀ that's beyond me; **⁀al** *adj.* [⁀'taːl] horizontal.

Hormon [hɔr'moːn] *n* (-s/-e) hormone.

Horn [hɔrn] *n* **1.** (-[e]s/⁀er) horn (*of bull*); ♪, *mot., etc.*: horn; ✕ bugle; peak; **2.** (-[e]s/-e) horn, horny matter; '**⁀haut** *f* horny skin; *anat.* cornea (*on eye*).

Hornisse *zo.* [hɔr'nisə] *f* (-/-n) hornet.

Hornist ♪ [hɔr'nist] *m* (-en/-en) horn-player; ✕ bugler.

Horoskop [hɔro'skoːp] *n* (-s/-e) horoscope; *j-m das* ⁀ *stellen* cast s.o.'s horoscope.

'**Hör|rohr** *n* ear-trumpet; ✂ stethoscope; '**⁀saal** *m* lecture-hall; '**⁀spiel** *n* radio play; '**⁀weite** *f*: *in* ⁀ within earshot.

Hose ['hoːzə] *f* (-/-n) (e-e *a pair of*) trousers *pl.* or *Am.* pants *pl.*; slacks *pl.*

'**Hosen|klappe** *f* flap; **⁀latz** [⁀lats] *m* (-es/-e) flap; fly; '**⁀tasche** *f* trouser-pocket; '**⁀träger** *m*: (*ein Paar*) ⁀ *pl.* (a pair of) braces *pl.* or *Am.* suspenders *pl.*

Hospital [hɔspi'taːl] *n* (-s/-e, ⁀er) hospital.

Hostie *eccl.* ['hɔstjə] *f* (-/-n) host, consecrated *or* holy wafer.

Hotel [ho'tɛl] *n* (-s/-s) hotel; **⁀besitzer** *m* hotel owner *or* proprietor;

~gewerbe n hotel industry; **~ier** [~'je:] m (-s/-s) hotel-keeper.

Hub ⊕ [hu:p] m (-[e]s/~e) mot. stroke (of piston); lift (of valve, etc.); **~raum** mot. m capacity.

hübsch adj. [hypʃ] pretty, nice; good-looking, handsome; attractive.

'Hubschrauber ✈ m (-s/-) helicopter.

Huf [hu:f] m (-[e]s/~e) hoof; **~eisen** n horseshoe; **~schlag** m hoof-beat; (horse's) kick; **~schmied** m farrier.

Hüft|e anat. ['hyftə] f (-/-n) hip; esp. zo. haunch; **~gelenk** n hip-joint; **~gürtel** m girdle; suspender belt, Am. garter belt.

Hügel ['hy:gəl] m (-s/-) hill(ock); **2ig** adj. hilly.

Huhn orn. [hu:n] n (-[e]s/~er) fowl, chicken; hen; junges ~ chicken.

Hühnchen ['hy:nçən] n (-s/-) chicken; ein ~ zu rupfen haben have a bone to pick (mit with).

Hühner|auge ⚕ ['hy:nər-] n corn; **~ei** n hen's egg; **~hof** m poultry-yard, Am. chicken yard; **~hund** zo. m pointer, setter; **~leiter** f chicken-ladder.

Huld [hult] f (-/no pl.) grace, favo(u)r; **2igen** ['~digən] v/i. (dat.) (ge-, h) pay homage to (sovereign, lady, etc.); indulge in (vice, etc.); **~igung** f (-/-en) homage; **2reich** adj., **2voll** adj. gracious.

Hülle ['hylə] f (-/-n) cover(ing), wrapper; letter, balloon, etc.: envelope; book, etc.: jacket; umbrella, etc.: sheath; **2n** v/t. (ge-, h) wrap, cover, envelope (a. fig.); sich in Schweigen ~ wrap o.s. in silence.

Hülse ['hylzə] f (-/-n) legume, pod (of leguminous plant); husk, hull (of rice, etc.); skin (of pea, etc.); ✄ case; **~nfrucht** f legume(n); leguminous plant; **~nfrüchte** f/pl. pulse.

human adj. [hu'ma:n] humane; **2i-tät** [~ani'tɛ:t] f (-/no pl.) humanity.

Hummel zo. ['huməl] f (-/-n) bumble-bee.

Hummer zo. ['humər] m (-s/-) lobster.

Humor [hu'mo:r] m (-s/~-e) humo(u)r; **~ist** [~o'rist] m (-en/-en) humorist; **2istisch** adj. [~o'ristiʃ] humorous.

humpeln ['humpəln] v/i. (ge-) 1. (sein) hobble (along), limp (along); 2. (h) (have a) limp, walk with a limp.

Hund [hunt] m (-[e]s/-e) zo. dog; ✄ tub; ast. dog, canis; auf den ~ kommen go to the dogs.

'Hunde|hütte f dog-kennel, Am. a. doghouse; **~kuchen** m dog-biscuit; **~leine** f (dog-)lead or leash; **~peitsche** f dog-whip.

hundert ['hundərt] 1. adj. a or one

hundred; 2. **2** n (-s/-e) hundred; fünf vom ~ five per cent; zu ~en by hundreds; **~fach** adj., **~fältig** adj. hundredfold; **2'jahrfeier** f centenary, Am. a. centennial; **~jährig** adj. ['~jɛ:riç] centenary, a hundred years old; **~st** adj. hundredth.

'Hunde|sperre f muzzling-order; **~steuer** f dog tax.

Hündi|n zo. ['hyndin] f (-/-nen) bitch, she-dog; **2sch** adj. doggish; fig. servile, cringing.

'hunds|ge'mein F adj. dirty, mean, scurvy; **~mise'rabel** F adj. rotten, wretched, lousy; **2tage** m/pl. dog-days pl.

Hüne ['hy:nə] m (-n/-n) giant.

Hunger ['huŋər] m (-s/no pl.) hunger (fig. nach for); ~ bekommen get hungry; ~ haben be or feel hungry; **~kur** f starvation cure; **~leider** F m (-s/-) starveling, poor devil; **~lohn** m starvation wages pl.; **2n** v/i. (ge-, h) hunger (fig. nach after, for); go without food; ~ lassen starve s.o.; **~snot** f famine; **~streik** m hunger-strike; **~tod** m death from starvation; **~tuch** fig. n: am ~ nagen have nothing to bite.

'hungrig adj. hungry (fig. nach for).

Hupe mot. ['hu:pə] f (-/-n) horn, hooter; klaxon; **2n** v/i. (ge-, h) sound one's horn, hoot.

hüpfen ['hypfən] v/i. (ge-, sein) hip, skip; gambol, frisk (about).

Hürde ['hyrdə] f (-/-n) hurdle; fold, pen; **~nrennen** n hurdle-race.

Hure ['hu:rə] f (-/-n) whore, prostitute.

hurtig adj. ['hurtiç] quick, swift; agile, nimble.

Husar ✕ [hu'za:r] m (-en/-en) hussar.

husch int. [huʃ] in or like a flash; shoo!; **~en** v/i. (ge-, sein) slip, dart; small animal: scurry, scamper, bat, etc.: flit.

hüsteln ['hy:stəln] 1. v/i. (ge-, h) cough slightly; 2. **2** n (-s/no pl.) slight cough.

husten ['hu:stən] 1. v/i. (ge-, h) cough; 2. **2** m (-s/~-) cough.

Hut [hu:t] 1. m (-[e]s/~e) hat; den ~ abnehmen take off one's hat; ~ ab vor (dat.)! hats off to ...!; 2. f (-/no pl.) care, charge; guard; auf der ~ sein be on one's guard (vor dat. against).

hüte|n ['hy:tən] v/t. (ge-, h) guard, protect, keep watch over; keep (secret); tend (sheep, etc.); das Bett ~ be confined to (one's) bed; sich ~ vor (dat.) beware of; **2r** m (-s/-) keeper, guardian; herdsman.

'Hut|futter n hat-lining; **~krempe** f hat-brim; **~macher** m (-s/-) hatter; **~nadel** f hat-pin.

Hütte ['hytə] f (-/-n) hut; cottage, cabin; ⊕ metallurgical plant; mount.

refuge; '**~nwesen** ⊕ *n* metallurgy, metallurgical engineering.

Hyäne *zo.* [hy'ɛːnə] *f* (-/-*n*) hy(a)ena.

Hyazinthe ♀ [hya'tsintə] *f* (-/-*n*) hyacinth. [hydrant.]

Hydrant [hy'drant] *m* (-*en*/-*en*)

Hydrauli|k *phys.* [hy'draʊlik] *f* (-/*no pl.*) hydraulics *pl.*; **2sch** *adj.* hydraulic.

Hygien|e [hy'gjeːnə] *f* (-/*no pl.*) hygiene; **2isch** *adj.* hygienic(al).

Hymne ['hymnə] *f* (-/-*n*) hymn.

Hypno|se [hyp'noːzə] *f* (-/-*n*) hypnosis; **2tisieren** [~oti'ziːrən] *v/t.* and *v/i.* (*no* -ge-, *h*) hypnotize.

Hypochond|er [hypo'xɔndər] *m* (-*s*/-) hypochondriac; **2risch** *adj.* hypochondriac.

Hypotenuse Ⱥ [hypote'nuːzə] *f* (-/-*n*) hypotenuse.

Hypothek [hypo'teːk] *f* (-/-*en*) mortgage; e-e **~** *aufnehmen* raise a mortgage; **2arisch** *adj.* [~e'kɑːriʃ]: **~e** *Belastung* mortgage.

Hypothe|se [hypo'teːzə] *f* (-/-*n*) hypothesis; **2tisch** *adj.* hypothetical.

Hyster|ie *psych.* [hyste'riː] *f* (-/-*n*) hysteria; **2isch** *psych. adj.* [~'teːriʃ] hysterical.

I

ich [iç] **1.** *pers. pron.* I; **2.** **2** *n* (-[*s*]/ -[*s*]) self; *psych. the* ego.

Ideal [ide'ɑːl] **1.** *n* (-*s*/-*e*) ideal; **2.** **2** *adj.* ideal; **2isieren** [~ali'ziːrən] *v/t.* (*no* -ge-, *h*) idealize; **~ismus** [~a'lismus] *m* (-/*Idealismen*) idealism; **~ist** [~a'list] *m* (-*en*/-*en*) idealist.

Idee [i'deː] *f* (-/-*n*) idea, notion.

identi|fizieren [identifi'tsiːrən] *v/t.* (*no* -ge-, *h*) identify; *sich* **~** identify *o.s.*; **~sch** *adj.* [i'dentiʃ] identical; **2tät** [~'tɛːt] *f* (-/*no pl.*) identity.

Ideolog|ie [ideolo'giː] *f* (-/-*n*) ideology; **2isch** *adj.* [~'loːgiʃ] ideological.

Idiot [idi'oːt] *m* (-*en*/-*en*) idiot; **~ie** [~o'tiː] *f* (-/-*n*) idiocy; **2isch** *adj.* [~'oːtiʃ] idiotic.

Idol [i'doːl] *n* (-*s*/-*e*) idol.

Igel *zo.* ['iːgəl] *m* (-*s*/-) hedgehog.

Ignor|ant [igno'rant] *m* (-*en*/-*en*) ignorant person, ignoramus; **~anz** [~ts] *f* (-/*no pl.*) ignorance; **2ieren** *v/t.* (*no* -ge-, *h*) ignore, take no notice of.

ihm *pers. pron.* [iːm] *p.* (to) him; *thing:* (to) it.

ihn *pers. pron.* [iːn] *p.* him; *thing:* it.

'ihnen *pers. pron.* (to) them; *Ihnen sg. and pl.* (to) you.

ihr [iːr] **1.** *pers. pron.*: (*2nd pl. nom.*) you; (*3rd sg. dat.*) (to) her; **2.** *poss. pron.*: her; their; *Ihr sg. and pl.* your; *der* (*die*, *das*) **~e** hers; theirs; *der* (*die*, *das*) *Ihre sg. and pl.* yours; **~erseits** ['~ɔr'zaɪts] *adv.* on her part; on their part; *Ihrerseits sg. and pl.* on your part; **'~es'gleichen** *pron.* (of) her *or* their kind, her *or* their equal; *Ihresgleichen sg.* (of) your kind, your equal; *pl.* (of) your kind, your equals; **'~et'wegen** *adv.* for her *or* their sake, on her *or* their account; *Ihretwegen sg. or pl.* for your sake, on your account; **'~et-willen** *adv.*: *um* **~** *s. ihretwegen*;

~ige *poss. pron.* ['~igə]: *der* (*die*, *das*) **~** hers; theirs; *der* (*die*, *das*) *Ihrige* yours.

illegitim *adj.* [ilegi'tiːm] illegitimate.

illusorisch *adj.* [ilu'zoːriʃ] illusory, deceptive.

illustrieren [ilu'striːrən] *v/t.* (*no* -ge-, *h*) illustrate.

Iltis *zo.* ['iltis] *m* (-*ses*/-*se*) fitchew, polecat.

im *prp.* [im] = *in dem*.

imaginär *adj.* [imagi'nɛːr] imaginary.

'Imbiß *m* light meal, snack; '**~stube** *f* snack bar.

Imker ['imkər] *m* (-*s*/-) bee-master, bee-keeper.

immatrikulieren [imatriku'liːrən] *v/t.* (*no* -ge-, *h*) matriculate, enrol(l); *sich* **~** *lassen* matriculate, enrol(l).

immer *adv.* ['imər] always; **~** *mehr* more and more; **~** *wieder* again *or* time and again; *für* **~** for ever, for good; **'2grün** ♀ *n* (-*s*/-*e*) evergreen; '**~hin** *adv.* still, yet; '**~zu** *adv.* always, continually.

Immobilien [imo'biːljən] *pl.* immovables *pl.*, real estate; **~händler** *m s. Grundstücksmakler.*

immun *adj.* [i'muːn] immune (*gegen* against, from); **2ität** [~uni'tɛːt] *f* (-/*no pl.*) immunity.

Imperativ *gr.* ['imperatiːf] *m* (-*s*/-*e*) imperative (mood).

Imperfekt *gr.* ['imperfɛkt] *n* (-*s*/-*e*) imperfect (tense), past tense.

Imperialis|mus [imperia'lismus] *m* (-/*no pl.*) imperialism; **~t** *m* (-*en*/-*en*) imperialist; **2tisch** *adj.* imperialistic.

impertinent *adj.* [imperti'nɛnt] impertinent, insolent.

impf|en ⚕ ['impfən] *v/t.* (ge-, *h*) vaccinate; inoculate; '**2schein** *m* certificate of vaccination *or* inoculation; '**2stoff** ⚕ *m* vaccine;

serum; '2ung *f* (-/-en) vaccination; inoculation.

imponieren [impo'ni:rən] *v/i.* (*no* -ge-, *h*): *j-m* ~ impress s.o.

Import ✝ [im'pɔrt] *m* (-[e]s/-e) import(ation); ~eur ✝ [~'tø:r] *m* (-s/-e) importer; ²ieren [~'ti:rən] *v/t.* (*no* -ge-, *h*) import.

imposant *adj.* [impo'zant] imposing, impressive.

imprägnieren [imprɛ'gni:rən] *v/t.* (*no* -ge-, *h*) impregnate; (water-) proof (*raincoat, etc.*).

improvisieren [improvi'zi:rən] *v/t. and v/i.* (*no* -ge-, *h*) improvise.

Im'puls *m* (-es/-e) impuls; **2iv** *adj.* [~'zi:f] impulsive.   [be able.\

imstande *adj.* [im'ʃtandə]: ~ *sein*\

in *prp.* (*dat.; acc.*) [in] **1.** *place:* in, at; within; into, in; *with names of important towns:* in, ↗ at, of; *with names of villages and less important towns:* at; *im Hause* in the house, indoors, in; *im ersten Stock on the first floor;* ~ *der Schule* (*im Theater*) at school (the theat[re, *Am.* -er); ~ *die Schule* (~s *Theater*) to school (the theat[re, *Am.* -er); ~ *England* in England; *waren Sie schon einmal in England?* have you ever been to England?; **2.** *time:* in, at; during; within; ~ *drei Tagen* (with)in three days; *heute* ~ *vierzehn Tagen* today fortnight; *im Jahre 1960* in 1960; *im Februar* in February; *im Frühling* in (the) spring; ~ *der Nacht* at night; ~ *letzter Zeit* lately, of late, recently; **3.** *mode:* ~ *großer Eile* in great haste; ~ *Frieden leben* live at peace; ~ *Reichweite* within reach; **4.** *condition, state:* *im Alter von fünfzehn Jahren* at (the age of) fifteen; ~ *Behandlung* under treatment.

'Inbegriff *m* (quint)essence; embodiment, incarnation; paragon; '2en *adj.* included, inclusive (of).

'Inbrunst *f* (-/*no pl.*) ardo(u)r, fervo(u)r.

'inbrünstig *adj.* ardent, fervent.

in'dem *cj.* whilst, while; by (*ger.*); ~ *er mich ansah, sagte er* looking at me he said.

Inder ['indər] *m* (-s/-) Indian.

in'des(sen) **1.** *adv.* meanwhile; **2.** *cj.* while; however.

Indianer [in'dja:nər] *m* (-s/-) (American *or* Red) Indian.

Indikativ *gr.* ['indikati:f] *m* (-s/-e) indicative (mood).

'indirekt *adj.* indirect.

'indisch *adj.* ['indiʃ] Indian.

'indiskret *adj.* indiscreet; **2ion** [~e'tsjo:n] *f* (-/-en) indiscretion.

indiskutabel *adj.* ['indiskuta:bəl] out of the question.

individu|ell *adj.* [individu'ɛl] individual; **2um** [~'vi:duum] *n* (-s/ Individuen) individual.

Indizienbeweis ↗ [in'di:tsjən-] *m* circumstantial evidence.

Indoss|ament ✝ [indɔsa'mɛnt] *n* (-s/-e) endorsement, indorsement; **2ieren** ✝ [~'si:rən] *v/t.* (*no* -ge-, *h*) indorse, endorse.

Industrialisierung [industriali'zi:ruŋ] *f* (-/-en) industrialization.

Industrie [indus'tri:] *f* (-/-n) industry; ~anlage *f* industrial plant; ~arbeiter *m* industrial worker; ~ausstellung *f* industrial exhibition; ~erzeugnis *n* industrial product; ~gebiet *n* industrial district *or* area; 2ll *adj.* [~i'ɛl] industrial; ~lle [~i'ɛlə] *m* (-n/-n) industrialist; ~staat *m* industrial country.

ineinander *adv.* [in'?ar'nandər] into one another; ~greifen ⊕ *v/i.* (*irr. greifen, sep.,* -ge-, *h*) gear into one another, interlock.

infam *adj.* [in'fa:m] infamous.

Infanter|ie ⚔ [infantə'ri:] *f* (-/-n) infantry; ~ist ⚔ *m* (-en/-en) infantryman.

Infektion ⚕ [infɛk'tsjo:n] *f* (-/-en) infection; ~skrankheit ⚕ *f* infectious disease.

Infinitiv *gr.* ['infiniti:f] *m* (-s/-e) infinitive (mood).

infizieren [infi'tsi:rən] *v/t.* (*no* -ge-, *h*) infect.   [flation.\

Inflation [infla'tsjo:n] *f* (-/-en) in-\

in'folge *prp.* (*gen.*) in consequence of, owing *or* due to; ~'dessen *adv.* consequently.

Inform|ation [infɔrma'tsjo:n] *f* (-/-en) information; **2ieren** [~'mi:rən] *v/t.* (*no* -ge-, *h*) inform; *falsch* ~ misinform.

Ingenieur [inʒe'njø:r] *m* (-s/-e) engineer.

Ingwer ['iŋvər] *m* (-s/*no pl.*) ginger.

Inhaber ['inha:bər] *m* (-s/-) owner, proprietor (*of business or shop*); occupant (*of flat*); keeper (*of shop*); holder (*of office, share, etc.*); bearer (*of cheque, etc.*).

'Inhalt *m* (-[e]s/-e) contents *pl.* (*of bottle, book, etc.*); tenor (*of speech*); *geom.* volume; capacity (*of vessel*).

'Inhalts|angabe *f* summary; '2los *adj.* empty, devoid of substance; '2reich *adj.* full of meaning; *life:* rich, full; '~verzeichnis *n* on *parcel:* list of contents; *in book:* table of contents.

Initiative [init̮sja'ti:və] *f* (-/*no pl.*) initiative; *die* ~ *ergreifen* take the initiative.

Ink:sso ✝ [in'kaso] *n* (-s/-s, *Inkassi*) collection.

'inkonsequen|t *adj.* inconsistent; **2z** ['~ts] *f* (-/-en) inconsistency.

In'krafttreten *n* (-s/*no pl.*) coming into force, taking effect (*of new law, etc.*).

'Inland *n* (-[e]s/*no pl.*) home (country); inland.

inländisch adj. ['inlɛndiʃ] native; inland; home; domestic; product: home-made.

Inlett ['inlɛt] n (-[e]s/-e) bedtick.

in'mitten prp. (gen.) in the midst of, amid(st).

'inne|haben v/t. (irr. haben, sep., -ge-, h) possess, hold (office, record, etc.); occupy (flat); **'_halten** v/i. (irr. halten, sep., -ge-, h) stop, pause.

innen adv. ['inən] inside, within; indoors; nach _ inwards.

'Innen|architekt m interior decorator; **'_ausstattung** f interior decoration, fittings pl., furnishing; **'_minister** m minister of the interior; Home Secretary, Am. Secretary of the Interior; **'_ministerium** n ministry of the interior; Home Office, Am. Department of the Interior; **'_politik** f domestic policy; **'_seite** f inner side, inside; **'_stadt** f city, Am. downtown.

inner adj. ['inər] interior; inner; ₰, pol. internal; **'_e** n (-n/no pl.) interior; Minister(ium) des Innern s. Innenminister(ium) **_eien** [‿'raiən] f/pl. offal(s pl.); **'_halb 1.** prp. (gen.) within; **2.** adv. within, inside; **'_lich** adv. inwardly; esp. ₰ internally.

innig adj. ['iniç] intimate, close; affectionate.

Innung ['inuŋ] f (-/-en) guild, corporation.

inoffiziell adj. ['inˀ-] unofficial.

ins prp. [ins] = in das.

Insasse ['inzasə] m (-n/-n) inmate; occupant, passenger (of car).

'Inschrift f inscription; legend (on coin, etc.).

Insekt zo. [in'zɛkt] n (-[e]s/-en) insect.

Insel ['inzəl] f (-/-n) island; **'_bewohner** m islander.

Inser|at [inzə'ra:t] n (-[e]s/-e) advertisement, F ad; **_ieren** [‿'ri:rən] v/t. and v/i. (no -ge-, h) advertise.

insge|'heim adv. secretly; **_'samt** adv. altogether.

in'sofern cj. so far; _ als in so far as.

insolvent ✝ adj. ['inzɔlvɛnt] insolvent.

Inspekt|ion [inspɛk'tsjo:n] f (-/-en) inspection; **_or** [in'spɛktɔr] m (-s/-en) inspector; surveyor; overseer.

inspirieren [inspi'ri:rən] v/t. (no -ge-, h) inspire.

inspizieren [inspi'tsi:rən] v/t. (no -ge-, h) inspect (troops, etc.); examine (goods); survey (buildings).

Install|ateur [instala'tø:r] m (-s/-e) plumber; (gas- or electrical) fitter; **_ieren** [‿'li:rən] v/t. (no -ge-, h) install.

instand adv. [in'ʃtant]: _ halten keep in good order; keep up; ⊕

maintain; _ setzen repair; **_haltung** f maintenance; upkeep.

'inständig adv.: j-n _ bitten implore or beseech s.o.

Instanz [in'stants] f (-/-en) authority; ₰₮ instance; **_enweg** ₰₮ m stages of appeal; auf dem _ through the prescribed channels.

Instinkt [in'stiŋkt] m (-[e]s/-e) instinct; **_iv** adv. [‿'ti:f] instinctively.

Institut [insti'tu:t] n (-[e]s/-e) institute.

Instrument [instru'mɛnt] n (-[e]s/-e) instrument.

inszenier|en esp. thea. [instse'ni:rən] v/t. (no -ge-, h) (put on the) stage; **_ung** thea. f (-/-en) staging, production.

Integr|ation [integra'tsjo:n] f (-/-en) integration; **_ieren** [‿'gri:rən] v/t. (no -ge-, h) integrate.

intellektuell adj. [intɛlɛktu'ɛl] intellectual, highbrow; **_e** m (-n/-n) intellectual, highbrow.

intelligen|t adj. [intɛli'gɛnt] intelligent; **_z** [‿ts] f (-/-en) intelligence.

Intendant thea. [intɛn'dant] m (-en/-en) director.

intensiv adj. [intɛn'zi:f] intensive; intense.

interess|ant adj. [intɛrɛ'sant] interesting; **_e** [‿'rɛsə] n (-s/-n) interest (an dat., für in); **_engebiet** [‿'rɛsən-] n field of interest; **_engemeinschaft** [‿'rɛsən-] f community of interests; combine, pool, trust; **_ent** [‿'sɛnt] m (-en/-en) interested person or party; ✝ prospective buyer, esp. Am. prospect; **_ieren** [‿'si:rən] v/t. (no -ge-, h) interest (für in); sich _ für take an interest in.

intern adj. [in'tɛrn] internal; **_at** [‿'na:t] n (-[e]s/-e) boardingschool.

international adj. [internatsjo'na:l] international.

inter|'nieren v/t. (no -ge-, h) intern; **_'nierung** f (-/-en) internment; **_'nist** ₰ m (-en/-en) internal specialist, Am. internist.

inter|pretieren [intɛrpre'ti:rən] v/t. (no -ge-, h) interpret; **_punktion** [‿puŋk'tsjo:n] f (-/-en) punctuation; **_vall** [‿'val] n (-s/-e) interval; **_venieren** [‿ve'ni:rən] v/i. (no -ge-, h) intervene; **_'zonenhandel** m interzonal trade; **_'zonenverkehr** m interzonal traffic.

intim adj. [in'ti:m] intimate (mit with); **_ität** [‿imi'tɛ:t] f (-/-en) intimacy.

'intoleran|t adj. intolerant; **_z** ['‿ts] f (-/-en) intolerance.

intransitiv gr. adj. ['intranziti:f] intransitive.

Intrig|e [in'tri:gə] f (-/-n) intrigue, scheme, plot; **_ieren** [‿'gi:rən] v/i. (no -ge-, h) intrigue, scheme, plot.

Invalid|e [inva'li:də] *m* (-n/-n) invalid; disabled person; **~enrente** *f* disability pension; **~ität** [~idi-'tɛ:t] *f* (-/*no pl.*) disablement, disability.

Inventar [invɛn'taːr] *n* (-s/-e) inventory, stock.

Inventur ✝ [invɛn'tuːr] *f* (-/-en) stock-taking; **~ machen** take stock.

invest|ieren ✝ [invɛs'tiːrən] *v/t.* (*no -ge-, h*) invest; **Qition** ✝ [~i'tsjoːn] *f* (-/-en) investment.

inwie|'fern *cj.* to what extent; in what way *or* respect; **~'weit** *cj.* how far, to what extent.

in'zwischen *adv.* in the meantime, meanwhile.

Ion *phys.* [i'oːn] *n* (-s/-en) ion.

ird|en *adj.* ['irdən] earthen; **~isch** *adj.* earthly; worldly; mortal.

Ire ['iːrə] *m* (-n/-n) Irishman; **die ~n** *pl.* the Irish *pl.*

irgend *adv.* ['irgənt] *in compounds:* some; any (*a.* negative *and in questions*); **wenn ich ~ kann** if I possibly can; **~'ein(e)** *indef. pron. and adj.* some(one) any(one); **~'einer** *indef. pron. s.* irgend jemand; **~'ein(e)s** *indef. pron.* some; any; **~ etwas** *indef. pron.* something; anything; **~ jemand** *indef. pron.* someone; anyone; **~'wann** *adv.* some time (or other); **~'wie** *adv.* somehow; anyhow; **~'wo** *adv.* somewhere; anywhere; **~'wo'her** *adv.* from somewhere; from anywhere; **~'wo'hin** *adv.* somewhere; anywhere.

'irisch *adj.* Irish.

Iron|ie [iro'niː] *f* (-/-n) irony; **Qisch** *adj.* [i'roːniʃ] ironic(al).

irre ['irə] **1.** *adj.* confused; **&** insane; mad; **2.** *Q f* (-/*no pl.*): **in die ~ gehen** go astray; **3.** *Q m, f* (-n/-n) lunatic; mental patient; **wie ein ~r** like a madman; **~'führen** *v/t.* (*sep., -ge-, h*) lead astray; *fig.* mislead; **'~gehen** *v/i.* (*irr.* gehen, *sep., -ge-, sein*) go astray, stray; lose one's way; **~'machen** *v/t.* (*sep., -ge-, h*) puzzle, bewilder; perplex; confuse;

~n 1. *v/i.* (*ge-, h*) err; wander; **2.** *v/refl.* (*ge-, h*) be mistaken (*in dat.* in *s.o.*, about *s.th.*); be wrong.

'Irren|anstalt **&** *f* lunatic asylum, mental home *or* hospital; **'~arzt** *m* alienist, mental specialist; **'~haus** **&** *n s.* Irrenanstalt.

'irrereden *v/i.* (*sep., -ge-, h*) rave.

'Irr|fahrt *f* wandering; Odyssey; **'~garten** *m* labyrinth; maze; **'~glaube** *m* erroneous belief; false doctrine, heterodoxy; heresy; **'Qgläubig** *adj.* heterodox; heretical; **'Qig** *adj.* erroneous, mistaken, false, wrong.

irritieren [iri'tiːrən] *v/t.* (*no -ge-, h*) irritate, annoy; confuse.

'Irr|lehre *f* false doctrine, heterodoxy; heresy; **'~licht** *n* will-o'-the-wisp, jack-o'-lantern; **'~sinn** *m* insanity; madness; **'Qsinnig** *adj.* insane; mad; *fig.:* fantastic; terrible; **'~sinnige** *m, f* (-n/-n) *s.* irre 3; **'~tum** *m* (-s/*~er*) error, mistake; **im ~ sein** be mistaken; **Qtümlich** ['~tyːmliç] **1.** *adj.* erroneous; **2.** *adv.* = **'Qtümlicherweise** *adv.* by mistake; mistakenly, erroneously; **'~wisch** *m s.* Irrlicht; *p.* flibbertigibbet.

Ischias **&** ['iʃias] *f, A a.: n, m* (-/*no pl.*) sciatica.

Islam ['islam, is'laːm] *m* (-s/*no pl.*) Islam.

Isländ|er ['iːslɛndər] *m* (-s/-) Icelander; **Qisch** *adj.* Icelandic.

Isolator **⚡** [izo'laːtɔr] *m* (-s/-en) insulator.

Isolier|band **⚡** [izo'liːr-] *n* insulating tape; **Qen** *v/t.* (*no -ge-, h*) isolate; **~masse** **⚡** *f* insulating compound; **~schicht** **⚡** *f* insulating layer; **~ung** *f* (-/-en) isolation (*a.* **&**); *ⅇ* quarantine; **⚡** insulation.

Isotop **🜨**, *phys.* [izo'toːp] *n* (-s/-e) isotope.

Israeli [isra'eːli] *m* (-s/-s) Israeli.

Italien|er [ital'jeːnər] *m* (-s/-) Italian; **Qisch** *adj.* Italian.

I-Tüpfelchen *fig.* ['iːtypfəlçən] *n* (-s/-): **bis aufs ~** to a T.

J

ja [jaː] **1.** *adv.* yes; **♣**, *parl.* aye, *Am. parl. a.* yea; **~ doch, ~ freilich** yes, indeed; to be sure; **da ist er ~!** well, there he is!; **ich sagte es Ihnen ~** I told you so; **tut es ~ nicht!** don't you dare do it!; **vergessen Sie es ~ nicht!** be sure not to forget it!; **2.** *cj.:* **~ sogar, ~ selbst** nay (even); **wenn ~** if so; **er ist ~ mein Freund** why, he is my friend; **3.** *int.:* **~, weißt du**

denn nicht, daß why, don't you know that.

Jacht **♣** [jaxt] *f* (-/-en) yacht; **'~klub** *m* yacht-club.

Jacke ['jakə] *f* (-/-n) jacket.

Jackett [ʒa'kɛt] *n* (-s/-e, -s) jacket.

Jagd [jaːkt] *f* (-/-en) hunt(ing); *with a gun:* shoot(ing); chase; *s.* Jagdrevier; **auf (die) ~ gehen** go hunting *or* shooting, *Am. a.* be gunning; **~ machen auf (acc.)** hunt after *or* for;

'~aufseher *m* gamekeeper, *Am.* game warden; **'~bomber** ✕ *m* (-s/-) fighter-bomber; **'~büchse** *f* sporting rifle; **'~flinte** *f* sporting gun; fowling-piece; **'~flugzeug** ✕ *n* fighter (aircraft); **'~geschwader** ✕ *n* fighter wing, *Am.* fighter group; **'~gesellschaft** *f* hunting *or* shooting party; **'~haus** *n* shooting-box *or* -lodge, hunting-box *or* -lodge; **'~hund** *m* hound; **'~hütte** *f* shooting-box, hunting-box; **'~pächter** *m* game-tenant; **'~rennen** *n* steeplechase; **'~revier** *n* hunting-ground, shoot; **'~schein** *m* shooting licen|ce, *Am.* -se; **'~schloß** *n* hunting seat; **'~tasche** *f* game-bag.

jagen ['jɑːgən] (ge-, h) **1.** *v/i.* go hunting *or* shooting, hunt; shoot; rush, dash; **2.** *v/t.* hunt; chase; *aus dem Hause* ~ turn *s.o.* out (of doors).

Jäger ['jɛːgər] *m* (-s/-) hunter huntsman, sportsman; ✕ rifleman; **'~latein** F *fig. n* huntsmen's yarn, tall stories *pl.* [jaguar.\

Jaguar *zo.* ['jɑːguɑːr] *m* (-s/-e)\

jäh *adj.* [jɛː] sudden, abrupt; precipitous, steep.

Jahr [jɑːr] *n* (-[e]s/-e) year; *ein halbes* ~ half a year, six months *pl.*; *einmal im* ~ once a year; *im* ~*e 1900* in 1900; *mit 18* ~*en*, *im Alter von 18* ~*en* at (the age of) eighteen; *letztes* ~ last year; *das ganze* ~ *hindurch or über* all the year round; ♀'*aus* *adv.*: ~, *jahrein* year in, year out; year after year; **'~buch** *n* yearbook, annual; **'~ein** *adv. s.* jahraus.

'jahrelang 1. *adv.* for years; **2.** *adj.*: ~*e Erfahrung* (many) years of experience.

jähren ['jɛːrən] *v/refl.* (ge-, h): *es jährt sich heute, daß* ... it is a year ago today that ..., it is a year today since ...

'Jahres|abonnement *n* annual subscription (*to magazine, etc.*); *thea.* yearly season ticket; **'~abschluß** *m* annual statement of accounts; **'~anfang** *m* beginning of the year; *zum* ~ *die besten Wünsche!* best wishes for the New Year; **'~bericht** *m* annual report; **'~einkommen** *n* annual *or* yearly income; **'~ende** *n* end of the year; **'~gehalt** *n* annual salary; **'~tag** *m* anniversary; **'~wechsel** *m* turn of the year; **'~zahl** *f* date, year; **'~zeit** *f* season, time of the year.

'Jahrgang *m* volume, year (*of periodical, etc.*); *p.* age-group; *univ., school:* year, class; *wine:* vintage.

Jahr'hundert *n* (-s/-e) century; **~feier** *f* centenary, *Am.* centennial; **~wende** *f* turn of the century.

jährig *adj.* ['jɛːriç] one-year-old.

jährlich ['jɛːrliç] **1.** *adj.* annual, yearly; **2.** *adv.* every year; yearly, once a year.

'Jahr|markt *m* fair; **~'tausend** *n* (-s/-e) millennium; **~'tausendfeier** *f* millenary; **~'zehnt** *n* (-[e]s/-e) decade.

'Jähzorn *m* violent (fit of) temper; irascibility; **'♀ig** *adj.* hot-tempered; irascible.

Jalousie [ʒaluˈziː] *f* (-/-n) (Venetian) blind, *Am. a.* window shade.

Jammer ['jamər] *m* (-s/*no pl.*) lamentation; misery; *es ist ein* ~ it is a pity.

jämmerlich *adj.* ['jɛmərliç] miserable, wretched; piteous; pitiable (*esp. contp.*).

jammer|n ['jamərn] *v/i.* (ge-, h) lament (*nach, um* for; *über acc.* over); moan; wail, whine; **'~schade** *adj.*: *es ist* ~ it is a thousand pities, it is a great shame.

Januar ['januɑːr] *m* (-[s]/-e) January.

Japan|er [jaˈpɑːnər] *m* (-s/-) Japanese; *die* ~ *pl.* the Japanese *pl.*; **♀isch** *adj.* Japanese.

Jargon [ʒarˈgõ] *m* (-s/-s) jargon, cant, slang.

Jasmin ♀ [jasˈmiːn] *m* (-s/-e) jasmin(e), jessamin(e).

'Jastimme *parl. f* ayc, *Am. a.* yea.

jäten ['jɛːtən] *v/t.* (ge-, h) weed.

Jauche ['jauxə] *f* (-/-n) ✗ liquid manure; sewage.

jauchzen ['jauxtsən] *v/i.* (ge-, h) exult, rejoice, cheer; *vor Freude* ~ shout for joy.

jawohl [jaˈvoːl] yes; yes, indeed; yes, certainly; that's right; ✕ *etc.*: yes, Sir!

'Jawort *n* consent; *j-m das* ~ *geben* accept *s.o.*'s proposal (of marriage).

je [jeː] **1.** *adv.* ever, at any time; always; *ohne ihn* ~ *gesehen zu haben* without ever having seen him; *seit eh und* ~ since time immemo ial, always; *distributive with numerals:* ~ *zwei* two at a time, two each, two by two, by *or* in twos; *sie bekamen* ~ *zwei Äpfel* they received two apples each; *für* ~ *zehn Wörter* for every ten words; *in Schachteln mit or zu* ~ *zehn Stück verpackt* packed in boxes of ten; **2.** *cj.*: ~ *nach Größe* according to *or* depending on size; ~ *nachdem* it depends; ~ *nachdem, was er für richtig hält* according as he thinks fit; ~ *nachdem, wie er sich fühlt* depending on how he feels; ~ *mehr, desto besser* the more the better; ~ *länger*, ~ *lieber* the longer the better; **3.** *prp.*: *die Birnen kosten e-e Mark* ~ *Pfund* the pears cost one mark a pound; *s. pro.*

jede|(r, -s) *indef. pron.* ['jeːdə(r, -s)] every; any; *of a group:* each; *of two persons:* either; jeder, der whoever; jeden zweiten Tag every other day; **'~n'falls** *adv.* at all events, in any case; '~rmann *indef. pron.* everyone, everybody; '~r'zeit *adv.* always, at any time; '~s'mal *adv.* each *or* every time; ~ wenn whenever.

jedoch *cj.* [je'dɔx] however, yet, nevertheless.

'**jeher** *adv.*: von *or* seit ~ at all times, always, from time immemorial.

jemals *adv.* ['je:mɑːls] ever, at any time.

jemand *indef. pron.* ['je:mant] someone, somebody; *with questions and negations:* anyone, anybody.

jene|(r, -s) *dem. pron.* ['je:nə(r, -s)] that (one); jene *pl.* those *pl.*

jenseitig *adj.* ['jenzaitiç] opposite.

'**jenseits 1.** *prp.* (*gen.*) on the other side of, beyond, across; **2.** *adv.* on the other side, beyond; **3.** ♀ *n* (-/no *pl.*) the other *or* next world, the world to come, the beyond.

jetzig *adj.* ['jetsiç] present, existing; *prices, etc.*: current.

jetzt *adv.* [jetst] now, at present; bis ~ until now; so far; eben ~ just now; erst ~ only now; für ~ for the present; gleich ~ at once, right away; noch ~ even now; von ~ an from now on.

jeweil|ig *adj.* ['je:vailiç] respective; ~s *adv.* ['~s] respectively, at a time; from time to time (*esp.* ½).

Joch [jɔx] *n* (-[e]s/-e) yoke; *in mountains:* col, pass, saddle; ⚓ bay; '~bein *anat.* *n* cheek-bone.

Jockei ['dʒɔki] *m* (-s/-s) jockey.

Jod ♂ [jo:t] *n* (-[e]s/no *pl.*) iodine.

jodeln ['jo:dəln] *v/i.* (ge-, h) yodel.

Johanni [jo'hani] *n* (-/no *pl.*), ~s [~s] *n* (-/no *pl.*) Midsummer day; ~s-beere *f* currant; rote ~ red currant; ~stag *m eccl.* St John's day; Midsummer day.

johlen ['jo:lən] *v/i.* (ge-, h) bawl, yell, howl.

Jolle ⚓ ['jɔlə] *f* (-/-n) jolly-boat, yawl, dinghy.

Jongl|eur [ʒõ'glø:r] *m* (-s/-e) juggler; ♀ieren *v/t.* and *v/i.* (no -ge-, h) juggle.

Journal [ʒur'nɑːl] *n* (-s/-e) journal; newspaper; magazine; diary; ⚓ log-book; ~ist [~a'list] *m* (-en/-en) journalist, *Am. a.* newspaperman.

Jubel ['ju:bəl] *m* (-s/no *pl.*) jubilation, exultation, rejoicing; cheering; '♀n *v/i.* (ge-, h) jubilate; exult, rejoice (*über acc.* at).

Jubil|ar [jubi'lɑːr] *m* (-s/-e) person celebrating his jubilee, *etc.*; ~äum [~ɛ:um] *n* (-s/ Jubiläen) jubilee.

Juchten ['juxtən] *m*, *n* (-s/no *pl.*), '~leder *n* Russia (leather).

jucken ['jukən] (ge-, h) **1.** *v/i.* itch; **2.** *v/t.* irritate, (make) itch; F sich ~ scratch (o.s.).

Jude ['ju:də] *m* (-n/-n) Jew; '♀n-feindlich *adj.* anti-Semitic; '~n-

tum *n* (-s/no *pl.*) Judaism; '~nver-folgung *f* persecution of Jews, Jew-baiting; pogrom.

Jüd|in ['jy:din] *f* (-/-nen) Jewess; '♀isch *adj.* Jewish.

Jugend ['ju:gənt] *f* (-/no *pl.*) youth; '~amt *n* youth welfare department; '~buch *n* book for the young; '~freund *m* friend of one's youth; school-friend; '~fürsorge *f* youth welfare; '~gericht *n* juvenile court; '~herberge *f* youth hostel; '~jahre *n/pl.* early years, youth; '~krimi-nalität *f* juvenile delinquency; '♀-lich *adj.* youthful, juvenile, young; '~liche *m*, *f* (-n/-n) young person; juvenile; young man, youth; young girl; teen-ager; '~liebe *f* early *or* first love, calf-love, *Am. a.* puppy love; old sweetheart *or* flame; '~schriften *f/pl.* books for the young; '~schutz *m* protection of children and young people; '~streich *m* youthful prank; '~werk *n* early work (*of author*); ~e *pl. a.* juvenilia *pl.*; '~zeit *f* (time *or* days of) youth.

Jugoslav|e [ju:go'slɑːvə] *m* (-en/-en) Jugoslav, Yugoslav; ♀isch *adj.* Jugoslav, Yugoslav.

Juli ['ju:li] *m* (-[s]/-s) July.

jung *adj.* [juŋ] young; youthful; *peas:* green; *beer, wine:* new; ~es Gemüse young *or* early vegetables *pl.*; F *fig.* young people, small fry.

'**Junge 1.** *m* (-n/-n) boy, youngster; lad; fellow, chap, *Am.* guy; *cards:* knave, jack; **2.** *n* (-n/-n) young; puppy (*of dog*); kitten (*of cat*); calf (*of cow, elephant, etc.*); cub (*of beast of prey*); ~ werfen bring forth young; ein ~s a young one; '♀nhaft *adj.* boyish; '~nstreich *m* boyish prank *or* trick.

jünger ['jyŋər] **1.** *adj.* younger, junior; er ist drei Jahre ~ als ich he is three years younger than I; **2.** ♀ *m* (-s/-) disciple.

Jungfer ['juŋfər] *f* (-/-n): alte ~ old maid *or* spinster.

'**Jungfern|fahrt** ⚓ *f* maiden voyage *or* trip; '~flug ✈ *m* maiden flight; '~rede *f* maiden speech.

'**Jung|frau** *f* maid(en), virgin; ♀-fräulich *adj.* ['~frɔyliç] virginal; *fig.* virgin; '~fräulichkeit *f* (-/no *pl.*) virginity, maidenhood; '~ge-selle *m* bachelor; '~gesellenstand *m* bachelorhood; '~gesellin *f* (-/-nen) bachelor girl.

Jüngling ['jyŋliŋ] *m* (-s/-e) youth, young man.

jüngst [jyŋst] **1.** *adj.* youngest; *time:* (most) recent, latest; das ♀e Ge-richt, der ♀e Tag Last Judg(e)ment, Day of Judg(e)ment; **2.** *adv.* recently, lately.

'**jungverheiratet** *adj.* newly married; '♀en *pl.* the newlyweds *pl.*

Juni ['ju:ni] *m* (-[s]/-s) June; '⁓käfer *zo. m* cockchafer, June-bug.
junior ['ju:njɔr] **1.** *adj.* junior; **2.** ⚥ *m* (-s/-en) junior (*a. sports*).
Jura ['ju:ra] *n/pl.*: ⁓ studieren read or study law.
Jurist [ju'rist] *m* (-en/-en) lawyer; law-student; ⚥isch *adj.* legal.
Jury [ʒy'ri:] *f* (-/-s) jury.
justier|en ⊕ [jus'ti:rən] *v/t.* (*no* -ge-, *h*) adjust; ⚥ung ⊕ *f* (-/-en) adjustment.
Justiz [jus'ti:ts] *f* (-/no *pl.*) (administration of) justice; ⁓beamte *m* judicial officer; ⁓gebäude *n* courthouse; ⁓inspektor *m* judicial officer; ⁓irrtum *m* judicial error; ⁓minister *m* minister of justice; Lord Chancellor, *Am.* Attorney General; ⁓ministerium *n* ministry of justice; *Am.* Department of Justice; ⁓mord *m* judicial murder.
Juwel [ju've:l] *m, n* (-s/-en) jewel, gem; ⁓en *pl.* jewel(le)ry; ⁓ier [⁓e-'li:r] *m* (-s/-e) jewel(l)er.
Jux F [juks] *m* (-es/-e) (practical) joke, fun, spree, lark; prank.

K

(Compare also C and Z)

Kabel ['ka:bəl] *n* (-s/-) cable.
Kabeljau *ichth.* ['ka:bəljau] *m* (-s/-e, -s) cod(fish).
'kabeln *v/t. and v/i.* (ge-, *h*) cable.
Kabine [ka'bi:nə] *f* (-/-n) cabin; *at hairdresser's, etc.*: cubicle; cage (*of lift*).
Kabinett *pol.* [kabi'nɛt] *n* (-s/-e) cabinet, government.
Kabriolett [kabrio'lɛt] *n* (-s/-e) cabriolet, convertible.
Kachel ['kaxəl] *f* (-/-n) (Dutch *or* glazed) tile; '⁓ofen *m* tiled stove.
Kadaver [ka'da:vər] *m* (-s/-) carcass.
Kadett [ka'dɛt] *m* (-en/-en) cadet.
Käfer *zo.* ['kɛ:fər] *m* (-s/-) beetle, chafer.
Kaffee ['kafe, ka'fe:] *m* (-s/-s) coffee; (')⁓bohne ♀ *f* coffee-bean; (')⁓kanne *f* coffee-pot; (')⁓mühle *f* coffee-mill *or* -grinder; (')⁓satz *m* coffee-grounds *pl.*; (')⁓tasse *f* coffee-cup.
Käfig ['kɛ:fiç] *m* (-s/-e) cage (*a. fig.*).
kahl *adj.* [ka:l] *p.* bald; *tree, etc.*: bare; *landscape, etc.*: barren, bleak; *rock, etc.*: naked; ⚥kopf *m* baldhead, baldpate; ⁓köpfig *adj.* ['⁓kœpfiç] bald(-headed).
Kahn [ka:n] *m* (-[e]s/⁼e) boat; riverbarge; ⁓ fahren go boating; '⁓fahren *n* (-s/no *pl.*) boating.
Kai [kai] *m* (-s/-e, -s) quay, wharf.
Kaiser ['kaizər] *m* (-s/-) emperor; '⁓krone *f* imperial crown; ⚥lich *adj.* imperial; '⁓reich *n*, '⁓tum *n* (-[e]s/⁼er) empire; '⁓würde *f* imperial status.
Kajüte ⚓ [ka'jy:tə] *f* (-/-n) cabin.
Kakao [ka'ka:o] *m* (-s/-s) cocoa; ♀ *a.* cacao.
Kakt|ee ♀ [kak'te:(ə)] *f* (-/-n), ⁓us ♀ ['⁓us] *m* (-/Kakteen, F Kaktusse) cactus.

Kalauer ['ka:lauər] *m* (-s/-) stale joke; pun.
Kalb *zo.* [kalp] *n* (-[e]s/⁼er) calf; ⚥en ['⁓bən] *v/i.* (ge-, *h*) calve; '⁓fell *n* calfskin; '⁓fleisch *n* veal; '⁓leder *n* calf(-leather).
'Kalbs|braten *m* roast veal; '⁓keule *f* leg of veal; '⁓leder *n* s. *Kalbleder*; '⁓nierenbraten *m* loin of veal.
Kalender [ka'lɛndər] *m* (-s/-) calendar; almanac; ⁓block *m* dateblock; ⁓jahr *n* calendar year; ⁓uhr *f* calendar watch *or* clock.
Kali ⚗ ['ka:li] *n* (-s/-s) potash.
Kaliber [ka'li:bər] *n* (-s/-) calib|re, *Am.* -er (*a. fig.*), bore (*of firearm*).
Kalk [kalk] *m* (-[e]s/-e) lime; *geol.* limestone; '⁓brenner *m* limeburner; ⚥en *v/t.* (ge-, *h*) whitewash (*wall, etc.*); 📐 lime (*field*); '⚥ig *adj.* limy; '⁓ofen *m* limekiln; '⁓stein *m* limestone; '⁓steinbruch *m* limestone quarry.
Kalorie [kalo'ri:] *f* (-/-n) calorie.
kalt *adj.* [kalt] *climate, meal, sweat, etc.*: cold; *p., manner, etc.*: cold, chilly, frigid; *mir ist* ⁓ I am cold; ⁓e Küche cold dishes *pl.* or *meat, etc.*; *j-m die* ⁓e *Schulter zeigen* give s.o. the cold shoulder; ⁓blütig *adj.* ['⁓bly:tiç] cold-blooded (*a. fig.*).
Kälte ['kɛltə] *f* (-/no *pl.*) cold; chill; coldness, chilliness (*both a. fig.*); *vor* ⁓ *zittern* shiver with cold; *fünf Grad* ⁓ five degrees below zero; '⁓grad *m* degree below zero; '⁓welle *f* cold spell.
'kalt|stellen *fig. v/t.* (*sep.*, -ge-, *h*) shelve, reduce to impotence; '⚥welle *f* cold wave.
kam [ka:m] *pret. of* kommen.
Kamel *zo.* [ka'me:l] *n* (-[e]s/-e) camel; ⁓haar *n textiles*: camel hair.
Kamera *phot.* ['kaməra] *f* (-/-s) camera.

Kamerad [kamə'rɑːt] m (-en/-en) comrade; companion; mate, F pal, chum; **~schaft** f (-/-en) comradeship, companionship; **2schaftlich** adj. comradely, companionable.

Kamille ♀ ['ka'milə] f (-/-n) camomile; **~ntee** m camomile tea.

Kamin [ka'miːn] m (-s/-e) chimney (a. mount.); fireplace, fireside; **~sims** m, n mantelpiece; **~vorleger** m hearth-rug; **~vorsetzer** m (-s/-) fender.

Kamm [kam] m (-[e]s/¤e) comb; crest (of bird or wave); crest, ridge (of mountain).

kämmen ['kemən] v/t. (ge-, h) comb; sich (die Haare) ~ comb one's hair.

Kammer ['kamər] f (-/-n) (small) room; closet; pol. chamber; board; ⅔ division (of court); **'~diener** m valet; **'~frau** f lady's maid; **'~gericht** ⅔ n supreme court; **'~herr** m chamberlain; **'~jäger** m vermin exterminator; **'~musik** f chamber music; **'~zofe** f chambermaid.

'Kamm|garn n worsted (yarn); **'~rad** ⊕ n cogwheel.

Kampagne [kam'panjə] f (-/-n) campaign.

Kampf [kampf] m (-[e]s/¤e) combat, fight (a. fig.); struggle (a. fig.); battle (a. fig.); fig. conflict; sports: contest, match; boxing: fight, bout; **'~bahn** f sports: stadium, arena; **'2bereit** adj. ready for battle.

kämpfen ['kempfən] v/i. (ge-, h) fight (gegen against; mit with; um for) (a. fig.); struggle (a. fig.); fig. contend, wrestle (mit with).

Kampfer ['kampfər] m (-s/no pl.) camphor.

Kämpfer ['kempfər] m (-s/-) fighter (a. fig.); ✕ combatant, warrior.

'Kampf|flugzeug n tactical aircraft; **'~geist** m fighting spirit; **'~platz** m battlefield; fig., sports: arena; **'~preis** m sports: prize; ✝ cut-throat price; **'~richter** m referee, judge, umpire; **'2unfähig** adj. disabled.

kampieren [kam'piːrən] v/i. (no -ge-, h) camp.

Kanal [ka'nɑːl] m (-s/¤e) canal; channel (a. ⊕, fig.); geogr. the Channel; sewer, drain; **~isation** [~aliza'tsjoːn] f (-/-en) river: canalization; town, etc.: sewerage; drainage; **2isieren** [~ali'ziːrən] v/t. (no -ge-, h) canalize; sewer.

Kanarienvogel orn. [ka'nɑːrjən-] m canary(-bird).

Kandare [kan'dɑːrə] f (-/-n) curb (-bit).

Kandid|at [kandi'dɑːt] m (-en/-en) candidate; applicant; **~atur** [~a'tuːr] f (-/-en) candidature, candidacy; **2ieren** [~'diːrən] v/i. (no -ge-, h) be a candidate (für for);

~ für apply for, stand for, Am. run for (office, etc.).

Känguruh zo. ['keŋguruː] n (-s/-s) kangaroo.

Kaninchen zo. [ka'niːnçən] n (-s/-) rabbit; **~bau** m rabbit-burrow.

Kanister [ka'nistər] m (-s/-) can.

Kanne ['kanə] f (-/-n) milk, etc.: jug; coffee, tea: pot; oil, milk: can; **'~gießer** F fig. m political wiseacre.

Kannibal|e [kani'baːlə] m (-n/-n) cannibal; **2isch** adj. cannibal.

kannte ['kantə] pret. of kennen.

Kanon ♪ ['kaːnɔn] m (-s/-s) canon.

Kanon|ade ✕ [kano'nɑːdə] f (-/-n) cannonade; **~e** [~'noːnə] f (-/-n) ✕ cannon, gun; F fig.: big shot; esp. sports: ace, crack.

Ka'nonen|boot ✕ n gunboat; **~donner** m boom of cannon; **~futter** fig. n cannon-fodder; **~kugel** f cannon-ball; **~rohr** n gun barrel.

Kanonier ✕ [kano'niːr] m (-s/-e) gunner.

Kant|e ['kantə] f (-/-n) edge; brim; **'~en** m (-s/-) end of loaf; **'2en** v/t. (ge-, h) square (stone, etc.); set on edge; tilt; edge (skis); **'2ig** adj. angular, edged; square(d).

Kantine [kan'tiːnə] f (-/-n) canteen.

Kanu ['kaːnu] n (-s/-s) canoe.

Kanüle ♫ [ka'nyːlə] f (-/-n) tubule, cannula.

Kanzel ['kantsəl] f (-/-n) eccl. pulpit; ✕ cockpit; ✕ (gun-)turret.; **'~redner** m preacher.

Kanzlei [kants'lai] f (-/-en) office.

'Kanzler m (-s/-) chancellor.

Kap geogr. [kap] n (-s/-s) headland.

Kapazität [kapatsi'teːt] f (-/-en) capacity; fig. authority.

Kapell|e [ka'pelə] f (-/-n) eccl. chapel; ♪ band; **~meister** m bandleader, conductor.

kaper|n ♴ ['kaːpərn] v/t. (ge-, h) capture, seize; **'2schiff** n privateer.

kapieren F [ka'piːrən] v/t. (no -ge-, h) grasp, get.

Kapital [kapi'tɑːl] 1. n (-s/-e, -ien) capital, stock, funds pl.; ~ und Zinsen principal and interest; 2. ♀ adj. capital; **~anlage** f investment; **~flucht** f flight of capital; **~gesellschaft** f joint-stock company; **2isieren** [~ali'ziːrən] v/t. (no -ge-, h) capitalize; **~ismus** [~a'lismus] m (-/no pl.) capitalism; **~ist** [~a'list] m (-en/-en) capitalist; **~markt** [~'tɑːl-] m capital market; **~verbrechen** n capital crime.

Kapitän [kapi'teːn] m (-s/-e) captain; ~ zur See naval captain; **~leutnant** m (senior) lieutenant.

Kapitel [ka'pitəl] n (-s/-) chapter (a. fig.).

Kapitul|ation ✕ [kapitula'tsjoːn] f (-/-en) capitulation, surrender; **2ieren** [~'liːrən] v/i. (no -ge-, h) capitulate, surrender.

Kaplan *eccl.* [ka'plɑːn] *m* (-s/-e) chaplain.

Kappe ['kapə] *f* (-/-n) cap; hood (a. ⊕); bonnet; '⊇n *v/t.* (ge-, h) cut (*cable*); lop, top (*tree*).

Kapriole [kapri'oːlə] *f* (-/-n) equitation: capriole; *fig.*: caper; prank.

Kapsel ['kapsəl] *f* (-/-n) case, box; ⊕, ⚕, *anat.*, *etc.*: capsule.

kaputt *adj.* [ka'put] broken; *elevator, etc.*: out of order; *fruit, etc.*: spoilt; *p.*: ruined; tired out, F fagged out; ⊸gehen *v/i.* (*irr. gehen, sep., -ge-, sein*) break, go to pieces; spoil.

Kapuze [ka'puːtsə] *f* (-/-n) hood; *eccl.* cowl.

Karabiner [kara'biːnər] *m* (-s/-) carbine.

Karaffe [ka'rafə] *f* (-/-n) carafe (*for wine or water*); decanter (*for liqueur, etc.*).

Karambol|age [karambo'laːʒə] *f* (-/-n) collision, crash; *billiards*: cannon, *Am. a.* carom; ⊇ieren *v/i.* (*no -ge-, sein*) cannon, *Am. a.* carom; F *fig.* collide.

Karat [ka'rɑːt] *n* (-[e]s/-e) carat.

Karawane [kara'vɑːnə] *f* (-/-n) caravan.

Karbid [kar'biːt] *n* (-[e]s/-e) carbide.

Kardinal *eccl.* [kardi'nɑːl] *m* (-s/=e) cardinal.

Karfreitag *eccl.* [kaːr'-] *m* Good Friday.

karg *adj.* [kark] *soil*: meagre; *vegetation*: scant, sparse; *meal*: scanty, meagre, frugal; ⊸en ['⊸gən] *v/i.* (ge-, h): ⊸ mit be sparing of.

kärglich *adj.* ['kerkliç] scanty, meagre; poor.

kariert *adj.* [ka'riːrt] check(ed), chequered, *Am.* checkered.

Karik|atur [karika'tuːr] *f* (-/-en) caricature, cartoon; ⊇ieren [⊸'kiːrən] *v/t.* (*no -ge-, h*) caricature, cartoon.

karmesin *adj.* [karme'ziːn] crimson.

Karneval ['karnəval] *m* (-s/-e, -s) Shrovetide, carnival.

Karo ['kaːro] *n* (-s/-s) square, check; *cards*: diamonds *pl*.

Karosserie *mot.* [karəsə'riː] *f* (-/-n) body.

Karotte ⚘ [ka'rɔtə] *f* (-/-n) carrot.

Karpfen *ichth.* ['karpfən] *m* (-s/-) carp.

Karre ['karə] *f* (-/-n) cart; wheelbarrow.

Karriere [kar'jɛːrə] *f* (-/-n) (successful) career.

Karte ['kartə] *f* (-/-n) card; postcard; map; chart; ticket; menu, bill of fare; list.

Kartei [kar'taɪ] *f* (-/-en) card-index; ⊸karte *f* index-card, filing-card; ⊸schrank *m* filing cabinet.

Kartell ⊤ [kar'tel] *n* (-s/-e) cartel.

'**Karten|brief** *m* letter-card; '⊸haus

n ⊕ chart-house; *fig.* house of cards; '⊸legerin *f* (-/-nen) fortune-teller from the cards; '⊸spiel *n* card-playing; card-game.

Kartoffel [kar'tɔfəl] *f* (-/-n) potato, F spud; ⊸brei *m* mashed potatoes *pl.*; ⊸käfer *m* Colorado *or* potato beetle, *Am. a.* potato bug; ⊸schalen *f/pl.* potato peelings *pl.*

Karton [kar'tõː, kar'tɔːn] *m* (-s/-s, -e) cardboard, pasteboard; cardboard box, carton. [*Kartei.*\]

Kartothek [karto'teːk] *f* (-/-en) *s.*\]

Karussell [karu'sel] *n* (-s/-s, -e) roundabout, merry-go-round, *Am. a.* car(r)ousel.

Karwoche *eccl.* ['kaːr-] *f* Holy *or* Passion Week.

Käse ['kɛːzə] *m* (-s/-) cheese.

Kasern|e ⚔ [ka'zernə] *f* (-/-n) barracks *pl.*; ⊸enhof *m* barrack-yard *or* -square; ⊇ieren [⊸'niːrən] *v/t.* (*no -ge-, h*) quarter in barracks, barrack.

'**käsig** *adj.* cheesy; *complexion*: pale, pasty.

Kasino [ka'ziːno] *n* (-s/-s) casino, club(-house); (officers') mess.

Kasperle ['kasperlə] *m, n* (-s/-) Punch; '⊸theater *n* Punch and Judy show.

Kasse ['kasə] *f* (-/-n) cash-box; till (*in shop, etc.*); cash-desk, pay-desk (*in bank, etc.*); pay-office (*in firm*); *thea., etc.*: box-office, booking-office; cash; *bei* ⊸ in cash.

'**Kassen|abschluß** ⊤ *m* balancing of the cash (accounts); '⊸anweisung *f* disbursement voucher; '⊸bestand *m* cash in hand; '⊸bote *m* bank messenger; '⊸buch *n* cash book; '⊸erfolg *m thea., etc.*: box-office success; '⊸patient ⚕ *m* panel patient; '⊸schalter *m bank, etc.*: teller's counter.

Kasserolle [kasə'rɔlə] *f* (-/-n) stewpan, casserole.

Kassette [ka'sɛtə] *f* (-/-n) box (*for money, etc.*); casket (*for jewels, etc.*); slip-case (*for books*); *phot.* plate-holder.

kassiere|n [ka'siːrən] (*no -ge-, h*) 1. *v/i. waiter, etc.*: take the money (*für for*); 2. *v/t.* take (*sum of money*); collect (*contributions, etc.*); annul; ⚖ quash (*verdict*); ⊇r *m* (-s/-) cashier; *bank*: *a.* teller; collector.

Kastanie ⚘ [ka'stɑːnjə] *f* (-/-n) chestnut.

Kasten ['kastən] *m* (-s/=, ⚘ -) box; chest (*for tools, etc.*); case (*for violin, etc.*); bin (*for bread, etc.*).

Kasus *gr.* ['kaːsus] *m* (-/-) case.

Katalog [kata'loːk] *m* (-[e]s/-e) catalogue, *Am. a.* catalog; ⊇isieren [⊸ogi'ziːrən] *v/t.* (*no -ge-, h*) catalogue, *Am. a.* catalog.

Katarrh ⚕ [ka'tar] *m* (-s/-e) (common) cold, catarrh.

katastroph|al adj. [katastro'fɑ:l] catastrophic, disastrous; **2e** [ˌˈstroː-fə] f (-/-n) catastrophe, disaster.

Katechismus eccl. [kate'çismus] m (-/Katechismen) catechism.

Katego|rie [katego'riː] f (-/-n) category; **2risch** adj. [ˌˈgoːriʃ] categorical.

Kater ['kɑːtər] m (-s/-) zo. male cat, tom-cat; fig. s. Katzenjammer.

Katheder [ka'teːdər] n, m (-s/-) lecturing-desk. [cathedral.)

Kathedrale [kate'drɑːlə] f (-/-n))

Katholi|k [kato'liːk] m (-en/-en) (Roman) Catholic; **2sch** adj. [ˌˈtoːliʃ] (Roman) Catholic.

Kattun [ka'tuːn] m (-s/-e) calico; cotton cloth or fabric; chintz.

Katze zo. ['katsə] f (-/-n) cat; '~n-jammer F fig. m hangover, morning-after feeling.

Kauderwelsch ['kaudərvɛlʃ] n (-[s]/ no pl.) gibberish, F double Dutch; **2en** v/i. (ge-, h) gibber, F talk double Dutch.

kauen ['kauən] v/t. and v/i. (ge-, h) chew.

kauern ['kauərn] (ge-, h) **1.** v/i. crouch; squat; **2.** v/refl. crouch (down); squat (down); duck (down).

Kauf [kauf] m (-[e]s/⸗e) purchase; bargain, F good buy; acquisition; purchasing, buying; '~brief m deed of purchase; **2en** v/t. (ge-, h) buy, purchase; acquire (by purchase); sich et. ~ buy o.s. s.th., buy s.th. for o.s.

Käufer ['kɔyfər] m (-s/-) buyer, purchaser; customer.

'Kauf|haus n department store; '~laden m shop, Am. a. store.

käuflich ['kɔyfliç] **1.** adj. for sale; purchasable; fig. open to bribery, bribable; venal; **2.** adv.: ~ erwerben (acquire by) purchase; ~ überlassen transfer by way of sale.

'Kauf|mann m (-[e]s/Kaufleute) businessman; merchant; trader, dealer; shopkeeper; Am. a. storekeeper; **2männisch** adj. [ˌˈmɛniʃ] commercial, mercantile; '~vertrag m contract of sale.

'Kaugummi m chewing-gum.

kaum adv. [kaum] hardly, scarcely, barely; ~ glaublich hard to believe.

'Kautabak m chewing-tobacco.

Kaution [kau'tsjoːn] f (-/-en) security, surety; ⚖ mst bail.

Kautschuk ['kautʃuk] m (-s/-e) caoutchouc, pure rubber.

Kavalier [kava'liːr] m (-s/-e) gentleman; beau, admirer.

Kavallerie ⚔ [kavalə'riː] f (-/-n) cavalry, horse.

Kaviar ['kɑːviar] m (-s/-e) caviar(e).

keck adj. [kɛk] bold; impudent, saucy, cheeky; '**2heit** f (-/-en) boldness; impudence, sauciness, cheekiness.

Kegel ['keːgəl] m (-s/-) games: skittle, pin; esp. ⚥, ⊕ cone; ~ schieben s. kegeln; '~bahn f skittle, alley, Am. bowling alley; **2förmig** adj. ['ˌfœrmiç] conic(al), coniform; tapering; '~n v/i. (ge-, h) play (at) skittles or ninepins, Am. bowl.

Kegler ['keːglər] m (-s/-) skittle-player, Am. bowler.

Kehl|e ['keːlə] f (-/-n) throat; '~kopf anat. m larynx.

Kehre ['keːrə] f (-/-n) (sharp) bend, turn; '**2n** v/t. (ge-, h) sweep, brush; turn (nach oben upwards); j-m den Rücken ~ turn one's back on s.o.

Kehricht ['keːriçt] m, n (-[e]s/no pl.) sweepings pl., rubbish.

'Kehrseite f wrong side, reverse; esp. fig. seamy side.

'kehrtmachen v/i. (sep., -ge-, h) turn on one's heel; ⚔ turn or face about.

keifen ['kaifən] v/i. (ge-, h) scold, chide.

Keil [kail] m (-[e]s/-e) wedge; gore, gusset; '~e F f (-/no pl.) thrashing, hiding; '~er zo. m (-s/-) wild-boar; ~erei F [ˌˈrai] f (-/-en) row, scrap; **2förmig** adj. ['ˌfœrmiç] wedge-shaped, cuneiform; '~kissen n wedge-shaped bolster; '~schrift f cuneiform characters pl.

Keim [kaim] m (-[e]s/-e) ⚥, biol. germ; ⚘: seed-plant; shoot; sprout; fig. seeds pl., germ, bud; '**2en** v/i. (ge-, h) ⚘ seeds, etc.: germinate; seeds, plants, potatoes, etc.: sprout; fig. b(o)urgeon; **2frei** adj. sterilized, sterile; '~träger ⚕ m (germ-)carrier; '~zelle f germ-cell.

kein indef. pron. [kain] as adj.: ~(e) no, not any; ~ anderer als none other but; as noun: ~er, ~e, ~(e)s none, no one, nobody; ~er von beiden neither (of the two); ~er von uns none of us; '~esfalls adv., '~eswegs adv. ['ˌˈveːks] by no means, not at all; '~mal adv. not once, not a single time.

Keks [keːks] m, n (-, -es/-, -e) biscuit, Am. cookie; cracker.

Kelch [kɛlç] m (-[e]s/-e) cup, goblet; eccl. chalice, communion-cup; ⚘ calyx.

Kelle ['kɛlə] f (-/-n) scoop; ladle; tool: trowel.

Keller ['kɛlər] m (-s/-) cellar; basement; ~ei [ˌˈrai] f (-/-en) wine-vault; '~geschoß n basement; '~meister m cellarman.

Kellner ['kɛlnər] m (-s/-) waiter; '~in f (-/-nen) waitress.

Kelter ['kɛltər] f (-/-n) winepress; '**2n** v/t. (ge-, h) press.

kenn|en ['kɛnən] v/t. (irr., ge-, h) know, be acquainted with; have knowledge of s.th.; '~enlernen v/t. (sep., -ge-, h) get or come to know;

make s.o.'s acquaintance, meet s.o.;
'2er m (-s/-) expert; connoisseur;
'~tlich adj. recognizable (an dat.
by); ~ machen mark; label; '2tnis f
(-/-se) knowledge; ~ nehmen von
take not(ic)e of; '2zeichen n mark,
sign; mot. registration (number),
Am. license number; fig. hallmark,
criterion; '~zeichnen v/t. (ge-, h)
mark, characterize.

kentern ⚓ ['kɛntərn] v/i. (ge-, sein)
capsize, keel over, turn turtle.

Kerbe ['kɛrbə] f (-/-n) notch, nick;
slot; '2n v/t. (ge-, h) notch, nick,
indent.

Kerker ['kɛrkər] m (-s/-) gaol, jail,
prison; '~meister m gaoler, jailer.

Kerl F [kɛrl] m (-s, ⚓ -es/-e, F -s)
man; fellow, F chap, bloke, esp.
Am. guy.

Kern [kɛrn] m (-[e]s/-e) kernel (of
nut, etc.); stone, Am. pit (of cherry,
etc.); pip (of orange, apple, etc.);
core (of the earth); phys. nucleus;
fig. core, heart, crux; Kern... s. a.
Atom...; '~energie f nuclear energy; '~forschung f nuclear research;
'~gehäuse n core; '2ge'sund adj.
thoroughly healthy, F as sound as
a bell; '2ig adj. full of pips; fig.:
pithy; solid; '~punkt m central or
crucial point; '~spaltung f nuclear
fission.

Kerze ['kɛrtsə] f (-/-n) candle; '~n-
licht n candle-light; '~nstärke f
candle-power.

keß F adj. [kɛs] pert, jaunty; smart.

Kessel ['kɛsəl] m (-s/-) kettle; caul-
dron; boiler; hollow.

Kette ['kɛtə] f (-/-n) chain; range
(of mountains, etc.); necklace; '2n
v/t. (ge-, h) chain (an acc. to).

'Ketten|hund m watch-dog; '~rau-
cher m chain-smoker; '~reaktion
f chain reaction.

Ketzer ['kɛtsər] m (-s/-) heretic; ~ei
[~'raɪ] f (-/-en) heresy; '2isch adj.
heretical.

keuch|en ['kɔʏçən] v/i. (ge-, h) pant,
gasp; '2husten ⚕ m (w)hooping
cough.

Keule ['kɔʏlə] f (-/-n) club; leg
(of mutton, pork, etc.).

keusch adj. [kɔʏʃ] chaste, pure;
'2heit f (-/no pl.) chastity, purity.

kichern ['kɪçərn] v/i. (ge-, h) giggle,
titter.

Kiebitz ['ki:bits] m (-es/-e) orn.
pe(e)wit; F fig. kibitzer; '2en F fig.
v/i. (ge-, h) kibitz.

Kiefer ['ki:fər] 1. anat. m (-s/-)
jaw(-bone); 2. ⚘ f (-/-n) pine.

Kiel [ki:l] m (-[e]s/-e) ⚓ keel; quill;
'~raum m bilge, hold; '~wasser n
wake (a. fig.).

Kieme zo. ['ki:mə] f (-/-n) gill.

Kies [ki:s] m (-es/-e) gravel; sl. fig.
dough; ~el ['ki:zəl] m (-s/-) pebble,
flint; '~weg m gravel-walk.

Kilo ['ki:lo] n (-s/-[s]), ~gramm
[kilo'gram] n kilogram(me); ~hertz
[~'hɛrts] n (-/no pl.) kilocycle per
second; ~meter ⚡ n kilomet|re, Am.
-er; ~watt n kilowatt.

Kimme ['kɪmə] f (-/-n) notch.

Kind [kɪnt] n (-[e]s/-er) child; baby.

'Kinder|arzt m p(a)ediatrician; ~ei
[~'raɪ] f (-/-en) childishness; childish trick; trifle; '~frau f nurse;
'~fräulein n governess; '~funk m
children's program(me); '~garten
m kindergarten, nursery school;
'~lähmung ⚕ f infantile paralysis,
polio(myelitis); '2leicht adj. very
easy or simple, F as easy as winking
or as ABC; '~lied n children's
song; '2los adj. childless; '~mäd-
chen n nurse(maid); '~spiel n
children's game; ein ~ s. kinderleicht; '~stube f nursery; fig.
manners pl., upbringing; '~wagen
m perambulator, F pram, Am. baby
carriage; '~zeit f childhood; '~zim-
mer n children's room.

'Kindes|alter n childhood, infancy;
'~beine n/pl.: von ~ an from childhood, from a very early age; '~kind
n grandchild.

'Kind|heit f (-/no pl.) childhood;
2isch adj. ['~dɪʃ] childish; '2lich
adj. childlike.

Kinn anat. [kɪn] n (-[e]s/-e) chin;
'~backe f, '~backen m (-s/-) jaw
(-bone); '~haken m boxing: hook
to the chin; uppercut; '~lade f
jaw(-bone).

Kino ['ki:no] n (-s/-s) cinema, F the
pictures pl., Am. motion-picture
theater, F the movies pl.; ins ~
gehen go to the cinema or F pictures,
Am. F go to the movies; '~besu-
cher m cinema-goer, Am. F
moviegoer; '~vorstellung f cine-
ma-show, Am. motion-picture
show.

Kippe F ['kɪpə] f (-/-n) stub, fag-end,
Am. a. butt; auf der ~ stehen or sein
hang in the balance; '2n (-/-n)
1. v/i. (sein) tip (over), topple (over),
tilt (over); 2. v/t. (h) tilt, tip over
or up.

Kirche ['kɪrçə] f (-/-n) church.

'Kirchen|älteste m (-n/-n) church-
warden, elder; '~buch n parochial
register; '~diener m sacristan,
sexton; '~gemeinde f parish;
'~jahr n ecclesiastical year; '~lied n
hymn; '~musik f sacred music;
'~schiff △ n nave; '~steuer f
church-rate; '~stuhl m pew; '~vor-
steher m churchwarden.

'Kirch|gang m church-going; ~gän-
ger ['~gɛŋər] m (-s/-) church-
goer; '~hof m churchyard; '2lich
adj. ecclesiastical; '~spiel n parish;
'~turm m steeple; ~weih ['~vaɪ] f
(-/-en) parish fair.

Kirsche ['kɪrʃə] f (-/-n) cherry.

Kissen ['kisən] n (-s/-) cushion; pillow; bolster, pad.
Kiste ['kistə] f (-/-n) box, chest; crate.
Kitsch [kitʃ] m (-es/no pl.) trash, rubbish; **'2ig** adj. shoddy, trashy.
Kitt [kit] m (-[e]s/-e) cement; putty.
Kittel ['kitəl] m (-s/-) overall; smock, frock.
'kitten v/t. (ge-, h) cement; putt.
kitz|eln ['kitsəln] (ge-, h) 1. v/t. tickle; 2. v/i.: meine Nase kitzelt my nose is tickling; **'~lig** adj. ticklish (a. fig.).
Kladde ['kladə] f (-/-n) rough note-book, waste-book.
klaffen ['klafən] v/i. (ge-, h) gape, yawn.
kläffen ['klɛfən] v/i. (ge-, h) yap, yelp.
klagbar ⚖ adj. ['klaːkbaːr] matter, etc.: actionable; debt, etc.: suable.
Klage ['klaːgə] f (-/-n) complaint; lament; ⚖ action, suit; **'2n** (ge-, h) 1. v/i. complain (über acc. of, about; bei to); lament; ⚖ take legal action (gegen against); 2. v/t.: j-m et. ~ complain to s.o. of or about s.th.
Kläger ⚖ ['klɛːgər] m (-s/-) plaintiff; complainant.
kläglich adj. ['klɛːkliç] pitiful, piteous, pitiable; cries, etc.: plaintive; condition: wretched, lamentable; performance, result, etc.: miserable, poor; failure, etc.: lamentable, miserable.
klamm [klam] 1. adj. hands, etc.: numb or stiff with cold, clammy; 2. ♀ f (-/-en) ravine, gorge, canyon.
Klammer ['klamər] f (-/-n) ⊕ clamp, cramp; (paper-)clip; gr., typ., ⚔ bracket, parenthesis; **'2n** (ge-, h) 1. v/t. clip together; ⚔ close (wound) with clips; sich ~ an (acc.) cling to (a. fig.); 2. v/i. boxing: clinch.
Klang [klaŋ] 1. m (-[e]s/-e) sound, tone (of voice, instrument, etc.); tone (of radio, etc.); clink (of glasses, etc.); ringing (of bells, etc.); timbre; 2. ♀ pret. of klingen; **'~fülle** ♪ f sonority; **'2los** adj. toneless; **'2voll** adj. sonorous.
Klappe ['klapə] f (-/-n) flap; flap, drop leaf (of table, etc.); shoulder strap (of uniform, etc.); tailboard (of lorry, etc.); ⊕, ♀, anat. valve; ♪ key; F fig.: bed; trap; **'2n** (ge-, h) 1. v/t.: nach oben ~ tip up; nach unten ~ lower, put down; 2. v/i. clap, flap; fig. come off well, work out fine, Am. sl. a. click.
Klapper ['klapər] f (-/-n) rattle; **'2ig** adj. vehicle, etc.: rattly, ramshackle; furniture: rickety; person, horse, etc.: decrepit; **'~kasten** F m wretched piano; rattletrap; **'2n** (ge-, h) clatter, rattle (mit et. s.th.); er klapperte vor Kälte mit den Zäh-

nen his teeth were chattering with cold; **'~schlange** zo. f rattlesnake, Am. a. rattler.
'Klapp|kamera phot. f folding camera; **'~messer** n clasp-knife, jack-knife; **'~sitz** m tip-up or flap seat; **'~stuhl** m folding chair; **'~tisch** m folding table, Am. a. gate-leg(ged) table; **~ult** ['klap-pult] n folding desk.
Klaps [klaps] m (-es/-e) smack, slap; **'2en** v/t. (ge-, h) smack, slap.
klar adj. [klaːr] clear; bright; transparent; limpid; pure; fig.: clear, distinct; plain; evident, obvious; sich ~ sein über (acc.) be clear about; ~en Kopf bewahren keep a clear head.
klären ['klɛːrən] v/t. (ge-, h) clarify; fig. clarify, clear up, elucidate.
'klar|legen v/t. (sep., -ge-, h), **'~stellen** v/t. (sep., -ge-, h) clear up.
'Klärung f (-/-en) clarification; fig. a. elucidation.
Klasse ['klasə] f (-/-n) class, category; school: class, form, Am. a. grade; (social) class.
'Klassen|arbeit f (test) paper; **'2be-wußt** adj. class-conscious; **'~be-wußtsein** n class-consciousness; **'~buch** n class-book; **'~haß** m class-hatred; **'~kamerad** m classmate; **'~kampf** m class-war(fare); **'~zim-mer** n classroom, schoolroom.
klassifizier|en [klasifi'tsiːrən] v/t. (no -ge-, h) classify; **2ung** f (-/-en) classification.
Klass|iker ['klasikər] m (-s/-) classic; **'2isch** adj. classic(al).
klatsch [klatʃ] 1. int. smack!, slap!; 2. ♀ m (-es/-e) smack, slap; F fig.: gossip; scandal; **2base** ['~baːzə] f (-/-n) gossip; **'2e** f (-/-n) fly-flap; **'~en** (ge-, h) 1. v/t. fling, hurl; Beifall ~ clap, applaud (j-m s.o.) 2. v/i. splash; applaud, clap; F fig. gossip; **'~haft** adj. gossiping, gossipy; **'2maul** F n s. Klatschbase; **'~naß** F adj. soaking wet.
Klaue ['klauə] f (-/-n) claw; paw; fig. clutch.
Klause ['klauzə] f (-/-n) hermitage; cell.
Klausel ⚖ ['klauzəl] f (-/-n) clause; proviso; stipulation.
Klaviatur ♪ [klavja'tuːr] f (-/-en) keyboard, keys pl.
Klavier ♪ [kla'viːr] n (-s/-e) piano (-forte); **~konzert** n piano concert or recital; **~lehrer** m piano teacher; **~sessel** m music-stool; **~stimmer** m (-s/-) piano-tuner; **~stunde** f piano-lesson.
kleb|en ['kleːbən] (ge-, h) 1. v/t. glue, paste, stick; 2. v/i. stick, adhere (an dat. to); **'~end** adj. adhesive; **'2epflaster** n adhesive or sticking plaster; **'~rig** adj. adhesive, sticky; **'2stoff** m adhesive; glue.

Klecks [klɛks] m (-es/-e) blot (of ink); mark (of dirt, grease, paint, etc.); spot (of grease, paint, etc.); stain (of wine, coffee, etc.); 'Ωen (ge-) 1. v/i. (h) make a mark or spot or stain; 2. v/i. (sein) ink, etc.: drip (down); 3. v/t. (h): et. auf et. ~ splash or spill s.th. on s.th.

Klee ♣ [kle:] m (-s/no pl.) clover, trefoil.

Kleid [klaɪt] n (-[e]s/-er) garment; dress, frock; gown; ~er pl. clothes pl.; Ωen ['~dən] v/t. (ge-, h) dress, clothe; sich ~ dress (o.s.); j-n gut ~ suit or become s.o.

Kleider|ablage ['klaɪdər-] f cloakroom, Am. a. checkroom; '~bügel m coat-hanger; '~bürste f clothesbrush; '~haken m clothes-peg; '~schrank m wardrobe; '~ständer m hat and coat stand; '~stoff m dress material.

'kleidsam adj. becoming.

Kleidung ['klaɪdʊŋ] f (-/-en) clothes pl., clothing; dress; '~sstück n piece or article of clothing; garment.

Kleie ['klaɪə] f (-/-n) bran.

klein [klaɪn] 1. adj. little (only attr.), small; fig. a. trifling, petty; 2. adv.: ~ schreiben write with a small (initial) letter; ~ anfangen start in a small or modest way; 3. noun: von ~ auf from an early age; 'Ωauto n baby or small car; 'Ωbahn f narrow-ga(u)ge railway; 'Ωbildkamera f miniature camera; 'Ωgeld n (small) change; 'Ωgläubig adj. of little faith; 'Ωhandel ♣ m retail trade; 'Ωhändler m retailer; 'Ωheit f (-/no pl.) smallness, small size; 'Ωholz n firewood, matchwood, kindling.

'Kleinigkeit f (-/-en) trifle, triviality; '~skrämer m pettifogger.

'Klein|kind n infant; 'Ωlaut adj. subdued; 'Ωlich adj. paltry; pedantic, fussy; '~mut m pusillanimity; despondency; Ωmütig adj. ['~my:tiç] pusillanimous; despondent; 'Ωschneiden v/t. (irr. schneiden, sep., -ge-, h) cut into small pieces; '~staat m small or minor state; '~stadt f small town; '~städter m small-town dweller, Am. a. small-towner; 'Ωstädtisch adj. small-town, provincial; '~vieh n small livestock.

Kleister ['klaɪstər] m (-s/-) paste; 'Ωn v/t. (ge-, h) paste.

Klemm|e ['klɛmə] f (-/-n) ⊕ clamp; ∮ terminal; F in der ~ sitzen be in a cleft stick, F be in a jam; 'Ωen v/t. (ge-, h) jam, squeeze, pinch; '~er m (-s/-) pince-nez; '~schraube ∮ f set screw.

Klempner ['klɛmpnər] m (-s/-) tinman, tin-smith, Am. a. tinner; plumber.

Klerus ['kle:rʊs] m (-/no pl.) clergy.

Klette ['klɛtə] f (-/-n) ♣ bur(r); fig. a. leech.

Kletter|er ['klɛtərər] m (-s/-) climber; 'Ωn v/i. (ge-, sein) climb, clamber (auf e-n Baum [up] a tree); '~pflanze f climber, creeper.

Klient [kli'ɛnt] m (-en/-en) client.

Klima ['kli:ma] n (-s/-s, -te) climate; fig. a. atmosphere; '~anlage f air-conditioning plant; Ωtisch adj. [~'ma:tiʃ] climatic.

klimpern ['klɪmpərn] v/i. (ge-, h) jingle, chink (mit et. s.th.); F strum or tinkle away (auf acc. on, at piano, guitar).

Klinge ['klɪŋə] f (-/-n) blade.

Klingel ['klɪŋəl] f (-/-n) bell, hand-bell; '~knopf m bell-push; 'Ωn v/i. (ge-, h) ring (the bell); doorbell, etc.: ring; es klingelt the doorbell is ringing; '~zug m bell-pull.

klingen ['klɪŋən] v/i. (irr., ge-, h) sound; bell, metal, etc.: ring; glasses, etc.: clink; musical instrument: speak.

Klini|k ['kli:nɪk] f (-/-en) nursing home; private hospital; clinic(al hospital); 'Ωsch adj. clinical.

Klinke ['klɪŋkə] f (-/-n) latch; (door-)handle.

Klippe ['klɪpə] f (-/-n) cliff; reef; crag; rock; fig. rock, hurdle.

klirren ['klɪrən] v/i. (ge-, h) window-pane, chain, etc.: rattle; chain, swords, etc.: clank, jangle; keys, spurs, etc.: jingle; glasses, etc.: clink, chink; pots, etc.: clatter; ~ mit rattle; jingle.

Klistier ⬧ [kli'sti:r] n (-s/-e) enema.

Kloake [klo'a:kə] f (-/-n) sewer, cesspool (a. fig.).

Klob|en ['klo:bən] m (-s/-) ⊕ pulley, block; log; 'Ωig adj. clumsy (a. fig.).

klopfen ['klɔpfən] (ge-, h) 1. v/i. heart, pulse: beat, throb; knock (at door, etc.); tap (on shoulder); pat (on cheek); es klopft there's a knock at the door; 2. v/t. knock, drive (nail, etc.).

Klöppel ['klœpəl] m (-s/-) clapper (of bell); lacemaking: bobbin; beetle; '~spitze f pillow-lace, bone-lace.

Klops [klɔps] m (-es/-e) meat ball.

Klosett [klo'zɛt] n (-s/-e, -s) lavatory, (water-)closet, W.C., toilet; ~papier n toilet-paper.

Kloß [klo:s] m (-es/⁼e) earth, clay, etc.: clod, lump; cookery: dumpling.

Kloster ['klo:stər] n (-s/⁼) cloister; monastery; convent, nunnery; '~bruder ♣ m friar; '~frau f nun; '~gelübde n monastic vow.

Klotz [klɔts] m (-es/⁼e) block, log (a. fig.).

Klub [klup] m (-s/-s) club; '~kamerad m clubmate; '~sessel m lounge-chair.

Kluft [klʊft] f 1. (-/⁼e) gap (a. fig.),

Kommand|ant ✕ [kɔmanˈdant] *m* (-en/-en), **~eur** ✕ [~ˈdøːr] *m* (-s/-e) commander, commanding officer; **2ieren** [~ˈdiːrən] (*no -ge-, h*) **1.** *v/i.* order, command, be in command; **2.** *v/t.* ✕ command, be in command of; order; **~itgesellschaft** ✝ [~ˈdiːt-] *f* limited partnership; **~o** [~ˈmando] *n* (-s/-s) ✕ command, order; order(s *pl.*), directive(s *pl.*); ✕ detachment; **~obrücke** ⚓ *f* navigating bridge.

kommen [ˈkɔmən] *v/i.* (*irr., ge-, sein*) come; arrive; **~** *lassen* send for *s.o.*, order *s.th.*; *et.* **~** *sehen* foresee; *an die Reihe* **~** it is one's turn; **~** *auf (acc.)* think of, hit upon; remember; *zu dem Schluß* **~**, *daß* decide that; *hinter et.* **~** find s.th. out; *um et.* **~** lose s.th.; *zu et.* **~** come by s.th.; *wieder zu sich* **~** come round or to; *wie* **~** *Sie dazu!* how dare you!

Komment|ar [kɔmɛnˈtaːr] *m* (-s/-e) commentary, comment; **~ator** [~ˈtɔr] *m* (-s/-en) commentator; **2ieren** [~ˈtiːrən] *v/t.* (*no -ge-, h*) comment on.

Kommissar [kɔmiˈsaːr] *m* (-s/-e) commissioner; superintendent; *pol.* commissar.

Kommißbrot F [kɔˈmis-] *n* army or ration bread, *Am. a.* G.I. bread.

Kommission [kɔmiˈsjoːn] *f* (-/-en) commission (*a.* ✝); committee; **~är** ✝ [~oˈnɛːr] *m* (-s/-e) commission agent.

Kommode [kɔˈmoːdə] *f* (-/-n) chest of drawers, *Am.* bureau.

Kommunis|mus *pol.* [kɔmuˈnismus] *m* (-/*no pl.*) communism; **~t** *m* (-en/-en) communist; **2tisch** *adj.* communist(ic).

Komöd|iant [kɔmøˈdjant] *m* (-en/-en) comedian; *fig.* play-actor; **~ie** [~ˈmøːdjə] *f* (-/-n) comedy; **~** *spielen* play-act.

Kompagnon ✝ [kɔmpanˈjõ] *m* (-s/-s) (business-)partner, associate.

Kompanie ✕ [kɔmpaˈniː] *f* (-/-n) company.

Kompaß [ˈkɔmpas] *m* (*Kompasses/Kompasse*) compass.

kompetent *adj.* [kɔmpeˈtɛnt] competent.

komplett *adj.* [kɔmˈplɛt] complete.

Komplex [kɔmˈplɛks] *m* (-es/-e) complex (*a. psych.*); block (*of houses*).

Kompliment [kɔmpliˈmɛnt] *n* (-[e]s/-e) compliment.

Komplize [kɔmˈpliːtsə] *m* (-n/-n) accomplice.

komplizier|en [kɔmpliˈtsiːrən] *v/t.* (*no -ge-, h*) complicate; **~t** *adj. machine, etc.*: complicated; *argument, situation, etc.*: complex; **~er** *Bruch* 🦴 compound fracture.

Komplott [kɔmˈplɔt] *n* (-[e]s/-e) plot, conspiracy.

kompo|nieren ♪ [kɔmpoˈniːrən] *v/t. and v/i.* (*no -ge-, h*) compose; **2'nist** *m* (-en/-en) composer; **2sition** [~zitsˈjoːn] *f* (-/-en) composition.

Kompott [kɔmˈpɔt] *n* (-[e]s/-e) compote, stewed fruit, *Am. a.* sauce.

komprimieren [kɔmpriˈmiːrən] *v/t.* (*no -ge-, h*) compress.

Kompromi|ß [kɔmproˈmis] *m* (*Kompromisses/Kompromisse*) compromise; **2ßlos** *adj.* uncompromising; **2ttieren** [~ˈtiːrən] *v/t.* (*no -ge-, h*) compromise.

Kondens|ator [kɔndɛnˈzaːtɔr] *m* (-s/-en) 🔋 capacitor, condenser (*a.* 🔧); **2ieren** [~ˈziːrən] *v/t.* (*no -ge-, h*) condense.

Kondens|milch [kɔnˈdɛns-] *f* evaporated milk; **~streifen** 🛩 *m* condensation or vapo(u)r trail; **~wasser** *n* water of condensation.

Konditor [kɔnˈdiːtɔr] *m* (-s/-en) confectioner, pastry-cook; **~ei** [~itoˈraɪ] *f* (-/-en) confectionery, confectioner's (shop); **~eiwaren** *f/pl.* confectionery.

Konfekt [kɔnˈfɛkt] *n* (-[e]s/-e) sweets *pl.*, sweetmeat, *Am. a.* soft candy; chocolates *pl.*

Konfektion [kɔnfɛkˈtsjoːn] *f* (-/-en) (manufacture of) ready-made clothing; **~sanzug** [kɔnfɛkˈtsjoːns-] *m* ready-made suit; **~sgeschäft** *n* ready-made clothes shop.

Konfer|enz [kɔnfeˈrɛnts] *f* (-/-en) conference; **2ieren** [~ˈriːrən] *v/i.* (*no -ge-, h*) confer (*über acc.* on).

Konfession [kɔnfɛˈsjoːn] *f* (-/-en) confession, creed; denomination; **2ell** *adj.* [~oˈnɛl] confessional, denominational; **~sschule** [~ˈsjoːns-] *f* denominational school.

Konfirm|and *eccl.* [kɔnfirˈmant] *m* (-en/-en) candidate for confirmation, confirmee; **~ation** [~ˈtsjoːn] *f* (-/-en) confirmation; **2ieren** [~ˈmiːrən] *v/t.* (*no -ge-, h*) confirm.

konfiszieren 🔏 [kɔnfisˈtsiːrən] *v/t.* (*no -ge-, h*) confiscate, seize.

Konfitüre [kɔnfiˈtyːrə] *f* (-/-n) preserve(s *pl.*), (whole-fruit) jam.

Konflikt [kɔnˈflikt] *m* (-[e]s/-e) conflict.

konform *adv.* [kɔnˈfɔrm]: **~** *gehen mit* agree or concur with.

konfrontieren [kɔnfrɔnˈtiːrən] *v/t.* (*no -ge-, h*) confront (*mit* with).

konfus *adj.* [kɔnˈfuːs] *p., a. ideas:* muddled; *p.* muddle-headed.

Kongreß [kɔnˈgrɛs] *m* (*Kongresses/ Kongresse*) congress; *Am. parl.* Congress; **~halle** *f* congress hall.

König [ˈkøːnɪç] *m* (-s/-e) king; **2lich** *adj.* [ˈ~k-] royal; regal; **2reich** [ˈ~k-] *n* kingdom; **~swürde** [ˈ~ks-] *f* royal dignity, kingship; **~tum** *n* (-s/~er) monarchy; kingship.

Konjug|ation *gr.* [kɔnjugaˈtsjoːn] *f*

(-/-en); Qieren [~'gi:rən] v/t. (no -ge-, h) conjugate.

Konjunkt|iv gr. ['kɔnjuŋkti:f] m (-s/-e) subjunctive (mood); ~ur ✝ [~'tu:r] f (-/-en) trade or business cycle; economic or business situation.

konkret adj. [kɔn'kre:t] concrete.

Konkurrent [kɔnku'rɛnt] m (-en/ -en) competitor, rival.

Konkurrenz [kɔnku'rɛnts] f (-/-en) competition; competitors pl., rivals pl.; sports: event; Qfähig adj. able to compete; competitive; ~geschäft n rival business or firm; ~kampf m competition.

konkur'rieren v/i. (no -ge-, h) compete (mit with; um for).

Konkurs ✝, ⚖ [kɔn'kurs] m (-es/-e) bankruptcy, insolvency, failure; ~ anmelden file a petition in bankruptcy; in ~ gehen or geraten become insolvent, go bankrupt; ~erklärung ⚖ f declaration of insolvency; ~masse ⚖ f bankrupt's estate; ~verfahren ⚖ n bankruptcy proceedings pl.; ~verwalter ⚖ m trustee in bankruptcy; liquidator.

können ['kœnən] 1. v/i. (irr., ge-, h): ich kann nicht I can't, I am not able to; 2. v/t. (irr., ge-, h) know, understand; e-e Sprache ~ know a language, have command of a language; 3. v/aux. (irr., no -ge-, h) be able to inf., be capable of ger.; be allowed or permitted to inf.; es kann sein it may be; du kannst hingehen you may go there; er kann schwimmen he can swim, he knows how to swim; 4. Q n (-s/no pl.) ability; skill; proficiency.

Konnossement ✝ [kɔnɔsə'mɛnt] n (-[e]s/-e) bill of lading.

konnte ['kɔntə] pret. of können.

konsequen|t adj. [kɔnze'kvɛnt] consistent; Qz [~ts] f (-/-en) consistency; consequence; die ~en ziehen do the only thing one can.

konservativ adj. [kɔnzɛrva'ti:f] conservative.

Konserven [kɔn'zɛrvən] f/pl. tinned or Am. canned foods pl.; ~büchse f, ~dose f tin, Am. can; ~fabrik f tinning factory, esp. Am. cannery.

konservieren [kɔnzɛr'vi:rən] v/t. (no -ge-, h) preserve.

Konsonant gr. [kɔnzo'nant] m (-en/ -en) consonant.

Konsortium ✝ [kɔn'zɔrtsjum] n (-s/Konsortien) syndicate.

konstruieren [kɔnstru'i:rən] v/t. (no -ge-, h) gr. construe; ⊕: construct; design.

Konstruk|teur ⊕ [kɔnstruk'tø:r] m (-s/-e) designer; ~tion ⊕ [~'tsjo:n] f (-/-en) construction; ~'tionsfehler ⊕ m constructional defect.

Konsul pol. ['kɔnzul] m (-s/-n) con-

sul; ~at pol. [~'la:t] n (-[e]s/-e) consulate; Q'tieren v/t. (no -ge-, h) consult, seek s.o.'s advice.

Konsum [kɔn'zu:m] m 1. (-s/no pl.) consumption; 2. (-s/-s) co-operative shop, Am. co-operative store, F co-op; 3. (-s/no pl.) consumers' co-operative society, F co-op; ~ent [~u'mɛnt] m (-en/-en) consumer; Qieren [~u'mi:rən] v/t. (no -ge-, h) consume; ~verein m s. Konsum 3.

Kontakt [kɔn'takt] m (-[e]s/-e) contact (a. ⚡); in ~ stehen mit be in contact or touch with.

Kontinent ['kɔntinɛnt] m (-[e]s/-e) continent.

Kontingent [kɔntiŋ'gɛnt] n (-[e]s/ -e) ⚔ contingent, quota (a. ✝).

Konto ✝ ['kɔnto] n (-s/Konten, Kontos, Konti) account; '~auszug ✝ m statement of account; ~korrentkonto ✝ [~ko'rɛnt-] n current account.

Kontor [kɔn'to:r] n (-s/-e) office; ~ist [~o'rist] m (-en/-en) clerk.

Kontrast [kɔn'trast] m (-es/-e) contrast.

Kontroll|e [kɔn'trɔlə] f (-/-n) control; supervision; check; Qieren [~'li:rən] v/t. (no -ge-, h) control; supervise; check.

Kontroverse [kɔntro'vɛrzə] f (-/-n) controversy.

konventionell adj. [kɔnvɛntsjo'nɛl] conventional.

Konversation [kɔnvɛrza'tsjo:n] f (-/-en) conversation; ~slexikon n encyclop(a)edia.

Konzentr|ation [kɔntsɛntra'tsjo:n] f (-/-en) concentration; Qieren [~'tri:rən] v/t. (no -ge-, h) concentrate, focus (attention, etc.) (auf acc. on); sich ~ concentrate (auf acc. on).

Konzern ✝ [kɔn'tsɛrn] m (-s/-e) combine, group.

Konzert ♪ [kɔn'tsɛrt] n (-[e]s/-e) concert; recital; concerto; ~saal ♪ m concert-hall.

Konzession [kɔntsɛ'sjo:n] f (-/-en) concession; licen|ce, Am. -se; Qieren [~o'ni:rən] v/t. (no -ge-, h) license.

Kopf [kɔpf] m (-[e]s/~e) head; top; brains pl.; pipe: bowl; ein fähiger ~ a clever fellow; ~ hoch! chin up!; j-m über den ~ wachsen outgrow s.o.; fig. get beyond s.o.; ~arbeit f brain-work; '~bahnhof 🚆 m terminus, Am. terminal; '~bedeckung f headgear, headwear.

köpfen ['kœpfən] v/t. (ge-, h) behead, decapitate; football: head (ball).

'Kopf|ende n head; '~hörer m headphone, headset; '~kissen n pillow; 'Qlos adj. headless; fig. confused; '~nicken n (-s/no pl.) nod; '~rechnen n (-s/no pl.) mental arithmetic; '~salat m cabbage-lettuce;

'~schmerzen *m/pl.* headache; '~sprung *m* header; '~tuch *n* scarf; ²'über *adv.* head first, headlong; '~weh *n* (-[e]s/-e) *s. Kopfschmerzen;* '~zerbrechen *n* (-s/no *pl.*): *j-m* ~ *machen* puzzle s.o.

Kopie [ko'pi:] *f* (-/-n) copy; dupli-cate; *phot., film:* print; ~rstift *m* indelible pencil.

Koppel ['kɔpəl] 1. *f* (-/-n) *hounds:* couple; *horses:* string; paddock; 2. ⚔ *n* (-s/-) belt; ²n *v/t.* (ge-, h) couple (*a.* ⊕, ⚓).

Koralle [ko'ralə] *f* (-/-n) coral; ~n-fischer *m* coral-fisher.

Korb [kɔrp] *m* (-[e]s/⸚e) basket; *fig.* refusal; *Hahn im* ~ cock of the walk; '~möbel *n/pl.* wicker furni-ture.

Kordel ['kɔrdəl] *f* (-/-n) string, twine; cord.

Korinthe [ko'rintə] *f* (-/-n) currant.

Kork [kɔrk] *m* (-[e]s/-e), '~en *m* (-s/-) cork; '~(en)zieher *m* (-s/-) corkscrew.

Korn [kɔrn] 1. *n* (-[e]s/⸚er) seed; grain; 2. *n* (-[e]s/-e) corn, cereals *pl.*; 3. *n* (-[e]s/⸚-e) front sight; 4. F *m* (-[e]s/-) (German) corn whisky.

körnig *adj.* ['kœrniç] granular; *in compounds:* ...-grained.

Körper ['kœrpər] *m* (-s/-) body (*a. phys.*, 🜍); ⚗ solid; '~bau *m* build, physique; ²behindert *adj.* ['~bə-hindərt] (physically) disabled, handi-capped; '~beschaffenheit *f* con-stitution, physique; '~fülle *f* cor-pulence; '~geruch *m* body-odo(u)r; '~größe *f* stature; '~kraft *f* physi-cal strength; ²lich *adj.* physical; corporal; bodily; '~pflege *f* care of the body, hygiene; '~schaft *f* (-/-en) body (corporate), corporation; '~verletzung 🜍🜍 *f* bodily harm, physical injury.

korrekt *adj.* [kɔ'rɛkt] correct; ²or [~ɔr] *m* (-s/-en) (proof-)reader; ²ur [~'tu:r] *f* (-/-en) correction; ²ur-bogen *m* proof-sheet.

Korrespond|ent [kɔrɛspɔn'dɛnt] *m* (-en/-en) correspondent; ~enz [~ts] *f* (-/-en) correspondence; ²ieren [~'di:rən] *v/i.* (no -ge-, h) corre-spond (*mit* with).

korrigieren [kɔri'gi:rən] *v/t.* (no -ge-, h) correct.

Korsett [kɔr'zɛt] *n* (-[e]s/-e, -s) corset, stays *pl.*

Kosename ['ko:zə-] *m* pet name.

Kosmetik [kɔs'me:tik] *f* (-/no *pl.*) beauty culture; ~erin *f* (-/-nen) beautician, cosmetician.

Kost [kɔst] *f* (-/no *pl.*) food, fare; board; diet; ²bar *adj.* present, *etc.*: costly, expensive; *health, time, etc.:* valuable; *mineral, etc.:* precious.

'kosten[1] *v/t.* (ge-, h) taste, try, sample.

'Kosten[2] 1. *pl.* cost(s *pl.*); expense(s *pl.*), charges *pl.*; *auf* ~ (*gen.*) at the expense of; 2. ² *v/t.* (ge-, h) cost; take, require (*time, etc.*); '~an-schlag *m* estimate, tender; ²frei 1. *adj.* free; 2. *adv.* free of charge; ²los *s. kostenfrei.*

Kost|gänger ['kɔstgɛŋər] *m* (-s/-) boarder; '~geld *n* board-wages *pl.*

köstlich *adj.* ['kœstliç] delicious.

'Kost|probe *f* taste, sample (*a. fig.*); ²spielig *adj.* ['~ʃpi:liç] expensive, costly.

Kostüm [kɔs'ty:m] *n* (-s/-e) cos-tume, dress; suit; ~fest *n* fancy-dress ball.

Kot [ko:t] *m* (-[e]s/no *pl.*) mud, mire; excrement.

Kotelett [kɔt(ə)'lɛt] *n* (-[e]s/-s, ⚒ -e) pork, veal, lamb: cutlet; *pork, veal, mutton:* chop; ~en *pl.* sidewhiskers *pl., Am. a.* sideburns *pl.*

'Kot|flügel *mot. m* mudguard, *Am. a.* fender; ²ig *adj.* muddy, miry.

Krabbe *zo.* ['krabə] *f* (-/-n) shrimp; crab.

krabbeln ['krabəln] *v/i.* (ge-, *sein*) crawl.

Krach [krax] *m* (-[e]s/-e, -s) crack, crash (*a.* ⚒); quarrel, *sl.* bust-up; F row; ~ *machen* kick up a row; ²en *v/i.* (ge-) 1. (h) *thunder:* crash; *cannon:* roar, thunder; 2. (*sein*) crash (*a.* ⚒), smash.

krächzen ['krɛçtsən] *v/t. and v/i.* (ge-, h) croak.

Kraft [kraft] 1. *f* (-/⸚e) strength; force (*a.* ⚔); power (*a.* ⚡, ⊕); energy; vigo(u)r; efficacy; *in* ~ *sein* (*setzen, treten*) be in (put into, come into) operation *or* force; *außer* ~ *setzen* repeal, abolish (*law*); 2. ² *prp.* (*gen.*) by virtue of; '~an-lage ⚡ *f* power plant; '~brühe *f* beef tea; '~fahrer *m* driver, motor-ist; '~fahrzeug *n* motor vehicle.

kräftig *adj.* ['krɛftiç] strong (*a. fig.*), powerful; *fig.* nutritious, rich; ~en ['~gən] (ge-, h) 1. *v/t.* strengthen; 2. *v/i.* give strength.

'kraft|los *adj.* powerless; feeble; weak; ²probe *f* trial of strength; ²rad *n* motor cycle; ²stoff *mot. m* fuel; '~voll *adj.* powerful (*a. fig.*); ²wagen *m* motor vehicle; '²werk ⚡ *n* power station.

Kragen ['kra:gən] *m* (-s/-) collar; '~knopf *m* collar-stud, *Am.* collar button.

Krähe *orn.* ['krɛ:ə] *f* (-/-n) crow; ²n *v/i.* (ge-, h) crow.

Kralle ['kralə] *f* (-/-n) claw (*a. fig.*); talon, clutch.

Kram [kra:m] *m* (-[e]s/no *pl.*) stuff, odds and ends *pl.*; *fig.* affairs *pl.*, business.

Krämer ['krɛ:mər] *m* (-s/-) shop-keeper.

Krampf ⚓ [krampf] m (-[e]s/⁼e)
cramp; spasm, convulsion; '~ader
⚓ f varicose vein; '⚓haft adj. ⚓
spasmodic, convulsive; laugh:
forced.

Kran ⊕ [kra:n] m (-[e]s/⁼e, -e)
crane.

krank adj. [kraŋk] sick; organ, etc.:
diseased; ~ sein p. be ill, esp. Am.
be sick; animal: be sick or ill; ~
werden p. fall ill or esp. Am. sick;
animal: fall sick; '⚓e m, f (-n/-n)
sick person, patient, invalid.

kränkeln ['krɛŋkəln] v/i. (ge-, h) be
sickly, be in poor health.

'kranken fig. v/i. (ge-, h) suffer (an
dat. from).

kränken ['krɛŋkən] v/t. (ge-, h)
offend, injure; wound or hurt s.o.'s
feelings; sich ~ feel hurt (über acc.
at, about).

'Kranken|bett n sick-bed; '~geld n
sick-benefit; '~haus n hospital; '~
kasse f health insurance (fund);
'~kost f invalid diet; '~lager n s.
Krankenbett; '~pflege f nursing;
'~pfleger m male nurse; '~schein
m medical certificate; '~schwester
f (sick-)nurse; '~versicherung f
health or sickness insurance; '~wa-
gen m ambulance; '~zimmer n
sick-room.

'krank|haft adj. morbid, patholog-
ical; '⚓heit f (-/-en) illness, sickness; disease.

'Krankheits|erreger ⚓ m path-
ogenic agent; '~erscheinung f
symptom (a. fig.).

'kränklich adj. sickly, ailing.

'Kränkung f (-/-en) insult, offen|ce,
Am. -se.

Kranz [krants] m (-es/⁼e) wreath;
garland.

Kränzchen fig. ['krɛntsçən] n (-s/-)
tea-party, F hen-party.

kraß adj. [kras] crass, gross.

kratzen ['kratsən] (ge-, h) 1. v/i.
scratch; 2. v/t. scratch; sich ~
scratch (o.s.).

kraulen ['kraulən] (ge-) 1. v/t. (h)
scratch gently; 2. v/i. (sein) sports:
crawl.

kraus adj. [kraus] curly, curled;
crisp; frizzy; die Stirn ~ ziehen knit
one's brow; '⚓e f (-/-n) ruff(le),
frill.

kräuseln ['krɔyzəln] v/t. (ge-, h)
curl, crimp (hair, etc.); pucker
(lips); sich ~ hair: curl; waves, etc.:
ruffle; smoke: curl or wreath up.

Kraut 🌿 [kraut] n 1. (-[e]s/⁼er)
plant; herb; 2. (-[e]s/no pl.) tops
pl.; cabbage; weed.

Krawall [kra'val] m (-[e]s/-e) riot,
shindy, F row, sl. rumpus.

Krawatte [kra'vatə] f (-/-n) (neck-)
tie.

Kreatur [krea'tu:r] f (-/-en) creature.

Krebs [kre:ps] m (-es/-e) zo. crayfish, Am. a. crawfish; ast. Cancer,
Crab; ⚓ cancer; ~e pl. 🦀 returns
pl.

Kredit ✝ [kre'di:t] m (-[e]s/-e) credit; auf ~ on credit; ⚓fähig ✝ adj.
credit-worthy.

Kreide ['kraidə] f (-/-n) chalk; paint.
crayon.

Kreis [krais] m (-es/-e) circle (a.fig.);
ast. orbit; ⚓ circuit; district, Am.
county; fig.: sphere, field; range.

kreischen ['kraiʃən] (ge-, h) 1. v/i.
screech, scream; squeal, shriek;
circular saw, etc.: grate (on the ear);
2. v/t. shriek, screech (insult, etc.).

Kreisel ['kraizəl] m (-s/-) (whip-
ping-)top; '~kompaß m gyro-com-
pass.

kreisen ['kraizən] v/i. (ge-, h) (move
in a) circle; revolve, rotate; ⚓,
bird: circle; bird: wheel; blood,
money: circulate.

kreis|förmig adj. ['kraisfœrmiç]
circular; '⚓lauf m physiol., money,
etc.: circulation; business, trade:
cycle; '⚓laufstörungen ⚓ f/pl.
circulatory trouble; '~rund adj.
circular; '~säge ⊕ f circular saw,
Am. a. buzz saw; '⚓verkehr m
roundabout (traffic).

Krempe ['krɛmpə] f (-/-n) brim (of
hat).

Krempel F ['krɛmpəl] m (-s/no pl.)
rubbish, stuff, lumber.

krepieren [kre'pi:rən] v/i. (no -ge-,
sein) shell: burst, explode; sl. kick
the bucket, peg or snuff out; animal: die, perish.

Krepp [krɛp] m (-s/-s, -e) crêpe;
crape; '~apier ['krɛppapi:r] n crêpe
paper; '~sohle f crêpe(-rubber)
sole.

Kreuz [krɔyts] 1. n (-es/-e) cross (a.
fig.); crucifix; anat. small of the
back; ⚓ sacral region; cards: club(s
pl.); ♩ sharp; zu ~e kriechen eat
humble pie; 2. ♀ adv.: ~ und quer
in all directions; criss-cross.

'kreuzen (ge-, h) 1. v/t. cross, fold
(arms, etc.); ⚓, zo. cross(-breed),
hybridize; sich ~ roads: cross, intersect; plans, etc.: clash; 2. ⚓ v/i.
cruise.

'Kreuzer ⚓ m (-s/-) cruiser.

'Kreuz|fahrer hist. m crusader;
'~fahrt f hist. crusade; ⚓ cruise;
'~feuer n ✕ cross-fire (a. fig.);
⚓igen ['~igən] v/t. (ge-, h) crucify;
'~igung f ['~iguŋ] f (-/-en) cruci-
fixion; '~otter f zo. ✝ common viper;
'~ritter hist. m knight of the Cross;
'~schmerzen m/pl. back ache; '~
spinne zo. f garden- or cross-spi-
der; '~ung f (-/-en) 🦀, roads, etc.:
crossing, intersection; roads: cross-
roads; ⚓, zo. cross-breeding, hy-
bridization; '~verhör ⚖ n cross-
examination; ins ~ nehmen cross-

examine; '**weise** adv. crosswise, crossways; '**worträtsel** n crossword (puzzle); '**zug** hist. m crusade.

kriech|en ['kri:çən] v/i. (irr., ge-, sein) creep, crawl; fig. cringe (vor dat. to, before); '**er** contp. m (-s/-) toady; **erei** contp. [**rai**] f (-/-en) toadyism.

Krieg [kri:k] m (-[e]s/-e) war; im **** at war; s. führen.

kriegen F ['kri:gən] v/t. (ge-, h) catch, seize; get.

Krieg|er ['kri:gər] m (-s/-) warrior; '**erdenkmal** n war memorial; '**erisch** adj. warlike; militant; '**führend** adj. belligerent; '**führung** f warfare.

'**Kriegs|beil** fig. n: das **** begraben bury the hatchet; **beschädigt** adj. ['**bəʃɛːdiçt**] war-disabled; '**beschädigte** m (-n/-n) disabled ex-serviceman; '**dienst** ⚔ m war service; '**dienstverweigerer** ⚔ m (-s/-) conscientious objector; '**erklärung** f declaration of war; '**flotte** f naval force; '**gefangene** m prisoner of war; '**gefangenschaft** ⚔ f captivity; '**gericht** ⚖ n court martial; **gewinnler** ['**gəvinlər**] m (-s/-) war profiteer; '**hafen** m naval port; '**kamerad** m wartime comrade; '**list** f stratagem; '**macht** f military forces pl.; '**minister** hist. m minister of war; Secretary of State for War, Am. Secretary of War; '**ministerium** hist. n ministry of war; War Office, Am. War Department; '**rat** m council of war; '**schauplatz** ⚔ m theat|re or Am. -er of war; '**schiff** n warship; '**schule** f military academy; '**teilnehmer** m combatant; ex-serviceman, Am. veteran; '**treiber** m (-s/-) warmonger; '**verbrecher** m war criminal; '**zug** m (military) expedition, campaign.

Kriminal|beamte [krimi'nɑːl-] m criminal investigator, Am. plainclothes man; **film** m crime film; thriller; **polizei** f criminal investigation department; **roman** m detective or crime novel, thriller, sl. whodun(n)it.

kriminell adj. [krimi'nɛl] criminal; **2e** m (-n/-n) criminal.

Krippe ['kripə] f (-/-n) crib, manger; crèche.

Krise ['kri:zə] f (-/-n) crisis.

Kristall [kris'tal] 1. m (-s/-e) crystal; 2. n (-s/no pl.) crystal(-glass); **2isieren** [..i'zi:rən] v/i. and v/refl. (no -ge-, h) crystallize.

Kriti|k [kri'ti:k] f (-/-en) criticism; ♩, thea., etc.: review, criticism; F unter aller **** beneath contempt; **** üben an (dat.) s. kritisieren; **ker** ['kri:tikər] m (-s/-) critic; books: re-

viewer; **2sch** adj. ['kri:tiʃ] critical (gegenüber of); **2sieren** [kriti'zi:rən] v/t. (no -ge-, h) criticize; review (book).

kritt|eln ['kritəln] v/t. (ge-, h) find fault (an dat. with), cavil (at); **2ler** ['**lər**] m (-s/-) fault-finder, caviller.

Kritzel|ei [kritsə'lai] f (-/-en) scrawl(ing), scribble, scribbling; '**2n** v/t. and v/i. (ge-, h) scrawl, scribble.

kroch [krɔx] pret. of kriechen.

Krokodil zo. [kroko'di:l] n (-s/-e) crocodile.

Krone ['kro:nə] f (-/-n) crown; coronet (of duke, earl, etc.).

krönen ['krø:nən] v/t. (ge-, h) crown (zum König king) (a. fig.).

'**Kron|leuchter** m chandelier; lust|re, Am. -er; electrolier; '**prinz** m crown prince; '**prinzessin** f crown princess.

'**Krönung** f (-/-en) coronation, crowning; fig. climax, culmination.

'**Kronzeuge** ⚖ m chief witness; King's evidence, Am. State's evidence.

Kropf 🌿 [krɔpf] goit|re, Am. -er.

Kröte zo. ['krø:tə] f (-/-n) toad.

Krücke ['krykə] f (-/-n) crutch.

Krug [kru:k] m (-[e]s/⁓e) jug, pitcher; jar; mug; tankard.

Krume ['kru:mə] f (-/-n) crumb; 🌱 topsoil.

Krümel ['kry:məl] m (-s/-) small crumb; '**2n** v/t. and v/i. (ge-, h) crumble.

krumm adj. [krum] p. bent, stooping; limb, nose, etc.: crooked; spine: curved; deal, business, etc.: crooked; '**beinig** adj. bandy- or bow-legged.

krümmen ['krymən] v/t. (ge-, h) bend (arm, back, etc.); crook (finger, etc.); curve (metal sheet, etc.); sich **** person, snake, etc.: writhe; worm, etc.: wriggle; sich vor Schmerzen **** writhe with pain; sich vor Lachen **** be convulsed with laughter.

'**Krümmung** f (-/-en) road, etc.: bend; arch, road, etc.: curve; river, path, etc.: turn, wind, meander; earth's surface, spine, etc.: curvature.

Krüppel ['krypəl] m (-s/-) cripple.

Kruste ['krustə] f (-/-n) crust.

Kübel ['ky:bəl] m (-s/-) tub; pail, bucket.

Kubik|meter [ku'bi:k-] n, m cubic met|re, Am. -er; **wurzel** ⅍ f cube root.

Küche ['kyçə] f (-/-n) kitchen; cuisine, cookery; s. kalt.

Kuchen ['ku:xən] m (-s/-) cake, flan; pastry.

'**Küchen|gerät** n, '**geschirr** n kitchen utensils pl.; '**herd** m (kitchen-)range; cooker, stove; '**schrank** m kitchen cupboard or cabinet; '**zettel** *m* bill of fare, menu.

Kuckuck *orn.* ['kukuk] *m* (-s/-e) cuckoo.

Kufe ['ku:fə] *f* (-/-n) ⚒ skid; *sleigh*, *etc.*: runner.

Küfer ['ky:fər] *m* (-s/-) cooper; cellarman.

Kugel ['ku:gəl] *f* (-/-n) ball; ⚒ bullet; ♈, *geogr.* sphere; *sports*: shot, weight; 2**förmig** *adj.* ['‿fœrmiç] spherical, ball-shaped, globular; '**‿gelenk** ⊕, *anat. n* ball-and-socket joint; '**‿lager** ⊕ *n* ball-bearing; '2n (ge-) 1. *v/i.* (*sein*) *ball*, *etc.*: roll; 2. *v/t.* (*h*) roll (*ball*, *etc.*); *sich* ‿ *children*, *etc.*: roll about; F double up (vor with *laughter*); '**‿schreiber** *m* ball(-point)-pen; '**‿stoßen** *n* (-s/*no pl.*) *sports*: putting the shot *or* weight.

Kuh *zo.* [ku:] *f* (-/‿e) cow.

kühl *adj.* [ky:l] cool (*a. fig.*); '2**anlage** *f* cold-storage plant; '2e *f* (-/*no pl.*) cool(ness); '**‿en** *v/t.* (ge-, *h*) cool (*wine*, *wound*, *etc.*); chill (*wine*, *etc.*); '2er *mot. m* (-s/-) radiator; '2**raum** *m* cold-storage chamber; '2**schrank** *m* refrigerator, F fridge.

kühn *adj.* [ky:n] bold (*a. fig.*), daring; audacious.

'**Kuhstall** *m* cow-house, byre, *Am. a.* cow barn.

Küken *orn.* ['ky:kən] *n* (-s/-) chick.

kulant ⚓ *adj.* [ku'lant] firm, *etc.*: accommodating, obliging; *price*, *terms*, *etc.*: fair, easy.

Kulisse [ku'lisə] *f* (-/-n) *thea.* wing, side-scene; *fig.* front; ‿n *pl. a.* scenery; *hinter den* ‿n behind the scenes.

Kult [kult] *m* (-[e]s/-e) cult, worship.

kultivieren [kulti'vi:rən] *v/t.* (*no* -ge-, *h*) cultivate (*a. fig.*).

Kultur [kul'tu:r] *f* (-/-en) ♪ cultivation; *fig.*: culture; civilization; 2**ell** *adj.* [‿u'rel] cultural; '**‿film** [‿'tu:r-] *m* educational film; **‿geschichte** *f* history of civilization; **‿volk** *n* civilized people.

Kultus ['kultus] *m* (-/Kulte) *s.* Kult; '**‿minister** *m* minister of education and cultural affairs; '**‿ministerium** *n* ministry of education and cultural affairs.

Kummer ['kumər] *m* (-s/*no pl.*) grief, sorrow; trouble, worry.

kümmer|lich *adj.* ['kymərliç] *life*, *etc.*: miserable, wretched; *conditions*, *etc.*: pitiful, pitiable; *result*, *etc.*: poor; *resources*: scanty; '**‿n** *v/t.* (ge-, *h*): es kümmert mich I bother, I worry; *sich* ‿ um look after, take care of; see to; meddle with.

'**kummervoll** *adj.* sorrowful.

Kump|an F [kum'pa:n] *m* (-s/-e) companion; F mate, chum, *Am.* F *a.*

buddy; '**‿el** ['‿pəl] *m* (-s/-, F -s) ⚒ pitman, collier; F work-mate; F *s.* Kumpan.

Kunde ['kundə] 1. *m* (-n/-n) customer, client; 2. *f* (-/-n) knowledge.

Kundgebung ['kunt-] *f* (-/-en) manifestation; *pol.* rally.

kündig|en ['kyndigən] (ge-, *h*) 1. *v/i.*: j-m ‿ give s.o. notice; 2. *v/t.* ⚓ call in (*capital*); ⚓ cancel (*contract*); *pol.* denounce (*treaty*); '2**ung** *f* (-/-en) notice; ⚓ calling in; ⚓ cancellation; *pol.* denunciation.

'**Kundschaft** *f* (-/-en) customers *pl.*, clients *pl.*; custom, clientele; '**‿er** ⚒ *m* (-s/-) scout; spy.

künftig ['kynftiç] 1. *adj.* event, years, *etc.*: future; *event*, *programme*, *etc.*: coming; *life*, *world*, *etc.*: next; 2. *adv.* in future, from now on.

Kunst [kunst] *f* (-/‿e) art; skill; '**‿akademie** *f* academy of arts; '**‿ausstellung** *f* art exhibition; '**‿druck** *m* art print(ing); '**‿dünger** *m* artificial manure, fertilizer; '2**fertig** *adj.* skilful, skilled; '**‿fertigkeit** *f* artistic skill; '**‿gegenstand** *m* objet d'art; '2**gerecht** *adj.* skilful; professional, expert; **‿geschichte** *f* history of art; '**‿gewerbe** *n* arts and crafts *pl.*; applied arts *pl.*; '**‿glied** *n* artificial limb; '**‿griff** *m* trick, dodge; artifice, knack; '**‿händler** *m* art-dealer; '**‿kenner** *m* connoisseur of *or* in art; '**‿leder** *n* imitation *or* artificial leather.

Künstler ['kynstlər] *m* (-s/-) artist; ♪, *thea.* performer; '2**isch** *adj.* artistic.

künstlich *adj.* ['kynstliç] eye, *flower*, *light*, *etc.*: artificial; *teeth*, *hair*, *etc.*: false; *fibres*, *dyes*, *etc.*: synthetic.

'**Kunst|liebhaber** *m* art-lover; '**‿maler** *m* artist, painter; '**‿reiter** *m* equestrian; circus-rider; '**‿schätze** ['‿ʃetsə] *m/pl.* art treasures *pl.*; '**‿seide** *f* artificial silk, rayon; '**‿stück** *n* feat, trick, F stunt; '**‿tischler** *m* cabinet-maker; '**‿verlag** *m* art publishers *pl.*; '2**voll** *adj.* artistic, elaborate; '**‿werk** *n* work of art.

kunterbunt F *fig. adj.* ['kuntər-] higgledy-piggledy.

Kupfer ['kupfər] *n* (-s/*no pl.*) copper; '**‿geld** *n* copper coins *pl.*, F coppers *pl.*; '2n *adj.* (of) copper; '2**rot** *adj.* copper-colo(u)red; '**‿stich** *m* copper-plate engraving.

Kupon [ku'põ:] *m* (-s/-s) *s.* Coupon.

Kuppe ['kupə] *f* (-/-n) rounded hilltop; *nail*: head.

Kuppel △ ['kupəl] *f* (-/-n) dome, cupola; **‿ei** ⚓ ['‿'lai] *f* (-/-en) procuring; '2n (ge-, *h*) 1. *v/t. s.* koppeln; 2. *mot. v/i.* declutch.

Kuppl|er ['kuplər] *m* (-s/-) pimp, procurer; '**‿ung** *f* (-/-en) ⊕ coupling (*a.* ⚒); *mot.* clutch.

Kur [ku:r] f (-/-en) course of treatment, cure.

Kür [ky:r] f (-/-en) sports: s. Kürlauf; voluntary exercise.

Kuratorium [kura'to:rium] n (-s/ Kuratorien) board of trustees.

Kurbel ⊕ ['kurbəl] f (-/-n) crank, winch, handle; '2n (ge-, h) 1. v/t. shoot (film); in die Höhe ~ winch up (load, etc.); wind up (car window, etc.); 2. v/i. crank.

Kürbis ⚘ ['kyrbis] m (-ses/-se) pumpkin.

'**Kur|gast** m visitor to or patient at a health resort or spa; '~haus n spa hotel.

Kurier [ku'ri:r] m (-s/-e) courier, express (messenger).

kurieren ⚕ [ku'ri:rən] v/t. (no -ge-, h) cure.

kurios adj. [kur'jo:s] curious, odd, strange, queer. [skating.)

'**Kürlauf** m sports: free (roller))

'**Kur|ort** m health resort; spa; '~pfuscher m quack (doctor); ~pfusche'rei f (-/-en) quackery.

Kurs [kurs] m (-es/-e) ✝ currency; ✝ rate, price; ⚓ and fig. course, class; '~bericht ✝ m market-report; '~buch 🚂 n railway guide, Am. railroad guide.

Kürschner ['kyrʃnər] m (-s/-) furrier.

kursieren [kur'zi:rən] v/i. (no -ge-, h) money, etc.: circulate, be in circulation; rumour, etc.: circulate, be afloat, go about.

Kursivschrift typ. [kur'zi:f-] f italics pl.

Kursus ['kurzus] m (-/Kurse) course, class.

'**Kurs|verlust** ✝ m loss on the stock exchange; '~wert ✝ m market value; '~zettel ✝ m stock exchange list.

Kurve ['kurvə] f (-/-n) curve; road, etc.: a. bend, turn.

kurz [kurts] 1. adj. space: short; time, etc.: short, brief; ~ und bündig brief, concise; ~e Hose shorts pl.; mit ~en Worten with a few words; den kürzeren ziehen get the worst of it; 2. adv. in short; ~ angebunden sein be curt or sharp; ~ und gut in short, in a word; ~ vor London short of London; sich ~ fassen be brief or concise; in ~em before long, shortly; vor ~em a short time ago; zu ~ kommen come off badly, get a raw deal; um es ~ zu sagen to cut a long story short; '2arbeit ✝ f short-

time work; '2arbeiter ✝ m short-time worker; '2atmig adj. ['~?a:t-miç] short-winded.

Kürze ['kyrtsə] f (-/no pl.) shortness; brevity; in ~ shortly, before long; '2n v/t. (ge-, h) shorten (dress, etc.) (um by); abridge, condense (book, etc.); cut, reduce (expenses, etc.).

'**kurz|er'hand** adv. without hesitation; on the spot; '2film m short (film); '2form f shortened form; '~fristig adj. short-term; ✝ bill, etc.: short-dated; '2geschichte f (short) short story; '~lebig adj. ['~le:biç] short-lived; '2nachrichten f/pl. news summary.

kürzlich adv. ['kyrtsliç] lately, recently, not long ago.

'**Kurz|schluß** ⚡ m short circuit, F short; '~schrift f shorthand, stenography; '2sichtig adj. short-sighted, near-sighted; 2'um adv. in short, in a word.

'**Kürzung** f (-/-en) shortening (of dress, etc.); abridg(e)ment, condensation (of book, etc.); cut, reduction (of expenses, etc.).

'**Kurz|waren** f/pl. haberdashery, Am. dry goods pl., notions pl.; '~weil f (-/no pl.) amusement, entertainment; '2weilig adj. amusing, entertaining; '~welle ⚡ f short wave; radio: short-wave band.

Kusine [ku'zi:nə] f (-/-n) s. Cousine.

Kuß [kus] m (Kusses/Küsse) kiss; '2echt adj. kiss-proof.

küssen ['kysən] v/t. and v/i. (ge-, h) kiss.

'**kußfest** adj. s. kußecht.

Küste ['kystə] f (-/-n) coast; shore.

'**Küsten|bewohner** m inhabitant of a coastal region; '~fischerei f inshore fishery or fishing; '~gebiet n coastal area or region; '~schiffahrt f coastal shipping.

Küster eccl. ['kystər] m (-s/-) verger, sexton, sacristan.

Kutsch|bock ['kutʃ-] m coach-box; '~e f (-/-n) carriage, coach; '~enschlag m carriage-door, coach-door; '~er m (-s/-) coachman; 2ieren [~'tʃi:rən] (no -ge-) 1. v/t. (h) drive s.o. in a coach; 2. v/i. (h) (drive a) coach; 3. v/i. (sein) (drive or ride in a) coach.

Kutte ['kutə] f (-/-n) cowl.

Kutter ⚓ ['kutər] m (-s/-) cutter.

Kuvert [ku'vert; ku've:r] n (-[e]s/-e; -s/-s) envelope; at table: cover.

Kux ⚒ [kuks] m (-es/-e) mining share.

L

Lab *zo.* [lɑːp] *n* (-[e]s/-e) rennet.

labil *adj.* [laˈbiːl] unstable (*a.* ⊕, ♣); *phys.*, ♪ labile.

Labor [laˈboːr] *n* (-s/-s, -e) *s.* **Laboratorium**; ~**ant** [laboˈrant] *m* (-en/-en) laboratory assistant; ~**atorium** [labora'toːrjum] *n* (-s/ *Laboratorien*) laboratory; **2ieren** [~oˈriːrən] *v/i.* (*no* -ge-, *h*): ~ *an* (*dat.*) labo(u)r under, suffer from.

Labyrinth [labyˈrint] *n* (-[e]s/-e) labyrinth, maze.

Lache [ˈlaxə] *f* (-/-n) pool, puddle.

lächeln [ˈlɛçəln] **1.** *v/i.* (ge-, *h*) smile (*über acc.* at); *höhnisch* ~ sneer (*über acc.* at); **2.** ♀ *n* (-s/*no pl.*) smile; *höhnisches* ~ sneer.

lachen [ˈlaxən] **1.** *v/i.* (ge-, *h*) laugh (*über acc.* at); **2.** ♀ *n* (-s/*no pl.*) laugh(ter).

lächerlich *adj.* [ˈlɛçərliç] ridiculous, laughable, ludicrous; absurd; derisory, scoffing; ~ make ridicule; *sich* ~ *machen* make a fool of o.s.

Lachs *ichth.* [laks] *m* (-es/-e) salmon.

Lack [lak] *m* (-[e]s/-e) (gum-)lac; varnish; lacquer, enamel; **2ieren** [laˈkiːrən] *v/t.* (*no* -ge-, *h*) lacquer, varnish, enamel; '~**leder** *n* patent leather; '~**schuhe** *m/pl.* patent leather shoes *pl.*, F patents *pl.*

Lade|fähigkeit [ˈlaːdə-] *f* loading capacity; '~**fläche** *f* loading area; '~**hemmung** ✗ *f* jam, stoppage; '~**linie** ⊕ *f* load-line.

laden[1] [ˈlaːdən] *v/t.* (*irr.*, ge-, *h*) load; load (*gun*), charge (*a.* ⚡); freight, ship; ⟂ cite, summon; invite, ask (*guest*).

Laden[2] [~] *m* (-s/=) shop, *Am.* store; shutter; '~**besitzer** *m s.* **Ladeninhaber**; '~**dieb** *m* shop-lifter; '~**diebstahl** *m* shop-lifting; '~**hüter** *m* drug on the market; '~**inhaber** *m* shopkeeper, *Am.* storekeeper; '~**kasse** *f* till; '~**preis** *m* selling-price, retail price; '~**schild** *n* shopsign; '~**schluß** *m* closing time; *nach* ~ after hours; '~**tisch** *m* counter.

'**Lade|platz** *m* loading-place; '~**rampe** *f* loading platform *or* ramp; '~**raum** *m* loading space; ⚓ hold; '~**schein** ⚓ *m* bill of lading.

'**Ladung** *f* (-/-en) loading; load, freight; ⚓ cargo; ⚡ charge (*a. of gun*); ⟂ summons.

lag [laːk] *pret. of* **liegen**.

Lage [ˈlaːgə] *f* (-/-n) situation, position; site, location (*of building*); state, condition; attitude; *geol.* layer, stratum; round (*of beer, etc.*); *in der* ~ *sein zu inf.* be able to *inf.*, be in a position to *inf.*; *versetzen*

Sie sich in meine ~ put yourself in my place.

Lager [ˈlaːgər] *n* (-s/-) couch, bed; den, lair (*of wild animals*); *geol.* deposit; ⊕ bearing; warehouse, storehouse, depot; store, stock (♦ *pl. a.* Läger); ✗, *etc.*: camp, encampment; *auf* ~ ♦ on hand, in stock; '~**buch** *n* stock-book; '~**feuer** *n* camp-fire; '~**geld** *n* storage; '~**haus** *n* warehouse; '2**n** (ge-, *h*) **1.** *v/i.* lie down, rest; ✗ (en)camp; ♦ be stored; **2.** *v/t.* lay down; ✗ (en)camp; ♦ store, warehouse; *sich* ~ lie down, rest; '~**platz** *m* ♦ depot; resting-place; ✗, *etc.*: camp-site; '~**raum** *m* store-room; '~**ung** *f* (-/-en) storage (*of goods*).

Lagune [laˈguːnə] *f* (-/-n) lagoon.

lahm *adj.* [laːm] lame; '~**en** *v/i.* (ge-, *h*) be lame.

lähmen [ˈlɛːmən] *v/t.* (ge-, *h*) (make) lame; paraly|se, *Am.* -ze (*a. fig.*).

'**lahmlegen** *v/t.* (*sep.*, -ge-, *h*) paraly|se, *Am.* -ze; obstruct.

'**Lähmung** ♣ *f* (-/-en) paralysis.

Laib [laip] *m* (-[e]s/-e) loaf.

Laich [laiç] *m* (-[e]s/-e) spawn; '2**en** *v/i.* (ge-, *h*) spawn.

Laie [ˈlaiə] *m* (-n/-n) layman; amateur; '~**nbühne** *f* amateur theat|re, *Am.* -er.

Lakai [laˈkai] *m* (-en/-en) lackey (*a. fig.*), footman.

Lake [ˈlaːkə] *f* (-/-n) brine, pickle.

Laken [ˈlaːkən] *n* (-s/-) sheet.

lallen [ˈlalən] *v/i. and v/t.* (ge-, *h*) stammer; babble.

Lamelle [laˈmɛlə] *f* (-/-n) lamella, lamina; ♀ gill (*of mushrooms*).

lamentieren [lamɛnˈtiːrən] *v/i.* (*no* -ge-, *h*) lament (*um* for; *über acc.* over).

Lamm *zo.* [lam] *n* (-[e]s/=er) lamb; '~**fell** *n* lambskin; '2**fromm** *adj.* (as) gentle *or* (as) meek as a lamb.

Lampe [ˈlampə] *f* (-/-n) lamp.

'**Lampen|fieber** *n* stage fright; '~**licht** *n* lamplight; '~**schirm** *m* lamp-shade.

Lampion [lãˈpjõː] *m, n* (-s/-s) Chinese lantern.

Land [lant] *n* (-[e]s/=er, *poet.* -e) land; country; territory; ground, soil; *an* ~ *gehen* go ashore; *auf dem* ~ *e* in the country; *aufs* ~ *gehen* go into the country; *außer* ~ *es gehen* go abroad; *zu* ~ *e* by land; '~**arbeiter** *m* farm-hand; '~**besitz** *m* landed property; ⟂ real estate; '~**besitzer** *m* landowner, landed proprietor; '~**bevölkerung** *f* rural population.

Lande|bahn ✈ [ˈlandə-] *f* runway; '~**deck** ✈ *n* flight-deck.

land'einwärts adv. upcountry, inland.

landen ['landən] (ge-) 1. v/i. (sein) land; 2. v/t. (h) ⚓ disembark (troups); ✈ land, set down (troups).

'Landenge f neck of land, isthmus.

Landeplatz ✈ ['landə-] m landing-field.

Ländereien [lendə'raɪən] pl. landed property, lands pl., estates pl.

Länderspiel ['lendər-] n sports: international match.

Landes|grenze ['landəs-] f frontier, boundary; '**~innere** n interior, inland, upcountry; '**~kirche** f national church; Brt. Established Church; '**~regierung** f government; in Germany: Land government; '**~sprache** f native language, vernacular; '2**üblich** adj. customary; '**~verrat** m treason; '**~verräter** m traitor to his country; '**~verteidigung** f national defen|ce, Am. -se.

'Land|flucht f rural exodus; '**~friedensbruch** ⚖ m breach of the public peace; '**~gericht** n appr. district court; '**~gewinnung** f (-/-en) reclamation of land; '**~gut** n country-seat, estate; '**~haus** n country-house, cottage; '**~karte** f map; '**~kreis** m rural district; 2**läufig** adj. ['~lɔyfiç] customary, current, common.

ländlich adj. ['lentliç] rural, rustic.

'Land|maschinen f/pl. agricultural or farm equipment; '**~partie** f picnic, outing, excursion into the country; '**~plage** iro. f nuisance; '**~rat** m (-[e]s/~e) appr. district president; '**~ratte** ⚓ f landlubber; '**~recht** n common law; '**~regen** m persistent rain.

'Landschaft f (-/-en) province, district, region; countryside, scenery; esp. paint. landscape; '2**lich** adj. provincial; scenic (beauty, etc.).

'Landsmann m (-[e]s/Landsleute) (fellow-)countryman, compatriot; was sind Sie für ein ~? what's your native country?

'Land|straße f highway, high road; '**~streicher** m (-s/-) vagabond, tramp, Am. sl. hobo; '**~streitkräfte** f/pl. land forces pl., the Army; ground forces pl.; '**~strich** m tract of land, region; '**~tag** m Landtag, Land parliament.

Landung ['landuŋ] f (-/-en) ⚓, ✈ landing; disembarkation; arrival; '**~sbrücke** ⚓ f floating: landing-stage; pier; '**~ssteg** ⚓ m gangway, gang-plank.

'Land|vermesser m (-s/-) surveyor; '**~vermessung** f land-surveying; 2**wärts** adv. ['~verts] landward(s); '**~weg** m: auf dem ~e by land; '**~wirt** m farmer, agriculturist; '**~wirtschaft** f agriculture, farming; 2**wirtschaftlich** adj. agri-

cultural; ~e Maschinen f/pl. s. Landmaschinen; '**~zunge** f spit.

lang [laŋ] 1. adj. long; p. tall; er machte ein ~es Gesicht his face fell; 2. adv. long; e-e Woche ~ for a week; über kurz oder ~ sooner or later; ~(e) anhaltend continuous; ~(e) entbehrt long-missed; ~(e) ersehnt long-wished-for; das ist schon ~(e) her that was a long time ago; ~ und breit at (full or great) length; noch ~(e) nicht not for a long time yet; far from ger.; wie ~e lernen Sie schon Englisch? how long have you been learning English?; ~atmig adj. ['~aːtmiç] long-winded; '~e adv. s. lang 2.

Länge ['leŋə] f (-/-n) length; tallness; geogr., ast. longitude; der ~ nach (at) full length, lengthwise.

langen ['laŋən] v/i. (ge-, h) suffice, be enough; ~ nach reach for.

'Längen|grad m degree of longitude; '**~maß** n linear measure.

'länger 1. adj. longer; ~e Zeit (for) some time; 2. adv. longer; ich kann es nicht ~ ertragen I cannot bear it any longer; je ~, je lieber the longer the better.

'Langeweile f (-, Langenweile/no pl.) boredom, tediousness, ennui.

'lang|fristig adj. long-term; '**~jährig** adj. of long standing; ~e Erfahrung (many) years of experience; '2**lauf** m skiing: cross-country run or race.

'länglich adj. longish, oblong.

'Langmut f (-/no pl.) patience, forbearance.

längs [leŋs] 1. prp. (gen., dat.) along(side of); ~ der Küste fahren ⚓ (sail along the) coast; 2. adv. lengthwise; '2**achse** f longitudinal axis.

'lang|sam adj. slow; 2**schläfer** ['~ʃlɛːfər] m (-s/-) late riser, lie-abed; '2**spielplatte** f long-playing record.

längst adv. [leŋst] long ago or since; ich weiß es ~ I have known it for a long time; '**~ens** adv. at the longest; at the latest; at the most.

'lang|stielig adj. long-handled; ♀ long-stemmed, long-stalked; '2**streckenlauf** m long-distance run or race; 2**weile** f (-, Langenweile/no pl.) s. Langeweile; '**~weilen** v/t. (ge-, h) bore; sich ~ be bored; '**~weilig** adj. tedious, boring, dull; ~e Person bore; '2**welle** f ♀ long wave; radio: long wave band; **~wierig** adj. ['~viːriç] protracted, lengthy; ♣ lingering.

Lanze ['lantsə] f (-/-n) spear, lance.

Lappalie [la'paːljə] f (-/-n) trifle.

Lapp|en ['lapən] m (-s/-) patch; rag; duster; (dish- or floor-)cloth; anat., ♀ lobe; '2**ig** adj. flabby.

läppisch adj. ['lepiʃ] foolish, silly.

Lärche ♀ ['lɛrçə] f (-/-n) larch.

Lärm [lɛrm] m (-[e]s/no pl.) noise; din; ~ schlagen give the alarm; '**2en** v/i. (ge-, h) make a noise; '**2end** adj. noisy.

Larve ['larfə] f (-/-n) mask; face (often iro.); zo. larva, grub.

las [lɑːs] pret. of lesen.

lasch F adj. [laʃ] limp, lax.

Lasche ['laʃə] f (-/-n) strap; tongue (of shoe).

lassen ['lasən] (irr., h) **1.** v/t. (ge-) let; leave; laß das! don't!; laß das Weinen! stop crying!; ich kann es nicht ~ I cannot help (doing) it; sein Leben ~ für sacrifice one's life for; **2.** v/i. (ge-): von et. ~ desist from s.th., renounce s.th.; do without s.th.; **3.** v/aux. (no -ge-) allow, permit, let; make, cause; drucken ~ have s.th. printed; gehen ~ let s.o. go; ich habe ihn dieses Buch lesen ~ I have made him read this book; von sich hören ~ send word; er läßt sich nichts sagen he won't take advice; es läßt sich nicht leugnen there is no denying (the fact).

lässig adj. ['lɛsiç] indolent, idle; sluggish; careless.

Last [last] f (-/-en) load; burden; weight; cargo, freight; fig. weight, charge, trouble; zu ~en von ✝ to the debit of; j-m zur ~ fallen be a burden to s.o.; j-m et. zur ~ legen lay s.th. at s.o.'s door or to s.o.'s charge; '**~auto** n s. Lastkraftwagen.

'lasten v/i. (ge-, h): ~ auf (dat.) weigh or press (up)on; '**2aufzug** m goods lift, Am. freight elevator.

Laster ['lastər] n (-s/-) vice.

Lästerer ['lɛstərər] m (-s/-) slanderer, backbiter.

'lasterhaft adj. vicious; corrupt.

Läster|maul ['lɛstər-] n s. Lästerer; '**2n** v/i. (ge-, h) slander, calumniate, defame; abuse; '**~ung** f (-/-en) slander, calumny.

lästig adj. ['lɛstiç] troublesome; annoying; uncomfortable, inconvenient.

'Last|kahn m barge, lighter; '**~kraftwagen** m lorry, Am. truck; '**~schrift** ✝ f debit; '**~tier** n pack animal; '**~wagen** m s. Lastkraftwagen.

Latein [la'taɪn] n (-s/no pl.) Latin; **2isch** adj. Latin.

Laterne [la'tɛrnə] f (-/-n) lantern; street-lamp; '**~npfahl** m lamp-post.

latschen F ['lɑːtʃən] v/i. (ge-, sein) shuffle (along).

Latte ['latə] f (-/-n) pale; lath; sports: bar; '**~nkiste** f crate; '**~nverschlag** m latticed partition; '**~nzaun** m paling, Am. picket fence.

Lätzchen ['lɛtsçən] n (-s/-) bib, feeder.

lau adj. [lau] tepid, lukewarm (a. fig.).

Laub [laup] n (-[e]s/no pl.) foliage, leaves pl.; '**~baum** m deciduous tree.

Laube ['laubə] f (-/-n) arbo(u)r, bower; '**~ngang** m arcade.

'Laub|frosch zo. m tree-frog; '**~säge** f fret-saw.

Lauch ♀ [laux] m (-[e]s/-e) leek.

Lauer ['lauər] f (-/no pl.): auf der ~ liegen or sein lie in wait or ambush, be on the look-out; '**2n** v/i. (ge-, h) lurk (auf acc. for); ~ auf (acc.) watch for; '**2nd** adj. louring, lowering.

Lauf [lauf] m (-[e]s/-e) run(ning); sports: a. run, heat; race; current (of water); course; barrel (of gun); ♪ run; im ~e der Zeit in (the course of time; '**~bahn** f career; '**~bursche** m errand-boy, office-boy; '**~disziplin** f sports: running event.

'laufen (irr., ge-) **1.** v/i. (sein) run; walk; flow; time: pass, go by, elapse; leak; die Dinge ~ lassen let things slide; j-n ~ lassen let s.o. go; **2.** v/t. (sein, h) run; walk; '**~d** adj. running; current; regular; ~en Monats ✝ instant; auf dem ~en sein be up to date, be fully informed.

Läufer ['lɔyfər] m (-s/-) runner (a. carpet); chess: bishop; football: half-back.

'Lauf|masche f ladder, Am. a. run; '**~paß** F m sack, sl. walking papers pl.; '**~planke** ♪ f gang-board, gang-plank; '**~schritt** m: im ~ running; '**~steg** m footbridge; ♪ gangway.

Lauge ['laugə] f (-/-n) lye.

Laun|e ['launə] f (-/-n) humo(u)r; mood; temper; caprice, fancy, whim; guter ~ in (high) spirits; '**2enhaft** adj. capricious; **2isch** adj. moody; wayward.

Laus zo. [laus] f (-/-e) louse; '**~bub** ['~buːp] m (-en/-en) young scamp, F young devil, rascal.

lausch|en ['lauʃən] v/i. (ge-, h) listen; eavesdrop; '**~ig** adj. snug, cosy; peaceful.

laut [laut] **1.** adj. loud (a. fig.); noisy; **2.** adv. aloud, loud(ly); (sprechen Sie) ~er! speak up!, Am. louder!; **3.** prp. (gen., dat.) according to; ✝ as per; **4.** ♀ m (-[e]s/-e) sound; '**2e** ♪ f (-/-n) lute; '**~en** v/i. (ge-, h) sound; words, etc.: run; read; ~ auf (acc.) passport, etc.: be issued to.

läuten ['lɔytən] (ge-, h) **1.** v/i. ring; toll; es läutet the bell is ringing; **2.** v/t. ring; toll.

'lauter adj. pure; clear; genuine; sincere; mere, nothing but, only.

läuter|n ['lɔytərn] v/t. (ge-, h) purify; ⊕ cleanse; refine; '**2ung** f (-/-en) purification; refining.

'laut|los adj. noiseless; mute; silent; silence: hushed; **'schrift** f phonetic transcription; **'sprecher** m loud-speaker; **'stärke** f sound intensity; radio: (sound-)volume; **stärkeregler** ['re:glər] m (-s/-) volume control.

'lauwarm adj. tepid, lukewarm.

Lava geol. ['la:va] f (-/Laven) lava.

Lavendel ♣ [la'vɛndəl] m (-s/-) lavender.

lavieren [la'vi:rən] v/i. (no -ge-, h, sein) ♣ tack (a. fig.).

Lawine [la'vi:nə] f (-/-n) avalanche.

lax adj. [laks] lax, loose; morals: a. easy.

Lazarett [latsa'rɛt] n (-[e]s/-e) (military) hospital.

leben¹ ['le:bən] (ge-, h) **1.** v/i. live; be alive; Sie wohl! good-bye!, farewell!; j-n hochleben lassen cheer s.o.; at table: drink s.o.'s health; von et. live on s.th.; hier lebt es sich gut it is pleasant living here; **2.** v/t. live (one's life).

Leben² [] n (-s/-) life; stir, animation, bustle; am bleiben remain alive, survive; am erhalten keep alive; ein neues beginnen turn over a new leaf; ins rufen call into being; sein aufs Spiel setzen risk one's life; sein lang all one's life; ums kommen lose one's life; perish.

lebendig adj. [le'bɛndiç] living; pred.: alive; quick; lively.

'Lebens|alter n age; **'anschauung** f outlook on life; **'art** f manners pl., behavio(u)r; **'auffassung** f philosophy of life; **'bedingungen** f/pl. living conditions pl.; **'beschreibung** f life, biography; **'dauer** f span of life; ⊕ durability; **'echt** adj. true to life; **'erfahrung** f experience of life; **'fähig** adj. ♣ and fig. viable; **'gefahr** f danger of life; ! danger (of death)!; unter at the risk of one's life; **'gefährlich** adj. dangerous (to life), perilous; **'gefährte** m life's companion; **'größe** f life-size; in at full length; **'kraft** f vital power, vigo(u)r, vitality; **'länglich** adj. for life, lifelong; **'lauf** m course of life; personal record, curriculum vitae; **'lustig** adj. gay, merry; **'mittel** pl. food (-stuffs pl.), provisions pl., groceries pl.; **'müde** adj. weary or tired of life; **'notwendig** adj. vital, essential; **'retter** m life-saver, rescuer; **'standard** m standard of living; **'unterhalt** m livelihood; s-n verdienen earn one's living; **'versicherung** f life-insurance; **'wandel** m life, (moral) conduct; **'weise** f mode of living, habits pl.; gesunde regimen; **'weisheit** f worldly wisdom; **'wichtig** adj. vital, essential; e Organe pl. vitals

pl.; **'zeichen** n sign of life; **'zeit** f lifetime; auf for life.

Leber anat. ['le:bər] f (-/-n) liver; **'fleck** m mole; **'krank** adj., **'leidend** adj. suffering from a liver-complaint; **'tran** m cod-liver oil; **'wurst** f liver-sausage, Am. liver-wurst.

'Lebewesen n living being, creature.

Lebe'wohl n (-[e]s/-e, -s) farewell.

leb|haft adj. ['le:phaft] lively; vivid; spirited; interest: keen; traffic: busy; **'kuchen** m gingerbread; **'los** adj. lifeless; **'zeiten** pl.: zu s-n in his lifetime.

lechzen ['lɛçtsən] v/i. (ge-, h): nach languish or yearn or pant for.

Leck [lɛk] **1.** n (-[e]s/-s) leak; **2.** ♀ adj. leaky; werden ♣ spring a leak.

lecken ['lɛkən] (ge-, h) **1.** v/t. lick; **2.** v/i. lick; leak.

lecker adj. ['lɛkər] dainty; delicious; **'bissen** m dainty, delicacy.

Leder ['le:dər] n (-s/-) leather; in gebunden leather-bound; **'n** adj. leathern, of leather.

ledig adj. ['le:diç] single, unmarried; child: illegitimate; **'lich** adv. ['k-] solely, merely.

Lee ♣ [le:] f (-/no pl.) lee (side).

leer [le:r] **1.** adj. empty; vacant; void; vain; blank; **2.** adv.: laufen ⊕ idle; **'e** f (-/no pl.) emptiness, void (a. fig.); phys. vacuum; **'en** v/t. (ge-, h) empty; clear (out); pour out; **'gut** ⚓ n empties pl.; **'lauf** m ⊕ idling; mot. neutral gear; fig. waste of energy; **'stehend** adj. flat: empty, unoccupied, vacant.

legal adj. [le'ga:l] legal, lawful.

Legat [le'ga:t] **1.** m (-en/-en) legate; **2.** n (-[e]s/-e) legacy.

legen ['le:gən] (ge-, h) **1.** v/t. lay; place, put; sich wind, etc.: calm down, abate; cease; Wert auf (acc.) attach importance to; **2.** v/i. hen: lay.

Legende [le'gɛndə] f (-/-n) legend.

legieren [le'gi:rən] v/t. (no -ge-, h) ⊕ alloy; cookery: thicken (mit with).

Legislative [le:gisla'ti:və] f (-/-n) legislative body or power.

legitim adj. [legi'ti:m] legitimate; **'ieren** [i'mi:rən] v/t. (no -ge-, h) legitimate; authorize; sich prove one's identity.

Lehm [le:m] m (-[e]s/-e) loam; mud; **'ig** adj. loamy.

Lehn|e ['le:nə] f (-/-n) support; arm, back (of chair); **'en** (ge-, h) **1.** v/i. lean (an dat. against); **2.** v/t. lean, rest (an acc., gegen against); sich an (acc.) lean against; sich auf (acc.) rest or support o.s. (up-)on; sich aus dem Fenster lean out of the window; **'sessel** m, **'stuhl** m armchair, easy chair.

Lehrbuch ['le:r-] *n* textbook.
Lehre ['le:rə] *f* (-/-n) rule, precept; doctrine; system; science; theory; lesson, warning; moral (*of fable*); instruction, tuition; ⊕ ga(u)ge; ⊕ pattern; *in der* ~ *sein* be apprenticed (*bei to*); *in die* ~ *geben* apprentice, article (*both: bei, zu* to); '**~n** *v/t.* (*ge- h*) teach, instruct; show.
'**Lehrer** *m* (-s/-) teacher; master, instructor; '**~in** *f* (-/-nen) (lady) teacher; (school)mistress; '**~kollegium** *n* staff (of teachers).
'**Lehr|fach** *n* subject; '**~film** *m* instructional film; '**~gang** *m* course (of instruction); '**~geld** *n* premium; '**~herr** *m* master, *sl.* boss; '**~jahre** *n/pl.* (years *pl.* of) apprenticeship; '**~junge** *m s.* Lehrling; '**~körper** *m* teaching staff; *univ.* professoriate, faculty; '**~kraft** *f* teacher; professor; '**~ling** *m* (-s/-e) apprentice; '**~mädchen** *n* girl apprentice; '**~meister** *m* master; '**~methode** *f* method of teaching; '**~plan** *m* curriculum, syllabus; 'Ǧreich *adj.* instructive; '**~satz** *m* ₳ theorem; doctrine; *eccl.* dogma; '**~stoff** *m* subject-matter, subject(s *pl.*); '**~stuhl** *m* professorship; '**~vertrag** *m* articles *pl.* of apprenticeship, indenture(s *pl.*); '**~zeit** *f* apprenticeship.
Leib [laɪp] *m* (-[e]s/-er) body; belly, *anat.* abdomen; womb; *bei lebendigem* ~*e* alive; *mit* ~ *und Seele* body and soul; *sich j-n vom* ~*e halten* keep s.o. at arm's length; '**~arzt** *m* physician in ordinary, personal physician; '**~chen** *n* (-s/-) bodice.
Leibeigen|e ['laɪp^Ɂaɪgənə] *m* (-n/-n) bond(s)man, serf; '**~schaft** *f* (-/no *pl.*) bondage, serfdom.
Leibes|erziehung ['laɪbəs-] *f* physical training; '**~frucht** *f* f(o)etus; '**~kraft** *f*: *aus Leibeskräften pl.* with all one's might; '**~übung** *f* bodily *or* physical exercise.
'**Leib|garde** *f* body-guard; '**~gericht** *n* favo(u)rite dish; Ǧhaftig *adj.* [~'haftiç]: *der* ~*e Teufel* the devil incarnate; 'Ǧlich *adj.* bodily, corpor(e)al; '**~rente** *f* life-annuity; '**~schmerzen** *m/pl.* stomach-ache, belly-ache, ⨝ colic; '**~wache** *f* body-guard; '**~wäsche** *f* underwear.
Leiche ['laɪçə] *f* (-/-n) (dead) body, corpse.
Leichen|beschauer ⚖ ['laɪçənbə-ʃaʊər] *m* (-s/-) *appr.* coroner; '**~bestatter** *m* (-s/-) undertaker, *Am. a.* mortician; '**~bittermiene** F *f* woebegone look *or* countenance; 'Ǧblaß *adj.* deadly pale; '**~halle** *f* mortuary; '**~schau** ⚖ *f appr.* (coroner's) inquest; '**~schauhaus** *n* morgue; '**~tuch** *n* (-[e]s/-er) shroud; '**~verbrennung** *f* cremation; '**~wagen** *m* hearse.

Leichnam ['laɪçnɑːm] *m* (-[e]s/-e) *s.* Leiche.
leicht [laɪçt] **1.** *adj.* light; easy; slight; *tobacco:* mild; **2.** *adv.:* *es* ~ *nehmen* take it easy; 'Ǧathlet *m* athlete; 'Ǧathletik *f* athletics *pl.*, *Am.* track and field events *pl.*; '**~fertig** *adj.* light(-minded); careless; frivolous, flippant; 'Ǧfertigkeit *f* levity; carelessness; frivolity, flippancy; 'Ǧgewicht *n* boxing: light-weight; '**~gläubig** *adj.* credulous; '**~hin** *adv.* lightly, casually; Ǧigkeit ['~iç] *f* (-/-en) lightness, ease, facility; '**~lebig** *adj.* easy-going; Ǧmetall *n* light metal; Ǧsinn *m* (-[e]s/no *pl.*) frivolity, levity; carelessness; '**~sinnig** *adj.* light-minded, frivolous; careless; '**~verdaulich** *adj.* easy to digest; '**~verständlich** *adj.* easy to understand.
leid [laɪt] **1.** *adv.:* *es tut mir* ~ I am sorry (*um* for), I regret; **2.** Ǧ *n* (-[e]s/no *pl.*) injury, harm; wrong; grief, sorrow; **~en** ['~dən] (*irr.*, *ge-, h*) **1.** *v/i.* suffer (*an dat.* from); **2.** *v/t.:* (*nicht*) ~ *können* (dis)like; Ǧen ['~dən] *n* (-s/-) suffering; ⚕ complaint; '**~end** *adj.* ['~dənt] ailing.
'**Leidenschaft** *f* (-/-en) passion; 'Ǧlich *adj.* passionate; ardent; vehement; 'Ǧslos *adj.* dispassionate.
'**Leidens|gefährte** *m*, '**~gefährtin** *f* fellow-sufferer.
leid|er *adv.* unfortunately; *int.* alas!; ~ *muß ich inf.* I'm (so) sorry to *inf.*; *ich muß* ~ *gehen* I am afraid I have to go; '**~ig** *adj.* disagreeable; '**~lich** *adj.* ['laɪt-] tolerable; fairly well; Ǧtragende ['laɪt-] *m, f* (-n/-n) mourner; *er ist der* ~ *dabei* he is the one who suffers for it; Ǧwesen ['laɪt-] *n* (-s/no *pl.*): *zu meinem* ~ to my regret.
Leier ♪ ['laɪər] *f* (-/-n) lyre; '**~kasten** *m* barrel-organ; '**~kastenmann** *m* organ-grinder.
Leih|bibliothek ['laɪ-] *f*, '**~bücherei** *f* lending *or* circulating library, *Am. a.* rental library; Ǧen *v/t.* (*irr., ge-, h*) lend; borrow (*von* from); '**~gebühr** *f* lending fee(s *pl.*); '**~haus** *n* pawnshop, *Am.* loan office; Ǧweise *adv.* as a loan.
Leim [laɪm] *m* (-[e]s/-e) glue; F *aus dem* ~ *gehen* get out of joint; F: *auf den* ~ *gehen* fall for it, fall into the trap; Ǧen *v/t.* (*ge-, h*) glue; size.
Lein ♀ [laɪn] *m* (-[e]s/-e) flax.
Leine ['laɪnə] *f* (-/-n) line, cord; (dog-)lead, leash.
leinen ['laɪnən] **1.** *adj.* (of) linen; **2.** Ǧ *n* (-s/-) linen; *in* ~ *gebunden* cloth-bound; 'Ǧschuh *m* canvas shoe.
'**Lein|öl** *n* linseed-oil; '**~samen** *m* linseed; '**~wand** *f* (-/no *pl.*) linen (cloth); *paint.* canvas; *film:* screen.

leise adj. ['laɪzə] low, soft; gentle; slight, faint; ~r stellen turn down (radio).

Leiste ['laɪstə] f (-/-n) border, ledge; ⚙ fillet; anat. groin.

leisten ['laɪstən] 1. v/t. (ge-, h) do; perform; fulfil(l); take (oath); render (service); ich kann mir das ~ I can afford it; 2. ♀ ⊕ m (-s/-) last; boot-tree, Am. a. shoetree; '2-**bruch** ⚙ m inguinal hernia.

'**Leistung** f (-/-en) performance; achievement; work(manship); result(s pl.); ⊕ capacity; output (of factory); benefit (of insurance company); '2**sfähig** adj. productive; efficient, ⊕ a. powerful; '~sfähig-keit f efficiency; ⊕ productivity; ⊕ capacity, producing-power.

Leit|artikel ['laɪt-] m leading article, leader, editorial; '~bild n image; example.

leiten ['laɪtən] v/t. (ge-, h) lead, guide; conduct (a. phys., ♪); fig. direct, run, manage, operate; preside over (meeting); '~d adj. leading; phys. conductive; ~e Stellung key position.

'**Leiter 1.** m (-s/-) leader; conductor (a. phys., ♪); guide; manager; 2. f (-/-n) ladder; '~in f (-/-nen) conductress, guide; manageress; '~wagen m rack-wag(g)on.

'**Leit|faden** m manual, textbook, guide; '~motiv ♪ n leit-motiv; '~spruch m motto; '~tier n leader; '~ung f (-/-en) lead(ing), conducting, guidance; management, direction, administration, Am. a. operation; phys. conduction; ∮ lead; circuit; tel. line; mains pl. (for gas, water, etc.); pipeline; die ~ ist besetzt teleph. the line is engaged or Am. busy.

'**Leitungs|draht** m conducting wire, conductor; '~rohr n conduit(-pipe); main (for gas, water, etc.); '~wasser n (-s/-) tap water.

'**Leitwerk** ✈ n tail unit or group, empennage.

Lekt|ion [lɛk'tsjoːn] f (-/-en) lesson; ~or ['lɛktɔr] m (-s/-en) lecturer; reader; ~üre [~'tyːrə] f 1. (-/no pl.) reading; 2. (-/-n) books pl.

Lende anat. ['lɛndə] f (-/-n) loin(s pl.).

lenk|bar adj. ['lɛŋkbaːr] guidable, manageable, tractable; docile; ⚓ steerable, dirigible; '~en v/t. (ge-, h) direct, guide; turn; rule; govern; drive (car); ⚓ steer; Aufmerksam-keit ~ auf (acc.) draw attention to; '2**rad** mot. n steering wheel; '2-**säule** mot. f steering column; '2-**stange** f handle-bar (of bicycle); '2**ung** mot. f (-/-en) steering-gear.

Lenz [lɛnts] m (-es/-e) spring.

Leopard zo. [leo'part] m (-en/-en) leopard.

Lepra ⚕ ['leːpra] f (-/no pl.) leprosy.

Lerche orn. ['lɛrçə] f (-/-n) lark.

lern|begierig adj. ['lɛrn-] eager to learn, studious; '~en v/t. and v/i. (ge-, h) learn; study.

Lese ['leːzə] f (-/-n) gathering; s. Weinlese; '~buch n reader; '~lampe f reading-lamp.

lesen ['leːzən] (irr., ge-, h) 1. v/t. read; ♪ gather; Messe ~ eccl. say mass; 2. v/i. read; univ. (give a) lecture (über acc. on); '~swert adj. worth reading.

'**Leser** m (-s/-), '~in f (-/-nen) reader; ♪ gatherer; vintager; '2**lich** adj. legible; '~zuschrift f letter to the editor.

'**Lesezeichen** n book-mark.

'**Lesung** parl. f (-/-en) reading.

letzt adj. [lɛtst] last; final; ultimate; ~e Nachrichten pl. latest news pl.; ~e Hand anlegen put the finishing touches (an acc. to); das ~e the last thing; der ~ere the latter; der (die, das) Letzte the last (one); zu guter Letzt last but not least; finally; '~ens adv., '~hin adv. lately, of late; '~lich adv. s. letztens; finally; ultimately.

Leucht|e ['lɔʏçtə] f (-/-n) (fig. shining) light, lamp (a. fig.), luminary (a. fig., esp. p.); '2**en** v/i. (ge-, h) (give) light, shine (forth); beam, gleam; '~en n (-s/no pl.) shining, light, luminosity; '2**end** adj. shining, bright; luminous; brilliant (a. fig.); '~er m (-s/-) candlestick; s. Kronleuchter; '~feuer n ♪, ✈, etc.: beacon(-light), flare (light); '~käfer zo. m glow-worm; '~kugel ✗ f Very light; flare; '~turm m light-house; '~ziffer f luminous figure.

leugnen ['lɔʏgnən] v/t. (ge-, h) deny; disavow; contest.

Leukämie ⚕ [lɔʏkɛ'miː] f (-/-n) leuk(a)emia.

Leumund ['lɔʏmunt] m (-[e]s/no pl.) reputation, repute; character; '~szeugnis ⚖ n character reference.

Leute ['lɔʏtə] pl. people pl.; persons pl.; ✗, pol. men pl.; workers: hands pl.; F folks pl.; domestics pl., servants pl.

Leutnant ✗ ['lɔʏtnant] m (-s/-s, ✈ -e) second lieutenant.

leutselig adj. ['lɔʏtze:lıç] affable.

Lexikon ['lɛksikɔn] n (-s/Lexika, Lexiken) dictionary; encyclop(a)e-dia.

Libelle zo. [li'bɛlə] f (-/-n) dragon-fly.

liberal adj. [libe'raːl] liberal.

Licht [lıçt] 1. n (-[e]s/-er) light; brightness; lamp; candle; hunt. eye; ~ machen ∮ switch or turn on the light(s pl.); das ~ der Welt er-blicken see the light, be born; 2. ♀ adj. light, bright; clear; '~er Augen-blick ⚕ lucid interval; '~anlage f lighting plant; '~bild n photo (-graph); '~bildervortrag m slide lecture; '~blick fig. m bright spot; '~bogen ⚡ m arc; '2durchlässig adj. translucent; '2echt adj. fast (to light), unfading; '2empfindlich adj. sensitive to light, phot. sensitive; ~ machen sensitize.

'lichten v/t. (ge-, h) clear (forest); den Anker ~ ⚓ weigh anchor; sich ~ hair, crowd: thin.

lichterloh adv. ['liçtər'lo:] blazing, in full blaze.

'Licht|geschwindigkeit f speed of light; '~hof m glass-roofed court; patio; halo (a. phot.); '~leitung f lighting mains pl.; '~maschine mot. f dynamo, generator; '~pause f blueprint; '~quelle f light source, source of light; '~reklame f neon sign; '~schacht m well; '~schalter m (light) switch; '~schein m gleam of light; '2scheu adj. shunning the light; '~signal n light or luminous signal; '~spieltheater n s. Filmtheater, Kino; '~strahl m ray or beam of light (a. fig.); '2undurchlässig adj. opaque.

'Lichtung f (-/-en) clearing, opening, glade.

'Lichtzelle f s. Photozelle.

Lid [li:t] n (-[e]s/-er) eyelid.

lieb adj. [li:p] dear; nice, kind; child: good; in letters: ~er Herr N. dear Mr N.; ~er Himmel! good Heavens!, dear me!; es ist mir ~, daß I am glad that; '2chen n (-s/-) sweetheart.

Liebe ['li:bə] f (-/no pl.) love (zu of, for); aus ~ for love; aus ~ zu for the love of; '2n (ge-, h) 1. v/t. love; be in love with; be fond of, like; 2. v/i. (be in) love; '~nde, f (-n/-n): die ~n pl. the lovers pl.

'liebens|wert adj. lovable; charming; '~würdig adj. lovable, amiable; das ist sehr ~ von Ihnen that is very kind of you; '2würdigkeit f (-/-en) amiability, kindness.

'lieber 1. adj. dearer; 2. adv. rather, sooner; ~ haben prefer, like better.

'Liebes|brief m love-letter; '~dienst m favo(u)r, kindness; good turn; '~erklärung f: e-e ~ machen declare one's love; '~heirat f love-match; '~kummer m lover's grief; '~paar n (courting) couple, lovers pl.; '~verhältnis n love-affair.

'liebevoll adj. loving, affectionate.

lieb|gewinnen ['li:p-] v/t. (irr. gewinnen, sep., no -ge-, h) get or grow fond of; '~haben v/t. (irr. haben, sep., -ge-, h) love, be fond of; '2haber m (-s/-) lover; beau; fig. amateur; 2haberei fig. [~'rai] f (-/-en) hobby; '2haberpreis m fancy price; '2haberwert m sentimental value; '~kosen v/t. (no -ge-, h) caress, fondle; '2kosung f (-/-en) caress;

'~lich adj. lovely, charming, delightful.

Liebling ['li:pliŋ] m (-s/-e) darling; favo(u)rite; esp. animals: pet; esp. form of address: darling, esp. Am. honey; '~sbeschäftigung f favo(u)rite occupation, hobby.

lieb|los adj. ['li:p-] unkind; careless; '2schaft f (-/-en) (love-)affair; '2ste m, f (-n/-n) sweetheart; darling.

Lied [li:t] n (-[e]s/-er) song; tune.

liederlich adj. ['li:dərliç] slovenly, disorderly; careless; loose, dissolute.

lief [li:f] pret. of laufen.

Lieferant [li:fə'rant] m (-en/-en) supplier, purveyor; caterer.

Liefer|auto ['li:fər-] n s. Lieferwagen; '2bar adj. to be delivered; available; '~bedingungen f/pl. terms pl. of delivery; '~frist f term of delivery; '2n v/t. (ge-, h) deliver; j-m et. ~ furnish or supply s.o. with s.th.; '~schein m delivery note; '~ung f (-/-en) delivery; supply; consignment; instal(l)ment (of book); '~ungsbedingungen f/pl. s. Lieferbedingungen; '~wagen m deliveryvan, Am. delivery wagon.

Liege ['li:gə] f (-/-n) couch; bedchair.

liegen ['li:gən] v/i. (irr., ge-, h) lie; house, etc.: be (situated); room: face; an wem liegt es? whose fault is it? es liegt an or bei ihm zu inf. it is for him to inf.; es liegt daran, daß the reason for it is that; es liegt mir daran zu inf. I am anxious to inf.; es liegt mir nichts daran it does not matter or it is of no consequence to me; '~bleiben v/i. (irr. bleiben, sep., -ge-, sein) stay in bed; break down (on the road, a. mot., etc.); work, etc.: stand over; fall behind; ✝ goods: remain on hand; '~lassen v/t. (irr. lassen, sep., [-ge-,] h) leave; leave behind; leave alone; leave off (work); j-n links ~ ignore s.o., give s.o. the cold shoulder; '2schaften f/pl. real estate.

'Liege|stuhl m deck-chair; '~wagen 🚂 m couchette coach.

lieh [li:] pret. of leihen.

ließ [li:s] pret. of lassen.

Lift [lift] m (-[e]s/-e, -s) lift, Am. elevator.

Liga ['li:ga] f (-/Ligen) league.

Likör [li'kø:r] m (-s/-e) liqueur, cordial.

lila adj. ['li:la] lilac.

Lilie ⚘ ['li:ljə] f (-/-n) lily.

Limonade [limo'na:də] f (-/-n) soft drink, fruit-juice; lemonade.

Limousine mot. [limu'zi:nə] f (-/-n) limousine, saloon car, Am. sedan.

lind adj. [lint] soft, gentle; mild.

Linde ⚘ ['lində] f (-/-n) lime(-tree), linden(-tree).

linder|n ['lindərn] *v/t.* (ge-, h) soften; mitigate; alleviate, soothe; allay, ease (*pain*); **'2ung** *f* (-/‰ -en) softening; mitigation; alleviation; easing.

Lineal [line'ɑːl] *n* (-s/-e) ruler.

Linie ['liːnjə] *f* (-/-n) line; **'‰papier** *n* ruled paper; **'‰nrichter** *m sports:* linesman; **'2ntreu** *pol. adj.:* ‰ **sein** follow the party line.

lin(i)ieren [li'niːrən; lini'iːrən] *v/t.* (*no* -ge-, h) rule, line.

link *adj.* [liŋk] left; ‰**e Seite** left (-hand) side; *of cloth:* wrong side; **'2e** *f* (-n/-n) the left (hand); *pol.* the Left (Wing); *boxing:* the left; **'‰isch** *adj.* awkward, clumsy.

links *adv.* on *or* to the left; **2händer** ['‰hɛndər] *m* (-s/-) left-hander, *Am. a.* southpaw.

Linse ['linzə] *f* (-/-n) ⚘ lentil; *opt.* lens.

Lippe ['lipə] *f* (-/-n) lip; **'‰nstift** *m* lipstick.

liquidieren [likvi'diːrən] *v/t.* (*no* -ge-, h) liquidate (*a. pol.*); wind up (*business company*); charge (*fee*).

lispeln ['lispəln] *v/i. and v/t.* (ge-, h) lisp; whisper.

List [list] *f* (-/-en) cunning, craft; artifice, ruse, trick; stratagem.

Liste ['listə] *f* (-/-n) list, roll.

'listig *adj.* cunning, crafty, sly.

Liter ['liːtər] *n, m* (-s/-) lit|re, *Am.* -er.

literarisch *adj.* [lite'rɑːriʃ] literary.

Literatur [litera'tuːr] *f* (-/-en) literature; **‰beilage** *f* literary supplement (*in newspaper*); **‰geschichte** *f* history of literature; **‰verzeichnis** *n* bibliography.

litt [lit] *pret. of* leiden.

Litze ['litsə] *f* (-/-n) lace, cord, braid; ∉ strand(ed wire).

Livree [li'vreː] *f* (-/-n) livery.

Lizenz [li'tsɛnts] *f* (-/-en) licen|ce, *Am.* -se; **‰inhaber** *m* licensee.

Lob [loːp] *n* (-[e]s/*no pl.*) praise; commendation; **2en** ['loːbən] *v/t.* (ge-, h) praise; **2enswert** *adj.* ['loːbəns-] praise-worthy, laudable; **‰gesang** ['loːp-] *m* hymn, song of praise; **‰hudelei** [loːphuːdə'laɪ] *f* (-/-en) adulation, base flattery.

löblich *adj.* ['løːpliç] *s.* lobenswert.

Lobrede ['loːp-] *f* eulogy, panegyric.

Loch [lɔx] *n* (-[e]s/‰er) hole; **'2en** *v/t.* (ge-, h) perforate, pierce; punch (*ticket, etc.*); **'‰er** *m* (-s/-) punch, perforator; **'‰karte** *f* punch(ed) card.

Locke ['lɔkə] *f* (-/-n) curl, ringlet.

'locken¹ *v/t. and v/refl.* (ge-, h) curl.

'locken² *v/t.* (ge-, h) *hunt.:* bait; decoy (*a. fig.*); *fig.* allure, entice.

'Locken|kopf *m* curly head; **‰wickler** ['‰viklər] *m* (-s/-) curler, roller.

locker *adj.* ['lɔkər] loose; slack; **'‰n**

v/t. (ge-, h) loosen; slacken; relax (*grip*); break up (*soil*); *sich* ‰ loosen, (be)come loose; give way; *fig.* relax.

'lockig *adj.* curly.

'Lock|mittel *n s.* Köder; **'‰vogel** *m* decoy (*a. fig.*), *Am. a.* stool pigeon (*a. fig.*).

lodern ['loːdərn] *v/i.* (ge-, h) flare, blaze.

Löffel ['lœfəl] *m* (-s/-) spoon; ladle; **'2n** *v/t.* (ge-, h) spoon up; ladle out; **'‰voll** *m* (-/-) spoonful.

log [loːk] *pret. of* lügen.

Loge ['loːʒə] *f* (-/-n) *thea.* box; freemasonry: lodge; **'‰nschließer** *thea. m* (-s/-) box-keeper.

logieren [lo'ʒiːrən] *v/i.* (*no* -ge-, h) lodge, stay, *Am. a.* room (*all:* bei with; *in dat.* at).

logisch *adj.* ['loːgiʃ] logical; **'‰erweise** *adv.* logically.

Lohn [loːn] *m* (-[e]s/‰e) wages *pl.*, pay(ment); hire; *fig.* reward; **'‰büro** *n* pay-office; **'‰empfänger** *m* wage-earner; **'2en** *v/t.* (ge-, h) compensate, reward; *sich* ‰ pay; *es lohnt sich zu inf.* it is worth while *ger.*, it pays to *inf.*; **'2end** *adj.* paying; advantageous; *fig.* rewarding; **‰erhöhung** *f* increase in wages, rise, *Am.* raise; **‰forderung** *f* demand for higher wages; **'‰steuer** *f* tax on wages *or* salary; **'‰stopp** *m* (-s/*no pl.*) wage freeze; **'‰tarif** *m* wage rate; **'‰tüte** *f* pay envelope.

lokal [lo'kɑːl] **1.** *adj.* local; **2.** **2** *n* (-[e]s/-e) locality, place; restaurant; public house, F pub, F local, *Am.* saloon.

Lokomotiv|e [lokomo'tiːvə] *f* (-/-n) (railway) engine, locomotive; **‰führer** [‰'tiːf-] *m* engine-driver, *Am.* engineer.

Lorbeer ⚘ ['lɔrbeːr] *m* (-s/-en) laurel, bay.

Lore ['loːrə] *f* (-/-n) lorry, truck.

Los¹ [loːs] *n* (-es/-e) lot; lottery ticket; *fig.* fate, destiny, lot; *das Große* ‰ *ziehen* win the first prize, *Am. sl.* hit the jackpot; *durchs* ‰ *entscheiden* decide by lot.

los² [‰] **1.** *pred. adj.* loose; free; *was ist* ‰? what is the matter?, F what's up?, *Am.* F what's cooking?; ‰ *sein* be rid of; **2.** *int.:* ‰! go (on *or* ahead)!

losarbeiten ['loːs‰-] *v/i.* (sep., -ge-, h) start work(ing).

lösbar *adj.* ['løːsbɑːr] soluble, ⚗ a. solvable.

'los|binden *v/t.* (*irr.* binden, *sep.*, -ge-, h) untie, loosen; **‰brechen** (*irr.* brechen, *sep.*, -ge-) **1.** *v/t.* (h) break off; **2.** *v/i.* (sein) break *or* burst out.

Lösch|blatt ['lœʃ-] *n* blotting-paper; **'2en** *v/t.* (ge-, h) extinguish, put out (*fire, light*); blot out (*writing*);

erase (*tape recording*); cancel (*debt*); quench (*thirst*); slake (*lime*); ⚓ unload; '**~er** *m* (-s/-) blotter; '**~papier** *n* blotting-paper.

lose *adj.* ['loːzə] loose.

'**Lösegeld** *n* ransom.

losen ['loːzən] *v/i.* (ge-, h) cast *or* draw lots (*um* for).

lösen ['løːzən] *v/t.* (ge-, h) loosen, untie; buy, book (*ticket*); solve (*task, doubt, etc.*); break off (*engagement*); annul (*agreement, etc.*); 🜍 dissolve; *ein Schuß löste sich* the gun went off.

'**los|fahren** *v/i.* (*irr.* fahren, *sep.,* -ge-, *sein*) depart, drive off;'**~gehen** *v/i.* (*irr.* gehen, *sep.,* -ge-, *sein*) go *or* be off; come off, get loose; *gun:* go off; begin, start; F *auf j-n ~* fly at s.o.; '**~haken** *v/t.* (*sep.,* -ge-, h) unhook; '**~kaufen** *v/t.* (*sep.,* -ge-, h) ransom, redeem; '**~ketten** *v/t.* (*sep.,* -ge-, h) unchain; '**~kommen** *v/i.* (*irr.* kommen, *sep.,* -ge-, *sein*) get loose *or* free; '**~lachen** *v/i.* (*sep.,* -ge-, h) laugh out; '**~lassen** *v/t.* (*irr.* lassen, *sep.,* -ge-, h) let go; release.

löslich 🜍 *adj.* ['løːsliç] soluble.

'**los|lösen** *v/t.* (*sep.,* -ge-, h) loosen, detach; sever; '**~machen** *v/t.* (*sep.,* -ge-, h) unfasten, loosen; *sich ~* disengange (o.s.) (*von* from); '**~reißen** *v/t.* (*irr.* reißen, *sep.,* -ge-, h) tear off; *sich ~* break away, *esp. fig.* tear o.s. away (*both: von* from); '**~sagen** *v/refl.* (*sep.,* -ge-, h): *sich ~ von* renounce; '**~schlagen** (*irr.* schlagen, *sep.,* -ge-, h) **1.** *v/t.* knock off; **2.** *v/i.* open the attack; *auf j-n ~* attack s.o.; '**~schnallen** *v/t.* (*sep.,* -ge-, h) unbuckle; '**~schrauben** *v/t.* (*sep.,* -ge-, h) unscrew, screw off; '**~sprechen** *v/t.* (*irr.* sprechen, *sep.,* -ge-, h) absolve (*von* of, from); acquit (*of*); free (from, of); '**~stürzen** *v/i.* (*sep.,* -ge-, *sein*): *~ auf* (*acc.*) rush at.

Losung ['loːzuŋ] *f* **1.** (-/-en) ✂ password, watchword; *fig.* slogan; **2.** *hunt.* (-/*no pl.*) droppings *pl.,* dung.

Lösung ['løːzuŋ] *f* (-/-en) solution; '**~smittel** *n* solvent.

'**los|werden** *v/t.* (*irr.* werden, *sep.,* -ge-, *sein*) get rid of, dispose of; '**~ziehen** *v/i.* (*irr.* ziehen, *sep.,* -ge-, *sein*) set out, take off, march away.

Lot [loːt] *n* (-[e]s/-e) plumb(-line), plummet.

löten ['løːtən] *v/t.* (ge-, h) solder.

Lotse ⚓ ['loːtsə] *m* (-n/-n) pilot; '**2n** *v/t.* (ge-, h) ⚓ pilot (*a. fig.*).

Lotterie [lɔtəˈriː] *f* (-/-n) lottery; '**~gewinn** *m* prize; '**~los** *n* lottery ticket.

Lotto ['lɔto] *n* (-s/-s) numbers pool, lotto.

Löwe zo. ['løːvə] *m* (-n/-n) lion.

'**Löwen|anteil** F *m* lion's share; '**~maul** ♀ *n* (-[e]s/*no pl.*) snapdragon; '**~zahn** ♀ *m* (-[e]s/*no pl.*) dandelion.

'**Löwin** zo. *f* (-/-nen) lioness.

loyal *adj.* [loaˈjaːl] loyal.

Luchs zo. [luks] *m* (-es/-e) lynx.

Lücke ['lykə] *f* (-/-n) gap; blank, void (*a. fig.*); '**~nbüßer** *m* stopgap; '**2nhaft** *adj.* full of gaps; *fig.* defective, incomplete; '**2nlos** *adj.* without a gap; *fig.*: unbroken; complete; **~er Beweis** close argument.

lud [luːt] *pret. of* laden.

Luft [luft] *f* (-/ᴴe) air; breeze; breath; *frische ~ schöpfen* take the air; *an die ~ gehen* go for an airing; *aus der ~ gegriffen* (totally) unfounded, fantastic; *es liegt et. in der ~* there is s.th. in the wind; *in die ~ fliegen* be blown up, explode; *in die ~ gehen* explode, *sl.* blow one's top; *in die ~ sprengen* blow up; F *j-n an die ~ setzen* turn s.o. out, *Am. sl.* give s.o. the air; *sich or s-n Gefühlen ~ machen* give vent to one's feelings.

'**Luft|alarm** *m* air-raid alarm; '**~angriff** *m* air raid; '**~aufnahme** *f* aerial photograph; '**~ballon** *m* (air-)balloon; '**~bild** *n* aerial photograph, airview; '**~blase** *f* air-bubble; '**~brücke** *f* air-bridge; *for supplies, etc.*: air-lift.

Lüftchen ['lyftçən] *n* (-s/-) gentle breeze.

'**luft|dicht** *adj.* air-tight; '**2druck** *phys. m* (-[e]s/*no pl.*) atmospheric *or* air pressure; '**2druckbremse** ⊕ *f* air-brake; '**~durchlässig** *adj.* permeable to air.

lüften ['lyftən] (ge-, h) **1.** *v/i.* air; **2.** *v/t.* air; raise (*hat*); lift (*veil*); disclose (*secret*).

'**Luft|fahrt** *f* aviation, aeronautics; '**~feuchtigkeit** *f* atmospheric humidity; '**2gekühlt** *adj.* air-cooled; '**~hoheit** *f* air sovereignty; '**2ig** *adj.* airy; breezy; flimsy; '**~kissen** *n* air-cushion; '**~klappe** *f* air-valve; '**~korridor** *m* air corridor; '**~krankheit** *f* airsickness; '**~krieg** *m* aerial warfare; '**~kurort** *m* climatic health resort; '**~landetruppen** *f/pl.* airborne troops *pl.*; '**2leer** *adj.* void of air, evacuated; **~er Raum** vacuum; '**~linie** *f* air line, bee-line; '**~loch** *n* ✂ air-pocket; vent(-hole); '**~post** *f* air mail; '**~pumpe** *f* air-pump; '**~raum** *m* airspace; '**~röhre** *anat. f* windpipe, trachea; '**~schacht** *m* air-shaft; '**~schaukel** *f* swing-boat; '**~schiff** *n* airship; '**~schloß** *n* castle in the air *or* in Spain; '**~schutz** *m* air-raid protection; '**~schutzkeller** *m* air-raid shelter; '**~sprünge** *f/pl.*: *~ machen* cut capers *pl.*; gambol; '**~stützpunkt** ✂ *m* air base.

'**Lüftung** f (-/-en) airing; ventilation.

'**Luft|veränderung** f change of air; '**∼verkehr** m air-traffic; '**∼verkehrsgesellschaft** f air transport company, airway, Am. airline; '**∼verteidigung** ✕ f air defen|ce, Am. -se; '**∼waffe** ✕ f air force; '**∼weg** m airway; auf dem ∼ by air; '**∼zug** m draught, Am. draft.

Lüge ['ly:gə] f (-/-n) lie, falsehood; j-n ∼n strafen give the lie to s.o.

'**lügen** v/i. (irr., ge-, h) (tell a) lie; '**∼haft** adj. lying, mendacious; untrue, false.

Lügner ['ly:gnər] m (-s/-), '**∼in** f (-/-nen) liar; '**☉isch** adj. s. lügenhaft.

Luke ['lu:kə] f (-/-n) dormer- or garret-window; hatch.

Lümmel ['lyməl] m (-s/-) lout, boor; saucy fellow; '**☉n** v/refl. (ge-, h) loll, lounge, sprawl.

Lump [lump] m (-en/-en) ragamuffin, beggar; cad, Am. sl. rat, heel; scoundrel.

'**Lumpen 1.** m (-s/-) rag; **2.** ☉ vb.: sich nicht ∼ lassen come down handsomely; '**∼pack** n rabble, riffraff; '**∼sammler** m rag-picker.

'**lumpig** adj. ragged; fig.: shabby, paltry; mean.

Lunge ['luŋə] f (-/-n) anat. lungs pl.; of animals: a. lights pl.

'**Lungen|entzündung** ☊ f pneumonia; '**∼flügel** anat. m lung; '**☉krank** ☊ adj. suffering from consumption, consumptive; '**∼kranke** ☊ m, f consumptive (patient); '**∼krankheit** ☊ f lung-disease; '**∼schwindsucht** ☊ f (pulmonary) consumption.

lungern ['luŋərn] v/i. (ge-, h) s. herumlungern.

Lupe ['lu:pə] f (-/-n) magnifying-glass; unter die ∼ nehmen scrutinize, take a good look at.

Lust [lust] f (-/∵e) pleasure, delight; desire; lust; ∼ haben zu inf. have a mind to inf., feel like ger.; haben Sie ∼ auszugehen? would you like to go out?

lüstern adj. ['lystərn] desirous (nach of), greedy (of, for); lewd, lascivious, lecherous.

'**lustig** adj. merry, gay; jolly, cheerful; amusing, funny; sich ∼ machen über (acc.) make fun of; '**☉keit** f (-/no pl.) gaiety, mirth; jollity, cheerfulness; fun.

Lüstling ['lystliŋ] m (-s/-e) voluptuary, libertine.

'**lust|los** adj. dull, spiritless; † flat; '**☉mord** m rape and murder; '**☉spiel** n comedy.

lutschen ['lutʃən] v/i. and v/t. (ge-, h) suck.

Luv ⏚ [lu:f] f (-/no pl.) luff, windward.

luxuriös adj. [luksu'rjø:s] luxurious.

Luxus ['luksus] m (-/no pl.) luxury (a. fig.); '**∼artikel** m luxury; '**∼ausgabe** f de luxe edition (of books); '**∼ware** f luxury (article); fancy goods pl.

Lymph|drüse anat. ['lymf-] f lymphatic gland; '**∼e** f (-/-n) lymph; ☊ vaccine; '**∼gefäß** anat. n lymphatic vessel.

lynchen ['lynçən] v/t. (ge-, h) lynch.

Lyrik ['ly:rik] f (-/no pl.) lyric verses pl., lyrics pl.; '**∼er** m (-s/-) lyric poet.

'**lyrisch** adj. lyric; lyrical (a. fig.).

M

Maat ⏚ [ma:t] m (-[e]s/-e[n]) (ship's) mate.

Mache F ['maxə] f (-/no pl.) make-believe, window-dressing, sl. eye-wash; et. in der ∼ haben have s.th. in hand.

machen ['maxən] (ge-, h) **1.** v/t. make; do; produce, manufacture; give (appetite, etc.); sit for, undergo (examination); come or amount to; make (happy, etc.); was macht das (aus)? what does that matter?; das macht nichts! never mind!, that's (quite) all right!; da(gegen) kann man nichts ∼ that cannot be helped; ich mache mir nichts daraus I don't care about it; mach, daß du fortkommst! off with you!; j-n ∼ lassen, was er will let s.o. do as he pleases; sich ∼ an (acc.) go or set

about; sich et. ∼ lassen have s.th. made; **2.** v/i.: na, mach schon! hurry up!; '**☉schaften** f/pl. machinations pl.

Macht [maxt] f (-/∵e) power; might; authority; control (über acc. of); an der ∼ pol. in power; '**∼befugnis** f authority, power; '**∼haber** pol. m (-s/-) ruler.

mächtig adj. ['mɛçtiç] powerful (a. fig.); mighty; immense, huge; ∼ sein (gen.) be master of s.th.; have command of (language).

'**Macht|kampf** m struggle for power; '**☉los** adj. powerless; '**∼politik** f power politics sg., pl.; policy of the strong hand; '**∼spruch** m authoritative decision; '**☉voll** adj. powerful (a. fig.); '**∼vollkommenheit** f authority; '**∼wort** n (-[e]s/-e) word of command; *ein ~ sprechen* put one's foot down.

'**Machwerk** *n* concoction, F put-up job; *elendes ~* bungling work.

Mädchen ['mɛ:tçən] *n* (-s/-) girl; maid(-servant); *~ für alles* maid of all work; *fig. a.* jack of all trades; '**2haft** *adj.* girlish; '**~name** *m* girl's name; maiden name; '**~schule** *f* girls' school.

Made *zo.* ['ma:də] *f* (-/-n) maggot, mite; *fruit:* worm.

Mädel ['mɛ:dəl] *n* (-s/-, F -s) girl, lass(ie).

madig *adj.* ['ma:dɪç] maggoty, full of mites; *fruit:* wormeaten.

Magazin [maga'tsi:n] *n* (-s/-e) store, warehouse; ⚔, *in rifle, periodical:* magazine.

Magd [ma:kt] *f* (-/=e) maid(-servant).

Magen ['ma:gən] *m* (-s/=, *a.* -) stomach, F tummy; *animals:* maw; '**~beschwerden** *f/pl.* stomach *or* gastric trouble, indigestion; '**~bitter** *m* (-s/-) bitters *pl.*; '**~geschwür** ꝰ *n* gastric ulcer; '**~krampf** *m* stomach cramp; '**~krebs** ꝰ *m* stomach cancer; '**~leiden** *n* gastric complaint; '**~säure** *f* gastric acid.

mager *adj.* ['ma:gər] meag|re, *Am.* -er (*a. fig.*); *p., animal, meat:* lean, *Am. a.* scrawny; '**2milch** *f* skim milk.

Magie [ma'gi:] *f* (-/*no pl.*) magic; **~r** ['ma:gjər] *m* (-s/-) magician.

magisch *adj.* ['ma:gɪʃ] magic(al).

Magistrat [magɪs'tra:t] *m* (-[e]s/-e) municipal *or* town council.

Magnet [ma'gne:t] *m* (-[e]s, -en/-e[n]) magnet (*a. fig.*); lodestone; **2isch** *adj.* magnetic; **2isieren** [~eti'zi:rən] *v/t.* (*no* -ge-, *h*) magnetize; '**~nadel** [~'gne:t-] *f* magnetic needle.

Mahagoni [maha'go:ni] *n* (-s/*no pl.*) mahogany (wood).

mähen ['mɛ:ən] *v/t.* (ge-, *h*) cut, mow, reap.

Mahl [ma:l] *n* (-[e]s/=er, -e) meal, repast.

'**mahlen** (*irr.*, ge-, *h*) 1. *v/t.* grind, mill; 2. *v/i. tyres:* spin.

'**Mahlzeit** *f s.* Mahl; F feed.

Mähne ['mɛ:nə] *f* (-/-n) mane.

mahn|en ['ma:nən] *v/t.* (ge-, *h*) remind, admonish (*both: an acc.* of); *j-n wegen e-r Schuld ~* press s.o. for payment, dun s.o.; '**2mal** *n* (-[e]s/-e) memorial; '**2ung** *f* (-/-en) admonition; ✝ reminder, dunning; '**2zettel** *m* reminder.

Mai [maɪ] *m* (-[e]s, -/-e) May; '**~baum** *m* maypole; '**~glöckchen** ꝰ ['~glœkçən] *n* (-s/-) lily of the valley; '**~käfer** *zo. m* cockchafer, may-beetle, may-bug.

Mais ꝰ [maɪs] *m* (-es/-e) maize, Indian corn, *Am.* corn.

Majestät [majɛ'stɛ:t] *f* (-/-en) majesty; **2isch** *adj.* majestic; **~s-beleidigung** *f* lese-majesty.

Major ⚔ [ma'jo:r] *m* (-s/-e) major.

Makel ['ma:kəl] *m* (-s/-) stain, spot; *fig. a.* blemish, fault; '**2los** *adj.* stainless, spotless; *fig. a.* unblemished, faultless, immaculate.

mäkeln F ['mɛ:kəln] *v/i.* (ge-, *h*) find fault (*an dat.* with), carp (at), F pick (at).

Makler ✝ ['ma:klər] *m* (-s/-) broker; '**~gebühr** ✝ *f* brokerage.

Makulatur ⊕ [makula'tu:r] *f* (-/-en) waste paper.

Mal[1] [ma:l] *n* (-[e]s/-e, =er) mark, sign; *sports:* start(ing-point), goal; spot, stain, mole.

Mal[2] [~] 1. *n* (-[e]s/-e) time; *für dieses ~* this time; *zum ersten ~e* for the first time; *mit e-m ~e* all at once, all of a sudden; 2. ♀ *adv.* times, multiplied by; *drei ~ fünf ist fünfzehn* three times five is *or* are fifteen; F *s. einmal.*

malen *v/t.* (ge-, *h*) paint; portray.

'**Maler** *m* (-s/-) painter; artist; **~ei** [~'raɪ] *f* (-/-en) painting; '**2isch** *adj.* pictorial, painting; *fig.* picturesque.

'**Malkasten** *m* paint-box.

'**malnehmen** ♀ *v/t.* (*irr. nehmen, sep.*, -ge-, *h*) multiply (*mit* by).

Malz [malts] *n* (-es/*no pl.*) malt; '**~bier** *n* malt beer.

Mama [ma'ma:, F 'mama] *f* (-/-s) mamma, mammy, F ma, *Am.* F *a.* mummy, mom.

man *indef. pron.* [man] one, you, we; they; people; *~ sagte mir* I was told.

Manager ['mɛnidʒər] *m* (-s/-) [manager.]

manch [manç], '**~er**, '**~e**, '**~es** *adj. and indef. pron.* many a; *~e pl.* some, several; *~erlei adj.* ['~ərlaɪ] diverse, different; all sorts of, ... of several sorts; *auf ~e Art* in various ways; *used as a noun:* many *or* various things; '**~mal** *adv.* sometimes, at times.

Mandant ꝛꝛ [man'dant] *m* (-en/-en) client.

Mandarine ꝰ [manda'ri:nə] *f* (-/-n) tangerine.

Mandat [man'da:t] *n* (-[e]s/-e) authorization; ꝛꝛ brief; *pol.* mandate; *parl.* seat.

Mandel ['mandəl] *f* (-/-n) ꝰ almond; *anat.* tonsil; '**~baum** ꝰ *m* almond-tree; '**~entzündung** ꝰ *f* tonsillitis.

Manege [ma'ne:ʒə] *f* (-/-n) (circus-)ring, manège.

Mangel[1] ['maŋəl] *m* 1. (-s/*no pl.*) want, lack, deficiency; shortage; penury; *aus ~ an* for want of; *~ leiden an* (*dat.*) be in want of; 2. (-s/=) defect, shortcoming.

Mangel[2] [~] *f* (-/-n) mangle; calender.

'**mangelhaft** adj. defective; deficient; unsatisfactory; '**2igkeit** f (-/no pl.) defectiveness; deficiency.

'**mangeln**[1] v/i. (ge-, h): es mangelt an Brot there is a lack or shortage of bread, bread is lacking or wanting; es mangelt ihm an (dat.) he is in need of or short of or wanting in, he wants or lacks.

'**mangeln**[2] v/t. (ge-, h) mangle (clothes, etc.); ⊕ calender (cloth, paper).

'**mangels** prp. (gen.) for lack or want of; esp. ⚖️ in default of.

'**Mangelware** † f scarce commodity; goods pl. in short supply.

Manie [ma'ni:] f (-/-n) mania.

Manier [ma'ni:r] f (-/-en) manner; **2lich** adj. well-behaved; polite, mannerly. [manifesto.]

Manifest [mani'fɛst] n (-es/-e)[

Mann [man] m (-[e]s/⁴er) man; husband.

'**mannbar** adj. marriageable; '**2-keit** f (-/no pl.) puberty, manhood.

Männchen ['mɛnçən] n (-s/-) little man; zo. male; birds: cock.

'**Mannes**|**alter** n virile age, manhood; '**∼kraft** f virility.

mannig|**fach** adj. ['maniç-], '**∼faltig** adj. manifold, various, diverse; '**2faltigkeit** f (-/no pl.) manifoldness, variety, diversity.

männlich adj. ['mɛnliç] male; gr. masculine; fig. manly; '**2keit** f (-/no pl.) manhood, virility.

'**Mannschaft** f (-/-en) (body of) men; ♣ crew; sports: team, side; '**∼führer** m sports: captain; '**∼geist** m (-es/no pl.) sports: team spirit.

Manöv|**er** [ma'nø:vər] n (-s/-) manœuvre, Am. maneuver; **2rieren** [∼'i:rən] v/i. (no -ge-, h) manœuvre, Am. maneuver.

Mansarde [man'zardə] f (-/-n) attic, garret; **∼nfenster** n dormer-window.

mansche|**n** F ['manʃən] (ge-, h) 1. v/t. mix, work; 2. v/i. dabble (in dat. in); '2**rei** F f (-/-en) mixing, F mess; dabbling.

Manschette [man'ʃɛtə] f (-/-n) cuff; '**∼nknopf** m cuff-link.

Mantel ['mantəl] m (-s/⁴) coat; overcoat, greatcoat; cloak, mantle (both a. fig.); ⊕ case, jacket; (outer) cover (of tyre).

Manuskript [manu'skript] n (-[e]s/-e) manuscript; typ. copy.

Mappe ['mapə] f (-/-n) portfolio, brief-case; folder; s. a. Schreibmappe, Schulmappe.

Märchen ['mɛːrçən] n (-s/-) fairytale; fig. (cock-and-bull) story, fib; '**∼buch** n book of fairy-tales; '**2haft** adj. fabulous (a. fig.).

Marder zo. ['mardər] m (-s/-) marten.

Marine [ma'ri:nə] f (-/-n) marine; ⚓ navy, naval forces pl.; **∼minister** m minister of naval affairs; First Lord of the Admiralty, Am. Secretary of the Navy; **∼ministerium** n ministry of naval affairs; the Admiralty, Am. Department of the Navy.

marinieren [mari'ni:rən] v/t. (no -ge-, h) pickle, marinade.

Marionette [mario'nɛtə] f (-/-n) puppet, marionette; **∼ntheater** n puppet-show.

Mark [mark] 1. f (-/-) coin: mark; 2. n (-[e]s/no pl.) anat. marrow; ♀ pith; fig. core.

markant adj. [mar'kant] characteristic; striking; (well-)marked.

Marke ['markə] f (-/-n) mark, sign, token; ⊗, etc.: stamp; † brand, trade-mark; coupon; '**∼nartikel** † m branded or proprietary article.

mar'kier|**en** (no -ge-, h) 1. v/t. mark (a. sports); brand (cattle, goods, etc.); 2. F fig. v/i. put it on; **2ung** f (-/-en) mark(ing).

'**markig** adj. marrowy; fig. pithy.

Markise [mar'ki:zə] f (-/-n) blind, (window-)awning.

'**Markstein** m boundary-stone, landmark (a. fig.).

Markt [markt] m (-[e]s/⁴e) † market; s. Marktplatz; fair; auf den bringen † put on the market; '**∼flecken** m small market-town; '**∼platz** m market-place; '**∼schreier** m (-s/-) quack; puffer.

Marmel|**ade** [marmə'la:də] f (-/-n) jam; marmalade (made of oranges).

Marmor ['marmor] m (-s/-e) marble; **2ieren** [∼o'i:rən] v/t. (no -ge-, h) marble, vein, grain; **2n** adj. ['∼orn] (of) marble. [whim, caprice.]

Marotte [ma'rotə] f (-/-n) fancy,[

Marsch [marʃ] 1. m (-es/⁴e) march (a. ♪); 2. f (-/-en) marsh, fen.

Marschall ['marʃal] m (-s/⁴e) marshal.

'**Marsch**|**befehl** ⚔ m marching orders pl.; **2ieren** [∼'ʃi:rən] v/i. (no -ge-, sein) march; '**∼land** n marshy land.

Marter ['martər] f (-/-n) torment, torture; '**2n** v/t. (ge-, h) torment, torture; '**∼pf∼hl** m stake.

Märtyrer ['mɛrtyrər] m (-s/-) martyr; '**∼tod** m martyr's death; '**∼tum** n (-s/no pl.) martyrdom.

Marxis|**mus** pol. [mar'ksismus] m (-/no pl.) Ma∼xism; **∼t** pol. m (-en/-en) Ma∼xian, Marxist; **2tisch** pol. adj. Ma∼xian, Marxist.

März [mɛrts] m (-[e]s/-e) March.

Marzipan [martsi'pa:n] n, ⚕ m (-s/-e) marzipan, marchpane.

Masche ['maʃə] f (-/-n) mesh; knitting: stitch; F fig. trick, line; '**2n-fest** adj. ladder-proof, Am. runproof.

Maschine [ma'ʃiːnə] f (-/-n) machine; engine.

maschinell adj. [maʃi'nɛl] mechanical; ~e Bearbeitung machining.

Ma'schinen|bau ⊕ m (-[e]s/no pl.) mechanical engineering; ~gewehr ✕ n machine-gun; **2mäßig** adj. mechanical; automatic; ~pistole ✕ f sub-machine-gun; ~schaden m engine trouble; ~schlosser m (engine) fitter; ~schreiberin f(-/-nen) typist; ~schrift f typescript.

Maschin|erie [maʃinə'riː] f (-/-n) machinery; ~ist [~'nist] m (-en/-en) machinist.

Masern ✕ ['maːzərn] pl. measles pl.

Mask|e ['maskə] f (-/-n) mask (a. fig.); ~enball m fancy-dress or masked ball; ~erade [~'raːdə] f (-/-n) masquerade; 2ieren [~'kiː-rən] v/t. (no -ge-, h) mask; sich ~ put on a mask; dress o.s. up (als as).

Maß [maːs] 1. n (-es/-e) measure; proportion; fig. moderation; ~e pl. und Gewichte pl. weights and measures pl.; ~e pl. room, etc.: measurements pl.; 2. f (-/-[e]) appr. quart (of beer); 3. 2 pret. of messen.

Massage [ma'saːʒə] f (-/-n) massage.

'Maßanzug m tailor-made or bespoke suit, Am. a. custom(-made) suit.

Masse ['masə] f (-/-n) mass; bulk; substance; multitude; crowd; ⚖ assets pl., estate; die breite ~ the rank and file; F e~e ~ a lot of, F lots pl. or heaps pl. of.

'Maßeinheit f measuring unit.

'Massen|flucht f stampede; '~grab n common grave; '~güter † ['~gyː-tər] n/pl. bulk goods pl.; '2haft adj. abundant; '~produktion † f mass production; '~versammlung f mass meeting, Am. a. rally; '2weise adv. in masses, in large numbers.

Masseu|r [ma'søːr] m (-s/-e) masseur; ~se [~zə] f (-/-n) masseuse.

'maß|gebend adj. standard; authoritative, decisive; board: competent; circles: influential, leading; '~halten v/i. (irr. halten, sep., -ge-, h) keep within limits, be moderate.

mas'sieren v/t. (no -ge-, h) massage, knead.

'massig adj. massy, bulky; solid.

mäßig adj. ['mɛːsiç] moderate; food, etc.: frugal; † price: moderate, reasonable; result, etc.: poor; ~en ['~gən] v/t. (ge-, h) moderate; sich ~ moderate or restrain o.s.; '2ung f (-/-en) moderation; restraint.

massiv [ma'siːf] 1. adj. massive, solid; 2. 2 geol. n (-s/-e) massif.

'Maß|krug m beer-mug, Am. a. stein; '2los adj. immoderate; boundless; exorbitant, excessive;

extravagant; ~nahme ['~naːmə] f (-/-n) measure, step, action; '2regeln v/t. (ge-, h) reprimand; inflict disciplinary punishment on; '~schneider m bespoke or Am. custom tailor; '~stab m measure, rule(r); maps, etc.: scale; fig. yardstick, standard; '2voll adj. moderate.

Mast¹ ⚓ [mast] m (-es/-e[n]) mast.

Mast² ✕ [~] f (-/-en) fattening; mast, food; '~darm anat. m rectum.

mästen ['mɛstən] v/t. (ge-, h) fatten, feed; stuff (geese, etc.).

'Mastkorb ⚓ m mast-head, crows-nest.

Material [mater'jaːl] n (-s/-ien) material; substance; stock, stores pl.; fig.: material, information; evidence; ~ismus phls. [~a'lismus] m (-/no pl.) materialism; ~ist [~a'list] m (-en/-en) materialist; 2istisch adj. [~a'listiʃ] materialistic.

Materie [ma'teːrjə] f (-/-n) matter (a. fig.), stuff; fig. subject; 2ll adj. [~er'jɛl] material.

Mathemati|k [matema'tiːk] f (-/no pl.) mathematics sg.; ~ker [~'maː-tikər] m (-s/-) mathematician; 2sch adj. [~'maːtiʃ] mathematical.

Matinee thea. [mati'neː] f (-/-n) morning performance.

Matratze [ma'tratsə] f (-/-n) mattress.

Matrone [ma'troːnə] f (-/-n) matron; 2nhaft adj. matronly.

Matrose ⚓ [ma'troːzə] m (-n/-n) sailor, seaman.

Matsch [matʃ] m (-es/no pl.), ~e F ['~ə] f (-/no pl.) pulp, squash; mud, slush; '2ig adj. pulpy, squashy; muddy, slushy.

matt adj. [mat] faint, feeble; voice, etc.: faint; eye, colour, etc.: dim; colour, light, † stock exchange, style, etc.: dull; metal: tarnished; gold, etc.: dead, dull; chess: mated; ✧ bulb: non-glare; ~ geschliffen glass: ground, frosted, matted; ~ setzen at chess: (check)mate s.o.

Matte ['matə] f (-/-n) mat.

'Mattigkeit f (-/no pl.) exhaustion, feebleness; faintness.

'Mattscheibe f phot. focus(s)ing screen; television: screen.

Mauer ['mauər] f (-/-n) wall; ~blümchen fig. ['~blyːmçən] n (-s/-) wall-flower; '2n (ge-, h) 1. v/i. make a wall, lay bricks; 2. v/t. build (in stone or brick); '~stein m brick; '~werk n masonry, brickwork.

Maul [maul] n (-[e]s/=er) mouth; sl.: halt's ~! shut up!; '2en F v/i. (ge-, h) sulk, pout; '~esel zo. m mule, hinny; '~held F m braggart; '~korb m muzzle; '~schelle F f box on the ear; '~tier zo. n mule;

'**~wurf** zo. m mole; '**~wurfshügel** m molehill.

Maurer ['maurər] m (-s/-) bricklayer, mason; '**~meister** m master mason; '**~polier** m bricklayers' foreman.

Maus zo. [maus] f (-/⁼e) mouse; **~efalle** ['~zə-] f mousetrap; **2en** ['~zən] (ge-, h) 1. v/i. catch mice; 2. F v/t. pinch, pilfer, F swipe.

Mauser ['mauzər] f (-/no pl.) mo(u)lt(ing); in der ~ sein be mo(u)lting; '**2n** v/refl. (ge-, h) mo(u)lt.

Maximum ['maksimum] n (-s/Maxima) maximum.

Mayonnaise [majɔ'nɛːzə] f (-/-n) mayonnaise.

Mechani|k [me'ça:nik] f 1. (-/no pl.) mechanics mst sg.; 2. ⊕ (-/-en) mechanism; '**~ker** m (-s/-) mechanic; **2sch** adj. mechanical; **2sieren** [~ani'zi:rən] v/t. (no -ge-, h) mechanize; **~sm⁀us** ⊕ [~a'nismus] m (-/Mechanismen) mechanism; clock, watch, etc.: works pl.

meckern ['mɛkərn] v/i. (ge-, h) bleat; fig. grumble (über acc. over, at, about), carp (at); nag (at); sl. grouse, Am. sl. gripe.

Medaill|e [me'daljə] f (-/-n) medal; **~on** [~'jɔ̃:] n (-s/-s) medallion; locket.

Medikament [medika'mɛnt] n (-[e]s/-e) medicament, medicine.

Medizin [medi'tsi:n] f 1. (-/no pl.) (science of) medicine; 2. (-/-en) medicine, F physic; **~er** m (-s/-) medical man; medical student; **2isch** adj. medical; medicinal.

Meer [me:r] n (-[e]s/-e) sea (a. fig.), ocean; '**~busen** m gulf, bay; '**~enge** f strait(s pl.); '**~esspiegel** m sea level; '**~rettich** ♀ m horse-radish; '**~schweinchen** zo. n guinea-pig.

Mehl [me:l] n (-[e]s/-e) flour; meal; '**~brei** m pap; '**2ig** adj. floury, mealy, farinaceous; '**~speise** f sweet dish, pudding; '**~suppe** f gruel.

mehr [me:r] 1. adj. more; er hat ~ Geld als ich he has (got) more money than I; 2. adv. more; nicht ~ no more, no longer, not any longer; ich habe nichts ~ I have nothing left; '**2arbeit** f additional work; overtime; '**2ausgaben** f/pl. additional expenditure; '**2betrag** m surplus; '**~deutig** adj. ambiguous; '**2einnahme(n** pl.) f additional receipts pl.; '**~en** v/t. (ge-, h) augment, increase; sich ~ multiply, grow; '**~ere** adj. and indef. pron. several, some; '**~fach 1.** adj. manifold, repeated; **2.** adv. repeatedly, several times; '**2gebot** n higher bid; '**2heit** f (-/-en) majority, plurality; '**2kosten** pl. additional expense; '**~malig** adj. repeated, reiterated;

~mals adv. ['~ma:ls] several times, repeatedly; '**~sprachig** adj. polyglot; '**~stimmig** ♪ adj.: ~er Gesang part-song; '**2verbrauch** m excess consumption; '**2wertsteuer** ♰ f (-/no pl.) value-added tax; '**2zahl** f majority; gr. plural (form); die ~ (gen.) most of.

meiden ['maidən] v/t. (irr., ge-, h) avoid, shun, keep away from.

Meile ['mailə] f (-/-n) mile; '**~nstein** m milestone.

mein poss. pron. ['main] my; der (die, das) ~e my; die **2en** pl. my family, F my people or folks pl.; ich habe das ~e getan I have done all I can; ~e Damen und Herren! Ladies and Gentlemen!

Meineid ♯ ['main?-] m perjury; '**2ig** adj. perjured.

meinen ['mainən] v/t. (ge-, h) think, believe, be of (the) opinion, Am. a. reckon, guess; say; mean; wie ~ Sie das? what do you mean by that?; ~ Sie das ernst? do you (really) mean it?; es gut ~ mean well.

meinetwegen adv. ['mainət'-] for my sake; on my behalf; because of me, on my account; for all I care; I don't mind or care.

'**Meinung** f (-/-en) opinion (über acc., von about, of); die öffentliche ~ (the) public opinion; meiner ~ nach in my opinion, to my mind; j-m (gehörig) die ~ sagen give s.o. a piece of one's mind; '**~saustausch** ['mainuŋs?-] m exchange of views (über acc. on); '**~sverschiedenheit** f difference of opinion (über acc. on); disagreement.

Meise orn. ['maizə] f (-/-n) titmouse.

Meißel ['maisəl] m (-s/-) chisel; '**2n** v/t. and v/i. (ge-, h) chisel; carve.

meist [maist] 1. adj. most; die ~en Leute most people; die ~e Zeit most of one's time; 2. adv.: s. meistens; am ~en most (of all); '**2bietende** ['~bi:təndə] m (-n/-n) highest bidder; '**~ens** adv. ['~əns], '**~en'teils** adv. mostly, in most cases; usually.

Meister ['maistər] m (-s/-) master, sl. boss; sports: champion; '**2haft 1.** adj. masterly; **2.** adv. in a masterly mann⁀er or way; '**2n** v/t. (ge-, h) mast⁀er; '**2schaft** f 1. (-/no pl.) mast⁀ y; **2.** (-/-en) sports: championship, title; '**~stück** n, '**~werk** n masterpi⁀ece.

'**Meistgebot** n highest bid, best offer.

Melancholie [melaŋko'li:] f (-/-n) melancholy; **2isch** [~'ko:liʃ] adj. melancholy; ~ sein F have the blues.

Melde|amt ['mɛldə-] n registration office; '**~liste** f sports: list of entries; '**2n** v/t. (ge-, h) announce; j-m et. ~ inᵢorm s.o. of s.th.; officially: notify s.th. to s.o.; j-n ~

enter s.o.'s name (*für, zu* for); *sich* ~ report o.s. (*bei* to); *school, etc.*: put up one's hand; answer the telephone; enter (one's name) (*für, zu* for *examination, etc.*); *sich* ~ *zu* apply for; *sich auf ein Inserat* ~ answer an advertisement.

'**Meldung** *f* (*-/-en*) information, advice; announcement; report; registration; application; *sports*: entry.

melke|n ['mɛlkən] *v/t.* ([*irr.,*] ge-, h) milk; '**2r** *m* (*-s/-*) milker.

Melod|ie ♪ [melo'di:] *f* (*-/-n*) melody; tune, air; **2isch** *adj.* [~'lo:diʃ] melodious, tuneful.

Melone [me'lo:nə] *f* (*-/-n*) ♀ melon; F bowler(-hat), *Am.* derby.

Membran [mɛm'brɑ:n] *f* (*-/-en*), ~**e** *f* (*-/-n*) membrane; *teleph. a.* diaphragm.

Memme F ['mɛmə] *f* (*-/-n*) coward; poltroon.

Memoiren [memo'ɑ:rən] *pl.* memoirs *pl.*

Menagerie [menaʒə'ri:] *f* (*-/-n*) menagerie.

Menge ['mɛŋə] *f* (*-/-n*) quantity; amount; multitude; crowd; *in großer* ~ in abundance; *persons, animals*: in crowds; e-e ~ *Geld* plenty of money, F lots *pl.* of money; *e-e* ~ *Bücher* a great many books; '**2n** *v/t.* (ge-, h) mix, blend; *sich* ~ mix (*unter acc.* with), mingle (with); *sich* ~ *in* (*acc.*) meddle *or* interfere with.

Mensch [mɛnʃ] *m* (*-en/-en*) human being; man; person, individual; *die* ~**en** *pl.* people *pl.*, the world, mankind; *kein* ~ nobody.

'**Menschen|affe** *zo.* *m* anthropoid ape; '~**alter** *n* generation, age; '~**feind** *m* misanthropist; '**2feindlich** *adj.* misanthropic; '~**fresser** *m* (*-s/-*) cannibal, man-eater; '~**freund** *m* philanthropist; '**2-freundlich** *adj.* philanthropic; '~**gedenken** *n* (*-s/no pl.*): *seit* ~ from time immemorial, within the memory of man; '~**geschlecht** *n* human race, mankind; '~**haß** *m* misanthropy; '~**kenner** *m* judge of men *or* human nature; '~**kenntnis** *f* knowledge of human nature; '~**leben** *n* human life; '**2leer** *adj.* deserted; '~**liebe** *f* philanthropy; '~**menge** *f* crowd (of people), throng; '**2möglich** *adj.* humanly possible; '~**raub** *m* kidnap(p)ing; '~**rechte** *n/pl.* human rights *pl.*; '**2scheu** *adj.* unsociable, shy; '~**seele** *f*: *keine* ~ not a living soul; '~**verstand** *m* human understanding; *gesunder* ~ common sense, F horse sense; '~**würde** *f* dignity of man.

'**Menschheit** *f* (*-/no pl.*) human race, mankind.

'**menschlich** *adj.* human; *fig.* hu-

mane; '**2keit** *f* (*-/no pl.*) human nature; humanity, humaneness.

Mentalität [mɛntali'tɛ:t] *f* (*-/-en*) mentality.

merk|bar *adj.* ['mɛrkbɑ:r] *s.* merklich; '**2blatt** *n* leaflet, instructional pamphlet; '**2buch** *n* notebook; '~**en** (ge-, h) **1.** *v/i.*: ~ *auf* (*acc.*) pay attention to, listen to; **2.** *v/t.* notice, perceive; find out, discover; *sich et.* ~ remember s.th.; bear s.th. in mind; '~**lich** *adj.* noticeable, perceptible; '**2mal** *n* (*-[e]s/-e*) mark, sign; characteristic, feature.

'**merkwürdig** *adj.* noteworthy, remarkable; strange, odd, curious; ~**erweise** *adv.* ['~gər'-] strange to say, strangely enough; '**2keit** *f* (*-/-en*) remarkableness; curiosity; peculiarity.

meßbar *adj.* ['mɛsbɑ:r] measurable.

Messe ['mɛsə] *f* (*-/-n*) ♱ fair; *eccl.* mass; ⚓, ⚓ mess.

messen ['mɛsən] *v/t.* (irr., ge-, h) measure; ⚓ gauge; *sich mit j-m* ~ compete with s.o.; *sich nicht mit j-m* ~ *können* be no match for s.o.; *gemessen an* (*dat.*) measured against, compared with.

Messer ['mɛsər] *n* (*-s/-*) knife; ⚕ scalpel; *bis aufs* ~ to the knife; *auf des* ~**s** *Schneide* on a razor-edge *or* razor's edge; '~**griff** *m* knife-handle; '~**held** *m* stabber; '~**klinge** *f* knife-blade; '~**schmied** *m* cutler; '~**schneide** *f* knife-edge; '~**stecher** *m* (*-s/-*) stabber; ~**stecherei** [~ʃtɛçə'raɪ] *f* (*-/-en*) knifing, knife-battle; '~**stich** *m* stab with a knife.

Messing ['mɛsiŋ] *n* (*-s/no pl.*) brass; '~**blech** *n* sheet-brass.

'**Meß|instrument** *n* measuring instrument; '~**latte** *f* surveyor's rod; '~**tisch** *m* surveyor's *or* plane table.

Metall [me'tal] *n* (*-s/-e*) metal; ~**arbeiter** *m* metal worker; **2en** *adj.* (of) metal, metallic; ~**geld** *n* coin(s *pl.*), specie; ~**glanz** *m* metallic lust|re, *Am.* -er; **2haltig** *adj.* metalliferous; ~**industrie** *f* metallurgical industry; ~**waren** *f/pl.* hardware.

Meteor *ast.* [mete'o:r] *n* (*-s/-e*) meteor; ~**ologe** [~oro'lo:gə] *m* (*-n/-n*) meteorologist; ~**ologie** [~orolo'gi:] *f* (*-/no pl.*) meteorology.

Meter ['me:tər] *n, m* (*-s/-*) met|re, *Am.* -er; '~**maß** *n* tape-measure.

Method|e [me'to:də] *f* (*-/-n*) method; ⊕ *a.* technique; **2isch** *adj.* methodical.

Metropole [metro'po:lə] *f* (*-/-n*) metropolis.)

Metzel|ei [mɛtsə'laɪ] *f* (*-/-en*) slaughter, massacre; '**2n** *v/t.* (ge-, h) butcher, slaughter, massacre.

Metzger ['mɛtsgər] *m* (*-s/-*) butcher; ~**ei** [~'raɪ] *f* (*-/-en*) butcher's (shop).

Meuchel|mord ['mɔʏçəl-] *m* assassination; '~**mörder** *m* assassin.

Meute ['mɔytə] f (-/-n) pack of hounds; *fig.* gang; ~**rei** [~'raı] f (-/-en) mutiny; ~**rer** m (-s/-) mutineer; **'2risch** *adj.* mutinous; **'2rn** v/i. (ge-, h) mutiny (gegen against).

mich *pers. pron.* [mıç] me; ~ (selbst) myself.

mied [mi:t] *pret. of* meiden.

Mieder ['mi:dər] n (-s/-) bodice; corset; **'~waren** f/pl. corsetry.

Miene ['mi:nə] f (-/-n) countenance, air; feature; *gute* ~ *zum bösen Spiel machen* grin and bear it; ~ *machen zu inf.* offer *or* threaten to *inf.*

mies F *adj.* [mi:s] miserable, poor; out of sorts, seedy.

Miet|e ['mi:tə] f (-/-n) rent; hire; *zur* ~ *wohnen* live in lodgings, be a tenant; **'2en** v/t. (ge-, h) rent (land, building, etc.); hire (horse, etc.); (take on) lease (land, etc.); ⚓, ✈ charter; **'~er** m (-s/-) tenant; lodger, *Am. a.* roomer; ⚖ lessee; **'2frei** *adj.* rent-free; **'~shaus** n block of flats, *Am.* apartment house; **'~vertrag** m tenancy agreement; lease; **'~wohnung** f lodgings *pl.*, flat, *Am.* apartment.

Migräne ✠ [mi'grɛ:nə] f (-/-n) migraine, megrim; sick headache.

Mikrophon [mikro'fo:n] n (-s/-e) microphone, F mike.

Mikroskop [mikro'sko:p] n (-s/-e) microscope; **2isch** *adj.* microscopic(al).

Milbe *zo.* ['mılbə] f (-/-n) mite.

Milch [mılç] f (-/no pl.) milk; milt, soft roe (of fish); **'~bar** f milk-bar; **'~bart** *fig.* m stripling; **'~brötchen** n (French) roll; **'~gesicht** n baby face; **'~glas** n frosted glass; **'2ig** *adj.* milky; **'~kanne** f milk-can; **'~kuh** f milk cow (a. fig.); **'~mädchen** f n milkmaid, dairymaid; **'~mann** F m milkman, dairyman; **'~pulver** n milk-powder; **'~reis** m rice-milk; **'~straße** *ast.* f Milky Way, Galaxy; **'~wirtschaft** f dairy-farm(ing); **'~zahn** m milk-tooth.

mild [mılt] 1. *adj. weather, punishment, etc.:* mild; *air, weather, light, etc.:* soft; *wine, etc.:* mellow, smooth; *reprimand, etc.:* gentle; 2. *adv.:* et. ~ *beurteilen* take a lenient view of s. th.

milde ['mıldə] 1. *adj. s.* mild 1; 2. *adv.:* ~ *gesagt* to put it mildly; 3. 2 f (-/no pl.) mildness; softness; smoothness; gentleness.

milder|n ['mıldərn] v/t. (ge-, h) soften, mitigate; soothe, alleviate (pain, etc.); **~de Umstände** ⚖ extenuating circumstances; **'2ung** f (-/-en) softening, mitigation; alleviation.

'mild|herzig *adj.* charitable; **'2herzigkeit** f (-/no pl.) charitableness;

'~tätig *adj.* charitable; **'2tätigkeit** f charity.

Milieu [mil'jø:] n (-s/-s) surroundings *pl.*, environment; class, circles *pl.*; local colo(u)r.

Militär [mili'tɛ:r] 1. n (-s/no pl.) military, armed forces *pl.*; army; 2. m (-s/-s) military man, soldier; **~attaché** [~ataʃe:] m (-s/-s) military attaché; **2dienst** m military service; **2isch** *adj.* military; **~musik** f military music; **~regierung** f military government; **~zeit** f (-/no pl.) term of military service.

Miliz ✠ [mi'li:ts] f (-/-en) militia; **~soldat** ✠ m militiaman.

Milliarde [mil'jardə] f (-/-n) thousand millions, milliard, *Am.* billion.

Millimeter [mili'-] n, m millimet|re, *Am.* -er.

Million [mil'jo:n] f (-/-en) million; **~är** [~o'nɛ:r] m (-s/-e) millionaire.

Milz *anat.* [mılts] f (-/-en) spleen, milt.

minder ['mındər] 1. *adv.* less; *nicht* ~ no less, likewise; 2. *adj.* less(er); smaller; minor; inferior; **'~begabt** *adj.* less gifted; **~bemittelt** *adj.* ['~bəmıtəlt] of moderate means; **2betrag** m deficit, shortage; **2einnahme** f shortfall in receipts; **2gewicht** n short weight; **'2heit** f (-/-en) minority; **~jährig** *adj.* ['~jɛ:rıç] under age, minor; **'2jährigkeit** f (-/no pl.) minority; **'~n** v/t. and v/refl. (ge-, h) diminish, lessen, decrease; **2ung** f (-/-en) decrease, diminution; **'~wertig** *adj.* inferior, of inferior quality; **'2wertigkeit** f (-/no pl.) inferiority; ✝ inferior quality; **'2wertigkeitskomplex** m inferiority complex.

mindest *adj.* ['mındəst] least; slightest; minimum; *nicht die* ~e *Aussicht* not the slightest chance; *nicht im* ~en not in the least, by no means; *zum* ~en at least; **'2alter** n minimum age; **'2anforderungen** f/pl. minumum requirements *pl.*; **'2betrag** m lowest amount; **'2einkommen** n minimum income; **'~ens** *adv.* at least; **'2gebot** n lowest bid; **'2lohn** m minimum wage; **'2maß** n minimum; *auf ein* ~ *herabsetzen* minimize; **'2preis** m minimum price.

Mine ['mi:nə] f (-/-n) ⚒, ✠, ⚓ mine; *pencil:* lead; *ball-point-pen:* refill.

Mineral [minə'ra:l] n (-s/-e, -ien) mineral; **2isch** *adj.* mineral; **~ogie** [~alo'gi:] f (-/no pl.) mineralogy; **~wasser** n (-s/⚌) mineral water.

Miniatur [minia'tu:r] f (-/-en) miniature; **~gemälde** n miniature.

Minirock ['mini-] m miniskirt.

Minister [mi'nıstər] m (-s/-) minister; Secretary (of State), *Am.* Secretary; **~ium** [~'te:rjum] *n* (-s/*Ministerien*) ministry; Office, *Am.* Department; **~präsident** *m* prime minister, premier; *in Germany, etc.*: minister president; **~rat** *m* (-[e]s/*~e*) cabinet council.

minus *adv.* ['mi:nus] minus, less, deducting.

Minute [mi'nu:tə] *f* (-/-n) minute; **~nzeiger** *m* minute-hand.

mir *pers. pron.* [mi:r] (to) me.

Misch|ehe ['miʃ?-] *f* mixed marriage; intermarriage; **2en** *v/t.* (ge-, h) mix, mingle; blend (*coffee, tobacco, etc.*); alloy (*metal*); shuffle (*cards*); sich **~** in (*acc.*) interfere in; join in (*conversation*); sich **~** unter (*acc.*) mix or mingle with (*the crowd*); **~ling** ['~liŋ] *m* (-s/-e) half-breed, half-caste; ♀, *zo.* hybrid; **~masch** F ['~maʃ] *m* (-es/-e) hotch-potch, jumble; **~ung** *f* (-/-en) mixture; blend; alloy.

miß|achten [mis'-] *v/t.* (no -ge-, h) disregard, ignore, neglect; slight, despise; **2achtung** *f* disregard, neglect; **~behagen 1.** *v/i.* (no -ge-, h) displease; **2.** **~** *n* discomfort, uneasiness; **2bildung** *f* malformation, deformity; **~billigen** *v/t.* (no -ge-, h) disapprove (of); **2billigung** *f* disapproval; **2brauch** *m* abuse; misuse; **~'brauchen** *v/t.* (no -ge-, h) abuse; misuse; **~bräuchlich** *adj.* ['~brɔʏçliç] abusive; improper; **~deuten** *v/t.* (no -ge-, h) misinterpret; **2deutung** *f* misinterpretation.

missen ['misən] *v/t.* (ge-, h) miss; do without, dispense with.

'Miß|erfolg *m* failure; fiasco; **~ernte** *f* bad harvest, crop failure.

Misse|tat ['misə-] *f* misdeed; crime; **~täter** *m* evil-doer, offender; criminal.

miß|'fallen *v/i.* (*irr. fallen*, no -ge-, h): j-m **~** displease s.o.; **2fallen** *n* (-s/no *pl.*) displeasure, dislike; **~fällig 1.** *adj.* displeasing; shocking; disparaging; **2.** *adv.*: sich **~** äußern über (*acc.*) speak ill of; **2geburt** *f* monster, freak (of nature), deformity; **2geschick** *n* bad luck, misfortune; mishap; **~gestimmt** *fig. adj.* ['~gəʃtimt] *s.* mißmutig; **~'glücken** *v/i.* (no -ge-, sein) fail; **~'gönnen** *v/t.* (no -ge-, h): j-m et. **~** envy or grudge s.o. s.th.; **2griff** *m* mistake, blunder; **2gunst** *f* envy, jealousy; **~günstig** *adj.* envious, jealous; **~'handeln** *v/t.* (no -ge-, h) ill-treat; maul, *sl.* manhandle; **2'handlung** *f* ill-treatment; mauling, *sl.* manhandling; ♯♯ assault and battery; **2'heirat** *f* misalliance; **~hellig** *adj.* dissonant, dissentient; **2helligkeit** *f* (-/-en) dissonance, dissension, discord.

Mission [mis'jo:n] *f* (-/-en) mission

(*a. pol. and fig.*); **~ar** [~o'na:r] *m* (-s/-e) missionary.

'Miß|klang *m* dissonance, discord (*both a. fig.*); **~kredit** *fig. m* (-[e]s/no *pl.*) discredit; in **~** bringen bring discredit upon *s.o.*

miß|'lang *pret. of* mißlingen; **~lich** *adj.* awkward; unpleasant; **~liebig** *adj.* ['~li:biç] unpopular; **~lingen** [~'liŋən] *v/i.* (*irr.*, no -ge-, sein) fail; **2lingen** *n* (-s/no *pl.*) failure; **2mut** *m* ill humo(u)r; discontent; **~mutig** *adj.* ill-humo(u)red; discontented; **~raten 1.** *v/i.* (*irr. raten*, no -ge-, sein) fail; turn out badly; **2.** *adj.* wayward; ill-bred; **2stand** *m* nuisance; grievance; **2stimmung** *f* ill humo(u)r; **2ton** *m* (-[e]s/*~e*) dissonance, discord (*both a. fig.*); **~trauen** *v/i.* (no -ge-, h): j-m **~** distrust or mistrust s.o.; **2trauen** *n* (-s/no *pl.*) distrust, mistrust; **~trauisch** *adj.* distrustful; suspicious; **2vergnügen** *n* (-s/no *pl.*) displeasure; **~vergnügt** *adj.* displeased; discontented; **2verhältnis** *n* disproportion; incongruity; **2verständnis** *n* misunderstanding; dissension; **~verstehen** *v/t.* (*irr. stehen*, no -ge-, h) misunderstand, mistake (*intention, etc.*); **2wirtschaft** *f* maladministration, mismanagement.

Mist [mist] *m* (-es/-e) dung, manure; dirt; F *fig.* trash, rubbish; **~beet** *n* hotbed.

Mistel ♀ ['mistəl] *f* (-/-n) mistletoe.

'Mist|gabel *f* dung-fork; **~haufen** *m* dung-hill.

mit [mit] **1.** *prp.* (*dat.*) with; **~** 20 Jahren at (the age of) twenty; **~** e-m Schlage at a blow; **~** Gewalt by force; **~** der Bahn by train; **2.** *adv.* also, too; **~** dabeisein be there too, be (one) of the party.

Mit|arbeiter ['mit?-] *m* co-worker; writing, art, etc.: collaborator; colleague; *newspaper, etc.*: contributor (*an dat.* to); **2benutzen** *v/t.* (*sep.*, no -ge-, h) use jointly or in common; **~besitzer** *m* joint owner; **~bestimmungsrecht** *n* right of co-determination; **~bewerber** *m* competitor; **~bewohner** *m* co-inhabitant, fellow-lodger; **2bringen** *v/t.* (*irr. bringen*, sep., -ge-, h) bring along (with one); **~bringsel** ['~briŋzəl] *n* (-s/-) little present; **~bürger** *m* fellow-citizen; **2einander** *adv.* [mit?ai'nandər] together, jointly; with each other, with one another; **2empfinden** ['mit?-] *n* (-s/no *pl.*) sympathy; **~erbe** ['mit?-] *m* co-heir; **~esser** ['mit?-] *m* (-s/-) blackhead; **2fahren** *v/i.* (*irr. fahren*, sep., -ge-, sein): mit j-m **~** drive or go with s.o.; j-n **~** lassen give s.o. a lift; **2fühlen**

v/i. (*sep.*, -ge-, *h*) sympathize (*mit* with); 'ℒgeben *v/t.* (*irr.* geben, *sep.*, -ge-, *h*) give along (*dat.* with); 'gefühl *n* sympathy; 'ℒgehen *v/i.* (*irr.* gehen, *sep.*, -ge-, *sein*): mit j-m ~ go with s.o.; 'gift *f* (-/-en) dowry, marriage portion.

'**Mitglied** *n* member; 'erversammlung *f* general meeting; 'erzahl *f* membership; 'sbeitrag *m* subscription; 'schaft *f* (-/*no pl.*) membership.

mit|'**hin** *adv.* consequently, therefore; ℒinhaber ['mitʔ-] *m* copartner; 'ℒkämpfer *m* fellow-combatant; 'kommen *v/i.* (*irr.* kommen, *sep.*, -ge-, *sein*) come along (*mit* with); *fig.* be able to follow; 'ℒläufer *pol. m* nominal member; *contp.* trimmer.

'**Mitleid** *n* (-[e]s/*no pl.*) compassion, pity; sympathy; *aus* ~ out of pity; ~ *haben mit* have or take pity on; 'enschaft *f* (-/*no pl.*): *in* ~ *ziehen* affect; implicate, involve; damage; 'ℒig *adj.* compassionate, pitiful; ℒ(s)los *adj.* ['t-] pitiless, merciless; ℒ(s)voll *adj.* ['t-] pitiful, compassionate.

'**mit**|**machen** (*sep.*, -ge-, *h*) **1.** *v/i.* make one of the party; **2.** *v/t.* take part in, participate in; follow, go with (*fashion*); go through (*hardships*); 'ℒmensch *m* fellow creature; 'nehmen *v/t.* (*irr.* nehmen, *sep.*, -ge-, *h*) take along (with one); *fig.* exhaust, wear out; *j-n* (*im Auto*) ~ give s.o. a lift; 'nichten *adv.* ['niçtən] by no means, not at all; 'rechnen *v/t.* (*sep.*, -ge-, *h*) include (in the account); *nicht* ~ leave out of account; *nicht mitgerechnet* not counting; 'reden (*sep.*, -ge-, *h*) **1.** *v/i.* join in the conversation; **2.** *v/t.*: *ein Wort or Wörtchen mitzureden haben* have a say (*bei* in); 'reißen *v/t.* (*irr.* reißen, *sep.*, -ge-, *h*) tear or drag along; *fig.* sweep along.

'**Mitschuld** *f* complicity (*an dat.* in); 'ℒig *adj.* accessary (*an dat.* to *crime*); 'ige *m* accessary, accomplice.

'**Mitschüler** *m* schoolfellow.

'**mitspiel**|**en** (*sep.*, -ge-, *h*) **1.** *v/i.* play (*bei* with); *sports*: be on the team; *thea.* appear, star (*in a play*); join in a game; *matter*: be involved; *j-m arg or übel* ~ play s.o. a nasty trick; **2.** *fig. v/t.* join in (*game*); 'ℒer *m* partner.

'**Mittag** *m* midday, noon; *heute* ℒ *at noon today*; *zu* ~ *essen* lunch, dine; 'essen *n* lunch(eon), dinner; 'ℒs *adv.* at noon.

'**Mittags**|**pause** *f* lunch hour; 'ruhe *f* midday rest; 'schlaf *m*, 'schläfchen *n* after-dinner nap, siesta; 'stunde *f* noon; 'tisch

fig. m lunch, dinner; 'zeit *f* noontide; lunch-time, dinner-time.

Mitte ['mitə] *f* (-/-n) middle; cent|re, *Am.* -er; *die goldene* ~ the golden *or* happy mean; *aus unserer* ~ from among us; ~ *Juli* in the middle of July; ~ *Dreißig* in the middle of one's thirties.

'**mitteil**|**en** *v/t.* (*sep.*, -ge-, *h*): *j-m et.* ~ communicate s.th. to s.o.; impart s.th. to s.o.; inform s.o. of s.th.; make s.th. known to s.o.; 'sam *adj.* communicative; 'ℒung *f* (-/-en) communication; information; communiqué.

Mittel ['mitəl] *n* (-s/-) means *sg.*, way; remedy (*gegen for*); average; ⅍ mean; *phys.* medium; ~ *pl. a.* means *pl.*, funds *pl.*, money; ~ *pl. und Wege* ways and means *pl.*; 'alter *n* Middle Ages *pl.*; 'ℒalterlich *adj.* medi(a)eval; 'ℒbar *adj.* mediate, indirect; 'ding *n*: *ein* ~ *zwischen* ... *und* ...; something between ... and ...; 'finger *m* middle finger; 'gebirge *n* highlands *pl.*; 'ℒgroß *adj.* of medium height; medium-sized; 'läufer *m sports*: centre half back, *Am.* center half back; 'ℒlos *adj.* without means, destitute; 'ℒmäßig *adj.* middling; mediocre; 'mäßigkeit *f* (-/*no pl.*) mediocrity; 'punkt *m* cent|re, *Am.* -er; *fig. a.* focus; 'ℒs *prp.* (*gen.*) by (means of), through; 'schule *f* intermediate school, *Am.* high school; 'smann *m* (-[e]s/ᵘer, *Mittelsleute*) mediator, go-between; 'stand *m* middle classes *pl.*; 'stürmer *m sports*: centre forward, *Am.* center forward; 'weg *fig. m* middle course; 'wort *gr. n* (-[e]s/ᵘer) participle.

mitten *adv.* ['mitən]: ~ *in or an or auf or unter* (*acc.*; *dat.*) in the midst *or* middle of; ~ *entzwei* right in two; ~ *im Winter* in the depth of winter; ~ *in der Nacht* in the middle *or* dead of night; ~ *ins Herz* right into the heart; ~'drin *F adv.* right in the middle; ~'durch *F adv.* right through *or* across.

Mitter|**nacht** ['mitər-] *f* midnight; *um* ~ at midnight; ℒnächtig *adj.* ['nɛçtiç], ℒnächtlich *adj.* midnight.

Mittler ['mitlər] **1.** *m* (-s/-) mediator, intercessor; **2.** ℒ *adj.* middle, central; average, medium; 'ℒ'weile *adv.* meanwhile, (in the) meantime.

Mittwoch ['mitvɔx] *m* (-[e]s/-e) Wednesday; 'ℒs *adv.* on Wednesday(s), every Wednesday.

mit|'**unter** *adv.* now and then, sometimes; 'verantwortlich *adj.* jointly responsible; 'ℒwelt *f* (-/*no pl.*): *die* ~ our, *etc.* contemporaries *pl.*

'mitwirk|en v/i. (sep., -ge-, h) co-operate (bei in), contribute (to), take part (in); '2ende m (-n/-n) thea. performer, actor, player (a. ♪); die ~n pl. the cast; '2ung f (-/no pl.) co(-)operation, contribution.

'Mitwisser m (-s/-) confidant; 2⁄₃ accessary.   [rechnen.]

'mitzählen v/t. (sep., -ge-, h) s. mit-

Mix|becher ['miks-] m (cocktail-) shaker; '2en v/t. (ge-, h) mix; ~tur [~'tu:r] f (-/-en) mixture.

Möbel ['mø:bəl] n (-s/-) piece of furniture; ~ pl. furniture; '~händ-ler m furniture-dealer; '~spedi-teur m furniture-remover; '~stück n piece of furniture; '~tischler m cabinet-maker; '~wagen m pan-technicon, Am. furniture truck.

mobil adj. [mo'bi:l] ✕ mobile; F active, nimble; ~ machen ✕ mobi-lize; 2iar [~il'ja:r] n (-s/-e) furni-ture; movables pl.; ~isieren [~ili-'zi:rən] v/t. (no -ge-, h) ✕ mobilize; ✝ realize (property, etc.); 2ma-chung ✕ [mo'bi:lmaxuŋ] f (-/-en) mobilization.

möblieren [mø'bli:rən] v/t. (no -ge-, h) furnish; möbliertes Zimmer furnished room, F bed-sitter.

mochte ['mɔxtə] pret. of mögen.

Mode ['mo:də] f (-/-n) fashion, vogue; use, custom; die neueste ~ the latest fashion; in ~ in fashion or vogue; aus der ~ kommen grow or go out of fashion; die ~ bestimmen set the fashion; '~artikel m/pl. fancy goods pl., novelties pl.; '~far-be f fashionable colo(u)r.

Modell [mo'dɛl] n (-s/-e) ⊕, fashion, paint.: model; pattern, design; ⊕ mo(u)ld; j-m ~ stehen paint. pose for s.o.; ~eisenbahn f model rail-way; 2ieren [~'li:rən] v/t. (no -ge-, h) model, mo(u)ld, fashion.

'Moden|schau f dress parade, fashion-show; '~zeitung f fashion magazine.

Moder ['mo:dər] m (-s/no pl.) must, putrefaction; '~geruch m musty smell; '2ig adj. musty, putrid.

modern¹ ['mo:dərn] v/i. (ge-, h) putrefy, rot, decay.

modern² adj. [mo'dɛrn] modern; progressive; up-to-date; fashion-able; ~isieren [~i'zi:rən] v/t. (no -ge-, h) modernize, bring up to date.

'Mode|salon m fashion house; '~schmuck m costume jewel(le)ry; '~waren f/pl. fancy goods pl.; '~zeichner m fashion-designer.

modifizieren [modifi'tsi:rən] v/t. (no -ge-, h) modify.

modisch adj. ['mo:diʃ] fashionable, stylish.   [liner.]

Modistin [mo'distin] f (-/-nen) mil-]

Mogel|ei F [mo:gə'lai] f (-/-en) cheat; '2n F v/i. (ge-, h) cheat.

mögen ['mø:gən] (irr., h) 1. v/i. (ge-) be willing; ich mag nicht I don't like to; 2. v/t. (ge-) want, wish; like, be fond of; nicht ~ dislike; not to be keen on (food, etc.); lieber ~ like better, prefer; 3. v/aux. (no -ge-) may, might; ich möchte wissen I should like to know; ich möchte lieber gehen I would rather go; das mag (wohl) sein that's (well) pos-sible; wo er auch sein mag wherever he may be; mag er sagen, was er will let him say what he likes.

möglich ['mø:kliç] 1. adj. possible; practicable, feasible; market, crim-inal, etc.: potential; alle ~en all sorts of things; alles ~e all sorts of things; sein ~stes tun do one's utmost or level best; nicht ~! you don't say (so)!; so bald etc. wie ~ = 2. adv.: ~st bald etc. as soon, etc., as possible; '~er'weise adv. possibly, if pos-sible; perhaps; '2keit f (-/-en) pos-sibility; chance; nach ~ if possible.

Mohammedan|er [mohame'da:-nər] m (-s/-) Muslim, Moslem, Mohammedan; 2isch adj. Muslim, Moslem, Mohammedan.

Mohn ♀ [mo:n] m (-[e]s/-e) poppy.

Möhre ♀ ['mø:rə] f (-/-n) carrot.

Mohrrübe ♀ ['mo:r-] f carrot.

Molch zo. [mɔlç] m (-[e]s/-e) sala-mander; newt.

Mole ⚓ ['mo:lə] f (-/-n) mole, jetty.

molk [mɔlk] pret. of melken.

Molkerei [mɔlkə'rai] f (-/-en) dairy; ~produkte n/pl. dairy products pl.

Moll ♪ [mɔl] n (-/-) minor (key).

mollig F adj. ['mɔliç] snug, cosy; plump, rounded.

Moment [mo'mɛnt] (-[e]s/-e) 1. m moment, instant; im ~ at the moment; 2. n motive; fact(or); ⊕ momentum; ⊕ impulse (a. fig.); 2an [~'ta:n] 1. adj. momentary; 2. adv. at the moment, for the time being; ~aufnahme phot. f snapshot, instantaneous photograph.

Monarch [mo'narç] m (-en/-en) monarch; ~ie [~'çi:] f (-/-n) mon-archy.

Monat ['mo:nat] m (-[e]s/-e) month; 2elang 1. adj. lasting for months; 2. adv. for months; 2lich 1. adj. monthly; 2. adv. monthly, a month.

Mönch [mœnç] m (-[e]s/-e) monk, friar.

'Mönchs|kloster n monastery; '~kutte f (monk's) frock; '~leben n monastic life; '~orden m monastic order; '~zelle f monk's cell.

Mond [mo:nt] m (-[e]s/-e) moon; hinter dem ~ leben be behind the times; '~fähre f lunar module; '~finsternis f lunar eclipse; '2hell adj. moonlit; '~schein m (-[e]s/no pl.) moonlight; '~sichel f crescent; '2süchtig adj. moonstruck.

Mono|log [mono'lo:k] m (-s/-e)

monologue, *Am.* *a.* monolog;
soliloquy; '**pol** ⚥ *n* (-s/-e) monop-
oly; ⚥**polisieren** [ˌoli'ziːrən] *v/t.*
(no -ge-, h) monopolize; ⚥'**ton** *adj.*
monotonous; ⚥**tonie** [ˌto'niː] *f*
(-/-n) monotony.

Monstrum ['mɔnstrum] *n* (-s/Mon-
stren, Monstra) monster.

Montag ['moːn-] *m* Monday; '⚥**s**
adv. on Monday(s), every Monday.

Montage ⊕ [mɔn'taːʒə] *f* (-/-n)
mounting, fitting; setting up; as-
semblage, assembly.

Montan|industrie [mɔn'taːn-] *f*
coal and steel industries *pl.*; ⚥**union**
f European Coal and Steel Community.

Mont|eur [mɔn'tøːr] *m* (-s/-e) ⊕
fitter, assembler; *esp.* mot., ⚡
mechanic; ⚥**euranzug** *m* overall;
⚥**ieren** [ˌti'ːrən] *v/t.* (no -ge-, h)
mount, fit; set up; assemble; ⚥**ur**
⚡ [ˌ'tuːr] *f* (-/-en) regimentals *pl.*

Moor [moːr] *n* (-[e]s/-e) bog; swamp;
'⚥**bad** *n* mud-bath; '⚥**ig** *adj.* boggy,
marshy.

Moos ⚥ [moːs] *n* (-es/-e) moss; '⚥**ig**
adj. mossy.

Moped *mot.* ['moːpɛt] *n* (-s/-s)
moped.

Mops *zo.* [mɔps] *m* (-es/⚥e) pug;
'⚥**en** *v/t.* (ge-, h) F pilfer, pinch; *sl.*:
sich ~ be bored stiff.

Moral [mo'raːl] *f* (-/⚥ -en) morality; morals *pl.*; moral; ⚡, *etc.*:
morale; ⚥**isch** *adj.* moral; ⚥**isieren**
[ˌali'ziːrən] *v/i.* (no -ge-, h) moral-
ize.

Morast [mo'rast] *m* (-es/-e, ⚥e)
slough, morass; *s.* Moor; mire, mud;
⚥**ig** *adj.* marshy; muddy, miry.

Mord [mɔrt] *m* (-[e]s/-e) murder
(*an dat.* of); *e-n ~* begehen commit
murder; '⚥**anschlag** *m* murderous
assault; ⚥**en** [ˌdən] *v/i.* (ge-, h)
commit murder(s).

Mörder ['mœrdər] *m* (-s/-) mur-
derer; ⚥**isch** *adj.* murderous;
climate, etc.: deadly; ⚡ *competition*:
cut-throat.

'**Mord|gier** *f* lust of murder, blood-
thirstiness; ⚥**gierig** *adj.* bloodthirsty; '⚥**kommission** *f* homicide
squad; '⚥**prozeß** ⚥⚡ *m* murder trial.

'**Mords|angst** *f* F blue funk, *sl.*
mortal fear; ⚥'**glück** F *n* stupendous
luck; '⚥**kerl** F *m* devil of a fellow';
⚥**spek'takel** F *m* hullabaloo.

Morgen ['mɔrgən] **1.** *m* (-s/-) morning; *measure*: acre; *am ~ s.* morgens;
2. ⚥ *adv.* tomorrow; *~ früh (abend)*
tomorrow morning (evening *or*
night); *~ in acht Tagen* tomorrow
week; '⚥**ausgabe** *f* morning edition; '⚥**blatt** *n* morning paper;
'⚥**dämmerung** *f* dawn, daybreak;
⚥**gebet** *n* morning prayer; '⚥**gym-
nastik** *f* morning exercises *pl.*;
⚥**land** *n* (-[e]s/*no pl.*) Orient, East;

'**rock** *m* peignoir, dressing-gown,
wrapper (*for woman*); '⚥**röte** *f*
dawn; '⚥**s** *adv.* in the morning; '⚥
zeitung *f* morning paper.

'**morgig** *adj.* of tomorrow.

Morphium *pharm.* ['mɔrfium] *n*
(-s/*no pl.*) morphia, morphine,

morsch *adj.* [mɔrʃ] rotten, decayed;
brittle.

Mörser ['mœrzər] *m* (-s/-) mortar
(*a.* ⚥).

Mörtel ['mœrtəl] *m* (-s/-) mortar.

Mosaik [moza'iːk] *n* (-s/-e) mosaic;
⚥**fußboden** *m* mosaic *or* tessellated
pavement.

Moschee [mɔ'ʃeː] *f* (-/-n) mosque.

Moschus ['mɔʃus] *m* (-/*no pl.*) musk.

Moskito *zo.* [mɔs'kiːto] *m* (-s/-s)
mosquito; ⚥**netz** *n* mosquito-net.

Moslem ['mɔslɛm] *m* (-s/-s) Mus-
lim, Moslem.

Most [mɔst] *m* (-es/-e) must, grape-
juice; *of apples*: cider; *of pears*:
perry.

Mostrich ['mɔstriç] *m* (-[e]s/*no pl.*)
mustard.

Motiv [mo'tiːf] *n* (-s/-e) motive,
reason; *paint.*, ⚥ motif; ⚥**ieren**
[ˌi'viːrən] *v/t.* (no -ge-, h) motivate.

Motor ['moːtɔr] *m* (-s/-en) engine,
esp. ⚥ motor; '⚥**boot** *n* motor boat;
'⚥**defekt** *m* engine *or* ⚥ motor
trouble; '⚥**haube** *f* bonnet, *Am.*
hood; ⚥**isieren** [motori'ziːrən] *v/t.*
(no -ge-, h) motorize; ⚥**isierung**
[motori'ziːruŋ] *f* (-/*no pl.*) motor-
ization; '⚥**rad** *n* motor (bi)cycle;
'⚥**radfahrer** *m* motor cyclist; '⚥**roller** *m* (motor) scooter; '⚥**sport** *m*
motoring.

Motte *zo.* ['mɔtə] *f* (-/-n) moth.

'**Motten|kugel** *f* moth-ball; ⚥**si-
cher** *adj.* mothproof; ⚥**zerfressen**
adj. moth-eaten.

Motto ['mɔto] *n* (-s/-s) motto.

Möwe *orn.* ['møːvə] *f* (-/-n) sea-gull,
(sea-)mew.

Mücke *zo.* ['mykə] *f* (-/-n) midge,
gnat, mosquito; *aus e-r ~ e-n Elefanten machen* make a mountain
out of a molehill; '⚥**nstich** *m* gnat-
bite.

Mucker ['mukər] *m* (-s/-) bigot,
hypocrite.

müd|e *adj.* ['myːdə] tired, weary;
e-r Sache ~ sein be weary *or* tired
of s.th.; ⚥**igkeit** *f* (-/*no pl.*) tired-
ness, weariness.

Muff [muf] *m* **1.** (-[e]s/-e) muff;
2. (-[e]s/*no pl.*) mo(u)ldy *or* musty
smell; '⚥**e** ⊕ *f* (-s/-n) sleeve, socket;
'⚥**eln** F *v/i.* (ge-, h) munch; mumble; '⚥**ig** *adj.* smell, *etc.*: musty,
fusty; *air*: close; *fig.* sulky, sullen.

Mühe ['myːə] *f* (-/-n) trouble, pains
pl.; *(nicht) der ~ wert* (not) worth
while; *j-m ~ machen* give s.o.
trouble; *sich ~ geben* take pains
(*mit over*, with *s.th.*); '⚥**los** *adj.*

effortless, easy; '2n v/refl. (ge-, h) take pains, work hard; '2voll adj. troublesome, hard; laborious.

Mühle ['my:lə] f (-/-n) mill.

'**Müh|sal** f (-/-e) toil, trouble; hardship; '2sam, '2selig 1. adj. toilsome, troublesome; difficult; 2. adv. laboriously; with difficulty.

Mulatte [mu'latə] m (-n/-n) mulatto.

Mulde ['muldə] f (-/-n) trough; depression, hollow.

Mull [mul] m (-[e]s/-e) mull.

Müll [myl] m (-[e]s/no pl.) dust, rubbish, refuse, Am. a. garbage; '~abfuhr f removal of refuse; '~eimer m dust-bin, Am. garbage can.

Müller ['mylər] m (-s/-) miller.

'**Müll|fahrer** m dust-man, Am. garbage collector; '~haufen m dust-heap; '~kasten m s. Mülleimer; '~kutscher m s. Müllfahrer; '~wagen m dust-cart, Am. garbage cart.

Multipli|kation [multiplika-'tsjo:n] f (-/-en) multiplication; 2zieren [~'tsi:rən] v/t. (no -ge-, h) multiply (mit by).

Mumie ['mu:mjə] f (-/-n) mummy.

Mumps [mumps] m, F f (-/no pl.) mumps.

Mund [munt] m (-[e]s/=er) mouth; den ~ halten hold one's tongue; den ~voll nehmen talk big; sich den ~ verbrennen put one's foot in it; nicht auf den ~ gefallen sein have a ready or glib tongue; j-m über den ~ fahren cut s.o. short; '~art f dialect; '2artlich adj. dialectal.

Mündel ['myndəl] m, n (-s/-), girl: a. f (-/-n) ward, pupil; '2sicher adj.: ~e Papiere n/pl. † gilt-edged securities pl.

münden ['myndən] v/i. (ge-, h): ~ in (acc.) river, etc.: fall or flow into; street, etc.: run into.

'**mund|faul** adj. too lazy to speak; '~gerecht adj. palatable (a. fig.); '2harmonika f f mouth-organ; '2höhle anat. f oral cavity.

mündig ['myndiç] adj.: ~ werden come of age; '2keit f (-/no pl.) majority.

mündlich ['myntliç] 1. adj. oral, verbal; 2. adv. a. by word of mouth.

'**Mund|pflege** f oral hygiene; '~raub m theft of comestibles; '~stück n mouthpiece (of musical instrument, etc.); tip (of cigarette); '2tot adj.: ~ machen silence or gag s.o.

'**Mündung** f (-/-en) mouth; a. estuary (of river); muzzle (of fire-arms).

'**Mund|vorrat** m provisions pl., victuals pl.; '~wasser n (-s/=) mouth-wash, gargle; '~werk F fig. n: ein gutes ~ haben have the gift of the gab.

Munition [muni'tsjo:n] f (-/-en) ammunition.

munkeln F ['muŋkəln] (ge-, h) 1. v/i. whisper; 2. v/t. whisper, rumo(u)r; man munkelt there is a rumo(u)r afloat. [lively; merry.\
munter adj. ['muntər] awake; fig.:\
Münz|e ['myntsə] f (-/-n) coin; (small) change; medal; mint; für bare ~ nehmen take at face value; j-m et. mit gleicher ~ heimzahlen pay s.o. back in his own coin; '~einheit f (monetary) unit, standard of currency; '2en v/t. (ge-, h) coin, mint; gemünzt sein auf (acc.) be meant for, be aimed at; '~fernsprecher teleph. m coin-box telephone; '~fuß m standard (of coinage); '~wesen n monetary system.

mürbe adj. ['myrbə] tender; pastry, etc.: crisp, short; meat: well-cooked; material: brittle; F fig. worn-out, demoralized; F j-n ~ machen break s.o.'s resistance; F ~ werden give in.

Murmel ['murməl] f (-/-n) marble; '2n v/i. and v/i. (ge-, h) mumble, murmur; '~tier zo. n marmot.

murren ['murən] v/i. (ge-, h) grumble, F grouch (both: über acc. at, over, about).

mürrisch adj. ['myriʃ] surly, sullen.

Mus [mu:s] n (-es/-e) pap; stewed fruit.

Muschel ['muʃəl] f (-/-n) zo.: mussel; shell, conch; teleph. ear-piece.

Museum [mu'ze:um] n (-s/Museen) museum.

Musik [mu'zi:k] f (-/no pl.) music; '~alienhandlung [~i'ka:ljən-] f music-shop; 2alisch adj. [~i'ka:liʃ] musical; ~ant [~i'kant] m (-en/-en) musician; '~automat m juke-box; ~er ['mu:zikər] m (-s/-) musician; bandsman; '~instrument n musical instrument; '~lehrer m music-master; '~stunde f music-lesson; '~truhe f radiogram(ophone), Am. radio-phonograph.

musizieren [muzi'tsi:rən] v/i. (no -ge-, h) make or have music.

Muskat ♀ [mus'ka:t] m (-[e]s/-e) nutmeg; ~nuß ♀ f nutmeg.

Muskel ['muskəl] m (-s/-n) muscle; '~kater F m stiffness and soreness, Am. a. charley horse; '~kraft f muscular strength; '~zerrung ♠ f pulled muscle.

Muskul|atur [muskula'tu:r] f (-/-en) muscular system, muscles pl.; 2ös adj. [~'lø:s] muscular, brawny.

Muß [mus] n (-/no pl.) necessity; es ist ein ~ it is a must.

Muße ['mu:sə] f (-/no pl.) leisure; spare time; mit ~ at one's leisure.

Musselin [musə'li:n] m (-s/-e) muslin.

müssen ['mysən] (irr., h) 1. v/i. (ge-): ich muß I must; 2. v/aux. (no -ge-): ich muß I must, I have to;

I am obliged *or* compelled *or* forced to; I am bound to; *ich habe gehen* ~ I had to go; *ich müßte (eigentlich) wissen* I ought to know.

müßig *adj.* ['myːsiç] idle; superfluous; useless; '2gang *m* idleness, laziness; 2gänger ['~gɛŋər] *m* (-s/-) idler, loafer; lazy-bones.

mußte ['mustə] *pret. of* müssen.

Muster ['mustər] *n* (-s/-) model; example, paragon; design, pattern; specimen; sample; '~betrieb *m* model factory *or* ✗ farm; '~gatte *m* model husband; '2gültig, '2haft **1.** *adj.* model, exemplary, perfect; **2.** *adv.*: *sich* ~ *benehmen* be on one's best behavio(u)r; '~kollektion ✝ *f* range of samples; '2n *v/t.* (ge-, h) examine; eye; ✗ inspect, review; figure, pattern (*fabric, etc.*); '~schutz *m* protection of patterns and designs; '~ung *f* (-/-en) examination; ✗ review; pattern (*of fabric, etc.*); '~werk *n* standard work.

Mut [muːt] *m* (-[e]s/*no pl.*) courage; spirit; pluck; ~ *fassen* pluck up courage, summon one's courage; *den* ~ *sinken lassen* lose courage *or* heart; *guten* ~(*e*)*s sein* be of good cheer; '2ig *adj.* courageous, plucky; '2los *adj.* discouraged; despondent; '~losigkeit *f* (-/*no pl.*) discouragement; despondency; 2maßen ['~maːsən] *v/t.* (ge-, h) suppose, guess, surmise; '2maßlich *adj.* presumable; supposed; *heir:* presumptive; '~maßung *f* (-/-en) supposition, surmise; *bloße* ~*en pl.* guesswork.

Mutter ['mutər] *f* **1.** (-/⁻) mother; **2.** ⊕ (-/-n) nut; '~brust *f* mother's breast; '~leib *m* womb.

mütterlich *adj.* ['mytərliç] motherly; maternal; ~erseits *adv.* ['~ər-'zaɪts] on *or* from one's mother's side; *uncle, etc.*: maternal.

Mutter|liebe *f* motherly love; '2los *adj.* motherless; '~mal *n* birth-mark, mole; '~milch *f* mother's milk; '~schaft *f* (-/*no pl.*) maternity, motherhood; '2'seelenal'lein *adj.* all *or* utterly alone; ~söhnchen ['~zøːnçən] *n* (-s/-) milksop, *sl.* sissy; '~sprache *f* mother tongue; '~witz *m* (-es/*no pl.*) mother wit.

Mutwill|e *m* wantonness; mischievousness; '2ig *adj.* wanton; mischievous; wilful.

Mütze ['mytsə] *f* (-/-n) cap.

Myrrhe ['myrə] *f* (-/-n) myrrh.

Myrte ⚘ ['myrtə] *f* (-/-n) myrtle.

mysteri|ös *adj.* [myster'jøːs] mysterious; 2um ['~'teːrjum] *n* (-s/*Mysterien*) mystery.

Mystifi|kation [mystifika'tsjoːn] *f* (-/-en) mystification; 2zieren [~'tsiːrən] *v/t.* (*no* -ge-, h) mystify.

Mysti|k ['mystik] *f* (-/*no pl.*) mysticism; 2sch *adj.* mystic(al).

Myth|e ['myːtə] *f* (-/-n) myth; '2isch *adj.* mythic; *esp. fig.* mythical; ~ologie [mytolo'giː] *f* (-/-n) mythology; 2ologisch *adj.* [myto-'loːgiʃ] mythological; ~os ['~ɔs] *m* (-/*Mythen*), ~us ['~us] *m* (-/*Mythen*) myth.

N

na *int.* [na] now!, then!, well!, *Am. a.* hey!

Nabe ['naːbə] *f* (-/-n) hub.

Nabel *anat.* ['naːbəl] *m* (-s/-) navel.

nach [naːx] **1.** *prp.* (*dat.*) direction, striving: after; to(wards), for (*a.* ~ ... *hin or zu*); *succession:* after; *time:* after, past; *manner, measure, example:* according to; ~ *Gewicht* by weight; ~ *deutschem Geld* in German money; *e-r* ~ *dem andern* one by one; *fünf Minuten* ~ *eins* five minutes past one; **2.** *adv.* after; ~ *und* ~ little by little, gradually; ~ *wie vor* now as before, still.

nachahm|en ['naːx⁹aːmən] *v/t.* (*sep.*, -ge-, h) imitate, copy; counterfeit; '~ens'wert *adj.* worthy of imitation, exemplary; '2er *m* (-s/-) imitator; '2ung *f* (-/-en) imitation; copy; counterfeit, fake.

Nachbar ['naxbaːr] *m* (-n, -s/-n), '~in *f* (-/-nen) neighbo(u)r; '~schaft *f* (-/-en) neighbo(u)rhood, vicinity.

'Nachbehandlung ✗ *f* after-treatment.

'nachbestell|en *v/t.* (*sep.*, *no* -ge-, h) repeat one's order for *s.th.*; '2ung *f* repeat (order).

'nachbeten *v/t.* (*sep.*, -ge-, h) echo.

'Nachbildung *f* copy, imitation; replica; dummy.

'nachblicken *v/i.* (*sep.*, -ge-, h) look after.

nachdem *cj.* [naːx'deːm] after, when; *je* ~ according as.

'nachdenk|en *v/i.* (*irr.* denken, *sep.*, -ge-, h) think (*über acc.* over, about); reflect, meditate (*über acc.* on); '2en *n* (-s/*no pl.*) reflection, meditation; musing; '~lich *adj.* meditative, reflecting; pensive.

'Nachdichtung *f* free version.

'Nachdruck *m* **1.** (-[e]s/*no pl.*) stress, emphasis; **2.** *typ.* (-[e]s/-e) reprint; *unlawfully*: piracy, pirated edition; '2en *v/t.* (*sep.*, -ge-, h) reprint; *unlawfully*: pirate.

nachdrücklich ['nɑːxdryklɪç] **1.** *adj.* emphatic, energetic; forcible; positive; **2.** *adv.*: ~ betonen emphasize.

nacheifern ['nɑːx⁹-] *v/i.* (*sep.*, -ge-, h) emulate *s.o.*

nacheinander *adv.* [nɑːx⁹aɪˈnandər] one after another, successively; by *or* in turns.

nachempfinden ['nɑːx⁹-] *v/t.* (*irr.* empfinden, *sep.*, no -ge-, h) s. nachfühlen.

nacherzähl|en ['nɑːx⁹-] *v/t.* (*sep.*, no -ge-, h) repeat; retell; *dem Englischen nacherzählt* adapted from the English; '2ung ['nɑːx⁹-] *f* repetition; story retold, reproduction.

'**Nachfolge** *f* succession; '2n *v/i.* (*sep.*, -ge-, sein) follow *s.o.*; *j-m im Amt* ~ succeed s.o. in his office; '~r *m* (-s/-) follower; successor.

'**nachforsch|en** *v/i.* (*sep.*, -ge-, h) investigate; search for; '2ung *f* investigation, inquiry, search.

'**Nachfrage** *f* inquiry; † demand; '2n *v/i.* (*sep.*, -ge-, h) inquire (*nach* after).

'**nach|fühlen** *v/t.* (*sep.*, -ge-, h): es *j-m* ~ feel *or* sympathize with s.o.; '~füllen *v/t.* (*sep.*, -ge-, h) fill up, refill; '~geben *v/i.* (*irr.* geben, *sep.*, -ge-, h) give way (*dat.* to); *fig.* give in, yield (to); '2gebühr ⚹ *f* surcharge; '~gehen *v/i.* (*irr.* gehen, *sep.*, -ge-, sein) follow (*s.o.*, *business*, *trade*, *etc.*); pursue (*pleasure*); attend to (*business*); investigate *s.th.*; *watch*: be slow; '2geschmack *m* (-[e]s/no *pl.*) after-taste.

nachgiebig *adj.* ['nɑːxɡiːbɪç] elastic, flexible; *fig.* a. yielding, compliant; '2keit *f* (-/-en) flexibility; compliance.

'**nachgrübeln** *v/i.* (*sep.*, -ge-, h) ponder, brood (*both*: *über acc.* over), muse (on).

nachhaltig *adj.* ['nɑːxhaltɪç] lasting, enduring.

nach'her *adv.* afterwards; then; *bis* ~*!* see you later!, so long!

'**Nachhilfe** *f* help, assistance; '~lehrer *m* coach, private tutor; '~unterricht *m* private lesson(s *pl.*), coaching.

'**nach|holen** *v/t.* (*sep.*, -ge-, h) make up for, make good; '2hut ⚔ *f* (-/-en) rear-(guard); *die* ~ *bilden* bring up the rear (*a. fig.*); '~jagen *v/i.* (*sep.*, -ge-, sein) chase *or* pursue *s.o.*; '~klingen *v/i.* (*irr.* klingen, *sep.*, -ge-, h) resound, echo.

'**Nachkomme** *m* (-n/-n) descendant; ~n *pl.* *esp.* ⚖ issue; '2n *v/i.* (*irr.* kommen, *sep.*, -ge-, sein) follow; come later; obey (*order*); meet (*liabilities*); '~nschaft *f* (-/-en) descendants *pl.*, *esp.* ⚖ issue.

'**Nachkriegs...** post-war.

Nachlaß ['nɑːxlas] *m* (*Nachlasses/Nachlasse, Nachlässe*) † reduction, discount; assets *pl.*, estate, inheritance (*of deceased*).

'**nachlassen** (*irr.* lassen, *sep.*, -ge-, h) **1.** *v/t.* reduce (*price*); **2.** *v/i.* deteriorate; slacken, relax; diminish; *pain*, *rain*, *etc.*: abate; *storm*: calm down; *strength*: wane; *interest*: flag.

'**nachlässig** *adj.* careless, negligent.

'**nach|laufen** *v/i.* (*irr.* laufen, *sep.*, -ge-, sein) run (*dat.* after); '~lesen *v/t.* (*irr.* lesen, *sep.*, -ge-, h) *in book*: look up; ✓ glean; '~liefern † *v/t.* (*sep.*, -ge-, h) deliver subsequently; repeat delivery of; '~lösen *v/t.* (*sep.*, -ge-, h): e-e Fahrkarte ~ take a supplementary ticket; buy a ticket en route; '~machen *v/t.* (*sep.*, -ge-, h) imitate (*j-m et. s.o. in s.th.*); copy; counterfeit, forge; '~messen *v/t.* (*irr.* messen, *sep.*, -ge-, h) measure again.

'**Nachmittag** *m* afternoon; '2s *adv.* in the afternoon; '~svorstellung *thea. f* matinée.

Nach|nahme ['nɑːxnɑːmə] *f* (-/-n) cash on delivery, *Am.* collect on delivery; *per* ~ *schicken* send C.O.D.; '~name *m* surname, last name; '~porto ⚹ *n* surcharge.

'**nach|prüfen** *v/t.* (*sep.*, -ge-, h) verify; check; '~rechnen *v/t.* (*sep.*, -ge-, h) reckon over again; check (*bill*).

'**Nachrede** *f*: üble ~ ⚖ defamation (of character); *oral*: slander, *written*: libel; '2n *v/t.* (*sep.*, -ge-, h): *j-m Übles* ~ slander s.o.

Nachricht ['nɑːxrɪçt] *f* (-/-en) news; message; report; information, notice; ~ *geben s. benachrichtigen*; '~enagentur *f* news agency; '~endienst *m* news service; ⚔ intelligence service; '~ensprecher *m* newscaster; '~enwesen *n* (-s/no *pl.*) communications *pl.*

'**nachrücken** *v/i.* (*sep.*, -ge-, sein) move along.

'**Nach|ruf** *m* obituary (notice); '~ruhm *m* posthumous fame.

'**nachsagen** *v/t.* (*sep.*, -ge-, h) repeat; *man sagt ihm nach, daß he is* said to *inf.*

'**Nachsaison** *f* dead *or* off season.

'**nachschicken** *v/t.* (*sep.*, -ge-, h) s. nachsenden.

'**nachschlage|n** *v/t.* (*irr.* schlagen, *sep.*, -ge-, h) consult (*book*); look up (*word*); '2werk *n* reference-book.

'**Nach|schlüssel** *m* skeleton key; '~schrift *f* in *letter*: postscript; '~schub *esp.* ⚔ *m* supplies *pl.*; '~schubweg ⚔ *m* supply line.

'**nach|sehen** (*irr.* sehen, *sep.*, -ge-, h) **1.** *v/i.* look after; ~, *ob* (go and) see whether; **2.** *v/t.* look after; examine, inspect; check; overhaul (*machine*); *s. nachschlagen*; *j-m et.* ~ indulge s.o. in s.th.; '~**senden** *v/t.* ([*irr. senden,*] *sep.*, -ge-, h) send after; send on, forward (*letter*) (*j-m to s.o.*).

'**Nachsicht** *f* indulgence; '2ig *adj.*, 2svoll *adj.* indulgent, forbearing.

'**Nachsilbe** *gr. f* suffix.

'**nach|sinnen** *v/i.* (*irr. sinnen*, *sep.*, -ge-, h) muse, meditate (*über acc.* [up]on); '~**sitzen** *v/i.* (*irr. sitzen*, *sep.*, -ge-, h) *pupil:* be kept in.

'**Nach|sommer** *m* St. Martin's summer, *esp. Am.* Indian summer; '~**speise** *f* dessert; '~**spiel** *fig. n* sequel.

'**nach|spionieren** *v/i.* (*sep.*, *no* -ge-, h) spy (*dat.* on); '~**sprechen** *v/i. and v/t.* (*irr. sprechen*, *sep.*, -ge-, h) repeat; '~**spülen** *v/t.* (*sep.*, -ge-, h) rinse; '~**spüren** *v/i.* (*sep.*, -ge-, h) (*dat.*) track, trace.

nächst [nɛːçst] **1.** *adj. succession*, *time:* next; *distance*, *relation:* nearest; **2.** *prp.* (*dat.*) next to, next after; '2'**beste** *m, f, n* (-n/-n): der (die) ~ anyone; das ~ anything; er fragte den ~n he asked the next person he met.

'**nachstehen** *v/i.* (*irr. stehen*, *sep.*, -ge-, h): *j-m in nichts* ~ be in no way inferior to s.o.

'**nachstell|en** (*sep.*, -ge-, h) **1.** *v/t.* place behind; put back (*watch*); ⊕ adjust (*screw, etc.*); **2.** *v/i.*: *j-m* ~ be after s.o.; '2**ung** *fig. f* persecution.

'**Nächstenliebe** *f* charity.

'**nächstens** *adv.* shortly, (very) soon, before long.

'**nach|streben** *v/i.* (*sep.*, -ge-, h) *s. nacheifern*; '~**suchen** *v/i.* (*sep.*, -ge-, h): ~ um apply for, seek.

Nacht [naxt] *f* (-/ᵋe) night; *bei* ~, *des* ~*s s. nachts*; '~**arbeit** *f* night-work; '~**asyl** *n* night-shelter; '~**ausgabe** *f* night edition (*of newspaper*); '~**dienst** *m* night-duty.

'**Nachteil** *m* disadvantage, drawback; *im* ~ *sein* be at a disadvantage; '2ig *adj.* disadvantageous.

'**Nacht|essen** *n* supper; '~**falter** *zo. m* (-s/-) moth; '~**gebet** *n* evening prayer; '~**geschirr** *n* chamberpot; '~**hemd** *n* night-gown, *Am. a.* night robe; *for men:* nightshirt.

Nachtigall *orn.* ['naxtigal] *f* (-/-en) nightingale.

'**Nachtisch** *m* (-es/*no pl.*) sweet, dessert.

'**Nachtlager** *n* (a) lodging for the night; bed.

nächtlich *adj.* ['nɛçtliç] nightly, nocturnal.

'**Nacht|lokal** *n* night-club; '~**mahl** *n* supper; '~**portier** *m* night-porter; '~**quartier** *n* night-quarters *pl.*

Nachtrag ['naːxtraːk] *m* (-[e]s/ᵋe) supplement; '2en *v/t.* (*irr. tragen*, *sep.*, -ge-, h) carry (*j-m et.* s.th. after s.o.); add; ✝ post up (*ledger*); *j-m et.* ~ bear s.o. a grudge; '2end *adj.* unforgiving, resentful.

nachträglich *adj.* ['naːxtrɛːkliç] additional; subsequent.

nachts *adv.* [naxts] at *or* by night.

'**Nacht|schicht** *f* night-shift; '2**schlafend** *adj.*: *zu* ~*er Zeit* in the middle of the night; '~**schwärmer** *fig. m* night-reveller; '~**tisch** *m* bedside table; '~**topf** *m* chamberpot; '~**vorstellung** *thea. f* night performance; '~**wache** *f* night-watch; '~**wächter** *m* (night-)watchman; '~**wandler** ['~vandlər] *m* (-s/-) sleep-walker; '~**zeug** *n* night-things *pl.*

'**nachwachsen** *v/i.* (*irr. wachsen*, *sep.*, -ge-, sein) grow again.

'**Nachwahl** *parl. f* by-election.

Nachweis ['naːxvais] *m* (-es/-e) proof, evidence; '2bar *adj.* demonstrable; traceable; 2en ['~zən] *v/t.* (*irr. weisen*, *sep.*, -ge-, h) point out, show; trace; prove; '2lich *adj. s. nachweisbar.*

'**Nach|welt** *f* posterity; '~**wirkung** *f* after-effect; consequences *pl.*; aftermath; '~**wort** *n* (-[e]s/-e) epilog(ue); '~**wuchs** *m* (-[e]s/*no pl.*) rising generation.

'**nach|zahlen** *v/t.* (*sep.*, -ge-, h) pay in addition; '~**zählen** *v/t.* (*sep.*, -ge-, h) count over (again), check; '2**zahlung** *f* additional payment.

Nachzügler ['naːxtsyːklər] *m* (-s/-) straggler, late-comer.

Nacken ['nakən] *m* (-s/-) nape (of the neck), neck.

nackt *adj.* [nakt] naked, nude; bare (*a. fig.*); *young birds:* unfledged; *truth:* plain.

Nadel ['naːdəl] *f* (-/-n) needle; pin; brooch; '~**arbeit** *f* needlework; '~**baum** ♀ *m* conifer(ous tree); '~**stich** *m* prick; stitch; *fig.* pinprick.

Nagel ['naːgəl] *m* (-s/ᵋ) *anat.*, ⊕ nail; *of wood:* peg; spike; stud; *die Arbeit brennt mir auf den Nägeln* it's a rush job; '~**haut** *f* cuticle; '~**lack** *m* nail varnish; '2n *v/t.* (ge-, h) nail (*an or auf acc.* to); ~**necessaire** ['~nesesɛːr] *n* (-s/-s) manicure-case; '2'**neu** F *adj.* bran(d)-new; '~**pflege** *f* manicure.

nage|n ['naːgən] (ge-, h) **1.** *v/i.* gnaw; ~ *an* (*dat.*) gnaw at; pick (*bone*); **2.** *v/t.* gnaw; '2**tier** *zo. n* rodent, gnawer.

nah *adj.* [naː] near, close (*bei* to); nearby; *danger:* imminent.

Näharbeit ['nɛː?-] *f* needlework, sewing.

'**Nahaufnahme** *f film:* close-up.

nahe *adj.* ['naːə] *s. nah.*

Nähe ['nɛːə] *f* (-/*no pl.*) nearness, proximity; vicinity; *in der ~* close by.

'nahe|gehen *v/i.* (*irr. gehen, sep., -ge-, sein*) (*dat.*) affect, grieve; **'~kommen** *v/i.* (*irr. kommen, sep., -ge-, sein*) (*dat.*) approach; get at (*truth*); **'~legen** *v/t.* (*sep., -ge-, h*) suggest; **'~liegen** *v/i.* (*irr. liegen, sep., -ge-, h*) suggest itself, be obvious.

nahen ['naːən] **1.** *v/i.* (*ge-, sein*) approach; **2.** *v/refl.* (*ge-, h*) approach (*j-m s.o.*).

nähen ['nɛːən] *v/t. and v/i.* (*ge-, h*) sew, stitch.

näher *adj.* ['nɛːər] nearer, closer; *road:* shorter; *das Nähere* (further) particulars *pl.* or details *pl.*

'Näherin *f* (-/*-nen*) seamstress.

'nähern *v/t.* (*ge-, h*) approach (*dat.* to); *sich ~* approach (*j-m s.o.*).

'nahe'zu *adv.* nearly, almost.

'Nähgarn *n* (sewing-)cotton.

'Nahkampf ✗ *m* close combat.

nahm [naːm] *pret. of* nehmen.

'Näh|maschine *f* sewing-machine; **'~nadel** *f* (sewing-)needle.

nähren ['nɛːrən] *v/t.* (*ge-, h*) nourish (*a. fig.*), feed; nurse (*child*); *sich ~* von live or feed on.

nahrhaft *adj.* ['naːrhaft] nutritious, nourishing.

'Nahrung *f* (-/*no pl.*) food, nourishment, nutriment.

'Nahrungs|aufnahme *f* intake of food; **'~mittel** *n/pl.* food(-stuff), victuals *pl.*

'Nährwert *m* nutritive value.

Naht [naːt] *f* (-/*-̈e*) seam; ✗ suture.

'Nahverkehr *m* local traffic.

'Nähzeug *n* sewing-kit.

naiv *adj.* [naˈiːf] naïve, naive, simple; **Lität** [naiviˈtɛːt] *f* (-/*no pl.*) naïveté, naivety, simplicity.

Name ['naːmə] *m* (-ns/*-n*) name; *im ~n* (*gen.*) on behalf of; *dem ~n nach* nominal(ly), in name only; *dem ~n nach kennen* know by name; *die Dinge beim rechten ~n nennen* call a spade a spade; *darf ich um Ihren ~n bitten?* may I ask your name?

'namen|los *adj.* nameless, anonymous; *fig.* unutterable; **'~s 1.** *adv.* named, by the name of, called; **2.** *prp.* (*gen.*) in the name of.

'Namens|tag *m* name-day; **'~vetter** *m* namesake; **'~zug** *m* signature.

namentlich ['naːməntlɪç] **1.** *adj.* nominal; **2.** *adv.* by name; especially, in particular.

'namhaft *adj.* notable; considerable; *~ machen* name.

nämlich ['nɛːmlɪç] **1.** *adj.* the same; **2.** *adv.* namely, that is (to say).

nannte ['nantə] *pret. of* nennen.

Napf [napf] *m* (-[e]s/*-̈e*) bowl, basin.

Narb|e ['narbə] *f* (-/*-n*) scar; **'Lig** *adj.* scarred; *leather:* grained.

Narko|se ✗ [narˈkoːzə] *f* (-/*-n*) narcosis; **Ltisieren** [̩ʊtiˈziːrən] *v/t.* (*no -ge-, h*) narcotize.

Narr [nar] *m* (-en/*-en*) fool; jester; *zum ~en halten* = **'Len** *v/t.* (*ge-, h*) make a fool of, fool.

'Narren|haus F *n* madhouse; **'~kappe** *f* fool's-cap; **'Lsicher** *adj.* foolproof.

'Narrheit *f* (-/*-en*) folly.

Närrin ['nɛrin] *f* (-/*-nen*) fool, foolish woman.

'närrisch *adj.* foolish, silly; odd.

Narzisse ♀ [narˈtsisə] *f* (-/*-n*) narcissus; *gelbe ~* daffodil.

nasal *adj.* [naˈzaːl] nasal; *~e Sprechweise* twang.

nasch|en ['naʃən] (*ge-, h*) **1.** *v/i.* nibble (*an dat.* at); *gern ~* have a sweet tooth; **2.** *v/t.* nibble; eat *s.th.* on the sly; **Lereien** [̩raɪən] *f/pl.* dainties *pl.*, sweets *pl.*; **'Lhaft** *adj.* fond of dainties *or* sweets.

Nase ['naːzə] *f* (-/*-n*) nose; *die ~ rümpfen* turn up one's nose (*über acc.* at).

näseln ['nɛːzəln] *v/i.* (*ge-, h*) speak through the nose, nasalize; snuffle.

'Nasen|bluten *n* (-s/*no pl.*) nosebleeding; **'~loch** *n* nostril; **'~spitze** *f* tip of the nose.

naseweis *adj.* ['naːzəvaɪs] pert, saucy.

nasführen ['naːs-] *v/t.* (*ge-, h*) fool, dupe.

Nashorn *zo.* ['naːs-] *n* rhinoceros.

naß *adj.* [nas] wet; damp, moist.

Nässe ['nɛsə] *f* (-/*no pl.*) wet(ness); moisture; ♈ humidity; **'Ln** (*ge-, h*) **1.** *v/t.* wet; moisten; **2.** ✗ *v/i.* discharge.

'naßkalt *adj.* damp and cold, raw.

Nation [naˈtsjoːn] *f* (-/*-en*) nation.

national *adj.* [natsjoˈnaːl] national; **Lhymne** *f* national anthem; **Lismus** [̩aˈlismus] *m* (-/*Nationalismen*) nationalism; **Lität** [̩aliˈtɛːt] *f* (-/*-en*) nationality; **Lmannschaft** *f* national team.

Natter ['natər] *f* (-/*-n*) *zo.* adder, viper; *fig.* serpent.

Natur [naˈtuːr] *f* **1.** (-/*no pl.*) nature; **2.** (-/*-en*) constitution; temper(ament), disposition, nature; *von ~* by nature.

Naturalien [natuˈraːljən] *pl.* natural produce *sg.*; *in ~* in kind.

naturalisieren [naturaliˈziːrən] *v/t.* (*no -ge-, h*) naturalize.

Naturalismus [naturaˈlismus] *m* (-/*no pl.*) naturalism.

Naturanlage [naˈtuːr-] *f* (natural) disposition.

Naturell [natuˈrɛl] *n* (-s/*-e*) natural disposition, nature, temper.

Na'tur|ereignis *n*, **~erscheinung** *f* phenomenon; **~forscher** *m* naturalist, scientist; 2gemäß adj. natural; ~geschichte f natural history; ~gesetz n law of nature, natural law; 2getreu adj. true to nature; life-like; ~kunde f (natural) science.

naturlich [na'ty:rliç] 1. adj. natural; genuine; innate; unaffected; 2. adv. naturally, of course.

Na'tur|produkte n/pl. natural products pl. or produce sg.; ~schutz m wild-life conservation; ~schutzgebiet n, ~schutzpark m national park, wild-life (p)reserve; ~trieb m instinct; ~wissenschaft f (natural) science; ~wissenschaftler m (natural) scientist.

Nebel ['ne:bəl] m (-s/-) fog; mist; haze; smoke; 2haft fig. adj. nebulous, hazy, dim; '~horn n fog-horn.

neben prp. (dat.; acc.) ['ne:bən] beside, by (the side of); near to; against, compared with; apart or Am. a. aside from, besides.

neben|'an adv. next door; close by; 2anschluß teleph. ['ne:bən?-] m extension (line); 2arbeit ['ne:bən?-] f extra work; 2ausgaben ['ne:bən?-] f/pl. incidental expenses pl., extras pl.; 2ausgang ['ne:bən?-] m side-exit, side-door; 2bedeutung f secondary meaning, connotation; ~'bei adv. by the way; besides; '2beruf m side-line; ~beruflich adv. as a side-line; in one's spare time; '2beschäftigung f s. Nebenberuf; 2buhler ['~bu:lər] m (-s/-) rival; ~ei'nander adv. side by side; ~ bestehen co-exist; 2eingang ['ne:bən?-] m side-entrance; 2einkünfte ['ne:bən?-] pl., 2einnahmen ['ne:bən?-] f/pl. casual emoluments pl., extra income; 2erscheinung ['ne:bən?-] f accompaniment; '2fach n subsidiary subject, Am. minor (subject); '2fluß m tributary (river); 2gebäude n annex(e); outhouse; '2geräusch n radio: atmospherics pl., interference, jamming; '2gleis 📖 n siding, side-track; '2handlung thea. f underplot; '2haus n adjoining house; ~'her adv., ~'hin adv. by his or her side; s. nebenbei; '2kläger ⚖ m co-plaintiff; '2kosten pl. extras pl.; '2mann m person next to one; '2produkt n by-product, '2rolle f minor part (a. thea.); '2sache f minor matter, side issue; '2sächlich adj. subordinate, incidental; unimportant; 2satz gr. m subordinate clause; '~stehend adj. in the margin; '2stelle f branch; agency; teleph. extension; '2straße f bystreet, by-road; '2strecke 📖 f branch line; '2tisch m next table; '2tür f side-door; '2verdienst m incidental or extra earnings pl.; '2zimmer n adjoining room.

'neblig adj. foggy, misty, hazy.

nebst prp. (dat.) [ne:pst] together with, besides; including.

neck|en ['nɛkən] v/t. (ge-, h) tease, banter, sl. kid; 2erei [~'raɪ] f (-/-en) teasing, banter; '~isch adj. playful; droll, funny.

Neffe ['nɛfə] m (-n/-n) nephew.

negativ [nega'ti:f] 1. adj. negative; 2. 2 n (-s/-e) negative.

Neger ['ne:gər] m (-s/-) negro; '~in f (-/-nen) negress.

nehmen ['ne:mən] v/t. (irr., ge-, h) take; receive; charge (money); zu sich ~ take, have (meal); j-m et. ~ take s.th. from s.o.; ein Ende ~ come to an end; es sich nicht ~ lassen zu inf. insist upon ger.; streng genommen strictly speaking.

Neid [naɪt] m (-[e]s/no pl.) envy; 2en ['naɪdən] v/t. (ge-, h): j-m et. ~ envy s.o. s.th.; ~er ['~dər] m (-s/-) envious person; ~hammel F ['naɪt-] m dog in the manger; 2isch adj. ['~diʃ] envious (auf acc. of); 2los adj. ['naɪt-] ungrudging.

Neige ['naɪgə] f (-/-n) decline; barrel: dregs pl.; glass: heeltap; zur ~ gehen (be on the) decline; esp. 🕈 run short; 2n (ge-, h) 1. v/t. and v/refl. bend, incline; 2. v/i.: er neigt zu Übertreibungen he is given to exaggeration.

'Neigung f (-/-en) inclination (a. fig.); slope, incline.

nein adv. [naɪn] no.

Nektar ['nɛkta:r] m (-s/no pl.) nectar.

Nelke ♀ ['nɛlkə] f (-/-n) carnation, pink; spice: clove.

nennen ['nɛnən] v/t. (irr., ge-, h) name; call; term; mention; nominate (candidate); sports: enter (für for); sich ... ~ be called ...; '~swert adj. worth mentioning.

'Nenn|er ♈ m (-s/-) denominator; '~ung f (-/-en) naming; mentioning; nomination (of candidates); sports: entry; '~wert m nominal or face value; zum ~ 🕈 at par.

Neon 🜍 ['ne:ɔn] n (-s/no pl.) neon; '~röhre f neon tube.

Nerv [nɛrf] m (-s/-en) nerve; j-m auf die ~en fallen or gehen get on s.o.'s nerves.

'Nerven|arzt m neurologist; '2aufreibend adj. trying; '~heilanstalt f mental hospital; '~kitzel m (-s/no pl.) thrill, sensation; '2krank adj. neurotic; '2leidend adj. neuropathic, neurotic; '~schwäche f nervous debility; '2stärkend adj. tonic; '~system n nervous system; '~zusammenbruch m nervous breakdown.

nerv|ig adj. ['nɛrviç] sinewy; '~ös adj. [~'vø:s] nervous; 2osität [~ozi'tɛ:t] f (-/no pl.) nervousness.

Nerz zo. [nɛrts] m (-es/-e) mink.

Nessel ♀ ['nɛsəl] f (-/-n) nettle.

Nest [nɛst] n (-es/-er) nest; F fig. bed; F fig. hick or one-horse town.

nett adj. [nɛt] nice; neat, pretty; Am. a. cute; pleasant; kind.

netto ✝ adv. ['nɛto] net, clear.

Netz [nɛts] n (-es/-e) net; fig. network; '~anschluß ⚡ m mains connection, power supply; '~haut anat. f retina; '~spannung ⚡ f mains voltage.

neu adj. [nɔy] new; fresh; recent; modern; ~ere Sprachen modern languages; ~este Nachrichten latest news; von ~em anew, afresh; ein ~es Leben beginnen turn over a new leaf; was gibt es Neues? what is the news?, Am. what is new?

'Neu|anschaffung f (-/-en) recent acquisition; '♀artig adj. novel; '~auflage typ. f, '~ausgabe typ. f new edition; reprint; '♀bearbeitet adj. revised; '~e m (-n/-n) new man; new-comer; novice; '♀entdeckt adj. recently discovered.

neuer|dings adv. ['nɔyər'dɪŋs] of late, recently; '♀er m (-s/-) innovator.

Neuerscheinung ['nɔy?-] f new book or publication.

'Neuerung f (-/-en) innovation.

'neu|geboren adj. new-born; '~gestalten v/t. (sep., -ge-, h) reorganize; '♀gestaltung f reorganization; '♀gier f, ♀gierde ['~də] f (-/no pl.) curiosity, inquisitiveness; '~gierig adj. curious (auf acc. about, of), inquisitive, sl. nos(e)y; ich bin ~, ob I wonder whether or if; '♀heit f (-/-en) newness, freshness; novelty.

'Neuigkeit f (-/-en) (e-e a piece of) news.

'Neu|jahr n New Year('s Day); '~land n (-[e]s/no pl.): ~ erschließen break fresh ground (a. fig.); '♀lich adv. the other day, recently; '♀ling m (-s/-e) novice; contp. greenhorn; '♀modisch adj. fashionable; '~mond m (-[e]s/no pl.) new moon.

neun adj. [nɔyn] nine; '~te adj. ninth; '♀tel n (-s/-) ninth part; '~tens adv. ninthly; '~zehn adj. nineteen; '~zehnte adj. nineteenth; '~zig adj. ['~tsɪç] ninety; '~zigste adj. ninetieth.

'Neu|philologe m student or teacher of modern languages; '~regelung f reorganization, rearrangement.

neutr|al adj. [nɔy'traːl] neutral; ♀alität [~ali'tɛːt] f (-/no pl.) neutrality; ♀um gr. ['~trum] n (-s/Neutra, Neutren) neuter.

'neu|vermählt adj. newly married; die ♀en pl. the newly-weds pl.; '♀wahl parl. f new election; '~wertig adj. as good as new; '♀zeit f (-/no pl.) modern times pl.

nicht adv. [nɪçt] not; auch ~ nor; ~ anziehend unattractive; ~ besser no better; ~ bevollmächtigt non-commissioned; ~ einlösbar ✝ inconvertible; ~ erscheinen fail to attend.

'Nicht|achtung f disregard; '♀amtlich adj. unofficial; '~angriffspakt pol. m non-aggression pact; '~annahme f non-acceptance; '~befolgung f non-observance.

Nichte ['nɪçtə] f (-/-n) niece.

'nichtig adj. null, void; invalid; vain, futile; für ~ erklären declare null and void, annul; '♀keit f (-/-en) nullity; vanity, futility.

'Nichtraucher m non-smoker.

nichts [nɪçts] 1. indef. pron. nothing, naught, not anything; 2. ♀ n (-/no pl.) nothing(ness); fig.: nonentity; void; '~ahnend adj. unsuspecting; ~destoweniger adv. nevertheless; ~nutzig adj. ['~nutsɪç] good-for-nothing, worthless; '~sagend adj. insignificant; ♀tuer ['~tuːər] m (-s/-) idler; '~würdig adj. vile, base, infamous.

'Nicht|vorhandensein n absence; lack; '~wissen n ignorance.

nick|en ['nɪkən] v/i. (ge-, h) nod; bow; '♀erchen F n (-s/-): ein ~ machen take a nap, have one's forty winks.

nie adv. [niː] never, at no time.

nieder ['niːdər] 1. adj. low; base, mean; vulgar; value, rank: inferior; 2. adv. down.

'Nieder|gang m decline; '♀gedrückt adj. dejected, downcast; '♀gehen v/i. (irr. gehen, sep., -ge-, sein) go down; ✈ descend; storm: break; '♀geschlagen adj. dejected, downcast; '♀hauen v/t. (irr. hauen, sep., -ge-, h) cut down; '♀kommen v/i. (irr. kommen, sep., -ge-, sein) be confined; be delivered (mit of); '~kunft ['~kunft] f (-/~e) confinement, delivery; '~lage f defeat; ✝ warehouse; branch; '♀lassen v/t. (irr. lassen, sep., -ge-, h) let down; sich ~ settle (down); bird: alight; sit down; establish o.s.; settle (in dat. at); '~lassung f (-/-en) establishment; settlement; branch, agency; '♀legen v/t. (sep., -ge-, h) lay or put down; resign (position); retire from (business); abdicate; die Arbeit ~ (go on) strike, down tools, Am. F a. walk out; sich ~ lie down, go to bed; '♀machen v/t. (sep., -ge-, h) cut down; massacre; '~schlag m 🜄 precipitate; sediment; precipitation (of rain, etc.); radio-active: fall-out; boxing: knock-down, knock-out; '♀schlagen v/t. (irr. schlagen, sep., -ge-, h) knock down; boxing: a. floor; cast down (eyes); suppress; put down, crush (rebellion); ⚖ quash; sich ~

precipitate; **ℓschmettern** *fig.*
v/t. (sep., -ge-, h) crush; **ℓsetzen**
v/t. (sep., -ge-, h) set *or* put down;
sich ~ sit down; *birds*: perch, alight;
ℓstrecken *v/t.* (sep., -ge-, h) lay
low, strike to the ground, floor;
ℓträchtig *adj.* base, mean; F
beastly; **'~ung** *f* (-/-en) lowlands *pl.*

niedlich *adj.* ['ni:tliç] neat, nice,
pretty, *Am. a.* cute.

Niednagel ['ni:t-] *m* agnail, hang-
nail.

niedrig *adj.* ['ni:driç] low (*a. fig.*);
moderate; *fig.* mean, base.

niemals *adv.* ['ni:mɑːls] never, at
no time.

niemand *indef. pron.* ['ni:mant]
nobody, no one, none; **ℓsland** *n*
(-[e]s/*no pl.*) no man's land.

Niere ['ni:rə] *f* (-/-n) kidney; **'~n-
braten** *m* loin of veal.

niesel|n F ['ni:zəln] *v/i.* (ge-, h)
drizzle; **ℓregen** F *m* drizzle.

niesen ['ni:zən] *v/i.* (ge-, h) sneeze.

Niet ⊕ ['ni:t] *m* (-[e]s/-e) rivet; **'~e** *f*
(-/-n) lottery: blank; F *fig.* wash-
out; **ℓen** ⊕ *v/t.* (ge-, h) rivet.

Nilpferd *zo.* ['ni:l-] *n* hippopotamus.

Nimbus ['nimbus] *m* (-/-se) halo (*a.
fig.*), nimbus.

nimmer *adv.* ['nimər] never; **'~-
mehr** *adv.* nevermore; **'ℓsatt** *m**
(-, -[e]s/-e) glutton; **ℓ'wiedersehen** F *n*: *auf ~* never to meet
again; *er verschwand auf ~* he left
for good.   [*dat.* at).]

nippen ['nipən] *v/i.* (ge-, h) sip (*an*)}

Nipp|es ['nipəs] *pl.*, **'~sachen** *pl.*
(k)nick-(k)nacks *pl.*

nirgend|s *adv.* ['nirgənts], **'~(s)'wo**
adv. nowhere.

Nische ['ni:ʃə] *f* (-/-n) niche, recess.

nisten ['nistən] *v/i.* (ge-, h) nest.

Niveau [ni'vo:] *n* (-s/-s) level; *fig. a.*
standard.

nivellieren [nive'li:rən] *v/t.* (no
-ge-, h) level, grade.

Nixe ['niksə] *f* (-/-n) water-nymph,
mermaid.

noch [nɔx] **1.** *adv.* still; yet; *~ ein*
another, one more; *~ einmal* once
more *or* again; *~ etwas* something
more; *~ etwas?* anything else?; *~
heute* this very day; *~ immer* still;
~ nicht not yet; *~ nie* never before;
~ so ever so; *~ im 19. Jahrhundert*
as late as the 19th century; *es wird
~ 2 Jahre dauern* it will take two
more *or* another two years; **2.** *cj.*:
s. weder; **~malig** *adj.* ['~mɑːliç]
repeated; **~mals** *adv.* ['~mɑːls]
once more *or* again.

Nomad|e [no'mɑːdə] *m* (-n/-n)
nomad; **ℓisch** *adj.* nomadic.

Nominativ *gr.* ['no:minati:f] *m*
(-s/-e) nominative (case).

nominieren [nomi'ni:rən] *v/t.* (no
-ge-, h) nominate.

Nonne ['nɔnə] *f* (-/-n) nun; **'~n-
kloster** *n* nunnery, convent.

Nord *geogr.* [nɔrt], **~en** ['~dən] *m*
(-s/*no pl.*) north; **ℓisch** *adj.* ['~diʃ]
northern.

nördlich *adj.* ['nœrtliç] northern,
northerly.

'Nord|licht *n* northern lights *pl.*;
~'ost(en *m*) north-east; **'~pol** *m*
North Pole; **ℓwärts** *adv.* ['~vɛrts]
northward(s), north; **~'west(en** *m*)
north-west.

nörg|eln ['nœrgəln] *v/i.* (ge-, h)
nag, carp (*an dat.* at); grumble;
ℓler ['~lər] *m* (-s/-) faultfinder,
grumbler.

Norm [nɔrm] *f* (-/-en) standard;
rule; norm.

normal *adj.* [nɔr'mɑːl] normal;
regular; *measure, weight, time*:
standard; **~isieren** [~ali'zi:rən]
v/refl. (no -ge-, h) return to normal.

'norm|en *v/t.* (ge-, h), **~ieren**
[~'mi:rən] *v/t.* (no -ge-, h) standardize.

Not [no:t] *f* (-/*~e) need, want; necessity; difficulty, trouble; misery,
danger, emergency, distress (*a. ⚓*);
~ leiden suffer privations; *in ~ geraten* become destitute, get into
trouble; *in ~ sein* be in trouble; *zur
~* at a pinch; *es tut not, daß* it is necessary that.

Notar [no'tɑːr] *m* (-s/-e) (public)
notary.

'Not|ausgang *m* emergency exit;
'~behelf *m* makeshift, expedient,
stopgap; **'~bremse** *f* emergency
brake; **'~brücke** *f* temporary
bridge; **~durft** ['~durft] *f* (-/*no pl.*):
s-e ~ verrichten relieve o.s.; **ℓdürf-
tig** *adj.* scanty, poor; temporary.

Note ['no:tə] *f* (-/-n) note (*a. ♪*);
pol. note, memorandum; *school*:
mark.

'Noten|bank ✝ *f* bank of issue; **'~-
schlüssel** ♪ *m* clef; **'~system** ♪ *n*
staff.

'Not|fall *m* case of need, emergency;
'ℓfalls *adv.* if necessary; **'ℓgedrun-
gen** *adv.* of necessity, needs.

notier|en [no'ti:rən] *v/t.* (no -ge-, h)
make a note of, note (down); ✝
quote; **ℓung** ✝ *f* (-/-en) quotation.

nötig *adj.* ['nø:tiç] necessary; *~ haben* need; **~en** ['~gən] *v/t.* (ge-, h)
force, oblige, compel; press, urge
(*guest*); **'~enfalls** *adv.* if necessary;
ℓung *f* (-/-en) compulsion; pressing; *⚖* intimidation.

Notiz [no'ti:ts] *f* (-/-en) notice; note,
memorandum; *~ nehmen von* take
notice of; pay attention to; *keine ~
nehmen von* ignore; *sich ~en machen* take notes; **~block** *m* pad,
Am. a. scratch pad; **~buch** *n* note-
book.

'Not|lage *f* distress; emergency;
'ℓlanden ✈ *v/i.* (ge-, sein) make

a forced *or* emergency landing; '**~landung** ✂ *f* forced *or* emergency landing; '**♀leidend** *adj.* needy, destitute; distressed; '**~lösung** *f* expedient; '**~lüge** *f* white lie.

notorisch *adj.* [no'to:riʃ] notorious.

'**Not|ruf** *teleph. m* emergency call; '**~signal** *n* emergency *or* distress signal; '**~sitz** *mot. m* dick(e)y(-seat), *Am. a.* rumble seat; '**~stand** *m* emergency; '**~standsarbeiten** *f/pl.* relief works *pl.*; '**~standsgebiet** *n* distressed area; '**~standsgesetze** *n/pl.* emergency laws *pl.*; '**~verband** *m* first-aid dressing; '**~verordnung** *f* emergency decree; '**~wehr** *f* self-defen|ce, *Am.* -se; '♀**wendig** *adj.* necessary; '**~wendigkeit** *f* (-/-en) necessity; '**~zucht** *f* (-/*no pl.*) rape.

Novelle [no'vɛlə] *f* (-/-n) short story, novella; *parl.* amendment.

November [no'vɛmbər] *m* (-[s]/-) November.

Nu [nu:] *m* (-/*no pl.*): im ~ in no time.

Nuance [ny'ã:sə] *f* (-/-n) shade.

nüchtern *adj.* ['nʏçtərn] empty, fasting, sober (*a. fig.*); matter-of-fact; *writings*: jejune; prosaic; cool; plain; '♀**heit** *f* (-/*no pl.*) sobriety; *fig.* soberness.

Nudel ['nu:dəl] *f* (-/-n) noodle.

null [nul] **1.** *adj.* null; nil; *tennis*: love; ~ *und* nichtig null and void; **2.** ♀ *f* (-/-en) nought, cipher (*a. fig.*); zero; '♀**punkt** *m* zero.

numerieren [numə'ri:rən] *v/t.* (*no* -ge-, h) number; *numerierter Platz* reserved seat.

Nummer ['numər] *f* (-/-n) number

(*a. newspaper, thea.*); size (*of shoes, etc.*); *thea.* turn; *sports*: event; '**~nschild** *mot. n* number-plate.

nun [nu:n] **1.** *adv.* now, at present; then; ~? well?; ~ *also* well then; **2.** *int.* now then!; '**~mehr** *adv.* now.

nur *adv.* [nu:r] only; (nothing) but; merely; ~ *noch* only.

Nuß [nus] *f* (-/'~*Nüsse*) nut; '**~kern** *m* kernel; '**~knacker** *m* (-s/-) nutcracker; '**~schale** *f* nutshell.

Nüstern ['ny:stərn] *f/pl.* nostrils *pl.*

nutz *adj.* [nuts] *s.* nütze; ♀**anwendung** *f* practical application; '**~bar** *adj.* useful; '**~bringend** *adj.* profitable.

nütze *adj.* ['nʏtsə] useful; *zu nichts* ~ *sein* be of no use, be good for nothing.

Nutzen ['nutsən] **1.** *m* (-s/-) use; profit, gain; advantage; utility; **2.** ♀ *v/i. and v/t.* (ge-, h) *s.* nützen.

nützen ['nʏtsən] (ge-, h) **1.** *v/i.*: zu et. ~ be of use *or* useful for s.th.; *j-m* ~ serve s.o.; *es nützt nichts zu inf.* it is no use ger.; **2.** *v/t.* use, make use of; put to account; avail o.s. of, seize (*opportunity*).

'**Nutz|holz** *n* timber; '**~leistung** *f* capacity.

nützlich *adj.* ['nʏtsliç] useful, of use; advantageous.

'**nutz|los** *adj.* useless; ♀**nießer** ['~ni:sər] *m* (-s/-) usufructuary; '♀**nießung** *f* (-/-en) usufruct.

'**Nutzung** *f* (-/-en) using; utilization.

Nylon ['naɪlɔn] *n* (-s/*no pl.*) nylon; **~strümpfe** ['~ʃtrʏmpfə] *m/pl.* nylons *pl.*, nylon stockings *pl.*

Nymphe ['nʏmfə] *f* (-/-n) nymph.

O

o *int.* [o:] oh!, ah!; ~ *weh!* alas!, oh dear (me)!

Oase [o'a:zə] *f* (-/-n) oasis.

ob *cj.* [ɔp] whether, if; *als* ~ as if, as though.

Obacht ['o:baxt] *f* (-/*no pl.*): ~ *geben auf* (*acc.*) pay attention to, take care of, heed.

Obdach ['ɔpdax] *n* (-[e]s/*no pl.*) shelter, lodging; '♀**los** *adj.* unsheltered, homeless; '**~lose** *m, f* (-n/-n) homeless person; '**~losenasyl** *n* casual ward.

Obdu|ktion ♀ [ɔpduk'tsjo:n] *f* (-/-en) post-mortem (examination), autopsy; ♀**zieren** ♀ ['~tsi:rən] *v/t.* (*no* -ge-, h) perform an autopsy on.

oben *adv.* ['o:bən] above; *mountain*: at the top; *house*: upstairs; on the surface; *von* ~ from above; *von* ~ *bis unten* from top to bottom;

von ~ *herab behandeln* treat haughtily; '**~an** *adv.* at the top; '**~auf** *adv.* on the top; on the surface; **~drein** *adv.* ['~'draɪn] into the bargain, at that; ~**erwähnt** *adj.* ['o:bən'ʔɛrvɛ:nt], ~**genannt** *adj.* above-mentioned, aforesaid; '**~hin** *adv.* superficially, perfunctorily.

ober ['o:bər] **1.** *adj.* upper, higher; *fig. a.* superior; **2.** ♀ *m* (-s/-) (head) waiter; *German cards*: queen.

Ober|arm ['o:bər'ʔ-] *m* upper arm; **~arzt** ['o:bər'ʔ-] *m* head physician; **~aufseher** ['o:bər'ʔ-] *m* superintendent; **~aufsicht** ['o:bər'ʔ-] *f* superintendence; '**~befehl** ✗ *m* supreme command; '**~befehlshaber** ✗ *m* commander-in-chief; '**~bekleidung** *f* outer garments *pl.*, outer wear; '**~bürgermeister** *m* chief burgomaster; Lord Mayor;

'~deck ⚓ n upper deck; '~fläche f surface; ²flächlich adj. ['~fleçliç] superficial; fig. a. shallow; '²halb prp. (gen.) above; '~hand fig. f: die ~ gewinnen über (acc.) get the upper hand of; '~haupt n head, chief; '~haus Brt. parl. n House of Lords; '~hemd n shirt; '~herrschaft f supremacy.

'Oberin f (-/-nen) eccl. Mother Superior; at hospital: matron.

ober|irdisch adj. ['o:bər?-] overground, above ground; ⚡ overhead; '²kellner m head waiter; '²kiefer anat. m upper jaw; '²körper m upper part of the body; '²land n upland; '²lauf m upper course (of river); '²leder n upper; '²leitung f chief management; ⚡ overhead wires pl.; '²leutnant ✗ m (Am. first) lieutenant; '²licht n skylight; '²lippe f upper lip; '²schenkel m thigh; '²schule f secondary school, Am. a. high school.

'oberst 1. adj. uppermost, topmost, top; highest (a. fig.); fig. chief, principal; rank, etc.: supreme; 2. ♀ ✗ m (-en, -s/-en, -e) colonel.
'Ober|'staatsanwalt ⚖ m chief public prosecutor; '~stimme ♪ f treble, soprano.

'Oberst'leutnant ✗ m lieutenant-colonel.

'Ober|tasse f cup; '~wasser fig. n: ~ bekommen get the upper hand.

obgleich cj. [ɔp'glaiç] (al)though.

'Obhut f (-/no pl.) care, guard; protection; custody; in (seine) ~ nehmen take care or charge of.

obig adj. ['o:biç] above(-mentioned), aforesaid.

Objekt [ɔp'jɛkt] n (-[e]s/-e) object (a. gr.); project; ✝ a. transaction.

objektiv [ɔpjɛk'ti:f] 1. adj. objective; impartial, detached; actual, practical; 2. ♀ n (-s/-e) object-glass, objective; phot. lens; ²ität [~ivi-'tɛ:t] f (-/no pl.) objectivity; impartiality.

obligat adj. [obli'ga:t] obligatory; indispensable; inevitable; ²ion ✝ [~a'tsjo:n] f (-/-en) bond, debenture; ~orisch adj. [~a'to:riʃ] obligatory (für on), compulsory, mandatory.

'Obmann m chairman; ⚖ foreman (of jury); umpire; ✝ shop-steward, spokesman.

Oboe ♪ [o'bo:ə] f (-/-n) oboe, hautboy.

Obrigkeit ['o:briçkait] f (-/-en) the authorities pl.; government; '²lich adj. magisterial, official; '~sstaat m authoritarian state.

ob'schon cj. (al)though.

Observatorium ast. [ɔpzɛrva'to:r-jum] n (-s/Observatorien) observatory.

Obst [o:pst] n (-es/no pl.) fruit;

'~bau m fruit-culture, fruit-growing; '~baum m fruit-tree; '~ernte f fruit-gathering; fruit-crop; '~garten m orchard; '~händler m fruiterer, Am. fruitseller; '~züchter m fruiter, fruit-grower.

obszön adj. [ɔps'tsø:n] obscene, filthy.

ob'wohl cj. (al)though.

Ochse zo. ['ɔksə] m (-n/-n) ox; bullock; '~nfleisch n beef.

öde ['ø:də] 1. adj. deserted, desolate; waste; fig. dull, tedious; 2. ♀ f (-/-n) desert, solitude; fig. dullness, tedium.

oder cj. ['o:dər] or.

Ofen ['o:fən] m (-s/ᵘ) stove; oven; kiln; furnace; '~heizung f heating by stove; '~rohr n stove-pipe.

offen adj. ['ɔfən] open (a. fig.); position: vacant; hostility: overt; fig. frank, outspoken.

'offen'bar 1. adj. obvious, evident; apparent; 2. adv. a. it seems that; ~en [ɔfən'-] v/t. (no -ge-, h) reveal, disclose; manifest; sich j-m ~ open one's heart to s.o.; ²ung [ɔfən'-] f (-/-en) manifestation; revelation; ²ungseid [ɔfən'ba:runs?-] m oath of manifestation.

'Offenheit fig. f (-/no pl.) openness, frankness.

'offen|herzig adj. open-hearted, sincere; frank; '~kundig adj. public; notorious; '~sichtlich adj. manifest, evident, obvious.

offensiv adj. [ɔfɛn'zi:f] offensive; ²e [~və] f (-/-n) offensive.

'offenstehen v/i. (irr. stehen, sep., -ge-, h) stand open; ✝ bill: be outstanding; fig. be open (j-m to s.o.); es steht ihm offen zu inf. he is free or at liberty to inf.

öffentlich ['œfəntliç] 1. adj. public; ~es Ärgernis public nuisance; ~er Dienst Civil Service; 2. adv. publicly, in public; ~ auftreten make a public appearance; '²keit f (-/no pl.) publicity; the public; in aller ~ in public.

offerieren [ɔfə'ri:rən] v/t. (no -ge-, h) offer.

Offerte [ɔ'fɛrtə] f (-/-n) offer; tender.

offiziell adj. [ɔfi'tsjɛl] official.

Offizier ✗ [ɔfi'tsi:r] m (-s/-e) (commissioned) officer; ~skorps ✗ [~sko:r] n (-/-) body of officers, the officers pl.; ~smesse f ✗ officers' mess; ⚓ a. wardroom.

offiziös adj. [ɔfi'tsjø:s] officious, semi-official.

öffn|en ['œfnən] v/t. (ge-, h) open; a. uncork (bottle); ⚕ dissect (body); sich ~ open; '²er m (-s/-) opener; '²ung f (-/-en) opening, aperture; '²ungszeiten f/pl. hours pl. of opening, business hours pl.

oft adv. [ɔft] often, frequently.

öfters *adv.* ['œftərs] *s.* oft.

'**oftmal|ig** *adj.* frequent, repeated; '∼s *adv. s.* oft.

oh *int.* [o:] o(h)!

ohne ['o:nə] **1.** *prp.* (*acc.*) without; **2.** *cj.*: ∼ daß, ∼ zu *inf.* without *ger.*; ∼'**dies** *adv.* anyhow, anyway; ∼'**glei- chen** *adv.* unequal(l)ed, matchless; ∼'**hin** *adv. s.* ohnedies.

'**Ohn|macht** *f* (-/-en) powerlessness; impotence; *⚔* faint, unconscious- ness; *in ∼ fallen* faint, swoon; ∼**machtsanfall** *⚔* ['o:nmaxts²-] *m* fainting fit, swoon; '2**mächtig** *adj.* powerless; impotent; *⚔* uncon- scious; ∼ *werden* faint, swoon.

Ohr [o:r] *n* (-[e]s/-en) ear; *fig. a.* hearing; *ein ∼ haben für* have an ear for; *ganz ∼ sein* be all ears; F *j-n übers ∼ hauen* cheat s.o., *sl.* do s.o. (in the eye); *bis über die ∼en* up to the ears *or* eyes.

Öhr [ø:r] *n* (-[e]s/-e) eye (*of needle*).

'**Ohren|arzt** *m* aurist, ear specialist; '2**betäubend** *adj.* deafening; '∼**lei- den** *n* ear-complaint; '∼**schmalz** *n* ear-wax; '∼**schmaus** *m* treat for the ears; '∼**schmerzen** *m/pl.* ear- ache; '∼**zeuge** *m* ear-witness.

'**Ohr|feige** *f* box on the ear(s), slap in the face (*a. fig.*); '2**feigen** *v/t.* (*ge-, h*): *j-n ∼* box s.o.'s ear(s), slap s.o.'s face; ∼**läppchen** ['∼lɛpçən] *n* (-s/-) lobe of ear; '∼**ring** *m* ear- ring.

Ökonom|ie [økono'mi:] *f* (-/-n) economy; 2**isch** *adj.* [∼'no:miʃ] economical.

Oktav [ɔk'ta:f] *n* (-s/-e) octavo; ∼**e** *f* [∼və] *f* (-/-n) octave.

Oktober [ɔk'to:bər] *m* (-[s]/-) October.

Okul|ar *opt.* [oku'la:r] *n* (-s/-e) eye- piece, ocular; 2**ieren** *⚔ v/t.* (*no -ge-, h*) inoculate, graft.

Öl [ø:l] *n* (-[e]s/-e) oil; ∼ *ins Feuer gießen* add fuel to the flames; *∼ auf die Wogen gießen* pour oil on the (troubled) waters; '∼**baum** ♀ *m* olive-tree; '∼**berg** *eccl. m* (-[e]s/*no pl.*) Mount of Olives; '2**en** *v/t.* (*ge-, h*) oil; ⊕ *a.* lubricate; '∼**farbe** *f* oil-colo(u)r, oil-paint; '∼**gemälde** *n* oil-painting; '∼**heizung** *f* oil heating; '2**ig** *adj.* oily (*a. fig.*).

Oliv|e ♀ [o'li:və] *f* (-/-n) olive; ∼**enbaum** ♀ *m* olive-tree; 2**grün** *adj.* olive(-green).

Öl|male'rei *f* oil-painting; '∼**quelle** *f* oil-spring, gusher; oil-well; '∼**ung** *f* (-/-en) oiling; ⊕ *a.* lubrication; *Letzte ∼ eccl.* extreme unction.

Olympi|ade [olymp'ja:də] *f* (-/-n) Olympiad; *a.* Olympic Games *pl.*; 2**sch** *adj.* [o'lympiʃ] Olympic; *Olym- pische Spiele pl.* Olympic Games *pl.*

'**Ölzweig** *m* olive-branch.

Omelett [ɔm(ə)'lɛt] *n* (-[e]s/-e, -s), ∼**e** [∼'lɛt] *f* (-/-n) omelet(te).

Om|en ['o:mən] *n* (-s/-, *Omina*) omen, augury; 2**inös** *adj.* [omi'nø:s] ominous.

Omnibus ['ɔmnibus] *m* (-ses/-se) (omni)bus; (motor-)coach; '∼**halte- stelle** *f* bus-stop.

Onkel ['ɔŋkəl] *m* (-s/-, F -s) uncle.

Oper ['o:pər] *f* (-/-n) *♪* opera; opera- house.

Operat|eur [opəra'tø:r] *m* (-s/-e) operator; *⚔* surgeon; ∼**ion** *⚔*, *⚔* [∼'tsjo:n] *f* (-/-en) operation; ∼**ions- saal** *⚔ m* operating room, *Am.* surgery; 2**iv** *⚔ adj.* [∼'ti:f] operative.

Operette *♪* [opə'rɛtə] *f* (-/-n) operetta.

operieren [opə'ri:rən] (*no -ge-, h*) **1.** *v/t.*: *j-n ∼ ⚔* operate (up)on s.o. (*wegen* for); **2.** *⚔*, *⚔ v/i.* operate; *sich ∼ lassen ⚔* undergo an opera- tion.

'**Opern|glas** *n*, ∼**gucker** F ['∼gukər] *m* (-s/-) opera-glass(es *pl.*); '∼**haus** *n* opera-house; '∼**sänger** *m* opera- singer, operatic singer; '∼**text** *m* libretto, book (of an opera).

Opfer ['ɔpfər] *n* (-s/-) sacrifice; offering; victim (*a. fig.*); *ein ∼ brin- gen* make a sacrifice; *j-m zum ∼ fallen* be victimized by s.o.; '∼**gabe** *f* offering; '2**n** (*ge-, h*) **1.** *v/t.* sacri- fice; immolate; *sich für et. ∼* sacri- fice o.s. for s.th.; **2.** *v/i.* (make a) sacrifice (*dat.* to); '∼**stätte** *f* place of sacrifice; '∼**tod** *m* sacrifice of one's life; '∼**ung** *f* (-/-en) sacrificing, sacrifice; immolation.

Opium ['o:pjum] *n* (-s/*no pl.*) opium.

opponieren [ɔpo'ni:rən] *v/i.* (*no -ge-, h*) be opposed (*gegen* to), resist.

Opposition [ɔpozi'tsjo:n] *f* (-/-en) opposition (*a. parl.*); ∼**führer** *parl. m* opposition leader; ∼**spartei** *parl. f* opposition party.

Optik ['ɔptik] *f* (-/∼-en) optics; *phot.* lens system; *fig.* aspect; '∼**er** *m* (-s/-) optician.

Optim|ismus [ɔpti'mismus] *m* (-/*no pl.*) optimism; ∼**ist** *m* (-en/-en) optimist; 2**istisch** *adj.* optimis- tic.

'**optisch** *adj.* optic(al); ∼**e** *Täu- schung* optical illusion.

Orakel [o'ra:kəl] *n* (-s/-) oracle; 2**haft** *adj.* oracular; 2**n** *v/i.* (*no -ge-, h*) speak oracularly; ∼**spruch** *m* oracle.

Orange [o'rã:ʒə] *f* (-/-n) orange; 2**farben** *adj.* orange(-colo[u]red); ∼**nbaum** ♀ *m* orange-tree.

Oratorium *♪* [ora'to:rjum] *n* (-s/ *Oratorien*) oratorio.

Orchester *♪* [ɔr'kɛstər] *n* (-s/-) orchestra.

Orchidee ♀ [ɔrçi'de:ə] *f* (-/-n) orchid.

Orden ['ɔrdən] *m* (-s/-) order (*a. eccl.*); order, medal, decoration.

'Ordens|band *n* ribbon (of an order); **'₂bruder** *eccl. m* brother, friar; **'₂gelübde** *eccl. n* monastic vow; **'₂schwester** *eccl. f* sister, nun; **'₂verleihung** *f* conferring (of) an order.

ordentlich *adj.* ['ɔrdəntliç] tidy; orderly; proper; regular; respectable; good, sound; ₂er *Professor univ.* professor in ordinary.

ordinär *adj.* [ɔrdi'nɛːr] common, vulgar, low.

ordn|en ['ɔrdnən] *v/t.* (ge-, h) put in order; arrange, fix (up); settle (*a. ✝ liabilities*); **'₂er** *m* (-s/-) at *festival, etc.*: steward; *for papers, etc.*: file.

'Ordnung *f* (-/-en) order; arrangement; system; rules *pl.*, regulations *pl.*; class; *in ₂ bringen* put in order.

'ordnungs|gemäß, '₂mäßig 1. *adj.* orderly, regular; 2. *adv.* duly; **'₂ruf** *parl. m* call to order; **'₂strafe** *f* disciplinary penalty; fine; '₂widrig *adj.* contrary to order, irregular; **'₂zahl** *f* ordinal number.

Ordonnanz ✗ [ɔrdo'nants] *f* (-/-en) orderly.

Organ [ɔr'gaːn] *n* (-s/-e) organ.

Organisat|ion [ɔrganiza'tsjoːn] *f* (-/-en) organization; **₂ionstalent** *n* organizing ability; **₂or** [₂'zaːtɔr] *m* (-s/-en) organizer; **₂orisch** *adj.* [₂a'toːriʃ] organizational, organizing.

or'ganisch *adj.* organic.

organi'sieren *v/t.* (*no* -ge-, *h*) organize; *sl.* scrounge; (*nicht*) *organisiert(er Arbeiter)* (non-)unionist.

Organismus [ɔrga'nismus] *m* (-/Organismen) organism; **✗** *a.* system.

Organist ♪ [ɔrga'nist] *m* (-en/-en) organist.

Orgel ♪ ['ɔrgəl] *f* (-/-n) organ, *Am. a.* pipe organ; '₂bauer *m* organ-builder; '₂pfeife *f* organ-pipe; '₂spieler ♪ *m* organist.

Orgie ['ɔrgjə] *f* (-/-n) orgy.

Oriental|e [orien'taːlə] *m* (-n/-n) oriental; **₂isch** *adj.* oriental.

orientier|en [orien'tiːrən] *v/t.* (*no* -ge-, *h*) inform, instruct; *sich ₂ orient(ate)* o.s. (*a. fig.*); inform o.s. (*über acc.* of); *gut orientiert sein über (acc.)* be well informed about, be familiar with; **₂ung** *f* (-/-en) orientation; *fig. a.* information; *die ₂ verlieren* lose one's bearings.

Origin|al [origi'naːl] 1. *n* (-s/-e) original; 2. ♀ *adj.* original; **₂alität** [₂ali'tɛːt] *f* (-/-en) originality; **₂ell** *adj.* [₂'nɛl] original; *design, etc.*: ingenious.

Orkan [ɔr'kaːn] *m* (-[e]s/-e) hur-
ricane; typhoon; **₂artig** *adj. storm*: violent; *applause*: thunderous, frenzied.

Ornat [ɔr'naːt] *m* (-[e]s/-e) robe(s *pl.*), vestment.

Ort [ɔrt] *m* (-[e]s/-e) place; site; spot, point; locality; place, village, town; *₂ der Handlung thea.* scene (of action); *an ₂ und Stelle* on the spot; *höher(e)n ₂(e)s* at higher quarters; **₂en** *v/t.* (ge-, *h*) locate.

ortho|dox *adj.* [ɔrto'dɔks] orthodox; **₂graphie** [₂gra'fiː] *f* (-/-n) orthography; **₂graphisch** *adj.* [₂'graːfiʃ] orthographic(al); **₂päde** [₂'pɛːdə] *m* (-n/-n) orthop(a)edist; **₂pädie** [₂pɛ'diː] *f* (-/no pl.) orthop(a)edics, orthop(a)edy; **₂pädisch** *adj.* [₂'pɛːdiʃ] orthop(a)edic.

örtlich *adj.* ['œrtliç] local; **✗** *a.* topical; **₂keit** *f* (-/-en) locality.

'Orts|angabe *f* statement of place; **'₂ansässig** *adj.* resident, local; **₂ansässige** ['₂gə] *m* (-n/-n) resident; **'₂beschreibung** *f* topography; **'₂besichtigung** *f* local inspection.

'Ortschaft *f* (-/-en) place, village.

'Orts|gespräch *teleph. n* local call; **'₂kenntnis** *f* knowledge of a place; **'₂kundig** *adj.* familiar with the locality; **'₂name** *m* place-name; **'₂verkehr** *m* local traffic; **'₂zeit** *f* local time.

Öse ['øːzə] *f* (-/-n) eye, loop; eyelet (*of shoe*).

Ost *geogr.* [ɔst] east; '₂en *m* (-s/no pl.) east; *the* East; *der Ferne (Nahe) ₂ the* Far (Near) East.

ostentativ *adj.* [ɔstenta'tiːf] ostentatious.

Oster|ei ['oːstar⁹-] *n* Easter egg; '₂fest *n* Easter; '₂hase *m* Easter bunny *or* rabbit; '₂lamm *n* paschal lamb; '₂n *n* (-/-) Easter.

Österreich|er ['øːstəraiçər] *m* (-s/-) Austrian; '₂isch *adj.* Austrian.

östlich *adj.* ['œstliç] 1. *adj.* eastern; *wind, etc.*: easterly; 2. *adv.:* ₂ *von* east of.

ost|wärts *adv.* ['ɔstverts] eastward(s); **₂wind** *m* east(erly) wind.

Otter *zo.* ['ɔtər] 1. *m* (-s/-) otter; 2. *f* (-/-n) adder, viper.

Ouvertüre ♪ [uver'tyːrə] *f* (-/-n) overture.

oval [o'vaːl] 1. *adj.* oval; 2. ♀ *n* (-s/-e) oval.

Ovation [ova'tsjoːn] *f* (-/-en) ovation; *j-m ₂en bereiten* give s.o. ovations.

Oxyd ⚗ ['ɔksyːt] *n* (-[e]s/-e) oxide; **₂ieren** [₂y'diːrən] (*no* -ge-) 1. *v/t.* (*h*) oxidize; 2. *v/i.* (*sein*) oxidize.

Ozean ['oːtseaːn] *m* (-s/-e) ocean.

P

Paar [pɑːr] **1.** *n* (-[e]s/-e) pair; couple; **2.** ♀ *adj.*: *ein ~* a few, some; *j-m ein ~ Zeilen schreiben* drop s.o. a few lines; '♀en *v/t.* (ge-, h) pair, couple; mate (*animals*); *sich ~* (form a) pair; *animals*: mate; *fig.* join, unite; '~lauf *m sports*: pair-skating; '~läufer *m sports*: pair-skater; '♀mal *adv.*: *ein ~* several or a few times; '~ung *f* (-/-en) coupling; mating, copulation; *fig.* union; '♀weise *adv.* in pairs or couples, by twos.

Pacht [paxt] *f* (-/-en) lease, tenure, tenancy; *money payment*: rent; '♀en *v/t.* (ge-, h) (take on) lease; rent.

Pächter ['pɛçtər] *m* (-s/-), '~in *f* (-/-nen) lessee, lease-holder; tenant.

'**Pacht|ertrag** *m* rental; '~geld *n* rent; '♀gut *n* farm; '~vertrag *m* lease; '♀weise *adv.* on lease.

Pack [pak] **1.** *m* (-[e]s/-e, ⁼e) *s. Packen²*; **2.** *n* (-[e]s/no *pl.*) rabble.

Päckchen ['pɛkçən] *n* (-s/-) small parcel, *Am. a.* package; *ein ~ Zigaretten* a pack(et) of cigarettes.

packen¹ ['pakən] (ge-, h) **1.** *v/t.* pack (up); seize, grip, grasp, clutch; collar; *fig.* grip, thrill; F *pack dich!* F clear out!, *sl.* beat it!; **2.** *v/i.* pack (up); **3.** ♀ *n* (-s/no *pl.*) packing.

Packen² [~] *m* (-s/-) pack(et), parcel; bale.

'**Packer** *m* (-s/-) packer; '~ei [~'raɪ] *f* **1.** (-/-en) packing-room; **2.** (-/no *pl.*) packing.

'**Pack|esel** *fig. m* drudge; '~material *n* packing materials *pl.*; '~papier *n* packing-paper, brown paper; '~pferd *n* pack-horse; '~ung *f* (-/-en) pack(age); packet; ♂ pack; *e-e ~ Zigaretten* a pack(et) of cigarettes; '~wagen *m s. Gepäck-wagen.*

Pädagog|e [pɛda'goːgə] *m* (-n/-n) pedagog(ue), education(al)ist; ~ik *f* (-/no *pl.*) pedagogics, pedagogy; ♀isch *adj.* pedagogic(al).

Paddel ['padəl] *n* (-s/-) paddle; '~boot *n* canoe; '♀n *v/i.* (ge-, h, sein) paddle, canoe.

Page ['pɑːʒə] *m* (-n/-n) page.

pah *int.* [pɑː] pah!, pooh!, pshaw!

Paket [pa'keːt] *n* (-[e]s/-e) parcel, packet, package; *Am. a.* package; ~annahme ♀ *f* parcel counter; ~karte ♀ *f* dispatch-note; ~post *f* parcel post; ~zustellung ♀ *f* parcel delivery.

Pakt [pakt] *m* (-[e]s/-e) pact; agreement; treaty.

Palast [pa'last] *m* (-es/⁼e) palace.

Palm|e ♀ ['palmə] *f* (-/-n) palm (-tree); '~öl *n* palm-oil; ~sonntag *eccl. m* Palm Sunday.

panieren [pa'niːrən] *v/t.* (no -ge-, h) crumb.

Pani|k ['pɑːnik] *f* (-/-en) panic; stampede; '♀sch *adj.* panic; *von ~em Schrecken erfaßt* panic-stricken.

Panne ['panə] *f* (-/-n) breakdown, *mot. a.* engine trouble; *tyres*: puncture; *fig.* blunder.

panschen ['panʃən] (ge-, h) **1.** *v/i.* splash (about); **2.** *v/t.* adulterate (*wine, etc.*).

Panther *zo.* ['pantər] *m* (-s/-) panther.

Pantine [pan'tiːnə] *f* (-/-n) clog.

Pantoffel [pan'tɔfəl] *m* (-s/-n, F -) slipper; *unter dem ~ stehen* be henpecked; ~held F *m* henpecked husband.

pantschen ['pantʃən] *v/i. and v/t.* (ge-, h) *s. panschen.*

Panzer ['pantsər] *m* (-s/-) armo(u)r; ✗ tank; *zo.* shell; '~abwehr ✗ *f* anti-tank defen|ce, *Am.* -se; '~glas *n* bullet-proof glass; '~hemd *n* coat of mail; '~kreuzer ✗ *m* armo(u)red cruiser; '♀n *v/t.* (ge-, h) armo(u)r; '~platte *f* armo(u)r-plate; '~schiff ✗ *n* ironclad; '~schrank *m* safe; '~ung *f* (-/-en) armo(u)r-plating; '~wagen *m* armo(u)red car; ✗ tank.

Papa [pa'pɑː, F 'papa] *m* (-s/-s) papa, F pa, dad(dy), *Am. a.* pop.

Papagei *orn.* [papa'gaɪ] *m* (-[e]s, -en/-e[n]) parrot.

Papier [pa'piːr] *n* (-s/-e) paper; ~e *pl.* papers *pl.*, documents *pl.*; papers *pl.*, identity card; *ein Bogen ~* a sheet of paper; ♀en *adj.* (of) paper; *fig.* dull; ~fabrik *f* paper-mill; ~geld *n* (-[e]s/no *pl.*) paper-money; banknotes *pl.*, *Am.* bills *pl.*; ~korb *m* waste-paper-basket; ~schnitzel F *n* or *m/pl.* scraps *pl.* of paper; ~tüte *f* paper-bag; ~waren *f/pl.* stationery.

'**Papp|band** *m* (-[e]s/⁼e) paperback; '~deckel *m* pasteboard, cardboard.

Pappe ['papə] *f* (-/-n) pasteboard, cardboard.

Pappel ♀ ['papəl] *f* (-/-n) poplar.

päppeln F ['pɛpəln] *v/t.* (ge-, h) feed (with pap).

papp|en F ['papən] (ge-, h) **1.** *v/t.* paste; **2.** *v/i.* stick; '~ig *adj.* sticky; '♀karton *m*, '♀schachtel *f* cardboard box, carton.

Papst [pɑːpst] *m* (-es/⁼e) pope.

päpstlich *adj.* ['pɛːpstliç] papal.

'**Papsttum** *n* (-s/no *pl.*) papacy.

Parade [pa'rɑːdə] *f* (-/-n) parade; ✗ review; *fencing*: parry.

Paradies [para'diːs] *n* (-es/-e) paradise; ♀isch *fig. adj.* [~'diːziʃ] heavenly, delightful.

paradox *adj.* [para'dɔks] paradoxical.

Paragraph [para'gra:f] *m* (-en, -s/-en) article, section; paragraph; section-mark.

parallel *adj.* [para'le:l] parallel; ℒe *f* (-/-n) parallel.

Paralys|e ℐ [para'ly:zə] *f* (-/-n) paralysis; ℒieren ℐ [͜y'zi:rən] *v/t.* (*no -ge-, h*) paralyse.

Parasit [para'zi:t] *m* (-en/-en) parasite.

Parenthese [paren'te:zə] *f* (-/-n) parenthesis.

Parforcejagd [par'fɔrs-] *f* hunt (-ing) on horseback (with hounds), *after hares:* coursing.

Parfüm [par'fy:m] *n* (-s/-e, -s) perfume, scent; ℒerie [͜ymə'ri:] *f* (-/-n) perfumery; ℒieren [͜y'mi:rən] *v/t.* (*no -ge-, h*) perfume, scent.

pari ♰ *adv.* ['pa:ri] par; *al* ͜ at par.

parieren [pa'ri:rən] (*no -ge-, h*) **1.** *v/t. fencing:* parry (*a. fig.*); pull up (*horse*); **2.** *v/i.* obey (*j-m s.o.*).

Park [park] *m* (-s/-s, -e) park; '͜anlage *f* park; '͜aufseher *m* parkkeeper; 'ℒen (*ge-, h*) **1.** *v/i.* park; ͜ *verboten!* no parking!; **2.** *v/t.* park.

Parkett [par'ket] *n* (-[e]s/-e) parquet; *thea.* (orchestra) stalls *pl.*, *esp. Am.* orchestra *or* parquet.

'**Park|gebühr** *f* parking-fee; '͜licht *n* parking light; '͜platz *m* (car-) park, parking lot; '͜uhr *mot. f* parking meter.

Parlament [parla'ment] *n* (-[e]s/-e) parliament; ℒarisch *adj.* [͜'ta:riʃ] parliamentary.

Parodie [paro'di:] *f* (-/-n) parody; ℒren *v/t.* (*no -ge-, h*) parody.

Parole [pa'ro:lə] *f* (-/-n) ✗ password, watchword; *fig.* slogan.

Partei [par'taɪ] *f* (-/-en) party (*a. pol.*); *j-s ͜ ergreifen* take s.o.'s part, side with s.o.; ͜apparat *pol. m* party machinery; ͜gänger [͜gɛŋər] *m* (-s/-) partisan; ℒisch *adj.*, ℒlich *adj.* partial (*für* to); prejudiced (*gegen* against); ͜los *pol. adj.* independent; ͜mitglied *pol. n* party member; ͜programm *pol. n* platform; ͜tag *pol. m* convention; ͜zugehörigkeit *pol. f* party membership.

Parterre [par'tɛr] *n* (-s/-s) ground floor, *Am.* first floor; *thea.:* pit, *Am.* parterre, *Am.* parquet circle.

Partie [par'ti:] *f* (-/-n) ♰ parcel, lot; outing, excursion; *cards, etc.:* game; ♩ part; *marriage:* match.

Partitur ♩ [parti'tu:r] *f* (-/-en) score.

Partizip *gr.* [parti'tsi:p] *n* (-s/-ien) participle.

Partner ['partnər] *m* (-s/-), '͜in *f* (-/-nen) partner; *film: a.* co-star; '͜schaft *f* (-/-en) partnership.

Parzelle [par'tsɛlə] *f* (-/-n) plot, lot, allotment.

Paß [pas] *m* (*Passes/Pässe*) pass; passage; *football, etc.:* pass; passport.

Passage [pa'sa:ʒə] *f* (-/-n) passage; arcade.

Passagier [pasa'ʒi:r] *m* (-s/-e) passenger, *in taxis: a.* fare; ͜flugzeug *n* air liner.

Passah ['pasa] *n* (-s/*no pl.*), '͜fest *n* Passover.

Passant [pa'sant] *m* (-en/-en), ͜in *f* (-/-nen) passer-by.

'**Paßbild** *n* passport photo(graph).

passen ['pasən] (*ge-, h*) **1.** *v/i.* fit (*j-m s.o.*); *auf acc. or für or zu et. s.th.*); suit (*j-m s.o.*), be convenient; *cards, football:* pass; ͜ *zu* go with, match (with); **2.** *v/refl.* be fit *or* proper; '͜d *adj.* fit, suitable; convenient (*für* for).

passier|bar *adj.* [pa'si:rba:r] passable, practicable; ͜en (*no -ge-*) **1.** *v/i.* (*sein*) happen; **2.** *v/t.* (*h*) pass (over *or* through); ℒschein *m* pass, permit.

Passion [pa'sjo:n] *f* (-/-en) passion; hobby; *eccl.* Passion.

passiv ['pasi:f] **1.** *adj.* passive; **2.** ℒ *gr. n* (-s/-e) *gr.* passive (voice); ℒa ♰ [pa'si:va] *pl.* liabilities *pl.*

Paste ['pastə] *f* (-/-n) paste.

Pastell [pas'tel] *n* (-[e]s/-e) pastel.

Pastete [pas'te:tə] *f* (-/-n) pie; ͜bäcker *m* pastry-cook.

Pate ['pa:tə] **1.** *m* (-n/-n) godfather; godchild; **2.** *f* (-/-n) godmother; ͜nkind *n* godchild; '͜nschaft *f* (-/-en) sponsorship.

Patent [pa'tent] *n* (-[e]s/-e) patent; ✗ commission; *ein ͜ anmelden* apply for a patent; ͜amt *n* Patent Office; ͜anwalt *m* patent agent; ℒieren [͜'ti:rən] *v/t.* (*no -ge-, h*) patent; *et. ͜ lassen* take out a patent for s.th.; ͜inhaber *m* patentee; ͜urkunde *f* letters patent.

Patient [pa'tsjent] *m* (-en/-en), ͜in *f* (-/-nen) patient.

Patin [pa'ti:n] *f* (-/-nen) godmother.

Patriot [patri'o:t] *m* (-en/-en), ͜in *f* (-/-nen) patriot.

Patron [pa'tro:n] *m* (-s/-e) patron, protector; *contp.* fellow, bloke, customer; ͜at [͜o'na:t] *n* (-[e]s/-e) patronage; ͜e [pa'tro:nə] *f* (-/-n) cartridge, *Am. a.* shell.

Patrouill|e ✗ [pa'truljə] *f* (-/-n) patrol; ℒieren ✗ [͜'ji:rən] *v/i.* (*no -ge-, h*) patrol.

Patsch|e F *fig.* ['patʃə] *f* (-/*no pl.*): *in der ͜ sitzen* be in a fix *or* scrape; 'ℒen F (*ge-*) **1.** *v/i.* (*h, sein*) splash; **2.** *v/t.* (*h*) slap; 'ℒ'naß *adj.* dripping wet, drenched.

patzig F *adj.* ['patsiç] snappish.

Pauke ♩ ['paʊkə] *f* (-/-n) kettledrum; 'ℒn F *v/i. and v/t.* (*ge-, h*) *school:* cram.

Pauschal|e [paʊ'ʃa:lə] *f* (-/-n), ͜summe *f* lump sum.

Pause ['pauzə] f (-/-n) pause, stop, interval; *school*: break, *Am.* recess; *thea.* interval, *Am.* intermission; ♪ rest; *drawing*: tracing; '₂n v/t. (ge-, h) trace; '₂nlos *adj.* uninterrupted, incessant; '₂nzeichen n *wireless*: interval signal.

pau'sieren v/i. (*no* -ge-, h) pause.

Pavian *zo.* ['pa:via:n] m (-s/-e) baboon.

Pavillon ['paviljõ] m (-s/-s) pavilion.

Pazifist [patsi'fist] m (-en/-en) pacif(ic)ist.

Pech [pɛç] n 1. (-[e]s /-e) pitch; 2. F *fig.* (-[e]s/*no pl.*) bad luck; '₂strähne F f run of bad luck; '₂vogel F m unlucky fellow.

pedantisch *adj.* [pe'dantiʃ] pedantic; punctilious, meticulous.

Pegel ['pe:gəl] m (-s/-) water-ga(u)ge.

peilen ['paɪlən] v/t. (ge-, h) sound (*depth*); take the bearings of (*coast*).

Pein [paɪn] f (-/*no pl.*) torment, torture, anguish; ₂igen ['₂igən] v/t. (ge-, h) torment; ₂iger ['₂igər] m (-s/-) tormentor.

'peinlich *adj.* painful, embarrassing; particular, scrupulous, meticulous.

Peitsche ['paɪtʃə] f (-/-n) whip; '₂n v/t. (ge-, h) whip; '₂nhieb m lash.

Pelikan *orn.* ['pe:lika:n] m (-s/-e) pelican.

Pell|e ['pɛlə] f (-/-n) skin, peel; '₂en v/t. (ge-, h) skin, peel; '₂kartoffeln f/pl. potatoes pl. (boiled) in their jackets *or* skins.

Pelz [pɛlts] m (-es/-e) fur; *garment*: *mst* furs pl.; '₂gefüttert *adj.* fur-lined; '₂händler m furrier; '₂handschuh m furred glove; '₂ig *adj.* furry; ♂ *tongue*: furred; '₂mantel m fur coat; '₂stiefel m fur-lined boot; '₂tiere n/pl. fur-covered animals pl.

Pendel ['pɛndəl] n (-s/-) pendulum; '₂n v/i. (ge-, h) oscillate, swing; 🚋 shuttle, *Am.* commute; '₂tür f swing-door; '₂verkehr 🚋 m shuttle service.

Pension [pã'sjõː, pɛn'zjo:n] f (-/-en) (old-age) pension, retired pay; board; boarding-house; ₂är [₂o-'nɛːr] m (-s/-e) (old-age) pensioner; boarder; ₂at [₂o'na:t] n (-[e]s/-e) boarding-school; ₂ieren [₂o'ni:rən] v/t. (*no* -ge-, h) pension (off); *sich ₂ lassen* retire; '₂gast m boarder.

Pensum ['pɛnzum] n (-s/Pensen, Pensa) task, lesson.

perfekt 1. *adj.* [pɛr'fɛkt] perfect; *agreement*: settled; 2. ♀ *gr.* ['₂] n (-[e]s/-e) perfect (tense).

Pergament [pɛrga'mɛnt] n (-[e]s/-e) parchment.

Period|e [per'jo:də] f (-/-n) period; ♂ *periods pl.*; ₂isch *adj.* periodic (-al).

Peripherie [perife'ri:] f (-/-n) circumference; outskirts pl. (*of town*).

Perle ['pɛrlə] f (-/-n) pearl; *of glass*: bead; '₂n v/i. (ge-, h) sparkle; '₂nkette f pearl necklace; '₂nschnur f string of pearls *or* beads.

'Perl|muschel *zo.* f pearl-oyster; ₂mutt ['₂mut] n (-s/*no pl.*), '₂mutter f (-/*no pl.*) mother-of-pearl.

Person [pɛr'zo:n] f (-/-en) person; *thea.* character.

Personal [pɛrzo'na:l] n (-s/*no pl.*) staff, personnel; ₂abteilung f personnel office; ₂angaben f/pl. personal data pl.; ₂ausweis m identity card; ₂chef m personnel officer *or* manager *or* director; ₂ien [₂jən] pl. particulars pl., personal data pl.; ₂pronomen gr. n personal pronoun.

Per'sonen|verzeichnis n list of persons; *thea.* dramatis personae pl.; ₂wagen m 🚋 (passenger-)carriage *or Am.* car, coach; *mot.* (motor-)car; ₂zug 🚋 m passenger train.

personifizieren [pɛrzonifi'tsi:rən] v/t. (*no* -ge-, h) personify.

persönlich *adj.* [pɛr'zø:nliç] personal; *opinion, letter*: a. private; ₂keit f (-/-en) personality; personage.

Perücke [pe'rykə] f (-/-n) wig.

Pest ♂ [pɛst] f (-/*no pl.*) plague.

Petersilie ♀ [petər'zi:ljə] f (-/-n) parsley.

Petroleum [pe'tro:leum] n (-s/*no pl.*) petroleum; *for lighting, etc.*: paraffin, *esp. Am.* kerosene.

Pfad [pfa:t] m (-[e]s/-e) path, track; '₂finder m boy scout; '₂finderin f (-/-nen) girl guide, *Am.* girl scout.

Pfahl [pfa:l] m (-[e]s/⁼e) stake, pale, pile.

Pfand [pfant] n (-[e]s/⁼er) pledge; ♈ deposit, security; *real estate*: mortgage; *game*: forfeit; '₂brief ♈ m debenture (bond).

pfänden ♂♂ ['pfɛndən] v/t. (ge-, h) seize *s.th.*; distrain upon *s.o. or s.th.*

'Pfand|haus n s. *Leihhaus*; '₂leiher m (-s/-) pawnbroker; '₂schein m pawn-ticket.

'Pfändung ♂♂ f (-/-en) seizure; distraint.

Pfann|e ['pfanə] f (-/-n) pan; '₂kuchen m pancake.

Pfarr|bezirk ['pfar-] m parish; '₂er m (-s/-) parson; *Church of England*: rector, vicar; *dissenters*: minister; '₂gemeinde f parish; '₂haus n parsonage; *Church of England*: rectory, vicarage; '₂kirche f parish church; '₂stelle f (church) living.

Pfau *orn.* [pfau] m (-[e]s/-en) peacock.

Pfeffer ['pfɛfər] m (-s/-) pepper; '₂gurke f gherkin; '₂ig *adj.* peppery; '₂kuchen m gingerbread;

~minze ⚥ ['~mintsə] f (-/no pl.) peppermint; '~minzplätzchen n peppermint; '⁓n v/t. (ge-, h) pepper; '~streuer m (-s/-) pepperbox, pepper-castor, pepper-caster.

Pfeife ['pfaɪfə] f (-/-n) whistle; ⚥ fife; pipe (of organ, etc.); (tobacco-) pipe; '⁓n (irr., ge-, h) 1. v/i. whistle (dat. to, for); radio: howl; pipe; 2. v/t. whistle; pipe; '~nkopf m pipe-bowl.

Pfeil [pfaɪl] m (-[e]s/-e) arrow.

Pfeiler ['pfaɪlər] m (-s/-) pillar (a. fig.); pier (of bridge, etc.).

'pfeil'schnell adj. (as) swift as an arrow; '⁓spitze f arrow-head.

Pfennig ['pfɛnɪç] m (-[e]s/-e) coin: pfennig; fig. penny, farthing.

Pferch [pfɛrç] m (-[e]s/-e) fold, pen; '⁓en v/t. (ge-, h) fold, pen; fig. cram.

Pferd zo. [pfe:rt] n (-[e]s/-e) horse; zu ~e on horseback.

Pferde|geschirr ['pfe:rdə-] n harness; '~koppel f (-/-n) paddock, Am. a. corral; '~rennen n horse-race; '~schwanz m horse's tail; hair-style: pony-tail; '~stall m stable; '~stärke ⊕ f horsepower.

pfiff¹ [pfɪf] pret. of pfeifen.

Pfiff² m (-[e]s/-e) whistle; fig. trick; '⁓ig adj. cunning, artful.

Pfingst|en eccl. ['pfɪŋstən] n (-/-), '~fest eccl. n Whitsun(tide); '~montag eccl. m Whit Monday; '~rose ⚥ f peony; '~sonntag eccl. m Whit Sunday.

Pfirsich ['pfɪrzɪç] m (-[e]s/-e) peach.

Pflanz|e ['pflantsə] f (-/-n) plant; '⁓en v/t. (ge-, h) plant, set; pot; '~enfaser f vegetable fib[re, Am. -er]; '~enfett n vegetable fat; '⁓enfressend adj. herbivorous; '~er m (-s/-) planter; '~ung f (-/-en) plantation.

Pflaster ['pflastər] n (-s/-) 🏥 plaster; road: pavement; '~er m (-s/-) paver, pavio(u)r; '⁓n v/t. (ge-, h) 🏥 plaster; pave (road); '~stein m paving-stone; cobble.

Pflaume ['pflaumə] f (-/-n) plum; dried: prune.

Pflege ['pfle:gə] f (-/-n) care; 🏥 nursing; cultivation (of art, garden, etc.); ⊕ maintenance; in ~ geben put out (child) to nurse; in ~ nehmen take charge of; '⁓bedürftig adj. needing care; '~befohlene ['~bəfo:lənə] m, f (-n/-n) charge; '~eltern pl. foster-parents pl.; '~heim n nursing home; '~kind n foster-child; '⁓n (ge-, h) 1. v/t. take care of; attend (to); foster (child); 🏥 nurse; maintain; cultivate (art, garden); 2. v/i.: ~ zu inf. be accustomed or used or wont to inf., be in the habit of ger.; sie pflegte zu sagen she used to say; '~r m (-s/-) fosterer; 🏥 male nurse;

trustee; 🏥 guardian, curator; '~rin f (-/-nen) nurse.

Pflicht [pflɪçt] f (-/-en) duty (gegen to); obligation; '⁓bewußt adj. conscious of one's duty; '⁓eifrig adj.zealous; '~erfüllung f performance of one's duty; '⁓fach n school, univ.: compulsory subject; '~gefühl n sense of duty; '⁓gemäß adj. dutiful; '⁓getreu adj. dutiful, loyal; '⁓schuldig adj. in duty bound; '⁓vergessen adj. undutiful, disloyal; '~verteidiger 🏥 m assigned counsel.

Pflock [pflɔk] m (-[e]s/⁓e) plug, peg.

pflücken ['pflʏkən] v/t. (ge-, h) pick, gather, pluck.

Pflug [pflu:k] m (-[e]s/⁓e) plough, Am. plow.

pflügen ['pfly:gən] v/t. and v/i. (ge-, h) plough, Am. plow.

Pforte ['pfɔrtə] f (-/-n) gate, door.

Pförtner ['pfœrtnər] m (-s/-) gate-keeper, door-keeper, porter, janitor.

Pfosten ['pfɔstən] m (-s/-) post.

Pfote ['pfo:tə] f (-/-n) paw.

Pfropf [pfrɔpf] m (-[e]s/-e) s. Pfropfen.

'Pfropfen 1. m (-s/-) stopper; cork; plug; 🏥 clot (of blood); 2. ⚥ v/t. (ge-, h) stopper; cork; fig. cram; ↗ graft.

Pfründe eccl. ['pfryndə] f (-/-n) prebend; benefice, (church) living.

Pfuhl [pfu:l] m (-[e]s/-e) pool, puddle; fig. sink, slough.

pfui int. [pfui] fie!, for shame!

Pfund [pfunt] n (-[e]s/-e) pound; ⚥ F adj. ['~dɪç] great, Am. swell; '⁓weise adv. by the pound.

pfusch|en F ['pfuʃən] (ge-, h) 1. v/i. bungle; 2. v/t. bungle, botch; '~erei F [~'raɪ] f (-/-en) bungle, botch.

Pfütze ['pfʏtsə] f (-/-n) puddle, pool.

Phänomen [fɛno'me:n] n (-s/-e) phenomenon; 2al adj. [~e'nɑ:l] phenomenal.

Phantasie [fanta'zi:] f (-/-n) imagination, fancy; vision; ♪ fantasia; 2ren (no -ge-, h) 1. v/i. dream; ramble; ♪ be delirious or raving; ♪ improvise; 2. v/t. dream; ♪ improvise.

Phantast [fan'tast] m (-en/-en) visionary, dreamer; 2isch adj. fantastic; F great, terrific.

Phase ['fɑ:zə] f (-/-n) phase (a. ⚡), stage.

Philanthrop [filan'tro:p] m (-en/-en) philanthropist.

Philolog|e [filo'lo:gə] m (-n/-n), '~in f (-/-nen) philologist; ~ie [~o-'gi:] f (-/-n) philology.

Philosoph [filo'zo:f] m (-en/-en) philosopher; ~ie [~o'fi:] f (-/-n) philosophy; 2ieren [~o'fi:rən] v/i. (no -ge-, h) philosophize (über acc. on); 2isch adj. [~'zo:fiʃ] philosophical.

Phlegma ['flɛgma] n (-s/no pl.) phlegm; **2tisch** adj. [~'maːtiʃ] phlegmatic.

phonetisch adj. [fo'neːtiʃ] phonetic.

Phosphor ⚗ ['fɔsfɔr] m (-s/no pl.) phosphorus.

Photo F ['foːto] **1.** n (-s/-s) photo; **2.** m (-s/-s) = '~apparat m camera.

Photograph [foto'graːf] m (-en/-en) photographer; ~ie [~a'fiː] f **1.** (-/-n) photograph, F: photo, picture; **2.** (-/no pl.) as an art: photography; **2ieren** [~a'fiːrən] (no -ge-, h) **1.** v/t. photograph; take a picture of; sich ~ lassen have one's photo(graph) taken; **2.** v/i. photograph; **2isch** adj. [~'graːfiʃ] photographic.

Photo|ko'pie f photostat; ~**ko'piergerät** n photostat; ~**zelle** f photoelectric cell.

Phrase ['fraːzə] f (-/-n) phrase.

Physik [fy'ziːk] f (-/no pl.) physics sg.; **2alisch** adj. [~i'kaːliʃ] physical; ~**er** ['fyːzikər] m (-s/-) physicist.

physisch adj. ['fyːziʃ] physical.

Pian|ist [pia'nist] m (-en/-en) pianist; ~**o** [pi'aːno] n (-s/-s) piano.

Picke ⊕ ['pikə] f (-/-n) pick(axe).

Pickel ['pikəl] m (-s/-) **1.** ⊕ pimple; ⊕ pick(axe); ice-pick; **2ig** adj. pimpled, pimply.

picken ['pikən] v/i. and v/t. (ge-, h) pick, peck.

picklig adj. ['pikliç] s. pickelig.

Picknick ['piknik] n (-s/-e, -s) picnic.

piekfein F adj. ['piːk'-] smart, tiptop, slap-up.

piep(s)en ['piːp(s)ən] v/i. (ge-, h) cheep, chirp, peep; squeak.

Pietät [pie'tɛːt] f (-/no pl.) reverence; piety; **2los** adj. irreverent; **2voll** adj. reverent.

Pik [piːk] **1.** m (-s/-e, -s) peak; **2.** F m (-s/-e): e-n ~ auf j-n haben bear s.o. a grudge; **3.** n (-s/-s) cards: spade(s pl.).

pikant adj. [pi'kant] piquant, spicy (both a. fig.); das Pikante the piquancy.

Pike ['piːkə] f (-/-n) pike; von der ~ auf dienen rise from the ranks.

Pilger ['pilgər] m (-s/-) pilgrim; '~**fahrt** f pilgrimage; **2n** v/i. (ge-, sein) go on or make a pilgrimage; wander.

Pille ['pilə] f (-/-n) pill.

Pilot [pi'loːt] m (-en/-en) pilot.

Pilz 🍄 [pilts] m (-es/-e) fungus, edible: mushroom, inedible: toadstool.

pimp(e)lig F adj. ['pimp(ə)liç] sickly; effeminate.

Pinguin orn. ['piŋguiːn] m (-s/-e) penguin.

Pinsel ['pinzəl] m (-s/-) brush; F fig. simpleton; **2n** v/t. and v/i. (ge-, h) paint; daub; '~**strich** m stroke of the brush.

Pinzette [pin'tsɛtə] f (-/-n) (e-e a pair of) tweezers pl.

Pionier [pio'niːr] m (-s/-e) pioneer, Am. a. trail blazer; ✕ engineer.

Pirat [pi'raːt] m (-en/-en) pirate.

Pirsch hunt. [pirʃ] f (-/no pl.) deerstalking, Am. a. still hunt.

Piste ['pistə] f (-/-n) skiing, etc.: course; ✈ runway.

Pistole [pis'toːlə] f (-/-n) pistol, Am. F a. gun, rod; ~**ntasche** f holster.

placieren [pla'siːrən] v/t. (no -ge-, h) place; sich ~ sports: be placed (second, etc.).

Plackerei F [plakə'raɪ] f (-/-en) drudgery.

plädieren [plɛ'diːrən] v/i. (no -ge-, h) plead (für for).

Plädoyer 🕮 [plɛdoa'jeː] n (-s/-s) pleading.

Plage ['plaːgə] f (-/-n) trouble, nuisance, F plague; torment; **2n** v/t. (ge-, h) torment; trouble, bother; F plague; sich ~ toil, drudge.

Plagiat [plag'jaːt] n (-[e]s/-e) plagiarism; ein ~ begehen plagiarize.

Plakat [pla'kaːt] n (-[e]s/-e) poster, placard, bill; ~**säule** f advertisement pillar.

Plakette [pla'kɛtə] f (-/-n) plaque.

Plan [plaːn] m (-[e]s/⁼e) plan; design, intention; scheme.

Plane ['plaːnə] f (-/-n) awning, tilt.

'planen v/t. (ge-, h) plan; scheme.

Planet [pla'neːt] m (-en/-en) planet.

planieren [pla'niːrən] v/t. (no -ge-, h) level.

Planke ['plaŋkə] f (-/-n) plank, board.

plänkeln ['plɛŋkəln] v/i. (ge-, h) skirmish (a. fig.).

'plan|los 1. adj. planless, aimless, desultory; **2.** adv. at random; '~**mäßig 1.** adj. systematic, planned; **2.** adv. as planned.

planschen ['planʃən] v/i. (ge-, h) splash, paddle.

Plantage [plan'taːʒə] f (-/-n) plantation.

Plapper|maul F ['plapər-] n chatterbox; **2n** F v/i. (ge-, h) chatter, prattle, babble.

plärren F ['plɛrən] v/i. and v/t. (ge-, h) blubber; bawl.

Plasti|k [plastik] **1.** f (-/no pl.) plastic art; **2.** f (-/-en) sculpture; ✍ plastic; **3.** ⊕ n (-s/-s) plastic; **2sch** adj. plastic; three-dimensional.

Platin [pla'tiːn] n (-s/no pl.) platinum.

plätschern ['plɛtʃərn] v/i. (ge-, h) dabble, splash; water: ripple, murmur.

platt adj. [plat] flat, level, even; fig. trivial, commonplace, trite; F fig. flabbergasted.

Plättbrett ['plɛt-] n ironing-board.

Platte ['platə] *f* (-/-n) plate; dish; sheet (*of metal, etc.*); flag, slab (*of stone*); *mountain*: ledge; top (*of table*); tray, salver; disc, record; F *fig.* bald pate; *kalte* ~ cold meat.

plätten ['plɛtən] *v/t.* (ge-, *h*) iron.

'Platten|spieler *m* record-player; **'~teller** *m* turn-table.

'Platt|form *f* platform; '~fuß *m* ⚕ flat-foot; F *mot.* flat; '~heit *fig.* *f* (-/-en) triviality; commonplace, platitude, *Am. sl. a.* bromide.

Platz [plats] *m* (-es/*~e*) place; spot, *Am. a.* point; room, space; site; seat; square; *round*: circus; *sports*: ground; *tennis*: court; ~ *behalten* remain seated; ~ *machen* make way *or* room (*dat.* for); ~ *nehmen* take a seat, sit down, *Am. a.* have a seat; *ist hier noch ~?* is this seat taken *or* engaged *or* occupied?; *den dritten ~ belegen sports*: be placed third, come in third; '~anweiserin *f* (-/-nen) usherette.

Plätzchen ['plɛtsçən] *n* (-s/-) snug place; spot; biscuit, *Am.* cookie.

'platzen *v/i.* (ge-, *sein*) burst; explode; crack, split.

'Platz|patrone *f* blank cartridge; '~regen *m* downpour.

Plauder|ei [plaudə'rai] *f* (-/-en) chat; talk; small talk; '2n *v/i.* (ge-, *h*) (have a) chat (*mit* with), talk (to); chatter.

plauz *int.* [plauts] bang!

Pleite F ['plaitə] **1.** *f* (-/-n) smash; *fig.* failure; **2.** ♀ F *adj.* (dead) broke, *Am. sl.* bust.

Plissee [pli'se:] *n* (-s/-s) pleating; ~rock *m* pleated skirt.

Plomb|e ['plɔmbə] *f* (-/-n) (lead) seal; stopping, filling (*of tooth*); 2ieren [~'bi:rən] *v/t.* (*no* -ge-, *h*) seal; stop, fill (*tooth*).

plötzlich *adj.* ['plœtslię] sudden.

plump *adj.* [plump] clumsy; ~s *int.* plump, plop; '~sen *v/i.* (ge-, *sein*) plump, plop, flop.

Plunder F ['plundər] *m* (-s/*no pl.*) lumber, rubbish, junk.

plündern ['plyndərn] (ge-, *h*) **1.** *v/t.* plunder, pillage, loot, sack; **2.** *v/i.* plunder, loot.

Plural *gr.* ['plu:ra:l] *m* (-s/-e) plural (number).

plus *adv.* [plus] plus.

Plusquamperfekt *gr.* ['pluskvamperfɛkt] *n* (-s/-e) pluperfect (tense), past perfect.

Pöbel ['pø:bəl] *m* (-s/*no pl.*) mob, rabble; '2haft *adj.* low, vulgar.

pochen ['pɔxən] *v/i.* (ge-, *h*) knock, rap, tap; *heart*: beat, throb, thump; *auf sein Recht* ~ stand on one's rights.

Pocke ⚕ ['pɔkə] *f* (-/-n) pock; '~n ⚕ *pl.* smallpox; '2nnarbig *adj.* pockmarked.

Podest [po'dɛst] *n*, *m* (-es/-e) pedestal (*a. fig.*).

Podium ['po:dium] *n* (-s/Podien) podium, platform, stage.

Poesie [poe'zi:] *f* (-/-n) poetry.

Poet [po'e:t] *m* (-en/-en) poet; 2isch *adj.* poetic(al).

Pointe [po'ɛ̃:tə] *f* (-/-n) point.

Pokal [po'ka:l] *m* (-s/-e) goblet; *sports*: cup; ~endspiel *n sports*: cup final; ~spiel *n football*: cup-tie.

Pökel|fleisch ['pø:kəl-] *n* salted meat; '2n *v/t.* (ge-, *h*) pickle, salt.

Pol [po:l] *m* (-s/-e) pole; ⚡ *a.* terminal; 2ar *adj.* [po'la:r] polar (*a.* ⚡).

Pole ['po:lə] *m* (-n/-n) Pole.

Polemi|k [po'le:mik] *f* (-/-en) polemic(s *pl.*); 2sch *adj.* polemic (-al); 2sieren [~emi'zi:rən] *v/i.* (*no* -ge-, *h*) polemize.

Police [po'li:s(ə)] *f* (-/-n) policy.

Polier ⊕ [po'li:r] *m* (-s/-e) foreman; 2en *v/t.* (*no* -ge-, *h*) polish, burnish; furbish.

Politi|k [poli'ti:k] *f* (-/~ -en) policy; politics *sg.*, *pl.*; ~ker [po'li:tikər] *m* (-s/-) politician; statesman; 2sch *adj.* [po'li:tiʃ] political; 2sieren [~iti'zi:rən] *v/i.* (*no* -ge-, *h*) talk politics.

Politur [poli'tu:r] *f* (-/-en) polish; lust|re, *Am.* -er, finish.

Polizei [poli'tsai] *f* (-/~ -en) police; ~beamte *m* police officer; ~knüppel *m* truncheon, *Am.* club; ~kommissar *m* inspector; 2lich *adj.* (of *or* by the) police; ~präsident *m* president of police; *Brt.* Chief Constable, *Am.* Chief of Police; ~präsidium *n* police headquarters *pl.*; ~revier *n* police-station; police precinct; ~schutz *m*: *unter* ~ *under* police guard; ~streife *f* police patrol; police squad; ~stunde *f* (-/*no pl.*) closing-time; ~verordnung *f* police regulation(s *pl.*); ~wache *f* police-station.

Polizist [poli'tsist] *m* (-en/-en) policeman, constable, *sl.* bobby, cop; ~in *f* (-/-nen) policewoman.

polnisch *adj.* ['pɔlniʃ] Polish.

Polster ['pɔlstər] *n* (-s/-) pad; cushion; bolster; *s. Polsterung*; '~möbel *n/pl.* upholstered furniture; upholstery; '2n *v/t.* (ge-, *h*) upholster, stuff; pad, wad; '~sessel *m*, '~stuhl *m* upholstered chair; '~ung *f* (-/-en) padding, stuffing; upholstery.

poltern ['pɔltərn] *v/i.* (ge-, *h*) make a row; rumble; *p.* bluster.

Polytechnikum [poly'tɛçnikum] *n* (-s/Polytechnika, Polytechniken) polytechnic (school).

Pommes frites [pɔm'frit] *pl.* chips *pl.*, *Am.* French fried potatoes *pl.*

Pomp [pɔmp] *m* (-[e]s/*no pl.*) pomp, splendo(u)r; '2haft *adj.*, 2ös *adj.* [~'pø:s] pompous, splendid.

Pony ['pɔni] **1.** *zo. n* (-s/-s) pony; **2.** *m* (-s/-s) hairstyle: bang, fringe.

popul|är *adj.* [popu'lɛːr] popular; **⊋arität** [ˌari'tɛːt] *f* (-/*no pl.*) popularity.

Por|e ['poːrə] *f* (-/-n) pore; **⊋ös** *adj.* [po'røːs] porous; permeable.

Portemonnaie[pɔrtmɔ'nɛː]*n*(-s/-s) purse.

Portier [pɔr'tjeː] *m* (-s/-s) *s.* **Pförtner**.

Portion [pɔr'tsjoːn] *f* (-/-en) portion, share; ✕ ration; helping, serving; *zwei* ~*en Kaffee* coffee for two.

Porto ['pɔrto] *n* (-s/-s, *Porti*) postage; **⊋frei** *adj.* post-free; prepaid, *esp. Am.* postpaid; **⊋pflichtig** *adj.* subject to postage.

Porträt [pɔr'trɛː; ~t] *n* (-s/-s; -[e]s/-e) portrait, likeness; **⊋ieren** [ˌɛ'tiːrən] *v/t.* (*no* -ge-, *h*) portray.

Portugies|e [pɔrtu'giːzə] *m* (-n/-n) Portuguese; *die* ~*n pl.* the Portuguese *pl.*; **⊋isch** *adj.* Portuguese.

Porzellan [pɔrtsə'laːn] *n* (-s/-e) porcelain, china.

Posaune [po'zaunə] *f* (-/-n) ♩ trombone; *fig.* trumpet.

Pose ['poːzə] *f* (-/-n) pose, attitude; *fig. a.* air.

Position [pozi'tsjoːn] *f* (-/-en) position; social standing; ⚓ station.

positiv *adj.* ['poːzitiːf] positive.

Postur [poni'tuːr] *f* (-/-en) posture; *sich in* ~ *setzen* strike an attitude.

Posse *thea.* ['pɔsə] *f* (-/-n) farce.

'Possen *m* (-s/-) trick, prank; **'⊋haft** *adj.* farcical, comical; **'~reißer** *m* (-s/-) buffoon, clown.

possessiv *gr. adj.* ['pɔsesiːf] possessive.

pos'sierlich *adj.* droll, funny.

Post [pɔst] *f* (-/*no pl.*) post, *Am.* mail; mail, letters *pl.*; post office; *mit der ersten* ~ by the first delivery; **'~amt** *n* post office; **'~anschrift** *f* mailing address; **'~anweisung** *f* postal order; **'~beamte** *m* post-office clerk; **'~bote** *m* postman, *Am.* mailman; **'~dampfer** *m* packet-boat.

Posten ['pɔstən] *m* (-s/-) post, place, station; job; ✕ sentry, sentinel; item; entry; *goods*: lot, parcel.

'Postfach *n* post-office box.

pos'tieren *v/t.* (*no* -ge-, *h*) post, station, place; *sich* ~ station o.s.

'Post|karte *f* postcard, *with printed postage stamp: Am. a.* postal card; **'~kutsche** *f* stage-coach; **'⊋lagernd** *adj.* to be (kept until) called for, poste restante, *Am.* (in care of) general delivery; **'~leitzahl** *f* postcode; **'~minister** *m* minister of post; *Brt. and Am.* Postmaster General; **'~paket** *n* postal parcel; **'~schalter** *m* (post-office) window; **'~scheck** *m* postal cheque, *Am.* postal check; **'~schließfach** *n*

post-office box; **'~sparbuch** *n* post-office savings-book; **'~stempel** *m* postmark; **'⊋wendend** *adv.* by return of post; **'~wertzeichen** *n* (postage) stamp; **'~zug** 🚂 *m* mail-train.

Pracht [praxt] *f* (-/✎ -en, ✎e) splendo(u)r, magnificence; luxury.

prächtig *adj.* ['prɛçtiç] splendid, magnificent; gorgeous; grand.

'prachtvoll *adj. s.* **prächtig**.

Prädikat [predi'kaːt] *n* (-[e]s/-e) *gr.* predicate; *school, etc.*: mark.

prägen ['prɛːgən] *v/t.* (ge-, *h*) stamp; coin (*word, coin*).

prahlen ['praːlən] *v/i.* (ge-, *h*) brag, boast (*mit* of); ~ *mit* show off *s.th.*

'Prahler *m* (-s/-) boaster, braggart; **~ei** [ˌ'rai] *f* (-/-en) boasting, bragging; **'⊋isch** *adj.* boastful; ostentatious.

Prakti|kant [prakti'kant] *m* (-en/-en) probationer; **'~ker** *m* (-s/-) practical man; expert; **~kum** ['~kum] *n* (-s/*Praktika, Praktiken*) practical course; **'⊋sch** *adj.* practical; useful, handy; ~*er Arzt* general practitioner; **⊋zieren** ✎, ⚕ [ˌ'tsiːrən] *v/i.* (*no* -ge-, *h*) practi|se, *Am.* -ce medicine *or* the law. [prelate.⟩

Prälat *eccl.* [prɛ'laːt] *m* (-en/-en)⟩

Praline [pra'liːnə] *f* (-/-n): ~*n pl.* chocolates *pl.*

prall *adj.* [pral] tight; plump; *sun:* blazing; **'~en** *v/t.* (ge-, *sein*) bounce *or* bound (*auf acc., gegen* against).

Prämi|e ['prɛːmjə] *f* (-/-n) ✎ premium; prize; bonus; **⊋(i)eren** [prɛ'miːrən, prɛmi'iːrən] *v/t.* (*no* -ge-, *h*) award a prize to.

prang|en ['praŋən] *v/i.* (ge-, *h*) shine, make a show; **⊋er** *m* (-s/-) pillory.

Pranke ['praŋkə] *f* (-/-n) paw.

pränumerando *adv.* [prɛːnumə'rando] beforehand, in advance.

Präpa|rat [prɛpa'raːt] *n* (-[e]s/-e) preparation; *microscopy:* slide; **⊋rieren** *v/t.* (*no* -ge-, *h*) prepare.

Präposition *gr.* [prɛpozi'tsjoːn] *f* (-/-en) preposition.

Prärie [prɛ'riː] *f* (-/-n) prairie.

Präsens *gr.* ['prɛːzɛns] *n* (-/*Präsentia, Präsenzien*) present (tense).

Präsi|dent [prɛzi'dɛnt] *m* (-en/-en) president; chairman; **⊋dieren** *v/i.* (*no* -ge-, *h*) preside (*über acc.* over); be in the chair; **~dium** [ˌ'ziːdjum] *n* (-s/*Präsidien*) presidency, chair.

prasseln ['prasəln] *v/i.* (ge-, *h*) *fire:* crackle; *rain:* patter.

prassen ['prasən] *v/i.* (ge-, *h*) feast, carouse.

Präteritum *gr.* [prɛ'teːritum] *n* (-s/*Präterita*) preterite (tense); past tense.

Praxis ['praksis] *f* **1.** (-/*no pl.*) practice; **2.** (-/*Praxen*) practice (*of doctor or lawyer*).

Präzedenzfall [prætse'dɛnts-] *m* precedent; ⅟₂ *a.* case-law.

präzis *adj.* [prɛ'tsi:s], ⁓e *adj.* [⁓zə] precise.

predig|en ['prɛ:digən] *v/i. and v/t.* (ge-, h) preach; '⁓er *m* (-s/-) preacher; clergyman; ⁓t ['⁓diçt] *f* (-/-en) sermon (*a. fig.*); *fig.* lecture.

Preis [prats] *m* (-es/-e) price; cost; *competition*: prize; award; reward; praise; *um jeden* ⁓ at any price *or* cost; '⁓ausschreiben *n* (-s/-) competition.

preisen ['praizən] *v/t.* (*irr.*, ge-, h) praise.

'Preis|erhöhung *f* rise *or* increase in price(s); '⁓gabe *f* abandonment; revelation (*of secret*); '⁓geben *v/t.* (*irr. geben, sep.*, -ge-, h) abandon; reveal, give away (*secret*); disclose; expose; '⁓gekrönt *adj.* prize-winning, prize (*novel, etc.*); '⁓gericht *n* jury; '⁓lage *f* range of prices; '⁓liste *f* price-list; '⁓nachlaß *m* price cut; discount; '⁓richter *m* judge, umpire; '⁓schießen *n* (-s/-) shooting competition; '⁓stopp *m* (-s/no pl.) price freeze; '⁓träger *m* prize-winner; '⁓wert *adj.*: ⁓ sein be a bargain.

prell|en ['prɛlən] *v/t.* (ge-, h) *fig.* cheat, defraud (*um of*); sich et. ⁓ 🐾 contuse *or* bruise s.th.; '⁓ung 🐾 *f* (-/-en) contusion.

Premier|e *thea.* [prəm'jɛːrə] *f* (-/-n) première, first night; ⁓minister [⁓'je:-] *m* prime minister.

Presse ['prɛsə] *f* 1. (-/-n) ⊕, *typ.* press; squeezer; 2. (-/no pl.) *newspapers generally: the* press; '⁓amt *n* public relations office; '⁓freiheit *f* freedom of the press; '⁓meldung *f* news item; '⁓n *v/t.* (ge-, h) press; squeeze; '⁓photograph *m* press-photographer; '⁓vertreter *m* reporter; public relations officer.

Preßluft ['prɛs-] *f* (-/no pl.) compressed air.

Prestige [prɛs'tiːʒə] *n* (-s/no pl.) prestige; ⁓ verlieren *a.* lose face.

Preuß|e ['prɔysə] *m* (-n/-n) Prussian; '⁓isch *adj.* Prussian.

prickeln ['prikəln] *v/i.* (ge-, h) prick(le), tickle; itch; *fingers*: tingle.

Priem [priːm] *m* (-[e]s/-e) quid.

pries [priːs] *pret. of* preisen.

Priester ['priːstər] *m* (-s/-) priest; '⁓in *f* (-/-nen) priestess; '⁓lich *adj.* priestly; sacerdotal; '⁓rock *m* cassock.

prim|a F *adj.* ['priːma] first-rate, F A 1; ✝ *a.* prime, F swell; ⁓är *adj.* [priːmɛ:r] primary.

Primel ♃ ['priːməl] *f* (-/-n) primrose.

Prinz [prints] *m* (-en/-en) prince; ⁓essin [⁓'tsɛsin] *f* (-/-nen) princess; '⁓gemahl *m* prince consort.

Prinzip [prin'tsiːp] *n* (-s/-ien)

principle; *aus* ⁓ on principle; *im* ⁓ in principle, basically.

Priorität [priori'tɛːt] *f* 1. (-/-en) priority; 2. (-/no pl.) *time*: priority.

Prise ['priːzə] *f* (-/-n) ⚓ prize; e-e ⁓ a pinch of (*salt, snuff*).

Prisma ['prisma] *n* (-s/Prismen) prism.

Pritsche ['pritʃə] *f* (-/-n) bat; plank-bed.

privat *adj.* [pri'vɑːt] private; ⁓adresse *f* home address; ⁓mann *m* (-[e]s/Privatmänner, Privatleute) private person *or* gentleman; ⁓patient 🐾 *m* paying patient; ⁓person *f* private person; ⁓schule *f* private school.

Privileg [privi'leːk] *n* (-[e]s/-ien, -e) privilege.

pro *prp.* [proː] per; ⁓ *Jahr* per annum; ⁓ *Kopf* per head; ⁓ *Stück* a piece.

Probe ['proːbə] *f* (-/-n) experiment; trial, test; *metall.* assay; sample; specimen; proof; probation; check; *thea.* rehearsal; audition; *auf* ⁓ on probation, on trial; *auf die* ⁓ *stellen* (put to the) test; '⁓abzug *typ.*, *phot. m* proof; '⁓exemplar *n* specimen copy; '⁓fahrt *f* ⚓ trial trip; *mot.* trial run; '⁓flug *m* test *or* trial flight; '⁓n *v/t.* (ge-, h) exercise; *thea.* rehearse; '⁓nummer *f* specimen copy *or* number; '⁓seite *typ. f* specimen page; '⁓sendung *f* goods on approval; '⁓weise *adv.* on trial; *p. a.* on probation; '⁓zeit *f* time of probation.

probieren [pro'biːrən] *v/t.* (no -ge-, h) try, test; taste (*food.*)

Problem [pro'bleːm] *n* (-s/-e) problem; ⁓atisch *adj.* [⁓e'mɑːtiʃ] problematic(al).

Produkt [pro'dukt] *n* (-[e]s/-e) product (*a.* ℞); ✍ produce; result; ⁓ion [⁓'tsjoːn] *f* (-/-en) production; output; ⁓iv *adj.* [⁓'tiːf] productive.

Produz|ent [produ'tsɛnt] *m* (-en/-en) producer; ⁓ieren [⁓'tsiːrən] *v/t.* (no -ge-, h) produce; sich ⁓ perform; *contp.* show off.

professionell *adj.* [profesio'nɛl] professional, by trade.

Profess|or [pro'fɛsor] *m* (-s/-en) professor; ⁓ur [⁓'suːr] *f* (-/-en) professorship, chair.

Profi ['proːfi] *m* (-s/-s) *sports*: professional, F pro. [*on tyre*: tread.\]

Profil [pro'fiːl] *n* (-s/-e) profile;\]

Profit [pro'fiːt] *m* (-[e]s/-e) profit; ⁓ieren [⁓i'tiːrən] *v/i.* (no -ge-, h) profit (*von* by).

Prognose [pro'gnoːzə] *f* (-/-n) 🐾 prognosis; *meteor.* forecast.

Programm [pro'gram] *n* (-s/-e) program(me); *politisches* ⁓ political program(me), *Am.* platform.

Projektion [projɛk'tsjoːn] *f* (-/-en) projection; ⁓sapparat [projɛk'tsjoːns?-] *m* projector.

proklamieren [prokla'mi:rən] *v/t.* (*no* -ge-, *h*) proclaim.

Prokur|a ✝ [pro'ku:ra] *f* (-/*Prokuren*) procuration; ‿**ist** [‿ku'rist] *m* (-*en*/-*en*) confidential clerk.

Proletari|er [prole'ta:rjər] *m* (-*s*/-) proletarian; 2**sch** *adj.* proletarian.

Prolog [pro'lo:k] *m* (-[*e*]*s*/-*e*) prolog(ue).

prominen|t *adj.* [promi'nɛnt] prominent; 2**z** [‿ts] *f* (-/*no pl.*) notables *pl.*, celebrities *pl.*; high society.

Promo|tion *univ.* [promo'tsjo:n] *f* (-/-*en*) graduation; 2**vieren** [‿'vi:rən] *v/i.* (*no* -ge-, *h*) graduate (*an dat.* from), take one's degree.

Pronomen *gr.* [pro'no:mɛn] *n* (-*s*/-, *Pronomina*) pronoun.

Propeller [pro'pɛlər] *m* (-*s*/-) ⚓, ✈ (screw-)propeller, screw; ✈ airscrew.

Prophe|t [pro'fe:t] *m* (-*en*/-*en*) prophet; 2**tisch** *adj.* prophetic; 2**zeien** [‿e'tsaiən] *v/t.* (*no* -ge-, *h*) prophesy; predict, foretell; ‿**zeiung** *f* (-/-*en*) prophecy; prediction.

Proportion [proporʹtsjo:n] *f* (-/-*en*) proportion.

Prosa ['pro:za] *f* (-/*no pl.*) prose.

prosit *int.* ['pro:zit] your health!, here's to you!, cheers!

Prospekt [pro'spɛkt] *m* (-[*e*]*s*/-*e*) prospectus; brochure, leaflet, folder.

prost *int.* [pro:st] *s.* **prosit**.

Prostituierte [prostitu'i:rtə] *f* (-*n*/-*n*) prostitute.

Protest [pro'tɛst] *m* (-*es*/-*e*) protest; ‿ *einlegen* or *erheben gegen* (enter a) protest against.

Protestant *eccl.* [protɛs'tant] *m* (-*en*/-*en*) Protestant; 2**isch** *adj.* Protestant.

protes'tieren *v/i.* (*no* -ge-, *h*): *gegen et.* ‿ protest against s.th., object to s.th.

Prothese ✠ [pro'te:zə] *f* (-/-*n*) pro(s)thesis; *dentistry:* a. denture; artificial limb.

Protokoll [proto'kɔl] *n* (-*s*/-*e*) record, minutes *pl.* (*of meeting*); *diplomacy:* protocol; *das* ‿ *aufnehmen* take down the minutes; *das* ‿ *führen* keep the minutes; *zu* ‿ *geben* ⚖ depose, state in evidence; *zu* ‿ *nehmen* take down, record; 2**ieren** [‿'li:rən] (*no* -ge-, *h*) **1.** *v/t.* record, take down (on record); **2.** *v/i.* keep the minutes.

Protz *contp.* [prɔts] *m* (-*en*, -*es*/-*e*[*n*]) braggart, F show-off; 2**en** *v/i.* (ge-, *h*) show off (*mit dat.* with); 2**ig** *adj.* ostentatious, showy.

Proviant [pro'vjant] *m* (-*s*/⚓-*e*) provisions *pl.*, victuals *pl.*

Provinz [pro'vints] *f* (-/-*en*) province; *fig. the* provinces *pl.*; 2**ial** *adj.* [‿'tsja:l], 2**iell** *adj.* [‿'tsjɛl] provincial.

Provis|ion ✝ [provi'zjo:n] *f* (-/-*en*) commission; 2**orisch** *adj.* [‿'zo:riʃ] provisional, temporary.

provozieren [provo'tsi:rən] *v/t.* (*no* -ge-, *h*) provoke.

Prozent [pro'tsɛnt] *n* (-[*e*]*s*/-*e*) per cent; ‿**satz** *m* percentage; proportion; 2**ual** [‿u'a:l] percental; ‿**er Anteil** percentage.

Prozeß [pro'tsɛs] *m* (*Prozesses*/*Prozesse*) process; ⚖: action, lawsuit; trial; (legal) proceedings *pl.*; *e-n* ‿ *gewinnen* win one's case; *e-n* ‿ *gegen j-n anstrengen* bring an action against s.o., sue s.o.; *j-m den* ‿ *machen* try s.o., put s.o. on trial; *kurzen* ‿ *machen mit* make short work of.

prozessieren [protse'si:rən] *v/i.* (*no* -ge-, *h*): *mit j-m* ‿ go to law against s.o., have the law of s.o.

Prozession [protse'sjo:n] *f* (-/-*en*) procession.

prüde *adj.* ['pry:də] prudish.

prüf|en ['pry:fən] *v/t.* (ge-, *h*) examine; try, test; quiz; check, verify; ‿**end** *adj. look:* searching, scrutinizing; 2**er** *m* (-*s*/-) examiner; 2**ling** *m* (-*s*/-*e*) examinee; 2**stein** *fig. m* touchstone; 2**ung** *f* (-/-*en*) examination; *school, etc.:* a. F exam; test; quiz; verification, checking, check-up; *e-e* ‿ *machen* go in for *or* sit for *or* take an examination.

'Prüfungs|arbeit *f*, ‿**aufgabe** *f* examination-paper; ‿**ausschuß** *m*, ‿**kommission** *f* board of examiners.

Prügel ['pry:gəl] **1.** *m* (-*s*/-) cudgel, club, stick; **2.** F *fig. pl.* beating, thrashing; ‿**ei** F [‿'lai] *f* (-/-*en*) fight, row; ‿**knabe** *m* scapegoat; 2**n** F *v/t.* (ge-, *h*) cudgel, flog; beat (up), thrash; *sich* ‿ (have a) fight.

Prunk [pruŋk] *m* (-[*e*]*s*/*no pl.*) splendo(u)r; pomp, show; 2**en** *v/i.* (ge-, *h*) make a show (*mit* of), show off (*mit et.* s.th.); 2**voll** *adj.* splendid, gorgeous.

Psalm *eccl.* [psalm] *m* (-*s*/-*en*) psalm.

Pseudonym [psɔ͟ydo'ny:m] *n* (-*s*/-*e*) pseudonym.

pst *int.* [pst] hush!

Psychi|ater [psyçi'a:tər] *m* (-*s*/-) psychiatrist, alienist; 2**sch** *adj.* ['psy:çiʃ] psychic(al).

Psycho|analyse [psyço˴ana'ly:zə] *f* (-/*no pl.*) psychoanalysis; ‿**analytiker** [‿tikər] *m* (-*s*/-) psychoanalist; ‿**loge** [‿'lo:gə] *m* (-*n*/-*n*) psychologist; ‿**se** [‿'ço:zə] *f* (-/-*n*) psychosis; panic.

Pubertät [puber'tɛ:t] *f* (-/*no pl.*) puberty.

Publikum ['pu:blikum] *n* (-*s*/*no pl.*) *the* public; audience; spectators *pl.*, crowd; readers *pl.*

publiz|ieren [publi'tsi:rən] *v/t.* (*no*

-ge-, h) publish; ℒist m (-en/-en) publicist; journalist.

Pudding ['pudiŋ] m (-s/-e, -s) cream.

Pudel zo. ['puːdəl] m (-s/-) poodle; 'ℒnaß F adj. dripping wet, drenched.

Puder ['puːdər] m (-s/-) powder; '~dose f powder-box; compact; 'ℒn v/t. (ge-, h) powder; sich ~ powder o.s. or one's face; '~quaste f powder-puff; '~zucker m powdered sugar.

Puff F [puf] m (-[e]s/~e, -e) poke, nudge; 'ℒen (ge-, h) **1.** F v/t. nudge; **2.** v/i. pop; '~er m (-s/-) buffer.

Pullover [pu'loːvər] m (-s/-) pullover, sweater.

Puls ℳ [puls] m (-es/-e) pulse; '~ader anat. f artery; ℒieren [~'ziːrən] v/i. (no -ge-, h) pulsate, throb; '~schlag ℳ m pulsation.

Pult [pult] n (-[e]s/-e) desk.

Pulv|er ['pulfər] n (-s/-) powder; gunpowder; F fig. cash, sl. brass, dough; 'ℒerig adj. powdery; ℒerisieren [~vəri'ziːrən] v/t. (no -ge-, h) pulverize; ℒrig adj. ['~friç] powdery.

Pump F [pump] m (-[e]s/-e): auf ~ on tick; '~e f (-/-n) pump; 'ℒen (ge-, h) **1.** v/i. pump; **2.** v/t. pump; F fig.: give s.th. on tick; borrow (et. von j-m s.th. from s.o.).

Punkt [puŋkt] m (-[e]s/-e) point (a. fig.); dot; typ., gr. full stop, period; spot, place; fig. item; article, clause (of agreement); der springende ~ the point; toter ~ deadlock, dead end; wunder ~ tender subject, sore point; ~ zehn Uhr on the stroke of ten, at 10 (o'clock) sharp; in vielen ~en on many points, in many respects; nach ~en siegen sports: win on points; ℒieren [~'tiːrən] v/t. (no -ge-, h) dot, point; ℳ puncture, tap; drawing, painting: stipple.

pünktlich adj. ['pyŋktliç] punctual; ~ sein be on time; 'ℒkeit f (-/no pl.) punctuality.

Punsch [punʃ] m (-es/-e) punch.

Pupille anat. [pu'pilə] f (-/-n) pupil.

Puppe ['pupə] f (-/-n) doll (a. fig.); puppet (a. fig.); tailoring: dummy; zo. chrysalis, pupa; '~nspiel n puppet-show; '~nstube f doll's room; '~nwagen m doll's pram, Am. doll carriage or buggy.

pur adj. [puːr] pure, sheer.

Püree [py're:] n (-s/-s) purée, mash.

Purpur ['purpur] m (-s/no pl.) purple; 'ℒfarben adj., 'ℒn adj., 'ℒrot adj. purple.

Purzel|baum ['purtsəl-] m somersault; e-n ~ schlagen turn a somersault; 'ℒn v/i. (ge-, sein) tumble.

Puste F ['puːstə] f (-/no pl.) breath; ihm ging die ~ aus he got out of breath.

Pustel ℳ ['pustəl] f (-/-n) pustule, pimple.

pusten ['puːstən] v/i. (ge-, h) puff, pant; blow.

Pute orn. ['puːtə] f (-/-n) turkey (-hen); '~r orn. m (-s/-) turkey (-cock); 'ℒr'rot adj. (as) red as a turkey-cock.

Putsch [putʃ] m (-es/-e) putsch, insurrection; riot; 'ℒen v/i. (ge-, h) revolt, riot.

Putz [puts] m (-es/-e) on garments: finery; ornaments pl.; trimming; △ roughcast, plaster; 'ℒen v/t. (ge-, h) clean, cleanse; polish, wipe; adorn; snuff (candle); polish, Am. shine (shoes); sich ~ smarten or dress o.s. up; sich die Nase ~ blow or wipe one's nose; sich die Zähne ~ brush one's teeth; '~frau f charwoman, Am. a. scrubwoman; 'ℒig adj. droll, funny; '~lappen m cleaning rag; '~zeug n cleaning utensils pl.

Pyjama [pi'dʒaːma] m (-s/-s) (ein a suit of) pyjamas pl. or Am. a. pajamas pl.

Pyramide [pyra'miːdə] f (-/-n) pyramid (a. ⚭); ✕ stack (of rifles); ℒnförmig adj. [~nfœrmiç] pyramidal.

Q

Quacksalber ['kvakzalbər] m (-s/-) quack (doctor); ~ei F [~'raɪ] f (-/-en) quackery; 'ℒn v/i. (ge-, h) (play the) quack.

Quadrat [kva'draːt] n (-[e]s/-e) square; 2 Fuß im ~ 2 feet square; ins ~ erheben square; ℒisch adj. square; ⚭ equation: quadratic; ~meile f square mile; ~meter n, m square metre, Am. -er; ~wurzel Ⱥ f square root; ~zahl Ⱥ f square number.

quaken ['kvaːkən] v/i. (ge-, h) duck: quack; frog: croak.

quäken ['kvɛːkən] v/i. (ge-, h) squeak.

Quäker ['kvɛːkər] m (-s/-) Quaker, member of the Society of Friends.

Qual [kvaːl] f (-/-en) pain; torment; agony.

quälen ['kvɛːlən] v/t. (ge-, h) torment (a. fig.); torture; agonize; fig. bother, pester; sich ~ toil, drudge.

Qualifikation [kvalifika'tsjo:n] *f* (-/-en) qualification.

qualifizieren [kvalifi'tsi:rən] *v/t. and v/refl.* (*no* -ge-, *h*) qualify (*zu* for).

Qualit|ät [kvali'tɛ:t] *f* (-/-en) quality; **~ativ** [~a'ti:f] **1.** *adj.* qualitative; **2.** *adv.* as to quality.

Quali'täts|arbeit *f* work of high quality; **~stahl** *m* high-grade steel; **~ware** *f* high-grade *or* quality goods *pl.*

Qualm [kvalm] *m* (-[e]s/*no pl.*) dense smoke; fumes *pl.*; vapo(u)r, steam; '**~en** (ge-, *h*) **1.** *v/i.* smoke, give out vapo(u)r *or* fumes; F *p.* smoke heavily; **2.** F *v/t.* puff (away) at (*cigar, pipe, etc.*); '**~ig** *adj.* smoky.

'**qualvoll** *adj.* very painful; *pain:* excruciating; *fig.* agonizing, harrowing.

Quantit|ät [kvanti'tɛ:t] *f* (-/-en) quantity; **~ativ** [~a'ti:f] **1.** *adj.* quantitative; **2.** *adv.* as to quantity.

Quantum ['kvantum] *n* (-s/*Quanten*) quantity, amount; quantum (*a. phys.*).

Quarantäne [karan'tɛ:nə] *f* (-/-n) quarantine; *in* ~ *legen* (put in) quarantine; [curd(s *pl.*).\

Quark [kvark] *m* (-[e]s/*no pl.*)|

Quartal [kvar'ta:l] *n* -s/-e) quarter (*of a year*); *univ.* term,

Quartett [kvar'tɛt] *n* (-[e]s/-e) ♪ quartet(te); *cards:* four.

Quartier [kvar'ti:r] *n* (-s/-e) accommodation; ✕ quarters *pl.*, billet.

Quaste ['kvastə] *f* (-/-n) tassel; (powder-)puff.

Quatsch F [kvatʃ] *m* (-es/*no pl.*) nonsense, fudge, *sl.* bosh, rot, *Am. sl. a.* baloney; '**~en** F *v/i.* (ge-, *h*) twaddle, blether, *sl.* talk rot; (have a) chat; '**~kopf** F *m* twaddler.

Quecksilber ['kvɛk-] *n* mercury, quicksilver.

Quelle ['kvɛlə] *f* (-/-n) spring, source (*a. fig.*); *oil:* well; *fig.* fountain, origin; '**~n** *v/i.* (*irr.*, ge-, *sein*) gush, well; **~nangabe** ['kvɛlən'-] *f*

mention of sources used; '**~n-forschung** *f* original research.

Quengel|ei F [kvɛŋə'laɪ] *f* (-/-en) grumbling, whining; nagging; '**~n** F *v/i.* (ge-, *h*) grumble, whine; nag.

quer *adv.* [kve:r] crossways, crosswise; F *fig.* wrong; F ~ *gehen* go wrong; ~ *über* (*acc.*) across.

'**Quer|e** *f* (-/*no pl.*): *der* ~ *nach* crossways, crosswise; F *j-m in die* ~ *kommen* cross s.o.'s path; *fig.* thwart s.o.'s plans; '**~frage** *f* cross-question; '**~kopf** *fig. m* wrong-headed fellow; **~schießen** F *v/i.* (*irr. schießen, sep.,* -ge-, *h*) try to foil s.o.'s plans; '**~schiff** ⌂ *n* transept; '**~schläger** ✕ *m* ricochet; '**~schnitt** *m* cross-section (*a. fig.*); '**~straße** *f* cross-road; *zweite* ~ *rechts* second turning to the right; '**~treiber** *m* (-s/-) schemer; **~treibe'rei** *f* (-/-en) intriguing, machination.

Querulant [kveru'lant] *m* (-en/-en) querulous person, grumbler, *Am. sl. a.* griper.

quetsch|en ['kvɛtʃən] *v/t.* (ge-, *h*) squeeze; *joint:* bruise, contuse; *sich den Finger* ~ jam one's finger; '**~ung** ✎ *f* (-/-en), '**~wunde** ✎ *f* bruise, contusion.

quick *adj.* [kvik] lively, brisk.

quieken ['kvi:kən] *v/i.* (ge-, *h*) squeak, squeal.

quietsch|en ['kvi:tʃən] *v/i.* (ge-, *h*) squeak, squeal; *door-hinge, etc.:* creak, squeak; *brakes, etc.:* screech; '**~ver'gnügt** F *adj.* (as) jolly as a sandboy.

Quirl [kvirl] *m* (-[e]s/-e) twirling-stick; '**~en** *v/t.* (ge-, *h*) twirl.

quitt *adj.* [kvit]: ~ *sein mit j-m* be quits *or* even with s.o.; *jetzt sind wir* ~ that leaves us even; **~ieren** [~'ti:rən] *v/t.* (*no* -ge-, *h*) receipt (*bill, etc.*); quit, abandon (*post, etc.*); '**~ung** *f* (-/-en) receipt; *fig.* answer; *gegen* ~ against receipt.

quoll [kvɔl] *pret. of quellen.*

Quot|e ['kvo:tə] *f* (-/-en) quota, share, portion; **~ient** ₳ [kvo'tsjɛnt] *m* (-en/-en) quotient.

R

Rabatt ✝ [ra'bat] *m* (-[e]s/-e) discount, rebate.

Rabe *orn.* ['ra:bə] *m* (-n/-n) raven; '**~n'schwarz** F *adj.* raven, jet-black.

rabiat *adj.* [ra'bja:t] rabid, violent.

Rache ['raxə] *f* (-/*no pl.*) revenge, vengeance; retaliation.

Rachen *anat.* ['raxən] *m* (-s/-) throat, pharynx; jaws *pl.*

rächen ['rɛçən] *v/t.* (ge-, *h*) avenge,

revenge; *sich* ~ *an* (*dat.*) revenge o.s. *or* be revenged on.

'**Rachen|höhle** *anat. f* pharynx; '**~katarrh** ✎ *m* cold in the throat.

'**rach|gierig** *adj.*, '**~süchtig** *adj.* revengeful, vindictive.

Rad [ra:t] *n* (-[e]s/*=er*) wheel; (bi)cycle, F bike; (*ein*) ~ *schlagen peacock:* spread its tail; *sports:* turn cart-wheels; *unter die Räder* *kommen* go to the dogs; '**~achse** *f* axle(-tree).

Radar ['raːdaːr, ra'daːr] *m, n* (-s/-s) radar.

Radau F [ra'dau] *m* (-s/*no pl.*) row, racket, hubbub.

radebrechen ['raːdə-] *v/t.* (ge-, h) speak (*language*) badly, murder (*language*).

radeln ['raːdəln] *v/i.* (ge-, sein) cycle, pedal, F bike.

Rädelsführer ['rɛːdəls-] *m* ringleader.

Räderwerk ⊕ ['rɛːdər-] *n* gearing.

'**rad|fahren** *v/i.* (irr. fahren, sep., -ge-, sein) cycle, (ride a) bicycle, pedal, F bike; '**²fahrer** *m* cyclist, Am. a. cycler or wheelman.

radier|en [ra'diːrən] *v/t.* (no -ge-, h) rub out, erase; *art:* etch; **²gummi** *m* (india-)rubber, *esp. Am.* eraser; **²messer** *n* eraser; **²ung** *f* (-/-en) etching.

Radieschen ♀ [ra'diːsçən] *n* (-s/-) (red) radish.

radikal *adj.* [radi'kaːl] radical.

Radio ['raːdjo] *n* (-s/-s) radio, wireless; *im* ~ on the radio, on the air; **²aktiv** *phys. adj.* [radjoak'tiːf] radio(-)active; ~*er Niederschlag* fall-out; '**~apparat** *m* radio or wireless (set).

Radium ⚛ ['raːdjum] *n* (-s/*no pl.*) radium.

Radius ⚕ ['raːdjus] *m* (-/*Radien*) radius.

'**Rad|kappe** *f* hub cap; '**~kranz** *m* rim; '**~rennbahn** *f* cycling track; '**~rennen** *n* cycle race; '**~sport** *m* cycling; '**~spur** *f* rut, track.

raffen ['rafən] *v/t.* (ge-, h) snatch up; gather (*dress*).

raffiniert *adj.* [rafi'niːrt] refined; *fig.* clever, cunning.

ragen ['raːgən] *v/i.* (ge-, h) tower, loom.

Ragout [ra'guː] *n* (-s/-s) ragout, stew, hash.

Rahe ⚓ ['raːə] *f* (-/-n) yard.

Rahm [raːm] *m* (-[e]s/*no pl.*) cream.

Rahmen ['raːmən] 1. *m* (-s/-) frame; *fig.*: frame, background, setting; scope; *aus dem* ~ *fallen* be out of place; 2. ♀ *v/t.* (ge-, h) frame.

Rakete [ra'keːtə] *f* (-/-n) rocket; *e-e* ~ *abfeuern or starten* launch a rocket; *dreistufige* ~ three-stage rocket; **~nantrieb** [ra'keːtən⁹-] *m* rocket propulsion; **~nflugzeug** *n* rocket(-propelled) plane; **~ntriebwerk** *n* propulsion unit.

Ramm|bär ⊕ ['ram-] *m*, '**~bock** *m*, '**~e** *f* (-/-n) ram(mer); '**²en** *v/t.* (ge-, h) ram.

Rampe ['rampə] *f* (-/-n) ramp, ascent; '**~nlicht** *n* footlights *pl.*; *fig.* limelight.

Ramsch [ramʃ] *m* (-es/♦ -e) junk,

trash; *im* ~ *kaufen* buy in the lump; '**~verkauf** *m* jumble-sale; '**~ware** *f* job lot.

Rand [rant] *m* (-[e]s/²er) edge, brink (a. fig.); *fig.* verge; border; brim (of hat, cup, etc.); rim (of plate, etc.), margin (of book, etc.); lip (of wound); *Ränder pl.* under the eyes: rings *pl.*, circles *pl.*; *vor Freude außer* ~ *und Band geraten* be beside o.s. with joy; *er kommt damit nicht zu* ~*e* he can't manage it; '**~bemerkung** *f* marginal note; *fig.* comment.

rang[1] [raŋ] *pret. of ringen.*

Rang[2] [~] *m* (-[e]s/²e) rank, order; ✗ rank; position; *thea.* tier; *erster* ~ *thea.* dress-circle, *Am.* first balcony; *zweiter* ~ *thea.* upper circle, *Am.* second balcony; *ersten* ~*es* first-class, first-rate; *j-m den* ~ *ablaufen* get the start or better of s.o.

Range ['raŋə] *m* (-n/-n), *f* (-/-n) rascal; romp.

rangieren [rã'ʒiːrən] (no -ge-, h) 1. ⚙ *v/t.* shunt, *Am. a.* switch; 2. *fig. v/i.* rank.

'**Rang|liste** *f sports, etc.:* ranking list; ✗ army-list, navy or air-force list; '**~ordnung** *f* order of precedence.

Ranke ♀ ['raŋkə] *f* (-/-n) tendril; runner.

Ränke ['rɛŋkə] *m/pl.* intrigues *pl.*

'**ranken** *v/refl.* (ge-, h) creep, climb.

rann [ran] *pret. of rinnen.*

rannte ['rantə] *pret. of rennen.*

Ranzen ['rantsən] *m* (-s/-) knapsack; satchel.

ranzig *adj.* ['rantsiç] rancid, rank.

Rappe *zo.* ['rapə] *m* (-n/-n) black horse.

rar *adj.* [raːr] rare, scarce.

Rarität [rari'tɛːt] *f* (-/-en) rarity; curiosity, curio.

rasch *adj.* [raʃ] quick, swift, brisk; hasty; prompt.

rascheln ['raʃəln] *v/i.* (ge-, h) rustle.

rasen[1] ['raːzən] *v/i.* (ge-) 1. (h) rage, storm, rave; 2. (sein) race, speed; '**~d** *adj.* raving; frenzied; *speed:* tearing; *pains:* agonizing; *headache:* splitting; *j-n* ~ *machen* drive s.o. mad.

Rasen[2] [~] *m* (-s/-) grass; lawn; turf; '**~platz** *m* lawn, grass-plot.

Raserei F [raːzə'rai] *f* (-/-en) rage, fury; frenzy, madness; F *mot.* scorching; *j-n zur* ~ *bringen* drive s.o. mad.

Rasier|apparat [ra'ziːr-] *m* (safety) razor; **²en** *v/t.* (no -ge-, h) shave; *sich* ~ (*lassen* get a) shave; **~klinge** *f* razor-blade; **~messer** *n* razor; **~pinsel** *m* shaving-brush; **~seife** *f* shaving-soap; **~wasser** *n* after-shave lotion; **~zeug** *n* shaving kit.

Rasse ['rasə] *f* (-/-n) race; *zo.* breed.

rasseln ['rasəln] *v/i.* (ge-, h) rattle.

*14**

'Rassen|frage *f* (*-/no pl.*) racial issue; **'~kampf** *m* race conflict; **'~problem** *n* racial issue; **'~schranke** *f* colo(u)r bar; **'~trennung** *f* (*-/no pl.*) racial segregation; **'~unruhen** *f/pl.* race riots *pl.*

'rasserein *adj.* thoroughbred, pure-bred.

'rassig *adj.* thoroughbred; *fig.* racy.

Rast [rast] *f* (-/-en) rest, repose; break, pause; **'2en** *v/i.* (ge-, h) rest, repose; **'2los** *adj.* restless; **'~platz** *m* resting-place; *mot.* picnic area.

Rat [ra:t] *m* **1.** (-[e]s/*no pl.*) advice, counsel; suggestion; *fig.* way out; *zu ~e ziehen* consult; *j-n um ~ fragen* ask s.o.'s advice; **2.** (-[e]s/"e) council, board; council(l)or, alderman.

Rate ['ra:tə] *f* (-/-n) instal(l)ment (*a.* ⚕); *auf ~n* ⚕ on hire-purchase.

'raten (*irr.*, ge-, h) **1.** *v/i.* advise, counsel (*j-m zu inf.* s.o. to *inf.*); **2.** *v/t.* guess, divine.

'raten|weise *adv.* by instal(l)ments; **'2zahlung** ⚕ *f* payment by instal(l)ments.

'Rat|geber *m* (-s/-) adviser, counsel(l)or; **'~haus** *n* town hall, *Am. a.* city hall.

ratifizieren [ratifi'tsi:rən] *v/t.* (*no* -ge-, h) ratify.

Ration [ra'tsjo:n] *f* (-/-en) ration, allowance; **2ell** *adj.* [~o'nɛl] rational; efficient; economical; **2ieren** [~o'ni:rən] *v/t.* (*no* -ge-, h) ration.

'rat|los *adj.* puzzled, perplexed, at a loss; **'~sam** *adj.* advisable; expedient; **'2schlag** *m* (piece of) advice, counsel.

Rätsel ['rɛ:tsəl] *n* (-s/-) riddle, puzzle; enigma, mystery; **'2haft** *adj.* puzzling; enigmatic(al), mysterious.

Ratte *zo.* ['ratə] *f* (-/-n) rat.

rattern ['ratərn] *v/i.* (ge-, h, *sein*) rattle, clatter.

Raub [raʊp] *m* (-[e]s/*no pl.*) robbery; kidnap(p)ing; piracy (*of intellectual property*); booty, spoils *pl.*; **'~bau** *m* (-[e]s/*no pl.*): *~ treiben* ⚘ exhaust the land; ⚒ rob a mine; *~ treiben mit* undermine (*one's health*); **2en** ['~bən] *v/t.* (ge-, h) rob, take by force, steal; kidnap; *j-m et. ~* rob *or* deprive s.o. of s.th.

Räuber ['rɔʏbər] *m* (-s/-) robber; **'~bande** *f* gang of robbers; **'2isch** *adj.* rapacious, predatory.

'Raub|fisch *ichth. m* fish of prey; **'~gier** *f* rapacity; **'2gierig** *adj.* rapacious; **'~mord** *m* murder with robbery; **'~mörder** *m* murderer and robber; **'~tier** *zo. n* beast of prey; **'~überfall** *m* hold-up, armed robbery; **'~vogel** *orn. m* bird of prey; **'~zug** *m* raid.

Rauch [raʊx] *m* (-[e]s/*no pl.*) smoke; fume; **'2en** (ge-, h) **1.** *v/i.* smoke; fume; *p.* (have a) smoke; **2.** *v/t.* smoke (*cigarette*); **'~er** *m* (-s/-) smoker; *s. Raucherabteil.*

Räucheraal ['rɔʏçər?-] *m* smoked eel.

Raucherabteil 🚃 ['raʊxər?-] *n* smoking-car(riage), smoking-compartment, smoker.

'Räucher|hering *m* red *or* smoked herring, kipper; **'2n** (ge-, h) **1.** *v/t.* smoke, cure (*meat, fish*); **2.** *v/i.* burn incense.

'Rauch|fahne *f* trail of smoke; **'~fang** *m* chimney, flue; **'~fleisch** *n* smoked meat; **'2ig** *adj.* smoky; **'~tabak** *m* tobacco; **'~waren** *f/pl.* tobacco products *pl.*; furs *pl.*; **'~zimmer** *n* smoking-room.

Räud|e ['rɔʏdə] *f* (-/-n) mange, scab; **'2ig** *adj.* mangy, scabby.

Rauf|bold *contp.* ['raʊfbɔlt] *m* (-[e]s/-e) brawler, rowdy, *Am. sl.* tough; **'2en** (ge-, h) **1.** *v/t.* pluck, pull; *sich die Haare ~* tear one's hair; **2.** *v/i.* fight, scuffle; **~erei** [~ə'raɪ] *f* (-/-en) fight, scuffle.

rauh *adj.* [raʊ] rough; rugged; *weather*: inclement, raw; *voice*: hoarse; *fig.*: harsh; coarse, rude; F: *in ~en Mengen* galore; **'2reif** *m* (-[e]s/*no pl.*) hoar-frost, *poet.* rime.

Raum [raʊm] *m* (-[e]s/"e) room, space; expanse; area; room; premises *pl.*; **'~anzug** *m* space suit.

räumen ['rɔʏmən] *v/t.* (ge-, h) remove, clear (away); leave, give up, *esp.* ⚔ evacuate; vacate (*flat*).

'Raum|fahrt *f* astronautics; **'~flug** *m* space flight; **'~inhalt** *m* volume, capacity; **'~kapsel** *f* capsule.

räumlich *adj.* ['rɔʏmliç] relating to space, of space, spatial.

'Raum|meter *n, m* cubic met|re, *Am.* -er; **'~schiff** *n* space craft *or* ship; **'~sonde** *f* space probe; **'~station** *f* space station.

'Räumung *f* (-/-en) clearing, removal; *esp.* ⚕ clearance; vacating (*of flat*), *by force*: eviction; ⚔ evacuation (*of town*); **'~sverkauf** ⚕ *m* clearance sale.

raunen ['raʊnən] (ge-, h) **1.** *v/i.* whisper, murmur; **2.** *v/t.* whisper, murmur; *man raunt* rumo(u)r has it.

Raupe *zo.* ['raʊpə] *f* (-/-n) caterpillar; **'~nschlepper** ⊕ *m* caterpillar tractor.

raus *int.* [raʊs] get out!, *sl.* beat it!, scram!

Rausch [raʊʃ] *m* (-es/"e) intoxication, drunkenness; *fig.* frenzy, transport(s *pl.*); *e-n ~ haben* be drunk; **'2en** *v/i.* (ge-) **1.** (h) *leaves, rain, silk*: rustle; *water, wind*: rush; *surf*: roar; *applause*: thunder; **2.** (*sein*) *movement*: sweep; **'~gift** *n* narcotic (drug), F dope.

räuspern ['rɔyspərn] *v/refl.* (ge-, h) clear one's throat.

Razzia ['ratsja] *f* (-/Razzien) raid, round-up.

reagieren [rea'giːrən] *v/i.* (no -ge-, h) react (auf *acc.* [up]on; to); *fig. and* ⊕ *a.* respond (to).

Reaktion [reak'tsjoːn] *f* (-/-en) reaction (*a. pol.*); *fig. a.* response (auf *acc.* to); **~är** [~o'nɛːr] **1.** *m* (-s/-e) reactionary; **2.** ♀ *adj.* reactionary.

Reaktor *phys.* [re'aktɔr] *m* (-s/-en) (nuclear) reactor, atomic pile.

real *adj.* [re'aːl] real; concrete; **~isieren** [reali'ziːrən] *v/t.* (no -ge-, h) realize; **♀ismus** [rea'lismus] *m* (-/no pl.) realism; **~istisch** *adj.* [rea'listiʃ] realistic; **♀ität** [reali'tɛːt] *f* (-/-en) reality; **♀schule** *f* non-classical secondary school.

Rebe ♀ ['reːbə] *f* (-/-n) vine.

Rebell [re'bɛl] *m* (-en/-en) rebel; **♀ieren** [~'liːrən] *v/i.* (no -ge-, h) rebel, revolt, rise; **♀isch** *adj.* rebellious.

Reb|huhn *orn.* ['rep-] *n* partridge; **~laus** *zo.* ['reːp-] *f* vine-fretter, phylloxera; **~stock** ♀ ['reːp-] *m* vine.

Rechen ['reçən] *m* (-s/-) rake; grid.

Rechen|aufgabe ['reçən-] *f* sum, (arithmetical) problem; **~fehler** *m* arithmetical error, miscalculation; **~maschine** *f* calculating-machine; **~schaft** *f* (-/no pl.): ~ ablegen give or render an account (über *acc.* of), account *or* answer (for); zur ~ ziehen call to account (wegen for); **~schieber** ♣ *m* slide-rule.

rechne|n ['reçnən] (ge-, h) **1.** *v/t.* reckon, calculate; estimate, value; charge; ~ zu rank with *or* among(st); **2.** *v/i.* count; ~ auf (*acc.*) *or* mit count *or* reckon *or* rely (up)on; **~risch** *adj.* arithmetical.

'Rechnung *f* (-/-en) calculation, sum, reckoning; account, bill; invoice (*of goods*); *in restaurant*: bill, *Am.* check; score; auf ~ on account; ~ legen render an account (über *acc.* of); e-r Sache ~ tragen make allowance for s.th.; es geht auf meine ~ *in restaurants*: it is my treat, *Am.* F this is on me; **~sprüfer** *m* auditor.

recht[1] [reçt] **1.** *adj.* right; real; legitimate; right, correct; zur ~en Zeit in due time, at the right moment; ein ~er Narr a regular fool; mir ist es ~ I don't mind; ~ haben be right; j-m ~ geben agree with s.o.; **2.** *adv.* right(ly), well; very; rather; really, correctly; ganz ~! quite (so)!; es geschieht ihm ~ it serves him right; ~ gern gladly, with pleasure; ~ gut quite good *or* well; ich weiß nicht ~ I wonder.

Recht[2] [~] *n* (-[e]s/-e) right (auf *acc.* to), title (to), claim (on), interest (in); privilege; power, authority; ⚖ law; justice; ~ sprechen administer justice; mit ~ justly.

'Rechte *f* (-n/-n) right hand; *boxing*: right; *pol. the* Right.

Rechteck ['reçt?-] *n* (-[e]s/-e) rectangle; **♀ig** *adj.* rectangular.

recht|fertigen ['reçtfɛrtigən] *v/t.* (ge-, h) justify; defend, vindicate; **♀fertigung** *f* (-/-en) justification; vindication, defen|ce, *Am.* -se; **~gläubig** *adj.* orthodox; **~haberisch** *adj.* ['~haːbəriʃ] dogmatic; **~lich** *adj.* legal, lawful, legitimate; honest, righteous; **~los** *adj.* without rights; outlawed; **♀losigkeit** *f* (-/no pl.) outlawry; **~mäßig** *adj.* legal, lawful, legitimate; **♀mäßigkeit** *f* (-/no pl.) legality, legitimacy.

rechts *adv.* [reçts] on *or* to the right (hand).

'Rechts|anspruch *m* legal right *or* claim (auf *acc.* on, to), title (to); **~anwalt** *m* lawyer, solicitor; barrister, *Am.* attorney (at law); **~außen** *m* (-/-) *football*: outside right; **~beistand** *m* legal adviser, counsel.

'recht|schaffen 1. *adj.* honest, righteous; **2.** *adv.* thoroughly, downright, F awfully; **♀schreibung** *f* (-/-en) orthography, spelling.

'Rechts|fall *m* case, cause; **~frage** *f* question of law; issue of law; **~gelehrte** *m* jurist, lawyer; **♀gültig** *adj. s.* rechtskräftig; **~kraft** *f* (-/no pl.) legal force *or* validity; **♀kräftig** *adj.* valid, legal; *judgement*: final; **~kurve** *f* right-hand bend; **~lage** *f* legal position *or* status; **~mittel** *n* legal remedy; **~nachfolger** *m* assign, assignee; **~person** *f* legal personality; **~pflege** *f* administration of justice, judicature.

'Rechtsprechung *f* (-/-en) jurisdiction.

'Rechts|schutz *m* legal protection; **~spruch** *m* legal decision; judg(e)ment; sentence; verdict (*of jury*); **~steuerung** *mot. f* (-/-en) right-hand drive; **~streit** *m* action, lawsuit; **~verfahren** *n* (legal) proceedings *pl.*; **~verkehr** *mot. m* right-hand traffic; **~verletzung** *f* infringement; **~vertreter** *m s.* Rechtsbeistand; **~weg** *m*: den ~ beschreiten take legal action, go to law; unter Ausschluß des ~es eliminating legal proceedings; **♀widrig** *adj.* illegal, unlawful; **~wissenschaft** *f* jurisprudence.

'recht|wink(e)lig *adj.* right-angled; **~zeitig 1.** *adj.* punctual; opportune; **2.** *adv.* in (due) time, punctually, *Am.* on time.

Reck [rɛk] n (-[e]s/-e) sports: horizontal bar.

recken ['rɛkən] v/t. (ge-, h) stretch; sich ~ stretch o.s.

Redakt|eur [redak'tøːr] m (-s/-e) editor; ~ion [~'tsjoːn] f (-/-en) editorship; editing, wording; editorial staff, editors pl.; editor's or editorial office; **2ionell** adj. [~tsjo'nɛl] editorial.

Rede ['reːdə] f (-/-n) speech; oration; language; talk, conversation; discourse; direkte ~ gr. direct speech; indirekte ~ gr. reported or indirect speech; e-e ~ halten make or deliver a speech; zur ~ stellen call to account (wegen for); davon ist nicht die ~ that is not the point; davon kann keine ~ sein that's out of the question; es ist nicht der ~ wert it is not worth speaking of; **2gewandt** adj. eloquent; '~kunst f rhetoric; **2n** (ge-, h) 1. v/t. speak; talk; 2. v/i. speak (mit to) talk (to), chat (with); discuss (über et. s.th.); sie läßt nicht mit sich ~ she won't listen to reason.

Redensart ['reːdəns?-] f phrase, expression; idiom; proverb, saying.

redigieren [redi'giːrən] v/t. (no -ge-, h) edit; revise.

redlich ['reːtlɪç] 1. adj. honest, upright; sincere; 2. adv.: sich ~ bemühen take great pains.

Redner ['reːdnər] m (-s/-) speaker; orator; '~bühne f platform; '2isch adj. oratorical, rhetorical; '~pult n speaker's desk.

redselig adj. ['reːtzeːlɪç] talkative.

reduzieren [redu'tsiːrən] v/t. (no -ge-, h) reduce (auf acc. to).

Reede ⚓ ['reːdə] f (-/-n) roads pl., roadstead; '~r m (-s/-) shipowner; ~'rei f (-/-en) shipping company or firm.

reell [re'ɛl] 1. adj. respectable, honest; business firm: solid; goods: good; offer: real; 2. adv.: ~ bedient werden get good value for one's money.

Refer|at [refe'raːt] n (-[e]s/-e) report; lecture; paper; ein ~ halten esp. univ. read a paper; ~endar [~ɛn'daːr] m (-s/-e) ⚖ junior lawyer; at school: junior teacher; ~ent [~'rɛnt] m (-en/-en) reporter, speaker; ~enz [~'rɛnts] f (-/-en) reference; **2ieren** [~'riːrən] v/i. (no -ge-, h) report (über acc. [up]on); (give a) lecture (on); esp. univ. read a paper (on).

reflektieren [reflek'tiːrən] (no -ge-, h) 1. phys. v/t. reflect; 2. v/i. (über acc. [up]on); ~ auf (acc.) ✝ think of buying; be interested in.

Reflex [re'flɛks] m (-es/-e) phys. reflection or reflexion; 💥 reflex (action); **2iv** gr. adj. [~'ksiːf] reflexive.

Reform [re'fɔrm] f (-/-en) reform; ~er m (-s/-) reformer; **2ieren** [~'miːrən] v/t. (no -ge-, h) reform.

Refrain [rə'frɛː] m (-s/-s) refrain, chorus, burden.

Regal [re'gaːl] n (-s/-e) shelf.

rege adj. ['reːgə] active, brisk, lively; busy.

Regel ['reːgəl] f (-/-n) rule; regulation; standard; physiol. menstruation, menses pl.; in der ~ as a rule; **2los** adj. irregular; disorderly; **2mäßig** adj. regular; **2n** v/t. (ge-, h) regulate, control; arrange, settle; put in order; **2recht** adj. regular; '~ung f (-/-en) regulation, control; arrangement, settlement; **2widrig** adj. contrary to the rules, irregular; abnormal; sports: foul.

regen¹ ['reːgən] v/t. and v/refl. (ge-, h) move, stir.

Regen² [~] m (-s/-) rain; vom ~ in die Traufe kommen jump out of the frying-pan into the fire, get from bad to worse; **2arm** adj. dry; '~bogen m rainbow; '~bogenhaut anat. f iris; **2dicht** adj. rain-proof; '~guß m downpour; '~mantel m waterproof, raincoat, mac(k)intosh, F mac; **2reich** adj. rainy; '~schauer m shower (of rain); '~schirm m umbrella; '~tag m rainy day; '~tropfen m raindrop; '~wasser n rain-water; '~wetter n rainy weather; '~wolke f rain-cloud; '~wurm zo. m earthworm, Am. a. angleworm; '~zeit f rainy season.

Regie [re'ʒiː] f (-/-en) management; thea., film: direction; unter der ~ von directed by.

regier|en [re'giːrən] (no -ge-, h) 1. v/i. reign; 2. v/t. govern (a. gr.), rule; **2ung** f (-/-en) government, Am. administration; reign.

Re'gierungs|antritt m accession (to the throne); **2beamte** m government official; Brt. Civil Servant; ~bezirk m administrative district; ~gebäude n government offices pl.

Regiment [regi'mɛnt] n 1. (-[e]s/-e) government, rule; 2. ⚔ (-[e]s/-er) regiment.

Regisseur [reʒɪ'søːr] m (-s/-e) thea. stage manager, director; film: director.

Regist|er [re'gɪstər] n (-s/-) register (a. ♪), record; index; ~ratur [~ra'tuːr] f (-/-en) registry; registration.

registrier|en [regɪs'triːrən] v/t. (no -ge-, h) register, record; **2kasse** f cash register.

reglos adj. ['reːkloːs] motionless.

regne|n ['reːgnən] v/i. (ge-, h) rain; es regnet in Strömen it is pouring with rain; '~risch adj. rainy.

Regreß ⚖ [re'grɛs] m (Regresses/Regresse) recourse; **2pflichtig** ⚖, ✝ adj. liable to recourse.

regulär adj. [regu'lɛːr] regular.

regulier|bar _adj._ [regu'li:rba:r] adjustable, controllable; **~en** _v/t._ (_no -ge-_, _h_) regulate, adjust; control.

Regung ['re:guŋ] _f_ (-/-en) movement, motion; emotion; impulse; **'2slos** _adj._ motionless.

Reh _zo._ [re:] _n_ (-[e]s/-e) deer, roe; _female:_ doe.

rehabilitieren [rehabili'ti:rən] _v/t._ (_no -ge-_, _h_) rehabilitate.

'Reh|bock _zo._ _m_ roebuck; **'2braun** _adj._, **'2farben** _adj._ fawn-colo(u)red; **~geiß** _zo._ _f_ doe; **'~kalb** _zo._ _n_, **~kitz** _zo._ ['~kits] _n_ (-es/-e) fawn.

Reib|e ['raibə] _f_ (-/-n), **~eisen** ['raip?-] _n_ grater.

reib|en ['raibən] (_irr._, _ge-_, _h_) **1.** _v/t._ rub (_an dat._ [up]on); **2.** _v/t._ rub, grate; pulverize; _wund ~_ chafe, gall; **2erei** F _fig._ ['~rai] _f_ (-/-en) (constant) friction; **'2ung** _f_ (-/-en) friction; **'~ungslos** _adj._ frictionless; _fig._ smooth.

reich[1] _adj._ [raiç] rich (_an dat._ in); wealthy; ample, abundant, copious.

Reich[2] [~] _n_ (-es/-e) empire; kingdom (_of animals, vegetables, minerals_); _poet._, _rhet._, _fig._ realm.

reichen ['raiçən] (_ge-_, _h_) **1.** _v/t._ offer; serve (_food_); _j-m et. ~_ hand or pass s.th. to s.o.; _sich die Hände ~_ join hands; **2.** _v/i._ reach; extend; suffice; _das reicht!_ that will do!

reich|haltig _adj._ ['raiçhaltiç] rich; abundant, copious; **'~lich 1.** _adj._ ample, abundant, copious, plentiful; _~ Zeit_ plenty of time; **2.** F _adv._ rather, fairly, F pretty, plenty; **'2tum** _m_ (-s/¤er) riches _pl._; wealth (_an dat._ of).

'Reichweite _f_ reach; ✠ range; _in ~_ within reach, near at hand.

reif[1] _adj._ [raif] ripe, mature.

Reif[2] [~] _m_ (-[e]s/_no pl._) white _or_ hoar-frost, _poet._ rime.

'Reife _f_ (-/_no pl._) ripeness, maturity.

'reifen[1] _v/i._ (_ge-_) **1.** (_sein_) ripen, mature; **2.** (_h_): _es hat gereift_ there is a white _or_ hoar-frost.

'Reifen[2] _m_ (-s/-) hoop; ring; tyre, (_Am. only_) tire; _as ornament:_ circlet; _~ wechseln mot._ change tyres; **'~panne** _mot._ _f_ puncture, _Am._ _a._ blowout.

'Reife|prüfung _f_ s. Abitur; **'~zeugnis** _n_ s. Abschlußzeugnis.

'reiflich _adj._ mature, careful.

Reihe ['raiə] _f_ (-/-n) row; line; rank; series; number; _thea._ row, tier; _der ~ nach_ by turns; _ich bin an der ~_ it is my turn.

'Reihen|folge _f_ succession, sequence; _alphabetische ~_ alphabetical order; **'~haus** _n_ terrace-house, _Am._ row house; **'2weise** _adv._ in rows.

Reiher _orn._ ['raiər] _m_ (-s/-) heron.

Reim [raim] _m_ (-[e]s/-e) rhyme; **'2en** (_ge-_, _h_) **1.** _v/i._ rhyme; **2.** _v/t._ and _v/refl._ rhyme (_auf acc._ with).

rein _adj._ [rain] pure; clean; clear; _~e Wahrheit_ plain truth; **'2ertrag** _m_ net proceeds _pl._; **'2fall** F _m_ letdown; **'2gewicht** _n_ net weight; **'2gewinn** _m_ net profit; **'2heit** _f_ (-/_no pl._) purity; cleanness.

'reinig|en _v/t._ (_ge-_, _h_) clean(se); _fig._ purify; **'2ung** _f_ (-/-en) clean(s)-ing; _fig._ purification; cleaners _pl._; _chemische ~_ dry cleaning; **'2ungs-mittel** _n_ detergent, cleanser.

'rein|lich _adj._ clean; cleanly; neat, tidy; **'2machefrau** _f_ charwoman; **'~rassig** _adj._ pedigree, thoroughbred, _esp. Am._ purebred; **'2schrift** _f_ fair copy.

Reis[1] ♀ [rais] _m_ (-es/-e) rice.

Reis[2] ♀ [~] _n_ (-es/-er) twig, sprig.

Reise ['raizə] _f_ (-/-n) journey, ⏚, ✈ voyage; travel; tour; trip; passage; **'~büro** _n_ travel agency _or_ bureau; **'~decke** _f_ travel(l)ing-rug; **'2fertig** _adj._ ready to start; **'~führer** _m_ guide(-book); **'~gepäck** _n_ luggage, _Am._ baggage; **'~gesellschaft** _f_ tourist party; **'~kosten** _pl._ travel(l)ing-expenses _pl._; **'~leiter** _m_ courier; **'2n** _v/i._ (_ge-_, _sein_) travel, journey; _~ nach_ go to; _ins Ausland ~_ go abroad; **'~nde** _m, f_ (-n/-n) (✠ commercial) travel(l)er; _in trains:_ passenger; _for pleasure:_ tourist; **'~necessaire** ['~nesesε:r] _n_ (-s/-s) dressing-case; **'~paß** _m_ passport; **'~scheck** _m_ traveller's cheque, _Am._ traveler's check; **'~schreibmaschine** _f_ portable typewriter; **'~tasche** _f_ travel(l)ing-bag, _Am._ grip(sack).

Reisig ['raiziç] _n_ (-s/_no pl._) brush-wood.

Reißbrett ['rais-] _n_ drawing-board.

reißen ['raisən] **1.** _v/t._ (_irr._, _ge-_, _h_) tear; pull; _an sich ~_ seize; _sich ~_ scratch o.s. (_an dat._ with); _sich ~ um_ scramble for; **2.** _v/i._ (_irr._, _ge-_, _sein_) break; burst; split; tear; _mir riß die Geduld_ I lost (all) patience; **3.** ♀ F _n_ (-s/_no pl._) rheumatism; **'~d** _adj._ rapid; _animal:_ rapacious; _pain:_ acute; _~en Absatz finden_ sell like hot cakes.

'Reiß|er F _m_ (-s/-) draw, box-office success; thriller; **'~feder** _f_ drawing-pen; **'~leine** ✈ _f_ rip-cord; **'~nagel** _m_ s. Reißzwecke; **'~schiene** _f_ (T-)square; **'~verschluß** _m_ zip-fastener, zipper, _Am._ _a._ slide fastener; **'~zeug** _n_ drawing instruments _pl._; **'~zwecke** _f_ drawing-pin, _Am._ thumbtack.

Reit|anzug ['rait-] _m_ riding-dress; **'~bahn** _f_ riding-school, manège; riding-track; **'2en** (_irr._, _ge-_) **1.** _v/i._ (_sein_) ride, go on horseback; **2.** _v/t._ (_h_) ride; **'~er** _m_ (-s/-) rider, horseman; ✠, _police:_ trooper; _filing:_ tab; **~e'rei** _f_ (-/-en) cavalry; **'~erin** _f_ (-/-nen) horsewoman; **'~gerte** _f_ riding-whip; '‿hose f (riding-) breeches pl.; '‿knecht m groom; '‿kunst f horsemanship; '‿lehrer m riding master; '‿peitsche f riding-whip; '‿pferd zo. n riding-horse, saddle-horse; '‿schule f riding-school; '‿stiefel m/pl. riding-boots pl.; '‿weg m bridle-path.

Reiz [raɪts] m (-es/-e) irritation; charm, attraction; allurement; '2-bar adj. sensitive; irritable, excitable, Am. sore; '2en (ge-, h) **1.** v/t. irritate (a. ♂⃗); excite; provoke; nettle; stimulate, rouse; entice, (al)lure, tempt, charm, attract; **2.** v/i. cards: bid; '2end adj. charming, attractive; Am. cute; lovely; '2los adj. unattractive; '‿mittel n stimulus; ♂⃗ stimulant; '‿ung f (-/-en) irritation; provocation; '2-voll adj. charming, attractive.

rekeln F ['reːkəln] v/refl. (ge-, h) loll, lounge, sprawl.

Reklamation [reklamaʦjoːn] f (-/-en) claim; complaint, protest.

Reklame [reˈklaːmə] f (-/-n) advertising; advertisement, F ad; publicity; ~ machen advertise; ~ machen für et. advertise s.th.

rekla'mieren (no -ge-, h) **1.** v/t. (re)claim; **2.** v/i. complain (wegen about).

Rekonvaleszen|t [rekonvalɛsˈtsɛnt] m (-en/-en), ‿tin f (-/-nen) convalescent; ‿z [‿ts] f (-/no pl.) convalescence.

Rekord [reˈkɔrt] m (-[e]s/-e) sports, etc.: record.

Rekrut [reˈkruːt] m (-en/-en) recruit; 2ieren ✕ [‿uˈtiːrən] v/t. (no -ge-, h) recruit.

Rektor ['rɛktɔr] m (-s/-en) headmaster, rector, Am. principal; univ. chancellor, rector, Am. president.

relativ adj. [relaˈtiːf] relative.

Relief [reˈljeːf] n (-s/-s, -e) relief.

Religi|on [reliˈgjoːn] f (-/-en) religion; 2ös adj. [‿øːs] religious; pious, devout; ‿osität [‿oziˈtɛːt] f (-/no pl.) religiousness; piety.

Reling ♣ ['reːlɪŋ] f (-/-s, -e) rail.

Reliquie [reˈliːkvi̯ə] f (-/-n) relic.

Ren zo. [ren; reːn] n (-s/-s; -s/-e) reindeer.

Renn|bahn ['rɛn-] f racecourse, Am. race track, horse-racing: a. the turf; mot. speedway; '‿boot n racing boat, racer.

rennen ['rɛnən] **1.** v/i. (irr., ge-, sein) run; race; **2.** v/t. (irr., ge-, h): j-n zu Boden ~ run s.o. down; **3.** 2 n (-s/-) run(ning); race; heat.

'**Renn|fahrer** m mot. racing driver, racer; racing cyclist; '‿läufer m ski racer; '‿mannschaft f race-crew; '‿pferd zo. n racehorse, racer; '‿rad n racing bicycle, racer; '‿sport m racing; horse-racing: a. the turf; '‿stall m racing stable;

renommiert adj. [renɔˈmiːrt] famous, noted (wegen for).

renovieren [renoˈviːrən] v/t. (no -ge-, h) renovate, repair; redecorate (interior of house).

rent|abel adj. [rɛnˈtaːbəl] profitable, paying; 2e f (-/-n) income, revenue; annuity; (old-age) pension; rent; 2enempfänger ['rɛntən?-] m s. Rentner; rentier.

Rentier zo. ['rɛn-] n s. Ren.

rentieren [rɛnˈtiːrən] v/refl. (no -ge-, h) pay.

Rentner ['rɛntnər] m (-s/-) (old-age) pensioner.

Reparatur [reparaˈtuːr] f (-/-en) repair; ‿werkstatt f repair-shop; mot. a. garage, service station.

repa'rieren v/t. (no -ge-, h) repair, Am. F fix.

Report|age [repɔrˈtaːʒə] f (-/-en) reporting, commentary, coverage; ‿er [reˈpɔrtər] m (-s/-) reporter.

Repräsent|ant [reprɛzɛnˈtant] m (-en/-en) representative; ‿antenhaus Am. parl. n House of Representatives; 2ieren (no -ge-, h) **1.** v/t. represent; **2.** v/i. cut a fine figure.

Repressalie [reprɛˈsaːli̯ə] f (-/-n) reprisal.

reproduzieren [reproduˈtsiːrən] v/t. (no -ge-, h) reproduce.

Reptil zo. [rɛpˈtiːl] n (-s/-ien, ⚹⃗ -e) reptile.

Republik [repuˈbliːk] f (-/-en) republic; ‿aner pol. [‿iˈkaːnər] m (-s/-) republican; 2anisch adj. [‿iˈkaːnɪʃ] republican.

Reserve [reˈzɛrvə] f (-/-n) reserve; ‿rad mot. n spare wheel.

reser'vier|en v/t. (no -ge-, h) reserve; ~ lassen book (seat, etc.); ‿t adj. reserved (a. fig.).

Resid|enz [reziˈdɛnts] f (-/-en) residence; 2ieren v/i. (no -ge-, h) reside.

resignieren [reziˈgniːrən] v/i. (no -ge-, h) resign.

Respekt [reˈspɛkt] m (-[e]s/no pl.) respect; 2ieren [‿ˈtiːrən] v/t. (no -ge-, h) respect; 2los adj. irreverent, disrespectful; 2voll adj. respectful.

Ressort [rɛˈsoːr] n (-s/-s) department; province.

Rest [rɛst] m (-es/-e, ♣⃗ -er) rest, remainder; residue (a. ♂⃗); esp. ♱ remnant (of cloth); leftover (of food); das gab ihm den ~ that finished him (off).

Restaurant [rɛstoˈrãː] n (-s/-s) restaurant.

'**Rest|bestand** m remnant; '‿betrag m remainder, balance; '2lich adj. remaining; '2los adv. completely; entirely; '**~zahlung** f payment of balance; final payment.

Resultat [rezul'taːt] n (-[e]s/-e) result, outcome; *sports:* score.

retten ['rɛtən] v/t. (ge-, h) save; deliver, rescue.

Rettich ♀ ['rɛtiç] m (-s/-e) radish.

'**Rettung** f (-/-en) rescue; deliverance; escape.

'**Rettungs|boot** n lifeboat; '**~gürtel** m lifebelt; '**2los** adj. irretrievable, past help or hope, beyond recovery; '**~mannschaft** f rescue party; '**~ring** m life-buoy.

Reu|e ['rɔyə] f (-/no pl.) repentance (*über acc.* of), remorse (at); '**2en** v/t. (ge-, h): *et. reut mich* I repent (of) s.th.; '**2evoll** adj. repentant; **2(müt)ig** adj. ['~(my:t)iç] repentant.

Revanche [re'vãːʃ(ə)] f (-/-n) revenge; **~spiel** n return match.

revan'chieren v/refl. (no -ge-, h) take or have one's revenge (*an dat.* on); return (*für et.* s.th.).

Revers 1. [re'vɛːr] m (-/-) lapel (*of coat*); 2. [re'vɛrs] m (-es/-e) declaration; ⚖ bond.

revidieren [revi'diːrən] v/t. (no -ge-, h) revise; check; ✝ audit.

Revier [re'viːr] n (-s/-e) district, quarter; s. *Jagdrevier.*

Revision [revi'zjoːn] f (-/-en) revision (*a. typ.*); ✝ audit; ⚖ appeal; *~ einlegen* ⚖ lodge an appeal.

Revolt|e [re'vɔltə] f (-/-n) revolt, uprising; **2ieren** [~'tiːrən] v/i. (no -ge-, h) revolt, rise (in revolt).

Revolution [revolu'tsjoːn] f (-/-en) revolution; **~är** [~o'nɛːr] 1. m (-s/-e) revolutionary; 2. 2 adj. revolutionary.

Revolver [re'vɔlvər] m (-s/-) revolver, *Am.* F a. gun.

Revue [rə'vyː] f (-/-n) review; *thea.* revue, (musical) show; *~ passieren lassen* pass in review.

Rezens|ent [retsen'zɛnt] m (-en/-en) critic, reviewer; **2ieren** v/t. (no -ge-, h) review, criticize; **~ion** [~'zjoːn] f (-/-en) review, critique.

Rezept [re'tsɛpt] n (-[e]s/-e) ⚕ prescription; *cooking:* recipe (*a. fig.*).

Rhabarber ♀ [ra'barbər] m (-s/no pl.) rhubarb.

rhetorisch adj. [re'toːriʃ] rhetorical.

rheumati|sch ⚕ adj. [rɔy'maːtiʃ] rheumatic; **2smus** ⚕ [~a'tismus] m (-/Rheumatismen) rheumatism.

rhythm|isch adj. ['rytmiʃ] rhythmic(al); **2us** ['~us] m (-/Rhythmen) rhythm.

richten ['riçtən] v/t. (ge-, h) set right, arrange, adjust; level, point (*gun*) (*auf acc.* at); direct (*gegen* at); ⚖ judge; execute; *zugrunde ~* ruin, destroy; *in die Höhe ~* raise, lift up; *sich ~ nach* conform to, act according to; take one's bearings from;

gr. agree with; depend on; *price:* be determined by; *ich richte mich nach Ihnen* I leave it to you.

'**Richter** m (-s/-) judge; '**2lich** adj. judicial; '**~spruch** m judg(e)ment, sentence.

'**richtig** 1. adj. right, correct, accurate; proper; true; just; *ein ~er Londoner* a regular cockney; 2. adv.: *~ gehen clock:* go right; '**2keit** f (-/no pl.) correctness; accuracy; justness; '**~stellen** v/t. (sep., -ge-, h) put or set right, rectify.

'**Richt|linien** f/pl. (general) directions pl., rules pl.; '**~preis** ✝ m standard price; '**~schnur** f ⊕ plumb-line; *fig.* rule (of conduct), guiding principle.

'**Richtung** f (-/-en) direction; course, way; *fig.* line; **~anzeiger** mot. ['riçtuŋs?~] m (-s/-) flashing indicator, trafficator; '**2weisend** adj. directive, leading, guiding.

'**Richtwaage** ⊕ f level.

rieb [riːp] pret. of *reiben.*

riechen ['riːçən] (irr., ge-, h) 1. v/i. smell (*nach* of; *an dat.* at); sniff (*an dat.* at); 2. v/t. smell; sniff.

rief [riːf] pret. of *rufen.*

riefeln ⊕ ['riːfəln] v/t. (ge-, h) flute, groove.

Riegel ['riːgəl] m (-s/-) bar, bolt; bar, cake (*of soap*); bar (*of chocolate*).

Riemen ['riːmən] m (-s/-) strap, thong; belt; ⚓ oar.

Ries [riːs] n (-es/-e) ream.

Riese ['riːzə] m (-n/-n) giant.

rieseln ['riːzəln] v/i. (ge-) 1. (sein) *small stream:* purl, ripple; trickle; 2. (h): *es rieselt* it drizzles.

ries|engroß adj. ['riːzən'~], '**~enhaft** adj., '**~ig** adj. gigantic, huge; '**2in** f (-/-nen) giantess.

riet [riːt] pret. of *raten.*

Riff [rif] n (-[e]s/-e) reef.

Rille ['rilə] f (-/-n) groove; ⊕ a. flute.

Rimesse ✝ [ri'mɛsə] f (-/-n) remittance.

Rind zo. [rint] n (-[e]s/-er) ox; cow; neat; *~er pl.* (horned) cattle pl.; *zwanzig ~er* twenty head of cattle.

Rinde ['rində] f (-/-n) ♀ bark; rind (*of fruit, bacon, cheese*); crust (*of bread*).

'**Rinder|braten** m roast beef; '**~herde** f herd of cattle; '**~hirt** m cowherd, *Am.* cowboy.

'**Rind|fleisch** n beef; '**~(s)leder** n neat's-leather, cow-hide; '**~vieh** n (horned) cattle pl., neat pl.

Ring [riŋ] m (-[e]s/-e) ring; circle; link (*of chain*); ✝ ring, pool, trust, *Am.* F combine; '**~bahn** f circular railway.

ringel|n ['riŋəln] v/refl. (ge-, h) curl, coil; '**2natter** zo. f ring-snake.

ring|en ['riŋən] (*irr.*, ge-, *h*) **1.** *v/i.* wrestle; struggle (*um* for); *nach Atem* ~ gasp (for breath); **2.** *v/t.* wring (*hands, washing*); '2er *m* (-s/-) wrestler.

ring|förmig *adj.* ['riŋfœrmiç] annular, ring-like; '2kampf *m sports:* wrestling(-match); '2richter *m boxing:* referee.

rings *adv.* [riŋs] around; '~he'rum *adv.*, '~um *adv.*, '~um'her *adv.* round about, all (a)round.

Rinn|e ['rinə] *f* (-/-n) groove, channel; gutter (*of roof or street*); gully; '2en *v/i.* (*irr.*, ge-, *sein*) run, flow; drip; leak; ~sal ['~za:l] *n* (-[e]s/-e) watercourse, streamlet; '~stein *m* gutter; sink (*of kitchen unit*).

Rippe ['ripə] *f* (-/-n) rib; △ groin; bar (*of chocolate*); '2n *v/t.* (ge-, *h*) rib; '~nfell *anat. n* pleura; '~nfell-entzündung *& f* pleurisy; '~n-stoß *m* dig in the ribs; nudge.

Risiko ['ri:ziko] *n* (-s/-s, Risiken) risk; *ein* ~ *eingehen* take a risk.

risk|ant *adj.* [ris'kant] risky; ~ieren *v/t.* (*no* -ge-, *h*) risk.

Riß [ris] **1.** *m* (Risses/Risse) rent, tear; split (*a. fig.*); crack; *in skin:* chap; scratch; ⊕ draft, plan; *fig.* rupture; **2.** 2 *pret. of* reißen.

rissig *adj.* ['risiç] full of rents; *skin, etc.*: chappy; ~ *werden* crack.

Rist [rist] *m* (-es/-e) instep; back of the hand; wrist.

Ritt [rit] **1.** *m* (-[e]s/-e) ride; **2.** 2 *pret. of* reiten.

Ritter *m* (-s/-) knight; *zum* ~ *schlagen* knight; '~gut *n* manor; '2lich *adj.* knightly, chivalrous; '~lichkeit *f* (-/-en) gallantry, chivalry.

rittlings *adv.* ['ritliŋs] astride (*auf e-m Pferd* a horse).

Ritz [rits] *m* (-es/-e) crack, chink; scratch; '~e *f* (-/-n) crack, chink; fissure; '2en *v/t.* (ge-, *h*) scratch; cut.

Rival|e [ri'va:lə] *m* (-n/-n), ~in *f* (-/-nen) rival; 2isieren [~ali'zi:rən] *v/i.* (*no* -ge-, *h*) rival (*mit j-m* s.o.); ~ität [~ali'tɛ:t] *f* (-/-en) rivalry.

Rizinusöl ['ri:tsinus?-] *n* (-[e]s/*no pl.*) castor oil.

Robbe *zo.* ['rɔbə] *f* (-/-n) seal.

Robe ['ro:bə] *f* (-/-n) gown; robe.

Roboter ['rɔbɔtər] *m* (-s/-) robot.

robust *adj.* [ro'bust] robust, sturdy, vigorous.

roch [rɔx] *pret. of* riechen.

röcheln ['rœçəln] (ge-, *h*) **1.** *v/i.* rattle; **2.** *v/t.* gasp out (*words*).

Rock [rɔk] *m* (-[e]s/¨e) skirt; coat, jacket; '~schoß *m* coat-tail.

Rodel|bahn ['ro:dəl-] *f* toboggan-run; '2n *v/i.* (ge-, *h*, *sein*) toboggan, *Am. a.* coast; '~schlitten *m* sled(ge), toboggan.

roden ['ro:dən] *v/t.* (ge-, *h*) clear (*land*); root up, stub (*roots*).

Rogen *ichth.* ['ro:gən] *m* (-s/-) roe, spawn.

Roggen & ['rɔgən] *m* (-s/-) rye.

roh *adj.* [ro:] raw; *fig.*: rough, rude; cruel, brutal; *oil, metal*: crude; '2bau *m* (-[e]s/-ten) rough brickwork; '2eisen *n* pig-iron.

Roheit ['ro:hart] *f* (-/-en) rawness; roughness (*a. fig.*); *fig.*: rudeness; brutality.

Roh|ling *m* (-s/-e) brute, ruffian; '~material *n* raw material; '~produkt *n* raw product.

Rohr [ro:r] *n* (-[e]s/-e) tube, pipe; duct; & reed; cane.

Röhre ['rø:rə] *f* (-/-n) tube, pipe; duct; *radio:* valve, *Am.* (electron) tube.

Rohr|leger *m* (-s/-) pipe fitter, plumber; '~leitung *f* plumbing; pipeline; '~post *f* pneumatic dispatch *or* tube; '~stock *m* cane; '~zucker *m* cane-sugar.

Rohstoff *m* raw material.

Rolladen ['rɔlla:dən] *m* (-s/¨, -) rolling shutter.

Rollbahn & *f* taxiway, taxi-strip.

Rolle ['rɔlə] *f* (-/-n) roll; roller; coil (*of rope, etc.*); pulley; *beneath furniture:* cast|or, -er; mangle; *thea.* part, role; *fig.* figure; ~ *Garn* reel of cotton, *Am.* spool of thread; *das spielt keine* ~ that doesn't matter, it makes no difference; *Geld spielt keine* ~ money (is) no object; *aus der* ~ *fallen* forget o.s.

rollen (ge-) **1.** *v/i.* (*sein*) roll; & taxi; **2.** *v/t.* (*h*) roll; wheel; mangle (*laundry*).

Rollenbesetzung *thea. f* cast.

Roller *m* (-s/-) *children's toy:* scooter; *mot.* (motor) scooter.

Roll|feld & *n* man(o)euvring area, *Am.* maneuvering area; '~film *phot. m* roll film; '~kragen *m* turtle neck; '~schrank *m* roll-fronted cabinet; '~schuh *m* roller-skate; '~schuhbahn *f* roller-skating rink; '~stuhl *m* wheel chair; '~treppe *f* escalator; '~wagen *m* lorry, truck.

Roman [ro'ma:n] *m* (-s/-e) novel, (work of) fiction; *novel of adventure and fig.*: romance; ~ist [~a'nist] *m* (-en/-en) Romance scholar *or* student; ~schriftsteller *m* novelist.

Romanti|k [ro'mantik] *f* (-/*no pl.*) romanticism; 2sch *adj.* romantic.

Röm|er ['rø:mər] *m* (-s/-) Roman; '2isch *adj.* Roman.

röntgen ['rœntgən] *v/t.* (ge-, *h*) X-ray; '2aufnahme *f*, '2bild *n* X-ray; '2strahlen *m/pl.* X-rays *pl.*

rosa *adj.* ['ro:za] pink.

Rose ['ro:zə] *f* (-/-n) & rose; *&* erysipelas.

Rosen|kohl & *m* Brussels sprouts *pl.*; '~kranz *eccl. m* rosary; '2rot *adj.* rose-colo(u)red, rosy; '~**stock** ♀ *m* (-[e]s/~e) rose-bush.

'**rosig** *adj.* rosy (*a. fig.*), rose-colo(u)red, roseate.

Rosine [ro'ziːnə] *f* (-/-n) raisin.

Roß *zo.* *n* (Rosses/Rosse, F *Rösser*) horse, *poet.* steed; '~**haar** *n* horsehair.

Rost [rɔst] *m* 1. (-es/*no pl.*) rust; 2. (-es/-e) grate; gridiron; grill; '~**braten** *m* roast joint.

'**rosten** *v/i.* (ge-, h, sein) rust.

rösten ['røːstən] *v/t.* (ge-, h) roast, grill; toast (*bread*); fry (*potatoes*).

'**Rost|fleck** *m* rust-stain; *in cloth:* iron-mo(u)ld; '2**frei** *adj.* rustless, rustproof; *esp. steel:* stainless; '2**ig** *adj.* rusty, corroded.

rot [roːt] 1. *adj.* red; 2. ♀ *n* (-s/-, F -s) red.

Rotationsmaschine *typ.* [rotaˈtsjoːns-] *f* rotary printing machine.

'**rot|backig** *adj.* ruddy; '~**blond** *adj.* sandy.

Röte ['røːtə] *f* (-/*no pl.*) redness, red (colo[u]r); blush; '2**n** *v/t.* (ge-, h) redden; paint or dye red; *sich* ~ redden; flush, blush.

'**rot|gelb** *adj.* reddish yellow; '~**glühend** *adj.* red-hot; '2**haut** *f* redskin.

rotieren [ro'tiːrən] *v/i.* (*no* -ge-, h) rotate, revolve.

Rot|käppchen ['roːtkɛpçən] *n* (-s/-) Little Red Riding Hood; '~**kehlchen** *orn.* *n* (-s/-) robin (redbreast).

rötlich *adj.* ['røːtliç] reddish.

'**Rot|stift** *m* red crayon or pencil; '~**tanne** ♀ *f* spruce (fir).

Rotte ['rɔtə] *f* (-/-n) band, gang.

'**Rot|wein** *m* red wine; claret; '~**wild** *zo.* *n* red deer.

Rouleau [ru'loː] *n* (-s/-s) *s.* *Rollladen*; blind, *Am.* (window) shade.

Route ['ruːtə] *f* (-/-n) route.

Routine [ru'tiːnə] *f* (-/*no pl.*) routine, practice.

Rübe ♀ ['ryːbə] *f* (-/-n) beet; *weiße* ~ (Swedish) turnip, *Am. a.* rutabaga; *rote* ~ red beet, beet(root); *gelbe* ~ carrot.

Rubin [ru'biːn] *m* (-s/-e) ruby.

ruch|bar *adj.* ['ruːxbaːr]: ~ *werden* become known, get about or abroad; '~**los** *adj.* wicked, profligate.

Ruck [ruk] *m* (-[e]s/-e) jerk, *Am.* F yank; jolt (*of vehicle*).

Rück|antwort ['ryk²-] *f* reply; *Postkarte mit* ~ reply postcard; *mit bezahlter* ~ *telegram:* reply paid; '2**bezüglich** *gr. adj.* reflexive; '~**blick** *m* retrospect(ive view) (*auf acc.* at); reminiscences *pl.*

rücken[1] ['rykən] (ge-) 1. *v/t.* (h) move, shift; 2. *v/i.* (sein) move; *näher* ~ near, approach.

Rücken[2] [~] *m* (-s/-) back; ridge (*of mountain*); '~**deckung** *fig.* *f* backing, support; '~**lehne** *f* back

(*of chair, etc.*); '~**mark** *anat.* *n* spinal cord; '~**schmerzen** *m/pl.* pain in the back, back ache; '~**schwimmen** *n* (-s/*no pl.*) backstroke swimming; '~**wind** *m* following or tail wind; '~**wirbel** *anat.* *m* dorsal vertebra.

Rück|erstattung ['ryk²-] *f* restitution; refund (*of money*), reimbursement (*of expenses*); '~**fahrkarte** *f* return (ticket), *Am. a.* round-trip ticket; '~**fahrt** *f* return journey or voyage; *auf der* ~ on the way back; '~**fall** *m* relapse; '2**fällig** *adj.*: ~ *werden* relapse; '~**flug** *m* return flight; '~**frage** *f* further inquiry; '~**gabe** *f* return, restitution; '~**gang** *fig.* *m* retrogression; ✝ recession, decline; '2**gängig** *adj.* retrograde; ~ *machen* cancel; '~**grat** *anat.* *n* (-[e]s/-e) spine, backbone (*both a. fig.*); '~**halt** *m* support; '2**haltlos** *adj.* unreserved, frank; '~**hand** *f* (-/*no pl.*) *tennis:* backhand (stroke); '~**kauf** *m* repurchase; '~**kehr** ['~keːr] *f* (-/*no pl.*) return; '~**kopp(e)lung** ⚡ *f* (-/-en) feedback; '~**lage** *f* reserve(s *pl.*); savings *pl.*; '2**läufig** *fig. adj.* ['~lɔyfiç] retrograde; '~**licht** *mot.* *n* tail-light, tail-lamp, rear-light; '~**lings** *adv.* backwards; from behind; '~**marsch** *m* march back or home; retreat; '~**porto** ⚡ *n* return postage; '~**reise** *f* return journey, journey back or home.

'**Rucksack** *m* knapsack, rucksack.

'**Rück|schlag** *m* backstroke; *fig.* setback; '~**schluß** *m* conclusion, inference; '~**schritt** *fig.* *m* retrogression, set-back; *pol.* reaction; '~**seite** *f* back, reverse; *a.* tail (*of coin*); '~**sendung** *f* return; '~**sicht** *f* respect, regard, consideration (*auf j-n* for s.o.); 2**sichtslos** *adj.* inconsiderate (*gegen* of), regardless (of); ruthless; reckless; ~*es Fahren mot.* reckless driving; '2**sichtsvoll** *adj.* regardful (*gegen* of); considerate, thoughtful; '~**sitz** *mot.* *m* back-seat; '~**spiegel** *mot.* *m* rearview mirror; '~**spiel** *n sports:* return match; '~**sprache** *f* consultation; ~ *nehmen mit* consult (*lawyer*), consult with (*fellow workers*); *nach* ~ *mit* on consultation with; '~**stand** *m* arrears *pl.*; backlog; 🜨 residue; *im* ~ *sein mit* be in arrears or behind with; '2**ständig** *fig. adj.* old-fashioned, backward; ~*e Miete* arrears of rent; '~**stoß** *m* recoil; kick (*of gun*); '~**strahler** *m* (-s/-) rear reflector, cat's eye; '~**tritt** *m* withdrawal, retreat; resignation; '~**trittbremse** *f* back-pedal brake, *Am.* coaster brake; '~**versicherung** *f* reinsurance; 2**wärts** *adv.* ['~verts] back, backward(s); '~**wärtsgang** *mot. m* reverse (gear); '**~weg** *m* way back, return.

'**ruckweise** *adv.* by jerks.

'**rück|wirkend** *adj.* reacting; *physiol., etc.*: retroactive, retrospective; '**~wirkung** *f* reaction; '**2zahlung** *f* repayment; '**2zug** *m* retreat.

Rüde ['ry:də] 1. *zo. m* (-n/-n) male dog *or* fox *or* wolf; large hound; 2. ♀ *adj.* rude, coarse, brutal.

Rudel ['ru:dəl] *n* (-s/-) troop; pack (*of wolves*); herd (*of deer*).

Ruder ['ru:dər] *n* (-s/-) oar; rudder (*a.* ✈); helm; '**~boot** *n* row(ing)-boat; '**~er** *m* (-s/-) rower, oarsman; '**~fahrt** *f* row; '**2n** (*ge-*) 1. *v/i.* (*h, sein*) row; 2. *v/t.* (*h*) row; '**~regatta** ['~regata] *f* (-/*Ruderregatten*) boat race, regatta; '**~sport** *m* rowing.

Ruf [ru:f] *m* (-[e]s/-e) call; cry, shout; summons; *univ.* call; reputation, repute; fame; standing, credit; '**2en** (*irr., ge-, h*) 1. *v/i.* call; cry, shout; 2. *v/t.* call; ~ *lassen* send for.

'**Ruf|name** *m* Christian *or* first name; '**~nummer** *f* telephone number; '**~weite** *f* (-/*no pl.*): in ~ within call *or* earshot.

Rüge ['ry:gə] *f* (-/-n) rebuke, censure, reprimand; '**2n** *v/t.* (*ge-, h*) rebuke, censure, blame.

Ruhe ['ru:ə] *f* (-/*no pl.*) rest, repose; sleep; quiet, calm; tranquillity; silence; peace; composure; *sich zur ~ setzen* retire; ~*! quiet!*, silence!; *immer mit der ~! take it easy!; lassen Sie mich in ~!* let me alone!; '**2bedürftig** *adj.*: ~ *sein* want *or* need rest; '**~gehalt** *n* pension; '**2los** *adj.* restless; '**2n** *v/i.* (*ge-, h*) rest, repose; sleep; *laß die Vergangenheit ~!* let bygones be bygones!; '**~pause** *f* pause; lull; '**~platz** *m* resting-place; '**~stand** *m* (-[e]s/*no pl.*) retirement; *im ~ retired; in den ~ treten retire; in den ~ versetzen* superannuate, pension off, retire; '**~stätte** *f*: *letzte ~* resting-place; '**~störer** *m* (-s/-) disturber of the peace, peacebreaker; '**~störung** *f* disturbance (of the peace), disorderly behavio(u)r, riot.

'**ruhig** *adj.* quiet; *mind, water*: tranquil, calm; silent; ⊕ smooth.

Ruhm [ru:m] *m* (-[e]s/*no pl.*) glory; fame, renown.

rühm|en ['ry:mən] *v/t.* (*ge-, h*) praise, glorify; *sich e-r Sache ~* boast of s.th.; '**~lich** *adj.* glorious, laudable.

'**ruhm|los** *adj.* inglorious; '**~reich** *adj.* glorious.

Ruhr ✠ [ru:r] *f* (-/*no pl.*) dysentery;

Rühr|ei ['ry:r⁹-] *n* scrambled egg; '**2en** (*ge-, h*) 1. *v/t.* stir, move; *fig.* touch, move, affect; *sich ~* stir, move, bustle; 2. *v/i.*: *an et. ~* touch s.th.; *wir wollen nicht daran ~* let sleeping dogs lie; '**2end**

adj. touching, moving; '**2ig** *adj.* active, busy; enterprising; nimble; '**2selig** *adj.* sentimental; '**~ung** *f* (-/*no pl.*) emotion, feeling.

Ruin [ru'i:n] *m* (-s/*no pl.*) ruin; decay; ~*e* *f* (-/-n) ruin(s *pl.*); *fig.* ruin, wreck; **2ieren** [rui'ni:rən] *v/t.* (*no -ge-, h*) ruin; destroy, wreck; spoil; *sich ~* ruin o.s.

rülpsen ['rylpsən] *v/i.* (*ge-, h*) belch.

Rumän|e [ru'mɛ:nə] *m* (-n/-n) Ro(u)manian; **2isch** *adj.* Ro(u)manian.

Rummel F ['rumǝl] *m* (-s/*no pl.*) hurly-burly, row; bustle; revel; *in publicity*: F ballyhoo; '**~platz** *m* fun fair, amusement park.

rumoren [ru'mo:rən] *v/i.* (*no -ge-, h*) make a noise *or* row; *bowels*: rumble.

Rumpel|kammer F ['rumpǝl-] *f* lumber-room; '**2n** F *v/i.* (*ge-, h, sein*) rumble.

Rumpf [rumpf] *m* (-[e]s/⁼e) *anat.* trunk, body; torso (*of statue*); ♪ hull, frame, body; ✈ fuselage, body.

rümpfen ['rympfən] *v/t.* (*ge-, h*): *die Nase ~* turn up one's nose, sniff (*über acc.* at).

rund [runt] 1. *adj.* round (*a. fig.*); circular; 2. *adv.* about; '**2blick** *m* panorama, view all (a)round; **2e** ['rundə] *f* (-/-n) round; *sports*: lap; *boxing*: round; round, patrol; beat (*of policeman*); *in der* *or* *die* ~ (a)round; ~**en** ['~dən] *v/refl.* (*ge-, h*) (grow) round; '**2fahrt** *f* drive round (*town, etc.*); *s. Rundreise*; '**2flug** *m* circuit (*über* of); '**2frage** *f* inquiry, poll.

'**Rundfunk** *m* broadcast(ing); broadcasting service; broadcasting company; radio, wireless; *im ~* over the wireless, on the radio *or* air; '**~anstalt** *f* broadcasting company; '**~ansager** *m* (radio) announcer; '**~gerät** *n* radio *or* wireless set; '**~gesellschaft** *f* broadcasting company; '**~hörer** *m* listener(-in); ~ *pl. a.* (radio) audience; '**~programm** *n* broadcast *or* radio program(me); '**~sender** *m* broadcast transmitter; broadcasting *or* radio station; '**~sendung** *f* broadcast; '**~sprecher** *m* broadcaster, broadcast speaker, (radio) announcer; '**~station** *f* broadcasting *or* radio station; '**~übertragung** *f* radio transmission, broadcast(ing); broadcast (*of programme*).

'**Rund|gang** *m* tour, round, circuit; '**~gesang** *m* glee, catch; '**2he'raus** *adv.* in plain words, frankly, plainly; '**2he'rum** *adv.* round about, all (a)round; '**2lich** *adj.* round(ish); rotund, plump; '**~reise** *f* circular tour *or* trip, sight-seeing trip, *Am. a.* round trip; '**~schau** *f* panorama;

newspaper: review; '~schreiben *n* circular (letter); '~weg *adv.* flatly, plainly.

Runz|el ['runtsəl] *f* (-/-n) wrinkle; '2elig *adj.* wrinkled; '2eln *v/t.* (ge-, h) wrinkle; *die Stirn* ~ knit one's brows, frown; '2lig *adj.* wrinkled.

Rüpel ['ry:pəl] *m* (-s/-) boor, lout; '2haft *adj.* coarse, boorish, rude.

rupfen ['rupfən] *v/t.* (ge-, h) pull up *or* out, pick; pluck (*fowl*) (*a. fig.*).

ruppig *adj.* ['rupiç] ragged, shabby; *fig.* rude.

Rüsche ['ry:ʃə] *f* (-/-n) ruffle, frill.

Ruß [ru:s] *m* (-es/*no pl.*) soot.

Russe ['rusə] *m* (-n/-n) Russian.

Rüssel ['rysəl] *m* (-s/-) trunk (*of elefant*); snout (*of pig*).

'ruß|en *v/i.* (ge-, h) smoke; '~ig *adj.* sooty.

'russisch *adj.* Russian.

rüsten ['rystən] (ge-, h) 1. *v/t. and v/refl.* prepare, get ready (*zu* for); 2. *esp.* ✗ *v/i.* arm.

rüstig *adj.* ['rystiç] vigorous, strong; '2keit *f* (-/*no pl.*) vigo(u)r.

'Rüstung *f* (-/-en) preparations *pl.*; ✗ arming, armament; armo(u)r; ~sindustrie ['rystuŋs?-] *f* armament industry.

'Rüstzeug *n* (set of) tools *pl.*, implements *pl.*; *fig.* equipment.

Rute ['ru:tə] *f* (-/-n) rod; switch; *fox's tail*: brush.

Rutsch [rutʃ] *m* (-es/-e) (land)slide; F short trip; '~bahn *f*, '~e *f* (-/-n) slide, chute; '2en *v/i.* (ge-, sein) glide, slide; slip; *vehicle*: skid; '2ig *adj.* slippery.

rütteln ['rytəln] (ge-, h) 1. *v/t.* shake, jog; jolt; 2. *v/i.* shake, jog; *car*: jolt; *an der Tür* ~ rattle at the door; *daran ist nicht zu* ~ that's a fact.

S

Saal [za:l] *m* (-[e]s/*Säle*) hall.

Saat [za:t] *f* (-/-en) sowing; standing *or* growing crops *pl.*; seed (*a. fig.*); '~feld *n* cornfield; '~gut *n* (-[e]s/*no pl.*) seeds *pl.*; '~kartoffel *f* seed-potato.

Sabbat ['zabat] *m* (-s/-e) Sabbath.

sabbern F ['zabərn] *v/i.* (ge-, h) slaver, slobber; *Am. a.* drool; twaddle, *Am. sl. a.* drool.

Säbel ['zɛ:bəl] *m* (-s/-) sab|re, *Am.* -er; *mit dem* ~ *rasseln pol.* rattle the sabre; '~beine *n/pl.* bandy legs *pl.*; '2beinig *adj.* bandy-legged; '~hieb *m* sabre-cut; '2n F *fig. v/t.* (ge-, h) hack.

Sabot|age [zabo'ta:ʒə] *f* (-/-n) sabotage; ~eur [~ø:r] *m* (-s/-e) saboteur; 2ieren *v/t.* (*no* -ge-, h) sabotage.

Sach|bearbeiter ['zax-] *m* (-s/-) official in charge; *social work*: case worker; '~beschädigung *f* damage to property; '2dienlich *adj.* relevant, pertinent; useful, helpful.

'Sache *f* (-/-n) thing; affair, matter, concern; ✗✗ case; point; issue; ~n *pl.* things *pl.*; *beschlossene* ~ foregone conclusion; *e-e* ~ *für sich a matter apart*; (*nicht*) *zur* ~ *gehörig* (ir)relevant, *pred. a.* to (off) the point; *bei der* ~ *bleiben* stick to the point; *gemeinsame* ~ *machen mit* make common cause with.

'sach|gemäß *adj.* appropriate, proper; '2kenntnis *f* expert knowledge; '~kundig *adj. s.* sachverständig; '2lage *f* state of affairs, situation; '~lich 1. *adj.* relevant,

pertinent, *pred. a.* to the point; matter-of-fact, business-like; unbias(s)ed; objective; 2. *adv.*: ~ *einwandfrei od. richtig* factually correct.

sächlich *gr. adj.* ['zɛçliç] neuter.

'Sachlichkeit *f* (-/*no pl.*) objectivity; impartiality; matter-of-factness.

'Sach|register *n* (subject) index; '~schaden *m* damage to property.

Sachse ['zaksə] *m* (-n/-n) Saxon.

sächsisch *adj.* ['zɛksiʃ] Saxon.

sacht *adj.* [zaxt] soft, gentle; slow.

Sach|verhalt ['zaxferhalt] *m* (-[e]s/-e) facts *pl.* (of the case); '2verständig *adj.* expert; '~verständige *m* (-n/-n) expert, authority; ✗✗ expert witness; '~wert *m* real value.

Sack [zak] *m* (-[e]s/=e) sack; bag; *mit* ~ *und Pack* with bag and baggage; '~gasse *f* blind alley, cul-de-sac, impasse (*a. fig.*), *Am. a.* dead end (*a. fig.*); *fig.* deadlock; '~leinwand *f* sackcloth.

Sadis|mus [za'dismus] *m* (-/*no pl.*) sadism; ~t *m* (-en/-en) sadist; 2tisch *adj.* sadistic.

säen ['zɛ:ən] *v/t. and v/i.* (ge-, h) sow (*a. fig.*).

Saffian ['zafia:n] *m* (-s/*no pl.*) morocco.

Saft [zaft] *m* (-[e]s/=e) juice (*of vegetables or fruits*); sap (*of plants*) (*a. fig.*); '2ig *adj. fruits, etc.*: juicy; *meadow, etc.*: lush; *plants*: sappy (*a. fig.*); *joke, etc.*: spicy, coarse; '2los *adj.* juiceless; sapless (*a. fig.*).

Sage ['za:gə] *f* (-/-n) legend, myth; *die* ~ *geht* the story goes.

Säge ['zɛːgə] *f* (-/-n) saw; '**blatt** *n* saw-blade; '**bock** *m* saw-horse, *Am. a.* sawbuck; '**fisch** *ichth. m* sawfish; '**mehl** *n* sawdust.

sagen ['zaːgən] (ge-, *h*) **1.** *v/t.* say; *j-m et.* ~ tell s.o. s.th., say s.th. to s.o.; *j-m* ~ *lassen, daß* send s.o. word that; *er läßt sich nichts* ~ he will not listen to reason; *das hat nichts zu* ~ that doesn't matter; *j-m gute Nacht* ~ bid s.o. good night; **2.** *v/i.* say; *es ist nicht zu* ~ it is incredible *or* fantastic; *wenn ich so* ~ *darf* if I may express myself in these terms; *sage und schreibe* believe it or not; no less than, as much as.

'sägen *v/t. and v/i.* (ge-, *h*) saw.

'sagenhaft *adj.* legendary, mythical; *F fig.* fabulous, incredible.

Säge|späne ['zɛːgəʃpɛːnə] *m/pl.* sawdust; '**werk** *n* sawmill.

sah [zaː] *pret. of sehen.*

Sahne ['zaːnə] *f* (-/*no pl.*) cream.

Saison [zɛ'zõ] *f* (-/-s) season; ℈**bedingt** *adj.* seasonal.

Saite ['zaɪtə] *f* (-/-n) string, chord (*a. fig.*); '**ninstrument** ['zaɪtən℈-] *n* stringed instrument.

Sakko ['zako] *m, n* (-s/-s) lounge coat; '**anzug** *m* lounge suit.

Sakristei [zakrɪs'taɪ] *f* (-/-en) sacristy, vestry.

Salat [za'laːt] *m* (-[e]s/-e) salad; ℈ lettuce.

Salb|e ['zalbə] *f* (-/-n) ointment; ℈**en** *v/t.* (ge-, *h*) rub with ointment; anoint; '**ung** *f* (-/-en) anointing, unction (*a. fig.*); ℈**ungsvoll** *fig. adj.* unctuous.

saldieren ✝ [zal'diːrən] *v/t.* (*no* -ge-, *h*) balance, settle.

Saldo ✝ ['zaldo] *m* (-s/*Salden, Saldos, Saldi*) balance; *den* ~ *ziehen* strike the balance; '**vortrag** ✝ *m* balance carried down.

Saline [za'liːnə] *f* (-/-n) salt-pit, salt-works.

Salmiak ℞ [zal'mjak] *m, n* (-s/*no pl.*) sal-ammoniac, ammonium chloride; '**geist** *m* (-es/*no pl.*) liquid ammonia.

Salon [za'lõː] *m* (-s/-s) drawing-room, *Am. a.* parlor; ⚓ saloon; ℈**fähig** *adj.* presentable; '**löwe** *fig. m* lady's man, carpet-knight; '**wagen** ☒ *m* saloon-car, saloon carriage, *Am.* parlor car.

Salpeter ℞ [zal'peːtər] *m* (-s/*no pl.*) saltpet|re *Am.* -er; nit|re, *Am.* -er.

Salto ['zalto] *m* (-s, -s, *Salti*) somersault; ~ *mortale* break-neck leap; *e-n* ~ *schlagen* turn a somersault.

Salut [za'luːt] *m* (-[e]s/-e) salute; ~ *schießen* fire a salute; ℈**ieren** [~u'tiːrən] *v/i.* (*no* -ge-, *h*) (stand at the) salute.

Salve ['zalvə] *f* (-/-n) volley; ⚓ broadside; salute.

Salz [zalts] *n* (-es/-e) salt; '**bergwerk** *n* salt-mine; '℈**en** *v/t.* (*irr.,*] ge-, *h*) salt; '**faß** *n*, '**fäßchen** ['~fɛsçən] *n* (-s/-) salt-cellar; '**gurke** *f* pickled cucumber; '℈**haltig** *adj.* saline, saliferous; '℈**hering** *m* pickled herring; '℈**ig** *adj.* salt(y); *s. salzhaltig*; '**säure** ℞ *f* hydrochloric *or* muriatic acid; '**wasser** *n* (-s/⸗) salt water, brine; '**werk** *n* salt-works, saltern.

Same ['zaːmə] *m* (-ns/-n), '**n** *m* (-s/-) ♣ seed (*a. fig.*); *biol.* sperm, semen; '**nkorn** ♣ *n* grain of seed.

Sammel|büchse ['zaməl-] *f* collecting-box; '**lager** *n* collecting point; *refugees, etc.*: assembly camp; '℈**n** (ge-, *h*) **1.** *v/t.* gather; collect (*stamps, etc.*); *sich* ~ gather; *fig.*: concentrate; compose o.s.; **2.** *v/i.* collect money (*für for*) '**platz** *m* meeting-place, place of appointment; ⚔, ⚓ rendezvous.

Sammler ['zamlər] *m* (-s/-) collector; '**ung** *f* **1.** (-/-en) collection; **2.** *fig.* (-/*no pl.*) composure; concentration.

Samstag ['zams-] *m* Saturday.

samt[1] [zamt] **1.** *adv.:* ~ *und sonders* one and all; **2.** *prp.* (*dat.*) together *or* along with.

Samt[2] [~] *m* (-[e]s/-e) velvet.

sämtlich ['zɛmtlɪç] **1.** *adj.* all (together); complete; **2.** *adv.* all (together *or* of them).

Sanatorium [zana'toːrjum] *n* (-s/*Sanatorien*) sanatorium, *Am. a.* sanitarium.

Sand [zant] *m* (-[e]s/-e) sand; *j-m* ~ *in die Augen streuen* throw dust into s.o.'s eyes; *im* ~*e verlaufen* end in smoke, come to nothing.

Sandale [zan'daːlə] *f* (-/-n) sandal.

'Sand|bahn *f sports:* dirt-track; '**bank** *f* sandbank; '**boden** *m* sandy soil; '**grube** *f* sand-pit; ℈**ig** *adj.* ['~dɪç] sandy; '**korn** *n* grain of sand; '**mann** *fig. m* (-[e]s/*no pl.*) sandman, dustman; '**papier** *n* sandpaper; '**sack** *m* sand-bag; '**stein** *m* sandstone.

sandte ['zantə] *pret. of senden.*

'Sand|torte *f* Madeira cake; '**uhr** *f* sand-glass; '**wüste** *f* sandy desert.

sanft *adj.* [zanft] soft; gentle, mild; smooth; *slope, death, etc.*: easy; ~*er Zwang* non-violent coercion; *mit* ~*er Stimme* softly, gently; '**mütig** *adj.* ['~myːtɪç] gentle, mild; meek.

sang [zaŋ] *pret. of singen.*

Sänger ['zɛŋər] *m* (-s/-) singer.

Sanguini|ker [zaŋgu'iːnikər] *m* (-s/-) sanguine person; ℈**sch** *adj.* sanguine.

sanier|en [za'niːrən] *v/t.* (*no* -ge-, *h*) improve the sanitary conditions of; *esp.* ✝: reorganize; readjust; ℈**ung** *f* (-/-en) sanitation; *esp.* ✝: reorganization; readjustment.

sanitär adj. [zani'tɛ:r] sanitary.

Sanität|er [zani'tɛ:tər] m (-s/-) ambulance man; ⚔ medical orderly.

sank [zaŋk] pret. of sinken.

Sankt [zaŋkt] Saint, St.

sann [zan] pret. of sinnen.

Sard|elle ichth. [zar'dɛlə] f (-/-n) anchovy; **~ine** ichth. [~'i:nə] f (-/-n) sardine.

Sarg [zark] m (-[e]s/-e) coffin, Am. a. casket; **~deckel** m coffin-lid.

Sarkas|mus [zar'kasmus] m (-/~, Sarkasmen) sarcasm; **2tisch** adj. [~tiʃ] sarcastic.

saß [za:s] pret. of sitzen.

Satan ['za:tan] m (-s/-e) Satan; fig. devil; **2isch** fig. adj. [za'ta:niʃ] satanic.

Satellit ast., pol. [zatɛ'li:t] m (-en/-en) satellite; **~enstaat** pol. m satellite state.

Satin [sa'tɛ̃:] m (-s/-s) satin; sateen.

Satir|e [za'ti:rə] f (-/-n) satire; **~iker** [~ikər] m (-s/-) satirist; **2isch** adj. satiric(al).

satt adj. [zat] satisfied, satiated, full; colour: deep, rich; sich ~ essen eat one's fill; ich bin ~ I have had enough; F et. ~ haben be tired or sick of s.th., sl. be fed up with s.th.

Sattel ['zatəl] m (-s/=) saddle; **~gurt** m girth; **2n** v/t. (ge-, h) saddle.

'Sattheit f (-/no pl.) satiety, fullness; richness, intensity (of colours).

sättig|en ['zɛtigən] (ge-, h) 1. v/t. satisfy, satiate; ?m phys. saturate; 2. v/i. food: be substantial; **2ung** f (-/-en) satiation; ?m fig. saturation.

Sattler ['zatlər] m (-s/-) saddler; **~ei** [~'raɪ] f (-/-en) saddlery.

'sattsam adv. sufficiently.

Satz [zats] m (-es/=e) gr. sentence, clause; phls. maxim; ♃ proposition, theorem; ♪ movement; tennis, etc.: set; typ. setting, composition; sediment, dregs pl., grounds pl.; rate (of prices, etc.); set (of stamps, tools, etc.); leap, bound.

'Satzung f (-/-en) statute, by-law; **2sgemäß** adj. statutory.

'Satzzeichen gr. n punctuation mark.

Sau [zaʊ] f 1. (-/=e) zo. sow; fig. contp. filthy swine; 2. hunt. (-/-en) wild sow.

sauber adj. ['zaʊbər] clean; neat (a. fig.), tidy; attitude: decent; iro. fine, nice; **2keit** f (-/no pl.) clean(li)ness; tidiness, neatness, decency (of attitude).

säuber|n ['zɔybərn] v/t. (ge-, h) clean(se); tidy, clean up (room, etc.); clear (von of); purge (of, from) (a. fig., pol.); **2ungsaktion** pol. f purge.

sauer ['zaʊər] 1. adj. sour (a. fig.), acid (a. ?m); cucumber: pickled; task, etc.: hard, painful; fig. morose,

surly; 2. adv.: ~ reagieren auf et. take s.th. in bad part.

säuer|lich adj. ['zɔyərliç] sourish, acidulous; **~n** v/t. (ge-, h) (make) sour, acidify (a. ?m); leaven (dough).

'Sauer|stoff ?m m (-[e]s/no pl.) oxygen; **~teig** m leaven.

saufen ['zaʊfən] v/t. and v/i. (irr., ge-, h) animals: drink; F p. sl. soak, lush.

Säufer F ['zɔyfər] m (-s/-) sot, sl. soak.

saugen ['zaʊgən] ([irr.,] ge-, h) 1. v/i. suck (an et. s.th.); 2. v/t. suck.

säuge|n ['zɔygən] v/t. (ge-, h) suckle, nurse; **2tier** n mammal.

Säugling ['zɔyklin] m (-s/-e) baby, suckling; **~sheim** n baby-farm, baby-nursery.

'Saug|papier n absorbent paper; **~pumpe** f suction-pump; **~wirkung** f suction-effect.

Säule ['zɔylə] f (-/-n) △, anat. column (a. of smoke, mercury, etc.); pillar, support (both a. fig.); **~ngang** m colonnade; **~nhalle** f pillared hall; portico.

Saum [zaʊm] m (-[e]s/=e) seam; hem; border, edge.

säum|en ['zɔymən] v/t. (ge-, h) hem; border, edge; die Straßen ~ line the streets; **~ig** adj. payer: dilatory.

'Saum|pfad m mule-track; **~tier** n sumpter-mule.

Säure ['zɔyrə] f (-/-n) sourness; acidity (a. ♁ of stomach); ?m acid.

Saure'gurkenzeit f silly or slack season.

säuseln ['zɔyzəln] (ge-, h) 1. v/i. leaves, wind: rustle, whisper; 2. v/t. p. say airily, purr.

sausen ['zaʊzən] v/i. (ge-) 1. (sein) F rush, dash; bullet, etc.: whiz(z), whistle; 2. (h) wind: whistle, sough.

'Saustall m pigsty; F fig. a. horrid mess.

Saxophon ♪ [zakso'fo:n] n (-s/-e) saxophone.

Schab|e ['ʃa:bə] f (-/-n) zo. cockroach; ⊕ s. Schabeisen; **~efleisch** n scraped meat; **~eisen** ⊕ n scraper, shaving-tool; **~emesser** ⊕ n scraping-knife; **2en** v/t. (ge-, h) scrape (a. ⊕), grate, rasp; scratch; **~er** ⊕ m (-s/-) scraper.

Schabernack ['ʃa:bərnak] m (-[e]s/-e) practical joke, hoax, prank.

schäbig adj. ['ʃɛ:biç] shabby (a. fig.), F seedy, Am. F a. dowdy, tacky; fig. mean.

Schablone [ʃa'blo:nə] f (-/-n) model, pattern; stencil; fig.: routine; cliché; **2nhaft** adj., **2nmäßig** adj. according to pattern; fig.: mechanical; attr. a. routine.

Schach [ʃax] n (-s/-s) chess; ~! check!; ~ und matt! checkmate!;

in or im ~ *halten* keep *s.o.* in check;
'~**brett** *n* chessboard.

schachern ['ʃaxərn] *v/i.* (ge-, h)
haggle (*um* about, over), chaffer
(about, over), *Am. a.* dicker; ~ *mit*
barter (away).

'**Schach|feld** *n* square; '~**figur** *f*
chess-man, piece; *fig.* pawn; '~-
'**matt** *adj.* (check)mated; *fig.* tired
out, worn out; '~**spiel** *n* game of
chess. [*a.* pit.]

Schacht [ʃaxt] *m* (-[e]s/ᵘe) shaft; 𝄞)
Schachtel ['ʃaxtəl] *f* (-/-n) box; F
alte ~ old frump.

'**Schachzug** *m* move (at chess); *ge-
schickter* ~ clever move (*a. fig.*).

schade *pred. adj.* ['ʃaːdə]: *es ist* ~
it is a pity; *wie* ~! what a pity!; *zu*
~ *für* too good for.

Schädel ['ʃɛːdəl] *m* (-s/-) skull,
cranium; '~**bruch** 𝄞 *m* fracture of
the skull.

schaden ['ʃaːdən] **1.** *v/i.* (ge-, h)
damage, injure, harm, hurt (*j-m*
s.o.); be detrimental (to s.o.); *das
schadet nichts* it does not matter,
never mind; **2.** ⚥ *m* (-s/ᵘ) damage
(*an dat.* to); injury, harm; infirmity; hurt; loss; **Qersatz** *m* indemnification, compensation; damages
pl.; ~ *verlangen* claim damages; ~
leisten pay damages; *auf* ~ (*ver*)*klagen* ⚖ sue for damages; '**Qfreude** *f*
malicious enjoyment of others'
misfortunes, schadenfreude; '~**froh**
adj. rejoicing over others' misfortunes.

schadhaft *adj.* ['ʃaːthaft] damaged;
defective, faulty; *building, etc.*:
dilapidated; *pipe, etc.*: leaking;
tooth, etc.: decayed.

schädig|en ['ʃɛːdigən] *v/t.* (ge-, h)
damage, impair; wrong, harm;
'**Qung** *f* (-/-en) damage (*gen.* to),
impairment (of); prejudice (to).

schädli|ch ['ʃɛːtliç] harmful,
injurious; noxious; detrimental,
prejudicial; '**Qng** [´~ŋ] *m* (-s/-e) *zo.*
pest; ♀ destructive weed; noxious
person; ~*e pl.* ⚥ *a.* vermin.

schadlos *adj.* ['ʃaːtloːs]: *sich* ~ *halten* recoup *or* indemnify o.s. (*für* for).

Schaf [ʃaːf] *n* (-[e]s/-e) *zo.* sheep;
fig. simpleton; '~**bock** *zo. m* ram.
Schäfer ['ʃɛːfər] *m* (-s/-) shepherd;
'~**hund** *m* sheep-dog; Alsatian
(wolf-hound).

Schaffell ['ʃaːfᵉ-] *n* sheepskin.

schaffen ['ʃafən] **1.** *v/t.* (irr., ge-, h)
create, produce; **2.** *v/t.* (ge-, h)
convey, carry, move; take, bring;
cope with, manage; **3.** *v/i.* (ge-, h)
be busy, work.

Schaffner ['ʃafnər] *m* (-s/-) 🚋
guard, *Am.* conductor; *tram, bus*:
conductor.

'**Schafhirt** *m* shepherd.

Schafott [ʃa'fɔt] *n* (-[e]s/-e) scaffold.

'**Schaf|pelz** *m* sheepskin coat;
'~**stall** *m* fold.

Schaft [ʃaft] *m* (-[e]s/ᵘe) shaft (*of
lance, column, etc.*); stick (*of flag*);
stock (*of rifle*); shank (*of tool, key,
etc.*); leg (*of boot*); '~**stiefel** *m*
high boot; ~ *pl. a.* Wellingtons *pl.*

'**Schaf|wolle** *f* sheep's wool;
'~**zucht** *f* sheep-breeding, sheep-
farming.

schäkern ['ʃɛːkərn] *v/i.* (ge-, h) jest,
joke; flirt.

schal¹ *adj.* [ʃaːl] insipid; stale; *fig.
a.* flat.

Schal² [~] *m* (-s/-e, -s) scarf, muffler; comforter.

Schale ['ʃaːlə] *f* (-/-n) bowl; ⊕
scale (*of scales*); shell (*of eggs, nuts,
etc.*); peel, skin (*of fruit*); shell, crust
(*of tortoise*); paring, peeling; F:
sich in ~ *werfen* doll o.s. up.

schälen ['ʃɛːlən] *v/t.* (ge-, h) remove
the peel *or* skin from; pare, peel
(*fruit, potatoes, etc.*); *sich* ~ *skin*:
peel *or* come off.

Schalk [ʃalk] *m* (-[e]s/-e, ᵘe) rogue,
wag; '**Qhaft** *adj.* roguish, waggish.

Schall [ʃal] *m* (-[e]s/-e, ᵘe) sound;
'~**dämpfer** *m* sound absorber;
mot. silencer, *Am.* muffler; silencer
(*on fire-arms*); '**Qdicht** *adj.* sound-
proof; '**Qen** *v/i.* ([irr.,] ge-, h)
sound; ring, peal; '**Qend** *adj.*: ~*es
Gelächter* roars *pl. or* a peal of
laughter; '~**mauer** *f* sound barrier;
'~**platte** *f* record, disc, disk;
'~**welle** *f* sound-wave.

schalt [ʃalt] *pret. of* schelten.

'**Schaltbrett** ⚡ *n* switchboard.

schalten ['ʃaltən] (ge-, h) **1.** *v/i.* ⚡
switch; *mot.* change *or* shift gears;
direct, rule; **2.** *v/t.* ⚡ actuate,
operate, control.

'**Schalter** *m* (-s/-) 🚋, *theatre, etc.*:
booking-office; ✉, *bank, etc.*:
counter; ⚡ switch; ⊕, *mot.* con-
troller.

'**Schalt|hebel** *m mot.* gear lever;
⊕, ⚡ control lever; ⚡ switch
lever; '~**jahr** *n* leap-year; '~**tafel**
⚡ *f* switchboard, control panel;
'~**tag** *m* intercalary day.

Scham [ʃaːm] *f* (-/no *pl.*) shame;
bashfulness, modesty; *anat.* privy
parts *pl.*, genitals *pl.*

schämen ['ʃɛːmən] *v/refl.* (ge-, h)
be *or* feel ashamed (*gen. or wegen* of).

'**Scham|gefühl** *n* sense of shame;
'**Qhaft** *adj.* bashful, modest; '~**haf-
tigkeit** *f* (-/no *pl.*) bashfulness,
modesty; '**Qlos** *adj.* shameless; impudent; '~**losigkeit** *f* (-/-en) shame-
lessness; impudence; '**Qrot** *adj.*
blushing; ~ *werden* blush; '~**röte** *f*
blush; '~**teile** *anat. m/pl.* privy
parts *pl.*, genitals *pl.*

Schande ['ʃandə] *f* (-/⚓ -n) shame,
disgrace.

schänden ['ʃɛndən] *v/t.* (ge-, h)

dishono(u)r, disgrace; desecrate, profane; rape, violate; disfigure.

Schandfleck *fig.* ['ʃant-] *m* blot, stain; eyesore.

schändlich *adj.* ['ʃentliç] shameful, disgraceful, infamous; **'2keit** *f* (-/-en) infamy.

'Schandtat *f* infamous act(ion).

'Schändung *f* (-/-en) dishono(u)ring; profanation, desecration; rape, violation; disfigurement.

Schanze ['ʃantsə] *f* (-/-n) ⚔ entrenchment; ⚓ quarter-deck; *sports*: ski-jump; **'2n** *v/i.* (ge-, h) throw up entrenchments, entrench.

Schar [ʃaːr] *f* (-/-en) troop, band; *geese, etc.*: flock; ⚘ ploughshare, *Am.* plowshare; **'2en** *v/t.* (ge-, h) assemble, collect; *sich ~ a.* flock (*um round*).

scharf [ʃarf] **1.** *adj.* sharp; *edge*: keen; *voice, sound*: piercing, shrill; *smell, taste*: pungent; *pepper, etc.*: hot; *sight, hearing, intelligence, etc.*: keen; *answer, etc.*: cutting; ⚔ ammunition: live; *sein auf (acc.)* be very keen on; **2.** *adv.*: *~ ansehen* look sharply at; *~ reiten* ride hard; **'2blick** *fig. m* (-[e]s/*no pl.*) clear-sightedness.

Schärfe ['ʃɛrfə] *f* (-/-n) sharpness; keenness; pungency; **'2n** *v/t.* (ge-, h) put an edge on, sharpen; strengthen (*memory*); sharpen (*sight, hearing, etc.*).

'Scharf|macher *fig. m* (-s/-) firebrand, agitator; **'~richter** *m* executioner; **'~schütze** ⚔ *m* sharpshooter, sniper; **'2sichtig** *adj.* sharp-sighted; *fig.* clear-sighted; **'~sinn** *m* (-[e]s/*no pl.*) sagacity; acumen; **'2sinnig** *adj.* sharpwitted, shrewd; sagacious.

Scharlach ['ʃarlax] *m* **1.** (-s/-e) scarlet; **2.** ⚕ (-s/*no pl.*) scarlet fever; **'2rot** *adj.* scarlet.

Scharlatan ['ʃarlatan] *m* (-s/-e) charlatan, quack (doctor); mountebank.

Scharmützel [ʃar'mytsəl] *n* (-s/-) skirmish.

Scharnier ⊕ [ʃar'niːr] *n* (-s/-e) hinge, joint.

Schärpe ['ʃɛrpə] *f* (-/-n) sash.

scharren ['ʃarən] (ge-, h) **1.** *v/i.* scrape (*mit den Füßen* one's feet); *hen, etc.*: scratch; *horse*: paw; **2.** *v/t. horse*: paw (*ground*).

Schart|e ['ʃartə] *f* (-/-n) notch, nick; *mountains*: gap, *Am.* notch; *e-e ~ auswetzen* repair a fault; wipe out a disgrace; **'2ig** *adj.* jagged, notchy.

Schatten ['ʃatən] *m* (-s/-) shadow (*a. fig.*); shade (*a. paint.*); **'~bild** *n* silhouette; **'2haft** *adj.* shadowy; **'~kabinett** *pol. n* shadow cabinet; **'~riß** *m* silhouette; **'~seite** *f* shady side; *fig.* seamy side.

schattier|en [ʃa'tiːrən] *v/t.* (*no -ge-, h*) shade, tint; **2ung** *f* (-/-en) shading; shade (*a. fig.*), tint.

'schattig *adj.* shady.

Schatz [ʃats] *m* (-es/⁻e) treasure; *fig.* sweetheart, darling; **'~amt** ✝ *n* Exchequer, *Am.* Treasury (Department); **'~anweisung** ✝ *f* Treasury Bond, *Am. a.* Treasury Note.

schätzen ['ʃetsən] *v/t.* (ge-, h) estimate; value (*auf acc.* at); price (at); rate; appreciate; esteem; *sich glücklich ~ zu inf.* be delighted to *inf.*; **'~swert** *adj.* estimable.

'Schatz|kammer *f* treasury; **'~meister** *m* treasurer.

'Schätzung *f* **1.** (-/-en) estimate, valuation; rating; **2.** (-/*no pl.*) appreciation, estimation; esteem.

'Schatzwechsel ✝ *m* Treasury Bill.

Schau [ʃau] *f* (-/-en) inspection; show, exhibition; *zur ~ stellen* exhibit, display.

Schauder ['ʃaudər] *m* (-s/-) shudder(ing), shiver, tremor; *fig.* horror, terror; **'2haft** *adj.* horrible, dreadful; F *fig. a.* awful; **'2n** *v/i.* (ge-, h) shudder, shiver (*both: vor dat.* at).

schauen ['ʃauən] *v/i.* (ge-, h) look (*auf acc.* at).

Schauer ['ʃauər] *m* (-s/-) rain, *etc.*: shower (*a. fig.*); shudder(ing), shiver; attack, fit; thrill; **'2lich** *adj.* dreadful, horrible; **'2n** *v/i.* (ge-, h) *s. schaudern*; **'~roman** *m* penny dreadful, thriller.

Schaufel ['ʃaufəl] *f* (-/-n) shovel; dust-pan; **'2n** *v/t. and v/i.* (ge-, h) shovel.

'Schaufenster *n* shop window, *Am. a.* show-window; **'~bummel** *m*: *e-n ~ machen* go window-shopping; **'~dekoration** *f* window-dressing; **'~einbruch** *m* smash-and-grab raid.

Schaukel ['ʃaukəl] *f* (-/-n) swing; **'2n** (ge-, h) **1.** *v/i.* swing; *ship, etc.*: rock; **2.** *v/t.* rock (*baby, etc.*); **'~pferd** *n* rocking-horse; **'~stuhl** *m* rocking-chair, *Am. a.* rocker.

Schaum [ʃaum] *m* (-[e]s/⁻e) foam; *beer, etc.*: froth, head; *soap*: lather; **'~bad** *n* bubble bath.

schäumen ['ʃɔymən] *v/i.* (ge-, h) foam, froth; lather; *wine, etc.*: sparkle.

'Schaum|gummi *n, m* foam rubber; **'2ig** *adj.* foamy, frothy; **'~wein** *m* sparkling wine.

'Schau|platz *m* scene (of action), *theat.*|re, *Am.* -er; **'~prozeß** ✝⁂ *m* show trial.

schaurig *adj.* ['ʃauriç] horrible, horrid.

'Schau|spiel *n* spectacle; *thea.* play; **'~spieler** *m* actor, player; **'~spielhaus** *n* playhouse, *theat.*|re, *Am.* -er; **'~spielkunst** *f* (-/*no pl.*) dra-

matic art, *the* drama; '**‿steller** *m*
(-s/-) showman.

Scheck ✝ [ʃɛk] *m* (-s/-s) cheque, *Am.*
check; '**‿buch** *n*, '**‿heft** *n* cheque-
book, *Am.* checkbook.

'**scheckig** *adj.* spotted; *horse:* piebald.

scheel [ʃeːl] **1.** *adj.* squint-eyed,
cross-eyed; *fig.* jealous, envious;
2. *adv.:* j~n ‿ ansehen look askance
at s.o.

Scheffel ['ʃɛfəl] *m* (-s/-) bushel; '**‿n**
v/t. (ge-, h) amass (*money, etc.*).

Scheibe ['ʃaɪbə] *f* (-/-n) disk, disc
(*a. of sun, moon*); *esp. ast.* orb; slice
(*of bread, etc.*); pane (*of window*);
shooting: target; '**‿nhonig** *m* honey
in combs; '**‿nwischer** *mot.* *m* (-s/-)
wind-screen wiper, *Am.* windshield
wiper.

Scheide ['ʃaɪdə] *f* (-/-n) sword, etc.:
sheath, scabbard; border, bound-
ary; '**‿münze** *f* small coin; '**‿n**
(*irr.*, ge-) **1.** *v/t.* (h) separate; 🔬
analyse; ⚖ divorce; *sich ‿ lassen
von* ⚖ divorce (*one's husband or
wife*); **2.** *v/i.* (sein) depart; part (*von*
with); *aus dem Dienst ‿* retire from
service; *aus dem Leben ‿* depart
from this life; '**‿wand** *f* partition;
'**‿weg** *fig. m* cross-roads *sg.*

'**Scheidung** *f* (-/-en) separation; ⚖
divorce; '**‿sgrund** ⚖ *m* ground for
divorce; '**‿sklage** ⚖ *f* divorce-suit;
die ‿ einreichen file a petition for
divorce.

Schein [ʃaɪn] *m* **1.** (-[e]s/*no pl.*)
shine; *sun, lamp, etc.:* light; *fire:*
blaze; *fig.* appearance; **2.** (-[e]s/-e)
certificate; receipt; bill; (bank-)
note; '**‿bar** *adj.* seeming, apparent;
'**‿en** *v/i.* (*irr.*, ge-, h) shine; *fig.*
seem, appear, look; '**‿grund** *m*
pretext, preten|ce, *Am.* -se; '**‿hei-
lig** *adj.* sanctimonious, hypocritical;
'**‿tod** *m* suspended animation;
'**‿tot** *adj.* in a state of suspended
animation; '**‿werfer** *m* (-s/-)
reflector, projector; ⚔, ⚓, 🚂
searchlight; *mot.* headlight; *thea.*
spotlight.

Scheit [ʃaɪt] *n* (-[e]s/-e) log, billet.

Scheitel ['ʃaɪtəl] *m* (-s/-) crown *or*
top of the head; *hair:* parting; summit, peak; *esp.* 📐 vertex; '**‿n** *v/t.*
(ge-, h) part (*hair*).

Scheiterhaufen ['ʃaɪtər-] *m* (funeral) pile; stake.

'**scheitern** *v/i.* (ge-, sein) ⚓ run
aground, be wrecked; *fig.* fail, mis-
carry.   [box on the ear.]

Schelle ['ʃɛlə] *f* (-/-n) (little) bell;]

'**Schellfisch** *ichth. m* haddock.

Schelm [ʃɛlm] *m* (-[e]s/-e) rogue;
'**‿enstreich** *m* roguish trick; '**‿isch**
adj. roguish, arch.

Schelte ['ʃɛltə] *f* (-/-n) scolding;
'**‿n** (*irr.*, ge-, h) **1.** *v/t.* scold, rebuke;
2. *v/i.* scold.

Schema ['ʃeːma] *n* (-s/-s, -ta, *Schemen*) scheme; model, pattern; arrangement; ⚖**tisch** *adj.* [ʃeˈmaːtiʃ]
schematic.

Schemel ['ʃeːməl] *m* (-s/-) stool.

Schemen ['ʃeːmən] *m* (-s/-) phantom, shadow; '**⚖haft** *adj.* shadowy.

Schenke ['ʃɛnkə] *f* (-/-n) public
house, F pub; tavern, inn.

Schenkel ['ʃɛŋkəl] *m* (-s/-) *anat.*
thigh; *anat.* shank; *triangle, etc.*:
leg; 📐 *angle:* side.

schenken ['ʃɛŋkən] *v/t.* (ge-, h)
give; remit (*penalty, etc.*); j-m et. ‿
give s.o. s.th., present s.o. with
s.th., make s.o. a present of s.th.

'**Schenkung** ⚖ *f* (-/-en) donation;
'**‿surkunde** ⚖ ['ʃɛŋkuŋsˀ-] *f* deed
of gift.

Scherbe ['ʃɛrbə] *f* (-/-n), '**‿n** *m*
(-s/-) (broken) piece, fragment.

Schere ['ʃeːrə] *f* (-/-n) (e-e a pair
of) scissors *pl.*; *zo.* crab, etc.: claw;
'**‿n** *v/t.* **1.** (*irr.*, ge-, h) shear (*a.
sheep*), clip; shave (*beard*); cut
(*hair*); clip, prune (*hedge*); **2.** (ge-,
h): *sich um et. ‿* trouble about s.th.;
'**‿nschleifer** *m* (-s/-) knife-grinder;
'**‿rei** [‿ˈraɪ] *f* (-/-en) trouble, bother.

Scherz [ʃɛrts] *m* (-es/-e) jest, joke;
‿ beiseite joking apart; *im ‿, zum ‿*
in jest *or* joke; *‿ treiben mit* make
fun of; '**‿en** *v/i.* (ge-, h) jest, joke;
'**⚖haft** *adj.* joking, sportive.

scheu [ʃɔʏ] **1.** *adj.* shy, bashful,
timid; *horse:* skittish; *‿ machen*
frighten; **2.** 2 *f* (-/*no pl.*) shyness;
timidity; aversion (*vor dat.* to).

scheuchen ['ʃɔʏçən] *v/t.* (ge-, h)
scare, frighten (away).

'**scheuen** (ge-, h) **1.** *v/i.* shy (*vor dat.*
at), take fright (at); **2.** *v/t.* shun,
avoid; fear; *sich ‿ vor* (*dat.*) shy at,
be afraid of.

Scheuer|lappen ['ʃɔʏər-] *m* scour-
ing-cloth, floor-cloth; '**‿leiste** *f*
skirting-board; '**‿n** (ge-, h) **1.** *v/t.*
scour, scrub; chafe; **2.** *v/i.* chafe.

'**Scheuklappe** *f* blinker, *Am.* a.
blinder.

Scheune ['ʃɔʏnə] *f* (-/-n) barn.

Scheusal ['ʃɔʏzaːl] *n* (-[e]s/-e)
monster.

scheußlich *adj.* ['ʃɔʏslɪç] hideous,
atrocious (F *a. fig.*), abominable (F
a. fig.); '**⚖keit** *f* **1.** (-/*no pl.*) hide-
ousness; **2.** (-/-en) abomination;
atrocity.

Schi [ʃiː] *m* (-s/-er) etc. s. Ski, etc.

Schicht [ʃɪçt] *f* (-/-en) layer; *geol.*
stratum (*a. fig.*); *at work:* shift;
(social) class, rank, walk of life;
'**⚖en** *v/t.* (ge-, h) arrange *or* put in
layers, pile up; classify; '**⚖weise**
adv. in layers; *work:* in shifts.

Schick [ʃɪk] *m* **1.** (-[e]s/*no pl.*) chic,
elegance, style; **2.** 2 *adj.* chic,
stylish, fashionable.

schicken ['ʃɪkən] *v/t.* (ge-, h) send

(nach, zu to); remit (money); nach j-m ~ send for s.o.; sich ~ für become, suit, befit s.o.; sich ~ in put up with, resign o.s. to s.th.

'**schicklich** adj. becoming, proper, seemly; **2keit** f (-/no pl.) propriety, seemliness.

'**Schicksal** n (-[e]s/-e) fate, destiny.

Schiebe|dach mot. ['ʃiːbə-] n sliding roof; '**.fenster** n sash-window; **2n** (irr., ge-, h) 1. v/t. push, shove; shift (blame) (auf acc. on to); F fig. sell on the black market; 2. F fig. v/i. profiteer; '**.r** m (-s/-) bolt (of door); ⊕ slide; fig. profiteer, black marketeer, sl. spiv; '**.tür** f sliding door.

'**Schiebung** fig. f (-/-en) black marketeering, profiteering; put-up job.

schied [ʃiːt] pret. of scheiden.

Schieds|gericht ['ʃiːts-] n court of arbitration, arbitration committee; '**.richter** m arbitrator; tennis, etc.: umpire; football, etc.: referee; **2richterlich** adj. arbitral; '**.spruch** m award, arbitration.

schief [ʃiːf] 1. adj. sloping, slanting; oblique; face, mouth: wry; fig. false, wrong; **.e Ebene** ⚡ inclined plane; 2. adv.: j-n ~ ansehen look askance at s.o.

Schiefer ['ʃiːfər] m (-s/-) slate; splinter; '**.stift** m slate-pencil; '**.tafel** f slate.

'**schiefgehen** v/i. (irr. gehen, sep., -ge-, sein) go wrong or awry.

schielen ['ʃiːlən] v/i. (ge-, h) squint, be cross-eyed; ~ auf (acc.) squint at; leer at.

schien [ʃiːn] pret. of scheinen.

Schienbein ['ʃiːn-] n shin(-bone), tibia.

Schiene ['ʃiːnə] f (-/-n) 🚃, etc.: rail; 🩹 splint; '**2n** 🩹 v/t. (ge-, h) splint.

schießen ['ʃiːsən] (irr., ge-) 1. v/t. (h) shoot; tot ~ shoot dead; ein Tor ~ score (a goal); Salut ~ fire a salute; 2. v/i. (h): auf j-n ~ shoot or fire at; gut ~ be a good shot; 3. v/i. (sein) shoot, dart, rush.

'**Schieß|pulver** n gunpowder; '**.scharte** ✕ f loop-hole, embrasure; '**.scheibe** f target; '**.stand** m shooting-gallery or -range.

Schiff [ʃif] n (-[e]s/-e) ⚓ ship, vessel; ⛪ church: nave.

Schiffahrt ['ʃiffaːrt] f (-/-en) navigation.

'**schiff|bar** adj. navigable; **2bau** m shipbuilding; **2bauer** m (-s/-) shipbuilder; **2bruch** m shipwreck (a. fig.); ~ erleiden be shipwrecked; fig. make or suffer shipwreck; '**.brüchig** adj. shipwrecked; '**2brücke** f pontoon-bridge; '**.er** v/i. (ge-, sein) navigate, sail; '**2er**

m (-s/-) sailor; boatman; navigator; skipper.

'**Schiffs|junge** m cabin-boy; '**.kapitän** m (sea-)captain; '**.ladung** f shipload; cargo; '**.makler** m shipbroker; '**.mannschaft** f crew; '**.raum** m hold; tonnage; '**.werft** f shipyard, engl. ✕ dockyard, Am. a. navy yard.

Schikan|e [ʃiˈkaːnə] f (-/-n) vexation, nasty trick; **2ieren** [**.kaˈniːrən**] v/t. (no -ge-, h) vex, ride.

Schild [ʃilt] 1. ✕ m (-[e]s/-e) shield, buckler; 2. n (-[e]s/-er) shop, etc.: sign(board), facia; name-plate; traffic: signpost; label; cap: peak; '**.drüse** anat. f thyroid gland.

'**Schilder|haus** n sentry-box; '**.maler** m sign-painter; '**2n** v/t. (ge-, h) describe, delineate; '**.ung** f (-/-en) description, delineation.

'**Schild|kröte** zo. f tortoise; turtle; '**.wache** ✕ f sentinel, sentry.

Schilf 🌱 [ʃilf] n (-[e]s/-e) reed; **2ig** adj. reedy; '**.rohr** n reed.

schillern ['ʃilərn] v/i. (ge-, h) show changing colo(u)rs; be iridescent.

Schimmel ['ʃiməl] m 1. zo. (-s/-) white horse; 2. 🌱 (-s/no pl.) mo(u)ld, mildew; '**2ig** adj. mo(u)ldy, musty; '**2n** v/i. (ge-, h) become mo(u)ldy, Am. a. mo(u)ld.

Schimmer ['ʃimər] m (-s/no pl.) glimmer, gleam (a. fig.); '**2n** v/i. (ge-, h) glimmer, gleam.

Schimpanse zo. [ʃimˈpanzə] m (-n/-n) chimpanzee.

Schimpf [ʃimpf] m (-[e]s/-e) insult; disgrace; mit ~ und Schande ignominiously; '**2en** (ge-, h) 1. v/i. rail (über acc., auf acc. at, against); 2. v/t. scold; j-n e-n Lügner ~ call s.o. a liar; '**2lich** adj. disgraceful (für to), ignominious (to); '**.name** m abusive name; '**.wort** n term of abuse; **.e** pl. a. invectives pl.

Schindel ['ʃindəl] f (-/-n) shingle.

schinden ['ʃindən] v/t. (irr., ge-, h) flay, skin (rabbit, etc.); sweat (worker); sich ~ drudge, slave, sweat.

'**Schinder** m (-s/-) knacker; fig. sweater, slave-driver; '**.ei** fig. ['.ˈraɪ] f (-/-en) sweating; drudgery, grind.

Schinken ['ʃinkən] m (-s/-) ham.

Schippe ['ʃipə] f (-/-n) shovel; '**2n** v/t. (ge-, h) shovel.

Schirm [ʃirm] m (-[e]s/-e) umbrella; parasol, sunshade; wind, television, etc.: screen; lamp: shade; cap: peak; visor; '**.futteral** n umbrella-case; '**.herr** m protector; patron; '**.herrschaft** f protectorate; patronage; unter der ~ von event: under the auspices of; '**.mütze** f peaked cap; '**.ständer** m umbrella-stand.

Schlacht ✕ [ʃlaxt] f (-/-en) battle (bei of); '**.bank** f shambles; '**2en** v/t. (ge-, h) slaughter, butcher.

Schlächter ['ʃlɛçtər] m (-s/-) butcher.

'Schlacht|feld ⚔ n battle-field; **'⁓haus** n, **'⁓hof** m slaughter-house, abattoir; **'⁓kreuzer** ⚓ m battle-cruiser; **'⁓plan** m ⚔ plan of action (a. fig.); **'⁓schiff** ⚓ n battleship; **'⁓vieh** n slaughter cattle.

Schlack|e ['ʃlakə] f (-/-n) wood, coal: cinder; metall. dross (a. fig.), slag; geol. scoria; **'2ig** adj. drossy, slaggy; F weather: slushy.

Schlaf [ʃlɑːf] m (-[e]s/no pl.) sleep; im ⁓(e) in one's sleep; e-n leichten (festen) ⁓ haben be a light (sound) sleeper; in tiefem ⁓e liegen be fast asleep; **'⁓abteil** 🚃 n sleeping-compartment; **'⁓anzug** m (ein a pair of) pyjamas pl. or Am. pajamas pl.

Schläfchen ['ʃlɛːfçən] n (-s/-) doze, nap, F forty winks pl.; ein ⁓ machen take a nap, F have one's forty winks.

'Schlafdecke f blanket.

Schläfe ['ʃlɛːfə] f (-/-n) temple.

'schlafen v/i. (irr., ge-, h) sleep; ⁓ gehen, sich ⁓ legen go to bed.

schlaff adj. [ʃlaf] slack, loose; muscles, etc.: flabby, flaccid; plant, etc.: limp; discipline, morals, etc.: lax; **'2heit** f (-/no pl.) slackness; flabbiness; limpness; fig. laxity.

'Schlaf|gelegenheit f sleeping accommodation; **'⁓kammer** f bedroom; **'⁓krankheit** ⚕ f sleeping-sickness; **'⁓lied** n lullaby; **'2los** adj. sleepless; **'⁓losigkeit** f (-/no pl.) sleeplessness; ⚕ insomnia; **'⁓mittel** ⚕ n soporific; **'⁓mütze** f nightcap; fig. sleepyhead.

schläfrig adj. ['ʃlɛːfriç] sleepy, drowsy; **'2keit** f (-/no pl.) sleepiness, drowsiness.

'Schlaf|rock m dressing-gown, Am. a. robe; **'⁓saal** m dormitory; **'⁓sack** m sleeping-bag; **'⁓stelle** f sleeping-place; night's lodging; **'⁓tablette** ⚕ f sleeping-tablet; **'2trunken** adj. very drowsy; **'⁓wagen** 🚃 m sleeping-car(riage), Am. a. sleeper; **'⁓wandler** ['⁓vandlər] m (-s/-) sleep-walker, somnambulist; **'⁓zimmer** n bedroom.

Schlag [ʃlɑːk] m (-[e]s/⁼e) blow (a. fig.); stroke (of clock, piston) (a. tennis, etc.); slap (with palm of hand); punch (with fist); kick (of horse's hoof); ⚡ shock; beat (of heart or pulse); clap (of thunder); warbling (of bird); door (of carriage); ⚕ apoplexy; fig. race, kind, sort; breed (esp. of animals); Schläge bekommen get a beating; ⁓ sechs Uhr on the stroke of six; **'⁓ader** anat. f artery; **'⁓anfall** ⚕ m (stroke of) apoplexy, stroke; **'2artig 1.** adj. sudden, abrupt; **2. adv.** all of a sudden; **'⁓baum** m turnpike.

schlagen ['ʃlɑːgən] (irr., ge-, h) **1.** v/t. strike, beat, hit; punch; slap;

beat, defeat; fell (trees); fight (battle); Alarm ⁓ sound the alarm; zu Boden ⁓ knock down; in den Wind ⁓ cast or fling to the winds; sich ⁓ (have a) fight; sich et. aus dem Kopf or Sinn ⁓ put s.th. out of one's mind, dismiss s.th. from one's mind; **2.** v/i. strike, beat; heart, pulse: beat, throb; clock: strike; bird: warble; das schlägt nicht in mein Fach that is not in my line; um sich ⁓ lay about one; **'⁓d** fig. adj. striking.

Schlager ['ʃlɑːgər] m (-s/-) ♪ song hit; thea. hit, draw, box-office success; book: best seller.

Schläger ['ʃlɛːgər] m (-s/-) rowdy, hooligan; cricket, etc.: batsman; horse: kicker; cricket, etc.: bat; golf: club; tennis, etc.: racket; hockey, etc.: stick; **⁓ei** [⁓'raɪ] f (-/-en) tussle, fight.

'schlag|fertig fig. adj. quick at repartee; **⁓e** Antwort repartee; **'2fertigkeit** fig. f (-/no pl.) quickness at repartee; **'2instrument** ♪ n percussion instrument; **'2kraft** f (-/no pl.) striking power (a. ⚔); **'2loch** n pot-hole; **'2mann** m rowing: stroke; **'2ring** m knuckle-duster, Am. a. brass knuckles pl.; **'2sahne** f whipped cream; **'2schatten** m cast shadow; **'2seite** ⚓ f list; ⁓ haben ⚓ list; F fig. be half-seas-over; **'2uhr** f striking clock; **'2werk** n clock: striking mechanism; **'2wort** n catchword, slogan; **'2zeile** f heading; banner headline, Am. banner; **'2zeug** ♪ n in orchestra: percussion instruments pl.; in band: drums pl., percussion; **'2zeuger** ♪ m (-s/-) in orchestra: percussionist; in band: drummer.

schlaksig adj. ['ʃlɑːkziç] gawky.

Schlamm [ʃlam] m (-[e]s/⚡ -e, ⁼e) mud, mire; **'⁓bad** n mud-bath; **'2ig** adj. muddy, miry.

Schlämmkreide ['ʃlɛm-] f (-/no pl.) whit(en)ing.

Schlamp|e ['ʃlampə] f (-/-n) slut, slattern; **'2ig** adj. slovenly, slipshod.

schlang [ʃlaŋ] pret. of schlingen.

Schlange ['ʃlaŋə] f (-/-n) zo. snake, rhet. serpent (a. fig.); fig.: snake in the grass; queue, Am. a. line; ⁓ stehen queue up (um for), Am. line up (for).

schlängeln ['ʃlɛŋəln] v/refl. (ge-, h): sich ⁓ durch person: worm one's way or o.s. through; path, river, etc.: wind (one's way) through, meander through.

'Schlangenlinie f serpentine line.

schlank adj. [ʃlaŋk] slender, slim; **'2heit** f (-/no pl.) slenderness, slimness; **'2heitskur** f: e-e ⁓ machen slim.

schlapp F adj. [ʃlap] tired, exhausted,

worn out; '2e F f (-/-n) reverse, setback; defeat; '~machen F v/i. (sep., -ge-, h) break down, faint.

schlau adj. [ʃlau] sly, cunning; crafty, clever, F cute.

Schlauch [ʃlaux] m (-[e]s/ᵘe) tube; hose; car, etc.: inner tube; '~boot n rubber dinghy, pneumatic boat.

Schlaufe ['ʃlaufə] f (-/-n) loop.

schlecht [ʃleçt] 1. adj. bad; wicked; poor; temper: ill; quality: inferior; ~e Laune haben be in a bad temper; ~e Aussichten poor prospects; ~e Zeiten hard times; mir ist ~ I feel sick; 2. adv. badly, ill; ~erdings adv. ['~ər'dɪŋs] absolutely, downright, utterly; ~gelaunt adj. ['~gəlaunt] ill-humo(u)red, in a bad temper; '~hin adv. plainly, simply; '2igkeit f (-/-en) badness; wickedness; ~en pl. base acts pl., mean tricks pl.; '~machen v/t. (sep., -ge-, h) run down, backbite; ~weg adv. ['~vɛk] plainly, simply.

schleich|en ['ʃlaiçən] v/i. (irr., ge-, sein) creep (a. fig.); sneak, steal; '2er m (-s/-) creeper; fig. sneak; '2handel m illicit trade; smuggling, contraband; '2händler m smuggler, contrabandist; black marketeer; '2weg m secret path.

Schleier ['ʃlaiər] m (-s/-) veil (a. fig.); mist: a. haze; den ~ nehmen take the veil; '2haft fig. adj. mysterious, inexplicable.

Schleife ['ʃlaifə] f (-/-n) loop (a. ⚛); slip-knot; bow; wreath: streamer; loop, horse-shoe bend.

'**schleif|en** v/t. (irr., ge-, h) whet (knife, etc.); cut (glass, precious stones); polish (a. fig.); 2. v/t. (ge-, h) ♪ slur; drag, trail; ⚔ raze (fortress, etc.); 3. v/i. (ge-, h) drag, trail; '2stein m grindstone, whetstone.

Schleim [ʃlaim] m (-[e]s/-e) slime; ⚕ mucus, phlegm; '~haut anat. f mucous membrane; '2ig adj. slimy (a. fig.); mucous.

schlemm|en ['ʃlemən] v/i. (ge-, h) feast, gormandize; '2er m (-s/-) glutton, gormandizer; 2erei [~'rai] f (-/-en) feasting; gluttony.

schlen|dern ['ʃlendərn] v/i. (ge-, sein) stroll, saunter; 2drian ['~dria:n] m (-[e]s/no pl.) jogtrot; beaten track.

schlenkern ['ʃlɛŋkərn] (ge-, h) 1. v/t. dangle, swing; 2. v/i.: mit den Armen ~ swing one's arms.

Schlepp|dampfer ['ʃlɛp-] m steam tug, tug(boat); '~e f (-/-n) train (of woman's dress); '2en (ge-, h) 1. v/t. carry with difficulty, haul, Am. F a. tote, ⚓, ⚔, mot. tow, haul; ⚓ tug; ✝ tout (customers); sich ~ drag o.s.; 2. v/i. dress: drag, trail; '2end adj. speech: drawling; gait: shuffling; style: heavy; con

versation, etc.: tedious; '~er ⚓ m (-s/-) steam tug, tug(boat); '~tau n tow(ing)-rope; ins ~ nehmen take in or on tow (a. fig.).

Schleuder ['ʃlɔydər] f (-/-n) sling, catapult (a. ⚔), Am. a. slingshot; spin drier; '2n (ge-, h) 1. v/t. fling, hurl (a. fig.); sling, catapult (a. ⚔); spin-dry (washing); 2. mot. v/i. skid; '~preis ✝ m ruinous or giveaway price; zu ~en dirt-cheap.

schleunig adj. ['ʃlɔyniç] prompt, speedy, quick.

Schleuse ['ʃlɔyzə] f (-/-n) lock, sluice; '2n v/t. (ge-, h) lock (boat) (up or down); fig. manœuvre, Am. maneuver.

schlich [ʃliç] pret. of schleichen.

schlicht adj. [ʃliçt] plain, simple; modest, unpretentious; hair: smooth, sleek; '~en v/t. (ge-, h) settle, adjust; settle by arbitration; '2er fig. m (-s/-) mediator; arbitrator.

schlief [ʃli:f] pret. of schlafen.

schließ|en ['ʃli:sən] (irr., ge-, h) 1. v/t. shut, close; shut down (factory, etc.); shut up (shop); contract (marriage); conclude (treaty, speech, etc.); parl. close (debate); in die Arme ~ clasp in one's arms; in sich ~ comprise, include; Freundschaft ~ make friends (mit with); 2. v/i. shut, close; school: break up; aus et. ~ auf (acc.) infer or conclude s.th. from s.th.; '2fach ⚓ n post-office box; '~lich adv. finally, eventually; at last; after all.

Schliff [ʃlif] 1. m (-[e]s/-e) polish (a. fig.); precious stones, glass: cut; 2. ⚓ pret. of schleifen 1.

schlimm [ʃlim] 1. adj. bad; evil, wicked, nasty; serious; F ⚕ bad, sore; ~er worse; am ~sten, das 2ste the worst; es wird immer ~er things are going from bad to worse; 2. adv.: daran sein be badly off; '~sten'falls adv. at (the) worst.

Schling|e ['ʃliŋə] f (-/-n) loop, sling (a. ⚕); noose; coil (of wire or rope); hunt. snare (a. fig.); den Kopf in die ~ stecken put one's head in the noose; '~el m (-s/-) rascal, naughty boy; '2en v/t. (irr., ge-, h) wind, twist; plait; die Arme ~ um (acc.) fling one's arms round; sich um et. ~ wind round; '~pflanze ⚘ f creeper, climber.

Schlips [ʃlips] m (-es/-e) (neck)tie.

Schlitten ['ʃlitən] m (-s/-) sled(ge); sleigh; sports: toboggan.

'**Schlittschuh** m skate; ~ laufen skate; '~läufer m skater.

Schlitz [ʃlits] m (-es/-e) slit, slash; slot; '2en v/t. (ge-, h) slit, slash.

Schloß [ʃlɔs] 1. n (Schlosses/Schlösser) lock (of door, gun, etc.); castle; palace; ins ~ fallen door: snap to;

hinter ~ und Riegel behind prison bars; 2. ⌀ pret. of schließen.

Schlosser ['ʃlɔsər] m (-s/-) locksmith; mechanic, fitter.

Schlot [ʃloːt] m (-[e]s/-e, ⹉e) chimney; flue; ⚓, ✈ funnel; '**~feger** m (-s/-) chimney-sweep(er).

schlotter|ig adj. ['ʃlɔtəriç] shaky, tottery, loose; '**~n** v/i. (ge-, h) garment: hang loosely; p. shake, tremble (both: vor dat. with).

Schlucht [ʃluxt] f (-/-en) gorge, mountain cleft; ravine, Am. a. gulch.

schluchzen ['ʃluxtsən] v/i. (ge-, h) sob.

Schluck [ʃluk] m (-[e]s/-e, ⹉e) draught, swallow; mouthful, sip; '**~auf** m (-s/no pl.) hiccup(s pl.).

'**schlucken** 1. v/t. and v/i. (ge-, h) swallow (a. fig.); 2. ⌀ m (-s/no pl.) hiccup(s pl.).

schlug [ʃluːk] pret. of schlagen.

Schlummer ['ʃlumər] m (-s/no pl.) slumber; '**~n** v/i. (ge-, h) slumber.

Schlund [ʃlunt] m (-[e]s/⹉e) anat. pharynx; fig. abyss, chasm, gulf.

schlüpf|en ['ʃlʏpfən] v/i. (ge-, sein) slip, slide; in die Kleider ~ slip on one's clothes; aus den Kleidern ~ slip out of or slip off one's clothes; '**⌀er** m (-s/-) (ein a pair of) knickers pl. or drawers pl. or F panties pl.; briefs pl.

Schlupfloch ['ʃlupf-] n loop-hole.

'**schlüpfrig** adj. slippery; fig. lascivious.

'**Schlupfwinkel** m hiding-place.

schlurfen ['ʃlurfən] v/i. (ge-, sein) shuffle, drag one's feet.

schlürfen ['ʃlʏrfən] v/t. and v/i. (ge-, h) drink or eat noisily; sip.

Schluß [ʃlus] m (Schlusses/Schlüsse) close, end; conclusion; parl. closing (of debate).

Schlüssel ['ʃlʏsəl] m (-s/-) key (zu of; fig. to); ♪ clef; fig.: code; quota; '**~bart** m key-bit; '**~bein** anat. n collar-bone, clavicle; '**~bund** m, n (-[e]s/-e) bunch of keys; '**~industrie** fig. f key industry; '**~loch** n keyhole; '**~ring** m key-ring.

'**Schlußfolgerung** f conclusion, inference; '**~formel** f in letter: complimentary close.

schlüssig adj. ['ʃlʏsiç] evidence: conclusive; sich ~ werden make up one's mind (über acc. about).

'**Schluß|licht** n 🚗, mot., etc.: tail-light; sports: last runner; bottom club; '**~rundel** f sports: final; '**~schein** † m contract-note.

Schmach [ʃmaːx] f (-/no pl.) disgrace; insult; humiliation.

schmachten ['ʃmaxtən] v/i. (ge-, h) languish (nach for); pine (for).

schmächtig adj. ['ʃmɛçtiç] slender, slim; ein ~er Junge a (mere) slip of a boy.

'**schmachvoll** adj. disgraceful; humiliating.

schmackhaft adj. ['ʃmakhaft] palatable, savo(u)ry.

schmäh|en ['ʃmɛːən] v/t. (ge-, h) abuse, revile; decry, disparage; slander, defame; '**~lich** adj. ignominious, disgraceful; '**⌀schrift** f libel, lampoon; '**⌀ung** f (-/-en) abuse; slander, defamation.

schmal adj. [ʃmaːl] narrow; figure: slender, slim; face: thin; fig. poor, scanty.

schmäler|n ['ʃmɛːlərn] v/t. (ge-, h) curtail; impair; belittle; '**⌀ung** f (-/-en) curtailment; impairment; detraction.

'**Schmal|film** phot. m substandard film; '**~spur** 🚗 f narrow ga(u)ge; '**~spurbahn** 🚗 f narrow-ga(u)ge railway; '**⌀spurig** 🚗 adj. narrow-ga(u)ge.

Schmalz [ʃmalts] n (-es/-e) grease; lard; '**⌀ig** adj. greasy; lardy; F fig. soppy, sentimental.

schmarotz|en [ʃma'rɔtsən] v/i. (no -ge-, h) sponge (bei on); **⌀er** m (-s/-) ⚕, zo. parasite; fig. a. sponge.

Schmarre F ['ʃmarə] f (-/-n) slash, cut; scar.

Schmatz [ʃmats] m (-es/-e) smack, loud kiss; '**⌀en** v/i. (ge-, h) smack (mit den Lippen one's lips); eat noisily.

Schmaus [ʃmaus] m (-es/⹉e) feast, banquet; fig. treat; **⌀en** ['~zən] v/i. (ge-, h) feast, banquet.

schmecken ['ʃmekən] (ge-, h) 1. v/t. taste, sample; 2. v/i.: ~ nach taste or smack of (both a. fig.); dieser Wein schmeckt mir I like or enjoy this wine.

Schmeichel|ei [ʃmaiçə'lai] f (-/-en) flattery; cajolery; '**⌀haft** adj. flattering; '**⌀n** v/i. (ge-, h): j-m ~ flatter s.o.; cajole s.o.

Schmeichler ['ʃmaiçlər] m (-s/-) flatterer; '**⌀isch** adj. flattering; cajoling.

schmeiß|en F ['ʃmaisən] (irr., ge-, h) 1. v/t. throw, fling, hurl; slam, bang (door); 2. v/i.: mit Geld um sich ~ squander one's money; '**⌀fliege** zo. f blowfly, bluebottle.

Schmelz [ʃmelts] m 1. (-es/-e) enamel; 2. fig. (-es/no pl.) bloom; ♪ sweetness, mellowness; '**⌀en** (irr., ge-) 1. v/i. (sein) melt (a. fig.); liquefy; fig. melt away, dwindle; 2. v/t. (h) melt; smelt, fuse (ore, etc.); liquefy; '**⌀erei** [~'rai] f (-/-en), '**~hütte** f foundry; '**~ofen** m smelting furnace; '**~tiegel** m melting-pot, crucible.

Schmerbauch ['ʃmeːr-] m paunch, pot-belly, F corporation, Am. sl. a. bay window.

Schmerz [ʃmerts] m (-es/-en) pain (a. fig.); ache; fig. grief, sorrow;

'‚en (ge-, h) 1. v/i. pain (a. fig.), hurt; ache; 2. v/t. pain (a. fig.); hurt; fig. grieve, afflict; '‚haft adj. painful; '‚lich adj. painful, grievous; '‚lindernd adj. soothing; '‚los adj. painless.

Schmetter|ling zo. ['ʃmɛtɔrliŋ] m (-s/-e) butterfly; '‚n (ge-, h) 1. v/t. dash (zu Boden to the ground); in Stücke to pieces); 2. v/i. crash; trumpet, etc.: bray, blare; bird: warble.

Schmied [ʃmiːt] m (-[e]s/-e) (black)-smith; ‚e ['‚də] f (-/-n) forge, smithy; ‚eisen ['‚dəʔ-] n wrought iron; '‚ehammer m sledge(-hammer); ‚en ['‚dən] v/t. (ge-, h) forge; make, devise, hatch (plans).

schmiegen ['ʃmiːgən] v/refl. (ge-, h) nestle (an acc. to).

schmiegsam adj. ['ʃmiːkzaːm] pliant, flexible; supple (a. fig.); '‚keit f (-/no pl.) pliancy, flexibility; suppleness (a. fig.).

Schmier|e ['ʃmiːrə] f (-/-n) grease; thea. contp. troop of strolling players, sl. penny gaff; '‚en v/t. (ge-, h) smear; ⊕ grease, oil, lubricate; butter (bread); spread (butter, etc.); scrawl, scribble; painter: daub; ‚enkomödiant ['‚kɔmødjant] m (-en/-en) strolling actor, barnstormer, sl. ham (actor); ‚erei [‚'raɪ] f (-/-en) scrawl; paint. daub; '‚ig adj. greasy; dirty; fig.: filthy; F smarmy; '‚mittel ⊕ n lubricant.

Schminke ['ʃmiŋkə] f (-/-n) make-up (a. thea.), paint; rouge; thea. grease-paint; '‚n v/t. and v/refl. (ge-, h) paint, make up; rouge (o.s.); put on lipstick.

Schmirgel ['ʃmirgəl] m (-s/no pl.) emery; '‚n v/t. (ge-, h) (rub with) emery; '‚papier n emery-paper.

Schmiß [ʃmis] 1. m (Schmisses/ Schmisse) gash, cut; (duelling-) scar; 2. F m (Schmisses/no pl.) verve, go, Am. sl. a. pep; 3. 2 pret. of schmeißen.

schmoll|en ['ʃmɔlən] v/i. (ge-, h) sulk, pout; '‚winkel m sulking-corner.

schmolz [ʃmɔlts] pret. of schmelzen.

Schmor|braten ['ʃmoːr-] m stewed meat; '‚en v/t. and v/i. (ge-, h) stew (a. fig.).

Schmuck [ʃmuk] 1. m (-[e]s/⚭-e) ornament; decoration; jewel(le)ry, jewels pl.; 2. 2 adj. neat, smart, spruce, trim.

schmücken ['ʃmykən] v/t. (ge-, h) adorn, trim; decorate.

'schmuck|los adj. unadorned; plain; '2sachen f/pl. jewel(le)ry, jewels pl.

Schmuggel ['ʃmugəl] m (-s/no pl.), ‚ei ['‚laɪ] f (-/-en) smuggling; '2n v/t. and v/i. (ge-, h) smuggle; '‚ware f contraband, smuggled goods pl.

Schmuggler ['ʃmuglər] m (-s/-) smuggler.

schmunzeln ['ʃmuntsəln] v/i. (ge-, h) smile amusedly.

Schmutz [ʃmuts] m (-es/no pl.) dirt; filth; fig. a. smut; '2en v/i. (ge-, h) soil, get dirty; '‚fink fig. m mudlark; '‚fleck m smudge, stain; fig. blemish; '2ig adj. dirty; filthy; fig. a. mean, shabby.

Schnabel ['ʃnaːbəl] m (-s/⁼) bill, esp. bird of prey: beak.

Schnalle ['ʃnalə] f (-/-n) buckle; '2n v/t. (ge-, h) buckle; strap.

schnalzen ['ʃnaltsən] v/i. (ge-, h): mit den Fingern ~ snap one's fingers; mit der Zunge ~ click one's tongue.

schnappen ['ʃnapən] (ge-, h) 1. v/i. lid, spring, etc.: snap; lock: catch; nach et. ~ snap or snatch at; nach Luft ~ gasp for breath; 2. F v/t. catch, sl. nab (criminal).

'Schnapp|messer n flick-knife; '‚schloß n spring-lock; '‚schuß phot. m snapshot.

Schnaps [ʃnaps] m (-es/⁼e) strong liquor, Am. hard liquor; brandy; ein (Glas) ~ a dram.

schnarchen ['ʃnarçən] v/i. (ge-, h) snore; '2er m (-s/-) snorer.

schnarren ['ʃnarən] v/i. (ge-, h) rattle; jar.

schnattern ['ʃnatərn] v/i. (ge-, h) cackle; fig. a. chatter, gabble.

schnauben ['ʃnaubən] (ge-, h) 1. v/i. snort; vor Wut ~ foam with rage; 2. v/t.: sich die Nase ~ blow one's nose.

schnaufen ['ʃnaufən] v/i. (ge-, h) pant, puff, blow; wheeze.

Schnauz|bart ['ʃnauts-] m m(o)ustache; '‚e f (-/-n) snout, muzzle; ⊕ nozzle; teapot, etc.: spout; sl. fig. potato-trap; '2en F v/i. (ge-, h) jaw.

Schnecke zo. ['ʃnɛkə] f (-/-n) snail; slug; ‚nhaus n snail's shell; '‚n-tempo n: im ~ at a snail's pace.

Schnee [ʃneː] m (-s/no pl.) snow; '‚ball m snowball; '‚ballschlacht f pelting-match with snowballs; 2bedeckt adj. ['‚bədɛkt] snow-covered, mountain-top: snow-capped; '2blind adj. snow-blind; '‚blindheit f snow-blindness; '‚brille f (e-e a pair of) snow-goggles pl.; '‚fall m snow-fall; '‚flocke f snow-flake; '‚gestöber n (-s/-) snow-storm; ‚glöckchen ⚭ ['‚glœkçən] n (-s/-) snowdrop; '‚grenze f snow-line; '‚mann m snow man; '‚pflug m snow-plough, Am. snowplow; '‚schuh m snow-shoe; '‚sturm m snow-storm, blizzard; '‚wehe f (-/-n) snow-drift; '2weiß adj. snow-white.

Schneid F [ʃnaɪt] m (-[e]s/no pl.) pluck, dash, sl. guts pl.

Schneide ['ʃnaɪdə] f (-/-n) edge; '‚mühle f sawmill; '2n (irr., ge-, h)

1. *v/t.* cut; carve (*meat*); pare, clip (*finger-nails, etc.*); 2. *v/i.* cut.

'**Schneider** *m* (-s/-) tailor; **~ei** [~'raɪ] *f* 1. (-/*no pl.*) tailoring; dressmaking; 2. (-/-en) tailor's shop; dressmaker's shop; '**~in** *f* (-/-nen) dressmaker; '**~meister** *m* master tailor; '£n (ge-, h) 1. *v/i.* tailor; do tailoring; do dressmaking; 2. *v/t.* make, tailor.

'**Schneidezahn** *m* incisor.

'**schneidig** *fig. adj.* plucky; dashing, keen; smart, *Am. sl. a.* nifty.

schneien ['ʃnaɪən] *v/i.* (ge-, h) snow.

schnell [ʃnɛl] 1. *adj.* quick, fast; rapid; swift, speedy; *reply, etc.*: prompt; sudden; 2. *adv.*: ~ fahren drive fast; ~ handeln act promptly *or* without delay; (*mach*) ~! be quick!, hurry up!

Schnelläufer ['ʃnɛlɔyfər] *m* sprinter; speed skater.

'**schnell|en** (ge-) *v/t.* (h) *and v/i.* (sein) jerk; '£feuer ⚔ *n* rapid fire; '£hefter *m* (-s/-) folder.

'**Schnelligkeit** *f* (-/*no pl.*) quickness, fastness; rapidity; swiftness; promptness; speed, velocity.

'**Schnell|imbiß** *m* snack (bar); '**~imbißstube** *f* snack bar; '**~kraft** *f* (-/*no pl.*) elasticity; '**~verfahren** *n* ṯ summary proceeding; ⊕ highspeed process; '**~zug** 🚋 *m* fast train, express (train).

schneuzen ['ʃnɔytsən] *v/refl.* (ge-, h) blow one's nose.

schniegeln ['ʃniːgəln] *v/refl.* (ge-, h) dress *or* smarten *or* spruce (o.s.) up.

Schnipp|chen ['ʃnɪpçən] *n:* F j-m ein ~ schlagen outwit *or* overreach s.o.; '£isch *adj.* pert, snappish, *Am.* F *a.* snippy.

Schnitt [ʃnɪt] 1. *m* (-[e]s/-e) cut; *dress, etc.*: cut, make, style; pattern; *book:* edge; 𝔸 (inter)section; *fig.*: average; F profit; 2. 2 *pret. of* schneiden; '**~blumen** *f/pl.* cut flowers *pl.*; '**~e** *f* (-/-n) slice; '**~er** *m* (-s/-) reaper, mower; '**~fläche** 𝔸 *f* section(al plane); '£ig *adj.* streamline(d); '**~muster** *n* pattern; '**~punkt** *m* (point of) intersection; '**~wunde** *f* cut, gash.

Schnitzel ['ʃnɪtsəl] 1. *n* (-s/-) schnitzel; 2. F *n, m* (-s/-) chip; *paper:* scrap; ~ *pl.* ⊕ parings *pl.*, shavings *pl.*; *paper: a.* clippings *pl.*; '£n *v/t.* (ge-, h) chip, shred, whittle.

schnitzen ['ʃnɪtsən] *v/t.* (ge-, h) carve, cut (in wood).

'**Schnitzer** *m* (-s/-) carver; F *fig.* blunder, *Am. sl. a.* boner; **~ei** [~'raɪ] *f* 1. (-/-en) carving, carved work; 2. (-/*no pl.*) carving.

schnöde *adj.* ['ʃnøːdə] contemptuous; disgraceful; base, vile; **~r** Mammon filthy lucre.

Schnörkel ['ʃnœrkəl] *m* (-s/-) flourish (*a. fig.*), scroll (*a.* ⚠).

schnorr|en F ['ʃnɔrən] *v/t. and v/i.* (ge-, h) cadge; '£er *m* (-s/-) cadger.

schnüff|eln ['ʃnyfəln] *v/i.* (ge-, h) sniff, nose (*both: an dat.* at); *fig.* nose about, *Am.* F *a.* snoop around; '£ler *fig. m* (-s/-) spy, *Am.* F *a.* snoop; F sleuth(-hound).

Schnuller ['ʃnʊlər] *m* (-s/-) dummy, comforter.

Schnulze F ['ʃnʊltsə] *f* (-/-n) sentimental song *or* film *or* play, F tearjerker.

Schnupf|en ['ʃnʊpfən] 1. *m* (-s/-) cold, catarrh; 2. 2 *v/i.* (ge-, h) take snuff; '**~er** *m* (-s/-) snuff-taker; '**~tabak** *m* snuff.

schnuppe F *adj.* ['ʃnʊpə]: *das ist mir ~* I don't care (F a damn); '**~rn** *v/i.* (ge-, h) sniff, nose (*both: an dat.* at).

Schnur [ʃnuːr] *f* (-/̈-e, ⚒ -en) cord; string, twine; line; ∉ flex.

Schnür|band ['ʃnyːr-] *n* lace; **~chen** ['~çən] *n* (-s/-): *wie am ~ like clockwork*; '£en *v/t.* (ge-, h) lace (up) (bind with) cord, tie up.

'**schnurgerade** *adj.* dead straight.

Schnurr|bart ['ʃnʊr-] *m* m(o)ustache; '£en (ge-, h) 1. *v/i. wheel, etc.*: whir(r); *cat:* purr (*a. fig.*); F *fig.* cadge; 2. F *fig. v/t.* cadge.

Schnür|senkel ['ʃnyːrzeŋkəl] *m* (-s/-) shoe-lace, shoe-string; '**~stiefel** *m* lace-boot.

schnurstracks *adv.* ['ʃnuːrʃtraks] direct, straight; on the spot, at once, *sl.* straight away.

schob [ʃoːp] *pret. of* schieben.

Schober ['ʃoːbər] *m* (-s/-) rick, stack.

Schock [ʃɔk] 1. *n* (-[e]s/-e) threescore; 2. 𝔰 *m* (-[e]s/-s, ⚒ -e) shock; £**ieren** [~'kiːrən] *v/t.* (*no* -ge-, h) shock, scandalize.

Schokolade [ʃokoˈlaːdə] *f* (-/-n) chocolate.

scholl [ʃɔl] *pret. of* schallen.

Scholle ['ʃɔlə] *f* (-/-n) clod (*of earth*), *poet.* glebe; floe (*of ice*); *ichth.* plaice.

schon *adv.* [ʃoːn] already; ~ *lange* for a long time; ~ *gut!* all right!; ~ *der Gedanke* the very idea; ~ *der Name* the bare name; *hast du ~ einmal ...?* have you ever ...?; *mußt du ~ gehen?* need you go yet?; ~ *um 8 Uhr* as early as 8 o'clock.

schön [ʃøːn] 1. *adj.* beautiful; *man:* handsome (*a. fig.*); *weather:* fair, fine (*a. iro.*); *das ~e Geschlecht* the fair sex; *die ~en Künste* the fine arts; ~*e Literatur* belles-lettres *pl.*; 2. *adv.*: ~ *warm* nice and warm; *du hast mich ~ erschreckt* you gave me quite a start.

schonen ['ʃoːnən] *v/t.* (ge-, h) spare (*j-n* s.o.; *j-s Leben* s.o.'s life); take care of; husband (*strength, etc.*); *sich* ~ take care of o.s., look after o.s.

'**Schönheit** *f* 1. (-/*no pl.*) beauty; *of woman*: a. pulchritude; 2. (-/-en) beauty; beautiful woman, belle; '~**spflege** *f* beauty treatment.

'**schöntun** *v/i.* (*irr. tun, sep., -ge-, h*) flatter (*j-m s.o.*); flirt (*dat.* with).

'**Schonung** *f* 1. (-/*no pl.*) mercy; sparing, forbearance; careful treatment; 2. (-/-en) tree-nursery; '**2slos** *adj.* unsparing, merciless, relentless.

Schopf [ʃɔpf] *m* (-[e]s/⸚e) tuft; *orn.* a. crest.

schöpfen ['ʃœpfən] *v/t.* (ge-, h) scoop, ladle; draw (*water at well*); draw, take (*breath*); take (*courage*); *neue Hoffnung* ~ gather fresh hope; *Verdacht* ~ become suspicious.

'**Schöpf|er** *m* (-s/-) creator; '**2e-risch** *adj.* creative; '~**ung** *f* (-/-en) creation.

schor [ʃoːr] *pret. of scheren.*

Schorf [ʃɔrf] *m* (-[e]s/-e) scurf; scab, crust; '**2ig** *adj.* scurfy; scabby.

Schornstein ['ʃɔrn-] *m* chimney, ⚓, 🚂 funnel; '~**feger** *m* (-s/-) chimney-sweep(er).

Schoß 1. [ʃoːs] *m* (-es/⸚e) lap; womb; *coat*: tail; 2. ⸚ [ʃɔs] *pret. of schießen.*

Schote ['ʃoːtə] *f* (-/-n) pod, husk.

Schott|e ['ʃɔtə] *m* (-n/-n) Scot, Scotchman, Scotsman; *die* ~*n pl.* the Scotch *pl.*; '~**en** *m* (-s/-) gravel; (road-)metal; '**2isch** *adj.* Scotch, Scottish.

schräg [ʃrɛːk] 1. *adj.* oblique, slanting; sloping; 2. *adv.:* ~ *gegenüber* diagonally across (von from).

schrak [ʃraːk] *pret. of schrecken 2.*

Schramme ['ʃramə] *f* (-/-n) scratch; *skin*: a. abrasion; '**2n** *v/t.* (ge-, h) scratch; graze, abrade (*skin*).

Schrank [ʃraŋk] *m* (-[e]s/⸚e) cupboard, *esp. Am.* closet; wardrobe.

'**Schranke** *f* (-/-n) barrier (a. *fig.*); 🚂 a. (railway-)gate; ⚖ bar; ~*n pl. fig.* bounds *pl.*, limits *pl.*; '**2nlos** *fig. adj.* boundless; unbridled; '~**n-wärter** *m* gate-keeper.

'**Schrankkoffer** *m* wardrobe trunk.

Schraube ['ʃraʊbə] *f* (-/-n) ⊕ screw; ⚓ screw(-propeller); '**2n** *v/t.* (ge-, h) screw.

'**Schrauben|dampfer** ⚓ *m* screw (steamer); '~**mutter** ⊕ *f* nut; '~**schlüssel** ⊕ *m* spanner, wrench; '~**zieher** ⊕ *m* screwdriver.

Schraubstock ⊕ ['ʃraʊp-] *m* vice, *Am.* vise.

Schrebergarten ['ʃreːbər-] *m* allotment garden.

Schreck [ʃrɛk] *m* (-[e]s/-e) fright, terror; consternation; '~**bild** *n* bugbear; '~**en** *m* (-s/-) fright, terror; consternation; '**2en** (ge-) 1. *v/t.* (h) frighten, scare; 2. *v/i.* (*irr.*, sein):

only in compounds; '~**ensbotschaft** *f* alarming *or* terrible news; '~**ens-herrschaft** *f* reign of terror; '**2haft** *adj.* fearful, timid; '**2lich** *adj.* terrible, dreadful (*both* a. F *fig.*); '~**schuß** *m* scare shot; *fig.* warning shot.

Schrei [ʃraɪ] *m* (-[e]s/-e) cry; shout; scream.

schreiben ['ʃraɪbən] 1. *v/t. and v/i.* (*irr.*, ge-, h) write (*j-m* to s.o.; *über acc.* on); *mit der Maschine* ~ type(write); 2. *v/t.* (*irr.*, ge-, h) spell; 3. ⸚ *n* (-s/-) letter.

'**Schreiber** *m* (-s/-) writer; secretary, clerk.

schreib|faul *adj.* ['ʃraɪp-] lazy in writing; '**2feder** *f* pen; '**2fehler** *m* mistake in writing *or* spelling, slip of the pen; '**2heft** *n* exercise-book; '**2mappe** *f* writing-case; '**2ma-schine** *f* typewriter; (*mit der*) ~ *schreiben* type(write); '**2material** *n* writing-materials *pl.*, stationery; '**2papier** *n* writing-paper; '**2-schrift** *typ. f* script; '**2tisch** *m* (writing-)desk; ⸚**ung** ['~bʊŋ] *f* (-/-en) spelling; '**2unterlage** *f* desk pad; '**2waren** *f/pl.* writing-materials *pl.*, stationery; '**2waren-händler** *m* stationer; '**2zeug** *n* writing-materials *pl.*

'**schreien** (*irr.*, ge-, h) 1. *v/t.* shout; scream; 2. *v/i.* cry (out) (*vor dat.* with *pain, etc.*; *nach* for *bread, etc.*); shout (*vor* with); scream (with); '~**d** *adj.* colour: loud; *injustice:* flagrant.

schreiten ['ʃraɪtən] *v/i.* (*irr.*, ge-, sein) step, stride (*über acc.* across); *fig.* proceed (*zu* to).

schrie [ʃriː] *pret. of schreien.*

schrieb [ʃriːp] *pret. of schreiben.*

Schrift [ʃrift] *f* (-/-en) (hand-) writing, hand; *typ.* type; character, letter; writing; publication; *die Heilige* ~ the (Holy) Scriptures *pl.*; '~**art** *f* type; '**2deutsch** *adj.* literary German; '~**führer** *m* secretary; '~**leiter** *m* editor; '**2lich** 1. *adj.* written, in writing; 2. *adv.* in writing; '~**satz** *m* ⚖ pleadings *pl.*; *typ.* composition, type-setting; '~**setzer** *m* compositor, type-setter; '~**sprache** *f* literary language; '~**steller** *m* (-s/-) author; writer; '~**stück** *n* piece of writing, paper, document; '~**tum** *n* (-s/*no pl.*) literature; '~**wechsel** *m* exchange of letters, correspondence; '~**zei-chen** *n* character, letter.

schrill *adj.* [ʃril] shrill, piercing.

Schritt [ʃrit] 1. *m* (-[e]s/-e) step (a. *fig.*); pace (a. *fig.*); ~*e unter-nehmen* take steps; 2. ⸚ *pret. of schreiten*; '**2macher** *m* (-s/-) *sports:* pace-maker; '**2weise** 1. *adj.* gradual; 2. *adv.* a. step by step.

schroff *adj.* [ʃrɔf] rugged, jagged;

steep, precipitous; *fig.* harsh, gruff; ~er Widerspruch glaring contradiction.

schröpfen ['ʃrœpfən] *v/t.* (ge-, h) 𝒮 cup; *fig.* milk, fleece.

Schrot [ʃroːt] *m, n* (-[e]s/-e) crushed grain; small shot; '~brot *n* wholemeal bread; '~flinte *f* shotgun.

Schrott [ʃrɔt] *m* (-[e]s/-e) scrap (-iron *or* -metal).

schrubben ['ʃrubən] *v/t.* (ge-, h) scrub.

Schrulle ['ʃrulə] *f* (-/-n) whim, fad.

schrumpf|en ['ʃrumpfən] *v/i.* (ge-, sein) shrink (*a.* ⊕, 𝒮, *fig.*); '2ung *f* (-/-en) shrinking, shrinkage.

Schub [ʃuːp] *m* (-[e]s/~e) push, shove; *phys.*, ⊕ thrust; *bread, people, etc.*: batch; '~fach *n* drawer; '~karren *m* wheelbarrow; '~kasten *m* drawer; '~kraft *phys.*, ⊕ *f* thrust; '~lade *f* (-/-n) drawer.

Schubs [ʃups] *m* (-es/-e) push; '2en F *v/t.* (ge-, h) push.

schüchtern *adj.* ['ʃyçtərn] shy, bashful, timid; *girl:* coy; '2heit *f* (-/*no pl.*) shyness, bashfulness, timidity; coyness (*of girl*).

schuf [ʃuːf] *pret.* of schaffen 1.

Schuft [ʃuft] *m* (-[e]s/-e) scoundrel, rascal; cad; '2en F *v/i.* (ge-, h) drudge, slave, plod; '2ig *adj.* scoundrelly, rascally, caddish.

Schuh [ʃuː] *m* (-[e]s/-e) shoe; *j-m et. in die* ~e schieben put the blame for s.th. on s.o.; *wissen, wo der* ~ drückt know where the shoe pinches; '~anzieher *m* (-s/-) shoehorn; '~band *n* shoe-lace *or* -string; '~creme *f* shoe-cream, shoe-polish; '~geschäft *n* shoe-shop; '~löffel *m* shoehorn; '~macher *m* (-s/-) shoemaker; '~putzer *m* (-s/-) shoeblack, *Am. a.* shoeshine; '~sohle *f* sole; '~spanner *m* (-s/-) shoetree; '~werk *n*, '~zeug F *n* foot-wear, boots and shoes *pl.*

'Schul|amt *n* school-board; '~arbeit *f* homework; '~bank *f* (school-) desk; '~beispiel *n* test-case, typical example; '~besuch *m* (-[e]s/*no pl.*) attendance at school; '~bildung *f* education; *höhere* ~ secondary education; '~buch *n* school-book.

Schuld [ʃult] *f* 1. (-/*no pl.*) guilt; fault, blame; *es ist s-e* ~ it is his fault, he is to blame for it; 2. (-/-en) debt; ~en machen contract *or* incur debts; '2bewußt *adj.* conscious of one's guilt; '2en ['~dən] *v/t.* (ge-, h): *j-m et.* ~ owe s.o. s.th.; *j-m Dank* ~ be indebted to s.o. (*für* for); '2haft *adj.* ['~thaft] culpable.

'Schuldiener *m* school attendant *or* porter.

schuldig *adj.* ['ʃuldiç] guilty (*e-r Sache* of s.th.); *respect, etc.:* due; *j-m et.* ~ sein owe s.o. s.th.; *Dank* ~ sein be indebted to s.o. (*für* for);

für ~ befinden 𝔱𝔱 find guilty; 2e ['~gə] *m, f* (-n/-n) guilty person; culprit; '2keit *f* (-/*no pl.*) duty, obligation.

'Schuldirektor *m* headmaster, *Am. a.* principal.

'schuld|los *adj.* guiltless, innocent; '2losigkeit *f* (-/*no pl.*) guiltlessness, innocence; '2ner ['~dnər] *m* (-s/-) debtor; '2schein *m* evidence of debt, certificate of indebtedness, IOU (= I owe you); '2verschreibung *f* bond, debt certificate.

Schule ['ʃuːlə] *f* (-/-n) school; *höhere* ~ secondary school, *Am. a.* high school; *auf* or *in der* ~ at school; *in die* ~ gehen go to school; '2n *v/t.* (ge-, h) train, school; *pol.* indoctrinate.

Schüler ['ʃyːlər] *m* (-s/-) schoolboy, pupil; *phls., etc.:* disciple; '~austausch *m* exchange of pupils; '~in *f* (-/-nen) schoolgirl.

'Schul|ferien *pl.* holidays *pl.*, vacation; '~fernsehen *n* educational TV; '~funk *m* educational broadcast; '~gebäude *n* school(house); '~geld *n* school fee(s *pl.*), tuition; '~hof *m* playground, *Am. a.* schoolyard; '~kamerad *m* schoolfellow; '~lehrer *m* schoolmaster, teacher; '~mappe *f* satchel; '2meistern *v/t.* (ge-, h) censure pedantically; '~ordnung *f* school regulations *pl.*; '2pflichtig *adj.* schoolable; '~rat *m* supervisor of schools, school inspector; '~schiff *n* training-ship; '~schluß *m* end of school; end of term; '~schwänzer *m* (-s/-) truant; '~stunde *f* lesson.

Schulter ['ʃultər] *f* (-/-n) shoulder; '~blatt *anat. n* shoulder-blade; '2n *v/t.* (ge-, h) shoulder.

'Schul|unterricht *m* school, lessons *pl.*; school instruction; '~versäumnis *f* (-/*no pl.*) absence from school; '~wesen *n* educational system; '~zeugnis *n* report.

schummeln F ['ʃuməln] *v/i.* (ge-, h) cheat, *Am.* F *a.* chisel.

Schund [ʃunt] 1. *m* (-[e]s/*no pl.*) trash, rubbish (*both a. fig.*); 2. 2 *pret.* of schinden; '~literatur *f* trashy literature; '~roman *m* trashy novel, *Am. a.* dime novel.

Schupp|e ['ʃupə] *f* (-/-n) scale; ~n *pl.* on head: dandruff; '~en 1. *m* (-s/-) shed; *mot.* garage; ✈ hangar; 2. 2 *v/t.* (ge-, h) scale (*fish*); *sich* ~ *skin:* scale off; '2ig *adj.* scaly.

Schür|eisen ['ʃyːr?-] *n* poker; '2en *v/t.* (ge-, h) poke; stoke; *fig.* fan, foment.

schürfen ['ʃyrfən] (ge-, h) 1. ⚒ *v/i.* prospect (*nach* for); 2. *v/t.* ⚒ prospect for; *sich den Arm* ~ graze one's arm.

Schurk|e ['ʃurkə] *m* (-n/-n) scoundrel, knave; ~erei [~'raɪ] *f* (-/-en)

rascality, knavish trick; '2isch adj.
scoundrelly, knavish.

Schürze ['ʃyrtsə] f (-/-n) apron;
children: pinafore; '2n v/t. (ge-, h)
tuck up (skirt); tie (knot); purse
(lips); '~njäger m skirt-chaser, Am.
sl. wolf.

Schuß [ʃus] m (Schusses/Schüsse)
shot (a. sports); ammunition: round;
sound: report; charge; wine, etc.:
dash (a. fig.); in ~ sein be in full
swing, be in full working order.

Schüssel ['ʃysəl] f (-/-n) basin (for
water, etc.); bowl, dish, tureen
(for soup, vegetables, etc.).

'Schuß|waffe f fire-arm; '~weite f
range; '~wunde f gunshot wound.

Schuster ['ʃuːstər] m (-s/-) shoemaker; '2n fig. v/i. (ge-, h) s. pfuschen.

Schutt [ʃut] m (-[e]s/no pl.) rubbish,
refuse; rubble, debris.

Schüttel|frost ['ʃytəl-] m shiver-
ing-fit; '2n v/t. (ge-, h) shake; den
Kopf ~ shake one's head; j-m die
Hand ~ shake hands with s.o.

schütten ['ʃytən] (ge-, h) 1. v/t.
pour; spill (auf acc. on); 2. v/i.:
es schüttet it is pouring with rain.

Schutz [ʃuts] m (-es/no pl.) protection (gegen, vor dat. against),
defen[ce, Am. -se (against, from);
shelter (from); safeguard; cover;
'~brille f (e-e a pair of) goggles pl.

Schütze ['ʃytsə] m (-n/-n) marksman,
shot; ⚔ rifleman; '2n v/t. (ge-, h)
protect (gegen, vor dat. against,
from); defend (against, from),
guard (against, from); shelter
(from); safeguard (rights, etc.).

Schutzengel ['ʃuts⁹-] m guardian
angel.

'Schützen|graben ⚔ m trench;
'~könig m champion shot.

'Schutz|haft ♗ f protective cus-
tody; '~heilige m patron saint;
'~herr m patron, protector; '~impf-
ung f protective inoculation;
smallpox: vaccination.

Schützling ['ʃytsliŋ] m (-s/-e) pro-
tégé, female: protégée.

'schutz|los adj. unprotected; de-
fen[celess, Am. -seless; '2mann m
(-[e]s/-er, Schutzleute) policeman,
(police) constable, sl. bobby, sl. cop;
'2marke f trade mark, brand; '2-
mittel n preservative; ♗ prophylactic; '2patron m patron saint;
'2umschlag m (dust-)jacket, wrapper; '~zoll m protective duty.

Schwabe ['ʃvaːbə] m (-n/-n) Swabian.

schwäbisch adj. ['ʃvɛːbiʃ] Swabian.

schwach adj. [ʃvax] resistance, team,
knees (a. fig.), eyes, heart, voice,
character, tea, gr. verb, ♗ demand,
etc.: weak; person, etc.: infirm;
person, recollection, etc.: feeble;
sound, light, hope, idea, etc.: faint;

consolation, attendance, etc.: poor;
light, recollection, etc.: dim; resemblance: remote; das ~e Geschlecht
the weaker sex; ~e Seite weak point
or side.

Schwäche ['ʃvɛçə] f (-/-n) weakness
(a. fig.); infirmity; fig. foible; e-e ~
haben für have a weakness for; '2n
v/t. (ge-, h) weaken (a. fig.); impair
(health).

'Schwach|heit f (-/-en) weakness;
fig. a. frailty; '~kopf m simpleton,
soft(y), Am. F a. sap(head); 2köp-
fig adj. ['~kœpfiç] weak-headed,
soft, Am. sl. a. sappy.

schwäch|lich adj. ['ʃvɛçliç] weakly,
feeble; delicate, frail; '2ling m
(-s/-e) weakling (a. fig.).

'schwach|sinnig adj. weak- or
feeble-minded; '2strom ⚡ m
(-[e]s/no pl.) weak current.

Schwadron ⚔ [ʃva'droːn] f (-/-en)
squadron; '2ieren [~o'niːrən] v/t.
(no -ge-, h) swagger, vapo(u)r.

Schwager ['ʃvaːgər] m (-s/ᵁ) broth-
er-in-law.

Schwägerin ['ʃvɛːgərin] f (-/-nen)
sister-in-law.

Schwalbe orn. ['ʃvalbə] f (-/-n)
[swallow.]

Schwall [ʃval] m (-[e]s/-e) swell,
flood; words: torrent.

Schwamm [ʃvam] 1. m (-[e]s/ᵁe)
sponge; ♗ fungus; ♗ dry-rot; 2. ♗
pret. of schwimmen; '2ig adj.
spongy; face, etc.: bloated.

Schwan orn. [ʃvaːn] m (-[e]s/ᵁe)
swan.

schwand [ʃvant] pret. of schwinden.

schwang [ʃvaŋ] pret. of schwingen.

schwanger adj. ['ʃvaŋər] pregnant,
with child, in the family way.

schwängern ['ʃvɛŋərn] v/t. (ge-, h)
get with child, impregnate (a. fig.).

'Schwangerschaft f (-/-en) preg-
nancy.

schwanken ['ʃvaŋkən] v/i. (ge-, h)
1. (h) earth, etc.: shake, rock; ♗
prices: fluctuate; branches, etc.:
sway; fig. waver, oscillate, vacillate;
2. (sein) stagger, totter.

Schwanz [ʃvants] m (-es/ᵁe) tail (a.
⚔, ast.); fig. train.

schwänz|eln ['ʃvɛntsəln] v/i. (ge-, h)
wag one's tail; fig. fawn (um [up]on);
'~en v/t. (ge-, h) cut (lecture, etc.);
die Schule ~ play truant, Am. a.
play hooky.

Schwarm [ʃvarm] m (-[e]s/ᵁe) bees,
etc.: swarm; birds: a. flight, flock;
fish: school, shoal; birds, girls,
etc.: bevy; F fig. fancy, craze; p.:
idol, hero; flame.

schwärmen ['ʃvɛrmən] v/i. (ge-, h)
bees, etc.: swarm; fig.: revel; rave
(von about, of), gush (over); ~ für
be wild about, adore s.o.

'Schwärmer m (-s/-) enthusiast;
esp. eccl. fanatic; visionary; fireworks: cracker, squib; zo. hawk-

moth; ~ei [~'raɪ] f (-/-en) enthusiasm (für for); idolization; ecstasy;
esp. eccl. fanaticism; '2isch adj.
enthusiastic; gushing, raving; ador-
ing; esp. eccl. fanatic(al).

Schwarte ['ʃvartə] f (-/-n) bacon:
rind; F fig. old book.

schwarz adj. [ʃvarts] black (a. fig.);
dark; dirty; ~es Brett notice-board,
Am. bulletin board; ~es Brot brown
bread; ~er Mann bog(e)y; ~er Markt
black market; ~ auf weiß in black
and white; auf die ~e Liste setzen
blacklist; '2arbeit f illicit work;
'2brot n brown bread; '2e m, f
(-n/-n) black.

Schwärze ['ʃvertsə] f (-/no pl.)
blackness (a. fig.); darkness; '2n
v/t. (ge-, h) blacken.

'**schwarz|fahren** F v/i. (irr. fahren,
sep., -ge-, sein) travel without a
ticket; mot. drive without a licence;
'2fahrer m fare-dodger; mot.
person driving without a licence;
'2fahrt f ride without a ticket; mot.
drive without a licence; '2handel
m illicit trade, black marketeering;
'2händler m black marketeer;
'2hörer m listener without a licence.

'**schwärzlich** adj. blackish.

'**Schwarz|markt** m black market;
~seher m pessimist; TV: viewer
without a licence; ~sender m
pirate broadcasting station; ~'weiß-
film m black-and-white film.

schwatzen ['ʃvatsən] v/i. (ge-, h)
chat; chatter, tattle.

schwätz|en ['ʃvetsən] v/i. (ge-, h) s.
schwatzen; '2er m (-s/-) chatterbox;
tattler, prattler; gossip.

'**schwatzhaft** adj. talkative, garrulous.

Schwebe fig. ['ʃveːbə] f (-/no pl.):
in der ~ sein be in suspense; law,
rule, etc.: be in abeyance; '~bahn f
aerial railway or ropeway; '2n v/i.
(ge-, h) be suspended; bird: hover
(a. fig.); glide; fig. be pending (a.
t'2); in Gefahr ~ be in danger.

Schwed|e ['ʃveːdə] m (-n/-n) Swede;
'2isch adj. Swedish.

Schwefel ['ʃveːfəl] m (-s/no pl.)
sulphur, Am. a. sulfur; ~säure
f (-/no pl.) sulphuric acid, Am. a.
sulfuric acid.

Schweif [ʃvaɪf] m (-[e]s/-e) tail (a.
ast.); fig. train; '2en (ge-) 1. v/i.
(sein) rove, ramble; 2. ⊕ v/t.
(h) curve; scallop.

schweigen ['ʃvaɪɡən] 1. v/i. (irr.,
ge-, h) be silent; 2. 2 n (-s/no pl.)
silence; '~d adj. silent.

schweigsam adj. ['ʃvaɪkzaːm] taciturn; '2keit f (-/no pl.) taciturnity.

Schwein [ʃvaɪn] n 1. (-[e]s/-e) zo.
pig, hog, swine (all a. contp. fig.);
2. F (-[e]s/no pl.): ~ haben be
lucky.

'**Schweine|braten** m roast pork;

'~fleisch n pork; '~hund F contp.
m swine; ~rei [~'raɪ] f (-/-en)
mess; dirty trick; smut(ty story);
'~stall m pigsty (a. fig.).

'**schweinisch** fig. adj. swinish;
smutty.

'**Schweinsleder** n pigskin.

Schweiß [ʃvaɪs] m (-es/-e) sweat,
perspiration; '2en ⊕ v/t. (ge-, h)
weld; '~er ⊕ m (-s/-) welder;
'~fuß m perspiring foot; '2ig adj.
sweaty, damp with sweat.

Schweizer ['ʃvaɪtsər] m (-s/-)
Swiss; on farm: dairyman.

schwelen ['ʃveːlən] v/i. (ge-, h)
smo(u)lder (a. fig.).

schwelg|en ['ʃvelɡən] v/i. (ge-, h)
lead a luxurious life; revel; fig.
revel (in dat. in); '2er m (-s/-)
revel(l)er; epicure; '2erei [~'raɪ] f
(-/-en) revel(ry), feasting; ~erisch
adj. luxurious; revel(l)ing.

Schwell|e ['ʃvelə] f (-/-n) sill, thresh-
old (a. fig.); ⊕ sleeper, Am. tie;
'2en 1. v/i. (irr., ge-, sein) swell
(out); 2. v/t. (ge-, h) swell; '~ung f
(-/-en) swelling.

Schwemme ['ʃvemə] f (-/-n)
watering-place; horse-pond; at
tavern, etc.: taproom; ✝ glut (of
fruit, etc.).

Schwengel ['ʃveŋəl] m (-s/-) clapper
(of bell); handle (of pump).

schwenk|en ['ʃveŋkən] (ge-) 1. v/t.
(h) swing; wave (hat, etc.); brandish
(stick, etc.); rinse (washing); 2. v/i.
(sein) turn, wheel; '2ung f (-/-en)
turn; fig. change of mind.

schwer [ʃveːr] 1. adj. heavy; problem, etc.: hard, difficult; illness,
mistake, etc.: serious; punishment,
etc.: severe; fault, etc.: grave; wine,
cigar, etc.: strong; ~e Zeiten hard
times; 2 Pfund ~ sein weigh two
pounds; 2. adv.: ~ arbeiten work
hard; ~ hören be hard of hearing;
'2e f (-/no pl.) heaviness; phys.
gravity (a. fig.); severity; '~fällig
adj. heavy, slow; clumsy; '2gewicht
n sports: heavy-weight; fig. main
emphasis; '2gewichtler m (-s/-)
sports: heavy-weight; '~hörig adj.
hard of hearing; '2industrie f
heavy industry; '2kraft phys. f
(-/no pl.) gravity; '~lich adv. hardly, scarcely; '2mut f (-/no pl.) melancholy; ~mütig adj. ['~myːtɪç]
melancholy; '2punkt m centre of
gravity, Am. center of gravity;
fig.: crucial point; emphasis.

Schwert [ʃveːrt] n (-[e]s/-er)
sword.

'**Schwer|verbrecher** m felon;
'2verdaulich adj. indigestible,
heavy; '2verständlich adj. difficult or hard to understand; '2ver-
wundet adj. seriously wounded;
'2wiegend fig. adj. weighty, mo-
mentous.

Schwester ['ʃvɛstər] f (-/-n) sister; nurse.

schwieg [ʃviːk] pret. of schweigen.

Schwieger|eltern ['ʃviːgər-] pl. parents-in-law pl.; '**～mutter** f mother-in-law; '**～sohn** m son-in-law; '**～tochter** f daughter-in-law; '**～vater** m father-in-law.

Schwiel|e ['ʃviːlə] f (-/-n) callosity; '**♀ig** adj. callous.

schwierig adj. ['ʃviːriç] difficult, hard; '♀keit f (-/-en) difficulty, trouble.

Schwimm|bad ['ʃvim-] n swimming-bath, Am. swimming pool; '♀en v/i. (irr., ge-) 1. (sein) swim; thing: float; ich bin über den Fluß geschwommen I swam across the river; in Geld ～ be rolling in money; 2. (h) swim; ich habe lange unter Wasser geschwommen I swam under water for a long time; '**～gür- tel** m swimming-belt; lifebelt; '**～haut** f web; '**～lehrer** m swimming-instructor; '**～weste** f life-jacket.

Schwindel ['ʃvindəl] m (-s/no pl.) ✶ vertigo, giddiness, dizziness; F fig.: swindle, humbug, sl. eyewash; cheat, fraud; '**～anfall** ✶ m fit of dizziness; '♀erregend adj. dizzy (a. fig.); '**～firma** ✝ f long firm, Am. wildcat firm; '♀n v/i. (ge-, h) cheat, humbug, swindle.

schwinden ['ʃvindən] v/i. (irr., ge-, sein) dwindle, grow less; strength, colour, etc.: fade.

'**Schwindl|er** m (-s/-) swindler, cheat, humbug; liar; '♀ig ✶ adj. giddy, dizzy.

Schwind|sucht ✶ ['ʃvint-] f (-/no pl.) consumption; '♀süchtig ✶ adj. consumptive.

Schwing|e ['ʃviŋə] f (-/-n) wing, poet. pinion; swingle; '♀en (irr., ge-, h) 1. v/t. swing; brandish (weapon); swingle (flax); 2. v/i. swing; ⊕ oscillate; sound, etc.: vibrate; '**～ung** f (-/-en) oscillation; vibration.

Schwips F [ʃvips] m (-es/-e): e-n ～ haben be tipsy, have had a drop too much.

schwirren ['ʃvirən] v/i. (ge-) 1. (sein) whir(r); arrow, etc.: whiz(z); insects: buzz; rumours, etc.: buzz, circulate; 2. (h): mir schwirrt der Kopf my head is buzzing.

'**Schwitz|bad** n sweating-bath, hot-air bath, vapo(u)r bath; '♀en (ge-, h) 1. v/i. sweat, perspire; 2. F fig. v/t.: Blut und Wasser ～ be in great anxiety.

schwoll [ʃvɔl] pret. of schwellen.

schwor [ʃvoːr] pret. of schwören.

schwören ['ʃvøːrən] (irr., ge-, h) 1. v/t. swear; e-n Meineid ～ commit perjury; j-m Rache ～ vow vengeance against s.o.; 2. v/i. swear (bei by);

～ auf (acc.) have great belief in, F swear by.

schwül adj. [ʃvyːl] sultry, oppressively hot; '♀e f (-/no pl.) sultriness.

Schwulst [ʃvulst] m (-es/⁼e) bombast.

schwülstig adj. ['ʃvylstiç] bombastic, turgid.

Schwund [ʃvunt] m (-[e]s/no pl.) dwindling; wireless, etc.: fading; ✶ atrophy.

Schwung [ʃvuŋ] m (-[e]s/⁼e) swing; fig. verve, go; flight (of imagination); buoyancy; '♀haft ✝ adj. flourishing, brisk; '**～rad** ⊕ n flywheel; watch, clock: balance-wheel; '♀voll adj. full of energy or verve; attack, translation, etc.: spirited; style, etc.: racy.

Schwur [ʃvuːr] m (-[e]s/⁼e) oath; '**～gericht** ✝✝ n England, Wales: appr. court of assize.

sechs [zɛks] 1. adj. six; 2. ♀ f (-/-en) six; '♀eck n (-[e]s/-e) hexagon; '**～eckig** adj. hexagonal; '**～fach** adj. sixfold, sextuple; '**～mal** adv. six times; '**～monatig** adj. lasting or of six months, six-months ...; '**～monatlich** 1. adj. six-monthly; 2. adv. every six months; '**～ständig** adj. ['-ʃtyndiç] lasting or of six hours, six-hour ...; ♀tagerennen n cycling: six-day race; '**～tägig** adj. ['-tɛːgiç] lasting or of six days.

sechs|te adj. ['zɛkstə] sixth; ♀tel n (-s/-) sixth (part); '**～tens** adv. sixthly, in the sixth place.

sech|zehn(te) adj.['zɛç-] sixteen(th); **～zig** adj. ['-tsiç] sixty; '**～zigste** adj. sixtieth.

See [zeː] 1. m (-s/-n) lake; 2. f (-/no pl.) sea; an die ～ gehen go to the seaside; in ～ gehen or stechen put to sea; auf ～ at sea; auf hoher ～ on the high seas; zur ～ gehen go to sea; 3. f (-/-n) sea, billow; '**～bad** n seaside resort; '**～fahrer** m sailor, navigator; '**～fahrt** f navigation; voyage; '♀fest adj. seaworthy; ～ sein be a good sailor; '**～gang** m (motion of the) sea; '**～hafen** m seaport; '**～handel** ✝ m maritime trade; '**～herrschaft** f naval supremacy; '**～hund** zo. m seal; '♀krank adj. seasick; '**～krankheit** f (-/no pl.) seasickness; '**～krieg** m naval war(fare).

Seele ['zeːlə] f (-/-n) soul (a. fig.); mit or von ganzer ～ with all one's heart.

'**Seelen|größe** f (-/no pl.) greatness of soul or mind; '**～heil** n salvation, spiritual welfare; '♀los adj. soulless; '**～qual** f anguish of mind, (mental) agony; '**～ruhe** f peace of mind; coolness.

'**seelisch** adj. psychic(al), mental.

'**Seelsorge** f (-/no pl.) cure of souls;

ministerial work; '~r *m* (-*s*/-) pastor, minister.

'See|macht *f* naval power; '~mann *m* (-[e]*s*/*Seeleute*) seaman, sailor; '~meile *f* nautical mile; '~not *f* (-/*no pl.*) distress (at sea); '~räuber *m* pirate; ~räuberei [~'raɪ] *f* (-/-*en*) piracy; '~recht *n* maritime law; '~reise *f* voyage; '~schiff *n* sea-going ship; '~schlacht *f* naval battle; '~schlange *f* sea serpent; '~sieg *m* naval victory; '~stadt *f* seaside town; '~streitkräfte *f*/*pl.* naval forces *pl.*; '~tüchtig *adj.* seaworthy; '~warte *f* naval observatory; '~weg *m* sea-route; *auf dem* ~ by sea; '~wesen *n* (-*s*/*no pl.*) maritime *or* naval affairs *pl.*

Segel ['ze:gəl] *n* (-*s*/-) sail; *unter* ~ *gehen* set sail; '~boot *n* sailing-boat, *Am.* sailboat; *sports:* yacht; '~fliegen *n* (-*s*/*no pl.*) gliding, soaring; '~flug *m* gliding flight, glide; '~flugzeug *n* glider; '²n (*ge*-) **1.** *v/i.* (*h*, *sein*) sail; *sports:* yacht; **2.** *v/t.* (*h*) sail; '~schiff *n* sailing-ship, sailing-vessel; '~sport *m* yachting; '~tuch *n* (-[e]*s*/-*e*) sail-cloth, canvas.

Segen ['ze:gən] *m* (-*s*/-) blessing (*a. fig.*), *esp. eccl.* benediction; '²s-reich *adj.* blessed.

Segler ['ze:glər] *m* (-*s*/-) sailing-vessel, sailing-ship; *fast, good, etc.* sailer; yachtsman.

segn|en ['ze:gnən] *v/t.* (*ge*-, *h*) bless; '²ung *f* (-/-*en*) *s.* Segen.

sehen ['ze:ən] (*irr.*, *ge*-, *h*) **1.** *v/i.* see; *gut* ~ have good eyes; ~ *auf* (*acc.*) look at; be particular about; ~ *nach* look for; look after; **2.** *v/t.* see; notice; watch, observe; '~swert *adj.* worth seeing; '²swürdigkeit *f* (-/-*en*) object of interest, curiosity; ~*en pl.* sights *pl.* (*of a place*).

Seher ['ze:ər] *m* (-*s*/-) seer, prophet; '~blick *m* (-[e]*s*/*no pl.*) prophetic vision; '~gabe *f* (-/*no pl.*) gift of prophecy.

'**Seh|fehler** *m* visual defect; '~kraft *f* vision, eyesight.

Sehne ['ze:nə] *f* (-/-*n*) *anat.* sinew, tendon; string (*of bow*); $\&$ chord.

'**sehnen** *v/refl.* (*ge*-, *h*) long (*nach* for), yearn (for, after); *sich danach* ~ *zu inf.* be longing to *inf.*

'**Sehnerv** *anat. m* visual *or* optic nerve.

'**sehnig** *adj.* sinewy (*a. fig.*), stringy.

'**sehn|lich** *adj.* longing; ardent; passionate; '²sucht *f* longing, yearning; '~süchtig *adj.*, ~suchts-voll *adj.* longing, yearning; *eyes, etc.:* a. wistful.

sehr *adv.* [ze:r] *before adj. and adv.:* very, most; *with vb.:* (very) much, greatly.

'**Seh|rohr** ⚓ *n* periscope; '~weite *f*

range of sight, visual range; *in* ~ within eyeshot *or* sight.

seicht *adj.* [zaɪçt] shallow; *fig. a.* superficial.

Seide ['zaɪdə] *f* (-/-*n*) silk.

'**seiden** *adj.* silk, silken (*a. fig.*); '²flor *m* silk gauze; '²glanz *m* silky lust|re, *Am.* -er; '²händler *m* mercer; '²papier *n* tissue(-paper); '²raupe *zo.* *f* silkworm; '²spinnerei *f* silk-spinning mill; '²stoff *m* silk cloth *or* fabric.

'**seidig** *adj.* silky.

Seife ['zaɪfə] *f* (-/-*n*) soap.

'**Seifen|blase** *f* soap-bubble; '~kistenrennen *n* soap-box derby; '~lauge *f* (soap-)suds *pl.*; '~pulver *n* soap-powder; '~schale *f* soap-dish; '~schaum *m* lather.

'**seifig** *adj.* soapy.

seih|en ['zaɪən] *v/t.* (*ge*-, *h*) strain, filter; '²er *m* (-*s*/-) strainer, colander.

Seil [zaɪl] *n* (-[e]*s*/-*e*) rope; '~bahn *f* funicular *or* cable railway; '~er *m* (-*s*/-) rope-maker; '~tänzer *m* rope-dancer.

sein[1] [zaɪn] **1.** *v/i.* (*irr.*, *ge*-, *sein*) be; exist; **2.** ☒ *n* (-*s*/*no pl.*) being; existence.

sein[2] *poss. pron.* [~] his, her, its (*in accordance with gender of possessor*); *der* (*die, das*) ~*e* his, hers, its; ~ *Glück machen* make one's fortune; *die Seinen pl.* his family *or* people.

'**seiner**|'**seits** *adv.* for his part; '~zeit *adv.* then, at that time; in those days.

'**seines**|'**gleichen** *pron.* his equal(s *pl.*); *j-n wie* ~ *behandeln* treat s.o. as one's equal; *er hat nicht* ~ he has no equal; there is no one like him.

seit [zaɪt] **1.** *prp.* (*dat.*): ~ *1945* since 1945; ~ *drei Wochen* for three weeks; **2.** *cj.* since; *es ist ein Jahr her,* ~ *...* it is a year now since *...*; ~**dem** [~'de:m] **1.** *adv.* since *or* from that time, ever since; **2.** *cj.* since.

Seite ['zaɪtə] *f* (-/-*n*) side (*a. fig.*); flank (*a.* ⚔, △); page (*of book*).

'**Seiten**|**ansicht** *f* profile, side-view; '~blick *m* side-glance; '~flügel △ *m* wing; '~hieb *fig. m* innuendo, sarcastic remark; '²s *prp.* (*gen.*) on the part of; by; '~schiff △ *n* *church:* aisle; '~sprung *fig. m* extra-marital adventure; '~straße *f* bystreet; '~stück *fig. n* counterpart (*zu* of); '~weg *m* by-way.

seit'**her** *adv.* since (then, that time).

'**seit**|**lich** *adj.* lateral; ~**wärts** *adv.* ['~verts] sideways; aside.

Sekret|**är** [zekre'tɛ:r] *m* (-*s*/-*e*) secretary; bureau; ~**ariat** [~ari'a:t] *n* (-[e]*s*/-*e*) secretary's office; secretariat(e); ~**ärin** *f* (-/-*nen*) secretary.

Sekt [zɛkt] m (-[e]s/-e) champagne.

Sekt|e ['zɛktə] f (-/-n) sect; **~ierer** [,'ti:rər] m (-s/-) sectarian.

Sektor ['zɛktɔr] m (-s/-en) ⚥, ✕, *pol.* sector; *fig.* field, branch.

Sekunde [ze'kundə] f (-/-n) second; **~nbruchteil** m split second; **~nzeiger** m second-hand.

selb adj. [zɛlp] same; **~er** F *pron.* [',~bər] s. selbst 1.

selbst [zɛlpst] 1. *pron.* self; personally; *ich* ~ I myself; *von* ~ *p.* of one's own accord; *thing:* by itself, automatically; 2. *adv.* even; 3. ♀ n (-/no pl.) (one's own) self; ego.

selbständig adj. ['zɛlpʃtɛndiç] independent; *sich* ~ *machen* set up for o.s.; **♀keit** f (-/no pl.) independence.

'Selbst|anlasser *mot.* m self-starter; **'~anschluß** *teleph.* m automatic connection; **'~bedienungsladen** m self-service shop; **'~beherrschung** f self-command, self-control; **'~bestimmung** f self-determination; **'~betrug** m self-deception; **'~bewußt** adj. self-confident, self-reliant; **'~bewußtsein** n self-confidence, self-reliance; **'~binder** m (-s/-) tie; **'~erhaltung** f self-preservation; **'~erkenntnis** f self-knowledge; **'~erniedrigung** f self-abasement; **'~gefällig** adj. (self-)complacent; **'~gefälligkeit** f (-/no pl.) (self-)complacency; **'~gefühl** n (-[e]s/no pl.) self-reliance; **♀gemacht** adj. ['~gəmaxt] homemade; **'♀gerecht** adj. self-righteous; **'~gespräch** n soliloquy, monolog(ue); **'♀herrlich** 1. adj. high-handed, autocratic(al); 2. adv. with a high hand; **'~hilfe** f self-help; **'~kostenpreis** ✝ m cost price; **'~laut** *gr.* m vowel; **'♀los** adj. unselfish, disinterested; **'~mord** m suicide; **'~mörder** m suicide; **'♀mörderisch** adj. suicidal; **'♀sicher** adj. self-confident, self-assured; **'~sucht** f (-/no pl.) selfishness, ego(t)ism; **'♀süchtig** adj. selfish, ego(t)istic(al); **'♀tätig** ⊕ adj. self-acting, automatic; **'~täuschung** f self-deception; **'~überwindung** f (-/no pl.) self-conquest; **'~unterricht** m self-instruction; **'~verleugnung** f self-denial; **'~versorger** m (-s/-) self-supporter; **'♀verständlich** 1. adj. self-evident, obvious; 2. adv. of course, naturally; **~l** a. by all means!; **'~verständlichkeit** f 1. (-/-en) matter of course; 2. (-/no pl.) matter-of-factness; **'~verteidigung** f self-defen|ce, *Am.* -se; **'~vertrauen** n self-confidence, self-reliance; **'~verwaltung** f self-government, autonomy; **'♀zufrieden** adj. self-satisfied; **'~zufriedenheit** f self-satisfaction; **'~zweck** m (-[e]s/no pl.) end in itself.

selig adj. ['ze:liç] *eccl.* blessed; late, deceased; *fig.* blissful, overjoyed; **'♀keit** fig. f (-/-en) bliss, very great joy.

Sellerie ♀ ['zɛləri:] m (-s/ [ɛ]), f (-/-) celery.

selten ['zɛltən] 1. adj. rare; scarce; 2. adv. rarely, seldom; **♀heit** f (-/-en) rarity, scarcity; rarity, curio(sity); **♀heitswert** m (-[e]s/no pl.) scarcity value.

Selterswasser ['zɛltərs-] n (-s/ᵘ) seltzer (water), soda-water.

seltsam adj. ['zɛltza:m] strange, odd.

Semester *univ.* [ze'mɛstər] n (-s/-) term.

Semikolon *gr.* [zemi'ko:lɔn] n (-s/-s, *Semikola*) semicolon.

Seminar [zemi'na:r] n (-s/-e) *univ.* seminar; seminary (*for priests*).

Senat [ze'na:t] m (-[e]s/-e) senate; *parl.* Senate.

send|en ['zɛndən] v/t. 1. ([irr.,] ge-, h) send; forward; 2. (ge-, h) transmit, broadcast, *Am. a.* radio(broadcast); telecast; **'♀er** m (-s/-) transmitter; broadcasting station.

'Sende|raum m (broadcasting) studio; **'~zeichen** n interval signal.

'Sendung f (-/-en) ✝ consignment, shipment; broadcast; telecast; *fig.* mission. {♀.}

Senf [zɛnf] m (-[e]s/-e) mustard (a.)

sengen ['zɛŋən] v/t. (ge-, h) singe, scorch; **'~d** adj. heat: parching.

senil adj. [ze'ni:l] senile; **♀ität** [~ili'tɛ:t] f (-/no pl.) senility.

senior adj. ['ze:niɔr] senior.

Senk|blei ['zɛŋk-] n ⚓ plumb, plummet; ♣ a. sounding-lead; **'♀e** *geogr.* f (-/-n) depression, hollow; **'♀en** v/t. (ge-, h) lower; sink (a. voice); let down; bow (head); cut (prices, etc.); *sich* ~ land, buildings, etc.: sink, subside; ceiling, etc.: sag; **'~fuß** ♣ m flat-foot; **'~fußeinlage** f arch support; **'~grube** f cesspool; **'♀recht** adj. vertical, esp. ⚥ perpendicular; **'~ung** f (-/-en) *geogr.* depression, hollow; lowering, reduction (of prices); ♣ sedimentation.

Sensation [zɛnza'tsjo:n] f (-/-en) sensation; **♀ell** adj. [~o'nɛl] sensational; **~slust** f (-/no pl.) sensationalism; **~spresse** f yellow press.

Sense ['zɛnzə] f (-/-n) scythe.

sensi|bel adj. [zɛn'zi:bəl] sensitive; **♀bilität** [~ibili'tɛ:t] f (-/no pl.) sensitiveness.

sentimental adj. [zɛntimɛn'ta:l] sentimental; **♀ität** [~ali'tɛ:t] f (-/-en) sentimentality.

September [zɛp'tɛmbər] m (-[s]/-) September.

Serenade ♪ [zere'nɑːdə] f (-/-n) serenade.

Serie ['zeːrjə] f (-/-n) series; set; *billiards*: break; '**⊸nmäßig 1.** *adj.* standard; **2.** *adv.:* ~ **herstellen** produce in mass; '**⊸nproduktion** f mass production.

seriös *adj.* [ze'rjøːs] serious; trustworthy, reliable.

Serum ['zeːrum] n (-s/Seren, Sera) serum.

Service[1] [zər'viːs] n (-s/-) service, set.

Service[2] ['zœːrvis] m, n (-/-s) service.

servier|en [zɛr'viːrən] v/t. (no -ge-, h) serve; **⊸wagen** m trolley(-table).

Serviette [zɛr'vjɛtə] f (-/-n) (table-) napkin.

Sessel ['zɛsəl] m (-s/-) armchair, easy chair; '**⊸lift** m chair-lift.

seßhaft *adj.* ['zɛshaft] settled, established; resident.

Setzei ['zɛts²-] n fried egg.

'**setzen** (ge-) **1.** v/t. (h) set, place, put; *typ.* compose; ♂ plant; erect, raise (*monument*); stake (*money*) (*auf acc.* on); *sich* ~ sit down, take a seat; *bird:* perch; *foundations of house, sediment, etc.:* settle; **2.** v/i. (h): ~ *auf* (*acc.*) back (*horse, etc.*); **3.** v/i. (sein): ~ *über* (*acc.*) leap (*wall, etc.*); clear (*hurdle, etc.*); take (*ditch, etc.*).

'**Setzer** *typ.* m (-s/-) compositor, type-setter; '**⊸ei** *typ.* [⸃'rai] f (-/-en) composing-room.

Seuche ['zɔyçə] f (-/-n) epidemic (disease).

seufz|en ['zɔyftsən] v/i. (ge-, h) sigh; '**⊸er** m (-s/-) sigh.

sexuell *adj.* [zɛksu'ɛl] sexual.

sezieren [ze'tsiːrən] v/t. (no -ge-, h) dissect (*a. fig.*).

sich *refl. pron.* [ziç] oneself; *sg.* himself, herself, itself; *pl.* themselves; *sg.* yourself, *pl.* yourselves; each other, one another; *sie blickte* ~ *um* she looked about her.

Sichel ['ziçəl] f (-/-n) sickle; *s.* Mondsichel.

sicher ['ziçər] **1.** *adj.* secure (*vor dat.* from), safe (from); proof (against); *hand:* steady; certain, sure; positive; *aus* ⸃er Quelle from a reliable source; e-r Sache ~ *sein* be sure of s.th.; **2.** *adv.* s. *sicherlich;* *um* ~ *zu gehen* to be on the safe side, to make sure.

'**Sicherheit** f (-/-en) security; safety; surety, certainty; positiveness; assurance (*of manner*); *in* ~ *bringen* place in safety; '**⊸snadel** f safety-pin; '**⊸sschloß** n safety-lock.

'**sicher|lich** *adv.* surely, certainly; undoubtedly; *er wird* ~ *kommen* he is sure to come; '**⊸n** v/t. (ge-, h) secure (*a.* ✂, ⊕); guarantee (*a.* †); protect, safeguard; *sich et.* ~ secure

(*prize, seat, etc.*); '**⊸stellen** v/t. (*sep.*, -ge-, h) secure; '**⊸ung** f (-/-en) securing; safeguard(ing); † security, guaranty; ⊕ safety device; ✐ fuse.

Sicht [ziçt] f (-/no pl.) visibility; view; *in* ~ *kommen* come in(to) view or sight; *auf lange* ~ in the long run; *auf* or *bei* ~ † at sight; '**⊸bar** *adj.* visible; '**⊸en** v/t. (ge-, h) ⊕ sight; *fig.* sift; '**⊸lich** *adv.* visibly; '**⊸vermerk** m visé, visa (*on passport*).

sickern ['zikərn] v/i. (ge-, sein) trickle, ooze, seep.

sie *pers. pron.* [ziː] *nom.: sg.* she, *pl.* they, *acc.: sg.* her, *pl.* them; **Sie** *nom. and acc.: sg. and pl.* you.

Sieb [ziːp] n (-[e]s/-e) sieve; riddle (*for soil, gravel, etc.*).

sieben[1] ['ziːbən] v/t. (ge-, h) sieve, sift; riddle.

sieben[2] [⸃] **1.** *adj.* seven; **2.** ⚲ f (-/-) (number) seven; *böse* ~ shrew, vixen; '**⊸fach** *adj.* sevenfold; '**⊸mal** *adv.* seven times; '**⊸'sachen** F f/pl. belongings *pl.*, F traps *pl.*; '**⊸te** *adj.* seventh; '**⊸tel** n (-s/-) seventh (part); '**⊸tens** *adv.* seventhly, in the seventh place.

sieb|zehn(te) *adj.* ['ziːp-] seventeen(th); '**⊸zig** *adj.* ['⸃tsiç] seventy; '**⊸zigste** *adj.* seventieth.

siech [ziːç] *adj.* sickly; '**⊸tum** n (-s/no pl.) sickliness, lingering illness.

Siedehitze ['ziːdə-] f boiling-heat.

siedeln ['ziːdəln] v/i. (ge-, h) settle; *Am. a.* homestead.

siede|n ['ziːdən] v/t. and v/i. ([irr.,] ge-, h) boil, simmer; '**⊸punkt** m boiling-point (*a. fig.*).

Siedler ['ziːdlər] m (-s/-) settler; *Am. a.* homesteader; '**⊸stelle** f settler's holding; *Am. a.* homestead.

'**Siedlung** f (-/-en) settlement; housing estate.

Sieg [ziːk] m (-[e]s/-e) victory (*über acc.* over); *sports: a.* win; *den* ~ *davontragen* win the day, be victorious.

Siegel ['ziːgəl] n (-s/-) seal (*a. fig.*); signet; '**⊸lack** m sealing-wax; '**⊸n** v/t. (ge-, h) seal; '**⊸ring** m signet-ring.

sieg|en ['ziːgən] v/i. (ge-, h) be victorious (*über acc.* over), conquer *s.o.*; *sports:* win; '**⊸er** m (-s/-) conqueror, *rhet.* victor; *sports:* winner.

Siegeszeichen ['ziːgəs-] n trophy.

'**siegreich** *adj.* victorious, triumphant.

Signal [zi'gnaːl] n (-s/-e) signal; **⊸isieren** [⸃ali'ziːrən] v/t. (no -ge-, h) signal.

Silbe ['zilbə] f (-/-n) syllable; '**⊸ntrennung** f syllabi(fi)cation.

Silber ['zilbər] n (-s/no pl.) silver; *s. Tafelsilber;* '**⊸n** *adj.* (of) silver;

'**~zeug** F *n* silver plate, *Am. a.* silverware.

Silhouette [zilu'etə] *f* (-/-n) silhouette; skyline.

Silvester [zil'vestər] *n* (-s/-), **~abend** *m* new-year's eve.

simpel ['zimpəl] **1.** *adj.* plain, simple; stupid, silly; **2.** ♀ *m* (-s/-) simpleton.

Sims [zims] *m, n* (-es/-e) ledge; sill (*of window*); mantelshelf (*of fireplace*); shelf; △ cornice.

Simul|ant [zimu'lant] *m* (-en/-en) *esp.* ✕, ⚓ malingerer; ♀**ieren** (*no* -ge-, *h*) **1.** *v/t.* sham, feign, simulate (*illness, etc.*); **2.** *v/i.* sham, feign; *esp.* ✕, ⚓ malinger.

Sinfonie ♪ [zinfo'ni:] *f* (-/-n) symphony.

sing|en ['ziŋən] *v/t. and v/i.* (*irr.*, ge-, *h*) sing; **vom Blatt ~** sing at sight; **nach Noten ~** sing from music; '♀**sang** *m* (-[e]s/*no pl.*) singsong; '♀**spiel** *n* musical comedy; '♀**stimme** ♪ *f* vocal part.

Singular *gr.* ['ziŋgula:r] *m* (-s/-e) singular (number).

'**Singvogel** *m* song-bird, songster.

sinken ['ziŋkən] *v/i.* (*irr.*, ge-, *sein*) sink; *ship:* a. founder, go down; ✝ *prices:* fall, drop, go down; **den Mut ~ lassen** lose courage.

Sinn [zin] *m* (-[e]s/-e) sense; taste (*für* for); tendency; sense, meaning; **von ~en sein** be out of one's senses; **im ~ haben** have in mind; **in gewissem ~e** in a sense; '**~bild** *n* symbol, emblem; '**~bildlich** *adj.* symbolic(al), emblematic; '♀**en** *v/i.* (*irr.*, ge-, *h*): **auf Rache ~** meditate revenge.

'**Sinnen|lust** *f* sensuality; '**~mensch** *m* sensualist; '**~rausch** *m* intoxication of the senses.

sinnentstellend *adj.* ['zin?-] garbling, distorting. [world.]

'**Sinnenwelt** *f* (-/*no pl.*) material]

'**Sinnes|änderung** *f* change of mind; '**~art** *f* disposition, mentality; '**~organ** *n* sense-organ; '**~täuschung** *f* illusion, hallucination.

'**sinn|lich** *adj.* sensual; material; '♀**lichkeit** *f* (-/*no pl.*) sensuality; '♀**los** *adj.* senseless; futile, useless; '♀**losigkeit** *f* (-/-en) senselessness; futility, uselessness; '**~reich** *adj.* ingenious; '**~verwandt** *adj.* synonymous.

Sippe ['zipə] *f* (-/-n) tribe; (blood-) relations *pl.*; family; '**~schaft** *contp. f* (-/-en) relations *pl.*; *fig.* clan, clique; **die ganze ~** the whole lot.

Sirene [zi're:nə] *f* (-/-n) siren.

Sirup ['zi:rup] *m* (-s/-e) syrup, *Am.* sirup; treacle, molasses *sg.*

Sitte ['zitə] *f* (-/-n) custom; habit; usage; **~n** *pl.* morals *pl.*; manners *pl.*

'**Sitten|bild** *n*, '**~gemälde** *n* genre (-painting); *fig.* picture of manners and morals; '**~gesetz** *n* moral law; '**~lehre** *f* ethics *pl.*; '♀**los** *adj.* immoral; '**~losigkeit** *f* (-/-en) immorality; '**~polizei** *f* *appr.* vice squad; '**~prediger** *m* moralizer; '**~richter** *fig. m* censor, moralizer; '♀**streng** *adj.* puritanic(al).

'**sittlich** *adj.* moral; '♀**keit** *f* (-/*no pl.*) morality; '♀**keitsverbrechen** *n* sexual crime.

'**sittsam** *adj.* modest; '♀**keit** *f* (-/*no pl.*) modesty.

Situation [zitua'tsjo:n] *f* (-/-en) situation.

Sitz [zits] *m* (-es/-e) seat (*a. fig.*); fit (*of dress, etc.*).

'**sitzen** *v/i.* (*irr.*, ge-, *h*) sit, be seated; *dress, etc.:* fit; *blow, etc.:* tell; F *fig.* do time; **~ bleiben** remain seated, keep one's seat; '**~bleiben** *v/i.* (*irr.* bleiben, sep., -ge-, *sein*) *girl at dance:* F be a wallflower; *girl:* be left on the shelf; *at school:* not to get one's remove; **~ auf** (*dat.*) be left with (*goods*) on one's hands; '**~d** *adj.* **~e Tätigkeit** sedentary work; '**~lassen** *v/t.* (*irr.* lassen, sep., [no] -ge-, *h*) leave *s.o.* in the lurch, let *s.o.* down; *girl:* jilt (*lover*); leave (*girl*) high and dry; **auf sich ~** pocket (*insult, etc.*).

'**Sitz|gelegenheit** *f* seating accommodation, seat(s *pl.*); **~ bieten für** seat; '**~platz** *m* seat; '**~streik** *m* sit-down *or* stay-in strike.

'**Sitzung** *f* (-/-en) sitting (*a. parl., paint.*); meeting, conference; '**~speriode** *f* session.

Skala ['ska:la] *f* (-/*Skalen, Skalas*) scale (*a.* ♪); dial (*of radio set*); *fig.* gamut; **gleitende ~** sliding scale.

Skandal [skan'da:l] *m* (-s/-e) scandal; row, riot; ♀**ös** *adj.* [~a'lø:s] scandalous.

Skelett [ske'lɛt] *n* (-[e]s/-e) skeleton.

Skep|sis ['skepsis] *f* (-/*no pl.*) scepticism, *Am. a.* skepticism; '**~tiker** ['~tikər] *m* (-s/-) sceptic, *Am. a.* skeptic; '♀**tisch** *adj.* sceptical, *Am. a.* skeptical.

Ski [ʃi:] *m* (-s/-er, ♘-) ski; **~ laufen** *or* **fahren** ski; '**~fahrer** *m*, '**~läufer** *m* skier; '**~lift** *m* ski-lift; '**~sport** *m* (-[e]s/*no pl.*) skiing.

Skizz|e ['skitsə] *f* (-/-n) sketch (*a. fig.*); ♀**ieren** [~'tsi:rən] *v/t.* (*no* -ge-, *h*) sketch, outline (*both a. fig.*).

Sklav|e ['skla:və] *m* (-n/-n) slave (*a. fig.*); '**~enhandel** *m* slave-trade; '**~enhändler** *m* slave-trader; **~e'rei** *f* (-/-en) slavery; '♀**isch** *adj.* slavish.

Skonto ✝ ['skɔnto] *m, n* (-s/-s, ♘ *Skonti*) discount.

Skrupel ['skru:pəl] *m* (-s/-) scruple; '♀**los** *adj.* unscrupulous.

Skulptur [skulp'tu:r] *f* (-/-en) sculpture.

Slalom ['slaːləm] *m* (-s/-s) skiing, *etc.*: slalom.

Slaw|e ['slaːvə] *m* (-n/-n) Slav; **'₂isch** *adj.* Slav(onic).

Smaragd [smaˈrakt] *m* (-[e]s/-e) emerald; **₂grün** *adj.* emerald.

Smoking ['smoːkiŋ] *m* (-s/-s) dinner-jacket, *Am. a.* tuxedo, F tux.

so [zoː] **1.** *adv.* so, thus; like this *or* that; as; ~ ein such a; ~ ... wie as ... as; nicht ~ ... wie not so ... as; ~ oder ~ by hook or by crook; **2.** *cj.* so, therefore, consequently; ~ daß so that; **₋bald** *cj.* [zoˈ-]: ~ (als) as soon as.

Socke ['zɔkə] *f* (-/-n) sock; **'₋l** *m* (-s/-) △ pedestal, socle; socket (*of lamp*); **₋n** *m* (-s/-) sock; **'₋nhalter** *m/pl.* suspenders *pl.*, *Am.* garters *pl.*

Sodawasser ['zoːdaː-] *n* (-s/⁼) soda(-water).

Sodbrennen ⚕ ['zoːt-] *n* (-s/no *pl.*) heartburn.

soeben *adv.* [zoˈ-] just (now).

Sofa ['zoːfa] *n* (-s/-s) sofa.

sofern *cj.* [zoˈ-] if, provided that; ~ nicht unless.

soff [zɔf] *pret. of* saufen.

sofort *adv.* [zoˈ-] at once, immediately, directly, right *or* straight away; **₋ig** *adj.* immediate, prompt.

Sog [zoːk] **1.** *m* (-[e]s/-e) suction; ⚓ wake (*a. fig.*), undertow; **2.** ⚲ *pret. of* saugen.

so|gar *adv.* [zoˈ-] even; **₋genannt** *adj.* ['zoˈ-] so-called; **₋gleich** *adv.* [zoˈ-] *s.* sofort.

Sohle ['zoːlə] *f* (-/-n) sole; bottom (*of valley, etc.*); ⚒ floor.

Sohn [zoːn] *m* (-[e]s/⁼e) son.

solange *cj.* [zoˈ-]: ~ (als) so *or* as long as. [such.)

solch *pron.* [zɔlç] such; *als* ~ e(r) as)

Sold ✠ [zɔlt] *m* (-[e]s/-e) pay.

Soldat [zɔlˈdaːt] *m* (-en/-en) soldier; der unbekannte ~ the Unknown Warrior *or* Soldier.

Söldner ['zœldnər] *m* (-s/-) mercenary.

Sole ['zoːlə] *f* (-/-n) brine, salt water.

solid *adj.* [zoˈliːt] solid (*a. fig.*); basis, *etc.*: sound; 🛠 firm, *etc.*: sound, solvent; prices: reasonable, fair; *p.* steady, staid, respectable.

solidarisch *adj.* [zoliˈdaːriʃ]: sich ~ erklären mit declare one's solidarity with.

solide *adj.* [zoˈliːdə] *s.* solid.

Solist [zoˈlist] *m* (-en/-en) soloist.

Soll 🛠 [zɔl] *n* (-[s]/-[s]) debit; (output) target.

'sollen (*h*) **1.** *v/i.* (ge-): ich sollte (eigentlich) I ought to; **2.** *v/aux.* (*irr., no* -ge-): er soll he shall; he is to; he is said to; ich sollte I should; er sollte (eigentlich) zu Hause sein he ought to be at home; er sollte seinen Vater niemals wiedersehen he was never to see his father again.

Solo ['zoːlo] *n* (-s/-s, Soli) solo.

somit *cj.* [zoˈ-] thus; consequently.

Sommer ['zɔmər] *m* (-s/-) summer; **'₋frische** *f* (-/-n) summer-holidays *pl.*; summer-resort; **'₂lich** *adj.* summer-like, summer(l)y; **'₋sprosse** *f* freckle; **'₂sprossig** *adj.* freckled; **'₋wohnung** *f* summer residence, *Am.* cottage, summer house; **'₋zeit f 1.** (-/-en) season: summertime; **2.** (-/no *pl.*) summer time, *Am.* daylight-saving time.

Sonate ♪ [zoˈnaːtə] *f* (-/-n) sonata.

Sonde ['zɔndə] *f* (-/-n) probe.

Sonder|angebot ['zɔndər-] *n* special offer; **₋ausgabe** *f* special (edition); **'₂bar** *adj.* strange, odd; **'₋beilage** *f* inset, supplement (*of newspaper*); **₋berichterstatter** *m* special correspondent; **'₂lich 1.** *adj.* special, peculiar; **2.** *adv.*: nicht ~ not particularly; **₋ling** *m* (-s/-e) crank, odd person; **'₂n 1.** *cj.* but; nicht nur, ~ auch not only, but (also); **2.** *v/t.* (ge-, h): die Spreu vom Weizen ~ sift the chaff from the wheat; **'₋recht** *n* privilege; **'₋zug** 🚂 *m* special (train).

sondieren [zɔnˈdiːrən] (*no* -ge-, h) **1.** *v/t.* ⚕ probe (*a. fig.*); **2.** *fig.* *v/i.* make tentative inquiries.

Sonn|abend ['zɔn-] *m* (-s/-e) Saturday; **₋e** *f* (-/-n) sun; **'₂en** *v/t.* (ge-, h) (expose to the) sun; sich ~ sun o.s. (*a. fig. in dat. in*), bask in the sun.

'Sonnen|aufgang *m* sunrise; **'₋bad** *n* sun-bath; **'₋brand** *m* sunburn; **'₋bräune** *f* sunburn, tan, *Am.* (sun)tan; **'₋brille** *f* (e-e a pair of) sunglasses *pl.*; **'₋finsternis** *f* solar eclipse; **'₋fleck** *m* sun-spot; **'₂klar** *fig. adj.* (as) clear as daylight; **'₋licht** *n* (-[e]s/no *pl.*) sunlight; **'₋schein** *m* (-[e]s/no *pl.*) sunshine; **'₋schirm** *m* sunshade, parasol; **'₋segel** *n* awning; **'₋seite** *f* sunny side (*a. fig.*); **'₋stich** ⚕ *m* sunstroke; **'₋strahl** *m* sunbeam; **'₋uhr** *f* sun-dial; **'₋untergang** *m* sunset, sundown; **'₂verbrannt** *adj.* sunburnt, tanned; **'₋wende** *f* solstice.

'sonnig *adj.* sunny (*a. fig.*).

'Sonntag *m* Sunday.

'Sonntags|anzug *m* Sunday suit *or* best; **'₋fahrer** *mot. contp. m* Sunday driver; **'₋kind** *n* person born on a Sunday; *fig.* person born under a lucky star; **'₋rückfahrkarte** 🚂 *f* week-end ticket; **'₋ruhe** *f* Sunday rest; **'₋staat** F *co. m* (-[e]s/no *pl.*) Sunday go-to-meeting clothes *pl.*

sonor *adj.* [zoˈnoːr] sonorous.

sonst [zɔnst] **1.** *adv.* otherwise, with *pron.* then; usually, normally; wer ~? who else?; wie ~ as usual; ~ nichts nothing else; **2.** *cj.* otherwise, or else; **'₋ig** *adj.* other; **'₋wie** *adv.*

in some other way; '~wo adv. elsewhere, somewhere else.

Sopran ♪ [zo'prɑ:n] m (-s/-e) soprano; sopranist; **~istin** ♪ [~a'nistin] f (-/-nen) soprano, sopranist.

Sorge ['zɔrgə] f (-/-n) care; sorrow; uneasiness, anxiety; ~ tragen für take care of; sich ~n machen um be anxious or worried about; mach dir keine ~n don't worry.

'**sorgen** (ge-, h) 1. v/i.: ~ für care for, provide for; take care of, attend to; dafür ~, daß take care that; 2. v/refl.: sich ~ um be anxious or worried about; '~frei adj., '~los adj. carefree, free from care; '~voll adj. full of cares; face: worried, troubled.

Sorg|falt ['zɔrkfalt] f (-/no pl.) care(fulness); ♀fältig adj. ['~fɛltiç] careful; ♀lich adj. careful, anxious; ♀los adj. carefree; thoughtless; negligent; careless; ♀sam adj. careful.

Sort|e ['zɔrtə] f (-/-n) sort, kind, species, Am. a. stripe; ♀ieren [~'ti:rən] v/t. (no -ge-, h) (as)sort; arrange; ~iment [~i'mɛnt] n (-[e]s/-e) assortment.

Soße ['zo:sə] f (-/-n) sauce; gravy.

sott [zɔt] pret. of sieden.

Souffl|eurkasten thea. [su'flø:r-] m prompt-box, promter's box; ~euse thea. [~zə] f (-/-n) prompter; ♀ieren thea. (no -ge-, h) 1. v/i. prompt (j-m s.o.); 2. v/t. prompt.

Souverän [suvə're:n] 1. m (-s/-e) sovereign; 2. ♀ adj. sovereign; fig. superior; ~ität [~ɛni'tɛːt] f (-/no pl.) sovereignty.

so|viel [zo'-] 1. cj. so or as far as; ~ ich weiß so far as I know; 2. adv.: doppelt ~ twice as much; '~'weit 1. cj.: ~ es mich betrifft in so far as it concerns me, so far as I am concerned; 2. adv.: ~ ganz gut not bad (for a start); '~'wieso adv. [zovi'zo:] in any case, anyhow, anyway.

Sowjet [zɔ'vjɛt] m (-s/-s) Soviet; ♀isch adj. Soviet.

sowohl cj. [zo'-]: ~ ... als (auch) ... both ... and ..., ... as well as ...

sozial adj. [zo'tsjɑ:l] social; ♀demokrat m social democrat; ~isieren [~ali'zi:rən] v/t. (no -ge-, h) socialize; ♀isierung [~ali'zi:ruŋ] f (-/-en) socialization; ♀ist m [~a'list] m (-en/-en) socialist; ~istisch adj. [~a'listiç] socialist.

Sozius ['zo:tsjus] m (-/-se) ♀ partner; mot. pillion-rider; '~sitz mot. m pillion.

sozusagen adv. [zotsu'zɑ:gən] so to speak, as it were.

Spachtel ['ʃpaxtəl] m (-s/-), f (-/-n) spatula.

spähe|n ['ʃpɛ:ən] v/i. (ge-, h) look

out (nach for); peer; '♀r m (-s/-) look-out; ✕ scout.

Spalier [ʃpa'li:r] n (-s/-e) trellis, espalier; fig. lane; ~ bilden form a lane.

Spalt [ʃpalt] m (-[e]s/-e) crack, split, rift, crevice, fissure; '~e f (-/-n) s. Spalt; typ. column; ♀en (ge-, h) v/t. ([irr.,] ge-, h) split (a. fig. hairs), cleave (block of wood, etc.); sich ~ split (up); '~ung f (-/-en) splitting, cleavage; fig. split; eccl. schism.

Span [ʃpɑ:n] m (-[e]s/♀e) chip, shaving, splinter.

Spange ['ʃpaŋə] f (-/-n) clasp; buckle; clip; slide (in hair); strap (of shoes); bracelet.

Span|ier ['ʃpɑ:njər] m (-s/-) Spaniard; '♀isch adj. Spanish.

Spann [ʃpan] 1. m (-[e]s/-e) instep; 2. ♀ pret. of spinnen; '~e f (-/-n) span; ✕, orn. spread (of wings); ✝ margin; ♀en (ge-, h) 1. v/t. stretch (rope, muscles, etc.); cock (rifle); bend (bow, etc.); tighten (spring, etc.); vor den Wagen ~ harness to the carriage; s. gespannt; 2. v/i. be (too) tight; '♀end adj. exciting, thrilling, gripping; '~kraft f (-/no pl.) elasticity; fig. energy; '~ung f (-/-en) tension (a. fig.); ∮ voltage; ⊕ strain, stress; △ span; fig. close attention.

Spar|büchse ['ʃpɑ:r-] f money-box; '♀en (ge-, h) 1. v/t. save (money, strength, etc.); put by; 2. v/i. save; economize, cut down expenses; ~ mit be chary of (praise, etc.); '~er m (-s/-) saver.

Spargel ♀ ['ʃpargəl] m (-s/-) asparagus.

'**Spar|kasse** f savings-bank; '~konto n savings-account.

spärlich adj. ['ʃpɛːrliç] crop, dress, etc.: scanty; population, etc.: sparse; hair: thin.

Sparren ['ʃparən] m (-s/-) rafter, spar.

'**sparsam** 1. adj. saving, economical (mit of); 2. adv.: ~ leben lead a frugal life, economize; ~ umgehen mit use sparingly, be frugal of; ♀keit f (-/no pl.) economy, frugality.

Spaß [ʃpɑ:s] m (-es/♀e) joke, jest; fun, lark; amusement; aus or im or zum ~ in fun; ~ beiseite joking apart; er hat nur ~ gemacht he was only joking; ♀en v/i. (ge-, h) joke, jest, make fun; damit ist nicht zu ~ that is no joking matter; '♀haft adj., '♀ig adj. facetious, waggish; funny; '~macher m (-s/-), '~vogel m wag, joker.

spät [ʃpɛːt] 1. adj. late; advanced; zu ~ too late; am ~en Nachmittag late in the afternoon; wie ~ ist es? what time is it?; 2. adv. late; er kommt 5 Minuten zu ~ he is five minutes late (zu for); ~ in der Nacht late at night.

Spaten ['ʃpaːtən] *m* (-s/-) spade.

'**späte|r 1.** *adj.* later; **2.** *adv.* later on; afterward(s); *früher oder* ~ sooner or later; **~stens** *adv.* ['~stəns] at the latest.

Spatz *orn.* [ʃpats] *m* (-en, -es/-en) sparrow.

spazieren [ʃpa'tsiːrən] *v/i.* (*no -ge-, sein*) walk, stroll; **~fahren** (*irr. fahren, sep., -ge-*) **1.** *v/i.* (*sein*) go for a drive; **2.** *v/t.* (*h*) take for a drive; take (*baby*) out (in pram); **~gehen** *v/i.* (*irr. gehen, sep., -ge-, sein*) go for a walk.

Spa'zier|fahrt *f* drive, ride; **~gang** *m* walk, stroll; *e-n* ~ *machen* go for a walk; **~gänger** [~gɛŋər] *m* (-s/-) walker, stroller; **~weg** *m* walk.

Speck [ʃpɛk] *m* (-[e]s/-e) bacon.

Spedi|teur [ʃpedi'tøːr] *m* (-s/-e) forwarding agent; (furniture) remover; **~tion** [~'tsjoːn] *f* (-/-en) forwarding agent *or* agency.

Speer [ʃpeːr] *m* (-[e]s/-e) spear; *sports:* javelin; **~werfen** *n* (-s/no *pl.*) javelin-throw(ing); **~werfer** *m* (-s/-) javelin-thrower.

Speiche ['ʃpaɪçə] *f* (-/-n) spoke.

Speichel ['ʃpaɪçəl] *m* (-s/no *pl.*) spit(tle), saliva; **~lecker** *fig. m* (-s/-) lickspittle, toady.

Speicher ['ʃpaɪçər] *m* (-s/-) granary; warehouse; garret, attic.

speien ['ʃpaɪən] (*irr., ge-, h*) **1.** *v/t.* spit out (*blood, etc.*); *volcano, etc.:* belch (*fire, etc.*); **2.** *v/i.* spit; vomit, be sick.

Speise ['ʃpaɪzə] *f* (-/-n) food, nourishment; meal; dish; '**~eis** *n* icecream; '**~kammer** *f* larder, pantry; '**~karte** *f* bill of fare, menu; '**2n** (ge-, h) **1.** *v/i. s.* essen **1**; *at restaurants:* take one's meals; **2.** *v/t.* feed; *⊕, ↯ a.* supply (*with* with); '**~nfolge** *f* menu; '**~röhre** *anat. f* gullet, (o)esophagus; '**~saal** *m* dining-hall; '**~schrank** *m* (meat-)safe; '**~wagen** 😄 *m* dining-car, diner; '**~zimmer** *n* dining-room.

Spektakel F [ʃpɛk'taːkəl] *m* (-s/-) noise, din.

Spekul|ant [ʃpeku'lant] *m* (-en/-en) speculator; **~ation** [~a'tsjoːn] *f* (-/-en) speculation; *↯ a.* venture; **2ieren** [~'liːrən] *v/i.* (*no -ge-, h*) speculate (*auf acc.* on).

Spelunke [ʃpe'luŋkə] *f* (-/-n) den; drinking-den, *Am.* F *a.* dive.

Spende ['ʃpɛndə] *f* (-/-n) gift; alms *pl.*; contribution; '**2n** *v/t.* (ge-, h) give; donate (*money to charity, blood, etc.*); *eccl.* administer (*sacraments*); bestow (*praise*) (*dat.* on); '**~r** *m* (-s/-) giver; donor.

spen'dieren *v/t.* (*no -ge-, h*): *j-m et.* ~ treat s.o. to s.th., stand s.o. s.th.

Sperling *orn.* ['ʃpɛrliŋ] *m* (-s/-e) sparrow.

Sperr|e ['ʃpɛrə] *f* (-/-n) barrier; 😄 barrier, *Am.* gate; toll-bar; ⊕ lock(ing device), detent; barricade; ✝, ⚓ embargo; 💥 blockade; *sports:* suspension; '**2en** (ge-, h) **1.** *v/t.* close; ✝, ⚓ embargo; cut off (*gas supply, electricity, etc.*); stop (*cheque, etc.*); *sports:* suspend; **2.** *v/i.* jam, be stuck; '**~holz** *n* plywood; '**~konto** ✝ *n* blocked account; '**~kreis** *⚡ m* embargo; wave-trap; '**~sitz** *thea. m* stalls *pl., Am.* orchestra; '**~ung** *f* (-/-en) closing; stoppage (*of cheque, etc.*); ✝, ⚓ embargo; 💥 blockade; '**~zone** *f* prohibited area.

Spesen ['ʃpeːzən] *pl.* expenses *pl.*, charges *pl.*

Spezial|ausbildung [ʃpe'tsjaːlʔ-] *f* special training; **~fach** *n* special(i)-ty; **~geschäft** ✝ *n* one-line shop, *Am.* specialty store; **2isieren** [~ali'ziːrən] *v/refl.* (*no -ge-, h*) specialize (*auf acc.* in); **~ist** [~'list] *m* (-en/-en) specialist; **~ität** [~ali'tɛːt] *f* (-/-en) special(i)ty.

speziell *adj.* [ʃpe'tsjɛl] specific, special, particular.

spezifisch *adj.* [ʃpe'tsiːfiʃ]: *~es Gewicht* specific gravity.

Sphäre ['sfɛːrə] *f* (-/-n) sphere (*a. fig.*).

Spick|aal ['ʃpik-] *m* smoked eel; '**2en** (ge-, h) **1.** *v/t.* lard; *fig.* (inter)lard (*mit* with); F: *j-n* ~ grease s.o.'s palm; **2.** F *fig. v/i.* crib.

spie [ʃpiː] *pret. of* speien.

Spiegel ['ʃpiːgəl] *m* (-s/-) mirror (*a. fig.*), looking-glass; *↯* reflected image; '**2blank** *adj.* mirror-like; **~ei** ['ʃpiːgəlʔ-] *n* fried egg; '**2glatt** *adj. water:* glassy, unrippled; *road, etc.:* very slippery; '**2n** (ge-, h) **1.** *v/i.* shine; **2.** *v/refl.* be reflected; '**~schrift** *f* mirror-writing.

Spieg(e)lung ['ʃpiːg(ə)luŋ] *f* (-/-en) reflection, reflexion; mirage.

Spiel [ʃpiːl] *n* (-[e]s/-e) play (*a. fig.*); game (*a. fig.*); match; 🎵 playing; *ein* ~ *Karten* a pack of playing-cards, *Am. a.* a deck; *auf dem* ~ *stehen* be at stake; *aufs* ~ *setzen* jeopardize, stake; '**~art** *♃, zo. f* variety; '**~ball** *m tennis:* game ball; *billiards:* red ball; *fig.* plaything, sport; '**~bank** *f* (-/-en) gaming-house; '**2en** (ge-, h) **1.** *v/i.* play; gamble; ~ *mit* play with; *fig. a.* toy with; **2.** *v/t.* play (*tennis, violin, etc.*); *thea.* act, play (*part*); *mit j-m Schach* ~ play s.o. at chess; *den Höflichen* ~ do the polite; '**2end** *fig. adv.* easily; '**~er** *m* (-s/-) player; gambler; **~e'rei** *f* (-/-en) pastime; child's amusement; '**~ergebnis** *n sports:* result, score; '**~feld** *n sports:* (playing-)field; pitch; '**~film** *m* feature film *or* picture; '**₋gefährte** *m* playfellow, playmate; '**₋karte** *f* playing-card; '**₋leiter** *m thea.* stage manager; cinematography: director; *sports:* referee; '**₋marke** *f* counter, *sl.* chip; '**₋plan** *m thea., etc.:* program(me); repertory; '**₋platz** *m* playground; '**₋raum** *fig. m* play, scope; '**₋regel** *f* rule (of the game); '**₋sachen** *f/pl.* playthings *pl.*, toys *pl.*; '**₋schuld** *f* gambling-debt; '**₋schule** *f* infant-school, kindergarten; '**₋tisch** *m* card-table; gambling-table; '**₋uhr** *f* musical box, *Am.* music box; '**₋verderber** *m* (-s/-) spoil-sport, killjoy, wet blanket; '**₋waren** *f/pl.* playthings *pl.*, toys *pl.*; '**₋zeit** *f thea.* season; *sports:* time of play; '**₋zeug** *n* toy(s *pl.*), plaything(s *pl.*).

Spieß [ʃpiːs] *m* (-es/-e) spear, pike; spit; den ~ umdrehen turn the tables; '**₋bürger** *m* bourgeois, Philistine, *Am. a.* Babbit; '**₋bürgerlich** *adj.* bourgeois, Philistine; '**₋er** *m* (-s/-) *s.* Spießbürger; '**₋geselle** *m* accomplice; '**₋ruten** *f/pl.*: ~ laufen run the gauntlet (*a. fig.*).

spinal *adj.* [ʃpiˈnaːl]: ~e Kinderlähmung *♂* infantile paralysis, poliomyelitis, F polio.

Spinat ♀ [ʃpiˈnaːt] *m* (-[e]s/-e) spinach.

Spind [ʃpint] *n*, *m* (-[e]s/-e) wardrobe, cupboard; ✕, *sports, etc.:* locker.

Spindel ['ʃpindəl] *f* (-/-n) spindle; '**2̣dürr** *adj.* (as) thin as a lath.

Spinn|e *zo.* ['ʃpinə] *f* (-/-n) spider; '**2en** (*irr.*, ge-, *h*) **1.** *v/t.* spin (*a. fig.*); hatch (*plot, etc.*); **2.** *v/i.* cat: purr; F *fig.* be crazy, *sl.* be nuts; '**₋engewebe** *n* cobweb; '**₋er** *m* (-s/-) spinner; F *fig.* silly; **₋e'rei** *f* (-/-en) spinning; spinning-mill; '**₋maschine** *f* spinning-machine; '**₋webe** *f* (-/-n) cobweb.

Spion [ʃpiˈoːn] *m* (-s/-e) spy, intelligencer; *fig.* judas; **₋age** [ⸯoˈnaːʒə] *f* (-/no *pl.*) espionage; **2̣ieren** [ⸯoˈniːrən] *v/i.* (no -ge-, *h*) (play the) spy.

Spiral|e [ʃpiˈraːlə] *f* (-/-n) spiral (*a. ♀*), helix; **2̣förmig** *adj.* [ⸯfœrmiç] spiral, helical.

Spirituosen [ʃpirituˈoːzən] *pl.* spirits *pl.*

Spiritus ['ʃpiːritus] *m* (-/-se) spirit, alcohol; '**₋kocher** *m* (-s/-) spirit stove.

Spital [ʃpiˈtaːl] *n* (-s/ᵘer) hospital; alms-house; home for the aged.

spitz [ʃpits] **1.** *adj.* pointed (*a. fig.*); ♗ angle: acute; *fig.* poignant; ~e Zunge sharp tongue; **2.** *adv.*: ~ zulaufen taper (off); '**2̣bube** *m* thief, rogue, rascal (*both a. co.*); **2̣büberei** [ⸯbyːbəˈraɪ] *f* (-/-en) roguery, ras-

cality (*both a. co.*); **₋bübisch** *adj.* ['ⸯbyːbiʃ] *eyes, smile, etc.:* roguish.

'**Spitz|e** *f* (-/-n) point (*of pencil, weapon, jaw, etc.*); tip (*of nose, finger, etc.*); nib (*of tool, etc.*); spire; head (*of enterprise, etc.*); lace; an der ~ liegen *sports:* be in the lead; j-m die ~ bieten make head against s.o.; auf die ~ treiben carry to an extreme; '**₋el** *m* (-s/-) (common) informer; '**2̣en** *v/t.* (ge-, *h*) point, sharpen; den Mund ~ purse (up) one's lips; die Ohren ~ prick up one's ears (*a. fig.*).

'**Spitzen|leistung** *f* top performance; ⊕ maximum capacity; '**₋lohn** *m* top wages *pl.*

'**spitz|findig** *adj.* subtle, captious; '**2̣findigkeit** *f* (-/-en) subtlety, captiousness; '**2̣hacke** *f* pickax(e), pick; '**₋ig** *adj.* pointed; *fig. a.* poignant; **2̣marke** *typ. f* head(ing); '**2̣name** *m* nickname.

Splitter ['ʃplitər] *m* (-s/-) splinter, shiver; chip; '**2̣frei** *adj. glass:* shatterproof; '**2̣ig** *adj.* splintery; '**2̣n** *v/i.* (ge-, *h, sein*) splinter, shiver; '**2̣'nackt** F *adj.* stark naked, *Am. a.* mother-naked; '**₋partei** *pol. f* splinter party.

spontan *adj.* [ʃpɔnˈtaːn] spontaneous.

sporadisch *adj.* [ʃpoˈraːdiʃ] sporadic.

Sporn [ʃpɔrn] *m* (-[e]s/Sporen) spur; die Sporen geben put or set spurs to (*horse*); sich die Sporen verdienen win one's spurs; '**2̣en** *v/t.* (ge-, *h*) spur.

Sport [ʃpɔrt] *m* (-[e]s/⸜-e) sport; *fig.* hobby; ~ treiben go in for sports; '**₋ausrüstung** *f* sports equipment; '**₋geschäft** *n* sporting-goods shop; '**₋kleidung** *f* sport clothes *pl.*, sportswear; '**₋lehrer** *m* games-master; '**2̣lich** *adj.* sporting, sportsmanlike; *figure:* athletic; '**₋nachrichten** *f/pl.* sports news *sg.*, *pl.*; '**₋platz** *m* sports field; stadium.

Spott [ʃpɔt] *m* (-[e]s/no *pl.*) mockery; derision; scorn; (s-n) ~ treiben mit make sport of; '**2̣billig** F *adj.* dirt-cheap.

Spötte|lei [ʃpœtəˈlaɪ] *f* (-/-en) raillery, sneer, jeer; '**2̣ln** *v/i.* (ge-, *h*) sneer (*über acc.* at), jeer (at).

'**spotten** *v/i.* (ge-, *h*) mock (*über acc.* at); jeer (at); jeder Beschreibung ~ beggar description.

Spötter ['ʃpœtər] *m* (-s/-) mocker, scoffer; **₋ei** [ⸯˈraɪ] *f* (-/-en) mockery.

'**spöttisch** *adj.* mocking; sneering; ironical.

'**Spott|name** *m* nickname; '**₋preis** *m* ridiculous price; für e-n ~ for a mere song; '**₋schrift** *f* lampoon, satire.

sprach [ʃpraːx] *pret. of* sprechen.

'**Sprache** *f* (-/-n) speech; language

(a. fig.); diction; zur ~ bringen bring up, broach; zur ~ kommen come up (for discussion).

'Sprach|eigentümlichkeit f idiom; '.fehler ⚔ m impediment (in one's speech); '.führer m language guide; '.gebrauch m usage; '.gefühl n (-[e]s/no pl.) linguistic instinct; ⚤kundig adj. ['.kundiç] versed in languages; '.lehre f grammar; '.lehrer m teacher of languages; ⚤lich adj. linguistic; grammatical; ⚤los adj. speechless; '.rohr n speaking-trumpet, megaphone; fig.: mouthpiece; organ; '.schatz m vocabulary; '.störung ⚔ f impediment (in one's speech); '.wissenschaft f philology, science of language; linguistics pl.; '.wissenschaftler m philologist; linguist; ⚤wissenschaftlich adj. philological; linguistic.

sprang [ʃpraŋ] pret. of springen.

Sprech|chor ['ʃprɛç-] m speaking chorus; ⚤en (irr., ge-, h) 1. v/t. speak (language, truth, etc.); ⚔⚔ pronounce (judgement); say (prayer); j-n zu ~ wünschen wish to see s.o.; j-n schuldig ~ ⚔⚔ pronounce s.o. guilty; F Bände ~ speak volumes (für for); 2. v/i. speak; talk (both: mit to, with; über acc., von of, about); er ist nicht zu ~ you cannot see him; '.er m (-s/-) speaker; radio: announcer; spokesman; '.fehler m slip of the tongue; '.stunde f consulting-hours pl.; '.übung f exercise in speaking; '.zimmer n consulting-room, surgery.

spreizen ['ʃpraitsən] v/t. (ge-, h) spread (out); a. straddle (legs); sich ~ pretend to be unwilling.

Spreng|bombe ✗ ['ʃprɛŋ-] f high-explosive bomb, demolition bomb; '.el eccl. m (-s/-) diocese, see; parish; ⚤en (ge-) 1. v/t. (h) sprinkle, water (road, lawn, etc.); blow up, blast (bridge, rocks, etc.); burst open (door, etc.); spring (mine, etc.); gambling: break (bank); break up (meeting, etc.); 2. v/i. (sein) gallop; '.stoff m explosive; '.ung f (-/-en) blowing-up, blasting; explosion; '.wagen m water(ing)-cart.

Sprenkel ['ʃprɛŋkəl] m (-s/-) speckle, spot; ⚤n v/t. (ge-, h) speckle, spot.

Spreu [ʃprɔy] f (-/no pl.) chaff; s. sondern 2.

Sprich|wort ['ʃpriç-] n (-[e]s/=er) proverb, adage; ⚤wörtlich adj. proverbial (a. fig.).

sprießen ['ʃpriːsən] v/i. (irr., ge-, sein) sprout; germinate.

Spring|brunnen ['ʃpriŋ-] m fountain; ⚤en v/i. (irr., ge-, sein) jump, leap; ball, etc.: bounce; swimming: dive; burst; crack; break; in die Augen ~ strike the eye; ~ über (acc.)

jump (over), leap, clear; '.er m (-s/-) jumper; swimming: diver; chess: knight; '.flut f spring tide.

Sprit [ʃprit] m (-[e]s/-e) spirit, alcohol; F mot. fuel, petrol, sl. juice, Am. gasoline, F gas.

Spritz|e ['ʃpritsə] f (-/-n) syringe (a. ⚔⚔), squirt; ⚕ fire-engine; j-m e-e ~ geben ⚕ give s.o. an injection; '⚤en (ge-) 1. v/t. (h) sprinkle, water (road, lawn, etc.); splash (water, etc.) (über acc. on, over); 2. v/i. (h) splash; pen: splutter; 3. v/i. (sein) F fig. dash, flit; ~ aus blood, etc.: spurt or spout from (wound, etc.); '.er m (-s/-) splash; '.tour F f: e-e ~ machen go for a spin.

spröde adj. ['ʃprøːdə] glass, etc.: brittle; skin: chapped, chappy; esp. girl: prudish, prim, coy.

Sproß [ʃprɔs] 1. m (Sprosses/Sprosse) ⚘ shoot, sprout, scion (a. fig.); fig. offspring; 2. ⚤ pret. of sprießen.

Sprosse ['ʃprɔsə] f (-/-n) rung, round, step.

Sprößling ['ʃprœsliŋ] m (-s/-e) ⚘ s. Sproß 1.; co. son.

Spruch [ʃprux] m (-[e]s/=e) saying; dictum; ⚔⚔ sentence; ⚔⚔ verdict; '.band n banner; '⚤reif adj. ripe for decision.

Sprudel ['ʃpruːdəl] m (-s/-) mineral water; '⚤n v/i. (ge-) 1. (h) bubble, effervesce; 2. (sein): ~ aus or von gush from.

sprüh|en ['ʃpryːən] (ge-) 1. v/t. (h) spray, sprinkle (liquid); throw off (sparks); Feuer ~ eyes: flash fire; 2. v/i. (h): ~ vor sparkle (with, etc.); es sprüht it is drizzling; 3. v/i. (sein) sparks: fly; '⚤regen m drizzle.

Sprung [ʃpruŋ] m (-[e]s/=e) jump, leap, bound; swimming: dive; crack, fissure; '.brett n sports: spring-board; fig. stepping-stone; '.feder f spiral spring.

Spuck|e F ['ʃpukə] f (-/no pl.) spit(tle); '⚤en (ge-, h) 1. v/t. spit (out) (blood, etc.); 2. v/i. spit; engine: splutter; '.napf m spittoon, Am. a. cuspidor.

Spuk [ʃpuːk] m (-[e]s/-e) apparition, ghost, co. spook; F fig. noise; '⚤en v/i. (ge-, h): ~ in (dat.) haunt (a place); hier spukt es this place is haunted.

Spule ['ʃpuːlə] f (-/-n) spool, reel; bobbin; ⚡ coil; '⚤n v/t. (ge-, h) spool, reel.

spülen ['ʃpyːlən] (ge-, h) 1. v/t. rinse (clothes, mouth, cup, etc.); wash up (dishes, etc.); an Land ~ wash ashore; 2. v/i. flush the toilet.

Spund [ʃpunt] m (-[e]s/=e) bung; plug; '.loch n bunghole.

Spur [ʃpuːr] f (-/-en) trace (a. fig.); track (a. fig.); print (a. fig.); rut (of wheels); j-m auf der ~ sein be on s.o.'s track.

spür|en ['ʃpyːrən] *v/t.* (ge-, h) feel; sense; perceive; '**2sinn** *m* (-[e]s/*no pl.*) scent; *fig. a.* flair (für for).

Spurweite 🚂 *f* ga(u)ge.

sputen ['ʃpuːtən] *v/refl.* (ge-, h) make haste, hurry up.

Staat [ʃtaːt] *m* **1.** ⚓ (-[e]s/*no pl.*) pomp, state; finery; ~ **machen mit** make a parade of; **2.** (-[e]s/-en) state; government; '**~enbund** *m* (-[e]s/ʉe) confederacy, confederation; '**2enlos** *adj.* stateless; '**2lich** *adj.* state; national; political; state.

'**Staats|angehörige** *m*, *f* (-n/-n) national, citizen, *esp. Brt.* subject; '**~angehörigkeit** *f* (-/*no pl.*) nationality, citizenship; '**~anwalt** ⚖️ *m* public prosecutor, *Am.* prosecuting attorney; '**~beamte** *m* Civil Servant, *Am. a.* public servant; '**~begräbnis** *n* state or national funeral; '**~besuch** *m* official or state visit; '**~bürger** *m* citizen; '**~bürgerkunde** *f* (-/*no pl.*) civics *sg.*; '**~bürgerschaft** *f* (-/-en) citizenship; '**~dienst** *m* Civil Service; '**2eigen** *adj.* state-owned; '**~feind** *m* public enemy; '**2feindlich** *adj.* subversive; '**~gewalt** *f* (-/*no pl.*) supreme power; '**~haushalt** *m* budget; '**~hoheit** *f* (-/*no pl.*) sovereignty; '**~kasse** *f* treasury, *Brt.* exchequer; '**~klugheit** *f* political wisdom; '**~kunst** *f* (-/*no pl.*) statesmanship; '**~mann** *m* statesman; '**2männisch** *adj.* ['~meniʃ] statesmanlike; '**~oberhaupt** *n* head of (the) state; '**~papiere** *n/pl.* Government securities *pl.*; '**~rat** *m* Privy Council; '**~recht** *n* public law; '**~schatz** *m* s. *Staatskasse*; '**~schulden** *f/pl.* national debt; '**~sekretär** *m* under-secretary of state; '**~streich** *m* coup d'état; '**~trauer** *f* national mourning; '**~vertrag** *m* treaty; '**~wesen** *n* polity; '**~wirtschaft** *f* public sector of the economy; '**~wissenschaft** *f* political science; '**~wohl** *n* public weal.

Stab [ʃtaːp] *m* (-[e]s/ʉe) staff (*a. fig.*); bar (*of metal, wood*); crosier, staff (*of bishop*); wand (*of magician*); relay-race, ♪ conducting: baton; *pole-vaulting*: pole.

stabil *adj.* [ʃtaˈbiːl] stable (*a.* ⚕); health: robust.

stabilisier|en [ʃtabiliˈziːrən] *v/t.* (*no* -ge-, h) stabilize (*a.* ⚕); **2ung** *f* (-/-en) stabilization (*a.* ⚕).

stach [ʃtaːx] *pret. of stechen*.

Stachel ['ʃtaxəl] *m* (-s/-n) prickle (*of plant, hedgehog, etc.*); sting (*of bee, etc.*); tongue (*of buckle*); spike (*of sports shoe*); *fig.*: sting; goad; '**~beere** ⚘ *f* gooseberry; '**~draht** *m* barbed wire; '**2ig** *adj.* prickly, thorny.

'**stachlig** *adj. s. stachelig*.

Stadi|on ['ʃtaːdjɔn] *n* (-s/Stadien) stadium; **~um** ['~um] *n* (-s/Stadien) stage, phase.

Stadt [ʃtat] *f* (-/ʉe) town; city.

Städt|chen ['ʃtɛːtçən] *n* (-s/-) small town; '**~ebau** *m* (-[e]s/*no pl.*) town-planning; '**~er** *m* (-s/-) townsman; ~ *pl.* townspeople *pl.*

'**Stadt|gebiet** *n* urban area; '**~gespräch** *n teleph.* local call; *fig.* town talk, talk of the town; '**~haus** *n* town house.

städtisch *adj.* ['ʃtɛːtiʃ] municipal.

'**Stadt|plan** *m* city map; plan (of a town); '**~planung** *f* town-planning; '**~rand** *m* outskirts *pl.* (of a town); '**~rat** *m* (-[e]s/ʉe) town council; town council(l)or; '**~teil** *m*, '**~viertel** *n* quarter.

Staffel ['ʃtafəl] *f* (-/-n) relay; relay-race; '**~ei** *paint.* [~ˈlaɪ] *f* (-/-en) easel; '**~lauf** *m* relay-race; '**2n** *v/t.* (ge-, h) graduate (*taxes, etc.*); stagger (*hours of work, etc.*).

Stahl[1] [ʃtaːl] *m* (-[e]s/ʉe, -e) steel.

stahl[2] [~] *pret. of stehlen*.

stählen ['ʃtɛːlən] *v/t.* (ge-, h) ⊕ harden (*a. fig.*), temper.

'**Stahl|feder** *f* steel pen; steel spring; '**~kammer** *f* strong-room; '**~stich** *m* steel engraving.

stak [ʃtaːk] *pret. of stecken 2*.

Stall [ʃtal] *m* (-[e]s/ʉe) stable (*a. fig.*); cow-house, cowshed; pigsty, *Am. a.* pigpen; shed; '**~knecht** *m* stableman; '**~ung** *f* (-/-en) stabling; **~en** *pl.* stables *pl.*

Stamm [ʃtam] *m* (-[e]s/ʉe) ⚘ stem (*a. gr.*), trunk; *fig.*: race; stock; family; tribe; '**~aktie** † *f* ordinary share, *Am.* common stock; '**~baum** *m* family or genealogical tree; pedigree (*a. zo.*); '**~buch** *n* album; book that contains the births, deaths, and marriages in a family; *zo.* studbook; '**2eln** (ge-, h) **1.** *v/t.* stammer (out); **2.** *v/i.* stammer; '**~eltern** *pl.* ancestors *pl.*, first parents *pl.*; '**2en** *v/i.* (ge-, sein): ~ **von** or **aus** come from (*town, etc.*), *Am. a.* hail from; date from (*certain time*); *gr.* be derived from; *aus gutem Haus* ~ be of good family; '**~gast** *m* regular customer or guest, *F* regular.

stämmig *adj.* ['ʃtɛmiç] stocky; thickset, squat(ty).

'**Stamm|kapital** † *n* share capital, *Am.* capital stock; '**~kneipe** F *f* one's favo(u)rite pub, local; '**~kunde** *m* regular customer, patron; '**~tisch** *m* table reserved for regular guests; '**~utter** *f* (-/ʉ) ancestress; '**~vater** *m* ancestor; '**2verwandt** *adj.* cognate, kindred; *pred.* of the same race.

stampfen ['ʃtampfən] (ge-) **1.** *v/t.* (h) mash (*potatoes, etc.*); *aus dem Boden* ~ conjure up; **2.** *v/i.* (h) stamp (one's foot); *horse:* paw;

3. v/i. (sein): ~ durch plod through;
✥ pitch through.

Stand [ʃtant] 1. m (-[e]s/=e) stand
(-ing), standing or upright position;
footing, foothold; s. Standplatz;
stall; fig.: level; state; station, rank,
status; class; profession; reading
(of thermometer, etc.); ast. position;
sports: score; auf den neuesten ~
bringen bring up to date; e-n
schweren ~ haben have a hard time
(of it); 2. ♀ pret. of stehen.

Standarte [ʃtan'dartə] f (-/-n) standard, banner.

'Standbild n statue.

Ständchen ['ʃtɛntçən] n (-s/-) serenade; j-m ein ~ bringen serenade
s.o.

Ständer ['ʃtɛndər] m (-s/-) stand;
post, pillar, standard.

'Standes|amt n registry (office),
register office; '2amtlich adj.: ~e
Trauung civil marriage; '~beamte
m registrar; '~dünkel m pride of
place; '2gemäß adj., '2mäßig adj.
in accordance with one's rank;
'~person f person of rank or position; '~unterschied m social difference.

'standhaft adj. steadfast; firm;
constant; ~ bleiben stand pat; resist
temptation; '2igkeit f (-/no pl.)
steadfastness; firmness.

'standhalten v/i. (irr. halten, sep.,
-ge-, h) hold one's ground; j-m or
e-r Sache ~ resist s.o. or s.th.

ständig adj. ['ʃtɛndiç] permanent;
constant; income, etc.: fixed.

'Stand|ort m position (of ship, etc.);
⚔ garrison, post; '~platz m stand;
'~punkt fig. m point of view, stand-
point, angle, Am. a. slant; '~quar-
tier ⚔ n fixed quarters pl.; '~recht
⚔ n martial law; '~uhr f grand-
father's clock.

Stange ['ʃtaŋə] f (-/-n) pole; rod,
bar (of iron, etc.); staff (of flag);
Anzug or Kleid von der ~ sl. reach-
me-down, Am. F hand-me-down.

stank [ʃtaŋk] pret. of stinken.

Stänker(er) contp. ['ʃtɛŋkər(ər)] m
(-s/-) mischief-maker, quarrel(l)er;
'2n F v/i. (ge-, h) make mischief.

Stanniol [ʃta'njo:l] n (-s/-e) tin foil.

Stanze ['ʃtantsə] f (-/-n) stanza; ⊕
punch, stamp, die; '2n ⊕ v/t. (ge-,
h) punch, stamp.

Stapel ['ʃta:pəl] m (-s/-) pile, stack;
✥ stocks pl.; vom or von ~ lassen
✥ launch; vom or von ~ laufen ✥ be
launched; '~lauf ✥ m launch; '2n
v/t. (ge-, h) pile (up), stack; '~platz
m dump; emporium.

stapfen ['ʃtapfən] v/i. (ge-, sein)
plod (durch through).

Star 1. [ʃta:r] m (-[e]s/-e) orn.
starling; ✥ cataract; j-m den ~ stechen open s.o.'s eyes; 2. [sta:r] m
(-s/-s) thea., etc.: star.

starb [ʃtarp] pret. of sterben.

stark [ʃtark] 1. adj. strong (a. fig.);
stout, corpulent; fig.: intense; large;
~e Erkältung bad cold; ~er Raucher
heavy smoker; ~e Seite strong point,
forte; 2. adv. very much; ~ erkältet
sein have a bad cold; ~ übertrieben
grossly exaggerated.

Stärke ['ʃtɛrkə] f (-/-n) strength (a.
fig.); stoutness, corpulence; fig.:
intensity; largeness; strong point,
forte; ⋔ starch; '2n v/t. (ge-, h)
strengthen (a. fig.); starch (linen,
etc.); sich ~ take some refresh-
ment(s).

'Starkstrom ⚡ m heavy current.

'Stärkung f (-/-en) strengthening;
fig. a. refreshment; '~smittel n
restorative; ✚ a. tonic.

starr [ʃtar] 1. adj. rigid (a. fig.),
stiff; gaze: fixed; ~ vor (dat.) numb
with (cold, etc.); transfixed with
(horror, etc.); dumbfounded with
(amazement, etc.); 2. adv.: j-n ~ ansehen stare at s.o.; '~en v/i. (ge-, h)
stare (auf acc. at); vor Schmutz ~ be
covered with dirt; '2heit f (-/no pl.)
rigidity (a. fig.), stiffness; '2kopf m
stubborn or obstinate fellow; '~köp-
fig fig. ['~kœpfiç] stubborn, obstinate; '2krampf ✚ m (-[e]s/no pl.)
tetanus; '2sinn m (-[e]s/no pl.)
stubbornness, obstinacy; '~sinnig
adj. stubborn, obstinate.

Start [ʃtart] m (-[e]s/-s, ✎-s) start
(a. fig.); ✎ take-off; '~bahn ✎ f
runway; '2bereit adj. ready to
start; ✎ ready to take off; '2en
(ge-) 1. v/i. (sein) start; ✎ take off;
2. v/t. (h) start; fig. a. launch; '~er
m (-s/-) sports: starter; '~platz m
starting-place.

Station [ʃta'tsjo:n] f (-/-en) station;
ward (of hospital); (gegen) freie ~
board and lodging (found); ~ machen break one's journey; '~svor-
steher ⛟ m station-master, Am. a.
station agent.

Statist [ʃta'tist] m (-en/-en) thea.
supernumerary (actor), F super;
film: extra; ~ik f (-/-en) statistics
pl., sg.; ~iker m (-s/-) statistician;
2isch adj. statistic(al).

Stativ [ʃta'ti:f] n (-s/-e) tripod.

Statt [ʃtat] 1. f (-/no pl.): an Eides ~
in lieu of an oath; an Kindes ~ annehmen adopt; 2. ♀ prp. (gen.) instead of; ~ zu inf. instead of ger.;
~ meiner in my place.

Stätte ['ʃtɛtə] f (-/-n) place, spot;
scene (of events).

'statt|finden v/i. (irr. finden, sep.,
-ge-, h) take place, happen; '~haft
adj. admissible, allowable; legal.

'Statthalter m (-s/-) governor.

'stattlich adj. stately; impressive;
sum of money, etc.: considerable.

Statue ['ʃta:tuə] f (-/-n) statue.

statuieren [ʃtatu'i:rən] v/t. (no -ge-,

h): ein Exempel ~ make an example (an dat. of).

Statur [ʃta'tuːr] f (-/-en) stature, size.

Statut [ʃta'tuːt] n (-[e]s/-en) statute, ~en pl. regulations pl.; ⚔ articles pl. of association.

Staub [ʃtaup] m (-[e]s/⊕ -e, ~e) dust; powder.

Staubecken ['ʃtauˀ-] n reservoir.

stauben ['ʃtaubən] v/i. (ge-, h) give off dust, make or raise a dust.

stäuben ['ʃtɔybən] (ge-, h) 1. v/t. dust; 2. v/i. spray.

'**Staub|faden** ⚘ m filament; '**_2ig** adj. ['-biç] dusty; **~sauger** ['~p-] m (-s/-) vacuum cleaner; **~tuch** ['~p-] n (-[e]s/~er) duster.

stauchen ⊕ ['ʃtauxən] v/t. (ge-, h) upset, jolt.

'**Staudamm** m dam.

Staude ⚘ ['ʃtaudə] f (-/-n) perennial (plant); head (of lettuce).

stau|en ['ʃtauən] v/t. (ge-, h) dam (up) (river, etc.); ⚓ stow; sich ~ waters, etc.: be dammed (up); vehicles: be jammed; '**2er** ⚓ m (-s/-) stevedore.

staunen ['ʃtaunən] 1. v/i. (ge-, h) be astonished (über acc. at); 2. ♀ n (-s/no pl.) astonishment; '**~swert** adj. astonishing. [temper.]

Staupe vet. ['ʃtaupə] f (-/-n) dis-]

'**Stau|see** m reservoir; '**~ung** f (-/-en) damming (up) (of water); stoppage; ⚕ congestion (a. of traffic); jam; ⚓ stowage.

stechen ['ʃteçən] (irr., ge-, h) 1. v/t. prick; insect, etc.: sting; flea, mosquito, etc.: bite; card: take, trump (other card); ⊕ engrave (in or auf acc. on); cut (lawn, etc.); sich in den Finger ~ prick one's finger; 2. v/i. prick, stab (nach at); insect, etc.: sting; flea, mosquito, etc.: bite; sun: burn; j-m in die Augen ~ strike s.o.'s eye; '**~d** adj. pain, look, etc.: piercing; pain: stabbing.

Steck|brief ⚖ ['ʃtek-] m warrant of apprehension; '**2brieflich** ⚖ adv.: er wird ~ gesucht a warrant is out against him; '**~dose** ∮ f (wall) socket; '**2en 1.** v/t. (ge-, h) put; esp. ⊕ insert (in acc. into); F stick; pin (an acc. to, on); ⚡ set, plant; **2.** v/i. ([irr.,] ge-, h) be; stick, be stuck; tief in Schulden ~ be deeply in debt; '**~en** m (-s/-) stick; '**2en- bleiben** v/i. (irr. bleiben, sep., -ge-, sein) get stuck; speaker, etc.: break down; '**~enpferd** n hobby-horse; fig. hobby; '**~er** ∮ m (-s/-) plug; '**~kontakt** ∮ m s. Steckdose; '**~na- del** f pin.

Steg [ʃteːk] m (-[e]s/-e) foot-bridge; ⚓ landing-stage; '**~reif** m (-[e]s/-e): aus dem ~ extempore, offhand (both a. attr.); aus dem ~ sprechen extemporize, F ad-lib.

stehen ['ʃteːən] v/i. (irr., ge-, h) stand; be; be written; dress: suit, become (j-m s.o.); ~ vor be faced with; gut ~ mit be on good terms with; es kam ihm or ihn teuer zu ~ it cost him dearly; wie steht's mit ...? what about ...?; wie steht das Spiel? what's the score?; ~ bleiben remain standing; '**~bleiben** v/i. (irr. bleiben, sep., -ge-, sein) stand (still), stop; leave off reading, etc.; '**~lassen** v/t. (irr. lassen, sep., [no] -ge-, h) turn one's back (up)on; leave (meal) untouched; leave (behind), forget; leave alone.

'**Steher** m (-s/-) sports: stayer.

'**Steh|kragen** m stand-up collar; '**~lampe** f standard lamp; '**~leiter** f (e-e a pair of) steps pl., step-ladder.

stehlen ['ʃteːlən] (irr., ge-, h) 1. v/t. steal; j-m Geld ~ steal s.o.'s money; 2. v/i. steal.

'**Stehplatz** m standing-room; '**~in- haber** m Am. F standee; in bus, etc.: straphanger.

steif adj. [ʃtaif] stiff (a. fig.); numb (vor Kälte with cold); '**~halten** v/t. (irr. halten, sep., -ge-, h): F die Ohren ~ keep a stiff upper lip.

Steig [ʃtaik] m (-[e]s/-e) steep path; '**~bügel** m stirrup.

steigen ['ʃtaigən] 1. v/i. (irr., ge-, sein) flood, barometer, spirits, prices, etc.: rise; mists, etc.: ascend; blood, tension, etc.: mount; prices, etc.: increase; auf e-n Baum ~ climb a tree; 2. ♀ n (-s/no pl.) rise; fig. a. increase.

steigern ['ʃtaigərn] v/t. (ge-, h) raise; increase; enhance; gr. compare.

'**Steigerung** f (-/-en) raising; increase; enhancement; gr. comparison; '**~sstufe** gr. f degree of comparison.

Steigung ['ʃtaiguŋ] f (-/-en) rise, gradient, ascent, grade.

steil adj. [ʃtail] steep; precipitous.

Stein [ʃtain] m (-[e]s/-e) stone (a. ⚘, 🦶), Am. F a. rock; s. Edel2; '**2'alt** F adj. (as) old as the hills; '**~bruch** m quarry; '**~druck** m 1. (-[e]s/no pl.) lithography; 2. (-[e]s/-e) lithograph; '**~drucker** m lithographer; '**2ern** adj. stone-..., of stone; fig. stony; '**~gut** n (-[e]s/-e) crockery, stoneware, earthenware; '**2ig** adj. stony; **2igen** ['~gən] v/t. (ge-, h) stone; '**~igung** ['~guŋ] f (-/-en) stoning; '**~kohle** f mineral coal; pit-coal; '**~metz** m (-en/ -en) stonemason; '**~obst** n stonefruit; '**2reich** F adj. immensely rich; '**~salz** n (-es/no pl.) rock-salt; '**~setzer** m (-s/-) pavio(u)r; '**~wurf** m throwing of a stone; fig. stone's throw; '**~zeit** f (-/no pl.) stone age.

Steiß [ʃtais] m (-es/-e) buttocks pl., rump; '**~bein** anat. n coccyx.

Stelldichein co. ['ʃtɛldiçʾaɪn] n (-[s]/-[s]) meeting, appointment, rendezvous, Am. F a. date.

Stelle ['ʃtɛlə] f (-/-n) place; spot; point; employment, situation, post, place, F job; agency, authority; passage (of book, etc.); freie ~ vacancy; an deiner ~ in your place, if I were you; auf der ~ on the spot; zur ~ sein be present.

'**stellen** v/t. (ge-, h) put, place, set, stand; regulate (watch, etc.); set (watch, trap, task, etc.); stop (thief, etc.); hunt down (criminal); furnish, supply, provide; Bedingungen ~ make conditions; e-e Falle ~ a. lay a snare; sich ~ give o.s. up (to the police); stand, place o.s. (somewhere); sich krank ~ feign or pretend to be ill.

'**Stellen|angebot** n position offered, vacancy; '~gesuch n application for a post; '2weise adv. here and there, sporadically.

'**Stellung** f (-/-en) position, posture; position, situation, (place of) employment; position, rank, status; arrangement (a. gr.); ✗ position; ~ nehmen give one's opinion (zu on), comment (upon); ~nahme ['~naːmə] f (-/-en) attitude (zu to[wards]); opinion (on); comment (on); '2slos adj. unemployed.

'**stellvertret|end** adj. vicarious, representative; acting, deputy; ~er Vorsitzender vice-chairman, deputy chairman; '2er m representative; deputy; proxy; '2ung f representation; substitution; proxy.

Stelz|bein contp. ['ʃtɛlts-] n wooden leg; '~e f (-/-n) stilt; '2en mst iro. v/i. (ge-, sein) stalk.

stemmen ['ʃtɛmən] v/t. (ge-, h) lift (weight); sich ~ press (gegen against); fig. resist or oppose s.th.

Stempel ['ʃtɛmpəl] m (-s/-) stamp; ⊕ piston; ♀ pistil; '~geld F n the dole; '~kissen n ink-pad; '2n (ge-, h) 1. v/t. stamp; hallmark (gold, silver); 2. v/i. F: ~ gehen be on the dole.

Stengel ♀ ['ʃtɛŋəl] m (-s/-) stalk, stem.

Steno F ['ʃtɛno] f (-/no pl.) s. Stenographie; ~'gramm n (-s/-e) stenograph; ~graph [~'graːf] m (-en/-en) stenographer; ~graphie [~a'fiː] f (-/-n) stenography, shorthand; 2graphieren [~a'fiːrən] (no -ge-, h) 1. v/t. take down in shorthand; 2. v/i. know shorthand; 2graphisch [~'graːfiʃ] 1. adj. shorthand, stenographic; 2. adv. in shorthand; ~typistin [~ty'pistin] f (-/-nen) shorthand-typist.

Stepp|decke ['ʃtɛp-] f quilt, Am. a. comforter; '2en (ge-, h) 1. v/t. quilt; stitch; 2. v/i. tap-dance.

Sterbe|bett ['ʃtɛrbə-] n deathbed; '~fall m (case of) death; '~kasse f burial-fund.

'**sterben** 1. v/i. (irr., ge-, sein) die (a. fig.) (an dat. of); esp. 🏿 decease; 2. ♀ n (-s/no pl.): im ~ liegen be dying.

sterblich ['ʃtɛrpliç] 1. adj. mortal; 2. adv.: ~ verliebt sein be desperately in love (in acc. with); '2keit f (-/no pl.) mortality; '2keitsziffer f death-rate, mortality.

stereotyp adj. [stereo'tyːp] typ. stereotyped (a. fig.); ~ieren typ. [~y'piːrən] v/t. (no -ge-, h) stereotype.

steril adj. [ʃte'riːl] sterile; ~isieren [~ili'ziːrən] v/t. (no -ge-, h) sterilize.

Stern [ʃtɛrn] m (-[e]s/-e) star (a. fig.); '~bild ast. n constellation; '~deuter m (-s/-) astrologer; '~deutung f astrology; '~enbanner n Star-Spangled Banner, Stars and Stripes pl., Old Glory; '~fahrt mot. f motor rally; '~gucker F m (-s/-) star-gazer; '2hell adj. starry, starlit; '~himmel m (-s/no pl.) starry sky; '~kunde f (-/no pl.) astronomy; '~schnuppe f (-/-n) shooting star; '~warte f observatory.

stet [ʃteːt], '~ig adj. continual, constant; steady; '2igkeit f (-/no pl.) constancy, continuity; steadiness; ~s adv. always; constantly.

Steuer ['ʃtɔʏər] 1. n (-s/-) ♣ helm, rudder; steering-wheel; 2. f (-/-n) tax; duty; rate, local tax; '~amt n s. Finanzamt; '~beamte m revenue officer; '~berater m (-s/-) tax adviser; '~bord ♣ n (-[e]s/-e) starboard; '~erhebung f levy of taxes; '~erklärung f tax-return; '~ermäßigung f tax allowance; '2frei adj. tax-free; goods: duty-free; '~freiheit f (-/no pl.) exemption from taxes; '~hinterziehung f tax-evasion; '~jahr n fiscal year; '~klasse f tax-bracket; '~knüppel ✗ m control lever or stick; '~mann m (-[e]s/~er, Steuerleute) ♣ helmsman, steersman, Am. a. wheelsman; coxwain (a. rowing); '2n 1. v/t. (h) ♣, ✗ steer, navigate, pilot; ⊕ control; fig. direct, control; 2. v/i. (h) check s.th.; 3. v/i. (sein): ~ in (acc.) ♣ enter (harbour, etc.); ~ nach ♣ be bound for; '2pflichtig adj. taxable; goods: dutiable; '~rad n steering-wheel; '~ruder ♣ n helm, rudder; '~satz m rate of assessment; '~ung f (-/-en) ♣, ✗ steering; ⊕, ⚡ control (a. fig.); ✗ controls pl.; '~veranlagung f tax assessment; '~zahler m (-s/-) taxpayer; ratepayer.

Steven ♣ ['ʃteːvən] m (-s/-) stem; stern-post.

Stich [ʃtiç] m (-[e]s/-e) prick (of needle, etc.); sting (of insect, etc.);

stab (*of knife, etc.*); *sewing*: stitch; *cards*: trick; ⊕ engraving; ⚙ stab; ~ halten hold water; *im* ~ *lassen* abandon, desert, forsake.

Stichel|ei *fig.* [ʃtiçəˈlaɪ] *f* (-/-en) gibe, jeer; '2n *fig. v/i.* (ge-, h) gibe (*gegen at*), jeer (*at*).

'Stich|flamme *f* flash; '2haltig *adj.* valid, sound; ~ *sein* hold water; '~probe *f* random test *or* sample, *Am. a.* spot check; '~tag *m* fixed day; '~wahl *f* second ballot; '~wort *n* 1. *typ.* (-[e]s/⸗er) head-word; 2. *thea.* (-[e]s/-e) cue; '~wunde *f* stab.

sticken ['ʃtɪkən] *v/t. and v/i.* (ge-, h) embroider.

'Stick|garn *n* embroidery floss; '~husten ⚙ *m* (w)hooping cough; '2ig *adj.* stuffy, close; '~stoff ⚗ *m* (-[e]s/*no pl.*) nitrogen.

stieben ['ʃtiːbən] *v/i.* (*irr.*,) ge-, h, sein) sparks, *etc.*: fly about.

Stief... ['ʃtiːf-] step...

Stiefel ['ʃtiːfəl] *m* (-s/-) boot; '~knecht *m* bootjack; '~schaft *m* leg of a boot.

'Stief|mutter *f* (-/⸗) stepmother; '~mütterchen ⚘ ['~mʏtərçən] *n* (-s/-) pansy; '~vater *m* stepfather.

stieg [ʃtiːk] *pret. of steigen.*

Stiel [ʃtiːl] *m* (-[e]s/-e) handle; helve (*of weapon, tool*); haft (*of axe*); stick (*of broom*); ⚘ stalk.

Stier [ʃtiːr] 1. *zo. m* (-[e]s/-e) bull; 2. ⚥ *adj.* staring; '2en *v/i.* (ge-, h) stare (*auf acc. at*); '~kampf *m* bull-fight.

stieß [ʃtiːs] *pret. of stoßen.*

Stift [ʃtɪft] 1. *m* (-[e]s/-e) pin; peg; tack; pencil, crayon; F *fig.*: young-ster; apprentice; 2. *n* (-[e]s/-e, -er) charitable institution; '2en *v/t.* (ge-, h) endow, give, *Am. a.* donate; found; *fig.* cause; make (*mischief, peace*); '~er *m* (-s/-) donor; founder; *fig.* author; '~ung *f* (-/-en) (charitable) endowment, donation; foundation.

Stil [ʃtiːl] *m* (-[e]s/-e) style (*a. fig.*); '2gerecht *adj.* stylish; 2isieren [ʃtiliˈziːrən] *v/t.* (*no* -ge-, h) stylize; 2istisch *adj.* [ʃtiˈlɪstɪʃ] stylistic.

still *adj.* [ʃtɪl] still, quiet; silent; ✝ dull, slack; secret; ~! silence!; *im* ~en secretly; ~er Gesellschafter ✝ sleeping or silent partner; der 2e Ozean the Pacific (Ocean); 2e *f* (-/*no pl.*) stillness, quiet(ness); silence; *in aller* ~ quietly, silently; privately; 2eben *paint.* ['ʃtɪlleːbən] *n* (-s/-) still life; ~egen ['ʃtɪlleːgən] *v/t.* (*sep.*, -ge-, h) shut down (*factory, etc.*); stop (*traffic*); '~en *v/t.* (ge-, h) soothe (*pain*); appease (*appetite*); quench (*thirst*); sta(u)nch (*blood*); nurse (*baby*); '~halten *v/i.* (*irr. halten, sep.*, -ge-, h) keep still; ~iegen ['ʃtɪlliːgən] *v/i.*

(*irr. liegen, sep.*, -ge-, h) *factory, etc.*: be shut down; *traffic*: be suspended; *machines, etc.*: be idle.

stillos *adj.* ['ʃtiːlloːs] without style.

'stillschweigen 1. *v/i.* (*irr. schweigen, sep.*, -ge-, h) be silent; ~ *zu et.* ignore *s.th.*; 2. ⚥ *n* (-s/*no pl.*) silence; secrecy; ~ *übergehen* observe secrecy; *et. mit* ~ *übergehen* pass *s.th.* over in silence; '~d *adj.* silent; *agreement, etc.*: tacit.

'Still|stand *m* (-[e]s/*no pl.*) standstill; *fig.*: stagnation (*a. ✝*); deadlock; 2stehen *v/i.* (*irr. stehen, sep.*, -ge-, h) stop; be at a standstill; *still-gestanden!* ⚔ attention!

'Still|möbel *n/pl.* period furniture; '2voll *adj.* stylish.

Stimm|band *anat.* ['ʃtɪm-] *n* (-[e]s/⸗er) vocal c(h)ord; '2berechtigt *adj.* entitled to vote; '~e *f* (-/-en) voice (*a. ♪, fig.*); vote; comment; ♪ part; '2en (ge-, h) 1. *v/t.* tune (*piano, etc.*); *j-n fröhlich* ~ put *s.o.* in a merry mood; 2. *v/i.* be true *or* right; *sum, etc.*: be correct; ~ *für* vote for; '~enmehrheit *f* majority *or* plurality of votes; '~enthaltung *f* abstention; '~enzählung *f* counting of votes; '~gabel ♪ *f* tuning-fork; '~recht *n* right to vote; *pol.* franchise; '~ung *f* (-/-en) ♪ tune; *fig.* mood, humo(u)r; '2ungsvoll *adj.* impressive; '~zettel *m* ballot, voting-paper.

stinken ['ʃtɪŋkən] *v/i.* (*irr.*, ge-, h) stink (*nach of*); F *fig.* be fishy.

Stipendium *univ.* [ʃtiˈpɛndjʊm] *n* (-s/*Stipendien*) scholarship; exhibition.

stipp|en ['ʃtɪpən] *v/t.* (ge-, h) dip, steep; '2visite F *f* flying visit.

Stirn [ʃtɪrn] *f* (-/-en) forehead, brow; *fig.* face, cheek; *j-m die* ~ *bieten* make head against *s.o.*; *s. runzeln*; '~runzeln *n* (-s/*no pl.*) frown(ing).

stob [ʃtoːp] *pret. of stieben.*

stöbern F ['ʃtøːbərn] *v/i.* (ge-, h) rummage (about) (*in dat. in*).

stochern ['ʃtɔxərn] *v/i.* (ge-, h): ~ *in* (*dat.*) poke (*fire*); pick (*teeth*).

Stock [ʃtɔk] *m* 1. (-[e]s/⸗e) stick; cane; ♪ baton; beehive; ⚘ stock; 2. (-[e]s/-) stor(e)y, floor; *im ersten* ~ on the first floor, *Am.* on the second floor; '2be'trunken F *adi.* dead drunk; '2'blind F *adj.* stone-blind; '2'dunkel F *adj.* pitch-dark.

Stöckelschuh ['ʃtœkəl-] *m* high-heeled shoe.

'stocken *v/i.* (ge-, h) stop; *liquid*: stagnate (*a. fig.*); *speaker*: break down; *voice*: falter; *traffic*: be blocked; *ihm stockte das Blut* his blood curdled.

'Stock|engländer F *m* thorough *or* true-born Englishman; '2'finster F *adj.* pitch-dark; '~fleck *m* spot of mildew; '2(fleck)ig adj. foxy, mildewy; '2'nüchtern F adj. (as) sober as a judge; '‿schnupfen ‿ m chronic rhinitis; '2'taub F adj. stone-deaf; '‿ung f (-/-en) stop (-page); stagnation (of liquid) (a. fig.); block (of traffic); '‿werk n stor(e)y, floor.

Stoff [ʃtɔf] m (-[e]s/-e) matter, substance; material, fabric, textile; material, stuff; fig.: subject(-matter); food; '2lich adj. material.

stöhnen ['ʃtøːnən] v/i. (ge-, h) groan, moan.

Stolle ['ʃtɔlə] f (-/-n) loaf-shaped Christmas cake; '‿n m (-s/-) s. Stolle; ‿ tunnel, gallery (a. ⚒).

stolpern ['ʃtɔlpərn] v/i. (ge-, sein) stumble (über acc. over), trip (over) (both a. fig.).

stolz [ʃtɔlts] 1. adj. proud (auf acc. of) (a. fig.); haughty; 2. 2 m (-es/no pl.) pride (auf acc. in); haughtiness; '‿ieren [‿'tsiːrən] v/i. (no -ge-, sein) strut, flaunt.

stopfen ['ʃtɔpfən] (ge-, h) 1. v/t. stuff; fill (pipe); cram (poultry, etc.); darn (sock, etc.); j-m den Mund ‿ stop s.o.'s mouth; 2. ‿ v/i. cause constipation.

'Stopf|garn n darning-yarn; '‿nadel f darning-needle.

Stoppel ['ʃtɔpəl] f (-/-n) stubble; '‿bart F m stubbly beard; '2ig adj. stubbly.

stopp|en ['ʃtɔpən] (ge-, h) 1. v/t. stop; time, F clock; 2. v/i. stop; '2licht mot. n stop-light; '2uhr f stop-watch.

Stöpsel ['ʃtœpsəl] m (-s/-) stopper, cork, plug (a. ⚡); F fig. whippersnapper; '2n v/t. (ge-, h) stopper, cork; plug (up).

Storch orn. [ʃtɔrç] m (-[e]s/-e) stork.

stören ['ʃtøːrən] (ge-, h) 1. v/t. disturb; trouble; radio: jam (reception); lassen Sie sich nicht ‿l don't let me disturb you!; darf ich Sie kurz ‿? may I trouble you for a minute?; 2. v/i. be intruding; be in the way; 2fried ['‿friːt] m (-[e]s/-e) troublemaker, mischief-maker.

störr|ig adj. ['ʃtœːrɪç], '‿isch adj. stubborn, obstinate; a. horse: restive.

'Störung f (-/-en) disturbance; trouble (a. ⊕); breakdown; radio: jamming, interference.

Stoß [ʃtoːs] m (-es/-e) push, shove; thrust (a. fencing); kick; butt; shock; knock, strike; blow; swimming, billiards: stroke; jolt (of car, etc.); pile, stock, heap; '‿dämpfer mot. m shock-absorber; '2en (irr., ge-) 1. v/t. (h) push, shove; thrust (weapon, etc.); kick; butt; knock, strike; pound (pepper, etc.); sich ‿ an (dat.) strike or knock against; fig. take offence at; 2. v/i. (h) thrust

(nach at); kick (at); butt (at); goat, etc.: butt; car: jolt; ‿an (acc.) adjoin, border on; 3. v/i. (sein): F ‿ auf (acc.) come across; meet with (opposition, etc.); ‿ gegen or an (acc.) knock or strike against.

'Stoß|seufzer m ejaculation; '‿stange mot. f bumper; '2weise adv. by jerks; by fits and starts; '‿zahn m tusk.

stottern ['ʃtɔtərn] (ge-, h) 1. v/t. stutter (out); stammer; 2. v/i. stutter; stammer; F mot. conk (out).

Straf|anstalt ['ʃtraːfʔ‿] f penal institution; prison; Am. penitentiary; '‿arbeit f imposition, F impo(t); '2bar adj. punishable, penal; '‿e f (-/-n) punishment; ⚖, ✝, sports, fig. penalty; fine; bei ‿ von on or under pain of; zur ‿ as a punishment; '2en v/t. (ge-, h) punish.

straff adj. [ʃtraf] tight; rope: a. taut; fig. strict, rigid.

'straf|fällig adj. liable to prosecution; '2gesetz n penal law; '2gesetzbuch n penal code.

sträf|lich adj. ['ʃtrɛːflɪç] culpable; reprehensible; inexcusable; 2ling ['‿lɪŋ] m (-s/-e) convict, Am. sl. a. lag.

'straf|los adj. unpunished; '2losigkeit f (-/no pl.) impunity; '2porto n surcharge; '2predigt f severe lecture; j-m e-e ‿ halten lecture s.o. severely; '2prozeß m criminal action; '2raum m football: penalty area; '2stoß m football: penalty kick; '2verfahren n criminal proceedings pl.

Strahl [ʃtraːl] m (-[e]s/-en) ray (a. fig.); beam; flash (of lightning, etc.); jet (of water, etc.); '2en v/i. (ge-, h) radiate; shine (vor dat. with); fig. beam (vor dat. with), shine (with); '‿ung f (-/-en) radiation, rays pl.

Strähne ['ʃtrɛːnə] f (-/-n) lock, strand (of hair); skein, hank (of yarn); fig. stretch.

stramm adj. [ʃtram] tight; rope: a. taut; stalwart; soldier: smart.

strampeln ['ʃtrampəln] v/i. (ge-, h) kick.

Strand [ʃtrant] m (-[e]s/‿-e, ‿-e) beach; '‿anzug m beach-suit; 2en ['‿dən] v/i. (ge-, sein) ⚓ strand, run ashore; fig. fail, founder; '‿gut n stranded goods pl.; fig. wreckage; '‿korb m roofed wicker chair for use on the beach; ‿promenade ['‿promənaːdə] f (-/-n) promenade, Am. boardwalk.

Strang [ʃtraŋ] m (-[e]s/‿-e) cord (a. anat.); rope; halter (for hanging s.o.); trace (of harness); 💀 track; über die Stränge schlagen kick over the traces.

Strapaz|e [ʃtra'paːtsə] f (-/-n) fatigue; toil; 2ieren [‿a'tsiːrən] v/t.

(no -ge-, h) fatigue, strain *(a. fig.)*; wear out *(fabric, etc.)*; **ierfähig** *adj.* [a'tsi:r-] long-lasting; **iös** *adj.* [a'tsjø:s] fatiguing.

Straße ['ʃtra:sə] *f (-/-n)* road, highway; street *(of town, etc.)*; strait; *auf der * on the road; in the street. '**Straßen|anzug** *m* lounge-suit, *Am.* business suit; '**bahn** *f* tram(way), tram-line, *Am.* street railway, streetcar line; *s.* Straßenbahnwagen; '**bahnhaltestelle** *f* tram stop, *Am.* streetcar stop; '**bahnwagen** *m* tram(-car), *Am.* streetcar; '**beleuchtung** *f* street lighting; '**damm** *m* roadway; '**händler** *m* hawker; '**junge** *m* street arab, *Am.* street Arab; '**kehrer** *m (-s/-)* scavenger, street orderly; '**kreuzung** *f* crossing, cross roads; '**reinigung** *f* street-cleaning, scavenging; '**rennen** *n* road-race.

strategisch *adj.* [ʃtra'te:giʃ] strategic(al).

sträuben ['ʃtrɔybən] *v/t. (ge-, h)* ruffle up *(its feathers, etc.)*; *sich hair:* stand on end; *sich gegen* kick against *or* at.

Strauch [ʃtraux] *m (-[e]s/er)* shrub; bush.

straucheln ['ʃtrauxəln] *v/i. (ge-, sein)* stumble *(über acc.* over, at), trip (over) *(both a. fig.)*.

Strauß [ʃtraus] *m* **1.** *orn. (-es/-e)* ostrich; **2.** *(-es/e)* bunch *(of flowers)*; bouquet; strife, combat.

Strebe ['ʃtre:bə] *f (-/-n)* strut, support, brace.

'**streben 1.** *v/i. (ge-, h):* *nach* strive for *or* after, aspire to *or* after; **2.** **** *n (-s/no pl.)* striving *(nach* for, after), aspiration (for, after); effort, endeavo(u)r.

'**Streber** *m (-s/-)* pusher, careerist; *at school: sl.* swot.

strebsam *adj.* ['ʃtre:pza:m] assiduous; ambitious; '**keit** *f (-/no pl.)* assiduity; ambition.

Strecke ['ʃtrɛkə] *f (-/-n)* stretch; route; tract, extent; distance *(a. sports)*; course; 🚂, *etc.:* section, line; *hunt.* bag; *zur bringen hunt.* bag, hunt down *(a. fig.)*; '**n** *v/t. (ge-, h)* stretch, extend; dilute *(fluid)*; *sich * stretch (o.s.); *die Waffen * lay down one's arms; *fig. a.* give in.

Streich [ʃtraɪç] *m (-[e]s/-e)* stroke; blow; *fig.* trick, prank; *j-m e-n spielen* play a trick on s.o.; **eln** ['əln] *v/t. (ge-, h)* stroke; caress; pat; '**en** *(irr., ge-)* **1.** *v/t. (h)* rub; spread *(butter, etc.)*; paint; strike out, delete, cancel *(a. fig.)*; strike, lower *(flag, sail)*; *sich * stretch *(um round)*; **3.** *v/i. (h):* mit der Hand über et. pass one's hand over s.th.; '**holz** *n* match; '**instrument** *n* stringed instrument;

'**orchester** *n* string band; '**riemen** *m* strop.

Streif [ʃtraɪf] *m (-[e]s/-e) s.* Streifen; '**band** *n (-[e]s/er)* wrapper; **e** *f (-/-n)* patrol; patrolman; raid. '**streifen** *(ge-)* **1.** *v/t. (h)* stripe, streak; graze, touch lightly in passing, brush; touch (up)on *(subject)*; **2.** *v/i. (sein):* *durch* rove, wander through; **3.** *v/i. (h):* *an (acc.)* graze, brush; *fig.* border *or* verge on; **4.** **** *m (-s/-)* strip; stripe; streak.

'**streif|ig** *adj.* striped; '**licht** *n* sidelight; '**schuß** ⚔ *m* grazing shot; '**zug** *m* ramble; ⚔ raid.

Streik [ʃtraɪk] *m (-[e]s/-s)* strike, *Am.* F *a.* walkout; *in den treten* go on strike, *Am.* F *a.* walk out; '**brecher** *m (-s/-)* strike-breaker, blackleg, scab; '**en** *v/i. (ge-, h)* (be on) strike; go on strike, *Am.* F *a.* walk out; **ende** ['əndə] *m, f (-n/-n)* striker; '**posten** *m* picket.

Streit [ʃtraɪt] *m (-[e]s/-e)* quarrel; dispute; conflict; ⚖ litigation; '**bar** *adj.* pugnacious; '**en** *v/i. and v/refl. (irr., ge-, h)* quarrel *(mit* with; *wegen* for; *über acc.* about); '**frage** *f* controversy, (point of) issue; '**ig** *adj.* debatable, controversial; *j-m et. machen* dispute s.o.'s right to s.th.; '**igkeiten** *f/pl.* quarrels *pl.*; disputes *pl.*; '**kräfte** ⚔ ['krɛftə] *f/pl.* (military *or* armed) forces *pl.*; '**lustig** *adj.* pugnacious, aggressive; '**süchtig** *adj.* quarrelsome; pugnacious.

streng [ʃtrɛŋ] **1.** *adj.* severe; stern; strict; austere; *discipline, etc.:* rigorous; *weather, climate:* inclement; *examination:* stiff; **2.** *adv.:* *vertraulich* in strict confidence; '**e** *f (-/no pl.) s.* streng 1: severity; sternness; strictness; austerity; rigo(u)r; inclemency; stiffness; '**genommen** *adv.* strictly speaking; '**gläubig** *adj.* orthodox.

Streu [ʃtrɔy] *f (-/-en)* litter; '**en** *v/t. (ge-, h)* strew, scatter; '**zucker** *m* castor sugar.

Strich [ʃtriç] **1.** *m (-[e]s/-e)* stroke; line; dash; tract *(of land)*; *j-m e-n durch die Rechnung machen* queer s.o.'s pitch; **2.** **** *pret. of* streichen; '**regen** *m* local shower; '**weise** *adv.* here and there.

Strick [ʃtrik] *m (-[e]s/-e)* cord; rope; halter, rope *(for hanging s.o.)*; F *fig.* (young) rascal; '**en** *v/t. and v/i. (ge-, h)* knit; '**garn** *n* knitting-yarn; '**jacke** *f* cardigan, jersey; '**leiter** *f* rope-ladder; '**nadel** *f* knitting-needle; '**waren** *f/pl.* knitwear; '**zeug** *n* knitting(-things *pl.*).

Striemen ['ʃtri:mən] *m (-s/-)* weal, wale.

Strippe F ['ʃtripə] *f (-/-n)* band; string; shoe-lace; *an der hängen* be on the phone.

stritt [ʃtrit] *pret. of* streiten; '~ig *adj.* debatable, controversial; ~er Punkt (point of) issue.

Stroh [ʃtroː] *n* (-[e]s/*no pl.*) straw; thatch; '~dach *n* thatch(ed roof); '~halm *m* straw; nach e-m ~ greifen catch at a straw; '~hut *m* straw hat; '~mann *m* man of straw; scarecrow; *fig.* dummy; '~sack *m* straw mattress; '~witwe F *f* grass widow.

Strolch [ʃtrɔlç] *m* (-[e]s/-e) scamp, F vagabond; '2en *v/i.* (ge-, sein): ~ durch rove.

Strom [ʃtroːm] *m* (-[e]s/*e) stream (*a. fig.*); (large) river; ≸ current (*a. fig.*); es regnet in Strömen it is pouring with rain; 2'ab(wärts) *adv.* down-stream; 2'auf(wärts) *adv.* up-stream.

strömen ['ʃtrøːmən] *v/i.* (ge-, sein) stream; flow, run; *rain:* pour; *people:* stream, pour (*aus* out of; *in acc.* into).

'**Strom|kreis** ≸ *m* circuit; '~linienform *f* (-/*no pl.*) streamline shape; '2linienförmig *adj.* streamline(d); '~schnelle *f* (-/-n) rapid, *Am. a.* riffle; '~sperre ≸ *f* stoppage of current.

'**Strömung** *f* (-/-en) current; *fig. a.* trend, tendency.

'**Stromzähler** ≸ *m* electric meter.

Strophe ['ʃtroːfə] *f* (-/-n) stanza, verse.

strotzen ['ʃtrɔtsən] *v/i.* (ge-, h): ~ von abound in; teem with (*blunders, etc.*); burst with (*health, etc.*).

Strudel ['ʃtruːdəl] *m* (-s/-) eddy, whirlpool; *fig.* whirl; '2n *v/i.* (ge-, h) swirl, whirl.   [ture.\

Struktur [ʃtrukˈtuːr] *f* (-/-en) struc-\

Strumpf [ʃtrumpf] *m* (-[e]s/*e) stocking; '~band *n* (-[e]s/*er) garter; '~halter *m* (-s/-) suspender, *Am.* garter; '~waren *f/pl.* hosiery.

struppig *adj.* ['ʃtrupiç] *hair:* rough, shaggy; *dog, etc.:* shaggy.

Stube ['ʃtuːbə] *f* (-/-n) room.

'**Stuben|hocker** *fig. m* (-s/-) stay-at-home; '~mädchen *n* chambermaid; '2rein *adj.* house-trained.

Stück [ʃtyk] *n* (-[e]s/-e) piece (*a. ♪*); fragment; head (*of cattle*); lump (*of sugar*); *thea.* play; aus freien ~en of one's own accord; in ~e gehen *or* schlagen break to pieces; '~arbeit *f* piece-work; '2weise *adv.* piece by piece; (by) piecemeal; † by the piece; '~werk *fig. n* patchwork.

Student [ʃtuˈdɛnt] *m* (-en/-en), ~in *f* (-/-nen) student, undergraduate.

Studie ['ʃtuːdjə] *f* (-/-n) study (*über acc., zu* of, in) (*a. art, literature*); *paint, etc.:* sketch; '~nrat *m* (-[e]s/*e) *appr.* secondary-school teacher; '~nreise *f* study trip.

studier|en [ʃtuˈdiːrən] (*no -ge-, h*) 1. *v/t.* study, read (*law, etc.*); 2. *v/i.*

study; be a student; 2zimmer *n* study.

Studium ['ʃtuːdjum] *n* (-s/Studien) study (*a. fig.*); studies *pl.*

Stufe ['ʃtuːfə] *f* (-/-n) step; *fig.:* degree; grade; stage.

'**Stufen|folge** *fig. f* gradation; '~leiter *f* step-ladder; *fig.* scale; '2weise 1. *adj.* gradual; 2. *adv.* gradually, by degrees.

Stuhl [ʃtuːl] *m* (-[e]s/*e) chair, seat; *in a church:* pew; *weaving:* loom; ≸ *s.* Stuhlgang; '~bein *n* leg of a chair; '~gang ≸ *m* (-[e]s/*no pl.*) stool; motion; '~lehne *f* back of a chair.

stülpen ['ʃtylpən] *v/t.* (ge-, h) put (*über acc.* over); clap (*hat*) (*auf acc.* on).

stumm *adj.* [ʃtum] dumb, mute; *fig. a.* silent; *gr.* silent, mute.

Stummel ['ʃtuməl] *m* (-s/-) stump, stub.

'**Stummfilm** *m* silent film.

Stümper F ['ʃtympər] *m* (-s/-) bungler; ~ei F [~ˈraɪ] *f* (-/-en) bungling; bungle; '2haft *adj.* bungling; botch; '2n F *v/i.* (ge-, h) bungle, botch.

stumpf [ʃtumpf] 1. *adj.* blunt; ⊼ *angle:* obtuse; *senses:* dull, obtuse; apathetic; 2. 2 *m* (-[e]s/*e) stump, stub; *mit* ~ *und* Stiel root and branch; '2sinn *m* (-[e]s/*no pl.*) stupidity, dul(l)ness; '~sinnig *adj.* stupid, dull.

Stunde ['ʃtundə] *f* (-/-n) hour; lesson, *Am. a.* period; '2n *v/t.* (ge-, h) grant respite for.

'**Stunden|kilometer** *m* kilometre per hour, *Am.* kilometer per hour; '2lang 1. *adj.:* nach ~em Warten after hours of waiting; 2. *adv.* for hours (and hours); '~lohn *m* hourly wage; '~plan *m* timetable, *Am.* schedule; '2weise 1. *adj.:* ~ Beschäftigung part-time employment; 2. *adv.* by the hour; '~zeiger *m* hour-hand.

stündlich ['ʃtyntliç] 1. *adj.* hourly; 2. *adv.* hourly, every hour; at any hour.

'**Stundung** *f* (-/-en) respite.

stur F *adj.* [ʃtuːr] *gaze:* fixed, staring; *p.* pigheaded, mulish.

Sturm [ʃturm] *m* (-[e]s/*e) storm (*a. fig.*); ⚓ gale.

stürm|en ['ʃtyrmən] (ge-) 1. *v/t.* (h) ⚔ storm (*a. fig.*); 2. *v/i.* (h) *wind:* storm, rage; es stürmt it is stormy weather; 3. *v/i.* (sein) rush; '2er *m* (-s/-) football, *etc.:* forward; '~isch *adj.* stormy; *fig.:* impetuous; tumultuous.

'**Sturm|schritt** ⚔ *m* double-quick step; '~trupp ⚔ *m* storming-party; '~wind *m* storm-wind.

Sturz [ʃturts] *m* (-es/*e) fall, tumble; overthrow (*of government, etc.*);

fig. ruin; ♁ slump; '⁓bach *m* torrent.

stürzen ['ʃtyrtsən] (ge-) 1. *v/i.* (*sein*) (have a) fall, tumble; *fig.* rush, plunge (*in acc.* into); 2. *v/t.* (*h*) throw; overthrow(*government, etc.*); *fig.* plunge (*in acc.* into), precipitate (into); *j-n ins Unglück* ⁓ ruin s.o.; *sich in Schulden* ⁓ plunge into debt.

'Sturz|flug 🛩 *m* (nose)dive; '⁓helm *m* crash-helmet.

Stute *zo.* ['ʃtuːtə] *f* (-/-n) mare.

Stütze ['ʃtytsə] *f* (-/-n) support, prop, stay (*all a. fig.*).

stutzen ['ʃtutsən] (ge-, h) 1. *v/t.* cut (*hedge*); crop (*ears, tail, hair*); clip (*hedge, wing*); trim (*hair, beard, hedge*); dock (*tail*); lop (*tree*); 2. *v/i.* start (*bei* at); stop dead *or* short.

'stützen *v/t.* (ge-, h) support, prop, stay (*all a. fig.*); ⁓ *auf* (*acc.*) base *or* found on; *sich* ⁓ *auf* (*acc.*) lean on; *fig.* rely (up)on; *argument, etc.*: be based on.

'Stutz|er *m* (-s/-) dandy, fop, *Am. a.* dude; '⁓ig *adj.* suspicious; ⁓ *machen* make suspicious.

'Stütz|pfeiler △ *m* abutment; '⁓punkt *m* *phys.* fulcrum; ⚔ base.

Subjekt [zup'jɛkt] *n* (-[e]s/-e) *gr.* subject; *contp.* individual; ⁀iv *adj.* [⁓'tiːf] subjective; ⁀ivität [⁓ivi'tɛːt] *f* (-/*no pl.*) subjectivity.

Substantiv *gr.* ['zupstanti:f] *n* (-s/-e) noun, substantive; ⁀isch *gr.* *adj.* ['⁓viʃ] substantival.

Substanz [zup'stants] *f* (-/-en) substance (*a. fig.*).

subtra|hieren ⚛ [zuptra'hiːrən] *v/t.* (*no* -ge-, *h*) subtract; ⁀ktion ⚛ [⁓k'tsjoːn] *f* (-/-en) subtraction.

Such|dienst ['zuːx-] *m* tracing service; '⁓e *f* (-/*no pl.*) search (*nach* for); *auf der* ⁓ *nach* in search of; '⁀en (ge-, h) 1. *v/t.* seek (*advice, etc.*); search for; look for; *Sie haben hier nichts zu* ⁓ you have no business to be here; 2. *v/i.*: ⁓ *nach* seek for *or* after; search for; look for; '⁓er *phot. m* (-s/-) view-finder.

Sucht [zuxt] *f* (-/-e) mania (*nach* for), rage (for), addiction (to).

süchtig *adj.* ['zyçtiç] having a mania (*nach* for); ⁓ *sein* be a drug addict; ⁀e ['⁓gə] *m, f* (-n/-n) drug addict *or* fiend.

Süd *geogr.* [zyːt], ⁀en ['⁓dən] *m* (-s/*no pl.*) south; ⁓früchte ['zyːtfryçtə] *f/pl.* fruits from the south; '⁀lich 1. *adj.* south(ern); southerly; 2. *adv.*: ⁓ *von* (to the) south of; ⁓'ost *geogr.*, ⁓'osten *m* (-s/*no pl.*) south-east; ⁀'östlich *adj.* south-east(ern); '⁀pol *geogr. m* (-s/*no pl.*) South Pole; ⁀wärts *adv.* ['⁓verts] southward(s); ⁓'west *geogr.*, ⁓'westen *m* (-s/*no pl.*) south-west;

⁀'westlich *adj.* south-west(ern); '⁓wind *m* south wind.

süffig F *adj.* ['zyfiç] palatable, tasty.

suggerieren [zuge'riːrən] *v/t.* (*no* -ge-, *h*) suggest.

suggestiv *adj.* [zugɛs'tiːf] suggestive.

Sühne ['zyːnə] *f* (-/-n) expiation, atonement; '⁀n *v/t.* (ge-, *h*) expiate, atone for.

Sülze ['zyltsə] *f* (-/-n) jellied meat.

summ|arisch *adj.* [zu'maːriʃ] summary (*a. fig.*); ⁀e *f* (-/-n) sum (*a. fig.*); (sum) total; amount.

'summen (ge-, h) 1. *v/i.* bees, *etc.*: buzz, hum; 2. *v/t.* hum (*song, etc.*).

sum'mieren *v/t.* (*no* -ge-, *h*) sum *or* add up; *sich* ⁓ run up.

Sumpf [zumpf] *m* (-[e]s/⁓e) swamp, bog, marsh; '⁀ig *adj.* swampy, boggy, marshy.

Sünd|e ['zyndə] *f* (-/-n) sin (*a. fig.*); '⁓enbock F *m* scapegoat; '⁓er *m* (-s/-) sinner; ⁀haft ['⁓t-] 1. *adj.* sinful; 2. *adv.*: F ⁓ *teuer* awfully expensive; ⁀ig ['⁓diç] *adj.* sinful; ⁀igen ['⁓digən] *v/i.* (ge-, *h*) (commit a) sin

Superlativ ['zuːperlatiːf] *m* (-s/-e) *gr.* superlative degree; *in* ⁓*en sprechen* speak in superlatives.

Suppe ['zupə] *f* (-/-n) soup; broth.

'Suppen|löffel *m* soup-spoon; '⁓schöpfer *m* soup ladle; '⁓schüssel *f* tureen; '⁓teller *m* soup-plate.

surren ['zurən] *v/i.* (ge-, h) whir(r); *insects*: buzz.

Surrogat [zuro'gaːt] *n* (-[e]s/-e) substitute.

suspendieren [zuspɛn'diːrən] *v/t.* (*no* -ge-, *h*) suspend.

süß *adj.* [zyːs] sweet (*a. fig.*); ⁀e *f* (-/*no pl.*) sweetness; '⁓en *v/t.* (ge-, h) sweeten; '⁀igkeiten *pl.* sweets *pl.*, sweetmeats *pl.*, *Am. a.* candy; '⁓lich *adj.* sweetish; mawkish (*a. fig.*); '⁀stoff *m* saccharin(e); '⁀wasser *n* (-s/-) fresh water.

Symbol [zym'boːl] *n* (-s/-e) symbol; ⁓ik *f* (-/*no pl.*) symbolism; ⁀isch *adj.* symbolic(al).

Symmetr|ie [zyme'triː] *f* (-/-n) symmetry; ⁀isch *adj.* [⁓'meːtriʃ] symmetric(al).

Sympath|ie [zympa'tiː] *f* (-/-n) liking; ⁀isch *adj.* [⁓'paːtiʃ] likable; *er ist mir* ⁓ I like him; ⁀isieren [⁓i'ziːrən] *v/i.* (*no* -ge-, h) sympathize (*mit* with).

Symphonie ♪ [zymfo'niː] *f* (-/-n) symphony; ⁓orchester *n* symphony orchestra.

Symptom [zymp'toːm] *n* (-s/-e) symptom; ⁀atisch *adj.* [⁓o'maːtiʃ] symptomatic (*für* of).

Synagoge [zyna'goːgə] *f* (-/-n) synagogue.

synchronisieren [zynkroni'ziːrən] *v/t.* (*no* -ge-, h) synchronize; dub.

Syndik|at [zyndi'kɑːt] *n* (-[e]s/-e) syndicate; **~us** ['zyndikus] *m* (-/-se, *Syndizi*) syndic.
Synkope ♪ [zyn'koːpə] *f* (-/-n) syncope.
synonym [zyno'nyːm] **1.** *adj.* synonymous; 2. ♫ *n* (-s/-e) synonym.
Syntax *gr.* ['zyntaks] *f* (-/-en) syntax.

synthetisch *adj.* [zyn'teːtiʃ] synthetic.
System [zys'teːm] *n* (-s/-e) system; scheme; **~atisch** *adj.* [~e'mɑːtiʃ] systematic(al), methodic(al).
Szene ['stseːnə] *f* (-/-n) scene (*a. fig.*); *in* ~ *setzen* stage; **~rie** [stsenə-'riː] *f* (-/-n) scenery.

T

Tabak ['tɑːbak, 'tabak, ta'bak] *m* (-s/-e) tobacco; (')**~händler** *m* tobacconist; (')**~sbeutel** *m* tobacco-pouch; (')**~sdose** *f* snuff-box; (')**~waren** *pl.* tobacco products *pl.*, F smokes *pl.*
tabellarisch [tabɛ'lɑːriʃ] **1.** *adj.* tabular; **2.** *adv.* in tabular form.
Tabelle [ta'bɛlə] *f* (-/-n) table; schedule.
Tablett [ta'blɛt] *n* (-[e]s/-e, -s) tray; *of metal:* salver; **~e** *pharm. f* (-/-n) tablet; lozenge.
Tachometer [taxo'-] *n*, *m* (-s/-) ⊕ tachometer; *mot. a.* speedometer.
Tadel ['tɑːdəl] *m* (-s/-) blame; censure; reprimand, rebuke, reproof; reproach; *at school:* bad mark; '**~los** *adj.* faultless, blameless; excellent, splendid; '**~n** *v/t.* (*ge-, h*) blame (*wegen* for); censure; reprimand, rebuke, reprove; scold; find fault with.
Tafel ['tɑːfəl] *f* (-/-n) table; plate (*a. book illustration*); slab; *on houses, etc.:* tablet, plaque; slate; blackboard; signboard, notice-board, *Am.* billboard; cake, bar (*of chocolate, etc.*); dinner-table; dinner; **~förmig** *adj.* ['~fœrmiç] tabular; '**~geschirr** *n* dinner-service, dinner-set; '**~land** *n* tableland, plateau; '**~n** *v/i.* (*ge-, h*) dine; feast, banquet; '**~service** *n s. Tafelgeschirr*; '**~silber** *n* silver plate, *Am.* silverware.
Täf(e)lung ['tɛːf(ə)luŋ] *f* (-/-en) wainscot, panelling.
Taft [taft] *m* (-[e]s/-e) taffeta.
Tag [tɑːk] *m* (-[e]s/-e) day; *officially:* a. date; *am or bei* ~*e* by day; *e-s* ~*es* one day; *den ganzen* ~ all day long; ~ *für* ~ day by day; *über* ~*e* ⚒ aboveground; *unter* ~*e* ⚒ underground; *heute vor acht* ~*en* a week ago; *heute in acht* (*vierzehn*) ~*en* today or this day week (fortnight), a week (fortnight) today; *denkwürdiger or freudiger* ~ red-letter day; *freier* ~ day off; *guten* ~*l* how do you do?; good morning!; good afternoon!; F hallo!, hullo!, *Am.* hello!; *am hellichten* ~*e* in broad daylight; *es wird* ~ it dawns; *an den*

~ *bringen* (*kommen*) bring (come) to light; *bis auf den heutigen* ~ to this day; ♀*aus adv.*: ~, *tagein* day in, day out.
Tage|blatt ['tɑːgə-] *n* daily (paper); '**~buch** *n* journal, diary.
tagein *adv.* [tɑː'kʼaɪn] *s. tagaus.*
tage|lang *adv.* ['tɑːgə-] day after day, for days together; ♀**lohn** *m* day's or daily wages *pl.*; ♀**löhner** ['~løːnər] *m* (-s/-) day-labo(u)rer; '**~n** *v/i.* (*ge-, h*) dawn; hold a meeting, meet, sit; 🜨 be in session; '♀**reise** *f* day's journey.
Tages|anbruch ['tɑːgəs?-] *m* daybreak, dawn; *bei* ~ at daybreak *or* dawn; '**~befehl** ⚔ *m* order of the day; '**~bericht** *m* daily report, bulletin; '**~einnahme** ✝ *f* receipts *pl. or* takings *pl.* of the day; '**~gespräch** *n* topic of the day; '**~kasse** *f thea.* box-office, booking-office; *s. Tageseinnahme*; '**~kurs** ✝ *m* current rate; *stock exchange:* quotation of the day; '**~licht** *n* daylight; '**~ordnung** *f* order of the day, agenda; *das ist an der* ~ that is the order of the day, that is quite common; '**~presse** *f* daily press; '**~zeit** *f* time of day; daytime; *zu jeder* ~ at any hour, at any time of the day; '**~zeitung** *f* daily (paper).
tage|weise *adv.* ['tɑːgə-] by the day; ♀**werk** *n* day's work; man-day.
täglich *adj.* ['tɛːkliç] daily.
tags *adv.* [tɑːks]: ~ *darauf* the following day, the day after; ~ *zuvor* (on) the previous day, the day before.
'**Tagschicht** *f* day shift.
tagsüber *adv.* ['tɑːks?-] during the day, in the day-time.
Tagung ['tɑːguŋ] *f* (-/-en) meeting.
Taille ['taljə] *f* (-/-n) waist; bodice (*of dress*).
Takel ⚓ ['tɑːkəl] *n* (-s/-) tackle; **~age** [takə'lɑːʒə] *f* (-/-n) rigging, tackle; '♀**n** ⚓ *v/t.* (*ge-, h*) rig (*ship*); '**~werk** ⚓ *n s. Takelage.*
Takt [takt] *m* **1.** (-[e]s/-e) ♪ time, measure; bar; *mot.* stroke; *den* ~ *halten* ♪ keep time; *den* ~ *schlagen* ♪ beat time; **2.** (-[e]s/*no pl.*) tact; '♀**fest** *adj.* steady in keeping time;

fig. firm; '~ik ✗ *f* (-/-en) tactics *pl. and sg.* (*a. fig.*); '~iker *m* (-s/-) tactician; '2isch *adj.* tactical; '2los *adj.* tactless; '~stock *m* baton; '~strich ♪ *m* bar; '2voll *adj.* tactful.

Tal [tɑ:l] *n* (-[e]s/-er) valley, *poet. a.* dale; *enges ~* glen.

Talar [ta'lɑ:r] *m* (-s/-e) ᵗᵗ₂, *eccl.* *univ.* gown; ᵗᵗ₂ robe.

Talent [ta'lɛnt] *n* (-[e]s/-e) talent, gift, aptitude, ability; 2iert *adj.* [~'tiːrt] talented, gifted.

'**Talfahrt** *f* downhill journey; ⚓ passage downstream.

Talg [talk] *m* (-[e]s/-e) suet; *melted:* tallow; '~drüse *anat. f* sebaceous gland; 2ig *adj.* ['~gɪç] suety; tallowish, tallowy; '~licht *n* tallow candle.

Talisman ['tɑ:lisman] *m* (-s/-e) talisman, (good-luck) charm.

'**Talsperre** *f* barrage, dam.

Tampon ♂ [tã'põː, 'tampɔn] *m* (-s/-s) tampon, plug.

Tang [taŋ] *m* (-[e]s/-e) seaweed.

Tank [taŋk] *m* (-[e]s/-s, -e) tank; '2en *v/i.* (ge-, 'h) get (some) petrol, *Am.* get (some) gasoline; '~er ⚓ *m* (-s/-) tanker; '~stelle *f* petrol station, *Am.* gas or filling station; '~wagen *m mot.* tank truck, *Am. a.* gasoline truck, tank trailer; ᵗᵗ₂ tank-car; ~wart ['~vart] *m* (-[e]s/-e) pump attendant.

Tanne ♀ ['tanə] *f* (-/-n) fir(-tree).

'**Tannen|baum** *m* fir-tree; '~nadel *f* fir-needle; '~zapfen *m* fir-cone.

Tante ['tantə] *f* (-/-n) aunt.

Tantieme [tã'tjɛ:mə] *f* (-/-n) royalty, percentage, share in profits.

Tanz [tants] *m* (-es/ᵘe) dance.

tänzeln ['tɛntsəln] *v/i.* (ge-, h, sein) dance, trip, frisk.

'**tanzen** (ge-) *v/i.* (h, sein) *and v/t.* (h) dance.

Tänzer ['tɛntsər] *m* (-s/-), '~in *f* (-/-nen) dancer; *thea.* ballet-dancer; partner.

'**Tanz|lehrer** *m* dancing-master; '~musik *f* dance-music; '~saal *m* dancing-room, ball-room, dancehall; '~schule *f* dancing-school; '~stunde *f* dancing-lesson.

Tapete [ta'pe:tə] *f* (-/-n) wallpaper, paper-hangings *pl.*

tapezier|en [tape'tsi:rən] *v/t.* (*no* -ge-, h) paper; 2er *m* (-s/-) paperhanger; upholsterer.

tapfer *adj.* ['tapfər] brave; valiant, heroic; courageous; 2keit *f* (-/*no pl.*) bravery, valo(u)r; heroism; courage.

tappen ['tapən] *v/i.* (ge-, sein) grope (about), fumble.   [awkward.]

täppisch *adj.* ['tɛpɪʃ] clumsy,

tapsen F ['tapsən] *v/i.* (ge-, sein) walk clumsily.

Tara ♀ ['tɑ:ra] *f* (-/*Taren*) tare.

Tarif [ta'ri:f] *m* (-s/-e) tariff, (table of) rates *pl.*, price-list; 2lich *adv.* according to tariff; ~lohn *m* standard wage(s *pl.*); ~vertrag *m* collective *or* wage agreement.

tarn|en ['tarnən] *v/t.* (ge-, h) camouflage; *esp. fig.* disguise; '2ung *f* (-/-en) camouflage.

Tasche ['taʃə] *f* (-/-n) pocket (*of garment*); (hand)bag; pouch; *s. Aktentasche, Schultasche.*

'**Taschen|buch** *n* pocket-book; '~dieb *m* pickpocket, *Am. sl.* dip; '~geld *n* pocket-money; *monthly:* allowance; '~lampe *f* (electric) torch, *esp. Am.* flashlight; '~messer *n* pocket-knife; '~spielerei *f* juggle(ry); '~tuch *n* (pocket) handkerchief; '~uhr *f* (pocket-)watch; '~wörterbuch *n* pocket dictionary.

Tasse ['tasə] *f* (-/-n) cup.

Tastatur [tasta'tu:r] *f* (-/-en) keyboard, keys *pl.*

Tast|e ['tastə] *f* (-/-n) key; '2en (ge-, h) 1. *v/i.* touch; grope (*nach* for, after), fumble (for); 2. *v/t.* touch, feel; *sich ~* feel *or* grope one's way; '~sinn *m* (-[e]s/*no pl.*) sense of touch.

Tat [tɑ:t] 1. *f* (-/-en) action, act, deed; offen|ce, *Am.* -se, crime; *in der ~* indeed, in fact, as a matter of fact, really; *auf frischer ~ ertappen* catch *s.o.* red-handed; *zur ~ schreiten* proceed to action; *in die ~ umsetzen* implement, carry into effect; 2. 2 *pret.* of *tun*; '~bestand ᵗᵗ₂ *m* facts *pl.* of the case; '2enlos *adj.* inactive, idle.

Täter ['tɛ:tər] *m* (-s/-) perpetrator; offender, culprit.

tätig *adj.* ['tɛ:tɪç] active; busy; *~ sein bei* work at; *be employed with*; ~en † ['~gən] *v/t.* (ge-, h) effect, transact; conclude; 2keit *f* (-/-en) activity; occupation, business, job; profession.

'**Tat|kraft** *f* (-/*no pl.*) energy; enterprise; 2kräftig *adj.* energetic, active.

tätlich *adj.* ['tɛ:tlɪç] violent; *~ werden gegen* assault; '2keiten *f/pl.* (acts *pl.* of) violence; ᵗᵗ₂ assault (and battery).

Tatort ᵗᵗ₂ ['tɑ:t?-] *m* (-[e]s/-e) place *or* scene of a crime.

tätowieren [teto'vi:rən] *v/t.* (*no* -ge-, h) tattoo.

'**Tat|sache** *f* (matter of) fact; '~sachenbericht *m* factual *or* documentary report, matter-of-fact account; '2sächlich *adj.* actual, real.

tätscheln ['tɛtʃəln] *v/t.* (ge-, h) pet, [pat.]

Tatze ['tatsə] *f* (-/-n) paw, claw.

Tau[1] [tau] *n* (-[e]s/-e) rope, cable.

Tau[2] [~] *m* (-[e]s/*no pl.*) dew.

taub *adj.* [taup] deaf (*fig.*: *gegen* to); *fingers, etc.*: benumbed, numb; *nut:*

deaf, empty; *rock*: dead; ∼es Ei
addle egg; *auf e-m Ohr* ∼ *sein* be
deaf of or in one ear.
Taube *orn.* ['taubə] *f* (-/-n) pigeon;
'∼nschlag *m* pigeon-house.
'**Taub|heit** *f* (-/*no pl.*) deafness;
numbness; '♀stumm *adj.* deaf and
dumb; '∼stumme *m, f* (-n/-n) deaf
mute.
tauch|en ['tauxən] (ge-) **1.** *v/t.*
(h) dip, plunge; **2.** *v/i.* (h, sein) dive,
plunge; dip; *submarine*: submerge;
'♀er *m* (-s/-) diver; '♀sieder *m* (-s/-)
immersion heater.
tauen ['tauən] *v/i.* (ge-) **1.** (h, sein):
der Schnee or es taut the snow or
it is thawing; *der Schnee ist von
den Dächern getaut* the snow has
melted off the roofs; **2.** (h): *es taut*
dew is falling.
Taufe ['taufə] *f* (-/-n) baptism,
christening; '♀n *v/t.* (ge-, h) baptize,
christen.
Täufling ['tɔyfliŋ] *m* (-s/-e) child *or*
person to be baptized.
'**Tauf|name** *m* Christian name, *Am.*
a. given name; '∼pate **1.** *m* godfather; **2.** *f* godmother; '∼patin *f*
godmother; '∼schein *m* certificate
of baptism.
taug|en ['taugən] *v/i.* (ge-, h) be
good, be fit, be of use (*all*: zu for);
(*zu*) *nichts* ∼ be good for nothing,
be of no good, be of no use; '♀enichts
m (-, -es/-e) good-for-nothing, *Am.*
sl. dead beat; '∼lich *adj.* ['tauk-]
good, fit, useful (*all*: für, zu for, to
inf.); able; ⚔, ⚓ able-bodied.
Taumel ['tauməl] *m* (-s/*no pl.*)
giddiness; rapture, ecstasy; '♀ig
adj. reeling; giddy; '♀n *v/i.* (ge-,
sein) reel, stagger; be giddy.
Tausch [tauʃ] *m* (-es/-e) exchange;
barter; '♀en *v/t.* (ge-, h) exchange;
barter (*gegen* for).
täuschen ['tɔyʃən] *v/t.* (ge-, h)
deceive, delude, mislead (on purpose); cheat; *sich* ∼ deceive o.s.; be
mistaken; *sich* ∼ *lassen* let o.s. be
deceived; '∼d *adj.* deceptive, delu-
sive; *resemblance*: striking.
'**Tauschhandel** *m* barter.
'**Täuschung** *f* (-/-en) deception,
delusion.
tausend *adj.* ['tauzənt] a thousand;
'∼fach *adj.* thousandfold; '♀fuß *zo.*
m, ♀füß(l)er *zo.* ['∼fy:s(l)ər] *m*
(-s/-) millepede, milliped(e), *Am. a.*
wireworm; '∼st *adj.* thousandth;
'♀stel *n* (-s/-) thousandth (part).
'**Tau|tropfen** *m* dew-drop; '∼wetter
n thaw.
Taxameter [taksa'-] *m* taximeter.
Taxe ['taksə] *f* (-/-n) rate; fee;
estimate; *s. Taxi.*
Taxi ['taksi] *n* (-[s]/-[s]) taxi(-cab),
cab, *Am. a.* hack.
ta'xieren *v/t.* (*no* -ge-, h) rate,
estimate; *officially*: value, appraise.

'**Taxistand** *m* cabstand.
Technik ['tɛçnik] *f* **1.** (-/*no pl.*)
technology; engineering; **2.** (-/-en)
skill, workmanship; technique,
practice; ♪ execution; '∼er *m* (-s/-)
(technical) engineer; technician;
∼um ['∼uum] *n* (-s/Technika, Tech-
niken) technical school.
'**technisch** *adj.* technical; ∼e *Hochschule* school of technology.
Tee [te:] *m* (-s/-s) tea; '∼büchse *f*
tea-caddy; '∼gebäck *n* scones *pl.*,
biscuits *pl., Am. a.* cookies *pl.*;
'∼kanne *f* teapot; '∼kessel *m* tea-
kettle; '∼löffel *m* tea-spoon.
Teer [te:r] *m* (-[e]s/-e) tar; '♀en *v/t.*
(ge-, h) tar.
'**Tee|rose** ♀ *f* tea-rose; '∼sieb *n*
tea-strainer; '∼tasse *f* teacup;
'∼wärmer *m* (-s/-) tea-cosy.
Teich [taiç] *m* (-[e]s/-e) pool,
pond.
Teig [taik] *m* (-[e]s/-e) dough, paste;
♀ig *adj.* ['∼giç] doughy, pasty;
'∼waren *f/pl.* farinaceous food;
noodles *pl.*
Teil [tail] *m, n* (-[e]s/-e) part; portion, share; component; ⚖ party;
zum ∼ partly, in part; *ich für mein*
∼ ... for my part I ...; '♀bar *adj.*
divisible; '∼chen *n* (-s/-) particle;
'♀en *v/t.* (ge-, h) divide; *fig.* share;
'♀haben *v/i.* (*irr. haben, sep.,* -ge-,
h) participate, (have a) share (*both*:
an dat. in); '∼haber *☂ m* (-s/-)
partner; '∼nahme ['∼na:mə] *f* (-/*no
pl.*) participation (*an dat.* in); *fig.*:
interest (in); sympathy (with);
♀nahmslos *adj.* ['∼na:mslo:s] indifferent, unconcerned; passive;
apathetic; '∼nahmslosigkeit *f*
(-/*no pl.*) indifference; passiveness;
apathy; ♀nehmen *v/i.* (*irr. nehmen,
sep.,* -ge-, h): ∼ *an* (*dat.*) take part *or*
participate in; join in; be present
at, attend at; *fig.* sympathize with;
'∼nehmer *m* (-s/-) participant;
member; *univ., etc.*: student; con-
testant; *sports*: competitor; *teleph.*
subscriber; ♀s *adv.* [∼s] partly;
'∼strecke *f* section; stage, leg; 🚌
fare stage; '∼ung *f* (-/-en) division;
'♀weise *adv.* partly, partially, in
part; '∼zahlung *f* (payment by)
instal(l)ments.
Teint [tɛ̃:] *m* (-s/-s) complexion.
Tele|fon [tele'fo:n] *n* (-s/-e) *etc. s.
Telephon, etc.*; '∼graf [∼'gra:f] *m*
(-en/-en) *etc. s. Telegraph, etc.*;
∼gramm [∼'gram] *n* (-s/-e) telegram, wire; *overseas*: cable(gram).
Telegraph [tele'gra:f] *m* (-en/-en)
telegraph; ∼enamt [∼ən?-] *n* telegraph office; ♀ieren [∼a'fi:rən] *v/t.
and v/i.* (*no* -ge-, h) telegraph, wire;
overseas: cable; ♀isch [∼a'fi:ʃ]
1. *adj.* telegraphic; **2.** *adv.* by telegram, by wire; by cable; ∼ist
[∼a'fist] *m* (-en/-en), ∼istin *f* (-/-nen)

telegraph operator, telegrapher, telegraphist.

Teleobjektiv phot. ['te:le-] n telephoto lens.

Telephon [tele'fo:n] n (-s/-e) telephone, F phone; am ~ on the (tele)phone; ans ~ gehen answer the (tele)phone; ~ haben be on the (tele)phone; ~anschluß m telephone connexion or connection; ~buch n telephone directory; ~gespräch n (tele)phone call; conversation or chat over the (tele-) phone; ~hörer m (telephone) receiver, handset; 2ieren [~o'ni:rən] v/i. (no -ge-, h) telephone, F phone; mit j-m ~ ring s.o. up, Am. call s.o. up; 2isch adv. [~'fo:niʃ] by (tele)phone, over the (tele)phone; ~ist [~o'nist] m (-en/-en), ~istin f (-/-nen) (telephone) operator, telephonist; ~vermittlung f s. Telephonzentrale; ~zelle f telephone kiosk or box, call-box, Am. telephone booth; ~zentrale f (telephone) exchange.

Teleskop opt. [tele'sko:p] n (-s/-e) telescope.

Teller ['telər] m (-s/-) plate.

Tempel ['tempəl] m (-s/-) temple.

Temperament [tempəra'ment] n (-[e]s/-e) temper(ament); fig. spirit(s pl.); 2los adj. spiritless; 2voll adj. (high-)spirited.

Temperatur [tempəra'tu:r] f (-/-en) temperature; j-s ~ messen take s.o.'s temperature.

Tempo ['tempo] n (-s/-s, Tempi) time; pace; speed; rate.

Tendenz [ten'dents] f (-/-en) tendency; trend; 2iös adj. [~'tsjø:s] tendentious.

Tennis ['tenis] n (-/no pl.) (lawn) tennis; ~ball m tennis-ball; ~platz m tennis-court; ~schläger m (tennis-)racket; ~spieler m tennis player; ~turnier n tennis tournament.

Tenor ♪ [te'no:r] m (-s/⁼e) tenor.

Teppich ['tepiç] m (-s/-e) carpet; ~kehrmaschine f carpet-sweeper.

Termin [ter'mi:n] m (-s/-e) appointed time or day; ꜰ, ♰ date, term; sports: fixture; äußerster ~ final date, dead(-)line; ~geschäfte ♰ n/pl. futures pl.; ~kalender m appointment book or pad; ꜰ causelist, Am. calendar; ~liste ꜰ f causelist, Am. calendar.

Terpentin [terpən'ti:n] n (-s/-e) turpentine.

Terrain [te'rɛ̃:] n (-s/-s) ground; plot; building site.

Terrasse [te'rasə] f (-/-n) terrace; 2nförmig [~nfœrmiç] terraced, in terraces.

Terrine [te'ri:nə] f (-/-n) tureen.

Territorium [teri'to:rjum] n (-s/ Territorien) territory.

Terror ['teror] m (-s/no pl.) terror; 2isieren [~ori'zi:rən] v/t. (no -ge-, h) terrorize.

Terz ♪ [terts] f (-/-en) third; ~ett ♪ [~'tset] n (-[e]s/-e) trio.

Testament [testa'ment] n (-[e]s/-e) (last) will, (often: last will and) testament; eccl. Testament; 2arisch [~'ta:riʃ] 1. adj. testamentary; 2. adv. by will; ~svollstrecker m (-s/-) executor; officially: administrator.

testen ['testən] v/t. (ge-, h) test.

teuer adj. ['tɔyər] dear (a. fig.), expensive; wie ~ ist es? how much is it?

Teufel ['tɔyfəl] m (-s/-) devil; der ~ the Devil, Satan; zum ~! dickens!, hang it!; wer zum ~? F who the devil or deuce?; der ~ ist los the fat's in the fire; scher dich zum ~! F go to hell!, go to blazes!; ~ei [~'lai] f (-/-en) devilment, mischief, devilry, Am. deviltry; ~skerl F m devil of a fellow.

'teuflisch adj. devilish, diabolic(al).

Text [tekst] m (-es/-e) text; words pl. (of song); book, libretto (of opera); ~buch n book; libretto.

Textil|ien [teks'ti:ljən] pl., ~waren pl. textile fabrics pl., textiles pl.

'textlich adv. concerning the text.

Theater [te'a:tər] n 1. (-s/-) theat|re, Am. -er; stage; 2. F (-s/no pl.) playacting; ~besucher m playgoer; ~karte f theatre ticket; ~kasse f box-office; ~stück n play; ~vorstellung f theatrical performance; ~zettel m playbill.

theatralisch adj. [tea'tra:liʃ] theatrical, stagy.

Theke ['te:kə] f (-/-n) at inn: bar, Am. a. counter; at shop: counter.

Thema ['te:ma] n (-s/Themen, Themata) theme, subject; topic (of discussion).

Theolog|e [teo'lo:gə] m (-n/-n) theologian, divine; ~ie [~o'gi:] f (-/-n) theology.

Theoret|iker [teo're:tikər] m (-s/-) theorist; 2isch adj. theoretic(al).

Theorie [teo'ri:] f (-/-n) theory.

Therapie ♰ [tera'pi:] f (-/-n) therapy. [spa.)

Thermalbad [ter'ma:l-] n (thermal)

Thermometer [termo'-] n (-s/-) thermometer; ~stand m (thermometer) reading.

Thermosflasche ['termɔs-] f vacuum bottle or flask, thermos (flask).

These ['te:zə] f (-/-n) thesis.

Thrombose ♰ [trɔm'bo:zə] f (-/-n) thrombosis.

Thron [tro:n] m (-[e]s/-e) throne; ~besteigung f accession to the throne; ~erbe m heir to the throne, heir apparent; '~folge f succession to the throne; ~folger m (-s/-) successor to the throne; '~rede parl. f Queen's or King's Speech.

17*

Thunfisch *ichth.* ['tuːn-] *m* tunny, tuna.

Tick F [tik] *m* (-[e]s/-s, -e) crotchet, fancy, kink; e-n ~ haben have a bee in one's bonnet.

ticken ['tikən] *v/i.* (ge-, h) tick.

tief [tiːf] **1.** *adj.* deep (*a. fig.*); *fig.*: profound; low; im ~sten Winter in the dead *or* depth of winter; **2.** *adv.*: bis ~ in die Nacht far into the night; das läßt ~ blicken that speaks volumes; zu ~ singen sing flat; **3.** ♀ *meteor.* *n* (-[e]s/-s) depression, low(-pressure area); '♀bau *m* civil *or* underground engineering; '♀-druckgebiet *meteor.* *n s.* Tief; '♀e *f* (-/-n) depth (*a. fig.*); *fig.* profundity; '♀ebene *f* low plain, lowland; '♀enschärfe *phot.* *f* depth of focus; '♀flug *m* low-level flight; '♀gang ⚓ *m* draught, *Am.* draft; ~gebeugt *fig. adj.* ['~gəbɔʏkt] deeply afflicted, bowed down; '~gekühlt *adj.* deep-frozen; '~greifend *adj.* fundamental, radical; '♀land *n* lowland(s *pl.*); '~liegend *adj.* eyes: sunken; *fig.* deep-seated; '♀schlag *m boxing*: low hit; '~schürfend *fig. adj.* profound; thorough; '♀see *f* deep sea; '~sinnig *adj.* thoughtful, pensive; F melancholy; '♀stand *m* (-[e]s/no *pl.*) low level.

Tiegel ['tiːgəl] *m* (-s/-) saucepan, stew-pan; ⊕ crucible.

Tier [tiːr] *n* (-[e]s/-e) animal; beast; brute; großes ~ *fig. sl.* bigwig, big bug, *Am.* big shot; '~arzt *m* veterinary (surgeon), F vet, *Am. a.* veterinarian; '~garten *m* zoological gardens *pl.*, zoo; '~heilkunde *f* veterinary medicine; '♀isch *adj.* animal; *fig.* bestial, brutish, savage; '~kreis *ast. m* zodiac; ~quälerei [~kvɛːlə'raɪ] *f* (-/-en) cruelty to animals; '~reich *n* (-[e]s/no *pl.*) animal kingdom; '~schutzverein *m* Society for the Prevention of Cruelty to Animals.

Tiger *zo.* ['tiːgər] *m* (-s/-) tiger; '~in *zo. f* (-/-nen) tigress.

tilgen ['tilgən] *v/t.* (ge-, h) extinguish; efface; wipe *or* blot out, erase; *fig.* obliterate; annul, cancel; discharge, pay (*debt*); redeem (*mortgage, etc.*); '♀ung *f* (-/-en) extinction; extermination; cancel(l)ing; discharge, payment; redemption.

Tinktur [tiŋk'tuːr] *f* (-/-en) tincture. [*sitzen* F be in a scrape.\]

Tinte ['tintə] *f* (-/-n) ink; *in der* ~|
'**Tinten|faß** *n* ink-pot, *desk*: inkwell; '~fisch *ichth. m* cuttle-fish; '~fleck *m*, '~klecks *m* (ink-)blot; '~stift *m* indelible pencil.

Tip [tip] *m* (-s/-s) hint, tip; '♀pen (ge-, h) **1.** *v/i.* F type; *fig.* guess; j-m auf die Schulter ~ tap s.o. on his shoulder; **2.** *v/t.* tip; foretell, predict; F type.

Tiroler [ti'roːlər] **1.** *m* (-s/-) Tyrolese; **2.** *adj.* Tyrolese.

Tisch [tiʃ] *m* (-es/-e) table; bei ~ at table; den ~ decken lay the table *or* cloth, set the table; reinen ~ machen make a clean sweep (*damit* of it); zu ~ bitten invite *or* ask to dinner *or* supper; bitte zu ~| dinner is ready!; '~decke *f* table-cloth; '♀fertig *adj. food*: ready-prepared; '~gast *m* guest; '~gebet *n*: das ~ sprechen say grace; '~gesellschaft *f* dinner-party; '~gespräch *n* table-talk; '~lampe *f* table-lamp; desk lamp.

Tischler ['tiʃlər] *m* (-s/-) joiner; carpenter; cabinet-maker; ~ei [~'raɪ] *f* (-/-en) joinery; joiner's workshop.

'**Tisch|platte** *f* top (of a table), table top; leaf (*of extending table*); '~rede *f* toast, after-dinner speech; '~tennis *n* table tennis, ping-pong; '~tuch *n* table-cloth; '~zeit *f* dinner-time.

Titan [ti'taːn] *m* (-en/-en) Titan; ♀isch *adj.* titanic.

Titel ['tiːtəl] *m* (-s/-) title; e-n ~ (inne)haben *sports*: hold a title; '~bild *n* frontispiece; cover picture (*of magazine, etc.*); '~blatt *n* title-page; cover (*of magazine*); '~halter *m* (-s/-) *sports*: title-holder; '~kampf *m boxing*: title fight; '~rolle *thea. f* title-role.

titulieren [titu'liːrən] *v/t.* (no -ge-, h) style, call, address as.

Toast [toːst] *m* (-es/-e, -s) toast (*a. fig.*).

tob|en ['toːbən] *v/i.* (ge-, h) rage, rave, storm, bluster; *children*: romp; ♀sucht ♬ ['toːp-] *f* (-/no *pl.*) raving madness, frenzy; '~süchtig *adj.* ['toːp-] raving mad, frantic.

Tochter ['tɔxtər] *f* (-/⁼) daughter; '~gesellschaft † *f* subsidiary company.

Tod [toːt] *m* (-[e]s/~-e) death; ⚖ decease.

Todes|angst ['toːdəsʔ-] *f* mortal agony; *fig.* mortal fear; Todesängste ausstehen be scared to death, be frightened out of one's wits; '~anzeige *f* obituary (notice); '~fall *m* (case of) death; Todesfälle *pl.* deaths *pl.*, ⚔ casualties *pl.*; '~kampf *m* death throes *pl.*, mortal agony; '~strafe *f* capital punishment, death penalty; bei ~ verboten forbidden *on or* under pain *or* penalty of death; '~ursache *f* cause of death; '~urteil *n* death *or* capital sentence, death-warrant.

'**Tod|feind** *m* deadly *or* mortal enemy; '♀krank *adj.* dangerously ill.

tödlich *adj.* ['tøːtliç] deadly; fatal; *wound: a.* mortal.

'**tod|'müde** *adj.* dead tired; '~

'**schick** F *adj.* dashing, gorgeous; '~'**sicher** F *adj.* cock-sure; '²**sünde** *f* deadly *or* mortal sin.

Toilette [toa'lɛtə] *f* (-/-n) dress(ing): toilet; lavatory, gentlemen's *or* ladies' room, *esp. Am.* toilet.

Toi'letten|artikel *m/pl.* toilet articles *pl., Am. a.* toiletry; ~**papier** *n* toilet-paper; ~**tisch** *m* toilet (-table), dressing-table, *Am. a.* dresser.

toleran|t *adj.* [tole'rant] tolerant (*gegen* of); ²**z** [~ts] *f* 1. (-/*no pl.*) tolerance, toleration (*esp. eccl.*); 2. ⊕ (-/-en) tolerance, allowance.

toll [tɔl] 1. *adj.* (raving) mad, frantic; mad, crazy, wild (*all a. fig.*); fantastic; *noise, etc.*: frightful, F awful; *das ist ja* ~ F that's (just) great; 2. *adv.*: es ~ *treiben* carry on like mad; *es zu* ~ *treiben* go too far; '~**en** *v/i.* (ge-, h, sein) *children*: romp; '²**haus** *fig. n* bedlam; '²**heit** *f* (-/-en) madness; mad trick; '~**kühn** *adj.* foolhardy, rash; '²**wut** *vet. f* rabies.

Tolpatsch F ['tɔlpatʃ] *m* (-es/-e) awkward *or* clumsy fellow; '²**ig** F *adj.* awkward, clumsy.

Tölpel F ['tœlpəl] *m* (-s/-) awkward *or* clumsy fellow; boob(y).

Tomate 💎 [to'maːtə] *f*(-/-n) tomato.

Ton¹ [toːn] *m* (-[e]s/-e) clay.

Ton² [~] *m* (-[e]s/=e) sound; ♪ tone (*a. of language*); ♪ *single*: note; accent, stress; *fig.* tone; *paint.* tone, tint, shade; *guter* ~ good form; *den* ~ *angeben* set the fashion; *zum guten* ~ *gehören* be the fashion; *große Töne reden* or F *spucken* F talk big, boast; '~**abnehmer** *m* pick-up; '²**angebend** *adj.* setting the fashion, leading; '~**arm** *m* pick-up arm (*of record-player*); '~**art** ♪ *f* key; '~**band** *n* recording tape; '~**bandgerät** *n* tape recorder.

tönen ['tøːnən] (ge-, h) 1. *v/i.* sound, ring; 2. *v/t.* tint, tone, shade.

tönern *adj.* ['tøːnərn] (of) clay, earthen.

'**Ton|fall** *m in speaking*: intonation, accent; '~**film** *m* sound film; '~**lage** *f* pitch; '~**leiter** ♪ *f* scale, gamut; '²**los** *adj.* soundless; *fig.* toneless; '~**meister** *m* sound engineer.

Tonne ['tɔnə] *f* (-/-n) *large*: tun; *smaller*: barrel, cask; ⚓ *measure of weight*: ton.

'**Tonsilbe** *gr. f* accented syllable.

Tonsur [tɔn'zuːr] *f* (-/-en) tonsure.

'**Tönung** *paint. f* (-/-en) tint, tinge, shade.

'**Tonwaren** *f/pl. s.* **Töpferware**.

Topf [tɔpf] *m* (-[e]s/=e) pot.

Töpfer ['tœpfər] *m* (-s/-) potter; stove-fitter; ~**ei** [~'raɪ] *f* (-/-en) pottery; '~**ware** *f* pottery, earthenware, crockery.

topp¹ *int.* [tɔp] done!, agreed!

Topp² ⚓ [~] *m* (-s/-e, -s) top, mast-head.

Tor¹ [toːr] *n* (-[e]s/-e) gate; gateway (*a. fig.*); *football*: goal; *skiing*: gate.

Tor² [~] *m* (-en/-en) fool.

Torf [tɔrf] *m* (-[e]s/*no pl.*) peat.

Torheit ['toːrhaɪt] *f* (-/-en) folly.

'**Torhüter** *m* gate-keeper; *sports*: goalkeeper.

töricht *adj.* ['tøːrɪçt] foolish, silly.

Törin ['tøːrɪn] *f* (-/-nen) fool(ish woman).

torkeln ['tɔrkəln] *v/i.* (ge-, h, sein) reel, stagger, totter.

'**Tor|latte** *f sports*: cross-bar; '~**lauf** *m skiing*: slalom; '~**linie** *f sports*: goal-line.

Tornister [tɔr'nɪstər] *m* (-s/-) knapsack; satchel.

torpedieren [tɔrpe'diːrən] *v/t.* (*no* -ge-, h) torpedo (*a. fig.*).

Torpedo [tɔr'peːdo] *m* (-s/-s) torpedo; ~**boot** *n* torpedo-boat.

'**Tor|pfosten** *m* gate-post; *sports*: goal-post; '~**schuß** *m* shot at the goal; '~**schütze** *m sports*: scorer.

Torte ['tɔrtə] *f* (-/-n) fancy cake, *Am.* layer cake; tart, *Am.* pie.

Tortur [tɔr'tuːr] *f* (-/-en) torture; *fig.* ordeal.

Tor|wart ['toːrvart] *m* (-[e]s/-e) *sports*: goalkeeper; '~**weg** *m* gateway.

tosen ['toːzən] *v/i.* (ge-, h, sein) roar, rage; '~**d** *applause*: thunderous.

tot *adj.* [toːt] dead (*a. fig.*); deceased; ~**er Punkt** ⊕ dead cent|re, *Am.* -er; *fig.*: deadlock; fatigue; ~**es Rennen** *sports*: dead heat.

total *adj.* [to'taːl] total, complete.

'**tot|arbeiten** *v/refl.* (*sep.*, -ge-, h) work o.s. to death; '²**e** (-n/-n) 1. *m* dead man; (dead) body, corpse; *die* ~**n** *pl.* the dead *pl.*, the deceased *pl.* or departed *pl.*; ✗ casualties *pl.*; 2. *f* dead woman.

töten ['tøːtən] *v/t.* (ge-, h) kill; destroy; murder; deaden (*nerve, etc.*).

'**Toten|bett** *n* deathbed; '²**blaß** *adj.* deadly *or* deathly pale; '~**blässe** *f* deadly paleness *or* pallor; '²**bleich** *adj. s.* totenblaß; '²**gräber** ['~grɛːbər] *m* (-s/-) grave-digger (*a. zo.*); '~**hemd** *n* shroud; '~**kopf** *m* death's-head (*a. zo.*); *emblem of death*: *a.* skull and cross-bones; '~**liste** *f* death-roll (*a.* ✗), *esp.* ✗ casualty list; '~**maske** *f* death-mask; '~**messe** *eccl. f* mass for the dead, requiem; '~**schädel** *m* death's-head, skull; '~**schein** *m* death certificate; '²**still** *adj.* (as) still as the grave; '~**stille** *f* dead(ly) silence, deathly stillness.

'**tot|geboren** *adj.* still-born; '²**geburt** *f* still birth; '~**lachen** *v/refl.* (*sep.*, -ge-, h) die of laughing.

Toto ['to:to] *m*, F *a. n* (-s/-s) football pools *pl.*

'**tot|schießen** *v/t.* (*irr. schießen, sep., -ge-, h*) shoot dead, kill; '**⁀schlag** ⚡ *m* manslaughter, homicide; '**⁀schlagen** *v/t.* (*irr. schlagen, sep., -ge-, h*) kill (*a. time*); slay; '**⁀schweigen** *v/t.* (*irr. schweigen, sep., -ge-, h*) hush up; '**⁀stechen** *v/t.* (*irr. stechen, sep., -ge-, h*) stab to death; '**⁀stellen** *v/refl.* (*sep., -ge-, h*) feign death.

'**Tötung** *f* (-/-en) killing, slaying; ⚡ homicide; *fahrlässige* ⁀ ⚡ manslaughter.

Tour [tu:r] *f* (-/-en) tour; excursion, trip; ⊕ turn, revolution; *auf* ⁀*en kommen mot.* pick up speed; '**⁀enwagen** *mot. m* touring car.

Tourist [tu'rist] *m* (-en/-en), **⁀in** *f* (-/-nen) tourist.

Tournee [tur'ne:] *f* (-/-s, -n) tour.

Trab [tra:p] *m* (-[e]s/*no pl.*) trot.

Trabant [tra'bant] *m* (-en/-en) satellite.

trab|en ['tra:bən] *v/i.* (*ge-, h, sein*) trot; **⁀rennen** ['tra:p-] *n* trotting race.

Tracht [traxt] *f* (-/-en) dress, costume; uniform; fashion; load; *e-e* (*gehörige*) ⁀ *Prügel* a (sound) thrashing; '**⁀en** *v/i.* (*ge-, h*): ⁀ *nach et.* strive for; *j-m nach dem Leben* ⁀ seek s.o.'s life.

trächtig *adj.* ['trɛçtiç] (big) with young, pregnant. [tradition.]

Tradition [tradi'tsjo:n] *f* (-/-en)

traf [tra:f] *pret. of* treffen.

Trag|bahre ['tra:k-] *f* stretcher, litter; '**⁀bar** *adj.* portable; *dress*: wearable; *fig.*: bearable; reasonable; *e-e* ['⁀gə] *f* (-/-n) hand-barrow; *s. Tragbahre.*

träge *adj.* ['trɛ:gə] lazy, indolent; *phys.* inert (*a. fig.*).

tragen ['tra:gən] (*irr., ge-, h*) **1.** *v/t.* carry; bear (*costs, name, responsibility, etc.*); bear, endure; support; bear, yield (*fruit,* ⁀ *interest, etc.*); wear (*dress, etc.*); *bei sich* ⁀ have about one; *sich gut* ⁀ *material*: wear well; *zur Schau* ⁀ show off; **2.** *v/i. tree*: bear, yield; *gun, voice*: carry; *ice*: bear.

Träger ['trɛ:gər] *m* (-s/-) carrier; porter (*of luggage*); holder, bearer (*of name, licence, etc.*); wearer (*of dress*); (shoulder-)strap (*of slip, etc.*); ⊕ support; △ girder.

Trag|fähigkeit ['tra:k-] *f* carrying or load capacity; ⚓ tonnage; '**⁀fläche** ✈ *f*, '**⁀flügel** ✈ *m* wing, plane.

Trägheit ['trɛ:khait] *f* (-/*no pl.*) laziness, indolence; *phys.* inertia (*a. fig.*).

tragisch *adj.* ['tra:giʃ] tragic (*a. fig.*); *fig.* tragical.

Tragödie [tra'gø:djə] *f* (-/-n) tragedy.

Trag|riemen ['tra:k-] *m* (carrying) strap; sling (*of gun*); '**⁀tier** *n* pack animal; '**⁀tüte** *f* carrier-bag; '**⁀weite** *f* range; *fig.* import(ance), consequences *pl.*; *von großer* ⁀ of great moment.

Train|er ['trɛ:nər] *m* (-s/-) trainer; coach; **⁀ieren** [⁀'ni:rən] (*no -ge-, h*) **1.** *v/t.* train; coach; **2.** *v/i.* train; **⁀ing** ['⁀iŋ] *n* (-s/-s) training; '**⁀ingsanzug** *m sports*: track suit.

traktieren [trak'ti:rən] *v/t.* (*no -ge-, h*) treat (badly).

Traktor ⊕ ['traktɔr] *m* (-s/-en) tractor.

trällern ['trɛlərn] *v/t. and v/i.* (*ge-, h*) troll.

trampel|n ['trampəln] *v/i.* (*ge-, h*) trample, stamp; '**⁀pfad** *m* beaten track.

Tran [tra:n] *m* (-[e]s/-e) train-oil, whale-oil.

Träne ['trɛ:nə] *f* (-/-n) tear; *in* ⁀*n ausbrechen* burst into tears; '**⁀en** *v/i.* (*ge-, h*) water; '**⁀ngas** *n* tear-gas.

Trank [traŋk] **1.** *m* (-[e]s/⁀e) drink, beverage; 🜹 potion; **2.** ♀ *pret. of* trinken.

Tränke ['trɛŋkə] *f* (-/-n) watering-place; '**⁀en** *v/t.* (*ge-, h*) water (*animals*); soak, impregnate (*material*).

Trans|formator ⚡ [transfɔr'ma:tɔr] *m* (-s/-en) transformer; **⁀fusion** 🜹 [⁀u'zjo:n] *f* (-/-en) transfusion.

Transistorradio [tran'zistɔr-] *n* transistor radio *or* set.

transitiv *gr. adj.* ['tranziti:f] transitive.

transparent [transpa'rɛnt] **1.** *adj.* transparent; **2.** ♀ *n* (-[e]s/-e) transparency; *in political processions, etc.*: banner.

transpirieren [transpi'ri:rən] *v/i.* (*no -ge-, h*) perspire.

Transplantation 🜹 [transplanta-'tsjo:n] *f* transplant (operation).

Transport [trans'pɔrt] *m* (-[e]s/-e) transport(ation), conveyance, carriage; **⁀abel** *adj.* [⁀'ta:bəl] (trans-)portable; **⁀er** *m* (-s/-) ⚓, ✈ (troop-)transport; ✈ transport (aircraft *or* plane); **⁀fähig** *adj.* transportable, *sick person*: a. transferable; **⁀ieren** [⁀'ti:rən] *v/t.* (*no -ge-, h*) transport, convey, carry; **⁀unternehmen** *n* carrier.

Trapez [tra'pe:ts] *n* (-es/-e) ⩤ trapezium, *Am.* trapezoid; *gymnastics*: trapeze.

trappeln ['trapəln] *v/i.* (*ge-, sein*) *horse*: clatter; *children, etc.*: patter.

Trass|ant ✝ [tra'sant] *m* (-en/-en) drawer; **⁀at** ✝ [⁀'sat] *m* (-en/-en) drawee; **⁀e** ⊕ *f* (-/-n) line; **⁀ieren** [⁀'si:rən] *v/t.* (*no -ge-, h*) ⊕ lay *or* trace out; ⁀ *auf* (*acc.*) ✝ draw on.

trat [trɑːt] pret. of treten.
Tratte ✝ ['tratə] f (-/-n) draft.
Traube ['traubə] f (-/-n) bunch of grapes; grape; cluster; '**~nsaft** m grape-juice; '**~nzucker** m grape-sugar, glucose.
trauen ['trauən] (ge-, h) **1.** v/t. marry; sich ~ lassen get married; **2.** v/i. trust (j-m s.o.), confide (dat. in); ich traute meinen Ohren nicht I could not believe my ears.
Trauer ['trauər] f (-/no pl.) sorrow, affliction; for dead person: mourning; '**~botschaft** f sad news; '**~fall** m death; '**~feier** f funeral ceremonies pl., obsequies pl.; '**~flor** m mourning-crape; '**~geleit** n funeral procession; '**~gottesdienst** m funeral service; '**~kleid** n mourning (-dress); '**~marsch** m funeral march; '**~n** v/i. (ge-, h) mourn (um for); be in mourning; '**~spiel** n tragedy; '**~weide** ♀ f weeping willow; '**~zug** m funeral procession.
Traufe ['traufə] f (-/-n) eaves pl.; gutter; s. Regen².
träufeln ['trɔyfəln] v/t. (ge-, h) drop, drip, trickle. [cosy, snug.]
traulich adj. ['traulic] intimate;
Traum [traum] m (-[e]s/=e) dream (a. fig.); reverie; das fällt mir nicht im ~ ein! I would not dream of (doing) it!; '**~bild** n vision; '**~deuter** m (-s/-) dream-reader.
träum|en ['trɔymən] v/i. and v/t. (ge-, h) dream; '**Ꞩer** m (-s/-) dreamer (a. fig.); **Ꞩerei** [~'rai] f (-/-en) dreaming; fig. a. reverie (a. ♪), day-dream, musing; '**~erisch** adj. dreamy; musing.
traurig adj. ['trauric] sad (über acc. at), Am. F blue; wretched.
'**Trau|ring** m wedding-ring; '**~schein** m marriage certificate or lines pl.; '**~ung** f (-/-en) marriage, wedding; '**~zeuge** m witness to a marriage.
Trecker ⊕ ['trɛkər] m (-s/-) tractor.
Treff [trɛf] n (-s/-s) cards: club (s pl.).
treffen¹ ['trɛfən] (irr., ge-) **1.** v/t. (h) hit (a. fig.), strike; concern, disadvantageously: affect; meet; nicht ~ miss; e-e Entscheidung ~ come to a decision; Maßnahmen ~ take measures or steps; Vorkehrungen ~ take precautions or measures; sich ~ happen; meet; gather, assemble; a. have an appointment (mit with), F have a date (with); das trifft sich gut! that's lucky!, how fortunate!; sich getroffen fühlen feel hurt; wen trifft die Schuld? who is to blame?; das Los traf ihn the lot fell on him; du bist gut getroffen paint., phot. this is a good likeness of you; vom Blitz getroffen struck by lightning; **2.** v/i. (h) hit; **3.** v/i. (sein): ~ auf (acc.) meet with; encounter (a. ⚔).

Treffen² [~] n (-s/-) meeting; rally; gathering; ⚔ encounter; '**Ꞩd** adj. remark: appropriate, to the point.
'**Treff|er** m (-s/-) hit (a. fig.); prize; '**~punkt** m meeting-place.
Treibeis ['traip9-] n drift-ice.
treiben¹ ['traibən] (irr., ge-) **1.** v/t. (h) drive; ⊕ put in motion, propel; drift (smoke, snow); put forth (leaves); force (plants); fig. impel, urge, press (j-n zu inf. s.o. to inf.); carry on (business, trade); Musik (Sport) ~ go in for music (sports); Sprachen ~ study languages; es zu weit ~ go too far; wenn er es weiterhin so treibt if he carries or goes on like that; was treibst du da? what are you doing there?; **2.** v/i. (sein) drive; float, drift; **3.** v/i. (h) ⚜ shoot; dough: ferment, work.
Treiben² [~] n (-s/no pl.) driving; doings pl., goings-on pl.; geschäftiges ~ bustle; '**Ꞩd** adj.: ~e Kraft driving force.
Treib|haus ['traip-] n hothouse; '**~holz** n drift-wood; '**~jagd** f battue; '**~riemen** m driving-belt; '**~stoff** m fuel; propell|ant, -ent (of rocket).
trenn|en ['trɛnən] v/t. (ge-, h) separate, sever; rip (seam); teleph., ⚡ cut off, disconnect; isolate, segregate; sich ~ separate (von from), part (from or with s.o.; with s.th.); '**Ꞩschärfe** f radio: selectivity; '**Ꞩung** f (-/-en) separation; disconne|xion, -ction; segregation (of races, etc.); '**Ꞩ(ungs)wand** f partition (wall). [(-bit).]
Trense ['trɛnzə] f (-/-n) snaffle
Treppe ['trɛpə] f (-/-n) staircase, stairway, (e-e a flight or pair of) stairs pl.; zwei ~n hoch on the second floor, Am. on the third floor.
'**Treppen|absatz** m landing; '**~geländer** n banisters pl.; '**~haus** n staircase; '**~stufe** f stair, step.
Tresor [tre'zoːr] m (-s/-e) safe; bank: strong-room, vault.
treten ['treːtən] (irr., ge-) **1.** v/i. (h) tread, step (j-n or j-m auf die Zehen on s.o.'s toes); **2.** v/i. (sein) tread, step (j-m auf die Zehen on s.o.'s toes); walk; ins Haus ~ enter the house; j-m unter die Augen ~ appear before s.o., face s.o.; j-m zu nahe ~ offend s.o.; zu j-m ~ step or walk up to s.o.; über die Ufer ~ overflow its banks; **3.** v/t. (h) tread; kick; mit Füßen ~ trample upon.
treu adj. [trɔy] faithful, loyal; '**Ꞩbruch** m breach of faith, perfidy; '**Ꞩe** f (-/no pl.) fidelity, faith(fulness), loyalty; **Ꞩhänder** ['~hɛndər] m (-s/-) trustee; '**~herzig** adj. guileless; ingenuous; simpleminded; '**~los** adj. faithless (gegen to), disloyal (to); perfidious.

Tribüne [tri'by:nə] f (-/-n) platform; sports, etc.: (grand) stand.

Tribut [tri'bu:t] m (-[e]s/-e) tribute.

Trichter ['triçtər] m (-s/-) funnel; made by bomb, shell, etc.: crater; horn (of wind instruments, etc.).

Trick [trik] m (-s/-e, -s) trick; '~film m animation, animated cartoon.

Trieb [tri:p] 1. m (-[e]s/-e) ♀ sprout, (new) shoot; driving force; impulse; instinct; (sexual) urge; desire; 2. ♀ pret. of treiben; '~feder f main-spring; fig. driving force, motive; '~kraft f motive power; fig. driving force, motive; '~wagen ⚙ m rail-car, rail-motor; '~werk ⊕ n gear (drive), (driving) mechanism, transmission; engine.

triefen ['tri:fən] v/i. ([irr.,] ge-, h) drip (von with); eye: run.

triftig adj. ['triftiç] valid.

Trigonometrie A [trigonome'tri:] f (-/no pl.) trigonometry.

Trikot [tri'ko:] (-s/-s) 1. m stockinet; 2. n tights pl.; vest; ~agen [~o'ta:ʒən] f/pl. hosiery.

Triller ♪ ['trilər] m (-s/-) trill, shake, quaver; '2n ♪ v/i. and v/t. (ge-, h) trill, shake, quaver; bird: a. warble.

trink|bar adj. ['triŋkba:r] drinkable; '2becher m drinking-cup; '~en (irr., ge-, h) 1. v/t. drink; take, have (tea, etc.); 2. v/i. drink; ~ auf (acc.) drink to, toast; '2er m (-s/-) drinker; drunkard; '2gelage n drinking-bout; '2geld n tip, gratuity; j-m e-e Mark ~ geben tip s.o. one mark; '2glas n drinking-glass; '2halle f at spa: pump-room; '2kur f: e-e ~ machen drink the waters; '2spruch m toast; '2wasser n (-s/no pl.) drinking-water.

Trio ['tri:o] n (-s/-s) trio (a. ♪).

trippeln ['tripəln] v/i. (ge-, sein) trip.

Tritt [trit] m (-[e]s/-e) tread, step; footprint; noise: footfall, (foot)step; kick; ⊕ treadle; s. Trittbrett, Trittleiter; im (falschen) ~ in (out of) step; ~ halten keep step; '~brett n step, footboard; mot. running-board; '~leiter f stepladder, (e-e pair or set of) steps pl.

Triumph [tri'umf] m (-[e]s/-e) triumph; 2al adj. [~'fa:l] triumphant; ~bogen m triumphal arch; 2ieren [~'fi:rən] v/i. (no -ge-, h) triumph (über acc. over).

trocken adj. ['trɔkən] dry (a. fig.); soil, land: arid; '2dock ⚓ n dry dock; '2haube f (hood of) hair-drier; '2heit f (-/no pl.) dryness; drought, aridity; '~legen v/t. (sep., -ge-, h) dry up; drain (land); change the napkins of, Am. change the diapers of (baby); '2obst n dried fruit.

trocknen ['trɔknən] (ge-) 1. v/i. (sein) dry; 2. v/t. (h) dry.

Troddel ['trɔdəl] f (-/-n) tassel.

Trödel F ['trø:dəl] m (-s/no pl.) second-hand articles pl.; lumber, Am. junk; rubbish; '2n F fig. v/i. (ge-, h) dawdle, loiter.

Trödler ['trø:dlər] m (-s/-) second-hand dealer, Am. junk dealer, junkman; fig. dawdler, loiterer.

troff [trɔf] pret. of triefen.

Trog¹ [tro:k] m (-[e]s/⁼e) trough.

trog² [~] pret. of trügen.

Trommel ['trɔməl] f (-/-n) drum; ⊕ a. cylinder, barrel; '~fell n drumskin; anat. ear-drum; '2n v/i. and v/t. (ge-, h) drum.

Trommler ['trɔmlər] m (-s/-) drummer.

Trompete [trɔm'pe:tə] f (-/-n) trumpet; 2n v/i. and v/t. (no -ge-, h) trumpet; ~r m (-s/-) trumpeter.

Tropen ['tro:pən]: die ~ pl. the tropics pl.

Tropf F [trɔpf] m (-[e]s/⁼e) simpleton; armer ~ poor wretch.

tröpfeln ['trœpfəln] (ge-) 1. v/i. (h) drop, drip, trickle; tap: a. leak; es tröpfelt rain: a few drops are falling; 2. v/i. (sein): ~ aus or von trickle or drip from; 3. v/t. (h) drop, drip.

tropfen¹ ['trɔpfən] (ge-) 1. v/i. (h) drop, drip, trickle; tap: a. leak; candle: gutter; 2. v/i. (sein): ~ aus or von trickle or drip from; 3. v/t. (h) drop, drip.

Tropfen² [~] m (-s/-) drop; ein ~ auf den heißen Stein a drop in the ocean or bucket; 2förmig adj. ['~fœrmiç] drop-shaped; '2weise adv. drop by drop, by drops.

Trophäe [tro'fɛ:ə] f (-/-n) trophy.

tropisch adj. ['tro:piʃ] tropical.

Trosse ['trɔsə] f (-/-n) cable; ⚓ a. hawser.

Trost [tro:st] m (-es/no pl.) comfort, consolation; das ist ein schlechter ~ that is cold comfort; du bist wohl nicht (recht) bei ~! F you must be out of your mind!

tröst|en ['trø:stən] v/t. (ge-, h) console, comfort; sich ~ console o.s. (mit with); ~ Sie sich! be of good comfort!, cheer up!; '~lich adj. comforting.

'trost|los adj. disconsolate, inconsolable; land, etc.: desolate; fig. wretched; '2losigkeit f (-/no pl.) desolation; fig. wretchedness; '2preis m consolation prize, booby prize; '~reich adj. consolatory, comforting.

Trott [trɔt] m (-[e]s/-e) trot; F fig. jogtrot, routine; '~el F m (-s/-) idiot, fool, ninny; '2en v/i. (ge-, sein) trot.

trotz [trɔts] 1. prp. (gen.) in spite of, despite; ~ alledem for all that; 2. 2 m (-es/no pl.) defiance; obstinacy; **~dem** *cj.* ['~de:m] nevertheless; (al)though; **~e** *v/i.* (*ge-, h*) (*dat.*) defy, dare; brave (*danger*); be obstinate; sulk; '**~ig** *adj.* defiant; obstinate; sulky.

trüb *adj.* [try:p], **~e** *adj.* ['~bə] *liquid:* muddy, turbid, thick; *mind, thinking:* confused, muddy, turbid; *eyes, etc.:* dim, dull; *weather:* dull, cloudy, dreary (*all a. fig.*); *experiences:* sad.

Trubel ['tru:bəl] *m* (-s/*no pl.*) bustle.

trüben ['try:bən] *v/t.* (ge-, h) make thick *or* turbid *or* muddy; dim; darken; spoil (*pleasures, etc.*); blur (*view*); dull (*mind*); **sich ~** *liquid:* become thick *or* turbid *or* muddy; dim, darken; *relations:* become strained.

Trüb|sal ['try:pza:l] *f* (-/~-e): ~ **blasen** mope, F be in the dumps, have the blues; '**2selig** *adj.* sad, gloomy, melancholy; wretched, miserable; dreary; '**~sinn** *m* (-[e]s/*no pl.*) melancholy, sadness, gloom; '**2sinnig** *adj.* melancholy, gloomy, sad; **~ung** ['~buŋ] *f* (-/-en) *liquid:* muddiness, turbidity (*both a. fig.*); dimming, darkening.

Trüffel ♀ ['tryfəl] *f* (-/-n), F *m* (-s/-) truffle.

Trug[1] [tru:k] *m* (-[e]s/*no pl.*) deceit, fraud; delusion (*of senses*).

trug[2] [~] *pret. of* tragen.

'**Trugbild** *n* phantom; illusion.

trüg|en ['try:gən] (*irr.*, ge-, h) **1.** *v/t.* deceive; **2.** *v/i.* be deceptive; '**~e-risch** *adj.* deceptive, delusive; treacherous.

'**Trugschluß** *m* fallacy, false conclusion.

Truhe ['tru:ə] *f* (-/-n) chest, trunk; *radio, etc.:* cabinet, console.

Trümmer ['trymər] *pl.* ruins *pl.*; rubble, debris, ⚓, ✈ wreckage; '**~haufen** *m* heap of ruins *or* rubble.

Trumpf [trumpf] *m* (-[e]s/~e) *cards:* trump (card) (*a. fig.*); **s-n ~ aus-spielen** play one's trump card.

Trunk [truŋk] *m* (-[e]s/~e) drink; draught; drinking; '**2en** *adj.* drunken; *pred.* drunk (*a. fig. von, vor* with); intoxicated; **~enbold** *contp.* ['~bolt] *m* (-[e]s/-e) drunkard, sot; '**~enheit** *f* (-/*no pl.*) drunkenness, intoxication; ~ *am Steuer* ⚖ drunken driving, drunkenness at the wheel; '**~sucht** *f* alcoholism, dipsomania; '**2süchtig** *adj.* addicted to drink, given to drinking.

Trupp [trup] *m* (-s/-s) troop, band, gang; ✕ detachment.

'**Truppe** *f* (-/-n) ✕ troop, body; ✕ unit; *thea.* company, troupe; **~n** *pl.* ✕ troops *pl.*, forces *pl.*; *die* **~n** *pl.* ✕ the (fighting) services *pl.*, the armed forces *pl.*

'**Truppen|gattung** *f* arm, branch, division; '**~schau** *f* military review;

~transporter ⚓, ✈ *m* (troop-) transport; '**~übungsplatz** *m* training area.

Truthahn *orn.* ['tru:t-] *m* turkey (-cock).

Tschech|e ['tʃɛçə] *m* (-n/-n), '**~in** *f* (-/-nen) Czech; '**2isch** *adj.* Czech.

Tube ['tu:bə] *f* (-/-n) tube.

tuberkul|ös ♣ *adj.* [tuberku'lø:s] tuberculous, tubercular; **2ose** ♣ [~o:zə] *f* (-/-n) tuberculosis.

Tuch [tu:x] *n* **1.** (-[e]s/-e) cloth; fabric; **2.** (-[e]s/~er) *head covering:* kerchief; shawl, scarf; *round neck:* neckerchief; duster; rag; '**~füh-lung** *f* (-/*no pl.*) close touch.

tüchtig ['tyçtiç] **1.** *adj.* able, fit; clever; proficient; efficient; excellent; good; thorough; **2.** *adv.* vigorously; thoroughly; F awfully; '**2keit** *f* (-/*no pl.*) ability, fitness; cleverness; proficiency; efficiency; excellency.

'**Tuchwaren** *f/pl.* drapery, cloths *pl.*

Tück|e ['tykə] *f* (-/-n) malice, spite; '**2isch** *adj.* malicious, spiteful; treacherous.

tüfteln F ['tyftəln] *v/i.* (ge-, h) puzzle (*an dat.* over).

Tugend ['tu:gənt] *f* (-/-en) virtue; **~bold** ['~bolt] *m* (-[e]s/-e) paragon of virtue; '**2haft** *adj.* virtuous.

Tüll [tyl] *m* (-s/-e) tulle.

Tulpe ♀ ['tulpə] *f* (-/-n) tulip.

tummel|n ['tuməln] *v/refl.* (ge-, h) *children:* romp; hurry; bestir o.s.; '**2platz** *m* playground; *fig.* arena.

Tümmler ['tymlər] *m* (-s/-) *orn.* tumbler; *zo.* porpoise.

Tumor ♣ ['tu:mor] *m* (-s/-en) tumo(u)r.

Tümpel ['tympəl] *m* (-s/-) pool.

Tumult [tu'mult] *m* (-[e]s/-e) tumult; riot, turmoil, uproar; row.

tun [tu:n] **1.** *v/t.* (*irr.*, ge-, h) do; make; put (*to school, into the bag, etc.*); *dazu* ~ add to it; contribute; *ich kann nichts dazu* ~ I cannot help it; *es ist mir darum zu* ~ I am anxious about (it); *zu* ~ *haben* have to do; be busy; *es tut nichts* it doesn't matter; **2.** *v/i.* (*irr.*, ge-, h) do; make; *so* ~ *als ob* make as if; pretend to *inf.*; *das tut gut!* that is a comfort!; that's good!; **3.** ♀ *n* (-s/*no pl.*) doings *pl.*; proceedings *pl.*; action; ~ *und Treiben* ways and doings *pl.*

Tünche ['tynçə] *f* (-/-n) whitewash (*a. fig.*); '**2n** *v/t.* (ge-, h) whitewash.

Tunichtgut ['tu:niçtgu:t] *m* (-, -[e]s/-e) ne'er-do-well, good-for-nothing.

Tunke ['tuŋkə] *f* (-/-n) sauce; '**2n** *v/t.* (ge-, h) dip, steep.

tunlichst *adv.* ['tu:nliçst] if possible.

Tunnel ['tunəl] *m* (-s/-, -s) tunnel; subway.

Tüpfel ['typfəl] *m, n* (-s/-) dot, spot; **'₂n** *v/t.* (ge-, h) dot, spot.

tupfen ['tupfən] **1.** *v/t.* (ge-, h) dab; dot, spot; **2.** **₂** *m* (-s/-) dot, spot.

Tür [ty:r] *f* (-/-en) door; *mit der ~ ins Haus fallen* blurt (things) out; *j-n vor die ~ setzen* turn s.o. out; *vor der ~ stehen* be near *or* close at hand; *zwischen ~ und Angel* in passing; **'₂angel** *f* (door-)hinge.

Turbine ⊕ [tur'bi:nə] *f* (-/-n) turbine; **₂nflugzeug** *n* turbo-jet.

Turbo-Prop-Flugzeug ['turbo-'prɔp-] *n* turbo-prop.

'Tür|flügel *m* leaf (of a door); **'₂-füllung** *f* (door-)panel; **'₂griff** *m* door-handle.

Türk|e ['tyrkə] *m* (-n/-n) Turk; **₂in** *f* (-/-nen) Turk(ish woman); **₂is** *min.* [~'ki:s] *m* (-es/-e) turquoise; **'₂isch** *adj.* Turkish.

'Türklinke *f* door-handle; latch.

Turm [turm] *m* (-[e]s/-e) tower; *a.* steeple (*of church*); *chess:* castle, rook.

Türm|chen ['tyrmçən] *n* (-s/-) turret; **'₂en** (ge-) **1.** *v/t.* (h) pile up; *sich ~* tower; **2.** F *v/i.* (sein) bolt, F skedaddle, *Am. sl. a.* skiddoo.

'turm|hoch *adv.: j-m ~ überlegen sein* stand head and shoulders above s.o.; **'₂spitze** *f* spire; **'₂-springen** *n* (-s/no *pl.*) swimming: high diving; **'₂uhr** *f* tower-clock, church-clock.

turnen ['turnən] **1.** *v/i.* (ge-, h) do gymnastics; **2.** **₂** *n* (-s/no *pl.*) gymnastics *f.*

'Turn|er *m* (-s/-), **'₂erin** *f* (-/-nen) gymnast; **'₂gerät** *n* gymnastic apparatus; **'₂halle** *f* gym(nasium); **'₂hemd** *n* (gym-)shirt; **'₂hose** *f* shorts *pl.*

Turnier [tur'ni:r] *n* (-s/-e) tournament.

'Turn|lehrer *m* gym master; **'₂-lehrerin** *f* gym mistress; **'₂schuh** *m* gym-shoe; **'₂stunde** *f* gym lesson; **'₂unterricht** *m* instruction in gymnastics; **'₂verein** *m* gymnastic *or* athletic club.

'Tür|pfosten *m* door-post; **'₂rahmen** *m* door-case, door-frame; **'₂schild** *n* door-plate.

Tusche ['tuʃə] *f* (-/-n) India(n) *or* Chinese ink; **'₂ln** *v/i.* (ge-, h) whisper; **'₂n** *v/t.* (ge-, h) draw in India(n) ink.

Tüte ['ty:tə] *f* (-/-n) paper-bag.

tuten ['tu:tən] *v/i.* (ge-, h) toot(le); *mot.* honk, blow one's horn.

Typ [ty:p] *m* (-s/-en) type; ⊕ *a.* model; **'₂e** *f* (-/-n) *typ.* type; F *fig.* (queer) character.

Typhus ૐ ['ty:fus] *m* (-/no *pl.*) typhoid (fever).

'typisch *adj.* typical (*für* of).

Tyrann [ty'ran] *m* (-en/-en) tyrant; **₂ei** [~'naɪ] *f* (-/no *pl.*) tyranny; **₂isch** *adj.* [ty'raniʃ] tyrannical; **₂isieren** [~i'zi:rən] *v/t.* (no -ge-, h) tyrannize (over) *s.o.*, oppress, bully.

U

U-Bahn ['u:-] *f s.* Untergrundbahn.

übel ['y:bəl] **1.** *adj.* evil, bad; *nicht ~* not bad, pretty good; *mir ist ~* I am *or* feel sick; **2.** *adv.* ill; *~ gelaunt sein* be in a bad mood; *es gefällt mir nicht ~* I rather like it; **3.** **₂** *n* (-s/-) evil; *s.* Übelstand; *das kleinere ~ wählen* choose the lesser evil; **'₂gelaunt** *adj.* ill-humo(u)red; **'₂keit** *f* (-/-en) sickness, nausea; **'₂nehmen** *v/t.* (*irr.* nehmen, sep., -ge-, h) take *s.th.* ill *or* amiss; **'₂-stand** *m* grievance; **'₂täter** *m* evil-doer, wrongdoer.

'übelwollen 1. *v/i.* (sep., -ge-, h): *j-m ~* wish s.o. ill; be ill-disposed towards s.o.; **2.** **₂** *n* (-s/no *pl.*) ill will, malevolence; **'₂d** *adj.* malevolent.

üben ['y:bən] (ge-, h) **1.** *v/t.* exercise; practi|se, *Am. a.* -ce; *Geduld ~* exercise patience; *Klavier ~* practise the piano; **2.** *v/i.* exercise; practi|se, *Am. a.* -ce.

über ['y:bər] **1.** *prp.* (dat.; acc.) over, above; across (*river, etc.*); via; by way of (*Munich, etc.*); *sprechen ~* (acc.) talk about *or* of; *~ Politik sprechen* talk politics; *nachdenken ~* (acc.) think about *or* of; *ein Buch schreiben ~* (acc.) write a book on; *~ Nacht bleiben* bei stay overnight at; *~ s-e Verhältnisse leben* live beyond one's income; *~ kurz oder lang* sooner *or* later; **2.** *adv.: die ganze Zeit ~* all along; *j-m in et. ~ sein* excel s.o. in *s.th.*

über'all *adv.* everywhere, anywhere, *Am. a.* all over.

über|'anstrengen *v/t.* (no -ge-, h) overstrain; *sich ~* overstrain o.s.; **~'arbeiten** *v/t.* (no -ge-, h) retouch (*painting, etc.*); revise (*book, etc.*); *sich ~* overwork o.s.

überaus *adv.* ['y:bər?-] exceedingly, extremely.

'überbelichten *phot. v/t.* (no -ge-, h) over-expose.

über'bieten *v/t.* (*irr.* bieten, no -ge-, h) *at auction:* outbid; *fig.:* beat; surpass.

Überbleibsel ['y:bərblaɪpsəl] *n*

(-s/-) remnant, *Am.* F *a.* holdover; ~ *pl. a.* remains *pl.*

'**Überblick** *fig. m* survey, general view (*both*: über *acc.* of).

über|'blicken *v/t.* (*no -ge-, h*) overlook; *fig.* survey, have a general view ot; ~'**bringen** *v/t.* (*irr. bringen, no -ge-, h*) deliver; **2'bringer** *m* (-s/-) bearer; ~'**brücken** *v/t.* (*no -ge-, h*) bridge; *fig.* bridge over *s.th.*; ~'**dachen** *v/t.* (*no -ge-, h*) roof over; ~'**dauern** *v/t.* (*no -ge-, h*) outlast, outlive; ~'**denken** *v/t.* (*irr. denken, no -ge-, h*) think *s.th.* over.

über'dies *adv.* besides, moreover.

über'drehen *v/t.* (*no -ge-, h*) overwind (*watch, etc.*); strip (*screw*).

'**Überdruck** *m* 1. (-[e]s/-e) overprint; ✠ *a.* surcharge; 2. ⊕ (-[e]s/-e) overpressure.

Über|druß ['y:bərdrus] *m* (Überdrusses/*no pl.*) satiety; *bis zum* ~ to satiety; **2drüssig** *adj.* (*gen.*) ['~y-siç] disgusted with, weary *or* sick of.

Übereif|er ['y:bər?-] *m* over-zeal; **2rig** *adj.* ['y:bər?-] over-zealous.

über'eil|en *v/t.* (*no -ge-, h*) precipitate, rush; *sich* ~ hurry too much; ~**t** *adj.* precipitate, rash.

übereinander [y:bər?ar'nandər] *adv.* one upon the other; ~**schlagen** *v/t.* (*irr. schlagen, sep., -ge-, h*) cross (*one's legs*).

über'ein|kommen *v/i.* (*irr. kommen, sep., -ge-, sein*) agree; **2kommen** *n* (-s/-), **2kunft** [~kunft] *f* (-/⍛e) agreement; ~**stimmen** *v/i.* (*sep., -ge-, h*) *p.* agree (*mit* with); *thing*: correspond (with, to); **2stimmung** *f* agreement; correspondence; *in* ~ *mit* in agreement *or* accordance with.

über|fahren 1. ['~fa:rən] *v/i.* (*irr. fahren, sep., -ge-, sein*) cross; 2. [~'fa:rən] *v/t.* (*irr. fahren, no -ge-, h*) run over; disregard (*traffic sign, etc.*); **2fahrt** *f* passage; crossing.

'**Überfall** *m* ✗ surprise; ✗ invasion (*auf acc.* of); ✗ raid; hold-up; assault ([up]on).

über'fallen *v/t.* (*irr. fallen, no -ge-, h*) ✗ surprise; ✗ invade; ✗ raid; hold up; assault.

'**über'fällig** *adj.* overdue; **2fallkommando** *n* flying squad, *Am.* riot squad.

über'fliegen *v/t.* (*irr. fliegen, no -ge-, h*) fly over *or* across; *fig.* glance over, skim (through); *den Atlantik* ~ fly (across) the Atlantic.

'**überfließen** *v/i.* (*irr. fließen, sep., -ge-, sein*) overflow.

über'flügeln *v/t.* (*no -ge-, h*) ✗ outflank; *fig.* outstrip, surpass.

'**Über|fluß** *m* (Überflusses/*no pl.*) abundance (*an dat.* of); superfluity (of); ~ *haben an* (*dat.*) abound in;

'**2flüssig** *adj.* superfluous; redundant.

über'fluten *v/t.* (*no -ge-, h*) overflow, flood (*a. fig.*).

'**Überfracht** *f* excess freight.

über'führen *v/t.* 1. ['~fy:rən] (*sep., -ge-, h*) convey (*dead body*); 2. [~'fy:rən] (*no -ge-, h*) *s.* 1; ✠✠ convict (*gen.* of); **2führung** *f* (-/-en) conveyance (*of dead body*); bridge, *Am.* overpass; ✠✠ conviction (*gen.* of). [*dat.* of).]

'**Überfülle** *f* superabundance (*an*∫

über'füllen *v/t.* (*no -ge-, h*) overfill; cram; overcrowd; *sich den Magen* ~ glut o.s.; ~'**füttern** *v/t.* (*no -ge-, h*) overfeed.

'**Übergabe** *f* delivery; handing over; surrender (*a.* ✗).

'**Übergang** *m* bridge; ✇ crossing; *fig.* transition (*a.* ♪); *esp.* ✠✠ devolution; '~**sstadium** *n* transition stage.

über'geben *v/t.* (*irr. geben, no -ge-, h*) deliver up; hand over; surrender (*a.* ✗); *sich* ~ vomit, be sick; ~**gehen** 1. [~'ge:ən] *v/i.* (*irr. gehen, sep., -ge-, sein*) pass over; *work, duties*: devolve (*auf acc.* [up]on); ~ *in* (*acc.*) pass into; ~ *zu et.* proceed to s.th.; 2. [~'ge:ən] *v/t.* (*irr. gehen, no -ge-, h*) pass over, ignore.

'**Übergewicht** *n* (-[e]s/*no pl.*) overweight; *fig. a.* preponderance (*über acc.* over).

über'gießen *v/t.* (*irr. gießen, no -ge-, h*): *mit Wasser* ~ pour water over *s.th.*; *mit Fett* ~ baste (*roasting meat*).

'**über|greifen** *v/i.* (*irr. greifen, sep., -ge-, h*): ~ *auf* (*acc.*) encroach (up)on (*s.o.'s rights*); *fire, epidemic, etc.*: spread to; '**2griff** *m* encroachment (*auf acc.* [up]on), inroad (on); '~**haben** F *v/t.* (*irr. haben, sep., -ge-, h*) have (*coat, etc.*) on; *fig.* have enough of, *sl.* be fed up with.

über'handnehmen *v/i.* (*irr. nehmen, sep., -ge-, h*) be rampant, grow *or* wax rife.

'**überhängen** 1. *v/i.* (*irr. hängen, sep., -ge-, h*) overhang; 2. *v/t.* (*sep., -ge-, h*) put (*coat, etc.*) round one's shoulders; sling (*rifle*) over one's shoulder.

über'häufen *v/t.* (*no -ge-, h*): ~ *mit* swamp with (*letters, work, etc.*); overwhelm with (*inquiries, etc.*).

über'haupt *adv.*: *wer will denn* ~, *daß er kommt?* who wants him to come anyhow?; *wenn* ~ if at all; ~ *nicht* not at all; ~ *kein* no ... whatever.

überheblich *adj.* [y:bər'he:pliç] presumptuous, arrogant; **2keit** *f* (-/✎-en) presumption, arrogance.

über|'hitzen *v/t.* (*no -ge-, h*) overheat (*a.* ⚚); ⊕ superheat; ~'**holen** *v/t.* (*no -ge-, h*) overtake (*a. mot.*);

esp. sports: outstrip (*a. fig.*); over-haul, *esp. Am. a.* service; ~'**holt** *adj.* outmoded; *pred. a.* out of date; ~'**hören** *v/t.* (*no -ge-, h*) fail to hear, miss; ignore.

'**überirdisch** *adj.* supernatural; un-earthly.

'**überkippen** *v/i.* (*sep., -ge-, sein*) p. overbalance, lose one's balance.

über'kleben *v/t.* (*no -ge-, h*) paste over.

'**Überkleidung** *f* outer garments *pl.*

'**überklug** *adj.* would-be wise, sapient.

'**überkochen** *v/i.* (*sep., -ge-, sein*) boil over; F *leicht* ~ be very irri-table.

über'kommen *v/t.* (*irr. kommen, no -ge-, h*): *Furcht überkam ihn* he was seized with fear; ~'**laden** *v/t.* (*irr. laden, no -ge-, h*) overload; overcharge (*battery, picture, etc.*).

'**Überland|flug** *m* cross-country flight; '~**zentrale** ⚡ *f* long-distance power-station.

über'lassen *v/t.* (*irr. lassen, no -ge-, h*): *j-m et.* ~ let s.o. have s.th.; *fig.* leave s.th. to s.o.; *j-n sich selbst* ~ leave s.o. to himself; *j-n s-m Schicksal* ~ leave *or* abandon s.o. to his fate; ~'**lasten** *v/t.* (*no -ge-, h*) overload; *fig.* overburden.

über'laufen 1. [ˈ~laʊfən] *v/i.* (*irr. laufen, sep., -ge-, sein*) run over; boil over; ⚡ desert (*zu* to); **2.** [~'laʊfən] *v/t.* (*irr. laufen, no -ge-, h*): *es überlief mich kalt* a shudder passed over me; *überlaufen werden von doctor, etc.*: be besieged by (*patients, etc.*); **3.** *adj.* [~'laʊfən] *place, profession, etc.*: overcrowded; '**2läufer** *m* ⚡ deserter; *pol.* rene-gade, turncoat.

'**überlaut** *adj.* too loud.

über'leben (*no -ge-, h*) **1.** *v/t.* survive, outlive; **2.** *v/i.* survive; **2de** *m, f* (*-n/-n*) survivor.

'**überlebensgroß** *adj.* bigger than life-size(d).

überlebt *adj.* [yːbərˈleːpt] outmod-ed, disused, out of date.

'**überlegen**[1] F *v/t.* (*sep., -ge-, h*) give (*child*) a spanking.

über'leg|en[2] **1.** *v/t. and v/refl.* (*no -ge-, h*) consider, reflect upon, think about; *ich will es mir* ~ I will think it over; *es sich anders* ~ change one's mind; **2.** *v/i.* (*no -ge-, h*): *er überlegt noch* he hasn't made up his mind yet; **3.** *adj.* superior (*dat. to; an dat. in*); **2enheit** *f* (*-/no pl.*) superiority; preponderance; ~**t** *adj.* [~kt] deliberate; prudent; **2ung** [~guŋ] *f* (*-/-en*) consideration, reflection; *nach reiflicher* ~ after mature deliberation.

über'lesen *v/t.* (*irr. lesen, no -ge-, h*) read *s.th.* through quickly, run over *s.th.*; overlook.

über'liefer|n *v/t.* (*no -ge-, h*) hand down *or* on (*dat.* to); **2ung** *f* tradi-tion.

über'listen *v/t.* (*no -ge-, h*) outwit, F outsmart.

'**Über|macht** *f* (*-/no pl.*) superiority; *esp.* ⚡ superior forces *pl.*; *in der* ~ *sein* be superior in numbers; '**2mächtig** *adj.* superior.

über'|malen *v/t.* (*no -ge-, h*) paint out; ~'**mannen** *v/t.* (*no -ge-, h*) overpower, overcome, overwhelm (*all. a. fig.*).

'**Über|maß** *n* (*-es/no pl.*) excess (*an dat.* of); '**2mäßig 1.** *adj.* excessive; immoderate; **2.** *adv.* excessively, *Am. a.* overly; ~ *trinken* drink to excess.

'**Übermensch** *m* superman; '**2lich** *adj.* superhuman.

über'mitt|eln *v/t.* (*no -ge-, h*) trans-mit; convey; **2lung** *f* (*-/-en*) trans-mission; conveyance.

'**übermorgen** *adv.* the day after tomorrow.

über'müd|et *adj.* overtired; **2ung** *f* (*-/~ -en*) overfatigue.

'**Über|mut** *m* wantonness; frolic-someness; '**2mütig** *adj.* [ˈ~myːtɪç] wanton; frolicsome.

'**übernächst** *adj. the* next but one; ~*e Woche* the week after next.

über'nacht|en *v/i.* (*no -ge-, h*) stay overnight (*bei* at a *friend's* [*house*], with *friends*), spend the night (at, with); **2ung** *f* (*-/-en*) spending the night; ~ *und Frühstück* bed and breakfast.

Übernahme [ˈyːbərnaːmə] *f* (*-/-n*) *field of application s.* übernehmen **1:** taking over; undertaking; assump-tion; adoption.

'**übernatürlich** *adj.* supernatural.

übernehmen *v/t.* **1.** [~'neːmən] (*irr. nehmen, no -ge-, h*) take over (*busi-ness, etc.*); undertake (*responsibility, etc.*); take (*lead, risk, etc.*); assume (*direction of business, office, etc.*); adopt (*idea, custom, etc.*); *sich* ~ overreach o.s.; **2.** ⚡ [ˈ~neːmən] (*irr. nehmen, sep., -ge-, h*) slope, shoul-der (*arms*).

über'|ordnen *v/t.* (*sep., -ge-, h*): *j-n j-m* ~ set s.o. over s.o.; '~**par-teilich** *adj.* non-partisan; '**2pro-duktion** *f* over-production.

über'prüf|en *v/t.* (*no -ge-, h*) reconsider; verify; check; review; screen *s.o.*; **2ung** *f* reconsideration; checking; review.

über'|queren *v/t.* (*no -ge-, h*) cross; ~'**ragen** *v/t.* (*no -ge-, h*) tower above (*a. fig.*), overtop; *fig.* sur-pass.

überrasch|en [yːbərˈrafən] *v/t.* (*no -ge-, h*) surprise; catch (*bei* at, in); **2ung** *f* (*-/-en*) surprise.

über'red|en *v/t.* (*no -ge-, h*) per-suade (*zu inf.* to *inf.*, into *ger.*);

talk (into *ger.*); ₂**ung** *f* (-/✎-en) persuasion.

über'reich|en *v/t.* (*no* -ge-, *h*) present; ₂**ung** *f* (-/✎-en) presentation.

über|'reizen *v/t.* (*no* -ge-, *h*) overexcite; **~'reizt** *adj.* overstrung; **~'rennen** *v/t.* (*irr.* rennen, *no* -ge-, *h*) overrun.

'Überrest *m* remainder; **~e** *pl.* remains *pl.*; sterbliche **~e** *pl.* mortal remains *pl.*

über'rump|eln *v/t.* (*no* -ge-, *h*) (take by) surprise; ₂(e)**lung** *f* (-/✎-en) surprise.

über'rund|en *v/t.* (*no* -ge-, *h*) *sports:* lap; *fig.* surpass; ₂**ung** *f* (-/-en) lapping.

übersät *adj.* [y:bər'zɛ:t] studded, dotted.

über'sättig|en *v/t.* (*no* -ge-, *h*) surfeit (*a. fig.*); 🜍 supersaturate; ₂**ung** *f* (-/-en) surfeit (*a. fig.*); 🜍 supersaturation.

'Überschallgeschwindigkeit *f* supersonic speed.

über|'schatten *v/t.* (*no* -ge-, *h*) overshadow (*a. fig.*); **~'schätzen** *v/t.* (*no* -ge-, *h*) overrate, overestimate.

'Überschlag *m gymnastics:* somersault; ≯ loop; ⚡ flashover; *fig.* estimate, approximate calculation; ₂**en** (*irr.* schlagen) 1. ['~ʃla:gən] *v/t.* (*sep.*, -ge-, *h*) cross (*one's legs*); 2. [~'ʃla:gən] *v/i.* (*sep.*, -ge-, *sein*) *voice:* become high-pitched; 3. [~'ʃla:gən] *v/t.* (*no* -ge-, *h*) skip (*page, etc.*); make a rough estimate of (*cost, etc.*); *sich* **~** fall head over heels; *car, etc.:* (be) turn(ed) over; ≯ loop the loop; *voice:* become high-pitched; *sich* **~** *vor* (*dat.*) outdo (*one's friendliness, etc.*); 4. *adj.* [~'ʃla:gən] lukewarm, tepid.

'überschnappen *v/i.* (*sep.*, -ge-, *sein*) *voice:* become high-pitched; F *p.* go mad, turn crazy.

über|'schneiden *v/refl.* (*irr.* schneiden, *no* -ge-, *h*) overlap; intersect; **~'schreiben** *v/t.* (*irr.* schreiben, *no* -ge-, *h*) superscribe; entitle; make *s.th.* over (*dat.* to); **~'schreiten** *v/t.* (*irr.* schreiten, *no* -ge-, *h*) cross; transgress (*limit, bound*); infringe (*rule, etc.*); exceed (*speed limit, one's instructions, etc.*); sie hat die 40 bereits überschritten she is on the wrong side of 40.

'Über|schrift *f* heading, title; headline; **'~schuh** *m* overshoe.

'Über|schuß *m* surplus, excess; profit; ₂**schüssig** *adj.* ['~ʃysiç] surplus, excess.

über'schütten *v/t.* (*no* -ge-, *h*): **~** *mit* pour (*water, etc.*) on; *fig.:* overwhelm with (*inquiries, etc.*); shower (*gifts, etc.*) upon.

überschwemm|en [y:bər'ʃvɛmən]

v/t. (*no* -ge-, *h*) inundate, flood (*both a. fig.*); ₂**ung** *f* (-/-en) inundation, flood(ing).

überschwenglich *adj.* ['y:bər-ʃvɛnliç] effusive, gushy.

'Übersee: *nach* **~** gehen go overseas; **'~dampfer** ⚓ *m* transoceanic steamer; **'~handel** *m* (-s/*no pl.*) oversea(s) trade.

über'sehen *v/t.* (*irr.* sehen, *no* -ge-, *h*) survey; overlook (*printer's error, etc.*); *fig.* ignore, disregard.

über'send|en *v/t.* ([*irr.* senden,] *no* -ge-, *h*) send, transmit; consign; ₂**ung** *f* sending, transmission; ✝ consignment.

'übersetzen[1] (*sep.*, -ge-) 1. *v/i.* (*sein*) cross; 2. *v/t.* (*h*) ferry.

über'setz|en[2] *v/t.* (*no* -ge-, *h*) translate (*in acc.* into), render (into); ⊕ gear; ₂**er** *m* (-s/-) translator; ₂**ung** *f* (-/-en) translation (*aus* from; *in acc.* into); rendering; ⊕ gear(ing), transmission.

'Übersicht *f* (-/-en) survey (*über acc.* of); summary; ₂**lich** *adj.* clear(ly arranged).

über|siedeln ['y:bərzi:dəln] *v/i.* (*sep.*, -ge-, *sein*) and [~'zi:dəln] *v/i.* (*no* -ge-, *sein*) remove (*nach* to); ₂**siedelung** [~'zi:dəluŋ] *f* (-/-en), ₂**siedlung** ['~zi:dluŋ, ~'zi:dluŋ] *f* (-/-en) removal (*nach* to).

'übersinnlich *adj.* transcendental; *forces:* psychic.

über'spann|en *v/t.* (*no* -ge-, *h*) cover (*mit* with); den Bogen **~** go too far; **~t** *adj.* extravagant; *p.* eccentric; *claims, etc.:* exaggerated; ₂**theit** *f* (-/✎-en) extravagance; eccentricity.

über'spitzt *adj.* oversubtle; exaggerated.

überspringen 1. ['~ʃpriŋən] *v/i.* (*irr.* springen, *sep.*, -ge-, *sein*) ⚡ spark: jump; *in a speech, etc.:* **~** *von ... zu ...* jump or skip from (*one subject*) to (*another*); 2. [~'ʃpriŋən] *v/t.* (*irr.* springen, *no* -ge-, *h*) jump, clear; skip (*page, etc.*); jump (*class*).

überstehen (*irr.* stehen) 1. ['~ʃte:ən] *v/i.* (*sep.*, -ge-, *h*) jut (out or forth), project; 2. [~'ʃte:ən] *v/t.* (*no* -ge-, *h*) survive (*misfortune, etc.*); weather (*crisis*); get over (*illness*).

über|'steigen *v/t.* (*irr.* steigen, *no* -ge-, *h*) climb over; *fig.* exceed; **~'stimmen** *v/t.* (*no* -ge-, *h*) outvote, vote down.

'überstreifen *v/t.* (*sep.*, -ge-, *h*) slip *s.th.* over.

überströmen 1. ['~ʃtrø:mən] *v/i.* (*sep.*, -ge-, *sein*) overflow (*vor dat.* with); 2. [~'ʃtrø:mən] *v/t.* (*no* -ge-, *h*) flood, inundate.

'Überstunden *f/pl.* overtime; **~** *machen* work overtime.

über'stürz|en *v/t.* (*no* -ge-, *h*) rush, hurry (up *or* on); *sich* **~** act rashly; *events*: follow in rapid succession; **~t** *adj.* precipitate, rash; **2ung** *f* (-/**~**-en) precipitancy.

über|'teuern *v/t.* (*no* -ge-, *h*) overcharge; **~'tölpeln** *v/t.* (*no* -ge-, *h*) dupe, take in; **~'tönen** *v/t.* (*no* -ge-, *h*) drown.

Übertrag ✝ ['y:bərtraːk] *m* (-[e]s/**~**e) carrying forward; sum carried forward.

über'trag|bar *adj.* transferable; ✝ negotiable; ✻ communicable; **~en** [**~**gən] 1. *v/t.* (*irr.* tragen, *no* -ge-, *h*) ✝ carry forward; make over (*property*) (*auf acc.* to); ✻ transfuse (*blood*); delegate (*rights, etc.*) (*dat.* to); render (*book, etc.*) (*in acc.* into); transcribe (*s.th. written in shorthand*); ✻, ⊕, *phys., radio*: transmit; *radio*: a. broadcast; *im Fernsehen* **~** televise; *ihm wurde eine wichtige Mission* **~** he was charged with an important mission; 2. *adj.* figurative; **2ung** [**~**guŋ] *f* (-/**~**-en) *field of application s.* übertragen 1: carrying forward; making over; transfusion; delegation; rendering; free translation; transcription; transmission; broadcast; **~** *im Fernsehen* telecast.

über'treffen *v/t.* (*irr.* treffen, *no* -ge-, *h*) excel *s.o.* (*an dat.* in; *in dat.* in, at); surpass (in), exceed (in).

über'treib|en (*irr.* treiben, *no* -ge-, *h*) 1. *v/t.* overdo; exaggerate, overstate; 2. *v/i.* exaggerate, draw the long bow; **2ung** *f* (-/**~**-en) exaggeration, overstatement.

'übertreten[1] *v/i.* (*irr.* treten, *sep.*, -ge-, *sei*n) *sports*: cross the take-off line; *fig.* go over (*zu* to); *zum Katholizismus* **~** turn Roman Catholic.

über'tret|en[2] *v/t.* (*irr.* treten, *no* -ge-, *h*) transgress, violate, infringe (*law, etc.*); *sich den Fuß* **~** sprain one's ankle; **2ung** *f* (-/**~**-en) transgression, violation, infringement.

'Übertritt *m* going over (*zu* to); *eccl.* conversion (to).

übervölker|n [y:bər'fœlkərn] *v/t.* (*no* -ge-, *h*) over-populate; **2ung** *f* (-/**~**-en) over-population.

über'vorteilen *v/t.* (*no* -ge-, *h*) overreach, F do.

über'wach|en *v/t.* (*no* -ge-, *h*) supervise, superintend; control; *police*: keep under surveillance, shadow; **2ung** *f* (-/**~**-en) supervision, superintendence; control; surveillance.

überwältigen [y:bər'vɛltigən] *v/t.* (*no* -ge-, *h*) overcome, overpower, overwhelm (*all a. fig.*); **~d** *fig. adj.* overwhelming.

über'weis|en *v/t.* (*irr.* weisen, *no* -ge-, *h*) remit (*money*) (*dat. or an acc.* to); (*zur Entscheidung etc.*) **~** refer (to); **2ung** *f* (-/**~**-en) remittance;

reference (*an acc.* to); *parl.* devolution.

überwerfen (*irr.* werfen) 1. ['**~**verfən] *v/t.* (*sep.*, -ge-, *h*) slip (*coat*) on; 2. [**~**'verfən] *v/refl.* (*no* -ge-, *h*) fall out (*mit* with).

über'wiegen (*irr.* wiegen, *no* -ge-, *h*) 1. *v/t.* outweigh; 2. *v/i.* preponderate; predominate; **~'wiegend** *adj.* preponderant; predominant; **~'winden** *v/t.* (*irr.* winden, *no* -ge-, *h*) overcome (*a. fig.*), subdue; *sich* **~** *zu inf.* bring o.s. to *inf.*; **~'wintern** *v/i.* (*no* -ge-, *h*) (pass the) winter.

'Über|wurf *m* wrap; **'~zahl** *f* (-/**~**-en) numerical superiority; *in der* **~** superior in numbers; **2zählig** *adj.* ['**~**tsɛːliç] supernumerary; surplus.

über'zeug|en *v/t.* (*no* -ge-, *h*) convince (*von* of); satisfy (of); **2ung** *f* (-/**~**-en) conviction.

überziehe|n *v/t.* (*irr.* ziehen) 1. ['**~**tsiːən] (*sep.*, -ge-, *h*) put on; 2. [**~**'tsiːən] (*no* -ge-, *h*) cover; put clean sheets on (*bed*); ✝ overdraw (*account*); *sich* **~** *sky*: become overcast; '2r *m* (-*s*/-) overcoat, topcoat.

'Überzug *m* cover; case, tick; ⊕ coat(ing).

üblich *adj.* ['y:pliç] usual, custom-[ary; normal.]

U-Boot ⚓, ✕ ['u:-] *n* submarine, *in Germany*: a. U-boat.

übrig *adj.* ['y:briç] left, remaining; *die* **~**e *Welt* the rest of the world; *die* **~**en *pl.* the others *pl.*, the rest; *im* **~**en for the rest; by the way; **~** *haben have s.th.* left; *keine Zeit* **~** *haben* have no time to spare; *etwas* **~** *haben für* care for, have a soft spot for; *ein* **~**es *tun* go out of one's way; '**~bleiben** *v/i.* (*irr.* bleiben, *sep.*, -ge-, *sein*) be left; remain; *es blieb ihm nichts anderes übrig* he had no (other) alternative (*als* but); **~ens** *adv.* ['**~**gəns] by the way; **~lassen** ['**~**s-] *v/t.* (*irr.* lassen, *sep.*, -ge-, *h*) leave; *viel zu wünschen* **~** leave much to be desired.

'Übung *f* (-/**~**-en) exercise; practice; drill; '**~shang** *m* skiing: nursery slope.

Ufer ['u:fər] *n* (-*s*/-) shore (*of sea, lake*); bank (*of river, etc.*).

Uhr [u:r] *f* (-/**~**-en) clock; watch; *um vier* **~** at four o'clock; '**~armband** *n* (-[e]s/**~**er) watch-strap; '**~feder** *f* watch-spring; '**~macher** *m* (-*s*/-) watch-maker; '**~werk** *n* clockwork; watch-work; '**~zeiger** *m* hand (*of clock or watch*); '**~zeigersinn** *m* (-[e]s/*no pl.*): *im* **~** clockwise; *entgegen dem* **~** counter-clockwise.

Uhu *orn.* ['u:hu:] *m* (-*s*/-*s*) eagle-owl.

Ulk [ulk] *m* (-[e]s/-e) fun, lark; '**2en** *v/i.* (*ge-, h*) (sky)lark, joke; '**2ig** *adj.* funny.

Ulme ♀ ['ulmə] *f* (-/-n) elm.

Ultimatum [ulti'maːtum] *n* (-*s*/-*Ul*-

timaten, -s) ultimatum; *j-m ein ~ stellen* deliver an ultimatum to s.o.

Ultimo † ['ultimo] *m (-s/-s)* last day of the month.

Ultrakurzwelle *phys.* [ultra'-] *f* ultra-short wave, very-high-frequency wave.

um [um] **1.** *prp. (acc.)* round, about; *~ vier Uhr* at four o'clock; *~ sein Leben laufen* run for one's life; *et. ~ einen Meter verfehlen* miss s.th. by a metre; *et. ~ zwei Mark verkaufen* sell s.th. at two marks; **2.** *prp.(gen.)*: *~ seinetwillen* for his sake; **3.** *cj.*: *~ so besser* all the better, so much the better; *~ so mehr (weniger)* all the more (less); *~ zu* (in order) to; **4.** *adv.*: *er drehte sich ~* he turned round.

um|ändern ['um⁹-] *v/t. (sep., -ge-, h)* change, alter; **~arbeiten** ['um⁹-] *v/t. (sep., -ge-, h)* make over *(coat, etc.)*; revise *(book, etc.)*; *~ zu* make into.

um'arm|en *v/t. (no -ge-, h)* hug, embrace; *sich ~* embrace; **2ung** *f (-/-en)* embrace, hug.

'Umbau *m (-[e]s/-e, -ten)* rebuilding; reconstruction; **2en** *v/t. (sep., -ge-, h)* rebuild; reconstruct.

'umbiegen *v/t. (irr. biegen, sep., -ge-, h)* bend; turn up *or* down.

'umbild|en *v/t. (sep., -ge-, h)* remodel, reconstruct; reorganize, reform; reshuffle *(cabinet)*; **'2ung** *f (-/-en)* remodel(l)ing, reconstruction; reorganization, *pol.* reshuffle.

'um|binden *v/t. (irr. binden, sep., -ge-, h)* put on *(apron, etc.)*; **'~blättern** *(sep., -ge-, h)* **1.** *v/t.* turn over; **2.** *v/i.* turn over the page; **~brechen** *v/t. (irr. brechen, sep., -ge-, h)* **1.** *⚘* ['~brɛçən] dig, break up *(ground)*; **2.** *typ.* ['brɛçən] *(no -ge-, h)* make up; **'~bringen** *v/t. (irr. bringen, sep., -ge-, h)* kill; *sich ~* kill o.s.; **'2bruch** *m typ.* make-up; *fig.*: upheaval; radical change; **'~buchen** *v/t. (sep., -ge-, h)* † transfer *or* switch to another account; book for another date; **'~disponieren** *v/i. (sep., no -ge-, h)* change one's plans.

'umdreh|en *v/t. (sep., -ge-, h)* turn; *s.* Spieß; *sich ~* turn round; **2ung** [um'-] *f (-/-en)* turn; *phys., ⊕* rotation, revolution.

um|fahren *(irr. fahren)* **1.** ['~fa:rən] *v/t. (sep., -ge-, h)* run down; **2.** ['~fa:rən] *v/i. (sep., -ge-, sein)* go a roundabout way; **3.** [~'fa:rən] *v/t. (no -ge-, h)* drive round; ⚓ sail round; ⚓ double *(cape)*; **'~fallen** *v/i. (irr. fallen, sep., -ge-, sein)* fall; collapse; *tot ~* drop dead.

'Umfang *m (-[e]s/no pl.)* circumference, circuit; perimeter; girth *(of body, tree, etc.)*; *fig.*: extent; volume; *in großem ~* on a large

scale; **'2reich** *adj.* extensive; voluminous; spacious.

um'fassen *v/t. (no -ge-, h)* clasp; embrace *(a. fig.)*; ✗ envelop; *fig.* comprise, cover, comprehend; **~d** *adj.* comprehensive, extensive; sweeping, drastic.

'umform|en *v/t. (sep., -ge-, h)* remodel, recast, transform *(a. ⚡)*; ⚡ convert; **'2er** *⚡ m (-s/-)* transformer; converter.

'Umfrage *f* poll; *öffentliche ~* public opinion poll.

'Umgang *m* **1.** *(-[e]s/¨e)* △ gallery; ambulatory; *eccl.* procession *(round the fields, etc.)*; **2.** *(-[e]s/no pl.)* intercourse *(mit* with); company; *~ haben mit* associate with.

umgänglich *adj.* ['umgɛŋliç] sociable, companionable, affable.

'Umgangs|formen *f/pl.* manners *pl.*; **'~sprache** *f* colloquial usage; *in der deutschen ~* in colloquial German.

um'garnen *v/t. (no -ge-, h)* ensnare.

um'geb|en *v/t.* **1.** *(irr. geben, no -ge-, h)* surround; *mit e-r Mauer ~* wall in; **2.** *adj.* surrounded *(von* with, by) *(a. fig.)*; **2ung** *f (-/-en)* environs *pl. (of town, etc.)*; surroundings *pl.*, environment *(of place, person, etc.)*.

umgeh|en *(irr. gehen)* **1.** ['~ge:ən] *v/i. (sep., -ge-, sein)* make a detour; *rumour, etc.*: go about, be afloat; *ghost*: walk; *~ mit* use s.th.; deal with s.o.; keep company with; *ein Gespenst soll im Schlosse ~* the castle is said to be haunted; **2.** [~'ge:ən] *v/t. (no -ge-, h)* go round; ✗ flank; bypass *(town, etc.)*; *fig.* avoid, evade; circumvent, elude *(law, etc.)*; **'~end** *adj.* immediate; **2ungsstraße** [um'ge:uŋs-] *f* bypass.

umgekehrt [umgə'ke:rt] **1.** *adj.* reverse, inverse, inverted; *in ~er Reihenfolge* in reverse order; *im ~en Verhältnis zu* in inverse proportion to; **2.** *adv.* vice versa.

'umgraben *v/t. (irr. graben, sep. -ge-, h)* dig (up).

um'grenzen *v/t. (no -ge-, h)* encircle; enclose; *fig.* circumscribe, limit.

'umgruppier|en *v/t. (sep., no -ge-, h)* regroup; **2ung** *f (-/-en)* regrouping.

'um|haben F *v/t. (irr. haben, sep., -ge-, h)* have *(coat, etc.)* on; **'2hang** *m* wrap; cape; **'~hängen** *v/t. (sep., -ge-, h)* rehang *(pictures)*; sling *(rifle)* over one's shoulder; *sich den Mantel ~* put one's coat round one's shoulders; **'~hauen** *v/t. (irr. hauen, sep., -ge-, h)* fell, cut down; F: *die Nachricht hat mich umgehauen* I was bowled over by the news.

um'her|blicken v/i. (sep., -ge-, h) look about (one); **~streifen** v/i. (sep., -ge-, sein) rove.

um'hinkönnen v/i. (irr. können, sep., -ge-, h): ich kann nicht umhin, zu sagen I cannot help saying.

um'hüll|en v/t. (no -ge-, h) wrap up (mit in), envelop (in); **2ung** f (-/-en) wrapping, wrapper, envelopment.

Umkehr ['umke:r] f (-/no pl.) return; **2en** (sep., -ge-) **1.** v/i. (sein) return, turn back; **2.** v/t. (h) turn out (one's pocket, etc.); invert (a. ♪); reverse (a. ♪, ♫); **~ung** f (-/-en) reversal; inversion.

'umkippen (sep., -ge-) **1.** v/t. (h) upset, tilt; **2.** v/i. (sein) upset, tilt (over); F faint.

um'klammer|n v/t. (no -ge-, h) clasp; boxing: clinch; **2ung** f (-/-en) clasp; boxing: clinch.

'umkleid|en v/refl. (sep., -ge-, h) change (one's clothes); **2eraum** m dressing-room.

'umkommen v/i. (irr. kommen, sep., -ge-, sein) be killed (bei in), die (in), perish (in); vor Langeweile ~ die of boredom.

'Umkreis m (-es/no pl.) ♫ circumscribed circle; im ~ von within a radius of. [round.]

um'kreisen v/t. (no -ge-, h) circle]

'um|krempeln v/t. (sep., -ge-, h) tuck up (shirt-sleeves, etc.); change (plan, etc.); (völlig) ~ turn s.th. inside out; **~laden** v/t. (irr. laden, sep., -ge-, h) reload; ✝, ⚓ transship.

'Umlauf m circulation; phys., ♫ rotation; circular (letter); in ~ setzen or bringen circulate, put into circulation; im ~ sein circulate, be in circulation; rumours: a. be afloat; außer ~ setzen withdraw from circulation; **~bahn** f orbit; **2en** (irr. laufen) **1.** ['~laufən] v/t. (sep., -ge-, h) knock over; **2.** ['~laufən] v/i. (sep., -ge-, sein) circulate; make a detour; **3.** [~'laufən] v/t. (no -ge-, h) run round.

'Umlege|kragen m turn-down collar; **2n** v/t. (sep., -ge-, h) lay down; ♫ throw (lever); storm, etc.: beat down (wheat, etc.); re-lay (cable, etc.); put (coat, etc.) round one's shoulders; apportion (costs, etc.); fig. sl. do s.o. in.

'umleit|en v/t. (sep., -ge-, h) divert; **2ung** f diversion, detour.

'umliegend adj. surrounding; circumjacent.

um'nacht|et adj.: geistig ~ mentally deranged; **2ung** f (-/-en): geistige ~ mental derangement.

'um|packen v/t. (sep., -ge-, h) repack; **~pflanzen** v/t. **1.** ['~pflantsən] (sep., -ge-, h) transplant; **2.** [~'pflantsən] (no -ge-, h): ~ mit

plant s.th. round with; **~pflügen** v/t. (sep., -ge-, h) plough, Am. plow.

um'rahmen v/t. (no -ge-, h) frame; musikalisch ~ put into a musical setting.

umrand|en [um'randən] v/t. (no -ge-, h) edge, border; **2ung** f (-/-en) edge, border.

um'ranken v/t. (no -ge-, h) twine (mit with).

'umrechn|en v/t. (sep., -ge-, h) convert (in acc. into); **2ung** f (-/no pl.) conversion; **2ungskurs** m rate of exchange.

umreißen v/t. (irr. reißen) **1.** ['~raisən] (sep., -ge-, h) pull down; knock s.o. over; **2.** [~'raisən] (no -ge-, h) outline. [round (a. fig.).]

um'ringen v/t. (no -ge-, h) sur-]

'Um|riß m outline (a. fig.), contour; **2rühren** v/t. (sep., -ge-, h) stir; **2satteln** (sep., -ge-, h) **1.** v/t. resaddle; **2.** F fig. v/i. change one's studies or occupation; ~ von ... auf (acc.) change from ... to ...; **~satz** ✝ m turnover; sales (pl.); return(s pl.); stock exchange: business done.

'umschalt|en (sep., -ge-, h) **1.** v/t. ♫ change over; ✗ commutate; ✗, ♫ switch; **2.** ✗, ♫ v/i. switch over; **2er** m ♫ change-over switch; ✗ commutator; **2ung** f (-/-en) ♫ change-over; ✗ commutation.

'Umschau f (-/no pl.): ~ halten nach look out for, be on the look-out for; **2en** v/refl. (sep., -ge-, h) look round (nach for); look about (for) (a. fig.), look about one.

'umschicht|en v/t. (sep., -ge-, h) pile afresh; fig. regroup (a. ✝); **~ig** adv. by or in turns; **2ung** fig. f (-/-en) regrouping; soziale ~en pl. social upheavals pl.

um'schiff|en v/t. (no -ge-, h) circumnavigate; double (cape); **2ung** f (-/✗-en) circumnavigation; doubling.

'Umschlag m envelope; cover, wrapper; jacket; turn-up, Am. a. cuff (of trousers); ✗ compress; ✗ poultice; trans-shipment (of goods); fig. change, turn; **2en** (irr. schlagen, sep., -ge-) **1.** v/t. (h) knock s.o. down; cut down, fell (tree); turn (leaf); turn up (sleeves, etc.); turn down (collar); trans-ship (goods); **2.** v/i. (sein) turn over, upset; ⚓ capsize, upset; wine, etc.: turn sour; fig. turn (in acc. into); **~hafen** m port of trans-shipment.

um'|schließen v/t. (irr. schließen, no -ge-, h) embrace, surround (a. ✗), enclose; ✗ invest; **~schlingen** v/t. (irr. schlingen, no -ge-, h) embrace.

'um|schmeißen F v/t. (irr. schmeißen, sep., -ge-, h) s. umstoßen; **'~**

schnallen v/t. (sep., -ge-, h) buckle on.

umschreib|en v/t. (irr. schreiben) 1. ['~ʃraɪbən] (sep., -ge-, h) re-write; transfer (property, etc.) (auf acc. to); 2. [~'ʃraɪbən] (no -ge-, h) ♣ circumscribe; paraphrase; ♀ung f (-/-en) 1. ['~ʃraɪbʊŋ] rewriting; transfer (auf acc. to); 2. [~'ʃraɪbʊŋ] ♣ circumscription; paraphrase.

'**Umschrift** f circumscription; phonetics: transcription.

'**umschütten** v/t. (sep., -ge-, h) pour into another vessel; spill.

'**Um|schweife** pl.: ~ machen beat about the bush; ohne ~ point-blank; '♀schwenken fig. v/i. (sep., -ge-, sein) veer or turn round; '~schwung fig. m revolution; revulsion (of public feeling, etc.); change (in the weather, etc.); reversal (of opinion, etc.).

um'seg|eln v/t. (no -ge-, h) sail round; double (cape); circumnavigate (globe, world); ♀(e)lung f (-/-en) sailing round (world, etc.); doubling; circumnavigation.

'**um|sehen** v/refl. (irr. sehen, sep., -ge-, h) look round (nach for); look about (for) (a. fig.), look about one; '~sein F v/i. (irr. sein, sep., -ge-, sein) time: be up; holidays, etc.: be over; '~setzen v/t. (sep., -ge-, h) transpose (a. ♪); ♂ transplant; ♰ turn over; spend (money) (in acc. on books, etc.); in die Tat ~ realize, convert into fact.

'**Umsicht** f (-/no pl.) circumspection; '♀ig adj. circumspect.

'**umsied|eln** (sep., -ge-) 1. v/t. (h) resettle; 2. v/i. (sein) (re)move (nach, in acc. to); '♀lung f (-/♣ -en) resettlement; evacuation; removal.

um'sonst adv. gratis, free of charge; in vain; to no purpose; nicht ~ not without good reason.

umspann|en v/t. 1. ['~ʃpanən] (sep., -ge-, h) change (horses); ♂ transform; 2. [~'ʃpanən] (no -ge-, h) span; fig. a. embrace; '♀er ♂ m (-s/-) transformer.

'**umspringen** v/i. (irr. springen, sep., -ge-, sein) shift, veer (round); ~ mit treat badly, etc.

'**Umstand** m circumstance; fact, detail; unter diesen Umständen in or under the circumstances; unter keinen Umständen in or under no circumstances, on no account; unter Umständen possibly; ohne Umstände without ceremony; in anderen Umständen sein be in the family way.

umständlich adj. ['umʃtɛntlɪç] story, etc.: long-winded; method, etc.: roundabout; p. fussy; das ist (mir) viel zu ~ that is far too much trouble (for me); '♀keit f (-/♣ -en) long-windedness; fussiness.

'**Umstands|kleid** n maternity robe; '~wort gr. n (-[e]s/⸫er) adverb.

'**umstehend** 1. adj.: auf der ~en Seite overleaf; 2. adv. overleaf; ♀en ['~dən] pl. the bystanders pl.

'**Umsteige|karte** f transfer; '♀n v/i. (irr. steigen, sep., -ge-, sein) change (nach for); ⛟ a. change trains (for).

Umsteigekarte ['umʃtaɪk-] f s. Umsteigekarte.

umstell|en v/t. 1. ['~ʃtɛlən] (sep., -ge-, h) transpose (a. gr.); shift (furniture) about or round; convert (currency, production) (auf acc. to); sich ~ change one's attitude; accommodate o.s. to new conditions; adapt o.s. (auf acc. to); 2. [~'ʃtɛlən] (no -ge-, h) surround; ♀ung ['~ʃtɛlʊŋ] f transposition; fig.: conversion; adaptation; change.

'**um|stimmen** v/t. (sep., -ge-, h) ♪ tune to another pitch; j-n ~ change s.o.'s mind, bring s.o. round; '~stoßen v/t. (irr. stoßen, sep., -ge-, h) knock over; upset; fig. annul; ♰ overrule, reverse; upset (plan).

um'stricken fig. v/t. (no -ge-, h) ensnare; ~stritten adj. [~'ʃtrɪtən] disputed; contested; controversial.

'**Um|sturz** m subversion, overturn; '♀stürzen (sep., -ge-) 1. v/t. (h) upset, overturn (a. fig.); fig. subvert; 2. v/i. (sein) overturn; fall down; ♀stürzlerisch adj. ['~lərɪʃ] subversive.

'**Umtausch** m (-es/♣ -e) exchange; ♰ conversion (of currency, etc.); '♀en v/t. (sep., -ge-, h) exchange (gegen for); ♰ convert.

'**umtun** F v/t. (irr. tun, sep., -ge-, h) put (coat, etc.) round one's shoulders; sich ~ nach look about for.

'**umwälz|en** v/t. (sep., -ge-, h) roll round; fig. revolutionize; '~end adj. revolutionary; '♀ung fig. f (-/-en) revolution, upheaval.

'**umwand|eln** v/t. (sep., -ge-, h) transform (in acc. into); ♰, ♰ convert (into); ♰ commute (into); '♀lung f transformation; ♂, ♰ conversion; ♰ commutation.

'**um|wechseln** v/t. (sep., -ge-, h) change; '♀weg m roundabout way or route; detour; auf ~en in a roundabout way; '~wehen v/t. (sep., -ge-, h) blow down or over; '♀welt f (-/♣ -en) environment; '~wenden 1. v/t. (sep., -ge-, h) turn over; 2. v/refl. ([irr. wenden,] sep., -ge-, h) look round (nach for).

um'werben v/t. (irr. werben, no -ge-, h) court, woo.

'**umwerfen** v/t. (irr. werfen, sep., -ge-, h) upset (a. fig.), overturn; sich ~ einen Mantel ~ throw a coat round one's shoulders.

um|'wickeln v/t. (no -ge-, h): et. mit Draht ~ wind wire round s.th.;

~**wölken** [~'vœlkən] *v/refl.* (*no* -ge-, *h*) cloud over (*a. fig.*); ~**zäunen** [~'tsɔʏnən] *v/t.* (*no* -ge-, *h*) fence (in).

umziehen (*irr. ziehen*) **1.** ['~tsiːən] *v/i.* (*sep.*, -ge-, *sein*) (re)move (*nach* to); move house; **2.** ['~tsiːən] *v/refl.* (*sep.*, -ge-, *h*) change (one's clothes); **3.** [~'tsiːən] *v/refl.* (*no* -ge-, *h*) cloud over.

umzingeln [um'tsiŋəln] *v/t.* (*no* -ge-, *h*) surround, encircle.

'**Umzug** *m* procession; move (*nach* to), removal (to); change of residence.

unab|änderlich *adj.* [un'ʔap'endərlɪç] unalterable; ~**hängig** ['~hɛŋɪç] **1.** *adj.* independent (*von* of); **2.** *adv.*: ~ *von* irrespective of; '2**hängigkeit** *f* (-/*no pl.*) independence (*von* of); ~**kömmlich** *adj.* ['~kœmlɪç]: er ist im Moment ~ we cannot spare him at the moment, we cannot do without him at the moment; ~'**lässig** *adj.* incessant, unremitting; ~**sehbar** *adj.* [~'zeːbaːr] incalculable; *in* ~*er Ferne* in a distant future; ~'**sichtlich** *adj.* unintentional; inadvertent; ~**wendbar** *adj.* [~'vɛntbaːr] inevitable, inescapable.

unachtsam *adj.* ['un ʔ-] careless, heedless; '2**keit** *f* (-/~-en) carelessness, heedlessness.

unähnlich *adj.* ['un ʔ-] unlike, dissimilar (*dat.* to).

unan|fechtbar *adj.* [un'ʔan'-] impeachable, unchallengeable, incontestable; '~**gebracht** *adj.* inappropriate; *pred. a.* out of place; '~**gefochten 1.** *adj.* undisputed; unchallenged; **2.** *adv.* without any hindrance; '~**gemessen** *adj.* unsuitable; improper; inadequate; '~**genehm** *adj.* disagreeable, unpleasant; awkward; troublesome; ~'**nehmbar** *adj.* unacceptable (*für* to); '2**nehmlichkeit** *f* (-/-en) unpleasantness; awkwardness; troublesomeness; ~*en pl.* trouble, inconvenience; '~**sehnlich** *adj.* unsightly; plain; '~**ständig** *adj.* indecent; obscene; '2**ständigkeit** *f* (-/-/ indecency; obscenity; ~'**tastbar** *adj.* unimpeachable; inviolable.

unappetitlich *adj.* ['un ʔ-] food, *etc.*: unappetizing; *sight, etc.*: distasteful, ugly.

Unart ['un ʔ-] **1.** *f* bad habit; **2.** *m* (-[e]s/-e) naughty child; '2**ig** *adj.* naughty; '2**igkeit** *f* (-/-en) naughty behavio(u)r, naughtiness.

unauf|dringlich *adj.* ['un ʔauf-] unobtrusive; unostentatious; '~**fällig** *adj.* inconspicuous; unobtrusive; ~**findbar** *adj.* [~'fɪntbaːr] undiscoverable, untraceable; ~**gefordert** ['~gəfɔrdərt] **1.** *adj.* un-

asked; **2.** *adv.* without being asked, of one's own accord; ~'**hörlich** *adj.* incessant, continuous, uninterrupted; '~**merksam** *adj.* inattentive; '2**merksamkeit** *f* (-/-en) inattention, inattentiveness; '~**richtig** *adj.* insincere; '2**richtigkeit** *f* (-/-en) insincerity; ~**schiebbar** *adj.* [~'ʃiːpbaːr] urgent; ~ *sein* brook no delay.

unaus|bleiblich *adj.* [un ʔaus'blaɪplɪç] inevitable; *das war* ~ that was bound to happen; ~'**führbar** *adj.* impracticable; ~**geglichen** *adj.* ['~gəglɪçən] unbalanced (*a.* ✝); ~'**löschlich** *adj.* indelible; *fig. a.* inextinguishable; ~'**sprechlich** *adj.* unutterable; unspeakable; inexpressible; ~'**stehlich** *adj.* unbearable, insupportable.

'**unbarmherzig** *adj.* merciless, unmerciful; '2**keit** *f* (-/*no pl.*) mercilessness, unmercifulness.

unbe|absichtigt *adj.* ['unbə ʔapzɪçtɪçt] unintentional, undesigned; '~**achtet** *adj.* unnoticed; ~**anstandet** ['unbə ʔ-] unopposed, not objected to; '~**baut** *adj.* ~ *un*-tilled; *land:* undeveloped; '~**dacht** *adj.* inconsiderate; imprudent; ~**denklich 1.** *adj.* unobjectionable; **2.** *adv.* without hesitation; '~**deutend** *adj.* insignificant; slight; '~**dingt 1.** *adj.* unconditional; *obedience, etc.:* implicit; **2.** *adv.* by all means; under any circumstances; ~'**fahrbar** *adj.* impracticable, impassable; '~**fangen** *adj.* unprejudiced, unbias(s)ed; ingenuous; unembarrassed; ~'**friedigend** *adj.* unsatisfactory; ~**friedigt** *adj.* ['~çt] dissatisfied; disappointed; '~**fugt** *adj.* unauthorized; incompetent; '2**fugte** *m* (-n/-n) unauthorized person; ~*n ist der Zutritt verboten!* no trespassing!; '~**gabt** *adj.* untalented; ~'**greiflich** *adj.* inconceivable, incomprehensible; ~'**grenzt** *adj.* unlimited; boundless; ~'**gründet** *adj.* unfounded; '2**hagen** *n* uneasiness; discomfort; ~'**haglich** *adj.* uneasy; uncomfortable; ~'**helligt** *adj.* [~'hɛlɪçt] unmolested; '~**herrscht** *adj.* lacking self-control; '2**herrschtheit** *f* (-/*no pl.*) lack of self-control; '~**hindert** *adj.* unhindered, free; ~**holfen** *adj.* ['~bə-hɔlfən] clumsy, awkward; '2**holfenheit** *f* (-/*no pl.*) clumsiness, awkwardness; ~'**irrt** *adj.* unswerving; '~**kannt** *adj.* unknown; ~*e Größe* ⚗ unknown quantity (*a. fig.*); ~'**kümmert** *adj.* unconcerned (*um, wegen* about), careless (of, about); '~**lebt** *adj.* inanimate; *street, etc.:* unfrequented; ~'**lehrbar** *adj.*: ~ *sein* take no advice; '~**liebt** *adj.* unpopular; *sich* ~ *machen* get o.s. disliked; '~**mannt** *adj.* unmanned;

'**merkt** adj. unnoticed; '**mittelt** adj. impecunious, without means; **nommen** adj. [**'**nɔmən]: es bleibt ihm ~ zu inf. he is at liberty to inf.; '**nutzt** adj. unused; '**quem** adj. uncomfortable; inconvenient; 'Q**quemlichkeit** f lack of comfort; inconvenience; '**rechtigt** adj. unauthorized; unjustified; **schadet** prp. (gen.) [**'**ʃa:dət] without prejudice to; **schädigt** adj. ['**çt] uninjured, undamaged; '**scheiden** adj. immodest; **scholten** adj. ['**ʃɔltən] blameless, irreproachable; '**schränkt** adj. unrestricted; absolute; **schreiblich** adj. [**'**fraıplıç] indescribable; **sehen** adv. unseen; without inspection; '**setzt** adj. unoccupied; vacant; **siegbar** adj. [**'**zi:kba:r] invincible; '**sonnen** adj. thoughtless, imprudent; rash; 'Q**sonnenheit** f (-/-en) thoughtlessness; rashness; '**ständig** adj. inconstant; unsteady; weather: changeable, unsettled (a. ♃); p. erratic; 'Q**ständigkeit** f (-/no pl.) inconstancy; changeability; **stätigt** adj. ['**çt] unconfirmed; letter, etc.: unacknowledged; **'stechlich** adj. incorruptible, unbribable; Q'**stechlichkeit** f (-/no pl.) incorruptibility; '**stimmt** adj. indeterminate (a. ♃); indefinite (a. gr.); uncertain; feeling, etc.: vague; 'Q**stimmtheit** f (-/no pl.) indeterminateness, indetermination; indefiniteness; uncertainty; vagueness; **'streitbar** adj. incontestable; **'stritten** adj. uncontested, undisputed; '**teiligt** adj. unconcerned (an dat. in); indifferent; **'trächtlich** adj. inconsiderable, insignificant. [flexible.]

unbeugsam adj. [un'bɔykza:m] in-]
'**unbe|wacht** adj. unwatched, unguarded (a. fig.); '**waffnet** adj. unarmed; eye: naked; '**weglich** adj. immovable; motionless; '**wiesen** adj. unproven; '**wohnt** adj. uninhabited; unoccupied, vacant; '**wußt** adj. unconscious; **'zähmbar** adj. indomitable.

'**Un|bilden** pl.: ~ der Witterung inclemency of the weather; '**bildung** f lack of education.

'**un|billig** adj. unfair; '**blutig** 1. adj. bloodless; 2. adv. without bloodshed.

unbotmäßig adj. insubordinate; 'Q**keit** f (-/-en) insubordination.

'**un|brauchbar** adj. useless; '**christlich** adj. unchristian.

und cj. [unt] and; F: na ~? so what?

'**Undank** m ingratitude; 'Q**bar** adj. ungrateful (gegen to); task, etc.: thankless; '**barkeit** f ingratitude, ungratefulness; fig. thanklessness.

un|'denkbar adj. unthinkable; inconceivable; **'denklich** adj.: seit **en** Zeiten from time immemorial; '**deutlich** adj. indistinct; speech: a. inarticulate; fig. vague, indistinct; '**deutsch** adj. un-German; '**dicht** adj. leaky; 'Q**dlng** n: es wäre ein ~, zu behaupten, daß ... it would be absurd to claim that ...

'**unduldsam** adj. intolerant; 'Q**keit** f intolerance.

undurch|'dringlich adj. impenetrable; countenance: impassive; **'führbar** adj. impracticable; **'lässig** adj. impervious, impermeable; '**sichtig** adj. opaque; fig. mysterious.

uneben adj. ['un?-] ground: uneven, broken; way, etc.: bumpy; 'Q**heit** f 1. (-/no pl.) unevenness; 2. (-/-en) bump.

un|echt adj. ['un?-] jewellery, etc.: imitation; hair, teeth, etc.: false; money, jewellery, etc.: counterfeit; picture, etc.: fake; ♃ fraction: improper; '**ehelich** adj. illegitimate.

Unehr|e ['un?-] f dishono(u)r; j-m ~ machen discredit s.o.; 'Q**enhaft** adj. dishono(u)rable; 'Q**lich** adj. dishonest; '**lichkeit** f dishonesty.

uneigennützig adj. ['un?-] disinterested, unselfish.

uneinig adj. ['un?-]: ~ sein be at variance (mit with); disagree (über acc. on); 'Q**keit** f variance, disagreement.

un|ein'nehmbar adj. impregnable; '**empfänglich** adj. insusceptible (für of, to).

unempfindlich adj. ['un?-] insensitive (gegen to); 'Q**keit** f insensitiveness (gegen to).

un'endlich 1. adj. endless, infinite (both a. fig.); 2. adv. infinitely (a. fig.); ~ lang endless; ~ viel no end of (money, etc.); Q**keit** f (-/no pl.) endlessness, infinitude, infinity (all a. fig.).

unent|behrlich adj. [un?ɛnt'be:rlıç] indispensable; **'geltlich** 1. adj gratuitous, gratis; 2. adv. gratis, free of charge; **'rinnbar** adj. ineluctable; '**schieden** 1. adj. undecided; ~ enden game: end in a draw or tie; 2. Q n (-s/-) draw, tie; '**schlossen** adj. irresolute; 'Q**schlossenheit** f irresoluteness, irresolution; **schuldbar** adj. [**'**ʃultba:r] inexcusable; **wegt** adv. [**'**ve:kt] untiringly; continuously; **'wirrbar** adj. inextricable.

uner|'bittlich adj. [un?er'bitlıç] inexorable; fact: stubborn; '**fahren** adj. inexperienced; **findlich** adj. [**'**fıntlıç] incomprehensible; **'forschlich** adj. inscrutable; '**freulich** adj. unpleasant; **'füllbar** adj. unrealizable; '**giebig** adj. unproductive (an dat. of); '**heb-**

lich *adj.* irrelevant (*für* to); inconsiderable; **~hört** *adj.* **1.** ['~hø:rt] unheard; **2.** [~'hø:rt] unheard-of; outrageous; '**~kannt** *adj.* unrecognized; **~'klärlich** *adj.* inexplicable; **~läßlich** *adj.* [~'lɛsliç] indispensable (*für* to, for); **~laubt** *adj.* ['~laupt] unauthorized; illegal, illicit; **~e** *Handlung* 𝔱𝔱 tort; **~ledigt** *adj.* ['~le:diçt] unsettled (*a.* ✝); **~meßlich** *adj.* [~'mɛsliç] immeasurable, immense; **~müdlich** *adj.* [~'my:tliç] *p.* indefatigable, untiring; *efforts, etc.*: untiring, unremitting; **~quicklich** *adj.* unpleasant, unedifying; **~'reichbar** *adj.* inattainable; inaccessible; *pred. a.* above *or* beyond *or* out of reach; **~'reicht** *adj.* unrival(l)ed, unequal(l)ed; **~sättlich** *adj.* [~'zɛtliç] insatiable, insatiate; **~'schöpflich** *adj.* inexhaustible.

unerschrocken *adj.* ['un⁹-] intrepid, fearless; '**2heit** *f* (-/*no pl.*) intrepidity, fearlessness.

uner|schütterlich *adj.* [un⁹ɛr'ʃʏtərliç] unshakable; **~'schwinglich** *adj.* *price*: prohibitive; *pred. a.* above *or* beyond *or* out of reach (*für* of); **~'setzlich** *adj.* irreplaceable; *loss, etc.*: irreparable; **~'träglich** *adj.* intolerable, unbearable; '**~wartet** *adj.* unexpected; '**~wünscht** *adj.* undesirable, undesired.

'unfähig *adj.* incapable (*zu inf.* of *ger.*); unable (to *inf.*); inefficient; '**2keit** *f* incapability (*zu inf.* of *ger.*); inability (to *inf.*); inefficiency.

'Unfall *m* accident; **e-n ~ haben** meet with *or* have an accident; '**~station** *f* emergency ward; '**~versicherung** *f* accident insurance.

un'faßlich *adj.* incomprehensible, inconceivable; *das ist mir ~* that is beyond me.

un'fehlbar **1.** *adj.* infallible (*a. eccl.*); *decision, etc.*: unimpeachable; *instinct, etc.*: unfailing; **2.** *adv.* without fail; inevitably; **2keit** *f* (-/*no pl.*) infallibility.

'un|fein *adj.* indelicate; *pred. a.* lacking in refinement; '**~fern** *prp.* (*gen. or von*) not far from; '**~fertig** *adj.* unfinished; *fig. a.* half-baked; **~flätig** *adj.* ['~flɛ:tiç] dirty, filthy.

'unfolgsam *adj.* disobedient; '**2keit** *f* disobedience.

un|förmig *adj.* ['unfœrmiç] misshapen; shapeless; '**~frankiert** *adj.* unstamped; '**~frei** *adj.* not free; ✍ unstamped; '**~freiwillig** *adj.* involuntary; *humour*: unconscious; '**~freundlich** *adj.* unfriendly (*zu* with), unkind (to); *climate, weather*: inclement; *room, day*: cheerless; '**2friede(n)** *m* discord.

'unfruchtbar *adj.* unfruitful; ster-

ile; '**2keit** *f* (-/*no pl.*) unfruitfulness; sterility.

Unfug ['unfu:k] *m* (-[e]s/*no pl.*) mischief.

Ungar ['uŋgar] *m* (-n/-n) Hungarian; '**2isch** *adj.* Hungarian.

'ungastlich *adj.* inhospitable.

unge|achtet *prp.* (*gen.*) ['ungə⁹axtət] regardless of; despite; **~ahnt** *adj.* ['ungə⁹-] undreamt-of; unexpected; **~bärdig** *adj.* ['~bɛ:rdiç] unruly; '**~beten** *adj.* uninvited, unasked; **~er** *Gast* intruder, *sl.* gatecrasher; '**~bildet** *adj.* uneducated; '**~bräuchlich** *adj.* unusual; '**~braucht** *adj.* unused; '**~bührlich** *adj.* improper, undue, unseemly; '**~bunden** *adj.* *book*: unbound; *fig.*: free; single; '**~deckt** *adj.* *table*: unlaid; *sports*, ✝: uncovered; *paper currency*: fiduciary.

'Ungeduld *f* impatience; '**2ig** *adj.* impatient.

'ungeeignet *adj.* unfit (*für* for *s.th.*, to do *s.th.*); *p. a.* unqualified; *moment*: inopportune.

ungefähr ['ungəfɛ:r] **1.** *adj.* approximate, rough; **2.** *adv.* approximately, roughly, about, *Am.* F *a.* around; *von ~* by chance; '**~det** *adj.* unendangered, safe; '**~lich** *adj.* harmless; *pred. a.* not dangerous.

'unge|fällig *adj.* disobliging; '**~halten** *adj.* displeased (*über* acc. at); '**~hemmt** **1.** *adj.* unchecked; **2.** *adv.* without restraint; '**~heuchelt** *adj.* unfeigned.

ungeheuer ['ungəhɔyər] **1.** *adj.* vast, huge, enormous; **2.** *2 n* (-*s*/-) monster; **~lich** *adj.* [~'hɔyərliç] monstrous.

'ungehobelt *adj.* not planed; *fig.* uncouth, rough.

'ungehörig *adj.* undue, improper; '**2keit** *f* (-/✍ -en) impropriety.

'ungehorsam **1.** *adj.* disobedient; **2.** *2 m* disobedience.

'unge|künstelt *adj.* unaffected; '**~kürzt** *adj.* unabridged.

'ungelegen *adj.* inconvenient, inopportune; '**2heiten** *f/pl.* inconvenience; trouble; *j-m ~ machen* put s.o. to inconvenience.

'unge|lehrig *adj.* indocile; '**~lenk** *adj.* awkward, clumsy; '**~lernt** *adj.* unskilled; '**~mütlich** *adj.* uncomfortable; *room*: *a.* cheerless; *p.* nasty; '**~nannt** *adj.* unnamed; *p.* anonymous.

'ungenau *adj.* inaccurate, inexact; '**2igkeit** *f* inaccuracy, inexactness.

'ungeniert *adj.* free and easy, unceremonious; undisturbed.

'unge|nießbar *adj.* ['ungəni:sba:r] uneatable; undrinkable; F *p.* unbearable; *pred. a.* in a bad humo(u)r; '**~nügend** *adj.* insufficient; '**~pflegt** *adj.* unkempt; '**~rade** *adj.* odd; '**~raten** *adj.* spoilt, undutiful.

'**ungerecht** *adj.* unjust (*gegen* to); '**Ɂigkeit** *f* (-/-en) injustice.

'**un|gern** *adv.* unwillingly, grudgingly; reluctantly; '**ˌgeschehen** *adj.*: ~ *machen* undo *s.th.*

'**Ungeschick** *n* (-[e]s/*no pl.*), '**ˌlichkeit** *f* awkwardness, clumsiness, maladroitness; '**Ɂt** *adj.* awkward, clumsy, maladroit.

unge|schlacht *adj.* ['ungəʃlaxt] hulking; uncouth; '**ˌschliffen** *adj.* unpolished, rough (*both a. fig.*); '**ˌschminkt** *adj.* not made up; *fig.* unvarnished.

'**ungesetzlich** *adj.* illegal, unlawful, illicit; '**Ɂkeit** *f* (-/-en) illegality, unlawfulness.

unge|sittet *adj.* uncivilized; unmannerly; '**ˌstört** *adj.* undisturbed, uninterrupted; '**ˌstraft 1.** *adj.* unpunished; **2.** *adv.* with impunity; ~ *davonkommen* get off *or* escape scot-free.

ungestüm ['ungəʃty:m] **1.** *adj.* impetuous; violent; **2.** **Ɂ** *n* (-[e]s/*no pl.*) impetuosity; violence.

unge|sund *adj. climate:* unhealthy; *appearance: a.* unwholesome; *food:* unwholesome; '**ˌteilt** *adj.* undivided (*a. fig.*); '**ˌtrübt** *adj.* ['ˌtry:pt] untroubled; unmixed; **Ɂtüm** ['ˌty:m] *n* (-[e]s/-e) monster; **ˌübt** *adj.* ['ˌ˄'y:pt] untrained; inexperienced; '**ˌwaschen** *adj.* unwashed.

'**ungewiß** *adj.* uncertain; *j-n im ungewissen lassen* keep s.o. in suspense; '**Ɂheit** *f* (-/-˄-en) uncertainty; suspense.

unge|wöhnlich *adj.* unusual, uncommon; '**ˌwohnt** *adj.* unaccustomed; unusual; '**ˌzählt** *adj.* numberless, countless; **Ɂziefer** ['ˌtsi:fər] *n* (-s/-) vermin; '**ˌziemend** *adj.* improper, unseemly; '**ˌzogen** *adj.* ill-bred, rude, uncivil; *child:* naughty; '**ˌzügelt** *adj.* unbridled.

'**ungezwungen** *adj.* unaffected, easy; '**Ɂheit** *f* (-/-˄-en) unaffectedness, ease, easiness.

'**Unglaube(n)** *m* unbelief, disbelief.

'**ungläubig** *adj.* incredulous, unbelieving (*a. eccl.*); infidel; '**Ɂe** *m, f* unbeliever; infidel.

unglaub|lich *adj.* [un'glauplɪç] incredible; '**ˌwürdig** *adj. p.* untrustworthy; *thing:* incredible; **ˌe** *Geschichte* cock-and-bull story.

'**ungleich 1.** *adj.* unequal, different; uneven; unlike; **2.** *adv.* (by) far, much; '**ˌartig** *adj.* heterogeneous; '**Ɂheit** *f* difference, inequality; unevenness; unlikeness; '**ˌmäßig** *adj.* uneven; irregular.

'**Unglück** *n* (-[e]s/˄-e) misfortune; bad *or* ill luck; accident; calamity, disaster; misery; '**Ɂlich** *adj.* unfortunate, unlucky; unhappy; **Ɂlicher'weise** *adv.* unfortunately,

unluckily; '**Ɂselig** *adj.* unfortunate; disastrous.

'**Unglücks|fall** *m* misadventure; accident; '**ˌrabe** F *m* unlucky fellow.

'**Un|gnade** *f* (-/*no pl.*) disgrace, disfavo(u)r; *in* ~ *fallen bei* fall into disgrace with, incur *s.o.'s* disfavo(u)r; '**Ɂgnädig** *adj.* ungracious, unkind.

'**ungültig** *adj.* invalid; *ticket:* not available; *money:* not current; **ʦ** (null and) void; '**Ɂkeit** *f* invalidity; **ʦ** *a.* voidness.

'**Un|gunst** *f* disfavo(u)r; inclemency (*of weather*); *zu meinen* ~*en* to my disadvantage; '**Ɂgünstig** *adj.* unfavo(u)rable; disadvantageous.

'**un|gut** *adj.*: ~*es Gefühl* misgiving; *nichts für* ~*!* no offen|ce, *Am.* -se!; '**ˌhaltbar** *adj. shot:* unstoppable; *theory, etc.:* untenable; '**ˌhandlich** *adj.* unwieldy, bulky.

'**Unheil** *n* mischief; disaster, calamity; '**Ɂbar** *adj.* incurable; '**Ɂvoll** *adj.* sinister, ominous.

'**unheimlich 1.** *adj.* uncanny (*a. fig.*), weird; sinister; F *fig.* tremendous, terrific; **2.** F *adv.*: ~ *viel* heaps of, an awful lot of.

'**unhöflich** *adj.* impolite, uncivil; '**Ɂkeit** *f* impoliteness, incivility.

Unhold ['unhɔlt] *m* (-[e]s/-e) fiend.

'**un|hörbar** *adj.* inaudible; '**ˌhygienisch** *adj.* unsanitary, insanitary.

Uni ['uni] *f* (-/-s) F varsity.

Uniform [uni'fɔrm] *f* (-/-en) uniform.

Unikum ['u:nikum] *n* (-s/*Unika, -s*) unique (thing); queer fellow.

uninteress|ant *adj.* ['unɁ-] uninteresting, boring; '**ˌiert** *adj.* uninterested (*an dat.* in).

Universität [univerzi'tɛ:t] *f* (-/-en) university.

Universum [uni'verzum] *n* (-s/*no pl.*) universe.

Unke ['uŋkə] *f* (-/-n) *zo.* fire-bellied toad; F *fig.* croaker; '**Ɂn** F *v/i.* (ge-, h) croak.

'**unkennt|lich** *adj.* unrecognizable; '**Ɂlichkeit** *f* (-/*no pl.*): *bis zur* ~ past all recognition; '**Ɂnis** *f* (-/*no pl.*) ignorance.

'**unklar** *adj.* not clear; *meaning, etc.:* obscure; *answer, etc.:* vague; *im* ~*en sein* be in the dark (*über acc.* about); '**Ɂheit** *f* want of clearness; vagueness; obscurity.

'**unklug** *adj.* imprudent, unwise.

'**Unkosten** *pl.* cost(s *pl.*), expenses *pl.*; *sich in (große)* ~ *stürzen* go to great expense.

'**Unkraut** *n* weed.

un|kündbar *adj.* ['unkyntbɑ:r] *loan, etc.:* irredeemable; *employment:* permanent; '**ˌkundig** *adj.* ['ˌkundiç] ignorant (*gen.* of); '**ˌlängst**

adv. lately, recently, the other day; '**⹂lauter** *adj. competition*: unfair; '**⹂leidlich** *adj.* intolerable, insufferable; '**⹂leserlich** *adj.* illegible; '**⹂leugbar** *adj.* ['⹂ɔykbɑːr] undeniable; '**⹂logisch** *adj.* illogical; '**⹂lösbar** *adj.* unsolvable, insoluble.

'**Unlust** *f* (-/no pl.) reluctance (*zu inf.* to *inf.*); '**⹂ig** *adj.* reluctant.

'**un|manierlich** *adj.* unmannerly; '**⹂männlich** *adj.* unmanly; '**⹂maßgeblich** *adj.* ['⹂geːpliç]: *nach m-r ⹀en Meinung* in my humble opinion; '**⹂mäßig** *adj.* immoderate; intemperate; '**⹂menge** *f* enormous *or* vast quantity *or* number.

'**Unmensch** *m* monster, brute; '**⹂lich** *adj.* inhuman, brutal; '**⹂lichkeit** *f* inhumanity, brutality.

'**un|mißverständlich** *adj.* unmistakable; '**⹂mittelbar** *adj.* immediate, direct; '**⹂möbliert** *adj.* unfurnished; '**⹂modern** *adj.* unfashionable, outmoded.

'**unmöglich** *adj.* impossible; '**⹂keit** *f* impossibility.

'**Unmoral** *f* immorality; '**⹂isch** *adj.* immoral.

'**unmündig** *adj.* under age.

'**un|musikalisch** *adj.* unmusical; '**⹂mut** *m* (-[e]s/no pl.) displeasure (*über acc.* at, over); '**⹂nachahmlich** *adj.* inimitable; '**⹂nachgiebig** *adj.* unyielding; '**⹂nachsichtig** *adj.* strict, severe; inexorable; **⹀nahbar** *adj.* inaccessible, unapproachable; '**⹂natürlich** *adj.* unnatural; affected; '**⹂nötig** *adj.* unnecessary, needless; '**⹂nütz** *adj.* useless; **⹀ordentlich** *adj.* ['un⁹-] untidy; *room, etc.*: *a.* disorderly; **⹂ordnung** ['un⁹-] *f* disorder, mess.

'**unpartei|isch** *adj.* impartial, unbias(s)ed; '**⹂ische** *m* (-n/-n) referee; umpire; '**⹂lichkeit** *f* impartiality.

'**un|passend** *adj.* unsuitable; improper; inappropriate; '**⹂passierbar** *adj.* impassable.

unpäßlich *adj.* ['unpeslıç] indisposed, unwell; '**⹂keit** *f* (-/-en) indisposition.

'**un|persönlich** *adj.* impersonal (*a. gr.*); '**⹂politisch** *adj.* unpolitical; '**⹂praktisch** *adj.* unpractical, *Am. a.* impractical; '**⹂rat** *m* (-[e]s/no pl.) filth; rubbish; **⹀ wittern** smell a rat.

'**unrecht 1.** *adj.* wrong; **⹀ haben** be wrong; *j-m ⹀ tun* wrong s.o.; **2. ⹀** *n* (-[e]s/no pl.): *mit or zu ⹀* wrongly; *ihm ist ⹀ geschehen* he has been wronged; '**⹂mäßig** *adj.* unlawful; '**⹂mäßigkeit** *f* unlawfulness.

'**unreell** *adj.* dishonest; unfair.

'**unregelmäßig** *adj.* irregular (*a. gr.*); '**⹂keit** *f* (-/-en) irregularity.

'**unreif** *adj.* unripe, immature (*both a. fig.*); '**⹂e** *f* unripeness, immaturity (*both a. fig.*).

'**un|rein** *adj.* impure (*a. eccl.*); unclean (*a. fig.*); '**⹂reinlich** *adj.* uncleanly; **⹀rettbar** *adv.*: *⹀ verloren* irretrievably lost; '**⹂richtig** *adj.* incorrect, wrong.

Unruh ['unruː] *f* (-/-en) balance (-wheel); '**⹂e** *f* (-/-en) restlessness, unrest (*a. pol.*); uneasiness; disquiet(ude); flurry; alarm; **⹀n** *pl.* disturbances *pl.*, riots *pl.*; '**⹂ig** *adj.* restless; uneasy; *sea*: rough, choppy.

'**unrühmlich** *adj.* inglorious.

uns *pers. pron.* [uns] us; *dat.*: *a.* to us; *⹀* (*selbst*) ourselves, *after prp.*: us; *ein Freund von ⹀* a friend of ours.

'**un|sachgemäß** *adj.* inexpert; '**⹂sachlich** *adj.* not objective; personal; **⹀säglich** *adj.* [⹀zeːklıç] unspeakable; untold; '**⹂sanft** *adj.* ungentle; '**⹂sauber** *adj.* dirty; *fig. a.* unfair (*a. sports*); '**⹂schädlich** *adj.* innocuous, harmless; '**⹂scharf** *adj.* blurred; *pred. a.* out of focus; **⹀schätzbar** *adj.* inestimable, invaluable; '**⹂scheinbar** *adj.* plain, *Am. a.* homely.

'**unschicklich** *adj.* improper, indecent; '**⹂keit** *f* (-/-en) impropriety, indecency.

unschlüssig *adj.* ['unʃlysıç] irresolute; '**⹂keit** *f* (-/no pl.) irresoluteness, irresolution.

'**un|schmackhaft** *adj.* insipid; unpalatable, unsavo(u)ry; '**⹂schön** *adj.* unlovely, unsightly; *fig.* unpleasant.

'**Unschuld** *f* (-/no pl.) innocence; '**⹂ig** *adj.* innocent (*an dat.* of).

'**unselbständig** *adj.* dependent (on others); '**⹂keit** *f* (lack of in)dependence.

unser ['unzər] **1.** *poss. pron.* our; *der* (*die, das*) *⹀e* ours; *die ⹀en pl.* our relations *pl.*; **2.** *pers. pron.* of us; *wir waren ⹀ drei* there were three of us.

'**unsicher** *adj.* unsteady; unsafe, insecure; uncertain; '**⹂heit** *f* unsteadiness; insecurity, unsafeness; uncertainty.

'**unsichtbar** *adj.* invisible.

'**Unsinn** *m* (-[e]s/no pl.) nonsense; '**⹂ig** *adj.* nonsensical.

'**Unsitt|e** *f* bad habit; abuse; '**⹂lich** *adj.* immoral; indecent (*a.* 🔃); '**⹂lichkeit** *f* (-/-en) immorality.

'**un|solid(e)** *adj. p.* easy-going; *life*: dissipated; † unreliable; '**⹂sozial** *adj.* unsocial, antisocial; '**⹂sportlich** *adj.* unsportsmanlike; unfair (*gegenüber* to).

'**unstatthaft** *adj.* inadmissible.

'**unsterblich** *adj.* immortal.

'**Un'sterblichkeit** *f* immortality.

'**un|stet** *adj.* unsteady; *character, life*: unsettled; **⹂stimmigkeit** ['⹀ʃtımiçkaıt] *f* (-/-en) discrepancy; dissension; '**⹂sträflich** *adj.* blameless; '**~streitig** adj. incontestable; '**~sympathisch** adj. disagreeable; er ist mir ~ I don't like him; '**~tätig** adj. inactive; idle.

'**untauglich** adj. unfit (a. ⚔); unsuitable; '**2keit** f (-/no pl.) unfitness (a. ⚔).

un'teilbar adj. indivisible.

unten adv. ['untən] below; downstairs; von oben bis ~ from top to bottom.

unter ['untər] **1.** prp. (dat.; acc.) below, under; among; ~ anderem among other things; ~ zehn Mark (for) less than ten marks; ~ Null below zero; ~ aller Kritik beneath contempt; ~ diesem Gesichtspunkt from this point of view; **2.** adj. lower; inferior; die ~en Räume the downstair(s) rooms.

Unter|abteilung ['untər⁹-] f subdivision; **~arm** ['untər⁹-] m forearm; '**~bau** m (-[e]s/-ten) 🏛 substructure (a. 🚉), foundation.

unter|'bieten v/t. (irr. bieten, no -ge-, h) underbid; ✝ undercut, undersell (competitor); lower (record); **~'binden** v/t. (irr. binden, no -ge-, h) 🩺 ligature; fig. stop; **~'bleiben** v/i. (irr. bleiben, no -ge-, sein) remain undone; not to take place.

unter'brech|en v/t. (irr. brechen, no -ge-, h) interrupt (a. ⚡); break, Am. a. stop over; ⚡ break (circuit); **2ung** f (-/-en) interruption; break, Am. a. stopover.   [mit.]

unter'breiten v/t. (no -ge-, h) sub-]

'**unterbring|en** v/t. (irr. bringen, sep., -ge-, h) place (a. ✝); accommodate, lodge; '**2ung** f (-/-en) accommodation; ✝ placement.

unterdessen adv. [untər'desən] (in the) meantime, meanwhile.

unter'drück|en v/t. (no -ge-, h) oppress (subjects, etc.); repress (revolt, sneeze, etc.); suppress (rising, truth, yawn, etc.); put down (rebellion, etc.); **2ung** f (-/-en) oppression; repression; suppression; putting down.

unterernähr|t adj. ['untər⁹-] underfed, undernourished; '**2ung** f (-/no pl.) underfeeding, malnutrition.

Unter'führung f subway, Am. underpass.

'**Untergang** m (-[e]s/⚓ ⸗e) ast. setting; ⚓ sinking; fig. ruin.

Unter'gebene m (-n/-n) inferior, subordinate; contp. underling.

'**untergehen** v/i. (irr. gehen, sep., -ge-, sein) ast. set; ⚓ sink, founder; fig. be ruined.

untergeordnet adj. ['untərgə⁹ɔrdnət] subordinate; importance: secondary.

'**Untergewicht** n (-[e]s/no pl.) underweight.

unter'graben fig. v/t. (irr. graben, no -ge-, h) undermine.

'**Untergrund** m (-[e]s/no pl.) subsoil; '**~bahn** f underground (railway), in London: tube; Am. subway; '**~bewegung** f underground movement.

'**unterhalb** prp. (gen.) below, underneath.

'**Unterhalt** m (-[e]s/no pl.) support, subsistence, livelihood; maintenance.

unter'halt|en v/t. (irr. halten, no -ge-, h) maintain; support; entertain, amuse; sich ~ converse (mit with; über acc. on, about), talk (with; on, about); sich gut ~ enjoy o.s.; **2ung** f maintenance, upkeep; conversation, talk; entertainment.

'**Unterhändler** m negotiator; ⚔ Parlementaire.

'**Unter|haus** parl. n (-es/no pl.) House of Commons; '**~hemd** n vest, undershirt; '**~holz** n (-es/no pl.) underwood, brushwood; '**~hose** f (e-e a pair of) drawers pl., pants pl.; '**2irdisch** adj. subterranean, underground (both a. fig.).

unter'joch|en v/t. (no -ge-, h) subjugate, subdue; **2ung** f (-/-en) subjugation.

'**Unter|kiefer** m lower jaw; '**~kleid** n slip; '**~kleidung** f underclothes pl., underclothing, underwear.

'**unterkommen 1.** v/i. (irr. kommen, sep., -ge-, sein) find accommodation; find employment; **2.** 2 n (-s/⸗) accommodation; employment, situation.

'**unter|kriegen** F v/t. (sep., -ge-, h) bring to heel; sich nicht ~ lassen not to knuckle down or under; '**2kunft** ['~kunft] f (-/⸗e) accommodation, lodging; ⚔ quarters pl.; '**2lage** f base; pad; fig.: voucher; **~n** pl. documents pl.; data pl.

unter'lass|en v/t. (irr. lassen, no -ge-, h) omit (zu tun doing, to do); neglect (to do, doing); fail (to do); **2ung** f (-/-en) omission; neglect; failure; **2ungssünde** f sin of omission.

'**unterlegen¹** v/t. (sep., -ge-, h) lay or put under; give (another meaning).

unter'legen² adj. inferior (dat. to); **2e** m (-n/-n) loser; underdog; **2heit** f (-/no pl.) inferiority.

'**Unterleib** m abdomen, belly.

unter'liegen v/i. (irr. liegen, no -ge-, sein) be overcome (dat. by); be defeated (by), sports: a. lose (to); fig.: be subject to; be liable to; es unterliegt keinem Zweifel, daß ... there is no doubt that ...

'**Unter|lippe** f lower lip; '**~mieter** m subtenant, lodger, Am. a. roomer.

unter'nehmen 1. v/t. (irr. nehmen, no -ge-, h) undertake; take (steps);

2. 2 *n* (-s/-) enterprise; ꝗ *a.* business; ꭙ operation.

unter'nehm|end *adj.* enterprising; **2er** ꝗ *m* (-s/-) entrepreneur; contractor; employer; **2ung** *f* (-/-en) enterprise, undertaking; ꭙ operation; **~ungslustig** *adj.* enterprising.

'Unter|offizier ꭙ *m* non-commissioned officer; **2ordnen** *v/t.* (*sep.*, -ge-, *h*) subordinate (*dat.* to); *sich ~* submit (to).

Unter'redung *f* (-/-en) conversation, conference.

Unterricht ['untəriçt] *m* (-[e]s/ꝗ -e) instruction, lessons *pl.*

unter'richten *v/t.* (*no* -ge-, *h*): *~ in* (*dat.*) instruct in, teach (*English*, *etc.*); *~ von* inform *s.o.* of.

'Unterrichts|ministerium *n* ministry of education; **'~stunde** *f* lesson, (teaching) period; **'~wesen** *n* (-s/*no pl.*) education; teaching.

'Unterrock *m* slip.

unter'sagen *v/t.* (*no* -ge-, *h*) forbid (*j-m et. s.o.* to do *s.th.*).

'Untersatz *m* stand; saucer.

unter'schätzen *v/t.* (*no* -ge-, *h*) undervalue; underestimate, underrate.

unter'scheid|en *v/t. and v/i.* (*irr.* *scheiden*, *no* -ge-, *h*) distinguish (*zwischen* between; *von* from); *sich ~* differ (*von* from); **2ung** *f* distinction.

'Unterschenkel *m* shank.

'unterschieb|en *v/t.* (*irr.* *schieben*, *sep.*, -ge-, *h*) push under; *fig.*: attribute (*dat.* to); substitute (*statt* for); **2ung** *f* substitution.

Unterschied ['untərʃiːt] *m* (-[e]s/-e) difference; distinction; *zum ~ von* in distinction from *or* to; **'2lich** *adj.* different; differential; variable, varying; **'2slos** *adj.* indiscriminate; undiscriminating.

unter'schlag|en *v/t.* (*irr.* *schlagen*, *no* -ge-, *h*) embezzle; suppress (*truth*, *etc.*); **2ung** *f* (-/-en) embezzlement; suppression.

'Unterschlupf *m* (-[e]s/ᵘe, -e) shelter, refuge.

unter'schreiben *v/t. and v/i.* (*irr.* *schreiben*, *no* -ge-, *h*) sign.

'Unterschrift *f* signature.

'Untersee|boot ⚓, ꭙ *n s.* U-Boot; **'~kabel** *n* submarine cable.

unter'setzt *adj.* thick-set, squat.

unterst *adj.* ['untərst] lowest, undermost.

'Unterstand ꭙ *m* shelter, dug-out.

unter'stehen *v/i.* (*irr.* *stehen*, *no* -ge-, *h*) 1. *v/i.* (*dat.*) be subordinate to; be subject to (*law*, *etc.*); 2. *v/refl.* dare; *untersteh dich!* don't you dare!; **~stellen** *v/t.* 1. ['~ʃtələn] (*sep.*, -ge-, *h*) put *or* place under; garage (*car*); *sich ~* take shelter (*vor dat.* from); 2. [~'ʃtelən] (*no* -ge-, *h*) (pre)suppose, assume; impute (*dat.*

to); *j-m ~* ꭙ put (*troops*, *etc.*) under *s.o.*'s command; **2'stellung** *f* (-/-en) assumption, supposition; imputation; **~'streichen** *v/t.* (*irr.* *streichen*, *no* -ge-, *h*) underline, underscore (*both a. fig.*).

unter'stütz|en *v/t.* (*no* -ge-, *h*) support; back up; **2ung** *f* (-/-en) support (*a.* ꭙ); assistance, aid; relief.

unter'such|en *v/t.* (*no* -ge-, *h*) examine (*a.* 🔬); inquire into, investigate (*a.* ⚖); explore; 🔬 try; analy|se, *Am.* -ze (*a.* 🏷); **2ung** *f* (-/-en) examination (*a.* 🔬); inquiry (*gen.* into), investigation (*a.* ⚖); exploration; analysis (*a.* 🏷).

Unter'suchungs|gefangene *m* prisoner on remand; **~gefängnis** *n* remand prison; **~haft** *f* detention on remand; **~richter** *m* investigating judge.

Untertan ['untərtaːn] *m* (-s, -en/ -en) subject.

untertänig *adj.* ['untərtɛːniç] submissive.

'Unter|tasse *f* saucer; **'2tauchen** (*sep.*, -ge-) 1. *v/i.* (*sein*) dive, dip; duck; *fig.* disappear; 2. *v/t.* (*h*) duck.

'Unterteil *n*, *m* lower part.

unter'teil|en *v/t.* (*no* -ge-, *h*) subdivide; **2ung** *f* subdivision.

'Unter|titel *m* subheading; subtitle; *a.* caption (*of film*); **'~ton** *m* undertone; **2vermieten** *v/t.* (*no* -ge-, *h*) sublet.

unter'wander|n *pol. v/t.* (*no* -ge-, *h*) infiltrate; **2ung** *pol. f* infiltration.

'Unterwäsche *f s.* Unterkleidung.

unterwegs *adv.* [untər'veːks] on the *or* one's way.

unter'weis|en *v/t.* (*irr.* *weisen*, *no* -ge-, *h*) instruct (*in dat.* in); **2ung** *f* instruction.

'Unterwelt *f* underworld (*a. fig.*).

unter'werf|en *v/t.* (*irr.* *werfen*, *no* -ge-, *h*) subdue (*dat.* to), subjugate (to); subject (to); submit (to); *sich ~* submit (to); **2ung** *f* (-/-en) subjugation, subjection; submission (*unter acc.* to).

unterworfen *adj.* [untər'vɔrfən] subject (*dat.* to).

unterwürfig *adj.* [untər'vyrfiç] submissive; subservient; **2keit** *f* (-/*no pl.*) submissiveness; subservience.

unter'zeichn|en *v/t.* (*no* -ge-, *h*) sign; **2er** *m* signer, *the* undersigned; subscriber (*gen.* to); signatory (*gen.* to *treaty*); **2erstaat** *m* signatory state; **2ete** *m, f* (-n/-n) *the* undersigned; **2ung** *f* signature, signing.

unterziehen *v/t.* (*irr.* *ziehen*) 1. ['~tsiːən] (*sep.*, -ge-, *h*) put on underneath; 2. [~'tsiːən] (*no* -ge-, *h*) subject (*dat.* to); *sich e-r Operation ~* undergo an operation; *sich e-r Prüfung ~* go in *or* sit for an examination; *sich der Mühe ~ zu inf.* take the trouble to *inf.*

'**Untiefe** *f* shallow, shoal.
'**Untier** *n* monster (*a. fig.*).
un|tilgbar *adj.* [un'tilkbɑːr] indelible; ✝ *government annuities*: irredeemable; ⁓'**tragbar** *adj.* unbearable, intolerable; *costs*: prohibitive; ⁓'**trennbar** *adj.* inseparable.
'**untreu** *adj.* untrue (*dat.* to), disloyal (to); *husband, wife*: unfaithful (to); '⁓e *f* disloyalty; unfaithfulness, infidelity.
un|'tröstlich *adj.* inconsolable, disconsolate; ⁓**trüglich** *adj.* [⁓'tryːklic] infallible, unerring.
'**Untugend** *f* vice, bad habit.
unüber|legt *adj.* ['unⁱyːbər-] inconsiderate, thoughtless; '⁓**sichtlich** *adj.* badly arranged; difficult to survey; involved; *mot. corner*: blind; ⁓'**trefflich** *adj.* unsurpassable; ⁓**windlich** *adj.* [⁓'vintlic] invincible; *fortress*: impregnable; *obstacle, etc.*: insurmountable; *difficulties, etc.*: insuperable.
unum|gänglich *adj.* [unⁱum'gɛnlic] absolutely necessary; ⁓**schränkt** *adj.* [⁓'frɛŋkt] absolute; ⁓**stößlich** *adj.* [⁓'ftøːslic] irrefutable; incontestable; irrevocable; ⁓**wunden** *adj.* ['⁓vundən] frank, plain.
ununterbrochen *adj.* ['unⁱuntərbrɔxən] uninterrupted; incessant.
unver|'änderlich *adj.* unchangeable; invariable; ⁓'**antwortlich** *adj.* irresponsible; inexcusable; ⁓'**besserlich** *adj.* incorrigible; '⁓**bindlich** *adj.* not binding *or* obligatory; *answer, etc.*: non-committal; ⁓**blümt** *adj.* [⁓'blyːmt] plain, blunt; ⁓**bürgt** *adj.* [⁓'byrkt] unwarranted; *news*: unconfirmed; '⁓**dächtig** *adj.* unsuspected; '⁓**daulich** *adj.* indigestible (*a. fig.*); '⁓**dient** *adj.* undeserved; '⁓**dorben** *adj.* unspoiled, unspoilt; *fig.*: uncorrupted; pure, innocent; '⁓**drossen** *adj.* indefatigable, unflagging; '⁓**dünnt** *adj.* undiluted, *Am. a.* straight; ⁓'**einbar** *adj.* incompatible; '⁓**fälscht** *adj.* unadulterated; *fig.* genuine; ⁓**fänglich** *adj.* ['⁓fɛŋlic] not captious; ⁓**froren** *adj.* ['⁓froːrən] unabashed, impudent; '⁓**frorenheit** *f* (-/-en) impudence, F cheek; '⁓**gänglich** *adj.* imperishable; '⁓**geßlich** *adj.* unforgettable; ⁓'**gleichlich** *adj.* incomparable; '⁓**hältnismäßig** *adj.* disproportionate; ⁓**heiratet** *adj.* unmarried, single; '⁓**hofft** *adj.* unhoped-for, unexpected; '⁓**hohlen** *adj.* unconcealed; '⁓**käuflich** *adj.* unsal(e)able; not for sale; ⁓**kennbar** *adj.* unmistakable; ⁓'**letzbar** *adj.* invulnerable; *fig. a.* inviolable; ⁓**meidlich** *adj.* [⁓'maɪtlic] inevitable; '⁓**mindert** *adj.* undiminished; '⁓**mittelt** *adj.* abrupt.

'**Unvermögen** *n* (-s/no *pl.*) inability; impotence; '⁓d *adj.* impecunious, without means.
'**unvermutet** *adj.* unexpected.
'**Unver|nunft** *f* unreasonableness, absurdity; '⁓**nünftig** *adj.* unreasonable, absurd; '⁓**richterdinge** *adv.* without having achieved one's object.
'**unverschämt** *adj.* impudent, impertinent; '⁓**heit** *f* (-/-en) impudence, impertinence.
'**unver|schuldet** *adj.* not in debt; through no fault of mine, *etc.*; '⁓**sehens** *adv.* unawares, suddenly, all of a sudden; ⁓**sehrt** *adj.* ['⁓zeːrt] uninjured; '⁓**söhnlich** *adj.* implacable, irreconcilable; '⁓**sorgt** *adj.* unprovided for; '⁓**stand** *m* injudiciousness; folly, stupidity; '⁓**ständig** *adj.* injudicious; foolish; '⁓**ständlich** *adj.* unintelligible; incomprehensible; *das ist mir* ⁓ that is beyond me; '⁓**sucht** *adj.*: *nichts* ⁓ *lassen* leave nothing undone; '⁓**träglich** *adj.* unsociable; quarrelsome; '⁓**wandt** *adj.* steadfast; ⁓**wundbar** *adj.* [⁓'vuntbaːr] invulnerable; ⁓**wüstlich** *adj.* [⁓'vyːstlic] indestructible; *fig.* irrepressible; ⁓**zagt** *adj.* ['⁓tsaːkt] intrepid, undaunted; ⁓'**zeihlich** *adj.* unpardonable; ⁓'**zinslich** *adj.* bearing no interest; non-interest-bearing; ⁓**züglich** *adj.* [⁓'tsyːklic] immediate, instant.
'**unvollendet** *adj.* unfinished.
'**unvollkommen** *adj.* imperfect; '⁓**heit** *f* imperfection.
'**unvollständig** *adj.* incomplete; '⁓**keit** *f* (-/no *pl.*) incompleteness.
'**unvorbereitet** *adj.* unprepared; extempore.
'**unvoreingenommen** *adj.* unbias(s)ed, unprejudiced; '⁓**heit** *f* freedom from prejudice.
'**unvor|hergesehen** *adj.* unforeseen; ⁓**schriftsmäßig** *adj.* irregular.
'**unvorsichtig** *adj.* incautious; imprudent; '⁓**keit** *f* incautiousness; imprudence.
'**unvor|'stellbar** *adj.* unimaginable; ⁓**teilhaft** *adj.* unprofitable; *dress, etc.*: unbecoming.
'**unwahr** *adj.* untrue; '⁓**heit** *f* untruth.
'**unwahrscheinlich** *adj.* improbable, unlikely; '⁓**keit** *f* (-/-en) improbability, unlikelihood.
'**un|wegsam** *adj.* pathless, impassable; '⁓**weit** *prp.* (*gen. or von*) not far from; '⁓**wesen** *n* (-s/no *pl.*) nuisance; *sein* ⁓ *treiben* be up to one's tricks; '⁓**wesentlich** *adj.* unessential, immaterial (*für* to); '⁓**wetter** *n* thunderstorm; '⁓**wichtig** *adj.* unimportant, insignificant.
unwider|legbar *adj.* [unvi'dər'leːk-

baːr] irrefutable; ‚'ruflich *adj.* irrevocable (*a.* ✝).

unwider'stehlich *adj.* irresistible; ‚keit *f* (-/*no pl.*) irresistibility.

unwieder'bringlich *adj.* irretrievable.

'Unwille *m* (-ns/*no pl.*), '‚en *m* (-s/*no pl.*) indignation (*über acc.* at), displeasure (at, over); '‚ig *adj.* indignant (*über acc.* at), displeased (at, with); unwilling; '‚kürlich *adj.* involuntary.

'unwirklich *adj.* unreal.

'unwirksam *adj.* ineffective, inefficient; *laws, rules, etc.*: inoperative; ⁀ₘ inactive; '‚keit *f* (-/*no pl.*) ineffectiveness, inefficiency; ⁀ₘ inactivity.

unwirsch *adj.* ['unvirʃ] testy.

unwirt|lich *adj.* inhospitable, desolate; '‚schaftlich *adj.* uneconomic(al).

'unwissen|d *adj.* ignorant; '‚heit *f* (-/*no pl.*) ignorance; '‚tlich *adj.* unwitting, unknowing.

'unwohl *adj.* unwell, indisposed; '‚sein *n* (-s/*no pl.*) indisposition.

'unwürdig *adj.* unworthy (*gen.* of).

un|zählig *adj.* ['un'tseːliç] innumerable; '‚zart *adj.* indelicate.

Unze ['untsə] *f* (-/-n) ounce.

'Unzeit *f*: zur ~ inopportunely; '‚gemäß *adj.* old-fashioned; inopportune; '‚ig *adj.* untimely; unseasonable; *fruit*: unripe.

unzer|'brechlich *adj.* unbreakable; ‚'reißbar *adj.* untearable; ‚'störbar *adj.* indestructible; ‚'trennlich *adj.* inseparable.

'un|ziemlich *adj.* unseemly; '‚zucht *f* (-/*no pl.*) lewdness; ⁂ sexual offen|ce, *Am.* -se; '‚züchtig *adj.* lewd; obscene.

'unzufrieden *adj.* discontented (*mit* with), dissatisfied (with, at); '‚heit *f* discontent, dissatisfaction.

'unzugänglich *adj.* inaccessible.

unzulänglich *adj.* ['untsulɛnliç] insufficient; '‚keit *f* (-/-en) insufficiency; shortcoming.

'unzulässig *adj.* inadmissible; *esp.* ⁂ *influence*: undue.

'unzurechnungsfähig *adj.* irresponsible; '‚keit *f* irresponsibility.

'unzu|reichend *adj.* insufficient; ‚'sammenhängend *adj.* incoherent; '‚träglich *adj.* unwholesome; '‚treffend *adj.* incorrect; inapplicable (*auf acc.* to).

'unzuverlässig *adj.* unreliable, untrustworthy; *friend*: *a.* uncertain; '‚keit *f* unreliability, untrustworthiness.

'unzweckmäßig *adj.* inexpedient; '‚keit *f* inexpediency.

'un|zweideutig *adj.* unequivocal; unambiguous; '‚zweifelhaft 1. *adj.* undoubted, undubitable; 2. *adv.* doubtless.

üppig *adj.* ['ypiç] ⚘ luxuriant, exuberant, opulent; *food*: luxurious, opulent; *figure*: voluptuous; '‚keit *f* (-/‚-en) luxuriance, luxuriancy, exuberance; voluptuousness.

ur|alt *adj.* ['uːrʔalt] very old; (as) old as the hills; ‚aufführung ['uːrʔ-] *f* world première.

Uran [u'raːn] *n* (-s/*no pl.*) uranium.

urbar *adj.* ['uːrbaːr] arable, cultivable; ~ *machen* reclaim; '‚machung *f* (-/-en) reclamation.

'Ur|bevölkerung *f* aborigines *pl.*; '‚bild *n* original, prototype; '‚eigen *adj.* one's very own; '‚enkel *m* great-grandson; '‚großeltern *pl.* great-grandparents *pl.*; '‚großmutter *f* great-grandmother; '‚großvater *m* great-grandfather.

'Urheber *m* (-s/-) author; '‚recht *n* copyright (*an dat.* in); '‚schaft *f* (-/*no pl.*) authorship.

Urin [u'riːn] *m* (-s/-e) urine; ‚ieren [‚i'niːrən] *v/i.* (*no* -ge-, *h*) urinate.

'Urkund|e *f* document; deed; '‚enfälschung *f* forgery of documents; ‚lich *adj.* ['‚tliç] documentary.

Urlaub ['uːrlaup] *m* (-[e]s/-e) leave (of absence) (*a.* ⚔); holiday(s *pl.*), *esp. Am.* vacation; ‚er ['‚bər] *m* (-s/-) holiday-maker, *esp. Am.* vacationist, vacationer.

Urne ['urnə] *f* (-/-n) urn; ballot-box.

'ur|plötzlich 1. *adj.* very sudden, abrupt; 2. *adv.* all of a sudden; '‚sache *f* cause; reason; *keine* ~l don't mention it, *Am. a.* you are welcome; '‚sächlich *adj.* causal; '‚schrift *f* original (text); '‚sprung *m* origin, source; ‚sprünglich *adj.* ['‚ʃprynliç] original; '‚stoff *m* primary matter.

Urteil ['urtail] *n* (-s/-e) judg(e)ment; ⁂ *a.* sentence; *meinem* ~ *nach* in my judg(e)ment; *sich ein* ~ *bilden* form a judg(e)ment (*über acc.* of, on); '‚en *v/i.* (ge-, *h*) judge (*über acc.* of; *nach* by, from); '‚kraft *f* (-/‚‚e) discernment.

'Ur|text *m* original (text); '‚wald *m* primeval *or* virgin forest; ‚wüchsig *adj.* ['‚vyːksiç] original; *fig.*: natural; rough; '‚zeit *f* primitive times *pl.*

Utensilien [uten'ziːljən] *pl.* utensils *pl.*

Utop|ie [uto'piː] *f* (-/-n) Utopia; ‚isch *adj.* [u'toːpiʃ] Utopian, utopian.

V

Vagabund [vaga'bunt] m (-en/-en) vagabond, vagrant, tramp, Am. hobo, F bum.

Vakuum ['vaːkuʔum] n (-s/Vakua, Vakuen) vacuum.

Valuta ✝ [va'luːta] f (-/Valuten) value; currency.

Vanille [va'niljə] f (-/no pl.) vanilla.

variabel adj. [vari'aːbəl] variable.

Varia|nte [vari'antə] f (-/-n) variant; ~tion [~'tsjoːn] f (-/-en) variation.

Varieté [varie'teː] n (-s/-s), ~theater n variety theatre, music-hall, Am. vaudeville theater.

variieren [vari'iːrən] v/i. and v/t. (no -ge-, h) vary.

Vase ['vaːzə] f (-/-n) vase.

Vater ['faːtər] m (-s/ᵘ) father; '~land n native country or land, mother country; '~landsliebe f patriotism.

väterlich adj. ['fɛːtərliç] fatherly, paternal.

'Vater|schaft f (-/no pl.) paternity, fatherhood; '~unser eccl. n (-s/-) Lord's Prayer.

Vati ['faːti] m (-s/-s) dad(dy).

Veget|arier [vege'taːrjər] m (-s/-) vegetarian; ~arisch adj. vegetarian; ~ation [~a'tsjoːn] f (-/-en) vegetation; ~ieren [~'tiːrən] v/i. (no -ge-, h) vegetate.

Veilchen ♀ ['failçən] n (-s/-) violet.

Vene anat. ['veːnə] f (-/-n) vein.

Ventil [ven'tiːl] n (-s/-e) valve (a. ♪); ♪ stop (of organ); fig. vent, outlet; ~ation [~ila'tsjoːn] f (-/-en) ventilation; ~ator [~i'laːtɔr] m (-s/-en) ventilator, fan.

verab|folgen [fɛr'ap-] v/t. (no -ge-, h) deliver; give; ⊕ administer (medicine); ~reden v/t. (no -ge-, h) agree upon, arrange; appoint, fix (time, place); sich ~ make an appointment, Am. F (have a) date; 2redung f (-/-en) agreement; arrangement; appointment, Am. F date; ~reichen v/t. (no -ge-, h) s. verabfolgen; ~scheuen v/t. (no -ge-, h) abhor, detest, loathe; ~schieden [~ʃiːdən] v/t. (no -ge-, h) dismiss; retire (officer); ⚔ discharge (troops); parl. pass (bill); sich ~ take leave (von of), say goodbye (to); 2schiedung f (-/-en) dismissal; discharge; passing.

ver|'achten v/t. (no -ge-, h) despise; ~ächtlich adj. [~'ɛçtliç] contemptuous; contemptible; 2achtung f contempt; ~allgemeinern [~ʔalgə'mainərn] v/t. (no -ge-, h) generalize; ~altet adj. antiquated, obsolete, out of date.

Veranda [ve'randa] f (-/Veranden) veranda(h), Am. a. porch.

veränder|lich adj. [fɛr'ɛndərliç] changeable; variable (a. Ⴟ, gr.); ~n v/t. and v/refl. (no -ge-, h) alter, change; vary; 2ung f change, alteration (in dat. in; an dat. to); variation.

verängstigt adj. [fɛr'ɛnstiçt] intimidated, scared.

ver'anlag|en v/t. (no -ge-, h) of taxation: assess; ~t adj. [~kt] talented; 2ung f (-/-en) assessment; fig. talent(s pl.); ⚕ predisposition.

ver'anlass|en v/t. (no -ge-, h) cause, occasion; arrange; 2ung f (-/-en) occasion, cause; auf m-e ~ at my request or suggestion.

ver|'anschaulichen v/t. (no -ge-, h) illustrate; ~'anschlagen v/t. (no -ge-, h) rate, value, estimate (all: auf acc. at).

ver'anstalt|en v/t. (no -ge-, h) arrange, organize; give (concert, ball, etc.); 2ung f (-/-en) arrangement; event; sports: event, meeting, Am. meet.

ver'antwort|en v/t. (no -ge-, h) take the responsibility for; account for; ~lich adj. responsible; j-n ~ machen für hold s.o. responsible for.

Ver'antwortung f (-/-en) responsibility; die ~ tragen be responsible; zur ~ ziehen call to account; 2slos adj. irresponsible.

ver|'arbeiten v/t. (no -ge-, h) work up; ⊕ process, manufacture (both: zu into); digest (food) (a. fig.); ~'ärgern v/t. (no -ge-, h) vex, annoy.

ver'arm|en v/i. (no -ge-, sein) become poor; ~t adj. impoverished.

ver|'ausgaben v/t. (no -ge-, h) spend (money); sich ~ run short of money; fig. spend o.s.; ~'äußern v/t. (no -ge-, h) sell; alienate.

Verb gr. [vɛrp] n (-s/-en) verb.

Ver'band m (-[e]s/ᵘe) ⚕ dressing, bandage; association, union; ⚔ formation, unit; ~(s)kasten m first-aid box; ~(s)zeug n dressing (material).

ver'bann|en v/t. (no -ge-, h) banish (a. fig.), exile; 2ung f (-/-en) banishment, exile.

ver|barrikadieren [fɛrbarika'diːrən] v/t. (no -ge-, h) barricade; block (street, etc.); ~'bergen v/t. (irr. bergen, no -ge-, h) conceal, hide.

ver'besser|n v/t. (no -ge-, h) improve; correct; 2ung f improvement; correction.

ver'beug|en v/i./refl. (no -ge-, h) bow (vor dat. to); 2ung f bow.

ver|'biegen v/t. (irr. biegen, no

-ge-, h) bend, twist, distort; ~
'**bieten** v/t. (irr. bieten, no -ge-, h)
forbid, prohibit; ~'**billigen** v/t.
(no -ge-, h) reduce in price,
cheapen.

ver'**bind|en** v/t. (irr. binden, no
-ge-, h) ⚕ dress; tie (together);
bind (up); link (mit to); join, unite,
combine; connect (a. teleph.);
teleph. put s.o. through (mit to);
j-m die Augen ~ blindfold s.o.; sich
~ join, unite, combine (a. 🜛); ich
bin Ihnen sehr verbunden I am
greatly obliged to you; falsch verbunden! teleph. wrong number!;
~**lich** adj. [~tliç] obligatory; obliging; 2**lichkeit** f (-/-en) obligation,
liability; obligingness, civility.

Ver'**bindung** f union; alliance;
combination; association (of ideas);
connexion, (Am. only) connection
(a. teleph., 🚂, ⚓, ⊕); relation;
communication (a. teleph.); 🜍
compound; geschäftliche ~ business relations pl.; teleph.: ~ bekommen (haben) get (be) through;
die ~ verlieren mit lose touch with;
in ~ bleiben (treten) keep (get) in
touch (mit with); sich in ~ setzen
mit communicate with, esp. Am.
contact s.o.; ~**straße** f communication road, feeder road; ~**stür** f
communication door.

ver'**bissen** adj. [fɛr'bisən] dogged;
crabbed; ~'**bitten** v/refl. (irr. bitten,
no -ge-, h) das verbitte ich mir!
I won't suffer or stand that!

ver'**bitter|n** v/t. (no -ge-, h) em-
bitter; 2**ung** f (-/✎-en) bitterness
(of heart).

verblassen [fɛr'blasən] v/i. (no
-ge-, sein) fade (a. fig.).

Verbleib [fɛr'blaɪp] m (-[e]s/no pl.)
whereabouts sg., pl.; 2**en** [~bən] v/i.
(irr. bleiben, no -ge-, sein) be left,
remain.

ver'**blend|en** v/t. (no -ge-, h) △
face (wall, etc.); fig. blind, delude;
2**ung** f (-/✎-en) △ facing; fig.
blindness, delusion. [faded.|

verblichen adj. [fɛr'bliçən] colour:)

verblüff|en [fɛr'blyfən] v/t. (no
-ge-, h) amaze; perplex, puzzle;
dumbfound; 2**ung** f (-/✎-en)
amazement, perplexity.

ver|'**blühen** v/i. (no -ge-, sein) fade,
wither; ~'**bluten** v/i. (no -ge-, sein)
bleed to death.

ver'**borgen** adj. hidden; secret;
2**heit** f (-/no pl.) concealment;
secrecy.

Verbot [fɛr'boːt] n (-[e]s/-e) prohibition; 2**en** adj. forbidden, pro-
hibited; Rauchen ~ no smoking.

Ver'**brauch** m (-[e]s/✎-e) consumption (an dat. of); 2**en** v/t. (no
-ge-, h) consume, use up; wear out;
~**er** m (-s/-) consumer; 2**t** adj. air:
stale; p. worn out.

ver'**brechen** 1. v/t. (irr. brechen,
no -ge-, h) commit; was hat er ver-
brochen? what is his offen|ce, Am.
-se?, what has he done?; 2. 2 n
(-s/-) crime, offen|ce, Am. -se.

Ver'**brecher** m (-s/-) criminal;
2**isch** adj. criminal; ~**tum** n (-s/no
pl.) criminality.

ver'**breit|en** v/t. (no -ge-, h) spread,
diffuse; shed (light, warmth, happiness); sich ~ spread; sich ~ über
(acc.) enlarge (up)on (theme); ~**ern**
v/t. and v/refl. (no -ge-, h) widen,
broaden; 2**ung** f (-/✎-en) spread
(-ing), diffusion.

ver'**brenn|en** (irr. brennen, no -ge-)
1. v/i. (sein) burn; 2. v/t. (h) burn
(up); cremate (corpse); 2**ung** f
(-/-en) burning, combustion;
cremation (of corpse); wound: burn.

ver'**bringen** m/t. (irr. bringen, no
-ge-, h) spend, pass.

verbrüder|n [fɛr'bryːdərn] v/refl.
(no -ge-, h) fraternize; 2**ung** f
(-/-en) fraternization.

ver|'**brühen** v/t. (no -ge-, h) scald;
sich ~ scald o.s.; ~'**buchen** v/t.
(no -ge-, h) book.

Verbum gr. ['vɛrbum] n (-s/Verba)
verb.

verbünden [fɛr'byndən] v/refl. (no
-ge-, h) ally o.s. (mit to, with).

Verbundenheit [fɛr'bundənhaɪt] f
(-/no pl.) bonds pl., ties pl.; solidarity; affection.

Ver'**bündete** m, f (-n/-n) ally, con-
federate; die ~n pl. the allies pl.

ver|'**bürgen** v/t. (no -ge-, h) guar-
antee, warrant; sich ~ für answer
or vouch for; ~'**büßen** v/t. (no -ge-,
h): e-e Strafe ~ serve a sentence,
serve (one's) time.

Verdacht [fɛr'daxt] m (-[e]s/no pl.)
suspicion; in ~ haben suspect.

verdächtig adj. [fɛr'dɛçtiç] sus-
pected (gen. of); pred. suspect;
suspicious; ~**en** [~gən] v/t. (no
-ge-, h) suspect s.o. (gen. of); cast
suspicion on; 2**ung** f [~guŋ] f (-/-en)
suspicion; insinuation.

verdamm|en [fɛr'damən] v/t. (no
-ge-, h) condemn, damn (a. eccl.);
2**nis** f (-/no pl.) damnation; ~**t**
1. adj. damned; F: ~! damn (it)!,
confound it!; 2. F adv.: ~ kalt
beastly cold; 2**ung** f (-/✎-en) condemnation, damnation.

ver|'**dampfen** (no -ge-) v/t. (h) and
v/i. (sein) evaporate; ~'**danken** v/t.
(no -ge-, h); j-m et. ~ owe s.th. to
s.o.

verdarb [fɛr'darp] pret. of verderben.

verdau|en [fɛr'daʊən] v/t. (no -ge-,
h) digest; ~**lich** adj. digestible;
leicht ~ easy to digest, light; 2**ung**
f (-/no pl.) digestion; 2**ungsstö-
rung** f indigestion.

Ver'**deck** n (-[e]s/-e) ⚓ deck;

hood (*of carriage, car, etc.*); top (*of vehicle*); 2en v/t. (*no -ge-, h*) cover; conceal, hide.

ver'denken v/t. (*irr. denken, no -ge-, h*): ich kann es ihm nicht ~, daß I cannot blame him for ger.

Verderb [fɛr'dɛrp] m (-[e]s/*no pl.*) ruin; 2en [.bən] 1. v/i. (*irr., no -ge-, sein*) spoil (*a. fig.*); rot; meat, etc.: go bad; fig. perish; 2. v/t. (*irr., no -ge-, h*) spoil; fig. a.: corrupt; ruin; er will es mit niemandem ~ he tries to please everybody; sich den Magen ~ upset one's stomach; ~en [.bən] n (-s/*no pl.*) ruin; 2lich adj. [.pliç] pernicious; food: perishable; ~nis [.pnis] f (-/%-se) corruption; depravity; 2t adj. [.pt] corrupted, depraved.

ver|'deutlichen v/t. (*no -ge-, h*) make plain or clear; ~'dichten v/t. (*no -ge-, h*) condense; sich ~ condense; suspicion: grow stronger; ~'dicken v/t. and v/refl. (*no -ge-, h*) thicken; ~'dienen v/t. (*no -ge-, h*) merit, deserve; earn (*money*).

Ver'dienst (-es/-e) 1. m gain, profit; earnings pl.; 2. n merit; es ist sein ~, daß it is owing to him that; 2voll adj. meritorious, deserving; ~spanne † f profit margin.

ver|'dient adj. p. of merit; (well-) deserved; sich ~ gemacht haben um deserve well of; ~'dolmetschen v/t. (*no -ge-, h*) interpret (*a. fig.*); ~'doppeln v/t. and v/refl. (*no -ge-, h*) double.

verdorben [fɛr'dɔrbən] 1. p.p. of verderben; 2. adj. meat: tainted; stomach: disordered, upset; fig. corrupt, depraved.

ver|dorren [fɛr'dɔrən] v/i. (*no -ge-, sein*) wither (up); ~'drängen v/t. (*no -ge-, h*) push away, thrust aside; fig. displace; psych. repress; ~'drehen v/t. (*no -ge-, h*) distort, twist (*both a. fig.*); roll (*eyes*); fig. pervert; j-m den Kopf ~ turn s.o.'s head; ~'dreht F fig. adj. crazy; ~'dreifachen v/t. and v/refl. (*no -ge-, h*) triple.

verdrießen [fɛr'dri:sən] v/t. (*irr., no -ge-, h*) vex, annoy; ~lich adj. vexed, annoyed; sulky; thing: annoying.

ver|droß [fɛr'drɔs] pret. of verdrießen; ~drossen [.'drɔsən] 1. p.p. of verdrießen; 2. adj. sulky; listless.

ver'drucken typ. v/t. (*no -ge-, h*) misprint.

Verdruß [fɛr'drus] m (Verdrusses/% Verdrusse) vexation, annoyance.

ver'dummen (*no -ge-*) 1. v/t. (*h*) make stupid; 2. v/i. (*sein*) become stupid.

ver'dunk|eln v/t. (*no -ge-, h*) darken, obscure (*both a. fig.*); black out (*window*); sich ~ darken;

2(e)lung f (-/%-en) darkening; obscuration; black-out; ⚡ collusion.

ver|'dünnen v/t. (*no -ge-, h*) thin; dilute (*liquid*); ~'dunsten v/i. (*no -ge-, sein*) volatilize, evaporate; ~'dursten v/i. (*no -ge-, sein*) die of thirst; ~dutzt adj. [.'dutst] nonplussed.

ver'ed|eln v/t. (*no -ge-, h*) ennoble; refine; improve; ⚡ graft; process (*raw materials*); 2(e)lung f (-/% -en) refinement; improvement; processing.

ver'ehr|en v/t. (*no -ge-, h*) revere, venerate; worship; admire, adore; 2er m (-s/-) worship(p)er; admirer, adorer; 2ung f (-/%-en) reverence, veneration; worship; adoration.

vereidigen [fɛr'aidigən] v/t. (*no -ge-, h*) swear (*witness*); at entrance into office: swear s.o. in.

Verein [fɛr'ain] m (-[e]s/-e) union; society, association; club.

ver'einbar adj. compatible (*mit with*), consistent (*with*); ~en v/t. (*no -ge-, h*) agree upon, arrange; 2ung f (-/-en) agreement, arrangement.

ver'einen v/t. (*no -ge-, h*) s. vereinigen.

ver'einfach|en v/t. (*no -ge-, h*) simplify; 2ung f (-/-en) simplification.

ver'einheitlichen v/t. (*no -ge-, h*) unify, standardize.

ver'einig|en v/t. (*no -ge-, h*) unite, join; associate; sich ~ unite, join; associate o.s.; 2ung f 1. (-/%-en) union; 2. (-/-en) union; society, association.

ver'ein|samen v/i. (*no -ge-, sein*) grow lonely or solitary; ~zelt adj. isolated; sporadic.

ver|'eiteln v/t. (*no -ge-, h*) frustrate; ~'ekeln v/t. (*no -ge-, h*): er hat mir das Essen verekelt he spoilt my appetite; ~'enden v/i. (*no -ge-, sein*) animals: die, perish; ~enge(r)n [.'ɛŋə(r)n] v/t. and v/refl. (*no -ge-, h*) narrow.

ver'erb|en v/t. (*no -ge-, h*) leave, bequeath; biol. transmit; sich ~ be hereditary; sich ~ auf (*acc.*) descend (up)on; 2ung f (-/%-en) biol. transmission; physiol. heredity; 2ungslehre f genetics.

verewig|en [fɛr'e:vigən] v/t. (*no -ge-, h*) perpetuate; ~t adj. [.çt] deceased, late.

ver'fahren 1. v/i. (*irr. fahren, no -ge-, sein*) proceed; ~ mit deal with; 2. v/t. (*irr. fahren, no -ge-, h*) mismanage, muddle, bungle; sich ~ miss one's way; 3. 2 n (-s/-) procedure; proceeding(s pl. ⚖); ⊕ process.

Ver'fall m (-[e]s/*no pl.*) decay, decline; dilapidation (*of house, etc.*);

$\frac{1}{2}t_2^2$ forfeiture; expiration; maturity (of bill of exchange); 2en 1. v/i. (irr. fallen, no -ge-, sein) decay; house: dilapidate; document, etc.: expire; pawn: become forfeited; right: lapse; bill of exchange: fall due; sick person: waste away; ~ auf (acc.) hit upon (idea, etc.); ~ in (acc.) fall into; j-m ~ become s.o.'s slave; 2. adj. ruinous; addicted (dat. to drugs, etc.); ~serscheinung [fɛr'fals⁹-] f symptom of decline; ~tag m day of payment.

ver|'fälschen v/t. (no -ge-, h) falsify; adulterate (wine, etc.); ~fänglich adj. [~'fɛŋliç] question: captious, insidious; risky; embarrassing; ~'färben v/refl. (no -ge-, h) change colo(u)r.

ver'fass|en v/t. (no -ge-, h) compose, write; 2er m (-s/-) author.

Ver'fassung f state, condition; pol. constitution; disposition (of mind); 2smäßig adj. constitutional; 2s-widrig adj. unconstitutional.

ver|'faulen v/i. (no -ge-, sein) rot, decay; ~'fechten v/t. (irr. fechten, no -ge-, h) defend, advocate.

ver'fehl|en v/t. (no -ge-, h) miss; 2ung f (-/-en) offen|ce, Am. -se.

ver|feinden [fɛr'faɪndən] v/t. (no -ge-, h) make enemies of; sich ~ mit make an enemy of; ~feinern [~'faɪnərn] v/t. and v/refl. (no -ge-, h) refine; ~fertigen [~'fɛrtɪgən] v/t. (no -ge-, h) make, manufacture; compose.

ver'film|en v/t. (no -ge-, h) film, screen; 2ung f (-/-en) film-version.

ver|'finstern v/t. (no -ge-, h) darken, obscure; sich ~ darken; ~'flachen (no -ge-) v/i. (sein) and v/refl. (h) (become) shallow (a. fig.); ~'flechten v/t. (irr. flechten, no -ge-, h) interlace; fig. involve; ~'fliegen (irr. fliegen, no -ge-) 1. v/i. (sein) evaporate; time: fly; fig. vanish; 2. v/refl. (h) bird: stray; ✈ lose one's bearings, get lost; ~'fließen v/i. (irr. fließen, no -ge-, sein) colours: blend; time: elapse; ~flossen adj. [~'flɔsən] time: past; F ein ~er Freund a late friend, an ex-friend.

ver'fluch|en v/t. (no -ge-, h) curse, Am. F cuss; ~t adj. damned; ~! damn (it)!, confound it!

ver|'flüchtigen [fɛr'flyçtɪgən] v/t. (no -ge-, h) volatilize; sich ~ evaporate (a. fig.); F fig. vanish; ~flüssigen [~'flysɪgən] v/t. and v/refl. (no -ge-, h) liquefy.

ver'folg|en v/t. (no -ge-, h) pursue; persecute; follow (tracks); trace; thoughts, dream: haunt; gerichtlich ~ prosecute; 2er m (-s/-) pursuer; persecutor; 2ung f (-/-en) pursuit; persecution; pursuance; gericht-liche ~ prosecution; 2ungswahn ♣ m persecution mania.

ver|frachten [fɛr'fraxtən] v/t. (no -ge-, h) freight, Am. a. ship (goods); ♣ ship; F j-n ~ in (acc.) bundle s.o. in(to) (train, etc.); ~'froren adj. chilled through; ~'früht adj. premature.

verfüg|bar adj. [fɛr'fy:kba:r] available; ~en [~gən] (no -ge-, h) 1. v/t. decree, order; 2. v/i.: ~ über (acc.) have at one's disposal; dispose of; 2ung [~guŋ] f (-/-en) decree, order; disposal; j-m zur ~ stehen (stellen) be (place) at s.o.'s disposal.

ver'führ|en v/t. (no -ge-, h) seduce; 2er m (-s/-) seducer; ~erisch adj. seductive; enticing, tempting; 2ung f seduction.

vergangen [fɛr'gaŋən] gone, past; im ~en Jahr last year; 2heit f (-/-en) past; gr. past tense.

vergänglich adj. [fɛr'gɛŋliç] transient, transitory.

vergas|en [fɛr'ga:zən] v/t. (no -ge-, h) gasify; gas s.o.; 2er mot. m (-s/-) carburet(t)or.

vergaß [fɛr'ga:s] pret. of vergessen.

ver'geb|en v/t. (irr. geben, no -ge-, h) give away (an j-n to s.o.); confer (on), bestow (on); place (order); forgive; sich et. ~ compromise one's dignity; ~ens adv. [~s] in vain; ~lich [~pliç] 1. adj. vain; 2. adv. in vain; 2ung [~buŋ] f (-/~-en) bestowal, conferment (both: an acc. on); forgiveness, pardon.

vergegenwärtigen [fɛrge:gən'vɛrtɪgən] v/t. (no -ge-, h) represent; sich et. ~ visualize s.th.

ver'gehen 1. v/i. (irr. gehen, no -ge-, sein) pass (away); fade (away); ~ vor (dat.) die of; 2. v/refl. (irr. gehen, no -ge-, h): sich an j-m ~ assault s.o.; violate s.o.; sich gegen das Gesetz ~ offend against or violate the law; 3. 2 n (-s/-) offen|ce, Am. -se.

ver'gelt|en v/t. (irr. gelten, no -ge-, h) repay, requite; reward; retaliate; 2ung f (-/-en) requital; retaliation; retribution.

vergessen [fɛr'gɛsən] 1. v/t. (irr., no -ge-, h) forget; leave; 2. p.p. of 1; 2heit f (-/no pl.): in ~ geraten sink or fall into oblivion.

vergeßlich adj. [fɛr'gɛsliç] forgetful.

vergeud|en [fɛr'gɔʏdən] v/t. (no -ge-, h) dissipate, squander, waste (time, money); 2ung f (-/~-en) waste.

vergewaltig|en [fɛrgə'valtɪgən] v/t. (no -ge-, h) violate; rape; 2ung f (-/-en) violation; rape.

ver|gewissern [fɛrgə'wɪsərn] v/refl. (no -ge-, h) make sure (e-r Sache of s.th.); ~'gießen v/t. (irr. gießen, no -ge-, h) shed (tears, blood); spill (liquid).

ver'gift|en v/t. (no -ge-, h) poison (a. fig.); sich ~ take poison; 2ung f (-/-en) poisoning.

Vergißmeinnicht ♀ [fɛr'gismaɪn-nɪçt] n (-[e]s/-[e]) forget-me-not.

vergittern [fɛr'gɪtərn] v/t. (no -ge-, h) grate.

Vergleich [fɛr'glaɪç] m (-[e]s/-e) comparison; ♈: agreement; compromise, composition; 2bar adj. comparable (mit to); 2en v/t. (irr. gleichen, no -ge-, h) compare (mit with, to); sich ~ mit ♈ come to terms with; verglichen mit as against, compared to; 2sweise adv. comparatively.

vergnügen [fɛr'gny:gən] 1. v/t. (no -ge-, h) amuse; sich ~ enjoy o.s.; 2. 2 n (-s/-) pleasure, enjoyment; entertainment; ~ finden an (dat.) take pleasure in; viel ~! have a good time! [gay.\
vergnügt adj. [fɛr'gny:kt] merry,/

Ver'gnügung f (-/-en) pleasure, amusement, entertainment; ~s-reise f pleasure-trip, tour; 2s-süchtig adj. pleasure-seeking.

ver|golden [fɛr'gɔldən] v/t. (no -ge-, h) gild; ~göttern fig. [~'gœ-tərn] v/t. (no -ge-, h) idolize, adore; ~'graben v/t. (irr. graben, no -ge-, h) bury (a. fig.); sich ~ bury o.s.; ~'greifen v/refl. (irr. greifen, no -ge-, h) sprain (one's hand, etc.); sich ~ an (dat.) lay (violent) hands on, attack, assault; embezzle (money); encroach upon (s.o.'s property); ~griffen adj. [~'grɪfən] goods: sold out; book: out of print.

vergrößer|n [fɛr'grø:sərn] v/t. (no -ge-, h) enlarge (a. phot.); opt. magnify; sich ~ enlarge; 2ung f 1. (-/-en) phot. enlargement; opt. magnification; 2. (-/♈-en) enlargement; increase; extension; 2ungs-glas n magnifying glass.

Vergünstigung [fɛr'gynstɪgʊŋ] f (-/-en) privilege.

vergüt|en [fɛr'gy:tən] v/t. (no -ge-, h) compensate (j-m et. s.o. for s.th.); reimburse (money spent); 2ung f (-/-en) compensation; reimbursement.

ver'haft|en v/t. (no -ge-, h) arrest; 2ung f (-/-en) arrest.

ver'halten 1. v/t. (irr. halten, no -ge-, h) keep back; catch or hold (one's breath); suppress, check; sich ~ thing: be; p. behave; sich ruhig ~ keep quiet; 2. 2 n (-s/no pl.) behavio(u)r, conduct.

Verhältnis [fɛr'hɛltnɪs] n (-ses/-se) proportion, rate; relation(s pl.) (zu with); F liaison, love-affair; F mistress; ~se pl. conditions pl., circumstances pl.; means pl.; 2mäßig

adv. in proportion; comparatively; ~wort gr. n (-[e]s/♈er) preposition.

Ver'haltungsmaßregeln f/pl. instructions pl.

ver'hand|eln (no -ge-, h) 1. v/i. negotiate, treat (über acc., wegen for); ♈ try (über et. s.th.); 2. v/t. discuss; 2lung f negotiation; discussion; ♈ trial, proceedings pl.

ver'häng|en v/t. (no -ge-, h) cover (over), hang; inflict (punishment) (über acc. upon); 2nis n (-ses/-se) fate; ~nisvoll adj. fatal; disastrous.

ver|härmt adj. [fɛr'hɛrmt] careworn; ~harren [~'harən] v/i. (no -ge-, h, sein) persist (auf dat., bei, in dat. in), stick (to); ~'härten v/t. and v/refl. (no -ge-, h) harden; ~haßt adj. [~'hast] hated; hateful, odious; ~'hätscheln v/t. (no -ge-, h) coddle, pamper, spoil; ~'hauen v/t. (irr. hauen, no -ge-, h) thrash.

verheer|en [fɛr'he:rən] v/t. (no -ge-, h) devastate, ravage, lay waste; ~end fig. adj. disastrous; 2ung f (-/-en) devastation.

ver|hehlen [fɛr'he:lən] v/t. (no -ge-, h) s. verheimlichen; ~'heilen v/i. (no -ge-, sein) heal (up).

ver'heimlich|en v/t. (no -ge-, h) hide, conceal; 2ung f (-/♈-en) concealment.

ver'heirat|en v/t. (no -ge-, h) marry (mit to); sich ~ marry; 2ung f (-/♈-en) marriage.

ver'heiß|en v/t. (irr. heißen, no -ge-, h) promise; 2ung f (-/-en) promise; ~ungsvoll adj. promising.

ver'helfen v/i. (irr. helfen, no -ge-, h): j-m zu et. ~ help s.o. to s.th.

ver'herrlich|en v/t. (no -ge-, h) glorify; 2ung f (-/♈-en) glorification.

ver|'hetzen v/t. (no -ge-, h) instigate; ~'hexen v/t. (no -ge-, h) bewitch.

ver'hinder|n v/t. (no -ge-, h) prevent; 2ung f (-/♈-en) prevention.

ver'höhn|en v/t. (no -ge-, h) deride, mock (at), taunt; 2ung f (-/-en) derision, mockery.

Verhör ♈ [fɛr'hø:r] n (-[e]s/-e) interrogation, questioning (of prisoners, etc.); examination; 2en v/t. (no -ge-, h) examine, hear; interrogate; sich ~ hear it wrong.

ver|'hüllen v/t. (no -ge-, h) cover, veil; ~'hungern v/i. (no -ge-, sein) starve; ~'hüten v/t. (no -ge-, h) prevent.

ver'irr|en v/refl. (no -ge-, h) go astray, lose one's way; ~t adj.: ~es Schaf stray sheep; 2ung fig. f (-/-en) aberration; error.

ver'jagen v/t. (no -ge-, h) drive away.

verjähr|en ♈ [fɛr'je:rən] v/i. (no -ge-, sein) become prescriptive;

Qung *f* (-/-en) limitation, (negative) prescription.

verjüngen [fɛr'jyŋən] *v/t. (no -ge-, h)* make young again, rejuvenate; reduce (*scale*); sich ~ grow young again, rejuvenate; taper off.

Ver'kauf *m* sale; Qen *v/t. (no -ge-, h)* sell; zu ~ for sale; sich gut ~ sell well.

Ver'käuf|er *m* seller; vendor; shop-assistant, salesman, *Am. a.* (sales-) clerk; ~erin *f* (-/-nen) seller; vendor; shop-assistant, saleswoman, shop girl, *Am. a.* (sales)clerk; Qlich *adj.* sal(e)able; for sale.

Ver'kaufs|automat *m* slot-machine, vending machine; ~schlager *m* best seller.

Verkehr [fɛr'ke:r] *m* (-[e]s/⚭-e) traffic; transport(ation); communication; correspondence ⚓, ⚒, ⚔, *etc.*: service; commerce, trade; intercourse (*a. sexually*); aus dem ~ ziehen withdraw from service; withdraw (*money*) from circulation; Qen (*no -ge-*, h) 1. *v/t.* convert (*in acc.* into), turn (into); 2. *v/i.* ship, bus, *etc.*: run, ply (*zwischen dat.* between); bei j-m ~ go to *or* visit s.o.'s house; ~ in (*dat.*) frequent (*public house, etc.*); ~ mit associate *or* mix with; have (sexual) intercourse with.

Ver'kehrs|ader *f* arterial road; ~ampel *f* traffic lights *pl.*, traffic signal; ~büro *n* tourist bureau; ~flugzeug *n* air liner; ~insel *f* refuge, island; ~minister *m* minister of transport; ~mittel *n* (means of) conveyance *or* transport, *Am.* transportation; ~polizist *m* traffic policeman *or* constable, *sl.* traffic cop; Qreich *adj.* congested with traffic, busy; ~schild *n* traffic sign; ~schutzmann *m s.* Verkehrspolizist; ~stauung *f*, ~stockung *f* traffic block, traffic jam; ~störung *f* interruption of traffic; ⚭, *etc.*: breakdown; ~straße *f* thoroughfare; ~teilnehmer *m* road user; ~unfall *m* traffic accident; ~verein *m* tourist agency; ~verhältnisse *pl.* traffic conditions *pl.*; ~vorschrift *f* traffic regulation; ~wesen *n* (-s/*no pl.*) traffic; ~zeichen *n* traffic sign.

ver'|kehrt *adj.* inverted, upside down; *fig.* wrong; ~'kennen *v/t.* (*irr.* kennen, *no -ge-*, h) mistake; misunderstand, misjudge.

Ver'kettung *f* (-/-en) concatenation (*a. fig.*).

ver'|klagen ⚖ *v/t. (no -ge-*, h) sue (*auf acc.*, *wegen* for); bring an action against *s.o.*; ~'kleben *v/t. (no -ge-*, h) paste *s.th.* up.

ver'kleid|en *v/t. (no -ge-*, h) disguise; ⊕: line; face; wainscot; encase; sich ~ disguise o.s.; Qung *f*

(-/-en) disguise; ⊕: lining; facing; panel(l)ing, wainscot(t)ing.

verkleiner|n [fɛr'klaɪnərn] *v/t. (no -ge-*, h) make smaller, reduce, diminish; *fig.* belittle, derogate; Qung *f* (-/-en) reduction, diminution; *fig.* derogation.

ver'|klingen *v/i.* (*irr.* klingen, *no -ge-, sein*) die away; ~knöchern [~'knœçərn] (*no -ge-*) 1. *v/t.* (h) ossify; 2. *v/i.* (sein) ossify; *fig. a.* fossilize; ~'knoten *v/t. (no -ge-*, h) knot; ~'knüpfen *v/t. (no -ge-*, h) knot *or* tie (together); *fig.* connect, combine; ~'kohlen (*no -ge-*) 1. *v/t.* (h) carbonize; char; F: j-n ~ pull s.o.'s leg; 2. *v/i.* (sein) char; ~'kommen 1. *v/i.* (*irr.* kommen, *no -ge-, sein*) decay; *p.*: go downhill *or* to the dogs; become demoralized; 2. *adj.* decayed; depraved, corrupt; ~'korken *v/t. (no -ge-*, h) cork (up).

ver'körper|n *v/t. (no -ge-*, h) personify, embody; represent; *esp. thea.* impersonate; Qung *f* (-/-en) personification, embodiment; impersonation.

ver'|krachen F *v/refl. (no -ge-*, h) fall out (*mit* with); ~'krampft *adj.* cramped; ~'kriechen *v/refl.* (*irr.* kriechen, *no -ge-*, h) hide; ~'krümmt *adj.* crooked; ~krüppelt *adj.* [~'krypəlt] crippled; stunted; ~krustet *adj.* [~'krustət] (en)crusted; caked; ~'kühlen *v/refl.* (*no -ge-*, h) catch (a) cold.

ver'kümmer|n *v/i. (no -ge-, sein)* ⚘, ⚘ become stunted; ⚘ atrophy; *fig.* waste away; ~t *adj.* stunted; atrophied; rudimentary (*a. biol.*).

verkünd|en [fɛr'kyndən] *v/t. (no -ge-*, h), ~igen *v/t. (no -ge-*, h) announce; publish, proclaim; pronounce (*judgement*); Qigung *f*, Qung *f* (-/-en) announcement; proclamation; pronouncement.

ver'|kuppeln *v/t. (no -ge-*, h) ⊕ couple; *fig.* pander; ~'kürzen *v/t. (no -ge-*, h) shorten; abridge; beguile (*time, etc.*); ~'lachen *v/t. (no -ge-*, h) laugh at; ~'laden *v/t.* (*irr.* laden, *no -ge-*, h) load; ship; ⚓ entrain (*esp. troops*).

Verlag [fɛr'la:k] *m* (-[e]s/-e) publishing house, *the* publishers *pl.*; im ~ von published by.

ver'lagern *v/t. (no -ge-*, h) displace; shift; sich ~ shift.

Ver'lags|buchhändler *m* publisher; ~buchhandlung *f* publishing house; ~recht *n* copyright.

ver'langen 1. *v/t. (no -ge-*, h) demand; require; desire; 2. *v/i. (no -ge-*, h): ~ nach ask for; long for; 3. Q *n* (-s/⚭-) desire; longing (*nach* for); demand, request; *auf* ~ by request, ✝ on demand; *auf* ~ von at the request of, at *s.o.'s* request.

verlänger|n [fɛr'lɛŋərn] *v/t. (no*

-ge-, h) lengthen; prolong, extend;
2ung f (-/-en) lengthening; pro-
longation, extension.

ver'langsamen v/t. (no -ge-, h)
slacken, slow down.

ver'lassen v/t. (irr. lassen, no -ge-,
h) leave; forsake, abandon, desert;
sich ~ auf (acc.) rely on; **2heit** f
(-/no pl.) abandonment; loneliness.

verläßlich adj. [fer'lɛsliç] reliable.

Ver'lauf m lapse, course (of time);
progress, development (of matter);
course (of disease, etc.); im ~ (gen.)
or von in the course of; e-n schlim-
men ~ nehmen take a bad turn; **2en**
(irr. laufen, no -ge-) 1. v/i. (sein)
time: pass, elapse; matter: take its
course; turn out, develop; road, etc.:
run, extend; 2. v/refl. (h) lose one's
way, go astray; crowd: disperse;
water: subside.

ver'lauten v/i. (no -ge-, sein): ~ lassen give to understand, hint; wie
verlautet as reported.

ver'leb|en v/t. (no -ge-, h) spend,
pass; ~t adj. [~pt] worn out.

ver'leg|en 1. v/t. (no -ge-, h) mislay;
transfer, shift, remove; ⊕ lay
(cable, etc.); bar (road); put off,
postpone; publish (book); sich ~ auf
(acc.) apply o.s. to; 2. adj. embarrassed; at a loss (um for answer,
etc.); **2enheit** f (-/~-en) embarrassment; difficulty; predicament;
2er m (-s/-) publisher; **2ung** f
(-/-en) transfer, removal; ⊕ laying;
time: postponement.

ver'leiden v/t. (no -ge-, h) s. ver-
ekeln.

ver'leih|en v/t. (irr. leihen, no -ge-,
h) lend, Am. a. loan; hire or let out;
bestow (right, etc.) (j-m on s.o.);
award (price); **2ung** f (-/-en) lend-
ing, loan; bestowal.

ver'leiten v/t. (no -ge-, h) mislead;
induce; seduce; ⅈ suborn; **~'lernen** v/t. (no -ge-, h) unlearn, forget;
~'lesen v/t. (irr. lesen, no -ge-, h)
read out; call (names) over; pick
(vegetables, etc.); sich ~ read wrong.

verletz|en [fɛr'lɛtsən] v/t. (no -ge-,
h) hurt, injure; fig. a.: offend;
violate; **~end** adj. offensive; **2te**
[~tə] m, f (-n/-n) injured person;
die ~n pl. the injured pl.; **2ung** f
(-/-en) hurt, injury, wound; fig.
violation.

ver'leugn|en v/t. (no -ge-, h) deny;
disown; renounce belief, principle,
etc.); sich ~ lassen have o.s. denied
(vor j-m to s.o.); **2ung** f (-/-en)
denial; renunciation.

verleumd|en [fɛr'lɔymdən] v/t. (no
-ge-, h) slander, defame; **~erisch**
adj. slanderous; **2ung** f (-/-en)
slander, defamation, in writing:
libel.

ver'lieb|en v/refl. (no -ge-, h): sich ~
in (acc.) fall in love with; **~t** adj.

[~pt] in love (in acc. with); amorous; **2theit** f (-/~-en) amorous-
ness.

verlieren [fɛr'li:rən] (irr., no -ge-, h)
1. v/t. lose; shed (leaves, etc.); sich ~
lose o.s.; disappear; 2. v/i. lose.

ver'lob|en v/t. (no -ge-, h) engage
(mit to); sich ~ become engaged;
2te [~ptə] (-n/-n) 1. m fiancé; die ~n
pl. the engaged couple sg.; 2. f
fiancée; **2ung** f (-/-en)
engagement.

ver'lock|en v/t. (no -ge-, h) allure,
entice; tempt; **~end** adj. tempting;
2ung f (-/-en) allurement, entice-
ment.

verlogen adj. [fɛr'lo:gən] mendacious; **2heit** f (-/~-en) mendac-
ity.

verlor [fɛr'lo:r] pret. of verlieren;
~en 1. p.p. of verlieren; 2. adj. lost;
fig. forlorn; **~e** Eier poached eggs;
~engehen v/i. (irr. gehen, sep.,
-ge-, sein) be lost.

ver'los|en v/t. (no -ge-, h) raffle;
2ung f (-/-en) lottery, raffle.

ver'löten v/t. (no -ge-, h) solder.

Verlust [fɛr'lust] m (-es/-e) loss; **~e**
pl. ⚔ casualties pl.

ver'machen v/t. (no -ge-, h) bequeath, leave s.th. (dat. to).

Vermächtnis [fɛr'mɛçtnis] n (-ses/
-se) will; legacy, bequest.

vermähl|en [fɛr'mɛ:lən] v/t. (no
-ge-, h) marry (mit to); sich ~ (mit)
marry (s.o.); **2ung** f (-/-en) wedding,
marriage.

ver'mehr|en v/t. (no -ge-, h) in-
crease (um by), augment; multiply;
add to; durch Zucht ~ propagate;
breed; sich ~ increase, augment;
multiply (a. biol.); propagate (itself), zo. breed; **2ung** f (-/~-en)
increase; addition (gen. to); prop-
agation.

ver'meid|en v/t. (irr. meiden, no
-ge-, h) avoid; **2ung** f (-/~-en)
avoidance.

ver|meintlich adj. [fɛr'maintliç]
supposed; **~'mengen** v/t. (no -ge-,
h) mix, mingle, blend.

Vermerk [fɛr'mɛrk] m (-[e]s/-e)
note, entry; **2en** v/t. (no -ge-, h)
note down, record.

ver'mess|en 1. v/t. (irr. messen, no
-ge-, h) measure; survey (land);
2. adj. presumptuous; **2enheit** f
(-/~-en) presumption; **2ung** f
(-/-en) measurement; survey (of
land).

ver'miete|n v/t. (no -ge-, h) let,
esp. Am. rent; hire (out); ⅈ lease;
zu ~ on or for hire; Haus zu ~ house
to (be) let; **2r** m landlord; ⅈ lessor;
letter, hirer.

ver'mindern v/t. (no -ge-, h)
diminish, lessen; reduce, cut.

ver'misch|en v/t. (no -ge-, h) mix,
mingle, blend; **~t** adj. mixed; news,

etc.: miscellaneous; 2*ung* *f* (-/-, -en) mixture.

ver'mi|ssen *v/t.* (*no* -ge-, h) miss; **~ßt** *adj.* [~'mist] missing; **2ßte** *m, f* (-n/-n) missing person; *die* **~n** *pl.* the missing *pl.*

vermitt|eln [fer'mitəln] (*no* -ge-, h) **1.** *v/t.* mediate (*settlement, peace*); procure, get; give (*impression, etc.*); impart (*knowledge*) (j-m to s.o.); **2.** *v/i.* mediate (*zwischen dat.* between); intercede (*bei* with, *für* for), intervene; **2ler** *m* mediator, go-between; **†** agent; **2lung** *f* (-/-en) mediation; intercession, intervention; *teleph.* (telephone) exchange.

ver'modern *v/i.* (*no* -ge-, *sein*) mo(u)lder, decay, rot.

ver'mögen 1. *v/t.* (*irr.* mögen, *no* -ge-, h); **~** zu *inf.* be able to *inf.*; et. **~** *bei* j-m have influence with s.o.; **2.** 2*n* (-s/-) ability, power; property; fortune; means *pl.*; **†** assets *pl.*; **~d** *adj.* wealthy; *pred.* well off; **2sverhältnisse** *pl.* pecuniary circumstances *pl.*

vermut|en [fer'mu:tən] *v/t.* (*no* -ge-, h) suppose, presume, *Am. a.* guess; conjecture, surmise; **~lich 1.** *adj.* presumable; **2.** *adv.* presumably; I suppose; **2ung** *f* (-/-en) supposition, presumption; conjecture, surmise.

vernachlässig|en [fer'na:xlɛsigən] *v/t.* (*no* -ge-, h) neglect; **2ung** *f* (-/-, -en) neglect(ing).

ver'narben *v/i.* (*no* -ge-, *sein*) cicatrize, scar over. [with.]

ver'narrt *adj.*: **~** *in* (*acc.*) infatuated]

ver'nehm|en *v/t.* (*irr.* nehmen, *no* -ge-, h) hear, learn; examine, interrogate; **~lich** *adj.* audible, distinct; **2ung** **†** *f* (-/-en) interrogation, questioning; examination.

ver'neig|en *v/refl.* (*no* -ge-, h) bow (*vor dat.* to); **2ung** *f* bow.

vernein|en [fer'naɪnən] (*no* -ge-, h) **1.** *v/t.* answer in the negative; deny; **2.** *v/i.* answer in the negative; **~end** *adj.* negative; **2ung** *f* (-/-en) negation; denial; *gr.* negative.

vernicht|en [fer'niçtən] *v/t.* (*no* -ge-, h) annihilate; destroy; dash (*hopes*); **~end** *adj.* destructive (*a. fig.*); *look*: withering; *criticism*: scathing; *defeat, reply*: crushing; **2ung** *f* (-/-, -en) annihilation; destruction.

ver|nickeln [fer'nikəln] *v/t.* (*no* -ge-, h) nickel(-plate); **~'nieten** *v/t.* (*no* -ge-, h) rivet.

Vernunft [fer'nunft] *f* (-/*no pl.*) reason; **~** annehmen listen to *or* hear reason; j-n zur **~** bringen bring s.o. to reason *or* to his senses.

vernünftig *adj.* [fer'nynftiç] rational; reasonable; sensible.

ver'öden (*no* -ge-) **1.** *v/t.* (h) make

desolate; **2.** *v/i.* (*sein*) become desolate.

ver'öffentlich|en *v/t.* (*no* -ge-, h) publish; **2ung** *f* (-/-en) publication.

ver'ordn|en *v/t.* (*no* -ge-, h) decree; order (*a.* **♯**); **♯** prescribe (j-m to *or* for s.o.); **2ung** *f* decree, order; **♯** prescription.

ver'pachten *v/t.* (*no* -ge-, h) rent, **†‡** lease (*building, land*).

Ver'pächter *m* landlord, **†‡** lessor.

ver'pack|en *v/t.* (*no* -ge-, h) pack (up); wrap up; **2ung** *f* packing (material); wrapping.

ver|'passen *v/t.* (*no* -ge-, h) miss (*train, opportunity, etc.*); **~patzen** F [~'patsən] *v/t.* (*no* -ge-, h) s. verpfuschen; **~'pesten** *v/t.* (*no* -ge-, h) *fumes*: contaminate (*the air*); **~'pfänden** *v/t.* (*no* -ge-, h) pawn, pledge (*a. fig.*); mortgage.

ver'pflanz|en *v/t.* (*no* -ge-, h) transplant (*a.* **♯**); **2ung** *f* transplantation; **♯** *a.* transplant.

ver'pfleg|en *v/t.* (*no* -ge-, h) board; supply with food, victual; **2ung** *f* (-/-, -en) board; food-supply; provisions *pl.*

ver'pflicht|en *v/t.* (*no* -ge-, h) oblige; engage; **2ung** *f* (-/-en) obligation, duty; **†**, **†‡** liability; engagement, commitment.

ver'pfusch|en F *v/t.* (*no* -ge-, h) bungle, botch; make a mess of; **~t** *adj.* *life*: ruined, wrecked.

ver'pön|t *adj.* [fer'pø:nt] taboo; **~'prügeln** F *v/t.* (*no* -ge-, h) thrash, flog, F wallop; **~'puffen** *fig.* *v/i.* (*no* -ge-, *sein*) fizzle out.

Ver'putz ▲ *m* (-es/-, -e) plaster; **2en** ▲ *v/t.* (*no* -ge-, h) plaster.

ver|quicken [fer'kvikən] *v/t.* (*no* -ge-, h) mix up; **~'quollen** *adj.* *wood*: warped; *face*: bloated; *eyes*: swollen; **~rammeln** [~'raməln] *v/t.* (*no* -ge-, h) bar(ricade).

Verrat [fer'ra:t] *m* (-[e]s/*no pl.*) betrayal (*an dat.* of); treachery (to); **†‡** treason (to); **2en** *v/t.* (*irr.* raten, *no* -ge-, h) betray, give *s.o.* away; give away (*secret*); sich **~** betray o.s., give o.s. away.

Verräter [fer'rɛ:tər] *m* (-s/-) traitor (*an dat.* to); **2isch** *adj.* treacherous; *fig.* telltale.

ver'rechn|en *v/t.* (*no* -ge-, h) reckon up; charge; settle; set off (*mit* against); account for; **~** *mit* offset against; sich **~** miscalculate, make a mistake (*a. fig.*); *fig.* be mistaken; sich um e-e Mark **~** be one mark out; **2ung** *f* settlement; clearing; booking *or* charging (*to account*); **2ungsscheck** *m* collection-only cheque *or* Am. check.

ver'regnet *adj.* rainy, rain-spoilt.

ver'reis|en *v/i.* (*no* -ge-, *sein*) go on a journey; **~t** *adj.* out of town; (*geschäftlich*) **~** away (on business).

verrenk|en [fɛr'rɛŋkən] v/t. (no -ge-, h) 🦵: wrench; dislocate, luxate; sich et. ~ 🦵 dislocate or luxate s.th.; sich den Hals ~ crane one's neck; 2ung 🦵 f (-/-en) dislocation, luxation.

ver'|richten v/t. (no -ge-, h) do, perform; execute; sein Gebet ~ say one's prayer(s); ~'riegeln v/t. (no -ge-, h) bolt, bar.

verringer|n [fɛr'rɪŋərn] v/t. (no -ge-, h) diminish, lessen; reduce, cut; sich ~ diminish, lessen; 2ung f (-/-en) diminution; reduction, cut.

ver'|rosten v/i. (no -ge-, sein) rust; ~rotten [~'rɔtən] v/i. (no -ge-, sein) rot.

ver'rück|en v/t. (no -ge-, h) displace, (re)move, shift; ~t adj. mad, crazy (both a. fig.: nach about); wie ~ like mad; j-n ~ machen drive s.o. mad; 2te (-n/-n) 1. m lunatic, madman; 2. f lunatic, madwoman; 2theit f (-/-en) madness; foolish action; craze.

Ver'ruf m (-[e]s/no pl.): in ~ bringen bring discredit (up)on; in ~ kommen get into discredit; 2en adj. ill-reputed, ill-famed.

ver'rutsch|en v/i. (no -ge-, sein) slip; shift; not straight.

Vers [fɛrs] m (-es/-e) verse.

ver'sagen 1. v/t. (no -ge-, h) refuse, deny (j-m et. s.o. s.th.); sich et. ~ deny o.s. s.th.; 2. v/i. (no -ge-, h) fail, break down; gun: misfire; 3. 2 n (-s/no pl.) failure. [ure.)

Ver'sager m (-s/-) misfire; p. fail-)

ver'salzen v/t. (irr. salzen, no -ge-, h) oversalt; F fig. spoil.

ver'samm|eln v/t. (no -ge-, h) assemble; sich ~ assemble, meet; 2lung f assembly, meeting.

Versand [fɛr'zant] m (-[e]s/no pl.) dispatch, Am. a. shipment; mailing; ~ ins Ausland a. export(ation); ~abteilung f forwarding department; ~geschäft n, ~haus n mailorder business or firm or house.

ver'säum|en v/t. (no -ge-, h) neglect (one's duty, etc.); miss (opportunity, etc.); lose (time); ~ zu inf. fail or omit to inf.; 2nis n (-ses/-se) neglect, omission, failure.

ver'|schachern F v/t. (no -ge-, h) barter (away); ~'schaffen v/t. (no -ge-, h) procure, get; sich ~ obtain, get; raise (money); sich Respekt ~ make o.s. respected; ~'schämt adj. bashful; ~'schanzen v/refl. (no -ge-, h) entrench o.s.; sich ~ hinter (dat.) (take) shelter behind; ~'schärfen v/t. (no -ge-, h) heighten, intensify; aggravate; sich ~ get worse; ~'scheiden v/i. (irr. scheiden, no -ge-, sein) pass away; ~'schenken v/t. (no -ge-, h) give s.th. away; make a present of; ~'scherzen v/t. and v/refl. (no

-ge-, h) forfeit; ~'scheuchen v/t. (no -ge-, h) frighten or scare away; fig. banish; ~'schicken v/t. (no -ge-, h) send (away), dispatch, forward.

ver'schieb|en v/t. (irr. schieben, no -ge-, h) displace, shift, (re)move; 🚂 shunt; put off, postpone; F fig. ✝ sell underhand; sich ~ shift; 2ung f shift(ing); postponement.

verschieden adj. [fɛr'ʃiːdən] different (von from); dissimilar, unlike; aus ~en Gründen for various or several reasons; Verschiedenes various things pl., esp. ✝ sundries pl.; ~artig adj. of a different kind, various; 2heit f (-/-en) difference; diversity, variety; ~tlich adv. repeatedly; at times.

ver'schiff|en v/t. (no -ge-, h) ship; 2ung f (-/-en) shipment.

ver'|schimmeln v/i. (no -ge-, sein) get mo(u)ldy, Am. mo(u)ld; ~'schlafen v/t. (irr. schlafen, no -ge-, h) miss by sleeping; sleep (afternoon, etc.) away; sleep off (headache, etc.) 2. v/i. (irr. schlafen, no -ge-, h) oversleep (o.s.); 3. adj. sleepy, drowsy.

Ver'schlag m shed; box; crate; 2en [~gən] 1. v/t. (irr. schlagen, no -ge-, h) board up; nail up; es verschlug ihm die Sprache it dum(b)founded him; 2. adj. cunning; eyes: a. shifty; ~enheit f (-/no pl.) cunning.

verschlechter|n [fɛr'ʃlɛçtərn] v/t. (no -ge-, h) deteriorate, make worse; sich ~ deteriorate, get worse; 2ung f (-/-en) deterioration; change for the worse.

ver'schleiern v/t. (no -ge-, h) veil (a. fig.).

Verschleiß [fɛr'ʃlaɪs] m (-es/-e) wear (and tear); 2en v/t. (irr.) no -ge-, h) wear out.

ver'|schleppen v/t. (no -ge-, h) carry off; pol. displace (person); abduct, kidnap; delay, protract; neglect (disease); ~'schleudern v/t. (no -ge-, h) dissipate, waste; ✝ sell at a loss, sell dirt-cheap; ~'schließen v/t. (irr. schließen, no -ge-, h) shut, close; lock (door); lock up (house).

verschlimmern [fɛr'ʃlɪmərn] v/t. (no -ge-, h) make worse, aggravate; sich ~ get worse.

ver'schlingen v/t. (irr. schlingen, no -ge-, h) devour; wolf (down) (one's food); intertwine, entwine, interlace; sich ~ intertwine, entwine, interlace.

verschli|ß [fɛr'ʃlɪs] pret. of verschleißen; ~ssen [~sən] p.p. of verschleißen.

verschlossen adj. [fɛr'ʃlɔsən] closed, shut; fig. reserved; 2heit f (-/no pl.) reserve.

ver'schlucken *v/t.* (*no -ge-, h*) swallow (up); *sich* ~ swallow the wrong way.

Ver'schluß *m* lock; clasp; lid; plug; stopper (*of bottle*); seal; fastener, fastening; *phot.* shutter; *unter* ~ under lock and key.

ver|'schmachten *v/i.* (*no -ge-, sein*) languish, pine away; *vor Durst* ~ *die or* be dying of thirst, be parched with thirst; **~'schmähen** *v/t.* (*no -ge-, h*) disdain, scorn.

ver'schmelz|en (*irr. schmelzen, no -ge-*) *v/t.* and *v/i.* (*sein*) melt, fuse (*a. fig.*); blend; *fig.:* amalgamate; merge (*mit in, into*); **2ung** *f* (*-/~-en*) fusion; **✝** merger; *fig.* amalgamation.

ver|'schmerzen *v/t.* (*no -ge-, h*) get over (the loss of); **~'schmieren** *v/t.* (*no -ge-, h*) smear (*over*); blur; **~schmitzt** *adj.* [~'ʃmɪtst] cunning; roguish; arch; **~'schmutzen** (*no -ge-*) **1.** *v/t.* (*h*) soil, dirty; pollute (*water*); **2.** *v/i.* (*sein*) get dirty; **~'schnaufen** F *v/i.* and *v/refl.* (*no -ge-, h*) stop for breath; **~'schneiden** *v/t.* (*irr. schneiden, no -ge-, h*) cut badly; blend (*wine, etc.*); geld, castrate; **~'schneit** *adj.* covered with snow; *mountains:* a. snow-capped; *roofs:* a. snow-covered.

Ver'schnitt *m* (*-[e]s/no pl.*) blend.

ver'schnupf|en F *fig. v/t.* (*no -ge-, h*) nettle, pique; **~t** *adj.:* ~ *sein* have a cold.

ver|'schnüren *v/t.* (*no -ge-, h*) tie up, cord; **~schollen** *adj.* [~'ʃɔlən] not heard of again; missing; **✝** presumed dead; **~'schonen** *v/t.* (*no -ge-, h*) spare; *j-n mit et.* ~ spare s.o. s.th.

verschöne(r)n [fɛr'ʃøːnə(r)n] *v/t.* (*no -ge-, h*) embellish, beautify; **2rung** *f* (*-/-en*) embellishment.

ver|schossen *adj.* [fɛr'ʃɔsən] *colour:* faded; F ~ *sein in* (*acc.*) be madly in love with; **~schränken** [~'ʃrɛŋkən] *v/t.* (*no -ge-, h*) cross, fold (*one's arms*).

ver|schreib|en *v/t.* (*irr. schreiben, no -ge-, h*) use up (*in writing*); **✍** prescribe (*j-m for s.o.*); **✍** assign (*j-m to s.o.*); *sich* ~ make a slip of the pen; *sich e-r Sache* ~ devote o.s. to s.th.; **2ung** *f* (*-/-en*) assignment; prescription.

ver|schroben *adj.* [fɛr'ʃroːbən] eccentric, queer, odd; **~'schrotten** *v/t.* (*no -ge-, h*) scrap; **~schüchtert** *adj.* [~'ʃʏçtərt] intimidated.

ver|schulden 1. *v/t.* (*no -ge-, h*) be guilty of; be the cause of; **2.** 2 *n* (*-s/no pl.*) fault.

ver|schuldet *adj.* indebted, in debt; **~'schütten** *v/t.* (*no -ge-, h*) spill (*liquid*); block (up) (*road*); bury *s.o.* alive; **~schwägert** *adj.* [~'ʃvɛːgərt] related by marriage;

~'schweigen *v/t.* (*irr. schweigen, no -ge-, h*) conceal (*j-m et. s.th. from s.o.*).

verschwend|en [fɛr'ʃvɛndən] *v/t.* (*no -ge-, h*) waste, squander (*an acc.* on); lavish (on); **2er** *m* (*-s/-*) spendthrift, prodigal; **~erisch** *adj.* prodigal, lavish (*both: mit* of); wasteful; **2ung** *f* (*-/~-en*) waste; extravagance.

verschwiegen *adj.* [fɛr'ʃviːgən] discreet; *place:* secret, secluded; **2heit** *f* (*-/no pl.*) discretion; secrecy.

ver|'schwimmen *v/i.* (*irr. schwimmen, no -ge-, sein*) become indistinct *or* blurred; **~'schwinden** *v/i.* (*irr. schwinden, no -ge-, sein*) disappear, vanish; F *verschwinde!* go away!, *sl.* beat it!; **2'schwinden** *n* (*-s/no pl.*) disappearance; **~schwommen** *adj.* [~'ʃvɔmən] vague (*a. fig.*); blurred; *fig.* woolly.

ver|'schwör|en *v/refl.* (*irr. schwören, no -ge-, h*) conspire; **2er** *m* (*-s/-*) conspirator; **2ung** *f* (*-/-en*) conspiracy, plot.

ver'sehen 1. *v/t.* (*irr. sehen, no -ge-, h*) fill (*an office*); look after (*house, etc.*); *mit et.* ~ furnish *or* supply with; *sich* ~ make a mistake; *ehe man sich's versieht* all of a sudden; **2.** 2 *n* (*-s/-*) oversight, mistake, slip; *aus* ~ = **~'tlich** *adv.* by mistake; inadvertently.

Versehrte [fɛr'zeːrtə] *m* (*-n/-n*) disabled person.

ver'send|en *v/t.* ([*irr. senden,*] *no -ge-, h*) send, dispatch, forward, *Am.* ship; *by water:* ship; *ins Ausland* ~ a. export; **2ung** *f* (*-/~-en*) dispatch, shipment, forwarding.

ver|'sengen *v/t.* (*no -ge-, h*) singe, scorch; **~'senken** *v/t.* (*no -ge-, h*) sink; *sich* ~ *in* (*acc.*) immerse o.s. in; **~sessen** *adj.* [~'zɛsən]: ~ *auf* (*acc.*) bent on, mad after.

ver'setz|en *v/t.* (*no -ge-, h*) displace, remove; transfer (*officer*); *at school:* remove, move up, *Am.* promote; transplant (*tree, etc.*); pawn, pledge; F *fig.* stand (*lover, etc.*) up; ~ *in* (*acc.*) put *or* place into (*situation, condition*); *j-m e-n Schlag* ~ give *or* deal s.o. a blow; *in Angst* ~ frighten *or* terrify *s.o.*; *in den Ruhestand* ~ pension *s.o.* off, retire *s.o.*; *versetzt werden* be transferred; *at school:* go up; ~ *Sie sich in m-e Lage* put *or* place yourself in my position; *Wein mit Wasser* ~ mix wine with water, add water to wine; *et.* ~ reply s.th.; **2ung** *f* (*-/-en*) removal; transfer; *at school:* remove, *Am.* promotion.

ver'seuch|en *v/t.* (*no -ge-, h*) infect; contaminate; **2ung** *f* (*-/~-en*) infection; contamination.

ver'sicher|n *v/t.* (*no -ge-, h*) assure

(*a. one's life*); protest, affirm; insure (*one's property or life*); sich ~ insure *or* assure o.s.; sich ~ (, daß) make sure (that); 2te *m*, *f* (-n/-n) insurant, *the* insured *or* assured, policy-holder; 2ung *f* assurance, affirmation; insurance; (life-)assurance; insurance company.

Ver'sicherungs|gesellschaft *f* insurance company; ~police *f*, ~schein *m* policy of assurance, insurance policy.

ver'|sickern *v/i.* (*no* -ge-, sein) trickle away; ~'siegeln *v/t.* (*no* -ge-, h) seal (up); ~'siegen *v/i.* (*no* -ge-, sein) dry up, run dry; ~'silbern *v/t.* (*no* -ge-, h) silver; F *fig.* realize, convert into cash; ~'sinken *v/i.* (*irr.* sinken, *no* -ge-, sein) sink; *s.* versunken; ~'sinnbildlichen *v/t.* (*no* -ge-, h) symbolize.

Version [ver'zjo:n] *f* (-/-en) version. **'Versmaß** *n* met|re, *Am.* -er.

versöhn|en [fer'zø:nən] *v/t.* (*no* -ge-, h) reconcile (*mit* to, with); sich (wieder) ~ become reconciled; ~lich *adj.* conciliatory; 2ung *f* (-/~-en) reconciliation.

ver'sorg|en *v/t.* (*no* -ge-, h) provide (*mit* with), supply (with); take care of, look after; ~t *adj.* [~kt] provided for; 2ung [~gun] *f* (-/-en) providing (*mit* with), supplying (with); supply, provision.

ver'spät|en *v/refl.* (*no* -ge-, h) be late; ~et *adj.* belated, late, *Am.* tardy; 2ung *f* (-/-en) lateness, *Am.* tardiness; ~ haben be late; *mit* 2 *Stunden* ~ two hours behind schedule.

ver'|speisen *v/t.* (*no* -ge-, h) eat (up); ~'sperren *v/t.* (*no* -ge-, h) lock (up); bar, block (up), obstruct (*a. view*); ~'spielen *v/t.* (*no* -ge-, h) at cards, *etc.*: los (*money*); ~'spielt *adj.* playful; ~'spotten *v/t.* (*no* -ge-, h) scoff at, mock (at), deride, ridicule; ~'sprechen *v/t.* (*irr.* sprechen, *no* -ge-, h) promise; sich ~ make a mistake in speaking; sich viel ~ von expect much of; 2'sprechen *n* (-s/~-) promise; ~'sprühen *v/t.* (*no* -ge-, h) spray; ~'spüren *v/t.* (*no* -ge-, h) feel; perceive, be conscious of.

ver'staatlich|en *v/t.* (*no* -ge-, h) nationalize; 2ung *f* (-/~-en) nationalization.

Verstand [fer'ftant] *m* (-[e]s/*no pl.*) understanding; intelligence, intellect, brains *pl.*; mind, wits *pl.*; reason; (common) sense.

Verstandes|kraft [fer'ftandəs-] *f* intellectual power *or* faculty; 2mäßig *adj.* rational; intellectual; ~mensch *m* matter-of-fact person.

verständ|ig *adj.* [fer'ftendiç] intelligent; reasonable, sensible; judi-

cious; ~igen [~gən] *v/t.* (*no* -ge-, h) inform (*von* of), notify (of); sich mit j-m ~ make o.s. understood to s.o.; come to an understanding with s.o.; 2igung [~gun] *f* (-/~-en) information; understanding, agreement; *teleph.* communication; ~lich *adj.* [~tliç] intelligible; understandable; j-m et. ~ machen make s.th. clear to s.o.; sich ~ machen make o.s. understood.

Verständnis [fer'ftentnis] *n* (-ses/~-se) comprehension, understanding; insight; appreciation (*für* of); ~ haben für appreciate; 2los *adj.* uncomprehending; *look, etc.*: blank; unappreciative; 2voll *adj.* understanding; appreciative; sympathetic; *look*: knowing.

ver'stärk|en *v/t.* (*no* -ge-, h) strengthen, reinforce (*a.* ⊕, ✕); amplify (*radio signals, etc.*); intensify; 2er *m* (-s/-) *in radio, etc.*: amplifier; 2ung *f* (-/~-en) strengthening, reinforcement (*a.* ✕); amplification; intensification.

ver'staub|en *v/i.* (*no* -ge-, sein) get dusty; ~t *adj.* [~pt] dusty.

ver'stauch|en *v/t.* (*no* -ge-, h) sprain; sich den Fuß ~ sprain one's foot; 2ung *f* (-/-en) sprain.

ver'stauen *v/t.* (*no* -ge-, h) stow away.

Versteck [fer'ftek] *n* (-[e]s/-e) hiding-place; *for gangsters, etc.*: *Am.* F *a.* hide-out; ~ spielen play at hide-and-seek; 2en *v/t.* (*no* -ge-, h) hide, conceal; sich ~ hide.

ver'stehen *v/t.* (*irr.* stehen, *no* -ge-, h) understand, see, F get; comprehend; realize; know (*language*); es ~ zu *inf.* know how to *inf.*; Spaß ~ take a joke; zu ~ geben intimate; ~ Sie? do you see?; ich ~! I see!; verstanden? (do you) understand?, F (do you) get me?; falsch ~ misunderstand; ~ Sie mich recht! don't misunderstand me!; was ~ Sie unter (*dat.*)? what do you mean *or* understand by ...?; er versteht et. davon he knows a thing or two about it; sich ~ understand one another; sich ~ auf (*acc.*) know well, be an expert at *or* in; sich mit j-m gut ~ get on well with s.o.; es versteht sich von selbst it goes without saying.

ver'steifen *v/t.* (*no* -ge-, h) ⊕ strut, brace; stiffen; sich ~ stiffen; sich ~ auf (*acc.*) make a point of, insist on.

ver'steiger|n *v/t.* (*no* -ge-, h) (sell by *or Am.* at) auction; 2ung *f* (sale by *or Am.* at) auction, auction-sale.

ver'steinern (*no* -ge-) *v/t.* (h) *and* *v/i.* (sein) turn into stone, petrify (*both a. fig.*).

ver'stell|bar *adj.* adjustable; ~en *v/t.* (*no* -ge-, h) shift; adjust; disarrange; bar, block (up), obstruct; disguise (*voice, etc.*); sich ~ play *or* act a part; dissemble, feign; 2ung *f* (-/~-en) disguise; dissimulation.

ver|'steuern *v/t.* (*no* -ge-, h) pay duty *or* tax on; ~stiegen *fig. adj.* [~'ſtiːɡən] eccentric.

ver'stimm|en *v/t.* (*no* -ge-, h) put out of tune; *fig.* put out of humo(u)r; ~t *adj.* out of tune; *fig.* out of humo(u)r; 2er *m* (-s/-) disagreement; ill humo(u)r; 2ung *f* ill humo(u)r; disagreement; ill feeling.

ver'stockt *adj.* stubborn, obdurate; 2heit *f* (-/no *pl.*) obduracy.

verstohlen *adj.* [fer'ſtoːlən] furtive.

ver'stopf|en *v/t.* (*no* -ge-, h) stop (up); clog, block (up), obstruct; jam, block (*passage, street*); ✻ constipate; 2ung ✻ *f* (-/~-en) constipation.

verstorben *adj.* [fer'ſtɔrbən] late, deceased; 2e *m, f* (-n/-n) *the* deceased, *Am.* ⚥ *a.* decedent; die ~n *pl.* the deceased *pl.*, the departed *pl.*

ver'stört *adj.* scared; distracted, bewildered; 2heit *f* (-/no *pl.*) distraction, bewilderment.

Ver'stoß *m* offen|ce, *Am.* -se; contravention (*gegen of law*); infringement (*on trade name, etc.*); blunder; 2en (*irr.* stoßen, *no* -ge-, h) 1. *v/t.* expel (*aus from*); repudiate, disown (*wife, child, etc.*); 2. *v/i.*: ~ gegen offend against; contravene (*law*); infringe (*rule, etc.*).

ver|'streichen (*irr.* streichen, *no* -ge-) 1. *v/i.* (sein) time: pass, elapse; expire; 2. *v/t.* (h) spread (*butter, etc.*); ~'streuen *v/t.* (*no* -ge-, h) scatter.

verstümmel|n [fer'ſtyməln] *v/t.* (*no* -ge-, h) mutilate; garble (*text, etc.*); 2ung *f* (-/-en) mutilation.

ver'stummen *v/i.* (*no* -ge-, sein) grow silent *or* dumb.

Verstümmlung [fer'ſtymluŋ] *f* (-/-en) mutilation.

Versuch [fer'zuːx] *m* (-[e]s/-e) attempt, trial; *phys., etc.*: experiment; e-n ~ machen mit give *s.o. or s.th.* a trial; try one's hand at *s.th.*, have a go at *s.th.*; 2en *v/t.* (*no* -ge-, h) try, attempt; taste; j-n ~ tempt *s.o.*; es ~ mit give *s.o. or s.th.* a trial.

Ver'suchs|anstalt *f* research institute; ~kaninchen *fig. n* guinea-pig; 2weise *adv.* by way of trial *or* (an) experiment; on trial; ~zweck *m*: zu ~en *pl.* for experimental purposes *pl.*

Ver'suchung *f* (-/-en) temptation; j-n in ~ bringen tempt *s.o.*; in ~ sein be tempted.

ver|'sündigen *v/refl.* (*no* -ge-, h) sin (*an dat.* against); ~sunken *fig. adj.* [~'zuŋkən]: ~ in (*acc.*) absorbed

or lost in; ~'süßen *v/t.* (*no* -ge-, h) sweeten.

ver'tag|en *v/t.* (*no* -ge-, h) adjourn; *parl.* prorogue; sich ~ adjourn, *Am. a.* recess; 2ung *f* adjournment; *parl.* prorogation.

ver'tauschen *v/t.* (*no* -ge-, h) exchange (*mit* for).

verteidig|en [fer'taɪdɪgən] *v/t.* (*no* -ge-, h) defend; sich ~ defend *o.s.*; 2er *m* (-s/-) defender; ⚥ *fig.* advocate; ⚥ counsel for the defen|ce, *Am.* -se, ⚥ *Am.* attorney for the defendant *or* defense; *football:* fullback; 2ung *f* (-/~-en) defen|ce, *Am.* -se.

Ver'teidigungs|bündnis *n* defensive alliance; ~minister *m* minister of defence; *Brt.* Minister of Defence, *Am.* Secretary of Defense; ~ministerium *n* ministry of defence; *Brt.* Ministry of Defence, *Am.* Department of Defense.

ver'teil|en *v/t.* (*no* -ge-, h) distribute; spread (*colour, etc.*); 2er *m* (-s/-) distributor; 2ung *f* (-/~-en) distribution.

ver'teuern *v/t.* (*no* -ge-, h) raise *or* increase the price of.

ver'tief|en *v/t.* (*no* -ge-, h) deepen (*a. fig.*); sich ~ deepen; sich ~ in (*acc.*) plunge in(to); become absorbed in; 2ung *f* (-/-en) hollow, cavity; recess.

vertikal *adj.* [verti'kaːl] vertical.

ver'tilg|en *v/t.* (*no* -ge-, h) exterminate; F consume, eat (up) (*food*); 2ung *f* (-/~-en) extermination.

ver'tonen ♩ *v/t.* (*no* -ge-, h) set to music.

Vertrag [fer'traːk] *m* (-[e]s/~-e) agreement, contract; *pol.* treaty; 2en [~gən] *v/t.* (*irr.* tragen, *no* -ge-, h) endure, bear, stand; diese Speise kann ich nicht ~ this food does not agree with me; sich ~ things: be compatible *or* consistent; *colours:* harmonize; *p.:* agree; get on with one another; sich wieder ~ be reconciled, make it up; 2lich [~klɪç] 1. *adj.* contractual, stipulated; 2. *adv.* as stipulated; ~ verpflichtet sein be bound by contract; sich ~ verpflichten contract (*zu* for *s.th.*; zu *inf.* to *inf.*).

verträglich *adj.* [fer'trɛːklɪç] sociable.

Ver'trags|bruch *m* breach of contract; 2brüchig *adj.*: ~ werden commit a breach of contract; ~entwurf *m* draft agreement; ~partner *m* party to a contract.

ver'trauen 1. *v/i.* (*no* -ge-, h) trust (*j-m s.o.*); ~ auf (*acc.*) trust *or* confide in; 2. 2 *n* (-s/no *pl.*) confidence, trust; im ~ confidentially, between you and me; ~erweckend *adj.* inspiring confidence; promising.

Ver'trauens|bruch *m* breach *or*

betrayal of trust; ~frage *parl. f*: *die ~ stellen* put the question of confidence; ~mann *m* (-[e]s/~er, *Vertrauensleute*) spokesman; shop-steward; confidential agent; ~sache *f*: *das ist ~* that is a matter of confidence; ~stellung *f* position of trust; 2voll *adj.* trustful, trusting; ~votum *parl. n* vote of confidence; 2würdig *adj.* trustworthy, reliable.

ver'traulich *adj.* confidential, in confidence; intimate, familiar; 2keit *f* (-/-en) confidence; intimacy, familiarity.

ver'traut *adj.* intimate, familiar; 2e (-n/-n) 1. *m* confidant, intimate friend; 2. *f* confidante, intimate friend; 2heit *f* (-/~-en) familiarity.

ver'treib|en *v/t.* (*irr.* treiben, *no* -ge-, *h*) drive away; expel (*aus* from); turn out; † sell, distribute (*goods*); *sich die Zeit ~* pass one's time, kill time; 2ung *f* (-/~-en) expulsion.

ver'tret|en *v/t.* (*irr.* treten, *no* -ge-, *h*) represent (*s.o., firm, etc.*); substitute for *s.o.*; attend to, look after (*s.o.'s interests*); hold (*view*); *parl.* sit for (*borough*); answer for *s.th.*; *j-s Sache ~* †† plead s.o.'s case *or* cause; *sich den Fuß ~* sprain one's foot; F *sich die Beine ~* stretch one's legs; 2er *m* (-s/-) representative; †† *a.* agent; proxy, agent; substitute, deputy; exponent; (sales) representative; door-to-door salesman; commercial travel(l)er, *esp. Am.* travel(l)ing salesman; 2ung *f* (-/-en) representation (*a. pol.*); †† agency; *in office*: substitution; *in ~* by proxy; *gen.*: acting for.

Vertrieb †† [fer'tri:p] *m* (-[e]s/-e) sale; distribution; ~ene [~bənə] *m,f* (-n/-n) expellee.

ver'trocknen *v/i.* (*no* -ge-, *sein*) dry up; ~'trödeln F *v/t.* (*no* -ge-, *h*) dawdle away, waste (*time*); ~'trösten *v/t.* (*no* -ge-, *h*) put off; ~'tuschen F *v/t.* (*no* -ge-, *h*) hush up; ~übeln *v/t.* (*no* -ge-, *h*) take *s.th.* amiss; ~üben *v/t.* (*no* -ge-, *h*) commit, perpetrate.

ver'unglück|en *v/i.* (*no* -ge-, *sein*) meet with *or* have an accident; F *fig.* fail, go wrong; *tödlich ~* be killed in an accident; 2te *m,f* (-n/-n) casualty.

verun|reinigen [fer'unrainigən] *v/t.* (*no* -ge-, *h*) soil, dirty; defile; contaminate (*air*); pollute (*water*); ~stalten [~ʃtaltən] *v/t.* (*no* -ge-, *h*) disfigure.

ver'untreu|en *v/t.* (*no* -ge-, *h*) embezzle; 2ung *f* (-/-en) embezzlement.

ver'ursachen *v/t.* (*no* -ge-, *h*) cause.

ver'urteil|en *v/t.* (*no* -ge-, *h*) condemn (*zu* to) (*a. fig.*), sentence (to);

convict (*wegen of*); 2te *m, f* (-n/-n) convict; 2ung *f* (-/-en) condemnation (*a. fig.*), conviction.

ver|vielfältigen [fer'fi:lfeltigən] *v/t.* (*no* -ge-, *h*) manifold; ~vollkommnen [~'folkomnən] *v/t.* (*no* -ge-, *h*) perfect; *sich ~* perfect *o.s.*

vervollständig|en [fer'folʃtendigən] *v/t.* (*no* -ge-, *h*) complete; 2ung *f* (-/~-en) completion.

ver|'wachsen 1. *v/i.* (*irr.* wachsen, *no* -ge-, *sein*): *miteinander ~* grow together; 2. *adj.* deformed; ♂ humpbacked, hunchbacked; ~'wackeln *phot. v/t.* (*no* -ge-, *h*) blur.

ver'wahr|en *v/t.* (*no* -ge-, *h*) keep; *sich ~ gegen* protest against; ~lost *adj.* [~lo:st] child, garden, *etc.*: uncared-for, neglected; degenerate; 2ung *f* keeping; charge; custody; *fig.* protest; *j-m et. in ~ geben* give s.th. into s.o.'s charge; *in ~ nehmen* take charge of.

verwaist *adj.* [fer'vaist] orphan(ed); *fig.* deserted.

ver'walt|en *v/t.* (*no* -ge-, *h*) administer, manage; 2er *m* (-s/-) administrator, manager; steward (*of estate*); 2ung *f* (-/-en) administration; management.

ver'wand|eln *v/t.* (*no* -ge-, *h*) change, turn, transform; *sich ~* change (*all: in acc.* into); 2lung *f* (-/-en) change; transformation.

verwandt *adj.* [fer'vant] related (*mit* to); *languages, tribes, etc.*: kindred; *languages, sciences*: cognate (with); *pred.* akin (to) (*a. fig.*); 2e *m, f* (-n/-n) relative, relation; 2schaft *f* (-/-en) relationship; relations *pl.*; *geistige ~* congeniality.

ver'warn|en *v/t.* (*no* -ge-, *h*) caution; 2ung *f* caution.

ver'wässern *v/t.* (*no* -ge-, *h*) water (down), dilute; *fig.* water down, dilute.

ver'wechs|eln *v/t.* (*no* -ge-, *h*) mistake (*mit* for); confound, mix up, confuse (*all: mit* with); 2(e)lung *f* (-/-en) mistake; confusion.

verwegen *adj.* [fer've:gən] daring, bold, audacious; 2heit *f* (-/~-en) boldness, audacity, daring.

ver|'wehren *v/t.* (*no* -ge-, *h*): *j-m et. ~* (de)bar s.o. from (doing) s.th.; *den Zutritt ~* deny *or* refuse admittance (*zu* to); ~'weichlicht *adj.* effeminate, soft.

ver'weiger|n *v/t.* (*no* -ge-, *h*) deny, refuse; disobey (*order*); 2ung *f* denial, refusal.

ver'weilen *v/i.* (*no* -ge-, *h*) stay, linger; *bei et. ~* dwell (up)on s.th.

Verweis [fɛr'vais] *m* (-es/-e) reprimand; rebuke, reproof; reference (*auf acc.* to); 2en [~zən] *v/t.* (*irr.* weisen, *no* -ge-, *h*): *j-n des Landes ~* expel s.o. from Germany, *etc.*;

j-m et. ~ reprimand s.o. for s.th.;
j-n ~ *auf (acc.)* or *an (acc.)* refer s.o.
to.

ver'welken *v/i. (no -ge-, sein)* fade,
wither (up).

ver'wend|en *v/t.* ([*irr.* wenden,] *no
-ge-, h)* employ, use; apply *(für
for)*; spend *(time, etc.) (auf acc.
on); sich bei j-m ~ für* intercede
with s.o. for; **2ung** *f (-/⅃-en)* use,
employment; application; *keine ~
haben für* have no use for.

ver'werf|en *v/t. (irr.* werfen, *no
-ge-, h)* reject; *r̄t̄* quash *(verdict)*;
⅃lich *adj.* abominable.

ver'werten *v/t. (no -ge-, h)* turn to
account, utilize.

verwes|en [fɛr'veːzən] *v/i. (no -ge-,
sein)* rot, decay; **2ung** *f (-/⅃-en)*
decay.

ver'wick|eln *v/t. (no -ge-, h)* entan-
gle *(in acc.* in); *sich ~* entangle o.s.
(in) (a. fig.); **⅃elt** *fig. adj.* complicated; **2(e)lung** *f (-/-en)* entanglement; *fig. a.* complication.

ver'wilder|n *v/i. (no -ge-, sein)* run
wild; **⅃t** *adj.* garden, *etc.:* uncultivated, weed-grown; *fig.* wild, unruly.

ver'winden *v/t. (irr.* winden, *no
-ge-, h)* get over s.th.

ver'wirklich|en *v/t. (no -ge-, h)*
realize; *sich ~* be realized, *esp. Am.*
materialize; come true; **2ung** *f
(-/⅃-en)* realization.

ver'wirr|en *v/t. (no -ge-, h)* entan-
gle; *j-n ~* confuse s.o.; embarrass
s.o.; **⅃t** *fig. adj.* confused; embarrassed; **2ung** *fig. f (-/-en)* confusion.

ver'wischen *v/t. (no -ge-, h)* wipe *or*
blot out; efface *(a. fig.);* blur,
obscure; cover up *(one's tracks).*

ver'witter|n *geol. v/i. (no -ge-, sein)*
weather; **⅃t** *adj. geol.* weathered;
weather-beaten *(a. fig.).*

ver'witwet *adj.* widowed.

verwöhn|en [fɛr'vøːnən] *v/t. (no
-ge-, h)* spoil; **⅃t** *adj.* fastidious,
particular.

verworren *adj.* [fɛr'vɔrən] *ideas,
etc.:* confused; *situation, plot:* intricate.

verwund|bar *adj.* [fɛr'vʊntbaːr]
vulnerable *(a. fig.);* **⅃en** [⅃dən] *v/t.
(no -ge-, h)* wound.

ver'wunder|lich *adj.* astonishing;
2ung *f (-/⅃-en)* astonishment.

Ver'wund|ete ⚔ *m (-n/-n)* wounded
(soldier), casualty; **⅃ung** *f (-/-en)*
wound, injury.

ver'wünsch|en *v/t. (no -ge-, h)*
curse; **2ung** *f (-/-en)* curse.

ver'wüst|en *v/t. (no -ge-, h)* lay
waste, devastate, ravage *(a. fig.);*
2ung *f (-/-en)* devastation, ravage.

verzag|en [fɛr'tsaːgən] *v/i. (no -ge-,
h)* despond *(an dat.* of); **⅃t** *adj.* [⅃kt]
despondent; **2theit** [⅃kt-] *f (-/no
pl.)* desponden|ce, -cy.

ver'|zählen *v/refl. (no -ge-, h)*
miscount; **⅃zärteln** [⅃'tsɛːrtəln]
v/t. (no -ge-, h) coddle, pamper;
⅃'zaubern *v/t. (no -ge-, h)* bewitch,
enchant, charm; **⅃'zehren** *v/t. (no
-ge-, h)* consume *(a. fig.).*

ver'zeichn|en *v/t. (no -ge-, h)* note
down; record; list; *fig.* distort; ~
können, zu ~ haben score *(success,
etc.);* **⅃et** *paint. adj.* out of drawing;
2is *n (-ses/-se)* list, catalog(ue);
register; inventory; index *(of book);*
table, schedule.

verzeih|en [fɛr'tsaɪən] *(irr., no -ge-,
h)* 1. *v/i.* pardon, forgive; ~ *Sie!*
I beg your pardon!; excuse me!;
sorry!; 2. *v/t.* pardon, forgive *(j-m
et. s.o. s.th.);* **⅃lich** *adj.* pardonable;
2ung *f (-/no pl.)* pardon; ~! I beg
your pardon!, sorry!

ver'zerr|en *v/t. (no -ge-, h)* distort;
sich ~ become distorted; **2ung** *f*
distortion.

ver'zetteln *v/t. (no -ge-, h)* enter on
cards; *sich ~* fritter away one's
energies.

Verzicht [fɛr'tsɪçt] *m (-[e]s/-e)*
renunciation *(auf acc.* of); **2en** *v/i.
(no -ge-, h)* renounce *(auf et.* s.th.);
do without (s.th.).

verzieh [fɛr'tsiː] *pret. of* verzeihen.

ver'ziehen[1] *(irr.* ziehen, *no -ge-)*
1. *v/i.* (sein) (re)move *(nach* to);
2. *v/t.* (h) spoil *(child);* distort; *das
Gesicht ~* make a wry face, screw
up one's face, grimace; *ohne e-e
Miene zu ~* without betraying the
least emotion; *sich ~ wood:* warp;
crowd, clouds: disperse; *storm,
clouds:* blow over; *F* disappear.

ver'ziehen[2] *p.p. of* verzeihen.

ver'zier|en *v/t. (no -ge-, h)* adorn,
decorate; **2ung** *f (-/-en)* decoration;
ornament.

verzins|en [fɛr'tsɪnzən] *v/t. (no
-ge-, h)* pay interest on; *sich ~* yield
interest; **2ung** *f (-/⅃-en)* interest.

ver'zöger|n *v/t. (no -ge-, h)* delay,
retard; *sich ~* be delayed; **2ung** *f
(-/-en)* delay, retardation.

ver'zollen *v/t. (no -ge-, h)* pay duty
on; *haben Sie et. zu ~?* have you
anything to declare?

verzück|t *adj.* [fɛr'tsʏkt] ecstatic,
enraptured; **2ung** *f (-/⅃-en)*
ecstasy, rapture; *in ~ geraten* go
into ecstasies *(wegen* over).

Ver'zug *m (-[e]s/no pl.)* delay; ✝
default; *in ~ geraten* ✝ come in
default; *im ~ sein* (be in) default.

ver'zweif|eln *v/i. (no -ge-, h, sein)*
despair *(an dat.* of); *es ist zum Verzweifeln* it is enough to drive one
mad; **⅃elt** *adj.* hopeless; desperate;
2lung [⅃luŋ] *f (-/no pl.)* despair;
j-n zur ~ bringen drive s.o. to despair.

verzweig|en [fɛr'tsvaɪgən] *v/refl.
(no -ge-, h)* ramify; *trees:* branch
(out); *road:* branch; *business firm,*

etc.: branch out; Ωung *f* (-/-en) ramification; branching.

verzwickt *adj.* [fɛr'tsvikt] intricate, complicated.

Veteran [vete'rɑːn] *m* (-en/-en) ✖ veteran (*a. fig.*), ex-serviceman.

Veterinär [veteri'nɛːr] *m* (-s/-e) veterinary (surgeon), F vet.

Veto ['veːto] *n* (-s/-s) veto; *ein* ~ *einlegen gegen* put a veto on, veto *s.th.*

Vetter ['fɛtɐr] *m* (-s/-n) cousin; '~nwirtschaft *f* (-/*no pl.*) nepotism.

vibrieren [vi'briːrən] *v/i.* (*no* -ge-, *h*) vibrate.

Vieh [fiː] *n* (-[e]s/*no pl.*) livestock, cattle; animal, brute, beast; F *fig.* brute, beast; '~bestand *m* livestock; '~händler *m* cattle-dealer; '~hof *m* stockyard; Ωisch *adj.* bestial, beastly, brutal; '~wagen 🚃 *m* stock-car; '~weide *f* pasture; '~zucht *f* stock-farming, cattle-breeding; '~züchter *m* stock-breeder, stock-farmer, cattle-breeder, *Am. a.* rancher.

viel [fiːl] **1.** *adj.* much; ~e *pl.* many; a lot (of), lots of; plenty of (*cake, money, room, time, etc.*); *so* ~e *Geld* all that money; *seine* ~en *Geschäfte pl.* his numerous affairs *pl.*; *sehr* ~e *pl.* a great many *pl.*; *ziemlich* ~ a good deal of; *ziemlich* ~e *pl.* a good many *pl.*; ~ *zuviel* far too much; *sehr* ~ a great *or* good deal; **2.** *adv.* much; ~ *besser* much *or* a good deal *or* a lot better; *et.* ~ *lieber tun* prefer to do *s.th.*

viel|beschäftigt *adj.* ['fiːlbəʃɛftiçt] very busy; '~deutig *adj.* ambiguous; ~erlei *adj.* ['~ɐrlaɪ] of many kinds, many kinds of; multifarious; ~fach ['~fax] **1.** *adj.* multiple; **2.** *adv.* in many cases, frequently; ~fältig *adj.* ['~fɛltiç] multiple, manifold, multifarious; '~leicht *adv.* perhaps, maybe; ~mals *adv.* ['~mɑːls]: *ich danke Ihnen* ~ many thanks, thank you very much; *sie läßt (dich)* ~ *grüßen* she sends you her kind regards; *ich bitte* ~ *um Entschuldigung* I am very sorry, I do beg your pardon; ~'mehr *cj.* rather; '~sagend *adj.* significant, suggestive; ~seitig *adj.* ['~zaɪtiç] many-sided, versatile; '~versprechend *adj.* (very) promising.

vier *adj.* [fiːr] four; *zu* ~t four of us *or* them; *auf allen* ~en on all fours; *unter* ~ *Augen* confidentially, privately; *um halb* ~ at half past three; '~beinig *adj.* four-legged; '~eck *n* square, quadrangle; '~eckig *adj.* square, quadrangular; ~erlei *adj.* ['~ɐrlaɪ] of four different kinds, four kinds of; ~fach *adj.* ['~fax] fourfold; ~e *Ausfertigung* four copies; Ωfüßer *zo.* ['~fyːsɐr] *m* (-s/-) quadruped; ~füßig *adj.* ['~fyːsiç]

four-footed; *zo.* quadruped; Ωfüßler *zo.* ['~fyːslɐr] *m* (-s/-) quadruped; ~händig *♪ adv.* ['~hɛndiç]: ~ *spielen* play a duet; ~jährig *adj.* ['~jɛːriç] four-year-old, of four; Ωlinge ['~liŋə] *m/pl.* quadruplets *pl.*, F quads *pl.*; '~mal *adv.* four times; ~schrötig *adj.* ['~ʃrøːtiç] square-built, thickset; ~seitig *adj.* ['~zaɪtiç] four-sided; ₳ quadrilateral; 'Ωsitzer *esp. mot. m* (-s/-) four-seater; ~stöckig *adj.* ['~ʃtœkiç] four-storeyed, four-storied; 'Ωtaktmotor *mot. m* four-stroke engine; '~te *adj.* fourth; '~teilen *v/t.* (ge-, *h*) quarter.

Viertel ['firtəl] *n* (-s/-) fourth (part); quarter; ~ *fünf, (ein)* ~ *nach vier* a quarter past four; *drei* ~ *vier* a quarter to four; '~jahr *n* three months *pl.*, quarter (of a year); 'Ωjährlich, Ω'jährlich **1.** *adj.* quarterly; **2.** *adv.* every three months, quarterly; '~note *♪ f* crotchet, *Am. a.* quarter note; '~pfund *n*, ~'pfund *n* quarter of a pound; '~stunde *f* quarter of an hour, *Am.* quarter hour.

vier|tens *adv.* ['firtəns] fourthly; Ω'vierteltakt *♪ m* common time.

vierzehn *adj.* ['firtseːn] fourteen; ~ *Tage pl.* a fortnight, *Am.* two weeks *pl.*; '~te *adj.* fourteenth.

vierzig *adj.* ['firtsiç] forty; '~ste *adj.* fortieth.

Vikar *eccl.* [vi'kɑːr] *m* (-s/-e) curate; vicar.

Villa ['vila] *f* (-/Villen) villa.

violett *adj.* [vio'lɛt] violet.

Violine *♪* [vio'liːnə] *f* (-/-n) violin.

Viper *zo.* ['viːpɐr] *f* (-/-n) viper.

virtuos *adj.* [virtu'oːs] masterly; Ωe [~zə] *m* (-n/-n), Ωin [~zin] *f* (-/-nen) virtuoso; Ωität [~ozi'tɛːt] *f* (-/*no pl.*) virtuosity.

Virus 🧬 ['viːrus] *n, m* (-/Viren) virus.

Vision [vi'zjoːn] *f* (-/-en) vision.

Visitation [vizita'tsjoːn] *f* (-/-en) search; inspection.

Visite 🧬 [vi'ziːtə] *f* (-/-n) visit; ~nkarte *f* visiting-card, *Am.* calling card.

Visum ['viːzum] *n* (-s/Visa, Visen) visa, visé.

Vitalität [vitali'tɛːt] *f* (-/*no pl.*) vitality. [min.]

Vitamin [vita'miːn] *n* (-s/-e) vita-

Vize|kanzler ['fiːtsə-] *m* vice-chancellor; '~könig *m* viceroy; '~konsul *m* vice-consul; '~präsident *m* vice-president.

Vogel ['foːgəl] *m* (-s/=) bird; F *e-n* ~ *haben* have a bee in one's bonnet, *sl.* have bats in the belfry; *den* ~ *abschießen* carry off the prize, *Am. sl.* take the cake; '~bauer *n, m* (-s/-) bird-cage; '~flinte *f* fowling-piece; 'Ωfrei *adj.* outlawed; '~futter *n* food for birds, bird-seed; '~kunde f (-/no pl.) ornithology; '**~liebhaber** m bird-fancier; '**~nest** n bird's nest, bird-nest; '**~perspektive** f (-/no pl.), '**~schau** f (-/no pl.) bird's-eye view; '**~scheuche** f (-/-n) scarecrow (a. fig.); ~'**StraußPolitik** f ostrich policy; ~ betreiben hide one's head in the sand (like an ostrich); '**~warte** f ornithological station; '**~zug** m passage or migration of birds.

Vokab|el [vo'ka:bəl] f (-/-n) word; **~ular** [~abu'la:r] n (-s/-e) vocabulary.

Vokal ling. [vo'ka:l] m (-s/-e) vowel.

Volk [fɔlk] n 1. (-[e]s/ᵘer) people; nation; swarm (of bees); covey (of partridges); 2. (-[e]s/no pl.) populace, the common people; contp. the common or vulgar herd; der Mann aus dem ~e the man in the street or Am. on the street.

Völker|bund ['fœlkər-] m (-[e]s/no pl.) League of Nations; '**~kunde** f (-/no pl.) ethnology; '**~recht** n (-[e]s/no pl.) international law, law of nations; '**~wanderung** f age of national migrations.

'**Volks|abstimmung** pol. f plebiscite; '**~ausgabe** f popular edition (of book); '**~bücherei** f free or public library; '**~charakter** m national character; '**~dichter** m popular or national poet; '**~entscheid** pol. ['~ɛntʃaɪt] m (-[e]s/-e) referendum; plebiscite; '**~fest** n fun fair, amusement park or grounds pl.; public merry-making; national festival; '**~gunst** f popularity; '**~herrschaft** f democracy; '**~hochschule** f adult education (courses pl.); '**~lied** n folk-song; '**~menge** f crowd (of people), multitude; '**~partei** f people's party; '**~republik** f people's republic; '**~schule** f elementary or primary school, Am. a. grade school; '**~schullehrer** m elementary or primary teacher, Am. grade teacher; '**~sprache** f vernacular; '**~stamm** m tribe, race; '**~stück** thea. n folk-play; '**~tanz** m folk-dance; '**~tracht** f national costume; **≈tümlich** adj. ['~ty:mliç] national; popular; '**~versammlung** f public meeting; '**~vertreter** parl. m deputy, representative; member of parliament, Brt. Member of Parliament, Am. Representative; '**~vertretung** parl. f representation of the people; parliament; '**~wirt** m (political) economist; '**~wirtschaft** f economics, political economy; **~wirtschaftler** ['~tlər] m (-s/-) s. Volkswirt; '**~zählung** f census.

voll [fɔl] 1. adj. full; filled; whole, complete, entire; figure, face: full, round; figure: buxom; ~er Knospen full of buds; aus ~em Halse at the top of one's voice; aus ~em Herzen from the bottom of one's heart; in ~er Blüte in full blossom; in ~er Fahrt at full speed; mit ~en Händen lavishly, liberally; mit ~em Recht with perfect right; um das Unglück ~zumachen to make things worse; 2. adv. fully, in full; ~ und ganz fully, entirely; j-n nicht für ~ ansehen or nehmen have a ~ poor opinion of s.o., think little of s.o.

'**voll|auf** adv., ~'**auf** adv. abundantly, amply, F plenty; '**~automatisch** adj. fully automatic; '**≈bad** n bath; '**≈bart** m beard; '**≈beschäftigung** f full employment; '**≈besitz** m full possession; '**≈blut(pferd)** zo. n thoroughbred (horse); '**~bringen** v/t. (irr. bringen, no -ge-, h) accomplish, achieve; perform; '**≈dampf** m full steam; F: mit ~ at or in full blast; '**~enden** v/t. (no -ge-, h) finish, complete; '**~endet** adj. perfect; **~ends** adv. ['~ɛnts] entirely, wholly, altogether; ≈'**endung** f (-/ᵏ-en) finishing, completion; fig. perfection.

Völlerei [fœlə'raɪ] f (-/ᵏ-en) gluttony.

voll|führen v/t. (no -ge-, h) execute, carry out; '**~füllen** v/t. (sep., -ge-, h) fill (up); '**≈gas** mot. n: ~ geben open the throttle; mit ~ with the throttle full open; at full speed; '**~gepfropft** adj. ['~gəpfrɔpft] crammed, packed; '**~gießen** v/t. (irr. gießen, sep., -ge-, h) fill (up); '**≈gummi** n, m solid rubber.

völlig adj. ['fœliç] entire, complete; silence, calm, etc.: dead.

voll|jährig adj. ['fɔljɛːriç]: ~ sein be of age; ~ werden come of age; '**≈jährigkeit** f (-/no pl.) majority; '**~kommen** adj. perfect; ≈'**kommenheit** f (-/ᵏ-en) perfection; '**≈kornbrot** n whole-meal bread; '**~machen** v/t. (sep., -ge-, h) fill (up); F soil, dirty; um das Unglück vollzumachen to make things worse; '**≈macht** f (-/-en) full power, authority; ᵗᵗ power of attorney; ~ haben be authorized; '**≈matrose** ⚓ m able-bodied seaman; '**≈milch** f whole milk; '**≈mond** m full moon; '**~packen** v/t. (sep., -ge-, h) stuff, cram; '**~schenken** v/t. (sep., -ge-, h) full board; '**~schenken** v/t. (sep., -ge-, h) fill (up); '**~schlank** adj. stout, corpulent; '**~ständig** adj. complete; '**~stopfen** v/t. (sep., -ge-, h) stuff, cram; sich ~ stuff o.s.; sich die Taschen ~ stuff one's pockets; '**~strecken** v/t. (no -ge-, h) execute; ≈'**streckung** f (-/-en) execution; '**~tönend** adj. sonorous, rich; '**≈treffer** m direct hit; '**≈versammlung** f plenary meeting or assembly; General Assembly (of the United Nations); '**~wertig** adj. equivalent,

equal in value; full; '.zählig adj.
complete; ziehen v/t. (irr. ziehen,
no -ge-, h) execute; consummate
(marriage); sich ~ take place;
Q'ziehung f (-/~ -en), Qzug m
(-[e]s/no pl.) execution.
Volontär[volɔn'tɛ:r]m(-s/-e) unpaid
assistant.
Volt £ [vɔlt] n (-, -[e]s/-) volt.
Volumen [vo'lu:mən] n (-s/-, Vo-
lumina) volume.
vom prp. [fɔm] = von dem
von prp. (dat.) [fɔn] space, time:
from; instead of gen.: of; passive:
by; ~ Hamburg from Hamburg;
~ nun an from now on; ~ morgen an
from tomorrow (on), beginning
tomorrow; ein Freund ~ mir a
friend of mine; die Einrichtung ~
Schulen the erection of schools; ~
dem or vom Apfel essen eat (some)
of the apple; der Herzog ~ Edinburgh the Duke of Edinburgh; ein
Gedicht ~ Schiller a poem by
Schiller; ~ selbst by itself; ~ selbst,
~ sich aus by oneself; ~ drei Meter
Länge three metres long; ein Betrag
~ 300 Mark a sum of 300 marks;
e-e Stadt ~ 10 000 Einwohnern a
town of 10,000 inhabitants; reden ~
talk of or about s.th.; speak on
(scientific subject); ~ mir aus as far
as I am concerned; I don't mind,
for all I care; das ist nett ~ ihm that
is nice of him; ich habe ~ ihm gehört I have heard of him; ~statten
adv. [~'ʃtatən]: gut ~ gehen go well.
vor prp. (dat.; acc.) [fo:r] space: in
front of, before; time: before; ~
langer Zeit a long time ago; ~ einigen Tagen a few days ago; (heute) ~
acht Tagen a week ago (today); am
Tage ~ (on) the day before, on the
eve of; 5 Minuten ~ 12 five minutes
to twelve, Am. five minutes of
twelve; fig. at the eleventh hour;
~ der Tür stehen be imminent,
be close at hand; ~ e-m Hintergrund
against a background; ~ Zeugen in
the presence of witnesses; ~ allen
Dingen above all; (dicht) ~ dem
Untergang stehen be on the brink
or verge of ruin; ~ Hunger sterben
die of hunger; ~ Kälte zittern
tremble with cold; schützen (verstecken) ~ protect (hide) from or
against; ~ sich gehen take place, pass
off; ~ sich hin lächeln smile to o.s.;
sich fürchten ~ be afraid of, fear.
Vor|abend['fo:rʔ-]m eve; '~ahnung
f presentiment, foreboding.
voran adv. [fo'ran] at the head (dat.
of), in front (of), before; Kopf ~
head first; ~gehen v/i. (irr. gehen,
sep., -ge-, sein) lead the way;
precede; ~kommen v/i. (irr. kommen, sep., -ge-, sein) make progress; fig. get on (in life).
Voran|schlag ['fo:rʔan-] m (rough)

estimate; '~zeige f advance notice;
film: trailer.
vorarbeite|n ['fo:rʔ-] v/t. and v/i.
(sep., -ge-, h) work in advance;
'Qr m foreman.
voraus adv. [fo'raus] in front (dat.
of), ahead (of); im ~ in advance,
beforehand; ~bestellen v/t. (sep.,
no -ge-, h) s. vorbestellen; ~bezah-
len v/t. (sep., no -ge-, h) pay in
advance, prepay; ~gehen v/i. (irr.
gehen, sep., -ge-, sein) go on before;
s. vorangehen; Qsage f prediction;
prophecy; forecast (of weather);
~sagen v/t. (sep., -ge-, h) foretell,
predict; prophesy; forecast (weather,
etc.); ~schicken v/t. (sep., -ge-, h)
send on in advance; fig. mention
beforehand, premise; ~sehen v/t.
(irr. sehen, sep., -ge-, h) foresee;
~setzen v/t. (sep., -ge-, h) (pre)sup-
pose, presume, assume; vorausgesetzt, daß provided that; Qsetzung
f (-/-en) (pre)supposition, assump-
tion; prerequisite; Qsicht f fore-
sight; aller ~ nach in all probability,
~sichtlich adj. presumable, prob-
able, likely; Qzahlung f advance
payment or instal(l)ment.
'Vor|bedacht 1. m (-[e]s/no pl.): mit
~ deliberately, on purpose; 2. Q adj.
premeditated; '~bedeutung f foreboding, omen, portent; '~bedin-
gung f prerequisite.
Vorbehalt ['fo:rbəhalt] m (-[e]s/-e)
reservation, reserve; Qen 1. v/t.
(irr. halten, sep., no -ge-, h): sich
~ reserve (right, etc.); 2. adj.: Än-
derungen ~ subject to change (without notice); 'Qlos adj. unreserved,
unconditional.
vorbei adv. [for'bai] space: along,
by, past (all: an dat. s.o., s.th.); time:
over, gone; 3 Uhr ~ past three
(o'clock); ~fahren v/i. (irr. fahren,
sep., -ge-, sein) drive past; ~gehen
v/i. (irr. gehen, sep., -ge-, sein) pass,
go by; pain: pass (off); storm:
blow over; ~ an (dat.) pass; im
Vorbeigehen in passing; ~kommen
v/i. (irr. kommen, sep., -ge-, sein)
pass by; F drop in; F ~ an (dat.)
get past (obstacle, etc.); ~lassen v/t.
(irr. lassen, sep., -ge-, h) let
pass.
'Vorbemerkung f preliminary remark or note.
'vorbereit|en v/t. (sep., no -ge-, h)
prepare (für, auf acc. for); 'Qung f
preparation (für, auf acc. for).
'Vorbesprechung f preliminary discussion or talk.
'vor|bestellen v/t. (sep., no -ge-, h)
order in advance; book (room, etc.);
'~bestraft adj. previously con-
victed.
'vorbeug|en (sep., -ge-, h) 1. v/i.
prevent (e-r Sache s.th.); 2. v/t.
and v/refl. bend forward; '~end

adj. preventive; ❊ *a.* prophylactic; '♀ung *f* prevention.

'**Vorbild** *n* model; pattern; example; prototype; '♀lich *adj.* exemplary; ⁓ung ['⁓duŋ] *f* preparatory training.

vor|bringen *v/t.* (*irr.* bringen, *sep.*, -ge-, h) bring forward, produce; advance (*opinion*); ⁜⁜ prefer (*charge*); utter, say, state; '⁓datieren *v/t.* (*sep.*, no -ge-, h) post-date.

vorder *adj.* ['fɔrdər] front, fore.

'**Vorder|achse** *f* front axle; '⁓ansicht *f* front view; '⁓bein *n* foreleg; '⁓fuß *m* forefoot; '⁓grund *m* foreground (*a. fig.*); '⁓haus *n* front building; '⁓mann *m* man in front (*of s.o.*); '⁓rad *n* front wheel; ⁓radantrieb *mot.* ['fɔrdərra:t'-] *m* front-wheel drive; '⁓seite *f* front (side); obverse (*of coin*); '⁓sitz *m* front seat; '♀st *adj.* foremost; '⁓teil *n, m* front (part); '⁓tür *f* front door; '⁓zahn *m* front tooth; '⁓zimmer *n* front room.

'**vordrängen** *v/refl.* (*sep.*, -ge-, h) press *or* push forward.

vordring|en *v/i.* (*irr.* dringen, *sep.*, -ge-, sein) advance; '⁓lich *adj.* urgent.   [blank.]

'**Vordruck** *m* (-[e]s/-e) form, *Am. a.*

voreilig *adj.* ['fo:r?-] hasty, rash, precipitate; ⁓e Schlüsse ziehen jump to conclusions.

voreingenommen *adj.* ['fo:r?-] prejudiced, bias(s)ed; '♀heit *f* (-/no *pl.*) prejudice, bias.

vor|enthalten ['fo:r?-] *v/t.* (*irr.* halten, *sep.*, no -ge-, h) keep back, withhold (*j-m et.* s.th. from s.o.); ♀entscheidung ['fo:r?-] *f* preliminary decision; ⁓erst *adv.* ['fo:r?-] for the present, for the time being.

Vorfahr ['fo:rfa:r] *m* (-en/-en) ancestor.

'**vorfahr|en** *v/i.* (*irr.* fahren, *sep.*, -ge-, sein) drive up; pass; *den Wagen* ⁓ *lassen* order the car; '♀t(srecht *n*) *f* right of way, priority.

'**Vorfall** *m* incident, occurrence, event; '♀en *v/i.* (*irr.* fallen, *sep.*, -ge-, sein) happen, occur.

'**vorfinden** *v/t.* (*irr.* finden, *sep.*, -ge-, h) find.

'**Vorfreude** *f* anticipated joy.

'**vorführ|en** *v/t.* (*sep.*, -ge-, h) bring forward, produce; bring (*dat.* before); show, display, exhibit; demonstrate (*use of s.th.*); show, present (*film*); '♀er *m* projectionist (*in cinema theatre*); '♀ung *f* presentation, showing; ⊕ demonstration; ⁜⁜ production (*of prisoner*); *thea.*, *film:* performance.

'**Vor|gabe** *f* *sports:* handicap; *athletics:* stagger; *golf, etc.*: odds *pl.*; '⁓gang *m* incident, occurrence, event; facts *pl.*; file, record(s *pl.*); *biol.*, ⊕ process; ⁓gänger ['⁓gɛŋər]

m (-s/-), '⁓gängerin *f* (-/-nen) predecessor; '⁓garten *m* front garden.

'**vorgeben** *v/t.* (*irr.* geben, *sep.*, -ge-, h) *sports:* give (*j-m s.o.*); *fig.* pretend, allege.

'**Vor|gebirge** *n* promontory, cape, headland; foot-hills *pl.*; '⁓gefühl *n* presentiment, foreboding.

'**vorgehen 1.** *v/i.* (*irr.* gehen, *sep.*, -ge-, sein) ✗ advance; F lead the way; go on before; *watch, clock:* be fast, gain (*fünf Minuten* five minutes); take precedence (*dat.* of, over), be more important (than); take action, act; proceed (*a.* ⁜⁜ gegen against); go on, happen, take place; **2.** ♀ *n* (-s/no *pl.*) action, proceeding.

'**Vor|geschmack** *m* (-[e]s/no *pl.*) foretaste; ⁓gesetzte ['⁓gəzɛtstə] *m* (-n/-n) superior; *esp. Am.* F boss; ♀gestern *adv.* the day before yesterday; '♀greifen *v/i.* (*irr.* greifen, *sep.*, -ge-, h) anticipate (*j-m or e-r* Sache s.o. *or* s.th.).

'**vorhaben 1.** *v/t.* (*irr.* haben, *sep.*, -ge-, h) intend, mean; be going to do *s.th.*; *nichts* ⁓ be at a loose end; *haben Sie heute abend et. vor?* have you anything on tonight?; *was hat er jetzt wieder vor?* what is he up to now?; *was hast du mit ihm vor?* what are you going to do with him?; **2.** ♀ *n* (-s/-) intention, purpose, ⁜⁜ intent; plan; project.

'**Vorhalle** *f* vestibule, (entrance-)hall; lobby; porch.

'**vorhalt|en** (*irr.* halten, *sep.*, -ge-, h) **1.** *v/t.*: *j-m et.* ⁓ hold s.th. before s.o.; *fig.* reproach s.o. with s.th.; **2.** *v/i.* last; '♀ung *f* remonstrance; *j-m* ⁓en machen remonstrate with s.o. (*wegen* on).

vorhanden *adj.* [for'handən] at hand, present; available (*a.* ✝); ✝ on hand, in stock; ⁓ *sein* exist; ♀sein *n* presence, existence.

'**Vor|hang** *m* curtain; '⁓hängeschloß *n* padlock.

'**vorher** *adv.* before, previously; in advance, beforehand.

vor'her|bestellen *v/t.* (*sep.*, no -ge-, h) *s.* vorbestellen; ⁓bestimmen *v/t.* (*sep.*, no -ge-, h) determine beforehand, predetermine; ⁓gehen *v/i.* (*irr.* gehen, *sep.*, -ge-, sein) precede; ⁓ig *adj.* preceding, previous.

'**Vorherr|schaft** *f* predominance; '♀schen *v/i.* (*sep.*, -ge-, h) predominate, prevail; '♀schend *adj.* predominant, prevailing.

Vor'her|sage *f s.* Voraussage; ♀sagen *v/t.* (*sep.*, -ge-, h) *s.* voraussagen; ♀sehen *v/t.* (*irr.* sehen, *sep.*, -ge-, h) foresee; ♀wissen *v/t.* (*irr.* wissen, *sep.*, -ge-, h) know beforehand, foreknow.

'vor|hin adv., ~'hin adv. a short while ago, just now.
'Vor|hof m outer court, forecourt; anat. auricle (of heart); '~hut ⚔ f vanguard.
'vor|ig adj. last; ~jährig adj. ['~jɛːrɪç] of last year, last year's.
'Vor|kämpfer m champion, pioneer; '~kehrung f (-/-en) precaution; ~en treffen take precautions; '~kenntnisse f/pl. preliminary or basic knowledge (in dat. of); mit guten ~n in (dat.) well grounded in.
'vorkommen 1. v/i. (irr. kommen, sep., -ge-, sein) be found; occur, happen; es kommt mir vor it seems to me; 2. ⒉ n (-s/-) occurrence.
'Vor|kommnis n (-ses/-se) occurrence; event; '~kriegszeit f prewar times pl.
'vorlad|en ⚖ v/t. (irr. laden, sep., -ge-, h) summon; '⒉ung ⚖ f summons.
'Vorlage f copy; pattern; parl. bill; presentation; production (of document); football: pass.
'vorlassen v/t. (irr. lassen, sep., -ge-, h) let s.o. pass, allow s.o. to pass; admit.
'Vorläuf|er m, '~erin f (-/-nen) forerunner; '⒉ig 1. adj. provisional, temporary; 2. adv. provisionally, temporarily; for the present, for the time being.
'vorlaut adj. forward, pert.
'Vorleben n past (life),antecedents pl.
'vorlege|n v/t. (sep., -ge-, h) put (lock) on; produce (document); submit (plans, etc. for discussion, etc.); propose (plan, etc.); present (bill, etc.); j-m et. ~ lay or place or put s.th. before s.o.; show s.o. s.th.; at table: help s.o. to s.th.; j-m e-e Frage ~ put a question to s.o.; sich ~ lean forward; '⒉r m (-s/-) rug.
'vorles|en v/t. (irr. lesen, sep., -ge-, h) read aloud; j-m et. ~ read (out) s.th. to s.o.; '⒉ung f lecture (über acc. on; vor dat. to); e-e ~ halten (give) a lecture.
'vorletzt adj. last but one; ~e Nacht the night before last.
'Vorlieb|e f (-/no pl.) predilection, preference; ⒉nehmen [~'li:p-] v/i. (irr. nehmen, sep., -ge-, h) be satisfied (mit with); ~ mit dem, was da ist at meals: take pot luck.
'vorliegen v/i. (irr. liegen, sep., -ge-, h) lie before s.o.; be there, exist; da muß ein Irrtum ~ there must be a mistake; was liegt gegen ihn vor? what is the charge against him?; '~d adj. present, in question.
'vor|lügen v/t. (irr. lügen, sep., -ge-, h): j-m et. ~ tell s.o. a lie; '~machen v/t. (sep., -ge-, h): j-m et. ~ show s.o. how to do s.th.; fig. impose upon s.o.; sich (selbst) et. ~ fool o.s.

'Vormacht f (-/⚔ ~e), '~stellung f predominance; supremacy; hegemony.
'Vormarsch ⚔ m advance.
'vormerken v/t. (sep., -ge-, h) note down, make a note of; reserve; sich ~ lassen für put one's name down for.
'Vormittag m morning, forenoon; '⒉s adv. in the morning.
'Vormund m (-[e]s/-e, ~er) guardian; '~schaft f (-/-en) guardianship.
vorn adv. [fɔrn] in front; nach ~ forward; von ~ from the front; ich sah sie von ~ I saw her face; von ~ anfangen begin at the beginning; noch einmal von ~ anfangen begin anew, make a new start.
'Vorname m Christian name, first name, Am. a. given name.
vornehm ['foːrneːm] 1. adj. of (superior) rank, distinguished; aristocratic; noble; fashioanble; ~e Gesinnung high character; 2. adv.: ~ tun give o.s. airs; '~en v/t. (irr. nehmen, sep., -ge-, h) take s.th. in hand; deal with; make (changes, etc.); take up (book); F sich j-n ~ take s.o. to task (wegen for, about); sich ~ resolve (up)on s.th.; resolve (zu inf. to inf.), make up one's mind (to inf.); sich vorgenommen haben a. be determined (zu inf. to inf.); '⒉heit f (-/no pl.) refinement; elegance; high-mindedness.
'vorn|herein adv., ~he'rein adv.: von ~ from the first or start or beginning.
Vorort ['foːr⁹-] m (-[e]s/-e) suburb; '~(s)verkehr m suburban traffic; '~(s)zug m local (train).
'Vor|posten m outpost (a. ⚔); '~rang m (-[e]s/no pl.) precedence (vor dat. of, over), priority (over); '~rat m store, stock (an dat. of); Vorräte pl. a. provisions pl., supplies pl.; ⒉rätig adj. ['~rɛːtɪç] available; ✝ a. on hand, in stock; '⒉rechnen v/t. (sep., -ge-, h) reckon up (j-m to s.o.); '~recht n privilege; '~rede f preface, introduction; '~redner m previous speaker; '~richtung ⊕ f contrivance, device; '⒉rücken (sep., -ge-) 1. v/t. (h) move (chair, etc.) forward; 2. v/i. (sein) advance; '~runde f sports: preliminary round; '⒉sagen v/i. (sep., -ge-, h): j-m ~ prompt s.o.; '~saison f off or dead season; '~satz m intention, purpose, design; ⒉sätzlich adj. ['~zɛtslɪç] intentional, deliberate; ~er Mord ⚖ wil(l)ful murder; '~schein m: zum ~ bringen bring forward, produce; zum ~ kommen appear, turn up; '⒉schieben v/t. (irr. schieben, sep., -ge-, h) push s.th. forward; slip (bolt); s. vorschützen; '⒉schießen

v/t. (*irr.* schießen, *sep.,* -ge-, *h*) advance (*money*).

'**Vorschlag** *m* proposition, proposal; suggestion; offer; ℒen ['∼gǝn] *v/t.* (*irr.* schlagen, *sep.,* -ge-, *h*) propose; suggest; offer.

'**Vor|schlußrunde** *f sports:* semifinal; 'ℒschnell *adj.* hasty, rash; 'ℒschreiben *v/t.* (*irr.* schreiben, *sep.,* -ge-, *h*): j-m et. ∼ write s.th. out for s.o.; *fig.* prescribe.

'**Vorschrift** *f* direction, instruction; prescription (*esp.* ✴); order (*a.* ✴); regulation(s *pl.*); 'ℒmäßig *adj.* according to regulations; ∼e Kleidung regulation dress; 'ℒswidrig *adj. and adv.* contrary to regulations.

'**Vor|schub** *m:* ∼ leisten (*dat.*) countenance (*fraud, etc.*); further, encourage; ⚖ aid and abet; '∼schule *f* preparatory school; '∼schuß *m* advance; *for barrister:* retaining fee, retainer; 'ℒschützen *v/t.* (*sep.,* -ge-, *h*) pretend, plead (*sickness, etc. as excuse*); 'ℒschweben *v/i.* (*sep.,* -ge-, *h*): mir schwebt et. vor I have s.th. in mind.

'**vorseh|en** *v/t.* (*irr.* sehen, *sep.,* -ge-, *h*) plan; design; ⚖ provide; sich ∼ take care, be careful; sich ∼ vor (*dat.*) guard against; 'ℒung *f* (-/∼ -en) providence.

'**vorsetzen** *v/t.* (*sep.,* -ge-, *h*) put forward; place *or* put *or* set before, offer.

'**Vorsicht** *f* caution; care; ∼! caution!, danger!; look out!, be careful!; ∼, Glas! Glass, with care!; ∼, Stufe! mind the step!; 'ℒig *adj.* cautious; careful; ∼! F steady!

'**vorsichts|halber** *adv.* as a precaution; 'ℒmaßnahme *f,* 'ℒmaßregel *f* precaution(ary measure); ∼n treffen take precautions.

'**Vorsilbe** *gr. f* prefix.

'**vorsingen** *v/t.* (*irr.* singen, *sep.,* -ge-, *h*): j-m et. ∼ sing s.th. to s.o.

'**Vorsitz** *m* (-es/*no pl.*) chair, presidency; den ∼ führen *or* haben be in the chair, preside (*bei* over; at); den ∼ übernehmen take the chair; ∼ende ['∼ǝndǝ] (-n/-n) 1. *m* chairman, president; 2. *f* chairwoman.

'**Vorsorg|e** *f* (-/*no pl.*) provision, providence; precaution; ∼ treffen make provision; 'ℒen *v/i.* (*sep.,* -ge-, *h*) provide; 'ℒlich ['∼kliç] 1. *adj.* precautionary; 2. *adv.* as a precaution.

'**Vorspeise** *f* appetizer, hors d'œuvre.

'**vorspieg|eln** *v/t.* (*sep.,* -ge-, *h*) pretend; j-m et. ∼ delude s.o. (with false hopes, *etc.*); 'ℒ(e)lung *f* preten|ce, *Am.* -se.

'**Vorspiel** *n* prelude; 'ℒen *v/t.* (*sep.,* -ge-, *h*): j-m et. ∼ play s.th. to s.o.

'**vor|sprechen** (*irr.* sprechen, *sep.,* -ge-, *h*) 1. *v/t.* pronounce (j-m et.

s.th. to *or* for s.o.); 2. *v/i.* call (*bei* on *s.o.*; at *an office*); *thea.* audition; '∼springen *v/i.* (*irr.* springen, *sep.,* -ge-, *sein*) jump forward; project; 'ℒsprung *m* △ projection; *sports:* lead; *fig.* start, advantage (vor *dat.* of); 'ℒstadt *f* suburb; '∼städtisch *adj.* suburban; 'ℒstand *m* board of directors, managing directors *pl.*

'**vorsteh|en** *v/i.* (*irr.* stehen, *sep.,* -ge-, *h*) project, protrude; *fig.:* direct; manage (*both:* e-r Sache s.th.); 'ℒer *m* director, manager; head, chief.

'**vorstell|en** *v/t.* (*sep.,* -ge-, *h*) put forward; put (*clock*) on; introduce (j-n j-m s.o. to s.o.); mean, stand for; represent; sich ∼ bei have an interview with; sich et. ∼ imagine *or* fancy s.th.; 'ℒung *f* introduction, presentation; interview (*of applicant for post*); *thea.* performance; *fig.:* remonstrance; idea, conception; imagination; 'ℒungsvermögen *n* imagination.

'**Vor|stoß** ✗ *m* thrust, advance; '∼strafe *f* previous conviction; 'ℒstrecken *v/t.* (*sep.,* -ge-, *h*) thrust out, stretch forward; advance (*money*); '∼stufe *f* first step *or* stage; 'ℒtäuschen *v/t.* (*sep.,* -ge-, *h*) feign, pretend.

Vorteil ['fɔrtaıl] *m* advantage (*a. sports*); profit; *tennis:* (ad)vantage; 'ℒhaft *adj.* advantageous (für to), profitable (to).

Vortrag ['fo:rtra:k] *m* (-[e]s/∼e) performance; execution (*esp.* ♪); recitation (*of poem*); ♪ recital; lecture; report; ✝ balance carried forward; e-n ∼ halten (give a) lecture (über *acc.* on); ℒen ['∼gǝn] *v/t.* (*irr.* tragen *sep.,* -ge-, *h*) ✝ carry forward; report on; recite (*poem*), perform, *esp.* ♪ execute; lecture on; state, express (*opinion*); ∼ende ['∼gǝndǝ] *m* (-n/-n) performer; lecturer; speaker.

vor|trefflich *adj.* [fo:r'trɛfliç] excellent; '∼treten *v/i.* (*irr.* treten, *sep.,* -ge-, *sein*) step forward; *fig.* project, protrude, stick out; 'ℒtritt *m* (-[e]s/*no pl.*) precedence.

vorüber *adv.* [fo:'ry:bǝr] *space:* by, past; *time:* gone by, over; ∼gehen *v/i.* (*irr.* gehen, *sep.,* -ge-, sein) pass, go by; ∼gehend *adj.* passing, temporary; ℒgehende [∼dǝ] *m* (-n/-n) passer-by; ∼ziehen *v/i.* (*irr.* ziehen, *sep.,* -ge-, sein) march past, pass by; *storm:* blow over.

Vor|übung ['fo:r?-] *f* preliminary practice; ∼untersuchung ⚖ ['fo:r?-] *f* preliminary inquiry.

Vorurteil ['fo:r?-] *n* prejudice; 'ℒslos *adj.* unprejudiced, unbias(s)ed.

'**Vor|verkauf** *thea. m* booking in advance; im ∼ bookable (*bei* at);

'Qverlegen v/t. (sep., no -ge-, h) advance; '₋wand m (-[e]s/‚e) pretext, preten|ce, Am. -se.

vorwärts adv. ['fo:rverts] forward, onward, on; ‚! go ahead!; '₋kommen v/i. (irr. kommen, sep., -ge-, sein) (make) progress; fig. make one's way, get on (in life).

vorweg adv. [for'vɛk] beforehand; ₋nehmen v/t. (irr. nehmen, sep., -ge-, h) anticipate.

vor|weisen v/t. (irr. weisen, sep., -ge-, h) produce, show; '₋werfen v/t. (irr. werfen, sep., -ge-, h) throw or cast before; j-m et. ₋ reproach s.o. with s.th.; '₋wiegend 1. adj. predominant, preponderant; 2. adv. predominantly, chiefly, mainly, mostly; '₋witzig adj. forward, pert; inquisitive.

'Vorwort n (-[e]s/-e) preface (by author); foreword.

'Vorwurf m reproach; subject (of drama, etc.); j-m e-n ₋ or Vorwürfe machen reproach s.o. (wegen with); 'Qsvoll adj. reproachful.

'vor|zählen v/t. (sep., -ge-, h) enumerate, count out (both: j-m to s.o.); 'Qzeichen n omen; '₋zeichnen v/t. (sep., -ge-, h): j-m et. ₋ draw or sketch s.th. for s.o.; show s.o. how to draw s.th.; fig. mark out, destine; '₋zeigen v/t. (sep., -ge-, h) produce, show.

'Vorzeit f antiquity; in literature often: times of old, days of yore; 'Qig adj. premature.

'vor|ziehen v/t. (irr. ziehen, sep., -ge-, h) draw forth; draw (curtains); fig. prefer; 'Qzimmer n antechamber, anteroom; waiting-room; 'Q-zug fig. m preference; advantage; merit; priority; '₋züglich adj. [₋'tsy:kliç] excellent, superior, exquisite.

'Vorzugs|aktie f preference share or stock, Am. preferred stock; '₋preis m special price; 'Qweise adv. preferably; chiefly.

Votum ['vo:tum] n (-s/Voten, Vota) vote.

vulgär adj. [vul'gɛ:r] vulgar.

Vulkan [vul'ka:n] m (-s/-e) volcano; 'Qisch adj. volcanic.

W

Waag|e ['va:gə] f (-/-n) balance, (e-e a pair of) scales pl.; die ₋ halten (dat.) counterbalance; 'Qerecht adj., 'Qrecht adj. ['va:k-] horizontal, level; '₋schale ['va:k-] f scale.

Wabe ['va:bə] f (-/-n) honeycomb.

wach adj. [vax] awake; hell₋ wide awake; ₋ werden awake, wake up; 'Qe f (-/-n) watch; guard; guardhouse, guardroom; police-station; sentry, sentinel; ₋ haben be on guard; '₋ halten keep watch; '₋en v/i. (ge-, h) (keep) watch (über acc. over); sit up (bei with); 'Qhund m watch-dog.

Wacholder ꝗ [va'xɔldər] m (-s/-) juniper.

'wach|rufen v/t. (irr. rufen, sep., -ge-, h) rouse, evoke; '₋rütteln v/t. (sep., -ge-, h) rouse (up); fig. rouse, shake up.

Wachs [vaks] n (-es/-e) wax.

'wachsam adj. watchful, vigilant; 'Qkeit f (-/no pl.) watchfulness, vigilance.

wachsen[1] ['vaksən] v/i. (irr., ge-, sein) grow; fig. increase.

wachsen[2] [₋] v/t. (ge-, h) wax.

wächsern adj. ['veksərn] wax; fig. waxen, waxy.

'Wachs|kerze f, '₋licht n wax candle; '₋tuch n waxcloth, oilcloth.

Wachstum ['vakstu:m] n (-s/no pl.) growth; fig. increase.

Wächte mount. ['vɛçtə] f (-/-n) cornice.

Wachtel orn. ['vaxtəl] f (-/-n) quail.

Wächter ['vɛçtər] m (-s/-) watcher, guard(ian); watchman.

'Wacht|meister m sergeant; '₋turm m watch-tower.

wackel|ig adj. ['vakəliç] shaky (a. fig.), tottery; furniture, etc.: rickety; tooth, etc.: loose; 'Qkontakt ꬴ m loose connexion or (Am. only) connection; '₋n v/i. (ge-, h) shake; table, etc.: wobble; tooth, etc.: be loose; tail, etc.: wag; ₋ mit wag s.th.

wacker adj. ['vakər] honest, upright; brave, gallant.

wacklig adj. ['vakliç] s. wackelig.

Wade ['va:də] f (-/-n) calf; '₋nbein anat. n fibula.

Waffe ['vafə] f (-/-n) weapon (a. fig.); ₋n pl. a. arms pl.

Waffel ['vafəl] f (-/-n) waffle; wafer.

'Waffen|fabrik f armaments factory, Am. a. armory; '₋gattung f arm; '₋gewalt f (-/no pl.): mit ₋ by force of arms; 'Qlos adj. weaponless, unarmed; '₋schein m firearm certificate, Am. gun license; '₋stillstand m armistice (a. fig.), truce.

Wage|hals ['va:gəhals] m daredevil; 'Qhalsig adj. daring, foolhardy; attr. a. daredevil; '₋mut m daring

wagen[1] ['va:gən] v/t. (ge-, h) venture; risk, dare; _sich ~_ venture (_an acc._ [up]on).

Wagen[2] [~] m (-s/-, =) carriage (_a._ 🚂); _Am._ 🚂 car; 🚂 coach; wag(g)on; cart; car; lorry, truck; van.

wägen ['vɛːgən] v/t. ([_irr._,] ge-, h) weigh (_a. fig._).

'Wagen|heber m (-s/-) (lifting) jack; '**~park** m (-[e]s/_no pl._) fleet of vehicles; '**~schmiere** f grease; '**~spur** f rut.

Waggon 🚂 [va'gõː] m (-s/-s) (railway) carriage, _Am._ (railroad) car.

wag|halsig adj. ['va:khalsiç] s. **wagehalsig**; '**~nis** n (-ses/-se) venture, risk.

Wahl [va:l] f (-/-en) choice; alternative; selection; _pol._ election; _e-e ~ treffen_ make a choice; _s-e ~ treffen_ take one's choice; _ich hatte keine (andere) ~_ I had no choice.

wählbar adj. ['vɛ:lba:r] eligible; '**2keit** f (-/_no pl._) eligibility.

wahl|berechtigt adj. ['va:lbərɛçtiçt] entitled to vote; '**2beteiligung** f percentage of voting, F turn-out; '**2bezirk** m constituency.

'wählen (ge-, h) 1. v/t. choose; _pol._ elect; _teleph._ dial; 2. v/i. choose, take one's choice; _teleph._ dial (the number).

'Wahlergebnis n election return.

'Wähler m (-s/-) elector, voter; '**2isch** adj. particular (_in dat._ in, about, as to), nice (about), fastidious, F choosy; '**~schaft** f (-/-en) constituency, electorate.

'Wahl|fach n optional subject, _Am. a._ elective; '**2fähig** adj. having a vote; eligible; '**~gang** m ballot; '**~kampf** m election campaign; '**~kreis** m constituency; '**~lokal** n polling station; '**2los** adj. indiscriminate; '**~recht** n (-[e]s/_no pl._) franchise; '**~rede** f electoral speech.

'Wählscheibe teleph. f dial.

'Wahl|spruch m device, motto; '**~stimme** f vote; '**~urne** f ballotbox; '**~versammlung** f electoral rally; '**~zelle** f polling-booth; '**~zettel** m ballot, voting-paper.

Wahn [va:n] m (-[e]s/_no pl._) delusion, illusion; mania; '**~sinn** m (-[e]s/_no pl._) insanity, madness (_both a. fig._); '**2sinnig** adj. insane, mad (_vor dat._ with) (_both a. fig._); **~sinnige** ['~gə] m (-n/-n) madman, lunatic; '**~vorstellung** f delusion, hallucination; '**~witz** m (-es/_no pl._) madness, insanity; '**2witzig** adj. mad, insane.

wahr [va:r] adj. true; real; genuine; '**~en** v/t. (ge-, h) safeguard (_interests, etc._); maintain (_one's dignity_); _den Schein ~_ keep up _or_ save appearances.

währen ['vɛ:rən] v/i. (ge-, h) last, continue.

während 1. _prp._ (_gen._) during; pending; 2. _cj._ while, whilst; while, whereas.

'wahrhaft adv. really, truly, indeed; '**~ig** [~'haftiç] 1. adj. truthful, veracious; 2. adv. really, truly, indeed.

'Wahrheit f (-/-en) truth; _in ~_ in truth; _j-m die ~ sagen_ give s.o. a piece of one's mind; '**2getreu** adj. true, faithful; '**~sliebe** f (-/_no pl._) truthfulness, veracity; '**2sliebend** adj. truthful, veracious.

'wahr|lich adv. truly, really; '**~nehmbar** adj. perceivable, perceptible; '**~nehmen** v/t. (irr. nehmen, sep., -ge-, h) perceive, notice; avail o.s. of (_opportunity_); safeguard (_interests_); '**2nehmung** f (-/-en) perception, observation; '**~sagen** v/i. (sep., -ge-, h) tell _or_ read fortunes; _sich ~ lassen_ have one's fortune told; '**2sagerin** f (-/-nen) fortuneteller; **~scheinlich** 1. adj. probable; likely; 2. adv.: _ich werde ~ gehen_ I am likely to go; **2'scheinlichkeit** f (-/🔔-en) probability, likelihood; _aller ~ nach_ in all probability _or_ likelihood.

'Wahrung f (-/_no pl._) maintenance; safeguarding.

Währung ['vɛːruŋ] f (-/-en) currency; standard; '**~sreform** f currency _or_ monetary reform.

'Wahrzeichen n landmark.

Waise ['vaizə] f (-/-n) orphan; '**~nhaus** n orphanage.

Wal zo. [va:l] m (-[e]s/-e) whale.

Wald [valt] m (-[e]s/=er) wood, forest; '**~brand** m forest fire; **2ig** adj. ['~diç] wooded, woody; **2reich** adj. ['~t-] rich in forests; '**~ung** ['~duŋ] f (-/-en) forest.

Walfänger ['va:lfɛŋər] m (-s/-) whaler.

walken ['valkən] v/t. (ge-, h) full (_cloth_); mill (_cloth, leather_).

Wall [val] m (-[e]s/=e) ⚔ rampart (_a. fig._); dam; mound.

Wallach ['valax] m (-[e]s/-e) gelding.

wallen ['valən] v/i. (ge-, h, sein) hair, articles of dress, etc.: flow; simmer; boil (_a. fig._).

wall|fahren ['valfa:rən] v/i. (ge-, sein) (go on a) pilgrimage; '**2fahrer** m pilgrim; '**2fahrt** f pilgrimage; '**~fahrten** v/i. (ge-, sein) (go on a) pilgrimage.

'Wallung f (-/-en) ebullition; 🩸 congestion; (_Blut_) _in ~ bringen_ make s.o.'s blood boil, enrage.

Walnuß ['val-] f walnut; '**~baum** ♣ m walnut(-tree).

Walroß zo. ['val-] n walrus.

walten ['valtən] v/i. (ge-, h): _s-s Amtes ~_ attend to one's duties; _Gnade ~ lassen_ show mercy.

Walze ['valtsə] f (-/-n) roller, cylinder; ⊕ a. roll; ⊕, ♪ barrel; '2n v/t. (ge-, h) roll (a. ⊕).

wälzen ['vɛltsən] v/t. (ge-, h) roll; roll (problem) round in one's mind; shift (blame) (auf acc. [up]on); sich ~ roll; wallow (in mud, etc.); welter (in blood, etc.).

Walzer ♪ ['valtsər] m (-s/-) waltz.

Wand [vant] 1. f (-/ᵸe) wall; partition; 2. 2 pret. of winden.

Wandel ['vandəl] m (-s/no pl.) change; '2bar adj. changeable; variable; '.gang m, '.halle f lobby; '2n (ge-) 1. v/i. (sein) walk; 2. v/refl. (h) change.

Wander|er ['vandərər] m (-s/-) wanderer; hiker; '.leben n (-s/no pl.) vagrant life; '2n v/i. (ge-, sein) wander; hike; '.niere ⚕ f floating kidney; '.prediger m itinerant preacher; '.preis m challenge trophy; '.schaft f (-/no pl.) wanderings pl.; auf (der) ~ on the tramp; '.ung f (-/-en) walking-tour; hike.

'**Wand|gemälde** n mural (painting); '.kalender m wall-calendar; '.karte f wall-map.

Wandlung ['vandluŋ] f (-/-en) change, transformation; eccl. transubstantiation; ⚖ redhibition.

'**Wand|schirm** m folding-screen; '.schrank m wall-cupboard; '~spiegel m wall-mirror; '.tafel f blackboard; '.teppich m tapestry; '.uhr f wall-clock.

wandte ['vantə] pret. of wenden 2.

Wange ['vaŋə] f (-/-n) cheek.

Wankel|mut ['vaŋkəlmu:t] m fickleness, inconstancy; 2mütig adj. ['.my:tiç] fickle, inconstant.

wanken ['vaŋkən] v/i. (ge-, h, sein) totter, stagger (a. fig.); house, etc.: rock; fig. waver.

wann adv. [van] when; s. dann; seit ~? how long?, since when?

Wanne ['vanə] f (-/-n) tub; bath (-tub), F tub; '.nbad n bath, F tub.

Wanze zo. ['vantsə] f (-/-n) bug, Am. a. bedbug.

Wappen ['vapən] n (-s/-) (coat of) arms pl.; '.kunde f (-/no pl.) heraldry; '.schild m, n escutcheon; '.tier n heraldic animal.

wappnen fig. ['vapnən] v/refl. (ge-, h): sich ~ gegen be prepared for; sich mit Geduld ~ have patience.

war [va:r] pret. of sein¹.

warb [varp] pret. of werben.

Ware ['va:rə] f (-/-n) commodity, article of trade; ~n pl. a. goods pl., merchandise, wares pl.

'**Waren|aufzug** m hoist; '.bestand m stock (on hand); '.haus n department store; '.lager n warehouse, Am. a. stock room; '.probe f sample; '.zeichen n trade mark.

warf [varf] pret. of werfen.

warm adj. [varm] warm (a. fig.); meal: hot; schön ~ nice and warm.

Wärme ['vɛrmə] f (-/ᵸ-n) warmth; phys. heat; '.grad m degree of heat; '2n v/t. (ge-, h) warm; sich die Füße ~ warm one's feet.

'**Wärmflasche** f hot-water bottle.

'**warmherzig** adj. warm-hearted.

Warm|wasser|heizung f hot-water heating; '.versorgung f hot-water supply.

warn|en ['varnən] v/t. (ge-, h) warn (vor dat. of, against), caution (against); '2signal n danger-signal (a. fig.); '2streik m token strike; '2ung f (-/-en) warning, caution; '2ungstafel ['varnuŋs-] f notice-board.

Warte fig. ['vartə] f (-/-n) point of view.

warten ['vartən] v/i. (ge-, h) wait (auf acc. for); be in store (for s.o.); j-n ~ lassen keep s.o. waiting.

Wärter ['vɛrtər] m (-s/-) attendant; keeper; (male) nurse.

'**Warte|saal** m, '.zimmer n waiting-room.

Wartung ⊕ ['vartuŋ] f (-/⚙-en) maintenance.

warum adv. [va'rum] why.

Warze ['vartsə] f (-/-n) wart; nipple.

was [vas] 1. interr. pron. what; ~ kostet das Buch? how much is this book?; F ~ rennst du denn so (schnell)? why are you running like this?; ~ für (ein) ...! what a(n) ...!; ~ für ein ...? what ...?; 2. rel. pron. what; ~ (auch immer), alles ~ ..., ~ ihn völlig kalt ließ ... which left him quite cold; 3. F indef. pron. something; ich will dir mal ~ sagen I'll tell you what.

wasch|bar adj. ['vaʃba:r] washable; '2becken n wash-basin, Am. washbowl.

Wäsche ['vɛʃə] f (-/-n) wash(ing); laundry; linen (a. fig.); underwear; in der ~ sein be at the wash; sie hat heute große ~ she has a large wash today.

waschecht adj. ['vaʃ⁹-] washable; colour: a. fast; fig. dyed-in-the-wool.

'**Wäsche|klammer** f clothes-peg, clothes-pin; '.leine f clothes-line.

'**waschen** v/t. (irr., ge-, h) wash; sich ~ (have a) wash; sich das Haar or den Kopf ~ wash or shampoo one's hair or head; sich gut ~ (lassen) wash well.

Wäscher|ei [vɛʃə'rai] f (-/-en) laundry; '.in f (-/-nen) washer-woman, laundress.

'**Wäscheschrank** m linen closet.

'**Wasch|frau** f s. Wäscherin; '~haus n wash-house; '.kessel m copper; '.korb m clothes-basket;

'~küche f wash-house; '~lappen m face-cloth, Am. washrag, wash-cloth; '~maschine f washing machine, washer; '~pulver n washing powder; '~raum m lavatory, Am. a. washroom; '~schüssel f wash-basin; '~tag m wash(ing)-day; '~ung f (-/-en) ⚓ wash; ablution; '~weib contp. n gossip; '~wanne f wash-tub.

Wasser ['vasər] n (-s/-, ⚓) water; ~ lassen make water; zu ~ und zu Land(e) by sea and land; '~ball m 1. beach-ball; water-polo ball; 2. (-[e]s/no pl.) water-polo; '~ballspiel n 1. (-[e]s/no pl.) water-polo; 2. water-polo match; '~behälter m reservoir, water-tank; '~blase ⚓ f water-blister; '~dampf m steam; '~dicht adj. waterproof; watertight; '~eimer m water-pail, bucket; '~fall m waterfall, cascade; cataract; '~farbe f water-colo(u)r; '~flugzeug n waterplane, seaplane; '~glas n 1. tumbler; 2. 🔬 (-es/no pl.) water-glass; '~graben m ditch; '~hahn m tap, Am. a. faucet; '~hose f waterspout.

wässerig adj. ['vɛsəriç] watery; washy (a. fig.); j-m den Mund ~ machen make s.o.'s mouth water. 'Wasser|kanne f water-jug, ewer; '~kessel m kettle; '~klosett n water-closet, W.C.; '~kraft f water-power; '~kraftwerk n hydroelectric power station or plant, water-power station; '~krug m water-jug, ewer; '~kur f water-cure, hydropathy; '~lauf m watercourse; '~leitung f water-supply; '~leitungsrohr n water-pipe; '~mangel m shortage of water; '⚓n v/i. (ge-, h) alight on water; splash down. [(salted herring, etc.).]
wässern ['vɛsərn] v/t. (ge-, h) soak/ 'Wasser|pflanze f aquatic plant; '~rinne f gutter; '~rohr n water-pipe; '~schaden m damage caused by water; '~scheide f watershed, Am. a. divide; '⚓scheu adj. afraid of water; '~schlauch m water-hose; '~spiegel m water-level; '~sport m aquatic sports pl.; '~spülung f (-/-en) flushing (system); '~stand m water-level; '~standsanzeiger ['vasərʃtants?-] m water-gauge; '~stiefel m/pl. waders pl.; '~stoff 🔬 m (-[e]s/no pl.) hydrogen; '~stoffbombe f hydrogen bomb, H-bomb; '~strahl m jet of water; '~straße f waterway; '~tier n aquatic animal; '~verdrängung f (-/-en) displacement; '~versorgung f water-supply; '~waage f spirit-level, water-level; '~weg m waterway; auf dem ~ by water; '~welle f water-wave; '~werk n waterworks sg., pl.; '~zeichen n watermark.

wäßrig adj. ['vɛsriç] s. wässerig.
waten ['va:tən] v/i. (ge-, sein) wade.
watscheln ['va:tʃəln] v/i. (ge-, sein, h) waddle.
Watt ⚡ [vat] n (-s/-) watt.
Watt|e ['vatə] f (-/-n) cotton-wool; surgical cotton; wadding; '~ebausch m wad; 2ieren [~'ti:rən] v/t. wad, pad.
weben ['ve:bən] v/t. and v/i. ([irr.,] ge-, h) weave.
'Weber m (-s/-) weaver; ~ei [~'raɪ] f 1. (-/no pl.) weaving; 2. (-/-en) weaving-mill.
Webstuhl ['ve:pʃtu:l] m loom.
Wechsel ['vɛksəl] m (-s/-) change; allowance; ✝ bill (of exchange); hunt. runway; eigener ~ ✝ promissory note; '~beziehung f correlation; '~fälle ['~fɛlə] pl. vicissitudes pl.; '~fieber ⚓ n (-s/no pl.) intermittent fever; malaria; '~frist ✝ f usance; '~geld n change; '~kurs m rate of exchange; '~makler ✝ m bill-broker; '2n (ge-, h) 1. v/t. change; vary; exchange (words, etc.); den Besitzer ~ change hands; die Kleider ~ change (one's clothes); 2. v/i. change; vary; alternate; '~nehmer ✝ m (-s/-) payee; 2seitig adj. ['~zaitiç] mutual, reciprocal; '~strom ⚡ m alternating current; '~stube f exchange office; '2weise adv. alternately, by or in turns; '~wirkung f interaction.
wecke|n ['vɛkən] v/t. (ge-, h) wake (up), waken; arouse (a. fig.); '2r m (-s/-) alarm-clock.
wedeln ['ve:dəln] v/i. (ge-, h): ~ mit wag (tail).
weder cj. ['ve:dər]: ~ ... noch neither ... nor.
Weg[1] [ve:k] m (-[e]s/-e) way (a.fig.); road (a. fig.); path; route; walk; auf halbem ~ half-way; am ~e by the roadside; aus dem ~e gehen steer clear of; aus dem ~e räumen remove (a. fig.); in die ~e leiten set on foot, initiate.
weg[2] adv. [vek] away, off; gone; geh ~! be off (with you)!; ~ mit ihm! off with him!; Hände ~! hands off!; F ich muß ~ I must be off; F ganz ~ sein be quite beside o.s.; '~bleiben F v/i. (irr. bleiben, sep., -ge-, sein) stay away; be omitted; '~bringen v/t. (irr. bringen, sep., -ge-, h) take away; a. remove (things).
wegen prp. (gen.) ['ve:gən] because of, on account of, owing to.
weg|fahren ['vek-] (irr. fahren, sep., -ge-) 1. v/t. (h) remove; cart away; 2. v/i. (sein) leave; '~fallen v/i. (irr. fallen, sep., -ge-, sein) be omitted; be abolished; '2gang m (-[e]s/no pl.) going away, departure; '~gehen v/i. (irr. gehen, sep., -ge-, sein) go away or off; merchandise:

sell; '~haben F v/t. (irr. haben, sep., -ge-, h): e-n ~ be tight; have a screw loose; er hat noch nicht weg, wie man es machen muß he hasn't got the knack of it yet; '~jagen v/t. (sep., -ge-, h) drive away; '~kommen F v/i. (irr. kommen, sep., -ge-, sein) get away; be missing; gut (schlecht) ~ come off well (badly); mach, daß du wegkommst! be off (with you)!; '~lassen v/t. (irr. lassen, sep., -ge-, h) let s.o. go; leave out, omit; '~laufen v/i. (irr. laufen, sep., -ge-, sein) run away; '~legen v/t. (sep., -ge-, h) put away; '~machen F v/t. (sep., -ge-, h) remove; a. take out (stains); '~müssen F v/i. (irr. müssen 1, sep., -ge-, h): ich muß weg I must be off; 2nahme ['~na:mə] f (-/-n) taking (away); '~nehmen v/t. (irr. nehmen, sep., -ge-, h) take up, occupy (time, space); j-m et. ~ take s.th. away from s.o.; '~raffen fig. v/t. (sep., -ge-, h) carry off.

Wegrand ['ve:k-] m wayside.

weg|räumen ['vek-] v/t. (sep., -ge-, h) clear away, remove; '~schaffen v/t. (sep., -ge-, h) remove; '~schicken v/t. (sep., -ge-, h) send away or off; '~sehen v/i. (irr. sehen, sep., -ge-, h) look away; ~ über (acc.) overlook, shut one's eyes to; '~setzen v/t. (sep., -ge-, h) put away; sich ~ über (acc.) disregard, ignore; '~streichen v/t. (irr. streichen, sep., -ge-, h) strike off or out; '~tun v/t. (irr. tun, sep., -ge-, h) put away or aside.

Wegweiser ['ve:kvaɪzər] m (-s/-) signpost, finger-post; fig. guide.

weg|wenden ['vek-] v/t. ([irr. wenden,] sep., -ge-, h) turn away, avert (one's eyes); sich ~ turn away; '~werfen v/t. (irr. werfen, sep., -ge-, h) throw away; '~werfend adj. disparaging; '~wischen v/t. (sep., -ge-, h) wipe off; '~ziehen (irr. ziehen, sep., -ge-) 1. v/t. (h) pull or draw away; 2. v/i. (sein) (re)move.

weh [ve:] 1. adj. sore; 2. adv.: ~ tun ache, hurt; j-m ~ tun pain or hurt s.o.; fig. a. grieve s.o.; sich ~ tun hurt o.s.; mir tut der Finger ~ my finger hurts.

Wehen¹ ♂ ['ve:ən] f/pl. labo(u)r, travail.

wehen² [~] (ge-, h) 1. v/t. blow; 2. v/i. blow; es weht ein starker Wind it is blowing hard.

'weh|klagen v/i. (ge-, h) lament (um for, over); '~leidig adj. snivel(l)ing; voice: plaintive; '2mut f (-/no pl.) wistfulness; '~mütig adj. ['~my:tiç] wistful.

Wehr [ve:r] 1. f (-/-en): sich zur ~ setzen offer resistance (gegen to), show fight; 2. n (-[e]s/-e) weir;

'~dienst ✗ m military service; '2en v/refl. (ge-, h) defend o.s.; offer resistance (gegen to); '2fähig ✗ adj. able-bodied; '2los adj. defenceless, Am. defenseless; '~pflicht ✗ f (-/no pl.) compulsory military service, conscription; '2pflichtig ✗ adj. liable to military service.

Weib [vaɪp] n (-[e]s/-er) woman; wife; '~chen zo. n (-s/-) female.

Weiber|feind ['vaɪbər-] m womanhater; '~held contp. m ladies' man; '~volk F n (-[e]s/no pl.) womenfolk.

weib|isch adj. ['vaɪbɪʃ] womanish, effeminate; ~lich adj. ['~p-] female; gr. feminine; womanly, feminine.

weich adj. [vaɪç] soft (a. fig.); meat, etc.: tender; egg: soft-boiled; ~ werden soften; fig. relent.

Weiche¹ ['vaɪçə] f (-/-n) switch; ~n pl. points pl.

Weiche² anat. [~] f (-/-n) flank, side.

weichen¹ ['vaɪçən] v/i. (irr., ge-, sein) give way, yield (dat. to); nicht von der Stelle ~ not to budge an inch; j-m nicht von der Seite ~ stick to s.o.

weichen² [~] v/i. (ge-, h, sein) soak.

'Weichensteller ⚙ m (-s/-) pointsman, switch-man.

'weich|herzig adj. soft-hearted, tender-hearted; '~lich adj. somewhat soft; fig. effeminate; 2ling ['~lɪŋ] m (-s/-e) weakling, milksop, molly(-coddle), sl. sissy; '2tier n mollusc.

Weide¹ ♀ ['vaɪdə] f (-/-n) willow.

Weide² ⚘ [~] f (-/-n) pasture; auf der ~ out at grass; '~land n pasture(-land); '2n (ge-, h) 1. v/t. feed, pasture, graze; sich ~ an (dat.) gloat over; feast on; 2. v/i. pasture, graze.

'Weiden|korb m wicker basket, osier basket; '~rute f osier switch.

weidmännisch hunt. adj. ['vaɪtmenɪʃ] sportsmanlike.

weiger|n ['vaɪgərn] v/refl. (ge-, h) refuse, decline; '2ung f (-/-en) refusal.

Weihe eccl. ['vaɪə] f (-/-n) consecration; ordination; '2n eccl. v/t. (ge-, h) consecrate; j-n zum Priester ~ ordain s.o. priest.

Weiher ['vaɪər] m (-s/-) pond.

'weihevoll adj. solemn.

Weihnachten ['vaɪnaxtən] n (-s/no pl.) Christmas, Xmas.

'Weihnachts|abend m Christmas eve; '~baum m Christmas-tree; '~ferien pl. Christmas holidays pl.; '~fest n Christmas; '~geschenk n Christmas present; '~gratifikation f Christmas bonus; '~karte f Christmas card; '~lied n carol, Christmas hymn; '~mann m Father Christmas, Santa Claus; '~markt m Christmas fair; '~zeit f

(-/no pl.) Christmas(-tide) (in Germany beginning on the first Advent Sunday).
'Weih|rauch eccl. m incense; '~wasser eccl. n (-s/no pl.) holy water.
weil cj. [vaɪl] because, since, as.
Weil|chen ['vaɪlçən] n (-s/-): ein ~ a little while, a spell; '~e f (-/no pl.): e-e ~ a while.
Wein [vaɪn] m (-[e]s/-e) wine; ♀ vine; wilder ~ ♀ Virginia creeper; '~bau m (-[e]s/no pl.) vine-growing, viticulture; '~beere f grape; '~berg m vineyard; '~blatt n vine-leaf.
wein|en ['vaɪnən] v/i. (ge-, h) weep (um, vor dat. for), cry (vor dat. for joy, etc., with hunger, etc.); '~erlich adj. tearful, lachrymose; whining.
'Wein|ernte f vintage; '~essig m vinegar; '~faß n wine-cask; '~flasche f wine-bottle; '~geist m (-[e]s/-e) spirit(s pl.) of wine; '~glas n wineglass; '~handlung f wine-merchant's shop; '~karte f wine-list; '~keller m wine-vault; '~kelter f winepress; '~kenner m connoisseur of or in wines.
'Weinkrampf ♀ m paroxysm of weeping.
'Wein|kühler m wine-cooler; '~lese f vintage; '~presse f winepress; '~ranke f vine-tendril; '~rebe f vine; '2rot adj. claret-colo(u)red; '~stock m vine; '~traube f grape, bunch of grapes.
weise¹ ['vaɪzə] 1. adj. wise; sage; 2. 2 m (-n/-n) wise man, sage.
Weise² [~] f (-/-n) ♪ melody, tune; fig. manner, way; auf diese ~ in this way.
weisen ['vaɪzən] (irr., ge-, h) 1. v/t.: j-m die Tür ~ show s.o. the door; von der Schule ~ expel from school; von sich ~ reject (idea, etc.); deny (charge, etc.); 2. v/i.: ~ auf (acc.) point at or to.
Weis|heit ['vaɪshaɪt] f (-/♀-en) wisdom; am Ende s-r ~ sein be at one's wit's end; '~heitszahn m wisdom-tooth; '2machen v/t. (sep., -ge-, h): j-m et. ~ make s.o. believe s.th.
weiß adj. [vaɪs] white; '2blech n tin(-plate); '2brot n white bread; '2e m (-n/-n) white (man); '~en v/t. (ge-, h) whitewash; '~glühend adj. white-hot, incandescent; '2kohl m white cabbage; '~lich adj. whitish; '2waren pl. linen goods pl.; '2wein m white wine.
Weisung ['vaɪzuŋ] f (-/-en) direction, directive.
weit [vaɪt] 1. adj. distant (von from); world, garment: wide; area, etc.: vast; garment: loose; journey, way: long; conscience: elastic; 2. adv.: ~ entfernt far away; ~ entfernt von a. a long distance from; fig. far from;

~ und breit far and wide; ~ über sechzig (Jahre alt) well over sixty; bei ~em (by) far; von ~em from a distance.
weit|ab adv. ['vaɪt-] far away (von from); '~aus adv. (by) far, much; '2blick m (-[e]s/no pl.) far-sightedness; '~blickend adj. far-sighted, far-seeing; '~en v/t. and v/refl. (ge-, h) widen.
'weiter 1. adj. particulars, etc.: further; charges, etc.: additional, extra; ~e fünf Wochen another five weeks; bis auf ~es until further notice; ohne ~es without any hesitation; off-hand; 2. adv. furthermore, moreover; ~! go on!; nichts ~ nothing more; und so ~ and so on; bis hierher und nicht ~ so far and no farther; '2e n (-n/no pl.) the rest; further details pl.
'weiter|befördern v/t. (sep., no -ge-, h) forward; '~bestehen v/i. (irr. stehen, sep., no -ge-, h) continue to exist, survive; '~bilden v/t. (sep., -ge-, h) give s.o. further education; sich ~ improve one's knowledge; continue one's education; '~geben v/t. (irr. geben, sep., -ge-, h) pass (dat., an acc. to); '~gehen v/i. (irr. gehen, sep., -ge-, sein) pass or move on, walk along; fig. continue, go on; '~hin adv. in (the) future; furthermore; et. ~ tun continue doing or to do s.th.; '~kommen v/i. (irr. kommen, sep., -ge-, sein) get on; '~können v/i. (irr. können, sep., -ge-, h) be able to go on; '~leben v/i. (sep., -ge-, h) live on, survive (a. fig.); '~machen v/t. and v/i. (sep., -ge-, h) carry on.
'weit|gehend adj. powers: large; support: generous; '~gereist adj. travel(l)ed; '~greifend adj. far-reaching; '~herzig adj. broadminded; '~hin adv. far off; '~läufig ['~lɔyfɪç] 1. adj. house, etc.: spacious; story, etc.: detailed; relative: distant; 2. adv.: ~ erzählen (tell in) detail; er ist ~ verwandt mit mir he is a distant relative of mine; '~reichend adj. far-reaching; '~schweifig adj. diffuse, prolix; '~sichtig adj. ♀ far-sighted; fig. a. far-seeing; '2sichtigkeit ♀ f (-/♀-en) far-sightedness; '2sprung m (-[e]s/no pl.) long jump, Am. broad jump; '~tragend adj. ⚔ long-range; fig. far-reaching; '~verbreitet adj. widespread.
Weizen ♀ ['vaɪtsən] m (-s/-) wheat; '2brot n wheaten bread; '~mehl n wheaten flour.
welch [vɛlç] 1. interr. pron. what; which; ~er? which one?; ~er von beiden? which of the two?; 2. rel. pron. who, that; which, that; 3. F indef. pron.: es gibt ~e, die sagen, daß ... there are some who say

that ...; *es sollen viele Ausländer hier sein, hast du schon* ~e *gesehen?* many foreigners are said to be here, have you seen any yet?

welk *adj.* [vɛlk] faded, withered; *skin*: flabby, flaccid; '~en *v/i.* (ge-, sein) fade, wither.

Wellblech ['vɛlblɛç] *n* corrugated iron.

Welle ['vɛlə] *f* (-/-n) wave (*a. fig.*); ⊕ shaft.

'**wellen** *v/t. and v/refl.* (ge-, h) wave; 'Qbereich ⚡ *m* wave-range; ~**förmig** *adj.* ['foermiç] undulating, undulatory; 'Qlänge ⚡ *f* wavelength; 'Qlinie *f* wavy line; 'Qreiten *n* (-s/*no pl.*) surf-riding.

'**wellig** *adj.* wavy.

'**Wellpappe** *f* corrugated cardboard *or* paper.

Welt [vɛlt] *f* (-/-en) world; *die ganze* ~ the whole world, all the world; *auf der* ~ in the world, *auf der ganzen* ~ all over the world; *zur* ~ *bringen* give birth to, bring into the world.

'**Welt|all** *n* universe, cosmos; '~**anschauung** *f* Weltanschauung; '~**ausstellung** *f* world fair; 'Qbekannt *adj.* known all over the world; 'Qberühmt *adj.* world-famous; '~**bürger** *m* cosmopolite; 'Qerschütternd *adj.* world-shaking; 'Qfremd *adj.* wordly innocent; '~**friede(n)** *m* universal peace; '~**geschichte** *f* (-/*no pl.*) universal history; 'Qgewandt *adj.* knowing the ways of the world; '~**handel** ⚡ *m* (-s/*no pl.*) world trade; '~**karte** *f* map of the world; 'Qklug *adj.* wordly-wise; '~**krieg** *m* world war; *der zweite* ~ World War II; '~**lage** *f* international situation; '~**lauf** *m* course of the world; 'Qlich **1.** *adj.* wordly, secular, temporal; **2.** *adv.*: ~ *gesinnt* wordly-minded; '~**literatur** *f* world literature; '~**macht** *f* world-power; 'Qmännisch *adj.* ['~mɛniʃ] man-of-the-world; '~**markt** *m* (-[e]s/*no pl.*) world market; '~**meer** *n* ocean; '~**meister** *m* world champion; '~**meisterschaft** *f* world championship; '~**raum** *m* (-[e]s/*no pl.*) (outer) space; '~**reich** *n* universal empire; *das Britische* ~ the British Empire; '~**reise** *f* journey round the world; '~**rekord** *m* world record; '~**ruf** *m* (-[e]s/*no pl.*) world-wide reputation; '~**schmerz** *m* Weltschmerz; '~**sprache** *f* world *or* universal language; '~**stadt** *f* metropolis; 'Qweit *adj.* world-wide; '~**wunder** *n* wonder of the world.

Wende ['vɛndə] *f* (-/-n) turn (*a. swimming*); *fig. a.* turning-point; '~**kreis** *m geogr.* tropic; *mot.* turning-circle.

Wendeltreppe ['vɛndəl-] *f* winding

staircase, (e-e a flight of) winding stairs *pl.*, spiral staircase.

'**Wende|marke** *f sports*: turning-point; 'Qn **1.** *v/t.* (ge-, h) turn (*coat, etc.*); turn (*hay*) about; **2.** *v/refl.* ([*irr.*,] ge-, h): *sich* ~ *an* (*acc.*) turn to; address o.s. to; apply to (*wegen* for); **3.** *v/i.* (ge-, h) ⚡, *mot.* turn; *bitte* ~! please turn over!; '~**punkt** *m* turning-point.

'**wend|ig** *adj.* nimble, agile (*both a. fig.*); *mot.*, ⚓ easily steerable; *mot.* flexible; 'Qung *f* (-/-en) turn (*a. fig.*); ⚔ facing; *fig.*: change; expression; idiom.

wenig ['ve:niç] **1.** *adj.* little; ~e *pl.* few *pl.*; ~er less; ~er *pl.* fewer; *ein klein* ~ *Geduld* a little bit of patience; *das* ~e the little; **2.** *adv.* little; ~er less; 𝔸 *a.* minus; *am* ~sten least (of all); 'Qkeit *f* (-/-en): *meine* ~ my humble self; '~**stens** *adv.* ['~stəns] at least.

wenn *cj.* [vɛn] when; if; ~ ... *nicht* if ... not, unless; ~ *auch* (al)though, even though; ~ *auch noch so however*; *und* ~ *nun* ...? what if ...?; *wie wäre es,* ~ *wir jetzt heimgingen?* what about going home now?

wer [ve:r] **1.** *interr. pron.* who; which; ~ *von euch?* which of you?; **2.** *rel. pron.* who; ~ *auch* (*immer*) who(so)ever; **3.** F *indef. pron.* somebody; anybody; *ist schon* ~ *gekommen?* has anybody come yet?

Werbe|abteilung ['vɛrbə-] *f* advertising *or* publicity department; '~**film** *m* advertising film.

'**werb|en** (*irr.*, ge-, h) **1.** *v/t.* canvass (*votes, subscribers, etc.*); ⚔ recruit, enlist; **2.** *v/i.*: ~ *für* advertise, *Am. a.* advertize; make propaganda for; canvass for; 'Qung *f* (-/-en) advertising, publicity, *Am. a.* advertizing; propaganda; canvassing; ⚔ enlistment, recruiting.

Werdegang ['ve:rdə-] *m* career; ⊕ process of manufacture.

'**werden 1.** *v/i.* (*irr.*, ge-, sein) become, get; grow; turn (*pale, sour, etc.*); *was ist aus ihm geworden?* what has become of him?; *was will er* (*einmal*) ~? what is he going to be?; **2.** Q ~ *n* (-s/*no pl.*): *noch im* ~ *sein* be in embryo.

werfen ['vɛrfən] (*irr.*, ge-, h) **1.** *v/t.* throw (*nach at*); *zo.* throw (*young*); cast (*shadow, glance, etc.*); *Falten* ~ fall in folds; set badly; **2.** *v/i.* throw; *zo.* litter; ~ *mit* throw (*auf acc., nach at*).

Werft ⚓ [vɛrft] *f* (-/-en) shipyard, dockyard.

Werk [vɛrk] *n* (-[e]s/-e) work; act; ⊕ works *pl.*; works *sg., pl.*, factory; *das* ~ *e-s Augenblicks* the work of a moment; *zu* ~e *gehen* proceed; '~**bank** ⊕ *f* work-bench; '~**meister** *m* foreman; ~**statt** ['~ʃtat] *f*

(-/=en) workshop; '⸸tag m work-day; '⸰tätig adj. working; '⸰zeug n tool; implement; instrument.
Wermut ['veːrmuːt] m (-[e]s/no pl.) ❧ wormwood; verm(o)uth.
wert [veːrt] **1.** adj. worth; worthy (gen. of); ⸰, getan zu werden worth doing; **2.** ⸰ m (-[e]s/-e) value (a. ♙, ♎ₘ, phys., fig.); worth (a. fig.); Brief-marken im ⸰ von 2 Schilling 2 shil-lings' worth of stamps; großen ⸰ legen auf (acc.) set a high value (up)on.
'Wert|brief m money-letter; '⸰en v/t. (ge-, h) value; appraise; '⸰ge-genstand m article of value; '⸰los adj. worthless, valueless; '⸰pa-piere n/pl. securities pl.; '⸰sachen pl. valuables pl.; '⸰ung f (-/-en) valuation; appraisal; sports: score; '⸰voll adj. valuable, precious.
Wesen ['veːzən] n **1.** (-s/no pl.) entity, essence; nature, character; viel ⸰s machen um make a fuss of; **2.** (-s/-) being, creature; '⸰los adj. unreal; '⸰tlich adj. essential, sub-stantial.
weshalb [ves'halp] **1.** interr. pron. why; **2.** cj. that's why.
Wespe zo. ['vɛspə] f (-/-n) wasp.
West geogr. [vɛst] west; '⸰en m (-s/no pl.) west; the West.
Weste ['vɛstə] f (-/-n) waistcoat, ✝ and Am. vest; e-e reine ⸰ haben have a clean slate.
'west|lich adj. west; westerly; western; '⸰wind m west(erly) wind.
Wett|bewerb ['vɛtbəvɛrp] m (-[e]s/-e) competition (a. ✝); '⸰büro n betting office; '⸰e f (-/-n) wager, bet; e-e ⸰ eingehen lay or make a bet; '⸰eifer m emulation, rivalry; '⸰eifern v/i. (ge-, h) vie (mit with; in dat. in; um for); '⸰en (ge-, h) **1.** v/t. wager, bet; **2.** v/i.: mit j-m um et. ⸰ wager or bet s.o. s.th.; ⸰ auf (acc.) wager or bet on, back.
Wetter[1] ['vɛtər] n (-s/-) weather.
Wetter[2] [⸰] m (-s/-) better.
'Wetter|bericht m weather-fore-cast; '⸰fest adj. weather-proof; '⸰karte f weather-chart; '⸰lage f weather-conditions pl.; '⸰leuchten n (-s/no pl.) sheet-lightning; '⸰vor-hersage f (-/-n) weather-forecast; '⸰warte f weather-station.
'Wett|kampf m contest, competi-tion; '⸰kämpfer m contestant; '⸰lauf m race; '⸰läufer m racer, runner; '⸰machen v/t. (sep., -ge-, h) make up for; '⸰rennen n race; '⸰rüsten n (-s/no pl.) armament race; '⸰spiel n match, game; '⸰streit m contest. [sharpen.]
wetzen ['vɛtsən] v/t. (ge-, h) whet,)
wich [viç] pret. of weichen[1].
Wichse ['viksə] f **1.** (-/-n) blacking; polish; **2.** F fig. (-/no pl.) thrashing; '⸰n v/t. (ge-, h) black; polish.

wichtig adj. ['viçtiç] important; sich ⸰ machen show off; '⸰keit f (-/♎-en) importance; ⸰tuer ['⸰tuː-ər] m (-s/-) pompous fellow; '⸰tue-risch adj. pompous.
Wickel ['vikəl] m (-s/-) roll(er); ⸼ₛ: compress; packing; '⸰n v/t. (ge-, h) wind; swaddle (baby); wrap.
Widder zo. ['vidər] m (-s/-) ram.
wider prp. (acc.) ['viːdər] against, contrary to; '⸰borstig adj. cross-grained; ⸰'fahren v/i. (irr. fahren, no -ge-, sein) happen (dat. to); '⸰haken m barb; ⸰hall ['⸰hal] m (-[e]s/-e) echo, reverberation; fig. response; ⸰'hallen v/i. (sep., -ge-, h) (re-)echo (von with), resound (with); ⸰'legen v/t. (no -ge-, h) refute, disprove; '⸰lich adj. repug-nant, repulsive; disgusting; '⸰na-türlich adj. unnatural; '⸰rechtlich adj. illegal, unlawful; '⸰rede f contradiction; '⸰ruf m ⸼⸼ revoca-tion; retraction; ⸰'rufen v/t. (irr. rufen, no -ge-, h) revoke; retract (a. ⸼⸼); '⸰ruflich adj. revocable; ⸰sacher ['⸰zaxər] m (-s/-) adversary; '⸰schein m reflection; ⸰'setzen v/refl. (no -ge-, h): sich e-r Sache ⸰ oppose or resist s.th.; ⸰'setzlich adj. refractory; insubordinate; '⸰sinnig adj. absurd; ⸰spenstig adj. ['⸰ʃpɛnstiç] refractory; ⸰spenstig-keit f (-/♎-en) refractoriness; '⸰spiegeln v/t. (sep., -ge-, h) reflect (a. fig.); sich ⸰ in (dat.) be reflected in; ⸰'sprechen v/i. (irr. sprechen, no -ge-, h): j-m ⸰ con-tradict s.o.; ⸰'spruch m contradic-tion; opposition; im ⸰ zu in con-tradiction to; ⸰sprüchlich adj. ['⸰ʃpryːçliç] contradictory; '⸰spruchslos **1.** adj. uncontradicted; **2.** adv. without contradiction; '⸰stand m resistance (a. ⸍); op-position; ⸰ leisten offer resistance (dat. to); auf heftigen ⸰ stoßen meet with stiff opposition; '⸰stands-fähig adj. resistant (a. ⊕); ⸰'ste-hen v/i. (irr. stehen, no -ge-, h) resist (e-r Sache s.th.); ⸰'streben v/i. (no -ge-, h): es widerstrebt mir, dies zu tun I hate doing or to do that, I am reluctant to do that; ⸰'strebend adv. reluctantly; '⸰streit m (-[e]s/♎-e) antagonism; fig. conflict; ⸰wärtig adj. ['⸰vɛrtiç] unpleasant, disagreeable; disgust-ing; '⸰wille m aversion (gegen to, for, from); dislike (to, of, for); disgust (at, for); reluctance, un-willingness; '⸰willig adj. reluctant, unwilling.
widm|en ['vitmən] v/t. (ge-, h) dedicate; '⸰ung f (-/-en) dedica-tion.
widrig adj. ['viːdriç] adverse; ⸰en-falls adv. ['⸰gən'-] failing which, in default of which.

wie [vi:] 1. *adv.* how; ~ *alt ist er?* what is his age?; ~ *spät ist es?* what is the time?; 2. *cj.*: *ein Mann* ~ *er* a man such as he, a man like him; ~ *er dies hörte* hearing this; *ich hörte,* ~ *er es sagte* I heard him saying so.

wieder *adv.* ['vi:dər] again, anew; *immer* ~ again and again; ♀'**aufbau** *m* (-[e]s/*no pl.*) reconstruction; rebuilding; ~'**aufbauen** *v/t.* (*sep.*, -ge-, *h*) reconstruct; ~'**aufleben** *v/i.* (*sep.*, -ge-, *sein*) revive; ♀'**aufleben** *n* (-s/*no pl.*) revival; ♀'**aufnahme** *f* resumption; ~'**aufnehmen** *v/t.* (*irr.* nehmen, *sep.*, -ge-, *h*) resume; '♀**beginn** *m* recommencement; re-opening; '~**bekommen** *v/t.* (*irr.* kommen, *sep.*, *no* -ge-, *h*) get back; '~**beleben** *v/t.* (*sep.*, *no* -ge-, *h*) resurrect; '~**belebung** *f* (-/-en) revival; *fig. a.* resurrection; '♀**belebungsversuch** *m* attempt at resuscitation; ~'**bringen** *v/t.* (*irr.* bringen, *sep.*, -ge-, *h*) bring back; restore, give back; ~'**einsetzen** *v/t.* (*sep.*, -ge-, *h*) restore; ~'**einstellen** *v/t.* (*sep.*, -ge-, *h*) re-engage; ♀**er-greifung** *f* reseizure; '~**erkennen** *v/t.* (*irr.* kennen, *sep.*, *no* -ge-, *h*) recognize (*an dat.* by); ~**erstatten** *v/t.* (*sep.*, *no* -ge-, *h*) restore; reimburse, refund (*money*); '~**geben** *v/t.* (*irr.* geben, *sep.*, -ge-, *h*) give back, return; render, reproduce; '**gutmachen** *v/t.* (*sep.*, -ge-, *h*) make up for; ♀'**gutmachung** *f* (-/-en) reparation; ~'**herstellen** *v/t.* (*sep.*, -ge-, *h*) restore; ~**holen** *v/t.* (*h*) 1. [~'ho:lən] (*no* -ge-) repeat; 2. ['~ho:lən] (*sep.*, -ge-) fetch back; ♀'**holung** *f* (-/-en) repetition; '~**käuen** [~'kɔyən] (*sep.*, -ge-, *h*) 1. *v/i.* ruminate, chew the cud; 2. F *fig. v/t.* repeat over and over; ♀**kehr** [~'ke:r] *f* (-/*no pl.*) return; recurrence; '~**kehren** *v/i.* (*sep.*, -ge-, *sein*) return; recur; '~**kommen** *v/i.* (*irr.* kommen, *sep.*, -ge-, *sein*) come back, return; '~**sehen** *v/t.* and *v/refl.* (*irr.* sehen, *sep.*, -ge-, *h*) see *or* meet again; '♀**sehen** *n* (-s/*no pl.*) meeting again; *auf* ~! good-bye!; '~**tun** *v/t.* (*irr.* tun, *sep.*, -ge-, *h*) do again, repeat; '**um** *adv.* again, anew; '~**vereinigen** *v/t.* (*sep.*, *no* -ge-, *h*) reunite; ♀**vereinigung** *f* reunion; *pol.* reunification; '♀**verheiratung** *f* remarriage; '♀**verkäufer** *m* reseller; retailer; ♀'**wahl** *f* re-election; '~**wählen** *v/t.* (*sep.*, -ge-, *h*) re-elect; ♀'**zulassung** *f* readmission.

Wiege ['vi:gə] *f* (-/-n) cradle.

wiegen[1] ['vi:gən] *v/t.* and *v/i.* (*irr.*, ge-, *h*) weigh.

wiegen[2] [~] *v/t.* (ge-, *h*) rock; *in Sicherheit* ~ rock in security, lull into (a false sense of) security.

'**Wiegenlied** *n* lullaby.

wiehern ['vi:ərn] *v/i.* (ge-, *h*) neigh.

Wiener ['vi:nər] *m* (-s/-) Viennese; ♀**isch** *adj.* Viennese.

wies [vi:s] *pret. of* weisen.

Wiese ['vi:zə] *f* (-/-n) meadow.

wie'**so** *interr. pron.* why; why so.

wie'**viel** *adv.* how much; *pl.* how many *pl.*; ~**te** *adv.* [~tə]: *den* ~**ten haben wir heute?** what's the date today?

wild [vilt] 1. *adj.* wild; savage; ~**es Fleisch** 🟉 proud flesh; ~**e Ehe** concubinage; ~**er Streik** † wildcat strike; 2. ♀ *n* (-[e]s/*no pl.*) game. '**Wild**|**bach** *m* torrent; ~**bret** ['~brɛt] *n* (-s/*no pl.*) game; venison.

Wilde ['vildə] *m* (-n/-n) savage.

Wilder|**er** ['vildərər] *m* (-s/-) poacher; '♀**n** *v/i.* (ge-, *h*) poach.

'**Wild**|**fleisch** *n s.* Wildbret; '♀**fremd** F *adj.* quite strange; '~**hüter** *m* gamekeeper; '~**leder** *n* buckskin; '♀**ledern** *adj.* buckskin; doeskin; '~**nis** *f* (-/-se) wilderness, wild (*a. fig.*); '~**schwein** *n* wildboar.

Wille ['vilə] *m* (-ns/🟉-n) will; *s-n* ~*n durchsetzen* have one's way; *gegen s-n* ~*n* against one's will; *j-m s-n* ~*n lassen* let s.o. have his (own) way; ♀**nlos** *adj.* lacking will-power.

'**Willens**|**freiheit** *f* (-/*no pl.*) freedom of (the) will; '~**kraft** *f* (-/*no pl.*) will-power; '~**schwäche** *f* (-/*no pl.*) weak will; '♀**stark** *adj.* strong-willed; '~**stärke** *f* (-/*no pl.*) strong will, will-power.

'**will**|**ig** *adj.* willing, ready; '~**kommen** *adj.* welcome; ♀**kür** ['~ky:r] *f* (-/*no pl.*) arbitrariness; '~**kürlich** *adj.* arbitrary.

wimmeln ['viməln] *v/i.* (ge-, *h*) swarm (*von* with), teem (with).

wimmern ['vimərn] *v/i.* (ge-, *h*) whimper, whine.

Wimpel ['vimpəl] *m* (-s/-) pennant, pennon, streamer.

Wimper ['vimpər] *f* (-/-n) eyelash.

Wind [vint] *m* (-[e]s/-e) wind; '~**beutel** *m* cream-puff; F *fig.* windbag.

Winde ['vində] *f* (-/-n) windlass; reel.

Windel ['vindəl] *f* (-/-n) diaper, (baby's) napkin; ~*n pl. a.* swaddling-clothes *pl.*

'**winden** *v/t.* (*irr.*, ge-, *h*) wind; twist, twirl; make, bind (*wreath*); *sich* ~ *vor* (*dat.*) writhe with.

'**Wind**|**hose** *f* whirlwind, tornado; '~**hund** *m* greyhound; ♀**ig** *adj.* ['~diç] windy; F *fig. excuse*: thin, lame; '~**mühle** *f* windmill; '~**pokken** 🟉 *pl.* chicken-pox; '~**richtung** *f* direction of the wind; '~**rose** ⚓ *f* compass card; '~**schutzscheibe** *f* wind-screen, *Am.* windshield; '~**stärke** *f* wind velocity; '2still *adj.* calm; '∼stille *f* calm; '∼stoß *m* blast of wind, gust.

'Windung *f* (-/-en) winding, turn; bend (*of way, etc.*); coil (*of snake, etc.*).

Wink [viŋk] *m* (-[e]s/-e) sign; wave; wink; *fig.*: hint; tip.

Winkel ['viŋkəl] *m* (-s/-) Å angle; corner, nook; '2ig *adj.* angular; *street*: crooked; '∼zug *m* subterfuge, trick, shift.

'winken *v/i.* (ge-, h) make a sign; beckon; *mit dem Taschentuch* ∼ wave one's handkerchief.

winklig *adj.* ['viŋkliç] *s.* winkelig.

winseln ['vinzəln] *v/i.* (ge-, h) whimper, whine.

Winter ['vintər] *m* (-s/-) winter; *im* ∼ in winter; '2lich *adj.* wintry; '∼schlaf *m* hibernation; '∼sport *m* winter sports *pl.*

Winzer ['vintsər] *m* (-s/-) vine-dresser; vine-grower; vintager.

winzig *adj.* ['vintsiç] tiny, diminutive.

Wipfel ['vipfəl] *m* (-s/-) top.

Wippe ['vipə] *f* (-/-n) seesaw; '2n *v/i.* (ge-, h) seesaw.

wir *pers. pron.* [vi:r] we; ∼ *drei* the three of us.

Wirbel ['virbəl] *m* (-s/-) whirl, swirl; eddy; flurry (*of blows, etc.*); *anat.* vertebra; '2ig *adj.* giddy, vertiginous; wild; '2n *v/i.* (ge-, h) whirl; *drums*: roll; '∼säule *anat. f* spinal *or* vertebral column; '∼sturm *m* cyclone, tornado, *Am. a.* twister; '∼tier *n* vertebrate; '∼wind *m* whirlwind (*a. fig.*).

wirk|en ['virkən] (ge-, h) 1. *v/t.* knit, weave; work (*wonders*); 2. *v/i.*: ∼ *als* act *or* function as; ∼ *auf* (*acc.*) produce an impression on; *beruhigend* ∼ have a soothing effect; '∼lich *adj.* real, actual; true, genuine; '2lichkeit *f* (-/-en) reality; *in* ∼ in reality; '∼sam *adj.* effective, efficacious; '2samkeit *f* (-/◣-en) effectiveness, efficacy; '2ung *f* (-/-en) effect.

'Wirkungs|kreis *m* sphere or field of activity; '2los *adj.* ineffective, inefficacious; '∼losigkeit *f* (-/no *pl.*) ineffectiveness, inefficacy; '2voll *adj. s.* wirksam.

wirr [vir] *adj.* confused; *speech*: incoherent; *hair*: dishevel(l)ed; '2en *pl.* disorders *pl.*; troubles *pl.*; 2warr ['∼var] *m* (-s/no *pl.*) confusion, muddle.

Wirsingkohl ['virzin-] *m* (-[e]s/no *pl.*) savoy.

Wirt [virt] *m* (-[e]s/-e) host; landlord; innkeeper.

'Wirtschaft *f* (-/-en) housekeeping; economy; trade and industry; economics *pl.*; *s.* Wirtshaus; F mess; '2en *v/i.* (ge-, h) keep house; economize; F bustle (about); '∼erin

f (-/-nen) housekeeper; '2lich *adj.* economic; economical.

'Wirtschafts|geld *n* housekeeping money; '∼jahr *n* financial year; '∼krise *f* economic crisis; '∼politik *f* economic policy; '∼prüfer *m* (-s/-) chartered accountant, *Am.* certified public accountant.

'Wirtshaus *n* public house, F pub.

Wisch [viʃ] *m* (-es/-e) wisp (*of straw, etc.*); *contp.* scrap of paper; '2en *v/t.* (ge-, h) wipe.

wispern ['vispərn] *v/t. and v/i.* (ge-, h) whisper.

Wiß|begierde ['vis-] *f* (-/no *pl.*) thirst for knowledge; '2begierig *adj.* eager for knowledge.

wissen ['visən] 1. *v/t.* (*irr.*, ge-, h) know; *man kann nie* ∼ you never know, you never can tell; 2. 2 *n* (-s/no *pl.*) knowledge; *meines* ∼s to my knowledge, as far as I know.

'Wissenschaft *f* (-/-en) science; knowledge; '∼ler *m* (-s/-) scholar; scientist; researcher; '2lich *adj.* scientific.

'Wissens|drang *m* (-[e]s/no *pl.*) urge *or* thirst for knowledge; '2-wert *adj.* worth knowing.

'wissentlich *adj.* knowing, conscious.

wittern ['vitərn] *v/t.* (ge-, h) scent, smell; *fig. a.* suspect.

'Witterung *f* (-/◣-en) weather; *hunt.* scent; '∼sverhältnisse ['∼sferheltnisə] *pl.* meteorological conditions *pl.*   [*m* (-s/-) widower.]

Witwe ['vitvə] *f* (-/-n) widow; '∼r)

Witz [vits] *m* 1. (-es/no *pl.*) wit; 2. (-es/-e) joke; ∼*e reißen* crack jokes; '∼blatt *n* comic paper; '2ig *adj.* witty; funny.

wo [vo:] 1. *adv.* where?; 2. *cj.*: F *ach* ∼*!* nonsense!

wob [vo:p] *pret. of* weben.

wo'bei *adv.* at what?; at which; in doing so.

Woche ['vɔxə] *f* (-/-n) week; *heute in e-r* ∼ today week.

'Wochen|bett *n* childbed; '∼blatt *n* weekly (paper); '∼ende *n* weekend; '2lang 1. *adj.*: *nach* ∼*em Warten* after (many) weeks of waiting; 2. *adv.* for weeks; '2lohn *m* weekly pay *or* wages *pl.*; '∼markt *m* weekly market; '∼schau *f* news-reel; '∼tag *m* week-day.

wöchentlich ['vœçəntliç] 1. *adj.* weekly; 2. *adv.* weekly, every week; *einmal* ∼ once a week.

Wöchnerin ['vœçnərin] *f* (-/-nen) woman in childbed.

wo'durch *adv.* by what?, how?; by which, whereby; ∼ *für adv.* for what?, what ... for?; (in return) for which.   [gen¹.]

wog [vo:k] *pret. of* wägen *and* wie-)

Woge ['vo:gə] *f* (-/-n) wave (*a. fig.*), billow; *die* ∼*n glätten* pour oil on troubled waters; '2n v/i. (ge-, h) surge (a. fig.), billow; *wheat: a.* wave; heave.

wo|'her adv. from where?, where ... from?; ~ wissen Sie das? how do you (come to) know that?; ~'hin adv. where (... to)?

wohl [vo:l] 1. adv. well; sich nicht ~ fühlen be unwell; ~ oder übel willy-nilly; leben Sie ~! farewell!; er wird ~ reich sein he is rich, I suppose; 2. 2 n (-[e]s/no pl.): ~ und Wehe weal and woe; auf Ihr ~! your health!, here is to you!

'Wohl|befinden n well-being; good health; '~behagen n comfort, ease; '2behalten adv. safe; '2bekannt adj. well-known; '~ergehen n (-s/no pl.) welfare, prosperity; 2er-zogen adj. ['~'ertso:gən] well-bred, well-behaved; '~fahrt f (-/no pl.) welfare; public assistance; '~ge-fallen n (-s/no pl.) pleasure; sein ~ haben an (dat.) take delight in; '2gemeint adj. well-meant, well-intentioned; 2gemut adj. ['~gə-mu:t] cheerful; '2genährt adj. well-fed; '~geruch m scent, perfume; '2gesinnt adj. well-disposed (j-m towards s.o.); '2habend adj. well-to-do; '2ig adj. comfortable, cosy, snug; '~klang m (-[e]s/no pl.) melodious sound, harmony; '2-klingend adj. melodious, harmonious; '~laut m s. Wohlklang; '~leben n (-s/no pl.) luxury; '2riechend adj. fragrant; '2schmeckend adj. savo(u)ry; '~sein n well-being; good health; '~stand m (-[e]s/no pl.) prosperity, wealth; '~tat f kindness, charity; fig. comfort, treat; '~täter m benefactor; '2tätig adj. charitable, beneficient; '~tä-tigkeit f charity; '2tuend adj. ['~tu:-ənt] pleasant, comfortable; '2tun v/i. (irr. tun, sep., -ge-, h) do good; '2verdient adj. well-deserved; p. of great merit; '~wollen n (-s/no pl.) goodwill; benevolence; favo(u)r; '2wollen v/i. (sep., -ge-, h) be well-disposed (j-m towards s.o.).

wohn|en ['vo:nən] v/i. (ge-, h) live (in dat. in, at; bei j-m with s.o.); reside (in, at; with); '2haus n dwelling-house; block of flats, Am. apartment house; '~haft adj. resident, living; '~lich adj. comfortable; cosy, snug; '2ort m dwelling-place, residence; esp. ‡‡ domicile; '2sitz m residence; mit ~ in resident in or at; ohne festen ~ without fixed abode; '2ung f (-/-en) dwelling, habitation; flat, Am. apartment.

'Wohnungs|amt n housing office; '~not f housing shortage; '~pro-blem n housing problem.

'Wohn|wagen m caravan, trailer; '~zimmer n sitting-room, esp. Am. living room.

wölb|en ['vœlbən] v/t. (ge-, h) vault; arch; sich ~ arch; '2ung f (-/-en) vault, arch; curvature.

Wolf zo. [vɔlf] m (-[e]s/⁺e) wolf.

Wolke ['vɔlkə] f (-/-n) cloud.

'Wolken|bruch m cloud-burst; '~kratzer m (-s/-) skyscraper; '2los adj. cloudless.

'wolkig adj. cloudy, clouded.

'Woll|decke ['vɔl-] f blanket; '~e f (-/-n) wool.

wollen[1] ['vɔlən] (h) 1. v/t. (ge-) wish, desire; want; lieber ~ prefer; nicht ~ refuse; er weiß, was er will he knows his mind; 2. v/i. (ge-): ich will schon, aber ... I want to, but ...; 3. v/aux. (no -ge-) be willing; intend, be going to; be about to; lieber ~ prefer; nicht ~ refuse; er hat nicht gehen ~ he refused to go.

woll|en[2] adj. [~] wool(l)en; '~ig adj. wool(l)y; '2stoff m wool(l)en.

Wol|lust ['vɔlust] f (-/⁺e) voluptuousness; 2lüstig adj. ['~lystiç] voluptuous.

'Wollwaren pl. wool(l)en goods pl.

wo|'mit adv. with what?, what ... with?; with which; ~'möglich adv. perhaps, maybe.

Wonn|e ['vɔnə] f (-/-n) delight, bliss; '2ig adj. delightful, blissful.

wo|ran adv. [vo:'ran]: ~ denkst du? what are you thinking of?; ich weiß nicht, ~ ich mit ihm bin I don't know what to make of him; ~ liegt es, daß ...? how is it that ...?; ~'rauf adv. on what?, what ... on?; whereupon, after which; ~ wartest du? what are you waiting for?; ~'raus adv. from what?; what ... of?; from which; ~rin adv. [~'rin] in what?; in which.

Wort [vɔrt] n 1. (-[e]s/⁺er) word; er kann seine Wörter noch nicht he hasn't learnt his words yet; 2. (-[e]s/-e) word; term, expression; ums ~ bitten ask permission to speak; das ~ ergreifen begin to speak; parl. rise to speak, address the House, esp. Am. take the floor; das ~ führen be the spokesman; ~ halten keep one's word; '2brüchig adj.: er ist ~ geworden he has broken his word.

'Wörter|buch ['vœrtər-] n dictionary; '~verzeichnis n vocabulary, list of words.

'Wort|führer m spokesman; '2ge-treu adj. literal; '2karg adj. taciturn; '~klauberei [~klaubə'raı] f (-/-en) word-splitting; '~laut m (-[e]s/no pl.) wording; text. [eral.]

wörtlich adj. ['vœrtliç] verbal, lit-

'Wort|schatz m (-es/no pl.) vocabulary; '~schwall m (-[e]s/no pl.) verbiage; '~spiel n pun (über acc., mit [up]on), play upon words; '~stellung gr. f word order, order of words; '~stamm ling. m stem; '~streit m, '~wechsel m dispute.

wo|rüber adv. [vo:'ry:bər] over or upon what?, what ... over or about or on?; over or upon which, about which; **~rum** adv. [~'rum] about what?, what ... about?; about or for which; ~ handelt es sich? what is it about?; **~runter** adv. [~'runtər] under or among what?, what ... under?; under or among which; **~'von** adv. of or from what?, what ... from or of?; about what?, what ... about?; of or from which; **~'vor** adv. of what?, what ... of?; of which; **~'zu** adv. for what?, what ... for?; for which.

Wrack [vrak] n (-[e]s/-e, -s) ⚓ wreck (a. fig.).

wrang [vraŋ] pret. of wringen.

wring|en ['vriŋən] v/t. (irr., ge-, h) wring; **'2maschine** f wringing-machine.

Wucher ['vu:xər] m. (-s/no pl.) usury; ~ treiben practise usury; **'~er** m (-s/-) usurer; **'~gewinn** m excess profit; **'2isch** adj. usurious; **'2n** v/i. (ge-, h) grow exuberantly; **'~ung** f (-/-en) ⚕ exuberant growth; ⚘ growth; **'~zinsen** m/pl. usurious interest.

Wuchs [vu:ks] 1. m (-es/⸚e) growth; figure, shape; stature; 2. ♀ pret. of wachsen.

Wucht [vuxt] f (-/⸚-en) weight; force; **'2ig** adj. heavy.

Wühl|arbeit fig. ['vy:l-] f insidious agitation, subversive activity; **'2en** v/i. (ge-, h) dig; pig: root; fig. agitate; ~ in (dat.) rummage (about) in; **'~er** m (-s/-) agitator.

Wulst [vulst] m (-es/⸚e), f (-/⸚e) pad; bulge; ⚠ roll(-mo[u]lding); ⊕ bead; **'2ig** adj. lips: thick.

wund adj. [vunt] sore; ~e Stelle sore; ~er Punkt tender spot; **2e** ['~də] f (-/-n) wound; alte ~n wieder aufreißen reopen old sores.

Wunder ['vundər] n (-s/-) miracle; fig. a. wonder, marvel; ~ wirken pills, etc.: work marvels; kein ~, wenn man bedenkt ... no wonder, considering ...; **'2bar** adj. miraculous; fig. a. wonderful, marvel-(l)ous; **'~kind** n infant prodigy; **'2lich** adj. queer, odd; **'2n** v/t. (ge-, h) surprise, astonish; sich ~ be surprised or astonished (über acc. at); **'2schön** adj. very beautiful; **'~tat** f wonder, miracle; **'~täter** m wonder-worker; **'2tätig** adj. wonder-working; **'2voll** adj. wonderful; **'~werk** n marvel, wonder.

'Wund|fieber ⚕ n wound-fever; **'~starrkrampf** ⚕ m tetanus.

Wunsch [vunʃ] m (-es/⸚e) wish, desire; request; auf ~ by or on request; if desired; nach ~ as desired; mit den besten Wünschen zum Fest with the compliments of the season.

Wünschelrute ['vynʃəl-] f divin-ing-rod, dowsing-rod; **~ngänger** ['~genər] m (-s/-) diviner, dowser.

wünschen ['vynʃən] v/t. (ge-, h) wish, desire; wie Sie ~ as you wish; was ~ Sie? what can I do for you?; **'~swert** adj. desirable.

'wunsch|gemäß adv. as requested or desired, according to one's wishes; **'2zettel** m list of wishes.

wurde ['vurdə] pret. of werden.

Würde ['vyrdə] f (-/-n) dignity; unter seiner ~ beneath one's dignity; **2los** adj. undignified; **'~nträger** m dignitary; **'2voll** adj. dignified; grave.

'würdig adj. worthy (gen. of); dignified; grave; **~en** ['~gən] v/t. (ge-, h) appreciate, value; mention hono(u)rably; laud, praise; j-n keines Blickes ~ ignore s.o. completely; **2ung** ['~guŋ] f (-/-en) appreciation, valuation.

Wurf [vurf] m (-[e]s/⸚e) throw, cast; zo. litter.

Würfel ['vyrfəl] m (-s/-) die; cube (a. ♉); **'~becher** m dice-box; **'2n** v/i. (ge-, h) (play) dice; **'~spiel** n game of dice; **'~zucker** m lump sugar. [tile.]

'Wurfgeschoß n missile, projec-)

würgen ['vyrgən] (ge-, h) 1. v/t. choke, strangle; 2. v/i. choke; retch.

Wurm zo. [vurm] m (-[e]s/⸚er) worm; **2en** F v/t. (ge-, h) vex; rankle (j-n in s.o.'s mind); **'2stichig** adj. worm-eaten.

Wurst [vurst] f (-/⸚e) sausage; F das ist mir ganz ~ I don't care a rap.

Würstchen ['vyrstçən] n (-s/-) sausage; heißes ~ hot sausage, Am. hot dog.

Würze ['vyrtsə] f (-/-n) seasoning, flavo(u)r; spice, condiment; fig. salt.

Wurzel ['vurtsəl] f (-/-n) root (a. gr., ♉); ~ schlagen strike or take root (a. fig.); **'2n** v/i. (ge-, h) (strike or take) root; ~ in (dat.) take one's root in, be rooted in.

'würz|en v/t. (ge-, h) spice, season, flavo(u)r; **'~ig** adj. spicy, well-seasoned, aromatic.

wusch [vu:ʃ] pret. of waschen.

wußte ['vustə] pret. of wissen.

Wust F [vu:st] m (-es/no pl.) tangled mass; rubbish; mess.

wüst adj. [vy:st] desert, waste; confused; wild, dissolute; rude; **'2e** f (-/-n) desert, waste; **2ling** ['~liŋ] m (-s/-e) debauchee, libertine, rake.

Wut [vu:t] f (-/no pl.) rage, fury; in ~ in a rage; **'~anfall** m fit of rage.

wüten ['vy:tən] v/i. (ge-, h) rage (a. fig.); **'~d** adj. furious, enraged (über acc. at; auf acc. with), esp. Am. F a. mad (über acc., auf acc. at).

Wüterich ['vy:tərıç] m (-[e]s/-e) berserker; bloodthirsty man.

'wutschnaubend adj. foaming with rage.

X, Y

X-Beine ['iks-] *n/pl.* knock-knees *pl.*; '**X-beinig** *adj.* knock-kneed.

x-beliebig *adj.* [iksbə'li:biç] any (... you please); *jede*(*r*, *-s*) *∼e* ... any ...

x-mal *adv.* ['iks-] many times, *sl.* umpteen times.

X-Strahlen ['iks-] *m/pl.* X-rays *pl.*

x-te *adj.* ['ikstə]: *zum ∼n Male* for the umpteenth time.

Xylophon ♪ [ksylo'fo:n] *n* (-s/-e) xylophone.

Yacht ⚓ [jaxt] *f* (-/-en) yacht.

Z

Zacke ['tsakə] *f* (-/-n) *s.* Zacken.

'**Zacken 1.** *m* (-s/-) (sharp) point; prong; tooth (*of comb, saw, rake*); jag (*of rock*); **2.** ♀ *v/t.* (ge-, h) indent, notch; jag.

'**zackig** *adj.* indented, notched; *rock*: jagged; pointed; ✕ F *fig.* smart.

zaghaft *adj.* ['tsa:khaft] timid; '**2igkeit** *f* (-/*no pl.*) timidity.

zäh *adj.* [tse:] tough, tenacious (*both a. fig.*); *liquid*: viscid, viscous; *fig.* dogged; '**∼flüssig** *adj.* viscid, viscous, sticky; '**2igkeit** *f* (-/*no pl.*) toughness, tenacity (*both a. fig.*); viscosity; *fig.* doggedness.

Zahl [tsa:l] *f* (-/-en) number; figure, cipher; '**2bar** *adj.* payable.

'**zählbar** *adj.* countable.

zahlen ['tsa:lən] (ge-, h) **1.** *v/i.* pay; *at restaurant*: ∼ (, *bitte*)! the bill, please!, *Am.* the check, please!; **2.** *v/t.* pay.

zählen ['tse:lən] (ge-, h) **1.** *v/t.* count, number; ∼ *zu* count or number among; **2.** *v/i.* count; ∼ *auf* (*acc.*) count (up)on, rely (up)on.

'**Zahlen|lotto** *n s.* Lotto; '**2mäßig 1.** *adj.* numerical; **2.** *adv.*: *j-m ∼ überlegen sein* outnumber s.o.

'**Zähler** *m* (-s/-) counter; ♠ numerator; *for gas, etc.*: meter.

'**Zahl|karte** *f* money-order form (*for paying direct into the postal cheque account*); '**2los** *adj.* numberless, innumerable, countless; '**∼meister** ✕ *m* paymaster; '**2reich 1.** *adj.* numerous; **2.** *adv.* in great number; '**∼tag** *m* pay-day; '**∼ung** *f* (-/-en) payment.

'**Zählung** *f* (-/-en) counting.

'**Zahlungs|anweisung** *f* order to pay; '**∼aufforderung** *f* request for payment; '**∼bedingungen** *f/pl.* terms *pl.* of payment; '**∼befehl** *m* order to pay; '**∼einstellung** *f* suspension of payment; '**2fähig** *adj.* solvent; '**∼fähigkeit** *f* solvency; '**∼frist** *f* term for payment; '**∼mittel** *n* currency; *gesetzliches ∼* legal tender; '**∼schwierigkeiten** *f/pl.* financial *or* pecuniary difficulties

pl.; '**∼termin** *m* date of payment; '**2unfähig** *adj.* insolvent; '**∼unfähigkeit** *f* insolvency.

'**Zahlwort** *gr. n* (-[e]s/*∼er*) numeral.

zahm *adj.* [tsa:m] tame (*a. fig.*), domestic(ated).

zähm|en ['tse:mən] *v/t.* (ge-, h) tame (*a. fig.*), domesticate; '**2ung** *f* (-/⚓-en) taming (*a. fig.*), domestication.

Zahn [tsa:n] *m* (-[e]s/*∼e*) tooth; ⊕ tooth, cog; *Zähne bekommen* cut one's teeth; '**∼arzt** *m* dentist, dental surgeon; '**∼bürste** *f* toothbrush; '**∼creme** *f* tooth-paste; '**2en** *v/i.* (ge-, h) teethe, cut one's teeth; '**∼ersatz** *m* denture; '**∼fäule** 🦷 ['∼fɔylə] *f* (-/*no pl.*) dental caries; '**∼fleisch** *n* gums *pl.*; '**∼füllung** *f* filling, stopping; '**∼geschwür** 🦷 *n* gumboil; '**∼heilkunde** *f* dentistry; '**2los** *adj.* toothless; '**∼lücke** *f* gap between the teeth; '**∼pasta** ['∼pasta] *f* (-/*Zahnpasten*), '**∼paste** *f* tooth-paste; '**∼rad** ⊕ *n* cog-wheel; '**∼radbahn** *f* rack-railway; '**∼schmerzen** *m/pl.* toothache; '**∼stocher** *m* (-s/-) toothpick.

Zange ['tsaŋə] *f* (-/-n) (e-e *a pair of*) tongs *pl. or* pliers *pl. or* pincers *pl.*; 🦷, *zo.* forceps *sg., pl.*

Zank [tsaŋk] *m* (-[e]s/*no pl.*) quarrel, F row; '**∼apfel** *m* bone of contention; '**2en** (ge-, h) **1.** *v/i.* scold (*mit j-m* s.o.); **2.** *v/refl.* quarrel, wrangle.

zänkisch *adj.* ['tseŋkiʃ] quarrelsome.

Zäpfchen ['tsepfçən] *n* (-s/-) small peg; *anat.* uvula.

Zapfen ['tsapfən] **1.** *m* (-s/-) plug; peg, pin; bung (*of barrel*); pivot; ♀ cone; **2.** ♀ *v/t.* (ge-, h) tap; '**∼streich** ✕ *m* tattoo, retreat, *Am. a.* taps *pl.*

'**Zapf|hahn** *m* tap, *Am.* faucet; '**∼säule** *mot. f* petrol pump.

zappel|ig *adj.* ['tsapəliç] fidgety; '**∼n** *v/i.* (ge-, h) struggle; fidget.

zart *adj.* [tsa:rt] tender; soft; gentle; delicate; '**∼fühlend** *adj.* delicate; '**2gefühl** *n* (-[e]s/*no pl.*) delicacy (of feeling).

zärtlich adj. ['tsɛːrtliç] tender; fond, loving; **2keit** f 1. (-/no pl.) tenderness; fondness; 2. (-/-en) caress.

Zauber ['tsaubər] m (-s/-) spell, charm, magic (all a. fig.); fig.: enchantment; glamo(u)r; **ei** [~'raɪ] f (-/-en) magic, sorcery; witchcraft; conjuring; **er** m (-s/-) sorcerer, magician; conjurer; **flöte** f magic flute; **formel** f spell; **2haft** adj. magic(al); fig. enchanting; **in** f (-/-nen) sorceress, witch; fig. enchantress; **kraft** f magic power; **kunststück** n conjuring trick; **2n** (ge-, h) 1. v/i. practise magic or witchcraft; do conjuring tricks; 2. v/t. conjure; **spruch** m spell; **stab** m (magic) wand; **wort** n (-[e]s/-e) magic word, spell.

zaudern ['tsaudərn] v/i. (ge-, h) hesitate; linger, delay.

Zaum [tsaum] m (-[e]s/=e) bridle; im ~ halten keep in check.

zäumen ['tsɔymən] v/t. (ge-, h) bridle.

'Zaumzeug n bridle.

Zaun [tsaun] m (-[e]s/=e) fence; **gast** m deadhead; **könig** orn. m wren; **pfahl** m pale.

Zebra zo. ['tseːbra] n (-s/-s) zebra; **streifen** m zebra crossing.

Zeche ['tsɛçə] f (-/-n) score, reckoning, bill; ⚒ mine; coal-pit, colliery; F die ~ bezahlen foot the bill, F stand treat; **2en** v/i. (ge-, h) carouse, tipple; **gelage** n carousal, carouse; **preller** m (-s/-) bilk(er).

Zeh [tseː] m (-[e]s/-en), **e** f (-/-n) toe; **enspitze** f point or tip of the toe; auf ~n on tiptoe.

zehn adj. [tseːn] ten; **2er** m (-s/-) ten; coin: F ten-pfennig piece; **fach** adj. ['~fax] tenfold; **jährig** adj. ['~jɛːriç] ten-year-old, of ten (years); **kampf** m sports: decathlon; **mal** adv. ten times; **te** ['~tə] 1. adj. tenth; 2. 2 † m (-n/-n) tithe; **2tel** ['~təl] n (-s/-) tenth (part); **tens** adv. ['~təns] tenthly.

zehren ['tseːrən] v/i. (ge-, h) make thin; ~ von live on s.th.; fig. live off (the capital); ~ an prey (up)on (one's mind); undermine (one's health).

Zeichen ['tsaɪçən] n (-s/-) sign; token; mark; indication, symptom; signal; zum ~ (gen.) in sign of, as a sign of; **block** m drawing-block; **brett** n drawing-board; **lehrer** m drawing-master; **papier** n drawing-paper; **setzung** gr. f (-/no pl.) punctuation; **sprache** f sign-language; **stift** m pencil, crayon; **trickfilm** m animation, animated cartoon; **unterricht** m drawing-lessons pl.

zeichn|en ['tsaɪçnən] (ge-, h) 1. v/t.

draw (plan, etc.); design (pattern); mark; sign; subscribe (sum of money) (zu to); subscribe for (shares); 2. v/i. draw; sie zeichnet gut she draws well; **2er** m (-s/-) draftsman, draughtsman; designer; subscriber (gen. for shares); **2ung** f (-/-en) drawing; design; illustration; zo. marking (of skin, etc.); subscription.

Zeige|finger ['tsaɪgə-] m forefinger, index (finger); **2n** (ge-, h) 1. v/t. show; point out; indicate; demonstrate; sich ~ appear; 2. v/i. ~ auf (acc.) point at; ~ nach point to; **r** m (-s/-) hand (of clock, etc.); pointer (of dial, etc.); **stock** m pointer.

Zeile ['tsaɪlə] f (-/-n) line; row; j-m ein paar ~n schreiben drop s.o. a line or a few lines.   [siskin.]

Zeisig orn. ['tsaɪzɪç] m (-[e]s/-e)

Zeit [tsaɪt] f (-/-en) time; epoch, era, age; period, space (of time); term; freie ~ spare time; mit der ~ in the course of time; von ~ zu ~ from time to time; vor langer ~ long ago, a long time ago; zur ~ (gen.) in the time of; at (the) present; zu meiner ~ in my time; zu s-r ~ in due course (of time); das hat ~ there is plenty of time for that; es ist höchste ~ it is high time; j-m ~ lassen give s.o. time; laß dir ~! take your time!; sich die ~ vertreiben pass the time, kill time. **'Zeit|abschnitt** m epoch, period; **alter** n age; **angabe** f exact date and hour; date; **aufnahme** phot. f time-exposure; **dauer** f length of time, period (of time); **enfolge** gr. f sequence of tenses; **geist** m (-es/no pl.) spirit of the time(s), zeitgeist; **2gemäß** adj. modern, up-to-date; **genosse** m contemporary; **2genössisch** adj. ['~gənœsiʃ] contemporary; **geschichte** f contemporary history; **gewinn** m gain of time; **2ig** 1. adj. early; 2. adv. on time; **karte** f season-ticket, Am. commutation ticket; **lang** f: e-e ~ for some time, for a while; **2lebens** adv. for life, all one's life; **2lich** 1. adj. temporal; 2. adv. as to time; ~ zusammenfallen coincide; **2los** adj. timeless; **lupe** phot. f slow motion; **lupenaufnahme** phot.f slow-motion picture; **2nah** adj. current, up-to-date; **ordnung** f chronological order; **punkt** m moment; time; date; **rafferaufnahme** phot. f time-lapse photography; **2raubend** adj. time-consuming; pred. a. taking up much time; **raum** m space (of time); period; **rechnung** f chronology; era; **schrift** f journal, periodical, magazine; review; **tafel** f chronological table.

'**Zeitung** f (-/-en) (news)paper, journal.

'**Zeitungs|abonnement** n subscription to a paper; '**~artikel** m newspaper article; '**~ausschnitt** m (press or newspaper) cutting, (Am. only) (newspaper) clipping; **~kiosk** ['~kiɔsk] m (-[e]s/-e) news-stand; '**~notiz** f press item; '**~papier** n newsprint; '**~verkäufer** m newsvendor; news-boy, news-man; '**~wesen** n journalism, the press.

'**Zeit|verlust** m loss of time; '**~verschwendung** f waste of time; **~vertreib** ['~fɛrtraɪp] m (-[e]s/-e) pastime; zum ~ to pass the time; **2weilig** adj. ['~vaɪlıç] temporary; '**2weise** adv. for a time; at times, occasionally; '**~wort** gr. n (-[e]s/=er) verb; '**~zeichen** n time-signal.

Zell|e ['tsɛlə] f (-/-n) cell; '**~stoff** m, **~ulose** ⊕ [~u'lo:zə] f (-/-n) cellulose.

Zelt [tsɛlt] n (-[e]s/-e) tent; '**2en** v/i. (ge-, h) camp; '**~leinwand** f canvas; '**~platz** m camping-ground.

Zement [tse'mɛnt] m (-[e]s/-e) cement; **2ieren** [~'ti:rən] v/t. (no -ge-, h) cement.

Zenit [tse'ni:t] m (-[e]s/no pl.) zenith (a. fig.).

zens|ieren [tsɛn'zi:rən] v/t. (no ge-, h) censor (book, etc.); at school: mark, Am. a. grade; **2or** ['~ɔr] m (-s/-en) censor; **2ur** [~'zu:r] f 1. (-/no pl.) censorship; 2. (-/-en) at school: mark, Am. a. grade; (school) report, Am. report card.

Zentimeter [tsɛnti'-] n, m centimet|re, Am. -er.

Zentner ['tsɛntnər] m (-s/-) (Brt. appr.) hundredweight.

zentral adj. [tsɛn'trɑ:l] central; **2e** f (-/-n) central office; teleph. (telephone) exchange, Am. a. central; **2heizung** f central heating.

Zentrum ['tsɛntrum] n (-s/Zentren) cent|re, Am. -er. [Am. -er.]

Zepter ['tsɛptər] n (-s/-) scept|re,]

zer|beißen [tsɛr'-] v/t. (irr. beißen, no -ge-, h) bite to pieces; **~'bersten** v/i. (irr. bersten, no -ge-, sein) burst asunder.

zer'brech|en (irr. brechen, no -ge-) 1. v/t. (h) break (to pieces); sich den Kopf ~ rack one's brains; 2. v/i. (sein) break; **~lich** adj. breakable, fragile.

zer|'bröckeln v/t. (h) and v/i. (sein) (no -ge-) crumble; **~'drücken** v/t. (no -ge-, h) crush; crease (dress).

Zeremon|ie [tseremo'ni:, ~'mo:njə] f (-/-n) ceremony; **2iell** adj. [~o'njɛl] ceremonial; **~iell** [~o'njɛl] n (-s/-e) ceremonial.

zer'fahren adj. road: rutted; p.: flighty, giddy; scatter-brained; absent-minded.

Zer'fall m (-[e]s/no pl.) ruin, decay;

disintegration; **2en** v/i. (irr. fallen, no -ge-, sein) fall to pieces, decay; disintegrate; in mehrere Teile ~ fall into several parts.

zer|'fetzen v/t. (no -ge-, h) tear in or to pieces; **~'fleischen** v/t. (no -ge-, h) mangle; lacerate; **~'fließen** v/i. (irr. fließen, no -ge-, sein) melt (away); ink, etc.: run; **~'fressen** v/t. (irr. fressen, no -ge-, h) eat away; 🜍 corrode; **~'gehen** v/i. (irr. gehen, no -ge-, sein) melt, dissolve; **~'gliedern** v/t. (no -ge-, h) dismember; anat. dissect; fig. analy|se, Am. -ze; **~'hacken** v/t. (no -ge-, h) cut (in)to pieces; mince, chop (up) (wood, meat); **~'kauen** v/t. (no -ge-, h) chew; **~'kleinern** v/t. (no -ge-, h) mince (meat); chop up (wood); grind.

zer'knirsch|t adj. contrite; **2ung** f (-/🜍-en) contrition.

zer|'knittern v/t. (no -ge-, h) (c)rumple, wrinkle, crease; **~'knüllen** v/t. (no -ge-, h) crumple up (sheet of paper); **~'kratzen** v/t. (no -ge-, h) scratch; **~'krümeln** v/t. (no -ge-, h) crumble; **~'lassen** v/t. (irr. lassen, no -ge-, h) melt; **~'legen** v/t. (no -ge-, h) take apart or to pieces; carve (joint); 🜍, gr., fig. analy|se, Am. -ze; **~'lumpt** adj. ragged, tattered; **~'mahlen** v/t. (irr. mahlen, no -ge-, h) grind; **~malmen** [~'malmən] v/t. (no -ge-, h) crush; crunch; **~'mürben** v/t. (no -ge-, h) wear down or out; **~'platzen** v/i. (no -ge-, sein) burst; explode; **~'quetschen** v/t. (no -ge-, h) crush, squash; mash (esp. potatoes).

Zerrbild ['tsɛr-] n caricature.

zer|'reiben v/t. (irr. reiben, no -ge-, h) rub to powder, grind down, pulverize; **~'reißen** (irr. reißen, no -ge-) 1. v/t. (h) tear, rip up; in Stücke ~ tear to pieces; 2. v/i. (sein) tear; rope, string: break.

zerren ['tsɛrən] (ge-, h) 1. v/t. tug, pull; drag; 🜍 strain; 2. v/i.: ~ an (dat.) pull at.

zer'rinnen v/i. (irr. rinnen, no -ge-, sein) melt away; fig. vanish.

'**Zerrung** 🜍 f (-/-en) strain.

zer|rütten [tsɛr'rytən] v/t. (no -ge-, h) derange, unsettle; disorganize; ruin, shatter (one's health or nerves); wreck (marriage); **~'sägen** v/t. (no -ge-, h) saw up; **~schellen** [~'ʃɛlən] v/i. (no -ge-, sein) be dashed or smashed; ⚓ be wrecked; ✈ crash; **~'schlagen** 1. v/t. (irr. schlagen, no -ge-, h) break or smash (to pieces); sich ~ come to nothing; 2. adj. battered; fig. knocked up; **~'schmettern** v/t. (no -ge-, h) smash, dash, shatter; **~'schneiden** v/t. (irr. schneiden, no -ge-, h) cut in two; cut up, cut to pieces.

zer'setz|en v/t. and v/refl. (no -ge-, h) decompose; 2ung f (-/≈ -en) decomposition.

zer|'spalten v/t. ([irr. spalten,] no -ge-, h) cleave, split; ≈'splittern (no -ge-) 1. v/t. (h) split (up), splinter; fritter away (one's energy, etc.); 2. v/i. (sein) split (up), splinter; ≈'sprengen v/t. (no -ge-, h) burst (asunder); disperse (crowd); ≈'springen v/i. (irr. springen, no -ge-, sein) burst; glass: crack; mein Kopf zerspringt mir I've got a splitting headache; ≈'stampfen v/t. (no -ge-, h) crush; pound.

zer'stäub|en v/t. (no -ge-, h) spray; 2er m (-s/-) sprayer, atomizer.

zer'stör|en v/t. (no -ge-, h) destroy; 2er m (-s/-) destroyer (a. ⊕); 2ung f destruction.

zer'streu|en v/t. (no -ge-, h) disperse, scatter; dissipate (doubt, etc.); fig. divert; sich ≈ disperse, scatter; fig. amuse o.s.; ≈t fig. adj. absent(-minded); 2theit f (-/≈ -en) absent-mindedness; 2ung f 1. (-/ -en) dispersion; diversion, amusement; 2. phys. (-/no pl.) dispersion (of light).

zerstückeln [tser'ʃtykəln] v/t. (no -ge-, h) cut up, cut (in)to pieces; dismember (body, etc.).

zer|'teilen v/t. and v/refl. (no -ge-, h) divide (in acc. into); ≈'trennen v/t. (no -ge-, h) rip (up) (dress); ≈'treten v/t. (irr. treten, no -ge-, h) tread down; crush; tread or stamp out (fire); ≈'trümmern v/t. (no -ge-, h) smash.

Zerwürfnis [tser'vyrfnis] n (-ses/ -se) dissension, discord.

Zettel ['tsetəl] m (-s/-) slip (of paper), scrap of paper; note; ticket; label, sticker; tag; s. Anschlagzettel; s. Theaterzettel; '≈ kartei f, '≈kasten m card index.

Zeug [tsɔʏk] n (-[e]s/-e) stuff (a. fig. contp.), material; cloth; tools pl.; things pl.

Zeuge ['tsɔʏgə] m (-n/-n) witness; '2n (ge-, h) 1. v/i. witness; ⚖ give evidence; für (gegen, von) et. ≈ testify for (against, of) s.th.; ≈ von be evidence of, bespeak (courage, etc.); 2. v/t. beget.

'Zeugen|aussage ⚖ f testimony, evidence; '≈bank f (-/≈ e) witness-box, Am. witness stand.

Zeugin ['tsɔʏgin] f (-/-nen) (female) witness.

Zeugnis ['tsɔʏknis] n (-ses/-se) ⚖ testimony, evidence; certificate; (school) report, Am. report card.

Zeugung ['tsɔʏguŋ] f (-/-en) procreation; 2sfähig adj. capable of begetting; '≈skraft f generative power; 2sunfähig adj. ['tsɔʏguŋs?-] impotent.

Zick|lein zo. ['tsiklaɪn] n (-s/-) kid;

≈zack ['≈tsak] m (-[e]s/-e) zigzag; im ≈ fahren etc. zigzag.

Ziege zo. ['tsi:gə] f (-/-n) (she-)goat, nanny(-goat).

Ziegel ['tsi:gəl] m (-s/-) brick; tile (of roof); '≈dach n tiled roof; ≈ei [≈'laɪ] f (-/-en) brickworks sg., pl., brickyard; '≈stein m brick.

'Ziegen|bock zo. m he-goat; '≈fell n goatskin; '≈hirt m goatherd; '≈ leder n kid(-leather); '≈peter ⚕ m (-s/-) mumps.

Ziehbrunnen ['tsi:-] m draw-well.

ziehen ['tsi:ən] (irr., ge-) 1. v/t. (h) pull, draw; draw (line, weapon, lots, conclusion, etc.); drag; ♀ cultivate; zo. breed; take off (hat); dig (ditch); draw, extract (tooth); ⚕ extract (root of number); Blasen ≈ ⚕ raise blisters; e-n Vergleich ≈ draw or make a comparison; j-n ins Vertrauen ≈ take s.o. into one's confidence; in Erwägung ≈ take into consideration; in die Länge ≈ draw out; fig. protract; Nutzen ≈ aus derive profit or benefit from; an sich ≈ draw to one; Aufmerksamkeit etc. auf sich ≈ attract attention, etc.; et. nach sich ≈ entail or involve s.th.; 2. v/i. (h) pull (an dat. at); chimney, cigar, etc.: draw; puff (an e-r Zigarre at a cigar); tea: infuse, draw; play: draw (large audiences); F ⚹ goods: draw (customers), take; es zieht there is a draught, Am. there is a draft; 3. v/i. (sein) move, go; march; (re)move (nach to); birds: migrate; 4. v/refl. (h) extend, stretch, run; wood: warp; sich in die Länge ≈ drag on.

'Zieh|harmonika ♪ f accordion; '≈ung f (-/-en) drawing (of lots).

Ziel [tsi:l] n (-[e]s/-e) aim (a. fig.); mark; sports: winning-post, goal (a. fig.); target; ⚔ objective; destination (of voyage); fig. end, purpose, target, object(ive); term; sein ≈ erreichen gain one's end(s pl.); über das ≈ hinausschießen overshoot the mark; zum ≈e führen succeed, be successful; sich zum ≈ setzen zu inf. aim at ger., Am. aim to inf.; '≈band n sports: tape; '2 bewußt adj. purposeful; '2en v/i. (ge-, h) (take) aim (auf acc. at); '≈fernrohr n telescopic sight; '2 los adj. aimless, purposeless; '≈ scheibe f target, butt; ≈ des Spottes butt or target (of derision); '2 strebig adj. purposive.

ziemlich ['tsi:mlɪç] 1. adj. fair, tolerable, considerable; 2. adv. pretty, fairly, tolerably; rather; about.

Zier [tsi:r] f (-/no pl.), ≈de ['≈də] f (-/-n) ornament; fig. a. hono(u)r (für to); '2en v/t. (ge-, h) ornament, adorn, decorate; sich ≈ be affected; esp. of woman: be prudish; refuse; '**‿lich** *adj.* delicate; neat; graceful, elegant; '**‿lichkeit** *f* (-/‿ -en) delicacy; neatness; gracefulness, elegance; '**‿pflanze** *f* ornamental plant.

Ziffer ['tsifər] *f* (-/-n) figure, digit; '**‿blatt** *n* dial(-plate), face.

Zigarette [tsiga'rɛtə] *f* (-/-n) cigaret(te); **‿nautomat** [‿n⁹-] *m* cigarette slot-machine; **‿netui** [‿n⁹-] *n* cigarette-case; **‿nspitze** *f* cigarette-holder; **‿nstummel** *m* stub, *Am. a.* butt.

Zigarre [tsi'garə] *f* (-/-n) cigar.

Zigeuner [tsi'gɔʏnər] *m* (-s/-), **‿in** *f* (-/-nen) gipsy, gypsy.

Zimmer ['tsimər] *n* (-s/-) room; apartment; '**‿antenne** *f* radio, *etc.*: indoor aerial, *Am. a.* indoor antenna; '**‿einrichtung** *f* furniture; '**‿flucht** *f* suite (of rooms); '**‿mädchen** *n* chamber-maid; '**‿mann** *m* (-[e]s/*Zimmerleute*) carpenter; '**‿n** (ge-, h) **1.** *v/t.* carpenter; *fig.* frame; **2.** *v/i.* carpenter; '**‿pflanze** *f* indoor plant; '**‿vermieterin** *f* (-/-nen) landlady.

zimperlich *adj.* ['tsimpərliç] prim; prudish; affected.

Zimt [tsimt] *m* (-[e]s/-e) cinnamon.

Zink [tsiŋk] *n* (-[e]s/*no pl.*) zinc; '**‿blech** *n* sheet zinc.

Zinke ['tsiŋkə] *f* (-/-n) prong; tooth (*of comb or fork*); '**‿n** *m* (-s/-) *s.* *Zinke.*

Zinn [tsin] *n* (-[e]s/*no pl.*) tin.

Zinne ['tsinə] *f* (-/-n) △ pinnacle; ⚔ battlement.

Zinnober [tsi'noːbər] *m* (-s/-) cinnabar; **‿rot** *adj.* vermilion.

Zins [tsins] *m* (-es/-en) rent; tribute; *mst ‿en pl.* interest; **‿en tragen** yield *or* bear interest; '**‿bringend** *adj.* bearing interest; **‿eszins** ['‿zəs-] *m* compound interest; '**‿frei** *adj.* rent-free; free of interest; '**‿fuß** *m*, '**‿satz** *m* rate of interest.

Zipf|el ['tsipfəl] *m* (-s/-) tip, point, end; corner (*of handkerchief, etc.*); lappet (*of garment*); '**‿elig** *adj.* having points *or* ends; '**‿elmütze** *f* jelly-bag cap; nightcap.

Zirkel ['tsirkəl] *m* (-s/-) circle (*a. fig.*); ⚙ (*ein a* pair of) compasses *pl. or* dividers *pl.*

zirkulieren [tsirku'liːrən] *v/i.* (*no* -ge-, h) circulate.

Zirkus ['tsirkus] *m* (-/-se) circus.

zirpen ['tsirpən] *v/i.* (ge-, h) chirp, cheep.

zisch|eln ['tsiʃəln] *v/t. and v/i.* (ge-, h) whisper; '**‿en** *v/i.* (ge-, h) hiss; whiz(z).

ziselieren [tsize'liːrən] *v/t.* (*no* -ge-, h) chase.

Zit|at [tsi'taːt] *n* (-[e]s/-e) quotation; **‿ieren** [‿'tiːrən] *v/t.* (*no* -ge-, h) summon; quote.

Zitrone [tsi'troːnə] *f* (-/-n) lemon;

‿nlimonade *f* lemonade; lemon squash; **‿npresse** *f* lemon-squeezer; **‿nsaft** *m* lemon juice.

zittern ['tsitərn] *v/i.* (ge-, h) tremble, shake (*vor dat.* with).

zivil [tsi'viːl] **1.** *adj.* civil; civilian; *price:* reasonable; **2.** ⌀ *n* (-s/*no pl.*) civilians *pl.*; *s. Zivilkleidung;* **2bevölkerung** *f* civilian population, civilians *pl.*; **2isation** [‿liza'tsjoːn] *f* (-/‿ -en) civilization; **‿isieren** [‿ili'ziːrən] *v/t.* (*no* -ge-, h) civilize; **2ist** [‿i'list] *m* (-en/-en) civilian; **2kleidung** *f* civilian *or* plain clothes *pl.*

Zofe ['tsoːfə] *f* (-/-n) lady's maid.

zog [tsoːk] *pret. of* ziehen.

zögern ['tsøːgərn] **1.** *v/i.* (ge-, h) hesitate; linger; delay; **2.** ⌀ *n* (-s/*no pl.*) hesitation; delay.

Zögling ['tsøːkliŋ] *m* (-s/-e) pupil.

Zoll [tsɔl] *m* **1.** (-[e]s/-) inch; **2.** (-[e]s/‿e) customs *pl.*, duty; *the* Customs *pl.*; '**‿abfertigung** *f* customs clearance; '**‿amt** *n* customhouse; '**‿beamte** *m* customs officer; '**‿behörde** *f* the Customs *pl.*; '**‿erklärung** *f* customs declaration; **2frei** *adj.* duty-free; '**‿kontrolle** *f* customs examination; **2pflichtig** *adj.* liable to duty; '**‿stock** *m* foot-rule; '**‿tarif** *m* tariff.

Zone ['tsoːnə] *f* (-/-n) zone.

Zoo [tsoː] *n* (-[s]/-s) zoo.

Zoolog|e [tsoⁿo'loːgə] *m* (-n/-n) zoologist; **‿ie** [‿o'giː] *f* (-/*no pl.*) zoology; **2isch** *adj.* [‿'loːgiʃ] zoological.

Zopf [tsɔpf] *m* (-[e]s/‿e) plait, tress; pigtail; *alter ‿* antiquated ways *pl. or* custom.

Zorn [tsɔrn] *m* (-[e]s/*no pl.*) anger; '**2ig** *adj.* angry (*auf j-n* with s.o.; *auf et.* at s.th.).

Zote ['tsoːtə] *f* (-/-n) filthy *or* smutty joke, obscenity.

Zott|el ['tsɔtəl] *f* (-/-n) tuft (of hair); tassel; '**2(e)lig** *adj.* shaggy.

zu [tsuː] **1.** *prp.* (*dat.*) *direction:* to; towards, up to; at; in; on; in addition to, along with; *purpose:* for; *~ Beginn* at the beginning *or* outset; *~ Weihnachten* at Christmas; *zum ersten Mal* for the first time; *~ e-m ... Preise* at a ... price; *~ Tausenden* by thousands; *~ Wasser* by water; *~ zweien* by twos; *zum Beispiel* for example; **2.** *adv.* too; *direction:* towards, to; F closed, shut; *with inf.:* to; *ich habe ~ arbeiten* I have to work.

'**zubauen** *v/t.* (*sep.*, -ge-, h) build up *or* in; block.

Zubehör ['tsuːbəhøːr] *n, m* (-[e]s/-e) appurtenances *pl.*, fittings *pl.*, *Am.* F fixings *pl.*; *esp.* ⊕ accessories *pl.*

'**zubereit|en** *v/t.* (*sep.*, *no* -ge-, h) prepare; **2ung** *f* preparation.

'zu|billigen v/t. (sep., -ge-, h) grant; '⁓binden v/t. (irr. binden, sep., -ge-, h) tie up; '⁓blinzeln v/i. (sep., -ge-, h) wink at s.o.; '⁓bringen v/t. (irr. bringen, sep., -ge-, h) pass, spend (time).

Zucht [tsuxt] f 1. (-/no pl.) discipline; breeding, rearing; rearing of bees, etc.: culture; ♀ cultivation; 2. (-/-en) breed, race; '⁓bulle zo. m bull (for breeding).

züchten ['tsyçtən] v/t. (ge-, h) breed (animals); grow, cultivate (plants); 'Ⅱer m (-s/-) breeder (of animals); grower (of plants).

'Zucht|haus n penitentiary; punishment: penal servitude; ⁓häusler ['⁓hɔyslər] m (-s/-) convict; '⁓hengst zo. m stud-horse, stallion.

züchtig adj. ['tsyçtiç] chaste, modest; ⁓en ['⁓gən] v/t. (ge-, h) flog.

'zucht|los adj. undisciplined; 'Ⅱlosigkeit f (-/⁓ -en) want of discipline; 'Ⅱstute zo. f brood-mare.

zucken ['tsukən] v/i. (ge-, h) jerk; move convulsively, twitch (all: mit et. s.th.); with pain: wince; lightning: flash.

zücken ['tsykən] v/t. (ge-, h) draw (sword); F pull out (purse, pencil).

Zucker ['tsukər] m (-s/no pl.) sugar; '⁓dose f sugar-basin, Am. sugar bowl; '⁓erbse ♀ f green pea; '⁓guß m icing, frosting; '⁓hut m sugarloaf; 'Ⅱig adj. sugary; 'Ⅱkrank adj. diabetic; 'Ⅱn v/t. (ge-, h) sugar; '⁓rohr ♀ n sugar-cane; '⁓rübe ♀ f sugar-beet; 'Ⅱsüß adj. (as) sweet as sugar; '⁓wasser n sugared water; '⁓zange f (e-e a pair of) sugar-tongs pl.

zuckrig adj. ['tsukriç] sugary.

'Zuckung ⚕ f (-/-en) convulsion.

'zudecken v/t. (sep., -ge-, h) cover (up).

zudem adv. [tsu'de:m] besides, moreover.

'zu|drehen v/t. (sep., -ge-, h) turn off (tap); j-m den Rücken ⁓ turn one's back on s.o.; '⁓dringlich adj. importunate, obtrusive; '⁓drücken v/t. (sep., -ge-, h) close, shut; '⁓erkennen v/t. (irr. kennen, sep., no -ge-, h) award (a. ⚖); adjudge (dat. to) (a. ⚖).

zuerst adv. [tsu'-] first (of all); at first; er kam ⁓ an he was the first to arrive.

'zufahr|en v/i. (irr. fahren, sep., -ge-, sein) drive on; ⁓ auf (acc.) drive to (-wards); fig. rush at s.o.; 'Ⅱt f approach; drive, Am. driveway; 'Ⅱtsstraße f approach (road).

'Zufall m chance, accident; durch ⁓ by chance, by accident; 'Ⅱen v/i. (irr. fallen, sep., -ge-, sein) eyes: be closing (with sleep); door: shut (of) itself; j-m ⁓ fall to s.o.('s share).

'zufällig 1. adj. accidental; attr.

chance; casual; 2. adv. accidentally, by chance.

'zufassen v/i. (sep., -ge-, h) seize (hold of) s.th.; (mit) ⁓ lend or give a hand.

'Zuflucht f (-/⁓ ⁓e) refuge, shelter, resort; s-e ⁓ nehmen zu have recourse to s.th., take refuge in s.th.

'Zufluß m afflux; influx (a. ⚕); affluent, tributary (of river); ⚕ supply.

'zuflüstern v/t. (sep., -ge-, h): j-m et. ⁓ whisper s.th. to s.o.

zufolge prp. (gen.; dat.) [tsu'fɔlgə] according to.

zufrieden adj. [tsu'-] content(ed), satisfied; 'Ⅱheit f (-/no pl.) contentment, satisfaction; ⁓lassen v/t. (irr. lassen, sep., -ge-, h) let s.o. alone; ⁓stellen v/t. (sep., -ge-, h) satisfy; ⁓stellend adj. satisfactory.

'zu|frieren v/i. (irr. frieren, sep., -ge-, sein) freeze up or over; '⁓fügen v/t. (sep., -ge-, h) add; do, cause; inflict (wound, etc.) (j-m [up]on s.o.); 'Ⅱfuhr f ['⁓fu:r] f (-/-en) supply; supplies pl.; influx; '⁓führen v/t. (sep., -ge-, h) carry, lead, bring; ⚕ feed; supply (a. ⚕).

Zug [tsu:k] m (-[e]s/⁓e) draw(ing), pull(ing); ⚕ traction; ✗ expedition, campaign; procession; migration (of birds); drift (of clouds); range (of mountains); ⚕⚕ train; feature; trait (of character); bent, tendency, trend; draught, Am. draft (of air); at chess: move; drinking: draught, Am. draft; at cigarette, etc.: puff.

'Zu|gabe f addition; extra; thea. encore; '⁓gang m entrance; access; approach; 'Ⅱgänglich adj. ['⁓gɛŋliç] accessible (für to); 'Ⅱgeben v/t. (irr. geben, sep., -ge-, h) add; fig.: allow; confess; admit.

zugegen adj. [tsu'-] present (bei at.).

'zugehen v/i. (irr. gehen, sep., -ge-, sein) door, etc.: close, shut; p. move on, walk faster; happen; auf j-n ⁓ go up to s.o., move or walk towards s.o.

'Zugehörigkeit f (-/no pl.) membership (zu to) (society, etc.); belonging (to).

Zügel ['tsy:gəl] m (-s/-) rein; bridle (a. fig.); 'Ⅱlos adj. unbridled; fig.: unrestrained; licentious; 'Ⅱn v/t. (ge-, h) rein (in); fig. bridle, check.

'Zuge|ständnis n concession; 'Ⅱstehen v/t. (irr. stehen, sep., -ge-, h) concede.

'zugetan adj. attached (dat. to).

'Zugführer ⚕⚕ m guard, Am. conductor. [-ge-, h) add.]

'zugießen v/t. (irr. gießen, sep.,)

zug|ig adj. ['tsu:giç] draughty, Am. drafty; 'Ⅱkraft ['⁓k-] f ⚕ traction; fig. attraction, draw, appeal; '⁓kräftig adj. ['⁓k-]: ⁓ sein be a draw.

zugleich adv. [tsu'-] at the same time; together.

'**Zug|luft** f (-/no pl.) draught, Am. draft; '**_maschine** f traction-engine, tractor; '**_pflaster** $\mathcal{S}^{\circ}$ n blister.

'**zu|greifen** v/i. (irr. greifen, sep., -ge-, h) grasp or grab at s.th.; at table: help o.s.; lend a hand; '**_griff** m grip, clutch.

zugrunde adv. [tsu'grundə]: ~ gehen perish; ~ richten ruin.

'**Zugtier** n draught animal, Am. draft animal.

zu|gunsten prp. (gen.) [tsu'gunstən] in favo(u)r of; '**_gute** adv.: j-m et. ~ halten give s.o. credit for s.th.; ~ kommen be for the benefit (dat. of).

'**Zugvogel** m bird of passage.

'**zuhalten** v/t. (irr. halten, sep., -ge-, h) hold (door) to; sich die Ohren ~ stop one's ears. [home.\

Zuhause [tsu'hauzə] n (-/no pl.)\

'**zu|heilen** v/i. (sep., -ge-, sein) heal up, skin over; '**_hören** v/i. (sep., -ge-, h) listen (dat. to).

'**Zuhörer** m hearer, listener; ~ pl. audience; '**_schaft** f (-/$\mathcal{R}$-en) audience.

'**zu|jubeln** v/i. (sep., -ge-, h) cheer; '**_kleben** v/t. (sep., -ge-, h) paste or glue up; gum (letter) down; '**_knallen** v/t. (sep., -ge-, h) bang, slam (door, etc.); '**_knöpfen** v/t. (sep., -ge-, h) button (up); '**_kommen** v/i. (irr. kommen, sep., -ge-, sein): auf j-n ~ come up to s.o.; j-m ~ be due to s.o.; j-m et. ~ lassen let s.o. have s.th.; send s.o. s.th.; '**_korken** v/t. (sep., -ge-, h) cork (up).

'**Zu|kunft** ['tsu:kunft] f (-/no pl.) future; gr. future (tense); '**_künftig** **1.** adj. future; ~er Vater father-to-be; **2.** adv. in future.

'**zu|lächeln** v/i. (sep., -ge-, h) smile at or (up)on; '**_lage** f extra pay, increase; rise, Am. raise (in salary or wages); '**_langen** v/i. (sep., -ge-, h) at table: help o.s.; '**_lassen** v/t. (irr. lassen, sep., -ge-, h) leave (door) shut; keep closed; fig.: admit s.o.; license; allow, suffer; admit of (only one interpretation, etc.); '**_lässig** adj. admissible, allowable; '**_lassung** f (-/-en) admission; per-mission; licen|ce, Am. -se.

'**zulegen** v/t. (sep., -ge-, h) add; F sich et. ~ get o.s. s.th.

zuleide adv. [tsu'laɪdə]: j-m et. ~ tun do s.o. harm, harm or hurt s.o.

'**zuleiten** v/t. (sep., -ge-, h) let in (water, etc.); conduct to; pass on to s.o.

zu|letzt adv. [tsu'-] finally, at last; er kam ~ he was the last to arrive; ~'**liebe** adv.: j-m ~ for s.o.'s sake.

zum prp. [tsum] = zu dem.

'**zumachen** v/t. (sep., -ge-, h) close, shut; button (up) (coat); fasten.

zumal cj. [tsu'-] especially, partic-ularly. [up.\

'**zumauern** v/t. (sep., -ge-, h) wall\

zumut|en ['tsu:mu:tən] v/t. (sep., -ge-, h): j-m et. ~ expect s.th. of s.o.; sich zuviel ~ overtask o.s., overtax one's strength, etc.; '**2ung** f (-/-en) exacting demand, exac-tion; fig. impudence.

zunächst [tsu'-] **1.** prp. (dat.) next to; **2.** adv. first of all; for the present.

'**zu|nageln** v/t. (sep., -ge-, h) nail up; '**_nähen** v/t. (sep., -ge-, h) sew up; '**2nahme** ['_nɑ:mə] f (-/-n) increase, growth; '**2name** m sur-name.

Zünd|en ['tsyndən] v/i. (ge-, h) kindle; esp. mot. ignite; fig. arouse enthusiasm.

Zünd|holz ['tsynt-] n match; '**_ker-ze** mot. f spark(ing)-plug, Am. spark plug; '**_schlüssel** mot. m ignition key; '**_schnur** f fuse; '**_stoff** fig. m fuel; '**_ung** mot. ['_duŋ] f (-/-en) ignition.

'**zunehmen** v/i. (irr. nehmen, sep., -ge-, h) increase (an dat. in); grow; put on weight; moon: wax; days: grow longer.

'**zuneig|en** (sep., -ge-, h) **1.** v/i. incline to(wards); **2.** v/refl. incline to(wards); sich dem Ende ~ draw to a close; '**2ung** f (-/$\mathcal{R}$ -en) affection.

Zunft [tsunft] f (-/=e) guild, corpora-tion.

Zunge ['tsuŋə] f (-/-n) tongue.

züngeln ['tsyŋəln] v/i. (ge-, h) play with its tongue; flame: lick.

'**zungen|fertig** adj. voluble; '**2fer-tigkeit** f (-/no pl.) volubility; '**2spitze** f tip of the tongue.

zunichte adv. [tsu'nɪçtə]: ~ machen or werden bring or come to nothing.

'**zunicken** v/i. (sep., -ge-, h) nod to.

zu|nutze adv. [tsu'nutsə]: sich et. ~ machen turn s.th. to account, utilize s.th.; ~'**oberst** adv. at the top, uppermost.

zupfen ['tsupfən] (ge-, h) **1.** v/t. pull, tug, twitch; **2.** v/i. pull, tug, twitch (all: an dat. at).

zur prp. [tsu:r] = zu der.

'**zurechnungsfähig** adj. of sound mind; $\frac{t}{t\hbar}$ responsible; '**2keit** $\frac{t}{t\hbar}$ f (-/no pl.) responsibility.

zurecht|finden [tsu'-] v/refl. (irr. finden, sep., -ge-, h) find one's way; '**_kommen** v/i. (irr. kommen, sep., -ge-, sein) arrive in time; ~ (mit) get on (well) (with); manage s.th.; '**_legen** v/t. (sep., -ge-, h) arrange; sich e-e Sache ~ think s.th. out; '**_machen** v/t. (sep., -ge-, h) get ready, prepare, Am. F fix; adapt (für to, for purpose); sich ~ of *woman*: make (o.s.) up; **~weisen** *v/t.* (*irr.* weisen, *sep.*, -ge-, h) reprimand; **2weisung** *f* reprimand. **'zu|reden** *v/i.* (*sep.*, -ge-, h): *j-m* ~ try to persuade s.o.; encourage s.o.; **'~reiten** *v/t.* (*irr.* reiten, *sep.*, -ge-, h) break in; **'~riegeln** *v/t.* (*sep.*, -ge-, h) bolt (up).

zürnen ['tsyrnən] *v/i.* (ge-, h) be angry (*j-m* with s.o.).

zurück *adv.* [tsu'ryk] back; backward(s); behind; **~behalten** *v/t.* (*irr.* halten, *sep.*, *no* -ge-, h) keep back, retain; **~bekommen** *v/t.* (*irr.* kommen, *sep.*, *no* -ge-, h) get back; **~bleiben** *v/i.* (*irr.* bleiben, *sep.*, -ge-, sein) remain *or* stay behind; fall behind, lag; **~blicken** *v/i.* (*sep.*, -ge-, h) look back; **~bringen** *v/t.* (*irr.* bringen, *sep.*, -ge-, h) bring back; **~datieren** *v/t.* (*sep.*, *no* -ge-, h) date back, antedate; **~drängen** *v/t.* (*sep.*, -ge-, h) push back; *fig.* repress; **~erobern** *v/t.* (*sep.*, *no* -ge-, h) reconquer; **~erstatten** *v/t.* (*sep.*, *no* -ge-, h) restore, return; refund (*expenses*); **~fahren** (*irr.* fahren, *sep.*, -ge-) **1.** *v/i.* (sein) drive back; *fig.* start; **2.** *v/t.* (h) drive back; **~fordern** *v/t.* (*sep.*, -ge-, h) reclaim; **~führen** *v/t.* (*sep.*, -ge-, h) lead back; ~ *auf* (*acc.*) reduce to (*rule*, *etc.*); refer to (*cause*, *etc.*); **~geben** *v/t.* (*irr.* geben, *sep.*, -ge-, h) give back, return, restore; **~gehen** *v/i.* (*irr.* gehen, *sep.*, -ge-, sein) go back; return; **~gezogen** *adj.* retired; **~greifen** *fig.* *v/i.* (*irr.* greifen, *sep.*, -ge-, h): ~ *auf* (*acc.*) fall back (up)on; **~halten** (*irr.* halten, *sep.*, -ge-, h) **1.** *v/t.* hold back; **2.** *v/i.*: ~ *mit* keep back; **~haltend** *adj.* reserved; **2haltung** *f* (-/~-en) reserve; **~kehren** *v/i.* (*sep.*, -ge-, sein) return; **~kommen** *v/i.* (*irr.* kommen, *sep.*, -ge-, sein) come back; return (*fig. auf acc.* to); **~lassen** *v/t.* (*irr.* lassen, *sep.*, -ge-, h) leave (behind); **~legen** *v/t.* (*sep.*, -ge-, h) lay aside; cover (*distance*, *way*); **~nehmen** *v/t.* (*irr.* nehmen, *sep.*, -ge-, h) take back; withdraw, retract (*words*, *etc.*); **~prallen** *v/i.* (*sep.*, -ge-, sein) rebound; start; **~rufen** *v/t.* (*irr.* rufen, *sep.*, -ge-, h) call back; *sich ins Gedächtnis* ~ recall; **~schicken** *v/t.* (*sep.*, -ge-, h) send back; **~schlagen** (*irr.* schlagen, *sep.*, -ge-, h) **1.** *v/t.* drive (*ball*) back; repel (*enemy*); turn down (*blanket*); **2.** *v/i.* strike back; **~schrecken** *v/i.* (*sep.*, -ge-, sein) **1.** (*irr.* schrecken) shrink back (*vor dat.* from *spectacle*, *etc.*); **2.** shrink (*vor dat.* from *work*, *etc.*); **~setzen** *v/t.* (*sep.*, -ge-, h) put back; *fig.* slight, neglect; **~stellen** *v/t.* (*sep.*, -ge-, h) put back (*a. clock*); *fig.* defer, postpone; **~strahlen** *v/t.* (*sep.*, -ge-, h) reflect;

~streifen *v/t.* (*sep.*, -ge-, h) turn *or* tuck up (*sleeve*); **~treten** *v/i.* (*irr.* treten, *sep.*, -ge-, sein) step *or* stand back; *fig.*: recede; resign; withdraw; **~weichen** *v/i.* (*irr.* weichen, *sep.*, -ge-, sein) fall back; recede (*a. fig.*); **~weisen** *v/t.* (*irr.* weisen, *sep.*, -ge-, h) decline, reject; repel (*attack*); **~zahlen** *v/t.* (*sep.*, -ge-, h) pay back (*a. fig.*); **~ziehen** (*irr.* ziehen, *sep.*, -ge-) **1.** *v/t.* (h) draw back; *fig.* withdraw; *sich* ~ retire, withdraw; ⚔ retreat; **2.** *v/i.* (sein) move *or* march back.

'Zuruf *m* call; **'2en** *v/t.* (*irr.* rufen, *sep.*, -ge-, h) call (out), shout (*j-m et. s.th.* to s.o.).

'Zusage *f* promise; assent; **'2n** (*sep.*, -ge-, h) **1.** *v/t.* promise; **2.** *v/i.* promise to come; *j-m* ~ *food*, *etc.*: agree with s.o.; accept s.o.'s invitation; suit s.o.

zusammen *adv.* [tsu'zamən] together; at the same time; *alles* ~ (all) in all; ~ *betragen* amount to, total (up to); **2arbeit** *f* (-/*no pl.*) co-operation; team-work; **~arbeiten** *v/i.* (*sep.*, -ge-, h) work together; co-operate; **~beißen** *v/t.* (*irr.* beißen, *sep.*, -ge-, h): *die Zähne* ~ set one's teeth; **~brechen** *v/i.* (*irr.* brechen, *sep.*, -ge-, sein) break down; collapse; **2bruch** *m* breakdown; collapse; **~drücken** *v/t.* (*sep.*, -ge-, h) compress, press together; **~fahren** *fig.* *v/i.* (*irr.* fahren, *sep.*, -ge-, sein) start (*bei* at; *vor dat.* with); **~fallen** *v/i.* (*irr.* fallen, *sep.*, -ge-, sein) fall in, collapse; coincide; **~falten** *v/t.* (*sep.*, -ge-, h) fold up; **~fassen** *v/t.* (*sep.*, -ge-, h) summarize, sum up; **2fassung** *f* (-/-en) summary; **~fügen** *v/t.* (*sep.*, -ge-, h) join (together); **~halten** (*irr.* halten, *sep.*, -ge-, h) **1.** *v/t.* hold together; **2.** *v/i.* hold together; *friends*: F stick together; **2hang** *m* coherence, coherency, connection; context; **~hängen** (*sep.*, -ge-, h) **1.** *v/i.* (*irr.* hängen) cohere; *fig.* be connected; **2.** *v/t.* hang together; **~klappen** *v/t.* (*sep.*, -ge-, h) fold up; close (*clasp-knife*); **~kommen** *v/i.* (*irr.* kommen, *sep.*, -ge-, sein) meet; **2kunft** [~kunft] *f* (-/-ᵉe) meeting; **~laufen** *v/i.* (*irr.* laufen, *sep.*, -ge-, sein) run *or* crowd together; ⚭ converge; *milk*: curdle; **~legen** *v/t.* (*sep.*, -ge-, h) lay together; fold up; club (*money*) (together); **~nehmen** *fig.* *v/t.* (*irr.* nehmen, *sep.*, -ge-, h) collect (*one's wits*); *sich* ~ be on one's good behavio(u)r; pull o.s. together; **~packen** *v/t.* (*sep.*, -ge-, h) pack up; **~passen** *v/i.* (*sep.*, -ge-, h) match, harmonize; **~rechnen** *v/t.* (*sep.*, -ge-, h) add up; **~reißen** F *v/refl.* (*irr.* reißen, *sep.*, -ge-, h) pull o.s. together; **~rollen**

v/t. and *v/refl.* (*sep.*, *-ge-*, *h*) coil (up); **⁓rotten** *v/refl.* (*sep.*, *-ge-*, *h*) band together; **⁓rücken** (*sep.*, *-ge-*) 1. *v/t.* (*h*) move together; 2. *v/i.* (*sein*) close up; **⁓schlagen** (*irr. schlagen, sep., -ge-*) 1. *v/t.* (*h*) clap (*hands*) (together); F smash to pieces; beat *s.o.* up; 2. *v/i.* (*sein*): **⁓ über** (*acc.*) close over; **⁓schließen** *v/refl.* (*irr. schließen, sep., -ge-*, *h*) join; unite; **2schluß** *m* union; **⁓schrumpfen** *v/i.* (*sep.*, *-ge-*, *sein*) shrivel (up), shrink; **⁓setzen** *v/t.* (*sep.*, *-ge-*, *h*) put together; compose; compound (*a.* **🐾**, *word*); ⊕ assemble; *sich* **⁓ aus** consist of; **2setzung** *f* (*-/-en*) composition; compound; ⊕ assembly; **⁓stellen** *v/t.* (*sep.*, *-ge-*, *h*) compile; combine; **2stoß** *m* collision (*a. fig.*); **✂** encounter; *fig.* clash; **⁓stoßen** *v/i.* (*irr. stoßen, sep., -ge-*, *sein*) collide (*a. fig.*); adjoin; *fig.* clash; **⁓ mit** knock (*heads, etc.*) together; **⁓stürzen** *v/i.* (*sep.*, *-ge-*, *sein*) collapse; house, *etc.*: fall in; **⁓tragen** *v/t.* (*irr. tragen, sep., -ge-*, *h*) collect; compile (*notes*); **⁓treffen** *v/i.* (*irr. treffen, sep., -ge-*, *sein*) meet; coincide; **2treffen** *n* (*-s/no pl.*) meeting; encounter (*of enemies*); coincidence; **⁓treten** *v/i.* (*irr. treten, sep., -ge-*, *sein*) meet; *parl. a.* convene; **⁓wirken** *v/i.* (*sep.*, *-ge-*, *h*) co-operate; **2wirken** *n* (*-s/no pl.*) co-operation; **⁓zählen** *v/t.* (*sep.*, *-ge-*, *h*) add up, count up; **⁓ziehen** *v/t.* (*irr. ziehen, sep., -ge-*, *h*) draw together; contract; concentrate (*troops*); *sich* **⁓** contract.

'**Zusatz** *m* addition; admixture, *metall.* alloy; supplement.

zusätzlich *adj.* ['tsu:zetsliç] additional.

'**zuschau|en** *v/i.* (*sep.*, *-ge-*, *h*) look on (*e-r Sache* at s.th.); *j-m* **⁓** watch s.o. (*bei* s.th.: doing s.th.); '**2er** *m* (*-s/-*) spectator, looker-on, onlooker; '**2erraum** *thea. m* auditorium.

'**zuschicken** *v/t.* (*sep.*, *-ge-*, *h*) send (*dat.* to); mail; consign (*goods*).

'**Zuschlag** *m* addition; extra charge; excess fare; **💰** surcharge; *at auction*: knocking down; **2en** ['⁓gən] (*irr. schlagen, sep., -ge-*) 1. *v/i.* (*h*) strike; 2. *v/i.* (*sein*) door: slam (to); 3. *v/t.* (*h*) bang, slam (*door*) (to); *at auction*: knock down (*dat.* to).

'**zu|schließen** *v/t.* (*irr. schließen, sep., -ge-*, *h*) lock (up); '**⁓schnallen** *v/t.* (*sep.*, *-ge-*, *h*) buckle (up); '**⁓schnappen** (*sep.*, *-ge-*) 1. *v/i.* (*h*) dog: snap; 2. *v/i.* (*sein*) door: snap to; '**⁓schneiden** *v/t.* (*irr. schneiden, sep., -ge-*, *h*) cut up; cut (*suit*) (to size); '**2schnitt** *m* (*-[e]s/⁓-e*) cut; styles; '**⁓schnüren** *v/t.* (*sep.*, *-ge-*, *h*) lace up; cord up; '**⁓schrauben** *v/t.*

(*sep.*, *-ge-*, *h*) screw up *or* tight; '**⁓schreiben** *v/t.* (*irr. schreiben, sep., -ge-*, *h*): *j-m et.* **⁓** ascribe *or* attribute s.th. to s.o.; '**2schrift** *f* letter.

zuschulden *adv.* [tsu'-]: *sich et.* **⁓** *kommen lassen* make o.s. guilty of s.th.

'**Zu|schuß** *m* allowance; subsidy, grant (*of government*); '**2schütten** *v/t.* (*sep.*, *-ge-*, *h*) fill up (*ditch*); F add; '**2sehen** *v/i.* (*irr. sehen, sep., -ge-*, *h*) *s. zuschauen*; **⁓**, *daß* see (to it) that; **2sehends** *adv.* ['⁓s] visibly; '**2senden** *v/t.* ([*irr. senden*], *sep.*, *-ge-*, *h*) *s. zuschicken*; '**2setzen** (*sep.*, *-ge-*, *h*) 1. *v/t.* add; lose (*money*); 2. *v/i.* lose money; *j-m* **⁓** press s.o. hard.

'**zusicher|n** *v/t.* (*sep.*, *-ge-*, *h*): *j-m et.* **⁓** assure s.o. of s.th.; promise s.o. s.th.; '**2ung** *f* promise, assurance.

'**zu|spielen** *v/t.* (*sep.*, *-ge-*, *h*) *sports*: pass (*ball*) (*dat.* to) '**⁓spitzen** *v/t.* (*sep.*, *-ge-*, *h*) point; *sich* **⁓** taper (off); *fig.* come to a crisis; '**2spruch** *m* (*-[e]s/no pl.*) encouragement; consolation; **✝** custom; '**2stand** *m* condition, state; *in gutem* **⁓** *house*: in good repair.

zustande *adv.* [tsu'ʃtandə]: **⁓** *bringen* bring about; **⁓** *kommen* come about; *nicht* **⁓** *kommen* not to come off.

'**zuständig** *adj.* competent; '**2keit** *f* (*-/-en*) competence.

zustatten *adv.* [tsu'ʃtatən]: *j-m* **⁓** *kommen* be useful to s.o.

'**zustehen** *v/i.* (*irr. stehen, sep., -ge-*, *h*) be due (*dat.* to).

'**zustell|en** *v/t.* (*sep.*, *-ge-*, *h*) deliver (*a.* **📬**); **⚖** serve (*j-m* on s.o.); '**2ung** *f* delivery; **⚖** service.

'**zustimm|en** *v/i.* (*sep.*, *-ge-*, *h*) agree (*dat.*: to *s.th.*; with *s.o.*); consent (*to s.th.*); '**2ung** *f* consent.

'**zustoßen** *fig. v/i.* (*irr. stoßen, sep., -ge-*, *sein*): *j-m* **⁓** happen to s.o.

zutage *adv.* [tsu'ta:gə]: **⁓** *treten* come to light.

Zutaten ['tsu:ta:tən] *f/pl.* ingredients *pl.* (*of food*); trimmings *pl.* (*of dress*); [fall to s.o.'s share.)

zuteil *adv.* [tsu'taɪl]: *j-m* **⁓** *werden*)

'**zuteil|en** *v/t.* (*sep.*, *-ge-*, *h*) allot, apportion; '**2ung** *f* allotment, apportionment; ration.

'**zutragen** *v/refl.* (*irr. tragen, sep.*, *-ge-*, *h*) happen.

'**zutrauen** 1. *v/t.* (*sep.*, *-ge-*, *h*): *j-m et.* **⁓** credit s.o. with s.th.; *sich zuviel* **⁓** overrate o.s.; 2. **2** *n* (*-s/no pl.*) confidence (*zu* in).

'**zutraulich** *adj.* confiding, trustful, trusting; *animal*: friendly, tame.

'**zutreffen** *v/i.* (*irr. treffen, sep.*, *-ge-*, *h*) be right, be true; **⁓** *auf* (*acc.*) be true of; '**⁓d** *adj.* right, correct; applicable.

'zutrinken v/i. (irr. trinken, sep., -ge-, h): j-m ~ drink to s.o.

'Zutritt m (-[e]s/no pl.) access; admission; ~ verboten! no admittance! [bottom.]

zuunterst adv. [tsu'-] right at the)

zuverlässig adj. ['tsu:ferlesiç] reliable; certain; 'Qkeit f (-/no pl.) reliability; certainty.

Zuversicht ['tsu:ferziçt] f (-/no pl.) confidence; 'Qlich adj. confident.

zuviel adv. [tsu'-] too much; e-r ~ one too many.

zuvor adv. [tsu'-] before, previously; first; ~kommen v/i. (irr. kommen, sep., -ge-, sein): j-m ~ anticipate s.o.; e-r Sache ~ anticipate or prevent s.th.; ~kommend adj. obliging; courteous.

Zuwachs ['tsu:vaks] m (-es/no pl.) increase; 'Qen v/i. (irr. wachsen, sep., -ge-, sein) become overgrown; wound: close.

zu|wege adv. [tsu've:gə]: ~ bringen bring about; ~'weilen adv. sometimes.

'zu|weisen v/t. (irr. weisen, sep., -ge-, h) assign; '~wenden v/t. (irr. wenden] sep., -ge-, h (dat.) turn to(wards); fig.: give; bestow on; sich ~ (dat.) turn to(wards).

zuwenig adv. [tsu'-] too little.

'zuwerfen v/t. (irr. werfen, sep., -ge-, h) fill up (pit); slam (door) (to); j-m ~ throw (ball, etc.) to s.o.; cast (look) at s.o.

zuwider prp. (dat.) [tsu'-] contrary to, against; repugnant, distasteful; ~handeln v/i. (sep., -ge-, h) (dat.) act contrary or in opposition to; esp. ~ contravene; Qhandlung ⚖ f contravention.

'zu|winken v/i. (sep., -ge-, h) (dat.) wave to; beckon to; '~zahlen v/t. (sep., -ge-, h) pay extra; '~zählen v/t. (sep., -ge-, h) add; '~ziehen (irr. ziehen, sep., -ge-) 1. v/t. (h) draw together; draw (curtains); consult (doctor, etc.); sich ~ incur (s.o.'s displeasure, etc.); ⚕ catch (disease); 2. v/i. (sein) move in; ~züglich prp. (gen.) ['~tsy:k-] plus.

Zwang [tsvaŋ] 1. m (-[e]s/⚓e) compulsion, coercion; constraint; ⚖ duress(e); force; sich ~ antun check or restrain o.s.; 2. Ꝗ pret. of zwingen.

zwängen ['tsvɛŋən] v/t. (ge-,h) press, force.

'zwanglos fig. adj. free and easy, informal; 'Qigkeit f (-/-en) ease, informality.

'Zwangs|arbeit f hard labo(u)r; '~jacke f strait waistcoat or jacket; '~lage f embarrassing situation; Qläufig fig. adj. ['~lɔyf-] necessary; '~maßnahme f coercive measure; '~vollstreckung ⚖ f distraint, execution; '~vorstellung ⚕ f

obsession, hallucination; 'Qweise adv. by force; '~wirtschaft f (-/⚓-en) controlled economy.

zwanzig adj. ['tsvantsiç] twenty; ~ste adj. ['~stə] twentieth.

zwar cj. [tsva:r] indeed, it is true; und ~ and that, that is.

Zweck [tsvɛk] m (-[e]s/-e) aim, end, object, purpose; design; keinen ~ haben be of no use; s-n ~ erfüllen answer its purpose; zu dem ~ (gen.) for the purpose of; 'Qdienlich adj. serviceable, useful, expedient.

Zwecke ['tsvɛkə] f (-/-n) tack; drawing-pin, Am. thumbtack.

'zweck|los adj. aimless, purposeless; useless; '~mäßig adj. expedient, suitable; 'Qmäßigkeit f (-/no pl.) expediency.

zwei adj. [tsvaɪ] two; '~beinig adj. two-legged; 'Qbettzimmer n double (bedroom); ~deutig adj. ['~dɔy-tiç] ambiguous; suggestive; ~erlei adj. ['~ɔr'laɪ] of two kinds, two kinds of; ~fach adj. ['~fax] double, twofold.

Zweifel ['tsvaɪfəl] m (-s/-) doubt; 'Qhaft adj. doubtful, dubious; 'Qlos adj. doubtless; 'Qn v/i. (ge-, h) doubt (an e-r Sache s.th.; an j-m s.o.).

Zweig [tsvaɪk] m (-[e]s/-e) branch (a. fig.); kleiner ~ twig; '~geschäft n, '~niederlassung f, '~stelle f branch.

zwei|jährig adj. ['tsvaɪjɛ:riç] two-year-old, of two (years); 'Qkampf m duel, single combat; '~mal adv. twice; '~malig adj. (twice) repeated; ~motorig adj. ['~moto:riç] two- or twin-engined; '~reihig adj. having two rows; suit: double-breasted; '~schneidig adj. double- or two-edged (both a. fig.); '~seitig adj. two-sided; contract, etc.: bilateral; fabric: reversible; 'Qsitzer esp. mot. m (-s/-) two-seater; '~sprachig adj. bilingual; '~stimmig adj. for two voices; '~stöckig adj. ['~ʃtœkiç] two-stor|eyed, -ied; '~stufig ⊕ adj. two-stage; ~stündig adj. ['~ʃtyndiç] of or lasting two hours, two-hour.

zweit adj. [tsvaɪt] second; ein ~er another; aus ~er Hand second-hand; zu ~ by twos; wir sind zu ~ there are two of us. [engine.]

'Zweitaktmotor mot. m two-stroke)

'zweit'best adj. second-best.

'zweiteilig adj. garment: two-piece.

zweitens adv. ['tsvaɪtəns] secondly.

'zweitklassig adj. second-class, second-rate.

Zwerchfell anat. ['tsvɛrç-] n diaphragm.

Zwerg [tsvɛrk] m (-[e]s/-e) dwarf; Qenhaft adj. ['~gən-] dwarfish.

Zwetsch(g)e ['tsvɛtʃ(g)ə] f (-/-n) plum.

Zwick|el ['tsvikəl] m (-s/-) *sewing*: gusset; 'en *v/t. and v/i.* (ge-, h) pinch, nip; 'er m (-s/-) (*ein a pair of*) eye-glasses *pl.*, pince-nez; 'mühle *fig. f* dilemma, quandary, fix.

Zwieback ['tsvi:bak] m (-[e]s/e, -e) rusk, zwieback.

Zwiebel ['tsvi:bəl] f (-/-n) onion; bulb (*of flowers, etc.*).

Zwie|gespräch ['tsvi:-] n dialog(ue); 'licht n (-[e]s/*no pl.*) twilight; 'spalt m (-[e]s/-e, e) disunion; conflict; spältig *adj.* ['ʃpɛltiç] disunited; *emotions*: conflicting; 'tracht f (-/*no pl.*) discord.

Zwilling|e ['tsviliŋə] m/pl. twins pl.; 'sbruder m twin brother; 'sschwester f twin sister.

Zwinge ['tsviŋə] f (-/-n) ferrule (*of stick, etc.*); ⊕ clamp; 'n *v/t.* (*irr.*, ge-, h) compel, constrain; force; 'nd *adj.* forcible; *arguments*: cogent, compelling; imperative; 'r m (-s/-) outer court; kennel(s pl.); bear-pit.

zwinkern ['tsviŋkərn] *v/i.* (ge-, h) wink, blink.

Zwirn [tsvirn] m (-[e]s/-e) thread, cotton; 'sfaden m thread.

zwischen *prp.* (*dat.*; *acc.*) ['tsviʃən] between (*two*); among (*several*); 'bilanz † f interim balance; 'deck ⊕ n steerage; 'durch F *adv.* in between; for a change; 'ergebnis n provisional result; 'fall m incident; 'händler † m middleman; 'landung ✈ f intermediate landing, stop, *Am. a.* stopover; (*Flug*) ohne non-stop (flight);

'pause f interval, intermission; 'prüfung f intermediate examination; 'raum m space, interval; 'ruf m (loud) interruption; 'spiel n interlude; 'staatlich *adj.* international; *Am. between States*: interstate; 'station f intermediate station; 'stecker ✓ m adapter; 'stück n intermediate piece, connexion, (*Am. only*) connection; 'stufe f intermediate stage; 'wand f partition (wall); 'zeit f interval; *in der* *in the meantime.*

Zwist [tsvist] m (-es/-e), 'igkeit f (-/-en) discord; disunion; quarrel.

zwitschern ['tsvitʃərn] *v/i.* (ge-, h) twitter, chirp.

Zwitter ['tsvitər] m (-s/-) hermaphrodite.

zwölf *adj.* [tsvœlf] twelve; *um* (*Uhr*) at twelve (o'clock); (*um*) *Uhr mittags* (at) noon; (*um*) *Uhr nachts* (at) midnight; 'finger-darm *anat.* m duodenum; te *adj.* ['tə] twelfth.

Zyankali [tsyan'ka:li] n (-s/*no pl.*) potassium cyanide.

Zyklus ['tsy:klus, 'tsyk-] m (-/Zyklen) cycle; course, set (*of lectures, etc.*).

Zylind|er [tsi'lindər, tsy'-] m (-s/-) Ä, ⊕ cylinder; chimney (*of lamp*); top hat; risch *adj.* [driʃ] cylindrical.

Zyni|ker ['tsy:nikər] m (-s/-) cynic; 'sch *adj.* cynical; smus [tsy-'nismus] m (-/Zynismen) cynicism.

Zypresse ♀ [tsy'prɛsə] f (-/-n) cypress.

Zyste ♀ ['tsystə] f (-/-n) cyst.

PART II

ENGLISH-GERMAN
DICTIONARY

A

a [ei, ə] *Artikel*: ein(e); per, pro, je; *all of a size* alle gleich groß; *twice a week* zweimal wöchentlich.

A 1 F [ei'wʌn] Ia, prima.

aback [ə'bæk] rückwärts; *taken ~ fig.* überrascht, verblüfft, bestürzt.

abandon [ə'bændən] auf-, preisgeben; verlassen; uberlassen; ~ed verworfen; ~ment [ʌnmənt] Auf-, Preisgabe *f*; Unbeherrschtheit *f*.

abase [ə'beis] erniedrigen, demütigen; ~ment [ʌsmənt] Erniedrigung *f*.

abash [ə'bæʃ] beschämen, verlegen machen; ~ment [ʌʃmənt] Verlegenheit *f*.

abate [ə'beit] *v/t.* verringern; *Mißstand* abstellen; *v/i.* abnehmen, nachlassen; ~ment [ʌtmənt] Verminderung *f*; Abschaffung *f*.

abattoir ['æbətwɑː] Schlachthaus *n*.

abb|ess ['æbis] Äbtissin *f*; ~ey ['æbi] Abtei *f*; ~ot ['æbət] Abt *m*.

abbreviat|e [ə'briːvieit] (ab)kürzen; ~ion [əbriːvi'eiʃən] Abkürzung *f*.

ABC ['eibiː'siː] Abc *n*, Alphabet *n*.

ABC weapons *pl.* ABC-Waffen *f/pl.*

abdicat|e ['æbdikeit] entsagen (*dat.*); abdanken; ~ion [æbdi-'keiʃən] Verzicht *m*; Abdankung *f*.

abdomen ['æbdəmen] Unterleib *m*, Bauch *m*.

abduct [æb'dʌkt] entführen.

aberration [æbə'reiʃən] Abweichung *f*; *fig.* Verirrung *f*.

abet [ə'bet] aufhetzen; anstiften; unterstützen; ~tor [ʌtə] Anstifter *m*; (Helfers)Helfer *m*.

abeyance [ə'beiəns] Unentschiedenheit *f*; *in ~ ɫtɫ* in der Schwebe.

abhor [əb'hɔː] verabscheuen; ~rence [əb'hɔrəns] Abscheu *m* (*of* vor *dat.*); ~rent □ [ʌnt] zuwider (*to dat.*); abstoßend.

abide [ə'baid] [*irr.*] *v/i.* bleiben (*by* bei); *v/t.* erwarten; (v)ertragen.

ability [ə'biliti] Fähigkeit *f*.

abject □ ['æbdʒekt] verächtlich, gemein.

abjure [əb'dʒuə] abschwören; entsagen (*dat.*).

able □ ['eibl] fähig, geschickt; *be ~* imstande sein, können; ~-bodied kräftig.

abnegat|e ['æbnigeit] ableugnen; verzichten auf (*acc.*); ~ion [æbni-'geiʃən] Ableugnung *f*; Verzicht *m*.

abnormal □ [æb'nɔːməl] abnorm.

aboard [ə'bɔːd] ⚓ an Bord (*gen.*); *all ~!* Am. 🚋 etc. einsteigen!

abode [ə'boud] 1. *pret. u. p.p. von abide*; 2. Aufenthalt *m*; Wohnung *f*.

aboli|sh [ə'bɔliʃ] abschaffen, aufheben; ~tion [æbə'liʃən] Abschaffung *f*, Aufhebung *f*; ~tionist [ʌnist] Gegner *m* der Sklaverei.

A-bomb ['eibɔm] = atomic bomb.

abomina|ble □ [ə'bɔminəbl] abscheulich; ~te [ʌneit] verabscheuen; ~tion [əbɔmi'neiʃən] Abscheu *m*.

aboriginal □ [æbə'ridʒənl] einheimisch; Ur...

abortion ⚕ [ə'bɔːʃən] Fehlgeburt *f*; Abtreibung *f*.

abortive □ [ə'bɔːtiv] vorzeitig; erfolglos, fehlgeschlagen; verkümmert.

abound [ə'baund] reichlich vorhanden sein; Überfluß haben (*in* an *dat.*).

about [ə'baut] 1. *prp.* um (...herum); bei; im Begriff; über (*acc.*); *I had no money ~ me* ich hatte kein Geld bei mir; *what are you ~?* was macht ihr da?; 2. *adv.* herum, umher; in der Nähe; etwa; ungefähr um, gegen; *bring ~* zustande bringen.

above [ə'bʌv] 1. *prp.* über; *fig.* erhaben über; ~ *all* vor allem; ~ *ground fig.* am Leben; 2. *adv.* oben; darüber; 3. *adj.* obig.

abreact [æbri'ækt] abreagieren.

abreast [ə'brest] nebeneinander.

abridg|e [ə'bridʒ] (ver)kürzen; ~(e)ment [ʌdʒmənt] (Ver)Kürzung *f*; Auszug *m*.

abroad [ə'brɔːd] im (ins) Ausland; überall(hin); *there is a report ~* es geht das Gerücht; *all ~* ganz im Irrtum.

abrogate ['æbrougeit] aufheben.

abrupt □ [ə'brʌpt] jäh; zs.-hanglos; schroff.

abscess ⚕ ['æbsis] Geschwür *n*.

abscond [əb'skɔnd] sich davonmachen.

absence ['æbsəns] Abwesenheit *f*; Mangel *m*; ~ *of mind* Zerstreutheit *f*.

absent 1. □ ['æbsənt] abwesend; nicht vorhanden; 2. [æb'sent]: ~ *o.s.* fernbleiben; ~-minded □ ['æbsənt'maindid] zerstreut, geistesabwesend.

absolut|e □ ['æbsəluːt] absolut; unumschränkt; vollkommen; unvermischt; unbedingt; ~ion [æbsə-'luːʃən] Lossprechung *f*.

absolve [əb'zɔlv] frei-, lossprechen.

absorb [əb'sɔːb] aufsaugen; *fig.* ganz in Anspruch nehmen.

absorption [əb'sɔːpʃən] Aufsaugung *f*; *fig.* Vertieftsein *n*.

abstain [əb'stein] sich enthalten.

abstemious □ [æb'sti:mjəs] enthaltsam; mäßig.
abstention [æb'stenʃən] Enthal-
tung f.
abstinen|ce ['æbstinəns] Enthalt-
samkeit f; ~t □ [~nt] enthaltsam.
abstract 1. □ ['æbstrækt] abstrakt;
2. [~] Auszug m; gr. Abstraktum n;
3. [æb'strækt] abstrahieren; ablenken; entwenden; *Inhalt* kurz
zs.-fassen; ~ed □ zerstreut; ~ion
[~kʃən] Abstraktion f; (abstrakter)
Begriff.
abstruse □ [æb'stru:s] *fig.* dunkel,
schwer verständlich; tiefgründig.
absurd [əb'sə:d] absurd, sinnwid-
rig; lächerlich.
abundan|ce [ə'bʌndəns] Überfluß
m; Fülle f; Überschwang m; ~t □
[~nt] reich(lich).
abus|e 1. [ə'bju:s] Mißbrauch m;
Beschimpfung f; **2.** [~u:z] mißbrauchen; beschimpfen; ~ive □
[~u:siv] schimpfend; Schimpf...
abut [ə'bʌt] (an)grenzen (*upon* an).
abyss [ə'bis] Abgrund m.
academic|(al □) [ækə'demik(əl)]
akademisch; ~ian [ækædə'miʃən]
Akademiemitglied n.
academy [ə'kædəmi] Akademie f.
accede [æk'si:d]: ~ *to* beitreten
(*dat.*); *Amt* antreten; *Thron* be-
steigen.
accelerat|e [æk'seləreit] beschleu-
nigen; *fig.* ankurbeln; ~or [æk'selə-
reitə] Gaspedal n.
accent 1. ['æksənt] Akzent m (*a. gr.*);
2. [æk'sent] *v/t.* akzentuieren, betonen; ~uate [~tjueit] akzentuieren,
betonen.
accept [ək'sept] annehmen; † ak-
zeptieren; hinnehmen; ~able □
[~təbl] annehmbar; ~ance [~əns]
Annahme f; † Akzept n.
access ['ækses] Zugang m; ⚕ Anfall
m; *easy of* ~ zugänglich; ~ *road* Zufahrtsstraße f; ~ary [æk'sesəri]
Mitwisser(in), Mitschuldige(r m) f;
= 'accessory 2; ~ible □ [~səbl] zugänglich; ~ion [~eʃən] Antritt m
(*to gen.*); Eintritt m (*to* in *acc.*); ~ *to
the throne* Thronbesteigung f.
accessory [æk'sesəri] **1.** □ zusätzlich; **2.** Zubehörteil n.
accident ['æksidənt] Zufall m; Un-
(glücks)fall m; ~al □ [æksi'dentl]
zufällig; nebensächlich.
acclaim [ə'kleim] *j-m* zujubeln.
acclamation [æklə'meiʃən] Zuruf
m.
acclimatize [ə'klaimətaiz] akklimatisieren, eingewöhnen.
acclivity [ə'kliviti] Steigung f;
Böschung f.
accommodat|e [ə'kɔmədeit] anpas-
sen; unterbringen; *Streit* schlichten; versorgen; *j-m* aushelfen (*with*
mit *Geld*); ~ion [əkɔmə'deiʃən] Anpassung f; Aushilfe f; Bequemlich-

keit f; Unterkunft f; Beilegung f;
seating ~ Sitzgelegenheit f; ~ *train
Am.* Personenzug m.
accompan|iment [ə'kʌmpənimənt]
Begleitung f; ~y [ə'kʌmpəni] begleiten; *accompanied with* verbunden mit.
accomplice [ə'kɔmplis] Komplice m.
accomplish [ə'kɔmpliʃ] vollenden;
ausführen; ~ed vollendet, perfekt;
~ment [~ʃmənt] Vollendung f;
Ausführung f; Tat f, Leistung f;
Talent n.
accord [ə'kɔ:d] **1.** Übereinstimmung f; *with one* ~ einstimmig; **2.**
v/i. übereinstimmen; *v/t.* gewähren; ~ance [~dəns] Übereinstimmung f; ~ant □ [~nt] übereinstimmend; ~ing [~diŋ]: ~ *to* gemäß (*dat.*); ~ingly [~ŋli] dem-
gemäß.
accost [ə'kɔst] *j-n bsd. auf der Straße*
ansprechen.
account [ə'kaunt] **1.** Rechnung f;
Berechnung f; † Konto n; Rechenschaft f; Bericht m; *of no* ~ ohne
Bedeutung; *on no* ~ auf keinen Fall;
on ~ *of* wegen; *take into* ~, *take* ~ *of*
in Betracht ziehen, berücksichtigen;
turn to ~ ausnutzen; *keep* ~s die
Bücher führen; *call to* ~ zur Rechenschaft ziehen; *give a good* ~ *of o.s.*
sich bewähren; *make* ~ *of* Wert auf
et. (*acc.*) legen; **2.** *v/i.*: ~ *for* Rechenschaft über *et.* (*acc.*) ablegen; (sich)
erklären; *be much* ~ed *of* hoch ge-
achtet sein; *v/t.* ansehen als; ~able
□ [~təbl] verantwortlich; erklärlich; ~ant [~ənt] Buchhalter m;
chartered ~, *Am. certified public* ~
vereidigter Bücherrevisor; ~ing
[~tiŋ] Buchführung f.
accredit [ə'kredit] beglaubigen.
accrue [ə'kru:] erwachsen (*from*
aus).
accumulat|e [ə'kju:mjuleit] (sich)
(an)häufen; ansammeln; ~ion
[əkju:mju'leiʃən] Anhäufung f.
accura|cy ['ækjurəsi] Genauigkeit f;
~te □ [~rit] genau; richtig.
accurs|ed [ə'kə:sid], ~t [~st] ver-
flucht, verwünscht.
accus|ation [ækju:(:)'zeiʃən] An-
klage f, Beschuldigung f; ~ative
gr. [ə'kju:zətiv] *a.* ~ *case* Akkusativ
m; ~e [ə'kju:z] anklagen, beschuldigen; ~er [~zə] Kläger(in).
accustom [ə'kʌstəm] gewöhnen (*to*
an *acc.*); ~ed gewohnt, üblich; gewöhnt (*to* an *acc.*, zu *inf.*).
ace [eis] As n (*a. fig.*); ~ *in the hole
Am.* F *fig.* Trumpf m in Reserve;
within an ~ um ein Haar.
acerbity [ə'sə:biti] Herbheit f.
acet|ic [ə'si:tik] essigsauer; ~ify
[ə'setifai] säuern.
ache [eik] **1.** schmerzen; sich sehnen
(*for* nach; *to* zu tun); **2.** anhal-
tende Schmerzen m/pl.

achieve [ə'tʃiːv] ausführen; erreichen; **~ment** [~vmənt] Ausführung f; Leistung f.

acid ['æsid] **1.** sauer; **2.** Säure f; **~ity** [ə'siditi] Säure f.

acknowledge [ək'nɔlidʒ] anerkennen; zugeben; ✝ bestätigen; **~(e)ment** [~dʒmənt] Anerkennung f; Bestätigung f; Eingeständnis n.

acme ['ækmi] Gipfel m; ✝ Krisis f.

acorn ✝ ['eikɔːn] Eichel f.

acoustics [ə'kuːstiks] pl. Akustik f.

acquaint [ə'kweint] bekannt machen; j-m mitteilen; be **~ed** with kennen; **~ance** [~təns] Bekanntschaft f; Bekannte(r m) f.

acquiesce [ækwi'es] (in) hinnehmen (acc.); einwilligen (in acc.).

acquire [ə'kwaiə] erwerben; **~ment** [~əmənt] Fertigkeit f.

acquisition [ækwi'ziʃən] Erwerbung f; Errungenschaft f.

acquit [ə'kwit] freisprechen; **~** o.s. of Pflicht erfüllen; **~** o.s. well s-e Sache gut machen; **~tal** [~tl] Freisprechung f, Freispruch m; **~tance** [~təns] Tilgung f.

acre ['eikə] Morgen m (4047 qm).

acrid ['ækrid] scharf, beißend.

across [ə'krɔs] **1.** adv. hin-, herüber; (quer) durch; drüben; überkreuz; **2.** prp. (quer) über (acc.); jenseits (gen.), über (dat.); come **~**, run **~** stoßen auf (acc.).

act [ækt] **1.** v/i. handeln; sich benehmen; wirken; funktionieren; thea. spielen; v/t. thea. spielen; **2.** Handlung f, Tat f; thea. Akt m; Gesetz n; Beschluß m; Urkunde f, Vertrag m; **~ing** ['æktiŋ] **1.** Handeln n; thea. Spiel(en) n; **2.** tätig, amtierend.

action ['ækʃən] Handlung f (a. thea.); Tätigkeit f; Tat f; Wirkung f; Klage f, Prozeß m; Gang m (Pferd etc.); Gefecht n; Mechanismus m; take **~** Schritte unternehmen.

activ|e □ ['æktiv] aktiv; tätig; rührig, wirksam; ✝ lebhaft; **~ity** [æk'tiviti] Tätigkeit f; Betriebsamkeit f; bsd. ✝ Lebhaftigkeit f.

act|or ['æktə] Schauspieler m; **~ress** ['æktris] Schauspielerin f.

actual □ ['æktjuəl] wirklich, tatsächlich, eigentlich.

actuate ['æktjueit] in Gang bringen.

acute □ [ə'kjuːt] spitz; scharf(sinnig); brennend (Frage); ✝ akut.

ad F [æd] = advertisement.

adamant fig. ['ædəmənt] unerbittlich.

adapt [ə'dæpt] anpassen (to, for dat.); Text bearbeiten (from nach); zurechtmachen; **~ation** [ædæp'teiʃən] Anpassung f, Bearbeitung f.

add [æd] v/t. hinzufügen; addieren; v/i.: **~** to vermehren; hinzukommen zu.

addict ['ædikt] Süchtige(r m) f; **~ed** [ə'diktid] ergeben (to dat.); **~** to e-m Laster verfallen.

addition [ə'diʃən] Hinzufügen n; Zusatz m; An-, Ausbau m; Addition f; in **~** außerdem; in **~** to außer, zu; **~al** □ [~nl] zusätzlich.

address [ə'dres] **1.** Worte richten (to an acc.); sprechen zu; **2.** Adresse f; Ansprache f; Anstand m, Manieren f/pl.; pay one's **~es** to a lady e-r Dame den Hof machen; **~ee** [ædre'siː] Adressat m, Empfänger m.

adept ['ædept] **1.** erfahren; geschickt; **2.** Eingeweihte(r m) f; Kenner m.

adequa|cy ['ædikwəsi] Angemessenheit f; **~te** □ [~kwit] angemessen.

adhere [əd'hiə] (to) haften (an dat.); fig. festhalten (an dat.); **~nce** [~ərəns] Anhaften n, Festhalten n; **~nt** [~nt] Anhänger(in).

adhesion [əd'hiːʒən] = adherence; fig. Einwilligung f.

adhesive [əd'hiːsiv] **1.** □ klebend; **~** plaster, **~** tape Heftpflaster n; **2.** Klebstoff m.

adjacent □ [ə'dʒeisənt] (to) anliegend (dat.); anstoßend (an acc.); benachbart.

adjective gr. ['ædʒiktiv] Adjektiv n, Eigenschaftswort n.

adjoin [ə'dʒɔin] angrenzen an (acc.).

adjourn [ə'dʒəːn] aufschieben; (v/i. sich) vertagen; **~ment** [~nmənt] Aufschub m; Vertagung f.

adjudge [ə'dʒʌdʒ] zuerkennen; verurteilen.

adjust [ə'dʒʌst] in Ordnung bringen; anpassen; Streit schlichten; Mechanismus u. fig. einstellen (to auf acc.); **~ment** [~tmənt] Anordnung f; Einstellung f; Schlichtung f.

administ|er [əd'ministə] verwalten; spenden; ✝ verabfolgen; **~** justice Recht sprechen; **~ration** [ədminis'treiʃən] Verwaltung f; Regierung f; bsd. Am. Amtsperiode f e-s Präsidenten; **~rative** [əd'ministrətiv] Verwaltungs...; **~rator** [~reitə] Verwalter m.

admir|able □ ['ædmərəbl] bewundernswert; (vor)trefflich; **~ation** [ædmə'reiʃən] Bewunderung f; **~e** [əd'maiə] bewundern; verehren.

admiss|ible □ [əd'misəbl] zulässig; **~ion** [~iʃən] Zulassung f; F Eintritt(sgeld n) m; Eingeständnis n.

admit [əd'mit] v/t. (her)einlassen (to, into in acc.), eintreten lassen; zulassen (to zu); zugeben; **~tance** [~təns] Einlaß m, Zutritt m.

admixture [əd'mikstʃə] Beimischung f, Zusatz m.

admon|ish [əd'mɔniʃ] ermahnen; warnen (of, against vor dat.); **~ition** [ædmə'niʃən] Ermahnung f; Warnung f.

ado [ə'du:] Getue *n*; Lärm *m*; Mühe *f*.

adolescen|ce [ædou'lesns] Adoleszenz *f*, Reifezeit *f*; **~t** [~nt] **1.** jugendlich, heranwachsend; **2.** Jugendliche(r *m*) *f*.

adopt [ə'dɔpt] adoptieren; sich aneignen; **~ion** [~pʃən] Annahme *f*.

ador|able □ [ə'dɔ:rəbl] verehrungswürdig; **~ation** [ædɔ:'reiʃən] Anbetung *f*; **~e** [ə'dɔ:] anbeten.

adorn [ə'dɔ:n] schmücken, zieren; **~ment** [~mənt] Schmuck *m*.

adroit □ [ə'drɔit] gewandt.

adult ['ædʌlt] **1.** erwachsen; **2.** Erwachsene(r *m*) *f*.

adulter|ate [ə'dʌltəreit] (ver)fälschen; **~er** [~rə] Ehebrecher *m*; **~ess** [~ris] Ehebrecherin *f*; **~ous** □ [~rəs] ehebrecherisch; **~y** [~ri] Ehebruch *m*.

advance [əd'vɑ:ns] **1.** *v/i.* vorrücken, vorgehen; steigen; Fortschritte machen; *v/t.* vorrücken; vorbringen; vorausbezahlen; vorschießen; (be)fördern; *Preis* erhöhen; beschleunigen; **2.** Vorrücken *n*; Fortschritt *m*; Angebot *n*; Vorschuß *m*; Erhöhung *f*; *in* ~ im voraus; **~d** vor-, fortgeschritten; ~ *in years* in vorgerücktem Alter; **~ment** [~smənt] Förderung *f*; Fortschritt *m*.

advantage [əd'vɑ:ntidʒ] Vorteil *m*; Überlegenheit *f*; Gewinn *m*; *take* ~ *of* ausnutzen; **~ous** □ [ædvən'teidʒəs] vorteilhaft.

adventur|e [əd'ventʃə] Abenteuer *n*, Wagnis *n*; Spekulation *f*; **~er** [~rə] Abenteurer *m*; Spekulant *m*; **~ous** □ [~rəs] abenteuerlich; wagemutig.

adverb *gr.* ['ædvə:b] Adverb *n*, Umstandswort *n*.

advers|ary ['ædvəsəri] Gegner *m*, Feind *m*; **~e** □ ['ædvə:s] widrig; feindlich; ungünstig, nachteilig (*to* für); **~ity** [əd'və:siti] Unglück *n*.

advertis|e ['ædvətaiz] ankündigen; inserieren; Reklame machen (für); **~ement** [əd'və:tismənt] Ankündigung *f*, Inserat *n*; Reklame *f*; **~ing** ['ædvətaiziŋ] Reklame *f*, Werbung *f*; ~ *agency* Annoncenbüro *n*; ~ *designer* Reklamezeichner *m*; ~ *film* Reklamefilm *m*; *screen* ~ Filmreklame *f*.

advice [əd'vais] Rat(schlag) *m*; (*mst pl.*) Nachricht *f*, Meldung *f*; *take medical* ~ e-n Arzt zu Rate ziehen.

advis|able □ [əd'vaizəbl] ratsam; **~e** [əd'vaiz] *v/t. j-n* beraten; *j-m* raten; † benachrichtigen, avisieren; *v/i.* (sich) beraten; **~er** [~zə] Ratgeber(in).

advocate 1. ['ædvəkit] Anwalt *m*; Fürsprecher *m*; **2.** [~keit] verteidigen, befürworten.

aerial ['ɛəriəl] **1.** □ luftig; Luft...;

~ *view* Luftaufnahme *f*; **2.** *Radio, Fernsehen:* Antenne *f*.

aero|... ['ɛərou] Luft...;~**cab** *Am.* F ['ɛərəkæb] Lufttaxi *n* (*Hubschrauber als Zubringer*); **~drome** [~ədroum] Flugplatz *m*; **~naut** [~ənɔ:t] Luftschiffer *m*; **~nautics** [ɛərə'nɔ:tiks] *pl.* Luftfahrt *f*; **~plane** ['ɛərəplein] Flugzeug *n*; **~stat** ['ɛəroustæt] Luftballon *m*.

aesthetic [i:s'θetik] ästhetisch; **~s** *sg.* Ästhetik *f*.

afar [ə'fɑ:] fern, weit (weg).

affable □ ['æfəbl] leutselig.

affair [ə'fɛə] Geschäft *n*; Angelegenheit *f*; Sache *f*; F Ding *n*; Liebschaft *f*.

affect [ə'fekt] (ein- *od.* sich aus-) wirken auf (*acc.*); (be)rühren; *Gesundheit* angreifen; gern mögen; vortäuschen, nachahmen; **~ation** [æfek'teiʃən] Vorliebe *f*; Ziererei *f*; Verstellung *f*; **~ed** □ gerührt; befallen (*von Krankheit*); angegriffen (*Augen etc.*); geziert, affektiert; **~ion** [~kʃən] Gemütszustand *m*; (Zu)Neigung *f*; Erkrankung *f*; **~ionate** □ [~ʃnit] liebevoll.

affidavit [æfi'deivit] *schriftliche* beeidigte Erklärung.

affiliate [ə'filieit] *als Mitglied* aufnehmen; angliedern; **~d** *company* Tochtergesellschaft *f*.

affinity [ə'finiti] *fig.* (geistige) Verwandtschaft *f*; ⚗ Affinität *f*.

affirm [ə'fə:m] bejahen; behaupten; bestätigen; **~ation** [æfə:'meiʃən] Behauptung *f*; Bestätigung *f*; **~ative** [ə'fə:mətiv] **1.** □ bejahend; **2.:** *answer in the* ~ bejahen.

affix [ə'fiks] (to) anheften (an *acc.*); befestigen (an *dat.*); *Siegel* aufdrücken (*dat.*); bei~, zufügen (*dat.*).

afflict [ə'flikt] betrüben; plagen; **~ion** [~kʃən] Betrübnis *f*; Leiden *n*.

affluen|ce ['æfluəns] Überfluß *m*; Wohlstand *m*; **~t** [~nt] **1.** □ reich (-lich); ~ *society* Wohlstandsgesellschaft *f*; **2.** Nebenfluß *m*.

afford [ə'fɔ:d] liefern; erschwingen; *I can* ~ *it* ich kann es mir leisten.

affront [ə'frʌnt] **1.** beleidigen; trotzen (*dat.*); **2.** Beleidigung *f*.

afield [ə'fi:ld] im Felde; (weit) weg.

afloat [ə'flout] ⚓ *u. fig.* flott; schwimmend; auf See; umlaufend; *set* ~ flottmachen; *fig.* in Umlauf setzen.

afraid [ə'freid] bange; *be* ~ *of* sich fürchten *od.* Angst haben vor (*dat.*).

afresh [ə'freʃ] von neuem.

African ['æfrikən] **1.** afrikanisch; **2.** Afrikaner(in); *Am. a.* Neger(in).

after ['ɑ:ftə] **1.** *adv.* hinterher; nachher; **2.** *prp.* nach; hinter (... her); ~ *all* schließlich (doch); **3.** *cj.* nachdem; **4.** *adj.* später; Nach...; **~crop** Nachernte *f*; **~glow** Abendrot *n*; **~math** [~əmæθ]

Nachwirkung(en *pl.*) *f*, Folgen *f*/*pl.*; ~noon [~ə'nu:n] Nachmittag *m*; ~ season Nachsaison *f*; ~taste Nachgeschmack *m*; ~thought nachträglicher Einfall; ~wards [~əwədz] nachher; später.

again [ə'gen] wieder(um); ferner; dagegen; an, vor (*dat. od. acc.*); *fig.* in Erwartung (*gen.*), für; as ~ verglichen mit.

age [eidʒ] 1. (Lebens)Alter *n*; Zeit (-alter *n*) *f*; Menschenalter *n*; (*old*) ~ Greisenalter *n*; of ~ mündig; over ~ zu alt; under ~ unmündig; wait for ~s F e-e Ewigkeit warten; 2. alt werden *od.* machen; ~d ['eidʒid] alt; [eidʒd]: ~ twenty 20 Jahre alt.

agency ['eidʒənsi] Tätigkeit *f*; Vermittlung *f*; Agentur *f*, Büro *n*.

agenda [ə'dʒendə] Tagesordnung *f*.

agent ['eidʒənt] Handelnde(r *m*) *f*; Agent *m*; wirkende Kraft, Agens *n*.

age-worn ['eidʒwɔ:n] altersschwach.

agglomerate [ə'glɔməreit] (sich) zs.-ballen; (sich) (an)häufen.

agglutinate [ə'glu:tineit] zs.-, an-, verkleben.

aggrandize [ə'grændaiz] vergrößern; erhöhen.

aggravate ['ægrəveit] erschweren; verschlimmern; F ärgern.

aggregate 1. ['ægrigeit] (sich) anhäufen; vereinigen (*to* mit); sich belaufen auf (*acc.*); 2. □ [~git] gehäuft; gesamt; 3. [~] Anhäufung *f*; Aggregat *n*.

aggress|ion [ə'greʃən] Angriff *m*; ~or [~esə] Angreifer *m*.

aggrieve [ə'gri:v] kränken; schädigen. [setzt.|

aghast [ə'ga:st] entgeistert, ent-|

agil|e □ ['ædʒail] flink, behend; ~ity [ə'dʒiliti] Behendigkeit *f*.

agitat|e ['ædʒiteit] *v/t.* bewegen, schütteln; *fig.* erregen; erörtern; *v/i.* agitieren; ~ion [ædʒi'teiʃən] Bewegung *f*, Erschütterung *f*; Aufregung *f*; Agitation *f*; ~or ['ædʒiteitə] Agitator *m*, Aufwiegler *m*.

ago [ə'gou]: a year ~ vor e-m Jahr.

agonize ['ægənaiz] (sich) quälen.

agony ['ægəni] Qual *f*, Pein *f*; Ringen *n*; Todeskampf *m*.

agree [ə'gri:] *v/i.* übereinstimmen; sich vertragen; einig werden (*on*, *upon* über *acc.*); übereinkommen; ~ *to* zustimmen (*dat.*); einverstanden sein mit; ~able □ [ə'griəbl] (*to*) angenehm (für); übereinstimmend (mit); ~ment [ə'gri:mənt] Übereinstimmung *f*; Vereinbarung *f*, Abkommen *n*; Vertrag *m*.

agricultur|al [ægri'kʌltʃərəl] land-

wirtschaftlich; ~e ['ægrikʌltʃə] Landwirtschaft *f*; ~ist [ægri'kʌltʃərist] Landwirt *m*.

aground ♱ [ə'graund] gestrandet; run ~ stranden, auflaufen.

ague 🜊 ['eigju:] Wechselfieber *n*; Schüttelfrost *m*.

ahead [ə'hed] vorwärts; voraus; vorn; *straight* ~ geradeaus.

aid [eid] 1. helfen (*dat.*; *in* bei *et.*); fördern; 2. Hilfe *f*, Unterstützung *f*.

ail [eil] *v/i.* kränkeln; *v/t.* schmerzen, weh(e) tun (*dat.*); *what* ~s *him?* was fehlt ihm?; ~ing ['eiliŋ] leidend; ~ment ['eilmənt] Leiden *n*.

aim [eim] 1. *v/i.* zielen (*at* auf *acc.*); ~ *at fig.* streben nach; ~ *to do bsd. Am.* beabsichtigen *od.* versuchen zu tun, tun wollen; *v/t.* ~ *at Waffe etc.* richten auf *od.* gegen (*acc.*); 2. Ziel *n*; Absicht *f*; ~less □ ['eimlis] ziellos.

air[1] [ɛə] 1. Luft *f*; Luftzug *m*; *by* ~ auf dem Luftwege; *in the open* ~ im Freien; *be in the* ~ *fig.* in der Luft liegen; ungewiß sein; *on the* ~ im Rundfunk (*senden*); *be on* (*off*) *the* ~ in (*außer*) Betrieb sein (*Sender*); *put on the* ~ im Rundfunk senden; 2. (aus)lüften; *fig.* an die Öffentlichkeit bringen; erörtern.

air[2] [~] Miene *f*; Aussehen *n*; *give o.s.* ~s vornehm tun.

air[3] ♪ [~] Arie *f*, Weise *f*, Melodie *f*.

air|-base ✕ ['ɛəbeis] Luftstützpunkt *m*; ~-bed Luftmatratze *f*; ~borne ✕ in der Luft (*Flugzeug*); ✕ Luftlande...; ~-brake Druckluftbremse *f*; ~-conditioned mit Klimaanlage; ~craft Flugzeug (-e *pl.*) *n*; ~field ✕ Flugplatz *m*; ~ force ✕ Luftwaffe *f*; ~ hostess ✕ Stewardess *f*; ~-jacket Schwimmweste *f*; ~-lift Luftbrücke *f*; ~ liner ✕ Verkehrsflugzeug *n*; ~ mail Luftpost *f*; ~man ✕ ['ɛəmən] Flieger *m*; ~plane *Am.* Flugzeug *n*; ~-pocket ✕ Luftloch *n*; ~port ✕ Flughafen *m*; ~raid ✕ Luftangriff *m*; ~-raid precautions *pl.* Luftschutz *m*; ~-raid shelter Luftschutzraum *m*; ~ route ✕ Luftweg *m*; ~-tight luftdicht; ~ *case sl.* todsicherer Fall; ~-tube Luftschlauch *m*; ~ umbrella ✕ Luftsicherung *f*; ~way ✕ Luftverkehrslinie *f*.

airy □ ['ɛəri] luftig; leicht(fertig).

aisle △ [ail] Seitenschiff *n*; Gang *m*.

ajar [ə'dʒa:] halb offen, angelehnt.

akin [ə'kin] verwandt (*to* mit).

alacrity [ə'lækriti] Munterkeit *f*; Bereitwilligkeit *f*, Eifer *m*.

alarm [ə'la:m] 1. Alarm(zeichen *n*) *m*; Angst *f*; 2. alarmieren; beunruhigen; ~-clock Wecker *m*.

albuminous [æl'bju:minəs] eiweißartig, -haltig.

alcohol ['ælkəhɔl] Alkohol *m*; ~ic

[ælkə'hɔlik] alkoholisch; ~ism ['æl-kəhɔlizəm] Alkoholvergiftung f.

alcove ['ælkouv] Nische f; Laube f.

alderman ['ɔːldəmən] Stadtrat m.

ale [eil] Ale n (Art engl. Bier).

alert [ə'ləːt] 1. □ wachsam; munter; 2. Alarm(bereitschaft f) m; on the ~ auf der Hut; in Alarmbereitschaft.

alibi ['ælibai] Alibi n; Am. F Entschuldigung f; Ausrede f.

alien ['eiljən] 1. fremd, ausländisch; 2. Ausländer(in); ~able [~nəbl] veräußerlich; ~ate [~neit] veräußern; fig. entfremden (from dat.); ~ist [~nist] Irrenarzt m, Psychiater m.

alight [ə'lait] 1. brennend; erhellt; 2. ab-, aussteigen; ✈ niedergehen, landen; sich niederlassen.

align [ə'lain] (sich) ausrichten (with nach); surv. abstecken; ~ o.s. with sich anschließen an (acc.).

alike [ə'laik] 1. adj. gleich, ähnlich; 2. adv. gleich; ebenso.

aliment ['ælimənt] Nahrung f; ~ary [æli'mentəri] nahrhaft; ~ canal Verdauungskanal m.

alimony ɡ [ˈ'ælimәni] Unterhalt m.

alive [ə'laiv] lebendig; in Kraft, gültig; empfänglich (to für); lebhaft; belebt (with von).

all [ɔːl] 1. adj. all; ganz; jede(r, -s); for ~ that dessenungeachtet, trotzdem; 2. pron. alles; alle pl.; at ~ gar, überhaupt; not at ~ durchaus nicht; for ~ (that) I care meinetwegen; for ~ I know soviel ich weiß; 3. adv. ganz, völlig; ~ at once auf einmal; ~ the better desto besser; ~ but beinahe, fast; ~ in Am. F fertig, ganz erledigt; ~ right (alles) in Ordnung.

all-American [ɔːlə'merikən] rein amerikanisch; die ganzen USA vertretend.

allay [ə'lei] beruhigen; lindern.

alleg|ation [æle'geiʃən] unerwiesene Behauptung f; ~e [ə'ledʒ] behaupten; ~ed angeblich.

allegiance [ə'liːdʒəns] Lehnspflicht f; (Untertanen)Treue f.

alleviate [ə'liːvieit] erleichtern, lindern.

alley ['æli] Allee f; Gäßchen n; Gang m; bsd. Am. schmale Zufahrtsstraße.

alliance [ə'laiəns] Bündnis n.

allocat|e ['æləkeit] zuteilen, anweisen; ~ion [ælə'keiʃən] Zuteilung f.

allot [ə'lɔt] zuweisen; ~ment [~t-mənt] Zuteilung f; Los n; Parzelle f.

allow [ə'lau] erlauben, bewilligen, gewähren, zugeben; ab-, anrechnen; vergüten; ~ for berücksichtigen; ~able □ [ə'lauəbl] erlaubt, zulässig; ~ance [~əns] Erlaubnis f; Bewilligung f; Taschengeld n, Zuschuß m; Vergütung f; Nachsicht f;

make ~ for s.th. et. in Betracht ziehen.

alloy 1. ['ælɔi] Legierung f; 2. [ə'lɔi] legieren; fig. verunedeln.

all-red ['ɔːl'red] rein britisch.

all-round ['ɔːl'raund] zu allem brauchbar; vielseitig.

all-star Am. ['ɔːl'staː] Sport u. thea.: aus den besten (Schau)Spielern bestehend.

allude [ə'luːd] anspielen (to auf acc.).

allure [ə'ljuə] (an-, ver)locken; ~ment [~mənt] Verlockung f.

allusion [ə'luːʒən] Anspielung f.

ally 1. [ə'lai] (sich) vereinigen, verbünden (to, with mit); 2. ['ælai] Verbündete(r m) f, Bundesgenosse m; the Allies pl. die Alliierten pl.

almanac ['ɔːlmənæk] Almanach m.

almighty [ɔːl'maiti] 1. □ allmächtig; 2 ♀ Allmächtige(r) m.

almond ♀ ['aːmənd] Mandel f.

almoner ['aːmənə] Krankenhausfürsorger(in).

almost ['ɔːlmoust] fast, beinahe.

alms [aːmz] sg. u. pl. Almosen n; ~-house ['aːmzhaus] Armenhaus n.

aloft [ə'lɔft] (hoch) (dr)oben.

alone [ə'loun] allein; let od. leave ~ in Ruhe od. bleiben lassen; let ~ ... abgesehen von ...

along [ə'lɔŋ] 1. adv. weiter, vorwärts, her; mit, bei (sich); all ~ die ganze Zeit; ~ with zs. mit; get ~ with you! F scher dich weg!; 2. prp. entlang, längs; ~side [~'said] Seite an Seite; neben.

aloof [ə'luːf] fern; weitab; stand ~ abseits stehen.

aloud [ə'laud] laut; hörbar.

alp [ælp] Alp(e) f; ♀s pl. Alpen pl.

already [ɔːl'redi] bereits, schon.

also ['ɔːlsou] auch; ferner.

altar ['ɔːltə] Altar m.

alter ['ɔːltə] (sich) (ver)ändern; ab-, umändern; ~ation [ɔːltə'reiʃən] Änderung f (to an dat.).

alternat|e 1. ['ɔːltəːneit] abwechseln (lassen); alternating current ⚡ Wechselstrom m; 2. □ [ɔːl'təːnit] abwechselnd; 3. [~] Am. Stellvertreter m; ~ion [ɔːltəː'neiʃən] Abwechslung f; Wechsel m; ~ive [ɔːl'təːnə-tiv] 1. □ nur eine Wahl zwischen zwei Möglichkeiten lassend; 2. Alternative f; Wahl f; Möglichkeit f.

although [ɔːl'ðou] obgleich.

altitude ['æltitjuːd] Höhe f.

altogether [ɔːltə'geðə] im ganzen (genommen), alles in allem; gänzlich.

aluminium [ælju'minjəm] Aluminium n.

aluminum Am. [ə'luːminəm] = aluminium.

always ['ɔːlwəz] immer, stets.

am [æm; im Satz əm] 1. sg. pres. von be.

amalgamate [ə'mælgəmeit] amalgamieren; (sich) verschmelzen.

amass [ə'mæs] (an-, auf)häufen.

amateur ['æmətə:] Amateur *m*; Liebhaber *m*; Dilettant *m*.

amaz|e [ə'meiz] in Staunen setzen, verblüffen; **~ement** [~zmənt] Staunen *n*, Verblüffung *f*; **~ing** □ [~ziŋ] erstaunlich, verblüffend.

ambassador [æm'bæsədə] Botschafter *m*, Gesandte(r) *m*.

amber ['æmbə] Bernstein *m*.

ambigu|ity [æmbi'gju(:)iti] Zwei-, Vieldeutigkeit *f*; **~ous** □ [æm-'bigjuəs] zwei-, vieldeutig; doppelsinnig.

ambitio|n [æm'biʃən] Ehrgeiz *m*; Streben *n* (of nach); **~us** □ [~ʃəs] ehrgeizig; begierig (of, for nach).

amble ['æmbl] 1. Paßgang *m*; 2. im Paßgang gehen *od.* reiten; schlendern.

ambulance ['æmbjuləns] Feldlazarett *n*; Krankenwagen *m*; **~ station** Sanitätswache *f*, Unfallstation *f*.

ambus|cade [æmbəs'keid], **~h** ['æmbuʃ] 1. Hinterhalt *m*; be *od.* lie in ambush for s.o. j-m auflauern; 2. auflauern (dat.); überfallen.

ameliorate [ə'mi:ljəreit] *v/t.* verbessern; *v/i.* besser werden.

amend [ə'mend] (sich) (ver)bessern; berichtigen; Gesetz (ab)ändern; **~ment** [~dmənt] Besserung *f*; ⚖ Berichtigung *f*; parl. Änderungsantrag *m*; Am. Zusatzartikel *m* zur Verfassung der USA; **~s** *sg.* (Schaden)Ersatz *m*.

amenity [ə'mi:niti] Annehmlichkeit *f*; Anmut *f*; amenities *pl.* angenehmes Wesen.

American [ə'merikən] 1. amerikanisch; **~ cloth** Wachstuch *n*; **~ plan** Hotelzimmervermietung mit voller Verpflegung; 2. Amerikaner(in); **~ism** [~nizəm] Amerikanismus *m*; **~ize** [~naiz] (sich) amerikanisieren.

amiable □ ['eimjəbl] liebenswürdig, freundlich.

amicable □ ['æmikəbl] freundschaftlich; gütlich.

amid(st) [ə'mid(st)] inmitten (gen.); (mitten) unter; mitten in (dat.).

amiss [ə'mis] verkehrt; übel; ungelegen; take ~ übelnehmen.

amity ['æmiti] Freundschaft *f*.

ammonia [ə'mounjə] Ammoniak *n*.

ammunition [æmju'niʃən] Munition *f*.

amnesty ['æmnesti] 1. Amnestie *f* (Straferlaß); 2. begnadigen.

among(st) [ə'mʌŋ(st)] (mitten) unter, zwischen; [in acc.].

amorous □ ['æmərəs] verliebt (of).

amount [ə'maunt] 1. (to) sich belaufen (auf acc.); hinauslaufen (auf acc.); 2. Betrag *m*, (Gesamt-)

Summe *f*; Menge *f*; Bedeutung *f*, Wert *m*.

amour [ə'muə] Liebschaft *f*; **~-propre** Selbstachtung *f*; Eitelkeit *f*.

ample □ ['æmpl] weit, groß; geräumig; reichlich.

ampli|fication [æmplifi'keiʃən] Erweiterung *f*; rhet. weitere Ausführung *f*; phys. Verstärkung *f*; **~fier** ['æmplifaiə] Radio: Verstärker *m*; **~fy** [~fai] erweitern; verstärken; weiter ausführen; **~tude** [~itju:d] Umfang *m*, Weite *f*, Fülle *f*.

amputate ['æmpjuteit] amputieren.

amuse [ə'mju:z] amüsieren; unterhalten; belustigen; **~ment** [~zmənt] Unterhaltung *f*; Zeitvertreib *m*.

an [æn, ən] Artikel: ein(e).

an(a)emia [ə'ni:mjə] Blutarmut *f*.

an(a)esthetic [ænis'θetik] 1. betäubend, Narkose...; 2. Betäubungsmittel *n*.

analog|ous □ [ə'næləgəs] analog, ähnlich; **~y** [~ədʒi] Ähnlichkeit *f*, Analogie *f*.

analys|e ['ænəlaiz] analysieren; zerlegen; **~is** [ə'næləsis] Analyse *f*.

anarchy ['ænəki] Anarchie *f*, Gesetzlosigkeit *f*; Zügellosigkeit *f*.

anatom|ize [ə'nætəmaiz] zergliedern; **~y** [~mi] Anatomie *f*; Zergliederung *f*, Analyse *f*.

ancest|or ['ænsistə] Vorfahr *m*, Ahn *m*; **~ral** [æn'sestrəl] angestammt; **~ress** ['ænsistris] Ahne *f*; **~ry** [~ri] Abstammung *f*; Ahnen *m/pl.*

anchor ['æŋkə] 1. Anker *m*; at ~ vor Anker; 2. (ver)ankern; **~age** [~əridʒ] Ankerplatz *m*.

anchovy ['æntʃəvi] Sardelle *f*.

ancient ['einʃənt] 1. alt, antik; uralt; 2. the ~s *pl.* hist. die Alten, die antiken Klassiker.

and [ænd, ənd] und.

anew [ə'nju:] von neuem.

angel ['eindʒəl] Engel *m*; **~ic(al** □) [æn'dʒelik(əl)] engelgleich.

anger ['æŋgə] 1. Zorn *m*, Ärger *m* (at über acc.); 2. erzürnen, ärgern.

angina [æn'dʒainə] Angina *f*, Halsentzündung *f*.

angle ['æŋgl] 1. Winkel *m*; fig. Standpunkt *m*; 2. angeln (for nach).

Anglican ['æŋglikən] 1. anglikanisch; Am. a. englisch; 2. Anglikaner(in).

Anglo-Saxon ['æŋglou'sæksən] 1. Angelsachse *m*; 2. angelsächsisch.

angry ['æŋgri] zornig, böse (a. ⚙) (with s.o., at s.th. über, auf acc.).

anguish ['æŋgwiʃ] Pein *f*, (Seelen-) Qual *f*, Schmerz *m*.

angular □ ['æŋgjulə] winkelig; Winkel...; fig. eckig.

animadver|sion [ænimæd'və:ʃən]

Verweis *m*, Tadel *m*; ~t [.ə:t] tadeln, kritisieren.

animal ['ænimǝl] **1.** Tier *n*; **2.** tierisch.

animat|e ['ænimeit] beleben; beseelen; aufmuntern; ~**ion** [æni-'meiʃǝn] Leben *n* (und Treiben *n*), Lebhaftigkeit *f*, Munterkeit *f*.

animosity [æni'mɔsiti] Feindseligkeit *f*.

ankle ['æŋkl] Fußknöchel *m*.

annals ['ænlz] *pl*. Jahrbücher *n/pl*.

annex 1. [ǝ'neks] anhängen; annektieren; **2.** ['æneks] Anhang *m*; Anbau *m*; ~**ation** [ænek'seiʃǝn] Annexion *f*, Aneignung *f*; Einverleibung *f*.

annihilate [ǝ'naiǝleit] vernichten; = annul.

anniversary [æni'vǝ:sǝri] Jahrestag *m*; Jahresfeier *f*.

annotat|e ['ænouteit] mit Anmerkungen versehen; kommentieren; ~**ion** [ænou'teiʃǝn] Kommentieren *n*; Anmerkung *f*.

announce [ǝ'nauns] ankündigen; ansagen; ~**ment** [.smǝnt] Ankündigung *f*; Ansage *f*; Radio: Durchsage *f*; Anzeige *f*; ~**r** [.sǝ] *Radio*: Ansager *m*.

annoy [ǝ'nɔi] ärgern; belästigen; ~**ance** [ǝ'nɔiǝns] Störung *f*; Plage *f*; Ärgernis *n*.

annual ['ænjuǝl] **1.** □ jährlich; Jahres...; **2.** einjährige Pflanze; Jahrbuch *n*. [Rente *f*.]

annuity [ǝ'nju(:)iti] (Jahres-)

annul [ǝ'nʌl] für ungültig erklären, annullieren; ~**ment** [.lmǝnt] Aufhebung *f*.

anodyne ['ænoudain] **1.** schmerzstillend; **2.** schmerzstillendes Mittel.

anoint [ǝ'nɔint] salben.

anomalous □ [ǝ'nɔmǝlǝs] anomal, unregelmäßig, regelwidrig.

anonymous □ [ǝ'nɔnimǝs] anonym, ungenannt.

another [ǝ'nʌðǝ] ein anderer; ein zweiter; noch ein.

answer ['ɑ:nsǝ] **1.** *v/t. et.* beantworten; *j-m* antworten; entsprechen (*dat.*); *Zweck* erfüllen; *dem Steuer* gehorchen; ~ *er Vorladung* Folge leisten; ~ *the bell od. door* (die Haustür) aufmachen; *v/i.* antworten (*to s.o.* j-m; *to a question* auf e-e Frage); entsprechen (*to dat.*); Erfolg haben; sich lohnen; ~ *for* einstehen für; bürgen für; **2.** Antwort *f* (*to* auf *acc.*); ~**able** □ [.ǝrǝbl] verantwortlich.

ant [ænt] Ameise *f*.

antagonis|m [æn'tægǝnizǝm] Widerstreit *m*; Widerstand *m*; Feindschaft *f*; ~t [.ist] Gegner(in).

antagonize [æn'tægǝnaiz] ankämpfen gegen; sich *j-n* zum Feind machen.

antecedent [ænti'si:dǝnt] **1.** □ vor-

hergehend; früher (*to* als); **2.** Vorhergehende(s) *n*.

anterior [æn'tiǝriǝ] vorhergehend; früher (*to* als); vorder.

ante-room ['æntirum] Vorzimmer *n*.

anthem ['ænθǝm] Hymne *f*.

anti|... ['ænti] Gegen...; gegen ... eingestellt *od.* wirkend; ~**aircraft** Fliegerabwehr...; ~**biotic** [.ibai-'ɔtik] Antibiotikum *n*.

antic ['æntik] Posse *f*; ~s *pl*. Mätzchen *n/pl*.; (tolle) Sprünge *m/pl*.

anticipat|e [æn'tisipeit] vorwegnehmen; zuvorkommen (*dat.*); voraussehen, ahnen; erwarten; ~**ion** [æntisi'peiʃǝn] Vorwegnahme *f*; Zuvorkommen *n*; Voraussicht *f*; Erwartung *f*; *in* ~ im voraus.

antidote ['æntidout] Gegengift *n*.

antipathy [æn'tipǝθi] Abneigung *f*.

antiqua|ry ['æntikwǝri] Altertumsforscher *m*; -händler *m*; ~**ted** [.kweitid] veraltet, überlebt.

antiqu|e [æn'ti:k] **1.** □ antik, alt (-modisch); **2.** alter Kunstgegenstand; ~**ity** [æn'tikwiti] Altertum *n*; Vorzeit *f*.

antiseptic [ænti'septik] **1.** antiseptisch; **2.** antiseptisches Mittel.

antlers ['æntlǝz] *pl*. Geweih *n*.

anvil ['ænvil] Amboß *m*.

anxiety [æŋ'zaiǝti] Angst *f*; *fig.* Sorge *f* (*for* um); ⚕ Beklemmung *f*.

anxious □ ['æŋkʃǝs] ängstlich, besorgt (*about* um, wegen); begierig, gespannt (*for* auf *acc.*); bemüht (*for* um).

any ['eni] **1.** *pron.* (irgend)einer; einige *pl.*; (irgend)welcher; (irgend) etwas; jeder (beliebige); *not* ~ keiner; **2.** *adv.* irgend(wie); ~**body** (irgend) jemand; jeder; ~**how** irgendwie; jedenfalls; ~**one** = anybody; ~**thing** (irgend) etwas, alles; ~ *but* alles andere als; ~**way** = anyhow; ohnehin; ~**where** irgendwo(hin); überall.

apart [ǝ'pɑ:t] einzeln; getrennt; für sich; beiseite; ~ *from* abgesehen von.

apartheid *pol.* [ǝ'pɑ:theit] Apartheid *f*, Rassentrennung(spolitik) *f*.

apartment [ǝ'pɑ:tmǝnt] Zimmer *n*, *Am. a.* Wohnung *f*; ~s *pl.* Wohnung *f*; ~ *house Am.* Mietshaus *n*.

apathetic [æpǝ'θetik] apathisch, gleichgültig.

ape [eip] **1.** Affe *m*; **2.** nachäffen.

aperient [ǝ'piǝriǝnt] Abführmittel *n*.

aperture ['æpǝtjuǝ] Öffnung *f*.

apiary ['eipiǝri] Bienenhaus *n*.

apiculture ['eipikʌltʃǝ] Bienenzucht *f*.

apiece [ǝ'pi:s] (für) das Stück; je.

apish □ ['eipiʃ] affig; äffisch.

apolog|etic [ǝpɔlǝ'dʒetik] (~ally) verteidigend; rechtfertigend; entschuldigend; ~**ize** [ǝ'pɔlǝdʒaiz] sich entschuldigen (*for* wegen; *to* bei); **~y** [~dʒi] Entschuldigung *f*; Rechtfertigung *f*; F Notbehelf *m*.

apoplexy ['æpəpleksi] Schlag(anfall) *m*.

apostate [ə'pɔstīt] Abtrünnige(r*m*)*f*.

apostle [ə'pɔsl] Apostel *m*.

apostroph|e [ə'pɔstrəfi] Anrede *f*; Apostroph *m*; **~ize** [~faiz] anreden, sich wenden an (*acc.*).

appal [ə'pɔːl] erschrecken.

apparatus [æpə'reitəs] Apparat *m*, Vorrichtung *f*, Gerät *n*.

apparel [ə'pærəl] **1.** Kleidung *f*; **2.** (be)kleiden.

appar|ent □ [ə'pærənt] anscheinend; offenbar; **~ition** [æpə'riʃən] Erscheinung *f*; Gespenst *n*.

appeal [ə'piːl] **1.** (*to*) appellieren (an *acc.*); sich berufen (auf *e-n Zeugen*); sich wenden (an *acc.*); wirken (auf *acc.*); Anklang finden (bei); **~ to the country** *parl.* Neuwahlen ausschreiben; **2.** ⚖ Revision *f*, Berufung(sklage) *f*; ⚖ Rechtsmittel *n*; *fig.* Appell *m* (*to* an *acc.*); Wirkung *f*, Reiz *m*; **~ for mercy** ⚖ Gnadengesuch *n*; **~ing** □ [~liŋ] flehend; ansprechend.

appear [ə'piə] (er)scheinen; sich zeigen; *öffentlich* auftreten; **~ance** [~ərəns] Erscheinen *n*, Auftreten *n*; Äußere(s) *n*, Erscheinung *f*; Anschein *m*; **~s** *pl.* äußerer Schein; **to** *od.* **by all ~s** allem Anschein nach.

appease [ə'piːz] beruhigen; beschwichtigen; stillen; mildern; beilegen.

appellant [ə'pelənt] **1.** appellierend; **2.** Appelant(in), Berufungskläger (-in).

append [ə'pend] anhängen; hinzu-, beifügen; **~age** [~didʒ] Anhang *m*; Anhängsel *n*; Zubehör *n*, *m*; **~icitis** [əpendi'saitis] Blinddarmentzündung *f*; **~ix** [ə'pendiks] Anhang *m*; *a. vermiform* **~** ⚕ Wurmfortsatz *m*, Blinddarm *m*.

appertain [æpə'tein] gehören (*to* zu).

appetite ['æpitait] (*for*) Appetit *m* (auf *acc.*); *fig.* Verlangen *n* (nach).

appetizing ['æpitaiziŋ] appetitanregend.

applaud [ə'plɔːd] applaudieren, Beifall spenden; loben.

applause [ə'plɔːz] Applaus *m*, Beifall *m*.

apple ['æpl] Apfel *m*; **~cart** Apfelkarren *m*; **upset s.o.'s ~** F j-s Pläne über den Haufen werfen; **~pie** gedeckter Apfelkuchen; **in ~ order** F in schönster Ordnung; **~sauce** Apfelmus *n*; *Am. sl.* Schmus *m*, Quatsch *m*.

appliance [ə'plaiəns] Vorrichtung *f*; Gerät *n*; Mittel *n*.

applica|ble ['æplikəbḷ] anwendbar

(*to* auf *acc.*); **~nt** [~ənt] Bittsteller (-in); Bewerber(in) (*for* um); **~tion** [æpli'keiʃən] (*to*) Auf-, Anlegung *f* (auf *acc.*); Anwendung *f* (auf *acc.*); Bedeutung *f* (für); Gesuch *n* (*for* um); Bewerbung *f*.

apply [ə'plai] *v/t.* (*to*) (auf)legen (auf *acc.*); anwenden (auf *acc.*); verwenden (für); **~ o.s. to** sich widmen(*dat.*); *v/i.* (*to*) passen, sich anwenden lassen (auf *acc.*); gelten (für); sich wenden (an *acc.*); (*for*) sich bewerben (um); nachsuchen (um).

appoint [ə'pɔint] bestimmen; festsetzen; verabreden; ernennen (*s.o. governor* j-n zum ...); berufen (*to* auf *e-n Posten*); **well ~ed** gut eingerichtet; **~ment** [~tmənt] Bestimmung *f*; Stelldichein *n*; Verabredung *f*; Ernennung *f*, Berufung *f*; Stelle *f*; **~s** *pl.* Ausstattung *f*, Einrichtung *f*.

apportion [ə'pɔːʃən] ver-, zuteilen; **~ment** [~nmənt] Verteilung *f*.

apprais|al [ə'preizəl] Abschätzung *f*; **~e** [ə'preiz] abschätzen, taxieren.

apprecia|ble □ [ə'priːʃəbl] (ab-) schätzbar; merkbar; **~te** [~ʃieit] *v/t.* schätzen; würdigen; dankbar sein für; *v/i.* im Werte steigen; **~tion** [əpriːʃi'eiʃən] Schätzung *f*, Würdigung *f*; Verständnis *n* (*of* für); Einsicht *f*; Dankbarkeit *f*; Aufwertung *f*.

apprehen|d [æpri'hend] ergreifen; fassen, begreifen; befürchten; **~sion** [~nʃən] Ergreifung *f*, Festnahme *f*; Fassungskraft *f*, Auffassung *f*; Besorgnis *f*; **~sive** □ [~nsiv] schnell begreifend (*of* *acc.*); ängstlich; besorgt (*of*, *for* um, wegen; *that* daß).

apprentice [ə'prentis] **1.** Lehrling *m*; **2.** in die Lehre geben (*to* *dat.*); **~ship** [~iʃip] Lehrzeit *f*; Lehre *f*.

approach [ə'prəutʃ] **1.** *v/i.* näherkommen, sich nähern; *v/t.* sich nähern (*dat.*), herangehen *od.* herantreten an (*acc.*); **2.** Annäherung *f*; *fig.* Herangehen *n*; Methode *f*; Zutritt *m*; Auffahrt *f*.

approbation [æprə'beiʃən] Billigung *f*, Beifall *m*.

appropriat|e 1. [ə'prəuprieit] sich aneignen; verwenden; *parl.* bewilligen; **2.** [~iit] (*to*) angemessen (*dat.*); passend (für); eigen (*dat.*); **~ion** [əprəupri'eiʃən] Aneignung *f*; Verwendung *f*.

approv|al [ə'pruːvəl] Billigung *f*, Beifall *m*; **~e** [~uːv] billigen, anerkennen; (**~ o.s.** sich) erweisen als; **~ed** □ bewährt.

approximate 1. [ə'prɔksimeit] sich nähern; **2.** □ [~mit] annähernd; ungefähr; nahe.

apricot ['eiprikɔt] Aprikose *f*.

April ['eiprəl] April *m*.

apron ['eiprən] Schürze f; **~-string** Schürzenband n; be tied to one's wife's (mother's) **~s** fig. unterm Pantoffel stehen (der Mutter am Rockzipfel hängen).

apt □ [æpt] geeignet, passend; begabt; ~ to geneigt zu; **~itude** ['æptitju:d], **~ness** ['æptnis] Neigung f (to zu); Befähigung f.

aquatic [ə'kwætik] Wasserpflanze f; **~s** pl. Wassersport m.

aque|duct ['ækwidʌkt] Aquädukt m, Wasserleitung f; **~ous** □ ['eikwiəs] wässerig.

aquiline ['ækwilain] Adler...; gebogen; ~ nose Adlernase f.

Arab ['ærəb] Araber(in); **~ic** [~bik] 1. arabisch; 2. Arabisch n.

arable ['ærəbl] pflügbar; Acker...

arbit|er ['a:bitə] Schiedsrichter m; fig. Gebieter m; **~rariness** [~trəri-nis] Willkür f; **~rary** □ [~trəri] willkürlich; eigenmächtig; **~rate** [~reit] entscheiden, schlichten; **~ration** [a:bi'treiʃən] Schiedsspruch m; Entscheidung f; **~rator** [ǎʒ ['a:bitreitə] Schiedsrichter m.

arbo(u)r ['a:bə] Laube f.

arc ast., ≠ etc. [a:k] (≠ Licht-) Bogen m; **~ade** [a:'keid] Arkade f; Bogen-, Laubengang m.

arch¹ [a:tʃ] 1. Bogen m; Gewölbe n; 2. (sich) wölben; überwölben.

arch² [~] erst; schlimmst; Haupt...; Erz...

arch³ □ [~] schelmisch.

archaic [a:'keiik] (~ally) veraltet.

archangel ['a:keindʒəl] Erzengel m.

archbishop ['a:tʃ'biʃəp] Erzbischof m.

archer ['a:tʃə] Bogenschütze m; **~y** [~əri] Bogenschießen n.

architect ['a:kitekt] Architekt m; Urheber(in), Schöpfer(in); **~onic** [a:kitek'tonik] (~ally) architektonisch; fig. aufbauend; **~ure** □ ['a:kitektʃə] Architektur f, Baukunst f.

archives ['a:kaivz] pl. Archiv n.

archway ['a:tʃwei] Bogengang m.

arc|-lamp ['a:klæmp], **~-light** ≠ Bogenlampe f.

arctic ['a:ktik] 1. arktisch, nördlich; Nord..., Polar...; 2. Am. wasserdichter Überschuh.

arden|cy ['a:dənsi] Hitze f, Glut f; Innigkeit f; **~t** □ [~nt] mst fig. heiß, glühend; fig. feurig; eifrig.

ardo(u)r ['a:də] fig. Glut f; Eifer m.

arduous □ ['a:djuəs] mühsam; zäh.

are [a:; im Satz ə] pres. pl. u. 2. sg. von be.

area ['ɛəriə] Areal n; (Boden-) Fläche f; Flächenraum m; Gegend f; Gebiet n; Bereich m.

Argentine ['a:dʒəntain] 1. argentinisch; 2. Argentinier(in); the ~ Argentinien n.

argue ['a:gju:] v/t. erörtern; beweisen; begründen; einwenden; ~

s.o. into j-n zu et. bereden; v/i. streiten; Einwendungen machen.

argument ['a:gjumənt] Beweis (-grund) m; Streit(frage f) m; Erörterung f; Thema n; **~ation** [a:gjumen'teiʃən] Beweisführung f.

arid ['ærid] dürr, trocken (a. fig.).

arise [ə'raiz] [irr.] sich erheben (a. fig.); ent-, erstehen (from aus); **~n** [ə'rizn] p.p von arise.

aristocra|cy [æris'tɔkrəsi] Aristokratie f (a. fig.), Adel m; **~t** ['æristəkræt] Aristokrat(in); **~tic(al** □) [æristə'krætik(əl)] aristokratisch.

arithmetic [ə'riθmətik] Rechnen n.

ark [a:k] Arche f.

arm¹ [a:m] Arm m; Armlehne f; keep s.o. at **~'s** length sich j-n vom Leibe halten; infant in **~s** Säugling m.

arm² [~] 1. Waffe f (mst pl.); Waffengattung f; be (all) up in **~s** in vollem Aufruhr sein; in Harnisch geraten; 2. (sich) (be)waffnen; (aus)rüsten; ⊕ armieren.

armada [a:'ma:də] Kriegsflotte f.

arma|ment ['a:məmənt] (Kriegs-aus)Rüstung f; Kriegsmacht f; ~ race Wettrüsten n; **~ture** ['a:mə-tjuə] Rüstung f; ⚡, phys. Armatur f.

armchair ['a:m'tʃɛə] Lehnstuhl m, Sessel m.

armistice ['a:mistis] Waffenstillstand m (a. fig.).

armo(u)r ['a:mə] 1. ✗ Rüstung f, Panzer m (a. fig., zo.); 2. panzern; **~ed car** Panzerwagen m; **~y** ['a:-məri] Rüstkammer f (a. fig.); Am. Rüstungsbetrieb m, Waffenfabrik f.

armpit ['a:mpit] Achselhöhle f.

army ['a:mi] Heer n, Armee f; fig. Menge f; ~ chaplain Militärgeistliche(r) m.

arose [ə'rouz] pret. von arise.

around [ə'raund] 1. adv. rund-(her)um; Am. F hier herum; 2. prp. um ... her(um), bsd. Am. F ungefähr, etwa (bei Zahlenangaben).

arouse [ə'rauz] aufwecken; fig. aufrütteln; erregen.

arraign [ə'rein] vor Gericht stellen, anklagen; fig. rügen.

arrange [ə'reindʒ] (an)ordnen, bsd. ♪ einrichten; festsetzen; Streit schlichten; vereinbaren; erledigen; **~ment** [~dʒmənt] Anordnung f; Disposition f; Übereinkommen n; Vorkehrung f; ♪ Arrangement n.

array [ə'rei] 1. (Schlacht)Ordnung f; fig. Aufgebot n; 2. ordnen, aufstellen; anreihen; kleiden, putzen.

arrear [ə'riə] mst pl. Rückstand m, bsd. Schulden f/pl.

arrest [ə'rest] 1. Verhaftung f; Haft f; Beschlagnahme f; 2. verhaften; beschlagnahmen; anhalten, hemmen.

arriv|al [ə'raivəl] Ankunft f; Auftreten n; Ankömmling m; **~s** pl. angekommene Personen *f/pl.*, Züge *m/pl.*, Schiffe *n/pl.*; ~e [ə'raiv] (an-) kommen, eintreffen; erscheinen; eintreten (*Ereignis*); ~ at erreichen (*acc.*).

arroga|nce ['ærəgəns] Anmaßung *f*; Überheblichkeit *f*; ~nt □ [~nt] anmaßend; überheblich; ~te *f*['ærougeit] sich *et.* anmaßen.

arrow ['ærou] Pfeil *m*; ~-head Pfeilspitze *f*; ~y ['æroui] pfeilartig.

arsenal ['ɑːsinl] Zeughaus *n*.

arsenic ['ɑːsnik] Arsen(ik) *n*.

arson *ʒ̣ʒ̣* ['ɑːsn] Brandstiftung *f*.

art [ɑːt] Kunst *f*; *fig.* List *f*; Kniff *m*; ~s *pl.* Geisteswissenschaften *f/pl.*; *Faculty of* ⌀s philosophische Fakultät *f*.

arter|ial [ɑː'tiəriəl] Pulsader...; ~ *road* Hauptstraße *f*; ~y ['ɑːtəri] Arterie *f*, Pulsader *f*; *fig.* Verkehrsader *f*.   [schmitzt.}

artful □ ['ɑːtful] schlau, ver-}

article ['ɑːtikl] Artikel *m*; *fig.* Punkt *m*; ~d *to* in der Lehre bei.

articulat|e 1. [ɑː'tikjuleit] deutlich (aus)sprechen; *Knochen* zs.-fügen; **2.** □ [~lit] deutlich; gegliedert; ~ion [ɑːtikju'leiʃən] deutliche Aussprache; *anat.* Gelenkfügung *f*.

artific|e ['ɑːtifis] Kunstgriff *m*, List *f*; ~ial □ [ɑː'tiˈfiʃəl] künstlich; *Kunst*...; ~ *person* *ʒ̣ʒ̣* juristische Person.

artillery [ɑː'tiləri] Artillerie *f*; ~man Artillerist *m*.

artisan [ɑː'tizæn] Handwerker *m*.

artist ['ɑːtist] Künstler(in); ~e [ɑː'tiːst] Artist(in); ~ic(al) □ [ɑː-'tistik(əl)] künstlerisch; *Kunst*...

artless □ ['ɑːtlis] ungekünstelt, schlicht; arglos.

as [æz, əz] **1.** *adv.* so; (ebenso) wie; (*in der Eigenschaft*) als; ~ *big* ~ so groß wie; ~ *well* ebensogut; auch; ~ *well* ~ sowohl...als auch; **2.** *cj.* (so-) wie; *ebenso*; (*zu der Zeit*) als, während; da, weil, indem; sofern; ~ *it were* sozusagen; *such* ~ *to* derart, daß; ~ *for*, ~ *to* was (an)betrifft; ~ *from* von...an.

ascend [ə'send] *v/i.* (auf-, empor-, hinauf)steigen; *zeitlich*: zurückgehen (*to* bis zu); *v/t.* be-, ersteigen; hinaufsteigen; *Fluß etc.* hinauffahren; ~ancy, ~ency [~dənsi] Überlegenheit *f*, Einfluß *m*; Herrschaft *f*.

ascension [ə'senʃən] Aufsteigen *n* (*bsd. ast.*); *Am. a.* Aufstieg *m* (*e-s Ballons etc.*); ⌀ (*Day*) Himmelfahrt(stag *m*) *f*.

ascent [ə'sent] Aufstieg *m*; Besteigung *f*; Steigung *f*; Aufgang *m*.

ascertain [æsə'tein] ermitteln.

ascetic [ə'setik] (~ally) asketisch.

ascribe [ə'skraib] zuschreiben.

aseptic *ʒ̣* [æ'septik] **1.** aseptisch; **2.** aseptisches Mittel.

ash¹ [æʃ] ⚭ Esche *f*; Eschenholz *n*.

ash² (~), *mst. pl.* ~es ['æʃiz] Asche *f*; *Ash Wednesday* Aschermittwoch *m*.

ashamed [ə'ʃeimd] beschämt; *be* ~ *of* sich e-r *Sache od. j-s* schämen.

ash can *Am.* ['æʃkæn] = *dust-bin*.

ashen ['æʃn] Aschen...; aschfahl.

ashore [ə'ʃɔː] am *od.* ans Ufer *od.* Land; *run* ~, *be driven* ~ stranden.

ash|-pan ['æʃpæn] Asch(en)kasten *m*; ~-tray Asch(en)becher *m*.

ashy ['æʃi] aschig; aschgrau.

Asiatic [eiʃi'ætik] **1.** asiatisch; **2.** Asiat(in).

aside [ə'said] **1.** beiseite (*a. thea.*); abseits; seitwärts; ~ *from Am.* abgesehen von; **2.** *thea.* Aparte *n*.

ask [ɑːsk] *v/t.* fragen (*s.th. nach et.*); verlangen (*of, from* s.o. von j-m); bitten (*s.o.* [*for*] *s.th.* j. um *et.*; *that* darum, daß); erbitten; ~ (*s.o.*) *a question* (j-m) e-e Frage stellen; *v/i.*: ~ *for* bitten um, fragen nach; *he* ~*ed for it od. for trouble* er wollte es ja so haben; *to be had for the* ~*ing* umsonst zu haben.

askance [əs'kæns], **askew** [əs'kjuː] von der Seite, seitwärts; schief.

asleep [ə'sliːp] schlafend; in den Schlaf; eingeschlafen, *be* ~ schlafen; *fall* ~ einschlafen.

asparagus ⚭ [əs'pærəgəs] Spargel *m*.

aspect ['æspekt] Äußere *n*; Aussicht *f*, Lage *f*; Aspekt *m*, Seite *f*, Gesichtspunkt *m*.

asperity [æs'periti] Rauheit *f*; Unebenheit *f*; *fig.* Schroffheit *f*.

asphalt ['æsfælt] **1.** Asphalt *m*; **2.** asphaltieren.

aspic ['æspik] Aspik *m*, Sülze *f*.

aspir|ant [əs'paiərənt] Bewerber (-in); ~ate *ling.* ['æspəreit] aspirieren; ~ation [æspə'reiʃən] Aspiration *f*; Bestrebung *f*; ~e [əs'paiə] streben, trachten (*to, after, at* nach).

ass [æs] Esel *m*.

assail [ə'seil] angreifen, überfallen (*a. fig.*); befallen (*Zweifel etc.*); ~ant [~lənt] Angreifer(in).

assassin [ə'sæsin] (Meuchel)Mörder(in); ~ate [~neit] (meuchlings) ermorden; ~ation [əsæsi'neiʃən] Meuchelmord *m*.

assault [ə'sɔːlt] **1.** Angriff *m* (*a. fig.*); **2.** anfallen, *et.* tätlich angreifen *od.* beleidigen; ✕ bestürmen (*a. fig.*).

assay [ə'sei] **1.** (Erz-, Metall-) Probe *f*; **2.** *v/t.* untersuchen; *v/i. Am.* Edelmetall enthalten.

assembl|age [ə'semblidʒ] (An-) Sammlung *f*; ⊕ Montage *f*; ~e [ə'sembl] (sich) versammeln; zs.-berufen; ⊕ montieren; ~y Versammlung *f*; Gesellschaft *f*; ⊕ Montage *f*; ~ *line* ⊕ Fließband *n*; ~ *man pol.* Abgeordnete(r) *m*.

assent [ə'sent] **1.** Zustimmung *f*; **2.** (*to*) zustimmen (*dat.*); billigen.

assert [ə'sə:t] (sich) behaupten; **∼ion** [ə'sə:ʃən] Behauptung *f*; Erklärung *f*; Geltendmachung *f*.

assess [ə'ses] besteuern; zur Steuer veranlagen (*at* mit); **∼able** □ [∼səbl] steuerpflichtig; **∼ment** [∼smənt] (Steuer)Veranlagung *f*; Steuer *f*.

asset ['æset] ✝ Aktivposten *m*; *fig.* Gut *n*, Gewinn *m*; **∼s** *pl.* Vermögen *n*; ✝ Aktiva *pl.*; ⚖ Konkursmasse *f*.

asseverate [ə'sevəreit] beteuern.

assiduous □ [ə'sidjuəs] emsig, fleißig; aufmerksam.

assign [ə'sain] an-, zuweisen; bestimmen; zuschreiben; **∼ation** [æsig'neiʃən] Verabredung *f*, Stelldichein *n*; = **∼ment** [ə'sainmənt] An-, Zuweisung *f*; bsd. Am. Auftrag *m*; ⚖ Übertragung *f*.

assimilat|e [ə'simileit] (sich) angleichen (*to*, *with dat.*); **∼ion** [əsimi'leiʃən] Assimilation *f*, Angleichung *f*.

assist [ə'sist] *j-m* beistehen, helfen; unterstützen; **∼ance** [∼təns] Beistand *m*; Hilfe *f*; **∼ant** [∼nt] **1.** behilflich; **2.** Assistent(in).

assize ⚖ [ə'saiz] (Schwur)Gerichtssitzung *f*; **∼s** *pl. periodisches* Geschworenengericht.

associa|te [ə'souʃieit] (sich) zugesellen (*with dat.*), (sich) vereinigen; Umgang haben (*with* mit); **2.** [∼ʃiit] verbunden; **3.** [∼] (Amts)Genosse *m*; Teilhaber *m*; **∼tion** [əsousi'eiʃən] Vereinigung *f*, Verbindung *f*; † *Handels- etc.* Gesellschaft *f*; Genossenschaft *f*; Verein *m*.

assort [ə'sɔ:t] *v/t.* sortieren, zs.-stellen; *v/i.* passen (*with* zu); **∼ment** [∼tmənt] Sortieren *n*; ✝ Sortiment *n*, Auswahl *f*.

assum|e [ə'sju:m] annehmen; vorgeben; übernehmen; **∼ption** [ə'sʌmpʃən] Annahme *f*; Übernahme *f*; *eccl.* ♀ (*Day*) Mariä Himmelfahrt *f*.

assur|ance [ə'ʃuərəns] Zu-, Versicherung *f*; Zuversicht *f*; Sicherheit *f*, Gewißheit *f*; Sicherheit *f*; Dreistigkeit *f*; **∼e** [ə'ʃuə] (*Leben etc.*)versichern; sicherstellen; **∼ed 1.** (*adv.* **∼edly** [∼əridli]) sicher; dreist; **2.** Versicherte(r *m*) *f*.

asthma ['æsmə] Asthma *n*.

astir [ə'stə:] auf (den Beinen) in Bewegung, rege.

astonish [əs'tɔniʃ] in Erstaunen setzen; verwundern; befremden; **be ∼ed** erstaunt sein (*at* über *acc.*); **∼ing** □ [∼ʃiŋ] erstaunlich; **∼ment** [∼ʃmənt] (Er)Staunen *n*; Verwunderung *f*.

astound [əs'taund] verblüffen.

astray [əs'trei] vom (rechten) Wege

ab (*a. fig.*); irre; **go ∼** sich verlaufen, fehlgehen.

astride [əs'traid] mit gespreizten Beinen; rittlings (*of* auf *dat.*).

astringent ⚕ [əs'trindʒənt] **1.** □ zs.-ziehend; **2.** zs.-ziehendes Mittel.

astro|logy [əs'trɔlədʒi] Astrologie *f*; **∼naut** ['æstrənɔ:t] Astronaut *m*, Raumfahrer *m*; **∼nomer** [əs'trɔnəmə] Astronom *m*; **∼nomy** [∼mi] Astronomie *f*.

astute □ [əs'tju:t] scharfsinnig; schlau; **∼ness** [∼tnis] Scharfsinn *m*.

asunder [ə'sʌndə] auseinander; entzwei.

asylum [ə'sailəm] Asyl *n*.

at [æt; *unbetont* ət] *prp.* an; auf; aus; bei; für; in; mit; nach; über; um; von; vor; zu; **∼ school** in der Schule; **∼ the age of** im Alter von.

ate [et] *pret. von* eat 1.

atheism ['eiθiizm] Atheismus *m*.

athlet|e ['æθli:t] (*bsd.* Leicht-)Athlet *m*; **∼ic(al** □) [æθ'letik(əl)] athletisch; **∼ics** *pl.* (*bsd.* Leicht-)Athletik *f*.

Atlantic [ət'læntik] **1.** atlantisch; **2.** *a.* **∼ Ocean** Atlantik *m*.

atmospher|e ['ætməsfiə] Atmosphäre *f* (*a. fig.*); **∼ic(al** □) [ætməs-'ferik(əl)] atmosphärisch.

atom ⚛ ['ætəm] Atom *n* (*a. fig.*); **∼ic** [ə'tɔmik] atomartig, Atom...; atomistisch; **∼ age** Atomzeitalter *n*; **∼** (*a. atom*) **bomb** Atombombe *f*; **∼ pile** Atomreaktor *m*; **∼-powered** durch Atomkraft betrieben; **∼ize** ['ætəmaiz] in Atome auflösen; atomisieren; **∼izer** [∼zə] Zerstäuber *m*.

atone [ə'toun]: **∼ for** büßen für *et.*; **∼ment** [∼mənt] Buße *f*; Sühne *f*.

atroci|ous □ [ə'trouʃəs] scheußlich, gräßlich; grausam; **∼ty** [ə'trɔsiti] Scheußlichkeit *f*, Gräßlichkeit *f*; Grausamkeit *f*.

attach [ə'tætʃ] *v/t.* (*to*) anheften (an, *acc.*), befestigen (an *dat.*); Wert, Wichtigkeit *etc.* beilegen (*dat.*); ⚖ *j-n* verhaften; *et.* beschlagnahmen; **∼ o.s. to** sich anschließen an (*acc.*); **∼ed:** **∼ to** gehörig zu; *j-m* zugetan, ergeben; **∼ment** [∼ʃmənt] Befestigung *f*; Bindung *f* (*to*, *for* an *acc.*); Anhänglichkeit *f* (an *acc.*), Neigung *f* (zu); Anhängsel *n* (*to gen.*); ⚖ Verhaftung *f*; Beschlagnahme *f*.

attack [ə'tæk] **1.** angreifen (*a. fig.*); befallen (*Krankheit*); *Arbeit* in Angriff nehmen; **2.** Angriff *m*; ✗ Anfall *m*; Inangriffnahme *f*.

attain [ə'tein] *v/t.* Ziel erreichen; *v/i.* **∼ to** gelangen zu, *-m* **∼ment** [∼nmənt] Erreichung *f*; *fig.* Aneignung *f*; **∼s** *pl.* Kenntnisse *f/pl.*; Fertigkeiten *f/pl.*

attempt [ə'tempt] **1.** versuchen; **2.** Versuch *m*; Attentat *n*.

attend [ə'tend] *v/t.* begleiten; be-

dienen; pflegen; ⚓ behandeln; *j-m*
aufwarten; beiwohnen (*dat.*); *Vor-*
lesung etc. besuchen; *v/i.* achten,
hören (*to auf acc.*); anwesend sein
(*at bei*); ~ to erledigen; **~ance**
[~dəns] Begleitung *f*; Aufwartung
f; Pflege *f*; ⚓ Behandlung *f*; Gefolge *n*; Anwesenheit *f* (*at bei*);
Besuch *m* (*der Schule etc.*); Be-
sucher(zahl *f*) *m/pl.*; Publikum *n*;
be in ~ zu Diensten stehen; **~ant**
[~nt] **1.** begleitend (*on, upon acc.*);
anwesend (*at bei*); **2.** Diener(in);
Begleiter(in); Wärter(in); Besu-
cher(in) (*at gen.*); ⊕ Bedienungs-
mann *m*; **~s** *pl.* Dienerschaft *f*.

attent|ion [ə'tenʃən] Aufmerksam-
keit *f* (*a. fig.*); ~! ✗ Achtung!;
~ive □ [~ntiv] aufmerksam.

attest [ə'test] bezeugen; beglaubigen; *bsd.* ✗ vereidigen.

attic ['ætik] Dachstube *f*. [dung *f*.\
attire [ə'taiə] **1.** kleiden; **2.** Klei-/
attitude ['ætitju:d] (Ein)Stellung *f*;
Haltung *f*; *fig.* Stellungnahme *f*.

attorney [ə'tə:ni] Bevollmächtig-
te(r) *m*; *Am.* Rechtsanwalt *m*;
power of ~ Vollmacht *f*; ♀ *General*
Generalstaats- *od.* Kronanwalt *m*,
Am. Justizminister *m*.

attract [ə'trækt] anziehen, *Auf-*
merksamkeit erregen; *fig.* reizen;
~ion [~kʃən] Anziehung(skraft) *f*;
fig. Reiz *m*; Zugartikel *m*; *thea.*
Zugstück *n*; **~ive** [~ktiv] anziehend;
reizvoll; zugkräftig; **~iveness**
[~vnis] Reiz *m*.

attribute 1. [ə'tribju:)t] beimessen,
zuschreiben; zurückführen (*to auf*
acc.); **2.** ['ætribju:t] Attribut *n*
(*a. gr.*), Eigenschaft *f*, Merkmal *n*.

attune [ə'tju:n] (ab)stimmen.

auburn ['ɔ:bən] kastanienbraun.

auction ['ɔ:kʃən] **1.** Auktion *f*; *sell*
by ~, *put up for* ~ versteigern;
2. *mst* ~ *off* versteigern; **~eer**
[ɔ:kʃə'niə] Auktionator *m*.

audaci|ous □ [ɔ:'deiʃəs] kühn; un-
verschämt; **~ty** [ɔ:'dæsiti] Kühnheit *f*; Unverschämtheit *f*.

audible □ ['ɔ:dəbl] hörbar; Hör...
audience ['ɔ:djəns] Publikum *n*,
Zuhörerschaft *f*; Leserkreis *m*;
Audienz *f*; Gehör *n*; *give* ~ *to* Gehör schenken (*dat.*).

audit ['ɔ:dit] **1.** Rechnungsprüfung
f; **2.** *Rechnung* prüfen; **~or** [~tə]
Hörer *m*; Rechnungs-, Buchprüfer
m; **~orium** [ɔ:di'tɔ:riəm] Hörsaal
m; *Am.* Vortrags-, Konzertsaal *m*.

auger ⊕ ['ɔ:gə] *großer* Bohrer.

aught [ɔ:t] (irgend) etwas; *for* ~ *I*
care meinetwegen; *for* ~ *I know*
soviel ich weiß.

augment [ɔ:g'ment] vergrößern;
~ation [~gmen'teiʃən] Vermeh-
rung *f*, Vergrößerung *f*; Zusatz *m*.

augur ['ɔ:gə] **1.** Augur *m*; **2.** weissagen, voraussagen (*well Gutes, ill*

Übles); **~y** ['ɔ:gjuri] Prophezeiung *f*; An-, Vorzeichen *n*; Vor-
ahnung *f*.

August¹ ['ɔ:gəst] *Monat* August *m*.
august² □ [ɔ:'gʌst] erhaben.

aunt [ɑ:nt] Tante *f*.

auspic|e ['ɔ:spis] Vorzeichen *n*; **~e**
pl. Auspizien *pl.*; Schirmherrschaft
f; **~ious** □ [ɔ:'spiʃəs] günstig.

auster|e □ [ɔ:'stiə] streng; herb;
hart; einfach; **~ity** [ɔs'teriti]
Strenge *f*; Härte *f*; Einfachheit *f*.

Australian [ɔs'treiljən] **1.** austra-
lisch; **2.** Australier(in).

Austrian ['ɔstriən] **1.** österreichisch;
2. Österreicher(in).

authentic [ɔ:'θentik] (**~ally**) authentisch; zuverlässig; echt.

author ['ɔ:θə] Urheber(in); Autor
(-in); Verfasser(in); **~itative** □
[ɔ:'θɔritətiv] maßgebend; gebieterisch; zuverlässig; **~ity** [ɔ:'θɔriti]
Autorität *f*; (Amts)Gewalt *f*, Vollmacht *f*; Einfluß *m* (*over auf acc.*);
Ansehen *n*; Glaubwürdigkeit *f*;
Quelle *f*; Fachmann *m*; Behörde *f*
(*mst pl.*); *on the* ~ *of auf j-s* Zeugnis
hin; **~ize** ['ɔ:θəraiz] *j-n* autorisieren,
bevollmächtigen; *et.* gutheißen;
~ship ['ɔ:θəʃip] Urheberschaft *f*.

autocar ['ɔ:touka:] Kraftwagen *m*.
autocra|cy [ɔ:'tɔkrəsi] Autokratie *f*;
~tic(al □) [ɔ:tə'krætik(əl)] auto-
kratisch, despotisch.

autogiro ✈ [ɔ:'tou'dʒaiərou] Autogiro *n*, Tragschrauber *m*.

autograph ['ɔ:təgrɑ:f] Autogramm
n. [Restaurant *n*.\
automat ['ɔ:təmæt] Automaten-/
automat|ic [ɔ:tə'mætik] (**~ally**)
1. automatisch; ~ *machine* (Verkaufs)Automat *m*; **2.** *Am.* Selbst-
ladepistole *f*, -gewehr *n*; **~ion**
[~'meiʃən] Automation *f*; **~on** *fig.*
[ɔ:'tɔmətən] Roboter *m*.

automobile *bsd. Am.* ['ɔ:təməbi:l]
Automobil *n*.

autonomy [ɔ:'tɔnəmi] Autonomie *f*.
autumn ['ɔ:təm] Herbst *m*; **~al** □
[ɔ:'tʌmnəl] herbstlich; Herbst...

auxiliary [ɔ:g'ziljəri] helfend;
Hilfs...

avail [ə'veil] **1.** nützen, helfen; ~
o.s. of sich *e-r S.* bedienen; **2.** Nutzen *m*; *of no* ~ nutzlos; **~able** □
[~əbl] benutzbar; verfügbar; *pred.*
erhältlich, vorhanden; gültig.

avalanche ['ævəlɑ:nʃ] Lawine *f*.

avaric|e ['ævəris] Geiz *m*; Habsucht
f; **~ious** □ [ævə'riʃəs] geizig; habgierig.

avenge [ə'vendʒ] rächen, *et.* ahn-
den; **~r** [~dʒə] Rächer(in).

avenue ['ævinju:] Allee *f*; Pracht-
straße *f*; *fig.* Weg *m*, Straße *f*.

aver [ə'və:] behaupten.

average ['ævəridʒ] **1.** Durchschnitt
m; ⚓ Havarie *f*; **2.** □ durchschnittlich; Durchschnitts...; **3.** durch-

schnittlich schätzen (*at* auf *acc.*); durchschnittlich betragen *od.* arbeiten *etc.*

avers|e □ [ə'və:s] abgeneigt (*to, from dat.*); widerwillig; **~ion** [ə'və:ʃən] Widerwille *m.*

avert [ə'və:t] abwenden (*a. fig.*).

aviat|ion ⚔ [eivi'eiʃən] Fliegen *n*; Flugwesen *n*; Luftfahrt *f*; **~or** ['eivieitə] Flieger *m.*

avid □ ['ævid] gierig (*of* nach; *for* auf *acc.*).

avoid [ə'vɔid] (ver)meiden; *j-m* ausweichen; ⅍ anfechten; ungültig machen; **~ance** [~dəns] Vermeidung *f.*

avouch [ə'vautʃ] verbürgen, bestätigen; = avow.

avow [ə'vau] bekennen, (ein)gestehen; anerkennen; **~al** [ə'vauəl] Bekenntnis *n*, (Ein)Geständnis *n*; **~edly** [ə'vauidli] eingestandenermaßen.

await [ə'weit] erwarten (*a. fig.*).

awake [ə'weik] **1.** wach, munter; be ~ to sich *e-r* *S.* bewußt sein; **2.** [*irr.*] *v/t.* (*mst* ~n [~kən]) (er-)wecken; *v/i.* erwachen; gewahr werden (*to s.th.* et.).

award [ə'wɔ:d] **1.** Urteil *n*, Spruch *m*; Belohnung *f*; Preis *m*; **2.** zuerkennen, *Orden etc.* verleihen.

aware [ə'wɛə]: be ~ wissen (*of* von *od. acc.*), sich bewußt sein (*of gen.*); become ~ of et. gewahr werden, merken.

away [ə'wei] (hin)weg; fort; immer weiter, darauflos; ~ back *Am.* F (schon) damals, weit zurück.

awe [ɔ:] **1.** Ehrfurcht *f*, Scheu *f* (*of* vor *dat.*); **2.** (Ehr)Furcht einflößen (*dat.*).

awful □ ['ɔ:ful] ehrfurchtgebietend; furchtbar; F *fig.* schrecklich.

awhile [ə'wail] e-e Weile.

awkward □ ['ɔ:kwəd] ungeschickt, unbeholfen; linkisch; unangenehm; dumm, ungünstig, unpraktisch.

awl [ɔ:l] Ahle *f*, Pfriem *m.*

awning ['ɔ:niŋ] Plane *f*; Markise *f.*

awoke [ə'wouk] *pret. u. p.p. von* awake 2.

awry [ə'rai] schief; *fig.* verkehrt.

ax(e) [æks] Axt *f*, Beil *n.*

axis ['æksis], *pl.* **axes** ['æksi:z] Achse *f.*

axle ⊕ ['æksl] *a.* **~-tree** (Rad-) Achse *f*, Welle *f.*

ay(e) [ai] Ja *n*; *parl.* Jastimme *f*; the ~s have it die Mehrheit ist dafür.

azure ['æʒə] azurn, azurblau.

B

babble ['bæbl] **1.** stammeln; (nach-) plappern; schwatzen; plätschern (*Bach*); **2.** Geplapper *n*; Geschwätz *n.*

baboon *zo.* [bə'bu:n] Pavian *m.*

baby ['beibi] **1.** Säugling *m*, kleines Kind, Baby *n*; *Am. sl.* Süße *f* (*Mädchen*); **2.** Baby...; Kinder...; klein; **~hood** [~ihud] *frühe* Kindheit.

bachelor ['bætʃələ] Junggeselle *m*; *univ.* Bakkalaureus *m* (*Grad*).

back [bæk] **1.** Rücken *m*; Rückseite *f*; Rücklehne *f*; Hinterende *n*; Fußball: Verteidiger *m*; **2.** *adj.* Hinter..., Rück...; hinter; rückwärtig; entlegen; rückläufig; rückständig; **3.** *adv.* zurück; **4.** *v/t.* mit e-m Rücken versehen; unterstützen; hinten anstoßen an (*acc.*); zurückbewegen; wetten *od.* setzen auf (*acc.*); ✝ indossieren; *v/i.* sich rückwärts bewegen, zurückgehen *od.* zurückfahren; ~ **alley** *Am.* finstere Seitengasse; **~bite** ['bækbait] (*irr.* (*bite*)] verleumden; **~bone** Rückgrat *n*; **~er** ['bækə] Unterstützer (-in); ✝ Indossierer *m*; Wetter(in); **~fire** *mot.* Frühzündung *f*; **~ground** Hintergrund *m*; ~ **number** alte Nummer (*e-r Zeitung*); **~**

pedal rückwärtstreten (*Radfahren*); **~ling** brake Rücktrittbremse *f*; **~side** Hinter-, Rückseite *f*; **~slapper** *Am.* [~slæpə] plump vertraulicher Mensch; **~slide** [*irr.* (*slide*)] rückfällig werden; **~stairs** Hintertreppe *f*; **~stop** *Am. Baseball:* Gitter *n hinter dem Fänger*; *Schießstand:* Kugelfang *m*; **~stroke** Rückenschwimmen *n*; **~talk** *Am.* freche Antworten; **~track** *Am.* F *fig.* e-n Rückzieher machen; **~ward** ['bækwəd] **1.** *adj.* Rück(wärts)...; langsam; zurückgeblieben, rückständig; zurückhaltend; **2.** *adv.* (*a.* **~wards** [~dz]) rückwärts, zurück; **~water** Stauwasser *n*; **~woods** *pl.* weit abgelegene Waldgebiete; *fig.* Provinz *f*; **~woodsman** Hinterwäldler *m.*

bacon ['beikən] Speck *m.*

bacteri|ologist [bæktiəri'ɔlədʒist] Bakteriologe *m*; **~um** [bæk'tiəriəm], *pl.* **~a** [~iə] Bakterie *f.*

bad □ [bæd] schlecht, böse, schlimm; falsch (*Münze*); faul (*Schuld*); he is ~ly off er ist übel dran; ~ly wounded schwerverwundet; want ~ly F dringend brauchen; be in ~ with *Am.* F in Ungnade bei.

bade [beid] *pret. von* bid 1.

badge [bædʒ] Ab-, Kennzeichen n.

badger ['bædʒə] **1.** zo. Dachs m; **2.** hetzen, plagen, quälen.

badlands Am. ['bædlændz] pl. Ödland n.

badness ['bædnis] schlechte Beschaffenheit; Schlechtigkeit f.

baffle ['bæfl] j-n verwirren; Plan etc. vereiteln, durchkreuzen.

bag [bæg] **1.** Beutel m, Sack m; Tüte f; Tasche f; ~ and baggage mit Sack und Pack; **2.** in e-n Beutel etc. tun, einsacken; hunt. zur Strecke bringen; (sich) bauschen.

baggage Am. ['bægidʒ] (Reise-) Gepäck n; ~ car Am. ⚏ Gepäckwagen m; ~ check Am. Gepäckschein m.

bagpipe ['bægpaip] Dudelsack m.

bail [beil] **1.** Bürge m; Bürgschaft f; Kaution f; admit to ~ ᵗᵗ gegen Bürgschaft freilassen; **2.** bürgen für; ~ out j-n freibürgen; ⚔ mit dem Fallschirm abspringen.

bailiff ['beilif] Gerichtsdiener m; (Guts)Verwalter m; Amtmann m.

bait [beit] **1.** Köder m; fig. Lockung f; **2.** v/t. Falle etc. beködern; hunt. hetzen; fig. quälen; reizen; v/i. rasten; einkehren.

bak|e [beik] **1.** backen; braten; Ziegel brennen; (aus)dörren; **2.** Am. gesellige Zusammenkunft; **~er** ['beikə] Bäcker m; **~ery** [~əri] Bäckerei f; **~ing-powder** [~kiŋpaudə] Backpulver n.

balance ['bæləns] **1.** Waage f; Gleichgewicht n (a. fig.); Harmonie f; ✝ Bilanz f, Saldo m, Überschuß m; Restbetrag m; F Rest m; a. ~ wheel Unruh(e) f der Uhr; ~ of power pol. Kräftegleichgewicht n; ~ of trade (Außen-) Handelsbilanz f; **2.** v/t. (ab-, er)wägen; im Gleichgewicht halten; ausgleichen; ✝ bilanzieren; saldieren; v/i. balancieren; sich ausgleichen.

balcony ['bælkəni] Balkon m.

bald [bɔːld] kahl; fig. nackt; dürftig.

bale ✝ [beil] Ballen m.

baleful [] ['beilful] verderblich; unheilvoll.

balk [bɔːk] **1.** (Furchen)Rain m; Balken m; Hemmnis n; **2.** v/t. (ver-) hindern; enttäuschen; vereiteln; v/i. stutzen, scheuen.

ball¹ [bɔːl] **1.** Ball m; Kugel f; (Hand-, Fuß)Ballen m; Knäuel m, n; Kloß m; Sport: Wurf m; keep the ~ rolling das Gespräch in Gang halten; play ~ Am. F mitmachen; **2.** (sich) (zs.-)ballen.

ball² [bɔːl] Ball m, Tanzgesellschaft f.

ballad ['bæləd] Ballade f; Lied n.

ballast ['bæləst] **1.** Ballast m; ⚏ Schotter m, Bettung f; **2.** mit Ballast beladen; ⚏ beschottern, betten.

ball-bearing(s pl.) ⊕ ['bɔːl'beəriŋ(z)] Kugellager n.

ballet ['bælei] Ballett n.

balloon [bə'luːn] **1.** Ballon m; **2.** im Ballon aufsteigen; sich blähen; **~ist** [~nist] Ballonfahrer m.

ballot ['bælət] **1.** Wahlzettel m; (geheime) Wahl; **2.** (geheim) abstimmen; ~ for losen um; **~-box** Wahlurne f.

ball(-point) pen ['bɔːl(point)pen] Kugelschreiber m.

ball-room ['bɔːlrum] Ballsaal m.

balm [bɑːm] Balsam m; fig. Trost m.

balmy [] ['bɑːmi] balsamisch (a. fig.).

baloney Am. sl. [bə'louni] Quatsch m.

balsam ['bɔːlsəm] Balsam m.

balustrade [bæləs'treid] Balustrade f, Brüstung f; Geländer n.

bamboo [bæm'buː] Bambus m.

bamboozle F [bæm'buːzl] beschwindeln.

ban [bæn] **1.** Bann m; Acht f; (amtliches) Verbot; **2.** verbieten.

banal [bə'nɑːl] banal, abgedroschen.

banana [bə'nɑːnə] Banane f.

band [bænd] **1.** Band n; Streifen m; Schar f; ♪ Kapelle f; **2.** zs.-binden; ~ o.s. sich zs.-tun od. zs.-rotten.

bandage ['bændidʒ] **1.** Binde f; Verband m; **2.** bandagieren; verbinden.

bandbox ['bændbɔks] Hutschachtel f.

bandit ['bændit] Bandit m.

band|-master ['bændmɑːstə] Kapellmeister m; **~stand** Musikpavillon m; **~ wagon** Am. Wagen m mit Musikkapelle; jump on the ~ sich der erfolgversprechenden Sache anschließen.

bandy ['bændi] Worte etc. wechseln; **~-legged** säbelbeinig.

bane [bein] Ruin m; **~ful** [] ['beinful] verderblich.

bang [bæŋ] **1.** Knall m; Ponyfrisur f; **2.** dröhnend (zu)schlagen; **~-up** Am. sl. ['bæŋ'ʌp] Klasse, prima.

banish ['bæniʃ] verbannen; **~ment** [~ʃmənt] Verbannung f.

banisters ['bænistəz] pl. Treppengeländer n.

bank [bæŋk] **1.** Damm m; Ufer n; (Spiel-, Sand-, Wolken- etc.)Bank f; ~ of issue Notenbank f; **2.** v/t. eindämmen; ✝ Geld auf die Bank legen; ⚔ in die Kurve bringen; v/i. Bankgeschäfte machen; ein Bankkonto haben; ⚔ in die Kurve gehen; ~ on sich verlassen auf (acc.); **~-bill** ['bæŋkbil] Bankwechsel m; Am. s. banknote; **~er** [~kə] Bankier m; **~ing** [~kiŋ] Bankgeschäft n; Bankwesen n; attr. Bank...; **~-note** Banknote f; Kassenschein m; **~-**

rate Diskontsatz m; ~rupt [~krəpt]
1. Bankrotteur m; 2. bankrott;
3. bankrott machen; ~ruptcy
[~tsi] Bankrott m, Konkurs m.
banner ['bænə] Banner n; Fahne f.
banns [bænz] pl. Aufgebot n.
banquet ['bæŋkwit] 1. Festmahl n;
2. v/t. festlich bewirten; v/i. tafeln.
banter ['bæntə] necken, hänseln.
baptism ['bæptizəm] Taufe f.
baptist ['bæptist] Täufer m.
baptize [bæp'taiz] taufen.
bar [ba:] 1. Stange f; Stab m;
Barren m; Riegel m; Schranke f;
Sandbank f; fig. Hindernis n; ⚔
Spange f; ♪ Takt(strich) m; (Gerichts)Schranke f; fig. Urteil n;
Anwaltschaft f; Bar f im Hotel etc.;
2. verriegeln; (ver-, ab)sperren;
verwehren; einsperren; (ver)hin-
dern; ausschließen.
barb [ba:b] Widerhaken m; ~ed
wire Stacheldraht m.
barbar|ian [ba:'bɛəriən] 1. bar-
barisch; 2. Barbar(in); ~ous □
['ba:bərəs] barbarisch; roh; grausam.
barbecue ['ba:bikju:] 1. großer
Bratrost; Am. Essen n (im Freien),
bei dem Tiere ganz gebraten
werden; 2. im ganzen braten.
barber ['ba:bə] (Herren)Friseur m.
bare [bɛə] 1. nackt, bloß; kahl; bar,
leer; arm, entblößt; 2. entblößen;
~faced □ ['bɛəfeist] frech; ~foot,
~footed barfuß; ~headed bar-
häuptig; ~ly ['bɛəli] kaum.
bargain ['ba:gin] 1. Geschäft n;
Handel m, Kauf m; vorteilhafter
Kauf; a (dead) ~ spottbillig; it's a ~!
F abgemacht!; into the ~ obendrein;
2. handeln, übereinkommen.
barge [ba:dʒ] Flußboot n, Lastkahn
m; Hausboot n; ~man ['ba:dʒmən]
Kahnführer m.
bark¹ [ba:k] 1. Borke f, Rinde f;
2. abrinden; Haut abschürfen.
bark² [~] 1. bellen; 2. Bellen n.
bar-keeper ['ba:ki:pə] Barbesitzer
m; Barkellner m.
barley ['ba:li] Gerste f; Graupe f.
barn [ba:n] Scheune f; bsd. Am.
(Vieh)Stall m; ~storm Am. pol.
['ba:nstɔ:m] herumreisen u. (Wahl-)
Reden halten.
barometer [bə'rɔmitə] Barometer n.
baron ['bærən] Baron m, Freiherr
m; ~ess [~nis] Baronin f.
barrack(s pl.) ['bærək(s)] (Miets-)
Kaserne f.
barrage ['bæra:ʒ] Staudamm m.
barrel ['bærəl] 1. Faß n, Tonne f;
Gewehr- etc. Lauf m; ⊕ Trommel
f; Walze f; 2. in Fässer füllen;
~organ ♪ Drehorgel f.
barren □ ['bærən] unfruchtbar;
dürr, trocken; tot (Kapital).
barricade [bæri'keid] 1. Barrikade
f; 2. verbarrikadieren; sperren.

barrier ['bæriə] Schranke f (a. fig.);
Barriere f, Sperre f; Hindernis
n.
barrister ['bæristə] (plädierender)
Rechtsanwalt, Barrister m.
barrow¹ ['bærou] Trage f; Karre f.
barrow² [~] Hügelgrab n, Tumulus
m.
barter ['ba:tə] 1. Tausch(handel)
m; 2. tauschen (for gegen); F
schachern.
base¹ □ [beis] gemein; unecht.
base² [~] 1. Basis f; Grundlage f;
Fundament n; Fuß m; ⚑ Base f;
Stützpunkt m; 2. gründen, stützen.
base|ball ['beisbɔ:l] Baseball m;
~born von niedriger Abkunft;
unehelich; ~less ['beislis] grundlos;
~ment ['beismənt] Fundament n;
Kellergeschoß n.
baseness ['beisnis] Gemeinheit f.
bashful □ ['bæʃful] schüchtern.
basic ['beisik] (~ally) grundlegend;
Grund...; ⚑ basisch.
basin ['beisn] Becken n; Schüssel f;
Tal-, Wasser-, Hafenbecken n.
bas|is ['beisis], pl. ~es ['beisi:z]
Basis f; Grundlage f; ⚔, ⚓ Stützpunkt m.
bask [ba:sk] sich sonnen (a. fig.).
basket ['ba:skit] Korb m; ~ball
Korbballspiel n) m; ~ dinner, ~
supper Am. Picknick n.
bass ♪ [beis] Baß m.
basso ♪ ['bæsou] Baß(sänger) m.
bastard ['bæstəd] 1. □ unehelich;
unecht; Bastard...; 2. Bastard m.
baste¹ [beist] Braten begießen;
durchprügeln.
baste² [~] lose nähen, (an)heften.
bat¹ [bæt] Fledermaus f; as blind
as a ~ stockblind.
bat² [~] Sport: 1. Schlagholz n;
Schläger m; 2. den Ball schlagen.
batch [bætʃ] Schub m Brote (a. fig.);
Stoß m Briefe etc. (a. fig.).
bate [beit] verringern; verhalten.
bath [ba:θ] 1. Bad n; ⚲ chair Rollstuhl m; 2. baden.
bathe [beið] baden.
bathing ['beiðiŋ] Baden n, Bad n;
attr. Bade...; ~suit Badeanzug m.
bath|robe Am. ['ba:θroub] Bade-
mantel m; ~room Badezimmer n;
~sheet Badelaken n; ~towel
Badetuch n; ~tub Badewanne f.
batiste ✝ [bæ'ti:st] Batist m.
baton ['bætən] Stab m; Taktstock
m.
battalion ⚔ [bə'tæljən] Bataillon n.
batten ['bætn] 1. Latte f; 2. sich
mästen.
batter ['bætə] 1. Sport: Schläger m;
Rührteig m; 2. heftig schlagen;
verbeulen; ~ down od. in Tür einschlagen; ~y ['bætri] Schlägerei f;
Batterie f; ⚡ Akku m; fig. Satz m;
assault and ~ ⚖ tätlicher Angriff.
battle ['bætl] 1. Schlacht f (of bei);

2. streiten, kämpfen; ~**ax(e)**
Streitaxt *f*; F Xanthippe *f*; ~**field**
Schlachtfeld *n*; ~**ments** [\lments]
pl. Zinnen *f*/*pl.*; ~**plane** ✕ Kriegs-
flugzeug *n*; ~**ship** ✕ Schlacht-
schiff *n*.

Bavarian [bə'vɛəriən] **1.** bay(e)-
risch; **2.** Bayer(in).

bawdy ['bɔ:di] unzüchtig.

bawl [bɔ:l] brüllen; johlen, grölen;
~ out auf-, losbrüllen.

bay¹ [bei] **1.** rotbraun; **2.** Braune(r)
m (*Pferd*).

bay² [\] Bai *f*, Bucht *f*; Erker *m*.

bay³ [\] Lorbeer *m*.

bay⁴ [\] **1.** bellen, anschlagen;
2. stand at ~ sich verzweifelt
wehren; *bring to* ~ *Wild etc.* stellen.

bayonet ✕ ['beiənit] **1.** Bajonett *n*;
2. mit dem Bajonett niederstoßen.

bayou *Am.* ['baiu:] sumpfiger
Nebenarm.

bay window ['bei'windou] Erker-
fenster *n*; *Am. sl.* Vorbau *m*
(*Bauch*).

baza(a)r [bə'zɑ:] Basar *m*.

be [bi:, bi] [*irr.*] **1.** *v/i.* sein; *there
is od.* are es gibt; *here you are again!*
da haben wir's wieder!; ~ *about* beschäftigt sein mit; ~ *at s.th.* et.
vorhaben; ~ *off* aus sein; sich fortmachen; **2.** *v/aux.*: ~ *reading* beim
Lesen sein, gerade lesen; *I am to
inform you* ich soll Ihnen mitteilen;
3. *v/aux.* mit *p.p.* zur Bildung des
Passivs: werden.

beach [bi:tʃ] **1.** Strand *m*; **2.** ⚓ auf
den Strand setzen *od.* ziehen;
~**comber** ['bi:tʃkoumə] *fig.* Nichtstuer *m*.

beacon ['bi:kən] Blinklicht *n*;
Leuchtfeuer *n*, Leuchtturm *m*.

bead [bi:d] Perle *f*; Tropfen *m*;
Visier-Korn *n*; ~s *pl. a.* Rosenkranz *m*.

beak [bi:k] Schnabel *m*; Tülle *f*.

beaker ['bi:kə] Becher(glas *n*) *m*.

beam [bi:m] **1.** Balken *m*; Waage-
balken *m*; Strahl *m*; Glanz *m*;
Radio: Richtstrahl *m*; **2.** (aus-)
strahlen.

bean [bi:n] Bohne *f*; *Am. sl.* Birne *f*
(*Kopf*); *full of* ~s F lebensprühend.

bear¹ [bɛə] Bär *m*; ✝ *sl.* Baissier *m*.

bear² [\] [*irr.*] *v/t.* tragen; hervorbringen, gebären; *Liebe etc.* hegen;
ertragen; ~ *down* überwältigen; ~
out unterstützen, bestätigen; *v/i.*
tragen; fruchtbar *od.* trächtig sein;
leiden, dulden; ~ up standhalten,
fest bleiben; ~ (up)on einwirken auf
(*acc.*); *bring to* ~ zur Anwendung
bringen, einwirken lassen, *Druck
etc.* ausüben.

beard [biəd] **1.** Bart *m*; ♀ Granne *f*;
2. *v/t. j-m* entgegentreten, trotzen.

bearer ['bɛərə] Träger(in); Über-
bringer(in), *Wechsel*-Inhaber(in).

bearing ['bɛəriŋ] (Er)Tragen *n*;

Betragen *n*; Beziehung *f*; Richtung *f*.

beast [bi:st] Vieh *n*, Tier *n*; Bestie
f; ~**ly** ['bi:stli] viehisch; scheußlich.

beat [bi:t] **1.** [*irr.*] *v/t.* schlagen;
prügeln; besiegen, *Am.* F *j-m* zuvorkommen; übertreffen; *Am.* ʃ
betrügen; ~ *it!* *Am. sl.* hau ab!;
~ *the band Am.* F wichtig *od.*
großartig sein; ~ *a retreat* den
Rückzug antreten; ~ *one's way Am.*
F sich durchschlagen; ~ *up* auf-
treiben; *v/i.* schlagen; ~ *about the
bush* wie die Katze um den heißen
Brei herumgehen; **2.** Schlag *m*;
♪ Takt(schlag) *m*; Pulsschlag *m*;
Runde *f*, Revier *n e-s Schutz-
mannes etc.*; *Am.* sensationelle
Erstmeldung *e-r Zeitung*; **3.** F baff,
verblüfft; ~**en** ['bi:tn] *p.p. von
beat* 1; (aus)getreten (*Weg*).

beatitude [bi(:)'ætitju:d] (Glück-)
Seligkeit *f*.

beatnik ['bi:tnik] Beatnik *m*, junger
Antikonformist und Bohemien.

beau [bou] Stutzer *m*; Anbeter *m*.

beautiful □ ['bju:təful] schön.

beautify ['bju:tifai] verschönern.

beauty ['bju:ti] Schönheit *f*; *Sleeping* ♀ Dornrös-chen *n*; ~ *parlo(u)r*,
~ *shop* Schönheitssalon *m*.

beaver ['bi:və] Biber *m*; Biberpelz *m*.

becalm [bi'kɑ:m] beruhigen.

became [bi'keim] *pret. von become.*

because [bi'kɔz] weil; ~ *of* wegen.

beckon ['bekən] (*j-m* zu)winken.

becom|e [bi'kʌm] [*irr.*] *v/i.* werden
(of aus); *v/t.* anstehen, ziemen
(*dat.*); sich schicken für; kleiden
(*Hut etc.*); ~**ing** □ [~miŋ] passend;
schicklich; kleidsam.

bed [bed] **1.** Bett *n*; Lager *n e-s
Tieres*; ♪ Beet *n*; Unterlage *f*;
2. betten.

bed-clothes ['bedklouðz] *pl.* Bett-
wäsche *f*.

bedding ['bediŋ] Bettzeug *n*; Streu *f.*

bedevil [bi'devl] behexen; quälen.

bedlam ['bedləm] Tollhaus *n*.

bed|rid(den) ['bedrid(n)] bett-
lägerig; ~**room** Schlafzimmer *n*;
~**spread** Bett-, Tagesdecke *f*;
~**stead** Bettstelle *f*; ~**time** Schla-
fenszeit *f*.

bee [bi:] *zo.* Biene *f*; *Am.* nachbar-
liches Treffen; Wettbewerb *m*;
have a ~ *in one's bonnet* F e-e fixe
Idee haben.

beech ♀ [bi:tʃ] Buche *f*; ~**nut** Buch-
ecker *f*.

beef [bi:f] **1.** Rindfleisch *n*; **2.** *Am.*
F nörgeln; ~ *tea* Fleischbrühe *f*;
~**y** ['bi:fi] fleischig; kräftig.

bee|hive ['bi:haiv] Bienenkorb *m*,
-stock *m*; ~**keeper** Bienenzüchter
m; ~**line** kürzester Weg; *make a
* ~ *for Am.* schnurstracks losgehen
auf (*acc.*).

been [bi:n, bin] *p.p. von* be.

beer [biə] Bier *n*; *small* ~ Dünnbier *n*. [Bete *f*.]

beet ⚥ [bi:t] (Runkel)Rübe *f*,⟩

beetle[1] ['bi:tl] Käfer *m*.

beetle[2] [~] 1. überhängend; buschig (*Brauen*); 2. *v/i.* überhängen.

beetroot ['bi:tru:t] rote Rübe.

befall [bi'fɔ:l] [*irr.* (*fall*)] *v/t.* zustoßen (*dat.*); *v/i.* sich ereignen.

befit [bi'fit] sich schicken für.

before [bi'fɔ:] 1. *adv. Raum*: vorn; voran; *Zeit*: vorher, früher; schon (früher); 2. *cj.* bevor, ehe, bis; 3. *prp.* vor; ~hand vorher, zuvor; voraus (*with dat.*).

befriend [bi'frend] sich *j-m* freundlich erweisen.

beg [beg] *v/t. et.* erbetteln; erbitten (*of von*); *j-n* bitten; ~ *the question* um den Kern der Frage herumgehen; *v/i.* betteln; bitten; betteln gehen; sich gestatten.

began [bi'gæn] *pret. von* begin.

beget [bi'get] [*irr.* (*get*)] (er)zeugen.

beggar ['begə] 1. Bettler(in); F Kerl *m*; 2. zum Bettler machen; *fig.* übertreffen; *it* ~*s all description* es spottet jeder Beschreibung.

begin [bi'gin] [*irr.*] beginnen (*at* bei, mit); ~**ner** [~nə] Anfänger(in); ~**ning** [~niŋ] Beginn *m*, Anfang *m*.

begone [bi'gɔn] fort!, F pack dich!

begot [bi'gɔt] *pret. von* beget; ~**ten** [~tn] 1. *p.p. von* beget; 2. *adj.* erzeugt.

begrudge [bi'grʌdʒ] mißgönnen.

beguile [bi'gail] täuschen; betrügen (*of, out of* um); *Zeit* vertreiben.

begun [bi'gʌn] *p.p. von* begin.

behalf [bi'hɑ:f]: *on* ~. *in* ~ *of* im Namen von; um ... (*gen.*) willen.

behav|**e** [bi'heiv] sich benehmen; ~**io(u)r** [~vjə] Benehmen *n*, Betragen *n*.

behead [bi'hed] enthaupten.

behind [bi'haind] 1. *adv.* hinten; dahinter; zurück; 2. *prp.* hinter; ~**hand** zurück, im Rückstand.

behold [bi'hould] [*irr.* (*hold*)] 1. erblicken; 2. siehe (da)!; ~**en** [~dən] verpflichtet, verbunden.

behoof [bi'hu:f]: *to* (*for, on*) *the* ~ *of* in *j-s* Interesse, um *j-s* willen.

behoove *Am.* [bi'hu:v] = behove.

behove [bi'houv]: *it* ~*s s.o. to inf.* es ist *j-s* Pflicht, zu *inf.*

being ['bi:iŋ] (Da)Sein *n*; Wesen *n*; *in* ~ lebend; wirklich (vorhanden).

belabo(u)r F [bi'leibə] verbleuen.

belated [bi'leitid] verspätet.

belch [beltʃ] 1. rülpsen; ausspeien; 2. Rülpsen *n*; Ausbruch *m*.

beleaguer [bi'li:gə] belagern.

belfry ['belfri] Glockenturm *m*, -stuhl *m*. [2. Belgier(in).⟩

Belgian ['beldʒən] 1. belgisch;⟩

belie [bi'lai] Lügen strafen.

belief [bi'li:f] Glaube *m* (*in an acc.*).

believable [bi'li:vəbl] glaubhaft.

believe [bi'li:v] glauben (*in an acc.*); ~**r** [~və] Gläubige(r *m*) *f*.

belittle *fig.* [bi'litl] verkleinern.

bell [bel] Glocke *f*; Klingel *f*; ~**boy** *Am.* ['belbɔi] Hotelpage *m*.

belle [bel] Schöne *f*, Schönheit *f*.

belles-lettres ['bel'letr] *pl.* Belletristik *f*, schöne Literatur.

bellhop *Am. sl.* ['belhɔp] Hotelpage *m*.

bellied ['belid] bauchig.

belligerent [bi'lidʒərənt] 1. kriegführend; 2. kriegführendes Land.

bellow ['belou] 1. brüllen; 2. Gebrüll *n*; ~*s pl.* Blasebalg *m*.

belly ['beli] 1. Bauch *m*; 2. (sich) bauchen; (an)schwellen.

belong [bi'lɔŋ] (an)gehören; ~ *to* gehören *dat. od.* zu; sich gehören für; *j-m* gebühren; ~**ings** [~ŋiŋz] *pl.* Habseligkeiten *f/pl.*

beloved [bi'lʌvd] 1. geliebt; 2. Geliebte(r *m*) *f*.

below [bi'lou] 1. *adv.* unten; 2. *prp.* unter.

belt [belt] 1. Gürtel *m*; ✕ Koppel *n*; Zone *f*; Bezirk *m*; ⊕ Treibriemen *m*; 2. umgürten; ~ *out Am.* F herausschmettern, loslegen (*singen*).

bemoan [bi'moun] betrauern, beklagen.

bench [bentʃ] Bank *f*; Richterbank *f*; Gerichtshof *m*; Arbeitstisch *m*.

bend [bend] 1. Biegung *f*, Kurve *f*; ⚓ Seemannsknoten *m*; 2. [*irr.*] (sich) biegen; *Geist etc.* richten (*to, on auf acc.*); (sich) beugen; sich neigen (*to vor dat.*).

beneath [bi'ni:θ] = below.

benediction [beni'dikʃən] Segen *m*.

benefact|**ion** [beni'fækʃən] Wohltat *f*; ~**or** ['benifæktə] Wohltäter *m*.

beneficen|**ce** [bi'nefisəns] Wohltätigkeit *f*; ~**t** □ [~nt] wohltätig.

beneficial □ [beni'fiʃəl] wohltuend; zuträglich; nützlich.

benefit ['benifit] 1. Wohltat *f*; Nutzen *m*, Vorteil *m*; Wohltätigkeitsveranstaltung *f*; (Wohlfahrts-) Unterstützung *f*; 2. nützen; begünstigen; Nutzen ziehen.

benevolen|**ce** [bi'nevələns] Wohlwollen *n*; ~**t** □ [~nt] wohlwollend; gütig, mildherzig.

benign □ [bi'nain] freundlich, gütig; zuträglich; ✝ gutartig.

bent [bent] 1. *pret. u. p.p. von* bend 2; ~ *on* versessen auf (*acc.*); 2. Hang *m*; Neigung *f*.

benzene 🜍 ['benzi:n] Benzol *n*.

benzine 🜍 ['benzi:n] Benzin *n*.

bequeath [bi'kwi:ð] vermachen.

bequest [bi'kwest] Vermächtnis *n*.

bereave [bi'ri:v] [*irr.*] berauben.

bereft [bi'reft] *pret. u. p.p. von* bereave.

beret ['berei] Baskenmütze *f*.

berry — 347 — **billy**

berry ['beri] Beere *f.*
berth [bə:θ] **1.** ⚓ Ankergrund *m*; Koje *f*; *fig.* (gute) Stelle; **2.** vor Anker gehen.
beseech [bi'si:tʃ] [*irr.*] ersuchen; bitten; um *et.* bitten; flehen.
beset [bi'set] [*irr.* (set)] umgeben; bedrängen; verfolgen.
beside *prp.* [bi'said] neben; weitab von; ~ o.s. außer sich (*with* vor); ~ the point, ~ the question nicht zur Sache gehörig; ~s [~dz] **1.** *adv.* außerdem; **2.** *prp.* abgesehen von, außer.
besiege [bi'si:dʒ] belagern.
besmear [bi'smiə] beschmieren.
besom ['bi:zəm] (Reisig)Besen *m.*
besought [bi'sɔ:t] *pret. u. p.p. von* beseech.
bespatter [bi'spætə] (be)spritzen.
bespeak [bi'spi:k] [*irr.* (speak)] vorbestellen; verraten; (an)zeigen; *bespoke tailor* Maßschneider *m.*
best [best] **1.** *adj.* best; höchst; größt, meist; ~ man Brautführer *m*; **2.** *adv.* am besten, aufs beste; **3.** Beste(r *m*, -s *n*) *f*, Besten *pl.*; to the ~ of ... nach bestem ...; make the ~ of tun, was man kann, mit; at ~ im besten Falle.
bestial □ ['bestjəl] tierisch, viehisch.
bestow [bi'stou] geben, schenken, verleihen (on, upon *dat.*).
bet [bet] **1.** Wette *f*; **2.** [*irr.*] wetten; you ~ F sicherlich.
betake [bi'teik] [*irr.* (take)]: ~ o.s. to sich begeben nach; fig. s-e Zuflucht nehmen zu.
bethink [bi'θiŋk] [*irr.* (think)]: ~ o.s. sich besinnen (of auf *acc.*); ~ o.s. to inf. sich in den Kopf setzen zu *inf.*
betimes [bi'taimz] beizeiten.
betray [bi'trei] verraten (*a. fig.*); verleiten; ~er [~eiə] Verräter(in).
betrothal [bi'trouðəl] Verlobung *f.*
better ['betə] **1.** *adj.* besser; he is ~ es geht ihm besser; **2.** Bessere(s) *n*; ~s *pl.* Höherstehenden *pl.*, Vorgesetzten *pl.*; get the ~ of die Oberhand gewinnen über (*acc.*); überwinden; **3.** *adv.* besser; mehr; so much the ~ desto besser; you had ~ go es wäre besser, wenn du gingest; **4.** *v/t.* (ver)bessern; *v/i.* sich bessern; ~ment [~əmənt] Verbesserung *f.*
between [bi'twi:n] (*a.* betwixt [bi'twikst]) **1.** *adv.* dazwischen; **2.** *prp.* zwischen, unter.
bevel ['bevəl] schräg, schief.
beverage ['bevəridʒ] Getränk *n.*
bevy ['bevi] Schwarm *m*; Schar *f.*
bewail [bi'weil] be-, wehklagen.
beware [bi'weə] sich hüten (of vor).
bewilder [bi'wildə] irremachen; verwirren; bestürzt machen; ~ment [~əmənt] Verwirrung *f*; Bestürzung *f.*

bewitch [bi'witʃ] bezaubern, behexen.
beyond [bi'jɔnd] **1.** *adv.* darüber hinaus; **2.** *prp.* jenseits, über (... hinaus); mehr als; außer.
bi... [bai] zwei ...
bias ['baiəs] **1.** *adj. u. adv.* schief, schräg; **2.** Neigung *f*; Vorurteil *n*; **3.** beeinflussen; ~sed befangen.
bib [bib] (Sabber)Lätzchen *n.*
Bible ['baibl] Bibel *f.*
biblical □ ['biblikəl] biblisch; Bibel...
bibliography [bibli'ɔgrəfi] Bibliographie *f.*
bicarbonate ⚗ [bai'kɑ:bənit] doppeltkohlensaures Natron.
biceps ['baiseps] Bizeps *m.*
bicker ['bikə] (sich) zanken; flakkern; plätschern; prasseln.
bicycle ['baisikl] **1.** Fahrrad *n*; **2.** radfahren, radeln.
bid [bid] **1.** [*irr.*] gebieten, befehlen; (ent)bieten; *Karten:* reizen; ~ fair versprechen; ~ farewell Lebewohl sagen; **2.** Gebot *n*, Angebot *n*; ~den ['bidn] *p.p. von* bid 1.
bide [baid] [*irr.*]: ~ one's time den rechten Augenblick abwarten.
biennial [bai'eniəl] zweijährig.
bier [biə] (Toten)Bahre *f.*
big [big] groß; erwachsen; schwanger; F wichtig(tuerisch); ~ business Großunternehmertum *n*; ~ shot F hohes Tier; ~ stick Am. Macht (-entfaltung) *f*; talk ~ den Mund vollnehmen.
bigamy ['bigəmi] Doppelehe *f.*
bigot ['bigət] Frömmler(in); blinder Anhänger; ~ry [~tri] Frömmelei *f.*
bigwig F ['bigwig] hohes Tier (*P.*).
bike F [baik] (Fahr)Rad *n.*
bilateral □ [bai'lætərəl] zweiseitig.
bile [bail] Galle *f* (*a. fig.*).
bilious □ ['biljəs] gallig (*a. fig.*).
bill[1] [bil] Schnabel *m*; Spitze *f.*
bill[2] [~] **1.** Gesetzentwurf *m*; Klage-, Rechtsschrift *f*; *a.* ~ of exchange Wechsel *m*; Zettel *m*; *Am.* Banknote *f*; ~ of fare Speisekarte *f*; ~ of lading Seefrachtbrief *m*, Konnossement *n*; ~ of sale Kaufvertrag *m*; ♀ of Rights englische Freiheitsurkunde (*1689*); *Am.* die ersten 10 Zusatzartikel zur Verfassung der USA; **2.** (durch Anschlag) ankündigen.
billboard *Am.* ['bil'bɔ:d] Anschlagbrett *n.*
billfold *Am.* ['bilfould] Brieftasche *f* für Papiergeld.
billiards ['biljədz] *pl. od. sg.* Billiard(spiel) *n.*
billion ['biljən] Billion *f*; *Am.* Milliarde *f.*
billow ['bilou] **1.** Woge *f* (*a. fig.*); **2.** wogen; ~y [~oui] wogend.
billy *Am.* ['bili] (Gummi)Knüppel *m.*

bin [bin] Kasten m, Behälter m.
bind [baind] [irr.] v/t. (an-, ein-, um-, auf-, fest-, ver)binden; verpflichten; Handel abschließen; Saum einfassen; v/i. binden; ~er ['baində] Binder m; Binde f; ~ing [~diŋ] 1. bindend; 2. Binden n; Einband m; Einfassung f.
binocular [bi'nɔkjulə] mst ~s pl. Feldstecher m, Fern-, Opernglas n.
biography [bai'ɔgrəfi] Biographie f.
biology [bai'ɔlədʒi] Biologie f.
biped zo. ['baiped] Zweifüßer m.
birch [bə:tʃ] 1. ♀ Birke f; (Birken-) Rute f; 2. mit der Rute züchtigen.
bird [bə:d] Vogel m; ~'s-eye ['bə:dzai]: ~ view Vogelperspektive f.
birth [bə:θ] Geburt f; Ursprung m; Entstehung f; Herkunft f; bring to ~ entstehen lassen, veranlassen; give ~ to gebären, zur Welt bringen; ~ control Geburtenregelung f; ~day ['bə:θdei] Geburtstag m; ~place Geburtsort m.
biscuit ['biskit] Zwieback m; Keks m, n; Biskuit n (Porzellan).
bishop ['biʃəp] Bischof m; Läufer m im Schach; ~ric [~prik] Bistum n.
bison zo. ['baisn] Wisent m.
bit [bit] 1. Bißchen n, Stückchen n; Gebiß n am Zaum; Schlüssel-Bart m; a (little) ~ ein (kleines) bißchen; 2. zäumen; zügeln; 3. pret. von bite 2.
bitch [bitʃ] Hündin f; V Hure f.
bite [bait] 1. Beißen n; Biß m; Bissen m; ♣ Fassen n; 2. [irr.] (an)beißen; brennen (Pfeffer); schneiden (Kälte); ⊕ fassen; fig. verletzen.
bitten ['bitn] p.p. von bite 2.
bitter ['bitə] 1. □ bitter; streng; fig. verbittert; 2. ~s pl. Magenbitter m.
biz F [biz] Geschäft n.
blab F [blæb] (aus)schwatzen.
black [blæk] 1. □ schwarz; dunkel; finster; ~ eye blaues Auge; 2. schwärzen; wichsen; ~ out verdunkeln; 3. Schwarz n; Schwärze f; Schwarze(r m) f (Neger); ~amoor ['blækəmuə] Neger m; ~berry Brombeere f; ~bird Amsel f; ~board Wandtafel f; ~en [~kən] v/t. schwärzen; fig. anschwärzen; v/i. schwarz werden; ~guard ['blæga:d] Lump m, Schuft m; 2. □ schuftig; ~head ♣ Mitesser m; ~ing [~kiŋ] Schuhwichse f; ~ish □ [~iʃ] schwärzlich; ~jack 1. bsd. Am. Totschläger m (Instrument); 2. niederknüppeln; ~leg Betrüger m; ~-letter typ. Fraktur f; ~mail 1. Erpressung f; 2. j-n erpressen; ~ market schwarzer Markt; ~ness [~nis] Schwärze f; ~out Verdunkelung f; ~ pudding Blutwurst f; ~smith Grobschmied m.

bladder anat. ['blædə] Blase f.
blade [bleid] Blatt n, ♀ Halm m; Säge-, Schulter- etc. Blatt n; Propellerflügel m; Klinge f.
blame [bleim] 1. Tadel m; Schuld f; 2. tadeln; be to ~ for schuld sein an (dat.); ~ful ['bleimful] tadelnswert; ~less □ [~mlis] tadellos.
blanch [bla:ntʃ] bleichen; erbleichen (lassen); ~ over beschönigen.
bland □ [blænd] mild, sanft.
blank [blæŋk] 1. □ blank; leer; unausgefüllt; unbeschrieben; ✝ Blanko...; verdutzt; ~ cartridge ✕ Platzpatrone f; 2. Weiße n; Leere f; leerer Raum; Lücke f; unbeschriebenes Blatt, Formular n; Niete f.
blanket ['blæŋkit] 1. Wolldecke f; wet ~ fig. Dämpfer m; Spielverderber m; 2. (mit e-r Wolldecke) zudecken; 3. Am. umfassend, Gesamt...
blare [blɛə] schmettern; grölen.
blasphem|e [blæs'fi:m] lästern (against über acc.); ~y ['blæsfimi] Gotteslästerung f.
blast [bla:st] 1. Windstoß m; Ton m e-s Blasinstruments; ⊕ Gebläse (-luft f) n; Luftdruck m e-r Explosion; ♀ Meltau m; 2. (in die Luft) sprengen; zerstören (a. fig.); ~ (it)! verdammt; ~-furnace ⊕ ['bla:stfə:nis] Hochofen m.
blatant □ ['bleitənt] lärmend.
blather Am. ['blæðə] schwätzen.
blaze [bleiz] 1. Flamme(n pl.) f; Feuer n; ~s pl. sl. Teufel m, Hölle f; heller Schein; fig. Ausbruch m; go to ~s! zum Teufel mit dir!; 2. v/i. brennen, flammen, lodern; leuchten; v/t. ~ abroad ausposaunen; ~r ['bleizə] Blazer m.
blazon ['bleizn] Wappen(kunde f) n.
bleach [bli:tʃ] bleichen; ~er ['bli:tʃe] Bleicher(in); mst ~s pl. Am. nichtüberdachte Zuschauerplätze.
bleak □ [bli:k] öde, kahl; rauh; fig. trüb, freudlos, finster.
blear [bliə] 1. trüb; 2. trüben; ~-eyed ['bliəraid] triefäugig.
bleat [bli:t] 1. Blöken n; 2. blöken.
bleb [bleb] Bläs-chen n, Pustel f.
bled [bled] pret. u. p.p. von bleed.
bleed [bli:d] [irr.] v/i. bluten; v/t. zur Ader lassen; fig. schröpfen; ~ing ['bli:diŋ] 1. Bluten n; Aderlaß m; 2. sl. verflixt.
blemish ['blemiʃ] 1. Fehler m; Makel m, Schande f; 2. verunstalten; brandmarken.
blench [blentʃ] v/i. zurückschrecken; v/t. die Augen schließen vor.
blend [blend] 1. [irr.] (sich) (ver-) mischen; Wein etc. verschneiden; 2. Mischung f; ✝ Verschnitt m.
blent [blent] pret. u. p.p. von blend 1.
bless [bles] segnen; preisen; be-

glücken; ~ me! herrje!; ~ed □ [pret. u. p.p. blest; adj. 'blesid] glückselig; gesegnet; ~ing [~siŋ] Segen m.

blew [blu:] pret. von blow² u. blow³1.

blight [blait] 1. ♀ Mehltau m; fig. Gifthauch m; 2. vernichten.

blind □ [blaind] 1. blind (fig. to gegen); geheim; nicht erkennbar; ~ alley Sackgasse f; ~ly fig. blindlings; 2. Blende f; Fenster-Vorhang m, Jalousie f; Am. Versteck n; Vorwand m; 3. blenden; verblenden (to gegen); abblenden; ~fold ['blaindfould] 1. blindlings; 2. j-m die Augen verbinden; ~worm Blindschleiche f.

blink [bliŋk] 1. Blinzeln n; Schimmer m; 2. v/i. blinzeln; blinken; schimmern; v/t. absichtlich übersehen; ~er ['bliŋkə] Scheuklappe f.

bliss [blis] Seligkeit f, Wonne f.

blister ['blistə] 1. Blase f (auf der Haut, im Lack); Zugpflaster n; 2. Blasen bekommen od. ziehen (auf dat.).

blithe □ mst poet. [blaið] lustig.

blizzard ['blizəd] Schneesturm m.

bloat [blout] aufblasen; aufschwellen; ~er ['bloutə] Bückling m.

block [blɔk] 1. (Häuser-, Schreibetc.)Block m; Klotz m; Druckstock m; Verstopfung f, Stockung f; 2. formen; verhindern; ~ in entwerfen, skizzieren; mst ~ up (ab-, ver-)sperren; blockieren.

blockade [blɔ'keid] 1. Blockade f; 2. blockieren.

block|head ['blɔkhed] Dummkopf m; ~ letters Druckschrift f.

blond(e f) [blɔnd] 1. blond; 2. Blondine f.

blood [blʌd] Blut n; fig. Blut n; Abstammung f; in cold ~ kalten Blutes, kaltblütig; ~-curdling ['blʌdkə:dliŋ] haarsträubend; ~-horse Vollblutpferd n; ~shed Blutvergießen n; ~shot blutunterlaufen; ~thirsty blutdürstig; ~-vessel Blutgefäß n; ~y □ ['blʌdi] blutig; blutdürstig.

bloom [blu:m] 1. Blüte f; Reif m auf Früchten; fig. Schmelz m; 2. (er-)blühen (a. fig.).

blossom ['blɔsəm] 1. Blüte f; 2. blühen.

blot [blɔt] 1. Klecks m; fig. Makel m; 2. v/t. beklecksen, beflecken; (ab-)löschen; ausstreichen; v/i. klecksen.

blotch [blɔtʃ] Pustel f; Fleck m.

blotter ['blɔtə] Löscher m; Am. Protokollbuch n. [Löschpapier n.)

blotting-paper ['blɔtiŋpeipə]]

blouse [blauz] Bluse f.

blow¹ [blou] Schlag m, Stoß m.

blow² [~] [irr.] blühen.

blow³ [~] 1. [irr.] v/i. blasen; wehen; schnaufen; ~ up in die Luft fliegen; v/t. (weg- etc.)blasen; wehen; ♂

durchbrennen; ~ one's nose sich die Nase putzen; ~ up sprengen; 2. Blasen n, Wehen n; ~er ['blouə] Bläser m.

blown [bloun] p.p. von blow² und blow³ 1.

blow|-out mot. ['blouaut] Reifenpanne f; ~pipe Gebläsebrenner m.

bludgeon ['blʌdʒən] Knüppel m.

blue [blu:] 1. □ blau; F trüb, schwermütig; 2. Blau n; 3. blau färben; blauen; ~bird ['blu:bə:d] amerikanische Singdrossel; ~ laws Am. strenge (puritanische) Gesetze; ~s [blu:z] pl. Trübsinn f; ♪ Blues m.

bluff [blʌf] 1. □ schroff; steil; derb; 2. Steilufer n; Irreführung f; 3. bluffen, irreführen.

bluish ['blu(:)iʃ] bläulich.

blunder ['blʌndə] 1. Fehler m, Schnitzer m; 2. e-n Fehler machen; stolpern; stümpern; verpfuschen.

blunt [blʌnt] 1. □ stumpf (a. fig.); plump, grob, derb; 2. abstumpfen.

blur [blə:] 1. Fleck(en) m; fig. Verschwommenheit f; 2. v/t. beflecken; verwischen; Sinn trüben.

blush [blʌʃ] 1. Schamröte f; Erröten n; flüchtiger Blick; 2. erröten; (sich) röten.

bluster ['blʌstə] 1. Brausen n, Getöse n; Prahlerei f; 2. brausen; prahlen.

boar [bɔ:] Eber m; hunt. Keiler m.

board [bɔ:d] 1. (Anschlag)Brett n; Konferenztisch m; Ausschuß m; Gremium n; Behörde f; Verpflegung f; Pappe f; on ~ a train Am. in e-m Zug; ♀ of Trade Handelsministerium n; 2. v/t. dielen, verschalen; beköstigen; an Bord gehen; ♣ entern; bsd. Am. einsteigen in (ein Fahr- od. Flugzeug); v/i. in Kost sein; ~er ['bɔ:də] Kostgänger(in); Internatsschüler(in); ~ing-house ['bɔ:diŋhaus] Pension f; ~ing-school ['bɔ:diŋsku:l] Internatsschule f; ~walk bsd. Am. Strandpromenade f.

boast [boust] 1. Prahlerei f; 2. (of, about) sich rühmen (gen.), prahlen (mit); ~ful □ ['boustful] prahlerisch.

boat [bout] Boot n; Schiff n; ~ing ['boutiŋ] Bootfahrt f.

bob [bɔb] 1. Quaste f; Ruck m; Knicks m; Schopf m; sl. Schilling m; 2. v/t. Haar stutzen; ~bed hair Bubikopf m; v/i. springen, tanzen; knicksen.

bobbin ['bɔbin] Spule f (a. ♂).

bobble Am. F ['bɔbl] Fehler m.

bobby sl. ['bɔbi] Schupo m, Polizist m.

bobsleigh ['bɔbslei] Bob(sleigh) m (Rennschlitten).

bode¹ [boud] prophezeien.

bode² [~] pret. von bide.

bodice ['bɔdis] Mieder n; Taille f.
bodily ['bɔdili] körperlich.
body ['bɔdi] Körper m, Leib m; Leichnam m; Körperschaft f; Hauptteil m; mot. Karosserie f; ✗ Truppenkörper m; ~guard Leibwache f.
Boer ['bouə] Bure m; attr. Buren...
bog [bɔg] 1. Sumpf m, Moor n; 2. im Schlamm versenken.
boggle ['bɔgl] stutzen; pfuschen.
bogus ['bougəs] falsch; Schwindel...
boil [bɔil] 1. kochen, sieden; (sich) kondensieren; 2. Sieden n; Beule f, Geschwür n; ~er ['bɔilə] (Dampf-)Kessel m.
boisterous □ ['bɔistərəs] ungestüm; heftig, laut; lärmend.
bold □ [bould] kühn; keck, dreist; steil; typ. fett; make ~ sich erkühnen; ~ness ['bouldnis] Kühnheit f; Keckheit f, Dreistigkeit f.
bolster ['boulstə] 1. Kopfkeil m; Unterlage f; 2. polstern; (unter-)stützen.
bolt [boult] 1. Bolzen m; Riegel m; Blitz(strahl) m; Ausreißen n; 2. adv. ~ upright kerzengerade; 3. v/t. verriegeln; F hinunterschlingen; sieben; v/i. eilen; durchgehen (Pferd); Am. pol. abtrünnig werden; ~er ['boultə] Ausreißer(in).
bomb [bɔm] 1. Bombe f; 2. mit Bomben belegen.
bombard [bɔm'baːd] bombardieren.
bombastic [bɔm'bæstik] schwülstig.
bomb-proof ['bɔmpruːf] bombensicher.
bond [bɔnd] Band n; Fessel f; Bündnis n; Schuldschein m; ✝ Obligation f; in ~ ✝ unter Zollverschluß; ~age ['bɔndidʒ] Hörigkeit f; Knechtschaft f; ~(s)man [~d(z)mən] Leibeigene(r) m.
bone [boun] 1. Knochen m; Gräte f; ~s pl. a. Gebeine n/pl.; ~ of contention Zankapfel m; make no ~s about F nicht lange fackeln mit; 2. die Knochen auslösen (aus); aus-, entgräten.
bonfire ['bɔnfaiə] Freudenfeuer n.
bonnet ['bɔnit] Haube f, Schute(nhut m) f; ⊕ (Motor)Haube f.
bonus ✝ ['bounəs] Prämie f; Gratifikation f; Zulage f.
bony ['bouni] knöchern; knochig.
boob Am. [buːb] Dummkopf m.
booby ['buːbi] Tölpel m.
book [buk] 1. Buch n; Heft n; Liste f; Block m; 2. buchen; eintragen; Fahrkarte etc. lösen; e-n Platz etc. bestellen; Gepäck aufgeben; ~burner Am. F ['bukbəːnə] intoleranter Mensch; ~case Bücherschrank m; ~ing-clerk ['bukiŋklaːk] Schalterbeamt|e(r) m, -in f; ~ing-office ['bukiŋɔfis] Fahrkartenausgabe f, -schalter m; thea.

Kasse f; ~ish □ [~iʃ] gelehrt; ~keeping Buchführung f; ~let ['buklit] Büchlein n; Broschüre f; ~seller Buchhändler m.
boom[1] [buːm] 1. ✝ Aufschwung m, Hochkonjunktur f, Hausse f; Reklamerummel m; 2. in die Höhe treiben od. gehen; für et. Reklame machen.
boom[2] [~] brummen; dröhnen.
boon[1] [buːn] Segen m, Wohltat f.
boon[2] [~] freundlich, munter.
boor fig. [buə] Bauer m, Lümmel m; ~ish □ ['buəriʃ] bäuerisch, lümmel-, flegelhaft.
boost [buːst] heben; verstärken (a. ⚡); Reklame machen.
boot[1] [buːt]: to ~ obendrein.
boot[2] [~] Stiefel m; Kofferraum m; ~black Am. ['buːtblæk] = shoeblack; ~ee ['buːtiː] Damen-Halbstiefel m.
booth [buːð] (Markt- etc.)Bude f; Wahlzelle f; Am. Fernsprechzelle f.
boot|lace ['buːtleis] Schnürsenkel m; ~legger Am. [~legə] Alkoholschmuggler m.
booty ['buːti] Beute f, Raub m.
border ['bɔːdə] 1. Rand m; Saum m; Grenze f; Einfassung f; Rabatte f; 2. einfassen; grenzen (upon an acc.).
bore[1] [bɔː] 1. Bohrloch n; Kaliber n; fig. langweiliger Mensch; Plage f; 2. bohren; langweilen; belästigen.
bore[2] [~] pret. von bear[2].
born [bɔːn] p.p. von bear[2] gebären.
borne [bɔːn] p.p. von bear[2] tragen.
borough ['bʌrə] Stadt(teil m) f; Am. a. Wahlbezirk m von New York City; municipal ~ Stadtgemeinde f.
borrow ['bɔrou] borgen, entleihen.
bosom ['buzəm] Busen m; fig. Schoß m.
boss F [bɔs] 1. Boss m, Chef m; bsd. Am. pol. (Partei)Bonze m; 2. leiten; ~y Am. F ['bɔsi] tyrannisch, herrisch.
botany ['bɔtəni] Botanik f.
botch [bɔtʃ] 1. Flicken m; Flickwerk n; 2. flicken; verpfuschen.
both [bouθ] beide(s); ~ ... and sowohl ... als (auch).
bother F ['bɔðə] 1. Plage f; 2. (sich) plagen, (sich) quälen.
bottle ['bɔtl] 1. Flasche f; 2. auf Flaschen ziehen.
bottom ['bɔtəm] 1. Boden m, Grund m; Grundfläche f, Fuß m, Ende m; F Hintern m; fig. Wesen n, Kern m; at the ~ ganz unten; fig. im Grunde; 2. grundlegend, Grund...
bough [bau] Ast m, Zweig m.
bought [bɔːt] pret. u. p.p von buy.
boulder ['bouldə] Geröllblock m.
bounce [bauns] 1. Sprung m, Rückprall m; F Aufschneiderei f; Auftrieb m; 2. (hoch)springen; F aufschneiden; ~r ['baunsə] F Mordskerl m; Am. sl. Rausschmeißer m.

bound[1] [baund] **1.** *pret. u. p.p von*
bind; **2.** *adj.* verpflichtet; bestimmt,
unterwegs (*for* nach).
bound[2] [‿] **1.** Grenze *f*, Schranke *f*;
2. begrenzen; beschränken.
bound[3] [‿] **1.** Sprung *m*; **2.** (hoch-)
springen; an-, abprallen.
boundary ['baundəri] Grenze *f*.
boundless □ ['baundlis] grenzenlos.
bount|eous □ ['bauntiəs], **‿iful** □
[‿iful] freigebig; reichlich.
bounty ['baunti] Freigebigkeit *f*;
Spende *f*; ✝ Prämie *f*.
bouquet ['bukei] Bukett *n*, Strauß
m; Blume *f des Weines*.
bout [baut] *Fecht-*Gang *m*; *Tanz-*
Tour *f*; ⚔ Anfall *m*; Kraftprobe *f*.
bow[1] [bau] **1.** Verbeugung *f*; **2.** *v/i.*
sich (ver)beugen; *v/t.* biegen; beugen.
bow[2] [‿] Bug *m*.
bow[3] [bou] **1.** Bogen *m*; Schleife *f*;
2. geigen.
bowdlerize ['baudləraiz] *Text* von
anstößigen Stellen reinigen.
bowels ['bauəlz] *pl.* Eingeweide *n*;
das Innere; *fig.* Herz *n*.
bower ['bauə] Laube *f*.
bowl[1] [boul] Schale *f*, Schüssel *f*;
*Pfeifen-*Kopf *m*.
bowl[2] [‿] **1.** Kugel *f*; **‿s** *pl.* Bowling
n; **2.** *v/t.* Ball *etc.* werfen; *v/i.*
rollen; kegeln.
box[1] [bɔks] Buchsbaum *m*; Büchse
f, Schachtel *f*, Kasten *m*; Koffer *m*;
⊕ Gehäuse *n*; *thea.* Loge *f*; *Ab-*
teilung *f*; **2.** in Kästen *etc.* tun.
box[2] [‿] **1.** boxen; **2.:** ‿ *on the ear*
Ohrfeige *f*.
Boxing-Day ['bɔksiŋdei] zweiter
Weihnachtsfeiertag.
box|-keeper ['bɔkski:pə] Logen-
schließer(in); **‿office** Theater-
kasse *f*.
boy [bɔi] Junge *m*, junger Mann;
Bursche *m* (*a. Diener*); **‿friend**
Freund *m*; **‿ scout** Pfadfinder *m*;
‿hood ['bɔihud] Knabenalter *n*;
‿ish □ ['bɔiiʃ] knabenhaft; kindisch.
brace [breis] **1.** ⊕ Strebe *f*; Stütz-
balken *m*; Klammer *f*; Paar *n*
(*Wild, Geflügel*); **‿s** *pl.* Hosenträger
m/pl.; **2.** absteifen; verankern;
(an)spannen; *fig.* stärken.
bracelet ['breislit] Armband *n*.
bracket ['brækit] **1.** ⚓ Konsole *f*;
Winkelstütze *f*; *typ.* Klammer *f*;
*Leuchter-*Arm *m*; *lower income* ‿
niedrige Einkommensstufe; **2.** ein-
klammern; *fig.* gleichstellen.
brackish ['brækiʃ] brackig, salzig.
brag [bræg] **1.** Prahlerei *f*; **2.** prahlen. [**2.** □ prahlerisch.]
braggart ['brægət] **1.** Prahler *m*;
braid [breid] **1.** *Haar-*Flechte *f*;
Borte *f*; Tresse *f*; **2.** flechten; mit
Borte besetzen.
brain [brein] **1.** Gehirn *n*; Kopf *m*

(*fig. mst* **‿s** = *Verstand*); **2.** *j-m* den
Schädel einschlagen; **‿pan** ['brein-
pæn] Hirnschale *f*; **‿(s)** trust *Am.*
[‿n(z)trʌst] Expertenrat *m* (*mst*
pol.); **‿wave** F Geistesblitz *m*.
brake [breik] **1.** ⊕ Bremse *f*;
2. bremsen; **‿(s)man** ⚙ ['breik(s)-
mən] Bremser *m*; *Am.* Schaffner *m*.
bramble ['bræmbl] Brombeer-
strauch *m*.
bran [bræn] Kleie *f*.
branch [brɑ:ntʃ] **1.** Zweig *m*; Fach
n; Linie *f des Stammbaumes*;
Zweigstelle *f*; **2.** sich ver-, ab-
zweigen.
brand [brænd] **1.** (Feuer)Brand *m*;
Brandmal *n*; Marke *f*; Sorte *f*;
2. einbrennen; brandmarken.
brandish ['brændiʃ] schwingen.
bran(d)-new ['bræn(d)'nju:] nagel-
neu.
brandy ['brændi] Kognak *m*; Wein-
brand *m*.
brass [brɑ:s] Messing *n*; F Unverschämtheit *f*; **‿ band** Blechblas-
kapelle *f*; **‿ knuckles** *pl. Am.* Schlag-
ring *m*.
brassière ['bræsiə] Büstenhalter *m*.
brave [breiv] **1.** tapfer; prächtig;
2. trotzen; mutig begegnen (*dat.*);
‿ry ['breivəri] Tapferkeit *f*;
Pracht *f*.
brawl [brɔ:l] **1.** Krakeel *m*, Krawall
m; **2.** krakeelen, Krawall machen.
brawny ['brɔ:ni] muskulös.
bray[1] [brei] **1.** Eselsschrei *m*;
2. schreien; schmettern; dröhnen.
bray[2] [‿] (zer)stoßen, zerreiben.
brazen ['breizn] bronzen; metallisch; *a.* **‿faced** unverschämt.
Brazilian [brə'ziljən] **1.** brasilia-
nisch; **2.** Brasilianer(in).
breach [bri:tʃ] **1.** Bruch *m*; *fig.* Verletzung *f*; ⚔ Bresche *f*; **2.** e-e
Bresche schlagen in (*acc.*).
bread [bred] Brot *n*; *know which*
side one's ‿ *is buttered* s-n Vorteil
(er)kennen.
breadth [bredθ] Breite *f*, Weite *f*,
Größe *f des Geistes*; *Tuch-*Bahn *f*.
break [breik] **1.** Bruch *m*; Lücke *f*;
Pause *f*; Absatz *m*; ✝ *Am.* (Preis-)
Rückgang *m*; *Tages-*Anbruch *m*;
a bad ‿ F e-e Dummheit; Pech *n*;
a lucky ‿ Glück *m*; **2.** [*irr.*] *v/t.*
(zer)brechen; unterbrechen; übertreten; *Tier* abrichten; *Bank* sprengen; *Brief* erbrechen; *Tür* aufbrechen; abbrechen; *Vorrat* an-
brechen; *Nachricht* schonend mitteilen; ruinieren; **‿ up** zerbrechen;
auflösen; *v/i.* (zer)brechen; aus-
los-, an-, auf-, hervorbrechen;
umschlagen (*Wetter*); **‿ away** sich
losreißen; **‿ down** zs.-brechen;
steckenbleiben; versagen; **‿able**
['breikəbl] zerbrechlich; **‿age**
[‿kidʒ] (*a.* ✝ *Waren*)Bruch *m*; **‿**
down Zs.-bruch *m*; Maschinen-

schaden *m*; *mot.* Panne *f*; ~fast
['brekfəst] 1. Frühstück *n*; 2. früh-
stücken; ~up ['breik'ʌp] Verfall
m; Auflösung *f*; Schulschluß *m*;
~water ['~kwɔːtə] Wellenbrecher
m.

breast [brest] Brust *f*; Busen *m*;
Herz *n*; *make a clean* ~ *of s.th.* et.
offen gestehen; ~stroke ['brest-
strouk] Brustschwimmen *n*.

breath [breθ] Atem(zug) *m*; Hauch
m; *waste one's* ~ s-e Worte verschwenden; ~e [briːð] *v/i.* atmen;
fig. leben; *v/t.* (aus-, ein)atmen;
hauchen; flüstern; ~less □ ['breθ-
lis] atemlos.

bred [bred] *pret. u. p.p. von*
breed 2.

breeches ['britʃiz] *pl.* Knie-, Reit-
hosen *f/pl.*

breed [briːd] 1. Zucht *f*; Rasse *f*;
Herkunft *f*; *Am.* Mischling *m bsd.*
weiß-indianisch; 2. [*irr.*] *v/t.* erzeugen; auf-, erziehen; züchten; *v/i.*
sich fortpflanzen; ~er ['briːdə] Er-
zeuger(in); Züchter(in); ~ing [~diŋ]
Erziehung *f*; Bildung *f*; (Tier-)
Zucht *f*.

breez|e [briːz] Brise *f*; ~y ['briːzi]
windig, luftig; frisch, flott.

brethren ['breðrin] *pl.* Brüder *m/pl.*

brevity ['breviti] Kürze *f*.

brew [bruː] 1. *v/t. u. v/i.* brauen;
zubereiten; *fig.* anzetteln; 2. Gebräu *n*; ~ery ['bruəri] Brauerei *f*.

briar ['braiə] = *brier*.

brib|e [braib] 1. Bestechung(sgeld
n, -sgeschenk *n*) *f*; 2. bestechen;
~ery ['braibəri] Bestechung *f*.

brick [brik] 1. Ziegel(stein) *m*; *drop*
a ~ *sl.* ins Fettnäpfchen treten;
2. mauern; ~layer ['brikleiə] Maurer *m*; ~works *sg.* Ziegelei *f*.

bridal □ ['braidl] bräutlich; Braut-
...; ~ *procession* Brautzug *m*.

bride [braid] Braut *f*, Neuvermählte
f; ~groom ['braidgrum] Bräutigam
m, Neuvermählte(r) *m*; ~smaid
[~dzmeid] Brautjungfer *f*.

bridge [bridʒ] 1. Brücke *f*; 2. e-e
Brücke schlagen über (*acc.*); *fig.*
überbrücken.

bridle ['braidl] 1. Zaum *m*; Zügel
m; 2. *v/t.* (auf)zäumen; zügeln; *v/i.*
a. ~ *up* den Kopf zurückwerfen;
~path, ~road Reitweg *m*.

brief [briːf] 1. □ kurz, bündig; 2. ɫ⅔
schriftliche Instruktion; *hold a* ~
for einstehen für; ~case ['briːf-
keis] Aktenmappe *f*.

brier ⚹ ['braiə] Dorn-, Hagebutten-
strauch *m*, wilde Rose.

brigade ✕ [bri'geid] Brigade *f*.

bright □ [brait] hell, glänzend, klar;
lebhaft; gescheit; ~en ['braitn] *v/t.*
auf-, erhellen; polieren; aufheitern;
v/i. sich aufhellen; ~ness [~nis]
Helligkeit *f*; Glanz *m*; Klarheit *f*;
Heiterkeit *f*; Aufgewecktheit *f*.

brillian|ce, ~cy ['briljəns, ~si]
Glanz *m*; ~t [~nt] 1. □ glänzend;
prächtig; 2. Brillant *m*.

brim [brim] 1. Rand *m*; Krempe *f*;
2. bis zum Rande füllen *od.* voll
sein; ~full, ~ful ['brim'ful] ganz
voll; ~stone † ['brimstən] Schwefel
m.

brindle(d) ['brindl(d)] scheckig.

brine [brain] Salzwasser *n*, Sole *f*.

bring [briŋ] [*irr.*] bringen; *j.* veranlassen; *Klage* erheben; *Grund etc.*
vorbringen; ~ *about*, ~ *to pass* zustande bringen; ~ *down Preis* herabsetzen; ~ *forth* hervorbringen; gebären; ~ *home to j.* überzeugen; ~
round wieder zu sich bringen; ~ *up*
auf-, erziehen.

brink [briŋk] Rand *m*.

brisk □ [brisk] lebhaft, munter;
frisch; flink; belebend.

bristl|e ['brisl] 1. Borste *f*; 2. (sich)
sträuben; hochfahren, zornig wer-
den; ~ *with fig.* starren von; ~ed,
~y [~li] gesträubt; struppig.

British ['britiʃ] britisch; *the* ~ *pl.* die
Briten *pl.*; ~er *bsd. Am.* [~ʃə] Ein-
wohner(in) Großbritanniens.

brittle ['britl] zerbrechlich, spröde.

broach [broutʃ] *Faß* anzapfen; vorbringen; *Thema* anschneiden.

broad □ [brɔːd] breit; weit; hell
(*Tag*); deutlich (*Wink etc.*); derb
(*Witz*); allgemein; weitherzig, liberal; ~cast ['brɔːdkɑːst] 1. weitverbreitet; 2. [*irr.* (*cast*)] weit verbreiten; *Radio*: senden; 3. Rundfunk
(-sendung *f*) *m*; ~cloth feiner
Wollstoff; ~minded großzügig.

brocade † [brɔ'keid] Brokat *m*.

broil [brɔil] 1. Lärm *m*, Streit *m*;
2. auf dem Rost braten; *fig.*
schmoren.

broke [brouk] 1. *pret. von break* 2;
2. *sl.* pleite, ohne e-n Pfennig; ~n
['broukən] 1. *p.p. von break* 2; 2.:
~ *health* zerrüttete Gesundheit.

broker ['broukə] Altwarenhändler
m; Zwangsversteigerer *m*; Makler
m.

bronc(h)o *Am.* ['brɔŋkou] (halb-)
wildes Pferd; ~buster [~oubʌstə]
Zureiter *m*.

bronze [brɔnz] 1. Bronze *f*; 2. bronzen, Bronze...; 3. bronzieren.

brooch [broutʃ] Brosche *f*; Spange *f*.

brood [bruːd] 1. Brut *f*; *attr.*
Zucht...; 2. brüten (*a. fig.*); ~er
Am. ['bruːdə] Brutkasten *m*.

brook [bruk] Bach *m*.

broom [brum] Besen *m*; ~stick
['brumstik] Besenstiel *m*.

broth [brɔθ] Fleischbrühe *f*.

brothel ['brɔθl] Bordell *n*.

brother ['brʌðə] Bruder *m*; ~(s) *and*
sister(s) Geschwister *pl.*; ~hood
[~hud] Bruderschaft *f*; ~-in-law
[~rinlɔː] Schwager *m*; ~ly [~əli]
brüderlich.

brought [brɔːt] *pret. u. p.p. von*
bring.

brow [brau] (Augen)Braue *f*; Stirn
f; Rand *m e-s Steilhanges*; **~beat**
['braubiːt] [*irr.* (*beat*)] einschüchtern; tyrannisieren.

brown [braun] 1. braun; 2. Braun *n*;
3. (sich) bräunen.

browse [brauz] 1. Grasen *n*; *fig.*
Schmökern *n*; 2. grasen, weiden;
fig. schmökern.

bruise [bruːz] 1. Quetschung *f*;
2. (zer)quetschen.

brunt [brʌnt] Hauptstoß *m*, (volle)
Wucht; *das* Schwerste.

brush [brʌʃ] 1. Bürste *f*; Pinsel *m*;
Fuchs-Rute *f*; Scharmützel *n*; Unterholz *n*; 2. *v/t.* (ab-, aus)bürsten;
streifen; *j.* abbürsten; **~ up** wieder
aufbürsten, *fig.* auffrischen; *v/i.*
bürsten; (davon)stürzen; **~ against**
s.o. j. streifen; **~wood** ['brʌʃwud]
Gestrüpp *n*, Unterholz *n*.

brusque □ [brusk] brüsk, barsch.

Brussels sprouts ♀ ['brʌsl'sprauts]
pl. Rosenkohl *m*.

brut|al □ ['bruːtl] viehisch; roh,
gemein; **~ality** [bruːˈtæliti] Bruta-
lität *f*, Roheit *f*; **~e** [bruːt] 1. tierisch; unvernünftig; gefühllos;
2. Vieh *n*; F Untier *n*, Scheusal *n*.

bubble ['bʌbl] 1. Blase *f*; Schwindel
m; 2. sieden; sprudeln.

buccaneer [bʌkəˈniə] Seeräuber *m*.

buck [bʌk] 1. *zo.* Bock *m*; Stutzer *m*;
Am. sl. Dollar *m*; 2. *v/i.* bocken;
~ for *Am.* sich bemühen um; **~ up**
F sich zs.-reißen; *v/t. Am.* F sich
stemmen gegen; *Am.* F die Oberhand gewinnen wollen über *et.*

bucket ['bʌkit] Eimer *m*, Kübel *m*.

buckle ['bʌkl] 1. Schnalle *f*; 2. *v/t.*
(an-, auf-, um-, zu)schnallen; *v/i.*
⊕ sich (ver)biegen; **~ to a task** sich
ernsthaft an eine Aufgabe machen.

buck|shot *hunt.* ['bʌkʃɔt] Rehposten
m; **~skin** Wildleder *n*.

bud [bʌd] 1. Knospe *f*; *fig.* Keim *m*;
2. *v/t.* ♠ veredeln; *v/i.* knospen.

buddy *Am.* F ['bʌdi] Kamerad *m*.

budge [bʌdʒ] (sich) bewegen.

budget ['bʌdʒit] Vorrat *m*; Staats-
haushalt *m*; *draft*~ Haushaltsplan *m*.

buff [bʌf] 1. Ochsenleder *n*; Leder-
farbe *f*; 2. lederfarben.

buffalo *zo.* ['bʌfəlou] Büffel *m*.

buffer ⚙ ['bʌfə] Puffer *m*; Prellbock
m.

buffet¹ ['bʌfit] 1. Puff *m*, Stoß *m*,
Schlag *m*; 2. puffen, schlagen;
kämpfen.

buffet² [~] Büfett *n*; Anrichte *f*.

buffet³ ['bufei] Büfett *n*, Theke *f*;
Tisch *m* mit Speisen u. Getränken;
Erfrischungsraum *m*.

buffoon [bʌˈfuːn] Possenreißer *m*.

bug [bʌg] Wanze *f*; *Am.* Insekt *n*,
Käfer *m*; *Am. sl.* Defekt *m*, Fehler
m; *big* **~** *sl.* hohes Tier.

bugle ['bjuːgl] Wald-, Signalhorn *n*.

build [bild] 1. [*irr.*] bauen; errichten; 2. Bauart *f*; Schnitt *m*; **~er**
['bildə] Erbauer *m*, Baumeister *m*;
~ing [~diŋ] Erbauen *n*; Bau *m*, Gebäude *n*; *attr.* Bau...

built [bilt] *pret. u. p.p. von* build 1.

bulb [bʌlb] ♀ Zwiebel *f*, Knolle *f*;
(Glüh)Birne *f*.

bulge [bʌldʒ] 1. (Aus)Bauchung *f*;
Anschwellung *f*; 2. sich (aus)bau-
chen; (an)schwellen; hervorquel-
len.

bulk [bʌlk] Umfang *m*; Masse *f*;
Hauptteil *m*; ⚓ Ladung *f*; *in* **~** lose;
in großer Menge; **~y** ['bʌlki] umfangreich; unhandlich; ⚓ sperrig.

bull¹ [bul] 1. Bulle *m*, Stier *m*; † *sl.*
Haussier *m*; 2. † *die Kurse* trei-
ben.

bull² [~] *päpstliche* Bulle.

bulldog ['buldɔg] Bulldogge *f*.

bulldoze *Am.* F ['buldouz] terrorisieren; **~r** ⊕ [~zə] Bulldozer *m*,
Planierraupe *f*.

bullet ['bulit] Kugel *f*, Geschoß *n*.

bulletin ['bulitin] Tagesbericht *m*;
~ board *Am.* Schwarzes Brett.

bullion ['buljən] Gold-, Silberbar-
ren *m*; Gold-, Silberlitze *f*.

bully ['buli] 1. Maulheld *m*; Tyrann
m; 2. prahlerisch; *Am.* F prima;
3. einschüchtern; tyrannisieren.

bulwark *mst fig.* ['bulwək] Bollwerk
n.

bum *Am.* F [bʌm] 1. Nichtstuer
m, Vagabund *m*; 2. *v/i.* nassauern.

bumble-bee ['bʌmblbiː] Hummel *f*.

bump [bʌmp] 1. Schlag *m*; Beule *f*;
fig. Sinn *m* (of für); 2. (zs.-)stoßen;
holpern; *Rudern:* überholen.

bumper ['bʌmpə] volles Glas
(*Wein*); F *et.* Riesiges; *mot.* Stoß-
stange *f*; **~ crop** Rekordernte *f*; **~
house** *thea.* volles Haus.

bun [bʌn] Rosinenbrötchen *n*;
Haar-Knoten *m*.

bunch [bʌntʃ] 1. Bund *n*; Büschel *n*;
Haufen *m*; **~ of grapes** Weintraube
f; 2. (zs.-)bündeln; bauschen.

bundle ['bʌndl] 1. Bündel *n*, Bund
n; 2. *v/t. a.* **~ up** (zs.-)bündeln.

bung [bʌŋ] Spund *m*.

bungalow ['bʌŋgəlou] Bungalow *m*
(*einstöckiges Haus*).

bungle ['bʌŋgl] 1. Pfuscherei *f*;
2. (ver)pfuschen.

bunion ♠ ['bʌnjən] entzündeter
Fußballen.

bunk¹ *Am. sl.* [bʌŋk] Quatsch *m*.

bunk² [~] Schlafkoje *f*.

bunny ['bʌni] Kaninchen *n*.

buoy ⚓ [bɔi] 1. Boje *f*; 2. *Fahrwas-
ser* betonnen; *mst* **~ up** *fig.* aufrechterhalten; **~ant** □ ['bɔiənt]
schwimmfähig; hebend; spannkräftig; *fig.* heiter.

burden ['bəːdn] 1. Last *f*; Bürde *f*;
⚓ Ladung *f*; ⚓ Tragfähigkeit *f*;

2. beladen; belasten; ~some [~nsəm] lästig; drückend.

bureau [bjuəˈrou] Büro *n*, Geschäftszimmer *n*; Schreibpult *n*; *Am.* Kommode *f*; ~cracy [~ˈrɔkrəsi] Bürokratie *f*.

burg *Am.* F [bəːg] Stadt *f*.

burgess [ˈbəːdʒis] Bürger *m*.

burglar [ˈbəːglə] Einbrecher *m*; ~y [~əri] Einbruch(sdiebstahl) *m*.

burial [ˈberiəl] Begräbnis *n*.

burlesque [bəːˈlesk] 1. possenhaft; 2. Burleske *f*, Posse *f*; 3. parodieren.

burly [ˈbəːli] stämmig, kräftig.

burn [bəːn] 1. Brandwunde *f*; Brandmal *n*; 2. [*irr.*] (ver-, an-)brennen; ~er [ˈbəːnə] Brenner *m*.

burnish [ˈbəːniʃ] polieren, glätten.

burnt [bəːnt] *pret. u. p.p. von* burn 2.

burrow [ˈbʌrou] 1. Höhle *f*, Bau *m*; 2. (sich ein-, ver)graben.

burst [bəːst] 1. Bersten *n*; Krach *m*; Riß *m*; Ausbruch *m*; 2. [*irr.*] *v/i.* bersten, platzen; zerspringen; explodieren; ~ *from* sich losreißen von; ~ *forth*, ~ *out* hervorbrechen; ~ *into tears* in Tränen ausbrechen; *v/t.* (zer)sprengen.

bury [ˈberi] be-, vergraben; beerdigen; verbergen.

bus F [bʌs] (Omni)Bus *m*; ~ *boy Am.* Kellnergehilfe *m*.

bush [buʃ] Busch *m*; Gebüsch *n*.

bushel [ˈbuʃl] Scheffel *m* (*36,37 Liter*).

bushy [ˈbuʃi] buschig.

business [ˈbiznis] Geschäft *n*; Beschäftigung *f*; Beruf *m*; Angelegenheit *f*; Aufgabe *f*; † Handel *m*; ~ *of the day* Tagesordnung *f*; *on* ~ geschäftlich; *have no* ~ *to inf.* nicht befugt sein zu *inf.*; *mind one's own* ~ sich um s-e eigenen Angelegenheiten kümmern; ~ *hours pl.* Geschäftszeit *f*; ~like geschäftsmäßig; sachlich; ~man Geschäftsmann *m*; ~tour, ~trip Geschäftsreise *f*.

bust[1] [bʌst] Büste *f*.

bust[2] *Am.* F [~] Bankrott *m*.

bustle [ˈbʌsl] 1. Geschäftigkeit *f*; geschäftiges Treiben; 2. *v/i.* (umher)wirtschaften; hasten; *v/t.* hetzen, jagen.

busy □ [ˈbizi] 1. beschäftigt; geschäftig; fleißig (*at* bei, an *dat.*); lebhaft; *Am. teleph.* besetzt; 2. (*mst* ~ *o.s.* sich) beschäftigen (*with*, *in*, *at*, *about*, *ger.* mit).

but [bʌt, bət] 1. *cj.* aber, jedoch, sondern; *a.* ~ *that* wenn nicht; indessen; 2. *prp.* außer; *the last* ~ *one* der vorletzte; *the next* ~ *one* der übernächste; ~ *for* wenn nicht ... gewesen wäre; ohne; 3. *nach Negation*: der (die *od.* das) nicht; *there is*

no one ~ *knows* es gibt niemand, der nicht wüßte; 4. *adv.* nur; ~ *just* soeben, eben erst; ~ *now* erst jetzt; *all* ~ fast, nahe daran; *nothing* ~ nur; *I cannot* ~ *inf.* ich kann nur *inf.*

butcher [ˈbutʃə] 1. Schlächter *m*, Fleischer *m*, Metzger *m*; *fig.* Mörder *m*; 2. (*fig.* ab-, hin)schlachten; ~y [~əri] Schlächterei *f*; Schlachthaus *n*.

butler [ˈbʌtlə] Butler *m*; Kellermeister *m*.

butt [bʌt] 1. Stoß *m*; *a.* ~ *end* (dickes) Ende *e-s Baumes etc.*; Stummel *m*, Kippe *f*; *Gewehr-*Kolben *m*; Schießstand *m*; (End)Ziel *n*; *fig.* Zielscheibe *f*; 2. (mit dem Kopf) stoßen.

butter [ˈbʌtə] 1. Butter *f*; F Schmeichelei *f*; 2. mit Butter bestreichen; ~cup Butterblume *f*; ~fingered tolpatschig; ~fly Schmetterling *m*; ~y [~əri] 1. butter(art)ig; Butter...; 2. Speisekammer *f*.

buttocks [ˈbʌtəks] *pl.* Gesäß *n*.

button [ˈbʌtn] 1. Knopf *m*; Knospe *f*; 2. an-, zuknöpfen.

buttress [ˈbʌtris] 1. Strebepfeiler *m*; *fig.* Stütze *f*; 2. (unter)stützen.

buxom [ˈbʌksəm] drall, stramm.

buy [bai] [*irr.*] *v/t.* (an-, ein)kaufen (*from* bei); ~er [ˈbaiə] (Ein)Käufer (-in).

buzz [bʌz] 1. Gesumm *n*; Geflüster *n*; ~ *saw Am.* Kreissäge *f*; 2. *v/i.* summen; surren; ~ *about* herumschwirren, herumeilen.

buzzard [ˈbʌzəd] Bussard *m*.

by [bai] 1. *prp. Raum*: bei; an, neben; *Richtung*: durch; über; an (*dat.*) entlang *od.* vorbei; *Zeit*: an, bei; spätestens bis, bis zu; *Urheber*, *Ursache*: von, durch (*bsd. beim pass.*); *Mittel*, *Werkzeug*: durch, mit; *Art u. Weise*: bei; *Schwur*: bei; *Maß*: um, bei; *Richtschnur*: gemäß, bei; ~ *the dozen* dutzendweise; ~ *o.s.* allein; ~ *land* zu Lande; ~ *rail* per Bahn; *day* ~ *day* Tag für Tag; ~ *twos* zu zweien; 2. *adv.* dabei; vorbei; beiseite; ~ *and* ~ nächstens, bald; nach und nach; ~ *the* ~ nebenbei bemerkt; ~ *and large Am.* im großen und ganzen; 3. *adj.* Neben...; Seiten...; ~election [ˈbaiilekʃən] Nachwahl *f*; ~gone vergangen; ~law Ortsstatut *n*; ~s *pl.* Satzung *f*, Statuten *n/pl.*; ~line *Am.* Verfasserangabe *f* *zu e-m Artikel*; ~name Bei-, Spitzname *m*; ~pass Umgehungsstraße *f*; ~path Seitenpfad *m*; ~product Nebenprodukt *n*; ~road Seitenweg *m*; ~stander Zuschauer *m*; ~street Neben-, Seitenstraße *f*; ~way Seitenweg *m*; ~word Sprichwort *n*; Inbegriff *m*; *be a* ~ *for* sprichwörtlich bekannt sein wegen.

C

cab [kæb] Droschke *f*, Mietwagen *m*, Taxi *n*; ⚓ Führerstand *m*.

cabbage ♀ ['kæbidʒ] Kohl *m*.

cabin ['kæbin] **1.** Hütte *f*; ⚓ Kabine *f*, Kajüte *f*; Kammer *f*; **2.** einpferchen; **~boy** Schiffsjunge *m*; **~ cruiser** ⚓ Kabinenkreuzer *m*.

cabinet ['kæbinit] Kabinett *n*, Ministerrat *m*; Schrank *m*, Vitrine *f*; (Radio)Gehäuse *n*; **~ council** Kabinettssitzung *f*; **~-maker** Kunsttischler *m*.

cable ['keibl] **1.** Kabel *n*; ⚓ Ankertau *n*; **2.** *tel.* kabeln; **~-car** Kabine *f*, Gondel *f*; Drahtseilbahn *f*; **~-gram** [‿lgræm] Kabeltelegramm *n*.

cabman ['kæbmən] Droschkenkutscher *m*, Taxifahrer *m*.

caboose [kə'bu:s] ⚓ Kombüse *f*; *Am.* ⚒ Eisenbahnerwagen *m am Güterzug.*

cab-stand ['kæbstænd] Taxi-, Droschkenstand *m*.

cacao ♀ [kə'ka:ou] Kakaobaum *m*, -bohne *f*.

cackle ['kækl] **1.** Gegacker *n*, Geschnatter *n*; **2.** gackern, schnattern.

cad [kæd] Prolet *m*; Kerl *m*.

cadaverous ☐ [kə'dævərəs] leichenhaft; leichenblaß.

cadence ♪ ['keidəns] Kadenz *f*; Tonfall *m*; Rhythmus *m*.

cadet [kə'det] Kadett *m*.

café ['kæfei] Café *n*.

cafeteria *bsd. Am.* [kæfi'tiəriə] Restaurant *n* mit Selbstbedienung.

cage [keidʒ] **1.** Käfig *m*; Kriegsgefangenenlager *n*; ⚒ Förderkorb *m*; **2.** einsperren.

cagey ☐ *bsd. Am.* F ['keidʒi] gerissen, raffiniert.

cajole [kə'dʒoul] *j-m* schmeicheln; *j-n* beschwatzen.

cake [keik] **1.** Kuchen *m*; Tafel *f* Schokolade, Riegel *m* Seife *etc.*; **2.** zs.-backen.

calamitous ☐ [kə'læmitəs] elend; katastrophal; **~ty** [‿ti] Elend *n*, Unglück *n*; Katastrophe *f*.

calcify ['kælsifai] (sich) verkalken.

calculate ['kælkjuleit] *v/t.* kalkulieren; be-, aus-, errechnen; *v/i.* rechnen (*on, upon auf acc.*); *Am.* F vermuten; **~ion** [kælkju'leiʃən] Kalkulation *f*, Berechnung *f*; Voranschlag *m*; Überlegung *f*.

caldron ['kɔ:ldrən] Kessel *m*.

calendar ['kælində] **1.** Kalender *m*; Liste *f*; **2.** registrieren.

calf [ka:f], *pl.* **calves** [ka:vz] Kalb *n*; Wade *f*; *a.* **~-leather** ['ka:fleðə] Kalbleder *n*; **~-skin** Kalbfell *n*.

calibre ['kælibə] Kaliber *n*.

calico ✝ ['kælikou] Kaliko *m*.

call [kɔ:l] **1.** Ruf *m*; *teleph.* Anruf *m*,

Gespräch *n*; *fig.* Berufung *f* (**to** in *ein Amt*; **auf** *e-n Lehrstuhl*); Aufruf *m*; Aufforderung *f*; Signal *n*; Forderung *f*; Besuch *m*; Nachfrage *f* (*for nach*); Kündigung *f v. Geldern*; **on ~** ✝ auf Abruf; **2.** *v/t.* (herbei-) rufen; (an)rufen; (ein)berufen; *Am. Baseball: Spiel* abbrechen; *fig.* berufen (**to** in *ein Amt*); nennen; wecken; *Aufmerksamkeit* lenken (**to auf** *acc.*); be **~ed** heißen; *s.o.* **names** *j.* beschimpfen, beleidigen; **~ down** *bsd. Am.* F anpfeifen; **~ in Geld** kündigen; **~ over Namen** verlesen; **~ up** aufrufen; *teleph.* anrufen; *v/i.* rufen; *teleph.* anrufen; vorsprechen (**at** *an e-m Ort*; **on** *s.o.* bei j-m); **~ at a port** *e-n* Hafen anlaufen; **~ for** rufen nach; *et.* fordern; abholen; **to be** (*left till*) **~ed for** postlagernd; **~ on** sich an *j.* wenden (*for wegen*); *j.* berufen, auffordern (**to** *inf.* zu); **~-box** ['kɔ:lbɔks] Fernsprechzelle *f*; **~er** ['kɔ:lə] *teleph.* Anrufer(in); Besucher(in).

calling ['kɔ:liŋ] Rufen *n*; Berufung *f*; Beruf *m*; **~ card** *Am.* Visitenkarte *f*.

call-office ['kɔ:lɔfis] Fernsprechstelle *f*.

callous ☐ ['kæləs] schwielig; *fig.* dickfellig; herzlos.

callow ['kælou] nackt (*ungefiedert*); *fig.* unerfahren.

calm [ka:m] **1.** ☐ still, ruhig; **2.** (Wind)Stille *f*, Ruhe *f*; **3.** (**~ down** sich) beruhigen; besänftigen.

caloric *phys.* [kə'lɔrik] Wärme *f*; **~e** *phys.* ['kæləri] Wärmeeinheit *f*.

column|iate [kə'lʌmnieit] verleumden; schmähen; **~iation** [kəlʌmni'eiʃən], **~y** ['kæləmni] Verleumdung *f*.

calve [ka:v] kalben; **~s** [ka:vz] *pl. von calf.*

cambric ✝ ['keimbrik] Batist *m*.

came [keim] *pret. von* **come.**

camel *zo.*, ⚓ ['kæməl] Kamel *n*.

camera ['kæmərə] Kamera *f*; **in ~** ⚖ unter Ausschluß der Öffentlichkeit.

camomile ♀ ['kæməmail] Kamille *f*.

camouflage ⚔ ['kæmufla:ʒ] **1.** Tarnung *f*; **2.** tarnen.

camp [kæmp] **1.** Lager *n*; ⚔ Feldlager *n*; **~ bed** Feldbett *n*; **2.** lagern; **~ out** zelten.

campaign [kæm'pein] **1.** Feldzug *m*; **2.** *e-n* Feldzug mitmachen *od.* führen.

camphor ['kæmfə] Kampfer *m*.

campus *Am.* ['kæmpəs] Universitätsgelände *n*.

can¹ [kæn] [*irr.*] *v/aux.* können, fähig sein zu; dürfen.

can² [‿] **1.** Kanne *f*; *Am.* Büchse *f*; **2.** *Am.* in Büchsen konservieren.

Canadian [kə'neidjən] **1.** kanadisch; **2.** Kanadier(in).

canal [kə'næl] Kanal m (a. ⚕).

canard [kæ'nɑ:d] (Zeitungs)Ente f.

canary [kə'nɛəri] Kanarienvogel m.

cancel ['kænsəl] (durch)streichen; entwerten; absagen; a. ~ out fig. aufheben; be ~led ausfallen.

cancer ast., ⚕ ['kænsə] Krebs m; ~ous [~ərəs] krebsartig.

candid □ ['kændid] aufrichtig; offen.

candidate ['kændidit] Kandidat m (for für), Bewerber m (for um).

candied ['kændid] kandiert.

candle ['kændl] Licht n, Kerze f; burn the ~ at both ends mit s-n Kräften Raubbau treiben; ~stick Leuchter m.

cando(u)r ['kændə] Aufrichtigkeit f.

candy ['kændi] **1.** Kandis(zucker) m; Am. Süßigkeiten f/pl.; **2.** v/t. kandieren.

cane [kein] **1.** ♀ Rohr n; (Rohr-) Stock m; **2.** prügeln.

canine ['keinain] Hunde...

canker ['kæŋkə] ⚕ Mundkrebs m; ♀ Brand m.

canned Am. [kænd] Büchsen...

cannery Am. ['kænəri] Konservenfabrik f.

cannibal ['kænibəl] Kannibale m.

cannon ['kænən] Kanone f.

cannot ['kænɔt] nicht können etc.; s. can¹.

canoe [kə'nu:] Kanu n; Paddelboot n.

canon ['kænən] Kanon m; Regel f; Richtschnur f; ~ize [~naiz] heiligsprechen.

canopy ['kænəpi] Baldachin m; fig. Dach n; △ Überdachung f.

cant¹ [kænt] **1.** Schrägung f; Stoß m; **2.** kippen, kanten.

cant² [~] **1.** Zunftsprache f; Gewäsch f; scheinheiliges Gerede; **2.** zunftmäßig od. scheinheilig reden.

can't F [kɑ:nt] = cannot.

cantankerous F □ [kən'tæŋkərəs] zänkisch, mürrisch.

canteen [kæn'ti:n] ✕ Feldflasche f; Kantine f; ✕ Kochgeschirr n; Besteckkasten m.

canton **1.** ['kæntən] Bezirk m; **2.** ✕ [kən'tu:n] (sich) einquartieren.

canvas ['kænvəs] Segeltuch n; Zelt (-e pl.) n; Zeltbahn f; Segel n/pl.; paint. Leinwand f; Gemälde n.

canvass [~] **1.** (Stimmen)Werbung f; Am. a. Wahlnachprüfung f; **2.** v/t. erörtern; v/i. (Stimmen, a. Kunden) werben.

caoutchouc ['kautʃuk] Kautschuk m.

cap [kæp] **1.** Kappe f; Mütze f; Haube f; ⊕ Aufsatz m; Zündhütchen n; set one's ~ at sich e-n Mann

angeln (Frau); **2.** mit e-r Kappe etc. bedecken; fig. krönen; F übertreffen; die Mütze abnehmen.

capab|ility [keipə'biliti] Fähigkeit f; ~le □ ['keipəbl] fähig (of zu).

capaci|ous □ [kə'peiʃəs] geräumig; ~ty [kə'pæsiti] Inhalt m; Aufnahmefähigkeit f; geistige (od. ⊕ Leistungs)Fähigkeit f (for ger. zu inf.); Stellung f; in my ~ as in meiner Eigenschaft als.

cape¹ [keip] Kap n, Vorgebirge n.

cape² [~] Cape n, Umhang m.

caper ['keipə] **1.** Kapriole f, Luftsprung m; cut ~s = **2.** Kapriolen od. Sprünge machen.

capital ['kæpitl] **1.** □ Kapital...; todeswürdig, Todes...; hauptsächlich, Haupt...; vortrefflich; ~ crime Kapitalverbrechen n; ~ punishment Todesstrafe f; **2.** Hauptstadt f; Kapital n; mst ~ letter Großbuchstabe m; ~ism [~təlizəm] Kapitalismus m; ~ize [kə'pitəlaiz] kapitalisieren.

capitulate [kə'pitjuleit] kapitulieren (to vor dat.).

capric|e [kə'pri:s] Laune f; ~ious □ [~iʃəs] kapriziös, launisch.

Capricorn ast. ['kæprikɔ:n] Steinbock m.

capsize [kæp'saiz] v/i. kentern; v/t. zum Kentern bringen.

capsule ['kæpsju:l] Kapsel f.

captain ['kæptin] Führer m; Feldherr m; ⚓ Kapitän m; ✕ Hauptmann m.

caption ['kæpʃən] **1.** Überschrift f; Titel m; Film: Untertitel m; **2.** v/t. Am. mit Überschrift etc. versehen.

captious □ ['kæpʃəs] spitzfindig.

captiv|ate ['kæptiveit] fig. gefangennehmen, fesseln; ~e ['kæptiv] **1.** gefangen, gefesselt; **2.** Gefangene(r m) f; ~ity [kæp'tiviti] Gefangenschaft f.

capture ['kæptʃə] **1.** Eroberung f; Gefangennahme f; **2.** (ein)fangen; erobern; erbeuten; ⚓ kapern.

car [kɑ:] Auto n; (Eisenbahn-, Straßenbahn)Wagen m; Ballonkorb m; Luftschiff-Gondel f; Kabine f e-s Aufzugs.

caramel ['kærəmel] Karamel m; Karamelle f.

caravan ['kærəvæn] Karawane f; Wohnwagen m.

caraway ♀ ['kærəwei] Kümmel m.

carbine ['kɑ:bain] Karabiner m.

carbohydrate ⚕ ['kɑ:bou'haidreit] Kohle(n)hydrat n.

carbon ['kɑ:bən] ⚕ Kohlenstoff m; ~ copy Brief-Durchschlag m; ~ paper Kohlepapier n.

carburet(t)or mot. ['kɑ:bjuretə] Vergaser m.

car|case, mst ~cass ['kɑ:kəs] (Tier-) Kadaver m; Fleischerei: Rumpf m.

card [kɑ:d] Karte f; have a ~ up

one's sleeve et. in petto haben;
~board ['ka:dɔ:d] Kartonpapier
n; Pappe f; ~ box Pappkarton m.
cardigan ['ka:digən] Wolljacke f.
cardinal □ ['ka:dinl] 1. Haupt...;
hochrot; ~ number Grundzahl f; 2.
Kardinal m.
card-index ['ka:dindeks] Kartei f.
card-sharper ['ka:dʃa:pə] Falschspieler m.
care [keə] 1. Sorge f; Sorgfalt f,
Obhut f, Pflege f; medical ~ ärztliche Behandlung; ~ of (abbr. c/o) ...
per Adresse, bei ...; take ~ of
acht(geb)en auf (acc.); with ~! Vorsicht!; 2. Lust haben (to inf. zu);
~ for sorgen für; sich kümmern um;
sich etwas machen aus; I don't ~!
F meinetwegen!; I couldn't ~ less F
es ist mir völlig egal; well ~d-for
gepflegt.   [bahn f; 2. rasen.]
career [kə'riə] 1. Karriere f; Lauf-]
carefree ['keəfri:] sorgenfrei.
careful □ ['keəful] besorgt (for um),
achtsam (of auf acc.); vorsichtig;
sorgfältig; ~ness [~lnis] Sorgsamkeit f; Vorsicht f; Sorgfalt f.
careless □ ['keəlis] sorglos; nachlässig; unachtsam; leichtsinnig;
~ness [~snis] Sorglosigkeit f; Nachlässigkeit f.
caress [kə'res] 1. Liebkosung f;
2. liebkosen; fig. schmeicheln.
caretaker ['keəteikə] Wärter(in)
(Haus)Verwalter(in).
care-worn ['keəwɔ:n] abgehärmt.
carfare Am. ['ka:feə] Fahrgeld n.
cargo ⚓ ['ka:gou] Ladung f.
caricature ['kærikə'tjuə] 1. Karikatur f; 2. karikieren.
carmine ['ka:main] Karmin(rot) n.
carn|al □ ['ka:nl] fleischlich; sinnlich; ~ation [ka:'neiʃən] 1. Fleischton m; ♀ Nelke f; 2. blaßrot.
carnival ['ka:nivəl] Karneval m.
carnivorous [ka:'nivərəs] fleischfressend.
carol ['kærəl] 1. Weihnachtslied n;
2. Weihnachtslieder singen.
carous|e [kə'rauz] 1. a. ~al [~ʒəl]
(Trink)Gelage n; 2. zechen.
carp [ka:p] Karpfen m.
carpent|er ['ka:pintə] Zimmermann m; ~ry [~tri] Zimmerhandwerk n; Zimmermannsarbeit f.
carpet ['ka:pit] 1. Teppich m;
bring on the ~ aufs Tapet bringen;
2. mit e-m Teppich belegen; ~bag
Reisetasche f; ~bagger [~tbægə]
politischer Abenteurer.
carriage ['kæridʒ] Beförderung f,
Transport m; Fracht f; Wagen m;
Fuhr-, Frachtlohn m; Haltung f;
Benehmen n; ~drive Anfahrt f
(vor e-m Hause); ~free, ~paid
frachtfrei; ~way Fahrbahn f.
carrier ['kæriə] Fuhrmann m;
Spediteur m; Träger m; Gepäckträger m; ~pigeon Brieftaube f.

carrion ['kæriən] Aas n; attr. Aas...
carrot ['kærət] Mohrrübe f.
carry ['kæri] 1. v/t. wohin bringen,
führen, tragen (a. v/i.), fahren, befördern; (bei sich) haben; Ansicht
durchsetzen; Gewinn, Preis davontragen; Zahlen übertragen; Ernte,
Zinsen tragen; Mauer etc. weiterführen; Benehmen fortsetzen; Antrag, Kandidaten durchbringen; ⚔
erobern; be carried angenommen
werden (Antrag); durchkommen
(Kandidat); ~ the day den Sieg
davontragen; ~ forward od. over ✝
übertragen; ~ on fortsetzen, weiterführen; Geschäft etc. betreiben; ~
out od. through durchführen; 2.
Trag-, Schußweite f.
cart [ka:t] 1. Karren m; Wagen m;
put the ~ before the horse fig. das
Pferd beim Schwanz aufzäumen;
2. karren, fahren; ~age ['ka:tidʒ]
Fahren m; Fuhrlohn m.
carter ['ka:tə] Fuhrmann m.
cartilage ['ka:tilidʒ] Knorpel m.
carton ['ka:tən] Karton m.
cartoon [ka:'tu:n] paint. Karton m;
⊕ Musterzeichnung f; Karikatur f;
Zeichentrickfilm m; ~ist [~nist]
Karikaturist m.
cartridge ['ka:tridʒ] Patrone f;
~paper Zeichenpapier n.
cart-wheel ['ka:twi:l] Wagenrad n;
Am. Silberdollar m; turn ~s radschlagen.
carve [ka:v] Fleisch vorschneiden,
zerlegen; schnitzen; meißeln; ~r
['ka:və] (Bild)Schnitzer m; Vorschneider m; Vorlegemesser n.
carving ['ka:viŋ] Schnitzerei f.
cascade [kæs'keid] Wasserfall m.
case¹ [keis] m Behälter m; Kiste f;
Etui n; Gehäuse n; Schachtel f;
Fach n; typ. Setzkasten m; 2. (ein-)
stecken; ver-, umkleiden.
case² [~] Fall m (a. gr., ✍, ⚕); gr.
Kasus m; ⚕ a. Kranke(r m) f; Am.
F komischer Kauz; ⚖ Schriftsatz
m; Hauptargument n; Sache f, Angelegenheit f.
case-harden ⊕ ['keisha:dn] hartgießen; ~ed fig. hartgesotten.
case-history ['keishistəri] Vorgeschichte f; Krankengeschichte f.
casement ['keismənt] Fensterflügel
m; ~ window Flügelfenster n.
cash [kæʃ] 1. Bargeld n, Kasse f;
~ down, for ~ gegen bar; ~ on delivery Lieferung f gegen bar; (per)
Nachnahme f; ~ register Registrierkasse f; 2. einkassieren, einlösen; ~book ['kæʃbuk] Kassabuch n; ~ier [kæ'ʃiə] Kassierer(in).
casing ['keisiŋ] Überzug m, Gehäuse n, Futteral n; ⚠ Verkleidung f.
cask [ka:sk] Faß n.
casket ['ka:skit] Kassette f; Am.
Sarg m.

casserole ['kæsərəul] Kasserolle *f.*

cassock *eccl.* ['kæsək] Soutane *f.*

cast [ka:st] 1. Wurf *m;* ⊕ Guß (-form *f*) *m;* Abguß *m,* Abdruck *m;* Schattierung *f,* Anflug *m;* Form *f,* Art *f;* ⚓ Auswerfen *n von Senkblei etc.;* *thea.* (Rollen)Besetzung *f;* 2. [*irr.*] *v/t.* (ab-, aus-, hin-, um-, weg)werfen; *zo.* Haut *etc.* abwerfen; *Zähne etc.* verlieren; verwerfen; gestalten; ⊕ gießen; *a.* ~ up aus-, zs.-rechnen; *thea.* Rolle besetzen; *Rolle* übertragen (*to dat.*); be ~ in a lawsuit ⚖ e-n Prozeß verlieren; ~ lots losen (for um); ~ in one's lot with s.o. j-s Los teilen; be ~ down niedergeschlagen sein; *v/i.* sich gießen lassen; ⊕ sich (ver)werfen; ~ about for sinnen auf (*acc.*); sich *et.* überlegen.

castanet [kæstə'net] Kastagnette *f.*

castaway ['ka:stəwei] 1. verworfen, ⚓ schiffbrüchig; 2. Verworfene(r *m*) *f;* Schiffbrüchige(r *m*) *f.*

caste [ka:st] Kaste *f* (*a. fig.*).

castigate ['kæstigeit] züchtigen; *fig.* geißeln.

cast iron ['ka:st'aiən] Gußeisen *n;* **cast-iron** gußeisern.

castle ['ka:sl] Burg *f,* Schloß *n;* *Schach:* Turm *m.*

castor[1] ['ka:stə]: ~ oil Rizinusöl *n.*

castor[2] [.] Laufrolle *f unter Möbeln;* (Salz-, Zucker- *etc.*) Streuer *m.*

castrate [kæs'treit] kastrieren.

cast steel ['ka:st'sti:l] Gußstahl *m;* **cast-steel** aus Gußstahl.

casual □ ['kæʒuəl] zufällig; gelegentlich; F lässig; **~ty** [.lti] Unfall *m;* ⚔ Verlust *m.*

cat [kæt] Katze *f;* ~ *burglar* Fassadenkletterer *m.*

catalo|gue, *Am.* **~g** ['kætələg] 1. Katalog *m; Am. univ.* Vorlesungsverzeichnis *n;* 2. katalogisieren.

catapult ['kætəpʌlt] Schleuder *f;* ✈ Katapult *m, n.*

cataract ['kætərækt] Katarakt *m,* Wasserfall *m;* ✚ grauer Star.

catarrh [kə'ta:] Katarrh *m;* Schnupfen *m.*

catastrophe [kə'tæstrəfi] Katastrophe *f.*

catch [kætʃ] 1. Fang *m;* Beute *f,* *fig.* Vorteil *m;* ♪ Rundgesang *m;* Kniff *m;* ⊕ Haken *m,* Griff *m,* Klinke *f;* 2. [*irr.*] *v/t.* fassen, F kriegen; fangen, ergreifen; ertappen; *Blick etc.* auffangen; *Zug etc.* erreichen; bekommen; sich *Krankheit* zuziehen; holen; *fig.* erfassen; ~ (*a*) *cold* sich erkälten; ~ *s.o.'s eye* j-m ins Auge fallen; ~ *up* auffangen; F *j.* unterbrechen; einholen; 3. *v/i.* sich verfangen, hängenbleiben; fassen, einschnappen (*Schloß etc.*); ~ *on* F Anklang finden; *Am.* F kapieren; ~ *up with* ∴ einholen; **~all** ['kætʃɔ:l] *Am.*

Platz *m od.* Behälter *m* für alles mögliche (*a. fig. u. attr.*); **~er** [.ʃə] Fänger(in); **~ing** [.ʃiŋ] packend; ✗ ansteckend; **~line** Schlagzeile *f;* **~word** Schlagwort *n;* Stichwort *n.*

catechism ['kætikizəm] Katechismus *m.*

categor|ical □ [kæti'gɔrikəl] kategorisch; **~y** ['kætigəri] Kategorie *f.*

cater ['keitə]: ~ *for* Lebensmittel liefern für; *fig.* sorgen für; **~ing** [.əriŋ] Verpflegung *f.*

caterpillar ['kætəpilə] *zo.* Raupe *f;* ⊕ Raupe(nschlepper *m*) *f.*

catgut ['kætgʌt] Darmsaite *f.*

cathedral [kə'θi:drəl] Dom *m,* Kathedrale *f.*

Catholic ['kæθəlik] 1. katholisch; 2. Katholik(in).

catkin ♀ ['kætkin] Kätzchen *n.*

cattish *fig.* ['kætiʃ] falsch.

cattle ['kætl] Vieh *n;* **~-breeding** Viehzucht *f;* **~-plague** *vet.* Rinderpest *f.* [catch 2.]

caught [kɔ:t] *pret. u. p.p. von*

ca(u)ldron ['kɔ:ldrən] Kessel *m.*

cauliflower ♀ ['kɔliflauə] Blumenkohl *m.*

caulk ⚓ [kɔ:k] kalfatern (*abdichten*).

caus|al □ ['kɔ:zəl] ursächlich; **~e** [kɔ:z] 1. Ursache *f,* Grund *m;* ⚖ Klage(grund *m*) *f;* Prozeß *m;* Angelegenheit *f,* Sache *f;* 2. verursachen, veranlassen; **~eless** □ ['kɔ:zlis] grundlos.

causeway ['kɔ:zwei] Damm *m.*

caustic ⨃ ['kɔ:stik] (~*ally*) ätzend; *fig.* beißend, scharf.

caution ['kɔ:ʃən] 1. Vorsicht *f;* Warnung *f;* Verwarnung *f;* ~ *money* Kaution *f;* 2. warnen; verwarnen.

cautious □ ['kɔ:ʃəs] behutsam, vorsichtig; **~ness** [.snis] Behutsamkeit *f,* Vorsicht *f.*

cavalry ✗ ['kævəlri] Reiterei *f.*

cave [keiv] 1. Höhle *f;* 2. *v/i.* ~ *in* einstürzen; klein beigeben.

cavern ['kævən] Höhle *f;* **~ous** *fig.* [.nəs] hohl.

cavil ['kævil] 1. Krittelei *f;* 2. kritteln (*at, about* an *dat.*).

cavity ['kæviti] Höhle *f;* Loch *n.*

cavort *Am.* F [kə'vɔ:t] sich aufbäumen, umherspringen.

caw [kɔ:] 1. krächzen; 2. Krächzen *n.*

cayuse *Am.* F ['kaiju:s] kleines (Indianer)Pferd.

cease [si:s] *v/i.* (*from*) aufhören (mit), ablassen (von); *v/t.* aufhören mit; **~less** □ ['si:slis] unaufhörlich.

cede [si:d] abtreten, überlassen.

ceiling ['si:liŋ] Zimmer-Decke *f;* *fig.* Höchstgrenze *f;* ~ *price* Höchstpreis *m.*

celebrat|e ['selibreit] feiern; **~ed** gefeiert, berühmt (*for* wegen); **~ion** [seli'breiʃən] Feier *f.*

celebrity [si'lebriti] Berühmtheit *f*.

celerity [si'leriti] Geschwindigkeit *f*.

celery ⚕ ['seləri] Sellerie *m, f*.

celestial □ [si'lestjəl] himmlisch.

cclibacy ['selibəsi] Ehelosigkeit *f*.

cell [sel] *allg.* Zelle *f*; ⚡ Element *n*.

cellar ['selə] Keller *m*.

cement [si'ment] 1. Zement *m*; Kitt *m*; 2. zementieren; (ver)kitten.

cemetery ['semitri] Friedhof *m*.

censor ['sensə] 1. Zensor *m*; 2. zensieren; **~ious** □ [sen'sɔːriəs] kritisch; kritt(e)lig; **~ship** ['sensəʃip] Zensur *f*; Zensoramt *n*.

censure ['senʃə] 1. Tadel *m*; Verweis *m*; 2. tadeln.

census ['sensəs] Volkszählung *f*.

cent [sent] Hundert *n*; *Am.* Cent *m* = ¹/₁₀₀ Dollar; *per* **~** Prozent *n*.

centenary [sen'tiːnəri] Hundertjahrfeier *f*.

centennial [sen'tenjəl] 1. hundertjährig; 2. hundertjähriges Jubiläum.

centi|grade ['sentigreid]: *10 degrees* **~** 10 Grad Celsius; **~metre**, *Am.* **~meter** Zentimeter *n, m*; **~pede** *zo.* [~ipiːd] Hundertfüßer *m*.

central □ ['sentrəl] zentral; **~ heating** Zentralheizung *f*; **~ office**, ⚡ **station** Zentrale *f*; **~ize** [~laiz] zentralisieren.

cent|re, *Am.* **~er** ['sentə] 1. Zentrum *n*, Mittelpunkt *m*; 2. zentral; 3. (sich) konzentrieren; zentralisieren; zentrieren.

century ['sentʃuri] Jahrhundert *n*.

cereal ['siəriəl] 1. Getreide...; 2. Getreide(pflanze *f*) *n*; Hafer-, Weizenflocken *f/pl.*; Corn-flakes *pl.*

cerebral *anat.* ['seribrəl] Gehirn...

ceremon|ial [seri'mounjəl] 1. □ *a.* **~ious** □ [~jəs] zeremoniell; förmlich; 2. Zeremoniell *n*; **~y** ['seriməni] Zeremonie *f*; Feierlichkeit *f*; Förmlichkeit(en *pl.*) *f*.

certain □ ['səːtn] sicher, gewiß; zuverlässig; bestimmt; gewisse(r, -s); **~ty** [~nti] Sicherheit *f*, Gewißheit *f*; Zuverlässigkeit *f*.

certi|ficate 1. [sə'tifikit] Zeugnis *n*, Schein *m*; **~** *of birth* Geburtsurkunde *f*; *medical* **~** ärztliches Attest; 2. [~keit] bescheinigen; **~fication** [səːtifi'keiʃən] Bescheinigung *f*; **~fy** ['səːtifai] *et.* bescheinigen; bezeugen; **~tude** [~itjuːd] Gewißheit *f*.

cessation [se'seiʃən] Aufhören *n*.

cession ['seʃən] Abtretung *f*.

cesspool ['sespuːl] Senkgrube *f*.

chafe [tʃeif] *v/t.* reiben; wundreiben; erzürnen; *v/i.* sich scheuern; sich wundreiben; toben.

chaff [tʃɑːf] 1. Spreu *f*; Häcksel *n*; F Neckerei *f*; 2. zu Häcksel schneiden; F necken.

chaffer ['tʃæfə] feilschen.

chaffinch ['tʃæfintʃ] Buchfink *m*.

chagrin ['ʃægrin] 1. Ärger *m*; 2. ärgern.

chain [tʃein] 1. Kette *f*; *fig.* Fessel *f*; **~** *store bsd. Am.* Kettenladen *m*, Zweiggeschäft *n*; 2. (an)ketten; *fig.* fesseln.

chair [tʃɛə] Stuhl *m*; Lehrstuhl *m*; Vorsitz *m*; *be in the* **~** den Vorsitz führen; **~man** ['tʃɛəmən] Vorsitzende(r) *m*; Präsident *m*.

chalice ['tʃælis] Kelch *m*.

chalk [tʃɔːk] 1. Kreide *f*; 2. mit Kreide (be)zeichnen; *mst* **~** *up* ankreiden; **~** *out* entwerfen.

challenge ['tʃælindʒ] 1. Herausforderung *f*; ⚔ Anruf *m*; *bsd.* ⚖ Ablehnung *f*; 2. herausfordern; anrufen; ablehnen; anzweifeln.

chamber ['tʃeimbə] *parl., zo.*, ⚕, ⊕, *Am.* Kammer *f*; **~s** *pl.* Geschäftsräume *m/pl.*; **~-maid** Zimmermädchen *n*.

chamois ['ʃæmwaː] 1. Gemse *f*; *a.* **~-leather** [*oft a.* 'ʃæmileðə] Wildleder *n*; 2. chamois (*gelbbraun*).

champagne [ʃæm'pein] Champagner *m*.

champion ['tʃæmpjən] 1. Vorkämpfer *m*, Verfechter *m*; Verteidiger *m*; *Sport*: Meister *m*; 2. verteidigen; kämpfen für; *fig.* stützen; 3. großartig; **~ship** Meisterschaft *f*.

chance [tʃɑːns] 1. Zufall *m*; Schicksal *n*; Glück(sfall *m*) *n*; Chance *f*; Aussicht *f* (*of* auf *acc.*); (günstige) Gelegenheit; Möglichkeit *f*; *by* **~** zufällig; *take a* **~** *take one's* **~** es darauf ankommen lassen; 2. zufällig; gelegentlich; 3. *v/i.* geschehen; sich ereignen; **~** *upon* stoßen auf (*acc.*); *v/t.* F wagen.

chancellor ['tʃɑːnsələ] Kanzler *m*.

chancery ['tʃɑːnsəri] Kanzleigericht *n*; *fig. in* **~** in der Klemme.

chandelier [ʃændi'liə] Lüster *m*.

chandler ['tʃɑːndlə] Krämer *m*.

change [tʃeindʒ] 1. Veränderung *f*, Wechsel *m*, Abwechs(e)lung *f*; Tausch *m*; Wechselgeld *n*; Kleingeld *n*; 2. *v/t.* (ver)ändern; (aus-) wechseln, (aus-, ver)tauschen (*for* gegen); **~** *trains* umsteigen; *v/i.* sich ändern, wechseln; sich umziehen; **~able** □ ['tʃeindʒəbl] veränderlich; **~less** □ [~dʒlis] unveränderlich; **~ling** [~liŋ] Wechselbalg *m*; **~over** Umstellung *f*.

channel ['tʃænl] 1. Kanal *m*; Flußbett *n*; Rinne *f*; *fig.* Weg *m*; 2. furchen; aushöhlen.

chant [tʃɑːnt] 1. (Kirchen)Gesang *m*; *fig.* Singsang *m*; 2. singen.

chaos ['keiɔs] Chaos *n*.

chap[1] [tʃæp] 1. Riß *m*, Sprung *m*; 2. rissig machen *od.* werden.

chap[2] F [~] Bursche *m*, Kerl *m*, Junge *m*.

chap³ [˅] Kinnbacken m; ˅s pl.
Maul n; ⊕ Backen f/pl.
chapel ['tʃæpəl] Kapelle f; Gottesdienst m.
chaplain ['tʃæplin] Kaplan m.
chapter ['tʃæptə] Kapitel n; Am.
Orts-, Untergruppe f e-r Vereinigung.
char [tʃɑː] verkohlen.
character ['kærɪktə] Charakter m;
Merkmal n; Schrift(zeichen n) f;
Sinnesart f; Persönlichkeit f; Original n; thea., Roman: Person f;
Rang m, Würde f; (bsd. guter) Ruf;
Zeugnis n; ˷istic [kærɪktə'ristik]
1. (˷ally) charakteristisch (of für);
2. Kennzeichen n; ˷ize ['kærɪktə-
raiz] charakterisieren.
charcoal ['tʃɑːkoul] Holzkohle f.
charge [tʃɑːdʒ] 1. Ladung f; fig.
Last f (on für); Verwahrung f,
Obhut f; Schützling m; Mündel m,
f, n; Amt n, Stelle f; Auftrag m,
Befehl m; Angriff m; Ermahnung f;
Beschuldigung f, Anklage f; Preis
m, Forderung f; ˷s pl. ✝ Kosten
pl.; be in ˷ of et. in Verwahrung
haben; mit et. beauftragt sein; für
et. sorgen; 2. v/t. laden; beladen,
belasten; beauftragen; j-m et. einschärfen, befehlen; ermahnen; beschuldigen, anklagen (with gen.);
zuschreiben (on, upon dat.); fordern, verlangen; an-, berechnen, in
Rechnung stellen (to dat.); angreifen (a. v/i.); behaupten.
chariot poet. od. hist. ['tʃæriət]
Streit-, Triumphwagen m.
charitable □ ['tʃæritəbl] mild(tätig),
wohltätig.
charity ['tʃæriti] Nächstenliebe f;
Wohltätigkeit f; Güte f; Nachsicht
f; milde Gabe.
charlatan ['ʃɑːlətən] Marktschreier
m.
charm [tʃɑːm] 1. Zauber m; fig.
Reiz m; 2. bezaubern; fig. entzücken; ˷ing □ ['tʃɑːmiŋ] be-
zaubernd.
chart [tʃɑːt] 1. ⚓ Seekarte f; Tabelle f; 2. auf e-r Karte einzeichnen.
charter ['tʃɑːtə] 1. Urkunde f;
Freibrief m; Patent n; Fracht-
vertrag m; 2. privilegieren; ⚓, ✈
chartern, mieten.
charwoman ['tʃɑːwumən] Putz-,
Reinemachefrau f.
chary □ ['tʃɛəri] vorsichtig.
chase [tʃeis] 1. Jagd f; Verfolgung f;
gejagtes Wild; 2. jagen, hetzen;
Jagd machen auf (acc.).
chasm ['kæzəm] Kluft f (a. fig.);
Lücke f.
chaste □ [tʃeist] rein, keusch, un-
schuldig; schlicht (Stil).
chastise [tʃæs'taiz] züchtigen.
chastity ['tʃæstiti] Keuschheit f.
chat³ [tʃæt] 1. Geplauder n, Plauderei f; 2. plaudern.

chattels ['tʃætlz] pl. mst goods and ˷
Hab n und Gut n; Vermögen n.
chatter ['tʃætə] 1. plappern; schnattern; klappern; 2. Geplapper n;
˷box F Plaudertasche f; ˷er [˷ərə]
Schwätzer(in).
chatty ['tʃæti] gesprächig.
chauffeur ['ʃoufə] Chauffeur m.
chaw sl. [tʃɔː] kauen; ˷ up Am.
mst fig. fix und fertig machen.
cheap □ [tʃiːp] billig; fig. gemein; ˷en ['tʃiːpən] (sich) ver-
billigen; fig. herabsetzen.
cheat [tʃiːt] 1. Betrug m, Schwindel
m; Betrüger(in); 2. betrügen.
check [tʃek] 1. Schach(stellung f) n;
Hemmnis n (on für); Zwang m,
Aufsicht f; Kontrolle f (on gen.);
Kontrollmarke f; Am. (Gepäck-)
Schein m; Am. ✝ = cheque; Am.
Rechnung f im Restaurant; ka-
rierter Stoff; 2. v/i. an-, innehalten,
Am. e-n Scheck ausstellen; ˷ in
Am. (in e-m Hotel) absteigen; ˷ out
Am. das Hotel (nach Bezahlung der
Rechnung) verlassen; v/t. hemmen;
kontrollieren; nachprüfen; Kleider
in der Garderobe abgeben; Am.
Gepäck aufgeben; ˷er ['tʃekə] Auf-
sichtsbeamte(r) m; ˷s pl. Am.
Damespiel n; ˷ing-room [˷kiŋrum]
Am. Gepäckaufbewahrung f; ˷
mate 1. Schachmatt n; 2. matt setzen; ˷up Am. scharfe Kontrolle.
cheek [tʃiːk] Backe f, Wange f; F
Unverschämtheit f; cheeky F
['tʃiːki] frech.
cheer [tʃiə] 1. Stimmung f, Fröhlichkeit f; Hoch(ruf m) n; Bei-
fall(sruf) m; Speisen f/pl., Mahl n;
three ˷s! dreimal hoch!; 2. v/t. a.
˷ up aufheitern; mit Beifall begrüßen; a. ˷ on anspornen; v/i.
hoch rufen; jauchzen; a. ˷ up Mut
fassen; ˷ful □ ['tʃiəful] heiter;
˷io [˷əri'ou] mach's gut!,
tschüs!; prosit!; ˷less [˷əlis]
freudlos; ˷y □ [˷əri] heiter, froh.
cheese [tʃiːz] Käse m.
chef [ʃef] Küchenchef m.
chemical ['kemikəl] 1. □ chemisch;
2. ˷s pl. Chemikalien pl.
chemise [ʃi'miːz] (Frauen)Hemd n.
chemist ['kemist] Chemiker(in);
Apotheker m; Drogist m; ˷ry [˷tri]
˷ Chemie f.
cheque ✝ [tʃek] Scheck m; crossed ˷
Verrechnungsscheck m.
chequer ['tʃekə] 1. mst ˷s pl. Karo-
muster n; 2. karieren; ˷ed ge-
würfelt; fig. bunt.
cherish ['tʃeriʃ] hegen, pflegen.
cherry ['tʃeri] Kirsche f.
chess [tʃes] Schach(spiel) n; ˷
board ['tʃesbɔːd] Schachbrett n;
˷man Schachfigur f.
chest [tʃest] Kiste f, Lade f; anat.
Brustkasten m; ˷ of drawers Kommode f.

chestnut ['tʃesnʌt] **1.** ⚘ Kastanie f; F alter Witz; **2.** kastanienbraun.

chevy F ['tʃevi] **1.** Hetzjagd f; Barlaufspiel n; **2.** hetzen, jagen.

chew [tʃu:] kauen; sinnen; ~ the fact od. rag Am. sl. die Sache durchkauen; ~ing-gum ['tʃu(:)ɪŋgʌm] Kaugummi m.

chicane [ʃi'kein] **1.** Schikane f; **2.** schikanieren.

chicken ['tʃikin] Hühnchen n, Küken n; ~hearted furchtsam, feige; ~pox ✲ [~npɔks] Windpocken f/pl.

chid [tʃid] pret. u. p.p. von chide; ~den ['tʃidn] p.p. von chide.

chide lit. [tʃaid] [irr.] schelten.

chief [tʃi:f] **1.** □ oberst; Ober...; Haupt...; hauptsächlich; ~ clerk Bürovorsteher m; **2.** Oberhaupt n, Chef m; Häuptling m; ...-in~ Ober...; ~tain ['tʃi:ftən] Häuptling m.

chilblain ['tʃilblein] Frostbeule f.

child [tʃaild] Kind n; from a ~ von Kindheit an; with ~ schwanger; ~birth ['tʃaildbə:θ] Niederkunft f; ~hood [~dhud] Kindheit f; ~ish □ [~diʃ] kindlich; kindisch; ~like kindlich; ~ren ['tʃildrən] pl. v. child.

chill [tʃil] **1.** eisig, frostig; **2.** Frost m, Kälte f; ✲ Fieberfrost m; Erkältung f; **3.** v/t. erkalten lassen; abkühlen; v/i. erkalten; erstarren; ~y ['tʃili] kalt, frostig.

chime [tʃaim] **1.** Glockenspiel n; Geläut n; fig. Einklang m; **2.** läuten; fig. harmonieren, übereinstimmen.

chimney ['tʃimni] Schornstein m; Rauchfang m; Lampen-Zylinder m; ~sweep(er) Schornsteinfeger m.

chin [tʃin] **1.** Kinn n; take it on the ~ Am. F es standhaft ertragen; **2.**: ~ o.s. Am. e-n Klimmzug machen.

china ['tʃainə] Porzellan n.

Chinese ['tʃai'ni:z] **1.** chinesisch; **2.** Chinese(n pl.) m, Chinesin f.

chink [tʃiŋk] Ritz m, Spalt m.

chip [tʃip] **1.** Schnitzel n, Stückchen n; Span m; Glas- etc. Splitter m; Spielmarke f; have a ~ on one's shoulder Am. F aggressiv sein; ~s pl. Pommes frites pl.; **2.** v/t. schnitzeln; an-, abschlagen; v/i. abbröckeln; ~muck ['tʃipmʌk], ~munk [~ʌŋk] nordamerikanisches gestreiftes Eichhörnchen.

chirp [tʃə:p] **1.** zirpen; zwitschern; **2.** Gezirp n.

chisel ['tʃizl] **1.** Meißel m; **2.** meißeln; sl. (be)mogeln.

chit-chat ['tʃittʃæt] Geplauder n.

chivalr|ous □ ['ʃivəlrəs] ritterlich; ~y [~ri] Ritterschaft f, Rittertum n; Ritterlichkeit f.

chive ⚘ ['tʃaiv] Schnittlauch m.

chlor|ine ['klɔ:ri:n] Chlor n; ~oform ['klɔrəfɔ:m] **1.** Chloroform n; **2.** chloroformieren.

chocolate ['tʃɔkəlit] Schokolade f.

choice [tʃɔis] **1.** Wahl f; Auswahl f; **2.** □ auserlesen, vorzüglich.

choir ['kwaiə] Chor m.

choke [tʃouk] **1.** v/t. (er)würgen, (a. v/i.) ersticken; ✄ (ab)drosseln; (ver)stopfen; mst ~ down hinunterwürgen; **2.** Erstickungsanfall m; ⊕ Würgung f; mot. Choke m, Starterklappe f.

choose [tʃu:z] [irr.] (aus)wählen; ~ to inf. vorziehen zu inf.

chop [tʃɔp] **1.** Hieb m; Kotelett n; ~s pl. Maul n, Rachen m; ⊕ Backen f/pl.; **2.** v/t. hauen, hacken; zerhacken; austauschen; v/i. wechseln; ~per ['tʃɔpə] Hackmesser n; ~py [~pi] unstet; unruhig (See); böig (Wind).

choral □ ['kɔ:rəl] chormäßig; Chor...; ~(e) ♪ [kɔ'rɑ:l] Choral m.

chord [kɔ:d] Saite f; Akkord m.

chore Am. [tʃɔ:] Hausarbeit f (mst pl.).

chorus ['kɔrəs] **1.** Chor m; Kehrreim m; **2.** im Chor singen od. sprechen.

chose [tʃouz] pret. von choose; ~n ['tʃouzn] p.p. von choose.

chow Am. sl. [tʃau] Essen n.

Christ [kraist] Christus m.

christen ['krisn] taufen; ~ing [~niŋ] Taufe f; attr. Tauf...

Christian ['kristjən] **1.** □ christlich; ~ name Vor-, Taufname m; **2.** Christ(in); ~ity [kristi'æniti] Christentum n.

Christmas ['krisməs] Weihnachten n.

chromium ['kroumjəm] Chrom n (Metall); ~plated verchromt.

chronic ['krɔnik] (~ally) chronisch (mst ✲), dauernd; sl. ekelhaft; ~le [~kl] **1.** Chronik f; **2.** aufzeichnen.

chronolog|ical □ [krɔnə'lɔdʒikəl] chronologisch; ~y [krɔ'nɔlədʒi] Zeitrechnung f; Zeitfolge f.

chubby F ['tʃʌbi] rundlich; pausbäckig; plump (a. fig.).

chuck¹ [tʃʌk] **1.** Glucken n; my ~! mein Täubchen!; **2.** glucken.

chuck² F [~] **1.** schmeißen; **2.** (Hinaus)Wurf m.

chuckle ['tʃʌkl] kichern, glucksen.

chum F [tʃʌm] **1.** (Stuben)Kamerad m; **2.** zs.-wohnen.

chump F [tʃʌmp] Holzklotz m.

chunk F [tʃʌŋk] Klotz m.

church [tʃə:tʃ] Kirche f; attr. Kirch(en)...; ~ service Gottesdienst m; ~warden ['tʃə:tʃ'wɔ:dn] Kirchenvorsteher m; ~yard Kirchhof m.

churl [tʃə:l] Grobian m; Flegel m; ~ish □ ['tʃə:liʃ] grob, flegelhaft.

churn [tʃə:n] **1.** Butterfaß n; **2.** buttern; aufwühlen.

chute [ʃu:t] Stromschnelle f; Gleit-, Rutschbahn f; Fallschirm m.

cider ['saidə] Apfelmost *m.*

cigar [si'ga:] Zigarre *f.*

cigarette [sigə'ret] Zigarette *f*; **~-case** Zigarettenetui *n.*

cigar-holder [si'ga:houldə] Zigarrenspitze *f.*

cilia ['siliə] *pl.* (Augen)Wimpern *f*|*pl.*

cinch *Am. sl.* [sintʃ] sichere Sache.

cincture ['siŋktʃə] Gürtel *m*, Gurt *m.*

cinder ['sində] Schlacke *f*; **~s** *pl.* Asche *f*; **Qella** [sində'relə] Aschenbrödel *n*; **~-path** *Sport*: Aschenbahn *f.*

cine-camera ['sini'kæmərə] Filmkamera *f.*

cinema ['sinəmə] Kino *n*; Film *m.*

cinnamon ['sinəmən] Zimt *m.*

cipher ['saifə] 1. Ziffer *f*; Null *f* (*a. fig.*); Geheimschrift *f*, Chiffre *f*; 2. chiffrieren; (aus)rechnen.

circle ['sə:kl] 1. Kreis *m*; *Bekanntenetc.* Kreis *m*; Kreislauf *m*; *thea.* Rang *m*; Ring *m*; 2. (um)kreisen.

circuit ['sə:kit] Kreislauf *m*; ⚡ Stromkreis *m*; Rundreise *f*; Gerichtsbezirk *m*; ⚡ Rundflug *m*; **short ~;** ⚡ Kurzschluß *m*; **~ous** □ [sə(:)'kju(:)itəs] weitschweifig; Um...

circular ['sə:kjulə] 1. □ kreisförmig; Kreis...; **~ letter** Rundschreiben *n*; **~ note** ⚡ Kreditbrief *m*; 2. Rundschreiben *n*; Laufzettel *m.*

circulat|e ['sə:kjuleit] *v/i.* umlaufen, zirkulieren; *v/t.* in Umlauf setzen; **~ing** [~tiŋ]: **~ library** Leihbücherei *f*; **~ion** [sə:kju'leiʃən] Zirkulation *f*, Kreislauf *m*; *fig.* Umlauf *m*; Verbreitung *f*; *Zeitungs-*Auflage *f.*

circum|... ['sə:kəm] (her)um...; **~ference** [sə'kʌmfərəns] (Kreis-) Umfang *m*, Peripherie *f*; **~jacent** [sə:kəm'dʒeisənt] umliegend; **~locution** [~mlə'kju:ʃən] Umständlichkeit *f*; Weitschweifigkeit *f*; **~navigate** [~m'nævigeit] umschiffen; **~scribe** ['sə:kəmskraib] ⚡ umschreiben; *fig.* begrenzen; **~spect** □ [~spekt] um-, vorsichtig; **~stance** [~stəns] Umstand *m* (~s *pl. a.* Verhältnisse *n*|*pl.*); Einzelheit *f*; Umständlichkeit *f*; **~stantial** □ [sə:kəm'stænʃəl] umständlich; **~ evidence** ⚡ Indizienbeweis *m*; **~vent** [~m'vent] überlisten; vereiteln.

circus ['sə:kəs] Zirkus *m*; (runder) Platz.

cistern ['sistən] Wasserbehälter *m.*

cit|ation [sai'teiʃən] Vorladung *f*; Anführung *f*, Zitat *n*; *Am. öffentliche* Ehrung; **~e** [sait] ⚡ vorladen; anführen; zitieren.

citizen ['sitizn] (Staats)Bürger(in); Städter(in); **~ship** [~nʃip] Bürgerrecht *n*, Staatsangehörigkeit *f.*

citron ['sitrən] Zitrone *f.*

city ['siti] 1. Stadt *f*; **the Q** die City, das Geschäftsviertel; 2. städtisch, Stadt...; **Q article** Börsen-, Handelsbericht *m*; **~ editor** *Am.* Lokalredakteur *m*; **~ hall** *Am.* Rathaus *n*; **~ manager** *Am.* Oberstadtdirektor *m.*

civic ['sivik] (staats)bürgerlich; städtisch; **~s** *sg.* Staatsbürgerkunde *f.*

civil □ ['sivl] bürgerlich, Bürger...; zivil; ⚡ zivilrechtlich; höflich; **Q Servant** Verwaltungsbeamt|e(r) *m*, -in *f*; **Q Service** Staatsdienst *m*; **~ian** ⚔ [si'viljən] Zivilist *m*; **~ity** [~liti] Höflichkeit *f*; **~ization** [sivilai'zeiʃən] Zivilisation *f*, Kultur *f*; **~ize** ['sivilaiz] zivilisieren.

clad [klæd] 1. *pret. u. p.p. von clothe*; 2. *adj.* gekleidet.

claim [kleim] 1. Anspruch *m*; Anrecht *n* (**to** auf *acc.*); Forderung *f*; *Am.* Parzelle *f*; 2. beanspruchen; fordern; sich berufen auf (*acc.*); **~ to be** sich ausgeben für; **~ant** ['kleimənt] Beanspruchende(r *m*) *f*; ⚡ Kläger *m.*

clairvoyant(e) [kleə'vɔiənt] Hellseher(in).

clamber ['klæmbə] klettern.

clammy □ ['klæmi] feuchtkalt, klamm.

clamo(u)r ['klæmə] 1. Geschrei *n*, Lärm *m*; 2. schreien (*for* nach).

clamp ⊕ [klæmp] 1. Klammer *f*; 2. verklammern; befestigen.

clan [klæn] Clan *m*, Sippe *f* (*a. fig.*).

clandestine □ [klæn'destin] heimlich; Geheim...

clang [klæŋ] 1. Klang *m*, Geklirr *n*; 2. schallen; klirren (lassen).

clank [klæŋk] 1. Gerassel *n*, Geklirr *n*; 2. rasseln, klirren (mit).

clap [klæp] 1. Klatschen *n*; Schlag *m*, Klaps *m*; 2. schlagen (mit) klatschen; **~board** *Am.* ['klæpbɔ:d] Schaltbrett *n*; **~trap** Effekthascherei *f.*

claret ['klærət] roter Bordeaux; *allg.* Rotwein *m*; Weinrot *n*; *sl.* Blut *n.*

clarify ['klærifai] *v/t.* (ab)klären; *fig.* klären; *v/i.* sich klären.

clarity ['klæriti] Klarheit *f.*

clash [klæʃ] 1. Geklirr *n*; Zs.-stoß *m*; Widerstreit *m*; 2. klirren (mit) zs.-stoßen.

clasp [kla:sp] 1. Haken *m*, Klammer *f*; Schnalle *f*; Spange *f*; *fig.* Umklammerung *f*; Umarmung *f*; 2. *v/t.* an-, zuhaken; *fig.* umklammern; umfassen; *v/i.* festhalten; **~-knife** ['kla:sp'naif] Taschenmesser *n.*

class [kla:s] 1. Klasse *f*; Stand *m*; (Unterrichts)Stunde *f*; Kurs *m*; *Am. univ.* Jahrgang *m*; 2. (in Klassen) einteilen, einordnen.

classic ['klæsik] Klassiker *m*; **~s**

pl. die alten Sprachen; ~(al □) [~k(əl)] klassisch.

classi|fication [klæsifi'keiʃən] Klassifizierung *f*, Einteilung *f*; ~**fy** ['klæsifai] klassifizieren, einstufen.

clatter ['klætə] 1. Geklapper *n*; 2. klappern (mit); *fig.* schwatzen.

clause [klɔ:z] Klausel *f*, Bestimmung *f*; *gr.* (Neben)Satz *m*.

claw [klɔ:] 1. Klaue *f*, Kralle *f*, Pfote *f*; *Krebs*-Schere *f*; 2. (zer-) kratzen; (um)krallen.

clay [klei] Ton *m*; *fig.* Erde *f*.

clean [kli:n] 1. *adj.* □ rein; sauber; 2. *adv.* rein, völlig; 3. reinigen (*of* von); sich waschen lassen (*Stoff etc.*); ~ up aufräumen; ~**er** ['kli:nə] Reiniger *m*; *mst* ~*s pl.* (chemische) Reinigung; ~**ing** [~niŋ] Reinigung *f*; ~**liness** ['klenlinis] Reinlichkeit *f*; ~**ly** 1. *adv.* ['kli:nli] rein; sauber; 2. *adj.* ['klenli] reinlich; ~**se** [klenz] reinigen; säubern.

clear [kliə] 1. □ klar; hell, rein; *fig.* rein (*from* von); frei (*of* von); ganz, voll; † rein, netto; 2. *v/t.* er-, aufhellen; (auf)klären; reinigen (*of, from* von); *Wald* lichten, roden; wegräumen (*a.* ~ *away od. off*); *Hindernis* nehmen; *Rechnung* bezahlen; † (aus)klarieren, verzollen; ⚖ freisprechen; befreien; rechtfertigen (*from* von); *v/i.* *a.* ~ *up* sich aufhellen; sich verziehen; ~**ance** ['kliərəns] Aufklärung *f*; Freilegung *f*; Räumung *f*; † Abrechnung *f*; ⚓, † Verzollung *f*; ~**ing** [~riŋ] Aufklärung *f*; Lichtung *f*, Rodung *f*; † Ab-, Verrechnung *f*; ⚓ *House* Ab-, Verrechnungsstelle *f*.

cleave[1] [kli:v] [*irr.*] (sich) spalten; *Wasser, Luft* (zer)teilen.

cleave[2] [~] *fig.* festhalten (*to an dat.*); treu bleiben (*dat.*).

cleaver ['kli:və] Hackmesser *n*.

clef ♪ [klef] Schlüssel *m*.

cleft [kleft] 1. Spalte *f*; Sprung *m*, Riß *m*; 2. *pret. u. p.p. von* cleave[1].

clemen|cy ['klemənsi] Milde *f*; ~**t** □ [~nt] mild.

clench [klentʃ] *Lippen etc.* fest zs.-pressen; *Zähne* zs.-beißen; *Faust* ballen; festhalten.

clergy ['klə:dʒi] Geistlichkeit *f*; ~**man** Geistliche(r) *m*.

clerical 1. □ geistlich; Schreib(er)...; 2. Geistliche(r) *m*.

clerk [klɑ:k] Schreiber(in), Büroangestellte(r *m*) *f*; Sekretär(in); † kaufmännische(r) Angestellte(r); *Am.* Verkäufer(in); Küster *m*.

clever □ ['klevə] gescheit; geschickt.

clew [klu:] Knäuel *m*, *n*; = clue.

click [klik] 1. Knacken *n*; ⊕ Sperrhaken *m*, -klinke *f*; 2. knacken; zu-, einschnappen; klappen.

client ['klaiənt] Klient(in); Kund|e

m, -in *f*; ~**ele** [kli:ã:n'teil] Kundschaft *f*.

cliff [klif] Klippe *f*; Felsen *m*.

climate ['klaimit] Klima *n*.

climax ['klaimæks] 1. *rhet.* Steigerung *f*; Gipfel *m*, Höhepunkt *m*; 2. (sich) steigern.

climb [klaim] (er)klettern, (er-) klimmen, (er)steigen; ~**er** ['klaimə] Kletterer *m*, Bergsteiger(in); *fig.* Streber(in); ♣ Kletterpflanze *f*; ~**ing** [~miŋ] Klettern *n*; *attr.* Kletter...

clinch [klintʃ] 1. ⊕ Vernietung *f*; Festhalten *n*; *Boxen:* Umklammerung *f*; 2. *v/t.* vernieten; festmachen; *s.* clench; *v/i.* festhalten.

cling [kliŋ] [*irr.*] (to) festhalten (an *dat.*), sich klammern (an *acc.*); sich (an)schmiegen (an *acc.*); *j-m* anhängen.

clinic ['klinik] Klinik *f*; klinisches Praktikum; ~**al** □ [~kəl] klinisch.

clink [kliŋk] 1. Geklirr *n*; 2. klingen, klirren (lassen); klimpern mit; ~**er** ['kliŋkə] Klinker(stein) *m*.

clip[1] [klip] 1. Schur *f*; *at one* ~ *Am.* F auf einmal; 2. ab-, aus-, beschneiden; *Schafe etc.* scheren.

clip[2] [~] Klammer *f*; Spange *f*.

clipp|er ['klipə]: (*a. pair of*) ~*s pl.* Haarschneide-, Schermaschine *f*; Klipper *m*; ⚓ Schnellsegler *m*; 🛪 Verkehrsflugzeug *n*; ~**ings** [~piŋz] *pl.* Abfälle *m/pl.*; *Zeitungs- etc.* Ausschnitte *m/pl.*

cloak [klouk] 1. Mantel *m*; 2. *fig.* bemänteln, verhüllen; ~-**room** ['kloukrum] Garderobe(nraum *m*) *f*; Toilette *f*; 🚉 Gepäckabgabe *f*.

clock [klɔk] *Schlag-, Wand*-Uhr *f*; ~**wise** ['klɔkwaiz] im Uhrzeigersinn; ~**work** Uhrwerk *n*; *like* ~ wie am Schnürchen.

clod [klɔd] Erdklumpen *m*; *a.* ~**hopper** [~hɔpə] (Bauern)Tölpel *m*.

clog [klɔg] 1. Klotz *m*; Holzschuh *m*, Pantine *f*; 2. belasten; hemmen; (sich) verstopfen.

cloister ['klɔistə] Kreuzgang *m*; Kloster *n*.

close 1. □ [klous] geschlossen; verborgen; verschwiegen; knapp, eng; begrenzt; nah, eng; bündig; dicht; gedrängt; schwül; knickerig; genau; fest (*Griff*); ~ *by*, ~ *to* dicht bei; ~ *fight*, ~ *quarters pl.* Handgemenge *n*, Nahkampf *m*; ~(*ed*) *season*, ~ *time hunt.* Schonzeit *f*; *sail* ~ *to the wind fig.* sich hart an der Grenze des Erlaubten bewegen; 2. [klouz] Schluß *m*; Abschluß *m*; [klous] Einfriedung *f*; Hof *m*; 3. [klouz] *v/t.* ab-, ein-, ver-, zu-schließen; beschließen; *v/i.* (sich) schließen; abschließen; handgemein werden; ~ *in* hereinbrechen (*Nacht*); kürzer werden (*Tage*); ~ *on* (*prp.*) sich schließen um, umfassen; ~ness ['klousnis] Genauig-keit f, Geschlossenheit f.

closet ['klɔzit] 1. Kabinett n; (Wand)Schrank m; = water-~; 2.: be ~ed with mit j-m e-e geheime Beratung haben. [nahme f.]

close-up ['klousʌp] Film: Großauf-|

closure ['klouʒə] Verschluß m; parl. (Antrag m auf) Schluß m e-r De-batte.

clot [klɔt] 1. Klümpchen n; 2. zu Klümpchen gerinnen (lassen).

cloth [klɔθ] Stoff m, Tuch n; Tisch-tuch n; Kleidung f, Amts-Tracht f; the ~ F der geistliche Stand; lay the ~ den Tisch decken; ~-binding Leineneinband m; ~-bound in Lei-nen gebunden.

clothe [klouð] [irr.] (an-, be)kleiden; einkleiden.

clothes [klouðz] pl. Kleider n/pl.; Kleidung f; Anzug m; Wäsche f; ~-basket ['klouðzbɑːskit] Wasch-korb m; ~-line Wäscheleine f; ~-peg Kleiderhaken m; Wäsche-klammer f; ~-pin bsd. Am. Wäsche-klammer f; ~-press Kleider-, Wäscheschrank m.

clothier ['klouðiə] Tuch-, Kleider-händler m.

clothing ['klouðiŋ] Kleidung f.

cloud [klaud] 1. Wolke f (a. fig.); Trübung f; Schatten m; 2. (sich) be-, umwölken (a. fig.); ~-burst ['klaudbəːst] Wolkenbruch m; ~-less □ ~dlis] wolkenlos; ~y □ ~di] wolkig; Wolken...; trüb; unklar.

clout [klaut] Lappen m; F Kopf-nuß f.

clove[1] [klouv] (Gewürz)Nelke f.

clove[2] [~] pret. von cleave[1]; ~n ['klouvn] 1. p.p. von cleave[1]; 2. adj. gespalten.

clover ♣ ['klouvə] Klee m.

clown [klaun] Hanswurst m; Tölpel m; ~ish □ ['klauniʃ] bäurisch; plump; clownhaft.

cloy [klɔi] übersättigen, überladen.

club [klʌb] 1. Keule f; (Gummi-)Knüppel m; Klub m; ~s pl. Karten: Kreuz n; 2. v/t. mit e-r Keule schlagen; v/i. sich zs.-tun; ~-foot ['klʌbfut] Klumpfuß m.

clue [kluː] Anhaltspunkt m, Finger-zeig m.

clump [klʌmp] 1. Klumpen m; Baum-Gruppe f; 2. trampeln; zs.-drängen.

clumsy □ ['klʌmzi] unbeholfen, un-geschickt; plump.

clung [klʌŋ] pret. u. p.p. von cling.

cluster ['klʌstə] 1. Traube f; Büschel n; Haufen m; 2. büschel-weise wachsen; (sich) zs.-drängen.

clutch [klʌtʃ] 1. Griff m; ⊕ Kupp-lung f; Klaue f; 2. (er)greifen.

clutter ['klʌtə] 1. Wirrwarr m; 2. durch-ea.-rennen; durch-ea.-bringen.

coach [koutʃ] 1. Kutsche f; ⛌ Wagen m; Reisebus m; Einpauker m; Trainer m; 2. in e-r Kutsche fahren; (ein)pauken; trainieren; ~man ['koutʃmən] Kutscher m.

coagulate [kou'ægjuleit] gerinnen (lassen).

coal [koul] 1. (Stein)Kohle f; carry ~s to Newcastle Eulen nach Athen tragen; 2. ♣ (be)kohlen.

coalesce [kouə'les] zs.-wachsen; sich vereinigen.

coalition [kouə'liʃən] Verbindung f; Bund m, Koalition f.

coal-pit ['koulpit] Kohlengrube f.

coarse □ [kɔːs] grob; ungeschliffen.

coast [koust] 1. Küste f; bsd. Am. Rodelbahn f; 2. die Küste entlang-fahren; im Freilauf fahren; rodeln; ~er ['koustə] Am. Rodelschlitten; ♣ Küstenfahrer m.

coat [kout] 1. Jackett n, Jacke f, Rock m; Mantel m; Pelz m, Ge-fieder n; Überzug m; ~ of arms Wappen(schild m, n) n; 2. über-ziehen; anstreichen; ~-hanger ['kouthæŋə] Kleiderbügel m; ~ing ['koutiŋ] Überzug m; Anstrich m; Mantelstoff m.

coax [kouks] schmeicheln (dat.); be-schwatzen (into zu).

cob [kɔb] kleines starkes Pferd; Schwan m; Am. Maiskolben m.

cobbler ['kɔblə] Schuhmacher m; Stümper m.

cobweb ['kɔbweb] Spinn(en)ge-webe n.

cock [kɔk] 1. Hahn m; Anführer m; Heuhaufen m; 2. a. ~ up aufrichten; Gewehrhahn spannen.

cockade [kɔ'keid] Kokarde f.

cockatoo [kɔkə'tuː] Kakadu m.

cockboat ['kɔkbout] Jolle f.

cockchafer ['kɔktʃeifə] Maikäfer m.

cock|-eyed sl. ['kɔkaid] schieläugig; Am. blau (betrunken); ~-horse Steckenpferd n.

cockney ['kɔkni] waschechter Lon-doner.

cockpit ['kɔkpit] Kampfplatz m für Hähne; ♣ Raumdeck n; ⚔ Führer-raum m, Kanzel f.

cockroach zo. ['kɔkroutʃ] Schabe f.

cock|sure F ['kɔk'ʃuə] absolut sicher; überheblich; ~tail Cocktail m; ~y □ F ['kɔki] selbstbewußt; frech.

coco ['koukou] Kokospalme f.

cocoa ['koukou] Kakao m.

coco-nut ['koukənʌt] Kokosnuß f.

cocoon [kə'kuːn] Seiden-Kokon m.

cod [kɔd] Kabeljau m.

coddle ['kɔdl] verhätscheln.

code [koud] 1. Gesetzbuch n; Kodex m; Telegramm-, Signal-Schlüssel m; 2. chiffrieren.

codger F ['kɔdʒə] komischer Kauz.

cod-liver ['kɔdlivə]: ~ oil Lebertran m.

co-ed *Am.* F ['kou'ed] Schülerin *f* e-r Koedukationsschule, *allg.* Studentin *f*.

coerc|e [kou'ə:s] (er)zwingen; **~ion** [kou'ə:ʃən] Zwang *m*.

coeval □ [kou'i:vəl] gleichzeitig; glcichalt(e)rig.

coexist ['kouig'zist] gleichzeitig bestehen.

coffee ['kɔfi] Kaffee *m*; **~-pot** Kaffeekanne *f*; **~-room** Speisesaal *m* e-s Hotels; **~-set** Kaffeeservice *n*.

coffer ['kɔfə] (Geld)Kasten *m*.

coffin ['kɔfin] Sarg *m*.

cogent □ ['koudʒənt] zwingend.

cogitate ['kɔdʒiteit] *v/i*. nachdenken; *v/t*. (er)sinnen.

cognate ['kɔgneit] verwandt.

cognition [kɔg'niʃən] Erkenntnis *f*.

cognizable ['kɔgnizəbl] erkennbar.

coheir ['kou'ɛə] Miterbe *m*.

coheren|ce [kou'hiərəns] Zs.-hang *m*; **~t** □ [~nt] zs.-hängend.

cohesi|on [kou'hi:ʒən] Kohäsion *f*; **~ve** [~i:siv] (fest) zs.-hängend.

coiff|eur [kwɑ:'fə:] Friseur *m*; **~ure** [~'fjuə] Frisur *f*.

coil [kɔil] **1.** *a.* **~ up** aufwickeln; (sich) zs.-rollen; **2.** Rolle *f*, Spirale *f*; Wicklung *f*; ⚡ Spule *f*; Windung *f*; ⊕ (Rohr)Schlange *f*.

coin [kɔin] **1.** Münze *f*; **2.** prägen (*a. fig.*); münzen; **~age** ['kɔinidʒ] Prägung *f*; Geld *n*, Münze *f*.

coincide [kouin'said] zs.-treffen; übereinstimmen; **~nce** [kou'insidəns] Zs.-treffen *n*; *fig.* Übereinstimmung *f*.

coke [kouk] Koks *m* (*a. sl.* = Kokain*); Am.* F Coca-Cola *n*, *f*.

cold [kould] **1.** □ kalt; **2.** Kälte *f*, Frost *m*; Erkältung *f*; **~ness** ['kouldnis] Kälte *f*.

coleslaw *Am.* ['koulslɔ:] Krautsalat *m*.

colic 𝒜 ['kɔlik] Kolik *f*.

collaborat|e [kə'læbəreit] zs.-arbeiten; **~ion** [kɔlæbə'reiʃən] Zs.-, Mitarbeit *f*; in ~ gemeinsam.

collaps|e [kə'læps] **1.** zs.-, einfallen; zs.-brechen; **2.** Zs.-bruch *m*; **~ible** [~səbl] zs.-klappbar.

collar ['kɔlə] **1.** Kragen *m*; Halsband *n*; Kum(me)t *n*; ⊕ Lager *n*; **2.** beim Kragen packen; *Fleisch* zs.-rollen; **~-bone** Schlüsselbein *n*; **~-stud** Kragenknopf *m*.

collate [kɔ'leit] *Texte* vergleichen.

collateral [kɔ'lætərəl] **1.** □ parallel laufend; Seiten..., Neben...; indirekt; **2.** Seitenverwandte(r *m*) *f*.

colleague ['kɔli:g] Kolleg|e *m*, -in *f*.

collect 1. *eccl.* ['kɔlekt] Kollekte *f*; **2.** *v/t.* [kə'lekt] (ein)sammeln; *Gedanken etc.* sammeln; einkassieren; abholen; *v/i.* sich (ver)sammeln; **~ed** □ *fig.* gefaßt; **~ion** [~kʃən] Sammlung *f*; Einziehung *f*; **~ive** [~ktiv] gesammelt; Sammel...; ~

bargaining Tarifverhandlungen *f/pl.*; **~ively** [~vli] insgesamt; zs.-fassend; **~or** [~tə] Sammler *m*; Steuereinnehmer *m*; ⚡ Fahrkartenabnehmer *m*; ⚡ Stromabnehmer *m*.

college ['kɔlidʒ] College *n* (*Teil e-r Universität*); höhere Schule *od.* Lehranstalt *f*; Hochschule *f*; Akademie *f*; Kollegium *n*.

collide [kə'laid] zs.-stoßen.

collie ['kɔli] Collie *m*, schottischer Schäferhund.

collier ['kɔliə] Bergmann *m*; ⚓ Kohlenschiff *n*; **~y** ['kɔljəri] Kohlengrube *f*.

collision [kə'liʒən] Zs.-stoß *m*.

colloquial □ [kə'loukwiəl] umgangssprachlich, familiär.

colloquy ['kɔləkwi] Gespräch *n*.

colon *typ.* ['koulən] Doppelpunkt *m*.

colonel ✕ ['kə:nl] Oberst *m*.

coloni|al [kə'lounjəl] Kolonial...; **~alism** *pol.* [~lizəm] Kolonialismus *m*; **~ze** ['kɔlənaiz] kolonisieren; (sich) ansiedeln; besiedeln.

colony ['kɔləni] Kolonie *f*; Siedlung *f*.

colossal □ [kə'lɔsl] kolossal.

colo(u)r ['kʌlə] **1.** Farbe *f*; *fig.* Färbung *f*; Anschein *m*; Vorwand *m*; **~s** *pl.* ✕ Fahne *f*, Flagge *f*; **2.** *v/t.* färben; anstreichen; *fig.* beschönigen; *v/i.* sich (ver)färben; erröten; **~-bar** Rassenschranke *f*; **~ed** gefärbt, farbig; ~ **man** Farbige(r) *m*; **~ful** [~əful] farbenreich, -freudig; lebhaft; **~ing** [~əriŋ] Färbung *f*; Farbton *m*; *fig.* Beschönigung *f*; **~less** □ [~əlis] farblos; ~ **line** *bsd. Am.* Rassenschranke *f*.

colt [koult] Hengstfüllen *n*; *fig.* Neuling *m*.

column ['kɔləm] Säule *f*; *typ.* Spalte *f*; ✕ Kolonne *f*; **~ist** *Am.* [~mnist] Kolumnist *m*.

comb [koum] **1.** Kamm *m*; ⊕ Hechel *f*; **2.** *v/t.* kämmen; striegeln; *Flachs* hecheln.

combat ['kɔmbət] **1.** Kampf *m*; single ~ Zweikampf *m*; **2.** (be-) kämpfen; **~ant** [~tənt] Kämpfer *m*.

combin|ation [kɔmbi'neiʃən] Verbindung *f*; *mst* **~s** *pl.* Hemdhose *f*; **~e** [kəm'bain] (sich) verbinden, vereinigen.

combust|ible [kəm'bʌstəbl] **1.** brennbar; **2.** **~s** *pl.* Brennmaterial *n*; *mot.* Betriebsstoff *m*; **~ion** [~tʃən] Verbrennung *f*.

come [kʌm] [*irr.*] kommen; to ~ künftig, kommend; ~ about zutragen; ~ across auf *j. od. et.* stoßen; ~ at erreichen; ~ by vorbeikommen; zu *et.* kommen; ~ down herunterkommen (*a. fig.*); *Am.* F erkranken (with *an dat.*); ~ for abholen; ~ off davonkommen; losgehen (*Knopf*), ausfallen (*Haare etc.*); stattfinden;

~ *round* vorbeikommen (*bsd. zu Besuch*); wiederkehren; F zu sich kommen; *fig.* einlenken; ~ *to adv.* dazukommen; ⚓ beidrehen; *prp.* betragen; ~ *up to* entsprechen (*dat.*); es *j-m* gleichtun; *Stand, Maß* erreichen; ~**back** ['kʌmbæk] Wiederkehr *f*, Comeback *n*; *Am. sl.* schlagfertige Antwort.

comedian [kə'miːdjən] Schauspieler(in); Komiker(in); Lustspieldichter *m*.

comedy ['kɔmidi] Lustspiel *n*.

comeliness ['kʌmlinis] Anmut *f*.

comfort ['kʌmfət] 1. Bequemlichkeit *f*; Behaglichkeit *f*; Trost *m*; *fig.* Beistand *m*; Erquickung *f*; 2. trösten; erquicken; beleben; ~**able** □ [~təbl] behaglich; bequem; tröstlich; ~**er** [~tə] Tröster *m*; *fig.* wollenes Halstuch; Schnuller *m*; *Am.* Steppdecke *f*; ⚓ ~**less** □ [~tlis] unbehaglich; trostlos; ~ **station** *Am.* Bedürfnisanstalt *f*.

comic(**al** □) ['kɔmik(əl)] komisch; lustig, drollig.

coming ['kʌmiŋ] 1. kommend; künftig; 2. Kommen *n*.

comma ['kɔmə] Komma *n*.

command [kə'maːnd] 1. Herrschaft *f*, Beherrschung *f* (*a. fig.*); Befehl *m*; ✗ Kommando *n*; be (*have*) *at* ~ zur Verfügung stehen (haben); 2. befehlen; ✗ kommandieren; verfügen über (*acc.*); beherrschen; ~**er** [~də] Kommandeur *m*, Befehlshaber *m*; ⚓ Fregattenkapitän *m*; ~**er-in-chief** [~ərin-'tʃiːf] Oberbefehlshaber *m*; ~**ment** [~dmənt] Gebot *n*.

commemorat|e [kə'meməreit] gedenken (*gen.*), feiern; ~**ion** [kəmemə'reiʃən] Gedächtnisfeier *f*.

commence [kə'mens] anfangen, beginnen; ~**ment** [~smənt] Anfang *m*.

commend [kə'mend] empfehlen;) [loben; anvertrauen.)

commensurable □ [kə'menʃərəbl] vergleichbar (*with, to* mit).

comment ['kɔment] 1. Kommentar *m*; Erläuterung *f*; An-, Bemerkung *f*; 2. (*upon*) erläutern (*acc.*); sich auslassen (über *acc.*); ~**ary** ['kɔməntəri] Kommentar *m*; ~**ator** ['kɔmənteitə] Kommentator *m*; *Radio:* Berichterstatter *m*.

commerc|e ['kɔmə(ː)s] Handel *m*; Verkehr *m*; ~**ial** □ [kə'məːʃəl] 1. kaufmännisch; Handels...; Geschäfts...; gewerbsmäßig; ~ *traveller* Handlungsreisende(r) *m*; 2. *bsd. Am. Radio, Fernsehen:* kommerzielle (Werbe)Sendung.

commiseration [kəmizə'reiʃən] Mitleid *n* (*for* mit).

commissary ['kɔmisəri] Kommissar *m*; ✗ Intendanturbeamte(r) *m*.

commission [kə'miʃən] 1. Auftrag *m*; Übertragung *f von Macht etc.*;

Begehung *f e-s Verbrechens*; Provision *f*; Kommission *f*; (Offiziers-) Patent *n*; 2. beauftragen; bevollmächtigen; ✗ bestallen; ⚓ in Dienst stellen; ~**er** [~ʃnə] Bevollmächtigte(r *m*) *f*; Kommissar *m*.

commit [kə'mit] anvertrauen; übergeben, überweisen; *Tat* begehen; bloßstellen; ~ (*o.s.* sich) verpflichten; ~ (*to prison*) in Untersuchungshaft nehmen; ~**ment** [~tmənt], ~**tal** [~tl] Überweisung *f*; Verpflichtung *f*; Verübung *f*; ~**tee** [~ti] Ausschuß *m*, Komitee *n*.

commodity [kə'mɔditi] Ware *f* (*mst pl.*), Gebrauchsartikel *m*.

common ['kɔmən] 1. □ (all)gemein; gewöhnlich; gemeinschaftlich; öffentlich; gemein (*niedrig*); ⚓ *Council* Gemeinderat *m*; 2. Gemeindewiese *f*; *in* ~ gemeinsam; *in* ~ *with fig.* genau wie; ~**er** [~ə] Bürger *m*, Gemeine(r) *m*; Mitglied *n* des Unterhauses; ~ *law* Gewohnheitsrecht *n*; ⚓ *Market* Gemeinsamer Markt; ~**place** 1. Gemeinplatz *m*; 2. gewöhnlich; F abgedroschen; ~**s** *pl.* das gemeine Volk; Gemeinschaftsverpflegung *f*; (*mst House of*) ⚓ Unterhaus *n*; ~ *sense* gesunder Menschenverstand; ~**wealth** [~nwelθ] Gemeinwesen *n*, Staat *m*; *bsd.* Republik *f*; *the British* ⚓ das Commonwealth.

commotion [kə'mouʃən] Erschütterung *f*; Aufruhr *m*; Aufregung *f*.

communal □ ['kɔmjunl] gemeinschaftlich; Gemeinde...

commune 1. [kə'mjuːn] sich vertraulich besprechen; 2. ['kɔmjuːn] Gemeinde *f*.

communicat|e [kə'mjuːnikeit] *v/t.* mitteilen; *v/i.* das Abendmahl nehmen, kommunizieren; in Verbindung stehen; ~**ion** [kəmjuːni'keiʃən] Mitteilung *f*; Verbindung *f*; ~**ive** [kə'mjuːnikətiv] gesprächig.

communion [kə'mjuːnjən] Gemeinschaft *f*; *eccl.* Kommunion *f*, Abendmahl *n*.

communis|m ['kɔmjunizəm] Kommunismus *m*; ~**t** [~ist] 1. Kommunist(in); 2. kommunistisch.

community [kə'mjuːniti] Gemeinschaft *f*; Gemeinde *f*; Staat *m*.

commut|ation [kɔmju(ː)'teiʃən] Vertauschung *f*; Umwandlung *f*; Ablösung *f*; Strafmilderung *f*; ~ *ticket Am.* Zeitkarte *f*; ~**e** [kə'mjuːt] ablösen; *Strafe* (mildernd) umwandeln; *Am.* pendeln *im Arbeitsverkehr.*

compact 1. ['kɔmpækt] Vertrag *m*; 2. [kəm'pækt] *adj.* dicht, fest; knapp, bündig; *v/t.* fest verbinden.

companion [kəm'pænjən] Gefährt|e *m*, -in *f*; Gesellschafter(in); ~**able** [~nəbl] gesellig; ~**ship** [~nʃip] Gesellschaft *f*.

company ['kʌmpəni] Gesellschaft f; Kompanie f; Handelsgesellschaft f; Genossenschaft f; ⚓ Mannschaft f; *thea.* Truppe f; *have* ~ Gäste haben; *keep* ~ *with* verkehren mit.

compar|able ☐ ['kɔmpərəbl] vergleichbar; ~ative [kəm'pærətiv] 1. ☐ vergleichend; verhältnismäßig; 2. *a.* ~ *degree gr.* Komparativ m; ~e [~'peə] 1.: *beyond* ~, *without* ~, *past* ~ unvergleichlich; 2. v/t. vergleichen; gleichstellen (*to* mit); v/i. sich vergleichen (lassen); ~ison [~'pærisn] Vergleich(ung f) m.

compartment [kəm'paːtmənt] Abteilung f; ⚔ Fach n; 🚂 Abteil m.

compass ['kʌmpəs] 1. Bereich m; ♪ Umfang m; Kompaß m; *oft pair of* ~es *pl.* Zirkel m; 2. herumgehen um; einschließen; erreichen; planen.

compassion [kəm'pæʃən] Mitleid n; ~ate ☐ [~nit] mitleidig.

compatible ☐ [kəm'pætəbl] vereinbar, verträglich; schicklich.

compatriot [kəm'pætriət] Landsmann m.

compel [kəm'pel] (er)zwingen.

compensat|e ['kɔmpenseit] *j-n* entschädigen; *et.* ersetzen; ausgleichen; ~ion [kɔmpən'seiʃən] Ersatz m; Ausgleich(ung f) m; Entschädigung f; *Am.* Vergütung f (*Gehalt*).

compère ['kɔmpeə] 1. Conférencier m; 2. ansagen (bei).

compete [kəm'piːt] sich mitbewerben (*for* um); konkurrieren.

competen|ce, ~**cy** ['kɔmpitəns, ~si] Befugnis f, Zuständigkeit f; Auskommen n; ~t ☐ [~nt] hinreichend; (leistungs)fähig; fachkundig; berechtigt, zuständig.

competit|ion [kɔmpi'tiʃən] Mitbewerbung f; Wettbewerb m; ♀ Konkurrenz f; ~ive [kəm'petitiv] wetteifernd; ~or [~tə] Mitbewerber (-in); Konkurrent(in).

compile [kəm'pail] zs.-tragen, zs.-stellen (*from* aus); sammeln.

complacen|ce, ~**cy** [kəm'pleisns, ~si] Selbstzufriedenheit f.

complain [kəm'plein] (sich be-) klagen; ~**ant** [~nənt] Kläger(in); ~t [~nt] Klage f, Beschwerde f; ⚕ Leiden n.

complaisan|ce [kəm'pleizənz] Gefälligkeit f; Entgegenkommen n; ~t ☐ [~nt] gefällig; entgegenkommend.

complement 1. ['kɔmplimənt] Ergänzung f; volle Anzahl; 2. [~ment] ergänzen.

complet|e [kəm'pliːt] 1. ☐ vollständig, ganz; vollkommen; 2. vervollständigen; vervollkommnen; abschließen; ~ion [~iːʃən] Vervollständigung f; Abschluß m; Erfüllung f.

complex ['kɔmpleks] 1. ☐ zs.-gesetzt; *fig.* kompliziert; 2. Gesamtheit f, Komplex m; ~ion [kəm'plekʃən] Aussehen n; Charakter m; Zug m; Gesichtsfarbe f, Teint m; ~ity [~ksiti] Kompliziertheit f.

complian|ce [kəm'plaiəns] Einwilligung f; Einverständnis n; *in* ~ *with* gemäß; ~t ☐ [~nt] gefällig.

complicate ['kɔmplikeit] komplizieren, erschweren.

complicity [kəm'plisiti] Mitschuld f (*in* an *dat.*).

compliment 1. ['kɔmplimənt] Kompliment n; Schmeichelei f; Gruß m; 2. [~ment] v/t. (*on*) beglückwünschen (zu); *j-m* Komplimente machen (über *acc.*); ~ary [kɔmpli'mentəri] höflich.

comply [kəm'plai] sich fügen; nachkommen, entsprechen (*with dat.*).

component [kəm'pounənt] 1. Bestandteil m; 2. zs.-setzend.

compos|e [kəm'pouz] zs.-setzen; komponieren, verfassen; ordnen; beruhigen; *typ.* setzen; ~ed ☐ ruhig, gesetzt; ~er [~zə] Komponist(in); Verfasser(in); ~ition [kɔmpə'ziʃən] Zs.-setzung f; Abfassung f; Komposition f; (Schrift-) Satz m; Aufsatz m; † Vergleich m; ~t ['kɔmpɔst] Kompost m; ~ure [kəm'pouʒə] Fassung f, Gemütsruhe f.

compound 1. ['kɔmpaund] zs.-gesetzt; ~ *interest* Zinseszinsen m/pl.; 2. Zs.-setzung f, Verbindung f; 3. [kəm'paund] v/t. zs.-setzen; *Streit* beilegen; v/i. sich einigen.

comprehend [kɔmpri'hend] umfassen; begreifen, verstehen.

comprehen|sible ☐ [kɔmpri'hensəbl] verständlich; ~sion [~nʃən] Verständnis n; Fassungskraft f; Umfang m; ~sive ☐ [~nsiv] umfassend.

compress [kəm'pres] zs.-drücken; ~ed *air* Druckluft f; ~ion [~eʃən] *phys.* Verdichtung f; ⊕ Druck m.

comprise [kəm'praiz] in sich fassen, einschließen, enthalten.

compromise ['kɔmprəmaiz] 1. Kompromiß m, n; 2. v/t. *Streit* beilegen; bloßstellen; v/i. e-n Kompromiß schließen.

compuls|ion [kəm'pʌlʃən] Zwang m; ~ory [~lsəri] obligatorisch; Zwangs...; Pflicht...

compunction [kəm'pʌŋkʃən] Gewissensbisse m/pl.; Reue f; Bedenken n.

comput|ation [kɔmpju(ː)'teiʃən] (Be)Rechnung f; ~e [kəm'pjuːt] (be-, er)rechnen; schätzen; ~er [~tə] Computer m.

comrade ['kɔmrid] Kamerad m.

con[1] *abbr.* [kɔn] = *contra.*

con² *Am. sl.* [⌣] **1.**: ~ man = confidence man; **2.** 'reinlegen (betrügen).

conceal [kən'si:l] verbergen; *fig.*
verhehlen, verheimlichen, ver-
schweigen.

concede [kən'si:d] zugestehen; ein-
räumen; gewähren, nachgeben.

conceit [kən'si:t] Einbildung *f*;
spitzfindiger Gedanke; übertriebe-
nes sprachliches Bild; ~ed □ eingebildet (of auf *acc.*).

conceiv|able □ [kən'si:vəbl] denk-
bar; begreiflich; ~e [kən'si:v] *v/i.*
empfangen (*schwanger werden*);
sich denken (of *acc.*); *v/t.* Kind
empfangen; sich denken; aussinnen.

concentrate ['kɔnsentreit] (sich)
zs.-ziehen, (sich) konzentrieren.

conception [kən'sepʃən] Begreifen
n; Vorstellung *f*, Begriff *m*, Idee *f*;
biol. Empfängnis *f*.

concern [kən'sə:n] **1.** Angelegenheit
f; Interesse *n*; Sorge *f*; Beziehung *f*
(with zu); ⚓ Geschäft *n*, (in-
dustrielles) Unternehmen; **2.** betreffen, angehen, interessieren; ~
o.s. about od. for sich kümmern um;
be ~ed in Betracht kommen; ~ed □
interessiert, beteiligt (in an *dat.*);
bekümmert; ~ing *prp.* [~niŋ] betreffend, über, wegen, hinsichtlich.

concert 1. ['kɔnsət] Konzert *n*;
2. [~sə(:)t] Einverständnis *n*;
3. [kən'sə:t] sich einigen, ~erab-
reden; ~ed gemeinsam; ♪ mehr-
stimmig.

concession [kən'seʃən] Zugeständ-
nis *n*; Erlaubnis *f*. [räumen.)

concessive □ [kən'sesiv] ein-)

conciliat|e [kən'silieit] aus-, ver-
söhnen; ausgleichen; ~or [~tə]
Vermittler *m*; ~ory [~iətəri] versöhnlich, vermittelnd.

concise □ [kən'sais] kurz, bündig,
knapp; ~ness [~snis] Kürze *f*.

conclude [kən'klu:d] schließen, beschließen; abschließen; folgern;
sich entscheiden; to be ~d Schluß
folgt.

conclusi|on [kən'klu:ʒən] Schluß *m*,
Ende *n*; Abschluß *m*; Folgerung *f*;
Beschluß *m*; ~ve □ [~u:siv]
schlüssig; endgültig.

concoct [kən'kɔkt] zs.-brauen; *fig.*
aussinnen; ~ion [~kʃən] Gebräu *n*;
fig. Erfindung *f*.

concord ['kɔnkɔ:d] Eintracht *f*;
Übereinstimmung *f* (*a. gr.*); ♪
Harmonie *f*; ~ant □ [kən'kɔ:dənt]
übereinstimmend; einstimmig; ♪
harmonisch.

concourse ['kɔnkɔ:s] Zusammen-,
Auflauf *m*; Menge *f*; *Am.* Bahn-
hofs-, Schalterhalle *f*.

concrete 1. ['kɔnkri:t] konkret; Beton...; **2.** [~] Beton *m*; **3.** [kən'kri:t]
zu e-r Masse verbinden; ['kɔnkri:t]
betonieren.

concur [kən'kə:] zs.-treffen, zs.-wir-
ken; übereinstimmen; ~rence [~-
'kʌrəns] Zusammentreffen *n*; Übereinstimmung *f*; Mitwirkung *f*.

concussion [kən'kʌʃən]: ~ of the
brain Gehirnerschütterung *f*.

condemn [kən'dem] verdammen;
verurteilen; verwerfen; *Kranke*
aufgeben; beschlagnahmen; ~a-
tion [kɔndem'neiʃən] Verurtei-
lung *f*; Verdammung *f*; Verwerfung *f*.

condens|ation [kɔnden'seiʃən] Ver-
dichtung *f*; ~e [kən'dens] (sich)
verdichten; ⊕ kondensieren; zs.-
drängen; ~er [~sə] ⊕ Konden-
sator *m*.

condescen|d [kɔndi'send] sich her-
ablassen; geruhen; ~sion [~ʃən]
Herablassung *f*.

condiment ['kɔndimənt] Würze *f*.

condition [kən'diʃən] **1.** Zustand *m*,
Stand *m*; Stellung *f*, Bedingung *f*;
~s *pl.* Verhältnisse *n/pl.*; **2.** bedingen; in e-n bestimmten Zustand
bringen; ~al □ [~nl] bedingt (on,
upon durch); Bedingungs...; ~
clause *gr.* Bedingungssatz *m*; ~
mood *gr.* Konditional *m*.

condol|e [kən'doul] kondolieren
(with *dat.*); ~ence [~ləns] Beileid *n*.

conduc|e [kən'dju:s] führen, dienen;
~ive [~siv] dienlich, förderlich.

conduct 1. ['kɔndəkt] Führung *f*;
Verhalten *n*, Betragen *n*; **2.** [kən-
'dʌkt] führen; ♪ dirigieren; ~ion
[~kʃən] Leitung *f*; ~or [~ktə]
Führer *m*; Leiter *m*; Schaffner *m*;
♪ Dirigent *m*; ⚡ Blitzableiter *m*.

conduit ['kɔndit] (Leitungs-)
Röhre *f*.

cone [koun] Kegel *m*; ♀ Zapfen *m*.

confabulation [kɔnfæbju'leiʃən]
Plauderei *f*.

confection [kən'fekʃən] Konfekt *n*;
~er [~ʃnə] Konditor *m*; ~ery
[~əri] Konfekt *n*; Konditorei *f*;
bsd. Am. Süßwarengeschäft *n*.

confedera|cy [kən'fedərəsi] Bünd-
nis *n*; the ⯒ *bsd. Am.* die 11 Südstaaten *bei der Sezession 1860—61*;
~te **1.** [~rit] verbündet; **2.** [~] Bundesgenosse *m*; **3.** [~reit] (sich) verbünden; ~tion [kɔnfedə'reiʃən]
Bund *m*, Bündnis *n*; the ⯒ *bsd. Am.*
die Staatenkonföderation *f* von
1781—1789.

confer [kən'fə:] *v/t.* übertragen, verleihen; *v/i.* sich besprechen; ~-
ence ['kɔnfərəns] Konferenz *f*.

confess [kən'fes] bekennen, gestehen; beichten; ~ion [~eʃən] Ge-
ständnis *n*; Bekenntnis *n*; Beichte
f; ~ional [~nl] Beichtstuhl *m*; ~or
[~esə] Bekenner *m*; Beichtvater *m*.

confide [kən'faid] *v/t.* anvertrauen;
v/i. vertrauen (in auf *acc.*); ~nce
['kɔnfidəns] Vertrauen *n*; Zuversicht *f*; ~nce man Schwindler *m*;

Hochstapler *m*; ∼nce trick Bauernfängerei *f*; ∼nt ☐ [∼nt] vertrauend; zuversichtlich; ∼ntial ☐ [konfi-'denʃəl] vertraulich.

confine [kən'fain] begrenzen; beschränken; einsperren; *be* ∼*d* niederkommen (*of* mit); *be* ∼*d to bed* das Bett hüten müssen; ∼ment [∼nmənt] Haft *f*; Beschränkung *f*; Entbindung *f*.

confirm [kən'fəːm] (be)kräftigen; bestätigen; konfirmieren; firmen; ∼ation [konfə'meiʃən] Bestätigung *f*; *eccl.* Konfirmation *f*; *eccl.* Firmung *f*.

confiscat|e ['kɔnfiskeit] beschlagnahmen; ∼ion [konfis'keiʃən] Beschlagnahme *f*.   [ßer Brand.)

conflagration [konflə'greiʃən] gro-)

conflict 1. ['kɔnflikt] Konflikt *m*; 2. [kən'flikt] im Konflikt stehen.

conflu|ence ['kɔnfluəns], ∼x [∼ʌks] Zs.-fluß *m*; Auflauf *m*; ∼ent [∼luənt] 1. zs.-fließend, zs.-laufend; 2. Zu-, Nebenfluß *m*.

conform [kən'fɔːm] (sich) anpassen; ∼able ☐ [∼məbl] (to) übereinstimmen (mit); entsprechend (*dat.*); nachgiebig (gegen); ∼ity [∼miti] Übereinstimmung *f*.

confound [kən'faund] vermengen; verwechseln; *j-n* verwirren; ∼ *it!* F verdammt!; ∼ed ☐ F verdammt.

confront [kən'frʌnt] gegenüberstellen; entgegentreten (*dat.*).

confus|e [kən'fjuːz] verwechseln; verwirren; ∼ion [∼'uːʒən] Verwirrung *f*; Verwechs(e)lung *f*.

confut|ation [konfjuː'teiʃən] Widerlegung *f*; ∼e [kən'fjuːt] widerlegen.

congeal [kən'dʒiːl] erstarren (lassen); gerinnen (lassen).

congenial ☐ [kən'dʒiːnjəl] (geistes-) verwandt (*with dat.*); zusagend.

congenital ☐ [kən'dʒenitl] angeboren.

congestion [kən'dʒestʃən] (Blut-) Andrang *m*; Stauung *f*; *traffic* ∼ Verkehrsstockung *f*.

conglomeration [kɔnglɔmə'reiʃən] Anhäufung *f*; Konglomerat *n*.

congratulat|e [kən'grætjuleit] beglückwünschen; *j-m* gratulieren; ∼ion [kəngrætju'leiʃən] Glückwunsch *m*.

congregat|e ['kɔngrigeit] (sich) (ver)sammeln; ∼ion [kɔngri'geiʃən] Versammlung *f*; *eccl.* Gemeinde *f*.

congress ['kɔngres] Kongreß *m*; ♀ Kongreß *m*, *gesetzgebende Körperschaft der USA*; ♀man, ♀woman *Am. pol.* Mitglied *n* des Repräsentantenhauses.

congruous ☐ ['kɔngruəs] angemessen (*to* für); übereinstimmend; folgerichtig.

conifer ['kounifə] Nadelholzbaum *m*.

conjecture [kən'dʒektʃə] 1. Mutmaßung *f*; 2. mutmaßen.

conjoin [kən'dʒɔin] (sich) verbinden; ∼t ['kɔndʒɔint] verbunden.

conjugal ☐ ['kɔndʒugəl] ehelich.

conjugat|e *gr.* ['kɔndʒugeit] konjugieren, beugen; ∼ion *gr.* [kɔndʒu-'geiʃən] Konjugation *f*, Beugung *f*.

conjunction [kən'dʒʌŋkʃən] Verbindung *f*; Zs.-treffen *n*; *gr.* Konjunktion *f*.

conjunctivitis [kɔndʒʌŋkti'vaitis] Bindehautentzündung *f*.

conjure[1] [kən'dʒuə] beschwören, inständig bitten.

conjur|e[2] [kʌndʒə] *v/t.* beschwören; *et. wohin* zaubern; *v/i.* zaubern; ∼er [∼rə] Zauber|er *m*, -in *f*; Taschenspieler(in); ∼ing-trick [∼riŋtrik] Zauberkunststück *n*; ∼or [∼rə] = *conjurer*.

connect [kə'nekt] (sich) verbinden; ⚡ schalten; ∼ed ☐ verbunden; zs.-hängend (*Rede etc.*); *be* ∼ *with* in Verbindung stehen mit *j-m*; ∼ion [∼kʃən] = *connexion*.

connexion [kə'nekʃən] Verbindung *f*; ⚡ Schaltung *f*; Anschluß *m* (*a.* 🚂, ✈); Zs.-hang *m*; Verwandtschaft *f*.

connive [kə'naiv]: ∼ *at* ein Auge zudrücken bei.

connoisseur [kɔni'səː] Kenner(in).

connubial ☐ [kə'njuːbjəl] ehelich.

conquer ['kɔŋkə] erobern; (be)siegen; ∼or [∼ərə] Eroberer *m*; Sieger *m*.

conquest ['kɔŋkwest] Eroberung *f*; Errungenschaft *f*; Sieg *m*.

conscience ['kɔnʃəns] Gewissen *n*.

conscientious ☐ [kɔnʃi'enʃəs] gewissenhaft; Gewissens...; ∼ *objector* Kriegsdienstverweigerer *m* aus Überzeugung; ∼ness [∼snis] Gewissenhaftigkeit *f*.

conscious ☐ ['kɔnʃəs] bewußt; *be* ∼ *of* sich bewußt sein (*gen.*); ∼ness [∼snis] Bewußtsein *n*.

conscript ✖ ['kɔnskript] Wehrpflichtige(r) *m*; ∼ion ✖ [kən'skripʃən] Einberufung *f*.

consecrat|e ['kɔnsikreit] weihen, einsegnen; heiligen; widmen; ∼ion [kɔnsi'kreiʃən] Weihung *f*, Einsegnung *f*; Heiligung *f*.

consecutive ☐ [kən'sekjutiv] aufea.-folgend; fortlaufend.

consent [kən'sent] 1. Zustimmung *f*; 2. einwilligen, zustimmen (*dat.*).

consequen|ce ['kɔnsikwəns] (*to*) Folge *f*, Konsequenz *f* (für); Wirkung *f*, Einfluß *m* (auf *acc.*); Bedeutung *f* (für); ∼t [∼nt] 1. folgend; 2. Folge(rung) *f*; ∼tial ☐ [kɔnsi-'kwenʃəl] sich ergebend (*on* aus); folgerichtig; wichtigtuerisch; ∼tly ['kɔnsikwəntli] folglich, daher.

conserv|ation [kɔnsə(ː)'veiʃən] Erhaltung *f*; ∼ative ☐ [kən'səːvətiv] 1. erhaltend (*of acc.*); konservativ; vorsichtig; 2. Konservative(r) *m*;

~atory [kən'sə:vətri] Treib-, Gewächshaus n; ♪ Konservatorium n; ~e [kən'sə:v] erhalten.

consider [kən'sidə] v/t. betrachten; erwägen; überlegen; in Betracht ziehen; berücksichtigen; meinen, glauben; v/i. überlegen; all things ~ed wenn man alles in Betracht zieht; ~able □ [~ərəbl] ansehnlich, beträchtlich; ~ably [~li] bedeutend, ziemlich, (sehr) viel; ~ate □ [~rit] rücksichtsvoll; ~ation [kənsidə'reiʃən] Betrachtung f, Erwägung f, Überlegung f; Rücksicht f; Wichtigkeit f; Entschädigung f; Entgelt n; be under ~ erwogen werden; in Betracht kommen; on no ~ unter keinen Umständen; ~ing □ [kən'sidəriŋ] 1. prp. in Anbetracht (gen.); 2. F adv. den Umständen entsprechend.

consign [kən'sain] übergeben, überliefern; anvertrauen; ✝ konsignieren; ~ment ✝ [~nmənt] Übersendung f; Konsignation f.

consist [kən'sist] bestehen (of aus); in Einklang stehen (with mit); ~ence, ~ency [~təns, ~si] Festigkeit(sgrad m) f; Übereinstimmung f; Konsequenz f; ~ent [~nt] fest; übereinstimmend, vereinbar (with mit); konsequent.

consol|ation [kənsə'leiʃən] Trost m; ~e [kən'soul] trösten.

consolidate [kən'səlideit] festigen; fig. vereinigen, zs.-legen.

consonan|ce [kɔnsənəns] Konsonanz f; Übereinstimmung f; ~t [~nt] 1. □ übereinstimmend; 2. gr. Konsonant m, Mitlaut m.

consort [kɔnsɔ:t] Gemahl(in); ⚓ Geleitschiff n.

conspicuous □ [kən'spikjuəs] sichtbar; auffallend; hervorragend; make o.s. ~ sich auffällig benehmen.

conspir|acy [kən'spirəsi] Verschwörung f; ~ator [~ətə] Verschwörer m; ~e [~'spaiə] sich verschwören.

constab|le ['kʌnstəbl] Polizist m; Schutzmann m; ~ulary [kən-'stæbjuləri] Polizei(truppe) f.

constan|cy ['kɔnstənsi] Standhaftigkeit f; Beständigkeit f; ~t □ [~nt] beständig, fest; unveränderlich; treu.

consternation [kɔnstə(:)'neiʃən] Bestürzung f.

constipation ⚕ [kɔnsti'peiʃən] Verstopfung f.

constituen|cy [kən'stitjuənsi] Wählerschaft f; Wahlkreis m; ~t [~nt] 1. wesentlich; Grund..., Bestand...; konstituierend; 2. wesentlicher Bestandteil; Wähler m.

constitut|e ['kɔnstitju:t] ein-, errichten; ernennen; bilden, ausmachen; ~ion [kɔnsti'tju:ʃən] Ein-, Errichtung f; Bildung f; Körper-

bau m; Verfassung f; ~ional □ [~nl] konstitutionell; natürlich; verfassungsmäßig.

constrain [kən'strein] zwingen; et. erzwingen; ~t [~nt] Zwang m.

constrict [kən'strikt] zs.-ziehen; ~ion [~kʃən] Zs.-ziehung f.

constringent [kən'strindʒənt] zs.-ziehend.

construct [kən'strʌkt] bauen, errichten; fig. bilden; ~ion [~kʃən] Konstruktion f; Bau m; Auslegung f; ~ive [~ktiv] aufbauend, schöpferisch, konstruktiv, positiv; Bau...; ~or [~tə] Erbauer m, Konstrukteur m.

construe [kən'stru:] gr. konstruieren; auslegen, auffassen; übersetzen.

consul ['kɔnsəl] Konsul m; ~-general Generalkonsul m; ~ate [~sjulit] Konsulat n (a. Gebäude).

consult [kən'sʌlt] v/t. konsultieren, um Rat fragen; in e-m Buch nachschlagen; v/i. sich beraten; ~ation [kɔnsəl'teiʃən] Konsultation f, Beratung f; Rücksprache f; ~ hour Sprechstunde f; ~ative [kən'sʌltətiv] beratend.

consume [kən'sju:m] v/t. verzehren; verbrauchen; vergeuden; ~r [~mə] Verbraucher m; Abnehmer m.

consummate 1. □ [kən'sʌmit] vollendet; 2. ['kɔnsʌmeit] vollenden.

consumpti|on [kən'sʌmpʃən] Verbrauch m; ⚕ Schwindsucht f; ~ve □ [~ptiv] verzehrend; ⚕ schwindsüchtig.

contact 1. ['kɔntækt] Berührung f; Kontakt m; ~ lenses pl. Haft-, Kontaktschalen f/pl.; 2. [kən'tækt] Fühlung nehmen mit.

contagi|on [kən'teidʒən] Ansteckung f; Verseuchung f; Seuche f; ~ous □ [~əs] ansteckend.

contain [kən'tein] (ent)halten, (um-)fassen; ~ o.s. an sich halten; ~er [~nə] Behälter m; Großbehälter m (im Frachtverkehr).

contaminat|e [kən'tæmineit] verunreinigen; fig. anstecken, vergiften; verseuchen; ~ion [kɔntæmi-'neiʃən] Verunreinigung f; (radioaktive) Verseuchung.

contemplat|e ['kɔntempleit] fig. betrachten; beabsichtigen; ~ion [kɔntəm'pleiʃən] Betrachtung f; Nachsinnen n; ~ive □ ['kɔntempleitiv] nachdenklich; [kən'templətiv] beschaulich.

contempora|neous □ [kəntempə-'reinjəs] gleichzeitig; ~ry [kən-'tempərəri] 1. zeitgenössisch; gleichzeitig; 2. Zeitgenoss|e m, -in f.

contempt [kən'tempt] Verachtung f; ~ible □ [~təbl] verachtenswert; ~uous □ [~tjuəs] geringschätzig (of gegen); verächtlich.

contend [kən'tend] v/i. streiten, ringen (for um); v/t. behaupten.

content [kən'tent] **1.** zufrieden; **2.** befriedigen; ~ o.s. sich begnügen; **3.** Zufriedenheit f; to one's heart's ~ nach Herzenslust; ['kɔntent] Umfang m; Gehalt m; ~s pl. stofflicher Inhalt; ~ed □ [kən'tentid] zufrieden; genügsam.

contention [kən'tenʃən] (Wort-) Streit m; Wetteifer m.

contentment [kən'tentmənt] Zufriedenheit f, Genügsamkeit f.

contest 1. ['kɔntest] Streit m; Wettkampf m; **2.** [kən'test] (be)streiten; anfechten; um et. streiten.   [m.]

context ['kɔntekst] Zusammenhang

contiguous □ [kən'tigjuəs] anstoßend (to an acc.); benachbart.

continent ['kɔntinənt] **1.** □ enthaltsam; mäßig; **2.** Kontinent m, Erdteil m; Festland n; ~al [kɔnti'nentl] **1.** □ kontinental; Kontinental...; **2.** Kontinentaleuropäer(in).

contingen|cy [kən'tindʒənsi] Zufälligkeit f; Zufall m; Möglichkeit f; ~t [~nt] **1.** □ zufällig; möglich (to bei); **2.** ✕ Kontingent n.

continu|al □ [kən'tinjuəl] fortwährend, unaufhörlich; ~ance [~əns] (Fort)Dauer f; ~ation [kən'tinju-'eiʃən] Fortsetzung f; Fortdauer f; ~ school Fortbildungsschule f; ~e [kən'tinju(:)] v/t. fortsetzen; beibehalten; to be ~d Fortsetzung folgt; v/i. fortdauern; fortfahren; ~ity [kɔnti'nju(:)iti] Kontinuität f; Film: Drehbuch n; Radio: verbindende Worte; ~ girl Skriptgirl n; ~ous □ [kən'tinjuəs] ununterbrochen.

contort [kən'tɔ:t] verdrehen; verzerren; ~ion [~ɔ:ʃən] Verdrehung f; Verzerrung f.

contour ['kɔntuə] Umriß m.

contra ['kɔntrə] wider.

contraband ['kɔntrəbænd] Schmuggelware f; Schleichhandel m; attr. Schmuggel...

contraceptive [kɔntrə'septiv] **1.** empfängnisverhütend; **2.** empfängnisverhütendes Mittel.

contract 1. [kən'trækt] v/t. zs.-ziehen; sich et. zuziehen; Schulden machen; Heirat etc. (ab)schließen; v/i. einschrumpfen; e-n Vertrag schließen; sich verpflichten; **2.** ['kɔntrækt] Kontrakt m, Vertrag m; ~ion [kən'trækʃən] Zs.-ziehung f; gr. Kurzform f; ~or [~ktə] Unternehmer m; Lieferant m.

contradict [kɔntrə'dikt] widersprechen (dat.); ~ion [~kʃən] Widerspruch m; ~ory □ [~ktəri] (sich) widersprechend.

contrar|iety [kɔntrə'raiəti] Widerspruch m; Widrigkeit f; ~y ['kɔntrəri] **1.** entgegengesetzt; widrig; ~ to zuwider (dat.); gegen; **2.** Gegenteil n; on the ~ im Gegenteil.

contrast 1. ['kɔntrɑ:st] Gegensatz m; **2.** [kən'trɑ:st] v/t. gegenüberstellen; vergleichen; v/i. sich unterscheiden, abstechen (with von).

contribut|e [kən'tribju(:)t] beitragen, beisteuern; ~ion [kɔntri'bju:ʃən] Beitrag m; ~or [kən'tribjutə] Beitragende(r m) f; Mitarbeiter(in) an e-r Zeitung; ~ory [~əri] beitragend.

contrit|e □ ['kɔntrait] reuevoll; ~ion [kən'triʃən] Zerknirschung f.

contriv|ance [kən'traivəns] Erfindung f; Plan m; Vorrichtung f; Kunstgriff m; Scharfsinn m; ~e [kən'traiv] v/t. ersinnen; planen; zuwegebringen; v/i. es fertig bringen (to inf. zu inf.); ~er [~və] Erfinder(in).

control [kən'troul] **1.** Kontrolle f, Aufsicht f; Befehl m; Zwang m; Gewalt f; Zwangswirtschaft f; Kontrollvorrichtung f; Steuerung f; ~ board ⊕ Schaltbrett n; **2.** ein-, beschränken; kontrollieren; beaufsichtigen, überwachen; beherrschen; (nach)prüfen; bewirtschaften; regeln; ✕ steuern (a. fig. dat.); ~ler [~lə] Kontrolleur m, Aufseher m; Leiter m; Rechnungsprüfer m.

controversial □ [kɔntrə'və:ʃəl] umstritten; streitsüchtig; ~sy [~sy] [kən'trɔvəsi] Streit(frage) f; ~t [~ə:t] bestreiten.

contumacious □ [kɔntju(:)'meiʃəs] widerspenstig; ✝✝ ungehorsam.

contumely ['kɔntju(:)mli] Beschimpfung f; Schmach f.

contuse ✱ [kən'tju:z] quetschen.

convalesce [kɔnvə'les] genesen; ~nce [~sns] Genesung f; ~nt [~nt] **1.** □ genesend; **2.** Genesende(r m) f.

convene [kən'vi:n] (sich) versammeln; zs.-rufen; ✝✝ vorladen.

convenien|ce [kən'vi:njəns] Bequemlichkeit f; Angemessenheit f; Vorteil m; Klosett n; at your earliest ~ möglichst bald; ~t [~nt] bequem; passend; brauchbar.

convent ['kɔnvənt] (Nonnen)Kloster n; ~ion [kən'venʃən] Versammlung f; Konvention f, Übereinkommen n, Vertrag m; Herkommen n; ~ional [~nl] vertraglich; herkömmlich, konventionell.

converge [kən'və:dʒ] konvergieren, zs.-laufen (lassen).

convers|ant [kən'və:sənt] vertraut; ~ation [kɔnvə'seiʃən] Gespräch n, Unterhaltung f; ~ational [~nl] Unterhaltungs...; umgangssprachlich; ~e [~və:s] umgekehrt; **2.** [kən'və:s] sich unterhalten; ~ion [~ə:ʃən] Um-, Verwandlung f; ⊕, ⚡ Umformung f; eccl. Bekehrung f; pol. Meinungswechsel m, Übertritt m; ✝ Konvertierung f; Umstellung f e-r Währung etc.

convert 1. ['kɔnvə:t] Bekehrte(r *m*) *f*, Konvertit *m*; **2.** [kən'və:t] (sich) um-, verwandeln; ⊕, ✠ umformen; *eccl.* bekehren; ✝ konvertieren; *Währung etc.* umstellen; **~er** ⊕, ✠ [⍳tə] Umformer *m*; **~ible 1.** □ [⍳təbl] um-, verwandelbar; ✝ konvertierbar; **2.** *mot.* Kabrio(lett) *n*.

convey [kən'vei] befördern, bringen, schaffen; übermitteln; mitteilen; ausdrücken; übertragen; **~ance** [⍳eiəns] Beförderung *f*; ✝ Spedition *f*; Übermittlung *f*; Verkehrsmittel *n*; Fuhrwerk *n*; Übertragung *f*; **~er, ~or** ⊕ [⍳eiə] *a.* **~ belt** Förderband *n*.

convict 1. ['kɔnvikt] Sträfling *m*; **2.** [kən'vikt] *j-n* überführen; **~ion** [⍳kʃən] ✝✝ Überführung *f*; Überzeugung *f* (of von).

convince [kən'vins] überzeugen.

convivial □ [kən'viviəl] festlich; gesellig.

convocation [kɔnvə'keiʃən] Einberufung *f*; Versammlung *f*.

convoke [kən'vouk] einberufen.

convoy ['kɔnvɔi] **1.** Geleit *n*; Geleitzug *m*; (Geleit)Schutz *m*; **2.** geleiten.

convuls|ion [kən'vʌlʃən] Zuckung *f*, Krampf *m*; **~ive** □ [⍳siv] krampfhaft, -artig, konvulsiv.

coo [ku:] girren, gurren.

cook [kuk] **1.** Koch *m*; Köchin *f*; **2.** kochen; *Bericht etc.* frisieren; **~book** *Am.* ['kukbuk] Kochbuch *n*; **~ery** ['kukəri] Kochen *n*; Kochkunst *f*; **~ie** *Am.* ['kuki] Plätzchen *n*; **~ing** [⍳iŋ] Küche *f* (*Kochweise*); **~y** *Am.* ['kuki] = *cookie*.

cool [ku:l] **1.** □ kühl; *fig.* kaltblütig, gelassen; unverfroren; **2.** Kühle *f*; **3.** (sich) abkühlen. **coolness** ['ku:lnis] Kühle *f* (*a. fig.*); Kaltblütigkeit *f*.

coon *Am.* F [ku:n] *zo.* Waschbär *m*; Neger *m*; (schlauer) Bursche.

coop [ku:p] **1.** Hühnerkorb *m*; **2. ~ up** *od.* **in** einsperren.

co-op F [kou'ɔp] = *co-operative* (*store*).

cooper ['ku:pə] Böttcher *m*, Küfer *m*.

co(-)operat|e [kou'ɔpəreit] mitwirken; zs.-arbeiten; **~ion** [kouɔpə'reiʃən] Mitwirkung *f*; Zs.-arbeit *f*; **~ive** [kou'ɔpərətiv] zs.-wirkend; **~ society** Konsumverein *m*; **~ store** Konsum(vereinsladen) *m*; **~or** [⍳reitə] Mitarbeiter *m*.

co-ordinat|e 1. □ [kou'ɔ:dnit] gleichgeordnet; **2.** [⍳dineit] koordinieren, gleichordnen; auf-ea. einstellen; **~ion** [kouɔ:di'neiʃən] Gleichordnung *f*, -schaltung *f*.

copartner ['kou'pɑ:tnə] Teilhaber *m*.

cope [koup]: **~ with** sich messen mit, fertig werden mit.

copious □ ['koupjəs] reich(lich); weitschweifig; **~ness** [⍳snis] Fülle *f*.

copper[1] ['kɔpə] **1.** Kupfer *n*; Kupfermünze *f*; **2.** kupfern; Kupfer...

copper[2] *sl.* [⍳] Polyp *m* (*Polizist*).

coppice, copse ['kɔpis, kɔps] Unterholz *n*, Dickicht *n*.

copy ['kɔpi] **1.** Kopie *f*; Nachbildung *f*; Abschrift *f*; Durchschlag *m*; Muster *n*; Exemplar *n* *e-s Buches*; *Zeitungs-*Nummer *f*; druckfertiges Manuskript; *fair od. clean* **~ Reinschrift** *f*; **2.** kopieren; abschreiben; nachbilden, nachahmen; **~book** Schreibheft *n*; **~ing** [⍳iŋ] Kopier...; **~ist** [⍳ist] Abschreiber *m*; Nachahmer *m*; **~right** Verlagsrecht *n*, Copyright *n*.

coral ['kɔrəl] Koralle *f*.

cord [kɔ:d] **1.** Schnur *f*, Strick *m*; *anat.* Strang *m*; **2.** (zu)schnüren, binden; **~ed** ['kɔ:did] gerippt.

cordial ['kɔ:djəl] **1.** □ herzlich; herzstärkend; **2.** (Magen)Likör *m*; **~ity** [kɔ:di'æliti] Herzlichkeit *f*.

cordon ['kɔ:dn] **1.** Postenkette *f*; **2. ~ off** abriegeln, absperren.

corduroy ['kɔ:dərɔi] Kord *m*; **~s** *pl.* Kordhosen *f/pl.*; **~ road** Knüppeldamm *m*.

core [kɔ:] **1.** Kerngehäuse *n*; *fig.* Herz *n*; Kern *m*; **2.** entkernen.

cork [kɔ:k] **1.** Kork *m*; **2.** (ver)korken; **~ing** *Am.* F ['kɔ:kiŋ] fabelhaft, prima; **~-jacket** Schwimmweste *f*; **~screw** Kork(en)zieher *m*.

corn [kɔ:n] **1.** Korn *n*; Getreide *n*; *a. Indian ~ Am.* Mais *m*; ✡ Hühnerauge *n*; **2.** einpökeln.

corner ['kɔ:nə] **1.** Ecke *f*, Winkel *m*; Kurve *f*; *fig.* Enge *f*; ✝ Aufkäufer-Ring *m*; **2.** Eck...; **3.** in die Ecke (*fig.* Enge) treiben; ✝ aufkaufen; **~ed** ...eckig.

cornet ♩ ['kɔ:nit] (kleines) Horn.

cornice △ ['kɔ:nis] Gesims *n*.

corn|-juice *Am. sl.* ['kɔ:ndʒu:s] Maisschnaps *m*; **~ pone** *Am.* ['kɔ:npoun] Maisbrot *n*; **~stalk** Getreidehalm *m*; *Am.* Maisstengel *m*; **~starch** *Am.* Maisstärke *f*.

coron|ation [kɔrə'neiʃən] Krönung *f*; **~er** ['kɔrənə] Leichenbeschauer *m*; **~et** [⍳nit] Adelskrone *f*.

corpor|al ['kɔ:pərəl] **1.** □ körperlich; **2.** ✕ Korporal *m*; **~ation** [kɔ:pə'reiʃən] Körperschaft *f*, Innung *f*, Zunft *f*; Stadtverwaltung *f*; *Am.* Aktiengesellschaft *f*.

corpse [kɔ:ps] Leichnam *m*.

corpulen|ce, ~cy ['kɔ:pjuləns, ~si] Beleibtheit *f*; **~t** [⍳nt] beleibt.

corral *Am.* [kɔ:'rɑ:l] **1.** Einzäunung *f*; **2.** zs.-pferchen, einsperren.

correct [kə'rekt] **1.** □ korrekt, richtig; **2.** *v/t.* korrigieren; zurechtweisen; strafen; **~ion** [⍳kʃən] Berichtigung *f*; Verweis *m*; Strafe *f*;

Korrektur f; *house of* ~ Besserungs-anstalt f.

correlate ['kɔrileit] in Wechselbe-ziehung stehen *od.* bringen.

correspond [kɔris'pɔnd] entspre-chen (*with, to dat.*); korrespondie-ren; ~ence [~dəns] Übereinstim-mung f; Briefwechsel m; ~ent [~nt] 1. □ entsprechend; 2. Briefschrei-ber(in); Korrespondent(in).

corridor ['kɔridɔ:] Korridor m; Gang m; ~ train D-Zug m.

corrigible ['kɔridʒəbl] verbesser-lich; zu verbessern(d).

corroborate [kə'rɔbəreit] stärken; bestätigen.

corro|de [kə'roud] zerfressen; weg-ätzen; ~sion [~'ʒən] Ätzen n, Zerfressen n; ⊕ Korrosion f; Rost m; ~sive [~'ousiv] 1. □ zerfressend, ätzend; 2. Ätzmittel n.

corrugate ['kɔrugeit] runzeln; ⊕ riefen; ~d iron Wellblech n.

corrupt [kə'rʌpt] 1. □ verdorben; verderbt; bestechlich; 2. *v/t.* ver-derben; bestechen; anstecken; *v/i.* (ver)faulen, verderben; ~ible [~'təbl] verderblich; bestechlich; ~ion [~pʃən] Verderbnis f, Verdor-benheit f; Fäulnis f; Bestechung f.

corsage [kɔ:'sa:ʒ] Taille f, Mieder n; *Am.* Ansteckblume(n *pl.*) f.

corset ['kɔ:sit] Korsett n.

coruscate ['kɔrəskeit] funkeln.

co-signatory ['kou'signətəri] 1. mit-unterzeichnend; 2. Mitunterzeich-ner m.

cosmetic [kɔz'metik] 1. kosme-tisch; 2. Schönheitsmittel n; Kos-metik f; ~ian [kɔzme'tiʃən] Kos-metiker(in).

cosmonaut ['kɔzmənɔ:t] Kosmo-naut m, Weltraumfahrer m.

cosmopolit|an [kɔzmə'pɔlitən], ~e [kɔz'mɔpəlait] 1. kosmopolitisch; 2. Weltbürger(in).

cost [kɔst] 1. Preis m; Kosten *pl.*; Schaden m; *first od.* prime ~ An-schaffungskosten *pl.*; 2. [*irr.*] ko-sten.

costl|iness ['kɔstlinis] Kostbarkeit f; ~y ['kɔstli] kostbar; kostspielig.

costume ['kɔstju:m] Kostüm n; Kleidung f; Tracht f.

cosy ['kouzi] 1. □ behaglich, gemüt-lich; 2. = tea-cosy.

cot [kɔt] Feldbett n; ♣ Hängematte f mit Rahmen, Koje f; Kinderbett n.

cottage ['kɔtidʒ] Hütte f; kleines Landhaus, Sommerhaus n; ~ cheese *Am.* Quark(käse) m; ~ piano Piani-no n; ~r [~dʒə] Häusler m; Hütten-bewohner m; *Am.* Sommergast m.

cotton ['kɔtn] 1. Baumwolle f; † Kattun m; Näh-Garn n; 2. baum-wollen; Baumwoll...; ~ wool Watte f; 3. F sich vertragen; sich an-schließen; ~-wood ♀ e-e amerika-nische Pappel.

couch [kautʃ] 1. Lager n; Couch f, Sofa n, Liege f; Schicht f; 2. *v/t.* Meinung *etc.* ausdrücken; Schrift-satz *etc.* abfassen; ♂ Star stechen; *v/i.* sich (nieder)legen; versteckt liegen; kauern.

cough [kɔf] 1. Husten m; 2. husten.

could [kud] *pret. von* can[1].

coulee *Am.* ['ku:li] (trockenes) Bachbett.

council ['kaunsl] Rat(sversammlung f) m; ~(l)or [~silə] Ratsmitglied n, Stadtrat m.

counsel ['kaunsəl] 1. Beratung f; Rat(schlag) m; ⚖ Anwalt m; ~ for the defense Verteidiger m; ~ for the prosecution Anklagevertreter m; 2. j-n beraten; j-m raten; ~(l)or [~slə] Ratgeber(in); Anwalt m; *Am.* Rechtsbeistand m.

count[1] [kaunt] 1. Rechnung f; Zahl f; ⚖ Anklagepunkt m; 2. *v/t.* zählen; rechnen; dazurechnen; *fig.* halten für; *v/i.* zählen; rechnen; gelten (*for little* wenig).

count[2] [kaunt] nichtbritischer Graf.

count-down ['kauntdaun] Count-down m, n, Startzählung f (*beim Raketenstart*).

countenance ['kauntinəns] 1. Ge-sicht n; Fassung f; Unterstützung f; 2. begünstigen, unterstützen.

counter[1] ['kauntə] Zähler m, Zähl-apparat m; Spielmarke f; Zahl-pfennig m; Ladentisch m; Schalter m.

counter[2] [~] 1. entgegen, zuwider (*to dat.*); Gegen...; 2. Gegenschlag m; 3. Gegenmaßnahmen treffen.

counteract [kauntə'rækt] zuwider-handeln (*dat.*).

counterbalance 1. ['kauntəbæləns] Gegengewicht n; 2. [kauntə'bæləns] aufwiegen; ✝ ausgleichen.

counter-espionage ['kauntər'espiə-na:ʒ] Spionageabwehr f.

counterfeit ['kauntəfit] 1. □ nach-gemacht; falsch, unecht; 2. Nach-ahmung f; Fälschung f; Falsch-geld n; 3. nachmachen; fälschen; heucheln.

counterfoil ['kauntəfɔil] Kontroll-abschnitt m.

countermand [kauntə'ma:nd] 1. Gegenbefehl m; Widerruf m; 2. widerrufen; abbestellen.

counter-move *fig.* ['kauntəmu:v] Gegenzug m, -maßnahme f.

counterpane ['kauntəpein] Bett-decke f.

counterpart ['kauntəpɑ:t] Gegen-stück n.

counterpoise ['kauntəpɔiz] 1. Ge-gengewicht n; 2. das Gleichgewicht halten (*dat.*) (*a. fig.*), ausbalancie-ren.

countersign ['kauntəsain] 1. Ge-genzeichen n; ✕ Losung(swort n) f; 2. gegenzeichnen.

countervail ['kauntəveil] aufwiegen.

countess ['kauntis] Gräfin f.

counting-house ['kauntiŋhaus] Kontor n.

countless ['kauntlis] zahllos.

countrified ['kʌntrifaid] ländlich; bäurisch.

country ['kʌntri] 1. Land n; Gegend f; Heimatland n; 2. Land(s)..., ländlich; ~man Landmann m (Bauer); Landsmann m; ~side Gegend f; Land(bevölkerung f) n.

county ['kaunti] Grafschaft f, Kreis m; ~ seat Am. = ~ town Kreisstadt f.

coup [ku:] Schlag m, Streich m.

couple ['kʌpl] 1. Paar n; Koppel f; 2. (ver)koppeln; ⊕ kuppeln; (sich) paaren; ~r [~lə] Radio: Koppler m.

coupling ['kʌpliŋ] Kupplung f; Radio: Kopplung f; attr. Kupplungs...

coupon ['ku:pɔn] Abschnitt m.

courage ['kʌridʒ] Mut m; ~ous □ [kə'reidʒəs] mutig, beherzt.

courier ['kuriə] Kurier m, Eilbote m; Reiseführer m.

course [kɔ:s] 1. Lauf m, Gang m; Weg m; ♫, fig. Kurs m; Rennbahn f; Gang m (Speisen); Kursus m; univ. Vorlesung f; Ordnung f, Folge f; of ~ selbstverständlich; 2. v/t. hetzen; jagen; v/i. rennen.

court [kɔ:t] 1. Hof m; Hofgesellschaft f; Gericht(shof m) n; General 2 Am. gesetzgebende Versammlung; pay (one's) ~ to j-m den Hof machen; 2. j-m den Hof machen; werben um; ~day ['kɔ:tdei] Gerichtstag m; ~eous □ ['kɔ:tjəs] höflich; ~esy ['kɔ:tisi] Höflichkeit f; Gefälligkeit f; ~house ['kɔ:t-'haus] Gerichtsgebäude n; Am. a. Amtshaus n e-s Kreises; ~ier ['kɔ:tjə] Höfling m; ~ly ['kɔ:tli] höfisch; höflich; ~ martial ✗ Kriegs-; ~-martial ✗ ['kɔ:t'ma:ʃəl] vor ein Kriegs- od. Militärgericht stellen; ~ room Gerichtssaal m; ~ship ['kɔ:tʃip] Werbung f; ~yard Hof m.

cousin ['kʌzn] Vetter m; Base f.

cove [kouv] 1. Bucht f; fig. Obdach n.

covenant ['kʌvinənt] 1. ⚖ Vertrag m; Bund m; 2. v/t. geloben; v/i. übereinkommen.

cover ['kʌvə] 1. Decke f; Deckel m; Umschlag m; Hülle f; Deckung f; Schutz m; Dickicht n; Deckmantel m; Decke f, Mantel m (Bereifung); 2. (be-, zu)decken; einschlagen; einwickeln; verbergen, verdecken; schützen; Weg zurücklegen; † decken; mit e-r Schußwaffe zielen nach; ✗ Gelände bestreichen; umfassen; fig. erfassen; Zeitung: berichten über (acc.); ~age [~əridʒ] Berichterstattung f (of über acc.); ~ing [~riŋ] Decke f; Bett-Bezug m; Überzug m; Bekleidung f; Bedachung f.

covert 1. □ ['kʌvət] heimlich, versteckt; 2. ['kʌvə] Schutz m; Versteck n; Dickicht n.

covet ['kʌvit] begehren; ~ous □ [~təs] (be)gierig; habsüchtig.

cow¹ [kau] Kuh f.

cow² [~] einschüchtern, ducken.

coward ['kauəd] 1. □ feig; 2. Feigling m; ~ice [~dis] Feigheit f; ~ly [~dli] feig(e).

cow|boy ['kaubɔi] Cowboy m (berittener Rinderhirt); ~-catcher Am. ⚙ Schienenräumer m.

cower ['kauə] kauern; sich ducken; cow|herd ['kauhə:d] Kuhhirt m; ~hide 1. Rind(s)leder n; 2. peitschen; ~house Kuhstall m.

cowl [kaul] Mönchskutte f; Kapuze f; Schornsteinkappe f.

cow|man ['kaumən] Melker m; Am. Viehzüchter m; ~-puncher Am. F ['kaupʌntʃə] Rinderhirt m; ~shed Kuhstall m; ~slip ⚘ Schlüsselblume f; Am. Sumpfdotterblume f.

coxcomb ['kɔkskoum] Geck m.

coxswain ['kɔkswein, ⚓ mst 'kɔksn] Bootsführer m; Steuermann m.

coy □ [kɔi] schüchtern; spröde.

crab [kræb] Krabbe f, Taschenkrebs m; ⊕ Winde f; F Querkopf m.

crab-louse ['kræblaus] Filzlaus f.

crack [kræk] 1. Krach m; Riß m, Sprung m; F derber Schlag; Versuch m; Witz m; 2. F erstklassig; 3. v/t. (zer)sprengen; knallen mit et.; (auf)knacken; ~ a joke e-n Witz reißen; v/i. platzen, springen; knallen; umschlagen (Stimme); ~ed geborsten; F verdreht; ~er ['krækə] Knallbonbon m, n; Schwärmer m; Am. Keks m (ungesüßt); ~le [~kl] knattern, knistern; ~up Zs.-stoß m; ✈ Bruchlandung f.

cradle ['kreidl] 1. Wiege f; Kindheit f (a. fig.); 2. (ein)wiegen.

craft [kra:ft] Handwerk n, Gewerbe n; Schiff(e pl.) n; Gerissenheit f; ~sman ['kra:ftsmən](Kunst)Handwerker m; ~y □ ['kra:fti] gerissen, raffiniert.

crag [kræg] Klippe f, Felsspitze f.

cram [kræm] (voll)stopfen; nudeln, mästen; F (ein)pauken.

cramp [kræmp] 1. Krampf m; ⊕ Klammer f; fig. Fessel f; 2. verkrampfen; einengen, hemmen.

cranberry ['krænbəri] Preiselbeere f.

crane [krein] 1. Kranich m; ⊕ Kran m; 2. (den Hals) recken; ~fly zo. ['kreinflai] Schnake f.

crank [kræŋk] 1. Kurbel f; Schwengel m; Wortspiel n; Schrulle f; komischer Kauz; fixe Idee; 2. (an-)kurbeln; ~-shaft ⊕ ['kræŋkʃa:ft]

Kurbelwelle *f*; ~y [᷄ki] wacklig; launisch; verschroben.

cranny [᷄kræni] Riß *m*, Ritze *f*.

crape [kreip] Krepp *m*, Flor *m*.

craps *Am.* [kræps] *pl. Würfelspiel.*

crash [kræʃ] 1. Krach *m* (*a.* †); ⚡ Absturz *m*; 2. *v/i.* krachen; ein-stürzen; ⚡ abstürzen; *mot.* zs.-stoßen; fahren, fliegen, stürzen (*into in, auf acc.*); *v/t.* zerschmettern; 3. *Am.* F blitzschnell ausge-führt; **~-helmet** [᷄kræʃhelmit] Sturzhelm *m*; **~-landing** Bruch-landung *f*.

crate [kreit] Lattenkiste *f*.

crater [᷄kreitə] Krater *m*; Trichter *m*.

crave [kreiv] *v/t.* dringend bitten *od.* flehen um; *v/i.* sich sehnen.

craven [᷄kreivən] feig.

crawfish [᷄krɔ:fiʃ] 1. Krebs *m*; 2. *Am.* F sich drücken.

crawl [krɔ:l] 1. Kriechen *n*; 2. krie-chen; schleichen; wimmeln; krib-beln; *Schwimmen*: kraulen; *it makes one's flesh* ~ man bekommt e-e Gänsehaut davon.

crayfish [᷄kreifiʃ] Flußkrebs *m*.

crayon [᷄kreiən] Zeichenstift *m*, *bsd.* Pastellstift *m*; Pastell(gemälde) *n*.

craz|e [kreiz] Verrücktheit *f*; F Fimmel *m*; *be the* ~ Mode sein; **~y** □ [᷄kreizi] baufällig; verrückt (*for, about* nach).

creak [kri:k] knarren.

cream [kri:m] 1. Rahm *m*, Sahne *f*; Creme *f*; Auslese *f*; *das Beste*; 2. den Rahm abschöpfen; **~ery** [᷄kri:məri] Molkerei *f*; Milchge-schäft *n*; **~y** □ [᷄mi] sahnig.

crease [kri:s] 1. (Bügel)Falte *f*; 2. (sich) kniffen, (sich) falten.

creat|e [kri(:)᷄eit] (er)schaffen; *thea.* *e-e Rolle* gestalten; verursachen; er-zeugen; ernennen; **~ion** [᷄eiʃən] Schöpfung *f*; Ernennung *f*; **~ive** [᷄eitiv] schöpferisch; *or* [᷄ətə] Schöpfer *m*; **~ure** [᷄kri:tʃə] Ge-schöpf *n*; Kreatur *f*.

creden|ce [᷄kri:dəns] Glaube *m*; **~tials** [kri᷄denʃəlz] *pl.* Beglaubi-gungsschreiben *n*; Unterlagen *f/pl.*

credible □ [᷄kredəbl] glaubwürdig; glaubhaft.

credit [᷄kredit] 1. Glaube(n) *m*; Ruf *m*, Ansehen *n*; Guthaben *n*; † Kredit *m*; † Kredit *m*; Einfluß *m*; Verdienst *n*, Ehre *f*; *Am. Schule*: (Anrechnungs)Punkt *m*; 2. *j-m* glauben; *j-m* trauen; † gutschrei-ben; ~ *s.o. with s.th.* j-m et. zu-trauen; **~able** □ [᷄təbl] achtbar; ehrenvoll (*to* für); **~or** [᷄ətə] Gläu-biger *m*.

credulous □ [᷄kredjuləs] leicht-gläubig.

creed [kri:d] Glaubensbekenntnis *n*.

creek [kri:k] Bucht *f*; *Am.* Bach *m*.

creel [kri:l] Fischkorb *m*.

creep [kri:p] [*irr.*] kriechen; *fig.* (sich ein)schleichen; kribbeln; *it makes my flesh* ~ ich bekomme e-e Gänsehaut davon; **~er** [᷄kri:pə] Kriecher(in); Kletterpflanze *f*.

cremator|ium [kremə᷄tɔ:riəm], *bsd. Am.* **~y** [᷄kremətəri] Kremato-rium *n*.

crept [krept] *pret. u. p.p. von* creep.

crescent [᷄kresnt] 1. zunehmend; halbmondförmig; 2. Halbmond *m*; 2 *City Am.* New Orleans.

cress ♀ [kres] Kresse *f*.

crest [krest] *Hahnen-, Berg- etc.* Kamm *m*; Mähne *f*; Federbusch *m*; *Heraldik: family* ~ Familien-wappen *n*; **~-fallen** [᷄krestfɔ:lən] niedergeschlagen.

crevasse [kri᷄væs] (Gletscher)Spalte *f*; *Am.* Deichbruch *m*.

crevice [᷄krevis] Riß *m*, Spalte *f*.

crew¹ [kru:] Schar *f*; ⚓, ⚡ Mann-schaft *f*.

crew² [᷄] *pret. von* crow 2.

crib [krib] 1. Krippe *f*; Kinderbett (-stelle *f*) *n*; F *Schule*: Klatsche *f*; *bsd. Am.* Behälter *m*; 2. einsperren; F mausen; F abschreiben.

crick [krik] Krampf *m*; ~ *in the neck* steifer Hals.

cricket [᷄krikit] *zo.* Grille *f*; *Sport*: Kricket *n*; *not* ~ F nicht fair.

crime [kraim] Verbrechen *n*.

criminal [᷄kriminl] 1. verbreche-risch; Kriminal..., Straf...; 2. Ver-brecher(in); **~ity** [krimi᷄næliti] Strafbarkeit *f*; Verbrechertum *n*.

crimp [krimp] kräuseln.

crimson [᷄krimzn] karmesin(rot).

cringe [krindʒ] sich ducken.

crinkle [᷄kriŋkl] 1. Windung *f*; Falte *f*; 2. (sich) winden; (sich) kräuseln.

cripple [᷄kripl] 1. Krüppel *m*; Lahme(r *m*) *f*; 2. verkrüppeln; *fig.* lähmen.

cris|is [᷄kraisis], *pl.* **~es** [᷄si:z] Krisis *f*, Krise *f*, Wende-, Höhe-punkt *m*.

crisp [krisp] 1. kraus; knusperig; frisch; klar; steif; 2. (sich) kräu-seln; knusperig machen *od.* wer-den; 3. **~s** *pl., a. potato* **~s** *pl.* Kar-toffelchips *pl.*

criss-cross [᷄kriskrɔs] 1. Kreuz-zeichen *n*; 2. (durch)kreuzen.

criteri|on [krai᷄tiəriən], *pl.* **~a** [᷄riə] Kennzeichen *n*, Prüfstein *m*.

criti|c [᷄kritik] Kritiker(in); **~cal** □ [᷄kəl] kritisch; bedenklich; **~cism** [᷄isizəm] Kritik *f* (*of an dat.*); **~cize** [᷄saiz] kritisieren; beurteilen; ta-deln; **~que** [kri᷄ti:k] kritischer Es-say; die Kritik.

croak [krouk] krächzen; quaken.

crochet [᷄krouʃei] 1. Häkelei *f*; 2. häkeln.

crock [krɔk] irdener Topf; **~ery** ['krɔkəri] Töpferware f.

crocodile zo. ['krɔkədail] Krokodil n.

crone F [kroun] altes Weib.

crony F ['krouni] alter Freund.

crook [kruk] **1.** Krümmung f; Haken m; Hirtenstab m; sl. Gauner m; **2.** (sich) krümmen; (sich) (ver)biegen; **~ed** ['krukid] krumm; bucklig; unehrlich; [krukt] Krück...

croon [kru:n] schmalzig singen; summen; **~er** ['kru:nə] Schnulzensänger m.

crop [krɔp] **1.** Kropf m; Peitschenstiel m; Reitpeitsche f; Ernte f; kurzer Haarschnitt; **2.** (ab-, be-) schneiden; (ab)ernten; Acker bebauen; **~ up** fig. auftauchen.

cross [krɔs] **1.** Kreuz n (a. fig. Leiden); Kreuzung f; **2.** □ sich kreuzend; quer (liegend, laufend etc.); ärgerlich, verdrießlich; entgegengesetzt; Kreuz..., Quer...; **3.** v/t. kreuzen; durchstreichen; fig. durchkreuzen; übequeren; in den Weg kommen (dat.); **~ o.s.** sich bekreuzigen; keep one's fingers **~ed** den Daumen halten; v/i. sich kreuzen; **~-bar** ['krɔsbɑ:] Fußball: Torlatte f; **~-breed** (Rassen)Kreuzung f; **~-country** querfeldein; **~-examination** Kreuzverhör n; **~-eyed** schieläugig; **~ing** [~siŋ] Kreuzung f; Übergang m; -fahrt f; **~-road** Querstraße f; **~-roads** pl. od. sg. Kreuzweg m; **~-section** Querschnitt m; **~-wise** kreuzweise; **~-word** (puzzle) Kreuzworträtsel n.

crotchet ['krɔtʃit] Haken m; ♪ Viertelnote f; wunderlicher Einfall.

crouch [krautʃ] **1.** sich ducken; **2.** Hockstellung f.

crow [krou] **1.** Krähe f; Krähen n; eat **~** Am. F zu Kreuze kriechen; **2.** [irr.] krähen; triumphieren; **~-bar** ['krouba:] Brecheisen n.

crowd [kraud] **1.** Haufen m, Menge f; Gedränge n; F Bande f; **2.** (sich) drängen; (über)füllen; wimmeln.

crown [kraun] **1.** Krone f; Kranz m; Gipfel m; Scheitel m; **2.** krönen; Zahn überkronen; to **~** all zu guter Letzt, zu allem Überfluß.

cruci|al □ ['kru:ʃəl] entscheidend; kritisch; **~ble** ['kru:sibl] Schmelztiegel m; **~fixion** [kru:si'fikʃən] Kreuzigung f; **~fy** ['kru:sifai] kreuzigen.

crude □ [kru:d] roh; unfertig; unreif; unfein; grob; Roh...; grell.

cruel □ ['kruəl] grausam; hart; fig. blutig; **~ty** [~lti] Grausamkeit f.

cruet ['kru(:)it] (Essig-, Öl)Fläschchen n.

cruise ♣ [kru:z] **1.** Kreuzfahrt f, Seereise f; **2.** kreuzen; **~r** ['kru:zə]

♣ Kreuzer m; Jacht f; Am. Funkstreifenwagen m.

crumb [krʌm] **1.** Krume f; Brocken m; **2.** panieren; zerkrümeln; **~le** ['krʌmbl] (zer)bröckeln; fig. zugrunde gehen.

crumple ['krʌmpl] v/t. zerknittern; fig. vernichten; v/i. (sich) knüllen.

crunch [krʌntʃ] (zer)kauen; zermalmen; knirschen.

crusade [kru:'seid] Kreuzzug m (a. fig.); **~r** [~də] Kreuzfahrer m.

crush [krʌʃ] **1.** Druck m; Gedränge n; (Frucht)Saft m; Am. sl. Schwarm m; have a **~** on s.o. in j-n verliebt od. verschossen sein; **2.** v/t. (zer-, aus)quetschen; zermalmen; fig. vernichten; v/i. sich drängen; **~barrier** ['krʌʃbæriə] Absperrgitter n.

crust [krʌst] **1.** Kruste f; Rinde f; Am. sl. Frechheit f; **2.** (sich) be-, überkrusten, verharschen; **~y** □ ['krʌsti] krustig; fig. mürrisch.

crutch [krʌtʃ] Krücke f.

cry [krai] **1.** Schrei m; Geschrei n; Ruf m; Weinen n; Gebell n; **2.** schreien; (aus)rufen; weinen; **~ for** verlangen nach.

crypt [kript] Gruft f; **~ic** ['kriptik] verborgen, geheim.

crystal ['kristl] Kristall m, n; Am. Uhrglas n; **~line** [~təlain] kristallen; **~lize** [~aiz] kristallisieren.

cub [kʌb] **1.** Junge(s) n; Flegel m; Anfänger m; **2.** (Junge) werfen.

cub|e [kju:b] Würfel m; Kubikzahl f; **~ root** Kubikwurzel f; **~ic(al** □) ['kju:bik(əl)] würfelförmig; kubisch; Kubik...

cuckoo ['kuku] Kuckuck m.

cucumber ['kju:kəmbə] Gurke f; as cool as a **~** fig. eiskalt, gelassen.

cud [kʌd] wiedergekäutes Futter; chew the **~** wiederkäuen; fig. überlegen.

cuddle ['kʌdl] v/t. (ver)hätscheln.

cudgel ['kʌdʒəl] **1.** Knüttel m; **2.** (ver)prügeln.

cue [kju:] Billard-Queue n; Stichwort n; Wink m.

cuff [kʌf] **1.** Manschette f; Handschelle f; (Ärmel-, Am. a. Hosen-) Aufschlag m; Faust-Schlag m; **2.** puffen, schlagen.

cuisine [kwi(:)'zi:n] Küche f (Art zu kochen).

culminate ['kʌlmineit] gipfeln.

culpable □ ['kʌlpəbl] strafbar.

culprit ['kʌlprit] Angeklagte(r m) f; Schuldige(r m) f, Missetäter(in).

cultivat|e ['kʌltiveit] kultivieren; an-, bebauen; ausbilden; pflegen; **~ion** [kʌlti'veiʃən] (An-, Acker)Bau m; Ausbildung f; Pflege f, Zucht f; **~or** ['kʌltiveitə] Landwirt m; Züchter m; ♂ Kultivator m (Maschine).

cultural □ ['kʌltʃərəl] kulturell.
culture ['kʌltʃə] Kultur f; Pflege f; Zucht f; ~d kultiviert.
cumb|er ['kʌmbə] überladen; belasten; ~ersome [~əsəm], ~rous □ [~brəs] lästig; schwerfällig.
cumulative □ ['kju:mjulətiv] (an-, auf)häufend; Zusatz...
cunning ['kʌniŋ] 1. □ schlau, listig; geschickt; Am. reizend; 2. List f, Schlauheit f; Geschicklichkeit f.
cup [kʌp] Becher m, Schale f, Tasse f; Kelch m; Sport: Pokal m; ~board ['kʌbəd] (Speise- etc.)Schrank m.
cupidity [kju(:)'piditi] Habgier f.
cupola ['kju:pələ] Kuppel f.
cur [kə:] Köter m; Schurke m, Halunke m.
curable ['kjuərəbl] heilbar.
curate ['kjuərit] Hilfsgeistliche(r) m.
curb [kə:b] 1. Kinnkette f; Kandare f (a. fig.); a. ~stone ['kə:bstoun] Bordschwelle f; 2. an die Kandare nehmen (a. fig.); fig. zügeln; ~market Am. Börse: Freiverkehr m; ~roof Mansardendach n.
curd [kə:d] 1. Quark m; 2. (mst ~le ['kə:dl]) gerinnen (lassen).
cure [kjuə] 1. Kur f; Heilmittel n; Seelsorge f; Pfarre f; 2. heilen; pökeln; räuchern; trocknen.
curfew ['kə:fju:] Abendglocke f; pol. Ausgehverbot n; ~bell Abendglocke f.
curio ['kjuəriou] Rarität f; ~sity [kjuəri'ɔsiti] Neugier f; Rarität f; ~us □ ['kjuəriəs] neugierig; genau; seltsam, merkwürdig.
curl [kə:l] 1. Locke f; 2. (sich) kräuseln; (sich) locken; (sich) ringeln; ~y ['kə:li] gekräuselt; lockig.
currant ['kʌrənt] Johannisbeere f; a. dried ~ Korinthe f.
curren|cy ['kʌrənsi] Umlauf m; ✝ Lauffrist f; Kurs m, Währung f; ~t [~nt] 1. □ umlaufend; ✝ kursierend (Geld); allgemein (bekannt); laufend (Jahr etc.); 2. Strom m (a. ⚡); Strömung f (a. fig.); Luftzug m.
curricul|um [kə'rikjuləm], pl. ~a [~lə] Lehr-, Stundenplan m; ~um vitae [~əm'vaiti:] Lebenslauf m.
curry¹ ['kʌri] Curry m, n.
curry² [~] Leder zurichten; Pferd striegeln.
curse [kə:s] 1. Fluch m; 2. (ver)fluchen; strafen; ~d □ ['kə:sid] verflucht.
curt □ [kə:t] kurz; knapp; barsch.
curtail [kə:'teil] beschneiden; fig. beschränken; kürzen (of um).
curtain ['kə:tn] 1. Vorhang m; Gardine f; 2. verhängen, verschleiern; ~lecture F Gardinenpredigt f.
curts(e)y ['kə:tsi] 1. Knicks m; m; 2. knicksen (to vor).

curvature ['kə:vətʃə] (Ver)Krümmung f.
curve [kə:v] 1. Kurve f; Krümmung f; 2. (sich) krümmen; (sich) biegen.
cushion ['kuʃən] 1. Kissen n; Polster n; Billard-Bande f; 2. polstern.
cuss Am. F [kʌs] 1. Nichtsnutz m; 2. fluchen.
custody ['kʌstədi] Haft f; (Ob)Hut f.
custom ['kʌstəm] Gewohnheit f, Brauch m; Sitte f; Kundschaft f; ~s pl. Zoll m; ~ary □ [~məri] gewöhnlich, üblich; ~er [~mə] Kund|e m, -in f; F Bursche m; ~house Zollamt n; ~made Am. maßgearbeitet.
cut [kʌt] 1. Schnitt m; Hieb m; Stich m; (Schnitt)Wunde f; Einschnitt m; Graben m; Kürzung f; Ausschnitt m; Wegabkürzung f (mst short~); Holz-Schnitt m; Kupfer-Stich m; Schliff m; Schnitte f, Scheibe f; Karten-Abheben n; Küche: cold ~s pl. Aufschnitt m; give s.o. the ~ (direct) F j. schneiden; 2. [irr.] v/t. schneiden; schnitzen; gravieren; ab-, an-, auf-, aus-, be-, durch-, zer-, zuschneiden; Edelstein etc. schleifen; Karten abheben; j. beim Begegnen schneiden; ~ teeth zahnen; ~ short j. unterbrechen; ~ back einschränken; ~ down fällen; mähen; beschneiden; Preis drücken; ~ out ausschneiden; Am. Vieh aussondern aus der Herde; fig. j. ausstechen; ❦ be ~ out for das Zeug zu e-r S. haben; v/i. ~ in sich einschieben; 3. adj. geschnitten etc.; s. cut 2.
cute □ F [kju:t] schlau; Am. reizend.
cuticle ['kju:tikl] Oberhaut f; ~ scissors pl. Hautschere f.
cutlery ['kʌtləri] Messerschmiedearbeit f; Stahlwaren f/pl.; Bestecke n/pl.
cutlet ['kʌtlit] Kotelett n; Schnitzel n.
cut|-off Am. ['kʌtɔ:f] Abkürzung f (Straße, Weg); ~out mot. Auspuffklappe f; ⚡ Sicherung f; Ausschalter m; Am. Ausschneidebogen m, -bild n; ~purse Taschendieb m; ~ter ['kʌtə] Schneidende(r m) f; Schnitzer m; Zuschneider(in) f; Film: Cutter m; ⚓ Schneidezeug n, -maschine f; ⚓ Kutter m; Am. leichter Schlitten; ~throat Halsabschneider m; Meuchelmörder m; ~ting ['kʌtiŋ] 1. □ schneidend; scharf; ⊕ Schneid..., Fräs...; 2. Schneiden n; ⊕ etc. Einschnitt m; ⚘ Steckling m; Zeitungs-Ausschnitt m; ~s pl. Schnipsel m, n/pl.; ⊕ Späne m/pl.
cycl|e ['saikl] 1. Zyklus m; Kreis (-lauf) m; Periode f; ⊕ Arbeitsgang

_m_; Fahrrad _n_; 2. radfahren; ~ist [~list] Radfahrer(in).

cyclone ['saikloun] Wirbelsturm _m_.

cylinder ['silində] Zylinder _m_, Walze _f_; ⊕ Trommel _f_.

cymbal ♪ ['simbəl] Becken _n_.

cynic ['sinik] 1. _a._ ~al □ [~kəl] zynisch; 2. Zyniker _m_.

cypress ♀ ['saipris] Zypresse _f_.

cyst ⚕ [sist] Blase _f_; Sackgeschwulst _f_; ~itis ⚕ [sis'taitis] Blasenentzündung _f_.

Czech [tʃek] 1. Tschech|e _m_, -in _f_; 2. tschechisch.

Czechoslovak ['tʃekou'slouvæk] 1. Tschechoslowak|e _m_, -in _f_; 2. tschechoslowakisch.

D

dab [dæb] 1. Klaps _m_; Tupf(en) _m_, Klecks _m_; 2. klapsen; (be)tupfen.

dabble ['dæbl] bespritzen; plätschern; (hinein)pfuschen.

dad F [dæd], ~dy F ['dædi] Papa _m_.

daddy-longlegs F _zo._ ['dædi'lɔŋlegz] Schnake _f_; _Am._ Weberknecht _m_.

daffodil ♀ ['dæfədil] gelbe Narzisse.

daft F [dɑːft] blöde, doof.

dagger ['dægə] Dolch _m_; be _at_ ~s drawn _fig._ auf Kriegsfuß stehen.

dago _Am. sl._ ['deigou] _contp. für_ Spanier, Portugiese, _mst Italiener._

daily ['deili] 1. täglich; 2. Tageszeitung _f_.

dainty ['deinti] 1. □ lecker; zart, fein; wählerisch; 2. Leckerei _f_.

dairy ['dɛəri] Molkerei _f_, Milchwirtschaft _f_; Milchgeschäft _n_; ~ cattle Milchvieh _n_; ~man Milchhändler _m_.

daisy ♀ ['deizi] Gänseblümchen _n_.

dale [deil] Tal _n_.

dall|iance ['dæliəns] Trödelei _f_; Liebelei _f_; ~y ['dæli] vertrödeln; schäkern.

dam [dæm] 1. Mutter _f von Tieren_; Deich _m_, Damm _m_; 2. (ab)dämmen.

damage ['dæmidʒ] 1. Schaden _m_; ~s _pl._ ⚖ Schadenersatz _m_; 2. (be-)schädigen.

damask ['dæməsk] Damast _m_.

dame [deim] Dame _f_; _sl._ Weib _n_.

damn [dæm] verdammen; verurteilen; ~ation [dæm'neiʃən] Verdammung _f_.

damp [dæmp] 1. feucht, dunstig; 2. Feuchtigkeit _f_, Dunst _m_; Gedrücktheit _f_; 3. _a._ ~en ['dæmpən] anfeuchten; dämpfen; niederdrükken; ~er [~pə] Dämpfer _m_.

danc|e [dɑːns] 1. Tanz _m_; Ball _m_; 2. tanzen (lassen); ~er ['dɑːnsə] Tänzer(in); ~ing [~siŋ] Tanzen _n_; _attr._ Tanz ... [zahn _m_.\]

dandelion ♀ ['dændilaiən] Löwen-\]

dandle _sl._ ['dændl] wiegen, schaukeln.

dandruff ['dændrəf] (Kopf)Schuppen _f_/_pl._

dandy ['dændi] 1. Stutzer _m_; F erstklassige Sache; 2. _Am._ F prima.

Dane [dein] Dän|e _m_, -in _f_.

danger ['deindʒə] Gefahr _f_; ~ous □ [~dʒrəs] gefährlich; ~-signal 🚦 Notsignal _n_.

dangle ['dæŋgl] baumeln (lassen); schlenkern (mit); _fig._ schwanken.

Danish ['deiniʃ] dänisch.

dank [dæŋk] dunstig, feucht.

Danubian [dæ'njuːbjən] Donau...

dapper □ F ['dæpə] nett; behend.

dapple ['dæpl] sprenkeln; ~d scheckig; ~-grey Apfelschimmel _m_.

dar|e [dɛə] _v/i._ es wagen; _v/t. et._ wagen; _j-n_ herausfordern; _j-m_ trotzen; ~e-devil ['dɛədevl] Draufgänger _m_; ~ing □ ['dɛəriŋ] 1. verwegen; 2. Verwegenheit _f_.

dark [dɑːk] 1. □ dunkel; brünett; schwerverständlich; geheim(nisvoll); trüb(selig); 2. Dunkel(heit _f_) _n_; _before (after)_ ~ vor (nach) Einbruch der Dunkelheit; ♀ Ages _pl._ _das_ frühe Mittelalter; ~en ['dɑːkən] (sich) (ver)dunkeln; (sich) verfinstern; ~ness ['dɑːknis] Dunkelheit _f_, Finsternis _f_; ~y F ['dɑːki] Schwarze(r _m_) _f_.

darling ['dɑːliŋ] 1. Liebling _m_; 2. Lieblings...; geliebt.

darn [dɑːn] stopfen; ausbessern.

dart [dɑːt] 1. Wurfspieß _m_; Wurfpfeil _m_; Sprung _m_, Satz _m_; ~s _pl._ Wurfpfeilspiel _n_; 2. _v/t._ schleudern; _v/i. fig._ schießen, (sich) stürzen.

dash [dæʃ] 1. Schlag _m_, (Zs.-)Stoß _m_; Klatschen _n_; Schwung _m_; Ansturm _m_; _fig._ Anflug _m_; Prise _f_; Schuß _m Rum etc._; _Feder_-Strich _m_; Gedankenstrich _m_; 2. _v/t._ schlagen, werfen, schleudern; zerschmettern; vernichten; (be)spritzen; vermengen; verwirren; _v/i._ stoßen, schlagen; stürzen; stürmen; jagen; ~-board mot. ['dæʃbɔːd] Armaturenbrett _n_; ~ing □ ['dæʃiŋ] schneidig, forsch; flott, F fesch.

dastardly ['dæstədli] heimtückisch; feig.

data ['deitə] _pl._, _Am. a. sg._ Angaben

f/pl.; Tatsachen f/pl.; **Unterlagen**
f/pl.; Daten pl.

date [deit] **1.** ♀ Dattel f; Datum n;
Zeit f; Termin m; Am. F Verabredung f; Freund(in); *out of* ~
veraltet, unmodern; *up to* ~ zeitgemäß, modern; auf dem laufenden; **2.** datieren; Am. F sich verabreden.

dative gr. ['deitiv] a. ~ *case* Dativ m.

daub [dɔːb] (be)schmieren; (be-)
klecksen.

daughter ['dɔːtə] Tochter f; ~-in-
law [~ɔrinlɔː] Schwiegertochter f.

daunt [dɔːnt] entmutigen; ~less
['dɔːntlis] furchtlos, unerschrocken.

daw orn. [dɔː] Dohle f.

dawdle F ['dɔːdl] (ver)trödeln.

dawn [dɔːn] **1.** Dämmerung f; fig.
Morgenrot n; **2.** dämmern, tagen;
it ~*ed upon him* fig. es wurde ihm
langsam klar.

day [dei] Tag m; *oft* ~*s pl.* (Lebens-)
Zeit f; ~ *off* dienst-freier Tag; *carry
od. win the* ~ den Sieg davontragen;
the other ~ neulich; *this* ~ *week*
heute in einer Woche; heute vor
einer Woche; *let's call it a* ~ machen wir Schluß für heute; ~**break**
['deibreik] Tagesanbruch m; ~-**la-
bo(u)rer** Tagelöhner m; ~-**star**
Morgenstern m.

daze [deiz] blenden; betäuben.

dazzle ['dæzl] blenden; ⚓ tarnen.

dead [ded] **1.** tot; unempfindlich
(*to* für); matt (*Farbe etc.*); blind
(*Fenster etc.*); erloschen (*Feuer*);
schal (*Getränk*); tief (*Schlaf*);
✝ tot (*Kapital etc.*); ~ *bargain*
Spottpreis m; ~ *letter* unzustellbarer
Brief; ~ *loss* Totalverlust m; a ~
shot ein Meisterschütze; ~ *wall*
blinde Mauer; ~ *wood* Reisig n;
Am. F Plunder m; **2.** adv. gänzlich,
völlig, total; durchaus; genau,
(haar)scharf; ~ *against* gerade od.
ganz und gar (ent)gegen; **3.** *the* ~
der Tote; die Toten pl.; Toten-
stille f; *in the* ~ *of winter* im tiefsten
Winter; *in the* ~ *of night* mitten in
der Nacht; ~**en** ['dedn] abstumpf-
fen; dämpfen; (ab)schwächen; ~
end Sackgasse f (a. fig.); ~-**line**
Am. Sperrlinie f im Gefängnis;
Schlußtermin m; Stichtag m;
~-**lock** Stockung f; fig. toter Punkt;
~**ly** [~li] tödlich.

deaf □ [def] taub; ~**en** ['defn] taub
machen; betäuben.

deal [diːl] **1.** Teil m; Menge f; Kar-
tengeben n; F Geschäft n; Abma-
chung f; *a good* ~ ziemlich viel;
a great ~ sehr viel; **2.** [irr.] v/t. (aus-,
ver-, zu)teilen; *Karten* geben; *e-n
Schlag* versetzen; v/i. handeln (*in
mit e-r Ware*) austeilen; verkehren; ~ *with* sich befassen mit, behandeln; ~**er** ['diːlə] Händler m;
Kartengeber m; ~**ing** ['diːliŋ] mst

~*s pl.* Handlungsweise f; Verfahren n; Verkehr m; ~**t** [delt] *pret. u
p.p. von* deal 2.

dean [diːn] Dekan m.

dear [diə] **1.** □ teuer; lieb; **2.** Liebling m; herziges Geschöpf n; **3.** *o(h)*
~!, ~ *me!* F du liebe Zeit!; *oh*
herrje!

death [deθ] Tod m; Todesfall m;
~-**bed** ['deθbed] Sterbebett n;
~-**duty** Erbschaftssteuer f; ~**less**
['deθlis] unsterblich; ~**ly** [~li] tödlich; ~-**rate** Sterblichkeitsziffer f;
~-**warrant** Todesurteil n.

debar [di'baː] ausschließen; hindern.

debarkation [diːbaːˈkeiʃən] Aus-
schiffung f.

debase [di'beis] verschlechtern; erniedrigen; verfälschen.

debat|able □ [di'beitəbl] strittig;
umstritten; ~**e** [di'beit] **1.** Debatte
f; **2.** debattieren; erörtern; überlegen.

debauch [di'bɔːtʃ] **1.** Ausschweifung f; **2.** verderben; verführen.

debilitate [di'biliteit] schwächen.

debit ✝ ['debit] **1.** Debet n, Schuld
f; **2.** j-n belasten; debitieren.

debris ['debri:] Trümmer pl.

debt [det] Schuld f; ~**or** ['detə]
Schuldner(in).

debunk ['diːˈbʌŋk] den Nimbus
nehmen (*dat.*).

début ['deibu:] Debüt n.

decade ['dekeid] Jahrzehnt n.

decadence ['dekədəns] Verfall m.

decamp [di'kæmp] aufbrechen; ausreißen; ~**ment** [~pmənt] Aufbruch
m.

decant [di'kænt] abgießen; umfül-
len; ~**er** [~tə] Karaffe f.

decapitate [di'kæpiteit] enthaupten; Am. F fig. absägen (*entlassen*).

decay [di'kei] **1.** Verfall m; Fäulnis
f; **2.** verfallen; (ver)faulen.

decease bsd. ⁂ [di'si:s] **1.** Ableben
n; **2.** sterben.

deceit [di'si:t] Täuschung f; Betrug
m; ~**ful** □ [~tful] (be)trügerisch.

deceive [di'si:v] betrügen; täuschen; verleiten; ~**r** [~və] Betrü-
ger(in).

December [di'sembə] Dezember m.

decen|cy ['di:snsi] Anstand m; ~**t**
□ [~nt] anständig; F annehmbar,
nett.

deception [di'sepʃən] Täuschung f.

decide [di'said] (sich) entscheiden;
bestimmen; ~**d** □ entschieden;
bestimmt; entschlossen.

decimal ['desiməl] Dezimalbruch
m; attr. Dezimal...

decipher [di'saifə] entziffern.

decisi|on [di'siʒən] Entscheidung f;
⁂ Urteil n; Entschluß m; Entschlossenheit f; ~**ve** □ [di'saisiv]
entscheidend; entschieden.

deck [dek] 1. ♣ Deck *n*; *Am.* Pack *m* Spielkarten; on ～ *Am.* F da(bei), bereit; 2. *rhet.* schmücken; **～-chair** ['dek'ʃɛə] Liegestuhl *m*.

declaim [di'kleim] vortragen; (sich er)eifern.

declar|able [di'klɛərəbl] steuer-, zollpflichtig; **～ation** [deklə'reiʃən] Erklärung *f*; *Zoll*-Deklaration *f*; **～e** [di'klɛə] (sich) erklären; behaupten; deklarieren.

declension [di'klenʃən] Abfall *m* (*Neigung*); Verfall *m*; *gr.* Deklination *f*.

declin|ation [dekli'neiʃən] Neigung *f*; Abweichung *f*; **～e** [di'klain] 1. Abnahme *f*; Niedergang *m*; Verfall *m*; 2. *v/t.* neigen, biegen; *gr.* deklinieren; ablehnen; *v/i.* sich neigen; abnehmen; verfallen.

declivity [di'kliviti] Abhang *m*.

declutch *mot.* ['di:'klʌtʃ] auskuppeln.

decode *tel.* ['di:'koud] entschlüsseln.

decompose [di:kəm'pouz] zerlegen; (sich) zersetzen; verwesen.

decontrol ['di:kən'troul] *Waren, Handel* freigeben.

decorat|e ['dekəreit] (ver)zieren; schmücken; **～ion** [dekə'reiʃən] Verzierung *f*; Schmuck *m*; Orden(sauszeichnung *f*) *m*; ♀ Day *Am.* Heldengedenktag *m*; **～ive** ['dekərətiv] dekorativ; Zier...; **～or** [～reitə] Dekorateur *m*, Maler *m*.

decor|ous □ ['dekərəs] anständig; **～um** [di'kɔ:rəm] Anstand *m*.

decoy [di'kɔi] 1. Lockvogel *m* (*a. fig.*); Köder *m*; 2. ködern; locken.

decrease 1. ['di:kri:s] Abnahme *f*; 2. [di:'kri:s] (sich) vermindern.

decree [di'kri:] 1. Dekret *n*, Verordnung *f*, Erlaß *m*; ᵗᵗ Entscheid *m*; 2. beschließen; verordnen, verfügen.

decrepit [di'krepit] altersschwach.

decry [di'krai] in Verruf bringen.

dedicat|e ['dedikeit] widmen; **～ion** [dedi'keiʃən] Widmung *f*.

deduce [di'dju:s] ableiten; folgern.

deduct [di'dʌkt] abziehen; **～ion** [～kʃən] Abzug *m*; ♀ Rabatt *m*; Schlußfolgerung *f*.

deed [di:d] 1. Tat *f*; Heldentat *f*; Urkunde *f*; 2. *Am.* urkundlich übertragen (to auf *acc.*).

deem [di:m] *v/t.* halten für; *v/i.* denken, urteilen (of über *acc.*).

deep [di:p] 1. □ tief; gründlich; schlau; vertieft; dunkel (*a. fig.*); verborgen; 2. Tiefe *f*; *poet.* Meer *n*; **～en** [di'pən] (sich) vertiefen; (sich) verstärken; **～freeze** 1. tiefkühlen; 2. Tiefkühlfach *n*, -truhe *f*; **～ness** ['di:pnis] Tiefe *f*.

deer [diə] Rotwild *n*; Hirsch *m*.

deface [di'feis] entstellen; unkenntlich machen; ausstreichen.

defalcation [di:fæl'keiʃən] Unterschlagung *f*.

defam|ation [defə'meiʃən] Verleumdung *f*; **～e** [di'feim] verleumden; verunglimpfen.

default [di'fɔ:lt] 1. Nichterscheinen *n* vor Gericht; Säumigkeit *f*; Verzug *m*; in ～ of which widrigenfalls; 2. s-n *etc.* Verbindlichkeiten nicht nachkommen.

defeat [di'fi:t] 1. Niederlage *f*; Besiegung *f*; Vereitelung *f*; 2. ✕ besiegen; vereiteln; vernichten.

defect [di'fekt] Mangel *m*; Fehler *m*; **～ive** □ [～tiv] mangelhaft; unvollständig; fehlerhaft.

defen|ce, *Am.* **～se** [di'fens] Verteidigung *f*; Schutzmaßnahme *f*; witness for the ～ Entlastungszeuge *m*; **～celess,** *Am.* **～seless** [～slis] schutzlos, wehrlos.

defend [di'fend] verteidigen; schützen (*from vor dat.*); **～ant** [～dənt] Angeklagte(r *m*) *f*; Beklagte(r *m*) *f*; **～er** [～də] Verteidiger(in).

defensive [di'fensiv] Defensive *f*; *attr.* Verteidigungs...

defer [di'fə:] auf-, verschieben; *Am.* ✕ zurückstellen; sich fügen; nachgeben; *payment on* ～red terms Ratenzahlung *f*; **～ence** ['defərəns] Ehrerbietung *f*; Nachgiebigkeit *f*; **～ential** □ [defə'renʃəl] ehrerbietig.

defian|ce [di'faiəns] Herausforderung *f*; Trotz *m*; **～t** □ [～nt] herausfordernd; trotzig.

deficien|cy [di'fiʃənsi] Unzulänglichkeit *f*; Mangel *m*; = deficit; **～t** [～nt] mangelhaft; unzureichend.

deficit ['defisit] Fehlbetrag *m*.

defile 1. ['di:fail] Engpaß *m*; 2. [di'fail] *v/i.* vorbeiziehen; *v/t.* beflecken; schänden.

defin|e [di'fain] definieren; erklären; genau bestimmen; **～ite** □ ['definit] bestimmt; deutlich; genau; **～ition** [defi'niʃən] (Begriffs-)Bestimmung *f*; Erklärung *f*; **～itive** □ [di'finitiv] bestimmt; entscheidend; endgültig.

deflect [di'flekt] ablenken; abweichen.

deform [di'fɔ:m] entstellen, verunstalten; **～ed** verwachsen; **～ity** [～miti] Unförmigkeit *f*; Mißgestalt *f*.

defraud [di'frɔ:d] betrügen (of um).

defray [di'frei] *Kosten* bestreiten.

defroster *mot.* [di:'frɔstə] Entfroster *m*.

deft □ [deft] gewandt, flink.

defunct [di'fʌŋkt] verstorben.

defy [di'fai] herausfordern; trotzen.

degenerate 1. [di'dʒenəreit] entarten; 2. □ [～rit] entartet.

degrad|ation [degrə'deiʃən] Absetzung *f*; **～e** [di'greid] *v/t.* absetzen; erniedrigen; demütigen.

degree [di'gri:] Grad *m*; *fig.* Stufe *f*,

Schritt *m*; Rang *m*, Stand *m*; by ~s allmählich; *in no* ~ in keiner Weise; *in some* ~ einigermaßen; *take one's* ~ sein Abschlußexamen machen.

dehydrated [di:'haidreitid] Trokken...

deify ['di:ifai] vergöttern; vergottlichen.

deign [dein] geruhen; gewähren.

deity ['di:iti] Gottheit *f*.

deject [di'dʒekt] entmutigen; ~ed □ niedergeschlagen; ~ion [~kʃən] Niedergeschlagenheit *f*.

delay [di'lei] 1. Aufschub *m*; Verzögerung *f*; 2. *v/t.* aufschieben; verzögern; *v/i.* zögern; trödeln.

delega|te 1. ['deligeit] abordnen; übertragen; 2. [~git] Abgeordnete(r *m*) *f*; ~tion [deli'geiʃən] Abordnung *f*; *Am. parl. die* Kongreßabgeordneten *m/pl. e-s Staates.*

deliberat|e 1. [di'libəreit] *v/t.* überlegen, erwägen; *v/i.* nachdenken; beraten; 2. □ [~rit] bedachtsam; wohlüberlegt; vorsätzlich; ~ion [dilibə'reiʃən] Überlegung *f*; Beratung *f*; Bedächtigkeit *f*.

delica|cy ['delikəsi] Wohlgeschmack *m*; Leckerbissen *m*; Zartheit *f*; Schwächlichkeit *f*; Feinfühligkeit *f*; ~te [~kit] schmackhaft; lecker; zart; fein; schwach; heikel; empfindlich; feinfühlig; wählerisch; ~tessen [delikə'tesn] Feinkost(geschäft *n*) *f*.

delicious [di'liʃəs] köstlich.

delight [di'lait] 1. Lust *f*, Freude *f*, Wonne *f*; 2. entzücken; (sich) erfreuen (*in an dat.*); ~ *to inf.* Freude daran finden, zu *inf.*; ~ful □ [~tful] entzückend; [schildern.]

delineate [di'linieit] entwerfen;

delinquen|cy [di'liŋkwənsi] Vergehen *n*; Kriminalität *f*; Pflichtvergessenheit *f*; ~t [~nt] 1. straffällig; pflichtvergessen; 2. Verbrecher(in).

deliri|ous □ [di'liriəs] wahnsinnig; ~um [~iəm] Fieberwahn *m*.

deliver [di'livə] befreien; über-, aus-, abliefern; *Botschaft* ausrichten; äußern; *Rede etc.* vortragen, halten; ⚔ entbinden; *Schlag* führen; werfen; ~ance [~ərəns] Befreiung *f*; (Meinungs)Äußerung *f*; ~er [~rə] Befreier(in); Überbringer(in); ~y [~ri] ⚔ Entbindung *f*; (Ab)Lieferung *f*; ⚕ Zustellung *f*; Übergabe *f*; Vortrag *m*; Wurf *m*; *special* ~ Lieferung *f* durch Eilboten; ~y-truck, ~y-van Lieferwagen *m*.

dell [del] kleines Tal.

delude [di'lu:d] täuschen; verleiten.

deluge ['delju:dʒ] 1. Überschwemmung *f*; 2. überschwemmen.

delus|ion [di'lu:ʒən] Täuschung *f*, Verblendung *f*; Wahn *m*; ~ive □ [~u:siv] (be)trügerisch; täuschend.

demand [di'mɑ:nd] 1. Verlangen *n*; Forderung *f*; Bedarf *m*; ✝ Nachfrage *f*; ⚖ Rechtsanspruch *m*; 2. verlangen, fordern; fragen (nach).

demean [di'mi:n]: ~ *o.s.* sich benehmen; sich erniedrigen; ~o(u)r [~nə] Benehmen *n*.

demented [di'mentid] wahnsinnig.

demerit [di:'merit] Fehler *m*.

demesne [di'mein] Besitz *m*.

demi... ['demi] Halb..., halb...

demijohn ['demidʒɔn] große Korbflasche, Glasballon *m*.

demilitarize ['di:'militəraiz] entmilitarisieren.

demise [di'maiz] 1. Ableben *n*; 2. vermachen.

demobilize [di:'moubilaiz] demobilisieren.

democra|cy [di'mɔkrəsi] Demokratie *f*; ~t ['deməkræt] Demokrat(in); ~tic(al □) [demə'krætik(əl)] demokratisch.

demolish [di'mɔliʃ] nieder-, abreißen; zerstören.

demon ['di:mən] Dämon *m*; Teufel *m*.

demonstrat|e ['demənstreit] anschaulich darstellen; beweisen; demonstrieren; ~ion [deməns'treiʃən] Demonstration *f*; anschauliche Darstellung; Beweis *m*; (Gefühls)Äußerung *f*; ~ive □ [di'mɔnstrətiv] überzeugend; demonstrativ; ausdrucksvoll; auffällig, überschwenglich.

demote [di:'mour] degradieren.

demur [di'mə:] 1. Einwendung *f*; 2. Einwendungen erheben.

demure □ [di'mjuə] ernst; prüde.

den [den] Höhle *f*; Grube *f*; *sl.* Bude *f*.

denial [di'naiəl] Leugnen *n*; Verneinung *f*; abschlägige Antwort.

denizen ['denizn] Bewohner *m*.

denominat|e [di'nɔmineit] (be-) nennen; ~ion [di'nɔmi'neiʃən] Benennung *f*; Klasse *f*; Sekte *f*, Konfession *f*.

denote [di'nout] bezeichnen; bedeuten.

denounce [di'nauns] anzeigen; brandmarken; *Vertrag* kündigen.

dens|e □ [dens] dicht, dick (*Nebel*); beschränkt; ~ity ['densiti] Dichte *f*; Dichtigkeit *f*.

dent [dent] 1. Kerbe *f*; Beule *f*; 2. ver-, einbeulen.

dent|al ['dentl] Zahn...; ~ *surgeon* Zahnarzt *m*; ~ist [~tist] Zahnarzt *m*.

denunciat|ion [dinʌnsi'eiʃən] Anzeige *f*; Kündigung *f*; ~or [di'nʌnsieitə] Denunziant *m*.

deny [di'nai] verleugnen; verweigern, abschlagen; *j-n* abweisen.

depart [di'pɑ:t] *v/i.* abreisen, abfahren; abstehen, (ab)weichen;

verscheiden; ~ment [~tmənt] Abteilung f; Bezirk m; † Branche f; Am. Ministerium n; State ♀ Am. Außenministerium n; ~ store Warenhaus n; ~ure [~tʃə] Abreise f, ⚙, ♣ Abfahrt f; Abweichung f.

depend [di'pend]: ~ (up)on abhängen von; angewiesen sein auf (acc.); sich verlassen auf (acc.); it ~s F es kommt (ganz) darauf an; ~able [~dəbl] zuverlässig; ~ant [~ənt] Abhängige(r m) f; Angehörige(r m) f; ~ence [~dəns] Abhängigkeit f; Vertrauen n; ~ency [~si] Schutzgebiet n; ~ent [~nt] 1. □ (on) abhängig (von); angewiesen (auf acc.); 2. Am. = dependant.

depict [di'pikt] darstellen; schildern.

deplete [di'pli:t] (ent)leeren; fig. erschöpfen.

deplor|able □ [di'plɔ:rəbl] beklagenswert; kläglich; jämmerlich; ~e [di'plɔ:] beklagen, bedauern.

deponent ⚖️ [di'pounənt] vereidigter Zeuge. [entvölkern.]

depopulate [di:'pɔpjuleit] (sich)

deport [di'pɔ:t] Ausländer abschieben; verbannen; ~ o.s. sich benehmen; ~ment [~tmənt] Benehmen n.

depose [di'pouz] absetzen; ⚖️ (eidlich) aussagen.

deposit [di'pɔzit] 1. Ablagerung f; Lager n; † Depot n; Bank-Einlage f; Pfand n; Hinterlegung f; 2. (nieder-, ab-, hin)legen; Geld einlegen, einzahlen; hinterlegen; (sich) ablagern; ~ion [depɔ'ziʃən] Ablagerung f; eidliche Zeugenaussage; Absetzung f; ~or [di'pɔzitə] Hinterleger m, Einzahler m; Kontoinhaber m.

depot ['depou] Depot n; Lagerhaus n; Am. Bahnhof m.

deprave [di'preiv] sittlich verderben.

deprecate ['deprikeit] ablehnen.

depreciate [di'pri:ʃieit] herabsetzen; geringschätzen; entwerten.

depredation [depri'deiʃən] Plünderung f.

depress [di'pres] niederdrücken; Preise etc. senken, drücken; bedrücken; ~ed fig. niedergeschlagen; ~ion [~eʃən] Senkung f; Niedergeschlagenheit f; † Flaute f, Wirtschaftskrise f; ⚕ Schwäche f; Sinken n.

deprive [di'praiv] berauben; entziehen; ausschließen (of von).

depth [depθ] Tiefe f; attr. Tiefen...

deput|ation [depju(:)'teiʃən] Abordnung f; ~e [di'pju:t] abordnen; ~y ['depjuti] Abgeordnete(r m) f; Stellvertreter m, Beauftragte(r) m.

derail ⚙ [di'reil] v/i. entgleisen; v/t. zum Entgleisen bringen.

derange [di'reindʒ] in Unordnung bringen; stören; zerrütten; (mentally) ~d geistesgestört; a ~d stomach eine Magenverstimmung.

derelict ['derilikt] 1. verlassen; bsd. Am. nachlässig; 2. herrenloses Gut; Wrack n; ~ion [deri'likʃən] Verlassen n; Vernachlässigung f.

deri|de [di'raid] verlachen, verspotten; ~sion [di'riʒən] Verspottung f; ~sive □ [di'raisiv] spöttisch.

deriv|ation [deri'veiʃən] Ableitung f; Herkunft f; ~e [di'raiv] herleiten; Nutzen etc. ziehen (from aus).

derogat|e ['derəgeit] schmälern (from acc.); ~ion [derə'geiʃən] Beeinträchtigung f; Herabwürdigung f; ~ory □ [di'rɔgətəri] (to) nachteilig (dat., für); herabwürdigend.

derrick ['derik] ⊕ Drehkran m; ♣ Ladebaum m; ⚒ Bohrturm m.

descend [di'send] (her-, nieder)steigen, herabkommen; sinken; ✈ niedergehen; ~ (up)on herfallen über (acc.); einfallen in (acc.); (ab)stammen; ~ant [~dənt] Nachkomme m.

descent [di'sent] Herabsteigen n; Abstieg m; Sinken n; Gefälle n; feindlicher Einfall; Landung f; Abstammung f; Abhang m.

describe [dis'kraib] beschreiben.

description [dis'kripʃən] Beschreibung f, Schilderung f; F Art f.

descry [dis'krai] wahrnehmen.

desecrate ['desikreit] entweihen.

desegregate Am. [di:'segrigeit] die Rassentrennung aufheben in (dat.).

desert[1] ['dezət] 1. verlassen; wüst, öde; Wüsten...; 2. Wüste f.

desert[2] [di'zə:t] v/t. verlassen; v/i. ausreißen; desertieren.

desert[3] [di'zə:t] Verdienst n.

desert|er [di'zə:tə] Fahnenflüchtige(r) m; ~ion [~ə:ʃən] Verlassen n; Fahnenflucht f.

deserv|e [di'zə:v] verdienen; sich verdient machen (of um); ~ing [~viŋ] würdig (of gen.); verdienstvoll.

design [di'zain] 1. Plan m; Entwurf m; Vorhaben n, Absicht f; Zeichnung f, Muster n; 2. ersinnen; zeichnen, entwerfen; planen; bestimmen.

designat|e ['dezigneit] bezeichnen; ernennen, bestimmen; ~ion [dezig'neiʃən] Bezeichnung f; Bestimmung f, Ernennung f.

designer [di'zainə] (Muster)Zeichner(in); Konstrukteur m.

desir|able □ [di'zaiərəbl] wünschenswert; angenehm; ~e [di'zaiə] 1. Wunsch m; Verlangen n; 2. verlangen, wünschen; ~ous □ [~ərəs] begierig.

desist [di'zist] abstehen, ablassen.

desk [desk] Pult n; Schreibtisch m.

desolat|e 1. ['desəleit] verwüsten; 2. □ [~lit] einsam; verlassen; öde; ~ion [desə'leiʃən] Verwüstung f; Einöde f; Verlassenheit f.

despair [dis'pɛə] 1. Verzweiflung f;

2. verzweifeln (*of* an *dat.*); ~ing
□ [„ɔriŋ] verzweifelt.
despatch [dis'pætʃ] = *dispatch.*
desperat|e *adj.* □ ['despərit] ver-
zweifelt; hoffnungslos; F schrecklich; ~ion [despə'reiʃən] Verzweiflung *f*; Raserei *f*.
despicable □ ['despikəbl] verächtlich.
despise [dis'paiz] verachten.
despite [dis'pait] 1. Verachtung *f*;
Trotz *m*; Bosheit *f*; *in* ~ *of* zum
Trotz, trotz; 2. *prp. a.* ~ *of* trotz.
despoil [dis'pɔil] berauben (*of gen.*).
despond [dis'pɔnd] verzagen, verzweifeln; ~ency [„dənsi] Verzagt-
heit *f*; ~ent □ [„nt] verzagt.
despot ['despɔt] Despot *m*, Tyrann
m; ~ism [„pətizəm] Despotismus
m.
dessert [di'zə:t] Nachtisch *m*, Dessert *n*; *Am.* Süßspeise *f*.
destin|ation [desti'neiʃən] Be-
stimmung(sort *m*) *f*; ~e ['destin]
bestimmen; ~y [„ni] Schicksal *n*.
destitute □ ['destitju:t] mittellos,
notleidend; entblößt (*of* von).
destroy [dis'trɔi] zerstören, vernichten; töten; unschädlich machen; ~er [„ɔiə] Zerstörer(in).
destruct|ion [dis'trʌkʃən] Zerstö-
rung *f*; Tötung *f*; ~ive □ [„ktiv]
zerstörend; vernichtend (*of, to*
acc.); ~or [„tə] (Müll)Verbren-
nungsofen *m.*
desultory □ ['desəltəri] unstet;
planlos; oberflächlich.
detach [di'tætʃ] losmachen, (ab-)
lösen; absondern; ✕ (ab)komman-
dieren; ~ed einzeln (stehend); unbeeinflußt; ~ment [„ʃmənt] Los-
lösung *f*; Trennung *f*; ✕ Abteilung *f*.
detail ['di:teil] 1. Einzelheit *f*; ein-
gehende Darstellung; ✕ Kom-
mando *n*; *in* ~ ausführlich; 2. genau
schildern; ✕ abkommandieren.
detain [di'tein] zurück-, auf-, abhalten; *j-n* in Haft behalten.
detect [di'tekt] entdecken; (auf-)
finden; ~ion [„kʃən] Entdeckung *f*;
~ive [„ktiv] Detektiv *m*; ~ *story*, ~
novel Kriminalroman *m.*
detention [di'tenʃən] Vorenthal-
tung *f*; Zurück-, Abhaltung *f*;
Haft *f*.   (von).|
deter [di'tə:] abschrecken (*from*)
detergent [di'tə:dʒənt] 1. reini-
gend; 2. Reinigungsmittel *n.*
deteriorat|e [di'tiəriəreit] (sich)
verschlechtern; entarten; ~ion
[ditiəriə'reiʃən] Verschlechterung *f*.
determin|ation [ditə:mi'neiʃən]
Bestimmung *f*; Entschlossenheit *f*;
Entscheidung *f*; Entschluß *m*; ~e
[di'tə:min] *v/t.* bestimmen; entscheiden; veranlassen; *Strafe* festsetzen; beendigen; *v/i.* sich entschließen; ~ed entschlossen.

deterrent [di'terənt] 1. abschrek-
kend; 2. Abschreckungsmittel *n*;
nuclear ~ *pol.* atomare Abschrek-
kung.
detest [di'test] verabscheuen; ~able
□ [„təbl] abscheulich; ~ation [di:-
tes'teiʃən] Abscheu *m.*
dethrone [di'θroun] entthronen.
detonate ['detouneit] explodieren
(lassen).
detour, détour ['deituə] 1. Umweg *m*; Umleitung *f*; 2. e-n Umweg machen.
detract [di'trækt]: ~ *from* s.th. et.
beeinträchtigen, schmälern; ~ion
[„kʃən] Verleumdung *f*; Herabset-
zung *f.*
detriment ['detrimənt] Schaden *m.*
deuce [dju:s] Zwei *f* *im Spiel*;
Tennis: Einstand *m*; F Teufel *m*;
the ~! zum Teufel!
devalu|ation [di:vælju'eiʃən] Ab-
wertung *f*; ~e ['di:'vælju:] abwer-
ten.
devastat|e ['devəsteit] verwüsten;
~ion [devəs'teiʃən] Verwüstung *f.*
develop [di'veləp] (sich) entwickeln;
(sich) entfalten; (sich) erweitern;
Gelände erschließen; ausbauen;
Am. (sich) zeigen; ~ment [„pmənt]
Entwicklung *f*, Entfaltung *f*; Erweiterung *f*; Ausbau *m.*
deviat|e ['di:vieit] abweichen; ~ion
[di:vi'eiʃən] Abweichung *f.*
device [di'vais] Plan *m*; Kniff *m*;
Erfindung *f*; Vorrichtung *f*; Muster *n*; Wahlspruch *m*; *leave s.o. to*
his own ~ *s* j. sich selbst überlassen.
devil ['devl] 1. Teufel *m* (*a. fig.*);
ᵗᵗ Hilfsanwalt *m*; Laufbursche *m*;
2. *v/t.* Gericht stark pfeffern; *Am.*
plagen, quälen; ~ish □ [„liʃ] teuflisch; ~(t)ry [„l(t)ri] Teufelei *f.*
devious □ ['di:vjəs] abwegig.
devise [di'vaiz] 1. ᵗᵗ Vermachen *n*;
Vermächtnis *n*; 2. ersinnen; ᵗᵗ vermachen.
devoid [di'vɔid]: ~ *of bar* (*gen.*), ohne.
devot|e [di'vout] weihen, widmen;
~ed □ ergeben; zärtlich; ~ion
[„ouʃən] Ergebenheit *f*; Hingebung
f; Frömmigkeit *f*; ~s *pl.* Andacht *f.*
devour [di'vauə] verschlingen.
devout □ [di'vaut] andächtig,
fromm; innig.
dew [dju:] 1. Tau *m*; 2. tauen; ~y
['dju:i] betaut; taufrisch.
dexter|ity [deks'teriti] Gewandtheit
f; ~ous □ ['dekstərəs] gewandt.
diabolic(al □) [daiə'bɔlik(əl)] teuflisch.
diagnose ['daiəgnouz] diagnosti-
zieren, erkennen.
diagram ['daiəgræm] graphische
Darstellung; Schema *n*, Plan *m.*
dial ['daiəl] 1. Sonnenuhr *f*; Zifferblatt *n*; *teleph.* Wähl(er)scheibe *f*;
Radio: Skala *f*; 2. *teleph.* wählen.
dialect ['daiəlekt] Mundart *f.*

dialo|gue, *Am. a.* ~g ['daiələg] Dialog *m*, Gespräch *n.*

dial-tone *teleph.* ['daiəltoun] Amtszeichen *n.*

diameter [dai'æmitə] Durchmesser *m.*

diamond ['daiəmənd] Diamant *m*; Rhombus *m*; *Am.* Baseball: Spielfeld *n*; *Karten:* Karo *n.*

diaper ['daiəpə] 1. Windel *f*; 2. *Am.* Baby trockenlegen, wickeln.

diaphragm ['daiəfræm] Zwerchfell *n*; *opt.* Blende *f*; *teleph.* Membran(e) *f.*

diarrh(o)ea ⚕ [daiə'riə] Durchfall *m.*

diary ['daiəri] Tagebuch *n.*

dice [dais] 1. *pl. von die*²; 2. würfeln; ~box ['daisbɔks] Würfelbecher *m.*

dick *Am. sl.* [dik] Detektiv *m.*

dicker *Am.* F ['dikə] (ver)schachern.

dick(e)y ['diki] 1. *sl.* schlecht, schlimm; 2. F Notsitz *m*; Hemdenbrust *f*; *a.* ~bird Piepvögelchen *n.*

dictat|e 1. ['dikteit] Diktat *n*, Vorschrift *f*; Gebot *n*; 2. [dik'teit] diktieren; *fig.* vorschreiben; ~ion [~'eiʃən] Diktat *n*; Vorschrift *f*; ~orship [~'eitəʃip] Diktatur *f.*

diction ['dikʃən] Ausdruck(sweise *f*) *m*, Stil *m*; ~ary [~nri] Wörterbuch *n.*

did [did] *pret. von* do.

die¹ [dai] sterben, umkommen; untergehen; absterben; F schmachten; ~ *away* ersterben; verhallen (*Ton*); ~ down hinsiechen; (dahin)schwinden; erlöschen.

die² [~], *pl.* dice [dais] Würfel *m*; *pl.* dies [daiz] ⊕ Preßform *f*; *Münz*-Stempel *m*; *lower* ~ Matrize *f.*

die-hard ['daihɑːd] Reaktionär *m.*

diet ['daiət] 1. Diät *f*; Nahrung *f*, Kost *f*; Landtag *m*; 2. *v/t.* Diät vorschreiben; beköstigen; *v/i.* diät leben.

differ ['difə] sich unterscheiden; anderer Meinung sein (*with, from* als); abweichen; ~ence ['difrəns] Unterschied *m*; ♈, ♉ Differenz *f*; Meinungsverschiedenheit *f*; ~ent □ [~nt] verschieden; anders, andere(r, -s) (*from* als); ~entiate [difə-'renʃieit] (sich) unterscheiden.

difficult □ ['difikəlt] schwierig; ~y [~ti] Schwierigkeit *f.*

diffiden|ce ['difidəns] Schüchternheit *f*; ~t □ [~nt] schüchtern.

diffus|e 1. *fig.* [di'fjuːz] verbreiten; 2. □ [~uːs] weitverbreitet, zerstreut (*bsd. Licht*); weitschweifig; ~ion [~uːʒən] Verbreitung *f.*

dig [dig] 1. [*irr.*] (um-, aus)graben; wühlen (*in in dat.*); 2. (Aus)Grabung(sstelle) *f*; ~s *pl.* F Bude *f*, Einzelzimmer *n*; F Stoß *m*, Puff *m.*

digest 1. [di'dʒest] *v/t.* ordnen; verdauen (*a. fig.* = *überdenken; verwinden*); *v/i.* verdaut werden;

2. ['daidʒest] Abriß *m*; Auslese *f*, Auswahl *f*; ♊♌ Gesetzsammlung *f*; ~ible [di'dʒestəbl] verdaulich; ~ion [~tʃən] Verdauung *f*; ~ive [~tiv] Verdauungsmittel *n.*

digg|er ['digə] (*bsd.* Gold)Gräber *m*; *sl.* Australier *m*; ~ings F ['diginz] *pl.* Bude *f* (*Wohnung*); *Am.* Goldmine(n *pl.*) *f.*

dignif|ied □ ['dignifaid] würdevoll; würdig; ~y [~fai] Würde verleihen (*dat.*); (be)ehren; *fig.* adeln.

dignit|ary ['dignitəri] Würdenträger *m*; ~y [~ti] Würde *f.*

digress [dai'gres] abschweifen.

dike [daik] 1. Deich *m*; Damm *m*; Graben *m*; 2. eindeichen; eindämmen. [(lassen).\]

dilapidate [di'læpideit] verfallen

dilat|e [dai'leit] (sich) ausdehnen; *Augen* weit öffnen; ~ory □ ['dilətəri] aufschiebend; saumselig.

diligen|ce ['dilidʒəns] Fleiß *m*; ~t □ [~nt] fleißig, emsig.

dilute [dai'ljuːt] 1. verdünnen; verwässern; 2. verdünnt.

dim [dim] 1. □ trüb; dunkel; matt; 2. (sich) verdunkeln; abblenden; (sich) trüben; matt werden.

dime *Am.* [daim] Zehncentstück *n.*

dimension [di'menʃən] Abmessung *f*; ~s *pl. a.* Ausmaß *n.*

dimin|ish [di'miniʃ] (sich) vermindern; abnehmen; ~ution [dimi-'njuːʃən] Verminderung *f*; Abnahme *f*; ~utive □ [di'minjutiv] winzig.

dimple ['dimpl] 1. Grübchen *n*; 2. Grübchen bekommen.

din [din] Getöse *n*, Lärm *m.*

dine [dain] (zu Mittag) speisen; bewirten; ~r [~'dainə] Speisende(r *m*) *f*; (Mittags)Gast *m*; 🚃 *bsd. Am.* Speisewagen *m*; *Am.* Restaurant *n.*

dingle ['diŋgl] Waldschlucht *f.*

dingy □ ['dindʒi] schmutzig.

dining|-car 🚃 ['daiɲiŋkɑː] Speisewagen *m*; ~room Speisezimmer *n.*

dinner ['dinə] (Mittag-, Abend-) Essen *n*; Festessen *n*; ~jacket Smoking *m*; ~pail *Am.* Essenträger *m* (*Gerät*); ~party Tischgesellschaft *f*; ~service, ~set Tafelgeschirr *n.*

dint [dint] 1. Beule *f*; *by* ~ *of* kraft, vermöge (*gen.*); 2. ver-, einbeulen.

dip [dip] 1. *v/t.* (ein)tauchen; senken; schöpfen; abblenden; *v/i.* (unter)tauchen, untersinken; sich neigen; sich senken; 2. Eintauchen *n*; F kurzes Bad; Senkung *f*, Neigung *f.* [*rie*.\]

diphtheria □ [dif'θiəriə] Diphthe-

diploma [di'ploumə] Diplom *n*; ~cy [~si] Diplomatie *f*; ~tic(al □) [diplə'mætik(əl)] diplomatisch; ~tist [di'ploumətist] Diplomat(in).

dipper ['dipə] Schöpfkelle *f*; *Am. Great od. Big* ♀ *ast. der* Große Bär.

dire ['daiə] gräßlich, schrecklich.

direct [di'rekt] 1. □ direkt; gerade; unmittelbar; offen, aufrichtig; deutlich; ~ current ⚡ Gleichstrom m; ~ train durchgehender Zug; 2. adv. geradeswegs; = ~ly 3. richten; lenken, steuern; leiten; anordnen; j-n (an)weisen; Brief adressieren; ~ion [~kʃən] Richtung f; Gegend f; Leitung f; Anordnung f; Adresse f; Vorstand m; ~ion-finder [~nfaində] Radio: (Funk)Peiler m; Peil-(funk)empfänger m; ~ion-indicator mot. Fahrtrichtungsanzeiger m; ⚡ Kursweiser m; ~ive [~ktiv] richtungweisend; leitend; ~ly [~tli] 1. adv. sofort; 2. cj. sobald, als.

director [di'rektə] Direktor m; Film: Regisseur m; board of ~s Aufsichtsrat m; ~ate [~ərit] Direktion f; ~y [~ri] Adreßbuch n; telephone ~ Telephonbuch f.

dirge [də:dʒ] Klage(lied n) f.

dirigible ['diridʒəbl] 1. lenkbar; 2. lenkbares Luftschiff.

dirt [də:t] Schmutz m; (lockere) Erde; ~-cheap F ['də:t'tʃi:p] spottbillig; ~y ['də:ti] 1. □ schmutzig (a. fig.); 2. beschmutzen; besudeln.

disability [disə'biliti] Unfähigkeit f.

disable [dis'eibl] (dienst-, kampf-) unfähig machen; ~d dienst-, kampfunfähig; körperbehindert; kriegsbeschädigt.

disabuse [disə'bju:z] e-s Besseren belehren (of über acc.).

disadvantage [disəd'vɑ:ntidʒ] Nachteil m; Schaden m; ~ous [disædvɑ:n'teidʒəs] nachteilig, ungünstig.

disagree [disə'gri:] nicht übereinstimmen; uneinig sein; nicht bekommen (with s.o. j-m); ~able □ [~riəbl] unangenehm; ~ment [~ri:mənt] Verschiedenheit f; Unstimmigkeit f; Meinungsverschiedenheit f.

disappear [disə'piə] verschwinden; ~ance [~ərəns] Verschwinden n.

disappoint [disə'pɔint] enttäuschen; vereiteln; j. im Stich lassen; ~ment [~tmənt] Enttäuschung f; Vereitelung f. [Mißbilligung f.]

disapprobation [disæprou'beiʃən]

disapprov|al [disə'pru:vəl] Mißbilligung f; ~e [~disə'pru:v] mißbilligen (of et.).

disarm [dis'ɑ:m] v/t. entwaffnen (a. fig.); v/i. abrüsten; ~ament [~məmənt] Entwaffnung f; Abrüstung f.

disarrange ['disə'reindʒ] in Unordnung bringen, verwirren.

disarray ['disə'rei] 1. Unordnung f; 2. in Unordnung bringen.

disast|er [di'zɑ:stə] Unglück(sfall m) n, Katastrophe f; ~rous □ [~trəs] unheilvoll; katastrophal.

disband [dis'bænd] entlassen; auflösen.

disbelieve ['disbi'li:v] nicht glauben.

disburse [dis'bə:s] auszahlen.

disc [disk] = disk.

discard 1. [dis'kɑ:d] Karten, Kleid etc. ablegen; entlassen; 2. ['diskɑ:d] Karten: Abwerfen n; bsd. Am. Abfall(haufen) m.

discern [di'sə:n] unterscheiden; erkennen; beurteilen; ~ing □ [~niŋ] kritisch, scharfsichtig; ~ment [~nmənt] Einsicht f; Scharfsinn m.

discharge [dis'tʃɑ:dʒ] 1. v/t. ent-, ab-, ausladen; entlassen, entbinden; abfeuern; Flüssigkeit absondern; Amt versehen; Pflicht etc. erfüllen; Zorn etc. auslassen (on an dat.); Schuld tilgen; quittieren; Wechsel einlösen; entlassen; freisprechen; v/i. sich entladen; eitern; 2. Entladung f; Abfeuern n; Ausströmen n; Ausfluß m, Eiter(ung f) m; Entlassung f; Entlastung f; Bezahlung f; Quittung f; Erfüllung f e-r Pflicht.

disciple [di'saipl] Schüler m; Jünger m.

discipline ['disiplin] 1. Disziplin f, Zucht f; Erziehung f; Züchtigung f; 2. erziehen; schulen; bestrafen.

disclaim [dis'kleim] (ab)leugnen; ablehnen; verzichten auf (acc.).

disclose [dis'klouz] aufdecken; erschließen, offenbaren, enthüllen.

discolo(u)r [dis'kʌlə] (sich) verfärben.

discomfiture [dis'kʌmfitʃə] Niederlage f; Verwirrung f; Vereitelung f.

discomfort [dis'kʌmfət] 1. Unbehagen n; 2. j-m Unbehagen verursachen.

discompose [diskəm'pouz] beunruhigen.

disconcert [diskən'sə:t] außer Fassung bringen; vereiteln.

disconnect ['diskə'nekt] trennen (a. ⚡); ⊕ auskuppeln; ⚡ ab-, ausschalten; ~ed □ zs.-hanglos.

disconsolate □ [dis'kɔnsəlit] trostlos.

discontent ['diskən'tent] Unzufriedenheit f; ~ed □ mißvergnügt, unzufrieden.

discontinue ['diskən'tinju(:)] aufgeben, aufhören mit; unterbrechen.

discord ['diskɔ:d], ~ance [dis'kɔ:dəns] Uneinigkeit f; ♪ Mißklang m.

discount ['diskaunt] 1. ✝ Diskont m; Abzug m, Rabatt m; 2. ✝ diskontieren; abrechnen; fig. absehen von; Nachricht mit Vorsicht aufnehmen; beeinträchtigen; ~enance [dis-'kauntinəns] mißbilligen; entmutigen.

discourage [dis'kʌridʒ] entmutigen;

abschrecken; **~ment** [~dʒmənt] Entmutigung *f*; Schwierigkeit *f*.

discourse [dis'kɔ:s] **1.** Rede *f*; Abhandlung *f*; Predigt *f*; **2.** reden, sprechen; e-n Vortrag halten.

discourte|ous □ [dis'kɔ:tjəs] unhöflich; **~sy** [~tisi] Unhöflichkeit *f*.

discover [dis'kʌvə] entdecken; ausfindig machen; **~y** [~əri] Entdeckung *f*.

discredit [dis'kredit] **1.** schlechter Ruf; Unglaubwürdigkeit *f*; **2.** nicht glauben; in Mißkredit bringen.

discreet □ [dis'kri:t] besonnen, vorsichtig; klug; verschwiegen.

discrepancy [dis'krepənsi] Widerspruch *m*; Unstimmigkeit *f*.

discretion [dis'kreʃən] Besonnenheit *f*, Klugheit *f*; Takt *m*; Verschwiegenheit *f*; Belieben *n*; *age (od. years) of ~* Strafmündigkeit *f* (*14 Jahre*); *surrender at ~* sich auf Gnade und Ungnade ergeben.

discriminat|e [dis'krimineit] unterscheiden; *~ against* benachteiligen; **~ing** □ [~tiŋ] unterscheidend; scharfsinnig; urteilsfähig; **~ion** [diskrimi'neiʃən] Unterscheidung *f*; unterschiedliche (*bsd.* nachteilige) Behandlung; Urteilskraft *f*.

discuss [dis'kʌs] erörtern, besprechen; **~ion** [~ʌʃən] Erörterung *f*.

disdain [dis'dein] **1.** Verachtung *f*; **2.** geringschätzen, verachten; verschmähen.

disease [di'zi:z] Krankheit *f*; **~d** krank.

disembark ['disim'ba:k] *v/t.* ausschiffen; *v/i.* landen, an Land gehen.

disengage ['disin'geidʒ] (sich) freimachen, (sich) lösen; ⊕ loskuppeln.

disentangle ['disin'tæŋgl] entwirren; *fig.* freimachen (*from* von).

disfavo(u)r ['dis'feivə] **1.** Mißfallen *n*, Ungnade *f*; **2.** nicht mögen.

disfigure [dis'figə] entstellen.

disgorge [dis'gɔ:dʒ] ausspeien.

disgrace [dis'greis] **1.** Ungnade *f*; Schande *f*; **2.** in Ungnade fallen lassen; *j-n* entehren; **~ful** □ [~sful] schimpflich.

disguise [dis'gaiz] **1.** verkleiden; *Stimme* verstellen; verhehlen; **2.** Verkleidung *f*; Verstellung *f*; Maske *f*.

disgust [dis'gʌst] **1.** Ekel *m*; **2.** anekeln; **~ing** □ [~tiŋ] ekelhaft.

dish [diʃ] **1.** Schüssel *f*, Platte *f*; Gericht *n* (*Speise*); *the ~es* das Geschirr; **2.** anrichten; *mst ~ up* auftischen; **~-cloth** ['diʃklɔθ] Geschirrspültuch *n*.

dishearten [dis'ha:tn] entmutigen.

dishevel(l)ed [di'ʃevəld] zerzaust.

dishonest □ [dis'ɔnist] unehrlich, unredlich; **~y** [~ti] Unredlichkeit *f*.

dishono(u)r [dis'ɔnə] **1.** Unehre *f*,

Schande *f*; **2.** entehren; schänden; *Wechsel* nicht honorieren; **~able** □ [~ərəbl] entehrend; ehrlos.

dish|-pan *Am.* ['diʃpæn] Spülschüssel *f*; **~rag** = *dish-cloth*; **~-water** Spülwasser *n*.

disillusion [disi'lu:ʒən] **1.** Ernüchterung *f*, Enttäuschung *f*; **2.** ernüchtern, enttäuschen.

disinclined ['disin'klaind] abgeneigt.

disinfect [disin'fekt] desinfizieren; **~ant** [~tənt] Desinfektionsmittel *n*.

disintegrate [dis'intigreit] (sich) auflösen; (sich) zersetzen.

disinterested □ [dis'intristid] uneigennützig, selbstlos.

disk [disk] Scheibe *f*; Platte *f*; Schallplatte *f*; *~ brake mot.* Scheibenbremse *f*; *~ jockey* Ansager *m* e-r Schallplattensendung.

dislike [dis'laik] **1.** Abneigung *f*; Widerwille *m*; **2.** nicht mögen.

dislocate ['disləkeit] aus den Fugen bringen; verrenken; verlagern.

dislodge [dis'lɔdʒ] vertreiben, verjagen; umquartieren.

disloyal □ ['dis'lɔiəl] treulos.

dismal □ ['dizməl] trüb(selig); öde; trostlos, elend.

dismantl|e [dis'mæntl] abbrechen, niederreißen; ⚓ abtakeln; ⊕ demontieren; **~ing** [~liŋ] Demontage *f*.

dismay [dis'mei] **1.** Schrecken *m*; Bestürzung *f*; **2.** *v/t.* erschrecken.

dismember [dis'membə] zerstückeln.

dismiss [dis'mis] *v/t.* entlassen, wegschicken; ablehnen; *Thema etc.* fallen lassen; ⚖ abweisen; **~al** [~səl] Entlassung *f*; Aufgabe *f*; ⚖ Abweichung *f*.

dismount ['dis'maunt] *v/t.* aus dem Sattel werfen; demontieren; ⊕ aus-ea.-nehmen; *v/i.* absteigen.

disobedien|ce [disə'bi:djəns] Ungehorsam *m*; **~t** □ [~nt] ungehorsam.

disobey ['disə'bei] ungehorsam sein.

disoblige ['disə'blaidʒ] ungefällig sein gegen; kränken.

disorder [dis'ɔ:də] **1.** Unordnung *f*; Aufruhr *m*; ⚕ Störung *f*; **2.** in Unordnung bringen; stören; zerrütten; **~ly** [~əli] unordentlich; ordnungswidrig; unruhig; aufrührerisch.

disorganize [dis'ɔ:gənaiz] zerrütten.

disown [dis'oun] nicht anerkennen, verleugnen; ablehnen.

disparage [dis'pæridʒ] verächtlich machen, herabsetzen.

disparity [dis'pæriti] Ungleichheit *f*.

dispassionate □ [dis'pæʃnit] leidenschaftslos; unparteiisch.

dispatch [dis'pætʃ] 1. (schnelle) Erledigung; (schnelle) Absendung; Abfertigung f; Eile f; Depesche f; 2. (schnell) abmachen, erledigen (a. fig. = töten); abfertigen; (eilig) absenden

dispel [dis'pel] vertreiben, zerstreuen.

dispensa|ble [dis'pensəbl] entbehrlich; ~ry [~əri] Apotheke f; ~tion [dispen'seiʃən] Austeilung f; Befreiung f (with von); göttliche Fügung.

dispense [dis'pens] v/t. austeilen; Gesetze handhaben; Arzneien anfertigen und ausgeben; befreien.

disperse [dis'pə:s] (sich) zerstreuen; auseinandergehen.

dispirit [di'spirit] entmutigen.

displace [dis'pleis] verschieben; absetzen; ersetzen; verdrängen.

display [dis'plei] 1. Entfaltung f; Aufwand m; Schaustellung f; Schaufenster-Auslage f; 2. entfalten; zur Schau stellen; zeigen.

displeas|e [dis'pli:z] j-m mißfallen; ~ed ungehalten; ~ure [~leʒə] Mißfallen n; Verdruß m.

dispos|al [dis'pouzəl] Anordnung f; Verfügung(srecht n) f; Beseitigung f; Veräußerung f; Übergabe f; ~e [~ouz] v/t. (an)ordnen, einrichten; geneigt machen, veranlassen; v/i. ~ of verfügen über (acc.); erledigen; verwenden; veräußern; unterbringen; beseitigen; ~ed geneigt; ...gesinnt; ~ition [dispə'ziʃən] Disposition f; Anordnung f; Neigung f; Sinnesart f; Verfügung f.

dispossess ['dispə'zes] (of) vertreiben (aus od. von); berauben (gen.).

dispraise [dis'preiz] tadeln.

disproof [dis'pru:f] Widerlegung f.

disproportionate [dis'prə'pɔ:ʃnit] unverhältnismäßig.

disprove ['dis'pru:v] widerlegen.

dispute [dis'pju:t] 1. Streit(igkeit f) m; Rechtsstreit m; beyond (all) ~, past ~ zweifellos; 2. (be)streiten.

disqualify [dis'kwɔlifai] unfähig od. untauglich machen; für untauglich erklären.

disquiet [dis'kwaiət] beunruhigen.

disregard ['disri'gɑ:d] 1. Nicht(be)achtung f; 2. unbeachtet lassen.

disr_put|able ['dis'repjutəbl] schimpflich; verrufen; ~e ['disri'pju:t] übler Ruf; Schande f.

disrespect ['disris'pekt] Nichtachtung f; Respektlosigkeit f; ~ful □ [~tful] respektlos; unhöflich.

disroot [dis'ru:t] entwurzeln.

disrupt [dis'rʌpt] zerreißen; spalten.

dissatis|faction ['dissætis'fækʃən] Unzufriedenheit f; ~factory [~ktəri] unbefriedigend; ~fy ['dis'sætisfai] nicht befriedigen; j-m mißfallen.

dissect [di'sekt] zerlegen; zergliedern.

dissemble [di'sembl] v/t. verhehlen; v/i. sich verstellen, heucheln.

dissen|sion [di'senʃən] Zwietracht f, Streit m, Uneinigkeit f; ~t [~nt] 1. abweichende Meinung; Nichtzugehörigkeit f zur Staatskirche; 2. andrer Meinung sein (from als).

dissimilar □ ['di'similə] (to) unähnlich (dat.); verschieden (von).

dissimulation [disimju'leiʃən] Verstellung f, Heuchelei f.

dissipat|e ['disipeit] (sich) zerstreuen; verschwenden; ~ion [disi'peiʃən] Zerstreuung f; Verschwendung f; ausschweifendes Leben.

dissociate [di'souʃieit] trennen; ~ o.s. sich distanzieren, abrücken.

dissoluble [di'sɔljubl] (auf)lösbar.

dissolut|e □ ['disəlu:t] liederlich, ausschweifend; ~ion [disə'lu:ʃən] Auflösung f; Zerstörung f; Tod m.

dissolve [di'zɔlv] v/t. (auf)lösen; schmelzen; v/i. sich auflösen; vergehen.

dissonant ['disənənt] ♪ mißtönend; abweichend; uneinig.

dissuade [di'sweid] j-m abraten.

distan|ce ['distəns] 1. Abstand m, Entfernung f; Ferne f; Strecke f; Zurückhaltung f; at a ~ von weitem; in e-r gewissen Entfernung; weit weg; keep s.o. at a ~ j-m gegenüber reserviert sein; 2. hinter sich lassen; ~t [~nt] entfernt; fern; zurückhaltend; Fern...; ~ control Fernsteuerung f.

distaste [dis'teist] Widerwille m; Abneigung f; ~ful [~tful] widerwärtig; ärgerlich.

distemper [dis'tempə] Krankheit f (bsd. von Tieren); (Hunde)Staupe f.

distend [dis'tend] (sich) ausdehnen; (auf)blähen; (sich) weiten.

distil [dis'til] herabtröpfeln (lassen); ⚗ destillieren; ~lery [~ləri] Branntweinbrennerei f.

distinct □ [dis'tiŋkt] verschieden; getrennt; deutlich, klar; ~ion [~kʃən] Unterscheidung f; Unterschied m; Auszeichnung f; Rang m; ~ive [~ktiv] unterscheidend; apart; kennzeichnend, bezeichnend.

distinguish [dis'tiŋgwiʃ] unterscheiden; auszeichnen; ~ed berühmt, ausgezeichnet; vornehm.

distort [dis'tɔ:t] verdrehen; verzerren.

distract ['dis'trækt] ablenken, zerstreuen; beunruhigen; verwirren; verrückt machen; ~ion [~kʃən] Zerstreutheit f; Verwirrung f; Wahnsinn m; Zerstreuung f.

distraught [dis'trɔ:t] verwirrt, bestürzt.

distress [dis'tres] 1. Qual f; Elend n, Not f; Erschöpfung f; 2. in Not

bringen; quälen; erschöpfen; **~ed** in Not befindlich; bekümmert; ~ *area* Notstandsgebiet *n*.
distribut|e [dis'tribju(:)t] verteilen; einteilen; verbreiten; **~ion** [distri'bju:ʃən] Verteilung *f*; *Film*-Verleih *m*; Verbreitung *f*; Einteilung *f*.
district ['distrikt] Bezirk *m*; Gegend *f*.
distrust [dis'trʌst] **1.** Mißtrauen *n*; **2.** mißtrauen (*dat.*); **~ful** □ [~tful] mißtrauisch; ~ (*of o.s.*) schüchtern.
disturb [dis'tə:b] beunruhigen; stören; **~ance** [~bəns] Störung *f*; Unruhe *f*; Aufruhr *m*; ~ *of the peace* ⚖ öffentliche Ruhestörung; **~er** [~bə] Störenfried *m*, Unruhestifter *m*.
disunite ['disju:'nait] (sich) trennen.
disuse ['dis'ju:z] nicht mehr gebrauchen.
ditch [ditʃ] Graben *m*.
ditto ['ditou] dito, desgleichen.
divan [di'væn] Diwan *m*; **~-bed** [*oft* 'daivænbed] Bettcouch *f*, Liege *f*.
dive [daiv] **1.** (unter)tauchen; *vom Sprungbrett* springen; e-n Sturzflug machen; eindringen in (*acc.*); **2.** *Schwimmen*: Springen *n*; (Kopf-)Sprung *m*; Sturzflug *m*; Kellerlokal *n*; *Am.* F Kaschemme *f*; **~r** ['daivə] Taucher *m*.
diverge [dai'və:dʒ] aus-ea.-laufen; abweichen; **~nce** [~dʒəns] Abweichung *f*; **~nt** □ [~nt] (von-ea.-)abweichend.
divers ['daivə(:)z] mehrere.
divers|e □ [dai'və:s] verschieden; mannigfaltig; **~ion** [~ə:ʃən] Ablenkung *f*; Zeitvertreib *m*; **~ity** [~ə:siti] Verschiedenheit *f*; Mannigfaltigkeit *f*.
divert [dai'və:t] ablenken; *j-n* zerstreuen; unterhalten; *Verkehr* umleiten.
divest [dai'vest] entkleiden (*a. fig.*).
divid|e [di'vaid] **1.** *v/t.* teilen; trennen; einteilen; Ꜳ dividieren (*by* durch); *v/i.* sich teilen; zerfallen; Ꜳ aufgehen; sich trennen *od.* auflösen; **2.** Wasserscheide *f*; **~end** ['dividend] Dividende *f*.
divine [di'vain] **1.** □ göttlich; ~ *service* Gottesdienst *m*; **2.** Geistliche(r) *m*; **3.** weissagen; ahnen.
diving ['daiviŋ] Kunstspringen *n*; *attr.* Taucher...
divinity [di'viniti] Gottheit *f*; Göttlichkeit *f*; Theologie *f*.
divis|ible □ [di'vizəbl] teilbar; **~ion** [~iʒən] Teilung *f*; Trennung *f*; Abteilung *f*; ⚔, Ꜳ Division *f*.
divorce [di'vɔ:s] **1.** (Ehe)Scheidung *f*; **2.** *Ehe* scheiden; sich scheiden lassen.
divulge [dai'vʌldʒ] ausplaudern; verbreiten; bekanntmachen.
dixie ⚔ *sl.* ['diksi] Kochgeschirr *n*; Feldkessel *m*; ♀ *Am.* die Südstaaten *pl.*; ♀*crat Am. pol.* opponierender Südstaatendemokrat.
dizz|iness ['dizinis] Schwindel *m*; **~y** □ ['dizi] schwind(e)lig.
do [du:] [*irr.*] *v/t.* tun; machen; (zu)bereiten; *Rolle, Stück* spielen; ~ *London sl.* London besichtigen; *have done reading* fertig sein mit Lesen; ~ *in* F um die Ecke bringen; ~ *into* übersetzen in; ~ *over* überstreifen, -ziehen; ~ *up* instand setzen; einpacken; *v/i.* tun; handeln; sich benehmen; sich befinden; genügen; *that will* ~ das genügt; *how* ~ *you* ~? guten Tag!, Wie geht's?; ~ *well* s-e Sache gut machen; gute Geschäfte machen; ~ *away with* weg-, abschaffen; *I could* ~ *with* ... ich könnte ... brauchen *od.* vertragen; ~ *without* fertig werden ohne; ~ *be quick* beeile dich doch; ~ *you like London?* — *I* ~ gefällt Ihnen London? — Ja.
docil|e ['dousail] gelehrig; fügsam; **~ity** [dou'siliti] Gelehrigkeit *f*.
dock[1] [dɔk] stutzen; *fig.* kürzen.
dock[2] [~] **1.** ⚓ Dock *n*; *bsd. Am.* Kai *m*, Pier *m*; ⚖ Anklagebank *f*; **2.** ⚓ docken.
dockyard ['dɔkja:d] Werft *f*.
doctor ['dɔktə] **1.** Doktor *m*; Arzt *m*; **2.** F verarzten; F *fig.* (ver)fälschen.
doctrine ['dɔktrin] Lehre *f*; Dogma *n*.
document **1.** ['dɔkjumənt] Urkunde *f*; **2.** [~ment] beurkunden.
dodge [dɔdʒ] **1.** Seitensprung *m*; Kniff *m*, Winkelzug *m*; **2.** *fig.* irreführen; ausweichen; Winkelzüge machen; **~r** ['dɔdʒə] Schieber(in); *Am.* Hand-, Reklamezettel *m*; *Am.* Maisbrot *n*, -kuchen *m*.
doe [dou] Hirschkuh *f*; Reh *n*; Häsin *f*.
dog [dɔg] **1.** Hund *m*; Haken *m*, Klammer *f*; **2.** nachspüren (*dat.*).
dogged □ ['dɔgid] verbissen.
dogma ['dɔgmə] Dogma *n*; Glaubenslehre *f*; **~tic(al** □) [dɔg'mætik(əl)] dogmatisch; bestimmt; **~tism** ['dɔgmətizəm] Selbstherrlichkeit *f*.
dog's-ear F ['dɔgziə] Eselsohr *n im Buch*.
dog-tired F ['dɔg'taiəd] hundemüde.
doings ['du(:)iŋz] *pl.* Dinge *n/pl.*; Begebenheiten *f/pl.*; Treiben *n*; Betragen *n*.
dole [doul] **1.** Spende *f*; F Erwerbslosenunterstützung *f*; **2.** verteilen.
doleful □ ['doulful] trübselig.
doll [dɔl] Puppe *f*.
dollar ['dɔlə] Dollar *m*.
dolly ['dɔli] Püppchen *n*.
dolorous ['dɔlərəs] schmerzhaft; traurig.
dolphin ['dɔlfin] Delphin *m*.
dolt [doult] Tölpel *m*.

domain [də'mein] Domäne f; fig. Gebiet n; Bereich m.

dome [doum] Kuppel f; ⊕ Haube f; ~d gewölbt.

Domesday Book ['du:mzdei'buk] Reichsgrundbuch n Englands.

domestic [də'mestik] 1. (~ally) häuslich; inländisch; einheimisch; zahm; ~ animal Haustier n; 2. Dienstbote m; ~s pl. Haushaltsartikel m/pl.; ~ate [~keit] zähmen; ~d wohnhaft.

domicile ['dɔmisail] Wohnsitz m; ~d wohnhaft.

domin|ant ['dɔminənt] (vor)herrschend; ~ate [~neit] (be)herrschen; ~ation [~'neiʃən] Herrschaft f; ~eer [~'niə] (despotisch) herrschen; ~eering □ [~əriŋ] herrisch, tyrannisch; überheblich.

dominion [də'minjən] Herrschaft f; Gebiet n; ⌀ Dominion n (im Brt. Commonwealth).

don [dɔn] anziehen; Hut aufsetzen.

donat|e Am. [dou'neit] schenken; stiften; ~ion [~'neiʃən] Schenkung f.

done [dʌn] 1. p.p. von do; 2. adj. abgemacht; fertig; gar gekocht.

donkey ['dɔŋki] zo. Esel m; attr. Hilfs...

donor ['dounə] (⅛ Blut)Spender m.

doom [du:m] 1. Schicksal n, Verhängnis n; 2. verurteilen, verdammen.

door [dɔ:] Tür f, Tor n; next ~ nebenan; ~-handle ['dɔ:hændl] Türgriff m; ~-keeper, Am. ~-man Pförtner m; Portier m; ~-way Türöffnung f; Torweg m; ~yard Am. Vorhof m, Vorgarten m.

dope [doup] 1. Schmiere f; bsd. ✕ Lack m; Aufputschmittel n; Rauschgift n; Am. sl. Geheimtip m; 2. lackieren; sl. betäuben, aufpulvern; Am. sl. herauskriegen.

dormant mst fig. ['dɔ:mənt] schlafend, ruhend; unbenutzt; † tot.

dormer(-window) ['dɔ:mə('windou)] Dachfenster n.

dormitory ['dɔ:mitri] Schlafsaal m; bsd. Am. Studenten(wohn)heim n.

dose [dous] 1. Dosis f, Portion f; 2. j-m e-e Medizin geben.

dot [dɔt] 1. Punkt m, Fleck m; 2. punktieren, tüpfeln; fig. verstreuen.

dot|e [dout]: ~ (up)on vernarrt sein in (acc.); ~ing ['doutiŋ] vernarrt.

double □ ['dʌbl] 1. doppelt; zu zweien; gekrümmt; zweideutig; 2. Doppelte(s) n; Doppelgänger(in); Tennis: Doppel(spiel) n; 3. v/t. verdoppeln; a. ~ up zs.-legen; zt. umfahren, umsegeln; ~d up zs.-gekrümmt; v/i. sich verdoppeln; a. ~ back e-n Haken schlagen (Hase); ~-breasted zweireihig (Jackett); ~-cross sl. Partner betrügen; ~-dealing Doppelzüngigkeit f; ~-edged zweischneidig; ~-entry doppelte Buchführung;

~-feature Am. Doppelprogramm n im Kino; ~-header Am. Baseball: Doppelspiel n; ~-park Am. verboten in zweiter Reihe parken.

doubt [daut] 1. v/i. zweifeln; v/t. bezweifeln; mißtrauen (dat.); 2. Zweifel m; no ~ ohne Zweifel; ~ful □ ['dautful] zweifelhaft; ~fulness [~lnis] Zweifelhaftigkeit f; ~less ['dautlis] ohne Zweifel.

douche [du:ʃ] 1. Dusche f; Irrigator m; 2. duschen; spülen.

dough [dou] Teig m; ~boy Am. F ['doubɔi] Landser m; ~nut Schmalzgebackenes.

dove [dʌv] Taube f; fig. Täubchen n.

dowel ⊕ ['dauəl] Dübel m.

down[1] [daun] Daune f; Flaum m; Düne f; ~s pl. Höhenrücken m.

down[2] [~] 1. adv. nieder; her-, hinunter, ab; abwärts; unten; be ~ upon F über j-n herfallen; 2. prp. herab, hinab, her-, hinunter; ~ the river flußabwärts; 3. adj. nach unten gerichtet; ~ platform Abfahrtsbahnsteig m (London); ~ train Zug m von London (fort); 4. v/t. niederwerfen; herunterholen; ~cast ['daunka:st] niedergeschlagen; ~easter Am. Neuengländer m bsd. von Maine; ~fall Fall m, Sturz m; Verfall m; ~-hearted niedergeschlagen; ~hill bergab; ~pour Regenguß m; ~right □ 1. adv. geradezu, durchaus; völlig; 2. adj. ehrlich; plump (Benehmen); richtig, glatt (Lüge etc.); ~stairs die Treppe hinunter, (nach) unten; ~stream stromabwärts; ~town bsd. Am. Hauptgeschäftsviertel n; ~ward(s) ['daunwəd(z)] abwärts (gerichtet).

downy ['dauni] flaumig; sl. gerissen.

dowry ['dauəri] Mitgift f (a. fig.).

doze [douz] 1. dösen; 2. Schläfchen n.

dozen ['dʌzn] Dutzend n.

drab [dræb] gelblichgrau; eintönig.

draft [dra:ft] 1. Entwurf m; † Tratte f; Abhebung f; ✕ (Sonder-) Kommando n; Einberufung f; = draught; 2. entwerfen; aufsetzen; ✕ abkommandieren; Am. einziehen; ~ee Am. ✕ [~'ti:] Dienstpflichtige(r) m; ~sman ['dra:ftsmən] (technischer) Zeichner; Verfasser m, Entwerfer m.

drag [dræg] 1. Schleppnetz n; Schleife f für Lasten; Egge f; 2. v/t. schleppen, ziehen; v/i. (sich) schleppen, schleifen; (mit e-m Schleppnetz) fischen; [Libelle f.]

dragon ['drægən] Drache m; ~-fly[

drain [drein] 1. Abfluß(graben m, -rohr n) m; F Schluck m; 2. v/t. entwässern; Glas leeren; a. ~ off abziehen; verzehren; v/i. ablaufen; ~age ['dreinidʒ] Abfluß m; Entwässerung(sanlage) f.

drake [dreik] Enterich *m.*
dram [dræm] Schluck *m*; *fig.*
Schnaps *m.*
drama ['drɑːmə] Drama *n*; **~tic**
[drə'mætik] (**~ally**) dramatisch;
~tist ['dræmətist] Dramatiker *m*;
~tize [**~**taiz] dramatisieren.
drank [dræŋk] *pret. von* drink 2.
drape [dreip] 1. drapieren; in Falten
legen; 2. *mst* **~s** *pl.* Vorhänge *m/pl.*;
~ry ['dreipəri] Tuchhandel *m*;
Tuchwaren *f/pl.*; Faltenwurf *m.*
drastic ['dræstik] (**~ally**) drastisch.
draught [drɑːft] Zug *m* (*Ziehen*;
Fischzug; *Zugluft*; *Schluck*); ⚓
Tiefgang *m*; **~s** *pl.* Damespiel *n*;
s. draft; **~ beer** Faßbier *n*; **~-horse**
['drɑːfthɔːs] Zugpferd *n*; **~sman**
[**~**tsmən] Damestein *m*; = draftsman; **~y** [**~**ti] zugig.
draw [drɔː] 1. [*irr.*] ziehen; an-,
auf-, ein-, zuziehen; (sich) zs.-
ziehen; in die Länge ziehen; dehnen; herausziehen, herauslocken;
entnehmen; *Geld* abheben; an-
locken, anziehen; abzapfen; aus-
fischen; *Geflügel* ausnehmen; zeichnen; entwerfen; *Urkunde* abfassen;
unentschieden spielen; *Luft* schöpfen; **~ near** heranrücken; **~ out** in
die Länge ziehen; **~ up** ab-, verfassen; **~** (up)on ✝ (e-n Wechsel)
ziehen auf (*acc.*); *fig.* in Anspruch
nehmen; 2. Zug *m* (*Ziehen*); *Lotterie:* Ziehung *f*; Los *n*; *Sport:* un-
entschiedenes Spiel; F Zugstück *n*,
-artikel *m*; **~back** ['drɔːbæk] Nachteil *m*; Hindernis *n*; ✝ Rückzoll *m*;
Am. Rückzahlung *f*; **~er** ['drɔːə]
Ziehende(r *m*) *f*; Zeichner *m*; ✝
Aussteller *m*, Trassant *m*; [drɔː]
Schublade *f*; (*a pair of*) **~s** *pl.* (eine)
Unterhose; (ein) Schlüpfer *m*; *mst
chest of* **~s** Kommode *f.*
drawing ['drɔːiŋ] Ziehen *n*; Zeichnen *n*; Zeichnung *f*; **~-account**
Girokonto *n*; **~-board** Reißbrett *n*;
~-room Gesellschaftszimmer *n.*
drawn [drɔːn] 1. *p.p. von* draw 1;
2. *adj.* unentschieden; verzerrt.
dread [dred] 1. Furcht *f*; Schrecken
m; 2. (sich) fürchten; **~ful** ☐
['dredful] schrecklich; furchtbar.
dream [driːm] 1. Traum *m*; 2. [*irr.*]
träumen; **~er** ['driːmə] Träumer
(-in); **~t** [dremt] *pret. u. p.p. von*
dream 2; **~y** ☐ ['driːmi] träume-
risch; verträumt.
dreary ☐ ['driəri] traurig; öde.
dredge [dredʒ] 1. Schleppnetz *n*;
Bagger(maschine *f*) *m*; 2. (aus-)
baggern.
dregs [dregz] *pl.* Bodensatz *m*,
Hefe *f.*
drench [drentʃ] 1. (Regen)Guß *m*;
2. durchnässen; *fig.* baden.
dress [dres] 1. Anzug *m*; Kleidung
f; Kleid *n*; 2. an-, ein-, zurichten;
✗ (sich) richten; zurechtmachen;

(sich) ankleiden; putzen; ✗ verbinden; frisieren; **~-circle** *thea.*
['dres'səːkl] erster Rang; **~er** [**~**ə]
Anrichte *f*; *Am.* Frisiertoilette *f.*
dressing ['dresiŋ] An-, Zurichten *n*;
Ankleiden *n*; Verband *m*; Appretur
f; *Küche:* Soße *f*; Füllung *f*; **~s** *pl.*
✗ Verbandzeug *n*; **~ down** Stand-
pauke *f*; **~-gown** Morgenrock *m*;
~-table Frisiertisch *m.*
dress|maker ['dresmeikə] Schnei-
derin *f*; **~-parade** Modenschau *f.*
drew ['druː] *pret. von* draw 1.
dribble ['dribl] tröpfeln, träufeln
(lassen); geifern; *Fußball:* drib-
beln.
dried [draid] getrocknet; Dörr...
drift [drift] 1. (Dahin)Treiben *n*;
fig. Lauf *m*; *fig.* Hang *m*; Zweck *m*;
(Schnee-, Sand)Wehe *f*; 2. *v/t.*
(zs.-)treiben, (zs.-)wehen; *v/i.* (dahin)treiben; sich anhäufen.
drill [dril] 1. Drillbohrer *m*; Furche
f; ✗ Drill-, Sämaschine *f*; ✗ Exerzieren *n* (*a. fig.*); 2. bohren; ✗
(ein)exerzieren (*a. fig.*).
drink [driŋk] 1. Trunk *m*; (geistiges)
Getränk; 2. [*irr.*] trinken.
drip [drip] 1. Tröpfeln *n*; Traufe *f*;
2. tröpfeln (lassen); triefen; **~-dry
shirt** ['drip'drai ʃəːt] bügelfreies
Hemd; **~ping** [**~**piŋ] Bratenfett *n.*
drive [draiv] 1. (Spazier)Fahrt *f*;
Auffahrt *f*, Fahrweg *m*; ⊕ Antrieb
m; *fig.* (Auf)Trieb *m*; Drang *m*;
Unternehmen *n*, Feldzug *m*; *Am.*
Sammelaktion *f*; 2. [*irr.*] *v/t.* (an-,
ein)treiben; *Geschäft* betreiben;
fahren; lenken; zwingen; vertreiben; *v/i.* treiben; fahren; **~ at** hin-
zielen auf.
drive-in *Am.* ['draiv'in] 1. *mst attr.*
Auto...; **~ cinema** Autokino *n*;
2. Autokino *n*; Autorestaurant *n.*
drivel ['drivl] 1. geifern; faseln;
2. Geifer *m*; Faselei *f.*
driven ['drivn] *p.p. von* drive 2.
driver ['draivə] Treiber *m*; *mot.*
Fahrer *m*, Chauffeur *m*; 🚂 Führer
m.
driving| licence ['draiviŋ laisəns]
Führerschein *m*; **~ school** Fahr-
schule *f.*
drizzle ['drizl] 1. Sprühregen *m*;
2. sprühen, nieseln.
drone [droun] 1. *zo.* Drohne *f*; *fig.*
Faulenzer *m*; 2. summen; dröhnen.
droop [druːp] *v/t.* sinken lassen; *v/i.*
schlaff niederhängen; den Kopf
hängen lassen; (ver)welken; schwinden.
drop [drɔp] 1. Tropfen *m*; Frucht-
bonbon *m*; *n*; Fall *m*; Falltür *f*;
thea. Vorhang *m*; **get** (**have**) **the ~
on** *Am.* F zuvorkommen; 2. *v/t.*
tropfen (lassen); niederlassen; fallen lassen; *Brief* einwerfen; *Fahrgast* absetzen; senken; **~ s.o. a few
lines** *pl.* j-m ein paar Zeilen schrei-

ben; *v/i.* tropfen; (herab)fallen; um-, hinsinken; ~ *in* unerwartet kommen.

dropsy ♂ ['drɔpsi] Wassersucht *f.*

drought [draut], **drouth** [drauθ] Trockenheit *f*, Dürre *f.*

drove [drouv] **1.** Trift *f Rinder*; Herde *f* (*a. fig.*); **2.** *pret. von* drive 2.

drown [draun] *v/t.* ertränken; überschwemmen; *fig.* übertäuben; übertönen; *v/i.* ertrinken.

drowse [drauz] schlummern, schläfrig sein *od.* machen; **~y** ['drauzi] schläfrig; einschläfernd.

drudge [drʌdʒ] **1.** *fig.* Sklave *m*, Packesel *m*, Kuli *m*; **2.** sich (ab-) placken.

drug [drʌg] **1.** Droge *f*, Arzneiware *f*; Rauschgift *n*; unverkäufliche Ware; **2.** mit (schädlichen) Zutaten versetzen; Arznei *od.* Rauschgift geben (*dat.*) *od.* nehmen; **~gist** ['drʌgist] Drogist *m*; Apotheker *m*; **~store** *Am.* Drugstore *m.*

drum [drʌm] **1.** Trommel *f*; Trommelfell *n*; **2.** trommeln; **~mer** ['drʌmə] Trommler *m*; *bsd. Am.* F Vertreter *m.*

drunk [drʌŋk] **1.** *p.p. von* drink 2; **2.** *adj.* (be)trunken; *get* ~ sich betrinken; **~ard** ['drʌŋkəd] Trinker *m*, Säufer *m*; **~en** *adj.* [~kən] (be-) trunken.

dry [drai] **1.** □ trocken; herb (*Wein*); F durstig; F antialkoholisch; ~ *goods pl. Am.* F Kurzwaren *f/pl.*; **2.** *Am.* F Alkoholgegner *m*; **3.** trocknen; dörren; ~ *up* austrocknen; verdunsten; **~-clean** ['drai'kli:n] chemisch reinigen; **~-nurse** Kinderfrau *f.*

dual □ ['dju(:)əl] doppelt; Doppel...

dubious □ ['dju:bjəs] zweifelhaft.

duchess ['dʌtʃis] Herzogin *f.*

duck [dʌk] **1.** *zo.* Ente *f*; *Am. sl.* Kerl *m*; Verbeugung *f*; Ducken *n*; (Segel)Leinen *n*; F Liebling *m*; **2.** (unter)tauchen; (sich) ducken; *Am. j-m* ausweichen.

duckling ['dʌkliŋ] Entchen *n.*

dude *Am.* [dju:d] Geck *m*; ~ *ranch Am.* Vergnügungsfarm *f.*

dudgeon ['dʌdʒən] Groll *m.*

due [dju:] **1.** schuldig; gebührend; gehörig; fällig; *in* ~ *time* zur rechten Zeit; *be* ~ *to j-m* gebühren; herrühren *od.* kommen von; *be* ~ *to inf.* sollen, müssen; *Am.* im Begriff sein zu; **2.** *adv.* ✦ gerade; genau; **3.** Schuldigkeit *f*; Recht *n*, Anspruch *m*; Lohn *m*; *mst* ~*s pl.* Abgabe(n *pl.*) *f*, Gebühr(en *pl.*) *f*; Beitrag *m*; **2.** sich duellieren.

duel □ ['dju(:)əl] **1.** Zweikampf *m*;

dug [dʌg] *pret. u. p.p. von* dig 1.

duke [dju:k] Herzog *m*; **~dom** ['dju:kdəm] Herzogtum *n*; Herzogswürde *f.*

dull [dʌl] **1.** □ dumm; träge;

schwerfällig; stumpf(sinnig); matt (*Auge etc.*); schwach (*Gehör*); langweilig; teilnahmslos; dumpf; trüb; ✝ flau; **2.** stumpf machen; *fig.* abstumpfen; (sich) trüben; **~ness** ['dʌlnis] Stumpfsinn *m*; Dummheit *f*; Schwerfälligkeit *f*; Mattheit *f*; Langweiligkeit *f*; Teilnahmslosigkeit *f*; Trübheit *f*; Flauheit *f.*

duly *adv.* ['dju:li] gehörig; richtig.

dumb □ [dʌm] stumm; sprachlos; *Am.* F doof, blöd; **~founded** [dʌm'faundid] sprachlos; **~waiter** ['dʌm'weitə] Drehtisch *m*; *Am.* Speisenaufzug *m.*

dummy ['dʌmi] Attrappe *f*; Schein *m*, Schwindel *m*; *fig.* Strohmann *m*; Statist *m*; *attr.* Schein...; Schwindel...

dump [dʌmp] **1.** *v/t.* auskippen; *Schutt etc.* abladen; *Waren* zu Schleuderpreisen ausführen; *v/i.* hinplumpsen; **2.** Klumpen *m*; Plumps *m*; Schuttabladestelle *f*; ✕ Munitionslager *n*; **~ing** ✝ ['dʌmpiŋ] Schleuderausfuhr *f*; **~s** *pl.*: (*down*) *in the* ~ niedergeschlagen.

dun [dʌn] mahnen, drängen.

dunce [dʌns] Dummkopf *m.*

dune [dju:n] Düne *f.*

dung [dʌŋ] **1.** Dung *m*; **2.** düngen.

dungeon ['dʌndʒən] Kerker *m.*

dunk *Am.* F [dʌŋk] (ein)tunken.

dupe [dju:p] anführen, täuschen.

duplex ⊕ ['dju:pleks] *attr.* Doppel...; *Am.* Zweifamilienhaus *n.*

duplic|ate 1. ['dju:plikit] doppelt; **2.** [~] Duplikat *n*; **3.** [~keit] doppelt ausfertigen; **~ity** [dju(:)'plisiti] Doppelzüngigkeit *f.*

dura|ble □ ['djuərəbl] dauerhaft; **~tion** [djuə'reiʃən] Dauer *f.*

duress(e) [djuə'res] Zwang *m.*

during *prp.* ['djuəriŋ] während.

dusk [dʌsk] Halbdunkel *n*, Dämmerung *f*; **~y** □ ['dʌski] dämmerig, düster (*a. fig.*); schwärzlich.

dust [dʌst] **1.** Staub *m*; **2.** abstauben; bestreuen; **~bin** ['dʌstbin] Mülleimer *m*; **~ bowl** *Am.* Sandstaubu. Dürregebiet *n im Westen der USA*; **~cart** Müllwagen *m*; **~er** [~tə] Staublappen *m*, -wedel *m*; *Am.* Staubmantel *m*; **~jacket** *Am.* Schutzumschlag *m e-s Buches*; **~man** Müllabfuhrmann *m*; **~y** □ [~ti] staubig.

Dutch [dʌtʃ] **1.** holländisch; ~ *treat Am.* F getrennte Rechnung; **2.** Holländisch *n*; *the* ~ die Holländer *pl.*

duty ['dju:ti] Pflicht *f*; Ehrerbietung *f*; Abgabe *f*, Zoll *m*; Dienst *m*; *off* ~ dienstfrei; **~-free** zollfrei.

dwarf [dwɔ:f] **1.** Zwerg *m*; **2.** in der Entwicklung hindern; verkleinern.

dwell [dwel] [*irr.*] wohnen; verweilen (*on, upon* bei); ~ (*up*)*on* bestehen auf (*acc.*); **~ing** ['dweliŋ] Wohnung *f.*

dwelt [dwelt] *pret. u. p.p. von* dwell.

dwindle ['dwindl] (dahin)schwinden, abnehmen; (herab)sinken.

dye [dai] 1. Farbe *f*; *of deepest* ~ *fig.* schlimmster Art; 2. färben.

dying ['daiiŋ] 1. □ sterbend; Sterbe...; 2. Sterben *n*.

dynam|ic [dai'næmik] dynamisch, kraftgeladen; ~ics [~ks] *mst sg.* Dynamik *f*; ~ite ['dainəmait] 1. Dynamit *n*; 2. mit Dynamit sprengen.

dysentery ℰ ['disntri] Ruhr *f*.

dyspepsia ℰ [dis'pepsiə] Verdauungsstörung *f*.

E

each [i:tʃ] jede(r, -s); ~ *other* einander, sich.

eager □ ['i:gə] (be)gierig; eifrig; ~ness [~'i:gənis] Begierde *f*; Eifer *m*.

eagle ['i:gl] Adler *m*; *Am.* Zehndollarstück *n*; ~eyed scharfsichtig.

ear [iə] Ähre *f*; Ohr *n*; Öhr *n*, Henkel *m*; *keep an* ~ *to the ground bsd. Am.* aufpassen, was die Leute sagen *od.* denken; ~drum ['iədrʌm] Trommelfell *n*.

earl [ə:l] *englischer* Graf.

early ['ə:li] früh; Früh...; Anfangs-...; erst; bald(ig); *as* ~ *as* schon in (*dat.*). [nen.]

ear-mark ['iəmɑ:k] (kenn)zeich-]

earn [ə:n] verdienen; einbringen.

earnest ['ə:nist] 1. □ ernst(lich, -haft); ernstgemeint; 2. Ernst *m*.

earnings ['ə:niŋz] Einkommen *n*.

ear|piece *teleph.* ['iəpi:s] Hörmuschel *f*; ~shot Hörweite *f*.

earth [ə:θ] 1. Erde *f*; Land *n*; 2. *v/t.* ℰ erden; ~en ['ə:θən] irden; ~enware [~nwεə] 1. Töpferware *f* Steingut *n*; 2. irden; ~ing ℰ ['ə:θiŋ] Erdung *f*; ~ly ['ə:θli] irdisch; ~quake Erdbeben *n*; ~worm Regenwurm *m*.

ease [i:z] 1. Bequemlichkeit *f*, Behagen *n*; Ruhe *f*; Ungezwungenheit *f*; Leichtigkeit *f*; *at* ~ bequem, behaglich; 2. *v/t.* erleichtern; lindern; beruhigen; bequem(er) machen; *v/i.* sich entspannen (*Lage*).

easel ['i:zl] Staffelei *f*.

easiness ['i:zinis] = ease 1.

east [i:st] 1. Ost(en *m*); Orient *m*; *the* ℒ *Am.* die Oststaaten *der USA*; 2. Ost...; östlich; ostwärts.

Easter ['i:stə] Ostern *n*; *attr.* Oster...

easter|ly ['i:stəli] östlich; Ost...; nach Osten; ~n [~ən] = *easterly*; orientalisch; ~ner [~nə] Ostländer (-in); Oriental|e *m*, -in *f*; ℒ *Am.* Oststaatler(in).

eastward(s) ['i:stwəd(z)] ostwärts.

easy ['i:zi] □ leicht; bequem; frei von Schmerzen; ruhig; willig; ungezwungen; *in* ~ *circumstances* wohlhabend; *on* ~ *street Am.* in guten Verhältnissen; *take it* ~! immer mit der Ruhe!; ~ *chair* Klubsessel *m*; ~going *fig.* bequem.

eat [i:t] 1. [*irr.*] essen; (zer)fressen; 2. ~s *pl. Am. sl.* Essen *n*, Eßwaren *f/pl.*; ~ables ['i:təblz] *pl.* Eßwaren *f/pl.*; ~er ['i:tn] *p.p. von* eat 1.

eaves [i:vz] *pl.* Dachrinne *f*, Traufe *f*; ~drop ['i:vzdrɔp] (er)lauschen; horchen.

ebb [eb] 1. Ebbe *f*; *fig.* Abnahme *f*; Verfall *m*; 2. verebben; *fig.* abnehmen, sinken; ~tide ['eb'taid] Ebbe *f*.

ebony ['ebəni] Ebenholz *n*.

ebullition [ebə'liʃən] Überschäumen *n*; Aufbrausen *n*.

eccentric [ik'sentrik] 1. exzentrisch; *fig.* überspannt; 2. Sonderling *m*.

ecclesiastic [ikli:zi'æstik] Geistliche(r) *m*; ~al □ [~kəl] geistlich, kirchlich.

echo ['ekou] 1. Echo *n*; 2. widerhallen; *fig.* echoen, nachsprechen.

eclipse [i'klips] 1. Finsternis *f*; 2. (sich) verfinstern, verdunkeln.

econom|ic(al □) [i:kə'nɔmik(əl)] haushälterisch; wirtschaftlich; Wirtschafts...; ~ics [~ks] *sg.* Volkswirtschaft(slehre) *f*; ~ist [i(:)'kɔnəmist] Volkswirt *m*; ~ize [~maiz] sparsam wirtschaften (mit); ~y [~mi] Wirtschaft *f*; Wirtschaftlichkeit *f*; Einsparung *f*; *political* ~ Volkswirtschaft(slehre) *f*.

ecsta|sy ['ekstəsi] Ekstase *f*, Verzückung *f*; ~tic [eks'tætik] (~ally) verzückt.

eddy ['edi] 1. Wirbel *m*; 2. wirbeln.

edge [edʒ] 1. Schneide *f*; Schärfe *f*; Rand *m*; Kante *f*; Tisch-Ecke *f*; *be on* ~ nervös sein; *have the* ~ *on s.o. bsd. Am.* F j-m über sein; 2. schärfen; (um)säumen; (sich) drängen; ~ways, ~wise ['edʒweiz, 'edʒwaiz] seitwärts; von der Seite.

edging ['edʒiŋ] Einfassung *f*; Rand.

edgy ['edʒi] scharf; F nervös. [*m.*]

edible ['edibl] eßbar.

edict ['i:dikt] Edikt *n*.

edifice ['edifis] Gebäude *n*.

edifying □ ['edifaiiŋ] erbaulich.

edit ['edit] *Text* herausgeben, redigieren; *Zeitung* als Herausgeber leiten; ~ion [i'diʃən] *Buch*-Ausgabe *f*; Auflage *f*; ~or ['editə] Herausgeber *m*; Redakteur *m*; ~orial [edi'tɔ:riəl] Leitartikel m; attr. Redaktions...; **~orship** ['editəʃip] Schriftleitung f, Redaktion f.

educat|e ['edju(:)keit] erziehen; unterrichten; **~ion** [edju(:)'keiʃən] Erziehung f; (Aus)Bildung f; Erziehungs-, Schulwesen n; Ministry of ♀ Unterrichtsministerium n; **~ional** □ [~nl] erzieherisch; Erziehungs...; Bildungs...; **~or** ['edju:keitə] Erzieher m.

eel [i:l] Aal m.

efface [i'feis] auslöschen; fig. tilgen.

effect [i'fekt] 1. Wirkung f; Folge f; ⊕ Leistung f; **~s** pl. Effekten pl.; Habseligkeiten f/pl.; be of ~ Wirkung haben; take ~ in Kraft treten; in ~ in der Tat; to the ~ des Inhalts; 2. bewirken, ausführen; **~ive** □ [~tiv] wirkend; wirksam; eindrucksvoll; wirklich vorhanden; ⊕ nutzbar; ~ date Tag m des Inkrafttretens; **~ual** □ [~tjuəl] wirksam, kräftig.

effeminate □ [i'feminit] verweichlicht; weibisch.

effervesce [efə'ves] (auf)brausen; **~nt** [~snt] sprudelnd, schäumend.

effete [e'fi:t] verbraucht; entkräftet.

efficacy ['efikəsi] Wirksamkeit f, Kraft f.

efficien|cy [i'fiʃənsi] Leistung(sfähigkeit) f; ~ expert Am. Rationalisierungsfachmann m; **~t** □ [~nt] wirksam; leistungsfähig; tüchtig.

efflorescence [əflɔ:'resns] Blütezeit f; 🜛 Beschlag m.

effluence ['efluəns] Ausfluß m.

effort ['efət] Anstrengung f, Bemühung f (at um); Mühe f.

effrontery [e'frʌntəri] Frechheit f.

effulgent □ [e'fʌldʒənt] glänzend.

effus|ion [i'fju:ʒən] Erguß m; **~ive** □ [~:siv] überschwenglich.

egg¹ [eg] mst ~ on aufreizen.

egg² [~] Ei n; put all one's ~s in one basket alles auf eine Karte setzen; as sure as ~s is ~s F todsicher; **~cup** ['egkʌp] Eierbecher m; **~head** Am. sl. Intellektuelle(r) m.

egotism ['egoutizəm] Selbstgefälligkeit f.

egregious iro. □ [i'gri:dʒəs] ungeheuer.

egress ['i:grəs] Ausgang m; Ausweg m.

Egyptian [i'dʒipʃən] 1. ägyptisch; 2. Ägypter(in).

eider ['aidə]: ~ down Eiderdaunen f/pl.; Daunendecke f.

eight [eit] 1. acht; 2. Acht f; behind the ~ ball Am. in der (die) Klemme; **~een** ['ei'ti:n] achtzehn; **~eenth** [~nθ] achtzehnt; **~fold** ['eitfould] achtfach; **~h** [eitθ] 1. achte(r, -s); 2. Achtel n; **~hly** ['eitθli] achtens; **~ieth** ['eitiiθ] achtzigste(r, -s); **~y** ['eiti] achtzig.

either ['aiðə] 1. adj. u. pron. einer

von beiden; beide; 2. cj. ~ ... or entweder ... oder; not (...) ~ auch nicht.

ejaculate [i'dʒækjuleit] Worte, Flüssigkeit ausstoßen.

eject [i(:)'dʒekt] ausstoßen; vertreiben, ausweisen; entsetzen (e-s Amtes).

eke [i:k]: ~ out ergänzen; verlängern; sich mit et. durchhelfen.

el Am. F [el] = elevated railroad.

elaborat|e 1. □ [i'læbərit] sorgfältig ausgearbeitet; kompliziert; 2. [~reit] sorgfältig ausarbeiten; **~eness** [~ritnis], **~ion** [ilæbə'reiʃən] sorgfältige Ausarbeitung.

elapse [i'læps] verfließen, verstreichen.

elastic [i'læstik] 1. (~ally) dehnbar; spannkräftig; 2. Gummiband n; **~ity** [elæs'tisiti] Elastizität f, Dehnbarkeit f; Spannkraft f.

elate [i'leit] (er)heben, ermutigen, froh erregen; stolz machen; **~d** in gehobener Stimmung, freudig erregt (at über acc.; with durch).

elbow ['elbou] 1. Ellbogen m; Biegung f; ⊕ Knie n; at one's ~ nahe, bei der Hand; out at ~s fig. heruntergekommen; 2. mit dem Ellbogen (weg)stoßen; ~ out verdrängen; **~grease** F Armschmalz n (Kraftanstrengung).

elder ['eldə] 1. älter; 2. der, die Ältere; (Kirchen)Älteste(r) m; ♀ Holunder m; **~ly** [~əli] ältlich.

eldest ['eldist] älteste(r, -s).

elect [i'lekt] 1. (aus)gewählt; 2. (aus-, er)wählen; **~ion** [~kʃən] Wahl f; **~ive** [~ktiv] 1. □ wählend; gewählt; Wahl...; Am. fakultativ; 2. Am. Wahlfach n; **~or** [~tə] Wähler m; Am. Wahlmann m; Kurfürst m; **~oral** [~ərəl] Wahl..., Wähler...; ~ college Am. Wahlmänner m/pl.; **~orate** [~rit] Wähler(schaft f) m/pl.

electric|(al □) [i'lektrik(əl)] elektrisch; Elektro...; fig. faszinierend; **~al engineer** Elektrotechniker m; ~ blue stahlblau; ~ chair elektrischer Stuhl; **~ian** [ilek'triʃən] Elektriker m; **~ity** [~isiti] Elektrizität f.

electri|fy [i'lektrifai], **~ze** [~raiz] elektrifizieren; elektrisieren.

electro|cute [i'lektrəkju:t] auf dem elektrischen Stuhl hinrichten; durch elektrischen Strom töten; **~metallurgy** Elektrometallurgie f.

electron [i'lektrɔn] Elektron n; **~ray tube** magisches Auge.

electro|plate [i'lektroupleit] galvanisch versilbern; **~type** galvanischer Druck; Galvano n.

elegan|ce ['eligəns] Eleganz f; Anmut f; **~t** □ [~nt] elegant; geschmackvoll; Am. erstklassig.

element ['elimənt] Element n; Urstoff m; (Grund)Bestandteil m; **~s** pl. Anfangsgründe m/pl.; **~al** □

[eli'mentl] elementar; wesentlich; ~ary [~təri] 1. □ elementar; Anfangs...; ~ school Volks-, Grundschule f; 2. elementaries pl. Anfangsgründe m/pl.

elephant ['elifənt] Elefant m.

elevat|e ['eliveit] erhöhen; fig. erheben; ~ed erhaben; ~ (railroad) Am. Hochbahn f; ~ion [eli'veiʃən] Erhebung f, Erhöhung f; Höhe f; Erhabenheit f; ~or ⊕ ['eliveitə] Aufzug m; Am. Fahrstuhl m; ⚓ Höhenruder n; (grain) ~ Am. Getreidespeicher m.

eleven [i'levn] 1. elf; 2. Elf f; ~th [~nθ] elfte(r, -s).

elf [elf] Elf(e f) m, Kobold m; Zwerg m.

elicit [i'lisit] hervorlocken, herausholen.

eligible □ ['elidʒəbl] geeignet, annehmbar; passend.

eliminat|e [i'limineit] aussondern, ausscheiden; ausmerzen; ~ion [ilimi'neiʃən] Aussonderung f; Ausscheidung f.

élite [ei'li:t] Elite f; Auslese f.

elk zo. [elk] Elch m.

ellipse ♉ [i'lips] Ellipse f.

elm ♉ [elm] Ulme f, Rüster f.

elocution [elə'kju:ʃən] Vortrag(skunst, -sweise f) m.

elongate [i'lɔŋgeit] verlängern.

elope [i'loup] entlaufen, durchgehen.

eloquen|ce ['eləkwəns] Beredsamkeit f; ~t □ [~nt] beredt.

else [els] sonst, andere(r, -s), weiter; ~where ['elswɛə] anderswo(hin).

elucidat|e [i'lu:sideit] erläutern; ~ion [ilu:si'deiʃən] Aufklärung f.

elude [i'lu:d] geschickt umgehen; ausweichen, sich entziehen (dat.).

elus|ive [i'lu:siv] schwer faßbar; ~ory [~səri] trügerisch.

emaciate [i'meiʃieit] abzehren, ausmergeln.

emanat|e ['eməneit] ausströmen; ausgehen (from von); ~ion [emə-'neiʃən] Ausströmen n; fig. Ausstrahlung f.

emancipat|e [i'mænsipeit] emanzipieren, befreien; ~ion [imænsi-'peiʃən] Emanzipation f; Befreiung f.

embalm [im'ba:m] (ein)balsamieren; be ~ed in fortleben in (dat.).

embankment [im'bæŋkmənt] Eindämmung f; Deich m; (Bahn-) Damm m; Uferstraße f, Kai m.

embargo [em'ba:gou] (Hafen-, Handels)Sperre f, Beschlagnahme f.

embark [im'ba:k] (sich) einschiffen (for nach); Geld anlegen; sich einlassen (in, on, upon in, auf acc.).

embarrass [im'bærəs] (be)hindern; verwirren; in (Geld)Verlegenheit bringen; verwickeln; ~ing □ [~siŋ]

unangenehm; unbequem; ~ment [~smənt] (Geld)Verlegenheit f; Schwierigkeit f.

embassy ['embəsi] Botschaft f; Gesandtschaft f.

embed [im'bed] (ein)betten, lagern.

embellish [im'beliʃ] verschönern; ausschmücken. [Asche.\

embers ['embəz] pl. glühende/

embezzle [im'bezl] unterschlagen; ~ment [~lmənt] Unterschlagung f.

embitter [im'bitə] verbittern.

emblazon [im'bleizən] mit e-m Wappenbild bemalen; fig. verherrlichen.

emblem ['embləm] Sinnbild n; Wahrzeichen n.

embody [im'bɔdi] verkörpern; vereinigen; einverleiben (in dat.).

embolden [im'bouldən] ermutigen.

embolism ⚕ ['embəlizəm] Embolie f.

embosom [im'buzəm] ins Herz schließen; ~ed with umgeben von.

emboss [im'bɔs] bossieren; mit dem Hammer treiben.

embrace [im'breis] 1. (sich) umarmen; umfassen; Beruf etc. ergreifen; Angebot annehmen; 2. Umarmung f.

embroider [im'brɔidə] sticken; ausschmücken; ~y [~əri] Stickerei f.

embroil [im'brɔil] (in Streit) verwickeln; verwirren.

emendation [i:men'deiʃən] Verbesserung f.

emerald ['emərəld] Smaragd m.

emerge [i'mə:dʒ] auftauchen; hervorgehen; sich erheben; sich zeigen; ~ncy [~dʒənsi] unerwartetes Ereignis; Notfall m; attr. Not...; ~ brake Notbremse f; ~ call Notruf m; ~ exit Notausgang m; ~ man Sport: Ersatzmann m; ~nt [~nt] auftauchend, entstehend; ~ countries Entwicklungsländer n/pl.

emersion [i(:)'mə:ʃən] Auftauchen n.

emigra|nt ['emigrənt] 1. auswandernd; 2. Auswanderer m; ~te [~reit] auswandern; ~tion [emi-'greiʃən] Auswanderung f.

eminen|ce ['eminəns] (An)Höhe f; Auszeichnung f; hohe Stellung; Eminenz f (Titel); ~t □ [~nt] fig. ausgezeichnet, hervorragend; ~tly [~tli] ganz besonders.

emissary ['emisəri] Emissär m.

emit [i'mit] von sich geben; aussenden, ausströmen; ↑ ausgeben.

emolument [i'mɔljumənt] Vergütung f; ~s pl. Einkünfte pl.

emotion [i'mouʃən] (Gemüts)Bewegung f; Gefühl(sregung f) n; Rührung f; ~al □ [~nl] gefühlsmäßig; gefühlvoll; gefühlsbetont; ~less [~nlis] gefühllos, kühl.

emperor ['empərə] Kaiser m.

empha|sis ['emfəsis] Nachdruck m; **~size** [˛saiz] nachdrücklich betonen; **~tic** [im'fætik] (**~ally**) nachdrücklich; ausgesprochen.

empire ['empaiə] (Kaiser)Reich n; Herrschaft f; the British ♀ das britische Weltreich.

empirical □ [em'pirikəl] erfahrungsgemäß.

employ [im'plɔi] **1.** beschäftigen, anstellen; an-, verwenden, gebrauchen; **2.** Beschäftigung f; in the ~ of angestellt bei; **~ee** [emplɔi'i:] Angestellte(r m) f; Arbeitnehmer(in); **~er** [im'plɔiə] Arbeitgeber m; ✝ Auftraggeber m; **~ment** [˛ɔimənt] Beschäftigung f; Arbeit f; **~ agency** Stellenvermittlungsbüro n; ♀ Exchange Arbeitsamt n.

empower [im'pauə] ermächtigen; befähigen.

empress ['empris] Kaiserin f.

empt|iness ['emptinis] Leere f; Hohlheit f; **~y** □ ['empti] **1.** leer; fig. hohl; **2.** (sich) (aus-, ent)leeren.

emul|ate ['emjuleit] wetteifern mit; nacheifern, es gleichtun (dat.); **~ation** [emju'leiʃən] Wetteifer m.

enable [i'neibl] befähigen, es j-m ermöglichen; ermächtigen.

enact [i'nækt] verfügen, verordnen; Gesetz erlassen; thea. spielen.

enamel [i'næməl] **1.** Email(le f) n, (Zahn)Schmelz m; Glasur f; Lack m; **2.** emaillieren; glasieren.

enamo(u)r [i'næmə] verliebt machen; **~ed** of verliebt in.

encamp ✕ [in'kæmp] (sich) lagern.

encase [in'keis] einschließen.

enchain [in'tʃein] anketten; fesseln.

enchant [in'tʃɑːnt] bezaubern; **~ment** [˛tmənt] Bezauberung f; Zauber m; **~ress** [˛tris] Zauberin f.

encircle [in'səːkl] einkreisen.

enclos|e [in'klouz] einzäunen; einschließen; beifügen; **~ure** [˛ouʒə] Einzäunung f; eingehegtes Grundstück; Bei-, Anlage f zu e-m Brief.

encompass [in'kʌmpəs] umgeben.

encore thea. [ɔŋ'kɔː] **1.** um e-e Zugabe bitten; **2.** Zugabe f.

encounter [in'kauntə] **1.** Begegnung f; Gefecht n; **2.** begegnen (dat.); auf Schwierigkeiten etc. stoßen; mit j-m zs.-stoßen.

encourage [in'kʌridʒ] ermutigen; fördern; **~ment** [˛dʒmənt] Ermutigung f; Unterstützung f.

encroach [in'kroutʃ] (on, upon) eingreifen, eindringen (in acc.); beschränken (acc.); mißbrauchen (acc.); **~ment** [˛fmənt] Ein-, Übergriff m.

encumb|er [in'kʌmbə] belasten; (be)hindern; **~rance** [˛brəns] Last f; fig. Hindernis n; Schuldenlast f; without ~ ohne (Familien)Anhang.

encyclop(a)edia [ensaiklou'piːdjə] Enzyklopädie f, Konversationslexikon n.

end [end] **1.** Ende n; Ziel n, Zweck m; no ~ of unendlich viel(e), unzählige; in the ~ am Ende, auf die Dauer; on ~ aufrecht; stand on ~ zu Berge stehen; to no ~ vergebens; go off the deep ~ fig. in die Luft gehen; make both ~s meet gerade auskommen; **2.** enden, beend(ig)en.

endanger [in'deindʒə] gefährden.

endear [in'diə] teuer machen; **~ment** [˛mənt] Liebkosung f, Zärtlichkeit f.

endeavo(u)r [in'devə] **1.** Bestreben n, Bemühung f; **2.** sich bemühen.

end|ing ['endiŋ] Ende n; Schluß m; gr. Endung f; **~less** □ ['endlis] endlos, unendlich; ⊕ ohne Ende.

endorse [in'dɔːs] ✝ indossieren; et. vermerken (on auf der Rückseite e-r Urkunde); gutheißen; **~ment** [˛smənt] Aufschrift f; ✝ Indossament n.

endow [in'dau] ausstatten; **~ment** [˛aumənt] Ausstattung f; Stiftung f.

endue fig. [in'djuː] (be)kleiden.

endur|ance [in'djuərəns] (Aus-)Dauer f; Ertragen n; **~e** [in'djuə] (aus)dauern; ertragen.

enema ✂ ['enimə] Klistier(spritze f) n.

enemy ['enimi] **1.** Feind m; the ♀ der Teufel; **2.** feindlich.

energ|etic [enə'dʒetik] (**~ally**) energisch; **~y** ['enədʒi] Energie f.

enervate ['enəːveit] entnerven.

enfeeble [in'fiːbl] schwächen.

enfold [in'fould] einhüllen; umfassen.

enforce [in'fɔːs] erzwingen; aufzwingen (upon dat.); bestehen auf (dat.); durchführen; **~ment** [˛smənt] Erzwingung f; Geltendmachung f; Durchführung f.

enfranchise [in'fræntʃaiz] das Wahlrecht verleihen (dat.); Sklaven befreien.

engage [in'geidʒ] v/t. anstellen; verpflichten; mieten; in Anspruch nehmen; ✕ angreifen; be ~d verlobt sein (to mit); beschäftigt sein (in mit); besetzt sein; ~ the clutch einkuppeln; v/i. sich verpflichten, versprechen, garantieren; sich beschäftigen (in mit); ✕ angreifen; ⊕ greifen (Zahnräder); **~ment** [˛dʒmənt] Verpflichtung f; Verlobung f; Verabredung f; Beschäftigung f; ✕ Gefecht n; Einrücken n e-s Ganges etc.

engaging □ [in'geidʒiŋ] einnehmend.

engender fig. [in'dʒendə] erzeugen.

engine ['endʒin] Maschine f, Motor m; ⬛ Lokomotive f; **~-driver** Lokomotivführer m.

engineer [endʒi'niə] **1.** Ingenieur m,

Techniker *m*; Maschinist *m*; *Am.* Lokomotivführer *m*; ✗ Pionier *m*; **2.** Ingenieur sein; bauen; ~**ing** [~əriŋ] **1.** Maschinenbau *m*; Ingenieurwesen *n*; **2.** technisch; Ingenieur...

English ['iŋgliʃ] **1.** englisch; **2.** Englisch *n*; the ~ *pl.* die Engländer *pl.*; *in plain ~ fig.* unverblümt; ~**man** Engländer *m*.

engrav|e [in'greiv] gravieren, stechen; *fig.* einprägen; ~**er** [~və] Graveur *m*; ~**ing** [~viŋ] (Kupfer-, Stahl)Stich *m*; Holzschnitt *m*.

engross [in'grous] an sich ziehen; ganz in Anspruch nehmen.

engulf *fig.* [in'gʌlf] verschlingen.

enhance [in'hɑ:ns] erhöhen.

enigma [i'nigmə] Rätsel *n*; ~**tic(al** □) [enig'mætik(əl)] rätselhaft.

enjoin [in'dʒɔin] auferlegen (*on j-m*).

enjoy [in'dʒɔi] sich erfreuen an (*dat.*); genießen; *did you ~ it?* hat es Ihnen gefallen?; *~ o.s.* sich amüsieren; *I ~ my dinner* es schmeckt mir; ~**able** [~ɔiəbl] genußreich, erfreulich; ~**ment** [~ɔimənt] Genuß *m*, Freude *f*.

enlarge [in'lɑ:dʒ] (sich) erweitern, ausdehnen; vergrößern; ~**ment** [~dʒmənt] Erweiterung *f*; Vergrößerung *f*.

enlighten [in'laitn] *fig.* erleuchten; *j-n* aufklären; ~**ment** [~nmənt] Aufklärung *f*.

enlist [in'list] *v/t.* ✗ anwerben; gewinnen; ~*ed men pl. Am.* ✗ Unteroffiziere *pl.* und Mannschaften *pl.*; *v/i.* sich freiwillig melden.

enliven [in'laivn] beleben.

enmity ['enmiti] Feindschaft *f*.

ennoble [i'noubl] adeln; veredeln.

enorm|ity [i'nɔ:miti] Ungeheuerlichkeit *f*; ~**ous** □ [~məs] ungeheuer.

enough [i'nʌf] genug.

enquire [in'kwaiə] = *inquire.*

enrage [in'reidʒ] wütend machen; ~**d** wütend (*at* über *acc.*).

enrapture [in'ræptʃə] entzücken.

enrich [in'ritʃ] be-, anreichern.

enrol(l) [in'roul] *in e-e* Liste eintragen; ✗ anwerben; aufnehmen; ~**ment** [~lmənt] Eintragung *f*; *bsd.* ✗ Anwerbung *f*, Einstellung *f*; Aufnahme *f*; Verzeichnis *n*; Schüler-, Studenten-, Teilnehmerzahl *f*.

ensign ['ensain] Fahne *f*; Flagge *f*; Abzeichen *n*; ♠ *Am.* ['ensn] Leutnant *m* zur See.

enslave [in'sleiv] versklaven; ~**ment** [~vmənt] Versklavung *f*.

ensnare *fig.* [in'snɛə] verführen.

ensue [in'sju:] folgen, sich ergeben.

ensure [in'ʃuə] sichern.

entail [in'teil] **1.** zur Folge haben; als unveräußerliches Gut vererben; **2.** (Übertragung *f* als) unveräußerliches Gut.

entangle [in'tæŋgl] verwickeln; ~**ment** [~lmənt] Verwicklung *f*; ✗ Draht-Verhau *m*.

enter ['entə] *v/t.* (ein)treten in (*acc.*); betreten; einsteigen, einfahren *etc.* in (*acc.*); eindringen in (*acc.*); eintragen, ✈ buchen; *Protest* einbringen; aufnehmen; anmelden; ~ *s.o. at school* j-n zur Schule anmelden; *v/i.* eintreten; sich einschreiben; *Sport:* sich melden; aufgenommen werden; ~ *into fig.* eingehen auf (*acc.*); ~ *(up)on Amt etc.* antreten; sich einlassen auf (*acc.*).

enterpris|e [in'təpraiz] Unternehmen *n*; Unternehmungslust *f*; ~**ing** □ [~ziŋ] unternehmungslustig.

entertain [entə'tein] unterhalten; bewirten; *in* Erwägung ziehen; *Meinung etc.* hegen; ~**er** [~nə] Gastgeber *m*; Unterhaltungskünstler *m*; ~**ment** [~nmənt] Unterhaltung *f*; Bewirtung *f*; Fest *n*, Gesellschaft *f*.

enthral(l) *fig.* [in'θrɔ:l] bezaubern.

enthrone [in'θroun] auf den Thron setzen.

enthusias|m [in'θju:ziæzəm] Begeisterung *f*; ~**t** [~æst] Schwärmer (-in); ~**tic** [inθju:zi'æstik] (~ally) begeistert (*at, about* von).

entice [in'tais] (ver)locken; ~**ment** [~smənt] Verlockung *f*, Reiz *m*.

entire □ [in'taiə] ganz; vollständig; ungeteilt; ~**ly** [~əli] völlig, lediglich; ~**ty** [~əti] Gesamtheit *f*.

entitle [in'taitl] betiteln; berechtigen.

entity ['entiti] Wesen *n*; Dasein *n*.

entrails ['entreilz] *pl.* Eingeweide *n/pl.*; Innere(s) *n.*

entrance ['entrəns] Ein-, Zutritt *m*; Einfahrt *f*, Eingang *m*; Einlaß *m.*

entrap [in'træp] (ein)fangen; verleiten.

entreat [in'tri:t] bitten, ersuchen; *et.* erbitten; ~**y** [~ti] Bitte *f*, Gesuch *n.*

entrench ✗ [in'trentʃ] (mit *od.* in Gräben) verschanzen.

entrust [in'trʌst] anvertrauen (*s. th. to s.o.* j-m *et.*); betrauen.

entry ['entri] Eintritt *m*; Eingang *m*; ⚖ Besitzantritt *m* (*on, upon gen.*); Eintragung *f*; *Sport:* Meldung *f*; ~ *permit* Einreisegenehmigung *f*; *book-keeping by double (single)* ~ doppelte (einfache) Buchführung.

enumerate [i'nju:məreit] aufzählen.

enunciate [i'nʌnsieit] verkünden; *Lehrsatz* aufstellen; aussprechen.

envelop [in'veləp] einhüllen; einwickeln; umgeben; ✗ einkreisen; ~**e** ['enviloup] Briefumschlag *m*; ~**ment** [in'veləpmənt] Umhüllung *f.*

envi|able □ ['enviəbl] beneidenswert; ~**ous** □ [~iəs] neidisch.

environ [in'vaiərən] umgeben; **~ment** [~nmənt] Umgebung f e-r Person; **~s** ['environz] pl. Umgebung f e-r Stadt.

envisage [in'vizidʒ] sich et. vorstellen.

envoy ['envoi] Gesandte(r) m; Bote m.

envy ['envi] 1. Neid m; 2. beneiden.

epic ['epik] 1. episch; 2. Epos n.

epicure ['epikjuə] Feinschmecker m.

epidemic [epi'demik] 1. (~ally) seuchenartig; ~ disease = 2. Seuche f.

epidermis [epi'də:mis] Oberhaut f.

epilepsy ['epilepsi] Epilepsie f.

epilogue ['epilɔg] Nachwort n.

episcopa|cy [i'piskəpəsi] bischöfliche Verfassung; **~l** [~əl] bischöflich; **~te** [~pit] Bischofswürde f; Bistum n.

epist|le [i'pisl] Epistel f; **~olary** [~stələri] brieflich; Brief...

epitaph ['epita:f] Grabschrift f.

epitome [i'pitəmi] Auszug m, Abriß m.

epoch ['i:pɔk] Epoche f.

equable ['ekwəbl] gleichförmig, gleichmäßig; fig. gleichmütig.

equal ['i:kwəl] 1. □ gleich, gleichmäßig; ~ to fig. gewachsen (dat.); 2. Gleiche(r m) f; 3. gleichen (dat.); **~ity** [i(:)'kwɔliti] Gleichheit f; **~ization** [i:kwəlai'zeiʃən] Gleichstellung f; Ausgleich m; **~ize** ['i:kwəlaiz] gleichmachen, gleichstellen; ausgleichen.

equanimity [i:kwə'nimiti] Gleichmut m.

equat|ion [i'kweiʃən] Ausgleich m; ⚕ Gleichung f; **~or** [~eitə] Äquator m.

equestrian [i'kwestriən] Reiter m.

equilibrium [i:kwi'libriəm] Gleichgewicht n; Ausgleich m.

equip [i'kwip] ausrüsten; **~ment** [~pmənt] Ausrüstung f; Einrichtung f.

equipoise ['ekwipɔiz] Gleichgewicht n; Gegengewicht n.

equity ['ekwiti] Billigkeit f; **equities** pl. ⚕ Aktien f/pl.

equivalent [i'kwivələnt] 1. gleichwertig; gleichbedeutend (to mit); 2. Äquivalent n, Gegenwert m.

equivoca|l [i'kwivəkəl] zweideutig, zweifelhaft; **~te** [~keit] zweideutig reden.

era ['iərə] Zeitrechnung f; -alter n.

eradicate [i'rædikeit] ausrotten.

eras|e [i'reiz] ausradieren, ausstreichen; auslöschen; **~er** [~zə] Radiergummi m; **~ure** [i'reiʒə] Ausradieren n; radierte Stelle.

ere [eə] 1. cj. ehe, bevor; 2. prp. vor.

erect [i'rekt] 1. □ aufrecht; 2. aufrichten; Denkmal etc. errichten; aufstellen; **~ion** [~kʃən] Auf-, Errichtung f; Gebäude n.

eremite ['erimait] Einsiedler m.

ermine zo. ['ə:min] Hermelin n.

erosion [i'rouʒən] Zerfressen n; Auswaschung f.

erotic [i'rɔtik] 1. erotisch; 2. erotisches Gedicht; **~ism** [~isizəm] Erotik f.

err [ə:] (sich) irren; fehlen, sündigen.

errand ['erənd] Botengang m, Auftrag m; **~boy** Laufbursche m.

errant □ ['erənt] (umher)irrend.

errat|ic [i'rætik] (~ally) wandernd; unberechenbar; **~um** [e'ra:təm], pl. **~a** [~tə] Druckfehler m.

erroneous □ [i'rounjəs] irrig.

error ['erə] Irrtum m, Fehler m; **~s** excepted Irrtümer vorbehalten.

erudit|e □ ['eru(:)dait] gelehrt; **~ion** [eru(:)'diʃən] Gelehrsamkeit f.

erupt [i'rʌpt] ausbrechen (Vulkan); durchbrechen (Zähne); **~ion** [~pʃən] Vulkan-Ausbruch m; ⚕ Hautausschlag m.

escalat|ion [eskə'leiʃən] Eskalation f (stufenweise Steigerung); **~or** ['eskəleitə] Rolltreppe f.

escap|ade [eskə'peid] toller Streich; **~e** [is'keip] 1. entschlüpfen, entgehen; entkommen, entrinnen; entweichen; j-m entfallen; 2. Entrinnen n; Entweichen n; Flucht f.

eschew [is'tʃu:] (ver)meiden.

escort [is'kɔ:t] Eskorte f; Geleit n; 2. [is'kɔ:t] eskortieren, geleiten.

escutcheon [is'kʌtʃən] Wappenschild m, n; Namenschild n.

especial [is'peʃəl] besonder; vorzüglich; **~ly** [~li] besonders.

espionage [espiə'na:ʒ] Spionage f.

espresso [es'presou] Espresso m (Kaffee); ~ **bar**, ~ **café** Espressobar f.

espy [is'pai] erspähen.

esquire [is'kwaiə] Landedelmann m, Gutsbesitzer m; auf Briefen: John Smith Esq. Herrn J. S.

essay 1. [e'sei] versuchen; probieren; 2. ['esei] Versuch m; Aufsatz m, kurze Abhandlung, Essay m, n.

essen|ce ['esns] Wesen n e-r Sache; Extrakt m; Essenz f; **~tial** [i'senʃəl] 1. □ (to für) wesentlich; wichtig; 2. Wesentliche(s) n.

establish [is'tæbliʃ] festsetzen; errichten, gründen; einrichten; einsetzen; ~ o.s. sich niederlassen; ⚲ed Church Staatskirche f; **~ment** [~ʃmənt] Festsetzung f; Gründung f; Er-, Einrichtung f; (bsd. großer) Haushalt; Anstalt f; Firma f.

estate [is'teit] Grundstück n; Grundbesitz m, Gut n; Besitz m; (Konkurs)Masse f, Nachlaß m; Stand m; real ~ Liegenschaften pl.; ~ **housing** ~ Wohnsiedlung f; ~ **agent** Grundstücksmakler m; ~ **car** Kombiwagen m; ~ **duty** Nachlaßsteuer f.

esteem [is'ti:m] 1. Achtung f, Ansehen n (with bei); 2. (hoch)achten, (hoch)schätzen; erachten für.

estimable ['estiməbl] schätzenswert.

estimat|e 1. ['estimeit] (ab)schätzen; veranschlagen; 2. [‿mit] Schätzung f; (Vor)Anschlag m; ‿ion [esti'meiʃən] Schätzung f; Meinung f; Achtung f.

estrange [is'treindʒ] entfremden.

estuary ['estjuəri] (den Gezeiten ausgesetzte) weite Flußmündung.

etch [etʃ] ätzen, radieren.

etern|al □ [i(:)'tə:nl] immerwährend, ewig; ‿ity [‿niti] Ewigkeit f.

ether ['i:θə] Äther m; ‿eal □ [i(:)'θiəriəl] ätherisch (a. fig.).

ethic|al □ ['eθikəl] sittlich, ethisch; ‿s [‿ks] sg. Sittenlehre f, Ethik f.

etiquette [eti'ket] Etikette f.

etymology [eti'mɔlədʒi] Etymologie f, Wortableitung f.

Eucharist ['ju:kərist] Abendmahl n.

euphemism ['ju:fimizəm] beschönigender Ausdruck.

European [juərə'pi(:)ən] 1. europäisch; 2. Europäer(in).

evacuate [i'vækjueit] entleeren; evakuieren; Land etc. räumen.

evade [i'veid] (geschickt) ausweichen (dat.); umgehen.

evaluate [i'væljueit] zahlenmäßig bestimmen, auswerten; berechnen.

evanescent [i:və'nesnt] (ver)schwindend.   [evangelisch.)

evangelic(al □) [i:væn'dʒelik(əl)])

evaporat|e [i'væpəreit] verdunsten, verdampfen (lassen); ‿ion [ivæpə-'reiʃən] Verdunstung f, Verdampfung f.

evasi|on [i'veiʒən] Umgehung f; Ausflucht f; ‿ve □ [i'veisiv] ausweichend; be ‿ ausweichen.

eve [i:v] Vorabend m; Vortag m; on the ‿ of unmittelbar vor (dat.), am Vorabend (gen.).

even ['i:vən] 1. adj. □ eben, gleich; gleichmäßig; ausgeglichen; glatt; gerade (Zahl); unparteiisch; get ‿ with s.o. fig. mit j-m abrechnen; 2. adv. selbst, sogar, auch; not ‿ nicht einmal; ‿ though, ‿ if wenn auch; 3. ebnen, glätten; gleichstellen; ‿-handed unparteiisch.

evening ['i:vniŋ] Abend m; ‿ dress Gesellschaftsanzug m; Frack m, Smoking m; Abendkleid n.

evenness ['i:vənnis] Ebenheit f; Geradheit f; Gleichmäßigkeit f; Unparteilichkeit f; Seelenruhe f.

evensong ['i:vənsɔŋ] Abendgottesdienst m.

event [i'vent] Ereignis n; Vorfall m; fig. Ausgang m; sportliche Veranstaltung; athletic ‿s pl. Leichtathletikwettkämpfe m/pl.; at all ‿s auf alle Fälle; in the ‿ of im Falle (gen.); ‿ful [‿tful] ereignisreich.

eventual □ [i'ventjuəl] etwaig, möglich; schließlich; ‿ly am Ende; im Laufe der Zeit; gegebenenfalls.

ever ['evə] je, jemals; immer; ‿ so noch so (sehr); as soon as ‿ I can sobald ich nur irgend kann; ‿ after, ‿ since von der Zeit an; ‿ and anon von Zeit zu Zeit; for ‿ für immer, auf ewig; Briefschluß: yours ‿ stets Dein ...; ‿glade Am. Sumpfsteppe f; ‿green 1. immergrün; 2. immergrüne Pflanze; ‿lasting □ [evə-'la:stiŋ] ewig; dauerhaft; ‿more ['evə'mɔ:] immerfort.

every ['evri] jede(r, -s); alle(s); ‿ now and then dann und wann; ‿ one of them jeder von ihnen; ‿ other day einen Tag um den anderen, jeden zweiten Tag; ‿body jeder (-mann); ‿day Alltags...; ‿one jeder(mann); ‿thing alles; ‿where überall.

evict [i(:)'vikt] exmittieren; ausweisen.

eviden|ce ['evidəns] 1. Beweis(material n) m; ⚖ Zeugnis n; Zeuge m; in ‿ als Beweis; deutlich sichtbar; 2. beweisen; ‿t □ [‿nt] augenscheinlich, offenbar, klar.

evil ['i:vl] 1. □ übel, schlimm, böse; the ⚹ One der Böse (Teufel); 2. Übel n, Böse(s) n; ‿-minded ['ivl'maindid] übelgesinnt, boshaft.

evince [i'vins] zeigen, bekunden.

evoke [i'vouk] (herauf)beschwören.

evolution [i:və'lu:ʃən] Entwicklung f; ✗ Entfaltung f e-r Formation.

evolve [i'vɔlv] (sich) entwickeln.

ewe [ju:] Mutterschaf n.

ex [eks] prp. ✝ ab Fabrik etc.; Börse: ohne; aus.

ex-... [‿] ehemalig, früher.

exact [ig'zækt] 1. □ genau; pünktlich; 2. Zahlung eintreiben; fordern; ‿ing [‿tiŋ] streng, genau; ‿itude [‿itju:d], ‿ness [‿tnis] Genauigkeit f; Pünktlichkeit f.

exaggerate [ig'zædʒəreit] übertreiben.

exalt [ig'zɔ:lt] erhöhen, erheben; verherrlichen; ‿ation [egzɔ:l'teiʃən] Erhöhung f, Erhebung f; Höhe f; Verzückung f.

exam Schul-sl. [ig'zæm] Examen n.

examin|ation [igzæmi'neiʃən] Examen n, Prüfung f; Untersuchung f; Vernehmung f; ‿e [ig'zæmin] untersuchen; prüfen, verhören.

example [ig'za:mpl] Beispiel n; Vorbild n, Muster n; for ‿ zum Beispiel.

exasperate [ig'za:spəreit] erbittern; ärgern; verschlimmern.

excavate ['ekskəveit] ausgraben, ausheben, ausschachten.

exceed [ik'si:d] überschreiten; übertreffen; zu weit gehen; ‿ing □ [‿diŋ] übermäßig; ‿ingly [‿ŋli] außerordentlich, überaus.

excel [ik'sel] *v/t.* übertreffen; *v/i.*
sich auszeichnen; **~lence** ['eksə-
ləns] Vortrefflichkeit *f*; hervorra-
gende Leistung; Vorzug *m*; **~lency**
[~si] Exzellenz *f*; **~lent** □ [~nt]
vortrefflich.

except [ik'sept] **1.** ausnehmen; *et.*
einwenden; **2.** *prp.* ausgenommen,
außer; ~ *for* abgesehen von; **~ing**
prp. [~tiŋ] ausgenommen; **~ion**
[~p∫ən] Ausnahme *f*; Einwendung
f (to gegen); by way of ~ ausnahms-
weise; *take* ~ *to* Anstoß nehmen an
(*dat.*); **~ional** [~nl] außergewöhn-
lich; **~ionally** [~∫nəli] un-, außer-
gewöhnlich.

excerpt ['eksə:pt] Auszug *m*.

excess [ik'ses] Übermaß *n*; Überschuß *m*; Ausschweifung *f*; *attr.*
Mehr...; ~ *fare* Zuschlag *m*; ~ *luggage* Übergewicht *n (Gepäck)*; ~
postage Nachgebühr *f*; **~ive** □
[~siv] übermäßig, übertrieben.

exchange [iks't∫eindʒ] **1.** (aus-, ein-,
um)tauschen (*for* gegen); wechseln;
2. (Aus-, Um)Tausch *m*; (*bsd.*
Geld)Wechsel *m; a. bill of ~* Wechsel *m; a.* ♀ Börse *f*; Fernsprechamt
n; foreign ~(s pl.) Devisen *f/pl.*;
(rate of) ~ Wechselkurs *m*.

exchequer [iks't∫ekə] Schatzamt *n*;
Staatskasse *f; Chancellor of the* ♀
(britischer) Schatzkanzler, Finanz-
minister *m*.

excise[1] [ek'saiz] indirekte Steuer;
Verbrauchssteuer *f*.

excise[2] [~] (her)ausschneiden.

excit|able [ik'saitəbl] reizbar; **~e**
[ik'sait] er-, anregen; reizen; **~e-
ment** [~tmənt] Auf-, Erregung *f*;
Reizung *f*; **~ing** [~tiŋ] erregend.

exclaim [iks'kleim] ausrufen; eifern.

exclamation [eksklə'mei∫ən] Aus-
ruf(ung *f*) *m*; **~s** *pl.* Geschrei *n*;
note of ~, *point of* ~, ~ *mark* Ausrufezeichen *n*.

exclude [iks'klu:d] ausschließen.

exclusi|on [iks'klu:ʒən] Ausschlie-
ßung *f*, Ausschluß *m*; **~ve** □
[~u:siv] ausschließlich; sich ab-
schließend; ~ *of* abgesehen von,
ohne.

excommunicat|e [ekskə'mju:ni-
keit] exkommunizieren; **~ion** ['eks-
kəmju:ni'kei∫ən] Kirchenbann *m*.

excrement ['ekskrimənt] Kot *m*.

excrete [eks'kri:t] ausscheiden.

excruciat|e [iks'kru:∫ieit] martern;
~ing □ [~tiŋ] qualvoll.

exculpate ['eksk∧lpeit] entschuldi-
gen; rechtfertigen; freisprechen
(*from* von).

excursion [iks'kə:∫ən] Ausflug *m*;
Abstecher *m*.

excursive □ [eks'kə:siv] abschwei-
fend.

excus|able □ [iks'kju:zəbl] ent-
schuldbar; **~e 1.** [iks'kju:z] ent-

schuldigen; ~ *s.o. s.th.* j-m et. erlassen; **2.** [~u:s] Entschuldigung *f*.

exeat ['eksiæt] *Schule etc.*: Urlaub
m.

execra|ble □ ['eksikrəbl] abscheu-
lich; **~te** ['eksikreit] verwünschen.

execut|e ['eksikju:t] ausführen; voll-
ziehen; ♪ vortragen; hinrichten;
Testament vollstrecken; **~ion** [eksi-
'kju:∫ən] Ausführung *f*; Vollzie-
hung *f*; (Zwangs)Vollstreckung *f*;
Hinrichtung *f*; ♪ Vortrag *m; put od.
carry a plan into* ~ e-n Plan ausführen *od.* verwirklichen; **~ioner**
[~∫nə] Scharfrichter *m*; **~ive** [ig-
'zekjutiv] **1.** □ vollziehend; ~ *committee* Vorstand *m*; **2.** vollziehende
Gewalt; *Am.* Staats-Präsident *m*;
♱ Geschäftsführer *m*; **~or** [~tə]
(Testaments)Vollstrecker *m*.

exemplary [ig'zempləri] vorbildlich.

exemplify [ig'zemplifai] durch Bei-
spiele belegen; veranschaulichen.

exempt [ig'zempt] **1.** befreit, frei;
2. ausnehmen, befreien.

exercise ['eksəsaiz] **1.** Übung *f*;
Ausübung *f; Schule*: Übungsarbeit
f; Leibesübung *f; take* ~ sich Bewegung machen; *Am.* **~s** *pl.* Feier-
lichkeit(en *pl.*) *f*; ✗ Manöver *n*;
2. üben; ausüben; (sich) Bewegung
machen; exerzieren.

exert [ig'zə:t] *Einfluß etc.* ausüben;
~ *o.s.* sich anstrengen *od.* bemühen;
~ion [~ʒən] Ausübung *f etc.*

exhale [eks'heil] ausdünsten, aus-
atmen; aushauchen; *Gefühlen* Luft
machen.

exhaust [ig'zɔ:st] **1.** erschöpfen;
entleeren; auspumpen; **2.** ⊕ Abgas
n, Abdampf *m*; Auspuff *m*; ~ *box*
Auspufftopf *m*; ~ *pipe* Auspuffrohr
n; **~ed** erschöpft (*a. fig.*); vergriffen
(*Auflage*); **~ion** [~t∫ən] Erschöpfung *f*; **~ive** □ [~tiv] erschöp-
fend.

exhibit [ig'zibit] **1.** ausstellen; zeigen, darlegen; aufweisen; **2.** Aus-
stellungsstück *n*; Beweisstück *n*;
~ion [eksi'bi∫ən] Ausstellung *f*;
Darlegung *f*; Zurschaustellung *f*;
Stipendium *n*.

exhilarate [ig'ziləreit] erheitern.

exhort [ig'zɔ:t] ermahnen.

exigen|ce, -cy ['eksidʒəns, ~si] drin-
gende Not; Erfordernis *n*; **~t** [~nt]
dringlich; anspruchsvoll.

exile ['eksail] **1.** Verbannung *f*, Exil
n; Verbannte(r *m*) *f*; **2.** verbannen.

exist [ig'zist] existieren, vorhanden
sein; leben; **~ence** [~təns] Existenz
f, Dasein *n*, Vorhandensein *n*; Leben *n; in* ~ = **~ent** [~nt] vorhanden.

exit ['eksit] **1.** Abgang *m;* Tod *m;*
Ausgang *m;* **2.** *thea.* (geht) ab.

exodus ['eksədəs] Auszug *m*.

exonerate [ig'zɔnəreit] *fig.* entlasten, entbinden, befreien; rechtfertigen.

exorbitant □ [ig'zɔ:bitənt] maßlos, übermäßig.

exorci|se, ~ze ['eksɔ:saiz] *Geister* beschwören, austreiben (*from* aus); befreien (*of* von).

exotic [eg'zɔtik] ausländisch, exotisch; fremdländisch.

expan|d [iks'pænd] (sich) ausbreiten; (sich) ausdehnen; (sich) erweitern; *Abkürzungen* (voll) ausschreiben; freundlich *od.* heiter werden; ~**se** [~ns], ~**sion** [~nʃən] Ausdehnung *f*; Weite *f*; Breite *f*; ~**sive** □ [~nsiv] ausdehnungsfähig; ausgedehnt, weit; *fig.* mitteilsam.

expatiate [eks'peiʃieit] sich weitläufig auslassen (*on* über *acc.*).

expatriate [eks'pætrieit] ausbürgern.

expect [iks'pekt] erwarten; F annehmen; *be* ~*ing* ein Kind erwarten; ~**ant** [~tənt] 1. erwartend (*of acc.*); ~ *mother* werdende Mutter; 2. Anwärter *m*; ~**ation** [ekspek'teiʃən] Erwartung *f*; Aussicht *f*.

expectorate [eks'pektəreit] *Schleim etc.* aushusten, auswerfen.

expedi|ent [iks'pi:djənt] 1. □ zweckmäßig; berechnend; 2. Mittel *n*; (Not)Behelf *m*; ~**tion** [ekspi'diʃən] Eile *f*; ⚔ Feldzug *m*; (Forschungs)Reise *f*; ~**tious** □ [~ʃəs] schnell, eilig, flink.

expel [iks'pel] (hin)ausstoßen; vertreiben, verjagen; ausschließen.

expen|d [iks'pend] *Geld* ausgeben; aufwenden; verbrauchen; ~**diture** [~ditʃə] Ausgabe *f*; Aufwand *m*; ~**se** [iks'pens] Ausgabe *f*; Kosten *pl.*; ~**s** *pl.* Unkosten *pl.*; Auslagen *f/pl.*; *at the* ~ *of* auf Kosten (*gen.*); *at any* ~ um jeden Preis; *go to the* ~ *of* Geld ausgeben für; ~**se account** Spesenrechnung *f*; ~**sive** □ [~siv] kostspielig, teuer.

experience [iks'piəriəns] 1. Erfahrung *f*; Erlebnis *n*; 2. erfahren, erleben; ~**d** erfahren.

experiment 1. [iks'perimənt] Versuch *m*; 2. [~iment] experimentieren; ~**al** □ [eksperi'mentl] Versuchs...; erfahrungsmäßig.

expert ['ekspə:t] 1. □ [*pred.* eks'pə:t] erfahren, geschickt; fachmännisch; 2. Fachmann *m*; Sachverständige(r *m*) *f*.

expiate ['ekspieit] büßen, sühnen.

expir|ation [ekspai'reiʃən] Ausatmung *f*; Ablauf *m*, Ende *n*; ~**e** [iks'paiə] ausatmen; verscheiden; ablaufen; ✝ verfallen; erlöschen.

explain [iks'plein] erklären, erläutern; *Gründe* auseinandersetzen; ~ *away* wegdiskutieren.

explanat|ion [eksplə'neiʃən] Erklärung *f*; Erläuterung *f*; ~**ory** □ [iks'plænətəri] erklärend.

explicable ['eksplikəbl] erklärlich.

explicit □ [iks'plisit] deutlich.

explode [iks'ploud] explodieren (lassen); ausbrechen; platzen (*with* vor).

exploit 1. ['eksplɔit] Heldentat *f*; 2. [iks'plɔit] ausbeuten; ~**ation** [eksplɔi'teiʃən] Ausbeutung *f*.

explor|ation [eksplɔ:'reiʃən] Erforschung *f*; ~**e** [iks'plɔ:] erforschen; ~**er** [~ɔ:rə] (Er)Forscher *m*; Forschungsreisende(r) *m*.

explosi|on [iks'plouʒən] Explosion *f*; Ausbruch *m*; ~**ve** [~ousiv] 1. □ explosiv; 2. Sprengstoff *m*.

exponent [eks'pounənt] Exponent *m*; Vertreter *m*.

export 1. [eks'pɔ:t] ausführen; 2. ['ekspɔ:t] Ausfuhr(artikel *m*) *f*; ~**ation** [ekspɔ:'teiʃən] Ausfuhr *f*.

expos|e [iks'pouz] aussetzen; *phot.* belichten; ausstellen; entlarven; bloßstellen; ~**ition** [ekspə'ziʃən] Ausstellung *f*; Erklärung *f*.

expostulate [iks'pɔstjuleit] protestieren; ~ *with j-m* Vorhaltungen machen.

exposure [iks'pouʒə] Aussetzen *n*; Ausgesetztsein *n*; Aufdeckung *f*; Enthüllung *f*, Entlarvung *f*; *phot.* Belichtung *f*; Bild *n*; Lage *f e-s Hauses*; ~ *meter* Belichtungsmesser *m*. [(legen.)]

expound [iks'paund] erklären, auseinanderlegen.

express [iks'pres] 1. □ ausdrücklich, deutlich; Expreß...; Eil...; ~ *company Am.* Transportfirma *f*; ~ *highway* Schnellverkehrsstraße *f*; 2. Eilbote *m*; *a.* ~ *train* Schnellzug *m*; *by* ~ = 3. *adv.* durch Eilboten; als Eilgut; 4. äußern, ausdrücken; auspressen; ~**ion** [~eʃən] Ausdruck *m*; ~**ive** □ [~esiv] ausdrückend (*of acc.*); ausdrucksvoll; ~**ly** [~sli] ausdrücklich, eigens; ~**way** *Am.* Autobahn *f*. [eignen.)]

expropriate [eks'prouprieit] enteignen.

expulsi|on [iks'pʌlʃən] Vertreibung *f*; ~**ve** [~lsiv] (aus)treibend.

expunge [eks'pʌndʒ] streichen.

expurgate ['ekspə:geit] säubern.

exquisite □ ['ekskwizit] auserlesen, vorzüglich; fein; heftig, scharf.

extant [eks'tænt] (noch) vorhanden.

extempor|aneous □ [ekstempə'reinjəs], ~**ary** [iks'tempərəri], ~**e** [eks'tempəri] aus dem Stegreif (vorgetragen).

extend [iks'tend] *v/t.* ausdehnen; ausstrecken; erweitern; verlängern; *Gunst etc.* erweisen; ⚔ (aus)schwärmen lassen; *v/i.* sich erstrecken.

extensi|on [iks'tenʃən] Ausdehnung *f*; Erweiterung *f*; Verlängerung *f*; Aus-, Anbau *m*; *teleph.* Nebenanschluß *m*; ~ *cord* ⚡ Verlängerungsschnur *f*; *University* ♀ Volkshochschule *f*; ~**ve** □ [~nsiv] ausgedehnt, umfassend.

extent [iks'tent] Ausdehnung *f*; Weite *f*, Größe *f*, Umfang *m*; Grad *m*; to the ~ of bis zum Betrage von; to some ~ einigermaßen.

extenuate [eks'tenjueit] abschwächen, mildern, beschönigen.

exterior [eks'tiəriə] 1. äußerlich; Außen...; außerhalb; 2. Äußere(s) *n*; *Film*: Außenaufnahme *f*.

exterminate [eks'tə:mineit] ausrotten, vertilgen.

external [eks'tə:nl] 1. □ äußere(r, -s), äußerlich; Außen...; 2. ~s *pl.* Äußere(s) *n*; *fig.* Äußerlichkeiten *f/pl.*

extinct [iks'tiŋkt] erloschen; ausgestorben.

extinguish [iks'tiŋgwiʃ] (aus)löschen; vernichten.

extirpate ['eksta:peit] ausrotten; *physiol.* Organ *etc.* entfernen.

extol [iks'tɔl] erheben, preisen.

extort [iks'tɔ:t] erpressen; abnötigen (*from dat.*); ~ion [~ɔ:ʃən] Erpressung *f*.

extra ['ekstrə] 1. Extra...; außer...; Neben...; Sonder...; ~ *pay* Zulage *f*; 2. *adv.* besonders; außerdem; 3. *et.* Zusätzliches; Zuschlag *m*; Extrablatt *n*; *thea.*, *Film*: Statist(in).

extract 1. ['ekstrækt] Auszug *m*; 2. [iks'trækt] (heraus)ziehen; herauslocken; ab-, herleiten; ~ion [~kʃən] (Heraus)Ziehen *n*; Herkunft *f*.

extradit|e ['ekstrədait] *Verbrecher* ausliefern (lassen); ~ion [ekstrə-'diʃən] Auslieferung *f*.

extraordinary □ [iks'trɔ:dnri]

außerordentlich; Extra...; ungewöhnlich; *envoy* ~ außerordentlicher Gesandter.

extra student ['ekstrə'stju:dənt] Gasthörer(in).

extravagan|ce [iks'trævigəns] Übertriebenheit *f*; Überspanntheit *f*; Verschwendung *f*, Extravaganz *f*; ~t □ [~nt] übertrieben, überspannt; verschwenderisch; extravagant.

extrem|e [iks'tri:m] 1. □ äußerst, größt, höchst; sehr streng; außergewöhnlich; 2. Äußerste(s) *n*; Extrem *n*; höchster Grad; ~ity [~remiti] Äußerste(s) *n*; höchste Not; äußerste Maßnahme; *extremities pl.* Gliedmaßen *pl.*

extricate ['ekstrikeit] herauswinden, herausziehen; befreien; *fig.* entwickeln.

extrude [eks'tru:d] ausstoßen.

exuberan|ce [ig'zju:bərəns] Überfluß *m*; Überschwenglichkeit *f*; ~t □ [~nt] reichlich; üppig; überschwenglich.

exult [ig'zʌlt] frohlocken.

eye [ai] 1. Auge *n*; Blick *m*; Öhr *n*; Öse *f*; up to the ~s in work bis über die Ohren in Arbeit; with an ~ to mit Rücksicht auf (*acc.*); mit der Absicht zu (*inf.*); 2. ansehen; mustern; ~ball ['aibɔ:l] Augapfel *m*; ~brow Augenbraue *f*; ~d ...äugig; ~glass Augenglas *n*; (*a pair of*) ~es *pl.* (ein) Kneifer; (e-e) Brille; ~lash Augenwimper *f*; ~lid Augenlid *n*; ~sight Augen(licht *n*) *pl.*; Sehkraft *f*; ~-witness Augenzeug|e *m*, -in *f*.

F

fable ['feibl] Fabel *f*; Mythen *pl.*, Legenden *pl.*; Lüge *f*.

fabric ['fæbrik] Bau *m*, Gebäude *n*; Struktur *f*; Gewebe *n*, Stoff *m*; ~ate [~keit] fabrizieren (*mst fig.* = erdichten, fälschen).

fabulous □ ['fæbjuləs] legendär; sagen-, fabelhaft.

façade △ [fə'sɑ:d] Fassade *f*.

face [feis] 1. Gesicht *n*; Anblick *m*; *fig.* Stirn *f*, Unverschämtheit *f*; (Ober)Fläche *f*; Vorderseite *f*; Zifferblatt *n*; ~ to ~ with Auge in Auge mit; save one's ~ das Gesicht wahren; on the ~ of it auf den ersten Blick; set one's ~ against sich gegen *et.* stemmen; 2. *v/t.* ansehen; gegenüberstehen (*dat.*); (hinaus)gehen auf (*acc.*); die Stirn bieten (*dat.*); einfassen; △ bekleiden; *v/i.* ~ about sich umdrehen; ~cloth ['feiskloθ] Waschlappen *m*.

facetious □ [fə'si:ʃəs] witzig.

facil|e ['fæsail] leicht; gewandt; ~itate [fə'siliteit] erleichtern; ~ity [~ti] Leichtigkeit *f*; Gewandtheit *f*; *mst facilities pl.* Erleichterung(en *pl.*) *f*, Möglichkeit(en *pl.*) *f*, Gelegenheit(en *pl.*) *f*.

facing ['feisiŋ] ⊕ Verkleidung *f*; ~s *pl. Schneiderei*: Besatz *m*.

fact [fækt] Tatsache *f*; Wirklichkeit *f*; Wahrheit *f*; Tat *f*. [keit *f.*]

faction ['fækʃən] Partei *f*; Uneinig-]

factitious □ [fæk'tiʃəs] künstlich.

factor ['fæktə] *fig.* Umstand *m*, Moment *n*, Faktor *m*; Agent *m*; Verwalter *m*; ~y [~əri] Fabrik *f*.

faculty ['fækəlti] Fähigkeit *f*; Kraft *f*; *fig.* Gabe *f*; *univ.* Fakultät *f*.

fad F *fig.* [fæd] Steckenpferd *n*.

fade [feid] (ver)welken (lassen), verblassen; schwinden; *Radio*: ~ in einblenden.

fag F [fæg] v/i. sich placken; v/t. erschöpfen, mürbe machen.

fail [feil] 1. v/i. versagen, mißlingen, fehlschlagen; versäumen; versiegen; nachlassen; Bankrott machen; durchfallen (Kandidat); he ~ed to do es mißlang ihm zu tun; he cannot ~ to er muß (einfach); v/t. im Stich lassen, verlassen; versäumen; 2. without ~ unfehlbar; ~ing ['feiliŋ] Fehler m, Schwäche f; ~ure [~ljə] Fehlen n; Ausbleiben n; Fehlschlag m; Mißerfolg m; Verfall m; Versäumnis n; Bankrott m; Versager m (P.).

faint [feint] 1. □ schwach, matt; 2. schwach werden; in Ohnmacht fallen (with vor); 3. Ohnmacht f; ~-hearted □ ['feint'ha:tid] verzagt.

fair¹ [fɛə] 1. adj. gerecht, ehrlich, anständig, fair; ordentlich; schön (Wetter), günstig (Wind); reichlich; blond; hellhäutig; freundlich; sauber, in Reinschrift; schön (Frau); 2. adv. gerecht, ehrlich, anständig, fair; in Reinschrift; direkt.

fair² [~] (Jahr)Markt m, Messe f.

fair|ly ['fɛəli] ziemlich; völlig; ~ness ['fɛənis] Schönheit f; Blondheit f; Gerechtigkeit f; Redlichkeit f; Billigkeit f; ~way ⚓ Fahrwasser n.

fairy ['fɛəri] Fee f; Zauberin f; Elf(e f) m; land Feen-, Märchenland n; ~-tale Märchen n.

faith [feiθ] Glaube m; Vertrauen n; Treue f; ~ful □ ['feiθful] treu; ehrlich; yours ~ly Ihr ergebener; ~less □ ['feiθlis] treulos; ungläubig.

fake sl. [feik] 1. Schwindel m; Fälschung f; Schwindler m; 2. a. ~ up fälschen.

falcon ['fɔ:lkən] Falke m.

fall [fɔ:l] 1. Fall(en n) m; Sturz m; Verfall m; Einsturz m; Am. Herbst m; Sinken n der Preise etc.; Fällen n; Wasserfall m (mst pl.); Senkung f, Abhang m; 2. [irr.] fallen; ab-, einfallen; sinken; sich legen (Wind); in e-n Zustand verfallen; ~ back zurückweichen; ~ back (up)on zurückkommen auf; ~ ill od. sick krank werden; ~ in love with sich verlieben in (acc.); ~ out sich entzweien; sich zutragen; ~ short knapp werden (of an dat.); ~ short of zurückbleiben hinter (dat.); ~ to sich machen an (acc.).

fallacious □ [fə'leiʃəs] trügerisch.

fallacy ['fæləsi] Täuschung f.

fallen ['fɔ:lən] p.p. von fall 2.

fall guy Am. sl. ['fɔ:l'gai] der Lackierte, der Dumme.

fallible □ ['fæləbl] fehlbar.

falling ['fɔ:liŋ] Fallen n; ~ sickness

Fallsucht f; ~ star Sternschnuppe f.

fallow ['fælou] zo. falb; ⚘ brach (-liegend).

false □ [fɔ:ls] falsch; ~hood ['fɔ:lshud], ~ness [~snis] Falschheit f.

falsi|fication ['fɔ:lsifi'keiʃən] (Ver-)Fälschung f; ~fy ['fɔ:lsifai] (ver-)fälschen; ~ty [~iti] Falschheit f.

falter ['fɔ:ltə] schwanken; stocken (Stimme); stammeln; fig. zaudern.

fame [feim] Ruf m, Ruhm m; ~d [~md] berühmt (for wegen).

familiar [fə'miljə] 1. □ vertraut; gewohnt; familiär; 2. Vertraute(r m) f; ~ity [fəmili'æriti] Vertrautheit f; (plumpe) Vertraulichkeit; ~ize [fə'miljəraiz] vertraut machen.

family ['fæmili] 1. Familie f; 2. Familien..., Haus...; in the ~ way in anderen Umständen; ~ allowance Kinderzulage f; ~ tree Stammbaum m.

fami|ne ['fæmin] Hungersnot f; Mangel m (of an dat.); ~sh [~iʃ] (aus-, ver)hungern.

famous □ ['feiməs] berühmt.

fan¹ [fæn] 1. Fächer m; Ventilator m; 2. (an)fächeln; an-, fig. entfachen.

fan² F [~] Sport- etc. Fanatiker m, Liebhaber m; Radio: Bastler m; ...narr m, ...fex m.

fanatic [fə'nætik] 1. a. ~al □ [~kəl] fanatisch; 2. Fanatiker(in).

fanciful □ ['fænsiful] phantastisch.

fancy ['fænsi] 1. Phantasie f; Einbildung(skraft) f; Schrulle f; Vorliebe f; Liebhaberei f; 2. Phantasie...; Liebhaber...; Luxus...; Mode...; ~ ball Maskenball m; ~ goods pl. Modewaren f/pl.; 3. sich einbilden; Gefallen finden an (dat.); just ~! denken Sie nur!; ~-work feine Handarbeit, Stickerei f.

fang [fæŋ] Fangzahn m; Giftzahn m.

fantas|tic [fæn'tæstik] (~ally) phantastisch; ~y ['fæntəsi] Phantasie f.

far [fɑ:] 1. adj. fern, entfernt; weit; 2. adv. fern; weit; (sehr) viel; as ~ as bis; in so ~ as insofern als; ~-away ['fɑ:rəwei] weit entfernt.

fare [fɛə] 1. Fahrgeld n; Fahrgast m; Verpflegung f, Kost f; 2. gut leben; he ~d well es (er)ging ihm gut; ~well ['fɛə'wel] 1. lebe(n Sie) wohl!; 2. Abschied m, Lebewohl n.

far|-fetched fig. ['fɑ:'fetʃt] weit hergeholt, gesucht; ~ gone F fertig (todkrank, betrunken etc.).

farm [fɑ:m] 1. Bauernhof m, -gut n, Gehöft n, Farm f; Züchterei f; chicken ~ Hühnerfarm f; 2. (ver-)pachten; Land bewirtschaften; ~er ['fɑ:mə] Landwirt m; Pächter m; ~hand Landarbeiter(in); ~house Bauern-, Gutshaus n; ~ing ['fɑ:miŋ]

1. Acker...; landwirtschaftlich; **2.** Landwirtschaft f; **~stead** Gehöft n; **~yard** Wirtschaftshof m e-s Bauernguts.

far-off ['fɑ:ɔ:f] entfernt, fern; **~sighted** fig. weitblickend.

farthe|r ['fɑ:ðə] comp. von far; **~st** ['fɑ:ðist] sup. von far.

fascinat|e ['fæsineit] bezaubern; **~ion** [fæsi'neiʃən] Zauber m, Reiz m.

fashion ['fæʃən] Mode f; Art f; feine Lebensart; Form f; Schnitt m; in (out of) ~ (un)modern; **2.** gestalten; Kleid machen; **~able** □ ['fæʃnəbl] modern, elegant.

fast[1] [fɑ:st] schnell; fest; treu; waschecht; flott; be ~ vorgehen (Uhr).

fast[2] [~] **1.** Fasten n; **2.** fasten.

fasten ['fɑ:sn] v/t. befestigen; anheften; fest (zu)machen; zubinden; Augen etc. heften (on, upon auf acc.); v/i. schließen (Tür); ~ upon fig. sich klammern an (acc.); **~er** [~nə] Verschluß m; Klammer f.

fastidious □ [fæs'tidiəs] anspruchsvoll, heikel, wählerisch, verwöhnt.

fat [fæt] **1.** □ fett; dick; fettig; **2.** Fett n; **3.** fett machen od. werden; mästen.

fatal □ ['feitl] verhängnisvoll (to für); Schicksals...; tödlich; **~ity** [fə'tæliti] Verhängnis n; Unglücks-, Todesfall m; Todesopfer n.

fate [feit] Schicksal n; Verhängnis n.

father ['fɑ:ðə] **1.** Vater m; **2.** der Urheber sein von; **~hood** [~hud] Vaterschaft f; **~-in-law** [~ərinlɔ:] Schwiegervater m; **~less** [~əlis] vaterlos; **~ly** [~li] väterlich.

fathom ['fæðəm] **1.** Klafter f (Maß); ♣ Faden m; **2.** ♣ loten; fig. ergründen; **~less** [~mlis] unergründlich.

fatigue [fə'ti:g] **1.** Ermüdung f; Strapaze f; **2.** ermüden; strapazieren.

fat|ness ['fætnis] Fettigkeit f; Fettheit f; **~ten** ['fætn] fett machen od. werden; mästen; Boden düngen.

fatuous □ ['fætjuəs] albern.

faucet Am. ['fɔ:sit] (Zapf)Hahn m.

fault [fɔ:lt] Fehler m; Defekt m; Schuld f; find ~ with et. auszusetzen haben an (dat.); be at ~ auf falscher Fährte sein; **~-finder** ['fɔ:ltfaində] Nörgler m; **~less** □ [~tlis] fehlerfrei, tadellos; **~y** [~ti] mangelhaft.

favo(u)r ['feivə] **1.** Gunst(bezeigung) f; Gefallen m; Begünstigung f; in ~ of zugunsten von od. gen.; do s.o. a ~ j-m e-n Gefallen tun; **2.** begünstigen; beehren; **~able** □ [~ərəbl] günstig; **~ite** [~rit] Günstling m; Liebling m; Sport: Favorit m; attr. Lieblings...

fawn[1] [fɔ:n] **1.** zo. (Dam)Kitz n; Rehbraun n; **2.** (Kitze) setzen.

fawn[2] [~] schwänzeln (Hund); kriechen (upon vor).

faze bsd. Am. F [feiz] durcheinanderbringen.

fear [fiə] **1.** Furcht f (of vor dat.); Befürchtung f; Angst f; **2.** (be-) fürchten; sich fürchten vor (dat.); **~ful** □ ['fiəful] furchtsam; furchtbar; **~less** □ ['fiəlis] furchtlos.

feasible ['fi:zəbl] ausführbar.

feast [fi:st] **1.** Fest n; Feiertag m; Festmahl n, Schmaus m; **2.** v/t. festlich bewirten; v/i. sich ergötzen; schmausen. [stück n.|

feat [fi:t] (Helden)Tat f; Kunst-|

feather ['feðə] **1.** Feder f; a. ~s Gefieder n; show the white ~ F sich feige zeigen; in high ~ in gehobener Stimmung; **2.** mit Federn schmücken; **~-bed** **1.** Feder-Unterbett n; **2.** verwöhnen; **~-brained**, **~-headed** unbesonnen; **~ed** be-, gefiedert; **~y** [~əri] feder(art)ig.

feature ['fi:tʃə] **1.** (Gesichts-, Grund-, Haupt-, Charakter)Zug m; (charakteristisches) Merkmal; Radio: Feature n; Am. Bericht m, Artikel m; **~s** pl. Gesicht n; Charakter m; **2.** kennzeichnen; sich auszeichnen durch; groß aufziehen; Film: in der Hauptrolle zeigen; ~ film Haupt-, Spielfilm m.

February ['februəri] Februar m.

fecund □ ['fi:kənd] fruchtbar.

fed [fed] pret. u. p.p. von feed 2.

federa|l ['fedərəl] Bundes...; **~lize** [~laiz] (sich) verbünden; **~tion** [fedə'reiʃən] Staatenbund m; Vereinigung f; Verband m.

fee [fi:] **1.** Gebühr f; Honorar n; Trinkgeld n; **2.** bezahlen.

feeble □ ['fi:bl] schwach.

feed [fi:d] **1.** Futter n; Nahrung f; Fütterung f; ⊕ Zuführung f; Speisung f; **2.** [irr.] v/t. füttern; speisen (a. ⊕), nähren; weiden; Material etc. zuführen; be fed up with et. od. j-n satt haben; well fed wohlgenährt; v/i. (fr)essen; sich nähren; ~er ['fi:də] Fütterer m; Am. Viehmäster m; Esser(in); **~er road** Zubringer(straße f m; **~ing-bottle** ['fi:diŋbɔtl] Saugflasche f.

feel [fi:l] **1.** [irr.] (sich) fühlen; befühlen; empfinden; sich anfühlen; I ~ like doing ich möchte am liebsten tun; **2.** Gefühl n; Empfindung f; **~er** ['fi:lə] Fühler m; **~ing** ['fi:liŋ] **1.** □ (mit)fühlend; gefühlvoll; **2.** Gefühl n; Meinung f.

feet [fi:t] pl. von foot 1.

feign [fein] heucheln; vorgeben.

feint [feint] Verstellung f; Finte f.

felicit|ate [fi'lisiteit] beglückwünschen; **~ous** □ [~təs] glücklich; **~y** [~ti] Glück(seligkeit f) n.

fell[1] [fel] **1.** pret. von fall 2; **2.** niederschlagen; fällen.

felloe ['felou] (Rad)Felge *f*.

fellow ['felou] Gefährt|e *m*, -in *f*, Kamerad(in); Gleiche(r, -s); Gegenstück *n*; *univ.* Fellow *m*, Mitglied *n* e-s *College*; Bursche *m*, Mensch *m*; *attr.* Mit...; *old* ~ F alter Junge; *the* ~ *of a glove* der andere Handschuh; **~country-man** Landsmann *m*; **~ship** [~ouʃip] Gemeinschaft *f*; Kameradschaft *f*; Mitgliedschaft *f*.

felly ['feli] (Rad)Felge *f*.

felon g♗ ['felən] Verbrecher *m*; **~y** [~ni] Kapitalverbrechen *n*.

felt¹ [felt] *pret. u. p.p. von* **feel** 1.

felt² [~] 1. Filz *m*; 2. (be)filzen.

female ['fi:meil] 1. weiblich; 2. Weib *n*; *zo.* Weibchen *n*.

feminine □ ['feminin] weiblich; weibisch.

fen [fen] Fenn *n*, Moor *n*; Marsch *f*.

fence [fens] 1. Zaun *m*; Fechtkunst *f*; *sl.* Hehler(nest *n*) *m*; *sit on the* ~ abwarten; 2. *v/t. a.* ~ *in* ein-, umzäunen; schützen; *v/i.* fechten; *sl.* hehlen.

fencing ['fensiŋ] Einfriedung *f*; Fechten *n*; *attr.* Fecht...

fend [fend]: ~ *off* abwehren; **~er** ['fendə] Schutzvorrichtung *f*; Schutzblech *n*; Kamingitter *n*, -vorsetzer *m*; Stoßfänger *m*.

fennel ♣ ['fenl] Fenchel *m*.

ferment 1. ['fə:ment] Ferment *n*; Gärung *f*; 2. [fə(:)'ment] gären (lassen); **~ation** [fə:men'teiʃən] Gärung *f*.

fern ♣ [fə:n] Farn(kraut *n*) *m*.

feroci|ous □ [fə'rouʃəs] wild; grausam; **~ty** [fə'rɔsiti] Wildheit *f*.

ferret ['ferit] 1. *zo.* Frettchen *n*; *fig.* Spürhund *m*; 2. (umher)stöbern; ~ *out* aufstöbern.

ferry ['feri] 1. Fähre *f*; 2. übersetzen; **~boat** Fährboot *n*, Fähre *f*; **~man** Fährmann *m*.

fertil|e □ ['fə:tail] fruchtbar; reich (*of, in an dat.*); **~ity** [fə:'tiliti] Fruchtbarkeit *f* (*a. fig.*); **~ize** ['fə:tilaiz] fruchtbar machen; befruchten; düngen; **~izer** [~zə] Düngemittel *n*.

ferven|cy ['fə:vənsi] Glut *f*; Inbrunst *f*; **~t** □ [~nt] heiß; inbrünstig, glühend; leidenschaftlich.

fervo(u)r ['fə:və] Glut *f*; Inbrunst *f*.

festal □ ['festl] festlich.

fester ['festə] eitern; verfaulen.

festiv|al ['festəvəl] Fest *n*; Feier *f*; Festspiele *n/pl.*; **~e** □ [~tiv] festlich; **~ity** [fes'tiviti] Festlichkeit *f*.

festoon [fes'tu:n] Girlande *f*.

fetch [fetʃ] holen; *Preis* erzielen; *Seufzer* ausstoßen; **~ing** □ F ['fetʃiŋ] reizend.

fetid □ ['fetid] stinkend.

fetter ['fetə] 1. Fessel *f*; 2. fesseln.

feud [fju:d] Fehde *f*; Leh(e)n *n*;

~al □ ['fju:dl] lehnbar; Lehns...; **~alism** [~delizəm] Lehnswesen *n*.

fever ['fi:və] Fieber *n*; **~ish** □ [~əriʃ] fieb(e)rig; *fig.* fieberhaft.

few [fju:] wenige; *a* ~ ein paar; *quite a* ~, *a good* ~ e-e ganze Menge.

fiancé [fi'ã:nsei] Verlobte(r) *m*; **~e** [~] Verlobte *f*.

fiat ['faiæt] Befehl *m*; ~ *money Am.* Papiergeld *n* (*ohne Deckung*).

fib F [fib] 1. Flunkerei *f*, Schwindelei *f*; 2. schwindeln, flunkern.

fib|re, *Am.* **~er** ['faibə] Faser *f*; Charakter *m*; **~rous** □ ['faibrəs] faserig.

fickle ['fikl] wankelmütig; unbeständig; **~ness** [~lnis] Wankelmut *m*.

fiction ['fikʃən] Erfindung *f*; Roman-, Unterhaltungsliteratur *f*; **~al** □ [~nl] erdichtet; Roman...

fictitious □ [fik'tiʃəs] erfunden.

fiddle F ['fidl] 1. Geige *f*, Fiedel *f*; 2. fiedeln; tändeln; **~r** [~lə] Geiger (-in); **~stick** Fiedelbogen *m*; **~s!** *fig.* dummes Zeug!

fidelity [fi'deliti] Treue *f*; Genauigkeit *f*.

fidget F ['fidʒit] 1. nervöse Unruhe; 2. nervös machen *od.* sein; **~y** [~ti] kribbelig.

fie [fai] pfui!

field [fi:ld] Feld *n*; (Spiel)Platz *m*; Arbeitsfeld *n*; Gebiet *n*; Bereich *m*; *hold the* ~ das Feld behaupten; **~day** ['fi:lddei] ✕ Felddienstübung *f*; Parade *f*; *fig.* großer Tag; *Am.* (Schul)Sportfest *n*; *Am.* Exkursionstag *m*; ~ *events pl. Sport:* Sprung- u. Wurfwettkämpfe *m/pl.*; **~glass**(es *pl.*) Feldstecher *m*; **~officer** Stabsoffizier *m*; **~sports** *pl.* Jagen *n u.* Fischen *n*.

fiend [fi:nd] böser Feind, Teufel *m*; **~ish** □ ['fi:ndiʃ] teuflisch, boshaft.

fierce □ [fiəs] wild; grimmig; **~ness** [~fiəsnis] Wildheit *f*; Grimm *m*.

fiery □ ['faiəri] feurig; hitzig.

fif|teen ['fif'ti:n] fünfzehn; **~teenth** [~nθ] fünfzehnte(r, -s); **~th** [fifθ] 1. fünfte(r, -s); 2. Fünftel *n*; **~thly** ['fifθli] fünftens; **~tieth** ['fiftiiθ] fünfzigste(r, -s); **~ty** [~ti] fünfzig; **~ty-fifty** F halb und halb.

fig [fig] Feige *f*; F Zustand *m*.

fight [fait] 1. Kampf *m*; Kampflust *f*; *show* ~ sich zur Wehr setzen; 2. [*irr.*] *v/t.* bekämpfen; erkämpfen; *v/i.* kämpfen, sich schlagen; **~er** ['faitə] Kämpfer *m*, Streiter *m*; ✕ Jagdflugzeug *n*; **~ing** ['faitiŋ] Kampf *m*.

figurative □ ['figjurətiv] bildlich.

figure ['figə] 1. Figur *f*; Gestalt *f*; Ziffer *f*; Preis *m*; be good at ~s gut im Rechnen sein; 2. *v/t.* abbilden; darstellen; sich *et.* vorstellen; beziffern; ~ *up od. out* berechnen; *v/i.* erscheinen; e-e Rolle spielen *as*) als); ~ on *Am. et.* überdenken; ~-**skating** [ˌɔskeitiŋ] Eiskunstlauf *m*.

filament ['filəmənt] Faden *m*, Faser *f*; ⚥ Staubfaden *m*; ⚡ Glüh-, Heizfaden *m*.

filbert ⚥ ['filbə(:)t] Haselnuß *f*.

filch [filtʃ] stibitzen (*from dat.*).

file¹ [fail] 1. Akte *f*, Ordner *m*; Ablage *f*; Reihe *f*; ⚔ Rotte *f*; on ~ bei den Akten; 2. *v/t.* aufreihen; *Briefe etc.* einordnen; ablegen; einreichen; *v/i.* hinter-ea. marschieren.

file² [ˌ] 1. Feile *f*; 2. feilen.

filial □ ['filjəl] kindlich, Kindes...

filibuster ['filibʌstə] 1. *Am.* Obstruktion(spolitiker *m*) *f*; 2. *Am.* Obstruktion treiben.

fill [fil] 1. (sich) füllen; an-, aus-, erfüllen; *Am. Auftrag* ausführen; ~ in *Formular* ausfüllen; 2. Fülle *f*, Genüge *f*; Füllung *f*.

fillet ['filit] Haarband *n*; Lendenbraten *m*; Roulade *f*; *bsd.* ⚓ Band *n*.

filling ['filiŋ] Füllung *f*; ~ **station** *Am.* Tankstelle *f*.

fillip ['filip] Nasenstüber *m*.

filly ['fili] (Stuten)Füllen *n*; *fig.* wilde Hummel.

film [film] 1. Häutchen *n*; Membran(e) *f*; Film *m*; Trübung *f des Auges*; Nebelschleier *m*; *take od.* shoot a ~ e-n Film drehen; 2. (sich) verschleiern; (ver)filmen.

filter ['filtə] 1. Filter *m*; 2. filtern.

filth [filθ] Schmutz *m*; ~**y** □ ['filθi] schmutzig; *fig.* unflätig.

filtrate ['filtreit] filtrieren.

fin [fin] Flosse *f* (*a. sl.* = Hand).

final ['fainl] 1. □ letzte(r, -s); endlich; schließlich; End...; endgültig; 2. Schlußprüfung *f*; *Sport*: Schlußrunde *f*, Endspiel *n*.

financ|e [fai'næns] 1. Finanzwesen *n*; ~s *pl.* Finanzen *pl.*; 2. *v/t.* finanzieren; *v/i.* Geldgeschäfte machen; ~**ial** □ [ˌnʃəl] finanziell; ~**ier** [ˌnsiə] Finanzmann *m*; Geldgeber *m*.

finch *orn.* [fintʃ] Fink *m*.

find [faind] 1. [*irr.*] finden; (an-)treffen; auf-, herausfinden; *schuldig etc.* befinden; beschaffen; versorgen; *all found* freie Station *f*; 2. Fund *m*; ~**ings** ['faindiŋz] *pl.* Befund *m*; Urteil *n*.

fine¹ □ [fain] 1. schön; fein; verfeinert; rein; spitz, dünn, scharf; geziert; vornehm; 2. *adv.* gut, bestens.

fine² [ˌ] 1. Geldstrafe *f*; 2. zu e-r Geldstrafe verurteilen.

fineness ['fainnis] Fein-, Zart-, Schönheit *f*, Eleganz *f*; Genauigkeit *f*.

finery ['fainəri] Glanz *m*; Putz *m*; Staat *m*.

finger ['fiŋgə] 1. Finger *m*; 2. betasten, (herum)fingern an (*dat.*);

~-**language** Zeichensprache *f*; ~-**nail** Fingernagel *m*; ~-**print** Fingerabdruck *m*.

fini|cal □ ['finikəl], ~**cking** [ˌkiŋ], ~**kin** [ˌin] geziert; wählerisch.

finish ['finiʃ] 1. *v/t.* beenden, vollenden; fertigstellen; abschließen; vervollkommnen; erledigen; *v/i.* enden; 2. Vollendung *f*, letzter Schliff (*a. fig.*); Schluß *m*.

finite □ ['fainait] endlich, begrenzt.

fink *Am. sl.* [fiŋk] Streikbrecher *m*.

Finn [fin] Finn|e *m*, -in *f*; ~**ish** ['finiʃ] finnisch.

fir [fəː] (Weiß)Tanne *f*; Fichte *f*; ~-**cone** ['fəːkoun] Tannenzapfen *m*.

fire ['faiə] 1. Feuer *n*; on ~ in Brand, in Flammen; 2. *v/t.* an-, entzünden; *fig.* anfeuern; abfeuern; *Ziegel etc.* brennen; F 'rausschmeißen (*entlassen*); heizen; *v/i.* Feuer fangen (*a. fig.*); feuern; ~-**alarm** ['faiərəlɑːm] Feuermelder *m*; ~-**brigade** Feuerwehr *f*; ~-**bug** *Am.* F Brandstifter *m*; ~-**cracker** Frosch *m* (*Feuerwerkskörper*); ~ **department** *Am.* Feuerwehr *f*; ~-**engine** ['faiərendʒin] (Feuer)Spritze *f*; ~-**escape** [ˌriskeip] Rettungsgerät *n*; Nottreppe *f*; ~-**extinguisher** [ˌrikstiŋgwiʃə] Feuerlöscher *m*; ~-**man** Feuerwehrmann *m*; Heizer *m*; ~-**place** Herd *m*; Kamin *m*; ~-**plug** Hydrant *m*; ~-**proof** feuerfest; ~-**screen** Ofenschirm *m*; ~-**side** Herd *m*; Kamin *m*; ~-**station** Feuerwache *f*; ~-**wood** Brennholz *n*; ~-**works** *pl.* Feuerwerk *n*.

firing ['faiəriŋ] Heizung *f*; Feuerung *f*.

firm [fəːm] 1. □ fest; derb; standhaft; 2. Firma *f*; ~**ness** ['fəːmnis] Festigkeit *f*.

first [fəːst] 1. *adj.* erste(r, -s); beste(r, -s); 2. *adv.* erstens; zuerst; ~ of all an erster Stelle; zu allererst; 3. Erste(r, -s); ~ of exchange ✝ Primawechsel *m*; at ~ zuerst, anfangs; *from the* ~ von Anfang an; ~-**born** ['fəːstbɔːn] erstgeboren; ~ **class** 1. Klasse (*e-s Verkehrsmittels*); ~-**class** erstklassig; ~**ly** [ˌtli] erstlich; erstens; ~ **name** Vorname *m*; Beiname *m*; ~-**papers** *Am.* vorläufige Einbürgerungspapiere; ~-**rate** ersten Ranges; erstklassig.

firth [fəːθ] Förde *f*; (Flut)Mündung *f*.

fish [fiʃ] 1. Fisch(e *pl.*) *m*; F Kerl *m*; 2. fischen; angeln; haschen; ~-**bone** ['fiʃboun] Gräte *f*.

fisher ['fiʃə], ~-**man** Fischer *m*; ~**y** [ˌəri] Fischerei *f*.

fishing ['fiʃiŋ] Fischen *n*; ~-**line** Angelschnur *f*; ~-**tackle** Angelgerät *n*. [händler *m*.]

fishmonger ['fiʃmʌŋgə] Fisch-

fiss|ion Ⓤ ['fiʃən] Spaltung *f*; ~**ure** ['fiʃə] Spalt *m*; Riß *m*.

fist [fist] Faust *f*; F Klaue *f*;
~icuffs ['fistikʌfs] *pl.* Faustschläge
m/pl.

fit¹ [fit] 1. □ geeignet, passend;
tauglich; *Sport*: in (guter) Form;
bereit; 2. *v/t.* passen für *od. dat.*;
anpassen, passend machen; befähigen; geeignet machen (*for, to* für,
zu); *a.* ~ *on* anprobieren; ausstatten;
~ *out* ausrüsten; ~ *up* einrichten;
montieren; *v/i.* passen; sich schik-
ken; sitzen (*Kleid*); 3. Sitz *m*
(*Kleid*).

fit² [~] Anfall *m*; ⚙ Ausbruch *m*;
Anwandlung *f*; *by* ~*s and starts*
ruckweise; *give s.o. a* ~ j-n hochbringen; j-m e-n Schock versetzen.

fit|ful □ ['fitful] ruckartig; *fig.* un-
stet; ~ness ['fitnis] Schicklichkeit *f*;
Tauglichkeit *f*; ~ter ['fitə] Mon-
teur *m*; Installateur *m*; ~ting ['fitiŋ]
1. passend; 2. Montage *f*; Anprobe
f; ~*s pl.* Einrichtung *f*; Armaturen
f/pl.

five [faiv] 1. fünf; 2. Fünf *f*.

fix [fiks] 1. *v/t.* befestigen, anheften;
fixieren; *Augen etc.* heften, richten;
fesseln; aufstellen; bestimmen,
festsetzen; *bsd. Am.* richten, *Bett
etc.* machen; ~ *o.s.* sich niederlassen;
~ *up* in Ordnung bringen, arrangie-
ren; *v/i.* fest werden; ~ *on* sich entschließen für; 2. F Klemme *f*; *Am.*
Zustand *m*; ~ed fest; bestimmt;
starr; ~ing ['fiksiŋ] Befestigen *n*;
Instandsetzen *n*; Fixieren *n*; Aufstellen *n*, Montieren *n*; Besatz *m*,
Versteifung *f*; *Am.* ~*s pl.* Zubehör
n, Extraausrüstung *f*; ~ture ['~stʃə]
fest angebrachtes Zubehörteil, feste
Anlage; Inventarstück *n*; *lighting* ~
Beleuchtungskörper *m*.

fizz [fiz] 1. zischen, sprudeln; 2. Zischen *n*; F Schampus *m* (*Sekt*).

flabbergast F ['flæbəgɑːst] verblüffen; *be* ~*ed* baff *od.* platt sein.

flabby □ ['flæbi] schlaff, schlapp.

flag [flæg] 1. Flagge *f*; Fahne *f*;
Fliese *f*; Schwertlilie *f*; 2. beflag-
gen; durch Flaggen signalisieren;
mit Fliesen belegen; ermatten;
mutlos werden; ~-day ['flægdei]
Opfertag *m*; *Flag Day Am.* Tag *m*
des Sternenbanners (*14. Juni*).

flagitious □ [flə'dʒiʃəs] schändlich.

flagrant □ ['fleigrənt] abscheulich;
berüchtigt; offenkundig.

flag|staff ['flægstɑːf] Fahnenstange
f; ~stone Fliese *f*.

flair [flɛə] Spürsinn *m*, feine Nase.

flake [fleik] 1. Flocke *f*; Schicht *f*;
2. (sich) flocken; abblättern.

flame [fleim] 1. Flamme *f*, Feuer *n*;
fig. Hitze *f*; 2. flammen, lodern.

flank [flæŋk] 1. Flanke *f*; Weiche *f
der Tiere*; 2. flankieren.

flannel ['flænl] Flanell *m*; Waschlappen *m*; ~*s pl.* Flanellhose *f*.

flap [flæp] 1. (Ohr)Läppchen *n*;

Rockschoß *m*; *Hut*-Krempe *f*;
Klappe *f*; Klaps *m*; (Flügel)Schlag
m; 2. *v/t.* klatschen(d schlagen); *v/i.*
lose herabhängen; flattern.

flare [flɛə] 1. flackern; sich nach
außen erweitern, sich bauschen;
~ *up* aufflammen; *fig.* aufbrausen;
2. flackerndes Licht; Lichtsignal *n*.

flash [flæʃ] 1. aufgedonnert; unecht; Gauner...; 2. Blitz *m*; *fig.*
Aufblitzen *n*; *bsd. Am. Zeitung*:
kurze Meldung; *in a* ~ im Nu; ~ *of
wit* Geistesblitz *m*; 3. (auf)blitzen;
auflodern (lassen); *Blick etc.* werfen; flitzen; funken, telegraphieren;
it ~*ed on me* mir kam plötzlich der
Gedanke; ~-back ['flæʃbæk] *Film*:
Rückblende *f*; ~-light *phot.* Blitz-
licht *n*; Blinklicht *n*; Taschenlampe
f; ~y □ ['~ʃi] auffallend.

flask [flɑːsk] Taschen-, Reiseflasche
f.

flat [flæt] 1. □ flach, platt; schal;
† flau; klar; glatt; ♪ um e-n halben
Ton erniedrigt; ~ *price* Einheits-
preis *m*; 2. *adv.* glatt; völlig; *fall* ~
danebengehen; *sing* ~ zu tief singen; 3. Fläche *f*, Ebene *f*; Flach-
land *n*; Untiefe *f*; (Miet)Wohnung
f; ♪ B *n*; F Simpel *m*; *mot. sl.* Plattfuß *m*; ~-foot ['flætfut] Plattfuß *m*;
Am. sl. Polyp *m* (*Polizist*); ~-footed
plattfüßig; *Am.* F *fig.* stur, eisern;
~-iron Plätteisen *n*; ~ness ['~tnis]
Flachheit *f*; Plattheit *f*; † Flauheit
f; ~ten ['~tn] (sich) ab-, verflachen.

flatter ['flætə] schmeicheln (*dat.*);
~er [~ərə] Schmeichler(in) *f*; ~y
[~ri] Schmeichelei *f*.

flavo(u)r ['fleivə] 1. Geschmack *m*;
Aroma *n*; Blume *f* (*Wein*); *fig.* Beigeschmack *m*; Würze *f*; 2. würzen;
~less [~əlis] geschmacklos, fad.

flaw [flɔː] 1. Sprung *m*, Riß *m*;
Fehler *m*; ♣ Bö *f*; 2. zerbrechen;
beschädigen; ~less □ ['flɔːlis] fehlerlos.

flax [flæks] ♀ Flachs *m*, Lein *m*.

flay [flei] die Haut abziehen (*dat.*).

flea [fliː] Floh *m*.

fled [fled] *pret. u. p.p. von* flee.

fledg|e [fledʒ] *v/i.* flügge werden;
v/t. befiedern; ~(e)ling ['fledʒliŋ]
Küken *n* (*a. fig.*); Grünschnabel *m*.

flee [fliː] [*irr.*] fliehen; meiden.

fleec|e [fliːs] 1. Vlies *n*; 2. scheren;
prellen; ~y ['fliːsi] wollig.

fleer [fliə] höhnen (*at* über *acc.*).

fleet [fliːt] 1. □ schnell; 2. Flotte *f*;
♀ *Street* die (Londoner) Presse.

flesh [fleʃ] 1. *lebendiges* Fleisch; *fig.*
Fleisch(eslust *f*) *n*; 2. *hunt.* Blut
kosten lassen; ~ly ['fleʃli] fleisch-
lich; irdisch; ~y [~ʃi] fleischig; fett.

flew [fluː] *pret. von* fly 2.

flexib|ility [fleksə'biliti] Biegsam-
keit *f*; ~le □ ['fleksəbl] flexibel,
biegsam; *fig.* anpassungsfähig.

flick [flik] schnippen; schnellen.

flicker ['flikə] 1. flackern; flattern; flimmern; 2. Flackern *n*, Flimmern *n*; Flattern *n*; *Am.* Buntspecht *m*.

flier ['flaiə] = *flyer*.

flight [flait] Flucht *f*; Flug *m* (*a. fig.*); Schwarm *m*; ✗, ⚔ Kette *f*; (~ *of stairs* Treppen)Flucht *f*; *put to* ~ in die Flucht schlagen; ~y □ ['flaiti] flüchtig; leichtsinnig.

flimsy ['flimzi] dünn, locker; schwach; *fig.* fadenscheinig.

flinch [flintʃ] zurückweichen; zukken.

fling [fliŋ] 1. Wurf *m*; Schlag *m*; *have one's* ~ sich austoben; 2. [*irr.*] *v/i.* eilen; ausschlagen (*Pferd*); *fig.* toben; *v/t.* werfen, schleudern; ~ *o.s.* sich stürzen; ~ *open* aufreißen.

flint [flint] Kiesel *m*; Feuerstein *m*.

flip [flip] 1. Klaps *m*; Ruck *m*; 2. schnippen; klapsen; (umher-) flitzen.

flippan|cy ['flipənsi] Leichtfertigkeit *f*; ~t □ [~nt] leichtfertig; vorlaut.

flirt [fləːt] 1. Kokette *f*; Weiberheld *m*; 2. flirten, kokettieren; = *flip* 2; ~ation [fləːˈteiʃən] Flirt *m*.

flit [flit] flitzen, wandern; umziehen

flivver *Am. sl.* ['flivə] 1. Nuckelpinne *f* (*billiges Auto*); 2. mißlingen.

float [flout] 1. Schwimmer *m*; Floß *n*; Plattformwagen *m*; 2. *v/t.* überfluten; flößen; tragen (*Wasser*); ⚓ flott machen, *fig.* in Gang bringen; ✝ gründen; verbreiten; *v/i.* schwimmen, treiben; schweben; umlaufen.

flock [flɔk] 1. Herde *f* (*a. fig.*); Schar *f*; 2. sich scharen; zs.-strömen.

floe [flou] (treibende) Eisscholle.

flog [flɔg] peitschen; prügeln.

flood [flʌd] 1. *a.* ~-*tide* Flut *f*; Überschwemmung *f*; 2. überfluten, überschwemmen; ~-**gate** ['flʌdgeit] Schleusentor *n*; ~**light** ⚡ Flutlicht *n*.

floor [flɔː] 1. Fußboden *m*; Stock (-werk *n*) *m*; ♪ Tenne *f*; ~ *leader Am.* Fraktionsvorsitzende(r) *m*; ~ *show* Nachtklubvorstellung *f*; *take the* ~ das Wort ergreifen; 2. dielen; zu Boden schlagen; verblüffen; ~-**cloth** ['flɔːklɔθ] Putzlappen *m*; ~**ing** ['flɔːriŋ] Dielung *f*; Fußboden *m*; ~-**lamp** Stehlampe *f*; ~-**walker** *Am.* ['flɔːwɔːkə] = *shopwalker*.

flop [flɔp] 1. schlagen; flattern; (hin)plumpsen (lassen); *Am.* versagen; 2. Plumps *m*; Versager *m*; ~*house Am. sl.* Penne *f*.

florid □ ['flɔrid] blühend.

florin ['flɔrin] Zweischillingstück *n*.

florist ['flɔrist] Blumenhändler *m*.

floss [flɔs] Florettseide *f*.

flounce[1] [flauns] Volant *m*.

flounce[2] [~] stürzen; zappeln.

flounder[1] *ichth.* ['flaundə] Flunder *f*.

flounder[2] [~] sich (ab)mühen.

flour ['flauə] (feines) Mehl.

flourish ['flʌriʃ] 1. Schnörkel *m*; Schwingen *n*; ♪ Tusch *m*; 2. *v/i.* blühen, gedeihen; *v/t.* schwingen.

flout [flaut] (ver)spotten.

flow [flou] 1. Fluß *m*; Flut *f*; 2. fließen, fluten; wallen.

flower ['flauə] 1. Blume *f*; Blüte *f* (*a. fig.*); Zierde *f*; 2. blühen; ~-**pot** Blumentopf *m*; ~**y** [~əri] blumig.

flown [floun] *p.p. von fly* 2.

flubdub *Am. sl.* ['flʌbdʌb] Geschwätz *n*.

fluctuat|e ['flʌktjueit] schwanken; ~**ion** [flʌktjuˈeiʃən] Schwankung *f*.

flu(e) F ['fluː] = *influenza*.

flue [fluː] Kaminrohr *n*; Heizrohr *n*.

fluen|cy *fig.* ['flu(ː)ənsi] Fluß *m*; ~**t** □ [~nt] fließend, geläufig (*Rede*).

fluff [flʌf] 1. Flaum *m*; Flocke *f*; *fig.* Schnitzer *m*; 2. *Kissen* aufschütteln; *Federn* aufplustern (*Vogel*); ~**y** ['flʌfi] flaumig; flockig.

fluid ['flu(ː)id] 1. flüssig; 2. Flüssigkeit *f*.

flung [flʌŋ] *pret. u. p.p. von fling* 2.

flunk *Am.* F *fig.* [flʌŋk] durchfallen (lassen).

flunk(e)y ['flʌŋki] Lakai *m*.

fluorescent [fluəˈresnt] fluoreszierend.

flurry ['flʌri] Nervosität *f*; Bö *f*; *Am. a.* (Regen)Schauer *m*; Schneegestöber *n*.

flush [flʌʃ] 1. ⊕ in gleicher Ebene; reichlich; (über)voll; 2. Erröten *n*; Übermut *m*; Fülle *f*; Wachstum *n*; *fig.* Blüte *f*; Spülung *f*; *Karten*: Flöte *f*; 3. über-, durchfluten (aus)spülen; strömen; sprießen (lassen); erröten (machen); übermütig machen; aufjagen.

fluster ['flʌstə] 1. Aufregung *f*; 2. *v/t.* aufregen.

flute [fluːt] 1. ♪ Flöte *f*; Falte *f*; 2. (auf der) Flöte spielen; riefeln; fälteln.

flutter ['flʌtə] 1. Geflatter *n*; Erregung *f*; F Spekulation *f*; 2. *v/t.* aufregen; *v/i.* flattern.

flux [flʌks] *fig.* Fluß *m*; ✗ Ausfluß *m*.

fly [flai] 1. *zo.* Fliege *f*; Flug *m*; *Am. Baseball*: hochgeschlagener Ball; Droschke *f*; 2. [*irr.*] (*a. fig.*) fliegen (lassen); entfliehen (*Zeit*); ⚔ führen; *Flagge* hissen; fliehen; ~ *überfliegen*; ~ *at* herfallen über; ~ *into a passion od.* rage in Zorn geraten.

flyer ['flaiə] Flieger *m*; Renner *m*; *take a* ~ *Am.* F Vermögen riskieren.

fly-flap ['flaiflæp] Fliegenklatsche *f*.

flying ['flaiiŋ] fliegend; Flug...; ~ *squad* Überfallkommando *n*.

fly-|over ['flaiouvə] (Straßen)Überführung *f*; ~-**weight** *Boxen*: Fliegengewicht *n*; **~-wheel** Schwung-rad *n*.

foal [foul] **1.** Fohlen *n*; **2.** fohlen.

foam [foum] **1.** Schaum *m*; **2.** schäumen; **~y** ['foumi] schaumig.

focus ['foukəs] **1.** Brennpunkt *m*; **2.** (sich) im Brennpunkt vereinigen; *opt.* einstellen (*a. fig.*); konzentrieren.

fodder ['fɔdə] (Trocken)Futter *n*.

foe *poet.* [fou] Feind *m*, Gegner *m*.

fog [fɔg] **1.** (dichter) Nebel; *fig.* Umnebelung *f*; *phot.* Schleier *m*; **2.** *mst fig.* umnebeln; *phot.* verschleiern.

fogey F ['fougi]: *old* ~ komischer alter Kauz.

foggy □ ['fɔgi] neb(e)lig; *fig.* nebelhaft.

fogy *Am.* ['fougi] = *fogey*.

foible *fig.* ['fɔibl] Schwäche *f*.

foil¹ [fɔil] Folie *f*; Hintergrund *m*.

foil² [~] **1.** vereiteln; **2.** Florett *n*.

fold¹ [fould] **1.** Schafhürde *f*; *fig.* Herde *f*; **2.** einpferchen.

fold² [~] **1.** Falte *f*; Falz *m*; **2.** ...fach, ...fältig; **3.** *v/t.* falten; falzen; *Arme* kreuzen; ~ (*up*) einwickeln; *v/i.* sich falten; *Am.* F eingehen; **~er** ['fouldə] Mappe *f*, Schnellhefter *m*; Faltprospekt *m*.

folding ['fouldiŋ] zs.-legbar; Klapp...; **~-bed** Feldbett *n*; **~-boat** Faltboot *n*; **~-door(s** *pl.*) Flügeltür *f*; **~-screen** spanische Wand; **~-seat** Klappsitz *m*.

foliage ['fouliidʒ] Laub(werk) *n*.

folk [fouk] *pl.* Leute *pl.*; ~*s pl.* Leute *pl.* (F *a. Angehörige*); **~lore** ['foukb:] Volkskunde *f*; Volkssagen *f/pl.*; **~-song** Volkslied *n*.

follow ['fɔlou] folgen (*dat.*); folgen auf (*acc.*); be-, verfolgen; *s-m Beruf etc.* nachgehen; **~er** [~ouə] Nachfolger(in); Verfolger(in); Anhänger(in); **~ing** [~ouiŋ] Anhängerschaft *f*, Gefolge *n*.

folly ['fɔli] Torheit *f*; Narrheit *f*.

foment [fou'ment] *j-m* warme Umschläge machen; *Unruhe* stiften.

fond □ [fɔnd] zärtlich; vernarrt (*of* in *acc.*); *be* ~ *of* gern haben, lieben; **~le** ['fɔndl] liebkosen; streicheln; (ver)hätscheln; **~ness** [~dnis] Zärtlichkeit *f*; Vorliebe *f*.

font [fɔnt] Taufstein *m*; *Am.* Quelle *f*.

food [fu:d] Speise *f*, Nahrung *f*; Futter *n*; Lebensmittel *n/pl.*; ~-**stuff** ['fu:dstʌf] Nahrungsmittel *n*.

fool [fu:l] **1.** Narr *m*, Tor *m*; Hanswurst *m*; *make a* ~ *of s.o.* j-n zum Narren halten; *make a* ~ *of o.s.* sich lächerlich machen; **2.** *Am.* F närrisch, dumm; **3.** *v/t.* narren; prellen (*out of* um *et.*); ~ *away* F vertrödeln; *v/i.* albern; (herum)spielen; ~ (*a*)*round bsd. Am.* Zeit vertrödeln.

fool|ery ['fu:ləri] Torheit *f*; **~hardy**

□ ['fu:lhɑ:di] tollkühn; **~ish** □ ['fu:liʃ] töricht; **~ishness** [~ʃnis] Torheit *f*; **~-proof** kinderleicht.

foot [fut] **1.** *pl.* **feet** [fi:t] Fuß *m* (*a. Maß*); Fußende *n*; ⚔ Infanterie *f*; *on* ~ zu Fuß; im Gange, in Gang; **2.** *v/t. mst* ~ *up* addieren; ~ *the bill* F die Rechnung bezahlen; *v/i.* ~ *it* zu Fuß gehen; **~board** ['futbɔ:d] Trittbrett *n*; **~boy** Page *m*; **~fall** Tritt *m*, Schritt *m*; **~gear** Schuhwerk *n*; **~hold** fester Stand; *fig.* Halt *m*.

footing ['futiŋ] Halt *m*, Stand *m*; Grundlage *f*, Basis *f*; Stellung *f*; fester Fuß; Verhältnis *n*; ⚔ Zustand *m*; Endsumme *f*; *be on a friendly* ~ *with s.o.* ein gutes Verhältnis zu j-m haben; *lose one's* ~ ausgleiten.

foot|lights *thea.* ['futlaits] *pl.* Rampenlicht(er *pl.*) *n*; Bühne *f*; **~man** Diener *m*; **~-passenger** Fußgänger (-in) *f*; **~-path** Fußpfad *m*; **~print** Fußstapfe *f*, -spur *f*; **~-sore** fußkrank; **~step** Fußstapfe *f*, Spur *f*; **~stool** Fußbank *f*; **~wear** = *foot-gear*.

fop [fɔp] Geck *m*, Fatzke *m*.

for [fɔ:, fər, fə] **1.** *prp. mst* für; *Zweck, Ziel, Richtung:* zu; nach; *warten, hoffen etc. auf* (*acc.*); *sich sehnen etc. nach; Grund, Anlaß:* aus, vor (*dat.*), wegen; *Zeitdauer:* ~ *three days* drei Tage (lang); *seit drei Tagen; Entfernung: I walked* ~ *a mile* ich ging eine Meile (weit); *Austausch:* (an)statt; *in der Eigenschaft* als; *I* ~ *one* ich zum Beispiel; ~ *sure* sicher!, gewiß!; **2.** *cj.* denn.

forage ['fɔridʒ] **1.** Futter *n*; **2.** (nach Futter) suchen.

foray ['fɔrei] räuberischer Einfall.

forbear¹ [fɔ:'bɛə] [*irr.* (*bear*)] *v/t.* unterlassen; *v/i.* sich enthalten (*from gen.*); Geduld haben.

forbear² ['fɔ:bɛə] Vorfahr *m*.

forbid [fə'bid] [*irr.* (*bid*)] verbieten; hindern; **~ding** □ [~diŋ] abstoßend.

force [fɔ:s] **1.** *mst* Kraft *f*, Gewalt *f*; Nachdruck *m*; Zwang *m*; Heer *n*; Streitmacht *f*; *the* ~ die Polizei; *armed* ~*s pl.* Streitkräfte *f/pl.*; *come* (*put*) *in* ~ in Kraft treten (setzen); **2.** zwingen, nötigen; erzwingen; aufzwingen; Gewalt antun (*dat.*); beschleunigen; aufbrechen; künstlich reif machen; ~ *open* aufbrechen; ~*d:* ~ *landing* Notlandung *f*; ~ *loan* Zwangsanleihe *f*; ~ *march* Eilmarsch *m*; **~ful** □ ['fɔ:sful] kräftig; eindringlich.

forceps 🕮 ['fɔ:seps] Zange *f*.

forcible □ ['fɔ:səbl] gewaltsam; Zwangs...; eindringlich; wirksam.

ford [fɔ:d] **1.** Furt *f*; **2.** durchwaten.

fore [fɔ:] **1.** *adv.* vorn; **2.** Vorderteil *m*, *n*; *bring* (*come*) *to the* ~ zum

Vorschein bringen (kommen); **3.** *adj.* vorder; Vorder...; **~bode** [fɔ:-ˈboud] vorhersagen; ahnen; **~boding** [~diŋ] (böses) Vorzeichen; Ahnung *f*; **~cast** [ˈfɔ:kɑ:st] **1.** Vorhersage *f*; **2.** *[irr. (cast)]* vorhersehen; voraussagen; **~father** Vorfahr *m*; **~finger** Zeigefinger *m*; **~foot** Vorderfuß *m*; **~go** [fɔ:ˈgou] *[irr. (go)]* vorangehen; **~gone** [fɔ:-ˈgɔn, *adj.* ˈfɔːgɔn] von vornherein feststehend; **~** *conclusion* Selbstverständlichkeit *f*; **~ground** Vordergrund *m*; **~head** [ˈfɔrid] Stirn *f*.

foreign [ˈfɔrin] fremd; ausländisch; auswärtig; **~er** [~nə] Ausländer(in), Fremde(r *m*) *f*; **♀ Office** Außenministerium *n*; **~ policy** Außenpolitik *f*; **~ trade** Außenhandel *m*.

fore|knowledge [ˈfɔːˈnɔlidʒ] Vorherwissen *n*; **~leg** [ˈfɔːleg] Vorderbein *n*; **~lock** Stirnhaar *n*; *fig.* Schopf *m*; **~man** *[~]* Obmann *m*; Vorarbeiter *m*, (Werk)Meister *m*; ⚒ Steiger *m*; **~most** vorderst, erst; **~name** Vorname *m*; **~noon** Vormittag *m*; **~runner** Vorläufer *m*, Vorbote *m*; **~see** [fɔːˈsiː] *[irr. (see)]* vorhersehen; **~shadow** ankündigen; **~sight** [ˈfɔːsait] Voraussicht *f*; Vorsorge *f*.

forest [ˈfɔrist] **1.** Wald *m* (*a. fig.*), Forst *m*; **2.** aufforsten.

forestall [fɔːˈstɔːl] *et.* vereiteln; *j-m* zuvorkommen.

forest|er [ˈfɔristə] Förster *m*; Waldarbeiter *m*; **~ry** [~tri] Forstwirtschaft *f*; Waldgebiet *n*.

fore|taste [ˈfɔːteist] Vorgeschmack *m*; **~tell** [fɔːˈtel] *[irr. (tell)]* vorhersagen; vorbedeuten; **~thought** [ˈfɔːθɔːt] Vorbedacht *m*; **~woman** Aufseherin *f*; Vorarbeiterin *f*; **~word** Vorwort *n*.

forfeit [ˈfɔːfit] **1.** Verwirkung *f*; Strafe *f*; Pfand *n*; **2.** verwirken; einbüßen; **~able** [~təbl] verwirkbar.

forge[1] [fɔːdʒ] *mst* **~** *ahead* sich vor(wärts)arbeiten.

forge[2] [~] **1.** Schmiede *f*; **2.** schmieden (*fig. ersinnen*); fälschen; **~ry** [ˈfɔːdʒəri] Fälschung *f*.

forget [fəˈget] *[irr.]* vergessen; **~ful** □ [~tful] vergeßlich; **~-me-not** ⚘ Vergißmeinnicht *n*.

forgiv|e [fəˈgiv] *[irr. (give)]* vergeben, verzeihen; *Schuld* erlassen; **~eness** [~vnis] Verzeihung *f*; **~ing** □ [~viŋ] versöhnlich; nachsichtig.

forgo [fɔːˈgou] *[irr. (go)]* verzichten auf (*acc.*); aufgeben.

forgot [fəˈgɔt] *pret. von* forget; **~ten** [~tn] *p.p. von* forget.

fork [fɔːk] **1.** Gabel *f*; **2.** (sich) gabeln; **~-lift** [ˈfɔːklift] Gabelstapler *m*.

forlorn [fəˈlɔːn] verloren, verlassen.

form [fɔːm] **1.** Form *f*; Gestalt *f*; Formalität *f*; Formular *n*; (Schul-)Bank *f*; *Schul-*Klasse *f*; Kondition *f*; geistige Verfassung; **2.** (sich) formen, (sich) bilden, gestalten; ✕ (sich) aufstellen.

formal □ [ˈfɔːməl] förmlich; formell; äußerlich; **~ity** [fɔːˈmæliti] Förmlichkeit *f*, Formalität *f*.

formati|on [fɔːˈmeiʃən] Bildung *f*; **~ve** [ˈfɔːmətiv] bildend; gestaltend; **~** *years pl.* Entwicklungsjahre *n/pl.*

former [ˈfɔːmə] vorig, früher; ehemalig, vergangen; erstere(r, -s); jene(r, -s); **~ly** [~əli] ehemals, früher.

formidable □ [ˈfɔːmidəbl] furchtbar, schrecklich; ungeheuer.

formula [ˈfɔːmjulə] Formel *f*; ⚗ Rezept *n*; **~te** [~leit] formulieren.

forsake [fəˈseik] *[irr.]* aufgeben; verlassen; **~n** [~kən] *p.p. von* forsake.

forsook [fəˈsuk] *pret. von* forsake.

forsooth *iro.* [fəˈsuːθ] wahrlich.

forswear [fɔːˈsweə] *[irr. (swear)]* abschwören. [werk *n*) *f*.]

fort ✕ [fɔːt] Fort *n*, Festungs-)

forth [fɔːθ] vor(wärts), voran; heraus, hinaus, hervor; weiter, fort(an); **~coming** [fɔːˈθˈkʌmiŋ] erscheinend; bereit; bevorstehend; F entgegenkommend; **~with** [ˈfɔːθˈwiθ] sogleich.

fortieth [ˈfɔːtiiθ] **1.** vierzigste(r, -s); **2.** Vierzigstel *n*.

forti|fication [fɔːtifiˈkeiʃən] Befestigung *f*; **~fy** [ˈfɔːtifai] ✕ befestigen; *fig.* (ver)stärken; **~tude** [~itjuːd] Seelenstärke *f*; Tapferkeit *f*.

fortnight [ˈfɔːtnait] vierzehn Tage.

fortress [ˈfɔːtris] Festung *f*.

fortuitous □ [fɔːˈtju(ː)itəs] zufällig.

fortunate [ˈfɔːtʃnit] glücklich; **~ly** [~tli] glücklicherweise.

fortune [ˈfɔːtʃən] Glück *n*; Schicksal *n*; Zufall *m*; Vermögen *n*; **~-teller** Wahrsager(in).

forty [ˈfɔːti] **1.** vierzig; **~-niner** *Am. kalifornischer Goldsucher von 1849*; **~** *winks pl.* F Nickerchen *n*; **2.** Vierzig *f*.

forward [ˈfɔːwəd] **1.** *adj.* vorder; bereit(willig); fortschrittlich; vorwitzig, keck; **2.** *adv.* vor(wärts); **3.** *Fußball:* Stürmer *m*; **4.** (be)fördern; (ab-, ver)senden.

forwarding-agent [ˈfɔːwədiŋeiˈdʒənt] Spediteur *m*.

foster [ˈfɔstə] **1.** *fig.* nähren, pflegen; **~** *up* aufziehen; **2.** Pflege...

fought [fɔːt] *pret. u. p.p. von* fight **2.**

foul [faul] **1.** □ widerwärtig; schmutzig (*a. fig.*); unehrlich; regelwidrig; übelriechend; faul, verdorben; widrig; schlecht (*Wetter*); *fall* **~** *of* mit *dem Gesetz* in Konflikt kommen; **2.** Zs.-stoß *m*; *Sport:* regelwidriges Spiel; *through fair and* **~** durch dick und dünn; **3.** beverschmutzen; (sich) verwickeln.

found [faund] 1. *pret. u. p.p. von find* 1; 2. (be)gründen; stiften; ⊕ gießen.

foundation [faun'deiʃən] Gründung *f*; Stiftung *f*; Fundament *n*.

founder ['faundə] 1. (Be)Gründer (-in), Stifter(in); Gießer *m*; 2. *v/i.* scheitern; lahmen.

foundling ['faundliŋ] Findling *m*.

foundry ⊕ ['faundri] Gießerei *f*.

fountain ['fauntin] Quelle *f*; Springbrunnen *m*; ~-**pen** Füllfederhalter *m*.

four [fɔ:] 1. vier; 2. Vier *f*; *Sport*: Vierer *m*; ~-**flusher** *Am. sl.* ['fɔ:-'flʌʃə] Hochstapler *m*; ~-**square** viereckig; *fig.* unerschütterlich; ~-**stroke** *mot.* Viert~kt...; ~-**teen** ['fɔ:'tin] vierzehn; ~**teenth** [~nθ] vierzehnte(r, -s); ~**th** [tɔ:θ] 1. vierte(r, -s); 2. Viertel *n*; ~**thly** ['fɔ:θli] viertens.

fowl [faul] Geflügel *n*; Huhn *n*; Vogel *m*; ~**ing-piece** ['fauliŋpi:s] Vogelflinte *f*.

fox [fɔks] 1. Fuchs *m*; 2. überlisten; ~**glove** ♀ ['fɔksglʌv] Fingerhut *m*; ~**y** ['fɔksi] fuchsartig; schlau.

fraction ['frækʃən] Bruch(teil) *m*.

fracture ['fræktʃə] 1. (*bsd.* Knochen)Bruch *m*; 2. brechen.

fragile ['frædʒail] zerbrechlich.

fragment ['frægmənt] Bruchstück *n*.

fragran|ce ['freigrəns] Wohlgeruch *m*, Duft *m*; ~**t** □ [~nt] wohlriechend.

frail □ [freil] ge-, zerbrechlich; schwach; ~**ty** *fig.* ['freilti] Schwäche *f*.

frame [freim] 1. Rahmen *m*; Gerippe *n*; Gerüst *n*; (Brillen)Gestell *n*; Körper *m*; (An)Ordnung *f*; *phot.* (Einzel)Bild *n*; ✍ Frühbeetkasten *m*; ~ *of mind* Gemütsverfassung *f*; 2. bilden, formen, bauen; entwerfen; (ein)rahmen; sich entwickeln; ~-**house** ['freimhaus] Holzhaus *n*; ~-**up** *bsd. Am.* F abgekartetes Spiel; ~**work** ⊕ Gerippe *n*; Rahmen *m*; *fig.* Bau *m*.

franchise ⚖ ['fræntʃaiz] Wahlrecht *n*; Bürgerrecht *n*; *bsd. Am.* Konzession *f*.

frank [fræŋk] 1. □ frei(mütig), offen; 2. *Brief* maschinell frankieren.

frankfurter ['fræŋkfətə] Frankfurter Würstchen.

frankness ['fræŋknis] Offenheit *f*.

frantic ['fræntik] (~ally) wahnsinnig.

fratern|al □ [frə'tə:nl] brüderlich; ~**ity** [~niti] Brüderlichkeit *f*; Brüderschaft *f*; *Am. univ.* Verbindung *f*.

fraud [frɔ:d] Betrug *m*; F Schwindel *m*; ~**ulent** □ ['frɔ:djulənt] betrügerisch.

fray [frei] 1. (sich) abnutzen; (sich) durchscheuern; 2. Schlägerei *f*.

frazzle *bsd. Am.* F ['fræzl] 1. Fetzen *m/pl.*; 2. zerfetzen.

freak [fri:k] Einfall *m*, Laune *f*.

freckle ['frekl] Sommersprosse *f*.

free [fri:] 1. □ *allg.* frei; freigebig (of mit); freiwillig; *he is ~ to inf.* es steht ihm frei, zu *inf.*; ~ *and easy* zwanglos; sorglos; *make ~* sich Freiheiten erlauben; *set ~* freilassen; 2. befreien; freilassen, *et.* freimachen; ~**booter** ['fri:bu:tə] Freibeuter *m*; ~**dom** ['fri:dəm] Freiheit *f*; freie Benutzung; Offenheit *f*; Zwanglosigkeit *f*; (plumpe) Vertraulichkeit; ~ *of a city* (Ehren-)Bürgerrecht *n*; ~**holder** Grundeigentümer *m*; ~-**man** freier Mann; Vollbürger *m*; ~**mason** Freimaurer *m*; ~-**wheel** Freilauf *m*.

freez|e [fri:z] 1. *irr.* *v/i.* (ge)frieren; erstarren; *v/t.* gefrieren lassen; ~**er** ['fri:zə] Eismaschine *f*; Gefriermaschine *f*; Gefriertruhe *f*; ~**ing** □ [~ziŋ] eisig; ~ *point* Gefrierpunkt *m*.

freight [freit] 1. Fracht(geld *n*) *f*; *attr. Am.* Güter...; 2. be-, verfrachten; ~-**car** *Am.* 🚃 ['freitka:] Güterwagen *m*; ~ *train Am.* Güterzug *m*.

French [frentʃ] 1. französisch; *take ~ leave* heimlich weggehen; ~ *window* Balkon-, Verandatür *f*; 2. Französisch *n*; *the ~ pl.* die Franzosen *pl.*; ~**man** ['frentʃmən] Franzose *m*.

frenz|ied ['frenzid] wahnsinnig; ~**y** [~zi] Wahnsinn *m*.

frequen|cy ['fri:kwənsi] Häufigkeit *f*; ⚡ Frequenz *f*; ~**t** 1. □ [~nt] häufig; 2. [fri'kwent] (oft) besuchen.

fresh □ [freʃ] frisch; neu; unerfahren; *Am.* F frech; ~ *water* Süßwasser *n*; ~**en** ['freʃn] frisch machen *od.* werden; ~**et** [~ʃit] Hochwasser *n*; *fig.* Flut *f*; ~**man** *univ.* Student *m* im ersten Jahr; ~**ness** [~ʃnis] Frische *f*; Neuheit *f*; Unerfahrenheit *f*; ~**water** Süßwasser...; ~ *college Am.* drittrangiges College.

fret [fret] 1. Aufregung *f*; Ärger *m*; ♪ Bund *m*, Griffleiste *f*; 2. zerfressen; (sich) ärgern; (sich) grämen; ~ *away*, ~ *out* aufreiben.

fretful □ ['fretful] ärgerlich.

fret-saw ['fretsɔ:] Laubsäge *f*.

fretwork ['fretwə:k] (geschnitztes) Gitterwerk; Laubsägearbeit *f*.

friar ['fraiə] Mönch *m*.

friction ['frikʃən] Reibung *f* (*a. fig.*).

Friday ['fraidi] Freitag *m*.

fridge F [fridʒ] Kühlschrank *m*.

friend [frend] Freund(in); Bekannte(r *m*) *f*; ~**ly** ['frendli] freund(schaft)lich; ~**ship** [~dʃip] Freundschaft *f*.

frigate ⚓ ['frigit] Fregatte *f*.

frig(e) F [fridʒ] = fridge.

fright [frait] Schreck(en) *m*; *fig.*
Vogelscheuche *f*; ~**en** ['fraitn] erschrecken; ~*ed at od.* of bange vor
(*dat.*); ~**ful** □ [~tful] schrecklich.
frigid □ ['fridʒid] kalt, frostig.
frill [fril] Krause *f*, Rüsche *f*.
fringe [frindʒ] 1. Franse *f*; Rand *m*;
a. ~**s** *pl.* Ponyfrisur *f*; 2. mit Fran-
sen besetzen.
frippery ['fripəri] Flitterkram *m.*
Frisian ['friziən] friesisch.
frisk [frisk] 1. Luftsprung *m*;
2. hüpfen; *sl. nach Waffen etc.* durchsuchen; ~**y** □ ['friski] munter.
fritter ['fritə] 1. Pfannkuchen *m*,
Krapfen *m*; 2.: ~ *away* verzetteln.
frivol|ity [fri'vɔliti] Frivolität *f*,
Leichtfertigkeit *f*; ~**ous** □ ['fri-
vələs] nichtig; leichtfertig.
frizzle ['frizl] *a.* ~ *up* (sich) kräuseln; *Küche*: brutzeln.
fro [frou]: *to and* ~ hin und her.
frock [frɔk] Kutte *f*; *Frauen*-Kleid
n; Kittel *m*; Gehrock *m.*
frog [frɔg] Frosch *m.*
frolic ['frɔlik] 1. Fröhlichkeit *f*;
Scherz *m*; 2. scherzen, spaßen;
~**some** □ [~ksəm] lustig, fröhlich.
from [frɔm, frəm] von; aus,
von ... her; von ... (an); aus, vor,
wegen; nach, gemäß; *defend* ~
schützen vor (*dat.*); ~ *amidst* mitten aus.
front [frʌnt] 1. Stirn *f*; Vorderseite
f; ✗ Front *f*; Hemdbrust *f*; Strandpromenade *f*; Kühnheit *f*, Frechheit *f*; *in* ~ vorn; *in* ~ *of* räumlich
vor; 2. Vorder...; 3. *a.* ~ *on*, ~
towards die Front haben nach;
gegenüberstehen, gegenübertreten
(*dat.*); ~**al** ['frʌntl] Stirn...; Front-
...; Vorder...; ~ **door** Haustür *f*;
~**ier** [~tjə] Grenze *f*, *bsd. Am. hist.*
Grenze zum Wilden Westen; *attr.*
Grenz...; ~**iersman** [~zmən]
Grenzbewohner *m*; *fig.* Pionier *m*;
~**ispiece** [~tispi:s] △ Vorderseite *f*;
typ. Titelbild *n*; ~ **man** *fig.* Aus-
hängeschild *n*; ~-**page** *Zeitung:*
Titelseite *f*; ~-**wheel drive** *mot.*
Vorderradantrieb *m.*
frost [frɔst] 1. Frost *m*; *a.* hoar ~,
white ~ Reif *m*; 2. (mit Zucker)
bestreuen; glasieren; mattieren;
~*ed glass* Milchglas *n*; ~-**bite** ☆
['frɔstbait] Erfrierung *f*; ~**y** □
[~ti] frostig; bereift.
froth [frɔθ] 1. Schaum *m*; 2. schäumen; zu Schaum schlagen; ~**y** □
['frɔθi] schaumig; *fig.* seicht.
frown [fraun] 1. Stirnrunzeln *n*;
finsterer Blick; 2. *v/i.* die Stirn
runzeln; finster blicken.
frow|sty □ ['frausti], ~**zy** ['frauzi]
moderig; schlampig.
froze [frouz] *pret. von* freeze; ~**n**
['frouzn] 1. *p.p. von* freeze; 2. *adj.*
(eis)kalt; (ein)gefroren.
frugal □ ['fru:gəl] mäßig; sparsam.

fruit [fru:t] 1. Frucht *f*; Früchte *pl.*;
Obst *n*; 2. Frucht tragen; ~**erer**
['fru:tərə] Obsthändler *m*; ~**ful** □
[~tful] fruchtbar; ~**less** □ [~tlis]
unfruchtbar.
frustrat|e [frʌs'treit] vereiteln;
enttäuschen; ~**ion** [~eiʃən] Vereitelung *f*; Enttäuschung *f.*
fry [frai] 1. Gebratene(s) *n*; Fisch-
brut *f*; 2. braten, backen; ~**ing-pan**
['fraiiŋpæn] Bratpfanne *f.*
fuchsia ♀ ['fju:ʃə] Fuchsie *f.*
fudge [fʌdʒ] 1. F zurechtpfuschen;
2. Unsinn *m*; Weichkaramelle *f.*
fuel [fjuəl] 1. Brennmaterial *n*;
Betriebs-, *mot.* Kraftstoff *m*; 2. *mot.*
tanken.
fugitive ['fju:dʒitiv] 1. flüchtig
(*a. fig.*); 2. Flüchtling *m.*
fulfil(l) [ful'fil] erfüllen; vollziehen;
~**ment** [~lmənt] Erfüllung *f.*
full [ful] 1. □ *allg.* voll; Voll...;
vollständig, völlig; reichlich; ausführlich; *of* ~ *age* volljährig; 2. *adv.*
völlig, ganz; genau; 3. Ganze(s) *n*;
Höhepunkt *m*; *in* ~ völlig; ausführlich; *to the* ~ vollständig; ~-
blooded ['ful'blʌdid] vollblütig;
kräftig; reinrassig; ~ **dress** Gesellschaftsanzug *m*; ~-**dress** ['fuldres]
formell, Gala...; *Am.* ausführlich;
~-**fledged** ['ful'fledʒd] flügge; voll
ausgewachsen; ~ **stop** Punkt *m.*
ful(l)ness ['fulnis] Fülle *f.*
full-time ['fultaim] vollbeschäftigt;
Voll...
fulminate *fig.* ['fʌlmineit] wettern.
fumble ['fʌmbl] tasten; fummeln.
fume [fju:m] 1. Dunst *m*, Dampf *m*;
2. rauchen; aufgebracht sein.
fumigate ['fju:migeit] ausräuchern,
desinfizieren.
fun [fʌn] Scherz *m*, Spaß *m*; *make* ~
of sich lustig machen über (*acc.*).
function ['fʌŋkʃən] 1. Funktion *f*;
Beruf *m*; Tätigkeit *f*; Aufgabe *f*;
Feierlichkeit *f*; 2. funktionieren;
~**ary** [~ʃnəri] Beamte(r) *m*; Funk-
tionär *m.*
fund [fʌnd] 1. Fonds *m*; ~**s** *pl.*
Staatspapiere *n*/*pl.*; Geld(mittel
n/*pl.*) *n*; Vorrat *m*; 2. *Schuld* fun-
dieren; *Geld* anlegen.
fundamental □ [fʌndə'mentl]
1. grundlegend; Grund...; ~**s** *pl.*
Grundlage *f*, -züge *m*/*pl.*, -begriffe
m/*pl.*
funer|al ['fju:nərəl] Beerdigung *f*;
attr. Trauer..., Begräbnis...; ~**eal** □
[fju:(:)'niəriəl] traurig, düster.
fun-fair ['fʌnfɛə] Rummelplatz
m.
funicular [fju:(:)'nikjulə] 1. Seil...;
2. *a.* ~ *railway* (Draht)Seilbahn *f.*
funnel ['fʌnl] Trichter *m*; Rauchfang *m*; ♨, 🚂 Schornstein *m.*
funnies *Am.* ['fʌniz] *pl.* Comics *pl.*
(*primitive Bildserien*).
funny □ ['fʌni] spaßig, komisch.

fur [fəː] **1.** Pelz *m*; Belag *m der Zunge*; Kesselstein *m*; ~s *pl.* Pelzwaren *pl.*; **2.** mit Pelz besetzen *od.* füttern.

furbish ['fəːbiʃ] putzen, polieren.

furious □ ['fjuəriəs] wütend; wild.

furl [fəːl] zs.-rollen; zs.-klappen.

furlough ✕ ['fəːlou] Urlaub *m*.

furnace ['fəːnis] Schmelz-, Hochofen *m*; (Heiz)Kessel *m*; Feuerung *f*.

furnish ['fəːniʃ] versehen (*with* mit); *et.* liefern; möblieren; ausstatten.

furniture ['fəːnitʃə] Möbel *pl.*, Einrichtung *f*; Ausstattung *f*; sectional ~ Anbaumöbel *pl.*

furrier ['fʌriə] Kürschner *m*.

furrow ['fʌrou] **1.** Furche *f*; **2.** furchen.

further ['fəːðə] **1.** *adj. u. adv.* ferner, weiter; **2.** fördern; ~ance [~ərəns] Förderung *f*; ~more [~əˈmɔː] ferner, überdies; ~most [~əmoust] weitest.

furthest ['fəːðist] = *furthermost*.

furtive □ ['fəːtiv] verstohlen.

fury ['fjuəri] Raserei *f*, Wut *f*; Furie *f*.

fuse [fjuːz] **1.** (ver)schmelzen; *⚡* durchbrennen; ausgehen (*Licht*); ✕ mit Zünder versehen; **2.** *⚡* (Schmelz)Sicherung *f*; ✕ Zünder *m*.

fuselage ['fjuːzilaːʒ] (Flugzeug-) Rumpf *m*.

fusion ['fjuːʒən] Schmelzen *n*; Verschmelzung *f*, Fusion *f*; ~ **bomb** ✕ Wasserstoffbombe *f*.

fuss F [fʌs] **1.** Lärm *m*; Wesen *n*, Getue *n*; **2.** viel Aufhebens machen (*about* um, von); (sich) aufregen.

fusty ['fʌsti] muffig; *fig.* verstaubt.

futile ['fjuːtail] nutzlos, nichtig.

future ['fjuːtʃə] **1.** (zu)künftig; **2.** Zukunft *f*; *gr.* Futur *n*, Zukunft *f*; ~s *pl.* † Termingeschäfte *n/pl.*

fuzz [fʌz] **1.** feiner Flaum; Fussel *f*; **2.** fusseln, (zer)fasern.

G

gab F [gæb] Geschwätz *n*; *the gift of the* ~ ein gutes Mundwerk.

gabardine ['gæbədiːn] Gabardine *m* (*Wollstoff*).

gabble ['gæbl] **1.** Geschnatter *n*, Geschwätz *n*; **2.** schnattern, schwatzen.

gaberdine ['gæbədiːn] Kaftan *m*; = *gabardine*.

gable ['geibl] Giebel *m*.

gad F [gæd]: ~ *about* sich herumtreiben.

gadfly *zo.* ['gædflai] Bremse *f*.

gadget *sl.* ['gædʒit] Dings *n*, Apparat *m*; Kniff *m*, Pfiff *m*.

gag [gæg] **1.** Knebel *m*; Witz *m*; **2.** knebeln; *pol.* mundtot machen.

gage[1] [geidʒ] Pfand *n*.

gage[2] [~] = *gauge*.

gaiety ['geiəti] Fröhlichkeit *f*.

gaily ['geili] *adv. von* gay.

gain [gein] **1.** Gewinn *m*; Vorteil *m*; **2.** *v/t.* gewinnen; erreichen; bekommen; *v/i.* vorgehen (*Uhr*); ~ *in* zunehmen an (*acc.*); ~**ful** □ ['geinful] einträglich.

gait [geit] Gang(art *f*) *m*; Schritt *m*.

gaiter ['geitə] Gamasche *f*.

gal *Am. sl.* [gæl] Mädel *n*.

gale [geil] Sturm *m*; steife Brise.

gall [gɔːl] **1.** Galle *f*; *⚕* Wolf *m*; Pein *f*; *bsd. Am. sl.* Frechheit *f*; **2.** wundreiben; ärgern.

gallant ['gælənt] **1.** □ stattlich; tapfer; galant, höflich; **2.** Kavalier *m*; **3.** galant sein; ~ry [~tri] Tapferkeit *f*; Galanterie *f*.

gallery ['gæləri] Galerie *f*; Empore *f*.

galley ['gæli] ♧ Galeere *f*; ♧ Kombüse *f*; ~**proof** Korrekturfahne *f*.

gallon ['gælən] Gallone *f* (*4,54 Liter, Am. 3,78 Liter*).

gallop ['gæləp] **1.** Galopp *m*; **2.** galoppieren (lassen).

gallows ['gælouz] *sg.* Galgen *m*.

galore [gəˈlɔː] in Menge.

gamble ['gæmbl] (um Geld) spielen; **2.** F Glücksspiel *n*; ~r [~lə] Spieler(in).

gambol ['gæmbəl] **1.** Luftsprung *m*; **2.** (fröhlich) hüpfen, tanzen.

game [geim] **1.** Spiel *n*; Scherz *m*; Wild *n*; **2.** F entschlossen; furchtlos; **3.** spielen; ~**keeper** ['geimkiːpə] Wildhüter *m*; ~**licence** Jagdschein *m*; ~**ster** ['geimstə] Spieler(in).

gander ['gændə] Gänserich *m*.

gang [gæŋ] **1.** Trupp *m*; Bande *f*; **2.** ~ *up* sich zs.-rotten *od.* zs.-tun; ~**board** ♧ ['gæŋbɔːd] Laufplanke *f*.

gangster *Am.* ['gæŋstə] Gangster *m*.

gangway ['gæŋwei] (Durch)Gang *m*; ♧ Fallreep *n*; ♧ Laufplanke *f*.

gaol [dʒeil], ~**bird** ['dʒeilbəːd], ~**er** ['dʒeilə] *s. jail etc.*

gap [gæp] Lücke *f*; Kluft *f*; Spalte *f*.

gape [geip] gähnen; klaffen; gaffen.

garage ['gæraːʒ] **1.** Garage *f*; Autowerkstatt *f*; **2.** *Auto* einstellen.

garb [gaːb] Gewand *n*, Tracht *f*.

garbage ['gaːbidʒ] Abfall *m*;

Schund *m*; ~ *can Am.* Mülltonne *f*; ~ *pail* Mülleimer *m*.

garden ['gɑːdn] **1.** Garten *m*; **2.** Gartenbau treiben; ~**er** [~nə] Gärtner(in); ~**ing** [~niŋ] Gartenarbeit *f*.

gargle ['gɑːgl] **1.** gurgeln; **2.** Gurgelwasser *n*.

garish □ ['gɛəriʃ] grell, auffallend.

garland ['gɑːlənd] Girlande *f*.

garlic ♀ ['gɑːlik] Knoblauch *m*.

garment ['gɑːmənt] Gewand *n*.

garnish ['gɑːniʃ] garnieren; zieren.

garret ['gærət] Dachstube *f*.

garrison ⚔ ['gærisn] **1.** Besatzung *f*; Garnison *f*; **2.** mit e-r Besatzung belegen.   [haft.\

garrulous □ ['gæruləs] schwatz-\

garter ['gɑːtə] Strumpfband *n*; *Am.* Socken-, Strumpfhalter *m*.

gas [gæs] **1.** Gas *n*; *Am.* = *gasoline*; **2.** *v/t.* vergasen; *v/i.* F faseln; ~**eous** ['geizjəs] gasförmig.

gash [gæʃ] **1.** klaffende Wunde; Hieb *m*; Riß *m*; **2.** tief (ein)schneiden in (*acc.*).

gas|-light ['gæslait] Gasbeleuchtung *f*; ~**-meter** Gasuhr *f*; ~**o-lene**, ~**oline** *Am. mot.* ['gæsəliːn] Benzin *n*.

gasp [gɑːsp] **1.** Keuchen *n*; **2.** keuchen; nach Luft schnappen.

gas|sed [gæst] gasvergiftet; ~**stove** ['gæs'stouv] Gasofen *m*, -herd *m*; ~**works** ['gæswəːks] *sg.* Gaswerk *n*, -anstalt *f*.

gat *Am. sl.* [gæt] Revolver *m*.

gate [geit] Tor *n*; Pforte *f*; Sperre *f*; ~**man** ⊞ ['geitmən] Schrankenwärter *m*; ~**way** Tor(weg *m*) *n*, Einfahrt *f*.

gather ['gæðə] **1.** *v/t.* (ein-, ver-) sammeln; ernten; pflücken; schließen (*from* aus); zs.-ziehen; kräuseln; ~ *speed* schneller werden *v/i.* sich (ver)sammeln; sich vergrößern; ☞ *u. fig.* reifen; **2.** Falte *f*; ~**ing** [~riŋ] Versammlung *f*; Zs.-kunft *f*.

gaudy □ ['gɔːdi] grell; protzig.

gauge [geidʒ] **1.** (Normal)Maß *n*; Maßstab *m*; ⊞ Lehre *f*; 🚃 Spurweite *f*; Meßgerät *n*; **2.** eichen; (aus)messen; *fig.* abschätzen.

gaunt □ [gɔːnt] hager; finster.

gauntlet ['gɔːntlit] *fig.* Fehdehandschuh *m*; *run the* ~ Spießruten laufen.

gauze [gɔːz] Gaze *f*.

gave [geiv] *pret. von give.*

gavel *Am.* ['gævl] Hammer *m* des Versammlungsleiters *od. Auktionators.*

gawk F [gɔːk] Tölpel *m*; ~**y** [gɔːʹki] tölpisch.

gay □ [gei] lustig, heiter; bunt, lebhaft, glänzend.

gaze [geiz] **1.** starrer *od.* aufmerksamer Blick; **2.** starren.

gazette [gəʹzet] **1.** Amtsblatt *n*; **2.** amtlich bekanntgeben.

gear [giə] **1.** ⊕ Getriebe *n*; *mot.* Gang *m*; Mechanismus *m*; Gerät *n*; *in* ~ mit eingelegtem Gang; in Betrieb; *out of* ~ im Leerlauf; außer Betrieb; *landing* ~ ✈ Fahrgestell *n*; *steering* ~ ⚓ Ruderanlage *f*; *mot.* Lenkung *f*; **2.** einschalten; ⊕ greifen; ~**ing** ['giəriŋ] (Zahnrad-) Getriebe *n*; Übersetzung *f*; ~ *lever*, *bsd. Am.* ~**-shift** Schalthebel *m*.

gee [dʒiː] **1.** *Kindersprache*: Hottehü *n* (*Pferd*); **2.** *Fuhrmannsruf*: hü! hott!; *Am.* nanu!, so was!

geese [giːs] *pl. von goose.*

gem [dʒem] Edelstein *m*; Gemme *f*; *fig.* Glanzstück *n*.

gender *gr.* ['dʒendə] Genus *n*, Geschlecht *n*.

general ['dʒenərəl] **1.** □ allgemein; gewöhnlich; Haupt..., General...; ~ *election* allgemeine Wahlen; **2.** ⚔ General *m*; Feldherr *m*; ~**ity** [dʒenəʹræliti] Allgemeinheit *f*; *die* große Masse; ~**ize** [dʒenərəʹlaiz] verallgemeinern; ~**ly** [~li] im allgemeinen, überhaupt; gewöhnlich.

general|te ['dʒenəreit] erzeugen; ~**ion** [dʒenəʹreiʃən] (Er)Zeugung *f*; Generation *f*; Menschenalter *n*; ~**or** ['dʒenəreitə] Erzeuger *m*; ⊕ Generator *m*; *bsd. Am. mot.* Lichtmaschine *f*.

gener|osity [dʒenəʹrɔsiti] Großmut *f*; Großzügigkeit *f*; ~**ous** □ ['dʒenərəs] großmütig, großzügig.

genial □ ['dʒiːnjəl] freundlich; anregend; gemütlich (*Person*); heiter.

genitive *gr.* ['dʒenitiv] *a.* ~ *case* Genitiv *m*.

genius ['dʒiːnjəs] Geist *m*; Genie *n*.

gent F [dʒent] Herr *m*.

genteel □ [dʒenʹtiːl] vornehm; elegant.

gentile ['dʒentail] **1.** heidnisch, nichtjüdisch; **2.** Heid|e *m*, -in *f*.

gentle □ ['dʒentl] sanft, mild; zahm; leise, sacht; vornehm; ~**man** Herr *m*; Gentleman *m*; ~**manlike**, ~**manly** [~li] gebildet; vornehm; ~**ness** [~lnis] Sanftheit *f*; Milde *f*, Güte *f*, Sanftmut *f*.

gentry ['dʒentri] niederer Adel; gebildete Stände *m/pl.*

genuine □ ['dʒenjuin] echt; aufrichtig.

geography [dʒiʹɔgrəfi] Geographie *f*.

geology [dʒiʹɔlədʒi] Geologie *f*.

geometry [dʒiʹɔmitri] Geometrie *f*.

germ [dʒəːm] **1.** Keim *m*; **2.** keimen.

German[1] ['dʒəːmən] **1.** deutsch; **2.** Deutsche(r *m*) *f*; Deutsch *n*.

german[2] [~] *brother* ~ leiblicher Bruder; ~**e** [dʒəːʹmein] (*to*) verwandt (mit); entsprechend (*dat.*).

germinate ['dʒəːmineit] keimen.

gesticulat|e [dʒes'tikjuleit] gestikulieren; **~ion** [dʒestikju'leiʃən] Gebärdenspiel *n*.

gesture ['dʒestʃə] Geste *f*, Gebärde *f*.

get [get] [*irr.*] *v/t.* erhalten, bekommen, F kriegen; besorgen; holen; bringen; erwerben; verdienen; ergreifen, fassen; (veran)lassen; *mit adv. mst* bringen, machen; *have got* haben; *~ one's hair cut* sich das Haar schneiden lassen; *~ by heart* auswendig lernen; *v/i.* gelangen, geraten, kommen; gehen; werden; *~ ready* sich fertig machen; *~ about* auf den Beinen sein; *~ abroad* bekannt werden; *~ ahead* vorwärtskommen; *~ at* (heran-) kommen an ... (*acc.*); zu *et.* kommen; *~ away* wegkommen; sich fortmachen; *~ in* einsteigen; *~ on with* s.o. *mit* j-m auskommen; *~ out* aussteigen; *~ to hear* (*know, learn*) erfahren; *~ up* aufstehen; **~up** ['getʌp] Aufmachung *f*; *Am.* F Unternehmungsgeist *m*.

ghastly ['gɑːstli] gräßlich; schrecklich; (toten)bleich; gespenstisch.

gherkin [gə'kin] Gewürzgurke *f*.

ghost [goust] Geist *m*, Gespenst *n*; *fig.* Spur *f*; **~like** ['goustlaik], **~ly** [~li] geisterhaft.

giant ['dʒaiənt] 1. riesig; 2.Riese *m*.

gibber ['dʒibə] kauderwelschen; **~ish** ['gibəriʃ] Kauderwelsch *n*.

gibbet ['dʒibit] 1. Galgen *m*; 2. hängen.

gibe [dʒaib] verspotten, aufziehen.

giblets ['dʒiblits] *pl.* Gänseklein *n*.

gidd|iness ['gidinis] ⚕ Schwindel *m*; Unbeständigkeit *f*; Leichtsinn *m*; **~y** □ ['gidi] schwind(e)lig; leichtfertig; unbeständig; albern.

gift [gift] Gabe *f*; Geschenk *n*; Talent *n*; **~ed** ['giftid] begabt.

gigantic [dʒai'gæntik] (*~ally*) riesenhaft, riesig, gigantisch.

giggle ['gigl] 1. kichern; 2. Gekicher *n*.

gild [gild] [*irr.*] vergolden; verschönen; **~ed youth** Jeunesse *f* dorée.

gill [gil] *ichth.* Kieme *f*; ♀ Lamelle *f*.

gilt [gilt] 1. *pret. u. p.p. von* gild; 2. Vergoldung *f*.

gimmick *Am. sl.* ['gimik] Trick *m*.

gin [dʒin] Gin *m* (*Wacholderschnaps*); Schlinge *f*; ⊕ Entkörnungsmaschine *f*.

ginger ['dʒindʒə] 1. Ingwer *m*; Lebhaftigkeit *f*; 2. *~ up in* Schwung bringen; 3. hellrot, rötlich-gelb; **~bread** Pfefferkuchen *m*; **~ly** [~əli] zimperlich; sachte.

gipsy ['dʒipsi] Zigeuner(in).

gird [gəːd] sticheln; [*irr.*] (um)gürten; umgeben.

girder ⊕ ['gəːdə] Tragbalken *m*.

girdle ['gəːdl] 1. Gürtel *m*; Hüfthalter *m*, -gürtel *m*; 2. umgürten.

girl [gəːl] Mädchen *n*; ♀ **Guide** ['gəːlgaid] Pfadfinderin *f*; **~hood** ['gəːlhud] Mädchenzeit *f*; Mädchenjahre *n/pl.*; **~ish** □ ['gəːliʃ] mädchenhaft; **~y** *Am.* F ['gəːli] mit spärlich bekleideten Mädchen (*Magazin, Varieté etc.*).

girt [gəːt] *pret. u. p.p. von* gird.

girth [gəːθ] (Sattel)Gurt *m*; Umfang *m*.

gist [dʒist] *das* Wesentliche.

give [giv] [*irr.*] *v/t.* geben; ab-, übergeben; her-, hingeben; überlassen; zum besten geben; schenken; gewähren; von sich geben; ergeben; *~ birth to* zur Welt bringen; *~ away* verschenken; F verraten; *~ forth* von sich geben; herausgeben; *~ in* einreichen; *~ up* *Geschäft etc.* aufgeben; j-n ausliefern; *v/i. mst ~ in* nachgeben; weichen; *~ into, ~ (up)on* hinausgehen auf (*acc.*) (*Fenster etc.*); *~ out* aufhören; versagen; **~ and take** [givən'teik] (Meinungs)Austausch *m*; Kompromiß *m*; **~-away** Preisgabe *f*; *~ show od. program bsd. Am. Radio, Fernsehen:* öffentliches Preisraten; **~n** ['givn] 1. *p.p. von* give; 2. *~ to* ergeben (*dat.*).

glaci|al □ ['gleisjal] eisig; Eis...; Gletscher...; **~er** ['glæsjə] Gletscher *m*.

glad □ [glæd] froh, erfreut; erfreulich; **~ly** gern; **~den** ['glædn] erfreuen.

glade [gleid] Lichtung *f*; *Am.* sumpfige Niederung.

gladness ['glædnis] Freude *f*.

glair [glɛə] Eiweiß *n*.

glamo|rous ['glæmərəs] bezaubernd; **~(u)r** ['glæmə] 1. Zauber *m*, Glanz *m*, Reiz *m*; 2. bezaubern.

glance [glɑːns] 1. Schimmer *m*, Blitz *m*; flüchtiger Blick; 2. hinweggleiten; *mst ~ off* abprallen; blitzen; glänzen; *~ at* flüchtig ansehen; anspielen auf (*acc.*).

gland *anat.* [glænd] Drüse *f*.

glare [glɛə] 1. grelles Licht; wilder, starrer Blick; 2. grell leuchten; wild blicken; (*at* an)starren.

glass [glɑːs] 1. Glas *n*; Spiegel *m*; Opern-, Fernglas *n*; Barometer *n*; (*a pair of*) **~es** *pl.* (eine) Brille; 2. gläsern; Glas...; 3. verglasen; **~case** ['glɑːskeis] Vitrine *f*; Schaukasten *m*; **~house** Treibhaus *n*; ✕ *sl.* Bau *m*; **~y** [~si] gläsern; glasig.

glaz|e [gleiz] 1. Glasur *f*; 2. *v/t.* verglasen; glasieren; polieren; *v/i.* trüb(e) *od.* glasig werden (*Auge*); **~ier** ['gleizjə] Glaser *m*.

gleam [gliːm] 1. Schimmer *m*, Schein *m*; 2. schimmern.

glean [gli:n] *v/t.* sammeln; *v/i.* Ähren lesen.

glee [gli:] Fröhlichkeit *f*; mehrstimmiges Lied; ~ club Gesangverein *m*.

glen [glen] Bergschlucht *f*.

glib □ [glib] glatt, zungenfertig.

glid|e [glaid] **1.** Gleiten *n*; ✈ Gleitflug *m*; **2.** (dahin)gleiten (lassen); e-n Gleitflug machen; **~er** ['glaidə] Segelflugzeug *n*.

glimmer ['glimə] **1.** Schimmer *m*; *min.* Glimmer *m*; **2.** schimmern.

glimpse [glimps] **1.** flüchtiger Blick (of auf *acc.*); Schimmer *m*; flüchtiger Eindruck; **2.** flüchtig (er)blicken.

glint [glint] **1.** blitzen, glitzern; **2.** Lichtschein *m*.

glisten ['glisn], **glitter** ['glitə] glitzern, glänzen.

gloat [glout]: ~ (up)on *od.* over sich weiden an (*dat.*).

globe [gloub] (Erd)Kugel *f*; Globus *m*.

gloom [glu:m], **~iness** ['glu:minis] Düsterkeit *f*, Dunkelheit *f*; Schwermut *f*; **~y** □ ['glu:mi] dunkel, düster; schwermütig; verdrießlich.

glori|fy ['glɔːrifai] verherrlichen; **~ous** □ [~iəs] herrlich; glorreich.

glory ['glɔːri] **1.** Ruhm *m*; Herrlichkeit *f*, Pracht *f*; Glorienschein *m*; **2.** frohlocken; stolz sein.

gloss [glɔs] **1.** Glosse *f*, Bemerkung *f*; Glanz *m*; **2.** Glossen machen (zu); Glanz geben (*dat.*); ~ over beschönigen.

glossary ['glɔsəri] Wörterverzeichnis *n*.

glossy □ ['glɔsi] glänzend, blank.

glove [glʌv] Handschuh *m*.

glow [glou] **1.** Glühen *n*; Glut *f*; **2.** glühen.

glower ['glauə] finster blicken.

glow-worm ['glouwə:m] Glühwürmchen *n*.

glucose ['glu:kous] Traubenzucker *m*.

glue [glu:] **1.** Leim *m*; **2.** leimen.

glum □ [glʌm] mürrisch.

glut [glʌt] überfüllen.

glutinous □ ['glu:tinəs] klebrig.

glutton ['glʌtn] Unersättliche(r *m*) *f*; Vielfraß *m*; **~ous** □ [~nəs] gefräßig; **~y** [~ni] Gefräßigkeit *f*.

G-man *Am.* F ['dʒi:mæn] FBI-Agent *m*.

gnarl [nɑːl] Knorren *m*, Ast *m*.

gnash [næʃ] knirschen (mit).

gnat [næt] (Stech)Mücke *f*.

gnaw [nɔː] (zer)nagen; (zer)fressen.

gnome [noum] Erdgeist *m*, Gnom *m*.

go [gou] **1.** *irr.* *allg.* gehen, fahren; vergehen (*Zeit*); werden; führen (to nach); sich wenden (to an); funktionieren, arbeiten; passen; kaputtgehen; let ~ loslassen; ~

shares teilen; ~ to *od.* and see besuchen; ~ at losgehen auf (*acc.*); ~ between vermitteln (zwischen); ~ by sich richten nach; ~ for gehen nach, holen; ~ for a walk, etc. einen Spaziergang *etc.* machen; ~ in for an examination e-e Prüfung machen; ~ on weitergehen; fortfahren; ~ through durchgehen; durchmachen; ~ without sich behelfen ohne; **2.** F Mode *f*; Schwung *m*, Schneid *m*; on the ~ auf den Beinen; im Gange; it is no ~ es geht nicht; in one ~ auf Anhieb; have a ~ at es versuchen mit.

goad [goud] **1.** Stachelstock *m*; *fig.* Ansporn *m*; **2.** *fig.* anstacheln.

go-ahead F ['gouəhed] **1.** zielstrebig; unternehmungslustig; **2.** *bsd. Am.* F Erlaubnis *f* zum Weitermachen.

goal [goul] Mal *n*; Ziel *n*; *Fußball:* Tor *n*; **~-keeper** ['goulki:pə] Torwart *m*.

goat [gout] Ziege *f*, Geiß *f*.

gob [gɔb] V Schleimklumpen *m*; F Maul *n*; *Am.* F Blaujacke *f* (*Matrose*).

gobble ['gɔbl] *gierig* verschlingen; **~dygook** *Am. sl.* [~ldiguk] Amts-, Berufsjargon *m*; Geschwafel *n*; **~r** [~lə] Vielfraß *m*; Truthahn *m*.

go-between ['goubitwi:n] Vermittler(in).

goblet ['gɔblit] Kelchglas *n*; Pokal *m*.

goblin ['gɔblin] Kobold *m*, Gnom *m*.

god, *eccl.* ♀ [gɔd] Gott *m*; *fig.* Abgott *m*; **~child** ['gɔdtʃaild] Patenkind *n*; **~dess** ['gɔdis] Göttin *f*; **~father** Pate *m*; **~head** Gottheit *f*; **~less** ['gɔdlis] gottlos; **~like** gottähnlich; göttlich; **~ly** [~li] gottesfürchtig; fromm; **~mother** Patin *f*.

go-getter *Am. sl.* F ['gou'getə] Draufgänger *m*.

goggle ['gɔgl] **1.** glotzen; **2.** **~s** *pl.* Schutzbrille *f*.

going ['gouiŋ] **1.** gehend; im Gange (befindlich); be ~ to *inf.* im Begriff sein zu *inf.*, gleich *tun* wollen *od.* werden; **2.** Gehen *n*; Vorwärtskommen *n*; Straßenzustand *m*; Geschwindigkeit *f*, Leistung *f*; **~s-on** F [~ŋz'ɔn] *pl.* Treiben *n*.

gold [gould] **1.** Gold *n*; **2.** golden; **~-digger** *Am.* ['goulddigə] Goldgräber *m*; **~en** *mst fig.* [~dən] golden, goldgelb; **~finch** *zo.* Stieglitz *m*; **~smith** Goldschmied *m*.

golf [gɔlf] **1.** Golf(spiel) *n*; **2.** Golf spielen; **~-course** ['gɔlfkɔːs], **~-links** *pl.* Golfplatz *m*.

gondola ['gɔndələ] Gondel *f*.

gone [gɔn] **1.** *p.p. von* go **1**; **2.** *adj.* fort; F futsch; vergangen; tot; F hoffnungslos.

good [gud] **1.** *allg.* gut; artig; gütig;

† zahlungsfähig; gründlich; ~ at geschickt in (dat.); 2. Gute(s) n; Wohl n, Beste(s) n; ~s pl. Waren f|pl.; Güter n|pl.; that's no ~ das nützt nichts; for ~ für immer; ~by(e) 1. [gud'bai] Lebewohl n; 2. ['gud'bai] (auf) Wiedersehen!; ♀ Friday Karfreitag m; ~ly ['gudli] anmutig, hübsch; fig. ansehnlich; ~natured gutmütig; ~ness [~nis] Güte f; das Beste; thank ~! Gott sei Dank!; ~will Wohlwollen n; † Kundschaft f; † Firmenwert m.

goody ['gudi] Bonbon m, n.

goon Am. sl. [gu:n] bestellter Schläger bsd. für Streik; Dummkopf m.

goose [gu:s], pl. **geese** [gi:s] Gans f (a. fig.); Bügeleisen n.

gooseberry ['guzbəri] Stachelbeere f.

goose|-flesh ['gu:sfleʃ], Am. ~pimples pl. fig. Gänsehaut f.

gopher bsd. Am. ['goufə] Erdeichhörnchen n.

gore [gɔ:] 1. (geronnenes) Blut; Schneiderei: Keil m; 2. durchbohren, aufspießen.

gorge [gɔ:dʒ] 1. Kehle f, Schlund m; enge (Fels)Schlucht; 2. (ver-)schlingen; (sich) vollstopfen.

gorgeous □ ['gɔ:dʒəs] prächtig.

gory □ ['gɔ:ri] blutig.

gospel [gɔspəl] Evangelium n.

gossip ['gɔsip] 1. Geschwätz n; Klatschbase f; 2. schwatzen.

got [gɔt] pret. u. p.p. von get.

Gothic ['gɔθik] gotisch; fig. barbarisch.

gotten Am. ['gɔtn] p.p. von get.

gouge [gaudʒ] 1. ⊕ Hohlmeißel m; 2. ausmeißeln; Am. F betrügen.

gourd ♀ [guəd] Kürbis m.

gout ♯ [gaut] Gicht f.

govern ['gʌvən] v/t. regieren, beherrschen; lenken, leiten; v/i. herrschen; ~ess [~nis] Erzieherin f; ~ment ['gʌvnmənt] Regierung(s-form) f; Leitung f; Herrschaft f (of über acc.); Ministerium n; Statthalterschaft f; attr. Staats...; ~mental [gʌvən'mentl] Regierungs...; ~or ['gʌvənə] Gouverneur m; Direktor m, Präsident m; F Alte(r) m (Vater, Chef).

gown [gaun] 1. (Frauen)Kleid n; Robe f, Talar m; 2. kleiden.

grab F [græb] 1. grapsen; an sich reißen, packen; 2. plötzlicher Griff; ⊕ Greifer m; ~bag bsd. Am. Glückstopf m.

grace [greis] 1. Gnade f; Gunst f; (Gnaden)Frist f; Grazie f, Anmut f; Anstand m; Zier(de) f; Reiz m; Tischgebet n; Your ♀ Euer Gnaden; 2. zieren, schmücken; begünstigen, auszeichnen; ~ful □ ['greisful] anmutig; ~fulness [~nis] Anmut f.

gracious □ ['greiʃəs] gnädig.

gradation [grə'deiʃən] Abstufung f.

grade [greid] 1. Grad m, Rang m; Stufe f; Qualität f; bsd. Am. = gradient; Am. Schule: Klasse f, Note f; make the ~ Am. Erfolg haben; ~ crossing bsd. Am. schienengleicher Bahnübergang; ~(d) school bsd. Am. Grundschule f; 2. abstufen; einstufen; ⊕ planieren.

gradient ⚙ etc. ['greidjənt] Steigung f.

gradua|l □ ['grædjuəl] stufenweise, allmählich; ~te 1. [~ueit] graduieren; (sich) abstufen; die Abschlußprüfung machen; promovieren; 2. univ. [~uit] Graduierte(r m) f; ~tion [grædju'eiʃən] Gradeinteilung f; Abschlußprüfung f; Promotion f.

graft [grɑ:ft] 1. ♠ Pfropfreis n; Am. Schiebung f; 2. ♠ pfropfen; ♯ verpflanzen; Am. fig. schieben.

grain [grein] (Samen)Korn n; Getreide n; Gefüge n; fig. Natur f; Gran n (Gewicht).

gram [græm] = gramme.

gramma|r ['græmə] Grammatik f; ~r-school höhere Schule, Gymnasium n; Am. a. Mittelschule f; ~tical □ [grə'mætikəl] grammati(kali)sch.

gramme [græm] Gramm n.

granary ['grænəri] Kornspeicher m.

grand □ [grænd] 1. fig. großartig; erhaben; groß; Groß..., Haupt...; ♀ Old Party Am. Republikanische Partei; ~ stand Sport: (Haupt-)Tribüne f; 2. ♪ a. ~ piano Flügel m; Am. sl. tausend Dollar pl.; ~child ['græntʃaild] Enkel(in); ~eur [~ndʒə] Größe f, Hoheit f; Erhabenheit f; ~father Großvater m.

grandiose □ ['grændious] großartig.

grand|mother ['grænmʌðə] Großmutter f; ~parents [~npɛərənts] pl. Großeltern pl.

grange [greindʒ] Gehöft n; Gut n; Am. Name für Farmerorganisation f.

granny F ['græni] Oma f.

grant [grɑ:nt] 1. Gewährung f; Unterstützung f; Stipendium n; 2. gewähren; bewilligen; verleihen; zugestehen; ♯ übertragen; take for ~ed als selbstverständlich annehmen.

granul|ate ['grænjuleit] (sich) körnen; ~e [~ju:l] Körnchen n.

grape [greip] Weinbeere f, -traube f; ~fruit ♀ ['greipfru:t] Pampelmuse f.

graph [græf] graphische Darstellung; ~ic(al □) ['græfik(əl)] graphisch; anschaulich; graphic arts pl. Graphik f; ~ite min. [~fait] Graphit m.

grapple ['græpl] entern; packen; ringen.

grasp [grɑːsp] **1.** Griff *m*; Bereich *m*; Beherrschung *f*; Fassungskraft *f*; **2.** (er)greifen, packen; begreifen.

grass [grɑːs] Gras *n*; Rasen *m*; **send to ~** auf die Weide schicken; **~hopper** ['grɑːshɔpə] Heuschrecke *f*; **~ roots** *pl. Am. pol.* die landwirtschaftlichen Bezirke, *die* Landbevölkerung; **~widow(er)** F Strohwitwe(r *m*) *f*; **~y** [~si] grasig; Gras...

grate [greit] **1.** (Kamin)Gitter *n*; (Feuer)Rost *m*; **2.** (zer)reiben; mit *et.* knirschen; *fig.* verletzen.

grateful □ ['greitful] dankbar.

grater ['greitə] Reibeisen *n*.

grati|fication [grætifi'keiʃən] Befriedigung *f*; Freude *f*; **~fy** ['grætifai] erfreuen; befriedigen.

grating ['greitiŋ] **1.** □ schrill; unangenehm; **2.** Gitter(werk) *n*.

gratitude ['grætitjuːd] Dankbarkeit *f*.

gratuit|ous □ [grə'tjuː(ː)itəs] unentgeltlich; freiwillig; **~y** [~ti] Abfindung *f*; Gratifikation *f*; Trinkgeld *n*.

grave [greiv] **1.** □ ernst; (ge)wichtig; gemessen; **2.** Grab *n*; **3.** [*irr.*] *mst fig.* (ein)graben; **~-digger** ['greivdigə] Totengräber *m*.

gravel ['grævəl] **1.** Kies *m*; *sᵍ* Harngrieß *m*; **2.** mit Kies bedecken.

graven ['greivən] *p.p. von* grave 3.

graveyard ['greivjɑːd] Kirchhof *m*.

gravitation [grævi'teiʃən] Schwerkraft *f*; *fig.* Hang *m*.

gravity ['græviti] Schwere *f*; Wichtigkeit *f*; Ernst *m*; Schwerkraft *f*.

gravy ['greivi] Fleischsaft *m*, Bratensoße *f*.

gray *bsd. Am.* [grei] grau.

graze [greiz] **1.** (ab)weiden; (ab)grasen; streifen, schrammen.

grease 1. [griːs] Fett *n*; Schmiere *f*; **2.** [griːz] (be)schmieren.

greasy □ ['griːzi] fettig; schmierig.

great □ [greit] *allg.* groß; Groß...; F großartig; **~coat** ['greit'kout] Überzieher *m*; **~-grandchild** Urenkel(in); **~-grandfather** Urgroßvater *m*; **~ly** [~tli] sehr; **~ness** [~tnis] Größe *f*; Stärke *f*.

greed [griːd] Gier *f*; **~y** □ ['griːdi] (be)gierig (*of, for* nach); habgierig.

Greek [griːk] **1.** griechisch; **2.** Griech|e *m*, -in *f*; Griechisch *n*.

green [griːn] **1.** □ grün (*a. fig.*); frisch (*Fisch etc.*); neu; Grün...; **2.** Grün *n*; Rasen *m*; Wiese *f*; **~s** *pl.* frisches Gemüse; **~back** *Am.* ['griːnbæk] Dollarnote *f*; **~grocer** Gemüsehändler(in); **~grocery** Gemüsehandlung *f*; **~horn** Grünschnabel *m*; **~house** Gewächshaus *n*; **~ish** [~niʃ] grünlich; **~sickness** Bleichsucht *f*.

greet [griːt] (be)grüßen; **~ing** ['griːtiŋ] Begrüßung *f*; Gruß *m*.

grenade ✕ [gri'neid] Granate *f*.

grew [gruː] *pret. von* grow.

grey [grei] **1.** □ grau; **2.** Grau *n*; **3.** grau machen *od.* werden; **~hound** ['greihaund] Windhund *m*.

grid [grid] Gitter *n*; ⚏, *ᵍ* Netz *n*; *Am. Fußball:* Spielfeld *n*; **~iron** ['gridaiən] (Brat)Rost *m*.

grief [griːf] Gram *m*, Kummer *m*; **come to ~** zu Schaden kommen.

griev|ance ['griːvəns] Beschwerde *f*; Mißstand *m*; **~e** [griːv] kränken; (sich) grämen; **~ous** □ ['griːvəs] kränkend, schmerzlich; schlimm.

grill [gril] **1.** grillen; braten (*a. fig.*); **2.** Bratrost *m*, Grill *m*; gegrilltes Fleisch; *a.* **~-room** Grillroom *m*.

grim □ [grim] grimmig; schrecklich.

grimace [gri'meis] **1.** Fratze *f*, Grimasse *f*; **2.** Grimassen schneiden.

grim|e [graim] Schmutz *m*; Ruß *m*; **~y** □ ['graimi] schmutzig; rußig.

grin [grin] **1.** Grinsen *n*; **2.** grinsen.

grind [graind] **1.** [*irr.*] (zer)reiben; mahlen; schleifen; Leierkasten *etc.* drehen; *fig.* schinden; mit *den* Zähnen knirschen; **2.** Schinderei *f*; **~stone** ['graindstoun] Schleif-, Mühlstein *f*.

grip [grip] **1.** packen, fassen (*a. fig.*); **2.** Griff *m*; Gewalt *f*; Herrschaft *f*; *Am.* = gripsack.

gripe [graip] Griff *m*; **~s** *pl.* Kolik *f*; *bsd. Am.* Beschwerden *f/pl.*

gripsack *Am.* ['gripsæk] Handtasche *f*, -köfferchen *n*.

grisly ['grizli] gräßlich, schrecklich.

gristle ['grisl] Knorpel *m*.

grit [grit] **1.** Kies *m*; Sand(stein) *m*; *fig.* Mut *m*; **2.** knirschen (mit).

grizzly ['grizli] **1.** grau; **2.** Graubär *m*.

groan [groun] seufzen, stöhnen.

grocer ['grousə] Lebensmittelhändler *m*; **~ies** [~əriz] *pl.* Lebensmittel *n/pl.*; **~y** [~ri] Lebensmittelgeschäft *n*.

groceteria *Am.* [grousi'tiəriə] Selbstbedienungsladen *m*.

groggy ['grɔgi] taumelig; wackelig.

groin *anat.* [grɔin] Leistengegend *f*.

groom [grum] **1.** Reit-, Stallknecht *m*; Bräutigam *m*; **2.** pflegen; *Am. pol. Kandidaten* lancieren.

groove [gruːv] **1.** Rinne *f*, Nut *f*; *fig.* Gewohnheit *f*; **2.** nuten, falzen.

grope [group] (be)tasten, tappen.

gross [grous] **1.** □ dick; grob; derb; † Brutto...; **2.** Gros *n* (12 Dutzend); in the **~** im ganzen.

grotto ['grɔtou] Grotte *f*.

grouch *Am.* F [grautʃ] **1.** quengeln, meckern; **2.** Griesgram *m*; schlechte Laune; **~y** ['grautʃi] quenglig.

ground[1] [graund] 1. *pret. u. p.p. von* **grind** 1; 2. ~ *glass* Mattglas *n*.

ground[2] [graund] 1. *mst* Grund *m*; Boden *n*; Gebiet *n*; *Spiel-* etc. Platz *m*; *Beweg-* etc. Grund *m*; ⚓ Erde *f*; ~s *pl.* Grundstück *n*, Park(s *pl.*) *m*, Gärten *m/pl.*; *Kaffee*-Satz *m*; on the ~(s) of auf Grund (*gen.*); stand *od.* hold *od.* keep one's ~ sich behaupten; 2. niederlegen; (be)gründen; j-m die Anfangsgründe beibringen; ⚓ erden; ~ **floor** ['graund'flɔ:] Erdgeschoß *n*; ~**hog** [⌂dhɔg] *bsd. Am.* Murmeltier *n*; ~**less** □ [⌂dlis] grundlos; ~**staff** ✠ Bodenpersonal *n*; ~**work** Grundlage *f*.

group [gru:p] 1. Gruppe *f*; 2. (sich) gruppieren.

grove [grouv] Hain *m*; Gehölz *n*.

grovel *mst fig.* ['grɔvl] kriechen.

grow [grou] [*irr.*] *v/i.* wachsen; werden; *v/t.* 🌱 anpflanzen, anbauen; ~**er** ['grouə] Bauer *m*, Züchter *m*.

growl [graul] knurren, brummen; ~**er** ['graulə] *fig.* Brummbär *m*; *Am. sl.* Bierkrug *m*.

grow|n [groun] 1. *p.p. von* **grow**; 2. *adj.* erwachsen; bewachsen; ~**n-up** ['grounʌp] 1. erwachsen; 2. Erwachsene(r *m*) *f*; ~**th** [grouθ] Wachstum *n*; (An)Wachsen *n*; Entwicklung *f*; Wuchs *m*; Gewächs *n*, Erzeugnis *n*.

grub [grʌb] 1. Raupe *f*, Larve *f*, Made *f*; *contp.* Prolet *m*; 2. graben; sich abmühen; ~**by** ['grʌbi] schmierig.

grudge [grʌdʒ] 1. Groll *m*; 2. mißgönnen; ungern geben *od.* tun *etc.*

gruel [gruəl] Haferschleim *m*.

gruff □ [grʌf] grob, schroff, barsch.

grumble ['grʌmbl] murren; (g)rollen; ~**r** *fig.* [⌂lə] Brummbär *m*.

grunt [grʌnt] grunzen.

guarant|ee [gærən'ti:] 1. Bürge *m*; = *guaranty*; 2. bürgen für; ~**or** [⌂'tɔ:] Bürge *m*; ~**y** ['gærənti] Bürgschaft *f*, Garantie *f*; Gewähr *f*.

guard [gɑ:d] 1. Wacht *f*; ✗ Wache *f*; Wächter *m*, Wärter *m*; 🚂 Schaffner *m*; Schutz(vorrichtung *f*) *m*; ⚔s *pl.* Garde *f*; be on (off) one's ~ (nicht) auf der Hut sein; 2. *v/t.* bewachen, (be)schützen (*from* vor *dat.*); *v/i.* sich hüten (*against* vor *dat.*); ~**ian** ['gɑ:djən] Hüter *m*, Wächter *m*; ⚚⚚ Vormund *m*; *attr.* Schutz...; ~**ianship** [⌂nʃip] Obhut *f*; Vormundschaft *f*.

guess [ges] 1. Vermutung *f*; 2. vermuten; (er)raten; *Am.* denken.

guest [gest] Gast *m*; ~**house** ['gesthaus] (Hotel)Pension *f*, Fremdenheim *n*; ~**room** Gast-, Fremdenzimmer *n*.

guffaw [gʌ'fɔ:] schallendes Gelächter.

guidance ['gaidəns] Führung *f*; (An)Leitung *f*.

guide [gaid] 1. Führer *m*; ⊕ Führung *f*; *attr.* Führungs...; 2. leiten; führen; lenken; ~**book** ['gaidbuk] Reiseführer *m*; ~**post** Wegweiser *m*.

guild [gild] Gilde *f*, Innung *f*; 2**hall** ['gild'hɔ:l] Rathaus *n* (*London*).

guile [gail] Arglist *f*; ~**ful** □ ['gailful] arglistig; ~**less** □ ['gaillis] arglos.

guilt [gilt] Schuld *f*; Strafbarkeit *f*; ~**less** □ ['giltlis] schuldlos; unkundig; ~**y** □ [⌂ti] schuldig; strafbar.

guinea ['gini] Guinee *f* (*21 Schilling*); ~**pig** Meerschweinchen *n*.

guise [gaiz] Erscheinung *f*, Gestalt *f*; Maske *f*.

guitar [gi'tɑ:] Gitarre *f*.

gulch *Am.* [gʌlʃ] tiefe Schlucht.

gulf [gʌlf] Meerbusen *m*, Golf *m*; Abgrund *m*; Strudel *m*.

gull [gʌl] 1. Möwe *f*; Tölpel *m*; 2. übertölpeln; verleiten (*into* zu).

gullet ['gʌlit] Speiseröhre *f*; Gurgel *f*.

gulp [gʌlp] Schluck *m*; Schlucken *n*.

gum [gʌm] 1. *a.* ~s *pl.* Zahnfleisch *n*; Gummi *n*; Klebstoff *m*; ~s *pl. Am.* Gummischuhe *m/pl.*; 2. gummieren; zukleben.

gun [gʌn] 1. Gewehr *n*; Flinte *f*; Geschütz *n*, Kanone *f*; *Am.* Revolver *m*; big ~ F *fig.* hohes Tier; 2. *Am.* auf die Jagd gehen; ~**boat** ['gʌnbout] Kanonenboot *n*; ~ **licence** Waffenschein *m*; ~**man** *Am.* Gangster *m*; ~**ner** ✗ ⚓ ['gʌnə] Kanonier *m*; ~**powder** Schießpulver *n*; ~**smith** Büchsenmacher *m*.

gurgle ['gə:gl] gluckern, gurgeln.

gush [gʌʃ] 1. Guß *m*; *fig.* Erguß *m*; 2. (sich) ergießen, schießen (*from* aus); *fig.* schwärmen; ~**er** ['gʌʃə] *fig.* Schwärmer(in); Ölquelle *f*.

gust [gʌst] Windstoß *m*, Bö *f*.

gut [gʌt] Darm *m*; ♪ Darmsaite *f*; ~s *pl.* Eingeweide *n/pl.*; *das* Innere; *fig.* Mut *m*.

gutter ['gʌtə] Dachrinne *f*; Gosse *f* (*a. fig.*), Rinnstein *m*.

guy [gai] 1. Halteseil *n*; F Vogelscheuche *f*; *Am.* F Kerl *m*; 2. verulken.

guzzle ['gʌzl] saufen; fressen.

gymnas|ium [dʒim'neizjəm] Turnhalle *f*, -platz *m*; ~**tics** [⌂'næstiks] *pl.* Turnen *n*; Gymnastik *f*.

gypsy *bsd. Am.* ['dʒipsi] = *gipsy*.

gyrate [dʒaiə'reit] kreisen; wirbeln.

gyroplane ['dʒaiərəplein] Hubschrauber *m*.

H

haberdasher ['hæbədæʃə] Kurz-warenhändler *m*; *Am.* Herrenarti-kelhändler *m*; **~y** [~əri] Kurzwaren (-geschäft *n*) *f*/*pl.*, *Am.* Herren-artikel *m*/*pl.*

habit ['hæbit] 1. (An)Gewohnheit *f*; Kleid(ung *f*) *n*; *fall od.* get into bad **~s** schlechte Gewohnheiten annehmen; 2. (an-) kleiden; **~able** [~təbl] bewohnbar; **~ation** [hæbi'teiʃən] Wohnung *f*.

habitual □ [hə'bitjuəl] gewohnt, gewöhnlich; Gewohnheits...

hack [hæk] 1. Hieb *m*; Einkerbung *f*; Miet-, Arbeitspferd *n* (*a. fig.*); *a.* ~ writer literarischer Lohn-schreiber *m*; 2. (zer)hacken.

hackneyed *fig.* ['hæknid] abge-droschen.

had [hæd] *pret. u. p.p. von* have.

haddock ['hædɔk] Schellfisch *m*.

h(a)emorrhage ['hemɔridʒ] Blut-sturz *m*.

hag [hæg] (*mst fig.* alte) Hexe.

haggard □ ['hægəd] verstört; ha-ger.

haggle ['hægl] feilschen, schachern.

hail [heil] 1. Hagel *m*; Anruf *m*; 2. (nieder)hageln (lassen); anrufen; (be)grüßen; ~ from stammen aus; **~stone** ['heilstoun] Hagelkorn *n*; **~storm** Hagelschauer *m*.

hair [hɛə] Haar *n*; **~-breadth** ['hɛəbredθ] Haaresbreite *f*; **~cut** Haarschnitt *m*; **~do** *Am.* Frisur *f*; **~dresser** (*bsd.* Damen)Friseur *m*; **~drier** [~draiə] Trockenhaube *f*; Fön *m*; **~less** ['hɛəlis] ohne Haare, kahl; **~pin** Haarnadel *f*; **~raising** ['hɛəreiziŋ] haarsträubend; **~split-ting** Haarspalterei *f*; **~y** ['hɛəri] haarig.

hale [heil] gesund, frisch, rüstig.

half [hɑːf] 1. *pl.* **halves** [hɑːvz] Hälfte *f*; *by halves* nur halb; *go halves* halbpart machen, teilen 2. halb; ~ *a crown* eine halbe Krone; **~back** ['hɑːf'bæk] *Fuß-ball:* Läufer *m*; **~breed** ['hɑːf-briːd] Halbblut *n*; **~caste** Halb-blut *n*; **~hearted** □ ['hɑːf'hɑːtid] lustlos, lau; **~length** Brustbild *n*; **~penny** ['heipni] halber Penny; **~time** ['hɑːf'taim] *Sport:* Halb-zeit *f*; **~way** halbwegs; **~witted** einfältig, idiotisch.

halibut *ichth.* ['hælibət] Heilbutt *m*.

hall [hɔːl] Halle *f*; Saal *m*; Vorraum *m*; Flur *m*; Diele *f*; Herren-, Guts-haus *n*; *univ.* Speisesaal *m*; ~ *of residence* Studentenwohnheim *n*.

halloo [hə'luː] (hallo) rufen.

hallow ['hælou] heiligen, weihen; **⊆mas** [~oumæs] Allerheiligenfest *n*.

halo ['heilou] *ast.* Hof *m*; Heiligen-schein *m*.

halt [hɔːlt] 1. Halt(estelle *f*) *m*; Stillstand *m*; 2. (an)halten; *mst fig.* hinken; schwanken.

halter ['hɔːltə] Halfter *f*; Strick *m*.

halve [hɑːv] halbieren; **~s** [hɑːvz] *pl. von* half 1.

ham [hæm] Schenkel *m*; Schinken *m*.

hamburger *Am.* ['hæmbəːgə] Fri-kadelle *f*; mit Frikadelle belegtes Brötchen.

hamlet ['hæmlit] Weiler *m*.

hammer ['hæmə] 1. Hammer *m*; 2. (be)hämmern.

hammock ['hæmək] Hängematte *f*.

hamper ['hæmpə] 1. Geschenk-, Eßkorb *m*; 2. verstricken; behin-dern.

hamster *zo.* ['hæmstə] Hamster *m*.

hand [hænd] 1. Hand *f* (*a. fig.*); Handschrift *f*; Handbreite *f*; (Uhr)Zeiger *m*; Mann *m*, Arbeiter *m*; *Karten:* Blatt *n*; *at* ~ bei der Hand; nahe bevorstehend; *at first* ~ aus erster Hand; *a good (poor)* ~ *at* (un)geschickt in (*dat.*); ~ *and glove* ein Herz und eine Seele; *change* ~*s* den Besitzer wechseln; *lend a* ~ (mit) anfassen; *off* ~ aus dem Hand-gelenk *od.* Stegreif; *on* ~ ✝ vor-rätig, auf Lager; *bsd. Am.* zur Stelle, bereit; *on one's* ~*s* auf dem Halse; *on the one* ~ einerseits; *on the other* ~ andererseits; ~ *to* ~ Mann gegen Mann; *come to* ~ sich bieten; einlaufen (*Briefe*); 2. reichen; ~ *about* herumreichen; ~ *down* vererben; ~ *in* einhändigen; einreichen; ~ *over* aushändigen; **~bag** ['hændbæg] Handtasche *f*; **~bill** Hand-, Reklamezettel *m*; **~brake** Handbremse *f*; **~cuff** Handfessel *f*; **~ful** [~dful] Hand-voll *f*; F Plage *f*; **~glass** Hand-spiegel *m*; Leselupe *f*.

handicap ['hændikæp] 1. Handikap *n*; Vorgaberennen *n*, Vorgabespiel *n*; (Extra)Belastung *f*; 2. (extra) belasten; beeinträchtigen.

handi|craft ['hændikrɑːft] Hand-werk *n*; Handfertigkeit *f*; **~crafts-man** Handwerker *m*; **~work** Hand-arbeit *f*; Werk *n*.

handkerchief ['hæŋkətʃi(ː)f] Ta-schentuch *n*; Halstuch *n*.

handle ['hændl] 1. Griff *m*; Stiel *m*; Henkel *m*; *Pumpen- etc.* Schwengel *m*; *fig.* Handhabe *f*; *fly off the* ~ F platzen vor Wut; 2. anfassen; hand-haben; behandeln; **~bar** Lenk-stange *f* e-s *Fahrrades*.

hand|-luggage ['hændlʌgidʒ] Handgepäck *n*; **~made** handgear-beitet; **~me-downs** *Am.* F *pl.* Fer-tigkleidung *f*; getragene Kleider *pl.*; **~rail** Geländer *n*; **~shake** Händedruck m; ~some □ ['hænsəm] ansehnlich; hübsch; anständig; ~work Handarbeit f; ~writing Handschrift f; ~y □ ['hændi] geschickt; handlich; zur Hand.

hang [hæŋ] 1. [irr.] v/t. hängen; auf-, einhängen; verhängen; (pret. u. p.p. mst ~ed) (er)hängen; hängen lassen; Tapete ankleben; v/i. hängen; schweben; sich neigen; ~ about (Am. around) herumlungern; sich an j-n hängen; ~ back sich zurückhalten; ~ on sich klammern an (acc.); fig. hängen an (dat.); 2. Hang m; Fall m e-r Gardine etc.; F Wesen n; F fig. Kniff m; Dreh m.

hangar ['hæŋə] Flugzeughalle f.

hang-dog ['hæŋdɔg] Armesünder...

hanger ['hæŋə] Aufhänger m; Hirschfänger m; ~-on fig. [~ər'ɔn] Klette f.

hanging ['hæŋiŋ] 1. Hänge...; 2. ~s pl. Behang m; Tapeten f/pl.

hangman ['hæŋmən] Henker m.

hang-nail ♣ ['hæŋneil] Niednagel m.

hang-over sl. ['hæŋouvə] Katzenjammer m, Kater m.

hanker ['hæŋkə] sich sehnen.

hap|hazard ['hæp'hæzəd] 1. Zufall m; at ~ aufs Geratewohl; 2. zufällig; ~less □ ['hæplis] unglücklich.

happen ['hæpən] sich ereignen, geschehen; he ~ed to be at home er war zufällig zu Hause; ~ (up)on zufällig treffen auf (acc.); ~ in Am. F hereinschneien; ~ing ['hæpniŋ] Ereignis n.

happi|ly ['hæpili] glücklicherweise; ~ness [~inis] Glück(seligkeit f) n.

happy □ ['hæpi] allg. glücklich; beglückt; erfreut; erfreulich; geschickt; treffend; F angeheitert; ~-go-lucky F unbekümmert.

harangue [hə'ræŋ] 1. Ansprache f, Rede f; 2. v/t. feierlich anreden.

harass ['hærəs] belästigen, quälen.

harbo(u)r ['ha:bə] 1. Hafen m; Zufluchtsort m; 2. (be)herbergen; Rache etc. hegen; ankern; ~age [~ɔridʒ] Herberge f; Zuflucht f.

hard [ha:d] 1. adj. allg. hart; schwer; mühselig; streng; ausdauernd; fleißig; heftig; Am. stark (Spirituosen); ~ of hearing schwerhörig; 2. adv. scharf; tüchtig; mit Mühe; ~ by nahe bei; ~ up in Not; ~-boiled ['ha:d'bɔild] hartgesotten; Am. gerissen; ~ cash Bargeld n; klingende Münze; ~en ['ha:dn] härten; hart machen od. werden; (sich) abhärten; fig. (sich) verhärten; ✝ sich festigen (Preise); ~headed nüchtern denkend; ~hearted □ hartherzig; ~ihood ['ha:dihud] Kühnheit f; ~iness [~inis] Widerstandsfähigkeit f; Härte f; ~ly ['ha:dli] kaum; streng;

mit Mühe; ~ness ['ha:dnis] Härte f; Schwierigkeit f; Not f; ~pan Am. harter Boden, fig. Grundlage f; ~ship ['ha:dʃip] Bedrängnis f, Not f; Härte f; ~ware Eisenwaren f/pl.; ~y □ ['ha:di] kühn; widerstandsfähig, hart; abgehärtet; winterfest (Pflanze).

hare [hɛə] Hase m; ~bell ♀ ['hɛəbel] Glockenblume f; ~brained zerfahren; ~lip anat. ['hɛə'lip] Hasenscharte f.

hark [ha:k] horchen (to auf acc.).

harlot ['ha:lət] Hure f.

harm [ha:m] 1. Schaden m; Unrecht n, Böse(s) n; 2. beschädigen, verletzen; schaden, Leid zufügen (dat.); ~ful □ ['ha:mful] schädlich; ~less □ ['ha:mlis] harmlos; unschädlich.

harmon|ic [ha:'mɔnik] (~ally), ~ious □ [ha:'mounjəs] harmonisch; ~ize ['ha:mənaiz] v/t. in Einklang bringen; v/i. harmonieren; ~y [~ni] Harmonie f.

harness ['ha:nis] 1. Harnisch m; Zug-Geschirr n; die in ~ in den Sielen sterben; 2. anschirren; bändigen; Wasserkraft nutzbar machen.

harp [ha:p] 1. Harfe f; 2. Harfe spielen; ~ (up)on herumreiten auf (dat.). [2. harpunieren.]

harpoon [ha:'pu:n] 1. Harpune f; 2.]

harrow ['hærou] 1. Egge f; 2. eggen; fig. quälen, martern.

harry ['hæri] plündern; quälen.

harsh □ [ha:ʃ] rauh; herb; grell; streng; schroff; barsch.

hart zo. [ha:t] Hirsch m.

harvest ['ha:vist] 1. Ernte(zeit) f; Ertrag m; 2. ernten; einbringen.

has [hæz] 3. sg. pres. von have.

hash [hæʃ] 1. gehacktes Fleisch; Am. F Essen n, Fraß m; fig. Mischmasch m; 2. (zer)hacken.

hast|e [heist] Eile f; Hast f; make ~ (sich be)eilen; ~en ['heisn] (sich be)eilen; j-n antreiben; et. beschleunigen; ~y □ ['heisti] (vor)eilig; hastig; hitzig; heftig.

hat [hæt] Hut m.

hatch [hætʃ] 1. Brut f, Hecke f; ⚓, 🔧 Luke f; serving ~ Durchreiche f; 2. (aus)brüten (a. fig.).

hatchet ['hætʃit] Beil n.

hatchway ⚓ ['hætʃwei] Luke f.

hat|e [heit] 1. Haß m; 2. hassen; ~eful □ ['heitful] verhaßt; abscheulich; ~red ['heitrid] Haß m.

haught|iness ['hɔ:tinis] Stolz m; Hochmut m; ~y □ ['hɔ:ti] stolz; hochmütig.

haul [hɔ:l] 1. Ziehen n; (Fisch-) Zug m; Am. Transport(weg) m; 2. ziehen; schleppen; transportieren; 🔧 fördern; ⚓ abdrehen; ~ down one's flag die Flagge streichen; fig. sich geschlagen geben.

haunch [hɔːntʃ] Hüfte *f*; Keule *f* von *Wild*.

haunt [hɔːnt] **1.** Aufenthaltsort *m*; Schlupfwinkel *m*; **2.** oft besuchen; heimsuchen; verfolgen; spuken in (*dat.*).

have [hæv] [*irr.*] *v/t.* haben; bekommen; *Mahlzeit* einnehmen; lassen; ~ *to do* tun müssen; *I* ~ *my hair cut* ich lasse mir das Haar schneiden; *he will* ~ *it that* ... er behauptet, daß ...; *I had better go* es wäre besser, wenn ich ginge; *I had rather go* ich möchte lieber gehen; ~ *about one* bei *od.* an sich haben; ~ *on* anhaben; ~ *it out with* sich auseinandersetzen mit; *v/aux.* haben; *bei v/i.* oft sein; ~ *come* gekommen sein.

haven [ˈheivn] Hafen *m* (*a. fig.*).

havoc [ˈhævək] Verwüstung *f*; *make* ~ *of*, *play* ~ *with od. among* verwüsten; übel zurichten.

haw ♀ [hɔː] Hagebutte *f*.

Hawaiian [haːˈwaiiən] **1.** hawaiisch; **2.** Hawaiier(in).

hawk [hɔːk] **1.** Habicht *m*; Falke *m*; **2.** sich räuspern; hausieren mit.

hawthorn ♀ [ˈhɔːθɔːn] Weißdorn *m*.

hay [hei] Heu *n*; **2.** heuen; ~**cock** [ˈheikɔk] Heuhaufen *m*; ~**fever** Heuschnupfen *m*; ~**loft** Heuboden *m*; ~**maker** *bsd. Am.* K.o.-Schlag *m*; ~**rick** = haycock; ~**seed** *bsd. Am.* F Bauerntölpel *m*; ~**stack** = haycock.

hazard [ˈhæzəd] **1.** Zufall *m*; Gefahr *f*, Wagnis *n*; Hasard(spiel) *n*; **2.** wagen; ~**ous** □ [~dəs] gewagt.

haze [heiz] **1.** Dunst *m*; **2.** ♣ *u. Am.* schinden; F schurigeln.

hazel [ˈheizl] **1.** ♀ Hasel(staude) *f*; **2.** nußbraun; ~**nut** Haselnuß *f*.

hazy □ [ˈheizi] dunstig; *fig.* unklar.

H-bomb ⚔ [ˈeitʃbɔm] H-Bombe *f*, Wasserstoffbombe *f*.

he [hiː] **1.** er; ~ *who* derjenige, welcher; **2.** Mann *m*; *zo.* Männchen *n*; **3.** *adj. in Zssgn*: männlich, ...männchen *n*; ~*-goat* Ziegenbock *m*.

head [hed] **1.** *allg.* Kopf *m* (*a. fig.*); Haupt *n* (*a. fig.*); *nach Zahlwort*: Mann *m* (*a. pl.*); Stück *n* (*a. pl.*); Leiter(in); Chef *m*; Kopfende *n e-s Bettes etc.*; Kopfseite *f e-r Münze*; Gipfel *m*; Quelle *f*; *Schiffs*-Vorderteil *n*; Hauptpunkt *m*, Abschnitt *m*; Überschrift *f*; *come to a* ~ eitern (*Geschwür*); *fig.* sich zuspitzen, zur Entscheidung kommen; *get it into one's* ~ *that* ... es sich in den Kopf setzen, daß; ~ *over heels* Hals über Kopf; **2.** erst; Ober...; Haupt...; **3.** *v/t.* (an)führen; an der Spitze von *et.* stehen; vorausgehen (*dat.*); mit e-r Überschrift versehen; ~ *off* ablenken; *v/i.* ♣ zusteuern (*for auf acc.*); *Am.* entspringen (*Fluß*); ~**ache** [ˈhedeik] Kopfweh *n*; ~

dress Kopfputz *m*; Frisur *f*; ~**gear** Kopfbedeckung *f*; Zaumzeug *n*; ~**ing** [ˈhediŋ] Titelkopf *m*, Rubrik *f*; Überschrift *f*, Titel *m*; *Sport*: Kopfball *m*; ~**land** [ˈhedlənd] Vorgebirge *n*; ~**light** *mot.* Scheinwerfer(licht *n*) *m*; ~**line** Überschrift *f*; Schlagzeile *f*; ~*s pl. Radio*: *das Wichtigste in Kürze*; ~**long 1.** *adj.* ungestüm; **2.** *adv.* kopfüber; ~**master** Direktor *m e-r Schule*; ~**phone** *Radio*: Kopfhörer *m*; ~**quarters** *pl.* ⚔ Hauptquartier *n*; Zentral(stell)e *f*; ~**strong** halsstarrig; eigensinnig; ~**waters** (*pl.*) Quellgebiet *n*; ~**way** Fortschritt(e *pl.*) *m*; *make* ~ vorwärtskommen; ~**word** Stichwort *n e-s Wörterbuchs*; ~**y** □ [ˈhedi] ungestüm; voreilig; zu Kopfe steigend.

heal [hiːl] heilen; ~ *up* zuheilen.

health [helθ] Gesundheit *f*; ~**ful** □ [ˈhelθful] gesund; heilsam; ~**resort** Kurort *m*; ~**y** □ [ˈhelθi] gesund.

heap [hiːp] **1.** Haufe(n) *m*; **2.** *a.* ~ *up* (auf)häufen; überhäufen.

hear [hiə] [*irr.*] hören; erfahren; anhören, *j-m* zuhören; erhören; *Zeugen* verhören; *Lektion* abhören; ~**d** [hɔːd] *pret. u. p.p. von hear*; ~**er** [ˈhiərə] (Zu)Hörer(in); ~**ing** [~riŋ] Gehör *n*; Audienz *f*; ⚖ Verhör *n*; Hörweite *f*; ~**say** Hörensagen *n*.

hearse [hɔːs] Leichenwagen *m*.

heart [hɑːt] *allg.* Herz *n* (*a. fig.*); Innere(s) *n*; Kern *m*; *fig.* Schatz *m*; *by* ~ auswendig; *out of* ~ mutlos; *lay to* ~ sich zu Herzen nehmen; *take* ~ sich ein Herz fassen; ~**ache** [ˈhɑːteik] Kummer *m*; ~**break** Herzeleid *n*; ~**breaking** □ [~kiŋ] herzzerbrechend; ~**broken** gebrochenen Herzens; ~**burn** Sodbrennen *n*; ~**en** [ˈhɑːtn] ermutigen; ~**failure** ⚕ Herzversagen *n*; ~**felt** innig, tief empfunden.

hearth [hɑːθ] Herd *m* (*a. fig.*).

heart|less □ [ˈhɑːtlis] herzlos; ~**rending** [ˈhɑːtrendiŋ] herzzerreißend; ~ **transplant** Herzverpflanzung *f*; ~**y** [ˈhɑːti] □ herzlich; aufrichtig; gesund; herzhaft.

heat [hiːt] **1.** *allg.* Hitze *f*; Wärme *f*; Eifer *m*; *Sport*: Gang *m*, einzelner Lauf; *zo.* Läufigkeit *f*; **2.** heizen; (sich) erhitzen (*a. fig.*); ~**er** ⊕ [ˈhiːtə] Erhitzer *m*; Ofen *m*.

heath [hiːθ] Heide *f*; ♀ Heidekraut *n*.

heathen [ˈhiːðən] **1.** Heid|e *m*, -in *f*; **2.** heidnisch.

heather ♀ [ˈheðə] Heide(kraut *n*) *f*.

heat|ing [ˈhiːtiŋ] Heizung *f*; *attr.* Heiz...; ~ **lightning** *Am.* Wetterleuchten *n*.

heave [hiːv] **1.** Heben *n*; Übelkeit *f*;

2. [*irr.*] *v/t.* heben; schwellen; *Seufzer* ausstoßen; *Anker* lichten; *v/i.* sich heben, wogen, schwellen.

heaven ['hevn] Himmel *m*; **~ly** [~nli] himmlisch.

heaviness ['hevinis] Schwere *f*, Druck *m*; Schwerfälligkeit *f*; Schwermut *f*.

heavy □ ['hevi] *allg.* schwer; schwermütig; schwerfällig; trüb; drückend; heftig (*Regen etc.*); unwegsam (*Straße*); Schwer...; **~ current** ⚡ Starkstrom *m*; **~-handed** ungeschickt; **~-hearted** niedergeschlagen; **~-weight** *Boxen:* Schwergewicht *n*.

heckle ['hekl] durch Zwischenfragen in die Enge treiben.

hectic ⚕ ['hektik] hektisch (*auszehrend*; *sl.* fieberhaft erregt).

hedge [hedʒ] **1.** Hecke *f*; **2.** *v/t.* einhegen, einzäunen; umgeben; **~ up** sperren; *v/i.* sich decken; sich nicht festlegen; **~hog** *zo.* ['hedʒhɔg] Igel *m*; *Am.* Stachelschwein *n*; **~row** Hecke *f*.

heed [hi:d] **1.** Beachtung *f*, Aufmerksamkeit *f*; *take ~ of*, *give ed*. *pay ~ to* achtgeben auf (*acc.*), beachten; **2.** beachten, achten auf (*acc.*); **~less** □ ['hi:dlis] unachtsam; unbekümmert (*of* um).

heel [hi:l] **1.** Ferse *f*; Absatz *m*; *Am. sl.* Lump *m*; *head over ~s* Hals über Kopf; *down at ~* mit schiefen Absätzen; *fig.* abgerissen; schlampig; **2.** mit e-m Absatz versehen; **~ed** *Am.* F finanzstark; **~er** *Am. sl. pol.* ['hi:lə] Befehlsempfänger *m*.

heft [heft] Gewicht *n*; *Am.* F Hauptteil *m*.

heifer ['hefə] Färse *f* (*junge Kuh*).

height [hait] Höhe *f*; Höhepunkt *m*; **~en** ['haitn] erhöhen; vergrößern.

heinous □ ['heinəs] abscheulich.

heir [ɛə] Erbe *m*; **~ apparent** rechtmäßiger Erbe; **~ess** ['ɛəris] Erbin *f*; **~loom** ['ɛəlu:m] Erbstück *n*.

held [held] *pret. u. p.p. von* hold 2.

helibus *Am.* F ['helibəs] Lufttaxi *n*.

helicopter ✈ ['helikɔptə] Hubschrauber *m*.

hell [hel] Hölle *f*; *attr.* Höllen...; *what the ~ ...?* F was zum Teufel ...?; *raise ~* Krach machen; **~-bent** ['helbent] *Am. sl.* unweigerlich entschlossen; **~ish** □ ['heliʃ] höllisch.

hello ['he'lou] hallo!

helm ⚓ [helm] (Steuer)Ruder *n*.

helmet ['helmit] Helm *m*.

helmsman ⚓ ['helmzmən] Steuermann *m*.

help [help] **1.** *allg.* Hilfe *f*; (Hilfs-) Mittel *n*; (Dienst)Mädchen *n*; **2.** *v/t.* (ab)helfen (*dat.*); unterlassen; *bei Tisch* geben, reichen;

~ o.s. sich bedienen, zulangen; *I could not ~ laughing* ich konnte nicht umhin zu lachen; *v/i.* helfen, dienen; **~er** ['helpə] Helfer(in), Gehilf|e *m*, -in *f*; **~ful** □ [~pful] hilfreich; nützlich; **~ing** [~piŋ] Portion *f*; **~less** □ [~plis] hilflos; **~lessness** [~snis] Hilflosigkeit *f*; **~mate**, **~meet** Gehilf|e *m*, -in *f*; Gattin *f*.

helter-skelter ['heltə'skeltə] holterdiepolter.

helve [helv] Stiel *m*, Griff *m*.

Helvetian [hel'vi:ʃjən] Helvetier (-in); *attr.* Schweizer...

hem [hem] **1.** Saum *m*; **2.** *v/t.* säumen; **~ in** einschließen; *v/i.* sich räuspern.

hemisphere ['hemisfiə] Halbkugel *f*.

hem-line ['hemlain] *Kleid:* Saum *m*.

hemlock ♣ ['hemlɔk] Schierling *m*; **~-tree** Schierlingstanne *f*.

hemp [hemp] Hanf *m*.

hemstitch ['hemstitʃ] Hohlsaum *m*.

hen [hen] Henne *f*; *Vogel*-Weibchen *n*.

hence [hens] weg; hieraus; daher; von jetzt an; *a year ~* heute übers Jahr; **~forth** ['hens'fɔ:θ], **~forward** [~'ɔ:wəd] von nun an.

hen|-coop ['henku:p] Hühnerstall *m*; **~pecked** unter dem Pantoffel (stehend).

hep *Am. sl.* [hep]: *to be ~ to* kennen; **~cat** *Am. sl.* ['hepkæt] Eingeweihte(r *m*) *f*; Jazzfanatiker(in).

her [hə:, hə] sie; ihr; ihr(e).

herald ['herəld] **1.** Herold *m*; **2.** (sich) ankündigen; **~ in** einführen; **~ry** [~dri] Wappenkunde *f*, Heraldik *f*.

herb [hə:b] Kraut *n*; **~age** ['hə:bidʒ] Gras *n*; Weide *f*; **~ivorous** [hə:-'bivərəs] pflanzenfressend.

herd [hə:d] **1.** Herde *f* (*a. fig.*); **2.** *v/t.* Vieh hüten; *v/i. a.* **~ together** in e-r Herde leben; zs.-hausen; **~er** ['hə:də], **~sman** ['hə:dzmən] Hirt *m*.

here [hiə] hier; hierher; **~'s to ...!** auf das Wohl von ...!

here|after [hiər'a:ftə] **1.** künftig; **2.** Zukunft *f*; **~by** ['hiə'bai] hierdurch.

heredit|ary [hi'reditəri] erblich; Erb...; **~y** [~ti] Erblichkeit *f*.

here|in ['hiər'in] hierin; **~of** [hiər'ɔv] hiervon.

heresy ['herəsi] Ketzerei *f*.

heretic ['herətik] Ketzer(in).

here|tofore ['hiətu'fɔ:] bis jetzt; ehemals; **~upon** [hiərə'pɔn] hierauf; **~with** hiermit.

heritage ['heritidʒ] Erbschaft *f*.

hermit ['hə:mit] Einsiedler *m*.

hero ['hiərou] Held *m*; **~ic(al** □) [hi'rouik(əl)] heroisch; heldenhaft;

Helden...; ~ine ['herouin] Heldin
f; ~ism [~izəm] Heldenmut m,
-tum n.

heron zo. ['herən] Reiher m.

herring ichth. ['heriŋ] Hering m.

hers [həːz] der (die, das) ihrige;
ihr.

herself [həː'self] (sie, ihr, sich)
selbst; sich; of ~ von selbst; by ~
allein.

hesitat|e ['heziteit] zögern, un-
schlüssig sein; Bedenken tragen;
~ion [hezi'teiʃən] Zögern n; Un-
schlüssigkeit f; Bedenken n.

hew [hjuː] [irr.] hauen, hacken; ~n
[hjuːn] p.p. von hew.

hey [hei] ei!; hei!; he!, heda!

heyday ['heidei] 1. heisa!; oho!;
2. fig. Höhepunkt m, Blüte f.

hi [hai] he!, heda!; hallo!

hicc|ough, ~up ['hikʌp] 1 Schluk-
ken m; 2. schlucken; den Schluk-
ken haben.

hid [hid] pret. u. p.p. von hide 2;
~den ['hidn] p.p. von hide 2.

hide [haid] 1. Haut f; 2. [irr.] (sich)
verbergen, verstecken; ~-and-seek
['haidənd'siːk] Versteckspiel n.

hidebound fig. ['haidbaund] engherzig.

hideous □ ['hidiəs] scheußlich.

hiding ['haidiŋ] F Tracht f Prügel;
Verbergen n; ~-place Versteck n.

hi-fi Am. ['hai'fai] = high-fidelity.

high [hai] 1. adj. □ allg. hoch; vornehm; gut, edel (Charakter); stolz;
hochtrabend; angegangen (Fleisch);
extrem; stark; üppig, flott (Leben);
Hoch...; Ober...; with a ~ hand
arrogant, anmaßend; in ~ spirits in
gehobener Stimmung, guter Laune;
ne; ~ life die vornehme Welt; ~
time höchste Zeit; ~ words heftige
Worte; 2. meteor. Hoch n; bsd. Am.
für Zssgn wie high school, etc.; 3.
adv. hoch; sehr, mächtig; ~ball
Am. ['haibɔːl] Whisky m mit Soda;
~-bred vornehm erzogen; ~-brow
F 1. Intellektuelle(r m) f; 2. betont
intellektuell; ~-class erstklassig;
~-fidelity mit höchster Wieder-
gabetreue, Hi-Fi; ~-grade hoch-
wertig; ~-handed anmaßend; ~
land ['hailənd] Hochland n; ~
lights pl. fig. Höhepunkte m/pl.;
~ly ['haili] hoch; sehr; speak ~ of
s.o. j-n loben; ~-minded hochher-
zig; ~ness ['hainis] Höhe f; fig.
Hoheit f; ~-pitched schrill (Ton);
steil (Dach); ~-power: ~ station
Großkraftwerk n; ~-road Land-
straße f; ~ school höhere Schule;
~-strung überempfindlich; ~ tea
frühes Abendessen mit Tee u.
Fleisch etc.; ~-water Hochwasser
n; ~way Hauptstr. f; fig. Weg m;
~ code Straßenverkehrsordnung f;
~wayman Straßenräuber m.

hike F [haik] 1. wandern; 2. Wan-

derung f; bsd. Am. F Erhöhung f
(Preis etc.); ~r ['haikə] Wanderer m.

hilarious □ [hi'lɛəriəs] ausgelassen.

hill [hil] Hügel m, Berg m; ~billy
Am. F ['hilbili] Hinterwäldler m;
~ock ['hilək] kleiner Hügel; ~side
['hil'said] Hang m; ~y ['hili] hüge-
lig.

hilt [hilt] Griff m (bsd. am Degen).

him [him] ihn; ihm; den, dem(je-
nigen); ~self [him'self] (er, ihm,
ihn, sich) selbst; sich; of ~ von
selbst; by ~ allein.

hind¹ zo. [haind] Hirschkuh f.

hind² [~] Hinter...; ~r 1. ['haində]
hintere(r, -s); Hinter...; 2. ['hində]
v/t. hindern (from an dat.); hemmen; ~most ['haindmoust] hinterst, letzt.

hindrance ['hindrəns] Hindernis n.

hinge [hindʒ] 1. Türangel f; Scharnier n; fig. Angelpunkt m; 2. ~
upon fig. abhängen von.

hint [hint] 1. Wink m; Anspielung f;
2. andeuten; anspielen (at auf acc.).

hinterland ['hintələnd] Hinterland
n.   [butte f.]

hip [hip] anat. Hüfte f; ♀ Hage-

hippopotamus zo. [hipə'potəməs]
Flußpferd n.

hire ['haiə] 1. Miete f; Entgelt m, n,
Lohn m; 2. mieten; j-n anstellen;
~ out vermieten.

his [hiz] sein(e); der (die, das) sei-
nige.

hiss [his] v/i. zischen; zischeln; v/t.
a. ~ off auszischen, auspfeifen.

histor|ian [his'tɔːriən] Historiker
m; ~ic(al □) [his'tɔrik(əl)] histo-
risch, geschichtlich; Geschichts...;
~y ['histəri] Geschichte f.

hit [hit] 1. Schlag m, Stoß m; fig.
(Seiten)Hieb m; (Glücks)Treffer
m; thea., ♪ Schlager m; 2. [irr.]
schlagen, stoßen; treffen; auf et.
stoßen; Am. F eintreffen in (dat.)
~ s.o. a blow j-m e-n Schlag versetzen; ~ it off with F sich vertragen
mit; ~ (up)on (zufällig) kommen od.
stoßen od. verfallen auf (acc.).

hitch [hitʃ] 1. Ruck m; ♣ Knoten m;
fig. Haken m, Hindernis n; 2. rük-
ken; (sich) festmachen, festhaken;
hängenbleiben; rutschen; ~-hike
F ['hitʃhaik] per Anhalter fahren.

hither lit. ['hiðə] hierher; ~to bisher.

hive [haiv] 1. Bienenstock m;
Bienenschwarm m; fig. Schwarm
m; 2. ~ up aufspeichern; zs.-woh-
nen.

hoard [hɔːd] 1. Vorrat m, Schatz m;
2. a. ~ up aufhäufen; horten.

hoarfrost ['hɔːfrɔst] (Rauh)Reif m.

hoarse □ [hɔːs] heiser, rauh.

hoary ['hɔːri] (alters)grau.

hoax [houks] 1. Täuschung f;
Falschmeldung f; 2. foppen.

hob [hɔb] = hobgoblin; raise ~ bsd.
Am. F Krach schlagen.

hobble ['hɔbl] 1. Hinken *n*, Humpeln *n*; F Klemme *f*, Patsche *f*; 2. *v/i.* humpeln, hinken (*a. fig.*); *v/t.* an den Füßen fesseln.

hobby ['hɔbi] *fig.* Steckenpferd *n*, Hobby *n*; **~-horse** Steckenpferd *n*; Schaukelpferd *n*.

hobgoblin ['hɔbgɔblin] Kobold *m*.

hobo *Am. sl.* ['houbou] Landstreicher *m*.

hock[1] [hɔk] Rheinwein *m*.

hock[2] *zo.* [~] Sprunggelenk *n*.

hod [hɔd] Mörteltrog *m*.

hoe ✏ [hou] 1. Hacke *f*; 2. hacken.

hog [hɔg] 1. Schwein *n* (*a. fig.*); 2. *Mähne* stutzen; *mot.* drauflos rasen; **~gish** □ ['hɔgiʃ] schweinisch; gefräßig.

hoist [hɔist] 1. Aufzug *m*; 2. hochziehen, hissen.

hokum *sl.* ['houkəm] Mätzchen *n/pl.*; Kitsch *m*; Humbug *m*.

hold [hould] 1. Halten *n*; Halt *m*, Griff *m*; Gewalt *f*, Einfluß *m*; ✠ Lade-, Frachtraum *m*; *catch* (*od.* get, lay, take, seize) ~ of erfassen, ergreifen; sich aneignen; *keep ~ of* festhalten; 2. [*irr.*] *v/t. allg.* halten; fest-, aufhalten; enthalten; *fig.* behalten; *Versammlung etc.* abhalten; (inne)haben; *Ansicht* vertreten; *Gedanken etc.* hegen; halten für; glauben; behaupten; ~ *one's ground,* ~ *one's own* sich behaupten; ~ *the line teleph.* am Apparat bleiben; ~ *on et.* (an s-m Platz fest)halten; ~ *over* aufschieben; ~ *up* aufrecht halten; (unter-) stützen; aufhalten; (räuberisch) überfallen *v/i.* (fest)halten; gelten; sich bewähren; standhalten; ~ *forth* Reden halten; ~ *good od.* *true* gelten; sich bestätigen; ~ *off* sich fernhalten; ~ *on* ausharren; fortdauern; sich festhalten; *teleph.* am Apparat bleiben; ~ *to* festhalten an (*dat.*); ~ *up* sich (aufrecht) halten; **~er** ['houldə] Pächter *m*; Halter *m* (*Gerät*); Inhaber(in) (*bsd.* ✝); **~ing** [~diŋ] Halten *n*; Halt *m*; Pachtgut *n*; Besitz *m*; ~ *company* Dachgesellschaft *f*; **~over** *Am.* Rest *m*; **~up** Raubüberfall *m*; Stauung *f*, Stockung *f*.

hole [houl] 1. Loch *n*; Höhle *f*; F *fig.* Klemme *f*; *pick* ~ *s in* bekritteln; 2. aushöhlen; durchlöchern.

holiday ['hɔlədi] Feiertag *m*; freier Tag; ~ *s pl.* Ferien *pl.*, Urlaub *m*; **~-maker** Urlauber(in).

holler *Am.* F ['hɔlə] laut rufen.

hollow ['hɔlou] 1. □ hohl; leer; falsch; 2. Höhle *f*, (Aus)Höhlung *f*; *Land*-Senke *f*; 3. aushöhlen.

holly ❧ ['hɔli] Stechpalme *f*.

holster ['houlstə] Pistolentasche *f*.

holy ['houli] heilig; ♀ *Thursday* Gründonnerstag *m*; ~ *water* Weihwasser *n*; ♀ *Week* Karwoche *f*.

homage ['hɔmidʒ] Huldigung *f*; *do od. pay od. render* ~ huldigen (*to dat.*).

home [houm] 1. Heim *n*; Haus *n*, Wohnung *f*; Heimat *f*; Mal *n*; *at* ~ zu Hause; 2. *adj.* (ein)heimisch, inländisch; wirkungsvoll; tüchtig (*Schlag etc.*); ♀ *Office* Innenministerium *n*; ~ *rule* Selbstregierung *f*; ♀ *Secretary* Innenminister *m*; ~ *trade* Binnenhandel *m*; 3. *adv.* heim, nach Hause; an die richtige Stelle; gründlich; *hit od. strike* ~ den rechten Fleck treffen; ♀ **Counties** *die* Grafschaften um London; ~ **economics** *Am.* Hauswirtschaftslehre *f*; **~-felt** ['houmfelt] tief empfunden; **~less** ['houmlis] heimatlos; **~like** anheimelnd, gemütlich; **~ly** [~li] anheimelnd, häuslich; *fig.* hausbacken; schlicht; anspruchslos; reizlos; **~-made** selbstgemacht; Hausmacher...; **~sickness** Heimweh *n*; **~stead** Anwesen *n*; ~ *team Sport:* Gastgeber *m/pl.*; **~ward(s)** ['houmwəd(z)] heimwärts (gerichtet); Heim...; ~ *work* Hausaufgabe(*n pl.*) *f*, Schularbeiten *f/pl.*

homicide ['hɔmisaid] Totschlag *m*; Mord *m*; Totschläger(in).

homogeneous □ [hɔmə'dʒiːnjəs] homogen, gleichartig.

hone ⊕ [houn] 1. Abziehstein *m*; 2. *Rasiermesser* abziehen.

honest □ ['ɔnist] ehrlich, rechtschaffen; aufrichtig; echt; **~y** [~ti] Ehrlichkeit *f*, Rechtschaffenheit *f*; Aufrichtigkeit *f*.

honey ['hʌni] Honig *m*; *fig.* Liebling *m*; **~comb** [~ikoum] (Honig-) Wabe *f*; **~ed** ['hʌnid] honigsüß; **~moon** 1. Flitterwochen *f/pl.*; 2. die Flitterwochen verleben.

honk *mot.* [hɔŋk] hupen, tuten.

honky-tonk *Am. sl.* ['hɔŋkitɔŋk] Spelunke *f*.

honorary ['ɔnərəri] Ehren...; ehrenamtlich.

hono(u)r ['ɔnə] 1. Ehre *f*; Achtung *f*; Würde *f*; *fig.* Zierde *f*; *Your* ♀ Euer Gnaden; 2. (be)ehren; ✝ honorieren; **~able** □ ['ɔnərəbl] ehrenvoll; redlich; ehrbar; ehrenwert.

hood [hud] 1. Kapuze *f*; *mot.* Verdeck *n*; *Am.* (Motor)Haube *f*; ⊕ Kappe *f*; 2. mit e-r Kappe *etc.* bekleiden; ein-, verhüllen.

hoodlum *Am.* F ['huːdləm] Strolch *m*.

hoodoo *bsd. Am.* ['huːduː] Unglücksbringer *m*; Pech *n* (*Unglück*).

hoodwink ['hudwiŋk] täuschen.

hooey *Am. sl.* ['huːi] Quatsch *m*.

hoof [huːf] Huf *m*; Klaue *f*.

hook [huk] 1. (*bsd.* Angel)Haken *m*; Sichel *f*; *by* ~ *or by crook* so oder so;

2. (sich) (zu-, fest)haken; angeln (*a. fig.*); **~y** ['huki] **1.** hakig; **2.**: *play* ~ *Am. sl.* (die Schule) schwänzen.

hoop [hu:p] **1.** *Faß- etc.* Reif(en) *m*; ⊕ Ring *m*; **2.** *Fässer* binden.

hooping-cough ♒ ['hu:piŋkɔf] Keuchhusten *m*.

hoot [hu:t] **1.** Geschrei *n*; **2.** *v/i.* heulen; johlen; *mot.* hupen; *v/t.* auspfeifen, auszischen.

Hoover ['hu:və] **1.** Staubsauger *m*; **2.** (mit e-m Staubsauger) saugen.

hop [hɔp] **1.** ♀ Hopfen *m*; Sprung *m*; F Tanzerei *f*; **2.** hüpfen, springen (*über acc.*).

hope [houp] **1.** Hoffnung *f*; **2.** hoffen (*for auf acc.*); ~ *in* vertrauen auf (*acc.*); **~ful** □ ['houpful] hoffnungsvoll; **~less** □ ['houplis] hoffnungslos; verzweifelt.

horde [hɔ:d] Horde *f*.

horizon [hə'raizn] Horizont *m*.

horn [hɔ:n] Horn *n*; Schalltrichter *m*; *mot.* Hupe *f*; **~s** *pl.* Geweih *n*; ~ *of plenty* Füllhorn *n*.

hornet *zo.* ['hɔ:nit] Hornisse *f*.

horn|swoggle *Am. sl.* ['hɔ:nswɔgl] *j-n* ʾreinlegen; **~y** ['hɔ:ni] hornig; schwielig.

horr|ible □ ['hɔrəbl] entsetzlich; scheußlich; **~id** □ ['hɔrid] gräßlich, abscheulich; schrecklich; **~ify** [~ifai] erschrecken; entsetzen; **~or** ['hɔrə] Entsetzen *n*, Schauder *m*; Schrecken *m*; Greuel *m*.

horse [hɔ:s] *zo.* Pferd *n*; Reiterei *f*; Bock *m*, Gestell *n*; **~back** ['hɔ:sbæk]: *on* ~ zu Pferde; **~hair** Roßhaar *n*; **~laugh** F wieherndes Lachen; **~man** Reiter *m*; **~manship** [~nʃip] Reitkunst *f*; ~ *opera Am. drittklassiger* Wildwestfilm; **~power** Pferdestärke *f*; **~radish** ♀ Meerrettich *m*; **~shoe** Hufeisen *n*.

horticulture ['hɔ:tikʌltʃə] Gartenbau *m*.

hose [houz] Schlauch *m*; Strumpfhose *f*; *coll.* Strümpfe *m/pl.*

hosiery['houʒəri]Strumpfwaren*f/pl.*

hospitable □ ['hɔspitəbl] gastfrei.

hospital ['hɔspitl] Krankenhaus *n*; ✗ Lazarett *n*; **~ity** [hɔspi'tæliti] Gastfreundschaft *f*, Gastlichkeit *f*.

host [houst] Wirt *m*; Gastgeber *m*; Gastwirt *m*; *fig.* Heer *n*; Schwarm *m*; *eccl.* Hostie *f*.

hostage ['hɔstidʒ] Geisel *m*, *f*.

hostel ['hɔstəl] Herberge *f*; *univ.* Studenten(wohn)heim *n*.

hostess ['houstis] Wirtin *f*; Gastgeberin *f*; = *air* ~.

hostil|e ['hɔstail] feindlich (gesinnt); **~ity** [hɔs'tiliti] Feindseligkeit *f* (*to gegen*).

hot [hɔt] heiß; scharf; beißend; hitzig, heftig; eifrig; warm (*Speise, Fährte*); *Am. sl.* falsch (*Scheck*); gestohlen; radioaktiv; **~bed** ['hɔtbed] Mistbeet *n*; *fig.* Brutstätte *f*.

hotchpotch ['hɔtʃpɔtʃ] Mischmasch *m*; Gemüsesuppe *f*. [chen.]

hot dog F ['hɔt ˈdɔg] heißes Würst-

hotel [hou'tel] Hotel *n*.

hot|head ['hɔthed] Hitzkopf *m*; **~house** Treibhaus *n*; **~pot** Irish Stew *n*; ~ *rod Am. sl. mot.* frisiertes altes Auto; **~spur** Hitzkopf *m*.

hound [haund] **1.** Jagd-, Spürhund *m*; *fig.* Hund *m*; **2.** jagen, hetzen

hour ['auə] Stunde *f*; Zeit *f*, Uhr *f*; **~ly** ['auəli] stündlich.

house 1. [haus] *allg.* Haus *n*; *the* ♌ das Unterhaus; die Börse; **2.** [hauz] *v/t.* unterbringen; *v/i.* hausen; **~agent** ['hauseidʒənt] Häusermakler *m*; **~breaker** ['hausbreikə] Abbrucharbeiter *m*; **~hold** Haushalt *m*; *attr.* Haushalts-; Haus...; **~holder** Hausherr *m*; **~keeper** Haushälterin *f*; **~keeping** Haushaltung *f*; **~maid** Hausmädchen *n*; **~warming** ['hauswɔ:miŋ] Einzugsfeier *f*; **~wife** ['hauswaif] Hausfrau *f*; ['hʌzif] Nähtäschchen *n*; **~wifery** ['hauswifəri] Haushaltung *f*; **~work** Haus(halts)arbeiten *f/pl.*

housing ['hauziŋ] Unterbringung *f*; Wohnung *f*; ~ *estate* Wohnsiedlung *f*.

hove [houv] *pret. u. p.p. von heave* 2.

hovel ['hɔvl] Schuppen *m*; Hütte *f*.

hover ['hɔvə] schweben; lungern; *fig.* schwanken; **~craft** Luftkissenfahrzeug *n*.

how [hau] wie; ~ *do you do? Begrüßungsformel bei der Vorstellung*; ~ *about* ...? wie steht's mit ...? **~ever** [hau'evə] **1.** *adv.* wie auch (immer); wenn auch noch so ...; **2.** *cj.* jedoch.

howl [haul] **1.** heulen, brüllen; **2.** Geheul *n*; **~er** ['haulə] Heuler *m*; *sl.* grober Fehler.

hub [hʌb] (Rad)Nabe *f*; *fig.* Mittel-, Angelpunkt *m*.

hubbub ['hʌbʌb] Tumult *m*, Lärm *m*.

hub(by) F [hʌb(i)] (Ehe)Mann *m*.

huckleberry ♀ ['hʌklberi] amerikanische Heidelbeere.

huckster ['hʌkstə] Hausierer(in).

huddle ['hʌdl] **1.** *a.* ~ *together* (sich) zs.-drängen, zs.-pressen; ~ (*o.s.*) *up* sich zs.-kauern; **2.** Gewirr *n*, Wirrwarr *m*. [*cry* Zetergeschrei *n.*]

hue [hju:] Farbe *f*; Hetze *f*; ~ *and*

huff [hʌf] **1.** üble Laune; **2.** *v/t.* grob anfahren; beleidigen; *v/i.* wütend werden; schmollen.

hug [hʌg] **1.** Umarmung *f*; **2.** an sich drücken, umarmen; *fig.* festhalten an (*dat.*); sich dicht am *Weg etc.* halten.

huge □ [hju:dʒ] ungeheuer, riesig; **~ness** ['hju:dʒnis] ungeheure Größe.

hulk *fig.* [hʌlk] Klotz *m*.

hull [hʌl] 1. ♀ Schale f; Hülse f; ⚓ Rumpf m; 2. enthülsen; schälen.
hullabaloo [hʌləbə'luː] Lärm m.
hullo ['hʌ'lou] hallo (bsd. teleph.).
hum [hʌm] summen; brumme(l)n; make things ~ F Schwung in die Sache bringen.
human ['hjuːmən] 1. □ menschlich; ~ly nach menschlichem Ermessen; 2. F Mensch m; ~e □ [hjuː)'mein] human, menschenfreundlich; ~i-tarian [hju(:)mæni'tɛəriən] 1. Menschenfreund m; 2. menschenfreundlich; ~ity [hjuː)'mæniti] menschliche Natur; Menschheit f; Humanität f; ~kind ['hjuːmən'kaind] Menschengeschlecht n.
humble ['hʌmbl] 1. □ demütig; bescheiden; 2. erniedrigen; demütigen.
humble-bee ['hʌmblbiː] Hummel f.
humbleness ['hʌmblnis] Demut f.
humbug ['hʌmbʌg] 1. (be)schwindeln; 2. Schwindel m.
humdinger Am. sl. [hʌm'diŋə] Mordskerl m, -sache f.
humdrum ['hʌmdrʌm] eintönig.
humid ['hjuːmid] feucht, naß; ~ity [hjuː)'miditi] Feuchtigkeit f.
humiliat|e [hjuː)'milieit] erniedrigen, demütigen; ~ion [hjuː)mili'eiʃən] Erniedrigung f, Demütigung f.
humility [hjuː)'militi] Demut f.
humming F ['hʌmiŋ] mächtig, gewaltig; ~bird zo. Kolibri m.
humorous □ ['hjuːmərəs] humoristisch, humorvoll; spaßig.
humo(u)r ['hjuːmə] 1. Laune f, Stimmung f; Humor m; das Spaßige; ⚕ hist. Körpersaft m; out of ~ schlecht gelaunt; 2. j-m s-n Willen lassen; eingehen auf (acc.).
hump [hʌmp] 1. Höcker m, Buckel m; 2. krümmen; ärgern, verdrießen; ~ o.s. Am. sl. sich dranhalten; ~back ['hʌmpbæk] = hunchback.
hunch [hʌntʃ] 1. Höcker m; großes Stück; Am. F Ahnung f; 2. a. ~ out, ~ up krümmen; ~back ['hʌntʃ-bæk] Bucklige(r m) f.
hundred ['hʌndrəd] 1. hundert; 2. Hundert n; ~th [~dθ] 1. hundertste; 2. Hundertstel n; ~weight englischer Zentner (50,8 kg).
hung [hʌŋ] 1. pret. u. p.p. von hang 1; 2. adj. abgehangen (Fleisch).
Hungarian [hʌŋ'gɛəriən] 1. ungarisch; 2. Ungar(in); Ungarisch n.
hunger ['hʌŋgə] 1. Hunger m (a. fig.; for nach); 2. v/i. hungern (for, after nach); v/t. durch Hunger zwingen (into zu).
hungry □ ['hʌŋgri] hungrig.
hunk F [hʌŋk] dickes Stück.
hunt [hʌnt] 1. Jagd f (for nach); Jagd(revier n) f; Jagd(gesellschaft) f; 2. jagen; Revier bejagen; hetzen; ~ out od. up aufspüren; ~ for, ~ after

Jagd machen auf (acc.); ~er ['hʌntə] Jäger m; Jagdpferd n; ~ing [~tiŋ] Jagen n; Verfolgung f; attr. Jagd...; ~ing-ground Jagdrevier n; ~sman [~tsmən] Jäger m; Rüdemann m (Meutenführer).
hurdle ['həːdl] Hürde f (a. fig.); ~r [~lə] Hürdenläufer(in); ~-race Hürdenrennen n.
hurl [həːl] 1. Schleudern n; 2. schleudern; Worte ausstoßen.
hurricane ['hʌrikən] Orkan m.
hurried □ ['hʌrid] eilig; übereilt.
hurry ['hʌri] 1. (große) Eile, Hast f; be in a ~ es eilig haben; not ... in a ~ F nicht so bald, nicht so leicht; 2. v/t. (an)treiben; drängen; et. beschleunigen; eilig schicken od. bringen; v/i. eilen, hasten; ~ up sich beeilen.
hurt [həːt] 1. Verletzung f; Schaden m; 2. [irr.] verletzen (a. fig.); weh tun (dat.); schaden (dat.).
husband ['hʌzbənd] 1. (Ehe)Mann m; 2. haushalten mit; verwalten; ~man Landwirt m; ~ry [~dri] Landwirtschaft f, Ackerbau m.
hush [hʌʃ] 1. still!; 2. Stille f; 3. v/t. zum Schweigen bringen; beruhigen; Stimme dämpfen; ~ up vertuschen; v/i. still sein; ~-money ['hʌʃmʌni] Schweigegeld n.
husk [hʌsk] 1. ♀ Hülse f, Schote f; Schale f (a. fig.); 2. enthülsen; ~y ['hʌski] 1. □ hülsig; trocken; heiser; F stramm, stämmig; 2. F stämmiger Kerl.
hussy ['hʌsi] Flittchen n; Range f.
hustle ['hʌsl] 1. v/t. (an)rempeln; stoßen; drängen; v/i. sich drängen; eilen; bsd. Am. mit Hochdruck arbeiten; 2. Hochbetrieb m; Rührigkeit f; ~ and bustle Gedränge und Gehetze n.
hut [hʌt] Hütte f; ✕ Baracke f.
hutch [hʌtʃ] Kasten m; bsd. Kaninchen-Stall m (a. fig.); Trog m.
hyacinth ♀ ['haiəsinθ] Hyazinthe f.
hyaena zo. [hai'iːnə] Hyäne f.
hybrid ⚕ ['haibrid] Bastard m, Mischling m; Kreuzung f; attr. Bastard...; Zwitter...; ~ize [~daiz] kreuzen.
hydrant ['haidrənt] Hydrant m.
hydro|... ['haidrou] Wasser...; ~carbon ⚕ Kohlenwasserstoff m; ~chloric acid [~rə'klɔrikæsid] Salzsäure f; ~gen ['haidʒən] Wasserstoff m; ~gen bomb Wasserstoffbombe f; ~pathy [hai'drɔpəθi] Wasserheilkunde f, Wasserkur f; ~phobia [haidrə'foubjə] Wasserscheu f; ⚕ Tollwut f; ~plane ['haidrouplein] Wasserflugzeug n; (Motor)Gleitboot n, Rennboot n.
hyena zo. [hai'iːnə] Hyäne f.
hygiene ['haidʒiːn] Hygiene f.
hymn [him] 1. Hymne f; Lobgesang m; Kirchenlied n; 2. preisen.

hyphen ['haifən] 1. Bindestrich *m*; 2. mit Bindestrich schreiben *od.* verbinden; **~ated** [~neitid] mit Bindestrich geschrieben; **~** *Americans pl.* Halb-Amerikaner *m*/*pl.* (*z. B. German-Americans*). [ren.]
hypnotize ['hipnətaiz] hypnotisie-
hypo|chondriac [haipou'kɔndriæk] Hypochonder *m*; **~crisy** [hi'pɔ-

krəsi] Heuchelei *f*; **~crite** ['hipə-krit] Heuchler(in); Scheinheilige(r *m*) *f*; **~critical** □ [hipə'kritikəl] heuchlerisch; **~thesis** [hai'pɔθisis] Hypothese *f*.
hyster|ia [his'tiəriə] Hysterie *f*; **~ical** □ [~'terikəl] hysterisch; **~ics** [~ks] *pl.* hysterischer Anfall; *go into* **~** hysterisch werden.

I

I [ai] ich.
ice [ais] 1. Eis *n*; 2. gefrieren lassen; *a.* **~** *up* vereisen; *Kuchen* mit Zuckerguß überziehen; in Eis kühlen; **~age** ['aiseidʒ] Eiszeit *f*; **~berg** ['aisbə:g] Eisberg *m* (*a. fig.*); **~bound** eingefroren; **~box** Eisschrank *m*; *Am. a.* Kühlschrank *m*; **~cream** Speiseeis *n*; **~floe** Eisscholle *f*.
icicle ['aisikl] Eiszapfen *m*.
icing ['aisiŋ] Zuckerguß *m*; Vereisung *f*.
icy □ ['aisi] eisig (*a. fig.*); vereist.
idea [ai'diə] Idee *f*; Begriff *m*; Vorstellung *f*; Gedanke *m*; Meinung *f*; Ahnung *f*; Plan *m*; **~l** [~əl] 1. □ ideell; eingebildet; ideal; 2. Ideal *n*.
identi|cal □ [ai'dentikəl] identisch, gleich(bedeutend); **~fication** [aidentifi'keiʃən] Identifizierung *f*; Ausweis *m*; **~fy** [ai'dentifai] identifizieren; ausweisen; erkennen; **~ty** [~iti] Identität *f*; Persönlichkeit *f*, Eigenart *f*; **~** *card* Personalausweis *m*, Kennkarte *f*; **~** *disk* Erkennungsmarke *f*.
ideological □ [aidiə'lɔdʒikəl] ideologisch.
idiom ['idiəm] Idiom *n*; Mundart *f*; Redewendung *f*.
idiot ['idiət] Idiot(in), Schwachsinnige(r *m*) *f*; **~ic** [idi'ɔtik] (**~ally**) blödsinnig.
idle ['aidl] 1. □ müßig, untätig; träg, faul; unnütz; nichtig; **~** *hours pl.* Mußestunden *f*/*pl.*; 2. *v*/*t. mst* **~** *away* vertrödeln; *v*/*i.* faulenzen; ⊕ leer laufen; **~ness** ['aidlnis] Muße *f*; Trägheit *f*; Nichtigkeit *f*; **~r** ['aidlə] Müßiggänger(in).
idol ['aidl] Idol *n*, Götzenbild *n*; *fig.* Abgott *m*; **~atrous** □ [ai'dɔlətrəs] abgöttisch; **~atry** [~ri] Abgötterei *f*; Vergötterung *f*; **~ize** ['aidəlaiz] vergöttern.
dyl(l) ['idil] Idyll(e *f*) *n*.
if [if] 1. wenn, falls; ob; 2. Wenn *n*; **~fy** *Am.* F ['ifi] zweifelhaft.
ignit|e [ig'nait] (sich) entzünden; zünden; **~ion** [ig'niʃən] ⚛ Entzündung *f*; *mot.* Zündung *f*.

ignoble □ [ig'noubl] unedel; niedrig, gemein.
ignominious □ [ignə'miniəs] schändlich, schimpflich.
ignor|ance ['ignərəns] Unwissenheit *f*; **~ant** [~nt] unwissend; unkundig; **~e** [ig'nɔ:] ignorieren, nicht beachten; ⚖ verwerfen.
ill [il] 1. *adj. u. adv.* übel, böse; schlimm, schlecht; krank; *adv.* kaum; *fall* **~**, *be taken* **~** krank werden; 2. Übel *n*; Üble(s) *n*, Böse(s) *n*.
ill-advised □ ['iləd'vaizd] schlecht beraten; unbesonnen, unklug; **~bred** ungebildet, ungezogen; **~** *breeding* schlechtes Benehmen.
illegal □ [i'li:gəl] ungesetzlich.
illegible □ [i'ledʒəbl] unleserlich.
illegitimate □ [ili'dʒitimit] illegitim; unrechtmäßig; unehelich.
ill-favo(u)red □ ['il'feivəd] häßlich; **~humo(u)red** übellaunig.
illiberal □ [i'libərəl] engstirnig; intolerant; knauserig.
illicit □ [i'lisit] unerlaubt.
illiterate □ [i'litərit] 1. ungelehrt, ungebildet; 2. Analphabet(in).
ill-judged ['il'dʒʌdʒd] unklug, unvernünftig; **~mannered** ungezogen; mit schlechten Umgangsformen; **~natured** □ boshaft, bösartig.
illness ['ilnis] Krankheit *f*.
illogical □ [i'lɔdʒikəl] unlogisch.
ill-starred ['il'stɑ:d] unglücklich; **~tempered** schlecht gelaunt; **~timed** ungelegen; **~treat** mißhandeln.
illuminat|e [i'lju:mineit] be-, erleuchten (*a. fig.*); erläutern; aufklären; **~ing** [~tiŋ] Leucht...; *fig.* aufschlußreich; **~ion** [ilju:mi'neiʃən] Er-, Beleuchtung *f*; Erläuterung *f*; Aufklärung *f*.
ill-use ['il'ju:z] mißhandeln.
illus|ion [i'lu:ʒən] Illusion *f*, Täuschung *f*; **~ive** [i'lu:siv], **~ory** □ [~səri] illusorisch, täuschend.
illustrat|e ['iləstreit] illustrieren; erläutern; bebildern; **~ion** ['iləs-'treiʃən] Erläuterung *f*; Illustration *f*; **~ive** □ ['iləstreitiv] erläuternd.

illustrious ☐ [i'lʌstriəs] berühmt.
ill will ['il'wil] Feindschaft f.
image ['imidʒ] Bild n; Standbild n; Ebenbild n; Vorstellung f; ~ry [~dʒəri] Bilder n/pl.; Bildersprache f, Metaphorik f.
imagin|able ☐ [i'mædʒinəbl] denkbar; ~ary [~əri] eingebildet; ~ation [imædʒi'neiʃən] Einbildung(skraft) f; ~ative ☐ [i'mædʒinətiv] ideen-, einfallsreich; ~e [i'mædʒin] sich et. einbilden od. vorstellen od. denken.
imbecile ☐ ['imbisi:l] **1.** geistesschwach; **2.** Schwachsinnige(r m) f.
imbibe [im'baib] einsaugen; fig. sich zu eigen machen.
imbue [im'bju:] (durch)tränken; tief färben; fig. erfüllen.
imitat|e ['imiteit] nachahmen; imitieren; ~ion [imi'teiʃən] **1.** Nachahmung f; **2.** künstlich, Kunst...
immaculate ☐ [i'mækjulit] unbefleckt, rein; fehlerlos.
immaterial ☐ [imə'tiəriəl] unkörperlich; unwesentlich (to für).
immature [imə'tjuə] unreif.
immeasurable ☐ [i'meʒərəbl] unermeßlich.
immediate ☐ [i'mi:djət] unmittelbar; unverzüglich, sofortig; ~ly [~tli] **1.** adv. sofort; **2.** cj. gleich nachdem.
immense ☐ [i'mens] ungeheuer.
immerse [i'mə:s] (ein-, unter)tauchen; fig. ~ o.s. in sich versenken od. vertiefen in (acc.).
immigra|nt ['imigrənt] Einwanderer(in); ~te [~greit] v/i. einwandern; v/t. ansiedeln (into in dat.); ~tion [imi'greiʃən] Einwanderung f.
imminent ☐ ['iminənt] bevorstehend, drohend.
immobile [i'moubail] unbeweglich.
immoderate ☐ [i'modərit] maßlos.
immodest ☐ [i'modist] unbescheiden; unanständig.
immoral ☐ [i'morəl] unmoralisch.
immortal [i'mo:tl] **1.** ☐ unsterblich; **2.** Unsterbliche(r m) f; ~ity [imo:'tæliti] Unsterblichkeit f.
immovable ☐ [i'mu:vəbl] **1.** ☐ unbeweglich; unerschütterlich; **2.** ~s pl. Immobilien pl.
immun|e & u. fig. [i'mju:n] immun, gefeit (from gegen); ~ity [~niti] Immunität f, Freiheit f (from von); Unempfänglichkeit f (für).
immutable ☐ [i'mju:təbl] unveränderlich.
imp [imp] Teufelchen n; Schelm m.
impact ['impækt] (Zs.-)Stoß m; Anprall m; Einwirkung f.
impair [im'peə] schwächen; (ver-)mindern; beeinträchtigen.
impart [im'pɑ:t] verleihen; weitergeben.
impartial [im'pɑ:ʃəl] unparteiisch; ~ity ['impɑ:ʃi'æliti] Unparteilichkeit f, Objektivität f.

impassable ☐ [im'pɑ:səbl] ungangbar, unpassierbar.
impassible ☐ [im'pæsibl] unempfindlich; gefühllos (to gegen).
impassioned [im'pæʃənd] leidenschaftlich.
impassive ☐ [im'pæsiv] unempfindlich; teilnahmslos; heiter.
impatien|ce [im'peiʃəns] Ungeduld f; ~t ☐ [~nt] ungeduldig.
impeach [im'pi:tʃ] anklagen (of, with gen.); anfechten, anzweifeln.
impeccable ☐ [im'pekəbl] sündlos; makellos, einwandfrei.
impede [im'pi:d] (ver)hindern.
impediment [im'pedimənt] Hindernis n.
impel [im'pel] (an)treiben.
impend [im'pend] hängen, schweben; bevorstehen, drohen.
impenetrable ☐ [im'penitrəbl] undurchdringlich; fig. unergründlich; fig. unzugänglich (to dat.).
impenitent ☐ [im'penitənt] unbußfertig, verstockt.
imperative [im'perətiv] **1.** ☐ notwendig, dringend, unbedingt erforderlich; befehlend; gebieterisch; gr. imperativisch; **2.** Befehl m; a. ~ mood gr. Imperativ m, Befehlsform f. [unermklich.\
imperceptible ☐ [impə'septəbl]\
imperfect [im'pə:fikt] **1.** ☐ unvollkommen; unvollendet; **2.** a. ~ tense gr. Imperfekt n.
imperial ☐ [im'piəriəl] kaiserlich; Reichs...; majestätisch; großartig; ~ism [~lizəm] Imperialismus m, Weltmachtpolitik f.
imperil [im'peril] gefährden.
imperious ☐ [im'piəriəs] gebieterisch, anmaßend; dringend.
imperishable ☐ [im'periʃəbl] unvergänglich.
impermeable ☐ [im'pə:mjəbl] undurchdringlich, undurchlässig.
impersonal ☐ [im'pə:snl] unpersönlich.
impersonate [im'pə:səneit] verkörpern; thea. darstellen.
impertinen|ce [im'pə:tinəns] Unverschämtheit f; Nebensächlichkeit f; ~t ☐ [~nt] unverschämt; ungehörig; nebensächlich.
imperturbable ☐ [impə(:)'tə:bəbl] unerschütterlich.
impervious ☐ [im'pə:vjəs] unzugänglich (to für); undurchlässig.
impetu|ous ☐ [im'petjuəs] ungestüm, heftig; ~s ['impitəs] Antrieb m.
impiety [im'paiəti] Gottlosigkeit f.
impinge [im'pindʒ] v/i. (ver)stoßen (on, upon, against gegen).
impious ☐ ['impiəs] gottlos; pietätlos; frevelhaft.
implacable ☐ [im'plækəbl] unversöhnlich, unerbittlich.
implant [im'plɑ:nt] einpflanzen.

implement 1. ['implimənt] Werkzeug *n*; Gerät *n*; **2.** [‿iment] ausführen.

implicat|e ['implikeit] verwickeln; in sich schließen; **‿ion** [impli'keiʃən] Verwick(e)lung *f*; Folgerung *f*.

implicit ☐ [im'plisit] mit eingeschlossen; blind (*Glaube etc.*).

implore [im'plɔ:] (an-, er)flehen.

imply [im'plai] mit einbegreifen, enthalten; bedeuten; andeuten.

impolite ☐ [impə'lait] unhöflich.

impolitic ☐ [im'pɔlitik] unklug.

import 1. ['impɔ:t] Bedeutung *f*; Wichtigkeit *f*; Einfuhr *f*; ‿s *pl.* Einfuhrwaren *f/pl.*; **2.** [im'pɔ:t] einführen; bedeuten; **‿ance** [‿təns] Wichtigkeit *f*; **‿ant** ☐ [‿nt] wichtig; wichtigtuerisch; **‿ation** [impɔ:-'teiʃən] Einfuhr(waren *f/pl.*) *f.*

importun|ate ☐ [im'pɔ:tjunit] lästig; zudringlich; **‿e** [im'pɔ:tju:n] dringend bitten; belästigen.

impos|e [im'pouz] *v/t.* auf(er)legen, aufbürden (*on, upon dat.*); *v/i.* ‿ *upon j-m* imponieren; *j-n* täuschen; **‿ition** [impə'ziʃən] Auf(er)legung *f*; Steuer *f*; Strafarbeit *f*; Betrügerei *f.*

impossib|ility [impɔsə'biliti] Unmöglichkeit *f*; **‿le** ☐ [im'pɔsəbl] unmöglich.

impost|or [im'pɔstə] Betrüger *m*; **‿ure** [‿tʃə] Betrug *m.*

impoten|ce ['impətəns] Unfähigkeit *f*; Machtlosigkeit *f*; **‿t** [‿nt] unvermögend, machtlos, schwach.

impoverish [im'pɔvəriʃ] arm machen; *Boden* auslaugen.

impracticable ☐ [im'præktikəbl] undurchführbar; unwegsam.

impractical [im'præktikəl] unpraktisch; theoretisch; unnütz.

imprecate ['imprikeit] *Böses* herabwünschen (*upon* auf *acc.*).

impregn|able ☐ [im'pregnəbl] uneinnehmbar; unüberwindlich; **‿ate** ['impregneit] schwängern; ♀ sättigen; ⊕ imprägnieren.

impress 1. ['impres] (Ab-, Ein-) Druck *m*; *fig.* Stempel *m*; **2.** [im-'pres] eindrücken, prägen; *Kraft etc.* übertragen; *Gedanken etc.* einprägen (*on dat.*); *j-n* beeindrucken; *j-n mit et.* erfüllen; **‿ion** [‿eʃən] Eindruck *m*; *typ.* Abdruck *m*; Abzug *m*; Auflage *f*; *be under the ‿ that* den Eindruck haben, daß; **‿ive** ☐ [‿esiv] eindrucksvoll.

imprint 1. [im'print] aufdrücken, prägen; *fig.* einprägen (*on, in dat.*); **2.** ['imprint] Eindruck *m*; Stempel *m* (*a. fig.*); *typ.* Druckvermerk *m.*

imprison [im'prizn] inhaftieren; **‿ment** [‿nment] Haft *f*; Gefängnis (-strafe *f*) *n.*

improbable ☐ [im'prɔbəbl] unwahrscheinlich.

improper ☐ [im'prɔpə] ungeeignet, unpassend; falsch; unanständig.

impropriety [imprə'praiəti] Ungehörigkeit *f*; Unanständigkeit *f.*

improve [im'pru:v] *v/t.* verbessern; veredeln; aus-, benutzen; *v/i.* sich (ver)bessern; ‿ *upon* vervollkommnen; **‿ment** [‿vmənt] Verbesserung *f*, Vervollkommnung *f*; Fortschritt *m* (*on, upon* gegenüber *dat.*).

improvise ['imprəvaiz] improvisieren.

imprudent ☐ [im'pru:dənt] unklug.

impuden|ce ['impjudəns] Unverschämtheit *f*, Frechheit *f*; **‿t** ☐ [‿nt] unverschämt, frech.

impuls|e ['impʌls], **‿ion** [im'pʌlʃən] Impuls *m*, (An)Stoß *m*; *fig.* (An)Trieb *m*; **‿ive** ☐ [‿lsiv] (an-) treibend; *fig.* impulsiv; rasch (handelnd).

impunity [im'pju:niti] Straflosigkeit *f*; *with ‿* ungestraft.

impure ☐ [im'pjuə] unrein (*a. fig.*); unkeusch.

imput|ation [impju(:)'teiʃən] Beschuldigung *f*; **‿e** [im'pju:t] zurechnen, beimessen; zur Last legen.

in [in] **1.** *prp. allg.* in (*dat.*); *engS.*: (‿ *the morning*, ‿ *number*, ‿ *itself*, *professor* ‿ *the university*) an (*dat.*); (‿ *the street*, ‿ *English*) auf (*dat.*); (‿ *this manner*) auf (*acc.*); (*coat* ‿ *velvet*) aus; (‿ *Shakespeare*, ‿ *the daytime*, ‿ *crossing the road*) bei; (*engaged* ‿ *reading*, ‿ *a word*) mit; (‿ *my opinion*) nach; (*rejoice* ‿ *s.th.*) über (*acc.*); (‿ *the circumstances*, ‿ *the reign of*, *one* ‿ *ten*) unter (*dat.*); (*cry out* ‿ *alarm*) vor (*dat.*); (*grouped* ‿ *tens*, *speak* ‿ *reply*, ‿ *excuse*, ‿ *honour of*) zu; ‿ *1949* im Jahre 1949; ‿ *that* ... insofern als, weil; **2.** *adv.* drin(nen); herein; hinein; *be* ‿ *for et.* zu erwarten haben; *e-e Prüfung etc.* vor sich haben; *F be well* ‿ *with* sich gut mit *j-m* stehen; **3.** *adj.* hereinkommend; Innen...

inability [inə'biliti] Unfähigkeit *f.*

inaccessible ☐ [inæk'sesəbl] unzugänglich.   [unrichtig.

inaccurate ☐ [in'ækjurit] ungenau;

inactiv|e ☐ [in'æktiv] untätig; ♀ lustlos; ♀ unwirksam; **‿ity** [inæk-'tiviti] Untätig-, Lustlosigkeit *f.*

inadequate ☐ [in'ædikwit] unangemessen; unzulänglich.

inadmissible ☐ [inəd'misəbl] unzulässig.

inadvertent ☐ [inəd'və:tənt] unachtsam; unbeabsichtigt, versehentlich.

inalienable ☐ [in'eiljənəbl] unveräußerlich.

inane ☐ [i'nein] *fig.* leer; albern.

inanimate ☐ [in'ænimit] leblos; *fig.* unbelebt; geistlos, langweilig.

inapproachable [inə'proutʃəbl] unnahbar, unzugänglich.

inappropriate ☐ [inə'proupriit] unangebracht, unpassend.

inapt ☐ [in'æpt] ungeeignet, untauglich; ungeschickt; unpassend.

inarticulate ☐ [inɑː'tikjulit] undeutlich; schwer zu verstehen(d); undeutlich sprechend.

inasmuch [inəz'mʌtʃ]: ~ *as* insofern als. [merksam.)

inattentive ☐ [inə'tentiv] unauf-)

inaudible ☐ [in'ɔːdəbl] unhörbar.

inaugura|l [i'nɔːgjurəl] Antrittsrede *f; attr.* Antritts...; **~te** [~reit] (feierlich) einführen, einweihen; beginnen; **~tion** [inɔːgju'reiʃən] Einführung *f,* Einweihung *f;* ♀ *Day Am.* Amtseinführung *f* des neugewählten Präsidenten der USA.

inborn ['in'bɔːn] angeboren.

incalculable ☐ [in'kælkjuləbl] unberechenbar; unzählig.

incandescent [inkæn'desnt] weiß glühend; Glüh...

incapa|ble ☐ [in'keipəbl] unfähig, ungeeignet (*of* zu); **~citate** [inkə-'pæsiteit] unfähig machen; **~city** [~ti] Unfähigkeit *f.*

incarnate [in'kɑːnit] Fleisch geworden; *fig.* verkörpert.

incautious ☐ [in'kɔːʃəs] unvorsichtig.

incendiary [in'sendjəri] **1.** brandstifterisch; *fig.* aufwieglerisch; **2.** Brandstifter *m;* Aufwiegler *m.*

incense¹ ['insens] Weihrauch *m.*

incense² [in'sens] in Wut bringen.

incentive [in'sentiv] Antrieb *m.*

incessant ☐ [in'sesnt] unaufhörlich.

incest ['insest] Blutschande *f.*

inch [intʃ] Zoll *m (2,54 cm); fig.* ein bißchen; *by* ~es allmählich; *every* ~ ganz (u. gar).

inciden|ce ['insidəns] Vorkommen *n;* Wirkung *f;* **~t** [~nt] **1.** (*to*) vorkommend (bei), eigen (*dat.*); **2.** Zu-, Vor-, Zwischenfall *m;* Nebenumstand *m;* **~tal** ☐ [insi'dentl] zufällig, gelegentlich; Neben...; *be* ~ *to* gehören zu; **~ly** nebenbei.

incinerate [in'sinəreit] einäschern; *Müll* verbrennen.

incis|e [in'saiz] einschneiden; **~ion** [in'siʒən] Einschnitt *m;* **~ive** ☐ [in'saisiv] (ein)schneidend, scharf; **~or** [~aizə] Schneidezahn *m.*

incite [in'sait] anspornen, anregen, anstiften; **~ment** [~tmənt] Anregung *f;* Ansporn *m;* Anstiftung *f.*

inclement [in'klemənt] rauh.

inclin|ation [inkli'neiʃən] Neigung *f (a. fig.);* **~e** [in'klain] **1.** *v/i.* sich neigen (*a. fig.*); ~ *to fig.* zu et. neigen; *v/t.* neigen; geneigt machen; **2.** Neigung *f,* Abhang *m.*

inclos|e [in'klouz], **~ure** [~ouʒə] *s. enclose, enclosure.*

inclu|de [in'kluːd] einschließen; enthalten; **~sive** ☐ [~uːsiv] einschließlich; alles einbegriffen; *be* ~ *of* einschließen; ~ *terms pl.* Pauschalpreis *m.*

incoheren|ce, ~cy [inkou'hiərəns, ~si] Zs.-hangslosigkeit *f;* Inkonsequenz *f;* **~t** ☐ [~nt] unzs.-hängend; inkonsequent.

income ['inkəm] Einkommen *n;* **~-tax** Einkommensteuer *f.*

incommode [inkə'moud] belästigen.

incommunica|do *bsd. Am.* [inkəmjuːni'kɑːdou] ohne Verbindung mit der Außenwelt; **~tive** ☐ [inkə'mjuːnikətiv] nicht mitteilsam, verschlossen.

incomparable ☐ [in'kɔmpərəbl] unvergleichlich.

incompatible ☐ [inkəm'pætəbl] unvereinbar; unverträglich.

incompetent [in'kɔmpitənt] unfähig; unzuständig, unbefugt.

incomplete ☐ [inkəm'pliːt] unvollständig; unvollkommen.

incomprehensible ☐ [inkɔmpri-'hensəbl] unbegreiflich.

inconceivable ☐ [inkən'siːvəbl] unbegreiflich, unfaßbar.

incongruous ☐ [in'kɔngruəs] nicht übereinstimmend; unpassend.

inconsequent ☐ [in'kɔnsikwənt] inkonsequent, folgewidrig; **~ial** [inkɔnsi'kwenʃəl] unbedeutend; = *inconsequent.*

inconsidera|ble ☐ [inkən'sidərəbl] unbedeutend; **~te** ☐ [~rit] unüberlegt; rücksichtslos.

inconsisten|cy [inkən'sistənsi] Unvereinbarkeit *f;* Inkonsequenz *f;* **~t** ☐ [~nt] unvereinbar; widerspruchsvoll; inkonsequent.

inconsolable ☐ [inkən'souləbl] untröstlich.

inconstant ☐ [in'kɔnstənt] unbeständig; veränderlich.

incontinent ☐ [in'kɔntinənt] unmäßig; ausschweifend.

inconvenien|ce [inkən'viːnjəns] **1.** Unbequemlichkeit *f;* Unannehmlichkeit *f;* **2.** belästigen; **~t** ☐ [~nt] unbequem; ungelegen; lästig.

incorporat|e 1. [in'kɔːpəreit] einverleiben (*into dat.*); (sich) vereinigen; *als Mitglied* aufnehmen; 🏛 *als Körperschaft* eintragen; **2.** [~rit] einverleibt; vereinigt; **~ed** (amtlich) eingetragen; **~ion** [inkɔːpə'reiʃən] Einverleibung *f;* Verbindung *f.* [fehlerhaft; ungehörig.)

incorrect ☐ [inkə'rekt] unrichtig;)

incorrigible ☐ [in'kɔridʒəbl] unverbesserlich.

increas|e 1. [in'kriːs] *v/i.* zunehmen; sich vergrößern *od.* vermehren; *v/t.* vermehren, vergrößern; erhöhen; **2.** [in'kriːs] Zunahme *f;* Vergrößerung *f;* Zuwachs *m;* **~ingly** [in'kriːsiŋli] zunehmend, immer (*mit folgendem comp.*); ~ *difficult* immer schwieriger.

incredible ☐ [in'kredəbl] unglaublich.

incredul|ity [inkri'dju:liti] Unglaube *m*; ~**ous** □ [in'kredjuləs] ungläubig, skeptisch.

incriminate [in'krimineit] beschuldigen; belasten.

incrustation [inkrʌs'teiʃən] Verkrustung *f*; Kruste *f*; ⊕ Belag *m*.

incub|ate ['inkjubeit] (aus)brüten; ~**ator** [~tə] Brutapparat *m*.

inculcate ['inkʌlkeit] einschärfen (*upon dat.*).

incumbent [in'kʌmbənt] obliegend; be ~ on *s.o.* j-m obliegen.

incur [in'kə:] sich *et.* zuziehen; geraten in (*acc.*); *Verpflichtung* eingehen; *Verlust* erleiden.

incurable [in'kjuərəbl] **1.** □ unheilbar; **2.** Unheilbare(r *m*) *f*.

incurious □ [in'kjuəriəs] gleichgültig, uninteressiert.

incursion [in'kə:ʃən] *feindlicher Einfall*.

indebted [in'detid] verschuldet; *fig.* (zu Dank) verpflichtet.

indecen|cy [in'di:snsi] Unanständigkeit *f*; ~**t** □ [~nt] unanständig.

indecisi|on [indi'siʒən] Unentschlossenheit *f*; ~**ve** □ [~'saisiv] nicht entscheidend; unbestimmt.

indecorous □ [in'dekərəs] unpassend; ungehörig.

indeed [in'di:d] **1.** *adv.* in der Tat, tatsächlich; wirklich; allerdings; **2.** *int.* so?; nicht möglich!

indefatigable □ [indi'fætigəbl] unermüdlich.

indefensible □ [indi'fensəbl] unhaltbar.

indefinite □ [in'definit] unbestimmt; unbeschränkt; ungenau.

indelible □ [in'delibl] untilgbar.

indelicate □ [in'delikit] unfein; taktlos.

indemni|fy [in'demnifai] sicherstellen; *j-m* Straflosigkeit zusichern; entschädigen; ~**ty** [~iti] Sicherstellung *f*; Straflosigkeit *f*; Entschädigung *f*.

indent 1. [in'dent] einkerben, auszacken; eindrücken; ⅍ *Vertrag* mit Doppel ausfertigen; ~ *upon s.o.* for *s.th.* ✝ et. bei j-m bestellen; **2.** ['indent] Kerbe *f*; Vertiefung *f*; ✝ Auslandsauftrag *m*; = *indenture*; ~**ation** [inden'teiʃən] Einkerbung *f*; ~**ure** [in'dentʃə] **1.** Vertrag *m*; Lehrbrief *m*; **2.** vertraglich verpflichten.

independen|ce [indi'pendəns] Unabhängigkeit *f*; Selbständigkeit *f*; Auskommen *n*; ♀ *Day Am.* Unabhängigkeitstag *m* (4. *Juli*); ~**t** □ [~nt] unabhängig; selbständig.

indescribable □ [indis'kraibəbl] unbeschreiblich.

indestructible □ [indis'trʌktəbl] unzerstörbar.

indeterminate □ [indi'tə:minit] unbestimmt.

index ['indeks] **1.** (An)Zeiger *m*; Anzeichen *n*; Zeigefinger *m*; Index *m*; (Inhalts-, Namen-, Sach)Verzeichnis *n*; **2.** *Buch* mit e-m Index versehen.

Indian ['indjən] **1.** indisch; indianisch; **2.** Inder(in); *a.* Red ~ Indianer(in), ~ **corn** Mais *m*; ~ **file:** *in* ~ im Gänsemarsch; ~ **pudding** *Am.* Maismehlpudding *m*; ~ **summer** Altweiber-, Nachsommer *m*.

Indiarubber ['indjə'rʌbə] Radiergummi *m*.

indicat|e ['indikeit] (an)zeigen; hinweisen auf (*acc.*); andeuten; ~**ion** [indi'keiʃən] Anzeige *f*; Anzeichen *n*; Andeutung *f*; ~**ive** [in'dikətiv] *a.* ~ **mood** *gr.* Indikativ *m*; ~**or** ['indikeitə] Anzeiger *m* (*a.* ⊕); *mot.* Blinker *m*.

indict [in'dait] anklagen (*for* wegen); ~**ment** [~tmənt] Anklage *f*.

indifferen|ce [in'difrəns] Gleichgültigkeit *f*; ~**t** □ [~nt] gleichgültig (*to* gegen); unparteiisch; (*nur*) mäßig; unwesentlich; unbedeutend.

indigenous [in'didʒinəs] eingeboren, einheimisch.

indigent □ ['indidʒənt] arm.

indigest|ible □ [indi'dʒestəbl] unverdaulich; ~**ion** [~tʃən] Verdauungsstörung *f*, Magenverstimmung *f*.

indign|ant □ [in'dignənt] entrüstet, empört, ungehalten; ~**ation** [indig'neiʃən] Entrüstung *f*; ~**ity** [in'digniti] Beleidigung *f*.

indirect □ [indi'rekt] indirekt; nicht direkt; *gr. a.* abhängig.

indiscre|et □ [indis'kri:t] unbesonnen; unachtsam; indiskret; ~**tion** [~reʃən] Unachtsamkeit *f*; Unbesonnenheit *f*; Indiskretion *f*.

indiscriminate □ [indis'kriminit] unterschieds-, wahllos.

indispensable □ [indis'pensəbl] unentbehrlich, unerläßlich.

indispos|ed [indis'pouzd] unpäßlich; abgeneigt; ~**ition** [indispə'ziʃən] Abneigung *f* (*to* gegen); Unpäßlichkeit *f*.

indisputable □ [indis'pju:təbl] unbestreitbar, unstreitig.

indistinct □ [indis'tiŋkt] undeutlich; unklar.

indistinguishable □ [indis'tiŋgwiʃəbl] nicht zu unterscheiden(d).

indite [in'dait] ab-, verfassen.

individual [indi'vidjuəl] **1.** □ persönlich, individuell; besondere(r, -s); einzeln; Einzel...; **2.** Individuum *n*; ~**ism** [~lizəm] Individualismus *m*; ~**ist** [~ist] Individualist *m*; ~**ity** [individju'æliti] Individualität *f*.

indivisible □ [indi'vizəbl] unteilbar.

indolen|ce ['indələns] Trägheit *f*;

∼t □ [∼nt] indolent, träge, lässig; ⚔ schmerzlos.

indomitable □ [in'dɔmitəbl] unbezähmbar.

indoor ['indɔ:] im Hause (befindlich); Haus..., Zimmer..., *Sport:* Hallen...; ∼s ['in'dɔ:z] zu Hause; im *od.* ins Haus.

indorse [in'dɔ:s] = *endorse etc.*

induce [in'dju:s] veranlassen; ∼ment [∼smənt] Anlaß *m*, Antrieb *m*.

induct [in'dʌkt] einführen; ∼ion [∼kʃən] Einführung *f*, Einsetzung *f in Amt, Pfründe; ⚡ Induktion *f*.

indulge [in'dʌldʒ] nachsichtig sein gegen *j-n*; *j-m* nachgeben; ∼ *with j-n* erfreuen mit; ∼ (*o.s.*) *in s.th.* sich et. gönnen; sich e-r S. hin- *od.* ergeben; ∼nce [∼dʒəns] Nachsicht *f*; Nachgiebigkeit *f*; Sichgehenlassen *n*; Vergünstigung *f*; ∼nt □ [∼nt] nachsichtig.

industri|al □ [in'dʌstriəl] gewerbetreibend, gewerblich; industriell; Gewerbe...; Industrie...; ∼ area Industriebezirk *m*; ∼ estate Industriegebiet *n e-r Stadt*; ∼ school Gewerbeschule *f*; ∼alist [∼list] Industrielle(r) *m*; ∼alize [∼laiz] industrialisieren; ∼ous □ [∼iəs] fleißig.

industry ['indəstri] Fleiß *m*; Gewerbe *n*; Industrie *f*.

inebriate 1. [i'ni:brieit] betrunken machen; **2.** [∼iit] Trunkenbold *m*.

ineffable □ [in'efəbl] unaussprechlich.

ineffect|ive [ini'fektiv], ∼ual □ [∼tjuəl] unwirksam, fruchtlos.

inefficient □ [ini'fiʃənt] wirkungslos; (leistungs)unfähig.

inelegant □ [in'eligənt] unelegant, geschmacklos.

ineligible □ [in'elidʒəbl] nicht wählbar; ungeeignet; *bsd.* ⚔ untauglich.

inept □ [i'nept] unpassend; albern.

inequality [ini(:)'kwɔliti] Ungleichheit *f*; Ungleichmäßigkeit *f*; Unebenheit *f*.

inequitable [in'ekwitəbl] unbillig.

inert □ [i'nə:t] träge, ∼ia [i'nə:ʃjə], ∼ness [i'nə:tnis] Trägheit *f*.

inescapable [inis'keipəbl] unentrinnbar.

inessential ['ini'senʃəl] unwesentlich (*to* für).

inestimable □ [in'estiməbl] unschätzbar.

inevitab|le □ [in'evitəbl] unvermeidlich; ∼ly [∼li] unweigerlich.

inexact □ [inig'zækt] ungenau.

inexcusable □ [iniks'kju:zəbl] unentschuldbar.

inexhaustible □ [inig'zɔ:stəbl] unerschöpflich; unermüdlich.

inexorable □ [in'eksərəbl] unerbittlich.

inexpedient □ [iniks'pi:djənt] unzweckmäßig, unpassend.

inexpensive □ [iniks'pensiv] nicht teuer, billig, preiswert.

inexperience [iniks'piəriəns] Unerfahrenheit *f*; ∼d [∼st] unerfahren.

inexpert □ [ineks'pə:t] unerfahren.

inexplicable □ [in'eksplikəbl] unerklärlich.

inexpressi|ble □ [iniks'presəbl] unaussprechlich; ∼ve [∼siv] ausdruckslos.

inextinguishable □ [iniks'tiŋgwiʃəbl] unauslöschlich.

inextricable □ [in'ekstrikəbl] unentwirrbar.

infallible □ [in'fæləbl] unfehlbar.

infam|ous □ ['infəməs] ehrlos; schändlich; verrufen; ∼y [∼mi] Ehrlosigkeit *f*; Schande *f*; Niedertracht *f*.

infan|cy ['infənsi] Kindheit *f*; ⚖ Minderjährigkeit *f*; ∼t [∼nt] Säugling *m*; (kleines) Kind; Minderjährige(r *m*) *f*.

infanti|le ['infəntail], ∼ne [∼ain] kindlich; Kindes..., Kinder...; kindisch.

infantry ⚔ ['infəntri] Infanterie *f*.

infatuate [in'fætjueit] betören; ∼d vernarrt (*with* in *acc.*).

infect [in'fekt] anstecken (*a. fig.*); infizieren, verseuchen, verpesten; ∼ion [∼kʃən] Ansteckung *f*; ∼ious □ [∼ʃəs], ∼ive [∼ktiv] ansteckend; Ansteckungs...

infer [in'fə:] folgern, schließen; ∼ence ['infərəns] Folgerung *f*.

inferior [in'fiəriə] **1.** untere(r, -s); minderwertig; ∼ to niedriger *od.* geringer als; untergeordnet (*dat.*); unterlegen (*dat.*); **2.** Geringere(r *m*) *f*; Untergebene(r *m*) *f*; ∼ity [infiəri'ɔriti] geringerer Wert *od.* Stand; Unterlegenheit *f*; Minderwertigkeit *f*.

infern|al □ [in'fə:nl] höllisch; ∼o [∼nou] Inferno *n*, Hölle *f*.

infertile [in'fə:tail] unfruchtbar.

infest [in'fest] heimsuchen; verseuchen; *fig.* überschwemmen.

infidelity [infi'deliti] Unglaube *m*; Untreue *f* (*to* gegen).

infiltrate [in'filtreit] *v/t.* durchdringen; *v/i.* durchsickern, eindringen.

infinite □ ['infinit] unendlich.

infinitive [in'finitiv] *a.* ∼ mood *gr.* Infinitiv *m*, Nennform *f*.

infinity [in'finiti] Unendlichkeit *f*.

infirm □ [in'fə:m] kraftlos, schwach; ∼ary [∼mɔri] Krankenhaus *n*; ∼ity [∼miti] Schwäche *f* (*a. fig.*); Gebrechen *n*.

inflame [in'fleim] entflammen (*mst fig.*); (sich) entzünden (*a. fig. u.* ⚔).

inflamma|ble □ [in'flæməbl] entzündlich; feuergefährlich; ∼tion [inflə'meiʃən] Entzündung *f*; ∼tory [inflə'meiʃən] [in'flæmətəri] entzündlich; *fig.* aufrührerisch; hetzerisch; Hetz...

inflat|e [in'fleit] aufblasen, aufblähen (*a. fig.*); **~ion** [~eiʃən] Aufblähung *f*; † Inflation *f*; *fig.* Aufgeblasenheit *f*.

inflect [in'flekt] biegen; *gr.* flektieren, beugen.

inflexi|ble □ [in'fleksəbl] unbiegsam; *fig.* unbeugsam, **~on** [~kʃən] Biegung *f*; *gr.* Flexion *f*, Beugung *f*; Modulation *f*.

inflict [in'flikt] auferlegen; zufügen; *Hieb* versetzen; *Strafe* verhängen; **~ion** [~kʃən] Auferlegung *f*; Zufügung *f*; Plage *f*.

influen|ce ['influəns] **1.** Einfluß *m*; **2.** beeinflussen; **~tial** □ [influ-'enʃəl] einflußreich.

influenza ♂ [influ'enzə] Grippe *f*.

influx ['inflʌks] Einströmen *n*; *fig.* Zufluß *m*, (Zu)Strom *m*.

inform [in'fɔ:m] *v/t.* benachrichtigen, unterrichten (*of* von); *v/i.* anzeigen (*against* s.o. j.); **~al** □ [~ml] formlos, zwanglos; **~ality** [infɔ:-'mæliti] Formlosigkeit *f*; Formfehler *m*; **~ation** [infə'meiʃən] Auskunft *f*; Nachricht *f*, Information *f*; **~ative** [in'fɔ:mətiv] informatorisch; lehrreich; mitteilsam; **~er** [in'fɔ:mə] Denunziant *m*; Spitzel *m*.

infrequent [in'fri:kwənt] selten.

infringe [in'frindʒ] *a.* **~ upon** *Vertrag etc.* verletzen; übertreten.

infuriate [in'fjuərieit] wütend machen.

infuse [in'fju:z] einflößen; aufgießen.

ingen|ious □ [in'dʒi:njəs] geist-, sinnreich; erfinderisch; raffiniert; genial; **~uity** [indʒi'nju(:)iti] Genialität *f*; **~uous** □ [in'dʒenjuəs] freimütig; unbefangen, naiv.

ingot ['iŋgət] *Gold- etc.* Barren *m*.

ingrati|ate [in'greiʃieit]: **~ o.s.** sich beliebt machen (*with* bei); **~tude** [~rætitju:d] Undankbarkeit *f*.

ingredient [in'gri:djənt] Bestandteil *m*.

ingrowing ['ingrouiŋ] nach innen wachsend; eingewachsen.

inhabit [in'hæbit] bewohnen; **~able** [~təbl] bewohnbar; **~ant** [~ənt] Bewohner(in), Einwohner(in).

inhal|ation [inhə'leiʃən] Einatmung *f*; **~e** [in'heil] einatmen.

inherent □ [in'hiərənt] anhaftend; innewohnend, angeboren (*in dat.*).

inherit [in'herit] (er)erben; **~ance** [~təns] Erbteil *n*, Erbe *n*; Erbschaft *f*; *biol.* Vererbung *f*.

inhibit [in'hibit] (ver)hindern; verbieten; zurückhalten; **~ion** [inhi-'biʃən] Hemmung *f*; Verbot *n*.

inhospitable □ [in'hɔspitəbl] ungastlich, unwirtlich.

inhuman □ [in'hju:mən] unmenschlich.

inimical □ [i'nimikəl] feindlich; schädlich.

inimitable □ [i'nimitəbl] unnachahmlich.

iniquity [i'nikwiti] Ungerechtigkeit *f*; Schlechtigkeit *f*.

initia|l [i'niʃəl] **1.** □ Anfangs...; anfänglich; **2.** Antangsbuchstabe *m*; **~te 1.** [~ʃiit] Eingeweihte(r *m*) *f*; **2.** [~ieit] beginnen; anbahnen; einführen, einweihen; **~tion** [iniʃi-'eiʃən] Einleitung *f*; Einführung *f*, Einweihung *f*; **~ fee** *bsd. Am.* Aufnahmegebühr *f* (*Vereinigung*); **~tive** [i'niʃiətiv] Initiative *f*; einleitender Schritt; Entschlußkraft *f*; Unternehmungsgeist *m*; Volksbegehren *n*; **~tor** [~ieitə] Initiator *m*, Urheber *m*.

inject [in'dʒekt] einspritzen; **~ion** [~kʃən] Injektion *f*, Spritze *f*.

injudicious □ [indʒu(:)'diʃəs] unverständig, unklug, unüberlegt.

injunction [in'dʒʌŋkʃən] gerichtliche Verfügung; ausdrücklicher Befehl.

injur|e ['indʒə] (be)schädigen; schaden (*dat.*); verletzen; beleidigen; **~ious** [in'dʒuəriəs] schädlich; ungerecht; beleidigend; **~y** ['indʒəri] Unrecht *n*; Schaden *m*; Verletzung *f*; Beleidigung *f*.

injustice [in'dʒʌstis] Ungerechtigkeit *f*; Unrecht *n*.

ink [iŋk] **1.** Tinte *f*; *mst printer's* **~** Druckerschwärze *f*; *attr.* Tinten...; **2.** (mit Tinte) schwärzen; beklecksen.

inkling ['iŋkliŋ] Andeutung *f*; dunkle *od.* leise Ahnung.

ink|pot ['iŋkpot] Tintenfaß *n*; **~stand** Schreibzeug *n*; **~y** ['iŋki] tintig; Tinten...; tintenschwarz.

inland 1. ['inlənd] inländisch; Binnen...; **2.** [~] Landesinnere(s) *n*, Binnenland *n*; **3.** [in'lænd] landeinwärts.

inlay 1. ['in'lei] [*irr.* (*lay*)] einlegen; **2.** ['inlei] Einlage *f*; Einlegearbeit *f*.

inlet ['inlet] Bucht *f*; Einlaß *m*.

inmate ['inmeit] Insass|e *m*, -in *f*; Hausgenoss|e *m*, -in *f*.

inmost ['inmoust] innerst.

inn [in] Gasthof *m*, Wirtshaus *n*.

innate □ [i'neit] angeboren.

inner ['inə] inner, inwendig; geheim; **~most** innerst; geheimst.

innervate ['inə:veit] Nervenkraft geben (*dat.*); kräftigen.

innings ['iniŋz] *Sport:* Dransein *n*.

innkeeper ['inki:pə] Gastwirt(in).

innocen|ce [in'nəsns] Unschuld *f*; Harmlosigkeit *f*; Einfalt *f*; **~t** [~nt] **1.** □ unschuldig; harmlos; **2.** Unschuldige(r *m*) *f*; Einfältige(r *m*) *f*.

innocuous □ [i'nɔkjuəs] harmlos.

innovation [inou'veiʃən] Neuerung *f*.

innoxious □ [i'nɔkʃəs] unschädlich.

innuendo [inju(:)'endou] Andeutung *f.*

innumerable ☐ [i'nju:mərəbl] unzählbar, unzählig.

inoccupation ['inɔkju'peiʃən] Beschäftigungslosigkeit *f.*

inoculate [i'nɔkjuleit] (ein)impfen.

inoffensive [inə'fensiv] harmlos.

inofficial [inə'fiʃəl] inoffiziell.

inoperative [in'ɔpərətiv] unwirksam.

inopportune ☐ [in'ɔpətju:n] unangebracht, zur Unzeit.

inordinate ☐ [i'nɔ:dinit] unmäßig.

in-patient ['inpeiʃənt] Krankenhauspatient *m*, stationärer Patient.

inquest 𝔱𝔥 ['inkwest] Untersuchung *f*; coroner's ~ Leichenschau *f.*

inquir|e [in'kwaiə] fragen, sich erkundigen (*of* bei *j-m*); ~ into untersuchen; **~ing** ☐ [~əriŋ] forschend; **~y** [~ri] Erkundigung *f*, Nachfrage *f*; Untersuchung *f*; Ermittlung *f.*

inquisit|ion [inkwi'ziʃən] Untersuchung *f*; **~ive** ☐ [in'kwizitiv] neugierig; wißbegierig.

inroad ['inroud] *feindlicher* Einfall; Ein-, Übergriff *m.*

insan|e ☐ [in'sein] wahnsinnig; **~ity** [in'sæniti] Wahnsinn *m.*

insatia|ble ☐ [in'seiʃjəbl], **~te** [~ʃiit] unersättlich (*of* nach).

inscribe [in'skraib] ein-, auf-, beschreiben; beschriften; *fig.* einprägen (*in, on dat.*); *Buch* widmen.

inscription [in'skripʃən] In-, Aufschrift *f*; ✝ Eintragung *f.*

inscrutable ☐ [in'skru:təbl] unerforschlich, unergründlich.

insect ['insekt] Insekt *n*; **~icide** [in-'sektisaid] Insektengift *n.*

insecure ☐ [insi'kjuə] unsicher.

insens|ate [in'senseit] gefühllos; unvernünftig; **~ible** ☐ [~səbl] unempfindlich; bewußtlos; unmerklich; gleichgültig; **~itive** [~sitiv] unempfindlich.

inseparable ☐ [in'sepərəbl] untrennbar; unzertrennlich.

insert 1. [in'sə:t] einsetzen, einschalten, einfügen; (hinein)stecken; *Münze* einwerfen; inserieren; 2. ['insə:t] Bei-, Einlage *f*; **~ion** [in'sə:ʃən] Einsetzung *f*, Einfügung *f*, Eintragung *f*; Einwurf *m e-r Münze*; Anzeige *f*, Inserat *n.*

inshore ⚓ ['in'ʃɔ:] *an od.* nahe der Küste (befindlich); Küsten...

inside [in'said] 1. Innenseite *f*; Innere(s) *n*; turn ~ out umkrempeln; auf den Kopf stellen; 2. *adj.* inner, inwendig; Innen...; 3. *adv.* im Innern; 4. *prp.* innerhalb.

insidious ☐ [in'sidiəs] heimtückisch.

insight ['insait] Einsicht *f*, Einblick *m.*

insignia [in'signiə] *pl.* Abzeichen *n/pl.*, Insignien *pl.*

insignificant [insig'nifikənt] bedeutungslos; unbedeutend.

insincere ☐ [insin'siə] unaufrichtig.

insinuat|e [in'sinjueit] unbemerkt hineinbringen; zu verstehen geben; andeuten; **~ion** [insinju'eiʃən] Einschmeichelung *f*; Anspielung *f*, Andeutung *f*; Wink *m.*

insipid [in'sipid] geschmacklos, fad.

insist [in'sist]: ~ (up)on bestehen auf (*dat.*); dringen auf (*acc.*); **~ence** [~təns] Bestehen *n*; Beharrlichkeit *f*; Drängen *n*; **~ent** ☐ [~nt] beharrlich; eindringlich.

insolent ☐ ['insələnt] unverschämt.

insoluble ☐ [in'sɔljubl] unlöslich.

insolvent [in'sɔlvənt] zahlungsunfähig. [keit *f.*]

insomnia [in'sɔmniə] Schlaflosig-ͭ

insomuch [insou'mʌtʃ]: ~ that dermaßen *od.* so sehr, daß.

inspect [in'spekt] untersuchen, prüfen, nachsehen; **~ion** [~kʃən] Prüfung *f*, Untersuchung *f*; Inspektion *f*; **~or** [~ktə] Aufsichtsbeamte(r) *m.*

inspir|ation [inspə'reiʃən] Einatmung *f*; Eingebung *f*; Begeisterung *f*; **~e** [in'spaiə] einatmen; *fig.* eingeben, erfüllen; *j-n* begeistern.

install [in'stɔ:l] einsetzen; (sich) niederlassen; ⊕ installieren; **~ation** [instə'leiʃən] Einsetzung *f*; ⊕ Installation *f*, Einrichtung *f*, ⚡ *etc.* Anlage *f.*

instal(l)ment [in'stɔ:lmənt] Rate *f*; Teil-, Ratenzahlung *f*; (Teil)Lieferung *f*; Fortsetzung *f.*

instance ['instəns] Ersuchen *n*; Beispiel *n*; (*besonderer*) Fall; 𝔱𝔥 Instanz *f*; for ~ zum Beispiel.

instant ☐ ['instənt] 1. dringend; sofortig; on the 10th ~ am 10. dieses Monats; 2. Augenblick *m*; **~aneous** ☐ [instən'teinjəs] augenblicklich; Moment...; **~ly** ['instəntli] sogleich.

instead [in'sted] dafür; ~ of anstatt.

instep ['instep] Spann *m.*

instigat|e ['instigeit] anstiften; aufhetzen; **~or** [~tə] Anstifter *m*, Hetzer *m.*

instil(l) [in'stil] einträufeln; *fig.* einflößen (*into dat.*).

instinct ['instiŋkt] Instinkt *m*; **~ive** ☐ [in'stiŋktiv] instinktiv.

institut|e ['institju:t] 1. Institut *n*; 2. einsetzen, stiften, einrichten; anverordnen; **~ion** [insti'tju:ʃən] Einsetzung *f*, Einrichtung *f*; An-, Verordnung *f*; Satzung *f*; Institut(ion *f*) *n*; Gesellschaft *f*; Anstalt *f*; **~ional** [~nl] Instituts..., Anstalts...

instruct [in'strʌkt] unterrichten; belehren; *j-n* anweisen; **~ion** [~kʃən] Vorschrift *f*; Unterweisung *f*; Anweisung *f*; **~ive** ☐ [~ktiv] lehrreich; **~or** [~tə] Lehrer *m*; Ausbilder *m*; *Am. univ.* Dozent *m.*

instrument ['instrumənt] Instrument *n*, Werkzeug *n* (*a. fig.*); ɟɪ̃ɟɟ Urkunde *f*; ~al □ [instru'mentl] als Werkzeug dienend; dienlich; ♪ Instrumental...; ~ality [instrumen-'tæliti] Mitwirkung *f*, Mittel *n*.

insubordinat|e [insə'bɔ:dnit] auf-sässig; ~ion ['insəbɔːdi'neiʃən] Auflehnung *f*.

insubstantial [insəb'stænʃəl] unwirklich; gebrechlich.

insufferable □ [in'sʌfərəbl] unerträglich, unausstehlich.

insufficient □ [insə'fiʃənt] unzulänglich, ungenügend.

insula|r □ ['insjulə] Insel...; *fig.* engstirnig; ~te [~leit] isolieren; ~tion [insju'leiʃən] Isolierung *f*.

insult 1. ['insʌlt] Beleidigung *f*; **2.** [in'sʌlt] beleidigen.

insupportable □ [insə'pɔːtəbl] unerträglich, unausstehlich.

insur|ance [in'ʃuərəns] Versicherung *f*; *attr.* Versicherungs...; ~ance policy Versicherungspolice *f*, -schein *m*; ~e [in'ʃuə] versichern.

insurgent [in'sɔːdʒənt] **1.** aufrührerisch; **2.** Aufrührer *m*.

insurmountable □ [insə(ː)'mauntəbl] unübersteigbar, *fig.* unüberwindlich.

insurrection [insə'rekʃən] Aufstand *m*, Empörung *f*.

intact [in'tækt] unberührt; unversehrt.

intangible □ [in'tændʒəbl] unfühlbar; unfaßbar; unantastbar.

integ|ral □ ['intigrəl] ganz, vollständig; wesentlich; ~rate [~reit] ergänzen; zs.-tun; einfügen; ~rity [in'tegriti] Vollständigkeit *f*; Redlichkeit *f*, Integrität *f*.

intellect ['intilekt] Verstand *m*; *konkr. die* Intelligenz; ~ual [inti-'lektjuəl] **1.** □ intellektuell; Verstandes...; geistig; verständlich; **2.** Intellektuelle(r *m*) *f*.

intelligence [in'telidʒəns] Intelligenz *f*; Verstand *m*; Verständnis *n*; Nachricht *f*, Auskunft *f*; ~ department Nachrichtendienst *m*.

intellig|ent □ [in'telidʒənt] intelligent; klug; ~ible □ [~dʒəbl] verständlich (*to* für).

intempera|nce [in'tempərəns] Unmäßigkeit *f*; Trunksucht *f*; ~te □ [~rit] unmäßig; zügellos; unbeherrscht; trunksüchtig.

intend [in'tend] beabsichtigen, wollen; ~ *for* bestimmen für *od.* zu; ~ed **1.** absichtlich; beabsichtigt, *a.* zukünftig; **2.** F Verlobte(r *m*) *f*.

intense □ [in'tens] intensiv; angestrengt; heftig; kräftig (*Farbe*).

intensify [in'tensifai] (sich) verstärken *od.* steigern.

intensity [in'tensiti] Intensität *f*.

intent [in'tent] **1.** □ gespannt; bedacht; beschäftigt (*on* mit); **2.** Absicht *f*; Vorhaben *n*; *to all* ~s and

purposes in jeder Hinsicht; ~ion [~nʃən] Absicht *f*; Zweck *m*; ~ional □ [~nl] absichtlich; ~ness [~ntnis] gespannte Aufmerksamkeit; Eifer *m*.

inter [in'tə:] beerdigen, begraben.

inter... ['intə(:)] zwischen; Zwischen...; gegenseitig, einander.

interact [intər'ækt] sich gegenseitig beeinflussen.

intercede [intə(:)'si:d] vermitteln.

intercept [intə(:)'sept] ab-, auffangen; abhören; aufhalten; unterbrechen; ~ion [~pʃən] Ab-, Auffangen *n*; Ab-, Mithören *n*; Unterbrechung *f*; Aufhalten *n*.

intercess|ion [intə'seʃən] Fürbitte *f*; ~or [~esə] Fürsprecher *m*.

interchange 1. [intə(:)'tʃeindʒ] *v/t.* austauschen, auswechseln; *v/i.* abwechseln; **2.** ['intə(:)'tʃeindʒ] Austausch *m*; Abwechs(e)lung *f*.

intercourse ['intə(:)kɔːs] Verkehr *m*.

interdict 1. [intə(:)'dikt] untersagen, verbieten (*s.th.* to s.o.; *s.o.* from doing j-m zu tun); **2.** ['intə(:)-dikt], ~ion [intə(:)'dikʃən] Verbot *n*; Interdikt *n*.

interest ['intrist] **1.** Interesse *n*; Anziehungskraft *f*; Bedeutung *f*; Nutzen *m*; ✝ Anteil *m*, Beteiligung *f*, Kapital *n*; Zins(en *pl.*) *m*; ~s *pl.* Interessenten *m/pl.*, Kreise *m/pl.*; *take an* ~ *in* sich interessieren für; *return a blow with* ~ noch heftiger zurückschlagen; *banking* ~s *pl.* Bankkreise *m/pl.*; **2.** *allg.* interessieren (*in* für *et.*); ~ing [~tiŋ] interessant.

interfere [intə'fiə] sich einmischen (*with* in *acc.*); vermitteln; (*ea.*) stören; ~nce [~ərəns] Einmischung *f*; Beeinträchtigung *f*; Störung *f*.

interim ['intərim] **1.** Zwischenzeit *f*; **2.** vorläufig; Interims...

interior [in'tiəriə] **1.** □ inner; innerlich; Innen...; ~ *decorator* Innenarchitekt *m*; Maler *m*, Tapezierer *m*; **2.** Innere(s) *n*; Interieur *n*; *pol.* innere Angelegenheiten; *Department of the* ♀ *Am.* Innenministerium *n*.

interjection [intə(:)'dʒekʃən] Ausruf *m*.

interlace [intə(:)'leis] *v/t.* durchflechten, -weben; *v/i.* sich kreuzen.

interlock [intə(:)'lɔk] in-ea.-greifen; in-ea.-schlingen; in-ea.-haken.

interlocut|ion [intə(:)lou'kju:ʃən] Unterredung *f*; ~or [~ə(:)'lɔkjutə] Gesprächspartner *m*.

interlope [intə(:)'loup] sich eindrängen; ~r ['intə(:)loupə] Eindringling *m*.

interlude ['intə(:)lu:d] Zwischenspiel *n*; Zwischenzeit *f*; ~s of bright weather zeitweilig schön.

intermarriage [intə(:)'mæridʒ] Mischehe *f*.

intermeddle [intə(:)'medl] sich einmischen (*with*, in in *acc.*).

intermedia|ry [intə(:)'mi:djəri]
1. = *intermediate*; vermittelnd;
2. Vermittler *m*; ~**te** □ [~ət] in der Mitte liegend; Mittel..., Zwischen...; ~**range** *ballistic missile* Mittelstreckenrakete *f*; ~ *school Am.* Mittelschule *f*.

interment [in'tə:mənt] Beerdigung *f*.

interminable □ [in'tə:minəbl] endlos, unendlich.

intermingle [intə(:)'miŋgl] (sich) vermischen.

intermission [intə(:)'miʃən] Aussetzen *n*, Unterbrechung *f*; Pause *f*.

intermit [intə(:)'mit] unterbrechen, aussetzen; ~**tent** □ [~tənt] aussetzend; ~ *fever* 𝔰 Wechselfieber *n*.

intermix [intə(:)'miks] (sich) vermischen.

intern[1] [in'tə:n] internieren.

intern[2] ['intə:n] Assistenzarzt *m*.

internal □ [in'tə:nl] inner(lich); inländisch.

international □ [intə(:)'næʃənl] international; ~ *law* Völkerrecht *n*.

interphone ['intəfoun] Haustelephon *n*; *Am.* 🕮 Bordsprechanlage *f*.

interpolate [in'tə:pouleit] einschieben.

interpose [intə(:)'pouz] *v/t. Veto* einlegen; *Wort* einwerfen; *v/i.* dazwischentreten; vermitteln.

interpret [in'tə:prit] auslegen, erklären, interpretieren; (ver)dolmetschen; darstellen; ~**ation** [intə:pri'teiʃən] Auslegung *f*; Darstellung *f*; ~**er** [in'tə:pritə] Ausleger (-in); Dolmetscher(in); Interpret (-in).

interrogat|e [in'terəgeit] (be-, aus-) fragen; verhören; ~**ion** [interə'geiʃən] (Be-, Aus)Fragen *n*, Verhör(en) *n*; Frage *f*; *note od. mark od. point of* ~ Fragezeichen *n*; ~**ive** □ [intə'rɔgətiv] fragend; Frage...

interrupt [intə'rʌpt] unterbrechen; ~**ion** [~pʃən] Unterbrechung *f*.

intersect [intə(:)'sekt] (sich) schneiden; ~**ion** [~kʃən] Durchschnitt *m*; Schnittpunkt *m*; Straßen- *etc.* Kreuzung *f*.

intersperse [intə(:)'spə:s] einstreuen; untermengen, durchsetzen.

interstate *Am.* [intə(:)'steit] zwischenstaatlich.

intertwine [intə(:)'twain] verflechten.

interval ['intəvəl] Zwischenraum *m*; Pause *f*; (Zeit)Abstand *m*.

interven|e [intə(:)'vi:n] dazwischenkommen; sich einmischen; einschreiten; dazwischenliegen; ~**tion** [~'venʃən] Dazwischenkommen *n*; Einmischung *f*; Vermitt(e)lung *f*.

interview ['intəvju:] **1.** Zusammenkunft *f*, Unterredung *f*; Interview *n*; **2.** interviewen.

intestine [in'testin] **1.** inner; **2.** Darm *m*; ~**s** *pl.* Eingeweide *n/pl.*

intima|cy ['intiməsi] Intimität *f*, Vertraulichkeit *f*; ~**te 1.** [~meit] bekanntgeben; zu verstehen geben; **2.** □ [~mit] intim; **3.** [~] Vertraute(r *m*) *f*; ~**tion** [inti'meiʃən] Andeutung *f*, Wink *m*; Ankündigung *f*.

intimidate [in'timideit] einschüchtern.

into *prp.* ['intu, *vor Konsonant* 'intə] in (*acc.*), in ... hinein.

intolera|ble □ [in'tɔlərəbl] unerträglich; ~**nt** □ [~ənt] unduldsam, intolerant.

intonation [intou'neiʃən] Anstimmen *n*; *gr.* Intonation *f*, Tonfall *m*.

intoxica|nt [in'tɔksikənt] **1.** berauschend; **2.** berauschendes Getränk; ~**te** [~keit] berauschen (*a. fig.*); ~**tion** [intɔksi'keiʃən] Rausch *m* (*a. fig.*).

intractable □ [in'træktəbl] unlenksam, störrisch; schwer zu bändigen(d).

intransitive □ *gr.* [in'trænsitiv] intransitiv.

intrastate *Am.* [intrə'steit] innerstaatlich.

intrench [in'trentʃ] = *entrench*.

intrepid [in'trepid] unerschrocken.

intricate □ ['intrikit] verwickelt.

intrigue [in'tri:g] **1.** Ränkespiel *n*, Intrige *f*; (Liebes)Verhältnis *n*; **2.** *v/i.* Ränke schmieden, intrigieren; ein (Liebes)Verhältnis haben; *v/t.* neugierig machen; ~**r** [~gə] Intrigant(in).

intrinsic(al □) [in'trinsik(əl)] inner(lich); wirklich, wahr.

introduc|e [intrə'dju:s] einführen (*a. fig.*); bekannt machen (*to* mit), vorstellen (*to j-m*); einleiten; ~**tion** [~'dʌkʃən] Einführung *f*; Einleitung *f*; Vorstellung *f*; *letter of* ~ Empfehlungsschreiben *n*; ~**tory** [~ktəri] einleitend, einführend.

introspection [introu'spekʃən] Selbstprüfung *f*; Selbstbetrachtung *f*.

introvert 1. [introu'və:t] einwärtskehren; **2.** *psych.* [~] ['introuvə:t] nach innen gekehrter Mensch.

intru|de [in'tru:d] hineinzwängen; (sich) ein- *od.* aufdrängen; ~**der** [~də] Eindringling *m*; ~**sion** [~u:ʒən] Eindringen *n*; Auf-, Zudringlichkeit *f*; ~**sive** □ [~u:siv] zudringlich.

intrust [in'trʌst] = *entrust*.

intuition [intju(:)'iʃən] unmittelbare Erkenntnis, Intuition *f*.

inundate ['inʌndeit] überschwemmen.

inure [i'njuə] gewöhnen (*to an acc.*).

invade [in'veid] eindringen in, ein-

fallen in (*acc.*); *fig.* befallen; ~r [~də] Angreifer *m*; Eindringling *m*.
invalid[1] ['invəli:d] **1.** dienstunfähig; kränklich; **2.** Invalide *m*.
invalid[2] [in'vælid] (rechts)ungültig; ~ate [~deit] entkräften; ⚕ ungültig machen. [~ɒchätzbar.|
invaluable □ [in'væljuəbl] un-⎰
invariab|le □ [in'vɛəriəbl] unver-änderlich; ~ly [~li] ausnahmslos.
invasion [in'veiʒən] Einfall *m*, Angriff *m*, Invasion *f*; Eingriff *m*; ⚔ Anfall *m*.
invective [in'vektiv] Schmähung *f*, Schimpfrede *f*, Schimpfwort *n*.
inveigh [in'vei] schimpfen (*against* über, auf *acc.*).
inveigle [in'vi:gl] verleiten.
invent [in'vent] erfinden; ~ion [~nʃən] Erfindung(sgabe) *f*; ~ive □ [~ntiv] erfinderisch; ~or [~tə] Erfinder(in); ~ory ['invəntri] **1.** Inventar *n*; Inventur *f*; **2.** inventarisieren.
invers|e □ ['in'və:s] umgekehrt; ~ion [in'və:ʃən] Umkehrung *f*; *gr.* Inversion *f*.
invert [in'və:t] umkehren; umstellen; ~ed *commas pl.* Anführungszeichen *n/pl.*
invest [in'vest] investieren, anlegen; bekleiden; ausstatten; umgeben (*with* von); ✠ belagern.
investigat|e [in'vestigeit] erforschen; untersuchen; nachforschen; ~ion [investi'geiʃən] Erforschung *f*; Untersuchung *f*; Nachforschung *f*; ~or [in'vestigeitə] Untersuchende(r *m*) *f*.
invest|ment ✠ [in'vestmənt] Kapitalanlage *f*; Investition *f*; ~or [~tə] Geldgeber *m*.
inveterate [in'vetərit] eingewurzelt.
invidious □ [in'vidiəs] verhaßt; gehässig; beneidenswert.
invigorate [in'vigəreit] kräftigen.
invincible □ [in'vinsəbl] unbesiegbar; unüberwindlich.
inviola|ble □ [in'vaiələbl] unverletzlich; ~te [~lit] unverletzt.
invisible [in'vizəbl] unsichtbar.
invit|ation [invi'teiʃən] Einladung *f*, Aufforderung *f*; ~e [in'vait] einladen; auffordern; (an)locken.
invoice ✠ ['invɔis] Faktura *f*, Warenrechnung *f*.
invoke [in'vouk] anrufen; zu Hilfe rufen (*acc.*); sich berufen auf (*acc.*); *Geist* heraufbeschwören.
involuntary □ [in'vɔləntəri] unfreiwillig; unwillkürlich.
involve [in'vɔlv] verwickeln, hineinziehen; in sich schließen, enthalten; mit sich bringen; ~ment [~vmənt] Verwicklung *f*; (*bsd.* Geld)Schwierigkeit *f*.
invulnerable □ [in'vʌlnərəbl] unverwundbar; *fig.* unanfechtbar.

inward ['inwəd] **1.** □ inner(lich); **2.** *adv. mst* ~s einwärts; nach innen; **3.** ~s *pl.* Eingeweide *n/pl.*
iodine ['aiədi:n] Jod *n*.
IOU ['aiou'ju:] (= *I owe you*) Schuldschein *m*.
irascible □ [i'ræsibl] jähzornig.
irate [ai'reit] zornig, wütend.
iridescent [iri'desnt] schillernd.
iris ['aiəris] *anat.* Regenbogenhaut *f*, Iris *f*; ⚘ Schwertlilie *f*.
Irish ['aiəriʃ] **1.** irisch; **2.** Irisch *n*; *the* ~ *pl.* die Iren *pl.*; ~man Ire *m*.
irksome ['ə:ksəm] lästig, ermüdend.
iron ['aiən] **1.** Eisen *n*; *a.* flat-~ Bügeleisen *n*; ~s *pl.* Fesseln *f/pl.*; *strike while the* ~ *is hot fig.* das Eisen schmieden, solange es heiß ist; **2.** eisern (*a. fig.*); Eisen...; **3.** bügeln; in Eisen legen; ~bound eisenbeschlagen; felsig; unbeugsam; ~clad **1.** gepanzert; **2.** Panzerschiff *n*; ~curtain *pol.* eiserner Vorhang; ~hearted *fig.* hartherzig.
ironic(al □) [ai'rɔnik(əl)] ironisch, spöttisch.
iron|ing ['aiəniŋ] Plätten *n*, Bügeln *n*; *attr.* Plätt..., Bügel...; ~ lung ⚙ eiserne Lunge; ~monger Eisenhändler *m*; ~mongery [~əri] Eisenwaren *f/pl.*; ~mo(u)ld Rostfleck *m*; ~work schmiedeeiserne Arbeit; ~works *mst sg.* Eisenhütte *f*.
irony[1] ['aiəni] eisenartig, -haltig.
irony[2] ['aiərəni] Ironie *f*.
irradiant [i'reidjənt] strahlend (*with* vor *Freude etc.*).
irradiate [i'reidieit] bestrahlen (*a.* ⚙); *fig.* aufklären; strahlen lassen.
irrational [i'ræʃənl] unvernünftig.
irreclaimable □ [iri'kleiməbl] unverbesserlich.
irrecognizable □ [i'rekəgnaizəbl] nicht (wieder)erkennbar.
irreconcilable □ [i'rekənsailəbl] unversöhnlich; unvereinbar.
irrecoverable □ [iri'kʌvərəbl] unersetzlich; unwiederbringlich.
irredeemable □ [iri'di:məbl] unkündbar; nicht einlösbar; unersetzlich.
irrefutable □ [i'refjutəbl] unwiderleglich, unwiderlegbar.
irregular □ [i'regjulə] unregelmäßig, regelwidrig; ungleichmäßig.
irrelevant □ [i'relivənt] nicht zur Sache gehörig; unzutreffend; unerheblich, belanglos (*to* für).
irreligious □ [iri'lidʒəs] gottlos.
irremediable □ [iri'mi:djəbl] unheilbar; unersetzlich.
irremovable □ [iri'mu:vəbl] nicht entfernbar; unabsetzbar.
irreparable □ [i'repərəbl] nicht wieder gutzumachen(d).
irreplaceable [iri'pleisəbl] unersetzlich.
irrepressible □ [iri'presəbl] ununterdrückbar; unbezähmbar.

irreproachable □ [iri'proutʃəbl] einwandfrei, untadelig.
irresistible □ [iri'zistəbl] unwiderstehlich.
irresolute □ [i'rezəlu:t] unentschlossen.
irrespective □ [iris'pektiv] (of) rücksichtslos (gegen); ohne Rücksicht (auf acc.); unabhängig (von).
irresponsible □ [iris'pɔnsəbl] unverantwortlich; verantwortungslos.
irretrievable □ [iri'tri:vəbl] unwiederbringlich, unersetzlich; nicht wieder gutzumachen(d).
irreverent □ [i'revərənt] respektlos, ehrfurchtslos.
irrevocable □ [i'revəkəbl] unwiderruflich; unabänderlich, endgültig.
irrigate [i'irigeit] bewässern.
irrita|ble □ ['iritəbl] reizbar; ~nt [~ənt] Reizmittel n; ~te [~teit] reizen; ärgern; ~ting □ [~tiŋ] aufreizend; ärgerlich (Sache); ~tion [iri'teiʃən] Reizung f; Gereiztheit f, Ärger m.
irrupt|ion [i'rʌpʃən] Einbruch m (mst fig.); ~ive [~ptiv] (her)einbrechend.
is [iz] 3. sg. pres. von be.
island ['ailənd] Insel f; Verkehrsinsel f; ~er [~də] Inselbewohner(in).
isle [ail] Insel f; ~t [ail] Inselchen n.
isolat|e ['aisəleit] absondern; isolieren; ~ed abgeschieden; ~ion [aisə'leiʃən] Isolierung f, Absonderung f; ~ ward ⚕ Isolierstation f; ~ionist Am. pol. [~ʃnist] Isolationist m.
issue ['isju:, Am. 'iʃu:] 1. Herauskommen n, Herausfließen n; Abfluß m; Ausgang m; Nachkommen (-schaft f) m/pl.; fig. Ausgang m, Ergebnis n; Streitfrage f; Ausgabe f v. Material etc., Erlaß m v. Befehlen; Ausgabe f, Exemplar n; Nummer f e-r Zeitung; ~ in law Rechtsfrage f; be at ~ uneinig sein; point at ~ strittiger Punkt; 2. v/i. herauskommen; herkommen, entspringen; endigen (in in acc.); v/t. von sich geben; Material etc. ausgeben; Befehl erlassen; Buch herausgeben.
isthmus ['isməs] Landenge f.
it [it] 1. es; nach prp. da... (z.B. by ~ dadurch; for ~ dafür); 2. das gewisse Etwas.
Italian [i'tæljən] 1. italienisch; 2. Italiener(in); Italienisch n.
italics typ. [i'tæliks] Kursivschrift f.
itch [itʃ] 1. 🅐 Krätze f; Jucken n; Verlangen n; 2. jucken; be ~ing to inf. darauf brennen, zu inf.; have an ~ing palm raffgierig sein; ~ing ['itʃiŋ] 1. juckend; n; fig. Gelüste n.
item ['aitem] 1. desgleichen; 2. Einzelheit f, Punkt m; Posten m; (Zeitungs)Artikel m; ~ize [~maiz] einzeln angeben od. aufführen.
iterate ['itəreit] wiederholen.
itiner|ant □ [i'tinərənt] reisend; umherziehend; Reise...; ~ary [ai'tinərəri] Reiseroute f, -plan m; Reisebericht m; attr. Reise...
its [its] sein(e); dessen, deren.
itself [it'self] (es, sich) selbst; sich; of ~ von selbst; in ~ an sich, an sich; by ~ für sich allein, besonders.
ivory ['aivəri] Elfenbein n.
ivy ♀ ['aivi] Efeu m.

J

jab F [dʒæb] 1. stechen; stoßen; 2. Stich m, Stoß m.
jabber ['dʒæbə] plappern.
jack [dʒæk] 1. Hebevorrichtung f, bsd. Wagenheber m; Malkugel f beim Bowlspiel; ⚓ Gösch f, kleine Flagge; Karten: Bube m; 2. a. ~ up aufbocken. [Handlanger m.]
jackal ['dʒækɔ:l] zo. Schakal m; fig.]
jack|ass ['dʒækæs] Esel m (a. fig.); ~boots Reitstiefel m/pl.; hohe Wasserstiefel m/pl.; ~daw orn. Dohle f.
jacket ['dʒækit] Jacke f; ⊕ Mantel m; Schutzumschlag m e-s Buches.
jack|-knife ['dʒæknaif] (großes) Klappmesser n; ♀ of all trades Hansdampf in allen Gassen; ♀ of all work Faktotum n; ~pot Poker: Einsatz m; hit the ~ Am. F großes Glück haben.
jade [dʒeid] (Schind)Mähre f, Klepper m; contp. Frauenzimmer n.
jag [dʒæg] Zacken m; sl. Sauferei f; ~ged ['dʒægid] zackig; gekerbt; bsd. Am. sl. voll (betrunken).
jaguar zo. ['dʒægjuə] Jaguar m.
jail [dʒeil] 1. Kerker m; 2. einkerkern; ~bird ['dʒeilbə:d] F Knastbruder m; Galgenvogel m; ~er ['dʒeilə] Kerkermeister m.
jalop(p)y coll. Am. F mot., ✈ [dʒə'lɔpi] Kiste f.
jam¹ [dʒæm] Marmelade f.
jam² [~] 1. Gedränge n; ⊕ Hemmung f; Radio: Störung f; traffic ~ Verkehrsstockung f; be in a ~ sl. in der Klemme sein; 2. (sich) (fest-, ver)klemmen; pressen, quetschen; versperren; Radio: stören; ~ the brakes mit aller Kraft bremsen.
jamboree [dʒæmbə'ri:] (bsd. Pfadfinder)Treffen n; sl. Vergnügen n, Fez m.

jangle ['dʒæŋgl] schrillen (lassen); laut streiten, keifen.

janitor ['dʒænitə] Portier *m*.

January ['dʒænjuəri] Januar *m*.

Japanese [dʒæpə'ni:z] **1.** japanisch; **2.** Japaner(in); Japanisch *n*; the ~ *pl.* die Japaner *pl.*

jar [dʒɑ:] **1.** Krug *m*; Topf *m*; Glas *n*; Knarren *n*, Mißton *m*; Streit *m*; mißliche Lage; **2.** knarren; unangenehm berühren; erzittern (lassen); streiten.

jaundice ['dʒɔ:ndis] Gelbsucht *f*; ~d [~st] gelbsüchtig; *fig.* neidisch.

jaunt [dʒɔ:nt] **1.** Ausflug *m*, Spritztour *f*; **2.** e-n Ausflug machen; ~y [] ['dʒɔ:nti] munter; flott.

javelin ['dʒævlin] Wurfspeer *m*.

jaw [dʒɔ:] Kinnbacken *m*, Kiefer *m*; ~s *pl.* Rachen *m*; Maul *n*; Schlund *m*; ⊕ Backen *f/pl.*; ~-bone ['dʒɔ:boun] Kieferknochen *m*.

jay *orn.* [dʒei] Eichelhäher *m*; ~walker *Am.* F ['dʒeiwɔ:kə] achtlos die Straße überquerender Fußgänger.

jazz [dʒæz] **1.** Jazz *m*; **2.** F grell.

jealous [] ['dʒeləs] eifersüchtig; besorgt (of um); neidisch; ~y [~si] Eifersucht *f*; Neid *m*.

jeans [dʒi:nz] *pl.* Jeans *pl.*, Niet(en)hose *f*.

jeep [dʒi:p] Jeep *m*.

jeer [dʒiə] **1.** Spott *m*, Spötterei *f*; **2.** spotten (*at* über *acc.*); (ver-)höhnen.

jejune [] [dʒi'dʒu:n] nüchtern, fad.

jelly ['dʒeli] **1.** Gallert(e *f*) *n*; Gelee *n*; **2.** gelieren; ~-fish *zo.* Qualle *f*.

jeopardize ['dʒepədaiz] gefährden.

jerk [dʒə:k] **1.** Ruck *m*; (Muskel-)Krampf *m*; **2.** rucken *od.* zerren (an *dat.*); schnellen; schleudern; ~water *Am.* ['dʒə:kwɔ:tə] **1.** 🚂 Nebenbahn *f*; **2.** F klein, unbedeutend; ~y ['dʒə:ki] **1.** [] ruckartig; holperig; **2.** *Am.* luftgetrocknetes Rindfleisch.

jersey ['dʒə:zi] Wollpullover *m*; wollenes Unterhemd.

jest [dʒest] **1.** Spaß *m*; **2.** scherzen; ~er ['dʒestə] Spaßmacher *m*.

jet [dʒet] **1.** (Wasser-, Gas)Strahl *m*; Strahlrohr *n*; ⊕ Düse *f*; Düsenflugzeug *n*; Düsenmotor *m*; **2.** hervorsprudeln; ~-propelled ['dʒetprəpeld] mit Düsenantrieb.

jetty ⚓ ['dʒeti] Mole *f*; Pier *m*...

Jew [dʒu:] Jude *m*; *attr.* Juden...

jewel ['dʒu:əl] Juwel *m*, *n*; ~(l)er [~lə] Juwelier *m*; ~(le)ry [~lri] Juwelen *pl.*, Schmuck *m*.

Jew|ess ['dʒu:(:)is] Jüdin *f*; ~ish ['dʒu:(:)iʃ] jüdisch.

jib ⚓ ['dʒib] Klüver *m*.

jibe *Am.* F [dʒaib] zustimmen.

jiffy F ['dʒifi] Augenblick *m*.

jig-saw ['dʒigsɔ:] Laubsägema-

schine *f*; ~ puzzle Zusammensetzspiel *n*.

jilt [dʒilt] **1.** Kokette *f*; **2.** *Liebhaber* versetzen.

Jim [dʒim]: ~ Crow *Am.* Neger *m*; *Am.* Rassentrennung *f*.

jingle ['dʒiŋgl] **1.** Geklingel *n*; **2.** klingeln, klimpern (mit).

jitney *Am. sl.* ['dʒitni] 5-Cent-Stück *n*; billiger Omnibus.

jive *Am. sl.* [dʒaiv] *heiße* Jazzmusik; Jazzjargon *m*.

job [dʒɔb] **1.** (Stück *n*) Arbeit *f*; Sache *f*, Aufgabe *f*; Beruf *m*; Stellung *f*; by the ~ stückweise; im Akkord; ~ lot F Ramschware *f*; ~ work Akkordarbeit *f*; **2.** *v/t.* *Pferd etc.* (ver)mieten; † vermitteln; *v/i.* im Akkord arbeiten; Maklergeschäfte machen; ~ber ['dʒɔbə] Akkordarbeiter *m*; Makler *m*; Schieber *m*.

jockey ['dʒɔki] **1.** Jockei *m*; **2.** prellen.

jocose [] [dʒə'kous] scherzhaft, spaßig.

jocular [] ['dʒɔkjulə] lustig; spaßig.

jocund [] ['dʒɔkənd] lustig, fröhlich.

jog [dʒɔg] **1.** Stoß(en *n*) *m*; Rütteln *n*; Trott *m*; **2.** *v/t.* (an)stoßen, (auf-)rütteln; *v/i. mst* ~ along, ~ on dahintrotten, dahinschlendern.

John [dʒɔn]: ~ Bull John Bull (*der Engländer*); ~ Hancock *Am.* F Friedrich Wilhelm *m* (*Unterschrift*).

join [dʒɔin] **1.** *v/t.* verbinden, zs.-fügen (*to* mit); sich vereinigen mit, sich gesellen zu; eintreten in (*acc.*); ~ battle den Kampf beginnen; ~ hands die Hände falten; sich die Hände reichen (*a. fig.*); *v/i.* sich verbinden, sich vereinigen; ~ in mitmachen bei; ~ up Soldat werden; **2.** Verbindung(sstelle) *f*.

joiner ['dʒɔinə] Tischler *m*; ~y [~əri] Tischlerhandwerk *n*; Tischlerarbeit *f*.

joint [dʒɔint] **1.** Verbindung(sstelle) *f*; Scharnier *n*; *anat.* Gelenk *n*; ⚕ Knoten *m*; Braten *m*; *Am. sl.* Spelunke *f*; *put out of* ~ verrenken; **2.** [] gemeinsam; Mit...; ~ heir Miterbe *m*; ~ stock † Aktienkapital *n*; **3.** zs.-fügen; zerlegen; ~ed ['dʒɔintid] gegliedert; Glieder...; ~-stock † Aktien...; ~ company Aktiengesellschaft *f*.

jok|e [dʒouk] **1.** Scherz *m*, Spaß *m*; *practical* ~ Streich *m*; **2.** *v/i.* scherzen; schäkern; *v/t.* necken (*about* mit); ~er ['dʒoukə] Spaßvogel *m*; *Karten:* Joker *m*; *Am.* versteckte Klausel; ~y [] ['dʒouki] spaßig.

jolly ['dʒɔli] lustig, fidel; F nett.

jolt [dʒoult] **1.** stoßen, rütteln; holpern; **2.** Stoß *m*; Rütteln *n*.

Jonathan ['dʒɔnəθən]: *Brother* ~ *der Amerikaner*.

josh *Am. sl.* [dʒɔʃ] **1.** Ulk *m*; **2.** aufziehen, auf die Schippe nehmen.

jostle ['dʒɔsl] **1.** anrennen; zs.-stoßen; **2.** Stoß *m*; Zs.-Stoß *m*.

jot [dʒɔt] **1.** Jota *n*, Pünktchen *n*; **2.** ~ *down* notieren.

journal ['dʒəːnl] Journal *n*; Tagebuch *n*; Tageszeitung *f*; Zeitschrift *f*; ⊕ Wellenzapfen *m*; **~ism** ['dʒəːnəlizəm] Journalismus *m*.

journey ['dʒəːni] **1.** Reise *f*; Fahrt *f*; **2.** reisen; **~man** Geselle *m*.

jovial □ ['dʒouvjəl] heiter; gemütlich.

joy [dʒɔi] Freude *f*; Fröhlichkeit *f*; **~ful** □ ['dʒɔiful] freudig; erfreut; fröhlich; **~less** □ ['dʒɔilis] freudlos; unerfreulich; **~ous** □ ['dʒɔiəs] freudig, fröhlich.

jubil|ant ['dʒuːbilənt] jubilierend, frohlockend; **~ate** [~leit] jubeln; **~ee** [~liː] Jubiläum *n*.

judge [dʒʌdʒ] **1.** Richter *m*; Schiedsrichter *m*; Beurteiler(in), Kenner(in); **2.** *v/i.* urteilen (*of* über *acc.*); *v/t.* richten; aburteilen; beurteilen (*by* nach); ansehen als.

judg(e)ment ['dʒʌdʒmənt] Urteil *n*; Urteilsspruch *m*; Urteilskraft *f*; Einsicht *f*; Meinung *f*; *göttliches* (Straf)Gericht; *Day of* ♀, ♀ *Day* Jüngstes Gericht.

judicature ['dʒuːdikətʃə] Gerichtshof *m*; Rechtspflege *f*.

judicial □ [dʒuː(ː)diʃəl] gerichtlich; Gerichts...; kritisch; unparteiisch.

judicious □ [dʒuː(ː)diʃəs] verständig, klug; **~ness** [~snis] Einsicht *f*.

jug [dʒʌg] Krug *m*, Kanne *f*.

juggle ['dʒʌgl] **1.** Trick *m*; Schwindel *m*; **2.** jonglieren (*a. fig.*); verfälschen; betrügen; **~r** [~lə] Jongleur *m*; Taschenspieler(in).

Jugoslav ['juːgou'slaːv] **1.** Jugoslaw|e *m*, -in *f*; **2.** jugoslawisch.

juic|e [dʒuːs] Saft *m*; *sl. mot.* Sprit *m*, Gas *n*; **~y** □ ['dʒuːsi] saftig; *F* interessant;   [sikautomat *m.*]

juke-box *Am.* F ['dʒuːkbɔks] Mu-

julep ['dʒuːlep] *süßes* (Arznei)Getränk; *bsd. Am.* alkoholisches Eisgetränk.

July [dʒuː(ː)'lai] Juli *m*.

jumble ['dʒʌmbl] **1.** Durcheinander *n*; **2.** *v/t.* durch-ea.-werfen; **~sale** Wohltätigkeitsbasar *m*.

jump [dʒʌmp] **1.** Sprung *m*; **~s** *pl.*

nervöses Zs.-fahren; *high* (*long*) ~ Hoch- (Weit)Sprung *m*; *get* (*have*) *the* ~ *on Am.* F zuvorkommen; **2.** *v/i.* (auf)springen; ~ *at* sich stürzen auf (*acc.*); ~ *to conclusions* übereilte Schlüsse ziehen; *v/t.* hinwegspringen über (*acc.*); überspringen; springen lassen; **~er** ['dʒʌmpə] Springer *m*; Jumper *m*; **~y** [~pi] nervös.

junct|ion ['dʒʌŋkʃən] Verbindung *f*; Kreuzung *f*; ⚡ Knotenpunkt *m*; **~ure** [~ktʃə] Verbindungspunkt *m*, -stelle *f*; (kritischer) Zeitpunkt; *at this* ~ bei diesem Stand der Dinge.

June [dʒuːn] Juni *m*.

jungle ['dʒʌŋgl] Dschungel *m*, *n*, *f*.

junior ['dʒuːnjə] **1.** jünger (*to* als); *Am. univ.* der Unterstufe (angehörend); ~ *high school Am.* Oberschule *f* mit Klassen 7, 8, 9; **2.** Jüngere(r *m*) *f*; *Am.* (Ober)Schüler *m od.* Student *m* im 3. Jahr; *F* Kleine(r) *m*.

junk [dʒʌŋk] ⚓ Dschunke *f*; Plunder *m*, alter Kram.

junket ['dʒʌŋkit] Quarkspeise *f*; *Am.* Party *f*; Vergnügungsfahrt *f*.

juris|diction [dʒuəris'dikʃən] Rechtsprechung *f*; Gerichtsbarkeit *f*; Gerichtsbezirk *m*; **~prudence** ['dʒuərispruː'dəns] Rechtswissenschaft *f*.

juror ['dʒuərə] Geschworene(r) *m*.

jury ['dʒuəri] *die* Geschworenen *pl.*; Jury *f*, Preisgericht *n*; **~man** Geschworene(r) *m*.

just □ [dʒʌst] **1.** *adj.* gerecht; rechtschaffen; **2.** *adv.* richtig; genau; (so)eben; nur; ~ *now* eben *od.* gerade jetzt.

justice ['dʒʌstis] Gerechtigkeit *f*; Richter *m*; Recht *n*; Rechtsverfahren *n*; *court of* ~ Gericht(shof *m*) *n*.

justification [dʒʌstifi'keiʃən] Rechtfertigung *f*.

justify ['dʒʌstifai] rechtfertigen.

justly ['dʒʌstli] mit Recht.

justness ['dʒʌstnis] Gerechtigkeit *f*, Billigkeit *f*; Rechtmäßigkeit *f*; Richtigkeit *f*.

jut [dʒʌt] *a.* ~ *out* hervorragen.

juvenile ['dʒuːvinail] **1.** jung, jugendlich; Jugend...; **2.** junger Mensch.

K

kale [keil] (bsd. Kraus-, Grün)Kohl m; Am. sl. Moos n (Geld).

kangaroo [kæŋgə'ru:] Känguruh n.

keel ⚓ [ki:l] 1. Kiel m; 2. ~ over od. kiel oben legen od. liegen; umschlagen.

keen □ [ki:n] scharf (a. fig.); eifrig, heftig; stark, groß (Appetit etc.); ~ on F scharf od. erpicht auf acc.; be ~ on hunting ein leidenschaftlicher Jäger sein; **~-edged** ['ki:ned3d] scharfgeschliffen; **~ness** ['ki:nnis] Schärfe f; Heftigkeit f; Scharfsinn m.

keep [ki:p] 1. (Lebens)Unterhalt m; for ~s F für immer; 2. [irr.] v/t. allg. halten; behalten; unterhalten; (er-) halten; einhalten; (ab)halten; Buch, Ware etc. führen; Bett etc. hüten; fest-, aufhalten; (bei)behalten; (auf)bewahren; ~ s.o. company j-m Gesellschaft leisten; ~ company with verkehren mit; ~ one's temper sich beherrschen; ~ time richtig gehen (Uhr); ♪, ✗ Takt, Schritt halten; ~ s.o. waiting j-n warten lassen; ~ away fernhalten; ~ s.th. from s.o. j-m et. vorenthalten; ~ in zurückhalten; Schüler nachsitzen lassen; ~ on Kleid anbehalten, Hut aufbehalten; ~ up aufrechterhalten; (Mut) bewahren; in Ordnung halten; hindern, zu Bett zu gehen; aufbleiben lassen; ~ it up (es) durchhalten; v/i. sich halten, bleiben; F sich aufhalten; ~ doing immer wieder tun; ~ away sich fernhalten; ~ from sich enthalten (gen.); ~ off sich fernhalten; ~ on talking fortfahren zu sprechen; ~ to sich halten an (acc.); ~ up sich aufrecht halten; sich aufrechterhalten; ~ up with Such halten mit; ~ up with the Joneses es den Nachbarn gleichtun.

keep|er ['ki:pə] Wärter m, Wächter m, Aufseher m; Verwalter m; Inhaber m; **~ing** ['ki:piŋ] Verwahrung f; Obhut f; Gewahrsam m, n; Unterhalt m; be in (out of) ~ with ... (nicht) übereinstimmen mit ...; **~sake** ['ki:pseik] Andenken n.

keg [keg] Fäßchen n.

kennel ['kenl] Gosse f, Rinnstein m; Hundehütte f, -zwinger m.

kept [kept] pret. u. p.p. von keep 2.

kerb [kə:b], **~stone** ['kə:bstoun] = curb etc.

kerchief ['kə:tʃif] (Kopf)Tuch n.

kernel ['kə:nl] Kern m (a. fig.); Hafer-, Mais- etc. Korn n.

kettle ['ketl] Kessel m; **~drum** ♪ Kesselpauke f.

key [ki:] 1. Schlüssel m (a. fig.); △ Schlußstein m; ⊕ Keil m; Schraubenschlüssel m; Klavier- etc. Taste f; ⚡ Taste f, Druck-

knopf m; ♪ Tonart f; fig. Ton m; 2. ~ up ♪ stimmen; erhöhen; fig. in erhöhte Spannung versetzen; **~board** ['ki:bɔ:d] Klaviatur f, Tastatur f; **~hole** Schlüsselloch n; **~man** Schlüsselfigur f; ~ **money** Ablösung f (für e-e Wohnung); **~note** ♪ Grundton m; **~stone** Schlußstein m; fig. Grundlage f.

kibitzer Am. F ['kibitsə] Kiebitz m, Besserwisser m.

kick [kik] 1. (Fuß)Tritt m; Stoß m; Schwung m; F Nervenkitzel m; get a ~ out of F Spaß finden an (dat.); 2. v/t. (mit dem Fuß) stoßen od. treten; Fußball: schießen; ~ out F hinauswerfen; v/i. (hinten) ausschlagen; stoßen (Gewehr); sich auflehnen; ~ in with Am. sl. Geld 'reinbuttern; ~ off Fußball: anstoßen; **~back** bsd. Am. F ['kikbæk] Rückzahlung f; **~er** ['kikə] Fußballspieler m.

kid [kid] 1. Zicklein n; sl. Kind n; Ziegenleder n; 2. sl. foppen; **~dy** sl. ['kidi] Kind n; ~ **glove** Glacéhandschuh m (a. fig.); **~-glove** sanft, zart.

kidnap ['kidnæp] entführen; **~(p)er** [~pə] Kindesentführer m, Kidnapper m.

kidney ['kidni] anat. Niere f; F Art f; ~ **bean** ♀ weiße Bohne.

kill [kil] 1. töten (a. fig.); fig. vernichten; parl. zu Fall bringen; ~ off abschlachten; ~ time die Zeit totschlagen; 2. Tötung f; Jagdbeute f; **~er** ['kilə] Totschläger m; **~ing** ['kiliŋ] 1. □ mörderisch; F komisch; 2. Am. F finanzieller Volltreffer.

kiln [kiln] Brenn-, Darrofen m.

kilo|gram(me) ['kiləgræm] Kilogramm n; **~metre**, Am. **~meter** Kilometer m.

kilt [kilt] Kilt m, Schottenrock m.

kin [kin] (Bluts)Verwandtschaft f.

kind [kaind] 1. □ gütig, freundlich; 2. Art f, Gattung f, Geschlecht n; Art und Weise f; pay in ~ in Naturalien zahlen; fig. mit gleicher Münze heimzahlen.

kindergarten ['kindəga:tn] Kindergarten m.

kind-hearted ['kaind'ha:tid] gütig.

kindle ['kindl] anzünden; (sich) entzünden (a. fig.).

kindling ['kindliŋ] Kleinholz n.

kind|ly ['kaindli] freundlich; günstig; **~ness** [~dnis] Güte f, Freundlichkeit f; Gefälligkeit f.

kindred ['kindrid] 1. verwandt, gleichartig; 2. Verwandtschaft f.

king [kiŋ] König m (a. fig. u. Schach, Kartenspiel); **~dom** ['kiŋdəm] Königreich n; bsd. ♀, zo. Reich n, Gebiet n; eccl. Reich n Gottes; **~like**

['kiŋlaik], **~ly** [~li] königlich; **~size** F ['kiŋsaiz] überlang, übergroß.

kink [kiŋk] Schlinge f, Knoten m; fig. Schrulle f, Fimmel m.

kin|ship ['kinʃip] Verwandtschaft f; **~sman** ['kinzmən] Verwandte(r) m.

kipper ['kipə] Räucherhering m Bückling m; sl. Kerl m.

kiss [kis] 1. Kuß m; 2. (sich) küssen.

kit [kit] Ausrüstung f (a. ✗ u. Sport); Handwerkszeug n, Werkzeug n; **~bag** ['kitbæg] ✗ Tornister m; Seesack m; Reisetasche f.

kitchen ['kitʃin] Küche f; **~ette** [kitʃi'net] Kochnische f; **~garden** ['kitʃin'gɑ:dn] Gemüsegarten m.

kite [kait] Papier-Drachen m.

kitten ['kitn] Kätzchen n.

Klan Am. [klæn] Ku-Klux-Klan m; **~sman** ['klænzmən] Mitglied n des Ku-Klux-Klan.

knack [næk] Kniff m, Dreh m; Geschicklichkeit f.   [Rucksack m.]

knapsack ['næpsæk] Tornister m;

knave [neiv] Schurke m; Kartenspiel: Bube m; **~ry** ['neivəri] Gaunerei f.

knead [ni:d] kneten; massieren.

knee [ni:] Knie n; ⊕ Kniestück n; **~cap** ['ni:kæp] Kniescheibe f; **~deep** bis an die Knie (reichend); **~joint** Kniegelenk n; **~l** [ni:l] [irr.] knien (to vor dat.).

knell [nel] Totenglocke f.

knelt [nelt] pret. u. p.p. von kneel.

knew [nju:] pret. von know.

knicker|bockers ['nikəbɔkəz] pl. Knickerbocker pl., Kniehosen f/pl.; **~s** F ['nikəz] pl. Schlüpfer m; = knickerbockers.

knick-knack ['niknæk] Spielerei f; Nippsache f.

knife [naif] 1. pl. knives [naivz] Messer n; 2. schneiden; (er)stechen.

knight [nait] 1. Ritter m; Springer m im Schach; 2. zum Ritter schlagen; **~errant** ['nait'erənt] fahrender Ritter; **~hood** ['naithud] Rittertum n; Ritterschaft f; **~ly** ['naitli] ritterlich.

knit [nit] [irr.] stricken; (ver)knüpfen; (sich) eng verbinden; **~ the brows** die Stirn runzeln; **~ting** ['nitiŋ] Stricken n; Strickzeug n; attr. Strick...

knives [naivz] pl. von knife 1.

knob [nɔb] Knopf m; Buckel m; Brocken m.

knock [nɔk] 1. Schlag m; Anklopfen n; mot. Klopfen n; 2. v/i. klopfen; pochen; stoßen; schlagen; **~ about** F sich herumtreiben; v/t. klopfen, stoßen, schlagen; Am. sl. bekritteln, schlechtmachen; **~ about** herumstoßen, übel zurichten; **~ down** niederschlagen; Auktion: zuschlagen; ⊕ aus-ea.-nehmen; be **~ed down** überfahren werden; **~ off** aufhören mit; F zs.-hauen (schnell erledigen); Summe abziehen; **~ out** Boxen: k.o. schlagen; **~er** ['nɔkə] Klopfende(r) m; Türklopfer m; Am. sl. Kritikaster m; **~kneed** ['nɔkni:d] x-beinig; fig. hinkend; **~out** Boxen: Knockout m, K.o. m; sl. tolle Sache od. Person.

knoll[1] [noul] kleiner Erdhügel.

knoll[2] [~] (bsd. zu Grabe) läuten.

knot [nɔt] 1. Knoten m; Knorren m; Seemeile f; Schleife f, Band n (a. fig.); Schwierigkeit f; 2. (ver)knoten, (ver)knüpfen (a. fig.); Stirn runzeln; verwickeln; **~ty** ['nɔti] knotig; knorrig; fig. verwickelt.

know [nou] [irr.] wissen; (er)kennen; erfahren; **~ French** Französisch können; come to **~** erfahren; get to **~** kennenlernen; **~ one's business**, **~ the ropes**, **~ a thing or two**, **~ what's what** sich auskennen, Erfahrung haben; you **~** (am Ende des Satzes) nämlich; **~ing** □ ['nouiŋ] erfahren; klug; schlau; verständnisvoll; wissentlich; **~ledge** ['nɔlidʒ] Kenntnis(se pl.) f; Wissen n; to my **~** meines Wissens; **~ n** [noun] p.p. von know; come to be **~** bekannt werden; make **~** bekanntmachen.

knuckle ['nʌkl] 1. Knöchel m; 2. **~ down**, **~ under** nachgeben.

Kremlin ['kremlin] der Kreml.

Ku-Klux-Klan Am. ['kju:klʌks-'klæn] Geheimbund in den USA.

L

label ['leibl] 1. Zettel m, Etikett n; Aufschrift f; Schildchen n; Bezeichnung f; 2. etikettieren, beschriften; fig. abstempeln (as als).

laboratory [lə'bɔrətəri] Laboratorium n; **~ assistant** Laborant(in).

laborious □ [lə'bɔ:riəs] mühsam; arbeitsam; schwerfällig (Stil).

labo(u)r ['leibə] 1. Arbeit f; Mühe f; (Geburts)Wehen f/pl.; Arbeiter m/pl.; Ministry of ♀ Arbeitsministerium n; hard **~** Zwangsarbeit f; 2. Arbeiter...; Arbeits...; 3. v/i. arbeiten; sich abmühen; **~ under** leiden unter (dat.), zu kämpfen haben mit; v/t. ausarbeiten; **~ed** schwerfällig (Stil); mühsam (Atem etc.); **~er** [~ərə] ungelernter Arbeiter; ♀ **Exchange** Arbeitsamt n; **Labour**

Party *pol.* Labour Party *f;* **labor union** *Am.* Gewerkschaft *f.*

lace [leis] **1.** Spitze *f;* Borte *f;* Schnur *f;* **2.** (zu)schnüren; mit Spitze *etc.* besetzen; *Schnur* durch-, einziehen; ~ (*into*) *s.o.* j-n verprügeln.

lacerate ['læsəreit] zerreißen; *fig.* quälen.

lack [læk] **1.** Fehlen *n,* Mangel *m;* **2.** *v/t.* ermangeln (*gen.*); he ~s money es fehlt ihm an Geld; *v/i.* be ~ing fehlen, mangeln; **~lustre** ['læklʌstə] glanzlos, matt.

laconic [lə'kɔnik] (~ally) lakonisch, wortkarg, kurz und prägnant.

lacquer ['lækə] **1.** Lack *m;* **2.** lakkieren.

lad [læd] Bursche *m,* Junge *m.*

ladder ['lædə] Leiter *f;* Laufmasche *f;* **~-proof** maschenfest (*Strumpf etc.*).

laden ['leidn] beladen.

lading ['leidiŋ] Ladung *f,* Fracht *f.*

ladle ['leidl] **1.** Schöpflöffel *m,* Kelle *f;* **2.** ~ out *Suppe* austeilen.

lady ['leidi] Dame *f;* Lady *f;* Herrin *f;* ~ doctor Ärztin *f;* **~bird** Marienkäfer *m;* **~like** damenhaft; **~love** Geliebte *f;* **~ship** [~ʃip]: her ~ die gnädige Frau; *Your* ♀ gnädige Frau, Euer Gnaden.

lag [læg] **1.** zögern; *a.* ~ *behind* zurückbleiben; **2.** Verzögerung *f.*

lager (beer) ['lɑːgə(biə)] Lagerbier *n.*

laggard ['lægəd] Nachzügler *m.*

lagoon [lə'guːn] Lagune *f.*

laid [leid] *pret. u. p.p. von* lay[3] **2;** ~ up bettlägerig (with mit, wegen).

lain [lein] *p.p. von* lie[2] **2.**

lair [lɛə] Lager *n* *e-s wilden Tieres.*

laity ['leiiti] Laien *m/pl.*

lake [leik] See *m;* rote Pigmentfarbe.

lamb [læm] **1.** Lamm *n;* **2.** lammen.

lambent ['læmbənt] leckend; züngelnd (*Flamme*); funkelnd.

lamb|kin ['læmkin] Lämmchen *n;* **~like** lammfromm.

lame [leim] **1.** □ lahm (*a. fig.* = *mangelhaft*); **2.** lähmen.

lament [lə'ment] **1.** Wehklage *f;* **2.** (be)klagen; trauern; **~able** □ ['læməntəbl] beklagenswert; kläglich; **~ation** [læmən'teiʃən] Wehklage *f.*

lamp [læmp] Lampe *f;* *fig.* Leuchte *f.*

lampoon [læm'puːn] **1.** Schmähschrift *f;* **2.** schmähen.

lamp-post ['læmppoust] Laternenpfahl *m.*

lampshade ['læmpʃeid] Lampenschirm *m.*

lance [lɑːns] **1.** Lanze *f;* Speer *m;* **2.** ✄ aufschneiden; **~-corporal** ✗ ['lɑːns'kɔːpərəl] Gefreite(r) *m.*

land [lænd] **1.** Land *n;* Grundstück *n;* by ~ auf dem Landweg; ~s *pl.*

Ländereien *f/pl.;* **2.** landen; ⚓ löschen; *Preis* gewinnen; **~-agent** ['lændeidʒənt] Grundstücksmakler *m;* Gutsverwalter *m;* **~ed** grundbesitzend; Land..., Grund...; **~holder** Grundbesitzer(in).

landing ['lændiŋ] Landung *f;* Treppenabsatz *m;* Anlegestelle *f;* **~field** ⚲ Landebahn *f;* **~gear** Fahrgestell *n;* **~stage** Landungsbrücke *f.*

land|lady ['lænleidi] Vermieterin *f,* Wirtin *f;* **~lord** [~lɔːd] Vermieter *m;* Wirt *m;* Haus-, Grundbesitzer *m;* **~lubber** ⚓ *contp.* Landratte *f;* **~mark** Grenz-, Markstein *m* (*a. fig.*); Wahrzeichen *n;* **~owner** Grundbesitzer(in); **~scape** ['lænskeip] Landschaft *f;* **~slide** Erdrutsch *m* (*a. pol.*); *a Democratic* ~ ein Erdrutsch zugunsten der Demokraten; **~slip** *konkr.* Erdrutsch *m.*

lane [lein] Feldweg *m;* Gasse *f;* Spalier *n; mot.* Fahrbahn *f,* Spur *f.*

language ['læŋgwidʒ] Sprache *f;* *strong* ~ Kraftausdrücke *m/pl.*

languid □ ['læŋgwid] matt; träg.

languish ['læŋgwiʃ] matt werden; schmachten; dahinsiechen.

languor ['læŋgə] Mattigkeit *f;* Schmachten *n;* Stille *f.*

lank □ [læŋk] schmächtig, dünn; schlicht; **~y** □ ['læŋki] schlaksig.

lantern ['læntən] Laterne *f;* **~slide** Dia(positiv) *n,* Lichtbild *n.*

lap [læp] **1.** Schoß *m;* ⊕ Vorstoß *m;* Runde *f;* **2.** über-ea.-legen; (ein)hüllen; (auf)lecken; schlürfen; plätschern (gegen) (*Wellen*).

lapel [lə'pel] Aufschlag *m am Rock.*

lapse [læps] **1.** Verlauf *m der Zeit;* Verfallen *n;* Versehen *n;* **2.** (ver)fallen; verfließen; fehlen.

larceny ['lɑːsni] Diebstahl *m.*

larch ♀ [lɑːtʃ] Lärche *f.*

lard [lɑːd] **1.** (Schweine)Schmalz *n;* **2.** spicken (*a. fig.*); **~er** ['lɑːdə] Speisekammer *f.*

large □ [lɑːdʒ] groß; weit; reichlich; weitherzig; flott; Groß...; *at* ~ auf freiem Fuß; ausführlich; als Ganzes; **~ly** ['lɑːdʒli] zum großen Teil, weitgehend; **~-minded** weitherzig; **~ness** ['lɑːdʒnis] Größe *f;* Weite *f;* **~-sized** groß(formatig).

lariat *Am.* ['læriət] Lasso *n, m.*

lark [lɑːk] *orn.* Lerche *f;* *fig.* Streich *m.*

larkspur ♀ ['lɑːkspə:] Rittersporn *m.*

larva *zo.* ['lɑːvə] Larve *f,* Puppe *f.*

larynx *anat.* ['læriŋks] Kehlkopf *m.*

lascivious □ [lə'siviəs] lüstern.

lash [læʃ] **1.** Peitsche(nschnur) *f;* Hieb *m;* Wimper *f;* **2.** peitschen; *fig.* geißeln; schlagen; anbinden.

lass, ~ie [læs, 'læsi] Mädchen *n.*

lassitude ['læsitjuːd] Mattigkeit *f,* Abgespanntheit *f;* Desinteresse *n.*

last¹ [lɑ:st] 1. adj. letzt; vorig; äußerst; geringst; ~ but one vorletzt; ~ night gestern abend; 2. Letzte(r m, -s n) f; Ende n; at ~ zuletzt, endlich; 3. adv. zuletzt; ~, but not least nicht zuletzt.

last² [~] dauern; halten (Farbe); ausreichen; ausdauern.

last³ [~] (Schuhmacher)Leisten m.

lasting □ ['lɑ:stiŋ] dauerhaft; beständig.

lastly ['lɑ:stli] zuletzt, schließlich.

latch [lætʃ] 1. Klinke f, Drücker m; Druckschloß n; 2. ein-, zuklinken.

late [leit] spät; (kürzlich)verstorben; ehemalig; jüngst; at (the) ~st spätestens; as ~ as noch (in dat.); of ~ letzthin; ~r on später; be ~ (zu) spät kommen; ~ly ['leitli] kürzlich.

latent ['leitənt] verborgen, latent; gebunden (Wärme etc.).

lateral □ ['lætərəl] seitlich; Seiten...

lath [lɑ:θ] 1. Latte f; 2. belatten.

lathe ⊕ [leið] Drehbank f; Lade f.

lather ['lɑ:ðə] 1. (Seifen)Schaum m; 2. v/t. einseifen; v/i. schäumen.

Latin ['lætin] 1. lateinisch; 2. Latein n.

latitude ['lætitju:d] Breite f; fig. Umfang m, Weite f; Spielraum m.

latter ['lætə] neuer; der (die, das) letztere; ~ly [~əli] neuerdings.

lattice ['lætis] a. ~-work Gitter n.

laud [lɔ:d] loben, preisen; ~able □ ['lɔ:dəbl] lobenswert, löblich.

laugh [lɑ:f] 1. Gelächter n, Lachen n; 2. lachen; ~ at j-n auslachen; he ~s best who ~s last wer zuletzt lacht, lacht am besten; ~able □ ['lɑ:fəbl] lächerlich; ~ter ['lɑ:ftə] Gelächter n, Lachen n.

launch [lɔ:ntʃ] 1. ⊕ Stapellauf m; Barkasse f; 2. vom Stapel laufen lassen; Boot aussetzen; schleudern (a. fig.); Schläge versetzen; Rakete starten, abschießen; fig. in Gang bringen; ~ing-pad ['lɔ:ntʃiŋpæd] (Raketen)Abschußrampe f.

launderette [lɔ:ndə'ret] Selbstbedienungswaschsalon m.

laund|ress ['lɔ:ndris] Wäscherin f; ~ry [~ri] Waschanstalt f; Wäsche f.

laurel ⚘ ['lɔrəl] Lorbeer m (a. fig.).

lavatory ['lævətəri] Waschraum m; Toilette f; public ~ Bedürfnisanstalt f.

lavender ⚘ ['lævində] Lavendel m.

lavish ['læviʃ] 1. □ freigebig, verschwenderisch; 2. verschwenden.

law [lɔ:] Gesetz n; (Spiel)Regel f; Recht(swissenschaft f) n; Gericht(sverfahren) n; go to ~ vor Gericht gehen; lay down the ~ den Ton angeben; ~-abiding ['lɔ:ə-baidiŋ] friedlich; ~-court Gericht(shof m) n; ~ful □ ['lɔ:ful] gesetzlich; gültig; ~less □ ['lɔ:lis] gesetzlos; ungesetzlich; zügellos.

lawn [lɔ:n] Rasen(platz) m; Batist m.

law|suit ['lɔ:sju:t] Prozeß m; ~yer ['lɔ:jə] Jurist m; (Rechts)Anwalt m.

lax □ [læks] locker; schlaff (a. fig.); lasch; ~ative ⚘ ['læksətiv] 1. abführend; 2. Abführmittel n.

lay¹ [lei] pret. von lie² 2.

lay² [~] weltlich; Laien...

lay³ [~] 1. Lage f, Richtung f; 2. [irr.] v/t. legen; umlegen; Plan etc. ersinnen; stellen, setzen; Tisch decken; lindern; besänftigen; auferlegen; Summe wetten; ~ before s.o. j-m vorlegen; ~ in einlagern, sich eindecken mit; ~ low niederwerfen; ~ open darlegen; ~ out auslegen; Garten etc. anlegen; ~ up Vorräte hinlegen, sammeln; be laid up ans Bett gefesselt sein; ~ with belegen mit; v/i. (Eier) legen; a. ~ a wager wetten.

lay-by ['leibai] Park-, Rastplatz m an e-r Fernstraße.

layer ['leiə] Lage f, Schicht f.

layman ['leimən] Laie m.

lay|off ['leiɔf] Arbeitsunterbrechung f; ~-out Anlage f; Plan m.

lazy □ ['leizi] faul.

lead¹ [led] Blei n; ⊕ Lot n, Senkblei n; typ. Durchschuß m.

lead² [li:d] 1. Führung f; Leitung f; Beispiel n; thea. Hauptrolle f; Kartenspiel: Vorhand f; ⚡ Leitung f; Hunde-Leine f; 2. [irr.] v/t. (an-)führen, leiten; bewegen (zu to); Karte ausspielen; ~ on (ver)locken; v/i. vorangehen; ~ off den Anfang machen; ~ up to überleiten zu.

leaden ['ledn] bleiern (a. fig.); Blei...

leader ['li:də] (An)Führer(in), Leiter(in); Erste(r) m; Leitartikel m; ~ship [~əʃip] Führerschaft f.

leading ['li:diŋ] 1. leitend; Leit...; Haupt...; 2. Leitung f, Führung f.

leaf [li:f], pl. leaves [li:vz] Blatt n; Tür- etc. Flügel m; Tisch-Platte f; ~let ['li:flit] Blättchen n; Flug-, Merkblatt n; ~y ['li:fi] belaubt.

league [li:g] 1. Liga f (a. hist. u. Sport); Bund m; mst poet. Meile f; 2. (sich) verbünden.

leak [li:k] 1. Leck n; 2. leck sein; tropfen; ~ out durchsickern; ~age ['li:kidʒ] Lecken n; ⚓ Leckage f; Verlust m (a. fig.), Schwund m; Durchsickern n; ~y ['li:ki] leck; undicht.

lean [li:n] 1. [irr.] (sich) (an)lehnen; (sich) stützen; (sich) (hin)neigen; 2. mager; 3. mageres Fleisch.

leant [lent] pret. u. p.p. von lean 1.

leap [li:p] 1. Sprung m; 2. [irr.] (über)springen; ~t [lept] pret. u. p.p. von leap 2; ~-year ['li:pjə:] Schaltjahr n.

learn [lə:n] [irr.] lernen; erfahren, hören; ~ from ersehen aus; ~ed ['lə:nid] gelehrt; ~er ['lə:nə] Anfänger(in); ~ing ['lɔ:niŋ] Lernen n; Gelehrsamkeit f; ~t [lə:nt] pret. u. p.p. von learn.

lease [li:s] 1. Verpachtung f, Vermietung f; Pacht f, Miete f; Pacht-, Mietvertrag m; 2. (ver-) pachten, (ver)mieten.

leash [li:ʃ] 1. Koppelleine f; Koppel f (3 Hunde etc.); 2. koppeln.

least [li:st] 1. adj. kleinst, geringst; wenigst, mindest; 2. adv. a. ~ of all am wenigsten; at ~ wenigstens; 3. das Mindeste, das Wenigste; to say the ~ gelinde gesagt.

leather ['leðə] 1. Leder n (fig.Haut); 2. a. ~n ledern; Leder...

leave [li:v] 1. Erlaubnis f; a. ~ of absence Urlaub m; Abschied m; 2. [irr.] v/t. (ver)lassen; zurück-, hinterlassen; übriglassen; überlassen; ~ off aufhören (mit); Kleid ablegen; v/i. ablassen; weggehen, abreisen (for nach).

leaven ['levn] Sauerteig m; Hefe f.

leaves [li:vz] pl. von leaf; Laub n.

leavings ['li:viŋz] pl. Überbleibsel n/pl.

lecherous ['letʃərəs] wollüstig.

lecture ['lektʃə] 1. Vorlesung f, Vortrag m; Strafpredigt f; 2. v/i. Vorlesungen od. Vorträge halten; v/t. abkanzeln; ~r [~ərə] Vortragende(r m) f; univ. Dozent(in).

led [led] pret. u. p.p. von lead² 2.

ledge [ledʒ] Leiste f; Sims m, n; Riff n.

ledger ✝ ['ledʒə] Hauptbuch n.

leech zo. [li:tʃ] Blutegel m; fig. Schmarotzer m.

leek ♣ [li:k] Lauch m, Porree m.

leer [liə] 1. (lüsterner od. finsterer) Seitenblick; 2. schielen (at nach).

lees [li:z] pl. Bodensatz m, Hefe f.

lee|ward ⚓ ['li:wəd] leewärts; ~way ['li:wei] ⚓ Abtrift f; make up ~ fig. Versäumtes nachholen.

left¹ [left] pret. u. p.p. von leave 2.

left² [~] 1. link(s); 2. Linke f; ~-handed ['left'hændid] linkshändig; linkisch.

left|-luggage office ['left'lʌgidʒɔfis] Gepäckaufbewahrung(sstelle) f; ~-overs pl. Speisereste m/pl.

leg [leg] Bein n; Keule f; (Stiefel-) Schaft m; ♣ Schenkel m; pull s.o.'s ~ j-n auf den Arm nehmen (hänseln).

legacy ['legəsi] Vermächtnis n.

legal □ ['li:gəl] gesetzlich; rechtsgültig; juristisch; Rechts...; ~ize [~laiz] rechtskräftig machen; beurkunden.

legation [li'geiʃən] Gesandtschaft f.

legend ['ledʒənd] Legende f; ~ary [~dəri] legendär, sagenhaft.

leggings ['leginz] pl. Gamaschen f/pl.

legible □ ['ledʒəbl] leserlich.

legionary ['li:dʒənəri] Legionär m.

legislat|ion [ledʒis'leiʃən] Gesetz-

gebung f; ~ive ['ledʒislətiv] gesetzgebend; ~or [~leitə] Gesetzgeber m.

legitima|cy [li'dʒitiməsi] Rechtmäßigkeit f; ~te 1. [~meit] legitimieren; 2. [~mit] rechtmäßig.

leisure ['leʒə] Muße f; at your ~ wenn es Ihnen paßt; ~ly [~əli] gemächlich.

lemon ['lemən] Zitrone f; ~ade [lemə'neid] Limonade f; ~ squash Zitronenwasser n.

lend [lend] [irr.] (ver-, aus)leihen; Hilfe leisten, gewähren.

length [leŋθ] Länge f; Strecke f; (Zeit)Dauer f; at ~ endlich, zuletzt; go all ~s aufs Ganze gehen; ~en ['leŋθən] (sich) verlängern, (sich) ausdehnen; ~wise [~θwaiz] der Länge nach; ~y □ [~θi] sehr lang.

lenient □ ['li:njənt] mild, nachsichtig.

lens opt. [lenz] Linse f.

lent [lent] pret. u. p.p. von lend.

Lent² [~] Fasten pl., Fastenzeit f.

leopard ['lepəd] Leopard m.

lepr|osy ♣ ['leprəsi] Aussatz m, Lepra f; ~ous [~əs] aussätzig.

less [les] 1. adj. u. adv. kleiner, geringer; weniger; 2. prp. minus.

lessen ['lesn] v/t. vermindern, schmälern; v/i. abnehmen.

lesser ['lesə] kleiner; geringer.

lesson ['lesn] Lektion f; Aufgabe f; (Unterrichts)Stunde f; Lehre f; ~s pl. Unterricht m.

lest [lest] damit nicht, daß nicht.

let [let] [irr.] lassen; vermieten, verpachten; ~ alone in Ruhe lassen; geschweige denn; ~ down j-n im Stich lassen; ~ go loslassen; ~ into einweihen in (acc.); ~ off abschießen; j-n laufen lassen; ~ out hinauslassen; ausplaudern; vermieten; ~ up aufhören.

lethal □ ['li:θəl] tödlich; Todes...

lethargy ['leθədʒi] Lethargie f.

letter ['letə] 1. Buchstabe m; Type f; Brief m; ~s pl. Literatur f, Wissenschaft f; attr. Brief...; to the ~ buchstäblich; 2. beschriften, betiteln; ~-box Briefkasten m; ~-card Kartenbrief m; ~-carrier Am. Briefträger m; ~-case Brieftasche f; ~-cover Briefumschlag m; ~ed (literarisch) gebildet; ~-file Briefordner m; ~ing [~əriŋ] Beschriftung f; ~-press Kopierpresse f.

lettuce ♣ ['letis] Lattich m, Salat m.

leuk(a)emia ♣ [lju:'ki:miə] Leukämie f.

levee¹ ['levi] Morgenempfang m.

levee² Am. [~] Uferdamm m.

level ['levl] 1. waag(e)recht; eben; gleich; ausgeglichen; my ~ best mein möglichstes; ~ crossing 🚂 schienengleicher Übergang; 2. ebene Fläche; (gleiche) Höhe, Niveau *n*, Stand *m*; *fig*. Maßstab *m*; Wasserwaage *f*; *sea* ~ Meeresspiegel *m*; *on the* ~ F offen, aufrichtig; **3.** *v/t.* gleichmachen, ebnen; *fig*. anpassen; richten, zielen mit; ~ *up* erhöhen; *v/i.* ~ *at, against* zielen auf (*acc.*); ~**-headed** vernünftig, nüchtern.

lever ['li:və] Hebel *m*; Hebestange *f*; ~**age** [~əridʒ] Hebelkraft *f*.

levity ['leviti] Leichtfertigkeit *f*.

levy ['levi] **1.** Erhebung *f von Steuern*; ⚔ Aushebung *f*; Aufgebot *n*; **2.** *Steuern* erheben; ⚔ ausheben.

lewd □ [lu:d] liederlich, unzüchtig.

liability [laiə'biliti] Verantwortlichkeit *f*; ⚖ Haftpflicht *f*; Verpflichtung *f*; *fig*. Hang *m*; *liabilities pl.* Verbindlichkeiten *f/pl.*, ⊹ Passiva *pl.*

liable □ ['laiəbl] verantwortlich; haftpflichtig; verpflichtet; ausgesetzt (*to dat.*); *be* ~ *to* neigen zu.

liar ['laiə] Lügner(in).

libel ['laibəl] **1.** Schmähschrift *f*; Verleumdung *f*; **2.** schmähen, verunglimpfen.

liberal ['libərəl] **1.** □ liberal (*a. pol.*); freigebig; reichlich; freisinnig; **2.** Liberale(r) *m*; ~**ity** [libə-'ræliti] Freigebigkeit *f*; Freisinnigkeit *f*.

liberat|e ['libəreit] befreien; freilassen; ~**ion** [libə'reiʃən] Befreiung *f*; ~**or** ['libəreitə] Befreier *m*.

libertine ['libə(:)tain] Wüstling *m*.

liberty ['libəti] Freiheit *f*; *take liberties* sich Freiheiten erlauben; *be at* ~ frei sein.

librar|ian [lai'brɛəriən] Bibliothekar(in); ~**y** ['laibrəri] Bibliothek *f*.

lice [lais] *pl. von louse.*

licen|ce, *Am.* ~**se** ['laisəns] **1.** Lizenz *f*; Erlaubnis *f*; Konzession *f*; Freiheit *f*; Zügellosigkeit *f*; *driving* ~ Führerschein *m*; **2.** lizenzieren, berechtigen; *et.* genehmigen; ~**see** [laisən'si:] Lizenznehmer *m*.

licentious □ [lai'senʃəs] unzüchtig; ausschweifend.

lichen ♀, ⚕ ['laikən] Flechte *f*.

lick [lik] **1.** Lecken *n*; Salzlecke *f*; F Schlag *m*; **2.** (be)lecken; F verdreschen; übertreffen; ~ *the dust* im Staub kriechen; fallen; geschlagen werden; ~ *into shape* zurechtstutzen.

licorice ['likəris] Lakritze *f*.

lid [lid] Deckel *m*; (Augen)Lid *n*.

lie¹ [lai] **1.** Lüge *f*; *give s.o. the* ~ j-n Lügen strafen; **2.** lügen.

lie² [~] **1.** Lage *f*; **2.** [*irr.*] liegen; ~ *by* still-, brachliegen; ~ *down* sich niederlegen; ~ *in wait for* j-m auflauern; *let sleeping dogs* ~ *fig*. daran rühren wir lieber nicht; ~**-down** [lai'daun] Nickerchen *n*; ~**-in:** *have a* ~ sich gründlich ausschlafen.

lien ⚖ ['liən] Pfandrecht *n*.

lieu [lju:]: *in* ~ *of* (an)statt.

lieutenant [lef'tenənt, ⚓ le'tenənt; *Am.* lu:'tenənt] Leutnant *m*; Statthalter *m*; ~**-commander** ⚓ Korvettenkapitän *m*.

life [laif], *pl.* **lives** [laivz] Leben *n*; Menschenleben *n*; Lebensbeschreibung *f*; *for* ~ auf Lebenszeit; *for one's* ~, *for dear* ~ ums (liebe) Leben; *to the* ~ naturgetreu; ~ *sentence* lebenslängliche Zuchthausstrafe; ~ **assurance** Lebensversicherung *f*; ~**belt** ['laifbelt] Rettungsgürtel *m*; ~**boat** Rettungsboot *n*; ~**guard** Leibwache *f*; Badewärter *m am Strand*; ~ **insurance** Lebensversicherung *f*; ~**jacket** ⚓ Schwimmweste *f*; ~**less** □ ['laiflis] leblos; matt (*a. fig.*); ~**-like** lebenswahr; ~**-long** lebenslänglich; ~**-preserver** *Am.* ['laif-prizə:və] Schwimmgürtel *m*; Totschläger *m* (*Stock mit Bleikopf*); ~**time** Lebenszeit *f*.

lift [lift] **1.** Heben *n*; *phys.*, ✈ Auftrieb *m*; *fig*. Erhebung *f*; Fahrstuhl *m*; *give s.o. a* ~ j-m helfen; j-n (im Auto) mitnehmen; **2.** *v/t.* (auf)heben; erheben; beseitigen; *sl.* klauen, stehlen; *v/i.* sich heben.

ligature ['ligətʃuə] Binde *f*; ✄ Verband *m.*

light¹ [lait] **1.** Licht *n* (*a. fig.*); Fenster *n*; Aspekt *m*, Gesichtspunkt *m*; Feuer *n*; Glanz *m*; *fig*. Leuchte *f*; ~*s pl.* Fähigkeiten *f/pl.*; *will you give me a* ~ darf ich Sie um Feuer bitten; *put a* ~ *to* anzünden; **2.** licht, hell; blond; **3.** [*irr.*] *v/t.* oft ~ *up* be-, erleuchten; anzünden; *v/i. mst* ~ *up* aufleuchten; ~ *out Am. sl.* schnell losziehen, abhauen.

light² [~] **1.** *adj.* □ *u. adv.* leicht (*a. fig.*); ~ *current* ⚡ Schwachstrom *m*; *make* ~ *of* et. leicht nehmen; **2.** ~ (*up)on* stoßen *od.* fallen auf (*acc.*), geraten an (*acc.*); sich niederlassen auf (*dat.*).

lighten ['laitn] blitzen; (sich) erhellen; leichter machen; (sich) erleichtern.

lighter ['laitə] Anzünder *m*; (Taschen)Feuerzeug *n*; ⚓ L(e)ichter *m.*

light|-headed ['lait'hedid] wirr im Kopf, irr; ~**hearted** □ [~'ha:tid] leichtherzig; fröhlich; ~**house** ['laithaus] Leuchtturm *m.*

lighting ['laitiŋ] Beleuchtung *f*; Anzünden *n.*

light|-minded ['lait'maindid] leichtsinnig; ~**ness** ['laitnis] Leichtigkeit *f*; Leichtsinn *m.*

lightning ['laitniŋ] Blitz *m*; ~ *bug Am. zo.* Leuchtkäfer *m*; ~**conductor,** ~**rod** ⚡ Blitzableiter *m.*

light-weight ['laitweit] *Sport:* Leichtgewicht *n.*

like [laik] **1.** gleich; ähnlich; wie; *such* ~ dergleichen; *feel* ~ F sich aufgelegt fühlen zu et.; ~ that so; what is he ~? wie sieht er aus?; wie ist er?; 2. Gleiche m, f, n; ~s pl. Neigungen f/pl.; his ~ seinesgleichen; the ~ der-, desgleichen; 3. mögen, gern haben; how do you ~ London? wie gefällt Ihnen L.?; I should ~ to know ich möchte wissen.

like|lihood ['laiklihud] Wahrscheinlichkeit f; ~ly ['laikli] wahrscheinlich; geeignet; he is ~ to die er wird wahrscheinlich sterben.

like|n ['laikən] vergleichen (to mit); ~ness ['laiknis] Ähnlichkeit f; (Ab-) Bild n; Gestalt f; ~wise ['laikwaiz] gleich-, ebenfalls.

liking ['laikiŋ] (for) Neigung f (für, zu), Gefallen n (an dat.).

lilac ['lailək] 1. lila; 2. ♀ Flieder m.

lily ♀ ['lili] Lilie f; ~ of the valley Maiglöckchen n; ~-white schneeweiß.

limb [lim] Körper-Glied n; Ast m.

limber ['limbə] 1. biegsam, geschmeidig; 2.: ~ up (sich) lockern.

lime [laim] Kalk m; Vogelleim m; ♀ Limone f; ♀ Linde f; ~light ['laimlait] Kalklicht n; thea. Scheinwerfer(licht n) m; fig. Mittelpunkt m des öffentlichen Interesses.

limit ['limit] 1. Grenze f; in (off) ~s Zutritt gestattet (verboten) (to für); that is the ~! F das ist der Gipfel!; das ist (doch) die Höhe!; go the ~ Am. F bis zum Äußersten gehen; 2. begrenzen, beschränken (to auf acc.); ~ation [limi'teiʃən] Begrenzung f, Beschränkung f; fig. Grenze f; ⚖ Verjährung f; ~ed □ (liability) company Gesellschaft f mit beschränkter Haftung; ~ in time befristet; ~less □ [~tlis] grenzenlos.

limp [limp] 1. hinken; 2. Hinken n; 3. schlaff; weich.

limpid □ ['limpid] klar, durchsichtig.

line [lain] 1. Linie f; Reihe f, Zeile f; Vers m; Strich m; Falte f, Furche f; (Menschen)Schlange f; Folge f; Verkehrsgesellschaft f; Eisenbahnlinie f; Strecke f; tel. Leitung f; Branche f, Fach n; Leine f, Schnur f; Äquator m; Richtung f; ✗ Linie(ntruppe) f; Front f; ~s pl. Richtlinien f/pl.; Grundlage f; ~ of conduct Lebensweise f; hard ~s pl. hartes Los, Pech n; in ~ with in Übereinstimmung mit; stand in ~ Schlange stehen; draw the ~ fig. nicht mehr mitmachen; hold the ~ teleph. am Apparat bleiben; 2. v/t. liniieren; aufstellen; Weg etc. säumen, einfassen; Kleid füttern; ~ out entwerfen; v/i. ~ up sich auf-, anstellen.

linea|ge ['liniid3] Abstammung f; Familie f; Stammbaum m; ~l □ [~iəl] gerade, direkt (Nachkomme

etc.); ~ment [~əmənt] (Gesichts-) Zug m; ~r ['liniə] geradlinig.

linen ['linin] 1. Leinen n, Leinwand f; Wäsche f; 2. leinen; ~-closet, ~-cupboard Wäscheschrank m; ~-draper [~ndreipə] Weißwarenhändler m, Wäschegeschäft n.

liner ['lainə] Linienschiff n, Passagierdampfer m; Verkehrsflugzeug n.

linger ['liŋgə] zögern; (ver)weilen; sich aufhalten; sich hinziehen; dahinsiechen; ~ at, ~ about sich herumdrücken an od. bei (dat.).

lingerie ['lɛ̃:nʒəri] Damenunterwäsche f. [Einreibemittel n.]

liniment ⚕ ['liniment] Liniment n.⎰

lining ['lainiŋ] Kleider- etc. Futter n; Besatz m; ⊕ Verkleidung f.

link [liŋk] 1. Ketten-Glied n, Gelenk n; Manschettenknopf m; fig. Bindeglied n; 2. (sich) verbinden.

links [liŋks] pl. Dünen f/pl.; a. golf-~ Golf(spiel)platz m.

linseed ['linsi:d] Leinsame(n) m; ~ oil Leinöl n.

lion ['laiən] Löwe m; fig. Größe f, Berühmtheit f; ~ess [~nis] Löwin f.

lip [lip] Lippe f; Rand m; sl. Unverschämtheit f; ~-stick ['lipstik] Lippenstift m.

liquefy ['likwifai] schmelzen.

liquid ['likwid] 1. flüssig; † liquid; klar (Luft etc.); 2. Flüssigkeit f.

liquidat|e ['likwideit] † liquidieren; bezahlen; ~ion [likwi'deiʃən] Abwicklung f, Liquidation f.

liquor ['likə] Flüssigkeit f; Alkohol m, alkoholisches Getränk.

liquorice ['likəris] Lakritze f.

lisp [lisp] 1. Lispeln n; 2. lispeln.

list [list] 1. Liste f, Verzeichnis n; Leiste f; Webkante f; 2. (in e-e Liste) eintragen; verzeichnen.

listen ['lisn] (to) lauschen, horchen (auf acc.); anhören (acc.), zuhören (dat.); hören (auf acc.); ~ in teleph., Radio: (mit)hören (to acc.); ~er [~nə] Zuhörer(in); a. ~-in (Rundfunk)Hörer(in).

listless ['listlis] gleichgültig; lustlos.

lists [lists] pl. Schranken f/pl.

lit [lit] pret. u. p.p. von light¹ 3.

literal □ ['litərəl] buchstäblich; am Buchstaben klebend; wörtlich.

litera|ry □ ['litərəri] literarisch; Literatur...; Schrift...; ~ture [~ritʃə] Literatur f.

lithe [laið] geschmeidig, wendig.

lithography [li'θɔgrəfi] Lithographie f, Steindruck m.

litigation [liti'geiʃən] Prozeß m.

lit|re, Am. ~er ['li:tə] Liter n, m.

litter ['litə] 1. Sänfte f; Tragbahre f; Streu f; Abfall m; Unordnung f; Wurf m junger Tiere; 2. ~ down mit Streu versehen; ~ up in Unordnung bringen; Junge werfen; ~-basket, ~-bin Abfallkorb m.

little ['litl] 1. *adj.* klein; gering(fügig); wenig; a ~ one ein Kleines (*Kind*); 2. *adv.* wenig; 3. Kleinigkeit *f*; a ~ ein bißchen; ~ by ~ nach und nach; *not* a ~ nicht wenig.

live 1. [liv] *allg.* leben; wohnen; ~ to see erleben; ~ s.th. down et. durch guten Lebenswandel vergessen machen; ~ through durchmachen, durchstehen, überleben; ~ up to s-m Ruf gerecht werden, s-n Grundsätzen gemäß leben; *Versprechen* halten; 2. [laiv] lebendig; richtig; aktuell; glühend; ⚔ scharf (*Munition*); ⚡ stromführend; *Radio*: Direkt..., Original...; **~lihood** ['laivlihud] Unterhalt *m*; **~liness** [~inis] Lebhaftigkeit *f*; **~ly** ['laivli] lebhaft; lebendig; aufregend; schnell; bewegt.

liver *anat.* ['livə] Leber *f*.

livery ['livəri] Livree *f*; (Amts-) Tracht *f*; *at* ~ in Futter (*stehen etc.*).

live|s [laivz] *pl. von* life; **~stock** ['laivstɔk] Vieh(bestand *m*) *n*.

livid ['livid] bläulich; fahl; F wild.

living ['livin] 1. □ lebend(ig); the ~ image *of* das genaue Ebenbild *gen.*; 2. Leben *n*; Lebensweise *f*; Lebensunterhalt *m*; *eccl.* Pfründe *f*; **~-room** Wohnzimmer *n*.

lizard *zo.* ['lizəd] Eidechse *f*.

load [loud] 1. Last *f*; Ladung *f*; 2. (be)laden; *fig.* überhäufen; überladen; **~ing** ['loudin] Laden *n*; Ladung *f*, Fracht *f*; *attr.* Lade...

loaf [louf] 1. *pl.* **loaves** [louvz] Brot-Laib *m*; (Zucker)Hut *m*; 2. herumlungern.

loafer ['loufə] Bummler *m*.

loam [loum] Lehm *m*, Ackerkrume *f*.

loan [loun] 1. Anleihe *f*, Darlehen *n*; Leihen *n*; Leihgabe *f*; *on* ~ leihweise; 2. *bsd. Am.* ausleihen.

loath □ [louθ] abgeneigt; **~e** [louð] sich ekeln vor (*dat.*); verabscheuen; **~ing** ['louðin] Ekel *m*; **~some** □ ['louðsəm] ekelhaft; verhaßt.

loaves [louvz] *pl. von* loaf 1.

lobby ['lɔbi] 1. Vorhalle *f*; *parl.* Wandelgang *m*; *thea.* Foyer *n*; 2. *parl.* s-n Einfluß geltend machen.

lobe *anat.*, ♀ [loub] Lappen *m*.

lobster ['lɔbstə] Hummer *m*.

local □ ['loukəl] 1. örtlich; Orts...; lokal; ~ government Gemeindeverwaltung *f*; 2. *Zeitung*: Lokalnachricht *f*; ~ train Vorortzug *m*; F Wirtshaus *n* (am Ort); **~ity** [lou'kæliti] Örtlichkeit *f*; Lage *f*; **~ize** ['loukəlaiz] lokalisieren.

locat|e [lou'keit] *v/t.* versetzen, verlegen, unterbringen; ausfindig machen; *Am.* an-, festlegen; *be* ~d gelegen sein; wohnen; *v/i.* sich niederlassen; **~ion** [~eiʃən] Lage *f*; Niederlassung *f*; *Am.* Anweisung *f* von Land; angewiesenes Land; Ort

m; *Film*: Gelände *n* für Außenaufnahmen.

loch *schott.* [lɔk] See *m*; Bucht *f*.

lock [lɔk] 1. *Tür-, Gewehr- etc.* Schloß *n*; Schleuse(nkammer) *f*; ⊕ Sperrvorrichtung *f*; Stauung *f*; Locke *f*; Wollflocke *f*; 2. (ver-) schließen (*a. fig.*), absperren; sich verschließen lassen; ⊕ blockieren, sperren, greifen; umschließen; ~ s.o. in j-n einsperren; ~ up wegschließen; abschließen; einsperren; *Geld* fest anlegen.

lock|er ['lɔkə] Schrank *m*, Kasten *m*; **~et** ['lɔkit] Medaillon *n*; **~out** Aussperrung *f* von Arbeitern; **~smith** Schlosser *m*; **~up** 1. Haftzelle *f*; ♱ zinslose Kapitalanlage; 2. verschließbar.

loco *Am. sl.* ['loukou] verrückt.

locomot|ion [loukə'mouʃən] Fortbewegung(sfähigkeit) *f*; **~ive** ['loukəmoutiv] 1. sich fortbewegend; beweglich; 2. *a.* ~ engine Lokomotive *f*.

locust ['loukəst] *zo.* Heuschrecke *f*; ♀ unechte Akazie.

lode|star ['loudsta:] Leitstern *m* (*a. fig.*); **~stone** Magnet(eisenstein) *m*.

lodg|e [lɔdʒ] 1. Häus-chen *n*; (Forst-, Park-, Pförtner)Haus *n*; Portierloge *f*; *Freimaurer*-Loge *f*; 2. *v/t.* beherbergen, aufnehmen; *Geld* hinterlegen; *Klage* einreichen; *Hieb* versetzen; *v/i.* (*bsd.* zur Miete) wohnen; logieren; **~er** ['lɔdʒə] (Unter)Mieter(in); **~ing** ['lɔdʒin] Unterkunft *f*; **~s** *pl.* möbliertes Zimmer; Wohnung *f*.

loft [lɔ:ft] (Dach)Boden *m*; Empore *f*; **~y** □ ['lɔfti] hoch; erhaben; stolz.

log [lɔg] Klotz *m*; Block *m*; gefällter Baumstamm; ♱ Log *n*; **~-cabin** ['lɔgkæbin] Blockhaus *n*; **~gerhead** ['lɔgəhed]: *be at* ~s sich in den Haaren liegen; **~-house**, **~-hut** Blockhaus *n*.

logic ['lɔdʒik] Logik *f*; **~al** □ [~kəl] logisch.

logroll *bsd. Am. pol.* ['lɔgroul] (sich gegenseitig) in die Hände arbeiten.

loin [lɔin] Lende(nstück *n*) *f*.

loiter ['lɔitə] trödeln, schlendern.

loll [lɔl] (sich) strecken; (sich) rekeln; ~ about herumlungern.

lone|liness ['lounlinis] Einsamkeit *f*; **~ly** □ ['lounli], **~some** □ ['lounsəm] einsam.

long¹ [lɔŋ] 1. Länge *f*; before ~ binnen kurzem; for ~ lange; take ~ lange brauchen *od.* dauern; 2. *adj.* lang; langfristig; langsam; *in the* ~ run am Ende; auf die Dauer; be ~ lange dauern *od.* brauchen; 3. *adv.* lang(e); so ~! bis dann! (*auf Wiedersehen*); (no) ~er (nicht) länger *od.* mehr.

long² [ᴧ] sich sehnen (for nach).
long|-distance['lɔŋ'distəns]Fern...,
Weit...; **~evity** [lɔn'dʒeviti] Lang-
lebigkeit f; langes Leben; **~hand**
['lɔŋhænd] Langschrift f.
longing ['lɔŋiŋ] 1. □ sehnsüchtig;
2. Sehnsucht f; Verlangen n.
longitude geogr. ['lɔndʒitju:d] Länge f.
long|-shore-man ['lɔŋʃɔ:mən] Ha-
fenarbeiterm; **~sighted**['lɔŋ'saitid]
weitsichtig; **~standing** seit langer
Zeit bestehend, alt; **~suffering 1.**
langmütig; 2. Langmut f; **~term**
['lɔŋtə:m] langfristig; **~winded** □
['lɔŋ'windid] langatmig.
look [luk] 1. Blick m; Anblick m;
oft **~s** pl. Aussehen n; have a **~** at
s.th. sich et. ansehen; I don't like
the **~** of it es gefällt mir nicht; 2. v/i.
sehen, blicken (at, on auf acc.,
nach); zusehen, daß od. wie ...; nachsehen, wer etc. ...; krank etc. aussehen; nach e-r Richtung liegen;
~ after sehen nach, sich kümmern
um; versorgen; nachsehen, nachblicken (dat.); **~** at ansehen; **~** for
erwarten; suchen; **~** forward to sich
freuen auf (acc.); **~** in als Besucher
hereinschauen (on bei); **~** into prüfen; erforschen; **~** on zuschauen
(dat.);betrachten (as als); liegen zu,
gehen auf (acc.) (Fenster); **~** out
vorsehen; **~** (up)on fig. ansehen (as
als); v/t. **~** disdain verächtlich
blicken; **~** over et. durchsehen; j-n
mustern; **~** up et. nachschlagen.
looker-on ['lukər'ɔn] Zuschauer(in).
looking-glass ['lukiŋglɑ:s] Spiegel
m.
look-out ['luk'aut] Ausguck m,
Ausblick m, Aussicht f (a. fig.);
that is my **~** F das ist meine Sache.
loom [lu:m] 1. Webstuhl m; 2. undeutlich zu sehen sein, sich ab-
zeichnen.
loop [lu:p] 1. Schlinge f, Schleife f,
Öse f; 2. v/t. in Schleifen legen;
schlingen; v/i. e-e Schleife machen;
sich winden; **~hole** ['lu:phoul]
Guck-, Schlupfloch n; ✂ Schieß-
scharte f.
loose [lu:s] 1. □ allg. lose, locker;
schlaff; weit; frei; un-zs.-hängend;
ungenau; liederlich; 2. lösen; aufbinden; lockern; **~n** ['lu:sn] (sich)
lösen, (sich) lockern.
loot [lu:t] 1. plündern; 2. Beute f.
lop [lɔp] Baum beschneiden; stutzen; schlaff herunterhängen (lassen); **~sided** ['lɔp'saidid] schief;
einseitig.
loquacious □ [lou'kweiʃəs] geschwätzig.
lord [lɔ:d] Herr m; Gebieter m;
Magnat m; Lord m; the ♀ der Herr
(Gott); my **~** ['mi'lɔ:d] Mylord,
Euer Gnaden; the ♀'s Prayer das
Vaterunser; the ♀'s Supper das

Abendmahl; **~ly** ['lɔ:dli] vornehm,
edel; großartig; hochmütig; **~ship**
['lɔ:dʃip] Lordschaft f (Titel).
lore [lɔ:] Lehre f, Kunde f.
lorry ['lɔri] Last(kraft)wagen m,
LKW m; ⬚ Lore f.
lose [lu:z] [irr.] v/t. verlieren; vergeuden; verpassen; abnehmen; **~**
o.s. sich verirren; v/i. verlieren;
nachgehen (Uhr).
loss [lɔs] Verlust m; Schaden m;
at a **~** in Verlegenheit; außerstande.
lost [lɔst] pret. u. p.p. von lose; be **~**
verlorengehen; verschwunden sein;
fig. versunken sein; **~property office**
Fundbüro n.
lot [lɔt] Los n (a. fig.); Anteil m;
♦ Partie f; Posten m; F Menge f;
Parzelle f; Am. Film: Atelierge-
lände n; a **~** of people F eine Menge
Leute; draw **~s** losen; fall to s.o.'s **~**
j-m zufallen.
loth □ [louθ] s. loath.
lotion ['louʃən] (Haut)Wasser n.
lottery ['lɔtəri] Lotterie f.
loud □ [laud] laut (a. adv.); fig.
schreiend, grell; **~speaker** ['laud-
'spi:kə] Lautsprecher m.
lounge [laundʒ] 1. sich rekeln; faulenzen; 2. Bummel m; Wohnzim-
mer n, -dicle f; Gesellschaftsraum
m e-s Hotels; thea. Foyer n; Chaiselongue f; **~chair** ['laundʒ'tʃeə]
Klubsessel m; **~suit** Straßenanzug
m.
lour ['lauə] finster blicken od. aussehen; die Stirn runzeln.
lous|e [laus], pl. **lice** [lais] Laus f;
~y ['lauzi] verlaust; lausig; Lause...
lout [laut] Tölpel m, Lümmel m.
lovable □ ['lʌvəbl] liebenswürdig,
liebenswert.
love [lʌv] 1. Liebe f (of, a. for, to,
towards zu); Liebschaft f; Ange-
betete f; Liebling m (als Anrede);
liebe Grüße m/pl.; Sport: nichts, null;
attr. Liebes...; give od. send one's **~**
~ to s.o. j-n freundlich grüßen
(lassen); in **~** with verliebt in (acc.);
fall in **~** with sich verlieben in (acc.);
make **~** to werben um; 2. lieben;
gern haben; **~** to do gern tun;
~affair ['lʌvəfeə] Liebschaft f;
~ly ['lʌvli] lieblich; entzückend,
reizend; **~r** ['lʌvə] Liebhaber m;
fig. Verehrer(in), Liebhaber(in).
loving □ ['lʌviŋ] liebevoll.
low¹ [lou] 1. niedrig; tief; gering;
leise; fig. niedergeschlagen;
schwach; gemein; **~est bid** Min-
destgebot n; 2. meteor. Tief(druck-
gebiet) n; bsd. Am. Tiefstand m,
-punkt m.
low² [ᴧ] brüllen, muhen (Rind).
low-brow F ['loubrau] 1. geistig anspruchslos, spießig; 2. Spießer m,
Banause m.
lower¹ ['louə] 1. niedriger; tiefer;
geringer; leiser; untere(r, -s); Un-

ter...; 2. v/t. nieder-, herunterlassen; senken; erniedrigen; abschwächen; *Preis etc.* herabsetzen; v/i. fallen, sinken.

lower² ['lauə] *s. lour.*

low|land ['loulənd] Tiefland *n*; ~**liness** ['loulinis] Demut *f*; ~**ly** ['louli] demütig; bescheiden; ~**necked** (tief) ausgeschnitten (*Kleid*); ~**spirited** niedergeschlagen. [Treue *f.*]

loyal □ ['lɔiəl] treu; ~**ty** [~lti]]

lozenge ['lɔzindʒ] Pastille *f.*

lubber ['lʌbə] Tölpel *m*, Stoffel *m.*

lubric|ant ['lu:brikənt] Schmiermittel *n*; ~**ate** [~keit] schmieren; ~**ation** [lu:bri'keiʃən] Schmieren *n*, ⊕ Ölung *f.*

lucid □ ['lu:sid] leuchtend, klar.

luck [lʌk] Glück(sfall *m*) *n*; Geschick *n*; *good* ~ Glück *n*; *bad* ~, *hard* ~, *ill* ~ Unglück *n*, Pech *n*; *worse* ~ unglücklicherweise; ~**ily** ['lʌkili] glücklicherweise, zum Glück; ~**y** □ ['lʌki] glücklich; Glücks...; *be* ~ Glück haben.

lucr|ative □ ['lu:krətiv] einträglich; ~**e** ['lu:kə] Gewinn(sucht *f*) *m.*

ludicrous □ ['lu:dikrəs] lächerlich.

lug [lʌg] zerren, schleppen.

luge [lu:ʒ] 1. Rodelschlitten *m*; 2. rodeln.

luggage ['lʌgidʒ] Gepäck *n*; ~**carrier** Gepäckträger *m am Fahrrad*; ~**office** □ Gepäckschalter *m*; ~**rack** Gepäcknetz *n*; ~**ticket** Gepäckschein *m.*

lugubrious □ [lu:'gju:briəs] traurig.

lukewarm ['lu:kwɔ:m] lau (*a. fig.*).

lull [lʌl] 1. einlullen; (sich) beruhigen; 2. (Wind)Stille *f*; Ruhepause *f.*

lullaby ['lʌləbai] Wiegenlied *n.*

lumbago ✻ [lʌm'beigou] Hexenschuß *m.*

lumber ['lʌmbə] 1. Bau-, Nutzholz *n*; Gerümpel *n*; 2. v/t. a. ~ up vollstopfen; v/i. rumpeln, poltern; sich (dahin)schleppen; ~**er** [~ərə], ~**jack**, ~**man** Holzfäller *m*, -arbeiter *m*; ~**mill** Sägewerk *n*; ~**room** Rumpelkammer *f*, ~**yard** Holzplatz *m*, -lager *n.*

lumin|ary ['lu:minəri] Himmelskörper *m*; Leuchtkörper *m*; *fig.* Leuchte *f*; ~**ous** □ [~nəs] leuchtend; Licht...; Leucht...; *fig.* lichtvoll.

lump [lʌmp] 1. Klumpen *m*; *fig.* Klotz *m*; Beule *f*; Stück *n* Zucker *etc.*; *in the* ~ in Bausch und Bogen; ~ *sugar* Würfelzucker *m*; ~ *sum*

Pauschalsumme *f*; 2. v/t. zs.-werfen, zs.-fassen; v/i. Klumpen bilden; ~**ish** ['lʌmpiʃ] schwerfällig; ~**y** □ [~pi] klumpig.

lunacy ['lu:nəsi] Wahnsinn *m.*

lunar ['lu:nə] Mond...

lunatic ['lu:nətik] 1. irr-, wahnsinnig; 2. Irre(r *m*) *f*; Wahnsinnige(r *m*) *f*; Geistesgestörte(r *m*) *f*; ~ *asylum* Irrenhaus *n*, -anstalt *f.*

lunch|(eon) ['lʌntʃ, 'lʌntʃən] 1. Lunch *m*, Mittagessen *n*; zweites Frühstück; 2. zu Mittag essen; *j-m* ein Mittagessen geben; ~**hour** Mittagszeit *f*, -pause *f.*

lung *anat.* [lʌŋ] Lunge(nflügel *m*) *f*; *the* ~*s pl.* die Lunge.

lunge [lʌndʒ] 1. *Fechten:* Ausfall *m*; 2. v/i. ausfallen (*at gegen*); (dahin)stürmen; v/t. stoßen.

lupin(e) ♀ ['lu:pin] Lupine *f.*

lurch [lə:tʃ] 1. taumeln, torkeln; 2.: *leave in the* ~ im Stich lassen.

lure [ljuə] 1. Köder *m*; *fig.* Lockung *f*; 2. ködern, (an)locken.

lurid ['ljuərid] unheimlich; erschreckend, schockierend; düster, finster.

lurk [lə:k] lauern; versteckt liegen.

luscious □ ['lʌʃəs] köstlich; üppig; süß(lich), widerlich.

lust [lʌst] (sinnliche) Begierde; *fig.* Gier *f*, Sucht *f.*

lust|re, *Am.* ~**er** ['lʌstə] Glanz *m*; Kronleuchter *m*; ~**rous** □ [~trəs] glänzend.

lusty □ ['lʌsti] rüstig; *fig.* lebhaft, kräftig.

lute¹ ♪ [lu:t] Laute *f.*

lute² [~] 1. Kitt *m*; 2. (ver)kitten.

Lutheran ['lu:θərən] lutherisch.

luxate ✻ ['lʌkseit] verrenken.

luxur|iant □ [lʌg'zjuəriənt] üppig; ~**ious** □ [~iəs] luxuriös, üppig; ~**y** ['lʌkʃəri] Luxus *m*, Üppigkeit *f*; Luxusartikel *m*; Genußmittel *n.*

lyceum [lai'siəm] Vortragsraum *m*; *bsd. Am.* Volkshochschule *f.*

lye [lai] Lauge *f.*

lying ['laiiŋ] 1. *p.pr. von lie¹ 2 u. lie² 2*; 2. *adj.* lügnerisch; ~**in** [~ŋ'in] Wochenbett *n*; ~ *hospital* Entbindungsheim *n.*

lymph ✻ [limf] Lymphe *f.*

lynch [lintʃ] lynchen; ~**law** ['lintʃlɔ:] Lynchjustiz *f.*

lynx *zo.* [liŋks] Luchs *m.*

lyric ['lirik] 1. lyrisch; 2. lyrisches Gedicht; ~*s pl.* (Lied)Text *m* (*bsd. e-s Musicals*); Lyrik *f*; ~**al** □ [~kəl] lyrisch, gefühlvoll; schwärmerisch, begeistert.

M

ma'am [mæm] Majestät f (*Anrede für die Königin*); Hoheit f (*Anrede für Prinzessinnen*); F [məm] gnä' Frau f (*von Dienstboten verwendete Anrede*).

macaroni [mækə'rouni] Makkaroni *pl.*

macaroon [mækə'ruːn] Makrone f.

machin|ation [mæki'neiʃən] Anschlag m; ~s *pl.* Ränke *pl.*; ~e [mə'ʃiːn] 1. Maschine f; Mechanismus m (a. fig.); 2. maschinell herstellen *od.* (be)arbeiten; ~e-made maschinell hergestellt; ~ery [~əri] Maschinen f/pl.; Maschinerie f; ~ist [~nist] Maschinist m; Maschinennäherin f.

mackerel *ichth.* ['mækrəl] Makrele f.

mackinow *Am.* ['mækinɔ:] Stutzer m (*Kleidungsstück*).

mackintosh ['mækintɔʃ] Regenmantel m.

mad □ [mæd] wahnsinnig; toll (-wütig); fig. wild; F wütend; go ~ verrückt werden; drive ~ verrückt machen.

madam ['mædəm] gnädige Frau, gnädiges Fräulein (*Anrede*).

mad|cap ['mædkæp] 1. toll; 2. Tollkopf m; Wildfang m; ~den ['mædn] toll *od.* rasend machen.

made [meid] *pret. u. p.p. von* make 1.

made-up ['meid'ʌp] zurechtgemacht; erfunden; fertig; ~ clothes *pl.* Konfektion f.

mad|house ['mædhaus] Irrenhaus n; ~man Wahnsinnige(r) m; ~ness ['mædnis] Wahnsinn m; (Toll)Wut f.

magazine [mægə'ziːn] Magazin n; (Munitions)Lager n; Zeitschrift f.

maggot *zo.* ['mægət] Made f.

magic ['mædʒik] 1. a. ~al □ [~kəl] magisch; Zauber...; 2. Zauberei f; fig. Zauber m; ~ian [me'dʒiʃən] Zauberer m.

magistra|cy ['mædʒistrəsi] Richteramt n; *die Richter* m/pl.; ~te [~rit] (Polizei-, Friedens)Richter m.

magnanimous □ [mæg'næniməs] großmütig.

magnet ['mægnit] Magnet m; ~ic [mæg'netik] (~ally) magnetisch.

magni|ficence [mæg'nifisns] Pracht f, Herrlichkeit f; ~ficent [~nt] prächtig, herrlich; ~fy ['mægnifai] vergrößern; ~tude [~itjuːd] Größe f, Wichtigkeit f.

magpie *orn.* ['mægpai] Elster f.

mahogany [mə'hɔgəni] Mahagoni (-holz) n.

maid [meid] *lit.* Mädchen n; (Dienst)Mädchen n; old ~ alte

Jungfer; ~ of all work Mädchen n für alles; ~ of honour Ehren-, Hofdame f.

maiden ['meidn] 1. = maid; 2. jungfräulich; unverheiratet; fig. Jungfern..., Erstlings...; ~ name Mädchenname m e-r Frau; ~head Jungfräulichkeit f; ~hood [~hud] Mädchenjahre n/pl.; ~ly [~nli] jungfräulich, mädchenhaft.

mail[1] [meil] (Ketten)Panzer m.

mail[2] [~] 1. Post(dienst m) f; Post(sendung) f; 2. *Am.* mit der Post schicken, aufgeben; ~able *Am.* ['meilabl] postversandfähig; ~-bag Briefträger-, Posttasche f; Postsack m; ~-box *bsd. Am.* Briefkasten m; ~ carrier *Am.* Briefträger m; ~man *Am.* Briefträger m; ~-order firm, *bsd. Am.* ~-order house (Post)Versandgeschäft n.

maim [meim] verstümmeln.

main [mein] 1. Haupt..., hauptsächlich; by ~ force mit voller Kraft; 2. Hauptrohr n, -leitung f; ~s *pl.* ⚡ (Strom)Netz n; in the ~ in der Hauptsache, im wesentlichen; ~land ['meinlənd] Festland n; ~ly [~li] hauptsächlich; ~spring Uhrfeder f; fig. Haupttriebfeder f; ~stay ⚓ Großstag n; fig. Hauptstütze f ⚓ Street *Am.* Hauptstraße f; ⚓ Streeter *Am.* Kleinstadtbewohner m.

maintain [men'tein] (aufrecht)erhalten; beibehalten; (unter)stützen; unterhalten; behaupten.

maintenance ['meintinəns] Erhaltung f; Unterhalt m; ⊕ Wartung f.

maize ♀ [meiz] Mais m.

majest|ic [mə'dʒestik] (~ally) majestätisch; ~y ['mædʒisti] Majestät f; Würde f, Hoheit f.

major ['meidʒə] 1. größer; wichtig(er); mündig; ♪ Dur n; ~ key Dur-Tonart f; ~ league *Am. Baseball:* Oberliga f; 2. ✗ Major m; Mündige(r m) f; *Am. univ.* Hauptfach n; ~-general ✗ Generalmajor m; ~ity [mə'dʒɔriti] Mehrheit f; Mündigkeit f; Majorsrang m.

make [meik] 1. [*irr.*] v/t. *allg.* machen; verfertigen, fabrizieren; bilden; (aus)machen; ergeben; (veran)lassen; gewinnen, verdienen; sich erweisen als, abgeben; Regel etc. aufstellen; Frieden etc. schließen; e-e Rede halten; ~ good wieder gutmachen; whar machen; do you ~ one of us? machen Sie mit?; ~ port ⚓ den Hafen anlaufen; ~ way vorwärtskommen; ~ into verarbeiten zu; ~ out ausfindig machen; erkennen; verstehen; entziffern; *Rechnung etc.* ausstellen; ~ over übertragen; ~ up ergänzen; vervoll-

ständigen; zs.-stellen; bilden, ausmachen; *Streit* beilegen; zurechtmachen, schminken; = ~ *up for*
(*v*/*i*.); ~ *up one's mind* sich entschließen; *v*/*i*. sich begeben;
gehen; ~ *away with* beseitigen;
Geld vertun; ~ *for* zugehen auf
(*acc*.); sich aufmachen nach; ~ *off*
sich fortmachen; ~ *up* sich zurechtmachen; sich schminken; ~ *up for*
nach-, aufholen; für *et.* entschädigen; 2. Mach-, Bauart *f*; Bau *m des*
Körpers; Form *f*; Fabrikat *n*, Erzeugnis *n*; **~believe** ['meikbili:v]
Schein *m*, Vorwand *m*, Verstellung
f; **~r** ['meikə] Hersteller *m*; ♀
Schöpfer *m* (*Gott*); **~shift** 1. Notbehelf *m*; 2. behelfsmäßig; **~up**
typ. Umbruch *m*; *fig*. Charakter *m*;
Schminke *f*, Make-up *n*.

maladjustment ['mælə'dʒʌstmənt]
mangelhafte Anpassung.

maladministration ['mælədmin-
nis'treiʃən] schlechte Verwaltung.

malady ['mælədi] Krankheit *f*.

malcontent ['mælkəntent] 1. unzufrieden; 2. Unzufriedene(r) *m*.

male [meil] 1. männlich; 2. Mann
m; *zo*. Männchen *n*.

malediction [mæli'dikʃən] Fluch
m.

malefactor ['mælifæktə] Übeltäter
m.

malevolen|ce [mə'levələns] Bös-
willigkeit *f*; **~t** □ [~nt] böswillig.

malice ['mælis] Bosheit *f*; Groll *m*.

malicious [mə'liʃəs] boshaft;
böswillig; **~ness** [~snis] Bosheit *f*.

malign [mə'lain] 1. □ schädlich;
2. verleumden; **~ant** □ [mə-
'lignənt] böswillig; ❀ bösartig;
~ity [~niti] Bosheit *f*; Schadenfreude *f*; *bsd*. ❀ Bösartigkeit *f*.

malleable ['mæliəbl] hämmerbar;
fig. geschmeidig.

mallet ['mælit] Schlegel *m*.

malnutrition ['mælnju(:)'triʃən]
Unterernährung *f*.

malodorous □ [mæ'loudərəs] übelriechend.

malpractice ['mæl'præktis] Übel-
tat *f*; ❀ falsche Behandlung.

malt [mɔ:lt] Malz *n*.

maltreat [mæl'tri:t] schlecht behandeln; mißhandeln.

mam(m)a [mə'mɑ:] Mama *f*.

mammal ['mæml] Säugetier *n*.

mammoth ['mæməθ] riesig.

mammy F ['mæmi] Mami *f*; *Am*.
farbiges Kindermädchen.

man [mæn, *in Zssgn* ...mən] 1. *pl*.
men [men] Mann *m*; Mensch(en
pl.) *m*; Menschheit *f*; Diener *m*;
Schach: Figur *f*; Damestein *m*;
2. männlich; 3. ✂, ⚓ bemannen;
~ *o.s.* sich ermannen.

manage ['mænidʒ] *v*/*t*. handhaben;
verwalten, leiten; *Menschen, Tiere*
lenken; mit *j-m* fertig werden; *et*.

fertigbringen; ~ *to inf.* es fertigbringen, zu *inf.*; *v*/*i*. die Aufsicht
haben, die Geschäfte führen; auskommen; F es schaffen; **~able** □
[~dʒəbl] handlich; lenksam; **~ment**
[~dʒmənt] Verwaltung *f*, Leitung *f*,
Direktion *f*, Geschäftsführung *f*;
geschickte Behandlung; **~r** [~dʒə]
Leiter *m*, Direktor *m*; Regisseur *m*;
Manager *m*; **~ress** [~əres] Leiterin
f, Direktorin *f*.

managing ['mænidʒiŋ] geschäfts-
führend; *Betriebs*...; ~ *clerk* Geschäftsführer *m*, Prokurist *m*.

mandat|e ['mændeit] Mandat *n*;
Befehl *m*; Auftrag *m*; Vollmacht *f*;
~ory [~dətəri] befehlend.

mane [mein] Mähne *f*.

maneuver [mə'nu:və] = *manoeuvre*.

manful □ ['mænful] mannhaft.

mange *vet.* [meindʒ] Räude *f*.

manger ['meindʒə] Krippe *f*.

mangle ['mæŋgl] 1. Wringmaschine
f; Wäschemangel *f*; 2. mangeln;
wringen; zerstückeln; *fig*. verstümmeln.

mangy ['meindʒi] räudig; *fig*.
schäbig.

manhood ['mænhud] Mannesalter
n; Männlichkeit *f*; die Männer *m/pl.*

mania ['meinjə] Wahnsinn *m*;
Sucht *f*, Manie *f*; **~c** ['meiniæk]
1. Wahnsinnige(r *m*) *f*; 2. wahnsinnig.

manicure ['mænikjuə] 1. Maniküre
f; 2. maniküren.

manifest ['mænifest] 1. □ offenbar;
2. ⚓ Ladungsverzeichnis *n*; 3. *v*/*t*.
offenbaren; kundtun; **~ation**
[mænifes'teiʃən] Offenbarung *f*;
Kundgebung *f*; **~o** [mæni'festou]
Manifest *n*.

manifold □ ['mænifould] 1. mannigfaltig; 2. vervielfältigen.

manipulat|e [mə'nipjuleit] (ge-
schickt) handhaben; **~ion** [məni-
pju'leiʃən] Handhabung *f*, Behandlung *f*, Verfahren *n*; Kniff *m*.

man|kind [mæn'kaind] die Mensch-
heit; ['mænkaind] die Männer *pl.*;
~ly ['mænli] männlich; mannhaft.

manner ['mænə] Art *f*, Weise *f*;
Stil(art *f*) *m*; Manier *f*; **~s** *pl*. Manieren *f/pl.*, Sitten *f/pl.*; *in a* ~
gewissermaßen; **~ed** [~əd] ...gear-
tet; gekünstelt; **~ly** [~əli] manier-
lich, gesittet.

manoeuvre, *Am. a.* **maneuver**
[mə'nu:və] 1. Manöver *n* (*a. fig.*);
2. manövrieren (lassen).

man-of-war ⚓ ['mænəv'wɔ:]
Kriegsschiff *n*.

manor ['mænə] Rittergut *n*; *lord of
the* ~ Gutsherr *m*; **~house** Herr-
schaftshaus *n*, Herrensitz *m*; Schloß
n.

manpower ['mænpauə] Men-
schenpotential *n*; Arbeitskräfte *f/pl.*

man-servant ['mænsəːvənt] Diener *m*.

mansion ['mænʃən] (herrschaftliches) Wohnhaus.

manslaughter ɡ̣ ['mænslɔːtə] Totschlag *m*, fahrlässige Tötung.

mantel|piece ['mæntlpiːs], **~shelf** Kaminsims *m*, -platte *f*.

mantle ['mæntl] 1. Mantel *m*; *fig*. Hülle *f*; Glühstrumpf *m*; 2. *v/t*. verhüllen; *v/i*. sich röten (*Gesicht*).

manual ['mænjuəl] 1. □ Hand...; mit der Hand (gemacht); 2. Handbuch *n*. [brik *f*.)

manufactory [mænjuˈfæktəri] Fa-)

manufactur|e [mænjuˈfæktʃə] 1. Fabrikation *f*; Fabrikat *n*; 2. fabrizieren; verarbeiten; **~er** [~ərə] Fabrikant *m*; **~ing** [~riŋ] Fabrik...; Gewerbe...; Industrie...

manure [məˈnjuə] 1. Dünger *m*; 2. düngen.

manuscript ['mænjuskript] Manuskript *n*; Handschrift *f*.

many ['meni] 1. viele; **~** *a* manche(r, -s); *be one too* **~** *for s.o.* j-m überlegen sein; 2. Menge *f*; *a good* **~** *a great* **~** ziemlich viele, sehr viele.

map [mæp] 1. (Land)Karte *f*; 2. aufzeichnen; **~** *out* planen; einteilen.

maple ♀ ['meipl] Ahorn *m*.

mar [maː] schädigen; verderben.

maraud [məˈrɔːd] plündern.

marble ['maːbl] 1. Marmor *m*; Murmel *f*; 2. marmorn.

March[1] [maːtʃ] März *m*.

march[2] [~] 1. Marsch *m*; Fortschritt *m*; Gang *m der Ereignisse etc.*; 2. marschieren (lassen); *fig*. vorwärtsschreiten.

marchioness ['maːʃənis] Marquise *f*.

mare [mɛə] Stute *f*; **~**'s *nest fig*. Schwindel *m*; (Zeitungs)Ente *f*.

marg|arine [maːdʒəˈriːn], *a*. **~e** F [maːdʒ] Margarine *f*.

margin ['maːdʒin] Rand *m*; Grenze *f*; Spielraum *m*; Verdienst-, Gewinn-, Handelsspanne *f*; **~al** □ [~nl] am Rande (befindlich); Rand...; **~** *note* Randbemerkung *f*.

marine [məˈriːn] Marineinfanterist *m*; Marine *f*; *paint*. Seestück *n*; *attr*. See...; Marine...; Schiffs...; **~r** ['mærinə] Seemann *m*.

marital □ ['mæritl] ehelich, Ehe...

maritime ['mæritaim] an der See liegend *od*. lebend; See...; Küsten-...; Schiffahrt(s)...

mark[1] [maːk] Mark *f* (*Geldstück*).

mark[2] [~] 1. Marke *f*, Merkmal *n*, Zeichen *n*; ✝ Preiszettel *m*; Fabrik-, Schutzmarke *f*; (Körper)Mal *n*; Norm *f*; *Schule*: Zensur *f*, Note *f*; Punkt *m*; *Sport*: Startlinie *f*; Ziel *n*; *a man of* **~** ein Mann von Bedeutung; *fig. up to the* **~** auf der Höhe;

beside the **~**, *wide of the* **~** den Kern der Sache verfehlend; unrichtig; 2. *v/t*. (be)zeichnen, markieren; *Sport*: anschreiben; kennzeichnen; be(ob)achten; sich *et*. merken; **~** *off* abtrennen; **~** *out* bezeichnen; abstecken; **~** *time* auf der Stelle treten; *v/i*. achtgeben; **~ed** □ auffallend; merklich; ausgeprägt.

market ['maːkit] 1. Markt(platz) *m*; Handel *m*; ✝ Absatz *m*; *in the* **~** auf dem Markt; *play the* **~** *Am. sl.* an der Börse spekulieren; 2. *v/t*. auf den Markt bringen, verkaufen; *v/i*. einkaufen gehen; **~able** □ [~təbl] marktfähig, -gängig; **~ing** [~tiŋ] ✝ Marketing *n*, Absatzpolitik *f*; Marktbesuch *m*.

marksman ['maːksmən] (guter) Schütze.

marmalade ['maːməleid] Orangenmarmelade *f*.

maroon [məˈruːn] 1. kastanienbraun; 2. *auf e-r einsamen Insel* aussetzen; 3. Leuchtrakete *f*.

marquee [maːˈkiː] (großes) Zelt.

marquis ['maːkwis] Marquis *m*.

marriage ['mæridʒ] Heirat *f*, Ehe (-stand *m*) *f*; Hochzeit *f*; *civil* **~** standesamtliche Trauung; **~able** [~dʒəbl] heiratsfähig; **~ articles** *pl*. Ehevertrag *m*; **~ lines** *pl*. Trauschein *m*; **~ portion** Mitgift *f*.

married ['mærid] verheiratet; ehelich; Ehe...; **~** *couple* Ehepaar *n*.

marrow ['mærou] Mark *n*; *fig*. Kern *m*, Beste(s) *n*; **~y** [~oui] markig.

marry ['mæri] *v/t*. (ver)heiraten; *eccl*. trauen; *v/i*. (sich ver)heiraten.

marsh [maːʃ] Sumpf *m*, Morast *m*.

marshal ['maːʃəl] 1. Marschall *m*; *hist*. Hofmarschall *m*; Zeremonienmeister *m*; *Am*. Bezirkspolizeichef *m*; Leiter *m* der Feuerwehr; 2. ordnen; führen; zs.-stellen.

marshy ['maːʃi] sumpfig.

mart [maːt] Markt *m*; Auktionsraum *m*.

marten *zo*. ['maːtin] Marder *m*.

martial □ ['maːʃəl] kriegerisch; Kriegs...; **~** *law* Stand-, Kriegsrecht *n*.

martyr ['maːtə] 1. Märtyrer(in) (*to gen.*); 2. (zu Tode) martern.

marvel ['maːvel] 1. Wunder *n*; 2. sich wundern; **~lous** □ ['maːviləs] wunderbar, erstaunlich.

mascot ['mæskət] Maskottchen *n*.

masculine ['maːskjulin] männlich.

mash [mæʃ] 1. Gemisch *n*; Maische *f*; Mengfutter *n*; 2. mischen; zerdrücken; (ein)maischen; **~ed** *potatoes* *pl*. Kartoffelbrei *m*.

mask [maːsk] 1. Maske *f*; 2. maskieren; *fig*. verbergen; tarnen; **~ed**: **~** *ball* Maskenball *m*.

mason ['meisn] Steinmetz *m*; Maurer *m*; Freimaurer *m*; **~ry** [~nri] Mauerwerk *n*.

masque [mɑːsk] Maskenspiel n.

masquerade [mæskə'reid] 1. Maskenball m; Verkleidung f; 2. fig. sich maskieren.

mass [mæs] 1. eccl. Messe f; Masse f; Menge f; ~ meeting Massenversammlung f; 2. (sich) (an)sammeln.

massacre ['mæsəkə] 1. Blutbad n; 2. niedermetzeln.

massage ['mæsɑːʒ] 1. Massage f; 2. massieren.

massif ['mæsiːf] (Gebirgs)Massiv n.

massive ['mæsiv] massiv; schwer.

mast ♣ [mɑːst] Mast m.

master ['mɑːstə] 1. Meister m; Herr m (a. fig.); Gebieter m; Lehrer m; Kapitän m e-s Handelsschiffs; Anrede: (junger) Herr; univ. Rektor m e-s College; ♀ of Arts Magister m Artium; ♀ of Ceremonies Conférencier m; 2. Meister...; fig. führend; 3. Herr sein od. werden über (acc.); Sprache etc. meistern, beherrschen; ~-builder Baumeister m; ~ful □ [~əful] herrisch; meisterhaft; ~key Hauptschlüssel f; ~ly [~əli] meisterhaft; ~piece Meisterstück n; ~ship [~əʃip] Meisterschaft f; Herrschaft f; Lehramt n; ~y [~əri] Herrschaft f; Vorrang m; Oberhand f; Meisterschaft f; Beherrschung f.

masticate ['mæstikeit] kauen.

mastiff ['mæstif] englische Dogge.

mat [mæt] 1. Matte f; Deckchen n; Unterlage f; 2. fig. bedecken; (sich) verflechten; 3. mattiert, matt.

match¹ [mætʃ] Streichholz n.

match² [~] 1. Gleiche(r m, -s n) f; Partie f; Wettspiel n, -kampf m; Heirat f; be a ~ for j-m gewachsen sein; meet one's ~ s-n Meister finden; 2. v/t. anpassen; passen zu; et. Passendes finden od. geben zu; es aufnehmen mit; verheiraten; well ~ed zs.-passend; v/i. zs.-passen; to ~ dazu passend; ~less □ ['mætʃlis] unvergleichlich, ohnegleichen; ~maker Ehestifter(in).

mate¹ [meit] Schach: matt (setzen).

mate² [~] 1. Gefährt|e m, -in f; Kamerad(in); Gatt|e m, -in f; Männchen n, Weibchen n von Tieren; Gehilf|e m, -in f; ♣ Maat m; 2. (sich) verheiraten; (sich) paaren.

material [mə'tiəriəl] 1. materiell; körperlich; materialistisch; wesentlich; 2. Material n, Stoff m; Werkstoff m; writing ~s pl. Schreibmaterial(ien pl.) n.

matern|al □ [mə'təːnl] mütterlich; Mutter...; mütterlicherseits; ~ity [~niti] Mutterschaft f; Mütterlichkeit f; mst ~ hospital Entbindungsanstalt f.

mathematic|ian [mæθimə'tiʃən] Mathematiker m; ~s [~'mætiks] mst sg. Mathematik f.

matriculate [mə'trikjuleit] (sich) immatrikulieren (lassen).

matrimon|ial □ [mætri'mounjəl] ehelich; Ehe...; ~y ['mætriməni] Ehe(stand m) f.

matrix ['meitriks] Matrize f.

matron ['meitrən] Matrone f; Hausmutter f; Oberin f.

matter ['mætə] 1. Materie f, Stoff m; ♣ Eiter m; Gegenstand m; Ursache f; Sache f; Angelegenheit f, Geschäft n; printed ~ ♣ Drucksache f; what's the ~? was gibt es?; what's the ~ with you? was fehlt Ihnen?; no ~ es hat nichts zu sagen; no ~ who gleichgültig wer; ~ of course Selbstverständlichkeit f; for that ~, for the ~ of that was dies betrifft; ~ of fact Tatsache f; 2. von Bedeutung sein; it does not ~, es macht nichts; ~-of-fact tatsächlich; sachlich.

mattress ['mætris] Matratze f.

matur|e [mə'tjuə] 1. □ reif; reiflich; ♣ fällig; 2. reifen; zur Reife bringen; ♣ fällig werden; ~ity [~əriti] Reife f; ♣ Fälligkeit f.

maudlin □ ['mɔːdlin] rührselig.

maul [mɔːl] beschädigen; fig. heruntermachen; roh umgehen mit.

Maundy Thursday eccl. ['mɔːndi 'θəːzdi] Gründonnerstag m.

mauve [mouv] 1. Malvenfarbe f; 2. hellviolett.

maw [mɔː] Tier-Magen m; Rachen m.

mawkish □ ['mɔːkiʃ] rührselig, sentimental.

maxim ['mæksim] Grundsatz m; ~um [~məm] Höchstmaß n, -stand m, -betrag m; attr. Höchst...

May¹ [mei] Mai m.

may² [~] [irr.] mag, kann, darf.

maybe Am. ['meibiː] vielleicht.

may|-beetle zo. ['meibiːtl], ~-bug Maikäfer m.

May Day ['meidei] der 1. Mai.

mayor [mɛə] Bürgermeister m.

maypole ['meipoul] Maibaum m.

maz|e [meiz] Irrgarten m, Labyrinth n; fig. Wirrnis f; in a ~ = ~ed [meizd] bestürzt, verwirrt; ~y □ ['meizi] labyrinthisch; wirr.

me [miː, mi] mich; mir; F ich.

mead [miːd] Met m; poet. = meadow.

meadow ['medou] Wiese f.

meag|re, Am. ~er □ ['miːgə] mager, dürr; dürftig.

meal [miːl] Mahl(zeit f) n; Mehl n.

mean¹ □ [miːn] gemein, niedrig, gering; armselig; knauserig.

mean² [~] 1. mittler, mittelmäßig; Durchschnitts...; in the ~ time inzwischen; 2. Mitte f; ~s pl. (Geld-)Mittel n/pl.; (a. sg.) Mittel n; by all ~s jedenfalls; by no ~s keineswegs; by ~s of mittels (gen.).

mean³ [~] [irr.] meinen; beabsich-

tigen; bestimmen; bedeuten; ~
well (*ill*) es gut (schlecht) meinen.
meaning ['mi:niŋ] **1.** □ bedeut-
sam; **2.** Sinn *m*, Bedeutung *f*; ~less
[~nlis] bedeutungslos; sinnlos.
meant [ment] *pret. u. p.p. von*
*mean*³.
mean|time ['mi:n'taim], ~while
mittlerweile, inzwischen.
measles 𝔰 ['mi:zlz] *sg.* Masern *pl.*
measure ['meʒə] **1.** Maß *n*; ♪ Takt
m; Maßregel *f*; ~ *of capacity* Hohl-
maß *n*; *beyond* ~ über alle Maßen;
in a great ~ großenteils; *made to* ~
nach Maß gemacht; **2.** (ab-, aus-,
ver)messen; *j-m* Maß nehmen; ~ *up*
Am. heranreichen; ~less □ [~əlis]
unermeßlich; ~ment [~əmənt]
Messung *f*; Maß *n*.
meat [mi:t] Fleisch *n*; *fig.* Gehalt *m*;
~ *tea* frühes Abendessen mit Tee;
~y ['mi:ti] fleischig; *fig.* gehaltvoll.
mechanic [mi'kænik] Handwerker
m; Mechaniker *m*; ~al □ [~kəl]
mechanisch; Maschinen...; ~ian
[mekə'niʃən] Mechaniker *m*; ~s
[mi'kæniks] *mst sg.* Mechanik *f*.
mechan|ism ['mekənizəm] Me-
chanismus *m*; ~ize [~naiz] mecha-
nisieren; ⚔ motorisieren.
medal ['medl] Medaille *f*; Orden
m.
meddle ['medl] sich einmischen
(*with, in* in *acc.*); ~some [~lsəm]
zu-, aufdringlich.
mediaeval □ [medi'i:vəl] mittelal-
terlich.
media|l □ ['mi:djəl], ~n [~ən]
Mittel..., in der Mitte (befindlich).
mediat|e ['mi:dieit] vermitteln;
~ion [mi:di'eiʃən] Vermittlung *f*;
~or ['mi:dieitə] Vermittler *m*.
medical □ ['medikəl] medizinisch,
ärztlich; ~ *certificate* Kranken-
schein *m*, Attest *n*; ~ *evidence* ärzt-
liches Gutachten; ~ *man* Arzt *m*,
Mediziner *m*; ~ *supervision* ärztliche Aufsicht.
medicate ['medikeit] medizinisch
behandeln; mit Arzneistoff versehen; ~d *bath* medizinisches Bad.
medicin|al □ [me'disinl] medizi-
nisch; heilend, heilsam; ~e ['med-
sin] Medizin *f*.
medieval □ [medi'i:vəl] = *mediae-*
val.
mediocre ['mi:dioukə] mittelmäßig.
meditat|e ['mediteit] *v/i.* nachden-
ken, überlegen; *v/t.* sinnen auf
(*acc.*); erwägen; ~ion [medi'teiʃən]
Nachdenken *n*; innere Betrachtung;
~ive □ ['meditətiv] nachdenklich,
meditativ.
Mediterranean [meditə'reinjən]
Mittelmeer *n*; *attr.* Mittelmeer-.
medium ['mi:djəm] **1.** Mitte *f*;
Mittel *n*; Vermittlung *f*; Medium
n; *Lebens-*Element *n*; **2.** mittler;
Mittel..., Durchschnitts...

medley ['medli] Gemisch *n*; ♪ Pot-
pourri *n*.
meek □ [mi:k] sanft-, demütig;
~ness ['mi:knis] Sanft-, Demut *f*.
meerschaum ['miəʃəm] Meer-
schaum(pfeife *f*) *m*.
meet¹ [mi:t] passend; schicklich.
meet² [~] [*irr.*] *v/t.* treffen; begegnen (*dat.*); abholen; stoßen auf
den Gegner; *Wunsch etc.* befriedigen; *e-r Verpflichtung* nachkommen; *Am. j-m* vorgestellt werden; ~
go to ~ s.o. j-m entgegengehen; *v/i.*
sich treffen; zs.-stoßen; *sich ver-*
sammeln; ~ *with* stoßen auf (*acc.*);
erleiden; ~ing ['mi:tiŋ] Begegnung
f; (Zs.-)Treffen *n*, Versammlung *f*;
Tagung *f*.
melancholy ['melənkəli] **1.** Schwermut *f*; **2.** melancholisch.
meliorate [mi:ljəreit] (sich) verbessern.
mellow ['melou] **1.** □ mürbe; reif;
weich; mild; **2.** reifen (lassen);
weich machen *od.* werden; (sich)
mildern.
melo|dious □ [mi'loudjəs] melo-
disch; ~dramatic [meloudrə-
'mætik] melodramatisch; ~dy
['melədi] Melodie *f*; Lied *n*.
melon 🜨 ['melən] Melone *f*.
melt [melt] (zer)schmelzen; *fig.* zer-
fließen; *Gefühl* erweichen.
member ['membə] (Mit)Glied *n*;
parl. Abgeordnete(r *m*) *f*; ~ship
[~əʃip] Mitgliedschaft *f*; Mitgliederzahl *f*.
membrane ['membrein] Mem-
bran(e) *f*, Häutchen *n*. [*n*.]
memento [mi'mentou] Andenken
memo ['mi:mou] = *memorandum*.
memoir ['memwa:] Denkschrift *f*;
~s *pl.* Memoiren *pl.*
memorable □ ['memərəbl] denk-
würdig.
memorandum [memə'rændəm]
Notiz *f*; *pol.* Note *f*; Schriftsatz *m*.
memorial [mi'mɔ:riəl] Denkmal *n*;
Gedenkzeichen *n*; Denkschrift *f*,
Eingabe *f*; *attr.* Gedächtnis..., Gedenk...
memorize ['meməraiz] auswendig
lernen, memorieren.
memory ['meməri] Gedächtnis *n*;
Erinnerung *f*; Andenken *n*; *commit*
to ~ dem Gedächtnis einprägen;
in ~ *of* zum Andenken an (*acc.*).
men [men] *pl. von man* **1**; Mannschaft *f*.
menace ['menəs] **1.** (be)drohen;
2. Gefahr *f*; Drohung *f*.
mend [mend] **1.** *v/t.* (ver)bessern;
ausbessern, flicken; besser machen;
~ *one's ways* sich bessern; *v/i.* sich
bessern; **2.** Flicken *m*; *on the* ~ auf
dem Wege der Besserung.
mendacious □ [men'deiʃəs] lügnerisch, verlogen.
mendicant ['mendikənt] **1.** bet-

telnd; Bettel...; 2. Bettler *m*; Bettel-
mönch *m*.
menial *contp.* ['mi:njəl] 1. □ knecht-
tisch; niedrig; 2. Knecht *m*; Lakai *m*.
meningitis ⚕ [menin'dʒaitis] Hirn-
hautentzündung *f*, Meningitis *f*.
mental □ ['mentl] geistig; Geistes...; ~ arithmetic Kopfrechnen *n*;
~ity [men'tæliti] Mentalität *f*.
mention ['menʃən] 1. Erwähnung *f*;
2. erwähnen; *don't* ~ *it!* bitte!
menu ['menju:] Speisenfolge *f*,
Menü *n*; Speisekarte *f*.
mercantile ['mə:kəntail] kaufmännisch; Handels...
mercenary ['mə:sinəri] 1. □ feil,
käuflich; gedungen; gewinnsüch-
tig; 2. ✗ Söldner *m*.
mercer ['mə:sə] Seidenwaren-,
Stoffhändler *m*.
merchandise ['mə:tʃəndaiz] Wa-
re(n *pl.*) *f*.
merchant ['mə:tʃənt] 1. Kaufmann
m; *Am.* (Klein)Händler *m*; 2. Handels..., Kaufmanns...; *law* ~ Han-
delsrecht *n*; ~man Handelsschiff *n*.
merci|ful □ ['mə:siful] barmher-
zig; ~less □ [~ilis] unbarmherzig.
mercury ['mə:kjuri] Quecksilber *n*.
mercy ['mə:si] Barmherzigkeit *f*;
Gnade *f*; *be at s.o.'s* ~ in j-s Gewalt sein.
mere [miə] rein, lauter; bloß;
~ly ['miəli] bloß, lediglich, allein.
meretricious □ [meri'triʃəs] aufdringlich; kitschig.
merge [mə:dʒ] verschmelzen (*in*
mit); ~r ['mə:dʒə] Verschmelzung *f*.
meridian [mə'ridiən] *geogr.* Meridian *m*; *fig.* Gipfel *m*; *attr.* Mittags...
merit ['merit] 1. Verdienst *n*; Wert
m; Vorzug *m*; *bsd.* ⚖ ~*s pl.* Haupt-
punkte *m/pl.*, Wesen *n e-r Sache*;
make a ~ *of* als Verdienst ansehen;
2. *fig.* verdienen; ~orious □
[meri'tɔ:riəs] verdienstvoll.
mermaid ['mə:meid] Nixe *f*.
merriment ['merimənt] Lustigkeit
f; Belustigung *f*.
merry ['meri] lustig, fröhlich;
make ~ lustig sein; ~ **andrew**
Hanswurst *m*; ~**go-round** Karussell *n*; ~**making** [~imeikiŋ] Lustbarkeit *f*.
mesh [meʃ] 1. Masche *f*; *fig.* oft ~es
pl. Netz *n*; *be in* ~ ⊕ (in-ea.-)grei-
fen; 2. in e-m Netz fangen.
mess¹ [mes] 1. Unordnung *f*;
Schmutz *m*, F Schweinerei *f*; F Patsche *f*; *make a* ~ *of* verpfuschen; 2.
v/t. in Unordnung bringen; verpfuschen; *v/i.* ~ *about* F herummurksen.
mess² [~] Kasino *n*, Messe *f*.
message ['mesidʒ] Botschaft *f*; *go
on a* ~ e-e Besorgung machen.
messenger ['mesindʒə] Bote *m*.
Messieurs, *mst* **Messrs.** ['mesəz]
(die) Herren *m/pl.*; Firma *f*.

met [met] *pret. u. p.p. von* meet².
metal ['metl] 1. Metall *n*; Schotter
m; 2. beschottern; ~lic [mi'tælik]
(~ally) metallisch; Metall...; ~lurgy
[me'tælədʒi] Hüttenkunde *f*.
metamorphose [metə'mɔ:fouz] verwandeln, umgestalten.
metaphor ['metəfə] Metapher *f*.
meteor ['mi:tjə] Meteor *m* (*a. fig.*);
~ology [mi:tjə'rɔlədʒi] Meteorologie *f*, Wetterkunde *f*.
meter ['mi:tə] Messer *m*, Zähler *m*;
Am. = metre.
methinks † [mi'θiŋks] mich dünkt.
method ['meθəd] Methode *f*; Art
u. Weise *f*; Verfahren *n*; Ordnung
f, System *n*; ~ic(al □) [mi'θɔ-
dik(əl)] methodisch.
methought [mi'θɔ:t] *pret. von*
methinks.
meticulous □ [mi'tikjuləs] peinlich
genau.
met|re, *Am.* ~er ['mi:tə] Meter *n*,
m; Versmaß *n*.
metric ['metrik] (~ally) metrisch;
~ system Dezimalsystem *n*.
metropoli|s [mi'trɔpolis] Haupt-
stadt *f*, Metropole *f*; ~tan [metrə-
'politən] hauptstädtisch.
mettle ['metl] Feuereifer *m*, Mut *m*;
be on one's ~ sein Bestes tun.
mews [mju:z] Stallung *f*; *daraus
entstandene* Garagen *f/pl. od.* Wohn-
häuser *n/pl.*
Mexican ['meksikən] 1. mexika-
nisch; 2. Mexikaner(in).
miaow [mi(:)'au] miauen; mauzen.
mice [mais] *pl. von* mouse.
Michaelmas ['miklməs] Michaelis
(-tag *m*) *n* (29. *September*).
micro... ['maikrou] klein..., Klein...
micro|phone ['maikrəfoun] Mikro-
phon *n*; ~scope Mikroskop *n*.
mid [mid] mittler; Mitt(el)...; *in* ~
air mitten in der Luft; *in* ~ *winter*
mitten im Winter; ~day ['middei]
1. Mittag *m*; 2. mittägig; Mittags...
middle ['midl] 1. Mitte *f*; Hüften
f/pl.; 2. mittler; Mittel...; ♀ *Ages
pl.* Mittelalter *n*; ~aged von mittlerem Alter; ~class Mittelstands-
...; ~ class(es *pl.*) Mittelstand *m*;
~man Mittelsmann *m*; ~ name
zweiter Vorname *m*; ~sized mittel-
groß; ~weight *Boxen:* Mittelge-
wicht *n*.
middling ['midliŋ] mittelmäßig;
leidlich; Mittel...
middy F ['midi] = midshipman.
midge [midʒ] Mücke *f*; ~t ['midʒit]
Zwerg *m*, Knirps *m*.
mid|land ['midlənd] 1. binnenlän-
disch; 2. the 2s *pl.* Mittelengland *n*;
~most mittelste(r, -s); ~night
Mitternacht *f*; ~riff ['midrif]
Zwerchfell *n*; ~shipman Leutnant
m zur See; *Am.* Oberfähnrich *m*
zur See; ~st [midst] Mitte *f*; *in the*
~ *of* inmitten (*gen.*); ~summer

Sommersonnenwende *f*; Hoch-
sommer *m*; ⁓way 1. halber Weg;
Am. Schaubudenstraße *f*; 2. *adj.*
in der Mitte befindlich; 3. *adv.* auf
halbem Wege; ⁓wife Hebamme *f*;
⁓wifery ['midwifəri] Geburtshilfe
f; ⁓winter Wintersonnenwende *f*;
Mitte *f* des Winters.

mien [miːn] Miene *f*.

might [mait] 1. Macht *f*, Gewalt *f*,
Kraft *f*; with ⁓ and main mit aller
Gewalt; 2. *pret. von* may²; ⁓y □
['maiti] mächtig, gewaltig.

migrat|e [mai'greit] (aus)wandern;
⁓ion [⁓eifən] Wanderung *f*; ⁓ory
['maigrətəri] wandernd; Zug...

mild □ [maild] mild, sanft; gelind.

mildew ♀ ['mildjuː] Mehltau *m*.

mildness ['maildnis] Milde *f*.

mile [mail] Meile *f* (1609.33 m).

mil(e)age ['maildʒ] Laufzeit *f in
Meilen*, Meilenstand *m e-s Autos*;
Kilometergeld *n*.

milestone ['mailstoun] Meilenstein
m.

milit|ary ['militəri] 1. □ militä-
risch; Kriegs...; ⚹ *Government*
Militärregierung *f*; 2. *das* Militär;
⁓ia [mi'lifə] Land-, Bürgerwehr *f*.

milk [milk] 1. Milch *f*; *it's no use
crying over spilt* ⁓ geschehen ist geschehen; 2. *v/t.* melken; *v/i.* Milch
geben; ⁓maid ['milkmeid] Melke-
rin *f*; Milchmädchen *n*; ⁓man
Milchmann *m*; ⁓powder Milch-
pulver *n*; ⁓shake Milchmischge-
tränk *n*; ⁓sop Weichling *m*; ⁓y ['mil-
ki] milchig; Milch...; ⚹ Way Milch-
straße *f*.

mill¹ [mil] 1. Mühle *f*; Fabrik *f*,
Spinnerei *f*; 2. mahlen; ⊕ fräsen;
Geld prägen; *Münze* rändeln.

mill² *Am.* [⁓] ¹⁄₁₀₀₀ Dollar *m*.

millepede *zo.* ['milipiːd] Tausend-
füß(l)er *m*.

miller ['milə] Müller *m*; ⊕ Fräs-
maschine *f*.

millet ♀ ['milit] Hirse *f*.

milliner ['milinə] Putzmacherin *f*,
Modistin *f*; ⁓y [⁓əri] Putz-, Mode-
waren(geschäft *n*) *pl*.

million ['miljən] Million *f*; ⁓aire
[miljə'nɛə] Millionär(in); ⁓th
['miljənθ] 1. millionste(r, -s);
2. Millionstel *n*.

mill|-pond ['milpɔnd] Mühlteich
m; ⁓stone Mühlstein *m*.

milt [milt] Milch *f der Fische*.

mimic ['mimik] 1. mimisch;
Schein...; 2. Mime *m*; 3. nachahmen; nachäffen; ⁓ry [⁓kri] Nach-
ahmung *f*; *zo.* Angleichung *f*.

mince· [mins] 1. *v/t.* zerhacken; *he
does not* ⁓ *matters* er nimmt kein
Blatt vor den Mund; *v/i.* sich zieren; 2. *a.* ⁓d *meat* Hackfleisch *n*;
⁓meat ['minsmiːt] *e-e* Torten-
füllung; ⁓pie Torte *f* aus *mince-
meat*; ⁓r [⁓ə] Fleischwolf *m*.

mincing-machine ['minsiŋməfiːn]
= *mincer*.

mind [maind] 1. Sinn *m*, Gemüt *n*;
Geist *m*, Verstand *m*; Meinung *f*;
Absicht *f*; Neigung *f*, Lust *f*; Gedächtnis *n*; Sorge *f*; *to my* ⁓ meiner
Ansicht nach; *out of one's* ⁓, *not
in one's right* ⁓ von Sinnen; *change
one's* ⁓ sich anders besinnen; *bear
s.th. in* ⁓ (immer) an et. denken;
have (half) a ⁓ *to* (beinahe) Lust
haben zu; *have s.th. on one's* ⁓ et.
auf dem Herzen haben; *make up
one's* ⁓ sich entschließen; 2. merken
od. achten auf (*acc.*); sich kümmern
um; etwas (einzuwenden) haben
gegen; ⁓! gib acht!; *never* ⁓! macht
nichts!; ⁓ *the step!* Achtung,
Stufe!; *I don't* ⁓ (it) ich habe nichts
dagegen; *do you* ⁓ *if I smoke?* stört
es Sie, wenn ich rauche?; *would
you* ⁓ *taking off your hat?* würden
Sie bitte den Hut abnehmen?; ⁓
your own business! kümmern Sie
sich um Ihre Angelegenheiten!;
⁓ful □ ['maindful] (*of*) eingedenk
(*gen.*); achtsam (auf *acc.*).

mine¹ [main] 1. der (die, das) mei-
nige; mein; 2. die Mein(ig)en
pl.

mine² [⁓] 1. Bergwerk *n*, Grube *f*;
fig. Fundgrube *f*; ⚔ Mine *f*; 2. *v/t.*
graben, minieren; *v/t.* graben;
⚒ fördern; ⚔ unterminieren; ⚔
verminen; ⁓r ['mainə] Bergmann *m*.

mineral ['minərəl] 1. Mineral *n*; ⁓s
pl. Mineralwasser *n*; 2. mineralisch.

mingle ['miŋgl] (ver)mischen; sich
mischen *od.* mengen (with unter).

miniature ['minjətfə] 1. Miniatur
(-gemälde *n*) *f*; 2. in Miniatur;
Miniatur...; Klein...; ⁓ *camera*
Kleinbildkamera *f*.

minikin ['minikin] 1. winzig; geziert; 2. Knirps *m*.

minim|ize ['minimaiz] möglichst
klein machen; *fig.* verringern; ⁓um
[⁓məm] Minimum *n*; Mindestmaß
n; Mindestbetrag *m*; *attr.* Mindest...

mining ['mainiŋ] Bergbau *m*; *attr.*
Berg(bau)...; Gruben...

minion ['minjən] Günstling *m*; *fig.*
Lakai *m*.

miniskirt ['miniskəːt] Minirock *m*.

minister ['ministə] 1. Diener *m*;
fig. Werkzeug *n*; Geistliche(r) *m*;
Minister *m*; Gesandte(r) *m*; 2. *v/t.*
darreichen; *v/i.* dienen; Gottesdienst halten.

ministry ['ministri] geistliches Amt;
Ministerium *n*; Regierung *f*.

mink *zo.* [miŋk] Nerz *m*.

minor ['mainə] 1. kleiner, geringer,
weniger bedeutend; ♪ Moll *n*; A ⁓
A-moll *n*; 2. Minderjährige(r *m*) *f*;
Am. univ. Nebenfach *n*; ⁓ity
[mai'nɔriti] Minderheit *f*; Un-
mündigkeit *f*.

minster ['minstə] Münster *n*.

minstrel ['minstrəl] Minnesänger *m*; ~s *pl.* Negersänger *m/pl.*

mint [mint] 1. ♀ Minze *f*; Münze *f*; *fig.* Goldgrube *f*; *a* ~ *of money* e-e Menge Geld; 2. münzen, prägen.

minuet ♪ [minju'et] Menuett *n.*

minus ['mainəs] 1. *prp.* weniger; F ohne; 2. *adj.* negativ.

minute 1. □ [mai'nju:t] sehr klein, winzig; unbedeutend; sehr genau; 2. ['minit] Minute *f*; Augenblick *m*; ~s *pl.* Protokoll *n*; ~ness [mai'nju:tnis] Kleinheit *f*; Genauigkeit *f.*

mirac|le ['mirəkl] Wunder *n*; ~ulous □ [mi'rækjuləs] wunderbar.

mirage ['mira:ʒ] Luftspiegelung *f.*

mire ['maiə] 1. Sumpf *m*; Kot *m*, Schlamm *m*; 2. mit Schlamm *od.* Schmutz bedecken.

mirror ['mirə] 1. Spiegel *m*; 2. (wider)spiegeln (*a. fig.*).

mirth [mə:θ] Fröhlichkeit *f*; ~ful □ ['mə:θful] fröhlich; ~less □ ['mə:θlis] freudlos.

miry ['maiəri] kotig.

mis... [mis] miß..., übel, falsch.

misadventure ['misəd'ventʃə] Mißgeschick *n*, Unfall *m.*

misanthrop|e ['mizənθroup], ~ist [mi'zænθrəpist] Menschenfeind *m.*

misapply ['misə'plai] falsch anwenden; [mißverstehen.]

misapprehend ['misæpri'hend])

misappropriate ['misə'prouprieit] unterschlagen, veruntreuen.

misbehave ['misbi'heiv] sich schlecht benehmen.

misbelief ['misbi'li:f] Irrglaube *m.*

miscalculate ['mis'kælkjuleit] falsch (be)rechnen.

miscarr|iage [mis'kæridʒ] Mißlingen *n*; Verlust *m* v. *Briefen*; Fehlgeburt *f*; ~ *of justice* Fehlspruch *m*; ~y [~ri] mißlingen; verlorengehen (*Brief*); fehlgebären.

miscellan|eous □ [misi'leinjəs] ge-, vermischt; vielseitig; ~y [mi'seləni] Gemisch *n*; Sammelband *m.*

mischief ['mistʃif] Schaden *m*, Unfug *m*; Mutwille *m*, Übermut *m*; ~-maker Unheilstifter(in).

mischievous □ ['mistʃivəs] schädlich; boshaft, mutwillig.

misconceive ['miskən'si:v] falsch auffassen *od.* verstehen.

misconduct 1. [miskən'dʌkt] schlechtes Benehmen; Ehebruch *m*; schlechte Verwaltung; 2. ['miskən'dʌkt] schlecht verwalten; ~ *o.s.* sich schlecht benehmen; e-n Fehltritt begehen.

misconstrue ['miskən'stru:] mißdeuten.

miscreant ['miskriənt] Schurke *m.*

misdeed ['mis'di:d] Missetat *f.*

misdemeano(u)r ⚖ [misdi'mi:nə] Vergehen *n.*

misdirect ['misdi'rekt] irreleiten; an die falsche Adresse richten.

misdoing ['misdu(:)iŋ] Vergehen *n* (*mst pl.*).

mise en scène *thea.* ['mi:zɑ:n'sein] Inszenierung *f.*

miser ['maizə] Geizhals *m.*

miserable □ ['mizərəbl] elend; unglücklich, erbärmlich.

miserly ['maizəli] geizig, filzig.

misery ['mizəri] Elend *n*, Not *f.*

misfit ['misfit] schlecht passendes Stück (*Kleid, Stiefel etc.*); Einzelgänger *m*, Eigenbrötler *m.*

misfortune [mis'fo:tʃən] Unglück(sfall *m*) *n*; Mißgeschick *n.*

misgiving [mis'giviŋ] böse Ahnung, Befürchtung *f.*

misguide ['mis'gaid] irreleiten.

mishap ['mishæp] Unfall *m*; *mot.* Panne *f.*

misinform ['misin'fo:m] falsch unterrichten. [deuten.)

misinterpret ['misin'tə:prit] miß-)

mislay [mis'lei] [*irr.* (*lay*)] verlegen.

mislead [mis'li:d] [*irr.* (*lead*)] irreführen; verleiten.

mismanage ['mis'mænidʒ] schlecht verwalten.

misplace ['mis'pleis] falsch stellen, verstellen; verlegen; falsch anbringen.

misprint 1. [mis'print] verdrucken; 2. ['mis'print] Druckfehler *m.*

misread ['mis'ri:d] [*irr.* (*read*)] falsch lesen *od.* deuten.

misrepresent ['misrepri'zent] falsch darstellen, verdrehen.

miss¹ [mis] *mst* ♀ Fräulein *n.*

miss² [~] 1. Verlust *m*; Fehlschuß *m*, -stoß *m*, -wurf *m*; 2. *v/t.* (ver-)missen; verfehlen; verpassen; auslassen; übersehen; überhören; *v/i.* fehlen (*nicht treffen*); fehlgehen.

misshapen ['mis'ʃeipən] verunstaltet; mißgestaltet.

missile ['misail] (Wurf)Geschoß *n*; Rakete *f.*

missing ['misiŋ] fehlend; ✕ vermißt; *be* ~ fehlen; vermißt werden.

mission ['miʃən] Sendung *f*; Auftrag *m*; Berufung *f*, Lebensziel *n*; Gesandtschaft *f*; *eccl., pol.* Mission *f*; ~ary ['miʃnəri] Missionar *m*; *attr.* Missions...

missive ['misiv] Sendschreiben *n.*

mis-spell ['mis'spel] [*irr.* (*spell*)] falsch buchstabieren *od.* schreiben.

mis-spend ['mis'spend] [*irr.* (*spend*)] falsch verwenden; vergeuden.

mist [mist] 1. Nebel *m*; 2. (um)nebeln; sich trüben; beschlagen.

mistake [mis'teik] 1. [*irr.* (*take*)] sich irren in (*dat.*), verkennen; mißverstehen; verwechseln (*for* mit); *be* ~n sich irren; 2. Irrtum *m*; Versehen *n*; Fehler *m*; ~n □ [~kən] irrig, falsch (verstanden).

mister ['mistə] Herr m (abbr. **Mr.**).

mistletoe ♀ ['misltou] Mistel f.

mistress ['mistris] Herrin f; Hausfrau f; Lehrerin f; Geliebte f; Meisterin f.

mistrust ['mis'trʌst] **1.** mißtrauen (dat.); **2.** Mißtrauen n; ∼ful □ [∼tful] mißtrauisch.

misty □ ['misti] neb(e)lig; unklar.

misunderstand ['misʌndə'stænd] [irr. (stand)] mißverstehen; ∼ing [∼diŋ] Mißverständnis n.

misus|age [mis'ju:zidʒ] Mißbrauch m; Mißhandlung f; ∼e **1.** ['mis'ju:z] mißbrauchen, mißhandeln; **2.** [∼u:s] Mißbrauch m.

mite [mait] zo. Milbe f; Heller m; fig. Scherflein n; Knirps m.

mitigate ['mitigeit] mildern, lindern (a. fig.).

mit|re, Am. ∼er ['maitə] Bischofsmütze f.

mitt [mit] Baseball-Handschuh m; F Boxhandschuh m; = mitten.

mitten ['mitn] Fausthandschuh m; Halbhandschuh m (ohne Finger); Am. sl. Tatze f (Hand).

mix [miks] (sich) (ver)mischen; verkehren (with mit); ∼ed gemischt; fig. zweifelhaft; ∼ up durch-ea.-bringen; be ∼ed up with in e-e S. verwickelt sein; ∼ture ['mikstʃə] Mischung f.

moan [moun] **1.** Stöhnen n; **2.** stöhnen.

moat [mout] Burg-, Stadtgraben m.

mob [mɔb] **1.** Pöbel m; **2.** anpöbeln.

mobil|e ['moubail] beweglich; ✕ mobil; ∼ization ✕ [moubilai'zeiʃən] Mobilmachung f; ∼ize ✕ ['moubilaiz] mobil machen.

moccasin ['mɔkəsin] weiches Leder; Mokassin m (Schuh).

mock [mɔk] **1.** Spott m; **2.** Schein...; falsch, nachgemacht; **3.** v/t. verspotten; nachmachen; täuschen; v/i. spotten (at über acc.); ∼ery ['mɔkəri] Spötterei f, Gespött n; Äfferei f.

mocking-bird orn. ['mɔkiŋbə:d] Spottdrossel f.

mode [moud] Art und Weise f; (Erscheinungs)Form f; Sitte f, Mode f.

model ['mɔdl] **1.** Modell n; Muster n; fig. Vorbild n; Vorführdame f; attr. Muster...; **2.** modellieren, (ab)formen; fig. modeln, bilden.

moderat|e **1.** □ ['mɔdərit] (mittel-)mäßig; **2.** [∼reit] (sich) mäßigen; ∼ion [mɔdə'reiʃən] Mäßigung f; Mäßigkeit f.

modern ['mɔdən] modern, neu; ∼ize [∼ɔ(:)naiz] (sich) modernisieren.

modest □ ['mɔdist] bescheiden; anständig; ∼y [∼ti] Bescheidenheit f.

modi|fication [mɔdifi'keiʃən] Ab-,

Veränderung f; Einschränkung f; ∼fy ['mɔdifai] (ab)ändern; mildern.

mods [mɔdz] pl. Halbstarke m/pl.

modulate ['mɔdjuleit] modulieren.

moiety ['mɔiəti] Hälfte f; Teil m.

moist [mɔist] feucht, naß; ∼en ['mɔisn] be-, anfeuchten; ∼ure ['mɔistʃə] Feuchtigkeit f.

molar ['moulə] Backenzahn m.

molasses [mə'læsiz] Melasse f; Sirup m.

mole[1] zo. [moul] Maulwurf m.

mole[2] [∼] Muttermal n.

mole[3] [∼] Mole f, Hafendamm m.

molecule ['mɔlikju:l] Molekül n.

molehill ['moulhil] Maulwurfshügel m; make a mountain out of a ∼ aus e-r Mücke e-n Elefanten machen.

molest [mou'lest] belästigen.

mollify ['mɔlifai] besänftigen.

mollycoddle ['mɔlikɔdl] **1.** Weichling m, Muttersöhnchen n; **2.** verzärteln.

molten ['moultən] geschmolzen.

moment ['moumənt] Augenblick m; Bedeutung f; = momentum; ∼ary □ [∼təri] augenblicklich; vorübergehend; ∼ous □ [mou'mentəs] (ge)wichtig, bedeutend; ∼um phys. [∼təm] Moment n; Triebkraft f.

monarch ['mɔnək] Monarch(in) f; ∼y [∼ki] Monarchie f.

monastery ['mɔnəstəri] (Mönchs-)Kloster n.

Monday ['mʌndi] Montag m.

monetary ['mʌnitəri] Geld...

money ['mʌni] Geld n; ready ∼ Bargeld n; ∼-box Sparbüchse f; ∼-changer [∼tʃeindʒə] (Geld-)Wechsler m; ∼-order Postanweisung f.

monger ['mʌŋgə] ...händler m, ...krämer m.

mongrel ['mʌŋgrəl] Mischling m, Bastard m; attr. Bastard...

monitor ['mɔnitə] ⊕ Monitor m; (Klassen)Ordner m.

monk [mʌŋk] Mönch m.

monkey ['mʌŋki] **1.** zo. Affe m (a. fig.); ⊕ Rammblock m; put s.o.'s ∼ up F j-n auf die Palme bringen; ∼ business Am. sl. fauler Zauber; **2.** F (herum)albern; ∼ with herummurksen an (dat.); ∼-wrench ⊕ Engländer m (Schraubenschlüssel); throw a ∼ in s.th. Am. sl. et. über den Haufen werfen.

monkish ['mʌŋkiʃ] mönchisch.

mono|... ['mɔnou] ein(fach)...; ∼cle ['mɔnɔkl] Monokel n; ∼gamy [mɔ'nɔgəmi] Einehe f; ∼logue, Am. a. ∼log ['mɔnəlɔg] Monolog m; ∼polist [mə'nɔpəlist] Monopolist m; ∼polize [∼laiz] monopolisieren; fig. an sich reißen; ∼poly [∼li] Monopol n (of auf acc.); ∼tonous □ [∼ɔtnəs] monoton, eintönig; ∼tony [∼ni] Monotonie f.

monsoon ['mɔn'su:n] Monsun *m*.

monster ['mɔnstə] Ungeheuer *n* (*a. fig.*); Monstrum *n*; *attr.* Riesen...

monstro|sity [mɔns'trɔsiti] Ungeheuer(lichkeit *f*) *n*; **~us** □ ['mɔnstrəs] ungeheuer(lich); gräßlich.

month [mʌnθ] Monat *m*; *this day* **~** heute in e-m Monat; **~ly** ['mʌnθli] **1.** monatlich; Monats...; **2.** Monatsschrift *f*.

monument ['mɔnjumənt] Denkmal *n*; **~al** □ [mɔnju'mentl] monumental; Gedenk...; großartig.

mood [mu:d] Stimmung *f*, Laune *f*; **~y** □ ['mu:di] launisch; schwermütig; übellaunig.

moon [mu:n] **1.** Mond *m*; *once in a blue* **~** F alle Jubeljahre einmal; **2.** *mst* **~** *about* F herumdösen; **~light** ['mu:nlait] Mondlicht *n*, -schein *m*; **~lit** mondhell; **~struck** mondsüchtig.

Moor[1] [muə] Maure *m*; Mohr *m*.

moor[2] [~] Ödland *n*, Heideland *n*.

moor[3] ⚓ [~] (sich) vertäuen; **~ings** ⚓ ['muəriŋz] *pl.* Vertäuungen *f/pl.*

moose *zo.* [mu:z] *a.* **~-***deer amerikanischer* Elch.

moot [mu:t]: **~** *point* Streitpunkt *m*.

mop [mɔp] **1.** Mop *m*; (Haar)Wust *m*; **2.** auf-, abwischen.

mope [moup] den Kopf hängen lassen.

moral ['mɔrəl] **1.** □ Moral...; moralisch; **2.** Moral *f*; Nutzanwendung *f*; **~s** *pl.* Sitten *f/pl.*; **~e** [mɔ'ra:l] *bsd.* ✕ Moral *f*, Haltung *f*; **~ity** [mɔ'ræliti] Moralität *f*; Sittlichkeit *f*, Moral *f*; **~ize** ['mɔrəlaiz] moralisieren.

morass [mə'ræs] Morast *m*, Sumpf *m*.

morbid □ ['mɔ:bid] krankhaft.

more [mɔ:] mehr; *once* **~** noch einmal, wieder; *so much od. all the* **~** um so mehr; *no* **~** nicht mehr.

morel ♀ [mɔ'rel] Morchel *f*.

moreover [mɔ:'rouvə] überdies, weiter, ferner.

morgue [mɔ:g] Leichenschauhaus *n*; Archiv *n*.

moribund ['mɔribʌnd] im Sterben (liegend), dem Tode geweiht.

morning ['mɔ:niŋ] Morgen *m*; Vormittag *m*; *tomorrow* **~** morgen früh; **~** *dress* Tagesgesellschaftsanzug *m*. [*m*) *f*.\

moron ['mɔ:rɔn] Schwachsinnige(r\

morose □ [mə'rous] mürrisch.

morph|ia ['mɔ:fjə], **~ine** ['mɔ:fi:n] Morphium *n*.

morsel ['mɔ:səl] Bissen *m*; Stückchen *n*, *das* bißchen.

mortal ['mɔ:tl] **1.** □ sterblich; tödlich; Tod(es)...; **2.** Sterbliche(r *m*) *f*; **~ity** [mɔ:'tæliti] Sterblichkeit *f*.

mortar ['mɔ:tə] Mörser *m*; Mörtel *m*.

mortgag|e ['mɔ:gidʒ] **1.** Pfandgut *n*; Hypothek *f*; **2.** verpfänden; **~ee** [mɔ:gə'dʒi:] Hypothekengläubiger *m*; **~er** ['mɔ:gidʒə], **~or** [mɔ:gə'dʒɔ:] Hypothekenschuldner *m*.

mortician *Am.* [mɔ:'tiʃən] Leichenbestatter *m*.

morti|fication [mɔ:tifi'keiʃən] Kasteiung *f*; Kränkung *f*; **~fy** ['mɔ:tifai] kasteien; kränken.

morti|se, **~ce** ⊕ ['mɔ:tis] Zapfenloch *n*.

mortuary ['mɔ:tjuəri] Leichenhalle *f*.

mosaic [mə'zeiik] Mosaik *n*.

mosque [mɔsk] Moschee *f*.

mosquito *zo.* [məs'ki:tou] Moskito *m*. [moosig.\

moss [mɔs] Moos *n*; **~y** ['mɔsi]\

most [moust] **1.** *adj.* □ meist; **2.** *adv.* meist, am meisten; höchst; **3.** *das* meiste; die meisten; Höchste(s) *n*; *at* (*the*) **~** höchstens; *make the* **~** *of* möglichst ausnutzen; **~ly** ['moustli] meistens.

moth [mɔθ] Motte *f*; **~-eaten** ['mɔθi:tn] mottenzerfressen.

mother ['mʌðə] **1.** Mutter *f*; **2.** bemuttern; **~ country** Vaterland *n*; Mutterland *n*; **~hood** [~hud] Mutterschaft *f*; **~-in-law** [~rinlɔ:] Schwiegermutter *f*; **~ly** [~li] mütterlich; **~-of-pearl** [~rəv'pə:l] Perlmutter *f*; **~-tongue** Muttersprache *f*.

motif [mou'ti:f] (Leit)Motiv *n*.

motion ['mouʃən] **1.** Bewegung *f*; Gang *m* (*a.* ⊕); *parl.* Antrag *m*; **2.** *v/t.* durch Gebärden auffordern *od.* andeuten; *v/i.* winken; **~less** [~nlis] bewegungslos; **~** *picture* Film *m*.

motivate ['moutiveit] motivieren, begründen.

motive ['moutiv] **1.** bewegend; **2.** Motiv *n*, Beweggrund *m*; **3.** veranlassen; **~less** [~vlis] grundlos.

motley ['mɔtli] (bunt)scheckig.

motor ['moutə] **1.** Motor *m*; treibende Kraft; Automobil *n*; 🚗 Muskel *m*; **2.** motorisch, bewegend; Motor...; Kraft...; Auto...; **3.** (im) Auto fahren; **~-assisted** [~rə'sistid] mit Hilfsmotor; **~** *bicycle*, **~bike** = *motor cycle*; **~** *boat* Motorboot *n*; **~** *bus* Autobus *m*; **~cade** *Am.* [~əkeid] Autokolonne *f*; **~-car** Auto(mobil) *n*; **~** *coach* Reisebus *m*; **~** *cycle* Motorrad *n*; **~ing** [~riŋ] Autofahren *n*; **~ist** [~rist] Kraftfahrer(in); **~ize** [~raiz] motorisieren; **~** *launch* Motorbarkasse *f*; **~-road**, **~way** Autobahn *f*.

mottled ['mɔtld] gefleckt.

mo(u)ld [mould] **1.** Gartenerde *f*; Schimmel *m*, Moder *m*; (Guß-)Form *f* (*a. fig.*); Abdruck *m*; Art *f*; **2.** formen, gießen (*on, upon* nach).

mo(u)lder ['mouldə] zerfallen.
mo(u)lding △ ['mouldiŋ] Fries *m*.
mo(u)ldy ['mouldi] schimm(e)lig, dumpfig, mod(e)rig.
mo(u)lt [moult] (*fig.* sich) mausern.
mound [maund] Erdhügel *m*, -wall *m*.
mount [maunt] 1. Berg *m*; Reitpferd *n*; 2. *v/i.* (empor)steigen; aufsteigen (*Reiter*); *v/t.* be-, ersteigen; beritten machen; montieren; aufziehen, aufkleben; *Edelstein* fassen.
mountain ['mauntin] 1. Berg *m*; ~s *pl.* Gebirge *n*; 2. Berg..., Gebirgs...; ~eer [maunti'niə] Bergbewohner(in); Bergsteiger(in); ~ous ['mauntinəs] bergig, gebirgig.
mountebank ['mauntibæŋk] Marktschreier *m*, Scharlatan *m*.
mourn [mɔːn] (be)trauern; ~er ['mɔːnə] Leidtragende(r *m*) *f*; ~ful □ ['mɔːnful] Trauer...; traurig; ~ing ['mɔːniŋ] Trauer *f*; *attr.* Trauer... [Maus *f*.]
mouse [maus], *pl.* **mice** [mais]]
moustache [məs'tɑːʃ] Schnurrbart *m*.
mouth [mauθ], *pl.* ~s [mauðz] Mund *m*; Maul *n*; Mündung *f*; Öffnung *f*; ~ful ['mauθful] Mundvoll *m*; ~organ Mundharmonika *f*; ~piece Mundstück *n*; *fig.* Sprachrohr *n*.
move [muːv] 1. *v/t. allg.* bewegen; in Bewegung setzen; (weg)rücken; (an)treiben; *Leidenschaft* erregen; *seelisch* rühren; beantragen; ~ *heaven and earth* Himmel und Hölle in Bewegung setzen; *v/i.* sich (fort)bewegen; sich rühren; *Schach:* ziehen; (um)ziehen (*Mieter*); ~ *for s.th. et.* beantragen; ~ *in* einziehen; ~ *on* weitergehen; ~ *out* ausziehen; 2. Bewegung *f*; *Schach:* Zug *m*; *fig.* Schritt *m*; *on the* ~ in Bewegung; *make a* ~ die Tafel aufheben; ~ment ['muːvmənt] Bewegung *f*; ♩ Tempo *n*; ♪ Satz *m*; ⊕ (Geh-)Werk *n*.
movies F ['muːviz] *pl.* Kino *n*.
moving □ ['muːviŋ] bewegend; beweglich; ~ *staircase* Rolltreppe *f*.
mow [mou] (*irr.*) mähen; ~er ['mouə] Mäher(in); Mähmaschine *f*; ~ing-machine ['mouiŋməʃiːn] Mähmaschine *f*; ~n [moun] *p.p. von* mow.
much [mʌtʃ] 1. *adj.* viel; 2. *adv.* sehr; viel; bei weitem; fast; ~ *as I would like* so gern ich möchte; *I thought as* ~ das dachte ich mir; *make* ~ *of* viel Wesens machen von; *I am not* ~ *of a dancer* ich bin kein großer Tänzer.
muck [mʌk] Mist *m* (F *a. fig.*); ~rake ['mʌkreik] 1. Mistgabel *f*; = ~r; 2. im Schmutz wühlen; ~raker [~kə] *Am.* Korruptionsschnüffler *m*.
mucus ['mjuːkəs] (Nasen)Schleim *m*.

mud [mʌd] Schlamm *m*; Kot *m*; ~dle ['mʌdl] 1. *v/t.* verwirren; *a.* ~ *up*, ~ *together* durcheinanderbringen; F benebeln; *v/i.* stümpern; ~ *through* F sich durchwursteln; 2. Wirrwarr *m*; F Wurstelei *f*; ~dy ['mʌdi] schlammig; trüb; ~guard Kotflügel *m*.
muff [mʌf] Muff *m*.
muffin ['mʌfin] Muffin *n* (*heißes Teegebäck*).
muffle ['mʌfl] *oft* ~ *up* ein-, umhüllen, umwickeln; *Stimme etc.* dämpfen; ~r [~lə] Halstuch *n*; Boxhandschuh *m*; *mot.* Auspufftopf *m*.
mug [mʌg] Krug *m*; Becher *m*.
muggy ['mʌgi] schwül.
mugwump *Am. iro.* ['mʌgwʌmp] großes Tier (*Person*); *pol.* Unabhängige(r) *m*.
mulatto [mju(ː)'lætou] Mulatt|e *m*, -in *f*.
mulberry ['mʌlbəri] Maulbeere *f*.
mule [mjuːl] Maultier *n*, -esel *m*; störrischer Mensch; ~teer [mjuːli'tiə] Maultiertreiber *m*.
mull¹ [mʌl] Mull *m*.
mull² [~]: ~ *over* überdenken.
mulled [mʌld]: ~ *wine* Glühwein *m*.
mulligan *Am.* F ['mʌligən] Eintopf *m aus Resten.*
mullion ['mʌliən] Fensterpfosten *m*.
multi|farious □ [mʌlti'fɛəriəs] mannigfaltig; ~form ['mʌltifɔːm] vielförmig; ~ple [~ipl] 1. vielfach; 2. Vielfache(s) *n*; ~plication [mʌltipli'keiʃən] Vervielfältigung *f*, Vermehrung *f*; Multiplikation *f*; *compound (simple)* ~ Großes (Kleines) Einmaleins; ~ *table* Einmaleins *n*; ~plicity [~i'plisiti] Vielfalt *f*; ~ply ['mʌltiplai] (sich) vervielfältigen; multiplizieren; ~tude ['mʌltitjuːd] Vielheit *f*, Menge *f*; ~tudinous [mʌlti'tjuːdinəs] zahlreich.
mum [mʌm] still.
mumble ['mʌmbl] murmeln, nuscheln; mummeln (*mühsam essen*).
mummery *contp.* ['mʌməri] Mummenschanz *m*.
mummify ['mʌmifai] mumifizieren.
mummy¹ ['mʌmi] Mumie *f*.
mummy² F [~] Mami *f*, Mutti *f*.
mumps [mʌmps] *sg.* Ziegenpeter *m*, Mumps *m*.
munch [mʌntʃ] mit vollen Backen (fr)essen, mampfen.
mundane □ ['mʌndein] weltlich.
municipal □ [mju(ː)'nisipəl] städtisch, Gemeinde..., Stadt...; ~ity [mjuːnisi'pæliti] Stadtbezirk *m*; Stadtverwaltung *f*.
municen|ce [mju(ː)'nifisns] Freigebigkeit *f*; ~t [~nt] freigebig.
munitions [mju(ː)'niʃənz] *pl.* Munition *f*.
mural ['mjuərəl] Mauer...
murder ['mɔːdə] 1. Mord *m*; 2. (er)-

morden; *fig.* verhunzen; **~er** [~ərə]
Mörder *m*; **~ess** [~ris] Mörderin *f*;
~ous □ [~rəs] mörderisch.
murky □ ['mə:ki] dunkel, finster.
murmur ['mə:mə] **1.** Gemurmel *n*;
Murren *n*; **2.** murmeln; murren.
murrain ['mʌrin] Viehseuche *f*.
musc|le ['mʌsl] **1.** Muskel *m*; **2.** ~ *in*
Am. sl. sich rücksichtslos eindrän-
gen; **~le-bound** mit Muskelkater;
be ~ Muskelkater haben; **~ular**
['mʌskjulə] Muskel...; muskulös.
Muse¹ [mju:z] Muse *f*.
muse² [~] (nach)sinnen, grübeln.
museum [mju(:)'ziəm] Museum *n*.
mush [mʌʃ] Brei *m*, Mus *n*; *Am.*
Polenta *f*, Maisbrei *m*.
mushroom ['mʌʃrum] **1.** Pilz *m*,
bsd. Champignon *m*; **2.** rasch wachsen; ~ *up* in die Höhe schießen.
music ['mju:zik] Musik *f*; Musik-
stück *n*; Noten *f/pl.*; *set to* ~ ver-
tonen; **~al** [~kəl] musikalisch;
Musik...; wohlklingend; ~ *box*
Spieldose *f*; ~ *box Am.* Spieldose *f*;
~-hall Varieté(theater) *n*; **~ian**
[mju(:)'ziʃən] Musiker(in); **~-stand**
Notenständer *m*; **~-stool** Klavier-
stuhl *m*.
musk [mʌsk] Moschus *m*, Bisam *m*;
~-deer *zo.* ['mʌsk'diə] Moschus-
tier *n*.
musket ['mʌskit] Muskete *f*.
musk-rat *zo.* ['mʌskræt] Bisamratte *f*.
muslin ['mʌzlin] Musselin *m*.
musquash ['mʌskwɔʃ] Bisamratte *f*;
Bisampelz *m*.
muss *bsd. Am.* F [mʌs] Durcheinander *n*.
mussel ['mʌsl] (Mies)Muschel *f*.
must¹ [mʌst] **1.** muß(te); darf;
durfte; *I* ~ *not* ich darf nicht; **2.**
Muß *n*.
must² [~] Schimmel *m*, Moder *m*.

must³ [~] Most *m*.
mustach|e *Am.* [məs'tæʃ], **~io** *Am.*
[məs'ta:ʃou] = *moustache*.
mustard ['mʌstəd] Senf *m*.
muster ['mʌstə] **1.** ✕ Musterung *f*;
fig. Heerschau *f*; **2.** ✕ mustern;
aufbieten, aufbringen.
musty ['mʌsti] mod(e)rig, muffig.
muta|ble □ ['mju:təbl] veränder-
lich; wankelmütig; **~tion** [mju(:)-
'teiʃən] Veränderung *f*.
mute [mju:t] **1.** □ stumm; **2.** Stum-
me(r *m*) *f*; Statist(in); **3.** dämpfen.
mutilate ['mju:tileit] verstümmeln.
mutin|eer [mju:ti'niə] Meuterer *m*;
~ous □ ['mju:tinəs] meuterisch;
~y [~ni] **1.** Meuterei *f*; **2.** meu-
tern.
mutter ['mʌtə] **1.** Gemurmel *n*;
Gemurre *n*; **2.** murmeln; murren.
mutton ['mʌtn] Hammelfleisch *n*;
leg of ~ Hammelkeule *f*; ~ *chop*
Hammelkotelett *n*.
mutual □ ['mju:tjuəl] gegenseitig;
gemeinsam.
muzzle ['mʌzl] **1.** Maul *n*, Schnauze
f; Mündung *f* e-r *Feuerwaffe*;
Maulkorb *m*; **2.** e-n Maulkorb anlegen (*dat.*); *fig.* den Mund stopfen
(*dat.*).
my [mai] mein(e).
myrrh ♮ [mə:] Myrrhe *f*.
myrtle ♮ ['mə:tl] Myrte *f*.
myself [mai'self] (ich) selbst; mir;
mich; *by* ~ allein.
myster|ious □ [mis'tiəriəs] ge-
heimnisvoll, mysteriös; **~y** ['mistəri]
Mysterium *n*; Geheimnis *n*; Rätsel
n.
mysti|c ['mistik] **1.** *a.* **~cal** □
[~kəl] mystisch, geheimnisvoll; **2.**
Mystiker *m*; **~fy** [~ifai] mystifizie-
ren, täuschen.
myth [miθ] Mythe *f*, Mythos *m*,
Sage *f*.

N

nab *sl.* [næb] schnappen, erwischen.
nacre ['neikə] Perlmutter *f*.
nadir ['neidiə] *ast.* Nadir *m* (*Fuß-
punkt*); *fig.* tiefster Stand.
nag [næg] **1.** F Klepper *m*; **2.** *v/i.*
nörgeln, quengeln; *v/t.* bekrit-
teln.
nail [neil] **1.** (Finger-, Zehen)Nagel
m; ⊕ Nagel *m*; *zo.* Kralle *f*, Klaue
f; **2.** (an-, fest)nageln; *Augen etc.*
heften (*to auf acc.*); **~-scissors**
['neilsizəz] *pl.* Nagelschere *f*; **~-
varnish** Nagellack *m*.
naïve □ [na:'i:v], **naive** □ [neiv]
naiv; ungekünstelt.
naked □ ['neikid] nackt, bloß; kahl;
fig. unverhüllt; *poet.* schutzlos;

~ness [~dnis] Nacktheit *f*, Blöße *f*;
Kahlheit *f*; Schutzlosigkeit *f*; *fig.*
Unverhülltheit *f*.
name [neim] **1.** Name *m*; Ruf *m*;
of od. by the ~ *of* ... namens ...;
call s.o. **~s** j-n beschimpfen; **2.** (be-)
nennen; erwähnen; ernennen; **~-
less** □ ['neimlis] namenlos; unbekannt; **~ly** [~li] nämlich; **~-plate**
Namens-, Tür-, Firmenschild *n*;
~sake ['neimseik] Namensvetter *m*.
nanny ['næni] Kindermädchen *n*;
~-goat Ziege *f*.
nap [næp] **1.** *Tuch-*Noppe *f*; Schläfchen *n*; *have od. take a* ~ ein
Nickerchen machen; **2.** schlummern.

nape [neip] *mst* ~ *of the neck* Genick *n.*

nap|kin ['næpkin] Serviette *f*; Windel *f*; *mst sanitary* ~ *Am.* Monatsbinde *f*; ~**py** F ['næpi] Windel *f.*

narcosis ⚕ [nɑː'kousis] Narkose *f.*

narcotic [nɑː'kɔtik] **1.** (~*ally*) narkotisch; **2.** Betäubungsmittel *n.*

narrat|e [næ'reit] erzählen; ~**ion** [~eiʃən] Erzählung *f*; ~**ive** ['nærətiv] **1.** □ erzählend; **2.** Erzählung *f*; ~**or** [næ'reitə] Erzähler *m.*

narrow ['nærou] **1.** eng, schmal; beschränkt; knapp *(Mehrheit, Entkommen)*; engherzig; **2.** ~**s** *pl.* Engpaß *m*; Meerenge *f*; **3.** (sich) verengen; beschränken; einengen; *Maschen* abnehmen; ~**chested** schmalbrüstig; ~**minded** □ engherzig; ~**ness** [~ounis] Enge *f*; Beschränktheit *f (a. fig.)*; Engherzigkeit *f.*

nary *Am.* F ['nɛəri] kein.

nasal □ ['neizəl] nasal; Nasen...

nasty □ ['nɑːsti] schmutzig; garstig; eklig, widerlich; häßlich; unflätig; ungemütlich.

natal ['neitl] Geburts...

nation ['neiʃən] Nation *f*, Volk *n.*

national ['næʃənl] **1.** □ national; Volks..., Staats...; **2.** Staatsangehörige(r *m*) *f*; ~**ity** [næʃə'næliti] Nationalität *f*; ~**ize** ['næʃnəlaiz] naturalisieren, einbürgern; verstaatlichen.

nation-wide ['neiʃənwaid] die ganze Nation umfassend.

native ['neitiv] **1.** □ angeboren; heimatlich, Heimat...; eingeboren; einheimisch; ~ *language* Muttersprache *f*; **2.** Eingeborene(r *m*) *f*; ~**born** (im Lande) geboren, einheimisch.

nativity [nə'tiviti] Geburt *f.*

natter F ['nætə] plaudern.

natural □ ['nætʃrəl] natürlich; *engS.*: angeboren; ungezwungen; unehelich *(Kind)*; ~ *science* Naturwissenschaft *f*; ~**ist** [~list] Naturalist *m*; Naturforscher *m*; Tierhändler *m*; ~**ize** [~laiz] einbürgern; ~**ness** [~lnis] Natürlichkeit *f.*

nature ['neitʃə] Natur *f.*

naught [nɔːt] Null *f*; set *at* ~ für nichts achten; ~**y** □ ['nɔːti] unartig.

nause|a ['nɔːsjə] Übelkeit *f*; Ekel *m*; ~**ate** ['nɔːsieit] *v/i.* Ekel empfinden; *v/t.* verabscheuen; *be* ~*d* sich ekeln; ~**ous** □ ['nɔːsjəs] ekelhaft.

nautical □ ['nɔːtikəl] nautisch; See...

naval ⚓ ['neivəl] See..., Marine...; ~ *base* Flottenstützpunkt *m.*

nave¹ [neiv] (Kirchen)Schiff *n.*

nave² [~] Rad-Nabe *f.*

navel ['neivəl] Nabel *m*; Mitte *f.*

naviga|ble □ ['nævigəbl] schiffbar; fahrbar; lenkbar; ~**te** [~geit] *v/i.* schiffen, fahren; *v/t. See etc.* befahren; steuern; ~**tion** [nævi'geiʃən]

Schiffahrt *f*; Navigation *f*; ~**tor** ['nævigeitə] Seefahrer *m.*

navy ['neivi] (Kriegs)Marine *f.*

nay † [nei] nein; nein vielmehr.

near [niə] **1.** *adj.* nahe; gerade *(Weg)*; nahe verwandt; verwandt; vertraut; genau; knapp; knauserig; ~ *at hand* dicht dabei; **2.** *adv.* nahe; **3.** *prp.* nahe *(dat.)*, nahe bei *od.* an; **4.** sich nähern *(dat.)*; ~**by** ['niəbai] in der Nähe (gelegen); nah; ~**ly** ['niəli] nahe; fast, beinahe; genau; ~**ness** ['niənis] Nähe *f*; ~**sighted** kurzsichtig.

neat □ [niːt] nett; niedlich; geschickt; ordentlich; sauber; rein; ~**ness** ['niːtnis] Nettigkeit *f*; Sauberkeit *f*; Zierlichkeit *f.*

nebulous □ ['nebjuləs] neblig.

necess|ary □ ['nesisəri] **1.** notwendig; unvermeidlich; **2.** *mst necessaries pl.* Bedürfnisse *n/pl.*; ~**itate** [ni'sesiteit] *et.* erfordern; zwingen; ~**ity** [~ti] Notwendigkeit *f*; Zwang *m*; Not *f.*

neck [nek] **1.** *(a. Flaschen)*Hals *m*; Nacken *m*, Genick *n*; Ausschnitt *m* *(Kleid)*; ~ *and* ~ Kopf an Kopf; ~ *or nothing* F alles oder nichts; **2.** *sl.* sich abknutschen; ~**band** ['nekbænd] Halsbund *m*; ~**erchief** ['nekətʃif] Halstuch *n*; ~**lace** ['neklis], ~**let** [~lit] Halskette *f*; ~**tie** Krawatte *f.*

necromancy ['nekroumænsi] Zauberei *f.*

née [nei] *bei Frauennamen:* geborene.

need [niːd] **1.** Not *f*; Notwendigkeit *f*; Bedürfnis *n*; Mangel *m*, Bedarf *m*; *be od. stand in* ~ *of* brauchen; **2.** nötig haben, brauchen; bedürfen *(gen.)*; müssen; ~**ful** ['niːdful] notwendig.

needle ['niːdl] **1.** Nadel *f*; Zeiger *m*; **2.** nähen; *bsd. Am.* irritieren; anstacheln.

needless □ ['niːdlis] unnötig.

needle|woman ['niːdlwumən] Näherin *f*; ~**work** Handarbeit *f.*

needy □ ['niːdi] bedürftig, arm.

nefarious □ [ni'fɛəriəs] schändlich.

negat|e [ni'geit] verneinen; ~**ion** [~eiʃən] Verneinung *f*; Nichts *n*; ~**ive** ['negətiv] **1.** □ negativ; verneinend; **2.** Verneinung *f*; *phot.* Negativ *n*; **3.** ablehnen.

neglect [ni'glekt] **1.** Vernachlässigung *f*; Nachlässigkeit *f*; **2.** vernachlässigen; ~**ful** [~tful] nachlässig.

negligen|ce ['neglidʒəns] Nachlässigkeit *f*; ~**t** □ [~nt] nachlässig.

negligible □ ['neglidʒəbl] nebensächlich; unbedeutend.

negotia|te [ni'gouʃieit] verhandeln (über *acc.*); zustande bringen; bewältigen; *Wechsel* begeben; ~**tion** [nigouʃi'eiʃən] Begebung *f e-s Wechsels etc.*; Ver-, Unterhandlung *f*; Bewältigung *f*; ~tor [ni'gouʃieitə] Unterhändler *m*.

negr|ess ['ni:gris] Negerin *f*; ~o [~rou], *pl.* ~oes Neger *m*.

neigh [nei] 1. Wiehern *n*; 2. wiehern.

neighbo(u)r ['neibə] Nachbar(in); Nächste(r *m*) *f*; ~hood [~hud] Nachbarschaft *f*; ~ing [~əriŋ] benachbart; ~ly [~əli] nachbarlich, freundlich; ~ship [~əʃip] Nachbarschaft *f*.

neither ['naiðə] 1. keiner (von beiden); 2. ~ ... nor ... weder ... noch ...; not ... auch nicht.

nephew ['nevju(:)] Neffe *m*.

nerve [nə:v] 1. Nerv *m*; Sehne *f*; *Blatt*-Rippe *f*; Kraft *f*, Mut *m*; Dreistigkeit *f*; get on one's ~s e-m auf die Nerven gehen; 2. kräftigen; ermutigen; ~less □ ['nə:vlis] kraftlos.

nervous □ ['nə:vəs] Nerven...; nervig, kräftig; nervös; ~ness [~snis] Nervigkeit *f*; Nervosität *f*.

nest [nest] 1. Nest *n* (*a. fig.*); 2. nisten; ~le ['nesl] *v/i.* (sich ein-) nisten; sich (an)schmiegen; *v/t.* schmiegen.

net¹ [net] 1. Netz *n*; 2. mit e-m Netz fangen *od.* umgeben.

net² [~] 1. netto; Rein...; 2. netto einbringen.

nether ['neðə] nieder; Unter...

nettle ['netl] 1. ⚘ Nessel *f*; 2. ärgern.

network ['netwə:k] (Straßen-, Kanal- *etc.*)Netz *n*; Sendergruppe *f*.

neurosis ⚕ [nju'rousis] Neurose *f*.

neuter ['nju:tə] 1. geschlechtslos; 2. geschlechtsloses Tier; *gr.* Neutrum *n*.

neutral ['nju:trəl] 1. neutral; unparteiisch; 2. Neutrale(r *m*) *f*; Null(punkt *m*) *f*; Leerlauf(stellung *f*) *m*; ~ity [nju(:)'træliti] Neutralität *f*; ~ize ['nju:trəlaiz] neutralisieren.

neutron *phys.* ['nju:trɔn] Neutron *n*.

never ['nevə] nie(mals); gar nicht; ~more [~ə'mɔ:] nie wieder; ~theless [nevəðə'les] nichtsdestoweniger.

new [nju:] neu; frisch; unerfahren; ~comer ['nju:'kʌmə] Ankömmling *m*; ~ly ['nju:li] neulich; neu.

news [nju:z] *mst. sg.* Neuigkeit(en *pl.*) *f*, Nachricht(en *pl.*) *f*; ~agent ['nju:zeidʒənt] Zeitungshändler *m*; ~boy Zeitungsausträger *m*; ~butcher *Am. sl.* Zeitungsverkäufer *m*; ~cast *Radio*: Nachrichten *f/pl.*; ~monger Neuigkeitskrämer *m*; ~paper Zeitung *f*; *attr.* Zeitungs...; ~print Zeitungspapier *n*; ~reel *Film*: Wochenschau *f*; ~room Lesezimmer *n*; *Am. Zeitung*: Nachrichtenredaktion *f*; ~stall, *Am.* ~stand Zeitungskiosk *m*.

new year ['nju:'jə:] *das* neue Jahr; New Year's Day Neujahr(stag *m*) *n*; New Year's Eve Silvester *n*.

next [nekst] 1. *adj.* nächst; ~ but one *der* übernächste; ~ door to *fig.* beinahe; ~ to nächst (*dat.*); 2. *adv.* zunächst, gleich darauf; nächstens.

nibble ['nibl] *v/t.* knabbern an (*dat.*); *v/i.* ~ at nagen *od.* knabbern an (*dat.*); (herum)kritteln an (*dat.*).

nice □ [nais] fein; wählerisch; peinlich (genau); heikel; nett; niedlich; hübsch; ~ly ['naisli] F (sehr) gut; ~ty ['naisiti] Feinheit *f*; Genauigkeit *f*; Spitzfindigkeit *f*.

niche [nitʃ] Nische *f*.

nick [nik] 1. Kerbe *f*; in the ~ of time gerade zur rechten Zeit; 2. (ein)kerben; *sl.* j-n schnappen.

nickel ['nikl] 1. *min.* Nickel *m* (*Am. a. Fünfcentstück*); 2. vernickeln.

nick-nack ['niknæk] = knick-knack.

nickname ['nikneim] 1. Spitzname *m*; 2. e-n Spitznamen geben (*dat.*).

niece [ni:s] Nichte *f*.

nifty *Am. sl.* ['nifti] elegant; stinkend.

niggard ['nigəd] Geizhals *m*; ~ly [~dli] geizig, knauserig; karg.

nigger F *mst contp.* ['nigə] Nigger *m* (*Neger*); ~ in the woodpile *Am. sl.* der Haken an der Sache.

night [nait] Nacht *f*; Abend *m*; by ~, in the ~, at ~ nachts; 2. *cap* ['naitkæp] Nachtmütze *f*; Nachttrunk *m*; ~club Nachtlokal *n*; ~dress (Damen)Nachthemd *n*; ~fall Einbruch *m* der Nacht; ~gown = night-dress; ~ingale *orn.* ['naitingeil] Nachtigall *f*; ~ly ['naitli] nächtlich; jede Nacht; ~mare Alptraum *m*; ~shirt (Herren)Nachthemd *n*; ~spot *Am.* Nachtlokal *n*; ~y ['naiti] F(Damen- *od.* Kinder)Nachthemd *n*.

nil [nil] *bsd. Sport:* nichts, null.

nimble □ ['nimbl] flink, behend.

nimbus ['nimbəs] Nimbus *m*, Heiligenschein *m*; Regenwolke *f*.

nine [nain] 1. neun; 2. Neun *f*; ~pins ['nainpinz] *pl.* Kegel(spiel *n*) *m/pl.*; ~teen ['nain'ti:n] neunzehn; ~ty ['nainti] neunzig.

ninny F ['nini] Dummkopf *m*.

ninth [nainθ] 1. neunte(r, -s); 2. Neuntel *n*; ~ly ['nainθli] neuntens.

nip [nip] 1. Kniff *m*; scharfer Frost; Schlückchen *n*; 2. zwicken; schneiden (*Kälte*); *sl.* flitzen; nippen; ~ in the bud im Keime ersticken.

nipper ['nipə] Krebsschere *f*; (a pair of) ~s *pl.* (eine) (Kneif)Zange.

nipple ['nipl] Brustwarze *f*.

Nisei *Am.* ['ni:'sei] (*a. pl.*) Japaner *m*, geboren in den USA.

nit|re, *Am.* ~er 🜍 ['naitə] Salpeter *m*.

nitrogen ['naitridʒən] Stickstoff *m*.

no [nou] **1.** *adj.* kein; *in ~ time* im Nu; *~ one* keiner; **2.** *adv.* nein; nicht; **3.** Nein *n.*

nobility [nou'biliti] Adel *m* (*a. fig.*).

noble ['noubl] **1.** □ adlig; edel, vornehm; vortrefflich; **2.** Adlige(r *m*) *f*; **~man** Adlige(r) *m*; **~-minded** edelmütig; **~ness** [.lnis] Adel *m*; Würde *f.*

nobody ['noubədi] niemand.

nocturnal [nɔk'tə:nl] Nacht...

nod [nɔd] **1.** nicken; schlafen; (sich) neigen; *~ding acquaintance* oberflächliche Bekanntschaft; **2.** Nicken *n*; Wink *m.*

node [noud] Knoten *m* (*a.* ♀ *u. ast.*); ♂ Überbein *n.*

noise [nɔiz] **1.** Lärm *m*; Geräusch *n*; Geschrei *n*; *big ~ bsd. Am.* F großes Tier (*Person*); **2.** *~ abroad* ausschreien; **~less** □ ['nɔizlis] geräuschlos.

noisome ['nɔisəm] schädlich; widerlich.

noisy □ ['nɔizi] geräuschvoll, lärmend; aufdringlich (*Farbe*).

nomin|al □ ['nɔminl] nominell; (nur) dem Namen nach (vorhanden); namentlich; *~ value* Nennwert *m*; **~ate** [.neit] ernennen; zur Wahl vorschlagen; **~ation** [nɔmi-'neiʃən] Ernennung *f*; Vorschlagsrecht *n.*

nominative ['nɔminətiv] *a. ~ case* gr. Nominativ *m.*

non [nɔn] *in Zssgn:* nicht, un..., Nicht...

nonage ['nounidʒ] Minderjährigkeit *f.*

non-alcoholic ['nɔnælkə'hɔlik] alkoholfrei.

nonce [nɔns]: *for the ~* nur für diesen Fall.

non-commissioned ['nɔnkə'miʃənd] nicht bevollmächtigt; *~ officer* ✗ Unteroffizier *m.*

non-committal ['nɔnkə'mitl] unverbindlich.

non-compliance ['nɔnkəm'plaiəns] Zuwiderhandlung *f*, Verstoß *m.*

non-conductor ⚡ ['nɔnkəndʌktə] Nichtleiter *m.*

nonconformist ['nɔnkən'fɔ:mist] Dissident(in), Freikirchler(in).

nondescript ['nɔndiskript] unbestimmbar; schwer zu beschreiben(d).

none [nʌn] **1.** keine(r, -s); nichts; **2.** keineswegs, gar nicht; *~ the less* nichtsdestoweniger.

nonentity [nɔ'nentiti] Nichtsein *n*; Unding *n*; Nichts *n*; *fig.* Null *f.*

non-existence ['nɔnig'zistəns] Nicht(da)sein *n.*

non-fiction ['nɔn'fikʃən] Sachbücher *n/pl.*

nonpareil ['nɔnpərəl] Unvergleichliche(r *m*, -s *n*) *f.*

non-party ['nɔn'pɑ:ti] parteilos.

non-performance ✗ ['nɔnpə-'fɔ:məns] Nichterfüllung *f.*

nonplus ['nɔn'plʌs] **1.** Verlegenheit *f*; **2.** in Verlegenheit bringen.

non-resident ['nɔn'rezidənt] nicht im Haus *od.* am Ort wohnend.

nonsens|e ['nɔnsəns] Unsinn *m*; **~ical** □ [nɔn'sensikəl] unsinnig.

non-skid ['nɔn'skid] rutschfest.

non-smoker ['nɔn'smoukə] Nichtraucher *m.*

non-stop 🚌, ✈ ['nɔn'stɔp] durchgehend; Ohnehalt...

non-union ['nɔn'ju:njən] nicht organisiert (*Arbeiter*).

non-violence ['nɔn'vaiələns] (Politik *f* der) Gewaltlosigkeit *f.*

noodle ['nu:dl] Nudel *f.*

nook [nuk] Ecke *f*, Winkel *m.*

noon [nu:n] Mittag *m*; *attr.* Mittags...; **~day** ['nu:ndei], **~tide**, **~time** = noon.

noose [nu:s] **1.** Schlinge *f*; **2.** (mit der Schlinge) fangen; schlingen.

nope *Am.* F [noup] nein.

nor [nɔ:] noch; auch nicht.

norm [nɔ:m] Norm *f*, Regel *f*; Muster *n*; Maßstab *m*; **~al** □ ['nɔ:məl] normal; **~alize** [.laiz] normalisieren; normen.

north [nɔ:θ] **1.** Nord(en *m*); **2.** nördlich; Nord...; **~east** ['nɔ:θ'i:st] **1.** Nordost *m*; **2.** *a.* **~eastern** nordöstlich; **~erly** ['nɔ:ðəli], **~ern** [.ən] nördlich; Nord...; **~erner** [.nə] Nordländer(in); *Am.* ♀ Nordstaatler(in); **~ward(s)** ['nɔ:θwəd(z)] *adv.* nördlich; nordwärts; **~west** ['nɔ:θ'west] **1.** Nordwest *m*; **2.** *a.* **~western** [.tən] nordwestlich.

Norwegian [nɔ:'wi:dʒən] **1.** norwegisch; **2.** Norweger(in); Norwegisch *n.*

nose [nouz] **1.** Nase *f*; Spitze *f*; Schnauze *f*; **2.** *v/t.* riechen; *~ one's way* vorsichtig fahren; *v/i.* schnüffeln; **~dive** ✈ ['nouzdaiv] Sturzflug *m*; **~gay** ['nouzgei] Blumenstrauß *m.*

nostalgia [nɔs'tældʒiə] Heimweh *n*, Sehnsucht *f.*

nostril ['nɔstril] Nasenloch *n*, Nüster *f.*

nostrum ['nɔstrəm] Geheimmittel *n*; Patentlösung *f.*

nosy F ['nouzi] neugierig.

not [nɔt] nicht.

notable ['noutəbl] **1.** □ bemerkenswert; **2.** angesehene Person.

notary ['noutəri] *oft ~ public* Notar *m.* [*f.*\]

notation [nou'teiʃən] Bezeichnung|

notch [nɔtʃ] **1.** Kerbe *f*, Einschnitt *m*; Scharte *f*; *Am.* Engpaß *m*, Hohlweg *m*; **2.** einkerben.

note [nout] **1.** Zeichen *n*; Notiz *f*; Anmerkung *f*; Briefchen *n*; (*bsd.* Schuld)Schein *m*; Note *f*; Ton *m*; Ruf *m*; Beachtung *f*; *take ~s* sich

Notizen machen; 2. be(ob)achten; besonders erwähnen; *a.* ~ *down* notieren; mit Anmerkungen versehen; ~**book** ['noutbuk] Notizbuch *n*; ~**d** bekannt; berüchtigt; ~**paper** Briefpapier *n*; ~**worthy** beachtenswert.

nothing ['nʌθiŋ] 1. nichts; 2. Nichts *n*; Null *f*; *for* ~ umsonst; *good for* ~ untauglich; *bring (come) to* ~ zunichte machen (werden).

notice ['noutis] 1. Notiz *f*; Nachricht *f*, Bekanntmachung *f*; Kündigung *f*; Warnung *f*; Beachtung *f*; *at short* ~ kurzfristig; *give* ~ *that* bekanntgeben, daß; *give a week's* ~ acht Tage vorher kündigen; *take* ~ *of* Notiz nehmen von; *without* ~ fristlos; 2. bemerken; be(ob)achten; ~**able** □ [~sǝbl] wahrnehmbar; bemerkenswert.

noti|fication [noutifi'keiʃǝn] Anzeige *f*; Meldung *f*; Bekanntmachung *f*; ~**fy** ['noutifai] *et.* anzeigen, melden; bekanntmachen.

notion ['nouʃǝn] Begriff *m*, Vorstellung *f*; Absicht *f*; ~**s** *pl. Am.* Kurzwaren *f*/*pl.*

notorious □ [nou'tɔːriǝs] all-, weltbekannt; notorisch; berüchtigt.

notwithstanding *prp.* [nɔtwiθ-'stændiŋ] ungeachtet, trotz (*gen.*).

nought [nɔːt] Null *f*, Nichts *n*.

noun *gr.* [naun] Hauptwort *n*.

nourish ['nʌriʃ] (er)nähren; *fig.* hegen; ~**ing** [~iŋ] nahrhaft; ~**ment** [~ʃmǝnt] Nahrung(smittel *n*) *f*.

novel ['nɔvǝl] 1. neu; ungewöhnlich; 2. Roman *m*; ~**ist** [~list] Romanschriftsteller(in), Romancier *m*; ~**ty** [~ti] Neuheit *f*.

November [nou'vembǝ] November *m*.

novice ['nɔvis] Neuling *m*; *eccl.* Novize *m*, *f*.

now [nau] 1. nun, jetzt; eben; *just* ~ soeben; ~ *and again od. then* dann u. wann; 2. *cj. a.* ~ *that* nun da.

nowadays ['nauǝdeiz] heutzutage.

nowhere ['nouwɛǝ] nirgends.

noxious □ ['nɔkʃǝs] schädlich.

nozzle ['nɔzl] ⊕ Düse *f*; Tülle *f*.

nuance [nju(ː)'ãːns] Nuance *f*, Schattierung *f*.

nub [nʌb] Knubbe(n *m*) *f*; *Am.* F springender Punkt *in e-r Sache.*

nucle|ar ['njuːkliǝ] Kern...; ~ *reactor* Kernreaktor *m*; ~ *research* (Atom-) Kernforschung *f*; ~**us** [~ǝs] Kern *m*.

nude [njuːd] 1. nackt; 2. *paint.* Akt *m*.

nudge F [nʌdʒ] 1. *j-n* heimlich anstoßen; 2. Rippenstoß *m*.

nugget ['nʌgit] (*bsd.* Gold)Klumpen *m*.

nuisance ['njuːsns] Mißstand *m*;

Ärgernis *n*; Unfug *m*; *fig.* Plage *f*; *what a* ~*!* wie ärgerlich!; *make o.s. od. be a* ~ lästig fallen.

null [nʌl] nichtig; nichtssagend; ~ *and void* null u. nichtig; ~**ify** ['nʌlifai] zunichte machen; aufheben, ungültig machen; ~**ity** [~iti] Nichtigkeit *f*, Ungültigkeit *f*.

numb [nʌm] 1. starr; taub (*empfindungslos*); 2. starr *od.* taub machen; ~**ed** erstarrt.

number ['nʌmbǝ] 1. Nummer *f*; (An)Zahl *f*; Heft *n*, Lieferung *f*, Nummer *f e-s Werkes*; *without* ~ zahllos; *in* ~ an der Zahl; 2. zählen; numerieren; ~**less** [~lis] zahllos; ~**plate** *mot.* Nummernschild *n*.

numera|l ['njuːmǝrǝl] 1. Zahl...; 2. Ziffer *f*; ~**tion** [njuːmǝ'reiʃǝn] Zählung *f*; Numerierung *f*.

numerical □ [nju(ː)'merikǝl] zahlenmäßig; Zahl...

numerous □ ['njuːmǝrǝs] zahlreich.

numskull F ['nʌmskʌl] Dummkopf *m*.

nun [nʌn] Nonne *f*; *orn.* Blaumeise *f*.

nunnery ['nʌnǝri] Nonnenkloster *n*.

nuptial ['nʌpʃǝl] 1. Hochzeits..., Ehe...; 2. ~**s** *pl.* Hochzeit *f*.

nurse [nǝːs] 1. Kindermädchen *n*, Säuglingsschwester *f*; *a.* wet-Amme *f*; (Kranken)Pflegerin *f*, (Kranken)Schwester *f*; *at* ~ in Pflege; *put out to* ~ in Pflege geben; 2. stillen, nähren; großziehen; pflegen; hätscheln; ~**ling** ['nǝːsliŋ] Säugling *m*; Pflegling *m*; ~**maid** ['nǝːsmeid] Kindermädchen *n*; ~**ry** ['nǝːsri] Kinderzimmer *n*; ♂ Pflanzschule *f*; ~ *rhymes* *pl.* Kinderlieder *n*/*pl.*, -reime *m*/*pl.*; ~ *school* Kindergarten *m*; ~ *slopes* *pl.* Ski: Idiotenhügel *m*/*pl.*

nursing ['nǝːsiŋ] Stillen *n*; (Kranken)Pflege *f*; ~ **bottle** Saugflasche *f*; ~ **home** Privatklinik *f*.

nursling ['nǝːsliŋ] = *nurseling.*

nurture ['nǝːtʃǝ] 1. Pflege *f*; Erziehung *f*; 2. aufziehen; nähren.

nut [nʌt] Nuß *f*; ⊕ (Schrauben-) Mutter *f*; *sl.* verrückter Kerl; ~**s** *pl.* Nußkohle *f*; ~**cracker** ['nʌtkrækǝ] Nußknacker *m*; ~**meg** ['nʌtmeg] Muskatnuß *f*.

nutriment ['njuːtrimǝnt] Nahrung *f*.

nutri|tion [nju(ː)'triʃǝn] Ernährung *f*; Nahrung *f*; ~**tious** [~ʃǝs], ~**tive** □ ['njuːtritiv] nahrhaft; Ernährungs...

nut|shell ['nʌtʃel] Nußschale *f*; *in a* ~ in aller Kürze; ~**ty** ['nʌti] nußreich; nußartig; *sl.* verrückt.

nylon ['nailǝn] Nylon *n*; ~**s** *pl.* Nylonstrümpfe *m*/*pl.*

nymph [nimf] Nymphe *f*.

O

o [ou] 1. oh!; ach!; 2. (*in Telefon-
nummern*) Null *f*.
oaf [ouf] Dummkopf *m*; Tölpel *m*.
oak [ouk] Eiche *f*.
oar [ɔː] 1. Ruder *n*; 2. rudern;
~sman [ˈɔːzmən] Ruderer *m*.
oas|is [ouˈeisis], *pl.* ~es [ouˈeisiːz]
Oase *f* (*a. fig.*).
oat [out] *mst* ~s *pl.* Hafer *m*; feel
one's ~s *Am.* F groß in Form sein;
sich wichtig vorkommen; sow one's
wild ~s sich austoben.
oath [ouθ], *pl.* ~s [ouðz] Eid *m*;
Schwur *m*; Fluch *m*; take (make,
swear) an ~ e-n Eid leisten, schwören.
oatmeal [ˈoutmiːl] Haferflocken
f/*pl*.
obdurate □ [ˈɔbdjurit] verstockt.
obedien|ce [əˈbiːdjəns] Gehorsam
m; ~t □ [~nt] gehorsam.
obeisance [ouˈbeisəns] Ehrerbietung *f*; Verbeugung *f*; do ~ huldigen.
obesity [ouˈbiːsiti] Fettleibigkeit *f*.
obey [əˈbei] gehorchen (*dat.*); *Befehl etc.* befolgen, Folge leisten
(*dat.*).
obituary [əˈbitjuəri] Totenliste *f*;
Todesanzeige *f*; Nachruf *m*;
attr. Todes..., Toten...
object 1. [ˈɔbdʒikt] Gegenstand *m*;
Ziel *n*, *fig.* Zweck *m*; Objekt *n* (*a.
gr.*); 2. [əbˈdʒekt] *v*/*t*. einwenden
(to gegen); *v*/*i*. et. dagegen haben
(to ger. daß).
objection [əbˈdʒekʃən] Einwand *m*;
~able □ [~ʃnəbl] nicht einwandfrei; unangenehm.
objective [əbˈdʒektiv] 1. □ objektiv,
sachlich; 2. ⚔ Ziel *n*.
object-lens *opt.* [ˈɔbdʒiktlenz] Objektiv *n*.
obligat|ion [ɔbliˈgeiʃən] Verpflich-
tung *f*; ✝ Schuldverschreibung *f*;
be under (an) ~ to s.o. j-m zu Dank
verpflichtet sein; be under ~ to inf.
die Verpflichtung haben, zu inf.;
~ory □ [ɔˈbligətəri] verpflichtend;
verbindlich.
oblig|e [əˈblaidʒ] (zu Dank) ver-
pflichten; nötigen; ~ s.o. j-m e-n
Gefallen tun; much ~d sehr verbunden; danke bestens; ~ing □
[~dʒiŋ] verbindlich, hilfsbereit,
gefällig.
oblique □ [əˈbliːk] schief, schräg.
obliterate [əˈblitəreit] auslöschen,
tilgen (*a. fig.*); *Schrift* ausstreichen;
Briefmarken entwerten.
oblivi|on [əˈbliviən] Vergessen(heit
f) *n*; ~ous □ [~iəs] vergeßlich.
oblong [ˈɔblɔŋ] länglich; recht-
eckig.
obnoxious □ [əbˈnɔkʃəs] anstößig;
widerwärtig, verhaßt.

30*

obscene □ [əbˈsiːn] unanständig.
obscur|e [əbˈskjuə] 1. □ dunkel
(*a. fig.*); unbekannt; 2. verdunkeln;
~ity [~ɔriti] Dunkelheit *f* (*a. fig.*);
Unbekanntheit *f*; Niedrigkeit *f der
Geburt.
obsequies [ˈɔbsikwiz] *pl.* Leichen-
begängnis *n*, Trauerfeier *f*.
obsequious □ [əbˈsiːkwiəs] unterwürfig (to gegen).
observ|able □ [əbˈzəːvəbl] be-
merkbar; bemerkenswert; ~ance
[~əns] Befolgung *f*; Brauch *m*;
~ant □ [~nt] beobachtend; achtsam; ~ation [ɔbzə(ː)ˈveiʃən]
Beobachtung *f*; Bemerkung *f*;
attr. Beobachtungs...; Aussichts...;
~atory [əbˈzəːvətri] Sternwarte *f*;
~e [əbˈzəːv] *v*/*t*. be(ob)achten;
acht(geb)en auf (*acc.*); bemerken;
v/*i*. sich äußern.
obsess [əbˈses] heimsuchen, quälen;
~ed by od. with besessen von; ~ion
[~eʃən] Besessenheit *f*.
obsolete [ˈɔbsəlit] veraltet.
obstacle [ˈɔbstəkl] Hindernis *n*.
obstina|cy [ˈɔbstinəsi] Hartnäckig-
keit *f*; ~te □ [~nit] halsstarrig;
eigensinnig; hartnäckig.
obstruct [əbˈstrakt] verstopfen,
versperren; hindern; ~ion [~kʃən]
Verstopfung *f*; Hemmung *f*; Hindernis *n*; ~ive □ [~ktiv] hinderlich.
obtain [əbˈtein] *v*/*t*. erlangen, erhalten, erreichen, bekommen; *v*/*i*.
sich erhalten (haben); ~able ✝
[~nəbl] erhältlich.
obtru|de [əbˈtruːd] (sich) aufdrän-
gen (on *dat.*); ~sive □ [~uːsiv] aufdringlich.   [schwerfällig.
obtuse □ [əbˈtjuːs] stumpf(sinnig);
obviate [ˈɔbvieit] vorbeugen (*dat.*).
obvious □ [ˈɔbviəs] offensichtlich,
augenfällig, einleuchtend.
occasion [əˈkeiʒən] 1. Gelegenheit
f; Anlaß *m*; Veranlassung *f*; F (fest-
liches) Ereignis; on the ~ of anläßlich (*gen.*); 2. veranlassen; ~al □
[~nl] gelegentlich; Gelegenheits...
occident [ˈɔksidənt] Westen *m*;
Okzident *m*, Abendland *n*; ~al □
[ɔksiˈdentl] abendländisch, westlich.
occult □ [ɔˈkalt] geheim, verborgen;
magisch, okkult.
occup|ant [ˈɔkjupənt] Besitzergrei-
fer(in); Bewohner(in); ~ation [ɔkju-
ˈpeiʃən] Besitz(ergreifung *f*) *m*; ⚔
Besetzung *f*; Beruf *m*; Beschäftigung *f*; ~y [ˈɔkjupai] einnehmen,
in Besitz nehmen, ⚔ besetzen; besitzen; innehaben; in Anspruch
nehmen; beschäftigen.
occur [əˈkəː] vorkommen; sich ereignen; it ~red to me es fiel mir ein;
~rence [əˈkarəns] Vorkommen *n*;
Vorfall *m*, Ereignis *n*.

ocean ['ouʃən] Ozean *m*, Meer *n*.

o'clock [ə'klɔk] Uhr (*bei Zeitangaben*); *five ~* fünf Uhr.

October [ɔk'toubə] Oktober *m*.

ocul|ar □ ['ɔkjulə] Augen...; **~ist** [~list] Augenarzt *m*.

odd □ [ɔd] ungerade (*Zahl*); einzeln; und einige *od*. etwas darüber; überzählig; gelegentlich; sonderbar, merkwürdig; **~ity** ['ɔditi] Seltsamkeit *f*; **~s** [ɔdz] *oft sg*. (Gewinn)Chancen *f/pl*.; Wahrscheinlichkeit *f*; Vorteil *m*; Vorgabe *f*, Handikap *n*; Verschiedenheit *f*; Unterschied *m*; Streit *m*; *be at ~ with s.o.* mit j-m im Streit sein; nicht übereinstimmen mit j-m; *~ and ends* Reste *m/pl*.; Krimskrams *m*.

ode [oud] Ode *f* (*Gedicht*).

odious □ ['oudjəs] verhaßt; ekelhaft.

odo(u)r ['oudə] Geruch *m*; Duft *m*.

of *prp*. [ɔv, əv] *allg*. von; *Ort*: bei (*the battle ~ Quebec*); um (*cheat s.o. ~ s.th.*); aus (*~ charity*); vor (*dat*.) (*afraid ~*); auf (*acc*.) (*proud ~*); über (*acc*.) (*ashamed ~*); nach (*smell ~ roses*; *desirous ~*); an (*acc*.) (*think ~ s.th.*); *nimble ~ foot* leichtfüßig.

off [ɔːf, ɔf] 1. *adv*. weg; ab; herunter; aus (*vorbei*) *Zeit*: hin (*3 months ~*); *~ and on* ab und an; hin und her; *be ~* fort sein, weg sein; *engS.*: (weg)gehen; zu sein (*Hahn etc*.); aus sein; *well etc. ~* gut *etc*. daran; 2. *prp*. von ... (weg, ab, herunter); frei von, ohne; unweit(*gen*.); neben; ⊕ auf der Höhe von; 3. *adj*. entfernt(er); abseitsliegend; Neben...; arbeits-, dienstfrei; ✝ *~ shade* Fehlfarbe *f*; 4. *int*. weg!, fort!, raus!

offal ['ɔfəl] Abfall *m*; Schund *m*; *~s pl. Fleischerei*: Innereien *f/pl*.

offen|ce, *Am*. **~se** [ə'fens] Angriff *m*; Beleidigung *f*, Kränkung *f*; Ärgernis *n*, Anstoß *m*; Vergehen *n*.

offend [ə'fend] *v/t*. beleidigen, verletzen; ärgern; *v/i*. sich vergehen; **~er** [~də] Übel-, Missetäter(in); Straffällige(r *m*) *f*; *first ~* noch nicht Vorbestrafte(r *m*) *f*.

offensive [ə'fensiv] 1. □ beleidigend; anstößig; ekelhaft; Offensiv..., Angriffs...; 2. Offensive *f*.

offer ['ɔfə] 1. Angebot *n*, Anerbieten *n*; *~ of marriage* Heiratsantrag *m*; 2. *v/t*. anbieten; *Preis*, *Möglichkeit etc*. bieten; *Gebet*, *Opfer* darbringen; versuchen; zeigen; *Widerstand* leisten; *v/i*. sich bieten; **~ing** ['ɔfəriŋ] Opfer *n*; Anerbieten *n*, Angebot *n*.

off-hand [ɔːf'hænd] aus dem Handgelenk *od*. Stegreif, unvorbereitet; ungezwungen, frei.

office ['ɔfis] Büro *n*; Geschäftsstelle

f; Ministerium *n*; Amt *n*, Pflicht *f*; *~s pl.* Hilfe *f*; *booking-~* Schalter *m*; *box-~* (Theater- *etc*.)Kasse *f*; *Divine ☾* Gottesdienst *m*; **~r** [~sə] Beamt|e(r) *m*, -in *f*; ⚔ Offizier *m*.

official [ə'fiʃəl] 1. □ offiziell, amtlich; Amts...; 2. Beamte(r) *m*.

officiate [ə'fiʃieit] amtieren.

officious □ [ə'fiʃəs] aufdringlich, übereifrig; offiziös, halbamtlich.

off|-licence ['ɔːflaisəns] Schankrecht *n* über die Straße; **~print** Sonderdruck *m*; **~set** ausgleichen; **~shoot** Sproß *m*; Wachstum *n*; **~side** ['ɔːf'said] *Sport*: abseits; **~spring** ['ɔːfspriŋ] Nachkomme(nschaft *f*) *m*; Ergebnis *n*.

often ['ɔːfn] oft(mals), häufig.

ogle ['ougl] liebäugeln *mit*.

ogre ['ougə] Menschenfresser *m*.

oh [ou] och!; ach!

oil [ɔil] 1. Öl *n*; Erdöl *n*, Petroleum *n*; 2. ölen; (*a. fig*.) schmieren; **~cloth** ['ɔilklɔθ] Wachstuch *n*; **~skin** Öleinwand *f*; *~s pl*. Ölzeug *n*; **~y** □ ['ɔili] ölig (*a. fig*.); fettig; schmierig (*a. fig*.).

ointment ['ɔintmənt] Salbe *f*.

O.K., okay F ['ou'kei] 1. richtig, stimmt!; gut, in Ordnung; 2. annehmen, gutheißen.

old [ould] alt; altbekannt; althergebracht; erfahren; *~ age* (das) Alter; *days of ~* alte Zeiten *f/pl*.; **~-age** ['ouldeidʒ] Alters...; **~-fashioned** ['ould'fæʃnd] altmodisch; altväterlich; ☾ *Glory* Sternenbanner *n*; **~ish** ['ouldiʃ] ältlich.

olfactory *anat*. [ɔl'fæktəri] Geruchs...

olive ['ɔliv] ⚘ Olive *f*; Olivgrün *n*.

Olympic Games [ou'limpik 'geimz] Olympische Spiele *pl*.

ominous □ ['ɔminəs] unheilvoll.

omission [ou'miʃən] Unterlassung *f*; Auslassung *f*.

omit [ou'mit] unterlassen; auslassen.

omnipoten|ce [ɔm'nipətəns] Allmacht *f*; **~t** □ [~nt] allmächtig.

omniscient □ [ɔm'nisiənt] allwissend.

on [ɔn] 1. *prp*. *mst* auf; *engS.*: an (*~ the wall*, *~ the Thames*); auf ... (los), nach ... (hin) (*march ~ London*); auf ... (hin) (*~ his authority*); *Zeit*: an (*~ the 1st of April*); (gleich) nach, bei (*~ his arrival*); über (*acc*.) (*talk ~ a subject*); nach (*~ this model*); *get ~ a train bsd. Am.* in e-n Zug einsteigen; *~ hearing it* als ich *etc*. es hörte; 2. *adv*. darauf; auf (*keep one's hat ~*), an (*have a coat ~*); voraus, vorwärts; weiter (*and so ~*); *be ~* im Gange sein; auf sein (*Hahn etc*.); an sein (*Licht etc*.); 3. *int*. drauf!, ran!

once [wʌns] 1. *adv*. einmal; einst (-mals); *at ~* (so)gleich, sofort; zugleich; ~ for all ein für allemal; ~ in a while dann und wann; this ~ dieses eine Mal; 2. cj. a. ~ that sobald.

one [wʌn] 1. ein; einzig; eine(r), ein; eins; man; ~ day eines Tages; 2. Eine(r) m; Eins f; the little ~s pl. die Kleinen pl.; ~ another einander; at ~ einig; ~ by ~ einzeln; I for ~ ich für meinen Teil.

onerous □ ['ɔnərəs] lästig.

one|self [wʌn'self] (man) selbst, sich; ~-sided □ ['wʌn'saidid] einseitig; ~-way ['wʌnwei]: ~ street Einbahnstraße f.

onion ['ʌnjən] Zwiebel f.

onlooker ['ɔnlukə] Zuschauer(in).

only ['ounli] 1. adj. einzig; 2. adv. nur; bloß; erst; ~ yesterday erst gestern; 3. cj. ~ (that) nur daß.

onrush ['ɔnrʌʃ] Ansturm m.

onset ['ɔnset], **onslaught** ['ɔnslɔ:t] Angriff m; bsd. fig. Anfall m; Anfang m.

onward ['ɔnwəd] 1. adj. fortschreitend; 2. a. ~s adv. vorwärts, weiter.

ooze [u:z] 1. Schlamm m; 2. v/i. (durch)sickern; ~ away schwinden; v/t. ausströmen, ausschwitzen.

opaque □ [ou'peik] undurchsichtig.

open ['oupən] 1. □ allg. offen; geöffnet, auf; frei (Feld etc.); öffentlich; offenstehend, unentschieden; aufrichtig; zugänglich (to dat.); aufgeschlossen (to gegenüber); mild (Wetter); 2. in the ~ (air) im Freien; come out into the ~ fig. an die Öffentlichkeit treten; 3. v/t. öffnen; eröffnen (a. fig.); v/i. (sich) öffnen; anfangen; ~ into führen in (acc.) (Tür etc.); ~ on to hinausgehen auf (acc.) (Fenster etc.); ~ out sich ausbreiten; ~-air ['oupn'ɛə] im Freien (stattfindend), Freiluft..., Frei(luft)...; ~-armed ['oupn'ɑ:md] herzlich, warm; ~er ['oupnə] (Er-)Öffner(in); (Dosen)Öffner m; ~eyed ['oupn'aid] wach; mit offenen Augen; aufmerksam; ~-handed ['oupn'hændid] freigebig, großzügig; ~-hearted ['oupən'ɑ:tid] offen(herzig), aufrichtig; ~ing ['oupniŋ] (Er)Öffnung f; Gelegenheit f; attr. Eröffnungs...; ~-minded fig. ['oupn'maindid] aufgeschlossen. [pl.] Opernglas n.

opera ['ɔpərə] Oper f; ~-glass(es)

operat|e ['ɔpəreit] v/t. ꝓ operieren; bsd. Am. in Gang bringen; Maschine bedienen; Unternehmen leiten; v/i. (ein)wirken; sich auswirken; arbeiten; ✝, ꝓ, ✗ operieren; ~ion [ɔpə'reiʃən] Wirkung f; Tätigkeit f; ꝓ, ✗, ✝ Operation f; be in ~ in Betrieb sein; in Kraft sein; ~ive ['ɔpərətiv] 1. □ wirksam, tätig; praktisch; ꝓ operativ; 2. Arbeiter m; ~or [~reitə] Operateur m; Telephonist(in); ⊕ Maschinist m.

opin|e [ou'pain] meinen; ~ion [ə'pinjən] Meinung f; Ansicht f; Stellungnahme f; Gutachten n; in my ~ meines Erachtens.

opponent [ə'pounənt] Gegner m.

opportun|e □ ['ɔpətju:n] passend; rechtzeitig; günstig; ~ity [ɔpə'tju:niti] (günstige) Gelegenheit.

oppos|e [ə'pouz] entgegen-, gegenüberstellen; bekämpfen; ~ed entgegengesetzt; to gegen ... sein; ~ite ['ɔpəzit] 1. □ gegenüberliegend; entgegengesetzt; 2. prp. u. adv. gegenüber; 3. Gegenteil n; ~ition [ɔpə'ziʃən] Gegenüberstehen n; Widerstand m; Gegensatz m; Widerspruch m, -streit m; ✝ Konkurrenz f; Opposition f.

oppress [ə'pres] be-, unterdrücken; ~ion [~eʃən] Unterdrückung f; Druck m; Bedrängnis f; Bedrücktheit f; ~ive [~esiv] (be)drückend; gewaltsam.

optic ['ɔptik] Augen..., Seh...; ~al □ [~kəl] optisch; ~ian [ɔp'tiʃən] Optiker m.

optimism ['ɔptimizəm] Optimismus m.

option ['ɔpʃən] Wahl(freiheit) f; ✝ Vorkaufsrecht n, Option f; ~al □ [~nl] freigestellt, wahlfrei.

opulence ['ɔpjuləns] Reichtum m.

or [ɔ:] oder; ~ else sonst, wo nicht.

oracular □ [ɔ'rækjulə] orakelhaft.

oral □ ['ɔ:rəl] mündlich; Mund...

orange ['ɔrindʒ] 1. Orange(farbe) f; Apfelsine f; 2. orangefarben; ~ade ['ɔrindʒ'eid] Orangenlimonade f.

orat|ion [ɔ:'reiʃən] Rede f; ~or ['ɔrətə] Redner m; ~ory [~əri] Redekunst f, Rhetorik f; Kapelle f.

orb [ɔ:b] Ball m; fig. Himmelskörper m; poet. Augapfel m; ~it ['ɔ:bit] 1. Planetenbahn f; Kreis-, Umlaufbahn f; Auge(nhöhle f) n; 2. sich in e-r Umlaufbahn bewegen.

orchard ['ɔ:tʃəd] Obstgarten m.

orchestra ♪ ['ɔ:kistrə] Orchester n.

orchid ♀ ['ɔ:kid] Orchidee f.

ordain [ɔ:'dein] an-, verordnen; bestimmen; Priester ordinieren.

ordeal fig. [ɔ:'di:l] schwere Prüfung.

order ['ɔ:də] 1. Ordnung f; Anordnung f; Befehl m; Regel f; ✝ Auftrag m; Zahlungsanweisung f; Klasse f, Rang m; Orden m (a. eccl.); take (holy) ~s in den geistlichen Stand treten; in ~ to inf. um zu inf.; in ~ that damit; make to ~ auf Bestellung anfertigen; standing ~s pl. parl. Geschäftsordnung f; 2. (an)ordnen; befehlen; ✝ bestellen; j-n beordern; ~ly ['ɔ:dəli] 1. ordentlich; ruhig; regelmäßig; 2. ✗ Ordonnanz f; ✗ Bursche m; Krankenpfleger m.

ordinal ['ɔ:dinl] 1. Ordnungs...; 2. a. ~ number Ordnungszahl f.

ordinance ['ɔ:dinəns] Verordnung f.

ordinary □ ['ɔːdnri] gewöhnlich.

ordnance ✕, ⚓ ['ɔːdnəns] Artillerie *f*, Geschütze *n/pl.*; Feldzeugwesen *n*.

ordure ['ɔːdjuə] Kot *m*, Schmutz *m*.

ore [ɔː] Erz *n*.

organ ['ɔːgən] ♪ Orgel *f*; Organ *n*; ~**grinder** [~ngraində] Leierkastenmann *m*; ~**ic** [ɔːˈgænik] (~ally) organisch; ~**ization** [ɔːgənaiˈzeiʃən] Organisation *f*; ~**ize** ['ɔːgənaiz] organisieren; ~**izer** [~zə] Organisator(in).

orgy ['ɔːdʒi] Ausschweifung *f*.

orient ['ɔːrient] 1. Osten *m*; Orient *m*, Morgenland *n*; 2. orientieren; ~**al** [ɔːriˈentl] 1. □ östlich; orientalisch; 2. Oriental|e *m*, -in *f*; ~**ate** ['ɔːrienteit] orientieren.

orifice ['ɔrifis] Mündung *f*; Öffnung *f*.

origin ['ɔridʒin] Ursprung *m*; Anfang *m*; Herkunft *f*.

original [əˈridʒənl] 1. □ ursprünglich; originell; Original...; ✝ Stamm...; 2. Original *n*; ~**ity** [əridʒiˈnæliti] Originalität *f*; ~**ly** [əˈridʒnəli] originell; ursprünglich, zuerst, anfangs, anfänglich.

originat|e [əˈridʒineit] *v/t.* hervorbringen, schaffen; *v/i.* entstehen; ~**or** [~tə] Urheber *m*.

ornament 1. ['ɔːnəmənt] Verzierung *f*; *fig.* Zierde *f*; 2. [~ment] verzieren; schmücken; ~**al** □ [ɔːnəˈmentl] zierend; schmückend.

ornate □ [ɔːˈneit] reich verziert; überladen.

orphan ['ɔːfən] 1. Waise *f*; 2. *a.* ~ed verwaist; ~**age** [~nidʒ] Waisenhaus *n*.

orthodox □ ['ɔːθədɔks] rechtgläubig; üblich; anerkannt.

oscillate ['ɔsileit] schwingen; *fig.* schwanken.

osier ♀ ['ouʒə] Korbweide *f*.

osprey *orn.* ['ɔspri] Fischadler *m*.

ossify ['ɔsifai] verknöchern.

ostensible □ [ɔsˈtensəbl] angeblich.

ostentatio|n [ɔstənˈteiʃən] Zurschaustellung *f*; Protzerei *f*; ~**us** □ [~ʃəs] prahlend, prahlerisch.

ostler ['ɔslə] Stallknecht *m*.

ostracize ['ɔstrəsaiz] verbannen; ächten.

ostrich *orn.* ['ɔstritʃ] Strauß *m*.

other ['ʌðə] andere(r, -s); the ~ day neulich; the ~ morning neulich morgens; every ~ day einen Tag; um den anderen, jeden zweiten Tag; ~**wise** ['ʌðəwaiz] anders; sonst.

otter *zo.* ['ɔtə] Otter(pelz) *m*.

ought [ɔːt] sollte; you ~ to have done it Sie hätten es tun sollen.

ounce [auns] Unze *f* (= 28,35 g).

our ['auə] unser; ~**s** ['auəz] der (die, das) unsrige; unsere(r, -s); *pred.* unser; ~**selves** [auəˈselvz] wir selbst; uns (selbst).

oust [aust] verdrängen, vertreiben, hinauswerfen; e-s *Amtes* entheben.

out [aut] 1. *adv.* aus; hinaus, heraus; draußen; außerhalb; (bis) zu Ende; be ~ with böse sein mit; ~ and ~ durch und durch; ~ and about wieder auf den Beinen; way ~ Ausgang *m*; 2. *Am.* F Ausweg *m*; the ~s *pl. parl.* die Opposition; 3. ✝ übernormal, Über...(*Größe*); 4. *prp.* ~ of aus, aus ... heraus; außerhalb; außer; aus, von.

out|balance [autˈbæləns] schwerer wiegen als; ~**bid** [~ˈbid] [*irr.* (bid)] überbieten; ~**board** ['autbɔːd] Außenbord...; ~**break** [~breik] Ausbruch *m*; ~**building** [~bildiŋ] Nebengebäude *n*; ~**burst** [~bəːst] Ausbruch *m*; ~**cast** [~kɑːst] 1. ausgestoßen; 2. Ausgestoßene(r *m*) *f*; ~**come** [~kʌm] Ergebnis *n*; ~**cry** [~krai] Aufschrei *m*, Schrei der Entrüstung; ~**dated** [autˈdeitid] zeitlich überholt; ~**distance** [~ˈdistəns] überholen; ~**do** [~ˈduː] [*irr.* (do)] übertreffen; ~**door** *adj.* ['autdɔː], ~**doors** *adv.* [~ˈdɔːz] Außen...; draußen, außer dem Hause; im Freien.

outer ['autə] äußer; Außen...; ~**most** [~moust] äußerst.

out|fit ['autfit] Ausrüstung *f*, Ausstattung *f*; *Am.* Haufen *m*, Trupp *m*, (Arbeits)Gruppe *f*; ~**going** [~gouiŋ] 1. weg-, abgehend; 2. Ausgehen *n*; ~**s** *pl.* Ausgaben *f/pl.*; ~**grow** [autˈgrou] [*irr.* (grow)] herauswachsen aus; hinauswachsen über (*acc.*); ~**house** ['authaus] Nebengebäude *n*; *Am.* Außenabort *m*.

outing ['autiŋ] Ausflug *m*, Tour *f*.

out|last [autˈlɑːst] überdauern; ~**law** ['autlɔː] 1. Geächtete(r *m*) *f*; 2. ächten; ~**lay** [~lei] Geld-Auslage(n *pl.*) *f*; ~**let** [~let] Auslaß *m*; Ausgang *m*; Abfluß *m*; ~**line** [~lain] 1. Umriß *m*; Überblick *m*; Skizze *f*; 2. umreißen; skizzieren; ~**live** [autˈliv] überleben; ~**look** ['autluk] Ausblick *m* (*a. fig.*); Auffassung *f*; ~**lying** [~laiiŋ] entlegen; ~**match** [autˈmætʃ] weit übertreffen; ~**number** [~ˈnʌmbə] an Zahl übertreffen; ~**patient** ⚕ ['autpeiʃənt] ambulanter Patient; ~**post** [~poust] Vorposten *m*; ~**pouring** [~pɔːriŋ] Erguß *m* (*a. fig.*); ~**put** [~put] Produktion *f*, Ertrag *m*.

outrage ['autreidʒ] 1. Gewalttätigkeit *f*; Attentat *n*; Beleidigung *f*; 2. gröblich verletzen; Gewalt antun (*dat.*); ~**ous** [autˈreidʒəs] abscheulich; empörend; gewalttätig.

out|reach [autˈriːtʃ] weiter reichen als; ~**right** [*adj.* 'autrait, *adv.* autˈrait] gerade heraus; völlig; ~**run** [~ˈrʌn] [*irr.* (run)] schneller laufen als; hinausgehen über (*acc.*); ~**set**

['autset] Anfang *m*; Aufbruch *m*;
~shine [aut'ʃain] [*irr.* (*shine*)] über-
strahlen; ~side ['aut'said] **1.** Au-
ßenseite *f*; *fig.* Äußerste(s) *n*; *at
the* ~ höchstens; **2.** Außen...; außen-
stehend; äußerst (*Preis*); **3.** (nach)
(dr)außen; **4.** *prp.* außerhalb; ~-
sider [~də] Außenseiter(in), -ste-
hende(r *m*) *f*; ~size [~saiz] Über-
größe *f*; ~skirts [~skəːts] *pl.* Außen-
bezirke *m/pl.*, (Stadt)Rand *m*;
~smart *Am.* F [aut'smɑːt] überver-
teilen; ~spoken [~'spoukən] frei-
mütig; ~spread ['aut'spred] ausgestreckt, ausgebreitet; ~standing
[aut'stændiŋ] hervorragend (*a. fig.*);
ausstehend (*Schuld*); offenstehend
(*Frage*); ~stretched ['autstretʃt] =
outspread; ~strip [aut'strip] überholen (*a. fig.*).

outward ['autwəd] **1.** äußer(lich);
nach (dr)außen gerichtet; **2.** *adv.
mst* ~s auswärts, nach (dr)außen;
~ly [~dli] äußerlich; an der Ober-
fläche.

out|weigh [aut'wei] überwiegen;
~wit [~'wit] überlisten; ~worn
['autwɔːn] erschöpft; *fig.* abgegrif-
fen; überholt.

oval ['ouvəl] **1.** oval; **2.** Oval *n*.

oven ['ʌvn] Backofen *m*.

over ['ouvə] **1.** *adv.* über; hin-, herüber; drüben; vorbei; übermäßig;
darüber; von Anfang bis zu Ende;
noch einmal; ~ *and above* neben,
zusätzlich zu; (*all*) ~ *again* noch
einmal (von vorn); ~ *against* gegenüber (*dat.*); *all* ~ ganz und gar;
~ *and* ~ *again* immer wieder; *read* ~
durchlesen; **2.** *prp.* über; *all* ~ *the
town* durch die ganze *od.* in der
ganzen Stadt.

over|act ['ouvər'ækt] übertreiben;
~all [~rɔːl] **1.** Arbeitsanzug *m*,
-kittel *m*; Kittel(schürze *f*) *m*; **2.** gesamt, Gesamt...; ~awe [ouvər'ɔː]
einschüchtern; ~balance [~-
'bæləns] **1.** Übergewicht *n*; **2.** umkippen; überwiegen; ~bearing □
[~'bɛəriŋ] anmaßend; ~board ⚓
['ouvəbɔːd] über Bord; ~cast
[~kɑːst] bewölkt; ~charge [~-
'tʃɑːdʒ] **1.** überladen; überfordern;
2. Überladung *f*; Überforderung *f*;
~coat [~kout] Mantel *m*; ~come
[ouvə'kʌm][*irr.*(*come*))überwinden,
überwältigen; ~crowd [~'kraud]
überfüllen; ~do [~'duː] [*irr.* (*do*)]
zu viel tun; übertreiben; zu sehr
kochen; überanstrengen; ~draw
[ouvə'drɔː] [*irr.* (*draw*)] übertreiben; † *Konto* überziehen; ~dress
[~'dres] (sich) übertrieben anziehen;
~due [~'djuː] (über)fällig; ~eat
[~'iːt] [*irr.* (*eat*)]: ~ *o.s.* sich
überessen; ~flow **1.** [ouvə'flou]
[*irr.* (*flow*)] *v/t.* überfluten; *v/i.* überfließen; **2.** ['ouvəflou] Überschwemmung *f*; Überfüllung *f*; ~grow

[~'grou] [*irr.* (*grow*)] *v/t.* überwu-
chern; *v/i.* zu sehr wachsen; ~
hang 1. [~'hæŋ] [*irr.* (*hang*)] *v/t.*
über (*acc.*) hängen; *v/i.* überhängen; **2.** [~hæŋ] Überhang *m*; ~
haul [ouvə'hɔːl] überholen; ~
head 1. *adv.* ['ouvə'hed] (dr)o-
ben; **2.** *adj.* [~hed] Ober...; †
allgemein (*Unkosten*); **3.** ~s *pl.* †
allgemeine Unkosten *pl.*; ~hear
[ouvə'hiə] [*irr.* (*hear*)] belauschen;
~joyed [~'dʒɔid] überglücklich;
~lap [~'læp] *v/t.* übergreifen auf
(*acc.*); überschneiden; *v/i.* inein-
andergreifen, überlappen; ~lay
[~'lei] [*irr.* (*lay*)] belegen; ⊕ über-
lagern; ~leaf ['ouvə'liːf] umseitig;
~load [~'loud] überladen; ~look
[ouvə'luk] übersehen; beaufsichtigen; ~master [~'mɑːstə] überwältigen; ~much ['ouvə'mʌtʃ] zu viel;
~night [~'nait] **1.** am Vorabend;
über Nacht; **2.** Nacht...; nächtlich;
Übernachtungs...; ~pay [~'pei] [*irr.*
(*pay*)] zu viel bezahlen; ~peopled
[ouvə'piːpld] übervölkert; ~plus
['ouvəplʌs] Überschuß *m*; ~power
[ouvə'pauə] überwältigen; ~rate
[~'reit] überschätzen; ~reach
[ouvə'riːtʃ] übervorteilen; ~ *o.s.* sich
übernehmen; ~ride *fig.* [~'raid]
[*irr.* (*ride*)] sich hinwegsetzen über
(*acc.*); umstoßen; ~rule [~'ruːl]
überstimmen; ⚖ verwerfen; ~run
[~'rʌn] [*irr.* (*run*)] überrennen;
überziehen; überlaufen; bedecken;
~sea ['ouvə'siː] **1.** *a.* ~s überseeisch;
Übersee...; **2.** ~s in *od.* nach Übersee; ~see [~'siː] [*irr.* (*see*)] beaufsichtigen; ~seer [~siə] Aufseher *m*;
~shadow [ouvə'ʃædou] überschat-
ten; ~sight ['ouvəsait] Versehen *n*;
~sleep [~'sliːp] [*irr.* (*sleep*)] verschlafen; ~state [~'steit] übertreiben; ~statement [~tmənt] Übertreibung *f*; ~strain **1.** [~'strein]
(sich) überanstrengen; *fig.* übertreiben; **2.** [~strein] Überanstren-
gung *f*.

overt ['ouvəːt] offen(kundig).

over|take [ouvə'teik] [*irr.* (*take*)]
einholen; *j-n* überraschen; ~tax
['ouvə'tæks] zu hoch besteuern; *fig.*
überschätzen; übermäßig in Anspruch nehmen; ~throw **1.** [ouvə-
'θrou] [*irr.* (*throw*)] (um)stürzen (*a.
fig.*); vernichten; **2.** ['ouvəθrou]
Sturz *m*; Vernichtung *f*; ~time
[~taim] Überstunden *f/pl.*

overture ['ouvətjuə] ♪ Ouvertüre *f*;
Vorspiel *n*; Vorschlag *m*, Antrag
m.

over|turn [ouvə'təːn] (um)stürzen;
~value ['ouvə'væljuː] zu hoch ein-
schätzen; ~weening [ouvə'wiːniŋ]
eingebildet; ~weight ['ouvəweit]
Übergewicht *n*; ~whelm ['ouvə-
'welm] überschütten (*a. fig.*); überwältigen; ~work ['ouvə'wəːk] **1.**

Überarbeitung f; 2. [irr. (work)] sich überarbeiten; **~wrought** [~-'rɔːt] überarbeitet; überreizt.

owe [ou] Geld, Dank etc. schulden, schuldig sein; verdanken.

owing ['ouiŋ] schuldig; **~ to** infolge.

owl orn. [aul] Eule f.

own [oun] 1. eigen; richtig; einzig, innig geliebt; 2. my **~** mein Eigentum; a house of one's **~** ein eigenes Haus; hold one's **~** standhalten;

3. besitzen; zugeben; anerkennen; sich bekennen (to zu).

owner ['ounə] Eigentümer(in); **~ship** ['ounəʃip] Eigentum(srecht) n.

ox [ɔks], pl. **oxen** ['ɔksən] Ochse m; Rind n.

oxid|ation 🔊 [ɔksi'deiʃən] Oxydation f, Oxydierung f; **~e** ['ɔksaid] Oxyd n; **~ize** ['ɔksidaiz] oxydieren.

oxygen 🔊 ['ɔksidʒən] Sauerstoff m.

oyster ['ɔistə] Auster f.

ozone 🔊 ['ouzoun] Ozon n.

P

pace [peis] 1. Schritt m; Gang m; Tempo n; 2. v/t. abschreiten; v/i. (einher)schreiten; (im) Paß gehen.

pacific [pə'sifik] (**~ally**) friedlich; the ♀ (Ocean) der Pazifik, der Pazifische od. Stille Ozean; **~ation** [pæsifi'keiʃən] Beruhigung f.

pacify ['pæsifai] beruhigen.

pack [pæk] 1. Pack(en) m; Paket n; Ballen m; Spiel n Karten; Meute f; Rotte f, Bande f; **Packung** f; 2. v/t. oft **~ up** (zs.-, ver-, ein)packen; a. **~ off** fortjagen; Am. F (bei sich) tragen (als Gepäck etc.); bepacken, vollstopfen; ⊕ dichten; v/i. oft **~ up** packen; sich packen (lassen); **~age** ['pækidʒ] Pack m, Ballen m; bsd. Am. Paket n; Packung f; Frachtstück n; **~er** ['pækə] Packer(in); Am. Konservenfabrikant m; **~et** ['pækit] Paket n; Päckchen n; a. **~-boat** Postschiff n.

packing ['pækiŋ] Packen n; Verpackung f; **~ house** Am. (bsd. Fleisch)Konservenfabrik f.

packthread ['pækθred] Bindfaden m.

pact [pækt] Vertrag m, Pakt m.

pad [pæd] 1. Polster n; Sport: Beinschutz m; Schreibblock m; Stempelkissen n; (Abschuß)Rampe f; 2. (aus)polstern; **~ding** ['pædiŋ] Polsterung f; fig. Lückenbüßer m.

paddle ['pædl] 1. Paddel(ruder) n; ⊕ (Rad)Schaufel f; 2. paddeln; planschen; **~wheel** Schaufelrad n.

paddock ['pædək] (Pferde)Koppel f; Sport: Sattelplatz m.

padlock ['pædlɔk] Vorhängeschloß n.

pagan ['peigən] 1. heidnisch; 2. Heid|e m, -in f.

page[1] [peidʒ] 1. Buch-Seite f; fig. Buch n; 2. paginieren.

page[2] [~] 1. (Hotel)Page m; Am. Amtsdiener m; 2. Am. (durch e-n Pagen) holen lassen.

pageant ['pædʒənt] historisches Festspiel; festlicher Umzug.

paid [peid] pret. u. p.p. von **pay** 2.

pail [peil] Eimer m.

pain [pein] 1. Pein f, Schmerz m; Strafe f; **~s** pl. Leiden n/pl.; Mühe f; on od. under **~** of death bei Todesstrafe; be in **~** leiden; take **~s** sich Mühe geben; 2. j-m weh tun; **~ful** □ ['peinful] schmerzhaft, schmerzlich; peinlich; mühevoll; **~less** □ ['peinlis] schmerzlos; **~staking** □ ['peinzteikiŋ] fleißig.

paint [peint] 1. Farbe f; Schminke f; Anstrich m; 2. (be)malen; anstreichen; (sich) schminken; **~brush** ['peintbrʌʃ] Malerpinsel m; **~er** [~tə] Maler(in); **~ing** [~tiŋ] Malen n; Malerei f; Gemälde n.

pair [peə] 1. Paar n; a **~** of scissors eine Schere; 2. (sich) paaren; zs.-passen; a. **~ off** paarweise weggehen.

pal sl. [pæl] Kumpel m, Kamerad m.

palace ['pælis] Palast m.

palatable □ ['pælətəbl] schmackhaft. [schmack m (a. fig.).\

palate ['pælit] Gaumen m; Ge-]

pale[1] [peil] 1. □ blaß, bleich; fahl; **~ ale** helles Bier; 2. (er)bleichen.

pale[2] [~] Pfahl m; fig. Grenzen f/pl.

paleness ['peilnis] Blässe f.

palisade [pæli'seid] 1. Palisade f; Staket n; **~s** pl. Am. Steilufer n; 2. umpfählen.

pall [pɔːl] schal werden; **~** (up)on j-n langweilen.

pallet ['pælit] Strohsack m.

palliat|e ['pælieit] bemänteln; lindern; **~ive** [~iətiv] Linderungsmittel n.

pall|id □ ['pælid] blaß; **~idness** [~dnis], a. ['pælə] Blässe f.

palm [pɑːm] 1. Handfläche f; ♀ Palme f; 2. in der Hand verbergen; **~** s.th. off upon s.o. j-m et. andrehen; **~tree** ['pɑːmtriː] Palme f.

palpable □ ['pælpəbl] fühlbar; fig. handgreiflich, klar, eindeutig.

palpitat|e ['pælpiteit] klopfen (Herz); **~ion** [pælpi'teiʃən] Herzklopfen n.

palsy ['pɔːlzi] **1.** Lähmung *f*; *fig.* Ohnmacht *f*; **2.** *fig.* lähmen.

palter ['pɔːltə] sein Spiel treiben.

paltry □ ['pɔːltri] erbärmlich.

pamper ['pæmpə] verzärteln.

pamphlet ['pæmflit] Flugschrift *f*.

pan [pæn] Pfanne *f*; Tiegel *m*.

pan... [_] all..., gesamt...; pan..., Pan...

panacea [pænə'siə] Allheilmittel *n*.

pancake ['pænkeik] Pfannkuchen *m*; ~ landing ✈ Bumslandung *f*.

pandemonium *fig.* [pændi'mounjəm] Hölle(nlärm *m*) *f*.

pander ['pændə] **1.** Vorschub leisten (to *dat.*); kuppeln; **2.** Kuppler *m*.

pane [pein] (Fenster)Scheibe *f*.

panegyric [pæni'dʒirik] Lobrede *f*.

panel ['pænl] **1.** ⚠ Fach *n*; Tür-Füllung *f*; ⚖ Geschworenen(liste *f*) *m/pl.*; Diskussionsteilnehmer *m/pl.*; Kassenarztliste *f*; **2.** täfeln.

pang [pæŋ] plötzlicher Schmerz, Weh *n*; *fig.* Angst *f*, Qual *f*.

panhandle ['pænhændl] **1.** Pfannenstiel *m*; *Am.* schmaler Fortsatz *e-s Staatsgebiets*; **2.** *Am.* F betteln.

panic ['pænik] **1.** panisch; **2.** Panik *f*.

pansy ♀ ['pænzi] Stiefmütterchen *n*.

pant [pænt] *nach Luft* schnappen; keuchen; klopfen (*Herz*); lechzen (for, after nach).

panther *zo.* ['pænθə] Panther *m*.

panties F ['pæntiz] (Damen)Schlüpfer *m*; (Kinder)Hös-chen *n*.

pantry ['pæntri] Vorratskammer *f*.

pants [pænts] *pl.* Hose *f*; ✞ lange) **pap** [pæp] Brei *m*.   [Unterhose.)

papa [pə'pɑː] Papa *m*.

papal □ ['peipəl] päpstlich.

paper ['peipə] **1.** Papier *n*; Zeitung *f*; Prüfungsaufgabe *f*; Vortrag *m*, Aufsatz *m*; ~*s pl.* (Ausweis)Papiere *n/pl.*; **2.** tapezieren; ~**back** Taschenbuch *n*, Paperback *n*; ~**bag** Tüte *f*; ~**clip** Büroklammer *f*; ~**fastener** Musterklammer *f*; ~**hanger** Tapezierer *m*; ~**mill** Papierfabrik *f*; ~**weight** Briefbeschwerer *m*.

pappy ['pæpi] breiig.

par [pɑː] ✞ Nennwert *m*, Pari *n*; at ~ zum Nennwert; be on a ~ with gleich *od.* ebenbürtig sein (*dat.*).

parable ['pærəbl] Gleichnis *n*.

parachute ['pærəʃuːt] Fallschirm *m*; ~**ist** [_tist] Fallschirmspringer(in).

parade [pə'reid] **1.** ✕ (Truppen-) Parade *f*; Zurschaustellung *f*; Promenade *f*; (Um)Zug *m*; *programme ~ Radio:* Programmvorschau *f*; make a ~ of *et.* zur Schau stellen; **2.** ✕ antreten (lassen); ✕ vorbeimarschieren (lassen); zur Schau stellen; ~**ground** ✕ Exerzier-, Paradeplatz *m*.

paradise ['pærədais] Paradies *n*.

paragon ['pærəgən] Vorbild *n*; Muster *n*.

paragraph ['pærəgrɑːf] Absatz *m*; Paragraph(zeichen *n*) *m*; kurze Zeitungsnotiz.

parallel ['pærəlel] **1.** parallel; **2.** Parallele *f* (*a. fig.*); Gegenstück *n*; Vergleich *m*; without (a) ~ ohnegleichen; **3.** vergleichen; entsprechen; gleichen; parallel laufen (mit).

paraly|se ['pærəlaiz] lähmen; *fig.* unwirksam machen; ~**sis** ✿ [pə'ræːlisis] Paralyse *f*, Lähmung *f*.

paramount ['pærəmaunt] oberst, höchst, hervorragend; größer, höher stehend (to als).

parapet ['pærəpit] ✕ Brustwehr *f*; Brüstung *f*; Geländer *n*.

paraphernalia [pærəfə'neiljə] *pl.* Ausrüstung *f*; Zubehör *n, m*.

parasite ['pærəsait] Schmarotzer *m*.

parasol [pærə'sɔl] Sonnenschirm *m*.

paratroops ✕ ['pærətruːps] Luftlandetruppen *f/pl.*

parboil ['pɑːbɔil] ankochen.

parcel ['pɑːsl] **1.** Paket *n*; Parzelle *f*; **2.** ~ out aus-, aufteilen.

parch [pɑːtʃ] rösten, (aus)dörren.

parchment ['pɑːtʃmənt] Pergament *n*.

pard *Am. sl.* [pɑːd] Partner *m*.

pardon ['pɑːdn] **1.** Verzeihung *f*; ⚖ Begnadigung *f*; **2.** verzeihen; *j.* begnadigen; ~**able** □ [_nəbl] verzeihlich.

pare [pɛə] (be)schneiden (*a. fig.*); schälen.

parent ['pɛərənt] Vater *m*, Mutter *f*; *fig.* Ursache *f*; ~*s pl.* Eltern *pl.*; ~**age** [_tidʒ] Herkunft *f*; ~**al** [pə'rentl] elterlich.

parenthe|sis [pə'renθisis], *pl.* ~**ses** [_siːz] Einschaltung *f*; *typ.* (runde) Klammer.

paring ['pɛəriŋ] Schälen *n*, Abschneiden *n*; ~*s pl.* Schalen *f/pl.*, Schnipsel *m/pl.*

parish ['pæriʃ] **1.** Kirchspiel *n*, Gemeinde *f*; **2.** Pfarr...; Gemeinde...; ~ council Gemeinderat *m*; ~**ioner** [pə'riʃənə] Pfarrkind *n*, Gemeindemitglied *n*.

parity ['pæriti] Gleichheit *f*.

park [pɑːk] **1.** Park *m*, Anlagen *f/pl.*; Naturschutzgebiet *n*; *mst car*-~ Parkplatz *m*; **2.** *mot.* parken; ~**ing** *mot.* ['pɑːkiŋ] Parken *n*; ~**ing lot** Parkplatz *m*; ~**ing meter** Parkuhr *f*.

parlance ['pɑːləns] Ausdrucksweise *f*.

parley ['pɑːli] **1.** Unterhandlung *f*; **2.** unterhandeln; sich besprechen.

parliament ['pɑːləmənt] Parlament *n*; ~**arian** [pɑːləmen'tɛəriən] Parlamentarier(in); ~**ary** □ [pɑːlə'mentəri] parlamentarisch; Parlaments...

parlo(u)r ['pɑːlə] Wohnzimmer n; Empfangs-, Sprechzimmer n; beauty ~ bsd. Am. Schönheitssalon m; ~ car 🚂 Am. Salonwagen m; ~maid Stubenmädchen n.

parochial □ [pə'roukjəl] Pfarr...; Gemeinde...; fig. engstirnig, beschränkt.

parole [pə'roul] 1. 🎵 mündlich; 2. ✕ Parole f; Ehrenwort n; put on ~ = 3. 🎵 bsd. Am. bedingt freilassen.

parquet ['pɑːkei] Parkett(fußboden m) n; Am. thea. Parkett n.

parrot ['pærət] 1. orn. Papagei m (a. fig.); 2. (nach)plappern.

parry ['pæri] abwehren, parieren.

parsimonious □ [pɑːsi'mounjəs] sparsam, karg; knauserig.

parsley ⚘ ['pɑːsli] Petersilie f.

parson ['pɑːsn] Pfarrer m; ~age [~nidʒ] Pfarrei f; Pfarrhaus n.

part [pɑːt] 1. Teil m; Anteil m; Partei f; thea., fig. Rolle f; 🎵 Einzel-Stimme f; Gegend f; a man of ~s ein fähiger Mensch; take ~ in s.th. an e-r Sache teilnehmen; take in good (bad) ~ gut (übel) aufnehmen; for my (own) ~ meinerseits; in ~ teilweise; on the ~ of von seiten (gen.); on my ~ meinerseits; 2. adv. teils; 3. v/t. (ab-, ein-, zer)teilen; Haar scheiteln; ~ company sich trennen (with von); v/i. sich trennen (with von); scheiden.

partake [pɑː'teik] [irr. (take)] teilnehmen, teilhaben; ~ of Mahlzeit einnehmen; grenzen an (acc.).

partial □ ['pɑːʃəl] Teil...; teilweise; partiell; parteiisch; eingenommen (to von, für); ~ity [pɑːʃi'æliti] Parteilichkeit f; Vorliebe f.

particip|ant [pɑː'tisipənt] Teilnehmer(in); ~ate [~peit] teilnehmen; ~ation [pɑːtisi'peiʃən] Teilnahme f.

participle gr. ['pɑːtsipl] Partizip n, Mittelwort n.

particle ['pɑːtikl] Teilchen n.

particular [pə'tikjulə] 1. □ mst besonder; einzeln; Sonder...; genau; eigen; wählerisch; 2. Einzelheit f; Umstand m; in ~ insbesondere; ~ity [pətikju'læriti] Besonderheit f; Ausführlichkeit f; Eigenheit f; ~ly [pə'tikjuləli] besonders.

parting ['pɑːtiŋ] 1. Trennung f; Teilung f; Abschied m; Haar-Scheitel m; ~ of the ways bsd. fig. Scheideweg m; 2. Abschieds...

partisan [pɑːti'zæn] Parteigänger (-in); ✕ Partisan m; attr. Partei...

partition [pɑː'tiʃən] 1. Teilung f; Scheidewand f; Verschlag m, Fach n; 2. mst ~ off (ab)teilen.

partly ['pɑːtli] teilweise, zum Teil.

partner ['pɑːtnə] 1. Partner(in); 2. (sich) zs.-tun mit, zs.-arbeiten mit; ~ship [~əʃip] Teilhaber-, Part-

nerschaft f; ✝ Handelsgesellschaft f.

part-owner ['pɑːtounə] Miteigentümer(in).

partridge orn. ['pɑːtridʒ] Rebhuhn n.

part-time ['pɑːttaim] 1. adj. Teilzeit..., Halbtags...; 2. adv. halbtags.

party ['pɑːti] Partei f; ✕ Trupp m, Kommando n; Party f, Gesellschaft f; Beteiligte(r) m; co. Type f, Individuum n; ~ line pol. Parteilinie f, -direktive f.

pass [pɑːs] 1. Paß m, Ausweis m; Passierschein m; Bestehen n e-s Examens; univ. gewöhnlicher Grad; (kritische) Lage; Fußball: Paß m; Bestreichung f, Strich m; (Gebirgs-) Paß m, Durchgang m; Karten: Passen n; free ~ Freikarte f; 2. v/i. passieren, geschehen; hingenommen werden; Karten: passen; (vorbei)gehen, (vorbei)kommen, (vorbei)fahren; vergehen (Zeit); sich verwandeln; angenommen werden (Banknoten); bekannt sein; vergehen; aussterben; a. ~ away sterben; durchkommen (Gesetz; Prüfling); ~ for gelten als; ~ off vonstatten gehen; ~ out F ohnmächtig werden; come to a ~ bringen; bring to ~ bewirken; v/t. vorbeigehen od. vorbeikommen od. vorbeifahren an (dat.); passieren; kommen od. fahren durch; verbringen; reichen, geben; Bemerkung machen, von sich geben; Banknoten in Umlauf bringen; Gesetz durchbringen, annehmen; Prüfling durchkommen lassen; Prüfung bestehen; (hinaus-) gehen über (acc.); Urteil abgeben; Meinung äußern; bewegen; streichen mit; Ball zuspielen; Truppen vorbeimaschieren lassen; ~able □ ['pɑːsəbl] passierbar; gangbar, gültig (Geld); leidlich.

passage ['pæsidʒ] Durchgang m, Durchfahrt f; Überfahrt f; Durchreise f; Korridor m, Gang m; Weg m; Annahme f e-s Gesetzes; 🎵 Passage f; Text-Stelle f; bird of ~ Zugvogel m.

passbook ✝ ['pɑːsbuk] Sparbuch n.

passenger ['pæsindʒə] Passagier m, Fahr-, Fluggast m, Reisende(r m) f.

passer-by ['pɑːsə'bai] Vorübergehende(r m) f, Passant(in).

passion ['pæʃən] Leidenschaft f; (Gefühls)Ausbruch m; Zorn m; 2 eccl. Passion f; be in a ~ zornig sein; in ~ 🎵 im Affekt; 2 Week eccl. Karwoche f; ~ate □ [~nit] leidenschaftlich.

passive □ ['pæsiv] passiv (a. gr.); teilnahmslos; untätig.

passport ['pɑːspɔːt] (Reise)Paß m.

password ✕ ['pɑːswəːd] Losung f.

past [pɑːst] 1. adj. vergangen; gr. Vergangenheits...; früher; for some

time ~ seit einiger Zeit; ~ *tense gr.*
Vergangenheit *f*; **2.** *adv.* vorbei;
3. *prp.* nach, über; über ... (*acc.*)
hinaus; an ... (*dat.*) vorbei; *half* ~
two halb drei; ~ *endurance* unerträglich; ~ *hope* hoffnungslos;
4. Vergangenheit *f* (*a. gr.*).

paste [peist] **1.** Teig *m*; Kleister *m*;
Paste *f*; **2.** (be)kleben; **~board**
['peistbɔːd] Pappe *f*; *attr.* Papp...

pastel [pæs'tel] Pastell(bild) *n*.

pasteurize ['pæstəraiz] pasteurisieren, keimfrei machen.

pastime ['pɑːstaim] Zeitvertreib *m*.

pastor ['pɑːstə] Pastor *m*; Seelsorger *m*; **~al** □ [~ərəl] Hirten...;
pastoral.

pastry ['peistri] Tortengebäck *n*,
Konditorwaren *f/pl.*; Pasteten *f/pl.*;
~cook Pastetenbäcker *m*, Konditor *m*.

pasture ['pɑːstʃə] **1.** *Vieh*-Weide *f*;
Futter *n*; **2.** (ab)weiden.

pat [pæt] **1.** Klaps *m*; Portion *f*
Butter; **2.** tätscheln; klopfen; **3.** gelegen, gerade recht; bereit.

patch [pætʃ] **1.** Fleck *m*; Flicken *m*;
Stück *n* Land; ✠ Pflaster *n*; **2.** flikken; **~work** ['pætʃwəːk] Flickwerk *n*.

pate F [peit] Schädel *m*.

patent ['peitənt, *Am.* 'pætənt] **1.** offenkundig; patentiert; Patent...;
letters ~ ['pætənt] *pl.* Freibrief *m*;
~ *leather* Lackleder *n*; **2.** Patent *n*;
Privileg *n*, Freibrief *m*; ~ *agent*
Patentanwalt *m*; **3.** patentieren;
~ee [peitən'tiː] Patentinhaber *m*.

patern|al □ [pə'təːnl] väterlich;
~ity [~niti] Vaterschaft *f*.

path [pɑːθ], *pl.* ~**s** [pɑːðz] Pfad *m*;
Weg *m*.

pathetic [pə'θetik] (~ally) pathetisch; rührend, ergreifend.

pathos ['peiθɔs] Pathos *n*.

patien|ce ['peiʃəns] Geduld *f*; Ausdauer *f*; Patience *f* (*Kartenspiel*);
~t [~nt] **1.** □ geduldig; **2.** Patient(in).

patio *Am.* ['pætiou] Innenhof *m*,
Patio *m*.

patrimony ['pætriməni] väterliches
Erbteil.

patriot ['peitriət] Patriot(in).

patrol ⚔ [pə'troul] **1.** Patrouille *f*,
Streife *f*; ~ *wagon Am.* Polizeigefangenenwagen *m*; **2.** (ab)patrouillieren; **~man** [~lmæn] patrouillierender Polizist; Pannenhelfer *m* e-s *Automobilclubs*.

patron ['peitrən] (Schutz)Patron *m*;
Gönner *m*; Kunde *m*; **~age** ['pætrənidʒ] Gönnerschaft *f*; Kundschaft *f*;
Schutz *m*; **~ize** [~naiz] beschützen;
begünstigen; Kunde sein bei; gönnerhaft behandeln.

patter ['pætə] *v/i.* platschen; trappeln; *v/t.* (her)plappern.

pattern ['pætən] **1.** Muster *n* (*a.*

fig.); Modell *n*; **2.** formen (*after, on*
nach).

paunch ['pɔːntʃ] Wanst *m*.

pauper ['pɔːpə] Fürsorgeempfänger(in); **~ize** [~əraiz] arm machen.

pause [pɔːz] **1.** Pause *f*; **2.** pausieren.

pave [peiv] pflastern; *fig.* Weg bahnen; **~ment** ['peivmənt] Bürgersteig *m*, Gehweg *m*; Pflaster *n*.

paw [pɔː] **1.** Pfote *f*, Tatze *f*; **2.** scharren; F befingern; rauh behandeln.

pawn [pɔːn] **1.** Bauer *m* im *Schach*;
Pfand *n*; *in od.* at ~ verpfändet; **2.**
verpfänden; **~broker** ['pɔːnbroukə]
Pfandleiher *m*; **~shop** Leihhaus *n*.

pay [pei] **1.** (Be)Zahlung *f*; Sold *m*,
Lohn *m*; **2.** [*irr.*] *v/t.* (be)zahlen;
(be)lohnen; sich lohnen für; *Ehre*
etc. erweisen; *Besuch* abstatten; ~
attention od. heed to achtgeben auf
(*acc.*); ~ *down* bar bezahlen; ~ *off j-n*
bezahlen u. entlassen; *j-n* voll
auszahlen; *v/i.* zahlen; sich lohnen;
~ *for* (für) *et.* bezahlen; **~able**
['peiəbl] zahlbar; fällig; **~-day**
Zahltag *m*; **~ee** ✝ [pei'iː] Zahlungsempfänger *m*; **~ing** ['peiŋ] lohnend; **~master** Zahlmeister *m*;
~ment ['peimənt] (Be)Zahlung *f*;
Lohn *m*, Sold *m*; **~-off** Abrechnung
f (*a. fig.*); *Am.* F Höhepunkt *m*;
~-roll Lohnliste *f*.

pea ♉ [piː] Erbse *f*.

peace [piːs] Frieden *m*, Ruhe *f*; at ~
friedlich; **~able** □ ['piːsəbl] friedliebend, friedlich; **~ful** □ ['piːsful]
friedlich; **~maker** Friedensstifter(in).

peach ♉ [piːtʃ] Pfirsich(baum) *m*.

pea|cock *orn.* ['piːkɔk] Pfau(hahn)
m; **~hen** *orn.* ['piːhen] Pfauhenne *f*.

peak [piːk] Spitze *f*; Gipfel *m*;
Mützen-Schirm *m*; *attr.* Spitzen...,
Höchst...; **~ed** [piːkt] spitz.

peal [piːl] **1.** Geläut *n*; Glockenspiel *n*; Dröhnen *n*; ~ *of laughter*
dröhnendes Gelächter; **2.** erschallen (lassen); laut verkünden; dröhnen.

peanut ['piːnʌt] Erdnuß *f*.

pear ♉ [peə] Birne *f*.

pearl [pəːl] **1.** Perle *f* (*a. fig.*); *attr.*
Perl(en)...; **2.** tropfen, perlen; **~y**
['pəːli] perlenartig.

peasant ['pezənt] **1.** Bauer *m*;
2. bäuerlich; **~ry** [~tri] Landvolk *n*.

peat [piːt] Torf *m*.

pebble ['pebl] Kiesel(stein) *m*.

peck [pek] **1.** Viertelscheffel *m*
(*9,087 Liter*); *fig.* Menge *f*; **2.** picken, hacken (*at* nach).

peculate ['pekjuleit] unterschlagen.

peculiar □ [pi'kjuːljə] eigen(tümlich); besonder; seltsam; **~ity**
[pikjuːli'æriti] Eigenheit *f*; Eigentümlichkeit *f*.

pecuniary [pi'kjuːnjəri] Geld...

pedagog|ics [pedə'gɔdʒiks] *mst sg.*

Pädagogik *f*; ~**ue** ['pedəgɔg] **Pädagoge** *m*; Lehrer *m*.

pedal ['pedl] 1. Pedal *n*; 2. Fuß...; 3. *Radfahren*: fahren, treten.

pedantic [pi'dæntik] (~*ally*) pedantisch.

peddle ['pedl] hausieren (mit); ~**r** *Am.* [~lə] = *pedlar*.

pedestal ['pedistl] Sockel *m* (*a. fig.*).

pedestrian [pi'destriən] 1. zu Fuß; nüchtern; 2. Fußgänger(in); ~ *crossing* Fußgängerübergang *m*.

pedigree ['pedigri] Stammbaum *m*.

pedlar ['pedlə] Hausierer *m*.

peek [pi:k] 1. spähen, gucken, lugen; 2. flüchtiger Blick.

peel [pi:l] 1. Schale *f*; Rinde *f*; 2. *a.* ~ *off* *v/t.* (ab)schälen; *Kleid* abstreifen; *v/i.* sich (ab)schälen.

peep [pi:p] 1. verstohlener Blick; Piepen *n*; 2. (verstohlen) gucken; *a.* ~ *out* (hervor(gucken *a. fig.*); piepen; ~**hole** ['pi:phoul] Guckloch *n*.

peer [piə] 1. spähen, lugen; ~ *at* angucken; 2. Gleiche(r *m*) *f*; Pair *m*; ~**less** □ ['piəlis] unvergleichlich.

peevish □ ['pi:viʃ] verdrießlich.

peg [peg] 1. Stöpsel *m*, Dübel *m*, Pflock *m*; *Kleider*-Haken *m*; 2. Wirbel *m*; *Wäsche*-Klammer *f*; *fig.* Aufhänger *m*; *take s.o.* down *a* ~ or two *j-n* demütigen; 2. festpflöcken; *Grenze* abstecken; ~ *away* od. *along* □ darauflosarbeiten; ~**top** ['pegtɔp] Kreisel *m*.

pelican *orn.* ['pelikən] Pelikan *m*.

pellet ['pelit] Kügelchen *n*; Pille *f*; Schrotkorn *n*.

pell-mell ['pel'mel] durcheinander.

pelt [pelt] 1. Fell *n*; † *rohe* Haut; 2. *v/t.* bewerfen; *v/i.* niederprasseln.

pelvis *anat.* ['pelvis] Becken *n*.

pen [pen] 1. (Schreib)Feder *f*; Hürde *f*; 2. schreiben; [*irr.*] einpferchen.

penal □ ['pi:nl] Straf...; strafbar; ~ *code* Strafgesetzbuch *n*; ~ *servitude* Zuchthausstrafe *f*; ~**ize** ['pi:nəlaiz] bestrafen; ~**ty** ['penlti] Strafe *f*; *Sport*: Strafpunkt *m*; ~ *area Fußball*: Strafraum *m*; ~ *kick Fußball*: Freistoß *m*.

penance ['penəns] Buße *f*.

pence [pens] *pl. von* penny.

pencil ['pensl] 1. Bleistift *m*; 2. zeichnen; (mit Bleistift) anzeichnen *od.* anstreichen; *Augenbrauen* nachzeichnen; ~**sharpener** Bleistiftspitzer *m*.

pendant ['pendənt] Anhänger *m*.

pending ['pendiŋ] 1. ⚖ schwebend; 2. *prp.* während; bis zu.

pendulum ['pendjuləm] Pendel *n*.

penetra|ble □ ['penitrəbl] durchdringbar; ~**te** [~reit] durchdringen; ergründen; eindringen (in *acc.*); vordringen (*to* bis zu); ~**tion** [peni-

'treiʃən] Durch-, Eindringen *n*; Scharfsinn *m*; ~**tive** □ ['penitrətiv] durchdringend (*a. fig.*); eindringlich; scharfsinnig.

pen-friend ['penfrend] Brieffreund (-in).

penguin *orn.* ['peŋgwin] Pinguin *m*.

penholder ['penhouldə] Federhalter *m*.

peninsula [pi'ninsjulə] Halbinsel *f*.

peniten|ce ['penitəns] Buße *f*, Reue *f*; ~**t** 1. □ reuig, bußfertig; 2. Büßer(in); ~**tiary** [peni'tenʃəri] Besserungsanstalt *f*; *Am.* Zuchthaus *n*.

pen|knife ['pennaif] Taschenmesser *n*; ~**man** Schönschreiber *m*; Schriftsteller *m*; ~**name** Schriftstellername *m*, Pseudonym *n*.

pennant ⚓ ['penənt] Wimpel *m*.

penniless ['penilis] ohne Geld.

penny ['peni], *pl. mst* **pence** [pens] (englischer) Penny ($^1/_{12}$ *Schilling*); *Am.* Cent *m*; Kleinigkeit *f*; ~**weight** *englisches* Pennygewicht ($1^1/_2$ *Gramm*).

pension ['penʃən] 1. Pension *f*, Ruhegehalt *n*; 2. *oft* ~ *off* pensionieren; ~**ary** [~nəri, ~nə] ~**er** [~nəri, ~nə] Pensionär(in).

pensive □ ['pensiv] gedankenvoll.

pent [pent] *pret. u. p.p. von* pen 2; ~*up* aufgestaut (*Zorn etc.*).

Pentecost ['pentikɔst] Pfingsten *n*.

penthouse ['penthaus] Schutzdach *n*; Dachwohnung *f auf e-m Hochhaus.*

penu|rious □ [pi'njuəriəs] geizig; ~**ry** ['penjuri] Armut *f*; Mangel *m*.

people ['pi:pl] 1. Volk *n*, Nation *f*; *coll.* die Leute *pl.*; man; 2. bevölkern.

pepper ['pepə] 1. Pfeffer *m*; 2. pfeffern; ~**mint** ⚘ Pfefferminze *f*; ~**y** □ [~əri] pfefferig; *fig.* hitzig.

per [pə:] per, durch, für; laut; je.

perambulat|e [pə'ræmbjuleit] (durch)wandern; bereisen; ~**or** ['præmbjuleitə] Kinderwagen *m*.

perceive [pə'si:v] (be)merken, wahrnehmen; empfinden; erkennen.

per cent [pə'sent] Prozent *n*.

percentage [pə'sentidʒ] Prozentsatz *m*; Prozente *n/pl.*; *fig.* Teil *m*.

percept|ible □ [pə'septəbl] wahrnehmbar; ~**ion** [~pʃən] Wahrnehmung(svermögen *n*) *f*; Erkenntnis *f*; Auffassung(skraft) *f*.

perch [pə:tʃ] 1. *ichth.* Barsch *m*; Rute *f* (5,029 *m*); (Sitz)Stange *f für Vögel*; 2. (sich) setzen; sitzen.

perchance [pə'tʃɑ:ns] zufällig; vielleicht.

percolate ['pə:kəleit] durchtropfen, durchsickern (lassen); sickern.

percussion [pə:'kʌʃən] Schlag *m*; Erschütterung *f*; ⚕ Abklopfen *n*.

perdition [pə:'diʃən] Verderben *n*.

peregrination [perigri'neiʃən] Wanderschaft *f*; Wanderung *f*.

peremptory ☐ [pə'remptəri] bestimmt; zwingend; rechthaberisch.

perennial ☐ [pə'renjəl] dauernd; immerwährend; ۵ perennierend.

perfect 1. ['pə:fikt] ☐ vollkommen; vollendet; gänzlich, völlig; **2.** [ۮ] *a.* ~ *tense gr.* Perfekt *n*; **3.** [pə'fekt] vervollkommnen; vollenden; ~**ion** [ۮkʃən] Vollendung *f*; Vollkommenheit *f*; *fig.* Gipfel *m*.

perfidious ☐ [pə:'fidiəs] treulos (*to* gegen), verräterisch.

perfidy ['pə:fidi] Treulosigkeit *f*.

perforate ['pə:fəreit] durchlöchern.

perforce [pə'fɔːs] notgedrungen.

perform [pə'fɔːm] verrichten; ausführen; tun; *Pflicht etc.* erfüllen; *thea.*, ♪ aufführen, spielen, vortragen (*a. v/i.*); ~**ance** [ۮməns] Verrichtung *f*; *thea.* Aufführung *f*; Vortrag *m*; Leistung *f*; ~**er** [ۮmə] Vortragende(r *m*) *f*.

perfume 1. ['pə:fjuːm] Wohlgeruch *m*; Parfüm *n*; **2.** [pə'fjuːm] parfümieren; ~**ry** [ۮməri] Parfümerie(n *pl.*) *f*.

perfunctory ☐ [pə'fʌŋktəri] mechanisch; oberflächlich.

perhaps [pə'hæps, præps] vielleicht.

peril ['peril] **1.** Gefahr *f*; **2.** gefährden; ~**ous** ☐ [ۮləs] gefährlich.

period ['piəriəd] Periode *f*; Zeitraum *m*; *gr.* Punkt *m*; langer Satz; (Unterrichts)Stunde *f*; *mst* ~*s pl.* ♀ Periode *f*; ~**ic** [piəri'ɔdik] periodisch; ~**ical** [ۮkəl] **1.** ☐ periodisch; **2.** Zeitschrift *f*.

perish ['periʃ] umkommen, zugrunde gehen; ~**able** ☐ [ۮʃəbl] vergänglich; leicht verderblich; ~**ing** ☐ [ۮʃiŋ] vernichtend, tödlich.

periwig ['periwig] Perücke *f*.

perjur|e ['pə:dʒə]: ~ *o.s.* falsch schwören; ~**y** [ۮri] Meineid *m*.

perk F [pə:k] *v/i. mst* ~ *up* selbstbewußt auftreten; sich wieder erholen; *v/t.* recken; ~ *o.s.* (*up*) sich putzen.

perky ☐ ['pə:ki] keck, dreist; flott.

perm F [pə:m] **1.** Dauerwelle *f*; **2.** *j-m* Dauerwellen machen.

permanen|ce ['pə:mənəns] Dauer *f*; ~**t** ☐ [ۮnt] dauernd, ständig; dauerhaft; Dauer...; ~ *wave* Dauerwelle *f*.

permea|ble ☐ ['pə:mjəbl] durchlässig; ~**te** ['pə:mieit] durchdringen; eindringen.

permissi|ble ☐ [pə'misəbl] zulässig; ~**on** [ۮʃən] Erlaubnis *f*.

permit 1. [pə'mit] erlauben, gestatten; **2.** ['pə:mit] Erlaubnis *f*, Genehmigung *f*; Passierschein *m*.

pernicious ☐ [pə:'niʃəs] verderblich; ♀ bösartig.

perpendicular ☐ [pə:pən'dikjulə] senkrecht; aufrecht; steil.

perpetrate ['pə:pitreit] verüben.

perpetu|al ☐ [pə'petjuəl] fortwährend, ewig; ~**ate** [ۮueit] verewigen.

perplex [pə'pleks] verwirren; ~**ity** [ۮsiti] Verwirrung *f*.

perquisites ['pə:kwizits] *pl.* Nebeneinkünfte *pl.*

persecut|e ['pə:sikjuːt] verfolgen; ~**ion** [pə:si'kjuːʃən] Verfolgung *f*; ~**or** ['pə:sikjuːtə] Verfolger *m*.

persever|ance [pə:si'viərəns] Beharrlichkeit *f*, Ausdauer *f*; ~**e** [pə:si'viə] beharren; aushalten.

persist [pə'sist] beharren (*in* auf *dat.*); ~**ence**, ~**ency** [ۮtəns, ۮsi] Beharrlichkeit *f*; ~**ent** ☐ [ۮnt] beharrlich.

person ['pə:sn] Person *f* (*a. gr.*); Persönlichkeit *f*; *thea.* Rolle *f*; ~**age** [ۮnidʒ] Persönlichkeit *f*; *thea.* Charakter *m*; ~**al** ☐ [ۮnl] persönlich (*a. gr.*); *attr.* Personal...; Privat...; eigen; ~**ality** [pə:sə'næliti] Persönlichkeit *f*; *personalities pl.* persönliche Bemerkungen *f/pl.*; ~**ate** ['pə:səneit] darstellen; sich ausgeben für; ~**ify** [pə:'sɔnifai] verkörpern; ~**nel** [pə:sə'nel] Personal *n*.

perspective [pə'spektiv] Perspektive *f*; Ausblick *m*, Fernsicht *f*.

perspex ['pə:speks] Plexiglas *n*.

perspicuous ☐ [pə'spikjuəs] klar.

perspir|ation [pə:spə'reiʃən] Schwitzen *n*; Schweiß *m*; ~**e** [pəs'paiə] (aus)schwitzen.

persua|de [pə'sweid] überreden; überzeugen; ~**sion** [ۮeiʒən] Überredung *f*; Überzeugung *f*; Glaube *m*; ~**sive** ☐ [ۮeisiv] überredend, überzeugend. [weis.)

pert ☐ [pə:t] keck, vorlaut, nase-)

pertain [pə:'tein] (*to*) gehören (*dat. od.* zu); betreffen (*acc.*).

pertinacious ☐ [pə:ti'neiʃəs] hartnäckig, zäh.

pertinent ☐ ['pə:tinənt] sachdienlich, -gemäß; zur Sache gehörig.

perturb [pə'tə:b] beunruhigen; stören.

perus|al [pə'ruːzəl] sorgfältige Durchsicht; ~**e** [ۮuːz] durchlesen; prüfen.

pervade [pə:'veid] durchdringen.

pervers|e ☐ [pə'və:s] verkehrt; ♂ pervers; eigensinnig; vertrackt (*Sache*); ~**ion** [ۮʃən] Verdrehung *f*; Abkehr *f*; ~**ity** [ۮsiti] Verkehrtheit *f*; ♂ Perversität *f*; Eigensinn *m*.

pervert 1. [pə'və:t] verdrehen; verführen; **2.** ♂ ['pə:və:t] perverser Mensch.

pessimism ['pesimizəm] Pessimismus *m*.

pest [pest] Pest *f*; Plage *f*; Schädling *m*; ~**er** ['pestə] belästigen.

pesti|ferous ☐ [pes'tifərəs] krankheiterregend; ~**lence** [ۮləns] Seuche *f*, *bsd.* Pest *f*; ~**lent** [ۮnt] gefährlich; *co.* verdammt; ~**lential**

□ [pesti'lenʃəl] pestartig; verderbenbringend.

pet [pet] **1.** üble Laune; zahmes Tier; Liebling *m*; **2.** Lieblings...; ~ **dog** Schoßhund *m*; ~ **name** Kosename *m*; **3.** (ver)hätscheln; knutschen.

petal ♀ ['petl] Blütenblatt *n*.

petition [pi'tiʃən] **1.** Bitte *f*; Bittschrift *f*, Eingabe *f*; **2.** bitten, ersuchen; **e-e** Eingabe machen.

petrify ['petrifai] versteinern.

petrol *mot.* ['petrəl] Benzin *n*; ~ **station** Tankstelle *f*.

petticoat ['petikout] Unterrock *m*.

pettish □ ['petiʃ] launisch.

petty □ ['peti] klein, geringfügig.

petulant ['petjulənt] gereizt.

pew [pju:] Kirchensitz *m*, -bank *f*.

pewter ['pju:tə] Zinn(gefäße *n/pl.*) *n*.

phantasm ['fæntæzəm] Trugbild *n*.

phantom ['fæntəm] Phantom *n*, Trugbild *n*; Gespenst *n*.

Pharisee ['færisi:] Pharisäer *m*.

pharmacy ['fɑ:məsi] Pharmazie *f*; Apotheke *f*. [Phasen.\

phase [feiz] Phase *f*; ~**d** [feizd] in]

pheasant *orn.* ['feznt] Fasan *m*.

phenomen|on [fi'nɔminən], *pl.* ~**a** [~nə] Phänomen *n*, Erscheinung *f*.

phial ['faiəl] Phiole *f*, Fläschchen *n*.

philander [fi'lændə] flirten.

philanthropist [fi'lænθrəpist] Menschenfreund(in).

philolog|ist [fi'lɔlədʒist] Philolog|e *m*, -in *f*; ~**y** [~dʒi] Philologie *f*.

philosoph|er [fi'lɔsəfə] Philosoph *m*; ~**ize** [~faiz] philosophieren; ~**y** [~fi] Philosophie *f*.

phlegm [flem] Schleim *m*; Phlegma *n*.

phone F [foun] *s. telephone.*

phonetics [fou'netiks] *pl.* Phonetik *f*, Lautbildungslehre *f*.

phon(e)y *Am. sl.* ['founi] **1.** Fälschung *f*; Schwindler *m*; **2.** unecht.

phosphorus ['fɔsfərəs] Phosphor *m*.

photograph ['foutəgrɑ:f] **1.** Photographie *f* (*Bild*); **2.** photographieren; ~**er** [fə'tɔgrəfə] Photograph (-in); ~**y** [~fi] Photographie *f*.

phrase [freiz] **1.** (Rede)Wendung *f*, Redensart *f*, Ausdruck *m*; **2.** ausdrücken.

physic|al □ ['fizikəl] physisch; körperlich; physikalisch; ~ **education**, ~ **training** Leibeserziehung *f*; ~**ian** [fi'ziʃən] Arzt *m*; ~**ist** ['fizisist] Physiker *m*; ~**s** [~iks] *sg.* Physik *f*.

physique [fi'zi:k] Körperbau *m*.

piano ['pjænou] Klavier *n*.

piazza [pi'ætsə] Piazza *f*, (Markt-)Platz *m*; *Am.* große Veranda.

pick [pik] Auswahl *f*; = *pick*axe; **2.** auf-~, wegnehmen; pflücken; (herum)stochern; *in der Nase* bohren; abnagen; *Schloß* knacken; *Streit* suchen; auswählen; (auf-)picken; bestehlen; ~ **out** auswählen;

herauschen; ~ **up** aufreißen, aufbrechen; aufnehmen, auflesen; sich *e-e Fremdsprache* aneignen; erfassen; (*im Auto*) mitnehmen, abholen; *Täter* ergreifen; gesund werden; ~**a-back** ['pikəbæk] huckepack; ~**axe** Spitzhacke *f*.

picket ['pikit] **1.** Pfahl *m*; ✕ Feldwache *f*; Streikposten *m*; **2.** einpfählen; an e-n Pfahl binden; mit Streikposten besetzen.

picking ['pikiŋ] Picken *n*, Pflücken *n*; Abfall *m*; *mst* ~**s** *pl.* Nebengewinn *m*.

pickle ['pikl] **1.** Pökel *m*; Eingepökelte(s) *n*, Pickles (*pl.*); F mißliche Lage; **2.** (ein)pökeln; ~**d herring** Salzhering *m*.

pick|lock ['piklɔk] Dietrich *m*; ~**pocket** Taschendieb *m*; ~**up** Ansteigen *n*; Tonabnehmer *m*; Kleinlieferwagen *m*; *sl.* Straßenbekanntschaft *f*.

picnic ['piknik] Picknick *n*.

pictorial [pik'tɔ:riəl] **1.** □ malerisch; illustriert; **2.** Illustrierte *f*.

picture ['piktʃə] **1.** Bild *n*, Gemälde *n*; *et.* Bildschönes; ~**s** *pl.* F Kino *n*; *attr.* Bilder...; *put s.o. in the* ~ j. ins Bild setzen, j. informieren; **2.** (aus-)malen; sich *et.* ausmalen; ~**post-card** Ansichtskarte *f*; ~**sque** [piktʃə'resk] malerisch.

pie [pai] Pastete *f*; Obsttorte *f*.

piebald ['paibɔ:ld] (bunt)scheckig.

piece [pi:s] **1.** Stück *n*; Geschütz *n*; Gewehr *n*; Teil *n* e-s *Services*; *Schach- etc.* Figur *f*; *a* ~ *of advice* ein Rat; *a* ~ *of news* e-e Neuigkeit; *of a* ~ gleichmäßig; *give s.o. a* ~ *of one's mind* j-m gründlich die Meinung sagen; *take to* ~**s** zerlegen; **2.** *a.* ~ *up* flicken, ausbessern; ~ *to-gether* zs.-stellen, -setzen, -stücken, -flicken; ~ *out* ausfüllen; ~**meal** ['pi:smi:l] stückweise; ~**work** Akkordarbeit *f*.

pieplant *Am.* ['paiplɑ:nt] Rhabarber *m*.

pier [piə] Pfeiler *m*; Wellenbrecher *m*; Pier *m*, *f*, Hafendamm *m*, Mole *f*, Landungsbrücke *f*.

pierce [piəs] durchbohren; durchdringen; eindringen (in *acc.*).

piety ['paiəti] Frömmigkeit *f*; Pietät *f*.

pig [pig] Ferkel *n*; Schwein *n*.

pigeon ['pidʒin] Taube *f*; ~**hole 1.** Fach *n*; **2.** in ein Fach legen.

pig|headed ['pig'hedid] dickköpfig; ~**iron** ['pigaiən] Roheisen *n*; ~**skin** Schweinsleder *n*; ~**sty** Schweinestall *m*; ~**tail** (Haar)Zopf *m*.

pike [paik] ✕ Pike *f*; Spitze *f*; *ichth.* Hecht *m*; Schlagbaum *m*; gebührenpflichtige Straße.

pile [pail] **1.** (Scheiter)Haufen *m*; Stoß *m* (*Holz*); großes Gebäude; ⚡ Batterie *f*; Pfahl *m*; Haar *n*;

Noppe *f*; ~s *pl.* ⚕ Hämorrhoiden *f/pl.*; *(atomic)* ~ *phys.* Atommeiler *m*, Reaktor *m*; **2.** *oft* ~ *up*, ~ *on* auf-, anhäufen, aufschichten.

pilfer ['pilfə] mausen, stibitzen.
pilgrim ['pilgrim] Pilger *m*; ~age [~midʒ] Pilgerfahrt *f*.
pill [pil] Pille *f*.
pillage ['pilidʒ] **1.** Plünderung *f*; **2.** plündern.
pillar ['pilə] Pfeiler *m*, Ständer *m*; Säule *f*; ~box Briefkasten *m*.
pillion *mot.* ['piljən] Soziussitz *m*.
pillory ['piləri] **1.** Pranger *m*; **2.** an den Pranger stellen; anprangern.
pillow ['pilou] (Kopf)Kissen *n*; ~case, ~slip (Kissen)Bezug *m*,
pilot ['pailət] **1.** ✈ Pilot *m*; ⚓ Lotse *m*; *fig.* Führer *m*; **2.** lotsen, steuern; ~balloon Versuchsballon *m*.
pimp [pimp] **1.** Kuppler(in); **2.** kuppeln.
pin [pin] **1.** (Steck-, Krawatten-, Hut- *etc.*)Nadel *f*; Reißnagel *m*; Pflock *m*; ♪ Wirbel *m*; Kegel *m*; **2.** (an)heften; befestigen; *fig.* festnageln.
pinafore ['pinəfɔ:] Schürze *f*.
pincers ['pinsəz] *pl.* Kneifzange *f*.
pinch [pintʃ] **1.** Kniff *m*; Prise *f* *(Tabak etc.)*; Druck *m*, Not *f*; **2.** *v/t.* kneifen, zwicken; F klauen; *v/i.* drücken; in Not sein; knausern.
pinch-hit *Am.* ['pintʃhit] einspringen *(for* für).
pincushion ['pinkuʃin] Nadelkissen *n*.
pine [pain] **1.** ♀ Kiefer *f*, Föhre *f*; **2.** sich abhärmen; sich sehnen, schmachten; ~apple ♀ ['painæpl] Ananas *f*; ~cone Kiefernzapfen *m*.
pinion ['pinjən] **1.** Flügel(spitze *f*) *m*; Schwungfeder *f*; ⊕ Ritzel *n* *(Antriebsrad)*; **2.** die Flügel beschneiden *(dat.)*; *fig.* fesseln.
pink [piŋk] **1.** ♀ Nelke *f*; Rosa *n*; *fig.* Gipfel *m*; **2.** rosa(farben).
pin-money ['pinmʌni] Nadelgeld *n*.
pinnacle ['pinəkl] △ Zinne *f*, Spitztürmchen *m*; (Berg)Spitze *f*; *fig.* Gipfel *m*.
pint [paint] Pinte *f* (0,57 *od. Am.* 0,47 *Liter*).
pioneer [paiə'niə] **1.** Pionier *m* (*a.* ✗); **2.** den Weg bahnen (für).
pious □ ['paiəs] fromm, religiös; pflichtgetreu.
pip [pip] *vet.* Pips *m*; *sl.* miese Laune; Obstkern *m*; Auge *n auf Würfeln etc.*; ✗ Stern *m* *(Rangabzeichen)*.
pipe [paip] **1.** Rohr *n*, Röhre *f*; Pfeife *f* (*a.* ♪); Flöte *f*; Lied *n e-s Vogels*; Luftröhre *f*; Pipe *f* *(Weinfaß* = 477,3 *Liter)*; **2.** pfeifen; quieken; ~layer ['paipleiə] Rohrleger *m*; *Am. pol.* Drahtzieher *m*;

~line Ölleitung *f*, Pipeline *f*; ~r ['paipə] Pfeifer *m*.
piping ['paipiŋ] **1.** pfeifend; schrill *(Stimme)*; ~ hot siedend heiß; **2.** Rohrnetz *n*; *Schneiderei:* Paspel *f*.
piquant □ ['pi:kənt] pikant.
pique [pi:k] **1.** Groll *m*; **2.** *j-n* reizen; ~ *o.s.* on sich brüsten mit.
pira|cy ['paiərəsi] Seeräuberei *f*; Raubdruck *m von Büchern*; ~te [~rit] **1.** Seeräuber(schiff *n*) *m*; Raubdrucker *m*; **2.** unerlaubt nachdrucken.
pistol ['pistl] Pistole *f*.
piston ⊕ ['pistən] Kolben *m*; ~rod Kolbenstange *f*; ~stroke Kolbenhub *m*.
pit [pit] **1.** Grube *f* (*a.* ✗, *anat.*); ♪ Miete *f*; *thea.* Parterre *n*; Pockennarbe *f*; (Tier)Falle *f*; *Am. Börse:* Maklerstand *m*; *Am.* Obst-Stein *m*; **2.** ♪ einmieten; mit Narben bedecken.
pitch [pitʃ] **1.** Pech *n*; Stand(platz) *m*; Tonhöhe *f*; Grad *m*, Stufe *f*; Steigung *f*, Neigung *f*; Wurf *m*; ⚓ Stampfen *n*; **2.** *v/t.* werfen; schleudern; Zelt *etc.* aufschlagen; ♪ stimmen (*a. fig.*); ~ too high *fig.* Ziel *etc.* zu hoch stecken; *v/i.* ✗ (sich) lagern; fallen; ⚓ stampfen; ~ into F herfallen über (*acc.*).
pitcher ['pitʃə] Krug *m*.
pitchfork ['pitʃfɔ:k] Heu-, Mistgabel *f*; ♪ Stimmgabel *f*.
piteous □ ['pitiəs] kläglich.
pitfall ['pitfɔ:l] Fallgrube *f*, Falle *f*.
pith [piθ] Mark *n*; *fig.* Kern *m*; Kraft *f*; ~y □ ['piθi] markig, kernig.
pitiable □ ['pitiəbl] erbärmlich.
pitiful □ ['pitiful] mitleidig; erbärmlich, jämmerlich *(a. contp.)*.
pitiless □ ['pitilis] unbarmherzig.
pittance ['pitəns] Hungerlohn *m*.
pity ['piti] **1.** Mitleid *n* (on mit); it is a ~ es ist schade; **2.** bemitleiden.
pivot ['pivət] **1.** ⊕ Zapfen *m*; (Tür-) Angel *f*; *fig.* Drehpunkt *m*; **2.** sich drehen (on, upon um). [verrückt.)
pixilated *Am.* F ['piksileitid] leicht)
placable □ ['plækəbl] versöhnlich.
placard ['plækɑ:d] **1.** Plakat *n*; **2.** anschlagen; mit e-m Plakat bekleben.
place [pleis] **1.** Platz *m*; Ort *m*; Stadt *f*; Stelle *f*; Stätte *f*; Stellung *f*; Aufgabe *f*; Anwesen *n*, Haus *n*, Wohnung *f*; ~ of delivery ✝ Erfüllungsort *m*; give ~ to *j-m* Platz machen; in ~ an Stelle (*gen.*); out of ~ fehl am Platz; **2.** stellen, legen, setzen; *j-n* anstellen; *Auftrag* erteilen; I can't place him *fig.* ich weiß nicht, wo ich ihn hintun soll (*identifizieren*).
placid □ ['plæsid] sanft; ruhig.
plagiar|ism ['pleidʒjərizəm] Plagiat *n*; ~ize [~raiz] abschreiben.

plague [pleig] 1. Plage *f*; Seuche *f*; Pest *f*; 2. plagen, quälen.

plaice *ichth.* [pleis] Scholle *f*.

plaid [plæd] *schottisches* Plaid.

plain [plein] 1. □ flach, eben; klar; deutlich; rein; einfach, schlicht; unscheinbar; offen, ehrlich; einfarbig; 2. *adv.* klar, deutlich; 3. Ebene *f*, Fläche *f*; *bsd. Am.* Prärie *f*; **~-clothes man** ['pleinklouðz mən] Geheimpolizist *m*; **~ dealing** ehrliche Handlungsweise; **~-dealing** ehrlich.

plainsman ['pleinzmən] Flachlandbewohner *m*; *Am.* Präriebewohner *m*.

plaint|iff ⚖ ['pleintif] Kläger(in); **~ive** □ [~iv] traurig, klagend.

plait [plæt, *Am.* pleit] 1. *Haar- etc.* Flechte *f*; Zopf *m*; 2. flechten.

plan [plæn] 1. Plan *m*; 2. e-n Plan machen von *od.* zu; *fig.* planen.

plane [plein] 1. flach, eben; 2. Ebene *f*, Fläche *f*; ⚔ Tragfläche *f*; Flugzeug *n*; *fig.* Stufe *f*; ⊕ Hobel *m*; 3. ebnen; (ab)hobeln; ⚔ fliegen.

plank [plæŋk] 1. Planke *f*, Bohle *f*, Diele *f*; *Am. pol.* Programmpunkt *m*; 2. dielen; verschalen; **~ down** *sl.*, *Am.* F *Geld* auf den Tisch legen.

plant [plɑːnt] 1. Pflanze *f*; ⊕ Anlage *f*; Fabrik *f*; 2. (an-, ein)pflanzen (*a. fig.*); (auf)stellen; anlegen; *Schlag* verpassen; bepflanzen; besiedeln; **~ation** [plæn'teiʃən] Pflanzung *f* (*a. fig.*); Plantage *f*; Besiedelung *f*; **~er** ['plɑːntə] Pflanzer *m*.

plaque [plɑːk] Platte *f*; Gedenktafel *f*.

plash [plæʃ] platschen.

plaster ['plɑːstə] 1. *pharm.* Pflaster *n*; ⊕ Putz *m*; *mst* **~ of Paris** Gips *m*, Stuck *m*; 2. bepflastern; verputzen.

plastic ['plæstik] 1. (~ally) plastisch; Plastik...; 2. *oft* **~s** *pl.* Plastik(material) *n*, Kunststoff *m*.

plat [plæt] *s. plait*; *s. plot* 1.

plate [pleit] 1. *allg.* Platte *f*; *Bild*-Tafel *f*; Schild *n*; *Kupfer*-Stich *m*; Tafelsilber *n*; Teller *m*; *Am. Baseball*: (Schlag)Mal *n*; ⊕ Grobblech *n*; 2. plattieren; ⚒, ⚓ panzern.

platform ['plætfɔːm] Plattform *f*; *geogr.* Hochebene *f*; 🚄 Bahnsteig *m*; *Am. bsd.* Plattform *f am Wagenende*; Rednerbühne *f*; *pol.* Parteiprogramm *n*; *bsd. Am. pol.* Aktionsprogramm *n im Wahlkampf*.

platinum *min.* ['plætinəm] Platin *n*.

platitude *fig.* ['plætitjuːd] Plattheit *f*.

platoon ⚔ [plə'tuːn] Zug *m*.

plat(t)en ['plætən] (Schreibmaschinen)Walze *f*.

platter ['plætə] (Servier)Platte *f*.

plaudit ['plɔːdit] Beifall *m*.

plausible □ ['plɔːzəbl] glaubhaft.

play [plei] 1. Spiel *n*; Schauspiel *n*; ⊕ Spiel *n*, Gang *m*; Spielraum *m*; 2. spielen; ⊕ laufen; **~ upon** einwirken auf (*acc.*); **~ off** *fig.* ausspielen (*against* gegen); **~ed out** erledigt; **~-bill** ['pleibil] Theaterzettel *m*; **~-book** *thea.* Textbuch *n*; **~-boy** Playboy *m*; **~er** ['pleiə] (Schau)Spieler(in); **~-piano** elektrisches Klavier; **~-fellow** Spielgefährt|e *m*, -in *f*; **~ful** □ [~ful] spielerisch, scherzhaft; **~goer** ['pleigouə] Theaterbesucher(in); **~ground** Spielplatz *m*; Schulhof *m*; **~house** Schauspielhaus *n*; *Am.* Miniaturhaus *n für Kinder*; **~mate** *s. playfellow*; **~thing** Spielzeug *n*; **~wright** Bühnenautor *m*, Dramatiker *m*.

plea [pliː] ⚖ Einspruch *m*; Ausrede *f*; Gesuch *n*; **on the ~ of** *od.* **that** unter dem Vorwand (*gen.*) *od.* daß.

plead [pliːd] *v/i.* plädieren; **~ for** für *j-n* sprechen; sich einsetzen für; **~ guilty** sich schuldig bekennen; *v/t. Sache* vertreten; als Beweis anführen; **~er** ⚖ ['pliːdə] Verteidiger *m*; **~ing** ⚖ [~diŋ] Schriftsatz *m*.

pleasant □ ['pleznt] angenehm; erfreulich; **~ry** [~tri] Scherz *m*, Spaß *m*.

please [pliːz] *v/i.* gefallen; belieben; **if you ~** *iro.* stellen Sie sich vor; **~ come in!** bitte, treten Sie ein!; *v/t. j-m* gefallen, angenehm sein; befriedigen; **~ yourself** tun Sie, was Ihnen gefällt; **be ~d to** *et.* gerne tun; **be ~d with** Vergnügen haben an (*dat.*); **~d** erfreut; zufrieden.

pleasing □ ['pliːziŋ] angenehm.

pleasure ['pleʒə] Vergnügen *n*, Freude *f*; Belieben *n*; *attr.* Vergnügungs...; **at ~** nach Belieben; **~-ground** (Vergnügungs)Park *m*.

pleat [pliːt] 1. (Plissee)Falte *f*; 2. fälteln, plissieren.

pledge [pledʒ] 1. Pfand *n*; Zutrinken *n*; Gelöbnis *n*; 2. verpfänden; *j-m* zutrinken; **he ~d himself** er gelobte.

plenary ['pliːnəri] Voll...

plenipotentiary [plenipə'tenʃəri] Bevollmächtigte(r *m*) *f* [reichlich.]

plenteous □ *poet.* ['plentjəs] voll,]

plentiful □ ['plentiful] reichlich.

plenty ['plenti] 1. Fülle *f*, Überfluß *m*; **~ of** reichlich; 2. F reichlich.

pliable □ ['plaiəbl] biegsam; *fig.* geschmeidig, nachgiebig.

pliancy ['plaiənsi] Biegsamkeit *f*.

pliers ['plaiəz] *pl.* (*a pair of ~ pl.* eine) (Draht-, Kombi)Zange.

plight [plait] 1. Ehre, Wort verpfänden; verloben; 2. Gelöbnis *n*; Zustand *m*, (Not)Lage *f*.

plod [plɔd] *a.* **~ along**, **~ on** sich dahinschleppen; sich plagen, schuften.

plot [plɔt] **1.** Platz *m*; Parzelle *f*; Plan *m*; Komplott *n*, Anschlag *m*; Intrige *f*; Handlung *f e-s Dramas etc.*; **2.** *v/t.* aufzeichnen; planen, anzetteln; *v/i.* intrigieren.

plough, *Am. mst.* **plow** [plau] **1.** Pflug *m*; **2.** pflügen; (*a. fig.*) furchen; ~ **man** ['plaumən] Pflüger *m*; ~**share** ['plauʃɛə] Pflugschar *f*.

pluck [plʌk] **1.** Mut *m*, Schneid *m*, *f*; Innereien *f/pl.*; Zug *m*, Ruck *m*; **2.** pflücken; *Vogel* rupfen (*a. fig.*); reißen; ~ *at* zerren an; ~ *up courage* Mut fassen; ~**y** *F* □ ['plʌki] mutig.

plug [plʌg] **1.** Pflock *m*; Dübel *m*; Stöpsel *m*; *≠* Stecker *m*; Zahn-Plombe *f*; Priem *m* (*Tabak*); *Am. Radio:* Reklamehinweis *m*; *alter Gaul:* ~ *socket* Steckdose *f*; **2.** *v/t.* zu-, verstopfen; *Zahn* plombieren; stöpseln; *Am. F im Rundfunk etc.* Reklame machen für *et.*

plum [plʌm] Pflaume *f*; Rosine *f* (*a. fig.*).

plumage ['plu:midʒ] Gefieder *n*.

plumb [plʌm] **1.** lotrecht; gerade; richtig; **2.** (Blei)Lot *n*; **3.** *v/t.* lotrecht machen; loten; sondieren (*a. fig.*); *F Wasser- od.* Gasleitungen legen in; *v/i. F als Rohrleger arbeiten; ~***er** ['plʌmə] Klempner *m*, Installateur *m*; ~**ing** [~miŋ] Klempnerarbeit *f*; Rohrleitungen *f/pl.*

plume [plu:m] **1.** Feder *f*; Federbusch *m*; **2.** mit Federn schmücken; *die Federn* putzen; ~ *o.s. on* sich brüsten mit.

plummet ['plʌmit] Senkblei *n*.

plump [plʌmp] **1.** *adj.* drall, prall, mollig; *F* □ glatt (*Absage etc.*); **2.** (hin)plumpsen (lassen); **3.** Plumps *m*; **4.** *F adv.* geradeswegs.

plum pudding ['plʌm'pudiŋ] Plumpudding *m*.

plunder ['plʌndə] **1.** Plünderung *f*; Raub *m*, Beute *f*; **2.** plündern.

plunge [plʌndʒ] **1.** (Unter)Tauchen *n*; (Kopf)Sprung *m*; Sturz *m*; *make od. take the* ~ den entscheidenden Schritt tun; **2.** (unter-) tauchen; (sich) stürzen (*into* in *acc.*); *Schwert etc.* stoßen; *♣* stampfen.

plunk [plʌŋk] *v/t. Saite* zupfen; *et.* hinplumpsen lassen, hinwerfen; *v/i.* (hin)plumpsen, fallen.

pluperfect *gr.* ['plu:'pɜ:fikt] Plusquamperfekt *n*.

plural *gr.* ['pluərəl] Plural *m*, Mehrzahl *f*; ~**ity** [pluə'ræliti] Vielheit *f*, Mehrheit *f*; Mehrzahl *f*.

plus [plʌs] **1.** *prp.* plus; **2.** *adj.* positiv; **3.** Plus *n*; Mehr *n*.

plush [plʌʃ] Plüsch *m*.

ply [plai] **1.** Lage *f Tuch etc.*; Strähne *f*; *fig.* Neigung *f*; **2.** *v/t.* fleißig anwenden; *j-m* zusetzen, *j-n* überhäufen; *v/i. regelmäßig* fahren; ~**wood** ['plaiwud] Sperrholz *n*.

pneumatic [nju(:)'mætik] **1.** (~*ally*) Luft...; pneumatisch; **2.** Luftreifen *m*.

pneumonia *≈* [nju(:)'mounjə] Lungenentzündung *f*.

poach [poutʃ] wildern; *Erde* zertreten; ~*ed eggs pl.* verlorene Eier *n/pl.*

poacher ['poutʃə] Wilddieb *m*.

pock *≈* [pɔk] Pocke *f*, Blatter *f*.

pocket ['pɔkit] **1.** Tasche *f*; *≍* Luft-Loch *n*; **2.** einstecken (*a. fig.*); *Am. pol. Gesetzesvorlage* nicht unterschreiben; *Gefühl* unterdrücken; **3.** Taschen...; ~**book** Notizbuch *n*; Brieftasche *f*; *Am.* Geldbeutel *m*; Taschenbuch *n*.

pod *♀* [pɔd] Hülse *f*, Schale *f*, Schote *f*.

poem ['pouim] Gedicht *n*.

poet ['pouit] Dichter *m*; ~**ess** [~tis] Dichterin *f*; ~**ic(al** □) [pou'etik(əl)] dichterisch; ~**ics** [~ks] *sg.* Poetik *f*; ~**ry** ['pouitri] Dichtkunst *f*; Dichtung *f*, *coll.* Dichtungen *f/pl.*

poignan|cy ['pɔinənsi] Schärfe *f*; ~**t** [~nt] scharf; *fig.* eindringlich.

point [pɔint] **1.** Spitze *f*; Pointe *f*; Landspitze *f*; *gr.*, *♀*, *phys. etc.* Punkt *m*; Fleck *m*, Stelle *f*; *♣* Kompaßstrich *m*; Auge *n auf Karten etc.*; Grad *m*; (springender) Punkt; Zweck *m*; *fig.* Eigenschaft *f*; ~*s pl. ♣* Weichen *f/pl.*; ~ *of view* Stand-, Gesichtspunkt *m*; *the* ~ *is that ...* die Sache ist die, daß ...; *make a* ~ *of s.th.* auf *et.* bestehen; *in* ~ *of* in Hinsicht auf (*acc.*); *off od. beside the* ~ nicht zur Sache (gehörig); *on the* ~ *of ger.* im Begriff zu *inf.*; *win on* ~*s* nach Punkten siegen; *to the* ~ zur Sache (gehörig); **2.** *v/t.* (zu)spitzen; *oft* ~ *out* zeigen, hinweisen auf (*acc.*); punktieren; ~ *at Waffe etc.* richten auf (*acc.*); *v/i.* ~ *at* weisen auf (*acc.*); ~ *to* nach *e-r Richtung* weisen; ~**ed** □ ['pɔintid] spitz(ig), Spitz...; *fig.* scharf; ~**er** [~tə] Zeiger *m*; Zeigestock *m*; Hühnerhund *m*; ~**less** [~tlis] stumpf; witzlos; zwecklos.

poise [pɔiz] **1.** Gleichgewicht *n*; Haltung *f*; **2.** *v/t.* im Gleichgewicht erhalten; *Kopf etc.* tragen, halten; *v/i.* schweben.

poison ['pɔizn] **1.** Gift *n*; **2.** vergiften; ~**ous** □ [~nəs] giftig (*a. fig.*).

poke [pouk] **1.** Stoß *m*, Puff *m*; **2.** *v/t.* stoßen; schüren; *Nase etc. in et.* stecken; ~ *fun at* sich über *j-n* lustig machen; *v/i.* stoßen; stochern.

poker ['poukə] Feuerhaken *m*.

poky ['pouki] eng; schäbig; erbärmlich. [*m.*]

polar ['poulə] polar; ~ *bear* Eisbär]

Pole¹ [poul] Pole *m*, Polin *f*.

pole² [~] Pol *m*; Stange *f*, Mast *m*; Deichsel *f*; (Sprung)Stab *m*.

polecat zo. ['poulkæt] Iltis m; Am. Skunk m.

polemic [pɔ'lemik], a. ~al □ [~kəl] polemisch; feindselig.

pole-star ['poulsta:] Polarstern m; fig. Leitstern m.

police [pə'li:s] 1. Polizei f; 2. überwachen; ~man Polizist m; ~office Polizeipräsidium n; ~officer Polizeibeamte(r) m, Polizist m; ~station Polizeiwache f.

policy ['pɔlisi] Politik f; (Welt-)Klugheit f; Police f; Am. Zahlenlotto n.

polio(myelitis) ♂ ['pouliou(maiə'laitis)] spinale Kinderlähmung.

Polish¹ ['pouliʃ] polnisch.

polish² ['pɔliʃ] 1. Politur f; fig. Schliff m; 2. polieren; fig. verfeinern.

polite □ [pə'lait] artig, höflich; fein; ~ness [~tnis] Höflichkeit f.

politic □ ['pɔlitik] politisch; schlau; ~al [pə'litikəl] politisch; staatlich; Staats..; ~ian [pɔli'tiʃən] Politiker m; ~s ['pɔlitiks] oft sg. Staatswissenschaft f, Politik f.

polka ['pɔlkə] Polka f; ~ dot Am. Punktmuster n auf Stoff.

poll [poul] 1. Wählerliste f; Stimmenzählung f; Wahl f; Stimmenzahl f; Umfrage f; co. Kopf m; 2. v/t. Stimmen erhalten; v/i. wählen; ~book ['poulbuk] Wählerliste f.

pollen ♀ ['pɔlin] Blütenstaub m.

polling-district ['poulindistrikt] Wahlbezirk m.

poll-tax ['poultæks] Kopfsteuer f.

pollute [pɔ'lu:t] beschmutzen, beflecken; entweihen.

polyp|(e) zo. ['pɔlip], ~us ♂ [~pəs] Polyp m.

pommel ['pʌml] 1. Degen-, Sattel-Knopf m; 2. knuffen, schlagen.

pomp [pɔmp] Pomp m, Gepränge n.

pompous □ ['pɔmpəs] prunkvoll; hochtrabend; pompös.

pond [pɔnd] Teich m, Weiher m.

ponder ['pɔndə] v/t. erwägen; v/i. nachdenken; ~able [~ərəbl] wägbar; ~ous □ [~rəs] schwer(fällig).

pontiff ['pɔntif] Hohepriester m; Papst m.

pontoon ✕ [pɔn'tu:n] Ponton m; ~bridge Schiffsbrücke f.

pony ['pouni] Pony n, Pferdchen n.

poodle ['pu:dl] Pudel m.

pool [pu:l] 1. Teich m; Pfütze f, Lache f; (Schwimm)Becken n; (Spiel)Einsatz m; ♥ Ring m, Kartell n; ~ room Am. Billardspielhalle f; Wettannahmestelle f; 2. ♥ zu e-m Ring vereinigen; Gelder zs.-werfen.

poop ♣ [pu:p] Heck n; Achterhütte f.

poor □ [puə] arm(selig); dürftig; schlecht; ~house ['puəhaus] Armenhaus n; ~-law ₰ Armenrecht

n; ~ly [~li] 1. adj. unpäßlich; 2. adv. dürftig; ~ness ['puənis] Armut f.

pop¹ [pɔp] 1. Knall m; F Sprudel m; F Schampus m; 2. v/t. knallen lassen; Am. Mais rösten; schnell wohin tun, stecken; v/i. puffen, knallen; mit adv. huschen; ~ in hereinplatzen.

pop² F [~] 1. populär, beliebt; 2. Schlager m; volkstümliche Musik.

pop³ Am. F [~] Papa m, alter Herr.

popcorn Am. ['pɔpkɔ:n] Puffmais m.

pope [poup] Papst m.

poplar ♀ ['pɔplə] Pappel f.

poppy ♀ ['pɔpi] Mohn m; ~cock Am. F Quatsch m.

popu|lace ['pɔpjuləs] Pöbel m; ~lar □ [~lə] Volks...; volkstümlich, populär; ~larity [pɔpju'læriti] Popularität f.

populat|e ['pɔpjuleit] bevölkern; ~ion [pɔpju'leiʃən] Bevölkerung f.

populous □ ['pɔpjuləs] volkreich.

porcelain ['pɔ:slin] Porzellan n.

porch [pɔ:tʃ] Vorhalle f, Portal n; Am. Veranda f.

porcupine zo. ['pɔ:kjupain] Stachelschwein n.

pore [pɔ:] 1. Pore f; 2. fig. brüten.

pork [pɔ:k] Schweinefleisch n; ~ barrel Am. sl. ['pɔ:kbærəl] politisch berechnete Geldzuwendung der Regierung; ~y F ['pɔ:ki] 1. fett, dick; 2. Am. = porcupine.

porous □ ['pɔ:rəs] porös.

porpoise ichth. ['pɔ:pəs] Tümmler m.

porridge ['pɔridʒ] Haferbrei m.

port [pɔ:t] 1. Hafen m; ♣ (Pfort-, Lade)Luke f; ♣ Backbord n; Portwein m; 2. ♣ das Ruder nach der Backbordseite umlegen.

portable ['pɔ:təbl] transportabel.

portal ['pɔ:tl] Portal n, Tor n.

portend [pɔ:'tend] vorbedeuten.

portent ['pɔ:tent] (bsd. üble) Vorbedeutung; Wunder n; ~ous □ [pɔ:'tentəs] unheilvoll; wunderbar.

porter ['pɔ:tə] Pförtner m; (Gepäck)Träger m; Porterbier n.

portion ['pɔ:ʃən] 1. (An)Teil m; Portion f Essen; Erbteil n; Aussteuer f; fig. Los n; 2. teilen; ausstatten.

portly ['pɔ:tli] stattlich.

portmanteau [pɔ:t'mæntou] Handkoffer m. [nis n.)

portrait ['pɔ:trit] Porträt n, Bild-)

portray [pɔ:'trei] (ab)malen, porträtieren; schildern; ~al [~eiəl] Porträtieren n; Schilderung f.

pose [pouz] 1. Pose f; 2. (sich) in Positur setzen; F sich hinstellen (as als); Frage aufwerfen.

posh sl. [pɔʃ] schick, erstklassig.

position [pə'ziʃən] Lage f, Stellung f (a. fig.); Stand m; fig. Standpunkt m.

positive ['pɔzətiv] **1.** □ bestimmt, ausdrücklich; feststehend, sicher; unbedingt; positiv; überzeugt; rechthaberisch; **2.** *das* Bestimmte; *gr.* Positiv *m*; *phot.* Positiv *n*.

possess [pə'zes] besitzen; beherrschen; *fig.* erfüllen; ~ *o.s. of et.* in Besitz nehmen; ~ed besessen; ~ion [~eʃən] Besitz *m*; *fig.* Besessenheit *f*; ~ive *gr.* [~esiv] **1.** □ besitzanzeigend; ~ *case* Genitiv *m*; **2.** Possessivpronomen *n*, besitzanzeigendes Fürwort; Genitiv *m*; ~or [~sə] Besitzer *m*.

possib|ility [pɔsə'biliti] Möglichkeit *f*; ~le ['pɔsəbl] möglich; ~ly [~li] möglicherweise, vielleicht; *if I* ~ *can* wenn ich irgend kann.

post [poust] **1.** Pfosten *m*; Posten *m*; Stelle *f*, Amt *n*; Post *f*; ~ *exchange Am.* ✕ Einkaufsstelle *f*; **2.** *v/t. Plakat etc.* anschlagen; postieren; eintragen; zur Post geben; per Post senden; ~ *up j-n* informieren; *v/i.* (dahin)eilen.

postage ['poustidʒ] Porto *n*; ~stamp Briefmarke *f*.

postal ['poustl] **1.** postalisch; Post...; ~ *order* Postanweisung *f*; **2.** *a.* ~ *card Am.* Postkarte *f*.

postcard ['poustka:d] Postkarte *f*.

poster ['poustə] Plakat *n*, Anschlag *m*.

posterior [pɔs'tiəriə] **1.** □ später (*to* als); hinter; **2.** Hinterteil *n*.

posterity [pɔs'teriti] Nachwelt *f*; Nachkommenschaft *f*.

post-free ['poust'fri:] portofrei.

post-graduate ['poust'grædjuit] **1.** nach beendigter Studienzeit; **2.** Doktorand *m*.

post-haste ['poust'heist] eilig(st).

posthumous □ ['pɔstjuməs] nachgeboren; hinterlassen.

post|man ['poustmən] Briefträger *m*; ~mark **1.** Poststempel *m*; **2.** abstempeln; ~master Postamtsvorsteher *m*.

post-mortem ['poust'mɔ:tem] **1.** nach dem Tode; **2.** Leichenschau *f*.

post|(-)office ['poustɔfis] Postamt *n*; ~ *box* Post(schließ)fach *n*; ~ *paid* frankiert.

postpone [poust'poun] ver-, aufschieben; ~ment [~nmənt] Aufschub *m*. [tum *n*.]

postscript ['pousskript] Postskript-)

postulate 1. ['pɔstjulit] Forderung *f*; **2.** [~leit] fordern; (als gegeben) voraussetzen.

posture ['pɔstʃə] **1.** Stellung *f*, Haltung *f des Körpers*; **2.** (sich) zurechtstellen; posieren.

post-war ['poust'wɔ:] Nachkriegs...

posy ['pouzi] Blumenstrauß *m*.

pot [pɔt] **1.** Topf *m*; Kanne *f*; Tiegel *m*; **2.** in e-n Topf tun; einlegen.

potation [pou'teiʃən] *mst* ~*spl.* Trinken *n*, Zecherei *f*; Trunk *m*.

potato [pə'teitou], *pl.* ~es Kartoffel *f*.

pot-belly ['pɔtbeli] Schmerbauch *m*.

poten|cy ['poutənsi] Macht *f*; Stärke *f*; ~t [~nt] mächtig; stark; ~tial [pə'tenʃəl] **1.** potentiell; möglich; **2.** Leistungsfähigkeit *f*.

pother ['pɔðə] Aufregung *f*.

pot|-herb ['pɔthə:b] Küchenkraut *n*; ~house Kneipe *f*.

potion ['pouʃən] (Arznei)Trank *m*.

potter[1] ['pɔtə]: ~ *about* herumwerkeln.

potter[2] [~] Töpfer *m*; ~y [~əri] Töpferei *f*; Töpferware(n *pl.*) *f*.

pouch [pautʃ] **1.** Tasche *f*; Beutel *m*; **2.** einstecken; (sich) beuteln.

poulterer ['poultərə] Geflügelhändler *m*.

poultice ['poultis] Packung *f*.

poultry ['poultri] Geflügel *n*.

pounce [pauns] **1.** Stoß *m*, Sprung *m*; **2.** sich stürzen (*on*, *upon* auf *acc.*).

pound [paund] **1.** Pfund *n*; ~ (*sterling*) Pfund *n* Sterling (*abbr.* £ = *20 shillings*); Pfandstall *m*; Tierasyl *n*; **2.** (zer)stoßen; stampfen; schlagen.

pounder ['paundə] ...pfünder *m*.

pour [pɔ:] *v/t.* gießen, schütten; ~ *out Getränke* eingießen; *v/i.* sich ergießen, strömen; *it never rains but it* ~*s fig.* ein Unglück kommt selten allein.

pout [paut] **1.** Schmollen *n*; **2.** *v/t. Lippen* aufwerfen; *v/i.* schmollen.

poverty ['pɔvəti] Armut *f*.

powder ['paudə] **1.** Pulver *n*; Puder *m*; **2.** pulverisieren; (sich) pudern; bestreuen; ~box Puderdose *f*.

power ['pauə] Kraft *f*; Macht *f*, Gewalt *f*; ⚡ Vollmacht *f*; ♃ Potenz *f*; *in* ~ an der Macht, im Amt; ~current Starkstrom *m*; ~ful □ ['pauəful] mächtig, kräftig; wirksam; ~less ['pauəlis] macht-, kraftlos; ~plant *s. power-station*; ~ politics *oft sg.* Machtpolitik *f*; ~station Kraftwerk *n*.

powwow ['pauwau] Medizinmann *m*; *Am.* F Versammlung *f*.

practica|ble □ ['præktikəbl] ausführbar; gangbar (*Weg*); brauchbar; ~l □ [~əl] praktisch; tatsächlich; eigentlich; sachlich; ~ *joke* Schabernack *m*; ~lly [~li] so gut wie.

practice ['præktis] **1.** Praxis *f*; Übung *f*; Gewohnheit *f*; Brauch *m*; Praktik *f*; *put into* ~ in die Praxis umsetzen; **2.** *Am.* = *practise*.

practise [~] *v/t.* in die Praxis umsetzen; ausüben; betreiben; üben; *v/i.* (sich) üben; praktizieren; ~ *upon j-s Schwäche* ausnutzen; ~d geübt (*P.*).

practitioner [præk'tiʃnə] a. general ~ praktischer Arzt; Rechtsanwalt m.

prairie Am. ['prɛəri] Grasebene f; Prärie f; ~-schooner Am. Planwagen m.

praise [preiz] 1. Preis m, Lob n; 2. loben, preisen.

praiseworthy □ ['preizwə:ði] lobenswert.

pram F [præm] Kinderwagen m.

prance [prɑːns] sich bäumen; paradieren; einherstolzieren.

prank [præŋk] Possen m, Streich m.

prate [preit] 1. Geschwätz n; 2. schwatzen, plappern.

prattle ['prætl] s. prate.

pray [prei] beten; (er)bitten; bitte!

prayer [prɛə] Gebet n; Bitte f; oft ~s pl. Andacht f; Lord's ♀ Vaterunser n; ~-book ['prɛəbuk] Gebetbuch n.

pre... [priː; pri] vor(her)...; Vor...; früher.

preach [priːtʃ] predigen; ~er ['priːtʃə] Prediger(in).

preamble [priːˈæmbl] Einleitung f.

precarious □ [priˈkɛəriəs] unsicher.

precaution [priˈkɔːʃən] Vorsicht(smaßregel) f; ~ary [~ʃnəri] vorbeugend.

precede [priˈsiːd] voraus-, vorangehen (dat.); ~nce, ~ncy [~dəns, ~si] Vortritt m, Vorrang m; ~nt ['presidənt] Präzedenzfall m.

precept ['priːsept] Vorschrift f, Regel f; ~or [priˈseptə] Lehrer m.

precinct ['priːsiŋkt] Bezirk m, bsd. Am. Wahlbezirk m, -kreis m; ~s pl. Umgebung f; Bereich m; Grenze f; pedestrian ~ Fußgängerzone f.

precious ['preʃəs] 1. □ kostbar; edel; F arg, gewaltig, schön; 2. F adv. recht, äußerst.

precipi|ce ['presipis] Abgrund m; ~tate 1. [priˈsipiteit] (hinab)stürzen; ᗧ fällen; überstürzen; 2. □ [~tit] übereilt, hastig; 3. [~] ᗧ Niederschlag m; ~tation [prisipiˈteiʃən] Sturz m; Überstürzung f, Hast f; ᗧ Niederschlag(en) n) m; ~tous □ [priˈsipitəs] steil, jäh.

précis [ˈpreisiː] gedrängte Übersicht, Zs.-fassung f.

precis|e □ [priˈsais] genau; ~ion [~ˈsiʒən] Genauigkeit f; Präzision f.

preclude [priˈkluːd] ausschließen; vorbeugen (dat.); j-n hindern.

precocious □ [priˈkouʃəs] frühreif; altklug.

preconceive ['priːkənˈsiːv] vorher ausdenken; ~d vorgefaßt (Meinung).

preconception ['priːkənˈsepʃən] vorgefaßte Meinung. [m.]

precursor [priˈkəːsə] Vorläufer.]

predatory ['predətəri] räuberisch.

predecessor ['priːdisesə] Vorgänger m.

predestin|ate [priˈdestineit]

vorherbestimmen; ~ed [~nd] auserkoren.

predetermine ['priːdiˈtəːmin] vorher festsetzen; vorherbestimmen.

predicament [priˈdikəmənt] (mißliche) Lage.

predicate 1. ['predikeit] aussagen; 2. gr. [~kit] Prädikat n, Satzaussage f.

predict [priˈdikt] vorhersagen; ~ion [~kʃən] Prophezeiung f.

predilection [priːdiˈlekʃən] Vorliebe f.

predispos|e ['priːdisˈpouz] vorher geneigt od. empfänglich machen (to für); ~ition [~spəˈziʃən] Geneigtheit f; bsd. ᗧ Anfälligkeit f (to für).

predomina|nce [priˈdɔminəns] Vorherrschaft f; Übergewicht n; Vormacht(stellung) f; ~nt □ [~nt] vorherrschend; ~te [~neit] die Oberhand haben; vorherrschen.

pre-eminent □ [priˈ(:)ˈeminənt] hervorragend.

pre-emption [priˈ(:)ˈempʃən] Vorkauf(srecht n) m.

pre-exist ['priːigˈzist] vorher dasein.

prefabricate ['priːˈfæbrikeit] vorfabrizieren.

preface ['prefis] 1. Vorrede f, Vorwort n, Einleitung f; 2. einleiten.

prefect ['priːfekt] Präfekt m; Schule: Vertrauensschüler m, Klassensprecher m.

prefer [priˈfəː] vorziehen; Gesuch etc. vorbringen; Klage einreichen; befördern; ~able □ ['prefərəbl] (to) vorzuziehen(d) (dat.); vorzüglicher (als); ~ably [~li] vorzugsweise; besser; ~ence [~rəns] Vorliebe f; Vorzug m; ~ential □ [prefəˈrenʃəl] bevorzugt; Vorzugs...; ~ment [priˈfəːmənt] Beförderung f.

prefix ['priːfiks] Präfix n, Vorsilbe f.

pregnan|cy ['pregnənsi] Schwangerschaft f; fig. Fruchtbarkeit f; Bedeutungsreichtum m; ~t □ [~nt] schwanger; fig. fruchtbar, inhaltsvoll.

prejud|ge ['priːˈdʒʌdʒ] vorher (ver)urteilen; ~ice ['predʒudis] 1. Voreingenommenheit f; Vorurteil n; Schaden m; 2. voreinnehmen; benachteiligen; e-r S. Abbruch tun; ~d (vor)eingenommen; ~icial □ [predʒuˈdiʃəl] nachteilig.

prelate ['prelit] Prälat m.

preliminary [priˈliminəri] 1. □ vorläufig; einleitend; Vor...; 2. Einleitung f.

prelude ♪ ['preljuːd] Vorspiel n.

premature □ [preməˈtjuə] fig. frühreif; vorzeitig; vorschnell.

premeditat|e [priˈ(:)ˈmediteit] vorher überlegen; ~ion [priˈ(:)mediˈteiʃən] Vorbedacht m.

premier ['premjə] **1.** erst; **2.** Premierminister *m*.

premises ['premisiz] *pl.* (Gebäude *pl.* mit) Grundstück *n*, Anwesen *n*; Lokal *n*.

premium ['pri:mjəm] Prämie *f*; Anzahlung *f*; † Agio *n*; Versicherungsprämie *f*; Lehrgeld *n*; *at a* ~ über pari; sehr gesucht.

premonition [pri:mə'niʃən] Warnung *f*; (Vor)Ahnung *f*.

preoccupied [pri(:)'ɔkjupaid] in Gedanken verloren; ~y [~pai] vorher in Besitz nehmen; ausschließlich beschäftigen; in Anspruch nehmen.

prep F [prep] = *preparation, preparatory school.*

preparation [prepə'reiʃən] Vorbereitung *f*; Zubereitung *f*; ~ory □ [pri'pærətəri] vorbereitend; ~ (*school*) Vorschule *f*.

prepare [pri'pɛə] *v/t.* vorbereiten; zurechtmachen; (zu)bereiten; (aus-) rüsten; *v/i.* sich vorbereiten; sich anschicken; ~d □ bereit.

prepay ['pri:'pei] (*irr.* (*pay*)) vorausbezahlen; frankieren.

preponderance [pri'pɔndərəns] Übergewicht *n*; ~nt □ [~nt] überwiegend; ~te [~reit] überwiegen.

preposition *gr.* [prepə'ziʃən] Präposition *f*, Verhältniswort *n*.

prepossess [pri:pə'zes] günstig stimmen; ~ing □ [~siŋ] einnehmend.

preposterous [pri'pɔstərəs] widersinnig, albern; grotesk.

prerequisite [pri:'rekwizit] Vorbedingung *f*, Voraussetzung *f*.

prerogative [pri'rɔgətiv] Vorrecht *n*.

presage ['presidʒ] **1.** Vorbedeutung *f*; Ahnung *f*; **2.** vorbedeuten; ahnen; prophezeien.

prescribe [pris'kraib] vorschreiben; ✗ verschreiben.

prescription [pris'kripʃən] Vorschrift *f*, Verordnung *f*; ✗ Rezept *n*.

presence ['prezns] Gegenwart *f*; Anwesenheit *f*; Erscheinung *f*; ~ *of mind* Geistesgegenwart *f*.

present¹ ['preznt] **1.** □ gegenwärtig; anwesend, vorhanden; jetzig; laufend (*Jahr etc.*); vorliegend (*Fall etc.*); ~ *tense gr.* Präsens *n*; **2.** Gegenwart *f*, *gr. a.* Präsens *n*; Geschenk *n*; *at* ~ jetzt; *for the* ~ einstweilen.

present² [pri'zent] präsentieren; (dar)bieten; (vor)zeigen; *j-n* vorstellen; vorschlagen; (über)reichen; (be)schenken.

presentation [prezen'teiʃən] Dar-, Vorstellung *f*; Ein-, Überreichung *f*; Schenkung *f*; Vorzeigen *n*, Vorlage *f*.

presentiment [pri'zentimənt] Vorgefühl *n*, Ahnung *f*.

presently ['prezntli] sogleich, bald (darauf), alsbald; *Am.* zur Zeit.

preservation [prezə(:)'veiʃən] Bewahrung *f*, Erhaltung *f*; ~ve [pri-'zə:vətiv] **1.** bewahrend; **2.** Schutz-, Konservierungsmittel *n*.

preserve [pri'zə:v] **1.** bewahren; behüten; erhalten; einmachen; *Wild* hegen; **2.** *hunt.* Gehege *n* (*a. fig.*); *mst* ~s *pl.* Eingemachte(s) *n*.   [ren (over bei).]

preside [pri'zaid] den Vorsitz füh-)

presidency ['prezidənsi] Vorsitz *m*; Präsidentschaft *f*; ~t [~nt] Präsident *m*, Vorsitzende(r) *m*; *Am.* † Direktor *m*.

press [pres] **1.** Druck *m der Hand*; (Wein- *etc.*)Presse *f*; *die* Presse (*Zeitungen*); Druckerei *f*; Verlag *m*; Druck(en *n*) *m*; *a.* printing-~ Druckerpresse *f*; Menge *f*; *fig.* Druck *m*, Last *f*, Andrang *m*; Schrank *m*; **2.** *v/t.* (aus)pressen; drücken; lasten auf (*dat.*); (be)drängen; dringen auf (*acc.*); aufdrängen (*on dat.*); bügeln; *be* ~*ed for time* es eilig haben; *v/i.* drücken; (sich) drängen; ~ *for* sich eifrig bemühen um; ~ *on* weitereilen; ~(*up*)on eindringen auf (*acc.*); ~ **agency** Nachrichtenbüro *n*; ~ **agent** Reklameagent *m*; ~ **button** Druckknopf *m*; ~ing □ ['presiŋ] dringend; ~ure ['preʃə] Druck *m* (*a. fig.*); Drang(sal *f*) *m*.

prestige [pres'ti:ʒ] Prestige *n*.

presumable □ [pri'zju:məbl] vermutlich; ~e [pri'zju:m] *v/t.* annehmen; vermuten; voraussetzen; *v/i.* vermuten; sich erdreisten; anmaßend sein; ~ (*up*)*on* pochen auf (*acc.*); ausnutzen, mißbrauchen.

presumption [pri'zʌmpʃən] Mutmaßung *f*; Wahrscheinlichkeit *f*; Anmaßung *f*; ~ive □ [~ptiv] mutmaßlich; ~uous □ [~tjuəs] überheblich; vermessen.

presuppose [pri:sə'pouz] voraussetzen; ~ition [pri:sʌpə'ziʃən] Voraussetzung *f*.

pretence, *Am.* ~se [pri'tens] Vortäuschung *f*; Vorwand *m*; Schein *m*, Verstellung *f*.

pretend [pri'tend] vorgeben; vortäuschen; heucheln; Anspruch erheben (*to auf acc.*); ~ed □ angeblich.

pretension [pri'tenʃən] Anspruch *m* (*to auf acc.*); Anmaßung *f*.

preterit(e) *gr.* ['pretərit] Präteritum *n*, Vergangenheitsform *f*.

pretext ['pri:tekst] Vorwand *m*.

pretty ['priti] **1.** □ hübsch, niedlich; nett; **2.** *adv.* ziemlich.

prevail [pri'veil] die Oberhand haben *od.* gewinnen; (vor)herrschen; maßgebend *od.* ausschlaggebend sein; ~ (*up*)*on s.o.* j-n dazu bewegen, *et.* zu tun; ~ing □ [~liŋ] (vor)herrschend.

prevalent □ ['prevələnt] vorherrschend, weit verbreitet.

prevaricate [pri'værikeit] Ausflüchte machen.

prevent [pri'vent] verhüten, *e-r S.* vorbeugen; *j-n* hindern; ∼**ion** [∼nʃən] Verhinderung *f;* Verhütung *f;* ∼**ive** [∼ntiv] **1.** □ vorbeugend; **2.** Schutzmittel *n.*

preview ['pri:'vju:] Vorschau *f;* Vorbesichtigung *f.*

previous □ ['pri:vjəs] vorhergehend; vorläufig; Vor...; ∼ *to* vor (*dat.*); ∼**ly** [∼sli] vorher, früher.

pre-war ['pri:'wɔ:] Vorkriegs...

prey [prei] **1.** Raub *m,* Beute *f; beast of* ∼ Raubtier *n; bird of* ∼ Raubvogel *m; be a* ∼ *to* geplagt werden von; **2.** ∼ (*up*)*on* rauben, plündern; fressen; *fig.* nagen an (*dat.*).

price [prais] **1.** Preis *m;* Lohn *m;* **2.** *Waren* auszeichnen; die Preise festsetzen für; (ab)schätzen; ∼**less** ['praislis] unschätzbar; unbezahlbar.

prick [prik] **1.** Stich *m;* Stachel *m* (*a. fig.*); **2.** *v/t.* (durch)stechen; *fig.* peinigen; *a.* ∼ *out Muster* punktieren; ∼ *up one's ears* die Ohren spitzen; *v/i.* stechen; ∼**le** ['prikl] Stachel *m,* Dorn *m;* ∼**ly** [∼li] stachelig.

pride [praid] **1.** Stolz *m;* Hochmut *m; take* ∼ *in* stolz sein auf (*acc.*); **2.** ∼ *o.s.* sich brüsten (*on, upon* mit).

priest [pri:st] Priester *m.*

prig [prig] Tugendbold *m,* selbstgerechter Mensch; Pedant *m.*

prim □ [prim] steif; zimperlich.

prima|**cy** ['praiməsi] Vorrang *m;* ∼**rily** [∼rili] in erster Linie; ∼**ry** □ [∼ri] **1.** ursprünglich; hauptsächlich; Ur...; Anfangs..., Haupt...; Elementar..., höchst; *⚡, ⚛* Primär...; **2.** *a.* ∼ *meeting Am.* Wahlversammlung *f;* ∼**ry school** Elementar-, Grundschule *f.*

prime [praim] **1.** □ ∼ erst; wichtigst; Haupt...; vorzüglich(st); ∼ *cost ✝* Selbstkosten *pl.;* ∼ *minister* Ministerpräsident *m;* ∼ *number* Primzahl *f;* **2.** *fig.* Blüte(zeit) *f;* Beste(s) *n;* höchste Vollkommenheit; **3.** *v/t.* vorbereiten; *Pumpe* anlassen; instruieren; F vollaufen lassen (*betrunken machen*); *paint.* grundieren.

primer ['praimə] Fibel *f,* Elementarbuch *n.* [lich; Ur...]

primeval [prai'mi:vəl] uranfang-]

primitive ['primitiv] **1.** □ erst, ursprünglich; Stamm...; primitiv; **2.** *gr.* Stammwort *n.*

primrose ♦ ['primrouz] Primel *f.*

prince [prins] Fürst *m;* Prinz *m;* ∼**ss** [prin'ses, *vor npr.* 'prinses] Fürstin *f;* Prinzessin *f.*

principal ['prinsəpl] **1.** □ hauptsächlich(st); Haupt...; ∼ *parts pl. gr.* Stammformen *f/pl. des vb.;*

2. Hauptperson *f;* Vorsteher *m; bsd. Am.* (Schul)Direktor *m,* Rektor *m;* ✝ Chef *m;* ⚖ Hauptschuldige(r) *m;* ✝ Kapital *n;* ∼**ity** [prinsi'pæliti] Fürstentum *n.*

principle ['prinsəpl] Prinzip *n;* Grund(satz) *m;* Ursprung *m; on* ∼ grundsätzlich, aus Prinzip.

print [print] **1.** Druck *m;* (Fingeretc.)Abdruck *m;* bedruckter Kattun, Druckstoff *m;* Stich *m; phot.* Abzug *m; Am.* Zeitungsdrucksache *f; out of* ∼ vergriffen; **2.** (ab-, auf-, be)drucken; *phot.* kopieren; *fig.* einprägen (*on dat.*); in Druckbuchstaben schreiben; ∼**er** ['printə] (Buch)Drucker *m.*

printing ['printiŋ] Druck *m;* Drucken *n; phot.* Abziehen *n,* Kopieren *n;* ∼**ink** Druckerschwärze *f;* ∼**office** (Buch)Druckerei *f;* ∼**press** Druckerpresse *f.*

prior ['praiə] **1.** früher, älter (*to* als); **2.** *adv.* ∼ *to* vor (*dat.*); **3.** *eccl.* Prior *m;* ∼**ity** [prai'ɔriti] Priorität *f;* Vorrang *m;* Vorfahrtsrecht *n.*

prism ['prizəm] Prisma *n.*

prison ['prizn] Gefängnis *n;* ∼**er** [∼nə] Gefangene(r *m*) *f,* Häftling *m; take s.o.* ∼ j-n gefangennehmen.

privacy ['praivəsi] Zurückgezogenheit *f;* Geheimhaltung *f.*

private ['praivit] **1.** □ privat; Privat...; persönlich; vertraulich; geheim; **2.** ⚔ (gewöhnlicher) Soldat; *in* ∼ privatim; im geheimen.

privation [prai'veiʃən] Mangel *m,* Entbehrung *f.*

privilege ['privilidʒ] **1.** Privileg *n;* Vorrecht *n;* **2.** bevorrechten.

privy ['privi] **1.** □ ∼ *to* eingeweiht in (*acc.*); ♀ *Council* Staatsrat *m;* ♀ *Councillor* Geheimer Rat; ♀ *Seal* Geheimsiegel *n;* **2.** Mitinteressent *m* (*to an dat.*); Abort *m.*

prize [praiz] **1.** Preis *m,* Prämie *f;* ⚓ Beute *f;* (Lotterie)Gewinn *m;* **2.** preisgekrönt, Preis...; **3.** (hoch-) schätzen; aufbrechen (öffnen); ∼ **fighter** ['praizfaitə] Berufsboxer *m.*

pro [prou] für.

probab|**ility** [prɔbə'biliti] Wahrscheinlichkeit *f;* ∼**le** □ ['prɔbəbl] wahrscheinlich.

probation [prə'beiʃən] Probe *f,* Probezeit *f;* ⚖ Bewährungsfrist *f;* ∼ *officer* Bewährungshelfer *m.*

probe [proub] **1.** ⚕ Sonde *f; fig.* Untersuchung *f; lunar* ∼ Mondsonde *f;* **2.** *a.* ∼ *into* sondieren; untersuchen.

probity ['proubiti] Redlichkeit *f.*

problem ['prɔbləm] Problem *n;* ⚖ Aufgabe *f;* ∼**atic(al** □) ['prɔbli'mætik(əl)] problematisch, zweifelhaft. [*n;* Handlungsweise *f.*]

procedure [prə'si:dʒə] Verfahren]

proceed [prə'si:d] weitergehen; fortfahren; vor sich gehen; vorgehen; *univ.* promovieren; ~ *from von od.* aus *et.* kommen; ausgehen *von*; ~ *to* zu *et.* übergehen; **~ing** [~diŋ] Vorgehen *n*; Handlung *f*; **~s** *pl.* ⚖ Verfahren *n*; Verhandlungen *f/pl.*, (Tätigkeits)Bericht *m*; **~s** ['prousi:dz] *pl.* Ertrag *m*, Gewinn *m*.

process ['prouses] 1. Fortschreiten *n*, Fortgang *m*; Vorgang *m*; Verlauf *m der Zeit*; Prozeß *m*, Verfahren *n*; *in* ~ *in the Gange; in* ~ *of construction* im Bau (befindlich); 2. gerichtlich belangen; ⊕ bearbeiten; **~ion** [prə'seʃən] Prozession *f*.

proclaim [prə'kleim] proklamieren; erklären; ausrufen.

proclamation [prɔklə'meiʃən] Proklamation *f*; Bekanntmachung *f*; Erklärung *f*.

proclivity [prə'kliviti] Neigung *f*.

procrastinate [prou'kræstineit] zaudern.

procreate ['proukrieit] (er)zeugen.

procuration [prɔkjuə'reiʃən] Vollmacht *f*; ✝ Prokura *f*; **~or** ['prɔkjuəreitə(r)] *m*.

procure [prə'kjuə] *v/t.* be-, verschaffen; *v/i.* Kuppelei treiben.

prod [prɔd] 1. Stich *m*; Stoß *m*; *fig.* Ansporn *m*; 2. stechen; stoßen; *fig.* anstacheln.

prodigal ['prɔdigəl] 1. ☐ verschwenderisch; *the* ~ *son* der verlorene Sohn; 2. Verschwender(in).

prodigious ☐ [prə'didʒəs] erstaunlich, ungeheuer; **~y** ['prɔdidʒi] Wunder *n* (*a. fig.*); Ungeheuer *n*; *oft infant* ~ Wunderkind *n*.

produce 1. [prə'dju:s] vorbringen, vorführen, vorlegen; beibringen; hervorbringen; produzieren, erzeugen; *Zinsen etc.* (ein)bringen; ⚖ verlängern; *Film etc.* herausbringen; 2. ['prɔdju:s] (Natur)Erzeugnis(se *pl.*) *n*, Produkt *n*; Ertrag *m*; **~r** [prə'dju:sə] Erzeuger *m*, Hersteller *m*; *Film*: Produzent *m*; *thea.* Regisseur *m*.

product ['prɔdəkt] Produkt *n*, Erzeugnis *n*; **~ion** [prə'dʌkʃən] Hervorbringung *f*; Vorlegung *f*, Beibringung *f*; Produktion *f*, Erzeugung *f*; *thea.* Herausbringen *n*; Erzeugnis *n*; **~ive** ☐ [~tiv] schöpferisch; produktiv, erzeugend; ertragreich; fruchtbar; **~iveness** [~vnis], **~ivity** [prɔdʌk'tiviti] Produktivität *f*.

prof *Am.* F [prɔf] Professor *m*.

profanation [prɔfə'neiʃən] Entweihung *f*; **~e** [prə'fein] 1. ☐ profan; weltlich; uneingeweiht; gottlos; 2. entweihen; **~ity** [~'fæniti] Gottlosigkeit *f*; Fluchen *n*.

profess [prə'fes] (sich) bekennen (zu); erklären; *Reue etc.* bekunden; *Beruf* ausüben; lehren; **~ed** ☐ erklärt; angeblich; Berufs...; **~ion** [~eʃən] Bekenntnis *n*; Erklärung *f*; Beruf *m*; **~ional** [~nl] 1. ☐ Berufs...; Amts...; berufsmäßig; freiberuflich; ~ *men* Akademiker *m/pl.*; 2. Fachmann *m*; *Sport*: Berufsspieler *m*; Berufskünstler *m*; **~or** [~esə] Professor *m*.

proffer ['prɔfə] 1. anbieten; 2. Anerbieten *n*.

proficiency [prə'fiʃənsi] Tüchtigkeit *f*; **~t** [~nt] 1. ☐ tüchtig; bewandert; 2. Meister *m*.

profile ['proufail] Profil *n*.

profit ['prɔfit] 1. Vorteil *m*, Nutzen *m*, Gewinn *m*; 2. *v/t. j-m* Nutzen bringen; *v/i.* ~ *by* Nutzen ziehen aus; ausnutzen; **~able** ☐ [~təbl] nützlich, vorteilhaft, einträglich; **~eer** [prɔfi'tiə] 1. Schiebergeschäfte machen; 2. Profitmacher *m*, Schieber *m*; **~-sharing** ['prɔfitʃeəriŋ] Gewinnbeteiligung *f*.

profligate ['prɔfligit] 1. ☐ liederlich; 2. liederlicher Mensch.

profound ☐ [prə'faund] tief; tiefgründig; gründlich; *fig.* dunkel.

profundity [prə'fʌnditi] Tiefe *f*.

profuse ☐ [prə'fju:s] verschwenderisch; übermäßig, überreich; **~ion** *fig.* [~u:ʒən] Überfluß *m*.

progenitor [prou'dʒenitə] Vorfahr *m*, Ahn *m*; **~y** ['prɔdʒini] Nachkommen(schaft *f*) *m/pl.*; Brut *f*.

prognosis ⚕ [prɔg'nousis], *pl.* **~es** [~si:z] Prognose *f*.

prognostication [prəgnɔsti'keiʃən] Vorhersage *f*.

program(me) ['prougræm] Programm *n*.

progress 1. ['prougres] Fortschritt(e *pl.*) *m*; Vorrücken *n* (*a.* ✕); Fortgang *m*; *in* ~ *im Gange*; 2. [prə'gres] fortschreiten; **~ion** [prə'greʃən] Fortschreiten *n*; ⚖ Reihe *f*; **~ive** [~esiv] 1. ☐ fortschreitend; fortschrittlich; 2. *pol.* Fortschrittler *m*.

prohibit [prə'hibit] verbieten; verhindern; **~ion** [proui'biʃən] Verbot *n*; Prohibition *f*; **~ionist** [~ʃnist] *bsd. Am.* Prohibitionist *m*; **~ive** ☐ [prə'hibitiv] verbietend; Sperr...; unerschwinglich.

project 1. ['prɔdʒekt] Projekt *n*; Vorhaben *n*, Plan *m*; 2. [prə'dʒekt] *v/t.* planen; (ent)werfen; ⚖ projizieren; *v/i.* vorspringen; **~ile** ['prɔdʒiktail] Projektil *n*, Geschoß *n*; **~ion** [prə'dʒekʃən] Werfen *n*; Entwurf *m*; Vorsprung *m*; ⚖, *ast.*, *phot.* Projektion *f*; **~or** [~ktə] ✝ Gründer *m*; *opt.* Projektor *m*.

proletarian [proule'teəriən] 1. proletarisch; 2. Proletarier(in).

prolific ☐ [prə'lifik] (~ally) fruchtbar.

prolix ☐ ['prouliks] weitschweifig.

prologue, *Am. a.* **~g** ['proulɔg] Prolog *m*.

prolong [prə'lɔŋ] verlängern.

promenade [prɔmi'nɑːd] **1.** Promenade *f*; **2.** promenieren.
prominent □ ['prɔminənt] hervorragend (*a. fig.*); *fig.* prominent.
promiscuous □ [prə'miskjuəs] unordentlich, verworren; gemeinsam; unterschiedslos.
promis|e ['prɔmis] **1.** Versprechen *n*; *fig.* Aussicht *f*; **2.** versprechen; **~ing** □ [~siŋ] vielversprechend; **~sory** [~səri] versprechend; **~ note** † Eigenwechsel *m*.
promontory ['prɔməntri] Vorgebirge *n*.
promot|e [prə'mout] *et.* fördern; *j-n* befördern; *bsd. Am. Schule*: versetzen; *parl.* unterstützen; † gründen; *bsd. Am. Verkauf durch Werbung* steigern; **~ion** [~ouʃən] Förderung *f*; Beförderung *f*; † Gründung *f*.
prompt [prɔmpt] **1.** □ schnell; bereit(willig); sofortig; pünktlich; **2.** *j-n* veranlassen; *Gedanken* eingeben; *j-m* vorsagen, soufflieren; **~er** ['prɔmptə] Souffleur *m*, -se *f*; **~ness** [~tnis] Schnelligkeit *f*; Bereitschaft *f*.
promulgate ['prɔməlgeit] verkünden, verbreiten.
prone □ [proun] mit dem Gesicht nach unten (liegend); hingestreckt; **~ to** *fig.* geneigt *od.* neigend zu.
prong [prɔŋ] Zinke *f*; Spitze *f*.
pronoun *gr.* ['prounaun] Pronomen *n*, Fürwort *n*.
pronounce [prə'nauns] aussprechen; verkünden; erklären (für).
pronto *Am.* F ['prɔntou] sofort.
pronunciation [prənʌnsi'eiʃən] Aussprache *f*.
proof [pruːf] **1.** Beweis *m*; Probe *f*, Versuch *m*; *typ.* Korrekturbogen *m*; *typ., phot.* Probeabzug *m*; **2.** fest; *in Zssgn*: ...fest, ...dicht, ...sicher; **~reader** *typ.* ['pruːfriːdə] Korrektor *m*.
prop [prɔp] **1.** Stütze *f* (*a. fig.*); **2.** *a.* **~ up** (unter)stützen.
propaga|te ['prɔpəgeit] (sich) fortpflanzen; verbreiten; **~tion** [prɔpə-'geiʃən] Fortpflanzung *f*; Verbreitung *f*.
propel [prə'pel] (vorwärts-, an-) treiben; **~ler** [~lə] Propeller *m*, (Schiffs-, Luft)Schraube *f*.
propensity [prə'pensiti] Neigung *f*.
proper □ ['prɔpə] eigen(tümlich); eigentlich; passend, richtig; anständig; **~ty** [~əti] Eigentum *n*, Besitz *m*; Vermögen *n*; Eigenschaft *f*.
prophe|cy ['prɔfisi] Prophezeiung *f*; **~sy** [~sai] prophezeien.
prophet ['prɔfit] Prophet *m*.
propi|tiate [prə'piʃieit] günstig stimmen, versöhnen; **~tious** □ [~ʃəs] gnädig; günstig.
proportion [prə'pɔːʃən] **1.** Verhältnis *n*; Gleichmaß *n*; (An)Teil *m*;

~s *pl.* (Aus)Maße *n/pl.*; **2.** in ein Verhältnis bringen; **~al** □ [~nl] im Verhältnis (to zu); **~ate** □ [~ʃnit] angemessen.
propos|al [prə'pouzəl] Vorschlag *m*, (*a.* Heirats)Antrag *m*; Angebot *n*; Plan *m*; **~e** [~ouz] *v/t.* vorschlagen; e-n Toast ausbringen auf (*acc.*); **~** to o.s. sich vornehmen; *v/i.* beabsichtigen; anhalten (to um); **~ition** [prɔpə'ziʃən] Vorschlag *m*, Antrag *m*; Behauptung *f*; Problem *n*.
propound [prə'paund] *Frage etc.* vorlegen; vorschlagen.
propriet|ary [prə'praiətəri] Eigentümer..., Eigentums...; Besitz(er)...; gesetzlich geschützt (*bsd. Arzneimittel*); **~or** [~tə] Eigentümer *m*; **~y** [~ti] Richtigkeit *f*; Schicklichkeit *f*; the proprieties *pl.* die Anstandsformen *f/pl.*   [*m.*\
propulsion ⊕ [prə'pʌlʃən] Antrieb]
prorate *Am.* [prou'reit] anteilmäßig verteilen.
prosaic [prou'zeiik] (~ally) *fig.* prosaisch (*nüchtern, trocken*).
proscribe [prous'kraib] ächten.
proscription [prous'kripʃən] Achtung *f*; Acht *f*; Verbannung *f*.
prose [prouz] **1.** Prosa *f*; **2.** prosaisch.
prosecut|e ['prɔsikjuːt] (*a.* gerichtlich) verfolgen; *Gewerbe etc.* betreiben; verklagen; **~ion** [prɔsi'kjuːʃən] Verfolgung *f* e-s Plans etc.; Betreiben *n* e-s Gewerbes etc.; gerichtliche Verfolgung; **~or** *z/z* [prɔsikjuːtə] Kläger *m*; Anklagevertreter *m*; *public* **~** Staatsanwalt *m*.
prospect 1. ['prɔspekt] Aussicht *f* (*a. fig.*); Anblick *m*; † Interessent *m*; **2.** [prɔs'pekt] ⚒ schürfen; bohren (*for nach Öl*); **~ive** □ [~tiv] vorausblickend; voraussichtlich; **~us** [~təs] (Werbe)Prospekt *m*.
prosper ['prɔspə] *v/i.* Erfolg haben, gedeihen, blühen; *v/t.* begünstigen, segnen; **~ity** [prɔs'periti] Gedeihen *n*; Wohlstand *m*; Glück *n*; *fig.* Blüte *f*; **~ous** □ ['prɔspərəs] glücklich, gedeihlich; *fig.* blühend; günstig.
prostitute ['prɔstitjuːt] **1.** Dirne *f*; **2.** zur Dirne machen; (der Schande) preisgeben, feilbieten (*a. fig.*).
prostrat|e 1. ['prɔstreit] hingestreckt; erschöpft; daniederliegend; demütig; gebrochen; **2.** [prɔs'treit] niederwerfen; *fig.* niederschmettern; entkräften; **~ion** [~eiʃən] Niederwerfung *f*; Fußfall *m*; *fig.* Demütigung *f*; Entkräftung *f*.
prosy *fig.* ['prouzi] prosaisch; langweilig.
protagonist [prou'tægənist] *thea.* Hauptfigur *f*; *fig.* Vorkämpfer(in).
protect [prə'tekt] (be)schützen; **~ion** [~kʃən] Schutz *m*; Wirtschaftsschutz *m*, Schutzzoll *m*; **~ive**

[⸗ktiv] schützend; Schutz...; ~ duty Schutzzoll m; ~or [⸗tə] (Be)Schützer m; Schutz-, Schirmherr m; ~orate [⸗ərit] Protektorat n.

protest 1. ['proutest] Protest m; Einspruch m; **2.** [prə'test] beteuern; protestieren; reklamieren.

Protestant ['protistənt] **1.** protestantisch; **2.** Protestant(in).

protestation [proutes'teifən] Beteuerung f; Verwahrung f.

protocol ['proutəkɔl] **1.** Protokoll n; **2.** protokollieren.

prototype ['proutətaip] Urbild n; Prototyp m, Modell n.

protract [prə'trækt] in die Länge ziehen, hinziehen.

protru|de [prə'tru:d] (sich) (her-)vorstrecken; (her)vorstehen, (her-)vortreten (lassen); ~sion [⸗u:ʒən] Vorstrecken n; (Her)Vorstehen n, (Her)Vortreten n.

protuberance [prə'tju:bərəns] Hervortreten n; Auswuchs m, Höcker m.

proud □ [praud] stolz (of auf acc.).

prove [pru:v] v/t. be-, er-, nachweisen; prüfen; erleben, erfahren; v/i. sich herausstellen od. erweisen (als); ausfallen; ~n ['pru:vən] erwiesen; bewährt.

provenance ['provinəns] Herkunftf.

provender ['provində] Futter n.

proverb ['provəb] Sprichwort n.

provide [prə'vaid] v/t. besorgen, beschaffen, liefern; bereitstellen; versehen, versorgen; 𝄞 vorsehen, festsetzen; v/i. (vor)sorgen; ~d (that) vorausgesetzt, daß; sofern.

providen|ce ['providəns] Vorsehung f; Voraussicht f; Vorsorge f; ~t □ [⸗nt] vorausblickend; vorsorglich; haushälterisch; ~tial □ [provi'denʃəl] durch die göttliche Vorsehung bewirkt; glücklich.

provider [prə'vaidə] Ernährer m der Familie; Lieferant m.

provinc|e ['provins] Provinz f; fig. Gebiet n; Aufgabe f; ~ial [prə'vinʃəl] **1.** provinziell; kleinstädtisch; **2.** Provinzbewohner(in).

provision [prə'viʒən] Beschaffungf; Vorsorge f; 𝄞 Bestimmung f; Vorkehrung f, Maßnahme f; Vorrat m; ~s pl. Proviant m, Lebensmittel pl.; ~al □ [⸗nl] provisorisch.

proviso [prə'vaizou] Vorbehalt m.

provocat|ion [provə'keiʃən] Herausforderung f; ~ive [prə'vɔkətiv] herausfordernd; (auf)reizend.

provoke [prə'vouk] auf-, anreizen; herausfordern.

provost ['provəst] Leiter m e-s College; schott. Bürgermeister m; ✕ [prə'vou]: ~ marshal Kommandeur m der Militärpolizei.

prow ⚓ [prau] Bug m, Vorschiff n.

prowess ['prauis] Tapferkeit f.

prowl [praul] **1.** v/i. umherstreifen; v/t. durchstreifen; **2.** Umherstreifen n; ~ car Am. ['praulkɑ:] Streifenwagen m der Polizei.

proximity [prɔk'simiti] Nähe f.

proxy ['proksi] Stellvertreter m; Stellvertretung f; Vollmacht f; by ~ in Vertretung.

prude [pru:d] Prüde f, Spröde f; Zimperliese f.

pruden|ce ['pru:dəns] Klugheit f, Vorsicht f; ~t □ [⸗nt] klug, vorsichtig.

prud|ery ['pru:dəri] Prüderie f, Sprödigkeit f; Zimperlichkeit f; ~ish □ [⸗diʃ] prüde, zimperlich, spröde.

prune [pru:n] **1.** Backpflaume f; **2.** ✗ beschneiden (a. fig.); a. ~ away, ~ off wegschneiden.

prurient □ ['pruəriənt] geil, lüstern.

pry [prai] **1.** neugierig gucken; ~ into s-e Nase stecken in (acc.); ~ open aufbrechen; ~ up hochheben; **2.** Hebel(bewegung f) m.

psalm [sɑ:m] Psalm m.

pseudo|... ['psju:dou] Pseudo..., falsch; ~nym [⸗dənim] Deckname m.

psychiatr|ist [sai'kaiətrist] Psychiater m (Nervenarzt); ~y [⸗ri] Psychiatrie f.

psychic(al □) ['saikik(əl)] psychisch, seelisch.

psycholog|ical □ [saikə'lɔdʒikəl] psychologisch; ~ist [sai'kɔlədʒist] Psycholog|e m, -in f; ~y [⸗dʒi] Psychologie f (Seelenkunde).

pub F [pʌb] Kneipe f, Wirtschaft f.

puberty ['pju:bəti] Pubertät f.

public ['pʌblik] **1.** □ öffentlich; staatlich, Staats...; allbekannt; ~ spirit Gemeinsinn m; **2.** Publikum n; Öffentlichkeit f; ~an [⸗kən] Gastwirt m; ~ation [pʌbli'keiʃən] Bekanntmachung f; Veröffentlichung f; Verlagswerk n; monthly ~ Monatsschrift f; ~ house Wirtshaus n; ~ity [pʌb'lisiti] Öffentlichkeit f; Propaganda f, Reklame f, Werbung f; ~ library Volksbücherei f; ~ relations pl. Verhältnis n zur Öffentlichkeit; Public Relations pl.; ~ school Public School f, Internatsschule f.

publish ['pʌbliʃ] bekanntmachen, veröffentlichen; Buch etc. herausgeben, verlegen; ~ing house Verlag m; ~er [⸗ʃə] Herausgeber m, Verleger m; ~s pl. Verlag(sanstalt f) m.

pucker ['pʌkə] **1.** Falte f; **2.** falten; Falten werfen; runzeln.

pudding ['pudiŋ] Pudding m; Süßspeise f; Auflauf m; Wurst f; black ~ Blutwurst f.

puddle ['pʌdl] Pfütze f.

pudent ['pju:dənt] verschämt.

puerile □ ['pjuərail] kindisch.

puff [pʌf] **1.** Hauch m; Zug m beim

Rauchen; (Dampf-, Rauch)Wölkchen _n;_ Puderquaste _f;_ (aufdringliche) Reklame; 2. _v/t._ (auf)blasen, pusten; paffen; anpreisen; ~ out sich (auf)blähen; ~ _up_ Preise hochtreiben; ~ed up _fig._ aufgeblasen; ~ed _eyes_ geschwollene Augen; _v/i._ paffen; pusten; ~-paste ['pʌfpeist] Blätterteig _m;_ ~y ['pʌfi] böig; kurzatmig; geschwollen; dick; bauschig.

pug [pʌg], **~-dog** ['pʌgdɔg] Mops _m._

pugnacious [pʌg'neiʃəs] kämpferisch; kampflustig; streitsüchtig.

pug-nose ['pʌgnouz] Stupsnase _f._

puissant ['pju(:)isnt] mächtig.

puke [pju:k] (sich) erbrechen.

pull [pul] 1. Zug _m;_ Ruck _m; typ._ Abzug _m;_ Ruderpartie _f;_ Griff _m;_ Vorteil _m;_ 2. ziehen; zerren; reißen; zupfen; pflücken; rudern; ~ _about_ hin- u. herzerren; ~ _down_ niederreißen; ~ _in_ einfahren (_Zug_); ~ _off_ zustande bringen; _Preis_ erringen; ~ _out_ heraus-, hinausfahren; ausscheren; ~ _round_ wiederherstellen; ~ _through j-n_ durchbringen; ~ _o.s. together_ sich zs.-nehmen; ~ _up Wagen_ anhalten; halten; ~ _up with,_ ~ _up to_ einholen.

pulley ['puli] Rolle _f;_ Flaschenzug _m;_ Riemenscheibe _f._

pull|-over ['pulouvə] Pullover _m;_ ~-up Halteplatz _m,_ Raststätte _f._

pulp [pʌlp] Brei _m;_ Frucht-, ZahnMark _n;_ ⊕ Papierbrei _m; a._ ~ _magazine Am._ Schundillustrierte _f._

pulpit ['pulpit] Kanzel _f._

pulpy □ ['pʌlpi] breiig; fleischig.

puls|ate [pʌl'seit] pulsieren; schlagen; ~e [pʌls] Puls(schlag) _m._

pulverize ['pʌlvəraiz] _v/t._ pulverisieren; _v/i._ zu Staub werden.

pumice ['pʌmis] Bimsstein _m._

pump [pʌmp] 1. Pumpe _f;_ Pumps _m;_ 2. pumpen; F _j-n_ aushorchen.

pumpkin ♀ ['pʌmpkin] Kürbis _m._

pun [pʌn] 1. Wortspiel _n;_ 2. ein Wortspiel machen.

Punch¹ [pʌntʃ] Kasperle _n, m._

punch² [~] 1. ⊕ Punze(n _m_) _f,_ Locheisen _n,_ Locher _m;_ Lochzange _f;_ (Faust)Schlag _m;_ Punsch _m;_ 2. punzen, durchbohren; lochen; knuffen, puffen; _Am._ Vieh treiben, hüten.

puncher ['pʌntʃə] Locheisen _n;_ Locher _m;_ F Schläger _m; Am._ Cowboy _m._

punctilious [pʌŋk'tiliəs] peinlich (genau), spitzfindig; förmlich.

punctual □ ['pʌŋktjuəl] pünktlich; ~ity [~'æliti] Pünktlichkeit _f._

punctuat|e ['pʌŋktjueit] (inter-) punktieren; _fig._ unterbrechen; ~ion _gr._ [pʌŋktju'eiʃən] Interpunktion _f._

puncture ['pʌŋktʃə] 1. Punktur _f,_

Stich _m;_ Reifenpanne _f;_ 2. (durch-) stechen; platzen (_Luftreifen_).

pungen|cy ['pʌndʒənsi] Schärfe _f;_ ~t [~nt] stechend, beißend, scharf.

punish ['pʌniʃ] (be)strafen; ~able □ [~ʃəbl] strafbar; ~ment [~ʃmənt] Strafe _f,_ Bestrafung _f._

punk _Am._ [pʌŋk] Zunderholz _n;_ Zündmasse _f;_ F _fig._ Mist _m,_ Käse _m._

puny □ ['pju:ni] winzig; schwächlich.

pupa _zo._ ['pju:pə] Puppe _f._

pupil ['pju:pl] _anat._ Pupille _f;_ Schüler(in); Mündel _m, n._

puppet ['pʌpit] Marionette _f (a. fig.);_ ~-show Puppenspiel _n._

pup(py) [pʌp, 'pʌpi] Welpe _m,_ junger Hund; _fig._ Laffe _m,_ Schnösel _m._

purchase ['pə:tʃəs] 1. (An-, Ein-) Kauf _m;_ Erwerb(ung _f) m;_ Anschaffung _f;_ ⊕ Hebevorrichtung _f; fig._ Ansatzpunkt _m; make_ ~s Einkäufe machen; 2. kaufen; _fig._ erkaufen; anschaffen; ⊕ aufwinden; ~r [~sə] Käufer(in).

pure □ [pjuə] _allg._ rein; _engS.:_ lauter; echt; gediegen; theoretisch; ~-bred _Am._ ['pjuəbred] reinrassig.

purgat|ive ♂ ['pə:gətiv] 1. abführend; 2. Abführmittel _n;_ ~ory [~təri] Fegefeuer _n._

purge [pə:dʒ] 1. ♂ Abführmittel _n; pol._ Säuberung _f;_ 2. _mst fig._ reinigen; _pol._ säubern; ♂ abführen.

purify ['pjuərifai] reinigen; läutern.

Puritan ['pjuəritən] 1. Puritaner (-in); 2. puritanisch.

purity ['pjuəriti] Reinheit _f (a. fig.)._

purl [pə:l] murmeln (_Bach_).

purlieus ['pə:lju:z] _pl._ Umgebung _f._

purloin [pə:'lɔin] entwenden.

purple ['pə:pl] 1. purpurn, purpurrot; 2. Purpur _m;_ 3. (sich) purpurn färben.

purport ['pə:pət] 1. Sinn _m;_ Inhalt _m;_ 2. besagen; beabsichtigen; vorgeben.

purpose ['pə:pəs] 1. Vorsatz _m;_ Absicht _f,_ Zweck _m;_ Entschlußkraft _f; for the_ ~ _of ger._ um zu _inf.; on_ ~ absichtlich; _to the_ ~ zweckdienlich; _to no_ ~ vergebens; 2. vorhaben, bezwecken; ~ful □ [~sful] zweckmäßig; absichtlich; zielbewußt; ~less □ [~slis] zwecklos; ziellos; ~ly [~li] vorsätzlich.

purr [pə:] schnurren (_Katze_).

purse [pə:s] 1. Börse _f,_ Geldbeutel _m;_ Geld(preis _m) n;_ _public_ ~ Staatssäckel _m;_ 2. _oft_ ~ _up Mund_ spitzen; _Stirn_ runzeln; _Augen_ zs.-kneifen.

pursuan|ce [pə'sju(:)əns] Verfolgung _f; in_ ~ _of_ zufolge (_dat._); ~t [~nt]: ~ _to_ zufolge, gemäß, entsprechend (_dat._).

pursu|e [pə'sju:] verfolgen (_a. fig._); streben nach; _e-m Beruf etc._ nachgehen; fortsetzen, fortfahren; ~er

[͜ju(:)ə] Verfolger(in); ͜it [͜juːt] Verfolgung f; mst ͜s pl. Beschäftigung f.

purvey [pəˈvei] *Lebensmittel* liefern; ͜or [͜eiə] Lieferant m.

pus [pʌs] Eiter m.

push [puʃ] 1. (An-, Vor)Stoß m; Schub m; Druck m; Notfall m; Energie f; Unternehmungsgeist m; Elan m; 2. stoßen; schieben; drängen; *Knopf* drücken; (an)treiben; a. ͜ through durchführen; *Anspruch etc.* durchdrücken; ͜ s.th. on s.o. j-m et. aufdrängen; ͜ one's way sich durch- *od.* vordrängen; ͜ along, ͜ on, ͜ forward weitermachen, -gehen, -fahren *etc.*; ͜-button ⚡ [ˈpuʃbʌtn] Druckknopf m; ͜-over *Am. fig.* Kinderspiel n; leicht zu beeinflussender Mensch.

pusillanimous ☐ [pjuːsiˈlæniməs] kleinmütig.

puss [pus] Kätzchen n, Katze f (a. fig. = *Mädchen*); ͜y [ˈpusi], a. ͜-cat Mieze f, Kätzchen n; ͜yfoot *Am.* F leisetreten, sich zurückhalten.

put [put] (*irr.*) v/t. setzen, legen, stellen, stecken, tun, machen; *Frage* stellen, vorlegen; werfen; ausdrücken, sagen; ͜ about *Gerüchte etc.* verbreiten; ⚓ wenden; ͜ across *sl.* drehen, schaukeln; ͜ back zurückstellen; ͜ by *Geld* zurücklegen; ͜ down niederlegen, -setzen, -werfen; aussteigen lassen; notieren; zuschreiben (to *dat.*); unterdrücken; ͜ forth *Kräfte* aufbieten; *Knospen etc.* treiben; ͜ forward *Meinung etc.* vorbringen; ͜ o.s. forward sich hervortun; ͜ in hinein-, hereinst(r)ecken; *Anspruch* erheben; *Gesuch* einreichen; *Urkunde* vorlegen; anstellen; ͜ off auf-, verschieben; vertrösten; abbringen; hindern; *fig.* ablegen; ͜ on *Kleid* anziehen, *Hut* aufsetzen; *fig.* annehmen; an-, einschalten;

vergrößern; ͜ on airs sich aufspielen; ͜ on weight zunehmen; ͜ out ausmachen, (aus)löschen; verrenken; (her)ausstrecken; verwirren; j-m Ungelegenheiten bereiten; *Kraft* aufbieten; *Geld* ausleihen; ͜ right in Ordnung bringen; ͜ through *teleph.* verbinden (to mit); ͜ to hinzufügen; ͜ to death hinrichten; ͜ to the rack *od.* torture auf die Folter spannen; ͜ up aufstellen *etc.*; errichten, bauen; *Waren* anbieten; *Miete* erhöhen; ver-, wegpacken; *Widerstand* leisten; *Kampf* liefern; *Gäste* unterbringen; *Bekanntmachung* anschlagen; v/i. off, ͜ on, to sea ⚓ auslaufen; ͜ in ⚓ einlaufen; ͜ up at einkehren *od.* absteigen in (dat.); ͜ up for sich bewerben um; ͜ up with sich gefallen lassen; sich abfinden mit.

putrefy [ˈpjuːtrifai] (ver)faulen.

putrid ☐ [ˈpjuːtrid] faul, verdorben; *sl.* scheußlich, saumäßig; ͜ity [pjuːˈtriditi] Fäulnis f.

putty [ˈpʌti] 1. Kitt m; 2. kitten.

puzzle [ˈpʌzl] 1. schwierige Aufgabe, Rätsel n; Verwirrung f; Geduldspiel n; 2. v/t. irremachen; j-m Kopfzerbrechen machen; ͜ out austüfteln; v/i. sich den Kopf zerbrechen; ͜-headed konfus.

pygm|(a)ean [pigˈmiːən] zwerghaft; ͜y [ˈpigmi] Zwerg m; attr. zwerghaft.

pyjamas [pəˈdʒɑːməz] pl. Schlafanzug m.

pyramid [ˈpirəmid] Pyramide f; ͜al ☐ [piˈræmidl] pyramidal.

pyre [ˈpaiə] Scheiterhaufen m.

pyrotechnic|(al ☐) [pairouˈteknik(əl)] pyrotechnisch, Feuerwerks...; ͜s pl. Feuerwerk n (a. fig.).

Pythagorean [paiθægəˈriː(ː)ən] 1. pythagoreisch; 2. Pythagoreer m.

pyx *eccl.* [piks] Monstranz f.

Q

quack [kwæk] 1. Quaken n; Scharlatan m; Quacksalber m, Kurpfuscher m; Marktschreier m; 2. quacksalbern; 3. quaken; quacksalbern (an dat.); ͜ery [ˈkwækəri] Quacksalberei f.

quadrangle [ˈkwɔdræŋgl] Viereck n; Innenhof m e-s College.

quadrennial ☐ [kwɔˈdreniəl] vierjährig; vierjährlich.

quadru|ped [ˈkwɔdruped] Vierfüßer m; ͜ple [͜pl] 1. ☐ vierfach; 2. (sich) vervierfachen; ͜plets [͜lits] pl. Vierlinge m/pl.

quagmire [ˈkwægmaiə] Sumpf (-land n) m, Moor n.

quail¹ *orn.* [kweil] Wachtel f.

quail² [͜] verzagen; beben.

quaint ☐ [kweint] anheimelnd, malerisch; putzig; seltsam.

quake [kweik] 1. beben, zittern (with, for vor dat.); 2. Erdbeben n.

Quaker [ˈkweikə] Quäker m.

quali|fication [kwɔlifiˈkeiʃən] (erforderliche) Befähigung; Einschränkung f; gr. nähere Bestimmung; ͜fy [ˈkwɔlifai] v/t. befähigen; (be-)nennen; gr. näher bestimmen; ein-

schränken, mäßigen; mildern; v/i.
seine Befähigung nachweisen; ~ty
[~iti] Eigenschaft f, Beschaffenheit
f; ✝ Qualität f; vornehmer Stand.

qualm [kwɔːm] plötzliche Übelkeit;
Zweifel m; Bedenken n.

quandary ['kwɔndəri] verzwickte
Lage, Verlegenheit f.

quantity ['kwɔntiti] Quantität f,
Menge f; großer Teil.

quantum ['kwɔntəm] Menge f,
Größe f, Quantum n; Anteil m.

quarantine ['kwɔrəntiːn] 1. Quarantäne f; 2. unter Quarantäne
stellen.

quarrel ['kwɔrəl] 1. Zank m, Streit
m; 2. (sich) zanken, streiten; ~some □ [~lsəm] zänkisch; streitsüchtig.

quarry ['kwɔri] 1. Steinbruch m;
fig. Fundgrube f; (Jagd)Beute f;
2. Steine brechen; fig. stöbern.

quart [kwɔːt] Quart n (1,136 l).

quarter ['kwɔːtə] 1. Viertel m, vierter Teil; bsd. Viertelstunde f; Vierteljahr n, Quartal n; Viertelzentner
m; Am. 25 Cent; Keule f, Viertel n
e-s geschlachteten Tieres; Stadtviertel n; (Himmels)Richtung f, Gegend f; ✕ Gnade f, Pardon m; ~s
pl. Quartier n (a. ✕), Unterkunft f;
fig. Kreise m/pl.; live in close ~s
beengt wohnen; at close ~s dicht
aufeinander; come to close ~s handgemein werden; 2. vierteln, vierteilen; beherbergen; ✕ einquartieren; ~back Am. Sport: Abwehrspieler m; ~day Quartalstag m;
~deck Achterdeck n; ~ly [~li]
1. vierteljährlich; 2. Vierteljahresschrift f; ~master ✕ Quartiermeister m. [n.]

quartet(te) ♩ [kwɔːˈtet] Quartett]

quarto ['kwɔːtou] Quart(format) n.

quash ⚖ [kwɔʃ] aufheben, verwerfen; unterdrücken.

quasi ['kwɑːziː(ː)] gleichsam, sozusagen; Quasi..., Schein...

quaver ['kweivə] 1. Zittern n; ♩
Triller m; 2. mit zitternder Stimme
sprechen od. singen; trillern.

quay [kiː] Kai m; Uferstraße f.

queasy □ ['kwiːzi] empfindlich
(Magen, Gewissen); heikel, mäkelig; ekelhaft.

queen [kwiːn] Königin f; ~ bee
Bienenkönigin f; ~like ['kwiːnlaik],
~ly [~li] wie eine Königin, königlich.

queer [kwiə] sonderbar, seltsam;
wunderlich; komisch; homosexuell.

quench [kwentʃ] fig. Durst etc. löschen, stillen; kühlen; Aufruhr
unterdrücken.

querulous □ ['kweruləs] quengelig,
mürrisch, unzufrieden.

query ['kwiəri] 1. Frage(zeichen n)
f; 2. (be)fragen; (be-, an)zweifeln.

quest [kwest] 1. Suche(n n) f, Nachforschen n; 2. suchen, forschen.

question ['kwestʃən] 1. Frage f;
Problem n; Untersuchung f; Streitfrage f; Zweifel m; Sache f, Angelegenheit f; beyond (all) ~ ohne
Frage; in ~ fraglich; call in ~ anzweifeln; that is out of the ~ das
steht außer od. kommt nicht in
Frage; 2. befragen; bezweifeln;
~able □ [~nəbl] fraglich; fragwürdig; ~er [~nə] Fragende(r m) f;
~mark Fragezeichen n; ~naire
[kwestiəˈnɛː] Fragebogen m.

queue [kjuː] 1. Reihe f v. Personen
etc., Schlange f; Zopf m; 2. mst ~
up (in e-r Reihe) anstehen, Schlange
stehen.

quibble ['kwibl] 1. Wortspiel n;
Spitzfindigkeit f; Ausflucht f; 2. fig.
ausweichen; witzeln.

quick [kwik] 1. schnell, rasch; voreilig; lebhaft; gescheit; beweglich;
lebendig; scharf (Gehör etc.); 2. lebendes Fleisch; the ~ die Lebenden; to the ~ (bis) ins Fleisch; fig.
(bis) ins Herz, tief; cut s.o. to the ~
j-n aufs empfindlichste kränken; ~en
['kwikn] v/t. beleben; beschleunigen; v/i. aufleben; sich regen; ~ly
[~kli] schnell, rasch; ~ness [~knis]
Lebhaftigkeit f; Schnelligkeit f;
Voreiligkeit f; Schärfe f des Verstandes etc.; ~sand Triebsand m;
~set ⚘ Setzling m, bsd. Hagedorn
m; a. ~ hedge lebende Hecke; ~sighted scharfsichtig; ~silver min.
Quecksilber n; ~witted schlagfertig.

quid[1] [kwid] Priem m (Kautabak).

quid[2] sl. [~] Pfund n Sterling.

quiescen|ce [kwaiˈesns] Ruhe f,
Stille f; ~t □ [~nt] ruhend; fig.
ruhig, still.

quiet ['kwaiət] 1. □ ruhig, still;
2. Ruhe f; on the ~ (sl. on the q.t.)
unter der Hand, im stillen; 3. a. ~
down (sich) beruhigen; ~ness
[~tnis], ~ude ['kwaiitjuːd] Ruhe f,
Stille f.

quill [kwil] 1. Federkiel m; fig. Feder f; Stachel m des Igels etc.;
2. rund fälteln; ~ing ['kwiliŋ]
Rüsche f, Krause f; ~pen Gänsefeder f zum Schreiben.

quilt [kwilt] 1. Steppdecke f;
2. steppen; wattieren.

quince ⚘ [kwins] Quitte f.

quinine pharm. [kwiˈniːn, Am.
ˈkwainain] Chinin n.

quinquennial □ [kwiŋˈkweniəl]
fünfjährig; fünfjährlich.

quinsy ⚕ ['kwinzi] Mandelentzündung f.

quintal ['kwintl] (Doppel)Zentner
m.

quintessence [kwinˈtesns] Quintessenz f, Kern m, Inbegriff m.

quintuple ['kwintjupl] 1. □ fünf-

fach; 2. (sich) verfünffachen; ~ts
[~lits] pl. Fünflinge m/pl.
quip [kwip] Stich(elei f) m; Witz
(-wort n) m; Spitzfindigkeit f.
quirk [kwə:k] Spitzfindigkeit f;
Witz(elei f) m; Kniff m; Schnörkel
m; Eigentümlichkeit f; △ Hohl-
kehle f.
quisling ['kwizliŋ] Quisling m, Kol-
laborateur m.
quit [kwit] 1. v/t. verlassen; aufgeben; Am. aufhören (mit); vergelten;
Schuld tilgen; v/i. aufhören; ausziehen (Mieter); give notice to ~
kündigen; 2. quitt; frei, los.
quite [kwait] ganz, gänzlich; recht;
durchaus; ~ a hero ein wirklicher
Held; ~ (so)!, ~ that! ganz recht;
~ the thing F große Mode.
quittance ['kwitəns] Quittung f.
quitter Am. F ['kwitə] Drückeberger m.
quiver[1] ['kwivə] zittern, beben.
quiver[2] [~] Köcher m.

quiz [kwiz] 1. Prüfung f, Test m;
Quiz n; belustigter Blick; 2. (aus-)
fragen; prüfen; necken, foppen;
anstarren, beäugen; ~zical □
['kwizikəl] spöttisch; komisch.
quoit [kɔit] Wurfring m; ~s pl.
Wurfringspiel n.
Quonset Am. ['kwɔnsit] a. ~ hut
Wellblechbaracke f.
quorum parl. ['kwɔ:rəm] beschluß-
fähige Mitgliederzahl.
quota ['kwoutə] Quote f, Anteil m,
Kontingent n.
quotation [kwou'teiʃən] Anführung
f, Zitat n; ✝ Preisnotierung f;
Kostenvoranschlag m; ~-marks pl.
Anführungszeichen n/pl.
quote [kwout] anführen, zitieren;
✝ berechnen, notieren (at mit).
quotient ⅍ ['kwouʃənt] Quotient
m.
quoth † [kwouθ]: ~ I sagte ich; ~
he sagte er.
quotidian [kwɔ'tidiən] (all)täglich.

R

rabbi ['ræbai] Rabbiner m.
rabbit ['ræbit] Kaninchen n.
rabble ['ræbl] Pöbel(haufen) m.
rabid □ ['ræbid] tollwütig (Tier);
fig. wild, wütend.
rabies vet. ['reibi:z] Tollwut f.
raccoon [rə'ku:n] = racoon.
race [reis] 1. Geschlecht n, Stamm
m; Rasse f, Schlag m; Lauf m (a.
fig.); Wettrennen n; Strömung f;
~s pl. Pferderennen n; 2. rennen;
rasen; um die Wette laufen (mit);
⊕ leer laufen; ~-course ['reiskɔ:s]
Rennbahn f, -strecke f; ~-horse
Rennpferd n; ~r ['reisə] Rennpferd n; Rennboot n; Rennwagen)
racial ['reiʃəl] Rassen... [m.]
racing ['reisiŋ] Rennsport m; attr.
Renn...
rack [ræk] 1. Gestell n; Kleider-
ständer m; Gepäcknetz n; Raufe f;
Futtergestell n; Folter(bank) f;
go to ~ and ruin völlig zugrunde
gehen; 2. strecken; foltern, quälen
(a. fig.); ~ one's brains sich den
Kopf zermartern.
racket ['rækit] 1. Tennis-Schläger m;
Lärm m; Trubel m; Am. F Schwin-
del(geschäft n) m; Strapaze f;
2. lärmen; sich amüsieren; ~eer
Am. [ræki'tiə] Erpresser m; ~eering
Am. [~ɔriŋ] Erpresserwesen n; ~y
['rækiti] ausgelassen.
racoon zo. [rə'ku:n] Waschbär m.
racy □ ['reisi] kraftvoll, lebendig;
stark; würzig; urwüchsig.
radar ['reidə] Radar(gerät) n.
radian|ce, ~cy ['reidjəns, ~si]

Strahlen n; ~t □ [~nt] strahlend,
leuchtend.
radiat|e ['reidieit] (aus)strahlen;
strahlenförmig ausgehen; ~ion [rei-
di'eiʃən] (Aus)Strahlung f; ~or
['reidieitə] Heizkörper m; mot.
Kühler m.
radical ['rædikəl] 1. □ Wurzel...,
Grund...; gründlich; eingewurzelt;
pol. radikal; 2. pol. Radikale(r m) f.
radio ['reidiou] 1. Radio n; Funk
(-spruch) m; ~ drama, ~ play Hör-
spiel n; ~ set Radiogerät n; 2. funken; ~(-)active radioaktiv; ~graph
[~ougra:f] 1. Röntgenbild n; 2. ein
Röntgenbild machen von; ~-tele-
gram Funktelegramm n; ~-thera-
py Strahlen-, Röntgentherapie f.
radish ⅋ ['rædiʃ] Rettich m; (red) ~
Radieschen n.
radius ['reidjəs] Radius m.
raffle ['ræfl] 1. Tombola f, Verlo-
sung f; 2. verlosen.
raft [ra:ft] 1. Floß n; 2. flößen; ~er
['ra:ftə] ⊕ (Dach)Sparren m.
rag[1] [ræg] Lumpen m; Fetzen m;
Lappen m.
rag[2] sl. [~] 1. Unfug m; Radau m;
2. Unfug treiben (mit); j-n aufziehen; j-n beschimpfen; herum-
tollen, Radau machen.
ragamuffin ['rægəmʌfin] Lumpen-
kerl m; Gassenjunge m.
rage [reidʒ] 1. Wut f, Zorn m,
Raserei f; Sucht f, Gier f (for
nach); Manie f; Ekstase f; it is all
the ~ es ist allgemein Mode;
2. wüten, rasen.

rag-fair ['rægfeə] Trödelmarkt *m.*
ragged ☐ ['rægid] rauh; zottig; zackig; zerlumpt.
ragman ['rægmən] Lumpensammler *m.*
raid [reid] 1. (feindlicher) Überfall, Streifzug *m;* (Luft)Angriff *m;* Razzia *f;* 2. einbrechen in (*acc.*); überfallen.
rail¹ [reil] schimpfen.
rail² [⸗] 1. Geländer *n;* Stange *f;* 🚃 Schiene *f;* off the ⸗s entgleist; *fig.* in Unordnung; by ⸗ per Bahn; 2. *a.* ⸗ in, ⸗ off mit e-m Geländer umgeben.
railing ['reiliŋ], *a.* ⸗s *pl.* Geländer *n;* Staket *n.*
raillery ['reiləri] Spötterei *f.*
railroad *Am.* ['reilroud] Eisenbahn *f.* [⸗man Eisenbahner *m.*\
railway ['reilwei] Eisenbahn *f;*\
rain [rein] 1. Regen *m;* 2. regnen; ⸗bow ['reinbou] Regenbogen *m;* ⸗coat Regenmantel *m;* ⸗fall Regenmenge *f;* ⸗proof 1. regendicht; 2. Regenmantel *m;* ⸗y ☐ ['reini] regnerisch; Regen...; *a* ⸗ day *fig.* Notzeiten *f/pl.*
raise [reiz] *oft* ⸗ up heben; (*oft fig.*) erheben; errichten; erhöhen (*a. fig.*); Geld *etc.* aufbringen; *Anleihe* aufnehmen; verursachen; *fig.* erwecken; anstiften; züchten, ziehen; *Belagerung etc.* aufheben.
raisin ['reizn] Rosine *f.*
rake [reik] 1. Rechen *m,* Harke *f;* Wüstling *m;* Lebemann *m;* 2. *v/t* (zs.-)harken; zs.-scharren; *fig.* (durch)stöbern; ⸗off *Am. sl.* ['reikɔːf] Schwindelprofit *m.*
rakish ☐ ['reikiʃ] schnittig; liederlich, ausschweifend; verwegen; salopp.
rally ['ræli] 1. Sammeln *n;* Treffen *n; Am.* Massenversammlung *f;* Erholung *f; mot.* Rallye *f;* 2. (sich ver)sammeln; sich erholen; necken.
ram [ræm] 1. *zo., ast.* Widder *m;* ⊕, ♣ Ramme *f;* 2. (fest)rammen; ♣ rammen.
ramble ['ræmbl] 1. Streifzug *m;* 2. umherstreifen; abschweifen; ⸗er [⸗lə] Wanderer *m;* ♣ Kletterrose *f;* ⸗ing [⸗liŋ] weitläufig.
ramify ['ræmifai] (sich) verzweigen.
ramp [ræmp] Rampe *f;* ⸗ant ☐ ['ræmpənt] wuchernd; *fig.* zügellos.
rampart ['ræmpɑːt] Wall *m.*
ramshackle ['ræmʃækl] wack(e)lig.
ran [ræn] *pret. von* run 1.
ranch [rɑːntʃ, *Am.* ræntʃ] Ranch *f,* Viehfarm *f;* ⸗er ['rɑːntʃə, *Am.* 'ræntʃə], ⸗man Rancher *m,* Viehzüchter *m;* Farmer *m.*
rancid ☐ ['rænsid] ranzig.
ranco(u)r ['ræŋkə] Groll *m,* Haß *m.*
random ['rændəm] 1. *at* ⸗ aufs Geratewohl, blindlings; 2. ziel-, wahllos; zufällig.

rang [ræŋ] *pret. von* ring 2.
range [reindʒ] 1. Reihe *f;* (Berg-)Kette *f;* ♱ Kollektion *f,* Sortiment *n;* Herd *m;* Raum *m;* Umfang *m,* Bereich *m;* Reichweite *f;* Schußweite *f;* (ausgedehnte) Fläche; Schießstand *m;* 2. *v/t.* (ein)reihen, ordnen; *Gebiet etc.* durchstreifen; ⚓ längs *et.* fahren; *v/i.* in e-r Reihe *od.* Linie stehen; (umher-) streifen; sich erstrecken, reichen; ⸗r ['reindʒə] Förster *m;* Aufseher *m* e-s Parks; *Am.* Förster *m;* ⚔ Nahkampfspezialist *m.*
rank [ræŋk] 1. Reihe *f,* Linie *f;* ⚔ Glied *n;* Klasse *f;* Rang *m,* Stand *m;* the ⸗s *pl.,* the ⸗ and file die Mannschaften *f/pl.; fig.* die große Masse; 2. *v/t.* (ein)reihen, (ein-) ordnen; *v/i.* sich reihen, sich ordnen; gehören (with zu); e-e Stelle einnehmen (above über *dat.*); ⸗ *as* gelten als; 3. üppig; ranzig; stinkend.
rankle *fig.* ['ræŋkl] nagen.
ransack ['rænsæk] durchwühlen, durchstöbern, durchsuchen; ausrauben.
ransom ['rænsəm] 1. Lösegeld *n;* Auslösung *f;* 2. loskaufen; erlösen.
rant [rænt] 1. Schwulst *m;* 2. Phrasen dreschen; mit Pathos vortragen.
rap [ræp] 1. Klaps *m;* Klopfen *n; fig.* Heller *m;* 2. schlagen, klopfen.
rapaci|ous ☐ [rə'peiʃəs] raubgierig; ⸗ty [rə'pæsiti] Raubgier *f.*
rape [reip] 1. Raub *m;* Entführung *f;* Notzucht *f,* Vergewaltigung *f;* ♣ Raps *m;* 2. rauben; vergewaltigen.
rapid ['ræpid] 1. ☐ schnell, reißend, rapid(e); steil; 2. *s. a.* ⸗s *pl.* Stromschnelle(n *pl.*) *f;* ⸗ity [rə'piditi] Schnelligkeit *f.*
rapprochement *pol.* [ræ'prɔʃmɑ̃ːŋ] Wiederannäherung *f.*
rapt [ræpt] entzückt; versunken; ⸗ure ['ræptʃə] Entzücken *n;* go into ⸗s in Entzücken geraten.
rare ☐ [reə] selten; *phys.* dünn.
rarebit ['reəbit]: *Welsh* ⸗ geröstete Käseschnitte.
rarefy ['reərifai] (sich) verdünnen.
rarity ['reəriti] Seltenheit *f;* Dünnheit *f.*
rascal ['rɑːskəl] Schuft *m; co.* Gauner *m;* ⸗ity [rɑːs'kæliti] Schurkerei *f;* ⸗ly ['rɑːskəli] schuftig; erbärmlich.
rash¹ ☐ [ræʃ] hastig, vorschnell; übereilt; unbesonnen; waghalsig.
rash² ☞ [⸗] Hautausschlag *m.*
rasher ['ræʃə] Speckschnitte *f.*
rasp [rɑːsp] 1. Raspel *f;* 2. raspeln; *j-m* weh(e) tun; kratzen; krächzen.
raspberry ['rɑːzbəri] Himbeere *f.*
rat [ræt] *zo.* Ratte *f; pol.* Überläufer *m;* smell *a* ⸗ Lunte *od.* den Braten riechen; ⸗s! Quatsch!
rate [reit] 1. Verhältnis *n,* Maß *n,*

Satz m; Rate f; Preis m, Gebühr f; Taxe f; (Gemeinde)Abgabe f, Steuer f; Grad m, Rang m; bsd. ⊕ Klasse f; Geschwindigkeit f; at any ~ auf jeden Fall; ~ of exchange (Umrechnungs)Kurs m; ~ of interest Zinsfuß m; 2. (ein)schätzen; besteuern; ~ among rechnen, zählen zu (dat.); ausschelten.

rather ['rɑːðə] eher, lieber; vielmehr; besser gesagt; ziemlich; ~! F und ob!; I had od. would ~ do ich möchte lieber tun.

ratify ['rætifai] ratifizieren.

rating ['reitiŋ] Schätzung f; Steuersatz m; ⊕ Dienstgrad m; ⊕ (Segel-) Klasse f; Matrose m; Schelte(n n) f.

ratio ⅋ etc. ['reiʃiou] Verhältnis n.

ration ['ræʃən] 1. Ration f, Zuteilung f; 2. rationieren.

rational □ ['ræʃənl] vernunftgemäß; vernünftig, (a. ⅋) rational; **~ity** [ræʃə'næliti] Vernunft(mäßigkeit) f; **~ize** ['ræʃnəlaiz] rationalisieren; wirtschaftlich gestalten.

rat race ['ræt 'reis] sinnlose Hetze; rücksichtsloses Aufstiegsstreben.

ratten ['rætn] sabotieren.

rattle ['rætl] 1. Gerassel n; Geklapper n; Geplapper n; Klapper f; (Todes)Röcheln n; 2. rasseln (mit); klappern; plappern; röcheln; ~ off herunterrasseln; **~brain**, **~pate** Hohl-, Wirrkopf m; **~snake** Klapperschlange f; **~trap** fig. Klapperkasten m (Fahrzeug).

rattling ['rætliŋ] 1. adj. rasselnd; fig. scharf (Tempo); 2. adv. sehr, äußerst.

raucous □ ['rɔːkəs] heiser, rauh.

ravage ['rævidʒ] 1. Verwüstung f; 2. verwüsten; plündern.

rave [reiv] rasen, toben; schwärmen (about, of von).

ravel ['rævəl] v/t. verwickeln; ~ (out) auftrennen; fig. entwirren; v/i. a. ~ out ausfasern, aufgehen.

raven orn. ['reivn] Rabe m.

raven|ing ['rævniŋ], **~ous** □ ['rævinəs] gefräßig; heißhungrig; raubgierig.

ravine [rə'viːn] Hohlweg m; Schlucht f.

ravings ['reiviŋz] pl. Delirien n/pl.

ravish ['ræviʃ] entzücken; vergewaltigen; rauben; **~ing** □ [~ʃiŋ] hinreißend, entzückend; **~ment** [~ʃmənt] Schändung f; Entzücken n.

raw □ [rɔː] roh, Roh...; wund; rauh (Wetter); ungeübt, unerfahren; **~boned** ['rɔːbound] knochig, hager; **~hide** Rohleder n.

ray [rei] Strahl m; fig. Schimmer m.

rayon ['reiən] Kunstseide f.

raze [reiz] Haus etc. abreißen; Festung schleifen; tilgen.

razor ['reizə] Rasiermesser n; Ra-

sierapparat m; **~blade** Rasierklinge f; **~edge** fig. des Messers Schneide f, kritische Lage.

razz Am. sl. [ræz] aufziehen.

re... [riː] wieder...; zurück...; neu...; um...

reach [riːtʃ] 1. Ausstrecken n; Griff m; Reichweite f; Fassungskraft f, Horizont m; Flußstrecke f; beyond ~, out of ~ unerreichbar; within easy ~ leicht erreichbar; 2. v/i. reichen; langen, greifen; sich erstrecken; v/t. (hin-, her)reichen, (hin-, her)langen; ausstrecken; erreichen.

react [riː'ækt] reagieren (to auf acc.); (ein)wirken (on, upon auf acc.); sich auflehnen (against gegen).

reaction [riː'ækʃən] Reaktion f (a. pol.); **~ary** [~'næri] 1. reaktionär; 2. Reaktionär(in).

reactor phys. [riː'æktə] Reaktor m.

read 1. [riːd] [irr.] lesen; deuten; (an)zeigen (Thermometer); studieren; sich gut etc. lesen; lernen; ~ to s.o. j-m vorlesen; 2. [red] pret. u. p.p. von 1; 3. [~] adj. belesen; **~able** □ ['riːdəbl] lesbar; leserlich; lesenswert; **~er** ['riːdə] (Vor)Leser(in); typ. Korrektor m; Lektor m; univ. Dozent m; Lesebuch n.

readi|ly ['redili] adv. gleich, leicht; gern; **~ness** [~inis] Bereitschaft f; Bereitwilligkeit f; Schnelligkeit f.

reading ['riːdiŋ] Lesen n; Lesung f (a. parl.); Stand m des Thermometers; Belesenheit f; Lektüre f; Lesart f; Auffassung f; attr. Lese...

readjust ['riːə'dʒʌst] wieder in Ordnung bringen; wieder anpassen; **~ment** [~tmənt] Wiederanpassung f; Neuordnung f.

ready □ ['redi] bereit, fertig; bereitwillig; im Begriff (to do zu tun); schnell; gewandt; leicht; zur Hand; ⊕ bar; ~ for use gebrauchsfertig; make od. get ~ (sich) fertig machen; **~made** fertig, Konfektions...

reagent ⅋ [riː'eidʒənt] Reagens n.

real □ [riəl] wirklich, tatsächlich; real; echt; ~ estate Grundbesitz m, Immobilien pl.; **~ism** ['riəlizəm] Realismus m; **~istic** [riə'listik] (~ally) realistisch; sachlich; wirklichkeitsnah; **~ity** [riː'æliti] Wirklichkeit f; **~ization** [riəlai'zeiʃən] Verwirklichung f; Erkenntnis f; ⊕ Realisierung f; **~ize** ['riəlaiz] sich klarmachen; erkennen; verwirklichen; realisieren; zu Geld machen; **~ly** [~li] wirklich, in der Tat.

realm [relm] Königreich n; Reich n.

realt|or Am. ['riəltə] Grundstücksmakler m; **~y** ⅋⅋ [~ti] Grundeigentum n.

reap [riːp] Korn schneiden; Feld

mähen; *fig.* ernten; **~er** ['ri:pə]
Schnitter(in); Mähmaschine *f.*

reappear ['ri:ə'piə] wieder erscheinen.

rear [riə] **1.** *v/t.* auf-, großziehen;
züchten; *v/i.* sich aufrichten;
2. Rück-, Hinterseite *f; mot.*, ⚓
Heck *n;* ✗ Nachhut *f; at the ~ of,
in (the) ~ of* hinter (*dat.*); **3.** Hinter...,
Nach...; **~** *wheel drive* Hinterrad-
antrieb *m;* **~-admiral** ⚓ ['riə-
'ædmərəl] Konteradmiral *m;*
~-guard ✗ Nachhut *f;* **~-lamp**
mot. Schlußlicht *n.*

rearm ['ri:'ɑ:m] (wieder)aufrüsten;
~ament [~məmənt] Aufrüstung *f.*

rearmost ['riəmoust] hinterst.

rearward ['riəwəd] **1.** *adj.* rückwärtig; **2.** *adv. a.* **~s** rückwärts.

reason ['ri:zn] **1.** Vernunft *f;* Verstand *m;* Recht *n,* Billigkeit *f;* Ursache *f,* Grund *m; by ~ of* wegen;
for this ~ aus diesem Grund; *listen
to ~* Vernunft annehmen; *it stands
to ~ that* es leuchtet ein, daß; **2.**
v/i. vernünftig denken; schließen;
urteilen; argumentieren; *v/t. a.*
~ *out* durchdenken; **~** *away* fort-
disputieren; **~** *s.o.* *into* (*out of*)
s.th. j-m et. ein- (aus)reden;
~able [~nəbl] vernünftig; billig;
angemessen; leidlich.

reassure [ri:ə'ʃuə] wieder versi-
chern; (wieder) beruhigen.

rebate [ri'beit] ✝ Rabatt *m,* Abzug
m; Rückzahlung *f.*

rebel 1. ['rebl] Rebell *m;* Aufrührer
m; **2.** [~] rebellisch; **3.** [ri'bel] sich
auflehnen; **~lion** [~ljən] Empörung
f; **~lious** [~jəs] = *rebel* **2.**

rebirth ['ri:'bə:θ] Wiedergeburt *f.*

rebound [ri'baund] **1.** zurückprallen; **2.** Rückprall *m,* Rückschlag *m.*

rebuff [ri'bʌf] **1.** Zurück-, Abwei-
sung *f;* **2.** zurück-, abweisen.

rebuild ['ri:'bild] [*irr.* (*build*)] wieder (auf)bauen.

rebuke [ri'bju:k] **1.** Tadel *m;*
2. tadeln.

rebut [ri'bʌt] zurückweisen.

recall [ri'kɔ:l] **1.** Zurückrufung *f;*
Abberufung *f;* Widerruf *m; beyond
~, past ~* unwiderruflich; **2.** zu-
rückrufen; ab(be)rufen; (sich) erinnern an (*acc.*); widerrufen; ✝
Kapital kündigen.

recapitulate [ri:kə'pitjuleit] kurz
wiederholen, zs.-fassen.

recapture ['ri:'kæptʃə] wieder (gefangen)nehmen; ✗ zurückerobern.

recast ['ri:kɑ:st] [*irr.* (*cast*)] ⊕ um-
gießen; umformen, neu gestalten.

recede [ri(:)'si:d] zurücktreten.

receipt [ri'si:t] **1.** Empfang *m;*
Eingang *m v. Waren;* Quittung *f;*
(Koch)Rezept *n;* **~s** *pl.* Einnahmen
f/pl.; **2.** quittieren.

receiv|able [ri'si:vəbl] annehmbar;
✝ noch zu fordern(d), ausstehend;

~e [ri'si:v] empfangen; erhalten,
bekommen; aufnehmen; anneh-
men; anerkennen; **~ed** anerkannt;
~er [~və] Empfänger *m; teleph.*
Hörer *m;* Hehler *m; Steuer- etc.*
Einnehmer *m; official ~* ⅜⅜ Masse-
verwalter *m.*

recent □ ['ri:snt] neu; frisch; modern; **~** *events pl. die* jüngsten Ereignisse *n/pl.;* **~ly** [~tli] neulich,
vor kurzem.

receptacle [ri'septəkl] Behälter *m.*

reception [ri'sepʃən] Aufnahme *f*
(*a. fig.*), (*a.* Radio)Empfang *m;*
Annahme *f;* **~ist** [~nist] Empfangs-
dame *f,* -herr *m;* **~-room** Emp-
fangszimmer *n.*

receptive □ [ri'septiv] empfänglich, aufnahmefähig (*of* für).

recess [ri'ses] Pause *f; bsd. parl.*
Ferien *pl.;* (entlegener) Winkel;
Nische *f;* **~es** *pl. fig.* Tiefe(n *pl.*) *f;*
~ion [~eʃən] Zurückziehen *n,* Zurücktreten *n;* ✝ Konjunkturrück-
gang *m,* rückläufige Bewegung.

recipe ['resipi] Rezept *n.*

recipient [ri'sipiənt] Empfänger(in).

reciproc|al [ri'siprəkəl] wechsel-,
gegenseitig; **~ate** [~keit] *v/i.* sich
erkenntlich zeigen; ⊕ sich hin- und
herbewegen; *v/t. Glückwünsche etc.*
erwidern; **~ity** [resi'prɔsiti] Ge-
genseitigkeit *f.*

recit|al [ri'saitl] Bericht *m;* Erzäh-
lung *f;* ♩ (Solo)Vortrag *m,* Konzert *n;* **~ation** [resi'teiʃən] Hersagen *n;* Vortrag *m;* **~e** [ri'sait] vortragen; aufsagen; berichten.

reckless □ ['reklis] unbekümmert;
rücksichtslos; leichtsinnig.

reckon ['rekən] *v/t.* rechnen; *a.* **~**
for, **~** *as* schätzen als, halten für; **~**
up zs.-zählen; *v/i.* rechnen; denken,
vermuten; **~** (*up*)*on* sich verlassen
auf (*acc.*); **~ing** ['rekniŋ] Rechnen
n; (Ab-, Be)Rechnung *f.*

reclaim [ri'kleim] wiedergewinnen;
j-n bessern; zivilisieren; urbar
machen.

recline [ri'klain] (sich) (zurück-)
lehnen; **~** *upon fig.* sich stützen auf.

recluse [ri'klu:s] Einsiedler(in).

recogni|tion [rekəg'niʃən] Anerken-
nung *f;* Wiedererkennen *n;* **~ze**
['rekəgnaiz] anerkennen; (wieder-)
erkennen.

recoil [ri'kɔil] **1.** zurückprallen;
2. Rückstoß *m,* -lauf *m.*

recollect[1] [rekə'lekt] sich erinnern
an (*acc.*).

re-collect[2] ['ri:kə'lekt] wieder sammeln; **~** *o.s.* sich fassen.

recollection [rekə'lekʃən] Erinnerung *f* (*of* an *acc.*); Gedächtnis *n.*

recommend [rekə'mend] empfehlen; **~ation** [rekəmen'deiʃən] Empfehlung *f;* Vorschlag *m.*

recompense ['rekəmpens] **1.** Belohnung *f,* Vergeltung *f;* Ersatz *m;*

2. belohnen, vergelten; entschädigen; ersetzen.

reconcil|e ['rekənsail] aus-, versöhnen; in Einklang bringen; schlichten; **~iation** [rekənsili'eiʃən] Ver-, Aussöhnung f.

recondition ['ri:kən'diʃən] wieder herrichten; ⊕ überholen.

reconn|aissance ⚔ [ri'kɔnisəns] Aufklärung f, Erkundung f; fig. Übersicht f; **~oitre**, Am. **~oiter** [rekə'nɔitə] erkunden, auskundschaften.

reconsider ['ri:kən'sidə] wieder erwägen; nochmals überlegen.

reconstitute ['ri:'kɔnstitju:t] wiederherstellen.

reconstruct ['ri:kəns'trʌkt] wiederaufbauen; **~ion** [~kʃən] Wiederaufbau m, Wiederherstellung f.

reconvert ['ri:kən'vɔ:t] umstellen.

record 1. ['rekɔ:d] Aufzeichnung f; ⟨t̯t̯⟩ Protokoll n; schriftlicher Bericht; Ruf m, Leumund m; Wiedergabe f; Schallplatte f; Sport: Rekord m; place on ~ schriftlich niederlegen; ⚖ Office Staatsarchiv n; off the ~ Am. inoffiziell; **2.** [ri'kɔ:d] auf-, verzeichnen; auf Schallplatte etc. aufnehmen; **~er** [~də] Registrator m; Stadtrichter m; Aufnahmegerät n, bsd. Tonbandgerät n; ♪ Blockflöte f; **~ing** [~diŋ] Radio: Aufzeichnung f, Aufnahme f; **~-player** Plattenspieler m.

recount [ri'kaunt] erzählen.

recoup [ri'ku:p] j-n entschädigen (for für); et. wieder einbringen.

recourse [ri'kɔ:s] Zuflucht f; have ~ to s-e Zuflucht nehmen zu.

recover [ri'kʌvə] v/t. wiedererlangen, wiederfinden; wieder einbringen, wiedergutmachen; Schulden etc. eintreiben; be ~ed wiederhergestellt sein; v/i. sich erholen; genesen; **~y** [~ɔri] Wiedererlangung f; Wiederherstellung f; Genesung f; Erholung f.

recreat|e ['rekrieit] v/t. erfrischen; v/i. a. ~ o.s. sich erholen; **~ion** [rekri'eiʃən] Erholung(spause) f.

recrimination [rikrimi'neiʃən] Gegenbeschuldigung f; Gegenklage f.

recruit [ri'kru:t] **1.** Rekrut m; fig. Neuling m; **2.** erneuern, ergänzen; Truppe rekrutieren; ⚔ Rekruten ausheben; sich erholen.

rectangle ⚥ ['rektæŋgl] Rechteck n.

recti|fy ['rektifai] berichtigen; verbessern; ⚡, Radio: gleichrichten; **~tude** [~itju:d] Geradheit f.

rector ['rektə] Pfarrer m; Rektor m; **~y** [~ɔri] Pfarre(i) f; Pfarrhaus n.

recumbent □ [ri'kʌmbənt] liegend.

recuperate [ri'kju:pəreit] wiederherstellen; sich erholen.

recur [ri'kə:] zurück-, wiederkehren (to zu), zurückkommen (to auf acc.); ~ to j-m wieder einfallen; **~rence**

[ri'kʌrəns] Wieder-, Rückkehr f; **~rent** □ [~nt] wiederkehrend.

red [red] **1.** rot; ~ heat Rotglut f; ~ herring Bückling m; ~ tape Amtsschimmel m; **2.** Rot n; (bsd. pol.) Rote(r m f); be in the ~ Am. F in Schulden stecken.

red|breast ['redbrest] a. robin ~ Rotkehlchen n; **~cap** Militärpolizist m; Am. Gepäckträger m; **~den** ['redn] (sich) röten; erröten; **~dish** ['rediʃ] rötlich.

redecorate ['ri:'dekəreit] Zimmer renovieren (lassen).

redeem [ri'di:m] zurück-, loskaufen; ablösen; Versprechen einlösen; büßen; entschädigen für; erlösen; 2er eccl. [~mə] Erlöser m, Heiland m.

redemption [ri'dempʃən] Rückkauf m; Auslösung f; Erlösung f.

red|-handed ['red'hændid]: catch od. take s.o. ~ j-n auf frischer Tat ertappen; **~head** Rotschopf m; Rotkopf m; **~-headed** rothaarig; **~-hot** rotglühend; fig. hitzig; 2 Indian Indianer(in); **~-letter day** Festtag m; fig. Freuden-, Glückstag m; **~ness** ['rednis] Röte f.

redolent ['redoulənt] duftend.

redouble [ri'dʌbl] (sich) verdoppeln.

redoubt ⚔ [ri'daut] Redoute f; **~able** rhet. [~təbl] fürchterlich.

redound [ri'daund]: ~ to beitragen od. gereichen zu, führen zu.

redress [ri'dres] **1.** Abhilfe f; Wiedergutmachung f; ⟨t̯t̯⟩ Entschädigung f; **2.** abhelfen (dat.); wiedergutmachen.

red|-tapism ['red'teipizəm] Bürokratismus m; **~-tapist** [~ist] Bürokrat m.

reduc|e [ri'dju:s] fig. zurückführen, bringen (to auf, in acc., zu); verwandeln (to in acc.); verringern, vermindern; einschränken; Preise herabsetzen; (be)zwingen; ⚥, ♎ reduzieren; ⚔ einrenken; ~ to writing schriftlich niederlegen; **~tion** [ri'dʌkʃən] Reduktion f; Verwandlung f; Herabsetzung f, (Preis)Nachlaß m, Rabatt m; Verminderung f; Verkleinerung f; ⚔ Einrenkung f.

redundant □ [ri'dʌndənt] überflüssig; übermäßig; weitschweifig.

reed [ri:d] Schilfrohr n; Rohrflöte f.

re-education ['ri:edju:(ː)'keiʃən] Umschulung f, Umerziehung f.

reef [ri:f] (Felsen)Riff n; ♫ Reff n.

reefer ['ri:fə] Seemannsjacke f; Am. sl. Marihuana-Zigarette f.

reek [ri:k] **1.** Rauch m, Dampf m; Dunst m; **2.** rauchen, dampfen (with von); unangenehm riechen.

reel [ri:l] **1.** Haspel f (Garn-, Film)Rolle f, Spule f; **2.** v/t. haspeln; wickeln, spulen; v/i. wirbeln; schwanken; taumeln.

re-elect ['ri:i'lekt] wiederwählen.
re-enter [ri:'entə] wieder eintreten (in acc.).
re-establish ['ri:is'tæbliʃ] wiederherstellen.
refection [ri'fekʃən] Erfrischung f.
refer [ri'fə:]: ~ to ver-, überweisen an (acc.); sich beziehen auf (acc.); erwähnen (acc.); zuordnen (dat.); befragen (acc.), nachschlagen in (dat.); zurückführen auf (acc.), zuschreiben (dat.); ~ee [refə'ri:] Schiedsrichter m; Boxen: Ringrichter f; ~ence ['refrəns] Referenz f, Empfehlung f, Zeugnis n; Verweisung f; Bezugnahme f; Anspielung f; Beziehung f; Auskunft (-geber m) f; in od. with ~ to in betreff (gen.), in bezug auf (acc.); ~ book Nachschlagewerk n; ~ library Handbibliothek f; ~ number Aktenzeichen n; make ~ to et. erwähnen.
referendum [refə'rendəm] Volksentscheid m.
refill 1. ['ri:fil] Nachfüllung f; Ersatzfüllung f; 2. ['ri:'fil] (sich) wieder füllen, auffüllen.
refine [ri'fain] (sich) verfeinern od. veredeln; ⊕ raffinieren; (sich) läutern (a. fig.); klügeln; ~ (up)on et. verfeinern, verbessern; ~ment [~nmənt] Verfeinerung f, Vered(e)-lung f; Läuterung f; Feinheit f, Bildung f; Spitzfindigkeit f; ~ry [~nəri] ⊕ Raffinerie f; metall. (Eisen)Hütte f.
refit ⚓ ['ri:'fit] v/t. ausbessern; neu ausrüsten; v/i. ausgebessert werden.
reflect [ri'flekt] v/t. zurückwerfen, reflektieren; zurückstrahlen, widerspiegeln (a. fig.); zum Ausdruck bringen; v/i. ~ (up)on nachdenken über (acc.); sich abfällig äußern über (acc.); ein schlechtes Licht werfen auf (acc.); ~ion [~kʃən] Zurückstrahlung f, Widerspiegelung f; Reflex m; Spiegelbild n; Überlegung f; Gedanke m; abfällige Bemerkung; Makel m; ~ive □ [~ktiv] zurückstrahlend; nachdenklich.
reflex ['ri:fleks] 1. Reflex...; 2.Widerschein m, Reflex m (a. physiol.).
reflexive □ [ri'fleksiv] zurückwirkend; gr. reflexiv, rückbezüglich.
reforest ['ri:'fɔrist] aufforsten.
reform¹ [ri'fɔ:m] 1. Verbesserung f, Reform f; 2. verbessern, reformieren; (sich) bessern.
re-form² ['ri:'fɔ:m] (sich) neu bilden; ⚔ sich wieder formieren.
reform|ation [refə'meiʃən] Umgestaltung f; Besserung f; eccl. ♎ Reformation f; ~atory [ri'fɔ:mətəri] 1. bessernd; 2. Besserungsanstalt f; ~er [ri'fɔ:mə] eccl. Reformator m; bsd. pol. Reformer m.

refract|ion [ri'frækʃən] Strahlenbrechung f; ~ory □ [~ktəri] widerspenstig; hartnäckig; ⊕ feuerfest.
refrain [ri'frein] 1. sich enthalten (from gen.), unterlassen (from acc.); 2. Kehrreim m, Refrain m.
refresh [ri'freʃ] (sich) erfrischen; auffrischen; ~ment [~ʃmənt] Erfrischung f (a. Getränk etc.).
refrigerat|e [ri'fridʒəreit] kühlen; ~or [~tə] Kühlschrank m, -raum m; ~ car Kühlwagen m.
refuel ['ri:'fjuəl] tanken.
refuge ['refju:dʒ] Zuflucht(sstätte) f; a. street-~ Verkehrsinsel f; ~e [refju(:)'dʒi:] Flüchtling m; ~ camp Flüchtlingslager n.
refulgent □ [ri'fʌldʒənt] strahlend.
refund [ri:'fʌnd] zurückzahlen.
refurbish ['ri:'fə:biʃ] aufpolieren.
refusal [ri'fju:zəl] abschlägige Antwort; (Ver)Weigerung f; Vorkaufsrecht n (of auf acc.).
refuse¹ [ri'fju:z] v/t. verweigern; abweisen, ablehnen; scheuen vor (dat.); v/i. sich weigern; scheuen (Pferd). [fall m, Müll m.]
refuse² ['refju:s] Ausschuß m; Ab-]
refute [ri'fju:t] widerlegen.
regain [ri'gein] wiedergewinnen.
regal □ ['ri:gəl] königlich; Königs...
regale [ri'geil] v/t. festlich bewirten; v/i. schwelgen (on in dat.).
regard [ri'gɑ:d] 1. fester Blick; (Hoch)Achtung f, Rücksicht f; Beziehung f; with ~ to im Hinblick auf (acc.); kind ~s herzliche Grüße; 2. ansehen; (be)achten; betrachten; betreffen; as ~s ... was ... anbetrifft; ~ing [~diŋ] hinsichtlich (gen.); ~less □ [~dlis]: ~ of ohne Rücksicht auf (acc.).
regenerate 1. [ri'dʒenəreit] (sich) erneuern; (sich) regenerieren; (sich) neu bilden; 2. [~rit] wiedergeboren.
regent ['ri:dʒənt] 1. herrschend; 2. Regent m.
regiment ⚔ ['redʒimənt] 1. Regiment n; 2. [~mənt] organisieren; ~als ⚔ [redʒi'mentlz] pl. Uniform f.
region ['ri:dʒən] Gegend f, Gebiet n; fig. Bereich m; ~al □ [~nl] örtlich; Orts...
register ['redʒistə] 1. Register n, Verzeichnis n; ⊕ Schieber m, Ventil n; ♪ Register n; Zählwerk n; cash ~ Registrierkasse f; 2. registrieren od. eintragen (lassen); (an-)zeigen, auf-, verzeichnen; Postsache einschreiben (lassen), Gepäck aufgeben; sich polizeilich melden.
registr|ar [redʒis'trɑ:] Registrator m; Standesbeamte(r) m; ~ation [~reiʃən] Eintragung f; ~ fee Anmeldegebühr f; ~y ['redʒistri] Eintragung f; Registratur f; Register n; ~ office Standesamt n.
regress, ~ion ['ri:gres, ri'greʃən] Rückkehr f; fig. Rückgang m.

regret [ri'gret] **1.** Bedauern *n*; Schmerz *m*; **2.** bedauern; *Verlust* beklagen; **~ful** □ [~tful] bedauernd; **~fully** [~li] mit Bedauern; **~table** □ [~təbl] bedauerlich.

regular □ ['regjulə] regelmäßig; regelrecht, richtig; ordentlich; pünktlich; ✕ regulär; **~ity** [regju-'læriti] Regelmäßigkeit *f*; Richtigkeit *f*, Ordnung *f*.

regulat|e ['regjuleit] regeln, ordnen; regulieren; **~ion** [regju'leiʃən] **1.** Regulierung *f*; Vorschrift *f*, Bestimmung *f*; **2.** vorschriftsmäßig.

rehash *fig.* ['ri:'hæʃ] **1.** wieder durchkauen *od.* aufwärmen; **2.** Aufguß *m*.

rehears|al [ri'həːsəl] *thea.*, ♪ Probe *f*; Wiederholung *f*; **~e** [ri'həːs] *thea.* proben; wiederholen; aufsagen.

reign [rein] **1.** Regierung *f*; *fig.* Herrschaft *f*; **2.** herrschen, regieren.

reimburse [ri:im'bəːs] *j-n* entschädigen; *Kosten* wiedererstatten.

rein [rein] **1.** Zügel *m*; **2.** zügeln.

reindeer *zo.* ['reindiə] Ren(tier)*n*.

reinforce [ri:in'fɔːs] verstärken; **~ment** [~smənt] Verstärkung *f*.

reinstate ['ri:in'steit] wieder einsetzen; wieder instand setzen.

reinsure ['ri:in'ʃuə] rückversichern.

reiterate [ri:'itəreit] (dauernd) wiederholen.

reject [ri'dʒekt] ver-, wegwerfen; ablehnen, ausschlagen; zurückweisen; **~ion** [~kʃən] Verwerfung *f*; Ablehnung *f*; Zurückweisung *f*.

rejoic|e [ri'dʒɔis] *v/t.* erfreuen; *v/i.* sich freuen (*at, in* über *acc.*); **~ing** [~siŋ] **1.** □ freudig; **2.** *oft* **~s** *pl.* Freude(nfest *n*) *f*.

rejoin ['ri:'dʒɔin] (sich) wieder vereinigen (mit); wieder zurückkehren zu; [ri'dʒɔin] erwidern.

rejuvenate [ri'dʒuːvineit] verjüngen. [entzünden.)

rekindle ['ri:'kindl] (sich) wieder)

relapse [ri'læps] **1.** Rückfall *m*; **2.** zurückfallen, rückfällig werden.

relate [ri'leit] *v/t.* erzählen; in Beziehung bringen; *v/i.* sich beziehen (*to* auf *acc.*); **~d** verwandt (*to* mit).

relation [ri'leiʃən] Erzählung *f*; Beziehung *f*; Verhältnis *n*; Verwandtschaft *f*; Verwandte(r *m*) *f*; *in* ~ *to* in bezug auf (*acc.*); **~ship** [~ʃip] Verwandtschaft *f*; Beziehung *f*.

relative ['relətiv] **1.** □ bezüglich (*to* gen.); *gr.* relativ; verhältnismäßig; entsprechend; **2.** *gr.* Relativpronomen *n*; Verwandte(r *m*) *f*.

relax [ri'læks] (sich) lockern; mildern; nachlassen (in *dat.*); (sich) entspannen, ausspannen; milder werden; **~ation** [ri:læk'seiʃən] Lockerung *f*; Nachlassen *n*; Entspannung *f*, Erholung *f*.

relay¹ [ri'lei] frisches Gespann; Ablösung *f*; ['riː'lei] ∉ Relais *n*; *Radio:* Übertragung *f*; **2.** [~] *Radio:* übertragen.

re-lay² ['riː'lei] *Kabel etc.* neu verlegen.

relay-race ['riːleireis] *Sport:* Staffellauf *m*.

release [ri'liːs] **1.** Freilassung *f*; *fig.* Befreiung *f*; Freigabe *f*; *Film:* oft *first* ~ Uraufführung *f*; ⊕, *phot.* Auslöser *m*; **2.** freilassen; erlösen; freigeben; *Recht* aufgeben, übertragen; *Film* uraufführen; ⊕ auslösen.

relegate ['religeit] verbannen; verweisen (*to an acc.*).

relent [ri'lent] sich erweichen lassen; **~less** □ [~tlis] unbarmherzig.

relevant ['relivənt] sachdienlich; zutreffend; wichtig, erheblich.

reliab|ility [rilaiə'biliti] Zuverlässigkeit *f*; **~le** □ [ri'laiəbl] zuverlässig.

reliance [ri'laiəns] Ver-, Zutrauen *n*; Verlaß *m*.

relic ['relik] Überrest *m*; Reliquie *f*; **~t** [~kt] Witwe *f*.

relief [ri'liːf] Erleichterung *f*; (angenehme) Unterbrechung; Unterstützung *f*; ✕ Ablösung *f*; Ersatz *m*; Hilfe *f*; △ *etc.* Relief *n*; ~ *works pl.* Notstandsarbeiten *f/pl.*

relieve [ri'liːv] erleichtern; mildern, lindern; *Arme etc.* unterstützen; ✕ ablösen; ✕ entsetzen; ⚖ (ab)helfen (*dat.*); befreien; hervortreten lassen; (angenehm) unterbrechen.

religion [ri'lidʒən] Religion *f*; Ordensleben *n*; *fig.* Ehrensache *f*.

religious □ [ri'lidʒəs] Religions...; religiös; *eccl.* Ordens...; gewissenhaft.

relinquish [ri'liŋkwiʃ] aufgeben; verzichten auf (*acc.*); loslassen.

relish ['reliʃ] **1.** (Bei)Geschmack *m*; Würze *f*; Genuß *m*; **2.** gern essen; Geschmack finden an (*dat.*); schmackhaft machen.

reluctan|ce [ri'lʌktəns] Widerstreben *n*; *bsd. phys.* Widerstand *m*; **~t** □ [~nt] widerstrebend, widerwillig.

rely [ri'lai] ~ (*up*)*on* sich verlassen (auf *acc.*), bauen auf (*acc.*).

remain [ri'mein] **1.** (ver)bleiben; übrigbleiben; **2.** ~s *pl.* Überbleibsel *n/pl.*, Überreste *m/pl.*; sterbliche Reste *m/pl.*; **~der** [~ndə] Rest *m*.

remand [ri'mɑːnd] **1.** (ṭ⅟₂ in die Untersuchungshaft) zurückschicken; **2.** (Zurücksendung *f* in die) Untersuchungshaft *f*; *prisoner on* ~ Untersuchungsgefangene(r *m*) *f*; ~ *home* Jugendstrafanstalt *f*.

remark [ri'mɑːk] **1.** Beachtung *f*; Bemerkung *f*; **2.** *v/t.* bemerken; *v/i.* sich äußern; **~able** □ [~kəbl] bemerkenswert; merkwürdig.

remedy ['remidi] **1.** (Heil-, Hilfs-, Gegen-, Rechts)Mittel *n*; (Ab-)Hilfe *f*; **2.** heilen; abhelfen (*dat.*).

rememb|er [ri'membə] sich erinnern an (*acc.*); denken an (*acc.*); beherzigen; ~ me to her grüße sie von mir; ~rance [~brəns] Erinnerung *f*; Gedächtnis *n*; Andenken *n*; ~s *pl.* Empfehlungen *f/pl.*, Grüße *m/pl.*

remind [ri'maind] erinnern (*of an acc.*); ~er [~də] Mahnung *f*.

reminiscen|ce [remi'nisns] Erinnerung *f*; ~t □ [~nt] (sich) erinnernd.

remiss □ [ri'mis] schlaff, (nach-)lässig; ~ion [~iʃən] *Sünden*-Vergebung *f*; Erlassung *f v.* Strafe etc.; Nachlassen *n*.

remit [ri'mit] *Sünden* vergeben; *Schuld etc.* erlassen; nachlassen in (*dat.*); überweisen; ~tance [~təns] (Geld)Sendung *f*; † Rimesse *f*.

remnant ['remnənt] (Über)Rest *m*.

remodel [ri:'mɔdl] umbilden.

remonstra|nce [ri'mɔnstrəns] Vorstellung *f*, Einwendung *f*; ~te [~treit] Vorstellungen machen (*on* über *acc.*; *with* s.o. j-m); einwenden.

remorse [ri'mɔːs] Gewissensbisse *m/pl.*; ~less □ [~slis] hart(herzig).

remote □ [ri'mout] entfernt, entlegen; ~ness [~tnis] Entfernung *f*.

remov|al [ri'muːvəl] Entfernen *n*; Beseitigung *f*; Umzug *m*; Entlassung *f*; ~ *van* Möbelwagen *m*; ~e [~uːv] **1.** *v/t.* entfernen; wegräumen, wegtun; beseitigen; entlassen; *v/i.* (aus-, um-, ver)ziehen; **2.** Entfernung *f*; Grad *m*; *Schule:* Versetzung *f*; Abteilung *f e-r* Klasse; ~er [~və] (Möbel)Spediteur *m*.

remunerat|e [ri'mjuːnəreit] (be-)lohnen; entschädigen; ~ive □ [~rətiv] lohnend.

Renaissance [rə'neisəns] Renaissance *f*.

renascen|ce [ri'næsns] Wiedergeburt *f*; Renaissance *f*; ~t [~nt] wieder wachsend.

rend [rend] [*irr.*] (zer)reißen.

render ['rendə] wieder-, zurückgeben; *Dienst etc.* leisten; *Ehre etc.* erweisen; *Dank* abstatten; übersetzen; ♪ vortragen; darstellen, interpretieren; *Grund* angeben; † *Rechnung* überreichen; übergeben; machen (zu); *Fett* auslassen; ~ing [~əriŋ] Wiedergabe *f*; Interpretation *f*; Übersetzung *f*, Wiedergabe *f*; △ Rohbewurf *m*.

rendition [ren'diʃən] Wiedergabe *f*.

renegade ['renigeid] Abtrünnige(r *m*) *f*.

renew [ri'njuː] erneuern; ~al [~u(ː)əl] Erneuerung *f*.

renounce [ri'nauns] entsagen (*dat.*); verzichten auf (*acc.*); verleugnen.

renovate ['renouveit] erneuern.

renown [ri'naun] Ruhm *m*, Ansehen *n*; ~ed [~nd] berühmt, namhaft.

rent[1] [rent] **1.** *pret. u. p.p. von* rend; **2.** Riß *m*; Spalte *f*.

rent[2] [~] **1.** Miete *f*; Pacht *f*; **2.** (ver)mieten, (ver)pachten; ~al ['rentl] (Einkommen *n* aus) Miete *f* od. Pacht *f*.

renunciation [rinʌnsi'eiʃən] Entsagung *f*; Verzicht *m* (*of auf acc.*).

repair[1] [ri'pɛə] **1.** Ausbesserung *f*, Reparatur *f*; ~s *pl.* Instandsetzungsarbeiten *f/pl.*; ~ *shop* Reparaturwerkstatt *f*; *in good* ~ in gutem (baulichen) Zustand, gut erhalten; *out of* ~ baufällig; **2.** reparieren, ausbessern; erneuern; wiedergutmachen.

repair[2] [~]: ~ *to* sich begeben nach.

reparation [repə'reiʃən] Ersatz *m*; Entschädigung *f*; *make* ~s *pol.* Reparationen leisten.

repartee [repɑː'tiː] schlagfertige Antwort; Schlagfertigkeit *f*.

repast [ri'pɑːst] Mahl(zeit *f*) *n*.

repay [riː'pei] [*irr.* (*pay*)] *et.* zurückzahlen; *fig.* erwidern; *et.* vergelten; *j-n* entschädigen; ~ment [~eimənt] Rückzahlung *f*.

repeal [ri'piːl] **1.** Aufhebung *f von* Gesetzen; **2.** aufheben, widerrufen.

repeat [ri'piːt] **1.** (sich) wiederholen; aufsagen; nachliefern; aufstoßen (*Essen*); **2.** Wiederholung *f*; *oft* ~ *order* Nachbestellung *f*; ♪ Wiederholungszeichen *n*.

repel [ri'pel] zurückstoßen, zurücktreiben, zurückweisen; *fig.* abstoßen.

repent [ri'pent] bereuen; ~ance [~təns] Reue *f*; ~ant [~nt] reuig.

repercussion [riːpəː'kʌʃən] Rückprall *m*; *fig.* Rückwirkung *f*.

repertory ['repətəri] *thea.* Repertoire *n*; *fig.* Fundgrube *f*.

repetition [repi'tiʃən] Wiederholung *f*; Aufsagen *n*; Nachbildung *f*.

replace [ri'pleis] wieder hinstellen od. einsetzen; ersetzen; an *j-s* Stelle treten; ~ment [~smənt] Ersatz *m*.

replant [riː'plɑːnt] umpflanzen.

replenish [ri'pleniʃ] wieder auffüllen; ~ment [~mənt] Auffüllung *f*; Ergänzung *f*.

replete [ri'pliːt] angefüllt, voll.

replica ['replikə] Nachbildung *f*.

reply [ri'plai] **1.** antworten, erwidern (*to auf acc.*); **2.** Erwiderung *f*, Antwort *f*.

report [ri'pɔːt] **1.** Bericht *m*; Gerücht *n*; *guter* Ruf; Knall *m*; *school* ~ (Schul)Zeugnis *n*; **2.** berichten (*über acc.*); (sich) melden; anzeigen; ~er [~tə] Berichterstatter(in).

repos|e [ri'pouz] **1.** *allg.* Ruhe *f*; **2.** *v/t.* ausruhen; (aus)ruhen lassen; ~ *trust etc. in* Vertrauen etc. setzen auf (acc.); v/i. a. ~ o.s. (sich) ausruhen; ruhen; beruhen (on auf dat.); ~itory [ri'pɔzitəri] Verwahrungsort m; Warenlager n; fig. Fundgrube f.

reprehend [repri'hend] tadeln.

represent [repri'zent] darstellen; verkörpern; thea. aufführen; schildern; bezeichnen (as als); vertreten; ~ation [reprizən'teiʃən] Darstellung f; thea. Aufführung f; Vorstellung f; Vertretung f; ~ative □ [repri'zentətiv] 1. dar-, vorstellend (of acc.); vorbildlich; (stell)vertretend; parl. repräsentativ; typisch; 2. Vertreter(in); House of ~s Am. parl. Repräsentantenhaus n.

repress [ri'pres] unterdrücken; ~ion [~eʃən] Unterdrückung f.

reprieve [ri'priːv] 1. (Gnaden)Frist f; Aufschub m; 2. j-m Aufschub od. eine Gnadenfrist gewähren.

reprimand ['reprimɑːnd] 1. Verweis m; 2. j-m e-n Verweis geben.

reprisal [ri'praizəl] Repressalie f.

reproach [ri'proutʃ] 1. Vorwurf m; Schande f; 2. vorwerfen (s.o. with s.th. j-m et.); Vorwürfe machen; ~ful □ [~fful] vorwurfsvoll.

reprobate ['reproubeit] 1. verkommen, verderbt; 2. verkommenes Subjekt; 3. mißbilligen; verdammen.

reproduc|e [riːprə'djuːs] wiedererzeugen; (sich) fortpflanzen; wiedergeben, reproduzieren; ~tion [~'dʌkʃən] Wiedererzeugung f; Fortpflanzung f; Reproduktion f.

reproof [ri'pruːf] Vorwurf m, Tadel m.

reprov|al [ri'pruːvəl] Tadel m, Rüge f; ~e [~uːv] tadeln, rügen.

reptile zo. ['reptail] Reptil n.

republic [ri'pʌblik] Republik f; ~an [~kən] 1. republikanisch; 2. Republikaner(in).

repudiate [ri'pjuːdieit] nicht anerkennen; ab-, zurückweisen.

repugnan|ce [ri'pʌgnəns] Abneigung f, Widerwille m; ~t □ [~nt] abstoßend; widerwärtig.

repuls|e [ri'pʌls] 1. Zurück-, Abweisung f; 2. zurück-, abweisen; ~ive □ [~siv] abstoßend; widerwärtig.

reput|able □ ['repjutəbl] achtbar; ehrbar, anständig; ~ation [repju(:)-'teiʃən] (bsd. guter) Ruf, Ansehen n; ~e [ri'pjuːt] 1. Ruf m; 2. halten für; ~ed vermeintlich; angeblich.

request [ri'kwest] 1. Gesuch n, Bitte f; Ersuchen n; ✝ Nachfrage f; by ~, on ~ auf Wunsch; in (great) ~ (sehr) gesucht, begehrt; ~ stop Bedarfshaltestelle f; 2. um et. bitten od. ersuchen; j-n bitten; et. erbitten.

require [ri'kwaiə] verlangen, fordern; brauchen; erfordern; ~d er-

forderlich; ~ment [~əmənt] (An-)Forderung f; Erfordernis n.

requisit|e ['rekwizit] 1. erforderlich; 2. Erfordernis n; Bedarfs-, Gebrauchsartikel m; toilet ~s pl. Toilettenartikel m/pl.; ~ion [rekwi-'ziʃən] 1. Anforderung f; ✕ Requisition f; 2. anfordern; ✕ requirieren.

requital [ri'kwaitl] Vergeltung f.

requite [ri'kwait] j-m et. vergelten.

rescind [ri'sind] aufheben.

rescission [ri'siʒən] Aufhebung f.

rescue ['reskjuː] 1. Rettung f; (gewaltsame) Befreiung; 2. retten; (gewaltsam) befreien.

research [ri'səːtʃ] Forschung f; Untersuchung f; Nachforschung f; ~er [~ʃə] Forscher m.

resembl|ance [ri'zembləns] Ähnlichkeit f (to mit); ~e [ri'zembl] gleichen, ähnlich sein (dat.).

resent [ri'zent] übelnehmen; ~ful □ [~tful] übelnehmerisch; ärgerlich; ~ment [~tmənt] Ärger m; Groll m.

reservation [rezə'veiʃən] Vorbehalt m; Am. Indianerreservation f; Vorbestellung f von Zimmern etc.

reserve [ri'zəːv] 1. Vorrat m; ✕ Rücklage f; Reserve f (a. fig., ✕); Zurückhaltung f, Verschlossenheit f; Vorsicht f; Vorbehalt m; Sport: Ersatzmann m; 2. aufbewahren, aufsparen; vorbehalten; zurücklegen; Platz etc. reservieren; ~d □ fig. zurückhaltend, reserviert.

reservoir ['rezəvwɑː] Behälter m für Wasser etc.; Sammel-, Staubekken n; fig. Reservoir n.

resid|e [ri'zaid] wohnen; (orts)ansässig sein; ~ in innewohnen (dat.); ~nce ['rezidəns] Wohnen n; Ortsansässigkeit f; (Wohn)Sitz m; Residenz f; ~ permit Aufenthaltsgenehmigung f; ~nt [~nt] 1. wohnhaft; ortsansässig; 2. Ortsansässige(r m) f; Einwohner(in).

residu|al [ri'zidjuəl] übrigbleibend; ~e ['rezidjuː] Rest m; Rückstand m; ✝ Reinnachlaß m.

resign [ri'zain] v/t. aufgeben; Amt niederlegen; überlassen; ~ o.s. to sich ergeben in (acc.), sich abfinden mit; v/i. zurücktreten; ~ation [rezig'neiʃən] Rücktritt m; Ergebung f; Entlassungsgesuch n; ~ed □ ergeben, resigniert.

resilien|ce [ri'ziliəns] Elastizität f; ~t [~nt] elastisch, fig. spannkräftig.

resin ['rezin] 1. Harz n; 2. harzen.

resist [ri'zist] widerstehen (dat.); sich widersetzen (dat.); ~ance [~təns] Widerstand m; attr. Widerstands...; line of least ~ Weg m des geringsten Widerstands; ~ant [~nt] widerstehend; widerstandsfähig.

resolut|e □ ['rezəluːt] entschlossen; ~ion [rezə'luːʃən] (Auf)Lösung f;

Entschluß *m*; Entschlossenheit *f*;
Resolution *f*.
resolve [ri'zɔlv] **1.** *v/t.* auflösen; *fig.*
lösen; *Zweifel etc.* beheben; entscheiden; *v/i. a.* ~ *o.s.* sich auflösen;
beschließen; ~ (*up*)*on* sich entschließen zu; **2.** Entschluß *m*; *Am.*
Beschluß *m*; ~**d** □ entschlossen.
resonan|ce ['reznəns] Resonanz *f*;
~**t** □ [~nt] nach-, widerhallend.
resort [ri'zɔːt] **1.** Zuflucht *f*; Besuch
m; Aufenthalt(sort) *m*; Erholungs-
ort *m*; *health* ~ Kurort *m*; *seaside* ~
Seebad *n*; *summer* ~ Sommerfrische *f*; **2.** ~ *to* oft besuchen;
seine Zuflucht nehmen zu. [sen].)
resound [ri'zaund] widerhallen(las-)
resource [ri'sɔːs] *natürlicher* Reichtum; Hilfsquelle *f*, -mittel *n*; Zuflucht *f*; Findigkeit *f*; Zeitvertreib
m, Entspannung *f*; ~**ful** □ [~sful]
findig.
respect [ris'pekt] **1.** Rücksicht *f* (*to,*
of auf *acc.*); Beziehung *f*; Achtung
f; ~**s** *pl.* Empfehlungen *f*/*pl.*; **2.** *v/t.*
(hoch)achten; Rücksicht nehmen
auf (*acc.*); betreffen; ~**able** □
[~təbl] achtbar; ansehnlich; anständig; *bsd.* ♀ solid; ~**ful** □ [~tful]
ehrerbietig; *yours* ~*ly* hochachtungsvoll; ~**ing** [~tiŋ] hinsichtlich
(*gen.*); ~**ive** □ [~iv] jeweilig; *we*
went to our ~ *places* wir gingen jeder
an seinen Platz; ~**ively** [~vli] beziehungsweise; je.
respirat|ion [respə'reiʃən] Atmen
n; Atemzug *m*; ~**or** ['respəreitə]
Atemfilter *m*; ⚕ Atemgerät *n*; Gas-
maske *f*.
respire [ris'paiə] atmen; aufat-
men.
respite ['respait] Frist *f*; Stundung *f*.
resplendent □ [ris'plendənt] glänzend.
respond [ris'pɔnd] antworten, erwidern; ~ *to* reagieren auf (*acc.*).
response [ris'pɔns] Antwort *f*, Erwiderung *f*; *fig.* Reaktion *f*.
responsi|bility [rispɔnsə'biliti] Ver-
antwortlichkeit *f*; Verantwortung *f*;
♱ Zahlungsfähigkeit *f*; ~**ble** [ris-
'pɔnsəbl] verantwortlich; verant-
wortungsvoll; ♱ zahlungsfähig.
rest [rest] **1.** Rest *m*; Ruhe *f*; Rast
f; Schlaf *m*; *fig.* Tod *m*; Stütze *f*;
Pause *f*; **2.** *v/i.* ruhen; rasten;
schlafen; (sich) lehnen, sich stützen
(*on* auf *acc.*); ~ *upon fig.* beruhen
auf (*dat.*); *in e-m Zustand* bleiben;
v/t. (aus)ruhen lassen; stützen.
restaurant ['restərɔ̃ːŋ, ~rɔnt] Gast-
stätte *f*.
rest-cure ⚕ ['restkjuə] Liegekur *f*.
restful ['restful] ruhig, geruhsam.
resting-place ['restiŋpleis] Ruhe-
platz *m*, -stätte *f*.
restitution [resti'tjuːʃən] Wiederherstellung *f*; Rückerstattung *f*.

restive □ ['restiv] widerspenstig.
restless ['restlis] ruhelos; rastlos;
unruhig; ~**ness** [~snis] Ruhelosig-
keit *f*; Rastlosigkeit *f*; Unruhe *f*.
restorat|ion [restə'reiʃən] Wieder-
herstellung *f*; Wiedereinsetzung *f*;
Rekonstruktion *f*, Nachbildung *f*;
~**ive** [ris'tɔrətiv] **1.** stärkend;
2. Stärkungsmittel *n*.
restore [ris'tɔː] wiederherstellen;
wiedereinsetzen (*to in acc.*); wieder-
geben; ~ *to health* wieder gesund
machen.
restrain [ris'trein] zurückhalten
(*from* von); in Schranken halten;
unterdrücken; einsperren; ~**t** [~nt]
Zurückhaltung *f*; Beschränkung *f*,
Zwang *m*; Zwangshaft *f*.
restrict [ris'trikt] be-, einschränken; ~**ion** [~kʃən] Be-, Einschränkung *f*; Vorbehalt *m*.
result [ri'zʌlt] **1.** Ergebnis *n*, Folge
f, Resultat *n*; **2.** folgen, sich ergeben
(*from* aus); ~ *in* hinauslaufen auf
(*acc.*), zur Folge haben.
resum|e [ri'zjuːm] wiedernehmen,
-erlangen; wiederaufnehmen; zs.-
fassen; ~**ption** [ri'zʌmpʃən] Zu-
rücknahme *f*; Wiederaufnahme *f*.
resurgent [ri'sɜːdʒənt] sich wieder-
erhebend, wieder aufkommend.
resurrection [rezə'rekʃən] Wieder-
aufleben *n*; ♀ *eccl.* (Wieder)Aufer-
stehung *f*.
resuscitate [ri'sʌsiteit] wiederer-
wecken, wiederbeleben.
retail 1. ['riːteil] Einzelhandel *m*;
by ~ im Einzelverkauf; **2.** [~] Ein-
zelhandels..., Detail...; **3.** [riːˈteil]
im kleinen verkaufen; ~**er** [~lə]
Einzelhändler(in).
retain [ri'tein] behalten (*a. fig.*);
zurück-, festhalten; beibehalten;
Anwalt nehmen.
retaliat|e [ri'tælieit] *v/t. Unrecht*
vergelten; sich rächen; ~**ion**
[ritæli'eiʃən] Vergeltung *f*.
retard [ri'taːd] verzögern; aufhalten; verspäten.
retention [ri'tenʃən] Zurück-, Behalten *n*; Beibehaltung *f*.
reticent ['retisənt] verschwiegen;
schweigsam; zurückhaltend.
retinue ['retinjuː] Gefolge *n*.
retir|e [ri'taiə] *v/t.* zurückziehen;
pensionieren; *v/i.* sich zurückziehen; zurück-, abtreten; in den
Ruhestand treten; ~**ed** □ zurück-
gezogen; im Ruhestand (lebend);
entlegen; ~ *pay* Pension *f.*; ~**ement**
[~əmənt] Sichzurückziehen *n*; Aus-,
Rücktritt *m*; Ruhestand *m*; Zurückgezogenheit *f*; ~**ing** [~əriŋ] zurückhaltend; schüchtern; ~ *pension*
Ruhegehalt *n.*
retort [ri'tɔːt] **1.** Erwiderung *f*; 🝆
Retorte *f*; **2.** erwidern.
retouch ['riːˈtʌtʃ] *et.* überarbeiten;
phot. retuschieren.

retrace [ri'treis] zurückverfolgen; ~ one's steps zurückgehen.

retract [ri'trækt] (sich) zurückziehen; ⊕ einziehen; widerrufen.

retread ['ri:tred] **1.** *Reifen* runderneuern; **2.** runderneuerter Reifen.

retreat [ri'tri:t] **1.** Rückzug *m*; Zurückgezogenheit *f*; Zuflucht(sort *m*) *f*; ✗. Zapfenstreich *m*; *beat a* ~ *fig.* es aufgeben; **2.** sich zurückziehen; *fig.* zurücktreten.

retrench [ri'trentʃ] (sich) einschränken; kürzen; *Wort etc.* streichen; ✗ verschanzen.

retribution [retri'bju:ʃən] Vergeltung *f*.

retrieve [ri'tri:v] wiederbekommen; wiederherstellen; wiedergutmachen; *hunt.* apportieren.

retro|... ['retrou] (zu)rück...; ~active [retrou'æktiv] rückwirkend; ~grade ['retrougreid] **1.** rückläufig; **2.** zurückgehen; ~gression [retrou'greʃən] Rück-, Niedergang *m*; ~spect ['retrouspekt] Rückblick *m*; ~spective □ [retrou'spektiv] zurückblickend; rückwirkend.

retry ♊ ['ri:'trai] Prozeß wiederaufnehmen.

return [ri'tə:n] **1.** Rückkehr *f*; Wiederkehr *f*; *parl.* Wiederwahl *f*; *oft* ~s *pl.* ✝ Gewinn *m*, Ertrag *m*; Umsatz *m*; ♊ Rückfall *m*; Rückgabe *f*; Rückzahlung *f*; Vergeltung *f*; Erwiderung *f*; Gegenleistung *f*; Dank *m*; *amtlicher* Bericht; Wahlergebnis *n*; Steuererklärung *f*; F Rückfahrkarte *f*; *attr.* Rück...; *many happy* ~s *of the day* herzliche Glückwünsche zum Geburtstag; *in* ~ dafür; *als Ersatz (for für); by* ~ *(of post)* postwendend; ~ *ticket* Rückfahrkarte *f*. **2.** *v/i.* zurückkehren; wiederkehren; *v/t.* zurückgeben; zurückzahlen; zurücksenden; *Dank* abstatten; erwidern; berichten, angeben; *parl.* wählen; *Gewinn* abwerfen.

reunification *pol.* ['ri:ju:nifi'keiʃən] Wiedervereinigung *f*.

reunion ['ri:'ju:njən] Wiedervereinigung *f*; Treffen *n*, Zs.-kunft *f*.

reval|orization ✝ [ri:vælərai'zeiʃən] Aufwertung *f*; ~uation [~lju-'eiʃən] Neubewertung *f*.

revamp ⊕ ['ri:'væmp] vorschuhen; *Am.* F aufmöbeln; erneuern.

reveal [ri'vi:l] enthüllen; offenbaren; ~ing [~liŋ] aufschlußreich.

revel ['revl] **1.** Lustbarkeit *f*; Gelage *n*; **2.** ausgelassen sein; schwelgen; zechen.

revelation [revi'leiʃən] Enthüllung *f*; Offenbarung *f*.

revel|(l)er ['revlə] Feiernde(r *m*) *f*; Zecher *m*; ~ry [~lri] Gelage *n*; Lustbarkeit *f*, Rummel *m*; Orgie *f*.

revenge [ri'vendʒ] **1.** Rache *f*;

Sport: Revanche *f*; **2.** rächen; ~ful □ [~dʒful] rachsüchtig; ~r [~dʒə] Rächer(in).

revenue ['revinju:] Einkommen *n*; ~s *pl.* Einkünfte *pl.*; ~ *board*, ~ *office* Finanzamt *n*.

reverberate [ri'və:bəreit] zurückwerfen; zurückstrahlen; widerhallen.

revere [ri'viə] (ver)ehren; ~nce ['revərəns] **1.** Verehrung *f*; Ehrfurcht *f*; **2.** (ver)ehren; ~nd [~nd] **1.** ehrwürdig; **2.** Geistliche(r) *m*.

reverent(ial) □ ['revərənt, revə-'renʃəl] ehrbietig, ehrfurchtsvoll.

reverie ['revəri] Träumerei *f*.

revers|al [ri'və:səl] Umkehrung *f*; Umschwung *m*; ♊ Umstoßung *f*; ⊕ Umsteuerung *f*; ~e [~ə:s] **1.** Gegenteil *n*; Kehrseite *f*; Rückschlag *m*; **2.** □ umgekehrt; Rück(wärts)...; ~ *(gear) mot.* Rückwärtsgang *m*; ~ *side* linke *Stoff*-Seite; **3.** umkehren, umdrehen; *Urteil* umstoßen; ⊕ umsteuern; ~ion [~ə:ʃən] Umkehrung *f*; Rückkehr *f*; ♊ Heimfall *m*; *biol.* Rückartung *f*.

revert [ri'və:t] um-, zurückkehren; *biol.* zurückarten; *Blick* wenden.

review [ri'vju:] **1.** Nachprüfung *f*; ♊ Revision *f*; ✗, ♣ Parade *f*; Rückblick *m*; Überblick *m*; Rezension *f*; Zeitschrift *f*; *pass s.th. in* ~ *et.* Revue passieren lassen; **2.** (über-nach)prüfen; zurückblicken auf *(acc.)*; überblicken; ✗, ♣ besichtigen; rezensieren; ~er [~u(:)ə] Rezensent *m*. [fen.)

revile [ri'vail] schmähen, beschimp-)

revis|e [ri'vaiz] überarbeiten, durchsehen, revidieren; ~ion [~'viʒən] Revision *f*; Überarbeitung *f*.

reviv|al [ri'vaivəl] Wiederbelebung *f*; Wiederaufleben *n*, Wiederaufblühen *n*; Erneuerung *f*; *fig.* Erweckung *f*; ~e [~aiv] wiederbeleben; wieder aufleben (lassen); erneuern; wieder aufblühen.

revocation [revə'keiʃən] Widerruf *m*; Aufhebung *f*.

revoke [ri'vouk] *v/t.* widerrufen; *v/i. Karten:* nicht bedienen.

revolt [ri'voult] **1.** Revolte *f*, Empörung *f*, Aufruhr *m*; **2.** *v/i.* sich empören; abfallen; *v/t. fig.* abstoßen.

revolution [revə'lu:ʃən] Umwälzung *f*, Umdrehung *f*; *pol.* Revolution *f*; ~ary [~ʃnəri] **1.** revolutionär; **2.** *a.* ~ist [~ʃnist] Revolutionär(in); ~ize [~ʃnaiz] aufwiegeln; umgestalten.

revolv|e [ri'vɔlv] *v/i.* sich drehen *(about, round um); v/t.* umdrehen; *fig.* erwägen; ~ing [~viŋ] sich drehend; Dreh...

revue *thea.* [ri'vju:] Revue *f*; Kabarett *n*.

revulsion [ri'vʌlʃən] *fig.* Umschwung *m*; ♊ Ableitung *f*.

reward [ri'wɔːd] 1. Belohnung f; Vergeltung f; 2. belohnen; vergelten.

rewrite ['riː'rait] [irr. (write)] neu (od. um)schreiben.

rhapsody ['ræpsədi] Rhapsodie f; fig. Schwärmerei f; Wortschwall m.

rhetoric ['retərik] Rhetorik f.

rheumatism ♀ ['ruːmətizəm] Rheumatismus m.

rhubarb ♧ ['ruːbɑːb] Rhabarber m.

rhyme [raim] 1. Reim m (to auf acc.); Vers m; without ~ or reason ohne Sinn u. Verstand; 2. (sich) reimen.

rhythm ['riðəm] Rhythmus m; ~ic(al □) ['riðmik(əl)] rhythmisch.

Rialto Am. [ri'æltou] Theaterviertel n e-r Stadt, bsd. in New York.

rib [rib] 1. Rippe f; 2. rippen; sl. aufziehen, necken.

ribald ['ribəld] lästerlich; unflätig; ~ry [~dri] Zoten f/pl.; derbe Späße m/pl.

ribbon ['ribən] Band n; Streifen m; ~s pl. Fetzen m/pl.; Zügel m/pl.; ~ building, ~ development Reihenbau m

rice [rais] Reis m.

rich [ritʃ] reich (in an dat.); reichlich; prächtig, kostbar; ergiebig, fruchtbar; voll (Ton); schwer (Speise, Wein, Duft); satt (Farbe); ~es ['ritʃiz] pl. Reichtum m, Reichtümer m/pl.; ~ness [~nis] Reichtum m; Fülle f.

rick ♪ [rik] (Heu)Schober m.

ricket|s ♀ ['rikits] sg. od. pl. Rachitis f; ~y [~i] [~ti] rachitisch; wack(e)lig (Möbel).

rid [rid] [irr.] befreien, frei machen (of von); get ~ of loswerden.

ridden ['ridn] 1. p.p. von ride 2; 2. in Zssgn: bedrückt od. geplagt von ...

riddle ['ridl] 1. Rätsel n; grobes Sieb; 2. sieben; durchlöchern.

ride [raid] 1. Ritt m; Fahrt f; Reitweg m; 2. [irr.] v/i. reiten; rittlings sitzen; fahren; treiben; schweben; liegen; v/t. Pferd etc. reiten; Land durchreiten; ~r ['raidə] Reiter(in) f; Fahrende(r m) f.

ridge [ridʒ] 1. (Gebirgs)Kamm m, Grat m; △ First m; ♪ Rain m; 2. (sich) furchen.

ridicul|e ['ridikjuːl] 1. Hohn m, Spott m; 2. lächerlich machen; ~ous □ [ri'dikjuləs] lächerlich.

riding ['raidiŋ] Reiten n; attr. Reit... [~ with voll von.]

rife □ [raif] häufig; vorherrschend;

riff-raff ['rifræf] Gesindel n.

rifle ['raifl] 1. Gewehr n; 2. (aus)plündern; ~man ⚔ Schütze m.

rift [rift] Riß m, Sprung m; Spalte f.

rig¹ [rig] 1. Markt etc. manipulieren; 2. Schwindelmanöver n.

rig² [~] 1. ♧ Takelung f; F Aufma-

chung f; 2. auftakeln; ~ s.o. out j-n versorgen od. ausrüsten; j-n herausputzen od. herrichten; ~ging ♧ ['rigiŋ] Takelage f.

right [rait] 1. □ recht; richtig; recht (Ggs. left); be ~ recht haben; all ~! alles in Ordnung!; ganz recht!; put od. set ~ in Ordnung bringen; berichtigen; 2. adv. recht, richtig; gerade; direkt; ganz (und gar); ~ away sogleich; ~ on geradeaus; 3. Recht n; Rechte f, rechte Seite od. Hand; the ~s and wrongs der wahre Sachverhalt; by ~ of auf Grund (gen.); on od. to the ~ rechts; ~ of way Wegerecht n; Vorfahrt(srecht n) f; 4. j-m Recht verschaffen; et. in Ordnung bringen; ♧ (sich) aufrichten; ~-down ['rait'daun] regelrecht, ausgemacht; wirklich; ~eous □ ['raitʃəs] rechtschaffen; ~ful □ ['raitful] recht(mäßig); gerecht.

rigid □ ['ridʒid] starr; fig. a. streng, hart; ~ity [ri'dʒiditi] Starrheit f; Strenge f, Härte f.

rigmarole ['rigməroul] Geschwätz n.

rigor ♀ ['raigə] Fieberfrost m.

rigo(u)r ['rigə] Strenge f, Härte f.

rigorous □ ['rigərəs] streng, rigoros.

rim [rim] 1. Felge f; Radkranz m; Rand m; 2. rändern; einfassen.

rime [raim] Reim m; Rauhreif m.

rind [raind] Rinde f, Schale f; Speck-Schwarte f.

ring¹ [riŋ] 1. Klang m; Geläut(e) n; Klingeln n; Rufzeichen n; Anruf m; give s.o. a ~ j-n anrufen; 2. [irr.] läuten; klingen (lassen); erschallen (with von); ~ again widerhallen; ~ off teleph. das Gespräch beenden; ~ the bell klingeln; ~ s.o. up j-n od. bei j-m anrufen.

ring² [~] 1. Ring m; Kreis m; 2. beringen; mst ~ in, ~ round, ~ about umringen; ~leader ['riŋliːdə] Rädelsführer m; ~let [~lit] (Ringel)Locke f.

rink [riŋk] Eisbahn f; Rollschuhbahn f.

rinse [rins] oft ~ out (aus)spülen.

riot ['raiət] 1. Tumult m; Aufruhr m; Orgie f (a. fig.); run ~ durchgehen; (sich aus)toben; 2. Krawall machen, im Aufruhr sein; toben; schwelgen; ~er [~tə] Aufrührer(in) f; Randalierer m; ~ous □ [~təs] aufrührerisch; lärmend; liederlich (Leben).

rip [rip] 1. Riß m; 2. (auf)trennen; (auf-, zer)reißen; (dahin)sausen.

ripe □ [raip] reif; ~n ['raipən] reifen; ~ness ['raipnis] Reife f.

ripple ['ripl] 1. kleine Welle; Kräuselung f; Geriesel n; 2. (sich) kräuseln; rieseln.

rise [raiz] 1. (An-, Auf)Steigen n;

Anschwellen *n*; (Preis-, Gehalts-) Erhöhung *f*; *fig.* Aufstieg *m*; Steigung *f*; Anhöhe *f*; Ursprung *m*; take (one's) ~ entstehen; entspringen; 2. [*irr.*] sich erheben, aufstehen; die Sitzung schließen; steigen; aufsteigen (*a. fig.*); auferstehen; aufgehen (*Sonne, Samen*); anschwellen; sich empören; entspringen (*Fluß*); ~ to sich e-r Lage gewachsen zeigen; ~n ['rizn] *p.p. von* rise 2; ~r ['raizə]: early ~ Frühaufsteher(in).

rising ['raiziŋ] 1. (Auf)Steigen *n*; Steigung *f*; *ast.* Aufgang *m*; Aufstand *m*; 2. heranwachsend (*Generation*).

risk [risk] 1. Gefahr *f*, Wagnis *n*; † Risiko *n*; run the ~ Gefahr laufen; 2. wagen, riskieren; ~y □ ['riski] gefährlich, gewagt.

rit|e [rait] Ritus *m*, Brauch *m*; ~ual ['ritjuəl] 1. rituell; 2. Ritual *n*.

rival ['raivəl] 1. Nebenbuhler(in); Rivale *m*; 2. rivalisierend; † Konkurrenz...; 3. wetteifern (mit); ~ry [~lri] Rivalität *f*; Wetteifer *m*.

rive [raiv] [*irr.*] (sich) spalten; ~n ['rivən] *p.p. von* rive.

river ['rivə] Fluß *m*; Strom *m* (*a. fig.*); ~side 1. Flußufer *n*; 2. am Wasser (gelegen).

rivet ['rivit] 1. ⊕ Niet(e *f*) *m*; 2. (ver)nieten; *fig.* heften (to an *acc.*; on, upon auf *acc.*); fesseln.

rivulet ['rivjulit] Bach *m*, Flüßchen *n*.

road [roud] Straße *f* (*a. fig.*), Weg *m*; *Am.* = railroad; *mst* ~s *pl.* ⚓ Reede *f*; ~stead ⚓ ['roudsted] Reede *f*; ~ster ⚓ [~tə] Roadster *m*, offener Sportwagen; ~way Fahrbahn *f*.

roam [roum] *v/i.* umherstreifen, wandern; *v/t.* durchstreifen.

roar [rɔː] 1. brüllen; brausen, tosen, donnern; 2. Gebrüll *n*; Brausen *n*; Krachen *n*, Getöse *n*; brüllendes Gelächter.

roast [roust] 1. rösten, braten; 2. geröstet; gebraten; ~ meat Braten *m*.

rob [rɔb] (be)rauben; ~ber ['rɔbə] Räuber *m*; ~bery [~əri] Raub (-überfall) *m*; Räuberei *f*.

robe [roub] (Amts)Robe *f*, Talar *m*; (Staats)Kleid *n*; *Am.* Morgenrock *m*.

robin *orn.* ['rɔbin] Rotkehlchen *n*.

robust □ [rə'bʌst] robust, kräftig.

rock [rɔk] 1. Felsen *m*; Klippe *f*; Gestein *n*; Zuckerstange *f*; ~ crystal Bergkristall *m*; 2. schaukeln; (ein)wiegen.

rocker ['rɔkə] Kufe *f*; *Am.* Schaukelstuhl *m*; Rocker *m*, Halbstarke(r) *m*.

rocket ['rɔkit] Rakete *f*; *attr.* Ra-

keten...; ~-powered mit Raketenantrieb; ~ry [~tri] Raketentechnik *f*.

rocking-chair ['rɔkiŋtʃeə] Schaukelstuhl *m*.

rocky ['rɔki] felsig; Felsen...

rod [rɔd] Rute *f*; Stab *m*; ⊕ Stange *f*; Meßrute *f* (5½ *yards*); *Am. sl.* Pistole *f*.

rode [roud] *pret. von* ride 2.

rodent ['roudənt] Nagetier *n*.

rodeo *Am.* [rou'deiou] Rodeo *m*; Zusammentreiben *n*; Cowboyturnier *n*.

roe[1] [rou] Reh *n*.

roe[2] *ichth.* [~] *a.* hard ~ Rogen *m*; soft ~ Milch *f*.

rogu|e [roug] Schurke *m*; Schelm *m*; ~ish ['rougiʃ] schurkisch; schelmisch.

roister ['rɔistə] krakeelen.

role, rôle *thea.* [roul] Rolle *f* (*a. fig.*).

roll [roul] 1. Rolle *f*; ⊕ Walze *f*; Brötchen *n*, Semmel *f*; Verzeichnis *n*; Urkunde *f*; (Donner)Rollen *n*; (Trommel)Wirbel *m*; ⚓ Schlingern *n*; 2. *v/t.* rollen; wälzen; walzen; *Zigarette* drehen; ~ up zs.-rollen; einwickeln; *v/i.* rollen; sich wälzen; wirbeln (*Trommel*); ⚓ schlingern; ~-call ✕ ['roulkɔːl] Appell *m*; ~er ['roulə] Rolle *f*, Walze *f*; Sturzwelle *f*; ~ coaster *Am.* Achterbahn *f*; ~ skate Rollschuh *m*.

rolliking ['rɔlikiŋ] übermütig.

rolling ['rouliŋ] rollend; Roll..., Walz...; ~ mill ⊕ Walzwerk *n*.

Roman ['roumən] 1. römisch; 2. Römer(in); *mst* 2 *typ.* Antiqua *f*.

romance[1] [rə'mæns] 1. (Ritter-, Vers)Roman *m*; Abenteuer-, Liebesroman *m*; Romanze *f* (*a. fig.*); *fig.* Märchen *n*; Romantik *f*; 2. *fig.* aufschneiden.

Romance[2] *ling.* [~]: ~ languages romanische Sprachen *f/pl.*

romancer [rə'mænsə] Romanschreiber(in); Aufschneider(in).

Romanesque [roumə'nesk] 1. romanisch; 2. romanischer Baustil.

romantic [rə'mæntik] (~ally) romantisch; ~ism [~isizəm] Romantik *f*; ~ist [~ist] Romantiker(in).

romp [rɔmp] 1. Range *f*, Wildfang *m*; Balgerei *f*; 2. sich balgen, toben; ~er(s) ['rɔmpə(z)] Spielanzug *m*.

rood [ruːd] Kruzifix *n*; Viertelmorgen *m* (10,117 *Ar*).

roof [ruːf] 1. Dach *n*; ~ of the mouth Gaumen *m*; 2. *a.* ~ over überdachen; ~ing ['ruːfiŋ] 1. Bedachung *f*; 2. Dach...; ~ felt Dachpappe *f*.

rook [ruk] 1. *Schach:* Turm *m*; *fig.* Gauner *m*; *orn.* Saatkrähe *f*; 2. betrügen.

room [rum] 1. Raum *m*; Platz *m*; Zimmer *n*; Möglichkeit *f*; ~s *pl.* Wohnung *f*; in my ~ an meiner Stelle; 2. *Am.* wohnen; ~er ['rumə] *bsd. Am.* Untermieter(in); **~ing-house** ['ruminhaus] *bsd. Am.* Miets-, Logierhaus *n*; **~mate** Stubenkamerad *m*; **~y** □ ['rumi] geräumig.

roost [ru:st] **1.** Schlafplatz *m e-s Vogels*; Hühnerstange *f*; Hühnerstall *m*; **2.** sich (zum Schlaf) niederhocken; *fig.* übernachten; **~er** ['ru:stə] Haushahn *m*.

root [ru:t] **1.** Wurzel *f*; **2.** (ein)wurzeln; (auf)wühlen; **~ for** *Am. sl.* Stimmung machen für; **~ out** *od. up* ausgraben; **~ out** *od. up* ausrotten; **~ed** ['ru:tid] eingewurzelt; **~er** *Am. sl.* ['ru:tə] Fanatiker *m für et.*

rope [roup] **1.** Tau *n*, Seil *n*; Strick *m*; Schnur *f Perlen etc.*; *be at the end of one's ~* F mit s-m Latein zu Ende sein; *know the ~s* sich auskennen; **2.** mit e-m Seil befestigen *od. (mst ~ in od. off od. out)* absperren; anseilen; **~way** ['roupwei] Seilbahn *f*.

ropy ['roupi] klebrig, zähflüssig.

rosary *eccl.* ['rouzəri] Rosenkranz *m*.

rose[1] [rouz] ♀ Rose *f*; (Gießkannen)Brause *f*; Rosenrot *n*.

rose[2] [~] *pret. von rise 2.*

rosebud ['rouzbʌd] Rosenknospe *f*; *Am.* hübsches Mädchen; Debütantin *f*.

rosin ['rɔzin] (Geigen)Harz *n*.

rostrum ['rɔstrəm] Rednertribüne *f*.

rosy □ ['rouzi] rosig.

rot [rɔt] **1.** Fäulnis *f*; *sl.* Quatsch *m*; **2.** *v/t.* faulen lassen; Quatsch machen mit *j-m*; *v/i.* verfaulen, vermodern.

rota|ry ['routəri] drehend; Rotations...; **~te** [rou'teit] (sich) drehen, (ab)wechseln; **~tion** [~ei∫ən] Umdrehung *f*; Kreislauf *m*; Abwechs(e)lung *f*; **~tory** ['routətəri] *s. rotary*; abwechselnd.

rote [rout]: *by ~* auswendig.

rotten □ ['rɔtn] verfault, faul(ig); mod(e)rig; morsch *(alle a. fig.)*; *sl.* saumäßig, dreckig.

rotund □ [rou'tʌnd] rund; voll *(Stimme)*; hochtrabend.

rouge [ru:ʒ] **1.** Rouge *n*; Silberputzmittel *n*; **2.** Rouge auflegen *(auf acc.)*.

rough [rʌf] **1.** □ rauh; roh; grob; *fig.* ungehobelt; ungefähr *(Schätzung)*; *~ and ready* grob (gearbeitet); Not..., Behelfs...; *~ copy* roher Entwurf; **2.** Rauhe *n*, Grobe *n*; Lümmel *m*; **3.** (an-, auf)rauhen; *~ it* sich mühsam durchschlagen; **~cast** ['rʌfkɑ:st] **1.** ⊕ Rohputz *m*; **2.** unfertig; **3.** ⊕ roh verputzen; roh entwerfen; **~en** ['rʌfən] rauh machen *od.* werden; **~neck** *Am. sl.* Rabauke *m*; **~ness** [~nis] Rauheit *f*; Roheit *f*; Grobheit *f*; **~shod**: *ride ~ over* rücksichtslos behandeln.

round [raund] **1.** □ rund; voll *(Stimme etc.)*; flott *(Gangart)*; abgerundet *(Stil)*; unverblümt; **~ game** Gesellschaftsspiel *n*; **~ trip** Rundreise *f*; **2.** *adv.* rund-, ringsum(her); *a. ~ about* in der Runde; *all ~* ringsum; *fig.* ohne Unterschied; *all the year ~* das ganze Jahr hindurch; **3.** *prp.* um ... herum; **4.** Rund *n*, Kreis *m*; Runde *f*; Kreislauf *m*; (Leiter)Sprosse *f*; Rundgesang *m*; *Lach- etc.* Salve *f*; *100 ~s* ✕ 100 Schuß; **5.** *v/t.* runden; herumgehen *od.* herumfahren um; *~ off* abrunden; *~ up* einkreisen; *v/i.* sich runden; sich umdrehen; **~ about** ['raundəbaut] **1.** umschweifig; **2.** Umweg *m*; Karussell *n*; Kreisverkehr *m*; **~ish** [~di∫] rundlich; **~up** Einkreisung *f*; Razzia *f*.

rous|e [rauz] *v/t.* wecken; ermuntern; aufjagen; (auf)reizen; *~ o.s.* sich aufraffen; *v/i.* aufwachen; **~ing** ['rauzin] brausend *(Beifall etc.)*.

roustabout *Am.* ['raustəbaut] ungelernter *(mst Hafen)*Arbeiter.

rout [raut] **1.** Rotte *f*; wilde Flucht; *a. put to ~* vernichtend schlagen; **2.** aufwühlen.

route [ru:t, ✕ *a.* raut] Weg *m*; ✕ Marschroute *f*.

routine [ru:'ti:n] **1.** Routine *f*; **2.** üblich; Routine...

rove [rouv] umherstreifen, umherwandern.

row[1] [rou] **1.** Reihe *f*; Ruderfahrt *f*; **2.** rudern.

row[2] F [rau] **1.** Spektakel *m*; Krach *m*; Schlägerei *f*; **2.** ausschimpfen.

row-boat ['roubout] Ruderboot *n*.

rower ['rouə] Ruder|er *m*, -in *f*.

royal □ ['rɔiəl] königlich; prächtig; **~ty** [~lti] Königtum *n*, -reich *n*; Königswürde *f*; königliche Persönlichkeit; Tantieme *f*.

rub [rʌb] **1.** Reiben *n*; Schwierigkeit *f*, *fig.* Stichelei *f*; Unannehmlichkeit *f*; **2.** *v/t.* reiben; (ab)wischen; (wund)scheuern; schleifen; *~ down* abreiben; *~ in* einreiben; *fig.* betonen; *~ off* abreiben; *~ out* auslöschen; *~ up* auffrischen; verreiben; *v/i.* sich reiben; *fig. ~ along od. on od. through* sich durchschlagen.

rubber ['rʌbə] **1.** Gummi *n, m*; Radiergummi *m*; Masseur *m*; Wischtuch *n*; *Whist:* Robber *m*; *~s pl. Am.* Gummischuhe *m/pl.*; **2.** Gummi...; *~ check Am. sl.* geplatzter Scheck; **~neck** *Am. sl.* **1.** Gaffer(in); **2.** sich den Hals verrenken; mithören; **~ stamp** Gummistempel *m*; *Am.* F *fig.* Nachbeter *m*; **~stamp** automatisch gutheißen.

rubbish ['rʌbi∫] Schutt *m*; Abfall *m*; Kehricht *m*; *fig.* Schund *m*; Unsinn *m*.

rubble ['rʌbl] Schutt *m*.

rube *Am.sl.* [ru:b] Bauernlümmel *m*.
ruby ['ru:bi] Rubin(rot *n*) *m*.
rucksack ['ruksæk] Rucksack *m*.
rudder ['rʌdə] ⚓ (Steuer)Ruder *n*;
✂ Seitenruder *n*.
rudd|iness ['rʌdinis] Röte *f*; ~y
['rʌdi] rot; rotbäckig.
rude □ [ru:d] unhöflich; unanständig; heftig, unsanft; ungebildet; einfach, kunstlos, robust; roh.
rudiment *biol.* ['ru:dimənt] Ansatz
m; ~s *pl.* Anfangsgründe *m/pl.*
rueful □ ['ru:ful] reuig; traurig.
ruff [rʌf] Halskrause *f*.
ruffian ['rʌfjən] Rohling *m*; Raufbold *m*; Schurke *m*.
ruffle ['rʌfl] 1. Krause *f*, Rüsche *f*;
Kräuseln *n*; *fig.* Unruhe *f*; 2. kräuseln; zerdrücken; zerknüllen; *fig.*
aus der Ruhe bringen; stören.
rug [rʌg] (Reise-, Woll)Decke *f*;
Vorleger *m*, Brücke *f*; ~ged □
['rʌgid] rauh (*a. fig.*); uneben; gefurcht.
ruin [ruin] 1. Ruin *m*, Zs.-bruch *m*;
Untergang *m*; *mst* ~s *pl.* Ruine(n
pl.) *f*, Trümmer *pl.*; 2. ruinieren;
zugrunde richten; zerstören; verderben; ~ous □ ['ruinəs] ruinenhaft, verfallen; verderblich, ruinös.
rul|e [ru:l] 1. Regel *f*; Vorschrift *f*;
Ordnung *f*; Satzung *f*; Herrschaft
f; Lineal *n*; *as a* ~ in der Regel; ~(s)
of the road Straßenverkehrsordnung *f*; 2. *v/t.* regeln; leiten; beherrschen; verfügen; liniieren; ~
out ausschließen; *v/i.* herrschen;
~er ['ru:lə] Herrscher(in); Lineal *n*.
rum [rʌm] Rum *m*; *Am.* Alkohol *m*.
Rumanian [ru(:)'meinjən] 1. rumänisch; 2. Rumän|e *m*, -in *f*; Rumänisch *n*.
rumble ['rʌmbl] 1. Rumpeln *n*; *a.*
~-seat *Am. mot.* Notsitz *m*; *Am.* F
Fehde *f* zwischen Gangsterbanden;
2. rumpeln, rasseln; grollen (*Donner*).
rumina|nt ['ru:minənt] 1. wiederkäuend; 2. Wiederkäuer *m*; ~te
[~neit] wiederkäuen; *fig.* nachsinnen.
rummage ['rʌmidʒ] 1. Durchsuchung *f*; Ramsch *m*, Restwaren
f/pl.; 2. *v/t.* durchsuchen, durchstöbern, durchwühlen; *v/i.* wühlen.
rumo(u)r ['ru:mə] 1. Gerücht *n*;
2. (als Gerücht) verbreiten; *it is* ~ed
es geht das Gerücht.   [*m*.]
rump *anat.* ['rʌmp] Steiß *m*; Rumpf)
rumple ['rʌmpl] zerknittern; zerren, (zer)zausen.
rum-runner *Am.* ['rʌmrʌnə] Alkoholschmuggler *m*.
run [rʌn] 1. [*irr.*] *v/i. allg.* laufen;
rennen (*Mensch, Tier*); eilen; zerlaufen (*Farbe etc.*); umgehen (*Gerücht etc.*); lauten (*Text*); gehen
(*Melodie*); ✝ sich stellen (*Preis*); ~
across s.o. j-m in die Arme laufen;

~ *away* davonlaufen; ~ *down* ablaufen (*Uhr etc.*); *fig.* herunterkommen; ~ *dry* aus-, vertrocknen; ~ *for
parl.* kandidieren für; ~ *into* geraten in (*acc.*); werden zu; *j-m* in die
Arme laufen; ~ *low* zur Neige gehen; ~ *mad* verrückt werden; ~ *off*
weglaufen; ~ *on* fortfahren; ~ *out*,
~ *short* zu Ende gehen; ~ *through*
durchmachen; durchlesen; ~ *to*
sich belaufen auf (*acc.*); sich entwickeln zu; ~ *up* to sich belaufen
auf (*acc.*); *v/t.* Strecke durchlaufen;
Weg einschlagen; laufen lassen;
Hand etc. gleiten lassen; stecken,
stoßen; transportieren; *Flut* ergießen; *Geschäft* betreiben, leiten;
hunt. verfolgen, hetzen; um die
Wette rennen mit; schmuggeln;
heften; ~ *the blockade* die Blockade
brechen; ~ *down* umrennen; zur
Strecke bringen; *fig.* schlecht machen; herunterwirtschaften; *be* ~
down abgearbeitet sein; ~ *errands*
Botengänge machen; ~ *in mot.* einfahren; F *Verbrecher* einbuchten; ~
off ablaufen lassen; ~ *out* hinausjagen; ~ *over* überfahren; *Text* überfliegen; ~ *s.o. through* j-n durchbohren; ~ *up Preis, Neubau etc.*
emportreiben; *Rechnung etc.* auflaufen lassen; 2. Laufen *n*, Rennen
n, Lauf *m*; Verlauf *m*; Fahrt *f* e-s
Schiffes; Reihe *f*; Folge *f*; Serie *f*;
Reise *f*, Ausflug *m*; ✝ Andrang *m*;
Ansturm *m*; *Am.* Bach *m*; *Am.*
Laufmasche *f*; *Vieh*-Trift *f*; freie
Benutzung; *Art f*, Schlag *m*; the
common ~ die große Masse; *have a*
~ *of 20 nights thea.* 20mal nacheinander gegeben werden; *in the long*
~ auf die Dauer, am Ende; *in the
short* ~ fürs nächste.
run|about *mot.* ['rʌnəbaut] kleiner
(Sport)Wagen; ~away Ausreißer *m*.
rune [ru:n] Rune *f*.
rung¹ [rʌŋ] *p.p. von* ring 2.
rung² [~] (Leiter)Sprosse *f* (*a. fig.*).
run-in ['rʌn'in] *Sport:* Einlauf *m*;
Am. F Krach *m*, Zs.-stoß *m* (*Streit*).
run|let ['rʌnlit], ~nel ['rʌnl] Rinnsal *n*; Rinnstein *m*.
runner ['rʌnə] Läufer *m*; Bote *m*;
(Schlitten)Kufe *f*; Schieber *m am
Schirm*; ⚭ Ausläufer *m*; ~-up
[~ər'ʌp] *Sport:* Zweitbeste(r *m*) *f*,
Zweite(r *m*) *f*.
running ['rʌniŋ] 1. laufend; *two
days* ~ zwei Tage nacheinander; ~
hand Kurrentschrift *f*; 2. Rennen
n; ~-board Trittbrett *n*.
runt [rʌnt] *zo.* Zwergrind *n*; *fig.*
Zwerg *m*; *attr.* Zwerg...
runway ['rʌnwei] ✂ Rollbahn *f*;
hunt. Wechsel *m*; Holzrutsche *f*; ~
watching Ansitzjagd *f*.
rupture ['rʌptʃə] 1. Bruch *m* (*a.* ✞);
2. brechen; sprengen.
rural □ ['ruərəl] ländlich; Land...

ruse [ruːz] List *f*, Kniff *m*.

rush [rʌʃ] 1. ♀ Binse *f*; Jagen *n*, Hetzen *n*, Stürmen *n*; (An)Sturm *m*; Andrang *m*; ✝ stürmische Nachfrage; ∼ hour(s *pl*.) Hauptverkehrszeit *f*; 2. *v/i*. stürzen, jagen, hetzen, stürmen; ∼ at sich stürzen auf (*acc*.); ∼ into print *et*. überstürzt veröffentlichen; *v/t*. jagen, hetzen; drängen; ✕ *u*. *fig*. stürmen; *sl*. neppen.

russet [ˈrʌsit] braunrot; grob.

Russian [ˈrʌʃən] 1. russisch; 2. Russ|e *m*, -in *f*; Russisch *n*.

rust [rʌst] 1. Rost *m*; 2. (ver-, ein-) rosten (lassen) (*a*. *fig*.).

rustic [ˈrʌstik] 1. (∼ally) ländlich; bäurisch; Bauern...; 2. Bauer *m*.

rustle [ˈrʌsl] 1. rascheln (mit *od*. in *dat*.); rauschen; *Am*. F sich ranhalten; *Vieh* stehlen; 2. Rascheln *n*.

rust|less [ˈrʌstlis] rostfrei; ∼y [ˌti] rostig; eingerostet (*a*. *fig*.); verschossen (*Stoff*); rostfarben.

rut [rʌt] Wagenspur *f*; *bsd*. *fig*. ausgefahrenes Geleise; *hunt*. Brunst *f*, Brunft *f*.

ruthless □ [ˈruːθlis] unbarmherzig; rücksichts-, skrupellos.

rutted [ˈrʌtid] ausgefahren (*Weg*).

rutty [ˈrʌti] ausgefahren (*Weg*).

rye ♀ [rai] Roggen *m*.

S

sable [ˈseibl] Zobel(pelz) *m*; Schwarz *n*. [2. sabotieren.]

sabotage [ˈsæbətɑːʒ] 1. Sabotage *f*;

sabre [ˈseibə] Säbel *m*.

sack [sæk] 1. Plünderung *f*; Sack *m*; *Am*. Tüte *f*; Sackkleid *n*; Sakko *m*, *n*; give (get) the ∼ F entlassen (werden); den Laufpaß geben (bekommen); 2. plündern; einsacken; F rausschmeißen; *j-m* den Laufpaß geben; ∼cloth [ˈsæklɔθ], ∼ing [ˈsækiŋ] Sackleinwand *f*.

sacrament *eccl*. [ˈsækrəmənt] Sakrament *n*.

sacred □ [ˈseikrid] heilig; geistlich.

sacrifice [ˈsækrifais] 1. Opfer *n*; at a ∼ ✝ mit Verlust; 2. opfern; ✝ mit Verlust verkaufen.

sacrileg|e [ˈsækrilidʒ] Kirchenraub *m*, -schändung *f*; Sakrileg *n*; ∼ious □ [sækriˈlidʒəs] frevelhaft.

sad □ [sæd] traurig; jämmerlich, kläglich; schlimm, arg; dunkel.

sadden [ˈsædn] (sich) betrüben.

saddle [ˈsædl] 1. Sattel *m*; 2. satteln; *fig*. belasten; ∼r [ˌlə] Sattler *m*.

sadism [ˈsædizəm] Sadismus *m*.

sadness [ˈsædnis] Traurigkeit *f*, Trauer *f*, Schwermut *f*.

safe [seif] 1. □ *allg*. sicher; unversehrt; zuverlässig; 2. Safe *m*, *n*, Geldschrank *m*; Speiseschrank *m*; ∼blower *Am*. [ˈseifblouə] Geldschrankknacker *m*; ∼ conduct freies Geleit; Geleitbrief *m*; ∼ guard 1. Schutz *m*; 2. sichern, schützen.

safety [ˈseifti] Sicherheit *f*; ∼belt *mot*. Sicherheitsgurt *m*; ∼ island Verkehrsinsel *f*; ∼lock Sicherheitsschloß *n*; ∼pin Sicherheitsnadel *f*; ∼ razor Rasierapparat *m*.

saffron [ˈsæfrən] Safran(gelb *n*) *m*.

sag [sæg] durchsacken; ⊕ durchhängen; ⚓ (ab)sacken (*a*. *fig*.).

sagaci|ous □ [səˈgeiʃəs] scharfsinnig; ∼ty [səˈgæsiti] Scharfsinn *m*.

sage [seidʒ] 1. □ klug, weise; 2. Weise(r) *m*; ♀ Salbei *m*, *f*.

said [sed] *pret*. *u*. *p.p*. *von* say 1.

sail [seil] 1. Segel *n*; Fahrt *f*; Windmühlenflügel *m*; (Segel-) Schiff(e *pl*.) *n*; set ∼ in See stechen; 2. *v/i*. (ab)segeln, fahren; *fig*. schweben; *v/t*. befahren; *Schiff* führen; ∼boat *Am*. [ˈseilbout] Segelboot *n*; ∼er [ˈseilə] Segler *m* (*Schiff*); ∼ing-ship [ˈseiliŋʃip], ∼ ing-vessel [ˌvesl] Segelschiff *n*; ∼or [ˈseilə] Seemann *m*, Matrose *m*; be a good (bad) ∼ (nicht) seefest sein; ∼plane Segelflugzeug *n*.

saint [seint] 1. Heilige(r *m*) *f*; [*vor npr*. snt] Sankt...; 2. heiligsprechen; ∼ly [ˈseintli] *adj*. heilig, fromm.

saith † *od*. *poet*. [seθ] 3. *sg*. *pres*. *von* say 1.

sake [seik]: for the ∼ of um ... (*gen*.) willen; for my ∼ meinetwegen; for God's ∼ um Gottes willen.

salad [ˈsæləd] Salat *m*.

salary [ˈsæləri] 1. Besoldung *f*; Gehalt *n*; 2. besolden; ∼earner [ˌiːənə] Gehaltsempfänger(in).

sale [seil] (Aus)Verkauf *m*; Absatz *m*; Auktion *f*; for ∼, on ∼ zum Verkauf, zu verkaufen, verkäuflich.

sal(e)able [ˈseiləbl] verkäuflich.

sales|man [ˈseilzmən] Verkäufer *m*; ∼woman Verkäuferin *f*.

salient □ [ˈseiljənt] vorspringend; *fig*. hervorragend, hervortretend; Haupt...

saline [ˈseilain] salzig; Salz...

saliva [səˈlaivə] Speichel *m*.

sallow [ˈsælou] blaß; gelblich.

sally [ˈsæli] 1. ✕ Ausbruch *m*; witziger Einfall; 2. *a*. ∼ out ✕ ausbrechen; ∼ forth, ∼ out sich aufmachen.

salmon *ichth*. [ˈsæmən] Lachs *m*, Salm *m*.

saloon [sə'lu:n] Salon *m*; (Gesellschafts)Saal *m*; erste Klasse *auf Schiffen*; *Am.* Kneipe *f*.

salt [sɔ:lt] 1. Salz *n*; *fig.* Würze *f*; *old* ~ alter Seebär; 2. salzig; gesalzen; Salz...; Pökel...; 3. (ein)salzen; pökeln, ~**cellar** ['sɔ:ltselə] Salzfäßchen *n*; ~**petre**, *Am.* ~**peter** [Λtpi:tə] Salpeter *m*; ~**water** Salzwasser...; ~y [Λi] salzig.

salubrious □ [sə'lu:briəs], **salutary** □ ['sæljutəri] heilsam, gesund.

salut|ation [sælju(:)'teiʃən] Gruß *m*, Begrüßung *f*; Anrede *f*; ~e [sə'lu:t] 1. Gruß *m*; *co.* Kuß *m*; ✕ Salut *m*; 2. (be)grüßen; ✕ salutieren.

salvage ['sælvidʒ] 1. Bergung(sgut *n*) *f*; Bergegeld *n*; 2. bergen.

salvation [sæl'veiʃən] Erlösung *f*; (Seelen)Heil *n*; *fig.* Rettung *f*; ♀ Army Heilsarmee *f*.

salve[1] [sælv] retten, bergen.

salve[2] [sɑ:v] 1. Salbe *f*; *fig.* Balsam *m*; 2. *mst fig.* (ein)salben; beruhigen.

salvo ['sælvou] Vorbehalt *m*; ✕ Salve *f* (*fig. Beifall*).

same [seim]: *the* ~ der-, die-, dasselbe; *all the* ~ trotzdem; *it is all the* ~ *to me* es ist mir (ganz) gleich.

samp *Am.* [sæmp] grobgemahlener Mais.

sample ['sɑ:mpl] 1. Probe *f*, Muster *n*; 2. bemustern; (aus)probieren.

sanatorium [sænə'tɔ:riəm] (*bsd.* Lungen)Sanatorium *n*; Luftkurort *m*.

sanct|ify ['sæŋktifai] heiligen; weihen; ~**imonious** □ [sæŋkti'mounjəs] scheinheilig; ~**ion** ['sæŋkʃən] 1. Sanktion *f*; Bestätigung *f*; Genehmigung *f*; Zwangsmaßnahme *f*; 2. bestätigen, genehmigen; ~**ity** [Λktiti] Heiligkeit *f*; ~**uary** [Λtjuəri] Heiligtum *n*; *das* Allerheiligste; Asyl *n*, Freistätte *f*.

sand [sænd] 1. Sand *m*; ~s *pl.* Sand (-massen *f/pl.*) *m*; Sandwüste *f*; Sandbank *f*; 2. mit Sand bestreuen.

sandal ['sændl] Sandale *f*.

sand|-glass ['sændglɑ:s] Sanduhr*f*; ~**hill** Sanddüne *f*; ~**piper** *orn.* Flußuferläufer *m*.

sandwich ['sænwidʒ] 1. Sandwich *n*; 2. *a.* ~ *in* einlegen, einklemmen.

sandy ['sændi] sandig; sandfarben.

sane [sein] geistig gesund; vernünftig (*Antwort etc.*).

sang [sæŋ] *pret. von sing*.

sanguin|ary □ ['sæŋgwinəri] blutdürstig; blutig; ~**e** [Λwin] leichtblütig; zuversichtlich; vollblütig.

sanitarium *Am.* [sæni'tɛəriəm] = *sanatorium*.

sanitary □ ['sænitəri] Gesundheits...; gesundheitlich; ⊕ Sanitär...; ~ *towel* Damenbinde *f*.

sanit|ation [sæni'teiʃən] Gesundheitspflege *f*; sanitäre Einrichtung; ~**y** ['sæniti] gesunder Verstand.

sank [sæŋk] *pret. von sink* 1.

Santa Claus [sæntə'klɔ:z] Nikolaus *m*.

sap [sæp] 1. ♀ Saft *m*; *fig.* Lebenskraft *f*; ✕ Sappe *f*; 2. untergraben (*a. fig.*); *sl.* büffeln; ~**less** ['sæplis] saft-, kraftlos; ~**ling** [Λliŋ] junger Baum; *fig.* Grünschnabel *m*.

sapphire *min.* ['sæfaiə] Saphir *m*.

sappy ['sæpi] saftig; *fig.* kraftvoll.

sarcasm ['sɑ:kæzəm] bitterer Spott.

sardine *ichth.* [sɑ:'di:n] Sardine *f*.

sash [sæʃ] Schärpe *f*; Fensterrahmen *m*. [befenster *n.*]

sash-window ['sæʃwindou] Schie-]

sat [sæt] *pret. u. p.p. von sit*.

Satan ['seitən] Satan *m*.

satchel ['sætʃəl] Schulmappe *f*.

sate [seit] (über)sättigen.

sateen [sæ'ti:n] Satin *m*.

satellite ['sætəlait] Satellit(enstaat) *m*.

satiate ['seiʃieit] (über)sättigen.

satin ['sætin] Seidensatin *m*.

satir|e ['sætaiə] Satire *f*; ~**ist** ['sætərist] Satiriker *m*; ~**ize** [Λraiz] verspotten.

satisfaction [sætis'fækʃən] Befriedigung *f*; Genugtuung *f*; Zufriedenheit *f*; Sühne *f*; Gewißheit *f*.

satisfactory □ [sætis'fæktəri] befriedigend, zufriedenstellend.

satisfy ['sætisfai] befriedigen; genügen (*dat.*); zufriedenstellen; überzeugen; *Zweifel* beheben.

saturate /Λ *u. fig.* ['sætʃəreit] sättigen.

Saturday ['sætədi] Sonnabend *m*, Samstag *m*.

saturnine ['sætə:nain] düster, finster.

sauce [sɔ:s] 1. (*oft kalte*) Soße; *Am.* Kompott *n*; *fig.* Würze *f*; F Frechheit *f*; 2. würzen; F frech werden zu *j-m*; ~**boat** ['sɔ:sbout] Soßenschüssel *f*; ~**pan** Kochtopf *m*; Kasserolle *f*; ~**r** [sɔ:sə] Untertasse *f*.

saucy □ F ['sɔ:si] frech; dreist.

saunter ['sɔ:ntə] 1. Schlendern *n*; Bummel *m*; 2. (umher)schlendern; bummeln.

sausage ['sɔsidʒ] Wurst *f*.

savage ['sævidʒ] 1. □ wild; roh, grausam; 2. Wilde(r *m*) *f*; *fig.* Barbar *m*; ~**ry** [Λdʒəri] Wildheit *f*; Barbarei *f*.

savant ['sævənt] Gelehrte(r) *m*.

save [seiv] 1. retten; erlösen; bewahren; (er)sparen; schonen; 2. *rhet. prp. u. cj.* außer; ~ *for* bis auf (*acc.*); ~ *that* nur daß.

saver ['seivə] Retter(in); Sparer(in).

saving ['seiviŋ] 1. □ sparsam; 2. Rettung *f*; ~s *pl.* Ersparnisse*f/pl.*

savings|-bank ['seiviŋzbæŋk] Sparkasse *f*; ~**deposit** Spareinlage *f*.

savio(u)r ['seivjə] Retter m; *Saviour eccl.* Heiland m.

savo(u)r ['seivə] 1. Geschmack m; *fig.* Beigeschmack m; 2. *fig.* schmecken, riechen (*of* nach).

savo(u)ry¹ □ ['seivəri] schmackhaft; appetitlich; pikant.

savo(u)ry² ♀ [‿] Bohnenkraut n.

saw¹ [sɔː] *pret. von* see.

saw² [‿] Spruch m.

saw³ [‿] 1. [*irr.*] sägen; 2. Säge f; **‿dust** ['sɔːdʌst] Sägespäne m/pl.; **‿mill** Sägewerk n; **‿n** [sɔːn] *p.p. von* saw³ 1.

Saxon ['sæksn] 1. sächsisch; *ling. oft* germanisch; 2. Sachse m, Sächsin f.

say [sei] 1. [*irr.*] sagen; hersagen; berichten; ‿ grace das Tischgebet sprechen; *that is to* ‿ das heißt; *you don't* ‿ *so!* was Sie nicht sagen!; *I* ‿ sag(en Sie) mal; ich muß schon sagen; *he is said to be ... of* soll ... sein; *no sooner said than done* gesagt, getan; 2. Rede f, Wort n; *it is my* ‿ now jetzt ist die Reihe zu reden an mir; *have a od. some* (*no*) ‿ *in s.th. et.* (nichts) zu sagen haben bei et.; **‿ing** ['seiiŋ] Rede f; Redensart f; Ausspruch m; *it goes without* ‿ es versteht sich von selbst.

scab [skæb] ⚚, ♀ Schorf m; *vet.* Räude f; *sl.* Streikbrecher m.

scabbard ['skæbəd] *Säbel*-Scheidef.

scabrous ['skeibrəs] heikel.

scaffold ['skæfəld] (Bau)Gerüst n; Schafott n; **‿ing** [‿diŋ] (Bau)Gerüst n.

scald [skɔːld] 1. Verbrühung f; 2. verbrühen; *Milch* abkochen.

scale¹ [skeil] 1. Schuppe f; Kesselstein m; ⚚ Zahnstein m; Waagschale f; (*a pair of*) ‿*s pl.* (eine) Waage f; 2. (sich) abschuppen, ablösen; ⊕ *Kesselstein* abklopfen; ⚚ *Zähne* vom Zahnstein reinigen; wiegen.

scale² [‿] 1. Stufenleiter f; ♪ Tonleiter f; Skala f; Maßstab m; *fig.* Ausmaß n; 2. ersteigen; ‿ *up* (*down*) maßstabsgetreu vergrößern (verkleinern).

scallop ['skɔləp] 1. *zo.* Kammuschel f; ⊕ Langette f; 2. ausbogen.

scalp [skælp] 1. Kopfhaut f; Skalp m; 2. skalpieren.

scaly ['skeili] schuppig; voll Kesselstein.

scamp [skæmp] 1. Taugenichts m; 2. pfuschen; **‿er** ['skæmpə] 1. (umher)tollen; hetzen; 2.*fig.* Hetzjagdf.

scan [skæn] *Verse* skandieren; absuchen; *fig.* überfliegen.

scandal ['skændl] Skandal m; Ärgernis n; Schande f; Klatsch m; Klippe [‿dəlaiz] Anstoß erregen bei *j-m*; **‿ous** □ [‿ləs] skandalös, anstößig; schimpflich; klatschhaft.

Scandinavian [skændi'neivjən]
1. skandinavisch; 2. Skandinavier (-in).

scant *lit.* [skænt] 1. knapp, kärglich; 2. knausern mit, sparen an (*dat.*); **‿y** □ ['skænti] knapp, spärlich, kärglich, dürftig.

scape|goat ['skeipgout] Sündenbock m; **‿grace** [‿greis] Taugenichts m.

scar [skaː] 1. Narbe f; *fig.* (Schand-) Fleck m, Makel m; Klippe f; 2. *v/t.* schrammen; *v/i.* vernarben.

scarc|e [skɛəs] knapp; rar; selten; **‿ely** ['skɛəsli] kaum; **‿ity** [‿siti] Mangel m; Knappheit f; Teuerung f.

scare [skɛə] 1. er-, aufschrecken; verscheuchen; **‿d** verstört; ängstlich; 2. Panik f; **‿crow** ['skɛəkrou] Vogelscheuche f (*a. fig.*); **‿head** (**-ing**) Riesenschlagzeile f.

scarf [skaːf] *pl.* **‿s**, **scarves** [‿fs, skaːvz] Schal m; Hals-, Kopftuch n; Krawatte f; ✂ Schärpe f.

scarlet ['skaːlit] 1. Scharlach(rot n) m; 2. scharlachrot; **‿** *fever* ⚚ Scharlach m; **‿** *runner* ♀ Feuerbohne f.

scarred [skaːd] narbig.

scarves [skaːvz] *pl. von* scarf.

scathing *fig.* ['skeiðiŋ] vernichtend.

scatter ['skætə] (sich) zerstreuen; aus-, verstreuen; (sich) verbreiten.

scavenger ['skævindʒə] Straßenkehrer m.

scenario [si'naːriou] *Film:* Drehbuch n.

scene [siːn] Szene f; Bühne(nbild n) f; Schauplatz m; **‿s** *pl.* Kulissen f/pl.; **‿ry** ['siːnəri] Szenerie f; Bühnenausstattung f; Landschaftf.

scent [sent] 1. (Wohl)Geruch m; Duft m; Parfüm n; *hunt.* Witterung(svermögen n) f; Fährte f; 2. wittern; parfümieren; **‿less** ['sentlis] geruchlos.

sceptic ['skeptik] Skeptiker(in); **‿al** □ [‿kəl] skeptisch.

scept|re, *Am.* **‿er** ['septə] Zepter n.

schedule ['ʃedjuːl, *Am.* 'skedjuːl] 1. Verzeichnis n; Tabelle f; *Am.* Fahrplan m; *on* ‿ fahrplanmäßig; 2. auf-, verzeichnen; festsetzen.

scheme [skiːm] 1. Schema n; Zs.-stellung f; Plan m; 2. *v/t.* planen; *v/i.* Pläne machen; Ränke schmieden.

schism ['sizəm] (Kirchen)Spaltung f.

scholar ['skɔlə] Gelehrte(r) m; *univ.* Stipendiat m; † Schüler(in); **‿ly** *adj.* [‿əli] gelehrt; **‿ship** [‿ʃip] Gelehrsamkeit f; Wissenschaftlichkeit f; *univ.* Stipendium n.

scholastic [skɔ'læstik] 1. (‿ally) *phls.* scholastisch; schulmäßig; Schul...; 2. *phls.* Scholastiker m.

school [skuːl] 1. Schwarm m; Schule f (*a. fig.*); *univ.* Fakultät f;

Disziplin f; Hochschule f; at ~ auf od. in der Schule; 2. schulen, erziehen; ~boy ['sku:lbɔi] Schüler m; ~fellow Mitschüler(in); ~girl Schülerin f; ~ing [~liŋ] (Schul-)Ausbildung f; ~master Lehrer m (bsd. e-r höheren Schule); ~mate Mitschüler(in); ~mistress Lehrerin f (bsd. e-r höheren Schule); ~teacher (bsd. Volksschul)Lehrer (-in).

schooner ['sku:nə] ⚓ Schoner m; Am. großes Bierglas; = prairieschooner.

science ['saiəns] Wissenschaft f; Naturwissenschaft(en pl.) f; Technik f.

scientific [saiən'tifik] (~ally) (engS. natur)wissenschaftlich; kunstgerecht.

scientist ['saiəntist] (bsd. Natur-) Wissenschaftler m.

scintillate ['sintileit] funkeln.

scion ['saiən] Sproß m, Sprößling m.

scissors ['sizəz] pl. (a pair of ~ pl. eine) Schere.

scoff [skɔf] 1. Spott m; 2. spotten.

scold [skould] 1. zänkisches Weib; 2. (aus)schelten, schimpfen.

scon(e) [skɔn] weiches Teegebäck.

scoop [sku:p] 1. Schaufel f, Schippe f; Schöpfeimer m, -kelle f; F Coup m, gutes Geschäft; F Exklusivmeldung f; 2. (aus)schaufeln; einscheffeln.

scooter ['sku:tə] (Kinder)Roller m; Motorroller m.

scope [skoup] Bereich m; geistiger Gesichtskreis; Spielraum m.

scorch [skɔːtʃ] v/t. versengen, verbrennen; v/i. F (dahin)rasen.

score [skɔː] 1. Kerbe f, Zeche f, Rechnung f; 20 Stück; Sport: Punktzahl f; (Tor)Stand m; Grund m; ♪ Partitur f; ~s of viele; four ~ achtzig; run up ~s Schulden machen; on the ~ of wegen (gen.); 2. (ein)kerben; anschreiben; Sport: (Punkte) machen; Fußball: ein Tor schießen; gewinnen; instrumentieren; Am. F scharfe Kritik üben an (dat.).

scorn [skɔːn] 1. Verachtung f; Spott m; 2. verachten; verschmähen; ~ful □ ['skɔːnful] verächtlich.

Scotch [skɔtʃ] 1.schottisch; 2.Schottisch n; the ~ die Schotten pl.; ~man ['skɔtʃmən] Schotte m.

scot-free ['skɔt'friː] straflos.

Scots [skɔts], ~man ['skɔtsmən] = Scotch(man).

scoundrel ['skaundrəl] Schurke m.

scour ['skauə] v/t. scheuern; reinigen; durchstreifen, absuchen; v/i. eilen.

scourge [skəːdʒ] 1. Geißel f; 2. geißeln.

scout [skaut] 1. Späher m, Kundschafter m; ⚓ Aufklärungsfahrzeug

n; ✈ Aufklärer m; mot. Mitglied n der Straßenwacht; (Boy) ♀ Pfadfinder m; ~ party ⚔ Spähtrupp m; 2. (aus)kundschaften, spähen; verächtlich zurückweisen.

scowl [skaul] 1. finsteres Gesicht; 2. finster blicken.

scrabble ['skræbl] (be)kritzeln; scharren; krabbeln.

scrag fig. [skræg] Gerippe n (dürrer Mensch etc.).

scramble ['skræmbl] 1. klettern; sich balgen (for um); ~d eggs pl. Rührei n; 2. Kletterei f; Balgerei f.

scrap [skræp] 1. Stückchen n; (Zeitungs)Ausschnitt m, Bild n zum Einkleben; Altmaterial n; Schrott m; ~s pl. Reste m/pl.; 2. ausrangieren; verschrotten; ~book ['skræpbuk] Sammelalbum n.

scrap|e [skreip] 1. Kratzen n, Scharren n; Kratzfuß m; Not f, Klemme f; 2. schrap(p)en; (ab-)schaben; (ab)kratzen; scharren; (entlang)streifen; ~er ['skreipə] Kratzeisen n.

scrap|-heap ['skræphiːp] Abfall-, Schrotthaufen m; ~iron Alteisen n, Schrott m.

scratch [skrætʃ] 1. Schramme f; Sport: Startlinie f; 2. zs.-gewürfelt; Zufalls...; Sport: ohne Vorgabe; 3. (zer)kratzen; (zer)schrammen; parl. u. Sport: streichen; ~ out ausstreichen.

scrawl [skrɔːl] 1. kritzeln; 2. Gekritzel n.

scrawny Am. F ['skrɔːni] dürr.

scream [skriːm] 1. Schrei m; Gekreisch n; he is a ~ F er ist zum Schreien komisch; 2. schreien, kreischen.

screech [skriːtʃ] s. scream; ~owl orn. ['skriːtʃaul] Käuzchen n.

screen [skriːn] 1. Wand-, Ofen-, Schutzschirm m; fig. Schleier m; (Film)Leinwand f; der Film; Sandsieb n; (Fliegen)Gitter n; 2. (ab-)schirmen; (be)schützen; ⚔ tarnen; auf der Leinwand zeigen; verfilmen; (durch)sieben; ~ play Drehbuch n; Fernsehfilm m.

screw [skruː] 1. Schraube f; ⚓ Propeller m; 2. (fest)schrauben; fig. bedrängen; ver-, umdrehen; ~ up festschrauben; ~ up one's courage Mut fassen; ~ball Am. sl. ['skruːbɔːl] komischer Kauz; ~driver Schraubenzieher m; ~jack Wagenheber m; ~propeller Schiffs-, Flugzeugschraube f.

scribble ['skribl] 1. Gekritzel n; 2. kritzeln. [skimp etc.\

scrimp [skrimp], ~y ['skrimpi] =

scrip ♱ [skrip] Interimsschein(e pl.) m.

script [skript] Schrift f; Schreibschrift f; Manuskript n; Film: Drehbuch n.

Scripture ['skriptʃə] *mst the Holy* ~s *pl.* die Heilige Schrift.

scroll [skroul] Schriftrolle *f*, Liste*f*; ⚠ Schnecke *f*; Schnörkel *m*.

scrub [skrʌb] **1.** Gestrüpp *n*; Zwerg *m*; *Am. Sport:* zweite (Spieler-) Garnitur; **2.** schrubben, scheuern.

scrubby ['skrʌbi] struppig; schäbig.

scrup|le ['skru:pl] **1.** Skrupel *m*, Zweifel *m*, Bedenken *n*; **2.** Bedenken haben; ~ulous □ [~pjuləs] (allzu) bedenklich; gewissenhaft; ängstlich.

scrutin|ize ['skru:tinaiz] (genau) prüfen; ~y [~ni] forschender Blick; genaue (*bsd.* Wahl)Prüfung.

scud [skʌd] **1.** (Dahin)Jagen *n*; (dahintreibende) Wolkenfetzen *m/pl.*; Bö *f*; **2.** eilen, jagen; gleiten.

scuff [skʌf] schlurfen, schlorren.

scuffle ['skʌfl] **1.** Balgerei *f*, Rauferei *f*; **2.** sich balgen, raufen.

scull ⚓ [skʌl] **1.** kurzes Ruder; **2.** rudern, skullen.

scullery ['skʌləri] Spülküche *f*.

sculptor ['skʌlptə] Bildhauer *m*.

sculpture ['skʌlptʃə] **1.** Plastik *f*; Bildhauerkunst *f*, Skulptur *f*; **2.** (heraus)meißeln, formen.

scum *fig.* [skʌm] (Ab)Schaum *m*.

scurf [skə:f] (Haut)Schuppen *f/pl.*

scurrilous ['skʌriləs] gemein.

scurry ['skʌri] hasten, rennen.

scurvy[1] 🌿 ['skə:vi] Skorbut *m*.

scurvy[2] 🌿 (hunds)gemein.

scuttle ['skʌtl] **1.** Kohlenbehälter *m*; **2.** eilen; *fig.* sich drücken.

scythe 🌾 [saið] Sense *f*.

sea [si:] See *f*, Meer *n* (*a. fig.*); hohe Welle; *at* ~ auf See; *fig.* ratlos; ~**board** ['si:bɔ:d] Küste(ngebiet *n*) *f*; ~**coast** Küste *f*; ~**faring** ['si:fɛəriŋ] seefahrend; ~**food** eßbare Seefische *m/pl.*; Meeresfrüchte *pl.*; ~**going** Hochsee...; ~**gull** (See)Möwe *f*.

seal [si:l] **1.** *zo.* Seehund *m*, Robbe *f*; Siegel *n*; Stempel *m*; Bestätigung *f*; **2.** versiegeln; *fig.* besiegeln; ~ *up* (fest) verschließen; ⊕ abdichten.

sea-level ['si:levl] Meeresspiegel *m*.

sealing-wax ['si:liŋwæks] Siegellack *m*.

seam [si:m] **1.** Saum *m*; (*a.* ⊕) Naht *f*; ⊕ Fuge *f*; *geol.* Flöz *n*; Narbe *f*; **2.** schrammen; furchen.

seaman ['si:mən] Seemann *m*, Matrose *m*.

seamstress ['semstris] Näherin *f*.

sea|-plane ['si:plein] Wasserflugzeug *n*; ~**power** Seemacht *f*.

sear [siə] **1.** dürr, welk; **2.** austrocknen, versengen; 🌿 brennen; *fig.* verhärten.

search [sə:tʃ] **1.** Suchen *n*, Forschen *n*; Unter-, Durchsuchung *f*; *in* ~ *of* auf der Suche nach; **2.** *v/t.* durch-, untersuchen; ~ sondieren; erfor-

schen; durchdringen; *v/i.* suchen, forschen (*for* nach); ~ *into* ergründen; ~**ing** □ ['sə:tʃiŋ] forschend, prüfend; eingehend (*Prüfung etc.*); ~**-light** (Such)Scheinwerfer *m*; ~**-warrant** 🏛 Haussuchungsbefehl *m*.

sea|-shore ['si:'ʃɔ:] Seeküste *f*; ~**sick** seekrank; ~**side** Strand *m*, Küste *f*; ~ *place*, ~ *resort* Seebad *n*; *go to the* ~ an die See gehen.

season ['si:zn] **1.** Jahreszeit *f*; (rechte) Zeit; Saison *f*; F *für* ~*-ticket; cherries are in* ~ jetzt ist Kirschenzeit; *out of* ~ zur Unzeit; *with the compliments of the* ~ mit den besten Wünschen zum Fest; **2.** *v/t.* reifen (lassen); würzen; abhärten (*to gegen*); *v/i.* ablagern; ~**able** □ [~nəbl] zeitgemäß; rechtzeitig; ~**al** □ [~'si:zənl] Saison...; periodisch; ~**ing** ['si:zniŋ] Würze *f*; ~**-ticket** 🚃 Zeitkarte *f*; *thea.* Abonnement *n*.

seat [si:t] **1.** Sitz *m* (*a. fig.*); Sessel *m*, Stuhl *m*, Bank *f*; (Sitz)Platz *m*; Landsitz *m*; Gesäß *n*; Schauplatz *m*; **2.** (hin)setzen; e-n Hosenboden einsetzen in (*acc.*); fassen, Sitzplätze haben für; ~**ed** sitzend; ...sitzig; be ~ed sitzen; sich setzen; ~**-belt** 🚗 ['si:tbelt] Sicherheitsgurt *m*.

sea|-urchin *zo.* ['si:'ə:tʃin] Seeigel *m*; ~**ward** ['si:wəd] **1.** *adj.* seewärts gerichtet; **2.** *adv. a.* ~s seewärts; ~**weed** 🌿 (See)Tang *m*; ~**worthy** seetüchtig.

secede [si'si:d] sich trennen.

secession [si'seʃən] Lossagung *f*; Abfall *m*; ~**ist** [~ʃnist] Abtrünnige(r *m*) *f*.

seclu|de [si'klu:d] abschließen, absondern; ~**ded** einsam; zurückgezogen; abgelegen; ~**sion** [~u:ʒən] Abgeschlossen-, Abgeschiedenheit *f*.

second ['sekənd] **1.** □ zweite(r, -s); nächste(r, -s); geringer (*to als*); *on* ~ *thoughts* bei genauerer Überlegung; **2.** Zweite(r, -s); Sekundant *m*; Beistand *m*; Sekunde *f*; ~s *pl.* Waren *pl.* zweiter Wahl; **3.** sekundieren (*dat.*); unterstützen; ~**ary** □ [~dəri] sekundär; untergeordnet; Neben...; Hilfs...; Sekundär...; ~**ary school** höhere Schule; weiterführende Schule; ~**-hand** aus zweiter Hand; gebraucht; antiquarisch; ~**ly** [~dli] zweitens; ~**-rate** zweiten Ranges; zweitklassig.

secre|cy ['si:krisi] Heimlichkeit *f*; Verschwiegenheit *f*; ~**t** [~it] **1.** □ geheim; Geheim...; verschwiegen; verborgen; **2.** Geheimnis *n*; *in* ~ insgeheim; *be in the* ~ eingeweiht sein; *be taken into the* ~ eingeweiht sein.

secretary ['sekrətri] Schriftführer *m*; Sekretär(in); ♀ *of State* Staats-

secretär m, Minister m; Am. Außen-
minister m.

secret|e [si'kri:t] verbergen; ab-
sondern; ~ion [~i:ʃən] Absonde-
rung f; ~ive [~i:tiv] fig. verschlossen; geheimtuerisch.

section ['sekʃən] ⚓ Sektion f;
(Durch)Schnitt m; Teil m; Abschnitt m, Paragraph m; typ. Absatz m; Abteilung f; Gruppe f.

secular □ ['sekjulə] weltlich.

secur|e [si'kjuə] 1. □ sicher; 2. (sich
et.) sichern; schützen; festmachen;
~ity [~əriti] Sicherheit f; Sorglosigkeit f; Gewißheit f; Schutz m;
Kaution f; securities pl. Wert-
papiere n/pl.

sedan [si'dæn] Limousine f; a.
~-chair Sänfte f.

sedate □ [si'deit] gesetzt; ruhig.

sedative mst ⚕ ['sedətiv] 1. beruhi-
gend; 2. Beruhigungsmittel n.

sedentary □ ['sedntəri] sitzend;
seßhaft.

sediment ['sedimənt] (Boden)Satz
m; geol. Ablagerung f.

sediti|on [si'diʃən] Aufruhr m; ~ous
□ [~ʃəs] aufrührerisch.

seduc|e [si'dju:s] verführen; ~tion
[si'dʌkʃən] Verführung f; ~tive □
[~ktiv] verführerisch.

sedulous □ ['sedjuləs] emsig.

see[1] [si:] [irr.] v/i. sehen; fig. einsehen; I ~ ich verstehe; ~ about
s.th. sich um et. kümmern; ~ through
s.o. od. s.th. j-n od. et. durch-
schauen; ~ to achten auf (acc.); v/t.
sehen; beobachten; einsehen; sorgen (daß et. geschieht); besuchen;
Arzt aufsuchen; ~ s.o. home j-n nach
Hause begleiten; ~ off Besuch etc.
wegbringen; ~ out Besuch hinaus-
begleiten; et. zu Ende erleben; ~
s.th. through et. durchhalten; ~ s.o.
through j-m durchhelfen; live to ~
erleben.

see[2] [~] (erz)bischöflicher Stuhl.

seed [si:d] 1. Same(n) m, Saat(gut n)
f; (Obst)Kern m; Keim m (a. fig.);
go od. run to ~ in Samen schießen;
fig. herunterkommen; 2. v/t. (be-)
säen; entkernen; v/i. in Samen
schießen; ~less ['si:dlis] kernlos
(Obst); ~ling ⚘ [~lin] Sämling m;
~y ['si:di] schäbig; F elend.

seek [si:k] [irr.] suchen (nach) begehren; trachten nach.

seem [si:m] (er)scheinen; ~ing □
['si:min] anscheinend; scheinbar;
~ly ['si:mli] schicklich.

seen [si:n] p.p. von see[1].

seep [si:p] durchsickern, tropfen.

seer ['si:(:)ə] Seher(in), Prophet(in).

seesaw ['si:sɔ:] 1. Wippen n; Wippe
f, Wippschaukel f; 2. wippen; fig.
schwanken.

seethe [si:ð] sieden, kochen.

segment ['segmənt] Abschnitt m.

segregat|e ['segrigeit] absondern,

33 SW E

trennen; ~ion [segri'geiʃən] Ab-
sonderung f; Rassentrennung f.

seiz|e [si:z] ergreifen, fassen; mit
Beschlag belegen; fig. erfassen; a.
~ upon sich e-r S. od. j-s bemächti-
gen; ~ure ['si:ʒə] Ergreifung f; 🕇🕇
Beschlagnahme f; ⚕ plötzlicher
Anfall.

seldom adv. ['seldəm] selten.

select [si'lekt] 1. auswählen, aus-
lesen, aussuchen; 2. auserwählt;
erlesen; exklusiv; ~ion [~kʃən]
Auswahl f, Auslese f; ~man Am.
Stadtrat m in den Neuenglandstaa-
ten.

self [self] 1. pl. selves [selvz] Selbst
n, Ich n; Persönlichkeit f; 2. pron.
selbst; ❡ od. F = myself etc.; 3. adj.
❡ einfarbig; ~-centered ['self-
'sentəd] egozentrisch; ~-command
Selbstbeherrschung f; ~-conceit
Eigendünkel m; ~-conceited dün-
kelhaft; ~-confidence Selbstver-
trauen n; ~-conscious befangen,
gehemmt; ~-contained (in sich)
abgeschlossen; fig. verschlossen;
~-control Selbstbeherrschung f;
~-defence, Am. ~-defense Selbst-
verteidigung f; in ~ in (der) Not-
wehr; ~-denial Selbstverleugnung
f; ~-employed selbständig (Handwerker etc.); ~-evident selbstverständlich; ~-government Selbst-
verwaltung f, Autonomie f; ~-in-
dulgent bequem; zügellos; ~-in-
terest Eigennutz m; ~-ish □ [~fiʃ]
selbstsüchtig; ~-possession Selbstbeherrschung f; ~-reliant [~'fri-
'laiant] selbstsicher; ~-righteous
selbstgerecht; ~-seeking [~f'si:kiŋ]
eigennützig; ~-willed eigenwillig.

sell [sel] [irr.] v/t. verkaufen (a. fig.);
Am. aufschwatzen; v/i. handeln,
gehen (Ware); ~ off, ~ out 🕇 ausver-
kaufen; ~er ['selə] Verkäufer m;
good etc. ~ 🕇 gut etc. gehende Ware.

selves [selvz] pl. von self 1.

semblance ['sembləns] Anschein
m; Gestalt f.

semi|... ['semi] halb...; Halb...;
~colon Strichpunkt m; ~-detached
house Doppelhaus(hälfte f) n;
~-final Sport: Vorschlußrunde f.

seminary ['seminəri] (Priester)Se-
minar m; fig. Schule f.

sempstress ['sempstris] Näherin f.

senate ['senit] Senat m.

senator ['senətə] Senator m.

send [send] [irr.] senden, schicken;
(mit adj. od. p.pr.) machen; ~ for
kommen lassen, holen (lassen); ~
forth aussenden; veröffentlichen;
~ in einsenden; einreichen; ~ up in
die Höhe treiben; ~ word mitteilen.

senil|e ['si:nail] greisenhaft, senil;
~ity [si'niliti] Greisenalter n.

senior ['si:njə] 1. älter; dienstälter;
Ober...; ~ partner 🕇 Chef m;
2. Ältere(r) m; Dienstältere(r) m;

Senior *m*; *he is my* ~ *by a year* er ist ein Jahr älter als ich; ~ity [si:ni-'oriti] höheres Alter *od.* Dienstalter.

sensation [sen'seiʃən] (Sinnes-) Empfindung *f*, Gefühl *n*; Eindruck *m*; Sensation *f*; ~al □ [~nl] Empfindungs...; sensationell.

sense [sens] 1. *allg.* Sinn *m* (*of* für); Empfindung *f*, Gefühl *n*; Verstand *m*; Bedeutung *f*; Ansicht *f*; *in* (*out of*) *one's* ~ bei (von) Sinnen; *bring s.o. to his* ~*s* j-n zur Vernunft bringen; *make* ~ Sinn haben (*S.*); *talk* ~ vernünftig reden; 2. spüren.

senseless □ ['senslis] sinnlos; bewußtlos; gefühllos; ~ness [~snis] Sinnlosigkeit *f*; Bewußt-, Gefühllosigkeit *f*.

sensibility [sensi'biliti] Sensibilität *f*, Empfindungsvermögen *n*; Empfindlichkeit *f*; sensibilities *pl.* Empfindsamkeit *f*, Zartgefühl *n*.

sensible □ ['sensəbl] verständig, vernünftig; empfänglich (*of* für); fühlbar; *be* ~ *of* sich e-r *S.* bewußt sein; *et.* empfinden.

sensitiv|e □ ['sensitiv] empfindlich (*to* für); Empfindungs...; feinfühlig; ~eness [~vnis], ~ity [sensi-'tiviti] Empfindlichkeit *f* (*to* für).

sensual □ ['sensjuəl] sinnlich.

sensuous □ ['sensjuəs] sinnlich; Sinnes...; sinnenfreudig.

sent [sent] *pret. u. p.p. von* send.

sentence ['sentəns] 1. ᵹᵗₛ Urteil *n*; *gr.* Satz *m*; *serve one's* ~ s-e Strafe absitzen; 2. verurteilen.

sententious □ [sen'tenʃəs] sentenziös; salbungsvoll; salbaderisch.

sentient ['senʃənt] empfindend.

sentiment ['sentimənt] (seelische) Empfindung, Gefühl *n*; Meinung *f*; *s. sentimentality*; ~al □ [senti'mentl] empfindsam; sentimental; ~ality [sentimen'tæliti] Sentimentalität *f*.

sent|inel ['sentinl], ~ry ⨯ [~tri] Schildwache *f*, Posten *m*.

separa|ble □ ['sepərəbl] trennbar; ~te 1. □ ['seprit] (ab)getrennt, gesondert, besonder, separat, für sich; 2. ['sepəreit] (sich) trennen; (sich) absondern; (sich) scheiden; ~tion [sepə'reiʃən] Trennung *f*, Scheidung *f*.

sepsis ⸎ ['sepsis] Sepsis *f*, Blutvergiftung *f*. [*m.*]

September [səp'tembə] September!

septic ⸎ ['septik] septisch.

sepul|chral [si'pʌlkrəl] Grab...; Toten...; *fig.* düster; ~chre, *Am.* ~cher [~] Grab(stätte *f*) *n*; ~ture [~ltʃə] Begräbnis *n*.

sequel ['si:kwəl] Folge *f*; Nachspiel *n*; (Roman)Fortsetzung *f*.

sequen|ce ['si:kwəns] Aufeinander-, Reihenfolge *f*; *Film:* Szene *f*; ~ *of tenses gr.* Zeitenfolge *f*; ~t [~nt] aufeinanderfolgend.

sequestrate ᵹᵗₛ [si'kwestreit] *Eigentum* einziehen; beschlagnahmen.

serenade [seri'neid] 1. ♩ Serenade *f*, Ständchen *n*; 2. *j-m* ein Ständchen bringen.

seren|e □ [si'ri:n] klar, heiter; ruhig; ~ity [si'reniti] Heiterkeit *f*; Ruhe *f*.

serf [sə:f] Leibeigene(r *m*) *f*, Hörige(r *m*) *f*; *fig.* Sklave *m*.

sergeant ['sɑ:dʒənt] ⨯ Feldwebel *m*, Wachtmeister *m*; (Polizei)Wachtmeister *m*.

serial □ ['siəriəl] 1. fortlaufend, reihenweise, Serien...; Fortsetzungs...; 2. Fortsetzungsroman *m*.

series ['siəri:z] *sg. u. pl.* Reihe *f*; Serie *f*; Folge *f*; *biol.* Gruppe *f*.

serious □ ['siəriəs] *allg.* ernst; ernsthaft, ernstlich; *be* ~ *es* im Ernst meinen; ~ness [~snis] Ernst (-haftigkeit *f*) *m*.

sermon ['sə:mən] (*iro.* Straf)Predigt *f*.

serpent ['sə:pənt] Schlange *f*; ~ine [~tain] schlangengleich, -förmig; Serpentinen...

serum ['siərəm] Serum *n*.

servant ['sə:vənt] Diener(in); *a.* domestic ~ Dienstbote *m*, Bedienstete(r *m*) *f*; Dienstmädchen *n*.

serve [sə:v] 1. *v/t.* dienen (*dat.*); *Zeit* abdienen; bedienen; *Speisen* reichen; *Speisen* auftragen; behandeln; nützen, dienlich sein (*dat.*); *Zweck* erfüllen; *Tennis:* angeben; (*it*) ~*s him right* (das) geschieht ihm recht; *s. sentence*; ~ *out et.* austeilen; *v/i.* dienen (*a.* ⨯; *as, for* als, zu); bedienen; nützen, zweckmäßig sein; ~ *at table* servieren; 2. *Tennis:* Aufschlag *m*.

service ['sə:vis] 1. Dienst *m*; Bedienung *f*; Gefälligkeit *f*; *a. divine* ~ Gottesdienst *m*; Betrieb *m*; Verkehr *m*; Nutzen *m*; Gang *m von Speisen*; Service *n*; ᵹᵗₛ Zustellung *f*; *Tennis:* Aufschlag *m*; *be at s.o.'s* ~ j-m zu Diensten stehen; 2. ⊕ warten, pflegen; ~able □ [~əbl] dienlich, nützlich; benutzbar; strapazierfähig; ~ station Tankstelle *f*; Werkstatt *f*.

servil|e □ ['sə:vail] sklavisch (*a. fig.*); unterwürfig; kriecherisch; ~ity [sə:'viliti] Unterwürfigkeit *f*, Kriecherei *f*.

serving ['sə:vin] Portion *f*.

servitude ['sə:vitju:d] Knechtschaft *f*; Sklaverei *f*.

session ['seʃən] (*a.* Gerichts)Sitzung *f*; *be in* ~ tagen.

set [set] 1. (*irr.*) *v/t.* setzen; stellen; legen; zurechtstellen, (ein)richten, ordnen; *Aufgabe, Wecker* stellen; *Messer* abziehen; *Edelstein* fassen; festsetzen; erstarren lassen; *Haar* legen; ⸎ *Knochenbruch* einrichten; ~ *s.o. laughing* j-n zum Lachen bringen; ~ an example ein Beispiel geben; ~ sail Segel setzen; ~ one's teeth die Zähne zs.-beißen; ~ aside beiseite stellen od. legen; fig. verwerfen; ~ at ease beruhigen; ~ at rest beruhigen; Frage entscheiden; ~ store by Wert legen auf (acc.); ~ forth darlegen; ~ off hervorheben; anrechnen; ~ up auf-, er-, einrichten; aufstellen; j-n etablieren; v/i. ast. untergehen; gerinnen, fest werden; laufen (Flut etc.); sitzen (Kleid etc.); ~ about s.th. sich an et. machen; ~ about s.o. F über j-n herfallen; ~ forth aufbrechen; ~ off aufbrechen; ~ (up)on anfangen; angreifen; ~ out aufbrechen; ~ to sich daran machen; ~ up sich niederlassen; ~ up for sich aufspielen als; 2. fest; starr; festgesetzt, bestimmt; vorgeschrieben; ~ (up)on versessen auf (acc.); ~ with besetzt mit; Barometer: ~ fair beständig; hard ~ in großer Not; ~ speech wohlüberlegte Rede; 3. Reihe f, Folge f, Serie f, Sammlung f, Satz m; Garnitur f; Service n; Radio-Gerät n; ✝ Kollektion f; Gesellschaft f; Sippschaft f; ✶ Setzling m; Tennis: Satz m; Neigung f; Richtung f; Sitz m e-s Kleides etc.; poet. Untergang m der Sonne; thea. Bühnenausstattung f.

set|-back ['setbæk] fig. Rückschlag m; ~down fig. Dämpfer m; ~off Kontrast m; fig. Ausgleich m.

settee [se'ti:] kleines Sofa.

setting ['setiŋ] Setzen n; Einrichten n; Fassung f e-s Edelsteins; Lage f; Schauplatz m; Umgebung f; thea. Ausstattung f; fig. Umrahmung f; ♪ Komposition f; (Sonnen- etc.) Untergang m; ⊕ Einstellung f.

settle ['setl] 1. Sitzbank f; 2. v/t. (fest)setzen; Kind etc. versorgen, ausstatten; j-n etablieren; regeln; Geschäft abschließen, abmachen, erledigen; Frage entscheiden; Rechnung begleichen; ordnen; beruhigen; Streit beilegen; Rente aussetzen; ansiedeln; Land besiedeln; v/i. sich senken (Haus); oft ~ down sich niederlassen; a. ~ in sich einrichten; sich legen (Wut etc.); beständig werden (Wetter); sich entschließen; ~ down to sich widmen (dat.); ~d fest; beständig; auf Rechnungen: bezahlt; ~ment [~lmənt] Erledigung f; Übereinkunft f; (Be)Siedlung f; ♔ (Eigentums)Übertragung f; ~r [~lə] Siedler m.

set|-to F ['set'tu:] Kampf m; Schlägerei f; ~up F Aufbau m; Am. sl. abgekartete Sache.

seven ['sevn] 1. sieben; 2. Sieben f; ~teen(th) [~n'ti:n(θ)] siebzehn (-te[r, -s]); ~th [~nθ] 1. ☐ sieben(en)te(r, -s); 2. Sieb(en)tel n; ~thly

[~θli] sieb(en)tens; ~tieth [~ntiiθ] siebzigste(r, -s); ~ty [~ti] 1. siebzig; 2. Siebzig f.

sever ['sevə] (sich) trennen; (auf-) lösen; zerreißen.

several ☐ ['sevrəl] mehrere, verschiedene; einige; einzeln; besonder; getrennt; ~ly [~li] besonders, einzeln.

severance ['sevərəns] Trennung f.

sever|e ☐ [si'viə] streng; rauh (Wetter); hart (Winter); scharf (Tadel); ernst (Mühe); heftig (Schmerz etc.); schlimm, schwer (Unfall etc.); ~ity [si'veriti] Strenge f, Härte f; Schwere f; Ernst m.

sew [sou] [irr.] nähen; heften.

sewage ['sju:(:)idʒ] Abwasser n.

sewer¹ ['souə] Näherin f.

sewer² ['sjuə] Abwasserkanal m; ~age [~əridʒ] Kanalisation f.

sew|ing ['souiŋ] Nähen n; Näherei f; attr. Näh...; ~n [soun] p.p. von sew.

sex [seks] Geschlecht n.

sexton ['sekstən] Küster m, Totengräber m.

sexual ☐ ['seksjuəl] geschlechtlich; Geschlechts...; sexuell; Sexual...

shabby ☐ ['∫æbi] schäbig; gemein.

shack Am. [∫æk] Hütte f, Bude f.

shackle ['∫ækl] 1. Fessel f (fig. mst pl.); 2. fesseln.

shade [∫eid] 1. Schatten m, Dunkel n (a. fig.); Lampen- etc. Schirm m; Schattierung f; Am. Rouleau n; fig. Spur f, Kleinigkeit f; 2. beschatten; verdunkeln (a. fig.); abschirmen; schützen; schattieren; ~ away, ~ off allmählich übergehen (lassen) (into in acc.).

shadow ['∫ædou] 1. Schatten m (a. fig.); Phantom n; Spur f, Kleinigkeit f; 2. beschatten; (mst ~ forth od. out) andeuten; versinnbildlichen; j-n beschatten, überwachen; ~y [~oui] schattig, dunkel; schattenhaft; wesenlos.

shady ['∫eidi] schattenspendend; schattig; dunkel; F zweifelhaft.

shaft [∫ɑ:ft] Schaft m; Stiel m; Pfeil m (a. fig.); poet. Strahl m; ⊕ Welle f; Deichsel f; ⚒ Schacht m.

shaggy ['∫ægi] zottig.

shake [∫eik] 1. [irr.] v/t. schütteln, rütteln; erschüttern; ~ down Stroh etc. hinunterschütten; ~ hands sich die Hände geben od. schütteln; ~ up Bett aufschütteln; fig. aufrütteln; v/i. zittern, beben, wackeln, wanken (with vor dat.); ♪ trillern; 2. Schütteln n; Erschütterung f; Beben n; ♪ Triller m; ~down ['∫eik'daun] 1. Notlager n; Am. sl. Erpressung f; 2. adj.: ~ cruise ⚓ Probefahrt f; ~-hands pl. Händedruck m; ~n ['∫eikən] 1. p.p. von shake 1; 2. adj. erschüttert.

shaky □ ['ʃeiki] wack(e)lig (*a. fig.*); (sch)wankend; zitternd, zitterig.

shall [ʃæl] [*irr.*] *v/aux.* soll; werde.

shallow ['ʃælou] **1.** seicht; flach; *fig.* oberflächlich; **2.** Untiefe *f*; **3.** (sich) verflachen.

sham [ʃæm] **1.** falsch; Schein...; **2.** Trug *m*; Täuschung *f*; Schwindler(in); **3.** *v/t.* vortäuschen; *v/i.* sich verstellen; simulieren; ~ *ill* (-*ness*) sich krank stellen.

shamble ['ʃæmbl] watscheln; ~s *pl. od. sg.* Schlachthaus *n*; *fig.* Schlachtfeld *n*.

shame [ʃeim] **1.** Scham *f*; Schande *f*; *for* ~!, ~ *on you!* pfui!, schäm dich!; *put to* ~ beschämen; **2.** beschämen; *j-m* Schande machen; ~faced □ ['ʃeimfeist] schamhaft, schüchtern; ~ful □ [~ful] schändlich, beschämend; ~less □ ['ʃeimlis] schamlos.

shampoo [ʃæm'pu:] **1.** Shampoo *n*; Haarwäsche *f*; **2.** *Haare* waschen.

shamrock ['ʃæmrɔk] Kleeblatt *n*.

shank [ʃæŋk] (Unter)Schenkel *m*; ⚕ Stiel *m*; (⚓ Anker)Schaft *m*.

shanty ['ʃænti] Hütte *f*, Bude *f*.

shape [ʃeip] **1.** Gestalt *f*, Form *f* (*a. fig.*); Art *f*; **2.** *v/t.* gestalten, formen, bilden; anpassen (*to dat.*); *v/i.* sich entwickeln; ~d ...förmig; ~less □ ['ʃeiplis] formlos; ~ly [~li] wohlgestaltet.

share [ʃɛə] **1.** (An)Teil *m*; Beitrag *m*; ✝ Aktie *f*; ⚔ Kux *m*; *have a* ~ *in* teilhaben an (*dat.*); *go* ~s teilen; **2.** *v/t.* teilen; *v/i.* teilhaben (*in an dat.*); ~cropper *Am.* ['ʃɛəkrɔpə] *kleiner* Farmpächter; ~holder ✝ Aktionär(in).

shark [ʃɑ:k] *ichth.* Hai(fisch) *m*; Gauner *m*; *Am. sl.* Kanone *f* (*Experte*).

sharp [ʃɑ:p] **1.** □ *allg.* scharf (*a. fig.*); spitz; schneidend, stechend; schrill; hitzig; schnell; pfiffig, schlau, gerissen; *C* ~ *♪* Cis *n*; **2.** *adv.* *♪* zu hoch; F pünktlich; *look* ~! (mach) schnell!; **3.** *♪* Kreuz *n*; durch ein Kreuz erhöhte Note; F Gauner *m*; ~en ['ʃɑ:pən] (ver-)schärfen; spitzen; ~ener ['ʃɑ:pnə] *Messer*-Schärfer *m*; *Bleistift*-Spitzer *m*; ~er ['ʃɑ:pə] Gauner *m*; ~ness ['ʃɑ:pnis] Schärfe *f* (*a. fig.*); ~set ['ʃɑ:p'set] hungrig; erpicht; ~sighted scharfsichtig; ~witted scharfsinnig.

shatter ['ʃætə] zerschmettern, zerschlagen; *Nerven etc.* zerrütten.

shave [ʃeiv] **1.** [*irr.*] (sich) rasieren; (ab)schälen; haarscharf vorbeigehen *od.* vorbeifahren *od.* vorbeikommen an (*dat.*); **2.** Rasieren *n*, Rasur *f*; *have a* ~ sich rasieren (lassen); *a close* ~ ein Entkommen mit knapper Not; ~n ['ʃeivn] *p.p. von shave 1.*

shaving ['ʃeiviŋ] **1.** Rasieren *n*; ~s *pl.* (*bsd.* Hobel)Späne *m/pl.*; **2.** Rasier...

shawl [ʃɔ:l] Schal *m*, Kopftuch *n*.

she [ʃi:] **1.** sie; **2.** Sie *f*; *zo.* Weibchen *n*; **3.** *adj. in Zssgn:* weiblich, ...weibchen *n*; ~dog Hündin *f*.

sheaf [ʃi:f], *pl.* **sheaves** [ʃi:vz] Garbe *f*; Bündel *n*.

shear [ʃiə] **1.** [*irr.*] scheren; *fig.* rupfen; **2.** ~s *pl.* große Schere.

sheath [ʃi:θ] Scheide *f*; ~e [ʃi:ð] (in die Scheide) stecken; einhüllen; ⊕ bekleiden, beschlagen.

sheaves [ʃi:vz] *pl. von sheaf.*

shebang *Am. sl.* [ʃə'bæŋ] Bude *f*, Laden *m*.

shed[1] [ʃed] [*irr.*] aus-, vergießen; verbreiten; *Blätter etc.* abwerfen.

shed[2] [~] Schuppen *m*; Stall *m*.

sheen [ʃi:n] Glanz *m* (*bsd.* Stoff).

sheep [ʃi:p] Schaf(e *pl.*) *n*; Schafleder *n*; ~cot ['ʃi:pkɔt] = sheepfold; ~dog Schäferhund *m*; ~fold Schafhürde *f*; ~ish □ ['ʃi:piʃ] blöd(e), einfältig; ~man *Am.* Schafzüchter *m*; ~skin Schaffell *n*; Schafleder *n*; F Diplom *n*.

sheer [ʃiə] rein; glatt; *Am.* hauchdünn; steil; senkrecht; direkt.

sheet [ʃi:t] Bett-, Leintuch *n*, Laken *n*; (*Glas- etc.*)Platte *f*; ⊕ ...blech *n*; Blatt *n*, Bogen *m Papier*; weite Fläche (*Wasser etc.*); ⚓ Schot(e) *f*; *the rain came down in* ~s es regnete in Strömen; ~ *iron* Eisenblech *n*; ~ *lightning* ['ʃi:t-laitniŋ] Wetterleuchten *n*.

shelf [ʃelf], *pl.* **shelves** [ʃelvz] Brett *n*, Regal *n*, Fach *n*; Riff *n*; *on the* ~ *fig.* ausrangiert.

shell [ʃel] **1.** Schale *f*, Hülse *f*, Muschel *f*; Gehäuse *n*; Gerippe *n e-s Hauses*; ⚔ Granate *f*; **2.** schälen, enthülsen; ⚔ bombardieren; ~fire ['ʃelfaiə] Granatfeuer *n*; ~fish *zo.* Schalentier *n*; ~proof bombensicher.

shelter ['ʃeltə] **1.** Schuppen *m*; Schutz-, Obdach *n*; *fig.* Schutz *m*, Schirm *m*; **2.** *v/t.* (be)schützen; (be)schirmen; Zuflucht gewähren (*dat.*); *v/i. a. take* ~ Schutz suchen.

shelve [ʃelv] mit Brettern *od.* Regalen versehen; auf ein Brett stellen; *fig.* zu den Akten legen; *fig.* beiseite legen; sich allmählich neigen.

shelves [ʃelvz] *pl. von shelf.*

shenanigan *Am.* F [ʃi'nænigən] Gaunerei *f*; Humbug *m*.

shepherd ['ʃepəd] **1.** Schäfer *m*, Hirt *m*; **2.** (be)hüten; leiten.

sherbet ['ʃə:bət] Brauselimonade *f*; (*Art*) (Speise)Eis *n*.

shield [ʃi:ld] **1.** (Schutz)Schild *m*; Wappenschild *m, n*; **2.** (be)schirmen (*from vor dat.*, *gegen*).

shift [ʃift] **1.** Veränderung *f*, Verschiebung f, Wechsel m; Notbehelf m; List f, Kniff m; Ausflucht f; (Arbeits)Schicht f; make ~ es möglich machen (to inf. zu inf.); sich behelfen; sich durchschlagen; 2. v/t. (ver-, weg)schieben; (ab)wechseln; verändern, Platz, Szene verlegen, verlagern; v/i. wechseln; sich verlagern; sich behelfen; ~ for o.s. sich selbst helfen; ~less □ ['ʃiftlis] hilflos; faul; ~y □ [~ti] fig. gerissen; unzuverlässig.

shilling [ʃiʃ] *englischer* Schilling.

shin [ʃin] 1. a. ~-bone Schienbein n; 2. ~ up hinaufklettern.

shine [ʃain] 1. Schein m; Glanz m; 2. [irr.] v/i. scheinen; leuchten; fig. glänzen, strahlen; v/t. blank putzen.

shingle ['ʃiŋgl] Schindel f; Am. F (Aushänge)Schild n; Strandkiesel m/pl.; ~s pl. ☞ Gürtelrose f.

shiny □ ['ʃaini] blank, glänzend.

ship [ʃip] 1. Schiff n; Am. F Flugzeug n; 2. an Bord nehmen od. bringen; verschiffen, versenden; ⚓ heuern; ~board ['ʃipbɔːd] on ~ ⚓ an Bord; ~ment ['ʃipmənt] Verschiffung f; Versand m; Schiffsladung f; ~owner Reeder m; ~ping ['ʃipiŋ] Verschiffung f; Schiffe n/pl., Flotte f; attr. Schiffs...; Verschiffungs..., Verlade...; ~wreck 1. Schiffbruch m; 2. scheitern (lassen); ~wrecked schiffbrüchig; ~yard Schiffswerft f. [schaft f.)

shire ['ʃaiə, *in Zssgn* ...ʃiə] Graf-)

shirk [ʃəːk] sich drücken (um *et.*); ~er ['ʃəːkə] Drückeberger m.

shirt [ʃəːt] Herrenhemd n; a. ~ waist Am. Hemdbluse f; ~sleeve ['ʃəːtsliːv] 1. Hemdsärmel m; 2. hemdsärmelig; informell; ~ diplomacy bsd. Am. offene Diplomatie.

shiver ['ʃivə] 1. Splitter m; Schauer m; 2. zersplittern; schau(d)ern; (er)zittern; frösteln; ~y [~əri] fröstelnd.

shoal [ʃoul] 1. Schwarm m, Schar f; Untiefe f; 2. flacher werden; 3. seicht.

shock [ʃɔk] 1. Garbenhaufen m; (Haar)Schopf m; Stoß m; Anstoß m; Erschütterung f, Schlag m; ☞ (Nerven)Schock m; 2. fig. verletzen; empören, Anstoß erregen bei; erschüttern; ~ing □ ['ʃɔkiŋ] anstößig; empörend; haarsträubend.

shod [ʃɔd] pret. u. p.p. von shoe 2.

shoddy ['ʃɔdi] 1. Reißwolle f; fig. Schund m; Am. Protz m; 2. falsch; minderwertig; Am. protzig.

shoe [ʃuː] 1. Schuh m; Hufeisen n; 2. [irr.] beschuhen; beschlagen; ~black ['ʃuːblæk] Schuhputzer m; ~blacking Schuhwichse f; ~horn Schuhanzieher m; ~lace Schnürsenkel m; ~maker Schuhmacher m; ~string Schnürsenkel m.

shone [ʃɔn] pret. u. p.p. von shine 2.

shook [ʃuk] pret. von shake 1.

shoot [ʃuːt] 1. fig. Schuß m; ⚘ Schößling m; 2. [irr.] v/t. (ab)schießen; erschießen; werfen, stoßen; Film aufnehmen, drehen; fig. unter o r Brücke etc. hindurchschießen, über et. hinwegschießen; ⚘ treiben; ☞ (ein)spritzen; v/i. schießen; stechen (Schmerz); daherschießen; stürzen; a. ~ forth ⚘ ausschlagen; ~ ahead vorwärtsschießen; ~er ['ʃuːtə] Schütze m.

shooting ['ʃuːtiŋ] 1. Schießen n; Schießerei f; Jagd f; Film: Dreharbeiten f/pl.; 2. stechend (Schmerz); ~gallery Schießstand m, -bude f; ~range Schießplatz m; ~ star Sternschnuppe f.

shop [ʃɔp] 1. Laden m, Geschäft n; Werkstatt f, Betrieb m; talk ~ fachsimpeln; 2. mst go ~ping einkaufen gehen; ~assistant ['ʃɔpəsistənt] Verkäufer(in); ~keeper Ladeninhaber(in); ~lifter ['ʃɔpliftə] Ladendieb m; ~man Ladengehilfe m; ~per ['ʃɔpə] Käufer(in); ~ping ['ʃɔpiŋ] Einkaufen n; attr. Einkaufs...; ~ centre Einkaufszentrum n; ~steward Betriebsrat m; ~walker ['ʃɔpwɔːkə] Aufsichtsherr m, -dame f; ~window Schaufenster n.

shore [ʃɔː] 1. Küste f, Ufer n; Strand m; Stütze f; on ~ an Land; 2. ~ up abstützen.

shorn [ʃɔːn] p.p. von shear 1.

short [ʃɔːt] 1. adj. kurz (a. fig.); klein; knapp; mürbe (Gebäck); wortkarg; in ~ kurz(um); ~ of knapp an (dat.); 2. adv. ~ of abgesehen von; come od. fall ~ of et. nicht erreichen; cut ~ plötzlich unterbrechen; run ~ (of) ausgehen (Vorräte); stop ~ of zurückschrecken vor (dat.); ~age ['ʃɔːtidʒ] Fehlbetrag m; Gewichtsverlust m; Knappheit f; ~coming Unzulänglichkeit f; Fehler m; Mangel m; ~cut Abkürzungsweg m; ~dated ☞ auf kurze Sicht; ~en ['ʃɔːtn] v/t. ab-, verkürzen; v/i. kürzer werden; ~ening [~niŋ] Backfett m; ~hand Kurzschrift f; ~ typist Stenotypistin f; ~ly ['ʃɔːtli] adv. kurz; bald; ~ness ['ʃɔːtnis] Kürze f; Mangel m; ~sighted kurzsichtig; ~term kurzfristig; ~winded kurzatmig.

shot [ʃɔt] 1. pret. u. p.p. von shoot 2; 2. Schuß m; Geschoß n, Kugel f; Schrot(korn) m; Schußweite f; Schütze m; Sport: Stoß m, Schlag m, Wurf m; phot., Film: Aufnahme f; ☞ Spritze f; have a ~ at et. versuchen; not by a long ~ F noch lange nicht; big ~ F großes Tier; ~gun ['ʃɔtgʌn] Schrotflinte f; ~ marriage Am. F Mußheirat f.

should [ʃud, ʃəd] pret. von shall.

shoulder ['ʃouldə] 1. Schulter f (a. v. Tieren; fig. Vorsprung); Achsel f; 2. auf die Schulter od. fig. auf sich nehmen; ✗ schultern; drängen; **~blade** anat. Schulterblatt n; **~strap** Träger m am Kleid; ✗ Schulter-, Achselstück n.

shout [ʃaut] 1. lauter Schrei od. Ruf; Geschrei n; 2. laut schreien.

shove [ʃʌv] 1. Schub m, Stoß m; 2. schieben, stoßen.

shovel ['ʃʌvl] 1. Schaufel f; 2. schaufeln.

show [ʃou] 1. [irr.] v/t. zeigen; ausstellen; erweisen; beweisen; **~ in** hereinführen; **~ off** zur Geltung bringen; **~ out** hinausgeleiten; **~ round** herumführen; **~ up** hinaufführen; entlarven; v/i. a. **~ up** sich zeigen; zu sehen sein; **~ off** angeben, prahlen, sich aufspielen; 2. Schau(stellung) f; Ausstellung f; Auf-, Vorführung f; Anschein m; **on ~** zu besichtigen; **~ business** ['ʃoubiznis] Unterhaltungsindustrie f; Schaugeschäft n; **~-case** Schaukasten m, Vitrine f; **~-down** Aufdecken n der Karten (bsd. Am. a. fig.); fig. Kraftprobe f.

shower ['ʃauə] 1. (Regen)Schauer m; Dusche f; fig. Fülle f; 2. v/t. herabschütten (a. fig.); überschütten; v/i. sich ergießen; **~y** ['ʃauəri] regnerisch.

show|n [ʃoun] p.p. von show 1; **~room** ['ʃourum] Ausstellungsraum m; **~-window** Schaufenster n; **~y** □ ['ʃoui] prächtig; protzig.

shrank [ʃræŋk] pret. von shrink.

shred [ʃred] 1. Stückchen n; Schnitz(el n) m; Fetzen m (a. fig.); 2. [irr.] (zer)schnitzeln; zerfetzen.

shrew [ʃru:] zänkisches Weib.

shrewd □ [ʃru:d] scharfsinnig schlau.

shriek [ʃri:k] 1. (Angst)Schrei m; Gekreisch n; 2. kreischen, schreien.

shrill [ʃril] 1. □ schrill, gellend; 2. schrillen, gellen; schreien.

shrimp [ʃrimp] zo. Krabbe f; fig. Knirps m.   [m.\

shrine [ʃrain] Schrein m; Altar\

shrink [ʃriŋk] [irr.] (ein-, zs.-) schrumpfen (lassen); einlaufen; sich zurückziehen; zurückschrecken (from, at vor dat.); **~age** ['ʃriŋkidʒ] Einlaufen n, Zs.-schrumpfen n; Schrumpfung f; fig. Verminderung f.

shrivel ['ʃrivl] einschrumpfen (lassen).

shroud [ʃraud] 1. Leichentuch n; fig. Gewand n; 2. in ein Leichentuch einhüllen; fig. hüllen.

Shrove|tide ['ʃrouvtaid] Fastnachtszeit f; **~ Tuesday** Fastnachtsdienstag m.

shrub [ʃrʌb] Strauch m; Busch m; **~bery** ['ʃrʌbəri] Gebüsch n.

shrug [ʃrʌg] 1. (die Achseln) zucken; 2. Achselzucken n.

shrunk [ʃrʌŋk] p.p. von shrink; **~en** ['ʃrʌŋkən] adj. (ein)geschrumpft.

shuck bsd. Am. [ʃʌk] 1. Hülse f, Schote f; **~s!** F Quatsch!; 2. enthülsen.

shudder ['ʃʌdə] 1. schaudern; (er-) beben; 2. Schauder m.

shuffle ['ʃʌfl] 1. schieben; Karten: mischen; schlurfen; Ausflüchte machen; **~ off** von sich schieben; abstreifen; 2. Schieben n; Mischen n; Schlurfen n; Ausflucht f; Schiebung f.

shun [ʃʌn] (ver)meiden.

shunt [ʃʌnt] 1. 🚂 Rangieren n; 🚂 Weiche f; ⚡ Nebenschluß m; 2. 🚂 rangieren; ⚡ nebenschließen; fig. verschieben.

shut [ʃʌt] [irr.] (sich) schließen; zumachen; **~ down** Betrieb schließen; **~ up** ein-, verschließen; einsperren; **~ up!** F halt den Mund!; **~ter** ['ʃʌtə] Fensterladen m; phot. Verschluß m.

shuttle ['ʃʌtl] 1. ⊕ Schiffchen n; Pendelverkehr m; 2. pendeln.

shy [ʃai] 1. □ scheu; schüchtern; 2. (zurück)scheuen (at vor dat.).

shyness ['ʃainis] Schüchternheit f; Scheu f.

shyster sl., bsd. Am. ['ʃaistə] gerissener Kerl; Winkeladvokat m.

Siberian [sai'biəriən] 1. sibirisch; 2. Sibirier(in).

sick [sik] krank (of an dat.; with vor dat.); übel; überdrüssig; be **~ for** sich sehnen nach; be **~ of** genug haben von; go **~**, report **~** sich krank melden; **~-benefit** ['sik-benifit] Krankengeld n; **~en** ['sikn] v/i. krank werden; kränkeln; **~** at sich ekeln vor (dat.); v/t. krank machen; anekeln.

sickle ['sikl] Sichel f.

sick|-leave ['sikli:v] Krankheitsurlaub m; **~ly** [-li] kränklich; schwächlich; bleich, blaß; ungesund (Klima); ekelhaft; matt (Lächeln); **~ness** ['siknis] Krankheit f; Übelkeit f.

side [said] 1. allg. Seite f; **~ by ~** Seite an Seite; take **~ with** Partei ergreifen für; 2. Seiten...; Neben...; 3. Partei ergreifen (with für); **~board** ['saidbɔ:d] Anrichte(tisch m) f, Sideboard n; **~-car** mot. Beiwagen m; **~d** ...seitig; **~-light** Streiflicht n; **~long** 1. adv. seitwärts; 2. adj. scitlich; Seiten...; **~-stroke** Seitenschwimmen n; **~-track** 1. 🚂 Nebengleis n; 2. auf ein Nebengleis schieben; bsd. Am. fig. aufschieben; beiseite schieben; **~walk** bsd. Am. Bürgersteig m; **~ward(s)** [~wəd(z)], **~ways** seitlich; seitwärts.

siding 🚂 ['saidiŋ] Nebengleis n.

sidle ['saidl] seitwärts gehen.

siege [si:dʒ] Belagerung *f*; *lay ~ to* belagern.

sieve [siv] 1. Sieb *n*; ~. (durch-) sieben.

sift [sift] sieben; *fig.* sichten; prüfen.

sigh [sai] 1. Seufzer *m*; 2. seufzen; sich sehnen (*after*, for nach).

sight [sait] 1. Sehvermögen *n*, Sehkraft *f*; *fig.* Auge *n*; Anblick *m*; Visier *n*; Sicht *f*· ~s *pl.* Sehenswürdigkeiten *f*/*pl.*; *at ~*, *a. on ~* beim Anblick; *♪ vom Blatt; ♱ nach* Sicht; *catch ~ of* erblicken, zu Gesicht bekommen; *lose ~ of* aus den Augen verlieren; *within ~* in Sicht; *know by ~* vom Sehen kennen; 2. sichten; (~n)visieren; ~ed ['saitid] ...sichtig; ~y ['saitli] ansehnlich, stattlich; ~seeing ['saitsi:iŋ] Besichtigung *f* von Sehenswürdigkeiten: ~seer Tourist(in).

sign [sain] 1. Zeichen *n*; Wink *m*; Schild *n*; *in ~ of* zum Zeichen(*gen.*); 2. *v*/*i.* winken, Zeichen geben; *v*/*t.* (unter)zeichnen, unterschreiben.

signal ['signl] 1. Signal *n*; Zeichen *n*; 2. ☐ bemerkenswert., außerordentlich; 3. signalisieren; ~ize [~nəlaiz] auszeichnen; = *signal* 3.

signat|ory ['signətəri] 1. Unterzeichner *m*; 2. unterzeichnend; ~ *powers pl.* Signatarmächte *f*/*pl.*; ~ure [~nitʃə] Signatur *f*; Unterschrift *f*; ~ *tune Radio*: Kennmelodie *f*.

sign|board ['sainbɔ:d] (Aushänge-) Schild *n*; ~er ['sainə] Unterzeichner(in).

signet ['signit] Siegel *n*.

signific|ance [sig'nifikəns] Bedeutung *f*; ~ant ☐ [~nt] bedeutsam; bezeichnend (*of für*); ~ation [signi-fi'keiʃən] Bedeutung *f*.

signify ['signifai] beze'chnen, andeuten; kundgeben; bedeuten.

signpost ['sainpoust] Wegweiser *m*.

silence ['sailəns] 1. (Still)Schweigen *n*; Stille *f*, Ruhe *f*; *~! Ruhe! put od. reduce to ~* = 2. zum Schweigen bringen; ~r [~sə] ⊕ Schalldämpfer *m*; *mot.* Auspuff·opí *m*.

silent ☐ ['sailənt] still; schweigend; schweigsam; stumm; ~ *partner ♱* stiller Teilhaber.

silk [silk] Seide *f*; *attr.* Seiden...; ~en ☐ ['silkən] seiden; ~stocking *Am.* vornehm; ~worm Seidenraupe *f*; ~y ☐ [~ki] seid(enart)ig.

sill [sil] Schwelle *f*; Fensterbrett *n*.

silly ☐ ['sili] albern, töricht.

silt [silt] 1. Schlamm *m*; 2. *mst ~ up* verschlammen.

silver ['silvə] 1. Silber *n*; 2. silbern; Silber...; 3. versilbern; silberig od. silberweiß werden (lassen); ~ware *Am.* Tafelsilber *n*; ~y [~əri] silberglänzend; silberhell.

similar ☐ ['similə] ähnlich, gleich; ~ity [simi'læriti] Ähnlichkeit *f*.

simile ['simili] Gleichnis *n*.

similitude [si'militju:d] Gestalt *f*; Ebenbild *n*; Gleichnis *n*.

simmer ['simə] sieden *od.* brodeln (lassen); *fig.* kochen, gären (*Gefühl, Aufstand*); ~ *down* ruhig(er) werden.

simper ['simpə] 1. einfältiges Lächeln; 2. einfältig lächeln.

simple ☐ ['simpl] einfach; schlicht; einfältig; arglos; ~-hearted, ~-minded naiv; ~ton [~ltən] Einfaltspinsel *m*.

simpli|city [sim'plisiti] Einfachheit *f*; Klarheit *f*; Schlichtheit *f*; Einfalt *f*; ~fication [simplifi'kei-ʃən] Vereinfachung *f*; ~fy ['simpli-fai] vereinfachen.

simply ['simpli] einfach; bloß.

simulate ['simjuleit] vortäuschen; (er)heucheln; sich tarnen als.

simultaneous ☐ [siməl'teinjəs] gleichzeitig.

sin [sin] 1. Sünde *f*; 2. sündigen.

since [sins] 1. *prp.* seit; 2. *adv.* seitdem; 3. *cj.* seit(dem); da (ja).

sincer|e ☐ [sin'siə] aufrichtig; *Yours ~ly* Ihr ergebener; ~ity [~'seriti] Aufrichtigkeit *f*.

sinew ['sinju:] Sehne *f*; *fig. mst.* ~s *pl.* Nerven(kraft *f*) *m*/*pl.*; Seele *f*; ~y [~ju(:)i] sehnig; nervig, stark.

sinful ☐ ['sinful] sündig, sündhaft, böse.

sing [siŋ] [*irr.*] singen; besingen; ~ *to s.o.* j-m vorsingen.

singe [sindʒ] (ver)sengen.

singer ['siŋə] Sänger(in).

singing ['siŋiŋ] Gesang *m.* Singen *n*; ~ *bird* Singvoge. *m.*

single ['siŋgl] 1. ☐ einzig; einzeln; Einzel...; einfach; ledig, unverheiratet; *book-keeping by ~ entry* einfache Buchführung; ~ *file* Gänsemarsch *m*; 2. einfache Fahrkarte, *mst* ~s *sg. Tennis:* Einzel *n*; 3. ~ *out* auswählen, aussuchen; ~-breasted einreihig (*Jacke etc.*); ~-engined ✈ einmotorig; ~-handed eigenhändig, allein; ~-hearted ☐, ~-minded ☐ aufrichtig; zielstrebig; ~t [~lit] Unterhemd *n*; ~-track eingleisig.

singular ☐ ['siŋgjulə] 1. ☐ einzigartig; eigenartig; sonderbar; 2. *a.* ~ *number gr.* Singular *m*, Einzahl *f*; ~ity [siŋgju'læriti] Einzigartigkeit *f*; Sonderbarkeit *f*.

sinister ☐ ['sinistə] unheilvoll; böse.

sink [siŋk] 1. [*irr.*] *v*/*i.* sinken; nieder-, unter-, versinken; sich senken; eindringen; erliegen; *v*/*t.* (ver)senken; *Brunnen* bohren; *Geld* festlegen; *Namen etc.* aufgeben; 2. Ausguß *m*; ~ing ['siŋkiŋ] (Ver-) Sinken *n*; Versenken *n*; ♣ Schwäche(gefühl *n*) *f*; Senkung *f*; ♱

Tilgung *f*; ~ **fund** (Schulden)Tilgungsfonds *m*.
sinless ['sinlis] sündenlos, -frei.
sinner ['sinə] Sünder(in).
sinuous □ ['sinjuəs] gewunden.
sip [sip] 1. Schlückchen *n*; 2. schlürfen; nippen; langsam trinken.
sir [sə:] Herr *m*; 2 Sir (*Titel*).
sire ['saiə] *mst poet.* Vater *m*; Vorfahr *m*; *zo.* Vater(tier *n*) *m*.
siren ['saiərin] Sirene *f*.
sirloin ['sə:loin] Lendenstück *n*.
sissy *Am.* ['sisi] Weichling *m*.
sister ['sistə] (*a.* Ordens-, Ober-) Schwester *f*; **~hood** [~hud] Schwesternschaft *f*; **~-in-law** [~ərinlɔ:] Schwägerin *f*; **~ly** [~əli] schwesterlich.
sit [sit] [*irr.*] *v/i.* sitzen; Sitzung halten, tagen; *fig.* liegen; ~ **down** sich setzen; ~ **up** aufrecht sitzen; aufbleiben; *v/t.* setzen; sitzen auf (*dat.*).
site [sait] Lage *f*; (Bau)Platz *m*.
sitting ['sitiŋ] Sitzung *f*; **~-room** Wohnzimmer *n*.
situat|ed ['sitjueitid] gelegen; be ~ liegen, gelegen sein; **~ion** [sitju-'eiʃən] Lage *f*; Stellung *f*.
six [siks] 1. sechs; 2. Sechs *f*; **~teen** ['siks'ti:n] sechzehn; **~teenth** [~nθ] sechzehnte(r, -s); **~th** [~θ] 1. sechste(r, -s); 2. Sechstel *n*; **~thly** ['siksθli] sechstens; **~tieth** [~stiiθ] sechzigste(r, -s); **~ty** [~ti] 1. sechzig; 2. Sechzig *f*.
size [saiz] 1. Größe *f*; Format *n*; 2. nach der Größe ordnen; ~ **up** F *j-n* abschätzen; **~d** von ... Größe.
siz(e)able □ ['saizəbl] ziemlich groß.
sizzle ['sizl] zischen; knistern; brutzeln; *sizzling hot* glühend heiß.
skat|e [skeit] 1. Schlittschuh *m*; *roller-* ~ Rollschuh *m*; 2. Schlittod. Rollschuh laufen; **~er** ['skeitə] Schlittschuh-, Rollschuhläufer(in).
skedaddle F [ski'dædl] abhauen.
skeesicks *Am.* F ['skiziks] Nichtsnutz *m*.
skein [skein] Strähne *f*, Docke *f*.
skeleton ['skelitn] Skelett *n*; Gerippe *n*; Gestell *n*; *attr.* Skelett...; ✗ Stamm...; ~ **key** Nachschlüssel *m*.
skeptic ['skeptik] *s.* **sceptic**.
sketch [sketʃ] 1. Skizze *f*; Entwurf *m*; Umriß *m*; 2. skizzieren, entwerfen.
ski [ski:] 1. *pl. a.* **ski** Schi *m*, Ski *m*; 2. Schi *od.* Ski laufen.
skid [skid] 1. Hemmschuh *m*, Bremsklotz *m*; ✗ (Gleit)Kufe *f*; Rutschen *n*; *mot.* Schleudern *n*; 2. *v/t.* hemmen; *v/i.* (aus)rutschen.
skiddoo *Am. sl.* [ski'du:] abhauen.
ski|er ['ski:ə] Schi-, Skiläufer(in); **~ing** ['ski:iŋ] Schi-, Skilauf(en *n*) *m*.
skilful □ ['skilful] geschickt; kundig.
skill [skil] Geschicklichkeit *f*, Fertigkeit *f*; **~ed** [skild] geschickt; gelernt; **~ worker** Facharbeiter *m*.
skillful *Am.* ['skilful] *s.* **skilful**.
skim [skim] 1. abschöpfen; abrahmen; dahingleiten über (*acc.*); *Buch* überfliegen; ~ **through** durchblättern; 2. ~ **milk** Magermilch *f*.
skimp [skimp] *j-n* knapp halten; sparen (mit *et.*); **~y** □ ['skimpi] knapp, dürftig.
skin [skin] 1. Haut *f*; Fell *n*; Schale *f*; 2. *v/t.* (ent)häuten; abbalgen; schälen; ~ **off** F abstreifen; *v/i. a.* ~ **over** zuheilen; **~-deep** ['skin'di:p] (nur) oberflächlich; **~flint** Knicker *m*; **~ny** [~ni] mager.
skip [skip] 1. Sprung *m*; 2. *v/i.* hüpfen, springen; seilhüpfen; *v/t.* überspringen.
skipper ['skipə] ⚓ Schiffer *m*; ⚓, ✈, *Sport*: Kapitän *m*.
skirmish ['skə:miʃ] 1. ✗ Scharmützel *n*; 2. plänkeln.
skirt [skə:t] 1. (Damen)Rock *m*; (Rock)Schoß *m*; *oft* **~s** *pl.* Rand *m*, Saum *m*; 2. umsäumen; (sich) entlangziehen (an *dat.*); entlangfahren; **~ing-board** ['skə:tiŋbɔ:d] Scheuerleiste *f*.
skit [skit] Stichelei *f*; Satire *f*; **~tish** □ ['skitiʃ] ungebärdig.
skittle ['skitl] Kegel *m*; *play* (*at*) **~s** Kegel schieben; **~alley** Kegelbahn *f*. (Gemeinheit *f*.)
skulduggery *Am.* F [skʌl'dʌgəri])
skulk [skʌlk] schleichen; sich verstecken; lauern; sich drücken; **~er** ['skʌlkə] Drückeberger *m*.
skull [skʌl] Schädel *m*.
sky [skai] *oft* **skies** *pl.* Himmel *m*; **~lark** ['skailɑ:k] 1. *orn.* Feldlerche *f*; 2. Ulk treiben; **~light** Oberlicht *n*; Dachfenster *n*; **~line** Horizont *m*; Silhouette *f*; **~rocket** F emporschnellen; **~scraper** Wolkenkratzer *m*; **~ward(s)** ['skaiwəd(z)] himmelwärts.
slab [slæb] Platte *f*; Scheibe *f*; Fliese *f*.
slack [slæk] 1. schlaff; locker; (nach)lässig; ♦ flau; 2. ⚓ Lose *n* (*loses Tauende*); ♦ Flaute *f*; Kohlengrus *m*; 3. = **slacken**; = **slake**; **~en** ['slækən] schlaff machen *od.* werden; verringern; nachlassen; (sich) lockern; (sich) entspannen; (sich) verlangsamen; **~s** *pl.* (lange) Hose.
slag [slæg] Schlacke *f*.
slain [slein] *p.p. von* **slay**.
slake [sleik] *Durst, Kalk* löschen; *fig.* stillen.
slam [slæm] 1. Zuschlagen *n*; Knall *m*; 2. *Tür etc.* zuschlagen, zuknallen; *et. auf den Tisch etc.* knallen.
slander ['slɑ:ndə] 1. Verleumdung *f*; 2. verleumden; **~ous** □ [~rəs] verleumderisch.

slang [slæŋ] 1. Slang *m*; Berufssprache *f*; lässige Umgangssprache; 2. *j-n* wüst beschimpfen.

slant [slɑːnt] 1. schräge Fläche; Abhang *m*; Neigung *f*; *Am.* Standpunkt *m*; 2. schräg legen *od.* liegen; sich neigen; **~ing** *adj.*, □ ['slɑːntiŋ], **~wise** *adv.* [~twaiz] schief, schräg.

slap [slæp] 1. Klaps *m*, Schlag *m*; 2. klapsen; schlagen; klatschen; **~jack** *Am.* ['slæpdʒæk] *Art* Pfannkuchen *m*; **~stick** (Narren)Pritsche *f*; *a.* ~ comedy *thea.* Posse *f*, Burleske *f*.

slash [slæʃ] 1. Hieb *m*; Schnitt *m*; Schlitz *m*; 2. (auf)schlitzen; schlagen, hauen; verreißen (*Kritiker*).

slate [sleit] 1. Schiefer *m*; Schiefertafel *f*; *bsd. Am.* Kandidatenliste *f*; 2. mit Schiefer decken; heftig kritisieren; *Am.* F *für e-n Posten* vorschlagen; **~pencil** ['sleit'pensl] Griffel *m*.

slattern ['slætə(ː)n] Schlampe *f*.

slaughter ['slɔːtə] 1. Schlachten *n*; Gemetzel *n*; 2. schlachten; niedermetzeln; **~house** Schlachthaus *n*.

Slav [slɑːv] 1. Slaw|e *m*, -in *f*; 2. slawisch.

slave [sleiv] 1. Sklav|e *m*, -in *f* (*a. fig.*); 2. F sich placken, schuften.

slaver ['slævə] 1. Geifer *m*, Sabber *m*; 2. (be)geifern, F (be)sabbern.

slav|ery ['sleivəri] Sklaverei *f*; F Plackerei *f*; **~ish** □ [~viʃ] sklavisch.

slay *rhet.* [slei] (*irr.*) erschlagen; töten.

sled [sled] = *sledge* 1.

sledge[1] [sledʒ] 1. Schlitten *m*; 2. Schlitten fahren.

sledge[2] [~] *a.* **~hammer** Schmiedehammer *m*.

sleek [sliːk] 1. □ glatt, geschmeidig; 2. glätten; **~ness** ['sliːknis] Glätte *f*.

sleep [sliːp] 1. (*irr.*) *v/i.* schlafen; (up)on *od.* over *et.* beschlafen; *v/t. j-n für die Nacht* unterbringen; ~ away Zeit verschlafen; 2. Schlaf *m*; go to ~ einschlafen; **~er** ['sliːpə] Schläfer(in); 👯 Schwelle *f*; Schlafwagen *m*; **~ing** [~piŋ] schlafend; Schlaf...; ♗ing **Beauty** Dornröschen *n*; **~ing-car(riage)** 👯 Schlafwagen *m*; **~ing partner** ♰ stiller Teilhaber; **~less** □ [~plis] schlaflos; **~walker** Schlafwandler(in); **~y** □ [~pi] schläfrig; verschlafen.

sleet [sliːt] 1. Graupelregen *m*; 2. graupeln; **~y** ['sliːti] graupelig.

sleeve [sliːv] Ärmel *m*; ⊕ Muffe *f*; **~link** ['sliːvliŋk] Manschettenknopf *m*.

sleigh [slei] 1. (*bsd.* Pferde)Schlitten *m*; 2. (im) Schlitten fahren.

sleight [slait]: **~of-hand** Taschenspielerei *f*; Kunststück *n*.

slender □ ['slendə] schlank; schmächtig; schwach; dürftig.

slept [slept] *pret. u. p.p. von sleep* 1.

sleuth [sluːθ], **~hound** ['sluːθhaund] Blut-, Spürhund *m* (*a. fig.*).

slew [sluː] *pret. von slay*.

slice [slais] 1. Schnitte *f*, Scheibe *f*, Stück *n*; Teil *m*, *n*; 2. (in) Scheiben schneiden; aufschneiden.

slick F [slik] 1. *adj.* glatt; *fig.* raffiniert; 2. *adv.* direkt; 3. *a.* ~ paper *Am. sl.* vornehme Zeitschrift; **~er** *Am.* F ['slikə] Regenmantel *m*; gerissener Kerl.

slid [slid] *pret. u. p.p. von slide* 1.

slide [slaid] 1. (*irr.*) gleiten (lassen); rutschen; schlittern; ausgleiten; geraten (*into* in *acc.*); let things ~ die Dinge laufen lassen; 2. Gleiten *n*; Rutsche *f*; ⊕ Schieber *m*; Diapositiv *n*; *a.* land~ Erdrutsch *m*; **~rule** ['slaidruːl] Rechenschieber *m*.

slight [slait] 1. □ schmächtig; schwach; gering, unbedeutend; 2. Geringschätzung *f*; 3. geringschätzig behandeln; unbeachtet lassen.

slim [slim] 1. □ schlank; dünn; schmächtig; dürftig; *sl.* schlau, gerissen; 2. e-e Schlankheitskur machen.

slim|e [slaim] Schlamm *m*; Schleim *m*; **~y** ['slaimi] schlammig; schleimig.

sling [sliŋ] 1. Schleuder *f*; Tragriemen *m*; ⚔ Schlinge *f*, Binde *f*; Wurf *m*; 2. (*irr.*) schleudern; auf~, umhängen; *a.* ~ up hochziehen.

slink [sliŋk] (*irr.*) schleichen.

slip [slip] 1. (*irr.*) *v/i.* schlüpfen, gleiten, rutschen; ausgleiten; ausrutschen; oft ~ away entschlüpfen; sich versehen; *v/t.* schlüpfen *od.* gleiten lassen; loslassen; entschlüpfen, entgleiten (*dat.*); ~ *in Bemerkung* dazwischenwerfen; ~ *into* hineinstecken *od.* hineinschieben in (*acc.*); ~ on (off) *Kleid* über-, (ab)streifen; have ~ped *s.o.'s memory* j-m entfallen sein; 2. (Aus)Gleiten *n*; Fehltritt *m* (*a. fig.*); Versehen *n* (Flüchtigkeits)Fehler *m*; Verstoß *m*; Streifen *m*; Zettel *m*; Unterkleid *n*; *a.* ~way ⚓ Helling *f*; (Kissen)Überzug *m*; ~s *pl.* Badehose *f*; give *s.o.* the ~ j-m entwischen; **~per** ['slipə] Pantoffel *m*, Hausschuh *m*; **~pery** □ [~əri] schlüpfrig; **~shod** [~ʃɔd] schlampig, nachlässig; **~t** [slipt] *pret. u. p.p. von slip* 1.

slit [slit] 1. Schlitz *m*; Spalte *f*; 2. (*irr.*) (auf-, zer)schlitzen.

sliver ['slivə] Splitter *m*.

slobber ['slɔbə] 1. Sabber *m*; Gesabber *n*; 2. F (be)sabbern.

slogan ['slougən] Schlagwort *n*, Losung *f*; (Werbe)Slogan *m*.

sloop ⚓ [sluːp] Schaluppe *f*.

slop [slɔp] **1.** Pfütze *f*; ~s *pl.* Spül-, Schmutzwasser *n*; Krankenspeise *f*; **2.** *v/t.* verschütten; *v/i.* überlaufen.

slope [sloup] **1.** (Ab)Hang *m*; Neigung *f*; **2.** schräg legen; ⊕ abschrägen; abfallen; schräg verlaufen; (sich) neigen.

sloppy □ ['slɔpi] naß, schmutzig; schlampig; F labb(e)rig; rührselig.

slops [slɔps] *pl.* billige Konfektionskleidung; ♣ Kleidung *f* u. Bettzeug *n*.

slot [slɔt] Schlitz *m*.

sloth [slouθ] Faulheit *f*; *zo.* Faultier *n*.

slot-machine ['slɔtməʃiːn] (Warenod. Spiel)Automat *m*.

slouch [slautʃ] **1.** faul herumhängen; F herumlatschen; **2.** schlaffe Haltung; ~ *hat* Schlapphut *m*.

slough[1] [slau] Sumpf(loch *n*) *m*.

slough[2] [slʌf] Haut abwerfen.

sloven ['slʌvn] unordentlicher Mensch; F Schlampe *f*; ~ly [~nli] liederlich.

slow [slou] **1.** □ langsam (*of* in *dat.*); schwerfällig; lässig; *be* ~ nachgehen (*Uhr*); **2.** *adv.* langsam; **3.** *oft* ~ *down od.* *up. off v/t.* verlangsamen; *v/i.* langsam(er) werden *od.* gehen *od.* fahren; ~coach ['sloukoutʃ] Langweiler *m*; altmodischer Mensch; ~-motion picture Zeitlupenaufnahme *f*; ~-worm *zo.* Blindschleiche *f*.

sludge [slʌdʒ] Schlamm *m*; Matsch *m*.

slug [slʌg] **1.** Stück *n* Rohmetall; *zo.* Wegschnecke *f*; *Am.* F (Faust-)Schlag *m*; **2.** *Am.* F hauen.

sluggard ['slʌgəd] Faulenzer(in); ~ish □ [~giʃ] träge, faul.

sluice [sluːs] **1.** Schleuse *f*; **2.** ausströmen (lassen); ausspülen; waschen.

slum [slʌm] schmutzige Gasse; ~s *pl.* Elendsviertel *n*, Slums *pl.*

slumber ['slʌmbə] **1.** *a.* ~s *pl.* Schlummer *m*; **2.** schlummern.

slump [slʌmp] *Börse:* **1.** fallen, stürzen; **2.** (Kurs-, Preis)Sturz *m*.

slung [slʌŋ] *pret. u. p.p. von* sling 2.

slunk [slʌŋk] *pret. u. p.p. von* slink.

slur [sləː] **1.** Fleck *m*; *fig.* Tadel *m*; ♪ Bindebogen *m*; **2.** *v/t.* oft ~ *over* übergehen; ♪ *Töne* binden.

slush [slʌʃ] Schlamm *m*; Matsch *m*; F Kitsch *m*.

slut [slʌt] F Schlampe *f*; Nutte *f*.

sly □ [slai] schlau, verschmitzt; hinterlistig; *on the* ~ heimlich.

smack [smæk] **1.** (Bei)Geschmack *m*; Prise *f* Salz *etc.*; *fig.* Spur *f*; Schmatz *m*; Schlag *m*, Klatsch *m*, ⎿aps *m*; **2.** schmecken (*of* nach), ⎿Geschmack haben; klatschen, ⎿mit); schmatzen (mit) ⎿geben.

⎿**1.** *allg.* klein; unbe-

deutend; *fig.* kleinlich; niedrig; wenig; *feel* ~, *look* ~ sich gedemütigt fühlen; *the* ~ *hours* die frühen Morgenstunden *f/pl.*; *in a* ~ *way* bescheiden; **2.** dünner Teil; ~s *pl.* F Leibwäsche *f*; ~ *of the back* anat. Kreuz *n*; ~-arms ['smɑːlɑːmz] *pl.* Handfeuerwaffen *f/pl.*; ~ change Kleingeld *n*; *fig.* triviale Bemerkungen *f/pl.*; ~ish [~liʃ] ziemlich klein; ~pox ☞ [~lpɔks] Pocken *f/pl.*; ~ talk Plauderei *f*; ~-time *Am.* F unbedeutend.

smart [smɑːt] **1.** □ scharf; gewandt; geschickt; gescheit; gerissen; schmuck, elegant, adrett; forsch; ~ *aleck Am.* F Neunmalkluge(r) *m*; **2.** Schmerz *m*; **3.** schmerzen; leiden; ~-money ['smɑːtmʌni] Schmerzensgeld *n*; ~ness [~tnis] Klugheit *f*; Schärfe *f*; Gewandtheit *f*; Gerissenheit *f*; Eleganz *f*.

smash [smæʃ] **1.** *v/t.* zertrümmern; *fig.* vernichten; (zer)schmettern; *v/i.* zerschellen; zs.-stoßen; *fig.* zs.-brechen; **2.** Zerschmettern *n*; Krach *m*; Zs.-bruch *m* (*a.* ✝); *Tennis:* Schmetterball *m*; ~-up ['smæʃʌp] Zs.-stoß *m*; Zs.-bruch *m*.

smattering ['smætəriŋ] oberflächliche Kenntnis.

smear [smiə] **1.** (be)schmieren; *fig.* beschmutzen; **2.** Schmiere *f*; Fleck *m*.

smell [smel] **1.** Geruch *m*; **2.** [*irr.*] riechen (*of* nach *et.*); *a.* ~ *at* riechen an (*dat.*); ~y ['smeli] übelriechend.

smelt[1] [smelt] *pret. u. p.p. von* smell 2.

smelt[2] [~] schmelzen.

smile [smail] **1.** Lächeln *n*; **2.** lächeln.

smirch [sməːtʃ] besudeln.

smirk [sməːk] grinsen.

smite [smait] [*irr.*] schlagen; heimsuchen; *schwer* treffen; quälen.

smith [smiθ] Schmied *m*.

smithereens ['smiðə'riːnz] *pl.* Stücke *n/pl.*, Splitter *m/pl*, Fetzen *m/pl.*

smithy ['smiði] Schmiede *f*.

smitten ['smitn] **1.** *p.p. von* smite; **2.** *adj.* ergriffen; betroffen; *fig.* hingerissen (with von).

smock [smɔk] **1.** fälteln; **2.** Kittel *m*; ~-frock ['smɔk'frɔk] Bauernkittel *m*.

smog [smɔg] Smog *m*, Gemisch *n* von Nebel und Rauch.

smoke [smouk] **1.** Rauch *m*; *have a* ~ (eine) rauchen; **2.** rauchen; dampfen; (aus)räuchern; ~-dried ['smoukdraid] geräuchert; ~r [~kə] Raucher *m*; ☞ F Raucherwagen *m*, -abteil *n*; ~-stack, ♣ Schornstein *m*.

smoking ['smoukiŋ] Rauchen *n*; *attr.* Rauch(er)...; ~-compartment ☞ Raucherabteil *n*.

smoky □ ['smouki] rauchig; verräuchert. [der.\

smolder *Am.* ['smouldə] = smoul-\

smooth [smu:ð] 1. □ glatt; *fig.* fließend; mild; schmeichlerisch; 2. glätten; ebnen (*a. fig.*); plätten; mildern; *a.* ~ over, ~ away *fig.* wegräumen; ~ness ['smu:ðnɪs] Glätte *f.*

smote [smout] *pret. von* smite.

smother ['smʌðə] ersticken.

smoulder ['smouldə] schwelen.

smudge [smʌdʒ] 1. (be)schmutzen; (be)schmieren; 2. Schmutzfleck *m.*

smug [smʌg] selbstzufrieden.

smuggle ['smʌgl] schmuggeln; ~r [~lə] Schmuggler(in).

smut [smʌt] Schmutz *m;* Ruß(fleck) *m;* Zoten *f/pl.*; 2. beschmutzen.

smutty □ ['smʌti] schmutzig.

snack [snæk] Imbiß *m;* ~-bar ['snækbɑː], ~-counter Snackbar *f,* Imbißstube *f.*

snaffle ['snæfl] Trense *f.*

snag [snæg] (Ast-, Zahn)Stumpf *m; fig.* Haken *m; Am.* Baumstumpf *m* (*bsd. unter Wasser*).

snail *zo.* [sneil] Schnecke *f.*

snake *zo.* [sneik] Schlange *f.*

snap [snæp] 1. Schnappen *n,* Biß *m;* Knack(s) *m;* Knall *m; fig.* Schwung *m,* Schmiß *m;* Schnappschloß *n; phot.* Schnappschuß *m; cold* ~ Kältewelle *f;* 2. *v/i.* schnappen (*at* nach); zuschnappen (*Schloß*); krachen; knacken; (zer)brechen; knallen; schnauzen; ~ *at s.o.* j-n anschnauzen; ~ *into it! Am. sl.* mach schnell!, Tempo!; ~ *out of it! Am. sl.* hör auf damit!; komm, komm!; *v/t.* (er)schnappen; (zu)schnappen lassen; *phot.* knipsen; zerbrechen; ~ *out* Wort hervorstoßen; ~ *up* wegschnappen; ~-fastener ['snæpfɑːsnə] Druckknopf *m;* ~-pish □ [~piʃ] bissig; schnippisch; ~-py [~pi] flott, bissig; F flott; ~-shot Schnappschuß *m,* Photo *n,* Momentaufnahme *f.*

snare [snɛə] 1. Schlinge *f;* 2. fangen; *fig.* umgarnen.

snarl [snɑːl] 1. knurren; murren; 2. Knurren *n;* Gewirr *n.*

snatch [snætʃ] 1. schneller Griff; Ruck *m;* Stückchen *n;* 2. schnappen; ergreifen; an sich reißen; nehmen; ~ *at* greifen nach.

sneak [sniːk] 1. *v/i.* schleichen; F petzen; *v/t.* F stibitzen; 2. Schleicher *m;* F Petzer *m;* ~ers ['sniːkəz] *pl.* F leichte Segeltuchschuhe *m/pl.*

sneer [sniə] 1. Hohnlächeln *n;* Spott *m;* 2. hohnlächeln; spotten; spötteln.

sneeze [sniːz] 1. niesen; 2. Niesen *n.*

snicker ['snikə] kichern; wiehern.

sniff [snif] schnüffeln, schnuppern; riechen; die Nase rümpfen.

snigger ['snigə] kichern.

snip [snip] 1. Schnitt *m;* Schnipsel

m, n; 2. schnippeln, schnipseln; knipsen.

snipe [snaip] 1. *orn.* (Sumpf-) Schnepfe *f;* 2. ✗ aus dem Hinterhalt (ab)schießen; ~r ✗ ['snaipə] Scharf-, Heckenschütze *m.*

snivel ['snivl] schniefen; schluchzen; plärren.

snob [snɔb] Großtuer *m;* Snob *m;* ~bish □ ['snɔbiʃ] snobistisch.

snoop *Am.* [snuːp] 1. *fig.* (herum-) schnüffeln; 2. Schnüffler(in).

snooze F [snuːz] 1. Schläfchen *n;* 2. dösen.

snore [snɔː] schnarchen.

snort [snɔːt] schnauben, schnaufen.

snout [snaut] Schnauze *f;* Rüssel *m.*

snow [snou] 1. Schnee *m;* 2. (be-) schneien; *be* ~*ed under fig.* erdrückt werden; ~-bound ['snoubaund] eingeschneit; ~-capped, ~-clad, ~-covered schneebedeckt; ~-drift Schneewehe *f;* ~-drop ♀ Schneeglöckchen *n;* ~-y □ ['snoui] schneeig; schneebedeckt, verschneit; schneeweiß.

snub [snʌb] 1. schelten, anfahren; 2. Verweis *m;* ~-nosed ['snʌbnouzd] stupsnasig.

snuff [snʌf] 1. Schnuppe *f e-r Kerze;* Schnupftabak *m;* 2. *a. take* ~ schnupfen; *Licht* putzen; ~le ['snʌfl] schnüffeln; näseln.

snug □ [snʌg] geborgen; behaglich; eng anliegend; ~gle ['snʌgl] (sich) schmiegen *od.* kuscheln (*to an acc.*).

so [sou] so; deshalb; also; *I hope* ~ ich hoffe es; *are you tired?* ~ *I am* bist du müde? Ja; *you are tired,* ~ *am I* du bist müde, ich auch; ~ *far* bisher.

soak [souk] *v/t.* einweichen; durchnässen; (durch)tränken; auf-, einsaugen; *v/i.* weichen; durchsickern.

soap [soup] 1. Seife *f;* soft ~ Schmierseife *f;* 2. (ein)seifen; ~-box ['soupbɔks] Seifenkiste *f;* improvisierte Rednertribüne; ~-y □ ['soupi] seifig; *fig.* unterwürfig.

soar [sɔː] sich erheben, sich aufschwingen; schweben; ✈ segelfliegen.

sob [sɔb] 1. Schluchzen *n;* 2. schluchzen.

sober ['soubə] 1. □ nüchtern; 2. (sich) ernüchtern; ~ness [~ənis], **sobriety** [sou'braiəti] Nüchternheit *f.*

so-called ['sou'kɔːld] sogenannt.

soccer F ['sɔkə] (Verbands)Fußball *m* (*Spiel*).

sociable ['souʃəbl] 1. □ gesellig; gemütlich; 2. geselliges Beisammensein.

social ['souʃəl] 1. □ gesellschaftlich; gesellig; sozial(istisch), Sozial...; ~ *insurance* Sozialversicherung *f;* ~ *services pl.* Sozialeinrichtungen *f/pl.*; 2. geselliges Beisammensein;

~ism [~lizəm] Sozialismus *m*; **~ist** [~ist] **1.** Sozialist(in); **2.** *a.* **~istic** [souʃə'listik] (~ally) sozialistisch; **~ize** ['souʃəlaiz] sozialisieren; verstaatlichen.

society [sə'saiəti] Gesellschaft *f*; Verein *m*, Klub *m*.

sociology [sousi'ɔlədʒi] Sozialwissenschaft *f*.

sock [sɔk] Socke *f*; Einlegesohle *f*.

socket ['sɔkit] (Augen-, Zahn)Höhle *f*; (Gelenk)Pfanne *f*; ⊕ Muffe *f*; ∮ Fassung *f*; ∮ Steckdose *f*.

sod [sɔd] **1.** Grasnarbe *f*; Rasen (-stück *n*) *m*; **2.** mit Rasen bedecken.

soda ['soudə] Soda *f*, *n*; **~-fountain** Siphon *m*; *Am.* Erfrischungshalle *f*, Eisdiele *f*.

sodden ['sɔdn] durchweicht; teigig.

soft [sɔft] **1.** □ *allg.* weich; *engS.*: mild; sanft; sacht, leise; zart, zärtlich; weichlich; F einfältig; ~ drink F alkoholfreies Getränk; **2.** *adv.* weich; **3.** F Trottel *m*; **~en** ['sɔfn] weich machen; (sich) erweichen; mildern; **~-headed** schwachsinnig; **~-hearted** gutmütig.

soggy ['sɔgi] durchnäßt; feucht.

soil [sɔil] **1.** Boden *m*, Erde *f*; Fleck *m*; Schmutz *m*; **2.** (be)schmutzen; beflecken.

sojourn ['sɔdʒəːn] **1.** Aufenthalt *m*; **2.** sich aufhalten.

solace ['sɔləs] **1.** Trost *m*; **2.** trösten.

solar ['soulə] Sonnen...

sold [sould] *pret. u. p.p. von* sell.

solder ['sɔldə] **1.** Lot *n*; **2.** löten.

soldier ['souldʒə] Soldat *m*; **~like**, **~ly** [~li] soldatisch; **~y** [~əri] Militär *n*.

sole¹ □ [soul] alleinig, einzig; ~ agent Alleinvertreter *m*.

sole² [~] **1.** Sohle *f*; **2.** besohlen.

solemn □ ['sɔləm] feierlich; ernst; **~ity** [sə'lemniti] Feierlichkeit *f*; Steifheit *f*; **~ize** ['sɔləmnaiz] feiern; feierlich vollziehen.

solicit [sə'lisit] (dringend) bitten; ansprechen, belästigen; **~ation** [səlisi'teiʃən] dringende Bitte; **~or** [sə'lisitə] ⚖ Anwalt *m*; *Am.* Agent *m*, Werber *m*; **~ous** □ [~təs] besorgt; ~ *of* begierig nach; ~ *to inf.* bestrebt zu *inf.*; **~ude** [~tju:d] Sorge *f*, Besorgnis *f*; Bemühung *f*.

solid ['sɔlid] **1.** □ fest; dauerhaft; haltbar; derb; massiv; A körperlich, Raum...; *fig.* gediegen; solid; triftig; solidarisch; *a* ~ *hour* e-e volle Stunde; **2.** (fester) Körper; **~arity** [sɔli'dæriti] Solidarität *f*; **~ify** [sə'lidifai] (sich) verdichten; **~ity** [~iti] Solidität *f*; Gediegenheit *f*.

soliloquy [sə'liləkwi] Selbstgespräch *n*, Monolog *m*.

solit|ary □ ['sɔlitəri] einsam; einzeln; einsiedlerisch; **~ude** [~tju:d]

Einsamkeit *f*; Verlassenheit *f*; Öde *f*.

solo ['soulou] Solo *n*; ≫ Alleinflug *m*; **~ist** [~ouist] Solist(in).

solu|ble ['sɔljubl] löslich; (auf)lösbar; **~tion** [sə'lu:ʃən] (Auf)Lösung *f*; ⊕ Gummilösung *f*.

solve [sɔlv] lösen; **~nt** ['sɔlvənt] **1.** (auf)lösend; ✝ zahlungsfähig; **2.** Lösungsmittel *n*.

somb|re, *Am.* **~er** □ ['sɔmbə] düster.

some [sʌm, səm] irgendein; etwas; einige, manche *pl.*; *Am.* F prima; ~ *20 miles* etwa 20 Meilen; *in* ~ *degree*, *to* ~ *extent* einigermaßen; **~body** ['sʌmbədi] jemand; ~ *day* eines Tages; **~how** irgendwie; ~ *or other* so oder so; **~one** jemand.

somersault ['sʌməsɔːlt] Salto *m*; Rolle *f*, Purzelbaum *m*; *turn a* ~ e-n Purzelbaum schlagen.

some|thing ['sʌmθiŋ] (irgend) etwas; ~ *like* so etwas wie, so ungefähr; ~ *time* **1.** einmal, dereinst; **2.** ehemalig; **~times** manchmal; **~what** etwas, ziemlich; **~where** irgendwo(hin).

somniferous □ [sɔm'nifərəs] einschläfernd.

son [sʌn] Sohn *m*.

song [sɔŋ] Gesang *m*; Lied *n*; Gedicht *n*; *for a mere od. an old* ~ für e-n Pappenstiel; **~-bird** ['sɔŋbəːd] Singvogel *m*; **~ster** ['sɔŋstə] Singvogel *m*; Sänger *m*.

sonic ['sɔnik] Schall...

son-in-law ['sʌninlɔː] Schwiegersohn *m*.

sonnet ['sɔnit] Sonett *n*.

sonorous □ [sə'nɔːrəs] klangvoll.

soon [su:n] bald; früh; gern; *as od. so* ~ *as* sobald als *od.* wie; **~er** ['su:nə] eher; früher; lieber; *no* ~ *... than* kaum ... als; *no* ~ *said than done* gesagt, getan.

soot [sut] **1.** Ruß *m*; **2.** verrußen.

sooth [su:θ]: *in* ~ in Wahrheit, fürwahr; **~e** [su:ð] beruhigen; mildern; **~sayer** ['su:θseiə] Wahrsager(in).

sooty □ ['suti] rußig.

sop [sɔp] **1.** eingeweichter Brocken; *fig.* Bestechung *f*; **2.** eintunken.

sophist|icate [sə'fistikeit] verdrehen; verfälschen; **~icated** kultiviert, raffiniert; intellektuell; blasiert; hochentwickelt, kompliziert; **~ry** ['sɔfistri] Spitzfindigkeit *f*.

sophomore *Am.* ['sɔfəmɔː] Student *m* im zweiten Jahr.

soporific [soupə'rifik] **1.** (~ally) einschläfernd; **2.** Schlafmittel *n*.

sorcer|er ['sɔːsərə] Zauberer *m*; **~ess** [~ris] Zauberin *f*; Hexe *f*; **~y** [~ri] Zauberei *f*.

sordid □ ['sɔːdid] schmutzig, schäbig (*bsd. fig.*).

sore [sɔː] **1.** □ schlimm, entzündet;

wund; weh; empfindlich; ~ throat
Halsweh n; 2. wunde Stelle; ~head
Am. F ['sɔːhed] 1. mürrischer
Mensch; 2. enttäuscht.

sorrel ['sɔrəl] 1. rötlichbraun (bsd.
Pferd); 2. Fuchs m (Pferd).

sorrow ['sɔrou] 1. Sorge f; Kummer m, Leid n; Trauer f; 2. trauern; sich grämen; ~ful □ ['sɔrəful]
traurig, betrübt; elend.

sorry □ ['sɔri] betrübt, bekümmert;
traurig; (I am) (so) ~! es tut mir
(sehr) leid; Verzeihung!; I am ~
for him er tut mir leid; we are ~ to
say wir müssen leider sagen.

sort [sɔːt] 1. Sorte f, Art f; what ~
of was für; of a ~, of ~s F so was
wie; ~ of F gewissermaßen; out of
~s F unpäßlich; verdrießlich; 2.
sortieren; ~ out (aus)sondern.

sot [sɔt] Trunkenbold m.

sough [sau] 1. Sausen n; 2. rauschen.

sought [sɔːt] pret. u. p.p. von seek.

soul [soul] Seele f (a. fig.).

sound [saund] 1. □ allg. gesund;
ganz; vernünftig; gründlich; fest;
✝ sicher; ♫ gültig; 2. Ton m,
Schall m, Laut m, Klang m; ♫
Sonde f; Meerenge f; Fischblase f;
3. (er)tönen, (er)klingen; erschallen
(lassen); sich gut etc. anhören; sondieren; ♫ loten; ♫ abhorchen;
~film ['saundfilm] Tonfilm m;
~ing ♫ [~diŋ] Lotung f; ~s pl.
lotbare Wassertiefe; ~less □ [~dlis]
lautlos; ~ness [~dnis] Gesundheit
f; ~proof schalldicht; ~track
Film: Tonspur f; ~wave Schall-
welle f.

soup¹ [suːp] Suppe f.

soup² Am. sl. mot. [~] 1. Stärke f;
2. ~ up Motor frisieren.

sour [sauə] 1. □ sauer; fig. bitter;
mürrisch; 2. v/t. säuern; fig. ver-,
erbittern; v/i. sauer (fig. bitter)
werden.

source [sɔːs] Quelle f; Ursprung m.

sour|ish □ ['sauəriʃ] säuerlich; ~
ness ['sauənis] Säure f; fig. Bitter-
keit f.

souse [saus] eintauchen; (mit Wasser) begießen; Fisch etc. einlegen,
einpökeln.

south [sauθ] 1. Süd(en m); 2. Süd...;
südlich; ~east ['sauθ'iːst] 1. Süd-
osten m; 2. a. ~eastern [sauθ-
'iːstən] südöstlich.

souther|ly ['sʌðəli] ~n [~ən] süd-
lich; Süd...; ~ner [~nə] Südlän-
der(in), Am. Südstaatler(in).

southernmost ['sʌðənmoust] süd-
lichst.

southpaw Am. ['sauθpɔː] Baseball:
Linkshänder m.

southward(s) adv. ['sauθwəd(z)]
südwärts, nach Süden.

south|-west ['sauθ'west] 1. Süd-
westen m; 2. südwestlich; ~-
wester [sauθ'westə] Südwestwind

m; ♫ Südwester m; ~westerly,
~western südwestlich.

souvenir ['suːvəniə] Andenken n.

sovereign ['sɔvrin] 1. □ höchst;
unübertrefflich; unumschränkt;
2. Herrscher(in); Sovereign m (20-
Schilling-Stück); ~ty [~rənti] Ober-
herrschaft f, Landeshoheit f.

soviet ['souviet] Sowjet m; attr.
Sowjet...

sow¹ [sau] zo. Sau f, (Mutter-)
Schwein n; ⊕ Sau f, Massel f.

sow² [sou] [irr.] (aus)säen, aus-
streuen; besäen; ~n [soun] p.p. von
sow².

spa [spaː] Heilbad n; Kurort m.

space [speis] 1. (Welt)Raum m;
Zwischenraum m; Zeitraum m;
2. typ. sperren; ~craft ['speis-
kraːft], ~ship Raumschiff n; ~
suit Raumanzug m.

spacious □ ['speiʃəs] geräumig,
weit, umfassend.

spade [speid] Spaten m; Kartenspiel: Pik n.

span¹ [spæn] 1. Spanne f; Spannweite f; Am. Gespann n; 2. (um-,
über)spannen; (aus)messen.

span² [~] pret. von spin 1.

spangle ['spæŋgl] 1. Flitter m;
2. (mit Flitter) besetzen; fig. über-
säen.

Spaniard ['spænjəd] Spanier(in).

Spanish ['spæniʃ] 1. spanisch; 2.
Spanisch n.

spank F [spæŋk] 1. verhauen;
2. Klaps m; ~ing ['spæŋkiŋ] 1. □
schnell, scharf; 2. F Haue f, Tracht
f Prügel.

spanner ⊕ ['spænə] Schraubenschlüssel m.

spar [spaː] 1. ♫ Spiere f; 🜨 Holm
m; 2. boxen; fig. sich streiten.

spare [spɛə] 1. □ spärlich, sparsam;
mager; überzählig; überschüssig;
Ersatz...; Reserve...; ~ hours Mußestunden f/pl.; ~ room Gastzimmer
n; ~ time Freizeit f; 2. ⊕ Ersatz-
teil m, n; 3. (ver)schonen; erübri-
gen; entbehren; (übrig)haben für;
(er)sparen; sparen mit.

sparing □ ['spɛəriŋ] sparsam.

spark [spaːk] 1. Funke(n) m; fig.
flotter Kerl; Galan m; 2. Funken
sprühen; ~(ing)-plug mot. ['spaːk-
(iŋ)plʌg] Zündkerze f.

sparkle ['spaːkl] 1. Funke(n) m;
Funkeln n; fig. sprühendes Wesen;
2. funkeln; blitzen; schäumen;
sparkling wine Schaumwein m.

sparrow orn. ['spærou] Sperling m,
Spatz m; ~hawk orn. Sperber m.

sparse □ [spaːs] spärlich, dünn.

spasm ♫ ['spæzəm] Krampf m;
~odic(al □) ♫ [spæz'mɔdik(əl)]
krampfhaft, -artig; fig. sprunghaft.

spat¹ [spæt] (Schuh)Gamasche f.

spat² [~] pret. u. p.p. von spit² 2.

spatter ['spætə] (be)spritzen.

spawn [spɔ:n] **1.** Laich *m*; *fig. contp.* Brut *f*; **2.** laichen; *fig.* aushecken.

speak [spi:k] [*irr.*] *v/i.* sprechen; reden; ~ *out*, ~ *up* laut sprechen; offen reden; ~ *to j-n od.* mit *j-m* sprechen; *v/t.* (aus)sprechen; äußern; ~**easy** *Am. sl.* ['spi:ki:zi] Flüsterkneipe *f* (*ohne Konzession*); ~**er** [~kə] Sprecher(in), Redner(in); *parl.* Vorsitzende(r) *m*; ~**ing-trumpet** [~kiŋtrʌmpit] Sprachrohr *n*.

spear [spiə] **1.** Speer *m*, Spieß *m*; Lanze *f*; **2.** (auf)spießen.

special ['speʃəl] **1.** □ besonder; Sonder...; speziell; Spezial...; **2.** Hilfspolizist *m*; Sonderausgabe *f*; Sonderzug *m*; *Am.* Sonderangebot *n*; *Am.* (Tages)Spezialität *f*; ~**ist** [~list] Spezialist *m*; ~**ity** [speʃi'æliti] Besonderheit *f*; Spezialfach *n*; ✝ Spezialität *f*; ~**ize** ['speʃəlaiz] besonders anführen; (sich) spezialisieren; ~**ty** [~lti] *s.* speciality.

specie ['spi:ʃi:] Metall-, Hartgeld *n*; ~**s** [~i:z] *pl. u. sg.* Art *f*, Spezies *f*.

speci|fic [spi'sifik] (~*ally*) spezifisch; besonder; bestimmt; ~**fy** ['spesifai] spezifizieren, einzeln angeben; ~**men** [~imin] Probe *f*, Exemplar *n*.

specious □ ['spi:ʃəs] blendend, bestechend; trügerisch; Schein...

speck [spek] **1.** Fleck *m*; Stückchen *n*; **2.** flecken; ~**le** ['spekl] **1.** Fleckchen *n*; **2.** flecken, sprenkeln.

spectacle ['spektəkl] Schauspiel *n*; Anblick *m*; (*a pair of*) ~**s** *pl.* (eine) Brille.

spectacular [spek'tækjulə] **1.** □ eindrucksvoll; auffallend, spektakulär; **2.** *Am.* F Galarevue *f*.

spectator [spek'teitə] Zuschauer *m*.

spect|ral □ ['spektrəl] gespenstisch; ~**re**, *Am.* ~**er** [~tə] Gespenst *n*.

speculat|e ['spekjuleit] grübeln, nachsinnen; ✝ spekulieren; ~**ion** [spekju'leiʃən] theoretische Betrachtung; Grübelei *f*; ✝ Spekulation *f*; ~**ive** □ ['spekjulətiv] grüblerisch; theoretisch; ✝ spekulierend; ~**or** [~leitə] Denker *m*; ✝ Spekulant *m*.

sped [sped] *pret. u. p.p. von* speed 2.

speech [spi:tʃ] Sprache *f*; Rede *f*, Ansprache *f*; *make a* ~ *e-e* Rede halten; ~**day** ['spi:tʃdei] *Schule:* (Jahres)Schlußfeier *f*; ~**less** □ [~ʃlis] sprachlos.

speed [spi:d] **1.** Geschwindigkeit *f*; Schnelligkeit *f*; Eile *f*; ⊕ Drehzahl *f*; **2.** [*irr.*] *v/i.* schnell fahren, rasen; ~ *up* (*pret. u. p.p.* ~*ed*) die Geschwindigkeit erhöhen; *v/t.* *j-m* Glück verleihen, befördern; ~ *up* (*pret. u. p.p.* ~*ed*) beschleunigen; ~**limit** ['spi:dlimit] Geschwindigkeitsbegrenzung *f*; ~**ometer** *mot.*

[spi'dɔmitə] Geschwindigkeitsmesser *m*, Tachometer *n*; ~**way** Motorradrennbahn *f*; *bsd. Am.* Schnellstraße *f*; ~**y** □ [~dj] schnell.

spell [spel] **1.** (Arbeits)Zeit *f*, ⊕ Schicht *f*; Weilchen *n*; Zauber (-spruch) *m*; **2.** abwechseln mit *j-m*; [*irr.*] buchstabieren; richtig schreiben; bedeuten; ~**binder** *Am.* ['spelbaində] fesselnder Redner; ~**bound** *fig.* (fest)gebannt; ~**er** *bsd. Am.* [~lə] Fibel *f*; ~**ing** [~liŋ] Rechtschreibung *f*; ~**ing-book** Fibel *f*.

spelt [spelt] *pret. u. p.p. von* spell 2.

spend [spend] [*irr.*] verwenden; (*Geld*) ausgeben; verbrauchen; verschwenden; verbringen; ~ *o.s.* sich erschöpfen; ~**thrift** ['spendθrift] Verschwender *m*.

spent [spent] **1.** *pret. u. p.p. von* spend; **2.** *adj.* erschöpft, matt.

sperm [spə:m] Same(n) *m*.

spher|e [sfiə] Kugel *f*; Erd-, Himmelskugel *f*; *fig.* Sphäre *f*; (Wirkungs)Kreis *m*; Bereich *m*; *fig.* Gebiet *n*; ~**ical** □ ['sferikəl] sphärisch; kugelförmig.

spice [spais] **1.** Gewürz(e *pl.*) *n*; *fig.* Würze *f*; Anflug *m*; **2.** würzen.

spick and span ['spikən'spæn] frisch u. sauber; schmuck; funkelnagelneu.

spicy □ ['spaisi] würzig; pikant.

spider *zo.* ['spaidə] Spinne *f*.

spiel *Am. sl.* [spi:l] Gequassel *n*.

spigot ['spigət] (Faß)Zapfen *m*.

spike [spaik] **1.** Stift *m*; Spitze *f*; Dorn *m*; Stachel *m*; *Sport:* Laufdorn *m*; *mot.* Spike *m*; ❧ Ähre *f*; **2.** festnageln; mit *eisernen* Stacheln versehen.

spill [spil] **1.** [*irr.*] *v/t.* verschütten; vergießen; F Reiter *etc.* abwerfen; schleudern; *v/i.* überlaufen; **2.** F Sturz *m*.

spilt [spilt] *pret. u. p.p. von* spill 1; *cry over* ~ *milk* über *et.* jammern, was doch nicht zu ändern ist. □

spin [spin] **1.** [*irr.*] spinnen (*a.fig.*); wirbeln; sich drehen; *Münze* hochwerfen; sich *et.* ausdenken; erzählen; ❧ trudeln; ~ *along* dahinsausen; ~ *s.th. out et.* in die Länge ziehen; **2.** Drehung *f*; Spritztour *f*; ❧ Trudeln *n*.

spinach ❧ ['spinidʒ] Spinat *m*.

spinal *anat.* ['spainl] Rückgrat...; ~ *column* Wirbelsäule *f*; ~ *cord*, ~ *marrow* Rückenmark *n*.

spindle ['spindl] Spindel *f*.

spin-drier ['spindraiə] Wäscheschleuder *f*.

spine [spain] *anat.* Rückgrat *n*; Dorn *m*; (Gebirgs)Grat *m*; (Buch-) Rücken *m*.

spinning|-mill ['spiniŋmil] Spinnerei *f*; ~**wheel** Spinnrad *n*.

spinster ['spinstə] unverheiratete Frau; (alte) Jungfer.
spiny ['spaini] dornig.
spiral ['spaiərəl] 1. □ spiralig; ~ staircase Wendeltreppe f; 2. Spirale f; fig. Wirbel m.
spire ['spaiə] Turm-, Berg- etc. Spitze f; Kirchturm(spitze f) m.
spirit ['spirit] 1. allg. Geist m; Sinn m; Temperament n, Leben n; Mut m; Gesinnung f; Spiritus n; Sprit m, Benzin n; ~s pl. Spirituosen pl.; high (low) ~s pl. gehobene (gedrückte) Stimmung f; 2. ~ away od. off wegzaubern; ~ed □ geistvoll; temperamentvoll; mutig; ~less □ [~tlis] geistlos; temperamentlos; mutlos.
spiritual □ ['spiritjuəl] geistig; geistlich; geistvoll; ~ism [~lizəm] Spiritismus m.
spirituous ['spiritjuəs] alkoholisch.
spirt [spə:t] (hervor)spritzen.
spit¹ [spit] 1. Bratspieß m; Landzunge f; 2. aufspießen.
spit² [~] 1. Speichel m; F Ebenbild n; 2. [irr.] (aus)spucken; fauchen; sprühen (fein regnen).
spite [spait] 1. Bosheit f; Groll m; in ~ of trotz (gen.); 2. ärgern; kränken; ~ful □ ['spaitful] boshaft, gehässig.
spitfire ['spitfaiə] Hitzkopf m.
spittle ['spitl] Speichel m, Spucke f.
spittoon [spi'tu:n] Spucknapf m.
splash [splæʃ] 1. Spritzfleck m; P(l)atschen n; 2. (be)spritzen; p(l)atschen; planschen; (hin)klecksen.
splay [splei] 1. Ausschrägung f; 2. auswärts gebogen; 3. v/t. ausschrägen; v/i. ausgeschrägt sein; ~foot ['spleifut] Spreizfuß m.
spleen [spli:n] anat. Milz f; üble Laune, Ärger m.
splend|id □ ['splendid] glänzend, prächtig, herrlich; ~o(u)r [~də] Glanz m, Pracht f, Herrlichkeit f.
splice [splais] (ver)spleißen.
splint [splint] 1. Schiene f; 2. schienen; ~er ['splintə] 1. Splitter m; 2. (zer)splittern.
split [split] 1. Spalt m, Riß m; fig. Spaltung f; 2. gespalten; 3. [irr.] v/t. (zer)spalten; zerreißen; (sich) et. teilen; ~ hairs Haarspalterei treiben; ~ one's sides with laughter sich totlachen; v/i. sich spalten; platzen; ~ting ['spliting] heftig, rasend (Kopfschmerz).
splutter ['splʌtə] s. sputter.
spoil [spoil] 1. oft ~s pl. Beute f, Raub m; fig. Ausbeute f; Schutt m; ~s pl. pol. bsd. Am. Futterkrippe f; 2. [irr.] (be)rauben; plündern; verderben; verwöhnen; Kind verziehen; ~sman Am. pol. ['spoilzmən]; Postenjäger m; ~sport Spieler-

derber(in); ~s system Am. pol. Futterkrippensystem n.
spoilt [spoilt] pret. u. p.p. von spoil 2.
spoke [spouk] 1. pret. von speak; 2. Speiche f; (Leiter)Sprosse f; ~n ['spoukən] p.p. von speak; ~sman [~ksmən] Wortführer m.
sponge [spʌndʒ] 1. Schwamm m; 2. v/t. mit e-m Schwamm (ab)wischen; ~ up aufsaugen; v/i. schmarotzen; ~cake ['spʌndʒ'keik] Biskuitkuchen m; ~r F fig. [~dʒə] Schmarotzer(in).
spongy ['spʌndʒi] schwammig.
sponsor ['spɔnsə] 1. Pate m; Bürge m; Förderer m; Auftraggeber m für Werbesendungen; 2. Pate stehen bei; fördern; ~ship [~ʃip] Paten-, Gönnerschaft f.
spontane|ity [spɔntə'ni:iti] Freiwilligkeit f; eigener Antrieb; ~ous □ [spɔn'teinjəs] freiwillig, von selbst (entstanden); Selbst...; spontan; unwillkürlich; unvermittelt.
spook [spu:k] Spuk m; ~y ['spu:ki] geisterhaft, Spuk...
spool [spu:l] 1. Spule f; 2. spulen.
spoon [spu:n] 1. Löffel m; 2. löffeln; ~ful ['spu:nful] Löffelvoll m.
sporadic [spə'rædik] (~ally) sporadisch, verstreut.
spore ♀ [spɔ:] Spore f, Keimkorn n.
sport [spɔ:t] 1. Sport m; Spiel n; fig. Spielball m; Scherz m; sl. feiner Kerl; ~s pl. allg. Sport m; Sportfest n; 2. v/i. sich belustigen; spielen; v/t. F protzen mit; ~ive □ ['spɔ:tiv] lustig; scherzhaft; ~sman [~tsmən] Sportler m.
spot [spɔt] 1. allg. Fleck m; Tupfen m; Makel m; Stelle f; ♀ Leberfleck m; ♀ Pickel m; Tropfen m; a ~ of F etwas; on the ~ auf der Stelle; sofort; 2. sofort liefer- od. zahlbar; 3. (be)flecken; ausfindig machen; erkennen; ~less □ ['spɔtlis] fleckenlos; ~light thea. Scheinwerfer(-licht n) m; ~ter [~tə] Beobachter m; Am. Kontrolleur m; ~ty [~ti] fleckig.
spouse [spauz] Gatte m; Gattin f.
spout [spaut] 1. Tülle f; Strahlrohr n; (Wasser)Strahl m; 2. (aus)spritzen; F salbadern.
sprain [sprein] 1. Verstauchung f; 2. verstauchen.
sprang [spræŋ] pret. von spring 2.
sprat ichth. [spræt] Sprotte f.
sprawl [sprɔ:l] sich rekeln; ausgestreckt daliegen; ♀ wuchern.
spray [sprei] 1. zerstäubte Flüssigkeit; Sprühregen m; Gischt m; Spray m, n; ~ser = sprayer; 2. zerstäuben; et. besprühen; ~er ['spreiə] Zerstäuber m.
spread [spred] 1. [irr.] v/t. a. ~ out ausbreiten; (aus)dehnen; verbreiten; belegen; Butter etc. aufstreichen; Brot etc. bestreichen; ~ the

table den Tisch decken; *v/i.* sich aus- *od.* verbreiten; 2. Aus-, Verbreitung *f*; Spannweite *f*; Fläche *f*; *Am. Bett-* etc. Decke *f*; *Brot-Aufstrich m*; F Festschmaus *m*.

spree F [spri:] Spaß *m*, Jux *m*; Zechgelage *n*; Orgie *f*; *Kauf-* etc. Welle *f*.

sprig [sprig] Sproß *m*, Reis *n* (*a. fig.*); ⊕ Zwecke *f*, Stift *m*.

sprightly ['spraitli] lebhaft, munter.

spring [spriŋ] 1. Sprung *m*, Satz *m*; (Sprung)Feder *f*; Federkraft *f*, Elastizität *f*; Triebfeder *f*; Quelle *f*; *fig.* Ursprung *m*; Frühling *m*; 2. [*irr.*] *v/t.* springen lassen; (zer-)sprengen; *Wild* aufjagen; ~ *a leak* ⊕ leck werden; ~ *a surprise on s.o.* j-n überraschen; *v/i.* springen; entspringen; ⚘ sprießen; ~ *up* aufkommen (*Ideen* etc.); **~board** ['spriŋbɔ:d] Sprungbrett *n*; ~ **tide** Springflut *f*; **~tide**, **~time** Frühling(szeit *f*) *m*; **~y** □ [~ŋi] federnd.

sprinkl|e ['spriŋkl] (be)streuen; (be)sprengen; **~er** [~lə] Berieselungsanlage *f*; Rasensprenger *m*; **~ing** [~liŋ] Sprühregen *m*; *a* ~ *of* ein wenig, ein paar.

sprint [sprint] *Sport:* 1. sprinten; spurten; 2. Sprint *m*; Kurzstreckenlauf *m*; Endspurt *m*; **~er** ['sprintə] Sprinter *m*, Kurzstreckenläufer *m*.

sprite [sprait] Geist *m*, Kobold *m*.

sprout [spraut] 1. sprießen, wachsen (lassen); 2. ⚘ Sproß *m*; (*Brussels*) ~ *pl.* Rosenkohl *m*.

spruce[1] □ [spru:s] schmuck, nett.

spruce[2] ⚘ [~] *a.* ~ *fir* Fichte *f*, Rottanne *f*.

sprung [sprʌŋ] *pret.* (⚘) *u. p.p.* von *spring* 2.

spry [sprai] munter, flink.

spun [spʌn] *pret. u. p.p. von spin* 1.

spur [spə:] 1. Sporn *m* (*a. zo.*, ⚘); *fig.* Ansporn *m*; Vorsprung *m*, Ausläufer *m e-s Berges*; *on the* ~ *of the moment* der Eingebung des Augenblicks folgend; spornstreichs; 2. (an)spornen.

spurious □ ['spjuəriəs] unecht, gefälscht.

spurn [spə:n] verschmähen, verächtlich zurückweisen.

spurt [spə:t] 1. alle s-e Kräfte zs.-nehmen; *Sport:* spurten; *s. spirt*; 2. plötzliche Anstrengung, Ruck *m*; *Sport:* Spurt *m*.

sputter ['spʌtə] 1. Gesprudel *n*; 2. (hervor)sprudeln; spritzen.

spy [spai] 1. Späher(in); Spion(in); 2. (er)spähen; erblicken; spionieren; **~glass** ['spaiglɑ:s] Fernglas *n*; **~hole** Guckloch *n*.

squabble ['skwɔbl] 1. Zank *m*, Kabbelei *f*; 2. (sich) zanken.

squad [skwɔd] Rotte *f*, Trupp *m*; **~ron** ['skwɔdrən] ✕ Schwadron *f*; ⚓ Staffel *f*; ⚓ Geschwader *n*.

squalid □ ['skwɔlid] schmutzig, armselig.

squall [skwɔ:l] 1. ⚓ Bö *f*; Schrei *m*; **~s** *pl.* Geschrei *n*; 2. schreien.

squalor ['skwɔlə] Schmutz *m*.

squander ['skwɔndə] verschwenden.

square [skwɛə] 1. □ viereckig; quadratisch; rechtwinklig; eckig; passend, stimmend; in Ordnung; direkt; quitt, gleich; ehrlich, offen; F altmodisch, spießig; ~ *measure* Flächenmaß *n*; ~ *mile* Quadratmeile *f*; 2. Quadrat *n*; Viereck *n*; *Schach-*Feld *n*; öffentlicher Platz; Winkelmaß *n*; F altmodischer Spießer; 3. *v/t.* viereckig machen; einrichten (*with* nach), anpassen (*dat.*); ⚘ be-, ausgleichen; *v/i.* passen (*with* zu); übereinstimmen; **~built** ['skwɛə'bilt] vierschrötig; ~ *dance* Quadrille *f*; **~toes** *sg.* F Pedant *m*.

squash[1] [skwɔʃ] 1. Gedränge *n*; Fruchtsaft *m*; Platsch(en *n*) *m*; Rakettspiel *n*; 2. (zer-, zs.-)quetschen; drücken.

squash[2] ⚘ [~] Kürbis *m*.

squat [skwɔt] 1. kauernd; untersetzt; 2. hocken, kauern; **~ter** ['skwɔtə] *Am.* Schwarzsiedler *m*; *Australien:* Schafzüchter *m*.

squawk [skwɔ:k] 1. kreischen, schreien; 2. Gekreisch *n*, Geschrei *n*.

squeak [skwi:k] quieken, quietschen.

squeal [skwi:l] quäken; gell schreien; quieken.

squeamish □ ['skwi:miʃ] empfindlich; mäkelig; heikel; penibel.

squeeze [skwi:z] 1. (sich) drücken, (sich) quetschen; auspressen; *fig.* (be)drängen; 2. Druck *m*; Gedränge *n*; **~r** ['skwi:zə] Presse *f*.

squelch F [skweltʃ] zermalmen.

squid *zo.* [skwid] Tintenfisch *m*.

squint [skwint] schielen; blinzeln.

squire ['skwaiə] 1. Gutsbesitzer *m*; (Land)Junker *m*; *Am.* F (Friedens-)Richter *m*; 2. *e-e Dame* begleiten.

squirm F [skwə:m] sich winden.

squirrel *zo.* ['skwirəl, *Am.* 'skwə:rəl] Eichhörnchen *n*.

squirt [skwə:t] 1. Spritze *f*; Strahl *m*; F Wichtigtuer *m*; 2. spritzen.

stab [stæb] 1. Stich *m*; 2. *v/t.* (er-)stechen; *v/i.* stechen (*at* nach).

stabili|ty [stə'biliti] Stabilität *f*; Standfestig-, Beständigkeit *f*; **~ze** ['steibilaiz] stabilisieren (*a.* ✈).

stable[1] □ ['steibl] stabil, fest.

stable[2] [~] 1. Stall *m*; 2. einstallen.

stack [stæk] 1. ✗ (Heu-, Stroh-, Getreide)Schober *m*; Stapel *m*; Schornstein(reihe *f*) *m*; Regal *n*; **~s** *pl. Am.* Hauptmagazin *n e-r*

Bibliothek; F Haufen *m*; 2. aufstapeln.

stadium ['steidjəm] *Sport*: Stadion *n*, Sportplatz *m*, Kampfbahn *f*.

staff [sta:f] 1. Stab *m* (a. ⚔); Stock *m*; Stütze *f*; ♪ Notensystem *n*; Personal *n*; Belegschaft *f*; Beamten-, Lehrkörper *m*; 2. (mit Personal, Beamten *od.* Lehrern) besetzen.

stag *zo.* [stæg] Hirsch *m*.

stage [steidჳ] 1. Bühne *f*, Theater *n*; *fig.* Schauplatz *m*; Stufe *f*, Stadium *n*; Teilstrecke *f*, Etappe *f*; Haltestelle *f*; Gerüst *n*, Gestell *n*; 2. inszenieren; **~coach** ['steidჳkoutʃ] Postkutsche *f*; **~craft** dramatisches Talent; Theatererfahrung *f*; **~ direction** Bühnenanweisung *f*; **~ fright** Lampenfieber *n*; **~ manager** Regisseur *m*.

stagger ['stægə] 1. *v/i.* (sch)wanken, taumeln; *fig.* stutzen; *v/t.* ins Wanken bringen; staffeln; 2. Schwanken *n*; Staffelung *f*.

stagna|nt □ ['stægnənt] stehend (*Wasser*); stagnierend; stockend; träg; † still; **~te** [~neit] stocken.

staid □ [steid] gesetzt, ruhig.

stain [stein] 1. Fleck(en) *m* (*a. fig.*); Beize *f*; 2. fleckig machen; *fig.* beflecken; beizen, färben; **~ed glass** buntes Glas; **~less** □ ['steinlis] ungefleckt; *fig.* fleckenlos; rostfrei.

stair [stɛə] Stufe *f*; **~s** *pl.* Treppe *f*, Stiege *f*; **~case** ['stɛəkeis], **~way** Treppe(nhaus *n*) *f*.

stake [steik] 1. Pfahl *m*; Marterpfahl *m*; (Spiel)Einsatz *m* (*a. fig.*); **~s** *pl. Pferderennen*: Preis *m*, Rennen *n*; *pull up* **~s** *Am.* F abhauen; *be at* **~** auf dem Spiel stehen; 2. (um)pfählen; aufs Spiel setzen; **~ out**, **~ off** abstecken.

stale □ [steil] alt; schal, abgestanden; verbraucht (*Luft*); fad.

stalk [stɔ:k] 1. Stengel *m*, Stiel *m*; Halm *m*; *hunt.* Pirsch *f*; 2. *v/i.* einherstolzieren; heranschleichen; *hunt.* pirschen; *v/t.* beschleichen.

stall [stɔ:l] 1. (Pferde)Box *f*; (Verkaufs)Stand *m*, Marktbude *f*; *thea.* Sperrsitz *m*; 2. *v/t.* einstallen; *Motor* abwürgen; *v/i. mot.* aussetzen.

stallion ['stæljən] Hengst *m*.

stalwart □ ['stɔ:lwət] stramm, stark.

stamina ['stæminə] Ausdauer *f*.

stammer ['stæmə] 1. stottern, stammeln; 2. Stottern *n*.

stamp [stæmp] 1. (Auf)Stampfen *n*; ⊕ Stampfe(r *m*) *f*; Stempel *m* (*a. fig.*); (Brief)Marke *f*; Gepräge *n*; Art *f*; 2. (auf)stampfen; prägen; stanzen; (ab)stempeln (*a. fig.*); frankieren.

stampede [stæm'pi:d] 1. Panik *f*, wilde Flucht; 2. *v/i.* durchgehen; *v/t.* in Panik versetzen.

stanch [sta:ntʃ] 1. hemmen; stillen; 2. □ fest; zuverlässig; treu.

stand [stænd] 1. [*irr.*] *v/i.* allg. stehen; sich befinden; beharren; *mst* **~ still** stillstehen, stehenbleiben; bestehen (bleiben); **~ against** *j-m* widerstehen; **~ aside** beiseite treten; **~ back** zurücktreten; **~ by** dabeistehen; *fig.* (fest) stehen zu; helfen; bereitstehen; **~ for** kandidieren für; bedeuten; eintreten für; F sich *et.* gefallen lassen; **~ in** einspringen; **~ in with** sich gut stellen mit; **~ off** zurücktreten (von); **~ off!** weg da!; **~ on** (*fig.* be)stehen auf; **~ out** hervorstehen; sich abheben (*against* gegen); standhalten (*dat.*); **~ over** stehen *od.* liegen bleiben; **~ pat** *Am.* F stur bleiben; **~ to** bleiben bei; **~ up** aufstehen; sich erheben; **~ up for** eintreten für; **~ up to** sich zur Wehr setzen gegen; standhalten (*dat.*); **~ upon** (*fig.* be)stehen auf (*dat.*); *v/t.* (hin)stellen; aushalten, (v)ertragen; über sich ergehen lassen; F spendieren; 2. Stand *m*; Standplatz *m*; Bude *f*; Standpunkt *m*; Stillstand *m*; Ständer *m*; Tribüne *f*; *bsd. Am.* Zeugenstand *m*; *make a od.* one's **~** *against* standhalten (*dat.*).

standard ['stændəd] 1. Standarte *f*, Fahne *f*; Standard *m*, Norm *f*; Regel *f*, Maßstab *m*; Niveau *n*; Stufe *f*; Münzfuß *m*; Währung *f*; Ständer *m*, Mast *m*; 2. maßgebend; Normal...; **~ize** [~daiz] norm(ier)en.

stand-by ['stændbai] Beistand *m*.

standee [stæn'di:] Stehende(r) *m*; *Am.* Stehplatzinhaber *m*.

standing ['stændiŋ] 1. □ stehend; fest; (be)ständig; **~ orders** *pl. parl.* Geschäftsordnung *f*; 2. Stellung *f*, Rang *m*, Ruf *m*; Dauer *f*; *of long* ~ alt; **~-room** Stehplatz *m*.

stand|off *Am.* ['stændɔ:f] Unentschieden *n*; Dünkel *m*; **~offish** [~d'ɔ:fiʃ] zurückhaltend; **~patter** *Am. pol.* [stænd'pætə] sturer Konservativer; **~point** ['stændpoint] Standpunkt *m*; **~still** Stillstand *m*; **~up**: ~ *collar* Stehkragen *m*.

stank [stæŋk] *pret. von* stink 2.

stanza ['stænzə] Stanze *f*; Strophe *f*.

staple[1] ['steipl] Haupterzeugnis *n*; Hauptgegenstand *m*; *attr.* Haupt...

staple[2] [~] Krampe *f*; Heftklammer *f*.

star [sta:] 1. Stern *m*; *thea.* Star *m*; **~s** *and Stripes pl. Am.* Sternenbanner *n*; 2. mit Sternen schmücken; *thea.*, *fig.* die Hauptrolle spielen.

starboard ⚓ ['sta:bəd] 1. Steuerbord *n*; 2. *Ruder* steuerbord legen.

starch [sta:tʃ] 1. (Wäsche)Stärke *f*; *fig.* Steifheit *f*; 2. stärken.

stare [stɛə] 1. Starren *n*; Staunen *n*; starrer Blick; 2. starren, staunen.

stark [stɑːk] **1.** *adj.* starr; bar, völlig (*Unsinn*); **2.** *adv.* völlig.

starlight ['stɑːlait] Sternenlicht *n.*

starling *orn.* ['stɑːliŋ] Star *m.*

starlit ['stɑːlit] sternenklar.

star|ry ['stɑːri] Stern(en)...; gestirnt; **~spangled** ['stɑːspæŋgld] sternenbesät; ♀ Banner Am. Sternenbanner *n.*

start [stɑːt] **1.** Auffahren *n,* Stutzen *n;* Ruck *m; Sport:* Start *m;* Aufbruch *m;* Anfang *m; fig.* Vorsprung *m; get the ~ of s.o.* j-m zuvorkommen; **2.** *v/i.* aufspringen, auffahren; stutzen; *Sport:* starten; abfahren; aufbrechen; *mot.* anspringen; anfangen (*on* mit; *doing* zu tun) *v/t.* in Gang bringen; *mot.* anlassen; *Sport:* starten (lassen); aufjagen; *fig.* anfangen; veranlassen (*doing* zu tun); **~er** ['stɑːtə] *Sport:* Starter *m;* Läufer *m; mot.* Anlasser *m.*

startl|e ['stɑːtl] (er-, auf)schrecken; **~ing** [~liŋ] bestürzend, überraschend, aufsehenerregend.

starv|ation [stɑːˈveiʃən] (Ver)Hungern *n,* Hungertod *m; attr.* Hunger...; **~e** [stɑːv] verhungern (lassen); *fig.* verkümmern (lassen).

state [steit] **1.** Zustand *m;* Stand *m;* Staat *m; pol. mst* ♀ Staat *m; attr.* Staats...; *in ~* feierlich; **2.** angeben; darlegen, darstellen; feststellen; melden; *Regel etc.* aufstellen; ♀ **Department** *Am. pol.* Außenministerium *n;* **~ly** ['steitli] stattlich; würdevoll; erhaben; **~ment** [~tmənt] Angabe *f;* Aussage *f;* Darstellung *f;* Feststellung *f;* Aufstellung *f;* ✝ (*~ of account* Konto-) Auszug *m;* **~room** Staatszimmer *n;* ♣ Einzelkabine *f;* **~side** *Am.* F **1.** *adj.* USA-..., Heimat...; **2.** *adv.: go ~* heimkehren; **~sman** [~smən] Staatsmann *m.*

static ['stætik] statisch, Ruhe...

station ['steiʃən] **1.** Stand(ort) *m;* Stelle *f;* Stellung *f;* ⚔, ♣, 🚉 Station *f;* Bahnhof *m;* Rang *m,* Stand *m;* **2.** aufstellen, postieren, stationieren; **~ary** □ [~ʃnəri] stillstehend; feststehend; **~ery** [~] Schreibwaren *f/pl.;* **~master** 🚉 Stationsvorsteher *m;* **~ wagon** *Am. mot.* Kombiwagen *m.*

statistics [stəˈtistiks] *pl.* Statistik *f.*

statu|ary ['stætjuəri] Bildhauer (-kunst *f*) *m;* **~e** [~ju:] Standbild *n,* Plastik *f,* Statue *f.*

stature ['stætʃə] Statur *f,* Wuchs *m.*

status ['steitəs] Zustand *m;* Stand *m.*

statute ['stætjuːt] Statut *n,* Satzung *f;* (Landes)Gesetz *n.*

staunch [stɔːntʃ] *s. stanch.*

stave [steiv] **1.** Faßdaube *f;* Strophe *f;* **2.** [*irr.*] *mst ~ in* ein Loch schlagen in (*acc.*); **~ off** abwehren.

stay [stei] **1.** ⚓ Stag *n;* ⊕ Strebe *f;*

Stütze *f;* Aufschub *m;* Aufenthalt *m;* **~s** *pl.* Korsett *n;* **2.** bleiben; wohnen; (sich) aufhalten; Ausdauer haben; hemmen; aufschieben; *Hunger* vorläufig stillen; stützen; **~er** ['steiə] *Sport:* Steher *m.*

stead [sted] Stelle *f,* Statt *f;* **~fast** □ ['stedfəst] fest, unerschütterlich; standhaft; unverwandt (*Blick*).

steady ['stedi] **1.** □ (be)ständig; stetig; sicher; fest; ruhig; gleichmäßig; unerschütterlich; zuverlässig; **2.** stetig *od.* sicher machen *od.* werden; (sich) festigen; stützen; (sich) beruhigen; **3.** *Am.* F feste Freundin, fester Freund.

steal [stiːl] **1.** [*irr.*] *v/t.* stehlen (*a. fig.*); *v/i.* sich stehlen *od.* schleichen; **2.** *Am.* Diebstahl *m.*

stealth [stelθ] Heimlichkeit *f; by ~* heimlich; **~y** □ ['stelθi] verstohlen.

steam [stiːm] **1.** Dampf *m;* Dunst *m; attr.* Dampf...; **2.** *v/i.* dampfen; **~ up** beschlagen (*Glas*); *v/t.* ausdünsten; dämpfen; **~er** ♣ ['stiːmə] Dampfer *m;* **~y** □ [~mi] dampfig; dampfend; dunstig.

steel [stiːl] **1.** Stahl *m;* **2.** stählern; Stahl...; **3.** (ver)stählen.

steep [stiːp] **1.** steil, jäh; F toll; **2.** einweichen; einlegen; eintauchen; tränken; *fig.* versenken.

steeple ['stiːpl] Kirchturm *m;* **~chase** *Sport:* Hindernisrennen *n.*

steer¹ [stiə] junger Ochse.

steer² [~] steuern; **~age** ♣ ['stiəridʒ] Steuerung *f;* Zwischendeck *n;* **~ing-wheel** [~riŋwiːl] Steuerrad *n;* *mot.* Lenkrad *n;* **~sman** ♣ [~zmən] Rudergänger *m.*

stem [stem] **1.** (Baum-, Wort-) Stamm *m;* Stiel *m;* Stengel *m;* ♣ Vordersteven *m;* **2.** *Am.* (ab)stammen (*from* von); sich stemmen gegen, ankämpfen gegen.

stench [stentʃ] Gestank *m.*

stencil ['stensl] Schablone *f; typ.* Matrize *f.* [graph(in).]

stenographer [steˈnɔgrəfə] Steno-]

step¹ [step] **1.** Schritt *m,* Tritt *m; fig.* Strecke *f;* Fußstapfe *f;* (Treppen)Stufe *f;* Trittbrett *n;* **~s** *pl.* Trittleiter *f;* **2.** *v/i.* schreiten, treten, gehen; **~ out** ausschreiten; *v/t.* **~ off,** **~ out** abschreiten; **~ up** ankurbeln.

step² [~] *in Zssgn* Stief...; **~father** ['stepfɑːðə] Stiefvater *m;* **~mother** Stiefmutter *f.*

steppe [step] Steppe *f.*

stepping-stone *fig.* ['stepiŋstoun] Sprungbrett *n.*

steril|e ['sterail] unfruchtbar; steril; **~ity** [steˈriliti] Sterilität *f;* **~ize** ['sterilaiz] sterilisieren.

sterling ['stɜːliŋ] vollwertig, echt; gediegen; ✝ Sterling *m* (*Währung*).

stern [stɜːn] **1.** □ ernst; finster, streng, hart; **2.** ♣ Heck *n;* **~ness**

['stə:nnis] Ernst *m*; Strenge *f*;
~-post ⚓ Hintersteven *m*.
stevedore ⚓ ['sti:vidɔ:] Stauer *m*.
stew [stju:] 1. schmoren, dämpfen;
2. Schmorgericht *n*; F Aufregung *f*.
steward [stjuəd] Verwalter *m*; ⚓,
🦌 Steward *m*; (Fest)Ordner *m*;
~ess ⚓, 🦌 ['stjuədis] Stewardeß *f*.
stick [stik] 1. Stock *m*; Stecken *m*;
Stab *m*; (Besen- *etc.*)Stiel *m*; Stange
f; F Klotz *m* (*unbeholfener Mensch*);
~s *pl.* Kleinholz *n*; the ~s *pl.* Am. F
die hinterste Provinz; 2. [*irr.*] *v/i.*
stecken (bleiben); haften; kleben
(to an *dat.*); ~ at nothing vor nichts
zurückscheuen; ~ out, ~ up hervorstehen; F standhalten; ~ to bleiben
bei; *v/t.* (ab)stechen; (an)stecken,
(an)heften; (an)kleben; F ertragen;
~ing-plaster ['stikiŋplɑ:stə] Heftpflaster *n*.
sticky □ ['stiki] kleb(e)rig; zäh.
stiff □ [stif] steif; starr; hart; fest;
mühsam; stark (*Getränk*); *be bored
~* F zu Tode gelangweilt sein; *keep
a ~ upper lip* die Ohren steifhalten;
~en ['stifn] (sich) (ver)steifen;
~-necked [~'nekt] halsstarrig.
stifle ['staifl] ersticken (*a. fig.*).
stigma ['stigmə] (Brand-, Schand-)
Mal *n*; Stigma *n*; **~tize** [~ətaiz]
brandmarken.
stile [stail] Zauntritt *m*, Zaunüber-
gang *m*.
still [stil] 1. *adj.* still; 2. *adv.* noch
(immer); 3. *cj.* doch, dennoch;
4. stillen; beruhigen; 5. Destillier-
apparat *m*; **~-born** ['stilbɔ:n] tot-
geboren; ~ *life* Stilleben *n*; **~ness**
Stille *f*, Ruhe *f*.
stilt [stilt] Stelze *f*; **~ed** ['stiltid]
gespreizt, hochtrabend, geschraubt.
stimul|ant ['stimjulənt] 1. 🩺 stimu-
lierend; 2. 🩺 Reizmittel *n*; Genuß-
mittel *n*; Anreiz *m*; **~ate** [~leit]
(an)reizen; anregen; **~ation** [stimju-
'leiʃən] Reizung *f*, Antrieb *m*; **~us**
['stimjuləs] Antrieb *m*; Reizmittel *n*.
sting [stiŋ] 1. Stachel *m*; Stich *m*,
Biß *m*; *fig.* Schärfe *f*; Antrieb *m*;
2. [*irr.*] stechen; brennen; schmerzen; (an)treiben.
sting|iness ['stindʒinis] Geiz *m*; **~y**
□ ['stindʒi] geizig; knapp, karg.
stink [stiŋk] 1. Gestank *m*; 2. [*irr.*]
v/i. stinken; *v/t.* verstänkern.
stint [stint] 1. Einschränkung *f*;
Arbeit *f*; 2. knausern mit; einschränken; *j-n* knapp halten.
stipend ['staipend] Gehalt *n*.
stipulat|e ['stipjuleit] *a.* ~ *for* aus-
bedingen, ausmachen, vereinbaren;
~ion [stipju'leiʃən] Abmachung *f*;
Klausel *f*, Bedingung *f*.
stir [stə:] 1. Regung *f*; Bewegung *f*;
Rühren *n*; Aufregung *f*; Aufsehen
n; 2. (sich) rühren; umrühren, bewegen; aufregen; ~ *up* aufrühren;
aufrütteln.

stirrup ['stirəp] Steigbügel *m*.
stitch [stitʃ] 1. Stich *m*; Masche *f*;
Seitenstechen *n*; 2. nähen; heften.
stock [stɔk] 1. (Baum)Strunk *m*;
Pfropfunterlage *f*; Griff *m*, Kolben
m e-s Gewehrs; Stamm *m*, Herkunft *f*; Rohstoff *m*; (Fleisch-,
Gemüse)Brühe *f*; Vorrat *m*, (Wa-
ren)Lager *n*; (Wissens)Schatz *m*;
a. live~ Vieh(bestand *m*) *n*; †
Stammkapital *n*; Anleihekapital *n*; ~s
pl. Effekten *pl.*; Aktien *f/pl.*; Staatspapiere *n/pl.*; ~s *pl.* ⚓ Stapel *m*; *in
(out of)* ~ (nicht) vorrätig; *take* ~ †
Inventur machen; *take* ~ *of fig.* sich
klarwerden über (*acc.*); 2. vorrätig;
ständig; gängig; Standard...; 3. versorgen; *Waren* führen; † vorrätig
haben.
stockade [stɔ'keid] Staket *n*.
stock|-breeder ['stɔkbri:də] Vieh-
züchter *m*; **~broker** † Börsen-
makler *m*; ~ *exchange* † Börse *f*;
~-farmer Viehzüchter *m*; **~holder**
† Aktionär(in).
stockinet [stɔki'net] Trikot *n*.
stocking ['stɔkiŋ] Strumpf *m*.
stock|jobber † ['stɔkdʒɔbə] Börsen-
makler *m*; **~-market** † Börse *f*;
~-still unbeweglich; **~-taking** Inventur *f*; **~y** ['stɔki] stämmig.
stog|ie, ~y Am. ['stougi] billige
Zigarre.
stoic ['stouik] 1. stoisch; 2. Stoiker
m.
stoker ['stoukə] Heizer *m*.
stole [stoul] *pret. von steal* 1; **~n**
['stoulən] *p.p. von steal* 1.
stolid □ ['stɔlid] schwerfällig;
gleichmütig; stur.
stomach ['stʌmək] Magen *m*;
Leib *m*, Bauch *m*; *fig.* Lust *f*; 2. verdauen, vertragen; *fig.* ertragen.
stomp Am. [stɔmp] (auf)stampfen.
stone [stoun] 1. Stein *m*; (Obst-)
Kern *m*; *Gewichtseinheit von 6,35 kg*;
2. steinern; Stein...; 3. steinigen;
entsteinen; **~-blind** ['stoun'blaind]
stockblind; **~-dead** mausetot;
~ware [~nwɛə] Steingut *n*.
stony ['stouni] steinig; *fig.* steinern.
stood [stud] *pret. u. p.p. von stand* 1.
stool [stu:l] Schemel *m*; 🩺 Stuhlgang *m*; **~-pigeon** Am. ['stu:l-
pidʒin] Lockvogel *m*; Spitzel *m*.
stoop [stu:p] 1. *v/i.* sich bücken;
sich erniedrigen *od.* herablassen;
krumm gehen; *v/t.* neigen; 2. ge-
beugte Haltung; *Am.* Veranda *f*.
stop [stɔp] 1. *v/t.* anhalten; hindern;
aufhören; *a.* ~ *up* (ver)stopfen;
Zahn plombieren; (ver)sperren;
Zahlung einstellen; *Lohn* einbehal-
ten; *v/i.* stehenbleiben; aufhören;
halten; F bleiben; ~ *dead*, ~ *short*
plötzlich anhalten; ~ *over* halt-
machen; 2. (Ein)Halt *m*; Pause *f*;
Hemmung *f*; ⊕ Anschlag *m*; Aufhören *n*, Ende *n*; Haltestelle *f*; *mst*

full ~ gr. Punkt *m*; **~gap** ['stɔpgæp]
Notbehelf *m*; **~page** [~pidʒ] Verstopfung *f*; (Zahlungs- *etc.*)Ein-
stellung *f*; Sperrung *f*; (Lohn)Ab-
zug *m*; Aufenthalt *m*; ⊕ Hemmung
f; Betriebsstörung *f*; (Verkehrs-)
Stockung *f*; **~per** [~pə] Stöpsel *m*;
~ping ⚓ [~piŋ] Plombe *f*.

storage ['stɔːridʒ] Lagerung *f*,
Aufbewahrung *f*; Lagergeld *n*.

store [stɔː] **1.** Vorrat *m*; *fig.* Fülle *f*;
Lagerhaus *n*; *Am.* Laden *m*; **~s** *pl.*
Kauf-, Warenhaus *n*; *in* ~ vorrätig,
auf Lager; **2.** *a.* ~ *up* (auf)speichern;
(ein)lagern; versorgen; **~house**
Lagerhaus *n*; *fig.* Schatzkammer *f*;
~keeper Lagerverwalter *m*; *Am.*
Ladenbesitzer *m*.

stor(e)y ['stɔːri] Stock(werk *n*) *m*.

storeyed ['stɔːrid] mit ... Stock-
werken, ...stöckig.

storied [~] *s.* storeyed.

stork [stɔːk] Storch *m*.

storm [stɔːm] **1.** Sturm *m*; Gewitter *n*; **2.** stürmen; toben; **~y** ['stɔː-
mi] stürmisch.

story ['stɔːri] Geschichte *f*; Erzählung *f*; Märchen *n*; *thea.* Handlung
f; F Lüge *f*; *short* ~ Kurzgeschich-
te *f*.

stout [staut] **1.** □ stark, kräftig;
derb; dick; tapfer; **2.** Starkbier *n*.

stove [stouv] **1.** Ofen *m*; Herd *m*;
2. *pret. u. p.p. von* stave 2.

stow [stou] (ver)stauen, packen;
~away ⚓ ['stouəwei] blinder Passagier.

straddle ['strædl] (die Beine) spreizen; rittlings sitzen auf (*dat.*); *Am.*
fig. es mit beiden Parteien halten;
schwanken.

straggl|e ['strægl] verstreut *od.* ein-
zeln liegen; umherstreifen; bum-
meln; *fig.* abschweifen; ⚘ wuchern;
~ing □ [~liŋ] weitläufig, lose.

straight [streit] **1.** *adj.* gerade; *fig.*
aufrichtig, ehrlich; glatt (*Haar*);
Am. pur, unverdünnt; *Am. pol.*
hundertprozentig; *put* ~ in Ordnung bringen; **2.** *adv.* gerade(wegs);
geradeaus; direkt; sofort; ~ *away*
sofort; ~ *out* rundheraus; **~en**
['streitn] gerade machen *od.* werden; ~ *out* in Ordnung bringen;
~forward □ [streit'fɔːwəd] gerade;
ehrlich, redlich.

strain [strein] **1.** Abstammung *f*;
Art *f*; ⊕ Spannung *f*; (Über)An-
strengung *f*; starke Inanspruchnahme (*on gen.*); Druck *m*; ⚚ Zerrung *f*; Ton *m*; *mst* ~*s pl.* ♪ Weise *f*;
Hang *m* (*of zu*); **2.** *v/t.* (an)spannen;
(über)anstrengen; überspannen; ⊕
beanspruchen; ⚚ zerren; durch-
seihen; *v/i.* sich spannen; sich anstrengen; sich abmühen (*after um*);
zerren (*at an dat.*); **~er** ['streinə]
Durchschlag *m*; Filter *m*; Sieb *n*.

strait [streit] (*in Eigennamen* ⚓*s pl.*)

Meerenge *f*, Straße *f*; **~s** *pl.* Not
(-lage) *f*; ~ *jacket* Zwangsjacke *f*;
~ened ['streitnd] dürftig; in Not.

strand [strænd] **1.** Strand *m*;
Strähne *f* (*a. fig.*); **2.** auf den Strand
setzen; *fig.* stranden (lassen).

strange □ [streindʒ] fremd (*a. fig.*);
seltsam; **~r** ['streindʒə] Fremde(r)
m.

strangle ['stræŋgl] erwürgen.

strap [stræp] **1.** Riemen *m*; Gurt *m*;
Band *m*; **2.** an-, festschnallen; mit
Riemen peitschen. [List *f*.]

stratagem ['strætidʒəm] (Kriegs-))

strateg|ic [strə'tiːdʒik] (~*ally*) stra-
tegisch; **~y** ['strætidʒi] Kriegs-
kunst *f*, Strategie *f*.

strat|um *geol.* ['strɑːtəm], *pl.* **~a**
[~tə] Schicht *f* (*a. fig.*), Lage *f*.

straw [strɔː] **1.** Stroh(halm *m*) *n*;
2. Stroh...; ~ *vote Am.* Probeab-
stimmung *f*; **~berry** ['strɔːbəri]
Erdbeere *f*.

stray [strei] **1.** irregehen; sich verirren; abirren; umherschweifen;
2. *a.* ~*ed* verirrt; vereinzelt; **3.** ver-
irrtes Tier.

streak [striːk] **1.** Strich *m*, Streifen
m; *fig.* Ader *f*, Spur *f*; kurze
Periode; ~ *of lightning* Blitzstrahl *m*;
2. streifen; jagen, F flitzen.

stream [striːm] **1.** Bach *m*; Strom
m; Strömung *f*; **2.** *v/i.* strömen;
triefen; flattern; *v/t.* strömen lassen; ausströmen; **~er** ['striːmə]
Wimpel *m*; (fliegendes) Band;
Lichtstrahl *m*; *typ.* Schlagzeile *f*.

street [striːt] Straße *f*; **~car** *Am.*
['striːtkɑː] Straßenbahn(wagen *m*) *f*.

strength [streŋθ] Stärke *f*, Kraft *f*;
on the ~ *of* auf ... hin, auf Grund
(*gen.*); **~en** ['streŋθən] *v/t.* stärken,
kräftigen; bestärken; *v/i.* erstarken.

strenuous □ ['strenjuəs] rührig,
emsig; eifrig; anstrengend.

stress [stres] **1.** Druck *m*; Nachdruck *m*; Betonung *f* (*a. gr.*);
fig. Schwergewicht *n*; Ton *m*; *psych.*
Stress *m*; **2.** betonen.

stretch [stretʃ] **1.** *v/t.* strecken;
(aus)dehnen; *mst* ~ *out* ausstrecken;
(an)spannen; *fig.* überspannen; *Gesetz* zu weit auslegen; *v/i.* sich (er-)
strecken; sich dehnen (lassen);
2. Strecken *n*; Dehnung *f*; (An-)
Spannung *f*; Übertreibung *f*,
Überschreitung *f*; Strecke *f*, Fläche
f; **~er** ['stretʃə] Tragbahre *f*;
Streckvorrichtung *f*.

strew [struː] [*irr.*] (be)streuen; **~n**
[~uːn] *p.p. von* strew.

stricken ['strikən] **1.** *p.p. von* strike
2; **2.** *adj.* ge-, betroffen.

strict [strikt] streng; genau; **~ly**
speaking strenggenommen; **~ness**
['striktnis] Genauigkeit *f*; Strenge *f*.

stridden ['stridn] *p.p. von* stride 1.

stride [straid] **1.** [*irr.*] *v/t.* über-,
durchschreiten; **2.** (weiter) Schritt.

strident □ ['straidnt] kreischend.

strife [straif] Streit *m*, Hader *m*.

strike [straik] **1.** Streik *m*; (Öl-, Erz)Fund *m*; *fig.* Treffer *m*; ✕ (Luft)Angriff *m auf ein Einzelziel*; *Am. Baseball:* Verlustpunkt *m*; be on ~ streiken; **2.** [*irr.*] *v/t.* treffen, stoßen; schlagen; gegen *od.* auf (*acc.*) schlagen *od.* stoßen; stoßen *od.* treffen auf (*acc.*); *Flagge etc.* streichen; *Ton anschlagen*; *anfallen* (*dat.*); ergreifen; *Handel* abschließen; *Streichholz, Licht* anzünden; *Wurzel* schlagen; *Pose* annehmen; *Bilanz* ziehen; ~ up ♪ anstimmen; *Freundschaft* schließen; *v/i.* schlagen; ♣ auf Grund stoßen; streiken; ~ home (richtig) treffen; ~r ['straikə] Streikende(r) *m.*

striking □ ['straikiŋ] Schlag...; auffallend; eindrucksvoll; treffend.

string [striŋ] **1.** Schnur *f*; Bindfaden *m*; Band *n*; *Am.* F Bedingung *f*; (Bogen)Sehne *f*; ♪ Faser *f*; ♪ Saite *f*; Reihe *f*, Kette *f*; ~s *pl.* ♪ Saiteninstrumente *n/pl.*, Streicher *m/pl.*; pull the ~s der Drahtzieher sein; **2.** [*irr.*] spannen; aufreihen; besaiten (*a. fig.*); bespannen; (ver-, zu)schnüren; *Bohnen* abziehen; *Am. sl.* j-n verkohlen; be strung up angespannt *od.* erregt sein; ~band♪ ['striŋbænd] Streichorchester *n.*

stringent □ ['strindʒənt] streng, scharf; bindend, zwingend; knapp.

stringy ['striŋi] faserig; zäh.

strip [strip] **1.** entkleiden (*a. fig.*); (sich) ausziehen; abziehen; *fig.* entblößen, berauben; ⊕ auseinandernehmen; ♣ abtakeln; *a.* ~ off ausziehen, abstreifen; **2.** Streifen *m.*

stripe [straip] Streifen *m*; ✕ Tresse *f.*

stripling ['stripliŋ] Bürschchen *n.*

strive [straiv] [*irr.*] streben; sich bemühen; ringen (*for* um); ~n ['strivn] *p.p. von* strive.

strode [stroud] *pret. von* stride 1.

stroke [strouk] **1.** Schlag *m* (*a.* ✕); Streich *m*; Stoß *m*; Strich *m*; ~ of luck Glücksfall *m*; **2.** streiche(l)n.

stroll [stroul] **1.** schlendern; umherziehen; **2.** Bummel *m*; Spaziergang *m*; ~er ['stroulə] Bummler(in), Spaziergänger(in); *Am.* (Falt)Sportwagen *m.*

strong □ [strɔŋ] *allg.* stark; kräftig; energisch, eifrig; fest; schwer (*Speise etc.*); ~box ['strɔŋbɔks] Stahlkassette *f*; ~hold Festung *f*; *fig.* Bollwerk *n*; ~room Stahlkammer *f*; ~willed eigenwillig.

strop [strɔp] **1.** Streichriemen *m*; **2.** *Messer* abziehen.

strove [strouv] *pret. von* strive.

struck [strʌk] *pret. u. p.p. von* strike 2.

structure ['strʌktʃə] Bau(werk *n*) *m*; Struktur *f*, Gefüge *n*; Gebilde *n.*

struggle ['strʌgl] **1.** sich (ab)mühen; kämpfen, ringen; sich sträuben; **2.** Kampf *m*; Ringen *n*; Anstrengung *f.*

strung [strʌŋ] *pret. u. p.p. von* string 2.

strut [strʌt] **1.** *v/i.* stolzieren; *v/t.* ⊕ abstützen; **2.** Stolzieren *n*; ⊕ Strebe(balken *m*) *f*; Stütze *f.*

stub [stʌb] **1.** (Baum)Stumpf *m*; Stummel *m*; *Am.* Kontrollabschnitt *m*; **2.** (aus)roden; sich den Fuß stoßen.

stubble ['stʌbl] Stoppel(n *pl.*) *f.*

stubborn □ ['stʌbən] eigensinnig; widerspenstig; stur; hartnäckig.

stuck [stʌk] *pret. u. p.p. von* stick 2; ~up ['stʌk'ʌp] F hochnäsig.

stud [stʌd] **1.** (Wand)Pfosten *m*; Ziernagel *m*; Knauf *m*; Manschetten-, Kragenknopf *m*; Gestüt *n*; **2.** beschlagen; besetzen; ~book ['stʌdbuk] Gestütbuch *n.*

student ['stju:dnt] Student(in).

studied □ ['stʌdid] einstudiert; gesucht; gewollt.

studio ['stju:diou] Atelier *n*; Studio *n*; *Radio:* Aufnahme-, Senderaum *m.*

studious □ ['stju:djəs] fleißig; bedacht; bemüht; geflissentlich.

study ['stʌdi] **1.** Studium *n*; Studier-, Arbeitszimmer *n*; *paint. etc.* Studie *f*; be in a brown ~ versunken sein; **2.** (ein)studieren; sich *et.* genau ansehen? sich bemühen um.

stuff [stʌf] **1.** Stoff *m*; Zeug *n*; *fig.* Unsinn *m*; **2.** *v/t.* (voll-, aus)stopfen; *~ed shirt Am. sl.* Fatzke *m*; *v/i.* sich vollstopfen; ~ing ['stʌfiŋ] Füllung *f*; ~y □ [~fi] dumpf(ig), muffig, stickig; *fig.* verärgert.

stultify ['stʌltifai] lächerlich machen, blamieren; *et.* hinfällig machen.

stumble ['stʌmbl] **1.** Stolpern *n*; Fehltritt *m*; **2.** stolpern; straucheln; ~ upon stoßen auf (*acc.*).

stump [stʌmp] **1.** Stumpf *m*, Stummel *m*; **2.** *v/t.* F verblüffen; *Am.* F herausfordern; ~ the country als Wahlredner im Land umherziehen; *v/i.* (daher)stapfen; ~y □ ['stʌmpi] gedrungen; plump.

stun [stʌn] betäuben (*a. fig.*).

stung [stʌŋ] *pret. u. p.p. von* sting 2.

stunk [stʌŋk] *pret. u. p.p. von* stink 2.

stunning □ F ['stʌniŋ] toll, famos.

stunt[1] [stʌnt] Kraft-, Kunststück *n*; (Reklame)Trick *m*; Sensation *f.*

stunt[2] [~] im Wachstum hindern; ~ed ['stʌntid] verkümmert.

stup|efy ['stju:pifai] *fig.* betäuben; verblüffen; verdummen; ~endous □ [stju(:)'pendəs] erstaunlich; ~id □ ['stju:pid] dumm, einfältig, stumpfsinnig; blöd; ~idity [stju(:)-'piditi] Dummheit *f*; Stumpfsinn *m*; ~or ['stju:(:)pə] Erstarrung *f*, Betäubung *f.*

sturdy ['stə:di] derb, kräftig, stark; stämmig; stramm; handfest.

stutter ['stʌtə] 1. stottern; 2. Stottern *n.*

sty[1] [stai] Schweinestall *m*, Koben *m.*

sty[2], **stye** ᵜ [ᴗ] Gerstenkorn *n am Auge.*

style [stail] 1. Stil *m*; Mode *f*; Betitelung *f*; 2. (be)nennen, betiteln.

stylish ☐ ['stailiʃ] stilvoll; elegant; ᴗness [ᴗnis] Eleganz *f.*

stylo F ['stailou], ᴗgraph [ᴗləgrɑ:f] Tintenkuli *m.*

suave ☐ [swɑ:v] verbindlich; mild.

sub... [sʌb] *mst* Unter..., unter...; Neben...; Hilfs...; fast ...

subdeb *Am.* F [sʌb'deb] Backfisch *m*, junges Mädchen.

subdivision ['sʌbdiviʒən] Unterteilung *f*; Unterabteilung *f.*

subdue [səb'dju:] unterwerfen; bezwingen; bändigen; unterdrücken; verdrängen; dämpfen.

subject ['sʌbdʒikt] 1. unterworfen; untergeben, abhängig; untertan; unterliegend (*to dat.*); be ᴗ to neigen zu; 2. *adv.* ᴗ to vorbehaltlich (*gen.*); 3. Untertan *m*, Staatsangehörige(r *m*) *f*; *phls.*, *gr.* Subjekt *n*; *a.* ᴗ *matter* Thema *n*, Gegenstand *m*; 4. [səb'dʒekt] unterwerfen; *fig.* aussetzen; ᴗion [ᴗkʃən] Unterwerfung *f.* [chen.]

subjugate ['sʌbdʒugeit] unterjo-

subjunctive *gr.* [səb'dʒʌŋktiv] *a.* ᴗ *mood* Konjunktiv *m.*

sub|lease ['sʌb'li:s], ᴗlet [*irr.* (let)] untervermieten.

sublime ☐ [sə'blaim] erhaben.

submachine-gun ['sʌbmə'ʃi:ŋgʌn] Maschinenpistole *f.*

submarine ['sʌbməri:n] 1. unterseeisch; 2. ⊕ Unterseeboot *n.*

submerge [səb'mə:dʒ] untertauchen; überschwemmen.

submiss|ion [səb'miʃən] Unterwerfung *f*; Unterbreitung *f*; ᴗive ☐ [ᴗisiv] unterwürfig.

submit [səb'mit] (sich) unterwerfen; anheimstellen; unterbreiten, einreichen; *fig.* sich fügen *od.* ergeben (*to in acc.*).

subordinate 1. ☐ [sə'bɔ:dnit] untergeordnet; untergeben; ᴗ *clause gr.* Nebensatz *m*; 2. [ᴗ] Untergebene(r *m*) *f*; 3. [ᴗdineit] unterordnen.

suborn ᴢᵗᵌ [sʌ'bɔ:n] verleiten.

subscribe [səb'skraib] *v/t.* Geld stiften (*to* für); *Summe* zeichnen; *s-n Namen* setzen (*to unter acc.*); unterschreiben mit; *v/i.* ᴗ *to Zeitung etc.* abonnieren; *e-r Meinung* zustimmen, *et.* unterschreiben; ᴗr [ᴗbə] (Unter)Zeichner(in); Abonnent(in); *teleph.* Teilnehmer(in).

subscription [səb'skripʃən] (Unter-)Zeichnung *f*; Abonnement *n.*

subsequent ☐ ['sʌbsikwənt] folgend; später; ᴗly hinterher.

subservient ☐ [səb'sə:vjənt] dienlich; dienstbar; unterwürfig.

subsid|e [səb'said] sinken, sich senken; *fig.* sich setzen; sich legen (*Wind*); ᴗ *into* verfallen in (*acc.*); ᴗiary [ᴗ'sidjəri] 1. ☐ Hilfs...; Neben...; untergeordnet; 2. Tochtergesellschaft *f*; Filiale *f*; ᴗize ['sʌbsidaiz] mit Geld unterstützen; subventionieren; ᴗy [ᴗdi] Beihilfe *f*; Subvention *f.*

subsist [səb'sist] bestehen; leben (*on*, *by* von); ᴗence [ᴗtəns] Dasein *n*; (Lebens)Unterhalt *m.*

substance ['sʌbstəns] Substanz *f*; Wesen *n*; *fig.* Hauptsache *f*; Inhalt *m*; Wirklichkeit *f*; Vermögen *n.*

substantial ☐ [səb'stænʃəl] wesentlich; wirklich; kräftig; stark; solid; vermögend; namhaft (*Summe*).

substantiate [səb'stænʃieit] beweisen, begründen, dartun.

substantive *gr.* ['sʌbstəntiv] Substantiv *n*, Hauptwort *n.*

substitut|e ['sʌbstitju:t] 1. an die Stelle setzen *od.* treten (for von); unterschieben (*for* statt); 2. Stellvertreter *m*; Ersatz *m*; ᴗion [sʌbsti'tju:ʃən] Stellvertretung *f*; Ersatz *m.*

subterfuge ['sʌbtəfju:dʒ] Ausflucht *f.*

subterranean ☐ [sʌbtə'reinjən] unterirdisch.

sub-title ['sʌbtaitl] Untertitel *m.*

subtle ☐ ['sʌtl] fein(sinnig); subtil; spitzfindig; ᴗty [ᴗlti] Feinheit *f.*

subtract ᴀᵗ [səb'trækt] abziehen, subtrahieren.

subtropical ['sʌb'trɔpikəl] subtropisch.

suburb ['sʌbə:b] Vorstadt *f*, Vorort *m*; ᴗan [sə'bə:bən] vorstädtisch.

subvention [səb'venʃən] 1. Subvention *f*; 2. subventionieren.

subver|sion [sʌb'və:ʃən] Umsturz *m*; ᴗsive [ᴗsiv] zerstörend (*of acc.*); subversiv; ᴗt [ᴗə:t] (um-)stürzen; untergraben.

subway ['sʌbwei] (*bsd.* Fußgänger-) Unterführung *f*; *Am.* Untergrundbahn *f.*

succeed [sək'si:d] Erfolg haben; glücken, gelingen; (nach)folgen (*dat.*); ᴗ to übernehmen; erben.

success [sək'ses] Erfolg *m*; ᴗful ☐ [ᴗsful] erfolgreich; ᴗion [ᴗeʃən] (Nach-, Erb-, Reihen)Folge *f*; Nachkommenschaft *f*; *in* ᴗ nacheinander; ᴗive [ᴗesiv] aufeinanderfolgend; ᴗor [ᴗsə] Nachfolger(in). [fen.]

succo(u)r ['sʌkə] 1. Hilfe *f*; 2. hel-

succulent ☐ ['sʌkjulənt] saftig.

succumb [sə'kʌm] unterliegen, erliegen.

such [sʌtʃ] solch(er, -e, -es); derartig; so groß; ᴗ *a man* ein solcher Mann; ᴗ *as* die, welche.

suck [sʌk] **1.** (ein)saugen; saugen an (dat.); aussaugen; lutschen; **2.** Saugen n; ~er ['sʌkə] Saugorgan n; ♀ Wurzelsproß m; Am. Einfaltspinsel m; ~le ['sʌkl] säugen, stillen; ~ling [~lɪŋ] Säugling m.

suction ['sʌkʃən] (An)Saugen n; Sog m; attr. Saug...

sudden □ ['sʌdn] plötzlich; all of a ~ ganz plötzlich.

suds [sʌdz] pl. Seifenlauge f; Seifenschaum m; ~y Am. ['sʌdzi] schaumig, seifig.

sue [sju:] v/t. verklagen; ~ out erwirken; v/i. nachsuchen (for um); klagen.

suède [sweid] (feines) Wildleder.

suet [sjuit] Nierenfett n; Talg m.

suffer ['sʌfə] v/i. leiden (from an dat.); v/t. erleiden, erdulden, (zu-)lassen; ~ance [~ərəns] Duldung f; ~er [~rə] Leidende(r m) f; Dulder(in); ~ing [~rɪŋ] Leiden n.

suffice [sə'faɪs] genügen; ~ it to say es sei nur gesagt.

sufficien|cy [sə'fɪʃənsi] genügende Menge; Auskommen n; ~t [~nt] genügend, ausreichend.

suffix gr. ['sʌfiks] **1.** anhängen; **2.** Nachsilbe f, Suffix n.

suffocate ['sʌfəkeit] ersticken.

suffrage ['sʌfridʒ] (Wahl)Stimme f; Wahl-, Stimmrecht n.

suffuse [sə'fju:z] übergießen; überziehen.

sugar ['ʃugə] **1.** Zucker m; **2.** zuckern; ~-basin, Am. ~-bowl Zuckerdose f; ~-cane ♀ Zuckerrohr n; ~-coat überzuckern, versüßen; ~y [~əri] zuckerig; zuckersüß.

suggest [sə'dʒest] vorschlagen, anregen; nahelegen; vorbringen; Gedanken eingeben; andeuten; denken lassen an (acc.); ~ion [~tʃən] Anregung f; Rat m, Vorschlag m; Suggestion f; Eingebung f; Andeutung f; ~ive □ [~tɪv] anregend; andeutend (of acc.); gehaltvoll; zweideutig.

suicide ['sjuisaid] **1.** Selbstmord m; Selbstmörder(in); Am. Selbstmord begehen.

suit [sju:t] **1.** (Herren)Anzug m; (Damen)Kostüm n; Anliegen n; (Heirats)Antrag m; Karten: Farbe f; ♱♱ Prozeß m; **2.** v/t. j-m passen, zusagen, bekommen; j-n kleiden, j-m stehen, passen zu (Kleidungsstück etc.); ~ oneself tun, was e-m beliebt; ~ s.th. to et. anpassen (dat.); be ~ed geeignet sein (for für), passen (to zu); v/i. passen; ~able □ ['sju:təbl] passend, geeignet; entsprechend; ~case (Hand)Koffer m; ~e [swi:t] Gefolge n; (Reihen)Folge f; ♪ Suite f; a. ~ of rooms Zimmerflucht f; Garnitur f, (Zimmer)Einrichtung f; ~or ['sju:tə] Freier m; ♱♱ Kläger(in).

sulk [sʌlk] schmollen, bocken; ~iness ['sʌlkinis] üble Laune; ~ pl. = sulkiness; ~y ['sʌlki] **1.** verdrießlich; launisch; schmollend; **2.** Sport: Traberwagen m, Sulky n.

sullen □ ['sʌlən] verdrossen, mürrisch.

sully ['sʌli] mst fig. beflecken.

sulphur ♔ ['sʌlfə] Schwefel m; ~ic [sʌl'fjuərik] Schwefel...

sultriness ['sʌltrinis] Schwüle f.

sultry □ ['sʌltri] schwül; fig. heftig, hitzig.

sum [sʌm] **1.** Summe f; Betrag m; fig. Inbegriff m, Inhalt m; Rechenaufgabe f; do ~s rechnen; **2.** mst ~ up zs.-rechnen; zs.-fassen.

summar|ize ['sʌməraiz] (kurz) zs.-fassen; ~y [~ri] **1.** □ kurz (zs.-gefaßt); ♱♱ Schnell...; **2.** (kurze) Inhaltsangabe, Auszug m.

summer ['sʌmə] Sommer m; ~ resort Sommerfrische f; ~ school Ferienkurs m; ~ly [~əli], ~y [~əri] sommerlich.

summit ['sʌmit] Gipfel m (a. fig.).

summon ['sʌmən] auffordern; (be-)rufen; ♱♱ vorladen; Mut etc. aufbieten; ~s Aufforderung f; ♱♱ Vorladung f.

sumptuous □ ['sʌmptjuəs] kostbar.

sun [sʌn] **1.** Sonne f; attr. Sonnen...; **2.** (sich) sonnen; ~-bath ['sʌnbɑ:θ] Sonnenbad n; ~beam Sonnenstrahl m; ~-burn Sonnenbräune f; Sonnenbrand m.

Sunday ['sʌndi] Sonntag m.

sun|-dial ['sʌndaiəl] Sonnenuhr f; ~down Sonnenuntergang m.

sundr|ies ['sʌndriz] pl. bsd. ♱ Verschiedene(s) n; Extraausgaben f/pl.; ~y [~ri] verschiedene.

sung [sʌŋ] pret. u. p.p. von sing.

sun-glasses ['sʌnglɑ:siz] pl. (a pair of ~ pl. eine) Sonnenbrille f.

sunk [sʌŋk] pret. u. p.p. von sink 1.

sunken ['sʌŋkən] **1.** p.p. von sink 1; **2.** adj. versunken; fig. eingefallen.

sun|ny □ ['sʌni] sonnig; ~rise Sonnenaufgang m; ~set Sonnenuntergang m; ~shade Sonnenschirm m; ~shine Sonnenschein m; ~stroke ♔ Sonnenstich m.

sup [sʌp] zu Abend essen.

super F ['sju:pə] erstklassig, prima, super.

super|... ['sju:pə] Über..., über...; Ober..., ober...; Groß...; ~abundant □ [sju:pərə'bʌndənt] überreichlich; überschwenglich; ~annuate [~ə'rænjueit] pensionieren; ~d ausgedient; veraltet (S.).

superb □ [sju:(:)'pə:b] prächtig; herrlich.

super|charger mot. ['sju:pətʃɑ:dʒə] Kompressor m; ~cilious [sju:pə-

'siliəs] hochmütig; ~ficial □ [~ə'fi-ʃəl] oberflächlich; ~fine ['sju:pə-'fain] extrafein; ~fluity [sju:pə-flu(:)iti] Überfluß m; ~fluous □ [sju(:)'pə:fluəs] überflüssig; ~heat ⊕ [sju:pə'hi:t] überhitzen; ~human □ [~'hju:mən] übermenschlich; ~impose ['sju:pərim'pouz] darauf-, darüberlegen; ~induce [~rin'dju:s] noch hinzufügen; ~intend [sju:prin'tend] die Oberaufsicht haben über (acc.); überwachen; ~intendent [~dənt] 1. Leiter m, Direktor m; (Ober)Aufseher m, Inspektor m; 2. aufsichtführend.

superior [sju(:)'piəriə] 1. □ ober; höher(stehend); vorgesetzt; besser, hochwertiger; überlegen (to dat.); vorzüglich; 2. Höherstehende(r m) f, bsd. Vorgesetzte(r m) f; eccl. Obere(r) m; mst Lady ♀, Mother ♀ eccl. Oberin f; ~ity [sju(:)piəri'ɔriti] Überlegenheit f.

super|lative [sju(:)'pə:lətiv] 1. □ höchst; übertragend; 2. a. ~ degree gr. Superlativ m; ~market Supermarkt m; ~natural □ [sju:pə'nætʃ-rəl] übernatürlich; ~numerary [~'nju:mərəri] 1. überzählig; 2. Überzählige(r m) f; thea. Statist (-in); ~scription [~ə'skripʃən] Über-, Aufschrift f; ~sede [~'si:d] ersetzen; verdrängen; absetzen; fig. überholen; ~sonic phys. ['sju:pə'sɔnik] Überschall...; ~stition [sju:pə'stiʃən] Aberglaube m; ~stitious □ [~ʃəs] abergläubisch; ~vene [~ə'vi:n] noch hinzukommen; unerwartet eintreten; ~vise ['sju:pəvaiz] beaufsichtigen, überwachen; ~vision [sju:pə'viʒən] (Ober)Aufsicht f; Beaufsichtigung f; ~visor ['sju:pəvaizə] Aufseher m, Inspektor m.

supper ['sʌpə] Abendessen n; the (Lord's) ♀ das Heilige Abendmahl.

supplant [sə'plɑ:nt] verdrängen.

supple ['sʌpl] geschmeidig (machen).

supplement 1. ['sʌplimənt] Ergänzung f; Nachtrag m; (Zeitungsetc.)Beilage f; 2. [~mənt] ergänzen; ~al □ [sʌpli'mentl], ~ary [~təri] Ergänzungs...; nachträglich; Nachtrags...

suppliant ['sʌpliənt] 1. □ demütig bittend, flehend; 2. Bittsteller(in).

supplicat|e ['sʌplikeit] demütig bitten, anflehen; ~ion [sʌpli'keiʃən] demütige Bitte.

supplier [sə'plaiə] Lieferant(in).

supply [sə'plai] 1. liefern; e-m Mangel abhelfen; e-e Stelle ausfüllen; vertreten; ausstatten, versorgen; ergänzen; 2. Lieferung f; Versorgung f; Zufuhr f; Vorrat m; Bedarf m; Angebot n; (Stell)Vertretung f; mst supplies pl. parl. Etat m.

support [sə'pɔ:t] 1. Stütze f; Hilfe f; ⊕ Träger m; Unterstützung f; Lebensunterhalt m; 2. (unter)stützen, unterhalten, sorgen für (Familie etc.); aufrechterhalten; (v)ertragen.

suppose [sə'pouz] annehmen; voraussetzen; vermuten; he is ~d to do er soll tun; ~ we go gehen wir; wie wär's, wenn wir gingen.

supposed □ [sə'pouzd] vermeintlich; ~ly [~zidli] vermutlich.

supposition [sʌpə'ziʃən] Voraussetzung f; Annahme f; Vermutung f.

suppress [sə'pres] unterdrücken; ~ion [~eʃən] Unterdrückung f.

suppurate ['sʌpjuəreit] eitern.

suprem|acy [sju'preməsi] Oberhoheit f; Vorherrschaft f; Überlegenheit f; Vorrang m; ~e □ [sju(:)'pri:m] höchst; oberst; Ober...; größt.

surcharge [sə:'tʃɑ:dʒ] 1. überladen; Zuschlag od. Nachgebühr erheben von j-m; 2. ['sə:tʃɑ:dʒ] Überladung f; (Straf)Zuschlag m; Nachgebühr f; Überdruck m auf Briefmarken.

sure □ [ʃuə] allg. sicher; to be ~!, ~ enough!, Am. ~! F sicher(lich)!; ~ly ['ʃuəli] sicherlich; ~ty ['ʃuəti] Bürge m.

surf [sə:f] Brandung f.

surface ['sə:fis] 1. (Ober)Fläche f; ✈ Tragfläche f; 2. ⊕ auftauchen (U-Boot).

surf|-board ['sə:fbɔ:d] Wellenreiterbrett n; ~boat Brandungsboot n.

surfeit ['sə:fit] 1. Übersättigung f; Ekel m; 2. (sich) überladen.

surf-riding ['sə:fraidiŋ] Sport: Wellenreiten n.

surge [sə:dʒ] 1. Woge f; 2. wogen.

surg|eon ['sə:dʒən] Chirurg m; ~ery [~əri] Chirurgie f; Sprechzimmer n; ~ hours pl. Sprechstunde(n pl.) f.

surgical □ ['sə:dʒikəl] chirurgisch.

surly □ ['sə:li] mürrisch; grob.

surmise 1. ['sə:maiz] Vermutung f; Argwohn m; 2. [sə:'maiz] vermuten; argwöhnen.

surmount [sə:'maunt] übersteigen; überragen; fig. überwinden.

surname ['sə:neim] Zu-, Nachname m.

surpass fig. [sə:'pɑ:s] übersteigen, übertreffen; ~ing [~siŋ] überragend.

surplus ['sə:pləs] 1. Überschuß m, Mehr n; 2. überschüssig; Über...

surprise [sə'praiz] 1. Überraschung f; ✕ Überrump(e)lung f; 2. überraschen; ✕ überrumpeln.

surrender [sə'rendə] 1. Übergabe f; Ergebung f; Kapitulation f; Aufgeben n; 2. v/t. übergeben; aufgeben; v/i. a. ~ o.s. sich ergeben.

surround [sə'raund] umgeben; ✕

umzingeln; ~ing [~diŋ] umliegend; ~ings pl. Umgebung f.

surtax ['səːtæks] Steuerzuschlag m.

survey 1. [səːˈvei] überblicken; mustern; begutachten; surv. vermessen; 2. ['səːvei] Überblick m (a. fig.); Besichtigung f; Gutachten n; surv. Vermessung f; ~or [sə(:)-'veiə] Land-, Feldmesser m.

surviv|al [səˈvaivəl] Über-, Fortleben n; Überbleibsel n; ~e [~aiv] überleben; noch leben; fortleben; am Leben bleiben; bestehen bleiben; ~or [~və] Überlebende(r m) f.

suscept|ible □ [səˈseptəbl], ~ive [~tiv] empfänglich (of, to für); empfindlich (gegen); be ~ of et. zulassen.

suspect 1. [səsˈpekt] (be)argwöhnen; in Verdacht haben, verdächtigen; vermuten, befürchten; 2. ['sʌspekt] Verdächtige(r m) f; 3. [~] = ~ed [səsˈpektid] verdächtig.

suspend [səsˈpend] (auf)hängen; aufschieben; in der Schwebe lassen; Zahlung einstellen; aussetzen; suspendieren, sperren; ~ed schwebend; ~er ['~də] Strumpf-, Sockenhalter m; ~s pl. Am. Hosenträger m/pl.

suspens|e [səsˈpens] Ungewißheit f; Unentschiedenheit f; Spannung f; ~ion [~nʃən] Aufhängung f; Aufschub m; Einstellung f; Suspendierung f, Amtsenthebung f; Sperre f; ~ion bridge Hängebrücke f; ~ive □ [~nsiv] aufschiebend.

suspici|on [səsˈpiʃən] Verdacht m; Argwohn m; fig. Spur f; ~ous □ [~ʃəs] argwöhnisch; verdächtig.

sustain [səsˈtein] stützen; fig. aufrechterhalten; aushalten; erleiden; ⚜ anerkennen; ~ed anhaltend; ununterbrochen.

sustenance ['sʌstinəns] (Lebens-) Unterhalt m; Nahrung f.

svelte [svelt] schlank (Frau).

swab [swɔb] 1. Aufwischmop m; ♣ Tupfer m; ♣ Abstrich m; 2. aufwischen.

swaddl|e ['swɔdl] Baby wickeln; ~ing-clothes mst fig. [~liŋkloudz] pl. Windeln f/pl.

swagger ['swægə] 1. stolzieren; prahlen, renommieren; 2. F elegant.

swale Am. [sweil] Mulde f, Niederung f.

swallow ['swɔlou] 1. orn. Schwalbe f; Schlund m; Schluck m; 2. (hinunter-, ver)schlucken; fig. Ansicht etc. begierig aufnehmen.

swam [swæm] pret. von swim 1.

swamp [swɔmp] 1. Sumpf m; 2. überschwemmen (a. fig.); versenken; ~y ['swɔmpi] sumpfig.

swan [swɔn] Schwan m.

swank sl. [swæŋk] 1. Angabe f,

Protzerei f; 2. angeben, protzen; ~y ['swæŋki] protzig, angeberisch.

swap F [swɔp] 1. Tausch m; 2. (ver-, aus)tauschen.

sward [swɔːd] Rasen m.

swarm [swɔːm] 1. Schwarm m; Haufe(n) m, Gewimmel n; 2. schwärmen; wimmeln (with von).

swarthy □ ['swɔːði] dunkelfarbig.

swash [swɔʃ] plan(t)schen.

swat [swɔt] Fliege klatschen.

swath ⚷ [swɔːθ] Schwade(n m) f.

swathe [sweið] (ein)wickeln.

sway [swei] 1. Schaukeln n; Einfluß m; Herrschaft f; 2. schaukeln; beeinflussen; beherrschen.

swear [swɛə] [irr.] (be)schwören; fluchen; ~ s.o. in j-n vereidigen.

sweat [swet] 1. Schweiß m; by the ~ of one's brow im Schweiße seines Angesichts; all of a ~ F in Schweiß gebadet (a. fig.); 2. [irr.] v/i. schwitzen; v/t. (aus)schwitzen; in Schweiß bringen; Arbeiter ausbeuten; ~er ['swetə] Sweater m, Pullover m; Trainingsjacke f; fig. Ausbeuter m; ~y [~ti] schweißig; verschwitzt.

Swede [swiːd] Schwed|e m, -in f.

Swedish ['swiːdiʃ] 1. schwedisch; 2. Schwedisch n.

sweep [swiːp] 1. [irr.] fegen (a. fig.), kehren; fig. streifen; bestreichen (a. ✕): (majestätisch) (dahin)rauschen; 2. (fig. Dahin)Fegen n; Kehren n; Schwung m; Biegung f; Spielraum m, Bereich m; Schornsteinfeger m; make a clean ~ reinen Tisch machen (of mit); ~er ['swiːpə] (Straßen)Feger m; Kehrmaschine f; ~ing □ [~piŋ] weitgehend; schwungvoll; ~ings pl. Kehricht m, Müll m.

sweet [swiːt] 1. □ süß; lieblich; freundlich; frisch; duftend; have a ~ tooth ein Leckermaul sein; 2. Liebling m; Süßigkeit f, Bonbon m, n; Nachtisch m; ~en ['swiːtn] (ver)süßen; ~heart Liebling m, Liebste(r m) f; ~ish [~tiʃ] süßlich; ~meat Bonbon m, n; kandierte Frucht; ~ness [~tnis] Süßigkeit f; Lieblichkeit f; ~ pea ⚘ Gartenwicke f.

swell [swel] 1. [irr.] v/i. (an)schwellen; sich blähen; sich (aus)bauchen; v/t. (an)schwellen lassen; aufblähen; 2. F fein; sl. prima; 3. Anschwellen n; Schwellung f; ♬ Dünung f; F feiner Herr; ~ing ['sweliŋ] Geschwulst f.

swelter ['sweltə] vor Hitze umkommen.

swept [swept] pret. u. p.p. von sweep 1.

swerve [swəːv] 1. (plötzlich) abbiegen; 2. plötzliche Wendung.

swift □ [swift] schnell, eilig, flink; ~ness ['swiftnis] Schnelligkeit f.

swill [swil] 1. Spülicht n; Schweinetrank m; 2. spülen; saufen.

swim [swim] 1. [irr.] (durch-) schwimmen; schweben; my head ~s mir schwindelt; 2. Schwimmen n; be in the ~ auf dem laufenden sein; ~ming ['swimiŋ] 1. Schwimmen n; 2. Schwimm...; ~-bath (bsd. Hallen)Schwimmbad n; ~-pool Schwimmbecken n; ~-suit Badeanzug m.

swindle ['swindl] 1. (be)schwindeln; 2. Schwindel m.

swine [swain] Schwein(e pl.) n.

swing [swiŋ] 1. [irr.] schwingen, schwanken; F baumeln; (sich) schaukeln; schwenken; sich drehen; 2. Schwingen n; Schwung m; Schaukel f; Spielraum m; in full ~ in vollem Gange; ~-door ['swiŋdɔː] Drehtür f.

swinish □ ['swainiʃ] schweinisch.

swipe [swaip] 1. aus vollem Arm schlagen; 2. starker Schlag.

swirl [swəːl] 1. (herum)wirbeln, strudeln; 2. Wirbel m, Strudel m.

Swiss [swis] 1. schweizerisch, Schweizer...; 2. Schweizer(in); the ~ pl. die Schweizer m/pl.

switch [switʃ] 1. Gerte f; ⚇ Weiche f; ⚡ Schalter m; falscher Zopf; 2. peitschen; ⚡ rangieren; ⚡ (um-) schalten; fig. wechseln, überleiten; ~ on (off) ⚡ ein- (aus)schalten; ~-board ⚡ ['switʃbɔːd] Schaltbrett n, -tafel f.

swivel ⊕ ['swivl] Drehring m; attr. Dreh...

swollen ['swoulən] p.p. von swell 1.

swoon [swuːn] 1. Ohnmacht f; 2. in Ohnmacht fallen.

swoop [swuːp] 1. ~ down on od. upon (herab)stoßen auf (acc.) (Raubvogel); überfallen; 2. Stoß m.

swop F [swɔp] s. swap.

sword [sɔːd] Schwert n, Degen m.

swordsman ['sɔːdzmən] Fechter m.

swore [swɔː] pret. von swear.

sworn [swɔːn] p.p. von swear.

swum [swʌm] p.p. von swim 1.

swung [swʌŋ] pret. u. p.p. von swing 1.

sycamore ⚘ ['sikəmɔː] Bergahorn m; Am. Platane f.

sycophant ['sikəfənt] Kriecher m.

syllable ['siləbl] Silbe f.

syllabus ['siləbəs] (bsd. Vorlesungs-) Verzeichnis n; (bsd. Lehr)Plan m.

sylvan ['silvən] waldig, Wald...

symbol ['simbəl] Symbol n, Sinnbild n; ~ic(al □) [sim'bɔlik(əl)] sinnbildlich; ~ism ['simbəlizəm] Symbolik f.

symmetr|ical □ [si'metrikəl] ebenmäßig; ~y ['simitri] Ebenmaß n.

sympath|etic [simpə'θetik] (~ally) mitfühlend; sympathisch; ~ strike Sympathiestreik m; ~ize ['simpəθaiz] sympathisieren, mitfühlen; ~y [~θi] Sympathie f, Mitgefühl n.

symphony ♪ ['simfəni] Symphonie f.

symptom ['simptəm] Symptom n.

synchron|ize ['siŋkrənaiz] v/i. gleichzeitig sein; v/t. als gleichzeitig zs.-stellen; Uhren auf-ea. abstimmen; Tonfilm: synchronisieren; ~ous □ [~nəs] gleichzeitig.

syndicate 1. ['sindikit] Syndikat n; 2. [~keit] zu e-m Syndikat verbinden.

synonym ['sinənim] Synonym n; ~ous □ [si'nɔniməs] sinnverwandt.

synop|sis [si'nɔpsis], pl. ~ses [~siːz] zs.-fassende Übersicht.

syntax gr. ['sintæks] Syntax f.

synthe|sis ['sinθisis], pl. ~ses [~siːz] Synthese f, Verbindung f; ~tic(al □) [sin'θetik(əl)] synthetisch.

syringe ['sirindʒ] 1. Spritze f; 2. (be-, ein-, aus)spritzen.

syrup ['sirəp] Sirup m.

system ['sistim] System n; Organismus m, Körper m; Plan m, Ordnung f; ~atic [sisti'mætik] (~ally) systematisch.

T

tab [tæb] Streifen m; Schildchen n; Anhänger m; Schlaufe f, Aufhänger m; F Rechnung f, Konto n.

table ['teibl] 1. Tisch m, Tafel f; Tisch-, Tafelrunde f; Tabelle f; Verzeichnis n; Bibel: Gesetzestafel f; s. ~-land; at ~ bei Tisch; turn the ~s den Spieß umdrehen (on gegen); 2. auf den Tisch legen; tabellarisch anordnen.

tableau ['tæblou], pl. ~x [~ouz] lebendes Bild.

table|-cloth ['teiblklɔθ] Tischtuch n; ~-land Tafelland n, Plateau n,

Hochebene f; ~-linen Tischwäsche f; ~-spoon Eßlöffel m.

tablet ['tæblit] Täfelchen n; (Gedenk)Tafel f; (Schreib- etc.)Block m; Stück n Seife; Tablette f.

table-top ['teibltɔp] Tischplatte f.

taboo [tə'buː] 1. tabu, unantastbar; verboten; 2. Tabu n; Verbot n; 3. verbieten.

tabulate ['tæbjuleit] tabellarisch ordnen.

tacit □ ['tæsit] stillschweigend; ~urn □ [~təːn] schweigsam.

tack [tæk] 1. Stift m, Zwecke f;

Heftstich *m*; ⚓ Halse *f*; ⚓ Gang *m*
beim Lavieren; *fig.* Weg *m*; **2.** *v/t.*
(an)heften; *fig.* (an)hängen; *v/i.* ⚓
wenden; *fig.* lavieren.

tackle ['tækl] **1.** Gerät *n*; ⚓ Takel-,
Tauwerk *n*; ⊕ Flaschenzug *m*;
2. (an)packen; in Angriff nehmen;
fertig werden mit; *j-n* angehen (for
um).

tacky ['tæki] klebrig; *Am.* F schäbig.

tact [tækt] Takt *m*, Feingefühl *n*;
~**ful** □ ['tæktful] taktvoll.

tactics ['tæktiks] Taktik *f*.

tactless □ ['tæktlis] taktlos.

tadpole *zo.* ['tædpoul] Kaulquappe*f*.

taffeta ['tæfitə] Taft *m*.

taffy *Am.* ['tæfi] = **toffee**; F Schmus
m, Schmeichelei *f*.

tag [tæg] **1.** (Schnürsenkel)Stift *m*;
Schildchen *n*, Etikett *n*; Redensart
f, Zitat *n*; Zusatz *m*; loses Ende;
Fangen *n* (*Kinderspiel*); **2.** etikettieren, auszeichnen; anhängen (to,
onto an *acc.*); ~ *after* herlaufen hinter (*dat.*); ~ *together* an-ea.-reihen.

tail [teil] **1.** Schwanz *m*; Schweif *m*;
hinteres Ende, Schluß *m*; ~*s pl.*
Rückseite *f* e-r Münze; F Frack *m*;
turn ~ davonlaufen; ~*s up* in Hoch-
stimmung; **2.** ~ *after* s.o. j-m nach-
laufen; ~ *s.o. Am.* j-n beschatten; ~
away, ~ *off* abflauen, sich verlieren;
zögernd enden; ~**coat** [teil'kout]
Frack *m*; ~**light** *mot. etc.* ['teillait]
Rück-, Schlußlicht *n*.

tailor ['teilə] **1.** Schneider *m*;
2. schneidern; ~**made** Schneider..., Maß...

taint [teint] **1.** Flecken *m*, Makel *m*;
⚕ Ansteckung *f*; *fig. krankhafter*
Zug; Verderbnis *f*; **2.** beflecken;
verderben; ⚕ anstecken.

take [teik] **1.** [*irr.*] *v/t.* nehmen; an-,
ab-, auf-, ein-, fest-, hin-, weg-
nehmen; (weg)bringen; *Speise* (zu
sich) nehmen; *Maßnahme, Gelegenheit* ergreifen; *Eid, Gelübde, Examen* ablegen; *phot.* aufnehmen; *et.
gut etc.* aufnehmen; *Beleidigung*
hinnehmen; fassen, ergreifen; fangen; *fig.* fesseln; sich *e-e Krankheit*
holen; erfordern; brauchen; *Zeit*
dauern; auffassen; halten, ansehen
(for für); *I* ~ *it that* ich nehme an,
daß; ~ *breath* verschnaufen; ~ *comfort* sich trösten; ~ *compassion on*
Mitleid empfinden mit; sich erbarmen (*gen.*); ~ *counsel* beraten; ~ *a
drive* e-e Fahrt machen; ~ *fire* Feuer
fangen; ~ *in hand* unternehmen; ~
hold of ergreifen; ~ *pity on* Mitleid
haben mit; ~ *place* stattfinden; ~
spielen (*Handlung*); ~ *a seat* Platz
nehmen; ~ *a walk* e-n Spaziergang
machen; ~ *my word for it* verlaß
dich drauf; ~ *about* herumführen;
~ *along* mitnehmen; ~ *down* her-
unternehmen; notieren; ~ *for* halten für; ~ *from j-m* wegnehmen;

abziehen von; ~ *in* enger machen;
Zeitung halten; aufnehmen (*als
Gast etc.*); einschließen; verstehen;
erfassen; F *j-n* reinlegen; ~ *off* ab-,
wegnehmen; *Kleid* ausziehen, *Hut*
abnehmen; ~ *on* an-, übernehmen;
Arbeiter etc. einstellen; *Fahrgäste*
zusteigen lassen; ~ *out* heraus-, entnehmen; *Fleck* entfernen; *j-n* ausführen; *Versicherung* abschließen;
~ *to pieces* auseinandernehmen; ~
up aufnehmen; sich *e-r S.* annehmen; *Raum, Zeit* in Anspruch nehmen; *v/i.* wirken, ein-, anschlagen;
gefallen, ziehen; ~ *after j-m* nachschlagen; ~ *off* abspringen; ✈ aufsteigen, starten; ~ *on* F Anklang
finden; ~ *over* die Amtsgewalt übernehmen; ~ *to* liebgewinnen; *fig.*
sich verlegen auf (*acc.*); Zuflucht
nehmen zu; sich ergeben (*dat.*); ~
up F sich bessern (*Wetter*); ~ *up
with* sich anfreunden mit; *that
won't* ~ *with me* das verfängt bei
mir nicht; **2.** Fang *m*; *Geld*-Ein-
nahme *f*; *Film:* Szene(naufnahme)
f; ~**in** F ['teik'in] Reinfall *m*; ~**n**
['teikən] *p.p. von* take 1; *be* ~ besetzt sein; *be* ~ *with* entzückt sein
von; *be* ~ *ill* krank werden; ~**off**
['teiko:f] Karikatur *f*; Absprung *m*;
✈ Start *m*.

taking ['teikiŋ] **1.** □ F anziehend,
fesselnd, einnehmend; ansteckend;
2. (An-, Ab-, Auf-, Ein-, Ent-,
Hin-, Weg- *etc.*)Nehmen *n*; Inbe-
sitznahme *f*; ⚔ Einnahme *f*; F Aufregung *f*; ~*s pl.* ✝ Einnahmen *f/pl.*

tale [teil] Erzählung *f*, Geschichte *f*;
Märchen *n*, Sage *f*; *it tells its own* ~
es spricht für sich selbst; ~**bearer**
['teilbɛərə] Zuträger(in).

talent ['tælənt] Talent *n*, Begabung
f, Anlage *f*; ~**ed** [~tid] talentvoll,
begabt.

talk [tɔ:k] **1.** Gespräch *n*; Unterredung *f*; Plauderei *f*; Vortrag *m*;
Geschwätz *n*; **2.** sprechen, reden
(*von et.*); plaudern; ~**ative** □ ['tɔ:-
kətiv] gesprächig, geschwätzig; ~**er**
['tɔ:kə] Schwätzer(in); Sprechen-
de(r *m*) *f*.

tall [tɔ:l] groß, lang, hoch; F übertrieben, unglaublich; *that's a* ~
order F das ist ein bißchen viel
verlangt.

tallow ['tælou] *ausgelassener* Talg.

tally ['tæli] **1.** Kerbholz *n*; Gegen-
stück *n* (of zu); Kennzeichen *n*;
2. übereinstimmen.

talon *orn.* ['tælən] Kralle *f*, Klaue
f.

tame [teim] **1.** □ zahm; folgsam;
harmlos; lahm, fad(e); **2.** (be)zäh-
men, bändigen.

Tammany *Am.* ['tæməni] New
Yorker Demokraten-Vereinigung.

tamper ['tæmpə]: ~ *with* sich (unbefugt) zu schaffen machen mit;

j-n zu bestechen suchen; *Urkunde* fälschen.

tan [tæn] **1.** Lohe *f*; Lohfarbe *f*; (Sonnen)Bräune *f*; **2.** lohfarben; **3.** gerben; bräunen.

tang [tæŋ] Beigeschmack *m*; *scharfer* Klang; ♣ Seetang *m*.

tangent ['tændʒənt] Å Tangente *f*; *fly od.* go off *at a ~* vom Gegenstand abspringen.

tangerine ♣ [tændʒə'ri:n] Mandarine *f*.

tangible □ ['tændʒəbl] fühlbar, greifbar (*a. fig.*); klar.

tangle ['tæŋgl] **1.** Gewirr *n*; Verwicklung *f*; **2.** (sich) verwirren, verwickeln.

tank [tæŋk] **1.** Zisterne *f*, Wasserbehälter *m*; ⊕, ✖ Tank *m*; **2.** tanken. [(Bier)Krug *m*.)

tankard ['tæŋkəd] Kanne *f*, *bsd.*)

tanner ['tænə] Gerber *m*; **~y** [**~**əri] Gerberei *f*.

tantalize ['tæntəlaiz] quälen.

tantamount ['tæntəmaunt] gleichbedeutend (mit).

tantrum F ['tæntrəm] Koller *m*.

tap [tæp] **1.** leichtes Klopfen; (Wasser-, Gas-, Zapf)Hahn *m*; Zapfen *m*; Schankstube *f*; F Sorte *f*; **~**s *pl. Am.* ✖ Zapfenstreich *m*; **2.** pochen, klopfen, tippen (auf, an, gegen *acc.*); an-, abzapfen; **~dance** ['tæpdɑ:ns] Stepptanz *m*.

tape [teip] schmales Band; *Sport:* Zielband *n*; *tel.* Papierstreifen *m*; Tonband *n*; *red ~* Bürokratismus *m*; **~measure** ['teipmeʒə] Bandmaß *n*.

taper ['teipə] **1.** dünne Wachskerze; **2.** *adj.* spitz (zulaufend); schlank; **3.** *v/i.* spitz zulaufen; *v/t.* zuspitzen.

tape| recorder ['teiprikɔ:də] Tonbandgerät *n*; **~ recording** Tonbandaufnahme *f*.

tapestry ['tæpistri] Gobelin *m*.

tapeworm ['teipwə:m] Bandwurm *m*.

tap-room ['tæprum] Schankstube *f*.

tar [tɑ:] **1.** Teer *m*; **2.** teeren.

tardy □ ['tɑ:di] langsam; spät.

tare ✝ [tɛə] Tara *f*.

target ['tɑ:git] (Schieß)Scheibe *f*; *fig.* Ziel(scheibe *f*) *n*; Ziel(leistung *f*) *n*; Soll *n*; *~ practice* Scheibenschießen *n*.

tariff ['tærif] (*bsd.* Zoll)Tarif *m*.

tarnish ['tɑ:niʃ] **1.** *v/t.* ⊕ trüb *od.* blind machen; *fig.* trüben; *v/i.* trüb werden, anlaufen; **2.** Trübung *f*; Belag *m*.

tarry[1] *lit.* ['tæri] säumen, zögern; verweilen.

tarry[2] ['tɑ:ri] teerig.

tart [tɑ:t] **1.** □ sauer, herb; *fig.* scharf, schroff; **2.** (Obst)Torte *f*; *sl.* Dirne *f*.

tartan ['tɑ:tən] Tartan *m*; Schottentuch *n*; Schottenmuster *n*.

task [tɑ:sk] **1.** Aufgabe *f*; Arbeit *f*; *take to ~* zur Rede stellen; **2.** beschäftigen; in Anspruch nehmen.

tassel ['tæsəl] Troddel *f*, Quaste *f*.

taste [teist] **1.** Geschmack *m*; (Kost)Probe *f*; Lust *f* (*for* zu); **2.** kosten, schmecken; versuchen; genießen; **~ful** □ ['teistful] geschmackvoll; **~less** □ [**~**tlis] geschmacklos.

tasty □ F ['teisti] schmackhaft.

ta-ta ['tæ'tɑ:] auf Wiedersehen!

tatter ['tætə] **1.** zerfetzen; **2.** **~**s *pl.* Fetzen *m/pl.*

tattle ['tætl] **1.** schwatzen; tratschen; **2.** Geschwätz *n*; Tratsch *m*.

tattoo [tə'tu:] **1.** ✖ Zapfenstreich *m*; Tätowierung *f*; **2.** *fig.* trommeln; tätowieren.

taught [tɔ:t] *pret. u. p.p. von* teach.

taunt [tɔ:nt] **1.** Stichelei *f*, Spott *m*; **2.** verhöhnen, verspotten.

taut ⚓ [tɔ:t] steif, straff; schmuck.

tavern ['tævən] Schenke *f*.

tawdry □ ['tɔ:dri] billig; kitschig.

tawny ['tɔ:ni] lohfarben.

tax [tæks] **1.** Steuer *f*, Abgabe *f*; *fig.* Inanspruchnahme *f* (*on, upon gen.*); **2.** besteuern; *fig.* stark in Anspruch nehmen; ⚖ *Kosten* schätzen; auf e-e harte Probe stellen; *j-n* zur Rede stellen; *~ s.o. with s.th.* j-n e-r S. beschuldigen; **~ation** [tæk'seiʃən] Besteuerung *f*; Steuer(n *pl.*) *f*; *bsd.* ⚖ Schätzung *f*.

taxi F ['tæksi] **1.** = **~**cab; **2.** mit e-m Taxi fahren; ✈ rollen; **~cab** Taxi *n*, (Auto)Droschke *f*.

taxpayer ['tækspeiə] Steuerzahler *m*.

tea [ti:] Tee *m*; *high ~*, *meat ~* frühes Abendbrot mit Tee.

teach [ti:tʃ] [*irr.*] lehren, unterrichten, *j-m et.* beibringen; **~able** □ ['ti:tʃəbl] gelehrig; lehrbar; **~er** [**~**ʃə] Lehrer(in); **~-in** [**~**ʃ'in] (politische) Diskussion *als Großveranstaltung.*

tea| -cosy ['ti:kouzi] Teewärmer *m*; **~cup** Teetasse *f*; *storm in a ~ fig.* Sturm *m* im Wasserglas; **~kettle** Wasserkessel *m*.

team [ti:m] Team *n*, Arbeitsgruppe *f*; Gespann *n*; *bsd. Sport:* Mannschaft *f*; **~ster** ['ti:mstə] Gespannführer *m*; *Am.* LKW-Fahrer *m*; **~work** Zusammenarbeit *f*, Teamwork *n*; Zusammenspiel *n*.

teapot ['ti:pot] Teekanne *f*.

tear[1] [tɛə] **1.** [*irr.*] zerren, (zer)reißen; rasen, stürmen; **2.** Riß *m*.

tear[2] [tiə] Träne *f*.

tearful □ ['tiəful] tränenreich.

tea-room ['ti:rum] Tearoom *m*. Teestube *f*, Café *n*.

tease [ti:z] **1.** necken, hänseln; quälen; **2.** Necker *m*; Quälgeist *m*.

teat [ti:t] Zitze *f*; Brustwarze *f*; (Gummi)Sauger *m*.

technic|al □ ['teknikəl] technisch; gewerblich, Gewerbe...; fachlich, Fach...; **~ality** [tekni'kæliti] technische Eigentümlichkeit od. Einzelheit; Fachausdruck m; **~ian** [tek-'niʃən] Techniker(in).

technique [tek'ni:k] Technik f, Verfahren n.

technology [tek'nɔlədʒi] Gewerbekunde f; school of **~** Technische Hochschule.

teddy boy F ['tedibɔi] Halbstarke(r) m.

tedious □ ['ti:djəs] langweilig, ermüdend; weitschweifig.

tee [ti:] Sport: Mal n, Ziel n; Golf: Abschlagmal n.

teem [ti:m] wimmeln, strotzen (with von).

teens [ti:nz] pl. Lebensjahre n/pl. von 13—19.

teeny F ['ti:ni] winzig.

teeth [ti:θ] pl. von tooth; **~e** [ti:ð] zahnen.

teetotal(l)er [ti:'toutlə] Abstinenzler(in).

telecast ['telika:st] 1. Fernsehsendung f; 2. [irr. (cast)] im Fernsehen übertragen.

telecourse Am. F ['telikɔ:s] Fernsehlehrgang m.

telegram ['teligræm] Telegramm n.

telegraph ['teligra:f] 1. Telegraph m; 2. Telegraphen...; 3. telegraphieren; **~ic** [teli'græfik] (**~ally**) telegraphisch; telegrammäßig (Stil); **~y** [ti'legrəfi] Telegraphie f.

telephon|e ['telifoun] 1. Telephon n, Fernsprecher m; 2. telephonieren; anrufen; **~e booth** Telephonzelle f; **~ic** [teli'fɔnik] (**~ally**) telephonisch; **~y** [ti'lefəni] Fernsprechwesen n.

telephoto phot. ['teli'foutou] a. **~ lens** Teleobjektiv n.

teleprinter ['teliprintə] Fernschreiber m.

telescope ['teliskoup] 1. opt. Fernrohr n; 2. (sich) ineinanderschieben.

teletype ['telitaip] Fernschreiber m.

televis|e ['telivaiz] im Fernsehen übertragen; **~ion** [**~**viʒən] Fernsehen n; watch **~** fernsehen; **~ion set**, **~or** [**~**vaizə] Fernsehapparat m.

tell [tel] [irr.] v/t. zählen; sagen, erzählen; erkennen; **~** s.o. to do s.th. j-m sagen, er solle et. tun; **~** off abzählen; auswählen; F abkanzeln; v/i. erzählen (of, about von); (aus)plaudern; sich auswirken; sitzen (Hieb etc.); **~er** [telə] (Er)Zähler m; **~ing** □ ['teliŋ] wirkungsvoll; **~tale** ['telteil] 1. Klatschbase f; ⊕ Anzeiger m; 2. fig. verräterisch.

temerity [ti'meriti] Unbesonnenheit f, Verwegenheit f.

temper ['tempə] 1. mäßigen, mildern; Kalk etc. anrühren; Stahl anlassen; 2. ⊕ Härte(grad m) f;

(Gemüts)Ruhe f, Gleichmut m; Temperament n, Wesen n; Stimmung f; Wut f; lose one's **~** in Wut geraten; **~ament** [**~**rəmənt] Temperament n; **~amental** □ [tempərə'mentl] anlagebedingt; launisch; **~ance** ['tempərəns] Mäßigkeit f; Enthaltsamkeit f; **~ate** □ [**~**rit] gemäßigt; zurückhaltend; maßvoll; mäßig; **~ature** [**~**pritʃə] Temperatur f.

tempest ['tempist] Sturm m; Gewitter n; **~uous** □ [tem'pestjəs] stürmisch; ungestüm.

temple ['templ] Tempel m; anat. Schläfe f.

tempor|al □ ['tempərəl] zeitlich; weltlich; **~ary** □ [**~**əri] zeitweilig; vorläufig; vorübergehend; Not..., (Aus)Hilfs..., Behelfs...; **~ize** [**~**raiz] Zeit zu gewinnen suchen.

tempt [tempt] j-n versuchen; verleiten; verlocken; **~ation** [temp'teiʃən] Versuchung f; Reiz m; **~ing** □ ['temptiŋ] verführerisch.

ten [ten] 1. zehn; 2. Zehn f.

tenable ['tenəbl] haltbar (Theorie etc.); verliehen (Amt).

tenaci|ous □ [ti'neiʃəs] zäh; festhaltend (of an dat.); gut (Gedächtnis); **~ty** [ti'næsiti] Zähigkeit f; Festhalten n; Verläßlichkeit f des Gedächtnisses.

tenant ['tenənt] Pächter m; Mieter m.

tend [tend] v/i. (to) gerichtet sein (auf acc.); hinstreben (zu); abzielen (auf acc.); neigen (zu); v/t. pflegen; hüten; ⊕ bedienen; **~ance** ['tendəns] Pflege f; Bedienung f; **~ency** [**~**si] Richtung f; Neigung f; Zweck m.

tender ['tendə] 1. □ zart; weich; empfindlich; heikel (Thema); zärtlich; 2. Angebot n; Kostenanschlag m; ⛟, ⚓ Tender m; legal **~** gesetzliches Zahlungsmittel; 3. anbieten; Entlassung einreichen; **~foot** Am. F Neuling m, Anfänger m; **~loin** bsd. Am. Filet n; Am. berüchtigtes Viertel; **~ness** [**~**nis] Zartheit f; Zärtlichkeit f.

tendon anat. ['tendən] Sehne f.

tendril ♀ ['tendril] Ranke f.

tenement ['tenimənt] Wohnhaus n; (bsd. Miet)Wohnung f; **~ house** Mietshaus n.

tennis ['tenis] Tennis(spiel) n; **~ court** Tennisplatz m.

tenor ['tenə] Fortgang m, Verlauf m; Inhalt m; ♪ Tenor m.

tens|e [tens] 1. gr. Zeit(form) f, Tempus n; 2. □ gespannt (a. fig.); straff; **~ion** [tenʃən] Spannung f.

tent [tent] 1. Zelt n; 2. zelten.

tentacle zo. ['tentəkl] Fühler m; Fangarm m e-s Polypen.

tentative □ ['tentətiv] versuchend; Versuchs...; **~ly** versuchsweise.

tenth [tenθ] 1. zehnte(r, -s); 2. Zehntel n; ~ly ['tenθli] zehntens.

tenuous □ ['tenjuəs] dünn; zart, fein; dürftig.

tenure ['tenjuə] Besitz(art f, -dauer f) m.

tepid □ ['tepid] lau(warm).

term [tə:m] 1. (bestimmte) Zeit, Frist f, Termin m; Zahltag m; Amtszeit f; ɪʦ Sitzungsperiode f; Semester n, Quartal n, Trimester n, Tertial n; Ⱥ, phls. Glied n; (Fach-)Ausdruck m, Wort n, Bezeichnung f; Begriff m; ~s pl. Bedingungen f/pl.; Beziehungen f/pl.; be on good (bad) ~s with gut (schlecht) stehen mit; come to ~s, make ~s sich einigen; 2. (be)nennen; bezeichnen (als).

termagant ['tə:məgənt] 1. □ zanksüchtig; 2. Zankteufel m (Weib).

termina|l ['tə:minl] 1. □ End...; letzt; ~ly terminweise; 2. Endstück n; ⚡ Pol m; Am. 🚂 Endstation f; ~te [~neit] begrenzen; (be)endigen; ~tion [tə:mi'neiʃən] Beendigung f; Ende n; gr. Endung f.

terminus ['tə:minəs] Endstation f.

terrace ['terəs] Terrasse f; Häuserreihe f; ~house Reihenhaus n; ~d [~st] terrassenförmig.

terrestrial □ [ti'restriəl] irdisch; Erd...; bsd. zo., ♀ Land...

terrible □ ['terəbl] schrecklich.

terri|fic [tə'rifik] (~ally) fürchterlich, schrecklich; F ungeheuer, großartig; ~fy ['terifai] v/t. u. erschrecken.

territor|ial [teri'tɔ:riəl] 1. □ territorial; Land...; Bezirks...; ♀ Army, ♀ Force Territorialarmee f; 2. ⚔ Angehörige(r) m der Territorialarmee; ~y ['teritəri] Territorium n, (Hoheits-, Staats)Gebiet n.

terror ['terə] Schrecken m, Entsetzen n; ~ize [~əraiz] terrorisieren.

terse □ [tə:s] knapp; kurz u. bündig.

test [test] 1. Probe f; Untersuchung f; (Eignungs)Prüfung f; Test m; 🧪 Reagens n; 2. probieren, prüfen, testen.

testament ['testəmənt] Testament n.

testicle anat. ['testikl] Hode(n m) [m, f.]

testify ['testifai] (be)zeugen; (als Zeuge) aussagen (on über acc.).

testimon|ial [testi'mounjəl] (Führungs)Zeugnis n; Zeichen n der Anerkennung; ~y ['testiməni] Zeugnis n; Beweis m.

test-tube 🧪 ['testtju:b] Reagenzglas n.

testy □ ['testi] reizbar, kribbelig.

tether ['teðə] 1. Haltestrick m; fig. Spielraum m; at the end of one's ~ fig. am Ende s-r Kraft; 2. anbinden.

text [tekst] Text m; Bibelstelle f;

~book ['tekstbuk] Leitfaden m, Lehrbuch n.

textile ['tekstail] 1. Textil..., Web...; 2. ~s pl. Webwaren f/pl., Textilien pl.

texture ['tekstʃə] Gewebe n; Gefüge n.

than [ðæn, ðən] als.

thank [θæŋk] 1. danken (dat.); ~ you, bei Ablehnung no, ~ you danke; 2. ~s pl. Dank m; ~s! vielen Dank!; danke (schön); ~s to dank (dat.); ~ful □ ['θæŋkful] dankbar; ~less □ [~klis] undankbar; ~sgiving [~ksgivin] Danksagung f; Dankfest n; ♀ (Day) bsd. Am. (Ernte)Dankfest n.

that [ðæt, ðət] 1. pl. those [ðouz] pron. jene(r, -s); der, die, das; der-, die-, das(jenige); welche(r, -s); 2. cj. daß; damit.

thatch [θætʃ] 1. Dachstroh n; Strohdach n; 2. mit Stroh decken.

thaw [θɔ:] 1. Tauwetter n; (Auf-)Tauen n; 2. (auf)tauen.

the [ði:; vor Vokalen ði; vor Konsonanten ðə] 1. art. der, die, das; 2. adv. desto, um so; ~ ... ~ ... je ... desto ...

theat|re, Am. ~er ['θiətə] Theater n; fig. (Kriegs)Schauplatz m; ~ric(al □) [θi'ætrik(əl)] Theater...; theatralisch.

thee Bibel, poet. [ði:] dich; dir.

theft [θeft] Diebstahl m.

their [ðeə] ihr(e); ~s [~z] der (die, das) ihrige od. ihre.

them [ðem, ðəm] sie (acc. pl.); ihnen.

theme [θi:m] Thema n; Aufgabe f.

themselves [ðem'selvz] sie (acc. pl.) selbst; sich selbst.

then [ðen] 1. adv. dann; damals; da; by ~ bis dahin; inzwischen; every now and ~ alle Augenblicke; there and ~ sogleich; now ~ nun denn; 2. cj. denn, also, folglich; 3. adj. damalig.

thence lit. [ðens] daher; von da.

theolog|ian [θiə'loudʒjən] Theologe m; ~y [θi'ɔlədʒi] Theologie f.

theor|etic(al □) [θiə'retik(əl)] theoretisch; ~ist ['θiərist] Theoretiker m; ~y [~ri] Theorie f.

therap|eutic [θerə'pju:tik] 1. (~ally) therapeutisch; 2. ~s mst. sg. Therapeutik f; ~y ['θerəpi] Therapie f, Heilbehandlung f.

there [ðeə] da, dort; darin; dorthin; na!; ~ is, ~ are es gibt, es ist, es sind; ~about(s) ['θeərəbaut(s)] da herum; so ungefähr ...; ~after [ðeər'a:ftə] danach; ~by ['ðeə'bai] dadurch, damit; ~fore ['ðeəfɔ:] darum, deswegen; deshalb, daher; ~upon ['θeərə'pɔn] darauf(hin); ~with [ðeə'wið] damit.

thermal ['θə:məl] 1. □ Thermal...; phys. Wärme...; 2. Aufwind m.

thermo|meter [θəˈmɔmitə] Thermometer *n*; ⚛ 8 [ˈθəːmɔs] *a.* ~ *flask*, ~ *bottle* Thermosflasche *f.*

these [ðiːz] *pl. von* this.

thes|is [ˈθiːsis], *pl.* ~es [ˈθiːsiːz] These *f*; Dissertation *f.*

they [ðei] sie (*pl.*).

thick [θik] 1. □ *allg.* dick; dicht; trüb; legiert (*Suppe*); heiser; dumm; *pred.* F dick befreundet; ~ *with* dicht besetzt mit; 2. dickster Teil; *fig.* Brennpunkt *m*; *in the* ~ *of* mitten in (*dat.*); ~**en** [ˈθikən] (sich) verdicken; (sich) verstärken; legieren; (sich) verdichten; ~**et** [ˈθikit] Dickicht *n*; ~**-headed** dumm; ~**ness** [ˈθiknis] Dicke *f*, Stärke *f*; Dichte *f*; ~**-set** dicht (gepflanzt); untersetzt; ~**-skinned** *fig.* dickfellig.

thief [θiːf], *pl.* **thieves** [θiːvz] Dieb(in); *fig.* **thieve** [θiːv] stehlen.

thigh [θai] (Ober)Schenkel *m.*

thimble [ˈθimbl] Fingerhut *m.*

thin [θin] 1. □ *allg.* dünn; leicht; mager; spärlich; dürftig; schwach; fadenscheinig (*bsd. fig.*); 2. verdünnen; (sich) lichten; abnehmen.

thine *Bibel, poet.* [ðain] dein; der (die, das) deinige *od.* deine.

thing [θiŋ] Ding *n*; Sache *f*; Geschöpf *n*; ~ *s* *pl.* Sachen *f/pl.*; die Dinge *n/pl.* (*Umstände*); the ~ F das Richtige; richtig; die Hauptsache; ~*s are going better* es geht jetzt besser.

think [θiŋk] [*irr.*] *v/i.* denken (*of* an *acc.*); nachdenken; sich besinnen; meinen, glauben; gedenken (*to inf.* zu *inf.*); *v/t.* (sich) *et.* denken; halten für; ~ *much etc. of* viel *etc.* halten von; ~ *s.th. over* (sich) *et.* überlegen, über *et.* nachdenken.

third [θəːd] 1. dritte(r, -s); 2. Drittel *n*; ~**ly** [ˈθəːdli] drittens; ~**rate** [ˈθəːdˈreit] drittklassig.

thirst [θəːst] 1. Durst *m*; 2. dürsten; ~**y** □ [ˈθəːsti] durstig; dürr (*Boden*).

thirt|een [ˈθəːˈtiːn] dreizehn; ~**eenth** [~ˈnθ] dreizehnte(r, -s); ~**ieth** [ˈθəːtiiθ] dreißigste(r, -s); ~**y** [ˈθəːti] dreißig.

this [ðis], *pl.* **these** [ðiːz] diese(r, -s); ~ *morning* heute morgen.

thistle ♣ [ˈθisl] Distel *f.*

thong [θɔŋ] (Leder-, Peitschen-) Riemen *m.*

thorn ♣ [θɔːn] Dorn *m*; ~**y** [ˈθɔːni] dornig, stach(e)lig; beschwerlich.

thorough □ [ˈθʌrə] vollkommen; vollständig; vollendet; gründlich; ~**ly** *a.* durchaus; ~**bred** Vollblüter *m*; *attr.* Vollblut...; ~**fare** Durchgang *m*, Durchfahrt *f*; Hauptverkehrsstraße *f*; ~**going** gründlich; tatkräftig.

those [ðouz] *pl. von* that 1.

thou *Bibel, poet.* [ðau] du.

though [ðou] obgleich, obwohl, wenn auch; zwar; aber, doch; freilich; *as* ~ als ob.

thought [θɔːt] 1. *pret. u. p.p. von* think; 2. Gedanke *m*; (Nach)Denken *n*; *on second* ~ *s* nach nochmaliger Überlegung; ~**ful** □ [ˈθɔːtful] gedankenvoll, nachdenklich; rücksichtsvoll (*of* gegen); ~**less** □ [ˈθɔːtlis] gedankenlos; unbesonnen; rücksichtslos (*of* gegen).

thousand [ˈθauzənd] 1. tausend; 2. Tausend *n*; ~**th** [~ntθ] 1. tausendste(r, -s); 2. Tausendstel *n.*

thrash [θræʃ] (ver)dreschen, (ver-) prügeln; (hin und her) schlagen; *s. thresh*; ~**ing** [ˈθræʃiŋ] Dresche *f*, Tracht *f* Prügel; *s. threshing.*

thread [θred] 1. Faden *m* (*a. fig.*); Zwirn *m*, Garn *n*; ⊕ (Schrauben-) Gewinde *n*; 2. einfädeln; sich durchwinden (durch); durchziehen; ~**bare** [ˈθredbɛə] fadenscheinig.

threat [θret] Drohung *f*; ~**en** [ˈθretn] (be-, an)drohen; ~**ening** [~niŋ] bedrohlich.

three [θriː] 1. drei; 2. Drei *f*; ~**fold** [ˈθriːfould] dreifach; ~**pence** [ˈθrepəns] Dreipence(stück *n*) *m/pl.*; ~**score** [ˈθriːˈskɔː] sechzig.

thresh [θreʃ] ♂ (aus)dreschen; *s. thrash*; ~ *out fig.* durchdreschen; ~**er** [ˈθreʃə] Drescher *m*; Dreschmaschine *f*; ~**ing** [~ʃiŋ] Dreschen *n*; ~**ing-machine** Dreschmaschine *f.*

threshold [ˈθreʃhould] Schwelle *f.*

threw [θruː] *pret. von* throw 1.

thrice [θrais] dreimal.

thrift [θrift] Sparsamkeit *f*, Wirtschaftlichkeit *f*; ~**less** □ [ˈθriftlis] verschwenderisch; ~**y** □ [~ti] sparsam; *poet.* gedeihend.

thrill [θril] 1. *v/t.* durchdringen, durchschauern; *fig.* packen, aufwühlen; aufregen; *v/i.* (er)beben; 2. Schauer *m*; Beben *n*; aufregendes Erlebnis; Sensation *f*; ~**er** F [ˈθrilə] Reißer *m*, Thriller *m*, Schauerroman *m*, Schauerstück *n*; ~**ing** [~liŋ] spannend.

thrive [θraiv] [*irr.*] gedeihen; *fig.* blühen; Glück haben; ~**n** [ˈθrivn] *p.p. von* thrive.

throat [θrout] Kehle *f*; Hals *m*; Gurgel *f*; Schlund *m*; *clear one's* ~ sich räuspern.

throb [θrɔb] 1. pochen, klopfen, schlagen; pulsieren; 2. Pochen *n*; Schlagen *n*; Pulsschlag *m.*

throes [θrouz] *pl.* Geburtswehen *f/pl.* [Thrombose *f.*]

thrombosis ♣ [θrɔmˈbousis]

throne [θroun] Thron *m.*

throng [θrɔŋ] 1. Gedränge *n*; Menge *f*, Schar *f*; 2. sich drängen (in *dat.*); anfüllen mit.

throstle *orn.* [ˈθrɔsl] Drossel *f.*

throttle [ˈθrɔtl] 1. erdrosseln; ⊕ (ab)drosseln; 2. ⊕ Drosselklappe *f.*

through [θru:] 1. durch; 2. Durchgangs...; durchgehend; **~out** [θru(:)'aut] 1. *prp.* überall in (*dat.*); 2. *adv.* durch u. durch, ganz und gar, durchweg.

throve [θrouv] *pret. von* thrive.

throw [θrou] 1. [*irr.*] (ab)werfen, schleudern; *Am.* F *Wettkampf etc.* betrügerisch verlieren; würfeln; ⊕ schalten; **~** off (die Jagd) beginnen; **~** over aufgeben; **~** up in die Höhe werfen; erbrechen; *fig.* hinwerfen; 2. Wurf *m*; **~n** [θroun] *p.p. von* throw 1.

thru *Am.* [θru:] = through.

thrum [θrʌm] klimpern (auf *dat.*).

thrush *orn.* [θrʌʃ] Drossel *f*.

thrust [θrʌst] 1. Stoß *m*; Vorstoß *m*; ⊕ Druck *m*, Schub *m*; 2. [*irr.*] stoßen; **~** *o.s.* into sich drängen in (*acc.*); **~** upon *s.o.* j-m aufdrängen.

thud [θʌd] 1. dumpf aufschlagen, F bumsen; 2. dumpfer (Auf)Schlag, F Bums *m*.

thug [θʌg] Strolch *m*.

thumb [θʌm] 1. Daumen *m*; Tom ♀ Däumling *m im Märchen*; 2. *Buch etc.* abgreifen; **~** a lift per Anhalter fahren; **~tack** *Am.* ['θʌmtæk] Reißzwecke *f*.

thump [θʌmp] 1. F Bums *m*; F Puff *m*; 2. *v/t.* F bumsen *od.* pochen auf (*acc.*) *od.* gegen; F knuffen, puffen; *v/i.* F (auf)bumsen.

thunder ['θʌndə] 1. Donner *m*; 2. donnern; **~bolt** Blitz *m* (*u.* Donner *m*); **~clap** Donnerschlag *m*; **~ous** □ [*~ərəs*] donnernd; **~storm** Gewitter *n*; **~struck** wie vom Donner gerührt.

Thursday ['θə:zdi] Donnerstag *m*.

thus [ðʌs] so; also, somit.

thwart [θwɔ:t] 1. durchkreuzen; hintertreiben; 2. Ruderbank *f*.

thy *Bibel, poet.* [ðai] dein.

tick¹ *zo.* [tik] Zecke *f*.

tick² [*~*] 1. Ticken *n*; (Vermerk-) Häkchen *n*; 2. *v/i.* ticken; *v/t.* anhaken; **~** off abhaken.

tick³ [*~*] Inlett *n*; Matratzenbezug *m*.

ticket ['tikit] 1. Fahrkarte *f*, -schein *m*; Flugkarte *f*; Eintrittskarte *f*; (Straf)Zettel *m*; (Preis- *etc.*)Schildchen *n*; *pol.* (Wahl-, Kandidaten-) Liste *f*; 2. etikettieren, *Ware* auszeichnen; **~machine** Fahrkartenautomat *m*; **~** office, **~** window *bsd. Am.* Fahrkartenschalter *m*.

tickl|e ['tikl] kitzeln (*a. fig.*); **~ish** □ [*~liʃ*] kitzlig; heikel.

tidal ['taidl]: **~** wave Flutwelle *f*.

tide [taid] 1. Gezeit(en *pl.*) *f*; Ebbe *f* und Flut *f*; *fig.* Strom *m*, Flut *f*; *in Zssgn:* rechte Zeit; high **~** Flut *f*; low **~** Ebbe *f*; 2. **~** over *fig.* hinwegkommen *od.* j-m hinweghelfen über (*acc.*).

tidings ['taidinz] *pl. od. sg.* Neuigkeiten *f/pl.*, Nachrichten *f/pl.*

tidy ['taidi] 1. ordentlich, sauber, reinlich; F ganz schön, beträchtlich (*Summe*); 2. Behälter *m*; Abfallkorb *m*; 3. *a.* **~** up zurechtmachen; ordnen; aufräumen.

tie [tai] 1. Band *n* (*a. fig.*); Schleife *f*; Krawatte *f*, Schlips *m*; Bindung *f*; *fig.* Fessel *f*, Verpflichtung *f*; *Sport:* Punkt-, *parl.* Stimmengleichheit *f*; *Sport:* Entscheidungsspiel *n*; 🚋 *Am.* Schwelle *f*; 2. *v/t.* (ver)binden; **~** down *fig.* binden (to an *acc.*); **~** up zu-, an-, ver-, zs.-binden; *v/i. Sport:* punktgleich sein.

tier [tiə] Reihe *f*; Rang *m*.

tie-up ['taiʌp] (Ver)Bindung *f*; ✝ Fusion *f*; Stockung *f*; *bsd. Am.* Streik *m*.

tiffin ['tifin] Mittagessen *n*.

tiger ['taigə] *zo.* Tiger *m*; *Am.* F Beifallsgebrüll *n*.

tight [tait] 1. □ dicht; fest; eng; knapp (sitzend); straff, prall, knapp; F beschwipst; *be in a* **~** *place od.* corner F in der Klemme sein; 2. *adv.* fest; *hold* **~** festhalten; **~en** ['taitn] *a.* **~** up (sich) zs.-ziehen; *Gürtel* enger schnallen; **~-fisted** knick(e)rig; **~ness** ['taitnis] Festigkeit *f*, Dichtigkeit *f*; Straffheit *f*; Knappheit *f*; Enge *f*; Geiz *m*; **~s** [taits] *pl.* Trikot *n*.

tigress ['taigris] Tigerin *f*.

tile [tail] 1. (Dach)Ziegel *m*; Kachel *f*; Fliese *f*; 2. mit Ziegeln *etc.* decken; kacheln; fliesen.

till¹ [til] Laden(tisch)kasse *f*.

till² [*~*] 1. *prp.* bis (zu); 2. *cj.* bis.

till³ ✗ [*~*] bestellen, bebauen; **~age** ['tilidʒ] (Land)Bestellung *f*; Ackerbau *m*; Ackerland *n*.

tilt [tilt] 1. Plane *f*; Neigung *f*, Kippe *f*; Stoß *m*; Lanzenbrechen *n* (*a. fig.*); 2. kippen; **~** against anrennen gegen.

timber ['timbə] 1. (Bau-, Nutz-) Holz *n*; Balken *m*; Baumbestand *m*, Bäume *m/pl.*; 2. zimmern.

time [taim] 1. Zeit *f*; Mal *n*; Takt *m*; Tempo *n*; **~** *and again* immer wieder; *at a* **~** zugleich; *for the being* einstweilen; *have a good* **~** es gut haben; sich amüsieren; *in* **~**, *on* **~** zur rechten Zeit, rechtzeitig; 2. zeitlich festsetzen; zeitlich abpassen; die Zeitdauer messen; **~-hono(u)red** ['taimɔnəd] altehrwürdig; **~ly** ['taimli] (recht)zeitig; **~piece** Uhr *f*; **~-sheet** Anwesenheitsliste *f*; **~-table** Terminkalender *m*; *Fahr-*, Stundenplan *m*.

tim|id □ ['timid], **~orous** □ ['timərəs] furchtsam; schüchtern.

tin [tin] 1. Zinn *n*; Weißblech *n*; (Konserven)Büchse *f*; 2. verzinnen; in Büchsen einmachen, eindosen.

tincture ['tiŋktʃə] 1. Farbe *f*; Tinktur *f*; *fig.* Anstrich *m*; 2. färben.

tinfoil ['tin'fɔil] Stanniol *n*.

tinge [tindʒ] 1. Färbung f; fig. Anflug m, Spur f; 2. färben; fig. e-n Anstrich geben (dat.).

tingle ['tiŋgl] klingen; prickeln.

tinker ['tiŋkə] basteln (at an dat.).

tinkle ['tiŋkl] klingeln (mit).

tin|-opener ['tinoupnə] Dosenöffner m; ~plate Weißblech n.

tinsel ['tinsəl] Flitter(werk n) m; Lametta n.

tin-smith ['tinsmiθ] Klempner m.

tint [tint] 1. Farbe f; (Farb)Ton m, Schattierung f; 2. färben; (ab-)tönen.

tiny ['taini] winzig, klein.

tip [tip] 1. Spitze f; Mundstück n; Trinkgeld n; Tip m, Wink m; leichter Stoß; Schuttabladeplatz m; 2. mit e-r Spitze versehen; (um-)kippen; j-m ein Trinkgeld geben; a. ~ off j-m e-n Wink geben.

tipple ['tipl] zechen, picheln.

tipsy ['tipsi] angeheitert.

tiptoe ['tiptou] 1. auf Zehenspitzen gehen; 2. on ~ auf Zehenspitzen.

tire[1] ['taiə] (Rad-, Auto)Reifen m.

tire[2] [~] ermüden, müde machen od. werden; ~d □ müde; ~less □ ['taiəlis] unermüdlich; ~some □ ['taiəsəm] ermüdend; lästig.

tiro ['taiərou] Anfänger m.

tissue ['tisju:, Am. 'tiʃu:] Gewebe n; ~paper Seidenpapier n.

tit[1] [tit] = teat.

tit[2] orn. [~] Meise f.

titbit ['titbit] Leckerbissen m.

titillate ['titileit] kitzeln.

title ['taitl] 1. (Buch-, Ehren)Titel m; Überschrift f; ⁊'ᵣ Anspruch m; 2. betiteln; ~d bsd. ad(e)lig.

titmouse orn. ['titmaus] Meise f.

titter ['titə] 1. kichern; 2. Kichern n.

tittle ['titl] Pünktchen n; fig. Tüttelchen n; ~-tattle [~ltætl] Schnickschnack m.

to [tu:, tu, tə] prp. zu (a. adv.); gegen, nach, an, in, auf; bis zu, bis an (acc.); um zu; für; ~ me etc. mir etc.; I weep ~ think of it ich weine, wenn ich daran denke; here's ~ you! auf Ihr Wohl!, Prosit!

toad zo. [toud] Kröte f; ~stool ['toudstu:l] (größerer Blätter)Pilz; Giftpilz m; ~y ['toudi] 1. Speichellecker m; 2. fig. vor j-m kriechen.

toast [toust] 1. Toast m, geröstetes Brot; Trinkspruch m; 2. toasten, rösten; fig. wärmen, trinken auf (acc.).

tobacco [tə'bækou] Tabak m; ~nist [~kənist] Tabakhändler m.

toboggan [tə'bɔgən] 1. Toboggan m; Rodelschlitten m; 2. rodeln.

today [tə'dei] heute. [teln.]

toddle ['tɔdl] unsicher gehen; zot-

toddy ['tɔdi] Art Grog m.

to-do F [tə'du:] Lärm m, Aufheben n.

toe [tou] 1. Zehe f; Spitze f; 2. mit den Zehen berühren.

toff|ee, ~y ['tɔfi] Sahnebonbon m, n, Toffee n.

together [tə'geðə] zusammen; zugleich; nacheinander.

toil [tɔil] 1. schwere Arbeit; Mühe f, F Plackerei f; 2. sich plagen.

toilet ['tɔilit] Toilette f; ~-paper Toilettenpapier n; ~-table Frisiertoilette f. [n.]

toils [tɔilz] pl. Schlingen f/pl., Netz

toilsome □ ['tɔilsəm] mühsam.

token ['toukən] Zeichen n; Andenken n, Geschenk n; ~ money Notgeld n; in ~ of zum Zeichen (gen.).

told [tould] pret. u. p.p. von tell.

tolera|ble □ ['tɔlərəbl] erträglich; ~nce [~əns] Duldsamkeit f; ~nt □ [~ənt] duldsam (of gegen); ~te [~reit] dulden; ertragen; ~tion [tɔlə'reiʃən] Duldung f.

toll [toul] 1. Zoll m (a. fig.); Wege-, Brücken-, Marktgeld n; fig. Tribut m; ~ of the road die Verkehrsopfer n/pl.; 2. läuten; ~-bar ['toulba:], ~-gate Schlagbaum m.

tomato ♀ [tə'ma:tou, Am. tə'meitou], pl. ~es Tomate f.

tomb [tu:m] Grab(mal) n.

tomboy ['tɔmbɔi] Range f.

tombstone ['tu:mstoun] Grabstein m.

tom-cat ['tɔm'kæt] Kater m.

tomfool ['tɔm'fu:l] Hansnarr m.

tomorrow [tə'mɔrou] morgen.

ton [tʌn] Tonne f (Gewichtseinheit).

tone [toun] 1. Ton m; Klang m; Laut m; out of ~ verstimmt; 2. e-n Ton geben (dat.); stimmen; paint. abtönen; ~ down (sich) abschwächen, mildern.

tongs [tɔŋz] pl. (a pair of ~ pl. eine) Zange.

tongue [tʌŋ] Zunge f; Sprache f; Landzunge f; (Schuh)Lasche f; hold one's ~ den Mund halten; ~-tied ['tʌŋtaid] sprachlos; schweigsam; stumm.

tonic ['tɔnik] 1. (~ally) tonisch; ⁓ stärkend; 2. ♩ Grundton m; ⁓ Stärkungsmittel n, Tonikum n.

tonight [tə'nait] heute abend od. nacht.

tonnage ⚓ ['tʌnidʒ] Tonnengehalt m; Lastigkeit f; Tonnengeld n.

tonsil anat. ['tɔnsl] Mandel f; ~litis ⁓ [tɔnsi'laitis] Mandelentzündung f.

too [tu:] zu, allzu; auch, noch dazu.

took [tuk] pret. von take 1.

tool [tu:l] Werkzeug n, Gerät n; ~-bag ['tu:lbæg], ~-kit Werkzeugtasche f.

toot [tu:t] 1. blasen, tuten; 2. Tuten n.

tooth [tu:θ] pl. teeth [ti:θ] Zahn m; ~ache ['tu:θeik] Zahnschmerzen pl.; ~brush Zahnbürste f; ~less □

['tu:θlis] zahnlos; ~-paste Zahnpasta *f*; ~pick Zahnstocher *m*; ~some □ ['tu:θsəm] schmackhaft.

top [tɔp] **1.** oberstes Ende; Oberteil *n*; Gipfel *m* (*a. fig.*); Wipfel *m*; Kopf *m* e-r Seite; *mot. Am.* Verdeck *n*; *fig.* Haupt *n*, Erste(r) *m*; *Stiefel*-Stulpe *f*; Kreisel *m*; *at the ~ of one's voice* aus voller Kehle; *on ~* obenauf; obendrein; **2.** ober(er, -e, -es); oberst; höchst; **3.** oben bedecken; *fig.* überragen; vorangehen in (*dat.*); als erste(r) stehen auf *e-r Liste*; ~**boots** ['tɔp'bu:ts] *pl.* Stulpenstiefel *m/pl.*

toper ['toupə] Zecher *m*.

tophat F ['tɔp'hæt] Zylinderhut *m*.

topic ['tɔpik] Gegenstand *m*, Thema *n*; ~**al** □ [~kəl] lokal; aktuell.

topmost ['tɔpmoust] höchst, oberst.

topple ['tɔpl] (um)kippen.

topsyturvy □ ['tɔpsi'tə:vi] auf den Kopf gestellt; das Oberste zuunterst; drunter und drüber.

torch [tɔ:tʃ] Fackel *f*; *electric ~* Taschenlampe *f*; ~**light** ['tɔ:tʃlait] Fackelschein *m*; ~ *procession* Fackelzug *m*.

tore [tɔ:] *pret. von* tear[1].

torment 1. ['tɔ:ment] Qual *f*, Marter *f*; **2.** [tɔ:'ment] martern, quälen.

torn [tɔ:n] *p.p. von* tear[1] 1.

tornado [tɔ:'neidou], *pl.* ~es Wirbelsturm *m*, Tornado *m*.

torpedo [tɔ:'pi:dou], *pl.* ~es **1.** Torpedo *m*; **2.** ⊕ torpedieren (*a. fig.*).

torpid [['tɔ:pid] starr; apathisch; träg; ~**idity** [tɔ:'piditi], ~**or** ['tɔ:pə] Erstarrung *f*, Betäubung *f*.

torrent ['tɔrənt] Sturz-, Gießbach *m*; (reißender) Strom; ~**ial** □ [tɔ'renʃəl] gießbachartig; strömend; *fig.* ungestüm.

torrid ['tɔrid] brennend heiß.

tortoise *zo.* ['tɔ:təs] Schildkröte *f*.

tortuous □ ['tɔ:tjuəs] gewunden.

torture ['tɔ:tʃə] **1.** Folter *f*, Marter *f*, Tortur *f*; **2.** foltern, martern.

toss [tɔs] **1.** Werfen *n*, Wurf *m*; Zurückwerfen *n* (*Kopf*); **2.** *a. ~ about* (sich) hin und her werfen; schütteln; (*mit adv.*) werfen; *a. ~ up* hochwerfen; ~ *off* Getränk hinunterstürzen; *Arbeit* hinhauen; *a. ~ up* losen (*for um*); ~**up** ['tɔsʌp] Losen *n*; *fig.* etwas Zweifelhaftes.

tot F [tɔt] Knirps *m* (*kleines Kind*).

total ['toutl] **1.** □ ganz, gänzlich; total; gesamt; **2.** Gesamtbetrag *m*; **3.** sich belaufen auf (*acc.*); summieren; ~**itarian** [toutæli'tɛəriən] totalitär; ~**ity** [tou'tæliti] Gesamtheit *f*.

totter ['tɔtə] wanken, wackeln.

touch [tʌtʃ] **1.** (sich) berühren; anrühren, anfassen; stoßen an (*acc.*); betreffen; *fig.* rühren; erreichen; ♪ anschlagen; *a bit ~ed fig.* ein biß-

chen verrückt; *~ at* ♣ anlegen in (*dat.*); *~ up* auffrischen; retuschieren; **2.** Berührung *f*; Gefühl(ssinn *m*) *n*; Anflug *m*, Zug *m*; Fertigkeit *f*; ♪ Anschlag *m*; (Pinsel-) Strich *m*; ~**and-go** ['tʌtʃən'gou] gewagte Sache; *it is ~* es steht auf des Messers Schneide; ~**ing** [~ʃiŋ] rührend; ~**stone** Prüfstein *m*; ~**y** [~ʃi] empfindlich; heikel.

tough [tʌf] zäh (*a. fig.*); schwer, hart; grob, brutal, übel; ~**en** [tʌfn] zäh machen *od.* werden; ~**ness** [~nis] Zähigkeit *f*.

tour [tuə] **1.** (Rund)Reise *f*, Tour (-nee) *f*; *conducted ~* Führung *f*; Gesellschaftsreise *f*; **2.** (be)reisen; ~**ist** ['tuərist] Tourist(in); ~ *agency*, ~ *bureau*, ~ *office* Reisebüro *n*; ~ *season* Reisezeit *f*. [*n.*]

tournament ['tuənəmənt] Turnier)

tousle ['tauzl] (zer)zausen.

tow [tou] **1.** Schleppen *n*; *take in ~* ins Schlepptau nehmen; **2.** (ab-) schleppen; treideln; ziehen.

toward(s) [tə'wɔ:d(z)] gegen; nach ... zu, auf ... (*acc.*) zu; (als Beitrag) zu.

towel ['tauəl] **1.** Handtuch *n*; **2.** abreiben; ~**rack** Handtuchhalter *m*.

tower ['tauə] **1.** Turm *m*; *fig.* Hort *m*, Bollwerk *n*; **2.** sich erheben; ~**ing** □ ['tauəriŋ] (turm)hoch; rasend (*Wut*).

town [taun] **1.** Stadt *f*; **2.** Stadt...; städtisch; ~ *clerk* Stadtsyndikus *m*; ~ *council* Stadtrat *m* (*Versammlung*); ~ *councillor* Stadtrat *m* (*Person*); ~ *hall* Rathaus *n*; ~**sfolk** ['taunzfouk] *pl.* Städter *pl.*; ~**ship** ['taunʃip] Stadtgemeinde *f*; Stadtgebiet *n*; ~**sman** ['taunzmən] (Mit)Bürger *m*; ~**speople** [~zpi:pl] *pl.* = townsfolk.

toxic(al □) ['tɔksik(əl)] giftig; Gift...; ~**n** [~in] Giftstoff *m*.

toy [tɔi] **1.** Spielzeug *n*; Tand *m*; ~**s** *pl.* Spielwaren *f/pl.*; **2.** Spiel(zeug)...; Miniatur...; Zwerg...; **3.** spielen; ~**book** ['tɔibuk] Bilderbuch *n*.

trace [treis] **1.** Spur *f* (*a. fig.*); Strang *m*; **2.** nachspüren (*dat.*); *fig.* verfolgen; herausfinden; (auf-) zeichnen; (durch)pausen.

tracing ['treisiŋ] Pauszeichnung *f*.

track [træk] **1.** Spur *f*; *Sport:* Bahn *f*; Rennstrecke *f*; Pfad *m*; Gleis *n*; ~ *events pl.* Laufdisziplinen *f/pl.*; **2.** nachspüren (*dat.*); verfolgen; ~ *down*, ~ *out* aufspüren.

tract [trækt] Fläche *f*, Strecke *f*, Gegend *f*; Traktat *n*, Abhandlung *f*.

tractable □ ['træktəbl] lenk-, fügsam.

tract|ion ['trækʃən] Ziehen *n*, Zug *m*; ~ *engine* Zugmaschine *f*; ~**or** ⊕ [~ktə] Trecker *m*, Traktor *m*.

trade [treid] 1. Handel *m*; Gewerbe *n*; Handwerk *n*; *Am.* Kompensationsgeschäft *n*; 2. Handel treiben; handeln; ~ on ausnutzen; ~ **mark** ✝ Warenzeichen *n*, Schutzmarke *f*; ~ **price** Händlerpreis *m*; ~**r** ['treidə] Händler *m*; ~**sman** [~dzmən] Geschäftsmann *m*; ~ **union** Gewerkschaft *f*; ~ **wind** ⚓ Passatwind *m*.

tradition [trə'diʃən] Tradition *f*, Überlieferung *f*; ~**al** □ [~nl] traditionell.

traffic ['træfik] 1. Verkehr *m*; Handel *m*; 2. handeln (*in* mit); ~ **jam** Verkehrsstauung *f*; ~ **light** Verkehrsampel *f*.

traged|ian [trə'dʒi:djən] Tragiker *m*; *thea.* Tragöd|e *m*, -in *f*; ~**y** ['trædʒidi] Tragödie *f*.

tragic(al □) ['trædʒik(əl)] tragisch.

trail [treil] 1. *fig.* Schweif *m*; Schleppe *f*; Spur *f*; Pfad *m*; 2. *v/t.* hinter sich (her)ziehen; verfolgen; *v/i.* (sich) schleppen; ♀ kriechen; ~ **blazer** *Am.* Bahnbrecher *m*; ~**er** ['treilə] (Wohnwagen)Anhänger *m*; ♀ Kriechpflanze *f*; *Film:* Vorschau *f*.

train [trein] 1. (Eisenbahn)Zug *m*; *allg.* Zug *m*; Gefolge *n*; Reihe *f*, Folge *f*, Kette *f*; Schleppe *f am Kleid*; 2. erziehen; schulen; abrichten; ausbilden; trainieren; (sich) üben; ~**ee** [trei'ni:] in der Ausbildung Begriffene(r) *m*; ~**er** ['treinə] Ausbilder *m*; Trainer *m*.

trait [trei] (Charakter)Zug *m*.

traitor ['treitə] Verräter *m*.

tram [træm] *s.* ~-*car*, ~*way*; ~-**car** ['træmka:] Straßenbahnwagen *m*.

tramp [træmp] 1. Getrampel *n*; Wanderung *f*; Tramp *m*, Landstreicher *m*; 2. trampeln, treten; (durch)wandern; ~**le** ['træmpl] (zer)trampeln.

tramway ['træmwei] Straßenbahn *f*.

trance [trɑːns] Trance *f*.

tranquil □ ['træŋkwil] ruhig; gelassen; ~**(l)ity** [træŋ'kwiliti] Ruhe *f*; Gelassenheit *f*; ~**(l)ize** ['træŋkwilaiz] beruhigen; ~**(l)izer** [~zə] Beruhigungsmittel *n*.

transact [træn'zækt] abwickeln, abmachen; ~**ion** [~kʃən] Verrichtung *f*; Geschäft *n*, Transaktion *f*; ~**s** *pl.* (Tätigkeits)Bericht(e *pl.*) *m*.

transalpine ['trænz'ælpain] transalpin(isch).

transatlantic ['trænzət'læntik] transatlantisch, Transatlantik...

transcend [træn'send] überschreiten, übertreffen; hinausgehen über (*acc.*); ~**ence**, ~**ency** [~dəns, ~si] Überlegenheit *f*; *phls.* Transzendenz *f*.

transcribe [træns'kraib] abschreiben; *Kurzschrift* übertragen.

transcript ['trænskript], ~**ion**

[træns'kripʃən] Abschrift *f*; Umschrift *f*.

transfer 1. [træns'fə:] *v/t.* übertragen; versetzen, verlegen; *v/i.* übertreten; *Am.* umsteigen; 2. ['trænsfə(:)] Übertragung *f*; ✝ Transfer *m*; Versetzung *f*, Verlegung *f*; *Am.* Umsteigefahrschein *m*; ~**able** [træns'fə:rəbl] übertragbar.

transfigure [træns'figə] umgestalten; verklären.

transfix [træns'fiks] durchstechen; ~**ed** *fig.* versteinert, starr (*with* vor *dat.*).

transform [træns'fɔ:m] umformen; um-, verwandeln; ~**ation** [trænsfə'meiʃən] Umformung *f*; Um-, Verwandlung *f*.

transfus|e [træns'fju:z] 웣 *Blut etc.* übertragen; *fig.* einflößen; *fig.* durchtränken; ~**ion** [~ʒən] (*bsd.* 웣 Blut)Übertragung *f*, Transfusion *f*.

transgress [træns'gres] *v/t.* überschreiten; übertreten, verletzen; *v/i.* sich vergehen; ~**ion** [~eʃən] Überschreitung *f*; Übertretung *f*; Vergehen *n*; ~**or** [~esə] Übertreter *m*.

transient ['trænziənt] 1. = *transitory*; 2. *Am.* Durchreisende(r *m*) *f*.

transit ['trænsit] Durchgang *m*; Durchgangsverkehr *m*.

transition [træn'siʒən] Übergang *m*.

transitive □ *gr.* ['trænsitiv] transitiv.

transitory □ ['trænsitəri] vorübergehend; vergänglich, flüchtig.

translat|e [træns'leit] übersetzen, übertragen; überführen; *fig.* umsetzen; ~**ion** [~eiʃən] Übersetzung *f*, Übertragung *f*; *fig.* Auslegung *f*; ~**or** [~eitə] Übersetzer(in).

translucent [trænz'lu:snt] durchscheinend; *fig.* hell.

transmigration [trænzmai'greiʃən] (Aus)Wanderung *f*; Seelenwanderung *f*.

transmission [trænz'miʃən] Übermittlung *f*; *biol.* Vererbung *f*; *phys.* Fortpflanzung *f*; *mot.* Getriebe *n*; *Radio:* Sendung *f*.

transmit [trænz'mit] übermitteln, übersenden; übertragen; senden; *biol.* vererben; *phys.* fortpflanzen; ~**ter** [~tə] Übermittler(in); *tel. etc.* Sender *m*.

transmute [trænz'mju:t] um-, verwandeln.

transparent □ [træns'pɛərənt] durchsichtig (*a. fig.*).

transpire [træns'paiə] ausdünsten, ausschwitzen; *fig.* durchsickern.

transplant [træns'plɑ:nt] um-, verpflanzen; ~**ation** [trænsplɑ:n'teiʃən] Verpflanzung *f*.

transport 1. [træns'pɔ:t] fortschaffen, befördern, transportieren; *fig.* hinreißen; 2. ['trænspɔ:t] Fortschaffen *n*; Beförderung *f*; Transport *m*; Verkehr *m*; Beförderungsmittel *n*; Transportschiff *n*; Verzückung *f*; *be in ~s* außer sich sein; **~ation** [trænspɔ:'teiʃən] Beförderung *f*, Transport *m*.

transpose [træns'pouz] versetzen, umstellen; ♪ transponieren.

transverse □ ['trænzvə:s] quer laufend; Quer...

trap [træp] **1.** Falle *f* (*a. fig.*); Klappe *f*; **2.** (in e-r Falle) fangen, in die Falle locken; *fig.* ertappen; **~door** ['træpdɔ:] Falltür *f*; *thea.* Versenkung *f*.

trapeze [trə'pi:z] *Zirkus:* Trapez *n*.

trapper ['træpə] Trapper *m*, Fallensteller *m*, Pelzjäger *m*.

trappings *fig.* ['træpiŋz] *pl.* Schmuck *m*, Putz *m*.

traps F [træps] *pl.* Siebensachen *pl.*

trash [træʃ] Abfall *m*; *fig.* Plunder *m*; Unsinn *m*, F Blech *n*; Kitsch *m*; **~y** [~i] wertlos, kitschig.

travel ['trævl] **1.** *v/i.* reisen; sich bewegen; wandern; *v/t.* bereisen; **2.** *das* Reisen; ⊕ Lauf *m*; **~s** *pl.* Reisen *f/pl.*; **~(l)er** [~lə] Reisende(r) *m*; **~'s cheque** (*Am.* check) Reisescheck *m*.

traverse ['trævə(:)s] **1.** Durchquerung *f*; **2.** (über)queren; durchqueren; *fig.* durchkreuzen.

travesty ['trævisti] **1.** Travestie *f*; Karikatur *f*; **2.** travestieren; verulken.

trawl [trɔ:l] **1.** (Grund)Schleppnetz *n*; **2.** mit dem Schleppnetz fischen; **~er** ['trɔ:lə] Trawler *m*.

tray [trei] (Servier)Brett *n*, Tablett *n*; Ablage *f*; *pen-~* Federschale *f*.

treacherous □ ['tretʃərəs] verräterisch, treulos; (heim)tückisch; trügerisch; **~y** [~ri] Verrat *m*, Verräterei *f*, Treulosigkeit *f*; Tücke *f*.

treacle ['tri:kl] Sirup *m*.

tread [tred] **1.** [*irr.*] treten; schreiten; **2.** Tritt *m*, Schritt *m*; Lauffläche *f*; **~le** ['tredl] Pedal *n*; Tritt *m*; **~mill** Tretmühle *f*.

treason ['tri:zn] Verrat *m*; **~able** □ [~nəbl] verräterisch.

treasure ['treʒə] **1.** Schatz *m*, Reichtum *m*; **~ trove** Schatzfund *m*; **2.** *Schätze* sammeln, aufhäufen; **~r** [~ərə] Schatzmeister *m*, Kassenwart *m*.

treasury ['treʒəri] Schatzkammer *f*; (*bsd.* Staats)Schatz *m*; ♀ **Bench** *parl.* Ministerbank *f*; ♀ **Board**, *Am.* ♀ **Department** Finanzministerium *n*.

treat [tri:t] **1.** *v/t.* behandeln; betrachten; *~ s.o. to s.th.* j-m et. spendieren; *v/i. ~ of* handeln von; *~ with* unterhandeln mit; **2.** Vergnügen *n*; *school ~* Schulausflug *m*; *it is my ~* es geht auf meine Rechnung; **~ise** ['tri:tiz] Abhandlung *f*;

~ment [~tmənt] Behandlung *f*; **Kur** *f*; *follow-up ~* Nachkur *f*; **~y** [~ti] Vertrag *m*.

treble ['trebl] **1.** □ dreifach; **2.** Dreifache(s) *n*; ♪ Diskant *m*, Sopran *m*; **3.** (sich) verdreifachen.

tree [tri:] Baum *m*.

trefoil ♣ ['trefoil] Klee *m*.

trellis ['trelis] **1.** ♪ Spalier *n*; **2.** vergittern; ♪ am Spalier ziehen.

tremble ['trembl] zittern.

tremendous □ [tri'mendəs] schrecklich, furchtbar; F kolossal, riesig.

tremor ['tremə] Zittern *n*, Beben *n*.

tremulous □ ['tremjuləs] zitternd, bebend.

trench [trentʃ] **1.** (Schützen)Graben *m*; Furche *f*; **2.** *v/t.* mit Gräben durchziehen; ♪ umgraben; *~ (up)on* eingreifen in (*acc.*); **~ant** □ ['trentʃənt] scharf.

trend [trend] **1.** Richtung *f*; *fig.* Lauf *m*; *fig.* Strömung *f*; Tendenz *f*; **2.** sich erstrecken, laufen.

trepidation [trepi'deiʃən] Zittern *n*, Beben *n*; Bestürzung *f*.

trespass ['trespəs] **1.** Übertretung *f*; **2.** unbefugt eindringen (*on, upon* in *acc.*); über Gebühr in Anspruch nehmen; **~er** ꝛᵵᵤ [~sə] Rechtsverletzer *m*; Unbefugte(r *m*) *f*.

tress [tres] Haarlocke *f*, -flechte *f*.

trestle ['tresl] Gestell *n*, Bock *m*.

trial ['traiəl] Versuch *m*; Probe *f*; Prüfung *f* (*a. fig.*); Plage *f*; ꝛᵵᵤ Verhandlung *f*, Prozeß *m*; *on ~* auf Probe; vor Gericht; *give s.o. a ~* es mit j-m versuchen; *~ run* Probefahrt *f*.

triangle ['traiæŋgl] Dreieck *n*; **~ular** □ [trai'æŋgjulə] dreieckig.

tribe [traib] Stamm *m*; Geschlecht *n*; *contp.* Sippe *f*; ♀, *zo.* Klasse *f*.

tribunal [trai'bju:nl] Richterstuhl *m*; Gericht(shof *m*) *n*; **~e** ['tribju:n] Tribun *m*; Tribüne *f*.

tributary ['tribjutəri] **1.** □ zinspflichtig; *fig.* helfend; Neben...; **2.** Nebenfluß *m*; **~e** [~ju:t] Tribut *m* (*a. fig.*), Zins *m*; Anerkennung *f*.

trice [trais]: *in a ~* im Nu.

trick [trik] **1.** Kniff *m*, List *f*, Trick *m*; Kunstgriff *m*, -stück *n*; Streich *m*; Eigenheit *f*; **2.** betrügen; herausputzen; **~ery** ['trikəri] Betrügerei *f*.

trickle ['trikl] tröpfeln, rieseln.

trickster ['trikstə] Gauner *m*; **~y** □ [~ki] verschlagen; F heikel; verzwickt, verwickelt, schwierig.

tricycle ['traisikl] Dreirad *n*.

trident ['traidənt] Dreizack *m*.

trifle ['traifl] **1.** Kleinigkeit *f*; Lappalie *f*; *a ~* ein bißchen, ein wenig, etwas; **2.** *v/i.* spielen, spaßen; *v/t. ~ away* verschwenden; **~ing** □ [~liŋ] geringfügig; unbedeutend.

trig [trig] **1.** hemmen; **2.** schmuck.

trigger ['trigə] Abzug *m am Gewehr*; *phot.* Auslöser *m*.

trill [tril] **1.** Triller *m*; gerolltes R; **2.** trillern; *bsd.* das R rollen.

trillion ['triljən] Trillion *f*; *Am.* Billion *f*.

trim [trim] **1.** □ ordentlich; schmuck; gepflegt; **2.** (richtiger) Zustand; Ordnung *f*; **3.** zurechtmachen; (~ *up* aus)putzen, schmükken; besetzen; stutzen; beschneiden; ✂, ⚓ trimmen; **~ming** ['trimiŋ] *mst* ~s *pl*. Besatz *m*, Garnierung *f*.

Trinity *eccl.* ['triniti] Dreieinigkeit *f*.

trinket ['triŋkit] wertloses Schmuckstück; ~s *pl*. F Kinkerlitzchen *pl*.

trip [trip] **1.** Reise *f*, Fahrt *f*; Ausflug *m*, Spritztour *f*; Stolpern *n*, Fallen *n*; Fehltritt *m* (*a. fig.*); *fig.* Versehen *n*, Fehler *m*; **2.** *v/i.* trippeln; stolpern; e-n Fehltritt tun (*a. fig.*); *fig.* e-n Fehler machen; *v/t. a.* ~ *up* j-m ein Bein stellen (*a. fig.*).

tripartite ['trai'pɑ:tait] dreiteilig.

tripe [traip] Kaldaunen *f/pl*.

triple □ ['tripl] dreifach; ~ts [~lits] *pl*. Drillinge *m/pl*.

triplicate 1. ['triplikit] dreifach; **2.** [~keit] verdreifachen.

tripod ['traipɔd] Dreifuß *m*; *phot.* Stativ *n*.

tripper F ['tripə] Ausflügler(in).

trite □ [trait] abgedroschen, platt.

triturate ['tritjureit] zerreiben.

triumph ['traiəmf] **1.** Triumph *m*, Sieg *m*; **2.** triumphieren; ~**al** [trai'ʌmfəl] Sieges..., Triumph...; ~**ant** □ [~ənt] triumphierend.

trivial □ ['triviəl] bedeutungslos; unbedeutend; trivial; alltäglich.

trod [trɔd] *pret. von* tread *1*; ~**den** ['trɔdn] *p.p. von* tread *1*.

troll [troul] (vor sich hin)trällern.

troll(e)y ['trɔli] Karren *m*; Draisine *f*; Servierwagen *m*; ⚡ Kontaktrolle *f* *e-s Oberleitungsfahrzeugs*; *Am.* Straßenbahnwagen *m*; ~ **bus** O(berleitungs)bus *m*.   [Hure *f*.\

trollop ['trɔləp] F Schlampe *f*.\

trombone ♪ [trɔm'boun] Posaune *f*.

troop [tru:p] **1.** Truppe *f*; Schar *f*; ✕ (Reiter)Zug *m*; **2.** sich scharen, sich sammeln; ~ *away*, ~ *off* abziehen; ~*ing the colour(s)* ✕ Fahnenparade *f*; ~**er** ✕ ['tru:pə] Kavallerist *m*.

trophy ['troufi] Trophäe *f*.

tropic ['trɔpik] Wendekreis *m*; ~s *pl*. Tropen *pl.*; ~(**al** □) [~k(əl)] tropisch.

trot [trɔt] **1.** Trott *m*, Trab *m*; **2.** traben (lassen).

trouble ['trʌbl] **1.** Unruhe *f*; Störung *f*; Kummer *m*, Not *f*; Mühe *f*; Plage *f*; Unannehmlichkeiten *f/pl.*; *ask od.* look for ~ sich (selbst) Schwierigkeiten machen; das

Schicksal herausfordern; take (the) ~ sich (die) Mühe machen; **2.** stören, beunruhigen, belästigen; quälen, plagen; Mühe machen (*dat.*); (sich) bemühen; ~ *s.o. for* j-n bemühen um, ~**man**, ~**-shooter** *Am.* F Störungssucher *m*; ~**some** □ [~lsəm] beschwerlich, lästig.

trough [trɔf] (Futter)Trog *m*; Backtrog *m*, Mulde *f*.

trounce F [trauns] *j-n* verhauen.

troupe *thea.* [tru:p] Truppe *f*.

trousers ['trauzəz] *pl*. (*a pair of* ~ *pl*. eine) (lange) Hose; Hosen *f/pl*.

trousseau ['tru:sou] Aussteuer *f*.

trout *ichth.* [traut] Forelle(n *pl*.) *f*.

trowel ['trauəl] Maurerkelle *f*.

truant ['tru:(:)ənt] **1.** müßig; **2.** Schulschwänzer *m*; *fig.* Bummler *m*.

truce [tru:s] Waffenstillstand *m*.

truck [trʌk] **1.** (offener) Güterwagen; Last(kraft)wagen *m*, Lkw *m*; Transportkarren *m*; Tausch (-handel) *m*; Verkehr *m*; Naturallohnsystem *n*; *Am.* Gemüse *n*; **2.** (ver)tauschen; ~**farm** *Am.* ['trʌkfɑ:m] Gemüsegärtnerei *f*.

truckle ['trʌkl] zu Kreuze kriechen.

truculent □ ['trʌkjulənt] wild, roh.

trudge [trʌdʒ] wandern; sich (dahin)schleppen, mühsam gehen.

true [tru:] wahr; echt, wirklich; treu; genau; richtig; *it is* ~ gewiß, freilich, zwar; *come* ~ sich bewahrheiten; in Erfüllung gehen; ~ *to nature* naturgetreu.

truism ['tru:(:)izəm] Binsenwahrheit *f*.

truly ['tru:li] wirklich; wahrhaft; aufrichtig; genau; treu; *Yours* ~ Hochachtungsvoll.

trump [trʌmp] **1.** Trumpf *m*; **2.** (über)trumpfen; ~ *up* erdichten; ~**ery** ['trʌmpəri] Plunder *m*.

trumpet ['trʌmpit] **1.** Trompete *f*; **2.** trompeten; *fig.* ausposaunen.

truncheon ['trʌntʃən] (Polizei-) Knüppel *m*; Kommandostab *m*.

trundle ['trʌndl] rollen.

trunk [trʌŋk] (Baum)Stamm *m*; Rumpf *m*; Rüssel *m*; *großer* Koffer; ~**call** *teleph.* ['trʌŋkkɔ:l] Ferngespräch *n*; ~**exchange** *teleph.* Fernamt *n*; ~**line** ✆ Hauptlinie *f*; *teleph.* Fernleitung *f*; ~s [trʌŋks] *pl*. Turnhose *f*; Badehose *f*; Herrenunterhose *f*.

trunnion ⚙ ['trʌnjən] Zapfen *m*.

truss [trʌs] **1.** Bündel *n*, Bund *n*; ♣ Bruchband *n*; △ Binder *m*, Gerüst *n*; **2.** (zs.-)binden; △ stützen.

trust [trʌst] **1.** Vertrauen *n*; Glaube *m*; Kredit *m*; Pfand *n*; Verwahrung *f*; ✝ Treuhand *f*; ✝ Ring *m*, Trust *m*; ~ *company* Treuhandgesellschaft *f*; *in* ~ zu treuen Händen; **2.** *v/t.* (ver)trauen (*dat.*); anvertrauen, übergeben (*s.o. with s.th., s.th. to s.o.* j-m et.); zuversichtlich hoffen;

v/i. vertrauen (*in*, *to* auf *acc.*); **~ee**
[trʌs'tiː] Sach-, Verwalter *m*; ɟɪ̄ɪ̄
Treuhänder *m*; **~ful** □ ['trʌstful],
~ing □ [~tiŋ] vertrauensvoll; **~worthy** [~twəːði] vertrauenswürdig; zuverlässig.

truth [truːθ], *pl.* **~s** [truːðz] Wahrheit *f*; Wirklichkeit *f*; Wahrhaftigkeit *f*; Genauigkeit *f*; **~ful** □
['truːθful] wahrhaft(ig).

try [trai] **1.** versuchen; probieren;
prüfen; ɟɪ̄ɪ̄ verhandeln über *et. od.*
gegen *j-n*; vor Gericht stellen; aburteilen; *die Augen etc.* angreifen;
sich bemühen *od.* bewerben; **~ on**
Kleid anprobieren; **2.** Versuch *m*;
~ing □ ['traiiŋ] anstrengend; kritisch.

Tsar [zɑː] Zar *m.*

T-shirt ['tiːʃəːt] kurzärmeliges
Sporthemd.

tub [tʌb] **1.** Faß *n*, Zuber *m*; Kübel
m; Badewanne *f*; F (Wannen)Bad *n.*

tube [tjuːb] Rohr *n*; (*Am. bsd.* Radio)Röhre *f*; Tube *f*; (Luft-)
Schlauch *m*; Tunnel *m*; F (Londoner) Untergrundbahn *f.*

tuber ♀ ['tjuːbə] Knolle *f*; **~culosis**
[tjuː(ː)bəːkju'lousis] Tuberkulose *f.*

tubular □ ['tjuːbjulə] röhrenförmig.

tuck [tʌk] **1.** Falte *f*; Abnäher *m*;
2. ab-, aufnähen; packen, stecken;
~ up hochschürzen, aufkrempeln; *in
e-e Decke etc.* einwickeln.

Tuesday ['tjuːzdi] Dienstag *m.*

tuft [tʌft] Büschel *n*, Busch *m*;
(Haar)Schopf *m.*

tug [tʌg] **1.** Zug *m*, Ruck *m*; ⚓
Schlepper *m*; *fig.* Anstrengung *f*;
2. ziehen, zerren; ⚓ schleppen;
sich mühen.

tuition [tjuː(ː)'iʃən] Unterricht *m*;
Schulgeld *n.*

tulip ♀ ['tjuːlip] Tulpe *f.*

tumble ['tʌmbl] **1.** *v/i.* fallen, purzeln; taumeln; sich wälzen; *v/t.*
werfen; zerknüllen; **2.** Sturz *m*;
Wirrwarr *m*; **~down** baufällig; **~r**
[~lə] Becher *m*; *orn.* Tümmler *m.*

tumid □ ['tjuːmid] geschwollen.

tummy F ['tʌmi] Bäuchlein *n*,
Magen *m.*

tumo(u)r ⚕ ['tjuːmə] Tumor *m.*

tumult ['tjuːmʌlt] Tumult *m*;
~uous □ [tjuː(ː)'mʌltjuəs] stürmisch.

tun [tʌn] Tonne *f*, Faß *n.*

tuna *ichth.* ['tuːnə] Thunfisch *m.*

tune [tjuːn] **1.** Melodie *f*, Weise *f*;
♪ Stimmung *f* (*a. fig.*); in **~** (gut-)
gestimmt; out of **~** verstimmt;
2. stimmen (*a. fig.*); **~ in** *Radio*:
einstellen; **~ out** *Radio*: ausschalten; **~ up** die Instrumente stimmen;
fig. Befinden etc. heben; *mot.* die
Leistung erhöhen; **~ful** □ ['tjuːnful] melodisch; **~less** □ [~nlis] unmelodisch.

tunnel ['tʌnl] **1.** Tunnel *m*; ⚒

Stollen *m*; **2.** e-n Tunnel bohren
(durch).

tunny *ichth.* ['tʌni] Thunfisch *m.*

turbid ['təːbid] trüb; dick.

turb|ine ⊕ ['təːbin] Turbine *f*;
~o-jet ['təːbou'dʒet] Strahlturbine
f; **~o-prop** [~ou'prɔp] Propellerturbine *f.*

turbot *ichth.* ['təːbət] Steinbutt
m.

turbulent □ ['təːbjulənt] unruhig;
ungestüm; stürmisch, turbulent.

tureen [tə'riːn] Terrine *f.*

turf [təːf] **1.** Rasen *m*; Torf *m*;
Rennbahn *f*; Rennsport *m*; **2.** mit
Rasen bedecken; **~y** ['təːfi] rasenbedeckt.

turgid □ ['təːdʒid] geschwollen.

Turk [təːk] Türk|e *m*, -in *f.*

turkey ['təːki] *orn.* Truthahn *m*,
-henne *f*, Pute(r *m*) *f*; *Am. sl. thea.*,
Film: Pleite *f*, Versager *m.*

Turkish ['təːkiʃ] türkisch.

turmoil ['təːmɔil] Aufruhr *m*, Unruhe *f*; Durcheinander *n.*

turn [təːn] **1.** *v/t.* drehen; (um)wenden, umkehren; lenken; verwandeln; abbringen; abwehren; übertragen; bilden; drechseln; verrückt
machen; **~ a corner** um eine Ecke
biegen; **~ s.o. against** j-n aufhetzen
gegen; **~ aside** abwenden; **~ away**
abwenden; abweisen; **~ down** umbiegen; *Gas etc.* kleinstellen; *Decke
etc.* zurückschlagen; ablehnen; **~ off**
ableiten (*a. fig.*); hinauswerfen;
wegjagen; **~ off (on)** ab-(an)drehen,
ab- (ein)schalten; **~ out** hinauswerfen; *Fabrikat* herausbringen; *Gas
etc.* ausdrehen; **~ over** umwenden;
fig. übertragen; ✝ umsetzen; überlegen; **~ up** nach oben richten;
hochklappen; umwenden; *Hose etc.*
auf-, umschlagen; *Gas etc.* aufdrehen; *v/i.* sich (um)drehen; sich
wenden; sich verwandeln; umschlagen (*Wetter etc.*); *Christ, grau
etc.* werden; *a.* **~ sour** sauer werden (*Milch*); **~ about** sich umdrehen; ✕ kehrtmachen; **~ back** zurückkehren; **~ in** einkehren; F zu
Bett gehen; **~ off** abbiegen; **~ on**
sich drehen um; **~ out** ausfallen,
ausgehen; sich herausstellen als; **~
to** sich zuwenden (*dat.*), sich wenden
an (*acc.*); werden zu; **~ up** auftauchen; **~ upon** sich wenden gegen;
2. (Um)Drehung *f*; Biegung *f*;
Wendung *f*; Neigung *f*; Wechsel *m*;
Gestalt *f*, Form *f*; Spaziergang *m*;
Reihe(nfolge) *f*; Dienst(leistung *f*)
m; F Schreck *m*; at every **~** auf
Schritt und Tritt; by *od.* in **~s** der
Reihe nach, abwechselnd; it is my
~ ich bin an der Reihe; take **~s**
mit-ea. abwechseln; does it serve
your **~**? entspricht das Ihren
Zwecken?; **~coat** ['təːnkout] Abtrünnige(r) *m*; **~er** ['təːnə] Drechs-

ler *m*; ~ery [~əri] Drechslerei *f*; Drechslerarbeit *f*.

turning ['tə:niŋ] Drechseln *n*; Wendung *f*; Biegung *f*; Straßenecke *f*; (Weg)Abzweigung *f*; Querstraße *f*; ~**point** *fig*. Wendepunkt *m*.

turnip ♀ ['tə:nip] (*bsd*. weiße) Rübe.

turn|key ['tə:nki:] Schließer *m*; ~**out** ['tə:n'aut] Ausstaffierung *f*; Arbeitseinstellung *f*; ✝ Gesamtproduktion *f*; ✝ Umsatz *m*; Verschiebung *f*; ~**pike** Schlagbaum *m*; (gebührenpflichtige) Schnellstraße; ~**stile** Drehkreuz *n*. [pentin *n*.\

turpentine ['tə:pəntain] Ter-]

turpitude ['tə:pitju:d] Schändlichkeit *f*.

turret ['tʌrit] Türmchen *n*; ⚔, ⚓ Panzerturm *m*; ✠ Kanzel *f*.

turtle ['tə:tl] *zo*. Schildkröte *f*; *orn. mst* ~**dove** Turteltaube *f*.

tusk [tʌsk] Fangzahn *m*; Stoßzahn *m*; Hauer *m*.

tussle ['tʌsl] **1.** Rauferei *f*, Balgerei *f*; **2.** raufen, sich balgen.

tussock ['tʌsək] Büschel *n*.

tut [tʌt] ach was!; Unsinn!

tutelage ['tju:tilidʒ] ⚖ Vormundschaft *f*; Bevormundung *f*.

tutor ['tju:tə] **1.** (Privat-, Haus-) Lehrer *m*; *univ*. Tutor *m*; *Am.univ*. Assistent *m mit Lehrauftrag*; ⚖ Vormund *m*; **2.** unterrichten; schulen, erziehen; *fig*. beherrschen; ~**ial** [tju(:)'tɔ:riəl] *univ*. Unterrichtsstunde *f e-s Tutors*; *attr*. Lehrer...; Tutoren...

tuxedo *Am*. [tʌk'si:dou] Smoking *m*.

TV ['ti:'vi:] Fernsehen *n*; Fernsehapparat *m*; *attr*. Fernseh...

twaddle ['twɔdl] **1.** Geschwätz *n*; **2.** schwatzen, quatschen.

twang [twæŋ] **1.** Schwirren *n*; *mst* nasal ~ näselnde Aussprache; **2.** schwirren (lassen); klimpern; näseln.

tweak [twi:k] zwicken.

tweet [twi:t] zwitschern.

tweezers ['twi:zəz] *pl*. (*a pair of ~ pl*. eine) Pinzette.

twelfth [twelfθ] **1.** zwölfte(r, -s); **2.** Zwölftel *n*; 2-**night** ['twelfθnait] Dreikönigsabend *m*.

twelve [twelv] zwölf.

twent|ieth ['twentiiθ] **1.** zwanzigste(r, -s); **2.** Zwanzigstel *n*; ~**y** [~ti] zwanzig.

twice [twais] zweimal.

twiddle ['twidl] (sich) drehen; mit *et*. spielen.

twig [twig] Zweig *m*, Rute *f*.

twilight ['twailait] Zwielicht *n*; Dämmerung *f* (*a. fig*.).

twin [twin] **1.** Zwillings...; doppelt; **2.** Zwilling *m*; ~**engined** ⚙ ['twinendʒind] zweimotorig.

twine [twain] **1.** Bindfaden *m*,

Schnur *f*; Zwirn *m*; **2.** zs.-drehen; verflechten; (sich) schlingen *od*. winden; umschlingen, umranken.

twinge [twindʒ] Zwicken *n*; Stich *m*; bohrender Schmerz.

twinkle ['twiŋkl] **1.** funkeln, blitzen; huschen; zwinkern; **2.** Funkeln *n*, Blitzen *n*; (Augen)Zwinkern *n*, Blinzeln *n*.

twirl [twə:l] **1.** Wirbel *m*; **2.** wirbeln.

twist [twist] **1.** Drehung *f*; Windung *f*; Verdrehung *f*; Verdrehtheit *f*; Neigung *f*; (Gesichts)Verzerrung *f*; Garn *n*; Kringel *m*, Zopf *m* (*Backwaren*); **2.** (sich) drehen *od*. winden; zs.-drehen; verdrehen, verziehen, verzerren.

twit *fig*. [twit] *j-n* aufziehen.

twitch [twitʃ] **1.** zupfen (an *dat*.); zucken; **2.** Zupfen *n*; Zuckung *f*.

twitter ['twitə] **1.** zwitschern; **2.** Gezwitscher *n*; *be in a* ~ zittern.

two [tu:] **1.** zwei; *in* ~ entzwei; *put* ~ *and* ~ *together* sich et. zs.-reimen; **2.** Zwei *f*; *in* ~*s* zu zweien; ~**bit** *Am*. F ['tu:bit] 25-Cent...; *fig*. unbedeutend, Klein...; ~**edged** ['tu:'edʒd] zweischneidig; ~**fold** ['tu:fould] zweifach; ~**pence** ['tʌpəns] zwei Pence; ~**penny** ['tʌpni] zwei Pence wert; ~**piece** ['tu:pi:s] zweiteilig; ~**seater** *mot*. ['tu:'si:tə] Zweisitzer *m*; ~**storey** ['tu:stɔ:ri], ~**storied** zweistöckig; ~**stroke** *mot*. Zweitakt...; ~**way** Doppel...; ~ *adapter* ⚡ Doppelstecker *m*; ~ *traffic* Gegenverkehr *m*.

tycoon *Am*. F [tai'ku:n] Industriekapitän *m*, Industriemagnat *m*.

tyke [taik] Köter *m*; Kerl *m*.

type [taip] Typ *m*; Urbild *n*; Vorbild *n*; Muster *n*; Art *f*; Sinnbild *n*; *typ*. Type *f*, Buchstabe *m*; *true to* ~ artecht; *set in* ~ setzen; ~**write** ['taiprait] [*irr*. (write)] (mit der) Schreibmaschine schreiben; ~**writer** Schreibmaschine *f*; ~ *ribbon* Farbband *n*.

typhoid ⚕ ['taifoid] **1.** typhös; ~ *fever* = **2.** (Unterleibs)Typhus *m*.

typhoon [tai'fu:n] Taifun *m*.

typhus ⚕ ['taifəs] Flecktyphus *m*.

typi|cal □ ['tipikəl] typisch; richtig; bezeichnend, kennzeichnend; ~**fy** [~ifai] typisch sein für; versinnbildlichen; ~**st** ['taipist] *a. shorthand* ~ Stenotypistin *f*.

tyrann|ic(al □) [ti'rænik(əl)] tyrannisch; ~**ize** ['tirənaiz] tyrannisieren; ~**y** [~ni] Tyrannei *f*.

tyrant ['taiərənt] Tyrann(in).

tyre ['taiə] *s*. tire *1*.

tyro ['taiərou] *s*. tiro.

Tyrolese [tirə'li:z] **1.** Tiroler(in); **2.** tirolisch, Tiroler...

Tzar [zɑ:] Zar *m*.

U

ubiquitous □ [ju(:)'bikwitəs] allgegenwärtig, überall zu finden(d).

udder ['ʌdə] Euter *n*.

ugly □ ['ʌgli] häßlich; schlimm.

ulcer ⚕ ['ʌlsə] Geschwür *n*; (Eiter-) Beule *f*; ~ate ⚕ [~əreit] eitern (lassen); ~ous ⚕ [~rəs] geschwürig.

ulterior □ [ʌl'tiəriə] jenseitig; *fig.* weiter; tiefer liegend, versteckt.

ultimate □ ['ʌltimit] letzt; endlich; End...; ~ly [~tli] zu guter Letzt.

ultimat|um [ʌlti'meitəm], *pl. a.* ~a [~tə] Ultimatum *n*.

ultimo ✝ ['ʌltimou] vorigen Monats.

ultra ['ʌltrə] übermäßig; Ultra..., ultra...; ~fashionable ['ʌltrə'fæʃənəbl] hypermodern; ~modern hypermodern.

umbel ⚘ ['ʌmbəl] Dolde *f*.

umbrage ['ʌmbridʒ] Anstoß *m* (*Ärger*); Schatten *m*.

umbrella [ʌm'brelə] Regenschirm *m*; *fig.* Schirm *m*, Schutz *m*; ✈ Abschirmung *f*.

umpire ['ʌmpaiə] 1. Schiedsrichter *m*; 2. Schiedsrichter sein.

un... [ʌn] un...; Un...; ent...; nicht...

unabashed ['ʌnə'bæʃt] unverfroren; unerschrocken.

unabated ['ʌnə'beitid] unvermindert. [stande.\
unable ['ʌn'eibl] unfähig, außer-/

unaccommodating ['ʌnə'kɔmədeitiŋ] unnachgiebig.

unaccountable □ ['ʌnə'kauntəbl] unerklärlich; seltsam; nicht zur Rechenschaft verpflichtet.

unaccustomed ['ʌnə'kʌstəmd] ungewohnt; ungewöhnlich.

unacquainted ['ʌnə'kweintid]: ~ with unbekannt mit, *e-r S* unkundig.

unadvised □ ['ʌnəd'vaizd] unbedacht; unberaten.

unaffected □ ['ʌnə'fektid] unberührt; ungerührt; ungekünstelt.

unaided ['ʌn'eidid] ohne Unterstützung; (ganz) allein; bloß (*Auge*).

unalter|able □ [ʌn'ɔːltərəbl] unveränderlich; ~ed ['ʌn'ɔːltəd] unverändert.

unanim|ity [juːnə'nimiti] Einmütigkeit *f*; ~ous □ [juː'nænməs] einmütig, einstimmig.

unanswer|able □ [ʌn'ɑːnsərəbl] unwiderleglich; ~ed ['ʌn'ɑːnsəd] unbeantwortet.

unapproachable □ [ʌnə'proutʃəbl] unzugänglich.

unapt □ [ʌn'æpt] ungeeignet.

unashamed □ ['ʌnə'ʃeimd] schamlos.

unasked ['ʌn'ɑːskt] unverlangt; ungebeten.

unassisted □ ['ʌnə'sistid] ohne Hilfe *od.* Unterstützung.

unassuming □ ['ʌnə'sjuːmiŋ] anspruchslos, bescheiden.

unattached ['ʌnə'tætʃt] nicht gebunden; ungebunden, ledig, frei.

unattractive □ ['ʌnə'træktiv] wenig anziehend, reizlos; uninteressant.

unauthorized ['ʌn'ɔːθəraizd] unberechtigt, unbefugt.

unavail|able ['ʌnə'veiləbl] nicht verfügbar; ~ing [~liŋ] vergeblich.

unavoidable □ [ʌnə'vɔidəbl] unvermeidlich.

unaware ['ʌnə'wɛə] ohne Kenntnis; *be* ~ *of et.* nicht merken; ~s [~ɛəz] unversehens, unvermutet; versehentlich.

unbacked ['ʌn'bækt] ohne Unterstützung; ungedeckt (*Scheck*).

unbag ['ʌn'bæg] aus dem Sack holen *od.* lassen.

unbalanced ['ʌn'bælənst] nicht im Gleichgewicht befindlich; unausgeglichen; geistesgestört.

unbearable □ [ʌn'bɛərəbl] unerträglich.

unbeaten ['ʌn'biːtn] ungeschlagen; unbetreten (*Weg*).

unbecoming □ [ʌnbi'kʌmiŋ] unkleidsam; unpassend, unschicklich.

unbeknown F ['ʌnbi'noun] unbekannt.

unbelie|f ['ʌnbi'liːf] Unglaube *m*; ~vable □ [ʌnbi'liːvəbl] unglaublich; ~ving □ ['ʌnbi'liːviŋ] ungläubig.

unbend ['ʌn'bend] [*irr.* (*bend*)] (sich) entspannen; freundlich werden, auftauen; ~ing □ [~diŋ] unbiegsam; *fig.* unbeugsam.

unbias(s)ed □ ['ʌn'baiəst] vorurteilsfrei, unbefangen, unbeeinflußt.

unbid(den) ['ʌn'bid(n)] ungeheißen, unaufgefordert; ungebeten.

unbind ['ʌn'baind] [*irr.* (*bind*)] losbinden, befreien; lösen.

unblushing □ [ʌn'blʌʃiŋ] schamlos. [boren.\
unborn ['ʌn'bɔːn] (noch) unge-/

unbosom [ʌn'buzəm] offenbaren.

unbounded □ [ʌn'baundid] unbegrenzt; schrankenlos.

unbroken □ [ʌn'broukən] ungebrochen; unversehrt; ununterbrochen.

unbutton ['ʌn'bʌtn] aufknöpfen.

uncalled-for [ʌn'kɔːldfɔː] ungerufen; unverlangt (*S.*); unpassend.

uncanny □ [ʌn'kæni] unheimlich.

uncared-for ['ʌn'kɛədfɔː] unbeachtet, vernachlässigt.

unceasing □ [ʌn'siːsiŋ] unaufhörlich.

unceremonious □ ['ʌnseri'mounjəs] ungezwungen; formlos.

uncertain □ [ʌnˈsəːtn] unsicher; ungewiß; unbestimmt; unzuverlässig; ~ty [~nti] Unsicherheit *f*.

unchallenged [ˈʌntʃælindʒd] unangefochten.

unchang|eable □ [ʌnˈtʃeindʒəbl] unveränderlich, unwandelbar; ~ed [ˈʌntʃeindʒd] unverändert; ~ing □ [ʌnˈtʃeindʒiŋ] unveränderlich.

uncharitable □ [ʌnˈtʃæritəbl] lieblos; unbarmherzig; unfreundlich.

unchecked [ʌnˈtʃekt] ungehindert.

uncivil □ [ˈʌnˈsivl] unhöflich; ~ized [~vilaizd] unzivilisiert.

unclaimed [ˈʌnˈkleimd] nicht beansprucht; unzustellbar (*bsd. Brief*).

unclasp [ˈʌnˈklɑːsp] auf-, loshaken, auf-, losschnallen; aufmachen.

uncle [ˈʌŋkl] Onkel *m*.

unclean □ [ˈʌnˈkliːn] unrein.

unclose [ˈʌnˈklouz] (sich) öffnen.

uncomely [ˈʌnˈkʌmli] reizlos; unpassend.

uncomfortable □ [ʌnˈkʌmfətəbl] unbehaglich, ungemütlich; unangenehm.

uncommon □ [ʌnˈkɔmən] ungewöhnlich.

uncommunicative □ [ˈʌnkəˈmjuːnikətiv] wortkarg, schweigsam.

uncomplaining □ [ˈʌnkəmˈpleiniŋ] klaglos; ohne Murren; geduldig.

uncompromising □ [ʌnˈkɔmprəmaiziŋ] kompromißlos.

unconcern [ˈʌnkənˈsəːn] Unbekümmertheit *f*; Gleichgültigkeit *f*; ~ed □ [~nd] unbekümmert; unbeteiligt.

unconditional □ [ˈʌnkənˈdiʃənl] unbedingt; bedingungslos.

unconfirmed [ˈʌnkənˈfəːmd] unbestätigt; *eccl.* nicht konfirmiert.

unconnected □ [ˈʌnkəˈnektid] unverbunden.

unconquer|able □ [ʌnˈkɔŋkərəbl] unüberwindlich; ~ed [ˈʌnˈkɔŋkəd] unbesiegt.

unconscionable □ [ʌnˈkɔnʃnəbl] gewissenlos; F unverschämt, übermäßig.

unconscious □ [ʌnˈkɔnʃəs] unbewußt; bewußtlos; ~ness [~snis] Bewußtlosigkeit *f*.

unconstitutional □ [ˈʌnkɔnstiˈtjuːʃənl] verfassungswidrig.

uncontroll|able □ [ˈʌnkənˈtroulabl] unkontrollierbar; unbändig; ~ed [ˈʌnkənˈtrould] unbeaufsichtigt; *fig.* unbeherrscht.

unconventional □ [ˈʌnkənˈvenʃənl] unkonventionell; ungezwungen.

unconvinc|ed [ˈʌnkənˈvinst] nicht überzeugt; ~ing [~siŋ] nicht überzeugend.

uncork [ˈʌnˈkɔːk] entkorken.

uncount|able [ˈʌnˈkauntəbl] unzählbar; ~ed [~tid] ungezählt.

uncouple [ˈʌnˈkʌpl] loskoppeln.

uncouth □ [ʌnˈkuːθ] ungeschlacht.

uncover [ʌnˈkʌvə] aufdecken, freilegen; entblößen.

unct|ion [ˈʌŋkʃən] Salbung *f* (*a. fig.*); Salbe *f*; ~uous □ [ˈʌŋktjuəs] fettig, ölig; *fig.* salbungsvoll.

uncult|ivated [ˈʌnˈkʌltiveitid], ~ured [~tʃəd] unkultiviert.

undamaged [ˈʌnˈdæmidʒd] unbeschädigt.

undaunted □ [ʌnˈdɔːntid] unerschrocken.

undeceive [ˈʌndiˈsiːv] *j-n* aufklären.

undecided □ [ˈʌndiˈsaidid] unentschieden; unentschlossen.

undefined □ [ˈʌndiˈfaind] unbestimmt; unbegrenzt.

undemonstrative □ [ˈʌndiˈmɔnstrətiv] zurückhaltend.

undeniable □ [ʌndiˈnaiəbl] unleugbar; unbestreitbar.

under [ˈʌndə] **1.** *adv.* unten; darunter; **2.** *prp.* unter; **3.** *adj.* unter; *in Zssgn:* unter...; Unter...; mangelhaft ...; ~bid [~ˈbid] [*irr.* (*bid*)] unterbieten; ~brush [~brʌʃ] Unterholz *n*; ~carriage ✈ (Flugzeug)Fahrwerk *n*; *mot.* Fahrgestell *n*; ~clothes, ~clothing Unterkleidung *f*, Unterwäsche *f*; ~cut [~ˈkʌt] *Preise* unterbieten; ~dog [~dɔg] Unterlegene(r) *m*; Unterdrückte(r) *m*; ~done [~ˈdʌn] nicht gar; ~estimate [~ərˈestimeit] unterschätzen; ~fed [~ˈfed] unterernährt; ~go [ʌndəˈgou] [*irr.* (*go*)] erdulden; sich unterziehen (*dat.*); ~graduate [~ˈgrædjuit] Student (-in); ~ground [ˈʌndəgraund] **1.** unterirdisch; Untergrund...; **2.** Untergrundbahn *f*; ~growth Unterholz *n*; ~hand unter der Hand; heimlich; ~lie [ʌndəˈlai] [*irr.* (*lie*)] zugrunde liegen (*dat.*); ~line [~ˈlain] unterstreichen; ~ling [ˈʌndəliŋ] Untergeordnete(r) *m*; ~mine [ʌndəˈmain] unterminieren; *fig.* untergraben; schwächen; ~most [ˈʌndəmoust] unterst; ~neath [ʌndəˈniːθ] **1.** *prp.* unter (-halb); **2.** *adv.* unten; darunter; ~pin [~ˈpin] untermauern; ~plot [ˈʌndəplɔt] Nebenhandlung *f*; ~privileged [~ˈprivilidʒd] benachteiligt; ~rate [ʌndəˈreit] unterschätzen; ~secretary [~ˈsekrətəri] Unterstaatssekretär *m*; ~sell ✝ [~ˈsel] [*irr.* (*sell*)] *j-n* unterbieten; *Ware* verschleudern; ~signed [~ˈsaind] Unterzeichnete(r) *m*; ~sized [~ˈsaizd] zu klein; ~staffed [ʌndəˈstɑːft] unterbesetzt; ~stand [~ˈstænd] [*irr.* (*stand*)] *allg.* verstehen; sich verstehen auf (*acc.*); (als sicher) annehmen; auffassen; (sinngemäß) ergänzen; *make o.s. understood* sich verständlich machen; *an understood thing* e-e abgemachte Sache; ~standable [~dəbl] verständlich; ~standing [~diŋ]

Verstand *m*; Einvernehmen *n*; Verständigung *f*; Abmachung *f*; Voraussetzung *f*; ~state ['ʌndə'steit] zu gering angeben; abschwächen; ~statement Unterbewertung *f*; Understatement *n*, Untertreibung *f*; ~take [ʌndə'teik] *irr. (take)* unternehmen; übernehmen; sich verpflichten; ~taker ['ʌndəteikə] Bestattungsinstitut *n*; ~taking [ʌndə'teikiŋ] Unternehmung *f*; Verpflichtung *f*; ['ʌndəteikiŋ] Leichenbestattung *f*; ~tone leiser Ton; ~value [~'vælju:] unterschätzen; ~wear [~weə] Unterkleidung *f*, Unterwäsche *f*; ~wood Unterholz *n*; ~write *irr. (write)* Versicherung abschließen; ~writer Versicherer *m*.

undeserv|ed □ ['ʌndi'zə:vd] unverdient; ~ing [~viŋ] unwürdig.

undesigned □ ['ʌndi'zaind] unbeabsichtigt, absichtslos.

undesirable ['ʌndi'zairəbl] 1. □ unerwünscht; 2. unerwünschte Person.

undeviating □ [ʌn'di:vieitiŋ] unentwegt.

undignified □ [ʌn'dignifaid] würdelos.

undisciplined [ʌn'disiplind] zuchtlos, undiszipliniert; ungeschult.

undisguised ['ʌndis'gaizd] unverkleidet; unverhohlen.

undisputed □ ['ʌndis'pju:tid] unbestritten.

undo [ʌn'du:] *irr. (do)* aufmachen; (auf)lösen; ungeschehen machen, aufheben; vernichten; ~ing [~u(:)iŋ] Aufmachen *n*; Ungeschehenmachen *n*; Vernichtung *f*; Verderben *n*; ~ne ['ʌn'dʌn] erledigt, vernichtet.

undoubted □ [ʌn'dautid] unzweifelhaft, zweifellos.

undreamt [ʌn'dremt]; ~of ungeahnt.

undress ['ʌn'dres] 1. (sich) entkleiden *od.* ausziehen; 2. Hauskleid *n*; ~ed unbekleidet; unangezogen; nicht zurechtgemacht.

undue □ ['ʌn'dju:] ungebührlich; übermäßig; ✝ noch nicht fällig.

undulat|e ['ʌnduleit] wogen; wallen; wellig sein; ~ion [ʌndju'leiʃən] wellenförmige Bewegung.

undutiful □ ['ʌn'dju:tiful] ungehorsam, pflichtvergessen.

unearth ['ʌn'ə:θ] ausgraben; *fig.* aufstöbern; ~ly [ʌn'ə:θli] überirdisch.

uneas|iness [ʌn'i:zinis] Unruhe *f*; Unbehagen *n*; ~y □ [ʌn'i:zi] unbehaglich; unruhig; unsicher.

uneducated ['ʌn'edjukeitid] unerzogen; ungebildet.

unemotional □ ['ʌni'mouʃənl] leidenschaftslos; passiv; nüchtern.

unemploy|ed ['ʌnim'plɔid] 1. unbeschäftigt; arbeitslos; unbenutzt; 2.: *the* ~ *pl.* die Arbeitslosen *pl.*; ~ment [~'ɔimənt] Arbeitslosigkeit *f*.

unending □ [ʌn'endiŋ] endlos.

unendurable □ ['ʌnin'djuərəbl] unerträglich.

unengaged ['ʌnin'geidʒd] frei.

unequal □ ['ʌn'i:kwəl] ungleich; nicht gewachsen (*to dat.*); ~(l)ed [~ld] unvergleichlich, unerreicht.

unerring □ ['ʌn'ə:riŋ] unfehlbar.

unessential □ ['ʌni'senʃəl] unwesentlich, unwichtig (*to für*).

uneven □ ['ʌn'i:vən] uneben; ungleich(mäßig); ungerade (*Zahl*).

uneventful □ ['ʌni'ventful] ereignislos; ohne Zwischenfälle.

unexampled [ʌnig'za:mpld] beispiellos.

unexceptionable □ [ʌnik'sepʃnəbl] untadelig; einwandfrei.

unexpected □ ['ʌniks'pektid] unerwartet.

unexplained ['ʌniks'pleind] unerklärt.

unfading □ [ʌn'feidiŋ] nicht welkend; unvergänglich; echt (*Farbe*).

unfailing □ [ʌn'feiliŋ] unfehlbar; nie versagend; unerschöpflich; *fig.* treu.

unfair □ ['ʌn'fɛə] unehrlich; unfair; ungerecht.

unfaithful □ ['ʌn'feiθful] un(ge)treu, treulos; nicht wortgetreu.

unfamiliar ['ʌnfə'miljə] unbekannt; ungewohnt.

unfasten ['ʌn'fɑ:sn] aufmachen; lösen; ~ed unbefestigt, lose.

unfathomable □ [ʌn'fæðəməbl] unergründlich.

unfavo(u)rable □ ['ʌn'feivərəbl] ungünstig.

unfeeling □ [ʌn'fi:liŋ] gefühllos.

unfilial □ ['ʌn'filjəl] respektlos, pflichtvergessen (*Kind*).

unfinished ['ʌn'finiʃt] unvollendet; unfertig.

unfit 1. □ ['ʌn'fit] ungeeignet, unpassend; 2. [ʌn'fit] untauglich machen.

unfix ['ʌn'fiks] losmachen, lösen.

unfledged ['ʌn'fledʒd] ungefiedert; (noch) nicht flügge; *fig.* unreif.

unflinching □ [ʌn'flintʃiŋ] fest entschlossen, unnachgiebig.

unfold ['ʌn'fould] (sich) entfalten *od.* öffnen; [ʌn'fould] klarlegen; enthüllen.

unforced □ ['ʌn'fɔ:st] ungezwungen.

unforeseen ['ʌnfɔ:'si:n] unvorhergesehen.

unforgettable □ [ʌnfə'getəbl] unvergeßlich.

unforgiving ['ʌnfə'giviŋ] unversöhnlich.

unforgotten ['ʌnfə'gɔtn] unvergessen.

unfortunate [ʌn'fɔ:tʃnit] 1. □ un-

glücklich; 2. Unglückliche(r *m*) *f*;
~ly [~tli] unglücklicherweise, leider.
unfounded □ ['ʌn'faundid] unbe-
gründet; grundlos.
unfriendly ['ʌn'frendli] unfreundlich; ungünstig.
unfurl [ʌn'fəːl] entfalten, aufrollen.
unfurnished ['ʌn'fəːniʃt] unmö-
bliert.
ungainly [ʌn'geinli] unbeholfen,
plump.
ungenerous □ ['ʌn'dʒenərəs] un-
edelmütig; nicht freigebig.
ungentle □ ['ʌn'dʒentl] unsanft.
ungodly □ [ʌn'gɔdli] gottlos.
ungovernable □ [ʌn'gʌvənəbl] unlenksam; zügellos, unbändig.
ungraceful □ ['ʌn'greisful] ungra-
ziös, ohne Anmut; unbeholfen.
ungracious □ ['ʌn'greiʃəs] ungnä-
dig; unfreundlich.
ungrateful □ [ʌn'greitful] undankbar.
unguarded □ ['ʌn'gaːdid] unbewacht; unvorsichtig; ungeschützt.
unguent ['ʌngwənt] Salbe *f*.
unhampered □ ['ʌn'hæmpəd] ungehindert.   [schön.]
unhandsome □ [ʌn'hænsəm] un-]
unhandy □ [ʌn'hændi] unhandlich;
ungeschickt; unbeholfen.
unhappy □ [ʌn'hæpi] unglücklich.
unharmed ['ʌn'haːmd] unversehrt.
unhealthy □ [ʌn'helθi] ungesund.
unheard-of [ʌn'həːdɔv] unerhört.
unheed|ed ['ʌn'hiːdid] unbeachtet,
unbewacht; ~ing [~diŋ] sorglos.
unhesitating □ [ʌn'heziteitiŋ] ohne
Zögern; unbedenklich.
unholy [ʌn'houli] unheilig; gottlos.
unhono(u)red ['ʌn'ɔnəd] ungeehrt;
uneingelöst (*Pfand, Scheck*).
unhook ['ʌn'huk] auf-, aushaken.
unhoped-for [ʌn'houptfɔː] unver-
hofft.
unhurt ['ʌn'həːt] unverletzt.
unicorn ['juːnikɔːn] Einhorn *n*.
unification [juːnifi'keiʃən] Vereinigung *f*; Vereinheitlichung *f*.
uniform ['juːnifɔːm] 1. □ gleichförmig, gleichmäßig; einheitlich;
2. Dienstkleidung *f*; Uniform *f*;
3. uniformieren; ~ity [juːni'fɔːmiti]
Gleichförmigkeit *f*, Gleichmäßigkeit *f*.
unify ['juːnifai] verein(ig)en; ver-
einheitlichen.
unilateral □ ['juːni'lætərəl] einseitig.
unimagina|ble □ [ʌni'mædʒinəbl]
undenkbar; ~tive □ ['ʌni'mædʒi-
nətiv] einfallslos.
unimportant □ ['ʌnim'pɔːtənt]
unwichtig.
unimproved ['ʌnim'pruːvd] nicht
kultiviert, unbebaut (*Land*); unver-
bessert.
uninformed ['ʌnin'fɔːmd] nicht
unterrichtet.

uninhabit|**able** ['ʌnin'hæbitəbl] un-
bewohnbar; ~ed [~tid] unbewohnt.
uninjured ['ʌn'indʒəd] unbeschädigt, unverletzt.
unintelligible □ ['ʌnin'telidʒəbl]
unverständlich.
unintentional □ ['ʌnin'tenʃənl] un-
absichtlich.
uninteresting □ ['ʌn'intristiŋ] uninteressant.
uninterrupted □ ['ʌnintə'rʌptid]
ununterbrochen.
union ['juːnjən] Vereinigung *f*; Verbindung *f*; Union *f*, Verband *m*;
Einigung *f*; Einigkeit *f*; Verein *m*,
Bund *m*; *univ.* (Debattier)Klub *m*;
Gewerkschaft *f*; ~ist [~nist] Ge-
werkschaftler *m*; ♀ Jack Union
Jack *m* (*britische Nationalflagge*); ~
suit *Am.* Hemdhose *f*.
unique □ [juː'niːk] einzigartig, ein-
malig.
unison ♪ *u. fig.* ['juːnizn] Einklang
m.
unit ['juːnit] Einheit *f*; Ⓐ Einer *m*;
~e [juː'nait] (sich) vereinigen, verbinden; ~ed vereinigt, vereint; ~y
['juːniti] Einheit *f*; Einigkeit *f*.
univers|**al** □ [juːni'vəːsəl] allge-
mein; allumfassend; Universal...,
Welt...; ~ality [juːnivəː'sæliti] Allgemeinheit *f*; umfassende Bildung,
Vielseitigkeit *f*; ~e [juːni'vəːs]
Weltall *n*, Universum *n*; ~ity [juː-
ni'vəːsiti] Universität *f*.
unjust □ ['ʌn'dʒʌst] ungerecht; ~i-
fiable □ [ʌn'dʒʌstifaiəbl] nicht zu
rechtfertigen(d), unverantwortlich.
unkempt ['ʌn'kempt] ungepflegt.
unkind □ [ʌn'kaind] unfreundlich.
unknow|**ing** □ ['ʌn'nouiŋ] unwis-
send; unbewußt; ~n [~oun] 1. unbekannt; unbewußt; ~ to me ohne
mein Wissen; 2. Unbekannte(r *m*,
-s *n*) *f*.
unlace ['ʌn'leis] aufschnüren.
unlatch ['ʌn'lætʃ] aufklinken.
unlawful □ ['ʌn'lɔːful] ungesetzlich; *weitS.* unrechtmäßig.
unlearn ['ʌn'ləːn] [*irr.* (*learn*)] ver-
lernen.
unless [ən'les] wenn nicht, außer
wenn; es sei denn, daß.
unlike ['ʌn'laik] 1. *adj.* □ ungleich;
2. *prp.* anders als; ~ly [ʌn'laikli]
unwahrscheinlich.
unlimited ['ʌn'limitid] unbegrenzt.
unload ['ʌn'loud] ent-, ab-, ausladen; *Ladung* löschen.
unlock ['ʌn'lɔk] aufschließen; *Waffe*
entsichern; ~ed unverschlossen.
unlooked-for [ʌn'luktfɔː] unerwartet.
unloose, ~n ['ʌn'luːs, ʌn'luːsn] lösen, losmachen.
unlov|**ely** ['ʌn'lʌvli] reizlos, un-
schön; ~ing □ [~viŋ] lieblos.
unlucky □ [ʌn'lʌki] unglücklich.

unmake ['ʌn'meik] [irr. (make)] vernichten; rückgängig machen; umbilden; Herrscher absetzen.

unman ['ʌn'mæn] entmannen.

unmanageable □ [ʌn'mænidʒəbl] unlenksam, widerspenstig.

unmarried ['ʌn'mærid] unverheiratet, ledig.

unmask ['ʌn'mɑ:sk] (sich) demaskieren; fig. entlarven.

unmatched ['ʌn'mætʃt] unerreicht; unvergleichlich.

unmeaning □ [ʌn'mi:niŋ] nichtssagend.

unmeasured [ʌn'meʒəd] ungemessen; unermeßlich.

unmeet ['ʌn'mi:t] ungeeignet.

unmentionable □ [ʌn'menʃnəbl] nicht zu erwähnen(d), unnennbar.

unmerited ['ʌn'meritid] unverdient.

unmindful □ [ʌn'maindful] unbedacht; sorglos; ohne Rücksicht.

unmistakable □ ['ʌnmis'teikəbl] unverkennbar; unmißverständlich.

unmitigated [ʌn'mitigeitid] ungemildert; richtig; fig. Erz...

unmolested ['ʌnmou'lestid] unbelästigt.

unmounted ['ʌn'mauntid] unberitten; nicht gefaßt (Stein); unaufgezogen (Bild); unmontiert.

unmoved □ ['ʌn'mu:vd] unbewegt, ungerührt.

unnamed ['ʌn'neimd] ungenannt.

unnatural □ [ʌn'nætʃrəl] unnatürlich.   [nötig.)

unnecessary □ [ʌn'nesisəri] un-)

unneighbo(u)rly ['ʌn'neibəli] nicht gutnachbarlich.

unnerve ['ʌn'nɔ:v] entnerven.

unnoticed ['ʌn'noutist] unbemerkt.

unobjectionable □ ['ʌnəb'dʒekʃnəbl] einwandfrei.

unobserv|ant □ ['ʌnəb'zɔ:vənt] unachtsam; ~ed □ [~vd] unbemerkt.

unobtainable ['ʌnəb'teinəbl] unerreichbar.

unobtrusive □ ['ʌnəb'tru:siv] unaufdringlich, bescheiden.

unoccupied ['ʌn'ɔkjupaid] unbesetzt; unbewohnt; unbeschäftigt.

unoffending ['ʌnə'fendiŋ] harmlos.

unofficial □ ['ʌnə'fiʃəl] nichtamtlich, inoffiziell.

unopposed ['ʌnə'pouzd] ungehindert.

unostentatious □ ['ʌnɔstən'teiʃəs] anspruchslos; unauffällig; schlicht.

unowned ['ʌn'ound] herrenlos.

unpack ['ʌn'pæk] auspacken.

unpaid ['ʌn'peid] unbezahlt; unbelohnt; & unfrankiert.

unparalleled ['ʌn'pærəleld] beispiellos, ohnegleichen.

unperceived □ ['ʌnpə'si:vd] unbemerkt.

unperturbed ['ʌnpə(:)'tə:bd] ruhig, gelassen.

unpleasant □ [ʌn'pleznt] unangenehm; unerfreulich; ~ness [~tnis] Unannehmlichkeit f.

unpolished ['ʌn'pɔliʃt] unpoliert; fig. ungebildet.

unpolluted ['ʌnpə'lu:tid] unbefleckt.

unpopular □ ['ʌn'pɔpjulə] unpopulär, unbeliebt; ~ity ['ʌnpɔpju-'læriti] Unbeliebtheit f.

unpracti|cal □ ['ʌn'præktikəl] unpraktisch; ~sed, Am. ~ced [ʌn'præktist] ungeübt.

unprecedented □ [ʌn'presidəntid] beispiellos; noch nie dagewesen.

unprejudiced □ [ʌn'predʒudist] unbefangen, unvoreingenommen.

unpremeditated □ ['ʌnpri'mediteitid] unbeabsichtigt.

unprepared □ ['ʌnpri'pɛəd] unvorbereitet.

unpreten|ding □ ['ʌnpri'tendiŋ], ~tious □ [~nʃəs] anspruchslos.

unprincipled ['ʌn'prinsəpld] ohne Grundsätze; gewissenlos.

unprivileged [ʌn'priviludʒd] sozial benachteiligt; arm.

unprofitable □ [ʌn'prɔfitəbl] unnütz.

unproved ['ʌn'pru:vd] unerwiesen.

unprovided ['ʌnprə'vaidid] nicht versehen (with mit); ~ for unversorgt, mittellos.

unprovoked □ ['ʌnprə'voukt] ohne Grund.

unqualified □ ['ʌn'kwɔlifaid] ungeeignet; unberechtigt; [ʌn'kwɔlifaid] unbeschränkt.

unquestion|able□[ʌn'kwestʃnəbl] unzweifelhaft, fraglos; ~ed [~nd] ungefragt; unbestritten.

unquote ['ʌn'kwout] Zitat beenden.

unravel [ʌn'rævəl] (sich) entwirren; enträtseln.

unready □ ['ʌn'redi] nicht bereit od. fertig; unlustig, zögernd.

unreal □ ['ʌn'riəl] unwirklich; ~istic ['ʌnriə'listik] (~ally) wirklichkeitsfremd, unrealistisch.

unreasonable □ [ʌn'ri:znəbl] unvernünftig; grundlos; unmäßig.

unrecognizable □ ['ʌn'rekəgnaizəbl] nicht wiederzuerkennen(d).

unredeemed □ ['ʌnri'di:md] unerlöst; uneingelöst; ungemildert.

unrefined ['ʌnri'faind] ungeläutert; fig. ungebildet.   [dankenlos.)

unreflecting □['ʌnri'flektiŋ] ge-)

unregarded ['ʌnri'gɑ:did] unbeachtet; unberücksichtigt.

unrelated ['ʌnri'leitid] ohne Beziehung (to zu).

unrelenting □ ['ʌnri'lentiŋ] erbarmungslos; unerbittlich.

unreliable ['ʌnri'laiəbl] unzuverlässig.

unrelieved □ ['ʌnri'li:vd] ungelindert; ununterbrochen.

unremitting □ [ʌnri'mitiŋ] unablässig, unaufhörlich; unermüdlich.

unrepining □ ['ʌnri'painiŋ] klaglos; unverdrossen.

unrequited □ ['ʌnri'kwaitid] unerwidert; unbelohnt.

unreserved □ ['ʌnri'zə:vd] rückhaltlos; unbeschränkt; ohne Vorbehalt.

unresisting □ ['ʌnri'zistiŋ] widerstandslos.

unresponsive ['ʌnris'ponsiv] unempfänglich (to für).

unrest ['ʌn'rest] Unruhe f.

unrestrained □ ['ʌnris'treind] ungehemmt; unbeschränkt.

unrestricted □ ['ʌnris'triktid] uneingeschränkt.

unriddle ['ʌn'ridl] enträtseln.

unrighteous □ ['ʌn'raitʃəs] ungerecht; unredlich.

unripe ['ʌn'raip] unreif.

unrival(l)ed [ʌn'raivəld] unvergleichlich, unerreicht, einzigartig.

unroll ['ʌn'roul] ent-, aufrollen.

unruffled ['ʌn'rʌfld] glatt; ruhig.

unruly [ʌn'ru:li] ungebärdig.

unsafe □ ['ʌn'seif] unsicher.

unsal(e)able ['ʌn'seiləbl] unverkäuflich.

unsanitary ['ʌn'sænitəri] unhygienisch.

unsatisf|actory □ ['ʌnsætis'fæktəri] unbefriedigend; unzulänglich; **~ied** ['ʌn'sætisfaid] unbefriedigt; **~ying** □ [~aiiŋ] = *unsatisfactory*.

unsavo(u)ry ['ʌn'seivəri] unappetitlich (*a. fig.*), widerwärtig.

unsay ['ʌn'sei] [*irr. (say)*] zurücknehmen, widerrufen.

unscathed ['ʌn'skeiðd] unversehrt.

unschooled ['ʌn'sku:ld] ungeschult; unverbildet.

unscrew ['ʌn'skru:] *v/t.* ab-, los-, aufschrauben; *v/i.* sich abschrauben lassen.

unscrupulous □ [ʌn'skru:pjuləs] bedenkenlos; gewissenlos; skrupellos.

unsearchable □ [ʌn'sə:tʃəbl] unerforschlich; unergründlich.

unseason|able □ [ʌn'si:znəbl] unzeitig; *fig.* ungelegen; **~ed** ['ʌn'si:znd] nicht abgelagert (*Holz*); *fig.* nicht abgehärtet; ungewürzt.

unseat ['ʌn'si:t] des Amtes entheben; abwerfen.

unseemly [ʌn'si:mli] unziemlich.

unseen ['ʌn'si:n] ungesehen; unsichtbar.

unselfish □ ['ʌn'selfiʃ] selbstlos, uneigennützig; **~ness** [~ʃnis] Selbstlosigkeit *f*.

unsettle ['ʌn'setl] in Unordnung bringen; verwirren; erschüttern; **~d** nicht festgesetzt; unbeständig; † unbezahlt; unerledigt; ohne festen Wohnsitz; unbesiedelt.

unshaken ['ʌn'ʃeikən] unerschüttert; unerschütterlich.

unshaven ['ʌn'ʃeivn] unrasiert.

unship ['ʌn'ʃip] ausschiffen.

unshrink|able ['ʌn'ʃriŋkəbl] nicht einlaufend (*Stoff*); **~ing** □ [ʌn'ʃriŋkiŋ] unverzagt.

unsightly [ʌn'saitli] häßlich.

unskil|(l)ful □ ['ʌn'skilful] ungeschickt; **~led** [~ld] ungelernt.

unsoci|able [ʌn'souʃəbl] ungesellig; **~al** [~əl] ungesellig; unsozial.

unsolder ['ʌn'sɔldə] los-, ablöten.

unsolicited ['ʌnsə'lisitid] nicht gefragt (*S.*); unaufgefordert (*P.*).

unsolv|able ['ʌn'sɔlvəbl] unlösbar; **~ed** [~vd] ungelöst.

unsophisticated ['ʌnsə'fistikeitid] unverfälscht; ungekünstelt; unverdorben, unverbildet.

unsound □ ['ʌn'saund] ungesund; verdorben; wurmstichig; morsch; nicht stichhaltig (*Beweis*); verkehrt.

unsparing □ [ʌn'spɛəriŋ] freigebig; schonungslos, unbarmherzig.

unspeakable □ [ʌn'spi:kəbl] unsagbar; unsäglich.

unspent ['ʌn'spent] unverbraucht; unerschöpft.

unspoil|ed, ~t ['ʌn'spɔilt] unverdorben; unbeschädigt; nicht verzogen (*Kind*).

unspoken ['ʌn'spoukən] ungesagt; **~of** unerwähnt.

unstable □ ['ʌn'steibl] nicht (stand)fest; unbeständig; unstet(ig); labil.

unsteady □ ['ʌn'stedi] unstet(ig), unsicher; schwankend; unbeständig; unsolid; unregelmäßig.

unstrained ['ʌn'streind] unfiltriert; *fig.* ungezwungen.

unstrap ['ʌn'stræp] los-, abschnallen.

unstressed ['ʌn'strest] unbetont.

unstring ['ʌn'striŋ] [*irr. (string)*] *Saite* entspannen.

unstudied ['ʌn'stʌdid] ungesucht, ungekünstelt, natürlich.

unsubstantial □ ['ʌnsəb'stænʃəl] wesenlos; gegenstandslos; inhaltlos; gehaltlos; dürftig.

unsuccessful □ ['ʌnsək'sesful] erfolglos, ohne Erfolg.

unsuitable □ ['ʌn'sju:təbl] unpassend; unangemessen.

unsurpassed ['ʌnsə(:)'pɑ:st] unübertroffen.

unsuspect|ed ['ʌnsəs'pektid] unverdächtig; unvermutet; **~ing** [~tiŋ] nichts ahnend; arglos.

unsuspicious □ ['ʌnsəs'piʃəs] nicht argwöhnisch, arglos.

unswerving □ [ʌn'swəːviŋ] unentwegt.

untangle ['ʌn'tæŋgl] entwirren.

untarnished ['ʌn'tɑːniʃt] unbefleckt; ungetrübt.

unteachable ['ʌn'tiːtʃəbl] unbelehrbar (P.); unlehrbar (S.).

untenanted ['ʌn'tənəntid] unvermietet, unbewohnt.

unthankful □ ['ʌn'θæŋkful] undankbar.

unthink|able [ʌn'θiŋkəbl] undenkbar; **~ing** □ ['ʌn'θiŋkiŋ] gedankenlos.

unthought [ʌn'θɔːt] unbedacht; **~of** unvermutet.

unthrifty □ ['ʌn'θrifti] verschwenderisch; nicht gedeihend.

untidy □ [ʌn'taidi] unordentlich.

untie ['ʌn'tai] aufbinden, aufknüpfen; *Knoten etc.* lösen; *j-n* losbinden.

until [ən'til] 1. *prp.* bis; 2. *cj.* bis (daß); *not ~* erst wenn *od.* als.

untimely [ʌn'taimli] unzeitig; vorzeitig; ungelegen. [lich.\

untiring □ [ʌn'taiəriŋ] unermüd-/

unto ['ʌntu] = to.

untold ['ʌn'tould] unerzählt; ungezählt; unermeßlich, unsäglich.

untouched ['ʌn'tʌtʃt] unberührt; *fig.* ungerührt; *phot.* unretuschiert.

untried ['ʌn'traid] unversucht; unerprobt; ⚖ noch nicht verhört.

untrod, ~den ['ʌn'trɔd, ~dn] unbetreten.

untroubled ['ʌn'trʌbld] ungestört.

untrue □ ['ʌn'truː] unwahr; untreu.

untrustworthy □ ['ʌn'trʌstwəːði] unzuverlässig, nicht vertrauenswürdig.

unus|ed ['ʌn'juːzd] ungebraucht; [ʌuːst] nicht gewöhnt (*to an acc.*; zu *inf.*); **~ual** □ [ʌn'juːʒuəl] ungewöhnlich; ungewohnt.

unutterable □ [ʌn'ʌtərəbl] unaussprechlich.

unvarnished *fig.* ['ʌn'vɑːniʃt] ungeschminkt.

unvarying □ [ʌn'vɛəriiŋ] unveränderlich.

unveil [ʌn'veil] entschleiern, enthüllen.

unversed ['ʌn'vəːst] unbewandert, unerfahren (*in* in *dat.*).

unvouched ['ʌn'vautʃt] *a.* **~for** unverbürgt, unbezeugt.

unwanted ['ʌn'wɔntid] unerwünscht.

unwarrant|able □ [ʌn'wɔrəntəbl] unverantwortlich; **~ed** [ʌtid] unberechtigt; ['ʌn'wɔrəntid] unverbürgt.

unwary □ [ʌn'wɛəri] unbedachtsam.

unwelcome [ʌn'welkəm] unwillkommen.

unwholesome ['ʌn'houlsəm] ungesund; schädlich.

unwieldy □ [ʌn'wiːldi] unhandlich; ungefüge; sperrig.

unwilling □ ['ʌn'wiliŋ] un-, widerwillig, abgeneigt.

unwind ['ʌn'waind] [*irr.* (*wind*)] auf-, loswickeln; (sich) abwickeln.

unwise □ ['ʌn'waiz] unklug.

unwitting □ [ʌn'witiŋ] unwissentlich; unbeabsichtigt.

unworkable ['ʌn'wəːkəbl] undurchführbar; ⊕ nicht betriebsfähig.

unworthy □ [ʌn'wəːði] unwürdig.

unwrap ['ʌn'ræp] auswickeln, auspacken, aufwickeln.

unwrought ['ʌn'rɔːt] unbearbeitet; roh; Roh...

unyielding □ [ʌn'jiːldiŋ] unnachgiebig.

up [ʌp] 1. *adv.* (her-, hin)auf; aufwärts, empor; oben; auf(gestanden); aufgegangen (*Sonne*); hoch; abgelaufen, um (*Zeit*); *Am. Baseball*: am Schlag; *~* and about wieder auf den Beinen; *be hard ~* in Geldschwierigkeiten sein; *~ against a task* e-r Aufgabe gewachsen; *~ to* bis (zu); *it is ~ to me* to do es ist an mir, zu tun; *what are you ~ to there?* was macht ihr da? *what's ~? sl.* was ist los? 2. *prp.* hinauf; *~ the river* flußaufwärts; *~* train Zug *m* nach der Stadt; 3. *adj.*: *~* train Zug *m* nach der Stadt; 4.: *the ~s and downs* das Auf und Ab, die Höhen und Tiefen *des Lebens*; 5. F (sich) erheben; hochfahren; hochtreiben.

up|-and-coming *Am.* F ['ʌpən'kʌmiŋ] unternehmungslustig; **~braid** [ʌp'breid] schelten; **~bringing** ['ʌpbriŋiŋ] Erziehung *f*; **~country** ['ʌp'kʌntri] landeinwärts (gelegen); **~heaval** [ʌp'hiːvl] Umbruch *m*; **~hill** ['ʌp'hil] bergan; mühsam; **~hold** [ʌp'hould] [*irr.* (*hold*)] aufrecht(er)halten; stützen; **~holster** [ʌp'houlstə] (auf)polstern; *Zimmer* dekorieren; **~holsterer** [ʌstərə] Tapezierer *m*, Dekorateur *m*, Polsterer *m*; **~holstery** [ʌri] Polstermöbel *n/pl.*; Möbelstoffe *m/pl.*; Tapezierarbeit *f*.

up|keep ['ʌpkiːp] Instandhaltung(skosten *pl.*) *f*; Unterhalt *m*; **~land** ['ʌplənd] Hoch-, Oberland *n*; **~lift** 1. [ʌp'lift] (empor-, er)heben; 2. ['ʌplift] Erhebung *f*; *fig.* Aufschwung *m*.

upon [ə'pɔn] = on.

upper ['ʌpə] ober; Ober...; **~most** oberst, höchst.

up|raise [ʌp'reiz] erheben; **~rear** [ʌp'riə] aufrichten; **~right** 1. □ ['ʌp'rait] aufrecht; *~ piano* ♩ Klavier *n*; *fig.* ['ʌprait] rechtschaffen; 2. Pfosten *m*; Ständer *m*; **~rising** [ʌp'raizin] Erhebung *f*, Aufstand *m*.

uproar ['ʌprɔː] Aufruhr *m*; **~ious** □ [ʌp'rɔːriəs] tobend; tosend.

up|root [ʌp'ruːt] entwurzeln; (her-) ausreißen; **~set** [ʌp'set] [*irr.* (set)] umwerfen; (um)stürzen; außer Fassung *od.* in Unordnung bringen; stören; verwirren; *be ~* außer sich sein; **~shot** [ʌpʃɔt] Ausgang *m*; **~side** [ʌpsaid] *adv.*: *~ down* das Oberste zuunterst; verkehrt; **~stairs** [ʌp'stɛəz] die Treppe hinauf, (nach) oben; **~start** [ʌpstaːt] Emporkömmling *m*; **~state** *Am.* [ʌp'steit] Hinterland *n e-s Staates*; **~stream** [ʌp'striːm] fluß-, stromaufwärts; **~-to-date** [ʌptə'deit] modern, neuzeitlich; **~town** [ʌp'taun] im *od.* in den oberen Stadtteil; *Am.* im Wohn- *od.* Villenviertel; **~turn** [ʌp'təːn] nach oben kehren; **~ward(s)** [ʌpwəd(z)] aufwärts (gerichtet).

uranium 🜍 [juə'reinjəm] Uran *n*.
urban [ʼəːbən] städtisch; Stadt...; **~e** □ [əː'bein] höflich; gebildet.
urchin [ʼəːtʃin] Bengel *m*.
urge [əːdʒ] **1.** *oft ~ on j-n* drängen, (an)treiben; dringen in *j-n*; dringen auf *et.*; *Recht* geltend machen; **2.** Drang *m*; **~ncy** [ʼəːdʒənsi] Dringlichkeit *f*; Drängen *n*; **~nt** □ [~nt] dringend; dringlich; eilig.
urin|al [ʼjuərinl] Harnglas *n*; Bedürfnisanstalt *f*; **~ate** [~neit] urinieren; **~e** [~in] Urin *m*, Harn *m*.
urn [əːn] Urne *f*; Tee- *etc.* Maschine *f*.
us [ʌs, əs] uns; *of ~* unser.
usage [ʼjuːzidʒ] Brauch *m*, Gepflogenheit *f*; Sprachgebrauch *m*; Behandlung *f*, Verwendung *f*, Gebrauch *m*.
usance 🜨 [ʼjuːzəns] Wechselfrist *f*.
use 1. [juːs] Gebrauch *m*; Benutzung *f*; Verwendung *f*; Gewohnheit *f*, Übung *f*; Brauch *m*; Nutzen *m*; (*of) no ~* unnütz, zwecklos; *have no ~ for* keine Verwendung haben

für; *Am.* F nicht mögen; **2.** [juːz] gebrauchen, benutzen, ver-, anwenden; behandeln; *~ up* ver-, aufbrauchen; *I ~d to do* ich pflegte zu tun, früher tat ich; *~d* [juːzd] gewöhnt; *~d* [juːst] gewöhnt (*to an acc.*); gewohnt (*to zu od. acc.*); **~ful** □ [ʼjuːsful] brauchbar; nützlich; Nutz...; **~less** □ [ʼjuːslis] nutz-, zwecklos, unnütz.

usher [ʼʌʃə] **1.** Türhüter *m*, Pförtner *m*; Gerichtsdiener *m*; Platzanweiser *m*; **2.** *mst. ~ in* (hin)einführen, anmelden; **~ette** [ʌʃə'ret] Platzanweiserin *f*.
usual □ [ʼjuːʒuəl] gewöhnlich; üblich; gebräuchlich.
usurer [ʼjuːʒərə] Wucherer *m*.
usurp [juːʼzəːp] sich *et.* widerrechtlich aneignen, an sich reißen; **~er** [~pə] Usurpator *m*.
usury [ʼjuːʒuri] Wucher(zinsen *pl.*) *m*.
utensil [juː(ː)'tensl] Gerät *n*; Geschirr *n*.
uterus *anat.* [ʼjuːtərəs] Gebärmutter *f*.
utility [juː(ː)'tiliti] **1.** Nützlichkeit *f*, Nutzen *m*; *public ~* öffentlicher Versorgungsbetrieb; **2.** Gebrauchs..., Einheits...
utiliz|ation [juːtilaiˈzeiʃən] Nutzbarmachung *f*; Nutzanwendung *f*; **~e** [ʼjuːtilaiz] sich *et.* zunutze machen.
utmost [ʼʌtmoust] äußerst.
Utopian [juːʼtoupjən] **1.** utopisch; **2.** Utopist(in), Schwärmer(in).
utter [ʼʌtə] **1.** □ *fig.* äußerst; völlig, gänzlich; **2.** äußern; *Seufzer etc.* ausstoßen, von sich geben; *Falschgeld etc.* in Umlauf setzen; **~ance** [ʼʌtərəns] Äußerung *f*, Ausdruck *m*; Aussprache *f*; **~most** [ʼʌtəmoust] äußerst.
uvula *anat.* [ʼjuːvjulə] Zäpfchen *n*.

V

vacan|cy [ʼveikənsi] Leere *f*; leerer *od.* freier Platz; Lücke *f*; offene Stelle; **~t** □ [~nt] leer (*a. fig.*); frei (*Zeit, Zimmer*); offen (*Stelle*); unbesetzt, vakant (*Amt*).
vacat|e [vəˈkeit, *Am.* ˈveikeit] räumen; *Stelle* aufgeben, aus *e-m Amt* scheiden; **~ion** [vəˈkeiʃən, *Am.* veiˈkeiʃən] **1.** (Schul)Ferien *pl.*; *bsd. Am.* Urlaub *m*; Räumung *f*; Niederlegung *f e-s Amtes*; **2.** *Am.* Urlaub machen; **~ionist** *Am.* [~nist] Ferienreisende(r *m*) *f*.
vaccin|ate [ʼvæksineit] impfen;

~ation [væksi'neiʃən] Impfung *f*; **~e** [ʼvæksiːn] Impfstoff *m*.
vacillate [ʼvæsileit] schwanken.
vacu|ous □ [ʼvækjuəs] *fig.* leer, geistlos; **~um** *phys.* [~uəm] Vakuum *n*; *~ cleaner* Staubsauger *m*; *~ flask, ~ bottle* Thermosflasche *f*.
vagabond [ʼvægəbɔnd] **1.** vagabundierend; **2.** Landstreicher *m*.
vagary [ʼveigəri] wunderlicher Einfall, Laune *f*, Schrulle *f*.
vagrant [ʼveigrənt] **1.** wandernd; *fig.* unstet; **2.** Landstreicher *m*, Vagabund *m*; Strolch *m*.
vague □ [veig] unbestimmt; unklar.

vain □ [vein] eitel, eingebildet; leer; nichtig; vergeblich; in ~ vergebens, umsonst; ~**glorious** □ [vein'glɔːriəs] prahlerisch.

vale [veil] *poet. od. in Namen*: Tal *n*.

valediction [væli'dikʃən] Abschied(sworte *n/pl.*) *m*.

valentine ['væləntain] Valentinsschatz *m*, -gruß *m* (*am Valentinstag, 14. Februar, erwählt, gesandt.*).

valerian ♀ [və'liəriən] Baldrian *m*.

valet ['vælit] 1. (Kammer)Diener *m*; 2. Diener sein bei *j-m*; *j-n* bedienen.

valetudinarian ['vælitju:di'nɛəriən] 1. kränklich; 2. kränklicher Mensch; Hypochonder *m*.

valiant □ ['væljənt] tapfer.

valid □ ['vælid] triftig, richtig, stichhaltig; (rechts)gültig; *be ~ gelten*; ~**ity** [və'liditi] Gültigkeit *f*; Triftig-, Richtigkeit *f*.

valise [və'liːz] Reisetasche *f*; ✕ Tornister *m*.

valley ['væli] Tal *n*.

valo(u)r ['vælə] Tapferkeit *f*.

valuable ['væljuəbl] 1. □ wertvoll; 2. ~s *pl*. Wertsachen *f/pl*.

valuation [vælju'eiʃən] Abschätzung *f*; Taxwert *m*.

value ['væljuː] 1. Wert *m*; Währung *f*; *give* (*get*) *good ~* (*for one's money*) ♰ reell bedienen (bedient werden); 2. (ab)schätzen; *fig*. schätzen; ~**less** [~julis] wertlos.

valve [vælv] Klappe *f*; Ventil *n*; *Radio*: Röhre *f*.

vamoose *Am. sl.* [və'muːs] *v/i.* abhauen; *v/t.* räumen (*verlassen*).

vamp F [væmp] 1. Vamp *m* (*verführerische Frau*); 2. neppen.

vampire ['væmpaiə] Vampir *m*.

van [væn] Möbelwagen *m*; Lieferwagen *m*; 🚃 Pack-, Güterwagen *m*; ✕ Vorhut *f*.

vane [vein] Wetterfahne *f*; (Windmühlen-, Propeller)Flügel *m*.

vanguard ✕ ['vænɡɑːd] Vorhut *f*.

vanilla ♀ [və'nilə] Vanille *f*.

vanish ['væniʃ] (ver)schwinden.

vanity ['væniti] Eitelkeit *f*, Einbildung *f*; Nichtigkeit *f*; ~ *bag* Kosmetiktäschchen *n*.

vanquish ['væŋkwiʃ] besiegen.

vantage ['vɑːntidʒ] *Tennis*: Vorteil *m*; ~**ground** günstige Stellung.

vapid □ ['væpid] schal, fad(e).

vapor|**ize** ['veipəraiz] verdampfen, verdunsten (lassen); ~**ous** □ [~rəs] dunstig; nebelhaft.

vapo(u)r ['veipə] Dunst *m*; Dampf *m*.

varia|**ble** □ ['vɛəriəbl] veränderlich; ~**nce** [~əns] Veränderung *f*; Uneinigkeit *f*; *be at ~* uneinig sein; (sich) widersprechen; *set at ~* entzweien; ~**nt** [~nt] 1. abweichend; 2. Variante *f*; ~**tion** [vɛəri'eiʃən]

Abänderung *f*; Schwankung *f*; Abweichung *f*; ♪ Variation *f*.

varicose ♬ ['værikous] Krampfader(n)...; ~ *vein* Krampfader *f*.

varie|**d** □ ['vɛərid] verschieden, verändert, mannigfaltig; ~**gate** [~igeit] bunt gestalten; ~**ty** [və'raiəti] Mannigfaltigkeit *f*, Vielzahl *f*; *biol.* Abart *f*; ♰ Auswahl *f*; Menge *f*; ~ *show* Varietévorstellung *f*; ~ *theatre* Varieté(theater) *n*.

various □ ['vɛəriəs] verschiedene, mehrere; mannigfaltig; verschiedenartig. [Racker.)

varmint *sl.* ['vɑːmint] *kleiner*)

varnish ['vɑːniʃ] 1. Firnis *m*, Lack *m*; *fig.* (äußerer) Anstrich; 2. firnissen, lackieren; *fig.* beschönigen.

vary ['vɛəri] (sich) (ver)ändern; wechseln (mit *et.*); abweichen.

vase [vɑːz] Vase *f*.

vassal ['væsəl] Vasall *m*; *attr.* Vasallen...

vast □ [vɑːst] ungeheuer, gewaltig, riesig, umfassend, weit.

vat [væt] Faß *n*; Bottich *m*; Kufe *f*.

vaudeville *Am.* ['voudəvil] Varieté *n*.

vault [vɔːlt] 1. Gewölbe *n*; Wölbung *f*; Stahlkammer *f*; Gruft *f*; *bsd. Sport*: Sprung *m*; *wine-~* Weinkeller *m*; 2. (über)wölben; *bsd. Sport*: springen (über *acc.*).

vaulting-horse ['vɔːltiŋhɔːs] *Turnen*: Pferd *n*.

vaunt *lit.* [vɔːnt] (sich) rühmen.

veal [viːl] Kalbfleisch *n*; *roast ~* Kalbsbraten *m*.

veer [viə] (sich) drehen.

vegeta|**ble** ['vedʒitəbl] 1. Pflanzen..., pflanzlich; 2. Pflanze *f*; *mst ~s pl.* Gemüse *n*; ~**rian** [vedʒi'tɛəriən] 1. Vegetarier(in); 2. vegetarisch; ~**te** ['vedʒiteit] vegetieren; ~**tive** □ [~tətiv] vegetativ; wachstumfördernd.

vehemen|**ce** ['viːiməns] Heftigkeit *f*; Gewalt *f*; ~**t** □ [~nt] heftig; ungestüm.

vehicle ['viːikl] Fahrzeug *n*, Beförderungsmittel *n*; *fig.* Vermittler *m*, Träger *m*; Ausdrucksmittel *n*.

veil [veil] 1. Schleier *m*; Hülle *f*; 2. (sich) verschleiern (*a. fig.*).

vein [vein] Ader *f* (*a. fig.*); Anlage *f*; Neigung *f*; Stimmung *f*.

velocipede [vi'lɔsipiːd] *Am.* (Kinder)Dreirad *n*; *hist.* Veloziped *n*.

velocity [vi'lɔsiti] Geschwindigkeit *f*.

velvet ['velvit] 1. Samt *m*; *hunt.* Bast *m*; 2. Samt...; samten; ~**y** [~ti] samtig.

venal ['viːnl] käuflich, feil.

vend [vend] verkaufen; ~**er**, ~**or** ['vendə, ~dɔː] Verkäufer *m*, Händler *m*.

veneer [vi'niə] 1. Furnier *n*; 2. furnieren; *fig.* bemänteln.

venera|ble □ ['venərəbl] ehrwürdig; **~te** [~reit] (ver)ehren; **~tion** [venə'reiʃən] Verehrung f.

venereal [vi'niəriəl] Geschlechts...

Venetian [vi'ni:ʃən] **1.** venetianisch; **~ blind** (Stab)Jalousie f; **2.** Venetianer(in).

vengeance ['vendʒəns] Rache f; **with a ~** F und wie, ganz gehörig.

venial □ ['vi:njəl] verzeihlich.

venison ['venzn] Wildbret n.

venom ['venəm] (bsd. Schlangen-) Gift n; fig. Gift n; Gehässigkeit f; **~ous** □ [~məs] giftig.

venous ['vi:nəs] Venen...; venös.

vent [vent] **1.** Öffnung f; Luft-, Spundloch n; Auslaß m; Schlitz m; **give ~ to** s-m Zorn etc. Luft machen; **2.** fig. Luft machen (dat.).

ventilat|e ['ventileit] ventilieren, (be-, ent-, durch)lüften; fig. erörtern; **~ion** [venti'leiʃən] Ventilation f, Lüftung f; fig. Erörterung f. **~or** ['ventileitə] Ventilator m.

ventral anat. ['ventrəl] Bauch...

ventriloquist [ven'triləkwist] Bauchredner m.

ventur|e ['ventʃə] **1.** Wagnis n; Risiko n; Abenteuer n; Spekulation f; **at a ~** auf gut Glück; **2.** (sich) wagen; riskieren; **~esome** □ [~səm], **~ous** □ [~ərəs] verwegen, kühn.

veracious □ [ve'reiʃəs] wahrhaft.

verb gr. [və:b] Verb(um) n, Zeitwort n; **~al** □ ['və:bəl] wörtlich; mündlich; **~iage** ['və:biidʒ] Wortschwall m; **~ose** □ [və:'bous] wortreich. [reif.]

verdant □ ['və:dənt] grün; fig. un-]

verdict ['və:dikt] ɪ̃tʒ (Urteils-) Spruch m der Geschworenen; fig. Urteil n; **bring in** od. **return a ~ of guilty** auf schuldig erkennen.

verdigris ['və:digris] Grünspan m.

verdure ['və:dʒə] Grün n.

verge [və:dʒ] **1.** Rand m, Grenze f; **on the ~ of** am Rande (gen.); dicht vor (dat.); **2.** sich (hin)neigen; **~ (up)on** grenzen an (acc.).

veri|fy ['verifai] (nach)prüfen; beweisen; bestätigen; **~similitude** [verisi'militju:d] Wahrscheinlichkeit f; **~table** □ ['veritəbl] wahr (-haftig).

vermic|elli [və:mi'seli] Fadennudeln f/pl.; **~ular** [və:'mikjulə] wurmartig.

vermilion [və'miljən] **1.** Zinnoberrot n; **2.** zinnoberrot.

vermin ['və:min] Ungeziefer n; hunt. Raubzeug n; fig. Gesindel n; **~ous** □ [~nəs] voller Ungeziefer.

vernacular [və'nækjulə] **1.** □ einheimisch; Volks...; **2.** Landes-, Muttersprache f; Jargon m.

versatile □ ['və:sətail] wendig.

verse [və:s] Vers(e pl.) m; Strophe f; Dichtung f; **~d** [və:st] bewandert.

versify ['və:sifai] v/t. in Verse bringen; v/i. Verse machen.

version ['və:ʃən] Übersetzung f; Fassung f, Darstellung f; Lesart f.

versus bsd. ɪ̃tʒ ['və:səs] gegen.

vertebra anat. ['və:tibrə], pl. **~e** [~ri:] Wirbel m.

vertical □ ['və:tikəl] vertikal, senkrecht.

vertig|inous □ [və:'tidʒinəs] schwindlig; schwindelnd (Höhe); **~o** ['və:tigou] Schwindel(anfall) m.

verve [veəv] Schwung m, Verve f.

very ['veri] **1.** adv. sehr; **the ~ best** das allerbeste; **2.** adj. wirklich; eben; bloß; **the ~ same** ebenderselbe; **in the ~ act** auf frischer Tat; gerade dabei; **the ~ thing** gerade das; **the ~ thought** der bloße Gedanke; **the ~ stones** sogar die Steine; **the veriest rascal** der größte Schuft.

vesicle ['vesikl] Bläs-chen n.

vessel ['vesl] Gefäß n (a. anat., &, fig.); ⚓ Fahrzeug n, Schiff n.

vest [vest] **1.** Unterhemd n; Weste f; **2.** v/t. bekleiden (with mit); j-n einsetzen (in in acc.); et. übertragen (in s.o. j-m); v/i. verliehen werden.

vestibule ['vestibju:l] Vorhof m (a. anat.); Vorhalle f; Hausflur m; bsd. Am. ⚅ Korridor m zwischen zwei D-Zug-Wagen; **~ train** D-Zug m.

vestige ['vestidʒ] Spur f.

vestment ['vestmənt] Gewand n.

vestry ['vestri] eccl. Sakristei f; Gemeindevertretung f; Gemeindesaal m; **~man** Gemeindevertreter m.

vet F [vet] **1.** Tierarzt m; Am. ⚔ Veteran m; **2.** co. verarzten; gründlich prüfen.

veteran ['vetərən] **1.** ausgedient; erfahren; **2.** Veteran m.

veterinary ['vetərinəri] **1.** tierärztlich; **2.** a. **~ surgeon** Tierarzt m.

veto ['vi:tou] **1.** pl. **~es** Veto n; **2.** sein Veto einlegen gegen.

vex [veks] ärgern; schikanieren; **~ation** [vek'seiʃən] Verdruß m; Ärger(nis n) m; **~atious** [~ʃəs] ärgerlich.

via [vaiə] über, via.

viaduct ['vaiədʌkt] Viadukt m, Überführung f.

vial ['vaiəl] Phiole f, Fläschchen n.

viand ['vaiənd] mst. **~s** pl. Lebensmittel n/pl.

vibrat|e [vai'breit] vibrieren; zittern; **~ion** [~eiʃən] Schwingung f, Zittern n, Vibrieren n, Erschütterung f.

vicar eccl. ['vikə] Vikar m; **~age** [~əridʒ] Pfarrhaus n.

vice¹ [vais] Laster n; Fehler m; Unart f; ⊕ Schraubstock m.

vice² prp. ['vaisi] an Stelle von.

vice³ [vais] F Stellvertreter m; attr. Vize..., Unter...; **~roy** ['vaisrɔi] Vizekönig m.

vice versa ['vaisi'və:sə] umgekehrt.

vicinity [vi'siniti] Nachbarschaft *f*; Nähe *f*.

vicious □ ['viʃəs] lasterhaft; bösartig; boshaft; fehlerhaft.

vicissitude [vi'sisitju:d] Wandel *m*, Wechsel *m*, ~s *pl*. Wechselfälle *m/pl*.

victim ['viktim] Opfer *n*; ~ize [~maiz] (hin)opfern; *fig. j-n* hereinlegen.

victor ['viktə] Sieger *m*; ♀ian *hist*. [vik'tɔ:riən] Viktorianisch; ~ious □ [~iəs] siegreich; Sieges...; ~y ['viktəri] Sieg *m*.

victual ['vitl] 1. (sich) verpflegen *od*. verproviantieren; 2. *mst* ~s *pl*. Lebensmittel *n/pl.*, Proviant *m*; ~(l)er [~lə] Lebensmittellieferant *m*.

video ['vidiou] Fernseh...

vie [vai] wetteifern.

Viennese [vie'ni:z] 1. Wiener(in); 2. Wiener..., wienerisch.

view [vju:] 1. Sicht *f*, Blick *m*; Besichtigung *f*; Aussicht *f* (*of* auf *acc*.); Anblick *m*; Ansicht *f* (*a. fig*.); Absicht *f*; *at first* ~ auf den ersten Blick; *in* ~ sichtbar, zu sehen; *in* ~ *of* im Hinblick auf (*acc*.); *fig*. angesichts (*gen*.); on ~ zu besichtigen; *with a* ~ *to inf. od. of ger*. in der Absicht zu *inf*.; have (keep) *in* ~ im Auge haben (behalten); 2. ansehen, besichtigen; *fig*. betrachten; ~er ['vju:ə] Betrachter(in), Zuschauer (-in); ~less ['vju:lis] ohne eigene Meinung; *poet*. unsichtbar; ~point Gesichts-, Standpunkt *m*.

vigil ['vidʒil] Nachtwache *f*; ~ance [~ləns] Wachsamkeit *f*; ~ant □ [~nt] wachsam.

vigo|rous □ ['vigərəs] kräftig; energisch; nachdrücklich; ~(u)r ['vigə] Kraft *f*; Vitalität *f*; Nachdruck *m*.

viking ['vaikiŋ] 1. Wiking(er) *m*; 2. wikingisch, Wikinger...

vile □ [vail] gemein; abscheulich.

vilify ['vilifai] verunglimpfen.

village ['vilidʒ] Dorf *n*; ~ green Dorfanger *m*, -wiese *f*; ~r [~dʒə] Dorfbewohner(in).

villain ['vilən] Schurke *m*, Schuft *m*, Bösewicht *m*; ~ous □ [~nəs] schurkisch; F scheußlich; ~y [~ni] Schurkerei *f*.

vim F [vim] Schwung *m*, Schneid *m*.

vindicat|e ['vindikeit] rechtfertigen (*from* gegen); verteidigen; ~ion [vindi'keiʃən] Rechtfertigung *f*.

vindictive □ [vin'diktiv] rachsüchtig.

vine [vain] Wein(stock) *m*, Rebe *f*; ~gar ['vinigə] (Wein)Essig *m*; ~-growing ['vaingrouiŋ] Weinbau *m*; ~yard ['vinjəd] Weinberg *m*.

vintage ['vintidʒ] 1. Weinlese *f*; (Wein)Jahrgang *m*; 2. klassisch; erlesen; altmodisch; ~ car *mot*. Veteran *m*; ~r [~dʒə] Winzer *m*.

viola ♪ [vi'oulə] Bratsche *f*.

violat|e ['vaiəleit] verletzen; *Eid etc*. brechen; vergewaltigen, schänden; ~ion [vaiə'leiʃən] Verletzung *f*; (Eid- *etc*.)Bruch *m*; Vergewaltigung *f*, Schändung *f*.

violen|ce ['vaiələns] Gewalt(samkeit, -tätigkeit) *f*; Heftigkeit *f*; ~t □ [~nt] gewaltsam; gewalttätig; heftig.

violet ♀ ['vaiəlit] Veilchen *n*.

violin ♪ [vaiə'lin] Violine *f*, Geige *f*.

V.I.P., VIP ['vi:ai'pi:] F hohes Tier.

viper *zo*. ['vaipə] Viper *f*, Natter *f*.

virago [vi'rɑ:gou] Zankteufel *m*.

virgin ['və:dʒin] 1. Jungfrau *f*; 2. *a*. ~al □ [~nl] jungfräulich; Jungfern...; ~ity [və:'dʒiniti] Jungfräulichkeit *f*.

viril|e ['virail] männlich; Mannes...; ~ity [vi'riliti] Männlichkeit *f*.

virtu [və:'tu:]: *article of* ~ Kunstgegenstand *m*; ~al □ ['və:tjuəl] eigentlich; ~ally [~li] praktisch; ~e ['və:tju:] Tugend *f*; Wirksamkeit *f*; Vorzug *m*, Wert *m*; *in virtue. by* ~ *of* kraft, vermöge (*gen*.); *make a* ~ *of necessity* aus der Not e-e Tugend machen; ~osity [və:tju'ɔsiti] Virtuosität *f*; ~ous □ ['və:tjuəs] tugendhaft.

virulent □ ['virulənt] giftig; ⚕ virulent; *fig*. bösartig.

virus ⚕ ['vaiərəs] Virus *n*; *fig*. Gift *n*.

visa ['vi:zə] Visum *n*, Sichtvermerk *m*; ~ed [~əd] mit e-m Sichtvermerk *od*. Visum versehen.

viscose ⚗ ['viskous] Viskose *f*; ~ silk Zellstoffseide *f*.

viscount ['vaikaunt] Vicomte *m*; ~ess [~tis] Vicomtesse *f*.

viscous □ ['viskəs] zähflüssig.

vise *Am*. [vais] Schraubstock *m*.

visé [vi:zei] = *visa*.

visib|ility [vizi'biliti] Sichtbarkeit *f*; Sichtweite *f*; ~le □ ['vizəbl] sichtbar; *fig*. (er)sichtlich; *pred*. zu sehen (*S*.); zu sprechen (*P*.).

vision ['viʒən] Sehvermögen *n*, Sehkraft *f*; *fig*. Seherblick *m*; Vision *f*, Erscheinung *f*; ~ary ['viʒnəri] 1. phantastisch; 2. Geisterseher(in); Phantast(in).

visit ['vizit] 1. *v/t*. besuchen; besichtigen; *fig*. heimsuchen; *et*. vergelten, *v/i*. Besuche machen; *Am*. sich unterhalten, plaudern (*with* mit); 2. Besuch *m*; ~ation [vizi'teiʃən] Besuch *m*; Besichtigung *f*; *fig*. Heimsuchung *f*; ~or ['vizitə] Besucher(in), Gast *m*; Inspektor *m*.

vista ['vistə] Durchblick *m* Rückod. Ausblick *m*.

visual □ ['vizjuəl] Seh...; Gesichts-...; ~ize [~laiz] (sich) vor Augen stellen, sich ein Bild machen von.

vital □ ['vaitl] 1. Lebens...; lebenswichtig, wesentlich; lebensgefährlich; ~ parts pl. = 2. ~s pl. lebenswichtige Organe n/pl.; edle Teile m/pl.; ~ity [vai'tæliti] Lebenskraft f; Vitalität f; ~ize ['vaitəlaiz] beleben.

vitamin(e) ['vitəmin] Vitamin n.

vitiate ['viʃieit] verderben; beeinträchtigen; hinfällig (g͡z ungültig) machen.

vitreous □ ['vitriəs] Glas...; gläsern.

vituperate [vi'tju:pəreit] schelten; schmähen, beschimpfen.

vivaci|ous □ [vi'veiʃəs] lebhaft; ~ty [vi'væsiti] Lebhaftigkeit f.

vivid □ ['vivid] lebhaft, lebendig.

vivify ['vivifai] (sich) beleben.

vixen ['viksn] Füchsin f; zänkisches Weib.

vocabulary [və'kæbjuləri] Wörterverzeichnis n; Wortschatz m.

vocal □ ['voukəl] stimmlich; Stimm...; gesprochen; laut; ♪ Vokal..., Gesang...; klingend; gr. stimmhaft; ~ist [~list] Sänger(in); ~ize [~laiz] (gr. stimmhaft) aussprechen; singen.

vocation [vou'keiʃən] Berufung f; Beruf m; ~al □ [~nl] beruflich; Berufs...

vociferate [vou'sifəreit] schreien.

vogue [voug] Beliebtheit f; Mode f.

voice [vɔis] 1. Stimme f; active (passive) ~ gr. Aktiv n (Passiv n); give ~ to Ausdruck geben (dat.); 2. äußern, ausdrücken; gr. stimmhaft aussprechen.

void [vɔid] 1. leer; g͡z ungültig; ~ of frei von; arm an (dat.); ohne; 2. Leere f; Lücke f; 3. entleeren; ungültig machen, aufheben.

volatile ['vɔlətail] 🜪 flüchtig (a. fig.); flatterhaft.

volcano [vɔl'keinou], pl. ~es Vulkan m.

volition [vou'liʃən] Wollen n; Wille(nskraft f) m.

volley ['vɔli] 1. Salve f; (Geschoß- etc.)Hagel m; fig. Schwall m; Tennis: Flugball m; 2. mst ~ out e-n Schwall von Worten etc. von sich geben; Salven abgeben; fig. hageln; dröhnen; ~ball Sport: Volleyball m, Flugball m.

volt 🜪 [voult] Volt n; ~age 🜪 ['voultidʒ] Spannung f; ~meter 🜪 Volt-, Spannungsmesser m.

volub|ility [vɔlju'biliti] Redegewandtheit f; ~le □ ['vɔljubl] (rede-)gewandt.

volum|e ['vɔljum] Band m e-s Buches; Volumen n; fig. Masse f,

große Menge; (bsd. Stimm)Umfang m; ~ of sound Radio: Lautstärke f; ~inous □ [və'lju:minəs] vielbändig; umfangreich, voluminös.

volunt|ary □ ['vɔləntəri] freiwillig; willkürlich; ~eer [vɔlən'tiə] 1. Freiwillige(r m) f; attr. Freiwilligen...; 2. v/i. freiwillig dienen; sich freiwillig melden; sich erbieten; v/t. anbieten; sich e-e Bemerkung erlauben.

voluptu|ary [və'lʌptjuəri] Wollüstling m; ~ous □ [~uəs] wollüstig; üppig.

vomit ['vɔmit] 1. (sich) erbrechen; fig. (aus)speien, ausstoßen; 2. Erbrochene(s) n; Erbrechen n.

voraci|ous □ [və'reiʃəs] gefräßig; gierig; ~ty [və'ræsiti] Gefräßigkeit f; Gier f.

vort|ex ['vɔ:teks], pl. mst ~ices ['vɔ:tisi:z] Wirbel m, Strudel m (mst fig.).

vote [vout] 1. (Wahl)Stimme f; Abstimmung f; Stimmrecht n; Beschluß m, Votum n; ~ of no confidence Mißtrauensvotum n; cast a ~ (s)eine Stimme abgeben; take a ~ on s.th. über et. abstimmen; 2. v/t. stimmen für; v/i. (ab)stimmen; wählen; ~ for stimmen für; F für et. sein; et. vorschlagen; ~r ['voutə] Wähler(in).

voting ['voutiŋ] Abstimmung f; attr. Wahl...; ~ machine Stimmenzählmaschine f; ~-paper Stimmzettel m; ~-power Stimmrecht n.

vouch [vautʃ] verbürgen; ~ for bürgen für; ~er ['vautʃə] Beleg m, Unterlage f; Gutschein m; Zeuge m; ~safe [vautʃ'seif] gewähren; geruhen.

vow [vau] 1. Gelübde n; (Treu-)Schwur m; 2. v/t. geloben.

vowel gr. ['vauəl] Vokal m, Selbstlaut m.

voyage ['vɔidʒ] 1. längere (See-, Flug)Reise; 2. reisen, fahren; ~r ['vɔidʒə] (See)Reisende(r m) f.

vulgar ['vʌlgə] 1. □ gewöhnlich, gemein, vulgär, pöbelhaft; ~ tongue Volkssprache f; 2.: the ~ der Pöbel; ~ism [~ərizəm] vulgärer Ausdruck; ~ity [vʌl'gæriti] Gemeinheit f; ~ize ['vʌlgəraiz] gemein machen; erniedrigen; populär machen.

vulnerable □ ['vʌlnərəbl] verwundbar; fig. angreifbar.

vulpine ['vʌlpain] Fuchs...; fuchsartig; schlau, listig.

vulture orn. ['vʌltʃə] Geier m.

vying ['vaiiŋ] wetteifernd.

W

wacky *Am. sl.* ['wæki] verrückt.

wad [wɔd] **1.** (Watte)Bausch *m*; Polster *n*; Pfropf(en) *m*; Banknotenbündel *n*; **2.** wattieren; polstern; zs.-pressen; zustopfen; **~ding** ['wɔdiŋ] Wattierung *f*; Watte *f*.

waddle ['wɔdl] watscheln, wackeln.

wade [weid] *v/i.* waten; *fig.* sich hindurcharbeiten; *v/t.* durchwaten.

wafer ['weifə] Waffel *f*; Oblate *f*; *eccl.* Hostie *f*.

waffle ['wɔfl] **1.** Waffel *f*; **2.** F quasseln.

waft [wɑːft] **1.** wehen, tragen; **2.** Hauch *m*.

wag [wæg] **1.** wackeln (mit); wedeln (mit); **2.** Schütteln *n*; Wedeln *n*; Spaßvogel *m*.

wage[1] [weidʒ] *Krieg* führen.

wage[2] [~] *mst* ~**s** *pl.* Lohn *m*; **~-earner** ['weidʒɜːnə] Lohnempfänger *m*.

wager ['weidʒə] **1.** Wette *f*; **2.** wetten.

waggish □ ['wægiʃ] schelmisch.

waggle F ['wægl] wackeln (mit).

wag(g)on ['wægən] (Roll-, Güter-)Wagen *m*; **~er** [~nə] Fuhrmann *m*.

wagtail *orn.* ['wægteil] Bachstelze *f*.

waif [weif] herrenloses Gut; Strandgut *n*; Heimatlose(r *m*) *f*.

wail [weil] **1.** (Weh)Klagen *n*; **2.** (weh)klagen.

wainscot ['weinskət] (Holz)Täfelung *f*.

waist [weist] Taille *f*; schmalste Stelle; ⊕ Mitteldeck *n*; **~coat** ['weiskout] Weste *f*; **~-line** ['weistlain] *Schneiderei*: Taille *f*.

wait [weit] **1.** *v/i.* warten (*for* auf *acc.*); *a.* ~ *at* (*Am.* on) *table* bedienen, servieren; ~ (*up*)on *j-n* bedienen; *j-n* besuchen; ~ *and see* abwarten; *v/t.* abwarten; *mit dem Essen* warten (*for* auf *j-n*); **2.** Warten *n*, Aufenthalt *m*; *lie in* ~ *for s.o.* j-m auflauern; **~er** ['weitə] Kellner *m*; Tablett *n*.

waiting ['weitiŋ] Warten *n*; Dienst *m*; *in* ~ diensttuend; **~-room** Wartezimmer *n*; 🚆 *etc.* Wartesaal *m*.

waitress ['weitris] Kellnerin *f*.

waive [weiv] verzichten auf (*acc.*), aufgeben; **~r** ⚖ ['weivə] Verzicht *m*.

wake [weik] **1.** ⊕ Kielwasser *n* (*a. fig.*); Totenwache *f*; Kirmes *f*; **2.** [*irr.*] *v/i. a.* ~ *up* aufwachen; *v/t. a.* ~ *up* (auf)wecken; erwecken; *fig.* wachrufen; **~ful** □ ['weikful] wachsam; schlaflos; **~n** ['weikən] *s.* wake **2.**

wale *bsd. Am.* [weil] Strieme *f*.

walk [wɔːk] **1.** *v/i.* (zu Fuß) gehen; spazierengehen; wandern; Schritt gehen; ~ *out* F streiken; ~ *out on sl.*

im Stich lassen; *v/t.* führen; *Pferd* Schritt gehen lassen; begleiten; (durch)wandern; umhergehen auf *od.* in (*dat.*); **2.** (Spazier)Gang *m*; Spazierweg *m*; ~ *of life* Lebensstellung *f*, Beruf *m*; **~er** ['wɔːkə] Fuß-, Spaziergänger(in).

walkie-talkie ⚔ ['wɔːki'tɔːki] tragbares Sprechfunkgerät.

walking ['wɔːkiŋ] Spazierengehen *n*, Wandern *n*; *attr.* Spazier...; Wander...; ~ *papers pl. Am.* F Entlassung(spapiere *n/pl.*) *f*; Laufpaß *m*; **~-stick** Spazierstock *m*; **~-tour** (Fuß)Wanderung *f*.

walk|-out *Am.* ['wɔːkaut] Ausstand *m*; **~-over** Kinderspiel *n*, leichter Sieg.

wall [wɔːl] **1.** Wand *f*; Mauer *f*; **2.** mit Mauern umgeben; ~ *up* zumauern.

wallet ['wɔlit] Ränzel *n*; Brieftasche *f*.

wallflower *fig.* ['wɔːlflauə] Mauerblümchen *n*.

wallop F ['wɔləp] *j-n* verdreschen.

wallow ['wɔlou] sich wälzen.

wall|-paper ['wɔːlpeipə] Tapete *f*; **~-socket** ⚡ Steckdose *f*.

walnut ♣ ['wɔːlnət] Walnuß(baum *m*) *f*.

walrus *zo.* ['wɔːlrəs] Walroß *n*.

waltz [wɔːls] **1.** Walzer *m*; **2.** Walzer tanzen.

wan □ [wɔn] blaß, bleich, fahl.

wand [wɔnd] (Zauber)Stab *m*.

wander ['wɔndə] wandern; umherschweifen, umherwandern; *fig.* abschweifen; irregehen; phantasieren.

wane [wein] **1.** abnehmen (*Mond*); *fig.* schwinden; **2.** Abnehmen *n*.

wangle *sl.* ['wæŋgl] *v/t.* deichseln, hinkriegen; *v/i.* mogeln.

want [wɔnt] **1.** Mangel *m* (of an *dat.*); Bedürfnis *n*; Not *f*; **2.** *v/i.*: *be ~ing* fehlen; es fehlen lassen (*in* an *dat.*); unzulänglich sein; ~ *for* Not leiden an (*dat.*); *it ~s of* es fehlt an (*dat.*); *v/t.* bedürfen (*gen.*), brauchen; nicht haben; wünschen, (haben) wollen; *it ~s s.th.* es fehlt an et. (*dat.*); *he ~s energy* es fehlt ihm an Energie; *~ed gesucht*; **~-ad** F ['wɔntæd] Kleinanzeige *f*; Stellenangebot *n*, -gesuch *n*.

wanton ['wɔntən] **1.** □ geil; üppig; mutwillig; **2.** Dirne *f*; **3.** umhertollen.

war [wɔː] **1.** Krieg *m*; *attr.* Kriegs...; *make* ~ Krieg führen (*upon* gegen); **2.** (ea. wider)streiten.

warble ['wɔːbl] trillern; singen.

ward [wɔːd] **1.** Gewahrsam *m*; Vormundschaft *f*; Mündel *n*; Schützling *m*; Gefängniszelle *f*; Abteilung *f*, Station *f*, Krankenzimmer *n*;

(Stadt)Bezirk *m*; ⊕ Einschnitt *m*
im Schlüsselbart; 2. ~ *off* abwehren;
~en ['wɔːdn] Aufseher *m*; (Luft-
schutz)Wart *m*; *univ.* Rektor *m*;
~er ['wɔːdə] (Gefangenen)Wärter
m; ~robe ['wɔːdroub] Garderobe *f*;
Kleiderschrank *m*; ~ trunk Schrankkoffer *m*.

ware [wɛə] Ware *f*; Geschirr *n*.

warehouse 1. ['wɛəhaus] (Waren-)
Lager *n*; Speicher *m*; 2. [~auz] auf
Lager bringen, einlagern.

war|fare ['wɔːfɛə] Krieg(führung *f*)
m; ~head ✕ Sprengkopf *m e-r
Rakete etc.*

wariness ['wɛərinis] Vorsicht *f*.

warlike ['wɔːlaik] kriegerisch.

warm [wɔːm] 1. ☐ warm (*a. fig.*);
heiß; *fig.* hitzig; 2. F Erwärmung *f*;
3. *v/t. a.* ~ *up* (auf-, an-, er)wär-
men; *v/i. a.* ~ *up* warm werden, sich
erwärmen; ~th [wɔːmθ] Wärme *f*.

warn [wɔːn] warnen (*of, against* vor
dat.); verwarnen; ermahnen; ver-
ständigen; ~ing ['wɔːniŋ] (Ver-)
Warnung *f*; Mahnung *f*; Kündigung *f*.

warp [wɔːp] *v/i.* sich verziehen
(*Holz*); *v/t. fig.* verdrehen, verzerren; beeinflussen; *j-n* abbringen
(*from* von).

warrant ['wɔrənt] 1. Vollmacht *f*;
Rechtfertigung *f*; Berechtigung *f*;
ಕೋ (Vollziehungs)Befehl *m*; Berech-
tigungsschein *m*; ~ *of arrest* ಕೋ
Haftbefehl *m*; 2. bevollmächtigen;
j-n berechtigen; *et.* rechtfertigen;
verbürgen; ✝ garantieren; ~y [~ti]
Garantie *f*; Berechtigung *f*.

warrior ['wɔriə] Krieger *m*.

wart [wɔːt] Warze *f*; Auswuchs *m*.

wary ☐ ['wɛəri] vorsichtig, behutsam; wachsam.

was [wɔz, wəz] *1. und 3. sg. pret.
von be*; *pret. pass. von be*; *he* ~ *to
have come er hätte kommen sollen*.

wash [wɔʃ] 1. *v/t.* waschen; (um-)
spülen; ~ *up* abwaschen, spülen;
v/i. sich waschen (lassen); waschecht sein (*a. fig.*); spülen, schlagen
(*Wellen*); 2. Waschen *n*; Wäsche *f*;
Wellenschlag *m*; Spülwasser *n*;
contp. Gewäsch *n*; *mouth-*~ Mund-
wasser *n*; ~able ['wɔʃəbl] wasch-
bar; ~-basin Waschbecken *n*; ~
cloth Waschlappen *m*; ~er ['wɔʃə]
Wäscherin *f*; Waschmaschine *f*;
⊕ Unterlagscheibe *f*; ~erwoman
Waschfrau *f*; ~ing ['wɔʃiŋ] 1. Waschen *n*; Wäsche *f*; ~s *pl.* Spülicht
n; 2. Wasch...; ~ing-up Abwaschen
n; ~rag *bsd. Am.* Waschlappen *m*;
~y ['wɔʃi] wässerig.

wasp [wɔsp] Wespe *f*.

wastage ['weistidʒ] Abgang *m*, Verlust *m*; Vergeudung *f*.

waste [weist] 1. wüst, öde; unbebaut; überflüssig; Abfall...; *lay* ~
verwüsten; ~ *paper* Altpapier *n*;

2. Verschwendung *f*, Vergeudung *f*;
Abfall *m*; Einöde *f*, Wüste *f*; 3. *v/t.*
verwüsten; verschwenden; verzeh-
ren; *v/i.* verschwendet werden;
~ful ☐ ['weistful] verschwenderisch; ~-paper-basket ['weist'pei-
pəbɑːskit] Papierkorb *m*; ~pipe
['weistpaip] Abflußrohr *n*.

watch [wɔtʃ] 1. Wache *f*; Taschen-
uhr *f*; 2. *v/i.* wachen; ~ *for* warten
auf (*acc.*); ~ *out* F aufpassen; *v/t.*
bewachen; beobachten; achtgeben
auf (*acc.*); *Gelegenheit* abwarten;
~dog ['wɔtʃdɔg] Wachhund *m*; ~
ful ☐ [~ʃful] wachsam, achtsam;
~-maker Uhrmacher *m*; ~man
(Nacht)Wächter *m*; ~word Losung
f.

water ['wɔːtə] 1. Wasser *n*; Gewässer *n*; *drink the* ~s Brunnen
trinken; 2. *v/t.* bewässern; (be-)
sprengen; (be)gießen; mit Wasser
versorgen; tränken; verwässern (*a.
fig.*); *v/i.* wässern (*Mund*); tränen
(*Augen*); Wasser einnehmen; ~
closet (Wasser)Klosett *n*; ~-col-
o(u)r Aquarell(malerei *f*) *n*; ~
course Wasserlauf *m*; ~cress *f*;
Brunnenkresse *f*; ~fall Wasserfall
m; ~front Ufer *n*, *bsd. Am. städti-
sches* Hafengebiet; ~-ga(u)ge ⊕
Wasserstands(an)zeiger *m*; Pegel *m*.

watering ['wɔːtəriŋ]: ~-can Gießkanne *f*; ~place Wasserloch *n*;
Tränke *f*; Bad(eort *m*) *n*; Seebad *n*;
~-pot Gießkanne *f*.

water|-level ['wɔːtəlevl] Wasser-
spiegel *m*; Wasserstand(slinie *f*) *m*;
⊕ Wasserwaage *f*; ~man Fähr-
mann *m*; Bootsführer *m*; Ruderer
m; ~proof 1. wasserdicht; 2. Regenmantel *m*; 3. imprägnieren;
~shed Wasserscheide *f*; Stromge-
biet *n*; ~side 1. Fluß-, Seeufer *n*;
2. am Wasser (gelegen); ~tight
wasserdicht; *fig.* unangreifbar; ~
way Wasserstraße *f*; ~works *oft
sg.* Wasserwerk *n*; ~y [~əri] wässerig.

watt ⚡ [wɔt] Watt *n*.

wattle ['wɔtl] 1. Flechtwerk *n*;
2. aus Flechtwerk herstellen.

wave [weiv] 1. Welle *f*; Woge *f*;
Winken *n*; 2. *v/t.* wellig machen;
wellen; schwingen; schwenken; ~
s.o. aside j-n beiseite winken; *v/i.*
wogen; wehen, flattern; winken;
~-length *phys.* ['weivlenθ] Wellen-
länge *f*.

waver ['weivə] (sch)wanken; flakkern.

wavy ['weivi] wellig wogend.

wax[1] [wæks] 1. Wachs *n*; Siegellack
m; Ohrenschmalz *n*; 2. wachsen;
bohnern.

wax[2] [~] [*irr.*] zunehmen (*Mond*).

wax|en *fig.* ['wæksən] wächsern;
~y ☐ [~si] wachsartig; weich.

way [wei] 1. *mst* Weg *m*; Straße *f*;

Art u. Weise *f*; *eigene* Art; Strecke *f*; Richtung *f*; F Gegend *f*; ⚓ Fahrt *f*; *fig.* Hinsicht *f*; Zustand *m*; ⚓ Helling *f*; ~ in Eingang *m*; ~ out Ausgang *m*; *fig.* Ausweg *m*; right of ~ 🚂 Wegerecht *n*; *bsd. mot.* Vorfahrt(srecht *n*) *f*; *this* ~ hierher, hier entlang; *by the* ~ übrigens; *by* ~ *of* durch; *on the* ~, *on one's* ~ unterwegs; *out of the* ~ ungewöhnlich; *under* ~ in Fahrt; *give* ~ zurückgehen; *mot.* die Vorfahrt lassen (*to dat.*); nachgeben; abgelöst werden (*to von*); sich hingeben (*to dat.*); *have one's* ~ *s-n* Willen haben; *lead the* ~ vorangehen; **2.** *adv.* weit; **~bill** ['weibil] Frachtbrief *m*; **~farer** ['weifəərə] Wanderer *m*; **~lay** [wei'lei] [*irr.* (lay)] *j-m* auflauern; **~side** 1. Wegrand *m*; 2. am Wege; ~ **station** *Am.* Zwischenstation *f*; ~ **train** *Am.* Bummelzug *m*; **~ward** □ ['weiwəd] starrköpfig, eigensinnig.

we [wi:, wij] wir.

weak □ [wi:k] schwach; schwächlich; dünn (*Getränk*); **~en** ['wi:kən] *v/t.* schwächen; *v/i.* schwach werden; **~ling** ['wi:kliŋ] Schwächling *m*; **~ly** [~li] schwächlich; **~minded** ['wi:k'maindid] schwachsinnig; **~ness** ['wi:knis] Schwäche *f*.

weal [wi:l] Wohl *n*; Strieme *f*.

wealth [welθ] Wohlstand *m*; Reichtum *m*; *fig.* Fülle *f*; **~y** □ ['welθi] reich; wohlhabend.

wean [wi:n] entwöhnen; ~ *s.o. from s.th.* j-m et. abgewöhnen.

weapon ['wepən] Waffe *f*.

wear [wɛə] 1. [*irr.*] *v/t.* am Körper tragen; zur Schau tragen; *a.* ~ *away*, ~ *down*, ~ *off*, ~ *out* abnutzen, abtragen, verbrauchen; erschöpfen; ermüden; zermürben; *v/i.* sich *gut etc.* tragen *od.* halten; *a.* ~ *off od. out* sich abnutzen *od.* abtragen; *fig.* sich verlieren; ~ *on* vergehen; 2. Tragen *n*; (Be)Kleidung *f*; Abnutzung *f*; *for hard* ~ strapazierfähig; *the worse for* ~ abgetragen; ~ *and tear* Verschleiß *m*.

wear|iness ['wiərinis] Müdigkeit *f*; Ermüdung *f*; *fig.* Überdruß *m*; **~some** □ [~isəm] ermüdend; langweilig; **~y** ['wiəri] 1. □ müde; *fig.* überdrüssig; ermüdend; anstrengend; 2. ermüden.

weasel *zo.* ['wi:zl] Wiesel *n*.

weather ['weðə] 1. Wetter *n*, Witterung *f*; 2. *v/t.* dem Wetter aussetzen; ⚓ *Sturm* abwettern; *fig.* überstehen; *v/i.* verwittern; **~beaten** vom Wetter mitgenommen; **~bureau** Wetteramt *n*; **~chart** Wetterkarte *f*; **~forecast** Wetterbericht *m*, -vorhersage *f*; **~worn** verwittert.

weav|e [wi:v] [*irr.*] weben; wirken; flechten; *fig.* ersinnen, erfinden;

sich schlängeln; **~er** ['wi:və] Weber *m*.

weazen ['wi:zn] verhutzelt.

web [web] Gewebe *n*; *orn.* Schwimmhaut *f*; **~bing** ['webiŋ] Gurtband *n*.

wed [wed] heiraten; *fig.* verbinden (*to mit*); **~ding** ['wediŋ] 1. Hochzeit *f*; 2. Hochzeits...; Braut...; Trau...; **~ring** Ehe-, Trauring *m*.

wedge [wedʒ] 1. Keil *m*; 2. (ver)keilen; *a.* ~ *in* (hin)einzwängen.

wedlock ['wedlɔk] Ehe *f*.

Wednesday ['wenzdi] Mittwoch *m*.

wee [wi:] klein, winzig; *a* ~ *bit* ein klein wenig.

weed [wi:d] 1. Unkraut *n*; 2. jäten; säubern (*of von*); ~ *out* ausmerzen; **~killer** ['wi:dkilə] Unkrautvertilgungsmittel *n*; **~s** *pl. mst widow's* ~ Witwenkleidung *f*; **~y** ['wi:di] voll Unkraut, verkrautet; *fig.* lang aufgeschossen.

week [wi:k] Woche *f*; *this day* ~ heute in *od.* vor e-r Woche; **~day** ['wi:kdei] Wochentag *m*; **~end** ['wi:k'end] Wochenende *n*; **~ly** ['wi:kli] 1. wöchentlich; 2. *a.* ~ *paper* Wochenblatt *n*, Wochen(zeit)schrift *f*.

weep [wi:p] [*irr.*] weinen; tropfen; **~ing** ['wi:piŋ] Trauer...; ~ *willow* ♀ Trauerweide *f*.

weigh [wei] *v/t.* (ab)wiegen, *fig.* ab-, erwägen; ~ *anchor* ⚓ den Anker lichten; ~ *ed down* niedergebeugt; *v/i.* wiegen (*a. fig.*); ausschlaggebend sein; ~ (*up*)*on* lasten auf (*dat.*).

weight [weit] 1. Gewicht *n* (*a. fig.*); Last *f* (*a. fig.*); *fig.* Bedeutung *f*; Wucht *f*; 2. beschweren; *fig.* belasten; **~y** □ ['weiti] (ge)wichtig; wuchtig.

weir [wiə] Wehr *n*; Fischreuse *f*.

weird [wiəd] Schicksals...; unheimlich; F sonderbar, seltsam.

welcome ['welkəm] 1. willkommen; *you are* ~ *to inf.* es steht Ihnen frei, zu *inf.*; (*you are*) ~! gern geschehen!, bitte sehr!; 2. Willkomm(en *n*) *m*; 3. willkommen heißen; *fig.* begrüßen.

weld ⊕ [weld] (zs.-)schweißen.

welfare ['welfɛə] Wohlfahrt *f*; ~ **centre** Fürsorgeamt *n*; ~ **state** Wohlfahrtsstaat *m*; ~ **work** Fürsorge *f*, Wohlfahrtspflege *f*; ~ **worker** Fürsorger(in).

well¹ [wel] 1. Brunnen *m*; *fig.* Quelle *f*; ⊕ Bohrloch *n*; Treppen-, Aufzugs-, Licht-, Luftschacht *m*; 2. quellen.

well² [~] 1. wohl; gut; ordentlich; gründlich; gesund; ~ *off* in guten Verhältnissen, wohlhabend; *I am not* ~ mir ist nicht wohl; *I am int.* nun!, F na!; **~being** ['wel'bi:iŋ] Wohl(sein) *n*; **~born** von guter

Herkunft; ~-bred wohlerzogen;
~-defined deutlich, klar umrissen;
~-favo(u)red gut aussehend; ~-
intentioned wohlmeinend; gut
gemeint; ~ known, ~-known bekannt; ~-mannered mit guten
Manieren; ~-nigh ['welnai] beinahe; ~ timed rechtzeitig; ~-to-do
['weltə'du:] wohlhabend; ~-wisher
Gönner m, Freund m; ~-worn abgetragen; fig. abgedroschen.
Welsh [welʃ] 1. walisisch; 2. Walisisch n; the ~ pl. die Waliser pl.; ~
rabbit überbackene Käseschnitte.
welt [welt] ⊕ Rahmen m, Schuh-
Rahmen m; Einfassung f; Strieme f.
welter ['weltə] 1. rollen, sich wälzen; 2. Wirrwarr m, Durcheinander n.
wench [wentʃ] Mädchen n; Dirne f.
went [went] pret. von go 1.
wept [wept] pret. u. p.p. von weep.
were [wə:, wə] 1. pret. pl. u. 2. sg.
von be; 2. pret. pass. von be;
3. subj. pret. von be.
west [west] 1. West(en m); 2. West...;
westlich; westwärts; ~erly ['wes-
təli], ~ern [~ən] westlich; ~erner
[~nə] Am. Weststaatler(in); Abend-
länder(in); ~ward(s) [~twəd(z)]
westwärts.
wet [wet] 1. naß, feucht; Am. den
Alkoholhandel gestattend; 2. Nässe
f; Feuchtigkeit f; 3. [irr.] naß
machen, anfeuchten.
wetback Am. sl. ['wetbæk] illegaler
Einwanderer aus Mexiko.
wether ['weðə] Hammel m.
wet-nurse ['wetnə:s] Amme f.
whack F [wæk] 1. verhauen; 2. Hieb
m.
whale [weil] Wal m; ~bone ['weil-
boun] Fischbein n; ~-oil Tran m;
~r ['weilə] Walfischfänger m.
whaling [weiliŋ] Walfischfang m.
wharf [wɔ:f], pl. a. wharves [wɔ:vz]
Kai m, Anlegeplatz m.
what [wɔt] 1. was; das, was; know
~'s ~ Bescheid wissen; 2. was?;
wie?; wieviel?; welch(er, -e, -es)?;
was für ein(e)?; ~ about ...? wie
steht's mit ...?; ~ for? wozu?; ~
of it? was ist denn dabei?; ~ next?
was sonst noch?; iro. was denn
noch alles?; ~ a blessing! was für
ein Segen!; 3. ~ with ... ~ with ...
teils durch ... teils durch ...; ~-
(so)ever [wɔt(sou)'evə] was od.
welcher auch (immer).
wheat ⊕ [wi:t] Weizen m.
wheedle ['wi:dl] beschwatzen; ~
s.th. out of s.o. j-m et. abschwatzen.
wheel [wi:l] 1. Rad n; Steuer n;
bsd. Am. F Fahrrad n; Töpfer-
scheibe f; Drehung f; ⨉ Schwen-
kung f; 2. rollen, fahren, schieben;
sich drehen; sich umwenden; ⨉
schwenken; F radeln; ~barrow

['wi:lbærou] Schubkarren m; ~
chair Rollstuhl m; ~ed mit Rä-
dern; fahrbar; ...räd(e)rig.
wheeze [wi:z] schnaufen, keuchen.
whelp [welp] 1. zo. Welpe m; allg.
Junge(s) n; F Balg m, n (ungezogenes
Kind); 2. (Junge) werfen.
when [wen] 1. wann?; 2. wenn;
als; während od. da doch; und da.
whence [wens] woher, von wo.
when(so)ever [wen(sou)'evə] immer od. jedesmal wenn; sooft (als).
where [wɛə] wo; wohin; ~about(s)
1. ['wɛərə'bauts] wo herum; 2. [~
əbauts] Aufenthalt m; ~as [~r'æz]
wohingegen, während (doch); ~at
[~'æt] wobei, worüber, worauf; ~by
[wɛə'bai] wodurch; ~fore ['wɛəfɔ:]
weshalb; ~in [wɛər'in] worin; ~of
[~r'ɔv] wovon; ~upon [~rə'pɔn]
worauf(hin); ~ver [~r'evə] wo(hin)
(auch) immer; ~withal ['wɛəwiðɔ:l]
Erforderliche(s) n; Mittel n/pl.
whet [wet] wetzen, schärfen; anstacheln.
whether ['weðə] ob; ~ or no so
oder so.
whetstone ['wetstoun] Schleifstein
m.
whey [wei] Molke f.
which [witʃ] 1. welche(r, -s)?;
2. der, die, das; was; ~ever
[~ʃ'evə] welche(r, -s) (auch) immer.
whiff [wif] 1. Hauch m; Zug m beim
Rauchen; Zigarillo n; 2. paffen.
while [wail] 1. Weile f; Zeit f;
for a ~ e-e Zeitlang; worth ~ der
Mühe wert; 2. mst ~ away Zeit verbringen; 2. a. whilst [wailst] während.
whim [wim] Schrulle f, Laune f.
whimper ['wimpə] wimmern.
whim|sical □ ['wimzikəl] wunder-
lich; ~sy ['wimzi] Grille f, Laune f.
whine [wain] winseln; wimmern.
whinny ['wini] wiehern.
whip [wip] 1. v/t. peitschen; geißeln
(a. fig.); j-n verprügeln; schlagen
(F a. fig.); umsäumen; werfen; reißen; ~ in parl. zs.-trommeln; ~ on
Kleidungsstück überwerfen; ~ up
antreiben; aufraffen; v/i. springen,
flitzen; 2. Peitsche f; Geißel f.
whippet zo. ['wipit] Whippet m
(kleiner englischer Rennhund).
whipping ['wipiŋ] Prügel pl.; ~-top
Kreisel m.
whippoorwill orn. ['wippuəwil]
Ziegenmelker m.
whirl [wə:l] 1. wirbeln; (sich) drehen; 2. Wirbel m, Strudel m; ~-
pool ['wə:lpu:l] Strudel m; ~wind
['wə:lwind] Wirbelwind m.
whir(r) [wə:] schwirren.
whisk [wisk] 1. Wisch m; Staub-
wedel m; Küche: Schneebesen m;
Schwung m; 2. v/t. (ab-, weg)wi-
schen, (ab-, weg)fegen; wirbeln
(mit); schlagen; v/i. huschen,

flitzen; ~er ['wiskə] Barthaar n;
mst ~s pl. Backenbart m.

whisper ['wispə] 1. flüstern; 2. Geflüster n.

whistle ['wisl] 1. pfeifen; 2. Pfeife f;
Pfiff m; F Kehle f; ~-stop Am.
🚉 Haltepunkt m; fig. Kaff n; pol.
kurzes Auftreten e-s Kandidaten im
Wahlkampf.

Whit [wit] in Zssgn: Pfingst...

white [wait] 1. allg. weiß; rein; F
anständig; Weiß...; 2. Weiß(e) n;
Weiße(r m) f (Rasse); ~-collar
['wait'kolə] geistig, Kopf..., Büro...;
~ workers pl. Angestellte pl.; ~ heat
Weißglut f; ~ lie fromme Lüge;
~n ['waitn] weiß machen od. werden; bleichen; ~ness [~nis] Weiße
f; Blässe f; ~wash 1. Tünche f;
2. weißen; fig. rein waschen.

whither lit. ['wiðə] wohin.

whitish ['waitiʃ] weißlich.

Whitsun ['witsn] Pfingst...; ~tide
Pfingsten pl.

whittle ['witl] schnitze(l)n; ~ away
verkleinern, beschneiden.

whiz(z) [wiz] zischen, sausen.

who [hu:, hu] 1. welche(r, -s); der,
die, das; 2. wer?

whodun(n)it sl. [hu:'dʌnit] Krimi
(-nalroman, -nalfilm) m.

whoever [hu(:)'evə] wer auch immer.

whole [houl] 1. □ ganz; heil, unversehrt; made out of ~ cloth Am.
F frei erfunden; 2. Ganze(s) n;
(up)on the ~ im ganzen; im allgemeinen; ~-hearted □ ['houl'ha:tid] aufrichtig; ~-meal bread
['houlmi:l bred] Vollkorn-, Schrotbrot n; ~sale 1. mst ~ trade Großhandel m; 2. Großhandels...; Engros...; fig. Massen...; ~ dealer =
~saler [~lə] Großhändler m; ~some
□ [~səm] gesund.

wholly adv. ['houli] ganz, gänzlich.

whom [hu:m, hum] acc. von who.

whoop [hu:p] 1. Schrei m, Geschrei
n; 2. laut schreien; ~ it up Am. sl.
laut feiern; ~ee Am. F ['wupi:]
Freudenfest n; make ~ auf die
Pauke hauen; ~ing-cough 🩺 ['hu:piŋkɔf] Keuchhusten m.

whore [hɔ:] Hure f.

whose [hu:z] gen. von who.

why [wai] 1. warum, weshalb; ~
so? wieso?; 2. eil, ja!; (je) nun.

wick [wik] Docht m.

wicked □ ['wikid] moralisch böse,
schlimm; ~ness [~dnis] Bosheit f.

wicker ['wikə] aus Weide geflochten; Weiden...; Korb...; ~ basket
Weidenkorb m; ~ chair Korbstuhl
m.

wicket ['wikit] Pförtchen n; Kricket:
Dreistab m, Tor n; ~-keeper Torhüter m.

wide [waid] a. □ u. adv. weit; ausgedehnt; weitgehend; großzügig;

breit; weitab; ~ awake völlig (od.
hell)wach; aufgeweckt (schlau);
3 feet ~ 3 Fuß breit; ~n ['waidn]
(sich) erweitern; ~-open ['waid'oupən] weit geöffnet; Am. sl. großzügig in der Gesetzesdurchführung;
~-spread weitverbreitet, ausgedehnt.

widow ['widou] Witwe f; attr.
Witwen...; ~er [~ouə] Witwer m.

width [widθ] Breite f, Weite f.

wield lit. [wi:ld] handhaben.

wife [waif], pl. wives [waivz] (Ehe-)
Frau f; Gattin f; Weib n; ~ly
['waifli] fraulich.

wig [wig] Perücke f.

wigging F ['wigiŋ] Schelte f.

wild [waild] 1. □ wild; toll; unbändig; abenteuerlich; planlos;
run ~ wild (auf)wachsen; talk ~
(wild) darauflos reden; ~ for od.
about (ganz) verrückt nach; 2. mst
~s pl. Wildnis f; ~-cat ['waildkæt]
1. zo. Wildkatze f; Am. Schwindelunternehmen n; bsd. Am. wilde Ölbohrung; 2. wild (Streik); Schwindel...; ~erness ['wildənis] Wildnis
f, Wüste f; Einöde f; ~-fire: like ~
wie ein Lauffeuer.

wile [wail] List f; mst ~s pl. Tücke f.

wil(l)ful □ ['wilful] eigensinnig;
vorsätzlich.

will [wil] 1. Wille m; Wunsch m;
Testament n; of one's own free ~
aus freien Stücken; 2. [irr.] v/aux.:
he ~ come er wird kommen; er
kommt gewöhnlich; I ~ do it ich
will es tun; 3. wollen; durch Willenskraft zwingen; entscheiden; ⚖ vermachen.

willing □ ['wiliŋ] willig, bereit
(-willig); pred. gewillt (to inf. zu);
~ness [~nis] (Bereit)Willigkeit f.

will-o'-the-wisp ['wiləðəwisp] Irrlicht n.

willow 🌿 ['wilou] Weide f.

willy-nilly ['wili'nili] wohl oder
übel.

wilt [wilt] (ver)welken.

wily □ ['waili] schlau, verschmitzt.

win [win] 1. [irr.] v/t. gewinnen;
erringen; erlangen, erreichen; j-n
dazu bringen (to do zu tun); ~ s.o.
over j-n für sich gewinnen; v/i.
gewinnen; siegen; 2. Sport: Sieg m.

wince [wins] (zs.-)zucken.

winch [wintʃ] Winde f; Kurbel f.

wind[1] [wind, poet.a. waind] 1. Wind
m; Atem m, Luft f; 🩺 Blähung f;
♪ Blasinstrumente n/pl.; 2. wittern;
außer Atem bringen; verschnaufen
lassen.

wind[2] [waind] [irr.] v/t. winden;
wickeln; Horn blasen; ~ up Uhr
aufziehen; Geschäft abwickeln; ⚖
liquidieren; v/i. sich winden; sich
schlängeln.

wind|bag ['windbæg] Schwätzer m;
~fall Fallobst n; Glücksfall m.

winding ['waindiŋ] **1.** Windung f; **2.** □ sich windend; ~ stairs pl. Wendeltreppe f; ~-sheet Leichentuch n.

wind-instrument ♪ ['windinstrumənt] Blasinstrument n.

windlass ⊕ ['windləs] Winde f.

windmill ['winmil] Windmühle f.

window ['windou] Fenster n; Schaufenster n; ~-dressing Schaufensterdekoration f; fig. Aufmachung f, Mache f; ~-shade Am. Rouleau n; ~-shopping Schaufensterbummel m.

wind|pipe ['windpaip] Luftröhre f; ~-screen, Am. ~-shield mot. Windschutzscheibe f; ~ wiper Scheibenwischer m.

windy □ ['windi] windig (a. fig. inhaltlos); geschwätzig.

wine [wain] Wein m; ~press ['wainpres] Kelter f.

wing [wiŋ] **1.** Flügel m (a. ✕ u. ⚑); Schwinge f; F co. Arm m; mot. Kotflügel m; ✈ Tragfläche f; ✕, ✕ Geschwader n; ~s pl. Kulissen f/pl.; take ~ weg-, auffliegen; on the ~ im Fluge; **2.** fig. beflügeln; fliegen.

wink [wiŋk] **1.** Blinzeln n, Zwinkern n; not get a ~ of sleep kein Auge zutun; s. forty; **2.** blinzeln, zwinkern (mit); ~ at ein Auge zudrücken bei et.; j-m zublinzeln.

winn|er ['winə] Gewinner(in); Sieger(in); ~ing ['winiŋ] **1.** □ einnehmend, gewinnend; **2.** ~s pl. Gewinn m.

winsome ['winsəm] gefällig, einnehmend.

wint|er ['wintə] **1.** Winter m; **2.** überwintern; ~ry ['~tri] winterlich; fig. frostig.

wipe [waip] (ab-, auf)wischen; reinigen; (ab)trocknen; ~ out wegwischen; (aus)löschen; fig. vernichten; tilgen.

wire ['waiə] **1.** Draht m; Leitung f; F Telegramm n; pull the ~s der Drahtzieher sein; s-e Beziehungen spielen lassen; **2.** (ver)drahten; telegraphieren; ~drawn ['waiədrɔːn] spitzfindig; ~less ['~lis] **1.** □ drahtlos; Funk...; **2.** a. ~ set Radio (-apparat m) n; on the ~ im Rundfunk; **3.** funken; ~-netting ['waiə-'netiŋ] Drahtgeflecht n.

wiry □ ['waiəri] drahtig, sehnig.

wisdom ['wizdəm] Weisheit f; Klugheit f; ~ tooth Weisheitszahn m.

wise [waiz] **1.** □ weise, verständig; klug; erfahren; ~ guy Am. sl. Schlauberger m; **2.** Weise f, Art f.

wise-crack F ['waizkræk] **1.** witzige Bemerkung; **2.** witzeln.

wish [wiʃ] **1.** wünschen; wollen; ~ for (sich) et. wünschen; ~ well (ill) wohl- (übel)wollen; **2.** Wunsch m;

~ful □ ['wiʃful] sehnsüchtig; ~ thinking Wunschdenken n.

wisp [wisp] Wisch m; Strähne f.

wistful □ ['wistful] sehnsüchtig.

wit [wit] **1.** Witz m; a. ~s pl. Verstand m; witziger Kopf; be at one's ~'s end mit s-r Weisheit zu Ende sein; keep one's ~s about one e-n klaren Kopf behalten; **2.**: to ~ nämlich, das heißt.

witch [witʃ] Hexe f, Zauberin f; ~craft ['witʃkrɑːft], ~ery ['~ʃəri] Hexerei f; ~hunt pol. Hexenjagd f (Verfolgung politisch verdächtiger Personen).

with [wið] mit; nebst; bei; von; durch; vor (dat.); ~ it sl. schwer auf der Höhe.

withdraw [wið'drɔː] [irr. (draw)] v/t. ab-, ent-, zurückziehen; zurücknehmen; Geld abheben; v/i. sich zurückziehen; abtreten; ~al ['~ɔːəl] Zurückziehung f; Rückzug m.

wither ['wiðə] v/i. (ver)welken; verdorren; austrocknen; v/t. welk machen.

with|hold [wið'hould] [irr. (hold)] zurückhalten; et. vorenthalten; ~in [wi'ðin] **1.** adv. lit. im Innern, drin(nen); zu Hause; **2.** prp. in(nerhalb); ~ doors im Hause; ~ call in Rufweite; call [wi'ðaut] **1.** adv. lit. (dr)außen; äußerlich; **2.** prp. ohne; lit. außerhalb; ~stand [wið'stænd] [irr. (stand)] widerstehen (dat.).

witness ['witnis] **1.** Zeug|e m, -in f; bear ~ Zeugnis ablegen (to für; of von); in ~ of zum Zeugnis (gen.); **2.** (be)zeugen; Zeuge sein von et.; ~-box, Am. ~ stand Zeugenstand m.

wit|ticism ['witisizəm] Witz m; ~ty □ ['witi] witzig; geistreich.

wives [waivz] pl. von wife.

wiz Am. sl. [wiz] Genie n; ~ard ['wizəd] Zauberer m; Genie n.

wizen(ed) ['wizn(d)] schrump(e)lig.

wobble ['wɔbl] schwanken; wackeln.

woe [wou] Weh n, Leid n; ~ is me! wehe mir!; ~begone ['woubigɔn] jammervoll; ~ful □ ['wouful] jammervoll, traurig, elend.

woke [wouk] pret. u. p.p. von wake 2; ~n ['woukən] p.p. von wake 2.

wold [would] (hügeliges) Heideland.

wolf [wulf] **1.** zo. pl. wolves [wulvz] Wolf m; **2.** verschlingen; ~ish □ ['wulfiʃ] wölfisch; Wolfs...

woman ['wumən], pl. women ['wimin] **1.** Frau f; Weib n; **2.** weiblich; ~ doctor Ärztin f; ~ student Studentin f; ~hood ['~nhud] die Frauen f/pl.; Weiblichkeit f; ~ish □ ['~niʃ] weibisch; ~kind ['~n'kaind] Frauen(welt f) f/pl.; ~like ['~nlaik] fraulich; ~ly ['~li] weiblich.

womb [wuːm] anat. Gebärmutter f; Mutterleib m; fig. Schoß m.

women ['wimin] *pl. von woman;*
~folk(s), ~kind die Frauen *f/pl.;* F
Weibervolk *n.*

won [wʌn] *pret. u. p.p. von win 1.*

wonder ['wʌndə] **1.** Wunder *n;*
Verwunderung *f;* **2.** sich wundern;
gern wissen mögen, sich fragen;
~ful □ [~sful] wunderbar, -voll;
~ing □ [~əriŋ] staunend, verwun-
dert.

won't [wount] = *will not.*

wont [~] **1.** *pred.* gewohnt; be ~ to
inf. pflegen zu *inf.;* **2.** Gewohnheit
f; ~ed ['wountid] gewohnt.

woo [wu:] werben um; locken.

wood [wud] Wald *m,* Gehölz *n;*
Holz *n;* Faß *n;* ♪ Holzblasinstrument
(-e *pl.*) *n;* touch ~! unberufen!; ~
chuck *zo.* ['wudtʃʌk] Waldmurmel-
tier *n;* ~**cut** Holzschnitt *m;* ~**cutter**
Holzfäller *m; Kunst:* Holzschneider
m; ~**ed** ['wudid] bewaldet; ~**en**
['wudn] hölzern (*a. fig.*); Holz...;
~**man** Förster *m;* Holzfäller *m;*
~**pecker** *orn.* ['wudpekə] Specht *m;*
~**sman** ['wudzmən] *s. woodman;*
~**wind** ♪ Holzblasinstrument *n; oft*
~**s** *pl.* ♪ Holzbläser *m/pl.;* ~**work**
Holzwerk *n;* ~**y** ['wudi] waldig;
holzig.

wool [wul] Wolle *f;* ~**gathering**
['wulgæðəriŋ] Geistesabwesenheit
f; ~(l)en ['wulin] **1.** wollen; Woll-
...; **2.** ~**s** *pl.* Wollsachen *f/pl.;*
~(l)y ['wuli] **1.** wollig; Woll...; be-
legt (*Stimme*); verschwommen;
2. woollies *pl.* F Wollsachen *f/pl.*

word [wə:d] **1.** *mst* Wort *n; eng S.:*
Vokabel *f;* Nachricht *f;* ✗ Lo-
sung(swort *n*) *f;* Versprechen *n;*
Befehl *m;* Spruch *m;* ~**s** *pl.* Wörter *n/pl.;* Worte *n/pl.; fig.* Wort-
wechsel *m;* Text *m e-s Liedes;*
have a ~ with *mit j-m* sprechen;
2. (in Worten) ausdrücken, (ab-)
fassen; ~**ing** ['wə:diŋ] Wortlaut *m,*
Fassung *f;* ~**splitting** Wortklau-
berei *f.*

wordy □ ['wə:di] wortreich; Wort...

wore [wɔ:] *pret. von wear 1.*

work [wə:k] **1.** Arbeit *f;* Werk *n;*
attr. Arbeits...; ~**s** *pl.* ⊕ (Uhr-,
Feder)Werk *n;* ✗ Befestigungen
pl.; ~**s** *sg.* Werk *n,* Fabrik *f;* ~ *of art*
Kunstwerk *n; at* ~ bei der Arbeit;
be in ~ Arbeit haben; be out of ~
arbeitslos sein; set to ~, set *od.* go
about one's ~ an die Arbeit gehen;
~**s** council Betriebsrat *m;* **2.** [*a. irr.*]
v/i. arbeiten (*a. fig.*); wirken; gären; sich *hindurch- etc.* arbeiten;
~ *at* arbeiten an (*dat.*); ~ *out* herauskommen (*Summe*); *v/t.* (be)arbei-
ten; arbeiten lassen; betreiben;
Maschine etc. bedienen; (be)wirken;
ausrechnen, lösen; *one's*
way sich durcharbeiten; ~ *off* abarbeiten; *Gefühl* abreagieren; † abstoßen; ~ *out* ausarbeiten; lösen;

ausrechnen; ~ *up* hochbringen; aufregen; verarbeiten (*into* zu).

work|able □ ['wə:kəbl] bearbei-
tungs-, betriebsfähig; ausführbar;
~**aday** [~ədei] Alltags...; ~**day**
Werktag *m;* ~**er** ['wə:kə] Arbeiter
(-in) *m;* ~**house** Armenhaus *n; Am.*
Besserungsanstalt *f,* Arbeitshaus
n.

working ['wə:kiŋ] **1.** Bergwerk *n;*
Steinbruch *m;* Arbeits-, Wirkungs-
weise *f;* **2.** arbeitend; Arbeits...;
Betriebs...; ~**class** Arbeiter...; ~
day Werk-, Arbeitstag *m;* ~ **hours**
pl. Arbeitszeit *f.*

workman ['wə:kmən] Arbeiter *m;*
Handwerker *m;* ~**like** [~nlaik]
kunstgerecht; ~**ship** [~nʃip] Kunst-
fertigkeit *f.*

work|out *Am.* F ['wə:kaut] *mst*
Sport: (Konditions)Training *n;*
Erprobung *f;* ~**shop** Werkstatt *f;*
~**woman** Arbeiterin *f.*

world [wə:ld] *allg.* Welt *f;* a ~ *of*
e-e Unmenge (von); bring (come)
into the ~ zur Welt bringen (kommen); *think the* ~ *of* alles halten
von; ~**ling** ['wə:ldliŋ] Weltkind *n.*

worldly ['wə:ldli] weltlich; Welt...;
~**wise** [~i'waiz] weltklug.

world|-power *pol.* ['wə:ldpauə]
Weltmacht *f;* ~**wide** weltweit;
weltumspannend; Welt...

worm [wə:m] **1.** Wurm *m* (*a. fig.*);
2. *ein Geheimnis* entlocken (*out of*
dat.); ~ *o.s.* sich schlängeln; *fig.*
sich einschleichen (*into* in *acc.*);
~**eaten** [~ə:mi:tn] wurmstichig.

worn [wə:n] *p.p. von wear 1;* ~**out**
['wə:n'aut] abgenutzt; abgetragen;
verbraucht (*a. fig.*); müde, erschöpft; abgezehrt; verhärmt.

worry ['wʌri] **1.** (sich) beunruhigen;
(sich) ärgern; sich sorgen; sich aufregen; bedrücken; zerren, (ab-)
würgen; plagen, quälen; **2.** Unruhe
f; Sorge *f;* Ärger *m;* Qual *f,*
Plage *f;* Quälgeist *m.*

worse [wə:s] schlechter; schlimmer;
~ *luck!* leider!; um so schlimmer!;
from bad to ~ vom Regen in die
Traufe; ~**n** ['wə:sn] (sich) verschlechtern.

worship ['wə:ʃip] **1.** Verehrung *f;*
Gottesdienst *m;* Kult *m;* **2.** ver-
ehren; anbeten; den Gottesdienst
besuchen; ~(p)er [~pə] Verehrer
(-in); Kirchgänger(in).

worst [wə:st] **1.** schlechtest; ärgst;
schlimmst; **2.** überwältigen.

worsted ['wustid] Kammgarn *n.*

worth [wə:θ] **1.** wert; ~ *reading*
lesenswert; **2.** Wert *m;* Würde *f;*
~**less** □ ['wə:θlis] wertlos; unwürdig; ~**while** ['wə:θ'wail] der
Mühe wert; ~**y** □ ['wə:ði] würdig.

would [wud] [*pret. von will 2*]
wollte; würde, möchte; pflegte;
~**be** ['wudbi:] angeblich, soge-

nannt; möglich, potentiell; Pseudo...

wound[1] [wu:nd] 1. Wunde f, Verwundung f, Verletzung f; fig. Kränkung f; 2. verwunden, verletzen (a. fig.).

wound[2] [waund] pret. u. p.p. von wind 2.

wove [wouv] pret. von weave; **~n** ['wouvən] p.p. von weave.

wow Am. [wau] 1. int. Mensch!; toll!; 2. sl. Bombenerfolg m.

wrangle ['ræŋgl] 1. streiten, (sich) zanken; 2. Streit m, Zank m.

wrap [ræp] 1. v/t. (ein)wickeln; fig. einhüllen; be **~ped up in** gehüllt sein in (acc.); ganz aufgehen in (dat.); v/i. **~ up** sich einhüllen; 2. Hülle f; engS.: Decke f; Schal m; Mantel m; **~per** ['ræpə] Hülle f, Umschlag m; a. postal **~** Streifband n; **~ping** ['ræpiŋ] Verpackung f.

wrath lit. [rɔ:θ] Zorn m, Grimm m.

wreak [ri:k] Rache üben, Zorn auslassen (upon an j-m).

wreath [ri:θ], pl. **~s** [ri:ðz] (Blumen)Gewinde n; Kranz m; Girlande f; Ring m, Kreis m; Schneewehe f; **~e** [ri:ð] [irr.] v/t. (um)winden; v/i. sich ringeln.

wreck [rek] 1. ⚓ Wrack n; Trümmer pl.; Schiffbruch m; fig. Untergang m; 2. zum Scheitern (🚂 Entgleisen) bringen; zertrümmern; vernichten; be **~ed** ⚓ scheitern; Schiffbruch erleiden; **~age** ['rekidʒ] Trümmer pl.; Wrackteile n/pl.; **~ed** schiffbrüchig; ruiniert; **~er** ['rekə] ⚓ Bergungsschiff n, -arbeiter m; Strandräuber m; Abbrucharbeiter m; Am. mot. Abschleppwagen m; **~ing** ['rekiŋ] Strandraub m; **~ company** Am. Abbruchfirma f; **~ service** Am. mot. Abschlepp-, Hilfsdienst m.

wren orn. [ren] Zaunkönig m.

wrench [rentʃ] 1. drehen; reißen; entwinden (from s.o. j-m); verdrehen (a. fig.); verrenken; **~ open** aufreißen; 2. Ruck m; Verrenkung f; fig. Schmerz m; ⊕ Schraubenschlüssel m.

wrest [rest] reißen; verdrehen; entreißen; **~le** ['resl] ringen (mit); **~ling** [**~**liŋ] Ringkampf m, Ringen n.

wretch [retʃ] Elende(r m) f; Kerl m. **wretched** □ ['retʃid] elend.

wriggle ['rigl] sich winden od. schlängeln; **~ out of** sich drücken von et.

wright [rait] ...macher m,...bauer m.

wring [riŋ] [irr.] Hände ringen; (aus)wringen; pressen; Hals umdrehen; abringen (from s.o. j-m); **~ s.o.'s heart** j-m zu Herzen gehen.

wrinkle ['riŋkl] 1. Runzel f; Falte f; Wink m; Trick m; 2. (sich) runzeln.

wrist [rist] Handgelenk n; **~ watch** Armbanduhr f; **~band** ['ristbænd] Bündchen n, (Hemd)Manschette f.

writ [rit] Erlaß m; (gerichtlicher) Befehl; Holy ⒉ Heilige Schrift.

write [rait] [irr.] schreiben; **~ down** auf-, niederschreiben; ausarbeiten; hervorheben; **~r** ['raitə] Schreiber (-in); Verfasser(in); Schriftsteller (-in).

writhe [raið] sich krümmen.

writing ['raitiŋ] Schreiben n; Aufsatz m; Werk n; Schrift f; Schriftstück n; Urkunde f; Stil m; attr. Schreib...; in **~** schriftlich; **~-case** Schreibmappe f; **~-desk** Schreibtisch m; **~-paper** Schreibpapier n.

written ['ritn] 1. p.p. von write; 2. adj. schriftlich.

wrong [rɔŋ] 1. □ unrecht; verkehrt, falsch; be **~** unrecht haben; in Unordnung sein; falsch gehen (Uhr); go **~** schiefgehen; on the **~** side of sixty über die 60 hinaus; 2. Unrecht n; Beleidigung f; 3. unrecht tun (dat.); ungerecht behandeln; **~doer** ['rɔŋ'duə] Übeltäter(in); **~ful** □ ['rɔŋful] ungerecht; unrechtmäßig.

wrote [rout] pret. von write.

wrought [rɔ:t] pret. u. p.p. von work 2; **~ iron** Schmiedeeisen n; **~-iron** ['rɔ:t'aiən] schmiedeeisern; **~-up** erregt.

wrung [rʌŋ] pret. u. p.p. von wring.

wry □ [rai] schief, krumm, verzerrt.

X, Y

Xmas ['krisməs] = Christmas.

X-ray ['eks'rei] 1. **~s** pl. Röntgenstrahlen m/pl.; 2. Röntgen...; 3. durchleuchten, röntgen.

xylophone ♪ ['zailəfoun] Xylophon n.

yacht ⚓ [jɔt] 1. (Motor)Jacht f; Segelboot n; 2. auf e-r Jacht fahren; segeln; **~-club** ['jɔtklʌb] Segel-, Jachtklub m; **~ing** ['jɔtiŋ] Segelsport m; attr. Segel...

Yankee F ['jæŋki] Yankee m (Amerikaner, bsd. der Nordstaaten).

yap [jæp] kläffen; F quasseln.

yard [jɑ:d] Yard n, englische Elle (= 0,914 m); ⚓ Rah(e) f; Hof m; (Bau-, Stapel)Platz m; Am. Garten m (um das Haus); **~-measure**

['jɑːdmeʒə], **~stick** Yardstock *m*, -maß *n*.

yarn [jɑːn] **1.** Garn *n*; F Seemannsgarn *n*; abenteuerliche Geschichte; **2.** F erzählen.

yawl ⚓ [jɔːl] Jolle *f*.

yawn [jɔːn] **1.** gähnen; **2.** Gähnen *n*.

ye †, *poet.*, *co.* [jiː] ihr.

yea †, *prov.* [jei] **1.** ja; **2.** Ja *n*.

year [jəː] Jahr *n*; **~ly** ['jəːli] jährlich.

yearn [jəːn] sich sehnen, verlangen; **~ing** ['jəːniŋ] **1.** Sehnen *n*, Sehnsucht *f*; **2.** □ sehnsüchtig.

yeast [jiːst] Hefe *f*; Schaum *m*.

yegg(man) *Am. sl.* ['jeg(mən)] Stromer *m*; Einbrecher *m*.

yell [jel] **1.** (gellend) schreien; aufschreien; **2.** (gellender) Schrei; anfeuernder Ruf.

yellow ['jelou] **1.** gelb; F hasenfüßig (*feig*); Sensations...; Hetz...; **2.** Gelb *n*; **3.** (sich) gelb färben; **~ed** vergilbt; **~ fever** 🏥 Gelbfieber *n*; **~ish** [~ouiʃ] gelblich.

yelp [jelp] **1.** Gekläff *n*; **2.** kläffen.

yen *Am. sl.* [jen] brennendes Verlangen.

yeoman ['joumən] freier Bauer.

yep *Am.* F [jep] ja.

yes [jes] **1.** ja; doch; **2.** Ja *n*.

yesterday ['jestədi] gestern.

yet [jet] **1.** *adv.* noch; bis jetzt; schon; sogar; *as ~* bis jetzt; *not ~* noch nicht; **2.** *cj.* (je)doch, dennoch, trotzdem.

yew ⚘ [juː] Eibe *f*, Taxus *m*.

yield [jiːld] **1.** *v/t.* hervorbringen, liefern; ergeben; *Gewinn* (ein)bringen; gewähren; übergeben; zugestehen; *v/i.* ♂ tragen; sich fügen; nachgeben; **2.** Ertrag *m*; **~ing** □ ['jiːldiŋ] nachgebend; *fig.* nachgiebig.

yip *Am.* F [jip] jaulen.

yod|el, ~le ['joudl] **1.** Jodler *m*; **2.** jodeln.

yoke [jouk] **1.** Joch *n* (*a. fig.*); Paar *n* (Ochsen); Schultertrage *f*; **2.** an-, zs.-spannen; *fig.* paaren (*to* mit).

yolk [jouk] (Ei)Dotter *m*, *n*, Eigelb *n*.

yon [jon], **~der** *lit.* ['jondə] **1.** jene(r, -s); jenseitig; **2.** dort drüben.

yore [jɔː]: *of ~* ehemals, ehedem.

you [juː, ju] ihr; du, Sie; man.

young [jʌŋ] **1.** □ jung; *von Kindern a.* klein; **2.** (Tier)Junge(s) *n*; (Tier)Junge *pl.*; *with ~* trächtig; **~ster** ['jʌŋstə] Junge *m*.

your [jɔː] euer(e); dein(e), Ihr(e); **~s** [jɔːz] der (die, das) eurige, deinige, Ihrige; euer; dein, Ihr; **~self** [jɔːˈself], *pl.* **~selves** [~lvz] (du, ihr, Sie) selbst; dich, euch, Sie (selbst), sich (selbst); *by ~* allein.

youth [juːθ], *pl.* **~s** [juːðz] Jugend *f*; Jüngling *m*; **~ hostel** Jugendherberge *f*; **~ful** □ ['juːθful] jugendlich.

yule *lit.* [juːl] Weihnacht *f*.

Z

zeal [ziːl] Eifer *m*; **~ot** ['zelət] Eiferer *m*; **~ous** □ [~əs] eifrig; eifrig bedacht (*for* auf *acc.*); innig, heiß.

zebra *zo.* ['ziːbrə] Zebra *n*; **~ crossing** Fußgängerüberweg *m*.

zenith ['zeniθ] Zenit *m*; *fig.* Höhepunkt *m*.

zero ['ziərou] Null *f*; Nullpunkt *m*.

zest [zest] **1.** Würze *f* (*a. fig.*); Lust *f*, Freude *f*; Genuß *m*; **2.** würzen.

zigzag ['zigzæg] Zickzack *m*.

zinc [ziŋk] **1.** *min.* Zink *n*; **2.** verzinken.

zip [zip] Schwirren *n*; F Schwung *m*; **~-fastener** ['zipfɑːsnə], **~per** ['zipə] Reißverschluß *m*.

zodiac *ast.* ['zoudiæk] Tierkreis *m*.

zone [zoun] Zone *f*; *fig.* Gebiet *n*.

Zoo F [zuː] Zoo *m*.

zoolog|ical □ [zouəˈlodʒikəl] zoologisch; **~y** [zouˈolədʒi] Zoologie *f*.

Alphabetical List of the German Irregular Verbs

Infinitive — Preterite — Past Participle

backen - backte (buk) - gebacken
bedingen - bedang (bedingte) - bedungen (*conditional*: bedingt)
befehlen - befahl - befohlen
beginnen - begann - begonnen
beißen - biß - gebissen
bergen - barg - geborgen
bersten - barst - geborsten
bewegen - bewog - bewogen
biegen - bog - gebogen
bieten - bot - geboten
binden - band - gebunden
bitten - bat - gebeten
blasen - blies - geblasen
bleiben - blieb - geblieben
bleichen - blich - geblichen
braten - briet - gebraten
brauchen - brauchte - gebraucht (*v*/*aux.* brauchen)
brechen - brach - gebrochen
brennen - brannte - gebrannt
bringen - brachte - gebracht
denken - dachte - gedacht
dreschen - drosch - gedroschen
dringen - drang - gedrungen
dürfen - durfte - gedurft (*v*/*aux.* dürfen)
empfehlen - empfahl - empfohlen
erlöschen - erlosch - erloschen
erschrecken - erschrak - erschrocken
essen - aß - gegessen
fahren - fuhr - gefahren
fallen - fiel - gefallen
fangen - fing - gefangen
fechten - focht - gefochten
finden - fand - gefunden
flechten - flocht - geflochten
fliegen - flog - geflogen
fliehen - floh - geflohen
fließen - floß - geflossen
fressen - fraß - gefressen
frieren - fror - gefroren
gären - gor (*esp. fig.* gärte) - gegoren (*esp. fig.* gegärt)
gebären - gebar - geboren
geben - gab - gegeben
gedeihen - gedieh - gediehen
gehen - ging - gegangen
gelingen - gelang - gelungen
gelten - galt - gegolten
genesen - genas - genesen
genießen - genoß - genossen
geschehen - geschah - geschehen
gewinnen - gewann - gewonnen

gießen - goß - gegossen
gleichen - glich - geglichen
gleiten - glitt - geglitten
glimmen - glomm - geglommen
graben - grub - gegraben
greifen - griff - gegriffen
haben - hatte - gehabt
halten - hielt - gehalten
hängen - hing - gehangen
hauen - haute (hieb) - gehauen
heben - hob - gehoben
heißen - hieß - geheißen
helfen - half - geholfen
kennen - kannte - gekannt
klingen - klang - geklungen
kneifen - kniff - gekniffen
kommen - kam - gekommen
können - konnte - gekonnt (*v*/*aux.* können)
kriechen - kroch - gekrochen
laden - lud - geladen
lassen - ließ - gelassen (*v*/*aux.* lassen)
laufen - lief - gelaufen
leiden - litt - gelitten
leihen - lieh - geliehen
lesen - las - gelesen
liegen - lag - gelegen
lügen - log - gelogen
mahlen - mahlte - gemahlen
meiden - mied - gemieden
melken - melkte (molk) - gemolken (gemelkt)
messen - maß - gemessen
mißlingen - mißlang - mißlungen
mögen - mochte - gemocht (*v*/*aux.* mögen)
müssen - mußte - gemußt (*v*/*aux.* müssen)
nehmen - nahm - genommen
nennen - nannte - genannt
pfeifen - pfiff - gepfiffen
preisen - pries - gepriesen
quellen - quoll - gequollen
raten - riet - geraten
reiben - rieb - gerieben
reißen - riß - gerissen
reiten - ritt - geritten
rennen - rannte - gerannt
riechen - roch - gerochen
ringen - rang - gerungen
rinnen - rann - geronnen
rufen - rief - gerufen
salzen - salzte - gesalzen (gesalzt)
saufen - soff - gesoffen

saugen - sog - gesogen
schaffen - schuf - geschaffen
schallen - schallte (scholl) - geschallt (*for erschallen a.* erschollen)
scheiden - schied - geschieden
scheinen - schien - geschienen
schelten - schalt - gescholten
scheren - schor - geschoren
schieben - schob - geschoben
schießen - schoß - geschossen
schinden - schund - geschunden
schlafen - schlief - geschlafen
schlagen - schlug - geschlagen
schleichen - schlich - geschlichen
schleifen - schliff - geschliffen
schließen - schloß - geschlossen
schlingen - schlang - geschlungen
schmeißen - schmiß - geschmissen
schmelzen - schmolz - geschmolzen
schneiden - schnitt - geschnitten
schrecken - schrak - † geschrocken
schreiben - schrieb - geschrieben
schreien - schrie - geschrie(e)n
schreiten - schritt - geschritten
schweigen - schwieg - geschwiegen
schwellen - schwoll - geschwollen
schwimmen - schwamm - geschwommen
schwinden - schwand - geschwunden
schwingen - schwang - geschwungen
schwören - schwor - geschworen
sehen - sah - gesehen
sein - war - gewesen
senden - sandte - gesandt
sieden - sott - gesotten
singen - sang - gesungen
sinken - sank - gesunken
sinnen - sann - gesonnen
sitzen - saß - gesessen
sollen - sollte - gesollt (*v/aux.* sollen)
spalten - spaltete - gespalten (gespaltet)
speien - spie - gespie(e)n
spinnen - spann - gesponnen
sprechen - sprach - gesprochen

sprießen - sproß - gesprossen
springen - sprang - gesprungen
stechen - stach - gestochen
stecken - steckte (stak) - gesteckt
stehen - stand - gestanden
stehlen - stahl - gestohlen
steigen - stieg - gestiegen
sterben - starb - gestorben
stieben - stob - gestoben
stinken - stank - gestunken
stoßen - stieß - gestoßen
streichen - strich - gestrichen
streiten - stritt - gestritten
tragen - trug - getragen
treffen - traf - getroffen
treiben - trieb - getrieben
treten - trat - getreten
triefen - triefte (troff) - getrieft
trinken - trank - getrunken
trügen - trog - getrogen
tun - tat - getan
verderben - verdarb - verdorben
verdrießen - verdroß - verdrossen
vergessen - vergaß - vergessen
verlieren - verlor - verloren
verschleißen - verschliß - verschlissen
verzeihen - verzieh - verziehen
wachsen - wuchs - gewachsen
wägen - wog (⬆ wägte) - gewogen (⬆ gewägt)
waschen - wusch - gewaschen
weben - wob - gewoben
weichen - wich - gewichen
weisen - wies - gewiesen
wenden - wandte - gewandt
werben - warb - geworben
werden - wurde - geworden (worden*)
werfen - warf - geworfen
wiegen - wog - gewogen
winden - wand - gewunden
wissen - wußte - gewußt
wollen - wollte - gewollt (*v/aux.* wollen)
wringen - wrang - gewrungen
ziehen - zog - gezogen
zwingen - zwang - gezwungen

* only in connexion with the past participles of other verbs, *e.g. er ist gesehen worden* he has been seen.

Alphabetical List of the English Irregular Verbs

Infinitive — Preterite — Past Participle

Irregular forms marked with asterisks (*) can be exchanged for the regular forms.

abide (*bleiben*) - abode* - abode*
arise (*sich erheben*) - arose - arisen
awake (*erwachen*) - awoke - awoke*
be (*sein*) - was - been
bear (*tragen; gebären*) - bore - *getragen*: borne - *geboren*: born
beat (*schlagen*) - beat - beat(en)
become (*werden*) - became - become
beget (*zeugen*) - begot - begotten
begin (*anfangen*) - began - begun
bend (*beugen*) - bent - bent
bereave (*berauben*) - bereft* - bereft*
beseech (*ersuchen*) - besought - besought
bet (*wetten*) - bet* - bet*
bid ([*ge*]*bieten*) - bade, bid - bid(den)
bide (*abwarten*) - bode* - bided
bind (*binden*) - bound - bound
bite (*beißen*) - bit - bitten
bleed (*bluten*) - bled - bled
blend (*mischen*) - blent* - blent*
blow (*blasen; blühen*) - blew - blown
break (*brechen*) - broke - broken
breed (*aufziehen*) - bred - bred
bring (*bringen*) - brought - brought
build (*bauen*) - built - built
burn (*brennen*) - burnt* - burnt*
burst (*bersten*) - burst - burst
buy (*kaufen*) - bought - bought
cast (*werfen*) - cast - cast
catch (*fangen*) - caught - caught
chide (*schelten*) - chid - chid(den)*
choose (*wählen*) - chose - chosen
cleave ([*sich*] *spalten*) cleft, clove* - cleft, cloven*
cling (*sich* [*an*]*klammern*) - clung - clung
clothe ([*an-, be*]*kleiden*) - clad* - clad*
come (*kommen*) - came - come
cost (*kosten*) - cost - cost
creep (*kriechen*) - crept - crept
crow (*krähen*) - crew* - crowed
cut (*schneiden*) - cut - cut
deal (*handeln*) - dealt - dealt
dig (*graben*) - dug - dug
do (*tun*) - did - done
draw (*ziehen*) - drew - drawn
dream (*träumen*) - dreamt* - dreamt*
drink (*trinken*) - drank - drunk
drive (*treiben; fahren*) - drove - driven
dwell (*wohnen*) - dwelt - dwelt

eat (*essen*) - ate, eat - eaten
fall (*fallen*) - fell - fallen
feed (*füttern*) - fed - fed
feel (*fühlen*) - felt - felt
fight (*kämpfen*) - fought - fought
find (*finden*) - found - found
flee (*fliehen*) - fled - fled
fling (*schleudern*) - flung - flung
fly (*fliegen*) - flew - flown
forbid (*verbieten*) - forbade - forbidden
forget (*vergessen*) - forgot - forgotten
forsake (*aufgeben; verlassen*) - forsook - forsaken
freeze ([*ge*]*frieren*) - froze - frozen
get (*bekommen*) - got - got, *Am.* gotten
gild (*vergolden*) - gilt* - gilt*
gird ([*um*]*gürten*) - girt* - girt*
give (*geben*) - gave - given
go (*gehen*) - went - gone
grave ([*ein*]*graben*) - graved - graven*
grind (*mahlen*) - ground - ground
grow (*wachsen*) - grew - grown
hang (*hängen*) - hung - hung
have (*haben*) - had - had
hear (*hören*) - heard - heard
heave (*heben*) - hove* - hove*
hew (*hauen, hacken*) - hewed - hewn*
hide (*verbergen*) - hid - hid(den)
hit (*treffen*) - hit - hit
hold (*halten*) - held - held
hurt (*verletzen*) - hurt - hurt
keep (*halten*) - kept - kept
kneel (*knien*) - knelt* - knelt*
knit (*stricken*) - knit* - knit*
know (*wissen*) - knew - known
lay (*legen*) - laid - laid
lead (*führen*) - led - led
lean ([*sich*] [*an*]*lehnen*) - leant* - leant*
leap ([*über*]*springen*) - leapt* - leapt*
learn (*lernen*) - learnt* - learnt*
leave (*verlassen*) - left - left
lend (*leihen*) - lent - lent
let (*lassen*) - let - let
lie (*liegen*) - lay - lain
light (*anzünden*) - lit* - lit*
lose (*verlieren*) - lost - lost
make (*machen*) - made - made
mean (*meinen*) - meant - meant
meet (*begegnen*) - met - met
mow (*mähen*) - mowed - mown*

pay (*zahlen*) - paid - paid
pen (*einpferchen*) - pent - pent
put (*setzen, stellen*) - put - put
read (*lesen*) - read - read
rend ([*zer*]*reißen*) - rent - rent
rid (*befreien*) - rid* - rid*
ride (*reiten*) - rode - ridden
ring (*läuten*) - rang - rung
rise (*aufstehen*) - rose - risen
rive ([*sich*] *spalten*) - rived - riven*
run (*laufen*) - ran - run
saw (*sägen*) - sawed - sawn*
say (*sagen*) - said - said
see (*sehen*) - saw - seen
seek (*suchen*) - sought - sought
sell (*verkaufen*) - sold - sold
send (*senden*) - sent - sent
set (*setzen*) - set - set
sew (*nähen*) - sewed - sewn*
shake (*schütteln*) - shook - shaken
shave ([*sich*] *rasieren*) - shaved - shaven*
shear (*scheren*) - sheared - shorn
shed (*ausgießen*) - shed - shed
shine (*scheinen*) - shone - shone
shoe (*beschuhen*) - shod - shod
shoot (*schießen*) - shot - shot
show (*zeigen*) - showed - shown*
shred ([*zer*]*schnitzeln, zerfetzen*) - shred* - shred*
shrink (*einschrumpfen*) - shrank - shrunk
shut (*schließen*) - shut - shut
sing (*singen*) - sang - sung
sink (*sinken*) - sank - sunk
sit (*sitzen*) - sat - sat
slay (*erschlagen*) - slew - slain
sleep (*schlafen*) - slept - slept
slide (*gleiten*) - slid - slid
sling (*schleudern*) - slung - slung
slink (*schleichen*) - slunk - slunk
slip (*schlüpfen, gleiten*) - slipt* - slipt*
slit (*schlitzen*) - slit - slit
smell (*riechen*) - smelt* - smelt*
smite (*schlagen*) - smote - smitten, smote
sow ([*aus*]*säen*) - sowed - sown*
speak (*sprechen*) - spoke - spoken
speed (*eilen*) - sped* - sped*
spell (*buchstabieren*) - spelt* - spelt*
spend (*ausgeben*) - spent - spent

spill (*verschütten*) - spilt* - spilt*
spin (*spinnen*) - spun - spun
spit ([*aus*]*spucken*) - spat - spat
split (*spalten*) - split - split
spoil (*verderben*) - spoilt* - spoilt*
spread (*verbreiten*) - spread - spread
spring (*springen*) - sprang - sprung
stand (*stehen*) - stood - stood
stave (*den Boden einschlagen*) - stove* - stove*
steal (*stehlen*) - stole - stolen
stick (*stecken*) - stuck - stuck
sting (*stechen*) - stung - stung
stink (*stinken*) - stank - stunk
strew ([*be*]*streuen*) - strewed - strewn*
stride (*über-, durchschreiten*) - strode - stridden
strike (*schlagen*) - struck - struck
string (*spannen*) - strung - strung
strive (*streben*) - strove - striven
swear (*schwören*) - swore - sworn
sweat (*schwitzen*) - sweat* - sweat*
sweep (*fegen*) - swept - swept
swell ([*an*]*schwellen*) - swelled - swollen
swim (*schwimmen*) - swam - swum
swing (*schwingen*) - swung - swung
take (*nehmen*) - took - taken
teach (*lehren*) - taught - taught
tear (*ziehen*) - tore - torn
tell (*sagen*) - told - told
think (*denken*) - thought - thought
thrive (*gedeihen*) - throve* - thriven*
throw (*werfen*) - threw - thrown
thrust (*stoßen*) - thrust - thrust
tread (*treten*) - trod - trodden
wake (*wachen*) - woke* - woke(n)*
wax (*zunehmen*) - waxed - waxen*
wear ([*Kleider*] *tragen*) - wore - worn
weave (*weben*) - wove - woven
weep (*weinen*) - wept - wept
wet (*nässen*) - wet* - wet*
win (*gewinnen*) - won - won
wind (*winden*) - wound - wound
work (*arbeiten*) - wrought* - wrought*
wreathe ([*um*]*winden*) - wreathed - wreathen*
wring ([*aus*]*wringen*) - wrung - wrung
write (*schreiben*) - wrote - written

German Proper Names

Aachen ['ɑːxən] *n* Aachen, Aix-la-Chapelle.

Adenauer ['aːdənauər] *first chancellor of the German Federal Republic.*

Adler ['aːdlər] *Austrian psychologist.*

Adria ['aːdria] *f* Adriatic Sea.

Afrika ['aːfrika] *n* Africa.

Ägypten [ɛ'gyptən] *n* Egypt.

Albanien [al'baːnjən] *n* Albania.

Algerien [al'geːrjən] *n* Algeria.

Algier ['alʒiːr] *n* Algiers.

Allgäu ['algɔy] *n* Al(l)gäu (*region of Bavaria*).

Alpen ['alpən] *pl.* Alps *pl.*

Amerika [a'meːrika] *n* America.

Anden ['andən] *pl.* the Andes *pl.*

Antillen [an'tilən] *f/pl.* Antilles *pl.*

Antwerpen [ant'verpən] *n* Antwerp.

Apenninen [ape'niːnən] *m/pl.* the Apennines *pl.*

Argentinien [argen'tiːnjən] *n* Argentina, the Argentine.

Ärmelkanal ['ɛrməlkanaːl] *m* English Channel.

Asien ['aːzjən] *n* Asia.

Athen [a'teːn] *n* Athens.

Äthiopien [ɛti'oːpjən] Ethiopia.

Atlantik [at'lantik] *m* Atlantic.

Australien [au'straːljən] *n* Australia.

Bach [bax] *German composer.*

Baden-Württemberg ['baːdən-'vyrtəmberk] *n Land of the German Federal Republic.*

Barlach ['barlax] *German sculptor.*

Basel ['baːzəl] *n* Bâle, Basle.

Bayern ['baiərn] *n* Bavaria (*Land of the German Federal Republic*).

Becher ['beçər] *German poet.*

Beckmann ['bɛkman] *German painter.*

Beethoven ['beːthoːfən] *German composer.*

Belgien ['bɛlgjən] *n* Belgium.

Belgrad ['belgraːt] *n* Belgrade.

Berg [berk] *Austrian composer.*

Berlin [ber'liːn] *n* Berlin.

Bermuda-Inseln [ber'muːda ?inzəln] *f/pl.* Bermudas *pl.*

Bern [bern] *n* Bern(e).

Bismarck ['bismark] *German statesman.*

Bloch [blɔx] *German philosopher.*

Böcklin ['bœkliːn] *German painter.*

Bodensee ['boːdənzeː] *m* Lake of Constance.

Böhm [bøːm] *Austrian conductor.*

Böhmen ['bøːmən] *n* Bohemia.

Böll [bœl] *German author.*

Bonn [bɔn] *n capital of the German Federal Republic.*

Brahms [braːms] *German composer.*

Brandt [brant] *German politician.*

Brasilien [bra'ziːljən] *n* Brazil.

Braunschweig ['braunʃvaik] *n* Brunswick.

Brecht [brɛçt] *German dramatist.*

Bremen ['breːmən] *n Land of the German Federal Republic.*

Bruckner ['bruknər] *Austrian composer.*

Brüssel ['brysəl] *n* Brussels.

Budapest ['buːdapest] *n* Budapest.

Bukarest ['buːkarest] *n* Bucharest.

Bulgarien [bul'gaːrjən] *n* Bulgaria.

Calais [ka'lɛ] *n*: Straße von ~ Straits of Dover.

Calvin [kal'viːn] *Swiss religious reformer.*

Chile ['tʃiːlə] *n* Chile.

China ['çiːna] *n* China.

Christus ['kristus] *m* Christ.

Daimler ['daimlər] *German inventor.*

Dänemark ['dɛːnəmark] *n* Denmark.

Deutschland ['dɔytʃlant] *n* Germany.

Diesel ['diːzəl] *German inventor.*

Döblin [dø'bliːn] *German author.*

Dolomiten [dolo'miːtən] *pl.* the Dolomites *pl.*

Donau ['doːnau] *f* Danube.

Dortmund ['dɔrtmunt] *n industrial city in West Germany.*

Dresden ['dreːsdən] *n capital of Saxony.*

Dublin ['dʌblin] *n* Dublin.

Dünkirchen ['dyːnkirçən] *n* Dunkirk.

Dürer ['dyːrər] *German painter.*

Dürrenmatt ['dyrənmat] *Swiss dramatist.*

Düsseldorf ['dysəldɔrf] *n capital of North Rhine-Westphalia.*

Ebert ['eːbərt] *first president of the Weimar Republic.*

Egk [ɛk] *German composer.*

Eichendorff ['aiçəndɔrf] *German poet.*

Eiger ['aigər] *Swiss mountain.*

Einstein ['ainʃtain] *German physicist.*

Elbe ['ɛlbə] *f German river.*

Elsaß ['ɛlzas] *n* Alsace.

Engels ['ɛŋəls] *German philosopher.*

England ['ɛŋlant] n England.
Essen ['ɛsən] n industrial city in West Germany.
Europa [ɔy'ro:pa] n Europe.

Feldberg ['fɛltbɛrk] German mountain.
Finnland ['finlant] n Finland.
Florenz [flo'rɛnts] n Florence.
Fontane [fɔn'ta:nə] German author.
Franken ['fraŋkən] n Franconia.
Frankfurt ['fraŋkfurt] n Frankfurt.
Frankreich ['fraŋkraɪç] n France.
Freud [frɔyt] Austrian psychologist.
Frisch [friʃ] Swiss author.

Garmisch ['garmiʃ] n health resort in Bavaria.
Genf [gɛnf] n Geneva; ⸤er See m Lake of Geneva.
Genua ['ge:nua] n Genoa.
Gibraltar [gi'braltar] n Gibraltar.
Goethe ['gø:tə] German poet.
Grass [gras] German author.
Graubünden [grau'byndən] n the Grisons.
Griechenland ['gri:çənlant] n Greece.
Grillparzer ['grilpartsər] Austrian dramatist.
Grönland ['grø:nlant] n Greenland.
Gropius ['gro:pjus] German architect.   [Great Britain.)
Großbritannien[gro:sbri'tanjən]n)
Großglockner [gro:s'glɔknər] Austrian mountain.
Grünewald ['gry:nəvalt] German painter.

Haag [ha:k]: Den ⸤ The Hague.
Habsburg hist. ['ha:psburk] n Hapsburg (German dynasty).
Hahn [ha:n] German chemist.
Hamburg ['hamburk] n Land of the German Federal Republic.
Händel ['hɛndəl] Handel (German composer).
Hannover [ha'no:fər] n Hanover (capital of Lower Saxony).
Hartmann ['hartman] German composer.
Harz [ha:rts] m Harz Mountains pl.
Hauptmann ['hauptman] German dramatist.
Haydn ['haɪdən] Austrian composer.
Hegel ['he:gəl] German philosopher.
Heidegger ['haɪdegər] German philosopher.
Heidelberg ['haɪdəlbɛrk] n university town in West Germany.
Heine ['haɪnə] German poet.
Heinemann ['haɪnəman] president of the German Federal Republic.
Heisenberg ['haɪzənbɛrk] German physicist.
Heißenbüttel ['haɪsənbytəl] German poet.
Helgoland ['hɛlgolant] n Heligoland.

Helsinki ['hɛlziŋki] n Helsinki.
Henze ['hɛntsə] German composer.
Hesse ['hɛsə] German poet.
Hessen ['hɛsən] n Hesse (Land of the German Federal Republic).
Heuß [hɔys] first president of the German Federal Republic.
Hindemith ['hindəmit] German composer.
Hohenzollern hist. [ho:ən'tsɔlərn] n German dynasty.
Hölderlin ['hœldərli:n] German poet.
Holland ['hɔlant] n Holland.

Indien ['indjən] n India.
Inn [in] m affluent of the Danube.
Innsbruck ['insbruk] n capital of the Tyrol.
Irak [i'ra:k] m Iraq, a. Irak.
Irland ['irlant] n Ireland.
Island ['i:slant] n Iceland.
Israel ['israɛl] n Israel.
Italien [i'ta:ljən] n Italy.

Japan ['ja:pan] n Japan.
Jaspers ['jaspərs] German philosopher.
Jesus ['je:zus] m Jesus.
Jordanien [jɔr'da:njən] n Jordan.
Jugoslawien [jugo'sla:vjən]n Yugoslavia.
Jung [juŋ] Swiss psychologist.
Jungfrau ['juŋfrau] f Swiss mountain.

Kafka ['kafka] Czech poet.
Kanada ['kanada] n Canada.
Kant [kant] German philosopher.
Karajan ['ka:rajan] Austrian conductor.
Karlsruhe [karls'ru:ə] n city in South-Western Germany.
Kärnten ['kɛrntən] n Carinthia.
Kassel ['kasəl] n Cassel.
Kästner ['kɛstnər] German author.
Kiel [ki:l] n capital of Schleswig-Holstein.
Kiesinger ['ki:ziŋər] German politician.
Klee [kle:] German painter.
Kleist [klaɪst] German poet.
Klemperer ['klɛmpərər] German conductor.
Koblenz ['ko:blɛnts] n Coblenz, Koblenz.
Kokoschka [ko'kɔʃka] German painter.
Köln [kœln] n Cologne.
Kolumbien [ko'lumbjən] n Columbia.
Kolumbus [ko'lumbus] m Columbus.
Königsberg ['kø:niçsbɛrk] n capital of East Prussia.
Konstanz ['kɔnstants] n Constance.
Kopenhagen [kopən'ha:gən] n Copenhagen.
Kordilleren [kɔrdil'je:rən] f/pl. the Cordilleras pl.

Kreml ['kreːməl] *m the* Kremlin.

Leibniz ['laɪbnits] *German philosopher.*
Leipzig ['laɪptsiç] *n* Leipsic.
Lessing ['lɛsiŋ] *German poet.*
Libanon ['liːbanɔn] *m* Lebanon.
Liebig ['liːbiç] *German chemist.*
Lissabon ['lisabɔn] *n* Lisbon.
London ['lɔndɔn] *n* London.
Lothringen ['loːtriŋən] *n* Lorraine.
Lübeck ['lyːbɛk] *n city in West Germany.*
Luther ['lutər] *German religious reformer.*
Luxemburg ['luksəmburk] *n* Luxemb(o)urg.
Luzern [lu'tsɛrn] *n* Lucerne.

Maas [mɑːs] *f* Meuse.
Madrid [ma'drit] *n* Madrid.
Mahler ['mɑːlər] *Austrian composer.*
Mailand ['maɪlant] *n* Milan.
Main [maɪn] *m German river.*
Mainz [maɪnts] *n* Mayence (*capital of Rhineland-Palatinate*).
Mann [man] *name of three German authors.*
Marokko [ma'rɔko] *n* Morocco.
Marx [marks] *German philosopher.*
Matterhorn ['matərhɔrn] *Swiss mountain.*
Meißen ['maɪsən] *n* Meissen.
Meitner ['maɪtnər] *German female physicist.*
Memel ['meːməl] *f frontier river in East Prussia.*
Menzel ['mɛntsəl] *German painter.*
Mexiko ['mɛksiko] *n* Mexico.
Mies van der Rohe ['miːsfandər-'roːə] *German architect.*
Mittelamerika ['mitəlʔa'meːrika] *n* Central America.
Mitteleuropa ['mitəlʔɔy'roːpa] *n* Central Europe.
Mittelmeer ['mitəlmeːr] *n* Mediterranean (Sea).
Moldau ['mɔldau] *f Bohemian river.*
Mörike ['møːrikə] *German poet.*
Mosel ['moːzəl] *f* Moselle.
Mössbauer ['mœsbauər] *German physicist.*
Moskau ['mɔskau] *n* Moscow.
Mozart ['moːtsart] *Austrian composer.*
München ['mynçən] *n* Munich (*capital of Bavaria*).

Neapel [ne'ɑːpəl] *n* Naples.
Neisse ['naɪsə] *f German river.*
Neufundland [nɔy'funtlant] *n* Newfoundland.
Neuseeland [nɔy'zeːlant] *n* New Zealand.
Niederlande ['niːdərlandə] *n/pl. the* Netherlands *pl.*
Niedersachsen ['niːdərzaksən] *n* Lower Saxony (*Land of the German Federal Republic*).

Nietzsche ['niːtʃə] *German philosopher.*
Nil [niːl] *m* Nile.
Nordamerika ['nɔrtʔa'meːrika] *n* North America.
Nordrhein-Westfalen ['nɔrtraɪn-vest'faːlən] *n* North Rhine-Westphalia (*Land of the German Federal Republic*).
Nordsee ['nɔrtzeː] *f* German Ocean, North Sea.
Norwegen ['nɔrveːgən] *n* Norway.
Nürnberg ['nyrnbɛrk] *n* Nuremberg.

Oder ['oːdər] *f German river.*
Orff [ɔrf] *German composer.*
Oslo ['ɔslo] *n* Oslo.
Ostasien ['ɔst'ɑːzjən] *n* Eastern Asia.
Ostende [ɔst'endə] *n* Ostend.
Österreich ['øːstəraɪç] *n* Austria.
Ostsee ['ɔstzeː] *f* Baltic.

Palästina [palɛ'stiːna] *n* Palestine.
Paris [pa'riːs] *n* Paris.
Persien ['pɛrzjən] *n* Persia.
Pfalz [pfalts] *f* Palatinate.
Philippinen [fili'piːnən] *f/pl.* Philippines *pl.,* Philippine Islands *pl.*
Planck [plaŋk] *German physicist.*
Polen ['poːlən] *n* Poland.
Pommern ['pɔmərn] *n* Pomerania.
Portugal ['pɔrtugal] *n* Portugal.
Prag [prɑːg] *n* Prague.
Preußen *hist.* ['prɔysən] *n* Prussia.
Pyrenäen [pyre'nɛːən] *pl.* Pyrenees *pl.*

Regensburg ['reːgənsburk] *n* Ratisbon.
Reykjavik ['raɪkjaviːk] *n* Reykjavik.
Rhein [raɪn] *m* Rhine.
Rheinland-Pfalz ['raɪnlant'pfalts] *n* Rhineland-Palatinate (*Land of the German Federal Republic*).
Rilke ['rilkə] *Austrian poet.*
Rom [roːm] *n* Rome.
Röntgen ['rœntgən] *German physicist.*
Ruhr [ruːr] *f German river;* **Ruhrgebiet** ['ruːrgəbiːt] *n industrial centre of West Germany.*
Rumänien [ru'mɛːnjən] *n* Ro(u)mania.
Rußland ['ruslant] *n* Russia.

Saale ['zɑːlə] *f German river.*
Saar [zɑːr] *f affluent of the Moselle;* **Saarbrücken** [zɑːr'brykən] *n capital of the Saar;* **Saarland** ['zɑːrlant] *n* Saar (*Land of the German Federal Republic*).
Sachsen ['zaksən] *n* Saxony.
Scherchen ['ʃɛrçən] *Swiss conductor.*
Schiller ['ʃilər] *German poet.*
Schlesien ['ʃleːzjən] *n* Silesia.
Schleswig-Holstein ['ʃleːsviç'hɔl-

ʃtaɪn] *n Land of the German Federal Republic.*

Schönberg [ˈʃøːnbɛrk] *Austrian composer.*

Schottland [ˈʃɔtlant] *n Scotland.*

Schubert [ˈʃuːbərt] *Austrian composer.*

Schumann [ˈʃuːman] *German composer.*

Schwaben [ˈʃvaːbən] *n Swabia.*

Schwarzwald [ˈʃvartsvalt] *m Black Forest.*

Schweden [ˈʃveːdən] *n Sweden.*

Schweiz [ʃvaɪts] *f: die ~ Switzerland.*

Sibirien [ziˈbiːrjən] *n Siberia.*

Siemens [ˈziːməns] *German inventor.*

Sizilien [ziˈtsiːljən] *n Sicily.*

Skandinavien [skandiˈnaːvjən] *n Scandinavia.*

Sofia [ˈzɔfja] *n Sofia.*

Sowjetunion [zɔˈvjɛtʔunjoːn] *f the Soviet Union.*

Spanien [ˈʃpaːnjən] *n Spain.*

Spitzweg [ˈʃpɪtsveːk] *German painter.*

Spranger [ˈʃpraŋər] *German philosopher.*

Steiermark [ˈʃtaɪərmark] *f Styria.*

Stifter [ˈʃtɪftər] *Austrian author.*

Stockholm [ˈʃtɔkhɔlm] *n Stockholm.*

Storm [ʃtɔrm] *German poet.*

Strauß [ʃtraʊs] *Austrian composer.*

Strauss [ʃtraʊs] *German composer.*

Stresemann [ˈʃtreːzəman] *German statesman.*

Stuttgart [ˈʃtutgart] *n capital of Baden-Württemberg.*

Südamerika [ˈzyːtʔaˈmeːrika] *n South America.*

Sudan [zuˈdaːn] *m S(o)udan.*

Syrien [ˈzyːrjən] *n Syria.*

Themse [ˈtɛmzə] *f Thames.*

Thoma [ˈtoːma] *German author.*

Thüringen [ˈtyːriŋən] *n Thuringia.*

Tirana [tiˈraːna] *n Tirana.*

Tirol [tiˈroːl] *n the Tyrol.*

Trakl [ˈtraːkəl] *Austrian poet.*

Tschechoslowakei [tʃɛçoslovaˈkaɪ] *f: die ~ Czechoslovakia.*

Türkei [tyrˈkaɪ] *f: die ~ Turkey.*

Ungarn [ˈuŋgarn] *n Hungary.*

Ural [uˈraːl] *m Ural (Mountains pl.).*

Vatikan [vatiˈkaːn] *m the Vatican.*

Venedig [veˈneːdiç] *n Venice.*

Vereinigte Staaten [vərˈaɪniçtə ˈʃtaːtən] *m/pl. the United States pl.*

Vierwaldstätter See [fiːrˈvaltʃtɛtər ˈzeː] *m Lake of Lucerne.*

Wagner [ˈvaːgnər] *German composer.*

Wankel [ˈvaŋkəl] *German inventor.*

Warschau [ˈvarʃaʊ] *n Warsaw.*

Weichsel [ˈvaɪksəl] *f Vistula.*

Weiß [vaɪs] *German dramatist.*

Weizsäcker [ˈvaɪtszɛkər] *German physicist.*

Werfel [ˈvɛrfəl] *Austrian author.*

Weser [ˈveːzər] *f German river.*

Westdeutschland *pol.* [ˈvɛstdɔʏtʃlant] *n West Germany.*

Wien [viːn] *n Vienna.*

Wiesbaden [ˈviːsbaːdən] *n capital of Hesse.*

Zeppelin [ˈtsɛpəliːn] *German inventor.*

Zuckmayer [ˈtsukmaɪər] *German dramatist.*

Zweig [tsvaɪg] *Austrian author.*

Zürich [ˈtsyːriç] *n Zurich.*

Zypern [ˈtsyːpərn] *n Cyprus.*

German Abbreviations

a. a. O. *am angeführten Ort* in the place cited, *abbr.* loc. cit., l. c.

Abb. *Abbildung* illustration.

Abf. *Abfahrt* departure, *abbr.* dep.

Abg. *Abgeordnete* Member of Parliament, *etc.*

Abk. *Abkürzung* abbreviation.

Abs. *Absatz* paragraph; *Absender* sender.

Abschn. *Abschnitt* paragraph, chapter. [dept.]

Abt. *Abteilung* department, *abbr.*

a. D. *außer Dienst* retired.

Adr. *Adresse* address.

AG *Aktiengesellschaft* joint-stock company, *Am.* (stock) corporation.

allg. *allgemein* general.

a. M. *am Main* on the Main.

Ank. *Ankunft* arrival.

Anm. *Anmerkung* note.

a. O. *an der Oder* on the Oder.

a. Rh. *am Rhein* on the Rhine.

Art. *Artikel* article.

atü *Atmosphärenüberdruck* atmospheric excess pressure.

Aufl. *Auflage* edition.

b. *bei* at; with; *with place names:* near, *abbr.* nr; care of, *abbr.* c/o.

Bd. *Band* volume, *abbr.* vol.; **Bde.** *Bände* volumes, *abbr.* vols.

beil. *beiliegend* enclosed.

Bem. *Bemerkung* note, comment, observation.

bes. *besonders* especially.

betr. *betreffend, betrifft, betreffs* concerning, respecting, regarding.

Betr. *Betreff, betrifft letter:* subject, re. [reference to.]

bez. *bezahlt* paid; *bezüglich* with

Bez. *Bezirk* district.

Bhf. *Bahnhof* station.

bisw. *bisweilen* sometimes, occasionally.

BIZ *Bank für Internationale Zahlungsausgleich* Bank for International Settlements.

Bln. *Berlin* Berlin.

BRD *Bundesrepublik Deutschland* Federal Republic of Germany.

BRT *Bruttoregistertonnen* gross register tons.

b. w. *bitte wenden* please turn over, *abbr.* P.T.O.

bzw. *beziehungsweise* respectively.

C *Celsius* Celsius, *abbr.* C.

ca. *circa, ungefähr, etwa* about, approximately, *abbr.* c.

cbm *Kubikmeter* cubic met|re, *Am.* -er.

ccm *Kubikzentimeter* cubic centimet|re, *Am.* -er, *abbr.* c.c.

CDU *Christlich-Demokratische Union* Christian Democratic Union.

cm *Zentimeter* centimet|re, *Am.* -er.

Co. *Kompagnon* partner; *Kompanie* Company.

CSU *Christlich-Soziale Union* Christian Social Union.

d. Ä. *der Ältere* senior, *abbr.* sen.

DB *Deutsche Bundesbahn* German Federal Railway.

DDR *Deutsche Demokratische Republik* German Democratic Republic.

DGB *Deutscher Gewerkschaftsbund* Federation of German Trade Unions.

dgl. *dergleichen, desgleichen* the like.

d. Gr. *der Große* the Great.

d. h. *das heißt* that is, *abbr.* i. e.

d. i. *das ist* that is, *abbr.* i. e.

DIN, Din *Deutsche Industrie-Norm (-en)* German Industrial Standards.

Dipl. *Diplom* diploma.

d. J. *dieses Jahres* of this year; *der Jüngere* junior, *abbr.* jr, jun.

DM *Deutsche Mark* German Mark.

d. M. *dieses Monats* instant, *abbr.* inst.

do. *dito* ditto, *abbr.* do.

d. O. *der (die, das) Obige* the above-mentioned.

dpa, DPA *Deutsche Presse-Agentur* German Press Agency.

Dr. *Doktor* Doctor, *abbr.* Dr; **~ jur.** *Doktor der Rechte* Doctor of Laws (LL.D.); **~ med.** *Doktor der Medizin* Doctor of Medicine (M.D.); **~ phil.** *Doktor der Philosophie* Doctor of Philosophy (D. ph[il]., Ph. D.); **~ theol.** *Doktor der Theologie* Doctor of Divinity (D. D.).

DRK *Deutsches Rotes Kreuz* German Red Cross.

dt(sch). *deutsch* German.

Dtz., Dtzd. *Dutzend* dozen.

d. Verf. *der Verfasser* the author.

ebd. *ebenda* in the same place.

ed. *edidit = hat (es) herausgegeben.*

eig., eigtl. *eigentlich* properly.

einschl. *einschließlich* including, inclusive, *abbr.* incl.

entspr. *entsprechend* corresponding.

Erl. *Erläuterung* explanation, (explanatory) note.

ev. *evangelisch* Protestant.

e. V. *eingetragener Verein* registered association, incorporated, *abbr.* inc.

evtl. *eventuell* perhaps, possibly.
EWG *Europäische Wirtschaftsgemeinschaft* European Economic Community, *abbr.* EEC.
exkl. *exklusive* except(ed), not included.
Expl. *Exemplar* copy.

Fa. *Firma* firm; *letter*: Messrs.
FDGB *Freier Deutscher Gewerkschaftsbund* Free Federation of German Trade Unions.
FDP *Freie Demokratische Partei* Liberal Democratic Party.
FD(-Zug) *Fernschnellzug* long-distance express.
ff. *sehr fein* extra fine; *folgende Seiten* following pages.
Forts. *Fortsetzung* continuation.
Fr. *Frau* Mrs.
frdl. *freundlich* kind.
Frl. *Fräulein* Miss.

g *Gramm* gram(me).
geb. *geboren* born; *geborene* ... née; *gebunden* bound.
Gebr. *Gebrüder* Brothers.
gef. *gefällig(st)* kind(ly).
gegr. *gegründet* founded.
geh. *geheftet* stitched.
gek. *gekürzt* abbreviated.
Ges. *Gesellschaft* association, company; society.   [registered.)
ges. gesch. *gesetzlich geschützt*
gest. *gestorben* deceased.
gez. *gezeichnet* signed, *abbr.* sgd.
GmbH *Gesellschaft mit beschränkter Haftung* limited liability company, *abbr.* Ltd., *Am.* closed corporation under German law.

ha *Hektar* hectare.
Hbf. *Hauptbahnhof* central *or* main station.
Hbg. *Hamburg* Hamburg.
h. c. *honoris causa* = ehrenhalber *academic title*: honorary.
Hr., Hrn. *Herr(n)* Mr.
hrsg. *herausgegeben* edited, *abbr.* ed.
Hrsg. *Herausgeber* editor, *abbr.* ed.

i. *im, in* in.
i. A. *im Auftrage* for, by order, under instruction.
i. allg. *im allgemeinen* in general, generally speaking.
i. Durchschn. *im Durchschnitt* on an average.
inkl. *inklusive, einschließlich* inclusive.
i. J. *im Jahre* in the year.
Ing. *Ingenieur* engineer.
Inh. *Inhaber* proprietor.
'Interpol *Internationale Kriminalpolizei-Kommission* International Criminal Police Commission, *abbr.* ICPC.
i. V. *in Vertretung* by proxy, as a substitute.

Jb. *Jahrbuch* annual.
jr., jun. *junior, der Jüngere* junior *abbr.* jr, jun.

Kap. *Kapitel* chapter.
kath. *katholisch* Catholic.
Kfm. *Kaufmann* merchant.
kfm. *kaufmännisch* commercial.
Kfz. *Kraftfahrzeug* motor vehicle.
kg *Kilogramm* kilogram(me).
KG *Kommanditgesellschaft* limited partnership.
Kl. *Klasse* class; *school*: form.
km *Kilometer* kilomet|re, *Am.* -er.
'Kripo *Kriminalpolizei* Criminal Investigation Department, *abbr.* CID.
Kto. *Konto* account, *abbr.* a/c.
kW *Kilowatt* kilowatt, *abbr.* kw.
kWh *Kilowattstunde* kilowatt hour.

l *Liter* lit|re, *Am.* -er.
LDP *Liberal-Demokratische Partei* Liberal Democratic Party.
lfd. *laufend* current, running.
lfde. Nr. *laufende Nummer* consecutive number.
Lfg., Lfrg. *Lieferung* delivery; instalment, part.
Lit. *Literatur* literature.
Lkw. *Lastkraftwagen* lorry, truck.
lt. *laut* according to.

m *Meter* met|re, *Am,* -er.
m. A. n. *meiner Ansicht nach* in my opinion.
M. d. B. *Mitglied des Bundestages* Member of the Bundestag.
m. E. *meines Erachtens* in my opinion.
MEZ *mitteleuropäische Zeit* Central European Time.
mg *Milligramm* milligram(me[s]), *abbr.* mg.
Mill. *Million(en)* million(s).
mm *Millimeter* millimet|re, *Am.* -er.
möbl. *möbliert* furnished.
MP *Militärpolizei* Military Police.
mtl. *monatlich* monthly.
m. W. *meines Wissens* as far as I know.

N *Nord(en)* north.
nachm. *nachmittags* in the afternoon, *abbr.* p. m.
n. Chr. *nach Christus* after Christ, *abbr.* A. D.
n. J. *nächsten Jahres* of next year.
n. M. *nächsten Monats* of next month.
No., Nr. *Numero, Nummer* number, *abbr.* N°.
NS *Nachschrift* postscript, *abbr.* P. S.

O *Ost(en)* east.
o. B. *ohne Befund* ♂ without findings.
od. *oder* or.

OEZ *osteuropäische Zeit* time of the East European zone.

OHG *Offene Handelsgesellschaft* ordinary partnership.

o. J. *ohne Jahr* no date.

p. Adr. *per Adresse* care of, *abbr.* c/o.

Pf *Pfennig* German coin: pfennig.

Pfd. *Pfund* German weight: pound.

PKW, Pkw. *Personenkraftwagen* (motor) car.

P. P. *praemissis praemittendis* omitting titles, to whom it may concern.

p.p., p.pa., ppa. *per procura* per proxy, *abbr.* per pro.

Prof. *Professor* professor.

PS *Pferdestärke(n)* horse-power, *abbr.* H.P., h.p.; *postscriptum, Nachschrift* postscript, *abbr.* P.S.

qkm *Quadratkilometer* square kilomet|re, *Am.* -er. [*Am.* -er.]

qm *Quadratmeter* square met|re,]

Reg. Bez. *Regierungsbezirk* administrative district.

Rel. *Religion* religion.

resp. *respektive* respectively.

S *Süd(en)* south.

S. *Seite* page.

s. *siehe* see, *abbr.* v., vid. (= vide).

s. a. *siehe auch* see also.

Sa. *Summa, Summe* sum, total.

s. d. *siehe dies* see this.

SED *Sozialistische Einheitspartei Deutschlands* United Socialist Party of Germany.

sen. *senior, der Ältere* senior.

sm *Seemeile* nautical mile.

s. o. *siehe oben* see above.

sog. *sogenannt* so-called.

SPD *Sozialdemokratische Partei Deutschlands* Social Democratic Party of Germany.

St. *Stück* piece; *Sankt* Saint.

St(d)., Stde. *Stunde* hour, *abbr.* h.

Str. *Straße* street, *abbr.* St.

s. u. *siehe unten* see below.

s. Z. *seinerzeit* at that time.

t *Tonne* ton.

tägl. *täglich* daily, per day.

Tel. *Telephon* telephone; *Telegramm* wire, cable.

TH *Technische Hochschule* technical university *or* college.

u. *und* and.

u. a. *und andere(s)* and others; *unter anderem or anderen* among other things, inter alia.

u. ä. *und ähnliche(s)* and the like.

U.A.w.g. *Um Antwort wird gebeten* an answer is requested, *répondez s'il vous plaît, abbr.* R.S.V.P.

u. dgl. (m.) *und dergleichen (mehr)* and the like.

u. d. M. *unter dem Meeresspiegel* below sea level; **ü. d. M.** *über dem Meeresspiegel* above sea level.

UdSSR *Union der Sozialistischen Sowjetrepubliken* Union of Soviet Socialist Republics.

u. E. *unseres Erachtens* in our opinion. [following.]

u. f., u. ff. *und folgende* and the]

UKW *Ultrakurzwelle* ultra-short wave, very high frequency, *abbr.* VHF.

U/min. *Umdrehungen in der Minute* revolutions per minute, r.p.m.

urspr. *ursprünglich* original(ly).

US(A) *Vereinigte Staaten (von Amerika)* United States (of America).

usw. *und so weiter* and so on, *abbr.* etc. [stances permitting.]

u. U. *unter Umständen* circum-]

v. *von, vom* of; from; by.

V *Volt* volt; *Volumen* volume.

V. *Vers* line, verse.

v. Chr. *vor Christus* before Christ, *abbr.* B. C.

VEB *Volkseigener Betrieb* People's Own Undertaking.

Verf., Vf. *Verfasser* author.

Verl. *Verlag* publishing firm; *Verleger* publisher.

vgl. *vergleiche* confer, *abbr.* cf.

v.g.u. *vorgelesen, genehmigt, unterschrieben* read, confirmed signed.

v. H. *vom Hundert* per cent.

v. J. *vorigen Jahres* of last year.

v. M. *vorigen Monats* of last month.

vorm. *vormittags* in the morning, *abbr.* a. m.; *vormals* formerly.

Vors. *Vorsitzender* chairman.

v. T. *vom Tausend* per thousand.

VW *Volkswagen* Volkswagen, People's Car.

W *West(en)* west; *Watt* watt(s).

WE *Wärmeeinheit* thermal unit.

WEZ *westeuropäische Zeit* Western European time (Greenwich time).

WGB *Weltgewerkschaftsbund* World Federation of Trade Unions, *abbr.* WFTU.

Wwe. *Witwe* widow.

Z. *Zahl* number; *Zeile* line.

z. *zu, zum, zur* at; to.

z. B. *zum Beispiel* for instance, *abbr.* e. g.

z. H(d). *zu Händen* attention of, to be delivered to, care of, *abbr.* c/o.

z. S. *zur See* of the navy.

z. T. *zum Teil* partly.

Ztg. *Zeitung* newspaper.

Ztr. *Zentner* centner.

Ztschr. *Zeitschrift* periodical.

zus. *zusammen* together.

zw. *zwischen* between; among.

z. Z(t). *zur Zeit* at the time, at present, for the time being.

American and British Proper Names

Aberdeen [æbə'di:n] *Stadt in Schottland.*
Africa ['æfrikə] Afrika *n.* [*U.S.A.*]
Alabama [ælə'bæmə] *Staat der*
Alaska [ə'læskə] *Staat der U.S.A.*
Albania [æl'beinjə] Albanien *n.*
Alberta [æl'bə:tə] *Provinz in Kanada.* [*U.S.A.*]
Alleghany ['æligeini] *Gebirge in*
Alsace ['ælsæs] Elsaß *n.*
America [ə'merikə] Amerika *n.*
Antilles [æn'tili:z] *die* Antillen.
Appalachians [æpə'leitʃjənz] *die* Appalachen (*Gebirge in U.S.A.*).
Arizona [æri'zounə] *Staat der U.S.A.* [*U.S.A.*]
Arkansas ['ɑ:kənsɔ:] *Staat der*
Arlington ['ɑ:liŋtən] *Nationalfriedhof bei Washington.*
Ascot ['æskət] *Stadt in England.*
Asia ['eiʃə] Asien *n.*
Athens ['æθinz] Athen *n.*
Australia [ɔs'treiljə] Australien *n.*
Austria ['ɔstriə] Österreich *n.*
Avon ['eivən] *Fluß in England.*
Azores [ə'zɔ:z] *die* Azoren.

Bacon ['beikən] *engl. Philosoph.*
Bahamas [bə'hɑ:məz] *die* Bahamainseln.
Balmoral [bæl'mɔrəl] *Königsschloß in Schottland.*
Bedford(shire) ['bedfəd(ʃiə)] *Grafschaft in England.*
Belfast [bel'fɑ:st] *Hauptstadt von Nordirland.*
Belgium ['beldʒəm] Belgien *n.*
Belgrade [bel'greid] Belgrad *n.*
Ben Nevis [ben'nevis] *höchster Berg in Großbritannien.*
Berkshire ['bɑ:kʃiə] *Grafschaft in England.*
Bermudas [bə:'mju:dəz] *die* Bermudainseln.
Bern(e) [bə:n] Bern *n.*
Birmingham ['bə:miŋəm] *Industriestadt in England* [Biskaya.]
Biscay ['biskei]: *Bay of* ~ *Golf m von*
Boston ['bɔstən] *Stadt in U.S.A.*
Bournemouth ['bɔ:nməθ] *Seebad in England.*
Brighton ['braitn] *Seebad in England.* [*land.*]
Bristol ['bristl] *Hafenstadt in Eng-*
Britten ['britn] *engl. Komponist.*
Brooklyn ['bruklin] *Stadtteil von New York.*
Brussels ['brʌslz] Brüssel *n.*
Bucharest ['bju:kərest] Bukarest *n.*
Buckingham(shire) ['bʌkiŋəm(ʃiə)] *Grafschaft in England.*

Budapest ['bju:də'pest] Budapest *n.*
Bulgaria [bʌl'geəriə] Bulgarien *n.*
Burns [bə:nz] *schott. Dichter.*
Byron ['baiərən] *engl. Dichter.*

California [kæli'fɔ.njə] Kalifornien *n* (*Staat der U.S.A.*).
Cambridge ['keimbridʒ] *engl. Universitätsstadt; Stadt in U.S.A.; a.* ~**shire** ['~ʃiə] *Grafschaft in England.*
Canada ['kænədə] Kanada *n.*
Canary Islands [kə'nɛəri 'ailəndz] *die* Kanarischen Inseln.
Canberra ['kænbərə] *Hauptstadt von Australien.* [*England.*]
Canterbury ['kæntəbəri] *Stadt in*
Capetown ['keiptaun] Kapstadt *n.*
Cardiff ['kɑ:dif] *Hauptstadt von Wales.*
Carinthia [kə'rinθiə] Kärnten *n.*
Carlyle [kɑ:'lail] *engl. Autor.*
Carolina [kærə'lainə]: *North* ~ Nordkarolina *n* (*Staat der U.S.A.*); *South* ~ Südkarolina *n* (*Staat der U.S.A.*).
Ceylon [si'lɔn] Ceylon *n.*
Chamberlain ['tʃeimbəlin, ~lein] *Name mehrerer brit. Staatsmänner.*
Cheshire ['tʃeʃə] *Grafschaft in England.*
Chicago [ʃi'kɑ:gou, *Am.* ʃi'kɔ:gou] *Industriestadt in U.S.A.*
China ['tʃainə] China *n.* [*mann.*]
Churchill ['tʃə:tʃil] *brit. Staats-*
Cleveland ['kli:vlənd] *Industrie- und Hafenstadt in U.S.A.*
Clyde [klaid] *Fluß in Schottland.*
Coleridge ['koulridʒ] *engl. Dichter.*
Colorado [kɔlə'rɑ:dou] *Staat der U.S.A.*
Columbia [kə'lʌmbiə] *Fluß in U.S.A.; Bundesdistrikt der U.S.A.*
Connecticut [kə'netikət] *Staat der U.S.A.*
Constance ['kɔnstəns]: *Lake of* ~ Bodensee *m.*
Cooper ['ku:pə] *amer. Autor.*
Copenhagen [koupn'heigən] Kopenhagen *n.* [*dilleren.*]
Cordilleras [kɔ:di'ljeərəz] *die* Kor-
Cornwall ['kɔ:nwəl] *Grafschaft in England.*
Coventry ['kɔvəntri] *Industriestadt in England.* [*mann.*]
Cromwell ['krɔmwəl] *engl. Staats-*
Cumberland ['kʌmbələnd] *Grafschaft in England.*
Cyprus ['saiprəs] Zypern *n.*
Czecho-Slovakia ['tʃekouslou'vækiə] *die* Tschechoslowakei.

Dakota [dɘ'koutɘ]: North ~ Norddakota n (Staat der U.S.A.); South ~ Süddakota n (Staat der U.S.A.).

Defoe [dɘ'fou] engl. Autor.

Delaware ['delɘwɛɘ] Staat der U.S.A.

Denmark ['denmaːk] Dänemark n.

Derby(shire) ['daːbi(ʃɘ)] Grafschaft in England.

Detroit [dɘ'trɔit] Industriestadt in U.S.A.

Devon(shire) ['devn(ʃiɘ)] Grafschaft in England.

Dickens ['dikinz] engl. Autor.

Dorset(shire) ['dɔːsit(ʃiɘ)] Grafschaft in England. [land.\

Dover ['douvɘ] Hafenstadt in Eng-\

Downing Street ['dauniŋ 'striːt] Straße in London mit der Amtswohnung des Prime Minister.

Dublin ['dʌblin] Hauptstadt von Irland.

Dunkirk [dʌn'kɔːk] Dünkirchen n.

Durham ['dʌrɘm] Grafschaft in England.

Edinburgh ['edinbɘrɘ] Edinburg n.

Edison ['edisn] amer. Erfinder.

Egypt ['iːdʒipt] Ägypten n.

Eire ['ɛɘrɘ] Republik Irland.

Eisenhower ['aizɘnhauɘ] Präsident der U.S.A.

Eliot ['eljɘt] engl. Dichter.

Emerson ['emɘsn] amer. Philosoph.

England ['iŋglɘnd] England n.

Epsom ['epsɘm] Stadt in England.

Erie ['iɘri]: Lake ~ Eriesee m.

Essex ['esiks] Grafschaft in England.

Eton ['iːtn] berühmte Public School.

Europe ['juɘrɘp] Europa n.

Falkland Islands ['fɔːlklɘnd 'ailɘndz] die Falklandinseln.

Faulkner ['fɔːknɘ] amer. Autor.

Finland ['finlɘnd] Finnland n.

Florida ['flɔridɘ] Staat der U.S.A.

Flushing ['flʌʃiŋ] Vlissingen n.

France [fraːns] Frankreich n.

Franklin ['fræŋklin] amer. Staatsmann und Physiker.

Galsworthy ['gɔːlzwɘːði] engl. Autor.

Geneva [dʒi'niːvɘ] Genf n; Lake of ~ Genfer See m.

Georgia ['dʒɔːdʒɘ] Staat der U.S.A.

Germany ['dʒɘːmɘni] Deutschland n. [nist.\

Gershwin ['gɘːʃwin] amer. Kompo-\

Gibraltar [dʒi'brɔːltɘ] Gibraltar n.

Glasgow ['glaːsgou] Hafenstadt in Schottland.

Gloucester ['glɔstɘ] Stadt in England; a. ~shire ['ˌʃiɘ] Grafschaft in England.

Great Britain ['greit 'britn] Großbritannien n.

Greece [griːs] Griechenland n.

Greene [griːn] engl. Autor.

Greenland ['griːnlɘnd] Grönland n.

Greenwich ['grinidʒ] Vorort von London.

Guernsey ['gɘːnzi] Kanalinsel.

Hague [heig]: The ~ Den Haag.

Hampshire ['hæmpʃiɘ] Grafschaft in England.

Harlem ['haːlem] Stadtteil von New York.

Harrow ['hærou] berühmte Public School.

Harvard University ['haːvɘd juː-ni'vɘːsiti] amer. Universität.

Harwich ['hæridʒ] Hafenstadt in England.

Hawaii [haː'waiiː] Staat der U.S.A.

Hebrides ['hebridiːz] die Hebriden.

Helsinki ['helsiŋki] Helsinki n.

Hemingway ['hemiŋwei] amer. Autor.

Hereford(shire) ['herifɘd(ʃiɘ)] Grafschaft in England.

Hertford(shire) ['haːtfɘd(ʃiɘ)] Grafschaft in England.

Hollywood ['hɔliwud] Filmstadt in Kalifornien, U.S.A.

Houston ['juːstɘn] Stadt in U.S.A.

Hudson ['hʌdsn] Fluß in U.S.A.

Hull [hʌl] Hafenstadt in England.

Hume [hjuːm] engl. Philosoph.

Hungary ['hʌŋgɘri] Ungarn n.

Huntingdon(shire) ['hʌntiŋdɘn (-ʃiɘ)] Grafschaft in England. [m.\

Huron ['hjuɘrɘn]: Lake ~ Huronsee\

Huxley ['hʌksli] engl. Autor.

Iceland ['aislɘnd] Island n.

Idaho ['aidɘhou] Staat der U.S.A.

Illinois [ili'nɔi] Staat der U.S.A.

India ['indjɘ] Indien n.

Indiana [indi'ænɘ] Staat der U.S.A.

Iowa ['aiouɘ] Staat der U.S.A.

Irak, Iraq [i'raːk] Irak m.

Iran [i'raːn] Iran m.

Ireland ['aiɘlɘnd] Irland n.

Irving ['ɘːviŋ] amer. Autor.

Italy ['itɘli] Italien n.

Jefferson ['dʒefɘsn] Präsident der U.S.A., Verfasser der Unabhängigkeitserklärung von 1776.

Johnson ['dʒɔnsn] 1. engl. Autor; 2. Präsident der U.S.A.

Kansas ['kænzɘs] Staat der U.S.A.

Kashmir [kæʃ'miɘ] Kaschmir n.

Keats [kiːts] engl. Dichter.

Kennedy ['kenidi] Präsident der U.S.A.; ~ Airport Flughafen von New York.

Kent [kent] Grafschaft in England.

Kentucky [ken'tʌki] Staat der U.S.A.

Kipling ['kipliŋ] engl. Dichter.

Klondike ['klɔndaik] Fluß und Landschaft in Kanada und Alaska.

Kremlin ['kremlin] der Kreml.

Labrador ['læbrədɔ:] *Halbinsel Nordamerikas.*

Lancashire ['læŋkəʃiə] *Grafschaft in England.*

Lancaster ['læŋkəstə] *Name zweier Städte in England und U.S.A.; s. Lancashire.* [*land.*\

Leeds [li:dz] *Industriestadt in England.*

Leicester ['lestə] *Stadt in England; a. ~shire ['~ʃiə] Grafschaft in England.*

Lincoln ['liŋkən] **1.** *Präsident der U.S.A.;* **2.** *a. ~shire ['~ʃiə] Grafschaft in England.*

Lisbon ['lizbən] *Lissabon n.*

Liverpool ['livəpu:l] *Hafen- und Industriestadt in England.*

Locke [lɔk] *engl. Philosoph.*

London ['lʌndən] *London n.*

Los Angeles [lɔs 'ændʒili:z] *Stadt in U.S.A.* [*U.S.A.*\

Louisiana [lu:izi'ænə] *Staat der*\

Lucerne [lu:'sə:n]: *Lake of ~ Vierwaldstätter See m.*

Luxemburg ['lʌksəmbə:g] *Luxemburg n.*

Madrid [mə'drid] *Madrid n.*

Maine [mein] *Staat der U.S.A.*

Malta ['mɔ:ltə] *Malta n.*

Manchester ['mæntʃistə] *Industriestadt in England.*

Manhattan [mæn'hætən] *Stadtteil von New York.* [*Kanada.*\

Manitoba [mæni'toubə] *Provinz in*\

Maryland ['mεərilənd, Am. 'merilənd] *Staat der U.S.A.*

Massachusetts [mæsə'tʃu:sits] *Staat der U.S.A.*

Melbourne ['mɔlbən] *Stadt in Australien.*

Miami [mai'æmi] *Badeort in Florida, U.S.A.*

Michigan ['miʃigən] *Staat der U.S.A.; Lake ~ Michigansee m.*

Middlesex ['midlseks] *Grafschaft in England.*

Miller ['milə] *amer. Dramatiker.*

Milton ['miltən] *engl. Dichter.*

Milwaukee [mil'wɔ:ki:] *Stadt in U.S.A.*

Minneapolis [mini'æpəlis] *Stadt in U.S.A.* [*U.S.A.*\

Minnesota [mini'soutə] *Staat der*\

Mississippi [misi'sipi] *Strom und Staat der U.S.A.*

Missouri [mi'zuəri] *Fluß und Staat der U.S.A.*

Monmouth(shire) ['mɔnməθ(ʃiə)] *Grafschaft in England.*

Monroe [mən'rou] *Präsident der U.S.A.* [*U.S.A.*\

Montana [mɔn'tænə] *Staat der*\

Montgomery [mənt'gɔməri] *brit. Feldmarschall.*

Montreal [mɔntri'ɔ:l] *Stadt in Kanada.*

Moore [muə] *engl. Bildhauer.*

Moscow ['mɔskou] *Moskau n.*

Nebraska [ni'bræskə] *Staat der U.S.A.*

Nelson ['nelsn] *engl. Admiral.*

Netherlands ['neðələndz] *die Niederlande.*

Nevada [ne'va:də] *Staat der U.S.A.*

New Brunswick [nju: 'brʌnzwik] *Provinz in Kanada.*

Newcastle ['nju:ka:sl] *Hafenstadt in England.* [*von Indien.*\

New Delhi [nju: 'deli] *Hauptstadt*\

New England [nju: 'iŋglənd] *Neuengland n.* [*Neufundland n.*\

Newfoundland [nju:fənd'lænd]\

New Hampshire [nju: 'hæmpʃiə] *Staat der U.S.A.*

New Jersey [nju: 'dʒə:si] *Staat der U.S.A.*

New Mexico [nju: 'meksikou] *Neumexiko n (Staat der U.S.A.).*

New Orleans [nju: 'ɔ:liəns] *Hafenstadt in U.S.A.*

Newton ['nju:tn] *engl. Physiker.*

New York ['nju: 'jɔ:k] *Stadt und Staat der U.S.A.*

New Zealand [nju: 'zi:lənd] *Neuseeland n.*

Niagara [nai'ægərə] *Niagara m.*

Nixon ['niksn] *Präsident der U.S.A.*

Norfolk ['nɔ:fək] *Grafschaft in England.*

Northampton [nɔ:'θæmptən] *Stadt in England; a. ~shire ['~ʃiə] Grafschaft in England.*

Northumberland [nɔ:'θʌmbələnd] *Grafschaft in England.*

Norway ['nɔ:wei] *Norwegen n.*

Nottingham ['nɔtiŋəm] *Stadt in England; a. ~shire ['~ʃiə] Grafschaft in England.*

Nova Scotia ['nouvə 'skouʃə] *Provinz in Kanada.*

Ohio [ou'haiou] *Staat der U.S.A.*

O'Neill [ou'ni:l] *amer. Dramatiker.*

Ontario [ɔn'tεəriou] *Provinz in Kanada; Lake ~ Ontariosee m.*

Oregon ['ɔrigən] *Staat der U.S.A.*

Orkney Islands ['ɔ:kni 'ailəndz] *die Orkneyinseln.*

Osborne ['ɔzbən] *engl. Dramatiker.*

Oslo ['ɔzlou] *Oslo n.*

Ostend [ɔs'tend] *Ostende n.*

Ottawa ['ɔtəwə] *Hauptstadt von Kanada.*

Oxford ['ɔksfəd] *engl. Universitätsstadt; a. ~shire ['~ʃiə] Grafschaft in England.*

Pakistan [pɑ:kis'tɑ:n] *Pakistan n.*

Paris ['pæris] *Paris n.*

Pearl Harbour ['pə:l 'hɑ:bə] *Hafenstadt auf Hawaii.*

Pennsylvania [pensil'veinjə] *Pennsylvanien n (Staat der U.S.A.).*

Philadelphia [filə'delfjə] *Stadt in U.S.A.*

Philippines ['filipi:nz] *die Philippinen.*

Pittsburg(h) ['pitsbə:g] *Stadt in U.S.A.*

Plymouth ['pliməθ] *Hafenstadt in England.*

Poe [pou] *amer. Autor.*

Poland ['poulənd] Polen *n.*

Portsmouth ['pɔ:tsməθ] *Hafenstadt in England.*

Portugal ['pɔ:tjugəl] Portugal *n.*

Prague [pra:g] Prag *n.*

Purcell ['pə:sl] *engl. Komponist.*

Quebec [kwi'bek] *Provinz und Stadt in Kanada.*

Reykjavik ['reikjəvi:k] Reykjavik *n.*

Rhode Island [roud 'ailənd] *Staat der U.S.A.*

Rocky Mountains ['rɔki 'mauntinz] *Gebirge in U.S.A.*

Rome [roum] Rom *n.*

Roosevelt ['rouzəvelt] *Name zweier Präsidenten der U.S.A.* [School.}

Rugby ['rʌgbi] *berühmte Public}

Rumania [ru:'meinjə] Rumänien *n.*

Russell ['rʌsl] *engl. Philosoph.*

Russia ['rʌʃə] Rußland *n.*

Rutland(shire) ['rʌtlənd(ʃiə)] *Grafschaft in England.*

San Francisco [sænfrən'siskou] *Hafenstadt in U.S.A.*

Saskatchewan [səs'kætʃiwən] *Provinz von Kanada.*

Scandinavia [skændi'neivjə] Skandinavien *n.*

Scotland ['skɔtlənd] Schottland *n.*

Shakespeare ['ʃeikspiə] *engl. Dichter.*

Shaw [ʃɔ:] *engl. Dramatiker.*

Shelley ['ʃeli] *engl. Dichter.*

Shetland Islands ['ʃetlənd 'ailəndz] *die Shetlandinseln.*

Shropshire ['ʃrɔpʃiə] *Grafschaft in England.*

Snowdon ['snoudn] *Berg in Wales.*

Sofia ['soufjə] Sofia *n.*

Somerset(shire) ['sʌməsit(ʃiə)] *Grafschaft in England.*

Southhampton [sauθ'æmptən] *Hafenstadt in England.*

Spain [spein] Spanien *n.*

Stafford(shire) ['stæfəd(ʃiə)] *Grafschaft in England.*

Stevenson ['sti:vnsn] *engl. Autor.*

St. Lawrence [snt'lɔrəns] *der St. Lorenz-Strom.*

St. Louis [snt'luis] *Industriestadt in U.S.A.* [n.}

Stockholm ['stɔkhoum] Stockholm}

Stratford ['strætfəd]: ~-on-Avon *Geburtsort Shakespeares.*

Suffolk ['sʌfək] *Grafschaft in England.* [rer See m.}

Superior [sju:'piəriə]: Lake ~ Obe-}

Surrey ['sʌri] *Grafschaft in England.*

Sussex ['sʌsiks] *Grafschaft in England.*

Sweden ['swi:dn] Schweden *n.*

Swift [swift] *engl. Autor.*

Switzerland ['switsələnd] *die Schweiz.* [tralien.}

Sydney ['sidni] *Hafenstadt in Aus-}

Tennessee [tene'si] *Staat der U.S.A.*

Tennyson ['tenisn] *engl. Dichter.*

Texas ['teksəs] *Staat der U.S.A.*

Thackeray ['θækəri] *engl. Autor.*

Thames [temz] Themse *f.*

Tirana [ti'ra:nə] Tirana *n.* [nada.}

Toronto [tə'rɔntou] *Stadt in Ka-}

Toynbee ['tɔinbi] *engl. Historiker.*

Trafalgar [trə'fælgə] *Vorgebirge bei Gibraltar.* [U.S.A.}

Truman ['tru:mən] *Präsident der}

Turkey ['tə:ki] *die Türkei.*

Twain [twein] *amer. Autor.*

Tyrol ['tirəl] Tirol *n.*

United States of America [ju:'naitid 'steitsəvə'merikə] *die Vereinigten Staaten von Amerika.*

Utah ['ju:ta:] *Staat der U.S.A.*

Vancouver [væn'ku:və] *Stadt in Kanada.*

Vermont [və:'mɔnt] *Staat der}

Vienna [vi'enə] Wien *n.* [U.S.A.}

Virginia [və'dʒinjə] Virginien *n (Staat der U.S.A.);* West ~ *Staat der U.S.A.*

Wales [weilz] Wales *n.*

Warsaw ['wɔ:sɔ:] Warschau *n.*

Warwick(shire) ['wɔrik(ʃiə)] *Grafschaft in England.*

Washington ['wɔʃiŋtən] **1.** *Präsident der U.S.A.;* **2.** *Staat der U.S.A.;* **3.** *Bundeshauptstadt der U.S.A.*

Wellington ['weliŋtən] *Hauptstadt von Neuseeland.*

Westmoreland ['westmələnd] *Grafschaft in England.*

White House ['wait 'haus] *das Weiße Haus.*

Whitman ['witmən] *amer. Dichter.*

Wilson ['wilsn] **1.** *Präsident der U.S.A.;* **2.** *brit. Premier.*

Wiltshire ['wiltʃiə] *Grafschaft in England.*

Wimbledon ['wimbldən] *Vorort von London.* [Kanada.}

Winnipeg ['winipeg] *Stadt in}

Wisconsin [wis'kɔnsin] *Staat der U.S.A.*

Worcester ['wustə] *Industriestadt in England;* a. ~shire ['~ʃiə] *Grafschaft in England.*

Wordsworth ['wə:dzwə:θ] *engl. Dichter.*

Yale University ['jeil ju:ni'və:siti] *amer. Universität.*

York [jɔ:k] *Stadt in England;* a. ~shire ['~ʃiə] *Grafschaft in England.*

Yugoslavia ['ju:gou'sla:vjə] Jugoslawien *n.*

American and British Abbreviations

abbr. *abbreviated* abgekürzt; *abbreviation* Abk., Abkürzung *f.*

A.B.C. *American Broadcasting Company* Amer. Rundfunkgesellschaft *f.* [strom *m.*]

A.C. *alternating current* Wechsel-

A.E.C. *Atomic Energy Commission* Atomenergie-Kommission *f.*

AFL-CIO *American Federation of Labor & Congress of Industrial Organizations* (größter amer. Gewerkschaftsverband).

A.F.N. *American Forces Network* (Rundfunkanstalt der amer. Streit-

Ala. *Alabama.* [kräfte).

Alas. *Alaska.*

a.m. *ante meridiem* (lateinisch = before noon) vormittags.

A.P. *Associated Press* (amer. Nachrichtenbüro). [Rotes Kreuz.

A.R.C. *American Red Cross* Amer.

Ariz. *Arizona.*

Ark. *Arkansas.*

arr. *arrival* Ank., Ankunft *f.*

B.A. *Bachelor of Arts* Bakkalaureus *m* der Philosophie.

B.B.C. *British Broadcasting Corporation* Brit. Rundfunkgesellschaft *f.*

B.E.A. *British European Airways* Brit.-Europäische Luftfahrtge-

Beds. *Bedfordshire.* [sellschaft.

Benelux *Belgium, Netherlands, Luxemburg* (Zollunion).

Berks. *Berkshire.*

B.F.N. *British Forces Network* (Sender der brit. Streitkräfte in Deutschland). [m des Rechts.

B.L. *Bachelor of Law* Bakkalaureus

B.M. *Bachelor of Medicine* Bakkalaureus *m* der Medizin.

B.O.A.C. *British Overseas Airways Corporation* Brit. Übersee-Luftfahrtgesellschaft *f.*

B.R. *British Railways.*

Br(it). *Britain* Großbritannien *n;* *British* britisch.

B.S. *Bachelor of Science* Bakkalaureus *m* der Naturwissenschaften.

Bucks. *Buckinghamshire.*

C. *Celsius, centigrade.*

c. *cent(s)* Cent *m; circa* ca., ungefähr, zirka; *cubic* Kubik...

Cal(if). *California.*

Cambs. *Cambridgeshire.*

Can. *Canada* Kanada *n; Canadian* kanadisch.

cf. *confer* vgl., vergleiche.

Ches. *Cheshire.*

C.I.C. *Counter Intelligence Corps* (Spionageabwehrdienst der U.S.A.).

C.I.D. *Criminal Investigation Department* (brit. Kriminalpolizei).

Co. *Company* Gesellschaft *f; County* Grafschaft *f,* Kreis *m.*

c/o *care of* p.A., per Adresse, bei.

Col(o). *Colorado.*

Conn. *Connecticut.*

cp. *compare* vgl., vergleiche.

Cumb. *Cumberland.* [ner *m.*

cwt. *hundredweight* (etwa 1) Zent-

d. *penny, pence.*

D.C. *direct current* Gleichstrom *m;* *District of Columbia* (mit der amer. Hauptstadt Washington).

Del. *Delaware.*

dep. *departure* Abf., Abfahrt *f.*

Dept. *Department* Abt., Abteilung *f.*

Derby. *Derbyshire.*

Devon. *Devonshire.*

Dors. *Dorsetshire.*

Dur(h). *Durham.*

dz. *dozen* Dutzend *n od. pl.*

E. *east* Ost(en *m); eastern* östlich; *English* englisch.

E.C. *East Central* (London) Mitte-Ost (Postbezirk).

ECOSOC *Economic and Social Council* Wirtschafts- und Sozialrat *m* (U.N.).

Ed., ed. *edition* Auflage *f; edited* hrsg., herausgegeben; *editor* Hrsg., Herausgeber *m.*

E.E.C. *European Economic Community* EWG, Europäische Wirtschaftsgemeinschaft.

E.F.T.A. *European Free Trade Association* EFTA, Europäische Freihandelsgemeinschaft *od.* -zone.

e.g. *exempli gratia* (lateinisch = for instance) z.B., zum Beispiel.

Enc. *enclosure(s)* Anlage(n *pl.*) *f.*

Ess. *Essex.*

F. *Fahrenheit.*

f. *fathom(s)* Faden *m,* Klafter *f, m, n;* *feminine* weiblich; *foot, pl. feet* Fuß *m od. pl.; following* folgend.

F.A.O. *Food and Agricultural Organization* Organisation *f* für Ernährung und Landwirtschaft (U.N.).

FBI *Federal Bureau of Investigation* (Bundeskriminalamt der U.S.A.).

fig. *figure(s)* Abb., Abbildung(en

Fla. *Florida.* [pl.) *f.*

F.O. *Foreign Office* brit. Auswärtiges

fr. *franc(s)* Frank(en *pl.*) *m.* [Amt.

ft. *foot, pl. feet* Fuß *m od. pl.*

g. gramme g, Gramm n; guinea Guinee f (21 Schilling).
Ga. Georgia.
gal. gallon Gallone f.
G.A.T.T. General Agreement on Tariffs and Trade Allgemeines Zoll- und Handelsabkommen.
G.B. Great Britain Großbritannien n.
G.I. government issue von der Regierung ausgegeben; Staatselgentum n; fig. der amer. Soldat.
Glos. Gloucestershire.
G.P.O. General Post Office Hauptpostamt n.
gr. gross brutto. [postamt n.]
Gt.Br. Great Britain Großbritannien n.

h. hour(s) Std., Stunde(n pl.) f.
Hants. Hampshire.
H.C. House of Commons Unterhaus n.
Heref. Herefordshire.
Herts. Hertfordshire.
hf. half halb.
H.I. Hawaiian Islands.
H.L. House of Lords Oberhaus n.
H.M. His (Her) Majesty Seine (Ihre) Majestät.
H.M.S. His (Her) Majesty's Service Dienst m, & Dienstsache f; His (Her) Majesty's Ship Seiner (Ihrer) Majestät Schiff n.
H.O. Home Office brit. Innenministerium n; [stärke f.]
H.P., h.p. horse-power PS, Pferde-]
H.Q., Hq. Headquarters Stab(squartier n) m, Hauptquartier n.
H.R. House of Representatives Repräsentantenhaus n (der U.S.A.).
H.R.H. His (Her) Royal Highness Seine (Ihre) Königliche Hoheit f.
Hunts. Huntingdonshire.

Ia. Iowa.
I.C.B.M. intercontinental ballistic missile interkontinentaler ballistischer Flugkörper.
I.D. Intelligence Department Nachrichtenamt n.
Id(a). Idaho. [d.h., das heißt.]
i.e. id est (lateinisch = that is to say)]
Ill. Illinois.
I.M.F. International Monetary Fund Weltwährungsfonds m.
in. inch(es) Zoll m od. pl. [gen.]
Inc. Incorporated (amtlich) eingetra-]
Ind. Indiana.
I.O.C. International Olympic Committee Internationales Olympisches Komitee.
Ir. Ireland Irland n; Irish irisch.
I.R.C. International Red Cross Internationales Rotes Kreuz.

J.P. Justice of the Peace Friedensrichter m.

Kan(s). Kansas.
k.o. knock(ed) out Boxen: k.o. (ge-) schlagen; fig. erledigen (erledigt).
Ky. Kentucky.

£ pound sterling Pfund n Sterling.
La. Louisiana.
Lancs. Lancashire. [wicht).]
lb. pound(s) Pfund n od. pl. (Ge-]
L.C. letter of credit Kreditbrief]
Leics. Leicestershire. [m.]
Lincs. Lincolnshire.
LP long-playing Langspiel...(Platte).
L.P. Labour Party (brit. Arbeiterpartei). [tung.]
Ltd. limited mit beschränkter Haf-]

m. male männlich; metre m, Meter n, m; mile Meile f; minute Min., Minute f. [Philosophie.]
M.A. Master of Arts Magister m der]
Mass. Massachusetts.
M.D. Medicinae Doctor (lateinisch = Doctor of Medicine) Dr. med., Doktor m der Medizin.
Md. Maryland.
Me. Maine.
mi. mile Meile f.
Mich. Michigan.
Middx. Middlesex.
Minn. Minnesota.
Miss. Mississippi.
Mo. Missouri.
M.O. money order Postanweisung f.
Mon. Monmouthshire.
Mont. Montana.
MP, M.P. Member of Parliament Parlamentsabgeordnete m; Military Police Militärpolizei f.
m.p.h. miles per hour Stundenmei-]
Mr Mister Herr m. [len pl.]
Mrs Mistress Frau f.
Mt. Mount Berg m.

N. north Nord(en m); northern nörd-]
n. noon Mittag m. lich.]
NASA National Aeronautics and Space Administration (amer. Luftfahrt- und Raumforschungsbehörde).
NATO North Atlantic Treaty Organization Nordatlantikpakt-Organisation f.
N.C. North Carolina.
N.D(ak). North Dakota.
Neb(r). Nebraska.
Nev. Nevada.
N.H. New Hampshire.
N.H.S. National Health Service Nationaler Gesundheitsdienst (brit. Krankenversicherung).
N.J. New Jersey.
N.M(ex). New Mexico.
Norf. Norfolk.
Northants. Northamptonshire.
Northumb. Northumberland.
Notts. Nottinghamshire.
nt. net netto.
N.Y. New York. [York.]
N.Y.C. New York City Stadt f New]

O. Ohio; order Auftrag m.
O.A.S. Organization of American States Organisation f amerikanischer Staaten.

O.E.E.C. *Organization of European Economic Co-operation* Organisation *f* für europäische wirtschaftliche Zusammenarbeit.
Okla. *Oklahoma.*
Ore(g). *Oregon.*
Oxon. *Oxfordshire.*

Pa. *Pennsylvania.*
P.A.A. *Pan-American Airways* Panamer. Luftfahrtgesellschaft *f.*
P.C. *police constable* Schutzmann *m.*
p.c. *per cent* %, Prozent *n od. pl.*
pd. *paid* bezahlt.
P.E.N., *mst* **PEN Club** *Poets, Playwrights, Editors, Essayists, and Novelists* Pen-Club *m, (Internationale Vereinigung von Dichtern, Dramatikern, Redakteuren, Essayisten und Romanschriftstellern).*
Penn(a). *Pennsylvania.*
Ph.D. *Philosophiae Doctor (lateinisch = Doctor of Philosophy)* Dr. phil., Doktor *m* der Philosophie.
p.m. *post meridiem (lateinisch = after noon)* nachmittags, abends.
P.O. *Post Office* Postamt *n; postal order* Postanweisung *f.*
P.O.B. *Post Office Box* Postschließfach *n.*
P.S. *Postscript* P.S., Nachschrift *f.*
P.T.O., p.t.o. *please turn over* b.w., bitte wenden.
PX *Post Exchange (Verkaufsläden der amer. Streitkräfte).*

R.A.F. *Royal Air Force* Königlich-Brit. Luftwaffe *f.*
Rd. *Road* Straße *f.*
ref(c). *(In) reference (to)* (in) Bezug *m* (auf); Empfehlung *f.*
regd. *registered* eingetragen; $\wp$ eingeschrieben. [tonne *f.*\
reg. tn. *register ton* RT, Register-/
resp. *respective(ly)* bzw., beziehungsweise.
ret. *retired* i.R., im Ruhestand.
Rev. *Reverend* Ehrwürden.
R.I. *Rhode Island.* Marine *f.*\
R.N. *Royal Navy* Königlich-Brit./
R.R. *Railroad Am.* Eisenbahn *f.*
Rutland. *Rutlandshire.*
Ry. *Railway* Eisenbahn *f.*

S. *south* Süd(en *m*); *southern* südlich.
s. *second(s)* Sek., Sekunde(n *pl.*) *f*; *shilling(s)* Schilling *m od. pl.*
$ *dollar* Dollar *m.*
S.A. *South Africa* Südafrika *n; South America* Südamerika *n.*
Salop *Shropshire.*
S.C. *South Carolina; Security Council* Sicherheitsrat *m (U.N.).*
S.D(ak). *South Dakota.*
SEATO *South East Asia Treaty Organization* Südostasienpakt-Organisation *f.*
sh. *shilling(s)* Schilling *m od. pl.*
Soc. *society* Gesellschaft *f*; Verein *m.*

Som. *Somersetshire.*
Sq. *Square* Platz *m.*
sq. *square* ... Quadrat...
Staffs. *Staffordshire.*
St(.) *Saint* ... Sankt ...; *Station* Bahnhof *m*; *Street* Straße *f.*
Suff. *Suffolk.*
suppl. *supplement* Nachtrag *m.*
Sur. *Surrey.*
Suss. *Sussex.*

t. *ton(s)* Tonne(n *pl.*) *f.*
Tenn. *Tennessee.*
Tex. *Texas.*
T.M.O. *telegraph money order* telegraphische Geldanweisung.
T.O. *Telegraph (Telephone) Office* Telegraphen- (Fernsprech)amt *n*
T.U. *Trade(s) Union(s)* Gewerkschaft(en *pl.*) *f.*
T.U.C. *Trade(s) Union Congress* brit. Gewerkschaftsverband *m.*

U.K. *United Kingdom* Vereinigtes Königreich *(England, Schottland, Wales und Nordirland).*
U.N. *United Nations* Vereinte Nationen *pl.*
UNESCO *United Nations Educational, Scientific, and Cultural Organization* Organisation *f* der Vereinten Nationen für Wissenschaft, Erziehung und Kultur.
U.N.S.C. *United Nations Security Council* Sicherheitsrat *m* der Vereinten Nationen.
U.P.I. *United Press International (amer. Nachrichtenagentur).*
U.S.(A.) *United States (of America)* Vereinigte Staaten *pl.* (von Amerika). [rika.)\
Ut. *Utah.*

Va. *Virginia.*
vol(s). *volume(s)* Band *m* (Bände\
Vt. *Vermont.* [*pl.*).\
V.T.O.(L.) *vertical take-off (and landing) (aircraft)* Senkrechtstart(er) *m.*

W. *west* West(en *m*); *western* west-\
War. *Warwickshire.* [lich.\
Wash. *Washington.*
W.C. *West Central (London)* Mitte-West *(Postbezirk).*
W.F.T.U. *World Federation of Trade Unions* Weltgewerkschaftsbund *m.*
W.H.O. *World Health Organization* Weltgesundheitsorganisation *f (U.N.).*
W.I. *West Indies* Westindien *n.*
Wilts. *Wiltshire.*
Wis. *Wisconsin.*
Worcs. *Worcestershire.*
wt. *weight* Gewicht *n.*
W.Va. *West Virginia.*
Wyo. *Wyoming.*

yd. *yard(s)* Elle(n *pl.*) *f.*
Yorks. *Yorkshire.*

German Weights and Measures

I. Linear Measure

1 mm   *Millimeter* millimet|re, *Am.* -er = 0.039 inch

1 cm   *Zentimeter* centimet|re, *Am.* -er = 10 mm = 0.394 inch

1 m   *Meter* met|re, *Am.* -er = 100 cm = 1.094 yards = 3.281 feet

1 km   *Kilometer* kilomet|re, *Am.* -er = 1000 m = 0.621 mile

1 sm   *Seemeile* nautical mile = 1852 m

II. Square Measure

1 mm²   *Quadratmillimeter* square millimet|re, *Am.* -er = 0.002 square inch

1 cm²   *Quadratzentimeter* square centimet|re, *Am.* -er = 100 mm² = 0.155 square inch

1 m²   *Quadratmeter* square met|re, *Am.* -er = 10000 cm² = 1.196 square yards = 10.764 square feet

1 a   *Ar* are = 100 m² = 119.599 square yards

1 ha   *Hektar* hectare = 100 a = 2.471 acres

1 km²   *Quadratkilometer* square kilomet|re, *Am.* -er = 100 ha = 247.11 acres = 0.386 square mile

III. Cubic Measure

1 cm³   *Kubikzentimeter* cubic centimet|re, *Am.* -er = 1000 mm³ = 0.061 cubic inch

1 m³   *Kubikmeter* cubic met|re, *Am.* -er = 1000000 cm³ = 35.315 cubic feet = 1.308 cubic yards

1 RT   *Registertonne* register ton = 2,832 m³ = 100 cubic feet

IV. Measure of Capacity

1 l   *Liter* lit|re, *Am.* -er = 1.760 pints = *U.S.* 1.057 liquid quarts *or* 0.906 dry quart

1 hl   *Hektoliter* hectolit|re, *Am.* -er = 100 l = 2.75 bushels = *U.S.* 26.418 gallons

V. Weight

1 g   *Gramm* gram(me) = 15.432 grains

1 Pfd.   *Pfund* pound (German) = 500 g = 1.102 pounds avdp.

1 kg   *Kilogramm* kilogram(me) = 1000 g = 2.205 pounds avdp. = 2.679 pounds troy

1 Ztr.   *Zentner* centner = 100 Pfd. = 0.984 hundredweight = 1.102 *U.S.* hundredweights

1 dz   *Doppelzentner* = 100 kg = 1.968 hundredweights = 2.204 *U.S.* hundredweights

1 t   *Tonne* ton = 1000 kg = 0.984 long ton = *U.S.* 1.102 short tons

American and British Weights and Measures

1. Linear Measure

1 inch (in.) = 2,54 cm
1 foot (ft)
 = 12 inches = 30,48 cm
1 yard (yd)
 = 3 feet = 91,439 cm
1 perch (p.)
 = 5$\frac{1}{2}$ yards = 5,029 m
1 mile (m.)
 = 1,760 yards = 1,609 km

2. Nautical Measure

1 fathom (f., fm)
 = 6 feet = 1,829 m
1 nautical mile
 = 6,080 feet = 1853,18 m

3. Square Measure

1 square inch (sq. in.)
 = 6,452 cm^2
1 square foot (sq. ft)
 = 144 square inches
 = 929,029 cm^2
1 square yard (sq. yd)
 = 9 square feet = 8361,26 cm^2
1 square perch (sq. p.)
 = 30$\frac{1}{4}$ square yards = 25,293m^2
1 rood
 = 40 square perches = 10,117 a
1 acre (a.) = 4 roods = 40,47 a
1 square mile
 = 640 acres = 258,998 ha

4. Cubic Measure

1 cubic inch (cu. in.)
 = 16,387 cm^3
1 cubic foot (cu. ft)
 = 1,728 cubic inches = 0,028 m^3
1 cubic yard (cu. yd)
 = 27 cubic feet = 0,765 m^3
1 register ton (reg. ton)
 = 100 cubic feet = 2,832 m^3

5. Measure of Capacity
Dry and Liquid Measure

1 British or imperial gill (gl, gi.)
 = 0,142 l
1 British or imperial pint (pt)
 = 4 gills = 0,568 l
1 British or imperial quart (qt)
 = 2 pints = 1,136 l
1British or imp. gallon (imp. gal.)
 = 4 imperial quarts = 4,546 l

Dry Measure

1 British or imperial peck (pk)
 = 2 imperial gallons = 9,092 l
1 Brit. or imp. bushel (bu., bus.)
 = 8 imperial gallons = 36,366 l

1 Brit. or imp. quarter (qr)
 = 8 imperial bushels = 290,935 l

Liquid Measure

1 Brit. or imp. barrel (bbl, bl)
 = 36 imperial gallons = 163,656 l

*

1 U.S. dry pint = 0,551 l
1 U.S. dry quart
 = 2 dry pints = 1,101 l
1 U.S. dry gallon
 = 4 dry quarts = 4,405 l
1 U.S. peck
 = 2 dry gallons = 8,809 l
1 U.S. bushel
 = 8 dry gallons = 35,238 l
1 U.S. gill = 0,118 l
1 U.S. liquid pint
 = 4 gills = 0,473 l
1 U.S. liquid quart
 = 2 liquid pints = 0,946 l
1 U.S. liquid gallon
 = 8 liquid pints = 3,785 l
1 U.S. barrel
 = 3$\frac{1}{2}$ liquid gallons = 119,228 l
1 U.S. barrel petroleum
 = 42 liquid gallons = 158,97 l

6. Avoirdupois Weight

1 grain (gr.) = 0,065 g
1 dram (dr.)
 = 27.344 grains = 1,772 g
1 ounce (oz.)
 = 16 drams = 28,35 g
1 pound (lb.)
 = 16 ounces = 453,592 g
1 quarter (qr)
 = 28 pounds = 12,701 kg
 (*U.S.A.* 25 pounds
 = 11,339 kg)
1 hundredweight (cwt.)
 = 112 pounds
 = 50,802 kg (*U.S.A.* 100 pounds
 = 45,359 kg)
1 ton (t.)
 (*a.* long ton) = 20 hundredweights = 1016,05 kg (*U.S.A.*,
 a. short ton, = 907,185 kg)
1 stone (st.) = 14 pounds = 6,35 kg

7. Troy Weight

1 grain = 0,065 g
1 pennyweight (dwt.)
 = 24 grains = 1,555 g
1 ounce
 = 20 pennyweights = 31,103 g
1 pound = 12 ounces = 373,242 g